HALSBURY'S
LAWS OF ENGLAND

ANNUAL ABRIDGMENT
2006

HALSBURY'S
Laws of England

FOURTH EDITION

ANNUAL ABRIDGMENT 2006

LEXISNEXIS BUTTERWORTHS

Members of the LexisNexis Group worldwide

UNITED KINGDOM	LexisNexis Butterworths, a Division of Reed Elsevier (UK) Ltd, Halsbury House, 35 Chancery Lane, **London**, WC2A 1EL, and London House, 20–22 East London Street, **Edinburgh**, EH7 4BQ
ARGENTINA	LexisNexis Argentina, **Buenos Aires**
AUSTRALIA	LexisNexis Butterworths, **Chatswood**, New South Wales
AUSTRIA	LexisNexis Verlag ARD Orac GmbH & Co KG, **Vienna**
BENELUX	LexisNexis Benelux, **Amsterdam**
CANADA	LexisNexis Canada, **Markham**, Ontario
CHILE	LexisNexis Chile Ltda, **Santiago**
CHINA	LexisNexis China, **Beijing** and **Shanghai**
FRANCE	LexisNexis SA, **Paris**
GERMANY	LexisNexis Deutschland GmbH, **Munster**
HONG KONG	LexisNexis Hong Kong, **Hong Kong**
INDIA	LexisNexis India, **New Delhi**
ITALY	Giuffrè Editore, **Milan**
JAPAN	LexisNexis Japan, **Tokyo**
MALAYSIA	Malayan Law Journal Sdn Bhd, **Kuala Lumpur**
MEXICO	LexisNexis Mexico, **Mexico**
NEW ZEALAND	LexisNexis NZ Ltd, **Wellington**
POLAND	Wydawnictwo Prawnicze LexisNexis Sp, **Warsaw**
SINGAPORE	LexisNexis Singapore, **Singapore**
SOUTH AFRICA	LexisNexis Butterworths, **Durban**
USA	LexisNexis, **Dayton**, Ohio

© Reed Elsevier (UK) Ltd 2007
Published by LexisNexis Butterworths

A CIP Catalogue record for this book is available from the British Library.

ISBN for this volume: 9781 405 724 579

ISBN 978-1-4057-2457-9

9 781405 724579

Typeset by Letterpart Ltd, Reigate, Surrey

Printed and bound in Great Britain by William Clowes Limited, Beccles, Suffolk

Visit LexisNexis Butterworths at www.lexisnexis.co.uk

Managing Editor

TANJA CLARKE LLM

Assistant Editors

NICOLA BURDON BSc
Solicitor

MARGARET CUNNINGHAM LLB
of Gray's Inn, Barrister

KIM DOLAN MA
Solicitor

Senior Sub-editors

NEIL JONES BA MPhil

NEIL KENNERLEY LLB

DANIEL WRIGHT LLB

Sub-editors

SULINA BANGAROO LLB

KAREN GIBBS LLB

TOM MACDONALD BA

Publisher

SIMON HETHERINGTON LLB

PUBLISHERS' NOTE

This is the thirty third *Annual Abridgment* and covers the year 2006. The *Abridgment* constitutes year by year a comprehensive and permanent survey of English case law, statute law and subordinate legislation. European Community law and decisions of Commonwealth courts are given attention commensurate with their importance. Further noteworthy items are derived from government papers, reports of committees and legal periodicals. The alphabetical arrangement and the comprehensive tables and index make the work an ideal aid to research.

Each *Annual Abridgment* is complete without recourse to any other publication. This volume is complementary to both the *Current Service* and the *Cumulative Supplement*.

When referring to this volume reference should be made to both the year and the relevant paragraph number: e g '2006 Abr para 2238'.

This volume covers the law made in 2006 and is compiled from sources available in London on 31 December 2006.

LEXISNEXIS BUTTERWORTHS

TABLE OF CONTENTS

The text of this *Abridgment* is arranged under the following titles. A list of titles currently used in *Halsbury's Laws* appears on page *11*.

Table of Contents

ARRANGEMENT OF TITLES
HALSBURY'S LAWS, FOURTH EDITION & REISSUE

The following is the title scheme of *Halsbury's Laws* as it stood as at May 2007, arranged by volume number and title. Where the titles used in the *Annual Abridgment* differ from those in the main work, the new titles appear in brackets.

In the *Annual Abridgment* the following are additional titles:

REFERENCES AND ABBREVIATIONS

The following is a list of abbreviations of the principal sources from which the *Annual Abridgment* is compiled. A full list of reports used in *Halsbury's Laws of England* may be found in volume 54(1) (Consolidated Table of Cases A–L) and volume 54(2) (Consolidated Table of Cases M-Z; ECJ Cases).

Abr	Halsbury's Abridgment
AC	Law Reports (Appeal Cases)
ACD	Administrative Court Digest
ADRLJ	Arbitration and Dispute Resolution Law Journal
All ER	All England Law Reports
All ER (Comm)	All England Law Reports Commercial Cases
All ER (EC)	All England Law Reports European Cases
All ER (D)	All England Law Reports Direct
BCLC	Butterworths Company Law Cases
BHRC	Butterworths Human Rights Cases
BLR	Building Law Reports
BMLR	Butterworths Medico-Legal Reports
BTR	British Tax Review
Ch	Law Reports (Chancery Division)
CJQ	Civil Justice Quarterly
CLJ	Cambridge Law Journal
CMLR	Common Market Law Reports
CML Rev	Common Market Law Review
Comms L	Communications Law
Comp Lawyer	Company Lawyer
Con LR	Construction Law Reports
Const LJ	Construction Law Journal
CPLR	Civil Procedure Law Reports
CR	Clinical Risk
Cr App Rep	Criminal Appeal Reports
Cr App Rep (S)	Criminal Appeal Reports (Sentencing)
Crim LR	Criminal Law Review
CTLR	Computer and Telecommunications Law Review
Ecc LJ	Ecclesiastical Law Journal
ECLR	European Competition Law Review
EG	Estates Gazette
EG (CS)	Estates Gazette Case Summaries
EHLR	Environmental Health Law Reports
EHRR	European Human Rights Reports
EHRLR	European Human Rights Law Review
EIPR	European Intellectual Property Review
ELJ	European Law Journal
ELM	Environmental Law and Management
ELR	Education Law Reports
EL Rev	European Law Review
EMLR	Entertainment and Media Law Reports
ENTLR	Entertainment Law Review
Env Law Mgmt	Environmental Law and Management
FCR	Family Court Reporter
FLR	Family Law Reports
FSR	Fleet Street Reports
Fam	Law Reports (Family Division)
Fam Law	Family Law
HC	House of Commons Paper
HLR	Housing Law Reports
IANL	Tolley's Immigration, Asylum and Nationality Law
ICCLR	International Company and Commercial Law Review
ICLQ	International and Comparative Law Quarterly
ICR	Industrial Cases Reports
ILJ	Industrial Law Journal
IP & T	Intellectual Property and Technology Cases

IP & T Law	Intellectual Property and Information Technology Law
IPQ	Intellectual Property Quarterly
IRLR	Industrial Relations Law Reports
IT CLJ	IT and Communications Law Journal
IT CLR	IT and Communications Law Reports
ITELR	International Trust and Estate Law Reports
ITLR	International Tax Law Reports
Imm AR	Immigration Appeal Reports
JBL	Journal of Business Law
JHL	Journal of Housing Law
JIBFL	Journal of International Banking and Financial Law
JP	Justice of the Peace Reports
JPIL	Journal of Personal Injury Law
JPL	Journal of Planning and Environment Law
JP Jo	Justice of the Peace Journal
JPL	Journal of Planning and Environmental Law
JSSL	Journal of Social Security Law
JSWFL	Journal of Social Welfare and Family Law
L & TR	Landlord and Tenant Reports
L & T Rev	Landlord and Tenant Review
LA	Legal Action
LGR	Butterworths Local Government Reports
LMCLQ	Lloyd's Maritime and Commercial Law Quarterly
LQR	Law Quarterly Review
LS Gaz	Law Society Gazette
Lloyd's Rep	Lloyd's Law Reports
Lloyd's Rep Bank	Lloyd's Law Reports Banking
Lloyd's Rep IR	Lloyd's Law Reports Insurance and Reinsurance
Lloyd's Rep Med	Lloyd's Law Reports Medical
MLR	Modern Law Review
MLRep	Manx Law Reports
Med LR	Medical Law Reports
NI	Northern Ireland Law Reports
NLJ	New Law Journal
NZFLR	New Zealand Family Law Reports
NZLR	New Zealand Law Reports
P & CR	Property, Planning and Compensation Reports
PCB	Private Client Business
PIQR	Personal Injuries and Quantum Reports
PLCR	Planning Law Case Reports
PLR	(Estates Gazette) Planning Law Reports
QB	Law Reports (Queen's Bench Division)
RA	Rating Appeals
RPC	Reports of Patent Cases
RTR	Road Traffic Reports
RVR	Rating and Valuation Reporter
SJ	Solicitors' Journal
SLT	Scots Law Times
STC	Simon's Tax Cases
STC (SCD)	Simon's Tax Cases (Special Commissioners' Decisions)
Stat LR	Statute Law Review
TCLR	Technology and Construction Law Reports
TR	Taxation Reports
Tax Cas	Tax Cases
V & DR	Value Added Tax and Duties Tribunal Reports
VATTR	Value Added Tax Tribunal Reports
WLR	Weekly Law Reports
WTLR	Wills and Trusts Law Reports

TABLE OF STATUTES

Table of Statutes

TABLE OF STATUTORY INSTRUMENTS

Table of Statutory Instruments

Table of Statutory Instruments

Table of Statutory Instruments

TABLE OF CASES

Decisions of the European Court of Human Rights and the European Court of Justice are listed numerically at the end of the main table.

A

B

Table of Cases

C

D

E

F

G

H

I

J

K

L

M

P

Q

R

Table of Cases

PARA

PARA

S

T

U

V

W

Table of Cases

Table of Cases

PARA

COMMAND PAPERS

PARA

TABLE OF PRACTICE DIRECTIONS

WORDS AND PHRASES

QUANTUM OF DAMAGES TABLE

This table refers to examples of awards of damages in personal injury or fatal accident cases that have been summarised in the Abridgment. Cases are arranged in the following order, with cases involving more than one injury being classified according to the major injury suffered.

Death	Dental negligence	Head
Brain damage	Internal injuries	Neck and shoulder
Paralysis	Industrial Disease	Back, chest and abdomen
Multiple injuries	Disease	Arm and hand
Psychological damage	Allergic reaction	Leg and foot
PTSD	Burns	Minor injuries
Medical negligence	Scarring	

For the purposes of this table the age of the plaintiff is at the date of the accident unless otherwise stated. In fatal accident cases, sex and age are those of the deceased unless otherwise stated.

INJURY	PSLA	SEX/AGE	CITATION & REVIEW PARA NUMBER
Brain damage	£170,000	Male/10	*J (A Child) v Jones (deceased)* (Queen's Bench Division), para 956
	£40,000	Male/18	*Madden v Ross* (Bodmin County Ct), para 957
	£30,000	Male/38	*S (A Patient) v Hopal* (Romford County Ct), para 958
Multiple injuries	£10,000	Female/32	*Porter v Mangham* (Northampton County Ct), para 959
	£6,500	Female/22	*Hussain v Rider Holdings Ltd* (Bradford County Ct), para 960
	£5,500	Male/35	*James v Border Counties Electronics* (Stoke-on-Trent County Ct), para 961
	£5,000	Female/60	*Thomason v The Village Café* (Warrington County Ct), para 962
	£4,500	Male/30	*Talbot v Guest* (Stoke-on-Trent County Ct), para 963
	£4,250	Male/56	*Stoor v Dean* (Oldham County Ct), para 964
Psychological damage	£15,250	Male/31	*Hirons v Kraft Foods plc* (Oxford County Ct), para 1011
	£14,000	Female/49	*Garrod v North Devon NHS Primary Care Trust* (Queen's Bench Division), para 965
	£5,000	Male/34	*Kalhar v Galatola* (Slough County Ct), para 992
	£2,500	Female/1	*S (A Child) v Begum* (Birmingham County Ct), para 966
	£2,250	Male/10	*K (A Child) v Arboretum Nursing Home* (Birmingham County Ct), para 967
	£1,800	Female/14	*C (A Child) v Dobbyn* (Leicester County Ct), para 968
	£1,640	Male/3	*J (A Child) v O'Connor* (Worcester County Ct), para 969

INJURY	PSLA	SEX/AGE	CITATION & REVIEW PARA NUMBER
	£1,250	Female/47	*Cobby v Griffiths* (Hastings County Ct), para 970
Post-traumatic stress disorder	£10,000	Female/33	*Sheath v GE Capital Fleet Services* (Oxford County Ct), para 1002
	£4,000	Female/36	*King v Hindley* (Liverpool County Ct), para 972
Medical negligence	£4,000	Female/4	*L (A Child) v The Royal Wolverhampton NHS Trust* (Birmingham County Ct), para 974
Food poisoning	£13,000	Male/24	*Willey v My Travel UK Ltd* (Walsall County Ct), para 975
Burns	£1,215	Male/14	*Z (A Child) v Attridge* (Dudley County Ct), para 976
Scarring	£5,500	Male/31	*Hamilton v Malcolm Group Ltd* (Birmingham County Ct), para 977
Head	£4,300	Male/26	*Trow v Haydes* (Cambridge County Ct), para 978
	£1,000	Male/6	*M (A Child) v JJB Sports* (Coventry County Ct), para 979
Neck	£7,800	Female/12	*J (A Child) v Kilroy* (Northampton County Ct), para 980
	£4,300	Male/26	*Trow v Haydes* (Cambridge County Ct), para 978
	£4,250	Male/80	*Carter v Hertfordshire CC* (Luton County Ct), para 982
	£3,600	Male/29	*Bunce v Lovatt* (Coventry County Ct), para 983
	£3,500	Female/50	*Jennings v Rehman* (Manchester County Ct), para 984
	(1)£2,800 (2)£3,250	Male Female	*Berry v Rustman* (Southend County Ct), para 981
	£2,500	Female/8	*G (A Child) v Bleasdell* (Edmonton County Ct), para 985
	£2,250	Female/38	*Mistry v Rajani* (Mansfield County Ct), para 986
	£1,900	Female/30	*Kemp v Barton* (Stockport County Ct), para 987
	£1,900	Female/9	*P (A Child) v Martin* (Watford County Ct), para 1040
	£1,150	Male/35	*Nolan v Pearson* (Liverpool County Ct), para 988
	£600	Male/14	*C (A Child) v Western* (Telford County Ct), para 989
Neck and back	£6,500	Male/25	*Gapper v Taviner* (Blackwood County Ct), para 991
	£5,000	Male/34	*Kalhar v Galatola* (Slough County Ct), para 992
	£2,500	Male/46	*Allen v Naeem* (Birkenhead County Ct), para 993

Quantum of Damages Table

INJURY	PSLA	SEX/AGE	CITATION & REVIEW PARA NUMBER
	£2,500	Female/14	*A (A Child) v Humphreys* (Edmonton County Ct), para 994
	£2,500	Male/36	*Towns v Morley* (Oldham County Ct), para 995
	£1,650	Male/12	*J (A Child) v Liu* (Medway County Ct), para 996
	£1,500	Female/41	*Keyte v Wheeler* (Ilford County Ct), para 997
Shoulder	£40,000	Male/18	*Madden v Ross* (Bodmin County Ct), para 957
	£6,500	Male/25	*Gapper v Taviner* (Blackwood County Ct), para 991
	£3,000	Female/7	*D (A Child) v Lavers* (Staines County Ct), para 998
Back	£14,500	Female/25	*Lane v Laing Construction Ltd* (Milton Keynes County Ct), para 1000
	£11,000	Female/36	*Shaw v Travel West Midlands* (Birmingham County Ct), para 1001
	£10,000	Female/33	*Sheath v GE Capital Fleet Services* (Oxford County Ct), para 1002
	£3,000	Female/12	*M (A Child) v Rhoden* (Birmingham County Ct), para 1003
	£2,650	Female/32	*Jacobs v Hodgson* (Leeds County Ct), para 1004
	£2,250	Male/41	*White v Birmingham City C* (Birmingham County Ct), para 1005
	£2,000	Male/13	*B (A Child) v Heath* (Coventry County Ct), para 1006
	£1,600	Male/38	*Lukhat v Grote* (Bolton County Ct), para 1007
	£1,250	Female/15	*G (A Child) v Kahzaei* (Wolverhampton County Ct), para 1009
	£1,250	Female/5	*L (A Child) v Woodburn* (Skipton County Ct), para 1008
Chest	£3,100	Female/36	*Carr v Midlands Counties Heating Services Ltd* (Birmingham County Ct), para 1010
Arm	£15,250	Male/31	*Hirons v Kraft Foods plc* (Oxford County Ct), para 1011
	£3,500	Male/22	*Sutton v Bridgend CBC* (Bridgend County Ct), para 1012
	£2,150	Female/1	*B (A Child) v Maidstone & Tunbridge Wells NHS Trust* (Tunbridge Wells County Ct), para 1013
Elbow	£15,250	Male/31	*Hirons v Kraft Foods plc* (Oxford County Ct), para 1011

Quantum of Damages Table

INJURY	PSLA	SEX/AGE	CITATION & REVIEW PARA NUMBER
	£3,650	Male/6	*R (A Child) v Barratt Developments plc* (Portsmouth County Ct), para 1014
	£1,500	Male/55	*Rigby v MFI UK Ltd* (Leeds County Ct), para 1018
Hand	£4,000	Male/57	*Slade v Corus (UK) Ltd* (Cardiff County Ct), para 1016
	£3,000	Male/52	*Dent v Corus (UK) Ltd* (Cardiff County Ct), para 1017
Thumb	£10,500	Female/26	*Shaw v Barber* (Bradford County Ct), para 1019
	£4,500	Female/42	*Pearson v Snax 24 Ltd* (Birmingham County Ct), para 1020
Leg	£70,000	Male/16	*Pimm v Paull* (settled out of court), para 1021
	£15,000	Male/6	*M (A Child) v Brown* (Birmingham County Ct), para 1022
	£4,000	Female/1	*B (A Child) v Connaught Cleaning Services* (Portsmouth County Ct), para 1023
Knee	£42,000	Female/25	*Sale v Sale,* (Cardiff County Ct), para 1024
	£8,000	Male/50	*Cavaney v Oakwood Leisure Ltd* (Swansea County Ct), para 1024
	£5,750	Male/46	*Tinkler v Siemens plc* (Birmingham County Ct), para 1026
Ankle	£5,750	Male/34	*Creed v Somerfield Stores Ltd* (Blackwood County Ct), para 1029
	£3,500	Female/10	*L (A Child) v Walsall MBC* (Birmingham County Ct), para 1030
	£3,250	Male/41	*Kenyon v Masters* (Birmingham County Ct), para 1031
	£2,500	Female/31	*Layland v Creative Print and Design Ltd* (Cardiff County Ct), para 1032
Foot	£4,000	Female/4	*L (A Child) v The Royal Wolverhampton NHS Trust* (Birmingham County Ct), para 974
	£2,000	Male/40	*O'Gorman v Bridgend CC* (Neath County Ct), para 1027
Toe	£6,000	Female/30	*Evans v Turner (t/a Able Van Hire)* (Doncaster County Ct), para 1033
Minor injuries	£2,700	Female/9	*V (A Child) v Ward* (Doncaster County Ct), para 1035

INJURY	PSLA	SEX/AGE	CITATION & REVIEW PARA NUMBER
	£2,500	Male/41	*Wakefield v Centrica plc* (Manchester County Ct), para 1036
	£2,500	Male/46	*Jones v Fletcher* (Bradford County Ct), para 1037
	£2,250	Female/13	*M (A Child) v Savill* (Edmonton County Ct), para 1038
	(1) £1,800	Female/8	*I (A Child) v Richardson*
	(2) £1,500	Male/6	(Huddersfield County Ct),
	(3) £1,200	Male/2	para 1034
	£1,700	Female/35	*Gagliardi v Makolli* (Manchester County Ct), para 1039
	£1,500	Male/4	*B (A Child) v Martin* (Cambridge County Ct), para 1040
	£1,300	Female/10	*S (A Child) v Blaney* (Edmonton County Ct), para 1041
	£1,300	Female/43	*Hillary v Arriva Trains Northern Ltd* (Newcastle County Ct), para 1042
	£1,100	Male/10	*L (A Child) v Murt* (Birkenhead County Ct), para 1043
	£1,000	Male/39	*Hardy v Johnson* (Manchester County Ct), para 1044
	£1,000	Female/5	*D (A Child) v Wicksteed Park Ltd* (Walsall County Ct), para 1045
	£800	Male/4	*W (A Child) v Hinton* (Walsall County Ct), para 1046

TABLE OF ARTICLES

What's the Point? Jeremy Nixon and Jonathan Goldsworthy (on the points-based immigration system for employees): 156 NLJ 577

BUILDING

Don't Be Alarmed by New Rules, Trevor Dean (on the Regulatory Reform (Fire Safety) Order 2005, SI 2005/1541 (2005 Abr para 1634)): [2006] 16 EG 144

High Energy, Andy Sloan (on the energy performance of buildings): 150 Sol Jo 390

BUILDING CONTRACTS, ARCHITECTS, ENGINEERS, VALUERS AND SURVEYORS

The Architect, the Banker, his Wife and the Adjudicator: Construction and the Changing Law of Unfair Contract Terms, Philip Britton: (2006) 22 Const LJ 23

Bitter-sweet Relations, Anna Robin (on construction industry payment practices): 156 NLJ 821

Constructive Criticism, Rupert Choat (on the Housing Grants, Construction and Regeneration Act 1996 (1996 Abr para 1559)): 156 NLJ 438

Courts v Construction: Accrual of a Cause of Action for Payment in Engineering Contracts, Wendy MacLaughlin: (2006) 22 Const LJ 445

Don't Pay the Penalty, James Levy (on liquidated damages clauses in building contracts): [2006] 22 EG 171

Freedom of Information: The New Law, Richard Honey (on the Freedom of Information Act 2000 (2000 Abr para 636)): (2006) 22 Const LJ 515

Into Extra Time and Out of Pocket, Jane Ryland (on the procurement and delivery methods of the 2012 Olympics): 156 NLJ 1494

Proper Jurisdiction, Stuart Pemble and Ruth Phillips (on *Carillion Construction Ltd v Devonport Royal Dockyard Ltd* [2005] EWCA Civ 1358, (2005) 104 BLR 1): [2006] 16 EG 141

Terminate with Extreme Prejudice, Nicholas Scott (on *Dalkia Utilities Services plc v Celtech International Ltd* [2006] EWHC 63 (Comm), [2006] 2 P & CR 173): 156 NLJ 872

A Test of Impartiality and Independence, Nicholas Cheffings (on the use of surveyors as experts): [2006] 10 EG 145

Third Way, Francis Ho (on the use of the Contracts (Rights of Third Parties) Act 1999 in the construction industry): 150 Sol Jo 150

Time and Loss and Expense in the Major Project Form: A Commentary, Nicholas Lane: (2006) 22 Const LJ 3

Value Judgment, Daniel Atkinson (on *ERDC Group Ltd v Brunel University* [2006] EWHC 687 (TCC), [2006] BLR 255, DC): 156 NLJ 1045

CAPITAL GAINS TAXATION

Balloons, Pizzas, Cats, Dogs & Rats, Patrick Cannon (on *Balloon Promotions Ltd v Wilson* (*Inspector of Taxes*) (3 March 2006, unreported)): Tax J, Issue 842, p 15

Industrial Buildings Allowances, Martin Wilson and Steven Bone: Tax J, Issue 853, p 13

The Ramsay Principle and Capital Loss Schemes, Sharon Anstey: [2006] PCB 10

Wood v Holden, John Carrell (on *Wood v Holden* [2006] EWCA Civ 26, [2006] 1 WLR 1393 (para 400)): Tax J, Issue 845, p 9

CARRIERS

The Rule Against Deduction from Freight Reconsidered, J C Sheppard: [2006] JBL 1

CHARITIES

Charitable Donation or Distribution? Maurice Parry-Wingfield (on *Noved Investment Co v Customs and Excise Comrs* (unreported)): Tax J, Issue 827, p 11

Charities and their Donors, Maurice Parry-Wingfield (on the Finance Act 2006): Tax J, Issue 850, p 9, Issue 851, p 5

Charity Members: Duties and Responsibilities, Jean Warburton: [2006] Conv 330

Charity's New Look, Douglas Cracknell (on the Charities Bill): 150 Sol Jo 684

Dispositions of Charitable Land, David Dennis: [2006] Conv 219

Formulating an Estate Strategy, James Spreckley and Stephen Claus (on the pitfalls for charities involved in property sales and development projects): New Law Journal Charities Appeal Supplement, 2006, p 20

Guard Against Fraud, Nick Sladden: New Law Journal Charities Appeal Supplement, 2006, p 32

Horses for Courses, Stephen Lloyd and Abbie Rumbold (on community interest companies and charitable incorporated organisations): New Law Journal Charities Appeal Supplement 2006, p 28

Legalising the London Marathon, Nick Bitel: New Law Journal Charities Appeal Supplement 2006, p 38

Looking After One's Own, Michael Hicks (on intellectual property rights held by charities and not-for-profit organisations): New Law Journal Charities Appeal Supplement 2006, p 20

Making Things Interesting, Trevor James (on charities' annual reports and trustees' annual reports): New Law Journal Charities Appeal Supplement 2006, p 24

CHILDREN AND YOUNG PERSONS

CIVIL PARTNERSHIP

CLUBS

COMPULSORY ACQUISITION OF LAND

COMPUTERS AND INFORMATION TECHNOLOGY

CONFIDENCE AND DATA PROTECTION

CONFLICT OF LAWS

CONSTITUTIONAL LAW

CORONERS

COSTS

COURTS

CRIMINAL EVIDENCE AND PROCEDURE

CRIMINAL LAW

CUSTOMS AND EXCISE

DAMAGES AND COMPENSATION

DISCRIMINATION

EQUITY

ESTOPPEL

EUROPEAN COMMUNITIES

EVIDENCE [CIVIL]

EXECUTORS AND ADMINISTRATORS

EXTRADITION

FINANCIAL SERVICES

FIRE SERVICES

FISHERIES

FOOD

FOREIGN RELATIONS LAW

FUEL AND ENERGY

GIFTS

GUARANTEE AND INDEMNITY

HEALTH AND SAFETY AT WORK

INCOME TAXATION

INHERITANCE TAX

INJUNCTIONS

INNS AND INNKEEPERS

INSURANCE

INTOXICATING LIQUOR

JURIES

LAND REGISTRATION

LANDLORD AND TENANT

LEGAL AID

NORTHERN IRELAND

NOTARIES

NUISANCE

OPEN SPACE AND ANCIENT MONUMENTS

PARLIAMENT

PARTNERSHIP

PATENTS AND REGISTERED DESIGN

PENSIONS AND SUPERANNUATION

PRESS, PRINTING AND PUBLISHING

PRISONS

PROTECTION OF ENVIRONMENT AND PUBLIC HEALTH

RAILWAYS, INLAND WATERWAYS AND PIPELINES

RATING AND COUNCIL TAX

REAL PROPERTY

TRADE, INDUSTRY AND INDUSTRIAL RELATIONS

TRADE MARKS AND TRADE NAMES

WAR AND ARMED CONFLICT

WATER

WILLS

Annual Abridgment 2006

ADMINISTRATIVE LAW

Halsbury's Laws of England (4th edn) vol 1(1) (2001 Reissue) paras 1–300

Articles

For articles relating to this title please refer to the Table of Articles at the beginning of the Abridgment.

1   Habeas corpus—application—sending of accused to Crown Court for trial—effective sending—remand in custody

See *R (on the application of Bentham) v Governor of HM Prison Wandsworth*, para 839.

2   Inquiries—evidence and procedure

The Inquiry Rules 2006, SI 2006/1838 (in force on 1 August 2006), deal with matters of evidence and procedure in relation to inquiries, the return or keeping after the end of an inquiry of documents given to or created by the inquiry and awards made by the chairman. In particular, the rules (1) deal with the designation of core participants by the chairman; (2) as a recognised legal representative, deal with the designation of a lawyer appointed by a core participant or a witness; (3) set out the circumstances in which one recognised legal representative should be appointed to represent two or more core participants; (4) are concerned with the collection of evidence by an inquiry panel and the conduct of any oral hearings that are held; (5) permit the recognised legal representative of a core participant to make opening and closing statements; (6) provide that, where there is an application that evidence should be withheld from the public domain by virtue of a restriction order, restriction notice or on grounds of public interest immunity, that evidence must be subject to the same restrictions as it would be subject to if the order sought had been granted, except that the chairman may show the evidence to another individual where he considers that disclosure is necessary for the determination of the application; (7) deal with the sending of warning letters to those who may be, or have been, criticised during inquiry proceedings or in an inquiry report or any interim report; (8) provide for the delivery of copies of any report which is to be published to core participants following delivery to the minister; (9) set out the chairman's records management obligations during an inquiry and provide for the transfer of custody of an inquiry record at the end of an inquiry; and (10) set out rules regarding the making and assessment of awards.

3   Judicial review—child in custody—local authority's duty to provide accommodation

See *R (on the application of M) v Gateshead Council*, para 435.

4   Judicial review—decision of asylum support adjudicator—refusal of asylum support

See *R (on the application of the Secretary of State for the Home Department) v Asylum Support Adjudicator*, para 337.

5   Judicial review—decision of Central Criminal Court—refusal to hear bail application in public

See *R (on the application of Malik) v Central Criminal Court*, para 106.

6   Judicial review—decision of Chief Asylum Support Adjudicator—hearing of asylum support appeal—failed asylum-seeker

See *R (on the application of the Secretary of State for the Home Department) v Chief Asylum Support Adjudicator*, para 336.

7   Judicial review—decision of chief constable—continuance criminal investigation

See *R (on the application of C) v Chief Constable of 'A' Police*, para 757.

8   Judicial review—decision of Civil Aviation Authority—issue of advice to air travel organisers

See *R (on the application of the Association of British Travel Agents Ltd) v Civil Aviation Authority*, para 266.

9   Judicial review—decision of commissioner of British overseas territory—order for removal of indigenous population

See *R (on the application of Bancoult) v Secretary of State for Foreign and Commonwealth Affairs*, para 509.

10   Judicial review—decision of Competition Commission—extent of Commission's power

See *Stericycle International LLC v Competition Commission*, para 2826.

11   Judicial review—decision of coroner—direction to jury—shooting by state agent—test for self-defence

See *R (on the application of Bennett) v Inner South London Coroner*, para 869.

12   Judicial review—decision of costs judge—failure to undertake detailed assessment of work done by attorney

See *R (on the application of Brewer) v Supreme Court Costs Office*, para 755.

13   Judicial review—decision of county court—refusal to vary or discharge restraining order—jurisdiction of Crown Court to hear appeal

See *R (on the application of Lee) v Crown Court at Leeds*, para 2563.

14   Judicial review—decision of court office—rejection of notice of appeal—time limits

See *R (on the application of Amoako) v DPP*, para 1313.

15   Judicial review—decision of Criminal Cases Review Commission—decision to refer cases to the Court of Appeal

See *R (on the application of Director of Revenue and Customs Prosecutions) v Criminal Cases Review Commission*, para 745.

16   Judicial review—decision of Criminal Injuries Compensation Appeals Panel—refusal of claim

See *R (on the application of M) v Criminal Injuries Compensation Appeals Panel*, para 852.

17   Judicial review—decision of Crown Court—extension of custody time limits

See *R (on the application of Thomas) v Central Criminal Court; R (on the application of Stubbs) v Central Criminal Court*, para 767.

18   Judicial review—decision of Crown Court—matter relating to trial on indictment— detention of witness

See *R (on the application of TH) v Crown Court at Wood Green*, para 752.

19   Judicial review—decision of Crown Court—refusal of bail—16-year-old offender— remand to young offender institution

See *R (on the application of M) v Crown Court at Inner London*, para 2365.

20   Judicial review—decision of Crown Prosecution Service—obligation of Director of Public Prosecutions to consider prosecution

See *R (on the application of Dennis) v DPP*, para 906.

21   Judicial review—decision of Department for Constitutional Affairs—refusal of leave to institute proceedings without oral hearing—vexatious litigant

See *R (on the application of Ewing) v Department for Constitutional Affairs*, para 2326.

22   Judicial review—decision of Department for Environment, Food and Rural Affairs— carbon dioxide emissions—allocation of allowances

See *R (on the application of Cemex UK Cement Ltd) v Department for Environment Food and Rural Affairs*, para 2394.

23   Judicial review—decision of Director of Serious Fraud Office—refusal to open investigation—power to determine forum—human rights

See *R (on the application of Bermingham) v Director of the Serious Fraud Office; Bermingham v Government of the United States of America*, para 1321.

24 Judicial review—decision of district judge—imposition of anti-social behaviour order—likelihood of causing harassment, alarm or distress

See *R (on the application of Gosport BC) v Fareham Magistrates' Court*, para 2526.

25 Judicial review—decision of doctor—medical treatment for mental disorder—treatment without consent

See *R (on the application of B) v Haddock*, para 1982.

26 Judicial review—decision of Environment Agency—liability for remediating contaminated land—successor to actual contaminator

See *R (on the application of National Grid Gas plc) v Environment Agency*, para 2369.

27 Judicial review—decision of executive—invasion of foreign territory—lawfulness

See *R (on the application of Gentle) v Prime Minister*, para 1536.

28 Judicial review—decision of justices—failure of child to attend school—prosecution of parent—burden of proof

See *R (on the application of P) v Liverpool City Magistrates*, para 1140.

29 Judicial review—decision of justices—failure to serve required notice—abuse of process

See *R (on the application of the Crown Prosecution Service) v City of London Magistrates' Court*, para 1877.

30 Judicial review—decision of licensing authority—application to vary opening hours

See *R (on the application of JD Wetherspoon plc) v Guildford BC*, para 1735.

31 Judicial review—decision of local authority—possession proceedings—eviction of travellers from unauthorised encampments

See *R (on the application of Casey) v Crawley BC*, para 1620.

32 Judicial review—decision of local authority—refusal to provide accommodation—asylum-seeker

See *R (on the application of B) v Southwark LBC*, para 334.

33 Judicial review—decision of local authority—refusal to provide accommodation—person in need of care and attention—asylum-seeker

See *R (on the application of M) v Slough BC*, para 2699.

34 Judicial review—decision of local authority—transfer of care homes to private sector operator

See *R (on the application of Johnson) v Havering LBC*, para 1534.

35 Judicial review—decision of local commissioner—refusal to exercise discretion to conduct investigation

See *R (on the application of M) v Comr for Local Administration in England*, para 1856.

36 Judicial review—decision of local education authority—re-organisation of school structure—consultation

See *R (on the application of Parents for Legal Action Ltd) v Northumberland CC*, para 1129.

37 Judicial review—decision of local housing authority—refusal to provide accommodation—homeless child

See *R (on the application of M) v Hammersmith and Fulham LBC*, para 1481.

38 Judicial review—decision of local housing authority—refusal to provide accommodation—intentionally homeless person

See *R (on the application of Conville) v Richmond upon Thames LBC*, para 1484.

39 Judicial review—decision of local housing authority—refusal to provide accommodation—person subject to immigration control

See *R (on the application of PB) v Haringey LBC*, para 1490.

40   Judicial review—decision of local housing authority—unilateral variation of secure tenancy agreement

See *R (on the application of Kilby) v Basildon DC*, para 1776.

41   Judicial review—decision of local planning authority—outline planning permission—environmental impact assessment

See *R (on the application of Barker) v Bromley LBC*, para 2787.

42   Judicial review—decision of magistrates' court—justices informed of defendant's previous convictions

See *R (on the application of Murchison) v Southend Magistrates' Court*, para 1879.

43   Judicial review—decision of magistrates' court—private prosecution

See *R (on the application of Charlson) v Guildford Magistrates' Court*, para 1871.

44   Judical review—decision of Metropolitan Police Commissioner—stop and search authorisations

See *R (on the application of Gillan) v Metropolitan Police Comr*, para 892.

45   Judicial review—decision of National Health Service trust—lack of consultation—closure of in-patient wards

See *R (on the application of Morris) v Trafford Healthcare NHS Trust*, para 2054.

46   Judicial review—decision of National Health Service trust—mental health patient—leave of absence from hospital

See *R (on the application of K) v West London Mental Health NHS Trust*, para 1979.

47   Judicial review—decision of panel of Parole Board—exclusion of prisoner from part of hearing—fairness of hearing

See *R (on the application of Gardner) v Parole Board*, para 2358.

48   Judicial review—decision of Parole Board—review of young offender's sentence—adult assistance

See *R (on the application of K) v Parole Board*, para 2352.

49   Judicial review—decision of planning authority—permitted development

See *R (on the application of Orange Personal Communications Services Ltd) v Islington LBC*, para 2793.

50   Judicial review—decision of police—anti-social behaviour—direction to disperse

See *R (on the application of Singh) v Chief Constable of West Midlands Police*, para 875.

51   Judicial review—decision of police commissioner—authorisation to remove child forcibly from dispersal area

See *R (on the application of W) v Metropolitan Police Comr*, para 874.

52   Judicial review—decision of Police Medical Appeal Board—member of police force—permanent disablement

See *R (on the application of Corkindale) v Police Medical Appeal Board*, para 2261.

53   Judicial review—decision of police officer—caution for possession of drugs

See *R (on the application of Mondelly) v Metropolitan Police Comr*, para 747.

54   Judicial review—decision of police officer—preventing breach of the peace—anti-war demonstration—power to prevent access to site

See *R (on the application of Laporte) v Chief Constable of Gloucestershire Constabulary*, para 2255.

55   Judicial review—decision of primary care trust—appointment of body to provide health services—failure to consult

See *R (on the application of Smith) v North Eastern Derbyshire Primary Care Trust*, para 2054.

56   Judicial review—decision of primary care trust—refusal to fund treatment using unlicensed drug

See *R (on the application of Rogers) v Swindon NHS Primary Care Trust*, para 2050.

57 Judicial review—decision of primary care trust—removal of doctor from performers list—procedure

See *R (on the application of S) v Knowsley NHS Primary Care Trust*, para 2049.

58 Judicial review—decision of primary care trust—suspension of medical practitioner—procedural requirements

See *R (on the application of Malik) v Waltham Forest Primary Care Trust*, para 1596.

59 Judicial review—decision of prison governor—release of prisoner on licence—administrative error

See *R (on the application of Lunn) v Governor of Moorland Prison*, para 2362.

60 Judicial review—decision of rail regulator—grant of track access rights

See *R (on the application of Great North Eastern Railway Ltd) v Office of Rail Regulation*, para 2430.

61 Judicial review—decision of recorder—reduction in costs of successful litigant

See *R (on the application of Galandauer) v Crown Court at Snaresbrook*, para 754.

62 Judicial review—decision of responsible medical officer—compulsory treatment of mentally ill patient

See *R (on the application of B) v S*, para 1981.

63 Judicial review—decision of returning officer in local election—rejection of candidate's nomination

See *R (on the application of Begum) v Tower Hamlets LBC*, para 1187.

64 Judicial review—decision of Secretary of State for Defence—imprisonment during war—applicable law

See *R (on the application of Al-Jedda) v Secretary of State for Defence*, para 1581.

65 Judicial review—decision of Secretary of State for Defence—prisoner of war compensation scheme—refusal to make payment

See *R (on the application of Elias) v Secretary of State for Defence*, para 2947.

66 Judicial review—decision of Secretary of State for Defence—protection of military remains—refusal to designate vessel

See *R (on the application of Fogg) v Secretary of State for Defence*, para 256.

67 Judicial review—decision of Secretary of State for the Environment, Food and Rural Affairs—public path extinguishment order—confirmation—refusal

See *R (on the application of Hertfordshire CC) v Secretary of State for Environment, Food and Rural Affairs*, para 1468.

68 Judicial review—decision of Secretary of State for the Foreign and Commonwealth Affairs—applicants detained by foreign state—refusal to request return of applicants

See *R (on the application of Al Rawi) v Secretary of State for Foreign and Commonwealth Affairs*, para 96.

69 Judicial review—decision of Secretary of State for Health—disclosure of unproven complaints against doctor

See *R (on the application of Dr D) v Secretary of State for Health*, para 1935.

70 Judicial review—decision of Secretary of State for Health—medical guidance—minors—advice and treatment on sexual matters

See *R (on the application of Axon) v Secretary of State for Health*, para 1949.

71 Judicial review—decision of Secretary of State for Health—vulnerable adults—care workers—allegation of misconduct

See *R (on the application of Wright) v Secretary of State for Health*, para 2710.

72 Judicial review—decision of Secretary of State for the Home Department—asylum-seeker—leave to remain in United Kingdom—revised policy—fairness

See *R (on the application of Rechachi) v Secretary of State for the Home Department*, para 333.

73   Judicial review—decision of Secretary of State for the Home Department— asylum-seeker—removal to safe third country—delay—right to family life

See *R (on the application of AA) (Afghanistan) v Secretary of State for the Home Department*, para 1600.

74   Judicial review—decision of Secretary of State for the Home Department—death of juvenile in custody—refusal to hold public inquiry

See *R (on the application of Scholes) v Secretary of State for the Home Department*, para 1587.

75   Judicial review—decision of Secretary of State for the Home Department—deportation of foreign prisoner

See *R (on the application of Christian) v Secretary of State for the Home Department*, para 2353.

76   Judicial review—decision of Secretary of State for the Home Department—designation of territory for extradition purposes—refusal to redesignate territory

See *R (on the application of Oliver) v Secretary of State for the Home Department*, para 1311.

77   Judicial review—decision of Secretary of State for the Home Department— discretionary immigration policy

See *S v Secretary of State for the Home Department*, para 346.

78   Judicial review—decision of Secretary of State for the Home Department—extradition— designation of category 2 territory

See *R (on the application of Norris) v Secretary of State for the Home Department*, para 1324.

79   Judicial review—decision of Secretary of State for the Home Department—inquiry into attempted suicide of prisoner—procedural requirements

See *R (on the application of D) v Secretary of State for the Home Department*, para 1586.

80   Judicial review—decision of Secretary of State for the Home Department—mental patient—recall to hospital

See *R (on the application of MM) v Secretary of State for the Home Department*, para 1978.

81   Judicial review—decision of Secretary of State for the Home Department—nomination of court to receive evidence requested by overseas authority

See *R (on the application of Hafner) v Secretary of State for the Home Department*, para 798.

82   Judicial review—decision of Secretary of State for the Home Department—person subject to immigration control—approval to marry

See *R (on the application of Baiai) v Secretary of State for the Home Department*, para 379.

83   Judicial review—decision of Secretary of State for the Home Department—recall to custody of prisoner on home detention curfew

See *R (on the application of Ramsden) v Secretary of State for the Home Department; R (on the application of Naylor) v Secretary of State for the Home Department*, para 2356.

84   Judicial review—decision of Secretary of State for the Home Department—recall to custody of prisoner on parole—failure to give reasons promptly

See *R (on the application of Hirst) v Secretary of State for the Home Department*, para 2359.

85   Judicial review—decision of Secretary of State for the Home Department—refusal of asylum—EC Association Agreement

See *R (on the application of Temiz) v Secretary of State for the Home Department*, para 369.

86   Judicial review—decision of Secretary of State for the Home Department—refusal of asylum—prior application in another member state

See *R (on the application of A) v Secretary of State for the Home Department*, para 330.

87   Judicial review—decision of Secretary of State for the Home Department—refusal to correct criminal records certificate

See *R (on the application of B) v Secretary of State for the Home Department*, para 763.

88   Judicial review—decision of Secretary of State for the Home Department—withdrawal of accommodation support

See *R (on the application of Rasul) v Asylum Support Adjudicator*, para 335.

89   Judicial review—decision of specialist training authority—application for inclusion on register of medical consultants

See *Malone v Specialist Training Authority of the Medical Royal Colleges*, para 1940.

90   Judicial review—decision of Treasury—refusal of social security benefit—spouse of person designated by United Nations Sanctions Committee

See *R (on the application of M) v HM Treasury*, para 2616.

91   Judicial review—decision of trial judge—criminal proceedings—refusal to grant bail

See *R (on the application of O) v Crown Court at Harrow; Re O (habeas corpus)*, para 1583.

92   Judicial review—jurisdiction—Court of Session—applicant located in Scotland and decision-maker located in England

Scotland
The claimant was a citizen of Iran who arrived in the United Kingdom and claimed asylum. After being temporarily housed, he was allocated more permanent accommodation in Glasgow. The Secretary of State refused his asylum application and his appeal against that refusal was dismissed by an adjudicator. The claimant's application for leave to appeal to the Immigration Appeal Tribunal was refused by the tribunal. The claimant presented an application for judicial review by the Court of Session of the determination of the adjudicator and the Immigration Appeal Tribunal. The impugned decisions were made under the Immigration and Asylum Act 1999, which extended to the whole of the United Kingdom. The Secretary of State took a preliminary plea of no jurisdiction on the ground that the hearings before the adjudicator and the Immigration Appeal Tribunal, and the determinations they made, were in England. The plea of no jurisdiction was sustained and the application was dismissed. The claimant appealed, contending that the Court of Session had concurrent jurisdiction with the High Court in England over determinations made by an adjudicator and the Immigration Appeal Tribunal. *Held*, the Court of Session had jurisdiction in the proceedings at common law. Provided that an application to the supervisory jurisdiction was competent and the Court of Session had jurisdiction over the exercise of the power that had been given to it by the decision maker, the court was bound to entertain the application. The mere fact that it had a supervisory jurisdiction which it shared with courts in other parts of the United Kingdom did not provide the Court of Session with a discretion as to whether it should exercise its jurisdiction when a claimant who could establish that it had jurisdiction to provide him with a remedy called on it to do so. For the supervisory jurisdiction to be exercised there had to be some connection between Scotland, within which the functions of the Court of Session as the Supreme Court were exercised, and the power or jurisdiction conferred on the decision maker. As a general rule the Court of Session had power to intervene where the excess or abuse of power gave rise to a wrong done or harm suffered in Scotland, but it could only do so in the case of a statutory tribunal which exercised its functions in Scotland or whose proceedings were governed by Scottish law. Accordingly, the appeal would be allowed.
Tehrani v Secretary of State for the Home Department (Scotland) [2006] UKHL 47, [2006] 1 All ER 559 (House of Lords: Lords Nicholls of Birkenhead, Hope of Craighead, Scott of Foscote, Rodger of Earlsferry and Carswell). Decision of Inner House 2004 SLT 97 (2004 Abr para 68) reversed.

93   Judicial review—jurisdiction—High Court—matter relating to trial on indictment

See *R (on the application of TH) v Crown Court at Wood Green*, para 752.

94   Judicial review—jurisdiction—liability order for child support—appeal

See *Giltinane v Child Support Agency*, para 440.

95   Judicial review—new legislation to replace existing legislation—failure to implement new legislation on repeal of existing legislation

See *R (on the application of the Crown Prosecution Service) v Bow Street Magistrates' Court*, para 2733.

96   Judicial review—principle of non-justiciability—act of foreign state—decision by Secretary of State not to intervene

The applicants were detained at a military detention camp by United States authorities. None of the applicants was a British national but they were all long-term residents of the United Kingdom where two of them had been granted asylum. The Secretary of State had made a formal request for the return to the United Kingdom of British nationals detained at the camp but had refused to make such a request for the return of the applicants. The Secretary of State considered that he was under no obligation to do so because the applicants were not United Kingdom nationals and that such a request would be counter-productive. The applicants sought judicial review of the Secretary of State's decision. *Held*, even where the arguments were made in the context of political debate, relief could be granted in restricted terms, such as requiring the Secretary of State to reconsider his decision, if he appeared to have failed to take into account any relevant material or where he had made an error of law. Nevertheless, the court could not require the Secretary of State to make a formal request. That would be an interference in the relationship between sovereign states which could only be justified if a clear duty in domestic or international law had been identified. There was a proper basis for making a distinction between British nationals and long-term residents who were not British nationals. Further, as the United Kingdom had never considered that the Refugee Convention imposed on it a like obligation in relation to consular assistance that it owed to British nationals, that could not be relied on by those applicants who had refugee status. International rights were not simply rights among nations generally, but also rights given by treaty or convention by one state to another which, in the case of the consular Convention between the United Kingdom and the United States of America was only concerned with nationals. Even if torture or a real risk of torture was established on the evidence, that would impose no duty on the United Kingdom government to do anything other than co-operate with other states to bring to an end through lawful means the circumstances which gave rise to that situation. International law imposed no further duty on an individual state to intervene, and the European Convention on Human Rights did not assist the applicants in that respect. The decisions made by the Secretary of State were quintessentially judgments taken in the context of a foreign policy decision which the court simply did not have the tools to evaluate. Accordingly, the applications would be dismissed.

R (on the application of Al Rawi) v Secretary of State for Foreign and Commonwealth Affairs [2006] EWHC 972 (Admin), [2006] All ER (D) 46 (May) (Queen's Bench Division: Latham LJ and Tugendhat J). *R v Jones; Ayliffe v DPP; Swain v DPP* [2006] UKHL 16, [2006] 2 All ER 741 (para 854) considered.

97   Legislative and Regulatory Reform Act 2006

The Legislative and Regulatory Reform Act 2006 enables provision to be made for the purpose of removing or reducing burdens resulting from legislation and promoting regulatory principles, makes provision in relation to the exercise of regulatory functions, and makes provision in relation to the interpretation of legislation relating to the European Communities and the European Economic Area. The Act received the royal assent on 8 November 2006 and came into force on 8 January 2007.

Part 1 (ss 1–20) Order-making powers
Sections 1, 2 provide powers for a minister of the Crown to make orders to remove or reduce burdens resulting from legislation and to promote regulatory principles. 'Burden' is defined by s 1 as a financial cost, an administrative inconvenience, an obstacle to efficiency, productivity or profitability, or a sanction, criminal or otherwise, which affects the carrying on of any lawful activity. The regulatory principles are that regulated activities should be carried out in a way which is transparent, accountable, proportionate and consistent, and should be targeted only at cases in which action is needed, and an order to promote regulatory principles may include provision which modifies the way in which a regulatory function is exercised by any person, amends the constitution of a body exercising regulatory functions which is established by or under an enactment, transfers, or provides for the delegation of, regulatory functions from one person to another, and amends or repeals any enactment: s 2. Section 3 sets out preconditions which a minister must consider before making an order containing provision under s 1 or 2. Section 4 provides that a function of legislating can only be conferred on or transferred to a minister, any person on or to whom functions are conferred or have been transferred by an enactment, such as a local authority or regulatory body, or a body which, or the holder of an office which, is created by the order. An order may not impose, abolish or vary any tax: s 5. The maximum penalties which may apply to a new offence created by an order or which may be applied to an existing offence by an order are specified by s 6. Section 7 prevents an order from making provision authorising forcible entry, search or seizure, or compelling the giving of evidence, although such a restriction does not apply to provision which is merely restating an enactment. By virtue of s 8, orders cannot make provision amending or repealing any provision of Pt 1 itself, or of the Human Rights Act 1998. The 2006 Act s 9 relates to Scotland and s 10 relates to Northern Ireland. Section 11 requires the agreement of the National Assembly for Wales for any provision in an order which confers a function on the Assembly, or modifies or removes a function of the Assembly. Section 12 provides that an order must be made by statutory instrument and that the minister must comply with the requirements of ss 13–18. Section 13 requires a minister to consult on his proposals for an order and s 14 requires him to lay a draft of the order and an explanatory document before Parliament. Section 15 sets out the procedure for determining whether the parliamentary procedure applicable to the order is to be the negative resolution procedure detailed in s 16, the affirmative resolution procedure detailed in s 17, or the super-affirmative resolution procedure detailed in s 18. The negative resolution procedure is where a minister may make an order in the terms of the draft he lays before Parliament, unless, within 40 days of the draft order being laid, either House of Parliament passes a resolution that the order may not be made. The affirmative resolution procedure is where a minister makes an order in the terms of the draft only if, after 40 days of the draft order being laid before Parliament, the draft order is approved by a resolution of each House of Parliament. The super-affirmative resolution procedure is a two-stage procedure during which there is an opportunity for the draft order to be revised by the

minister. Section 19 provides for the calculation of time periods in relation to the procedure for resolutions in which the Houses of Parliament must resolve, and s 20 enables the order-making powers to be exercise together with the order-making powers under the European Communities Act 1972.

Part 2 (ss 21–24) Regulators
The 2006 Act s 21 sets out principles to which a person must have regard when exercising certain regulatory functions. A minister is able to issue and revise a code of practice to the exercise of regulatory functions: s 22. Section 23 sets out the procedure which the minister must follow when he proposes to revise a code of practice. Section 24 makes provision for orders to specify the regulatory functions to which the duties in ss 21, 22 apply.

Part 3 (ss 25–29) Legislation relating to the European Communities
Section 25 makes provision to simplify the drafting of legislation which refers to Community instruments. Section 26 sets out the purpose of the EEA agreement and provides that references to an EEA state have a standard definition. Section 27 allows the European Communities Act 1972 s 2(2) to be used in combination with delegated powers in other legislation which enable the making of orders, rules or schemes. The 2006 Act s 28 confers a power on a minister to make ambulatory references to Community instruments and s 29 makes provision to enable the power conferred by the 1972 Act s 2(2) to be combined with delegated powers in other legislation where the procedures in each case are different.

Part 4 (ss 30–35) Supplementary and general
The 2006 Act s 30 and the Schedule deal with repeals and savings and s 31 makes consequential amendments. Section 32 provides for interpretation, s 33 deals with commencement, s 34 with extent and s 35 with short title.

Amendments, repeals and revocations
The lists below, which are not exhaustive, mention amendments and repeals which are or will be effective when the Act is fully in force.

Specific provisions of a number of Acts are added and amended. These include: European Communities Act 1972 ss 1A, 2, Schs 2, 2A–2C; Interpretation Act 1978 ss 20A, 22(1), 24, Sch 1; Government of Wales Act 1998 s 29; Deregulation and Contracting Out Act 1994 s 6(7); Local Government Act 2003 s 100; and Civil Partnership Act 2004 s 35(1).

Specific provisions of a number of Acts are also repealed. These include: Regulatory Reform Act 2001 ss 1–12, 13–15 (in part); Education Act 2002 s 2(9); Human Fertilisation and Embryology (Deceased Fathers) Act 2003 s 2(2), (3); Health and Social Care (Community Health and Standards) Act 2003 s 189(4); Criminal Justice Act 2003 Sch 27 para 8; Gender Recognition Act 2004 s 24 (in part), Sch 3 para 11; Statute Laws (Repeals) Act 2004 s 1(3); Asylum and Immigration (Treatment of Claimants, etc) Act 2004 s 20(6); Railways Act 2005 Sch 3 para 14; and Wireless Telegraphy Act 2006 Sch 8 para 9.

98   Natural justice—fair hearing—application to institute proceedings—refusal of application without oral hearing—vexatious litigant

See *R (on the application of Ewing) v Department for Constitutional Affairs*, para 2326.

99   Natural justice—fair hearing—bias—apparent bias—medical member of disability appeal tribunal—previous dealings with Benefits Agency

Scotland
The claimant's application for renewal of disability living allowance was refused by a disability appeal tribunal. The claimant appealed, alleging that the medical member of the tribunal was biased because she had provided reports for the Benefits Agency as an examining medical practitioner for several years and spent the majority of her working week either examining claimants and preparing reports or sitting as a tribunal member. *Held*, there was no basis for a finding that there was a reasonable apprehension of bias on the ground that the doctor had a predisposition to favour the interests of the Agency. The common law test for bias was whether the fair-minded and informed observer, having considered the facts, would conclude that there was a real possibility that the tribunal was biased. The allegation was therefore that the doctor would not evaluate reports by other doctors who acted as examining medical practitioners objectively and impartially against the other evidence. A fair-minded observer who had considered the facts properly would appreciate that the doctor's professional detachment and ability to exercise her own independent judgment on medical issues lay at the heart of her relationship with the Agency, and would also find that she was just as capable of exercising those qualities when sitting as the medical member of a tribunal. As to the question of whether there were grounds for thinking that the doctor was unconsciously biased because of a disposition to prefer the views of other examining medical practitioners, the fair-minded observer would appreciate that the doctor's knowledge and experience would make her just as well-placed to find weaknesses as to find strengths in those practitioners' reports. There was no reason to think that she would not apply her medical knowledge and experience as impartially when sitting as a tribunal

member as when acting as an examining medical practitioner. The test for disqualification on the ground of apparent bias had not been made out and, accordingly, the appeal would be dismissed.

Gillies v Secretary of State for Work and Pensions [2006] UKHL 2, [2006] 1 All ER 731 (House of Lords: Lords Nicholls of Birkenhead, Hope of Craighead, Rodger of Earlsferry and Walker of Gestingthorpe and Baroness Hale of Richmond). *Porter v Magill* [2001] UKHL 67, [2002] 2 AC 537 (2001 Abr para 2107) applied.

100 Natural justice—fair hearing—bias—judge—recusal

An employee brought claims of race discrimination before an employment tribunal. The hearing was adjourned and, before the proceedings were resolved, the employee made a second claim, which was stayed pending the resolution of the first action. The employer made an application for the second proceedings, which was heard before the same chairman at the tribunal, to be struck out on the basis that the issues had already been determined in the first action. At a pre-hearing review of the second action, an issue arose as to whether the chairman ought to have recused himself from the hearing because of complaints against him of apparent bias in respect of the first hearing. *Held*, as a matter of policy, courts should not yield too easily to applications for recusal. Even if it was appropriate for one judge to recuse himself because of the particular nature of the complaint made, it should not become a principle that every judge had to recuse himself simply because a complaint was made. There was no distinction between a complaint that a judge or tribunal could of, and had, acted perversely in reaching an earlier decision hostile to the party making the application for recusal, and one where the complaint was of bias or misconduct in so doing. If the objection was based on whether the fair-minded observer would conclude that there was a real possibility that the tribunal would not bring objective judgment to bear then there had to be something of substance to cause that observer to reach that conclusion. It was not necessarily more likely that a judge would be decided to have a closed mind if he was accused by the party in front of him of having previously been biased, than if he was accused by that party of having made a decision which was so stupid that no reasonable person could possibly have arrived at it. In the present case, the existence and nature of the complaints did not render it necessary that the chairman should stand down or decline to hear the case. Judgment would be given accordingly.

Ansar v Lloyds TSB Bank plc (No 2) [2006] All ER (D) 277 (Jul) (Employment Appeal Tribunal: Burton J presiding).

This decision has been affirmed on appeal: [2006] EWCA Civ 1462, [2007] IRLR 211.

101 Natural justice—fair hearing—bias—judge—witness known to judge

While pre-reading a case, the judge noticed that one of the claimant's witnesses was well known to him. He alerted the parties to the fact, and the defendant applied to the judge to recuse himself. The claimant contended that the potential problem was resolved by the claimant's decision not to call the witness to give evidence. In applying the test of apparent bias, the judge balanced whether the apparent role of the witness in the case led to the risk that such a changed picture might emerge against the undoubted disruption of the administration of justice generally caused by having to find a new judge to try a case of such length at short notice, and also the inevitable further cost imposed on the parties resulting from the ensuing delay. He concluded that he should not recuse himself. The defendant appealed. *Held*, disqualification of a judge for apparent bias was not a discretionary matter. Inconvenience, costs and delay did not count in a case where the principle of judicial impartiality was properly invoked. That was because it was the fundamental principle of justice, both at common law and under the European Convention on Human Rights art 6. If, on an assessment of all the relevant circumstances, the conclusion was that the principle either had been, or would be, breached, the judge was automatically disqualified from hearing the case. In the unfortunate circumstances in which the judge had been placed, through no fault of his own, he should have recused himself. The possibility of apparent bias was not so small that the court would be justified in taking the risk of allowing the judge to try the action. By far the safer course was to remove all possibility of apparent bias by the recusal of the judge before the trial even began. Accordingly, the appeal would be allowed.

AWG Group Ltd v Morrison [2006] EWCA Civ 6, [2006] 1 All ER 967 (Court of Appeal: Mummery, Latham and Carnwath LJJ). *Locabail (UK) Ltd v Bayfield Properties Ltd* [2000] 1 All ER 65, CA (1999 Abr para 1857); *Re Medicaments and Related Classes of Goods (No 2)* [2001] 1 WLR 700 (2000 Abr para 118); *Porter v Magill; Weeks v Magill* [2001] UKHL 67, [2002] 2 AC 357 (2001 Abr para 2107); *Taylor v Lawrence* [2002] EWCA Civ 90, [2002] 2 All ER 353 (2002 Abr para 2361); and *Lawal v Northern Spirit Ltd* [2003] UKHL 35, [2004] 1 All ER 187 (2003 Abr para 64) applied.

102 Natural justice—fair hearing—bias—member of freemasons

An agricultural society applied for planning permission to use agricultural land as a show-ground and to erect a pavilion. That application was supported by a business plan, which stated that a masonic lodge would provide a substantial capital injection towards the development and would contribute to the running costs. The defendant council approved the application. Two members of the council, who had declared their membership of the Masonic Society, voted in favour of granting permission. Neither councillor was a member of the masonic lodge involved in the application. The claimant applied for judicial review of the defendant's decision, submitting that it was unlawful because of apparent bias. *Held*, in order to determine whether a fair-minded observer would not have concluded that there was a real possibility of apparent bias, the following factors had to be taken into account: (1) the fundamental principle that everyone who entered freemasonry was strictly forbidden to countenance any act which might have a tendency to subvert the peace and good order of society and had to pay due obedience to the law of the state clearly extended to the discharge of public duties under the Local Government Act 2000; (2) the information and guidance given to masons included advice on the need for declarations of interest to be made; (3) the councillors, being masons, were governed in their conduct by the various obligations and standards of conduct dictated by freemasonry as well as by the declarations signed by them in accordance with the council's Code of Conduct established by statute; (4) freemasonry, by the standards it required, underpinned the requirements of impartiality and fairness set by the law; and (5) case law that stated that, ordinarily, masonic associations would not have required a judge to recuse himself from a case. In the circumstances, membership by the two councillors of the general body of freemasonry had not given rise to apparent bias in connection with the defendant's decision. Accordingly, the application would be dismissed.

R (on the application of Port Regis School Ltd) v North Dorset DC [2006] EWHC 742 (Admin), [2006] LGR 696 (Queen's Bench Division: Newman J). *Locabail (UK) Ltd v Bayfield Properties Ltd* [2000] QB 451, CA (1999 Abr para 1857), considered.

103 Natural justice—fair hearing—bias—planning permission application—statement made to objector

A developer submitted a planning application for permission to carry out opencast mining and related removal and reclamation operations at a certain site. Due to the amount of local opposition to the development, a public inquiry was held, after which the inspector recommended that permission be granted subject to conditions. The defendant delegated its decision on the application to a planning decision committee, which decided to follow the inspector's recommendation. A formal grant of permission was duly made. The claimant, who was one of the objectors to the development, appealed under the Town and Country Planning Act 1990 s 288 against the grant of permission. One of the grounds of appeal was that the chair of committee was alleged to have remarked to another objector before the committee made its decision that he intended to follow the inspector's report. The judge decided that that gave rise to an appearance of bias on the part of the committee, and he therefore allowed the appeal. The defendant appealed. *Held*, in deciding whether an allegation of apparent bias had been made out, the relevant circumstances were those apparent to the court on investigation, and were not restricted to the circumstances available to the hypothetical observer at the original hearing. The judge had fallen into error by either disregarding or giving inappropriate weight to relevant circumstances. He appeared to have concentrated unduly on the remarks alleged to have been made and how they would have appeared to an observer at the time, rather than taking into account the totality of circumstances apparent to the court on investigation. A fair-minded and informed observer, having considered all the facts as they were now known, would not conclude that there was a real possibility that the chair himself or the committee as a whole had been biased when reaching the decision to grant planning permission. Viewed in its wider context, the brief remark by the chair that was at the centre of the case provided an insufficient basis for the suggestion that the decision had been approached with a closed mind and without impartial consideration of all relevant planning issues. Accordingly, the appeal would be allowed.

Condron v National Assembly for Wales [2006] EWCA Civ 1573, [2007] LGR 87 (Court of Appeal: Ward, Wall and Richards LJJ). *Porter v Magill; Weeks v Magill* [2001] UKHL 67, [2002] 2 AC 357 (2001 Abr para 2107); and *Flaherty v National Greyhound Racing Club Ltd* [2005] EWCA Civ 1117, [2005] All ER (D) 70 (Sep) (2005 Abr para 98) applied.

104 Natural justice—fair hearing—bias—recorder hearing case against current client— right to object—waiver

The claimant's personal injury claim was dismissed. Shortly before the hearing, the claimant had been told that the recorder was the head of the chambers to which both his counsel and counsel for the defendant company belonged, and that the recorder was currently acting for companies in the same group as the defendant. The claimant's counsel had advised him that he could seek to have the case transferred to another judge on the ground that the recorder acted for the defendant. However, he advised strongly against that course, stating that it was an advantage that the recorder was a member of his chambers as he knew the recorder's qualities and the nature of his approach. He reassured the claimant that he could expect a fair trial and that there would be no question of bias. The claimant's counsel failed to advise him that he could object to the hearing being conducted by the recorder because both counsel and the recorder were in the same chambers. The claimant appealed against the dismissal of his personal injury claim and contended that the judgment should be set aside because there was an appearance that the recorder was biased. *Held*, there could be circumstances where a recorder could be financially affected by a ruling made against counsel in his chambers, such as where expenses of the chambers were shared by reference to earnings and where the members acted under conditional fee agreements. However, none of those considerations applied on the facts. It was plain that the recorder considered that the defendant was a longstanding and a current lay client, and, in those circumstances, in the absence of waiver by the claimant, the recorder should not have tried the case. A waiver would not be valid unless the party waiving was aware of all the material facts, of the consequences of the choice open to him and had a fair opportunity to reach a decision without pressure. Where there was an appearance of bias on the part of the judge, counsel should advise his client of all the implications of the situation, but it would not be appropriate for him to expound on his knowledge of the personal integrity of the individual judge. Although counsel had thought that he was acting in his client's best interests, his reassurance and the strong advice he had given to the claimant was directed at encouraging the claimant to waive his right to object. For those reasons, the claimant's decision to agree to the recorder continuing to try his case had not been made freely. Further, the recorder should have explained to the claimant what the options were at the outset, and made quite sure that he was content that the recorder should try the case. Accordingly, the appeal would be allowed.

Smith v Kvaerner Cementation Foundations Ltd (Bar Council intervening) [2006] EWCA Civ 242, [2006] 3 All ER 593 (Court of Appeal: Lord Phillips of Worth Matravers CJ, Sir Anthony Clarke MR and May LJ). *Metropolitan Properties v Lannon* [1968] 3 All ER 304, CA, applied.

105 Natural justice—fair hearing—perception of injustice—justices informed of defendant's previous convictions

See *R (on the application of Murchison) v Southend Magistrates' Court*, para 1879.

106 Natural justice—judicial proceedings—openness—bail application

The claimant, who had been charged with possession of a record of information likely to be useful to a person committing or preparing an act of terrorism contrary to the Terrorism Act 2000 s 58(1)(b), applied to the Common Serjeant of London, sitting at the Central Criminal Court, the first defendant, to have his application for bail heard in public. The second defendant, the prosecution, opposed the application on the ground that the normal practice of the first defendant was that bail applications were made in chambers. The Common Serjeant refused the application on the grounds that the rules were clear and there was nothing that distinguished the case from any other so that the application for bail should be decided in chambers. Bail was subsequently refused. The claimant sought judicial review of the Common Serjeant's decision not to hear the application in public. *Held*, a hearing in open court of an application directly affecting personal liberty was in the first instance a matter not of private or individual right, and certainly not of judicial discretion, but of public obligation. The role of private or individual right, which would be prominent in bail applications, obliged a court to consider whether it was necessary to depart from the ordinary rule of open justice in the interest of justice itself. An application to hear a bail application in public had to start from the fundamental presumption in favour of open justice. The court's decision was an exercise not of discretion, which implied a judicial choice between two or more equally proper courses, but of judgment as to whether a departure from the norm was justified. The Common Serjeant had erred in not starting from the presumption in favour of open justice. Accordingly, the application would be allowed and a rehearing of the bail application would be ordered.

R (on the application of Malik) v Central Criminal Court [2006] EWHC 1539 (Admin), [2006] All ER (D) 305 (Jun) (Queen's Bench Division: Sedley LJ and Gray J). *Scott v Scott* [1913] AC 417, HL, applied.

107 Non-judicial redress—Public Services Ombudsman for Wales—general

The Public Services Ombudsman (Wales) Act 2005 (Transitional Provisions and Consequential Amendments) Order 2006, SI 2006/362 (in force on 1 April 2006), revokes SI 1999/1791, 2001/2275 and 2004/2359 consequential to the establishment of the Public Services Ombudsman for Wales and the abolition of the Welsh Administration Ombudsman, the Health Service Commissioner for Wales and the Social Housing Ombudsman for Wales by the Public Services Ombudsman (Wales) Act 2005. SI 1990/200, 1992/1812, 1993/3228, 1995/201, 1996/709, 2001/2281, 2283, 2284, 2288, 2289, 2291, 2003/437 and 2005/1313 are amended.

108 Non-judicial redress—Public Services Ombudsman for Wales—jurisdiction

The Public Services Ombudsman for Wales (Jurisdiction and Transitional Provisions and Savings) Order 2006, SI 2006/363 (in force on 1 April 2006), amends the Public Services Ombudsman (Wales) Act 2003 by adding to the lists of matters that the Public Services Ombudsman for Wales is not entitled to investigate action under specified enactments which is or has been the subject of an inquiry under the Inquiries Act 2005. The order also brings the Board of Community Health Councils in Wales and valuation tribunals in Wales within the Ombudsman's remit.

109   Parliamentary Commissioner—bodies subject to investigation

The Parliamentary Commissioner Order 2006, SI 2006/3328 (in force on 22 January 2007), further amends the Parliamentary Commissioner Act 1967 by amending the list of departments and authorities which are subject to investigation by the Parliamentary Commissioner for Administration in the exercise of its administrative functions. The following bodies are added to the list: Animal Welfare Advisory Committee; Advisory Committee on Animal Feedingstuffs; Advisory Committee on Hazardous Substances; Advisory Committee on Microbiological Safety of Food; Advisory Group on Medical Countermeasures; Central Advisory Committee on War Pensions; Competition Service; Cycling England; Defence Nuclear Advisory Committee; Defence Scientific Advisory Committee; England Implementation Group; Firebuy Limited; Herbal Medicines Advisory Committee; National Victims Advisory Panel; Nuclear Liabilities Fund; Nuclear Research Advisory Council; The Quality Improvement Agency; The School Food Trust; Technology Strategy Board; Union Modernisation Fund Supervisory Board; and UK Chemical Weapons Convention National Authority Advisory Committee. The following bodies are removed from the list: Dental Vocational Training Authority; Intellectual Property Advisory Committee; National Health Service-wide Clearing Service; Standing Medical Advisory Committee; Standing Nursing and Midwifery Advisory Committee; Standing Pharmaceutical Advisory Committee; Wider Health Working Group; and Wine Standards Board. Further, the references to the Independent Review body for the Advertising of Medicines and the Independent Review Panel on the Classification of Borderline Medicines are replaced by references to the Independent Review Panel for Advertising and the Independent Review Panel on the Classification of Borderline Products respectively. The Order also deletes the Dental Vocational Training Authority Appeal Body and the Registered Inspectors of Schools Appeal Tribunals from the list of bodies whose administrative functions may be subject to investigation by the Commissioner under the terms of the 1967 Act s 5(7). SI 1968/1859, 1970/1535, 1972/1716, 1975/1033, 1977/816, 1978/616, 1979/915, 1705, 1981/1537, 1986/1889, 1988/585, 1985, 1995/1615, 1996/1914, 2601, 1999/277, 2028, 2000/739, 2003/2921, 2004/2670 are revoked.

AGENCY

Halsbury's Laws of England (4th edn) vol 2(1) (Reissue) paras 1–300

Articles

For articles relating to this title please refer to the Table of Articles at the beginning of the Abridgment.

110   Commercial agent—meaning—continuing authority—self-employed intermediary under single contract—contract renewed annually

EC Council Directive 86/653 art 1(2) defines 'commercial agent' as a self-employed intermediary who has continuing authority to negotiate the sale or the purchase of goods on behalf of another person, or to negotiate and conclude such transactions on behalf of and in the name of that person.

The applicant acted as intermediary in the charter of a ship concluded between the first respondent and another company. The charter was extended annually for several years until contractual relations were terminated. The applicant brought proceedings in the Netherlands against the respondents under the contract, which the respondents attempted to resist by contending that the applicant was not a commercial agent as it had negotiated only one contract. The Dutch court stayed the proceedings and sought a preliminary ruling from the European Court of Justice on whether a self-employed intermediary with authority to conclude a single charter for a ship, subsequently extended over several years, was a commercial agent within the meaning of Directive 86/653 art 1(2). The applicant argued that the peculiarity of there being a single contract was not decisive where the intermediary had continuing authority, and that the renewal of the contract demonstrated that it had such authority. *Held*, art 1(2) was to be interpreted as meaning that, where a self-employed intermediary had authority to conclude a single contract, subsequently extended over several years, the requirement that the authority be continuing was only fulfilled where the principal conferred continuing authority on that intermediary to negotiate successive extensions to that contract. It was for the national court to make the requisite findings in that regard. The mere fact that the intermediary maintained relations with the principal throughout the contractual period was, in itself, insufficient to demonstrate such authority.

Case C-3/04 *Poseidon Chartering BV v Marianne Zeeschip VOF* [2006] 2 Lloyd's Rep 105 (ECJ: First Chamber).

111   Commercial agent—termination of principal's business—compensation under agency contract—calculation of compensation

The claimant had been a commercial agent for the defendant company for 13 years when the claimant's agency was terminated as a result of the closure of the defendant's business. The Commercial Agents (Council Directive) Regulations 1993, SI 1993/3053, gave the claimant a right to compensation on the termination of the agency, but the parties could not agree on the amount. Although the defendant paid the claimant a sum in respect of compensation, the claimant issued proceedings seeking a larger payment. The claimant submitted that where the agency had persisted over a reasonable period of time and the agent had been competent, he should receive compensation of an amount equal to two years' gross commission. The judge assessed compensation at a lower figure than that paid by the defendant to the claimant. On the claimant's appeal, *held,* the 1993 Regulations gave the agent a right to receive compensation for any damage he had suffered. They did not simply provide for him to receive payment of any amount that was fair and reasonable having regard to all the circumstances. There was no basis for construing the 1993 Regulations in a way that would entitle the court to award an amount of compensation unrelated to the damage which the agent had suffered, much less a conventional sum largely unrelated to the particular circumstances of the case. Therefore, the two years' compensation rule could not be supported even as a broad guideline. Further, neither the duration of the agency nor the quality of the agent's performance were necessarily important factors in the assessment of compensation. In the present case, the judge had directed himself correctly on the principles to be applied. Accordingly, the appeal would be dismissed.

Lonsdale (*t/a Lonsdale Agencies*) *v Howard & Hallam Ltd* [2006] EWCA Civ 63, [2006] 1 WLR 1281 (Court of Appeal: Jacob, Moore-Bick and Hallett LJJ).

AGRICULTURE

Halsbury's Laws of England (4th edn) vol 1(2) (Reissue) paras 301–1133

Articles

For articles relating to this title please refer to the Table of Articles at the beginning of the Abridgment.

112   Agricultural holdings—agricultural subsidies and grants schemes—appeals—Wales

The Agricultural Subsidies and Grants Schemes (Appeals) (Wales) Regulations 2006, SI 2006/3342 (in force on 1 January 2007), enable the National Assembly for Wales to establish one or more appeals procedures for farmers who dispute decisions it has taken in connection with the funding of certain elements of the common agricultural policy and schemes related to it. Any appeal procedure may take the form of oral or written submission to persons appointed by the Assembly with a view to such persons making a recommendation to the Assembly as to how the matter should be finally determined. The Assembly may pay remuneration and allowances to persons so appointed and to charge a fee in respect of the costs of the procedure. SI 2004/2919 is revoked and minor amendments are made to SI 1987/2026, 2027, 1988/1291, 1992/905, 1993/1210, 1211, 1994/238, 239, 3099–3102, 1997/829 and 2001/2537.

113   Agricultural holdings—tenancy—regulatory reform

The Regulatory Reform (Agricultural Tenancies) (England and Wales) Order 2006, SI 2006/2805 (in force on 19 October 2006), amends the Agricultural Holdings Act 1986 and the Agricultural Tenancies Act 1995, which regulate tenancies of agricultural land in England and Wales, so as to give the parties to agricultural tenancies greater freedom of contract in the areas of rent reviews, succession, end of tenancy compensation, arbitration, new tenancies and notice periods. The effect of the amendments to the 1986 Act are that (1) where the rent payable in respect of a holding is referred to arbitration, the arbitrator must now determine the rent properly payable at the next termination date rather than at the date of reference; (2) where the 1986 Act applies by virtue of the 1995 Act s 4(1)(g), the references to 'substantial part' mean a substantial part by reference to either area or value; (3) agricultural work, or other work, carried out by the potential successor from the holding or an agricultural unit of which the holding forms part, is included as a condition in relation to the eligibility for succession to a 1986 Act tenancy; (4) the provisions relating to successive tenancies in relation to improvements and deterioration also apply where the earlier tenancy was of a holding which comprised the whole or a substantial part of the land comprised in the holding; (5) the provisions relating to the appointment of an arbitrator, applications to the President of the Royal Institution of Charted Surveyors to make such an appointment, and to the effect of certain agreements relating to compensation, are modified; and (6) where the 1986 Act applies to a new tenancy by virtue of the 1995 Act s 4(1)(g), and the rent payable is unchanged from the rent payable under the previous tenancy, disregarding any changes resulting from adjustments to the boundary of the holding, the three-year rent review cycle is uninterrupted. The amendments to the 1995 Act are that (a) the scope of when the 1986 Act applies to tenancies granted under the doctrine of surrender and re-grant are widened; (b) parties are allowed to apply the 1986 Act to a tenancy by express provision in the contract of tenancy, provided the tenant previously held a 1986 Act tenancy of all or a substantial part of the holding; (c) the 1986 Act applies to a new tenancy where there is an agreed succession; (d) the 24-month upper limit on notice periods for farm business tenancies is removed;

(e) the exceptions to rent review provisions that apply to farm business tenancies are extended; (f) on a statutory rent review, the arbitrator must not take into account those terms of the tenancy which would preclude a reduction in rent; (g) landlords and tenants are given an option of agreeing an upper limit to the amount of end of tenancy compensation payable where the tenant has increased the value of the holding attributable to the improvement; (h) where the landlord and tenant agree that there should be such a limit but are unable to agree on the amount of the limit, the amount is the cost to the tenant of making the improvement; and (i) where the parties have agreed to a compensation limit, the tenant has received some compensation in respect of the improvement at the time he gave up the part, and the tenant is entitled to further compensation in respect of the improvement at the time he gave up the part and at the end of the tenancy, the total amount of compensation he receives does not exceed the compensation limit. The order also makes consequential repeals and amendments and revokes SI 1990/1472.

114   Agricultural holdings—units of production—England

The Agricultural Holdings (Units of Production) (England) Order 2006, SI 2006/2628 (in force on 7 November 2006), replaces the 2005 Order, SI 2005/2867. The order (1) prescribes units of production for the assessment of the productive capacity of agricultural land situated in England; (2) sets out the amount which is to be regarded as the net annual income from each unit for the year commencing on 7 November 2006; (3) provides that, in determining the annual income figure, whenever a particular listed farming use is relevant to the assessment of the productive capacity of the land in question, the units of production and the net annual income will form the basis of that assessment; and (4) specifies net annual income figures for land which was, in 2005, an eligible hectare for the purposes of EC Council Regulation 1782/2003, and separate figures for moorland, severely disadvantaged land excluding moorland, disadvantaged land and other land, in addition to separate figures for land which was set aside from production in 2005.

115   Agricultural holdings—units of production—Wales

The Agricultural Holdings (Units of Production) (Wales) Order 2006, SI 2006/2796 (in force on 27 October 2006), replaces the 2004 Order, SI 2004/1218. The order prescribes units of production for the assessment of the productive capacity of agricultural land situated in Wales and sets out the amount which is to be regarded as the net annual income from each such unit for the years 12 September 2004 to 11 September 2005 and 12 September 2005 to 11 September 2006 inclusive. In assessing the productive capacity of the land, the total production in the course of a year is to be taken account of so as to include income derived from a unit which may be on the land for only part of the year and where there may be more than one production cycle in the year.

116   Common agricultural policy—payments to agricultural producers—paying agency—
National Assembly for Wales

The Paying Agency (National Assembly for Wales) (Amendment) Regulations 2006, SI 2006/2698 (in force on 16 October 2006), amend the 1999 Regulations, SI 1999/2223, by updating references made to European legislation so as to refer to EC Commission Regulation 885/2006, laying down detailed rules on the accreditation of paying agencies, and EC Council Regulation 1290/2005, on the financing of the common agricultural policy.

117   Common agricultural policy—rural development programme—closure of project-based
schemes—England

The England Rural Development Programme (Closure of Project-Based Schemes) Regulations 2006, SI 2006/2298 (in force on 1 October 2006), provide that the Secretary of State must not consider any applications received on or after the date of enforcement for approval of a project under the Energy Crops Regulations 2000, SI 2000/3042, the Rural Enterprise Regulations 2000, SI 2000/3043, the Vocational Training Grants (Agriculture and Forestry) Regulations 2000, SI 2000/3045, and the Agricultural Processing and Marketing Grants Regulations 2000, SI 2000/3046.

118   Common agricultural policy—rural development programme—Wales

The Rural Development Programmes (Wales) Regulations 2006, SI 2006/3343 (in force on 1 January 2007), make provision in relation to the Rural Development Programmes, established under the EC Council Regulations 1698/2005 and 1257/1999. In particular, the regulations (1) empower the National Assembly for Wales to approve operations for the receipt of financial assistance, to attach conditions to any such approval and to pay financial assistance; (2) set out the circumstances in which approval of an operation may be revoked and financial assistance may be withheld or recovered; (3) make provision for powers of entry and inspection to authorised persons in relation to land on which an approved operation is situated or documents relating to an approved operation are held; (4) require beneficiaries of financial assistance to keep records relating to the approved operation, to supply such information relating to the approved operations as the Assembly requires, and to assist an authorised person in the exercise of his powers; (5) allow the Assembly to demand interest on sums due to it and provide that sums payable to the Assembly are recoverable as a debt; (6) provide for offences and penalties; and (7) enable the Assembly to require a beneficiary to give undertakings. SI 1996/529, 1999/1176, 2001/424, 496, 1154, 2446, 3806 and 2006/41 are revoked.

119   Common agricultural policy—single payment and support schemes—cross compliance—England

The Common Agricultural Policy Single Payment and Support Schemes (Cross-compliance) (England) (Amendment) Regulations 2006, SI 2006/3254 (in force on 1 January 2007), amend the 2005 Regulations, SI 2005/3459, by (1) adding to the list of agri-environment commitments to include commitments under EC Council Regulation 1698/2005 and the Natural Environment and Rural Communities Act 2006 s 7; (2) amending the definition of 'authorised person'; (3) updating definitions of EC legislation; (4) designating the Secretary of State as the competent control authority in relation to certain statutory management requirements, and the Environment Agency as the competent control authority in relation to certain other such requirements; (5) empowering Natural England to carry out inspections where requested to do so by the Secretary of State or the Rural Payments Agency; (6) conferring further powers on inspectors so as to provide for inspections relating to new animal welfare requirements which apply to farmers; (7) removing the requirement to retain soils protection guidance; and (8) making changes in relation to post-harvest management of land, overgrazing and supplementary feeding and sites of special scientific interest.

120   Common agricultural policy—single payment and support schemes—cross compliance—Wales

The Common Agricultural Policy Single Payment and Support Schemes (Cross Compliance) (Wales) (Amendment) Regulations 2006, SI 2006/2831 (in force on 1 November 2006), further amend the 2004 Regulations, SI 2004/3280, by designating the Secretary of State as a specialised control body who bears the responsibility of carrying out controls in respect of the statutory management requirements specified. The regulations also update references to certain Community instruments.

121   Common agricultural policy—single payment and support schemes—England

The Common Agricultural Policy Single Payment and Support Schemes (Amendment) Regulations 2006, SI 2006/239 (in force on 2 March 2006), further amend the 2005 Regulations, SI 2005/219, so as to provide that a farmer may choose up to two start dates for the beginning of the relevant ten-month period in respect of his holding, and if no such date is chosen, for the ten-month period in respect of his holding to start on 1 February of the year of application.

The Common Agricultural Policy Single Payment and Support Schemes (Amendment No 2) Regulations 2006, SI 2006/301 (in force on 14 February 2006), further amend the 2005 Regulations supra so as to change the definition of 'moorland' in order to refer to the Moorland Map of England 2006.

The Common Agricultural Policy Single Payment and Support Schemes (Amendment) (No 3) Regulations 2006, SI 2006/989 (in force on 1 April 2006), further amend the 2005 Regulations by reducing, from six weeks to three weeks, the amount of notice which a transferor is required to give the relevant competent authority of a transfer of payment entitlements, provided that he gives such notice on or before 23 April 2006. Where a transferor gives the relevant competent authority notice of a transfer of payment entitlements after 23 April 2006, he is still required to give at least six weeks notice of the transfer.

122   Common agricultural policy—single payment and support schemes—reductions from payments—England

The Common Agricultural Policy Single Payment and Support Schemes (Reductions from Payments) (England) Regulations 2006, SI 2006/169 (in force on 26 February 2006), implement EC Commission Regulation 1954/2005 so as to disapply art 1 in relation to payments to be made in respect of the year 2005 under the single payment scheme and various other aid schemes.

123   Common agricultural policy—single payment and support schemes—Wales

The Common Agricultural Policy Single Payment and Support Schemes (Wales) (Amendment) Regulations 2006, SI 2006/357 (in force on 20 February 2006), amend the 2005 Regulations, SI 2005/360, so as to (1) update references to Community legislation; (2) authorise farmers to make use of the possibility to fix two different dates for the beginning of the ten-month period in respect of which parcels of eligible land have to be at a farmer's disposal for the purposes of the single payment scheme; and (3) allow the period within which payment entitlement transfers are to be communicated to the National Assembly for Wales, to be determined in accordance with the discretionary powers granted to the Assembly, as a competent authority of the member state under EC Commission Regulation 795/2004.

124 Common agricultural policy—single payment scheme—set-aside—Wales

The Common Agricultural Policy Single Payment Scheme (Set-aside) (Wales) (Amendment) Regulations 2006, SI 2006/3101 (in force on 1 December 2006), amend the 2005 Regulations, SI 2005/45 Sch 1 in relation to the good agricultural and environmental conditions that apply to land set aside under the single payment scheme. In particular, the regulations (1) add further exemptions from the requirement to establish a green cover by the commencement of the current green cover season; (2) add a provision allowing farmers to cultivate land set aside from production on or after 1 May which is organic land, for the purposes of controlling weeds; (3) remove the restriction on grazing after the set-aside period where the green cover has been replaced; and (4) prohibit the use of pesticides and herbicides on land set aside from production except in the circumstances set out.

125 Common agricultural policy—wine—production and marketing—England

The Common Agricultural Policy (Wine) (England and Northern Ireland) (Amendment) Regulations 2006, SI 2006/1499 (in force on 1 July 2006), further amend the 2001 Regulations, SI 2001/686, by (1) replacing references to the Wine Standards Board with references to the Food Standards Agency, thereby making the Food Standards Agency responsible for the enforcement functions under the 2001 Regulations; (2) putting in place a different procedure for the review of prohibitions on the movement of wine-sector products; and (3) making consequential amendments.

126 Common agricultural policy—wine—production and marketing—Wales

The Common Agricultural Policy (Wine) (Wales) (Amendment) Regulations 2006, SI 2006/1716 (in force on 1 July 2006), further amend the 2001 Regulations, SI 2001/2193, by (1) replacing references to the Wine Standards Board with references to the Food Standards Agency, thereby making the Agency responsible for the enforcement functions under the 2001 Regulations; (2) updating the definition of 'the Commissioners'; (3) updating references to European Community legislation; (4) adopting a procedure for the review of prohibitions on the movement of wine-sector products; and (5) adding Gamay and Gewurztraminer to the list of vine varieties that may be used in the production of wines in Wales.

127 Dairies—dairy produce—quotas—general provisions

The Dairy Produce Quotas (Amendment) Regulations 2006, SI 2006/120 (in force on 31 March 2006), amend the 2005 Regulations, SI 2005/465, by (1) correcting an error preventing the transfer of quota necessary to cover production taking place before the date of transfer so that the quota may be transferred, but cannot be identified as unused; (2) revising provisions requiring dairy producers and purchasers to provide information to the Secretary of State on or before a specified date; and (3) penalising purchasers who send inaccurate summaries of production causing an overstatement or an understatement of deliveries made to him, by providing that the producer is liable to pay to the Secretary of State a penalty equivalent to the theoretical amount of levy that would be due on 0·5 per cent of the quantity by volume of milk which comprises the overstatement or understatement.

128 Dairies—dairy produce—quotas—Wales

The Dairy Produce Quotas (Wales) (Amendment) Regulations 2006, SI 2006/762 (in force on 31 March 2006), amend the 2005 Regulations, SI 2005/537, by (1) correcting an error preventing the transfer of quota necessary to cover production taking place before the date of transfer, providing that the quota may be transferred, but cannot be identified as unused quota; (2) revising provisions requiring dairy producers and purchasers to provide information to the National Assembly for Wales on or before a specified date; (3) penalising purchasers who send inaccurate summaries of production by requiring payment to the National Assembly of a sum equivalent to the theoretical amount of levy that would be due on 0·5 per cent of the quantity by volume of milk that comprises the overstatement or understatement; and (4) providing that the penalty for purchasers who fail to submit a summary before 1 July in the year in which it is required applies 30 days after the service of a notice by the National Assembly to this effect.

129 Eggs—marketing standards

The Eggs (Marketing Standards) (Amendment) (England and Wales) Regulations 2006, SI 2006/1540 (in force on 15 June 2006), further amend the 1995 Regulations, SI 1995/1544, by (1) revoking provisions relating to the United Kingdom official mark; and (2) replacing the Schedule with an updated schedule of Community provisions.

130   Feeding stuffs—general provisions—England

The Feeding Stuffs and the Feeding Stuffs (Sampling and Analysis) (Amendment) (England) Regulations 2006, SI 2006/113 (in force on 16 February 2006), implement EC Commission Directives 2005/6, 2002/7, and 2002/8 (1) amend the Feeding Stuffs (England) 2005, SI 2005/3281 so as to make changes in relation to certain entries for lead, fluorine and mercury; and (2) amend the Feeding Stuffs (Sampling and Analysis) Regulations 1999, SI 1999/1663, so as to (a) reflect that as from 1 January 2006 the general obligation on member states to ensure that sampling and analysis carried out in pursuit of official controls follows prescribed Community methods are now given effect by the European Parliament and EC Council Regulation 882/2004; and (b) provide for requirements regarding expanded measurement uncertainty and correction for recovery when analysing and reporting on the analysis of animal feed to determine the levels of undesirable substances.

The Feeding Stuffs (England) (Amendment) Regulations 2006, SI 2006/2808 (in force on 17 November 2006), amend the 2005 Regulations, SI 2005/3281, so as to require the percentage of each feed material contained in a compound feed to be declared, within a tolerance of plus or minus 15 per cent, on the label of the compound feed or on an accompanying document. The regulations also revoke a provision in the 2000 Regulations, SI 2000/2481, requiring the exact percentage of each feed material in a compound feed to be disclosed to customers on request.

131   Feeding stuffs—general provisions—Wales

The Feeding Stuffs (Wales) Regulations 2006, SI 2006/116 (in force on 25 January 2006), which apply to farmed creatures and pet animals and to animals living in the wild, replace the 2001 Regulations, SI 2001/343, and implement Community legislation. In particular, the regulations (1) provide that any material useable as a feeding stuff, additive or premixture is prescribed material; (2) make provision that sellers of prescribed materials are required to give to purchasers statutory statements covering the composition of the material and information on storage, handling and use; (3) provide that materials held for sale must be marked with information under head (2); (4) prescribe the content and form of the statutory statement and other declarations; (5) provide attribution of meanings to the names of certain materials for the purposes of the Agriculture Act 1970 s 70; (6) prescribe the way in which compound feeds may be sealed and packaged; (7) provide for the way in which feed materials may be put into circulation or used; (8) restrict the putting into circulation or use of feeding stuffs containing specified undesirable substances; (9) prohibit the putting into circulation or use of any feeding stuff containing certain prescribed substances; (10) restrict the marketing and use of certain protein sources and non-protein nitrogenous compounds in feeds; (11) prescribe the iron content of milk replacer feeds; (12) prohibit the putting into circulation of compound feeding stuffs in which the amount of ash insoluble in hydrochloric acid exceeds specified levels; (12) provide for marketing of feeds intended for particular nutritional purposes; (13) make provision for enforcement of EC Regulation 1831/2003 on additives for use in animal nutrition; (14) provide for the enforcement of requirements where the legal basis is the European Communities Act 1972; and (15) amend the 1970 Act s 74A so as to provide for offences and penalties in relation to the regulations.

The Feeding Stuffs (Wales) (Amendment) Regulations 2006, SI 2006/2928 (in force on 17 November 2006), amend the 2006 Regulations supra so as to insert a provision requiring the percentage of each feed material contained in a compound feed to be declared, within a tolerance of plus or minus 15 per cent, on the label of the compound feed or on an accompanying document. The regulations also revoke a provision in the 2001 Regulations, SI 2001/343, requiring the exact percentage of each feed material in a compound feed to be disclosed to customers on request.

The Feeding Stuffs and the Feeding Stuffs (Sampling and Analysis) (Amendment) (Wales) Regulations 2006, SI 2006/617 (in force on 10 March 2006), implement EC Commission Directives 2005/6, 2002/7, and 2002/8 (1) amend the 2006 Regulations supra so as to make changes in relation to certain entries for lead, fluorine and mercury; and (2) amend the Feeding Stuffs (Sampling and Analysis) Regulations 1999, SI 1999/1663, so as to (a) reflect that as from 1 January 2006 the general obligation on member states to ensure that sampling and analysis carried out in pursuit of official controls follows prescribed Community methods are now given effect by the European Parliament and EC Council Regulation 882/2004; and (b) provide for requirements regarding expanded measurement uncertainty and correction for recovery when analysing and reporting on the analysis of animal feed to determine the levels of undesirable substances.

132   Feeding stuffs—sampling and analysis—England

See para 130.

133   Feeding stuffs—sampling and analysis—Wales

See para 131.

134   Feeding stuffs—specified undesirable substances—England

The Feed (Specified Undesirable Substances) (England) Regulations 2006, SI 2006/3120 (in force on 26 December 2006), further amend the Feeding Stuffs (England) Regulations 2005, SI 2005/3281, and the Feed (Hygiene and Enforcement) (England) Regulations 2005, SI 2005/3280, so as to provide for the implementation of EC Commission Directives 2005/86, 2005/87 and 2006/13. The regulations also implement a provision contained in EC Council Directive 79/373 on the circulation of compound feeding stuffs, which relates to the limits of variation for the declaration of the moisture content of compound pet foods. The regulations amend SI 2005/3281 by (1) adding limits of variation for declarations of the moisture content of compound pet foods; (2) revising the existing entries for cadmium, dioxin, fluorine and lead, and by adding new entries relating to the sum of dioxins and dioxin-like PCBs; and (3) revising the existing entries for camphechlor. The regulations amend SI 2005/3280 by (a) adding a new provision to give authorised officers of a feed authority powers of entry, sampling, inspection and associated activities in order to carry out the investigative functions required by EC Directive 2002/32; and (b) extending its application to sampling in the course of carrying out investigations.

135   Feeding stuffs—specified undesirable substances—Wales

The Feed (Specified Undesirable Substances) (Wales) Regulations 2006, SI 2006/3256 (in force on 26 December 2006), further amend the Feeding Stuffs (Wales) Regulations 2006, SI 2006/116, and the Feed (Hygiene and Enforcement) (Wales) Regulations 2005, SI 2005/3368, so as to provide for the implementation of EC Commission Directives 2005/86, 2005/87 and 2006/13. The regulations also implement a provision contained in EC Council Directive 79/373 on the circulation of compound feeding stuffs, which relates to the limits of variation for the declaration of the moisture content of compound pet foods. The regulations amend the 2006 Regulations by (1) adding limits of variation for declarations of the moisture content of compound pet foods; (2) revising the existing entries for cadmium, dioxin, fluorine and lead, and by adding new entries relating to the sum of dioxins and dioxin-like PCBs; and (3) revising the existing entries for camphechlor. The regulations amend the 2005 Regulations by (a) adding a new provision to give authorised officers of a feed authority powers of entry, sampling, inspection and associated activities in order to carry out the investigative functions required by EC Directive 2002/32; and (b) extending its application to sampling in the course of carrying out investigations.

136   Fertilisers—EC fertilisers

The EC Fertilisers (England and Wales) Regulations 2006, SI 2006/2486 (in force on 11 October 2006), implement European Parliament and EC Council Regulation 2003/2003 and create offences for breaches by manufacturers of the requirements of Regulation 2003/2003 regarding designation, compositional tolerances, identification, marking, labelling and packaging of fertilisers designated as EC fertilisers. In particular, the regulations (1) provide that manufacturers are required to keep specified records; (2) provide the Secretary of State or the National Assembly for Wales with the power to serve compliance notices; (3) provide that local authorities are responsible for enforcing the regulations and appointing inspectors for that purpose; powers of entry, inspection and offences of obstruction of inspectors are included; (4) make provision for the authorisation of laboratories competent to analyse samples and for the taking and analysis of samples for the purpose of the regulations; (5) provide that inspectors have powers to require remedial action to be taken regarding fertiliser designated as EC fertiliser in respect of which they think an offence under the regulations is being committed, or to seize the fertiliser; (6) provide the Secretary of State and the National Assembly for Wales with a power to give directions for the mitigation or elimination of risk in circumstances where either of them has justifiable grounds for believing that an EC designated fertiliser, although complying with the requirements of Regulation 2003/2003, constitutes a risk to safety or health of humans, animals or plants or a risk to the environment; (7) set out penalties for offences under the regulations; and (8) disapply the provisions of (a) the Agriculture Act 1970 Pt IV (ss 66–87); (b) the Fertilisers Regulations 1991, SI 1991/2197; and (c) the Fertilisers (Sampling and Analysis) Regulations 1996, SI 1996/1342.

137   Fishing quotas

See FISHERIES.

138   Gangmasters—appeals

The Gangmasters (Appeals) Regulations 2006, SI 2006/662 (in force on 6 April 2006), provide for an appeals procedure against decisions of the Gangmasters Licensing Authority, under the Gangmasters (Licensing) Act 2004, to refuse to grant a licence, to impose conditions to which a licence is subject, to modify or revoke a licence, or to refuse to transfer a licence. In particular the regulations: (1) provide for the appointment and remuneration of an appointed person from members of the panel of Employment Tribunal Chairmen to hear and determine appeals; (2) provide for the establishment of a Secretariat to administer the appeals process and provide administrative assistance to appointed persons; (3) set out the decisions which may be appealed against; (4) set out the procedure to be followed when making or replying to an appeal; (5) provide for the determination of an appeal without an oral hearing if both parties agree and the appointed person considers it appropriate; (6) set out the procedure up to and at the hearing; and (7) make provision for a register of decisions to be kept by the Secretariat.

139   Gangmasters—licensing—conditions

The Gangmasters (Licensing Conditions) (No 2) Rules 2006, SI 2006/2373 (in force on 1 October 2006), replace the 2006 Rules, SI 2006/660, and establish the procedure for licensing gangmasters covered by the provisions of the Gangmasters (Licensing) Act 2004. In particular, the rules (1) set out the information to be provided on application for a gangmaster's licence; (2) specify the licence conditions that apply to licence holders; (3) provide that an applicant or licence holder is fit and proper to hold a gangmaster's licence if he complies with the criteria set out in the rules and with the obligations contained in the Gangmasters (Licensing Authority) Regulations 2005, SI 2005/448, reg 12(2), which establish a general principle governing the determination of criteria assessing the fitness of applicants for licences and the terms of licence conditions; (4) specify when a new application is required; and (5) prescribe the licence fee, the renewal fee and the charge for inspection at the point of application.

140   Gangmasters—licensing—exclusions

The Gangmasters Licensing (Exclusions) Regulations 2006, SI 2006/658 (in force on 6 April 2006), make provision for the circumstances in which a licence to act as a gangmaster is not required.

141   Gangmasters (Licensing) Act 2004—commencement

The Gangmasters (Licensing) Act 2004 (Commencement No 3) Order 2006, SI 2006/2406, brings into force, on 1 October 2006, ss 11, 13(3), 14 and, for certain purposes, ss 6(1), 12 and 27.

The Gangmasters (Licensing) Act 2004 (Commencement No 4) Order 2006, SI 2006/2906, brings s 13(1), (2), (4) into force for certain purposes on 1 December 2006.

For a summary of the Act, see 2004 Abr para 108. See also the commencement table in the title STATUTES.

142   Home-Grown Cereals Authority—levy scheme—rate of levy

The Home-Grown Cereals Authority (Rate of Levy) Order 2006, SI 2006/1357 (in force on 1 July 2006), specifies, for the year beginning on 1 July 2006, the rates of dealer levy, grower levy and processor levies which appear to the Secretary of State for Environment, Food and Rural Affairs and the National Assembly for Wales to be sufficient to meet the amount apportioned to certain cereals and certain oilseeds grown in the United Kingdom, to finance the non-trading functions of the Home-Grown Cereals Authority.

143   Land in care scheme—Tir Gofal—Wales

The Tir Gofal (Wales) (Amendment) Regulations 2006, SI 2006/1717 (in force on 16 October 2006), amend the Land in Care Scheme (Tir Gofal) (Wales) Regulations 1999, 1999/1176, so as to effect a transfer of responsibility for the administration of the Land in Care (Tir Gofal) agri-environment scheme, from the Countryside Council for Wales to the National Assembly for Wales. In particular, the regulations (1) provide that all references to Countryside Council are replaced by references to the National Assembly; (2) provide for the transfer of rights and liabilities in connection with Tir Gofal scheme arrangements entered into by the Countryside Council to be transferred to the National Assembly; (3) update references in the 1999 Regulations to certain Community instruments; and (4) make a minor consequential provision.

144   Livestock—bovine animals—enzootic bovine leukosis—Wales

See para 190.

145   Livestock—cattle—brucellosis—Wales

See para 191.

146   Livestock—cattle—database

The Cattle Database (Amendment) Regulations 2006, SI 2006/1539 (in force on 15 June 2006), further amend the 1998 Regulations, SI 1998/1796, by replacing references to (1) EC Council Regulation 820/97 with references to EC Council Regulation 1760/2000; and (2) EC Commission Regulation 2629/97 with references to EC Commission Regulation 911/2004.

147 Livestock—cattle—identification

The Cattle Identification (Amendment) Regulations 2006, SI 2006/1538 (in force on 15 June 2006), further amend the 1998 Regulations, SI 1998/871, by replacing references to (1) EC Council Regulation 820/97 with references to EC Council Regulation 1760/2000; and (2) EC Commission Regulation 2629/97 with references to EC Commission Regulation 911/2004.

148 Livestock—cattle—older animals—disposal—Wales

The Older Cattle (Disposal) (Wales) Regulations 2006, SI 2006/62 (in force on 23 January 2006), make provision for the enforcement of certain of the requirements of EC Commission Regulation 716/96, which introduced a scheme authorising the purchase of older bovine animals born or reared in the United Kingdom which do not exhibit any clinical sign of BSE. The regulations (1) create offences in respect of breaches of the Commission Regulation; (2) provide for their enforcement by the Secretary of State, and require him to appoint inspectors for this purpose; (3) provide for the powers of inspectors; (4) provide for the offence of obstructing a person executing the regulations; and (5) provide for penalties in respect of offences under the regulations.

149 Natural Environment and Rural Communities Act 2006

See para 2109.

150 Organic products—inspection system

The Environmental Stewardship (England) and Organic Products (Amendment) Regulations 2006, SI 2006/2075 (in force on 4 September 2006), further amend the Organic Products Regulations 2004, SI 2004/1604, and the Environmental Stewardship (England) Regulations 2005, SI 2005/621, by replacing the definition of 'the Council Regulation' so that it refers to the latest amending instrument, and by updating references to the Compendium of United Kingdom Organic Standards. SI 2005/2003 is revoked.

151 Pesticides—maximum residue levels—crops, food and feeding stuffs

The Pesticides (Maximum Residue Levels in Crops, Food and Feeding Stuffs) (England and Wales) (Amendment) Regulations 2006, SI 2006/985 (in force in part on 27 April 2006, in part on 10 May 2006 and in part on 21 April 2007), implement EC Commission Directives 2005/70, 2005/74 and 2005/76, and amend the 2005 Regulations, SI 2005/3286, by substituting new maximum residue levels for specified pesticides and by replacing and adding specified pesticides.

The Pesticides (Maximum Residue Levels in Crops, Food and Feeding Stuffs) (England and Wales) (Amendment) (No 2) Regulations 2006, SI 2006/1742 (in force in part on 27 July 2006, and in part on 15 September 2006), further amend the principal 2005 Regulations supra and implement EC Commission Directives 2006/4, 2006/9, and 2006/30. The effects of the amendments to the 2005 Regulations are that (1) new maximum residue levels for residues of the pesticides, Carbofuran and Diquat, are substituted; (2) the entry for the pesticide group Benomyl, Carbendazim and Thiophanate-methyl are replaced with two entries, one for Benomyl and Carbendazim, and a separate one for Thiophanate-methyl; and (3) new maximum residue levels for residues of such pesticides are substituted.

The Pesticides (Maximum Residue Levels in Crops, Food and Feeding Stuffs) (England and Wales) (Amendment) (No 3) Regulations 2006, SI 2006/2922 (in force on various dates in 2006 and 2007), further amend the principal 2005 Regulations supra and implement EC Commission Directives 2006/53, 2006/59, and 2006/60 and 2006/61, by substituting or adding (1) new residue definitions for certain pesticides which identify the pesticide residues that are taken into account in the measuring of residue levels for each pesticide; and (2) new maximum residue levels for specified pesticides.

152 Pigs—salmonella—England

See para 202.

153 Plant breeders' rights—exemption—prior use—Wales

The Plant Breeders' Rights (Discontinuation of Prior Use Exemption) (Wales) Order 2006, SI 2006/1261 (in force on 12 May 2006), discontinues the prior use exemption in the Plant Varieties Act 1997 s 9(5).

154 Plant breeders' rights—naming and fees

The Plant Breeders' Rights (Naming and Fees) Regulations 2006, SI 2006/648 (in force on 31 March 2006), replace, in part, the Plant Breeders' Rights Regulations 1978, SI 1978/294. In particular, the regulations (1) require the Controller of Plant Variety Rights, in deciding whether to accept a proposed name, to have regard to the suitability criteria set out in EC Council Regulation 2100/94 and EC Commission Regulation 930/2000; (2) update the procedural provisions for approving the name; (3) enable the Controller to charge a fee for costs reasonably incurred in respect of specified matters relating to plant breeders' rights arising under the Plant Varieties Act 1997. SI 1998/1021 and 2002/1677 are revoked.

155 Plant health—control of pests—Dryocosmus kuriphilus Yasumatsu

The Plant Health (Forestry) (Amendment) Order 2006, SI 2006/2696 (in force on 6 November 2006), amend the 2005 Regulations, SI 2005/2517, so as to implement EC Commission Decision 2006/464 on provisional emergency measures to prevent the introduction into, and spread within, the Community of the plant pest *Dryocosmus kuriphilus* Yasumatsu, by (1) revising (a) the definition of 'Europe' to clarify the geographical area of Russia which it includes; and (b) the requirements to notify the likely entry into, or presence in, a free zone, of tree pests or relevant material, to make it clear that the obligation to confirm a notice in writing only applies where the notice was given orally; (2) requiring a registered trader to retain plant passports for one year from the date he created or received them; and (3) prohibiting the landing in and spread within Great Britain of *Dryocosmus kuriphilus* Yasumatsu, and imposing additional requirements on the landing of *Castanea* Mill intended for planting.

156 Plant health—control of pests—Phytophthora ramorum—Wales

The Plant Health (Phytophthora ramorum) (Wales) Order 2006, SI 2006/1344 (in force on 24 May 2006), replaces SI 2002/2762 and implements EC Commission Decisions 2002/757 and 2004/426 in relation to plants other than forest trees, by prohibiting the introduction and spread of the plant pest Phytophthora ramorum and controlling the importation and movement of specified species of plants susceptible to the pest. The order also implements EC Commission Decision 2004/278 on the Community position on the amendment of the Agreement between the European Community and the Swiss Confederation on trade and agricultural products in so far as it relates to camellia, rhododendron and viburnum, by requiring such plants produced in Wales or originating anywhere else in the Community or Switzerland to be accompanied by a plant passport when they are moved, and subjecting them to further controls on their movement.

157 Plant health—export certification—Wales

The Plant Health (Export Certification) (Wales) Order 2006, SI 2006/1701 (in force on 30 June 2006), makes provision for the issue of phytosanitary certificates and reforwarding phytosanitary certificates for the export of plants, plant products or other objects to third countries to satisfy the requirements of those countries' phytosanitary regulations. In particular, the order (1) provides for the making of applications for and the issue of phytosanitary certificates and phytosanitary certificates for re-export; (2) provides for the making of applications for pre-export services and the carrying out of such services by authorised officers; (3) prescribes the fees payable by applicants for such certificates; and (4) makes it an offence to knowingly or recklessly make a false statement or intentionally fail to disclose material information for the purpose of obtaining the issue of a certificate.

158 Plant health—forestry—fees

The Plant Health (Fees) (Forestry) Regulations 2006, SI 2006/2697 (in force on 6 November 2006), replace the Plant Health (Fees) (Forestry) (Great Britain) Regulations 1996, SI 1996/2291 (as amended), and implement EC Council Directive 2000/29 on protective measures against the introduction into the Community of organisms harmful to plants or plant products and against their spread within the Community, so as to (1) make provision for payment to the Forestry Commissioners of an increased fee in respect of inspections carried out in relation to the (a) grant, variation or suspension of, or the monitoring of compliance with, an authority to issue plant passports; and (b) grant, extension or variation of, or the monitoring of compliance with, licence terms and conditions; and (2) require (a) an importer to pay the fee specified, in respect of consignments of certain isolated bark or wood of a type listed under the Plant Health (Forestry) Order 2005, SI 2005/2517, for plant health checks, documentary checks and identity checks carried out on those consignments; and (b) a person to pay the fee specified in respect of any remedial work carried out or monitored by an inspector in accordance with the provisions of the 2005 Order, relating to a consignment of certain isolated bark or wood of a listed type. The fee payable for applications remains the same as in the 1996 Regulations.

159 Plant health—forestry—wood packaging material marking

The Plant Health (Wood Packaging Material Marking) (Forestry) Order 2006, SI 2006/2695 (in force on 6 November 2006), implements the International Standard for Phytosanitary Measures No 15 of March 2002 on Guidelines for regulating wood packaging material in international trade ('ISPM No 15'), so as to provide (1) that no person may (a) apply an ISPM No 15 mark to any wood packaging material except as authorised by a certificate issued under the order; (b) apply any mark other than an ISPM No 15 mark to wood packaging material for the purpose of indicating that it has been subject to an approved measure; or (c) without the authorisation of the Forestry Commissioners, manufacture, remanufacture, recycle or repair any wood without first removing any existing ISPM No 15 mark; (2) procedures for (a) applications for certificates, renewal of certificates, or reassessment following the refusal of an application for or renewal of a certificate, including the fees payable in respect of those applications, and for the issue and validity of certificates; (3) that a inspector (a) has powers to enter premises reasonably believed to be used for the manufacture, collection, storage, trade, transportation or importation of wood packaging material, and to carry out certain investigations for the purpose of ascertaining whether an approved measure has been properly carried out on wood packaging material to which an ISPM No 15 mark has been applied, or for any other purpose of the order, including checking for compliance with it; and (b) may remove, or require another to remove, a mark if he has reasonable grounds for suspecting that it has been applied to wood packaging material other than in accordance with the provisions of the order; (4) that an inspector may seize items he knows or suspects were used to apply a mark to wood packaging material other than in accordance with provisions of the order, or were intended to be so used; (5) for claims to be made against seizure, for referral to the court and the destruction of seized items; (6) that the Forestry Commissioners may, orally or in writing, withdraw a certificate issued under the order if it their opinion that a wood packaging material manufacturer to whom a certificate has been issued has not properly carried out an approved measure to which the certificate relates or has not complied with the provisions of the order; (7) that it is an offence to (a) contravene any of the provisions in respect of restrictions on the marking of wood packaging material; (b) contravene a notice prohibiting the movement of seized items; (c) intentionally obstruct an inspector in the exercise of his powers; (d) knowingly or recklessly make a false statement or intentionally fail to disclose any material information for the purposes of procuring the issue of a certificate; (e) dishonestly alter a certificate; or (f) dishonestly create an instrument which purports to be a certificate; and (8) that a person found guilty of an offence is liable on summary conviction to a fine of up to level five on the standard scale.

160 Plant health—general provisions—England

The Plant Health (England) (Amendment) Order 2006, SI 2006/2307 (in force on 1 October 2006), amends the 2005 Order, SI 2005/2530, so as to implement EC Commission Directives 2005/77 and 2006/35, and EC Commission Decision 2005/870, 2006/473 and 2006/464. In particular, the order (1) makes provision as to the matters in respect of which an inspector must be satisfied before he may discharge any material which is destined for a protected zone from an area of plant health control ; (2) provides that the local movement exemption is a discretionary exemption which takes account of plant health risk; (3) requires certain commercial users of plant material to retain plant passports for one year; (4) enables a registered plant trader to issue passports for the movement of relevant material from any premises; (5) makes it clear that, in relation to the requirements to notify pests, the obligation to confirm a notice in writing only applies where the notice was given orally; (6) makes it an offence to fail to comply with the requirements for plant passports or certain provisions relating to certain solanaceous species; (7) prohibits the landing in and spread within England of *Dryocosmus kuriphilus* Yasumatsu and imposes additional requirements on the landing and movement of *Castanea* Mill intended for planting; (8) exempts tubers of *Solanum* L which originate in Bulgaria from the prohibition on landing in England; (9) make provision in relation to countries and areas recognised as free from *Xanthomonas campestris*, *Cercospora angolensis* and *Guignardia citricarpa*; (10) requires seeds of all *Solanaceae* and certain plants coming from Switzerland to be accompanied by a phytosanitary certificate; and (11) limits the circumstances in which the Secretary of State is required to publish the demarcation of zones for the control of *Ralstonia solanacearum*.

161 Plant health—general provisions—Wales

The Plant Health (Wales) Order 2006, SI 2006/1643 (in force on 27 June 2006), revokes and consolidates with amendments the Plant Health (Great Britain) Order 1993, SI 1993/1320, and implements EC Council Directive 2002/89, EC Commission Directives 2004/103, 2004/105, 2005/16, 2005/17, 2005/77, 2006/35 and Commission Decisions 2005/260 and 2005/870. In particular, the order (1) contains general prohibitions and restrictions on any plant, plant product, soil or growing medium ('relevant material') being landed in Wales; (2) requires importers to provide the National Assembly for Wales with advance notice of landing of relevant material; (3) imposes requirements for relevant material to be accompanied by a phytosanitary certificate; (4) exempts certain relevant material which is brought into Wales in a person's baggage from these prohibitions and requirements; (5) imposes requirements relating to the contents, display and presentation of documents required to accompany relevant material; (6) provides that certain relevant material must not be removed from an area of plant health control until, having satisfied himself as to the matters specified, an inspector has discharged that material; (7) provides for an officer for Revenue and Customs to be able to detain relevant material from which an inspector considers a plant pest may spread; (8) contains general requirements to be met by phytosanitary documentation; (9) introduces provisions to allow relevant material to be inspected at its place of destination provided that place is approved by the relevant authorities and the material is accompanied by a plant health movement document; (10) contains prohibitions and restrictions that apply to relevant material coming to Wales from another part of the European Community, which includes other parts of the United Kingdom, and on the movement of that material within Wales; (11) imposes a requirement on plant traders to be registered in respect of their activities and provides for the National Assembly to be able to authorise them to issue plant passports; (12) contains special arrangements governing trade in relevant material between Wales and Switzerland; (13) contains general enforcement powers given to plant health inspectors; (14) imposes additional requirements in respect of certain solanaceous species (potatoes and tomatoes); (15) provides for the National Assembly to be able to license activities that would otherwise be prohibited by the order; (16) imposes requirements to notify the presence of certain pests to the National Assembly; and (17) contains offences for non-compliance with the order or with requirements imposed under it.

162 Plant health—import inspection fees—England

The Plant Health (Import Inspection Fees) (England) Regulations 2006, SI 2006/1879 (in force on 4 August 2006), replace the 2005 Regulations, SI 2005/906, and, in particular, (1) require an importer to pay, on import of a consignment to which the regulations apply, a specified fee or a reduced specified fee, as appropriate; (2) provide that such a fee is payable regardless of whether an inspection is carried out on the particular consignment, except in the case of the fees payable for an inspection carried out at the request of an importer outside daytime working hours; and (3) require an importer to pay the specified fee for documentary checks and identity checks.

163 Plant health—import inspection fees—Wales

The Plant Health (Import Inspection Fees) (Wales) (No 2) Regulations 2006, SI 2006/2832 (in force on 31 October 2006), replace the 2006 Regulations, SI 2006/171, which implemented EC Council Directive 2000/29 in part, and (1) require an importer to pay, on import of a consignment to which the regulations apply, a specified fee or reduced rate fee, as appropriate; (2) provide that such a fee is payable regardless of whether an inspection is carried out on the particular consignment, except in the case of the fees payable for an inspection carried out at the request of an importer outside daytime working hours; and (3) require an importer to pay the specified fee for documentary checks and identity checks.

164 Plant protection—products

The Plant Protection Products (Amendment) Regulations 2006, SI 2006/1295 (in force on various dates in 2006 and 2007), further amend the 2005 Regulations, SI 2005/1435, by adding to the list of directives which specify active substances which can be used in products capable for being approved for placing on the market.

The Plant Protection Products (Amendment) (No 2) Regulations 2006, SI 2006/2933 (in force in part on 16 December 2006 and in part on 1 February 2007), further amend the 2005 Regulations supra by adding to the list of directives which specify active substances which can be used in products capable for being approved for placing on the market.

165 Potatoes—seed potatoes—England

The Seed Potatoes (England) Regulations 2006, SI 2006/1161 (in force on 16 May 2006), replace the 1991 Regulations, SI 1991/2206, and give effect to EC Council Directive 2002/56 and EC Commission Decision 2004/842. The regulations control the production with a view to marketing, the certification and the marketing of seed potatoes in England, other than those intended for export outside the European Community, so as to (1) prohibit the marketing of any seed potatoes unless they have been certified as either pre-basic, basic or certified seed potatoes; or authorised for marketing for scientific purposes, selection work or for test and trial purposes; (2) restrict the marketing of seed potatoes within a protected region to the marketing of pre-basic seed potatoes, or basic seed potatoes satisfying specified requirements; (3) prohibit the marketing of seed potatoes unless they comply with the specified size requirements; (4) allow the Secretary of State to authorise the marketing of small quantities of seed potatoes for scientific purposes or selection work, and seed potatoes for tests or trials purposes; (5) provide (a) that seed potatoes, other than retail sales of small quantities of seed potatoes meeting specified conditions, may only be marketed in properly labelled and sealed packages or containers; (b) that no person may market genetically modified seed potatoes unless any marketing information provided, and any label or document affixed to, accompanying or relating to the seed potatoes, clearly indicates that they have been genetically modified; (c) for the taking of samples of seed potatoes as part of the certification process or to ensure compliance with the provisions of the regulations; and (d) the Secretary of State with powers of examination and production of seed potatoes and relevant documents; and (6) allow the Secretary of State to withdraw official labels or official documents relating to seed potatoes which are found not to comply with specified requirements.

The Seed Potatoes (Fees) (England) Regulations 2006, SI 2006/1160 (in force on 17 May 2006), replace the 2004 Regulations, SI 2004/1316, so as to reflect changes in terminology made by SI 2006/1161 supra in relation to certain categories of seed potatoes.

166   Potatoes—seed potatoes—Wales

The Seed Potatoes (Wales) Regulations 2006, SI 2006/2929 (in force on 15 November 2006), replace the 1991 Regulations, SI 1991/2206, and give effect to EC Council Directive 2002/56 and EC Commission Decision 2004/842. The regulations control the production with a view to marketing, the certification and the marketing of seed potatoes in Wales, other than those intended for export outside the European Community, so as to (1) prohibit the marketing of any seed potatoes unless they have been certified as either pre-basic, basic or certified seed potatoes; or authorised for marketing for scientific purposes, selection work or for test and trial purposes; (2) restrict the marketing of seed potatoes within a protected region to the marketing of pre-basic seed potatoes, or basic seed potatoes satisfying specified requirements; (3) prohibit the marketing of seed potatoes unless they comply with the specified size requirements; (4) allow the National Assembly for Wales to authorise the marketing of small quantities of seed potatoes for scientific purposes or selection work, and seed potatoes for tests or trials purposes; (5) provide (a) that seed potatoes, other than retail sales of small quantities of seed potatoes meeting specified conditions, may only be marketed in properly labelled and sealed packages or containers; (b) that no person may market genetically modified seed potatoes unless any marketing information provided, and any label or document affixed to, accompanying or relating to the seed potatoes, clearly indicates that they have been genetically modified; (c) for the taking of samples of seed potatoes as part of the certification process or to ensure compliance with the provisions of the regulations; and (d) the National Assembly with powers of examination and production of seed potatoes and relevant documents; and (6) allow the National Assembly to withdraw official labels or official documents relating to seed potatoes which are found not to comply with specified requirements.

The Seed Potatoes (Fees) (Wales) (No 2) Regulations 2006, SI 2006/2961 (in force on 16 November 2006), replace the 1998 Regulations, SI 1998/1228, and (1) prescribe the fees payable by applicants for certification of seed potatoes under the Seed Potatoes (Wales) Regulations 2006, SI 2006/2929; and (2) introduce new categories of fee for the inspection of pre-basic seed potatoes and for the inspection of seed potatoes under a scheme or arrangement. SI 2006/519 is revoked.

167   Poultry—broiler flocks—salmonella—Wales

See para 201.

168   Poultry—turkey flocks—salmonella—England

See para 202.

169   Products of animal origin—third country imports—veterinary checks—England

The Products of Animal Origin (Third Country Imports) (England) Regulations 2006, SI 2006/2841 (in force on 24 November 2006), replace the 2004 Regulations, SI 2004/3388, so as to implement EC Council Directive 97/78 laying down the principles governing the organisation of veterinary checks on products entering the Community from third countries. The products to which the regulations apply must comply with the requirements listed by reference to the relevant Community legislation. In particular, the regulations (1) provide for specified exemptions; (2) define the authorities that enforce the regulations; usually, these are port health authorities, who appoint official veterinary surgeons and official fish inspectors to conduct veterinary checks at each border inspection post in their area; (3) make provision that the Commissioners for Her Majesty's Revenue and Customs is to enforce the prohibition on the introduction of products at points of entry other than border inspection posts; (4) enable local authority enforcement officers who are not authorised officers to take hold of any products of animal origin they suspect of having been illegally imported until an authorised officer is able to take charge of it; (5) create a new offence relating to the unlawful disclosure of information received from Her Majesty's Revenue and Customs; (6) confer the necessary enforcement powers on the enforcement authorities; (7) enable the approval of border inspection posts to be suspended in part; previously only a full suspension of approval was permitted; (8) provide that the bringing into England of products that do not comply with the specified requirements is prohibited, unless they are being transported across England; (9) provide that products must be brought in at border inspection posts, that advance notice of their introduction must be given and that they must be made available for inspection, together with required documentation, at a border inspection post; (10) bring requirements for pre-notification of imported consignments to border inspection posts into line with Commission Regulation 136/2004 laying down procedures for veterinary checks at Community border inspection posts on products imported from third countries; (11) deal with products that are rejected at inspection, are brought in illegally or present a risk to animal health or public health; (12) implement procedures for the direct movement of consignments, intended as food for passengers or crew, that do not meet EU import requirements from border inspection posts to ships operating internationally; (13) deal with the calculation and payment of charges for the veterinary checks provided for in the regulations; (14) confer on the Secretary of State and the Food Standards Agency power to prohibit the bringing of products into England from non-EEA countries in which there is an outbreak of animal disease; (15) establish offences and penalties; (16) deal with the service of notices and with notification of decisions; (17) provide that certain existing provisions do not apply to products to which the regulations apply; and (18) in relation to salmonella testing, enable border inspection posts to charge for such tests carried out in accordance with Community legislation. SI 2006/844 is revoked.

170 Products of animal origin—third country imports—veterinary checks—Wales

The Products of Animal Origin (Third Country Imports) (Wales) (Amendment) Regulations 2006, SI 2006/767 (in force on 16 March 2006), amend the 2005 Regulations, SI 2005/666, so as to give effect to the restrictions on the importation of products derived from birds contained in EC Commission Decision 2005/760, concerning certain protection measures in relation to highly pathogenic avian influenza in certain third countries for the import of captive birds. SI 2005/3395 is revoked.

The Products of Animal Origin (Third Country Imports) (Wales) (Amendment) (No 2) Regulations 2006, SI 2006/1349 (in force on 31 May 2006), further amend the 2005 Regulations supra so as to give effect to the restrictions on the importation of products derived from birds contained in EC Commission Decision 2006/7, concerning certain protection measures in relation to the import of feathers from certain third countries.

171 Seeds—cereal seed and fodder plant seed—England

The Cereal Seed (England) and Fodder Plant Seed (England) (Amendment) Regulations 2006, SI 2006/1678 (in force on 19 July 2006), amend the Cereal Seed (England) Regulations 2002, SI 2002/3173, and the Fodder Plant Seed (England) Regulations 2002, SI 2002/3172, so as to implement EC Commission Directive 2006/55 on the maximum weight of seed lots, with the effect that the maximum weight of a seed lot of species of cereal seed, except for maize, and the maximum weight of a mixed seed lot, where more than 50 per cent of that lot is increased by virtue of these provisions, is increased from 25 to 30 tonnes.

172 Seeds—cereal seed and fodder plant seed—Wales

The Cereal Seed (Wales) and Fodder Plant Seed (Wales) (Amendment) Regulations 2006, SI 2006/3250 (in force on 20 December 2006), implement EC Commission Directive 2006/55 on the maximum weight of seed lots, and amend the Cereal Seed (Wales) Regulations 2005, SI 2005/3036, by increasing, from 25 to 30 tonnes, the maximum weight of a seed lot of species of cereal seed, except for maize. The regulations also amend the Fodder Plant Seed (Wales) Regulations 2005, SI 2005/1207, so as to ensure that, where more than 50 per cent of a seed lot comprising a mixture of fodder plant seed and seed for which the maximum weight of a seed lot is increased by the regulations to 30 tonnes, the maximum weight of the mixed seed lot is also 30 tonnes.

173 Seeds—tests and trials—England

The Seed (England) (Amendments for Tests and Trials etc) Regulations 2006, SI 2006/2314 (in force on 23 September 2006), further amend the Beet Seed (England) Regulations 2002, SI 2002/3171, the Cereal Seed (England) Regulations 2002, SI 2002/3173, the Fodder Plant Seed (England) Regulations 2002, SI 2002/3172, the Oil and Fibre Seed (England) Regulations 2002, SI 2002/3174, and the Vegetable Seed (England) Regulations 2002, SI 2002/3175, to give effect to European Commission Decision 2004/842 concerning the authorisation of the placing on the market of seed belonging to varieties for which an application for entry in the national catalogue of varieties of agricultural plant species or vegetable species has been submitted, which sets out the conditions under which beet, cereal, fodder plant, oil and fibre plant and vegetable seed which have not yet been added to a national list may be marketed for test and trial purposes or, in the case of vegetable seed, for purposes of gaining knowledge from practical experience during cultivation.

ANIMALS

Halsbury's Laws of England (4th edn) vol 2(1) (Reissue) paras 501–970

174 Animal by-products—Wales

The Animal By-Products (Wales) Regulations 2006, SI 2006/1293 (in force on 12 May 2006), make provision in Wales for the administration and enforcement of EC European Parliament and Council Regulation 1774/2002 laying down health rules concerning animal by-products not intended for human consumption and replace the 2003 Regulations, SI 2003/2756, so as to (1) make it an offence, other than in accordance with Regulation 1774/2002 to (a) categorise, collect, transport, dispose, store, process or use, category 1, category 2 or category 3 material; and (b) collect, transport, identify or store animal by-products; (2) specify that a mixture of mammalian and non-mammalian by-products are to be treated as mammalian by-products; (3) enforce restrictions on the feeding of catering waste and processed animal protein; (4) prohibit the feeding to farmed animals of other unprocessed animal by-products; (5) restrict access to catering waste and other animal by-products; (6) enforce restrictions on the application of organic fertiliser to pasture land; (7) provide for the approval of premises for the different types of treatment of animal by-products; (8) make provision that composting on premises where the composted material originated does not need approval if specified conditions are complied with; (9) provide for checks at plants, sampling and approved laboratories; (10) make provision to regulate the placing on the market of various products derived from animal by-products; (11) provide derogations relating to the use of animal by-products for taxidermy and feeding certain specified animals; (12) permit the burial of pet animals; (13) permit burial and burning on Bardsey Island and Caldy Island; (14) provide for burial or burning in the event of a disease outbreak and for burning and burial of bees and apiculture products; (15) make provision for record keeping; (16) provide for applications for approvals, authorisations and registrations, their suspension or revocation and for representations against a notice to amend, suspend or revoke them; (17) authorise an inspector to serve a notice requiring the disposal of animal by-products or catering waste and requiring cleansing and disinfection of any vehicle, container or premises; (18) confer on inspectors, powers of entry and provide that it is an offence to obstruct an inspector; (19) make provision for biogas and composting plants; (20) provide for the disposal of fluid from rendering ruminant animal by-products; (21) provide for testing methods; and (22) provide that the regulations are enforced by the local authority, except in specified premises, and that breach of the regulations is an offence punishable on summary conviction to a fine up to the statutory maximum or three months imprisonment and that on indictment the penalty is an unlimited fine or two years imprisonment. The Dogs Act 1906 s 6 and provisions relating to knackers' yard under the Slaughterhouses Act 1974 are repealed.

175 Animal gatherings—England

The Animal Gatherings (England) Order 2006, SI 2006/2211 (in force on 31 August 2006), replaces the 2004 Order, SI 2004/1202, and (1) requires a licence for animal gatherings; (2) prohibits an animal gathering from taking place until 27 days or more after the last animal has left the premises and when the premises and equipment on the premises have been cleaned of visible contamination; (3) where a gathering takes place on paved premises, makes provision for the cleansing and disinfection of the premises, and enables a gathering to take place inside the normal time limits; (4) imposes a 48-hour time limit on animal gatherings for the purpose of sale on paved premises and sheep autumn breeding sales and onward consignments on any premises; (5) imposes duties on persons attending an animal gathering; (6) imposes restrictions following an animal gathering; and (7) provides for enforcement of the order.

176 Animal health—animals and animal products—import and export—England

The Animals and Animal Products (Import and Export) (England) Regulations 2006, SI 2006/1471 (in force on 29 June 2006), replace the 2005 Regulations, SI 2005/2002, and implement EEC Council Directives 90/452, 91/496 and EC Commission Decision 2000/666. In particular, the regulations (1) make it an offence to export, import or transport for intra-Community trade any animal or animal product to which Directive 90/425 applies except in accordance with the directive; (2) provide a statutory basis for the Poultry Health Scheme, which is a means of approving and monitoring poultry establishments engaging in intra-Community trade of poultry and hatching eggs and prohibit exports unless the commodities originate from an establishment which is a member of the Scheme and conforms to the requirements of EEC Council Directive 90/539; (3) set out the procedures and requirements for the registration of dealers in animals and animal products and the approval of centres and teams engaging in intra-Community trade in animals and animal products; (4) provide for approval of laboratories to carry out specified poultry health tests and provide for the approval of assembly centres; (5) provide for checks on intra-Community trade at the place of destination; (6) impose duties on consignees of animals and animal products and specify the procedure to be followed in cases of illegal consignments; (7) prohibit the importation of any animal from a third country unless the conditions of Directive 91/496 are complied with; (8) prescribe the third countries from which animals may be imported; (9) specify the places at which animals may be imported through border inspection posts and provide for the procedure for such importation; (10) require that, at the place of destination, certain animals may not be released until authorised by an authorised officer of the Secretary of State; (11) provide for post-import controls; (12) make provision for imports from third countries which undergo the requisite veterinary border checks on arrival at another member state; (13) confer powers on the Secretary of State to take action in the event of an outbreak of disease in another state and make provision for the notification of decisions, inspectors' powers of entry and the recovery of expenses; (14) provide for offences and penalties; (15) provide for the arrangements for quarantine of captive birds imported from third countries;

(16) impose requirements on quarantine managers as to the running of quarantine centres and facilities; (17) make general prohibitions applying to any persons in respect of entry to a quarantine centre or facility and removal of birds and carcases from quarantine without the authorisation of a veterinary inspector; (18) confer supplementary powers of entry on inspectors and powers of inspection and sampling; (19) provide for the Veterinary Laboratories Agency to act as the official laboratory and make charges for laboratory testing; (20) prescribe measures which must be taken when avian influenza, Newcastle disease or Chlamydia psittaci is found in an imported captive bird at a quarantine centre or facility; and (21) specifically identify special conditions on exports of cattle to Germany, Denmark, Italy, Austria, Finland and Sweden.

The Animals and Animal Products (Import and Export) (England) (Amendment) Regulations 2006, SI 2006/2126 (in force in part on 1 August 2006 and in part on 1 September 2006), amend SI 2006/1471 supra to give effect to the extension of the European Union ban, under EC Commission Decision 2005/760, on the import of captive birds from third countries until 1 January 2007.

177 Animal health—animals and animal products—import and export—Wales

The Animals and Animal Products (Import and Export) (Wales) Regulations 2006, SI 2006/1536 (in force on 15 June 2006), replace the 2005 Regulations, SI 2005/1158, and implement EEC Council Directives 90/452, 91/496 and EC Commission Decision 2000/666. In particular, the regulations (1) make it an offence to export, import or transport for intra-Community trade any animal or animal product to which Directive 90/425 applies except in accordance with that Directive; (2) provide a statutory basis for the Poultry Health Scheme, which is a means of approving and monitoring poultry establishments engaging in intra-Community trade of poultry and hatching eggs and prohibit exports unless the commodities originate from an establishment which is a member of the Scheme and conforms to the requirements of EEC Council Directive 90/539; (3) set out the procedures and requirements for the registration of dealers in animals and animal products and the approval of centres and teams engaging in intra-Community trade in animals and animal products; (4) provide for approval of laboratories to carry out specified poultry health tests and provide for the approval of assembly centres; (5) provide for checks on intra-Community trade at the place of destination; (6) impose duties on consignees of animals and animal products and specify the procedure to be followed in cases of illegal consignments; (7) prohibit the importation of any animal from a third country unless the conditions of Directive 91/496 are complied with; (8) prescribe the third countries from which animals may be imported; (9) specify the places at which animals may be imported through border inspection posts and provide for the procedure for such importation; (10) require that, at the place of destination, certain animals may not be released until authorised by an authorised officer of the National Assembly for Wales; (11) provide for post-import controls; (12) make provision for imports from third countries which undergo the requisite veterinary border checks on arrival at another member state; (13) confer powers on the National Assembly to take action in the event of an outbreak of disease in another state and make provision for the notification of decisions, inspectors' powers of entry and the recovery of expenses; (14) provide for offences and penalties; (15) provide for the arrangements for quarantine of captive birds imported from third countries; (16) impose requirements on quarantine managers as to the running of quarantine centres and facilities; (17) make general prohibitions applying to any persons in respect of entry to a quarantine centre or facility and removal of birds and carcases from quarantine without the authorisation of a veterinary inspector; (18) confer supplementary powers of entry on inspectors and powers of inspection and sampling; (19) provide for the Veterinary Laboratories Agency to act as the official laboratory and make charges for laboratory testing; (20) prescribe measures which must be taken when avian influenza, Newcastle disease or Chlamydia psittaci is found in an imported captive bird at a quarantine centre or facility; and (21) specifically identify special conditions on exports of cattle to Germany, Denmark, Italy, Austria, Finland and Sweden.

The Animals and Animal Products (Import and Export) (Wales) (Amendment) Regulations 2006, SI 2006/2128 (in force on 1 August 2006), amend SI 2006/1536 supra to give effect to the extension of the European Union ban, under EC Commission Decision 2005/760, on the import of captive birds from third countries until 1 January 2007.

The Animals and Animal Products (Import and Export) (Wales) (Amendment) (No 2) Regulations 2006, SI 2006/3452 (in force on 31 December 2006), further amend SI 2006/1536 to give effect to the extension of the European Union ban, under EC Commission Decision 2005/760 (as amended), on the import of captive birds from third countries until 31 March 2007.

178 Animal health—diseases of animals—approved disinfectants—England

The Diseases of Animals (Approved Disinfectants) (Amendment) (England) Order 2006, SI 2006/1394 (in force on 16 June 2006), further amends the 1978 Order, SI 1978/32, so as to list disinfectants approved by the Secretary of State and disinfectants which, although no longer approved, may continue to be used as approved disinfectants until 15 September 2006. SI 2005/1908 is revoked.

179 Animal health—diseases of animals—approved disinfectants—Wales

The Diseases of Animals (Approved Disinfectants) (Amendment) (Wales) Order 2006, SI 2006/3166 (in force on 30 November 2006), further amends the 1978 Order, SI 1978/32, so as to list disinfectants approved by the National Assembly for Wales and disinfectants which, although no longer approved, may continue to be used as approved disinfectants until 28 February 2007. SI 2005/583 is revoked.

180 Animal health—diseases of animals—avian influenza—H5N1 in poultry—England

The Avian Influenza (H5N1 in Poultry) (England) Order 2006, SI 2006/3247 (in force on 30 December 2006), transposes EC Commission Decision 2006/415 concerning certain protection measures in relation to highly pathogenic avian influenza of subtype H5N1 in poultry in the Community and repealing EC Commission Decision 2006/135. The order also supplements the general measures to control avian influenza set out in the Avian Influenza and Influenza of Avian Origin in Mammals (England) (No 2) Order 2006, SI 2006/2702. In particular, the order (1) specifies which zones declared under SI 2006/2702 are zones A and B for the purposes of the Decision 2006/135; (2) requires the Secretary of State to declare temporary control zones or temporary movement restriction zones under SI 2006/2702 if highly pathogenic avian influenza of subtype H5N1 is suspected in poultry; (3) relates to the location and size of such zones; (4) requires the Secretary of State to declare a restricted zone under SI 2006/2702 on confirmation of highly pathogenic avian influenza of subtype H5N1 in poultry; (5) provides additional measures which restrict movements of the following: (a) poultry and other captive birds from restricted zones; (b) hatching eggs from restricted zones; (c) wild game bird products from protection, surveillance and restricted zones; and (d) by-products from any bird in a protection, surveillance or restricted zone; (5) bans bird gatherings in restricted zones; (6) contains general measures relating to enforcement of the order; and (7) sets out the mark to be applied to meat and meat products from wild game birds from protection, surveillance and restricted zones.

181 Animal health—diseases of animals—avian influenza—H5N1 in poultry—Wales

The Avian Influenza (H5N1 in Poultry) (Wales) Order 2006, SI 2006/3309 (in force on 13 December 2006), transposes EC Commission Decision 2006/415 concerning certain protection measures in relation to highly pathogenic avian influenza of subtype H5N1 in poultry in the Community and repealing EC Commision Decision 2006/135. The order also supplements the general measures to control avian influenza set out in the Avian Influenza and Influenza of Avian Origin in Mammals (Wales) (No 2) Order 2006, SI 2006/2927. In particular, the order (1) specifies which zones declared under SI 2006/2927 are zones A and B for the purposes of the Decision 2006/135; (2) requires the National Assembly for Wales to declare temporary control zones or temporary movement restriction zones under SI 2006/2927 if highly pathogenic avian influenza of subtype H5N1 is suspected in poultry; (3) relates to the location and size of such zones; (4) requires the National Assembly to declare a restricted zone under SI 2006/2927 on confirmation of highly pathogenic avian influenza of subtype H5N1 in poultry; (5) provides additional measures which restrict movements of the following: (a) poultry and other captive birds from restricted zones; (b) hatching eggs from restricted zones; (c) wild game bird products from protection, surveillance and restricted zones; and (d) by-products from any bird in a protection, surveillance or restricted zone; (5) bans bird gatherings in restricted zones; and (6) contains general measures relating to enforcement of the order.

182 Animal health—diseases of animals—avian influenza—H5N1 in wild birds—England

The Avian Influenza (H5N1 in Wild Birds) (England) Order 2006, SI 2006/3249 (in force on 30 December 2006), implements (1) EC Commission Decision 2006/563 concerning certain protection measures in relation to highly pathogenic avian influenza in wild birds in the Community and repealing EC Commission Decision 2006/115; and (2) the Commission Decision establishing an alternative health mark pursuant to EC Council Directive 2002/99. In particular, the order (1) provides that if the Chief Veterinary Officer advises the Secretary of State that avian influenza of subtype H5 is present in a wild bird or a wild bird carcase and that she suspects or confirms that the neuraminidase type is N1, the Secretary of State must, subject to a derogation, declare a wild bird control area and a wild bird monitoring area; (2) sets out the circumstances in which the Secretary of State can amend a declaration so that certain measures do not apply in respect of those areas; (3) provides that the Secretary of State may, in his declaration of a wild bird control area or a wild bird monitoring area, impose additional measures to those set out; (4) provides that the Secretary of State must ensure that veterinary inspectors inspect commercial premises in a wild bird control area or a wild bird monitoring area to monitor the spread of avian influenza; (5) sets out the circumstances in which the Secretary of State can either amend a declaration of a wild bird control area so that it becomes part of the wild bird monitoring area or revoke the declaration of either area; (6) relates to the provision of information and reasonable assistance, record keeping and to compliance with requirements laid down under the order; (7) provides for the feeding and tending of animals or poultry which cannot be moved on termination of a right of occupation because of a restriction imposed by the order; (8) makes provision in relation to cleansing and disinfection; (9) makes provision related to offences and enforcement including the conferring of general powers on inspectors to take action to prevent spread of the disease; (10) sets out the measures that are to apply in respect of a wild bird control area including measures relating to the movement of birds, the movement of hatching eggs, the movement of meat, the movement of poultry by-products and the use or movement of manure, the hunting or release of birds and bird gatherings and other provisions relating to the measures to be taken at premises receiving birds or their products from the area; (11) sets out the measures that are to apply in respect of a wild bird monitoring area including measures relating to the movement of birds and prohibitions on bird gatherings and the hunting or release of birds; and (12) sets out the biosecurity measures that are to apply in respect of premises where poultry or other captive birds are kept in a wild bird control area or a wild bird monitoring area.

183 Animal health—diseases of animals—avian influenza—H5N1 in wild birds—Wales

The Avian Influenza (H5N1 in Wild Birds) (Wales) Order 2006, SI 2006/3310 (in force on 13 December 2006), implements (1) EC Commission Decision 2006/563 concerning certain protection measures in relation to highly pathogenic avian influenza in wild birds in the Community and repealing EC Commission Decision 2006/115; and (2) the Commission Decision establishing an alternative health mark pursuant to EC Council Directive 2002/99. In particular, the order (1) provides that if the Chief Veterinary Officer advises the National Assembly for Wales that avian influenza of subtype H5 is present in a wild bird or a wild bird carcase and that he suspects or confirms that the neuraminidase type is N1, the National Assembly must, subject to a derogation, declare a wild bird control area and a wild bird monitoring area; (2) sets out the circumstances in which the National Assembly can amend a declaration so that certain measures do not apply in respect of those areas; (3) provides that the National Assembly may, in its declaration of a wild bird control area or a wild bird monitoring area, impose additional measures to those set out; (4) provides that the National Assembly must ensure that veterinary inspectors inspect commercial premises in a wild bird control area or a wild bird monitoring area to monitor the spread of avian influenza; (5) sets out the circumstances in which the National Assembly can either amend a declaration of a wild bird control area so that it becomes part of the wild bird monitoring area or revoke the declaration of either area; (6) relates to the provision of information and reasonable assistance, record keeping and to compliance with requirements laid down under the order; (7) provides for the feeding and tending of animals or poultry which cannot be moved on termination of a right of occupation because of a restriction imposed by the order; (8) makes provision in relation to cleansing and disinfection; (9) makes provision related to offences and enforcement including the conferring of general powers on inspectors to take action to prevent spread of the disease; (10) sets out the measures that are to apply in respect of a wild bird control area including measures relating to the movement of birds, the movement of hatching eggs, the movement of meat, the movement of poultry by-products and the use or movement of manure, the hunting or release of birds and bird gatherings and other provisions relating to the measures to be taken at premises receiving birds or their products from the area; (11) sets out the measures that are to apply in respect of a wild bird monitoring area including measures relating to the movement of birds and prohibitions on bird gatherings and the hunting or release of birds; and (12) sets out the biosecurity measures that are to apply in respect of premises where poultry or other captive birds are kept in a wild bird control area or a wild bird monitoring area.

184 Animal health—diseases of animals—avian influenza—preventive measure—England

The Avian Influenza (Preventive Measures) (England) Regulations 2006, SI 2006/2701 (in force on 13 November 2006), replace, in relation to England, the 2005 Regulations, SI 2005/3394, so as to (1) prohibit any person from (a) arranging an unlicensed gathering of poultry or other captive birds unless the Secretary of State licenses him to do so; and (b) bringing poultry or captive birds to a bird gathering which he knows or suspects is unlicensed; (2) require the keeper of 50 or more poultry on any one premises, not just commercial premises, to notify the Secretary of State within the specified notification period of certain information relating to each premises, or to notify the Secretary of State of specified changes to the information provided; (3) make provision in relation to the vaccination of zoo birds; (4) provide a general prohibition on the unauthorised vaccination of zoo birds; (5) allow the Secretary of State, following a risk assessment, to (a) vaccinate zoo birds; (b) require the vaccination of zoo birds; or (c) license the vaccination of zoo birds; (6) make provision for restrictions on the movement of vaccinated zoo birds; and (7) provide (a) general duties relating to the execution of the 2006 Regulations supra; (b) for the powers of inspectors; and (c) for offences and enforcement. Provision is made for the continued effect of the general licence for bird gatherings issued by the Secretary of State under the 2005 Regulations supra, reg 5.

185 Animal health—diseases of animals—avian influenza—preventive measures—Wales

The Avian Influenza (Preventive Measures) (Wales) Regulations 2006, SI 2006/2803 (in force on 13 November 2006), replace SI 2005/3384 and 3385, and give effect to EC Commission Decision

2005/734, as amended. The regulations (1) prohibit any person from arranging an unlicensed gathering of poultry or other captive birds, or from bringing such birds to a bird gathering which he knows or suspects is unlicensed; (2) require keepers of 50 or more poultry on any one premises to notify the National Assembly for Wales of specified information relating to those poultry, and of specified changes to this information; (3) allow the Assembly to require and licence vaccination of susceptible birds in zoos and prohibit the unlicensed movement of vaccinated zoo birds; (4) make provision to ensure the effective operation of the regulations; (5) provide for the powers of inspectors; and (6) make provision in relation to enforcement and offences.

186   Animal health—diseases of animals—avian influenza—vaccination—England

The Avian Influenza (Vaccination) (England) Regulations 2006, SI 2006/2703 (in force on 14 November 2006), transpose EC Council Directive 2005/94 on Community measures for the control of avian flu. The regulations (1) impose a general prohibition on the vaccination of birds against avian influenza except where required or licensed by the Secretary of State; (2) permit the Secretary of State to (a) take emergency or preventive measures, if he considers it necessary to reduce the risk of the spread of avian influenza, by declaring vaccination zones in areas that contain poultry and other captive birds, or to serve a vaccination notice on premises where poultry or captive birds are kept, requiring vaccination in the zones or on the premises, provided that the measures are carried out in accordance with a vaccination plan approved by the European Commission and following a risk assessment that has indicated that there is a significant and immediate threat of avian influenza spreading within or into England; and (b) take preventive measures by granting a licence to the occupier of any premises to vaccinate poultry, other captive birds or any category of poultry or other captive birds on the premises, provided that a risk assessment indicates that the birds on the premises are exposed to a risk of avian influenza, and the measures are carried out in accordance with a vaccination plan approved by the European Commission; (3) provide (a) for measures applying in a vaccination zone or premises that are the subject of a vaccination notice or a vaccination licence; and (b) that where emergency vaccination is undertaken before the approval of an emergency vaccination plan by the European Commission, there is a general prohibition on the movement of poultry, other captive birds, their carcasses or any eggs from one premises within an emergency vaccination zone to another within an emergency vaccination zone, into or out of any emergency zone and into or out of any premises that is the subject of a vaccination notice, unless the movement is (i) one of the permitted movements specified and the movement is licensed by a veterinary inspector or an inspector acting under his direction; (ii) for the purpose of retail distribution of poultry eggs; or (iii) to move carcases or eggs for disposal; and (4) make provision in relation to the powers of inspectors, offences and enforcement.

187   Animal health—diseases of animals—avian influenza—vaccination—Wales

The Avian Influenza (Vaccination) (Wales) (No 2) Regulations 2006, SI 2006/2932 (in force on 14 November 2006), transpose, in relation to Wales, EC Council Directive 2005/94 on Community measures for the control of avian influenza. In particular, the regulations (1) impose a general prohibition on vaccination of birds against avian influenza except where required or licensed by the National Assembly for Wales; (2) permit the National Assembly, if it considers it necessary to reduce the risk of the spread of avian influenza, to declare vaccination zones in areas that contain poultry or other captive birds that it considers should be vaccinated, or to serve vaccination notices on premises where such birds are kept; (3) give the National Assembly the power to require vaccination in these zones or on such premises; (4) provide that such measures can only be carried out in accordance with a vaccination plan approved by the European Commission and where a risk assessment has been carried out that has indicated that there is a significant and immediate threat of avian influenza spreading within or into Wales, or that certain areas or birds are in any event exposed to a risk of avian influenza; (5) permit the National Assembly to grant licences to occupiers of premises that permit vaccination of birds, or certain categories of birds, on those premises; (6) provide for measures applying in a vaccination zone or premises that are the subject of a vaccination notice or a vaccination licence; (7) provide that where emergency vaccination is undertaken before the European Commission has approved the national emergency vaccination plan, there is a general prohibition on the movement of poultry, other captive birds and their eggs from one premises within an emergency vaccination zone to another within an emergency vaccination zone, into or out of any emergency vaccination zone and into or out of any premises that is the subject of a vaccination notice unless the movement is one of the permitted movements listed in the Schedule and the movement is licensed; and (8) make provision relating to offences and enforcement. SI 2006/1761 is revoked.

188   Animal health—diseases of animals—avian influenza and influenza of avian origin in mammals—England

The Avian Influenza and Influenza of Avian Origin in Mammals (England) (No 2) Order 2006, SI 2006/2702 (in force on 13 November 2006), (1) extends the slaughter power to any infection in mammals caused by influenza virus of avian origin; (2) sets out preventive measures to reduce the risk of the transmission of avian influenza and provides for surveillance of the disease; (3) specifies measures to be taken where there is (a) a suspected outbreak of avian influenza; (b) a confirmed outbreak of highly pathogenic avian influenza at premises other than regulated places; (c) a suspected or confirmed outbreak of highly pathogenic avian influenza in regulated places and vehicles; and (d) a confirmed outbreak of low pathogenic avian influenza; (4) makes provision to reduce the risk of the spread of avian influenza virus to pigs and other mammals by the testing or slaughter of mammals on affected or suspected premises, and the movement of uninfected animals off the premises where a license to do so is gained from a veterinary inspector, and (5) makes failure to comply an offence under the Animal Health Act 1981. SI 2006/1197 is revoked.

189   Animal health—diseases of animals—avian influenza and influenza of avian origin in mammals—Wales

The Avian Influenza and Influenza of Avian Origin in Mammals (Wales) (No 2) Order 2006, SI 2006/2927 (in force on 13 November 2006), replaces, with amendments, the 2006 Order, SI 2006/1762. It continues to transpose EC Council Directive 2005/94 on Community measures for the control of avian influenza, and also implements, in part (1) EC Commission Decision 2005/734 laying down biosecurity measures to reduce the risk of transmission of highly pathogenic avian influenza caused by influenza A virus of subtype H5N1 from birds living in the wild to poultry and other captive birds and providing for an early detection system in areas at particular risk; and (2) EC Commission Decision 2006/474 concerning measures to prevent the spread of highly pathogenic avian influenza caused by influenza A virus of subtype H5N1 to birds kept in zoos and approved bodies, institutes and centres in the member states. In particular, the order (a) sets out preventive measures to reduce the risk of the transmission of avian influenza and provides for surveillance for the disease; (b) sets out measures to deal with any suspected outbreak of avian influenza at premises other than slaughterhouses, border inspection posts and in vehicles; (c) provides for the declaration of protection zones, surveillance zones and restricted zones around infected premises; (d) prescribes measures for when highly pathogenic avian influenza is confirmed at such premises and at slaughterhouses, border inspection posts and in vehicles; (e) prescribes measures for when low pathogenic avian influenza is confirmed at premises other than slaughterhouses, border inspection posts and in vehicles, including the declaration of the low pathogenic avian influenza zones; (f) sets out measures to reduce the risk of the spread of avian influenza viruses to pigs and other mammals; (g) sets out general measures applicable on suspicion or confirmation of avian influenza; and (h) provides for inspection, enforcement and offences. The effects of the main substantive changes to SI 2006/1762 introduced by the order are that the order (i) requires any person examining any mammal or carcase or analysing a sample taken from any mammal or carcase to inform the divisional veterinary manager if he or she suspects influenza of avian origin or antibodies to the disease in the mammal or carcase; (ii) allows the National Assembly for Wales to apply some rather than all the measures applicable to suspect and infected premises to contact premises; (iii) permits derogations from certain measures applicable to laboratories where low pathogenic avian influenza virus is kept; (iv) makes clear that the duty on the occupier of premises where poultry or other captive birds are kept to keep records of visitors to those premises does not extend to trespassers and those on rights of way; and (v) allows inspectors appointed by local authorities as well as veterinary inspectors appointed by the National Assembly to serve notices in certain circumstances.

190   Animal health—diseases of animals—bovine animals—enzootic bovine leukosis—Wales

The Enzootic Bovine Leukosis (Wales) Order 2006, SI 2006/867 (in force on 31 March 2006), replaces the 1997 Order, SI 1997/757, and implements EEC Council Directives 64/432, 77/391 in relation to milk. In particular, the order (1) introduces changes relating to the arrangements for testing milk for evidence of enzootic bovine leukosis and the removal of the list of approved laboratories contained in the 1997 Order; (2) requires notice to be given to the Divisional Veterinary Manager if any animal, carcase or laboratory sample is found to be infected with enzootic bovine leukosis; (3) sets out the duties of purchasers of milk for resale to ensure that milk is sent for testing to an approved laboratory; (4) requires the person in charge of an approved laboratory to notify the National Assembly for Wales of any positive test results within 24 hours and of any negative test results within one month; and (5) requires such a person to maintain records of all the tests carried out for a period of one year from the date of the test.

191   Animal health—diseases of animals—cattle—brucellosis—Wales

The Brucellosis (Wales) Order 2006, SI 2006/866 (in force on 31 March 2006), replaces the 1997 Order, SI 1997/758, and implements the provisions relating to milk of EEC Council Directives 64/432, 77/391, which require the operation of a monitoring and testing programme to maintain the officially brucellosis-free status of Great Britain under EEC Council Directive 64/432. In particular, the order (1) introduces changes relating to the arrangements for testing milk for evidence of brucellosis and the removal of the list of approved laboratories contained in the 1997 Order;

(2) sets out the duties of those who buy milk for resale to ensure that milk is sent for testing to an approved laboratory; (3) requires the person in charge of an approved laboratory to notify the National Assembly for Wales within 24 hours if the result of any test for brucellosis is positive, and within one month if the result is negative; (4) requires such a person to maintain records of all the tests carried out for a period of one year; and (5) provides for enforcement by the local authority.

192 Animal health—diseases of animals—cattle—compensation—England

The Cattle Compensation (England) Order 2006, SI 2006/168 (in force on 1 February 2006), replaces the 2005 Order, SI 2005/3433, and provides for the rates of compensation payable where the Secretary of State causes a bovine animal to be slaughtered under the Animal Health Act 1981 s 32 in its application to brucellosis, tuberculosis or enzootic bovine leukosis. In particular, the order provides that the amount of compensation payable is, in the case of buffalo or bison, the market value of the animal, and, in the case of a bovine animal of the genus Bos, either the average market price for the bovine category into which the slaughtered animal falls at the relevant date, or the market value of the animal. SI 1978/1483, 1980/80, 1981/1412, 1996/1352 and 1998/2073 are revoked.

193 Animal health—diseases of animals—control—bees—England

The Bee Diseases and Pests Control (England) Order 2006, SI 2006/342 (in force on 17 March 2006), replaces the Bee Diseases Control Order 1982, SI 1982/107, and provides for the notification of the presence or suspected presence of a notifiable disease or a notifiable pest to the Secretary of State so as to trigger a prohibition on the movement of things that might spread the disease or pest. In particular, the order (1) provides that where an authorised person has reasonable grounds for suspecting the presence of a notifiable disease or pest, he must serve a notice prohibiting the movement of certain items; (2) sets out the measures that apply on confirmation of the presence of a notifiable disease or pest; (3) provides that the Secretary of State may declare, by notice, an area to be an infected area if it is satisfied that a notifiable pest is present in that area; (4) requires the provision of facilities and the giving of information to authorised persons in certain circumstances; (5) prohibits the use of substances that may disguise the presence of or render difficult the detection of a notifiable disease other than in accordance with a notice requiring treatment; and (6) provides that where any person has not complied with a notice served an authorised person may arrange for it to be complied with at the expense of the person on whom the notice is served. SI 1997/310 is revoked.

194 Animal health—diseases of animals—control—bees—Wales

The Bee Diseases and Pests Control (Wales) Order 2006, SI 2006/1710 (in force on 1 July 2006), replaces the Bee Diseases Control Order 1982, SI 1982/107, and provides for the notification of the presence or suspected presence of a notifiable disease or a notifiable pest to the National Assembly for Wales so as to trigger a prohibition on the movement of things that might spread the disease or pest. In particular, the order (1) provides that where an authorised person has reasonable grounds for suspecting the presence of a notifiable disease or pest, he must serve a notice prohibiting the movement of certain items; (2) sets out the measures that apply on confirmation of the presence of a notifiable disease or pest; (3) provides that the National Assembly may declare, by notice, an area if it is satisfied that a notifiable pest is present in that area; (4) requires the provision of facilities and the giving of information to authorised persons in certain circumstances; (5) prohibits the use of substances that may disguise the presence of or render difficult the detection of a notifiable disease other than in accordance with a notice requiring treatment; and (6) provides that where any person has not complied with a notice served an authorised person may arrange for it to be complied with at the expense of the person on whom the notice is served. SI 1997/310 is revoked.

195 Animal health—diseases of animals—equine infectious anaemia—compensation—England

The Equine Infectious Anaemia (Compensation) (England) Order 2006, SI 2006/2740 (in force on 6 November 2006), provides that where the Secretary of State causes a diseased equine animal to be slaughtered under the Animal Health Act 1981 s 32 in its application to equine infectious anaemia, the amount of compensation payable in relation to that animal is £1.

196 Animal health—diseases of animals—foot-and-mouth disease—control—England

The Foot-and-Mouth Disease (England) Order 2006, SI 2006/182 (in force on 23 February 2006), replaces the 1983 Order, SI 1983/1950, and makes provision for the control of foot-and-mouth disease ('the disease'). In particular, the order (1) provides for notification of the disease or suspicion of it; (2) imposes restrictions on premises where the disease exists or is suspected of existing; (3) provides for veterinary investigation into the presence or suspicion of the disease; (4) allows premises to be separated into separate production units, so that only part of the premises may be subject to restrictions; (5) requires the Secretary of State to trace the possible spread of the disease; (6) provides for the declaration of a temporary control zone on suspicion of existence of the disease; (7) requires the Secretary of State to trace items from susceptible animals originating on infected premises, and either arrange for the treatment or disposal of those items; (8) makes provision relating to the slaughter of animals, including the place of slaughter, movement and disposal of carcases and faecal material, isolation of things which may spread the disease, and cleansing and disinfection of the premises; (9) provides for the declaration of protection and surveillance zones around infected premises and sets out the measures which apply in those zones; (10) provides for the declaration of restricted zones on confirmation of the disease and for measures applicable in relation to those zones; (11) provides for the declaration of a wild animal infected zone and for the measures applying there in such a zone; (12) requires licences granted for the movement of susceptible animals to be produced before animals are unloaded; (13) requires the Secretary of State to take steps to prevent spread of the disease to certain premises; (14) requires the local authority to erect signs indicating the perimeters of zones declared under the order; (15) sets out the method to be used when cleansing and disinfecting vehicles transporting susceptible animals; (16) requires occupiers to provide facilities, equipment and materials where cleansing and disinfection of vehicles is required on their premises; (17) ensures that where animals cannot be moved on termination of a right of occupation because of a restriction imposed by the order, those animals may be fed and tended to; (18) makes provision in relation to offences and enforcement; and (19) empowers veterinary inspectors to take action to prevent spread of the disease. SI 1978/32, 2001/2734 and 2003/1729 are amended, and SI 1983/3119, 2001/571, 680, 974, 1078, 1241, 1407, 1514, 1862, 2238, 2735, 2814, 2994, 3140, 3722 and 4029 are revoked.

197   Animal health—diseases of animals—foot-and-mouth disease—control—Wales

The Foot-and-Mouth Disease (Wales) Order 2006, SI 2006/179 (in force on 1 February 2006), replaces the 1983 Order, SI 1983/1950, and makes provision for the control of foot-and-mouth disease ('the disease'). In particular, the order (1) provides for notification of the disease or suspicion of it; (2) imposes restrictions on premises where the disease exists or is suspected of existing; (3) provides for veterinary investigation into the presence or suspicion of the disease; (4) allows premises to be separated into separate production units, so that only part of the premises may be subject to restrictions; (5) requires the National Assembly for Wales to trace the possible spread of the disease; (6) provides for the declaration of a temporary control zone on suspicion of existence of the disease; (7) requires the Assembly to trace items from susceptible animals originating on infected premises, and either arrange for the treatment or disposal of those items; (8) makes provision relating to the slaughter of animals, including the place of slaughter, movement and disposal of carcases and faecal material, isolation of things which may spread the disease, and cleansing and disinfection of the premises; (9) provides for the declaration of protection and surveillance zones around infected premises and sets out the measures which apply in those zones; (10) provides for the declaration of restricted zones on confirmation of the disease and for measures applicable in relation to those zones; (11) provides for the declaration of a wild animal infected zone and for the measures applying there in such a zone; (12) requires licences granted for the movement of susceptible animals to be produced before animals are unloaded; (13) requires the Assembly to take steps to prevent spread of the disease to certain premises; (14) requires the local authority to erect signs indicating the perimeters of zones declared under the order; (15) sets out the method to be used when cleansing and disinfecting vehicles transporting susceptible animals; (16) requires occupiers to provide facilities, equipment and materials where cleansing and disinfection of vehicles is required on their premises; (17) ensures that where animals cannot be moved on termination of a right of occupation because of a restriction imposed by the order, those animals may be fed and tended to; (18) makes provision in relation to offences and enforcement; and (19) empowers veterinary inspectors to take action to prevent spread of the disease. SI 1978/32, 2001/2771 and 2003/1966 are amended, and SI 1983/3119, 2001/572, 658, 968, 1033, 1234, 1406, 1509, 1874, 2236, 2813, 2981, 3145, 3706 and 4009 are revoked.

198   Animal health—diseases of animals—foot-and-mouth disease—vaccination—England

The Foot-and-Mouth Disease (Control of Vaccination) (England) Regulations 2006, SI 2006/183 (in force on 23 February 2006), replace the Foot-and-Mouth Disease (Infected Areas) (Vaccination) Order 1972, SI 1972/1509, and the 2001 Regulations, SI 2001/2375, and make provision for a programme of vaccination against foot-and-mouth disease. Vaccination must be carried out under licence granted by the Secretary of State unless it is carried out as authorised scientific research. Provision is made (1) requiring the place or area where a programme of vaccination is undertaken to be declared a vaccination zone and requiring an additional area surrounding the vaccination zone to be declared a vaccination surveillance zone; (2) requiring keepers of animals to facilitate their vaccination; (3) controlling movement of animals from premises where vaccination is being undertaken; (4) providing for the identification of vaccinated animals; (5) dealing with animals which should have been vaccinated but which have not been or are not identified as having being vaccinated; (6) providing for the survey of premises; and (7) specifying inspectors' powers. Contravention of the regulations is an offence. The regulations are to be enforced by the Secretary of State or a local authority.

199   Animal health—diseases of animals—foot-and-mouth disease—vaccination—Wales

The Foot-and-Mouth Disease (Control of Vaccination) (Wales) Regulations 2006, SI 2006/180 (in force on 1 February 2006), replace the Foot-and-Mouth Disease (Infected Areas) (Vaccination) Order 1972, SI 1972/1509, and the Foot-and-Mouth Disease (Prohibition of Vaccination) (Wales) Regulations 2006, SI 2001/2374, and make provision for a programme of vaccination against foot-and-mouth disease. Vaccination must be carried out under licence granted by the National Assembly for Wales unless it is carried out as authorised scientific research. Provision is made (1) requiring the place or area where a programme of vaccination is undertaken to be declared a vaccination zone and requiring an additional area surrounding the vaccination zone to be declared a vaccination surveillance zone; (2) requiring keepers of animals to facilitate their vaccination and controls movement of animals from premises where vaccination is being undertaken; (3) providing for the identification of vaccinated animals; (4) dealing with animals which should have been vaccinated but which have not or are not identified as having being vaccinated; (5) providing for the survey of premises; and (6) specifying inspectors' powers. Contravention of the regulations is an offence. The regulations are to be enforced by the National Assembly or a local authority.

200   Animal health—diseases of animals—salmonella—pigs—England

See para 202.

201   Animal health—diseases of animals—salmonella—poultry—broiler flocks—Wales

The Salmonella in Broiler Flocks (Survey Powers) (Wales) Regulations 2006, SI 2006/1511 (in force on 14 June 2006), provide that the National Assembly for Wales is responsible for selection of holdings for sampling for the purposes of EC Commission Decision 2005/636. In particular, the regulations (1) require the occupier or person in charge of a holding used for the keeping or rearing of broiler chickens to provide information to the Assembly to assist it with the selection of holdings to be included in a survey; (2) empower inspectors to enter premises and take samples of faecal material, to examine records and to make inquiries of any person; (3) prescribe offences and penalties; and (4) provide for enforcement of the regulations by the local authority or, where it so directs, by the Assembly.

202   Animal health—diseases of animals—salmonella—poultry—turkey flocks—England

The Salmonella in Turkey Flocks and Slaughter Pigs (Survey Powers) (England) Regulations 2006, SI 2006/2821 (in force on 17 November 2006), replace the Salmonella in Laying Flocks (Survey Powers) (England) Regulations 2005, SI 2005/359, and the Salmonella in Broiler Flocks (Survey Powers) (England) Regulations 2006, SI 2006/864, and designate the Secretary of State as the competent authority for the purposes of EC Commission Decisions 2006/662 and 2006/668. In particular, the regulations (1) provide that the occupier or person in charge of a turkey holding must, within seven days of a request, send information to the Secretary of State to assist him with the survey of turkey flocks; (2) provide that the occupier or person in charge of a slaughterhouse must, within seven days of a request, send information to the Secretary of State to assist him with the survey of slaughter pigs; (3) empower inspectors to enter premises, to take samples, to examine records and to make inquiries of any person; (4) prescribe offences and penalties; and (5) provide for enforcement of the regulations by the local authority or, where he so directs, by the Secretary of State.

203   Animal health—diseases of animals—specified diseases—notification and slaughter— England

The Specified Diseases (Notification and Slaughter) Order 2006, SI 2006/2166 (in force on 29 August 2006), further amends the 1992 Order, SI 1992/3159, and the Specified Diseases (Notification) Order 1996, SI 1996/2628, by adding equine infectious anaemia to the list of diseases.

204   Animal health—diseases of animals—specified diseases—notification and slaughter— Wales

The Specified Diseases (Notification and Slaughter) (Wales) Order 2006, SI 2006/2237 (in force on 29 August 2006), further amends the 1992 Order, SI 1992/3159, and the Specified Diseases (Notification) Order 1996, SI 1996/2628, by adding inquine infectious anaemia to the list of diseases.

205   Animal health—diseases of animals—transmissible spongiform encephalopathies—control and eradication—England

The Transmissible Spongiform Encephalopathies (No 2) Regulations 2006, SI 2006/1228 (in force on 3 May 2006), which apply in relation to England only, replace the TSE (England) Regulations 2002, SI 2002/843, and implement European Parliament and EC Council Regulation 999/2001 on the prevention, control and eradication of certain transmissible spongiform encephalopathies ('TSEs'). The regulations, in particular, (1) provide that the Secretary of State is the competent authority for most purposes of Regulation 999/2001; (2) make provision for approvals, authorisations, licences and registrations, occupier's duties, suspension, amendment and revocations of approvals, appeals, and valuations; (3) entitle the Secretary of State and local authorities to appoint inspectors, and specify the powers the inspectors have; (4) make provision for a notice procedure; (5) provide for licences permitting movement during a movement restriction; (6) deal with obstruction of an inspector, penalties, and offences by a body corporate; (7) specify the persons responsible for enforcement; (8) make provision with regard to monitoring for TSEs, including that (a) the Secretary of State must be notified of fallen stock that is required to be tested for TSE under Regulation 999/2001; (b) it is an offence to consign an over-age animal to a slaughterhouse for human consumption or to slaughter such an animal for human consumption; (c) brain stem samples of bovine animals must be taken in prescribed circumstances; (d) anyone slaughtering animals over 30 months old for human consumption must have a 'Required Method of Operation', which must describe certain prescribed matters; (e) there are requirements in relation to the retention of products and their disposal; and (f) compensation is payable where an animal tests positive; (9) provide for the control and eradication of TSEs in bovine animals by (a) requiring suspect animals to be notified to the Secretary of State; (b) providing for the restriction and slaughter of the suspect; (c) making provision for the offspring and cohorts of the suspect; (d) requiring compensation to be paid where an animal dies under restriction; and (e) making it an offence to place an infected animal on the market; (10) deal with the control and eradication of TSEs in sheep and goats, by making provision in relation to (a) the notification of a suspect animal to the Secretary of State; (b) the restriction and slaughter of the suspect; (c) movement restrictions; (d) action following confirmation; (e) time for appeals; (f) killing and destruction; (g) infected animals from another holding, common grazing and multiple flocks on a holding; (h) subsequent occupiers of the land; (i) the procedure to be followed after the killing or destruction; (j) restrictions on the introduction of animals onto a holding; (k) the use of ovine germinal products; (l) the movement of animals from a holding; (m) time limits on restrictions; (n) the notification of animals that die while under restriction; (o) the placing on the market of progeny; (p) the notification of the Secretary of State before the consigning for slaughter of sheep aged over 18 months; (q) derogations from the requirement for the killing and destruction of sheep and goats; and (r) compensation; (11) impose requirements in relation to feedingstuffs, in particular with regard to (a) the prohibition on the feeding of specified feedingstuffs to ruminant and non-ruminant animals, subject to exceptions; (b) movement restrictions and the slaughter of animals suspected of having been fed prohibited feedingstuffs; (c) the provision of compensation; (d) the prohibition on the slaughter for human consumption of restricted animals; (e) the control of the production and use of fishmeal for feeding to non-ruminant animals; (f) the regulation of feedingstuffs containing dicalcium phosphate or tricalcium phosphate; (g) the regulation of feedingstuffs containing blood products and blood meal; (h) changes in the use of equipment; (i) control of the manufacture, storage and transport of processed animal protein and products containing it; (j) exports; (k) fertilisers derived from animal protein; (l) records; and (m) cross-contamination; (12) make provision in connection with specified risk material, mechanically recovered meat and slaughtering techniques, specifically by (a) appointing the Food Standards Agency as the competent authority; (b) imposing certain duties on local authorities in relation to butcher shops; (c) making provision for the training of slaughterhouse, cutting plant and butcher shop staff; (d) imposing requirements in relation to pithing, tongue harvesting and head meat harvesting; (e) controlling the removal of specified risk material; (f) dealing with bovine animals and sheep and goats at a slaughterhouse, with young lamb and goat stamps; (g) regulating the removal of spinal cord from sheep and goats; (h) providing for the authorisation of cutting plants; (i) controlling the removal of specified risk material at cutting plants; (j) providing for the removal at unauthorised cutting plants of vertebral column that is specified risk material; (k) providing for the authorisation and registration of butcher shops; (l) regulating the removal of specified risk material at such shops; (m) dealing with meat from other member states; (n) requiring the staining of specified risk material; (o) providing for the security of specified risk material; and (o) prohibiting the supply of specified risk material for human consumption; and (13) prohibit the dispatch of certain live animals, bovine heads, specified risk material and meat containing such material to other member states and to third countries. SI 1999/1103, SI 2005/404 and SI 2006/1228 are revoked.

206   Animal health—diseases of animals—transmissible spongiform encephalopathies—control and eradication—Wales

The Transmissible Spongiform Encephalopathies (Wales) Regulations 2006, SI 2006/1226 (in force on 3 May 2006) substantially replace the TSE (Wales) Regulations 2002, SI 2002/1416 (as amended), and implement European Parliament and EC Council Regulation 999/2001 on the prevention, control and eradication of certain transmissible spongiform encephalopathies ('TSEs'). The regulations, in particular, (1) provide that the National Assembly for Wales is the competent authority for most purposes of Regulation 999/2001; (2) make provision for approvals, authorisations, licences and registrations, occupier's duties, suspension, amendment and revocations of approvals, appeals, and valuations; (3) entitle National Assembly and local authorities to appoint inspectors, and specify the powers the inspectors have; (4) make provision for a notice procedure; (5) provide for licences permitting movement during a movement restriction; (6) deal with obstruction of an inspector, penalties, and offences by a body corporate; (7) specify the persons responsible for enforcement; (8) make provision with regard to monitoring for TSEs, including that (a) the National Assembly must be notified of fallen stock that is required to be tested for TSE under Regulation 999/2001; (b) it is an offence to consign an over-age animal to a slaughterhouse for human consumption or to slaughter such an animal for human consumption; (c) brain stem samples of bovine animals must be taken in prescribed circumstances; (d) anyone slaughtering animals over 30 months old for human consumption must have a 'Required Method of Operation', which must describe certain prescribed matters; (e) there are requirements in relation to the retention of products and their disposal; and (f) compensation is payable where an animal tests positive; (9) provide for the control and eradication of TSEs in bovine animals by (a) requiring suspect animals to be notified to the National Assembly; (b) providing for the restriction and slaughter of the suspect; (c) making provision for the offspring and cohorts of the suspect; and (d) requiring compensation to be paid where an animal dies under restriction; (10) deal with the control and eradication of TSEs in sheep and goats, by making provision in relation to (a) the notification of a suspect animal to the National Assembly; (b) the restriction and slaughter of the suspect; (c) movement restrictions; (d) action following confirmation; (e) time for appeals; (f) killing and destruction; (g) infected animals from another holding, common grazing and multiple flocks on a holding; (h) subsequent occupiers of the land; (i) the procedure to be followed after the killing or destruction; (j) restrictions on the introduction of animals onto a holding; (k) the use of ovine germinal products; (l) the movement of animals from a holding; (m) time limits on restrictions; (n) the notification of animals that die while under restriction; (o) the placing on the market of progeny; (p) the notification of the National Assembly before the consigning for slaughter of sheep aged over 18 months; and (q) derogations from the requirement for the killing and destruction of sheep and goats; (11) impose requirements in relation to feedingstuffs, in particular with regard to (a) the prohibition on the feeding of specified feedingstuffs to ruminant and non-ruminant animals, subject to exceptions; (b) movement restrictions and the slaughter of animals suspected of having been fed prohibited feedingstuffs; (c) the provision of compensation; (d) the prohibition on the slaughter for human consumption of restricted animals; (e) the control of the production and use of fishmeal for feeding to non-ruminant animals; (f) the regulation of feedingstuffs containing dicalcium phosphate or tricalcium phosphate; (g) the regulation of feedingstuffs containing blood products and blood meal; (h) changes in the use of equipment; (i) control of the manufacture, storage and transport of processed animal protein and products containing it; (j) exports; (k) fertilisers derived from animal protein; (l) records; and (m) cross-contamination; (12) make provision in connection with specified risk material, mechanically recovered meat and slaughtering techniques, specifically by (a) appointing the Food Standards Agency as the competent authority; (b) imposing certain duties on local authorities in relation to butcher shops; (c) making provision for the training of slaughterhouse, cutting plant and butcher shop staff; (d) imposing requirements in relation to pithing, tongue harvesting and head meat harvesting; (e) controlling the removal of specified risk material; (f) dealing with bovine animals and sheep and goats at a slaughterhouse, with young lamb and goat stamps; (g) regulating the removal of spinal cord from sheep and goats; (h) providing for the authorisation of cutting plants; (i) controlling the removal of specified risk material at cutting plants; (j) providing for the removal at unauthorised cutting plants of vertebral column that is specified risk material; (k) providing for the authorisation and registration of butcher shops; (l) regulating the removal of specified risk material at such shops; (m) dealing with meat from other member states; (n) requiring the staining of specified risk material; (o) providing for the security of specified risk material; and (o) prohibiting the supply of specified risk material for human consumption; and (13) prohibit the dispatch of certain live animals, bovine heads, specified risk material and meat containing such material to other member states and to third countries. SI 1997/2964, SI 1997/2965 (as amended), SI 2001/1303 and SI 2001/2780 are revoked.

The Bovine Spongiform Encephalopathy (BSE) Compensation (Wales) Regulations 2006, SI 2006/1512 (in force on 14 June 2006) provide for rates of compensation to be paid when the National Assembly for Wales causes a bovine animal to be slaughtered under the Transmissible Spongiform Encephalopathies (Wales) Regulations 2006 supra. The amount of compensation payable on the slaughter of a bovine animal is the average price paid in Great Britain for that age and category of animal in the previous six months in the case of a pedigree animal, and for any other bovine animal in the previous month. The compensation for buffalo and bison is the market price.

The Sheep and Goats Transmissible Spongiform Encephalopathy (TSE) Compensation (Wales) Regulations 2006, SI 2006/1513 (in force on 14 June 2006) replace provision made by the TSE

(Wales) Regulations 2002 supra in relation to the amount of compensation payable on the slaughter of a sheep or goat killed following infection with transmissible spongiform encephalopathy ('TSE'). The amount of compensation payable on the slaughter of a sheep or goat depends on whether it is a suspect animal or is killed as a result of it being confirmed as being affected with a TSE. If the owner of an animal killed following confirmation of TSE considers that the compensation to be paid is unreasonable, then the owner may notify the National Assembly for Wales and obtain a valuation. If the National Assembly considers that the compensation to be paid to the owner of an animal killed following confirmation of TSE is unreasonable, it may obtain a valuation.

207   Animal health—diseases of animals—tuberculosis—England

The Tuberculosis (England) Order 2006, SI 2006/394 (in force in part on 18 February 2006 and in part on 27 March 2006), replaces the 1984 Order, SI 1984/1943. In particular, the order (1) introduces an obligation to test certain animals before movement; (2) includes a reactor within the definition of suspected animal rather than affected animal; (3) provides that the definitions of premises, carcase, inspector and veterinary inspector are those that apply to the Animal Health Act 1981; (4) adds buffalo and bison to the definition of bovine animal; (5) removes exclusions in relation to imported animals; (6) requires that notice of an affected or suspected animal must be given to the Divisional Veterinary Manager; (7) provides that the duty to notify in relation to carcases applies to all farmed animals, including bovine animals and pets; (8) requires that notice under the order must comply with specified provisions; (9) provides that licences under the order may be general or specific; (10) clarifies the power of the Secretary of State to (a) require tuberculosis testing by a certain date, which applies to routine testing of herds according to the testing frequency of the parish in which they are located, and to additional testing which may be required for different purposes; and (b) impose movement restrictions where there has been a failure to test by a specified date; (11) makes provision that where a skin test has been administered but not yet read, or where a blood test has been taken but the result is not yet known, the movement of an animal, until a negative test result has been obtained, is prohibited; (12) provides that it is an offence to interfere with any tuberculosis test; (13) requires all bovine animals to be skin tested not more than 60 days before movement and have a negative result before they move from one premises to another; (14) provides that the requirement under head (13) does not apply to animals falling within specified categories; (15) sets out movements which are exempt from the requirement for pre-movement testing; (16) imposes a duty to (i) retain records of certain tuberculosis tests; and (ii) notify the Veterinary Laboratories Agency of the presence of *M bovis* where this has been isolated in any laboratory sample, except where it has been deliberately introduced in the course of research; (17) makes provision relating to manure and slurry; and (18) provides that breach of the order is an offence under the 1981 Act s 73. SI 2005/3446 is revoked.

208   Animal health—diseases of animals—tuberculosis—Wales

The Tuberculosis (Wales) Order 2006, SI 2006/1053 (in force on 2 May 2006), replaces the 1984 Order, SI 1984/1943. In particular, the order (1) introduces an obligation to test certain animals before movement; (2) includes a reactor within the definition of suspected animal rather than affected animal; (3) provides that the definitions of premises, carcase, inspector and veterinary inspector are those that apply to the Animal Health Act 1981; (4) adds buffalo and bison to the definition of bovine animal; (5) removes exclusions in relation to imported animals; (6) requires that notice of an affected or suspected animal must be given to the Divisional Veterinary Manager; (7) provides that the duty to notify in relation to carcases applies to all farmed animals, including bovine animals and pets; (8) requires that notice under the order must comply with specified provisions; (9) provides that licences under the order may be general or specific; (10) clarifies the power of the National Assembly for Wales to (a) require tuberculosis testing by a certain date, which applies to routine testing of herds according to the testing frequency of the parish in which they are located, and to additional testing which may be required for different purposes; and (b) impose movement restrictions where there has been a failure to test by a specified date; (11) makes provision that where a skin test has been administered but not yet read, or where a blood test has been taken but the result is not yet known, the movement of an animal, until a negative test result has been obtained, is prohibited; (12) provides that it is an offence to interfere with any tuberculosis test; (13) requires all bovine animals to be skin tested not more than 60 days before movement and have a negative result before they move from one premises to another; (14) provides that the requirement under head (13) does not apply to animals falling within specified categories; (15) sets out movements which are exempt from the requirement for pre-movement testing; (16) imposes a duty to (i) retain records of certain tuberculosis tests; and (ii) notify the Veterinary Laboratories Agency of the presence of *M bovis* where this has been isolated in any laboratory sample, except where it has been deliberately introduced in the course of research; (17) makes provision relating to manure and slurry; and (18) provides that breach of the order is an offence under the 1981 Act s 73.

209   Animal pathogens—possession or introduction into animal—licence—England

The Specified Animal Pathogens (Amendment) (England) Order 2006, SI 2006/1506 (in force on 4 July 2006), amends the 1998 Order, SI 1998/463, by (1) adding Nipah disease virus, West Nile virus and St Louis equine encephalomyelitis virus to the list of pathogens requiring a licence for possession or introduction into an animal; (2) updating certain terms to reflect those more commonly used by the scientific community and certain references to veterinary medicines legislation; and (3) clarifying the controls applicable to specified animal pathogens.

210 Animal pathogens—possession or introduction into animal—licence—Wales

The Specified Animal Pathogens (Amendment) (Wales) Order 2006, SI 2006/2981 (in force on 24 November 2006), amends the 1998 Order, SI 1998/463, so as to (1) add Nipah disease virus, West Nile virus and St. Louis equine encephalomyelitis virus to the to the list of pathogens requiring a licence for possession or introduction into an animal; (2) update certain terms to reflect those more commonly used by the scientific community and certain references to veterinary medicines legislation; and (3) clarify the controls applicable to specified animal pathogens.

211 Animal Welfare Act 2006

The Animal Welfare Act 2006 makes provision about animal welfare. The Act received the royal assent on 8 November 2006 and certain provisions came into force on that day. The remaining provisions come into force on a day or days to be appointed. For details of commencement, see the commencement table in the title STATUTES.

Section 1 specifies animals to which the Act applies. Section 2 defines 'protected animal'. In the Act, references to a person responsible for an animal are to a person responsible for an animal whether on a permanent or temporary basis: s 3. A person commits an offence if he (1) causes unnecessary suffering to an animal (s 4); (2) carries out a prohibited procedure on a protected animal or he causes such a procedure to be carried out on such an animal (s 5); (3) removes the whole or any part of a dog's tail, other than for the purposes of its medical treatment (s 6); (4) administers any poisonous or injurious drug or substance to a protected animal, knowing it to be poisonous or injurious, without lawful authority or reasonable excuse (s 7); (5) causes an animal fight to take place, or attempts to do so (s 8); and (6) if he does not take such steps as are reasonable in all the circumstances to ensure that the needs of an animal for which he is responsible are met to the extent required by good practice (s 9). Under s 10, if an inspector is of the opinion that a person is failing to comply with s 9 he may serve on him an improvement notice. There is a prohibition on the transfer of animals by way of sale or prize to persons under the age of 16: s 11. Section 12 enables the appropriate national authority to make such provision by regulations as the authority thinks fit for the purpose of promoting the welfare of animals for which a person is responsible, or the progeny of such animals.

Under s 13, Sch 1, regulations made for the purpose of promoting animal welfare may require certain animal-related activities to be licensed by the local authority or appropriate national authority.

The appropriate national authority may issue, and may from time to time revise, codes of practice for the purpose of providing practical guidance in respect of any provision made by or under the Act: s 14. Under ss 15, 16, where the Secretary of State or National Assembly for Wales proposes to issue or revise such a code of practice he or it must prepare a draft of the code, consult about the draft such persons appearing to him or it to represent any interests concerned as he or it considers appropriate and consider any representations made by them. The appropriate national authority may, by order, revoke a code of practice: s 17. By virtue of s 18, if an inspector or a constable reasonably believes that a protected animal is suffering, he may take, or arrange for the taking of, such steps as appear to him to be immediately necessary to alleviate the animal's suffering. An inspector or a constable may enter premises for the purposes of searching for a protected animal and of exercising any power under s 18 in relation to it if he reasonably believes that there is a protected animal on the premises and that the animal is suffering or, if the circumstances of the animal do not change, it is likely to suffer: s 19. Where an animal has been taken into possession under s 18 and the animal is being retained, s 20 enables a magistrates' court to make an order for the treatment, giving up, disposal or destruction of the animal. Where such an order is made, the owner of the animal to which the order relates may appeal against the order to the Crown Court: s 21. Under s 22, a constable may seize an animal if it appears to him that it is one in relation to which a fighting offence has been committed. On the application of an inspector or constable, a justice of the peace may issue a warrant authorising an inspector or a constable to enter premises, if necessary using reasonable force, in order to search for evidence of the commission of a relevant offence: s 23. Section 24 adds the most serious offences under the Act to the list of offences in respect of which a police officer has power to enter and search premises to arrest a person. An inspector may require the holder of a licence to produce for inspection any records which he is required to keep by a condition of the licence: s 25. Under s 26, an inspector may carry out an inspection in order to check compliance with the conditions subject to which a licence is granted, or provision made by or under the Act, which is relevant to the carrying on of an activity to which a licence relates. By virtue of s 27, an inspector may carry out an inspection in order to check compliance with provision made by or under the Act which is relevant to the carrying on of an activity to which a registration for the purposes of s 13 relates. Provision is also made for the inspection of farm premises: s 28. An inspector may carry out an inspection in order to check compliance with regulations under s 12 that implement a Community obligation: s 29. Under s 30, a local authority in England or Wales may prosecute proceedings for any offence under the Act. By virtue of s 31, a magistrates' court may try an information relating to an offence under the Act if the information is laid before the end of the period of three years beginning with the date of the commission of the offence, and before the end of the period of six months beginning with the date on which evidence which the prosecutor thinks is sufficient to justify the proceedings comes to his knowledge.

Section 32 prescribes the penalties for offences under the Act. Section 33 enables the courts to confiscate an animal from an owner who has been convicted of an offence in relation to that animal. Section 34 enables a court to disqualify a person from owning animals, keeping animals, participating in the keeping of animals and being party to an arrangement under which he is entitled to control or influence the way in which animals are kept. Sections 35, 36 make provision for the seizure of animals in connection with disqualification. The court by or before which a person is convicted of an offence may order the destruction of an animal in relation to which the offence was committed if it is satisfied that it is appropriate to do so in the interests of the animal: s 37. Section 38 deals with the destruction of animals involved in fighting offences. Under s 39, the court, by or before which a person is convicted of a specified offence, may order the offender or another person to reimburse any expenses incurred by the police in connection with the keeping of an animal in relation to which the offence was committed. Section 40 makes provision in connection with the forfeiture of equipment used in offences. By virtue of s 41, the operation of various orders relating to animals and equipment under the Act is suspended until the possibility of a successful appeal has expired. Where a person is convicted of certain offences, the court may make an order cancelling any licence held by him or make an order disqualifying him, for such period as it thinks fit, from holding a licence: s 42. Section 43 provides that a person who is disqualified by virtue of an order under s 34 or s 42 may apply to the appropriate court for the termination of the order. Where an order is made under specified provisions, the expenses that are required by the order to be reimbursed are not to be regarded for the purposes of the Magistrates' Courts Act 1980 as a sum adjudged to be paid by a summary conviction, but are to be recoverable summarily as a civil debt: 2006 Act s 44. Section 45 provides that there is a right of appeal against an order for the reimbursement of expenses for a non-offender. Sections 46–50 apply to Scotland.

Section 51 deals with the appointment of inspectors. Section 52 provides the conditions for the grant of a warrant. Supplementary powers of entry, inspection and search are provided by s 53, Sch 2. Section 54 deals with the power to stop and detain vehicles. Power to detain vessels, aircraft and hovercraft is provided by s 55. Section 56 deals with the obtaining of documents in connection with carrying out orders and s 57 with offences by bodies corporate. Nothing in the Act applies to anything lawfully done under the Animals (Scientific Procedures) Act 1986: 2006 Act s 58. Section 59 provides that nothing in the Act applies in relation to anything which occurs in the normal course of fishing. The Act and regulations and orders made under it bind the Crown: s 60. Section 61 provides for the making of orders and regulations and s 62 with interpretation. Section 63 contains financial provisions. Sections 64, 65, Schs 3, 4 make minor and consequential amendments and repeals. Section 66 deals with transitional provision. Sections 67–69 deal with extent, commencement and short title.

Amendments, repeals and revocations
The list below, which is not exhaustive, mentions repeals and amendments which are or will be effective when the Act is fully in force.

Specific provisions of a number of Acts are amended or repealed. These include: Performing Animals (Regulation) Act 1925 s 4; Cinematograph Films (Animals) 1937 s 1; Pet Animals Act 1951 ss 2, 5; Animal Boarding Establishments Act 1963 ss 1, 3; Riding Establishments Act 1964 ss 1, 4; Breeding of Dogs Act 1973 s 3; Guard Dogs Act 1975 s 3; Dangerous Wild Animals Act 1976 s 6; Magistrates' Courts Act 1980 s 108; Zoo Licensing Act 1981 s 4; Animals (Scientific Procedures) Act 1986 ss 22, 26, 29; Criminal Justice and Police Act 2001 s 57, 66, Sch 1; Metropolitan Police Act 1839 s 47; Town Police Clauses Act 1847 s 36; Protection of Animals Act 1911 ss 1–3, 5–5B, 7, 9, 11–14; Protection of Animals Act 1934; Docking and Nicking of Horses ss 1, 3; Pet Animals Act 1951 ss 2, 3; Cockfighting Act 1952; Protection of Animals (Amendment) Act 1954 ss 1, 2, 4; Protection of Animals (Anaesthetics) Act 1954; Abandonment of Animals Act 1960; Animals (Cruel Poisons) Act 1962 s 4; Protection of Animals (Anaesthetics) Act 1964; Agriculture (Miscellaneous Provisions) Act 1968 Pt 1 (ss 1–8); Animal Health Act 1981 ss 37–39, Sch 5; Animals (Scientific Procedures) Act 1986 Sch 3; Protection of Animals (Penalties) Act 1987; Protection of Animals (Amendment) Act 1988 ss 1, 2; Protection against Cruel Tethering Act 1988; Protection of Animals (Amendment) Act 2000.

212   Dogs—control orders—non-application—designated land—England

The Controls on Dogs (Non-application to Designated Land) Order 2006, SI 2006/779 (in force on 6 April 2006), designates (1) any land that is placed at the disposal of the Forestry Commissioners under the Forestry Act 1967 s 39(1); and (2) any land over which a road passes as descriptions of land to which the Clean Neighbourhoods and Environment Act 2005 Pt 6 Ch 1 (ss 55–67) does not apply, for specified purposes relating to the making of dog control orders under s 55.

213 Dogs—control orders—prescribed offences and penalties—England

The Dog Control Orders (Prescribed Offences and Penalties, etc) Regulations 2006, SI 2006/1059 (in force on 6 April 2006), (1) prescribe, for the purpose of the Clean Neighbourhoods and Environment Act 2005 s 55, the offences which may be provided for in a dog control order; (2) prescribe the maximum penalty which may be provided for in such an order; and (3) specify the wording that must be used in providing for an offence in an order.

214 Dogs—control orders—procedures—England

The Dog Control Orders (Procedures) Regulations 2006, SI 2006/798 (in force on 6 April 2006), prescribe the procedures to be observed by a primary or secondary authority, as described in the Clean Neighbourhoods and Environment Act 2005, in making dog control orders or when amending or revoking such orders. In particular, the regulations (1) require an authority, before making an order, to consult on its proposal by publishing a notice in a newspaper circulating in the area where the land to which the order would apply is situated, and to consult every other authority which has the power to make an order in respect of all or part of the same land; (2) specify additional consultees, where any land to which a proposed order would apply is access land as defined in the Countryside and Rights of Way Act 2000; (3) require an authority to publicise the making and effect of an order before it comes into force; (4) apply the same consultation and information requirements to the making of any amendment to an order; and (5) prescribe similar consultation and information requirements for the revocation of an order.

215 Horses—zootechnical standards—England

The Horses (Zootechnical Standards) (England) Regulations 2006, SI 2006/1757 (in force on 28 July 2006), replace the 1992 Regulations, SI 1992/3045, and implement EC Commission Decisions 92/353 and 96/78. The regulations (1) specify the criteria which an organisation or association must satisfy in order to become recognised by the Secretary of State for the purpose of maintaining a stud book; (2) provide that any organisation or association which satisfies the criteria will be granted official recognition; (3) set out the circumstances in which the Secretary of State may refuse to grant recognition to, or withdraw recognition from, an organisation or association and provide that such refusal or withdrawal must be communicated in writing; (4) allow a person to make representations to the Secretary of State where recognition has been refused or withdrawn; (5) permit a recognised organisation to divide the main section of its stud book into different classes according to the horses' merits, but prohibits it from doing so for any other purpose; (6) specify the circumstances in which a recognised organisation must enter a horse in the main section of its stud book; and (7) permit a recognised organisation to (a) enter a horse in a supplementary section of its stud book where that horse meets certain minimum criteria; (b) enter a horse in the main section of its stud book to take part in a cross-breeding programme; and (c) enter a horse registered in another stud book in the main section of its own stud book.

216 Horses—zootechnical standards—Wales

The Horses (Zootechnical Standards) (Wales) Regulations 2006, SI 2006/2607 (in force on 30 September 2006), replace the 1992 Regulations, SI 1992/3045, and implement EC Commission Decisions 92/353 and 96/78. The regulations (1) specify the criteria which an organisation or association must satisfy in order to become recognised by the National Assembly for Wales for the purpose of maintaining a stud book; (2) provide that any organisation or association which satisfies the criteria will be granted official recognition; (3) set out the circumstances in which the National Assembly may refuse to grant recognition to, or withdraw recognition from, an organisation or association and provide that such refusal or withdrawal must be communicated in writing; (4) allow a person to make representations to the National Assembly where recognition has been refused or withdrawn; (5) permit a recognised organisation to divide the main section of its stud book into different classes according to the horses' merits, but prohibits it from doing so for any other purpose; (6) specify the circumstances in which a recognised organisation must enter a horse in the main section of its stud book; and (7) permit a recognised organisation to (a) enter a horse in a supplementary section of its stud book where that horse meets certain minimum criteria; (b) enter a horse in the main section of its stud book to take part in a cross-breeding programme; and (c) enter a horse registered in another stud book in the main section of its own stud book.

217 Hunting—legislation—validity

The claimants brought judicial review proceedings challenging the legal validity of the Hunting Act 2004. The application was dismissed and, on the claimants' appeal, various arguments were advanced at common law and in reliance on the European Convention on Human Rights and the EC Treaty. The claimants submitted that no legislative aim could be derived from the 2004 Act, and that the court had consciously defined an objective wider than that intended by the legislature. In relation to the Convention, the claimants contended that the ban on hunting infringed their right under art 8 to respect for their personal autonomy, their culture, community and lifestyle, and their home and their use of that home. That contention included the argument that the hunting ban would cause a decline in hunting activities, which might then place in jeopardy the claimants' homes and livelihood. The claimants also submitted that there was an infringement of art 11 (freedom of assembly) on the basis that the ban prohibited hunting meetings. A submission was also made in relation to the First Protocol art 1 (protection of property rights). With regard to the EC Treaty, the claimants argued that the free movement provisions contained in arts 28 and 49 were infringed by the 2004 Act. *Held*, the objective of the 2004 Act was a composite one of preventing or reducing unnecessary suffering to wild mammals, based on the view that causing suffering for sport was unethical. It was manifest from the available background material that the legislature had framed the statute with such an ethical sentiment in mind. Moreover, none of the claims under the Convention could be accepted. Article 8 was not broad enough to encompass the contentions made by the claimants. The ban did not infringe art 11 as it prohibited merely a particular activity that could be undertaken by an assembled group, but did not prohibit the assembly itself. In terms of the First Protocol art 1, the claimants were relying on interests which could not be said to be 'property' for the purposes of that provision. The aim pursued by the 2004 Act was legitimate, the ban was proportionate to the aim pursued, and the passing of the ban was a permissible course of action for the state to take considering the significant margin of discretion accorded to it in such circumstances. The contentions under the EC Treaty also failed. To begin with, art 28 was not wide enough to encompass the ban, since the ban was not a restriction aimed at products from other member states, or at products at all, and did not have a discriminatory effect on imported products. Likewise, art 49 was not engaged by the ban since to be infringing a measure had to have a direct inhibiting effect on the free movement of services rather than merely decrease the demand for a particular service within a member state. Accordingly, the appeal would be dismissed.

R (on the application of the Countryside Alliance) v A-G; R (on the application of Derwin) v A-G [2006] EWCA Civ 817, [2006] 3 WLR 1017 (Court of Appeal: Sir Anthony Clarke MR, Brooke and Buxton LJJ). Decision of Queen's Bench Divisional Court [2005] EWHC 1677 (Admin), [2005] All ER (D) 482 (Jul) (2005 Abr para 182) affirmed.

218 Liability of keeper—horse—normal characteristics of species in unusual circumstances

The Animals Act 1971 s 2(2) provides that where damage is caused by an animal which does not belong to a dangerous species, a keeper of the animal is liable for the damage, except as otherwise provided by the 1971 Act, if (a) the damage is of a kind which the animal, unless restrained, was likely to cause or which, if caused by the animal, was likely to be severe; and (b) the likelihood of the damage or of its being severe was due to characteristics of the animal which are not normally found in animals of the same species or are not normally so found except at particular times or in particular circumstances.

As the claimant's car had been about to pass the defendant's horse, the horse had moved into the road and collided with the car. The claimant brought proceedings against the defendant in negligence and under s 2. The defendant counterclaimed alleging that it was the claimant who had been negligent. The judge held that neither party had been negligent, but found the defendant liable under s 2. On the defendant's appeal, *held,* the judge had erred in not considering whether the damage caused by the horse was damage which the horse, unless restrained, was likely to cause. Instead, he had concluded that the alternative limb of s 2(2)(a) was satisfied, namely that if the horse caused damage, it was likely to be severe, due to the horse's weight. The judge ought to have asked himself, with regard to s 2(2)(b), whether the likelihood of the damage being severe was due to characteristics of the animal not normally found in animals of the same species. The relevant characteristic was the weight of the animal. Had the judge asked that question, he would have concluded that the horse's weight was a normal characteristic of its species, so that the requirement was not satisfied. However, instead of identifying the horse's weight as the relevant characteristic, the judge had identified the propensity of a horse 'in particular times and in particular circumstances' to 'assert an inclination to move otherwise than as directed'. It was doubtful whether such a propensity could be described as a characteristic of an animal, and even if it could, the judge's assertion that it was one that was not normally found in horses 'except at particular times and in particular circumstances' was questionable. The accident had been an unlikely mischance for which no-one had been to blame, and which attracted no liability under the provisions of s 2. Accordingly, the appeal would be allowed.

Bowlt v Clark [2006] All ER (D) 295 (Jun) (Court of Appeal: Lord Phillips of Worth Matravers CJ, Buxton and Sedley LJJ).

219 Natural Environment and Rural Communities Act 2006

See para 2109.

220 Protection of animals—causing unnecessary suffering—cat—untreated injury

The defendant, who was aged 15, owned a cat which had injured its tail. The defendant did not seek veterinary care herself but did tell her father that the cat should go to the vet. Her father, however, decided only to call the vet if the cat's condition worsened. The claimant charged the father and the defendant with an offence of causing unnecessary suffering to an animal contrary to the Animals Act 1911 s 1(1)(a). The father pleaded guilty to the offence but the defendant pleaded not guilty. The justices held that she had realised that the cat needed treatment and had told her father that but that her father, as head of the house, had decided that it was not necessary to seek veterinary attention and they accepted that it was reasonable for the defendant, being a young person, not to go against her father's decision. The defendant was acquitted. The claimant appealed, contending that the defendant's age and her position in the family were factors which were not to be taken into account. They stated that the correct test was to establish whether the defendant acted as a reasonably competent, reasonably caring owner. *Held*, the test to establish whether the defendant had acted unreasonably by permitting unnecessary suffering to be caused to her cat was not to be confined so that it had to be applied objectively. It could include a subjective element. Although the suffering of the animal had to be judged objectively, it was for the justices to decide whether any explanation given by the defendant was or was not reasonable by having regard to subjective considerations. The justices were entitled, indeed obliged, to take account of the defence that the defendant was putting forward as to why she had failed to act and to accede to the submissions that she was a youth and had relied on the decisions and actions of her father in determining whether she had not acted unreasonably in the matter. Accordingly, the appeal would be dismissed.

Royal Society for the Prevention of Cruelty to Animals v C [2006] EWHC 1069 (Admin), (2006) 170 JP 463 (Queen's Bench Division: Newman and Burton JJ). *RSPCA v Isaac* [1994] Crim LR 517, DC, considered.

221 Protection of animals—transportation of animals—welfare—England

The Welfare of Animals (Transport) (England) Order 2006, SI 2006/3260 (in force on 5 January 2007), replaces the 1997 Order, SI 1997/1480, and makes provision for the administration and enforcement of EC Council Regulations 1255/97 and 1/2005 on Community criteria for staging points and the protection of animals during transport and related operations. In particular, the order (1) makes general provision in relation to the protection of animals during transport; (2) enforces requirements in relation to transport, transporters, roll-on-roll-off vessels, organisers, keepers, assembly centres and control posts; (3) provides for derogations from specified requirements in respect of journeys undertaken by road and not exceeding 12 hours from origin to final destination; (4) identifies the Secretary of State as the competent authority for specified purposes; (5) makes provision in relation to the amendment, suspension and revocation of approvals, authorisations and certificates of competence, and allows for written representations to be made against refusals, conditions, amendments, suspensions and revocations; (6) empowers inspectors to ensure compliance with the order; (7) requires owners and charterers of vessels used to transport animals to produce specified information on demand to an officer of the Secretary of State; and (8) makes provision in relation to offences and enforcement. SI 2003/1724 is amended. SI 1975/1024, 1981/1051, 1998/2537, 1999/1622 and 2000/646 are revoked.

222 Sheep and goats—records, identification and movement—England

The Sheep and Goats (Records, Identification and Movement) (England) (Amendment) Order 2006, SI 2006/2987 (in force on 11 December 2006), amends the 2005 Order, SI 2005/3100, so as to (1) remove the possibility of marking an animal moved to another member state of the European Union with an 'X tag'; (2) provide that, in the case of an animal moved from a holding to an assembly centre for consignment to another member state, a second eartag must be applied before the animal leaves the holding; (3) provide that, on the replacement of removed, lost or illegible eartags or tattoos, a replacement eartag or tattoo must be applied as soon as possible after the removal or the discovery of the loss or illegibility of the eartag or tattoo, but in any event within 28 days and before the animal leaves the holding; (4) insert new enforcement provisions which give a range of powers to inspectors, including a power to prohibit the movement of a flock of sheep or a herd of goats to or from a holding, by notice served on a keeper, if they are satisfied that the prohibition is necessary for the proper enforcement of the 2005 Order in relation to that flock or herd; new provisions relate to the provision of false or misleading information and to offences committed by bodies corporate; and (5) substitute the prescribed form for recording animal movements; the new form contains a field to record the expected duration of the journey.

223 Sheep and goats—records, identification and movement—Wales

The Sheep and Goats (Records, Identification and Movement) (Wales) Order 2006, SI 2006/1036 (in force on 5 April 2006), makes provision for the administration and enforcement of EC Council Regulation 21/2004. The order (1) provides for a system for identifying and registering sheep and goats and tracing their movement; (2) sets out the information that must be entered in the register;

(3) sets out the information that must be entered in movement documents and imposes a requirement for a copy to be sent to the local authority; (4) makes provision concerning ear tags, tattoos and electronic devices; (5) provides for the allocation of lot numbers to animals at a market and prohibits the buying or selling of animals unless all animals in the lot are bought or sold; and (6) provides for enforcement by the local authority, or where the National Assembly for Wales so directs, by the Assembly. SI 2003/1966 is amended. SI 2002/2302, 2003/167, 946 are revoked.

The Sheep and Goats (Records, Identification and Movement) (Wales) (Amendment) Order 2006, SI 2006/2926 (in force on 1 January 2007), amends the 2006 Order supra, so as to (1) remove the possibility of marking an animal moved to another member state of the European Union with an 'X tag'; (2) provide that, in the case of an animal moved from a holding to an assembly centre for consignment to another member state, a second eartag must be applied before the animal leaves the holding; (3) provide that, on the replacement of removed, lost or illegible eartags or other means of identification, a replacement means of identification must be applied as soon as possible, but no later than 28 days, after the removal or the discovery of the loss or illegibility of the identification, but in any event before the animal leaves the holding; (4) insert new enforcement provisions which give a range of powers to inspectors, including a power to prohibit the movement of animals on, to or from a holding, by notice served on a keeper, if satisfied that the prohibition is necessary for the proper enforcement of the 2006 Order; new provisions relate to the giving of reasonable assistance to a person acting under the 2006 Order, to the provision of false or misleading information, and to offences committed by bodies corporate; and (5) substitute the prescribed form for recording animal movements; the new form contains a field to record the expected duration of the journey.

224 Veterinary medicines

See MEDICINAL PRODUCTS AND DRUGS.

225 Veterinary surgeons and veterinary practitioners—registration

The Veterinary Surgeons and Veterinary Practitioners (Registration) (Amendment) Regulations Order of Council 2006, SI 2006/3255 (in force on 1 April 2007), approves the Veterinary Surgeons and Veterinary Practitioners (Registration) (Amendment) Regulations 2006 made by the Council of the Royal College of Veterinary Surgeons under the Veterinary Surgeons Act 1966 s 11. The regulations provide for an increase in fees payable for annual registration and retention of names on the registers of the Royal College of Veterinary Surgeons. The increase in fees for all categories of membership is 5 per cent except for restoration of a name to the supplementary register, the fee for which is not increased. No fee is charged for non-practising veterinary surgeons over 70 years of age on 1 April of the year in which a fee would otherwise be due.

226 Welfare of animals—methods of killing—England

The Welfare of Animals (Slaughter or Killing) (Amendment) (England) Regulations 2006, SI 2006/1200 (in force on 29 April 2006), further amend the 1995 Regulations, SI 1995/731, so as to permit ventilation shutdown as a method of killing birds for the purpose of disease control.

ARBITRATION

Halsbury's Laws of England (4th edn) vol 2(3) (Reissue) paras 1–200

Articles

For articles relating to this title please refer to the Table of Articles at the beginning of the Abridgment.

227 Arbitrator—bias—process for determining jurisdiction

The first defendant had been the legal advisor to both the claimant, and his brother, the second defendant, as well as to their companies and trust. Disputes arose between the claimant and his brother in relation to the trust, which the first defendant tried, but failed, to resolve through mediation. An agreement was signed by the parties which appointed the first defendant as arbitrator, and waived the parties' rights, on any ground that they might have, to challenge the appointment of the arbitrator, and that the agreement was governed by Swiss law and that the seat of the arbitration would be Geneva. The claimant contended, stating that the agreement was void or had been avoided by him as it had been procured by misrepresentations. He sought an injunction to restrain the first defendant from acting as arbitrator on the ground that he was in breach of duty by promoting and accepting appointment as arbitrator in a matter from two existing clients with conflicting interests for whom he had acted previously in connected matters. The first defendant stated he intended to hold a hearing in Geneva to determine his jurisdiction. The claimant applied for an interim injunction to stop the first defendant acting as arbitrator in anyway. The application was dismissed and the claimant appealed. *Held*, it was common for arbitrators to face submissions of incompetence on the basis of bias, in such circumstances, where the seat of arbitration was in a nation where courts exercised an appropriate supervisory jurisdiction over arbitration, such as Switzerland, the arbitrator's decision would not be final. The first defendant's consideration of his own jurisdiction was only the first step in determining the question. There was nothing untoward in him doing so, whether the subsequent steps took place in Switzerland or England. Accordingly, the appeal would be dismissed.

Weissfisch v Julius [2006] EWCA Civ 218, [2006] 2 All ER (Comm) 504 (Court of Appeal: Lord Phillips of Worth Matravers CJ, Sir Anthony Clarke MR, and Moses LJ).

228 Arbitrator—jurisdiction—transaction set-off—set-off in respect of sums owed in separate contract

The first contract between the claimant and the defendant for the supply of satellite capacity and voice termination services was governed by Danish law and provided for arbitration in Denmark. A second contract between them for the supply of telephony services stated that the contract was governed by the laws of the United Kingdom and that disputes were to be resolved by arbitration under UNCITRAL Arbitration Rules. The defendant refused to pay the full amount invoiced by the claimant under the second contract. The defendant admitted that it owed the amount claimed, but asserted that the right to a transaction set-off in respect of sums owed under the first contract. The arbitrators made a partial award, but held that they had no jurisdiction to determine the transaction set-off defence because the second contract provided only for disputes under that contract to be resolved by arbitration, and because the UNCITRAL Arbitration Rules art 19(3) restricted a party's right to claim a set-off to a claim which arose out of the same contract. The defendant challenged the arbitrators' ruling. *Held*, an arbitral tribunal's jurisdiction depended on the scope of the arbitration agreement, and the clear meaning of art 19(3) was that a party's right of set-off arose only where it was founded on a claim which arose out of the same contract as that on which the other party's claim was based. There was no rule that the governing law prevailed over any conflicting procedural rules. It followed that the transaction set-off claimed by the defendant was excluded and, accordingly, the application would be dismissed.

Econet Satellite Services Ltd v Vee Networks Ltd [2006] EWHC 1664 (Comm), [2006] 2 All ER (Comm) 1000 (Queen's Bench Division: Field J).

229 Award—appeal—permission to appeal—question of law—evidence

The respondent contractor engaged the appellant as a sub-contractor under a modified standard agreement. One of the standard terms provided that the parties agreed to appeals on questions of law arising out of an arbitrator's award being brought under the Arbitration Act 1996 s 69. A dispute arose over several items in the appellant's final account and the matter was referred to arbitration. The arbitrator made an award in the appellant's favour, but the appellant was of the opinion that the award should have been significantly more and appealed on points of law under s 69(2)(a). Issues arose as to the evidence that the court could receive on an appeal under s 69, as to whether a philosophy or ethos of non-intervention, having regard to the general principles in s 1, should dissuade the court from allowing an appeal under s 69(2)(a), and as to whether the decision of an arbitrator was to be afforded any deference. *Held*, although the principal document that had to be considered in any appeal under s 69 was the arbitrator's award, the court should also receive any document referred to therein that was necessary to determine any question of law arising out of that award. The autonomy of parties was a general principle of Pt 1 (ss 1–84), and the parties had agreed, in the exercise of their autonomy, to an appeal to the court on a question of law. Finally, having regard to previous authorities, where an arbitrator's experience assisted in the determination of a question of law, such as documents passing between members of his own trade, the court would afford his decision a measure of deference and would only reverse that decision where, despite the benefit of his relevant experience, the arbitrator had come to the wrong conclusion. The court should read an arbitral award as a whole in a fair and reasonable way without engaging in minute textual analysis. Judgment would be given accordingly.

Kershaw Mechanical Services Ltd v Kendrick Construction Ltd [2006] EWHC 727 (TCC), [2006] 4 All ER 79 (Queen's Bench Division: Jackson J).

230 Award—appeal—permission to appeal—question of law—right to appeal—exclusion

The claimant's predecessor in title entered into a contract with the defendant, an international organisation, to design a website. The contract provided for arbitration by the Commonwealth Secretariat Arbitration Tribunal, whose statute provided that the tribunal's judgment was final and unappealable. A dispute over ownership of the website was referred to the tribunal, which found in favour of the defendant. The claimant applied to the court, under the Arbitration Act 1996 s 69, for permission to appeal against the award on the basis of an error of law. The claimant argued that the right to appeal under s 69 could not be excluded by reference rather than by expressly stating it on the face of the agreement. *Held*, s 69(1) permitted the incorporation of exclusion agreements by reference without spelling them out in the body of the arbitration clause. The 1996 Act was intended to reflect and preserve the twin objectives of finality and party autonomy, and the right to contract out under s 69 presented an optional and consensual facility directed at reinforcing those two key objectives. Further, an express reference to such an exclusion clause in a case where one of the parties was a public authority was not necessary in order to comply with the European Convention on Human Rights art 6. Parties entering into an arbitration agreement containing such an exclusion clause were not, by agreeing to such restrictions, acting inconsistently with the human rights of the opposing party. There was an effective and enforceable exclusion agreement and the court had no jurisdiction to entertain an application, under the 1996 Act s 69, for leave to appeal. Accordingly, the application would be dismissed.

Sukuman Ltd v Commonwealth Secretariat [2006] EWHC 304 (Comm), [2006] 1 All ER (Comm) 621 (Queen's Bench Division: Colman J).

This decision has been affirmed on appeal: [2007] EWCA Civ 243, (2007) Times, 13 April.

231   Award—appeal—permission to appeal—residual jurisdiction of Court of Appeal—unfairness

The Arbitration Act 1996 s 69(8) provides that the decision of the court on an arbitral appeal must be treated as a judgment of the court for the purposes of a further appeal, but that no such appeal lies without the leave of the court, and leave must not be given unless the court considers that the question is one of general importance or is one which for some other special reason should be considered by the Court of Appeal.

A dispute between the claimant insurer and the defendant reinsurers went to arbitration. An award was made in favour of the claimant, and the defendants appealed. The judge allowed the appeal, and the claimant applied to the judge for permission to appeal to the Court of Appeal. The judge refused permission, and the claimant applied to the Court of Appeal for permission to appeal. The defendants submitted that the 1996 Act s 69(8) imposed a statutory and thus jurisdictional bar on any possibility of the Court of Appeal granting permission to appeal or entertaining any form of appellate proceedings in circumstances where the judge himself had not given permission to appeal. The claimant submitted that there was case authority for the existence of a residual discretion to permit an appeal, despite the judge's refusal of permission, where that refusal could be challenged on the grounds of unfairness pursuant to the European Convention on Human Rights art 6, and that there was such unfairness in the present case. *Held*, a residual jurisdiction existed for reviewing on appeal the misconduct or unfairness of a first instance judge's determination concerning the grant or refusal of leave to appeal. There were all sorts of contexts in which, for good reason, Parliament had provided that there should be restrictions on the appeal process, and a limit to appellate jurisdiction. In such situations it was natural to conclude that, even in the absence of express language, the statute intended the lower court's discretion as to whether to give permission to appeal to a higher court to be exclusive and final. However, there was no similar rationale, it might be said no good reason at all, for thinking that a court's unfairness was to be left incapable of appellate review. However, on the facts of the present case, there was no cause for thinking that the judge's refusal of leave to appeal was unfair. Accordingly, the application would be dismissed.

AstraZeneca Insurance Co Ltd v CGU International Insurance plc [2006] EWCA Civ 1340, [2006] All ER (D) 176 (Oct) (Court of Appeal: Sir Anthony Clarke MR, Rix and Longmore LJJ). *North Range Shipping Ltd v Seatrans Shipping Corpn* [2002] EWCA Civ 405, [2002] 4 All ER 390 (2002 Abr para 254) followed.

232   Award—challenge—failure to deal with question of costs

In the present case, the first interim award had been made but the remaining costs had been reserved by the arbitration tribunal. An application was made by the applicant to determine whether the Arbitration Act 1996 s 57 applied if, after a claim had been presented to the tribunal for determination at the hearing, the tribunal failed to deal with it. The applicant contended that a reservation of the issue for further consideration did not deal with the claim. *Held*, for the purposes of s 57, the tribunal addressing its collective mind to the question of costs and determining that they would be the subject of another award, was 'dealing' with the claim. It was neither the purpose nor the effect of s 57 to impose on the tribunal or the parties a timetable within which the tribunal had to produce a second award on an aspect of the matters referred to the tribunal which differed from those the subject of the first award and which the tribunal had purposely left for determination on a separate occasion. Section 57 was a remedial section, enabling the arbitral process to correct itself rather than requiring an application to the court. Section 57 would be applicable in a case where the arbitrator had failed to deal with the question of the parties' costs at all. Accordingly, the application would be refused.

Sea Trade Maritime Corpn v Hellenic Mutual War Risks Association (Bermuda) Ltd, The Athena [2006] EWHC 578 (Comm), [2006] 2 All ER (Comm) 648 (Queen's Bench Division: Clarke J).

233   Award—challenge—lack of substantive jurisdiction—bilateral agreement—rights in international law

By virtue of a contract between a state-owned corporation in Ecuador and the defendant, a Californian corporation, the defendant had exclusive rights to carry out hydrocarbon exploration and exploitation in a region of the Ecuadorian Amazon basin. A dispute arose between the defendant and the Ecuadorian internal revenue service concerning the entitlement of the defendant to refunds of value added tax payments made on purchases of goods and services in connection with the production of oil. Arbitral proceedings were subsequently initiated pursuant to a bilateral investment treaty between Ecuador (the claimant) and the United States, in which the defendant argued that the actions of the revenue service constituted breaches by the claimant of its obligations under the treaty and under public international law. The arbitrator made an award in the defendant's favour. In reliance on the Arbitration Act 1996 ss 67 and 68, the claimant sought to challenge that award by arguing that the arbitrators had ruled on a matter which was outside the scope of the treaty, and had exceeded their powers in such a way as to constitute a serious procedural irregularity in the arbitral proceedings, which had resulted in a substantial injustice to the claimant. *Held*, it had already been decided by the courts that, from the moment when an investor submitted a dispute with a state party to arbitration under the treaty, the treaty conferred or created rights in international law in favour of the investor. The arbitral tribunal was therefore dealing with the rights of the defendant in international law and the obligations that the claimant owed. It had to follow that, if the tribunal concluded that international law rights of the defendant had been violated by the claimant, the tribunal would have to consider what remedies were available in international law to repair any damage caused to the defendant by those breaches. In the absence of any express agreement between the parties to the arbitration in which the international law rights and obligations of the parties were to be determined, the remedies that the tribunal could grant had to be those that were generally available to deal with breaches of international law as determined by the tribunal. It followed that the tribunal had had jurisdiction for the purposes of s 67 and had not exceeded its powers within the terms of s 68. In any event, the claimant had not suffered substantial injustice even if the tribunal had exceeded its powers. Accordingly, the application would be dismissed.

Republic of Ecuador v Occidental Exploration and Production Co (No 2) [2006] EWHC 345 (Comm), [2006] 1 Lloyd's Rep 773 (Queen's Bench Division: Aikens J). For earlier related proceedings see *Republic of Ecuador v Occidental Exploration and Production Co* [2005] EWCA Civ 1116, [2006] 2 All ER 225 (2005 Abr para 195).

234   Award—enforcement—foreign arbitration award—refusal—defendant unable to present case

The Arbitration Act 1996 s 103(2)(c) provides that enforcement of an award may be refused if the person against whom it is invoked proves that he was unable to present his case.

The claimants alleged that a company of which the defendant was a majority shareholder owed money to one of them. However, there was no allegation that the defendant had failed to make any payments to anyone. The claimants brought arbitration proceedings in India. The defendant stated that he was not in a position to respond due to ill health and the arbitration took place in his absence. A ruling was made that the award should not be enforced against the defendant because it had been impossible for him to present his case. On appeal, the claimants alleged that the defendant had acted in bad faith, but accepted that no notice of that allegation had been given to the defendant at any previous stage. *Held*, it was clear on the natural wording of the 1996 Act s 103(2)(c) that a party to an arbitration was unable to present his case if he had not been informed of the case that he was required to meet. The defendant had never been given the opportunity to meet the actual case against him. The claimants' submission that the court should not exercise its discretion under s 103(2)(c) to refuse to enforce the award could not be accepted: even if the court had such a discretion, it would not exercise it. There was good ground for refusing to enforce the award and, accordingly, the appeal would be dismissed.

Kanoria v Guinness [2006] EWCA Civ 222, [2006] 2 All ER (Comm) 413 (Court of Appeal: Lord Phillips of Worth Matravers CJ, Sir Anthony Clarke MR and May LJ). *Minmetals Germany Gmbh v Ferco Steel Ltd* [1999] 1 All ER (Comm) 315 (1999 Abr para 180) considered.

235   Award—enforcement—foreign arbitration award—state immunity—waiver

See *Svenska Petroleum Exploration AB v Government of the Republic of Lithuania*, para 1398.

236   Court—powers—determination of question of law—power to refuse

The Arbitration Act 1996 s 45(1) provides that, unless otherwise agreed by the parties, the court may on the application of a party to arbitral proceedings determine any question of law arising in the course of the proceedings which the court is satisfied substantially affects the rights of one or more of the parties.

The claimants purchased buildings which required extensive design, remedial and conversion works, and the project was put out to tender. The defendant made a bid, which stated by way of 'clarification' that any repairs to external elevations over and above the percentage specified in the tender might be subject to additional cost. Following correspondence between the parties, the defendant offered a provisional sum in relation to the external elevations and the claimants sought confirmation that the 'clarification' should be deemed to have been removed from the tender. The defendant made such a confirmation in writing, and a contract was duly signed. The defendant had to carry out significant structural works and sought change orders from the claimants in order that

that work could be valued. The claimants took the view that the work was in fact within the scope of the defendant's original contractual obligations. The matter was referred to arbitration, and issues arose as to whether the court had discretion to refuse to determine a question of law under the 1996 Act s 45, and whether the claimants had retained the risk that unforeseen structural work might be necessary before carrying out the contract works. *Held*, the use of the word 'may' in s 45 was a clear indication that the court had the relevant discretion. It was essentially a speedy procedure designed to interrupt the arbitration to the minimum possible extent and it was an exception to the general rule that the courts did not intervene in the course of an arbitration. In all the circumstances, it was appropriate to exercise that discretion to determine the question of law. Party autonomy was a cornerstone of modern arbitration and, although the arbitrator was the parties' chosen tribunal of fact, the court was their chosen tribunal of law. Moreover, in all the circumstances, the correspondence had the effect of removing the 'clarification' altogether. Judgment would be given accordingly.

Taylor Woodrow v Barnes & Elliott [2006] EWHC 1693 (TCC), [2006] 2 All ER (Comm) 735 (Queen's Bench Division: Jackson J). *Babanaft International Co SA v Avant Petroleum Inc; The Oltenia* [1982] 3 All ER 244, CA (1982 Abr para 232), applied.

237   Court—powers—orders supporting arbitral proceedings—without notice application

The shareholders of a Nigerian company had a shareholders' agreement which provided that, if any shareholder wished to sell shares, a right of pre-emption was given to other shareholders, who were entitled to exercise their right of first refusal within 15 days from the receipt of intention to sell, and the price was to be paid within 30 days from the date of the notice. The agreement was subject to Nigerian law and provided for arbitration in Nigeria by three arbitrators. An offer by a second company to buy the respondent's shares was matched by the applicant company, one of the shareholders. The applicant's request for an extension of time in which to pay, as the transaction documents were not in an acceptable form, was refused. The applicant made an application to the English court, as the share purchase agreement provided for the agreement to be resolved by arbitration in London, without notice to the respondents, for urgent relief on the basis that the failure by the respondents to provide proper transaction documents was a breach of express and implied terms of the shareholders' agreement. Arbitration had not commenced, and the court granted an injunction under the Arbitration Act 1996 s 44. The respondents sought to have the injunction set aside. *Held*, there had been no justification for rushing the proceedings through without notice to the respondents as there had been sufficient time to notify them. While the share purchase agreement would have the seat of arbitration in London, the agreement did not apply before completion of the share sale to the applicant. In the circumstances, the English court was not the appropriate forum for an application for an injunction in aid of arbitration. There was no good arguable case that there was an English arbitration clause, the seat of the arbitration was in Nigeria and English law was not the procedural law of the arbitration, and none of the assets were in England. Accordingly, the injunction would be set aside.

Econet Wireless Ltd v VEE Networks Ltd [2006] EWHC 1568 (Comm), [2006] 2 All ER (Comm) 989 (Queen's Bench Division: Morison J).

ARMED FORCES

Halsbury's Laws of England (4th edn) vol 2(2) (Reissue) paras 1–554

Articles

For articles relating to this title please refer to the Table of Articles at the beginning of the Abridgment.

238   Armed Forces Act 2001—commencement

The Armed Forces Act 2001 (Commencement No 6) Order 2006, SI 2006/235, brings into force, on 3 February 2006, ss 32(1)–(8), (9) (so far as not already in force), 33 and Sch 5 (so far as not already in force).

The Armed Forces Act 2001 (Commencement No 7) Order 2006, SI 2006/2309, brings s 29, which gives effect to Sch 4, and s 30 into force on 25 August 2006.

For a summary of the Act, see 2001 Abr para 2755. See also the commencement table in the title STATUTES.

239   Armed Forces Act 2006

The Armed Forces Act 2006 makes provision with respect to the armed forces. The Act received the royal assent on 8 November 2006 and came into force in part on that day. The remaining provisions come into force on a day or days to be appointed. For details of commencement, see the commencement table in the title STATUTES.

First Group of Parts (Pts 1–13) Discipline

Part 1 (ss 1–49) Offences
Section 1 makes it an offence for a person subject to service law to assist intentionally an enemy in a number of ways, such as communicating with an enemy or providing the enemy with supplies. When a person subject to service law is taking part in operations against an enemy, or is in the vicinity of an enemy, he commits an offence if he is found to be guilty of misconduct in specified circumstances: s 2. Under s 3, a person subject to service law is guilty of an offence if he intentionally or recklessly puts an operation of Her Majesty's forces at risk, or intentionally delays or discourages such an operation. Service personnel and civilians subject to service discipline may be guilty of looting in defined circumstances: s 4. Under s 5, it is an offence for service personnel who have been captured by an enemy to fail to escape where they could reasonably be expected to take steps to do so, or intentionally to prevent or discourage a member of Her Majesty's forces from taking reasonable steps to do so. A person subject to service law commits the offence of mutiny if he takes part in concerted action to overthrow or resist the authority of those in command or to disobey authority in such a way as to undermine discipline: s 6. Section 7 provides that it is an offence if persons subject to service law fail to do what can reasonably be expected of them to prevent or stop the concerted actions of resisting or overthrowing authority or disobeying authority so as to undermine discipline. Under s 8, a person subject to service law commits an offence of desertion if is absent without leave and either intends to remain permanently so absent or to avoid service on operations against an enemy, or service abroad on operations to protect life or property, or service on military occupation of a foreign country or territory. A person subject to service law commits an offence if he is absent from duty without leave: s 9. Under s 10, it is an offence if a person subject to service law fails to do what can reasonably be expected of him to cause a deserter or absentee without leave, or a person attempting to commit either offence, to be detained. Section 11 penalises misconduct towards a superior officer by a person subject to service law. A person subject to service law who intentionally or recklessly disobeys a lawful command commits an offence: s 12. Section 13 provides that a breach of standing orders by a person subject to service law or a civilian subject to service discipline is an offence, but only if he is aware, or could reasonably be expected to be aware, of the order in question. It is an offence for a person subject to service law to use force against a sentry or, by the threat of force, to compel a sentry to let him or any other person pass: s 14. A person subject to service law commits an offence if he fails to attend for, or perform any, duty: s 15. Section 16 makes it an offence for a person subject to service law to avoid service either by pretending to be ill or injured or by harming himself, or arranging for someone else to harm him. A person subject to service law commits an offence if, without lawful authority, he discloses information which he knows or has reasonable cause to believe would or might be useful to an enemy: s 17. The making of false official records, the interference with or the suppression of official documents, and the failure, with intent to deceive, to make an official record when under a duty to do so are offences under s 18. Section 19 penalises conduct which is prejudicial to good order and service discipline. A person subject to service law who is unfit to be entrusted with his duty or whose behaviour is disorderly or likely to discredit the armed forces due to the influence of alcohol or any drug commits an offence: s 20. Fighting or threatening, abusive, insulting or provocative behaviour, without reasonable excuse, by a person subject to service law is an offence under s 21. Section 22 penalises intentional ill-treatment and recklessness on the part of a superior officer where he enforces excessively harsh discipline on a subordinate. Cruel or indecent conduct by service personnel is an offence if the circumstances, motive or other factors render it disgraceful: s 23. Section 24 deals with offences concerning damage or loss caused by service personnel to public or service property or to the property of another member of the armed forces. The misapplication or wasting of any public or service property by a person subject to service law is an offence: s 25. Section 26 defines 'public property' and 'service property' for the purposes of ss 24, 25. Section 27 provides that a person subject to service law or a civilian subject to service discipline commits an offence if he intentionally obstructs, or fails to assist when called on to do so, a service policeman carrying out his duties or a member of the armed forces acting under the authority of a provost officer. Section 28 penalises service personnel or civilians subject to service discipline who use or threaten violence towards a person who has a duty to apprehend them, and who know or have reasonable cause to believe that the person has a duty to apprehend them. It is an offence for a member of the armed forces or a civilian subject to service discipline who is in lawful custody to escape, or to use or threaten violence against a person in whose lawful custody he is: s 29. It is an offence for a person subject to service law to allow the escape or unlawful release of a person in his charge, or whom it is his duty to guard, when he has no reasonable cause to believe that he has authority to do so: s 30. It is an offence under s 31 for service personnel to cause a ship to be at risk, with the aim of causing damage to or the stranding of the ship, or causing it to sink, without a lawful excuse, or to cause a ship to be at risk through recklessness or negligence. It is an offence for service personnel to give a false air signal intentionally: s 32. Under s 33, it is an offence for a member of the armed forces to do something when flying or using an aircraft, or in relation to an aircraft or aircraft material, which causes, or is likely to cause death or injury, if he intends to cause, or is reckless or negligent about causing, death or injury. A person subject to service law who breaches regulations

governing minimum heights for flying commits an offence (s 34), and annoyance caused by such a person by flying an aircraft is also an offence (s 35). Under s 36, it is an offence for a person subject to service law to make or sign a certificate without having first checked that it is correct. It is an offence if a person in command of a service ship or aircraft unlawfully fails to ensure that all papers which identify a captured ship or aircraft are sent to a court which can determine whether the ship, aircraft or goods are prize, and bring the ship, aircraft or goods to a convenient place for adjudication: s 37. It is also an offence to ill-treat, or unlawfully take anything from, a person on board a ship or aircraft captured as prize: s 38. Under s 39, it is an offence for a person subject to service law to attempt to commit a service offence, or for a civilian subject to service discipline to attempt to commit a specified offence. It is an offence for a person subject to service law to incite another person to commit a service offence, or for a civilian subject to service discipline to incite another person to commit an offence specified in s 39: s 40. Under s 41, it is an offence for a person subject to service law to aid, abet, counsel or procure the commission of a service offence, or for a civilian subject to service discipline to aid, abet, counsel or procure the commission of an offence specified in s 39. Further, it is an offence for a person subject to service law, or a civilian subject to service discipline, to do something which is an offence under the criminal law of England and Wales or would be such an offence if done in England and Wales: s 42. Sections 43–48 modify the law relating to criminal attempts and to conspiring to commit, inciting, aiding, abetting, counselling or procuring criminal conduct. Certain acts in relation to military aircraft done by a person subject to service law or by a civilian subject to service discipline that would if done in relation to a civil aircraft amount to prescribed air navigation order offences may be treated for the purposes of s 42 as punishable by the law of England and Wales: s 49.

Part 2 (ss 50–66) Jurisdiction and Time Limits

Chapter 1 (ss 50–54) Jurisdiction
Section 50 confers jurisdiction on the Court Martial to try any service offence; its jurisdiction is set out in s 51. Section 52 defines what is meant by references in the Act to charges capable of being heard summarily. Section 53, Sch 1 Pt 1 detail offences that may be heard summarily. An officer may not hear summarily a charge in respect of an offence listed in Sch 1 Pt 2, or an attempt to commit such an offence, without the permission of higher authority, unless he is of or above the rank of rear admiral, major-general or air vice-marshal: s 54.

Chapter 2 (ss 55–62) Time Limits for Commencing Proceedings
Sections 55–62 make provision as to time limits for commencing proceedings.

Chapter 3 (ss 63–66) Double Jeopardy
Sections 63–66 make provision as to the circumstances in which a trial is to be barred on the ground of double jeopardy.

Part 3 (ss 67–97) Powers of Arrest, Search and Entry

Chapter 1 (ss 67–74) Arrest etc
Sections 67, 68 set out the powers of arrest when it is reasonably suspected that a service offence has been or is being committed. A service policeman has the power to arrest a person if he reasonably suspects the person is about to commit a service offence: s 69. Section 70 permits a service policeman to search an arrested person if he has reasonable grounds to believe that the arrested person may present a danger to himself or others or who may be concealing anything which might help him escape or which may be evidence relating to a service offence. A person, other than a service policeman, who is exercising a power of arrest may search the arrested person if he has reasonable grounds for believing that the arrested person may present a danger to himself or others: s 71. Section 72 describes the extent of the powers conferred by ss 70, 71. Section 73 sets out when persons exercising a power of search may seize and retain anything found. The Secretary of State may make provision conferring power to search the premises at which a person is arrested: s 74.

Chapter 2 (ss 75–82) Stop and Search
Section 75 gives a service policeman the power to stop and search certain persons and vehicles for stolen goods or controlled drugs. Section 76 confers stop and search powers on persons other than service policemen, s 77 provides definitions for the purposes of ss 75, 76, and s 78 describes the places in which powers under ss 75, 76 may be exercised. Section 79 sets out limitations in respect of the search of persons in certain gardens or on certain other land, and s 80 sets out the safeguards with regard to the conduct of the search. The Secretary of State is permitted by s 81 to make further provision about searches under ss 75, 76. Section 82 applies the provisions of ss 75–82 to ships and aircraft.

Chapter 3 (ss 83–93) Powers of Entry, Search and Seizure
Section 83 enables judge advocates to issue warrants authorising the entry and search of relevant residential premises on the application of a service policeman, and s 84 defines terms used in s 83. Section 85 enables the Secretary of State by order to make provision for the use of live television links for hearing an application for an entry and search warrant. Under s 86, the Secretary of State may by order establish procedures to enable service policemen investigating a service offence to apply to a judge advocate for a warrant for access to excluded or special procedure material that is

held in any relevant residential premises. Commanding officers are given a limited power to authorise a service policeman to search relevant residential premises without a warrant: s 87. Section 88 gives the commanding officer a similar power to authorise a member of Her Majesty's forces who is not a service policeman to conduct the search. Section 89 requires that where any search authorised by a commanding officer under s 87 or 88 has resulted in anything being seized and retained, a judge advocate must be asked to review the search, seizure and retention as soon as practicable. Section 90 sets out the circumstances in which a service policeman may, without a warrant, enter and search service living accommodation or other premises occupied by a person subject to service law or a civilian subject to service discipline to arrest a person if he has reasonable grounds for believing that the person is on the premises. Section 91 enables a commanding officer to authorise a person subject to service law, other than a service policeman, to exercise the powers of entry for the purposes of arrest conferred on a service policeman by s 90. Section 92 gives the Secretary of State power to make provision dealing with the entry and search of premises controlled by a person arrested under s 67 who is being held in service custody without being charged. The Secretary of State has the power to make provision dealing with seizure and the power to retain property seized: s 93.

Chapter 4 (ss 94–97) Supplementary
Sections 94–97 make provision as to property in the possession of service police or a commanding officer, make certain savings, define particular terms used in Pt 3, and permit the use of reasonable force in the exercise of a power conferred by or under Pt 3.

Part 4 (ss 98–112) Custody

Chapter 1 (ss 98–104) Custody without Charge
Section 98 states the general principle that a person who is arrested for a service offence may not be kept in custody without charge except in accordance with the provisions of ss 99–102. The circumstances in which a person may be held in custody without charge are set out in s 99. Section 100 sets out the duties of a commanding officer who, under s 99, has authorised the continued custody without charge of a person arrested for a service offence. Sections 101, 102 are concerned with the extension by a judge advocate of periods of custody without charge. The circumstances in which the provisions of ss 98–102 are to apply other than when a person has been arrested under s 67 are set out: s 103, and s 104 empowers the Secretary of State to provide for further matters concerned with custody without charge.

Chapter 2 (ss 105–111) Custody etc after Charge
An accused person must be brought before a judge advocate as soon as practicable: s 105. Section 106 sets out conditions which the judge advocate must consider when deciding whether to authorise keeping the accused in custody under s 105, and a condition which applies when a judge advocate is considering whether to remand an accused into service custody during court proceedings. Section 107 concerns the situation where the judge advocate decides that custody is not appropriate, in which case the accused must be released. If a judge advocate has authorised custody, a review must be carried out by a judge advocate no later than the end of the authorised period: s 108. Section 109 is concerned with keeping an accused in custody during proceedings before the Court Martial or the Service Civilian Court. Section 110 provides that where an accused has not been kept in custody but his commanding officer is satisfied that taking him into custody is justified the commanding officer may order the arrest of the accused. Where an accused who is not in custody has been arraigned before the Court Martial or Service Civilian Court but the proceedings have not concluded and a judge advocate becomes satisfied that taking the accused into custody is justified, he may direct that the accused be arrested: s 111.

Chapter 3 (s 112) Custody Proceedings Rules
Section 112 confers power on the Secretary of State to make custody proceedings rules.

Part 5 (ss 113–128) Investigation, Charging and Mode of Trial

Chapter 1 (s 113–118) Investigation
Under s 113, if an officer becomes aware of allegations or circumstances indicating that a serious offence, described in Sch 2, has or may have been committed, he must ensure that the service police are aware of the matter. Section 114 requires specified officers to ensure as soon as reasonably practicable that the service police are aware of certain circumstances. Section 115 deals with situations in which a commanding officer becomes aware of allegations or circumstances which would indicate to a reasonable person that a person within the commanding officer's command may have committed a service offence. The duties of the service police, after an investigation, in relation to a case which they have investigated or which has been referred to them by a United Kingdom police force or by an overseas police force are dealt with by s 116. Section 117 applies where such an investigation involves more than one incident or more than one suspect. A service policeman who refers a case about a person to the Director of Service Prosecutions has a duty under s 118 to notify the person's commanding officer.

Chapter 2 (s 119–126) Charging and Mode of Trial
Section 119 specifies the circumstances in which a commanding officer has initial powers, defined in
s 120, in relation to a case; those powers are to bring charges or to refer the case to the Director of
Service Prosecutions. Section 121 gives powers to the Director of Service Prosecutions where he has
had a case referred to him by a service policeman. Section 122 requires a commanding officer to
bring any charge which he is directed, under s 121, by the Director of Service Prosecutions to bring.
Where, under his initial powers under s 120, a commanding officer charges a person with an offence
triable summarily, the commanding officer has certain powers under s 123 in relation to the charge.
Section 124 requires an accused's commanding officer to hear charges which are allocated for
summary hearing. Sections 125, 126 give the Director of Service Prosecutions certain powers in
respect of charges allocated for Court Martial or Service Civilian Court trial.

Chapter 3 (ss 127, 128) Supplementary
Section 127 provides for a direction by the Director of Service Prosecutions barring further
proceedings, and s 128 enables the Secretary of State to make regulations for the purposes of Pt 5.

Part 6 (ss 129–153) Summary Hearing and Appeals and Review

Chapter 1 (ss 129–139) Summary Hearing
Section 129 requires a commanding officer, before hearing a charge summarily, to give the accused
the opportunity of electing Court Martial trial of the charge. Section 130 prevents the Director of
Service Prosecutions from taking certain actions, without the written consent of the accused, where
the accused has elected Court Martial trial. Section 131 gives the commanding officer certain
powers in respect of summary hearings. The punishments which are available to a commanding
officer who has found a charge proved are listed in s 132. Limits are placed by s 133 on the amount
of detention a commanding officer may award and the circumstances in which he may do so.
Section 134 prevents a commanding officer from awarding forfeiture of seniority unless he has
extended powers for the purpose. Section 135 sets limits on the powers of a commanding officer to
award reduction in rank or disrating. Section 136 deals with a commanding officer's powers to award
a fine. The maximum amount for a service compensation order that may be awarded by a
commanding officer is set out in s 137. Section 138 prohibits the award of certain punishments in
combination with each other. Section 139 places restrictions on the punishments which may be
awarded by a commanding officer where he is hearing a criminal conduct charge.

Chapter 2 (ss 140–151) The Summary Appeal Court
The Summary Appeal Court is established by s 140. A person who has had a charge against him
proven at a summary hearing may appeal to the Summary Appeal Court: s 141. For the purpose of
an appeal, the Summary Appeal Court is to consist of a judge advocate and two other members:
s 142. By virtue of s 143, officers and warrant officers are generally qualified for membership of the
Summary Appeal Court. The categories of officers and warrant officers who, by virtue of any
involvement in the case which is the subject of the appeal or any command relationship with the
accused person, are ineligible for membership of the court for that particular appeal are set out:
s 144. Subject to any provision made by rules, the Summary Appeal Court must sit in open court:
s 145. An appeal against a finding is to be by way of a rehearing of the charge: s 146. At a rehearing
of a charge, the Summary Appeal Court may confirm, quash or substitute the finding with another
charge having been proved: s 147. Unless it directs otherwise, any punishment substituted by the
Summary Appeal Court is deemed to have been awarded on the day on which the original
punishment was awarded: s 148. Section 149 provides that decisions of the Summary Appeal Court
are to be made on the basis of a majority of the votes of the members of the court. A witness before
the Summary Appeal Court is entitled to the same immunities and privileges as a witness before the
High Court: s 150. The Secretary of State may make rules with respect to the Summary Appeal
Court: s 151.

Chapter 3 (s 152) Review of Summary Findings and Punishment
Under s 152, a finding or punishment awarded at a summary hearing may be reviewed at any time.

Chapter 4 (s 153) Summary Hearings etc Rules
The Secretary of State may make regulations with respect to the summary hearing of charges by
commanding officers and hearings as regards the making of orders activating suspended sentences of
service detention passed on an offender by a commanding officer: s 153.

Part 7 (ss 154–172) Trial by Court Martial

Chapter 1 (ss 154–157) The Court Martial
Section 154 establishes the Court Martial as a standing court which may sit anywhere within or
outside the United Kingdom. Section 155 provides for the membership of the court for Court
Martial proceedings. As a general principle, officers and warrant officers may be members of the
Court Martial: s 156. Section 157 provides for the circumstances in which officers and warrant
officers who are otherwise qualified are nevertheless ineligible for membership of the Court Martial
for a particular trial.

Chapter 2 (ss 158–163) Court Martial Proceedings
As a general principle, the Court Martial must sit in open court: s 158. Where the Court Martial consists of a judge advocate and other persons, rulings and directions on questions of law, procedure or practice are to be given by the judge advocate: s 159. The finding of the Court Martial on a charge and any sentence passed by it must be determined by a majority of the members of the court: s 160. When the Court Martial finds a person not guilty of an offence but the allegations on the charge sheet amount to allegations of another service offence, including an attempted offence, the court may convict him of that offence: s 161. A witness before the Court Martial is entitled to the same immunities and privileges as a witness before the High Court: s 162. The Secretary of State may make rules with respect to the Court Martial: s 163.

Chapter 3 (ss 164, 165) Punishments Available to Court Martial
Section 164, Sch 3 specify the punishments that may be awarded by the Court Martial. Section 165 limits the powers of punishment of the Court Martial where it tries a person as the result of his electing to be tried by that court.

Chapter 4 (ss 166–172) Findings of Unfitness to Stand Trial and Insanity
On a trial by the Court Martial, the issue of whether the defendant is fit to stand trial must be decided, subject to certain exceptions, as soon as it arises: s 166. Where a judge advocate has determined that a person is unfit to stand trial, the trial must not proceed further but the court must determine whether it is satisfied that the defendant did the act charged against him: s 167. If on a trial by the Court Martial the court is satisfied that the defendant did the act charged against him, and that at the time of the act he was insane, the court must find the defendant not guilty by reason of insanity: s 168. Section 169, Sch 4 provide for the powers of the Court Martial where there is a finding of unfitness to stand trial or not guilty by reason of insanity. Section 170 defines service supervision orders and sets out the conditions that must be satisfied for them to be made. Under s 171, the Secretary of State, if he is satisfied that a person who is the subject of a hospital order with a restriction order is no longer unfit to stand trial, may remit the person for trial by the Court Martial. Section 172 makes provision supplementary to ss 166 and 168.

Part 8 (ss 173–236) Sentencing Powers and Mandatory etc Sentences

Chapter 1 (ss 173–187) Definition etc of Certain Sentences
Section 173 defines a service supervision and punishment order. A commanding officer must review such an order made in respect of a person under his command: s 174. Section 175 defines a service compensation order. Compensation awarded in favour of a person need not be paid to him until the expiry of the period allowed for an appeal: s 176. A service compensation order may be reviewed, on application by the person against whom it is made, by the Court Martial or by the person's commanding officer: s 177. Sections 178–181, Sch 5 Pt 1 concern service community orders, and ss 182–184, Sch 5 Pt 2, Sch 6, concern overseas community orders. Section 185 defines a conditional discharge and an absolute discharge. Section 186 provides for dealing with a person who has been conditionally discharged who commits a further offence during the period of conditional discharge. Section 187 details the effect of the discharge of a person.

Chapter 2 (ss 188, 189) Consecutive Sentences
Sections 188, 189 provide for consecutive custodial sentences and consecutive sentences of service detention.

Chapter 3 (ss 190–195) Suspended Sentence of Service Detention
When passing a sentence of service detention, a court or officer may suspend the sentence: s 190. Sections 191–194 make provision as to the activation of a suspended sentence. Section 195 enables an offender to appeal against an order activating the sentence.

Chapter 4 (ss 196–207) Imprisonment for Term of Under 12 Months
Section 196 extends certain provisions of the Criminal Justice Act 2003 to service courts. The 2006 Act s 197 enables a service court to pass an immediate sentence of imprisonment for less than 12 months that does not include a custody plus order. Section 198 deals with the transfer to Scotland or Northern Ireland of a custody plus order. In the case of a custody plus order made by a service court, the civilian court in England and Wales with power to amend or revoke the order is the Crown Court: s 199. Section 200 provides that a service court has power to make a suspended sentence order either with or without community requirements. Section 201 ensures that provisions relating to community requirements do not apply to a suspended sentence order without such requirements. Section 202 disapplies certain provisions in relation to a suspended sentence order with community requirements. Where a service court makes a suspended sentence order with community requirements and provides for periodic review, the court required to review the order is the Crown Court: s 203. Section 204 deals with the transfer to Scotland or Northern Ireland of a suspended sentence order. If a suspended sentence order with community requirements has been made by a service court, the court with power to amend it is the Crown Court: s 205. Section 206, Sch 7 make modifications as to civilian provisions regarding further conviction or breach of community requirements. Section 207 provides definitions for the purposes of ss 196–206.

Chapter 5 (ss 208–216) Young Offenders: Custodial Sentences Available to Service Courts
Section 208 prohibits the imposition by the Court Martial or Service Civilian Court of a sentence of imprisonment on a person aged under 18 at the date of conviction. Where a person aged under 18 is convicted by the Court Martial of an offence under s 42, s 209 enables the court in certain circumstances to pass a sentence of detention for any period up to the maximum term of imprisonment that would have been available in the case of an adult. Section 210 allows a person sentenced under s 208 to be detained in a place determined by, or under the authority of, the Secretary of State. Section 211 enables the Court Martial or the Service Civilian Court to pass a sentence resembling the detention and training order available to civilian courts, and s 212 restricts the period for which such an order may be made. Section 213 applies to orders made under s 211 provisions relating to civilian detention and training orders. Section 214 concerns offences committed during the currency of a detention and training order. Section 215 provides definitions for the purposes of s 214. Section 216 enables an offender to appeal against an order for his detention under s 214 as if it were a new sentence for the original offence.

Chapter 6 (ss 217–228) Mandatory etc Custodial Sentences for Certain Offences
The court is required to pass a sentence of life imprisonment where such a sentence would be mandatory in the case of the corresponding civilian offence: s 217. Under s 218, where life imprisonment is mandatory in the case of the corresponding civilian offence but the offender was under 18 at the time of the offence, the court must sentence him to be detained during Her Majesty's pleasure. Section 219 concerns the sentencing of dangerous offenders aged 18 or over. Section 220 relates to certain violent or sexual offences committed by offenders aged 18 or over. Where s 219 would apply but for the offender being under 18, s 221 requires the court to pass a sentence of detention for life under s 209 if certain conditions are met. Where s 220 would apply but for the offender being under 18, or s 221 applies but the court does not think that a sentence of detention for public protection is necessary, s 222 requires the court to pass an extended sentence of detention. Section 223 requires the Court Martial, in determining what sentence is required by ss 219–222, to apply criteria similar to those that a civilian court would be required to apply. Section 224 deals with the place of detention under certain sentences. Unless there are particular circumstances which would make it unjust, s 225 requires the Court Martial to impose a sentence of at least seven years' imprisonment on an adult convicted of a third class A drug trafficking offence. Unless there are particular circumstances which would make it unjust, s 226 requires the Court Martial to impose a sentence of at least three years' imprisonment on an adult convicted of a third domestic burglary. Section 227 makes similar provision with regard to firearms offences. Section 228 allows an offender extra time to appeal against his sentence if the court took account of a previous conviction which has since been set aside on appeal.

Chapter 7 (ss 229–236) Court Orders Other Than Sentences
Sections 229, 230 concern service restraining orders, and ss 231, 232 deal with appeals against the making of a service restraining order and the variation or revocation of such an order. Section 233 enables the court to ask a parent or guardian to enter into a recognisance to take proper care of the offender and exercise proper control over him. Sections 234–236 make further provision regarding recognisances and fines under s 233 including appeals, variation, revocation and forfeiture of recognisances.

Part 9 (ss 237–271) Sentencing: Principles and Procedures

Chapter 1 (ss 237–254) Principles and Procedures applying to Service Courts and Summary Hearings
A service court or officer, when dealing with an offender for a service offence, must have regard to the purposes of sentencing (s 237) and, when determining the seriousness of an offence, must take into account certain matters (s 238). Section 239 provides for a reduction in sentence for an offender who has pleaded guilty. That an offence is racially or religiously motivated must be treated as an aggravating factor: s 240. A court or officer must treat as an aggravating factor the fact that the offender demonstrated hostility based on the victim's sexual orientation or disability: s 241. Section 242 prohibits a court from passing a sentence of service detention unless the offence is serious enough to warrant such a sentence. Where a sentence of service detention is passed by a court, it must be for the shortest term commensurate with the seriousness of the offence: s 243. Sections 244, 245 place a limit on the length of a combined term of sentences of service detention. Sections 246, 247 require credit to be given for time spent in service custody. Section 248 prohibits a court from passing a sentence of forfeiture of seniority, reduction in rank or disrating unless the offence and any associated offences are serious enough to warrant such a sentence. Section 249 requires a court or officer, when fixing a fine in respect of a service offence, to inquire into the offender's financial circumstances. A court or officer must have regard to the offender's financial circumstances when deciding whether to make a service compensation order: s 250. Section 251 allows a court or officer imposing a fine or a service compensation order to make a further order allowing time to pay, or directing payment by instalments. Section 252 requires a court or officer passing sentence to explain the reasons for the sentence, and s 253 specifies particular matters which a court or officer must mention or explain in complying with the s 252 duty. Section 254 makes savings for powers to mitigate sentence.

Chapter 2 (ss 255–270) Principles and Procedures applying to Service Courts Only
Both the Court Martial and the Service Civilian Court must pass a separate sentence for each offence: s 255. Sections 256, 257 deal with the requirement for pre-sentence reports. Section 258 requires a service court to consider a medical report before passing a custodial sentence on an offender who is mentally disordered. A service court must have regard to relevant guidelines issued by the Sentencing Guidelines Council: s 259. There are restrictions on passing a custodial sentence unless a service court thinks the offence was so serious that no less severe sentence can be justified: s 260. Where a service court passes a custodial sentence, s 261 requires the sentence to be for the shortest term commensurate with the seriousness of the offence. A service court, when passing a sentence of imprisonment for 12 months or more, may recommend particular conditions that in its view should be included in the offender's licence when he is released: s 262. Section 263 makes restrictions on imposing a custodial sentence or service detention on an unrepresented offender. Section 264 makes it clear that, where any provision of the Act requires a court to pass a particular custodial sentence in respect of an offence, the court is not thereby prevented from including in its sentence any other authorised punishment. Section 265 makes provision about restrictions on passing a sentence of dismissal. Section 266 enables a service court to order an offender to give the court a statement of his financial circumstances before it passes sentence. Section 267 enables a service court to reduce or remit a fine if it did not have full information about the offender's financial circumstances when it imposed the fine. Where an offender was aged under 18 when convicted, he is a civilian subject to service discipline, and he has a parent or guardian who is subject to service law or who is a civilian subject to service discipline, s 268 enables the court to order that parent or guardian to pay any fine or compensation awarded against the offender. Section 269 varies provisions of the Act relating to the fixing of fines and compensation orders in light of s 268. Section 270 deals with general restrictions on community punishments.

Chapter 3 (s 271) Supplementary
Section 271 provides for the modification of certain provisions where a civilian court is dealing with an offender for a service offence.

Part 10 (ss 272–276) Court Martial Decisions: Appeals and Review

Chapter 1 (s 272) Appeals from Court Martial
Section 272, Sch 8 rename the Courts-Martial Appeal Court as the Court Martial Appeal Court.

Chapter 2 (ss 273–275) Review of Court Martial Sentence
Section 273 gives the Attorney General power to refer a case to the Court Martial Appeal Court if he considers that the sentence passed by the Court Martial in respect of the offence is unduly lenient. Section 274 allows the Attorney General or the offender to refer to the Supreme Court a point of law involved in any sentence passed in the proceedings, and s 275 enables the Secretary of State to make supplementary provision about review of sentence.

Chapter 3 (s 276) Compensation for Miscarriage of Justice
Provision is made by s 276, Sch 9 for the payment of compensation where a person has suffered a miscarriage of justice by the Court Martial.

Part 11 (ss 277–288) The Service Civilian Court
Sections 277, 278, Sch 10 establish a court to be known as the Service Civilian Court and provide for its constitution and proceedings. Before the charge is put and a plea entered, the Service Civilian Court must decide whether it or the Court Martial should try the charge: s 279. Where the Service Civilian Court decides that it should try a charge, the defendant must be given the opportunity before arraignment to elect to be tried by the Court Martial: s 280. The Service Civilian Court has the power to convict a person of an offence other than that with which he has been charged: s 281. Punishments available to the Service Civilian Court are provided by s 282. Section 283 prevents the Service Civilian Court from passing a sentence of imprisonment for more than 12 months in respect of a single offence. The Service Civilian Court may not impose a fine of more than the prescribed sum for any one offence: s 284. Section 285 provides that a person convicted by the Service Civilian Court may appeal to the Court Martial. An appeal against conviction is to be by way of rehearing of the charge so that all of the evidence is reheard by the Court Martial: s 286. By virtue of s 287, any finding made or sentence passed by the Court Martial on an appeal replaces the finding or sentence of the Service Civilian Court. The Secretary of State has power to make rules in relation to the Service Civilian Court: s 288.

Part 12 (ss 289–304) Service and Effect of Certain Sentences
A sentence passed by the Court Martial or the Service Civilian Court takes effect from the beginning of the day on which it is passed, unless some other provision enables the court to direct otherwise: s 289. Section 290 postpones the point at which an award of service detention made by a commanding officer takes effect. Unless the offender elects to start the new sentence as soon as the old one expires, the new one does not take effect until the old one has expired and the appeal period has expired or any appeal has been disposed of: s 291. Section 292 deals with the commencement of a suspended sentence which is activated by a commanding officer. Where a warrant officer or non-commissioned officer is given a custodial sentence for a service offence or is sentenced to

service detention, his rank or rate is automatically reduced: s 293. A warrant officer or non-commissioned officer serving a custodial sentence or a sentence of service detention is to be treated as holding the lowest rank or rate for the service to which he belongs: s 294. If an offender is sentenced to dismissal or dismissal with disgrace, his commission is forfeit and he automatically ceases to be a member of the forces: s 295. A person sentenced to service detention may be detained in service custody but may not be detained in prison: s 296. Where a person is sentenced to a custodial sentence for a service offence, he must serve his sentence in a civilian institution but, by virtue of s 297, he may be detained in service custody until he is committed to the appropriate civilian institution. If a person is outside England and Wales when a custodial sentence is passed on him, or when an order under s 214 is made in respect of him, he must be removed to England and Wales as soon as practicable: s 298. Section 299 confers a duty on the governor of a civilian prison in England or Wales to receive and confine, for the duration of his sentence, any person who has been sent to the prison in accordance with service custody rules made under s 300. Section 300 empowers the Secretary of State to make rules about service custody and the service of sentences imposed by service courts. The duration of a sentence may be adjusted where the sentenced person spends any period of the sentence unlawfully at large or on temporary release: s 301. Where a person is already serving a relevant sentence and, during that sentence, he is sentenced in separate proceedings to a custodial sentence, either in respect of a service offence or by a civilian criminal court, the unserved balance of the relevant sentence is remitted: s 302. Section 303 empowers a service policeman to arrest a person sentenced to service detention who is unlawfully at large, and s 304 makes supplementary provision as to sentences passed by civilian courts.

Part 13 (ss 305–327) Discipline: Miscellaneous and Supplementary

Chapter 1 (ss 305–308) Testing for Alcohol and Drugs
Section 305 permits testing for drugs, and s 306 permits testing for alcohol and drugs after a serious incident. Section 307 provides definitions for the purposes of s 306, and s 308 authorises the Defence Council to make regulations governing the obtaining and analysis of samples.

Chapter 2 (ss 305–308) Contempt of Court
Section 309 confers power on a qualifying service court to deal with a person for contempt of court. Where that power is not immediately exercised, the court has power to take the person into service custody and to order his detention there until the court rises: s 310. Section 311 applies where a person does an act in relation to proceedings before a qualifying service court that would constitute contempt of court if the court were a civilian court with power to commit for contempt. Section 312 provides that the rules relating to findings by the Court Martial and the Service Appeal Court do not apply to ss 309–311.

Chapter 3 (ss 313–320) Arrest and Detention by Civil Authorities
Section 313 deals with arrest by civilian police under the warrant of a judge advocate. Section 314 permits the civilian police in the United Kingdom or a British overseas territory to arrest without a warrant a suspected absentee. A person who surrenders himself to a police officer of a United Kingdom or British overseas territory police force as being a deserter or absent without leave must be taken to a police station: s 315. Section 316 details the duties of a summary court in the United Kingdom, the Isle of Man or a British overseas territory when a person admits to being illegally absent or where the court is in possession of evidence that he is illegally absent. When a suspect is released from custody subject to specified conditions and he fails to meet those conditions, a warrant may be issued for his arrest: s 317. Section 318 provides that a person who has been sentenced to service detention and is unlawfully at large may be arrested without a warrant by a member of a United Kingdom police force or British overseas territory police force and may be taken to the place where he is required to be detained. Section 319 allows the Secretary of State to make provision requiring a certificate in respect of a person who, having been apprehended by the civil authorities, is either delivered into service custody or released by them. Where a power of arrest is conferred on any person by virtue of ss 313–320, he may use reasonable force, if necessary, in the exercise of the power: s 320.

Chapter 4 (s 321) Contempt of Court
Section 321, Sch 11 confer powers on the Criminal Cases Review Commission in relation to convictions by service courts.

Chapter 5 (s 322–327) Supplementary
Sections 322–324 make supplementary provision in relation to financial penalty enforcement orders and the power to make provision in consequence of criminal justice enactments. Further provision is made with regard to the evidential burden as respects excuses (s 325), the exclusion of enactments requiring the consent of the Attorney General or the Director of Public Prosecutions in relation to proceedings for a sevice offence (326) and local probation boards (s 327).

Second Group of Parts (Pts 14–17) Miscellaneous Matters

Part 14 (ss 328–340) Enlistment, Terms of Service etc
Section 328 confers power on the Defence Council to make regulations about the process of enlistment into the regular forces. The Defence Council may make regulations about the terms and

conditions of service of a person who is about to enlist or a person who has already enlisted (s 329), with respect to confessions by members of the regular forces to the offence of desertion including whether a trial may be dispensed with in such cases (s 330) and conferring a right on warrant officers to discharge following reduction in rank or rate (s 331). Section 332 places limitations on the power to reduce administratively a person's rank or rate. Section 333 makes harmonised provision with respect to pay, bounty and allowances for members of the regular or reserve forces. Section 334 allows a person who is, or who has previously been, subject to service law to make a complaint if he thinks himself wronged in any matter relating to his service. Section 335 permits the Defence Council to delegate to a panel the Council's responsibilities under s 334. Section 336 sets out the eligibility criteria for membership of a service complaint panel. Section 337 lays down certain conditions that must be satisfied for an officer to have his complaint referred to Her Majesty. Under s 338, the Service Complaints Commissioner may receive from any person allegations that a member of the armed forces has been the victim of certain types of wrong in relation to his service, or that a former member was the victim of such a wrong while in the armed forces. The Commissioner must provide the Secretary of State with an annual report on the efficiency, effectiveness and fairness of the redress system: s 339. Section 340 prevents aliens from being members of the regular forces or of Her Majesty's forces raised under the law of a British overseas territory.

Part 15 (ss 341, 342) Forfeitures and Deductions
Section 341 prohibits forfeiture of the pay of a person subject to service law unless authorised by statute, but s 342 enables the Secretary of state to make provision for the Defence Council or authorised officers to make orders authorising forfeiture of pay of a relevant person for a period of prescribed absence from duty or to authorise deductions from the pay of a relevant person in specified circumstances.

Part 16 (s 343) Inquiries
Section 343 enables the Secretary of State to make regulations for causing service inquiries to be held in prescribed circumstances in relation to matters connected with any of Her Majesty's forces.

Part 17 (ss 344–359) Miscellaneous
Offences which can be committed by any person, as opposed to offences which can only be committed by a person who is subject to service law, of aiding or abetting desertion or absence without leave (s 344), aiding or abetting malingering (s 345) and obstructing persons subject to service law in the course of duty (s 346) are set out, and s 347 makes supplementary provision in respect of ss 344–346. Section 348 concerns sentences that may be imposed in a British overseas territory following a conviction for an offence under ss 344–346. Section 349 preserves the exemption from tolls or charges for vehicles belonging to or in the service of Her Majesty's forces in respect of their passing over roads or bridges and through tunnels. Section 350 exempts items used by a serviceman in the course of his duty from being taken in execution of a court order. Section 351, Sch 12 make provision for admitting persons suffering from mental disorder to service hospitals outside the British Islands, and detaining them there temporarily for assessment or treatment. Where an otherwise qualified person may not be available, s 352 authorises certain officers outside the United Kingdom to take affidavits or declarations from a person subject to service law or service discipline. Section 353, Sch 13 amend the Armed Forces Act 1991 with regard to provision for the protection of the children of service families abroad. The 2006 Act s 354 extends certain powers of command that are dependent on rank or rate. The Secretary of State may make regulations allowing the service of process on relevant persons in connection with prescribed proceedings: s 355. Section 356 makes void assignments of, or charges on a serviceman's pay, pension, bounty, grant or allowances. Section 357 concerns the power of a British overseas territory to apply the provisions of the 2006 Act. Section 358, Sch 14 make amendments to certain legislation relating to the reserve forces. Pardons are conferred by s 359 on servicemen executed for certain disciplinary offences committed between 4 August 1914 and 11 November 1918: 2006 Act s 359.

Third Group of Parts (Pts 18, 19) Supplementary

Part 18 (ss 360–366) Commanding Officer and Other Persons with Functions under Act
Sections 360, 361 define 'commanding officer' and 'higher authority'. References to 'judge advocate' mean the Judge Advocate General: s 362. Section 363 creates the post of the court administration officer, s 364 provides for the appointment of the Director of Service Prosecutions who may, under s 365, appoint officers to be prosecuting officers, and s 366 provides for there to be a Service Complaints Commissioner.

Part 19 (ss 367–386) Supplementary

Chapter 1 (ss 367–371) Application of Act
Sections 367–371, Sch 15 make provision as to when persons are subject to service law (s 367), about who is a member of the regular forces (s 368), about members of British overseas territories' forces serving with United Kingdom forces (s 369), civilians subject to service discipline (s 370) and concerning naval chaplains (s 371).

Chapter 2 (ss 372, 373) Other Supplementary Provisions
Sections 372, 373 give the Secretary of State power to make provision with respect to evidence in proceedings before civilian courts and provide for the making of orders, regulations and rules.

Chapter 3 (ss 374–377) Interpretation
Section 374 provides definitions for the purposes of the whole Act, and ss 375, 376 deal with interpretation.

Chapter 4 (ss 378–386) Final Provisions
Section 378, Schs 16, 17 make minor and consequential amendments and repeals, s 379 confers power to make further amendments and repeals, and s 380 deals with transitional and transitory provision. Sections 381, 382 deal with the alignment of other Acts with the 2006 Act. Sections 383–386 deal with commencement, extent and short title.

Amendments, repeals and revocations
The list below, which is not exhaustive, mentions repeals and amendments which are or will be effective when the Act is fully in force.

Specific provisions of a number of Acts are amended or repealed. These include: Courts-Martial (Appeals) Act 1968 ss 4, 5, 8, 10–12, 14, 14A, 15–18, 20–29, 31–34, 36–39, 43, 47, 48A, 50, 52, 57, 58, 61, Schs 3, 4; Reserve Forces Act 1980 ss 10, 11, 18, 19, 19A, 21, 21A, 24–26, 30–32, 34, 39, 44, 139–146, 156, Sch 8; Reserve Forces Act 1996 ss 2, 4, 7, 13, 15, 24, 25, 27, 53, 55, 57, 66, 72, 95–99, 102, 104–108, 124, 126, 127, Schs 1–3, 7, 9, 10; Metropolitan Police Act 1860 s 2; Naval and Marine Pay and Pensions Act 1865 ss 3, 9; Naval Pensions Act 1884 s 2; Foreign Marriage Act 1892 s 22; Regimental Debts Act 1893 ss 23, 29. Uniforms Act 1894 s 4; Criminal Evidence Act 1898 s 6.

240 Armed forces and reserve forces compensation scheme—benefits

The Armed Forces and Reserve Forces (Compensation Scheme) (Amendment) Order 2006, SI 2006/1438 (in force in part on 30 June 2006 and in part on 26 July 2006), amends the Armed Forces and Reserve Forces Compensation Scheme 2005 ('the Scheme') which is set out in the 2005 Order, SI 2005/439, and provides for benefits to be payable to or in respect of a person by reason of his illness or injury, whether physical or mental, or his death, which is caused, wholly or partly, by his service in the armed forces or the reserve forces. In particular, the order amends the Scheme so as to provide that (1) for benefit to be payable for injuries made worse by service, service must be the predominant cause of the worsening of the injury; (2) the included activities for which benefit may be payable where injury or death occurs also apply where an injury is worsened; (3) no benefit will be payable by reason of the associated conditions of excluded illnesses; (4) where more than one injury is sustained in one incident and one or more of those injuries is an injury to a like part of the body or the same part of the body as that injured in a previous incident, the appropriate calculation will take place prior to the multiple injury calculation; (5) the recipient of a temporary award will have no right to seek a reconsideration or review of that award; (6) the Secretary of State will issue a decision, within one year of a temporary award being made, either making, or refusing to make, a permanent award; (7) where a member of the forces, who is a member of the Scheme, dies leaving more than one surviving spouse entitled to the bereavement grant, the amount to which each surviving spouse is entitled will be the difference between the salary of the member of the forces on the day on which he dies and the bereavement grant divided by the number of surviving spouses; (8) on the death of a member or a former member of the forces' sole surviving spouse, civil partner or surviving adult dependant, who had been in receipt of a survivor's guaranteed income payment, any child's payments will be recalculated as if the member or former member of the forces had died without leaving a spouse or civil partner or surviving adult dependant; (9) any guaranteed income payment and survivor's guaranteed income payment will cease to be paid to a former member of the forces on his admission to the Royal Hospital Chelsea; (10) the Secretary of State has discretion to extend, by one year, the time limits for making a claim; (11) the Secretary of State, when writing to inform a claimant of the decision on any claim, is obliged to inform him of any right to reconsideration or any right to appeal that the claimant may have; (12) there is no right to seek reconsideration of a decision to make either an interim award or a temporary award; and (13) the requirement that an application for a review to be on a form approved by the Secretary of State is removed. The order also incorporates additional table entries and amends the contents of certain pre-existing table entries in relation to the tariff tables which list the various forms of injury or disease for which compensation is available under the Scheme.

241 Armed forces and reserve forces compensation scheme—excluded benefits for tax purposes

The Armed Forces and Reserve Forces (Compensation Scheme) (Excluded Benefits for Tax Purposes) Regulations 2006, SI 2006/132 (in force on 6 April 2006), prescribe any benefit which is provided under the Armed Forces and Reserve Forces (Compensation Scheme) Order 2005, SI 2005/439 as an excluded benefit under the Income Tax and Pensions Act 2003 s 393B(3)(d).

242 Armed forces and reserve forces compensation scheme—pensions appeal tribunal—right of appeal

The Pensions Appeal Tribunals (Armed Forces and Reserve Forces Compensation Scheme) (Rights of Appeal) Amendment Regulations 2006, SI 2006/2892 (in force on 31 October 2006), amend the 2005 Regulations, SI 2005/1029, so as to (1) provide that a decision by the Secretary of State which determines whether a permanent award of compensation is made is a specified decision, which decision consequently attracts a right of appeal; and (2) provide that a decision by the Secretary of State which determines whether a temporary award should be made is not a specified decision, which decision does not therefore attract a right of appeal.

243 Armed Forces Pension Scheme

The Armed Forces Pension Scheme etc Amendment Order 2006, SI 2006/717 (in force on 6 April 2006), amends the Armed Forces Pension Scheme Order 2005, SI 2005/438, and amends the Armed Forces Pension Scheme 2005 by (1) altering a condition relating to the definition of eligible children so that where a child is suffering from mental or physical impairment, the child must be under 23 years of age and dependant on the deceased member at the date of his death; (2) removing the requirement that the child be engaged in gainful employment; (3) making minor amendments to ill-health pensions and lump sums that are payable early; (4) making minor amendments to the option for members in serious ill-health to exchange a whole pension for a lump sum; (5) clarifying that the Secretary of State may take advice before determining questions that arise under the Scheme; (6) removing the requirement that the Secretary of State must consult the Scheme medical adviser in certain cases; (7) removing the references to pension credit members in relation to the early payment of pensions with actuarial reduction; (8) restricting the amount of pension that a member may allocate to 37·5 per cent or such lower percentage of the pension as will not risk a breach of the pension death benefit rules; (9) altering the formula for calculating children's pensions in cases where a pensioner member leaves a surviving adult dependant and two or more children, so as to increase those pensions in cases where the member has allocated some pension to the surviving dependant; (10) extending the rule that applications for a transfer-in payment to be accepted by the Scheme to be made in relation to members joining the Scheme on or after 6 April 2006 and to existing members from 6 April 2007, within one year of the member becoming eligible, so that it also applies to transfers-in from personal pension arrangements or involving rights under an occupational pension scheme that derive from voluntary contributions; (11) providing for payment of the lifetime allowance charge on behalf of members and for transfer values or benefits to be reduced where such a payment has been made without the member having made a payment to the Scheme to cover the tax; (12) providing for the payment of special lump sum death benefits charge; (13) simplifying the entitlement to pensions and transfers-in rules by removing references to specific kinds of scheme; and (14) clarifying which members are excluded from the Scheme. The order also amends the Armed Forces Early Departure Payments Scheme Order 2005, SI 2005/437, so that the requirements for the payment of lump sums where ill-health occurs match those of the Scheme relating to payments in the event of ill-health.

See para 2209.

244 Armed Forces Redundancy Scheme

The Armed Forces Redundancy Scheme Order 2006, SI 2006/55 (in force on 6 April 2006), establishes the Armed Forces Redundancy Scheme 2006, and provides (1) that a member of the armed services is eligible for payment if the Secretary of State has notified him that he will be treated as having become redundant when he leaves service and he leaves service accordingly; (2) for entitlement to an immediate lump sum payment to arise on leaving the service; (3) for the way in which the amount of payment is calculated in relation to (a) the circumstances where the leaver's terms of service commit him to serve for a period at the end of which he would be entitled to payments under the Armed Forces Early Departure Payments Scheme Order 2005, SI 2005/437, or would have attained the age of 55; and (b) leavers with short service commitments; (4) for a limit on the amount that can be paid where the leaver is entitled to count 40 years' reckonable service in the 2005 Pension Scheme; (5) that, where a person is entitled to a payment and rejoins the armed forces or enters certain reserve forces service after a short break, the person must repay a relevant fraction of the payment made to him; and (6) that, where a person entitled to a payment rejoins the armed forces and becomes entitled to further payment when the new service ceases, the old service is ignored for the purpose of the calculation of the further payment.

245 Courts-martial—independent and impartial tribunal—application of military law to civilians

The applicant was a minor who lived with his family in Germany where his father was serving in the army. The applicant was charged with murder and, as a family member residing with a member of the armed forces, was subject to military law in accordance with the provisions of the Army Act 1955. The court-martial board was composed of a president and six ordinary members. Four of the members were senior officers, all of whom were subordinate in rank to the convening officer and the president and one of whom was within the convening officer's chain of command. Two members were civilian civil servants who came from the United Kingdom solely for the purpose of the trial, and were placed under the convening officer's command while in Germany, although they did not report to him. The applicant submitted that his trial by court-martial was inherently unfair and oppressive and thus an abuse of process. The Vice-Judge Advocate General, a senior judge appointed by the Lord Chancellor, rejected that submission and the applicant was convicted. His appeals to the Courts-Martial Appeal Court the House of Lords were dismissed. The applicant complained to the European Court of Human Rights that his right to an independent and impartial tribunal, guaranteed by the European Convention on Human Rights art 6(1), had been violated. *Held*, only in very exceptional circumstances would the determination of criminal charges against civilians in military courts be held to be compatible with art 6. The power of military criminal justice should not extend to civilians unless there were compelling reasons justifying such a situation, and then only on a clear and foreseeable legal basis. The existence of such reasons had to be substantiated in each specific case; it was not sufficient for the national legislation to allocate certain categories of offence to military courts in abstracto. Moreover, the mere presence of civilians during the proceedings would not of itself provide adequate guarantees of independence and impartiality. While the power to try the applicant had a clear and foreseeable legal basis, the structure and procedure of the applicant's court-martial were in themselves sufficient to raise in him legitimate fears as to its lack of independence and impartiality. The civilians, including the Vice-Judge Advocate General, participating in the applicant's court-martial process might have contributed somewhat to its independence, but they did not have sufficient influence over the proceedings as a whole, including over the military members of the court-martial, to satisfy the requirements of art 6.

Application 40426/98 *Martin v United Kingdom* [2006] All ER (D) 306 (Oct) (European Court of Human Rights). Application 124/1996/743/942 *Findlay v United Kingdom* (1997) 24 EHRR 221, ECtHR (1997 Abr para 1800); Application 48843/99 *Cooper v United Kingdom* [2003] All ER (D) 283 (Dec), ECtHR (2003 Abr para 169); and Application 57067/00 *Grieves v United Kingdom* (2004) 39 EHRR 51, ECtHR (2003 Abr para 169), considered. For previous proceedings see *R v Martin* [1998] AC 917, HL (1997 Abr para 2891).

246   Courts-martial—procedure—evidence—young, disabled, vulnerable or intimidated witnesses

The Youth Justice and Criminal Evidence Act 1999 (Application to Courts-Martial) Order 2006, SI 2006/2886 (in force on 6 December 2006), applies with modifications, the Youth Justice and Criminal Evidence Act 1999, which contains a range of measures designed to help young, disabled, vulnerable or intimidated witnesses give evidence in criminal proceedings, to courts-martial. The order also contains modifications to certain provisions dealing with reporting restrictions.

The Youth Justice and Criminal Evidence Act 1999 (Application to the Courts-Martial Appeal Court) Order 2006, SI 2006/2887 (in force on 6 December 2006), applies with modifications, the Youth Justice and Criminal Evidence Act 1999, which contains a range of measures designed to help young, disabled, vulnerable or intimidated witnesses give evidence in criminal proceedings, to proceedings before the Courts-Martial Appeal Court.

The Courts-Martial (Royal Navy, Army and Royal Air Force) (Evidence) Rules 2006, SI 2006/2889 (in force on 6 December 2006), make provision for a range of measures designed to help young, disabled, vulnerable or intimidated witnesses give evidence in court-martial proceedings. In particular, the rules (1) provide for an application for a special measures direction to be made in the prescribed form; (2) provide rules for extending the time for making an application and for late applications; (3) provide for an application to be made to vary or discharge a special measures direction which has already been made and for renewal applications where a material change of circumstances has occurred since an application was refused; (4) impose additional requirements where the application relates either to the giving of evidence by means of live television link or the admission of a video recording of an interview with a witness as evidence in chief of the witness; (5) provide for the mutual disclosure between parties of expert evidence to be adduced in connection with the application for the special measures direction and set out the declaration required to be made by an intermediary; (6) set out the procedure for the judge advocate to notify the accused that he is prevented from cross-examining the witness and the procedure required for the accused to appoint a legal representative to conduct the cross-examination; (7) deal with the appointment of a legal representative by the judge advocate and with the appointment of that legal representative by the accused; (8) make provision for the prosecutor to make an application to the judge advocate to give a direction that the accused be prevented from cross-examining a witness; (9) make provision for an application to adduce evidence or ask questions about a complainant's sexual history; (10) contain provisions relating to applications for reporting directions in respect of adult witnesses; (11) provide for applications for a reporting direction to be made using the prescribed form; (12) make provision for any party to the proceedings to oppose an application and for urgent applications to be made in exceptional circumstances; (13) contain provision for applications to be made for an excepting direction to dispense with the restrictions imposed by a reporting direction; (14) contain provisions relating to applications for the revocation of reporting directions or the variation or revocation of an excepting direction and provision for applications for an extension of time; (15) set out the procedure for determining applications for reporting directions; and (16) contain consequential revocations and amendments to existing courts-martial rules.

247 Courts-martial—procedure—inferences from accused's silence—application to armed forces

The Criminal Justice and Public Order Act 1994 (Application to the Armed Forces) Order 2006, SI 2006/2326 (in force on 26 September 2006), applies to the armed forces, with appropriate modifications, the provisions of the Criminal Justice and Public Order Act which prohibit the drawing of inferences from an accused's silence if he has not been allowed an opportunity to consult a solicitor in circumstances where ss 34, 36 and 37 would otherwise apply.

248 Courts-Martial Appeal Court—prosecution appeals

The Courts-Martial (Prosecution Appeals) Order 2006, SI 2006/1786 (in force on 5 July 2006), (1) establishes the right of appeal for the prosecution in relation to a trial by a court-martial and provides that such an appeal, subject to the granting of leave, lies to the Courts-Martial Appeal Court ('CMAC'); (2) establishes a right of appeal for the prosecution against a ruling of a judge advocate at a court-martial which either is terminating of itself or which would otherwise have the effect of terminating proceedings in that the prosecution would offer no, or no further, evidence; (3) makes provision in relation to appeals following either an expedited or non-expedited route; (4) allows for proceedings to continue in respect of any charge which is not subject of an appeal; (5) establishes powers for the CMAC to confirm, reverse or vary any ruling to which the appeal relates; (6) provides for a legal test that must be met before the CMAC may reverse a ruling from a judge advocate at a court-martial; (7) provides for a right to appeal to lie to the House of Lords against any decision of the CMAC in relation to an appeal under the order and provides for the granting of bail to an accused who has so appealed to the House of Lords; and (8) imposes restrictions on reporting of appeals provides the contravention of any such restriction is an offence.

The Courts-Martial (Prosecution Appeals) (Supplementary Provisions) Order 2006, SI 2006/1788 (in force on 1 August 2006), makes procedural provision in relation to appeals by the prosecution in the service courts which corresponds to equivalent provision in the civilian courts.

249 Criminal investigations—entry, search and seizure

The Armed Forces (Entry, Search and Seizure) Order 2006, SI 2006/3243 (in force on 1 January 2007), makes provision in relation to powers of seizure of service police. In particular, the order (1) permits a service policeman to remove material from premises being searched where there are reasonable grounds for believing that the material is, or contains, material which that policeman is entitled to seize, and permits the seizure by a service policeman of material which the policeman is entitled to seize but which is attached to other material from which it cannot be separated in a reasonably practicable manner; (2) makes similar provision in relation to material found by a service policeman while undertaking a lawful search of an individual; (3) requires notices to be given to specified persons, in the manners prescribed, where material is seized in exercise of the above powers; (4) requires any material so seized to be examined, and any property whose retention is not authorised to be returned, as soon as is reasonably practicable; (5) stipulates, with exceptions, that any seized property which is subject to legal privilege or which consists of or includes excluded or special procedure material must be returned as soon as is reasonably practicable; (6) allows the retention of seized property where there are reasonable grounds for believing that it is the proceeds of, or evidence of, an offence and that it is necessary to retain it so as to prevent its being concealed, lost, damaged, altered or destroyed; (7) provides that any property to be returned is to be returned to the person from whom it was seized, unless the person obliged to return it is satisfied that someone else has a better right to it; (8) permits a person with an interest in property seized in the purported exercise of certain powers to apply to a judicial officer for its return; (9) imposes, with exceptions, a duty to secure seized material from being examined, copied or used where an application to a judicial officer for the return of the material has been made on the grounds that the material is, or contains, property subject to legal privilege, special procedure material or excluded material; (10) imposes a similar prohibition in respect of seized property which would have to be returned if it were not inextricably linked to property which has been lawfully retained; and (11) makes provision in relation to copies.

The Armed Forces (Entry, Search and Seizure) (Amendment) Order 2006, SI 2006/3244 (in force on 1 January 2007), amends the 2003 Order, SI 2003/2273, so as to (1) enable service policemen to apply for warrants authorising entry and search of named premises on more than one occasion, on grounds which must be stated in any such warrant; (2) require such warrants to specify whether the maximum number of entries allowed is unlimited or limited to a specified maximum; (3) permit the making of as many copies as may be required of multiple entry warrants; (4) give a person accompanying a service policeman on a search of premises the same powers of search and seizure as that service policeman; (5) impose a three-month time limit on the execution of a warrant for entry and search; and (6) require approval from a senior policeman not below a specified rank to be obtained in order to execute any multiple entry warrant.

250 Criminal investigations—questioning and treatment by police—legislation—application to armed forces

The Police and Criminal Evidence Act 1984 (Application to the Armed Forces) Order 2006, SI 2006/2015 (in force on 31 December 2006), applies to investigations conducted by service policemen, subject to modifications, the Police and Criminal Evidence Act 1984 Pt V (ss 53–65).

251 Discipline—air force—flying offence—low flying

The Air Force Act 1955 s 51 provides that any person subject to air force law who, being the pilot of one of Her Majesty's aircraft, flies it at a height less than such height as may be provided by any regulations issued under the authority of the Defence Council, except while taking off or alighting, or in such other circumstances as may be so provided, is liable, on conviction by court-martial, to imprisonment for a term not exceeding two years or any less punishment provided by the 1955 Act.

The defendant was charged with unlawful low flying, contrary to the 1955 Act s 51. At his trial, he submitted that the offence was one of full mens rea and that the prosecution had to prove that he had either known that he was flying under the minimum height or that he had been reckless. He argued that he was not guilty because the instrument which informed him at what height he was flying was unreliable. The prosecution contended that the offence was one of strict liability. The judge ruled that the offence was indeed one of strict liability, referring to the rationale behind the creation of such offences, namely that they generally covered conduct that was of itself potentially dangerous to the public. Following the ruling, the defendant pleaded guilty but appealed against conviction, arguing that the judge had erred in making his ruling. *Held*, the offence of unlawful low flying contrary to s 51 was an offence of strict liability. Low flying created a serious hazard and risk of serious danger to person and property and was one where the strictest possible standards had to be imposed to ensure the avoidance of such danger occurring. When Parliament had legislated in the field of civil aviation some years after the commencement of the 1955 Act, it had created an offence of low flying that was an offence of strict liability. Other sections of the 1955 Act that concerned flying included elements of mens rea. Section 51 was not unique in imposing the sanction of imprisonment for the commission of an offence of strict liability. The authorities provided an example of a situation where even more serious penalties than those available under s 51 did not prevent an offence of strict liability being upheld. Those entrusted with the responsibility of handling lethal equipment of the nature that was entrusted to service personnel could not complain if they were made subject to more severe penalties than their civilian counterparts. That was a responsibility which went with the privilege of serving in the armed forces. The training that such personnel received and general common sense dictated that pilots flying at extremely low levels should have a good idea of the level at which they were flying, regardless of whether their instruments were faulty, particularly if they were actually flying below the top of some potential hazard on the ground. Accordingly, the appeal would be dismissed.

R v Jackson [2006] EWCA Crim 2380, [2006] All ER (D) 193 (Oct) (Courts-Martial Appeal Court: Hooper LJ, Keith and Lloyd Jones JJ).

252 Discipline—armed forces—legislation—continuation

The Army, Air Force and Naval Discipline Acts (Continuation) Order 2006, SI 2006/1910 (in force on 19 July 2006), provides for the Service Discipline Acts to continue in force until 31 December 2006 instead of expiring on 31 August 2006.

253 Discipline—service courts—evidence

The Criminal Justice Act 1988 (Application to Service Courts) (Evidence) Order 2006, SI 2006/2890 (in force on 6 December 2006), revokes the 1996 Order, SI 1996/2592, but makes savings, with modifications, for service courts for the Criminal Justice Act 1988 s 32(1)(a), (3), which allows a witness who is not in the country where the court is sitting to give evidence by live television link.

254 Pensions—disablement and death

The Naval, Military and Air Forces etc (Disablement and Death) Service Pensions Order 2006, SI 2006/606 (in force on 10 April 2006), replaces the 1983 Order, SI 1983/883 (as amended), which made provision for pensions and other awards in respect of disablement or death due to service in the naval, military or air forces. The changes of substance effected by the 2006 Order are (1) a person in receipt of a retirement pension (other than a retirement pension which consists of certain additions) may be eligible for unemployability allowances; (2) deductions from constant attendance allowance and severe disablement occupational allowance must only be made while a person to whom those allowances are paid is in hospital or an institution; (3) the Secretary of State is empowered to suspend a pension, gratuity or supplement where a person, having been required to provide evidence or information or to attend for a medical examination, fails to do so after being given reasonable notice; (4) the Secretary of State must cancel an award which has been so suspended where the person fails either to provide the evidence or information required or to attend for a medical examination within the period of 12 months starting with the date on which the notice is given or sent to him; and (5) the rates of retired pay, pensions, gratuities and allowances payable in respect of disablement due to service, and the rates of pension and allowances payable to spouses and civil partners of members of the armed forces and to persons who lived as spouses or civil partners of members of the armed forces, are up-rated.

The Naval, Military and Air Forces Etc (Disablement and Death) Service Pensions (Amendment) (No 2) Order 2006, SI 2006/1455 (in force on 21 June 2006), amends the principal regulations, SI 2006/606, supra by correcting certain errors and omissions.

255 Protection of military remains—vessels and controlled sites—designation

The Protection of Military Remains Act 1986 (Designation of Vessels and Controlled Sites) Order 2006, SI 2006/2616 (in force on 1 November 2006), (1) designates various vessels as vessels to which the Protection of Military Remains Act 1986 applies, with the effect that the places containing the remains of those vessels are protected places within the meaning of the 1986 Act; and (2) provides that the places containing the remains of HMS A7, HMS Affray, HMS Bulwark, HMS Dasher, HMS Exmouth, HMS Formidable, HMS H5, HMS Hampshire, HMS Natal, HMS Royal Oak, HMS Vanguard and UB-81 are controlled sites within the meaning of the 1986 Act. SI 2002/1761 (as amended) is revoked.

256 Protection of military remains—war—vessel on military service—vessel lost on convoy

The Protection of Military Remains Act 1986 s 9(2)(a) provides that a vessel is to be regarded as having been in military service at a particular time if at that time it was in service with, or being used for the purposes of, any of the armed forces of the United Kingdom.

The applicants' father had died on a merchant ship which had been owned by the Ministry of War Transport when it was sunk by enemy action while part of a convoy. The applicants became concerned that the wreck was being dived on and successfully applied for judicial review against the decision of the Secretary of State that the wreck of the ship that the applicants' father had died on was not capable of designation under the 1986 Act. The Secretary of State appealed. *Held*, the essential issue was whether 'in service with' any of the armed forces meant vessels which were at the disposition of those forces, in that they could be directed to perform such services as the armed forces required, or whether the words applied to all vessels that at the time of their loss were serving with the armed forces, in the sense of engaging in an activity or performing a function jointly with those forces. The wider construction adopted by the judge was to be preferred, as the ship was at least capable of being regarded as being in the service of the armed forces when she was sunk, even though the question was one that was ultimately for the Secretary of State to decide. The ship was, to a significant extent, under the control of the Admiralty or the Royal Navy. The Secretary of State had too narrowly applied the 1986 Act when refusing the applicants' application. The judge had been correct in that more had to be shown than that the ship furthered the war effort generally, and that the Secretary of State did not take account of the role played by the Admiralty in connection with the convoy and did not take sufficient account of the fact that the ship was armed and manned by military gunners, not just for her own safety but for that of the convoy, for which the Royal Navy was responsible. Accordingly, the appeal would be dismissed.

R (on the application of Fogg) v Secretary of State for Defence [2006] EWCA Civ 1270, [2006] 3 WLR 931 (Court of Appeal: Sir Anthony Clarke MR, Rix and Longmore LJJ). Decision of Newman J [2005] EWHC 2888 (Admin), [2006] 3 WLR 53 affirmed.

257 Royal Marines—terms of service

The Royal Marines Terms of Service Regulations 2006, SI 2006/2917 (in force on 1 December 2006), replace the 1988 Regulations, SI 1988/1395 (as amended), and make provision as to the terms of enlistment for other ranks in the Royal Marines. The 2006 Regulations (1) provide for terms to be either (a) of 18 years' duration from the date of attestation or until the date of the recruit's 40th birthday, if that date is later; or (b) between six months and 17 years from the date of attestation; (2) enable persons in the Royal Marines to transfer to the reserve, subject to restrictions by agreement; (3) confer on recruits the right to claim discharge from the Royal Marines within six months of the date of attestation; and (4) enable persons who have completed periods of service in the Royal Marines to remain in the Royal Marines for a further period or periods of at least 12 months' duration but not exceeding 15 years in total.

258   Royal Navy—terms of service

The Royal Navy Terms of Service (Ratings) Regulations 2006, SI 2006/2918 (in force on 1 December 2006), replace the 1982 Regulations, SI 1982/834 (as amended), and make provision as to terms of service for ratings in the Royal Navy. The 2006 Regulations (1) provide for terms to be either (a) of 18 years' duration from the date of entry to the Royal Navy or until the date of the recruit's 40th birthday, if that date is later; or (b) between 6 months and 17 years from the date of attestation; (2) enable persons in the Royal Navy to transfer to the reserve, subject to restrictions by agreement; (3) confer the right on recruits to claim discharge from the Royal Navy in the first six months from the date of entry to the service; and (4) enable persons who have completed periods of service in the Royal Navy to remain in the service for a further period or periods of at least 12 months' duration but not exceeding 15 years in total.

259   Standing civilian courts—procedure—evidence—young, disabled, vulnerable or intimidated witnesses

The Youth Justice and Criminal Evidence Act 1999 (Application to Standing Civilian Courts) Order 2006, SI 2006/2888 (in force on 6 December 2006), applies to standing civilian courts, with modifications, the Youth Justice and Criminal Evidence Act 1999, which contains a range of measures designed to help young, disabled, vulnerable or intimidated witnesses give evidence in criminal proceedings. The order also contains modifications to certain provisions dealing with reporting restrictions.

The Standing Civilian Courts (Evidence) Rules 2006, SI 2006/2891 (in force on 6 December 2006), make provision for a range of measures designed to help young, disabled, vulnerable or intimidated witnesses give evidence in proceedings in a standing civilian court. In particular, the rules (1) provide for an application for a special measures direction to be made in the prescribed form; (2) provide rules for extending the time for making an application for a special measures direction; (3) provide for late applications; (4) provide for an application to be made to vary or discharge a special measures direction which has already been made; (5) provide for renewal applications where a material change of circumstances has occurred since an application was refused; (6) provide that additional requirements are imposed where the application relates either to the giving of evidence by means of live television link or the admission of a video recording of an interview with a witness as evidence in chief of the witness; (7) provide for the mutual disclosure between parties of expert evidence to be adduced in connection with the application for the special measures direction and set out the declaration required to be made by an intermediary; (8) provide for applications for a reporting direction to be made using the specified form or orally; (9) make provision for any party to the proceedings to oppose an application and make provision for urgent applications to be made in exceptional circumstances; (10) contain provisions for applications to be made using the specified form for an excepting direction to dispense with the restrictions imposed by a reporting direction; (11) contain provisions relating to applications for the revocation of reporting directions or the variation or revocation of an excepting direction and contain provisions for applications for an extension of time; (12) set out the procedure for determining applications for reporting directions; and (13) contain a consequential revocation to the Standing Civilian Courts Order 1997, SI 1997/172.

AVIATION

Halsbury's Laws of England (4th edn) vol 2(3) (Reissue) paras 301–1113

Articles

For articles relating to this title please refer to the Table of Articles at the beginning of the Abridgment.

260   Air navigation—data

The Air Navigation (Amendment) Order 2006, SI 2006/2316 (in force on 30 September 2006), amends the 2005 Order, SI 2005/1970, so as to enable the Secretary of State to direct an operator of an aircraft to make data relating to passengers and crew available electronically to authorities in a country outside the European Economic Area to which the aircraft is being flown.

261   Air navigation—general

The Air Navigation (General) Regulations 2006, SI 2006/601 (in force on 30 March 2006), replace the 2005 Regulations, SI 2005/1980, principally to rectify defective drafting in the 2005 Regulations. The regulations make provision as to (1) load sheets; (2) weighing requirements; (3) aircraft performance; (4) noise and vibration caused by aircraft on aerodromes; (5) repairs and maintenance which pilots must be capable of carrying out; (6) aerodrome facilities; (7) mandatory reporting of prescribed occurrences and birdstrikes; (8) navigation performance equipment; and (9) airborne collision avoidance systems.

262 Air navigation—overseas territories—general

The Air Navigation (Overseas Territories) (Amendment) Order 2006, SI 2006/1911 (in force on 21 August 2006), further amends the 2001 Order, SI 2001/2128, and (1) introduces a process for certification of aerodromes that provide facilities for certain types of aircraft operations as to their compliance with the requirements of the Chicago Convention; and (2) provides for a new definition of 'government aerodrome' so as to exclude from the requirement for certification aerodromes under the control of Her Majesty's armed forces or any visiting force.

263 Air passenger duty—qualifying territories

The Air Passenger Duty (Rate) (Qualifying Territories) Order 2006, SI 2006/2693 (in force on 1 November 2006), extends the destinations to which the lower rates of air passenger duty in the Finance Act 1994 s 30(3A) apply by adding Croatia to the list of qualifying territories.

264 Airports—slot allocation

The Airports Slot Allocation Regulations 2006, SI 2006/2665 (in force on 1 January 2007) replace the 1993 Regulations, SI 1993/1067 (as amended). In particular, the regulations (1) provide (a) that an airport formerly designated as (i) a co-ordinated airport is to be treated as if it had been designated as a schedules facilitated airport; and (ii) a fully co-ordinated airport is to be treated as if it had been designated as a co-ordinated airport; and (b) that a capacity analysis is to be conducted at other airports in specified circumstances; (2) require the appointment of schedules facilitators or co-ordinators, and set out the conditions to be complied with in respect of appointments, providing that (a) any person previously appointed as a co-ordinator for an airport formerly designated as co-ordinated is to be treated as if he had been appointed as a schedules facilitator for that airport; and (b) any person previously appointed as a co-ordinator for an airport formerly designated as fully co-ordinated is to be treated as if he had been appointed as a co-ordinator for that airport; (3) require the operators of co-ordinated airports to (a) establish co-ordination committees; and (b) determine slot allocation parameters biannually; (4) permit a co-ordinator or a schedules facilitator to impose financial penalties on any air carrier or managing body of an airport with no designation status where that person fails to provide information requested without reasonable excuse, or knowingly or recklessly provides false information; (5) require (a) the operators of co-ordinated airports and co-ordinators to notify the Secretary of State of local guidelines and rules which are required to be notified to the European Commission; (b) co-ordinators to comply with slot reservations made for the purpose of public service obligations; (c) the operators of co-ordinated airports to convene a meeting of the local co-ordination committee in certain circumstances; and (d) that co-ordinators and air carriers observe any measures that the Secretary of State is required to take by the European Commission; (6) protect co-ordinators and schedules facilitators from civil claims, except in cases of gross negligence or wilful default; (7) prohibit the misuse of slots at co-ordinated airports; (8) permit a co-ordinator to impose non-criminal sanctions in the form of financial penalties; (9) establish an enforcement procedure with which a co-ordinator or schedules facilitator must comply; (10) oblige a co-ordinator or schedules facilitator to adopt an enforcement code and make provision as to its content, amendment, revocation and modification; and (11) make provision for the appointment of an independent reviewer to whom enforcement decisions of a co-ordinator or schedules facilitator may be appealed; and for offences.

265 Carriage by air—dangerous goods

The Air Navigation (Dangerous Goods) (Amendment) Regulations 2006, SI 2006/1092 (in force on 21 April 2006), further amend the 2002 Regulations, SI 2002/2786, so as to include a further addendum and corrigendum to the 2005–2006 edition of the Technical Instructions for the Safe Transport of Dangerous Goods by Air, approved and published by decision of the Council of the International Civil Aviation Organisation on 18 August 2005.

266 Carriage by air—licensing—air travel organiser—Civil Aviation Authority guidance—validity

Under the Civil Aviation (Air Travel Organisers' Licensing) Regulations 1995, SI 1995/1054, reg 3(1A), a person must not make available flight accommodation which constitutes a component of a package either in the capacity of an agent for a licence holder except where all the components of the package are made available under a single contract between the licence holder and the customer or in the capacity of a ticket provider.

A guidance note issued by the respondent gave advice on the need to provide consumer protection on the sale of air package arrangements. The advice was intended to help travel organisers and travel agents understand the definition of 'air package' set out in the 1995 Regulations and in the Civil Aviation (Air Travel Organisers' Licensing) (Amendment) Regulations 2003, SI 2003/1741. The applicant, a trade association of travel organisers and travel agents, sought judicial review of the decision to issue the guidance note. The application succeeded and the respondent appealed. *Held*, the cumulative effect of certain potentially misleading statements was that the guidance note was likely to give the uninformed reader a misleading impression as to the circumstances in which the 1995 Regulations reg 3(1A) required that the agent be a licence holder. It was not satisfactory that the uninformed reader of the note might be led to think that reg 3(1A) had a wider reach than, on a proper interpretation, it could be given. It was clear that the difficulties of interpretation of the 1995 Regulations had tried to be addressed in the 2003 Regulations but that was at best a compromise that did not really meet the need for consumer protection in the changed market conditions. Accordingly, the appeal would be dismissed and the guidance note withdrawn.

R (on the application of the Association of British Travel Agents Ltd) v Civil Aviation Authority [2006] EWCA Civ 1299, [2006] All ER (D) 191 (Oct) (Court of Appeal: Sir Mark Potter P, Chadwick and Arden LJJ). Decision of Goldring J [2006] EWHC 13 (Admin), [2006] All ER (D) 54 (Jan) affirmed.

267   Civil aviation—denied boarding, compensation and assistance—prosecutions—notice

See para 2510.

268   Civil aviation—provision of information to passengers

The Civil Aviation (Provision of Information to Passengers) Regulations 2006, SI 2006/3303 (in force on 16 January 2007), create offences for the purposes of enforcing the obligations set out in EC Parliament and Council Regulation 2111/2005, which require air passengers to be informed of the identity of the operating air carrier or carriers, and to have a right of reimbursement or re-routing if the air carrier is subject to an operating ban. In particular, the regulations provide that (1) anyone failing to comply with the specified provisions are liable on summary conviction to a fine; (2) it is a defence for a person to demonstrate that all reasonable steps have been taken to avoid the commission of the offence, except where the person has unreasonably relied on information provided to him; and (3) specified officers of bodies corporate and limited partnerships may be liable to prosecution in certain circumstances.

269   Civil aviation—safety—third-country aircraft

The Civil Aviation (Safety of Third-Country Aircraft) Regulations 2006, SI 2006/1384 (in force on 30 June 2006), make provision to comply with EC European Parliament and Council Directive 2004/36 on the safety of aircraft from outside the Community using Community airports. In particular, the regulations (1) require the Secretary of State to ensure that aircraft to which the regulations apply are subject to a ramp inspection and that such specific inspections and measures are performed; (2) permit the Secretary of State to authorise a person to perform a ramp inspection or carry out other surveillance measures which must be carried out at the Secretary of State's request or direction; (3) set out matters which the Secretary of State must take into account in determining whether a third-country aircraft is suspected of non-compliance with international safety standards; (4) place an obligation on an authorised person to perform a ramp inspection in accordance with specified requirements; (5) require the Secretary of State to inform the operator of an aircraft and that operator's regulatory authority that a ramp inspection has revealed significant safety deficiencies; (6) provide for the collection and retention of safety-related information by the Secretary of State; (7) provide for the use of ramp inspection reports and safety reports by the Secretary of State; (8) place an obligation on the Secretary of State to provide certain types of information to the competent authorities in a member state; (9) provide that the Secretary of State may only disclose a ramp inspection report or safety report that he has received from the competent authority of another member state to a limited category of people and that recipients of such information must not disclose the report further; (10) make amendments to the Air Navigation Order 2005, SI 2005/1970, so as to (a) provide for the detention by an authorised person of a third-country aircraft that does not comply with international safety standards, the notification of the relevant competent authority, and certain conditions under which a direction to detain such an aircraft may be revoked; and (b) provide for a penalty for the contravention of a direction to detain an aircraft; and (11) provide for the powers of entry available to an authorised person.

270   Civil Aviation Act 2006

The Civil Aviation Act 2006 makes further provision about civil aviation, including provision about the funding of the Air Travel Trust. The Act received the royal assent on 8 November 2006 and came into force in part on that day. The remaining provisions come into force on a day or days to be appointed. For details of commencement, see the commencement table in the title STATUTES.

Section 1 enables an authority which owns or manages a licensed aerodrome to fix its charges, for certain prescribed purposes, by reference to specified factors. Under s 2, the powers of the Secretary of State to give to the manager of a designated aerodrome such directions as the Secretary of State considers appropriate for the purposes of avoiding, limiting or mitigating the effect of noise and vibration either generally or in any particular area or areas are extended. Powers to levy financial penalties on an aircraft operator, in respect of any breach by it of noise abatement requirements imposed by the Secretary of State, are conferred by s 3 on the manager of a designated aerodrome. Section 4 makes provision in relation to the implementation of noise control schemes by aerodrome operators, so that operators of non-designated aerodromes are provided with powers to regulate noise and vibration from aircraft, and to impose penalties where the noise control scheme which it is permitted to establish is not complied with. The prohibition on a local authority owned airport company, or any subsidiary, from engaging in activities in which none of its shareholding local authorities have the power to engage is removed by s 5 in relation to activities specified by the Secretary of State as activities considered to be incidental to or connected with the business of operating a commercial airport. Section 6, Sch 1, amend certain provisions concerning the policing of airports designated by the Secretary of State. Under s 7, the right of appeal to the Secretary of State against a route licence decision of the Civil Aviation Authority ('CAA') is removed, so that affected parties will instead be able to challenge a decision of the CAA in the courts by way of judicial review. The general duties of the Secretary of State relating to civil aviation are extended by s 8 to include measures for safeguarding the health of people on board an aircraft. Section 9 replaces references to documents which are no longer in use by references to the current correct description. Air travel organisers are required by s 10 to contribute to the funding of the Air Travel Trust Fund. Under s 11, the Secretary of State is obliged to lay before Parliament a copy of every report received from the trustees of the Air Travel Trust in accordance with the terms of the trust deed, and no court may vary the terms of the deed establishing the Air Travel Trust unless the variation is sought by, or with the consent of, the Secretary of State. Section 12 applies to Scotland. Section 13, Sch 2, deal with consequential amendments, and s 14 with short title, commencement and extent.

Amendments, repeals and revocations
The list below, which is not exhaustive, mentions repeals and amendments which are or will be effective when the Act is fully in force.

Specific provisions of a number of Acts are amended or repealed. These include: Civil Aviation Act 1982 ss 1(1), 16, 38, 69A, 71, 78, 96; Airports Act 1986 s 17; and Aviation Security Act 1982 ss 2, 25, 29.

271 Civil Aviation Authority—functions—air navigation services—single European sky

The Single European Sky (Functions of the National Supervisory Authority) Regulations 2006, SI 2006/3104 (in force on 21 December 2006), confer on the Civil Aviation Authority (the 'CAA'), additional functions. In particular, the regulations (1) specify the CAA as the competent authority for the purpose of EC European Parliament and Council Regulation 550/2004 on the provision of air navigation services in the single European sky, so that the CAA has a right of access to the accounts of those providing air navigation services in United Kingdom airspace; (2) confer on the CAA the functions of designating those providing, or those who wish to provide, air traffic services and meteorological services in the United Kingdom and its airspace; in addition, the CAA is to inform the European Commission and other member states of any designations of air traffic services or meteorological services it has made and to approve the working relationships between air navigation service providers; (3) require the CAA to recognise any certificate that has been issued by a member state to an air navigation service provider; and (4) confer on the CAA the function of approving the establishment or modification of routes and sectors in upper airspace for which the United Kingdom is responsible.

272 Security—electronic communications
See para 2878.

BAILMENT
Halsbury's Laws of England (4th edn) vol 3(1) (2005 Reissue) paras 1–100

Articles
For articles relating to this title please refer to the Table of Articles at the beginning of the Abridgment.

273 Bailor—chattel—damage to bailed chattel—right to recover
The claimant owned rolling stock which was leased to a train operating company. The company used the railway track owned by the defendant. Under the lease from the claimant the company assumed all risk of loss, damage or destruction of the rolling stock. In the event of total loss, the company was obliged to pay the claimant 'the agreed value' which was defined as the projected replacement value for insurance purposes. An all risks insurance policy was taken out in the names of the claimant and the company for their rights under which any proceeds of the policy payable as a result of a total loss were to be paid to the claimant and applied by it in discharging the company's outstanding obligations to pay the agreed value. As a result of a train derailment some of the claimant's railway carriages were damaged beyond economic repair and others were damaged so as to require repair. In relation to the carriages which were constructive total losses, the insurer made payment to the claimant. Repair of the other carriages was paid for by the company and reimbursement of those

payments was made by the insurer to the company. The claimant brought proceedings in negligence against the defendant for damages representing the cost of repairs and the value of carriages beyond repair. The judge held that the claimant could not recover, holding that a lessor or bailor of chattels who was not entitled to possession during the term of the lease could only sue for damage to his reversionary interest. On the claimant's appeal, *held*, although a bailee in possession could sue for the full value of goods, it did not follow that the bailor had a similar right to sue for the full value, being accountable to the bailee to the extent that the loss was that of the bailee. A bailee could recover the full value of goods from a tortfeasor who damaged or destroyed them because, as between a bailee and a stranger, possession gave absolute and complete ownership. A bailor without possession, or the immediate right to possession, only had a limited interest. In the present case, the claimant's reversionary interest had not been damaged. Therefore, it was not entitled to recover the value of the unrepairable carriages or the cost of repairing the repairable carriages. The position as to the insurance payment was that the claimant had suffered no damage to its reversionary interest because the company had fully indemnified it, not because it had been indemnified by insurance. Accordingly, the appeal would be dismissed.

HSBC Rail (UK) Ltd v Network Rail Infrastructure Ltd (formerly Railtrack plc) [2005] EWCA Civ 1437, [2006] 1 All ER 343 (Court of Appeal: Sir Andrew Morritt C, Longmore and Lloyd LJJ).

BANKING

Halsbury's Laws of England (4th edn) vol 3(1) (2005 Reissue) paras 101–300

Articles

For articles relating to this title please refer to the Table of Articles at the beginning of the Abridgment.

274   Bank—duty of care—freezing order prohibiting disposals from bank account

See *Customs and Excise Comrs v Barclays Bank plc*, para 2072.

275   Money laundering

See CRIMINAL LAW.

276   National Savings Bank—investment accounts

The National Savings Bank (Amendment) Regulations 2006, SI 2006/1066 (in force in part on 6 June 2006 and in part on 1 October 2006), further amend the 1972 Regulations, SI 1972/764, (1) by removing the one month period of notice required before depositors may make withdrawals from NS&I Investment Accounts; (2) by enabling the Director of Savings to impose an upper limit of £2,000 on the amount which may be withdrawn in cash from NS&I Ordinary and Investment Accounts at a post office; and (3) by changing the manner in which cash may be withdrawn from NS&I Ordinary and Investment Accounts, by providing for uncrossed warrants to be replaced by cash payment advices.

BANKRUPTCY AND INDIVIDUAL INSOLVENCY

Halsbury's Laws of England (4th edn) vol 3(2) (2002 Reissue) paras 1–911

Articles

For articles relating to this title please refer to the Table of Articles at the beginning of the Abridgment.

277   Bankruptcy—order—annulment—appeal—likelihood of additional creditors

The Insolvency Act 1986 s 282(1) empowers the court to annul a bankruptcy order if at any time it appears that (1) on the grounds existing at the time the order was made, the order ought not to have been made; or (2) to the extent required by the rules, the bankruptcy debts and the expenses of the bankruptcy have all, since the making of the order, been either paid or secured for to the satisfaction of the court. In relation to an application under s 282, all bankruptcy debts which have been proved must have been paid in full, and, where security has been given in the case of an untraced creditor, the court may direct that particulars of the alleged debt, and the security, be advertised in such manner as it thinks fit: Insolvency Rules 1986, SI 1986/1925, r 6.211(2), (4).

A bankruptcy order was made in respect of a person. At the time of the order, the bankrupt's only asset of substance was a half share in a house which was encumbered by a mortgage exceeding the value of his half share in the property. Only four creditors proved in the bankrupt's bankruptcy. Twelve years after the bankruptcy order was made, the Official Receiver appointed a trustee in bankruptcy. The trustee in bankruptcy and the Official Receiver did not advertise for any other creditors of the bankrupt. The bankrupt then applied for an annulment of the bankruptcy pursuant to the 1986 Act s 282. By the time of that application, the value of his half share in the house exceeded the amount of his debts and any costs payable to the trustee in bankruptcy. The district judge allowed the bankrupt's application, taking the view that it was unlikely that any unidentified creditors would come forward at that stage. He also took into consideration the fact that the value of the bankrupt's half share in the house would ensure that the identified creditors were paid and that their interests were secured. The trustee in bankruptcy appealed against that decision, contending that the judge had wrongly exercised his discretion by failing to adequately consider the effect of s 282 on the 1986 Rules r 6.211. *Held*, there was no error of law in the district judge's exercise of his discretion. The district judge had not exceeded the band within which reasonable people would disagree with his decision. In the circumstances, he had been entitled to take the view that advertising for unidentified creditors of the bankrupt would be pointless and that debts of that age would be unlikely to be brought forward at that date. Accordingly, the appeal would be dismissed.

Savage v Howard [2006] All ER (D) 13 (Feb) (Chancery Division: Lewison J).

278 Bankruptcy—transaction at an undervalue—victim of transaction

The Insolvency Act 1986 s 423(2) provides that where a person has entered into a transaction at an undervalue, the court may make such order as it thinks fit for (a) restoring the position to what it would have been if the transaction had not been entered into, and (b) protecting the interests of persons who are victims of the transaction. Where a person has entered into such a transaction, an order may be made if the court is satisfied that it was entered into by him for the purpose of putting assets beyond the reach of a person who is making, or may at some time make, a claim against him, or of otherwise prejudicing the interests of such a person in relation to the claim which he is making or may make: s 423(3). In relation to a transaction at an undervalue, references to a victim of the transaction are to a person who is, or is capable of being, prejudiced by it, and in ss 424 and 425 the person entering into the transaction is referred to as 'the debtor'.

On an application by a trustee in bankruptcy for relief pursuant to the 1986 Act s 423 in relation to a settlement, the judge declared that certain legal charges and an assignment made by the bankrupt to the trustees of the settlement constituted transactions within s 423(3) that should be set aside and that the application was not statute-barred as a claim under s 423 was a specialty so that the Limitation Act 1980 s 8(1), under which the limitation period was 12 years, applied. The trustees of the settlement appealed. *Held*, Arden LJ dissenting in part, the 1986 Act s 423(2), in conjunction with the definition of 'victim' in s 423(5), made prejudice or potential prejudice a condition for obtaining relief. That prejudice did not have to be achieved by the purpose with which the transaction had been entered into. Section 423(3) required that the purpose should be one which was to prejudice 'the interests' of a claimant or prospective claimant. In a case where the applicant relied on s 423(2)(b), the crucial step was to identify the interests of the person that were said to be prejudiced. If the transaction under s 423 was entered into with the requisite purpose, the fact that some other event needed to occur did not mean that the transaction could not itself be within s 423(3). It was entry into the transaction, not the transaction itself, which had to have the necessary purpose. Further, under s 424(1)(c), a victim could bring an application under s 423 at any time. If he did so, he was deemed to bring the claim on behalf of every victim of the transaction. A victim who brought an application under s 423 was not enforcing a remedy for prejudice to himself alone because he, like the trustee in bankruptcy, was deemed to bring the proceedings on behalf of all the victims. Notwithstanding that, it was the policy of the statute of limitations that there should be an end to litigation and that that was in the public interest. On that basis, there was no reason why claims under s 423 should not be subject to some time limit. In so far as the relief sought was not for 'the recovery of a sum recoverable by virtue of an enactment' within the 1980 Act s 9, it was an action for a specialty within s 8. Once there had been a statutory period for non-monetary claims based on a statute, that period should apply. Furthermore, the 1986 Act ss 423–425 were drafted in wide terms and, although it was correct that the court would normally consider that it was not proportionate to hear an application unless it could be shown at that date that there was a person who could benefit by a positive finding under s 423, there were bound to be cases where that could not be shown. Judgment would be given accordingly.

Hill v Spread Trustee Co Ltd [2006] EWCA Civ 542, [2007] 1 All ER 1106 (Court of Appeal: Waller and Arden LJJ and Sir Martin Nourse).

279 Bankruptcy—trustee in bankruptcy—property vesting in trustee—matrimonial home— wife's beneficial ownership

See *Supperstone v Hurst*, para 2882.

280 Bankruptcy—trustee in bankruptcy—property vesting in trustee—property over which charging order made—sale—limitation period

See *Gotham v Doodes*, para 1827.

281 Bankruptcy—trusts of land—dwelling house—rights of co-owner in occupation—balancing exercise

The Insolvency Act 1986 s 335A(2) provides that, on an application by a trustee of a bankrupt's estate under the Trusts of Land and Appointment of Trustees Act 1996 s 14 for an order for the sale of land, the court must make such order as it thinks just and reasonable having regard to (1) the interests of the bankrupt's creditors; (2) where the application is made in respect of land which includes a dwelling house which is the home of the bankrupt's spouse, the conduct of the spouse, so far as contributing to the bankruptcy, and the needs and financial resources of the spouse; and (3) all other circumstances of the case.

The respondent and her husband were the joint owners of a house. The respondent lived in the property and had joint ownership of a second house with her brother, who lived there. The husband was adjudged bankrupt and the applicant was appointed as his trustee in bankruptcy. The applicant sought declaratory relief as to the extent of the beneficial interests of the respondent and her husband, and for an order for sale of their house pursuant to the 1996 Act s 14. The district judge declared that the property was held beneficially in equal shares by the applicant and the respondent, and further ordered that the property should be placed on the market for sale. The respondent appealed, contending that the judge had attached too much weight to the interests of the creditors, whose identities and particular needs had not been ascertained. *Held*, an appellate court could only interfere with the balancing exercise carried out by the district judge pursuant to the 1986 Act s 335A if he had erred in law in his interpretation of that provision or in some other respect. The judge had considered the possibility of the respondent realising her interest in the second house and the possible consequential effect on her brother, although there was next to no evidence about his position. In relation to the creditors, it was taken to be almost axiomatic that what they wanted was to be paid their money as soon as possible. It was not necessary for a trustee in bankruptcy to do very much by way of positive evidence as to the creditors' interests and their interests should not be dismissed as having no weight where there was little or no specific evidence as to their identity and as to their concerns. The judge had not committed any error which would allow an appellate court to interfere with his discretion as to what was just and reasonable for the purposes of s 335A. Accordingly, the appeal would be dismissed.

Nicholls v Lan [2006] EWHC 1255 (Ch), [2006] All ER (D) 16 (Jun) (Chancery Division: Paul Morgan QC).

282 Disqualification from office

The Enterprise Act 2002 (Disqualification from Office: General) Order 2006, SI 2006/1722 (in force on 29 June 2006), amends and revokes various disqualification provisions which prevent individuals who are bankrupts from being elected or appointed to, or holding, certain offices or positions, or from becoming or remaining a member of a body or group, thereby reducing the class of bankrupts to whom the provisions apply.

283 Insolvency—corporate insolvency

See COMPANY AND PARTNERSHIP INSOLVENCY.

284 Insolvency—cross-border insolvency—proceedings

See para 562.

285 Insolvency—fees

The Insolvency Proceedings (Fees) (Amendment) Order 2006, SI 2006/561 (in force on 1 April 2006), further amends the 2004 Order, SI 2004/593, so as to (1) increase the amount of the various deposits payable; (2) reduce the deposit payable in connection with the registration of an individual voluntary arrangement and the performance by the official receiver of the functions of nominee in relation to such an arrangement; (3) reduce from £35 to £15 the fee currently payable to the Secretary of State to register an individual voluntary arrangement; (4) provide that certain fees continue to apply to cases that were commenced after 29 December 1986 and for which a winding up or bankruptcy order was made before 1 April 2004; (5) provide that after 1 April 2006 no fees are payable in any case where £100,000 or more has been paid into the Insolvency Services Account before the commencement date; and (6) make provision that any case where less than £100,000 has been paid into the Insolvency Services Account before 1 April 2006 fees are payable in relation to that proportion of payments into that account on or after the commencement date which takes the balance of sums paid into that account up to £100,000 and no further fees are then payable; and (6) prescribe the percentage fees that are payable in relation to the first £100,000 paid into the Insolvency Services Account in old cases.

286 Winding up

See COMPANY AND PARTNERSHIP INSOLVENCY.

BARRISTERS

Halsbury's Laws of England (4th edn) vol 3(1) (2005 Reissue) paras 401–702

Articles

For articles relating to this title please refer to the Table of Articles at the beginning of the Abridgment.

287   Conduct of cases—sentencing—duty to assist judge

See *R v Cain*, para 2566.

288   Rights of audience—right to conduct litigation—Association of Law Costs Draftsmen

See para 2721.

BETTING, GAMING AND LOTTERIES

Halsbury's Laws of England (4th edn) vol 4(1) (2002 Reissue) paras 1–300

Articles

For articles relating to this title please refer to the Table of Articles at the beginning of the Abridgment.

289   Betting—call centre services—provision of facilities for placing bets—activities exempt from value added tax

See Case C-89/05 *United Utilities plc v Comrs of Customs and Excise*, para 2889.

290   Finance Act 2006

See para 2465.

291   Gambling—functions of licensing authority—policy statement

The Gambling Act 2005 (Licensing Authority Policy Statement) (England and Wales) Regulations 2006, SI 2006/636 (in force on 31 March 2006), set out requirements as to the form and publication of a policy statement, or a revision of such a statement, which must be produced by a licensing authority at least every three years in accordance with the Gambling Act 2005 s 349. In particular, the regulations (1) provide that the form of a statement or any revision is for the authority producing it to determine; (2) require a statement or revision to include an introductory section summarising the matters contained in it, describing the geographical area in respect of which the authority exercises functions under the 2005 Act and listing the persons consulted in preparing the statement or revision; (3) require a statement to include four sections setting out the principles which the authority will apply in exercising its powers under specified provisions of the Act; and (4) set out requirements relating to the advertisement and publication of a statement or revision.

The Gambling Act 2005 (Licensing Authority Policy Statement) (First Appointed Day) Order 2006, SI 2006/637 (in force on 31 March 2006), prescribes 31 January 2007 as the first day of the initial three-year period for the purposes of the 2005 Act s 349.

292   Gambling—Gambling Appeals Tribunal—appeals procedure

The Gambling Appeals Tribunal Rules 2006, SI 2006/3293 (in force on 1 January 2007), regulate the procedure for appeals to the Gambling Appeals Tribunal by (1) providing (a) for the bringing of an appeal by the appellant filing an appeal notice with the Tribunal; (b) that a statement of case must be filed by the Gambling Commission in support of its determination, containing the information specified and accompanied by a list and a copy of certain material; and (c) that the appellant must reply to that statement of case no later than 28 days after the date on which the appellant received a copy of the statement, or if the Commission amends its statement of case, the date on which the appellant received a copy of the amended statement of case; (2) allowing a party to request that a document that they are otherwise obliged to disclose is exempted from such disclosure on the ground that it would not be in the public interest, that the document contains commercially sensitive information, that the document is privileged or that it is disproportionate to the case to order such disclosure; (3) specifying that the Tribunal may make directions to ensure the just, expeditious and economical determination of the appeal, listing examples of particular directions that the Tribunal may give; (4) providing (a) that the Tribunal may direct that a hearing to determine a preliminary question of law or fact is to take place before the substantive hearing of the appeal takes place; (b) for the circumstances in which the Tribunal directs that a pre hearing review of the case is to be held; (c) that the Tribunal may determine an appeal without an oral hearing, giving consideration to whether it is undesirable to publish the whole or part of its final determination, taking into account the circumstances of the case, such as whether there are matters of commercial sensitivity, or personal details relating to key personnel in an organisation or relating to a personal licence holder; and (d) an exemption to the general rule that all hearings must be held in public, directing the tribunal to look at the particular circumstances of the case and allow the hearing to take place without the attendance of the press and public when it considers that it is in the interests of justice to do so; (5) allowing the Tribunal to (a) consider whether it would be undesirable to publish the whole or part of its final determination when the whole or part of the hearing was held in private; and (b) make a costs order against the appellant or the Commission in relation to the bringing of the appeal or its conduct; and (6) providing that, where a person seeks permission from the Tribunal to bring an appeal against the Tribunal's final determination, the application for permission must be decided without an oral hearing unless the application is made immediately following the hearing, or the Tribunal considers that a hearing is desirable.

293   Gambling—Gambling Appeals Tribunal—fees

The Gambling Appeals Tribunal Fees Regulations 2006, SI 2006/3287 (in force on 1 January 2007), (1) prescribe various levels of fee payable for bringing an appeal before the Gambling Appeal Tribunal under the Gambling Act 2005 s 141; (2) provide that no such fee is payable by an appellant who is in receipt of a qualifying benefit, or an appellant for whom payment of the fee would involve undue financial hardship; and (3) make provision in relation to refunds where the relevant fee has been paid.

294   Gambling—operating licences—fees

The Gambling (Operating Licence and Single-Machine Permit Fees) Regulations 2006, SI 2006/3284 (in force in part on 1 January 2007 and in part on 1 September 2007), prescribe application, annual and other fees relating to operating licences and application fees relating to single-machine supply and maintenance permits. In particular, the regulations (1) define the units of division by which different kinds of operating licence are assigned to categories for the purposes of prescribing fees; (2) set out categories of non-remote casino operating licences and prescribe fees for each of those categories; (3) provide that the first annual fee payable in respect of a non-remote operating licence is 75 per cent of the usual annual fee payable in respect of that licence; (4) prescribe categories of remote operating licences and application and annual fees in respect of each category; (5) prescribe special application and annual fees which are payable where a person holds or applies for (a) a combined operating licence, which combines more than one kind of remote or more than one kind of non-remote operating licence; or (b) two separate operating licences, one of which is remote and the other non-remote; (6) provide that the first annual fee payable in respect of a combined non-remote operating licence is subject to a 25 per cent discount; (7) provide that, where a person applies for or holds two operating licences simultaneously, the lesser of the ordinary annual or application fees payable in respect of those licences is discounted by a specified amount; (8) prescribe fees payable (a) when a person makes a change of corporate control application; (b) on an application to vary a licence; (c) for a copy of an operating licence; and (d) on application for a single-machine supply and maintenance permit; and (9) require the first annual fee payable in respect of an operating licence to be paid within 30 days of the date on which such a licence is issued.

295   Gambling—personal licences—exclusion and modification of provisions

The Gambling (Personal Licences) (Modification of Part 5 of the Gambling Act 2005) Regulations 2006, SI 2006/3267 (in force on 1 January 2007), specify the provisions of the Gambling Act 2005 Pt 5 (ss 65–126) which do not apply to personal licences and modify further specified provisions of Pt 5 as they apply to personal licences.

296   Gambling—personal licences—fees

The Gambling (Personal Licence Fees) Regulations 2006, SI 2006/3285 (in force on 1 January 2007), prescribe application, maintenance and other fees relating to personal licences issued under the Gambling Act 2005 Pt 6 (ss 127–139). In particular, the regulations (1) prescribe two categories of personal licence, namely personal management licences and personal functional licences, for the purposes of prescribing fees; (2) prescribe different application fees in respect of each category of personal licence; (3) provide for a discounted application fee where an application for a personal licence is made through the Gambling Commission's website; (4) prescribe maintenance fees payable in respect of each category of personal licence, and specify when payment of maintenance fees is to be made; (5) prescribe the fees payable in respect of an application to vary a personal licence; and (6) provide that the fee for issuing a copy of a personal licence is not to exceed £25.

297 Gambling—personal or operating licence—relevant offences

The Gambling Act 2005 (Relevant Offences) (Amendment) Order 2006, SI 2006/3391 (in force on 8 January 2007), amends the list of offences that are treated as relevant offences for the purpose of the grant and maintenance of operating and personal licences under the Gambling Act 2005 Pts 5 and 6 (ss 65–139).

298 Gambling—single-machine permits—fees

See para 294.

299 Gambling—small-scale operators—definition

The Gambling Act 2005 (Definition of Small-scale Operator) Regulations 2006, SI 2006/3266 (in force on 1 January 2007), provide that the holder of an operating licence qualifies as a small-scale operator for the purposes of the Gambling Act 2005 s 129 if, in relation to the relevant licensed activities, there are no more than three qualifying positions which are occupied by a qualified person. The regulations also provide that a small-scale operator only ceases to be such an operator if he fails to comply with the conditions imposed for a period of more than 28 days or for two periods of more than 14 days each occurring within 28 days of each other.

300 Gambling Act 2005—commencement

The Gambling Act 2005 (Commencement No 3) Order 2006, SI 2006/631, brings ss 166 and 349 into force on 31 March 2006.

The Gambling Act 2005 (Commencement No 4) Order 2006, SI 2006/2964, brings into force, on 13 November 2006, ss 154(1) (for certain purposes), (2)(b) (for certain purposes), 247(2), (3) (in part), 289(2), (3) (in part), Sch 10 paras 1, 7(1), (2), (3) (in part), Sch 14 paras 1, 8(1), (2), (3) (in part).

The Gambling Act 2005 (Commencement No 5) Order 2006, SI 2006/3220, brings Sch 7 para 23 into force on 5 December 2006.

The Gambling Act 2005 (Commencement No 6 and Transitional Provisions) Order 2006, SI 2006/3272, amended by SI 2006/3361, brings into force (1) on 1 January 2007, ss 28 (in part), 65–74 (for certain purposes), 75 (so far as not already in force), 76 (so far as not already in force), 77, 78, 79 (so far as not already in force), 80 (so far as not already in force), 81, 84–88, 89(1), (4)–(7), 90–107, 109, 113–115, 116(2)(b), (c), (3)–(5), 117–120 (for certain purposes), 122, 124–126, 128 (for certain purposes), 129, 130 (for certain purposes), 132, 133, 136, 140–149, 235 (in part), 237–241, 248(2), 251–257, 288, 291 (for certain purposes), 341 (in part), 342 (in part), 345 (in part), 350, 351, 353, 356(1) (in part), (2) (in part), (4) (in part), (5) (in part), Sch 7 (for all remaining purposes), Sch 8, Sch 16 para 12 (for certain purposes) and certain repeals in Sch 17; (2) on 30 April 2007, ss 7(5)–(7), 150–153, 154 (so far as not already in force), 155–158, 159–165 (for certain purposes), 167–171, 174(1), 176(1), (2), 181, 184, 186–190, 192, 194–196, 204 (for certain purposes), 205–213, 235 (so far as not already in force), 236, 247(3) (in part), 289(3), 303, 304, 309(1), 311(1), 313(1), 317–326, 342 (so far as not already in force), 343, 346(1)(l), (2), (3), Sch 10 paras 2–6 (for certain purposes), 7(3) (so far as not already in force), 8–11 (for certain purposes), 12(a), 13, 15–17, 21, 22 (for certain purposes), 23, 24, Sch 14 paras 2, 3–7 (for certain purposes), 8(3) (so far as not already in force), 9–12 (for certain purposes), 13(a), 14–17, 21, 22 (for certain purposes), 23, 24; (3) on 1 June 2007, ss 159–165 (for certain purposes), 175, 204 (so far as not already in force), 266–268, 271(2), 273(2), 274, 276–278, 283(2), (5) (for certain purposes), 284, 310(1), 312(4), Sch 9, Sch 12 paras 1–11 (for certain purposes), 15–21, 23, 25 (for certain purposes), 26–31, Sch 13 paras 1–7 (for certain purposes), 11–20, 21 (for certain purposes), 22, 23; and (4) on 1 September 2007, certain repeals in Sch 17 and, so far as they are not already in force, the remaining provisions of the Act. Transitional provision is also made.

For a summary of the Act, see 2005 Abr para 642. See also the commencement table in the title STATUTES.

301 Gaming—fees—variation

The Gaming Act 1968 (Variation of Fees) Order 2006, SI 2006/541 (in force on 1 April 2006), increases the fees to be charged under the Gaming Act 1968 for the matters specified in the order. SI 2004/531 and 2005/567 are revoked.

The Gaming Act 1968 (Variation of Fees) (England and Wales) Order 2006, SI 2006/543 (in force on 1 April 2006), increases the fees to be charged under the Gaming Act 1968 for the matters specified in the order. SI 2005/566 is amended.

302 Gaming—gaming duty—rates

The Gaming Duty (Amendment) Regulations 2006, SI 2006/1999 (in force on 1 October 2006), further amend the 1997 Regulations, SI 1997/2196, in relation to the calculation of payments on account of gaming duty. SI 2004/2243 is revoked.

303 Gaming—gaming machines—monetary limits

The Gaming Act 1968 (Variation of Monetary Limits) Order 2006, SI 2006/2663 (in force on 27 October 2006), replaces the 2005 Regulations, SI 2005/2776, and (1) increases the limit on the charge for play where jackpot gaming machines are used on all other premises, other than in a casino; (2) increases the maximum charge for play on amusement with prizes machines; and (3) increases the limits on prizes payable in respect of a particular type of amusement with prizes machine. SI 2001/3971 is revoked.

304 Gaming—licences—transitional provisions

The Gambling Act 2005 (Transitional Provisions) Order 2006, SI 2006/1038 (in force on 29 April 2006), makes transitional provision in connection with the commencement of the Gambling Act 2005, so as to restrict the circumstances in which, during the period between 29 April 2006 and the date on which the relevant provision of the Gaming Act 1968 is repealed, the Gambling Commission may issue a certificate of consent relating to an application for a casino licence. The order also makes incidental modifications to the powers of the Commission to revoke certificates of consent.

The Gambling Act 2005 (Transitional Provisions) (No 2) Order 2006, SI 2006/1758 (in force on 1 August 2006), makes further transitional provision in connection with the commencement of the Gambling Act 2005, and, in particular, about the grant or renewal of certain licences and permits issued under the Betting, Gaming and Lotteries Act 1963, the Gaming Act 1968 and the Lotteries and Amusements Act 1976, all of which are repealed by the 2005 Act, during the period before the repeal of those Acts.

305 Lottery—Gambling Commission—fees

The Lotteries (Gambling Commission Fees) Order 2006, SI 2006/542 (in force on 1 April 2006), replaces the Lotteries (Gaming Board Fees) Order 2005, SI 2005/568, and makes provision as to the fees payable to the Gambling Commission by specified societies, local authorities and lottery managers.

306 Lotteries—Olympics—payments out of Fund

The Olympic Lotteries (Payments out of Fund) Regulations 2006, SI 2006/655 (in force on 31 March 2006), provide (1) for payments from the Olympic Lottery Distribution Fund in respect of expenses (a) of the Secretary of State in connection with functions under the Horserace Betting and Olympic Lottery Act 2004 Pt 3 (ss 21–37); and (b) expenses incurred, or to be incurred, by the National Debt Commissioner in making investments under s 27; (2) that payments under head (1) will be at such times and for such amounts as the Secretary of State determines to be appropriate and may only be made with the consent of the Treasury; (3) for payments from the Olympic Lottery Distribution Fund into the Consolidated Fund for the purpose of meeting payments made, or to be made, under the National Lottery etc Act 1993 Sch 2A para 10; (4) that payments under head (3) will be at such times and for such amounts as the Secretary of State determines to be appropriate, taking into account sums paid or to be paid into the Consolidated Fund; (5) for all fees received by the National Lottery Commission to be paid into the Consolidated Fund; and (6) for payments out of the National Lottery Distribution Fund into the Consolidated Fund in respect of the expenses of the National Lottery Commission

307 National Lottery—awards for all—joint scheme—England

The Awards for All (England) Joint Scheme (Authorisation) Order 2006, SI 2006/565 (in force on 1 April 2006), replaces the 2005 Regulations, SI 2005/374, and authorises a modification to the Awards for All (England) joint scheme so as to extend the duration of the scheme to 31 March 2007 and to increase the maximum amount that may be distributed under the scheme to £60m in one year.

308 National lottery—Big Lottery Fund—prescribed expenditure

The Big Lottery Fund (Prescribed Expenditure) Order 2006, SI 2006/3202 (in force on 1 December 2006), prescribes the descriptions of charitable expenditure for the purposes of the National Lottery etc Act 1993 and thereby defines the extent of the power of the Big Lottery Fund to distribute Lottery money in the fund allocated to prescribed expenditure that is charitable and connected with health, education or the environment. In particular, the order prescribes descriptions of expenditure which are to have effect in relation to each of England, Scotland, Wales, Northern

Ireland and the Isle of Man. The Fund's functions in relation to Scottish, Welsh and Northern Ireland devolved expenditure will be exercised by the committees established under the 1993 Act and will be subject to the directions given by Scottish Ministers, the National Assembly for Wales and the Northern Ireland Department of Culture, Arts and Leisure. The order also (1) prescribes a further description of devolved expenditure relating to small grants under which the Awards for All programme will continue to be funded; and (2) prescribes a description of non-devolved expenditure which allows the Fund to make grants for expenditure on or connected with projects which are intended to transform communities, regions or the nation as a whole. The Fund's functions in relation to this description of expenditure will be exercised by the main board and will be subject to directions given by the Secretary of State under the 1993 Act. The maximum amount that may be distributed by the Fund by 1 April 2008 for this description of expenditure is also prescribed.

309   National Lottery—distribution fund—allocations of funds—sport

The National Lottery etc Act 1993 (Amendment of Section 23) Order 2006, SI 2006/654 (in force on 1 April 2006), amends the National Lottery etc Act 1993 s 23(2) by (1) increasing the percentage held for the United Kingdom Sports Council from 9·2 per cent to 22·8 per cent and make a corresponding decrease in the percentage held for the English Sports Council; and (2) transferring £7m from the amount held in the National Lottery Distribution Fund for distribution by the English Sports Council to be held for distribution by the United Kingdom Sports Council.

310   National Lottery—distributors—dissolution

The National Lottery Distributors Dissolution Order 2006, SI 2006/2915 (in force on 17 November 2006), dissolved the National Lottery Charities Board, also known as the Community Fund, the Millennium Commission and the New Opportunities Fund on 1 December 2006, on the date when the Big Lottery Fund (Prescribed Expenditure) Order 2006, SI 2006/3202 came into force. The Big Lottery Fund is the successor body of the three lottery distributors. SI 1999/1878, 2000/3355, 2003/2869, 3033, 2005/1102, 2470, 3235 are revoked.

311   National Lottery—transformational grants joint scheme

The Transformational Grants Joint Scheme (Revocation) Order 2006, SI 2006/3146 (in force on 1 December 2006), revokes the Transformational Grants Joint Scheme (Authorisation) Order 2005, SI 2005/608, which authorised a joint scheme entered into between the National Lottery Charities Board and the New Opportunities Fund. Those bodies are dissolved and replaced by the Big Lottery Fund established by the National Lottery Act 2006 s 14.

312   National Lottery Act 2006

The National Lottery Act 2006 amends the National Lottery etc Act 1993 so as to make provision about the National Lottery. The Act received the royal assent on 11 July 2006 and came into force in part on that day. Further provisions came into force on and between 1 August 2006 and 1 December 2006: SI 2006/2177, 2630, 3201. The remaining provisions come into force on a date to be appointed. For details of commencement see the commencement table in the title STATUTES.

Section 1 provides that the number of members of the New Opportunities Fund and the Millennium Commission must be five or more, that the Secretary of State appoints the chairman of the National Lottery Commission ('the Commission'), and allows the Secretary of State to appoint the chief executive and another employee of the Commission as members of the Commission, in line with normal commercial arrangements. The Commissioners for Her Majesty's Revenue and Customs and the Commission are allowed to share information, and the wrongful disclosure of information received from the Commissioners relating to identifiable person is to be a criminal offence carrying a maximum penalty for up to two years of imprisonment and an unlimited fine: s 2. By virtue of s 3, the Commission may grant licences to run the National Lottery and to promote lotteries to any person rather than only to a body corporate. Section 4 provides that such a licence cannot exceed or be extended beyond 15 years, and may include provision allowing the Commission to extend the period of the licence or provision, or allowing the licence to be extended with the agreement of the relevant licensee. The holders of licences must, under s 5, pay annual fees, to be set out in regulations, which reflect the expenses incurred by the Commission in the exercise of all its functions to the Commission. Section 6 provides for Sch 1, which sets out the reserve licensing structure to allow the Commission to issue more than one licence to operate and promote the lotteries forming part of the National Lottery. Fifty per cent of all sums paid into the National Lottery Distribution Fund ('the fund') by the licensee who runs the National Lottery must be allocated for expenditure prescribed by the Secretary of State that is charitable or connected with health, education or the environment: s 7. By virtue of s 8, The Secretary of State may, by order, reallocate sums paid into the fund for particular good causes and distributors, from one lottery distributor to another body but not from one good cause to another. Section 9 provides that proceeds from investments of money held in the fund are allocated according to the same percentage shares as money entered the fund. Lottery distributors are permitted under s 10 to take account of the opinions expressed or information supplied as a result of consultation with any person about making a decision about distributing lottery money. Section 11 clarifies that lottery distributors can publicise the National Lottery. All lottery distributors are required to include a statement in their annual reports of their policy and practice in relation to the principle that proceeds of the National Lottery should be used to fund projects, or aspects of projects, for which funds would be unlikely to be made available by the government or the devolved administrations: s 12. A body may distribute money, under s 13, to meet expenditure which relates to the Isle of Man or any of the Channel Islands. Under s 14 the Big Lottery Fund is established as a corporate body and Sch 2 makes detailed provision in relation to the Big Lottery Fund's constitution, proceedings and money. Section 15 allows and makes provision for the Big Lottery Fund to distribute the money in the fund allocated to prescribed expenditure that is charitable and connected with health, education or the environment. The Secretary of State may appoint a day or days by order on which the Community Fund, the Millennium Commission and the New Opportunities Fund will cease to exist: s 16. Provision is made under s 17 for the property, rights and liabilities of the Community Fund, the Millennium Fund and the New Opportunities Fund to be transferred to the Big Fund and for the Big Lottery Fund to have the power to do anything for the purpose of giving effect to any decision, agreement or undertaking of the dissolved Lottery distributors. Money held in the fund for the Millennium Commission, the Community Fund and the New Opportunities Fund is now held for distribution by the Big Lottery Fund: s 18. Consequential amendments are made under s 19. Section 20 defines 'charitable expenditure' as expenditure for a charitable, benevolent or philanthropic purpose, s 21, Sch 3 deals with repeals, s 22 with commencement, s 23 with extent and s 24 with short title.

Amendments, repeals and revocations
The list below, which is not exhaustive, mentions repeals and amendments which are or will be effective when the Act is fully in force.

Specific provisions of a number of Acts are amended or repealed. These include: National Lottery Act etc 1993 ss 7(5), (6), 22, 25, 32, 34, 37–43D, Sch 2A para 2(1), 4, Schs 5–6A; National Lottery Act 1998 ss 6(2)–(7), (9), (10), 7, 8(1), (3)–(7), 11(5), (6), 14, Sch 2; Government of Wales Act 1998, Sch 5 para 34; and National Lottery (Funding of Endowments) Act 2003 s 1(5)–(7).

BOUNDARIES

Halsbury's Laws of England (4th edn) vol 4(1) (2002 Reissue) paras 901–989

313   Delineation of boundary—evidence—reliance on extrinsic evidence

The claimants brought an action for adverse possession over an area of land lying south of their property, to which the defendant held title. The issue to be decided was the precise boundary of land where it abutted the claimants' property. The judge dismissed the claim and the claimants appealed. *Held*, where information contained in a conveyance of land was unclear or ambiguous, regard to extraneous evidence could be permitted, including evidence of subsequent conduct, subject to such evidence being of probative value in determining what the parties to the original conveyance intended, as opposed to their successors in title. Evidence of physical features which were in existence after the execution of the original conveyance were of no relevance unless there was some reason to think they existed at the time of that conveyance. The judge had been entitled to reject the claimants' evidence. Accordingly, the appeal would be dismissed.

Ali v Lane [2006] EWCA Civ 1532, [2006] All ER (D) 271 (Nov) (Court of Appeal: Waller, Carnwath and Maurice Kay LJJ). *Watcham v A-G of the East African Protectorate* [1919] AC 533, PC, applied.

314   Party wall—dispute—award—appeal—statutory appeal

See *Zissis v Lukomski*, para 2277.

BRITISH NATIONALITY, IMMIGRATION AND ASYLUM

Halsbury's Laws of England (4th edn) vol 4(2) (2002 Reissue) paras 1–300

Articles

For articles relating to this title please refer to the Table of Articles at the beginning of the Abridgment.

315   Asylum—appeal—appeal by Secretary of State from adjudicator—grounds of appeal

The claimant, a citizen of Zimbabwe, had an uncle who had associations with an opposition political party in Zimbabwe. A house owned by the uncle was raided by activists of the governing party while the claimant was staying there. She alleged that she had been assaulted, held captive for three days and interrogated about the activities of the opposition party. She was later brought to a safe-house, but the police took no interest in her allegations. She subsequently came to the United Kingdom and claimed asylum. The Secretary of State refused to believe her story and denied the claim, but that decision was overturned on the claimant's appeal to an adjudicator. The Secretary of State applied for permission to appeal to the Asylum and Immigration Tribunal on the grounds that the adjudicator had failed to state how the claimant had satisfied the burden of proof on her to show that she would be at risk if returned to Zimbabwe, and that his conclusion that she would be at risk had been pure speculation, unjustified by the evidence. The vice-president of the tribunal granted permission to appeal on the basis that there was a point of law as to whether the adjudicator's decision had been perverse. Permission was granted to appeal on all the grounds of appeal advanced. Subsequently, the tribunal allowed the Secretary of State's appeal on the ground that the adjudicator's decision had been perverse. The claimant appealed, submitting that the tribunal had lacked the jurisdiction to entertain the appeal since leave had been granted to argue a point of law not set out in the Secretary of State's grounds of appeal. *Held*, in considering whether to grant permission to appeal, the tribunal should limit itself to the grounds settled. If it identified other grounds of appeal on points of law, it was for the Secretary of State to apply for permission to amend his grounds of appeal. No suggestion had been made that the grounds of appeal should be amended, and no application to amend had been made by the Secretary of State. The vice-president had none the less granted permission to appeal on a ground not identified, namely, that the adjudicator's conclusion had been perverse. That had not and had never been a ground of appeal, and the vice-president had wholly erred in granting permission to appeal on that basis. Only one sentence saved the decision to grant permission to appeal: the statement that permission would be granted on all the grounds of appeal advanced. However, the appeal should never have been brought because the adjudicator had made no error of law in reaching his conclusions. Accordingly, the appeal would be allowed.

M v Secretary of State for the Home Department [2006] All ER (D) 384 (May) (Court of Appeal: Rix, Moses and Hedley LJJ). *B v Secretary of State for Home Department* [2005] EWCA Civ 61, [2005] All ER (D) 15 (Feb) (2005 Abr para 345) followed.

316   Asylum—appeal—appeal to Asylum and Immigration Tribunal—tribunal's power to identify issues of law

The Asylum and Immigration Tribunal allowed the Secretary of State's appeal against an adjudicator's decision that the claimant should be granted asylum. On appeal, the question arose whether the Secretary of State's grounds of appeal to the tribunal had raised a question of law. *Held*, appeal to the tribunal lay only on questions of law. Where the appeal rested on taking issue with the adjudicator's findings of fact, in order to take on a legal dimension, there had to be a sufficient argument that the findings were demonstrably unfounded or erroneous and capable of affecting the outcome. The Secretary of State's appeal had raised some issues of law, and the tribunal had not gone beyond its remit in revealing an issue of law as to whether the adjudicator had established truly exceptional circumstances. The tribunal was entitled to extract a point of law from nebulously expressed grounds of appeal or, in exceptional cases, to identify an obvious issue of law missed by the appellant. The tribunal should be rigorous in only letting issues of law to arise, but it should be prepared to help identify such issues where they arguably arose. The Court of Appeal could not support the tribunal's reasons and, accordingly, the appeal would be allowed.

Krasniqi v Secretary of State for the Home Department [2006] EWCA Civ 391, (2006) Times, 20 April (Court of Appeal: Chadwick, Sedley and Arden LJJ). *R v Secretary of State for the Home Department, Ex parte Robinson* [1998] QB 929, CA (1997 Abr para 253), applied.

317   Asylum—appeal—application to appeal out of time—removal directions—court's power to stay direction

The applicant was a Turkish Kurd whose claim for asylum was refused by the Immigration and Appeal Tribunal. His application to the new Asylum and Immigration Tribunal for permission to appeal was out of time and the tribunal informed the applicant that it had no jurisdiction to consider the application. He filed a note of appeal at the Civil Appeals Office. Removal directions had been set, and the court made an order staying the directions until after the application for an extension of time and for permission to appeal had been determined. It fell to be determined whether the court had the power to issue such a stay, and if so, by what procedural mechanism. *Held*, the Court of Appeal had an inherent jurisdiction to stay a removal direction for a claimant between the time when an out-of-time application for permission to appeal was filed at the Civil Appeals Office and the time when the application was determined. The court's assessment of the likelihood that the applications would be granted would be a very important factor in determining whether the jurisdiction was exercised. In order to grant an extension of time for two months or more, the court would have to be satisfied that a significant injustice had probably occurred. The court was not so satisfied and, accordingly, the application would be dismissed.

YD (Turkey) v Secretary of State for the Home Department [2006] EWCA Civ 52, [2006] 1 WLR 1646 (Court of Appeal: Brooke, Moore-Bick and Wilson LJJ).

318   Asylum—appeal—Asylum and Immigration Tribunal—jurisdiction

Consequent to a failed application for asylum, the claimant sought exceptional leave to remain on human rights grounds, claiming that he might face torture or inhuman or degrading treatment. His application was dismissed and he appealed citing fresh evidence in relation to his human rights claim. The immigration judge found that he had no jurisdiction to consider the human rights claim, and dismissed the appeal. On further appeal, *held*, the transitional provisions of the Asylum and Immigration (Treatment of Claimants) Act 2004 limited the Asylum and Immigration Tribunal's jurisdiction on a reconsideration. The immigration judge could only deal with those aspects of the case which had been remitted to him by the tribunal, and he could not deal with the whole claim afresh. Accordingly, the appeal would be dismissed.

Mogos v Secretary of State for the Home Department (2006) Times, 25 January (Court of Appeal: Auld, Laws and Richards LJJ).

319   Asylum—appeal—country guidance

The Home Secretary refused the claimant's asylum application on the ground that he was at risk of persecution if he returned to Eritrea as he was of draft age. His appeal to the Asylum and Immigration Tribunal against the rejection of his appeal to an adjudicator was dismissed. He appealed further. *Held*, the tribunal had previously determined in a country guidance case that not all returnees of draft age were at risk of persecution on return. As the claimant had not submitted relevant fresh evidence that the country guidance was incorrect, the tribunal had been obliged to follow that guidance. Accordingly, the appeal would be dismissed.

Ariaya v Secretary of State for the Home Department [2006] EWCA Civ 48, [2006] All ER (D) 93 (Feb) (Court of Appeal: Laws and Richards LJJ and Coleridge J). *IN (Draft Evaders: Evidence of Risk) Eritrea* [2005] UKIAT 00106 applied.

320   Asylum—appeal—decision of special adjudicator in England—availability of judicial review in Scottish courts

See *Tehrani v Secretary of State for the Home Department (Scotland)*, para 92.

321   Asylum—appeal—evidence—belief in claimant's story

The claimant, a citizen of Sierra Leone, made an asylum claim on the ground that he feared persecution by members of a society because of his partial initiation and subsequent escape. His claim was refused and his appeal dismissed as the Immigration Appeal Tribunal did not believe part of his evidence. He further appealed. *Held*, the Court of Appeal was normally precluded from interfering with conclusions based on findings of primary fact in appeals from the tribunal. However, a mistake of fact which gave rise to unfairness could be a separate challenge in appeal on a point of law. In many asylum cases a claimant's story might seem in part, or even mostly, inherently unlikely, but that did not mean it was untrue. The story as a whole and its ingredients had to be considered against the available country evidence, reliable expert evidence and other factors such as consistency with what the claimant had previously said and with any other factual evidence. While inherent probability might be helpful in domestic cases, it could be a dangerous and wholly inappropriate factor to rely on in some asylum cases. Much of the evidence would be referable to societies with customs and circumstances which were very different from those of which the members of the fact-finding tribunals had any, even second-hand experience. Taken as a whole, the reasons for which the tribunal had rejected the story simply could not stand. Accordingly, the appeal would be allowed.

HK v Secretary of State for the Home Department [2006] EWCA Civ 1037, [2006] All ER (D) 281 (Jul) (Court of Appeal: Chadwick, Jacob and Neuberger LJJ).

322   Asylum—appeal—human rights grounds—risk of persecution by border control authorities

The applicant, a Palestinian refugee, had been arrested and detained by Israeli authorities on three occasions. He claimed that he and his family had been targeted by the authorities and that they wanted him to collaborate and spy against his own people. He fled to Jordan and then to the United Kingdom where he claimed asylum. He was refused leave to enter and was informed that the Secretary of State proposed to give directions for his removal to Palestine, although no removal directions had been given. The applicant challenged the decision under the Nationality, Immigration and Asylum Act 2002 s 84(1)(g) on the grounds that his removal to Palestine would not be possible, thereby rendering him a stateless person, and that his human rights were in danger of being infringed by the actions of the Israeli authorities' border controls if such a removal was attempted. The appeal tribunal found that there was no evidence to show that the applicant would be refused entry to his former territory of residence, and that he had provided no credible evidence to support his claim that his human rights would be violated if he were returned to Palestine. The applicant appealed. *Held*, there was no difference in principle between consideration of the position within the territory and consideration of the position at the border of the territory when determining an appeal under s 84(1)(g). Where the applicant claimed to fear persecution or ill-treatment in violation of the

European Convention on Human Rights art 3 by reason of the conduct of the Israeli authorities at the occupied territories' border, there was no reason why the claim should not have been examined by the appeal tribunal in the same way as a claim of fear of persecution or ill-treatment by reason of the conduct of the authorities within that territory. Both circumstances fell within the ambit of the 2002 Act s 84(1)(g). Further, the applicant's case was that he would have been denied re-entry whatever route or method the Secretary of State might have chosen. The issue had not been dependent on some future variable or contingency. In those circumstances, the appeal tribunal had had jurisdiction to consider the applicant's claims in that respect. Furthermore, the appeal tribunal had not erred in finding that the applicant's removal to his former habitual residence would not have been impossible. It had carefully examined and considered all the evidence placed before it and had reached the conclusion that, with the correct documentation, the applicant's removal could have been effected. In those circumstances, it was a finding that the appeal tribunal had been entitled to make so that the applicant's appeal fell at the first substantive hurdle. Accordingly, the appeal would be dismissed.

AK v Secretary of State for the Home Department [2006] EWCA Civ 1117, [2006] All ER (D) 470 (Jul) (Court of Appeal: Sir Mark Potter P, Moore-Bick and Richards LJJ). *GH v Secretary of State for the Home Department* [2005] EWCA Civ 1182, [2005] All ER (D) 113 (Oct) distinguished.

323   Asylum—appeal—indefinite leave to remain as dependent relative—refusal of leave—right to family life

The claimant, a citizen of Yemen, was given six months' leave to remain in the United Kingdom. He gave false information in order to obtain a visa and subsequently applied out of time for indefinite leave to remain as a dependent relative. The claimant's two former wives, seven of his children and numerous other family members lived in the United Kingdom. The application was refused. By the time the claimant's appeal came before an adjudicator, the medical condition from which the claimant suffered had deteriorated. His doctor stated that the claimant was not mentally or physically capable of giving evidence and that he would not be able to survive without someone to care for him. The adjudicator held that there would be a violation of the European Convention on Human Rights art 8 if the claimant was returned to Yemen but that there was a good reason for the violation, namely the requirements of immigration control. However, the adjudicator decided that it would not be proportionate to return the claimant to Yemen. The appeal of the defendant, the Secretary of State, was allowed on the ground that the adjudicator's decision had been erroneous in law. The case was transferred for a new hearing on the merits. The judge agreed with the adjudicator that the only issue was proportionality but found that it was not a truly exceptional case. The claimant appealed. *Held*, the defendant had not identified any grounds to support the conclusion that the adjudicator's decision was wrong in law. Factual judgments of the kind involved in the present case were often difficult but were not made easier by excessive legal or linguistic analysis. It was the nature of such judgments that different tribunals, without illegality or irrationality, might reach different conclusions on the same case, as was illustrated by the judge's decision. The fact that one tribunal had reached what might seem an unusually generous view of the facts of a particular case did not mean that it had made an error of law, so as to justify an appeal under the old system, or an order for reconsideration under the new. Further, it did not create any precedent so as to limit the defendant's right to argue for a more restrictive approach on a similar case. However, on the facts of the particular case, the decision of the adjudicator should be respected. Accordingly, the appeal would be allowed.

Mukarkar v Secretary of State for the Home Department [2006] EWCA Civ 1045, [2006] All ER (D) 367 (Jul) (Court of Appeal: Auld, Sedley and Carnwath LJJ).

324   Asylum—appeal—permission to appeal—extension of time

The claimant's application for asylum and a subsequent appeal were turned down. A further claim to submit fresh reports was refused, and an application for judicial review of that decision was dismissed on the ground that the new evidence was not significantly different from that which had already been presented. The claimant then sought to make a fresh appeal, but owing to a series of delays the claim was brought more than six months out of time. The delays were the combined fault of the claimant's solicitors, the Legal Services Commission and the official transcribers. The claimant sought permission to appeal and an extension of time. *Held*, it was settled law that delays of more than two months in filing a notice of appeal would only be overlooked in rare and limited cases where the facts justifying such a long extension of time could be strictly proved and the Court of Appeal was satisfied that a significant injustice had probably occurred. In the circumstances, while it was quite clear that no blame for the delay could be attributed to the claimant himself, there was no trace of injustice. His claim for asylum had been rejected on the facts that were personal to his particular case, and there was no evidence that the previous decisions reached represented a significant injustice such as to justify the grant of a long extension of time for appealing. Moreover, there was no real prospect of success on the appeal. Accordingly, the application would be dismissed.

R (on the application of RG) v Secretary of State for the Home Department [2006] EWCA Civ 396, [2006] All ER (D) 141 (Apr) (Court of Appeal: Brooke and Buxton LJJ). *YD (Turkey) v Secretary of State for the Home Department* [2006] EWCA Civ 52, [2006] 1 WLR 1646 (para 317) applied.

325   Asylum—appeal—procedure—power to remit case to Asylum and Immigration Tribunal for further reasons

The claimant, a Burundi national, arrived in the United Kingdom and claimed asylum. The defendant rejected her claim and the claimant appealed to the Asylum and Immigration Tribunal, which dismissed the appeal. She applied for permission to appeal to the Court of Appeal, and an issue arose as to whether the Court of Appeal had jurisdiction, at the stage of applying for permission to appeal, to remit a case to the Asylum and Immigration Tribunal for further reasoning. *Held*, the Court of Appeal did not, at the stage of applying for permission to appeal, have jurisdiction to remit a case to the Asylum and Immigration Tribunal to supplement its reasons. Although there was such a power in employment cases, the statutory scheme regulating the Employment Appeal Tribunal was different from that regulating the Asylum and Immigration Tribunal and there was no equivalent power in respect of the latter. Judgment would be given accordingly.

Hatungimana v Secretary of State for the Home Department [2006] All ER (D) 281 (Feb) (Court of Appeal: Brooke, Jonathan Parker and Maurice Kay LJJ). *Barke v SEETEC Business Technology Centre Ltd* [2005] EWCA Civ 578, [2005] ICR 1373 distinguished.

326   Asylum—appeal—reasons for decision—adequacy of reasons

The claimant, an Afghan national, entered the United Kingdom and claimed asylum on the basis that he had a well-founded fear of persecution if he was to return to Afghanistan. He contended that his father had been a Taliban commander before the Taliban regime was overthrown, and that the bodies of his father and brother had been found in a hospital, showing signs of torture. The claimant argued that he would face the same fate if he returned to his homeland. The Secretary of State refused his claim for asylum and humanitarian protection, deciding that the claimant's argument was not credible. Appeals to an adjudicator and the Asylum and Immigration Tribunal were dismissed and, on the claimant's further appeal, he argued that the appeal tribunal had erred in law by failing to give adequate reasons for rejecting his account. *Held*, inadequate reasoning could, in some circumstances, undermine the validity of a decision. However, where reasons were given, the essential question for the court to answer was whether the decision was one to which no tribunal could sensibly have come. Since the reasons a tribunal had given might well provide a good guide to whether a decision was one to which a tribunal could properly have come, it followed that inadequate reasons could also be a guide. The ultimate question was whether a tribunal was entitled to reach its conclusion on the evidence before it. In the instant case, although the appeal tribunal's conclusion was not one all would agree with, there were no reasons justifying the conclusion that it was perverse. Accordingly, the appeal would be dismissed.

Barikzai v Secretary of State for the Home Department [2006] All ER (D) 302 (May) (Court of Appeal: Latham, Carnwath and Hughes LJJ).

327   Asylum—application—delay in processing—effect of delay—conspicuous unfairness

See *R (on the application of Rechachi) v Secretary of State for the Home Department*, para 333.

328   Asylum—application—fresh claim—approach of court

The Immigration Rules para 353 provides that a decision maker in an asylum claim must consider whether submissions made after a claim has been refused amount to a fresh claim, which requires that the submissions are significantly different from the material that has previously been considered and create a realistic prospect of success.

In two conjoined cases, the claimants unsuccessfully applied for asylum and then sought to make a fresh claim pursuant to the Immigration Rules para 353 on the ground that fresh evidence had become available. Issues arose as to the proper approach of the Secretary of State when making a decision under para 353 and the proper approach of the court when reviewing such a decision. *Held*, in assessing the reliability of fresh material, the Secretary of State could, of course, have in mind both how the fresh material related to material already found to be reliable by an adjudicator, and, where it was relevantly probative, any finding as to the honesty or reliability of the applicant that was made by the adjudicator. However, the latter might be of little relevance where the fresh material did not emanate from the applicant himself and thus could not be said to be automatically suspect because it had come from a tainted source. The considerations of the Secretary of State, the adjudicator and the court had to be informed by the anxious scrutiny of the material that was axiomatic in decisions that, if made incorrectly, might lead to the applicant's exposure to persecution. When reviewing a decision of the Secretary of State as to whether a fresh claim existed, the court had to consider whether the Secretary of State had asked himself whether there was a realistic prospect of an adjudicator, applying the rule of anxious scrutiny, concluding that the applicant would be exposed to a real risk of persecution on his return. The Secretary of State could, and no doubt logically should, treat his own views of the merits as a starting point, but only a starting point in the consideration of a question that was distinctly different from the exercise of the Secretary of State making up his own mind. The court also had to consider whether the Secretary of State, in addressing that question both in respect of the evaluation of the facts and in respect of the legal conclusions to be drawn from those facts, had satisfied the requirement of anxious scrutiny. If the answer to both questions was not in the affirmative, judicial review would have to be granted. While the decision remained that of the Secretary of State, and the test was one of irrationality, a decision would be irrational if it was not taken on the basis of anxious scrutiny. Judgment would be given accordingly.

WM (Democratic Republic of Congo) v Secretary of State for the Home Department; AR (Afghanistan) v Secretary of State for the Home Department [2006] EWCA Civ 1495, [2006] All ER (D) 109 (Nov) (Court of Appeal: Buxton, Jonathan Parker and Moore-Bick LJJ). *R v Secretary of State for the Home Department, ex p Onibiyo* [1996] QB 768, CA (1996 Abr para 276); and *Cakabay v Secretary of State for the Home Department (No 2)* [1999] Imm AR 176, CA, applied. *Razgar v Secretary of State for the Home Department* [2004] UKHL 27, [2004] 2 AC 368 (2004 Abr para 271) considered.

329   Asylum—application—grounds—Convention right—qualified right

The claimant, a Lebanese citizen, arrived in the United Kingdom with her son and claimed asylum. In divorce proceedings she had been granted custody of her son by the Lebanese court until the son was seven years old, when custody would pass to the father, in accordance with Shari'a law. Her claim was refused and she appealed on asylum grounds and that to return to Lebanon would be a breach of her right to family life guaranteed under the European Convention on Human Rights art 8. Her appeal, and reconsideration of appeal, were unsuccessful and she further appealed. *Held*, the correct test in cases where it was claimed that the conduct of the state in removing a person from its territory to another territory would lead to a violation of the person's Convention rights in that other territory was whether the right would be completely denied or nullified. In such a case the word 'flagrant', in the test of a 'flagrant denial or gross violation' of her right, was not used as a definitive test, but to illustrate the extreme circumstances which would be needed to bring the Convention into play. Custody was but one important aspect of the right to family life under art 8, and the claimant's right would not be completely denied. Accordingly, the appeal would be dismissed.

EM (Lebanon) v Secretary of State for the Home Department [2006] EWCA Civ 1531, [2006] All ER (D) 276 (Nov) (Court of Appeal: Carnwath and Gage LJJ and Bodey J). *R (on the application of Ullah) v Special Adjudicator* [2004] UKHL 26, [2004] 3 All ER 785 (2004 Abr para 262) applied.

330   Asylum—application—prior application in another member state—state responsible for deciding application

The claimant, a Somali national, arrived in Italy and claimed asylum. He then travelled to the United Kingdom illegally and claimed asylum. He informed the United Kingdom asylum authorities that he was 16 years old and that he had an adult half-sister and a full brother with refugee status in the United Kingdom. He had given a different age to the Italian authorities, and it was disputed whether they had been informed of the existence or whereabouts of his siblings. The Secretary of State made a request to the Italian authorities to take back the claimant. As the Italian authorities failed to reply to that request within two weeks, they subsequently admitted that, pursuant to EC Council Regulation 343/2003 art 20(1)(c), they were deemed to have accepted responsibility for the claimant. The claimant's application to defer his removal to Italy was refused. He applied for judicial review of that decision, arguing that, pursuant to arts 5 and 15, the issue of which member state should consider his asylum application fell to be determined in the light of the further information that had come to light and the importance attached to family unity. *Held*, the screening process under Regulation 343/2003 fell to be conducted only once, and should be undertaken by reference to the inquiry conducted by the member state with which the application for asylum was first lodged and at the time it was lodged. The objective of Regulation 343/2003 was the speedy identification of a single state with responsibility for the substantive consideration of an asylum claim. It would be inconsistent with that objective to allow an asylum-seeker who was dissatisfied with the result of the screening process conducted by one member state to move to other member states, and, by reference to the purported emergence of new facts, demand that that screening process be undertaken again. Moreover, it was also inconsistent with the provisions for taking back asylum-seekers. The importance attached to family unity was adequately protected by the provisions of art 15, and it remained open to the claimant to apply to the Italian authorities under art 15. Accordingly, the application would be dismissed.

R (on the application of A) v Secretary of State for the Home Department [2006] All ER (D) 178 (Oct) (Court of Appeal: Laws, Maurice Kay LJJ and Bodey J). *R (on the application of G) v Secretary of State for the Home Department* [2004] EWHC 2848 (Admin), [2004] All ER (D) 289 (Nov) (2004 Abr para 263) followed.

331   Asylum—asylum-seeker—detention at reception centre

See Application 13229/03 *Saadi v United Kingdom*, para 1580.

332   Asylum—asylum-seeker—offence—obtaining services by deception—availability of defence

The defendant, an Ethiopian, was travelling to the United States to seek asylum. She stopped at a United Kingdom airport, and passed through immigration using a forged passport. She was then given another forged passport and a ticket for a flight to Washington. She was arrested and charged with using a false instrument with intent, contrary to the Forgery and Counterfeiting Act 1981 s 3, and with attempting to obtain services by deception. She successfully raised the statutory defence available to refugees under the Immigration and Asylum Act 1999 s 31 to the charge under the 1981 Act, but, as no such defence applied to the deception charge, she was convicted of that offence. She was sentenced to nine months' imprisonment, and she appealed, arguing that her prosecution on the deception charge amounted to an abuse of process. The prosecution accepted that the defendant should have been entitled to a defence to the deception charge under the Refugee Convention art 31, but that the failure of Parliament to enact such a defence in the 1999 Act meant the law was simply being enforced as it stood. *Held*, it was not possible to reach any firm conclusion as to why, in cases such as the instant case, the prosecution combined the two counts. However, irrespective of whether there was merit in the defendant's argument that there had been an abuse of process, the fair course was to order that the defendant should be absolutely discharged pursuant to the Powers of Criminal Courts (Sentencing) Act 2000 s 12. That would mean, by virtue of s 14, that she would not in the future be deemed to have had a conviction for any purpose. When sentencing the defendant, the judge should have had regard to the circumstances and consequences of the dishonesty. There was no suggestion that the defendant's ticket was not properly purchased, nor any evidence that, had she been carried to Washington, the airline would in fact have been exposed to the risk of any penalty. The judge's reasoning for imposing the custodial sentence was not merely inappropriate in the light of the offence for which the defendant fell to be sentenced, but was at odds with the principle reflected by the Convention art 31 and the 1999 Act s 31, assuming that each had the ambit which the prosecution had accepted. Judgment would be given accordingly.

R v Asfaw [2006] All ER (D) 311 (Mar) (Court of Appeal: Lord Phillips of Worth Matravers CJ, McCombe and Gross JJ). *R v Uxbridge Magistrates' Court, ex p Adimi* [2001] QB 667, DC (1999 Abr para 304); and *R (on the application of Pepushi) v Crown Prosecution Service* [2004] EWHC 798 (Admin), [2004] All ER (D) 129 (May), DC (2004 Abr para 299), considered.

333   Asylum—asylum-seeker—period of leave to remain—revised policy—fairness

At the time of the claimants' applications for asylum in the United Kingdom, the Secretary of State's policy in relation to individuals whose asylum applications succeeded was to grant indefinite leave to remain. Shortly afterwards, the Home Office published an intention to revise the policy, with the result that leave to remain would be granted for an initial period of five years, after which the situation in an applicant's country of origin would be reassessed with a view to returning the applicant if appropriate. The revised policy became operative approximately six months later, by which time the claimants had successfully claimed asylum. However, the status papers of the first and second claimants were not processed until after the introduction of the revised policy, and the decisions to grant asylum to the third and fourth claimants were only confirmed after the date of policy implementation, following a challenge from the Secretary of State. The status of all four claimants, therefore, was determined under the revised procedure, and all were granted leave to remain in the United Kingdom for five years. The claimants sought judicial review of the decisions, claiming that the delays in processing their status had been unreasonable so as to have caused conspicuous unfairness, and that the implementation of the new policy had been unlawful on account of a failure to provide for transitional arrangements in respect of individuals whose determination had been pending at the date of implementation. *Held*, in determining whether a delay had been unreasonable so as to cause conspicuous unfairness, the consequences of the delay fell to be assessed in making the determination. While the claimants' applications had been subject to delays, those delays had not been unreasonable. The claimants' status as refugees had been afforded the necessary protection demanded by the terms of the Geneva Convention Relating to the Status of Refugees 1951 and, therefore, there had been no conspicuous unfairness. The question of whether the implementation of the revised policy should have contained transitional arrangements for individuals in the situation in which the claimants found themselves had been a question of policy for the Secretary of State, who had concluded that no such arrangements were required. Provision had been made for exceptional cases, but the claimants' situations had not brought them within the scope of that provision. The change in policy had been lawful and, accordingly, the applications would be dismissed.

R (on the application of Rechachi) v Secretary of State for the Home Department [2006] All ER (D) 341 (Dec) (Queen's Bench Division: Davis J). *R (on the application of Mambakasa) v Secretary of State for the Home Department* [2003] EWHC 319 (Admin), [2003] All ER (D) 04 (Mar) considered.

334   Asylum—asylum-seeker—provision of accommodation—refusal by local authority

The claimant was a Ugandan national who entered the United Kingdom at the age of 15 using a false passport. He was referred to a local authority by the refugee council as a child in need, and was treated by the authority as a child who was to be accommodated under the Children Act 1989 s 20. He made an unsuccessful claim for asylum, and his appeal against that decision was dismissed by the Immigration Appeal Tribunal. After he had reached the age of 18, the claimant made a further application for leave, alleging that, if he were to be removed, it would lead to such a deterioration in his health as to amount to a breach of his rights under the European Convention on Human Rights art 8. He was subsequently admitted to hospital, suffering from paranoid delusions, and was discharged after a week with a supply of medication to last him for two weeks. There was also medical evidence that the claimant was suffering from high blood pressure. Pursuant to the Nationality, Immigration and Asylum Act 2002 Sch 3 para 1, the authority decided to withdraw its continuing support for the claimant, on the basis that it would not be a breach of the Convention art 8 to compel the claimant to return to Uganda. The claimant applied for judicial review of the authority's decision. *Held*, where a claimant had an outstanding application with the Home Office that a return to his country of origin would violate his art 8 rights, the local authority, in considering whether to cease providing support under the 2002 Act, should do no more than to ask itself whether that application was manifestly unfounded. The expertise and responsibility for making difficult judgments as to whether to grant leave to enter or remain lay with the Home Office (and the Asylum and Immigration Tribunal on appeal), and it was only in the clearest cases that local authorities should make their decisions on the predicate that the application in question would be dismissed by the immigration authorities. In the instant case, the local authority had effectively been asking itself the same question as the Secretary of State would ask when deciding whether the claimant should be allowed to remain in the United Kingdom so as to avoid a breach of his rights under the Convention art 8. It was quite clear that it had not asked the very different question of whether the claimant's art 8 application was manifestly unfounded. It could not be said that the outcome of a reconsideration by the local authority would inevitably be a decision that the application was manifestly unfounded. Accordingly, the application would be allowed.

R (on the application of B) v Southwark LBC [2006] EWHC 2254 (Admin), [2006] All ER (D) 83 (Sep) (Queen's Bench Division: Andrew Nicol QC). *R (on the application of AW) v Croydon LBC; R (on the application of A, D and Y) v Hackney LBC* [2005] EWHC 2950 (Admin), [2005] All ER (D) 251 (Dec) (2005 Abr para 313) applied. *R v Wandsworth LBC, ex p O; R v Leicester City Council, ex p Bhikha* [2000] 4 All ER 590, CA (2000 Abr para 1711); and *R (on the application of Kimani) v Lambeth LBC* [2003] EWCA Civ 1150, [2004] 1 WLR 272 (2003 Abr para 263) considered.

335 Asylum—asylum-seeker—viable route of return—withdrawal of accommodation support

The claimant, a citizen of Iraq, arrived in the United Kingdom but was unsuccessful in claiming asylum. He applied to the Secretary of State for accommodation support. This was authorised on the ground that the claimant was destitute and there was no viable route of return to Iraq available, pursuant to the Immigration and Asylum (Provision of Accommodation to Failed Asylum-Seekers) Regulations 2005, SI 2005/930, reg 3. Subsequently, the Secretary of State contacted the claimant and told him that in his opinion there was now a viable route of return to Iraq and that accommodation support would be withdrawn unless the claimant made representations that any of the other conditions in reg 3(2) existed so as to require continuing support. In the absence of any representations, the Secretary of State informed the claimant that support would cease. The claimant sought judicial review of the dismissal of his appeal by an asylum support adjudicator and of the decision of the Secretary of State to cease support. Issues arose as to the jurisdiction of the adjudicator over the question as to whether a failed asylum-seeker had a viable route of return from the United Kingdom under reg 3(2)(c), and whether the Secretary of State had acted unlawfully in refusing to continue to provide accommodation support. *Held*, the adjudicator's jurisdiction was limited to whether the Secretary of State's opinion was truly held rather than whether there was a viable route of return. On the statutory construction of reg 3(2)(c), the Secretary of State's opinion was formed as a matter of policy to be applied to whether there was a viable route of return to a country generally rather than in respect of an individual case. It followed that the claim had fundamentally misconceived the nature of the decision-making process provided by the 2005 Regulations. The Secretary of State had not acted unlawfully in refusing to continue to provide accommodation support to the claimant. Accordingly, the application would be dismissed.

R (on the application of Rasul) v Asylum Support Adjudicator [2006] All ER (D) 364 (Feb) (Queen's Bench Division: Wilkie J).

336 Asylum—asylum support—appeal—jurisdiction of asylum support adjudicator—failed asylum-seeker

The Immigration and Asylum Act 1999 s 103 provides that, if, on an application for support under s 95, the Secretary of State decides that the applicant does not qualify for support, the applicant may appeal to an adjudicator.

The interested party's application for asylum support pursuant to the 1999 Act s 95 was refused by the Secretary of State on the basis that she was no longer an asylum-seeker. She appealed to the defendant, the Chief Asylum Support Adjudicator, but before the appeal was determined the

Secretary of State wrote to the defendant asserting that s 103 was not applicable so that the defendant had no jurisdiction to hear the appeal. The defendant disagreed with that view, and went on to hear the appeal, which was dismissed. The Secretary of State applied for judicial review of the decision to hear the appeal, submitting that the defendant did not have jurisdiction to hear the appeal as the interested party was not entitled to receive support under s 95, as she was a failed asylum-seeker. *Held*, an adjudicator would have jurisdiction to entertain an appeal under s 103, which related to the existence or otherwise of the factual circumstances permitting the grant of support under s 95, irrespective of the fact that the Secretary of State had deemed the applicant a failed asylum-seeker. Section 103 provided an applicant with a general right of appeal against a Secretary of State's decision which refused support under s 95. To hold otherwise would equate to a rewriting of the statute, which was an illegitimate exercise. It was plain that s 95 described the class of persons to whom the Secretary of State could offer support, and the purpose of s 103 was to enable the adjudication of disputes on those support applications. Section 103 was not limited to asylum-seekers, but extended to persons who had previously applied for s 95 support and failed. It followed that the Secretary of State had misunderstood the nature of the asylum support and appeals process. Accordingly, the application would be dismissed.

R (on the application of the Secretary of State for the Home Department) v Chief Asylum Support Adjudicator [2006] All ER (D) 414 (Nov) (Queen's Bench Division: Judge Gilbart QC).

337   Asylum—asylum support—entitlement to benefits—asylum-seeker—medical condition preventing departure from United Kingdom

Three failed asylum-seekers who were destitute and suffering from tuberculosis applied to the claimant Secretary of State for support and accommodation, pursuant to the Immigration and Asylum Act 1999 s 4. The claimant refused their applications and they appealed. Adjudicators allowed the asylum-seekers' appeals on the ground that, as a result of their medical condition, each person was unable to leave the United Kingdom and therefore satisfied the conditions for support contained in the Immigration and Asylum (Provision of Accommodation to Failed Asylum-Seekers) Regulations 2005, SI 2005/2044, reg 3(2). The claimant applied for judicial review of those decisions. *Held*, the proper approach to be adopted by decision makers when applying reg 3(2) was to take a careful and deliberate two-step approach. The first question was to ask whether an applicant was unable to leave the United Kingdom. If the answer to that was in the affirmative, then the decision maker should go on to ask whether that inability was by reason of a physical impediment to travel or for some other medical reason. In the circumstances, the adjudicators had fallen into error by failing to adopt that approach to the application of the condition. Accordingly, the application would be allowed.

R (on the application of the Secretary of State for the Home Department) v Asylum Support Adjudicator [2006] All ER (D) 237 (May) (Queen's Bench Division: Holman J).

338   Asylum—asylum support—payments

The Asylum Support (Amendment) Regulations 2006, SI 2006/733 (in force on 10 April 2006), further amend the 2000 Regulations, SI 2000/704, by increasing the cash amounts payable, as a general rule, in respect of a person's essential living needs. SI 2005/738 is revoked.

339   Asylum—decision of adjudicator—implementation—delay by Secretary of State for the Home Department

See *S v Secretary of State for the Home Department*, para 346.

340   Asylum—fear of persecution—membership of particular social group

Two appeals were heard together which each concerned whether an asylum-seeker belonged to a particular social group within the meaning of the Refugee Convention art 1A(2). In the first case, the appellant left Iran after a protracted period of harassment from the authorities which included her husband being detained in prison without charge, herself being insulted and raped, and her and husband's house being searched. She claimed asylum in the United Kingdom, but the court rejected her contention that she had a well-founded fear of persecution for reasons of her membership of a particular social group, the group in question being her husband's family. The appellant in the second case was a 15-year-old citizen of Sierra Leone who claimed asylum in the United Kingdom on the ground that she would be at risk of subjection to female genital mutilation if she was returned to her home country. The court decided that young, single women in Sierra Leone did not constitute a particular social group meriting protection under the Refugee Convention, because female genital mutilation was not, in the circumstances in which it was practised in Sierra Leone, discriminatory in such a way as to set those who underwent it apart from society. On the appeal of the appellants in both cases, *held*, it was common ground that a family might be a particular social group for purposes of art 1A(2), and it was certainly open to the adjudicator in the first case to regard the appellant as having a well-founded fear of persecution for reasons of her membership of her husband's family. There was no basis for an appellate court to second-guess the adjudicator on that matter. In terms of the second case, it was clear that women in Sierra Leone were a group of persons sharing the common characteristic of being perceived by society as inferior, a position that would not change unless there was a significant alteration in social mores. That was true of all women, those who accepted or willingly embraced their inferior position and those who did not. To define the group in that way was not to define it by reference to the persecution complained of: it was a characteristic which would exist even if female genital mutilation were not practised, although such a practice was an extreme and very cruel expression of male dominance. The fact that it was carried out by women was irrelevant. Accordingly, the appeals in both cases would be allowed.

K v Secretary of State for the Home Department; Fornah v Secretary of State for the Home Department [2006] UKHL 46, [2006] 1 All ER 671 (House of Lords: Lords Bingham of Cornhill, Hope of Craighead and Rodger of Earlsferry, Baroness Hale of Richmond and Lord Brown of Eaton-under-Heywood). *R v Immigration Appeal Tribunal ex p Shah* [1999] 2 AC 629, HL (1999 Abr para 305), applied. Decisions of Court of Appeal at [2004] EWCA Civ 986, [2004] All ER (D) 516 (Jul) and at [2005] EWCA Civ 680, [2005] 1 WLR 3773 (2005 Abr para 321) reversed.

341 Asylum—fear of persecution—persecution by state authority

In four conjoined appeals, asylum-seekers had been refused entry to the United Kingdom on the ground that they could reasonably be expected to relocate internally in their home countries. On their respective appeals, an issue arose as to whether, in judging reasonableness and undue harshness in that context, account should be taken of any disparity between the civil, political and socio-economic human rights which the claimant would enjoy under the leading international human rights conventions and covenants and those which he would enjoy at the place of relocation. In three of the appeals, the question also arose as to the approach to be followed where the persecution suffered or to be suffered was or would be sanctioned or connived at by the authorities of the country of the claimants' nationality. *Held*, when considering an application for asylum based on the Refugee Convention rather than the European Convention on Human Rights, the consequences to the asylum-seeker of settling in the place of relocation in comparison to his previous home was the matter that was relevant to the question of whether internal relocation was reasonable, and not the comparison between his situation in the United Kingdom and the place of relocation. There was no absolute rule that internal relocation was never an available option where persecution was by the authorities of the country of nationality. The decision-maker, taking account of all relevant circumstances pertaining to the claimant and his country of origin, had to decide whether it was reasonable to expect the claimant to relocate or whether that would be unduly harsh. The source of the persecution giving rise to the claimant's well-founded fear in his place of ordinary domicile might be agents of the state authorised or directed by the state to persecute; or they might be agents of the state whose persecution was connived at or tolerated by the state, or not restrained by the state; or the persecution might be by those who were not agents of the state, but whom the state did not or could not control. The more closely the persecution in question was linked to the state, and the greater the control of the state over those acting or purporting to act on its behalf, the more likely, other things being equal, that a victim of persecution in one place would be similarly vulnerable in another place within the state. Judgment would be given accordingly.

Januzi v Secretary of State for the Home Department; Hamid v Secretary of State for the Home Department; Gaafar v Secretary of State for the Home Department [2006] UKHL 5, [2006] 2 AC 426 (House of Lords: Lords Bingham of Cornhill, Nicholls of Birkenhead, Hope of Craighead, Carswell and Mance).

342 Asylum—fear of persecution—person of draft age

See *Ariaya v Secretary of State for the Home Department*, para 319.

343 Asylum—fear of persecution—risk of persecution on deportation, but not on voluntary return

It has been held that a person who can return to his country voluntarily without being put at risk of persecution there is not a refugee, notwithstanding that he will be at risk if he is deported.

AA v Secretary of State for the Home Department; LK v Secretary of State for the Home Department [2006] EWCA Civ 401, [2006] All ER (D) 176 (Apr) (Court of Appeal: Brooke and Laws LJJ and Sir Christopher Staughton).

344 Asylum—former asylum-seeker—provision of accommodation

See *Ozbek v Ipswich BC*, para 1482.

345 Asylum—international protection—refugee or person in need

The Refugee or Person in Need of International Protection (Qualification) Regulations 2006, SI 2006/2525 (in force on 9 October 2006), implement, in part, EC Council Directive 2004/83 on minimum standards for the qualification and status of third country nationals or stateless persons as refugees or as persons who otherwise need international protection. The regulations apply to any person who is not a British citizen who makes an application for asylum on or after 9 October 2006, and to any application for asylum and any relevant immigration appeal which has not been decided.

In deciding whether a person is a refugee or person eligible for humanitarian protection the actors that can commit persecution or serious harm include (1) the state; (2) any party or organisation controlling the state or a substantial part of the state; (3) any non-state actor if the state, a party controlling the state or a substantial part of it, or any international organisation, is unable or unwilling to provide protection against persecution or serious harm. In deciding whether a person is a refugee or person eligible for humanitarian protection, protection from persecution or serious harm can be provided by the state or any person or organisation, including any international organisation, controlling the state or a substantial part of the state's territory. The regulations also prescribe which acts constitute persecution and the forms that persecution can take, and provide that, in determining whether a person is a refugee, certain factors must be taken into consideration when looking at the reasons for persecution in the Geneva Convention.

346   Asylum—refusal—discretionary leave policy—validity

The Immigration Act 1971 Sch 2 para 2(3) provides that a person, on being examined by an immigration officer, may be required in writing by him to submit to further examination. A person who may be required to submit to examination under Sch 2 para 2 may be detained under the authority of an immigration officer pending the person's examination and pending a decision to give or refuse him leave to enter: Sch 2 para 16(1). A person liable to detention under Sch 2 para 16 may be temporarily admitted to the United Kingdom: Sch 2 para 21.

The claimant arrived in the United Kingdom on an aircraft which he and others had hijacked in Afghanistan. His conviction for hijacking was subsequently quashed. The defendant Secretary of State refused the claimant leave to enter the United Kingdom on either asylum or human rights grounds. The claimant's appeal to an immigration panel was allowed on the grounds that to return him to Afghanistan would expose him to a real risk of harm, contrary to the European Convention on Human Rights art 3. Pursuant to the asylum policy instruction on discretionary leave in force at the time, a person whose removal, notwithstanding his actions, would breach the Convention, and who did not qualify for any other form of leave to enter the United Kingdom, would normally be granted six months' discretionary leave. However, nothing was heard from the defendant for over a year and the claimant sought judicial review of the defendant's decision refusing him leave to enter. The defendant subsequently refused to grant discretionary leave by reference to an amended policy whereby a discretion was reserved to the Secretary of State to refuse to grant such leave, in which case the individual would be kept or placed on temporary admission or temporary release. Having regard to the 1971 Act, the judge ruled that the status of 'temporary admission or temporary release' had no parliamentary sanction in the present context. The application for judicial review was allowed and the defendant appealed. He argued that the claimant came within the concept of 'temporary admission' pursuant to Sch 2 paras 16(1) and 21 as a person who might be required to submit to further examination for the purposes of Sch 2 para 2(3). *Held*, it was not open to the defendant to determine, without obtaining the necessary authority from Parliament, that someone in the position of the claimant could be kept or placed on temporary admission. It was beyond the powers of the defendant to introduce a new category of 'persons temporarily admitted' of his own motion without parliamentary sanction. Parliament had created that status for those persons identified in Sch 2 para 21(1), which did not include a person in the position of the claimant. A person would not be a person who might be required to submit to further examination within the meaning of Sch 2 para 2(3) unless and until a notice in writing was given to him so to submit. That might occur, for instance, if there was some change in circumstances into which it was considered expedient to conduct a further examination. It would be very far-fetched, however, to regard everyone who had an entitlement to discretionary leave as being a person who might be required to submit to further examination, even when no change of circumstances was in question. Such a person could hardly be detained pending his examination when no examination was in prospect. Accordingly, the appeal would be dismissed.

S v Secretary of State for the Home Department (sub nom R (on the application of GG) v Secretary of State for the Home Department) [2006] EWCA Civ 1157, [2006] All ER (D) 30 (Aug) (Court of Appeal, Civil Division: Sir Anthony Clarke MR, Brooke and Neuberger LJJ). *R (on the application of Gillan) v Metropolitan Police Comr* [2004] EWCA Civ 1067, [2005] 1 All ER 970 (2004 Abr para 827) (affirmed on appeal [2006] UKHL 12, [2006] 2 AC 307 (para 892)) considered. *R (on the application of Khadir) v Secretary of State for the Home Department* [2005] UKHL 39, [2005] 4 All ER 114 (2005 Abr para 308) distinguished. Decision of Sullivan J [2006] EWHC 1111 (Admin), [2006] All ER (D) 143 (May) affirmed.

347   Asylum—removal directions—delay—right to family life

See *R (on the application of AA) (Afghanistan) v Secretary of State for the Home Department*, para 1600.

348   Asylum—unfounded claim—designated states

The Asylum (Designated States) (Amendment) Order 2006, SI 2006/3215 (in force on 1 January 2007), amends the Nationality, Immigration and Asylum Act 2002, so as to remove Bulgaria and Romania from the list of states in s 94(4).

The Asylum (Designated States) (Amendment) (No 2) Order 2006, SI 2006/3275 (in force on 13 December 2006), amends the 2002 Act supra, so as to remove Sri Lanka from the list of states in s 94(4).

349   Asylum and Immigration (Treatment of Claimants, etc) Act 2004—commencement

The Asylum and Immigration (Treatment of Claimants, etc) Act 2004 (Commencement No 6) Order 2006, SI 2006/1517, brings s 13 into force on 29 June 2006. For a summary of the Act, see 2004 Abr para 284. See also the commencement table in the title STATUTES.

350   Asylum and Immigration Tribunal—procedure

The Asylum and Immigration Tribunal (Procedure) (Amendment) Rules 2006, SI 2006/2788 (in force in part on 13 November 2006 and in part on the day on which the Immigration, Asylum and Nationality Act 2006 s 8 comes into force), further amend the 2005 Rules, SI 2005/230, so as to (1) revise the requirement that an appeal must be in the appropriate prescribed form, providing instead that the appeal must be made in a form approved by the President of the Tribunal; (2) require the Tribunal to provide reasons for a decision in relation to a late notice of appeal; (3) provide for an appeal to be treated as withdrawn, or for the Tribunal to direct that the personal representative of the appellant may continue the proceedings in place of the appellant, if an appellant dies before his appeal has been considered by the Tribunal; (4) revise the provision on abandonment of appeals, providing a procedure for appellants to notify the Tribunal that they wish their appeal to continue in circumstances in which it would otherwise be abandoned; (5) extend the time limits within which the Tribunal must fix a date for a hearing, or determine an appeal without a hearing, from 28 days to 35 days; and (6) make provision for (a) a notice of appeal, which is signed by a representative, to be deemed to constitute notification to the Tribunal and the other party that the representative is acting for a party; and (b) the President of the Tribunal to review and set aside orders, notices of decision and determinations in circumstances where they are wrongly made as a result of administration errors at the Tribunal.

The Asylum and Immigration Tribunal (Fast Track Procedure) (Amendment) Rules 2006, SI 2006/2789 (in force on 13 November 2006), amend the 2005 Rules, SI 2005/560, so as to bring the rules into line with the Asylum and Immigration Tribunal (Procedure) Rules 2005, SI 2005/230.

The Asylum and Immigration Tribunal (Fast Track Procedure) (Amendment No 2) Rules 2006, SI 2006/2898 (in force on 27 November 2006), amend SI 2006/2789 supra in consequence of a defect.

351   Asylum and Immigration Tribunal—reconsideration—scope of reconsideration on ground of error of law—guidance

The Asylum and Immigration Tribunal (Procedure) Rules 2005, SI 2005/230, r 32(2) provides that if a party wishes to ask the Asylum and Immigration Tribunal to consider evidence which was not submitted on any previous occasion when the appeal was considered, he must file with the Tribunal and serve on the other party written notice to that effect, which must indicate the nature of the evidence and explain why it was not submitted on any previous occasion.

A number of appeals were heard together in order for the Court of Appeal to give guidance on the scope of reconsideration by the Asylum and Immigration Tribunal, on the ground of an error of law, of a decision of an immigration judge, and the procedures that should be adopted by the tribunal in dealing with the reconsideration. *Held*, in relation to the identification of any error or errors of law, that should normally be restricted to those grounds on which the immigration judge ordered reconsideration, and any point which properly fell within the category of an obvious or manifest point of Convention jurisprudence. Although nothing in either the Asylum and Immigration (Treatment of Claimants, etc) Act 2004 or the 2005 Rules expressly precluded an applicant from raising points of law in respect of which he had not been successful at the application stage itself, it should be very much the exception that a tribunal would permit other grounds to be argued. Where a body was asked to reconsider a decision on the ground of any identified error of law, any factual findings and conclusions or judgments arising from those findings which were unaffected by the error of law need not be revisited. Other than in the most exceptional cases, any such challenge would only be on the basis of new evidence or new material as to which the usual principles as to the reception of such evidence would apply, as envisaged in r 32(2). In a straightforward case, identification of the error of law should enable the tribunal to resolve the substance of the reconsideration without the need for any evidence or new material, and without the need for any adjournment. However, in other cases that might be wholly inappropriate because it failed to give either party a fair opportunity to deal with the substance of the reconsideration. When considering the application for reconsideration, the immigration judge could give directions for the reconsideration as to how the reconsideration should be dealt with in the event that the tribunal agreed with him as to the error of law which he had identified, even though the tribunal was not bound to follow those directions. If a party had not filed a notice under r 32(2), the tribunal was entitled to assume that there was no further evidence or material it wished to put before the tribunal for the purposes of the reconsideration. If the party other than the one whose application the reconsideration had been ordered failed to file a reply, the tribunal was entitled to assume that he did not wish to rely on any arguments or material other than those on which the original decision had been based. If the tribunal considered that it was necessary to determine the first stage separately, and then adjourn the second stage, it was imperative that the written reasons for its finding should be to enable the parties to understand how the tribunal's conclusion would impact on the scope of the second stage of the reconsideration.

DK (*Serbia*) *v Secretary of State for the Home Department* [2006] EWCA Civ 1747, [2006] All ER (D) 312 (Dec) (Court of Appeal: Latham, Longmore, and Moore-Bick LJJ).

352   British nationality—citizenship by descent—parent in designated service overseas

The British Citizenship (Designated Service) Order 2006, SI 2006/1390 (in force on 16 June 2006), replaces the 1982 Order, SI 1982/1004, and designates various types of service for the purpose of the British Nationality Act 1981 s 2 which provides for the acquisition of British citizenship by persons born outside the United Kingdom by a person whose father or mother is serving in designated service.

353   British nationality—paternity—proof of paternity

The British Nationality (Proof of Paternity) Regulations 2006, SI 2006/1496 (in force on 1 July 2006), prescribe requirements as to proof of paternity for the purposes of the British Nationality Act 1981 s 50(9A), that the person must either be named on a birth certificate issued within one year of the birth of the child or satisfy the Secretary of State that he is the father of the child. The regulations also provide that in determining whether a person is the father of a child, the Secretary of State may have regard to any relevant evidence, including, but not limited to DNA test reports and court orders.

354   Identity Cards Act 2006

See para 619.

355   Immigration—accession states—entitlement to work and reside—Bulgaria and Romania

The Accession (Immigration and Worker Authorisation) Regulations 2006, SI 2006/3317 (in force on 1 January 2007), make provision in relation to the entitlement of nationals of Bulgaria and Romania to reside and work in the United Kingdom on the accession of those states to the European Union by (1) defining 'accession state national subject to worker authorisation,' with the effect that Bulgarian and Romanian nationals who are accession state nationals subject to authorisation will require authorisation during the accession period to be able to work in the United Kingdom; (2) derogating during the accession period from the free movement of worker provisions of European Community law as provided by the Accession Treaty for Bulgaria and Romania; (3) providing (a) that Bulgarian and Romanian workers who are subject to the worker authorisation scheme will only have a right to reside in the United Kingdom by virtue of their worker status while they are working in accordance with that scheme, a work seeker or ex-worker status being insufficient to confer this right; (b) for the issuing of European Community residence documents to Bulgarian and Romanian nationals and their family members; and (c) that an accession state national subject to worker authorisation is only authorised to work in the United Kingdom if he holds an accession worker authorisation document to work in the United Kingdom, leave granted under the Immigration Act 1971 before accession or a seasonal agricultural worker card also counting as such a document, and is working in accordance with the conditions set out in the document; (4) setting out the procedure for the issuing of an accession worker card, which will only be issued in relation to the authorised categories of employment, covering the categories of employment in relation to which leave to enter or remain is issued under the 1971 Act, or to an authorised family member, defined as a person who will be authorised to work on the basis that a member of his family has already been authorised to work in the United Kingdom, or he has a right to reside as a self-employed or self-sufficient person or as a student; (5) making it an offence for (a) an employer to employ an accession state national subject to worker authorisation in breach of the worker authorisation scheme; (b) an accession state national subject to worker authorisation to work in breach of the scheme; and (c) a person to obtain, or seek to obtain, an accession worker card by deception; and (6) providing for (a) the issuing of penalty notices offering the opportunity for a person to discharge his liability to conviction by paying a penalty; and (b) enforcement powers of search, entry and arrest.

356   Immigration—appeal—Asylum and Immigration Tribunal—issue estoppel—applicability

The claimant and his daughter, who were Columbian nationals, arrived in the United Kingdom and claimed asylum, alleging that they had received death threats from a Columbian guerrilla organisation. The Secretary of State refused the applications. At a hearing before a special adjudicator, the decision in respect of the claimant's daughter was overturned. The claimant's own appeal subsequently came before the Asylum and Immigration Tribunal. The Secretary of State sought to undermine the claimant's credibility by adducing a copy of a record of an interview with him demonstrating material inconsistencies with the account he had later given in support of his daughter's successful appeal. The Secretary of State maintained that it was new and compelling evidence that could not have been placed before the adjudicator in the daughter's appeal, since asylum applications were made in confidence and the interviews conducted with applicants were confidential to that application. The tribunal took the view that it was entitled to consider the new evidence, and decided that the claimant and his daughter were not credible witnesses so that the claimant's appeal would be dismissed. The claimant appealed, submitting that the principles of res judicata and issue estoppel applied to the daughter's refugee status as a result of the adjudicator's acceptance of her evidence, and that the adjudicator's decision was, unless impeached in an appropriate court and not obtained by fraud or collusion, conclusive evidence on the matters actually decided. *Held*, it was doubtful whether the principles of res judicata or issue estoppel had any application to appeals before immigration tribunals, any more than they did to successive claims for judicial review, while allowing for the possibility of abuse of process as a means of preventing a matter being raised. The guidelines applicable to second appeals concerning the same claimant, raising the same or similar issues, were relevant to cases where the parties involved were not the same but where there was a material overlap of evidence. Clearly, the guidance might need adaptation according to the nature of the new evidence, the circumstances in which it had been given or not given in the earlier proceedings and its materiality to securing a just outcome in the second appeal, along with consistency in the maintenance of firm immigration control. The admission of new evidence might, as a matter of fairness, operate for, as well as against, a claimant for asylum. As a matter of common sense and fairness, the tribunal had rightly taken into account the material inconsistencies in the claimant's two accounts, the second of which had not been before the adjudicator in his daughter's appeal and which logically affected the outcome of his appeal. Reliance by the Secretary of State on the new evidence had not been a collateral attack on her refugee status or an abuse of process. Accordingly, the appeal would be dismissed.

Ocampo v Secretary of State for the Home Department [2006] EWCA Civ 1276, [2006] All ER (D) 59 (Oct) (Court of Appeal: Auld, Rix and Hooper LJJ).

357   Immigration—appeal—Asylum and Immigration Tribunal—procedure—guidance

The Court of Appeal has given the following guidance as to the approach to be adopted by the Asylum and Immigration Tribunal on reconsideration of an appeal when it has concluded that there is an error of law in the original decision which vitiates all findings of fact made by the immigration judge. The judge should normally receive the original decision where the Tribunal has transferred proceedings to him for reconsideration of an appeal. Issues in the original decision may assist the judge, even if the findings of fact are invalidated for a reason of law, but he must be careful not to be influenced by the discredited findings. There may arise on rare occasions special circumstances where the interests of justice require that proceedings be transferred to a judge who is not aware of the terms of the original decision. In such a case, the panel of the Tribunal which identified the error of law may direct that the proceedings be transferred to a judge who is not provided with the original decision. In the absence of such an order, the parties should proceed on the premise that the judge to whom the matter is transferred will have received the original decision. An application to him not to read it must be made promptly after the transfer is ordered and must give proper grounds.

Swash v Secretary of State for the Home Department [2006] EWCA Civ 1093, (2006) Times, 14 August (Court of Appeal: Lord Phillips of Worth Matravers CJ, Buxton and Sedley LJJ).

358   Immigration—control zones—extension to France

The Nationality, Immigration and Asylum Act 2002 (Juxtaposed Controls) (Amendment) Order 2006, SI 2006/2908 (in force on 18 November 2006), amends the 2003 Order, SI 2003/2812, so as to give effect to two provisions of English law in control zones in France. The order extends, to control zones (1) the power to take and destroy fingerprints under the Immigration and Asylum Act 1999; and (2) the provisions under the Immigration, Asylum and Nationality Act 2006, which allows the Secretary of State to authorise persons other than immigration officers to search a ship, aircraft or vehicle or other thing for the purpose of satisfying himself whether there are individuals whom an immigration officer might wish to examine for the purposes of considering whether the person should enter the United Kingdom. The order also makes consequential amendments.

359   Immigration—deportation—asylum or human rights claim—list of safe countries

The Asylum (First List of Safe Countries) (Amendment) Order 2006, SI 2006/3393 (in force on 1 January 2007), adds Bulgaria and Romania to the list of countries in the Asylum and Immigration (Treatment of Claimants, etc) Act 2004 Sch 3 Pt 2 which are to be treated as safe for the purpose of determining whether a third country national, who has made an asylum or human rights claim in the United Kingdom, may be removed to one of them.

360   Immigration—deportation—obstacles in relocating to home country—British citizenship of claimant's child

The claimant, a Vietnamese national, was granted entry to the United Kingdom as a student. She subsequently gave birth to a son, the father of whom was a United Kingdom resident. The child was registered as a British citizen. The claimant applied for asylum, which was refused. The claimant appealed to an adjudicator against the Secretary of State's decision to remove her from the United Kingdom. The adjudicator allowed the appeal, finding that it was disproportionate for the claimant to be removed and that any such removal would therefore breach the European Convention on Human Rights art 8. The Secretary of State's appeal to the Asylum and Immigration Tribunal was allowed on the ground that the adjudicator had erred in law. The claimant appealed. *Held*, the tribunal had been entitled to find an error of law by the adjudicator. The adjudicator had clearly followed an approach that had been rejected in established authority. It was not possible to extrapolate a finding of disproportionality on the test of exceptionality within the meaning of that authority. The test needed to be confronted squarely and a reference to reasonable responses and disproportionality could not amount to a finding that the test had been applied. The present case was not one in which it could be said that the circumstances were truly exceptional. However, the tribunal had not properly confronted the obstacles that the claimant and child might face in relocating to Vietnam, exacerbated by the fact that the child was a British citizen. Further, the fact that the child was a British citizen ought to have been taken into account. Therefore, the matter would be remitted to the tribunal. Accordingly, the appeal would be allowed.

Nguyen v Secretary of State for the Home Department [2006] All ER (D) 380 (Mar) (Court of Appeal: Pill, Scott Baker and Neuberger LJJ).

361   Immigration—deportation order—recommendation by court—duty to consider human rights

See *R v Carmona*, para 2545.

362   Immigration—designation of travel bans

The Immigration (Designation of Travel Bans) (Amendment) Order 2006, SI 2006/3277 (in force on 13 December 2006), further amends the 2000 Order, SI 2000/2724, by substituting a new Schedule of designated instruments. Any person named by or under a designated instrument will be excluded from the United Kingdom subject to certain exception under the Immigration Act 1971 s 8B(1)–(3). SI 2005/3310 is revoked.

363   Immigration—European Economic Area

The Immigration (European Economic Area) Regulations 2006, SI 2006/1003 (in force on 30 April 2006), revoke the 2000 Regulations, SI 2000/2326, and amend the Channel Tunnel (International Arrangements) Order 1993, SI 1993/1813, the Immigration (Notices) Regulations 2003, SI 2003/658, the Nationality, Immigration and Asylum Act 2002 (Juxtaposed Controls) Order 2003, SI 2003/2818, the Immigration and Asylum Act 1999 (Part V Exemption: Relevant Employers) Order 2003, SI 2003/3214, the Immigration (Restrictions on Employment) Order 2004, SI 2004/755, the Accession (Immigration and Worker Registration) Regulations 2004, SI 2004/1219, the Immigration (European Economic Area) and Accession (Amendment) Regulations 2004, SI 2004/1236, the Asylum and Immigration Tribunal (Procedure) Rules 2005, SI 2005/230, and the Travel Restriction Order (Prescribed Removal Powers) Order 2002, SI 2002/313. The regulations also implement European Parliament and Council Directive 2004/38 on the right of citizens of the Union and their family members to move and reside freely within the territory of the member states, amend EEC Council Regulation 1612/68 and repeal EEC Council Directives 64/221, 68/360, 72/194, 73/148, 75/34, 75/35, 90/364, 90/365 and 93/96. The 2006 Regulations also (1) set out the free movement rights conferred on EEA nationals, in particular (a) the right of EEA nationals and their family members to be admitted to the United Kingdom provided they have the relevant documents; (b) the right of EEA nationals and their family members to reside in the United Kingdom for an initial period of three months; (c) the right of a 'qualified person' (a jobseeker, worker, self-employed person, self-sufficient person or student), a family member a qualified person, and a 'family member who has retained the right of residence' (for example, a family member of a deceased qualified person who satisfies specified conditions) to reside in the United Kingdom for as long as they have this status; and (d) the right of EEA nationals and their family members to permanent residence in the United Kingdom in specified circumstances, (2) provide for the issue of residence documentation, which can be used as proof of the rights of residence provided for in the regulations, (3) provide for the exclusion and removal of EEA nationals and their family members, (4) contain procedural provisions relating to persons who claim admission under the regulations, who are refused admission, or are being removed, and (5) set out the appeal rights in relation to decisions taken under the regulations.

364 Immigration—freedom of movement—non-Community national married to Community national—residence in third country—work permit

The applicants, a married couple, lived in Belgium. The first applicant, the wife, was a Luxembourg national who had completed professional training while in Belgium. The second applicant, the husband, was a national of a non-member state. His application for a work permit in Luxembourg was refused on the basis that EC Council Regulation 1612/68 did not apply to the first applicant as she did not work in Luxembourg. It fell to be determined whether the spouse of a Community national who lived and had completed professional training in a member state other than her own was exempt from the requirement to obtain a work permit in the spouse's member state. *Held*, the right of a national from a non-member state who was married to a national from a member state to access to the labour market of a member state depended on the rights of the spouse. It was for a national court to verify whether the wife pursued a genuine and effective activity as an employed person in the course of her professional training in such a way that she could be regarded as a worker within the meaning of the EC Treaty art 39. Regulation 1612/68 art 11 provided that the right of a national of non-member state of access to the labour market could only be relied on in the member state where the Community national pursued an activity as an employed or self-employed person. The right was not a direct one, but for the benefit of the migrant worker whose family included a spouse or dependent child who was a non-member state national. As the first applicant was not pursuing any such activity in a member state other than Belgium, the second applicant could only rely on the right of access to the labour market there.

Case C-10/05 *Mattern v Ministre du Travail et de l'Emploi* [2006] 2 CMLR 1080, (ECJ: First Chamber). Case C-131/85 *Gül v Regierungsprasident Düsseldorf* [1986] ECR 1573, ECJ (1986 Abr para 3002); Case C-66/85 *Lawrie Blum* [1986] ECR 2121, ECJ (1986 Abr para 3006); and Case C-109/04 *Kranemann v Land Nordrhein-Westfalen*, [2005] All ER (D) 287 (Mar), ECJ, considered.

365 Immigration—illegal entrant—right to marry—certificate of approval

The claimants sought to challenge the legality of the regime, introduced by the Asylum and Immigration (Treatment of Claimants etc) Act 2004 ss 19–25 and the Immigration (Procedure for Marriage) Regulations 2005, SI 2005/15, to prevent sham marriages among persons subject to immigration control. In judicial review proceedings, the court decided that the legislation in question was incompatible with the right to marry, enshrined in the European Convention on Human Rights art 12, and that it constituted direct discrimination on the grounds of religion and nationality, in violation of art 14, which was not justified in the interests of immigration control. A further issue arose subsequently as to the Convention compatibility of the decision of the Secretary of State to refuse to grant to the first claimant a certificate of approval to marry under the 2004 Act s 19 on the ground that he was unlawfully in the United Kingdom. *Held*, when an illegal entrant's Convention right to marry was under consideration, it had to be considered in the light of special factors which were not relevant in the case of a person subject to immigration control who was lawfully resident in the United Kingdom. Having regard to the need to have a proper and fair system of immigration control, which precluded any form of queue-jumping by illegal entrants over those having to apply from abroad for permission to come to the United Kingdom, it followed that a policy of precluding illegal immigrants from obtaining certificates of approval, and in consequence from obtaining further rights, was rationally connected to the policy of immigration control. It would otherwise be manifestly unfair to other would-be entrants. Accordingly, the application would be dismissed.

R (on the application of Baiai) v Secretary of State for the Home Department [2006] EWHC 1454 (Admin), [2006] 4 All ER 555 (Queen's Bench Division: Silber J). For earlier related proceedings see *R (on the application of Baiai) v Secretary of State for the Home Department* [2006] EWHC 823 (Admin), [2006] 2 FCR 131 (para 379).

366 Immigration—Immigration Services Commissioner—designated professional body—fees

The Immigration Services Commissioner (Designated Professional Body) (Fees) Order 2006, SI 2006/400 (in force on 16 March 2006), specifies the fee to be paid by the designated professional bodies to the Immigration Services Commissioner for the purpose of meeting the costs incurred by him in discharging his functions under the Immigration and Asylum Act 1999 Pt V.

367 Immigration—leave to enter—continuation—notices

The Immigration (Continuation of Leave) (Notices) Regulations 2006, SI 2006/2170 (in force on 31 August 2006), specify when an application for variation of leave is decided for the purposes of the Immigration Act 1971 s 3C.

368 Immigration—leave to remain—prescribed forms and procedures

The Immigration (Leave to Remain) (Prescribed Forms and Procedures) Regulations 2006, SI 2006/1421 (in force on 22 June 2006), replace the 2005 Order, SI 2005/2358, and prescribe the forms to be used for applications for leave to remain in the United Kingdom and the procedures to be followed in relation to an application for which a form is prescribed.

The Immigration (Leave to Remain) (Prescribed Forms and Procedures) (Amendment) Regulations 2006, SI 2006/1548 (in force on 22 June 2006), amend SI 2006/1421 supra so as to correct errors in certain of the forms prescribed by those regulations.

The Immigration (Leave to Remain) (Prescribed Forms and Procedures) (Amendment No 2) Regulations 2006, SI 2006/2899 (in force on 8 November 2006), further amend SI 2006/1421 so as to (1) prescribe a form for applications for limited leave to remain in the United Kingdom for (a) work permit employment; (b) as a seasonal agricultural worker; (c) for the purposes of the Sectors-Based Scheme; and (d) for Home Office approved training or work experience; and (2) omit from the form any reference to highly skilled migrants and prescribe another form for applications for limited leave to remain in the United Kingdom as a highly skilled migrant.

369   Immigration—non-European Union citizen—right of establishment—Association Agreement—person without leave to enter

The claimant, a Turkish national, was caught trying to enter the United Kingdom illegally. He claimed asylum, informing the authorities that he had travelled directly from Turkey. In fact he had already claimed asylum in Italy. Italy duly accepted responsibility for the claimant whose asylum claim and human rights claim in the United Kingdom were dismissed. He failed to attend an interview at which arrangements were due to be made for his removal, and later started an off-licence business. He was subsequently detained pending his removal, and he applied for judicial review of the decision to dismiss his asylum claim, relying on the Association Agreement between the European Union and Turkey. The Agreement contained a standstill clause which obliged the contracting parties to refrain from introducing between themselves any new restrictions on the freedom of establishment and the freedom to provide services. *Held*, previous authority had decided no more than that the standstill clause meant that the domestic law applicable was that in force in January 1973. Unlawful presence, whether as an illegal entrant or an overstayer, could justify a refusal to permit an in-country application under the Agreement. Further, if the opportunity to engage in business had been created by working in breach of the terms of any temporary admission or when overstaying so that the unlawfulness of the applicant's conduct went beyond mere unlawful presence, there was a further justification for refusing the application. Accordingly, the application would be dismissed.

R (on the application of Temiz) v Secretary of State for the Home Department [2006] EWHC 2450 (Admin), [2006] All ER (D) 156 (Oct) (Queen's Bench Division: Collins J). *R (on the application of Tum) v Secretary of State for the Home Department; R (on the application of Dari) v Secretary of State for the Home Department* [2004] EWCA Civ 788, [2004] 2 CMLR 1131 (2004 Abr para 313) considered.

370   Immigration—notices

The Immigration (Notices) (Amendment) Regulations 2006, SI 2006/2168 (in force on 31 August 2006), amend the 2003 Regulations, SI 2003/658, by specifying that (1) the decision-maker must provide a written notice of a decision that a person is no longer a refugee if as a result of that decision a right of appeal arises under the Nationality, Immigration and Asylum Act 2002 s 83A(2); (2) if the notice relates to an immigration decision specified in s 82(2)(ia), it must state the country to which it is proposed to remove the person; and (3) where the decision-maker feels that the affected party may be removable to more than one country or territory, any such countries or territories may be specified in the notice of decision.

371   Immigration—offences—defence—Refugee Convention

Following the dismissal of an appeal against conviction and the refusal of leave to appeal to the House of Lords, the Court of Appeal has certified that there is a point of law of general public importance in the question as to what extent a defendant charged with an offence not specified in the Immigration and Asylum Act 1999 s 31(3) is entitled to rely on the protections afforded by the United Nations Convention Relating to the Status of Refugees 1951 art 31.

R v Asfaw [2006] EWCA Crim 2197, [2006] All ER (D) 10 (Nov) (Court of Appeal: Lord Phillips of Worth Matravers CJ, McCombe and Gross JJ). For earlier related proceedings see *R v Asfaw* [2006] All ER (D) 311 (Mar), CA (para 332).

372   Immigration—offences—failure to provide immigration document—entry on false passport—inability to obtain genuine immigration document

The Asylum and Immigration (Treatment of Claimants, etc) Act 2004 s 2(1) provides that a person commits an offence if at an asylum interview he does not have with him an immigration document. However, a person does not commit such an offence if within the period of three days beginning with the date of the interview the person provides such a document: s 2(3)(b). Where the charge for an offence under s 2(1) relates to an interview which takes place after the defendant has entered the

United Kingdom, it is a defence for the defendant to prove that he has a reasonable excuse for not providing a document in accordance with s 2(3): s 2(6)(b).

The defendant was a Burmese national who had been unable to obtain a genuine passport in Burma. He entered the United Kingdom on a false passport supplied by a facilitator. Once he had cleared immigration control he handed the passport back to the facilitator. The defendant subsequently attended a number of asylum screening interviews, and was unable to produce either a genuine passport or the document which he had used to gain entry to the United Kingdom. He was charged with an offence contrary to the 2004 Act s 2(1), and he sought to rely on the defence in s 2(6)(b) that he had a reasonable excuse for not providing an immigration document because of his inability to obtain one. The trial judge rejected this contention and convicted the defendant. On appeal, *held*, the offence under s 3(1) concerned the failure to possess an immigration document at an asylum interview. An immigration document was defined by s 2(12), and s 2(13) drew a distinction between an immigration document and a false immigration document. It was therefore clear that s 2(3) and (6), which referred only to immigration documents, had no application to false immigration documents such as the one used by the defendant. The defendant had satisfied the trial judge that it was impossible for him to obtain a passport in his country of origin, and so he clearly had a reasonable excuse for not providing a genuine immigration document within three days of his asylum interview. In those circumstances, he had a valid defence to the charge under s 3(6)(b). Accordingly, the appeal would be allowed.

Thet v DPP [2006] EWHC 2701 (Admin), [2006] All ER (D) 09 (Nov) (Queen's Bench Division: Lord Phillips of Worth Matravers CJ and Roderick Evans J).

373   Immigration—passenger transit visa

The Immigration (Passenger Transit Visa) (Amendment) Order 2006, SI 2006/493 (in force on 2 March 2006), further amends the 2003 Order, SI 2003/1185, by adding Malawi to the list of countries whose nationals or citizens must have a transit visa in order to pass through the United Kingdom.

374   Immigration—physical data

The Immigration (Provision of Physical Data) Regulations 2006, SI 2006/1743 (in force on 4 July 2006), replace the 2003 Regulations, SI 2003/1875, and (1) provide that an authorised person may require a person who makes an application for entry clearance or leave to enter to provide a record of his fingerprints and a photograph of his face; (2) provide that an authorised person may require the applicant to attend a British diplomatic mission or a British consular post, a diplomatic mission or consular post of another state or other premises so nominated for his fingerprints or photograph to be taken; (3) provide that an individual's application for entry clearance or leave to enter may be treated as being invalid or may be refused where the individual fails to comply with any requirement specified in the regulations; (4) provide that, as fingerprints or a photograph can only be taken from an applicant under the age of 16 in the presence of a responsible adult and satisfied by an authorised person, an adult who takes responsibility for the applicant must not be an authorised person, an officer of the Secretary of State or any other person acting on behalf of the authorised person; (5) require that any record of fingerprints, photograph or a copy of fingerprints or a photograph held by the Secretary of State to be destroyed within ten years or as soon as reasonably practicable if the person proves he is a British citizen or a Commonwealth citizen with a right of abode; and (6) make provision for electronic data which relate to any record of fingerprints or photograph to be destroyed or erased, or access to the data blocked.

375   Immigration—right of abode—certificate of entitlement

The Immigration (Certificate of Entitlement to Right of Abode in the United Kingdom) Regulations 2006, SI 2006/3145 (in force on 21 December 2006), provide the procedure under which a person can apply for and obtain a Certificate of Entitlement to Right of Abode in the United Kingdom. In particular, the regulations (1) set out the authority to which an application for a certificate must be submitted; (2) provide that an application must be accompanied by certain documents; (3) define what is required in order for a passport to be valid for the purposes of an application; (4) provide when and how a certificate will be issued; (5) provide for when a certificate will expire and the circumstances in which a certificate can be revoked; and (6) provide a saving for certificates that have been issued prior to the regulations coming into force.

376   Immigration—right of residence—child—need for health insurance

The appellants, who were Chinese citizens, left China and entered the United Kingdom and later the Republic of Ireland illegally. While living in the Republic, they had a child, who was therefore a citizen of the Republic and, pursuant to the EC Treaty art 17, the European Union. The appellants subsequently returned to the United Kingdom and applied unsuccessfully for asylum. Before the Immigration Appeal Tribunal, the appellants argued that, since the child could not assert her rights to free movement within the European Union without their assistance, they were entitled to bring her to the United Kingdom for that purpose. EEC Council Directive 90/364 art 1 provided that the right of movement and residence of a citizen of the European Union was subject to cover by sickness insurance and possession of resources sufficient to avoid becoming a burden on the social assistance system of the host state, and that spouses of a person having a right to install themselves in another member state and their descendants who were dependents, and dependent relatives in the ascending line of his or her spouse, had the right to install themselves. The appeal tribunal therefore dismissed the claim on the ground that the family lacked the necessary health insurance. On the appellant's appeal, *held,* the residence of the accompanying parents in the member state was simply a consequence of the child's right, and the child's right was a right to reside only in such circumstances as would not place on the member state a financial burden arising out of his residence. Therefore, in order to qualify under Directive 90/364, the accompanying family members had to have medical insurance and sufficient resources for themselves and the child. If it were otherwise, the exercise of the right of residence would in fact impose a financial burden on the member state. The absence of health insurance was fatal to the appellants' claim and, accordingly, the appeal would be dismissed.

W (China) v Secretary of State for the Home Department [2006] EWCA Civ 1494, [2006] All ER (D) 97 (Nov) (Court of Appeal: Buxton, Sedley and Dyson LJJ). Case C-200/02 *Chen v Secretary of State for the Home Department* [2005] QB 325, ECJ (2004 Abr para 314), considered.

377   Immigration—right of residence—European Union citizen—parent—derivative right

The appellant, a Somali national, arrived in the United Kingdom and claimed asylum for himself and also for a dependent son who had been born in the Netherlands. The Secretary of State refused the claim and the appellant appealed. In addition to the asylum claim, the appellant contended that he had rights of residence in the United Kingdom under European law and that to remove him would breach his right to family life under the European Convention on Human Rights art 8. The judge accepted that the appellant was the father of the son, who was a Dutch citizen, and that the appellant had a family relationship with the son's mother, but not that they were living together. Further, she considered that the son's mother was not a worker within the meaning of the EC Treaty art 39. The judge held that the fact that the son was at school in the United Kingdom did not give the appellant a right of residence in the United Kingdom. The appellant did not obtain permission to appeal on the asylum claim, and therefore, his appeal was confined to the points with regard to art 39 and the Convention art 8. *Held,* the judge had applied the correct burden of proof when determining the question of whether the appellant was married. Further, the son's right of residence by virtue of the EC Treaty art 18 was not unfettered, and therefore, a Dutch citizen receiving education in the United Kingdom did not of itself provide any right of residence. It followed that the parent of such a child could not obtain any derivative right. In the present case, the fact that the son was receiving education in the United Kingdom did not alter the fact that he was not a recipient of services. Accordingly, the appeal would be dismissed.

Ali v Secretary of State for the Home Department [2006] EWCA Civ 484, [2006] All ER (D) 28 (May) (Court of Appeal: May, Keene and Wall LJJ).

378   Immigration—right of residence—European Union national—condition—financial resources—legality

Belgian domestic law required nationals from other European Union member states who sought to reside in Belgium to demonstrate that they possessed sufficient resources so that they would not become a burden on the public authorities. European Union foreign nationals coming to Belgium in order to pursue an activity as an employed or self-employed person had to be registered and issued with a certificate valid for five months. Registration would be refused if the conditions were not met, and anyone failing to meet the requirements would be automatically ordered to leave Belgian territory if they did not produce relevant documentation. The European Commission received complaints that various persons had been ordered to leave Belgium despite holding undertakings from other persons demonstrating that they possessed adequate resources. The Commission took the view that resources other than the personal resources of the individual in question could be taken into account, but the Belgian authorities disagreed. The Commission decided that Belgium had failed to fulfil its obligations under EEC Council Directive 90/364 on the right to reside, and brought proceedings in the European Court of Justice. *Held,* by excluding the income of a partner residing in the host member state in the absence of an agreement concluded before a notary and containing an assistance clause, Belgium had failed to fulfil its obligations under Directive 90/364. The condition in art 1(1) concerning the sufficiency of resources was met where the financial resources were provided by a partner residing in the host member state. To require the income of another person to be taken into account only if legally connected with the beneficiary was disproportionate in that it went beyond what was necessary to achieve the purpose of the legislation, which was the protection of the public funds in the host member state. Moreover, automatic deportation did not allow account to be taken of the reasons why the person concerned did not take the necessary administrative measures to establish that he fulfilled the conditions attaching to his residence.

Case C-408/03 *European Commission v Belgium* [2006] All ER (EC) 725 (ECJ: Grand Chamber).

379   Immigration—right to marry—non-Church of England marriage—certificate of approval—human rights

In three linked applications for judicial review, an issue arose as to whether the regime to prevent sham marriages introduced by the Asylum and Immigration (Treatment of Claimants, etc) Act 2004 s 19, by which a person who was subject to immigration control and who wished to enter into a civil marriage other than one according to the rites of the Church of England had to apply to the Secretary of State for a certificate of approval to marry, was compatible with the right to marry guaranteed by the European Convention on Human Rights art 12 and with the non-discrimination requirement of art 14. *Held*, the measures adopted by the Secretary of State were not rationally connected to their legislative objective because they automatically deemed all marriages of a party who required a certificate of approval to be actual or potential marriages of convenience. There was no basis for assuming that all marriages conducted in religious ceremonies other than Church of England ones were automatically to be treated as sham marriages and so require a certificate of approval while, in contrast, all those marriages conducted according to Church of England rites were to be regarded as automatically not being sham marriages and therefore not requiring a certificate of approval. Moreover, the regime constituted direct discrimination because the group targeted by that scheme as requiring certificates of approval were those who, because of their religious convictions or lack of them, were unable or unwilling to marry pursuant to the rites of the Church of England while those who wished to marry pursuant to those rights were exempted from the scheme. That discrimination was not justified because there was no evidence that those who married in non-Anglican religious ceremonies were more likely to engage in sham marriages than those who married in Anglican religious ceremonies. It followed that the regime infringed the Convention arts 12, 14 and, accordingly, the applications would be allowed.

R (*on the application of Baiai*) *v Secretary of State for the Home Department* [2006] EWHC 823 (Admin), [2006] 3 All ER 608 (Queen's Bench Division: Silber J). R (*on the application of Carson*) *v Secretary of State for Work and Pensions; R* (*on the application of Reynolds*) *v Secretary of State for Work and Pensions* [2005] UKHL 37, [2005] 4 All ER 545 (2005 Abr para 1715) considered.

380   Immigration—rules

The Statement of Changes in Immigration Rules 1994 (HC 395) is further amended (see HC Paper (2005–06) no 949), so that, with effect from 2 March 2006, nationals or citizens of Malawi require a visa to travel to the United Kingdom and, with effect from 22 March 2006, nationals or citizens of Croatia no longer require such a visa.

The Statement of Changes in Immigration Rules 1994 supra is further amended (see HC Paper (2005–06) no 1016), with effect from 3 April 2006, so that (1) the qualifying period for indefinite leave to remain in the United Kingdom for all employment-related categories of entry to the United Kingdom is five years; (2) only postgraduate doctors and dentists who have completed their medical or dental degree in the United Kingdom are eligible for leave to remain in the United Kingdom and then only in order to complete the two-year foundation programme; (3) the Science and Engineering Graduates scheme is extended to enable all Master's and PhD students to apply to work in the United Kingdom for twelve months after they have completed their studies, regardless of the subject they have studied; (4) a non-visa national in the United Kingdom as a visitor may not transfer into the student category for a course above degree level; (5) an omission from the civil partnership provisions is rectified so as to extend to proposed civil partners; (6) leave to enter under the ancestry provisions may be granted for up to five years at a time; and (7) a prospective student must have sought prior entry clearance if he wishes subsequently to transfer to student status in the United Kingdom.

The Statement of Changes in Immigration Rules 1994 is further amended (see HC Paper (2005–06) no 1053), with effect from 30 April 2006, so as to apply to all European Economic Area nationals and their family members the right, contained in European Parliament and Council Directive 2004/38, to acquire a right of permanent residence under certain conditions and generally after five years of residence in the host member state under Community law.

The Statement of Changes in Immigration Rules 1994 is further amended (see HC Paper (2005–06) no 1337), with effect from 20 July 2006, to make it clear that, where a person is liable to deportation, the presumption is that the public interest requires deportation and that it is only in exceptional circumstances that such public interest will be outweighed in a case where it would not be contrary to the European Convention on Human Rights and the Refugee Convention to deport.

The Statement of Changes in Immigration Rules 1994 is further amended (see Cm 6918), with effect from 9 October 2006, by the addition of provisions which implement in part EC Council Directive 2004/83 on minimum standards for the qualification and status of third country nationals or stateless persons as refugees or as persons who otherwise need international protection and the content of the protection granted.

The Statement of Changes in Immigration Rules 1994 is further amended (see HC Paper (2005–06) no 1702), with effect from 5 December 2006, by a number of changes to the rules relating to the Highly Skilled Migrant Programme.

The Statement of Changes in Immigration Rules 1994 is further amended (see HC Paper (2006–07) no 130), with effect from 1 January 2007, in consequence of the accession of Bulgaria and Romania to the European Union on 1 January 2007, by (1) the removal of those countries from the list of countries whose nationals may submit applications under the au pair rules; (2) the deletion of the rules relating to leave to enter and limited leave to remain under the European Community Association Agreements with Bulgaria and Romania; and (3) the removal of Bulgaria and Romania from the list of countries whose nationals require a visa to come to the United Kingdom, such individuals now having a right under European Community law to be admitted to the United Kingdom on production of their ID cards and passports, and no longer requiring leave under the Immigration Rules.

381 Immigration, Asylum and Nationality Act 2006

The Immigration, Asylum and Nationality Act 2006 makes provision about immigration, asylum and nationality. The Act received the royal assent on 30 March 2006 and certain provisions came into force on that day. Further provisions came into force on and between 16 June 2006 and 4 December 2006: SI 2006/1497, 2226, 2838. The remaining provisions come into force on a day or days to be appointed. For details of commencement, see the commencement table in the title STATUTES.

Section 1 introduces a new right of appeal against a decision to curtail or refuse to extend limited leave to enter or remain for people who are no longer recognised as refugees but are permitted to stay in the United Kingdom on another basis, and s 3 provides that such an appeal may only be brought on the ground that the appellant's removal would breach the United Kingdom's obligations under the United Nations Convention relating to the Status of Refugees 1951 ('the Refugee Convention'). Section 2 provides for a right of appeal against a decision to remove persons whose indefinite leave to enter or remain has been revoked. All appeals against refusal of entry clearance are limited to the grounds of human rights and race discrimination: ss 4–6. Section 7 provides that an appeal against a decision to make a deportation order on national security grounds will normally only be able to be brought from outside the United Kingdom. Provision is made in relation to legal aid (s 8), the abandonment of appeals (s 9) and the abolition of grants to organisations giving advice in relation to appeals (s 10). Section 11 provides for the continuation of leave to enter or remain while an in-country appeal against revocation or curtailment of such leave may be brought or is pending. Asylum claims and human rights claims are no longer required to be made in person at a place designated by the Secretary of State: s 12. Section 13 allows the Secretary of State to make regulations which limit his power to certify clearly unfounded human rights or asylum claims, and s 14, Sch 1, make consequential amendments. By virtue of s 15, a penalty notice can be served on any person who employs an adult subject to immigration control and without leave to enter or remain, and s 16 sets out the procedure for employers to object in relation to such a penalty notice. Sections 17, 18 deal with appeals and enforcement. The Secretary of State must issue codes of practice specifying the factors to be considered in determining the amount of a penalty and specifying how employers may avoid contravening race discrimination legislation when acting to avoid a penalty under s 15: ss 19, 23. Section 20 makes further provision as to the Secretary of State's order-making powers under ss 15, 16 and 19, and s 21 creates an offence of employing a person knowing that they are an adult subject to immigration control and without leave to enter or remain. Section 22 makes provision for offences by bodies corporate, officers of bodies and members of partnerships. A person granted temporary admission or release from detention is to be treated for the purposes of ss 15 and 21 as having been granted leave to enter and remain: s 24. Sections 25, 26 deal with interpretation of ss 15–24 and repeal previous legislation relating to restrictions on the employment of persons subject to immigration control and without leave to enter or remain. Immigration officers may in certain circumstances require entrants to the United Kingdom to provide biometric information so that their identity can be ascertained: s 27. Provision is also made in relation to the taking of fingerprints (s 28) and a person's attendance for the purpose of having his fingerprints taken (s 29). Section 30 changes the way in which a person seeking leave to enter the United Kingdom and claim a right of abode must prove that right, and s 31 empowers immigration officers to collect passenger lists and crew information on or before the arrival of a ship or aircraft into the United Kingdom. Similar powers are conferred on police in relation to passengers and crew (s 32) and freight (s 33), and it is an offence for a person to fail to provide such information when requested (s 34). Similar powers are also conferred on Revenue and Customs by s 35. Sections 36–39 provide for the sharing and disclosure of information held by the Border Services. Provision is made by ss 40, 41 for the contracting out of vehicle searches for individuals whom an immigration officer may wish to examine. An immigration officer may examine embarking passengers for the purpose of establishing further prescribed information: s 42. Section 43 empowers local authorities to provide accommodation in accordance with further arrangements made by the Secretary of State. The Secretary of State is empowered by s 44 to repeal legislation relating to the withdrawal of support for failed asylum-seekers, and may, by virtue of s 45, make integration loans to refugees who have been given limited leave to enter or remain. Section 46 introduces a statutory inspection regime in respect of short-term holding facilities. Section 47 provides for the making of an appealable decision to remove a person from the United Kingdom during a period in which he enjoys continuing leave to enter or remain, and s 48 provides for the invalidation of leave to enter or remain on the notification of a decision to remove a person from the United Kingdom. Provision is made in relation to a person's capacity on the making of an application to be naturalised or to renounce or resume citizenship: s 49. Section 50 empowers the Secretary of State to prescribe, in the immigration rules, forms to be used and procedures to be followed when making an immigration-related application, and ss 51, 52, Sch 2 make provision in relation to the designation of immigration-related applications and claims for which a fee may be charged. The circumstances in which certain powers of arrest arise in deportation cases are clarified by s 53. Provision is made in relation to the construction of the Refugee Convention (s 54) and to certification that an appellant is not entitled to its protection (s 55). The Secretary of State may deprive a person of citizenship status or a right of abode in the United Kingdom if satisfied that it is conducive to the public good to do so: ss 56, 57. Section 58 requires applicants for citizenship or British subject status under specified provisions to satisfy requirements as to proof of good character. Immigration detainees are exempted from the national minimum wage in respect of work done in a removal centre by s 59. Section 60 deals with money, s 61, Sch 3 with repeals and ss 62–64 with commencement, extent and citation.

Amendments, repeals and revocations
The list below, which is not exhaustive, mentions repeals and amendments which are or will be effective when the Act is fully in force.

Specific provisions of a number of Acts are added, amended or repealed. These include: Prison Act 1952 ss 5A, 55; Immigration Act 1971 ss 2A, 3, 3C, 3D, 31A, 32, Sch 2; British Nationality Act 1981 ss 40, 41, 42A, 44A; Asylum and Immigration Act 1996 ss 8, 8A; National Minimum Wage Act 1998 s 45B; Immigration and Asylum Act 1999 ss 5, 10, 27, 99, 118, 141, 142, 153A; Anti-terrorism, Crime and Security Act 2001 s 33; Nationality, Immigration and Asylum Act 2002 ss 10, 23, 82, 83A, 88A, 89–91, 97A, 104, 110, 122, 158; Asylum and Immigration (Treatment of Claimants, etc) Act 2004 ss 13, 25, 44; Civil Partnership Act 2004 Sch 23.

382 Nationality, Immigration and Asylum Act 2002—commencement

The Nationality, Immigration and Asylum Act 2002 (Commencement No 11) Order 2006, SI 2006/1498, brings s 9 into force on 5 June 2006, for regulation-making purposes, and on 1 July 2006, for remaining purposes. The date appointed for the purpose of s 162(5) is 1 July 2006.

The Nationality, Immigration and Asylum Act 2002 (Commencement No 12) Order 2006, SI 2006/3144, brings s 10(5)(b) into force on 21 December 2006.

For a summary of the Act, see 2002 Abr para 368. See also the commencement table in the title STATUTES.

BUILDING

Halsbury's Laws of England (4th edn) vol 4(2) (2002 Reissue) paras 301–457

Articles

For articles relating to this title please refer to the Table of Articles at the beginning of the Abridgment.

383 Sports grounds—safety—designated grounds

The Safety of Sports Grounds (Designation) Order 2006, SI 2006/218 (in force on 1 March 2006), amends the 1986 Order, SI 1986/1296, by removing the Ellis Sports Ground in Workington, Cumbria from the list of designated sports stadia so that it no longer requires a safety certificate under the Safety of Sports Grounds Act 1975.

The Safety of Sports Grounds (Designation) (No 2) Order 2006, SI 2006/1662 (in force on 17 July 2006), further amends the 1986 Order supra by removing St Helen's Ground in Swansea from the list of designated sports stadia so that it no longer requires a safety certificate under the 1975 Act supra. The order also designates the Sixways Stadium in Worcester, occupied by Worcester Rugby Football Club; Sophia Gardens in Cardiff, occupied by Glamorgan County Cricket Club; and the Emirates Stadium in London, occupied by Arsenal Football Club, as sports grounds which require safety certificates under the 1975 Act.

The Safety of Sports Grounds (Designation) (No 3) Order 2006, SI 2006/1971 (in force on 11 August 2006), designates the Fraser Eagle Stadium in Accrington, occupied by Accrington Stanley Football Club, as a sports ground which requires a safety certificate under the 1975 Act.

The Safety of Sports Grounds (Designation) (No 4) Order 2006, SI 2006/3168 (in force on 20 December 2006), designates the Keepmoat Stadium in Doncaster, occupied by Doncaster Rovers Football Club, as a sports ground which requires a safety certificate under the 1975 Act.

384   Sustainable and Secure Buildings Act 2004—commencement

The Sustainable and Secure Buildings Act 2004 (Commencement No 1) Order 2006, SI 2006/224, brings into force, on 1 February 2006, ss 2, 7 (for the purpose only of conferring power to make regulations), 8 and 9. For a summary of the Act, see 2004 Abr para 337. See also the commencement table in the title STATUTES.

BUILDING CONTRACTS, ARCHITECTS, ENGINEERS, VALUERS AND SURVEYORS

Halsbury's Laws of England (4th edn) vol 4(3) (Reissue) paras 1–400

Articles

For articles relating to this title please refer to the Table of Articles at the beginning of the Abridgment.

385   Approved inspectors

The Building and Approved Inspectors (Amendment) (No 2) Regulations 2006, SI 2006/3318 (in force in part on 15 January 2007 and in part on 6 April 2007), further amend (1) the Building Regulations 2000, SI 2000/2531, by (a) requiring a person carrying out work to a building or part of a building to which the Regulatory Reform (Fire Safety) Order 2005, SI 2005/1541, applies, or will apply, to give fire safety information in relation to that building to the responsible person not later than the earlier of the date of completion of the work or the date of occupation; (b) revising the provision in relation to completion certificates, to add compliance with the requirements concerning fire safety information and target CO2 emission rates for new buildings to matters which a local authority may specify in a completion order; (c) requiring the provision of automatic fire suppression systems to inhibit fire spread within buildings where reasonably necessary; and (d) adding new bodies who are able to register persons for the purposes of self-certification schemes; and (2) the Building (Approved Inspectors etc) Regulations 2000, SI 2000/2532, by (a) adding compliance with the fire safety information provision of the Building Regulations 2000, SI 2000/2531, to the matters which an approved inspector must monitor while an initial notice remains in force; and (b) restoring the eight week limit between the occupation of a building comprising only flats and common parts and the expiry notice.

386   Architect—duty of care—recommendations—letter of intent

The claimant engaged the defendant architect in respect of the refurbishment of a listed building. The defendant sent out invitations to tender. One of the tenders was chosen by the claimant on the defendant's advice. The work was to go ahead on the JCT standard form of contracts for minor works. A letter of intent authorised certain preparatory works to a financial limit but the project was delayed, partly due to the wording of an escrow agreement. The contractor ended its involvement in the project before the contract had been finalised. The defendant ceased work due to non-payment of fees and obtained an award from an adjudicator in respect of them. It sought to enforce the award. The claimant commenced negligence proceedings and the actions were consolidated. *Held*, if a contract administrator liked and understood the way a particular standard form worked, then, unless there was a very good reason why he should not use it in a particular instance, it was to everybody's advantage if he recommended that form for use on his projects. The recommendation as to which standard form of building contract should be used for a particular project would normally depend on the consultant's personal preference and his previous experience. Such a subjective choice was entirely reasonable. In all the circumstances, the defendant had not been negligent in recommending the standard form or in its conduct regarding the appointment of the original contractor. Further, a letter of intent could be appropriate when the price was either agreed or there was a clear mechanism in place for it to be agreed, the contract terms were, or were very likely to be, agreed and there were good reasons to start work in advance of the finalisation of all the contract documents. Although the failure to enter into a principal contract was an inevitable risk of any letter of intent that created respective rights and obligations, the point of careful drafting was to minimise that risk. In all the circumstances, the letter of intent had not been premature. The overwhelming cause of the delay to the project was the failure to agree the wording of the escrow agreement for which the claimant was responsible. The claimant had failed to establish any negligence on the part of the defendant which was entitled to recover its fees as awarded by the adjudicator. Accordingly, judgment would be given for the defendant.

Cunningham v Collett [2006] EWHC 1771 (TCC), [2006] All ER (D) 233 (Jul) (Queen's Bench Division: Judge Peter Coulson QC). *British Steel Corpn v Cleveland Bridge and Engineering Co Ltd* [1984] 1 All ER 504 (1981 Abr para 567) considered.

387 Construction contract—adjudication—award—enforcement—reliance on document—separate document relied on to establish jurisdiction

The defendant employed the claimant to carry out certain construction works, but no formal contract was executed. The claimant later purported to refer a dispute to adjudication, and the defendant contended that the adjudicator had no jurisdiction because any contract between the parties was not in writing within the meaning of the Housing Grants, Construction and Regeneration Act 1996 s 107. The claimant relied on a particular document and an oral agreement to rebut the defendant's argument. The adjudicator, in a non-binding decision, ruled that he had jurisdiction to hear the claim, and subsequently made an award in the claimant's favour. The defendant failed to pay, and the claimant brought proceedings to enforce the award, relying on other documents as establishing a contract in writing. *Held*, the claimant could not go beyond the matters it had relied on in the adjudication in order to support the adjudicator's decision that he had jurisdiction. The claimant could not disavow its submissions to the adjudicator. Applying settled principles, a party who had taken some benefit under an instrument could not disavow that instrument in order to obtain a further benefit. Similarly, it would not be just to allow the claimant, having elected to put its argument in a particular way in order to obtain a benefit, namely the decision of an adjudicator in its favour, to resile from that election, irrespective of whether the same benefits could have been obtained by other arguments. On the material relied on before the adjudicator, there was no contract in writing within the meaning of s 107. It followed that the adjudicator had no jurisdiction to hear the reference, and, accordingly, the application would be dismissed.

Redworth Construction Ltd v Brookdale Healthcare Ltd [2006] EWHC 1994 (TCC), [2006] All ER (D) 04 (Aug) (Queen's Bench Division: Judge Richard Havery QC). *Banque des Marchands de Moscou (Koupetschesky) v Kindersley* [1950] 2 All ER 549, CA, applied.

388 Construction contract—adjudication—discontinuance—costs

A firm of architects and a developer entered into a contract which was compliant with the adjudication provisions of the Housing Grants, Construction and Regeneration Act 1996 s 108. The parties incorporated into their contract the standard printed terms of the Construction Industry Council's model adjudication procedure. Under the model procedure, each party was to bear its own costs involved in the adjudication. However, the parties incorporated a slightly amended version, under which the adjudicator could at his discretion direct the payment of legal costs and expenses of one party by another as part of his decision. A dispute arose between the parties and the developer sent the architect a formal notice of adjudication, claiming damages and the costs of the adjudication pursuant to the agreement. The adjudication did not proceed to a substantive decision, and the architect claimed its legal costs from the developer, and asked the adjudicator to direct that the developer should pay them. The developer argued that the adjudicator had no power to make such a direction, because the contract only empowered him to do so as part of his substantive decision, which he would not make as the adjudication had been discontinued. The adjudicator decided that he did have power to direct that the developer pay the architect's costs, and made a direction accordingly. The developer did not pay, and the architect issued proceedings. The judge decided that the developer's construction of the contract was correct, and the architect appealed. *Held*, the natural meaning of the adjudication clause, and certainly the commercially sensible meaning, was that the words 'as part of his decision' meant 'as part of what he had to decide'. It would seem to be very odd indeed if the parties by their agreement had given the adjudicator power to direct the payment of legal costs, which could be substantial, only if he were to make a substantive contested decision. Other terms of the agreement contemplated that he might not do that. The oddity arose because there could be no reason why parties, who had agreed that they should be at risk as to the other party's costs, should draw the line where the construction of the agreement contended for by the developer drew it. It would mean that either party, having generated legal costs by referring an unmeritorious claim to adjudication, or by responding with an unmeritorious defence, could throw in their hand at the eleventh hour without being at risk of paying the legal costs which their conduct had generated. Accordingly, the appeal would be allowed.

John Roberts Architects Ltd v Parkcare Homes (No 2) Ltd [2006] EWCA Civ 64, [2006] BLR 106 (Court of Appeal: May, Keene and Scott Baker LJJ). Decision of Judge Richard Havery QC [2005] EWHC 1637 (TCC), [2005] BLR 484 (2005 Abr para 370) reversed.

389 Construction contract—contractual term—standard form contract—insurance requirement during works by contractor

The claimant had employed the defendant contractor to carry out various works on a building of which the claimant was the leasehold owner. The parties' agreement incorporated the standard terms of the Joint Contracts Tribunal Agreement for Minor Building Works ('JCT agreement'). This included a clause which required the employer to insure in the joint names of the employer and contractor against loss or damage to existing structures and to the works, and provided that if any loss or damage occurred then the architect or contract administrator would issue instructions for reinstatement and make good such loss or damage. Following heavy rainfall part of the building was flooded as a result of part of a drainpipe not having yet been replaced by the contractor. The employer alleged that the flood was caused by the contractor's breach of contract and/or negligence. The judge found that the claimant's contractual obligation to insure in the parties' joint names continued for the duration of the defects liability period and that the claimant's claim for damages was barred by the contract. The claimant appealed. *Held*, there was no clear indication from guidance on how long the JCT agreement believed or intended that the insurance obligation would last, and it was uncertain whether it would have been admissible had it existed. The obligation applied, in relation to unfixed materials and goods intended for the works, to a period before practical completion and this also applied in relation to the works which includes the work and materials required by the contract to bring the project to its finished state and not the finished state itself. It could not have been intended that the obligation to insure against loss or damage to the existing structures and contents should be for a different period. Also, it could not have been intended that the architect should be authorised to issue instructions after practical completion. Accordingly, the appeal would be allowed.

TFW Printers Ltd v Interserve Project Services Ltd [2006] EWCA Civ 875, [2006] BLR 299 (Court of Appeal: Sedley, Dyson and Carnwath LJJ). *Investors' Compensation Scheme Ltd v West Bromwich Building Society* [1998] 1 All ER 98, HL (1998 Abr para 464); and *Bank of Credit and Commerce International SA (in liquidation) v Ali* [2001] UKHL 8, [2002] 1 AC 251 (2001 Abr para 1334) considered.

390   Construction contract—dispute—arbitration—transfer of engagements by registered society—transfer without written consent

See *Co-operative Group (CWS) Ltd v Stansell Ltd*, para 1699.

391   Construction contract—dispute—decision-maker—impartiality

The defendant engaged the claimant under a construction contract to install cladding on buildings. The contract provided for a design team and a construction manager to certify certain matters and to make decisions as to extensions of time for the completion of the works. The contract specified the identity of the construction manager in a section that also included a power to appoint 'any further or other person'. When the defendant purported to appoint itself as construction manager in place of the manager specified in the contract a dispute arose between the parties and the defendant sought a declaration that it was entitled to appoint itself as construction manager. A preliminary issue arose as to whether the defendant could appoint itself to that role having regard to the decision-making functions of the construction manager. *Held*, a decision-maker in a construction contract, who was not independent of the employer, had to use his professional skills and best endeavours to reach the right decision rather than a decision favouring the interests of the employer. The appointment of the employer itself as construction manager was such an unusual state of affairs that it could only be achieved by an express term of the contract. While the employer was not incapable of acting independently, it would be more difficult for it to make a decision contrary to its own interests than for one of its employees nominated to the task. Further, from the claimant's point of view, a contract in which the defendant was also construction manager was very different to that which it had priced. The whole structure of the contract proceeded on the basis that the employer and construction manager were different entities and endless anomalies were created if they were the same entity. Finally, on the defendant's construction, it would be entitled to dismiss the entire design team and stand in their stead, utterly transforming the agreement between the parties. Thus, the defendant was not entitled to appoint itself as construction manager. Accordingly, the application would be refused.

Scheldebouw BV v St James Homes (Grosvenor Dock) Ltd [2006] EWHC 89 (TCC), [2006] BLR 113 (Queen's Bench Division: Jackson J).

392   Construction contract—dispute—reference to adjudication—right to refer—existence of dispute

By a concession agreement, the second claimant Secretary of State granted to the first claimant the right to design, build and operate the M6 toll road. The first claimant engaged a joint venture vehicle formed of the four defendants as main contractor under a separate contract. Both contracts provided for the adjudication of disputes in certain circumstances and for any matter arising out of an adjudicator's determination to be referred to the court for determination. A dispute arose concerning the entitlement of the defendants to any direct or indirect costs occasioned by mitigating the delay that would otherwise have been caused by a particular change to the works. At an adjudication, the defendants sought to withdraw the assessment of indirect costs from the adjudicator because, following a decision of the High Court, it had no articulated claim in that regard that could succeed. The adjudicator was of the opinion that there was no dispute as to the indirect costs and that there was no reason why a particular claim could not be abandoned or withdrawn, in whole or in part, by a referring party. The defendants referred to the court the question of the scope of the adjudication.

Issues arose as to whether the adjudicator had been right to conclude that no dispute existed in relation to indirect costs and whether the defendants were entitled to withdraw that issue from the adjudicator having regard to the Housing Grants, Construction and Regeneration Act 1996, the scheme for construction contracts set out in the Scheme for Construction Contracts (England and Wales) Regulations 1998, SI 1998/649, and the terms of the contracts. *Held*, in all the circumstances, the adjudicator had been right to conclude that there was no dispute between the parties. At no relevant stage of the adjudication in question did there exist a quantified claim for the indirect costs that was capable of being disputed. Although there was a dispute as to whether, in principle, the defendants had any entitlement to indirect costs, no one had asked for that issue to be determined in isolation. Judgment would be given accordingly.

Midland Expressway v Carillion Construction [2006] EWHC 1505 (TCC), (2006) 107 Con LR 205 (Queen's Bench Division: Jackson J).

393 Construction contract—public works contract—award without tender—award to undertaking in which contracting authority has shareholding

A dispute arose out of the award of a contract for the supply of fuel and for the maintenance, modification and upgrading of the heating installations in the buildings of a particular municipality. The contract was awarded to a joint stock company in which the awarding municipality had a majority shareholding. The claimants contended that the award was contrary to EC Council Directive 93/36 on the co-ordination of the procedures for the award of public service contracts. The national court stayed the proceedings and referred the question to the European Court of Justice pursuant to the EC Treaty art 234. *Held*, Directive 93/36 precluded the direct award of a public supply and service contract, the main value of which lay in supply, to a joint stock company whose board of directors had ample managerial powers which it might exercise independently and whose share capital was, currently, held entirely by another joint stock company whose majority shareholder was, in turn, the contracting authority. Moreover, EC Council Directive 93/38 art 13 should not be applied in the assessment of the requirement relating to the inapplicability of Directive 93/36, according to which the undertaking to which a supply contract was awarded directly had to carry out the essential part of its activities with the controlling authority. In order to determine whether an undertaking carried out the essential part of its activities with the controlling authority for the purpose of deciding on the applicability of Directive 93/36, account had to be taken of all the activities which that undertaking carried out on the basis of an award made by the contracting authority, regardless of who paid for those activities, whether it be the contracting authority itself or the user of the services provided.

Case C-340/04 *Carbotermo SpA v Comune di Busto Arsizio* [2006] 3 CMLR 195 (ECJ: First Chamber).

394 Engineers—qualifications—mutual recognition

See Case C-330/03 *Colegio de Ingenieros de Caminos, Canales y Puertos v Administracion del Estrado*, para 3007.

395 Public procurement—award of contracts—general

The Public Contracts Regulations 2006, SI 2006/5 (in force on 31 January 2006), implement European Parliament and EC Council Directive 2004/18 on the co-ordination of procedures for the award of public works contracts, public supply contracts and public services contracts. The regulations specify the procedures to be followed in relation to the award of such contracts and provide remedies for breaches of the requirements. SI 1991/2680, SI 1993/3228 and SI 1995/201 are revoked.

396 Public procurement—award of contracts—utilities—procedure

The Utilities Contracts Regulations 2006, SI 2006/6, (in force on 31 January 2006), replace the 1996 Regulations, SI 1996/2911, and implement EC European Parliament and Council Directive 2004/17. The regulations specify the procedures to be followed in relation to the award of supply, works and services contracts by utilities for the purposes of carrying out activities in the water, energy, transport and postal services sectors. The regulations deal with the treatment to be accorded to suppliers, contractors and service providers who are nationals of or established in other member states. Specified contracts are excluded from the regulations. The regulations also make provision in relation to (1) the time allowed for the response by potential providers to invitations and for obtaining relevant documents; (2) a qualification system for providers; (3) the selection of providers; (4) tenders by a consortium; (5) the criteria for the award of a contract; (6) the rejection of third country offers; (7) contract award notices and information about contract awards; (8) design contests; (9) obligations relating to taxes, environmental protection, employment protection and working conditions; (10) the preservation of records; (11) statistical and other reports; (12) the provision of reports; (13) the publication of notices; (14) confidentiality of information; (15) sub-contracting; (16) the enforcement of obligations; and (17) conciliation.

397   Public service contracts—freedom to provide services—tendering procedure—failure to meet prescribed obligations

The Italian Ministry of Defence sought tenders for the provision to it of catering services. The applicants, three Italian companies, were excluded from the tendering procedure. Two applicants were excluded on the ground that they had not fulfilled their social security obligations and the third applicant was excluded for having failed to comply with its tax obligations. Under an Italian law, which implemented EC Council Directive 92/50 relating to the co-ordination of procedures for the award of public service contracts, participation in contracts was excluded by candidates who were not in compliance in respect of obligations relating to the payment of social security contributions for employees or payment of taxes. The applicants sought the annulment of the decision to exclude them, contending that the first two applicants' social security contributions had been regularised and a tax amnesty had allowed for the third applicant to pay its outstanding taxes in instalments. It fell to be determined whether Italian law was entitled to be more permissive by accepting tenders from applicants who could show that their positions had been regularised. *Held*, Directive 92/50 provided that member states could not provide for grounds of exclusion other than those laid down within the directive. This allowed member states to make the criteria less onerous and flexible. While Directive 92/50 referred to a service provider who had not fulfilled obligations and the Italian legislation referred to those who were not in compliance with their obligations, Directive 92/50 did not intend there to be a Community-wide definition. There was no difference in content between the two expressions. The particular provision was not intended to be applied uniformly across member states. It was for national rules to determine the date by which tenderers had to fulfil their obligations and prove the fulfilment of the conditions for subsequent regularisation. If, before the tender period, the candidate had made all the payments relating to the obligation, then it would be regarded as fulfilled. Anything less was not sufficient in order to avoid infringing the principle of equal treatment of candidates. However, Directive 92/50 did not prevent a national law or administrative practice where a candidate for a contract could subsequently regularise his position following a tax amnesty, or leniency measures adopted by the member state, or an administrative arrangement of payment in instalments, or debt relief, where he provided evidence that he had benefited from such measures or arrangement or that he had brought such proceedings within the period for submitting the tender.

Case C-226/04 *La Cascina Soc Coop arl v Ministero della Difesa*; Case C-228/04 *Consorzio GFM v Ministero della Difesa* [2006] 2 CMLR 1029 (ECJ: First Chamber). Case C-470/99 *Universale-Bau v Entsorgungsbetriebe Simmering GmbH* [2002] All ER (D) 177(Dec), ECJ; and Case C-421/01 *Traunfellner GmbH v Osterreichische Autobahnen-und Scnellstrassen Finanzierungs AG* [2003] All ER (D) 302 (Oct), ECJ, considered.

CAPITAL GAINS TAXATION

Halsbury's Laws of England (4th edn) vol 5(1) (2004 Reissue) paras 1–500

Articles

For articles relating to this title please refer to the Table of Articles at the beginning of the Abridgment.

398   Authorised investment funds—general

See para 1641.

399   Disposal of assets—distributions of proceeds of sale of property—part disposal—restriction on allowable losses

The taxpayer invested in an enterprise zone property unit trust, and the trustees used the money to purchase land and buildings. To the extent that the investment was spent on buildings, in contrast with land, 100 per cent first year capital allowances were obtained by the taxpayer and other unit holders. The taxpayer claimed that the allowance was set off against his general income for the year. Subsequently, the trustees realised a substantial consideration from the sale of a property, which was effected by a set of transactions designed to avoid balancing charges. In relation to two tax years, the taxpayer's distributions fell to be treated, for capital gains tax, as part disposals by the taxpayer of his units, but those part disposals would have given rise to allowable losses in the taxpayer's hands for the purposes of the Taxation of Chargeable Gains Act 1992 s 41(2). The taxpayer contended that s 41(2) did not operate to restrict the losses accruing to him, but the Commissioners for Her Majesty's Revenue and Customs disagreed. A Special Commissioner found in favour of the taxpayer, and the Commissioners appealed. The central question was whether part of the sum subscribed by the taxpayer for his units was expenditure in respect of which a capital allowance had been made in such a way as to fall within s 41(2) in computing the taxpayer's loss on such disposal. *Held*, in respect of s 39(1), the expenditure giving rise to the capital allowances available to unit holders was not excluded from the sums allowable as a deduction in computing the gain accruing to unit holders on distributions from the scheme. It would be illogical to reach a different conclusion in relation to ss 39(1), 41(2), and there was nothing in s 41 that would drive the court to reach a different conclusion. For capital gains tax purposes, the 1992 Act applied as if the scheme were a company and as if the rights of the unit holders were shares in the company. The capital allowance had been obtained not because of the payment of the subscription money to the trustees but because of the acquisition of the property by the trustees. Further, since the 1992 Act was to apply as if the scheme were a company, that expenditure was not part of the consideration that fell within s 38(1) in relation to notional shares. Accordingly, the appeal would be dismissed.

Smallwood v Revenue and Customs Comrs [2006] EWHC 1653 (Ch), [2006] STC 2050 (Chancery Division: Warren J).

400 Disposal of assets—group of companies—residence of company for purposes of United Kingdom tax law—central control and management test

The taxpayers had been assessed to tax on gains accrued on a disposal of shares in a United Kingdom company. The disposal had been made by a company registered in the British Virgin Islands, to a company incorporated in the Netherlands. The Revenue considered that whilst the British Virgin Islands company was not resident in the United Kingdom, the Netherlands' company was. Therefore the Revenue considered that the whole of the purchase consideration was a chargeable gain. The taxpayers appealed to the Special Commissioners. It was common ground that the question whether the Netherlands' company was resident in the United Kingdom at the relevant time turned on the issue of where its real business and central management and control were carried on. The commissioners considered that there was no indication that any effective management decisions had been taken in the Netherlands and dismissed the appeal. On further appeal by the taxpayers the judge held that the commissioners had erred in the proper application of the law and that the company had been resident in the Netherlands. The appeal was allowed and the Revenue appealed. *Held*, in seeking to determine where central management and control of a company incorporated outside the United Kingdom lay, it was essential to recognise the distinction between cases where management and control of the company were exercised through its own constitutional organs and cases where the functions of those constitutional organs were usurped, in the sense that management and control were exercised independently of those constitutional organs. In cases which fell within the former class, it was essential to recognise the distinction between the role of an outsider in proposing and influencing the decisions which the constitutional organs took in fulfilling their functions and the role of an outsider who dictated the decisions which were to be taken. The judge had been correct that the only conclusion open to the commissioners, on the facts that they had found, was that the company was resident in the Netherlands. The facts included the finding that the company's directors had not been by-passed since their representatives had signed or executed documents, and that the directors had accepted the agreement. Accordingly, the appeal would be dismissed.

Wood v Holden (Inspector of Taxes) [2006] EWCA Civ 26, [2006] 1 WLR 1393 (Court of Appeal: Chadwick and Moore-Bick LJJ and Sir Christopher Staughton). Decision of Park J [2005] EWHC 547 (Ch), [2005] STC 789 (2005 Abr para 379) affirmed.

401 Exemptions and reliefs—annual exempt amount

The Capital Gains Tax (Annual Exempt Amount) Order 2006, SI 2006/871 (made on 22 March 2006), provides that for the year 2006–07 an individual is exempt from capital gains tax on taxable gains not exceeding £8,800. This applies unless Parliament determines otherwise.

402 Exemption and reliefs—gilt-edged securities

The Taxation of Chargeable Gains (Gilt-edged Securities) Order 2006, SI 2006/184 (in force on 30 January 2006), specifies five further gilt-edged securities, disposals of which are exempt from tax on chargeable gains in accordance with the Taxation of Chargeable Gains Act 1992 s 115.

The Taxation of Chargeable Gains (Gilt-edged Securities) (No 2) Order 2006, SI 2006/3170 (made on 28 November 2006), specifies five further gilt-edged securities, disposals of which are exempt from tax on chargeable gains in accordance with the Taxation of Chargeable Gains Act 1992 s 115.

403 Finance Act 2006

See para 2465.

404 Permanent interest-bearing share—definition

The Capital Gains Tax (Definition of Permanent Interest Bearing Share) Regulations 2006, SI 2006/3291 (in force on 1 January 2007), amend the definition of 'permanent interest-bearing share' in the Taxation of Chargeable Gains Act 1992 s 117(11)(b) by replacing the reference to the Prudential Sourcebook for Building Societies with a reference to the General Prudential Sharebook issued by the Financial Services Authority under the Financial Services and Markets Act 2000.

CARRIERS

Halsbury's Laws of England (4th edn) vol 5(1) (Reissue) paras 501–703

Articles

For articles relating to this title please refer to the Table of Articles at the beginning of the Abridgment.

405　Carriage by air

See AVIATION.

406　Carriage by rail

See RAILWAYS, INLAND WATERWAYS AND PIPE-LINES.

407　Carriage by sea

See SHIPPING AND NAVIGATION.

CHARITIES

Halsbury's Laws of England (4th edn) vol 5(2) (2001 Reissue) paras 1–581

Articles

For articles relating to this title please refer to the Table of Articles at the beginning of the Abridgment.

408　Charities Act 2006

The Charities Act 2006 makes provision for the establishment and functions of the Charity Commission for England and Wales and the Charity Tribunal and makes other amendments to the law about charities, including provision about charitable incorporated organisations and public charitable collections and other fund raising carried on in connection with charities and other institutions. The Act received the royal assent on 8 November 2006 and came into force in part on that day. The remaining provisions come into force on a day or days to be appointed. For details of commencement, see the commencement table in the title STATUTES.

Part 1 (ss 1–5) Meaning of 'charity' and 'charitable purpose'
Section 1 provides for the first time a general statutory definition of charity for the purposes of the law. There is also the first statutory definition of 'charitable purpose': s 2. The public benefit test is dealt with by s 3. Section 4 requires the Charity Commission to issue guidance in pursuance of the objective of promoting understanding and awareness of the operation of the public benefit requirement. By virtue of s 5, facilities made available to men only are to be regarded as charitable on the same basis as facilities made available to the public as a whole or to women only.

Part 2 (ss 6–44) Regulation of charities
Section 6, Schs 1, 2 create a new body corporate called the Charity Commission for England and Wales, to be known in Wales as Comisiwn Elusennau Cymru a Lloegr, which will be a non-ministerial government department with a significant degree of independence in the performance of its functions. The Commission is provided with objectives which describe what the Commission is to seek to achieve: s 7.
　　Section 8, Schs 3, 4 create a new tribunal to act as the court of first instance for appeals and applications in respect of certain decisions of the new Commission and enable the Charity Tribunal to consider matters referred to it by the Attorney General or the Commission. By virtue of s 9, there continues to be a register of charities, which is to be kept by the Commission and in which every charity must be registered unless it belongs to one of the four classes or descriptions of charity that are not required to be registered. The Minister for the Cabinet Office may change the threshold for registration of small charities before he brings into force the general rule that every charity must be registered: s 10. Under s 11, specified institutions are no longer exempt charities. Section 12, Sch 5 concern the Commission's power to institute inquires into exempt charities on the request of a charity's principal regulator. By virtue of s 13, the Minister for the Cabinet Office may make regulations prescribing a body or a minister of the Crown as the principal regulator of an exempt charity. Before exercising any of its specific powers in relation to an exempt charity the Commission must consult the principal regulator of the charity : s 14. Under s 15, the Commission, when making a scheme to alter the purposes for which charity property is to be applied, must take into account not only the spirit of the gift of the property but also the social and economic circumstances prevailing at the time of the proposed alteration in the purpose.
　　Section 16 gives the Commission the power to decide whether property is to be treated as belonging to donors who cannot be identified. Provision is made by s 17 for the application cy-près

of gifts made in response to certain solicitations. Section 18 alters the cy-près rule so that the court or the Commission, when making a scheme changing the charitable purposes for which particular property given to a charity is held, must have regard to the desirability of choosing new purposes which are close to the original purposes. Under s 19, the Commission has power to suspend from membership of a charity a trustee, charity trustee, officer, agent or employee of the charity who has been suspended or removed from office. Section 20 allows the Commission, after it has instituted a statutory inquiry with respect to a charity, to give specific directions for the protection of the charity. The Commission, in certain circumstances, may make an order directing a person who is in possession or control of charity property to apply that property in a specified way: s 21. Changes are made by s 22 to expedite the formal procedure for the making of schemes and orders by the Commission and to reduce the cost to charities, by making the advertising of such schemes and orders a matter of Commission discretion: s 22. Section 23 relates to Scottish and Northern Irish charities. By s 24, provision is made to preserve the Commission's existing power to give advice and guidance, and to add a more general power to give advice. Section 25 gives the Commission power to determine membership of a charity. The Commission, under the authority of a warrant issued by a justice of the peace, may enter premises and seize documents for certain purposes: s 26. Under s 27, the restrictions on the mortgaging of charity land are extended. Section 28 removes from the requirement for an annual audit or examination of accounts of a charity which is not a company any references to the expenditure of the charity so that the level of its expenditure is no longer relevant in determining whether its accounts must be audited. By s 29, the duty of auditors of registered charities to report to the Commission abuse or significant breaches of charity law or regulation is extended to independent examiners. Section 30, Sch 6 require a charity which has subsidiaries under its control to prepare annual accounts relating to the whole group consisting of the parent and all of its subsidiaries.

Section 31 limits the occasions on which alteration of a charitable company's memorandum or articles of association require the prior written consent of the Commission. Under s 32, the audit thresholds for charitable companies and unincorporated charities are revised. Section 33 extends to persons acting as auditors of charitable companies the duties, powers and protection given to auditors and independent examiners. Section 34, Sch 7 make provision for charitable incorporated organisations, a new legal form, whose purpose is to avoid the need for a charity wishing to benefit from incorporation to register as a company and be liable to dual regulation by Companies House and the Commission. The Commission must grant an application for a waiver from disqualification to a person who has been disqualified for more than five years unless it is satisfied that there are special circumstances: s 35. Provision is made by s 36 for the remuneration of a person who is either a trustee of a charity or connected with a trustee of the charity who might receive a benefit as a result of the connected person's remuneration: s 36. Where a trustee or connected person is entitled to receive remuneration under an agreement, s 37 provides that the trustee is disqualified from acting as a trustee in relation to decisions or other matters about the agreement. Section 38 empowers the Commission to grant relief where it believes that a trustee has acted honestly and reasonably and ought fairly to be excused from liability for breach of trust or duty. Charity trustees are provided with a power to purchase trustee indemnity insurance and to pay the premiums with the charity's money: s 39. Sections 40–42 extend the powers of unincorporated charities to transfer all of their property, to replace their purposes and to modify their powers or procedures. Section 43 provides powers for small unincorporated charities to spend capital or far larger unincorporated charities to spend capital given for a particular purpose and for the spending of capital subject to special trusts. The register of charity mergers is established by s 44.

Part 3 (ss 45–71) Funding for charitable, benevolent or philanthropic institutions
Section 45 defines collections in a public place and door to door collections as the two types of public charitable collection. Charitable appeals that are not public charitable collections are defined: s 46. Section 47 provides further definitions relating to public charitable collections. Section 48 sets out the restrictions on collecting in a public place. A collection by means of visits door to door cannot be undertaken unless the organisation holds a public collections certificate: s 49. Section 50 sets out the conditions under which a collection is exempt from the requirement to obtain a public collections certificate and a permit to collect. A person proposing to undertake public charitable collections may apply to the Commission for a public collections certificate: s 51. By virtue of s 52, on receiving such an application, the Commission may make such inquiries as it thinks fit and determine the application by either issuing the certificate or refusing the application. Section 53 sets out the grounds on which the Commission may rely for refusing to award a public collections certificate. Section 54 provides a power for the Commission to request information or documents held by applicants. There is a fast-track method for unincorporated charities to transfer a public collections certificate between trustees: s 55. Section 56 enables the Commission to withdraw or suspend a public collections certificate. Section 57 sets out the rights of appeal against Commission decisions relating to public collections certificates. The process for applications to local authorities for a permit to conduct a collection in a public place is set out: s 58. Section 59 describes the process for the determination of applications and the issue of permits to collect in a public place. Section 60 provides that the only ground on which a local authority may refuse to award a permit to conduct a

collection in a public place is that the proposed collection would cause undue inconvenience to members of the public. A local authority may withdraw a permit, or attach or vary conditions to a permit: s 61. Section 62 sets out the rights of appeal to magistrates' courts against local authority decisions. Section 63 confers regulation-making powers on the Minister for the Cabinet Office in relation to public charitable collections. Offences are created by s 64 in respect of charitable collections. Section 65 specifies the circumstances in which the officers of a corporate body as well as the corporate body itself are guilty of an offence. The requirements for serving notices to persons or corporate bodies are specified: s 66.

Section 67 requires a professional fund raiser to state the amount of his remuneration in connection with an appeal. Where a paid employee, officer, or trustee of a charity is acting as a collector in respect of a public charitable collection, he must indicate the institutions benefiting and the arrangements for his remuneration: s 68. A power to make regulations to control charity fund raising if the Minister for the Cabinet Office deems it necessary or desirable is provided by s 69. Section 70 confers power on the Secretary of State or the Minister for the Cabinet Office to give financial assistance to charitable, benevolent or philanthropic institutions. The National Assembly for Wales is given an equivalent power: s 71.

Part 4 (ss 72–80) Miscellaneous and general
Section 72 concerns disclosure of information to and by the Northern Ireland regulator. Section 73 requires the Minister for the Cabinet Office within five years after royal assent to institute a review of the operation of the 2006 Act. Section 74 deals with the making of orders or regulations under the Act, s75, Schs 8–10 deal with amendments, repeals and transitional provisions, and s 76 with pre-consolidation amendments. Section 77 enables the Minister for the Cabinet Office to amend the Charities Act 1993 and the 2006 Act to reflect changes in company law audit provisions. Section 78 deals with interpretation. Section 79 provides for commencement and s 80 with short title.

Amendments, repeals and revocations
The list below, which is not exhaustive, mentions repeals and amendments which are or will be effective when the Act is fully in force.

Specific provisions of a number of Acts are amended, added or repealed. These include: Recreational Charities Act 1958 ss 1, 2; Companies Act 1985 s 249A; Charities Act 1992 ss 60, 60A, 60B, 64A; Charities Act 1993 ss 1A, 1B, 2A–2D, 13, 14, 14A, 14B, 18A, 19A, 19B, 20, 20A, 24, 25, 29A, 31A, 43, 49A, 64, 73F, 75C–75F, 86A, Schs 1A, 1C, 1D, 5A.

409 Charity Commissioners—powers—power to authorise action by charity trustees—constitutional and membership issues

Under the Charities Act 1993 s 26(1), where it appears to the Charity Commissioners that any action proposed or contemplated in the administration of a charity is expedient in the interests of the charity, they may by order sanction that action, whether or not it would otherwise be within the powers exercisable by the charity trustees in the administration of the charity; and anything done under the authority of such an order must be deemed to be properly done in the exercise of those powers.

The articles of association of a citizens advice bureau provided for one-third of the members of the bureau's management committee to retire at the annual general meeting, when new members would be chosen and elected. The applicant sought a declaration that he was a member of the committee and should be permitted to attend meetings. An injunction to restrain the holding of any meetings was granted but later discharged and the action was stayed pending the applicant's obtaining permission from the defendants, the Charity Commissioners, to continue the action. The applicant applied, pursuant to the 1993 Act s 33, for permission to continue the action. Having investigated the bureau's records, the defendants concluded that it was particularly difficult to identify the members of the committee without a full trial of the issue. In order to provide a practical solution to the problem, pursuant to their powers under s 26, the defendants proposed a method for identifying those members, and refused the applicant leave to continue with the action. The applicant applied to the High Court for such leave. It fell to be determined whether s 26 applied to constitutional and membership issues. *Held*, s 26 gave particulars of transactions which might be authorised by the defendants under the general power in s 26. It was fair to say that those particulars were directed to transactions relating to property of a charity rather than to constitutional issues or membership issues. However, the final words of s 26 should not be cut down by reference to the latter words of s 26. More particularly, the wording of s 26 where reference was made to 'any action proposed or contemplated in the administration of a charity is expedient in the interests of the charity' was wide enough to encompass the matters to be dealt with by the proposed exercise of the defendants' powers. The defendants had the power to proceed as they proposed to do pursuant to their powers under s 26. Accordingly, the application would be dismissed and leave to proceed with the action would be refused.

Seray-Wurie v Charity Comrs for England and Wales [2006] All ER (D) 43 (Aug) (Chancery Division: David Richards J).

410   Registration—social landlord—housing association—business

See *Riverside Housing Association Ltd v Revenue and Customs Comrs*, para 2942.

CHILDREN AND YOUNG PERSONS

Halsbury's Laws of England (4th edn) vol 5(3) (Reissue) paras 1–1824

Articles

For articles relating to this title please refer to the Table of Articles at the beginning of the Abridgment.

411   Adoption—application—hearing—notice of hearing—birth parents

The applicants sought to adopt two brothers, aged five and seven, pursuant to the Adoption and Children Act 2002. The two children had been subject to care orders under the Children Act 1989 Pt IV (ss 31–42), but they had been freed for adoption pursuant to the Adoption Act 1976 s 18, and placed for adoption with the applicants by the adoption agency. Under the 1976 Act, there was no requirement for birth parents to be given notice of the adoption application hearing. However, an issue arose as to whether the position was different for birth parents whose children were freed for adoption under the 1976 Act, but who were the subject of adoption proceedings under the 2002 Act. The judge decided that the 2002 Act reflected a more enlightened approach to birth parents, and that, in the circumstances, it would be wholly wrong for the birth parents to be kept ignorant of the applications for the adoption of their children. He therefore ordered that the birth parents be given notice of the adoption hearing, and the opportunity to file and serve a written statement as well as attend or be represented at the hearing if they so wished. The applicants appealed. *Held*, where proceedings for adoption were brought under the 2002 Act in respect of a child who had been freed for adoption under the 1976 Act, the court would follow the procedure laid down in the 1976 Act, as prescribed by the 2002 Act Sch 4 para 7(1), unless any provision of the 2002 Act or the Family Procedure (Adoption) Rules 2005, SI 2005/2795, required the court to do otherwise. Nothing in either the 2002 Act or the 2005 Rules required the court to give notice of the proceedings to the children's birth parents. The 1976 Act s 19, which limited the duties of the adoption agency to notifying the birth parents that the children had been placed for adoption and/or adopted expressly, continued to apply. It followed that the judge had been plainly wrong to hold that the children's birth parents had a right to be notified of the final hearing of the adoption proceedings. Accordingly, the appeal would be allowed.

Re F (Children) (Adoption: Notice of Hearing) [2006] EWCA Civ 1345, [2006] All ER (D) 205 (Oct) (Court of Appeal: Ward and Wall LJJ).

412   Adoption—confidentiality—identity of adopters—local authority's duty to maintain confidentiality

See *B v A CC*, para 2081.

413   Adoption—freeing order—dispensing with parental agreement—parent unreasonably withholding agreement

Scotland

A local authority had been closely involved in the care of a child since he was four months old. He had not lived with his parents since he was one year and ten months old and had no direct contact with them since he was four years old. The authority sought an order freeing the child for adoption, and dispensing with the agreement of his parents on the ground that they were unreasonably withholding their agreement. Initially the petition was dismissed, but on appeal the court found that the child had no significant attachment to his birth parents, that direct contact was not in the child's best interests and that they had been unreasonably withholding their agreement to adoption. The father appealed, contending that there had been an undue delay in the proceedings and that the authority had breached its statutory duty to consider alternatives to adoption. *Held*, the length of the delay in the proceedings had not been unreasonable and had not contravened the European Convention on Human Rights art 6. Part of the delay had resulted from the authority's decision to appeal, which it was entitled to do and which it did in a legally impeccable manner. The remainder consisted of time taken by the appellant deciding whether he should appeal. The findings of fact showed that the authority and the other agencies involved had considered all practicable options before the authority decided to apply for a freeing order. Further, the conclusion that the appellant was unreasonably withholding consent was supported by the finding that direct contact with him would not be in the child's best interests. Accordingly, the appeal would be dismissed.

Dundee CC v K 2006 SLT 63 (Inner House).

414   Adoption—independent review of determinations—Wales

The Independent Review of Determinations (Adoption) (Wales) Regulations 2006, SI 2006/3100 (in force on 31 December 2006), replace the 2005 Regulations, SI 2005/1819, and make provision for the review by an independent panel in two types of case, which are (1) a determination made by an adoption agency under the Adoption Agencies (Wales) Regulations 2005, SI 2005/1313, that it does not propose to approve a prospective adopter as suitable to adopt a child or decides on review that a prospective adopter is no longer suitable to adopt a child; and (2) a determination made by an adoption agency under the Access to Information (Post-Commencement Adoptions) (Wales) Regulations 2005, SI 2005/2689. The regulations also (a) make provision for the constitution and membership of panels, their functions and the payment of fees, meetings and record keeping of the panels which are appointed by the National Assembly for Wales to review qualifying determinations; and (b) make provision for the procedure to be followed when a review of a qualifying determination by a constituted panel is sought.

415   Adoption—placement for adoption—recommendation—approval by local authority—procedure

A local authority had devised several care plans in respect of a child but subsequently came to the conclusion that adoption would be the best solution for the child. The court granted both a care order and a placement order and the parents appealed. An issue arose as to the meaning of the requirement in the Adoption and Children Act 2002 s 22 that a local authority was to apply for a placement order if it was satisfied that a child ought to be placed for adoption, more specifically whether a local authority was acting in accordance with the provisions of the Children Act 1989 Pt III (ss 17–30) and Pt IV (ss 31–42) or as an adoption agency under the terms of the 2002 Act. *Held*, it was in its role as an adoption agency that a local authority had to be satisfied that a child ought to be placed for adoption. That process could not be achieved until there had been complete compliance with the requirements of the Adoption Agencies Regulations 2005, SI 2005/389, which included the positive decision of the authority's appointed officer to indorse the recommendation of the adoption panel. The authority might reach a decision that adoption was the right future for the child, and so declare that in the care plan. The case would then be presented to the panel, which had to reach its recommendation within the terms of the 2005 Regulations. If the decision of the panel supported the provisional decision of the authority acting in accordance with the 1989 Act Pt IV, then that decision had to be considered independently by the authority as an adoption agency under the provisions of the 2005 Regulations. Once that was done, the way was clear for the issue of an application for a placement order. Before that point an application would be premature. Judgment would be given accordingly.

Re P-B (A Child) (Adoption: Application for Placement Order) [2006] EWCA Civ 1016, [2006] Fam Law 9 (Court of Appeal: Thorpe, Arden and Wilson LJJ).

416   Adoption—proceedings—rules of court

Sir Mark Potter, President of the Family Division, has issued 22 *Practice Directions*, with the concurrence of the Lord Chancellor, which supplement the Family Procedure (Adoption) Rules 2005, SI 2005/2795, and will apply to proceedings under the Adoption and Children Act 2002, whether at first instance or on appeal in the High Court, county courts and magistrates' courts. The *Practice Directions* deal with:

1. Hearings by a single justice of the peace
2. Court documents
3. Civil restraint orders
4. Forms
5. Who receives a copy of the application form for orders in proceedings
6. The first directions hearing – adoptions with a foreign element
7. Reports by the adoption agency or local authority
8. Reports by registered medical practitioner
9. Service
10. Service out of the jurisdiction
11. Litigation friends
12. Communication of information relating to proceedings
13. Disclosing information to adopted adult
14. Other applications in proceedings
15. Alternative procedure for applications
16. Human rights, joining the Crown
17. Interim injunctions
18. Evidence
19. Depositions and court attendance by witnesses
20. Experts
21. Change of solicitor
22. Appeals

1. Practice Direction – Hearings by a Single Justice of the Peace

This *Practice Direction* supplements the 2005 Rules Pt 2 r 7(1)(c)(ii)(bb).

Functions of the court that may be dealt with by a single justice of the peace.

1.1 Rule 7(1)(c) provides that a single justice of the peace who is a member of the family panel may deal with an application under the 2002 Act s 41(2) (recovery orders) made without notice.

1.2 A single justice of the peace who is a member of the family panel may also perform the functions of the court listed in:

(a) column 2 of table 1 in accordance with the rules listed in column 1; and

(b) column 2 of table 2 in accordance with the paragraph of the *Practice Direction* listed in column 1.

Table 1

Rule	Nature of function
12(2)(a)–(c), (e), (g), (i), (j), (m), (n)	Case management powers, in accordance with the 2005 Rules r 13 (except paras (5), (7), if exercised of own initiative).
14(b)	Step to be taken by court instead of court officer.
20(3)	Direction that serial number be removed.
21(1), (2)	Direction to reveal personal details.
23(2)	Direction that child be made a respondent.
23(3)	Direction that any other person or body be made a respondent or cease to be a respondent.
23(4)	Consequential directions following the addition or removal of a party.
24(1)(a)(ii)	Set date for first directions hearing.
24(1)(a)(vi)	Set date for final hearing.
24(2)(a)(i)	Ask that relevant forms of consent to an adoption order or the 2002 Act s 84 order be filed.
24(2)(a)(ii)	Ask that the local authority prepare a report on the suitability of the prospective adopters.
24(2)(b)(i)	Ask that the adoption agency file relevant forms of consent.
24(2)(b)(ii) and (iii)	Ask that any statements made under s 20(4)(a) or (b) be filed.
24(2)(b)(iv)	Ask that the adoption agency prepare a report on the suitability of the prospective adopters.
24(3)(a)	Direction that local authority prepare report giving their reasons for placing the child for adoption.
24(3)(b)	Ask that relevant forms of consent to the child being placed for adoption be filed.
24(4)	Giving directions instead of setting date for first directions hearing.
25	Direction that first directions hearing may be more than four weeks after the date on which the application is issued.
26(1), (4)	Giving directions at first directions hearing.
26(5)	Giving directions at any stage of the proceedings.
26(6)(a)	Setting a date for a further directions hearing or other hearing.
26(7)	Monitoring compliance with timetable and directions given.
27(4)(b)(ii)	Direction that an application under the 2005 Rules r 55(3) (litigation friend) be made.
29(4)	Request to adoption agency or local authority for further report or for assistance.
32(4)	Direction that person must attend final hearing.
32(7)	Direction that child or applicant need not attend final hearing.
34(b)	Direction that the provisions in Pt 6 do not apply to the service of a document.
35(3)	Direction that service be effected by an alternative method.
36(1)(b)	Direction that document be served by someone other than court officer.
36(2)	Decision as to which method of service to use.

Rule	Nature of function
37(4)	Direction that document be served on child, patient or some other person other than person specified in table.
37(5)	Direction that, although document served on someone other than the person specified in table, it is to be treated as properly served.
39	Direction that service of a document is dispensed with.
55(3)	Direction that an application under r 55(3) (litigation friend) be made by a party.
55(5)	Direction that person appointed as litigation friend will not be treated as a party for the purpose of any provision in the 2005 Rules regarding service.
57(2)	Direction that court officer need not send application to patient.
59	Appointment of children's guardian.
60(1)(a)	Recording reasons for refusal to appoint children's guardian.
61(1), (2)	Terminating appointment of children's guardian and recording the reasons for doing so.
63(1)	Direction regarding investigations conducted by children's guardian.
63(3)(b)	Consideration that child of sufficient understanding to instruct a solicitor direct.
64(2)(a), (b)	Directions about children's guardian performing duties and role in proceedings where child instructing solicitor direct.
64(2)(c)	Giving permission for children's guardian to have legal representation.
65(1)	Direction that children's guardian or solicitor need not attend directions hearing.
65(3)	Direction that advice from children's guardian to be given to the court in a particular way.
65(4)(a)	Direction that children's guardian need not file written report on the interests of the child.
66(2)(b)(ii)	Direction that children's guardian need not bring documents/records to attention of parties.
68(5)	Terminating appointment of solicitor and recording the reasons for doing so.
68(6)	Recording the appointment of or refusal to appoint a solicitor for the child.
69	Appointment of reporting officer.
72(4)	Direction that reporting officer need not attend directions hearing.
73(1)	Request to children and family reporter to prepare report on the welfare of the child.
74(1)	Direction regarding investigations conducted by children and family reporter.
74(3)(a)	Direction that children and family reporter need not attend directions hearing.
77	Direction that confidential report be disclosed to party.
78(1)(a)	Giving permission to communicate information relating to proceedings held in private.
78(1)(b)	Direction that information relating to proceedings held in private is not to be disclosed in accordance with the relevant *practice direction*.
83	Direction that document or order be open to inspection or given to any person.
84(2)	Removing protected information from document before disclosing to adopted adult.
85(1)(a)	Direction that translation of document may be provided by party other than the applicant.

This *Practice Direction* supplements the 2005 Rules Pt 2 r 9(4).

Form of Documents

1.1 Documents drafted by a legal representative should bear his or her signature and if they are drafted by a legal representative as a member or employee of a firm they should be signed in the name of the firm.

1.2 Every document prepared by a party for filing or use at the court must:

(a) unless the nature of the document renders it impracticable, be on A4 paper of durable quality having a margin, not less than 3.5 centimetres wide;

(b) be fully legible and should normally be typed;

(c) where possible be bound securely in a manner which would not hamper filing or otherwise each page should be endorsed with the case number;

(d) have the pages numbered consecutively;

(e) be divided into numbered paragraphs;

(f) have all numbers, including dates, expressed as figures; and

(g) give in the margin the reference of every document mentioned that has already been filed.

1.3 A document which is a copy produced by a colour photostat machine or other similar device may be filed at the court office provided that the coloured date seal of the court is not reproduced on the copy.

Documents for filing at court

2.1 The date on which a document was filed at court must be recorded on the document. This may be done by a seal or a receipt stamp.

2.2 Particulars of the date of delivery at a court office of any document for filing and the title of the proceedings in which the document is filed must be entered in court records, on the court file or on a computer kept in the court office for the purpose. Except where a document has been delivered at the court office through the post, the time of delivery should also be recorded.

2.3 Where the court orders any document to be lodged in court, the document must, unless otherwise directed, be deposited in the office of that court.

2.4 A document filed, lodged or held in any court office must not be taken out of that office without the permission of the court unless the proceedings are transferred to another court in accordance with the Children (Allocation of Proceedings) Order 1991, SI 1991/1677.

3. Practice Direction – Civil Restraint Orders

This *Practice Direction* supplements the 2005 Rules Pt 3 r 16.

Introduction

1 This *Practice Direction* applies where the court is considering whether to make:

(a) a limited civil restraint order;

(b) an extended civil restraint order; or

(c) a general civil restraint order,

against a party who has made applications which are totally without merit.

Rules 13(7), 96 provide that where an application is dismissed and is totally without merit, the court order must specify that fact and the court must consider whether to make a civil restraint order. Rule 180(5) makes similar provision where the appeal court strikes out an appellant's notice or dismisses an appeal.

Limited civil restraint orders

2.1 A limited civil restraint order may be made by a judge or district judge, including a district judge of the principal registry of the Family Division, of the High Court or a county court where a party has made two or more applications which are totally without merit.

2.2 Where the court makes a limited civil restraint order, the party against whom the order is made:

(1) will be restrained from making any further applications in the proceedings in which the order is made without first obtaining the permission of a judge identified in the order;

(2) may apply for amendment or discharge of the order provided he has first obtained the permission of a judge identified in the order; and

(3) may apply for permission to appeal the order and if permission is granted, may appeal the order.

2.3 Where a party who is subject to a limited civil restraint order:

(1) makes a further application in the proceedings in which the order is made without first obtaining the permission of a judge identified in the order, such application will automatically be dismissed

(a) without the judge having to make any further order; and

(b) without the need for the other party to respond to it; and

(2) repeatedly makes applications for permission pursuant to that order which are totally without merit, the court may direct that if the party makes any further application for permission which is totally without merit, the decision to dismiss the application will be final and there will be no right of appeal, unless the judge who refused permission grants permission to appeal.

2.4 Unless the court directs otherwise, a party who is subject to a limited civil restraint order may not make an application for permission under heads 2.2(1) or (2), above, without first serving notice of the application on the other party in accordance with head 2.5, below.

2.5 A notice under head 2.4, above, must:

(1) set out the nature and grounds of the application; and

(2) provide the other party with at least seven days within which to respond.

2.6 An application for permission under heads 2.2(1) or (2), above:

(1) must be made in writing;

(2) must include the other party's written response, if any, to the notice served under head 2.4, above; and

(3) will be determined without a hearing.

2.7 An order under head 2.3(2), above, may only be made by a High Court judge.

2.8 Where a party makes an application for permission under heads 2.2(1) or (2), above, and permission is refused, any application for permission to appeal:

(1) must be made in writing; and

(2) will be determined without a hearing.

2.9 A limited civil restraint order:

(1) is limited to the particular proceedings in which it is made;

(2) will remain in effect for the duration of the proceedings in which it is made, unless the court otherwise orders; and

(3) must identify the judge or judges to whom an application for permission under heads 2.2(1), 2.2(2) or 2.8, above, should be made.

Extended civil restraint orders

3.1 An extended civil restraint order may be made by a judge of the High Court where a party has persistently made applications which are totally without merit.

3.2 Unless the court otherwise orders, where the court makes an extended civil restraint order, the party against whom the order is made:

(1) will be restrained from making applications in any court concerning any matter involving or relating to or touching on or leading to the proceedings in which the order is made without first obtaining the permission of a judge identified in the order;

(2) may apply for amendment or discharge of the order provided he has first obtained the permission of a judge identified in the order; and

(3) may apply for permission to appeal the order and if permission is granted, may appeal the order.

3.3 Where a party who is subject to an extended civil restraint order:

(1) makes an application in a court identified in the order concerning any matter involving or relating to or touching on or leading to the proceedings in which the order is made without first obtaining the permission of a judge identified in the order, the application will automatically be struck out or dismissed

(a) without the judge having to make any further order; and

(b) without the need for the other party to respond to it; and

(2) repeatedly makes applications for permission pursuant to that order which are totally without merit, the court may direct that if the party makes any further application for permission which is totally without merit, the decision to dismiss the application will be final and there will be no right of appeal, unless the judge who refused permission grants permission to appeal.

3.4 Unless the court otherwise directs, a party who is subject to an extended civil restraint order may not make an application for permission under heads 3.2(1) or (2), above, without first serving notice of the application on the other party in accordance with head 3.5, below.

3.5 A notice under head 3.4, above, must:

(1) set out the nature and grounds of the application; and

(2) provide the other party with at least seven days within which to respond.

3.6 An application for permission under heads 3.2(1) or (2), above:

(1) must be made in writing;

(2) must include the other party's written response, if any, to the notice served under head 3.4, above; and

(3) will be determined without a hearing.

3.7 An order under head 3.3(2), above, may only be made by a High Court judge.

3.8 Where a party makes an application for permission under heads 3.2(1) or (2), above, and permission is refused, any application for permission to appeal:

(1) must be made in writing; and

(2) will be determined without a hearing.

3.9 An extended civil restraint order:

(1) will be made for a specified period not exceeding two years;

(2) must identify the courts in which the party against whom the order is made is restrained from making applications; and

(3) must identify the judge or judges to whom an application for permission under heads 3.2(1), 3.2(2) or 3.8, above should be made.

3.10 The court may extend the duration of an extended civil restraint order, if it considers it appropriate to do so, but it must not be extended for a period greater than two years on any given occasion.

General civil restraint orders

4.1 A general civil restraint order may be made by a judge of the High Court where, the party against whom the order is made persists in making applications which are totally without merit, in circumstances where an extended civil restraint order would not be sufficient or appropriate.

4.2 Unless the court otherwise orders, where the court makes a general civil restraint order, the party against whom the order is made:

(1) will be restrained from making any application in any court without first obtaining the permission of a judge identified in the order;

(2) may apply for amendment or discharge of the order provided he has first obtained the permission of a judge identified in the order; and

(3) may apply for permission to appeal the order and if permission is granted, may appeal the order.

4.3 Where a party who is subject to a general civil restraint order:

(1) makes an application in a court identified in the order without first obtaining the permission of a judge identified in the order, the application will automatically be struck out or dismissed

(a) without the judge having to make any further order; and

(b) without the need for the other party to respond to it; and

(2) repeatedly makes applications for permission pursuant to that order which are totally without merit, the court may direct that if the party makes any further application for permission which is totally without merit, the decision to dismiss that application will be final and there will be no right of appeal, unless the judge who refused permission grants permission to appeal.

4.4 Unless the court directs otherwise, a party who is subject to a general civil restraint order may not make an application for permission under heads 4.2(1) or (2), above, without first serving notice of the application on the other party in accordance with head 4.5, below.

4.5 A notice under head 4.4 must:

(1) set out the nature and grounds of the application; and

(2) provide the other party with at least seven days within which to respond.

4.6 An application for permission under heads 4.2(1) or (2), above:

(1) must be made in writing;

(2) must include the other party's written response, if any, to the notice served under head 4.4, above; and

(3) will be determined without a hearing.

4.7 An order under head 4.3(2), above, may only be made by a High Court judge.

4.8 Where a party makes an application for permission under heads 4.2(1) or (2), above, and permission is refused, any application for permission to appeal:

(1) must be made in writing; and

(2) will be determined without a hearing.

4.9 A general civil restraint order:

(1) will be made for a specified period not exceeding two years;

(2) must identify the courts in which the party against whom the order is made is restrained from making applications; and

(3) must identify the judge or judges to whom an application for permission under heads 4.2(1), 4.2(2) or 4.8, above, should be made.

4.10 The court may extend the duration of a general civil restraint order, if it considers it appropriate to do so, but it must not be extended for a period greater than two years on any given occasion.

General

5.1 The other party or parties to the proceedings may apply for any civil restraint order.

5.2 An application under head 5.1, above, must be made using the procedure in the 2005 Rules Pt 9 unless the court otherwise directs and the application must specify which type of civil restraint order is sought.

4. Practice Direction – Forms

This *Practice Direction* supplements the 2005 Rules Pt 4 r 17, Pt 5, r 28.

1.1 This *Practice Direction* lists the forms to be used in proceedings under the 2002 Act.

1.2 This *Practice Direction* contains two tables:

(a) Table 1 lists forms required or permitted by the 2005 Rules r 17;

(b) Table 2 lists forms required by r 28 (consent).

Table 1

No	Title
A50	Application for a placement order
A51	Application for variation of a placement order
A52	Application for revocation of a placement order
A53	Application for a contact order
A54	Application for variation or revocation of a contact order
A55	Application for permission to change a child's surname
A56	Application for permission to take a child out of the United Kingdom
A57	Application for a recovery order
A58	Application for an adoption order
A59	Application for an adoption order (Convention adoption)
A60	Application for an adoption order (foreign element)
A61	Application for an order under the 2002 Act s 84 (parental responsibility prior to adoption abroad)
A62	Application for a direction under s 88
A63	Application for an order under s 89
A64	Application to receive information from court records
A65	Confidential information
FP1	Application under the 2005 Rules Pt 10
FP1A	Application under the 2005 Rules Pt 10 – notes for applicant
FP1B	Application under the 2005 Rules Pt 10 – notes for respondent
FP2	Application Notice 2005 Rules Pt 9
FP3	Injunction application
FP5	Acknowledgment of service – Pt 10 application
FP6	Certificate of service
FP8	Notice of change of solicitor
FP9	Certificate of suitability of litigation friend
FP25	Witness summons

Table 2

No	Title
A100	Consent to placement for adoption with any prospective adopters
A101	Consent to placement for adoption with identified prospective adopters
A102	Consent to placement for adoption with identified prospective adopters and, if the placement breaks down, with any prospective adopters
A103	Advance consent to adoption
A104	Consent to adoption
A105	Consent to the making of an order under the 2002 Act s 84
A106	Withdrawal of consent

5. *Practice Direction* – Who receives a copy of the Application Form for Orders in Proceedings
This *Practice Direction* supplements the 2005 Rules Pt 5 r 24(1)(b)(ii).

1. In relation to each type of proceedings in column 1 of the following table, column 2 sets out which persons are to receive a copy of the application form.

Proceeding for	Who Receives a Copy of the Application Form
An adoption order (the 2002 Act s 46); or a s 84 order	Any appointed children's guardian, children and family reporter and reporting officer; the local authority to whom notice under s 44 (notice of intention to apply to adopt or apply for a s 84 order) has been given; the adoption agency which placed the child for adoption with the applicants; any other person directed by the court to receive a copy.
A placement order (s 21); or an order varying a placement order (s 23)	Each parent with parental responsibility for the child or guardian of the child; any appointed children's guardian, children and family reporter and reporting officer; any other person directed by the court to receive a copy.
An order revoking a placement order (s 24)	Each parent with parental responsibility for the child or guardian of the child; any appointed children's guardian and children and family reporter; the local authority authorised by the placement order to place the child for adoption; any other person directed by the court to receive a copy.
A contact order (s 26); an order varying or revoking a contact order (s 27); an order permitting the child's name to be changed or the removal of the child from the United Kingdom (s 28(2)); a recovery order (s 41(2)); a s 89 order; and a s 88 direction	All the parties; any appointed children's guardian and children and family reporter; any other person directed by the court to receive a copy.

6. *Practice Direction*—The First Directions Hearing—Adoptions with a Foreign Element
This *Practice Direction* supplements the 2005 Rules Pt 5 r 26(3).

1. This *Practice Direction* applies to proceedings for:

(a) a Convention adoption order;

(b) a 2002 Act s 84 order;

(c) a s 88 direction;

(d) a s 89 order; and

(e) an adoption order where the child has been brought into the United Kingdom in the circumstances where s 83(1) applies.

2 At the first directions hearing the court will, in addition to any matters referred to in the 2005 Rules r 26(1):

(a) consider whether the requirements of the 2002 Act and the Adoptions with a Foreign Element Regulations 2005, SI 2005/392, appear to have been complied with and, if not, consider whether or not it is appropriate to transfer the case to the High Court;

(b) consider whether all relevant documents are translated into English and, if not, fix a timetable for translating any outstanding documents;

(c) consider whether the applicant needs to file an affidavit setting out the full details of the circumstances in which the child was brought to the United Kingdom, of the attitude of the parents to the application and confirming compliance with the requirements of the 2005 Regulations;

(d) give directions about

(i) the production of the child's passport and visa;

(ii) the need for the Official Solicitor and a representative of the Home Office to attend future hearings; and

(iii) personal service on the parents, via the Central Authority in the case of an application for a Convention Adoption Order, including information about the role of the Official Solicitor and availability of legal aid to be represented within the proceedings; and

(e) consider fixing a further directions appointment no later than six weeks after the date of the first directions appointment and timetable a date by which the Official Solicitor should file an interim report in advance of that further appointment.

7. *Practice Direction* – Reports by the Adoption Agency or Local Authority
This *Practice Direction* supplements the 2005 Rules Pt 5 r 29(3).

Matters to be contained in reports

1.1 The matters to be covered in the report on the suitability of the applicant to adopt a child are set out in Annex A to this *Practice Direction*.

1.2 The matters to be covered in a report on the placement of the child for adoption are set out in Annex B to this *Practice Direction*.

1.3 Where a matter to be covered in the reports set out in Annex A and Annex B does not apply to the circumstances of a particular case, the reasons for not covering the matter should be given.

[Editor's note: Annexes A and B not reproduced in this summary.]

8. *Practice Direction*—Reports by a Registered Medical Practitioner ('Health Reports')
This *Practice Direction* supplements the 2005 Rules Pt 5 r 30(2).

Matters to be contained in health reports

1.1 Rule 30(1) requires that health reports must be attached to an application for an adoption order or a 2002 Act s 84 order except where:

(a) the child was placed for adoption with the applicant by an adoption agency;

(b) the applicant or one of the applicants is a parent of the child; or

(c) the applicant is the partner of a parent of the child.

1.2 The matters to be contained in the health reports are set out in the Annex to this *Practice Direction*.

1.3 Where a matter to be contained in the health report does not apply to the circumstances of a particular case, the reasons for not covering the matter should be given.

[Editor's note: Annex not reproduced in this summary.]

9. *Practice Direction*—Service
This *Practice Direction* supplements the 2005 Rules Pt 6 s 1.

Methods of Service

1.1 The various methods of service are set out in r 35.

1.2 The following provisions apply to the specific methods of service referred to.

Service by Document Exchange

2.1 Service by document exchange (DX) may take place only where:

(1) the legal representative's address for service includes a numbered box at a DX; or

(2) the writing paper of the legal representative sets out the DX box number; and

(3) the legal representative has not indicated in writing that they are unwilling to accept service by DX. 'Legal representative' is defined in r 6.

2.2 Service by DX is effected by leaving the document addressed to the numbered box:

(1) at the DX of the legal representative; or

(2) at a DX which sends documents to that legal representative's DX every business day.

Service by the court

3 Where the court effects service of a document in accordance with r 36, the method will normally be by first class post.

Service on members of HM Forces

4.1 Where a person to be served (the 'serviceman') is known to be serving or to have recently served as a member of H.M. Forces the applicant's legal representative may obtain the address for service of proceedings under the 2002 Act from the appropriate officer of the Ministry of Defence as specified in the table in head 4.7, below.

4.2 The letter of inquiry should in every case show that the writer is a legal representative and that the inquiry is made solely with a view to the service of legal documents in those proceedings.

4.3 In all cases the letter should give the full name, service number, rank or rating, and Ship, Arm or Trade, Regiment or Corps and Unit or as much of this information as is available. Failure to quote the service number and the rank or rating may result either in failure to identify the serviceman or in considerable delay.

4.4 The letter should contain an undertaking by the legal representative that if the address is given, it will be used solely for the purpose of issuing and serving documents in the proceedings and that so far as is possible the legal representative will disclose the address only to the court and not to the applicant or any other person, except in the normal course of the proceedings. A legal representative in the service of a public authority or private company should undertake that the address will be used solely for the purpose of issuing and serving documents in the proceedings and that the address will not be disclosed so far as is possible to any other part of his employing organisation or to any other person but only to the court. Normally on receipt of the required information and undertaking the appropriate office will give the service address.

4.5 If the legal representative does not give the undertaking, the only information he will receive will be whether the serviceman is at that time serving in England or Wales, Scotland, Northern Ireland or outside the United Kingdom.

4.6 It should be noted that a serviceman's address which ends with a British Forces Post Office address and reference (BFPO) will nearly always indicate that he is serving outside the United Kingdom.

4.7 The letter of inquiry should be addressed as follows:
Royal Navy Officers The Naval Secretary
Room 161
Victory Building
HM Naval Base
Portsmouth
Hants PO1 3LS

Royal Navy Officers The Naval Secretary
Room 161
Victory Building
HM Naval Base
Portsmouth
Hants PO1 3LS

RN Ratings Commodore Naval Drafting
Centurion Building
Grange Road
Gosport
Hants PO13 9XA

Royal Navy Officers The Naval Secretary
Room 161
Victory Building
HM Naval Base
Portsmouth
Hants PO1 3LS

RN Medical and Dental Officers The Medical Director General (Naval)
Room 114
Victory Building
HM Naval Base
Portsmouth
Hants PO1 3LS

Officers of Queen Alexandra's Royal Naval Nursing Service The Matron-in-Chief
QARNNS
Room 139
Victory Building
HM Naval Base
Portsmouth
Hants PO1 3LS

Naval Chaplains Director General Naval
Chaplaincy Service
Room 201
Victory Building
HM Naval Base
Portsmouth
Hants PO1 3LS

Royal Marine Officers and Ranks Personnel Section
West Battery
Whale Island
Portsmouth
Hants PO2 8DX

RM Ranks HQRM (DRORM)
West Battery
Whale Island
Portsmouth
Hants PO2 8DX

Army Officers and other ranks Army Personnel Centre
Secretariat, Public Enquiries
RM CD424
Kentigern House
65 Brown Street
Glasgow G2 8EH

Royal Air Force Officers and Other Ranks Personnel Management Agency (RAF)
Building 248
RAF Innsworth
Gloucester GL3 1EZ

4.8 Once the applicant's legal representative has learnt the serviceman's address, that address may be used for service by post, in cases where this method of service is allowed by the 2005 Rules.

10. Practice Direction—Service out of the Jurisdiction
This *Practice Direction* supplements the 2005 Rules Pt 6, r 2.

Service in other Member States of the European Union

1.1 Where service is to be effected in another member of state of the European Union, EC Council Regulation 1348/2000 on the service in the Member States of judicial and extrajudicial documents in civil or commercial matters applies.

1.2 Regulation 1348/2000 is annexed to this *Practice Direction*.

(Article 20(1) provides that Regulation 1348/2000 prevails over other provisions contained in bilateral or multilateral agreements or arrangements concluded by the member of states and in particular art IV of the protocol to the Brussels Convention of 1968 and the Hague Convention of 15 November 1965).

Originally published in the official languages of the European Community in the Official Journal of the European Communities by the Office for Official Publications of the European Communities

Documents to be filed under the 2005 Rules 46(2)(d)

2.1 A duplicate of the application form and of any translation required by r 43 must be provided for each party to be served out of the jurisdiction.

2.2 The documents to be served in certain countries require legalisation and the Foreign Process Section (Room E02), Royal Courts of Justice will advise on request. Some countries require legalisation and some require a formal letter of request.

Service in Scotland, Northern Ireland, the Channel Islands, the Isle of Man, Commonwealth countries and United Kingdom Overseas Territories

3.1 Where r 45(3) applies, service should be effected by the applicant or his agent direct except in the case of a Commonwealth State where the judicial authorities have required service to be in accordance with r 44(1)(b)(i). These are presently Malta and Singapore.

3.2 For the purposes of r 45(3)(c), the following countries are United Kingdom Overseas Territories:
(a) Anguilla;
(b) Bermuda;
(c) British Antarctic Territory;
(d) British Indian Ocean Territory;
(e) Cayman Islands;
(f) Falkland Islands;
(g) Gibraltar;
(h) Montserrat;
(i) Pitcairn, Henderson, Ducie and Oeno;
(j) St. Helena and Dependencies;
(k) South Georgia and the South Sandwich Islands;
(l) Sovereign Base Areas of Akrotiri and Dhekelia;
(m) Turks and Caicos Islands; and
(n) Virgin Islands.

Service of application notices and orders

4.1 The provisions of Pt 6 r 2 (special provisions about service out of the jurisdiction) also apply to service out of the jurisdiction of an application notice or order.

4.2 Where an application notice is to be served out of the jurisdiction in accordance Pt 6 r 2 the court must have regard to the country in which the application notice is to be served in setting the date for the hearing of the application and giving any direction about service of the respondent's evidence.

Period for responding to an application

5. Where a Pt 10 application needs to be served out of the jurisdiction, the period for responding to service is seven days less than the number of days listed in the Table.

Table

Place or country	Number of days
Abu Dhabi	22
Afghanistan	23
Albania	25
Algeria	22
Angola	22
Anguilla	31
Antigua	23
Antilles (Netherlands)	31
Argentina	22
Armenia	21

Place or country	Number of days
Ascension	31
Australia	25
Austria	21
Azores	23
Bahamas	22
Bahrain	22
Balearic Islands	21
Bangladesh	23
Barbados	23
Belarus	21
Belgium	21
Belize	23
Benin	25
Bermuda	31
Bhutan	28
Bolivia	23
Bosnia–Hercegovina	21
Botswana	23
Brazil	22
Brunei	25
Bulgaria	23
Burkina Faso	23
Burma	23
Burundi	22
Cameroon	22
Canada	22
Canary Islands	22
Cape Verde Islands	25
Caroline Islands	31
Cayman Islands	31
Central African Republic	25
Chad	25
Chile	22
China	24
Christmas Island	27
Cocos (Keeling) Islands	41
Colombia	22
Comoros	23
Congo (People's Republic)	25
Corsica	21
Costa Rica	23
Croatia	21
Cuba	24
Cyprus	31
Cyrenaica (see Libya)	21
Czech Republic	21
Denmark	21
Djibouti	22
Dominica	23
Dominican Republic	23
Dubai	22

Place or country	Number of days
Ecuador	22
Egypt (Arab Republic)	22
El Salvador (Republic of)	25
Equatorial Guinea	23
Estonia	21
Ethiopia	22
Falkland Islands and Dependencies	31
Faroe Islands	31
Fiji	23
Finland	24
France	21
French Guiana	31
French Polynesia	31
French West Indies	31
Gabon	25
Gambia	22
Georgia	21
Germany	21
Ghana	22
Gibraltar	31
Greece	21
Greenland	31
Grenada	24
Guatemala	24
Guernsey	18
Guyana	22
Haiti	23
Holland (Netherlands)	21
Honduras	24
Hong Kong	31
Hungary	22
Iceland	22
India	23
Indonesia	22
Iran	22
Iraq	22
Ireland (Republic of)	21
Ireland (Northern)	21
Isle of Man	18
Israel	22
Italy	21
Ivory Coast	22
Jamaica	22
Japan	23
Jersey	18
Jordan	23
Kampuchea	38
Kazakhstan	21
Kenya	22
Kirgizstan	21
Korea (North)	28

Place or country	Number of days
Korea (South)	24
Kuwait	22
Laos	30
Latvia	21
Lebanon	22
Lesotho	23
Liberia	22
Libya	21
Liechtenstein	21
Lithuania	21
Luxembourg	21
Macau	31
Macedonia	21
Madagascar	23
Madeira	31
Malawi	23
Malaya	24
Maldive Islands	26
Mali	25
Malta	21
Mariana Islands	26
Marshall Islands	32
Mauritania	23
Mauritius	22
Mexico	23
Moldova	21
Monaco	21
Montserrat	31
Morocco	22
Mozambique	23
Nauru Island	36
Nepal	23
Netherlands	21
Nevis	24
New Caledonia	31
New Hebrides (now Vanuatu)	29
New Zealand	26
New Zealand Island Territories	50
Nicaragua	24
Niger (Republic of)	25
Nigeria	22
Norfolk Island	31
Norway	21
Oman (Sultanate of)	22
Pakistan	23
Panama (Republic of)	26
Papua New Guinea	26
Paraguay	22
Peru	22
Philippines	23
Pitcairn Island	31

Place or country	Number of days
Poland	21
Portugal	21
Portuguese Timor	31
Puerto Rico	23
Qatar	23
Reunion	31
Romania	22
Russia	21
Rwanda	23
Sabah	23
St. Helena	31
St. Kitts–Nevis	24
St. Lucia	24
St. Pierre and Miquelon	31
St. Vincent and the Grenadines	24
Samoa (U.S.A. Territory) (See also Western Samoa)	30
Sarawak	28
Saudi Arabia	24
Scotland	21
Senegal	22
Seychelles	22
Sharjah	24
Sierra Leone	22
Singapore	22
Slovakia	21
Slovenia	21
Society Islands (French Polynesia)	31
Solomon Islands	29
Somali Democratic Republic	22
South Africa (Republic of)	22
South Georgia (Falkland Island Dependencies)	31
South Orkneys	21
South Shetlands	21
Spain	21
Spanish Territories of North Africa	31
Sri Lanka	23
Sudan	22
Suriname	22
Swaziland	22
Sweden	21
Switzerland	21
Syria	23
Taiwan	23
Tajikistan	21
Tanzania	22
Thailand	23
Tibet	34
Tobago	23
Togo	22
Tonga	30
Tortola	31

Place or country	Number of days
Trinidad & Tobago	23
Tristan Da Cunha	31
Tunisia	22
Turkey	21
Turkmenistan	21
Turks & Caicos Islands	31
Uganda	22
Ukraine	21
United States of America	22
Uruguay	22
Uzbekistan	21
Vanuatu	29
Vatican City State	21
Venezuela	22
Vietnam	28
Virgin Islands – British (Tortola)	31
Virgin Islands – U.S.A	24
Wake Island	25
Western Samoa	34
Yemen (Republic of)	30
Yugoslavia (except for Bosnia-Hercegovina Croatia Macedonia and Slovenia)	21
Zaire	25
Zambia	23
Zimbabwe	22

Further information

6. Further information concerning service out of the jurisdiction can be obtained from the Foreign Process Section, Room E02, Royal Courts of Justice, Strand, London WC2A 2LL (telephone 020 7947 6691).

[Editor's note: Annex, not reproduced in this summary, contains EC Council Regulations 1348/2000.]

11. *Practice Direction*—Litigation Friends
This *Practice Direction* supplements the 2005 Rules Pt 7 s 1.

General

1.1 In this *Practice Direction* 'non-subject child' means a person under 18 years old who is a party to the proceedings but is not the subject of the proceedings and 'patient' means a person who by reason of mental disorder within the meaning of the Mental Health Act 1983 is incapable of managing and administering his property and affairs.

1.2 A patient must have a litigation friend to conduct proceedings on his behalf (see head 2, below, for the definition of a litigation friend).

1.3 In the proceedings referred to in head 1.2, above, the patient should be referred to in the title as 'A.B. (by C.D. his litigation friend)'.

1.4 A non-subject child must have a litigation friend to conduct proceedings on his behalf unless the 2005 Rules r 51 applies.

1.5 A child who does not have a children's guardian must have a litigation friend to conduct proceedings on his behalf unless r 51 applies and any reference to non-subject child in this *Practice Direction* is to be taken as including a child.

1.6 Where:

(1) the non-subject child has a litigation friend, he or she should be referred to in the title to proceedings as 'A.B. (a child by C.D. his litigation friend)'; and

(2) the non-subject child is conducting proceedings on his own behalf, he or she should be referred to in the title as 'A.B. (a child)'.

The Litigation friend

2.1 It is the duty of a litigation friend fairly and competently to conduct proceedings on behalf of a non-subject child or patient. He must have no interest in the proceedings adverse to that of the non-subject child or patient and all steps and decisions he takes in the proceedings must be taken for the benefit of the non-subject child or patient.

2.2 A person may become a litigation friend of a non-subject child or a patient:

(a) without a court order under the provisions of r 54; or

(b) by a court order under r 55.

2.3 In order to become a litigation friend without a court order the person who wishes to act as litigation friend must:

(1) if he wishes to act on behalf of a patient, file an official copy of the order or other document which constitutes the authorisation to act under the Mental Health Act 1983 Pt VII; or

(2) if he wishes to act on behalf of a non-subject child, or on behalf of a patient without the authorisation referred to in head (1) above, file a certificate of suitability in form FP9:

(a) stating that he consents to act;

(b) stating that he knows or believes that the [applicant] [respondent] is a [non-subject child] [patient];

(c) in the case of a patient, stating the grounds of his belief and if his belief is based on medical opinion attaching any relevant document to the certificate;

(d) stating that he can fairly and competently conduct proceedings on behalf of the non-subject child or patient and has no interest adverse to that of the non-subject child or patient;

(e) undertaking to pay any costs which the non-subject child or patient may be ordered to pay in relation to the proceedings, subject to any right he may have to be repaid from the assets of the non-subject child or patient; and

(f) which he has signed in verification of its contents.

2.4 Head 2.3, above, does not apply to the Official Solicitor, an officer of the Service or a Welsh family proceedings officer.

2.5 The court officer will send the certificate of suitability:

(1) in the case of a non-subject child (who is not also a patient) to one of the non-subject child's parents or guardians or if there is no parent or guardian, to the person with whom the non-subject child resides or in whose care the non-subject child is; and

(2) in the case of a patient to the person authorised under the Mental Health Act 1983 Pt VII to conduct proceedings on behalf of the patient or if there is no person so authorised, to the person with whom the patient resides or in whose care the patient is.

2.6 The court officer is not required to send the documents referred to in head 2.3(2)(c), above, when he sends the certificate of suitability to the person to be served under head 2.5, above.

2.7 The litigation friend must file either the certificate of suitability or the authority referred to in head 2.3(1), above, at a time when he first takes a step in the proceedings on behalf of the non-subject child or patient.

Application for a court order appointing a litigation friend

3.1 The 2005 Rules r 55 sets out who may apply for an order appointing a litigation friend.

3.2 An application should be made in accordance with Pt 9 and must be supported by evidence.

3.3 The court officer must serve the application notice:

(1) on the persons referred to in head 2.5, above; and

(2) where the application is in respect of a patient, on the patient unless the court directs otherwise.

3.4 The evidence in support must satisfy the court that the proposed litigation friend:

(1) consents to act;

(2) can fairly and competently conduct proceedings on behalf of the non-subject child or patient;

(3) has no interest adverse to that of the non-subject child or patient; and

(4) undertakes to pay any costs which the non-subject child or patient may be ordered to pay in relation to the proceedings, subject to any right he may have to be repaid from the assets of the non-subject child or patient.

3.5 Head 3.4(4), above, does not apply to the Official Solicitor, an officer of the Service or a Welsh family proceedings officer.

3.6 The proposed litigation friend must satisfy the conditions in heads 3.4(1)–(3), above, and may be one of the persons referred to in head 2.5, above, where appropriate, or otherwise may be the Official Solicitor, an officer of the Service or a Welsh family proceedings officer. Where it is sought to appoint the Official Solicitor, an officer of the Service or a Welsh family proceedings officer, provision should be made for payment of his charges.

Change of litigation friend and prevention of person acting as litigation friend

4.1 Rule 56(1) states that the court may:

(1) direct that a person may not act as a litigation friend;

(2) terminate a litigation friend's appointment; or

(3) substitute a new litigation friend for an existing one.

4.2 Where an application is made for an order under r 56(1), the application notice must set out the reasons for seeking it. The application must be supported by evidence.

4.3 Subject to head 3.5, above, if the order sought is the substitution of a new litigation friend for an existing one, the evidence must satisfy the court of the matters set out in head 3.4, above.

4.4 The court officer will serve the application notice on:

(1) the persons referred to in head 2.5, above; and

(2) the litigation friend or person purporting to act as litigation friend.

Procedure where the need for a litigation friend has come to an end

5.1 Rule 58 deals with the situation where the need for a litigation friend comes to an end during the proceedings because either:

(1) a non-subject child who is not also a patient reaches the age of 18 (full age) during the proceedings; or

(2) a patient ceases to be a patient (recovers).

5.2 The court officer will send a notice to the other parties informing them that the appointment of a non-subject child or patient's litigation friend has ceased.

5.3 A non-subject child who reaches full age will subsequently be described in the proceedings as 'A.B. (formerly a child but now of full age)'.

5.4 Where a patient recovers, an application under r 58(3) must be made for an order under r 58(2) that the litigation friend's appointment has ceased.

5.5 The application must be supported by the following evidence:

(1) a medical report indicating that the patient has recovered and that he is capable of managing and administering his property and affairs; and

(2) where the patient's affairs were under the control of the Court of Protection, a copy of the order or notice discharging the patient.

12. Practice Direction—Communication of Information relating to Proceedings
This *Practice Direction* supplements the 2005 Rules Pt 8 r 78(1)(b).

1.1 Rule 78 deals with the communication of information, whether or not it is recorded in any form, relating to proceedings.

1.2 Subject to any direction of the court, information may be communicated for the purposes of the law relating to contempt in accordance with heads 1.3 or 1.4, above.

1.3 A person specified in the first column of the following table may communicate to a person listed in the second column such information as is specified in the third column for the purpose or purposes specified in the fourth column.

Communication of information without permission of the court.

Communicated by	To	Information	Purpose
A party	A lay adviser or a McKenzie Friend	Any information relating to the proceedings	To enable the party to obtain advice or assistance in relation to the proceedings.

Communicated by	To	Information	Purpose
A party	The party's spouse, civil partner, cohabitant or close family member		For the purpose of confidential discussions enabling the party to receive support from his spouse, civil partner, cohabitant or close family member.
A party	A health care professional or a person or body providing counselling services for children or families		To enable the party or any child of the party to obtain health care or counselling.
A party or any person lawfully in receipt of information	The Children's Commissioner or the Children's Commissioner for Wales		To refer an issue affecting the interests of children to the Children's Commissioner or the Children's Commissioner for Wales.
A party or a legal representative	A mediator		For the purpose of mediation in relation to the proceedings.
A party, any person lawfully in receipt of information or a proper officer	A person or body conducting an approved research project		For the purpose of an approved research project.
A party, a legal representative or a professional legal adviser	A person or body responsible for investigating or determining complaints in relation to legal representatives or professional legal advisers		For the purposes of making a complaint or the investigation or determination of a complaint in relation to a legal representative or a professional legal adviser.
A legal representative or a professional legal adviser	A person or body assessing quality assurance systems		To enable the legal representative or professional legal adviser to obtain a quality assurance assessment.
A legal representative or a professional legal adviser	An accreditation body	Any information relating to the proceedings providing that it does not, or is not likely to, identify any person involved in the proceedings	To enable the legal representative or professional legal adviser to obtain accreditation.

Communicated by	To	Information	Purpose
A party	An elected representative or peer	The text or summary of the whole or part of a judgment	To enable the elected representative or peer to give advice, investigate any complaint or raise any question of policy or procedure.
A party	The General Medical Council		For the purpose of making a complaint to the General Medical Council.
A party	A police officer		For the purpose of a criminal investigation.
A party or any person lawfully in receipt of information	A member of the Crown Prosecution Service		To enable the Crown Prosecution Service to discharge its functions under any enactment.

1.4 A person in the second column of the table in head 1.3, above, may only communicate information relating to the proceedings received from a person in the first column for the purpose or purposes:

(a) for which he received that information, or

(b) of professional development or training, providing that any communication does not, or is not likely to, identify any person involved in the proceedings without that person's consent.

1.5 In this *Practice Direction*:

(1) 'accreditation body' means:

(a) The Law Society,

(b) Resolution, or

(c) The Legal Services Commission;

(2) 'approved research project' means a project of research:

(a) approved in writing by a Secretary of State after consultation with the President of the Family Division,

(b) approved in writing by the President of the Family Division, or

(c) conducted under the 1989 Act s 83 or the Criminal Justice and Court Services Act 2000 s 13;

(3) 'body assessing quality assurance systems' includes:

(a) The Law Society,

(b) The Legal Services Commission, or

(c) The General Council of the Bar;

(4) 'body or person responsible for investigating or determining complaints in relation to legal representatives or professional legal advisers' means –

(a) The Law Society,

(b) The General Council of the Bar,

(c) The Institute of Legal Executives, or

(d) The Legal Services Ombudsman;

(5) 'cohabitant' means one of two persons who are neither married to each other nor civil partners of each other but are living together as husband and wife or as if they were civil partners;

(6) 'criminal investigation' means an investigation conducted by police officers with a view to it being ascertained:

(a) whether a person should be charged with an offence, or

(b) whether a person charged with an offence is guilty of it;

(7) 'elected representative' means:

(a) a member of the House of Commons,

(b) a member of the National Assembly for Wales, or

(c) a member of the European Parliament elected in England and Wales;

5.3 A direction under head 5.1, above, will not normally be made unless every party entitled to be given notice of the application and to be heard at the hearing has consented to the order.

5.4

(1) Where a party entitled to be heard at the hearing of the application is acting in person, the court:

(a) may not make a direction under head 5.1, above, except on condition that arrangements will be made for the party acting in person to be attended at the telephone hearing by a responsible person to whom the party acting in person is known and who can confirm to the court the identity of the party; and

(b) may not give effect to a direction under head 5.1, above, unless the party acting in person is accompanied by a responsible person who at the commencement of the hearing confirms to the court the identity of the party;

(2) the 'responsible person' may be a barrister, solicitor, legal executive, doctor, clergyman, police officer, prison officer or other person of comparable status; and

(3) if the court makes a direction under head 5.1, above, it will give any directions necessary for a telephone hearing.

5.5 No representative of a party to an application being heard by telephone may attend the court in person while the application is being heard unless the other parties to the application have agreed that he may do so.

5.6 If an application is to be heard by telephone the following directions will apply, subject to any direction to the contrary:

(1) the applicant's legal representative must arrange the telephone conference for precisely the time fixed by the court. The telecommunications provider must be capable of connecting the parties and the court;

(2) he must tell the operator the telephone numbers of all those participating in the conference call and the sequence in which they are to be called;

(3) it is the responsibility of the applicant's legal representative to ascertain from all the other parties whether they have instructed counsel, and whether the legal representative and counsel will be on the same or different telephone numbers;

(4) the sequence in which they are to be called will be:

(a) the applicant's legal representative and (if on a different number) his counsel

(b) the legal representative (or counsel) for all other parties; and

(c) the judge, district judge or justices, as the case may be;

(5) the applicant's legal representative must arrange for the conference to be recorded on tape by the telecommunications provider whose system is being used and must send the tape to the court;

(6) each speaker is to remain on the line after being called by the operator setting up the conference call. The call may be two or three minutes before the time fixed for the application;

(7) when the judge, district judge or justices have been connected the applicant's legal representative (or his counsel) will introduce the parties in the usual way;

(8) if the use of a 'speaker phone' by any party causes the court or any other party difficulty in hearing what is said the court may require the party to use a hand held telephone; and

(9) the telephone charges debited to the account of the party initiating the conference call will be treated as part of the costs of the application.

6. Video conferencing

Where the parties to a matter wish to use video conferencing facilities, and those facilities are available in the relevant court, they should apply to the court for directions.

(Head 27 and Annex 3 of the *Practice Direction* supplementing Pt 15 provide guidance on the use of video conferencing).

7. Note of proceedings

The court or court officer should keep, either by way of a note or a tape recording, brief details of all proceedings before the court, including the dates of the proceedings and a short statement of the decision taken at each hearing.

8. Evidence

8.1 The requirement for evidence in certain types of applications is set out in some of the rules and *Practice Directions*. Where there is no specific requirement to provide evidence it should be borne in mind that, as a practical matter, the court will often need to be satisfied by evidence of the facts that are relied on in support of or for opposing the application.

8.2 The court may give directions for the filing of evidence in support or opposing a particular application. The court may also give directions for the filing of evidence in relation to any hearing that it fixes on its own initiative. The directions may specify the form that evidence is to take and when it is to be served.

8.3 Where it is intended to rely on evidence which is not contained in the application itself, the evidence, if it has not already been served, should be served with the application.

8.4 Where a respondent to an application wishes to rely on evidence it must be filed in accordance with any directions the court may have given and a court officer will serve the evidence on the other parties, unless the court directs otherwise.

8.5 If it is necessary for the applicant to file any evidence in reply the court officer will serve it on the other parties, unless the court directs otherwise.

8.6 Evidence must be filed with the court as well as served on the parties. Exhibits should not be filed unless the court otherwise directs.

8.7 The contents of an application notice may be used as evidence provided that the contents have been verified by a statement of truth.

9. Consent orders

9.1 The parties to an application for a consent order must ensure that they provide the court with any material it needs to be satisfied that it is appropriate to make the order. Subject to any rule or *practice direction* a letter will generally be acceptable for this purpose.

9.2 Where a judgment or order has been agreed in respect of an application where a hearing date has been fixed, the parties must inform the court immediately.

10. Other applications considered without a hearing

10.1 Where r 92(b) applies the parties should so inform the court in writing and each should confirm that all evidence and other material on which he relies has been disclosed to the other parties to the application.

10.2 Where r 92(c) applies the court will treat the application as if it were proposing to make an order on its own initiative.

11. Miscellaneous

11.1 Except in the most simple application the applicant should bring to any hearing a draft of the order sought. If the case is proceeding in the High Court and the order is unusually long or complex it should also be supplied on disk for use by the court office.

11.2 Where r 95 applies the power to re-list the application in r 95(2) is in addition to any other powers of the court with regard to the order (for example to set aside, vary, discharge or suspend the order).

12. Costs

Attention is also drawn to CPR 44.13(i) which provides that if an order makes no mention of costs, none are payable in respect of the proceedings to which it relates.

15. Practice Direction—Alternative Procedure for Applications

This *Practice Direction* supplements the 2005 Rules Pt 10.

1. Types of application in which Pt 10 procedure may be used

1.1 An applicant must use the Pt 10 procedure if the application is for an order under:

(a) 2002 Act s 60(3), to prevent disclosure of information to an adopted person;

(b) s 79(4), to require the Registrar General to provide information; or

(c) 2005 Rules r 108, to request directions of the High Court regarding fathers without parental responsibility.

1.2 An applicant may use the Pt 10 procedure if Pt 9 does not apply and if:

(a) there is no prescribed form in which to make the application; or

(b) he seeks the court's decision on a question which is unlikely to involve a substantial dispute of fact.

1.3 An applicant may also use the Part 10 procedure if a *practice direction* permits or requires its use for the type of proceedings concerned.

1.4 The *practice directions* referred to in head 1.3, above, may in some respects modify or disapply the Pt 10 procedure and, where that is so, it is those *Practice Directions* that must be complied with.

1.5 The types of application for which the Pt 10 procedure may be used include an application for an order or direction which is unopposed by each respondent before the commencement of proceedings and the sole purpose of the application is to obtain the approval of the court to the agreement.

1.6 The court may at any stage order the application to continue as if the applicant had not used the Part 10 procedure and, if it does so, the court will give such directions as it considers appropriate.

2. The application

2.1 Where an applicant uses the Pt 10 procedure, application form FP1 should be used and must state the matters set out in r 98 and, if heads 1.3 or 1.4, above, apply, must comply with the *Practice Direction* in question. In particular, the application must state that Pt 10 applies. A Pt 10 application means an application which so states.

2.2 An application:

(a) in accordance with r 108, to ask the High Court for directions on the need to give a father without parental responsibility notice of the intention to place a child for adoption; or

(b) under the 2002 Act s 60(3), for an order to prevent disclosure of information to an adopted person

may be issued without naming a respondent.

3. Responding to the application

3.1 Where a respondent who wishes to respond to a 2005 Rules Pt 10 application is required to file an acknowledgment of service, that acknowledgment of service should be in form FP5 but can, alternatively, be given in an informal document such as a letter.

3.2 Rule 100 sets out provisions relating to an acknowledgment of service of a Pt 10 application.

3.3 Rule 101 sets out the consequence of failing to file an acknowledgment of service.

3.4 Where a respondent believes that the Pt 10 procedure should not be used because there is a substantial dispute of fact or, as the case may be, because its use is not authorised by any rule or *practice direction*, he must state his reasons in writing when he files his acknowledgment of service.

4. Managing the application

4.1 The court may give directions immediately a Pt 10 application is issued either on the application of a party or on its own initiative. The directions may include fixing a hearing date where:

(a) there is no dispute; or

(b) where there may be a dispute but a hearing date could conveniently be given.

4.2 Where the court does not fix a hearing date when the application is issued, it will give directions for the disposal of the application as soon as practicable after each respondent has acknowledged service of the application or, as the case may be, after the period for acknowledging service has expired.

4.3 Certain applications may not require a hearing.

4.4 The court may convene a directions hearing before giving directions.

5. Evidence

5.1 An applicant wishing to rely on written evidence should file it with his Pt 10 application (unless the evidence is contained in the application form itself).

5.2 Evidence will normally be in the form of a witness statement or an affidavit but an applicant may rely on the matters set out in the application provided that it has been verified by a statement of truth.

5.3 A respondent wishing to rely on written evidence should file it with his acknowledgment of service.

5.4 Rule 102 sets out the times and provisions for filing and serving written evidence.

5.5 The court may give a party an extension of time to serve and file evidence under r 102 or may give permission to serve and file additional evidence under r 103(1).

16. Practice Direction—Human Rights, joining the Crown

This *Practice Direction* supplements the 2005 Rules Pt 13.

1. Human Rights Act 1998 s 4

1.1 Where a party has informed the court about:

(a) a claim for a declaration of incompatibility in accordance with s 4; or

(b) an issue for the court to decide which may lead to the court considering making a declaration then the court may at any time consider whether notice should be given to the Crown as required by the 1998 Act and give directions for the content and service of the notice. The rule allows a period of 21 days before the court will make the declaration but the court may vary this period of time.

1.2 The court will normally consider the issues and give the directions referred to in head 1.1, above, at a directions hearing.

1.3 The notice must be served on the person named in the list published under the Crown Proceedings Act 1947 s 17.

1.4 The notice will be in the form directed by the court and will normally include the directions given by the court. The notice will also be served on all the parties.

1.5 The court may require the parties to assist in the preparation of the notice.

1.6 Unless the court orders otherwise, the Minister or other person permitted by the 1998 Act to be joined as a party must, if he wishes to be joined, give notice of his intention to be joined as a party to the court and every other party. Where the Minister has nominated a person to be joined as a party the notice must be accompanied by the written nomination.

(Section 5(2)(a) permits a person nominated by a Minister of the Crown to be joined as a party. The nomination may be signed on behalf of the Minister.)

2. The 1998 Act 8 s 9

2.1 The procedure in heads 1.1–1.6, above, also applies where a claim is made under ss 7(1)(a), 9(3) for damages in respect of a judicial act.

2.2 Notice must be given to the Lord Chancellor and should be served on the Treasury Solicitor on his behalf.

2.3 The notice will also give details of the judicial act, which is the subject of the claim for damages, and of the court that made it.

(Section 9(4) provides that no award of damages may be made against the Crown as provided for in s 9(3) unless the appropriate person is joined in the proceedings. The appropriate person is the Minister responsible for the court concerned or a person or department nominated by him (s 9(5)).

17. *Practice Direction*—Interim Injunctions
This *Practice Direction* supplements the 2005 Rules Pt 14.

1. Making an application

1.1 The application notice must state:

(1) the order sought; and

(2) the date, time and place of the hearing.

1.2 Unless the court directs otherwise, the application notice and evidence in support must be served as soon as practicable after issue and in any event not less than seven days before the court is due to hear the application.

1.3 The applicant should file sufficient copies of the application notice and evidence in support for the court and for each respondent.

1.4 Whenever possible a draft of the order sought should be filed with the application notice and a disk containing the draft should also be available to the court in a format compatible with the word processing software used by the court. This will enable the court officer to arrange for any amendments to be incorporated and for the speedy preparation and sealing of the order.

2. Evidence

2.1 Applications for interim injunctions must be supported by evidence set out in either:

(1) a witness statement; or

(2) the application notice provided that it is verified by a statement of truth

unless the court, an Act, a rule or a *practice direction* requires evidence by affidavit.

2.2 The evidence must set out the facts on which the applicant relies for the application being made against the respondent, including all material facts of which the court should be made aware.

2.3 Where an application is made without notice to the respondent, the evidence must also set out why notice was not given.

(See Pt 15 and the *Practice Direction* that supplements it for information about evidence.)

3. Urgent applications and applications without notice

3.1 These fall into two categories:

(1) applications where an application form in proceedings has already been issued; and

(2) applications where an application form in proceedings has not yet been issued;

and, in both cases, where notice of the application has not been given to the respondent.

3.2 These applications are normally dealt with at a court hearing but cases of extreme urgency may be dealt with by telephone.

3.3 Applications dealt with at a court hearing after issue of an application form:

(1) the application notice, evidence in support and a draft order (as in head 1.4, above) should be filed with the court two hours before the hearing wherever possible;

(2) if an application is made before the application notice has been issued, a draft order (as in head 1.4, above) should be provided at the hearing, and the application notice and evidence in support must be filed with the court on the same or next working day or as ordered by the court; and

(3) except in cases where secrecy is essential, the applicant should take steps to notify the respondent informally of the application.

3.4 Applications made before the issue of an application form:

(1) in addition to the provisions set out at head 3.3, above, unless the court orders otherwise, either the applicant must undertake to the court to issue an application notice immediately or the court will give directions for the commencement of the application; and

(2) an order made before the issue of an application form should state in the title after the names of the applicant and respondent 'the Applicant and Respondent in Intended Proceedings'.

3.5 Applications made outside normal working hours:

(1) where an application is made outside normal working hours the applicant should either:

(a) telephone the Royal Courts of Justice on 020 7947 6000 where he will be put in contact with the clerk to the appropriate duty judge in the High Court (or the appropriate area Circuit Judge where known); or

(b) the Urgent Court Business Officer of the appropriate Circuit who will contact the local duty judge;

(2) where the facility is available it is likely that the judge will require a draft order to be faxed to him;

(3) the application notice and evidence in support must be filed with the court on the same or next working day or as ordered, together with two copies of the order for sealing; and

(4) injunctions will be heard by telephone only where the applicant is acting by counsel or solicitors.

4. Orders for injunctions

4.1 Any order for an injunction, unless the court orders otherwise, must contain:

(1) an undertaking by the applicant to the court to pay any damages which the respondent, or any other party served with or notified of the order, sustain which the court considers the applicant should pay;

(2) if made without notice to any other party, an undertaking by the applicant to the court to serve on the respondent the application notice, evidence in support and any order made as soon as practicable;

(3) if made without notice to any other party, a return date for a further hearing at which the other party can be present;

(4) if made before filing the application notice, an undertaking to file and pay the appropriate fee on the same or next working day, and

(5) if made before issue of an application form in proceedings:

(a) an undertaking to issue and pay the appropriate fee on the same or next working day; or

(b) directions for the commencement of the proceedings.

4.2 An order for an injunction made in the presence of all parties to be bound by it or made at a hearing of which they have had notice, may state that it is effective until final hearing or further order.

4.3 Any order for an injunction must set out clearly what the respondent must do or not do.

18. Practice Direction—Evidence
This *Practice Direction* supplements the 2005 Rules Pt 15.

1. Evidence in general

1.1 Rule 124 sets out how evidence is to be given and facts are to be proved.

1.2 Evidence at a hearing other than the final hearing should normally be given by witness statement (see head 17 onwards).

1.3 Application forms and application notices may also be used as evidence provided that their contents have been verified by a statement of truth.

(For information regarding evidence by deposition see Pt 16 and the *Practice Direction* which supplements it.)

1.4 Affidavits must be used as evidence in the following instances:

(1) where sworn evidence is required by an enactment, rule, order or *practice direction*;

(2) in any application for an order against anyone for alleged contempt of court.

1.5 If a party believes that sworn evidence is required by a court in another jurisdiction for any purpose connected with the proceedings, he may apply to the court for a direction that evidence shall be given only by affidavit on any applications to be heard before the final hearing.

1.6 The court may give a direction under r 134 that evidence must be given by affidavit instead of or in addition to a witness statement:

(1) on its own initiative; or

(2) after any party has applied to the court for such a direction.

1.7 An affidavit, where referred to in the 2005 Rules or a *Practice Direction*, also means an affirmation unless the context requires otherwise.

2. Deponent

A deponent is a person who gives evidence by affidavit or affirmation.

3. Heading

3.1 The affidavit should be headed with the title of the proceedings where the proceedings are between several parties with the same status it is sufficient to identify the parties, subject to head 4.2, below, as follows:

Number:

A.B. (and others)

Applicants

C.D. (and others)

Respondents

(as appropriate)

3.2 Subject to head 4.2, below, at the top right hand corner of the first page, and on the backsheet, there should be clearly written—

(1) the party on whose behalf it is made;

(2) the initials and surname of the deponent;

(3) the number of the affidavit in relation to that deponent;

(4) the identifying initials and number of each exhibit referred to; and

(5) the date sworn.

4. Body of Affidavit

4.1 Subject to head 4.2, below, and r 21, the affidavit must, if practicable, be in the deponent's own words, the affidavit should be expressed in the first person and the deponent should:

(1) commence 'I (full name) of (address) state on oath …';

(2) if giving evidence in his professional, business or other occupational capacity, give the address at which he works in head (1) above, the position he holds and the name of his firm or employer;

(3) give his occupation or, if he has none, his description; and

(4) state if he is a party to the proceedings or employed by a party to the proceedings, if it be the case.

4.2 If a serial number has been assigned under r 20, the affidavit must be framed so that it does not disclose the identity of the applicant.

(Rule 21 provides that unless the court directs otherwise, a party is not required to reveal the address of his private residence)

4.3 An affidavit must indicate:

(1) which of the statements in it are made from the deponent's own knowledge and which are matters of information or belief; and

(2) the source for any matters of information or belief.

4.4 Where a deponent:

(1) refers to an exhibit or exhibits, he should state 'there is now shown to me marked '...' the (description of exhibit)'; and

(2) makes more than one affidavit (to which there are exhibits) in the same proceedings; the numbering of the exhibits should run consecutively throughout and not start again with each affidavit.

5. Jurat

5.1 The jurat of an affidavit is a statement set out at the end of the document which authenticates the affidavit.

5.2 It must:

(1) be signed by all deponents;

(2) be completed and signed by the person before whom the affidavit was sworn whose name and qualification must be printed beneath his signature;

(3) contain the full address of the person before whom the affidavit was sworn; and

(4) follow immediately on from the text and not be put on a separate page.

5.3 If a serial number has been assigned under r 20 or the name of the witness is not being revealed in accordance with r 21, the signature of the deponent will be edited from the affidavit before it is served on any other party.

6. Format of Affidavits

6.1 An affidavit should:

(1) be produced on durable quality A4 paper with a 3.5cm margin;

(2) be fully legible and should normally be typed on one side of the paper only;

(3) where possible, be bound securely in a manner which would not hamper filing, or otherwise each page should be endorsed with the case number and should bear the initials of the deponent and of the person before whom it was sworn;

(4) have the pages numbered consecutively as a separate document (or as one of several documents contained in a file);

(5) be divided into numbered paragraphs;

(6) have all numbers, including dates, expressed in figures; and

(7) give the reference to any document or documents mentioned either in the margin or in bold text in the body of the affidavit.

6.2 It is usually convenient for an affidavit to follow the chronological sequence of events or matters dealt with; each paragraph of an affidavit should as far as possible be confined to a distinct portion of the subject.

7. Inability of Deponent to read or sign Affidavit

7.1 Where an affidavit is sworn by a person who is unable to read or sign it, the person before whom the affidavit is sworn must certify in the jurat that:

(1) he read the affidavit to the deponent;

(2) the deponent appeared to understand it; and

(3) the deponent signed or made his mark, in his presence.

7.2 If that certificate is not included in the jurat, the affidavit may not be used in evidence unless the court is satisfied that it was read to the deponent and that he appeared to understand it. Two versions of the form of jurat with the certificate are set out at Annex 1 to this *Practice Direction*.

8. Alterations to Affidavits

8.1 Any alteration to an affidavit must be initialled by both the deponent and the person before whom the affidavit was sworn.

8.2 An affidavit which contains an alteration that has not been initialled may be filed or used in evidence only with the permission of the court.

9. Who may administer oaths and take Affidavits

9.1 Only the following may administer oaths and take affidavits

(1) Commissioners for oaths;

(2) Practising solicitors;

(3) other persons specified by statute;

(4) certain officials of the Supreme Court;

(5) a circuit judge or district judge;

(6) any justice of the peace; and

(7) certain officials of any county court appointed by the judge of that court for the purpose.

9.2 An affidavit must be sworn before a person independent of the parties or their representatives.

10. Filing of Affidavits

10.1 If the court directs that an affidavit is to be filed, it must be filed in the court or Division, or Office or Registry of the court or Division where the action in which it was or is to be used, is proceeding or will proceed.

10.2 Where an affidavit is in a foreign language:

(1) the party wishing to rely on it:

(a) must have it translated; and

(b) must file the foreign language affidavit with the court; and

(2) the translator must sign the translation to certify that it is accurate.

11. Manner of Exhibiting Documents

11.1 A document used in conjunction with an affidavit should be –

(1) produced to and verified by the deponent, and remain separate from the affidavit; and

(2) identified by a declaration of the person before whom the affidavit was sworn.

11.2 The declaration should be headed with the name of the proceedings in the same way as the affidavit.

11.3 The first page of each exhibit should be marked:

(1) as in paragraph 3.2; and

(2) with the exhibit mark referred to in the affidavit.

12. Letters

12.1 Copies of individual letters should be collected together and exhibited in a bundle or bundles. They should be arranged in chronological order with the earliest at the top, and firmly secured.

12.2 When a bundle of correspondence is exhibited, the exhibit should have a front page attached stating that the bundle consists of original letters and copies. They should be arranged and secured as above and numbered consecutively.

13. Other documents

13.1 Photocopies instead of original documents may be exhibited provided the originals are made available for inspection by the other parties before the hearing and by the court at the hearing.

13.2 Court documents must not be exhibited (official copies of such documents prove themselves).

13.3 Where an exhibit contains more than one document, a front page should be attached setting out a list of the documents contained in the exhibit; the list should contain the dates of the documents.

14. Exhibits other than documents

14.1 Items other than documents should be clearly marked with an exhibit number or letter in such a manner that the mark cannot become detached from the exhibit.

14.2 Small items may be placed in a container and the container appropriately marked.

15. General provisions

15.1 Where an exhibit contains more than one document:

(1) the bundle should not be stapled but should be securely fastened in a way that does not hinder the reading of the documents; and

(2) the pages should be numbered consecutively at bottom centre.

15.2 Every page of an exhibit should be clearly legible; typed copies of illegible documents should be included, paginated with 'a' numbers.

15.3 Where affidavits and exhibits have become numerous, they should be put into separate bundles and the pages numbered consecutively throughout.

15.4 Where on account of their bulk the service of exhibits or copies of exhibits on the other parties would be difficult or impracticable, the directions of the court should be sought as to arrangements for bringing the exhibits to the attention of the other parties and as to their custody pending final hearing.

16. Affirmations

16.1 All provisions in this or any other *practice direction* relating to affidavits apply to affirmations with the following exceptions—

(1) the deponent should commence 'I (name) of (address) do solemnly and sincerely affirm … ; and

(2) in the jurat the word 'sworn' is replaced by the word 'affirmed'.

17. Witness statements

17.1 The witness statement should be headed with the title of the proceedings; where the proceedings are between several parties with the same status it is sufficient to identify the parties, subject to paragraph 18.2, as follows—

Number—

A.B. (and others)

Applicants

C.D. (and others)

Respondents

(as appropriate)

17.2 Subject to head 18.2, below, at the top right hand corner of the first page there should be clearly written:

(1) the party on whose behalf it is made;

(2) the initials and surname of the witness;

(3) the number of the statement in relation to that witness;

(4) the identifying initials and number of each exhibit referred to; and

(5) the date the statement was made.

18. Body of Witness Statement

18.1 Subject to head 18.2, below, and r 21, the witness statement must, if practicable, be in the intended witness's own words, the statement should be expressed in the first person and should also state:

(1) the full name of the witness;

(2) his place of residence or, if he is making the statement in his professional, business or other occupational capacity, the address at which he works, the position he holds and the name of his firm or employer;

(3) his occupation, or if he has none, his description; and

(4) the fact that he is a party to the proceedings or is the employee of such a party if it be the case.

18.2 If a serial number has been assigned under r 20, the witness statement must be framed so that it does not disclose the identity of the applicant.

(Rule 21 provides that unless the court directs otherwise, a party is not required to reveal the address of his private residence)

18.3 A witness statement must indicate:

(1) which of the statements in it are made from the witness's own knowledge and which are matters of information or belief; and

(2) the source for any matters of information or belief.

18.4 An exhibit used in conjunction with a witness statement should be verified and identified by the witness and remain separate from the witness statement.

18.5 Where a witness refers to an exhibit or exhibits, he should state 'I refer to the (description of exhibit) marked '…'.

18.6 The provisions of heads 11.3–15.4, above, (exhibits) apply similarly to witness statements as they do to affidavits.

18.7 Where a witness makes more than one witness statement to which there are exhibits, in the same proceedings, the numbering of the exhibits should run consecutively throughout and not start again with each witness statement.

19. Format of Witness Statement

19.1 A witness statement should

(1) be produced on durable quality A4 paper with a 3.5cm margin;

(2) be fully legible and should normally be typed on one side of the paper only;

(3) where possible, be bound securely in a manner which would not hamper filing, or otherwise each page should be endorsed with the case number and should bear the initials of the witness;

(4) have the pages numbered consecutively as a separate statement (or as one of several statements contained in a file);

(5) be divided into numbered paragraphs;

(6) have all numbers, including dates, expressed in figures; and

(7) give the reference to any document or documents mentioned either in the margin or in bold text in the body of the statement.

19.2 It is usually convenient for a witness statement to follow the chronological sequence of the events or matters dealt with, each paragraph of a witness statement should as far as possible be confined to a distinct portion of the subject.

20. Statement of Truth

20.1 A witness statement is the equivalent of the oral evidence which that witness would, if called, give in evidence; it must include a statement by the intended witness that he believes the facts in it are true.

20.2 To verify a witness statement the statement of truth is as follows:

'I believe that the facts stated in this witness statement are true'.

20.3 Attention is drawn to r 133 which sets out the consequences of verifying a witness statement containing a false statement without an honest belief in its truth.

20.4 If a serial number has been assigned under r 20 or the name of the witness is not being revealed in accordance with r 21, the signature of the witness will be edited from the affidavit before it is served on any other party.

21. Inability of witness to read or sign statement

21.1 Where a witness statement is made by a person who is unable to read or sign the witness statement, it must contain a certificate made by an authorised person.

21.2 An authorised person is a person able to administer oaths and take affidavits but need not be independent of the parties or their representatives.

21.3 The authorised person must certify:

(1) that the witness statement has been read to the witness;

(2) that the witness appeared to understand it and approved its content as accurate;

(3) that the declaration of truth has been read to the witness;

(4) that the witness appeared to understand the declaration and the consequences of making a false witness statement; and

(5) that the witness signed or made his mark in the presence of the authorised person.

21.4 The form of the certificate is set out at Annex 2 to this *Practice Direction*.

22. Alterations to witness statements

22.1 Any alteration to a witness statement must be initialled by the person making the statement or by the authorised person where appropriate (see head 21.1, above).

22.2 A witness statement which contains an alteration that has not been initialled may be used in evidence only with the permission of the court.

23. Filing of witness statements

23.1 If the court directs that a witness statement is to be filed, it must be filed in the court or Division, or Office or Registry of the court or Division where the action in which it was or is to be used, is proceeding or will proceed.

23.2 Where the court has directed that a witness statement in a foreign language is to be filed:

(1) the party wishing to rely on it must

(a) have it translated; and

(b) file the foreign language witness statement with the court; and

(2) the translator must sign the translation to certify that it is accurate.

24. Defects in affidavits, witness statements and exhibits

24.1 Where:

(1) an affidavit;

(2) a witness statement; or

(3) an exhibit to either an affidavit or a witness statement;

does not comply with Pt 15 or this *Practice Direction* in relation to its form, the court may refuse to admit it as evidence and may refuse to allow the costs arising from its preparation.

24.2 Permission to file a defective affidavit or witness statement or to use a defective exhibit may be obtained from the court where the case is proceeding.

25. Agreed bundles for hearings

25.1 The court may give directions requiring the parties to use their best endeavours to agree a bundle or bundles of documents for use at any hearing.

25.2 All documents contained in bundles which have been agreed for use at a hearing will be admissible at that hearing as evidence of their contents, unless:

(1) the court directs otherwise; or

(2) a party gives written notice of objection to the admissibility of particular documents.

26. Penalty

26.1

(1) Where a party alleges that a statement of truth is false the party must refer that allegation to the court dealing with the application in which the statement of truth has been made.

(2) the court may:

(a) exercise any of its powers under the rules;

(b) initiate steps to consider if there is a contempt of court and, where there is, to punish it;

(RSC Order 52 and CCR Order 29 (CPR Schs 1, 2) make provision where committal to prison is a possibility if contempt is proved)

(c) direct the party making the allegation to refer the matter to the Attorney General with a request to him to consider whether he wishes to bring proceedings for contempt of court.

26.2

(1) An application to the Attorney General should be made to his chambers at 9 Buckingham Gate London SW1E 6JP in writing. The Attorney General will initially require a copy of the order recording the direction of the judge or district judge referring the matter to him and information which:

(a) identifies the statement said to be false; and

(b) explains:

(i) why it is false; and

(ii) why the maker knew it to be false at the time he made it; and

(c) explains why contempt proceedings would be appropriate in the light of the overriding objective in Pt 1.

(2) The practice of the Attorney General is to prefer an application that comes from the court, and so has received preliminary consideration by a judge or district judge, to one made direct to him by a party to the application in which the alleged contempt occurred without prior consideration by the court. An application to the Attorney General is not a way of appealing against, or reviewing, the decision of the judge or district judge.

26.3 Where a party makes an application to the court for permission for that party to commence proceedings for contempt of court, it must be supported by written evidence containing the information specified in head 27.2(1), below, and the result of the application to the Attorney General made by the applicant.

26.4 The rules do not change the law of contempt or introduce new categories of contempt. A person applying to commence such proceedings should consider whether the incident complained of does amount to contempt of court and whether such proceedings would further the overriding objective in Pt 1.

27. Video conferencing

27.1 Guidance on the use of video conferencing in courts is set out at Annex 3 to this *Practice Direction*.

27.2 A list of the sites which are available for video conferencing can be found on Her Majesty's Courts Service website at www.hmcourts-service.gov.uk.

[Editor's note: Annexes 1–3 have not been reproduced in this summary]

19. Practice Direction—Depositions and Court Attendance by Witnesses
This *Practice Direction* supplements the 2005 Rules Pt 16.

1. Issue of witness summons

1.1 A witness summons may require a witness to:

(1) attend court to give evidence;

(2) produce documents to the court; or

(3) both;

on either a date fixed for the hearing or such date as the court may direct

1.2 Two copies of the witness summons should be filed with the court for sealing, one of which will be retained on the court file.

1.3 A mistake in the name or address of a person named in a witness summons may be corrected if the summons has not been served.

1.4 The corrected summons must be re-sealed by the court and marked 'Amended and Re-Sealed'.

2. Magistrates' courts proceedings

2.1 An application for the issue of a summons or warrant under the Magistrates' Courts Act 1980 s 97 may be made by the applicant in person or by his legal representative.

2.2 An application for the issue of such a summons may be made by delivering or sending the application in writing to the court officer for the magistrates' court.

3. Travelling expenses and compensation for loss of time

3.1 When a witness is served with a witness summons he must be offered a sum to cover his travelling expenses to and from the court and compensation for his loss of time.

3.2 If the witness summons is to be served by the court, the party issuing the summons must deposit with the court:

(1) a sum sufficient to pay for the witness's expenses in travelling to the court and in returning to his home or place of work; and

(2) a sum in respect of the period during which earnings or benefit are lost, or such lesser sum as it may be proved that the witness will lose as a result of his attendance at court in answer to the witness summons.

3.3 The sum referred to in head 3.2(2), above, is to be based on the sums payable to witnesses attending the Crown Court.

4. Depositions to be taken in England and Wales for use as evidence in proceedings in courts in England and Wales

4.1 A party may apply for an order for a person to be examined on oath before:

(1) a judge or district judge (including a district judge of the principal registry of the Family Division;

(2) an examiner of the court; or

(3) such other person as the court may appoint.

4.2 The party who obtains an order for the examination of a deponent before an examiner of the court must:

(1) apply to the Foreign Process Section of the Masters' Secretary's Department at the Royal Courts of Justice for the allocation of an examiner;

(2) when allocated, provide the examiner with copies of all documents in the proceedings necessary to inform the examiner of the issues; and

(3) pay the deponent a sum to cover his travelling expenses to and from the examination and compensation for his loss of time.

4.3 In ensuring that the deponent's evidence is recorded in full, the court or the examiner may permit it to be recorded on audiotape or videotape, but the deposition must always be recorded in writing by him or by a competent shorthand writer or stenographer.

4.4 If the deposition is not recorded word for word, it must contain, as nearly as may be, the statement of the deponent; the examiner may record word for word any particular questions and answers which appear to him to have special importance.

4.5 If a deponent objects to answering any question or where any objection is taken to any question, the examiner must:

(1) record in the deposition or a document attached to it:

(a) the question;

(b) the nature of and grounds for the objection; and

(c) any answer given; and

(2) give his opinion as to the validity of the objection and must record it in the deposition or a document attached to it.

The court will decide as to the validity of the objection and any question of costs arising from it.

4.6 Documents and exhibits must:

(1) have an identifying number or letter marked on them by the examiner, and

(2) be preserved by the party or his legal representative who obtained the order for the examination, or as the court or the examiner may direct.

4.7 The examiner may put any question to the deponent as to:

(1) the meaning of any of his answers; or

(2) any matter arising in the course of the examination.

4.8 Where a deponent:

(1) fails to attend the examination; or

(2) refuses to:

(a) be sworn; or

(b) answer any lawful question; or

(c) produce any document;

the examiner will sign a certificate of such failure or refusal and may include in his certificate any comment as to the conduct of the deponent or of any person attending the examination.

4.9 The party who obtained the order for the examination must file the certificate with the court and may apply for an order that the deponent attend for examination or produce any document, as the case may be. The application may be made without notice.

4.10 The court will make such order on the application as it thinks fit including an order for the deponent to pay any costs resulting from his failure or refusal.

4.11 A deponent who wilfully refuses to obey an order made against him under Pt 16 may be proceeded against for contempt of court.

4.12 A deposition must:

(1) be signed by the examiner;

(2) have any amendments to it initialled by the examiner and the deponent;

(3) be endorsed by the examiner with:

(a) a statement of the time occupied by the examination; and

(b) a record of any refusal by the deponent to sign the deposition and of his reasons for not doing so; and

(4) be sent by the examiner to the court where the proceedings are taking place for filing on the court file.

4.13 Rule 151 deals with the fees and expenses of an examiner.

5. Depositions to be taken abroad for use as evidence in proceedings before courts in England and Wales (where England and Wales EC Council Regulation 1206/2001 does not apply)

5.1 Where a party wishes to take a deposition from a person outside the jurisdiction, the High Court may order the issue of a letter of request to the judicial authorities of the country in which the proposed deponent is.

5.2 An application for an order referred to in head 5.1, above, should be made by application notice in accordance with the 2005 Rules Pt 9.

5.3 The documents which a party applying for an order for the issue of a letter of request must file with his application notice are set out in r 150(7). They are as follows:

(1) a draft letter of request in the form set out in Annex A to this *Practice Direction*;

(2) a statement of the issues relevant to the proceedings;

(3) a list of questions or the subject matter of questions to be put to the proposed deponent;

(4) a translation of the documents in heads (1), (2) and (3), above, unless the proposed deponent is in a country of which English is an official language; and

(5) an undertaking to be responsible for the expenses of the Secretary of State In addition to the documents listed above the party applying for the order must file a draft order.

5.4 The above documents should be filed with the Masters' Secretary in Room E214, Royal Courts of Justice, Strand, London WC2A 2LL.

5.5 The application will be dealt with by the Senior Master of the Queen's Bench Division of the High Court who will, if appropriate, sign the letter of request.

5.6 Attention is drawn to the provisions of r 94 (application to vary or discharge an order made without notice).

5.7 If parties are in doubt as to whether a translation under paragraph 5.3(4) is required, they should seek guidance from the Foreign Process Section of the Masters' Secretary's Department.

5.8 A special examiner appointed under r 150(5) may be the British Consul or the Consul-General or his deputy in the country where the evidence is to be taken if:

(1) there is in respect of that country a Civil Procedure Convention providing for the taking of evidence in that country for the assistance of proceedings in the High Court or other court in this country; or

(2) the Secretary of State has consented.

5.9 The provisions of heads 4.1–4.12, above, apply to the depositions referred to in this paragraph.

6. Taking of evidence between EU Member States

6.1 Where evidence is to be taken from a person in another Member State of the European Union for use as evidence in proceedings before courts in Regulation 1206/2001 on co-operation between the courts of the member states in the taking of evidence in civil or commercial matters applies.

6.2 Regulation 1206/2001is annexed to this *Practice Direction* as Annex B.

6.3 Regulation 1206/2001 does not apply to Denmark. In relation to Denmark, therefore, the 2005 Rules r 150 will continue to apply.

(Regulation 1206/2001 Art 21(1) provides that Regulation 1206/2001 prevails over other provisions contained in bilateral or multilateral agreements or arrangements concluded by the member states)

Originally published in the official languages of the European Community in the Official Journal of the European Communities by the Office for Official Publications of the European Communities.

7. Meaning of 'designated court'

7.1 In accordance with Regulation 1206/2001, each regulation state has prepared a list of courts competent to take evidence in accordance with Regulation 1206/2001 indicating the territorial and, where appropriate, special jurisdiction of those courts.

7.2 Where the 2005 Rules Pt 16 and the 2002 Act s 2 refers to a 'designated court' in relation to another regulation state, the reference is to the court, referred to in the list of competent courts of that state, which is appropriate to the application in hand.

7.3 Where the reference is to the 'designated court' in England and Wales, the reference is to the appropriate competent court in the jurisdiction. The designated courts for England and Wales are listed in Annex C to this *Practice Direction*.

8. Central Body

8.1 Regulation 1206/2001 stipulates that each regulation state must nominate a central body responsible for:

(a) supplying information to courts;

(b) seeking solutions to any difficulties which may arise in respect of a request; and

(c) forwarding, in exceptional cases, at the request of a requesting court, a request to the competent court.

8.2 The United Kingdom has nominated the Senior Master, Queen's Bench Division, to be the Central Body for England and Wales.

8.3 The Senior Master, as central body, has been designated responsible for taking decisions on requests pursuant to Regulation 1206/2001 Art 17. Article 17 allows a court to submit a request to the central body or a designated competent authority in another regulation state to take evidence directly in that state.

9. Evidence to be taken in another regulation state for use in England and Wales

9.1 Where a person wishes to take a deposition from a person in another regulation state, the court where the proceedings are taking place may order the issue of a request to the designated court in the regulation state (2005 Rules r 153(2)). The form of request is prescribed as Form A in Regulation 1206/2001.

9.2 An application to the court for an order under r 153(2) should be made by application notice in accordance with Pt 9.

9.3 Rule 153(3) provides that the party applying for the order must file a draft form of request in the prescribed form. Where completion of the form requires attachments or documents to accompany the form, these must also be filed.

9.4 If the court grants an order under r 153(2), it will send the form of request directly to the designated court.

9.5 Where the taking of evidence requires the use of an expert, the designated court may require a deposit in advance towards the costs of that expert. The party who obtained the order is responsible for the payment of any such deposit which should be deposited with the court for onward transmission. Under the provisions of the Regulation 1206/2001, the designated court is not required to execute the request until such payment is received.

9.6 Regulation 1206/2001 Art 17 permits the court where proceedings are taking place to take evidence directly from a deponent in another regulation state if the conditions of the article are satisfied. Direct taking of evidence can only take place if evidence is given voluntarily without the need for coercive measures. The 2005 Rules r 153(5) provides for the court to make an order for the submission of a request to take evidence directly. The form of request is Form I annexed to Regulation 1206/2001 and the 2005 Rules r 153(6) makes provision for a draft of this form to be filed by the party seeking the order. An application for an order under r 153(5) should be by application notice in accordance with Pt 9.

9.7 Attention is drawn to the provisions of r 94 (application to vary or discharge an order made without notice).

[Editor's note: Annexes A–C have not been reproduced in this summary]

20. Practice Direction—Experts
This *Practice Direction* supplements the 2005 Rules Pt 17. Pt 17 is intended to limit the use of oral expert evidence to that which is reasonably required. In addition, where possible, matters requiring expert evidence should be dealt with by a single expert. Permission of the court is always required either to call an expert or to put an expert's report in evidence.

1. Expert evidence—general requirements

1.1 It is the duty of an expert to help the court on matters within his own expertise: r 156(1). This duty is paramount and overrides any obligation to the person from whom the expert has received instructions or by whom he is paid: r 156(2).

1.2 Expert evidence should be the independent product of the expert uninfluenced by the pressures of litigation.

1.3 An expert should assist the court by providing objective, unbiased opinion on matters within his expertise, and should not assume the role of an advocate.

1.4 An expert should consider all material facts, including those which might detract from his opinion.

1.5 An expert should make it clear:

(a) when a question or issue falls outside his expertise; and

(b) when he is not able to reach a definite opinion, for example because he has insufficient information.

1.6 If, after producing a report, an expert changes his view on any material matter, such change of view should be communicated to all the parties without delay, and when appropriate to the court.

2. Form and content of expert's reports

2.1 An expert's report should be addressed to the court and not to the party from whom the expert has received his instructions.

2.2 An expert's report must:

(1) give details of the expert's qualifications;

(2) give details of any literature or other material which the expert has relied on in making the report;

(3) contain a statement setting out the substance of all facts and instructions given to the expert which are material to the opinions expressed in the report or on which those opinions are based;

(4) make clear which of the facts stated in the report are within the expert's own knowledge;

(5) say who carried out any examination, measurement, test or experiment which the expert has used for the report, give the qualifications of that person, and say whether or not the test or experiment has been carried out under the expert's supervision;

(6) where there is a range of opinion on the matters dealt with in the report:

(a) summarise the range of opinion, and

(b) give reasons for his own opinion;

(7) contain a summary of the conclusions reached;

(8) if the expert is not able to give his opinion without qualification, state the qualification; and

(9) contain a statement that the expert understands his duty to the court, and has complied and will continue to comply with that duty.

2.3 An expert's report must be verified by a statement of truth as well as containing the statements required in heads 2.2(8), (9), above.

2.4 The form of the statement of truth is as follows:

'I confirm that insofar as the facts stated in my report are within my own knowledge I have made clear which they are and I believe them to be true, and that the opinions I have expressed represent my true and complete professional opinion.'

2.5 Attention is drawn to r 133 which sets out the consequences of verifying a document containing a false statement without an honest belief in its truth.

3. Information

Under r 162 the court may direct a party with access to information which is not reasonably available to another party to prepare and file a document which records the information. A court officer will then send a copy of that document to the other party. The document must include sufficient details of all the facts, tests, experiments and assumptions which underlie any part of the information to enable the party on whom it is served to make, or to obtain, a proper interpretation of the information and an assessment of its significance.

4. Instructions

The instructions referred to in head 2.2(3), above, will not be protected by privilege (see r 163(4)). But cross-examination of the expert on the contents of his instructions will not be allowed unless the court permits it (or unless the party who gave the instructions consents to it). Before it gives permission the court must be satisfied that there are reasonable grounds to consider that the statement in the report of the substance of the instructions is inaccurate or incomplete. If the court is so satisfied, it will allow the cross-examination where it appears to be in the interests of justice to do so.

5. Questions to experts

5.1 Questions asked for the purpose of clarifying the expert's report (see r 159) should be put, in writing, to the expert not later than five days after receipt of the expert's report (see heads 1.2–1.5, above, as to verification).

5.2 Where a party sends a written question or questions direct to an expert, a copy of the questions should, at the same time, be sent to the court and, unless the court directs otherwise, a court officer will send them to the other party or parties.

5.3 The party or parties instructing the expert must pay any fees charged by that expert for answering questions put under r 159. This does not affect any decision of the court as to the party who is ultimately to bear the expert's costs.

6. Single expert

Where the court has directed that the evidence on a particular issue is to be given by one expert only (r 160) but there are a number of disciplines relevant to that issue, a leading expert in the dominant discipline should be identified as the single expert. He should prepare the general part of the report and be responsible for annexing or incorporating the contents of any reports from experts in other disciplines.

7. Orders

Where a direction requires an act to be done by an expert, or otherwise affects an expert, the party instructing that expert must serve a copy of the direction on the expert instructed by him. In the case of a jointly instructed expert, unless the court directs otherwise, the applicant must serve the direction.

21. Practice Direction—Change of Solicitor
This *Practice Direction* supplements the 2005 Rules Pt 18.

1. Solicitor acting for a party

1.1 Subject to r 168(6) (where the certificate of a LSC funded client or assisted person is revoked or discharged), where a party has changed his solicitor or intends to act in person, the former solicitor will be considered to be the party's solicitor unless or until:

(1) a notice of the change is:

(a) filed with the court; and

(b) served on the former solicitor; and

(c) served on every other party in accordance with directions of the court; or

(2) the court makes an order under r 169 and the order is served on the former solicitor and every other party in accordance with directions of the court.

1.2 A solicitor appointed to represent a party only as an advocate at a hearing will not be considered to be acting for that party within the meaning of Pt 18.

2. Notice of change of solicitor

2.1 Rule 168(1) sets out the circumstances following which a notice of the change must be filed and served.

2.2 A notice of the change must also be filed and served in accordance with the court's directions where, under r 168(6):

(1) the certificate of a LSC funded client or assisted person is revoked or discharged; and

(2) the LSC funded client or the assisted person wishes either to act in person or appoint another solicitor to act on his behalf.

2.3 Form FP8 should be used to give notice of any change. The notice should be filed in the court office in which the application is proceeding.

3. Application for an order that a solicitor has ceased to act

3.1 A solicitor may apply under r 169 for an order declaring that he has ceased to be the solicitor acting for a party.

3.2 The application should be made in accordance with Pt 9 and must be supported by evidence. Unless the court directs otherwise the application notice must be served on the party.

3.3 The court will give directions about serving an order made under r 169 on every party. Where the order is not served by the court, the person serving must file a certificate of service in practice form FP6.

4. Application by another party to remove a solicitor

4.1 Rule 170 sets out circumstances in which any other party may apply for an order declaring that a solicitor has ceased to be the solicitor acting for another party in the proceedings.

4.2 The application should be made in accordance with Pt 9 and must be supported by evidence. Unless the court directs otherwise the application notice must be served on the party to whose solicitor the application relates.

4.3 The court will give directions about serving an order made under r 170 on every other party to the proceedings. Where the order is not served by the court, the person serving must file a certificate of service in practice form FP6.

22. *Practice Direction*—Appeals
This *Practice Direction* supplements the 2005 Rules Pt 19.

1. Introduction

This *Practice Direction* applies to all appeals to which Pt 19 applies and in this *Practice Direction* a reference to a 'judge' includes a district judge, including a district judge of the principal registry of the Family Division.

2. Routes of appeal

2.1 The following table sets out to which court or judge an appeal is to be made (subject to obtaining any necessary permission)

Decision of	Appeal made to
Magistrates' court	High Court
District judge of a county court	Circuit judge
District judge of the High Court	High Court judge
District judge of the principal registry of the Family Division	High Court judge
Costs judge	High Court judge
Circuit judge or recorder	Court of Appeal
High Court judge	Court of Appeal

(The Supreme Court Act 1981 s 16(1); the County Courts Act 1984 s 77(1); the Children Act 1989 s 94 and the Access to Justice Act 1999 (Destination of Appeals) (Family Proceedings) Order 2005, SI 2005/3276, set out the provisions governing routes of appeal.)

2.2 Where the decision to be appealed is a decision in a 2005 Rules Pt 10 application on a point of law in a case which did not involve any substantial dispute of fact, the court to which the appeal lies, where that court is the High Court or a county court and unless the appeal would lie to the Court of Appeal in any event, must consider whether to order the appeal to be transferred to the Court of Appeal under r 182.

3. Grounds for appeal

3.1 Rule 181(3) sets out the circumstances in which the appeal court will allow an appeal.

3.2 The grounds of appeal should:

(1) set out clearly the reasons why r 181(3)(a) or (b) is said to apply; and

(2) specify, in respect of each ground, whether the ground raises an appeal on a point of law or is an appeal against a finding of fact.

4. Permission to appeal

4.1 Rule 173 sets out the circumstances when permission to appeal is required.

(The requirement of permission to appeal may be imposed by a *Practice Direction*—see r 173(1)(b).)

Court to which permission to appeal application should be made

4.2 An application for permission should be made orally at the hearing at which the decision to be appealed against is made, where that decision is made by the High Court or a county court.

4.3 Where:

(a) no application for permission to appeal is made at the hearing;

(b) the decision being appealed was made by a magistrates' court; or

(c) the lower court refuses permission to appeal,

an application for permission to appeal may be made to the appeal court in accordance with rr 173(2), (3).

(Rule 171(3) defines 'lower court'.)

4.4 There is no appeal from a decision of the appeal court to allow or refuse permission to appeal to that court, although where the appeal court, without a hearing, refuses permission to appeal, the person seeking permission may request that decision to be reconsidered at a hearing. See section the Access to Justice Act 1999 54(4) and the 2005 Rules r 173(2), (3), (4), (5).

Consideration of Permission without a hearing

4.5 Applications for permission to appeal may be considered by the appeal court without a hearing.

4.6 If permission is granted without a hearing the parties will be notified of that decision and the procedure in heads 6.1–6.8, above, will then apply.

4.7 If permission is refused without a hearing the parties will be notified of that decision with the reasons for it. The decision is subject to the appellant's right to have it reconsidered at an oral hearing. This may be before the same judge.

4.8 A request for the decision to be reconsidered at an oral hearing must be filed at the appeal court within seven days after service of the notice that permission has been refused. A copy of the request must be served on the respondent. Unless the court directs otherwise, a court officer will effect service.

Permission hearing

4.9 Where an appellant, who is represented, makes a request for a decision to be reconsidered at an oral hearing, the appellant's advocate must, at least four days before the hearing, in a brief written statement:

(a) inform the court and the respondent of the points which he proposes to raise at the hearing;

(b) set out his reasons why permission should be granted notwithstanding the reasons given for the refusal of permission; and

(c) confirm, where applicable, that the requirements of head 4.12, below, have been complied with (appellant in receipt of services funded by the Legal Services Commission).

4.10 Notice of a permission hearing will be given to the respondent but he is not required to attend unless the court requests him to do so.

4.11 If the court requests the respondent's attendance at the permission hearing, a copy of the appeal bundle will be supplied to the respondent (see head 5.9, below) within seven days of being notified of the request, or such other period as the court may direct. The costs of providing that bundle shall be borne by the appellant initially, but will form part of the costs of the permission application. Unless the court directs otherwise, a court officer will supply the appeal bundle.

Appellants in receipt of services funded by the Legal Services Commission applying for permission to appeal

4.12 Where the appellant is in receipt of services funded by the Legal Services Commission, or legally aided, and permission to appeal has been refused by the appeal court without a hearing, the appellant must send a copy of the reasons the appeal court gave for refusing permission to the relevant office of the Legal Services Commission as soon as it has been received from the court. The court will require confirmation that this has been done if a hearing is requested to re-consider the question of permission.

Limited permission

4.13 Where a court under r 173(7) gives permission to appeal on some issues only, it will:

(1) refuse permission on any remaining issues; or

(2) reserve the question of permission to appeal on any remaining issues to the court hearing the appeal.

4.14 If the court reserves the question of permission under head 4.13(2), above, the appellant must, within 14 days after service of the court's order, inform the appeal court in writing whether he intends to pursue the reserved issues. A court officer will inform the respondent whether the appellant intends to pursue the reserved issues. If the appellant does intend to pursue the reserved issues, the parties must include in any time estimate for the appeal hearing, their time estimate for the reserved issues.

4.15 If the appeal court refuses permission to appeal on the remaining issues without a hearing and the applicant wishes to have that decision reconsidered at an oral hearing, the time limit in r 173(5) will apply. Any application for an extension of this time limit should be made promptly. The court hearing the appeal on the issues for which permission has been granted will not normally grant, at the appeal hearing, an application to extend the time limit in r 173(5) for the remaining issues.

4.16 If the appeal court refuses permission to appeal on remaining issues at or after an oral hearing, the application for permission to appeal on those issues cannot be renewed at the appeal hearing. See the Access to Justice Act 1999 s 54(4).

Respondents' costs of permission applications

4.17 In most cases, applications for permission to appeal will be determined without the court requesting:

(1) submissions from; or

(2) if there is an oral hearing, attendance by,

the respondent.

4.18 Where the court does not request submissions from or attendance by the respondent, costs will not normally be allowed to a respondent who volunteers submissions or attendance.

4.19 Where the court does request:

(1) submissions from; or

(2) attendance by the respondent,

the court will normally allow the respondent his costs if permission is refused.

5. Appellant's notice

5.1 An appellant's notice must be filed and served in all cases. Where an application for permission to appeal is made to the appeal court it must be applied for in the appellant's notice.

Human Rights

5.2 Where the appellant seeks:

(a) to rely on any issue under the Human Rights Act 1998; or

(b) a remedy available under the 1998 Act,

for the first time in an appeal, he must include in his appeal notice the information required by the 2005 Rules r 116(1).

5.3 The *Practice Direction* supplementing Pt 13 will apply as if references to the directions hearing were to the application for permission to appeal.

Extension of time for filing appellant's notice

5.4 If an appellant requires an extension of time for filing his notice the application must be made in the appellant's notice. The notice should state the reason for the delay and the steps taken prior to the application being made.

5.5 Where the appellant's notice includes an application for an extension of time and permission to appeal has been given or is not required the respondent has the right to be heard on that application.

A copy of the appeal bundle must be served on the respondent (see head 5.9, below). Unless the court directs otherwise, a court officer will effect service. However, a respondent who unreasonably opposes an extension of time runs the risk of being ordered to pay the appellant's costs of that application.

5.6 If an extension of time is given following such an application the procedure at heads 6.1–6.8, below, applies.

Applications

5.7 Notice of an application to be made to the appeal court for a remedy incidental to the appeal (e.g. an interim injunction under r 118) may be included in the appeal notice or in a Pt 9 application notice.

(Head 9, below, of this *Practice Direction* contains other provisions relating to applications.)

Documents

5.8 The appellant must file the following documents together with an appeal bundle (see head 5.9, below) with his appellant's notice:

(a) two additional copies of the appellant's notice for the appeal court;

(b) one copy of the appellant's notice for each of the respondents;

(c) one copy of his skeleton argument for each copy of the appellant's notice that is filed (see head 5.9, below);

(d) a sealed or stamped copy of the order being appealed or a copy of the notice of the making of an order;

(e) a copy of any order giving or refusing permission to appeal, together with a copy of the judge's reasons for allowing or refusing permission to appeal; and

(f) any witness statements or affidavits in support of any application included in the appellant's notice.

5.9 An appellant must include the following documents in his appeal bundle:

(a) a sealed or stamped copy of the appellant's notice;

(b) a sealed or stamped copy of the order being appealed, or a copy of the notice of the making of an order;

(c) a copy of any order giving or refusing permission to appeal, together with a copy of the judge's reasons for allowing or refusing permission to appeal;

(d) any affidavit or witness statement filed in support of any application included in the appellant's notice;

(e) a copy of his skeleton argument;

(f) a transcript or note of judgment or, in a magistrates' court, written reasons for the courts decision (see head 5.23, below), and in cases where permission to appeal was given by the lower court or is not required those parts of any transcript of evidence which are directly relevant to any question at issue on the appeal;

(g) the application form;

(h) any application notice (or case management documentation) relevant to the subject of the appeal;

(i) any other documents which the appellant reasonably considers necessary to enable the appeal court to reach its decision on the hearing of the application or appeal; and

(j) such other documents as the court may direct.

5.10 All documents that are extraneous to the issues to be considered on the application or the appeal must be excluded. The appeal bundle may include affidavits, witness statements, summaries, experts' reports and exhibits but only where these are directly relevant to the subject matter of the appeal.

5.11 Where the appellant is represented, the appeal bundle must contain a certificate signed by his solicitor, counsel or other representative to the effect that he has read and understood head 5.10, above, and that the composition of the appeal bundle complies with it.

5.12 Where it is not possible to file all the above documents, the appellant must indicate which documents have not yet been filed and the reasons why they are not currently available. The appellant must then provide a reasonable estimate of when the missing document or documents can be filed and file them as soon as reasonably practicable.

Skeleton arguments

5.13 The appellant's notice must, subject to heads 5.14, 5.15, above, be accompanied by a skeleton argument. Alternatively the skeleton argument may be included in the appellant's notice. Where the skeleton argument is so included it will not form part of the notice for the purposes of r 178.

5.14 Where it is impracticable for the appellant's skeleton argument to accompany the appellant's notice it must be filed and served on all respondents within 14 days of filing the notice. Unless the court directs otherwise, a court officer will effect service.

5.15 An appellant who is not represented need not file a skeleton argument but is encouraged to do so since this will be helpful to the court.

5.16 A skeleton argument must contain a numbered list of the points which the party wishes to make. These should both define and confine the areas of controversy. Each point should be stated as concisely as the nature of the case allows.

5.17 A numbered point must be followed by a reference to any document on which the party wishes to rely.

5.18 A skeleton argument must state, in respect of each authority cited:

(a) the proposition of law that the authority demonstrates; and

(b) the parts of the authority (identified by page or paragraph references) that support the proposition.

5.19 If more than one authority is cited in support of a given proposition, the skeleton argument must briefly state the reason for taking that course.

5.20 The statement referred to in head 5.19, above, should not materially add to the length of the skeleton argument but should be sufficient to demonstrate, in the context of the argument:

(a) the relevance of the authority or authorities to that argument; and

(b) that the citation is necessary for a proper presentation of that argument.

5.21 The cost of preparing a skeleton argument which:

(a) does not comply with the requirements set out in this paragraph; or

(b) was not filed within the time limits provided by this *Practice Direction*, or any further time granted by the court,

will not be allowed on assessment except to the extent that the court otherwise directs.

5.22 The appellant should consider what other information the appeal court will need. This may include a list of persons who feature in the case or glossaries of technical terms. A chronology of relevant events will be necessary in most appeals.

Suitable record of the judgment

5.23 Where the judgment to be appealed has been officially recorded by the court, an approved transcript of that record should accompany the appellant's notice. Photocopies will not be accepted for this purpose. However, where there is no officially recorded judgment, the following documents will be acceptable:

Written judgments

Where the judgment was made in writing a copy of that judgment endorsed with the judge's signature.

Written reasons

Where, in a magistrates' court, reasons for the court's decision are given in writing, a copy of those reasons.

Note of judgment

When judgment was not officially recorded or made in writing a note of the judgment (agreed between the appellant's and respondent's advocates) should be submitted for approval to the judge whose decision is being appealed. If the parties cannot agree on a single note of the judgment, both versions should be provided to that judge with an explanatory letter. For the purpose of an application for permission to appeal the note need not be approved by the respondent or the lower court judge.

Advocates' notes of judgments where the appellant is unrepresented

When the appellant was unrepresented in the lower court it is the duty of any advocate for the respondent to make his/her note of judgment promptly available, free of charge to the appellant where there is no officially recorded judgment or if the court so directs. Where the appellant was represented in the lower court it is the duty of his own former advocate to make his/her note available in these circumstances. The appellant should submit the note of judgment to the appeal court.

5.24 An appellant may not be able to obtain an official transcript or other suitable record of the lower court's decision within the time within which the appellant's notice must be filed. In such cases the appellant's notice must still be completed to the best of the appellant's ability on the basis of the documentation available. However it may be amended subsequently with the permission of the appeal court in accordance with r 178.

Advocates' notes of judgments

5.25 Advocates' brief (or, where appropriate, refresher) fee includes:

(1) remuneration for taking a note of the judgment of the court;

(2) having the note transcribed accurately;

(3) attempting to agree the note with the other side if represented;

(4) submitting the note to the judge for approval where appropriate;

(5) revising it if so requested by the judge;

(6) providing any copies required for the appeal court, instructing solicitors and lay client; and

(7) providing a copy of his note to an unrepresented appellant.

Transcripts or Notes of Evidence

5.26 When the evidence is relevant to the appeal an official transcript of the relevant evidence must be obtained. Transcripts or notes of evidence are generally not needed for the purpose of determining an application for permission to appeal.

Notes of evidence

5.27 If evidence relevant to the appeal was not officially recorded, a typed version of the judge's or justices' clerk's/assistant clerk's notes of evidence must be obtained.

Transcripts at public expense

5.28 Where the lower court or the appeal court is satisfied that an unrepresented appellant is in such poor financial circumstances that the cost of a transcript would be an excessive burden the court may certify that the cost of obtaining one official transcript should be borne at public expense.

5.29 In the case of a request for an official transcript of evidence or proceedings to be paid for at public expense, the court must also be satisfied that there are reasonable grounds for appeal. Whenever possible a request for a transcript at public expense should be made to the lower court when asking for permission to appeal.

Filing and service of appellant's notice

5.30 Rule 174 sets out the procedure and time limits for filing and serving an appellant's notice. The appellant must file the appellant's notice at the appeal court within such period as may be directed by the lower court, where that court is the High Court or a county court, which should not normally exceed 28 days or, where the lower court directs no such period or the lower court is a magistrates' court, within 14 days of the date of the decision that the appellant wishes to appeal.

5.31 Where the lower court judge announces his decision and reserves the reasons for his judgment or order until a later date, he should, in the exercise of powers under r 174(2)(a), fix a period for filing the appellant's notice at the appeal court that takes this into account.

5.32 Except where the appeal court orders otherwise a sealed or stamped copy of the appellant's notice, including any skeleton arguments must be served on all respondents in accordance with the timetable prescribed by r 174(3) except where this requirement is modified by head 5.14, above, in which case the skeleton argument should be served as soon as it is filed.

5.33 Except where the appeal court orders otherwise, a sealed or stamped copy of the appellant's notice, including any skeleton arguments, must also be served on:

(a) any children's guardian, reporting officer or children and family reporter; and

(b) where the appeal is from a magistrates' court, the court officer.

Unless the court directs otherwise, a court officer will effect service.

5.34 Unless the court otherwise directs a respondent need not take any action when served with an appellant's notice until such time as notification is given to him that permission to appeal has been given.

5.35 The court may dispense with the requirement for service of the notice on a respondent.

5.36 Where the appellant is applying for permission to appeal in his appellant's notice, his appellant's notice and skeleton argument (but not the appeal bundle) must be served on the respondents, unless the appeal court directs otherwise.

5.37 Where permission to appeal:

(a) has been given by the lower court; or

(b) is not required,

the appeal bundle must be served on the respondents and the persons mentioned in head 5.33, above, with the appellant's notice. Unless the court directs otherwise, a court officer will effect service.

Amendment of Appeal Notice

5.38 An appeal notice may be amended with permission. Such an application to amend and any application in opposition will normally be dealt with at the hearing unless that course would cause unnecessary expense or delay in which case a request should be made for the application to amend to be heard in advance. If the application to amend relates to an appeal from a magistrates' court it may be heard by a district judge of the appeal court.

6. Procedure after permission is obtained

6.1 This paragraph sets out the procedure where—

(1) permission to appeal is given by the appeal court; or

(2) the appellant's notice is filed in the appeal court and:

(a) permission was given by the lower court; or

(b) permission is not required.

6.2 If the appeal court gives permission to appeal, the appeal bundle must be served on each of the respondents within seven days beginning with the date that the order giving permission to appeal is made. Unless the court directs otherwise, a court officer will effect service.

6.3 The appeal court will send the parties:

(1) notification of the date of the hearing or the period of time (the 'listing window') during which the appeal is likely to be heard;

(2) where permission is granted by the appeal court a copy of the order giving permission to appeal; and

(3) any other directions given by the court.

6.4 Where the appeal court grants permission to appeal, the appellant must add the following documents to the appeal bundle:

(a) the respondent's notice and skeleton argument (if any);

(b) those parts of the transcripts of evidence which are directly relevant to any question at issue on the appeal;

(c) the order granting permission to appeal and, where permission to appeal was granted at an oral hearing, the transcript (or note) of any judgment which was given; and

(d) any document which the appellant and respondent have agreed to add to the appeal bundle in accordance with head 7.16, below.

6.5 Where permission to appeal has been refused on a particular issue, the appellant must remove from the appeal bundle all documents that are relevant only to that issue.

Time estimates

6.6 If the appellant is legally represented, the appeal court must be notified, in writing, of the advocate's time estimate for the hearing of the appeal.

6.7 The time estimate must be that of the advocate who will argue the appeal. It should exclude the time required by the court to give judgment.

6.8 A court officer will notify the respondent of the appellant's time estimate and if the respondent disagrees with the time estimate he must inform the court within 7 days of the notification. In the absence of such notification the respondent will be deemed to have accepted the estimate proposed on behalf of the appellant.

7. Respondent

7.1 A respondent who wishes to ask the appeal court to vary the order of the lower court in any way must appeal and permission will be required on the same basis as for an appellant.

(Head 3.2, above, applies to grounds of appeal by a respondent.)

7.2 A respondent who wishes to appeal or who wishes to ask the appeal court to uphold the order of the lower court for reasons different from or additional to those given by the lower court must file a respondent's notice.

7.3 If the respondent does not file a respondent's notice, he will not be entitled, except with the permission of the court, to rely on any reason not relied on in the lower court.

7.4 Heads 5.2–5.4, above, of this *Practice Direction* (Human Rights and extension for time for filing appellant's notice) also apply to a respondent and a respondent's notice.

Time limits

7.5 The time limits for filing a respondent's notice are set out in r 175(4), (5).

7.6 Where an extension of time is required the extension must be requested in the respondent's notice and the reasons why the respondent failed to act within the specified time must be included.

7.7 Except where head 7.8, above, applies, the respondent must file a skeleton argument for the court in all cases where he proposes to address arguments to the court. The respondent's skeleton argument may be included within a respondent's notice. Where a skeleton argument is included within a respondent's notice it will not form part of the notice for the purposes of r 178.

7.8 A respondent who:

(a) files a respondent's notice; but

(b) does not include his skeleton argument within that notice,

must file his skeleton argument within 14 days of filing the notice.

7.9 A respondent who does not file a respondent's notice but who files a skeleton argument must file that skeleton argument at least seven days before the appeal hearing.

(Rule 175(4) sets out the period for filing a respondent's notice.)

7.10 A respondent who is not represented need not file a skeleton argument but is encouraged to do so in order to assist the court.

7.11 The respondent's skeleton argument must be served on—

(a) the appellant; and

(b) any other respondent.

Unless the court directs otherwise, a court officer will effect service.

7.12 A respondent's skeleton argument must conform to the directions at heads 5.16–5.22 with any necessary modifications. It should, where appropriate, answer the arguments set out in the appellant's skeleton argument.

Applications within respondent's notices

7.13 A respondent may include an application within a respondent's notice in accordance with head 5.7, above.

Filing respondent's notices and skeleton arguments.

7.14 The respondent must file the following documents with his respondent's notice in every case:

(a) two additional copies of the respondent's notice for the appeal court; and

(b) one copy each for the appellant and any other respondents.

7.15 The respondent may file a skeleton argument with his respondent's notice and:

(a) where he does so he must file two copies; and

(b) where he does not do so he must comply with head 7.8, above.

7.16 If the respondent wishes to rely on any documents which he reasonably considers necessary to enable the appeal court to reach its decision on the appeal in addition to those filed by the appellant, any amendments to the appeal bundle should be agreed with the appellant if possible.

7.17 If the representatives for the parties are unable to reach agreement, the respondent may prepare a supplemental bundle.

7.18 If the respondent prepares a supplemental bundle he must file it, together with the requisite number of copies for the appeal court, at the appeal court:

(a) with the respondent's notice; or

(b) if a respondent's notice is not filed, within 21 days after he is served with the appeal bundle.

7.19 The following documents must be served:

(1) the respondent's notice;

(2) his skeleton argument (if any); and

(3) the supplemental bundle (if any),

on:

(a) the appellant; and

(b) any other respondent,

as soon as practicable and in any event not later than seven days after the respondent's notice was filed. Unless the court directs otherwise, a court officer will effect service.

8. Appeals to the High Court

Application

8.1 This paragraph applies where an appeal lies to the High Court from the decision of a magistrates' court.

8.2 The appellant's notice must be filed in:

(a) the principal registry of the Family Division; or

(b) the district registry, being in the same place as an adoption centre or an intercountry adoption centre within the meaning of the Children (Allocation of Proceedings) Order 1991, SI 1991/1677, art 2(d), (e) which is nearest to the court from which the appeal lies.

8.3 A respondent's notice must be filed at the court where the appellant's notice was filed.

8.4 In the case of appeals from district judges of the High Court, appeals, applications for permission and any other applications in the appeal may be heard and directions in the appeal may be given by a High Court Judge or by any person authorised under the Supreme Court Act 1981 s 9 to act as a judge of the High Court.

Appeals to a judge of a county court from a district judge

8.5 The Designated Family Judge in consultation with the Family Division Liaison Judges has responsibility for allocating appeals from decisions of district judges to circuit judges.

9. Applications

9.1 Where a party to an appeal makes an application whether in an appeal notice or by Pt 9 application notice, the provisions of Pt 9 will apply.

9.2 The applicant must file the following documents with the notice:

(1) one additional copy of the application notice for the appeal court and one copy for each of the respondents;

(2) where applicable a sealed or stamped copy of the order which is the subject of the main appeal or a copy of the notice of the making of an order;

(3) a bundle of documents in support which should include:

(a) the Pt 9 application notice; and

(b) any witness statements and affidavits filed in support of the application notice.

10. Disposing of applications or appeals by consent

10.1 Where an appellant does not wish to pursue an application or an appeal, he may request the appeal court for an order that his application or appeal be dismissed. Such a request must state whether the appellant is a child, non-subject child or patient.

10.2 The request must be accompanied by a consent signed by the other parties stating whether the respondent is a child, non-subject child or patient and consents to the dismissal of the application or appeal.

10.3 Where the application relates to an appeal from a magistrates' court, the application may be heard by a district judge of the appeal court.

11. Allowing unopposed appeals or applications on paper

11 The appeal court will not normally make an order allowing an appeal unless satisfied that the decision of the lower court was wrong, but the appeal court may set aside or vary the order of the lower court with consent and without determining the merits of the appeal, if it is satisfied that there are good and sufficient reasons for doing so. Where the appeal court is requested by all parties to allow an application or an appeal the court may consider the request on the papers. The request should state whether any of the parties is a child, non-subject child or patient and set out the relevant history of the proceedings and the matters relied on as justifying the proposed order and be accompanied by a copy of the proposed order.

12. Withdrawal of appeal

12 An application to withdraw an appeal from a decision of a magistrates' court may be heard by a district judge of the appeal court.

13. Summary assessment of costs

13.1 Costs are likely to be assessed by way of summary assessment at the following hearings:

(1) contested directions hearings;

(2) applications for permission to appeal at which the respondent is present;

(3) appeals from case management decisions or decisions made at directions hearings; and

(4) appeals listed for one day or less.

(Provision for summary assessment of costs is made by head 13 of the *Practice Direction* supplementing CPR Pt 44.)

13.2 Parties attending any of the hearings referred to in head 13.1, above, should be prepared to deal with the summary assessment.

14. Reopening of final appeals

14.1 This paragraph applies to applications under r 183 for permission to reopen a final determination of an appeal.

14.2 In this paragraph, 'appeal' includes an application for permission to appeal.

14.3 Permission must be sought from the court whose decision the applicant wishes to reopen.

14.4 The application for permission must be made by application notice and supported by written evidence, verified by a statement of truth.

14.5 A copy of the application for permission must not be served on any other party to the original appeal unless the court so directs.

14.6 Where the court directs that the application for permission is to be served on another party, that party may within 14 days of the service on him of the copy of the application file a written statement either supporting or opposing the application which, unless the court directs otherwise, a court officer will serve on the other parties.

14.7 The application for permission, and any written statements supporting or opposing it, will be considered on paper by a single judge, and will be allowed to proceed only if the judge so directs.

417   Care order—interim order—residential assessment—procedure and costs

The following guidance has been given regarding the factors that should be taken into account and the steps that should be taken in relation to applications for residential assessments under the Children Act 1989 s 38(6): (1) s 38(6) directions should not be made until the court has had an opportunity to examine in appropriate detail the scope and nature of the proposed assessment; (2) to facilitate that, the proposed assessment provider needs to be told before the application for the s 38(6) direction that what is required, assuming that to be the case, is an assessment of the child, and that that can include an assessment of the child's relationship with the carer, of the carer's ability to meet the child's various needs, and of the carer's present capacity to change in the reasonably foreseeable future in order to eliminate or improve deficient parenting; but that the cost of specific teaching, training, therapy or other educative work, if it was instructed to be done, or if it was an integral and substantive part of the providers' method of work, would not be paid for under the court order, and so would need to be separately negotiated, for example, with the local authority; (3) the parties also need already to have obtained from the proposed assessment provider clear information as to the nature of the work which it expects to undertake, together with the overall cost per week and the number of weeks likely to be required; (4) if and in so far as therapy, training or treatment is to be specifically commissioned, or is regarded by the proposed assessment provider as an integral and substantive part of its modus operandi, then the hourly rate and likely number of hours for that particular element and type of work should be separately stated by the proposed assessment provider; (5) on receipt of that information, and using a collaborative approach, all parties should endeavour to agree, subject to the courts' approval, whether and how the costs of the proposed assessment should be apportioned; (6) if the court does have to rule on a contested funding issue, then it would do so by applying the guidelines laid down by the courts to the information obtained under heads (3), (4) above and to the overall facts of the case; (7) when an assessment is genuinely of a mixed nature, the court should identify the work which is outside s 38(6) and which could not therefore be ordered to be done or paid for; the remainder of the assessment work can then be ordered and the costs apportioned appropriately, according to the authorities and to the overall circumstances of the case; (8) the issue of funding ought to be determined at the same hearing as that at which the application for permission to commission the assessment is determined; if that is not possible then the assessment-provider needs to be told clearly that specific teaching elements of therapy and training and so on would not or might not be ordered by the court, nor ordered to be paid for by any party; and (9) where a proposed residential assessment appears on the face of it to be an assessment of the child under s 38(6), the party seeking to say that the assessment would in fact contain elements of teaching, training or therapy, should be in a position to establish that to the satisfaction of the court, otherwise the very strong probability is that the costs would be apportioned between the parties.

Sheffield CC v V [2006] EWHC 1861 (Fam), [2006] Fam Law 833 (Family Division: Bodey J).

418   Care order—prescribed orders—Northern Ireland, Guernsey and Isle of Man

The Children (Prescribed Orders—Northern Ireland, Guernsey and Isle of Man) Amendment Regulations 2006, SI 2006/837 (in force on 12 April 2006), amend the 1991 Regulations, SI 1991/2032, in consequence of the coming into force of certain enactments so that certain care orders made in Northern Ireland and the Isle of Man are to have effect in England and Wales.

419   Care order—threshold criteria—responsibility for injury

The Children Act 1989 s 31(2) entitles a court to make a care order or supervision order only if it is satisfied that (1) the child concerned is suffering, or is likely to suffer, significant harm; and (2) the harm, or likelihood of harm, is attributable to the care given to the child, or likely to be given to him if the order were not made, not being what it would be reasonable to expect a parent to give to him.

A local authority took care proceedings relating to a child because of the injuries he had suffered when seven weeks old, which included a fractured skull. At a fact finding hearing, the local authority contended that the injuries had been caused non-accidentally. The parents maintained that the injuries were accidental, but admitted that they had not been entirely truthful in their earlier explanations of what had happened. The judge decided that she was unable on the evidence to find how the injuries to the child had occurred, save that they had been incurred while he was in the care of his parents, and that either the mother or father or both were responsible, but that she was unable to indicate who was likely to be the more culpable. However, on the basis that at least one of the parents had been responsible and that the other had colluded to prevent that fact from becoming known, the judge found that the threshold criteria under the 1989 Act s 31 had been satisfied. On the mother's appeal, *held*, translated into everyday language and experience, the words of s 31(2) meant that, in order to satisfy the threshold criteria, the local authority had to prove that an injury was non-accidental. Once that finding could properly be made, the question arose of who the perpetrator was. In cases where the judge could not identify the perpetrator, it was often sufficient to satisfy the threshold criteria to show that the child had been non-accidentally injured in the care of his parents and that either or both had been responsible. Such considerations did not apply when the local authority could not satisfy the court that injuries had been inflicted non-accidentally. It had not been open to the local authority to use the fact of the injuries to the child as a basis for submitting that the threshold criteria had been established in relation to the injuries, and that one or both of the parents was responsible. In so far as the judge had found the threshold criteria satisfied because either the mother or father was responsible for the child's injuries, she had been wrong to do so. The injuries had simply not satisfied the threshold criteria, and it was not open to the judge to allocate responsibility or guilt or to say that one or other of the parents had caused them. Judgment would be given accordingly.

Re L (A Child) (Care Proceedings: Responsibility for Child's Injury) [2006] EWCA Civ 49, [2006] 1 FCR 285 (Court of Appeal: Wall LJ and Coleridge J).

420 Care proceedings—decision-making process—departure from good practice

See *Re J (Care: Assessment: Fair Trial)*, para 1558.

421 Care proceedings—disclosure of medical records—foster parent infected with HIV— local authority's duty of disclosure to parents

See *Brent LBC v N (Foster Carers)*, para 586.

422 Care proceedings—paternity of child—determination—retained criminal DNA evidence

The Police and Criminal Evidence Act 1984 s 64(1A) provides that where samples are taken from a person in connection with the investigation of an offence, they may be retained after they have fulfilled the purposes for which they were taken but must not be used by any person except for the purposes related to the prevention or detection of crime, the investigation of an offence, or the conduct of a prosecution.

The deceased had been killed by the husband of the deceased's former partner. When the deceased had been treated in hospital, a pre-transfusion blood sample had been taken for the purpose of the police investigation of the offence. In care proceedings by a local authority, the authority sought a direction for the release by the police of the DNA evidence available from the sample, in order to establish the paternity of the child who was the subject of the proceedings. The child believed the deceased to be his father but the child's mother denied this. It was clear that the husband was not the child's father. The authority's care plan was to place the child with the deceased's mother. *Held*, there was no absolute right under the European Convention on Human Rights art 8, which guaranteed the right to respect for private and family life, to establish one's identity in that there was no absolute right of access to genetic information. The state could control access to such information in accordance with the restrictions allowed under art 8(2). It would be inconsistent with the public policy underpinning the 1984 Act, as well as contrary to its specific wording, to allow the use of retained DNA samples for any purpose other than those specified. The prohibition of other uses was proportionate interference. Parliament had not authorised the sample to be seized and retained for the establishment of paternity and the court had no power to order disclosure. Accordingly, the application would be dismissed.

Lambeth LBC v S [2006] EWHC 326 (Fam), [2006] Fam Law 843 (Family Division: Ryder J).

423 Care proceedings—representations procedure—England

The Children Act 1989 Representations Procedure (England) Regulations 2006, SI 2006/1738 (in force on 1 September 2006), replace the Representations Procedure (Children) Regulations 1991, SI 1991/894, and regulate the procedure which local authorities are to follow in the consideration of representations made to them about the discharge of certain functions under the Children Act 1989 and the Adoption and Children Act 2002. In particular, the regulations (1) specify some of the matters about which a person may make representations; (2) provide for the application of the procedure, with modifications, to representations made to voluntary organisations providing accommodation for children and about fostering limits; (3) provide for a procedure for (a) making representations about the discharge by a local authority of its functions under the 1989 Act; and (b) considering representations about specified local authority functions under the 1989 Act and the 2002 Act; (4) make provision for functions to do with special guardianship support services; (5) permit a local authority not to consider representations, in whole or in part, if the local authority decide that to do so might prejudice any of certain proceedings; (6) provide that a complainant may make his representations to the local authority no later than one year after the grounds to make the representations arose; (7) make provision for where the representations are made outside the one year time limit that the local authority may still consider them if it thinks that it would not be reasonable to expect the complainant to have made the representations within a year and that it is still possible to consider the representations effectively and fairly; (8) require local authorities to give complainants information about the representations procedure when they first make representations and to give information about advocacy services where relevant; (9) set out how local authorities are to deal with representations which are made by persons whom the local authority consider to have sufficient interest in the child concerned to warrant their representations being considered; (10) provide that local authorities must decide whether to consider representations under head (9) and are required to take into account the views of the child if they think it appropriate to do so; (11) provide for the first stage for considering representations, which involves an informal attempt at resolving the problem unless the complainant and the local authority agree otherwise; (12) require that whether the representations have been considered under stage one or not they must be set down in writing where they have only been made orally before going to the second stage; (13) provide for the second stage for considering representations which involves consideration by an independent person; (14) make provision for the third stage of consideration by a panel of three independent persons, which can be requested by the complainant or his advocate, which has to make recommendations within five working days of considering the representations and the local authority have 15 working days to consider the recommendations and decide what to do; (15) require voluntary organisations who are providing accommodation for a child to have a procedure for considering representations made to them by specified persons; (16) require every local authority to establish a procedure for considering any representations made to them about the discharge of their functions in relation to the exemption of people from the limit on the number of children they may foster; and (17) provide for the procedure local authorities must follow in carrying out consideration of a representation under head (16).

424   Care Standards Tribunal—proceedings
See para 485.

425   Child abduction and custody—extension to Jersey
The Child Abduction and Custody Act 1985 (Jersey) Order 2006, SI 2006/1917 (in force on 21 August 2006), provides that references made in the 1985 Act to orders made, proceedings brought and other things done in relation to the Hague Convention on the Civil Aspects of International Child Abduction 1980 and the European Convention on Recognition and Enforcement of Decisions concerning Custody of Children 1980 in the United Kingdom are to have effect as if they included a reference to orders made, proceedings brought and other things done in Jersey.

426   Child abduction and custody—long-term shared custody arrangement—habitual residence
New Zealand
Two children were born in Australia and were Australian citizens. Consequent to the mother's decision to move to New Zealand, she made a long-term shared custody agreement with the father under which both of them would retain parental responsibility and each of them would have custody of the children for alternate two-year periods. After the mother removed the children to New Zealand under the agreement, she sought sole custody of them. The authorities then applied for the return of the children to Australia. It was held that the children were habitually resident in New Zealand and the application was refused. On appeal, *held*, it was clear that the father neither intended nor consented to a change in the children's habitual residence in terms of the Hague Convention. Although the long-term shared custody agreement involved the alternation of actual residence, for Hague Convention purposes children who were the subjects of such agreements could have only one habitual residence. It was unlikely that it was intended that the protection of the Hague Convention would be lost to parents who agreed to what they saw as reasonable arrangements. It followed that long-term shared custody agreements should be construed to uphold the Hague Convention's stated purposes of securing the return of children removed to contracting states and ensuring that rights of custody and access under the law of one contracting state were effectively respected in other contracting states. The correct forum for this case was Australia which remained

the place of the children's habitual residence for the purposes of the Hague Convention given that they were born there, had Australian citizenship and the agreement had been made in Australia. Accordingly, the appeal would be allowed.

Secretary for Justice v P (Habitual Residence) [2006] NZFLR 255 (New Zealand High Court).

427   Child abduction and custody—wrongful removal—application to add child as party to proceedings—exceptional circumstances test

The mother of a 15-year-old child commenced proceedings under the Child Abduction and Custody Act 1985 Pt I (ss 1–11) and the Hague Convention on the Civil Aspects of International Child Abduction after the child refused to return to South Africa, where she and her mother were habitually resident, after visiting her father in the United Kingdom. The child applied to be added as a party to the proceedings. The judge, applying settled authority, stated that only in exceptional circumstances would a child be joined to such proceedings, and refused the application, finding that no such exceptional circumstances existed. The child appealed, submitting that the exceptional circumstances test should no longer be applied to applications to join a child as a party to Hague Convention proceedings, since in family proceedings a child would be joined to proceedings, if able to understand them and give instructions in relation to them, pursuant to the Family Proceedings Rules 1991, SI 1991/1247, r 9.2A. *Held*, the suggestion that the exceptional circumstances test should be in any way relaxed would be firmly rejected. Rule 9.2A only regulated the participation of children in proceedings after they had cleared the hurdle of obtaining party status. Moreover, in most, if not all, of the rare reported cases in which a child had been granted separate representation in Hague Convention proceedings, there had been something close to a public law dimension. Accordingly, the appeal would be dismissed.

Re H (A Child: Child Abduction) [2006] EWCA Civ 1247, [2007] 1 FCR 345 (Court of Appeal: Thorpe and Wall LJJ). *Re M (Minors) (Child Abduction)* [1994] 2 FCR 750, CA (1994 Abr para 354), applied.

428   Child abduction and custody—wrongful removal—determination by court of another Convention state

A child was born in Romania to Romanian parents, who were married and later divorced. The mother brought the child to England without the knowledge or consent of the father. Proceedings under the Child Abduction and Custody Act 1985 and the Hague Convention on the Civil Aspects of International Child Abduction 1980 were commenced, and a dispute arose as to the effect of orders made in Romania about the child when his parents divorced. The judge was unable to resolve a difference of opinion between two experts, and directed that a determination be obtained from the Romanian court pursuant to the Convention art 15. The Romanian court ruled that the removal of the child to England had not been wrongful under Romanian law. However, when the case came back before the English court, it was ordered that further evidence on Romanian law be obtained from an expert jointly instructed by both parents. The expert reached a different conclusion to the Romanian court. At the eventual hearing, the judge ordered the child's immediate return to Romania on certain undertakings by the father. The mother appealed, arguing that the father had at most rights of access rather than rights of custody so that, pursuant to arts 3 and 12, the removal of the child from Romania was not wrongful and there was no duty to return him to his home country. The appeal was dismissed and, on the mother's further appeal, *held*, art 3 made it quite clear that what mattered was whether the removal of a child breached the custody rights of a person under the laws of the country in which the child had been habitually resident before the removal. Plainly, therefore, one had to ask first what rights that person had under the law of the home country, and second whether those rights were rights of custody within the meaning of the Convention. Article 15 contemplated that, if the court in a requested state was uncertain of the answers to those questions, it might seek a determination from the authorities of the requesting state, as had been done in the present case. The foreign court was much better placed than the English court to understand the true meaning and effect of its own laws in Convention terms. Only if its characterisation of the parent's rights was clearly out of line with the international understanding of the Convention's terms should the court in the requested state decline to follow it. It could not be said that the father had rights of custody when the child was removed. Accordingly, the appeal would be allowed.

Re D (A Child) (Abduction: Foreign Custody Rights) [2006] UKHL 51, [2007] 1 All ER 783 (House of Lords: Lords Nicholls of Birkenhead and Hope of Craighead, Baroness Hale of Richmond, Lords Carswell and Brown of Eaton-under-Heywood). Decision of Court of Appeal [2006] All ER (D) 355 (May) reversed.

429   Child abduction and custody—wrongful removal—determination by court of another Convention state—jurisdiction of English court

The parties were married in Greece and had a child the following year. They later separated, and the mother, a citizen of the United Kingdom, filed a petition for divorce. The mother was granted temporary custody of the child, and decided to return with the child to the United Kingdom. The father, a Greek national, made an application pursuant to the Hague Convention on the Civil Aspects of International Child Abduction 1980 for the child to be returned to Greece, arguing that the provisional and exclusive award of care to the mother did not entitle her to select a place of residence for the child outside the jurisdiction of the Greek court. The mother contended that she had removed the child lawfully under Greek law. *Held*, the father had failed to demonstrate that the mother's removal of the child had been wrongful in Greek law. Having determined the rights of the remaining parent under domestic law, it was then a matter of English law whether the removal was in breach of Convention rights of custody. Rights of custody involved rights relating to the care of the child and, crucially, the right to determine the child's place of residence. A right to be consulted without an associated right to object did not amount to rights relating to the care of the child. Where both parents had equal and separate rights of custody under their domestic law then, even if the removal was not in breach of that domestic law, the removal would be in breach of the remaining parent's rights of custody. The question was not whether there was a breach of domestic law, but whether the rights possessed by the remaining party, if any, amounted to rights of custody. Where, on the other hand, one parent did not have parental responsibility, and no right to stop the other parent taking a child abroad but a right to watch over the child's education, instruction, and living conditions, and a right to access, but only a right to apply to stop the other parent removing the child, the position was changed. A removal by the parent with responsibility would not be in breach of the parent without responsibility's rights of custody. Accordingly, the application would be dismissed.

M v P [2006] EWHC 2227 (Fam), [2006] All ER (D) 54 (Oct) (Family Division: Sumner J). *Re M (A Minor) (Abduction)* [1995] 3 FCR 99 (1995 Abr para 381) applied.

430 Child abduction and custody—wrongful removal—order for return of child—stay of proceedings—appropriateness

A mother and her child moved from England to Hungary with the father's agreement. On a subsequent visit by the child to England, the father refused to allow the child to return to Hungary and sought a residence order in respect of the child. The mother applied for the return of the child pursuant to the Hague Convention on the Civil Aspects of International Child Abduction 1980. An English judge ordered the immediate return of the child to Hungary, and stayed the residence proceedings initiated by the father. However, the judge also decided that it would be appropriate to lift the stay for one day in order to make detailed provisions for a three-day hearing in the High Court. The mother appealed against that decision. *Held*, the paramount concern in child abduction cases was that any steps within the litigation were taken expeditiously. The issuing of proceedings by the father compounded his wrong of retaining the child, rather than mitigated it, as the judge appeared to believe. It was imperative in such cases that no orders should be made in England which might be said by inference to challenge the jurisdiction of another member state or to suggest that an English court was in a superior position to decide welfare issues. While it might in some circumstances be appropriate to impose a general stay on domestic proceedings rather than dismiss them outright, no such stay could be justified in the present case. Accordingly, the appeal would be allowed.

Re EC (Child Abduction: Stayed Proceedings) (2006) Times, 19 July (Court of Appeal: Thorpe, Dyson and Hallett LJJ).

431 Child abduction and custody—wrongful removal—recognition of foreign judgment

A married couple, who were British citizens and had two children, moved to Spain and became resident there. They subsequently separated and, without the mother's consent, the father took the children to England. The mother began proceedings in Spain for separation, custody and return of the children, but the Spanish court ruled that care and custody of the children should be granted to the father. The mother then issued proceedings in England applying for the return of the children to Spain pursuant to the Child Abduction and Custody Act 1985. The father accepted that the removal of the children had been wrongful for the purposes of the Hague Convention on the Civil Aspects of International Child Abduction 1980, but contended that the judgment of the Spanish court should be followed pursuant to EC Council Regulation 2201/2003 art 60(e), by virtue of which judgments of courts of member states were to be recognised by domestic courts in priority to the Hague Convention. *Held*, if the court made an order for the return of the children to Spain, it would be failing to give effect to its recognition of the Spanish judgment and thus failing to accord precedence to Regulation 2201/2003 over the Hague Convention in that respect. The primary rationale underlying the Hague Convention was to ensure that decisions as to the welfare of children, and questions where and with which parent they should reside, were taken in the country of the child's habitual residence. By the time the instant matter came before the English court for decision as to whether an order for the return of the child should be granted under the terms of the Hague Convention, those purposes would have been achieved, in the sense that there had been a full and careful hearing of the issue by a Spanish court in possession of all the relevant facts going to its welfare decisions, as well as the full circumstances of the father's removal of the children. The Spanish court had specifically vested interim custody in the father on the basis that the children should continue to reside in England with the father as their main carer, and with appropriate and beneficial educational arrangements, pending a full and final hearing. By virtue of the relevant Spanish law, that interim custody order was not capable of appeal and would remain in place till the resolution of the divorce and/or separation proceedings. In those circumstances, if the court was obliged to return the children, it would defeat rather than assist the overall purpose of the Hague Convention. However, by application of the provisions of Regulation 2201/2003, such a result was avoided. Accordingly, the application would be dismissed.

Re T (Children) (Abduction: Recognition of Foreign Judgment) [2006] EWHC 1472 (Fam), [2006] 3 FCR 333 (Family Division: Sir Mark Potter P).

432 Child abduction and custody—wrongful removal—request for return of child— procedure

On the separation of an unmarried French couple, a French court ordered that their son should reside with the mother and that the father should be allowed contact. Neither party was to leave France, or to leave France with their son, without the other's express consent. The father went to England and, on a subsequent trip to France, removed his son to England without the mother's consent. Proceedings were issued under the Child Abduction and Custody Act 1985, which incorporated EC Council Regulation 2201/2003, although the trial did not take place until after the date prescribed by Regulation 2201/2003. The mother's summons for the return of her son was dismissed and she appealed. *Held*, an application under Regulation 2201/2003 should be headed under the 1985 Act and Regulation 2201/2003. The court file should be clearly marked on the outside to draw attention to the nature of the application. It should also state the date by which Regulation 2201/2003 required the matter to be resolved for the court administration as in order to comply with Regulation 2201/2003, a previously fixed case would have to be removed. The welfare investigations and conclusions had to be taken in France and could not be introduced in the court's discretionary conclusions. The nature and strengths of the son's objections to returning to his mother had to be weighed against the policy of Regulation 2201/2003. Accordingly, the appeal would be allowed.

Vigreux v Michel [2006] EWCA Civ 630, [2006] 2 FLR 1180 (Court of Appeal: Thorpe and Wall LJJ).

433 Child abduction and custody—wrongful retention—retention in foreign state— jurisdiction—habitual residence

See *Re A (A Child) (Wardship: Habitual Residence)*, para 603.

434 Child abuse—misdiagnosis of abuse—negligence—duty of care owed to parents

See *Lawrence v Pembrokeshire CC*, para 2083.

435 Child in need—local authority—duty to provide accommodation—child in custody

The Children Act 1989 s 21(2)(b) provides that every local authority must receive and provide accommodation for children whom it is requested to receive under the Police and Criminal Evidence Act 1984 s 38(6).

The claimant, a 16-year-old girl, was arrested for alleged wounding with intent and charged with the offence late at night. The police contacted social services in order to find secure accommodation for her overnight but none was found and she was detained overnight at the police station under the 1984 Act s 38(6). She sought judicial review of the local authority's failure to provide secure accommodation overnight. Her application failed and she appealed. *Held*, under the language of the 1989 Act s 21(2)(b), the local authority which received a custody officer's request to provide accommodation had a duty to do so. Parliament might have wished for the police to have the choice of which local authority to make the request to. There was an absolute duty to provide accommodation, but it was impossible to say whether there was an absolute duty to provide secure accommodation when it was requested. However, this did not mean that when an authority received a request for secure accommodation under the 1984 Act s 38(6) it could ignore it. In this instance the authority had not been in breach of its duty by failing to provide secure accommodation at the time. Accordingly, the appeal would be dismissed.

R (on the application of M) v Gateshead MBC [2006] EWCA Civ 221, [2006] QB 650 (Court of Appeal: Thorpe, Dyson and Moore-Brick LJJ).

436 Child in need—local authority—duty to provide accommodation—priority need

See *R (on the application of M) v Hammersmith and Fulham LBC*, para 1481.

437 Child minding and day care—registration fees—England

The Day Care and Child Minding (Registration Fees) (England) (Amendment) Regulations 2006, SI 2006/2081 (in force on 2 October 2006), amend the 2005 Regulations, SI 2005/2301, by increasing the prescribed fee (1) for an application for registration as a day care provider from £121 to £150 where the provider provides at least four hours care a day and from £14 to £18 where the provider provides less than four hours a day; (2) for an application for registration as a child minder from £14 to £18; (3) payable by registered day care providers from £94 to £120 (where at least four hours care is provided) and from £11 to £14 where less than four hours care is provided; and (4) payable by registered child minders from £11 to £14.

438   Child support—financial relief—modification of pre-existing agreement

The claimant mother gave birth to a daughter following an affair with a married man. The relationship ended and she obtained a periodical payments order against him under the Children Act 1989 s 15. She began another affair with the defendant, a wealthy man who assumed financial responsibility for her daughter. The claimant gave birth to the defendant's son, but then the relationship ended and the parties reached an agreement on financial arrangements which was expressed to be comprehensive and to make provision for the foreseeable future. They agreed that it was not necessary for the agreement to be made the subject of a court order. Subsequently, the claimant brought proceedings against the defendant for a settlement of property order, a lump sum order and a maintenance order. The judge ordered the defendant to set up a housing trust fund to provide for the son during his minority, to pay a lump sum to clear the claimant's debts, and to make periodical payments. The defendant appealed. *Held*, the court was empowered, under the Sch 1 para 10(3)(b), to alter an agreement provided it was satisfied that it did not contain proper financial arrangements with respect to the child. Such an alteration had to be just having regard to all the circumstances and the agreement itself, which would be the starting point of the court's assessment. If the court conceived that the claimant was capricious or unreasonable in the attempt to depart from the terms of the agreement then the dismissal of the application would naturally follow. The judge had been right to make such greater financial provision for the son's future as he considered to be just in all the circumstances and to reject the defendant's reliance on the argument that the claimant's claims should be dismissed on the ground that she had negotiated with the best legal advice an agreement intended to be final and comprehensive of all her claims. The court's jurisdiction under Sch 1 para 1 was limited to making an order against the father as a parent of a child. The only child of the defendant in the application was his son and so the court had no jurisdiction to make an order against him to the mother for the benefit of the daughter. It could not be said in relation to either the housing fund or the periodical payments order that the judge should have ordered only a portion against the defendant leaving the mother to apply against the daughter's father for the balance. However, the lump sum order would be reduced as it was plain that part of the responsibility for the mother's overall debt rested with the daughter's father. Accordingly, the appeal would be allowed in part.

Morgan v Hill [2006] EWCA Civ 1602, [2006] 3 FCR 620 (Court of Appeal: Thorpe, Keene and Hughes LJJ). *Edgar v Edgar* [1980] 3 All ER 887, CA (1980 Abr para 958), considered.

439   Child support—functions—contracting out

The Contracting Out (Functions Relating to Child Support) Order 2006, SI 2006/1692 (in force on 3 July 2006), enables the Secretary of State to authorise another person to exercise functions relating to child support, not including functions under the Child Support Act 1991 ss 15, 35, 39A and 40B, and those excluded from contracting out by the Deregulation and Contracting Out Act 1994 s 71.

440   Child support—liability order—appeal—expiry of time limit—miscarriage of justice

A liability order under the Child Support Act 1981 s 33 was made against the claimant. The claimant sought to appeal against the order on the ground that the defendant body had misled the court concerning the extent of the liability. However, the claimant failed to bring his appeal within the time limit prescribed by the Magistrates' Courts Act 1980. An issue arose as to whether the claimant was entitled to appeal. *Held*, where a claimant had failed to bring his appeal against a liability order in time but there had been an obvious miscarriage of justice, he was entitled to appeal by way of judicial review. A miscarriage of justice had clearly occurred in the instant case, and in such circumstances the court had the power to provide an avenue of appeal and a remedy in the form of judicial review. Judgment would be given accordingly.

Giltinane v Child Support Agency [2006] 2 FLR 857 (Family Division: Munby J).

441   Child support—maintenance assessment—treatment of income of absent parent's partner—partner of same sex—discrimination

See *M v Secretary of State for Work and Pensions*, para 1621.

442   Child support—maintenance calculation—self-employed father—total taxable profits

On a father's appeal against a decision of a social security commissioner, it fell to be determined whether capital allowances should be included in calculating the net income of a self-employed absent parent for the purposes of assessing child support. Under the Child Support (Maintenance

Assessment and Special Cases) Regulations 1992, SI 1992/1815, Sch 1 Pt 1 Ch 2 para 3, 'earnings' meant the gross receipts of the employment less certain expenses, but it was expressly provided that such expenses did not include any capital expenditure or depreciation of any capital assets. Changes were introduced by amendments to Sch 1 Pt 1 Ch 2, so that in para 2A, 'earnings' were defined as the total taxable profits as submitted to the Inland Revenue in accordance with their requirements. The 1992 Regulations were silent as to whether capital expenditure and depreciation were to be deducted. The father's appeal succeeded. The claimant, the mother, appealed. *Held*, in calculating a self-employed trader's earnings for child support purposes, he was not entitled to any deduction for capital allowances. Before the introduction of Sch 1 Pt 1 Ch 2 para 2A there would have been no question of deducting capital allowances. The changes were described as making administrative improvements, not changes of substance. The interpretation which the Secretary of State argued for would be a substantial change. The economic reality was that capital allowances had enabled the father to build up a profitable business while paying very little income tax. It was unfair that he had had the benefit of that but that his children had had the burden of it. Accordingly, the appeal would be allowed.

Smith v Secretary of State for Work and Pensions [2006] UKHL 35, [2006] 3 All ER 907 (House of Lords: Lords Nicholls of Birkenhead, Rodger of Earlsferry and Walker of Gestingthorpe, Baroness Hale of Richmond and Lord Carswell). Decision of Court of Appeal [2004] EWCA Civ 1318, [2005] 1 FLR 606 (2004 Abr para 390) reversed.

443 Child support—maintenance calculation—variation in contact order—increase in one parent's liability for child support—anomalies in legislation

See *Re B* (*A Child*) (*Contact: Parent's Liability to Pay Child Support*), para 456.

444 Child support—maintenance payments—arrears—jurisdiction of magistrates' court to inquire into liability

The Child Support Act 1991 s 33(4) provides that, on an application by the Secretary of State for a liability order in respect of the non-payment of child support by a person, the court must not question the maintenance calculation under which the payments of child support maintenance fell to be made.

The claimant Secretary of State applied for a liability order to be made in relation to the defendant on the basis that he had failed to pay an amount of child support. Before the magistrates, the defendant conceded that the amounts of maintenance were unpaid, but argued that the maintenance assessments had not been lawfully made as there was a pre-existing written maintenance agreement. The justices rejected that submission and made the liability order as sought, deciding that they had no power to inquire whether the Secretary of State had authority to make the maintenance assessments sought to be enforced by him. The defendant's appeal was dismissed, but a subsequent judicial review application challenging the magistrates' ruling was allowed, the court ruling that the magistrates'' court had an adjudicative function under 33 as to whether the parent was a liable person. The claimant appealed against that decision. *Held*, the language of s 33(4), read in the context of s 33 as a whole, admitted of only one interpretation: on an application for a liability order the magistrates' court had to proceed on the basis that the maintenance assessment in question was lawfully and properly made. The court was precluded from questioning that assessment. The magistrates' court's function was to check that the assessment related to the defendant brought before the court and that the payments in question had become payable and had not been paid. The provisions of ss 11, 18 and 20 provided an effective means by which an absent parent could challenge the claimant's jurisdiction to make a maintenance assessment. There was thus no justification for reading s 33 as requiring or permitting the magistrates' court to entertain such a challenge. Given the existence of that statutory right of review and appeal, it would be surprising and undesirable if the magistrates' court was to have a parallel jurisdiction to adjudicate on the same question. Accordingly, the appeal would be allowed.

Farley v Secretary of State for Work and Pensions [2006] UKHL 31, [2006] 3 All ER 935 (House of Lords: Lords Nicholls of Birkenhead, Hope of Craighead, Hutton, Walker of Gestingthorpe and Mance). Decision of Court of Appeal [2005] EWCA Civ 869, [2005] 3 FCR 343 (2005 Abr para 469) reversed.

445 Child support—miscellaneous provisions

The Child Support (Miscellaneous Amendments) Regulations 2006, SI 2006/1520 (in force on 12 July 2006), further amend (1) the Child Support (Information, Evidence and Disclosure) Regulations 1992, SI 1992/1812, by making provision for credit reference agencies to be required to furnish information to the Secretary of State; (2) the Child Support (Collection and Enforcement) Regulations 1992, SI 1992/1989, so as to (a) extend the range of arrangements for collection of child support by adding payment by credit card and voluntary deduction from earnings arrangement; (b) provide a basis for calculating the protected earnings proportion in relation to a deduction from earnings order which relates only to arrears of child support maintenance; and (c) removes the six year limitation period for an application for a liability order, but only in relation to amounts that became due after 12 July 2000; (3) the Social Security and Child Support (Decisions and Appeals) Regulations 1999, SI 1999/991, by revoking the provision which specifies an effective date in a case where a default maintenance decision is revised as if it were a maintenance calculation under the Child Support Act 1991 s 11; (4) the Child Support (Maintenance Calculation Procedure) Regulations 2000, SI 2001/157, by providing for an interim effective date for the initial calculation of child support maintenance in cases where the available information does not cover the whole of the relevant period; and (5) the Child Support (Collection and Enforcement and Miscellaneous Amendments) Regulations 2000, SI 2001/162, so as to (a) bring fully into force, for both old and new scheme cases, the amendments which make provision for collection of child support maintenance by debit card; and (b) modify the savings provision so that, in cases which have been converted from the old scheme to the new scheme, all arrears of child support maintenance, whenever they accrued, are treated the same for collection and enforcement purposes.

446   Child support—proposals for new system of child maintenance—consultation

The Secretary of State for Work and Pensions has presented to Parliament a White Paper, *A new system of child maintenance* (Cm 6979), on which consultation is sought. It is proposed that a non-departmental public body, the Child Maintenance and Enforcement Commission, should be established to replace the Child Support Agency and to operate a new scheme for assessing and collecting child maintenance. The changes which are envisaged would end the requirement that parents with care who claim benefits are treated as applying for child maintenance. This would effectively overturn any extant maintenance arrangements. The changes would extend in 2008 to all parents with care the right to keep up to £10 of child maintenance each week before affecting their benefits, and would significantly increase, from 2010–11, the amount of maintenance which parents on benefit could keep before it affected their level of benefits. The new scheme for child maintenance would be based on fixed-term awards normally for one year at a time, primarily based on the most recent tax information and calculated by reference to gross weekly income. Enforcement powers would be strengthened by the imposition of a loss of driving licence or a curfew, by means of electronic tagging, on parents who failed to make payments, and the removal of the requirement to apply to the court for a liability order before taking enforcement action. The removal of the requirement to apply to the court for a charging order is to be considered, as is the possibility of administratively issuing interim orders withdrawing a driving licence or surrendering a passport pending application to the court, and introducing administrative deduction orders authorising financial institutions to deduct maintenance from a non-resident parent's account. It is further proposed that the names of both parents should normally be entered on a birth certificate. The Child Maintenance and Enforcement Commission, when established, would be responsible for the management of existing cases and debts, putting the new scheme for child maintenance into practice, and helping parents to make private arrangements for maintenance or to join the new scheme. The Commission is also expected to be given power to factor debts. Some debts that may not be recoverable may be written off.

447   Child trust funds—accounts and account providers

The Child Trust Funds (Amendment) Regulations 2006, SI 2006/199 (in force on 7 February 2006), amend the 2004 Regulations, SI 2004/1450, so as to allow extra flexibility in opening accounts close to the expiry date on the voucher and so as to provide that, if a completed application to open an account has been made on or before the expiry date, there is an extra period of seven days for the voucher to be delivered to the account provider.

The Child Trust Funds (Amendment No 2) Regulations 2006, SI 2006/2684 (in force on 31 October 2006), further amend the 2004 Regulations supra so as to (1) add a further requirement to the details which local authorities are required to provide in their monthly returns, with respect to looked after children, which is details of the child's mother, or failing that, father, to assist with identification of the child; (2) extend the period within which the local authority has to make its monthly returns, from five to ten days; (3) set out the additional circumstance in which an official solicitor will administer the child trust fund account of a child, which is where the child has been placed for adoption in England and Wales; and (4) remove the requirement for providers to pay daily interest on cash deposits for a stakeholder account where the cash is held temporarily on deposit while dealing in investments.

The Child Trust Funds (Amendment No 3) Regulations 2006, SI 2006/3195 (in force on 1 January 2007), further amend the 2004 Regulations so as to exempt from tax, annual bonuses that are paid to building society members who hold a Child Trust Fund account ('CTF'), so far as the bonus is calculated by reference to assets in their CTF. In particular, the regulations (1) insert a definition of 'building society bonus', normally excluding any bonus paid on the demutualisation of a building society; (2) exempt the bonus from income tax so far as it is calculated by reference to CTF assets, and provide that bonuses paid directly into the CTF do not count against the annual subscription limit; and (3) similarly exempt the bonus from capital gains tax.

448 Childcare Act 2006

The Childcare Act 2006 makes provision about (1) the powers and duties of local authorities and other bodies in England in relation to the improvement of the well-being of young children; (2) the powers and duties of local authorities in England and Wales in relation to the provision of childcare and the provision of information to parents and other persons; and (3) the regulation and inspection of childcare provision in England. The Act received the royal assent on 11 July 2006 and certain provisions came into force on that day. Further provisions came into force on 20 December 2006: SI 2006/3360. The remaining provisions come into force on a day or days to be appointed. For details of commencement, see the commencement table in the title STATUTES.

Part 1 (ss 1–21) General functions of local authority: England
Section 1 places a duty on local authorities in England to improve the well-being of all young children in their area and to reduce inequalities between those achieving the poorest outcomes and the rest. Local authorities are required under s 3 to deliver the improved outcomes set out in s 1 by ensuring that early childhood services (as defined by s 2) are delivered in an integrated way that facilitates access to services and maximises the benefits to children, parents and prospective parents. A reciprocal duty is created by s 4 between the local authority and relevant partners in the National Health Service and Jobcentre Plus to work together in delivering integrated early childhood services to improve outcomes and reduce inequalities in achievement. The Secretary of State is entitled to alter, by order, the definition of 'early childhood services' and to make any consequential changes to ss 2–4: s 5. By virtue of s 6, local authorities in England are under a duty to secure sufficient childcare to meet the requirements of parents in their area who require childcare in order to work or to undertake training or education to prepare for work. An English local authority has a duty under s 7 to secure prescribed early years provision free of charge. Under s 8, a local authority may make arrangements with childcare providers and provide support to them, including financial support. Section 9 requires local authorities to exercise their powers to ensure that any providers with whom they enter into a financial agreement in relation to childcare provision meet requirements imposed on them. Local authorities are permitted by s 10 to enter into agreements which impose a charge for the provision of childcare by the authority. Local authorities are under a duty to assess, at least every three years, whether childcare provision in their area is sufficient, and to keep assessments under review: s 11. Local authorities must, by virtue of s 12, establish and maintain a service providing information, advice and assistance in relation to childcare provision. Under s 13, an English local authority has a duty to provide information, advice and training to childcare providers. The childcare duties and functions of a local authority are to be subject to inspection by Her Majesty's Chief Inspector of Schools and subject to the powers of the Secretary of State to secure proper performance: ss 14, 15. The functions under Pt 1 are brought by s 16 within the responsibility of the director of children's services. Under s 17, regulations may be made prescribing the circumstances in which the prohibition on charging for education does not apply in respect of early years provision. For the purposes of Pt 1, 'childcare' is defined by s 18 as any form of care for a child, including education and any supervised activity, but excluding education (or any other supervised activity) provided in school hours for a registered pupil at a school who is not a young child. Sections 19–21 make further provision relating to interpretation.

Part 2 (ss 22–30) General functions of local authority: Wales
Section 22 places a duty on local authorities in Wales to secure sufficient childcare to meet the requirements of parents in their area who require childcare in order to work or to undertake training or education to prepare for work. Under s 23, a Welsh local authority may make arrangements with childcare providers and provide support to them, including financial support. Welsh local authorities are required by s 24 to exercise their powers to ensure that any providers with whom they enter into a financial agreement in relation to childcare provision meet any conditions imposed on them by local authorities. Welsh local authorities may enter into agreements which impose a charge for the provision of childcare by the authority: s 25. Section 26 empowers the Welsh Assembly to make regulations placing a duty on local authorities in Wales to assess whether childcare provision in their area is sufficient. By virtue of s 27, Welsh local authorities are under a duty to establish and maintain a service providing information, advice and assistance to parents and prospective parents in relation to childcare. The childcare duties of a Welsh local authority are subject to inspection by Her Majesty's Chief Inspector of Education and Training in Wales and are to be subject to the powers of the Assembly to secure proper performance: ss 28, 29. Section 30 deals with interpretation.

Part 3 (ss 31–98) Regulation of provision of childcare in England
Chapter 1 (ss 31, 32) General functions of Chief Inspector
Section 31 sets out the general functions of Her Majesty's Chief Inspector of Schools, which include keeping the Secretary of State informed about the quality and standards of early years provision. By virtue of s 32, the Chief Inspector is required to maintain a register of early years providers and a general childcare register.

Chapter 2 (ss 33–51) Regulation of early years provision
A person is prohibited from providing early years childminding unless he is registered in the early years register: s 33. The requirement for early years providers, other than childminders, to be

registered are set out in s 34. Provision is made for applications for registration by early years childminders who are required to be registered (s 35), and by other early years providers (s 36). Section 37 requires the Chief Inspector to place successful applicants in the early years register and to issue them with certificates of registration. Under s 38, the Chief Inspector may impose conditions on registration for compulsorily registered early years providers. The Secretary of State has a duty pursuant to s 39 to specify certain learning and development requirements, known as the Early Years Foundation Stage, for the purpose of promoting the well-being of young children who are receiving early years provision. The providers who are required to implement the Early Years Foundation Stage are specified in s 40, and the areas which may and may not be covered by a learning and development order made by the Secretary of State under s 39 are detailed in s 41. The Secretary of State is entitled, when making a learning and development order under s 39, to confer or impose functions on specified persons: s 42. The matters that may be covered by regulations made by the Secretary of State under s 39 are outlined in s 43. Section 44 makes supplementary provision in relation to learning and development orders. Mandatory consultation procedures are imposed by s 45 for when the Secretary of State proposes to make an order specifying the early learning goals or educational programmes for the Early Years Foundation Stage. Under s 46, the Secretary of State is permitted to confer exemptions from the learning and development requirements in certain prescribed circumstances. Section 47 provides that the independent school standards prescribed by regulations do not apply in relation to early years provision for pupils of independent schools who have not attained the age of three. Section 48, Sch 1 make consequential amendments. The Chief Inspector must inspect early years provision at prescribed intervals and on request from the Secretary of State (s 49), and must produce and distribute copies of reports of the inspections (s 50). Section 51 deals with interpretation.

Chapter 3 (ss 52–61) Regulation of later years provision for children under 8
Under s 52, a person is prohibited from providing later years childminding for children up to the age of eight unless he is registered in Part A of the general childcare register as a childminder. Later years providers (other than childminders) providing childcare for children up to the age of eight must be registered in respect of particular premises: s 53. Sections 54, 55 require applicants for registration as a later years provider for children under eight to give certain information to the Chief Inspector and pay any prescribed fee. By virtue of s 56, the Chief Inspector must enter successful applicants in Part A of the general childcare register and give them a registration certificate. The Chief Inspector must also, on request, register a person in Part A of the general childcare register if he is already registered as an early years provider in the early years register: s 57. The Chief Inspector is entitled under s 58 to impose conditions on registration for compulsorily registered later years providers. Section 59 allows the Secretary of State to make regulations governing the activities of compulsorily registered later years providers. The Chief Inspector must inspect compulsorily registered later years provision at any time when the Secretary of State requires it, and may do so at any other appropriate time: s 60. Under s 61, the Chief Inspector may produce a report regarding such an inspection.

Chapter 4 (ss 62–67) Voluntary registration
Sections 62, 63 enable childminders and other childcare providers who do not need to be registered to apply for voluntary registration in Part B of the general register. The Chief Inspector must by virtue of s 64 give persons so registered a registration certificate containing information about prescribed matters. Under s 65, the Chief Inspector must register on Part B of the general childcare register any person who is already registered either as an early years provider on the early years register or as a later years provider on Part A of the general childcare register, if that person so requests. The Chief Inspector may place conditions on the registration of voluntarily registered providers: s 66. Section 67 allows the Secretary of State, after consulting the Chief Inspector, to make regulations governing the activities of voluntarily registered providers.

Chapter 5 (ss 68–98) Common provisions
Section 68 details when the Chief Inspector is required or permitted to cancel registration of a childcare provider. The Secretary of State is entitled under s 69 to make regulations allowing a person's registration to be suspended in certain circumstances. Registered providers may give notice to the Chief Inspector when they wish to be removed from either of the registers: s 70. Section 71 allows the Secretary of State to make regulations specifying a period of time after which voluntary registration expires. Under s 72, the Chief Inspector is permitted to apply to a Justice of the Peace for an order cancelling registration, varying or removing a condition on registration or imposing a condition. Procedures are set out in s 73 for taking certain steps such as refusing an application for registration, imposing, varying, removing or refusing to remove conditions on registration and cancelling registration. Section 74 sets out the procedure for appeals, and s 75 makes provision for disqualification from registration. The consequences of a childcare provider being disqualified are prescribed by s 76.
    Under s 77, powers are granted to specified persons to enter premises where there is a reasonable cause to suspect childcare provision is being provided in contravention of the registration requirements. Section 78 prescribes powers of entry in relation to domestic premises, and s 79 outlines when a police constable is authorised to assist in the exercise of a power of entry under s 77

or 78. Provision is made in s 80 for reports to be combined in appropriate circumstances. The Chief Inspector must include an account of the exercise of his functions relating to early years and later years provision in his annual report to the Secretary of State: s 81. By virtue of s 82, the Chief Inspector may require from a registered person information about his activities as an early years or later years provider. Section 83 requires the Chief Inspector to provide Her Majesty's Revenue and Customs and the relevant local authority information when he takes certain steps under Pt 3, such as adding or removing a name from a register. The Chief Inspector is permitted by s 84 to make prescribed information about registered persons available for the purpose of assisting parents in choosing a childcare provider or protecting children from harm and neglect. It is an offence for any person applying for registration to knowingly make a false or misleading statement in his application: s 85. Time limits for the bringing of proceedings are specified in s 86. Provision is made for where a childcare offence is committed by a body corporate (s 87), and for how childcare providers who are unincorporated associations are to be treated for the purposes of proceedings for offences relating to registration (s 88).

Section 89 allows the Secretary of State to prescribe in regulations the amounts of fees to be paid to the Chief Inspector and the timing of payment. The Secretary of State is entitled under s 90 to make regulations allowing the Chief Inspector to refuse or to cancel registration if consent to the disclosure of information by third parties is withheld or withdrawn. The requirements relating to co-operation by the local authority with the Chief Inspector are set out in s 91. Where appropriate, the Chief Inspector may combine any two or more certificates in a single document: s 92. Section 93 provides for the methods by which the Chief Inspector may give certain notices to registered providers or applicants, for instance in respect of decisions to refuse registration, impose conditions or cancel registration. The Chief Inspector is empowered by s 94 to allow applications for registration by persons other than childminders to be made in respect of more than one set of premises. By virtue of s 95, institutions that only provide early years provision and are not maintained nursery schools are not to be regarded as schools. Definitions of 'early years provision' and 'later years provision' are given in s 96. By virtue of s 97, where an early years or later years provider employs an individual to care for a child, the employee cannot be registered. Section 98 deals with interpretation.

Part 4 (ss 99–111) Miscellaneous and general
Under s 99, regulations may be made requiring all registered early years providers, and school-based providers who are exempt from the registration requirements, to provide individual child information to the Secretary of State or any prescribed person. Section 100 makes transitional provision. Regulations may be made under s 101 requiring childminders, providers of day care and providers of funded nursery education in Wales to provide individual child information to the Assembly or any prescribed person. Section 102 revises the categories of persons who may be disqualified from being registered to provide day care or childminding. Section 103, Schs 2 and 3 make consequential amendments and various repeals. Powers to make subordinate legislation are provided for in ss 104, 105. Section 106 deals with interpretation, and s 107 makes financial provision. Special provision for the Isles of Scilly is made by s 108. Sections 109 and 110 deal with commencement, and s 111 deals with extent and the short title.

Amendments, repeals and revocations
The list below, which is not exhaustive, mentions repeals and amendments which are or will be effective when the Act is fully in force.

Specific provisions of a number of Acts are amended or repealed. These include: Children Act 1989 ss 79B, 79C, 79H, 79N, 79Q, 79R, Sch 9A para 4; Education Act 1996 ss 4, 451; Education Act 1997 s 23; School Standards and Framework Act 1998 ss 118A, 119, Sch 26; Education Act 2002 ss 76–81, 83, 87, 89, 90, 93, 94, 96, 149, 150, 157, 171, 210; and Children Act 2004 ss 18, 23.

449 Children—private arrangements for fostering—Wales

The Children (Private Arrangements for Fostering) (Wales) Regulations 2006, SI 2006/940 (in force on 1 April 2006), replace the 1991 Regulations, SI 1991/ 2050, and (1) require any person proposing to privately foster a child, any person involved, whether directly or not, in arranging for the child to be privately fostered, and a parent of the child or other person with parental responsibility for the child who knows that it is proposed to privately foster the child, to notify the local authority in advance of the arrangement starting; (2) require notification by the proposed private foster carer to be given at least six weeks before the private fostering arrangement begins, or where the arrangement is to begin within six weeks, then given immediately; (3) set out the requirement to notify the local authority of the arrangement where such notification has not been given; (4) set out the requirement to notify the local authority when a private fostering arrangement of which they have been notified actually starts; (5) provide for the local authority to send an officer to carry out visits once such notification has been received; (6) require private foster carers to notify the local authority of certain changes in circumstances; (7) provide for the notification of the end of the arrangement; and (8) require local authorities to monitor the way in which they discharge their functions in respect of privately fostered children and to appoint an officer of the local authority for that purpose.

450   Children Act 2004—commencement

The Children Act 2004 (Commencement No 6) (Wales) Order 2006, SI 2006/885, brings into force in relation to Wales (1) on 31 March 2006, s 26; (2) on 1 April 2006, ss 28(1)(a)–(c), (i), (2) (in part), (3), (4), 44, 48, 53–55, 61, Sch 4 (in part), and certain repeals in Sch 5; (3) on 1 September 2006, s 27, and certain repeals in Sch 5; and (4) on 1 October 2006, ss 30, 32–34, 50, 52, 56.

The Children Act 2004 (Commencement No 7) (Wales) Order 2006, SI 2006/870, brings into force, in relation to Wales, (1) on 1 September 2006, s 25; and (2) on 1 October 2006, s 31.

The Children Act 2004 (Commencement No 8) Order 2006, SI 2006/927, brings into force on 1 April 2006, so far as they are not already in force, ss 13–16, and s 56 (in part).

For a summary of the Act, see 2004 Abr para 395. See also the commencement table in the title STATUTES.

451   Children and Adoption Act 2006

The Children and Adoption Act 2006 makes provision as regards contact with children, family assistance orders, risk assessments and adoptions with a foreign element. The Act received the royal assent on 21 June 2006 and came into force in part on that day. The remaining provisions come into force on a day or days to be appointed. For details of commencement, see the commencement table in the title STATUTES.

Part 1 (ss 1–8) Orders with respect to children in family proceedings
Section 1 makes provision enabling courts to make orders for contact activity directions where there is some dispute about the provision about contact that the court is considering whether to make, and enables the court to make a contact activity condition when making or varying a contact order. Provision is made by s 2 allowing a court to ask an officer of the Children and Family Court Advisory and Support Service ('CAFCASS') to monitor compliance with a contact order and to report to the court on such matters relating to compliance as the court may specify, for a period of up to a year. Whenever a court makes or varies a contact order, it must attach a notice warning of the consequences of failing to comply with it: s 3. A court may make an enforcement order imposing an unpaid work requirement on a person who has breached a contact order where it is satisfied beyond reasonable doubt that the person has, without reasonable excuse, breached the contact order, and where it is satisfied that the making of the order is necessary to secure compliance with the contact order and that the order is proportionate: s 4. Section 4 also allows the court to ask a CAFCASS officer to monitor a person's compliance with an enforcement order, and introduces Sch 1, which makes detailed provision about enforcement orders. Provision is made by s 5 allowing the court to require an individual who has caused financial loss to another individual as a result of breaching a contact order to pay compensation up to the amount of the loss. Section 6 removes the requirement that family assistance orders may be made only in exceptional circumstances and increases the maximum duration of such orders from six to twelve months. CAFCASS officers must carry out a risk assessment and provide it to the court if, in the course of carrying out any function in private law family proceedings under the Children Act 1989 (which include applications for residence and contact orders and applications for enforcement of contact orders), the officer is given cause to suspect that the child concerned is at risk of harm: 2006 Act s 7. Section 8 makes transitional provision.

Part 2 (ss 9–14) Adoptions with a foreign element
Section 9 empowers the Secretary of State to impose special restrictions on intercountry adoptions from countries and territories where he has determined that it would be contrary to public policy to further the bringing into the United Kingdom of children by British residents in cases where there have been, or would have been, adoption proceedings in the other country. The Secretary of State must publish a list of countries and territories to which the special restrictions apply: s 9. Section 10 requires the Secretary of State to keep the list of restricted countries and territories under review. Except in exceptional cases, the appropriate authority may not process intercountry adoption cases from the restricted country or territory: s 11. Under s 12, the Secretary of State may impose extra conditions that must be met in relation to adoptions from any restricted country or territory, and a person who brings or causes another to bring a child into the United Kingdom without meeting those conditions is guilty of an offence. Section 13 empowers the Secretary of State or the National Assembly for Wales to charge a fee to adopters or prospective adopters for services provided or to be provided in relation to intercountry adoptions. Certain legislation concerning intercountry adoption is amended by s 14.

Part 3 (ss 15–17) Miscellaneous and final
Section 15, Sch 2 deal with minor and consequential amendments, and Sch 3 deals with repeals. Section 16 deals with the making of regulations and orders, and s 17 provides for short title, commencement and extent.

Amendments, repeals and revocations
The list below, which is not exhaustive, mentions repeals and amendments which are or will be effective when the Act is fully in force.
Specific provisions of a number of Acts are added, amended or repealed. These include: Domestic and Matrimonial Proceedings Act 1973 Sch 1 para 11; Family Law Act 1986 ss 5, 29, 30, 31; Children Act 1989 ss 11A–11P, 14B, 16, 16A, 91, 104, 105, Sch 8; Family Law Act 1996 Sch 3 para 9; and Adoption and Children Act 2002 ss 26, 83.

452 Children in care—arrangements to assist children to live abroad—placement with prospective adopters—period before parental responsibility order made

The Children Act 1989 Sch 2 para 19(1) provides that a local authority may only arrange for, or assist in arranging for, any child in its care to live outside England and Wales with the approval of the court. Schedule 2 para 19(1) does not apply to a local authority placing a child for adoption with prospective adopters: Sch 2 para 19(9).

The first respondent was unable to care for her baby son, the second respondent, owing to drug-related problems. An interim care order was made in respect of the second respondent, and the local authority expressed its intention that he should live in Germany with close family members, with a view to those family members eventually adopting him. The authority issued an application for a parental responsibility order under the Adoption Act 1976 s 55, and an issue arose as to whether the placement of the second respondent with family members abroad, which was clearly in his best interests, could go ahead legitimately in advance of a s 55 order being made. The first respondent argued that the proposed relocation of her child to Germany amounted to placing him with prospective adopters with a view to adoption, meaning that the authority's prospective care plan could not be approved under the 1989 Act Sch 2 para 19 because of the exception contained in Sch 2 para 19(9). *Held*, the local authority could not 'place a child for adoption with prospective adopters' until it had decided, following consideration by the appropriate adoption panel, that the proposed adoptive match with the particular family that had been chosen was the right one for the child. The authority had not reached that point in its decision making. If authority could not be given under Sch 2 para 19 for the second respondent to live in Germany, either the family would have had to take up temporary residence in the United Kingdom for at least six months so that the child could live with them, satisfying the residence requirement under the 1976 Act s 55, or the s 55 application might have to be abandoned and an application under the Adoption and Children Act 2002 s 84 made instead. Alternatively, the placement would have to be for something other than adoption. It followed that the 1989 Act Sch 2 para 19(9) was not an obstacle to the court giving approval for the second respondent to live in Germany. Judgment would be given accordingly.

A London Borough Council v M [2006] EWHC 1907 (Fam), [2006] All ER (D) 416 (Jul) (Family Division: Black J).

453 Children in care—assault by foster parent—victim and offender living together—entitlement to compensation

See *R (on the application of M) v Criminal Injuries Compensation Appeals Panel*, para 852.

454 Contact order—application by father—domestic violence—findings of fact—guidance

A mother and father separated permanently two years after the birth of their child. Thereafter, the father had no contact with the child. The mother's case was that the father subjected her to a serious assault which required her to have hospital treatment on the day of their separation. The father obtained a contact order. On appeal, the mother complained that the judge had made errors as to the findings of fact he had made at an earlier hearing and that he had failed to apply the relevant authorities in reaching his decision. *Held*, it was clear that the judge had looked at his earlier judgment, but there were several errors in the later judgment as to his findings of fact. It was wholly unacceptable that the judge had not followed guidance given in a seminal decision of the Court of Appeal and had failed to have regard to the principles identified in the psychiatric report written for the court in that case, even though a witness had given powerful evidence about their applicability. The critical areas of the guidelines which the judge did not appear to have addressed were 'the capacity of the parent seeking contact to appreciate the effect of past and future violence on the other parent and the children concerned' and 'the attitude of the parent seeking contact to past violent conduct … in particular whether that parent has the capacity to change'. The judge simply had not applied his mind to the father's capacity to appreciate the effect of his violence on the mother and the child. Many of the views expressed by the judge were partial, distorted, and not based on the evidence. In these circumstances, it should be open to another judge on a re-hearing not to be bound by the findings made. Accordingly, the appeal would be allowed.

Re H (A Child) (Contact: Domestic Violence) [2005] EWCA Civ 1404, [2006] 1 FCR 102 (Court of Appeal: Thorpe, Dyson and Wall LJJ). *Re L (A Child) (Contact: Domestic Violence)* [2001] Fam 260, CA (2000 Abr para 470), applied.

455   Contact order—history of domestic violence by father—indirect contact with father through child welfare body—need to safeguard mother's whereabouts

The father of a child had inflicted violence on the child's mother in the periods when they were together but had at all times loved and shown affection for the child. While the child had frequently witnessed the violence, it had never been directed towards her. In care proceedings in respect of the child, the judge made a defined contact order which was designed to ensure that the contact arrangements would not require the father and mother to meet and a non-molestation order to protect the mother. The father was prosecuted for a large number of breaches of both orders and was sentenced to four months' imprisonment. Unknown to the father, the mother and child moved to new accommodation and assumed fresh identities. The father made every effort to track down the mother and child, which included taking measures which lead to him receiving a further five-month custodial sentence. The child's guardian had recommended that contact should be restricted to indirect contact, as long as it could be managed in a safe way and did not compromise the child's situation, but changed her view because she did not think that the child's location could be safeguarded if indirect contact were permitted. The court made an order for indirect contact allowing certain specified communications between the father and the child that were to be sent through the Children and Family Court Advisory and Support Service ('CAFCASS'), which would vet the contents to ensure that they were appropriate. The mother appealed against the contact order. *Held*, the judge had been aware of the paramount necessity of preventing the father from tracing the whereabouts of the mother, and he stated that he had been able to make suitable arrangements with CAFCASS to ensure that that did not occur. The judge had understood the guardian's view, which was that she favoured indirect contact in principle and had only changed her view because she did not think that the child's location could be safeguarded if such contact were permitted. The paramount concern of the court had to be for the child's welfare. Accordingly, the appeal would be dismissed.

Re F (A Child) (Indirect Contact Through Third Party) [2006] EWCA Civ 1426, [2006] 3 FCR 553 (Court of Appeal: Lord Phillips of Worth Matravers CJ, Thorpe and Wilson LJJ).

456   Contact order—variation—consequential increase in one parent's liability for child support—relevance to child's welfare

An order for contact was made between a child and her father. The child's mother successfully applied to vary the order. The only substantive variation was to reduce the number of nights to be spent by the child with the father. This had the effect of increasing the father's liability to child support under the Child Support Act 1991. The father appealed against the order. His grounds of appeal were based on anomalies in the child support legislation, and the fact that the reduction in his disposable income by reason of the increase in child support rendered him unable to make direct payments for the benefit of the child at the level at which he would otherwise have made them, so that the order did not serve the child's welfare, even though that should have been the recorder's paramount consideration under the Children Act 1989 s 1(1). *Held*, while the arguments based on anomalies in the current child support legislation could properly be said to give rise to substantial injustice, they were irrelevant to determination of the optimum level of a parent's contact with a child. Further, it would be impracticable for a court which heard an issue as to contact or shared residence to discern the beneficial or detrimental effect on the child of the consequences under the 1991 Act of alternative possible orders, and it would also be wrong in principle for the court to attempt to do so. Accordingly, the appeal would be dismissed.

Re B (A Child) (Contact: Parent's Liability to Pay Child Support) [2006] EWCA Civ 1574, [2006] All ER (D) 327 (Nov) (Court of Appeal: Mummery and Wilson LJJ).

457   Criminal proceedings—child witness—competence to give evidence

See *R v MacPherson*, para 800.

458   Criminal proceedings against children—young offenders—sentencing

See SENTENCING.

459   Cruelty to a child—mitigation—no malice—deluded belief

See *R v P; R v K; R v M*, para 2537.

460   Family proceedings—allocation of proceedings

The Children (Allocation of Proceedings) (Amendment) Order 2006, SI 2006/1541 (in force on 6 July 2006), further amends the 1991 Order, SI 1991/1677, so as to confer family hearing centre status on the Clerkenwell & Shoreditch County Court.

461   Family proceedings—confidence and confidentiality—transparency and privacy—government consultation

The Lord Chancellor has presented to Parliament a consultation paper, *Confidence and confidentiality: Improving transparency and privacy in family courts* (Cm 6886), which calls for greater openness in proceedings in the family courts. It is suggested that there should be introduced changes based on ensuring public confidence in the family justice system through public scrutiny, improving the understanding of decisions made by those courts, protecting the privacy of the families, particularly the children, concerned, ensuring that there are strong sanctions and rigorous enforcement where privacy is breached, and providing arrangements which are simple, easily understood, consistent and workable. The proposals on which consultation is sought include changes to the attendance and reporting restrictions to make them consistent across all family proceedings. It is suggested that the media should be allowed to attend proceedings as of right, although the courts would be able in appropriate cases to exclude the media or to place restrictions on the reporting of evidence. Other persons should be able to attend hearings on application to the court concerned, or on the court's own motion, reporting restrictions should provide anonymity for the persons involved, but should be flexible to allow the restrictions to be enhanced or relaxed in any particular case. A new criminal offence is suggested for breaches of the reporting restrictions. It is further suggested that adoption proceedings should be treated as a special case. Transparency should be allowed up to the placement order, but thereafter the proceedings should remain private.

462   Family proceedings—dependent territories—custody orders

The Family Law Act 1986 (Dependent Territories) (Amendment) Order 2006, SI 2006/1456 (in force on 10 July 2006), amends the 1991 Order, SI 1991/1723, by adding Jersey to the list of territories to which the scheme of jurisdiction of courts applies, so as to provide for the recognition and enforcement of custody orders made by a court in Jersey in the United Kingdom.

463   Family proceedings—hearings—court bundles

1. Sir Mark Potter P, has issued the following *Practice Direction (Family Proceedings: Court Bundles)* [2006] 2 FCR 834 to achieve consistency across the country in all family courts, other than the Family Proceedings Court, in the preparation of court bundles and in respect of other related matters on 27 July 2006.

2.1 Except as specified in head 2.4, below, and subject to specific directions given in any particular case, the following *Practice Direction* applies to (a) all hearings of whatever nature, including but not limited to hearings in family proceedings, CPR 7, 8 claims and appeals, before a judge of the Family Division of the High Court wherever the court may be sitting; (b) all hearings in family proceedings in the Royal Courts of Justice ('RCJ'); (c) all hearings in the Principal Registry of the Family Division ('PRFD') at First Avenue House; and (d) all hearings in family proceedings in all other courts except for Family Proceedings Courts.

2.2 'Hearings' includes all appearances before a judge or district judge, whether with or without notice to other parties and whether for directions or for substantive relief.

2.3 This *Practice Direction* applies whether a bundle is being lodged for the first time or is being re-lodged for a further hearing, see head 9.2, below.

2.4 This *Practice Direction* does not apply to (a) cases listed for one hour or less at a court referred to in heads 2.1(c) or 2.1(d), above, or (b) the hearing of any urgent application if and to the extent that it is impossible to comply with it.

2.5 The designated family judge responsible for any court referred to in heads 2.1(c) or 2.1(d), above, might, after such consultation as is appropriate, but in the case of hearings in the PRFD at First Avenue House only with the agreement of the senior district judge, direct that in that court this *Practice Direction* applies to all family proceedings irrespective of the length of hearing.

3.1 A bundle for the use of the court at the hearing is to be provided by the party in the position of applicant at the hearing, or, if there are cross-applications, by the party whose application was first in time, or, if that person is a litigant in person, by the first listed respondent who is not a litigant in person.

3.2 The party preparing the bundle must paginate it. If possible the contents of the bundle are to be agreed by all parties.

4.1 The bundle must contain copies of all documents relevant to the hearing, in chronological order from the front of the bundle, paginated and indexed, and divided into separate sections, each section being separately paginated, as follows: (a) preliminary documents (see head 4.2, below) and any other case management documents required by any other *Practice Direction*; (b) applications and orders; (c) statements and affidavits, which must be dated in the top right corner of the front page; (d) care plans, where appropriate; (e) experts' reports and other reports, including those of a guardian, children's guardian or litigation friend; and (f) other documents, divided into further sections as may be appropriate. Copies of notes of contact visits should normally not be included in the bundle unless directed by a judge.

4.2 At the commencement of the bundle there must be inserted the following documents (the preliminary documents): (a) an up-to-date summary of the background to the hearing confined to those matters which are relevant to the hearing and the management of the case and limited, if practicable, to one A4 page; (b) a statement of the issue or issues to be determined (i) at that hearing; and (ii) at the final hearing; (c) a position statement by each party including a summary of the order or directions sought by that party (A) at that hearing; and (B) at the final hearing; (d) an up-to-date chronology, if it is a final hearing or if the summary under (a) is insufficient; (e) skeleton arguments, if appropriate, with copies of all authorities relied on; and (f) a list of essential reading for that hearing.

4.3 Each of the preliminary documents must state on the front page immediately below the heading the date when it was prepared and the date of the hearing for which it was prepared.

4.4 The summary of the background, statement of issues, chronology, position statement and any skeleton arguments must be cross-referenced to the relevant pages of the bundle.

4.5 The summary of the background, statement of issues, chronology and reading list must in the case of a final hearing, and, so far as practicable in the case of any other hearing, is to each consist of a single document in a form agreed by all parties. Where the parties disagree as to the content the fact of their disagreement and their differing contentions are to be set out at the appropriate places in the document.

4.6 Where the nature of the hearing is such that a complete bundle of all documents is unnecessary, the bundle, which need not be repaginated, may comprise only those documents necessary for the hearing, but (a) the summary (head 4.2(a), above) must commence with a statement that the bundle is limited or incomplete; and (b) the bundle if reasonably practicable is to be in a form agreed by all parties.

4.7 Where the bundle is re-lodged in accordance with head 9.2, below, before it is re-lodged (a) the bundle must be updated as appropriate; and (b) all superseded documents, and in particular all outdated summaries, statements of issues, chronologies, skeleton arguments and similar documents, are to be removed from the bundle.

5.1 The bundle is to be contained in one or more A4 size ring binders or lever arch files, each lever arch file being limited to 350 pages.

5.2 All ring binders and lever arch files are to have clearly marked on the front and the spine (a) the title and number of the case; (b) the court where the case has been listed; (c) the hearing date and time; (d) if known, the name of the judge hearing the case; and (e) where there is more than one ring binder or lever arch file, a distinguishing letter (A, B, C etc).

6.1 The party preparing the bundle, whether or not the bundle has been agreed, is to provide a paginated index to all other parties not less than four working days before the hearing, in relation to a case management conference to which the provisions of the *Public Law Protocol* [2003] 2 FLR 719 apply, not less than five working days before the case management conference.

6.2 Where counsel is to be instructed at any hearing, a paginated bundle, if not already in counsel's possession, is to be delivered to counsel by the person instructing that counsel not less than three working days before the hearing.

6.3 The bundle, with the exception of the preliminary documents if and insofar as they are not then available, is to be lodged with the court not less than two working days before the hearing, or at such other time as may be specified by the judge.

6.4 The preliminary documents are to be lodged with the court no later than 11 am on the day before the hearing and, where the hearing is before a judge of the High Court and the name of the judge is known, must at the same time be sent by e-mail to the judge's clerk.

7.1 The bundle is to be lodged at the appropriate office. If the bundle is lodged in the wrong place the judge may (a) treat the bundle as having not been lodged; and (b) take the steps referred to in head 12, below.

7.2 Unless the judge has given some other direction as to where the bundle in any particular case is to be lodged, for example a direction that the bundle is to be lodged with the judge's clerk, the bundle must be lodged (a) for hearings in the RCJ, in the office of the Clerk of the Rules, Room TM 9.09, Royal Courts of Justice, Strand, London WC2A 2LL (DX 44450 Strand); (b) for hearings in the PRFD at First Avenue House, at the List Office counter, 3rd floor, First Avenue House, 42/49 High Holborn, London, WC1V 6NP (DX 396 Chancery Lane); and (c) for hearings at any other court, at such place as may be designated by the designated family judge or other judge at that court and in default of any such designation at the court office of the court where the hearing is to take place.

7.3 Any bundle sent to the court by post, DX or courier must be clearly addressed to the appropriate office and must show the date and place of the hearing on the outside of any packaging as well as on the bundle itself.

8.1 In the case of hearings at the RCJ or First Avenue House, parties must (a) if the bundle or preliminary documents are delivered personally, ensure that they obtain a receipt from the clerk accepting it or them; and (b) if the bundle or preliminary documents are sent by post or DX, ensure that they obtain proof of posting or despatch. The receipt, or proof of posting or despatch, as the case may be, must be brought to court on the day of the hearing and must be produced to the court if requested. If the receipt, or proof of posting or despatch, cannot be produced to the court the judge may (i) treat the bundle as having not been lodged; and (ii) take the steps referred to in head 12, below.

8.2 For hearings at the RCJ (a) bundles or preliminary documents delivered after 11 am on the day before the hearing will not be accepted by the Clerk of the Rules and must be delivered (i) in a case where the hearing is before a judge of the High Court, directly to the clerk of the judge hearing the case; (ii) in a case where the hearing is before a circuit judge, deputy High Court judge or recorder, directly to the messenger at the judge's entrance to the Queen's Building (with telephone notification to the personal assistant to the designated family judge, 020 7947 7155, that this has been done); (b) on learning before which judge a hearing is to take place, the clerk to counsel, or other advocate, representing the party in the position of applicant must no later than 3 pm the day before the hearing (A) in a case where the hearing is before a judge of the High Court, telephone the clerk of the judge hearing the case; (B) in a case where the hearing is before a circuit judge, deputy High Court judge or recorder, telephone the personal assistant to the designated family judge, to ascertain whether the judge has received the bundle, including the preliminary documents, and, if not, must organise prompt delivery by the applicant's solicitor.

9.1 Following completion of the hearing the party responsible for the bundle must retrieve it from the court immediately or, if that is not practicable, is to collect it from the court within five working days. Bundles which are not collected in due time may be destroyed.

9.2 The bundle must be re-lodged for the next and any further hearings in accordance with the provisions of this *Practice Direction* and in a form which complies with head 4.7, above.

10.1 In every case a time estimate, which must be inserted at the front of the bundle, is to be prepared which, so far as practicable, is be agreed by all parties and must (a) specify separately (i) the time estimated to be required for judicial pre-reading; (ii) the time required for hearing all evidence and submissions; and (iii) the time estimated to be required for preparing and delivering judgment; and (b) be prepared on the basis that before they give evidence all witnesses will have read all relevant filed statements and reports.

10.2 Once a case has been listed, any change in time estimates is to be notified immediately by telephone, and then immediately confirmed in writing (a) in the case of hearings in the RCJ, to the Clerk of the Rules; (b) in the case of hearings in the PRFD at First Avenue House, to the List Officer at First Avenue House; and (c) in the case of hearings elsewhere, to the relevant listing officer.

11. As soon as it becomes known that a hearing will no longer be effective, whether as a result of the parties reaching agreement or for any other reason, the parties and their representatives must immediately notify the court by telephone and by letter. The letter, which must wherever possible be a joint letter sent on behalf of all parties with their signatures applied or appended, must include (a) a short background summary of the case; (b) the written consent of each party who consents and, where a party does not consent, details of the steps which have been taken to obtain that party's consent and, where known, an explanation of why that consent has not been given; (c) a draft of the order being sought; and (d) enough information to enable the court to decide (i) whether to take the case out of the list; and (ii) whether to make the proposed order.

12. Failure to comply with any part of this *Practice Direction* may result in the judge removing the case from the list or putting the case further back in the list and may also result in a wasted costs order in accordance with CPR 48.7 or some other adverse costs order.

13. This *Practice Direction* replaces *Practice Direction (Family Proceedings: Court Bundles)* [2000] 2 All ER 287 (2000 Abr para 489) and is to have effect from 2 October 2006.

14. Any reference in any other *Practice Direction* to *Practice Direction (Family Proceedings: Court Bundles)* [2000] 2 All ER 287 (2000 Abr para 489) must be read as if substituted by a reference to this *Practice Direction*.

15. This *Practice Direction* should where appropriate be read in conjunction with *Practice Direction (Human Rights Act 1998)* [2000] 4 All ER 288 (2000 Abr para 490) and with *Practice Direction (Care Cases: Judicial Continuity and Judicial Case Management)* [2002] 3 All ER 603 (2002 Abr para 2395) appended to the *Public Law Protocol* [2003] 2 FLR 719. In particular, nothing in this *Practice Direction* is to be read as removing or altering any obligation to comply with the requirements of the *Public Law Protocol*. This *Practice Direction* is issued (a) in relation to family proceedings, by the President of

the Family Division, as the nominee of the Lord Chief Justice, with the agreement of the Lord Chancellor; and (b) to the extent that it applies to proceedings to which the Civil Procedure Act 1997 s 5 applies, by the Master of the Rolls as the nominee of the Lord Chief Justice, with the agreement of the Lord Chancellor.

464   Family proceedings—jurisdiction

See CONFLICT OF LAWS.

465   Family proceedings—order restricting right to initiate—guidelines

The Children Act 1989 s 91(14) provides that on disposing of an order under the Act, the court may order that no application for an order of any specified kind can be made with respect to the child concerned by any named person without the leave of the court.

The applicants, who were the fathers of two children, were subject to an order under the 1989 Act s 91(14). In the course of the proceedings, questions arose as to whether it was permissible to attach conditions to a s 91(14) order, the approach to be taken when an application for permission to apply was made, and the circumstances in which it was appropriate to make a s 91(14) order without limit of time. *Held*, while the court was permitted to impose conditions when it made a contact order under s 8, it was not permissible to attach conditions to a s 91(14) order other than stating how long it was to last and identifying the type of relief to which it applied. In particular it was not permissible to require a party to undergo treatment as a pre-condition to making an application for permission to apply. A s 91(14) order could be made without limit of time or for the period of time that the court had jurisdiction to make orders in relation to children, generally until the age of 16, under s 8. Orders without limit of time and those expressed to last until a child was 16 should be the exception rather than the rule and where they were made, the reasons for making them should be fully and carefully set out. Before a s 91(14) order was made, the party affected by it should have had a proper opportunity to consider it and be heard on it. Where the need for such an order became apparent during proceedings or at relatively short notice, the court had to ensure that the party affected had full opportunity to consider the making of such an order and to voice objections to it, particularly if he was a litigant in person. It would not necessarily be the case that an application for permission to apply should be treated inter partes. On making a s 91(14) order it was open to the judge to direct that any application for permission to apply during its operation should not in the first instance be served on the respondent to it, but should be considered by the judge on paper.

Re S (Permission to Seek Relief); Re E (Permission to Seek Relief) [2006] EWCA Civ 1190, (2006) Times, 13 September (Court of Appeal: Thorpe and Wall LJJ). *Re P (A Child) (Residence Order: Restriction Order)* [1999] 3 All ER 734, CA (1999 Abr para 449); *Re N (Residence Order: Appeal)* [1996] 1 FLR 356, CA (1996 Abr para 469); *Re A (A Minor) (Contact: Parent's Application for Leave)* [1998] 1 FLR 1, CA (1998 Abr para 1245), considered.

466   Family proceedings—proceedings relating to children—appointment of guardians

Anthony Douglas, Chief Executive of CAFCASS and Dafydd Ifans, Chief Executive of CAFCASS Cymru, have jointly issued the *Practice Note (CAFCASS and the National Assembly for Wales: Appointment of Guardians in Private Law Proceedings)* [2006] 2 FLR 143.

Introduction

1. This Practice Note applies to both England and Wales and supersedes the CAFCASS *Practice Note* dated 6 April 2004 found at [2004] 1 FLR 1190 (2004 Abr para 419). It is issued with the approval of the President of the Family Division and should be read together with the *President's Practice Direction (Family Proceedings: Representation of Children)* [2004] 2 All ER 459 (2004 Abr para 419) dated 5 April 2004.

2. The term 'CAFCASS Legal' throughout the *Practice Note* refers to the CAFCASS in house lawyers; the term 'the CAFCASS High Court Team' refers to the team of CAFCASS practitioners known by that name at the address given at head 11, below; the term 'CAFCASS Cymru' refers to the division of the National Assembly for Wales to whom the functions of the Assembly under the Children Act 2004 Pt 4 have been delegated; the term 'Assembly lawyers' refers to lawyers employed by the National Assembly for Wales to provide legal advice, support and representation to Welsh family proceedings officers.

Appointment of CAFCASS officers and Welsh family proceedings officers in private law proceedings pursuant to the Family Proceedings Rules 1991, SI 1991/1247, r 9.5

3. Where the court has decided to appoint an officer of CAFCASS or Welsh family proceedings officer as guardian ad litem ('guardian') the order should simply state that: '[name of the child] is made party to the proceedings and pursuant to r 9.5 an officer of CAFCASS/a Welsh family proceedings officer be appointed as his/her guardian.'

4. Courts are to endeavour to send orders to CAFCASS or to CAFCASS Cymru as appropriate on the day of the hearing but in any event no less than two working days following the hearing, or two working days following the order being received by the court office/associate. Where suitable

arrangements exist, orders are to be sent by email. Where it is not possible to email orders they should be faxed or sent by first class post. Documents in adoption proceedings and Human Fertilisation and Embryology Act 1990 proceedings are not to be sent by email.

5. The decision about which particular officer of CAFCASS or Welsh family proceedings officer to allocate as guardian is a matter for CAFCASS or CAFCASS Cymru as appropriate. However, it is helpful if the court records whether there is any reason why any CAFCASS officer or Welsh family proceedings officer who has dealt with the matter so far should not continue to deal with it in the role of guardian.

County court

6. In cases proceeding in the county court, the order making the 1991 Rules r 9.5 appointment should be sent to the CAFCASS/CAFCASS Cymru office responsible for private law cases in the area for which the child is currently living. For county court cases proceeding in the Principal Registry, the order and the court file should be sent to the CAFCASS office at the Principal Registry for referral to the relevant local office or directly to CAFCASS Cymru.

7. The CAFCASS High Court Team does not undertake work proceeding in the county court.

High Court

8. In private law cases proceeding in the High Court where a guardian is appointed, the case will be referred either to the CAFCASS High Court Team, where child is resident in England; the Assembly lawyers, where child is resident in Wales, or to the relevant local CAFCASS office. Guidance as to which cases should be referred to the CAFCASS High Court Team/the Assembly lawyers is set out at head 10, below.

9. In proceedings brought under the Child Abduction and Custody Act 1985, the CAFCASS team based at the Principal Registry will continue to assist the High Court and provide reports in cases where the child is usually resident in England. Where the child is usually resident in Wales, the matter should be referred to the relevant regional office of CAFCASS Cymru (National Office (North), Porthdy Grosvenor, 1 Grosvenor Road, Wrexham, LL11 1BS, telephone 01978 368479; National Office (South), Llys y Delyn, 107–111 Cowbridge Road East, Cardiff, CF11 9AG, telephone 02920 647 926.

10. The following categories of case involving an appointment pursuant to the 1991 Rules r 9.5 or otherwise where the child is a party, should be referred to the CAFCASS High Court Team/Assembly lawyers:

(a) reporting restriction orders arising in a children's case;

(b) exceptionally complex adoption cases including exceptionally complex cases involving inter country adoption;

(c) all medical treatment cases where the child is old enough to have views which need to be taken into account, or where there are particularly difficult ethical issues such as the withdrawal of treatment, unless the issue arises in existing proceedings already being handled locally when the preferred arrangement will usually be for the matter to continue to be dealt with locally but with additional advice provided by CAFCASS Legal/Assembly lawyers if necessary;

(d) any freestanding human rights applications pursuant to the Human Rights Act 1998 s 7(1)(a) in which it is thought that it may be possible and appropriate for any part to be played by CAFCASS/CAFCASS Cymru or its officers;

(e) exceptionally complex international cases particularly where there is a dispute as to which country's courts should have jurisdiction over the child's affairs;

(f) applications in wardship and applications made under the High Court's inherent jurisdiction.

11. In cases referred to the CAFCASS High Court Team, a copy of the court file, including the order appointing the CAFCASS officer and the record of the court's reasons, should be sent for the attention of The Manager, CAFCASS High Court Team, 8th Floor, South Quay Plaza 3, 189 Marsh Wall, London E14 9SH (Fax no: 0207 510 7104) or by Document Exchange to DX 42691 Isle of Dogs. If the appointment is urgent then the judge or a member of the Court Service is encouraged, if possible, to telephone on 020 7510 7089 to discuss the matter before an order is made.

12. In cases referred to the Assembly lawyers a copy of the court file, including the order appointing the Welsh family proceedings officer and the record of the court's reasons, should be sent for the attention of the Social Care Team, Directorate of Legal Services, National Assembly for Wales, Cathays Park, Cardiff CF10 3NQ (Fax no: 02920 823834). If the appointment is urgent then the judge or a member of the Court Service is encouraged, if possible, to telephone on 02920 826813 to discuss the matter before an order is made.

13. In cases falling outside the categories at head 10, above, the order making the appointment should be sent to the CAFCASS office/CAFCASS Cymru office for the area where the child is currently living. The exception to this is cases proceeding in the Principal Registry when the order

together with the court file should be sent to the CAFCASS office at the Principal Registry for referral to the relevant local office or directly to CAFCASS Cymru.

14. The office that is to be responsible for the matter will notify the court of the name and professional address and telephone number of the particular officer who will act as guardian. If for whatever reason there is likely to be any significant delay in an officer being made available CAFCASS/CAFCASS Cymru will notify the court accordingly to enable the court to consider whether some other proper person should instead be appointed as guardian.

15. If the officer to be appointed as guardian is a member of the CAFCASS High Court Team there may be no need for a solicitor for the child also to be appointed as the litigation may be conducted in house pursuant to the Criminal Justice and Court Services Act 2000 s 15.

CAFCASS Legal or Assembly lawyers acting as advocate to the court

16. CAFCASS Legal or Assembly lawyers may be invited to act or instruct counsel as advocate to the court in family proceedings in which the welfare of children is or may be in question.

Provision of general assistance by CAFCASS Legal and Assembly lawyers

17. CAFCASS Legal and Assembly lawyers are available to offer advice to judges and other professionals engaged in family proceedings in which the welfare of children is or may be in question without necessarily being appointed as advocate to the court.

18. Lawyers at CAFCASS Legal take it in turn to carry a mobile telephone through which they can be contacted any day of the year by the High Court out of hours duty judge if their help is needed, for instance in relation to a medical treatment emergency.

467 Family proceedings—publicity—claim of miscarriage of justice—previous media attention

Care orders were made in respect of three siblings consequent to an allegation that one or more of the children had been physically abused by their parents. The children were subsequently adopted. The parents alleged that they had been the victims of a miscarriage of justice and that the case received publicity from the media. The mother had a fourth child in respect of whom the local authority initiated care proceedings which attracted further media attention. An order was made prohibiting the publication of any information relating to the child. The parents and interested parties from the media applied for a variation of the order to allow media reporting of the case. *Held*, the Children Act 1989 s 97, which provided for privacy for children in family proceedings, had to be read in a Convention-compliant way, as s 97 constituted a specific restriction on the media's rights under the European Convention on Human Rights art 10. The power under the 1989 Act s 97(4) to dispense with reporting restrictions about the identity of the child therefore had to be construed as not being limited to those occasions where the welfare of the child required it, but as extending to every occasion where proper compliance with the Convention so required. The same approach applied in relation to the Family Proceedings Rules 1991, SI 1991/1247, r 4.16(7), which provided that, unless the court otherwise directed, certain hearings concerning children should be in chambers. Rule 4.16(7) had to be regarded as a default provision and not as a provision that indicated some heavy presumption in favour of privacy. A judge had to be alert to the dangers inherent in the strong inherited convention of privacy and careful not to be prejudiced by the tradition or a subconscious preference for a hearing in chambers. There had been a claim that the case involved a miscarriage of justice, the parents themselves sought publicity, there had already been very extensive publicity and, in the circumstances, there was a need for the full facts and the truth to emerge in a way which would command public confidence. The contention that privacy was necessary in the interests of the child was speculative and involved a disproportionate interference with the applicants' rights. In these circumstances, the order would be replaced with an order allowing the media to attend the hearing and report the names of the parents and child. Accordingly, the application would be allowed.

Re Webster (A Child) [2006] EWHC 2733 (Fam), [2007] EMLR 199 (Family Division: Munby J).

468 Family proceedings—publicity—need for transparency—perceived gender bias against fathers

The applicants were both fathers whose applications for contact with their children had been dismissed. They both sought permission to appeal. *Held*, like every other judgment of the Court of Appeal, applications for permission to appeal in family proceedings were delivered in open court and in public, and if a single Lord Justice refused permission he should give reasons for doing so. One advantage of transparency was the opportunity to dispel the myth that there was a gender bias against fathers in the family justice system which, in particular, improperly denied non-residential fathers contact with their children. From the findings of the trial judges it was clear that the reason why contact had been denied was the applicants' behaviour. It was idle for them to blame the system or the mothers. Accordingly, the application would be dismissed.

Re B (A Child); Re O (Children) [2006] EWCA Civ 1199, [2007] Fam Law 19 (Court of Appeal: Wall LJ).

469 Family proceedings—urgent and out of hours cases—procedure

Laurence Oates, the Official Solicitor, the Chief Executive of CAFCASS and the Chief Executive of CAFCASS Cymru on behalf of the National Assembly for Wales, have jointly issued the following *Practice Note (Official Solicitor, CAFCASS and the National Assembly for Wales: Urgent and Out of Hours Cases in the Family Division of the High Court)* [2006] 2 FLR 354, which describes the procedure to be followed in respect of urgent and out of hours cases in which a decision is sought by a judge of the Family Division of the High Court, on 28 July 2006.

1. In some cases, urgent or out of hours applications become necessary because applications to the court have not been pursued sufficiently promptly. This is undesirable, in particular because urgent applications may be founded on incomplete evidence, inquiries and under-prepared advocacy, and should be avoided where possible. A judge who has concerns that the urgent or out of hours facilities may have been abused may require a representative of the claimant to attend at a subsequent directions hearing to provide an explanation.

2. Whenever possible, urgent applications should be made within court hours. The earliest possible liaison is required with the Clerk of the Rules. It will usually be possible to accommodate a genuinely urgent application, at least for initial directions, in the Family Division applications court, from which the matter may, if necessary and possible, be referred to another judge.

3. When it is not possible to apply within court hours, contact should be made with the security office at the Royal Courts of Justice (020 7947 6000) who will refer the matter to the urgent business officer. The urgent business officer can contact the duty judge. The judge may agree to hold a hearing, either convened at court or elsewhere, or by telephone. When the hearing is to take place by telephone it should be by tape-recorded conference call arranged, and paid for in the first instance, by the claimant's solicitors. Solicitors acting for NHS trusts or other potential claimants should have standing arrangements with their telephone service providers under which such conference calls can be arranged. All parties, especially the judge, should be informed that the call is being recorded by the service provider. The claimant should order a transcript of the hearing from the service provider.

Adult Medical Treatment and Welfare Cases

4. The Official Solicitor will act in urgent cases under the inherent jurisdiction concerning medical treatment to, or the welfare of, an adult who lacks capacity to make decisions for himself. His office should be contacted at the earliest possible opportunity if an urgent application is envisaged. Where cases arise out of hours the urgent business officer will be able to contact him or his representative. As with cases dealt with on a less urgent basis, evidence is required of incapacity and as to best interests. When written evidence is not available, oral evidence of incapacity must be available. When there is a telephone hearing, oral evidence must be given as part of the conference call.

5. When final evidence either as to capacity or best interest is not available, the court may be willing to grant an interim declaration, see CPR 25.1(1)(b) and *NHS Trust v T (Adult Patient: Refusal of Medical Treatment)* [2004] EWHC 1279 (Fam), [2005] 1 All ER 387 (2004 Abr para 1989). Evidence establishing on the balance of probability that the patient is under incapacity and that the treatment proposed is in his best interest must be adduced. An interim injunction to restrain treatment may be granted, see *Re C (Adult) (Refusal of Treatment)* [1994] 1 WLR 290.

6. An adult patient must be a party and must be represented through a litigation friend, see CPR 21.3. Notice of an application must be given to the patient, or his litigation friend. The claimant may be an NHS trust, local authority, relative, carer, or the patient. The Official Solicitor stands ready to accept appointment as litigation friend, usually for the patient as defendant, if the conditions for his appointment are shown, either on an interim or final basis, to exist. Should a declaration be made without notice, it is of no effect and my be set aside, see *St George's Healthcare NHS Trust v S; R (on the application of S) v Collins* [1999] Fam 26 (1998 Abr para 2207).

Children Medical Treatment and Welfare Cases

7. It may be desirable for a child who is the subject of such proceedings to be made a party and represented through a guardian ad litem, usually an officer of CAFCASS or a Welsh Family Proceedings Officer. CAFCASS and CAFCASS Cymru stand ready to arrange for an officer to accept appointment as guardian ad litem. They should be contacted at the earliest opportunity where an urgent application is envisaged. For urgent out of hours applications, the urgent business officer is able to contact a representative of CAFCASS. CAFCASS Cymru is not able to deal with cases that arise out of office hours and those cases should be referred to CAFCASS who will deal with the matter on behalf of CAFCASS Cymru until the next working day. A child of sufficient understanding to instruct his or her own solicitor should be made a party and given notice of any application.

8. Interim declarations/orders under the wardship jurisdiction, or the Children Act 1989, may be made on application either by an NHS trust, a local authority, an interested adult, where necessary with the leave of the court, or by the child if he has sufficient understanding to make the application.

General Issues

9. Parents, carers or other necessary respondents should be given the opportunity to have independent legal advice or at least to have access to support or counselling.

10. In suitable cases, application may be made for direction providing for anonymity of the parties and others involved in the matter in any order of subsequent listing of the case. Exceptionally, a reporting restriction order may be sought, see the *President's Practice Direction (Applications for Reporting Restriction Orders)* [2005] Fam Law 397 (2005 Abr para 499) issued on 18 March 2005.

11. Either the Official Solicitor or CAFCASS, as the case may be, may be appointed by the court as advocate to the court, see Memorandum from the Lord Chief Justice and the Attorney General reproduced in The White Book service 2006, Civil Procedure (Sweet and Maxwell, 2006) at 39.8.2, especially at 39.8.5.

12. Draft standard form orders for use in urgent and out of hours medical treatment cases are annexed to this note [Editor's note: not reproduced in this summary]. They should be adapted to suit the individual circumstances of each case.

Consultation with CAFCASS, CAFCASS Cymru and the Official Solicitor

13. Members of the Official Solicitor's legal staff, CAFCASS, and CAFCASS Cymru are prepared to discuss medical cases before proceedings are issued. In all cases in which the urgent and out of hours procedures are to be used it would be helpful if the Official Solicitor, CAFCASS or CAFCASS Cymru have had some advance notice of the application and its circumstances. Inquiries about adult medical and welfare cases should be addressed to a family and medical litigation lawyer at the office of the Official Solicitor, 81 Chancery Lane, London, WC2A, telephone 0207 911 7127, fax number: 0207 911 7105, email: inquiries@offsol.gsi.gov.uk. Inquiries about children medical cases should be directed to the duty lawyer at CAFCASS, 8th Floor, South Quay Plaza 2, 189 Marsh Wall, London, E14 9SH, telephone: 0207 510 7000, fax number: 0207 510 7104. Inquiries about children medical cases in Wales should be directed to the Social Care Team, Legal Services, National Assembly for Wales, Cathays Park, Cardiff, CF10 3NQ, telephone: 02920 826813, fax no: 02920 823834.

470   Financial support for children—parent's financial resources—separate representation for child

The appellant had been awarded a sum from which to provide housing for herself and her child. This meant moving to a cheaper area while the father lived in a house with an estimated value of over three times the sum awarded to the appellant. On appeal, *held*, the judge had erred in using a higher value multi-million pound financial provision case as a benchmark from which to proportionately scale down the award made to the applicant. He should have asked whether it was necessary for the child to move area as well as assessing the risk of harm to his welfare. Without a representative of the child constantly urging his needs and interests, it was easy to see how the crux of the case could be lost, and the case provided an illustration of the advantage of separate representation of the child. Accordingly, the appeal would be allowed.

Re S (A Child: Unmarried Parents: Financial Provision) [2006] EWCA Civ 479, [2006] 2 FLR 950 (Court of Appeal: Thorpe, Laws, and Hallett LJJ). *P (A Child) (Financial Provision)* [2003] EWCA Civ 837, [2003] 2 FCR 481 (2003 Abr para 406) considered.

471   Information sharing index—England

The Information Sharing Index (England) Regulations 2006, SI 2006/983 (in force on 6 April 2006), (1) require a children's services authority in England to provide information to the Secretary of State within 14 days if so requested; (2) permit disclosure of information by the Secretary of State to a person or body who has been authorised by the by the Secretary of State to process data on his behalf; (3) provide that any disclosure under heads (1), (2) supra, or any provision of information by the Secretary of State may be made, even if a rule of common law might otherwise prohibit or restrict the disclosure or provision of information; (4) place certain conditions on the processing of information; and (5) limit to three years the time that the Secretary of State may keep information.

472   Legal capacity—contract—representation agreement for minor

See *Proform Sports Management Ltd v Proactive Sports Management Ltd*, para 2774.

473   Local safeguarding children boards—England

The Local Safeguarding Children Boards Regulations 2006, SI 2006/90 (in force on 1 April 2006), make provision for local safeguarding children boards and, in particular, (1) provide for representation of children's services authorities and their board partners; (2) provide for the appointment of a person to chair a board; and (3) prescribe the functions of a board.

474 Local safeguarding children boards—Wales

The Local Safeguarding Children Boards (Wales) Regulations 2006, SI 2006/1705 (in force on 1 October 2006), provide for the functions of Welsh local safeguarding children boards in relation to the objective set for them by the Children Act 2004 s 32. In particular, the regulations (1) make provision about the carrying out of serious case reviews; (2) prescribe the membership of a board; and (3) deal with a board's procedures and confer functions on children's services authorities in relation to their boards.

475 Medical treatment—gravely ill child—declaration by court concerning treatment

See *An NHS Trust v MB (A Child Represented by CAFCASS as Guardian ad Litem)*, para 1948.

476 Medical treatment—treatment without parental knowledge or consent—sexual matters

See *R (on the application of Axon) v Secretary of State for Health*, para 1949.

477 Parentage—child conceived by artificial insemination by donor—parties to marriage—purported marriage between two women

The parties went through a ceremony of marriage. The husband suffered from gender dysmorphia and, although he had long been living as a man, he had been registered at birth as a female and at the date of the marriage was, both in fact and in law, a woman. The parties lived for many years as husband and wife although the wife was unaware that the husband was a woman. The wife gave birth to a child by way of artificial insemination, and subsequently filed a petition for divorce. During the proceedings, she saw a copy of the husband's birth certificate and realised that he was a woman. A decree of nullity was pronounced and the wife later remarried. The husband issued proceedings under the Children Act 1989 s 8 for a prohibited steps order that the child should not be informed of her parentage, save at such time and in a manner advised by a specified consultant psychiatrist. It fell to be determined as preliminary issues whether the husband needed leave pursuant to s 10(9) to bring the proceedings and, if he did, whether it should be given. The judge made a declaration that the husband was not a 'parent' of the child within the meaning of s 10(4)(a) and that he required leave under s 10(1)(a)(ii) to make an application for an order under s 8. The judge applied the Human Fertilisation and Embryology Act 1990 s 28, having accepted the argument that s 28 applied because the child was being carried by the wife after 1 August 1991, the commencement date of s 28. He refused leave, the wife having given an undertaking that she would take the advice of the specified psychiatrist. The husband appealed but, shortly before the determination of the preliminary issues, he obtained a gender recognition certificate under the Gender Recognition Act 2004, which showed him to be male as from 1 June 2005. He had also obtained a fresh birth certificate giving his sex as male. *Held*, the judge had erred in applying the 1990 Act s 28. The applicable provision was the Family Law Reform Act 1987 s 27. The critical date for the application of the 1990 Act s 28 was the date of artificial insemination, which had resulted in the child being carried by the wife. That date was plainly before 1 August 1991. The fact that the child was 'being carried' by the wife after that date was thus immaterial. Further, having regard to the words 'a party to a marriage' in the 1987 Act s 27(1)(a), and the corresponding words 'the other party to that marriage' in s 27(1)(b), if marriage was exclusively the union of a man and a woman which, in English law, it plainly was, 'the other party to that marriage' had to be a man in order for there to be a marriage. In 1991 the husband was a woman, so that he could not fulfil the definition of 'the other party to that marriage', and could not, therefore, be the child's father. It followed that, although the judge had been directed to, and had construed, the wrong statute, he had reached the right conclusion and the declaration he had made was correct. Accordingly, the appeal would be dismissed.

J v C [2006] EWCA Civ 551, [2007] Fam 1 (Court of Appeal: Thorpe, Wall and Richards LJJ).

478 Parental responsibility—order sought by father—mother in same-sex relationship

The first and second respondents were a lesbian couple who advertised for a man to father a child. The applicant responded and together with the first respondent fathered a daughter. The first respondent, being the daughter's mother, had parental responsibility, as did the second respondent, pursuant to a joint residence order made by the court. The applicant also sought parental responsibility. His application was adjourned and subsequently, on the rehearing of his application, he offered to undertake not to exercise his parental responsibility to involve himself without the first and second respondents' consent in particular areas of the daughter's life where they might anticipate that problems might be caused, namely her medical treatment and her schooling. The respondents objected to the grant of parental responsibility, fearing the applicant's influence on the stability of their family and relationship. *Held*, on the facts, the applicant would be granted parental responsibility for the daughter. Pursuant to his undertaking, the applicant would not visit or contact the daughter's school for any purpose and would not contact any health professional involved in the daughter's care without the prior written consent of the first or second respondent. Accordingly, the application would be allowed.

Re D (Contact and Parental Responsibility: Lesbian Mothers and Known Father) [2006] EWHC 2 (Fam), [2006] 1 FCR 556 (Family Division: Black J). *Re H* [1991] 2 All ER 185; *Re RH* [1998] 2 FCR 89; *Re G (Children) (Shared Residence Order: Parental Responsibility)* [2005] All ER (D) 25 (Apr) (2005 Abr para 524) considered.

479   Parental responsibility—proceedings—jurisdiction—deemed acceptance

See *C v C*, para 604.

480   Paternity—proof of paternity—British nationality

See para 353.

481   Procedure—appeals—split hearings—clarification of issues in first part of hearing

After its dismissal of an application for permission to appeal against a care order, the Court of Appeal drew attention to a number of procedural points relevant to cases where the court was contemplating a split hearing in a case which involved children. Firstly, it was essential that the issues which were to be resolved in the first limb of the hearing were clearly defined and that the consequences of any such findings were fully understood by the parties. If the court was dealing with a single-issue case in which the facts found would determine the threshold criteria under the Children Act 1989 s 31(2), directions given by the court must identify precisely that the purpose of the hearing was to decide whether the threshold criteria were established and identify with as much precision as possible the facts on which the authority relied and which it asserted would, if proved, establish the criteria. Alternatively, if the question concerned the resolution of an issue of fact which would affect the manner in which subsequent assessments of the parties were to be made, the issues which the court had to resolve and the facts which it was being invited to find had to be clearly spelled out. Once the first limb of the hearing had been completed and the judge had delivered judgment, it would usually be sensible for there to be a short discussion in court between counsel and the judge to clarify the consequences of the findings.

Re A (Children: Split Hearings) [2006] EWCA Civ 714, [2007] Fam Law 16 (Court of Appeal: Chadwick, Wall and Moore-Bick LJJ).

482   Protection of children—child involved in proceedings—identification—restraint on publication

The Children Act 1989 s 97(2) provides that no person may publish to the public at large or any section of the public any material which is intended, or likely, to identify any child as being involved in any proceedings in which any power under the 1989 Act may be exercised by the court with respect to that or any other child.

The parties separated and care of their daughter was shared between them. Contact and residence proceedings were commenced, but before they could be resolved the father abducted the child and took her abroad. The father was subsequently convicted of child abduction on his return to the United Kingdom and was only able to resume contact with the child four months after his release from prison following proceedings brought under the Children Act 1989. The father then expressed an intention of recording a video diary documenting his time spent with his daughter in Portugal and the perceived failings of the legal aid system, the care proceedings process and the services of the Children and Family Court Advisory and Support Service. The mother successfully applied for an order restraining the father from communicating any matter relating to the education, maintenance, financial circumstances or family circumstances of the child other than with specified persons. A shared care agreement was subsequently reached in the care proceedings and the father applied for the injunction to be lifted in its totality. The judge declined to discharge the injunction, being satisfied that the need to ensure that the child had peace and freedom from publicity outweighed the father's right to freedom of speech, and that that approach broadly reflected the policy of the 1989 Act s 97. The father appealed. *Held*, while the prohibition on publication contained in s 97 prevented identification of children involved in proceedings under the 1989 Act while the proceedings continued, such prohibition ended when the proceedings were concluded. However, that did not mean the restriction on publication of information relating to proceedings under the 1989 Act contained in the Administration of Justice Act 1960 s 12 was affected. Nor did it prevent the judge from making an injunction or order which prohibited the identification of the child for a period extending beyond that specified in the 1989 Act s97(2) in the interests of the child. The court was necessarily required to conduct a balancing exercise between the child's interests and freedom of speech in relation to any long-term injunction, however. Accordingly, the appeal would be allowed.

Clayton v Clayton [2006] EWCA Civ 878, [2006] Fam 83 (Court of Appeal: Sir Mark Potter P, Arden and Wall LJJ).

483 Protection of children—emergency protection order—approach of local authority and court

A case conference was held in relation to the care requirements of a child. No mention was made at the conference of the child being removed as a matter of urgency. However, shortly after the conference the local authority applied to the court for an emergency protection order in connection with the child. As a result, the child was placed in foster care and remained there for the next 14 months. An issue arose as to the correctness of the approach of the authority and the court. *Held*, as an emergency protection order was a harsh measure, it should not be made unless the court was satisfied that no other less radical form of order would achieve the end of promoting the child's welfare. The authority and the court should pay particular attention to guidance which had already been issued by the court, to ensuring that evidence came from the best available source, to fully recording proceedings and reasons, and to determining, with reasons, whether the hearing should proceed on a without notice basis. Judgment would be given accordingly.

Re X (A Child: Emergency Protection Orders) [2006] EWHC 510 (Fam), [2007] 1 FCR 551 (Family Division: McFarlane J).

484 Protection of children—injunction to prevent identification—television documentary identifying social workers—consequential identification of children

Allegations of satanic and ritual abuse were made against certain families, but the court found that the allegations had not been made out. The court ordered injunctions to protect the identities of the children. The terms of the injunctions prevented the publication of details or pictures which might lead to the identification of the children as having been wards of court. Solicitation of information concerning the children from identified parties was also forbidden. The professionals involved were publicly named, except for two social workers, who were granted anonymity, because publishing their names could lead to the children being identified. Subsequently, the applicant television company sought an order that would lead to the disclosure of evidence given in the proceedings to the applicant, and disclosure of the identities of the social workers, in order to make a documentary. The defendant local authority made an application to restrain the applicant from publishing any material that might lead to the identification of the social workers. However, the children, via their representatives, sought to exercise their right under the European Convention on Human Rights art 8 to share their privacy with the world, and, together with the applicant, their art 10 right to tell their story. *Held*, as a matter of general principle there was nothing, in the absence of an order to the contrary, to prevent the identification of a witness who had given evidence in a case. The general practice of affording privacy in children's cases did not extend to preserving the privacy of expert witnesses. While the Administration of Justice Act 1960 s 12 prevented publication of witness evidence, including expert evidence, in children's cases, there could not be an expectation that the evidence would remain confidential in all circumstances. There was a public interest in encouraging frankness which was essential in cases involving children's welfare, which included promoting rather than deterring witnesses, including professional witnesses, from giving evidence. The children's right to tell their story was protected by the Convention arts 8, 10 since, once a protected child achieved adulthood and was not incompetent, the court's role in the maintenance or enforcement of their anonymity was necessarily limited. Accordingly, the application for an injunction would be refused.

British Broadcasting Corpn v Rochdale MBC [2005] EWHC 2862 (Fam), [2006] EMLR 117 (Family Division: Ryder J).

485 Protection of children—tribunal—proceedings

The Protection of Children and Vulnerable Adults and Care Standards Tribunal (Review of Disqualification Orders) Regulations 2006, SI 2006/1929 (in force on 15 August 2006), make provision regarding the conduct of proceedings of the Care Standards Tribunal. In particular, the regulations (1) make provision as to the constitution of the Tribunal, in respect of the powers and functions that may be exercised by the President and the Secretary; (2) make provision in relation to applications and determinations and set out the procedural steps involved in the making and acknowledgment of an application; (3) enable misconceived applications to be struck out; (4) provide for the grant or refusal of leave to proceed with an application and the reconsideration of a refusal of such leave; (5) make provision in relation to the appointment of the Tribunal; (6) make provision regarding directions and preliminary issues and the conduct of hearings, the summoning of witnesses and particular arrangements applying to child and vulnerable adult witnesses; (7) allow for the provision of expert evidence and set out the circumstances where medical reports may be withheld from disclosure; (8) provide for the exclusion of the press and public from hearings and for restricted reporting orders; (9) make provision in relation to decisions of the Tribunal, its power to review decisions either on its own initiative or at the request of the applicant, its powers on such a review and the publication of Tribunal decisions; and (10) provide for the method of sending documents, dealing with any irregularities, cases where the applicant dies, withdrawal of applications, proof of documents and certifying of decisions and extending or reducing time limits.

The Protection of Children and Vulnerable Adults and Care Standards Tribunal (Amendment) Regulations 2006, SI 2006/1930 (in force on 1 October 2006), further amend the 2002

Regulations, SI 2002/816, by revising (1) the definition of 'working day' in order to clarify that the term 'bank holiday' refers only to such holidays in England and Wales; (2) the provisions concerning multiple appeals, in order to permit the Tribunal President (or nominated chairman), on the application of either party or on his own initiative, to hear together cases that share the same factual background; and (3) the procedure for appeals to provide that (a) where a person is appealing against a decision of the registration authority to refuse his application for registration as a childminder or day care provider, then the period within which such an appeal must be lodged is three months after the applicant has received notice of the decision to refuse his application for registration, instead of 28 days; and (b) where a person is appealing against a decision of a council to refuse his application for registration as a social worker, then the period within which such an appeal must be lodged is three months after the applicant has received notice of the decision to refuse his application for registration, instead of 28 days.

486   Residence order—best interests of child—risk of damage to child if returned to natural parent—child's ability to form attachment to foster family

The parents of a child were Indian. The child had been born following the mother's return from a period living in India, during which, she alleged, she was ill treated and virtually imprisoned by the father. The mother informed the local authority that she wanted the child to be adopted, and the child was placed into foster care with the fourth respondents. The father expressed a wish to care for the child but it took nearly two years for him to arrive in the United Kingdom. He then faced obstacles in his application to become primary carer, namely the language barrier and questions over his parenting skills. The father's sister, the third respondent, also expressed a wish to help the father look after the child. The mother opposed the child going to her paternal family and, as a result, the authority issued care proceedings. The authority, the father and the third respondent sought a residence order in favour of the father and third respondent on the ground that they were her family and because of the prospective adolescent problems of her identity and culture in being brought up in a trans-racial placement. The mother, the fourth respondents and the guardian, acting for the child, supported a residence order in favour of the fourth respondents. *Held*, in care proceedings, as with wardship proceedings, the starting point was that, other things being equal, there was a strong presumption that it was in the interests of a child that he should be brought up by his natural parents. That was not an absolute right either of the child or its parents, but compelling reasons to depart from such a strong presumption had to be established. In the instant case, the risks attached to moving the child to her paternal family heavily outweighed all the advantages of such a placement. The risk of damage to her by such a move at the present time would be so great that it provided a compelling reason for not implementing the care plan proposed by the authority. The child's ability to attach in her new home was a primary factor and the very great importance of being raised within the natural family, with all its ethnic and cultural advantages, had to take second place to that consideration. On the evidence, the court was satisfied that the child would not form an attachment either to the father, or her family. Judgment would be given accordingly.

A Local Authority v D [2006] EWHC 295 (Fam), [2006] All ER (D) 392 (Feb) (Family Division: Sumner J).

487   Residence order—shared residence order—appropriateness

The parents of a child separated and arranged to share the care of their six-year-old child. The mother was subsequently granted a residence order, but because of generous contact arrangements with the father, the child's time was divided almost equally between the parents' two homes. The father later applied for a shared residence order. The judge expressed concern that the granting of that order would affect the issue of control and power between the parents, and would empower the father in a way contrary to the interests of the child. He therefore refused to grant the order. The father appealed. *Held*, the judge's reasons for refusing the order were unsatisfactory, and the anxieties that had driven his decision were incomprehensible. There was no evidence of either parent having interfered with the exercise of the responsibility and judgment of the parent in possession of the child. There had been a plain case for a shared residence order, which would reflect the reality that the parents had established, to their credit and to the child's advantage, in making two homes for her. Accordingly, the appeal would be allowed.

Re P (Children) (Shared Residence Order) [2005] EWCA Civ 1639, [2006] 1 FCR 309 (Court of Appeal: Thorpe, Scott Baker and Wall LJJ).

488   Residence order—shared residence order—same-sex couple—children born to one party—relevance of biological relationship

The appellant and the respondent cohabited in a lesbian relationship for a number of years during which the appellant twice underwent anonymous donor insemination which resulted in the birth of two daughters. The relationship broke down and the appellant and her two daughters moved to a different property. The respondent obtained a shared residence order and, after the appellant and her new partner relocated to a different part of the country, obtained a new shared residence order under which she was the primary carer. The appellant appealed on the basis that her connection with the children as their only biological and legal parent was a dominating factor in the welfare balancing exercise. *Held*, the authorities which referred to the importance of the natural bond and relationship between parent and child concerned disputes between a parent and a non-parent. No general proposition drawn from these authorities could legitimately be extended so that the position of one parent should be enhanced on grounds of a biological connection. Examples of families which involved a parent who was not the genetic parent included cases where a heterosexual couple had a child after a donated egg fertilised by the father was implanted in the woman, where a fertilised egg of one party to a lesbian relationship was implanted in the other's womb, and where a male homosexual couple entered into a surrogacy agreement in order to parent. The question was who was the natural parent. In the eyes of a child, his natural parent might be a non-biological parent who, by virtue of long settled care, had become the child's psychological parent. Where, as in the present case, the care of a newborn and then developing baby had broadly been shared, the children would not distinguish between one woman and the other on the grounds of a biological relationship. The psychological attachment to each parent might be more or less equal or more to the biological parent or more to the non-biological parent. The judge had been entitled to reach the decision which she had reached. Accordingly, the appeal would be dismissed.

Re G (Children) (Residence: Same-Sex Partner) [2006] EWCA Civ 372, [2006] 1 FCR 681 (Court of Appeal: Thorpe, Laws and Hallett LJJ). *J v C* [1970] AC 668, HL; and *Re KD* [1988] AC 806, HL (1988 Abr para 1589), distinguished. For earlier proceedings see *Re G (Residence: Same-Sex Partner)* [2005] EWCA Civ 462, [2006] 1 FCR 436 (2005 Abr para 524).

489   Residence order—shared residence order—same-sex couple—rights of the natural mother

The applicant and respondent had been in a same-sex relationship for several years. During the relationship the respondent had been artificially inseminated and bore two children. After the parties separated, the applicant sought a shared residence order, which was rejected on the ground of the hostility between the parties, but was granted on appeal. The respondent had moved the children away without informing the applicant, and the applicant applied for the children's primary residence to be with her. The court maintained the shared residence order but reversed the time in each home. The respondent further appealed following the failure of her appeal. *Held*, there was no question of a parental right. The lower courts had allowed the unusual context of the case to distract them from the principles of universal application, which were (1) the respondent was the natural mother of the children in every sense of the term, which was an important and significant factor in determining what would be best for the children now and in the future, although it would not raise any presumption in her favour; and (2) while it might be in the interests of the children to change their living arrangements if one parent was frustrating their relationship with the other parent who was able to provide a good and loving home, that it was unlikely to be the case where that relationship was being maintained in accordance with the court's order. Accordingly, the appeal would be allowed.

Re G (Children (Residence: Same Sex Partner)) [2006] UKHL 43, (2006) Times, 27 July (Lords Nicholls of Birkenhead, Scott of Foscote, Rodger of Earlsferry and Walker of Gestingthorpe and Baroness Hale of Richmond). *Re H (a Minor) (Custody: Interim Care and Control)* [1991] 2 FLR 109, CA (1991 Abr para 235), considered. Decision of Court of Appeal [2005] EWCA Civ 462, [2005] 1 FCR 436 (2005 Abr para 524) reversed.

490   Safeguarding Vulnerable Groups Act 2006

The Safeguarding Vulnerable Groups Act 2006 makes provision in connection with the protection of children and vulnerable adults. The Act received the royal assent on 8 November 2006 and came into force in part on that day. The remaining provisions come into force on a day or days to be appointed. For details of commencement, see the commencement table in the title STATUTES.

Section 1 establishes the Independent Barring Board which is to take over responsibility for vetting people who wish to work with children or vulnerable adults. Section 1 also gives effect to Sch 1, which details the composition and procedure of the Board, and Sch 2, which provides for the transfer of staff and property to the Board. The Board must maintain the 'children's barred list' and the 'adults' barred list', inclusion on either of which can be (1) automatic, where certain criteria are satisfied; (2) subject to consideration of representations; (3) based on concerns regarding a person's behaviour; or (4) due to a perceived risk that a person will cause harm to children or vulnerable adults: s 2, Sch 3. By virtue of s 3, a person is barred from regulated activity relating to children or vulnerable adults if he is included on the children's barred list or the adults' barred list, as the case may be. A right of appeal is granted by s 4 against a decision of the Board to include or keep a person on either of the lists. Section 5 gives effect to Sch 4, which defines 'regulated activity', and 'regulated activity provider' is defined by s 6. Under s 7, a person commits an offence if he engages in regulated activity from which he is barred, or seeks or offers to engage in such activity. Section 8 makes it an offence for a person to engage in regulated activity with the permission of a regulated activity provider, if he is not subject to monitoring in relation to that activity. It is also an offence (a) to permit an individual to engage in regulated activity, if it is known or there is reasonable belief that the individual is barred from the activity (s 9); (b) for a regulated activity provider to permit an individual who is known or reasonably believed not to be subject to monitoring in relation to a regulated activity to engage in that activity (s 10); (c) for a regulated activity provider to permit a person to engage in regulated activity without first ascertaining whether he is subject to monitoring in relation to that activity (s 11, Sch 5); (d) for an employment business to fail to register an interest in an individual prior to supplying the individual to engage in regulated activity (s 12, Sch 6); and (e) for a prescribed officer to fail within a specified period to make a check in accordance with s 15 in relation to a person who is appointed to the governing body of a relevant educational establishment (s 13). The Secretary of State is empowered by s 14 to create offences in connection with the carrying out of regulated activities by office holders. Section 15 sets out how checks of governors of educational institutions and prescribed officers are to be made. In relation to vulnerable adults, certain regulated activity is exempt from the obligation to make an appropriate check under s 11 and from the offence under s 10: s 16. Under s 17, special provision is made for regulated activity providers who employ people in relevant National Health Service employment. By virtue of s 18, persons in charge of corporate bodies or partnerships may be held liable for specified offences committed by the body. Provision for circumstances in which a person acts, or appears to act, on behalf of a regulated activity provider is made by s 19, and s 20 outlines various defences to the offences created by s 19.

Under ss 21 and 22, controlled activity relating to children or vulnerable adults means any activity in specified sectors that is carried out frequently, or on three or more days in a 30-day period, and involves the opportunity for contact with children or vulnerable adults, as the case may be, or access to their medical records, and is not a regulated activity. The Secretary of State is empowered by s 23 to make regulations regarding the steps that must be taken by employers when engaging an individual in controlled activity. Various criteria must be satisfied for a person to be subject to monitoring in relation to a regulated activity, and the Secretary of State is entitled to set a fee to be paid by applicants for monitoring: s 24. Section 25 provides for the payment of fees in relation to monitoring under s 24. Provision is made in s 26 for ceasing the monitoring of an individual in prescribed circumstances. It is an offence to require an individual or a third party to produce the record of information given to an individual pursuant to the duty to provide disclosable information to an individual who is subject to monitoring: s 27. Section 28 provides for the appointment of an independent monitor to report on matters connected with the disclosure or non-disclosure of information under specified provisions. The code of practice issued under the Police Act 1997 s 122 applies to provisions relating to the carrying out of any function by a body or person registered with the Criminal Records Bureau for the purpose of accessing the disclosure service under Pt V (ss 112–127): 2006 Act s 29.

Section 30, Sch 7 deal with the making of applications for relevant vetting information concerning relevant individuals, and s 31 prescribes what relevant information is for that purpose. Under s 32, there is to be a system pursuant to which persons may register an interest to be notified if an individual ceases to be subject to monitoring. Such registration must cease once the Secretary of State has notified the person that the individual is no longer monitored or when the person who registered his interest requests that it ceases: s 33. By virtue of s 34, it is an offence to make a false declaration under s 30 or 32. Section 35 requires a regulated activity provider and a responsible person to provide the Board with prescribed information about an individual in certain prescribed circumstances, and s 36 makes equivalent provision in relation to personnel suppliers. Under s 37, the Board may require regulated activity providers, responsible persons or personnel suppliers to provide it with certain information. It is an offence to fail to comply with the requirements of s 35, 36 or 37: s 38. A local is authority is required by ss 39 and 40, and a keeper of a relevant register by ss 41 and 42, to provide the Board with information relating to a person if certain conditions are satisfied. Sections 43, 44 make provision for the sharing of information by the Secretary of State and the Board with the General Teaching Councils for England and Wales, the General Social Care Council and the Care Council for Wales. Sections 45–50 make provision for supervisory authorities, which are various official bodies designated to oversee the vetting process. Supervisory authorities (1) must provide prescribed information to the Board in certain circumstances (ss 45, 46); (2) may request vetting information from the Secretary of State (s 47), (3) are to be notified when a person is newly included on a children's barred list (s 48) or vulnerable adults' barred list (s 49); and (4) are entitled to information from the Board relevant to the carrying out of their functions (s 50).

Provision is made by s 51 for the application to the Crown of the duties and rights under the 2006 Act. Section 52 provides that, for certain purposes, it is immaterial that there is a finding of fact in any proceedings. Under s 53, it is an offence for a barred person to act as a local authority foster carer, foster carer employed by a voluntary organisation, or a person who fosters a child for reward or through the arrangements made by a person other than a member of the child's family. Sections 54, 55 apply to Scotland and Northern Ireland. Various secondary legislative powers are transferred by s 56 to the Welsh ministers in relation to the exercise of the powers in Wales. No claim for damages may be made as a result of a person's inclusion in, or the fact that he is not included in, a barred list: s 57. By virtue of s 58, the 2006 Act does not apply to activity carried out during the course of family relationships. Sections 59, 60 deal with interpretation. Requirements for the making of orders are detailed in s 61, and transitional provision is made by s 62, Sch 8. Section 63 gives effect to Sch 9, which makes amendments to various primary legislation, and to Sch 10, which makes various repeals. Supplementary and consequential provision is made by s 64. Section 65 deals with commencement, s 66 deals with extent, and s 67 specifies the short title.

Amendments, repeals and revocations
The list below, which is not exhaustive, mentions repeals and amendments which are or will be effective when the Act is fully in force.

Specific provisions of a number of Acts are amended or repealed. These include: Police Act 1997 ss 113C–113F; Teaching and Higher Education Act 1998 ss 15, 15A; Protection of Children Act 1990 ss 1–4C, 7, 13; and Care Standards Act 2000 ss 80–89, 91–99, 101.

491 Secure accommodation—approval—Wales

The Children (Secure Accommodation) (Amendment) (Wales) Regulations 2006, SI 2006/2986 (in force on 16 November 2006), further amend the 1991 Regulations, SI 1991/1505, in relation to Wales, so as to revoke the provision for the approval by the Secretary of State of secure accommodation in a children's home.

492 Special guardianship order—application—permission to apply

A child was taken into the interim care of a local authority owing to the inability of her parents to care for her. It was the authority's position that the child should be placed with adoptive parents who were not members of her family, but the child's mother believed it was in the best interests of the child for her to be placed with her maternal grandparents under a special guardianship order. Such an order could only be made if the grandparents had obtained leave pursuant to the Children Act 1989 s 14A(7). A judge ordered that the authority undertake an assessment of the grandparents under s 14A(9), despite the grandparents not at that point having obtained the court's leave to make the application for the guardianship order. The authority maintained that the judge could not require the authority to undertake the assessment, as the grandparents had neither applied for the order nor made an application to apply for leave. *Held*, it was not open to an individual who needed the leave of the court to make an application for a special guardianship order to give notice to the local authority of his intention to apply for such an order prior to the leave being obtained. On the relevant date, the grandparents had not obtained leave, and they plainly could not therefore at that point make an application for a special guardianship order. All they could do was to apply for permission to make an application for an order. The court order was plainly in error in recording their undertaking to make an application for a special guardianship order within seven days. Judgment would be given accordingly.

Birmingham CC v R (2006) Times, 29 December (Court of Appeal: Thorpe, Tuckey and Wall LJJ).

493 Wardship—jurisdiction—liability of local authority

The applicant, a girl of 17, obtained a visa and came to the United Kingdom from Ghana. She began living with a woman who she believed was her mother. Subsequently the relationship with the mother broke down and the applicant was placed with foster carers. The applicant was made a ward of court, a litigation friend was appointed and the local authority was ordered to prepare a report under the Children Act 1989 s 37(1). The report concluded that the authority had no grounds to issue care proceedings. The mother wanted the applicant to return to Ghana but she refused to go, and an application for a review of the s 37 assessment was made. The mother then declared that she was the applicant's sister rather than her mother and that the applicant was over 20 years old. An age assessment concluded that the applicant was between 20 and 22 years old and the authority decided that it had no duty to the applicant as a child in terms of accommodation or support and her foster placement was terminated. The authority sought a declaration that the applicant was not a child because, if she were, she would be a 'relevant child' for the purposes of access to resources and support. *Held*, where the question of the age of a putative child became an issue in wardship proceedings, the court should not decline to deal with it simply because a authority had conducted an earlier assessment on the basis of more limited evidence and for a more limited statutory purpose. The court differed from the age assessment of the authority and concluded that the applicant was 17 years old. The evidence she gave as to her age was credible and convincing. There was no reason to doubt that the date on her birth certificate was other than true and there was nothing in the school report to suggest that the applicant was not an age-appropriate member of her year group. Therefore, the wardship would not be discharged until the applicant's eighteenth birthday and the court would retain oversight of her welfare for the remainder of her minority. Judgment would be given accordingly.

E v London Borough of X [2005] EWHC 2811 (Fam), [2006] 1 FLR 730 (Family Division: Sir Mark Potter P).

CHOSES IN ACTION

Halsbury's Laws of England (4th edn) vol 6 (2003 Reissue) paras 1–100

494   Assignment—debts of assignor's customers—security for loan

See *MBNA Europe Bank Ltd v Revenue and Customs Comrs*, para 2923.

495   Assignment—express assignment—benefit of covenant

See *Sugarman v Porter*, para 1285.

496   Assignment—lease—indemnity covenant for payment of rent

See *Scottish & Newcastle v Raguz*, para 1750.

497   Assignment—personal contract—conditional fee agreement

See *Jenkins v Young Brothers Transport Ltd*, para 689.

CIVIL PARTNERSHIP

Halsbury's Laws of England (4th edn) vol 6 (Supp) paras 100A–100Q

Articles

For articles relating to this title please refer to the Table of Articles at the beginning of the Abridgment.

498   Ancillary relief—financial provision—division of assets—property—adults lacking in capacity

See para 1886.

499   Civil Partnership Act 2004—commencement

The Civil Partnership Act 2004 (Commencement No 3) Order 2006, SI 2006/639 brings Sch 5 Pt 7 (paras 30–37) and Sch 7 para 10(4)(b), (5)(b), (9)(c) into force on 6 April 2006.

500   Police—pensions—civil partnership

See para 2259.

501   Relationships arising through civil partnership—statutory references

The Civil Partnership Act 2004 (Relationships Arising Through Civil Partnership) Order 2006, SI 2006/1121 (in force on 11 May 2006), applies the Civil Partnership Act 2004 s 246 to the Social Security (Categorisation of Earners) Regulations 1978, SI 1978/1689, Sch 1 Pt III para 7.

502   Same-sex partners—form of marriage recognised abroad—validity of partnership in England

See *Wilkinson v Kitzinger*, para 705.

CLUBS

Halsbury's Laws of England (4th edn) vol 6 (2003 Reissue) paras 101–400

Articles

For articles relating to this title please refer to the Table of Articles at the beginning of the Abridgment.

503   Gaming licence—application—notice—invitation to make objections—relevant date

The claimant applied to the defendant for casino licences. Pursuant to the Gaming Act 1968 Sch 2 para 6, an applicant had to publish notice of its application. The notice was required to state that any persons wishing to object were required to do so before a date specified in the notice, and such a date had to be not be earlier than 14 days after the publication of the notice. The claimant's notice was published in a local newspaper on 26 January 2006, and stated that any person who wished to object to its application should do so by 9 February 2006. At a subsequent directions hearing, the interested party and another contended that the date specified by the claimant in its notice should have been no earlier than 10 February 2006. On that basis, they argued that the defect in the claimant's notice rendered the proceedings a nullity with the result that the defendant had no jurisdiction to hear the claimant's application. The defendant agreed with those submissions and declined to hear the claimant's application. The claimant sought permission to apply for judicial review in order to challenge the defendant's decision. *Held*, the general rule in relation to the computation of time in which an act might be done was that the day of service was not included, but the later date of the later event was included. However, when a period was fixed before the expiration of which an act might not be done, the person for whose benefit the delay was prescribed had the benefit of the entire period, and therefore the day from which it ran as well as the day on which it expired should be excluded. Following that rule, the date specified in the claimant's notice fell within the statutory provisions, as it was not 'earlier than' 14 days after the date of publication of the notice, but was 14 days 'after' such publication. The defendant was in error in declaring the proceedings a nullity or in finding that it had no jurisdiction in the matter. Accordingly, the application would be allowed.

R (on the application of TC Projects Ltd) v Gaming Licensing Committee [2006] All ER (D) 241 (Apr) (Queen's Bench Division: Gibbs J). *R v Long* [1959] 3 All ER 559, CA, considered.

504 Licence—licensing authority—policy statement

See para 292.

COMMONHOLD

Halsbury's Laws of England (4th edn) vol 7(1) (2004 Reissue) paras 1–200

Articles

For articles relating to this title please refer to the Table of Articles at the beginning of the Abridgment.

COMMONS

Halsbury's Laws of England (4th edn) vol 6 (2003 Reissue) paras 401–700

Articles

For articles relating to this title please refer to the Table of Articles at the beginning of the Abridgment.

505 Common land—registration—town or village green

In the Commons Registration Act 1965 'town or village green' means land which has been allotted by or under any Act for the exercise or recreation of the inhabitants of any locality or on which the inhabitants of any locality have a customary right to indulge in lawful sports and pastimes or which falls within s 22(1A): s 22(1). Land falls within s 22(1A) if it is land on which for not less than 20 years a significant number of the inhabitants of any locality, or of any neighbourhood within a locality, have indulged in lawful sports and pastimes as of right, and either continue to do so, or have ceased to do so for not more than such period as may be prescribed, or determined in accordance with prescribed provisions: s 22(1A).

On an application to register certain land as a town or village green under the 1965 Act s 13, issues arose as to whether (1) the relevant inhabitants had rights to indulge in lawful sports and pastimes on land which had become a green as defined in s 22(1A); (2) land which had become a green as so defined fell within the scope of the Inclosure Act 1857 s 12 and the Commons Act 1876 s 29; (3) the words 'continue to do so' in the definition of a green meant that the lawful sports and pastimes had to continue up to the date of the application to register or the date of registration or some other date; (4) all applications for registration of land made on or after 30 January 2001 automatically engaged the 1965 Act s 22(1A) definition; (5) an application was bound to fail if it specified a date earlier than that immediately preceding the date of the application; (6) the registration authority had power to treat the application as if a different date, namely that immediately preceding the date of the application, had been specified, and to determine the application on that basis; and (7) as a matter of law, it was open to the registration authority to permit the application to be amended so as to refer to some lesser area or, without such an amendment, to register as a green only part of the land included in the application. *Held*, the amended s 22, with the addition of the words 'and ... continue to do so' meant until the date of the application to register. As the register was conclusive, land did not become a village green until it was registered. The mere fact that it would at some earlier time have come within the statutory definition was irrelevant if it was not registered as such. The rational construction of s 10 was that land registered as a town or village green could be used generally for sports and pastimes. It did not interfere with property rights, as the primary purpose of the 1965 Act, as applied to town and village greens, was not to create new rights which override those of the owner, it was to create a register of town and village greens which would include all land over which statutory or customary rights of recreation existed or probably existed. The effect of s 10 was to apply the Inclosure Act 1857 s 12 and the Commons Act 1876 s 29 to land registered as a town or village green. There was no special definition of a town and village green in the 1857 or 1876 Acts that might suggest that when the 1965 Act s 10 said that registration was to be conclusive evidence of the matters registered, and the matter registered was that the land was a village green, Parliament did not intend that it should be a village green for the purposes of the 1857 and 1876 Acts. Neither Act was intended to prevent the owner from using the land consistently with the rights of the inhabitants. That construction would not infringe any of a landowner's right to property as guaranteed by the European Convention on Human Rights. Finally, the registration authority had power to allow amendments to the application form and to register an area of land different from that originally claimed and should be guided by the general principle of being fair to the parties. It also was entitled, without any amendment of the application, to register only that part of the subject premises which the applicant had proved to have been used for the necessary period. There was no rule that the lesser area had to be substantially the same or bear any particular relationship to the area originally claimed.

Oxfordshire CC v Oxford City Council [2006] UKHL 25, [2006] 2 AC 674 (House of Lords: Lords Hoffmann, Scott of Foscote, Rodger of Earlsferry and Walker of Gestingthorpe and Baroness Hale of Richmond). Decision of Court of Appeal [2005] EWCA Civ 175, [2006] Ch 43 (2005 Abr para 576) reversed in part.

506   Common land—severance of rights—England

The Commons (Severance of Rights) (England) Order 2006, SI 2006/2145 (in force on 9 September 2006), which applies in relation to England only, provides that a right of common to graze animals, to which the Commons Act 2006 s 9(1) applies, may be temporarily severed from the land to which the right is attached by the leasing or licensing of the right to a third party for no more than two years, or by a lease or licence of the land without the right of common.

507   Commons Act 2006

The Commons Act 2006 makes provision about common land and town or village greens. The Act received the royal assent on 19 July 2006 and came into force in part on that day. Further provisions came into force on 19 September and 1 October 2006: SI 2006/2504. The remaining provisions come into force on a day or days to be appointed. For details of commencement, see the commencement table in the title STATUTES.

Part 1 (ss 1–25) Registration
Section 1 requires commons registration authorities to continue to keep commons registers. The purpose of the register of common land is explained by s 2. Section 3 provides that the land registered under s 2 is to be the same land as was registered as common land under the Commons Registration Act 1965. By virtue of the 2006 Act s 4, the continued appointment of certain local authorities as commons registration authorities is provided for. Section 5 provides that Pt 1 applies to all land in England and Wales, subject to specific exceptions. Section 6 makes it impossible, apart from by statute, to create a new right other than by express grant and then only if the newly created right is attached to land. Under s 7, a right of common is to be regarded as varied if it is altered as specified. Regulations may be made regarding the amendment of the commons registers where rights of common are to be apportioned: s 8. Section 9 effects a prohibition on the severance of rights of common, subject to the exceptions specified in Sch 1 or under any other Act. By virtue of s 10, rights of common held in gross may be attached to land. Section 11 enables a right of common attached to a dominant tenement to be concentrated on part of the dominant tenement where another part is to be developed for non-agricultural use. By virtue of s 12, the transfer of any right of common held in gross is required to comply with such requirements as to form and content as regulations may provide. Section 13 requires the surrender of any right of common to be effected in a prescribed form, and delays the effect of the surrender until the right has been deleted from the commons registers. The appropriate national authority may make regulations to provide for amendment of the commons registers consequent on a disposition arising under statute: s 14. Section 15 sets out the circumstances in which land may be newly registered as a town or village green. Provision is made for the owner of any land registered as common land or as a town or village green to apply to the appropriate national authority for the land to cease to be so registered: s 16. By virtue of s 17, where the appropriate national authority grants an application under s 16 it must make an order requiring the commons registration authority to remove the release land from its register of common land or town or village greens. Where land is registered as subject to a right, it is deemed to have become subject to the right on its registration if it would not otherwise have been so subject: s 18. By virtue of s 19, commons registration authorities may correct certain errors in the commons registers. Section 20 provides for a right of public access to the commons registers, and to records held in connection with applications for registration under Pt 1 or under the 1965 Act. Provision is made by the 2006 Act s 21 for the admissibility in evidence, and the issue, of official copies. Section 22 introduces Sch 2 which makes provision for the rectification of mistakes and other matters in the commons registers prepared under the 1965 Act. The 2006 Act s 23 enables the appropriate national authority to make transitional provisions and savings in connection with the coming into force of Pt 1, and introduces Sch 3. The appropriate national authority may make

regulations regarding the making and determination of applications for the amendment of the registers under Pt 1: s 24. By virtue of s 25, the appropriate national authority may make regulations permitting or requiring commons registration authorities to maintain commons registers in an electronic form.

Part 2 (ss 26–37) Management
Section 26 provides a power for the appropriate national authority, by order, to establish commons councils in relation to land registered as common land. The procedural requirements to be followed by the appropriate national authority when seeking to establish a commons council are set out: s 27. Under s 28, provision is made about the status of commons councils. Section 29 requires the appropriate national authority to prescribe by regulations standard terms for use in the constitution of a commons council. By virtue of s 30, an illustrative list of matters which may appear in either the standard constitution or the order under s 26 establishing the council is provided. Section 31 sets out the functions which may be conferred on a commons council in an order made under s 26. A commons council is given ancillary powers to enable it to carry out its functions: s 32. Section 33 makes it clear that where the consent of a person with an interest in the land is required for the commons council to do anything on the land for which it is established, nothing in Pt 2 authorises a commons council to do anything on the land without that consent. Section 34 sets out the consequences of not complying with rules made by a commons council. Further provision is made in relation to the making of rules by a commons council: s 35. Section 36 makes consequential provision for when the functions given to a council might overlap with those of some other body. The procedure to be followed where the appropriate national authority wishes to wind up a commons council because it is no longer operating effectively is described by s 37.

Part 3 (ss 38–44) Works
Section 38 prohibits the carrying out of restricted works without the consent of the appropriate national authority on registered common land and on certain other land. Under s 39, the criteria that the appropriate national authority must take into account when determining an application for consent for works are set out. Section 40 enables regulations to be made setting out the procedures for making and determining applications under ss 38, 39(5). Contravention of the controls on works in s 38 leaves the works open to civil enforcement action, as set out in s 41, but not to criminal prosecution. Section 42 clarifies the situation in relation to commons which are subject to schemes of regulation and management under the Commons Act 1899 or the Metropolitan Commons Act 1866. The 2006 Act s 43 gives the appropriate national authority the power to make an order exempting certain works from the controls in s 38. Section 44 enables the appropriate national authority to amend, by order, local or personal Acts enacted before the 2006 Act, in order to ensure that any provision in those Acts about consent for works, or about enforcement against unlawful works on registered common land is consistent with provision in Pt 3, and also introduces Sch 4 which contains supplementary provisions about works on common land.

Part 4 (ss 45–51) Miscellaneous
Section 45 confers powers on a local authority to protect land registered as common land or a town or village green where the land has no owner recorded in the register of title at the Land Registry, and the local authority cannot identify the owner of the land. By virtue of s 46, the appropriate national authority may stop unauthorised agricultural activities on registered common land or certain greens, which are detrimental to the interest of persons with rights over the land or those who own or occupy the land, or to the public interest. Section 47 repeals the Commons Act 1285 which conferred statutory powers on landowners to inclose land surplus to the needs of commoners, the 2006 Act s 48 repeals various powers to inclose land and s 49 repeals the Commons Act 1876 s 31 and amends the Metropolitan Commons Act 1878 s 3 which require notice to be advertised of the approvement or inclosure of common land subject to rights of common. The 2006 Act s 50 updates and broadens the purpose for which a scheme for the regulation and management of a common may be made. Section 51 repeals the Countryside and Rights of Way Act 2000 s 68.

Part 5 (ss 52–63) Supplementary and general
The 2006 Act s 52 gives effect to the minor and consequential amendments set out in Sch 5, and s 53 gives effect to the repeals set out in Sch 6. By virtue of s 54, the appropriate national authority may amend, by order, public Acts for the purposes of modifying their application to common land or town or village greens. Section 55 confers a power to amend local or personal Acts, and provisional order confirmation Acts, where they confer functions on the national authority in relation to common land, or require consultation of, or the consent of, the national authority in relation to common land, or require consultation of, or the consent of, the national authority in respect of activities relating to common land. Section 56 provides for commencement, and s 57 makes transitional provision. Under s 58, any reference to Natural England is to be read as a reference to English Nature. Section 59 provides that an order or regulations under the Act may make transitional, consequential, incidental and supplemental provision or savings. By virtue of s 60, the Act binds the Crown. Section 61 deals with interpretation, s 62 with short title and s 63 with extent.

Amendments, repeals and revocations
The list below, which is not exhaustive, mentions repeals and amendments which are or will be effective when the Act is fully in force.

Specific provisions of a number of Acts are amended, added or repealed. These include: Commons Act 1285; Inclosure Act 1845 s 147; Gifts for Churches Act 1811 s 2; School Sites Act 1841 s 2; Literary and Scientific Institutions Act 1854 s 1; Commons Act 1876 s 31; Metropolitan Commons Act 1878 s 3; Commons Act 1899 ss 1, 1A, 2, 9, 10; Countryside and Rights of Way Act 2000 s 68.

COMMONWEALTH

Halsbury's Laws of England (4th edn) vol 6 (2003 Reissue) paras 701–882

Articles

For articles relating to this title please refer to the Table of Articles at the beginning of the Abridgment.

508   Bahamas—restraint order—non-appearance of applicant—re-instatement of proceedings

See *Gaydamak v UBS Bahamas Ltd*, para 816.

509   British Indian Ocean Territory—order for exclusion of indigenous population—validity

The Chagos islanders, one of whom was the claimant, were exiled from the British Indian Ocean Territory by virtue of the British Indian Ocean Territory (Constitution) Order 2004 and the Immigration Order 2004 in order to ensure and maintain the availability and effective use of the territory for the defence purposes of the governments of the United Kingdom and the United States of America. While the source of the power to make the Constitution Order was the royal prerogative, the order was in reality an act of the executive by the defendant Secretary of State, although the Queen formally assented to it. An earlier decision had found that the islanders had been unlawfully expelled from the territory by a 1971 Ordinance made in similar terms to the Constitution Order. The claimant sought judicial review of the order, on the ground that it was irrational for the defendant to have made it, and a declaration that its provisions were unlawful. The defendant submitted that it should be judged by reference to the interests of the United Kingdom and that, by virtue of the common law and the Colonial Laws Validity Act 1865, the order was not justiciable and was, therefore, immune from judicial review. *Held*, irrationality had to be judged by reference to the interests of the territory which were, primarily, those of the people whose rights of abode and unrestricted right to enter and remain were being in effect removed; something that the Constitution Order had conspicuously failed to do. While the order was made by the Queen in right of the government of the territory, it was, on its face, not concerned with the interests of the territory, but with the interests of the United Kingdom and the United States of America. In the circumstances, the exclusion of the islanders from the territory by the order was irrational as a matter of public law and was, therefore, unlawful. The challenge to the order by way of judicial review had involved matters on which the court could adjudicate, the interests of the territory, and therefore the order was amenable to judicial review. Moreover, the 1865 Act had not precluded the public law rationality challenge and, as the act in question was the act of the executive, it was amenable to judicial review. The order could be challenged by way of judicial review. Accordingly, the application would be allowed and the order quashed.

R (on the application of Bancoult) v Secretary of State for Foreign and Commonwealth Affairs [2006] EWHC 1038 (Admin), [2006] All ER (D) 149 (May) (Queen's Bench Division: Hooper LJ and Cresswell J). *Council of Civil Service Unions v Minister for the Civil Service* [1985] AC 374, HL (1984 Abr para 2789); *R (on the application of Quark Fishing Ltd) v Secretary of State for Foreign and Commonwealth Affairs* [2005] UKHL 57, [2005] 3 WLR 837 (2005 Abr para 1686); and *R (on the application of Bancoult) v Secretary of State for Foreign and Commonwealth Affairs* [2001] 2 WLR 1219, DC (2000 Abr para 521), considered.

510   British Virgin Islands—criminal law—theft

See *Wheatley v Comr of Police of the British Virgin Islands*, para 903.

511   Cayman Islands—criminal proceedings—right to fair trial

See *Ebanks v R*, para 788.

512   Cayman Islands—insolvency—liquidator's remuneration—court ruling—jurisdiction of Attorney General to intervene

Cayman Islands
Joint official liquidators applied to the Grand Court of the Cayman Islands for orders providing for their remuneration by the four companies of which they had been appointed official liquidators

pursuant to an order of the court. The Grand Court gave various directions regarding the fees, including for the fees to be submitted to creditors' committees and for the agreed fees to be submitted thereafter to the Grand Court for approval. The liquidators appealed to the Court of Appeal of the Cayman Islands against that ruling, arguing that the procedure for fixing the remuneration of Cayman Island liquidators was governed by English insolvency law and that no recourse to the court was required and no requirement existed for a liquidator to apply to the court to sanction fees approved by a liquidation committee. The appeal was allowed, and the Attorney General sought the Court of Appeal's leave to intervene and to appeal to the Privy Council. A preliminary issue arose concerning the Attorney General's standing to bring the appeal. The Attorney General contended that the appeal raised a general issue of public importance relating to the remuneration of court-appointed liquidators, and that he could bring the appeal in his quasi-judicial role as the guardian of the public interest in order to correct a fundamental error of law. *Held*, the Attorney General had standing to intervene where he had a sufficient interest in his capacity as guardian of the public interest. As a matter of principle and in the light of case authority, one set of circumstances in which it might be appropriate to grant the Attorney General, as guardian of the public interest, leave to intervene was where there was an issue of general public importance going to the jurisdiction of lower courts and their consequent ability to do justice according to the law. The Court of Appeal's decision in the present case satisfied that test. It had erred in its understanding of the role of the Grand Cayman Court under the existing statutory scheme and there was an important public interest in establishing the correct position for the future. It followed that the Attorney General had sufficient standing to apply to intervene and appeal. Judgment would be given accordingly.

A-G of the Cayman Islands v James Cleaver & Co [2006] UKPC 28, [2006] 1 WLR 2245 (Privy Council: Lords Bingham of Cornhill, Clyde, Hope of Craighead, Carswell and Mance).

513   Mauritius—trial—delay—validity of proceedings

See *Boolell v The State*, para 829.

514   New Zealand—child abduction and custody—Hague Convention

See *Secretary for Justice v P (Habitual Residence)*, para 426.

515   Pitcairn—criminal proceedings—validity of incorporated legislation

Pitcairn

The Pitcairn Order 1970, SI 1970/1434, provides for a governor to make laws for Pitcairn and requires all such laws to be published in such manner and at such place or places in Pitcairn as the governor may from time to time direct. The Judicature Ordinance 1970, made under the 1970 Order, provides for common law, equity and statutes of general application in force in England to be in force in Pitcairn, but so far only as the local circumstances and the limits of local jurisdiction permit.

The appellants, who were inhabitants of Pitcairn, were convicted of rape and sexual assault under the Sexual Offences Act 1956. They submitted, on appeal to the Privy Council, that the language of the 1970 Ordinance was too imprecise to incorporate the 1956 Act as part of the law of Pitcairn, that the 1956 Act could not apply because it had not been published in accordance with the 1970 Order, and that the prosecution was an abuse of process because of the failure to publish the 1956 Act. *Held*, there could be no doubt that the 1956 Act was a statute of general application, and that there were no local circumstances which made it inappropriate to apply the provisions about rape, indecent assault and incest. Although the 1956 Act had not been published in Pitcairn under the 1970 Order, it would be unrealistic to interpret the order as applying not only to laws made by the governor but also to laws incorporated by an ordinance made by the governor. The 1970 Ordinance incorporated not only statutes but also common law and the rules of equity, which did not lend themselves easily to publication. While the fact that a law had not been published and could not reasonably have been known to exist might be a ground for staying a prosecution for contravention of that law as an abuse of process, the Privy Council would not interfere with the way in which the lower courts had exercised their discretion on the matter. The offences were serious, and the balance between the public interest in ensuring that those who were charged with grave crimes should be tried, and the competing public interest in not conveying an impression that the end justified the means, came down firmly in favour of bringing the appellants before a court of justice. Accordingly, the appeals would be dismissed.

Christian v R [2006] UKPC 47, [2006] All ER (D) 358 (Oct) (Privy Council: Lords Hoffmann, Woolf, Steyn, Hope of Craighead and Carswell).

516   Restrictive measures

See FOREIGN RELATIONS LAW.

517   Trinidad and Tobago—constitution—human rights—due process of law—appeal against acquittal

Trinidad and Tobago

In a fight outside a night club, the defendant struck the victim on the head. The victim fell to the ground and was taken unconscious to hospital where he underwent emergency surgery, before developing aspiration pneumonia and being put on a ventilator. He remained in a coma and later died. The defendant was charged with manslaughter. At trial, medical evidence was submitted to show that certain incidents which had taken place at the hospital, rather than the blow to the victim's head, had been the cause of death. A pathologist called by the prosecution gave evidence that the victim had died as a result of complications arising from the head injury he had sustained. However, the judge decided that the pathologist was not qualified as an expert for the purpose of giving an opinion on the cause of death and that his evidence was inadmissible. He also ruled that other medical evidence advanced by the prosecution did not provide a sufficient basis for a finding that the defendant had caused the victim's death and directed that the defendant be acquitted. The prosecution appealed against the decision, pursuant to a statutory provision, which allowed it to appeal against a verdict of acquittal resulting from a decision of the trial judge. The defendant challenged the court's jurisdiction in relation to the provision, arguing that it was inconsistent with the fundamental human right not to be deprived of liberty except by due process of law, as declared by the Constitution of Trinidad and Tobago. The appeal court accepted the defendant's submission, but dismissed the appeal on other grounds. On appeal by the prosecution, *held*, the concept of 'due process' incorporated observance of all the mandatory requirements of criminal procedure, but 'due process of law' also had a narrower constitutional meaning, namely those fundamental principles which were necessary for a fair system of justice. However, there was nothing fundamentally unfair or unjust about a statutory rule which enabled an appellate court to correct an error of law by which an accused person had been wrongly acquitted and order that the question of his guilt or innocence be properly determined according to law. It followed that the appeal court had been wrong to rule that the statutory provision was unconstitutional. Judgment would be given accordingly.

State of Trinidad and Tobago v Boyce [2006] UKPC 1, [2006] 2 AC 76 (Privy Council: Lords Bingham of Cornhill, Hoffmann, Hutton, Scott of Foscote and Brown of Eaton-under-Heywood).

518   Trinidad and Tobago—conviction—insufficient grounds—fairness

See *State of Trinidad and Tobago v Boyce1*, para 517.

519   Trinidad and Tobago—criminal procedure—order of closing speeches—fairness

Trinidad and Tobago

It has been held that, in jurisdictions where the prosecutor's closing speech follows the closing speech of all defence counsel, it is particularly important that the tone and content of the prosecutor's speech conform to the standards expected in a criminal trial. If the judge does not make a specific caveat regarding any improper aspect of a prosecutor's closing speech, such as where the prosecutor expresses views that he is not entitled to express, there may be a material irregularity rendering the conviction unsafe notwithstanding that the summing up is fair.

Ramdhanie v State of Trinidad and Tobago [2005] UKPC 47, [2006] 1 WLR 796 (Privy Council: Lords Hoffmann, Rodger of Earlsferry, Walker of Gestingthorpe, Brown of Eaton-under-Heywood and Mance).

520   Turks and Caicos Islands—Constitution

The Turks and Caicos Islands Constitution Order 2006, SI 2006/1913 (in force on a date to be notified in the Gazette), establishes a new Constitution of the Turks and Caicos Islands. The new Constitution sets out a modernised chapter on fundamental rights and freedoms of the individual. It provides for a Governor as Her Majesty's representative in the Islands. It provides for a House of Assembly composed of elected and appointed members, and for a cabinet and ministers appointed from among the members of the House. It also provides for the judiciary, the public service and a Complaints Commissioner for the Islands. The 1988 Order, SI 1988/247, to which the current Constitution is scheduled, is revoked.

COMPANIES

Halsbury's Laws of England (4th edn) vol 7(1) (2004 Reissue) paras 201–1000, vol 7(2) (2004 Reissue) paras 1001–2008

Articles

For articles relating to this title please refer to the Table of Articles at the beginning of the Abridgment.

521 Charge—floating charge—enforcement by debenture holder—taking possession—preferential debts

The Companies Act 1985 s 196(2) provides that if possession is taken by or on behalf of the holders of any of the debentures of any property comprised in or subject to a floating charge, and the company is not at that time in the course of being wound up, the company's preferential debts must be paid out of assets coming to the hands of the person taking possession in priority to any claims in respect of the debentures.

A company granted a debenture to the defendant bank, which created fixed and floating charges over the company's business. The company experienced financial problems and sold certain of its business and assets to two subsidiaries specially formed for the purpose. The subsidiaries were then sold to a third party. Under a contractual arrangement between the company and the defendant, money received from the sale was used to repay debt due to the defendant and, on receipt of the money, the defendant released the assets transferred to the subsidiaries from the charges created by its debenture. The company's board then decided that the company should cease trading because it was insolvent, and the shareholders resolved that the company should be wound up. The Commissioners for Her Majesty's Revenue and Customs commenced proceedings, arguing that, in the circumstances, the effect of the 1985 Act s 196 was that the preferential creditors fell to be paid out of the money received from the sale of the assets of the company in preference to the defendant. The latter contended that the Commissioners' claim had no real prospect of success and sought summary judgment. *Held*, it would be wrong to suppose that s 196 had the consequence that every payment to a debenture holder whose rights were secured by a floating charge carried with it an obligation on the part of that debenture holder to apply all sums received to pay preferential creditors. Some line had to be drawn between acts which were, in substance, acts by which the charge holder realised the security and acts which were no more than the ordinary discharge of the debtor's liability. If s 196 was to be effective, attention had to be paid to the substance of what was done and not merely to its form. Where, for example, the debenture holder was positively and actively involved in a transaction where payment was made to it of money which was subject to its floating charge, then this might amount to 'taking possession'. No release of its floating charge would be necessary. The company could dispose of its assets in the ordinary course of its business and then pay the debenture holder out of the proceeds. However, if the debenture holder agreed to release its charge over certain assets in anticipation that, on the sale by the company of those assets, the floating charge would crystallise, and the debenture holder and the company came to an arrangement where particular money which was subject to the floating charge would be earmarked to repay debt owed to the debenture holder, then it could be said to be taking possession of that money. Such an arrangement would put the parties in the same position as if a receiver had been appointed and had taken possession of those assets. This was the nature of the arrangement between the company and the defendant. It followed that the transaction was caught by s 196(2), with the consequence that the preferential creditors had priority over the sums paid to the defendant. Judgment would be given accordingly.

Re Oval 1742 Ltd (in creditors voluntary liquidation) v Royal Bank of Scotland [2006] All ER (D) 57 (Nov) (Chancery Division: Susan Prevezer QC). *IRC v Goldblatt* [1972] Ch 498 considered.

522 Charge—registration—certificate—conclusiveness—certificate issued contrary to implied direction of the court

The claimant creditor sought an order, under the Companies Act 1985 s 404, for an extension of time for the registration of a charge which he claimed the defendant company had granted him to secure a loan. An order was made granting the extension of time but which provided that the defendant, its administrators or any unsecured creditor should have permission to apply within 14 days to set it aside. The registrar of companies then issued a certificate of registration which, by virtue of s 401(2), was conclusive evidence that the requirements as to registration had been satisfied. The second defendant applied for the order granting the extension of time to be set aside. *Held*, s 404(2) empowered the court to impose terms and conditions on an extension of time for registration. Where a court granted an extension of time for registration and gave other interested parties permission to apply to have the order set aside, by implication it also directed the registrar not to issue a certificate of registration until either the time for a party to apply for review had expired, or the court had confirmed the extension. The registrar had therefore breached that implied direction. However, the circumstances in which the certificate was issued did not affect its conclusiveness, and so there would be no point in setting aside the order for the extension of time. Accordingly, the application would be dismissed.

Ali v Top Marques Car Rental Ltd [2006] EWHC 109 (Ch), (2006) Times, 10 February (Chancery Division: Michael Furness QC).

523 Community requirements—right of establishment—cross-border merger—no provision in domestic legislation

The applicant German company had a merger contract with a Luxembourg company which provided for merger by way of the absorption of the Luxembourg company and its dissolution without liquidation. The applicant applied for the registration of the merger to the German authorities but was refused on the ground that domestic legislation only provided for mergers between legal entities established in Germany. The domestic company brought proceedings against the decision, and the court referred the question to the European Court of Justice whether it was contrary to the freedom of establishment for companies under the EC Treaty arts 43 and 48 to refuse the registration of a proposed merger of a company registered in another member state and a German company on the ground that German legislation only provided for the transformation of legal entities established in Germany. *Held*, arts 43 and 48 excluded the refusal in general of registration in the national commercial register of the merger by dissolution without liquidation of one company and transfer of the whole of its assets to another company by a member state where one of the companies was established in another member state, where such registration would be possible in the case of two companies established in the first member state. Cross-border merger operations responded to the need for co-operation and consolidation between companies established in different member states. They constituted particular methods of the exercise of the freedom of establishment, important for the proper functioning of the internal market and were therefore among the economic activities which member states were required to comply with by the freedom of establishment laid down by art 43. By establishing a difference in treatment between companies according to the internal or cross-border nature of a merger, German domestic legislation was likely to deter the exercise of the freedom of establishment. The different treatment constituted a restriction of the freedom of establishment within the meaning of arts 43 and 48. While it was not possible to exclude the possibility that imperative reasons in the public interest could, in certain circumstances, justify a measure restricting the freedom of establishment, such a measure would have to be appropriate for ensuring the attainment of the objective pursued and not go beyond what was necessary to attain them. The refusal to generally register a merger between a company established in a member state and a company in another member state had the effect of preventing the realisation of cross-border mergers, even if imperative reasons in the public interest were not threatened, and the domestic legislation went beyond what was necessary to protect those interests.

Case C-411/03 *Re SEVIC Systems AG* [2006] 2 BCLC 510 (ECJ: Grand Chamber).

524 Companies Act 2006

The Companies Act 2006 reforms company law and restates the greater part of the enactments relating to companies, makes other provision relating to companies and other forms of business organisation, makes provision about directors' disqualification, business names, auditors and actuaries and amends the Enterprise Act 2002 Pt 9 (ss 237–247). The Act received the royal assent on 8 November 2006 and came into force in part on that day. Further provisions came into force on and between 1 January 2007 and 6 April 2007: SI 2006/3428. The remaining provisions come into force on a day or days to be appointed. For details of commencement, see the commencement table in the title STATUTES.

Part 1 (ss 1–6) General introductory provisions
Sections 1–6 deal with interpretation, and consolidate provision made by the Companies Act 1985 ss 1 and 15.

Part 2 (ss 7–16) Company formation
Sections 7–16 consolidate provision made by the Companies Act 1985 ss 2, 3, 10, 12 and 13. A memorandum of association is now simply a memorandum stating that the subscribers wish to form a company under the 2006 Act, agree to become members of the company and, in the case of a company that is to have a share capital, to take at least one share each: s 8. Section 10 sets out the requirements of the statement of capital and initial shareholdings that must be delivered in the case of a company that is to have a share capital. Under s 12, where an application is made for registration, a service address must be provided for each director who is a natural person, and there is no requirement for a private company to have a company secretary. Section 13 provides that a paper application for registration of a company must now be accompanied by a statement of compliance.

Part 3 (ss 17–38) A company's constitution

Chapter 1 (s 17) Introductory
Section 17 defines 'a company's constitution'.

Chapter 2 (ss 18–28) Articles of association
Sections 18–28 consolidate provision made by the Companies Act 1985 ss 7–9, 16 and 18. By virtue of the 2006 Act ss 18, 19, some types of company that are required to register articles with the relevant registrar of companies may rely on the relevant model articles for that description of company instead of registering. Section 22 permits companies to provide in their articles that specified provisions may be amended or repealed only if conditions are met that are more restrictive than would apply in the case of a special resolution. A company must give notice to the registrar when an entrenching provision is included in its articles (s 23), or when it amends its articles where it has made provision for entrenchment or there are other restrictions on the power to amend (s 24). Section 27 gives the registrar greater powers to ensure that a company complies with its duty to send the registrar a copy of amended articles.

Chapter 3 (ss 29, 30) Resolutions and agreements affecting a company's constitution
Sections 29, 30 consolidate provision made by the Companies Act 1985 s 380.

Chapter 4 (ss 31–38) Miscellaneous and supplementary provisions
Sections 31–38 consolidate provision made by the Companies Act 1985 ss 14, 15, 18, 19 and 380. By virtue of the 2006 Act s 31, companies have unrestricted objects unless the objects are specifically restricted by the articles. A mechanism for registering alterations which are made to a company's constitution by an order of the court or other authority is created by s 25.

Part 4 (ss 39–52) A company's capacity and related matters
Sections 39–52 consolidate provision made by the Companies Act 1985 ss 35–40, 322A and 350 and the Charities Act 1993 s 65.

Part 5 (ss 53–85) A company's name

Chapter 1 (ss 53–57) General requirements
Sections 53–56 consolidate provision made by the Companies Act 1985 ss 26 and 29. Under the 2006 Act s 57, regulations may be made specifying the letters and symbols that may be used in a company's registered name, and the form the name may take.

Chapter 2 (ss 58–65) Indications of company type or legal form
Sections 58–65 consolidate provision made by the Companies Act 1985 ss 25–27, 30 and 31.

Chapter 3 (ss 66–74) Similarity to other names
Sections 66–68 consolidate provision made by the Companies Act 1985 ss 26 and 28. Under the 2006 Act s 69, any person may object to a company names adjudicator if a company's name is similar to a name in which the objector has goodwill. The Secretary of State may appoint company names adjudicators and their staff and finance their activities (s 70), and is entitled to make rules for the proceedings before a company names adjudicator (s 71). Section 72 requires the adjudicator to publish his decisions and his reasons for them. If an objection made under s 69 is upheld, then, by virtue of s 73, the adjudicator is to direct the company with the offending name to change its name to one that does not similarly offend. An appeals system is established by s 74.

Chapter 4 (ss 75, 76) Other powers of the Secretary of State
Sections 75 and 76 consolidate provision made by the Companies Act 1985 ss 28 and 32.

Chapter 5 (ss 77–81) Change of name
Sections 77, 80 and 81 consolidate provision made by the Companies Act 1985 ss 28 and 32. The 2006 Act s 78 requires a company to notify the registrar of a change of name when it has been agreed by special resolution. Under s 79, a company must provide the registrar with both a notice of the name change and a statement that the change has been made in accordance with the company's articles.

Chapter 6 (ss 82–85) Trading disclosures
Sections 82–84 consolidate provision made by the Companies Act 1985 ss 348, 349 and 351 and the Business Names Act 1985 ss 4, 5 and 7. Under the 2006 Act s 85, a company's name as used to comply with the disclosure requirements need not be exactly the same as the registered name.

Part 6 (ss 86–88) A company's registered office
Sections 86–88 consolidate provision made by the Companies Act 1985 ss 2 and 287.

Part 7 (ss 89–111) Re-registration as a means of altering a company's status
Sections 89–111 consolidate provision made by the Companies Act 1985 ss 43–55. By virtue of the 2006 Act s 95, where a private company is proposing to re-register as a public company and the company does not already have a company secretary, the application for re-registration must include details of the person or persons who will act as company secretary or joint secretaries on re-registration. Where a company which has re-registered from unlimited having a share capital to private limited by shares, it must in certain circumstances file a statement of capital with the registrar: s 108. Section 109 enables a public company to re-register as a private unlimited company with a share capital without first having to re-register as a private limited company. The contents of the application for re-registration where a company is proposing to re-register from public to unlimited private and the information that must accompany the application are prescribed by s 110. Under s 111, the registrar must issue a new certificate of incorporation if he is satisfied that a public company is entitled to register as private and unlimited.

Part 8 (ss 112–144) A company's members

Chapter 1 (s 112) The members of a company
Section 112 replaces the Companies Act 1985 s 22.

Chapter 2 (ss 113–128) Register of members
Sections 113–128 consolidate provision made by the Companies Act 1985 ss 352–356, 359–361. The 2006 Act s 117 sets out a procedure by which a company can refer the matter to the court if it thinks that a request for inspection of the register of members may not be for a proper purpose. It is an offence knowingly or recklessly to make a statement that is misleading, false or deceptive in response

to a request for information in the register of members: s 119. Section 120 requires companies to inform anyone exercising his right of inspection or right to demand a copy of the register or index as to whether the information is up-to-date.

Chapter 3 (ss 129–135) Overseas branch registers
Sections 129–135 replace the Companies Act 1985 s 362.

Chapter 4 (ss 136–144) Prohibition on subsidiary being member of its holding company
Sections 136–144 replace provision made by the Companies Act 1985 s 23, Sch 2.

Part 9 (ss 145–153) Exercise of members' rights
A company may specify in its articles that a member is entitled to identify another person or persons as entitled to enjoy or exercise all or any specified rights of a member: s 145. Section 146 provides for new rights for members of companies whose shares are traded on regulated markets to nominate those on whose behalf they hold shares to receive information which is sent to members direct from the company and to exercise certain rights. Provision is made by s 147 for the way in which information is to be provided to a nominated person. Under s 148, a nomination ceases to have effect on the request of the nominated person or the member, or on the death, bankruptcy or winding up of the nominated person or the member. When sending a meeting notice to nominated persons, a company must include a statement that the nominated person may have voting rights which he can exercise through the person who nominated him: s 149. Section 150 provides that it is the member, rather than the nominated person, who can enforce the rights arising from the nomination. By virtue of s 151, the Secretary of State is empowered to amend ss 146–150. Under ss 152 and 153, indirect investors may be permitted, through the registered member, to exercise voting and requisition rights.

Part 10 (ss 154–259) A company's directors

Chapter 1 (ss 154–169) Appointment and removal of directors
Sections 154–169 consolidate provision made by the Companies Act 1985 ss 282, 285, 288, 289, 292, 303 and 304. By virtue of the 2006 Act s 155, every company must have at least one director who is a natural person, and s 156 contains enforcement provision in relation to this requirement. A person must be aged 16 or above to be a director (s 157), unless provision is made otherwise in regulations by the Secretary of State (s 158). Section 159 requires companies to keep a register of the usual residential addresses of directors who are individuals. Under s 160, the Secretary of State is permitted to make regulations that add or remove items from the particulars that have to be entered in a company's register of directors and register of directors' residential addresses.

Chapter 2 (ss 170–181) General duties of directors
Section 170 provides that the duties owed by directors at common law are replaced by the statutory ones specified in ss 171–177. A director has a duty (1) to act in accordance with the company's constitution (s 171); (2) to act in a way he considers would be most likely to promote the success of the company (s 172); (3) to exercise his powers independently (s 173); (4) to exercise reasonable care, skill and diligence (s 174); (5) to avoid conflicts of interest (s 175); (6) not to accept benefits from third parties (s 176); and (7) to disclose any interest that he has in relation to a proposed transaction or arrangement with the company (s 177). By virtue of s 178, the consequences of a breach of any of the duties are the same as would apply if the corresponding common law rule or equitable principle applied. Section 179 provides that more than one of the general duties may apply in any given case. Under s 180, in a case where the duty to avoid conflicts of interest or the duty to declare an interest in a proposed transaction or arrangement is complied with, the transaction or arrangement is not liable to be set aside by virtue of any common law rule or equitable principle requiring the consent or approval of the members of the company. Modified provision is made by s 181 in relation to the duties owed by directors of charitable companies.

Chapter 3 (ss 182–187) Declaration of interest in existing transaction or arrangement
Sections 182–187 replace the Companies Act 1985 s 317. The 2006 Act s 184 provides a new written procedure for the declarations of interest in an existing transaction or arrangement.

Chapter 4 (ss 188–226) Transactions with directors requiring approval of members
Sections 188–226 consolidate provision made by the Companies Act 1985 ss 312–322 and 330–341.

Chapter 5 (ss 227–230) Directors' service contracts
Sections 227–230 replace the Companies Act 1985 s 318.

Chapter 6 (s 231) Contracts with sole members who are directors
Section 231 replaces the Companies Act 1985 s 322B.

Chapter 7 (ss 232–239) Directors' liabilities
Sections 232–239 consolidate provision made by the Companies Act 1985 ss 309A–309C. Any decision by a company to ratify conduct by a director amounting to negligence, default, breach of duty or breach of trust in relation to the company must now be taken by the members, and without reliance on the votes in favour by the director or any connected person: 2006 Act s 239.

Chapter 8 (ss 240–246) Directors' residential addresses: protection from disclosure
Section 240 sets out the information that will be protected under a new scheme restricting the disclosure of director's residential addresses. A company is prohibited from using or disclosing an individual director's home address except in certain circumstances: s 241. Section 242 provides for the protection to be given by the registrar of information to the information covered by s 240, and s 243 provides for the certain kinds of permitted use or disclosure of protected information. Under s 244, the court may require the company to disclose protected information if the service address is not effective or if the home address is needed for the enforcement of an order or decree of the court. Provision is made in ss 245 and 246 for when the director's home address is to be put on the public record.

Chapter 9 (ss 247–259) Supplementary provisions
Sections 247–259, Sch 1 consolidate provision made by the Companies Act 1985 ss 345–347, 382 and 719.

Part 11 (ss 260–269) Derivative claims and proceedings by members

Chapter 1 (ss 260–264) Derivative claims in England and Wales or Northern Ireland
Section 261 specifies the circumstances in which a member of a company may bring a derivative claim on behalf of the company. By virtue of s 262, a member may in appropriate circumstances apply to the court to continue a claim as a derivative claim where the claim was originally brought by the company. The criteria to be taken into account by the court in considering whether to give permission to continue a derivative claim are prescribed by s 263. Provision is made by s 264 for transferring a derivative claim from one member to another.

Chapter 2 (ss 265–269) Derivative proceedings in Scotland
Sections 265–269 deal with derivative proceedings in Scotland.

Part 12 (ss 270–280) Company secretaries
Sections 270–280 consolidate provision made by the Companies Act 1985 ss 283–286 and 288–290. The 2006 Act s 272 enables enforcement of the continuing requirement for a public company to have a secretary. Under s 279, the Secretary of State has the power to make regulations that add or remove items from the particulars that have to be entered in a company's register of secretaries.

Part 13 (ss 281–361) Resolutions and meetings

Chapter 1 (ss 281–287) General provisions about resolutions
Sections 281–287 consolidate provision made by the Companies Act 1985 ss 370 and 378. Under the 2006 Act s 281, members' resolutions must satisfy certain requirements in order to be passed. Section 285 sets out specific requirements on votes of members, which the company's articles may not override. New provision is made by s 287 preserving the right for a company to require objections to votes to be made in accordance with procedures in its articles.

Chapter 2 (ss 288–300) Written resolutions
Section 288 defines 'written resolution' as the term applies to private companies, and makes other general provision about such resolutions. Provision is made by s 289 to ensure that the same shares cannot be used more than once to vote on a written resolution. Under s 290, the circulation date of a written resolution is the date on which copies are sent or submitted to members. A company must circulate a written resolution to its members (s 291), and members of a private company may require the company to circulate a resolution that may properly be moved and is proposed to be moved as a written resolution (s 292). Section 293 specifies what a company must do when it is required under s 292 to circulate a resolution and accompanying statement. By virtue of s 294, the expenses of complying with s 293 are to be paid by the members who requested the circulation of the resolution unless the company resolves otherwise. Section 295 enables the court to relieve the company of an obligation to circulate a members' statement. Under s 296, a member may signify agreement to a written resolution in hard copy or electronic form. The time limit for passing a written resolution is 28 days, unless the company's articles specify a different period: s 297. Section 298 provides for the sending of documents relating to written resolutions by electronic means. A company is entitled, by virtue of s 299, to publish a written resolution on a website rather than send it to a member individually, provided certain conditions are met. Section 300 ensures that a company's articles cannot remove the ability of a private company and its members to propose and pass a statutory resolution using the statutory written resolutions procedures.

Chapter 3 (ss 301–335) Resolutions at meetings
Sections 301–335 consolidate provision made by the Companies Act 1985 ss 368–381.

Chapter 4 (ss 336–340) Public companies: additional requirements for AGMs
Sections 336–340 consolidate provision made by the Companies Act 1985 ss 366, 369, 376 and 377.

Chapter 5 (ss 341–354) Additional requirements for quoted companies
Under s 341, quoted companies must disclose on a website the results of all polls taken at a general meeting. Members of a quoted company have the right to require an independent report of any poll taken, or to be taken, at a general meeting: s 342. The appointment of an independent assessor must, by virtue of s 343, be made within one week of the members' request. Section 344 precludes a

person from acting as an independent assessor on a poll if he is too closely connected to the company or an associated undertaking of the company, and s 345 defines 'associate' for this purpose. Provision is made by s 346 for where a partnership that is not a legal person is appointed as an independent assessor on a poll. The minimum information the independent assessor's report must contain is specified in s 347. The independent assessor is entitled to attend the meeting at which the poll or polls may be taken and to be provided with information relating to the meeting (s 348), and to access company records relating to any poll on which he is to report and to the meeting at which the poll or polls may be taken (s 349). Under s 350, it is an offence to fail to comply with the requirement to provide information or explanation relating to the poll on which the independent assessor is preparing a report. Section 351 requires the company to publish on a website the independent assessor's report of the poll or polls, as well as other specified information. By virtue of s 352, ss 341–351 also apply in relation to a meeting of holders of a class of shares of a quoted company. Section 353 sets out the minimum requirements that apply to information to be published on a quoted company's website under ss 341 and 351. The Secretary of State has power to limit or extend the types of company to which Pt 12 Ch 5 applies: s 354.

Chapter 6 (ss 355–359) Records of resolutions and meetings
Sections 355–359 consolidate provision made by the Companies Act 1985 ss 382–383.

Chapter 7 (ss 360, 361) Supplementary provisions
Section 360 specifies matters that must be excluded when calculating periods of notice, or periods before a meeting by which a request must be received or sum deposited or tendered. Section 361 deals with interpretation.

Part 14 (ss 362–379) Control of political donations and expenditure
Sections 362–379 consolidate provision made by the Companies Act 1985 ss 347A–347K.

Part 15 (ss 380–474) Accounts and reports
Sections 380–474 consolidate provision made by the Companies Act 1985 Pt 7 (ss 221–262A) relating to accounts and reports. The principal substantive changes effected are that (a) the time limit for private companies to file their accounts is reduced from ten months to nine months after the year end; (b) the time limit for public companies to lay full financial statements before the company in a general meeting and file them is reduced from seven months to six months after the year end; (c) there is a new requirement for quoted companies to publish their annual accounts and reports on a website; and (d) the general power of the Secretary of State to alter accounting requirements is replaced by a general power of amendment by regulations and more specific powers in relation to specific sections.

Part 16 (ss 475–539) Audit

Chapter 1 (ss 475–484) Requirement for audited accounts
Sections 475–484 consolidate provision made by the Companies Act 1985 ss 235, 249A–249B and 257. The 2006 Act ss 482 and 483 provide that certain non-commercial, public sector bodies constituted as companies that are audited by a public sector auditor are not required to be audited under the 2006 Act.

Chapter 2 (ss 485–494) Appointment of auditors
Sections 485–494 consolidate provision made by the Companies Act 1985 ss 384, 385, 387, 388, 390A and 390B. By virtue of the 2006 Act s 487, the end of the term of office of the auditor of a private company is to be the end of the next period for appointing an auditor. Section 488 enables members with at least 5 per cent of the voting rights in a private company to prevent, by giving notice to the company, an auditor being automatically re-appointed. A new power is granted to the Secretary of State by s 493 to require companies to disclose information about the terms on which they engage their auditors.

Chapter 3 (ss 495–509) Functions of auditor
Sections 495–509 consolidate provision made by the Companies Act 1985 ss 235–237, 389A–390. Under the 2006 Act s 506, a company is not required to include the names of the auditor in both the published and filed copies of the audit report if it passes a resolution not to reveal the names because it considers on reasonable grounds that revealing them would lead to a serious risk of violence or intimidation. It is an offence knowingly or recklessly to cause an auditor's report to include anything that is misleading, false or deceptive, or to omit a required statement of a problem with the accounts or audit: s 507. Section 508 enables the Secretary of State to issue guidance about handling matters where the same behaviour by an auditor could give rise both to disciplinary proceedings by a regulatory body and to prosecution for an offence under s 507.

Chapter 4 (ss 510–526) Removal, resignation, etc of auditors
Sections 510–526 consolidate provision made by the Companies Act 1985 ss 388, 391–394A. The 2006 Act s 514 sets out the procedure for changing an auditor from one financial year to the next by written resolution. Departing auditors are required to send copies of their leaving statements to an appropriate audit authority: s 522. A company is obliged by s 523 to notify the appropriate audit

authority whenever an auditor leaves office before the end of his term. Section 524 sets out the duty of the audit authorities to give the accounting authorities information about an auditor's departure.

Chapter 5 (ss 527–531) Quoted companies: right of members to raise audit concerns at accounts meeting
By virtue of s 527, the members of a quoted company may, in certain circumstances, ask the company to publish on a website a statement raising questions about the accounts, or about the departure of an auditor, that they propose to bring up at the next meeting where the accounts are to be discussed. Section 528 sets out the requirements which the company must meet in making the shareholders' statements available on a website. Quoted companies must draw attention to the possibility of a website statement in the notice of the accounts meeting: s 529. Under s 530, a company commits an offence if it fails to comply with s 528 or 529. Section 531 deals with interpretation.

Chapter 6 (ss 532–538) Auditors' liability
Sections 532–538 replace the Companies Act 1985 s 310. The 2006 Act s 535 contains rules about the terms of a liability limitation agreement, which is defined by s 534 as an agreement that seeks to limit the liability of an auditor to a company whose accounts he audits. The way in which members of a company must give their approval to a liability limitation agreement, without which approval the agreement will not be effective, is prescribed by s 536. A liability limitation agreement is not effective to limit an auditor's liability if the limitation will result in the company recovering an amount that is less than what is fair and reasonable: s 538. Section 539 requires companies to disclose any liability limitation agreement they have made with their auditor in accordance with any regulations made by the Secretary of State.

Chapter 7 (s 539) Supplementary provisions
Section 539 deals with interpretation.

Part 17 (ss 540–657) A company's share capital

Chapter 1 (ss 540–548) Shares and share capital of a company
Sections 540–548 consolidate provision made by the Companies Act 1985 ss 182, 737 and 744. The 2006 Act s 542 requires the shares in a limited company having a share capital to have a fixed nominal value, and permits shares to be denominated in any currency.

Chapter 2 (ss 549–559) Allotment of shares: general provisions
Sections 549–559 consolidate provision made by the Companies Act 1985 ss 80, 88, 97, 98 and 128. Under the 2006 Act s 550, directors do not need the prior authority of the company's members to allot shares where the company is a private company which will have only one class of shares after the proposed allotment. The directors must register an allotment of shares as soon as practicable, but in any event within two months of the date of allotment: s 554.

Chapter 3 (ss 560–577) Allotment of equity securities: existing shareholders' right of pre-emption
Sections 560–577 consolidate provision made by the Companies Act 1985 ss 89–96.

Chapter 4 (ss 578, 579) Public companies: allotment where issue not fully subscribed
Sections 578, 579 replace the Companies Act 1985 ss 84 and 85.

Chapter 5 (ss 580–592) Payment for shares
Sections 580–592 consolidate provision made by the Companies Act 1985 ss 99–102, 106, 107, 112–115 and 119.

Chapter 6 (ss 593–609) Public companies: independent valuation of non-cash consideration
Sections 593–609 consolidate provision made by the Companies Act 1985 ss 103–105 and 107–115.

Chapter 7 (ss 610–616) Share premiums
Sections 610–616 consolidate provision made by the Companies Act 1985 ss 130–134.

Chapter 8 (ss 617–628) Alteration of share capital
Sections 617–621 consolidate provision made by the Companies Act 1985 ss 121 and 122. The 2006 Act s 622 prescribes a simplified procedure under which a company limited by shares may redenominate its share capital. The method for calculating the new nominal value of a share which has been redenominated from one currency to another is specified by s 623. A redenomination of a company's share capital, or any class of it, does not affect any rights or obligations that the members may have under the company's constitution: s 624. Section 625 sets out the requirements as to notice where a company redenominates its share capital, or any class of it. By virtue of s 626, a company may renominalise the value of its shares by cancelling part of its share capital. The notice requirements where a company reduces its share capital in connection with a redenomination of its share capital are set out in s 627. Sums transferred to the redenomination reserve following a reduction in share capital under s 626 may be used by the company in paying up shares to be allotted to existing members as fully paid bonus shares: s 628.

Chapter 9 (ss 629–640) Classes of share and class rights
Sections 629–640 consolidate provision made by the Companies Act 1985 ss 125–129. The 2006 Act s 631 extends the statutory provisions on variation of class rights to companies without a share

capital. Section 634 enables members in companies not having a share capital, and who did not consent to or vote in favour of the resolution approving a variation of class rights, to apply to the court to have the variation cancelled.

Chapter 10 (ss 641–653) Reduction of share capital
Sections 641–653 consolidate provision made by the Companies Act 1985 ss 135–141. The 2006 Act s 642 sets out the conditions that must be satisfied in order for a private company limited by shares to reduce its share capital using the new solvency statement procedure. Supplementary provision in relation solvency statements is made by ss 643 and 644.

Chapter 11 (ss 654–657) Miscellaneous and supplementary provisions
Sections 654–657 consolidate provision made by the Companies Act 1985 ss 111A and 142. Under the 2006 Act s 654, the Secretary of State may specify the circumstances in which a reserve arising from a reduction of capital will be distributable.

Part 18 (ss 658–737) Acquisition by limited company of its own shares
Sections 658–737 consolidate, with minor substantive changes, provision made by the Companies Act 1985 ss 122, 143–154, 159–181, Schs 2 and 15A.

Part 19 (ss 738–754) Debentures
Sections 738–754 consolidate provision made by the Companies Act 1985 ss 190–197. A company is obliged to register an allotment of debentures as soon as practicable, but in any event within two months after their allotment: 2006 Act s 741. Section 745 provides a procedure by which a company can refer the matter to the court if it considers a request to inspect the register of debenture holders is not for a proper purpose. Under s 747, it is an offence knowingly or recklessly to make a statement that is misleading, false or deceptive when responding to a request to inspect the register, or to cause information received in response to such a request to be disclosed to another person knowing or having reason to suspect that the other person may use the information for an improper purpose.

Part 20 (ss 755–767) Private and public companies

Chapter 1 (ss 755–760) Prohibition of public offers by private companies
Sections 755–760 consolidate provision made by the Companies Act 1985 ss 58, 81 and 742A. The 2006 Act s 757 enables members, creditors or the Secretary of State to apply to the court for an order restraining a private company from carrying out any proposed contravention of the prohibition on offering shares or debentures to the public. A new civil enforcement procedure is introduced by s 758 for where a private company breaches the prohibition on offering securities to the public.

Chapter 2 (ss 761–767) Minimum share capital requirement for public companies
Sections 761–767 replace the Companies Act 1985 ss 117 and 118. The 2006 Act s 765 makes new provision prescribing how the authorised minimum share capital required for a public company is to be met. The Secretary of State is entitled to prescribe how references to the authorised minimum are to be applied where a public company has its share capital denominated in more than one currency, or where it redenominates its share capital from one currency to another: s 766.

Part 21 (ss 768–790) Certification and transfer of securities

Chapter 1 (ss 768–782) Certification and transfer of securities: general
Sections 768–782 consolidate provision made by the Companies Act 1985 Pt 5 (ss 183–189). The 2006 Act s 771 requires the directors either to register a transfer of shares or debentures or to provide the transferee with reasons for their refusal to register. It is an offence under s 780 to fail to complete and have ready for delivery a certificate of the shares specified in the warrant within two months from the date of surrender.

Chapter 2 (ss 783–790) Evidencing and transfer of title to securities without written instrument
Sections 783–790 replace the Companies Act 1985 s 207, and make new provision in relation to the making of regulations about the transfer of title to securities without a written instrument.

Part 22 (ss 791–828) Information about interests in a company's shares
Sections 791–828 consolidate provision made by the Companies Act 1985 ss 198–219 and 454–457.

Part 23 (ss 829–853) Distributions
Sections 829–853 consolidate provision made by the Companies Act 1985 Pt 8 (ss 263–281) and the Income and Corporation Taxes Act 1988 ss 838 and 842.

Part 24 (ss 854–859) A company's annual return
Sections 854–859 consolidate provision made by the Companies Act 1985 ss 363–365.

Part 25 (ss 860–894) Company charges

Chapter 1 (ss 860–877) Companies registered in England and Wales or in Northern Ireland
Sections 860–877 consolidate provision made by the Companies Act 1985 ss 395–408.

Chapter 2 (ss 878–892) Companies registered in Scotland
Sections 878–892 consolidate provision made by the Companies Act 1985 ss 410–423.

Chapter 3 (ss 893, 894) Powers of the Secretary of State
By virtue of s 893, the Secretary of State is entitled to make an order providing that, where a charge is registered in another register, the registrar may not register it, but it is to be treated as if it had been registered in accordance with the requirements of Pt 25. Section 894 empowers the Secretary of State to amend Pt 25.

Part 26 (ss 895–901) Arrangements and reconstructions
Sections 895–901 consolidate provision made by the Companies Act 1985 ss 425–427. The 2006 Act s 901 requires a company to deliver to the registrar any court order that alters the company's constitution.

Part 27 (ss 902–941) Mergers and divisions of public companies
Sections 902–941 consolidate provision made by the Companies Act 1985 s 427A, Sch 15B.

Part 28 (ss 942–992) Takeovers etc

Chapter 1 (ss 942–965) The Takeover Panel
Section 942 confers on the Panel on Takeovers and Mergers certain prescribed regulatory functions relating to takeovers. The Panel is empowered to make rules in relation to takeover regulation: ss 943, 944. By virtue of s 945, the Panel is authorised to make rulings on the interpretation, application or effect of such rules. The Panel is entitled under s 946 to make provision in its rules for it to give a direction preventing a person from breaching the rules. The Panel is entitled to require the production of such documents and information as it may reasonably require in the exercise of its functions: s 947. Sections 948, 949, Sch 2 prohibit the disclosure of confidential information obtained by the Panel in the exercise of its functions. The Panel is obliged by s 950 to co-operate with overseas takeover and financial services regulatory authorities. Procedures for the review of and appeal against decisions taken by the Panel in connection with its regulatory functions are provided for by s 951. Section 952 confers on the Panel the power to make rules for imposing sanctions for breach of its rules or directions given under s 946. By virtue of s 953, new offences are created in relation to takeover bid documentation. The Panel is permitted to make rules providing for financial redress in consequence of a breach of rules which require monetary payments to be made: s 954. Section 955 provides a mechanism by which the Panel may, if necessary, apply to the court in order to enforce rule-based requirements as well as requests for documents and information under s 947. Contravention of a rule-based requirement does not make a transaction void or unenforceable: s 956. The Panel is entitled under s 957 to make rules for the payment of fees or charges to itself for the purposes of meeting its expenses. Section 958 enables the Secretary of State to make regulations imposing a levy for meeting the costs of the Panel. An amount payable under s 957 or 958 constitutes a debt owed by the specified person to the Panel and is recoverable by the Panel as a debt: s 959. By virtue of s 960, the Panel may bring or defend proceedings in its own name. Section 961 confers limited immunity on the Panel and those involved in carrying out its regulatory activities. Under s 962, a statement made by a person to the Panel, or a person authorised on its behalf, in compliance with a requirement to provide information under s 947 or a court order made to secure compliance with such a requirement under s 955, cannot be used against that person in most types of criminal proceedings. The Panel is required to publish annual reports containing annual accounts and setting out how the Panel's functions were discharged in the year in question: s 963. Consequential amendments are made by s 964. Provision relating to the Panel may be extended to the Isle of Man or any of the Channel Islands: s 965.

Chapter 2 (ss 966–973) Impediments to takeovers
Sections 966 and 967 specify the requirements that must be satisfied where a company wishes to opt in to or out of European Parliament and EC Council Directive 2004/25 art 11, which makes provision for overriding the defensive mechanisms that a company may implement prior to a takeover bid. The effect on contractual restrictions in relation to an opted-in company are set out in the 2006 Act s 968. Where a takeover bid is made for an opted-in company, the offeror may in certain circumstances require the directors to call a general meeting of the company: s 969. Under s 970, a company passing an opting-in or opting-out resolution must notify the Panel of that fact. Section 971 deals with interpretation, and s 972 makes transitional provision.

Chapter 3 (ss 974–991) 'Squeeze-out' and 'sell-out'
Sections 974–991 consolidate provision made by the Companies Act 1985 ss 428–430F.

Chapter 4 (s 992) Amendments to Part 7 of the Companies Act 1985
Section 992 requires companies admitted to trading on a regulated market to provide in their annual reports detailed information relating to matters such as the control and share structures of the company.

Part 29 (s 993) Fraudulent trading
Section 993 replaces the Companies Act 1985 s 458, and increases, from seven years' imprisonment to ten years' imprisonment, the maximum sentence for the offence of fraudulent trading.

Part 30 (ss 994–999) Protection of members against unfair prejudice
Sections 994–998 consolidate provision made by the Companies Act 1985 ss 459–461. The 2006 Act s 999 ensures that, if the court makes an order under Pt 30 amending a company's articles, updated articles are registered and a copy of the court order is supplied with any copies of the articles that are issued by the company, unless they already incorporate the amendments.

Part 31 (ss 1000–1034) Dissolution and restoration to the register

Chapter 1 (ss 1000–1011) Striking off
Sections 1000–1011 consolidate provision made by the Companies Act 1985 ss 652–654.

Chapter 2 (ss 1012–1023) Property of dissolved company
Sections 1012–1023 consolidate provision made by the Companies Act 1985 ss 656–658.

Chapter 3 (ss 1024–1034) Restoration to the register
Section 1024 provides that an application may be made to the registrar to restore a company that has been struck off the register under s 1000 or 1001. In order to be restored, the company must have been carrying on business or have been in operation at the time of its striking off, the Crown representative must have given any relevant consent, and the applicant must have delivered any necessary documents and paid any outstanding penalties: s 1025. By virtue of s 1026, an application for restoration must be accompanied by a statement that the applicant has the necessary standing to make the application and that the requirements for administrative restoration have been met. If the decision is made to restore the company to the register, the restoration takes effect from the date of the registrar's notice of the decision: s 1027. Under s 1028, the effect of restoration is that the company is deemed to have continued in existence as if it had not been struck off. Section 1029 provides that an application may be made to the court for the restoration of a company which has been dissolved or is deemed to be dissolved. The time limit for making a court application for restoration is, in general, six years: s 1030. Section 1031 specifies the circumstances in which the court may order restoration. By virtue of s 1032, the effect of the court deciding to restore a company to the register is that the company is deemed to have continued in existence as if it had not been struck off and, under s 1033, the company is restored in the name it had before it was struck off. Where a company's property has passed to the Crown and been disposed of, the Crown, in reimbursing the newly restored company, may deduct the reasonable costs of sale that were incurred: s 1034.

Part 32 (ss 1035–1039) Company investigations: amendments
Under s 1035, the Secretary of State has the power to give mandatory directions to inspectors. Provision is made by s 1036 for the resignation or revocation of an inspector's appointment and for his replacement. Under s 1037, where an inspector resigns or has his appointment revoked, the Secretary of State may direct him to hand over documents which he has obtained or generated during the course of his investigation. Section 1038 ensures that there is a consistent approach in existing investigation provisions where there is a requirement to produce documents. By virtue of s 1039, decisions on whether to take action to disqualify company directors may be taken on the basis of information that was obtained or generated by an inspector as a result of his investigation.

Part 33 (ss 1040–1043) UK companies not formed under companies legislation

Chapter 1 (ss 1040–1042) Companies not formed under companies legislation but authorised to register
Sections 1040, 1041 consolidate provision made by the Companies Act 1985 ss 680 and 683. Under the 2006 Act s 1042, the Secretary of State is entitled to make regulations in connection with the registration of a company following an application under s 1040.

Chapter 2 (s 1043) Unregistered companies
Section 1043 replaces the Companies Act 1985 s 718.

Part 34 (ss 1044–1059) Overseas companies
Section 1044 defines 'overseas company'. Under s 1045, the Secretary of State may make provision applying to overseas companies rules relating to company contracts and the execution of documents. The Secretary of State may make regulations requiring overseas companies to register with the registrar of companies (s 1046), and to deliver to the registrar certain particulars and documents (s 1047). An overseas company is entitled, by virtue of s 1048, to be registered under a name other than its corporate name. Section 1049 confers on the Secretary of State a power to make regulations requiring overseas companies to prepare accounts and directors' reports, and to obtain an auditor's report. Under s 1050, the Secretary of State is authorised to make regulations in respect of accounts and directors' reports by credit or financial institutions incorporated or formed outside the United Kingdom that have a branch in the United Kingdom. Regulations may also be made in relation to the information which overseas companies must display in specified locations, include in specified documents or communications, or provide to those who make a request in the course of business (s 1051), in relation to the registration by overseas companies of charges which they grant over property in the United Kingdom (s 1052), and in relation to the delivery of returns to the registrar by overseas companies if they are being wound up or subjected to insolvency proceedings (s 1053). Provision is made by s 1054 for offences in connection with regulations made under Pt 34.

Section 1055 provides that, if regulations under s 1046 require an overseas company to register an individual's usual residential address, the regulations must also provide for its protection from disclosure. Under s 1056, every overseas company required to register must register particulars identifying every person resident in the United Kingdom who is authorised to accept service of documents on the company's behalf, or make a statement that there is no such person. Section 1057 provides for the delivery of documents by overseas companies which are required to register. Regulations may be made requiring an overseas company to give notice that it has ceased to have a registrable presence in the United Kingdom: s 1058. For the purposes of Pt 34, the relocation of a branch from one part of the United Kingdom to another is to be treated, by virtue of s 1059, as the closing of the branch in one part and the opening in another.

Part 35 (ss 1060–1120) The registrar of companies
Sections 1060–1067 consolidate provision made by the Companies Act 1985 ss 704–705A, 708–711. The registrar of companies has the power to make rules about the form, authentication and manner of delivery of documents: 2006 Act s 1068. Under s 1069, the Secretary of State is authorised to provide for electronic-only delivery of certain classes of document. Section 1070 sets out the power of the registrar to make agreements with companies to deliver information only electronically. Rules governing the receipt and delivery of documents to the registrar are prescribed by ss 1071–1074. In limited circumstances, the registrar is permitted to correct information in a document by informal means: s 1075. The circumstances in which the registrar may accept a replacement document that was not properly delivered in the first place are set out in s 1076. Under ss 1077 and 1078, the receipt by the registrar of certain documents must be made public, and s 1079 specifies the consequences of a failure to provide such notice. The registrar has a duty to keep a record of material received: s 1080. Section 1081 sets out the circumstances in which the registrar has a duty to annotate information or to provide supplementary information. The Secretary of State is empowered by s 1082 to make regulations enabling unique identifiers to be allocated to company officers such as directors, so that searchers can distinguish between persons of the same name. The hard copies of documents and records delivered to the registrar must be retained for at least three years, providing the information contained in them has been transferred to the register: s 1083. Under s 1084, records may be transferred to the Public Records Office two years after a company has been dissolved. Any person may, by virtue of s 1085, inspect the register and, under s 1086, any person is entitled to a copy of material on the register. Section 1087 lists various exceptions to the rights under ss 1085 and 1086. The Secretary of State is empowered to make regulations providing for applications to remove addresses from the public record held by Companies House: s 1088. By virtue of s 1089, the registrar may specify the form and manner in which an application is to be made to inspect the register or for a copy of material on it. Section 1090 provides that the applicant is entitled to insist on receiving the copies in either hard copy or electronic form. Under s 1091, only copies of information provided in hard copy must be certified. Legal proceedings relating to the production of a record by the registrar may only be undertaken with the permission of the court: s 1092. Section 1093 enables the registrar to notify a company of an apparent inconsistency in the information on the register. Under s 1094, the registrar has the power to remove from the register information that there was power, but no duty, to include. The Secretary of State is authorised by s 1095 to make regulations under which, following a successful application, the registrar may be required to remove certain kinds of material from the register. The registrar is also required to remove material from the register where there is a court order for its removal: s 1096. Section 1097 specifies the powers of the court when ordering the removal of material from the register. The registrar has a duty under s 1098 to notify the public where certain specified material is removed from the register. The registrar must keep an index of the names of companies incorporated under the Companies Acts, of business entities formed under other legislation, and of overseas companies with a United Kingdom branch: s 1099. By virtue of s 1100, the public has a right to inspect the index of company names. Section 1101 enables the Secretary of State to amend the rules for the names which may be adopted by other business entities on the index of company names. Sections 1102 and 1103 provide that, subject to specified exceptions, all documents required under the Companies Acts must be in English. Circumstances in which the Welsh language may be used are specified in s 1104, and those in which other languages may be used are specified in s 1105. A company may deliver to the registrar one or more certified translations of any document relating to the company that is or has been delivered to the registrar: s 1106. Under s 1107, a 'certified translation' is one that has been certified in a manner prescribed by the registrar. Sections 1108 and 1109 make provision for the transliteration of the names and addresses of directors of overseas companies used in documents delivered to the registrar, where the character set used would be unfamiliar to most people using the register. The Secretary of State is empowered by s 1110 to make regulations relating to the certification of the transliteration of names and addresses. Where documents delivered to the registrar require certification or validation, the registrar is authorised under s 1111 to impose requirements as to who must provide the relevant certification or verification. It is an offence knowingly or recklessly to deliver to the registrar information which is misleading, false or deceptive in a material particular: s 1112. Section 1113 provides the mechanism for ensuring that companies comply with their obligations to file documents or give notices to the

registrar. Interpretative provision relating to documents and delivery is made by s 1114. Under s 1115, the registrar may require those who choose to file electronically to accept electronic communications from the registrar. Section 1116 enables the Secretary of State to specify alternative mechanisms through which the registrar can fulfil his obligation to publish certain statutory notices. The power of the registrar to make rules is provided for by s 1117, and s 1118 deals with payments into the Consolidated Fund. Section 1119 makes provision in relation to the contracting out of the registrar's functions, and s 1120 provides that, where appropriate, Pt 35 applies equally to overseas companies.

Part 36 (ss 1121–1133) Offences under the Companies Acts
Sections 1121–1133 consolidate provision made by the Companies Act 1985 ss 721, 730–734. Where a company is an officer of another company, liability for an offence can be fixed on the company as an officer in default only if one of its officers is in default: 2006 Act s 1122. By virtue of s 1123, s 1121 applies to persons in bodies other than companies where their role is equivalent to that of an officer of a company. Section 1124, Sch 3 amend provision in the Companies Act 1985 relating to offences.

Part 37 (ss 1134–1157) Companies: supplementary provisions
Sections 1134–1139 consolidate provision made by the Companies Act 1985 ss 695, 722–725. The 2006 Act s 1140 ensures that the address on the public record for any director or secretary is effective for the service of documents on that person. 'Service address' is defined by s 1141, by virtue of which a requirement to give an address means a requirement to give a service address, unless a different address is specified. Under s 1143, the provision made by ss 1144–1148, Schs 4, 5 applies to any provision of the Companies Acts that authorises or requires documents or information to be sent or supplied by or to a company. Section 1144, Schs 4 and 5 make provision in connection with documents and information sent to or supplied by a company, and in relation to communications by a company and between companies. Individual members or debenture holders have the right to require information to be sent in paper copy form: s 1145. Section 1146 details the requirements in relation to the authentication of a document sent or information sent or supplied by a person to a company. Rules prescribing when communications from a company are deemed to have been delivered are set out in s 1147. Section 1148 deals with interpretation in relation to provision concerning company communications. Section 1149 specifies the scope of the application of the independent valuation provision made by ss 1150–1153. The qualifications required of a person carrying out an independent valuation are prescribed by ss 1150 and 1151. Section 1152 defines 'associate' for the purposes of s 1151. An independent valuer is entitled to require from the company any information necessary to carry out the valuation: s 1153. Under s 1154, the registrar must be notified of certain appointments, and it is an offence contrary to s 1155 to fail to give such notification. Section 1156 defines 'the court' for the purposes of the Companies Acts, and s 1157 entitles an officer of a company or an auditor to apply to the court for relief from liability for negligence, default, breach of duty or breach of trust.

Part 38 (ss 1158–1174) Companies: interpretation
Sections 1158–1174, Schs 6–8 define terms used in the 2006 Act, replacing interpretative provision made by the Companies Act 1985.

Part 39 (ss 1175–1181) Companies: minor amendments
Sections 1175–1181, Sch 9 repeal various provisions of the Companies Act 1985 and the 1989 Act.

Part 40 (ss 1182–1191) Company directors: foreign disqualification etc
Section 1182 defines what is meant by references in Pt 40 to a person being subject to foreign restrictions, and s 1183 defines 'the court' and 'UK company'. The Secretary of State is permitted under s 1184 to make regulations disqualifying a person subject to foreign restrictions from being the director of a United Kingdom company, acting as a receiver of a United Kingdom company's property, or, in any way, taking part in the promotion, formation or management of a United Kingdom company. Supplementary provision in relation to such regulations is made by s 1185. By virtue of s 1186, regulations made under s 1184 may provide that a person disqualified under Pt 40 who acts in breach of the disqualification commits an offence. Section 1187 provides for a disqualified person to be made personally responsible for the debts and liabilities of the company. Regulations may require a person who is not disqualified under Pt 40 but who is subject to foreign restrictions to send a statement to the registrar if he does anything that, if done by a disqualified person, would be a breach of the disqualification (s 1188), and require a disqualified director to provide an additional statement where he has received approval from the court to act in a capacity that would otherwise be in breach of the disqualification (s 1189). By virtue of s 1190, such regulations must state whether statements made are to be on the public register, and the circumstances in which they may be withheld from public inspection or removed from the register. Section 1191 creates offences for breaches of s 1188 or 1189.

Part 41 (ss 1192–1208) Business names
Sections 1192–1208 replace, with minor substantive changes, the Business Names Act 1985.

Part 42 (ss 1209–1264) Statutory auditors

Chapter 1 (ss 1209–1211) Introductory
The principal purposes of Pt 42 are specified by s 1209 as being to secure that only persons who are properly supervised and appropriately qualified are appointed as statutory auditors, and to secure that audits by persons so appointed are carried out properly, with integrity and with a proper degree of independence. Section 1210 deals with interpretation, and s 1211 states the provisions according to which eligibility for appointment as an auditor are to be determined.

Chapter 2 (ss 1212–1225) Individuals and firms
Sections 1212–1225, Schs 10 and 11 consolidate provision made by the 1989 Act ss 25–39, 48, Schs 11 and 12.

Chapter 3 (ss 1226–1238) Auditors General
Section 1226 defines 'Auditor General' as the Comptroller and Auditor General or the Auditor General for Wales, and provides that an Auditor General is eligible for appointment as a statutory auditor. An Auditor General must ensure that the individuals within his charge, who are carrying out statutory audits on his behalf, are, in their own right, eligible for appointment as a statutory auditor by virtue of the prescribed qualifications and requirements: s 1227. Under s 1228, the Secretary of State must appoint a body to be the Independent Supervisor of Auditors General in respect of the exercise of statutory audit functions. Section 1229 sets the framework for the supervision arrangements to be carried out by the Independent Supervisor. Each Auditor General must comply with the standards set by, as well as the monitoring arrangements and decisions of, the independent supervision arrangements: s 1230. The Independent Supervisor must, by virtue of s 1231, provide at least one report in each calendar year to the Secretary of State and to the Assembly First Secretary in Wales. Under s 1232, an Auditor General must notify the Independent Supervisor in writing of events that the Independent Supervisor may specify. Section 1233 enables the Independent Supervisor to require an Auditor General to provide information. The Independent Supervisor has the power to suspend an Auditor General's eligibility for appointment as a statutory auditor: s 1234. An Auditor General must not, by virtue of s 1235, act as a statutory auditor of a particular person if he is suspended in relation to that person. Section 1236 confers power on the Independent Supervisor to take an Auditor General to court if he fails to comply with any obligation imposed by or by virtue of Pt 42. Under s 1237, where the Independent Supervisor is an unincorporated association, it may take proceedings in the name of the body corporate under which it is constituted. By virtue of s 1238, the body which carries out the functions of the Independent Supervisor is eligible for grants from the Secretary of State to meet the expenditure of the body and any subsidiary.

Chapter 4 (ss 1239, 1240) The register of auditors etc
Section 1239 replaces the Companies Act 1985 s 35. Under the 2006 Act s 1240, the Secretary of State may make regulations requiring statutory auditors to make certain information available to the public.

Chapter 5 (ss 1241–1247) Registered third country auditors
Section 1241 provides definitions, including 'third country auditor' and 'registered third country auditor'. Registered third country auditors are to be subject to systems of independent monitoring and discipline in the United Kingdom: s 1242, Sch 12. Sections 1243 and 1244 replicate for registered third country auditors the requirements in ss 1223 and 1224 for the notification of information to the Secretary of State. The Secretary of State is entitled by virtue of s 1245 to apply to the court for an order to make a registered third country auditor comply with its obligations and, by virtue of s 1246, to make provision as to the removal, in certain circumstances, of third country auditors from the register of auditors. Under s 1247, the body that carries out the monitoring and investigation functions in relation to third country auditors is eligible for grants from the Secretary of State.

Chapter 6 (ss 1248–1264) Supplementary and general
Sections 1248–1264, Schs 13 and 14 make supplementary provision in relation to statutory auditors.

Part 43 (ss 1265–1273) Transparency obligations and related matters
Section 1265 adds a definition of 'the transparency obligations directive', which is European Parliament and EC Council Directive 2004/109 on the harmonisation of transparency requirements in relation to information about issuers whose securities are traded on a regulated market, and in implementation of which the 2006 Act s 1266 sets out transparency obligations. By virtue of s 1267, the Financial Services Authority is authorised to call for information from specified persons, including issuers of shares and their auditors and directors. Section 1268 sets out the Authority's powers where the transparency obligations are infringed. The Authority is entitled to make rules implementing, enabling the implementation of or dealing with matters arising out of, Community obligations on corporate governance of issuers on a regulated market: s 1269. Under s 1270, a regime is established for civil liability to third parties by issuers admitted to trading on a regulated market in respect of disclosures made public in response to provisions implementing obligations imposed by Directive 2004/109. The 2006 Act s 1271 sets out the Authority's ability to exercise

powers in relation to infringements of prospectus rules and transparency rules or related provisions where the issuer's home state is not the United Kingdom. Section 1272, Sch 15, make minor and consequential amendments. The Secretary of State may make regulations for the purposes of implementing, enabling the implementation of or dealing with matters arising out of, Community obligations on corporate governance for United Kingdom companies whose securities are traded on a regulated market in the United Kingdom or elsewhere in the EEA: s 1273.

Part 44 (ss 1274–1283) Miscellaneous provisions
Under s 1274, the list of matters carried on by bodies eligible for grants includes activities concerned with the setting of actuarial standards, compliance with those standards, oversight of the actuarial profession and related matters. By virtue of s 1275, the administrators of a public service pension scheme and the trustees and managers of an occupational or personal pension scheme are added to the list of persons by whom a levy may be payable. Section 1276 applies to Scotland and Northern Ireland. The Secretary of State and the Treasury may make regulations requiring certain categories of institutional investor to provide information about the exercise of their voting rights: s 1277. The categories of institutions in relation to which the power conferred by s 1277 is exercisable are listed in s 1278. Section 1279 confers the power to specify by regulations the descriptions of shares in relation to which the information provisions apply, and s 1280 specifies the information that may be required by such regulations. Section 1281 allows a public authority to disclose prescribed information to any person for the purposes of certain civil proceedings. Property subject to a floating charge may, where necessary, be used to fund the general expenses of winding up in priority to the floating charge holder and to any preferential creditors entitled to be paid out of that property: s 1282. Under s 1283, the application of the provision whereby an alteration of the memorandum or articles of association of a commonhold association has no effect until the altered version is registered is limited to alterations made at a time when the land the association is established to manage is commonhold land.

Part 45 (ss 1284–1287) Northern Ireland
Sections 1284–1287 apply to Northern Ireland.

Part 46 (ss 1288–1297) General supplementary provisions
Provision for the making of regulations and orders under the 2006 Act is made by ss 1288–1292. Section 1293 defines 'enactment' for the purposes of the 2006 Act, and s 1294 gives the Secretary of State the power to make consequential amendments. Section 1294, Sch 16, repeal various primary legislation, including most of the Companies Act 1985 and the 1989 Act. The 2006 Act ss 1296 and 1297 make transitional provision.

Part 47 (ss 1298–1300) Final provisions
Section 1298 specifies the short title, s 1299 deals with extent, and s 1300 makes provision for commencement.

Amendments, repeals and revocations
The list below, which is not exhaustive, mentions repeals and amendments which are or will be effective when the Act is fully in force.

Specific provisions of a number of Acts are amended or repealed. These include: Companies Act 1985 ss 1–430F, 458–461, 651–746, Schs 1–15B, 20–25; Business Names Act 1985; Companies Act 1989 ss 1–22, 24–54, 92–110, 113–138, 141–143, Schs 1–9, 11–13, 15–17; Deregulation and Contracting Out Act 1994 s 13(1), Sch 5; Financial Services and Markets Act 2000 ss 143, 263; and Companies (Audit, Investigations and Community Enterprise) Act 2004 ss 1–10, 12, 13, 19, 20, Sch 1.

DESTINATION TABLE

1. The table identifies the provisions of the Companies Act 1985 (c 6) that are repealed and re-enacted (with or without changes) by the Companies Act 2006 and identifies the corresponding provisions in that Act.

2. The table is based on the table of origins. So it only shows a provision of the 2006 Act as a destination of a provision of the 1985 Act if the latter is cited in that table as an origin for the new provision.

3. A repealed provision of the 1985 Act may not be listed in this table because the provision is spent or it is otherwise unnecessary to re-enact it, because the new provision is fundamentally different from the existing provision or because as a matter of policy it has been decided to repeal the existing provision without replacing it.

4. There is no entry for the 1985 Act Sch 24 (punishment of offences) in the table. This is cited in the table of origins as the origin for a large number of provisions in the 2006 Act.

5. A section at the end of the table identifies the substantive provisions of the Companies Act 1989 (c 40) that are repealed and re-enacted by the 2006 Act.

Companies Act 1985

Provision of Companies Act 1985	Destination in Companies Act 2006
1 Mode of forming incorporated company	
(1)	s 7(1), (2) (changed)
(2)	s 3(1)–(4)
(3)	s 4(1)–(3)
(4)	s 5(1), (2)
2 Requirements with respect to memorandum	
(1)	s 9(2)
(2)	ss 9(2), 88(2)
(3)	s 9(2) (changed)
(4)	s 11(3) (changed)
3 Forms of memorandum	
(1)	s 8(2)
7 Articles prescribing regulations for companies	
(1)	s 18(2) (changed)
(3)	s 18(3) (changed)
8 Tables A, C, D and E	
(1)	s 19(1)–(3) (changed)
(2)	s 20(1), (2) (changed)
(3)	s 19(4)
(4)	s 19(1)–(3) (changed)
(5)	s 19(5)
9 Alteration of articles by special resolution	
(1), (2)	s 21(1)
10 Documents to be sent to registrar	
(1)	s 9(1), (5), (6) (changed)
(2)	s 12(1) (changed)
(3)	s 12(3)
(4)	s 9(3)
(6)	s 9(5)
12 Duty of registrar	
(1), (2)	s 14
(3), (3A)	s 13(1), (2) (changed)
13 Effect of registration	
(1)	s 15(1)
(2)	s 15(3)
(3)	s 16(2) (changed)
(4)	s 16(3)
(5)	s 16(6)
(7)	s 15(4)
14 Effect of memorandum and articles	
(1)	s 33(1) (changed)
(2)	s 33(2) (changed)
15 Memorandum and articles of company limited by guarantee	
(1)	s 37
(2)	s 5(3)
16 Effect of alteration on company's members	
(1)	s 25(1)
(2)	s 25(2)
18 Amendments of memorandum or articles to be registered	
(1)	s 34(2) (changed)

Provision of Companies Act 1985	Destination in Companies Act 2006
(2)	ss 26(1), 34(3) (changed)
(3)	ss 26(3), (4), 34(5), (6)
19 Copies of memorandum and articles to be given to members	
(1)	s 32(1) (changed)
(2)	s 32(3), (4) (changed)
22 Definition of 'member'	
(1)	s 112(1) (changed)
(2)	s 112(2)
23 Membership of holding company	
(1)	s 136(1)
(2)	s 138(1), (2)
(3)	s 141(1), (2)
(3A)	s 141(3)
(3B)	s 141(4)
(3BA)	s 141(5)
(3C)	s 142(1), (2)
(4), (5)	s 137(1), (2)
(6)	s 137(3), (4)
(7)	s 144
(8)	s 143
25 Name as stated in memorandum	
(1)	s 58(1), (2)
(2)	s 59(1), (2), (3)
26 Prohibition on registration of certain names	
(1)	ss 53, 65(1)–(5), 66(1) (changed)
(2)	ss 54(1)–(3) and 55(1) (changed)
(3)	s 66(2), (3) (changed)
27 Alternatives of statutory designations	
(4)	ss 58(1), (2), 59(1), (2)
28 Change of name	
(1)	s 77(1)
(2)	ss 67(1), 68(2), (3)
(3)	s 75(1), (2), (4)
(4)	ss 68(3), 75(3)
(5)	ss 68(5), (6), 75(5), (6)
(6)	ss 80(1)–(3), 81(1)
(7)	s 81(2), (3)
29 Regulations about names	
(1)	ss 55(1), 56(1)
(2)	s 56(2)
(3)	s 56(3), (4) (changed)
(6)	s 55(2)
30 Exemption from requirement of 'limited' as part of the name	
(2), (3)	ss 61(1)–(4), 62(1)–(3) (changed)
(4)	s 60(3)
(5B)	s 60(2)
31 Provisions applying to company exempt under s 30	
(1)	s 63(1)
(2)	s 64(1)–(4) (changed)
(3)	s 64(7)
(5)	s 63(2), (3)

Provision of Companies Act 1985	*Destination in Companies Act 2006*
(6)	s 64(5), (6)
32 Power to require company to abandon misleading name	
(1)	s 76(1)
(2)	s 76(3)
(3)	s 76(4), (5)
(4)	s 76(6), (7) (changed)
(5)	ss 80(1)–(3), 81(1)
(6)	s 81(2), (3)
35 A company's capacity not limited by its memorandum	
(1)	s 39(1) (changed)
(4)	s 39(2)
35A Power of directors to bind the company	
(1)	s 40(1)
(2)	s 40(2)
(3)	s 40(3)
(4)	s 40(4)
(5)	s 40(5)
(6)	s 40(6)
35B No duty to inquire as to capacity of company or authority of directors	
	s 40(2)
36 Company contracts: England and Wales	
(1), (2)	s 43(1), (2)
36A Execution of documents: England and Wales	
(2)	ss 44(1)
(3)	s 45(1)
(4)	s 44(2), (3), (4)
(4A)	s 44(6)
(6)	s 44(5)
(7)	s 44(8)
(8)	s 44(7)
36AA Execution of deeds: England and Wales	
(1)	s 46(1)
(2)	s 46(2)
36B Execution of documents by companies	
(1)	s 48(2)
(2)	s 48(3)
36C Pre-incorporation contracts, deeds and obligations	
(1)	s 51(1)
(2)	s 51(2)
37 Bills of exchange and promissory notes	
	s 52
38 Execution of deeds abroad	
(1)	s 47(1) (changed)
(2)	s 47(2)
(3)	s 47(1)
39 Power of company to have official seal for use abroad	
(1)	s 49(1), (2) (changed)
(2), (2A)	s 49(3)
(3)	s 49(4)
(4)	s 49(5)
(5)	s 49(6)

Provision of Companies Act 1985	*Destination in Companies Act 2006*
40 Official seal for share certificates, etc	
(1)	s 50(1), (2)
42 Events affecting a company's status	
(1)	s 1079(1)–(3)
43 Re-registration of private company as public	
(1)	s 90(1), (2) (changed)
(2)	s 90(3)
(3)	ss 92(1), (2), 94(2), (3)
(4)	s 92(1)
44 Consideration for shares recently allotted to be valued	
(1)	s 93(1)
(2)	s 93(2), (7)
(4), (5)	s 93(3)–(5)
(6)	s 93(6)
(7)	s 93(6), (7)
45 Additional requirements relating to share capital	
(1)–(4)	s 91(1)
46 Meaning of 'unqualified report' in s 43(3)	
(2)	s 92(3)
(3)	s 92(4)
(4)	s 92(5), (6)
47 Certificate of re-registration under s 43	
(1)	s 96(1), (2)
(2)	s 94(4)
(3)	s 91(5) (changed)
(4)	s 96(4)
(5)	s 96(5)
48 Modification for unlimited company re-registering	
(1), (2)	s 90(4)
(5)	s 91(2)
(6)	s 91(3)
(7)	s 91(4)
49 Re-registration of limited company as unlimited	
(1)	s 102(1)
(2)	s 102(2)
(4)	s 102(1)
(5)–(7)	s 102(3)
(8)	ss 102(1), 103(2)–(4) (changed)
(8A)	s 103(3), (4) (changed)
(9)	s 102(4)
50 Certificate of re-registration under s 49	
(1)	s 104(1), (2)
(2)	s 104(4)
(3)	s 104(5)
51 Re-registration of unlimited company as limited	
(1)	s 105(1) (changed)
(2)	s 105(2)
(3)	s 105(3), (4)
(5)	s 106(2)
52 Certificate of re-registration under s 51	
(1)	s 107(1), (2)

Provision of Companies Act 1985	Destination in Companies Act 2006
(2)	s 107(4)
(3)	s 107(5)
53 Re-registration of public company as private	
(1)	ss 97(1), 100(2) (changed)
(2)	s 97(3)
54 Litigated objection to resolution under s 53	
(1)	s 98(1)
(2)	ss 98(1), 370(3) (changed)
(3)	s 98(2)
(4)	s 99(1), (2) (changed)
(5)	s 98(3), (4)
(6)	s 98(5), (6)
(7)	s 99(3)
(8)	s 98(6)
(10)	s 99(4), (5)
55 Certificate of re-registration under s 53	
(1)	s 101(1), (2)
(2)	s 101(4)
(3)	s 101(5)
58 Document offering shares etc for sale deemed a prospectus	
(3)	s 755(2)
80 Authority of company required for certain allotments	
(1)	s 549(1),s 551(1) (changed)
(2)	ss 549(1)–(3), 551(1), 559
(3)	s 551(2)
(4)	s 551(3), (4)
(5)	s 551(5)
(6)	s 551(6)
(7)	s 551(7)
(8)	s 551(8)
(9)	s 549(4), (5)
(10)	s 549(6) (changed)
81 Restriction on public offers by private company	
(1)	s 755(1)
(3)	s 760
84 Allotment where issue not fully subscribed	
(1)	s 578(1)
(2)	s 578(2)
(3)	s 578(3) (changed)
(4)	s 578(4), (5)
(5)	s 578(5)
(6)	s 578(6)
85 Effect of irregular allotment	
(1)	s 579(1), (2)
(2)	s 579(3)
(3)	s 579(4)
88 Return as to allotments, etc	
(1)	s 555(1)
(2)	s 555(2) (changed)
(5)	s 557(1), (2)
(6)	ss 557(3), 597(5), (6)

Provision of Companies Act 1985	*Destination in Companies Act 2006*
89 Offers to shareholders to be on pre-emptive basis	
(1)	s 561(1)
(2)	s 568(1)
(3)	s 568(1), (2)
(4)	ss 561(2), 565
(5)	s 566
(6)	s 561(4)
90 Communication of pre-emption offers to shareholders	
(1)	s 562(1)
(2)	s 568(3)
(5)	s 562(3) (changed)
(6)	s 562(4), (5) (changed)
91 Exclusion of ss 89, 90 by private company	
(1)	s 567(1), (2)
(2)	s 567(3), (4)
92 Consequences of contravening ss 89, 90	
(1)	ss 563(1), (2), 568(4)
(2)	ss 563(3), 568(5)
93 Saving for other restrictions as to offers	
(1)	s 575(1)
(2)	s 575(2)
94 Definitions for ss 89–96	
(2)	ss 560(1), 564, 577
(3)	ss 560(2), 561(3)
(3A)	s 560(2)
(5)	s 560(1)
(7)	s 574(1), (2)
95 Disapplication of pre-emption rights	
(1)	ss 570(1), (2), 573(2), (3), (5)
(2)	ss 571(1), (2), 573(4)
(2A)	s 573(1)–(5])
(3)	ss 570(3), 571(3)
(4)	ss 570(4), 571(4), 573(3), (5)
(5)	ss 571(5)–(7), 573(5) (changed)
(6)	572(1)–(3)
96 Saving for company's pre-emption procedure operative before 1982	
(1), (2)	s 576(1)
(3)	s 576(2)
(4)	s 576(3)
97 Power of company to pay commissions	
(1)	s 553(1)
(2)	s 553(2)
98 Apart from s 97, commissions and discounts barred	
(1)	s 552(1)
(2)	s 552(2)
(3)	s 552(3)
(4)	s 553(3)
99 General rules as to payment for shares on allotment	
(1)	s 582(1), (3)
(2)	s 585(1)
(3)	s 585(2)

Provision of Companies Act 1985	Destination in Companies Act 2006
(4)	s 582(2)
(5)	s 585(3)
100 Prohibition on allotment of shares at a discount	
(1)	s 580(1)
(2)	s 580(2)
101 Shares to be allotted as at least one-quarter paid-up	
(1)	s 586(1)
(2)	s 586(2)
(3), (4)	s 586(3)
(5)	s 586(4)
102 Restriction on payment by long-term undertaking	
(1)	s 587(1)
(2)	s 587(2)
(3), (4)	s 587(3)
(5), (6)	s 587(4)
(7)	s 587(5)
103 Non-cash consideration to be valued before allotment	
(1)	s 593(1)
(2)	s 593(2)
(3)	s 594(1)–(3)
(4)	s 594(4), (5)
(5)	s 595(1), (2)
(6)	s 593(3)
(7)	ss 594(6), 595(3)
104 Transfer to public company of non-cash asset in initial period	
(1)	s 598(1)
(2)	s 598(2)
(3)	s 603
(4)	ss 599(1), (3), 601(1)–(3) (changed)
(5)	s 599(2), (4)
(6)	s 598(4), (5)
105 Agreements contravening s 104	
(1)	s 604(1)
(2)	s 604(2)
(3)	s 604(3)
106 Shares issued to subscribers of memorandum	
	s 584
107 Meaning of 'the appropriate rate'	
	ss 592(1), (2), 609(1), (2)
108 Valuation and report (s 103)	
(1)	s 1150(1) (changed)
(2)	s 1150(2)
(3)	s 1150(3)
(4)	s 596(2)
(5)	s 1150(4)
(6)	ss 596(3), 600(3)
(7)	s 596(4), (5)
109 Valuation and report (s 104)	
(2)	s 600(2), (3)
(3)	s 600(4), (5)
110 Entitlement of valuer to full disclosure	

Provision of Companies Act 1985	*Destination in Companies Act 2006*
(1)	s 1153(1)
(2)	s 1153(2), (4)
(3)	s 1153(3)
111 Matters to be communicated to registrar	
(1)	s 597(1), (2)
(2)	s 602(1)
(3)	s 597(3)–(6)
(4)	s 602(2), (3)
111A Right to damages, &c not affected	
	s 655
112 Liability of subsequent holders of shares allotted	
(1)	ss 588(1), 605(1)
(2)	s 605(2)
(3)	ss 588(2), 605(3)
(4)	ss 588(3), 605(4)
(5)	s 588(1), (4)
113 Relief in respect of certain liabilities under ss 99 ff	
(1)	ss 589(1), (2), 606(1)
(2)	ss 589(3), 606(2) (changed)
(3)	ss 589(3), 606(2)
(4)	ss 589(4), 606(3)
(5)	ss 589(5), 606(4)
(6), (7)	ss 589(6), 606(5)
(8)	s 606(6)
114 Penalty for contravention	
	ss 590(1), (2), 607(2), (3)
115 Undertakings to do work, etc	
(1)	ss 591(1), (2), 608(1), (2)
117 Public company share capital requirements	
(1)	s 761(1)
(2)	s 761(2) (changed)
(3)	s 762(1) (changed)
(4)	s 761(3)
(5)	s 762(3)
(6)	s 761(4) (changed)
(7)	s 767(1), (2)
(8)	s 767(3)
118 The authorised minimum	
(1)	ss 763(1), 764(1) (changed)
(2)	s 764(3)
(3)	s 764(4)
119 Provision for different amounts to be paid on shares	
	s 581
121 Alteration of share capital (limited companies)	
(1)	s 617(1) (changed)
(2)	ss 617(2), (3), 618(1), 620(1) (changed)
(3)	s 618(2)
(4)	ss 618(3), 620(2) (changed)
122 Notice to registrar of alteration	
(1)	ss 619(1)–(3), 621(1), 663(1), 689(1) (changed)

Provision of Companies Act 1985	Destination in Companies Act 2006
(2)	ss 619(4), (5), 621(4), (5), 663(4), (5), 689(4), (5)
125 Variation of class rights	
(1)	s 630(1)
(2)	s 630(2)–(4) (changed)
(6)	s 334(1)–(4), (6) (changed)
(7)	ss 334(7), 630(5)
(8)	s 630(6)
126 Saving for court's powers under other provisions	
	s 632
127 Shareholders' right to object to variation	
(1)	s 633(1)
(2)	s 633(2), (3)
(2A)	s 633(2)
(3)	s 633(4)
(4)	s 633(5)
(5)	s 635(1)–(3)
(6)	s 633(6)
128 Registration of particulars of special rights	
(1)	s 556(1)–(3) (changed)
(2)	ss 556(1), (4), 629(2)
(3)	s 637(1) (changed)
(4)	s 636(1) (changed)
(5)	ss 557(1), (2), 636(2), (3), 637(2), (3) (changed)
129 Registration of newly created class rights	
(1)	s 638(1) (changed)
(2)	s 640(1) (changed)
(3)	s 639(1) (changed)
(4)	ss 638(2), (3), 639(2), (3), 640(2), (3)
130 Application of share premiums	
(1)	s 610(1)
(2)	s 610(2), (2) (changed)
(3)	s 610(4)
(4)	s 610(5), (6)
131 Merger relief	
(1)	s 612(1), (4)
(2)	s 612(2)
(3)	s 612(3)
(4)	s 613(2), (3)
(5)	s 613(4)
(6)	s 613(5)
(7)	s 616(1)
132 Relief in respect of group reconstructions	
(1)	s 611(1)
(2)	s 611(2)
(3)	s 611(3)
(4)	s 611(4)
(5)	s 611(5)
(8)	s 612(4)
133 Provisions supplementing ss 131, 132	
(1)	s 615

Provision of Companies Act 1985	Destination in Companies Act 2006
(2)	s 616(2)
(3)	s 616(3)
(4)	s 616(1)
134 Provision for extending or restricting relief from s 130	
(1)	s 614(1)
(3)	s 614(2)
135 Special resolution for reduction of share capital	
(1)	s 641(1)–(3) (changed)
(2)	s 641(4)
136 Application to court for order of confirmation	
(1)	s 645(1)
(2)	ss 645(2), (4), 646(4)
(3)	s 646(1)
(4)	s 646(2), (3)
(5)	s 646(4), (5)
(6)	s 645(2), (3)
137 Court order confirming reduction	
(1)	s 648(1), (2)
(2)	s 648(3), (4)
(3)	s 648(4)
138 Registration of order and minute of reduction	
(1)	s 649(1) (changed)
(2)	s 649(3) (changed)
(3)	s 649(4) (changed)
(4)	s 649(5), (6) (changed)
139 Public company reducing capital below authorised minimum	
(1)	s 650(1)
(2)	s 650(2)
(3)	s 651(1), (2)
(4)	s 651(3) (changed)
(5)	s 651(4), (6), (7)
140 Liability of members on reduced shares	
(1)	s 652(1) (changed)
(2)	s 653(1)
(3)	s 653(2)
(4)	s 653(3)
(5)	s 653(3)
141 Penalty for concealing name of creditor, etc	
	s 647(1), (2) (changed)
142 Duty of directors on serious loss of capital	
(1)	s 656(1)–(3)
(2)	s 656(4), (5) (changed)
(3)	s 656(6)
143 General rule against company acquiring own shares	
(1)	s 658(1)
(2)	s 658(2), (3)
(2A)	s 725(4)
(3)	s 659(1), (2)
144 Acquisition of shares by company's nominee	
(1)	s 660(1), (2) (changed)
(2)	s 661(1), (2) (changed)

Provision of Companies Act 1985	Destination in Companies Act 2006
(3)	s 661(3)
(4)	s 661(4)
145 Exceptions from s 144	
(1)	s 660(3)
(2)	ss 660(3), 661(5)
(3)	s 671
146 Treatment of shares held by or for public company	
(1)	ss 662(1), 671
(2)	s 662(2), (3)
(3)	s 662(3)
(4)	s 662(5), (6)
147 Matters arising out of compliance with s 146(2)	
(2)	s 664(1), (2)
(3)	s 664(4) (changed)
(4)	s 665(1), (2), (4), (5) (changed)
148 Further provisions supplementing ss 146, 147	
(1)	s 668(1), (2)
(2)	s 668(3)
(3)	s 671
(4)	s 669(1), (2)
149 Sanctions for non-compliance	
(1)	s 666(1), (2)
(2)	s 667(1)–(3)
150 Charges of public companies on own shares	
(1)	s 670(1)
(2)	s 670(2)
(3)	s 670(3)
(4)	s 670(4)
151 Financial assistance generally prohibited	
(1)	ss 678(1), 679(1) (changed)
(2)	ss 678(3), 679(3) (changed)
(3)	s 680(1), (2)
152 Definitions for this Chapter	
(1)	ss 677(1), 683(1)
(2)	s 677(2), (3)
(3)	s 683(2)
153 Transactions not prohibited by s 151	
(1)	ss 678(2), 679(2) (changed)
(2)	ss 678(4), 679(4)
(3)	s 681(1), (2)
(4)	s 682(1), (2)
(5)	s 682(5)
154 Special restriction for public companies	
(1)	s 682(1)
(2)	ss 682(3), (4), 840(4), (5)
159 Power to issue redeemable shares	
(1)	s 684(1), (3) (changed)
(2)	s 684(4)
(3)	ss 686(1)–(3) (changed), 691(1), (2)
160 Financing etc of redemption	
(1)	ss 687(1)–(3), (6), 692(1), (2), (5)

Provision of Companies Act 1985	Destination in Companies Act 2006
(2)	ss 687(4), (5), 692(3), (4)
(4)	ss 688, 706 (changed)
162 Power of company to purchase own shares	
(1)	s 690(1) (changed)
(2)	ss 691(1), (2), 692(1)–(5)
(2A)	s 706
(2B)	ss 706, 724(1)
(3)	s 690(2)
(4)	s 724(2)
162A Treasury shares	
(1)	s 724(3)
(2)	s 724(4)
(3)	s 724(5)
162B Treasury shares: maximum holdings	
(1)	s 725(1)
(2)	s 725(2)
(3)	s 725(4)
162C Treasury shares: voting and other rights	
(1)	s 726(1)
(2), (3)	s 726(2)
(4)	s 726(3)
(5)	s 726(4)
(6)	s 726(5)
162D Treasury shares: disposal and cancellation	
(1)	ss 727(1), 729(1)
(2)	s 727(2) (changed)
(3)	s 727(3)
(4)	s 729(4)
(5)	s 729(5)
162E Treasury shares: mandatory cancellation	
(1)	s 729(2)
(2)	s 729(3)
162F Treasury shares: proceeds of sale	
(1)	s 731(1)
(2)	s 731(2)
(3)	s 731(3)
(4), (5)	s 731(4)
162G Treasury shares: penalty for contravention	
	s 732(1), (2) (changed)
163 Definitions of 'off-market' and 'market' purchase	
(1)	s 693(2)
(2)	s 693(3)
(3)	s 693(4)
(4), (5)	s 693(5)
164 Authority for off-market purchase	
(1)	ss 693(1), 694(1)
(2)	s 694(2) (changed)
(3)	ss 694(4), 697(3), 700(3)
(4)	ss 694(5), 697(4), 700(4)
(5)	ss 694(1), (3), (4), 698(1), (3), (4), 700(5)
(6)	ss 696(1)–(5), 699(1)–(6), 700(5) (changed)

Provision of Companies Act 1985	Destination in Companies Act 2006
(7)	ss 697(1)–(4), 698(1), (3), (4), 699(1)–(6), 700(3)–(5)
165 Authority for contingent purchase contract	
(1)	s 694(3)
(2)	ss 694(2), (4), (5), 695(1), (3), (5), 696(1)–(5)
166 Authority for market purchase	
(1)	ss 693(1), 701(1)
(2)	s 701(2)
(3)	s 701(3), (5)
(4)	s 701(4), (5)
(5)	s 701(6)
(6)	s 701(7)
(7)	s 701(8)
167 Assignment or release of company's right to purchase own shares	
(1)	s 704
(2)	s 700(1)–(5)
168 Payments apart from purchase price to be made out of distributable profits	
(1)	s 705(1)
(2)	s 705(2)
169 Disclosure by company of purchase of own shares	
(1)	ss 707(1)–(3), 708(1) (changed)
(1A)	ss 707(1)–(3), 708(1) (changed)
(1B)	ss 707(1)–(3), 708(1) (changed)
(2)	s 707(4)
(3)	s 707(5)
(4)	s 702(1)–(4) (changed)
(5)	s 702(6)
(6)	ss 707(6), (7), 708(4), (5)
(7)	s 703(1), (2) (changed)
(8)	s 703(3)
(9)	s 702(7)
169A Disclosure by company of cancellation or disposal of treasury shares	
(1)	ss 728(1), 730(1)
(2)	ss 728(2), 730(2)
(3)	ss 728(3), 730(3)
(4)	ss 728(4), (5), 730(6), (7)
170 The capital redemption reserve	
(1)	s 733(1), (2), (4)
(2), (3)	s 733(3)
(4)	s 733(5), (6)
171 Power of private companies to redeem or purchase own shares out of capital	
(1)	s 709(1) (changed)
(2)	s 709(2)
(3)	s 710(1), (2)
(4)	s 734(2)
(5)	s 734(3)
(6)	s 734(4)
172 Availability of profits for purposes of s 171	
(1)	s 711(1), (2)
(2)	s 712(2)
(3)	s 712(6)

Provision of Companies Act 1985	Destination in Companies Act 2006
(4)	s 712(3)
(5)	s 712(4)
(6)	s 712(7)
173 Conditions for payment out of capital	
(1)	s 713(1), (2)
(2)	s 716(1)
(3)	s 714(1)–(3)
(4)	s 714(4) (changed)
(5)	s 714(5), (6) (changed)
(6)	s 715(1), (2)
174 Procedure for special resolution under s 173	
(1)	ss 716(2), 723(1)
(2)	s 717(3)
(3)	s 717(4)
(4)	s 718(2), (3) (changed)
(5)	s 717(5)
175 Publicity for proposed payment out of capital	
(1)	s 719(1)
(2)	s 719(2)
(3)	s 719(3)
(4)	ss 719(4), 720(1)
(5)	s 719(4)
(6)	s 720(1), (2), (4) (changed)
(7)	s 720(5), (6)
(8)	s 720(7)
176 Objections by company's members or creditors	
(1)	s 721(1), (2)
(2)	s 721(2)
(3)	s 722(2), (3)
(4)	s 722(4), (5)
177 Powers of court on application under s 176	
(1)	s 721(3)
(2)	s 721(4), (5)
(3)	s 721(6)
(4)	s 721(7)
178 Effect of company's failure to redeem or purchase	
(1)	s 735(1)
(2)	s 735(2)
(3)	s 735(2), (3)
(4)	s 735(4)
(5)	s 735(5)
(6)	s 735(6)
181 Definitions for Chapter VII	
	s 736
182 Nature, transfer and numbering of shares	
(1)	ss 541, 544(1), (2)
(2)	s 543(1), (2)
183 Transfer and registration	
(1)	s 770(1)
(2)	s 770(2)
(3)	s 773

Provision of Companies Act 1985	Destination in Companies Act 2006
(4)	s 772
184 Certification of transfers	
(1)	s 775(1), (2)
(2)	s 775(3)
(3)	s 775(4)
185 Duty of company as to issue of certificates	
(1)	ss 769(1), (2), 776(1), (3)
(2)	s 776(2)
(3)	s 777(1), (2)
(4)	ss 769(2), 776(3), 778(1)
(4A)	s 778(1)
(4B), (4C)	s 778(2)
(4D)	s 778(3)
(5)	ss 769(3), (4), 776(5), (6)
(6)	s 782(1)
(7)	s 782(2), (3)
186 Certificate to be evidence of title	
(1)	s 768(1), (2)
(2)	s 768(2)
187 Evidence of grant of probate or confirmation as executor	
	s 774
188 Issue and effect of share warrant to bearer	
(1)	s 779(1)
(2)	s 779(2)
(3)	s 779(3)
189 Offences in connections with share warrants (Scotland)	
(1)	s 781(1), (3)
(2)	s 781(2), (4)
190 Register of debenture holders	
(1)	s 743(6)
(5)	s 743(2), (6) (changed)
(6)	s 743(3)
191 Right to inspect register	
(1)	s 744(1)
(2)	s 744(2)
(3)	s 749(1)
(4)	ss 746(1), (2), 749(2), (3)
(5)	ss 746(3), 749(4)
(6)	s 744(5)
(7)	s 748(1), (2) (changed)
192 Liability of trustees of debentures	
(1)	s 750(1), (3)
(2)	s 750(2)
(3)	s 751(1), (2)
(4)	s 751(3), (4)
193 Perpetual debentures	
	s 739(1), (2)
194 Power to re-issue redeemed debentures	
(1)	s 752(1)
(2)	s 752(2)
(3)	s 753

Provision of Companies Act 1985	Destination in Companies Act 2006
(4)	s 752(3)
(5)	s 752(4)
195 Contract to subscribe for debentures	
	s 740
196 Payment of debts out of assets subject to floating charge (England and Wales)	
(1)	s 754(1)
(2)	s 754(2)
(3)	s 754(3)
(4)	s 754(4)
197 Debentures to bearer (Scotland)	
	s 742
198 Obligation of disclosure: the cases in which it may arise and 'the relevant time'	
(2)	s 792(1), (2) (changed)
203 Notification of family and corporate interests	
(1)	s 822(1), (2)
(2)	s 823(1)
(3)	s 832(2)
(4)	s 823(3)
204 Agreement to acquire interests in a particular company	
(1)	s 824(1)
(2)	ss 824(1), (2), 988(4)
(3)	ss 824(3), 988(6)
(4)	s 824(4)
(5)	ss 824(5), 988(7)
(6)	ss 824(6), 988(5)
205 Obligation of disclosure arising under s 204	
(1)	s 825(1)
(2)	s 825(2)
(3)	s 825(3)
(4)	s 825(4)
207 Interests in shares by attribution	
(1)	ss 783, 785(1)
(2)	s 785(2)
(3)	s 785(3)
(4)	s 785(4)
(5)	s 785(5)
(6)	s 785(6)
(7)	s 788
(9)	s 784(3)
(10)	s 783
208 Interests in shares which are to be notified	
(1)	s 820(1)
(2)	s 820(2)
(3)	s 820(3)
(4)	s 820(4)
(5)	s 820(6)
(6)	s 820(5)
(7)	s 820(7)
(8)	s 820(8)
210A Power to make further provision by regulations	
(1)	s 828(1), (2)

Provision of Companies Act 1985	Destination in Companies Act 2006
(5)	s 828(3)
211 Register of interests in shares	
(3)	s 808(2)
(4)	s 808(7)
(5)	s 808(4)
(6)	s 810(1)–(3)
(7)	s 819(1)
(8)	ss 809(1), 810(4), 811(1), (2), 813(1)–(3) (changed)
(9)	s 826(1)
(10)	ss 808(5), (6), 819(2), (3)
212 Company investigations	
(1)	s 793(1), (2) (changed)
(2)	s 793(3), (4), (6)
(3)	s 793(5)
(4)	s 793(7)
(5)	ss 820(1)–(8), 822(1), (2), 823(1)–(3), 824(1)–(6), 825(1)–(4)
(6)	s 821(1), (2)
213 Registration of interests disclosed under s 212	
(1)	s 808(1)–(3) (changed)
(3)	ss 808(2), (4)–(7), 809(1), 810(1)–(4), 811(1), (2), 813(1)–(3), 819(1)–(3), 826(1)
214 Company investigation on requisition by members	
(1)	s 803(1), (2) (changed)
(2)	s 803(3) (changed)
(4)	s 804(1)
(5)	s 804(2), (3) (changed)
215 Company report to members	
(1)	s 805(1)
(2)	s 805(2), (3)
(3)	s 805(1), (3)
(4)	s 826(1), (2)
(5)	s 805(6)
(6)	s 805(7)
(7)	ss 805(4), 807(1)–(5)
(8)	s 806(3), (4)
216 Penalty for failure to provide information	
(1)	s 794(1)
(1A)	s 794(3)
(1B)	s 794(2)
(3)	s 795(1), (3)
(4)	s 795(2)
(5)	s 796(1), (2)
217 Removal of entries from register	
(1)	s 816 (changed)
(2)	s 817(1) (changed)
(3)	s 817(2), (3)
(4)	s 818(1), (2)
(5)	ss 817(4), 818(3)
218 Otherwise, entries not to be removed	

Provision of Companies Act 1985	*Destination in Companies Act 2006*
(1)	s 815(1)
(2)	s 815(2)
(3)	s 815(3), (4)
219 Inspection of register and reports	
(1)	s 807(1), 811(1)
(2)	s 807(2), 811(2)
(3)	ss 807(3), (4), 813(1), (2) (changed)
(4)	ss 807(5), 813(3)
220 Definitions for Part VI	
(2)	s 827
221 Duty to keep accounting records	
(1)	s 386(1), (2)
(2)–(4)	s 386(3)–(5)
(5)	s 387(1), (2)
(6)	s 387(3)
222 Where and for how long records to be kept	
(1)–(3)	s 388(1)–(3)
(4)	s 389(1), (2), (4)
(5)	s 388(4), (5)
(6)	s 389(3), (4)
223 A company's financial year	
(1)–(5)	s 390(1)–(5)
224 Accounting reference periods and accounting reference date	
(1)	s 391(1)
(2), (3)	s 391(2)
(3A)	s 391(4)
(4)–(6)	s 391(5)–(7)
225 Alteration of accounting reference date	
(1)	s 392(1)
(3)–(7)	s 392(2)–(6)
226 Duty to prepare individual accounts	
(1)	s 394
(2)–(6)	s 395(1)–(5)
226A Companies Act individual accounts	
(1), (2)	s 396(1), (2)
(3)	s 396(3) (changed)
(4)	s 396(4)
(5), (6)	s 396(5)
226B IAS individual accounts	
	s 397
227 Duty to prepare group accounts	
(1)	s 399(2)
(2)–(7)	s 403(1)–(6)
(8)	s 399(2), (3)
227A Companies Act group accounts	
(1), (2)	s 404(1), (2)
(3)	s 404(3) (changed)
(4)	s 404(4)
(5), (6)	s 404(5)
227B IAS group accounts	
	s 406

Provision of Companies Act 1985	Destination in Companies Act 2006
227C Consistency of accounts	
(1)–(5)	s 407(1)–(5)
228 Exemption for parent companies included in accounts of larger group	
(1), (2)	s 400(1), (2)
(3)	s 400(4)
(4)	s 400(5)
(5)	s 400(3)
(6)	s 400(6)
228A Exemption for parent companies included in non-EEA group accounts	
(1), (2)	s 401(1), (2)
(3)	s 401(4)
(4)	s 401(5)
(5)	s 401(3)
(6)	s 401(6)
229 Subsidiary undertakings included in the consolidation	
(1), (2)	s 405(1), (2)
(3)	s 405(3), (4)
(5)	s 402
230 Treatment of individual profit and loss account where group accounts prepared	
(1)	s 408(1) (changed)
(2)	s 408(2) (changed)
(3), (40	s 408(3), (4)
231 Disclosure required in notes to accounts: related undertakings	
(1), (2)	s 409(1), (2) (changed)
(3)	s 409(3), (4) (changed)
(4)	s 409(5)
(5)	s 410(1), (2)
(6)	s 410(3)
(7)	s 410(4), (5)
231A Disclosure required in notes to annual accounts: particulars of staff	
(1)	s 411(1)
(2)–(4)	s 411(3)–(5)
(5)	s 411(2)
(6)	s 411(7)
(7)	s 411(6)
232 Disclosure required in notes to accounts: emoluments and other benefits of directors and others	
(3)	s 412(5)
(4)	s 412(6)
233 Approval and signing of accounts	
(1), (2)	ss 414(1), (2), 450(1), (2)
(3)	ss 433(1)–(3), 436(1), (2),
(4)	ss 444(6), 445(5), 446(3), 447(3) (changed)
(5)	ss 414(4), (5) (changed)
(6)(a)	s 433(4), (5),
234 Duty to prepare directors' report	
(1)	ss 415(1), 417(1), 418(2)
(2), (3)	s 415(2), (3)
(5)	ss 415(4), (5), 419(3), (4)
234ZZA Directors' report: general requirements	
(1)	s 416(1), (3)

Provision of Companies Act 1985	Destination in Companies Act 2006
(2)	s 416(2)
(3), (4)	s 416(4) (changed)
234ZZB Directors' report: business review	
(1), (2)	s 417(3), (4)
(3)	s 417(6)
(4)	s 417(8)
(5)	s 417(6)
(6)	s 417(9)
234ZA Statement as to disclosure of information to auditors	
(1)–(4)	s 418(1)–(4)
(6)	s 418(5), (6)
234A Approval and signing of directors' report	
(1)	s 419(1)
(2)	ss 433(1)–(3), 436(1), (2)
(3)	ss 444(6), 445(5), 446(3), 447(3)
(4)	ss 419(3), (4), 433(4), (5)
234B Duty to prepare directors' remuneration report	
(1)	ss 420(1), 421(1), (2)
(2)	s 421(1), (2)
(3), (4)	s 420(2), (3)
(5), (6)	s 421(3), (4)
234C Approval and signing of directors' remuneration report	
(1)	s 422(1)
(2)	ss 433(1)–(3), 436(1), (2)
(3)	s 447(3)
(4)	s 422(2), (3)
235 Auditors' report	
(1)	ss 475(1), 495(1)
(1A)	s 495(2)
(1B), (2)	s 495(3)
(2A)	s 495(4)
(3)	s 496
(4), (5)	s 497(1), (2)
236 Signature of auditors' report	
(1)	s 503(1), (2)
(2)	s 505(1), (2) (changed)
(3)	s 444(7) (changed)
(4)	s 505(3), (4)
237 Duties of auditors	
(1)–(4)	s 498(1)–(4)
(4A)	s 498(5)
238 Persons entitled to receive copies of accounts and reports	
(1), (1A)	ss 423(1), 424(1)–(3) (changed)
(3)	s 423(4)
(4)	s 424(4) (changed)
(5)	s 425(1), (2)
(6)	s 423(5)
239 Right to demand copies of accounts and reports	
(1), (2)	ss 431(1), (2), 432(1), (2)
(3)	ss 431(3), (4), 432(3), (4)
240 Requirements in connection with publication of accounts	

Provision of Companies Act 1985	Destination in Companies Act 2006
(1)	s 434(1) (changed)
(2)	s 434(2) (changed)
(3)	s 435(1), (2) (changed)
(4)	s 436(1), (2) (changed)
(5)	ss 434(3), 435(3) (changed)
(6)	s 435(5), (6)
241 Accounts and reports to be laid before company in general meeting	
(1)	s 437(1) (changed)
(2)	ss 437(2), 438(1), (4)
(3), (4)	s 438(2), (3)
241A Members' approval of directors' remuneration report	
(1), (3)	s 439(1)
(4)	s 439(2)
(5)	s 439(3)
(6)	s 439(4)
(7)	s 439(3)
(8)	s 439(5)
(9)	s 440(1), (4)
(10)	s 440(2)–(4)
(11)	s 440(2), (3)
(12)	s 439(6)
242 Accounts and reports to be delivered to the registrar	
(1)	s 441(1), 444(1), (2), 445(1), (2), 446(1), (2), 447(1), (2) (changed)
(2)	s 451(1)
(3)	s 452(1), (2)
(4), (5)	s 451(2), (3)
242A Civil penalty for failure to deliver accounts	
(1)	s 453(1)
(2)	s 453(2) (changed)
(3), (4)	s 453(3), (4)
242B Delivery and publication of accounts in ECUs	
(1)–(4)	s 469(1)–(4)
244 Period allowed for laying and delivering accounts and reports	
(1), (2)	s 442(2), (3) (changed)
(4), (5)	s 442(4), (5)
(6)	s 442(7)
245 Voluntary revision of annual accounts or directors' report	
(1)–(3)	s 454(1)–(3)
(4)	s 454(4) (changed)
(5)	s 454(5)
245A Secretary of State's notice in respect of annual accounts	
(1)	s 455(1), (2)
(2)–(4)	s 455(3)–(5)
245B Application to court in respect of defective accounts	
(1)–(3)	s 456(1)–(3)
(3A)	s 456(4)
(4)–(7)	s 456(5)–(8)
245C Other persons authorised to apply to court	
(1)	s 457(1)
(1A)	s 457(5)

Provision of Companies Act 1985	*Destination in Companies Act 2006*
(2), (3)	s 457(2), (3)
(4)	s 457(7)
(4A)	s 457(5)
(4B)	s 457(4)
(5)	s 457(6)
245D Disclosure of information held by Inland Revenue to persons authorised to apply to court	
(1)	s 458(1)
(2)	s 458(2)
(3)	s 458(1)
245E Restrictions on use and further disclosure of information disclosed under section 245D	
(1), (2)	s 458(3)
(3)	s 458(4), (5)
(4)	s 458(4) (changed)
(5)	ss 1126, 1130
245F Power of authorised persons to require documents, information and explanations	
(1)–(8)	s 459(1)–(8)
245G Restrictions on further disclosure of information obtained under section 245F	
(1), (2)	s 460(1), (2)
(3)	ss 460(3), 461(1)–(6)
(4)–(6)	s 462(1)–(3)
(7)	s 460(4), (5)
(8)	s 460(4)
(9)	ss 1126, 1130
(10)	s 460(3)
(11)	s 461(7)
246 Special provisions for small companies	
(3)	s 411(1)
(4)	ss 416(3), 417(1)
(5)	s 444(1), (3) (changed)
(6)	s 444(3) (changed)
(7)	ss 444(6), 450(1), (2)
(8)	ss 414(3), 419(2), 444(5), 450(3)
246A Special provisions for medium-sized companies	
(1)	s 445(1)
(2)	s 445(3) (changed)
(2A)	s 417(7)
(3)	s 445(3) (changed)
(4)	s 450(3)
247 Qualification of company as small or medium-sized	
(1)(a)	ss 382(1), 465(1)
(1)(b), (2)	ss 382(2), 465(2)
(3), (4)	ss 382(3), (4), 465(3), (4)
(5)	ss 382(5), 465(5) (changed)
(6)	ss 382(6), 465(6)
247A Cases in which special provisions do not apply	
(1)–(1B)	ss 384(1), 467(1)
(2)	ss 384(2), 467(2) (changed)
(2A)	ss 384(3), 467(3)
(3)	ss 383(1), 466(1)
247B Special auditors' report	
(1)	s 449(1)

Provision of Companies Act 1985	Destination in Companies Act 2006
(2)	ss 444(4), 445(4), 449(2)
(3)–(5)	s 449(3)–(5)
248 Exemption for small and medium-sized groups	
(1), (2)	ss 398, 399(1), (2) (changed)
249 Qualification of group as small or medium-sized	
(1)(a)	s 466(2)
(1)(b), (2)	s 466(3)
(3)	s 466(4)
(4)	s 466(5), (6)
(5), (6)	s 466(7)
249A Exemptions from audit	
(1)	s 477(1)
(3)	s 477(2), (4)
(6)	s 477(3)
(7)	s 477(4)
249AA Dormant companies	
(1), (2)	s 480(1), (2)
(3)	s 481
(4)	s 1169(1)
(5)–(7)	s 1169(2), (3)
249B Cases where exemptions not available	
(1)	ss 478, 479(1)–(3)
(1A)	s 479(3)
(1B)	s 479(1)–(3)
(1C)	s 479(2), (5), (6)
(2), (3)	s 476(1)–(3)
(4)	s 475(2), (3)
(5)	s 475(4)
249E Effect of exemptions	
(1)(b)	ss 444(2), 445(2), 446(2) (changed)
251 Provision of summary financial statement to shareholders	
(1)	ss 426(1), 427(1)
(2)	s 426(2), (3)
(3)	ss 427(2), 428(2)
(3A)	ss 427(3), 428(3)
(4)	ss 427(4), 428(4)
(5)	ss 427(6), 428(6)
(6)	s 429(1), (2)
(7)	ss 434(6), 435(7)
254 Exemption from requirement to deliver accounts and reports	
(1)–(3)	s 448(1)–(3)
(4)	s 448(4)
255A Special provisions for banking and insurance groups	
(4)	s 1164(5)
(5)	s 1165(5)
(5A)	ss 1164(5), 1165(6)
255D Power to apply provisions to banking partnerships	
(1)	s 470(1)
(2), (2A)	s 470(2)
(4)	s 470(4)
(5)	s 470(3)

Provision of Companies Act 1985	*Destination in Companies Act 2006*
256 Accounting standards	
(1), (2)	s 464(1), (2)
(4)	s 464(3)
257 Power of Secretary of State to alter accounting requirements	
(1)	s 484(1)
(2)	ss 473(1)–(4) (changed), 484(3)
(3)	s 484(4)
(4)(c)	s 484(2)
258 Parent and subsidiary undertakings	
(1)–(6)	s 1162(1)–(6)
259 Meaning of 'undertaking' and related expressions	
(1)	ss 1161(1), 1173 'parent company'
(2)–(5)	s 1161(2)–(5)
261 Notes to the accounts	
(1), (2)	s 472(1), (2)
262 Minor definitions	
(1)	ss 474(1), 539, 835(6), 1173 'credit institution' (changed)
(2)	s 474(2)
(3)	s 853(4), (5)
263 Certain distributions prohibited	
(1)	s 830(1)
(2)	s 829(1), (2)
(3)	s 830(2), (3)
(4)	s 849
(5)	s 850(1)–(3)
264 Restriction on distribution of assets	
(1)	s 831(1), (6)
(2)	s 831(2), (3)
(3)	s 831(4)
(4)	s 831(5)
265 Other distributions by investment companies	
(1)	s 832(1)–(3)
(2)	s 832(4)
(3)	s 832(7)
(4)	s 832(5)
(4A)	s 832(6)
(5)	s 832(6)
(6)	s 832(5)
266 Meaning of 'investment company'	
(1)	s 833(1)
(2)	ss 833(2), 834(1)
(2A)	s 833(3)
(3)	s 833(4), (5)
(4)	s 834(2)–(5)
267 Extension of ss 265, 266 to other companies	
(1)	s 835(1)
(2)	s 835(2)
268 Realised profits of insurance company with long term business	
(1)	s 843(1), (2), (4), (5)
(2)	s 843(3), (4)

Provision of Companies Act 1985	*Destination in Companies Act 2006*
(3)	s 843(6), (7)
(4)	s 843(7)
269 Treatment of development costs	
(1)	s 844(1)
(2)	s 844(2), (3)
270 Distribution to be justified by reference to company's accounts	
(1), (2)	s 836(1)
(3)	ss 836(2), 837(1)
(4)	ss 836(2), 838(1), 839(1)
(5)	s 836(3), (4)
271 Requirements for last annual accounts	
(2)	s 837(2)
(3)	s 837(3), (4)
(4)	s 837(4)
(5)	s 837(5)
272 Requirements for interim accounts	
(1)	s 838(2)
(2)	s 838(3)
(3)	ss 838(4), (5), 839(4)
(4), (5)	s 838(6)
273 Requirements for initial accounts	
(1)	s 839(2)
(2)	s 839(3)
(3)	s 839(4)
(4)	s 839(5), (6)
(5)	s 839(6)
(6), (7)	s 839(7)
274 Method of applying s 270 to successive distributions	
(1)	s 840(1)
(2)	s 840(1), (2)
(3)	s 840(3)–(5)
275 Treatment of assets in the relevant accounts	
(1)	s 841(1), (2)
(1A)	s 841(3)
(2)	s 841(5)
(3)	s 842
(4)–(6)	s 841(4)
276 Distributions in kind	
	s 846(1), (2) (changed)
277 Consequences of unlawful distribution	
(1)	s 847(1), (2)
(2)	s 847(3), (4)
278 Saving for provision in articles operative before Act of 1980	
	s 848(1), (2)
280 Definitions for Part VIII	
(1)	s 853(1)
(2)	s 853(2)
(3)	s 853(3)
281 Saving for other restraints on distribution	
	ss 851, 852 (changed)
282 Directors	

Provision of Companies Act 1985	Destination in Companies Act 2006
(1)	s 154(2) (changed)
(3)	s 154(1)
283 Secretary	
(1)	s 271 (changed)
(3)	ss 270(3), 274 (changed)
284 Acts done by person in dual capacity	
	s 280
285 Validity of acts of directors	
	s 161(1), (2) (changed)
286 Qualifications of company secretaries	
(1)	s 273(1), (2) (changed)
(2)	s 273(3)
287 Registered office	
(1)	s 86
(3)	s 87(1)
(4)	s 87(2)
(5)	s 87(3)
(6)	s 87(4)
288 Register of directors and secretaries	
(1)	ss 162(1)–(3), 275(1)–(3) (changed)
(2)	ss 167(1), (2), 276(1), (2)
(3)	ss 162(5), 275(5)
(4)	ss 162(6), (7), 167(4), (5), 275(6), (7), 276(3), (4)
(5)	ss 162(8), 275(8)
(6)	s 162(6), 167(4), 275(6), 276(3)
289 Particulars of directors to be registered under s 288	
(1)	ss 163(1), 164 (changed)
(2)	ss 163(2), (4), 277(2), (4) (changed)
290 Particulars of secretaries to be registered under s 288	
(1)	ss 277(1), 278(1) (changed)
(2)	s 278(2)
(3)	s 277(2), (4)
292 Appointment of directors to be voted on individually	
(1)	s 160(1)
(2)	s 160(2)
(3)	s 160(3)
(4)	s 160(4)
303 Resolution to remove director	
(1)	s 168(1) (changed)
(2)	s 168(2)
(3)	s 168(3)
(4)	s 168(4)
(5)	s 168(5)
304 Director's right to protest removal	
(1)	s 169(1), (2)
(2)	s 169(3)
(3)	s 169(4)
(4)	s 169(5)
(5)	s 169(6)
309 Directors to have regard to interests of employees	

Provision of Companies Act 1985	Destination in Companies Act 2006
(1)	s 172(1)
309A Provisions protecting directors from liability	
(1)	s 232(1), (2)
(2)	s 232(1)
(3)	s 232(2)
(4)	s 234(1)
(5)	s 233
(6)	s 232(3)
309B Qualifying third party indemnity provisions	
(1), (2)	s 234(2)
(3)	s 234(3)
(4)	s 234(3), (6)
(5)	s 234(4)
(6), (7)	s 234(5)
309C Disclosure of qualifying third party indemnity provisions	
(1)	s 236(1) (changed)
(2)	s 236(2), (3)
(3)	s 236(4), (5) (changed)
(4)	s 237(1)
(5)	ss 237(1)–(3), (5)–(8), 238(1), (3)–(5)
310 Provisions protecting auditors from liability	
(1)	s 532(1), (3) (changed)
(2)	s 532(2)
(3)	s 533
312 Payment to director for loss of office, etc	
	ss 215(1), 217(1), (3) (changed)
313 Company approval for property transfer	
(1)	ss 215(1), 218(1), (3) (changed)
(2)	s 222(2)
314 Director's duty of disclosure on takeover, etc	
(1)	ss 215(1), 219(1) (changed)
315 Consequences of non-compliance with s 314	
(1)	ss 219(1), (2), 222(3) (changed)
(3)	s 219(5)
316 Provisions supplementing ss 312 to 315	
(1)	ss 218(5), 219(7)
(2)	s 216(1), (2) (changed)
(3)	s 220(1)
317 Directors to disclose interest in contracts	
(1)	s 182(1) (changed)
(2)	s 182(2) (changed)
(3)	s 185(1), (2) (changed)
(4)	s 185(4)
(5)	s 185(1) (changed)
(7)	s 183(1), (2)
(8)	s 187(1)–(4)
318 Director's service contracts to be open to inspection	
(1)	ss 228(1), 237(2)
(2), (3)	ss 228(2), 237(3) (changed)
(4)	ss 228(4), 237(5)
(6)	s 230

Provision of Companies Act 1985	Destination in Companies Act 2006
(7)	ss 229(1), 238(1)
(8)	ss 228(5), (6), 229(3), (4), 237(6), (7), 238(3), (4) (changed)
(9)	ss 229(5), 238(5) (changed)
(10)	ss 228(7), 237(8)
319 Director's contract of employment for more than 5 years	
(1)	s 188(1), (3) (changed)
(2)	s 188(4) (changed)
(3)	s 188(2) (changed)
(4)	s 188(6)
(5)	s 188(5)
(6)	s 189
(7)	ss 188(7), 223(1)
320 Substantial property transactions involving directors, etc	
(1)	s 190(1), (2) (changed)
(2)	s 191(1)–(5) (changed)
(3)	s 223(1)
321 Exceptions from s 320	
(1)	s 190(4)
(2)	ss 192, 193(1), (2) (changed)
(3)	s 192
(4)	s 194(1), (2)
322 Liabilities arising from contravention of s 320	
(1)	s 195(1), (2)
(2)	ss 195(2) and 196
(3)	s 195(1), (3), (4)
(4)	s 195(3), (5), (8)
(5)	s 195(6)
(6)	s 195(7)
322A Invalidity of certain transactions involving directors, etc	
(1)	s 41(1), (2)
(2)	s 41(2)
(3)	s 41(3)
(4)	s 41(1)
(5)	s 41(4)
(6)	s 41(5)
(7)	s 41(6)
(8)	s 41(7)
322B Contracts with sole members who are directors	
(1)	s 231(1), (2) (changed)
(2)	s 231(1)
(3)	s 231(5)
(4)	s 231(3), (4) (changed)
(5)	s 231(7)
(6)	s 231(6)
325 Register of directors' interests notified under s 324	
(5)	s 809(2), (3)
330 General restriction on loans etc to directors and persons connected with them	
(2)	s 197(1) (changed)
(3)	ss 198(1), (2) (changed), 200(1), (2)
(4)	s 201(1), (2) (changed)

Provision of Companies Act 1985	Destination in Companies Act 2006
(5)	s 223(1)
(6)	s 203(1), (6) (changed)
(7)	s 203(1) (changed)
331 Definitions for ss 330 ff	
(3)	s 199(1)
(4)	s 199(2), (3)
(6)	ss 198(1), 200(1), 201(1)
(7)	s 202(1)
(8)	s 202(3)
(9)	ss 202(2), 212
(10)	s 202(3)
333 Inter-company loans in same group	
	s 208(1) (changed)
334 Loans of small amounts	
	s 207(1) (changed)
335 Minor and business transactions	
(1)	s 207(2) (changed)
(2)	s 207(3)
336 Transactions at behest of holding company	
	208(1), (2) (changed)
337 Funding of director's expenditure on duty to company	
(1), (2)	s 204(1) (changed)
(3)	s 204(2) (changed)
337A Funding of director's expenditure on defending proceedings	
(1)	s 205(1) (changed)
(2)	s 205(5)
(3)	s 205(1) (changed)
(4)	s 205(2)
(5)	s 205(3)
(6)	s 205(4)
338 Loan or quasi-loan by money-lending company	
(1)	s 209(1)
(2)	s 209(2)
(3)	s 209(1)
(6)	s 209(3), (4)
339 'Relevant amounts' for purposes of ss 334 ff	
(1)	ss 204(2), 207(1), (2), 210(1)
(2)	ss 204(2), 207(1), (2), 210(2)–(4)
(3)	s 210(3), (4)
(5)	s 210(5)
(6)	s 211(1)
340 'Value' of transactions and arrangements	
(2)	s 211(2)
(3)	s 211(3)
(4)	s 211(5)
(5)	s 211(6)
(6)	s 211(4)
(7)	s 211(7) (changed)
341 Civil remedies for breach of s 330	
(1)	s 213(1), (2)
(2)	s 213(3), (4)

Provision of Companies Act 1985	*Destination in Companies Act 2006*
(3)	s 213(5), (8)
(4)	s 213(6)
(5)	s 213(7)
345 Power to increase financial limits	
(1)	s 258(1)
(2)	s 258(2)
(3)	s 258(3)
346 'Connected persons', etc	
(1)	ss 252(1), 254(1), 255(1)
(2), (3)	ss 252(2), (3), 253(2) (changed)
(4)	s 254(2), (5)
(5)	s 255(2), (5)
(6)	ss 254(6), 255(6)
(7)	ss 254(3), 255(3)
(8)	ss 254(4), 255(4)
347 Transactions under foreign law	
	s 259
347A Introductory provisions	
(1)	s 362 (changed)
(3)	s 379(1)
(4)	s 364(2)
(5)	s 365(1) (changed)
(6)	s 363(1), (2)
(7)	s 363(1), (2) (changed)
(8)	s 379(1)
(9)	s 363(1)
(10)	ss 366(5), 379(2)
347B Exemptions	
(1)	s 375(1)
(2)	s 375(2) (changed)
(3)	s 376(1), (2)
(4)	s 378(1) (changed)
(5)	s 378(3)
(6), (7)	s 378(1) (changed)
(8)	s 377(1)
(9)	s 377(3)
(10)	s 377(2)
(11)	s 377(4)
347C Prohibition on donations and political expenditure by companies	
(1)	s 366(1), (2), (5) (changed)
(2)	s 367(3), (6) (changed)
(3)	s 368(1), (2)
(4)	s 367(5)
(6)	s 366(6)
347D Special rules for subsidiaries	
(1)	s 366(2)
(2)	s 366(2), (5) (changed)
(3)	s 366(2), (3), (5) (changed)
(4)	s 367(3), (6) (changed)
(5)	s 368(1), (2)
(6)	s 367(5)

Provision of Companies Act 1985	Destination in Companies Act 2006
(9)	s 366(6)
347F Remedies for breach of prohibitions on company donations etc	
(1)	s 369(1)
(2)	s 369(2), (3) (changed)
(3)	s 369(2), (5)
(4)	s 369(2)
(5)	s 369(6)
(6)	s 369(3) (changed)
347I Enforcement of directors' liabilities by shareholder action	
(1)	s 370(1), (2) (changed)
(2)	s 370(3)
(3)	ss 370(4), 371(1)
(4), (5)	s 371(2)
(6)	s 371(3)
(7)	s 371(4)
(8)	s 371(5)
347J Costs of shareholder action	
(1)	s 372(1)
(2)	s 372(2)
(3)	s 372(3)
(4), (5)	s 372(4)
(6)	s 372(5)
347K Information for purposes of shareholder action	
(1)	s 373(1)
(2)	s 373(2)
348 Company name to appear outside place of business	
(1)	s 82(1), (2)
(2)	s 84(1), (2)
349 Company's name to appear in its correspondence, etc	
(1)	s 82(1), (2)
(2), (3)	s 84(1), (2)
350 Company seal	
(1)	s 45(2), (3) (changed)
(2)	s 45(4), (5)
351 Particulars in correspondence etc	
(1), (2)	s 82(1), (2)
(5)	s 84(1), (2)
352 Obligation to keep and enter up register	
(1)	s 113(1)
(2)	s 113(2)
(3)	s 113(3), (4)
(4)	s 113(6)
(5)	s 113(7), (8)
(6)	s 121 (changed)
(7)	s 128(1), (2)
352A Statement that company has only one member	
(1)	s 123(2) (changed)
(2)	s 123(3) (changed)
(3)	s 123(4), (5)
(3A)	s 124(1), (2)
353 Location of register	

Provision of Companies Act 1985	Destination in Companies Act 2006
(1)	s 114(1) (changed)
(2)	s 114(2)
(3)	s 114(3), (4)
(4)	s 114(5), (6)
354 Index of members	
(1)	s 115(1), (2)
(2)	s 115(3)
(3)	s 115(4) (changed)
(4)	s 115(5), (6)
355 Entries in register in relation to share warrants	
(1)	s 122(1) (changed)
(2)	s 122(4)
(3)	s 122(5)
(4)	s 122(2), (6)
(5)	s 122(3)
356 Inspection of register and index	
(1)	s 116(1) (changed)
(3)	s 116(2)
(5)	s 118(1), (2) (changed)
(6)	s 118(3)
359 Power of court to rectify register	
(1)	s 125(1)
(2)	s 125(2)
(3)	s 125(3)
(4)	s 125(4)
360 Trusts not to be entered on register in England and Wales	
	s 126
361 Register to be evidence	
	s 127
362 Overseas branch registers	
(1)	s 129(1)
(2)	s 129(1), (5)
(3)	ss 130(1)–(3), 131(1), (4), 132(1)–(4), 133(1)–(3), 134(1)–(3), 135(1)–(5)
363 Duty to deliver annual returns	
(1)	s 854(1), (2)
(2)	s 854(3) (changed)
(3)	s 858(1)–(3)
(4)	s 858(1), (2), (4) (changed)
364 Contents of annual return: general	
(1)	s 855(1) (changed)
(2)	s 855(2)
(3)	s 855(3)
364A Contents of annual return: particulars of share capital and shareholders	
(1)	s 856(1)
(2)	s 856(2)
(3)	s 856(2) (changed)
(4)	s 856(3)
(5)	s 856(4)
(6)	s 856(5)
(8)	s 856(6)

Provision of Companies Act 1985	*Destination in Companies Act 2006*
365 Supplementary provisions: regulations and interpretation	
(1)	s 857(1), (2)
(2)	s 857(3)
(3)	s 859
366 Annual general meeting	
(1)	ss 336(1), 337(1)
(4)	s 336(3), (4)
368 Extraordinary general meeting on members' requisition	
(1)	s 303(1), (2)
(2)	s 303(2), (3) (changed)
(2A)	s 303(2)
(3)	s 303(4), (6) (changed)
(4)	ss 304(1), 305(1), (3)
(5)	s 305(4)
(6)	s 305(6), (7)
(7)	s 304(4)
(8)	s 304(1)
369 Length of notice for calling meetings	
(1), (2)	s 307(2), (3) (changed)
(3)	ss 307(4), 337(2) (changed)
(4)	s 307(5), (6) (changed)
(4A)	s 308 (changed)
(4B)	ss 308, 309(1), (3) (changed)
(4C)	s 309(2)
370 General provisions as to meetings and votes	
(1)	ss 284(4), 310(4), 318(2), 319(2)
(2)	s 310(1)
(4)	s 318(2) (changed)
(5)	s 319(1)
(6)	s 284(1), (3)
370A Quorum at meetings of the sole member	
	s 318(1), (3) (changed)
371 Power of court to order meeting	
(1)	s 306(1), (2)
(2)	s 306(3), (4)
(3)	s 306(5)
372 Proxies	
(1)	s 324(1)
(2)	s 324(2) (changed)
(3)	s 325(1) (changed)
(4)	s 325(3), (4)
(5)	s 327(1), (2) (changed)
(6)	s 326(1)–(4) (changed)
373 Right to demand a poll	
(1)	s 321(1), (2) (changed)
(2)	s 329(1), (2) (changed)
374 Voting on a poll	
	s 322
375 Representation of corporations at meetings	
(1)	s 323(1)
(2)	s 323(2), (3) (changed)

Provision of Companies Act 1985	*Destination in Companies Act 2006*
376 Circulation of members' resolutions	
(1)	ss 314(1), (4), 315(2), 316(2), 338(1), (4), 339(2), 340(2)
(2)	ss 314(2), (3), 338(3)
(3)	ss 315(1), 339(1)
(5)	ss 315(1), 339(1)
(6)	s 339(3)
(7)	ss 315(3), (4), 339(4), (5)
377 In certain cases, compliance with s 376 not required	
(1)	ss 314(4), 316(2), 338(4), 340(2) (changed)
(3)	s 317(1), (2) (changed)
378 Extraordinary and special resolutions	
(1)	s 283(1), (4), (5) (changed)
(2)	s 283(1), (4)–(6) (changed)
(4)	s 320(1), (3)
(5)	s 283(5) (changed)
(6)	s 301 (changed)
379 Resolution requiring special notice	
(1)	s 312(1)
(2)	s 312(2), (3) (changed)
(3)	s 312(4)
380 Registration, etc of resolutions and agreements	
(1)	s 30(1)
(2)	s 36(1), (2) (changed)
(4)	s 29(1) (changed)
(4A)	s 29(2)
(5)	s 30(2), (3)
(6)	s 36(3), (4) (changed)
(7)	ss 30(4), 36(5)
381 Resolution passed at adjourned meeting	
	s 332
381A Written resolutions of private companies	
(1)	ss 288(1), 289(1) (changed)
(2)	s 296(1) (changed)
(4)	s 288(5)
(7)	s 288(2)
381C Written resolutions: supplementary provisions	
(1)	s 300
382 Minutes of meetings	
(1)	ss 248(1), 355(1)
(2)	ss 249(1), 356(4)
(4)	ss 249(2), 356(5)
(5)	ss 248(3), (4), 355(3), (4) (changed)
382A Recording of written resolutions	
(1)	s 355(1) (changed)
(2)	s 356(2), (3)
382B Recording of decisions by the sole member	
(1)	s 357(1), (2)
(2)	s 357(3), (4)
(3)	s 357(5)
383 Inspection of minute books	

Provision of Companies Act 1985	Destination in Companies Act 2006
(1)	s 358(1), (3) (changed)
(3)	s 358(4) (changed)
(4)	s 358(5), (6) (changed)
(5)	s 358(7)
384 Duty to appoint auditors	
(1)	ss 485(1), 489(1) (changed)
(2)	s 489(2)
385 Appointment at general meeting at which accounts laid	
(2)	ss 489(2), (4), 491(1) (changed)
(3)	s 489(3) (changed)
(4)	s 489(4) (changed)
387 Appointment by Secretary of State in default of appointment by company	
(1)	ss 486(1), 490(1)
(2)	ss 486(2)–(4), 490(2)–(4)
388 Filling of casual vacancies	
(1)	ss 489(3), 526
389A Rights to information	
(1)	s 499(1)
(2)	s 499(2)
(3)	s 500(1)
(4)	s 500(2)
(5)	s 500(3)
(6)	ss 499(3), 500(4)
(7)	ss 499(4) 500(5)
389B Offences relating to the provision of information to auditors	
(1)	s501(1), (2)
(2)	s 501(3)
(3)	s 501(3) (changed)
(4)	s 501(4), (5)
(5)	s 501(6)
390 Right to attend company meetings, &c	
(1)	s 502(2)
(2)	s 502(1)
(3)	s 502(2)
390A Remuneration of auditors	
(1)	s 492(1)
(2)	s 492(2), (3)
(4)	s 492(4)
(5)	s 492(5)
390B Disclosure of services provided by auditors or associates and related remuneration	
(1)	ss 494(1), 501(1), (2)
(2)	s 494(2)
(3)	s 494(3)
(4)	s 494(4)
(5)	s 494(5)
(8)	s 494(1)
(9)	s 494(6)
391 Removal of auditors	
(1)	s 510(1), (2)
(2)	s 512(1)–(3)
(3)	s 510(3)

Provision of Companies Act 1985	*Destination in Companies Act 2006*
(4)	s 513(1), (2)
391A Rights of auditors who are removed or not re-appointed	
(1)	ss 511(1), 515(1), (2) (changed)
(2)	ss 511(2), 515(3)
(3)	ss 511(3), 515(4)
(4)	ss 511(4), 515(5)
(5)	ss 511(5), 515(6)
(6)	ss 511(6), 515(7)
392 Resignation of auditors	
(1)	s 516(1), (2)
(2)	s 516(3)
(3)	s 517(1)–(3)
392A Rights of resigning auditors	
(1)	s 518(1)
(2)	s 518(2)
(3)	s 518(3)
(4)	s 518(4)
(5)	s 518(5)–(7)
(6)	s 518(8)
(7)	s 518(9)
(8)	s 518(10)
394 Statement by person ceasing to hold office as auditor	
(1)	s 519(1)–(3), (7) (changed)
(2)	s 519(4) (changed)
(3)	s 520(2)
(4)	s 520(3)
(5)	s 521(1)
(6)	s 520(4)
(7)	ss 520(5), 521(2) (changed)
394A Offences of failing to comply with s 394	
(1)	ss 519(5), 521(3)–(5)
(2)	ss 519(6), 521(4)
(4)	s 520(6), (8) (changed)
395 Certain charges void if not registered	
(1)	ss 860(1), 861(5), 870(1). 874(1), (2)
(2)	s 874(3)
396 Charges which have to be registered	
(1)	ss 860(7), 861(2)
(2)	s 861(3)
(3)	s 861(1)
(3A)	s 861(4)
(4)	s 861(5)
397 Formalities of registration (debentures)	
(1)	ss 863(1)–(4), 870(3)
(2)	s 864(1), (3)
(3)	s 864(2)
398 Verification of charge on property outside United Kingdom	
(1)	s 866(1)
(2)	s 870(1)
(3)	s 866(2)

Provision of Companies Act 1985	Destination in Companies Act 2006
(4)	s 867(1), (2)
399 Company's duty to register charges it creates	
(1)	ss 860(1), (2), 863(5)
(2)	ss 860(3), 863(5)
(3)	ss 860(4)–(6),s 863(5)
400 Charges existing on property acquired	
(1)	ss 861(5), 862(1)
(2)	ss 862(2), (3), 870(2)
(3)	s 870(2)
(4)	s 862(4), (5) (changed)
401 Register of charges to be kept by registrar of companies	
(1)	s 869(1), (2), (4)
(2)	s 869(5), (6)
(3)	s 869(7)
402 Endorsement of certificate on debentures	
(1)	s 865(1)
(2)	s 865(2)
(3)	s 865(3), (4)
403 Entries of satisfaction and release	
(1)	s 872(1), (2) (changed)
(2)	s 872(3)
404 Rectification of register of charges	
(1)	s 873(1)
(2)	s 873(2)
405 Registration of enforcement of security	
(1)	s 871(1), (3)
(2)	s 871(2), (3)
(4)	s 871(4), (5)
406 Companies to keep copies of instrument creating charges	
(1)	ss 875(1), 877(2) (changed)
(2)	s 875(2)
407 Company's register of charges	
(1)	ss 876(1), 877(2) (changed)
(2)	s 876(2)
(3)	s 876(3), (4)
408 Right to inspect instruments which create charges, etc	
(1)	s 877(1), (2), (4) (changed)
(2)	s 877(2) (changed)
(3)	s 877(5), (6)
(4)	s 877(7)
410 Charges void unless registered	
(1)	s 878(1)
(2)	ss 886(1), 889(1)
(3)	s 889(2)
(4)	ss 878(7), 879(1), (3)
(5)	s 879(5), (6)
411 Charges on property outside United Kingdom	
(1)	s 886(1)
(2)	s 884
412 Negotiable instrument to secure book debts	
	s 879(4)

Provision of Companies Act 1985	Destination in Companies Act 2006
413 Charges associated with debentures	
(1)	s 879(2)
(2)	ss 882(1)–(4), 886(3)
(3)	s 883(1)–(3)
414 Charge by way of ex facie absolute disposition, etc	
(1)	s 881(1)
(2)	s 881(2), (3)
415 Company's duty to register charges created by it	
(1)	ss 878(1), (2), 882(5)
(2)	s 878(3), 882(5)
(3)	s 878(4)–(6), 882(5)
416 Duty to register charges existing on property acquired	
(1)	ss 880(1), (2), 886(2)
(2)	s 886(2)
(3)	s 880(3), (4) (changed)
417 Register of charges to be kept by registrar of companies	
(1)	s 885(1)
(2)	s 885(2)
(3)	s 885(3)
(4)	s 886(6)
418 Certificate of registration to be issued	
(1)	s 885(4)
(2)	s 885(4), (5)
419 Entries of satisfaction and release	
(1)	s 887(1), (3) (changed)
(1B)	s 887(2)
(2)	s 887(4)
(3)	s 887(2) (changed)
(4)	s 887(5)
420 Rectification of register	
	s 888(1), (2)
421 Copies of instruments creating charges to be kept by company	
(1)	ss 890(1), 892(2) (changed)
(2)	s 890(2)
422 Company's register of charges	
(1)	ss 891(1), 892(2) (changed)
(2)	s 891(2)
(3)	s 891(3), (4)
423 Right to inspect copies of instruments, and company's register	
(1)	s 892(1), (2), (4) (changed)
(2)	s 892(4) (changed)
(3)	s 892(5), (6)
(4)	s 892(7)
425 Power of company to compromise with creditors and members	
(1)	ss 895(1), 896(1), (2)
(2)	ss 899(1), (3), 907(1), 922(1)
(3)	s 899(4), 901(3), (4) (changed)
(4)	s 901(5) and 96)
(6)	s 895(2)
426 Information as to compromise to be circulated	
(1)	s 897(1)

Provision of Companies Act 1985	Destination in Companies Act 2006
(2)	s 897(1), (2)
(3)	s 897(1)
(4)	s 897(3)
(5)	s 897(4)
(6)	ss 895(1), 897(5)–(8)
(7)	s 898(1)–(3)
427 Provisions for facilitating company reconstruction or amalgamation	
(1)	s 900(1)
(2)	s 900(1), (2)
(3)	s 900(2)
(4)	s 900(3), (4)
(5)	s 900(6)–(8)
(6)	ss 900(5), 941
427A Application of ss 425–427 to mergers and divisions of public companies	
(1)	ss 902(1), 903(1), 907(2), 922(2)
(2)	ss 904(1), 919(1)
(3)	s 938(1), (2)
(4)	s 902(3)
(8)	s 941
428 Takeover offers	
(1)	s 974(1)–(3)
(2)	s 974(4), (5)
(2A)	s 974(6)
(3)	s 976(1)
(4)	s 976(3)
(5)	s 975(1), (2) (changed)
(6)	s 975(3) (changed)
(7)	s 974(7)
(8)	s 991(1)
429 Right of offeror to buy out minority shareholders	
(1)	s 979(1), (2) (changed)
(2)	s 979(3), (4) (changed)
(3)	s 980(2) (changed)
(4)	s 980(1), (4)
(5)	s 980(5)
(6)	s 980(6), (8)
(7)	s 980(7)
(8)	ss 977(1), 979(8)–(10) (changed)
430 Effect of notice under s 429	
(1)	s 981(1)
(2)	s 981(2)
(3)	s 981(3)
(4)	s 981(4), (5) (changed)
(5)	s 981(6)
(6)	s 981(7)
(7)	s 981(8(
(8)	s 981(6)
(9)	s 981(9)
(10)	s 982(2), (3)
(11)	s 982(4), (5)
(12)	s 982(6)

Provision of Companies Act 1985	Destination in Companies Act 2006
(13)	s 982(7)
(14)	s 982(8)
(15)	s 982(9)
430A Right of minority shareholder to be bought out by offeror	
(1)	ss 983(1)–(3), 984(1)
(1A)	s 983(1)
(2)	s 983(4)
(2A)	s 983(5)
(3)	s 984(3)
(4)	s 984(2)
(5)	s 984(4)
(6)	s 984(5), (7)
(7)	s 984(6)
430B Effect of requirement under s 430A	
(1)	s 985(1)
(2)	s 985(2)
(3)	s 985(3)
(4)	s 985(4), (5) (changed)
430C Applications to the court	
(1)	s 986(1), (2)
(2)	s 986(2)
(3)	s 986(3)
(4)	s 986(5)
(5)	s 986(9), (10)
430D Joint offers	
(1)	s 987(1)
(2)	s 987(2), (3) (changed)
(3)	s 987(5), (6)
(4)	s 987(4), (7)
(5)	s 987(8)
(6)	s 987(9)
(7)	s 987(10)
430E Associates	
(1)	ss 975(4), 977(2) (changed)
(2)	s 979(9)
(3)	s 983(8)
(4)	s 988(1), (4)
(5)	s 988(2)
(6)	s 988(3)
(7)	s 988(3), (5), (7)
(8)	s 988(1)
430F Convertible securities	
(1)	s 989(1)
(2)	s 989(2)
458 Punishment for fraudulent trading	
	s 993(1)–(3)
459 Order on application of company member	
(1)	s 994(1)
(2)	s 994(2)
(3)	s 994(3)
460 Order on application of Secretary of State	

Provision of Companies Act 1985	*Destination in Companies Act 2006*
(1)	s 995(2), (3)
(1A)	s 995(1)
(2)	s 995(4)
461 Provisions as to petitions and orders under this Part	
(1)	s 996(1)
(2)	s 996(2)
(3)	s 996(2)
(5)	s 998(1)–(4)
(6)	s 997
652 Registrar may strike defunct company off register	
(1)	s 1000(1)
(2)	s 1000(2)
(3)	s 1000(3)
(4)	s 1001(1)
(5)	ss 1000(4)–(6), 1001(2)–(4)
(6)	ss 1000(7), 1001(5)
(7)	s 1002(1)–(3)
652A Registrar may strike private company off register on application	
(1)	s 1003(1) (changed)
(2)	s 1003(2) (changed)
(3)	s 1003(3)
(4)	s 1003(4)
(5)	s 1003(5)
(6)	s 1003(6)
(7)	s 1003(6)
652B Duties in connection with making application under section 652A	
(1)	s 1004(1)
(2)	s 1004(2)
(3)	s 1005(1)
(4)	s 1005(2)
(5)	s 1005(3)
(6)	s 1006(1)
(7)	s 1006(2)
(8)	s 1006(3)
(9)	s 1004(3)
652C Directors' duties following application under section 652A	
(1)	s 1007(1)
(2)	s 1007(2)
(3)	s 1007(3)
(4)	s 1009(1)
(5)	s 1009(2)
(6)	s 1009(4)
(7)	s 1009(3)
652D Sections 652B and 652C: supplementary provisions	
(1)	s 1008(1), (2)
(2)	s 1008(3)
(3)	s 1008(3)
(4)	s 1008(4)
(5)(c)	ss 1004(4), 1006(1), 1007(2), 1009(4)
(6)	s 1010
(8)	s 1011

Provision of Companies Act 1985	Destination in Companies Act 2006
652E Sections 652B and 652C: enforcement	
(1)	ss 1004(5), (7), 1005(4), (6), 1006(4), (6), 1007(4), (6), 1009(5), (7)
(2)	ss 1006(4), (7), 1007(4), (7)
(3)	ss 1004(6), 1005(5)
(4)	s1006(5)
(5)	ss 1007(5), 1009(6)
s654 Property of dissolved company to be bona vacantia	
(1)	s 1012(1)
(2)	s 1012(2)
655 Effect on s 654 of company's revival after dissolution	
(1)	s 1034(1)
(2)	s 1034(2)
(3)	s 1034(4)
(4)	s 1034(5)
656 Crown disclaimer of property vesting as bona vacantia	
(1)	s 1013(1)
(2)	s 1013(2) (changed)
(3)	s 1013(3)–(5) (changed)
(5)	s 1013(6), (7)
(6)	s 1013(8)
657 Effect of Crown disclaimer under s 656	
(1)	s 1014(1)
(2)	ss 1015(1), (2), 1016(1), (2), 1017(1)–(5), 1018(1)–(5), 1019
(4)	s 1020(1), (2)
(5)	s 1021(1), (2)
(6)	s 1021(3)
658 Liability for rentcharge on company's land after dissolution	
(1)	s 1023(1), (2)
(2)	s 1023(3)
680 Companies capable of being registered under this Chapter	
(1)(a), (b)	s 1040(1)
(1) (closing words)	s 1040(2), (3), (6)
(1A)	s 1040(1)
(2)	s 1040(1)
(3)	s 1040(4)
(4)	s 1040(4)
(5)	s 1040(5)
683 Definition of 'joint stock company'	
(1)	s 1041(1)
(2)	s 1041(2)
694 Regulation of oversea companies in respect of their names	
(4)	s 1048(1), (2) (changed)
(5)	s 1048(3)–(5)
695 Service of documents on oversea company	
(1), (2)	s 1139(2) (changed)
695A Registrar to whom documents to be delivered: companies to which section 690A applies	
(4)	s 1059
699A Credit and financial institutions to which the Bank Branches Directive (89/117/ EEC) applies	

Provision of Companies Act 1985	Destination in Companies Act 2006
(3) ('financial institution')	s 1173(1)
704 Registration offices	
(2)	s 1060(1), (2)
(4)	s 1062 (changed)
(7), (8)	s 1119(1), (2)
705 Companies' registered numbers	
(1)–(3)	s 1066(1)–(3)
(4)	s 1066(4), (5)
(5)(za)	s 1066(6)
705A Registration of branches of oversea companies	
(1)	s 1067(1) (changed)
(2)	s 1067(1)
(3)	s 1067(2)
(4)	s 1067(3)
(5)	s 1067(4), (5)
707A The keeping of company records by the registrar	
(1)	s 1080(4)
(2)	s 1083(1) (changed)
(3)	s 1084(1)–(3) (changed), (5)
(4)	s 1084(4)
708 Fees payable to registrar	
(1)	s 1063(1)–(3) (changed)
(2), (3)	s 1063(4) (changed)
(4)	s 1063(6)
(5)	s 1063(5) (changed)
709 Inspection, &c. of records kept by the registrar	
(1) opening words	s 1085(1) ands 1100
(1)(a), (b)	s 1086(1)
(2)	s 1085(2) (changed)
(3)	s 1091(3)
(4)	s 1091(5)
(5)	s 1092(1), (2)
710 Certificate of incorporation	
	s 1065
710A Provision and authentication by registrar of documents in non-legible form	
(2)	s 1115(2)
710B Documents relating to Welsh companies	
(1)–(3)	s 1104(1), (2)
(4)	s 1104(3)
(5)	s 1104(4)
711 Public notice by registrar of receipt and issue of certain documents	
(1)	ss 1064(1)–(3), 1077(1)–(3), 1078(2), (3) (changed)
(2)	s 1079(4) (changed)
713 Enforcement of company's duty to make returns	
(1)	s 1113(1)–(3)
(2), (3)	s 1113(4), (5)
714 Registrar's index of company and corporate names	
(1)	s 1099(1)–(3) (changed)
(2)	s 1099(4), (5)
715A Interpretation	

Provision of Companies Act 1985	Destination in Companies Act 2006
(1) ('document'), (2)	s 1114(1)
718 Unregistered companies	
(1)	s 1043(1), (3), (5) (changed)
(2)	s 1043(1)
(3)	s 1043(2), (5) (changed)
(5)	s 1043(4)
(6)	s 1043(6)
719 Power of company to provide for employees on cessation or transfer of business	
(1)	s 247(1)
(2)	s 247(2) (changed)
(3)	s 247(4)–(6) (changed)
(4)	s 247(7) (changed)
721 Production and inspection of books where offence suspected	
(1)	s 1132(1), (2)
(2)–(4)	s 1132(3)–(5)
722 Form of company registers, etc	
(1)	ss 1134 and 1135(1) (changed)
(2)	s 1138(1)
(3)	s 1138(2), (3)
723 Use of computers for company records	
(1)	s 1135(1) (changed)
(2)	s 1135(5)
723A Obligations of company as to inspections of registers, &c.	
(1)	s 1137(1), (2)
(2)	s 1137(3)
(3)	s 1137(3)
(4)	s 1137(4)
(6), (7)	s 1137(5), (6)
725 Service of documents	
(1)	s 1139(1)
(2)	s 1139(4)
(3)	s 1139(4)
727 Power of court to grant relief in certain cases	
(1)–(3)	s 1157(1)–(3)
730 Punishment of offences	
(4)	s 1125(2)
(5)	ss 1121(1), (3) (changed)
731 Summary proceedings	
(1)	s 1127(1), (2)
(2)	s 1128(1)
(3)	s 1128(2)
(4)	s 1128(4)
732 Prosecution by public authorities	
(1)	s 1126(1)
(2)	s 1126(2) (changed)
(3)	s 1129 (changed)
734 Criminal proceedings against unincorporated bodies	
(1)	s 1130(1), (2) (changed)
(2)	s 1130(3)
(3)	s 1130(2)
(4)	s 1130(2)

Provision of Companies Act 1985	Destination in Companies Act 2006
735 'Company', etc	
(1)(a), (b)	s 1(1)
(1)(c)	s 1171 (changed)
(3)	s 1171
736 'Subsidiary'; 'holding company' and 'wholly-owned subsidiary'	
(1), (2)	s 1159(1), (2)
(3)	s 1159(4)
736A Provisions supplementing s 736	
(1)–(11)	s 1159(3), Sch 6
736B Power to amend ss 736 and 736A	
(1)	s 1160(1)
(3)–(5)	s 1160(2)–(4)
737 'Called-up share capital'	
(1), (2)	s 547
738 'Allotment' and 'paid up'	
(1)	s 558
(2)	s 583(2)–(3)(d)
(3)	s 583(5)
(4)	s 583(6)
739 'Non-cash asset'	
(1), (2)	s 1163(1), (2)
741 'Director' and 'shadow director'	
(1)	s 250
(2)	s 251(1), (2)
(3)	s 251(3)
742 Expressions used in connection with accounts	
(1) ('fixed assets')	s 853(6)
(1) ('parent company')	s 1173(1)
(2)	s 853(4), (5)
742A Meaning of 'offer to the public'	
(1)	s 756(1), (2)
(2)	s 756(3)
(3)	s 756(4), (5)(a)–(d) (changed)
(4)	s 756(4)
(5)	s 756(4)
(6)	s 756(5)(e), (6)
742B Meaning of 'banking company'	
(1)–(3)	s 1164(1)–(3)
742C Meaning of 'insurance company' and 'authorised insurance company'	
(1)–(4)	s 1165(2)–(4)
(5)	s 1165(8)
743 'Employees' share scheme'	
	s 1166
744 Expressions used generally in this Act	
'articles'	s 18(4)
'the Companies Acts'	s 2(1), (2) (changed)
'the court'	s 1156(1)–(3) (changed)
'debenture'	s 738
'EEA State'	s 1170
'equity share capital'	s 548
'the Gazette'	s 1173(1)

Provision of Companies Act 1985	Destination in Companies Act 2006
'hire-purchase agreement'	s 1173(1)
'insurance market activity'	s 1165(7)
'officer'	ss 1121(2), 1173(1)
'oversea company'	s 1044 (changed)
'prescribed'	s 1167
'the registrar of companies' and 'the registrar'	s 1060(3)
'regulated activity'	s 1173(1)
'share'	s 540(1), (4)
744A Index of defined expressions	
	Sch 8

Sch 2 Interpretation of references to 'beneficial interest'
Part 1 References in sections 23, 145, 146 and 148

para 1(1)	ss 139(1), 672(1)
para 1(2)	ss 139(2), 672(2)
para 1(3)	ss 139(3), 672(3)
para 1(4)	ss 139(4), 672(4)
para 2(3)	s 672(5)
para 2(4)	s 672(6)
para 3(1), (2)	ss 140(1), (2), 673(1), (2)
para 4(1)	ss 138(1), (2), 674
para 4(2)	s 138(1)
para 4(3)	s 674
para 5(1)	ss 675(1), (2), 676
para 5(2)	ss 139(5), (6), 140(3), 675(1), (2)
para 5(3)	ss 139(6), 140(4), 676

Sch 4 Form and content of company accounts
Part 3 Notes to the accounts

para 56(2), (3)	ss 382(6), 465(6)

Part 7 Interpretation of Schedule

para 94(1), (2)	s 411(6)

Sch 7B Specified persons, descriptions of disclosures etc for the purposes of section 245G
Part 1 Specified persons

	s 461(1)

Part 2 Specified descriptions of disclosures

	s 461(4)

Part 3 Overseas regulatory bodies

	s 461(5), (6)

Sch 10A Parent and subsidiary undertakings: supplementary provisions

para 1	Sch 7, para 1
para 2(1)	Sch 7, para 2(1)
para 2(2)	Sch 7, para 2(2)
para 3(1)	Sch 7, para 3(1)
para 3(2)	Sch 7, para 3(2)
para 3(2)	Sch 7, para 3(3)
para 4(1)	Sch 7, para 4(1)
para 4(2)	Sch 7, para 4(2)
para 4(3)	Sch 7, para 4(3)
para 5(1)	Sch 7, para 5(1)
para 5(2)	Sch 7, para 5(2)
para 6	Sch 7, para 6

Provision of Companies Act 1985	Destination in Companies Act 2006
para 7(1)	Sch 7, para 7(1)
para 7(2)	Sch 7, para 7(2)
para 8	Sch 7, para 8
para 9(1)	Sch 7, para 9(1)
para 9(2)	Sch 7, para 9(2)
para 9(3)	Sch 7, para 9(3)
para 10	Sch 7, para 10
para 11	Sch 7, para 11

Sch 13 Provisions supplementing and interpreting sections 324 to 328
Part 4 Provisions with respect to register of directors' interests to be kept under section 325

para 27	s 809(2), (3)

Sch 14 Overseas branch registers
Part 1 Countries and territories in which overseas branch register may be kept

	s 129(2)

Part 2 General provisions with respect to overseas branch registers

para 1(1), (2)	ss 130(1), 135(3)
para 1(3)	ss 130(2), (3), 135(4), (5)
para 2(1)	s 131(1)
para 3(1)	s 134(1), (2) (changed)
para 3(2)	s 134(3)
para 4(1)	s 132(1), (2) (changed)
para 4(2)	s 132(3), (4)
para 5	s 133(1), (2)
para 6	s 135(1), (2)
para 7	s 131(4)

Sch 15A Written resolutions of private companies
Part 1 Exceptions

para 1	s 288(2)

Part 2 Adaptation of procedural requirements

para 3(1), (2)	ss 571(7), 573(5)
para 5(1), (2)	ss 695(2), 698(2)
para 5(3), (4)	ss 696(2), 699(2)
para 6(1)	ss 717(2), 718(2)
para 6(2)	s 717(2)
para 6(3)	s 718(2)
para 7	s 188(5)

Sch 15B Provisions subject to which ss 425–427 have effect in their application to mergers and divisions of public companies

para 1	ss 907(1), (2), 922(1), (2)
para 2(1)	ss 905(1), 906(1)–(3), 920(1), 921(1)–(4)
para 2(2)	ss 905(2), (3), 920(2)
para 2(3)	s 920(3)
para 3	ss 908(1), (3), 909(1), (7), 911(1), (2), (4), 912, 923(1), (4), 924(1), (7), 925(5), 926(1), (2), (4), 927(1)–(3), 928
para 4(1)	ss 908(2), 923(2)
para 4(2)	s 923(3)
para 5(1)	ss 909(2), (3), 924(2), (3)
para 5(2)	ss 909(3), 924(3)
para 5(3)	ss 909(4), 924(4)
para 5(4)	s 935(1) (changed)

Provision of Companies Act 1985	Destination in Companies Act 2006
para 5(6)	s 935(2)
para 5(7)	ss 909(5), 924(5)
para 5(8)	ss 909(6), 924(6)
para 6(1)	ss 910(1), 911(3), 925(1), 926(3)
para 6(2)	ss 910(2), 925(2)
para 6(3)	ss 910(3), 925(3) (changed)
para 6(4)	ss 910(4), 925(4),
para 7	ss 914, 930
para 8(1)	ss 913(1), 929(1)
para 8(2)	ss 913(2), 929(2)
para 9(1)	s 939(1)
para 9(2)	s 939(1), (2)
para 9(3)	s 939(3), (4)
para 9(4)	s 939(5)
para 10(1)	ss 918(1), 932(1)
para 10(2)	ss 916(3)–(5), 918(2)–(4), 932(2)–(5)
para 11(1)	s 933(1)–(3), 934(1)
para 11(2)	s 933(1)–(3)
para 11(3)	s 934(1)
para 11(4)	s 934(2)–(4)
para 12(1)	ss 915(1), (6), 917(1), (6)
para 12(2)	s 915(2)
para 12(3)	s 915(3)–(5)
para 12(4)	s 917(2)
para 12(5)	ss 917(3) to 95), 931(3), (5)
para 13(1)	s 931(1)
para 13(2)	s 931(2)
para 13(3)	s 931(3), (4), (6)
para 14(1)	s 916(1)
para 14(2)	s 916(2)
para 14(3)	s 916(3)–(5)
para 15(1)	s 940(1)
para 15(2)	s 940(2)
para 15(3)	s 940(3)
Sch 20 Vesting of disclaimed property; protection of third parties	
Part 2 Crown disclaimer under section 656 (Scotland only)	
para 5	s 1022(1)
para 6	s 1022(2)
para 7	s 1022(3)
para 8	s 1022(4), (5)
para 9	s 1022(6)

COMPANIES ACT 1989

1. The Companies Act 1989 s 130(6) (power by regulations to apply provisions relating to company contracts and execution of documents by companies to overseas companies) is re-enacted in the Companies Act 2006 s 1045.

2. The 1989 Act s 207 (transfer of securities) is re-enacted in the 2006 Act ss 783, 784(3), 785, 788.

TABLE OF ORIGINS

1. This table shows the origin of the company law provisions of the Companies Act 2006 by reference to the enactments in force on the date that Act received royal assent (subject to the note to

the origins for Pt 28). The Act received Royal Assent on 8 November 2006. Where an enactment had been amended before that date, the reference is to the text at that date; the table does not show the source of such amendments.

2. The origin of a provision of the 2006 Act in the Companies (Northern Ireland) Order 1986 is acknowledged where it makes significantly different provision in relation to Northern Ireland than in relation to England and Wales or, as the case may be, Great Britain.

3. In the table—

'1985'	means the Companies Act 1985 (c 6);
'IA 1986'	means the Insolvency Act 1986 (c 45);
'1986'	means the Companies (Northern Ireland) Order 1986, SI 1096/1032 (NI 6);
'ICTA'	means the Income and Corporation Taxes Act 1988 (c 1);
'1989'	means the Companies Act 1989 (c 40).

4. The entry 'drafting' indicates a new provision of a mechanical or editorial nature—for example, a provision defining an expression to avoid repetition or indicating where other relevant provisions are to be found.

5. A reference followed by '(changed)' means that the provision referred to has been re-enacted with one or more changes. In general, a change is noted only in the primary context affected and not in every provision where a consequential change results. The table does not show changes in the maximum penalties for offences.

6. The entry 'new' indicates a provision which has no predecessor in the repealed legislation or which is fundamentally different from its predecessor.

7. The entries in the table are intended only as a general indication of what has changed and what is new. They should not be read as expressing any view as to the application or otherwise of any provision relating to enactments repealed and re-enacted.

Section of 2006 Act	Origin
Part 1 General Introductory Provisions	
1	
(1)	1985, s 735(1)(a), (b)
(2), (3)	drafting
2	
(1), (2)	1985, s 744 (changed)
3	
(1)–(4)	1985, s 1(2)
4	
(1), (2)	1985, s 1(3)
(3)	1985, s 1(3), 1986 art 12(3)
(4)	drafting
5	
(1)	1985, s 1(4)
(2)	1985, s 1(4), 1986 art 12(4)
(3)	1985, s 15(2)
6	
(1), (2)	drafting
Part 2 Company Formation	
7	
(1), (2)	1985, s 1(1) (changed)
8	
(1)	new
(2)	1985, s 3(1)
9	
(1)	1985, s 10(1) (changed)
(2)	1985, s 2(1)(a), (b), (2), (3) (changed)
(3)	1985, s 10(4)
(4)	new
(5)	1985, s 10(1), (6)

Section of 2006 Act	Origin
(6)	1985, s 10(1)
10	
(1)–(5)	new
11	
(1)	drafting
(2)	new
(3)	1985, s 2(4) (changed)
12	
(1)	1985, s 10(2) (changed)
(2)	new
(3), first sentence	1985, s 10(3)
(3), second sentence	new
13	
(1), (2)	1985, s 12(3), (3A) (changed)
14	1985, s 12(1), (2)
15	
(1)	1985, s 13(1)
(2)	new
(3)	1985, s 13(2)
(4)	1985, s 13(7)(a)
16	
(1)	drafting
(2)	1985, s 13(3) (changed)
(3)	1985, s 13(4)
(4)	new
(5)	new
(6)	1985, s 13(5)
Part 3 A Company's Constitution	
Chapter 1 Introductory	
17	new
Chapter 2 Articles of association	
18	
(1)	new
(2)	1985, s 7(1) (changed)
(3)	1985, s 7(3) (changed)
(4)	1985, s 744
19	
(1)–(3)	1985, s 8(1), (4) (changed)
(4)	1985, s 8(3)
(5)	1985, s 8(5)
20	
(1), (2)	1985, s 8(2) (changed)
21	
(1)	1985, s 9(1)
(2), (3)	drafting
22	
(1)–(3)	new
23	
(1), (2)	new
24	
(1)–(4)	new

Section of 2006 Act	Origin
25	
(1)	1985, s 16(1)
(2)	1985, s 16(2)
26	
(1)	1985, s 18(2) (changed)
(2)	new
(3), (4)	1985, s 18(3) and, Sch 24
27	
(1)–(5)	new
28	
(1)–(3)	new
Chapter 3 Resolutions and agreements affecting a company's constitution	
29	
(1)	1985, s 380(4) (changed)
(2)	1985, s 380(4A)
30	
(1)	1985, s 380(1)
(2), (3)	1985, s 380(5) and, Sch 24
(4)	1985, s 380(7)
Chapter 4 Miscellaneous and supplementary provisions	
31	
(1)–(5)	new
32	
(1)	1985, s 19(1) (changed)
(2)	new
(3), (4)	1985, s 19(2) (changed) and, Sch 24
33	
(1)	1985, s 14(1) (changed)
(2)	1985, s 14(2) (changed)
34	
(1)	drafting
(2)	1985, s 18(1) (changed)
(3)	1985, s 18(2) (changed)
(4)	new
(5), (6)	1985, s 18(3) and, Sch 24
35	
(1)–(5)	new
36	
(1), (2)	1985, s 380(2) (changed)
(3), (4)	1985, s 380(6) (changed) and, Sch 24
(5)	1985, s 380(7)
37	1985, s 15(1)
38	Companies (Single Member Private Limited Companies) Regulations 1992 (SI 1992/1699) (changed)
Part 4 A Company's Capacity and Related Matters	
39	
(1)	1985, s 35(1) (changed)
(2)	1985, s 35(4)
40	
(1)	1985, s 35A(1)
(2)	1985, s 35A(2) and 35B

Section of 2006 Act	Origin
(3)	1985, s 35A(3)
(4)	1985, s 35A(4)
(5)	1985, s 35A(5)
(6)	1985, s 35A(6)
41	
(1)	1985, s 322A(1), (4)
(2)	1985, s 322A(1), (2)
(3)	1985, s 322A(3)
(4)	1985, s 322A(5)
(5)	1985, s 322A(6)
(6)	1985, s 322A(7)
(7)	1985, s 322A(8)
42	
(1)	Charities Act 1993, s 65(1)
(2)	Charities Act 1993, s 65(2)
(3)	Charities Act 1993, s 65(3)
(4)	Charities Act 1993, s 65(4)
(5)	drafting
43	
(1), (2)	1985, s 36
44	
(1)	1985, s 36A(1)–(3)
(2)(a), (3), (4)	1985, s 36A(4)
(2)(b)	new
(5)	1985, s 36A(6) (changed)
(6)	1985, s 36A(4A)
(7)	1985, s 36A(8)
(8)	1985, s 36A(7)
45	
(1)	1985, s 36A(3)
(2)	1985, s 350(1)
(3)	1985, s 350(1) (changed)
(4), (5)	1985, s 350(2) and, Sch 24
(6)	drafting
46	
(1)	1985, s 36AA(1)
(2)	1985, s 36AA(2)
47	
(1)	1985, s 38(1) (changed), (3)
(2)	1985, s 38(2) (changed)
48	
(1)	Requirements of Writing (Scotland) Act 1995 (c 7), s 15(3)
(2)	1985, s 36B(1)
(3)	1985, s 36B(2)
49	
(1)	1985, s 39(1) (changed)
(2)	1985, s 39(1)
(3)	1985, s 39(2), (2A)
(4)	1985, s 39(3)
(5)	1985, s 39(4)

Section of 2006 Act	Origin
(6)	1985, s 39(5)
50	
(1), (2)	1985, s 40(1)
51	
(1)	1985, s 36C(1)
(2)	1985, s 36C(2)
52	1985, s 37
Part 5 A Company's Name	
Chapter 1 General requirements	
53	1985, s 26(1)(d), (e)
54	
(1)–(3)	1985, s 26(2)(a) and second sentence (changed)
55	
(1)	1985, s 26(2)(b) and 29(1)(a)
(2)	1985, s 29(6)
56	
(1)	1985, s 29(1)(b) (changed)
(2)	1985, s 29(2)
(3), (4)	1985, s 29(3) (changed)
(5)	drafting
57	
(1)–(5)	new
Chapter 2 Indications of company type or legal form	
58	
(1)	1985, s 25(1) and 27(4)(b)
(2)	1985, s 25(1) and 27(4)(d)
(3)	drafting
59	
(1)	1985, s 25(2) (opening words) and 27(4)(a)
(2)	1985, s 25(2)(b) and 27(4)(c)
(3)	1985, s 25(2)(a)
(4)	drafting
60	
(1)(a), (b)	new
(1)(c)	drafting
(2)	1985, s 30(5B)
(3)	1985, s 30(4)
(4)	new
61	
(1)	1985, s 30(2), 1986 art.40(2)
(2)–(4)	1985, s 30(2), (3) (changed)
62	
(1)–(3)	1985, s 30(2), (3) (changed)
63	
(1)	1985, s 31(1)
(2), (3)	1985, s 31(5) and, Sch 24
(4), (5)	new
64	
(1)–(3)	1985, s 31(2) first sentence
(4)	1985, s 31(2) second sentence (changed)
(5), (6)	1985, s 31(6) and, Sch 24

Section of 2006 Act	Origin
(7)	1985, s 31(3)
65	
(1)–(5)	1985, s 26(1)(a), (b), (bb), (bbb) (changed)
Chapter 3 Similarity to other names	
66	
(1)	1985, s 26(1)(c)
(2), (3)	1985, s 26(3) (changed)
(4)–(6)	new
67	
(1)	1985, s 28(2)
(2)–(6)	new
68	
(1)	drafting
(2)	1985, s 28(2) full out
(3)	1985, s 28(4)
(4)	1985, s 28(2) full out and (4)
(5), (6)	1985, s 28(5) and, Sch 24
69	
(1)–(7)	new
70	
(1)–(6)	new
71	
(1)–(4)	new
72	
(1), (2)	new
73	
(1)–(6)	new
74	
(1)–(5)	new
Chapter 4 Other powers of the Secretary of State	
75	
(1), (2)	1985, s 28(3)
(3)	1985, s 28(4)
(4)	1985, s 28(3)
(5), (6)	1985, s 28(5) and, Sch 24
76	
(1)	1985, s 32(1)
(2)	new
(3)	1985, s 32(2)
(4), (5)	1985, s 32(3)
(6), (7)	1985, s 32(4) (changed) and, Sch 24
Chapter 5 Change of name	
77	
(1)(a)	1985, s 28(1)
(1)(b)	new
(2)	drafting
78	
(1)–(3)	new
79	
(1), (2)	new
80	

Section of 2006 Act	Origin
(1), (2)	1985, s 28(6) and 32(5) (changed)
(3)	1985, s 28(6) and 32(5)
81	
(1)	1985, s 28(6) and 32(5)
(2), (3)	1985, s 28(7) and 32(6)
Chapter 6 Trading disclosures	
82	
(1), (2)	1985, s s 348(1), 349(1), 351(1), (2), Business Names Act 1985, s 4(1) (changed)
(3)–(5)	new
83	
(1), (2)	Business Names Act 1985, s 5(1)
(3)	Business Names Act 1985, s 5(2)
84	
(1), (2)	1985, s s 348(2), 349(2), (3), 351(5), Business Names Act 1985, s 7 (changed)
(3)	new
85	
(1), (2)	new
Part 6 A Company's Registered Office	
86	1985, s 287(1)
87	
(1)	1985, s 287(3)
(2)	1985, s 287(4)
(3)	1985, s 287(5)
(4)	1985, s 287(6)
88	
(1)	drafting
(2)	1985, s 2(2)
(3), (4)	new
Part 7 Re-Registration as a Means of Altering a Company's Status	
89	drafting
90	
(1)	1985, s 43(1) (changed)
(2)	1985, s 43(1); drafting
(3)	1985, s 43(2)
(4)	1985, s 48(1), (2)
91	
(1)	1985, s 45(1)–(4)
(2)	1985, s 45(5), 1986 art.55(5)
(3)	1985, s 45(6)
(4)	1985, s 45(7)
(5)	1985, s 47(3) (changed)
92	
(1)	1985, s 43(3)(b), (c), (4)
(2)	1985, s 43(e)(ii)
(3), (4)	1985, s 46(2), (3)
(5), (6)	1985, s 46(4)
93	
(1)	1985, s 44(1)
(2)	1985, s 44(2), drafting

Section of 2006 Act	Origin
(3)–(5)	1985, s 44(4), (5)
(6)	1985, s 44(6), (7)(b)
(7)	1985, s 44(2), (7)(a)
94	
(1)	new
(2)	1985, s 43(3)(a)–(d)
(3)	1985, s 43(e)(i)
(4)	1985, s 47(2)
95	
(1)–(3)	new
96	
(1), (2)	1985, s 47(1)
(3)	new
(4), (5)	1985, s 47(4), (5)
97	
(1)	1985, s 53(1) (changed)
(2)	new
(3)	1985, s 53(2)
98	
(1)	1985, s 54(1), (2)
(2)	1985, s 54(3)
(3), (4)	1985, s 54(5)
(5)	1985, s 54(6)
(6)	1985, s 54(8)
99	
(1), (2)	1985, s 54(4) (changed)
(3)	1985, s 54(7)
(4), (5)	1985, s 54(10), Sch 24
100	
(1)	new
(2)	1985, s 53(1)(b) (changed)
(3), (4)	new
101	
(1), (2)	1985, s 55(1)
(3)	new
(4), (5)	1985, s 55(2), (3)
102	
(1)	1985, s 49(1), (4), (8)(a) (changed)
(2)	1985, s 49(2)
(3)	1985, s 49(5)–(7) (changed)
(4)	1985, s 49(9)
(5)	new
103	
(1)	new
(2)	1985, s 49(8)(a), (c), (d)
(3), (4)	1985, s 49(8)(b), (8A) (changed)
(5)	new
104	
(1), (2)	1985, s 50(1)(b)
(3)	new
(4), (5)	1985, s 50(2), (3)

Section of 2006 Act	Origin
105	
(1)	1985, s 51(1) (changed)
(2)	1985, s 51(2)
(3), (4)	1985, s 51(3)
106	
(1)	new
(2)	1985, s 51(5) (changed)
(3)–(5)	new
107	
(1), (2)	1985, s 52(1)
(3)	new
(4), (5)	1985, s 52(2), (3)
108	
(1)–(5)	new
109	
(1)–(5)	new
110	
(1)–(5)	new
111	
(1)–(5)	new
Part 8 A Company's Members	
Chapter 1 The members of a company	
112	
(1)	1985, s 22(1) (changed)
(2)	1985, s 22(2)
Chapter 2 Register of members	
113	
(1), (2)	1985, s 352(1), (2)
(3), (4)	1985, s 352(3)
(5)	new
(6)	1985, s 352(4)
(7), (8)	1985, s 352(5), Sch 24
114	
(1)	1985, s 353(1) (changed)
(2)	1985, s 353(2)
(3)	1985, s 353(3)
(4)	1985, s 353(3), 1986 art.361(3)
(5), (6)	1985, s 353(4), Sch 24
115	
(1), (2)	1985, s 354(1)
(3)	1985, s 354(2)
(4)	1985, s 354(3) (changed)
(5), (6)	1985, s 354(4), Sch 24
116	
(1)	1985, s 356(1) (changed)
(2)	1985, s 356(3) first branch
(3), (4)	new
117	
(1)–(5)	new
118	
(1), (2)	1985, s 356(5), Sch 24 (changed)

Section of 2006 Act	*Origin*
(3)	1985, s 356(6)
119	
(1)–(3)	new
120	
(1)–(4)	new
121	1985, s 352(6) (changed)
122	
(1)	1985, s 355(1) (changed)
(2)	1985, s 355(4)
(3)	1985, s 355(5)
(4), (5)	1985, s 355(2), (3)
(6)	1985, s 355(4)
123	
(1)	new
(2), (3)	1985, s 352A(1), (2) (changed)
(4), (5)	1985, s 352A(3), Sch 24
124	
(1), (2)	1985, s 352(3A)
125	
(1)–(4)	1985, s 359(1)–(4)
126	1985, s 360
127	1985, s 361
128	
(1), (2)	1985, s 352(7)
Chapter 3 Overseas branch registers	
129	
(1)	1985, s 362(1), (2) opening words
(2)	1985, Sch 14, Pt 1
(3), (4)	new
(5)	1985, s 362(2)(b), (c)
130	
(1)	1985, s 362(3), Sch 14, Pt 2, para 1(1), (2)
(2), (3)	1985, s 362(3), Sch 14, Pt 2, para 1(3), Sch 24
131	
(1)	1985, s 362(3), Sch 14, Pt 2, para 2(1)
(2), (3)	new
(4)	1985, s 362(3), Sch 14, Pt 2, para 7
132	
(1), (2)	1985, s 362(3), Sch 14, Pt 2, para 4(1) (changed)
(3), (4)	1985, s 362(3), Sch 14, Pt 2, para 4(2), Sch 24
133	
(1), (2)	1985, s 362(3), Sch 14, Pt 2, para 5
(3)	1985, s 362(3), Sch 14, Pt 2, para 8
134	
(1), (2)	1985, s 362(3), Sch 14, Pt 2, para 3(1) (changed)
(3)	1985, s 362(3), Sch 14, Pt 2, para 3(2)
135	
(1), (2)	1985, s 362(3), Sch 14, Pt 2, para 6
(3)	1985, s 362(3), Sch 14, Pt 2, para 1(1), (2)
(4), (5)	1985, s 362(3), Sch 14, Pt 2, para 1(3), Sch 24

Chapter 4 Prohibition on subsidiary being member of its holding company

Section of 2006 Act	Origin
136	
(1)	1985, s 23(1)
(2)	drafting
137	
(1)	1985, s 23(4), (5)
(2)	1985, s 23(4), 1986 art.33(4)
(3), (4)	1985, s 23(6)
138	
(1), (2)	1985, s 23(2), Sch 2, para 4(1), (2); drafting
139	
(1)–(4)	1985, Sch 2, para 1(1)–(4)
(5)	1985, Sch 2, para 5(2)
(6)	1985, Sch 2, para 5(2), (3)
140	
(1), (2)	1985, Sch 2, para 3(1), (2)
(3), (4)	1985, Sch 2, para 5(2), (3)
141	
(1), (2)	1985, s 23(3)
(3), (4)	1985, s 23(3A), (3B)
(5)	1985, s 23(3BA)
142	
(1), (2)	1985, s 23(3C)
143	1985, s 23(8)
144	1985, s 23(7)
Part 9 Exercise of Members' Rights	
145	
(1)–(4)	new
146	
(1)–(5)	new
147	
(1)–(6)	new
148	
(1)–(8)	new
149	
(1)–(3)	new
150	
(1)–(7)	new
151	
(1)–(3)	new
152	
(1)–(4)	new
153	
(1), (2)	new
Part 10 A Company's Directors	
Chapter 1 Appointment and removal of directors	
154	
(1)	1985, s 282(3)
(2)	1985, s 282(1) (changed)
155	
(1), (2)	new
156	

Section of 2006 Act	Origin
(1)–(7)	new
157	
(1)–(6)	new
158	
(1)–(5)	new
159	
(1)–(4)	new
160	
(1)–(4)	1985, s 292(1)–(4)
161	
(1), (2)	1985, s 285 (changed)
162	
(1)–(3)	1985, s 288(1) (changed)
(4)	new
(5)	1985, s 288(3)
(6)	1985, s 288(4), (6)
(7)	1985, s 288(4), Sch 24
(8)	1985, s 288(5)
163	
(1)	1985, s 289(1)(a) (changed)
(2)	1985, s 289(2)(a)
(3)	new
(4)	1985, s 289(2)(b) (changed)
(5)	new
164	1985, s 289(1)(b) (changed)
165	
(1)–(6)	new
166	
(1), (2)	new
167	
(1), (2)	1985, s 288(2) (changed)
(3)	new
(4)	1985, s 288(4), (6)
(5)	1985, s 288(4), Sch 24
168	
(1)	1985, s 303(1) (changed)
(2)–(5)	1985, s 303(2)–(5)
169	
(1), (2)	1985, s 304(1)
(3), (4)	1985, s 304(2), (3)
(5)	1985, s 304(4) (changed)
(6)	1985, s 304(5)
Chapter 2 General duties of directors	
170	
(1)–(5)	new
171	new
172	
(1)	1985, s 309(1) (changed)
(2), (3)	new
173	
(1), (2)	new

Section of 2006 Act	Origin
174	
(1), (2)	new
175	
(1)–(7)	new
176	
(1)–(5)	new
177	
(1)–(6)	new
178	
(1), (2)	new
179	new
180	
(1)–(5)	new
181	
(1)–(5)	new

Chapter 3 Declaration of interest in existing transaction or arrangement

182	
(1)	1985, s 317(1), (5) (changed)
(2)	1985, s 317(2) (changed)
(3)–(6)	new
183	
(1)	1985, s 317(7)
(2)	1985, s 317(7), Sch 24
184	
(1)–(5)	new
185	
(1), (2)	1985, s 317(3) (changed)
(3)	new
(4)	1985, s 317(4)
186	
(1), (2)	new
187	
(1)–(4)	1985, s 317(8) (changed)

Chapter 4 Transactions with directors requiring approval of members

188	
(1)	1985, s 319(1) (changed)
(2)	1985, s 319(3) (changed)
(3)	1985, s 319(1) (changed)
(4)	1985, s 319(2) (changed)
(5)	1985, s 319(5), para 7 of Sch 15A (changed)
(6)	1985, s 319(4)
(7)	1985, s 319(7)(a)
189	1985, s 319(6)
190	
(1), (2)	1985, s 320(1) (changed)
(3)	new
(4)	1985, s 321(1)
(5), (6)	new
191	
(1)–(5)	1985, s 320(2) (changed)
192	1985, s 321(2)(a), (3) (changed)

Section of 2006 Act	Origin
193	
(1), (2)	1985, s 321(2)(b) (changed)
194	
(1), (2)	1985, s 321(4)
195	
(1)	1985, s 322(1), (3)
(2)	1985, s 322(1), (2)(a), (b)
(3)	1985, s 322(3), (4)
(4)	1985, s 322(3)
(5)	1985, s 322(4)
(6)	1985, s 322(5)
(7)	1985, s 322(6)
(8)	1985, s 322(4)
196	1985, s 322(2)(c)
197	
(1)	1985, s 330(2) (changed)
(2)–(5)	new
198	
(1)	1985, s 330(3), s 331(6)
(2)	1985, s 330(3)(a), (c) (changed)
(3)–(6)	new
199	
(1)	1985, s 331(3)
(2), (3)	1985, s 331(4)
200	
(1)	1985, s 330(3), s 331(6)
(2)	1985, s 330(3)(b), (c) (changed)
(3)–(6)	new
201	
(1)	1985, s 330(4), s 331(6)
(2)	1985, s 330(4) (changed)
(3)–(6)	new
202	
(1)	1985, s 331(7)
(2)	1985, s 331(9)(b)
(3)	1985, s 331(8), (10)
203	
(1)	1985, s 330(6), (7) (changed)
(2)–(5)	new
(6)	1985, s 330(6)
204	
(1)	1985, s 337(1), (2) (changed)
(2)	1985, s 337(3), s 339(1), (2) (changed)
205	
(1)	1985, s 337A(1), (3) (changed)
(2)	1985, s 337A(4)
(3)	1985, s 337A(5)
(4)	1985, s 337A(6)
(5)	1985, s 337A(2)
206	new
207	

Section of 2006 Act	Origin
(1)	1985, s 334, s 339(1), (2) (changed)
(2)	1985, s 335(1), s 339(1), (2) (changed)
(3)	1985, s 335(2)
208	
(1)	1985, s 333, s 336(a) (changed)
(2)	1985, s 336(b) (changed)
209	
(1)	1985, s 338(1), (3)
(2)	1985, s 338(2)
(3), (4)	1985, s 338(6) (changed)
210	
(1)	1985, s 339(1)
(2)	1985, s 339(2)
(3)	1985, s 339(2), (3)
(4)	1985, s 339(2), (3)
(5)	1985, s 339(5)
211	
(1)	1985, s 339(6) and, s 340(1)
(2)	1985, s 340(2)
(3)	1985, s 340(3)
(4)	1985, s 340(6)
(5)	1985, s 340(4)
(6)	1985, s 340(5)
(7)	1985, s 340(7) (changed)
212	1985, s 331(9)(a)–(d)
213	
(1), (2)	1985, s 341(1)
(3), (4)	1985, s 341(2)
(5)	1985, s 341(3)
(6)	1985, s 341(4)
(7)	1985, s 341(5)
(8)	1985, s 341(3)
214	new
215	
(1)	1985, s 312, s 313(1), s 314(1) (changed)
(2)–(4)	new
216	
(1), (2)	1985, s 316(2) (changed)
217	
(1)	1985, s 312
(2)	new
(3)	1985, s 312 (changed)
(4)	new
218	
(1)	1985, s 313(1)
(2)	new
(3)	1985, s 313(1) (changed)
(4)	new
(5)	1985, s 316(1)
219	
(1)	1985, s 314(1), s 315(1)(b) (changed)

Section of 2006 Act	Origin
(2)	1985, s 315(1)(b)
(3), (4)	new
(5)	1985, s 315(3)
(6)	new
(7)	1985, s 316(1)
220	
(1)	1985, s 316(3) (changed)
(2)–(5)	new
221	
(1)–(4)	new
222	
(1)	new
(2)	1985, s 313(2)
(3)	1985, s 315(1)
(4), (5)	new
223	
(1)	1985, s 319(6), 320(3), 330(5)
(2)	new
224	
(1) and (2)	new
225	
(1)–(3)	new
226	new
Chapter 5 Directors' service contracts	
227	new
228	
(1)	1985, s 318(1)
(2)	1985, s 318(2), (3) (changed)
(3)	new
(4)	1985, s 318(4)
(5)	1985, s 318(8) (changed)
(6)	1985, s 318(8), Sch 24
(7)	1985, s 318(10)
229	
(1)	1985, s 318(7)
(2)	new
(3)	1985, s 318(8) (changed)
(4)	1985, s 318(8), Sch 24
(5)	1985, s 318(9) (changed)
230	1985, s 318(6)
Chapter 6 Contracts with sole members who are directors	
231	
(1)	1985, s 322B(1), (2) (changed)
(2)	1985, s 322B(1)
(3)	1985, s 322B(4) (changed)
(4)	1985, s 322B(4), Sch 24
(5)	1985, s 322B(3)
(6)	1985, s 322B(6)
(7)	1985, s 322B(5)
Chapter 7 Directors' liabilities	
232	

Section of 2006 Act	Origin
(1)	1985, s 309A(1), (2)
(2)	1985, s 309A(1), (3) (changed)
(3)	1985, s 309A(6)
(4)	new
233	1985, s 309A(5)
234	
(1)	1985, s 309A(4)
(2)	1985, s 309B(1), (2)
(3)	1985, s 309B(3), (4)
(4)	1985, s 309B(5)
(5)	1985, s 309B(6), (7)
(6)	1985, s 309B(4)(c)
235	
(1)–(6)	new
236	
(1)	1985, s 309C(1) (changed)
(2), (3)	1985, s 309C(2)
(4), (5)	1985, s 309C(3)
237	
(1)	1985, s 309C(4), (5)
(2)	1985, s 309C(5), s 318(1)
(3)	1985, s 309C(5), s 318(2), (3) (changed)
(4)	new
(5)	1985, s 309C(5), s 318(4)
(6)	1985, s 309C(5), s 318(8) (changed).
(7)	1985, s 309C(5), s 318(8), Sch 24
(8)	1985, s 309C(5), s 318(10)
(9)	new
238	
(1)	1985, s 309C(5), s 318(7)
(2)	new
(3)	1985, s 309C(5), s 318(8) (changed)
(4)	1985, s 309C(5), 1985, s 318(8), Sch 24
(5)	1985, s 309C(5), s 318(9) (changed)
239	
(1)–(7)	new
Chapter 8 Directors' residential addresses: protection from disclosure	
240	
(1)–(3)	new
241	
(1), (2)	new
242	
(1)–(3)	new
243	
(1)–(8)	new
244	
(1)–(4)	new
245	
(1)–(6)	new
246	
(1)–(7)	new

Section of 2006 Act	*Origin*
Chapter 9 Supplementary provisions	
247	
(1)	1985, s 719(1)
(2)	1985, s 719(2) (changed)
(3)	new
(4)	1985, s 719(3)
(5)	1985, s 719(3) (changed)
(6)	1985, s 719(3)
(7)	1985, s 719(4) (changed)
248	
(1)	1985, s 382(1)
(2)	new
(3)	1985, s 382(5) (changed)
(4)	1985, s 382(5), Sch 24
249	
(1)	1985, s 382(2)
(2)	1985, s 382(4)
250	1985, s 741(1)
251	
(1), (2)	1985, s 741(2)
(3)	1985, s 741(3)
252	
(1)	1985, s 346(1)
(2)	1985, s 346(2), (3) (changed)
(3)	1985, s 346(2)
253	
(1)	drafting
(2)	1985, s 346(2), (3) (changed)
(3)	new
254	
(1)	1985, s 346(1)
(2)	1985, s 346(4)
(3)	1985, s 346(7)
(4)	1985, s 346(8)
(5)	1985, s 346(4)
(6)	1985, s 346(6)
255	
(1)	1985, s 346(1)
(2)	1985, s 346(5)
(3)	1985, s 346(7)
(4)	1985, s 346(8)
(5)	1985, s 346(5)
(6)	1985, s 346(6)
256	new
257	
(1), (2)	new
258	
(1)	1985, s 345(1)
(2)	1985, s 345(2)
(3)	1985, s 345(3)
259	1985, s 347

Section of 2006 Act	Origin
Part 11 Derivative Claims and Proceedings by Members	
Chapter 1 Derivative claims in England and Wales or Northern Ireland	
260	
(1)–(5)	new
261	
(1)–(4)	new
262	
(1)–(5)	new
263	
(1)–(7)	new
264	
(1)–(5)	new
Chapter 2 Derivative proceedings in Scotland	
265	
(1)–(7)	new
266	
(1)–(5)	new
267	
(1)–(5)	new
268	
(1)–(6)	new
269(1)–(5)	new
Part 12 Company Secretaries	
270	
(1), (2)	new
(3)	1985, s 283(3) (changed)
271	1985, s 283(1) (changed)
272	
(1)–(7)	new
273	
(1), (2)	1985, s 286(1) (changed)
(3)	1985, s 286(2)
274	1985, s 283(3) (changed)
275	
(1)–(3)	1985, s 288(1) (changed)
(4)	new
(5)	1985, s 288(3)
(6)	1985, s 288(4), (6)
(7)	1985, s 288(4), Sch 24
(8)	1985, s 288(5)
276	
(1), (2)	1985, s 288(2)
(3)	1985, s 288(4), (6) (changed)
(4)	1985, s 288(4), Sch 24
277	
(1)	1985, s 290(1)(a) (changed)
(2)	1985, s 289(2)(a), s 290(3)
(3)	new
(4)	1985, s 289(2)(b), s 290(3) (changed)
(5)	new
278	

Section of 2006 Act	Origin
(1)	1985, s 290(1)(b) (changed)
(2)	1985, s 290(2)
279	
(1), (2)	new
280	1985, s 284
Part 13 Resolutions and Meetings	
Chapter 1 General provisions about resolutions	
281	
(1)–(4)	new
282	
(1)–(5)	new
283	
(1)	1985, s 378(1), (2) (changed)
(2), (3)	new
(4)	1985, s 378(1), (2) (changed)
(5)	1985, s 378(1), (2), (5) (changed)
(6)	1985, s 378(2) (changed)
284	
(1)	1985, s 370(6)
(2)	Table A, para 54 (changed)
(3)	1985, s 370(6), Table A, para 54 (changed)
(4)	1985, s 370(1), Table A, para 54
285	
(1)–(3)	new
286	
(1)–(3)	Table A, para 55
287	new
Chapter 2 Written resolutions	
288	
(1)	new
(2)	1985, s 381A(7), Sch 15A, para 1
(3)	new
(4)	1985, s 381A(1) (changed)
(5)	1985, s 381A(4)
289	
(1)	1985, s 381A(1) (changed)
(2)	new
290	new
291	
(1)–(7)	new
292	
(1)–(6)	new
293	
(1)–(7)	new
294	
(1), (2)	new
295	
(1), (2)	new
296	
(1)	1985, s 381A(2) (changed)
(2)–(4)	new

Section of 2006 Act	Origin
297	
(1), (2)	new
298	
(1), (2)	new
299	
(1), (2)	new
300	1985, s 381C(1)
Chapter 3 Resolutions at meetings	
301	1985, s 378(6) (changed)
302	Table A, para 37
303	
(1)	1985, s 368(1)
(2)	1985, s 368(1), (2), (2A)
(3)	1985, s 368(2) (changed)
(4)	1985, s 368(3) (changed)
(5)	new
(6)	1985, s 368(3) (changed)
304	
(1)	1985, s 368(4), (8)
(2), (3)	new
(4)	1985, s 368(7)
305	
(1)	1985, s 368(4)
(2)	new
(3)	1985, s 368(4)
(4)	1985, s 368(5)
(5)	new
(6), (7)	1985, s 368(6)
306	
(1), (2)	1985, s 371(1)
(3), (4)	1985, s 371(2)
(5)	1985, s 371(3)
307	
(1)	new
(2)	1985, s 369(1), (2) (changed)
(3)	1985, s 369(1), (2)
(4)	1985, s 369(3) (changed)
(5), (6)	1985, s 369(4) (changed)
(7)	drafting
308	1985, s 369(4A), (4B) (changed)
309	
(1)	1985, s 369(4B)
(2)	1985, s 369(4C) (changed)
(3)	1985, s 369(4B)(d)
310	
(1)	1985, s 370(2), Table A, para 38 (changed)
(2)	Table A, para 38 (changed)
(3)	new
(4)	1985, s 370(1), Table A, para 38
311	
(1), (2)	Table A, para 38

Section of 2006 Act	Origin
312	
(1)	1985, s 379(1)
(2)	1985, s 379(2)
(3)	1985, s 379(2) (changed)
(4)	1985, s 379(3)
313	
(1), (2)	1985 Table A, para 39 (changed)
314	
(1)	1985, s 376(1)(b)
(2), (3)	1985, s 376(2) (changed)
(4)	1985, s 376(1), s 377(1)(a) (changed)
315	
(1)	1985, s 376(3), (5)
(2)	1985, s 376(1)
(3)	1985, s 376(7)
(4)	1985, s 376(7), Sch 24
316	
(1)	new
(2)	1985, s 376(1), s 377(1)(b) (changed)
317	
(1)	1985, s 377(3) (changed)
(2)	1985, s 377(3)
318	
(1)	1985, s 370A
(2)	1985, s 370(1), (4) (changed)
(3)	1985, s 370A (changed)
319	
(1)	1985, s 370(5)
(2)	1985, s 370(1)
320	
(1)	1985, s 378(4), Table A, para 47
(2)	Table A, para 47
(3)	1985, s 378(4), Table A, para, s 47 and 48 (changed)
321	
(1)	1985, s 373(1)(a)
(2)	1985, s 373(1)(b) (changed)
322	1985, s 374
323	
(1)	1985, s 375(1)(a)
(2), (3)	1985, s 375(2) (changed)
(4)	new
324	
(1)	1985, s 372(1) (changed)
(2)	1985, s 372(2)(b) (changed)
325	
(1)	1985, s 372(3) (changed)
(2)	new
(3)	1985, s 372(4)
(4)	1985, s 372(4), Sch 24
326	
(1), (2)	1985, s 372(6)

Section of 2006 Act	Origin
(3)	1985, s 372(6) (changed)
(4)	1985, s 372(6), Sch 24
327	
(1)	1985, s 372(5)
(2)	1985, s 372(5) (changed)
(3)	new
328	
(1), (2)	new
329	
(1)	1985, s 373(2)
(2)	1985, s 373(2) (changed)
330	
(1)–(7)	Table A, para 63 (changed)
331	new
332	1985, s 381
333	
(1)–(4)	new
334	
(1)–(3)	1985, s 125(6) (changed)
(4)	1985, s 125(6)(a)
(5)	new
(6)	1985, s 125(6)(b)
(7)	1985, s 125(7), (8)
335	
(1)–(6)	new

Chapter 4 Public companies: additional requirements for AGMs

336	
(1)	1985, s 366(1) (changed)
(2)	new
(3)	1985, s 366(4) (changed)
(4)	1985, s 366(4), Sch 24
337	
(1)	1985, s 366(1)
(2)	1985, s 369(3)(a)
338	
(1)	1985, s 376(1)(b)
(2)	new
(3)	1985, s 376(2) (changed)
(4)	1985, s 376(1), s 377(1)(a), (2) (changed)
339	
(1)	1985, s 376(3), (5)
(2)	1985, s 376(1)
(3)	1985, s 376(6)
(4)	1985, s 376(7)
(5)	1985, s 376(7), Sch 24
340	
(1)	new
(2)	1985, s 376(1), s 377(1)(b) (changed)

Chapter 5 Additional requirements for quoted companies

341	
(1)–(6)	new

Section of 2006 Act	Origin
342	
(1)–(4)	new
343	
(1)–(6)	new
344	
(1)–(4)	new
345	
(1)–(6)	new
346	
(1)–(5)	new
347	
(1)–(4)	new
348	
(1)–(4)	new
349	
(1)–(5)	new
350	
(1)–(5)	new
351	
(1)–(5)	new
352	
(1), (2)	new
353	
(1)–(5)	new
354	
(1)–(4)	new
Chapter 6 Records of resolutions and meetings	
355	
(1)	1985, s 382(1), s 382A(1) (changed)
(2)	new
(3)	1985, s 382(5) (changed)
(4)	1985, s 382(5), Sch 24
356	
(1)	drafting
(2), (3)	1985, s 382A(2)
(4)	1985, s 382(2)
(5)	1985, s 382(4)
357	
(1), (2)	1985, s 382B(1)
(3)	1985, s 382B(2)
(4)	1985, s 382B(2), Sch 24
(5)	1985, s 382B(3)
358	
(1)	1985, s 383(1) (changed)
(2)	new
(3)	1985, s 383(1)
(4)	1985, s 383(3) (changed)
(5)	1985, s 383(4) (changed)
(6)	1985, s 383(4), Sch 24
(7)	1985, s 383(5)
359	new

Section of 2006 Act	Origin
Chapter 7 Supplementary provisions	
360	
(1), (2)	new
361	new
Part 14 Control of Political Donations and Expenditure	
362	1985, s 347A(1) (changed)
363	
(1)	1985, s 347A(6), (7)(a), (9)
(2)	1985, s 347A(6)(b), (7)(b), (c) (changed)
(3)	new
(4)	drafting
364	
(1)	drafting
(2)	1985, s 347A(4)
(3)	new
(4)	new
365	
(1)	1985, s 347A(5) (changed)
(2)	new
366	
(1)	1985, s 347C(1) (changed)
(2)	1985, s 347C(1), 347D(1), (2), (3) (changed)
(3)	1985, s 347D(3) (changed)
(4)	new
(5)	1985, s 347A(10), s 347C(1), s 347D(2), (3)
(6)	1985, s 347C(6), s 347D(9)
367	
(1), (2)	new
(3)	1985, s 347C(2), s 347D(4) (changed)
(4)	new
(5)	1985, s 347C(4), s 347D(6)
(6)	1985, s 347C(2), s 347D(4) (changed)
(7)	new
368	
(1)	1985, s 347C(3)(b), s 347D(5)
(2)	1985, s 347C(3), s 347D(5)
369	
(1)	1985, s 347F(1)
(2)	1985, s 347F(2), (3), (4)
(3)	1985, s 347F(2), (6) (changed)
(4)	new
(5)	1985, s 347F(3)
(6)	1985, s 347F(5)
370	
(1)	1985, s 347I(1) (changed)
(2)	1985, s 347I(1)
(3)	1985, s 54(2), s 347I(2) (changed)
(4)	1985, s 347I(3)
(5)	new
371	
(1)	1985, s 347I(3)

Section of 2006 Act	Origin
(2)	1985, s 347I(4), (5)
(3)	1985, s 347I(6)
(4)	1985, s 347I(7)
(5)	1985, s 347I(8)
372	
(1)	1985, s 347J(1)
(2)	1985, s 347J(2)
(3)	1985, s 347J(3)
(4)	1985, s 347J(4), (5)
(5)	1985, s 347J(6)
373	
(1)	1985, s 347K(1)
(2)	1985, s 347K(2)
374	
(1)–(3)	new
375	
(1)	1985, s 347B(1)
(2)	1985, s 347B(2) (changed)
376	
(1), (2)	1985, s 347B(3)
377	
(1)	1985, s 347B(8)
(2)	1985, s 347B(10)
(3)	1985, s 347B(9)
(4)	1985, s 347B(11)
378	
(1)	1985, s s 347B(4), (6), (7) (changed)
(2)	new
(3)	1985, s 347B(5)
379	
(1)	1985, s 347A(3), (8)
(2)	1985, s 347A(10)
Part 15 Accounts and Reports	
Chapter 1 Introduction	
380	
(1)–(4)	drafting
381	drafting
382	
(1)	1985, s 247(1)(a)
(2)	1985, s 247(1)(b), (2)
(3), (4)	1985, s 247(3), (4)
(5)	1985, s 247(5) (changed)
(6)	1985, s 247(6), Sch 4, para 56(2), (3)
(7)	drafting
383	
(1)	1985, s 247A(3)
(2)	1985, s 249(1)(a)
(3)	1985, s 249(1)(b), (2)
(4)	1985, s 249(3)
(5), (6)	1985, s 249(4)
(7)	1985, s 249(5), (6)

Section of 2006 Act	Origin
384	
(1)	1985, s 247A(1)–(1B)
(2)	1985, s 247A(2) (changed)
(3)	1985, s 247A(2A)
385	
(1)	new
(2)	1985, s 262(1) 'quoted company'
(3)	drafting
(4)–(6)	new
Chapter 2 Accounting records	
386	
(1), (2)	1985, s 221(1)
(3)–(5)	1985, s 221(2)–(4)
387	
(1), (2)	1985, s 221(5)
(3)	1985, s 221(6), Sch 24
388	
(1)–(3)	1985, s 222(1)–(3)
(4), (5)	1985, s 222(5)
389	
(1), (2)	1985, s 222(4)
(3)	1985, s 222(6)
(4)	1985, s 222(4), (6), Sch 24
Chapter 3 A company's financial year	
390	
(1)–(5)	1985, s 223(1)–(5)
391	
(1)	1985, s 224(1)
(2)	1985, s 224(2), (3)
(3)	1986 art.232(2), (3)
(4)	1985, s 224(3A), 1986 art.232(3A)
(5)–(7)	1985, s 224(4)–(6)
392	
(1)	1985, s 225(1)
(2)–(6)	1985, s 225(3)–(7)
Chapter 4 Annual accounts	
393	
(1), (2)	new
394	1985, s 226(1)
395	
(1)–(5)	1985, s 226(2)–(6)
396	
(1), (2)	1985, s 226A(1), (2)
(3)	1985, s 226A(3) (changed)
(4)	1985, s 226A(4)
(5)	1985, s 226A(5), (6)
397	1985, s 226B
398	1985, s s 227(8), 248(1) (changed)
399	
(1), (2)	1985, s s 227(1), (8), 248(1), (2) (changed)
(3)	1985, s 227(8)

Section of 2006 Act	Origin
(4)	new
400	
(1), (2)	1985, s 228(1), (2)
(3)	1985, s 228(5)
(4)	1985, s 228(3)
(5)	1985, s 228(4)
(6)	1985, s 228(6)
401	
(1), (2)	1985, s 228A(1), (2)
(3)	1985, s 228A(5)
(4)	1985, s 228A(3)
(5)	1985, s 228A(4)
(6)	1985, s 228A(6)
402	1985, s 229(5)
403	
(1)–(6)	1985, s 227(2)–(7)
404	
(1), (2)	1985, s 227A(1), (2)
(3)	1985, s 227A(3) (changed)
(4)	1985, s 227A(4)
(5)	1985, s 227A(5), (6)
405	
(1), (2)	1985, s 229(1), (2)
(3), (4)	1985, s 229(3)
406	1985, s 227B
407	
(1)–(5)	1985, s 227C(1)–(5)
408	
(1)	1985, s 230(1) (changed)
(2)	1985, s 230(2) (changed)
(3), (4)	1985, s 230(3), (4)
409	
(1), (2)	1985, s 231(1), (2) (changed)
(3), (4)	1985, s 231(3) (changed)
(5)	1985, s 231(4)
410	
(1), (2)	1985, s 231(5)
(3)	1985, s 231(6)
(4), (5)	1985, s 231(7), Sch 24
411	
(1)	1985, s s 231A(1), 246(3)(b)(ai)
(2)	1985, s 231A(5)
(3)–(5)	1985, s 231A(2)–(4)
(6)	1985, s 231A(7), Sch 4, para 94(1), (2)
(7)	1985, s 231A(6)
412	
(1)–(4)	new
(5)	1985, s 232(3)
(6)	1985, s 232(4), Sch 24
413	
(1)–(8)	new

Section of 2006 Act	Origin
414	
(1), (2)	1985, s 233(1), (2)
(3)	1985, s 246(8)
(4), (5)	1985, s 233(5) (changed), Sch 24
Chapter 5 Directors' report	
415	
(1)	1985, s 234(1)
(2), (3)	1985, s 234(2), (3)
(4), (5)	1985, s 234(5), Sch 24
416	
(1)	1985, s 234ZZA(1)(a), (b)
(2)	1985, s 234ZZA(2)
(3)	1985, s s 234ZZA(1)(c), 246(4)(a)
(4)	1985, s 234ZZA(3), (4) (changed)
417	
(1)	1985, s s 234(1)(a), 246(4)(a)
(2)	new
(3), (4)	1985, s 234ZZB(1), (2)
(5)	new
(6)	1985, s 234ZZB(3), (5)
(7)	1985, s 246A(2A)
(8)	1985, s 234ZZB(4)
(9)	1985, s 234ZZB(6)
(10), (11)	new
418	
(1)	1985, s 234ZA(1)
(2)	1985, s s 234(1)(b), 234ZA(2)
(3), (4)	1985, s 234ZA(3), (4)
(5), (6)	1985, s 234ZA(6), Sch 24
419	
(1)	1985, s 234A(1)
(2)	1985, s 246(8)(b)
(3), (4)	1985, s s 234(5), 234A(4) (changed), Sch 24
Chapter 6 Quoted companies: directors' remuneration report	
420	
(1)	1985, s 421(1)
(2)	1985, s 234B(3), (4) (changed)
(3)	1985, s 234B(3), Sch 24
421	
(1), (2)	1985, s 234B(1), (2) (changed)
(3)	1985, s 234B(5), (6)
(4)	1985, s 234B(6), Sch 24
422	
(1)	1985, s 234C(1)
(2), (3)	1985, s 234C(4) (changed), Sch 24
Chapter 7 Publication of accounts and reports	
423	
(1)	1985, s 238(1), (1A)
(2), (3)	new
(4)	1985, s 238(3)
(5)	1985, s 238(6)

Section of 2006 Act	Origin
(6)	drafting
424	
(1)–(3)	1985, s 238(1) (changed)
(4)	1985, s 238(4) (changed)
(5)	new
(6)	drafting
425	
(1), (2)	1985, s 238(5), Sch 24
426	
(1)	1985, s 251(1)
(2), (3)	1985, s 251(2)
(4)	drafting
(5)	new
(6)	1985, s 251(5)
427	
(1)	1985, s 251(1) 'summary financial statement'
(2)	1985, s 251(3)
(3)	1985, s 251(3A)
(4)	1985, s 251(4)
(5)	new
(6)	1985, s 251(5)
428	
(1)	1985, s 251(1) 'summary financial statement'
(2)	1985, s 251(3)
(3)	1985, s 251(3A)
(4)	1985, s 251(4)
(5)	new
(6)	1985, s 251(5)
429	
(1), (2)	1985, s 251(6), Sch 24
430	
(1)–(7)	new
431	
(1), (2)	1985, s 239(1), (2)
(3), (4)	1985, s 239(3), Sch 24
432	
(1), (2)	1985, s 239(1), (2)
(3), (4)	1985, s 239(3), Sch 24
433	
(1)–(3)	1985, s s 233(3), 234A(2) and 234C(2)
(4), (5)	1985, s s 233(6)(a), 234A(4)(a) and 234C(4)(a), Sch 24
434	
(1)	1985, s 240(1) (changed)
(2)	1985, s 240(2) (changed)
(3)	1985, s 240(5)
(4), (5)	1985, s 240(6), Sch 24
(6)	1985, s 251(7)
435	
(1), (2)	1985, s 240(3) (changed)
(3)	1985, s 240(5) (changed)
(4)	new

Section of 2006 Act	Origin
(5), (6)	1985, s 240(6), Sch 24
(7)	1985, s 251(7)
436	
(1), (2)	1985, s s 233(3), 234A(2), 234C(2), 240(4) (changed)

Chapter 8 Public companies: laying of accounts and reports before general meeting

437	
(1)	1985, s 241(1) (changed)
(2)	1985, s 241(2)
(3)	drafting
438	
(1)–(3)	1985, s 241(2)–(4)
(4)	1985, s 241(2), Sch 24

Chapter 9 Quoted companies: members' approval of directors' remuneration report

439	
(1)	1985, s 241A(1), (3)
(2)	1985, s 241A(4)
(3)	1985, s 241A(5), (7)
(4)	1985, s 241A(6)
(5)	1985, s 241A(8)
(6)	1985, s 241A(2), (12)
440	
(1)	1985, s 241A(9)
(2), (3)	1985, s 241A(10), (11)
(4)	1985, s 241A(9), (10), Sch 24
(5)	1985, s 241A(2), (12)

Chapter 10 Filing of accounts and reports

441	
(1)	1985, s 242(1)
(2)	drafting
442	
(1)	drafting
(2), (3)	1985, s 244(1), (2) (changed)
(4), (5)	1985, s 244(4), (5)
(6)	new
(7)	1985, s 244(6)
443	
(1)–(5)	new
444	
(1)	1985, s s 242(1)(a), (b), 246(5)
(2)	1985, s s 242(1)(d), 249E(1)(b) (changed)
(3)	1985, s 246(5), (6) (changed)
(4)	1985, s 247B(2)
(5)	1985, s 246(8)
(6)	1985, s s 233(4), 234A(3), 246(7)
(7)	1985, s 236(3)
445	
(1)	1985, s s 242(1)(a), (b), 246A(1)
(2)	1985, s s 242(1)(d), 249E(1)(b) (changed)
(3)	1985, s 246A(2), (3) (changed)
(4)	1985, s 247B(2)
(5)	1985, s s 233(4), 234A(3) (changed)

Section of 2006 Act	*Origin*
(6)	new
(7)	drafting
446	
(1)	1985, s 242(1)(a), (b)
(2)	1985, s s 242(1)(d), 249E(1)(b)
(3)	1985, s s 233(4), 234A(3) (changed)
(4)	new
(5)	drafting
447	
(1)	1985, s 242(1)(a), (b), (c)
(2)	1985, s s 242(1)(d)
(3)	1985, s s 233(4), 234A(3), 234C(3) (changed)
(4)	new
448	
(1)–(3)	1985, s 254(1)–(3)
(4)	1985, s 254(4)
(5)	1985, s 244(6)
449	
(1)–(5)	1985, s 247B(1)–(5)
450	
(1), (2)	1985, s s 233(1), (2), 246(7)
(3)	1985, s 246(8), 246A(4)
(4), (5)	1985, s 233(5), Sch 24
451	
(1)	1985, s 242(2)
(2), (3)	1985, s 242(4), (5)
(4)	1985, s 242(2), Sch 24
452	
(1), (2)	1985, s 242(3)
453	
(1)	1985, s 242A(1)
(2)	1985, s 242A(2) (changed)
(3), (4)	1985, s 242A(3), (4)
(5)	new
Chapter 11 Revision of defective accounts and reports	
454	
(1)–(3)	1985, s 245(1)–(3)
(4)	1985, s 245(4) (changed)
(5)	1985, s 245(5)
455	
(1), (2)	1985, s 245A(1)
(3)–(5)	1985, s 245A(2)–(4)
456	
(1)–(3)	1985, s 245B(1)–(3)
(4)	1985, s 245B(3A)
(5)–(8)	1985, s 245B(4)–(7)
457	
(1)	1985, s 245C(1)
(2), (3)	1985, s 245C(2), (3)
(4)	1985, s 245C(4B)
(5)	1985, s 245C(1A), (4A)

Section of 2006 Act	Origin
(6)	1985, s 245C(5)
(7)	1985, s 245C(4)
458	
(1)	1985, s 245D(1), (3)
(2)	1985, s 245D(2)
(3)	1985, s 245E(1), (2)
(4)	1985, s 245E(3), (4) (changed)
(5)	1985, s 245E(3), Sch 24
459	
(1)–(8)	1985, s 245F(1)–(8)
460	
(1), (2)	1985, s 245G(1), (2)
(3)	drafting; 1985, s 245G(3), (10)
(4)	1985, s 245G(7)(a), (8)
(5)	1985, s 245G(7)(b), Sch 24
461	
(1)	1985, s 245G(3)
(2)	1985, s 245G(3)(a)
(3)	1985, s 245G(3)(b), Sch 7B, Pt 1
(4)	1985, s 245G(3)(c), Sch 7B, Pt 2
(5), (6)	1985, s 245G(3)(d), Sch 7B, Pt 3
(7)	1985, s 245G(11)
462	
(1)–(3)	1985, s 245G(4)–(6)
Chapter 12 Supplementary provisions	
463	
(1)–(6)	new
464	
(1), (2)	1985, s 256(1), (2)
(3)	1985, s 256(4)
465	
(1)	1985, s 247(1)(a)
(2)	1985, s 247(1)(b), (2)
(3), (4)	1985, s 247(3), (4)
(5)	1985, s 247(5) (changed)
(6)	1985, s 247(6), Sch 4, para 56(2), (3)
(7)	drafting
466	
(1)	1985, s 247A(3)
(2)	1985, s 249(1)(a)
(3)	1985, s 249(1)(b), (2)
(4)	1985, s 249(3)
(5), (6)	1985, s 249(4)
(7)	1985, s 249(5), (6)
467	
(1)	1985, s 247A(1)–(1B)
(2)	1985, s 247A(2)
(3)	1985, s 247A(2A)
468	
(1)–(5)	new
469	

Section of 2006 Act	Origin
(1)–(4)	1985, s 242B(1)–(4) (changed)
470	
(1)	1985, s 255D(1)
(2)	1985, s 255D(2), (2A)
(3)	1985, s 255D(5)
(4)	1985, s 255D(4)
471	
(1)	1985, s 262(1) 'annual accounts'
(2), (3)	1985, s 238(1A); drafting
472	
(1), (2)	1985, s 261(1), (2)
473	
(1)–(4)	1985, s 257(2), (3) (changed)
474	
(1)	1985, s s 262(1), 744 'regulated activity'
(2)	1985, s 262(2)
Part 16 Audit	
Chapter 1 Requirement for audited accounts	
475	
(1)	1985, s 235(1) (changed)
(2), (3)	1985, s 249B(4)
(4)	1985, s 249B(5)
476	
(1)–(3)	1985, s 249B(2)
477	
(1)	1985, s 249A(1)
(2)	1985, s 249A(3)
(3)	1985, s 249A(6)
(4)	1985, s 249A(3)(a), (7)
(5)	drafting
478	1985, s 249B(1)(a)–(e)
479	
(1)–(3)	1985, s 249B(1)(f), (1A)–(1C)
(4)	drafting
(5), (6)	1985, s 249B(1)(C)
480	
(1), (2)	1985, s 249AA(1), (2)
(3)	drafting
481	1985, s 249AA(3)
482	
(1)–(4)	new
483	
(1)–(5)	new
484	
(1)	1985, s 257(1)
(2)	1985, s 257(4)(c)
(3)	1985, s 257 (2)(b), (d)
(4)	1985, s 257 (3)
Chapter 2 Appointment of auditors	
485	
(1)	1985, s 384(1)

Section of 2006 Act	Origin
(2)–(5)	new
486	
(1), (2)	1985, s 387(1), (2)
(3), (4)	1985, s 387(2), Sch 24
487	
(1)–(4)	new
488	
(1)–(3)	new
489	
(1)	1985, s 384(1) (changed)
(2)	1985, s s 384(2), 385(2)
(3)	1985, s s 385(3), 388(1) (changed)
(4)	1985, s 385(2), (4) (changed)
(5)	drafting
490	
(1), (2)	1985, s 387(1), (2)
(3), (4)	1985, s 387(2), Sch 24
491	
(1)	1985, s 385(2) (changed)
(2)	drafting
492	
(1)	1985, s 390A(1)
(2), (3)	1985, s 390A(2)
(4), (5)	1985, s 390A(4), (5)
493	
(1)–(4)	new
494	
(1)	1985, s 390B(1), (8)
(2)–(4)	1985, s 390B(2)–(4)
(5)	1985, s 390B(5)(a)
(6)	1985, s 390B(9)
Chapter 3 Functions of auditor	
495	
(1)	1985, s 235(1); drafting
(2)	1985, s 235(1A)
(3)	1985, s 235(1B), (2)
(4)	1985, s 235(2A)
496	1985, s 235(3)
497	
(1), (2)	1985, s 235(4), (5)
498	
(1)–(4)	1985, s 237(1)–(4)
(5)	1985, s 237(4A)
499	
(1), (2)	1985, s 389A(1), (2)
(3)	1985, s 389A(6)
(4)	1985, s 389A(7)
500	
(1)–(3)	1985, s 389A(3)–(5)
(4)	1985, s 389A(6)
(5)	1985, s 389A(7)

Section of 2006 Act	Origin
501	
(1)	1985, s 389B(1)
(2)	1985, s 389B(1), Sch 24
(3)	1985, s 389B(2), (3) (changed)
(4)	1985, s 389B(4)
(5)	1985, s 389B(4), Sch 24
(6)	1985, s 389B(5)
502	
(1)	1985, s 390(2)
(2)	1985, s 390(1)
(3)	1985, s 390(3)
503	
(1), (2)	1985, s 236(1)
(3)	new
504	
(1)–(4)	new
505	
(1), (2)	1985, s 236(2) (changed)
(3), (4)	1985, s 236(4), Sch 24
506	
(1), (2)	new
507	
(1)–(4)	new
508	
(1)–(4)	new
509	
(1)–(4)	new
Chapter 4 Removal, resignation, etc of auditors	
510	
(1), (2)	1985, s 391(1); drafting
(3)	1985, s 391(3)
(4)	drafting
511	
(1)	1985, s 391A(1)(a)
(2)–(6)	1985, s 391A(2)–(6)
512	
(1)	1985, s 391(2)
(2), (3)	1985, s 391(2), Sch 24
513	
(1), (2)	1985, s 391(4)
514	
(1)–(8)	new
515	
(1)	1985, s 391A(1)(b)
(2)	1985, s 391A(1) opening words (changed)
(3)–(7)	1985, s 391A(2)–(6)
516	
(1), (2)	1985, s 392(1)
(3)	1985, s 392(2)
517	
(1)	1985, s 392(3)

Section of 2006 Act	Origin
(2), (3)	1985, s 392(3), Sch 24
518	
(1)–(4)	1985, s 392A(1)–(4)
(5)	1985, s 392A(5)
(6), (7)	1985, s 392(5), Sch 24
(8)–(10)	1985, s 392A(6)–(8)
519	
(1)–(3)	1985, s 394(1) (changed)
(4)	1985, s 394(2) (changed)
(5), (6)	1985, s 394A(1), (2)
(7)	1985, s 394(1), Sch 24
520	
(1)	drafting
(2), (3)	1985, s 394(3), (4)
(4)	1985, s 394(6)
(5)	1985, s 394(7) (changed)
(6)	1985, s 394A(4)
(7)	new
(8)	1985, s 394A(4), Sch 24 (changed)
521	
(1)	1985, s 394(5)
(2)	1985, s 394(7)
(3), (4)	1985, s 394A(1), (2)
(5)	1985, s 394A(1), Sch 24
522	
(1)–(8)	new
523	
(1)–(6)	new
524	
(1) to 4)	new
525	
(1)–(3)	new
526	1985, s 388(2)

Chapter 5 Quoted companies: right of members to raise audit concerns at accounts meeting

527	
(1)–(6)	new
528	
(1)–(5)	new
529	
(1)–(4)	new
530	
(1), (2)	new
531	
(1), (2)	new

Chapter 6 Auditors' liability

532	
(1)	1985, s 310(1) (changed)
(2)	1985, s 310(2), drafting
(3)	1985, s 310(1)
(4)	new
533	1985, s 310(3)(b)

Section of 2006 Act	Origin
534	
(1)–(3)	new
535	
(1)–(5)	new
536	
(1)–(5)	new
537	
(1)–(3)	new
538	
(1)–(3)	new
Chapter 7 Supplementary provisions	
539	1985, s s 262(1)
Part 17 A Company's Share Capital	
Chapter 1 Shares and share capital of a company	
540	
(1)	1985, s 744 ('share')
(2), (3)	new
(4)	1985, s 744 ('share'), drafting
541	1985, s 182(1)(a)
542	
(1)–(5)	new
543	
(1), (2)	1985, s 182(2)
544	
(1), (2)	1985, s 182(1)(b)
(3)	drafting
545	new
546	
(1), (2)	new
547	1985, s 737(1), (2)
548	1985, s 744 ('equity share capital')
Chapter 2 Allotment of shares: general provisions	
549	
(1)	1985, s 80(1), (2) (changed)
(2), (3)	1985, s 80(2)
(4)	1985, s 80(9)
(5)	1985, s 80(9), Sch 24
(6)	1985, s 80(10) (changed)
550	new
551	
(1)	1985, s 80(1), (2)
(2)	1985, s 80(3)
(3)	1985, s 80(4)
(4)	1985, s 80(4), (5)
(5)	1985, s 80(5)
(6)	1985, s 80(6)
(7)	1985, s 80(7)
(8)	1985, s 80(8)
(9)	drafting
552	
(1)	1985, s 98(1)

Section of 2006 Act	Origin
(2)	1985, s 98(2)
(3)	1985, s 98(3)
553	
(1)	1985, s 97(1)
(2)	1985, s 97(2)(a)
(3)	1985, s 98(4)
554	
(1)–(5)	new
555	
(1)	1985, s 88(1)
(2)	1985, s 88(2) (changed)
(3), (4)	new
556	
(1)	1985, s 128(1), (2) (changed)
(2), (3)	1985, s 128(1)
(4)	1985, s 128(2)
557	
(1)	1985, s 88(5), s 128(5) (changed)
(2)	1985, s 88(5), s 128(5), Sch 24
(3)	1985, s 88(6) (changed)
558	1985, s 738(1)
559	1985, s 80(2)(a)

Chapter 3 Allotment of equity securities: existing shareholders' right of pre-emption

Section of 2006 Act	Origin
560	
(1)	1985, s 94(2), (5)
(2)	1985, s 94(3), (3A)
561	
(1)	1985, s 89(1)
(2)	1985, s 89(4)
(3)	1985, s 94(3)
(4)	1985, s 89(6)
(5)	drafting
562	
(1)	1985, s 90(1)
(2)	new
(3)	1985, s 90(5) (changed)
(4)	1985, s 90(6)
(5)	1985, s 90(6) (changed)
(6), (7)	new
563	
(1), (2)	1985, s 92(1)
(3)	1985, s 92(2)
564	1985, s 94(2)
565	1985, s 89(4)
566	1985, s 89(5)
567	
(1), (2)	1985, s 91(1)
(3), (4)	1985, s 91(2)
568	
(1)	1985, s 89(2), (3)
(2)	1985, s 89(3)

Section of 2006 Act	Origin
(3)	1985, s 90(1)
(4)	1985, s 92(1)
(5)	1985, s 92(2)
569	
(1), (2)	new
570	
(1), (2)	1985, s 95(1)
(3)	1985, s 95(3)
(4)	1985, s 95(4)
571	
(1), (2)	1985, s 95(2)
(3)	1985, s 95(3)
(4)	1985, s 95(4)
(5), (6)	1985, s 95(5)
(7)	1985, s 95(5), Sch 15A, para 3(1), (2)
572	
(1), (2)	1985, s 95(6)
(3)	1985, s 95(6), Sch 24
573	
(1)	1985, s 95(2A)
(2)	1985, s 95(1), (2A)
(3)	1985, s 95(1), (2A), (4)
(4)	1985, s 95(2), (2A)
(5)	1985, s 95(1), (2A), (4), (5), Sch 15A, para 3(1), (2)
574	
(1), (2)	1985, s 94(7)
575	
(1)	1985, s 93(1)
(2)	1985, s 93(2)
576	
(1)	1985, s 96(1), (2)
(2)	1985, s 96(3)
(3)	1985, s 96(4)
577	1985, s 94(2)
Chapter 4 Public companies: allotment where issue not fully subscribed	
578	
(1)	1985, s 84(1)
(2)	1985, s 84(2)
(3)	1985, s 84(3) (changed)
(4)	1985, s 84(4)
(5)	1985, s 84(4), (5)
(6)	1985, s 84(6)
579	
(1), (2)	1985, s 85(1)
(3)	1985, s 85(2)
(4)	1985, s 85(3)
Chapter 5 Payment for shares	
580	
(1)	1985, s 100(1)
(2)	1985, s 100(2)
581	1985, s 119

Section of 2006 Act	Origin
582	
(1)	1985, s 99(1)
(2)	1985, s 99(4)
(3)	1985, s 99(1)
583	
(1)	drafting
(2)–(3)(d)	1985, s 738(2)
(3)(e), (4)	new
(4)	new
(5)	1985, s 738(3)
(6)	1985, s 738(4)
(7)	new
584	1985, s 106
585	
(1)	1985, s 99(2)
(2)	1985, s 99(3)
(3)	1985, s 99(5)
586	
(1)	1985, s 101(1)
(2)	1985, s 101(2)
(3)	1985, s 101(3), (4)
(4)	1985, s 101(5)
587	
(1)	1985, s 102(1)
(2)	1985, s 102(2)
(3)	1985, s 102(3), (4)
(4)	1985, s 102(5), (6)
(5)	1985, s 102(7)
588	
(1)	1985, s 112(1), (5)(a)
(2)	1985, s 112(3)
(3)	1985, s 112(4)
(4)	1985, s 112(5)(b)
589	
(1), (2)	1985, s 113(1)
(3)	1985, s 113(2), (3) (changed)
(4)	1985, s 113(4)
(5)	1985, s 113(5)
(6)	1985, s 113(6), (7)
590	
(1)	1985, s 114
(2)	1985, s 114., Sch 24
591	
(1), (2)	1985, s 115(1)
592	
(1), (2)	1985, s 107
Chapter 6 Public companies: independent valuation of non-cash consideration	
593	
(1)	1985, s 103(1)
(2)	1985, s 103(2)
(3)	1985, s 103(6)

Section of 2006 Act	Origin
(4)	drafting
594	
(1)–(3)	1985, s 103(3)
(4), (5)	1985, s 103(4)
(6)	1985, s 103(7)
595	
(1), (2)	1985, s 103(5)
(3)	1985, s 103(7)(b)
596	
(1)	drafting
(2)	1985, s 108(4)
(3)	1985, s 108(6)
(4), (5)	1985, s 108(7)
597	
(1), (2)	1985, s 111(1)
(3), (4)	1985, s 111(3), Sch 24
(5), (6)	1985, s s 88(6), 111(3)
598	
(1)	1985, s 104(1)
(2)	1985, s 104(2)
(3)	drafting
(4)	1985, s 104(6)(a)
(5)	1985, s 104(6)(b)
599	
(1)	1985, s 104(4)(a), (b), (d)
(2)	1985, s 104(5)(a)
(3)	1985, s 104(4)(d)
(4)	1985, s 104(5)(b)
600	
(1)	drafting
(2)	1985, s 109(2)(a), (b)
(3)	1985, s 108(6)(a), (b), (c), 109(2)(c), (d)
(4), (5)	1985, s 109(3)
601	
(1), (2)	1985, s 104(4)(c), (d)
(3)	1985, s 104(4)(c) (changed)
602	
(1)	1985, s 111(2)
(2), (3)	1985, s 111(4), Sch 24
603	1985, s 104(3)
604	
(1)	1985, s 105(1)
(2)	1985, s 105(2)
(3)	1985, s 105(3)
605	
(1)	1985, s 112(1)
(2)	1985, s 112(2)
(3)	1985, s 112(3)
(4)	1985, s 112(4)
606	
(1)	1985, s 113(1)

Section of 2006 Act	Origin
(2)	1985, s 113(2), (3) (changed)
(3)	1985, s 113(4)
(4)	1985, s 113(5)
(5)	1986, s 113(6), (7)
(6)	1986, s 113(8)
607	
(1)	drafting
(2)	1985, s 114
(3)	1985, s 114, Sch 24
608	
(1), (2)	1985, s 115(1)
609	
(1), (2)	1985, s 107
Chapter 7 Share premiums	
610	
(1)	1985, s 130(1)
(2), (3)	1985, s 130(2) (changed)
(4)	1985, s 130(3)
(5), (6)	1985, s 130(4)
611	
(1)	1985, s 132(1)
(2)	1985, s 132(2)
(3)	1985, s 132(3)
(4)	1985, s 132(4)
(5)	1985, s 132(5)
612	
(1)	1985, s 131(1)
(2)	1985, s 131(2)
(3)	1985, s 131(3)
(4)	1985, s 131(1), 132(8)
613	
(1)	drafting
(2), (3)	1985, s 131(4)
(4)	1985, s 131(5)
(5)	1985, s 131(6)
614	
(1)	1985, s 134(1)
(2)	1985, s 134(3)
615	1985, s 133(1)
616	
(1)	1985, s 131(7), 133(4)
(2)	1985, s 133(2)
(3)	1985, s 133(3)
Chapter 8 Alteration of share capital	
617	
(1)	1985, s 121(1) (changed)
(2)	1985, s 121(2)(a) (changed)
(3)	1985, s 121(2)(b), (c), (d) (changed)
(4), (5)	new
618	
(1)	1985, s 121(2)(b), (d)

Section of 2006 Act	Origin
(2)	1985, s 121(3) (changed)
(3)	1985, s 121(4) (changed)
(4), (5)	new
619	
(1)	1985, s 122(1)(a), (d)
(2), (3)	1985, s 122(1) (changed)
(4)	1985, s 122(2)
(5)	1985, s 122(2), Sch 24
620	
(1)	1985, s 121(2)(c) (changed)
(2)	1985, s 121(4) (changed)
(3)	new
621	
(1)	1985, s 122(1)(c)
(2), (3)	new
(4)	1985, s 122(2)
(5)	1985, s 122(2), Sch 24
622	
(1)–(8)	new
623	new
624	
(1)–(3)	new
625	
(1)–(5)	new
626	
(1)–(6)	new
627	
(1)–(8)	new
628	
(1)–(3)	new
Chapter 9 Classes of share and class rights	
629	
(1)	new
(2)	1985, s 128(2)
630	
(1)	1985, s 125(1)
(2)–(4)	1985, s 125(2) (changed)
(5)	1985, s 125(7)
(6)	1985, s 125(8)
631	
(1)–(6)	new
632	1985, s 126 (changed)
633	
(1)	1985, s 127(1)(b)
(2)	1985, s 127(2), (2A)
(3)	1985, s 127(2)
(4)	1985, s 127(3)
(5)	1985, s 127(4)
(6)	1985, s 127(6)
634	
(1)–(6)	new

Section of 2006 Act	Origin
635	
(1)–(3)	1985, s 127(5)
636	
(1)	1985, s 128(4) (changed)
(2)	1985, s 128(5)
(3)	1985, s 128(5), Sch 24
637	
(1)	1985, s 128(3) (changed)
(2)	1985, s 128(5)
(3)	1985, s 128(5), Sch 24
638	
(1)	1985, s 129(1) (changed)
(2)	1985, s 129(4)
(3)	1985, s 129(4), Sch 24
639	
(1)	1985, s 129(3) (changed)
(2)	1985, s 129(4)
(3)	1985, s 129(4), Sch 24
640	
(1)	1985, s 129(2) (changed)
(2)	1985, s 129(4)
(3)	1985, s 129(4), Sch 24
Chapter 10 Reduction of share capital	
641	
(1)–(3)	1985, s 135(1) (changed)
(4)	1985, s 135(2)
(5), (6)	new
642	
(1)–(4)	new
643	
(1)–(5)	new
644	
(1)–(9)	new
645	
(1)	1985, s 136(1)
(2)	1985, s 136(2), (6)
(3)	1985, s 136(6)
(4)	1985, s 136(2)
646	
(1)	1985, s 136(3)
(2), (3)	1985, s 136(4)
(4), (5)	1985, s 136(5)
647	
(1)	1985, s 141 (changed)
(2)	1985, s 141, Sch 24
648	
(1), (2)	1985, s 137(1)
(3)	1985, s 137(2)(b)
(4)	1985, s 137(2)(a), (3)
649	
(1)	1985, s 138(1) (changed)

Section of 2006 Act	Origin
(2)	new
(3)	1985, s 138(2) (changed)
(4)	1985, s 138(3) (changed)
(5)	1985, s 138(4) (changed)
(6)	1985, s 138(4)
650	
(1)	1985, s 139(1)
(2)	1985, s 139(2)
(3)	drafting
651	
(1), (2)	1985, s 139(3)
(3)	1985, s 139(4) (changed)
(4)	1985, s 139(5)
(5)	new
(6)	1985, s 139(5)(a)
(7)	1985, s 139(5)(b)
652	
(1)	1985, s 140(1) (changed)
(2)	drafting
(3)	1985, s 140(5)
653	
(1)	1985, s 140(2)
(2)	1985, s 140(3)
(3)	1985, s 140(4)
(4)	drafting
Chapter 11 Miscellaneous and supplementary provisions	
654	
(1)–(3)	new
655	1985, s 111A
656	
(1)–(3)	1985, s 142(1)
(4)	1985, s 142(2) (changed)
(5)	1985, s 142(2), Sch 24
(6)	1985, s 142(3)
657	
(1)–(4)	new
Part 18 Acquisition by Limited Company of its Own Shares	
Chapter 1 General provisions	
658	
(1)	1985, s 143(1)
(2)	1985, s 143(2)
(3)	1985, s 143(2), Sch 24
659	
(1), (2)	1985, s 143(3)
660	
(1), (2)	1985, s 144(1) (changed)
(3)	1985, s 145(1), (2)(a)
661	
(1), (2)	1985, s 144(2) (changed)
(3)	1985, s 144(3)
(4)	1985, s 144(4)

Section of 2006 Act	Origin
(5)	1985, s 145(2)(a)
662	
(1)	1985, s 146(1)
(2)	1985, s 146(2)
(3)	1985, s 146(2), (3)
(4)	1985, s 147(1)
(5), (6)	1985, s 146(4)
663	
(1)	1985, s 122(1)(f)
(2), (3)	new
(4)	1985, s 122(2)
(5)	1985, s 122(2), Sch 24
664	
(1), (2)	1985, s 147(2) (changed)
(3)	new
(4)	1985, s 147(3) (changed)
(5), (6)	new
665	
(1), (2)	1985, s 147(4)
(3)	new
(4)	1985, s 147(4)(a) (changed)
(5)	1985, s 147(4)(b)
666	
(1), (2)	1985, s 149(1)
667	
(1), (2)	1985, s 149(2)
(3)	1985, s 149(2), Sch 24
668	
(1), (2)	1985, s 148(1)
(3)	1985, s 148(2)
669	
(1), (2)	1985, s 148(4)
670	
(1)	1985, s 150(1)
(2)	1985, s 150(2)
(3)	1985, s 150(3)
(4)	1985, s 150(4)
671	1985, s 145(3), s 146(1), s 148(3)
672	
(1)	1985, Sch 2, para 1(1)
(2)	1985, Sch 2, para 1(2)
(3)	1985, Sch 2, para 1(3)
(4)	1985, Sch 2, para 1(4)
(5)	1985, Sch 2, para 2(3)
(6)	1985, Sch 2, para 2(4)
673	
(1)	1985, Sch 2, para 3(1)(a), (2)
(2)	1985, Sch 2, para 3(1)(b), (2)(a)
674	1985, Sch 2, para 4(1), (3)
675	
(1), (2)	1985, Sch 2, para 5(1), (2)

Section of 2006 Act	Origin
676	1985, Sch 2, para 5(1), (3)

Chapter 2 Financial assistance for purchase of own shares

677	
(1)	1985, s 152(1)(a)
(2), (3)	1985, s 152(2)
678	
(1)	1985, s 151(1) (changed)
(2)	1985, s 153(1)
(3)	1985, s 151(2) (changed)
(4)	1985, s 153(2)
(5)	drafting
679	
(1)	1985, s 151(1) (changed)
(2)	1985, s 153(1) (changed)
(3)	1985, s 151(2) (changed)
(4)	1985, s 153(2) (changed)
(5)	drafting
680	
(1)	1985, s 151(3)
(2)	1985, s 151(3), Sch 24
681	
(1), (2)	1985, s 153(3)
682	
(1)	1985, s 153(4), s 154(1)
(2)	1985, s 153(4)
(3), (4)	1985, s 154(2)
(5)	1985, s 153(5)
683	
(1)	1985, s 152(1)(b), (c)
(2)	1985, s 152(3)

Chapter 3 Redeemable shares

684	
(1)	1985, s 159(1) (changed)
(2)	new
(3)	1985, s 159(1) (changed)
(4)	1985, s 159(2)
685	
(1)–(4)	new
686	
(1)–(3)	1985, s 159(3) (changed)
687	
(1)–(3)	1985, s 160(1)
(4), (5)	1985, s 160(2)
(6)	1985, s 160(1)
688	1985, s 160(4) (changed)
689	
(1)	1985, s 122(1)(e)
(2), (3)	new
(4)	1985, s 122(2)
(5)	1985, s 122(2), Sch 24

Chapter 4 Purchase of own shares

Section of 2006 Act	Origin
690	
(1)	1985, s 162(1) (changed)
(2)	1985, s 162(3)
691	
(1), (2)	1985, s 159(3), s 162(2)
692	
(1), (2)	1985, s 160(1), s 162(2)
(3), (4)	1985, s 160(2), s 162(2)
(5)	1985, s 160(1), s 162(2)
693	
(1)	1985, s 164(1), s 166(1)
(2)	1985, s 163(1)
(3)	1985, s 163(2)
(4)	1985, s 163(3)
(5)	1985, s 163(4), (5)
694	
(1)	1985, s 164(1)
(2)	1985, s 164(2), s 165(2) (changed)
(3)	1985, s 165(1)
(4)	1985, s 164(3), 165(2)
(5)	1985, s 164(4), 165(2)
(6)	drafting
695	
(1)	1985, s 164(5), 165(2)
(2)	1985, Sch 15A, para 5(1), (2)
(3), (4)	1985, s 164(5), s 165(2)
696	
(1)	1985, s 164(6), s 165(2)
(2)	1985, s 164(6), s 165(2), Sch 15A, para 5(3), (4)
(3)–(5)	1985, s 164(6), s 165(2)
697	
(1), (2)	1985, s 164(7)
(3)	1985, s 164(3), (7)
(4)	1985, s 164(4), (7)
(5)	drafting
698	
(1)	1985, s 164(5), (7)
(2)	1985, Sch 15A, para 5(1), (2)
(3), (4)	1985, s 164(5), (7)
699	
(1)	1985, s 164(6), (7)
(2)	1985, s 164(6), (7), Sch 15A, para 5(3)
(3)–(6)	1985, s 164(6), (7)
700	
(1), (2)	1985, s 167(2)
(3)	1985, s 164(3), (7), s 167(2)
(4)	1985, s 164(4), (7), s 167(2)
(5)	1985, s 164(5), (6), (7), s 167(2)
701	
(1)	1985, s 166(1)
(2)	1985, s 166(2)

Section of 2006 Act	Origin
(3)	1985, s 166(3)(a), (b)
(4)	1985, s 166(4)
(5)	1985, s 166(3)(c), (4)
(6)	1985, s 166(5)
(7)	1985, s 166(6)
(8)	1985, s 166(7)
702	
(1)–(4)	1985, s 169(4) (changed)
(5)	new
(6)	1985, s 169(5)
(7)	1985, s 169(9)
703	
(1)	1985, s 169(7) (changed)
(2)	1985, s 169(7), Sch 24
(3)	1985, s 169(8)
704	1985, s 167(1)
705	
(1)	1985, s 168(1)
(2)	1985, s 168(2)
706	1985, s 160(4), s 162(2), (2B)
707	
(1)–(3)	1985, s 169(1), (1A), (1B) (changed)
(4)	1985, s 169(2)
(5)	1985, s 169(3)
(6)	1985, s 169(6)
(7)	1985, s 169(6), Sch 24
708	
(1)	1985, s 169(1), (1A), (1B) (changed)
(2), (3)	new
(4)	1985, s 169(6)
(5)	1985, s 169(6), Sch 24
Chapter 5 Redemption or purchase by private company out of capital	
709	
(1)	1985, s 171(1) (changed)
(2)	1985, s 171(2)
710	
(1), (2)	1985, s 171(3)
711	
(1), (2)	1985, s 172(1)
712	
(1)	drafting
(2)	1985, s 172(2)
(3)	1985, s 172(4)
(4)	1985, s 172(5)
(5)	drafting
(6)	1985, s 172(3)
(7)	1985, s 172(6)
713	
(1), (2)	1985, s 173(1)
714	
(1)–(3)	1985, s 173(3) (changed)

Section of 2006 Act	Origin
(4)	1985, s 173(4) (changed)
(5), (6)	1985, s 173(5) (changed)
715	
(1)	1985, s 173(6)
(2)	1985, s 173(6), Sch 24
716	
(1)	1985, s 173(2)
(2)	1985, s 174(1)
(3)	drafting
717	
(1)	drafting
(2)	1985, Sch 15A, para 6(1), (2)
(3)	1985, s 174(2)
(4)	1985, s 174(3), (5)
718	
(1)	drafting
(2)	1985, s 174(4), Sch 15A, para 6(1), (3)
(3)	1985, s 174(4)
719	
(1)	1985, s 175(1)
(2)	1985, s 175(2)
(3)	1985, s 175(3)
(4)	1985, s 175(4), (5)
720	
(1)	1985, s 175(4), (6)(a)
(2)	1985, s 175(6)(a) (changed)
(3)	new
(4)	1985, s 175(6)(b)
(5)	1985, s 175(7) (changed)
(6)	1985, s 175(7), Sch 24
(7)	1985, s 175(8)
721	
(1)	1985, s 176(1)
(2)	1985, s 176(1), (2)
(3)	1985, s 177(1)
(4), (5)	1985, s 177(2)
(6)	1985, s 177(3)
(7)	1985, s 177(4)
722	
(1)	new
(2)	1985, s 176(3)(a)
(3)	1985, s 176(3)(b)
(4)	1985, s 176(4)
(5)	1985, s 176(4), Sch 24
723	
(1)	1985, s 174(1)
(2)	drafting
Chapter 6 Treasury shares	
724	
(1)	1985, s 162(2B)
(2)	1985, s 162(4)

Section of 2006 Act	Origin
(3)	1985, s 162A(1)
(4)	1985, s 162A(2)
(5)	1985, s 162A(3)
725	
(1)	1985, s 162B(1)
(2)	1985, s 162B(2)
(3)	1985, s 162B(3)
(4)	1985, s 143(2A)
726	
(1)	1985, s 162C(1)
(2)	1985, s 162C(2), (3)
(3)	1985, s 162C(4)
(4)	1985, s 162C(5)
(5)	1985, s 162C(6)
727	
(1)	1985, s 162D(1)(a), (b)
(2)	1985, s 162D(2) (changed)
(3)	1985, s 162D(3)
(4), (5)	new
728	
(1)	1985, s 169A(1)(b)(ii), (2)
(2)	1985, s 169A(2)
(3)	1985, s 169A(3)
(4)	1985, s 169A(4)
(5)	1985, s 169A(4), Sch 24
729	
(1)	1985, s 162D(1)(c)
(2)	1985, s 162E(1)
(3)	1985, s 162E(2)
(4)	1985, s 162D(4)
(5)	1985, s 162D(5)
730	
(1)	1985, s 169A(1)(b)(i), (2)
(2)	1985, s 169A(2)
(3)	1985, s 169A(3)
(4), (5)	new
(6)	1985, s 169A(4)
(7)	1985, s 169A(4), Sch 24
731	
(1)	1985, s 162F(1)
(2)	1985, s 162F(2)
(3)	1985, s 162F(3)
(4)	1985, s 162F(4), (5)
732	
(1)	1985, s 162G (changed)
(2)	1985, s 162G
Chapter 7 Supplementary provisions	
733	
(1), (2)	1985, s 170(1)
(3)	1985, s 170(2), (3)
(4)	1985, s 170(1)

Section of 2006 Act	Origin
(5), (6)	1985, s 170(4)
734	
(1)	drafting
(2)	1985, s 171(4)
(3)	1985, s 171(5)
(4)	1985, s 171(6)
735	
(1)	1985, s 178(1)
(2)	1985, s 178(2), (3)
(3)	1985, s 178(3)
(4)	1985, s 178(4)
(5)	1985, s 178(5)
(6)	1985, s 178(6)
736	1985, s 181(a)
737	
(1)–(4)	new
Part 19 Debentures	
738	1985, s 744 ('debenture')
739	
(1), (2)	1985, s 193
740	1985, s 195
741	
(1)–(4)	new
742	1985, s 197
743	
(1)	new
(2)	1985, s 190(5) (changed)
(3)	1985, s 190(6)
(4), (5)	new
(6)	1985, s 190(1), (5)
744	
(1)	1985, s 191(1)
(2)	1985, s 191(2)
(3), (4)	new
(5)	1985, s 191(6)
(6)	new
745	
(1)–(5)	new
746	
(1)	1985, s 191(4) (changed)
(2)	1985, s 191(4), Sch 24
(3)	1985, s 191(5)
747	
(1)–(3)	new
748	
(1)	1985, s 191(7) (changed)
(2)	1985, s 191(7)
749	
(1)	1985, s 191(3)
(2)	1985, s 191(4)
(3)	1985, s 191(4), Sch 24

Section of 2006 Act	Origin
(4)	1985, s 191(5)
750	
(1)	1985, s 192(1)
(2)	1985, s 192(2)
(3)	1985, s 192(1)
751	
(1)	1985, s 192(3)
(2)	1985, s 192(3), 1986 art.201(3)
(3), (4)	1985, s 192(4)
752	
(1)	1985, s 194(1)
(2)	1985, s 194(2)
(3)	1985, s 194(4)
(4)	1985, s 194(5)
753	1985, s 194(3)
754	
(1)	1985, s 196(1)
(2)	1985, s 196(2)
(3)	1985, s 196(3)
(4)	1985, s 196(4)

Part 20 Public and Private Companies

Chapter 1 Prohibition of public offers by private companies

755	
(1)	1985, s 81(1) (changed)
(2)	1985, s 58(3)
(3), (4)	new
(5)	drafting
756	
(1), (2)	1985, s 742A(1)
(3)	1985, s 742A(2)
(4)	1985, s 742A(3), (4), and (5)
(5)	1985, s 742A(3)(a), (6)(b) (changed)
(6)	1985, s 742A(6)(a)
757	
(1)–(3)	new
758	
(1)–(4)	new
759	
(1)–(5)	new
760	1985, s 81(3)

Chapter 2 Minimum share capital requirement for public companies

761	
(1)	1985, s 117(1)
(2)	1985, s 117(2) (changed)
(3)	1985, s 117(4)
(4)	1985, s 117(6) (changed)
762	
(1)	1985, s 117(3) (changed)
(2)	new
(3)	1985, s 117(5)
763	

Section of 2006 Act	Origin
(1)	1985, s 118(1) (changed)
(2)–(6)	new
764	
(1)	1985, s 118(1) (changed)
(2)	new
(3)	1985, s 118(2)
(4)	1985, s 118(3)
765	
(1)–(4)	new
766	
(1)–(6)	new
767	
(1)	1985, s 117(7)
(2)	1985, s 117(7), Sch 24
(3)	1985, s 117(8)
(4)	new

Part 21 Certification and Transfer of Securities

Chapter 1 Certification and transfer of securities: general

768	
(1)	1985, s 186(1)(a)
(2)	1985, s 186(1)(b), (2)
769	
(1)	1985, s 185(1)(a)
(2)	1985, s 185(1), (4)(a), (b)
(3)	1985, s 185(5)
(4)	1985, s 185(5), Sch 24
770	
(1)	1985, s 183(1)
(2)	1985, s 183(2)
771	
(1)–(6)	new
772	1985, s 183(4)
773	1985, s 183(3)
774	1985, s 187
775	
(1), (2)	1985, s 184(1)
(3)	1985, s 184(2)
(4)	1985, s 184(3)
776	
(1)	1985, s 185(1)(b)
(2)	1985, s 185(2)
(3)	1985, s 185(1), (4)(c)
(4)	drafting
(5)	1985, s 185(5)
(6)	1985, s 185(5), Sch 24
777	
(1), (2)	1985, s 185(3)
778	
(1)	1985, s 185(4), (4A)
(2)	1985, s 185(4B), (4C)
(3)	1985, s 185(4D)

Section of 2006 Act	Origin
779	
(1)	1985, s 188(1)
(2)	1985, s 188(2)
(3)	1985, s 188(3)
780	
(1)–(4)	new
781	
(1)	1985, s 189(1)
(2)	1985, s 189(2)
(3)	1985, s 189(1), Sch 24
(4)	1985, s 189(2), Sch 24
782	
(1)	1985, s 185(6)
(2), (3)	1985, s 185(7)
Chapter 2 Evidencing and transfer of title to securities without written instrument	
783	1989, s 207(1), (10)
784	
(1), (2)	new
(3)	1989, s 207(9)
785	
(1)	1989, s 207(1)
(2)	1989, s 207(2)
(3)	1989, s 207(3)
(4)	1989, s 207(4)
(5)	1989, s 207(5)
(6)	1989, s 207(6)
786	
(1)–(5)	new
787	
(1)–(3)	new
788	1989, s 207(7)
789	new
790	new
Part 22 Information about Interests in a Company's Shares	
791	new
792	
(1)	1985, s 198(2) (changed)
(2)	1985, s 198(2)(b)
793	
(1), (2)	1985, s 212(1) (changed)
(3)	1985, s 212(2)(a)
(4)	1985, s 212(2)(b)
(5)	1985, s 212(3)
(6)	1985, s 212(2)(c)
(7)	1985, s 212(4)
794	
(1)	1985, s 216(1)
(2)	1985, s 216(1B)
(3)	1985, s 216(1A)
(4)	drafting
795	

Section of 2006 Act	Origin
(1)	1985, s 216(3)
(2)	1985, s 216(4)
(3)	1985, s 216(3), Sch 24
796	
(1), (2)	1985, s 216(5)
797	
(1)	1985, s 454(1)
(2)	1985, s 454(2)
(3)	1985, s 454(3)
(4)	1985, s 454(2), (3)
798	
(1), (2)	1985, s 455(1)
(3)	1985, s 455(2)
(4)	1985, s 455(2), Sch 24
(5)	1985, s 455(1), (2)
799	
(1)	1985, s 456(1A)
(2)	1985, s 456(2)
(3)	1985, s 456(1A)
800	
(1)	1985, s 456(1)
(2)	1985, s 456(2)
(3)	1985, s 456(3)
(4)	1985, s 456(6)
(5)	1985, s 456(7)
801	
(1), (2)	1985, s 456(4)
(3), (4)	1985, s 456(5)
(5)	1985, s 457(3)
802	
(1), (2)	1985, s 457(1)
(3)	1985, s 457(2)
(4)	1985, s 457(3)
803	
(1), (2)	1985, s 214(1) (changed)
(3)	1985, s 214(2) (changed)
804	
(1)	1985, s 214(4)
(2)	1985, s 214(5) (changed)
(3)	1985, s 214(5), Sch 24
805	
(1)	1985, s 215(1), (3)
(2)	1985, s 215(2)
(3)	1985, s 215(2), (3)
(4)	1985, s 215(7) (changed)
(5)	new
(6)	1985, s 215(5)
(7)	1985, s 215(6)
806	
(1), (2)	new
(3)	1985, s 215(8) (changed)

Section of 2006 Act	Origin
(4)	1985, s 215(8), Sch 24
807	
(1)	1985, s 215(7)(b), s 219(1)
(2)	1985, s 215(7)(b), s 219(2)
(3)	1985, s 215(7)(b), s 219(3)
(4)	1985, s 215(7)(b), s 219(3), Sch 24
(5)	1985, s 215(7)(b), s 219(4)
808	
(1)	1985, s 213(1)
(2)	1985, s 211(3), s 213(1), (3)
(3)	1985, s 213(1) (changed)
(4)	1985, s 211(5), s 213(3)
(5)	1985, s 211(10), s 213(3)
(6)	1985, s 211(10), s 213(3), Sch 24
(7)	1985, s 211(4), s 213(3)
809	
(1)	1985, s 211(8), s 213(3) (changed)
(2), (3)	, s 211(8), s 213(3), s 325(5), Sch 13, para 27
(4), (5)	new
810	
(1)–(3)	1985, s 211(6), s 213(3)
(4)	1985, s 211(8), s 213(3)
(5), (6)	new
811	
(1)	1985, s 211(8)(b), s 213(3), s 219(1)
(2)	1985, s 211(8)(b), s 213(3), s 219(2) (changed)
(3)	new
(4)	new
812	
(1)–(7)	new
813	
(1)	1985, s 211(8)(b), s 213(3), s 219(3) (changed)
(2)	1985, s 211(8)(b), s 213(3), s 219(3), Sch 24
(3)	1985, s 211(8)(b), s 213(3), s 219(4)
814	
(1)–(3)	new
815	
(1)	1985, s 218(1)
(2)	1985, s 218(2)
(3)	1985, s 218(3)
(4)	1985, s 218(3), Sch 24
816	1985, s 217(1) (changed)
817	
(1)	1985, s 217(2) (changed)
(2), (3)	1985, s 217(3)
(4)	1985, s 217(5)
818	
(1), (2)	1985, s 217(4)
(3)	1985, s 217(5)
819	
(1)	1985, s 211(7), s 213(3)

Section of 2006 Act	Origin
(2)	1985, s 211(10), s 213(3)
(3)	1985, s 211(10), s 213(3), Sch 24
820	
(1)	1985, s 208(1), s 212(5)
(2)	1985, s 208(2), s 212(5)
(3)	1985, s 208(3), s 212(5)
(4)	1985, s 208(4), s 212(5)
(5)	1985, s 208(6), s 212(5)
(6)	1985, s 208(5), s 212(5)
(7)	1985, s 208(7), s 212(5)
(8)	1985, s 208(8), s 212(5)
821	
(1), (2)	1985, s 212(6)
822	
(1), (2)	1985, s 203(1), s 212(5)
823	
(1)	1985, s 203(2), s 212(5)
(2)	1985, s 203(3), s 212(5)
(3)	1985, s 203(4), s 212(5)
824	
(1)	1985, s 204(1), (2), s 212(5)
(2)	1985, s 204(2), s 212(5)
(3)	1985, s 204(3), s 212(5)
(4)	1985, s 204(4), s 212(5)
(5)	1985, s 204(5), s 212(5)
(6)	1985, s 204(6), s 212(5)
825	
(1)	1985, s 205(1), s 212(5)
(2)	1985, s 205(2), s 212(5)
(3)	1985, s 205(3), s 212(5)
(4)	1985, s 205(4), s 212(5)
826	
(1)	1985, s 211(9), s 213(3), s 215(4)
(2)	1985, s 215(4)
827	1985, s 220(2) (changed)
828	
(1), (2)	1985, s 210A(1)
(3)	1985, s 210A(5)

Part 23 Distributions

Chapter 1 Restrictions on when distributions may be made

829	
(1), (2)	1985, s 263(2)
830	
(1)	1985, s 263(1)
(2), (3)	1985, s 263(3)
831	
(1)	1985, s 264(1)
(2), (3)	1985, s 264(2)
(4)	1985, s 264(3)
(5)	1985, s 264(4)
(6)	1985, s 264(1)

Section of 2006 Act	Origin
832	
(1)–(3)	1985, s 265(1)
(4)	1985, s 265(2)
(5)	1985, s 265(4), (6)
(6)	1985, s 265(4A), (5)
(7)	1985, s 265(3)
833	
(1)	1985, s 266(1)
(2)	1985, s 266(2)
(3)	1985, s 266(2A)
(4), (5)	1985, s 266(3)
834	
(1)	1985, s 266(2)(b)
(2)	1985, s 266(4), ICTA, s 842(1A)
(3)	1985, s 266(4), ICTA, s 842(2)
(4)	1985, s 266(4), ICTA, s 842(3)
(5)	1985, s 266(4), ICTA, s 838, s 842(1A), (4)
835	
(1)	1985, s 267(1)
(2)	1985, s 267(2)(b)
Chapter 2 Justification of distribution by reference to accounts	
836	
(1)	1985, s 270(1), (2)
(2)	1985, s 270(3), (4)
(3), (4)	1985, s 270(5)
837	
(1)	1985, s 270(3)
(2)	1985, s 271(2)
(3)	1985, s 271(3)
(4)	1985, s 271(3), (4)
(5)	1985, s 271(5)
838	
(1)	1985, s 270(4)
(2)	1985, s 272(1)
(3)	1985, s 272(2)
(4), (5)	1985, s 272(3)
(6)	1985, s 272(4), (5)
839	
(1)	1985, s 270(4)
(2)	1985, s 273(1)
(3)	1985, s 273(2)
(4)	1985, s 272(3), s 273(3)
(5)	1985, s 273(4)
(6)	1985, s 273(4), (5)
(7)	1985, s 273(6), (7)
840	
(1)	1985, s 274(1), (2)
(2)	1985, s 274(2)
(3)	1985, s 274(3) ('financial assistance')
(4)	1985, s 154(2)(a), s 274(3) ('net assets' and 'net liabilities')

Section of 2006 Act	Origin
(5)	1985, s 154(2)(b), s 274(3) ('net liabilities')
Chapter 3 Supplementary provisions	
841	
(1), (2)	1985, s 275(1)
(3)	1985, s 275(1A)
(4)	1985, s 275(4), (5), (6)
(5)	1985, s 275(2)
842	1985, s 275(3)
843	
(1)	1985, s 268(1)
(2)	1985, s 268(1)(a)
(3)	1985, s 268(2)(aa), (a)
(4)	1985, s 268(1)(b), (2)(b)
(5)	1985, s 268(1)
(6)	1985, s 268(3)(a)
(7)	1985, s 268(3)(b), (4)
844	
(1)	1985, s 269(1)
(2), (3)	1985, s 269(2)
845	
(1)–(5)	new
846	
(1), (2)	1985, s 276 (changed)
847	
(1), (2)	1985, s 277(1)
(3), (4)	1985, s 277(2)
848	
(1)	1985, s 278
(2)	1985, s 278, 1986 art.286
849	1985, s 263(4)
850	
(1), (2)	1985, s 263(5)
(3)	1985, s 263(5), 1986 art.271(5)
851	
(1)	1985, s 281 (changed)
(2), (3)	new
852	1985, s 281
853	
(1)	1985, s 280(1)
(2)	1985, s 280(3)
(3)	1985, s 280(2)
(4), (5)	1985, s 262(3), s 742(2)
(6)	1985, s 262(1), s 742(1)
Part 24 A Company's Annual Return	
854	
(1), (2)	1985, s 363(1)
(3)	1985, s 363(2) (changed)
855	
(1)	1985, s 364(1) (changed)
(2)	1985, s 364(2)
(3)	1985, s 364(3)

Section of 2006 Act	Origin
856	
(1)	1985, s 364A(1)
(2)	1985, s 364A(2), (3) (changed)
(3)	1985, s 364A(4) (changed)
(4)	1985, s 364A(5)
(5)	1985, s 364A(6)
(6)	1985, s 364A(8)
857	
(1), (2)	1985, s 365(1)
(3)	1985, s 365(2)
858	
(1)	1985, s 363(3), (4) (changed)
(2)	1985, s 363(3), (4), Sch 24
(3)	1985, s 363(3)
(4)	1985, s 363(4)
(5)	new
859	1985, s 365(3)
Part 25 Company Charges	
Chapter 1 Companies registered in England and Wales or in Northern Ireland	
860	
(1)	1985, s s 395(1), 399(1)
(2)	1985, s 399(1)
(3)	1985, s 399(2)
(4)–(6)	1985, s 399(3), Sch 24 (changed)
(7)	1985, s 396(1)
861	
(1)	1985, s 396(3)
(2)	1985, s 396(1)(d)
(3)	1985, s 396(2)
(4)	1985, s 396(3A)
(5)	1985, s s 395(1) ('company'), 396(4) ('charge'), 400(1) ('company')
862	
(1)	1985, s 400(1)
(2), (3)	1985, s 400(2)
(4), (5)	1985, s 400(4), Sch 24 (changed)
863	
(1)–(4)	1985, s 397(1)
(5)	1985, s 399(1)–(3)
864	
(1)	1985, s 397(2)
(2)	1985, s 397(3)
(3)	1985, s 397(2)
865	
(1)	1985, s 402(1)
(2)	1985, s 402(2)
(3), (4)	1985, s 402(3), Sch 24
866	
(1)	1985, s 398(1)
(2)	1985, s 398(3)
867	

Section of 2006 Act	Origin
(1), (2)	1985, s 398(4)
868	
(1), (2)	1986 art.408(1)
(3)	1986 art.408(2)
(4)	1986 art.408(3)
(5)	Drafting
869	
(1)	1985, s 401(1) (opening words)
(2)	1985, s 401(1)(a)
(3)	1986 art.409(2)(b)
(4)	1985, s 401(1)(b)
(5), (6)	1985, s 401(2)
(7)	1985, s 401(3)
870	
(1)	1985, s s 395(1), 398(2)
(2)	1985, s 400(2), (3)
(3)	1985, s 397(1)
871	
(1)	1985, s 405(1)
(2)	1985, s 405(2)
(3)	1985, s 405(1), (2)
(4), (5)	1985, s 405(4), Sch 24
872	
(1), (2)	1985, s 403(1) (changed)
(3)	1985, s 403(2)
873	
(1)	1985, s 404(1)
(2)	1985, s 404(2)
874	
(1), (2)	1985, s 395(1)
(3)	1985, s 395(2)
875	
(1)	1985, s 406(1), 1986 art.414(1)
(2)	1985, s 406(2)
876	
(1)	1985, s 407(1)
(2)	1985, s 407(2)
(3), (4)	1985, s 407(3), Sch 24
877	
(1)	1985, s 408(1)
(2)	1985, s s 406(1), 407(1), 408(1) (changed)
(3)	new
(4)	1985, s 408(1), (2) (changed)
(5), (6)	1985, s 408(3), Sch 24 (changed)
(7)	1985, s 408(4)
Chapter 2 Companies registered in Scotland	
878	
(1)	1985, s s 410(2), 415(1)
(2)	1985, s 415(1)
(3)	1985, s 415(2)
(4)–(6)	1985, s 415(3), Sch 24 (changed)

Section of 2006 Act	Origin
(7)	1985, s 410(4)
879	
(1)	1985, s 410(4)(a)
(2)	1985, s 413(1)
(3)	1985, s 410(4)(a)
(4)	1985, s 412
(5)	1985, s 410(5)
(6)	1985, s 410(5) ('company')
880	
(1), (2)	1985, s 416(1)
(3), (4)	1985, s 416(3), Sch 24 (changed)
881	
(1)	1985, s 414(1)
(2), (3)	1985, s 414(2)
882	
(1)–(4)	1985, s 413(2)
(5)	1985, s 415(1)–(3)
883	
(1)–(3)	1985, s 413(3)
884	1985, s 411(2)
885	
(1)	1985, s 417(1)
(2)	1985, s 417(2)
(3)	1985, s 417(3)
(4)	1985, s 418(1), (2)(b)
(5)	1985, s 418(2)(a), (c)
(6)	1985, s 417(4)
886	
(1)	1985, s s 410(2), 411(1)
(2)	1985, s 416(1), (2)
(3)	1985, s 413(2)
887	
(1)	1985, s 419(1) (changed)
(2)	1985, s 419(1B)(a), (c), (3) (changed)
(3)	1985, s 419(1)
(4)	1985, s 419(2)
(5)	1985, s 419(4)
888	
(1), (2)	1985, s 420
889	
(1)	1985, s 410(2)
(2)	1985, s 410(3)
890	
(1)	1985, s 421(1)
(2)	1985, s 421(2)
891	
(1)	1985, s 422(1)
(2)	1985, s 422(2)
(3), (4)	1985, s 422(3), Sch 24
892	
(1)	1985, s 423(1)

Section of 2006 Act	Origin
(2)	1985, s s 421(1), 422(1), 423(1) (changed)
(3)	new
(4)	1985, s 423(1), (2) (changed)
(5), (6)	1985, s 423(3), Sch 24 (changed)
(7)	1985, s 423(4)
Chapter 3 Powers of the Secretary of State	
893	
(1)–(9)	new
894	
(1), (2)	new
Part 26 Arrangements and Reconstructions	
895	
(1)	1985, s 425(1)
(2)	1985, s s 425(6), 427(6)
(3)	drafting
896	
(1), (2)	1985, s 425(1)
897	
(1)	1985, s 426(1), (2), (3)
(2)	1985, s 426(2)
(3)	1985, s 426(4)
(4)	1985, s 426(5)
(5)–(8)	1985, s 426(6), Sch 24
898	
(1)–(3)	1985, s 426(7), Sch 24
899	
(1)	1985, s 425(2)
(2)	new
(3)	1985, s 425(2)
(4)	1985, s 425(3)
900	
(1)	1985, s 427(1), (2)
(2)	1985, s 427(2), (3)
(3), (4)	1985, s 427(4)
(5)	1985, s 427(6)
(6)–(8)	1985, s 427(5), Sch 24
901	
(1), (2)	new
(3), (4)	1985, s 425(3) (changed)
(5), (6)	1985, s 425(4), Sch 24
Part 27 Mergers and Divisions of Public Companies	
Chapter 1 Introductory	
902	
(1)	1985, s 427A(1)
(2)	drafting
(3)	1985, s 427A(4)
903	
(1)	1985, s 427A(1)
(2), (3)	drafting
Chapter 2 Merger	
904	

Section of 2006 Act	Origin
(1)	1985, s 427A(2) Cases 1 and 2
(2)	drafting
905	
(1)	1985, Sch 15B, para 2(1)(a)
(2), (3)	1985, Sch 15B, para 2(2)
906	
(1), (2)	1985, Sch 15B, para 2(1)(b)
(3)	1985, Sch 15B, para 2(1)(c)
907	
(1)	1985, s 425(2), Sch 15B, para 1
(2)	1985, s 427A(1) closing words, Sch 15B, para 1 opening words
908	
(1)	1985, Sch 15B, para 3(a)
(2)	1985, Sch 15B, para 4(1)
(3)	1985, Sch 15B, para 3 opening words
909	
(1)	1985, Sch 15B, para 3(d)
(2)	1985, Sch 15B, para 5(1)
(3)	1985, Sch 15B, para 5(1), (2)
(4)	1985, Sch 15B, para 5(3)
(5)	1985, Sch 15B, para 5(7)
(6)	1985, Sch 15B, para 5(8)
(7)	1985, Sch 15B, para 3 opening words
910	
(1)	1985, Sch 15B, para 6(1)(e)
(2)	1985, Sch 15B, para 6(2)
(3)	1985, Sch 15B, para 6(3) (changed)
(4)	1985, Sch 15B, para 6(4)
911	
(1), (2)	1985, Sch 15B, para 3(e)
(3)	1985, Sch 15B, para 6(1)
(4)	1985, Sch 15B, para 3 opening words
912	1985, Sch 15B, para 3(f)
913	
(1)	1985, Sch 15B, para 8(1)
(2)	1985, Sch 15B, para 8(2)
914	1985, Sch 15B, para 7
915	
(1)	1985, Sch 15B, para 12(1)
(2)	1985, Sch 15B, para 12(2)
(3)–(5)	1985, Sch 15B, para 12(3)
(6)	1985, Sch 15B, para 12(1)(a), (b)
916	
(1)	1985, Sch 15B, para 14(1)
(2)	1985, Sch 15B, para 14(2)
(3)–(5)	1985, Sch 15B para, s 10(2), 14(3)
(6)	1985, Sch 15B para14(1)(a), (b)
917	
(1)	1985, Sch 15B, para 12(1)

Section of 2006 Act	Origin
(2)	1985, Sch 15B, para 12(4)
(3)–(5)	1985, Sch 15B, para 12(5)
(6)	1985, Sch 15B, para 12(1)(a), (b)
918	
(1)	1985, Sch 15B, para 10(1)
(2)–(4)	1985, Sch 15B, para 10(2)
Chapter 3 Division	
919	
(1)	1985, s 427A(2) Case 3
(2)	drafting
920	
(1)	1985, Sch 15B, para 2(1)(a)
(2)	1985, Sch 15B, para 2(2)
(3)	1985, Sch 15B, para 2(3)
921	
(1), (2)	1985, Sch 15B, para 2(1)(b)
(3)	1985, Sch 15B, para 2(1)(c)
(4)	1985, Sch 15B, para 2(1)(b), (c) opening words
922	
(1)	1985, s 425(2), Sch 15B, para 1
(2)	1985, s 427A(1) closing words, Sch 15B, para 1 opening words
923	
(1)	1985, Sch 15B, para 3(a)
(2)	1985, Sch 15B, para 4(1)
(3)	1985, Sch 15B, para 4(2)
(4)	1985, Sch 15B, para 3 opening words
924	
(1)	1985, Sch 15B, para 3(d)
(2)	1985, Sch 15B, para 5(1)
(3)	1985, Sch 15B, para 5(1), (2)
(4)	1985, Sch 15B, para 5(3)
(5)	1985, Sch 15B, para 5(7)
(6)	1985, Sch 15B, para 5(8)
(7)	1985, Sch 15B, para 3 opening words
925	
(1)	1985, Sch 15B, para 6(1)(e)
(2)	1985, Sch 15B, para 6(2)
(3)	1985, Sch 15B, para 6(3) (changed)
(4)	1985, Sch 15B, para 6(4)
(5)	1985, Sch 15B, para 3 opening words
926	
(1), (2)	1985, Sch 15B, para 3(e)
(3)	1985, Sch 15B, para 6(1)
(4)	1985, Sch 15B, para 3 opening words
927	
(1)	1985, Sch 15B, para 3(b)
(2)	1985, Sch 15B, para 3(c)
(3)	1985, Sch 15B, para 3 opening words
928	1985, Sch 15B, para 3(f)
929	

Section of 2006 Act	Origin
(1)	1985, Sch 15B, para 8(1)
(2)	1985, Sch 15B, para 8(2)
930	1985, Sch 15B, para 7
931	
(1)	1985, Sch 15B, para 13(1)
(2)	1985, Sch 15B, para 13(2)
(3)	1985, Sch 15B para, s 12(5)(a), 13(3)(a)
(4)	1985, Sch 15B, para 13(3)(b)
(5)	1985, Sch 15B para, s 12(5)(c), 13(3)(a)
(6)	1985, Sch 15B, para 13(3)(c)
932	
(1)	1985, Sch 15B, para 10(1)
(2)–(4)	1985, Sch 15B, para 10(2)
(5)	1985, Sch 15B, para 10(2) opening words
933	
(1)–(3)	1985, Sch 15B, para 11(1), (2)
934	
(1)	1985, Sch 15B, para 11(1), (3)
(2)	1985, Sch 15B, para 11(4)(a), (b)
(3)	1985, Sch 15B, para 11(4)(c)
(4)	1985, Sch 15B, para 11(4)(d)
Chapter 4 Supplementary provisions	
935	
(1)	1985, Sch 15B, para 5(4) (changed)
(2)	1985, Sch 15B, para 5(6)
936	
(1)–(4)	new
937	
(1)–(6)	new
938	
(1), (2)	1985, s 427A(3)
939	
(1)	1985, Sch 15B, para 9(1), (2)
(2)	1985, Sch 15B, para 9(2)
(3), (4)	1985, Sch 15B, para 9(3)
(5)	1985, Sch 15B, para 9(4)
940	
(1)	1985, Sch 15B, para 15(1)
(2)	1985, Sch 15B, para 15(2)
(3)	1985, Sch 15B, para 15(1)
941	1985, s s 427(6), 427A(8)

Part 28 Takeovers etc

[Note: The Takeovers Directive (Interim Implementation) Regulations 2006, SI 2006/1183 are based on the provisions of this Part. So although the regulations came into force on 20 May 2006 and so before the date of royal assent to the Companies Act 2006, they are not cited as origins for those provisions]

Chapter 1 The Takeover Panel

942	
(1)–(3)	new
943	
(1)–(9)	new

Section of 2006 Act	Origin
944	
(1)–(7)	new
945	
(1), (2)	new
946	new
947	
(1)–(10)	new
948	
(1)–(9)	new
949	
(1)–(3)	new
950	
(1), (2)	new
951	
(1)–(5)	new
952	
(1)–(8)	new
953	
(1)–(9)	new
954	
(1), (2)	new
955	
(1)–(4)	new
956	
(1)–(3)	new
957	
(1), (2)	new
958	
(1)–(8)	new
959	new
960	new
961	
(1)–(3)	new
962	
(1), (2)	new
963	
(1), (2)	new
964	
(1)–(6)	new
965	new
Chapter 2 Impediments to takeovers	
966	
(1)–(8)	new
967	
(1)–(7)	new
968	
(1)–(8)	new
969	
(1)–(3)	new
970	
(1)–(4)	new

Section of 2006 Act	Origin
971	
(1), (2)	new
972	
(1)–(4)	new
973	new
Chapter 3 'Squeeze-out' and 'sell-out'	
974	
(1)–(3)	1985, s 428(1), drafting
(4), (5)	1985, s 428(2)
(6)	1985, s 428(2A)
(7)	1985, s 428(7)
975	
(1), (2)	1985, s 428(5) (changed)
(3)	1985, s 428(6) (changed)
(4)	1985, s 430E(1)
976	
(1)	1985, s 428(3)
(2)	new
(3)	1985, s 428(4)
977	
(1)	1985, s 429(8) (changed)
(2)	1985, s 430E(1) (changed)
(3)	drafting
978	
(1)–(3)	new
979	
(1), (2)	1985, s 429(1) (changed)
(3), (4)	1985, s 429(2) (changed)
(5)–(7)	new
(8)	1985, s 429(8) (changed)
(9)	1985, s s 429(8), 430E(2) (changed)
(10)	1985, s 429(8) (changed)
980	
(1)	1985, s 429(4)
(2)	1985, s 429(3) (changed)
(3)	new
(4)	1985, s 429(4)
(5)	1985, s 429(5)
(6)	1985, s 429(6)
(7)	1985, s 429(7)
(8)	1985, s 429(6), Sch 24
981	
(1)	1985, s 430(1)
(2)	1985, s 430(2)
(3)	1985, s 430(3)
(4)	1985, s 430(4)
(5)	1985, s 430(4) (changed)
(6)	1985, s 430(5), (8)
(7)	1985, s 430(6)
(8)	1985, s 430(7)
(9)	1985, s 430(9), drafting

Section of 2006 Act	Origin
982	
(1)	drafting
(2), (3)	1985, s 430(10)
(4), (5)	1985, s 430(11)
(6)	1985, s 430(12)
(7)	1985, s 430(13)
(8)	1985, s 430(14)
(9)	1985, s 430(15)
983	
(1)	1985, s 430A(1), (1A)
(2), (3)	1985, s 430A(1) (changed)
(4)	1985, s 430A(2) (changed)
(5)	1985, s 430A(2A)
(6), (7)	new
(8)	1985, s 430E(3)
984	
(1)	1985, s 430A(1)
(2)	1985, s 430A(4) (changed)
(3)	1985, s 430A(3)
(4)	1985, s 430A(5)
(5)	1985, s 430A(6)
(6)	1985, s 430A(7)
(7)	1985, s 430A(6), Sch 24
985	
(1)	1985, s 430B(1)
(2)	1985, s 430B(2)
(3)	1985, s 430B(3)
(4)	1985, s 430B(4)
(5)	1985, s 430B(4) (changed)
986	
(1)	1985, s 430C(1)
(2)	1985, s 430C(1), (2)
(3)	1985, s 430C(3)
(4)	new
(5)	1985, s 430C(4)
(6)–(8)	new
(9), (10)	1985, s 430C(5)
987	
(1)	1985, s 430D(1)
(2), (3)	1985, s 430D(2) (changed)
(4)	1985, s 430D(4) (changed)
(5), (6)	1985, s 430D(3)
(7)	1985, s 430D(4)
(8)	1985, s 430D(5)
(9)	1985, s 430D(6)
(10)	1985, s 430D(7)
988	
(1)	1985, s 430E(4), (8)
(2)	1985, s 430E(5)
(3)	1985, s 430E(6), (7)
(4)	1985, s s 204(2)(a), 430E(4)(d)

Section of 2006 Act	Origin
(5)	1985, s s 204(6), 430E(7)
(6)	1985, s 204(3)
(7)	1985, s s 204(5), 430E(7)
989	
(1)	1985, s 430F(1)
(2)	1985, s 430F(2)
990	
(1)–(3)	new
991	
(1)	1985, s 428(8) ('the company' and 'the offeror'), new ('date of the offer', 'non-voting shares', 'voting rights' and 'voting shares')
(2)	new
Chapter 4 Amendments to Part 7 of the Companies Act 1985	
992	
(1)–(6)	new (amends 1985 Pt 7)
Part 29 Fraudulent Trading	
993	
(1)–(3)	1985, s 458, Sch 24
Part 30 Protection of Members against Unfair Prejudice	
994	
(1)	1985, s 459(1)
(2)	1985, s 459(2)
(3)	1985, s 459(3)
995	
(1)	1985, s 460(1A)
(2), (3)	1985, s 460(1)
(4)	1985, s 460(2)
996	
(1)	1985, s 461(1)
(2)	1985, s 461(2), (3)
997	1985, s 461(6)
998	
(1)–(4)	1985, s 461(5)
999	
(1)–(5)	new
Part 31 Dissolution and Restoration to the Register	
Chapter 1 Striking off	
1000	
(1)	1985, s 652(1)
(2)	1985, s 652(2)
(3)	1985, s 652(3)
(4)–(6)	1985, s 652(5)
(7)	1985, s 652(6)
1001	
(1)	1985, s 652(4)
(2)–(4)	1985, s 652(5)
(5)	1985, s 652(6)
1002	
(1)–(3)	1985, s 652(7)
1003	

Section of 2006 Act	Origin
(1)	1985, s 652A(1) (changed)
(2)	1985, s 652A(2) (changed)
(3)	1985, s 652A(3)
(4)	1985, s 652A(4)
(5)	1985, s 652A(5)
(6)	1985, s 652A(6), (7)
1004	
(1)	1985, s 652B(1)
(2)	1985, s 652B(2)
(3)	1985, s 652B(9)
(4)	1985, s 652D(5)(c)
(5)	1985, s 652E(1)
(6)	1985, s 652E(3)
(7)	1985, s 652E(1), Sch 24
1005	
(1)	1985, s 652B(3)
(2)	1985, s 652B(4)
(3)	1985, s 652B(5)
(4)	1985, s 652E(1)
(5)	1985, s 652E(3)
(6)	1985, s 652E(1), Sch 24
1006	
(1)	1985, s s 652B(6), 652D(5)(c)
(2)	1985, s 652B(7)
(3)	1985, s 652B(8)
(4)	1985, s 652E(1), (2)
(5)	1985, s 652E(4)
(6)	1985, s 652E(1), Sch 24
(7)	1985, s 652E(2), Sch 24
1007	
(1)	1985, s 652C(1)
(2)	1985, s s 652C(2), 652D(5)(c)
(3)	1985, s 652C(3)
(4)	1985, s 652E(1), (2)
(5)	1985, s 652E(5)
(6)	1985, s 652E(1), Sch 24
(7)	1985, s 652E(2), Sch 24
1008	
(1), (2)	1985, s 652D(1)
(3)	1985, s 652D(2), (3)
(4)	1985, s 652D(4)
1009	
(1)	1985, s 652C(4)
(2)	1985, s 652C(5)
(3)	1985, s 652C(7)
(4)	1985, s s 652C(6), 652D(5)(c)
(5)	1985, s 652E(1)
(6)	1985, s 652E(5)
(7)	1985, s 652E(1), Sch 24
1010	1985, s 652D(6)
1011	1985, s 652D(8)

Section of 2006 Act	*Origin*
Chapter 2 Property of dissolved company	
1012	
(1)	1985, s 654(1)
(2)	1985, s 654(2)
1013	
(1)	1985, s 656(1)
(2)	1985, s 656(2) (changed)
(3)–(5)	1985, s 656(3) (changed)
(6), (7)	1985, s 656(5)
(8)	1985, s 656(6)
1014	
(1)	1985, s 657(1)
(2)	drafting
1015	
(1), (2)	1985, s 657(2), IA 1986, s 178(4)
1016	
(1)	1985, s 657(2), IA 1986, s 179(1)
(2)	1985, s 657(2), IA 1986, s 179(2)
(3)	drafting
1017	
(1)	1985, s 657(2), 1A 1986, s 181(2), (3)
(2)	1985, s 657(2), 1A 1986, s 181(3)
(3)	1985, s 657(2), 1A 1986, s 181(4)
(4)	1985, s 657(2), 1A 1986, s 181(3)
(5)	1985, s 657(2), 1A 1986, s 181(6)
1018	
(1)	1985, s 657(2), 1A 1986, s 182(1)
(2)	1985, s 657(2), 1A 1986, s 182(2)
(3)	1985, s 657(2), 1A 1986, s 182(4)
(4), (5)	1985, s 657(2), 1A 1986, s 182(3)
1019	1985, s 657(2), 1A 1986, s 180(1), (2)
1020	
(1), (2)	1985, s 657(4)
1021	
(1), (2)	1985, s 657(5)
(3)	1985, s 657(6)
1022	
(1)	1985, Sch 20, para 5
(2)	1985, Sch 20, para 6
(3)	1985, Sch 20, para 7
(4), (5)	1985, Sch 20, para 8
(6)	1985, Sch 20, para 9
1023	
(1)	1985, s 658(1), IA, s 180(1)
(2)	1985, s 658(1), IA, s 180(2)
(3)	1985, s 658(2)
Chapter 3 Restoration to the register	
1024	
(1)–(4)	new
1025	
(1)–(6)	new

Section of 2006 Act	Origin
1026	
(1)–(3)	new
1027	
(1)–(4)	new
1028	
(1)–(4)	new
1029	
(1), (2)	new
1030	
(1)–(6)	new
1031	
(1)–(4)	new
1032	
(1)–(5)	new
1033	
(1)–(7)	new
1034	
(1)	1985, s 655(1)
(2)	1985, s 655(2)
(3)	new
(4)	1985, s 655(3)
(5)	1985, s 655(4)
(6)	drafting

Part 32 Company Investigations: Amendments

1035	
(1)–(5)	new (inserts 1985, s s 446A and 446B; amends 1985 s, s 431, 432, 437 and 442)
1036	new (inserts 1985, s s 446C and 446D)
1037	
(1)–(3)	new (inserts 1985, s 446E; amends 1985, s s 451A and 452)
1038	
(1), (2)	new (amends 1985, s s 434 and 447)
1039	new (amends Company Directors Disqualification Act 1986, s 8)

Part 33 UK Companies not formed under the Companies Legislation

Chapter 1 Companies not formed under companies legislation but authorised to register

1040	
(1)	1985, s 680(1)(a), (b), (1A), (2)
(2), (3)	1985, s 680(1) (closing words)
(4)	1985, s 680(3), (4)
(5)	1985, s 680(5)
(6)	1985, s 680(1) (closing words)
1041	
(1)	1985, s 683(1)
(2)	1985, s 683(2)
1042	
(1)–(3)	new

Chapter 2 Unregistered companies

1043	
(1)	1985, s 718(1), (2)

Section of 2006 Act	Origin
(2)	1985, s 718(3) (changed)
(3)	1985, s 718(1) (changed)
(4)	1985, s 718(5)
(5)	1985, s 718(1), (3)
(6)	1985, s 718(6)
Part 34 Overseas Companies	
1044	1985, s 744 ('overseas company') (changed)
1045	
(1), (2)	1989, s 130(6)
1046	
(1)–(8)	new
1047	
(1)–(6)	new
1048	
(1), (2)	1985, s 694(4) (changed)
(3)–(5)	1985, s 694(5)
1049	
(1)–(4)	new
1050	
(1)–(6)	new
1051	
(1)–(5)	new
1052	
(1)–(6)	new
1053	
(1)–(6)	new
1054	
(1)–(4)	new
1055	new
1056	new
1057	
(1)–(3)	new
1058	
(1)–(4)	new
1059	1985, s 695A(4)
Part 35 The Registrar of Companies	
1060	
(1), (2)	1985, s 704(2)
(3)	1985, s 744 ('the registrar of companies' and 'the registrar')
(4)	drafting
1061	
(1)–(3)	drafting
1062	1985, s 704(4) (changed)
1063	
(1)–(3)	1985, s 708(1) (changed)
(4)	1985, s 708(2), (3) (changed)
(5)	1985, s 708(5) (changed)
(6)	1985, s 708(4)
(7)	new
1064	

Section of 2006 Act	Origin
(1)–(3)	1985, s 711(1)(a) (changed)
1065	1985, s 710
1066	
(1)–(3)	1985, s 705(1)–(3)
(4), (5)	1985, s 705(4)
(6)	1985, s 705(5)(za)
1067(1)	1985, s 705A(1), (2) (changed)
(2)	1985, s 705A(3)
(3)	1985, s 705A(4)
(4), (5)	1985, s 705A(5)
1068	
(1)–(7)	new
1069	
(1)–(3)	new
1070	
(1)–(3)	new
1071	
(1), (2)	new
1072	
(1), (2)	new
1073	
(1)–(6)	new
1074	
(1)–(5)	new
1075	
(1)–(7)	new
1076	
(1)–(4)	new
1077	
(1)	1985, s 711(1) opening words
(2), (3)	new
1078	
(1)	drafting
(2), (3)	1985, s 711(1) (changed)
(4)	new
(5), (6)	new
1079	
(1)–(3)	1985, s 42(1)
(4)	1985, s 711(2) (changed)
1080	
(1), (2)	drafting
(3)	new
(4)	1985, s 707A(1)
(5)	new
1081	
(1)–(7)	new
1082	
(1)–(5)	new
1083	
(1)	1985, s 707A(2) (changed)
(2), (3)	new

Section of 2006 Act	Origin
1084	
(1)–(3)	1985, s 707A(3) (changed)
(4)	1985, s 707A(4)
(5)	1985, s 707A(3)
1085	
(1)	1985, s 709(1) opening words
(2)	1985, s 709(2) (changed)
(3)	drafting
1086	
(1)	1985, s 709(1)(a), (b)
(2)	new
(3)	drafting
1087	
(1)–(3)	new
1088	
(1)–(6)	new
1089	
(1), (2)	new
1090	
(1)–(4)	new
1091	
(1), (2)	new
(3)	1985, s 709(3)
(4)	new
(5)	1985, s 709(4)
1092	
(1), (2)	1985, s 709(5)
1093	
(1)–(4)	new
1094	
(1)–(5)	new
1095	
(1)–(6)	new
1096	
(1)(1)–(6)	new
1097	
(1)–(5)	new
1098	
(1), (2)	new
1099	
(1)–(3)	1985, s 714(1) (changed)
(4), (5)1985, s 714(2)	
1100	1985, s 709(1) opening words
1101	
(1), (2)	new
1102	
(1)–(4)	new
1103	
(1), (2)	new
1104	
(1), (2)	1985, s 710B(1)–(3)

Section of 2006 Act	Origin
(3)	1985, s 710B(4)
(4)	1985, s 710B(5)
(5)	drafting
1105	
(1)–(3)	new
1106	
(1)–(6)	new
1107	
(1)	drafting
11107	
(2), (3)	new
1108	
(1)–(3)	new
1109	
(1), (2)	new
1110	
(1)–(3)	new
1111	
(1)–(3)	new
1112	
(1), (2)	new
1113	
(1)–(3)	1985, s 713(1)
(4), (5)	1985, s 713(2), (3)
1114	
(1)	1985, s 715A(1) 'document', (2)
(2)	new
1115	
(1)	new
(2)	1985, s 710A(2)
1116	
(1)–(6)	new
1117	
(1)–(3)	new
1118	drafting
1119	
(1), (2)	1985, s 704(7), (8)
(3)	new
1120	new
Part 36 Offences under the Companies Acts	
1121	
(1)	1985, s 730(5)
(2)	1985, s 744 'officer'
(3)	1985, s 730(5) (changed)
1122	
(1)–(3)	new
1123	
(1)–(4)	new
1124 and, Sch 3	new (amend 1985 Act)
1125	
(1)	drafting

Section of 2006 Act	Origin
(2)	1985, s 730(4)
1126	
(1)	1985, s 732(1)
(2)	1985, s 732(2) (changed)
(3)	1986 art.680(2) (changed)
1127	
(1), (2)	1985, s 731(1)
1128	
(1)	1985, s 731(2)
(2)	1985, s 731(3)
(3)	1986 art.679(2)
(4)	1985, s 731(4), 1986 art.679(3)
1129	1985, s 732(3) (changed)
1130	
(1)	1985, s 734(1) (changed)
(2)	1985, s 734(1), (3), (4)
(3)	1985, s 734(2)
1131	
(1), (2)	new
1132	
(1), (2)	1985, s 721(1)
(3)–(5)	1985, s 721(2)–(4)
(6)	drafting
1133	new
Part 37 Companies: Supplementary Provisions	
1134	1985, s 722(1) (changed)
1135	
(1)	1985, s s 722(1), 723(1) (changed)
(2)	new
(3), (4)	new
(5)	1985, s 723(2)
1136	
(1)–(7)	new
1137	
(1), (2)	1985, s 723A(1)
(3)	1985, s 723A(2), (3)
(4)	1985, s 723A(4)
(5), (6)	1985, s 723A(6), (7)
1138	
(1)	1985, s 722(2)
(2), (3)	1985, s 722(3), Sch 24
(4)	new
1139	
(1)	1985, s 725(1)
(2)	1985, s 695(1), (2) (changed)
(3)	new
(4)	1985, s 725(2), (3)
(5)	drafting
1140	
(1)–(8)	new
1141	

Section of 2006 Act	Origin
(1)	drafting
(2), (3)	new
1142	new
1143	
(1)–(4), Sch, s 4 and 5	new
1144	
(1)–(3)	new
1145	
(1)–(5)	new
1146	
(1)–(4)	new
1147	
(1)–(6)	new
1148	
(1)–(3)	new
1149	drafting
1150	
(1)	1985, s 108(1) (changed)
(2), (3)	1985, s 108(2), (3)
(4)	1985, s 108(5)
1151	
(1)–(4)	new
1152	
(1)–(6)new	
1153	
(1)	1985, s 110(1)
(2), (3)	1985, s 110(2), (3)
(4)	1985, s 110(2), Sch 24
1154	
(1)–(4)	new
1155	
(1), (2)	new
1156	
(1)–(3)	1985, s 744 'the court', IA 1986, s 117 (changed)
1157	
(1)–(3)	1985, s 727(1)–(3)
(3), (4)	
Part 38 Companies: Interpretation	
1158	drafting
1159	
(1), (2)	1985, s 736(1), (2)
(3) and, Sch 6	1985, s 736A(1)–(11)
(4)	1985, s s 736(3), 736A(12)
1160	
(1)	1985, s 736B(1)
(2)–(4)	1985, s 736B(3)–(5)
1161	
(1)–(5)	1985, s 259(1)–(5)
1162	
(1)–(5)	1985, s 258(1)–(5)
(6) and, Sch 7	1985, s 258(6) and, Sch 10A

Section of 2006 Act	Origin
1163	
(1), (2)	1985, s 739(1), (2)
1164	
(1)–(3)	1985, s 742B(1)–(3)
(4)	1985, s 255A(4)
(5)	1985, s 255A(5A)
1165	
(1)	drafting
(2)–(4)	1985, s 742C(1)–(4)
(5)	1985, s 255A(5)
(6)	1985, s 255A(5A)
(7)	1985, s 744 'insurance market activity'
(8)	1985, s 742C(5)
1166	1985, s 743
1167	1985, s 744 'prescribed'
1168	
(1)–(7)	new
1169	
(1)	1985, s 249AA(4)
(2), (3)	1985, s 249AA(5)–(7)
(4)	drafting
1170	1985, s 744 'EEA State', drafting
1171'the former Companies Acts'	1985, s 735(1)(c) (changed)
'the Joint Stock Companies Acts'	1985, s 735(3)
1172	drafting
1173	
(1) 'body corporate' and 'corporation'	new
'credit institution'	1985, s 262 'credit institution' (changed)
'financial institution'	1985, s 699A(3) 'financial institution'
'firm'	new
'the Gazette'	1985, s 744 'the Gazette'
'hire-purchase agreement'	1985, s 744 'hire purchase agreement'
'officer'	1985, s 744 'officer'
'parent company'	1985, s s 258(1) and 742(1)
'regulated activity'	1985, s 744 'regulated activity'
'regulated market'	1985 passim (changed)
'working day'	drafting
(2)	drafting
1174 and, Sch 8	drafting
Part 39 Companies: Minor Amendments	
1175(1), (2), Sch 9	new (amend 1985, Pt 7 and 1986, Pt 8)
1176	
(1)–(3)	new (repeals 1985, s 438, amends 1985, s s 439 and 453)
1177	new (repeals 1985, s s 311, 323 and 327, 324 to 326, 328 to 329, Pts 2 to 4 of, Sch 13 and, s s 343 and 344)
1178	new (repeals 1985, s 720 and, Sch 23)
1179	new (repeals 1985, s 729)
1180	new (repeals 1985, Pt 4)
1181	
(1)–(4)	new (power to amend)

525 Director—disqualification—de facto director—necessary level of involvement in company's affairs

The second defendant was the only director of a company which was in the business of providing corporate directors to business people who wished to form limited companies. The company became corporate director of one company ('the client company'), of which the first defendant and another person became the only salaried directors. The client company later ceased trading and was placed in insolvent liquidation. The Secretary of State commenced proceedings against the directors of the client company, seeking their disqualification from acting as directors pursuant to the Companies Director Disqualification Act 1986 s 6. The case against the second defendant proceeded on the basis that he was being held responsible for his own company's inaction in relation to the affairs of the client company. The Secretary of State submitted that the office of director required positive action and that a person in a position to control the actions of a company could constitute himself a de facto director of that company notwithstanding that he might not have ever actually exercised the powers pertinent to his position. The second defendant challenged the jurisdiction of the court to make a disqualification order against him on the basis that he had never been appointed a director of the client company. *Held*, the crucial issue was whether the individual in question had assumed the status and functions of a company director so as to make himself responsible under the 1986 Act as if he were a de jure director. It seemed that, in order to be constituted a de facto director of a subject company, a director of a corporate de jure director had to cause the corporate director to take actions with relation to the subject company as would have constituted it a de facto director of that company. For that purpose, the degree of control which the director of the corporate director exercised over that company would be of relevance. The second defendant had not, either individually or through his control of his own company, taken any step that indicated that he or his company had assumed the status and functions of a director of the client company. Indeed, they had positively declined to do so. It followed that the second defendant (in contrast to his company) had never been under a duty to ensure that the client company kept proper books of account or made proper returns to the companies' registry. Accordingly, the application would be dismissed.

Secretary of State for Trade and Industry v Hall [2006] EWHC 1995 (Ch), [2006] All ER (D) 432 (Jul) (Chancery Division: Evans-Lombe J).

The first defendant was registered as the director of a company which provided vehicle accident and breakdown recovery services. He was married to the fourth defendant and was the father of the second and third defendants. The Secretary of State sought disqualification orders against the defendants pursuant to the Companies Directors Disqualification Act 1986 s 8. The Secretary of State contended that the second to fourth defendants had acted as de facto directors of companies associated with the company of which the first defendant was director. An issue arose as to the level of involvement in the affairs of a company that was required to support a finding that a person was a de facto director. *Held*, a de facto director was one who claimed to act and purported to act as a director, although not validly appointed as such. The touchstone was whether a person had been part of the corporate governing structure, and inherent in that touchstone was the distinction between someone who participated, or had the right to participate in collective decision making on corporate policy and strategy and its implementation, on the one hand, and others who might advise or act on behalf of, or otherwise for the benefit of, the company, but did not participate in decision making as part of the corporate governance of the company. The issue whether a person had acted so as to become a de facto director was to be judged objectively in the light of all relevant facts. Judgment would be given accordingly.

Secretary of State for Trade and Industry v Hollier [2006] EWHC 1804 (Ch), [2006] All ER (D) 232 (Jul) (Chancery Division: Etherton J).

526 Director—disqualification—proceedings—deliberate wrongdoing

Following a report made pursuant to the Companies Act 1985 s 437 the Secretary of State made an application under the Company Directors Disqualification Act 1986 s 8 for a disqualification order against the defendant, who was the director and chief executive of a company. Following the defendant's acquittal in respect of criminal charges made against him, the Secretary of State concluded that it remained in the public interest that the defendant be disqualified and that no application would be made to withdraw or amend any part of the Secretary of State's case. The defendant did not resist the application and filed no evidence dealing with the allegations against him, although he made it clear that he did not accept any of them. *Held*, on the evidence, there was deliberate wrongdoing by the defendant. Therefore, the Secretary of State's allegations were established. Those allegations amounted to deliberate and dishonest conduct on the part of the defendant in the performance of his duties as a company director. They were very serious matters which made inevitable a substantial period of disqualification. The top bracket of disqualification for 10 to 15 years was invoked in particularly serious cases, of which the present case was one. In all the circumstances, a period of disqualification for nine and a half years was appropriate. Accordingly, the application would be granted.

Secretary of State for Trade and Industry v Carr [2006] EWHC 2110 (Ch), [2006] All ER (D) 59 (Aug) (Chancery Division: David Richards J).

527 Director—disqualification—undertaking—declaration that undertaking should not have been offered

The claimant applied to have disqualification proceedings against him struck out. The proceedings had been begun eight years previously, and the claimant contended that, by virtue of the delay, his right to a fair trial within a reasonable time under the European Convention on Human Rights art 6 had been infringed. The application and several subsequent applications were dismissed. During the time that these applications were being made, the claimant signed a disqualification undertaking, which was accepted by the Secretary of State. Subsequently, the claimant obtained a judgment from the European Court of Human Rights in his favour on the art 6 issue. The claimant then applied in the domestic courts for a declaration that the undertaking should not have been offered by him or accepted by the Secretary of State. *Held*, the basis for his claim to the declaration was to give effect to the judgment of the European Court. His entitlement under that judgment was already fully satisfied, and the right which he had established there could in no way justify the declaration sought. Further, the jurisdiction of the court to grant declarations could only be exercised in respect of legal rights and duties. A declaration that the claimant should not have offered the undertaking could not sensibly mean that he was under a legal duty not to offer it. What it did mean was unclear. All that was clear was that it did not form the proper subject matter of a declaration. In any event the declaration sought was wrong, for it was quite clear that the claimant had been legally entitled to offer the disqualification undertaking and the Secretary of State had been, pursuant to the Insolvency Act 1986, legally entitled to accept. The Secretary of State had fairly and properly considered that the public interest had been given effect to by the prosecution of the disqualification proceedings and that it was expedient in the public interest. Accordingly, the application would be dismissed.

Re Blackspur Group plc (No 4); Eastaway v Secretary of State for Trade and Industry [2006] EWHC 299 (Ch), [2006] 2 BCLC 489 (Chancery Division: Lightman J).

528 Director—disqualification—undertaking—variation

The applicant and her husband were directors of a company which sold arts and crafts products. The applicant commenced divorce proceedings, and shortly afterwards the company went into administrative receivership. The Secretary of State gave notice to the parties of his intention to apply for disqualification orders under the Company Directors Disqualification Act 1986 s 6 in respect of their conduct as directors of the company. The applicant agreed to provide a disqualification undertaking for a period of five years and she signed an undertaking enclosing a schedule of unfit conduct. She subsequently applied pursuant to s 8A to vary the disqualification undertaking and for a declaration that it should immediately cease to have effect on the grounds that the proceedings had been discontinued against her husband. The Secretary of State opposed the application, contending that it was not permissible for an applicant under s 8A to seek to controvert the facts agreed at the time of the undertaking and that the agreed schedule of facts had the status of a private law contract between the parties. *Held*, there was no good reason why the court should not, in the exercise of its jurisdiction under s 8A, treat the agreement as binding on the applicant unless either some ground of public interest was shown that would be sufficient to discharge a private law contract or some ground of public interest was shown that outweighed the importance of holding a party to his agreement. The applicant was not able to show that any of the facts relied on by the Secretary of State were incorrect, but simply that they might be capable of challenge in whole or in part. The possibility of challenge arose not from the emergence of some new information unavailable at the date of the original undertaking, but from the fact that the Secretary of State had subsequently decided not to test the potentially contentious issues of fact in the proceedings against the husband. That did not provide the applicant with a justification for resiling from her agreement not to dispute those facts. However, the undertakings regime would be undermined if a director who had given an undertaking was able, in an unrestricted way and without having to show some special circumstances, to apply to the court to be relieved of it. Such special circumstances existed in the present case. The discovery that, in the light of evidence presented by the alleged perpetrator, the Secretary of State no longer believed that it was in the public interest for the husband to be subject to a disqualification order was a new event, uncontemplated at the date of the applicant's undertaking, which entitled the applicant to ask the court to consider whether there remained any good reason why she should continue to be subject to the undertaking which she had voluntarily given. Accordingly, the application would be allowed.

Re INS Realisations Ltd; Secretary of State for Trade and Industry v Jonkler [2006] EWHC 135 (Ch), [2006] 2 All ER 902 (Chancery Division: Hart J).

529 Director—fiduciary duty—breach—establishment of competing business

The defendants were former directors and employees of the claimant company. Prior to their resignation, the defendants had promoted the establishment of another company which the claimant alleged was a competing business. The claimant brought proceedings for damages, an account of profits and other relief against the defendants for various breaches of duty and contract. *Held*, it was the fiduciary duty of a director to act in good faith and in the best interests of the company, and not to place himself in a position where his own interests conflicted with those of the company. The precise point at which preparations for the establishment of a competing business became unlawful would depend on the facts of any particular case. In each case, the standard for what was permissible and impermissible, unless consent was obtained from the company or employer after full disclosure, was what would be a breach of the fiduciary duty owed by a director, or in breach of the obligation of fidelity owed by an employee. By promoting the establishment of the competing business prior to their resignation, the defendants were in breach of their fiduciary duties and their obligations of loyalty to the claimant. Judgment would be given accordingly.

Shepherds Investments Ltd v Walters [2006] EWHC 836 (Ch), [2007] IRLR 110 (Chancery Division: Etherton J). *British Midland Tool Ltd v Midland International Tooling Ltd* [2003] EWHC 466 (Ch), [2003] 2 BCLC 523 applied.

530 Director—fiduciary duty—shadow director—board of directors—act only on instructions of individual

A limited company, the claimant, and a public limited company were competitors in the market for the manufacture of conservatories. The defendants were the majority shareholders in the public limited company. A dispute arose between the claimant and the public limited company relating to the ownership of businesses in the field of the design of a conservatory roof system originally developed by a third party. The roof system was exploited by two companies, one of which became the licensor of the intellectual property rights in the system. In time, the third party was adjudged bankrupt and the two companies were acquired by the claimant. The claimant alleged that the defendants had stolen the business and assets of the two companies. The claimant contended that the third party had lied about the ownership of the two companies, and so had prevented the third party's trustee in bankruptcy from realising the assets for the benefit of the third party's creditors. Further, the claimant asserted that a dishonest story had prevented it from taking control of the companies until after the defendants had stripped them of their value. A number of actions arose out of the dispute and the issues to be decided included whether one of the defendants became a shadow director, within the meaning of the Companies Act 1985 s 741(2), or de facto director of the companies, and what duties, if any, were owed by a shadow director. *Held,* a person who effectively controlled the activities of a company was to be subject to the same statutory liabilities as a person who was a de jure director. Since a de jure director was subject to those liabilities even if he was non-executive, or even inactive, it would undermine the principle if the fact that an inactive director did not act on the instructions of an alleged shadow director could prevent that person from being a shadow director, even though in reality he controlled the activities of the company. Therefore, a person at whose direction a governing majority of the board was accustomed to act was capable of being a shadow director. The boards of the two companies had not been accustomed to act on the instructions of the majority shareholder at the relevant time and, therefore, he had not been a shadow director in relation to either company. Judgment would be given accordingly.

Ultraframe (UK) Ltd v Fielding (No 2) [2005] EWHC 1638 (Ch), [2006] FSR 293 (Chancery Division: Lewison J).

531 Director—loan by company—joint and several liability—knowledge of individual payments

In the course of administration proceedings, a complaint was made against the defendants, two former directors, that they had operated their directors' loan accounts so as to cause or allow the company to loan money to them in contravention of the Companies Act 1985 s 330. Summary judgment was given against both defendants for an amount standing to the credit of the company on each defendant's own loan account in accordance with s 341(1), and the defendants were found jointly and severally liable for the amount outstanding to the company, in accordance with s 341(2)(b). The judge rejected the first defendant's argument, under s 341(5), against joint and several liability on the basis that he had been unaware of or had not approved and authorised the making of loans to his co-director at least until the point when the relevant accounts were signed off because the accounts could only have been signed when the first defendant was still a director. The first defendant appealed. *Held,* a director who knowingly allowed a practice to continue, under which lending by the company to his co-director was treated as acceptable, had authorised the individual payments which were made in accordance with that practice notwithstanding that he did not have actual knowledge of each individual payment at the time that it was made. The complaint made by the administrator went beyond a complaint that individual payments had been made to the defendants by way of loan. Properly understood, it was a complaint that both defendants had allowed a practice to arise and continue under which lending by the company to the defendants was acceptable. Accordingly, the appeal would be dismissed.

Neville v Krikorian [2006] EWCA Civ 943, [2007] 1 BCLC 1 (Court of Appeal: Chadwick and Dyson LJJ and Sir Martin Nourse).

532 Director—use of prohibited name—personal liability for debts—disapplication by notice

See *First Independent Factors and Finance Ltd v Churchill*, para 557.

533   Disclosure of information—designated authorities

The Companies (Disclosure of Information) (Designated Authorities) Order 2006, SI 2006/1644 (in force on 1 October 2006), amends the Companies Act 1985 and the Companies act 1989 by adding a disclosure to the list of permitted disclosures of information, for the purpose of enabling or assisting the Gambling Commission to exercise its functions under the Gambling Act 2005.

534   Distributions—legality—entitlement to repayment—knowledge of law

Under the Companies Act 1985 s 277(1), where a distribution is made by a company to one of its members in contravention of Pt VIII (ss 263–281), which prohibits a distribution except out of profits, and, at the time of the distribution, the member knows or has reasonable grounds for believing that it is so made, he is liable to repay it to the company.

A company made trading losses for two years but, nevertheless, paid dividends to the defendants, its directors and shareholders, in respect or those years. The company went into voluntary liquidation and sought the return of the dividends under the 1985 Act s 277(1). Its application was dismissed and it appealed. *Held*, s 277(1) had to be interpreted as meaning that the shareholder could not claim that he was not liable to return a distribution because he did not know of the restrictions in the Act on the making of distributions. He would be liable if he knew or ought reasonably to have known of the facts which meant that the distribution contravened the requirements of the Act. Section 277(1) also had to be interpreted in conformity with EC Council Directive 77/91 art 16, which it was designed to implement. Accordingly, the appeal would be allowed.

It's a Wrap (UK) Ltd v Gula [2006] EWCA Civ 544, [2006] 2 BCLC 634 (Court of Appeal: Chadwick, Sedley and Arden LJJ). Decision of Nicolas Davidson QC [2005] EWHC 2015 (Ch), [2006] 1 BCLC 143 (2005 Abr para 614) reversed.

535   European Co-operative Societies—general

The European Co-operative Society Regulations 2006, SI 2006/2078 (in force on 18 August 2006), give effect to EC Council Regulation 1435/2003 on European Co-operative Societies. The regulations (1) designate the Financial Services Authority as the competent authority in relation to European Co-operative Societies and cooperatives which have their registered office in Great Britain; (2) permit bodies whose head offices are outside the EC to participate in the formation of a European Co-operative Society, subject to certain conditions; (3) prescribe the information and documents that a cooperative must provide if it wishes to form a European Co-operative Society by merger or conversion; (4) enable the competent authority to oppose the participation of a cooperative in the formation of a European Co-operative Society by merger; (5) provide for the establishment and maintenance of a register of European Co-operative Societies by the competent authority; (6) specify the process by which a European Co-operative Society may register with the competent authority; (7) list the documents that a European Co-operative Society must send to the competent authority while it continues to be registered; (8) prescribe the circumstances in which the competent authority must or may cancel a European Co-operative Society's registration; (9) specify the information that European Co-operative Societies with registered offices outside the United Kingdom and which open a branch in the United Kingdom must send to the competent authority; (10) require the relevant organ of a European Co-operative Society to make a solvency statement concerning the European Co-operative Society's liabilities before its registered office is transferred to another EEA state; (11) prescribe the information and documents that a European Co-operative Society must provide before its registered office is transferred to another EEA state; (12) enable the competent authority to oppose the transfer of a European Co-operative Society's registered office to another EEA state; (13) prescribe the process by which a cooperative or European Co-operative Society may appeal against a decision taken by the competent authority; (14) regulate the conversion of a European Co-operative Society into another cooperative form; (15) empower the competent authority to (a) require information or documents from a European Co-operative Society; (b) order an inspection of a European Co-operative Society's accounts; (c) order an inquiry into a European Co-operative Society's business affairs; and (d) direct a European Co-operative Society to comply with certain other obligations under Regulation 1435/2003 and enforce the direction through an application for an injunction; (16) amend the Insolvency Act 1986 s 124 to enable the Financial Services Authority to petition for a European Co-operative Society that has its registered office in Great Britain to be wound up on certain specified grounds; (17) make it an offence to breach the requirements to provide information, to make a solvency statement where the maker of the statement has no reasonable grounds for the opinion expressed in that statement, to fail to use the required terminology in the title of a European Co-operative Society, to use the term 'European Co-operative Society' in relation to an entity that is not such, or to carry on the business of a European Co-operative Society after that European Co-operative Society's registration has been cancelled; (18) make provision for the publication and inspection of certain information; and (19) empower the competent authority to charge fees.

536   European Co-operative Societies—involvement of employees

The European Co-operative Society (Involvement of Employees) Regulations 2006, SI 2006/2059 (in force on 18 August 2006), implement EC Council Directive 2003/72 with regard to the involvement of employees in European Co-operative Societies. The 2006 Regulations (1) create an exemption to the application of the requirements in the case of certain formations below a specified size threshold; (2) provide that the requirements apply to formerly exempt European Co-operative Societies which increase in size to fall above the threshold, or if a request is made by a sufficient proportion of the workforce; (3) impose a duty on participating individuals or legal entities involved in forming a European Co-operative Society to provide information to the employees or their representatives, who may complain to the Central Arbitration Committee ('CAC') if such information is not provided correctly; (4) define the function of the special negotiating body and its composition; (5) create a right of complaint if the special negotiating body is not established in accordance with specified requirements; (6) set out details of the arrangements for and conduct of the ballot by which members of the body should be elected; (7) provide that, in certain circumstances, members are to be appointed by a consultative committee instead of being elected by a ballot; (8) provide for a right of complaint to the CAC on the ground that the consultative committee is not correctly constituted; (9) set out when an individual is to be treated as an employee representative after being elected or appointed; (10) set out the timing of the requirement to negotiate the agreement; (11) prescribe the content and scope of the agreement; (12) make provision for the decision-making procedure of the special negotiating body and the consequences of a decision not to open or to terminate negotiations with the participating individuals or legal entities; (13) provide that decisions of the special negotiating body may be subject to complaint to the CAC; (14) set out standard rules on employee involvement, which are to apply either if the parties so agree or have reached the end of the negotiation period without an agreement being reached and certain other criteria apply; (15) allow complaints to be brought before the CAC where the terms of the employee involvement agreement or the information and consultation provisions have not been complied with; (16) provide that, if the complaint is well founded, a penalty notice may be issued by the Appeal Tribunal; (17) authorise the bringing of a complaint over the misuse of procedures; (18) provide that it is a breach of statutory duty for a recipient of confidential information to disclose it except in accordance with the terms on which it was disclosed to him; (19) make provision for the withholding of information in certain circumstances; (20) provide for rights to remuneration for time off, protection from unfair dismissal and protection from detriment; (21) provide for recourse to an employment tribunal for breach of such rights; and (22) impose restrictions on contracting out of the requirements.

537   Insider dealing—purchase of shares by third party—subsequent sale of shares—Community law

An employee-elected member of the board of a financial institution disclosed to the general secretary of a trade union, which represented workers employed in the financial sector, the institution's plan to enter into merger negotiations with a bank. The general secretary passed on the information to a colleague who bought shares in the institution. Subsequently, the merger was made public and the institution's share price increased. The colleague sold the shares at a profit and was later sentenced to six months' imprisonment for insider dealing. Criminal proceedings were brought against the member of the board and the general secretary on the ground that they had disclosed insider information contrary to a Danish law which implemented EC Council Directive 89/592. It fell to be determined whether art 3(a) precluded a person from disclosing inside information in a case where he received the inside information in his capacity as an employee-elected member of the board of the undertaking to which the inside information related and such information was disclosed to the general secretary of the trade union which organised the employees who elected the person concerned as a board member. *Held,* the exception in art 3(a) to the prohibition on disclosing inside information that applied to its disclosure by a person in the normal course of exercising his employment, profession or duties had to be interpreted strictly. Therefore, disclosure of inside information by a person who received it in his capacity as an employee representative to the general secretary of the professional organisation which organised those employees could only be justified if the disclosure was strictly necessary for the exercise of the employment, profession or duties of the person concerned and complied with the principle of proportionality. The same principles applied to whether art 3(a) allowed the general secretary of a professional organisation who received inside information to disclose that information to his colleagues.

Case C-384/02 *Criminal proceedings against Grongaard* [2006] 1 CMLR 785 (ECJ: Grand Chamber).

Directive 89/592 replaced by EC Council Directive 2003/6.

538   Insolvency

See COMPANY AND PARTNERSHIP INSOLVENCY.

539   Parent company—requirement to be based in European Union—dividends— corporation tax

See *NEC Semi-Conductors Ltd v Revenue and Customs Comrs*, para 1638.

540   Register of companies—provision of information to registrar

The Companies (Registrar, Languages and Trading Disclosures) Regulations 2006, SI 2006/3429 (in force on 1 January 2007), make provision in relation to disclosure requirements in respect of certain types of companies, in implementation of EC Parliament and Council Directive 2003/58. In particular, the regulations (1) provide that, where the registrar of companies provides a copy in electronic form of material on the register and the recipient requests the copy to be certified as a true copy, the registrar's certificate must be certified by an electronic signature uniquely linked to the registrar; (2) amend the Companies Act 1985 so that copies of certain documents delivered to the registrar are no longer required to be hard copies; (3) stipulate that a contract for the allotment of shares paid up other than in cash need not be in English when delivered to the registrar, but must be accompanied by a certified English translation; (4) enable the voluntary filing of transactions, under the Companies Act 2006 s 1106, to be carried out in any official European Union language if accompanied by a certified English translation; and (5) amend the 1985 Act supra and the Insolvency Act 1986 so as to require company websites and electronic documents to include a company's name, registered number, registered office and, if applicable, a statement that the company is being wound up.

541   Scheme of arrangement—sanction of court—convening of meeting—jurisdiction

The applicant company and its subsidiaries provided support services to the energy sector. Its principal businesses had been the manufacture of asbestos products. The applicant faced a number of claims for damages for asbestos-related personal injuries. Although the applicant was solvent, the uncertainty as to future asbestos-related claims posed a real but unquantifiable risk that in the future the applicant or its subsidiaries could become insolvent. Therefore, the applicant developed proposals in order to protect the group from asbestos claims. The group made an application, under the Companies Act 1985 s 425(1), to convene meetings to consider a scheme of arrangement containing such proposals. Issues arose as to whether the court had jurisdiction to sanction such a scheme and whether by excluding or restricting the liability of the subsidiaries for personal injury and death, the scheme fell foul of the Unfair Contracts Terms Act 1977. *Held,* the word 'arrangement' in the 1985 Act s 425 had a wide meaning. It was accepted that a scheme of arrangement could contain provisions which could be contained in a contract and that the machinery of s 425 was available where individual assent was impossible or not reasonably practicable. Although there were strong reasons why in most cases the court was unlikely to exercise its jurisdiction to sanction a scheme with provision for future amendments, the circumstances of a case might make it appropriate. In the present case, the need to provide for asbestos-related claims was clear. The claims were likely to continue for 40 or more years and it was predictable that there would be legal, medical and financial developments with a significant impact on the arrangement, but it was impossible to know what they would be. Therefore, it would not be right to refuse to make orders convening the meetings on the grounds that the scheme or ancillary documents contained provisions permitting future amendment. Further such a scheme was not a contract or notice within the meaning of the 1977 Act s 2(1). Although it might bind the parties, to the same extent as if they had made a contract, it was a statutory procedure involving the proposal, approval and sanction of the scheme. Accordingly, the application would be granted.

Re Cape plc [2006] EWHC 1316 (Ch), [2006] 3 All ER 1222 (Chancery Division: David Richards J).

542   Scheme of arrangement—sanction of court—objection by shareholder or creditor— costs

See *Re Peninsular & Oriental Steam Navigation Co*, para 697.

543   Shareholder—minority shareholder—derivative action—power of court to intervene

The claimant was a minority shareholder in a company. A subsidiary of that company developed a product known as 'E-plate', a device which enabled vehicles to be monitored. The claimant was notified of a proposal that a third company would acquire a licence to manufacture and market E-plate technology. The claimant sought to satisfy himself as to why the venture was not being pursued through the parent company or its subsidiary and that it was a bona fide transaction for those companies. The claimant was not satisfied with the response obtained. Three further proposals were put forward. The defendants, the shareholders and directors of the parent company, were of the view that the fourth proposal satisfied the claimant's concerns. The claimant disagreed. Meanwhile the claimant issued proceedings alleging breaches of fiduciary duty by the defendants. That action was a derivative action and as such, under CPR 19.9(3), the claimant required and applied for permission to carry on the claim on behalf of the parent company and its subsidiary. The defendants accepted that the claimant had a prima facie case, but contended that no independent board acting reasonably would consider it in the interests of either company to bring the claim. *Held*, in order to determine whether it was appropriate to grant permission for a derivative action to proceed it was not for the court to assert its own view of what it would do if it was the board. The court merely had to be satisfied that a reasonable independent board could take the view that it was appropriate to bring the proceedings. Only if no reasonable board would bring proceedings should the court not sanction the bringing of a shareholder's derivative action. It would not be right to shut out a minority shareholder on the basis of the court's possibly inadequate assessment. In the present case, a reasonable independent board would press for some sort of benefit for the company. It might threaten proceedings, but it would withdraw proceedings if a reasonable offer was received. The fourth proposal was not sufficient to protect the claimant's interests. It would, however, be appropriate to allow a period of time in order to see whether agreement could be reached on a proposal which would adequately protect the claimant's interests. If such a proposal were forthcoming, the claimant would not be allowed to proceed. Accordingly, the action would be stayed in order to allow that process to take place.

Airey v Cordell [2006] All ER (D) 111 (Aug) (Chancery Division: Warren J).

544 Small companies—accounts and audit

The Companies Act 1985 (Small Companies Accounts and Audit) Regulations 2006, SI 2006/2782 (in force on 8 November 2006), amend (1) the Companies Act 1985 Pt 7 (ss 221–262A) concerning accounting and auditing, so as to extend the accounting, reporting and auditing exemptions to small companies which have permission under the Financial Services and Markets Act 2000 Pt 4 (ss 40–55) to carry on a regulated activity, unless such companies are (a) authorised insured companies; (b) banking companies; (c) e-money issuers; (d) ISD investment firms; or (e) UCITS management companies; and (2) the Limited Liability Partnerships Regulations 2001, SI 2001/1090, so as to make similar provision in relation to limited liability partnerships.

545 Takeovers—interim implementation

The Takeovers Directive (Interim Implementation) Regulations 2006, SI 2006/1183 (in force on 20 May 2006), implement EC European Parliament and Council Directive 2004/25. In particular, the regulations (1) make provision for the operation of regulatory activities of the Panel on Takeovers and Mergers ('the Panel') so as to (a) give effect to the rules in the City Code on Takeovers and Mergers and the Rules of Procedure of the Panel's Hearing Committee; (b) confer powers on the Panel including the power to require information and to apply to the court to secure compliance with certain requirements; and (c) provide for new offences relating to disclosure and failure to comply with rules about bid documentation; (2) provide for defensive devices that may be adopted by a company prior to a takeover bid to be overridden in certain circumstances and provide that such a provision is optional for companies; (3) set out additional information that must be contained in a directors' report of certain companies; (4) amend the Companies Act 1985 s 251 in relation to summary financial statements so as to provide for the explanatory material either to be included in any summary financial statement or to accompany it; (5) contain provisions designed to address the problem of and for residual minority shareholders following a successful takeover bid; and (6) provide that certain provisions apply (a) to takeover bids covered by Directive 2004/25 for all companies with securities traded on a regulated market and in the United Kingdom or for companies registered in the United Kingdom whose securities are traded on a regulated market in one or more member states of the European Economic Area, other than the United Kingdom; and (b) only to companies registered under the 1985 Act and to unregistered companies.

546 Unfair prejudice to members—minority shareholder—management of company and profits—exclusion

The Companies Act 1985 s 459(1) provides that a member of a company may apply to the court by petition for an order under Pt XVII (ss 459–461) on the ground that the company's affairs are being or have been conducted in a manner which is unfairly prejudicial to the interests of its members generally or of some part of its members (including at least himself) or that any actual or proposed act or omission of the company (including an act or omission on its behalf) is or would be so prejudicial.

The claimant owned a large minority stake in a company from whose management and in whose profits, he alleged, he had been unfairly excluded. He brought a petition under the 1985 Act s 459, submitting that the unfairness stemmed from the agreement by which he had become a shareholder. *Held*, where an agreement between members of a company did not cover a change in circumstances which arose in relation to the management of the company's business, the conduct of the affairs of the company could be unfairly prejudicial within the meaning of s 459 and the court could intervene. However, for the court to intervene, the change in circumstances had to be such that it was not reasonable to require the former association to remain as it had been, and such that the court's intervention was required to adjust matters. In the present case, some of the failures to consult had been prejudicial for the purposes of s 459 and had been unfair. However, although the claimant could legitimately have expected a proper share of the company's profits, his stake in those profits depended on the state of the business. Losses had been made by the company and, unless the claimant could establish that those losses should not have been made, he could not complain about a failure to pay him income on his investment. It followed that the failure to pay the claimant any part of the profits had not been unfair conduct. On an overall assessment, the situation had not been shown to be based on a degree of unfairness which required or justified the intervention of the court. The court would not order a buy-out under s 459. Accordingly, the claim would be dismissed.

Re Metropolis Motorcycles; Hale v Waldock [2006] EWHC 364 (Ch), [2006] All ER (D) 68 (Mar) (Chancery Division: Mann J).

547   Unfair prejudice to members—purchase of shares of prejudiced member—date of purchase

The issued share capital of the first company, a family company concerned with heating and boilers and having significant property assets, was owned in equal shares by the petitioner and the respondent. Their common intention and shared assumption was that they would be involved in the management of the first company, would be paid equal salaries by it, and would enjoy equal rights and benefits from the first company. In the course of their involvement with the first company, the respondent, without the prior consent of the first company or the petitioner, took money for his own private purposes from the first company and rent money due to it. Personal animosity within the family led to the petitioner leaving the business. He formed a second company through which he commenced trading in heating parts. Thereafter, the respondent incorporated a third company to which he transferred the first company's business without any payment for goodwill. He further caused the first company to grant to the third company's successor company a long lease of part of the first company's property, without having regard as to whether that was in the first company's best interests. The parties neared a point at which they could resolve their differences by a separation of their affairs and written heads of agreement, marked 'subject to contract', were drawn up, containing a proposed split of the business and assets of the first company. However, the heads of agreement were not successfully taken forward. The respondent subsequently signed a special notice of an extraordinary general meeting of the first company removing the petitioner as a director and appointing new auditors. The petitioner applied, pursuant to the Companies Act 1985 s 459, for an order that the respondent purchase his shares in the first company at a fair price to be determined. Held, an interest in a going concern should be valued at the date on which it was ordered to be purchased, subject to the overriding requirement that the valuation should be fair on the facts of the particular case. In deciding what valuation date was fair on the facts of the particular case, there were two main considerations which the court had to bear in mind. One was that the shares should be valued on a date as close as possible to the actual sale so as to reflect the value of what the shareholder was selling. However, there were many cases in which fairness, to one side or the other, required the court to take another date. The affairs of the first company were being, or had been, conducted in a manner which had been unfairly prejudicial to the interests of its members, including the petitioner, and there had been acts or omissions of the first company that were so prejudicial. The court had jurisdiction, under s 461, to make such order as it saw fit for giving relief in respect of the matters complained of, and there was no doubt that the court should exercise that jurisdiction. The court would order that the respondent buy the petitioner's one-half interest in the first company at a price equal to one-half of the value of the first company at a convenient and suitable date after the date of the heads of agreement, and assuming that the first company enjoyed the goodwill of the business transferred to the third company. The first company would then sell its property interests to the petitioner at a price equal to the value of that property at a convenient and suitable date after the date of the heads of agreement. Accordingly, the application was allowed.

Re Adlink Ltd [2006] All ER (D) 198 (Oct) (Chancery Division: Robert Knowles QC). Profinance Trust SA v Gladstone [2001] EWCA Civ 1031, [2002] 1 WLR 1024 (2001 Abr para 569) considered.

548   Unfair prejudice to members—purchase of shares of prejudiced member—quasi-partnership—valuation of shares

The claimant took over the management of a company owned entirely by the defendant, eventually becoming managing director. The parties agreed that the claimant would have an option to purchase all the defendant's shares at a price per share based on a certain valuation of the company. The claimant was advised by his accountant that the valuation was too high. A second option was subsequently granted under which the claimant could buy up to ten per cent of the shares out of his bonuses, at a lower price than under the first option but again at a price which the claimant's advisors believed to be above the true value. The claimant decided to exercise the second option. He was later dismissed from his employment with the company and resigned as a director. He asked the defendant to buy his shares at their full value on a non-discounted basis. The defendant declined, and the claimant presented a petition for relief from unfair prejudice under the Companies Act 1985 s 459, based on his exclusion from management and the defendant's failure to buy out his shares at their full value. The judge found that the company was a 'quasi-partnership', and that the defendant's failure to offer to buy the claimant's shares at their non-discounted value following his dismissal from the company amounted to unfair prejudice for the purposes of s 459. He therefore ordered the defendant to buy the claimant's shares at their non-discounted value. The defendant appealed. *Held*, the judge had been entitled on the evidence to conclude that the relationship between the claimant and the defendant had developed into the relationship of quasi-partnership, and that there were equitable considerations which bound the defendant to purchase the claimant's shares on a non-discounted basis once the claimant had been dismissed by the company. In truth, the relationship between the parties was multi-layered and multi-faceted, involving aspects arising from the claimant's employment, his right under the options and his participation in the management of the company's business. Moreover, the terms of the option agreements did not inevitably mean that the parties had adopted the position of vendor and purchaser under a commercial contract. On the contrary, the defendant had considered that, under the terms of the second option, he was giving the claimant the opportunity to acquire shares in the company at a price representing about half their value, something he was most unlikely to have done if the relationship was purely commercial. Also, the second option opened the door to the claimant becoming a shareholder without having acquired all the shares under the first option, which again was something the defendant would hardly have wanted to do under a purely commercial contract of sale and purchase. The claimant's departure from the company was involuntary. He had been prevented from continuing to participate in management. Moreover, he had invested his bonuses in buying the shares. He was not able to benefit from any increase in the value of those shares by staying in the company and contributing to its profitability (if such was achievable). In those circumstances fairness demanded that he should be entitled to claim back not merely the cost of acquiring the shares but their value at the date of the buy-out order. Accordingly, the appeal would be dismissed.

Strahan v Wilcock [2006] EWCA Civ 13, [2006] 2 BCLC 555 (Court of Appeal: Mummery, Arden and Richards LJJ). *Ebrahimi v Westbourne Galleries Ltd* [1973] AC 360, HL; *Re Bird Precision Bellows Ltd* [1986] Ch 658, CA (1985 Abr para 313); and *O'Neill v Phillips* [1999] 2 All ER 961, HL (1999 Abr para 553), applied.

The court had held by an earlier decision that the petitioners had suffered unfair prejudice as a result of the management of the company by the first respondent and ordered the first respondent to purchase the petitioners' shares in the company. A dispute arose as to the valuation of the shares. The petitioners alleged that, in the working out of the buy-out order, the petitioners' shareholding in the company should be valued on a pro-rata, non-discounted basis. The first respondent submitted that a minority shareholding would be valued on a non-discounted basis only where the relevant company was a quasi-partnership and that, in the present circumstances, the valuation should be on a discounted basis. *Held*, a minority shareholding, even where the extent of the minority was slight, was to be valued as a minority shareholding unless a good reason existed to attribute to it a pro-rata share of the overall value of the company. Short of a quasi-partnership or some other exceptional circumstance, there was no reason to accord to it a quality which it lacked. In the present case, the company was not a quasi-partnership and there were no exceptional circumstances. Therefore the shares would be valued on a discounted basis. Judgment would be given accordingly.

Irvine v Irvine [2006] EWHC 583 (Ch), [2006] 4 All ER 102 (Chancery Division: Blackburne J). *Strahan v Wilcock* [2006] EWCA Civ 13, [2006] 2 BCLC 555 (supra) applied.

549 Unfair prejudice to members—refusal to pay agreed dividend—dismissal of director—requirement to buy out shares

The claimant owned 25 per cent of the shares in a company of which he was also a director. The remaining shares were owned by the respondents, the other directors of the company. At an annual general meeting of the company, the parties agreed to pay a dividend to themselves as shareholders, to be divided equally between them. The claimant later alleged that the respondents had subsequently decided, without his knowledge or consent and contrary to what had previously been agreed, that the claimant was not to receive a dividend. The respondents also purported to remove the claimant as a director. The claimant brought proceedings pursuant to the Companies Act 1985 s 459, seeking an order under s 461 requiring the respondents to purchase his shares at a price to be determined by the court. The judge held that unfair prejudice had been established in respect of the failure to pay the dividend in accordance with what had been agreed but that the respondents had had sufficient cause to justify the claimant's removal as a director because he had been negotiating to acquire another company dealing in the same line of business as their company, and had therefore put himself in a position of actual or potential conflict with his duties as a director. The judge also declined to make an order requiring the respondents to purchase the claimant's shares. The claimant appealed. *Held*, the judge had been right to find that the claimant's conduct had justified his dismissal as a director but he had exercised his discretion under s 461 on too narrow a basis, and the factors which he had taken into account as reasons for not making the buy-out order did not justify the conclusion which he had reached. It was appropriate that the respondents should be required to purchase the claimant's shares at a price to be determined by the court. Accordingly, the appeal would be allowed in part.

Grace v Biagioli [2005] EWCA Civ 1222, [2006] 2 BCLC 70 (Court of Appeal: Mummery and Mance LJJ and Patten J).

COMPANY AND PARTNERSHIP INSOLVENCY

Halsbury's Laws of England (4th edn) vol 7(3) (2004 Reissue) paras 1–628, vol 7(4) (2004 Reissue) paras 629–1310

Articles

For articles relating to this title please refer to the Table of Articles at the beginning of the Abridgment.

550 Charge—floating charge—enforcement—appointment of administrative receiver—validity—facility agreement

The Insolvency Act 1986 s 72A prohibits the holder of a qualifying charge in respect of a company's property from appointing an administrative receiver of the company. Section 72A does not prevent the appointment of an administrative receiver of a project company of a project which is a financed project, and for this purpose a project is 'financed' if, under an agreement relating to the project, a project company incurs or, when the agreement is entered into, is expected to incur, a debt of at least £50m for the purposes of carrying out the project: s 72E(1), (2)(a).

The claimants were among the five founders of the fourth defendant, a limited liability partnership, which entered into a facility agreement with a bank under which the bank agreed to make available capital to fund a project involving the exploitation by the fourth defendant of certain licences. Pursuant to a power contained in a debenture granted by the fourth defendant to the third defendant, the first two defendants were appointed administrative receivers of the fourth defendant. The claimants brought proceedings challenging the validity of that appointment, contending that, at the date when the appointment was made, there had been no 'insolvency event' as defined in the debenture so that the power to appoint receivers had not arisen, and that in any event the 1986 Act prohibited any exercise of the power. The judge decided that the appointment of the receivers was prohibited by the 1986 Act and was therefore invalid. The third defendant appealed, arguing that the judge had wrongly construed s 72E(2)(a). *Held*, s 72E(2) addressed a situation in which the precise amount of the debt incurred 'under' a relevant agreement was not ascertainable as at the date of that agreement, as, for example, where a project company entered into a facility agreement with a bank where the precise amount of the draw-down within the permitted limit was dependant on future contingencies. It followed that it was under the facility agreement that the fourth defendant was or was not 'expected to incur' an indebtedness above the specified threshold, and therefore that the judge had been right to conclude that the date for assessing whether the requisite expectation existed was that set out in the facility agreement. Accordingly, the appeal would be dismissed.

Feetum v Levy [2005] EWCA Civ 1601, [2006] 3 WLR 427 (Court of Appeal: Ward and Jonathan Parker LJJ and Sir Peter Gibson).

551 Company insolvency—administration—priority of expenses—entitlement to declaration where substantive relief not sought

A local authority issued an application seeking, among other things, a declaration that non-domestic rates which had accrued to it in respect of premises owned by a company, together with interest thereon, fell within the Insolvency Rules 1986, SI 1986/1925, r 2.67(1)(a) or (f). Rule 2.67(1) detailed the order of priority of the expenses of the administration. By the time the application came before the judge for directions, the alternative forms of relief sought by the authority in its application were not pressed as the original administrators were no longer the administrators. That meant that the judge was faced with a bare application for a declaration that the rates fell within r 2.67(1)(a) or (f). The administrators therefore applied to be removed as parties to the application and for the claim for relief against them to be struck out. The judge acceded to the administrators' application, and the authority appealed. It subsequently emerged that the administrators had paid themselves a large sum in respect of their remuneration during the course of the administration, which had not been repaid. The administrators submitted that a claim for declaratory relief had to be coupled with a claim for substantive relief. *Held*, had it not been for the emergence of the matter of the administrators' remuneration, it was possible that their submissions might have prevailed. However, the consequence was that, at the date of the hearing before the judge, the authority had by virtue of r 2.67 a potential right to claim or to be awarded priority over the administrators to the extent of the amount that had been taken by them by way of remuneration. Since that raised an issue between them, it was and remained a sufficient basis for the authority to claim the declaration it sought against the administrators, notwithstanding that it was not coupled with any claim for substantive relief. Accordingly, the appeal would be allowed.

Re Trident Fashions plc; Exeter CC v Bairstow [2006] EWCA Civ 203, [2006] All ER (D) 140 (Mar) (Court of Appeal: Rix and Maurice Kay LJJ and Sir Martin Nourse).

552   Company insolvency—administration—priority of expenses—insurer's claims handling expenses

The Insolvency Act 1986 s 19(5) provides that any sums payable in respect of debts or liabilities incurred by the former administrator of a company, while he was administrator, under contracts entered into by him in the carrying out of his functions are to be charged on and paid out of property of the company which is in his custody or under his control in priority to a charge in respect of his remuneration and expenses.

A company faced a large number of tortious claims arising out of the use of asbestos in its products. It appeared likely that it would be unable to pay its debts and it obtained an administration order. The company had the benefit of an asbestos liability policy under which it was entitled to be indemnified against certain losses. It was a condition of the policy that, after the occurrence of an insolvency event, which included the presentation of an administration petition, the insurers had the exclusive right to handle and defend claims. It was accepted that, in handling claims, the insurers acted as agents for the company and were entitled to reimbursement for their expenses. The question arose whether the insurers' right to reimbursement of expenses incurred after the appointment of the administrators had priority over other costs of the administration pursuant to the 1986 Act s 19(5). The administrators sought directions from the court and it was held that the insurers' expenses did not have priority. The insurers' appeal succeeded and the administrators appealed further. *Held*, the purpose of administration under the 1986 Act was simply to impose a moratorium to allow time to find a way of saving the business or realising it to better advantage than in a liquidation. It was not intended to alter substantive rights or priorities more than was necessary to enable that objective to be achieved. The provisions of s 19(4) and (5) entrusted to the administrator, subject to the supervision of the court, the power to decide what expenditure was necessary for the purposes of the administration and should therefore receive priority. The company had conferred on the insurers the power to make contracts on its behalf, which the administrator had no power to revoke. However, such contracts were made on behalf of the company and not on behalf of the administrator as required by s 19(5). There was no reason to extend that priority to expenditure which neither the administrator nor the court had specifically approved. The court had a broad discretion to authorise or direct the administrators to make payments or enter into contracts for the purposes of the administration. In the exercise of that power, the court could direct the administrator to authorise or ratify particular claims handling expenditure by the insurers, with the result that their rights to reimbursement would have priority under s 19(5). It would however be unusual for the court to make such a decision, involving questions of business judgment, contrary to the opinion of the administrator that such expenditure, while no doubt in the interests of the insurers, was not necessary for the very limited purposes of the administration. Accordingly, the appeal would be allowed.

Centre Reinsurance International Co v Freakley; Freakley v Centre Reinsurance International Co [2006] UKHL 45, [2006] 4 All ER 1153 (House of Lords: Lords Hoffmann, Hope of Craighead, Phillips of Worth Matravers, Walker of Gestingthorpe and Brown of Eaton-under-Heywood). Decision of Court of Appeal [2005] EWCA Civ 115, [2005] 2 All ER (Comm) 65 (2005 Abr para 1893) reversed in part.

1986 Act s 19(5) now Sch B1 para 99(4).

553   Company insolvency—administration—transition to liquidation—registration of notice—registration when administrators no longer in office

The Insolvency Act 1986 Sch B1 para 83(6) provides that, on the registration of a notice that the total amount which each secured creditor of a company is likely to receive has been paid to him or set aside for him, and that a distribution is to be made to unsecured creditors of the company, the appointment of an administrator in respect of the company ceases to have effect, and the company must be wound up as if a resolution for voluntary winding up under s 84 were passed on the day on which the notice is registered.

In each of two conjoined cases administrators were appointed in respect of a company. In both cases it was decided to adopt the procedure prescribed by the 1986 Act Sch B1 para 83, with the administrators becoming the liquidators. The administrators sent the appropriate notices under Sch B1 para 83(3) to the registrar of companies. However, in each case the notice was not registered until after the administrators' appointment had ceased to have effect. An issue arose as to whether the registration of the notice, and therefore the transition of the companies from administration to liquidation under the terms of Sch B1 para 83(6), were effective. *Held*, on its proper construction, Sch B1 para 83(6) was to be applied in accordance with its express and mandatory terms so that, on registration of a notice sent by administrators while still in office, the company should be wound up. If by the date of registration the administrators had already ceased to hold office, the first part of Sch B1 para 83(6) would simply not have any effect. It followed that, in the instant cases, the companies had been wound up on the date of registration of the relevant notice and that the liquidators of each company were its former administrators. Judgment would be given accordingly.

Re E Squared Ltd; Re Sussex Pharmaceutical Ltd [2006] EWHC 532 (Ch), [2006] 3 All ER 779 (Chancery Division: David Richards J). *Re Powerstore (Trading) Ltd; Re Homepower Stores Ltd* [1998]

1 All ER 121 (1997 Abr para 491); *Re Norditrack (UK) Ltd* [2000] 1 All ER 369 (1999 Abr para 507); and *Re Ballast plc (in administration)* [2004] EWHC 2356 (Ch), [2005] 1 All ER 630 (2004 Abr para 492) considered.

554   Company insolvency—administration order—distribution without company voluntary arrangement or compulsory liquidation—power of court to sanction distribution

The administrators of a company made proposals which envisaged the company entering into a company voluntary arrangement once the assets had been realised. However, the administrators believed that it would be cheaper if the creditors were to be paid early, with the preferential creditors paid in full and the unsecured creditors paid on the same basis as if the payments had been made in the course of a compulsory liquidation. The administrators therefore applied for the proposed distribution to be sanctioned. The judge decided, however, that he had no jurisdiction to sanction the distribution, on the basis that the Insolvency Act 1986, prior to its amendment by the Enterprise Act 2002, had given neither the administrators power to make such a distribution, nor the court power to sanction or order the making of such a distribution. He concluded that, if he had had jurisdiction, he would have sanctioned the proposed distribution, on the basis that the creditors had either supported it or had not objected to it, and it would result in an enhanced payment, at least to the unsecured creditors. The administrators appealed, and an issue arose as to whether the court had the jurisdiction to sanction the distribution to the creditors under the 1986 Act s 14(3) or 18(3). *Held*, although s 14(3) envisaged the court giving the administrator 'directions', those directions had to be in connection with the carrying out of his functions, which did not extend to paying out creditors. While s 14(3) did extend to giving the court what might be characterised as an inherent jurisdiction over the actions of an administrator, which might be invoked in the same sort of circumstances as in relation to liquidators, it could properly and fairly be said to justify the court sanctioning a course of action which was wholly outside the ambit of an administrator's powers. It followed that the judge had had no jurisdiction under s 14(3) to make an order sanctioning the administrator to make payments to the creditors. Moreover, s 18(3) only came into play on the hearing of an application under s 18, namely, an application to discharge, vary or add an additional purpose to an administration order pursuant to s 18(1). The variation contemplated could not extend to sanctioning an action by an administrator which was not contemplated or permitted by some other provision of the 1986 Act. The court could, however, under s 18(3), sanction administrators paying money directly to a class of creditors (and therefore to all creditors), at least if it was to facilitate a desirable exit route from the administration. In the present case, there was no question of a variation or additional purpose, and therefore the jurisdiction under s 18(3) could only be invoked if the administrators had been making an application for discharge, which they had not. Judgment would be given accordingly.

Re Lune Metal Products Ltd (in administration) [2006] EWCA Civ 1720, [2006] All ER (D) 225 (Dec) (Court of Appeal: Tuckey, Carnwarth and Neuberger LJJ).

555   Company insolvency—administration order—failure to obtain approval of administrator's proposals—failure to obtain approval of revised proposals

The Insolvency Act 1986 Sch B1 para 55(2)(a) provides that where an administrator reports to the court that an initial creditors' meeting has failed to approve the administrator's proposals presented to it, or a creditors' meeting has failed to approve a revision of the administrator's proposals presented to it, the court may provide that the appointment of an administrator will cease to have effect from a specified time.

The proceedings concerned three applications by the joint administrators of the company, namely an application under the 1986 Act Sch B1 para 55(2)(a) that their appointment should cease to have effect due to the creditors' rejection of their proposals, an application under Sch B1 para 98(2)(c) for their discharge from liability in respect of any of their actions and an application under the Insolvency Rules 1986, SI 1986/1925, r 2.106(6) fixing remuneration. *Held*, in the absence of any authority or rules of procedure applicable to applications under the 1986 Act Sch B1 para 55, for an administration order to cease to have effect, the 1986 Rules r 2.114, relating to analogous provisions under the 1986 Act Sch B1 para 79, should apply. The court would adjourn the application under Sch B1 para 55(2)(a) and direct that the administrators comply with the 1986 Rules r 2.114(1), (3). Specifically, a progress report should be attached to the application for an order ending the administration, and notice should be given to the creditors of the administrators' intention to make such an application. The administrators should notify the creditors that an application for remuneration to be fixed would be made. Judgment would be given accordingly.

Re ML Design Group [2006] All ER (D) 75 (Jan) (Chancery Division: Richard Sheldon QC).

556   Company insolvency—banks—former authorised institutions

The Banks (Former Authorised Institutions) (Insolvency) Order 2006, SI 2006/3107 (in force on 15 December 2006), makes provision for the modified application of the Insolvency Act 1986 Pt II (ss 8–27), Sch B1, to any company within the meaning of the Companies Act 1985 s 735(1) that (1) has a liability in respect of a deposit which it accepted in accordance with the Banking Act 1979 or Banking Act 1987, but (2) does not have permission under the Financial Services and Markets Act 2000 Pt IV (ss 40–55) to accept deposits. In particular, the order sets out modifications of the 1986 Act Sch B1 in its application to such companies; broadly speaking these confer rights on the Financial Services Authority to participate in administration proceedings that are commenced as a result of the application of the order. SI 1989/1276 is revoked.

557 Company insolvency—company name—restriction on re-use—liability of successor company's directors—notice to creditors

The Insolvency Rules 1986, SI 1986/1925, r 4.228(1) provides that where a successor company acquires the business of an insolvent company, under arrangements made by an insolvency practitioner, the successor company may give notice to the insolvent company's creditors. Such a notice must specify the name which the successor company has assumed, or proposes to assume for the purpose of carrying on the business, if that name is or will be a prohibited name: r 4.228(2)(b). The notice may also name a person to whom provisions restricting the re-use of company names may apply as having been a director of the insolvent company, and may give particulars as to the nature and duration of that directorship, with a view to his being a director of the successor company: r 4.228(3).

The defendants were the directors of a company which went into insolvent liquidation. At the date of liquidation, the defendants were also the directors of a second, similarly named, company. The first company, acting by its liquidator, sold its goodwill to the second company. The claimant brought proceedings for debts of the second company on the basis that the defendants were jointly and severally liable for those debts by virtue of the Insolvency Act 1986 ss 216, 217. Where the new company had a prohibited name and none of the prescribed exceptions applied, the effect of those sections was that a person who was a director of a company when it went into insolvent liquidation became liable for the debts and liabilities of a new company of which he was a director. While the defendants accepted that the name of the second company was a prohibited name, they argued that a prescribed exception applied in their case, which was that they had given notice to creditors under the 1986 Rules r 4.228. The claimant obtained summary judgment and the defendants appealed. *Held*, r 4.228 operated only where directors of the company in liquidation were not the directors of, or involved in the management of, the successor company at the date when the notice was given. Rule 4.228 contained no express provision that it was intended to have retrospective effect, and the expression in r 4.228(3) 'with a view to his being a director' plainly had a prospective flavour to it. Indeed, r 4.229 strongly suggested the opposite to be the case. The purpose of r 4.228 was to alert creditors of a company in liquidation to the fact that a person who had been involved in the management of that company was also to be involved in the management of a successor company, so that such creditors could make an informed assessment of the risk of extending credit to the successor company. To ensure that that purpose was achieved, a person had to give notice to such creditors before starting to involve himself in the management of the successor company. Accordingly, the appeal would be dismissed.

First Independent Factors and Finance Ltd v Churchill [2006] EWCA Civ 1623, [2006] All ER (D) 427 (Nov) (Court of Appeal: Ward, Jonathan Parker and Moore-Bick LJJ).

558 Company insolvency—foreign company—power to remit proceeds of assets to foreign liquidator

Winding-up petitions were presented in England against companies which had formed part of a large Australian insurance group. The companies, which were incorporated in Australia and registered in England as overseas companies, were also ordered to be wound up by an Australian court. During the insolvency proceedings an issue arose as to whether, where a foreign company was in liquidation both in its country of incorporation and in England, and there were material assets among the unsecured creditors under the laws of the two countries, the English court had the power to direct the English liquidator to remit the proceeds of the assets to the foreign liquidator for distribution by him in accordance with the law of that country. The court ruled that, in an English liquidation of a foreign company, the court had no power to direct the liquidator to transfer funds for distribution in the principal liquidation, if the scheme for pari passu distribution in that liquidation was not substantially the same as under English law. On appeal, *held*, if the companies were in liquidation in England, the court in England would have jurisdiction to entertain a request under the Insolvency Act 1986 s 426 for directions to the liquidators in England to transfer the assets collected by them to the liquidators in the principal liquidation even though the result of such transfer would be to interfere with the statutory scheme imposed on those assets by the 1986 Act. Whether to sanction such a transfer would be a matter for the discretion of the court, and would involve a consideration of all the circumstances, including whether the transfer sought would prejudice the creditors of any class of them and whether there would be other advantages sufficient to counteract such prejudice. In the instant case, the court would have jurisdiction to consider the request, but would not, in the exercise of its discretion, direct a transfer of the English assets by the English provisional liquidators to the Australian liquidators because, subject to certain exceptions, that would prejudice the interests of all the creditors. The fact that there were no winding up orders in England at the present was no reason to take a different view of the propriety of the direction for transfers currently sought by the Australian liquidators or the Australian insurance creditors. Accordingly, the appeal would be dismissed.

Re HIH Casualty and General Insurance Ltd; McMahon v McGrath [2006] EWCA Civ 732, [2007] 1 All ER 177 (Court of Appeal: Sir Andrew Morritt C, Tuckey and Carnwath LJJ). Decision of David Richards J [2005] EWHC 2125 (Ch), [2005] All ER (D) 74 (Oct) (2005 Abr para 637) affirmed.

559   Company insolvency—proof of debts—deed of indemnity

A group of companies traded primarily as retailers of petrol. The parent company was in charge of bank borrowing, and lent to the subsidiaries such funds as were necessary for their trading. There were, therefore, significant inter-company debts. The group went into liquidation, and the liquidators brought proceedings to determine the effect of a deed of indemnity entered into between a creditor of the group and various members of the group. The creditor contended that, by virtue of the deed of indemnity, the debt of one of the subsidiaries to the parent was subordinated to that owed to the creditor, so that nothing could be paid on account of those inter-company debts unless and until the creditor had been paid in full. The judge decided that the deed did prohibit the parent from proving for its inter-company debt due from the subsidiary and from receiving a dividend in respect of such debt in the liquidation of the subsidiary at a time when the debt to the creditor remained unpaid. The parent company and its liquidators appealed. *Held*, the restriction in the deed, which had the effect that the parent could not prove in the liquidation of the subsidiary, did not impede the liquidators of the parent in discharging their functions in the parent's liquidation. The reasons given by the judge, namely that, although the deed was detrimental to the creditors of the parent, that was not because it imposed on the parent continuing financial obligations, that it did not give rise to prospective liabilities, and that it did not require performance over a substantial period of time or involve expenditure, was correct. Also, the parent should not be permitted to prove in the liquidation of the subsidiary. It was commercially important that, if group companies entered into subordination agreements with their creditors while solvent, they and the creditors should be held to the bargain when the event for which the agreement was intended to provide, in other words insolvency, occurred. The liquidators of the subsidiary were correct in their contention that, if the parent was to prove in the liquidation of the subsidiary, it would be required to bring into account the whole of the subsidiary's claims for indemnity as a contribution to the whole fund distributable in the liquidation of the subsidiary. On the figures that had been put before the court, that requirement would have the effect, prima facie, that the dividend which would be payable on the parent's proof would be less than the amount of that contribution. If so, the parent would receive nothing in the liquidation of the subsidiary. Accordingly, the appeal would be dismissed.

Squires (liquidators of SSSL Realisations (2002) Ltd)) v AIG Europe (UK) Ltd [2006] EWCA Civ 7, [2006] 2 WLR 1369 (Court of Appeal: Chadwick and Jonathan Parker LJJ and Etherton J).

560   Company insolvency—rules

The Insolvency (Amendment) Rules 2006, SI 2006/1272 (in force on 1 June 2006), further amend the 1986 Rules, SI 1986/1925, by extending the category of debts provable in a winding up or administration so as to include claims founded in tort where all of the elements required to bring an action against the company exist at the time the company goes into liquidation or enters administration.

561   Company insolvency—voluntary arrangement—creditors' meeting—notice

The administrators of a company and the United States parties involved in the administration proceedings entered into a settlement agreement. The court gave directions that the administrators could propose voluntary arrangements and/or schemes of arrangement in respect of such companies as they considered appropriate in accordance with the terms of the settlement agreement. By virtue of the Insolvency Act 1986 s 3, in summoning meetings of creditors, the administrators were required to give notice to all the creditors of whose claims they were aware. The notice had to be in writing and accompanied by certain documents and a form of proxy. In relation to convening the proposed meetings, an issue arose as to whether the Insolvency Rules 1986, SI 1986/1925, rr 12.10–12.12 were applicable. Rule 12.10 provided for service of notice by post, r 12.11 contained general provisions for service, and r 12.12 provided for service out of the jurisdiction. *Held*, rr 12.10 and 12.11 were applicable to notices of meetings, but r 12.12 did not apply to notices of meetings. In relation to r 12.10, 'service' clearly applied to the delivery of documents other than in court proceedings. There needed to be some provision for deeming the date on which notice was given of a meeting when the notice was sent by post. Likewise, in terms of r 12.11, an analysis of the provisions in which the expression 'giving of notice' was used indicated that it was not necessarily restricted to court proceedings. If rr 12.10 and 12.11 were restricted to service of documents in court proceedings, they would more naturally be included in that part of the 1986 Rules which dealt with court procedure and practice. However, it did not follow that r 12.12 applied to notices of meetings. Firstly, provision was made in the CPR for the permission of the court to be required for service of documents in court proceedings out of the jurisdiction. Secondly, the provisions of the Insolvency Act 1986 dealing with meetings required notice to be given to all creditors known to those convening the meeting. Those provisions clearly applied as much to foreign creditors as to domestic creditors. There would therefore be no point in applying to the court for leave to serve the notice, as the court could not refuse leave. Moreover, the terms of the 1985 Rules r 12.12 contemplated court proceedings. It followed that there was no requirement for an application to the court, or for the permission of the court, in order for notice of the meetings to be given to foreign creditors. Judgment would be given accordingly.

Re T&N Ltd [2006] EWHC 842 (Ch), [2006] 1 WLR 2831 (Chancery Division: David Richards J). *Re a Debtor (No 64 of 1992)* [1994] 2 All ER 177 (1993 Abr para 195); *Beverley Group plc v McClue* [1995] 2 BCLC 407 (1995 Abr para 541); and *Skipton Building Society v Collins* [1998] BPIR 267 followed.

562 Cross-border insolvency—proceedings

The Cross-Border Insolvency Regulations 2006, SI 2006/1030 (in force on 4 April 2006), (1) give effect to the United Nations Commission on International Trade Law Model Law on cross-border insolvency; (2) set out the procedural matters in relation to proceedings under the Model Law; (3) make provision in relation to notices delivered to the registrar of companies; and (4) contain forms prescribed for use in connection with proceedings.

563 Partnership insolvency—administration by court order

The Insolvent Partnerships (Amendment) Order 2006, SI 2006/622 (in force on 6 April 2006), further amends the 1994 Order, SI 1994/2421, so as to correct errors introduced by the 2005 Order, SI 2005/1516. The order also provides that the priority between agricultural floating charges for the purposes of the appointment of an administrator by the holder of a floating charge is to be determined in accordance with the provisions of the Agricultural Credits Act 1928, and amends the application of the Insolvency Act 1986 s 221, so as to ensure that the requirement to set aside a prescribed part does not apply in the winding up of an insolvent partnership.

564 Winding-up—freezing order—application to pursue substantial claim if company wound up

See *Revenue and Customs Comrs v Egleton*, para 1706.

COMPULSORY ACQUISITION OF LAND

Halsbury's Laws of England (4th edn) vol 8(1) (2003 Reissue) paras 1–400

Articles

For articles relating to this title please refer to the Table of Articles at the beginning of the Abridgment.

565 Compensation—costs—conduct of parties

See *Blakes Estates Ltd v Government of Montserrat*, para 684.

566 Compulsory purchase order—clearance area—properties demolished following designation of clearance area—exclusion from order

See *Rowe v First Secretary of State; Burnley BC v First Secretary of State*, para 1475.

567 Home loss payments—displacement from dwelling—England

The Home Loss Payments (Prescribed Amounts) (England) Regulations 2006, SI 2006/1658 (in force on 1 September 2006), increase the amount of home loss payments payable under the Land Compensation Act 1973 s 30, with the effect that (1) where a person occupying a dwelling on the date of displacement has an owner's interest, the maximum amount payable increases from £38,000 to £40,000, and the minimum amount payable from £3,800 to £4,000; and (2) the amount payable, in relation to any other case, increases from £3,800 to £4,000. SI 2005/1635 is revoked.

568 Home loss payments—displacement from dwelling—Wales

The Home Loss Payments (Prescribed Amounts) (Wales) Regulations 2006, SI 2006/1789 (in force on 1 September 2006), replace the 2005 Regulations, SI 2005/1808, and increase the amount of home loss payments payable to a person displaced from a dwelling by compulsory purchase or in other specified circumstances so that (1) where a person occupying a dwelling on the date of displacement has an owner's interest the maximum payment is £40,000 and the minimum payment is £4,000; and (2) in all other cases the payment is £4,000.

COMPUTERS AND INFORMATION TECHNOLOGY

Articles

For articles relating to this title please refer to the Table of Articles at the beginning of the Abridgment.

569　Computers—computer hacked from foreign country—place where tort occurred

See *Ashton Investments Ltd v OJSC Russian Aluminium (RUSAL)*, para 2332.

570　Computers—computers removed in accordance with search order—objectionable images discovered—modification of privilege against self-incrimination

See *C v P (Secretary of State for the Home Office)*, para 578.

571　Electronic communications—transport security

See para 2878.

572　E-mail—disclosure of confidential information—sending information to personal e-mail account

See *Freshtime UK Ltd v Wayne*, para 585.

573　E-mail—interception—person with right to control communication system

See *R v Stanford*, para 862.

574　E-mail—unsigned e-mail—capability of constituting enforceable guarantee or agreement

See *J Pereira Fernandes SA v Metha*, para 1439.

575　Internet—download of images—indecent photographs of children

See *R (on the application of C) v Chief Constable of 'A' Police,* para 757.

576　Internet—download of images—indecent photographs of children—deleted images— person in possession—images on computer's hard drive

See *R v Porter*, para 861.

577　Internet—statements on website—communication via internet service provider— determination of libel

See *Bunt v Tilley*, para 1794.

CONFIDENCE AND DATA PROTECTION

Halsbury's Laws of England (4th edn) vol 8(1) (2003 Reissue) paras 401–617

Articles

For articles relating to this title please refer to the Table of Articles at the beginning of the Abridgment.

578　Confidence—breach—search order—privilege against self-incrimination—modification of privilege

A search order was made in an action in which the claimant claimed breach of confidence and copyright infringement. The respondent stated that he would rely on his privilege against self-incrimination in respect of any material which the search disclosed. During the search, a number of computers were removed and placed in the hands of an independent computer expert. In the course of documenting their contents, the expert uncovered highly objectionable images of children. He applied to the court for directions as to what he should do with the offending material. A question arose as to what materials the privilege against self-incrimination might extend. *Held*, the public's right under the European Convention on Human Rights arts 2, 3 and 8 to be protected from the effect of criminal activity, when balanced against the respondent's right to domestic privilege against self-incrimination, which would otherwise operate to prevent the court from directing that the offending material be passed to the police, required the court to modify the respondent's right so as to enable the material to be so transferred. The current anomaly between the scope of the privilege in civil proceedings and the scope of privilege in criminal proceedings would disappear, putting to an end what appeared to be an irrational difference between the scope of domestic and European privilege against self-incrimination and removing or reducing the anomalies in the application of domestic privilege against self-incrimination presently imposed on disclosure in civil proceedings. The potential offence revealed by the offending material was serious enough having regard to the inhuman treatment of children which its production had to have involved. Further, it was strongly arguable that the present case was an exceptional case which fell within the partial exception to the rule that it was by the decisions of national courts that the domestic standard had initially to be set, and to those decisions that the ordinary rules of precedent should apply. The case was one where the court could modify the application of domestic privilege against self-incrimination so as to exclude from its ambit material constituting free standing evidence which was not created by the respondent to the search order under compulsion. Accordingly, the court would direct delivery of the offending material to the police, staying the order pending an appeal.

C plc v P (*Secretary of State for the Home Office*) [2006] EWHC 1226 (Ch), [2006] Ch 549 (Chancery Division: Evans-Lombe J). *Kay v Lambeth LBC; Leeds City Council v Price* [2006] UKHL 10, [2006] 2 WLR 570 (para 1539) applied.

579   Confidential information—disclosure—identification of social workers—consequential identification of children

See *British Broadcasting Corpn v Rochdale MBC*, para 484.

580   Confidential information—disclosure—journalist—source of information

An article published in a newspaper concerned a patient within the claimant trust's care. The claimant's action against the newspaper succeeded and a disclosure order was obtained against the publisher. As a result of the order, the defendant, an investigative journalist, was identified as an intermediary source who had supplied the information contained in the article. The claimant brought proceedings against the defendant for an order to disclose the source of the information which he had obtained about the patient. Although the patient appeared to have supported the claimant's action against the newspaper, the patient had informed his solicitors that he was now willing to give evidence against the claimant. The patient purported to give the defendant permission to use any of the documents held by the patient's solicitors. *Held*, it had not been established that there was a pressing social need that the source should be identified. An order for disclosure of the defendant's source would not be proportionate to the pursuit of the claimant's legitimate aim to seek redress against the source, given the vital public interest in the protection of a journalist's source. Even within such a sensitive category of information such as medical records, there was a range of sensitivity. Although the information disclosed was plainly private or confidential, it was not information that could be described as intimate or highly sensitive. Regardless of whether the source had been employed by the claimant, if the source was a person who had had access to the records when he had been permitted to be in the hospital for any reason, it was plain that he would have obtained the information subject to obligations owed by him, both to the patient and to the hospital, not to use or to disclose the information without authorisation or otherwise than for any purposes for which he had been permitted to have access to them. It was not an essential part of the claimant's case that it should establish that there had been a breach of duty to the patient. It was quite possible that the patient had encouraged or authorised the leak of information and, as between the source and the patient, the source had done no wrong to the patient. In the circumstances of the case, there had been no public interest justification for the disclosure which was in fact made by the source. Furthermore, the defendant had a good record of fulfilling the role of the press in a free society. He was a responsible journalist whose purpose had been to act in the public interest and it was in the public interest that his sources should not be deterred from communicating with him. Judgment would be given accordingly.

Ackroyd v Mersey Care NHS Trust (No 2) [2006] EWHC 107 (QB), (2006) 88 BMLR 1 (Queen's Bench Division: Tugendhat J). *Norwich Pharmacal Co v Customs and Excise Comrs* [1974] AC 133, HL; and *Ashworth Hospital Authority v MGN Ltd* 2002] UKHL 29, [2002] 4 All ER 193 (2002 Abr para 587) considered.

581   Confidential information—disclosure—public interest defence

See *Harrods Ltd v Times Newspapers Ltd*, para 2293.

582   Confidential information—disclosure—sensitive personal data—adulterous relationship

The claimant conducted an adulterous relationship for some months with the defendant's wife. The defendant then made it clear that he wished to reveal information about the relationship to the world at large, partly out of revenge and partly to make money for himself by selling the story to the media. The claimant issued proceedings to prevent the defendant from telling anyone about the relationship on the basis that any such communication would be a breach of confidence. The defendant contended that a party to an adulterous relationship could never, as a matter of law, obtain injunctive relief against the wronged party preventing the latter from disclosing the relationship. Issues were also raised as to the parties' competing rights to privacy and freedom of expression under the European Convention on Human Rights arts 8, 10. *Held*, there could be no rule of generality that an adulterer could never obtain an injunction to restrain the publication of matters relating to his adulterous relationship, and even an adulterous relationship might attract a legitimate expectation of privacy. There was also no rule which automatically exempted a 'wronged' husband from restraint of publication, although, in any given situation, there might be particular respects in which his right to free speech should be afforded greater priority. While the defendant's art 10 rights were clearly engaged, the same was true of the claimant's art 8 rights, which had become engaged on the defendant's threat to publish to the world at large the fact of the claimant's sexual relationship and its conduct. The wife's art 8 rights also had to be taken into account and an appropriate balance between the competing rights struck. Therefore, the injunction would be granted. Accordingly, the application would be allowed.

CC v AB [2006] EWHC 3083 (QB), [2006] All ER (D) 39 (Dec) (Queen's Bench Division: Eady J). *Campbell v MGN Ltd* [2004] UKHL 22, [2004] 2 All ER 995 (2004 Abr para 536) considered.

583 Confidential information—disclosure—sensitive personal data—public interest

A newspaper published by the defendant printed substantial extracts from a handwritten journal kept by the claimant which related to his visit to Hong Kong during the period in which it was being handed over to the Republic of China. The journal contained his views and impressions of the visit, and had come into the possession of the defendant after being handed to an intermediary by one of the claimant's employees, in breach of her contract of employment. The claimant commenced an action against the defendant for breach of confidence and infringement of copyright. He applied for summary judgment under CPR 24 in relation to that part of the claim which concerned the publication of the journal. The judge granted summary judgment, and on the defendant's appeal, an issue arose as to whether the principles permitting publication of information disclosed in breach of an obligation of confidence needed to be revised in order to give full effect to the right to freedom of expression under the European Convention on Human Rights art 10. *Held*, the test to be applied when considering whether it was necessary to restrict freedom of expression in order to prevent disclosure of information received in confidence was not simply whether the information was a matter of public interest but whether, in all the circumstances, it was in the public interest that the duty of confidence should be breached. The court would need to consider whether, having regard to the nature of the information and all the relevant circumstances, it was legitimate for the owner of the information to seek to keep it confidential or whether it was in the public interest that the information should be made public. The information in the journal had been disclosed to the newspaper by a person employed in the claimant's private office in circumstances and under a contract that placed her under a duty to keep the contents of the journal confidential. Moreover, in the instant case, the significance of the interference with the claimant's art 8 rights effected by the newspaper's publication of information in the journal outweighed the significance of the interference with the newspaper's art 10 rights that would have been involved had the newspaper been prevented from publishing the information. Thus, even if the fact that the information published had been revealed by the employee in breach of confidence were ignored, the judge had been correct to hold that the claimant had an unanswerable claim for breach of privacy. When the breach of a confidential relationship was added to the balance, his case was overwhelming. Accordingly, the appeal would be dismissed.

HRH Prince of Wales v Associated Newspapers Ltd [2006] All ER (D) 335 (Dec) (Court of Appeal: Lord Phillips of Worth Matravers CJ, Sir Anthony Clarke MR and May LJ). Decision of Blackburne J [2006] EWHC 522 (Ch), [2006] IP&T 648 affirmed.

584 Confidential information—disclosure—sensitive personal data—public interest—balance between right to privacy and freedom of expression

The claimant was an international folk musician. The first defendant wrote a book about the claimant's personal and sexual relationships. The claimant brought proceedings seeking to prevent the publication of certain material. The judge agreed and prohibited further publication of a significant part of the work complained of. The defendants appealed. The defendants objected to the judge's approach in carrying out a balancing exercise between the claimant's right to privacy under the European Convention of Human Rights art 8 and the defendants' right to freedom of information under art 10. The first defendant also submitted that information which she had stated to be true, but was later found to be untrue would provide her with a complete defence to the claim of breach of confidence. *Held*, the judge had not erred in carrying out the balancing exercise between the claimant's right to privacy and the defendants' right to freedom of information under the Convention. The information complained of was private, and therefore protected by art 8. The judge had also correctly found that the untrue information would not provide the first defendant with a complete defence to the claim of breach of confidence, as the matter complained of attracted the law of breach of confidence and although the information was untrue, the claimant could not be deprived of her right to privacy under the Convention. Accordingly, the appeal would be dismissed.

McKennitt v Ash [2006] EWCA Civ 1714, [2007] EMLR 113 (Court of Appeal: Buxton, Latham and Longmore LJJ). *A v B plc* [2002] EWCA Civ 337, [2003] QB 195 (2002 Abr para 585);

Application 59320/00 *Von Hannover v Germany* (2004) 16 BHRC 545, ECHR (2004 Abr para 1559); and *Campbell v MGN Ltd* [2004] UKHL 22, [2004] 2 AC 457 (2004 Abr para 536), considered. Decision of Eady J [2005] EWHC 3003 (QB), [2006] IP&T 605 affirmed.

585 Confidential information—former employee—breach of confidence—injunction to restrain

The defendant's terms of employment included provisions precluding her from divulging information about the business, products, employees or other affairs to third parties. She subsequently obtained employment with one of the claimant company's competitors. The claimant discovered that the defendant had sent three work-related e-mails to her personal e-mail account. The claimant took the view that that information was confidential and confronted the defendant with the discovery. The defendant claimed that she had sent the e-mails in error and offered to let the claimant view her personal e-mails. The claimant wrote to the defendant, alleging a fundamental implied or express breach of contract and requesting the delivery up of all the claimant's materials in her possession. It further alleged that it had a good claim for breach of confidence. The defendant stated that the e-mails had not been sent to anyone else and that once the error had been discovered, she had never opened them. Although the claimant did not reply to that letter, three days later it issued proceedings against the defendant, accompanied by a request for an interim injunction, alleging that by sending the e-mails to her personal account she had used confidential information in breach of her contractual terms and had failed, as required by that contract, to immediately deliver up the materials in question. *Held*, confidential information contained in an e-mail that remained unopened could not be said to have been used. Although the defendant had not delivered up the required materials immediately, she had previously offered to deliver them up and to delete them. The information complained of was utterly innocuous and the claimant's reaction had been wholly disproportionate. Accordingly, the claim would be dismissed.

Freshtime UK Ltd v Wayne [2006] All ER (D) 255 (Oct) (Chancery Division: Levenson J).

586 Confidential information—information held by local authority—medical records—duty to inform adoptive parents that foster parent HIV positive

A local authority obtained an interim care order in respect of a child, placed her with foster parents and proposed that she should live with her father, his partner and her child. The authority learned that one of the foster parents was HIV positive and sought the court's permission to disclose this to the father and his partner. Medical evidence indicated that the risk of HIV transmission to the child was negligible. *Held*, in general there was an obligation on a local authority to share relevant information relating to a child in its care with the parents, including the state of the child's health and his exposure to serious infectious diseases. However, the interests of the parents had to be balanced against the right of the foster carer to respect for his private life. Where the risk was negligible and disclosure was opposed, disclosure of confidential details about the foster carer's health would breach the authority's duty of confidentiality to him. As the medical evidence showed that the risk was negligible, the authority should not disclose the fact of the foster carer's HIV infection. Accordingly, the application would be refused.

Brent LBC v N (Foster Carers) [2005] EWHC 1676 (Fam), [2006] 1 FLR 310 (Family Division: Sumner J).

587 Data protection—expose security breach failings—hacking into computer system—action done to confirm belief—failure to comply with legal obligation

See *Evans v Bolton School*, para 1269.

588 Data protection—information—processing of information—professional body—information about member—review—fairness

The claimant was a consultant orthopaedic surgeon and a member of the defendant Medical Defence Union. His membership was terminated as a result of a resolution by the defendant not to renew his membership on the expiry of his then current annual subscription. As a result, his professional indemnity cover automatically terminated. The claimant was given no warning of possible termination of his membership and was not, nor had he ever been, the subject of a claim for alleged professional negligence. He sought reasons for the resolution but none were provided. He alleged that the defendant had unfairly processed his personal data and commenced proceedings for damages, pursuant to the Data Protection Act 1998 s 13. It fell to be determined whether the risk review conducted by the defendant involved processing of the claimant's personal data and, if so, whether the processing was unfair. *Held*, the fairness of the processing of a member's personal data had to be considered in the context of the contractual relationship between the defendant organisation and its members. The defendant was entitled first to determine its policy and, having done so, to ensure that any processing of members' data in line with that policy was carried out fairly. It followed that it was not open to the court to hold that the defendant's risk assessment policy was unfair. In respect of the actual information which was held by the defendant on file, unfair processing, in the form of misstatement of information, was found in relation to only two of the 17 files which the defendant held. However, those files had played an immaterial part in the making of the committee's ultimate decision to terminate the claimant's membership of the defendant. Accordingly, the action would be dismissed.

Johnson v Medical Defence Union Ltd [2006] EWHC 321 (Ch), (2006) 89 BMLR 43 (Chancery Division: Rimer J).

589   Data protection—personal data—disclosure—passenger name record of air passengers

The European Commission adopted EC Decision 2004/535 on the adequate protection of personal data contained in the passenger name record of air passengers transferred to the United States Bureau of Customs and Border Protection, and the European Council adopted EC Decision 2004/496 on the conclusion of an agreement between the European Community and the United States of America on the processing and transfer of passenger name record data by air carriers to the United States of America. The European Parliament sought the annulment of that agreement as well as the decision on adequacy. The European Parliament contended that the adoption of the decision was ultra vires on the ground that the provisions laid down in EC Directive 95/46 on the protection of individuals with regard to the processing of personal data and on the free movement of such data had not been complied with. In particular, art 3(2) first indent, relating to the exclusion of activities which fell outside the scope of Community law, had been infringed. It also contended that EC Treaty art 95 was an incorrect legal basis for the agreement. *Held*, the decision on adequacy concerned processing of personal data as referred to in Directive 95/46 art 3(2). Therefore, it did not fall within the scope of Directive 95/46. The agreement related to the same transfer of data as the decision on adequacy and therefore to data processing operations which were excluded from the scope of Directive 95/46. Consequently, the agreement could not have been validly adopted on the basis of EC Treaty art 95. It followed that Directive 95/46 had been infringed and the agreement had to be annulled. Judgment would be given accordingly.

Joined Cases C-317/04 and C-318/04 *European Parliament v European Council* [2007] All ER (EC) 278 (ECJ: Full Court).

590   Data protection—sensitive personal data—processing

The Data Protection (Processing of Sensitive Personal Data) Order 2006, SI 2006/2068 (in force on 26 July 2006), specifies, pursuant to the Data Protection Act 1998 Sch 3 para 10, the circumstances in which the processing of sensitive personal data may be carried out if it falls outside the scope of the prohibition on the processing of such material enshrined in the first data protection principle in Sch 1 para 1. In particular, the order specifies that information about a criminal conviction or caution may be processed for the purpose of administering an account relating to a payment card, or for cancelling a payment card, used in the commission of one of the listed offences relating to indecent images of children and for which the data subject has been convicted or cautioned under the relevant legislation.

591   Interception of communications

See CRIMINAL LAW.

CONFLICT OF LAWS

Halsbury's Laws of England (4th edn) vol 8(3) (Reissue) paras 1–509

Articles

For articles relating to this title please refer to the Table of Articles at the beginning of the Abridgment.

592   Applicable law—reinsurance contract—nature of contract

The claimants entered into a contract of reinsurance with the defendant in respect of an excess liability policy, which was stated to be subject to United States law. Provision was made for the contract of reinsurance to be interpreted and governed by English law. Following a number of claims under the policy in respect of which the claimants refused to indemnify the defendant, a dispute arose and the parties commenced arbitration. A preliminary issue arose as to the law applicable to the claims. The arbitrators held that, since the terms of the policy had been incorporated into the contract of reinsurance, the extent of the claimants' obligations was to be construed as having the same meaning as in the policy, and United States law therefore governed the contract of reinsurance. The claimants appealed. *Held*, reinsurance was prima facie a contract of indemnity, under which the reinsurer indemnified the reinsured against a specified amount of the risk which the reinsured had insured. It was incorrect to equate it with liability insurance. It was an independent contract between the reinsured and the reinsurer in which the subject matter of the insurance was the risk insured. The contract of reinsurance was to be interpreted in accordance with English law, as specifically provided for in the contract. Accordingly, the appeal would be allowed.

CGU International Insurance plc v AstraZeneca Insurance Co Ltd [2005] EWHC 2755 (Comm), [2006] Lloyd's Rep IR 409 (Queen's Bench Division: Cresswell J). *Forsikringsaktieselskapet Vesta v Butcher* [1989] AC 852, HL (1989 Abr para 286); *Charter Reinsurance Co Ltd v Fagan* [1997] AC 313, HL (1996 Abr para 1777); and *Toomey v Eagle Star Reinsurance Co Ltd* [1994] 1 Lloyd's Rep 516, CA, applied.

593 Applicable law—tort—assessment of damages—substantive or procedural issue

The claimant, who was English, was left severely disabled as a result of an accident in a vehicle being driven by the defendant, an Australian national. The accident occurred in New South Wales, but proceedings were initiated against the defendant in England, where the parties had been living together in a settled relationship. The defendant conceded liability, and a preliminary issue arose as to whether English or New South Wales law applied to the assessment of damages. The judge held that the general rule under the Private International Law (Miscellaneous Provisions) Act 1995 s 11, by virtue of which the applicable law was that of the country where the injury giving rise to the claim occurred, was displaced as, pursuant to s 12, in all the circumstances of the case it was substantially more appropriate for English law to apply. On the defendant's appeal, an issue arose whether, under s 14, the relevant New South Wales law provisions were substantive or procedural for the purposes of English law. Section 14 specified that the application of the law of a country outside the forum as the applicable law for determining issues arising in any claim was not authorised in so far as it would affect any rules of evidence, pleading or practice or would authorise questions of procedure in any proceedings to be determined otherwise than in accordance with the law of the forum. The court decided that the matter was substantive, and the claimant appealed. *Held*, the phrase 'questions of procedure' in s 14(3)(b) included the assessment of damages and therefore the quantification of damages was to be determined in accordance with English law. Section 14(3) was expressed to be without prejudice to the generality of s 14(2), which said that nothing in Pt III (ss 9–15) was to affect any rules of law except those abolished by s 10. Section 10 was concerned with the rules which determined whether a tort was actionable, and not with the rules concerning the remedies available for actionable injury. Moreover, Parliament had simply provided that the law chosen in accordance with ss 11 and 12 was to be used to determine certain issues while the law of the forum was to continue to be used to determine others. The matters in respect of which the United Kingdom courts were to continue to use the law of the forum were spelt out in s 14(3). Furthermore, Parliament meant the expression 'questions of procedure' to be understood in the way that it would be understood in the field of private international law because it was being used in a statute on private international law. By the time Parliament legislated in 1995, it was generally understood that, for the purposes of private international law, questions relating to quantification of damages for actionable heads of claim related to remedy and so were classified as procedural. Moreover, the provisions of the relevant New South Wales legislation were, for the purposes of private international law, prima facie procedural in nature. That being so, they fell to be ignored when the English court awarded damages for the claimant's injuries. Accordingly, the appeal would be allowed.

Harding v Wealands [2006] UKHL 32, [2006] 4 All ER 1 (House of Lords: Lords Bingham of Cornhill, Woolf, Hoffmann, Rodger of Earlsferry and Carswell). *Roerig v Valiant Trawlers Ltd* [2002] EWCA Civ 21, [2002] 1 All ER 961 (2002 Abr para 606); and *Stevens v Head* (1993) 112 ALR 7 considered. Decision of Court of Appeal [2004] EWCA Civ 1735, [2005] 1 All ER 415 (2004 Abr para 551) reversed.

594 Applicable law—tort—tort committed abroad—displacement of general rule

The claimant, a Dutch company, sold a cargo of oil to a Korean company. When the cargo arrived in South Korea it was discharged without production of the bills of lading and released to the Korean company. The defendant, a Korean bank, was the issuing bank of a letter of credit in favour of the claimant. The claimant received payment under the letter of credit through a bank in London. When the Korean company became insolvent and failed to reimburse the defendant for the price of the cargo financed by the letter of credit, the defendant brought proceedings in Korea against the claimant. The defendant alleged that the claimant had breached obligations owed to the defendant and was liable under the Korean civil code. Meanwhile the claimant commenced proceedings in England seeking a declaration of non-liability and an anti-suit injunction to prevent the defendant from continuing the Korean proceedings. It was held that England was the appropriate forum to decide the claimant's English proceedings and the defendant's claim in Korea because the letter of credit was governed by English law. However, it was also held that the claimant's application for an anti-suit injunction fell short of the standard required for the grant of such an injunction. The defendant argued that its claims in Korea were tortious and the choice of English law in the letter of credit did not compel English law to govern the claim for the purposes of the Private International Law (Miscellaneous Provisions) Act 1995 s 12. *Held*, s 12(1) invited the court to make a comparison of the significance of the factors that connected a tort with the country whose law would be the applicable law under the general rule. Section 12(2) provided that the court could take into account factors relating to the parties as factors that might connect the tort with another country. The phrase 'factors relating to the parties' could include the fact of a pre-existing relationship between the parties, whether contractual or otherwise. It would also include the law that the parties had chosen for that pre-existing relationship. The governing law of a contract was a 'factor' for consideration under s 12. The claims brought by the defendant were brought in tort. However, the governing law, on the facts, was English law, and thus in principle the claimant was entitled to a declaration of non-liability in the English action. Judgment would be given accordingly.

Trafigura Beheer BV v Kookmin Bank Co [2006] EWHC 1450 (Comm), [2006] 2 All ER (Comm) 1008 (Queen's Bench Division: Aikens J).

595   Domicile—change of domicile—proof

A husband and wife had been married for over 20 years. They had moved from England to France ten years earlier, and had sold all their properties in England. They had eight children, all of whom were educated in French schools. The husband's only income was derived from one day of work a fortnight in England, and both the husband and the wife remained domiciled in England for tax purposes. The wife kept many connections with England, including her driving licence, her passport and sole nationality, her bank accounts and credit cards and vehicle licence plates. The husband filed for divorce in England, and the wife sought to stay the petition on the basis that she was domiciled in France. *Held*, the standard of proof required to establish loss of domicile was a heavy one which went beyond the mere balance of probabilities. Apart from her residence, the wife had demonstrated very little from which a real connection with France could be inferred. It had not been proved, even on a balance of probabilities, that she had formed a fixed and settled intention to abandon her English domicile of origin and settle permanently in France. Accordingly, the application would be dismissed.

R v R (Divorce: Jurisdiction: Domicile) [2006] 1 FLR 389 (Family Division: Philip Sapsford QC). *Henderson v Henderson* [1967] P 77 applied.

596   Foreign judgment—enforcement—recognition—submission to foreign court

Turkish forces had previously invaded the Republic of Cyprus and occupied the north of the island. The Turkish Republic of North Cyprus ('TRNC') was declared, but was not recognised by any country save Turkey. During negotiations for the accession of Cyprus to the European Union it was hoped that a settlement could be reached between the Greek and Turkish communities so that the whole island could be brought within the European Union. That had not occurred by the time of the signing of the Treaty of Accession. In those circumstances, the European Council reached a decision, given effect by the Treaty of Accession Protocol 10, to suspend the application of European Union legislation in those areas controlled by the TRNC. The respondent, a Greek Cypriot, had owned land in the area which subsequently came under the TRNC's control but had fled the Turkish invasion. The appellant, a British citizen, purchased land in the area controlled by the TRNC to which the respondent held title. The respondent issued proceedings in Nicosia for an order that the appellant deliver up the land to him and pay damages for trespass. Judgment was entered in default, and a judgment subsequently given refusing to set aside the earlier decision. Both judgments were registered in, and declared enforceable by, the High Court pursuant to EC Council Regulation 44/2001. The appellant appealed against those registrations. The issues to be decided included whether Regulation 44/2001 had effect in relation to the area controlled by the TRNC. *Held*, the effect of the Treaty of Accession Protocol 10 was that the Regulation 44/2001 was of no effect in relation to matters which related to the area controlled by the TRNC. Just as the respondent could not rely on the European Union legislation against his own government in relation to human rights arising from matters relating to the area controlled by the TRNC, he could not use it against the appellant to enforce the judgment against him. That was the answer which avoided the conflict which would otherwise arise in cases concerning the situation in northern Cyprus, and the enforcement of judgments such as that in the present case against new owners of Greek Cypriot property who had assets elsewhere in the European Union. It followed that the respondent could not enforce in the English court the judgments which he had obtained in the Cypriot court. Accordingly, the appeal would be allowed.

Orams v Apostolides [2006] EWHC 2226 (QB), [2006] All ER (D) 20 (Sep) (Queen's Bench Division: Jack J).

597   Jurisdiction—Convention jurisdiction—choice of court agreement—acceptance of jurisdiction by third party

The claimant owned a vessel which it chartered to an American company. The charterers agreed by the terms of the charterparty not to allow a lien or incumbrance over the vessel and undertook that, during the charter period, they would not procure any supplies on the credit of the owners. During the charter period, the charterers ordered bunkers from the defendant, a Danish company. The agreement for the sale of the bunkers contained an English jurisdiction clause. A sales notice provided for the bunkers to be for the account of the charterers, and the defendant billed the charterers for payment. However, as the charterers had gone into bankruptcy, the defendant sought to recover the debt from the claimant. The claimant started proceedings in the English courts seeking negative declaratory relief that it had no liability to the defendant. The defendant challenged the jurisdiction of the English court, arguing that, as the claimant was not a party to the agreement, then, pursuant to the Brussels Convention on Jurisdiction and the Enforcement of Judgments in Civil and Commercial Matters 1968 art 17, the English jurisdiction clause did not apply to it. The claimant contended that art 17 applied where a person who was not party to the contract with the choice of jurisdiction clause in it, and had not succeeded to the rights, had otherwise accepted the jurisdiction clause in question. *Held*, agreement to a jurisdiction clause had to be clearly and precisely demonstrated not just by looking at the words of the contract but at all the circumstances. It might be possible for an acceptance to be demonstrated by the issue of proceedings in the chosen jurisdiction, but the claimant could not be said to have accepted, let alone accepted clearly and precisely, the jurisdiction clause when the purpose of the proceedings was to deny that it was bound by the contract which contained the clause. Before a jurisdiction clause could be accepted within the meaning of art 17, there had to have been some kind of offer capable of being accepted. All that was on offer in the present case was acceptance of the contract as a whole, or nothing. In the circumstances, the claimant had not accepted that it was bound by the clause and it was very doubtful whether it was open to it to accept the clause without accepting everything else, including the obligation to pay. It followed that the court did not have jurisdiction to hear the claimant's case. Judgment would be given accordingly.

Andromeda Marine SA v OW Bunker & Trading A/S [2006] EWHC 777 (Comm), [2006] 2 All ER (Comm) 331 (Queen's Bench Division: Morison J).

598   Jurisdiction—Convention jurisdiction—matters relating to contract—place of delivery and performance

EC Council Regulation 44/2001 art 5(1)(a) provides that a person domiciled in a member state may be sued in another member state in matters relating to a contract in the courts for the place of performance. The place of performance is, in the case of the sale of goods, the place in a member state where, under the contract, the goods were delivered or should have been delivered: art 5(1)(b).

The claimant agreed to sell and the defendant agreed to buy a quantity of cider, which was shipped from England to Cyprus. The contract of sale was governed by English law and stated that shipment would be from Liverpool and delivery cfr Limassol. The sellers subsequently issued proceedings in England for the price of the cider. The buyers disputed the jurisdiction of the English courts on the ground that the contract expressly provided for delivery in Cyprus and that, for the purposes of EC Council Regulation 44/2001 art 5, Cyprus was the place of performance. The judge held that the English court had jurisdiction and the buyers appealed. *Held*, in accordance with the well-known rules in relation to c & f (or cfr) and cif contracts, possession would prima facie be transferred to the buyers on shipment on terms that the sellers would procure for the buyers a contract to carry the goods to the specified destination. There was no question of the title being retained until payment, or transfer of documents. Risk, title and possession had all been intended to pass on shipment at latest. Article 5(1)(b) was an example of the selection of the place of performance of the obligation in question as constituting that close connecting factor which justified an alternative jurisdiction in that place. Therefore, the place where, under the contract, the goods were delivered ought to reflect a matter of obligatory performance under the contract. In a c & f or cif contract, unlike an ex ship contract, the seller had no obligation to deliver to the ultimate destination, only to procure the shipment of goods for carriage to destination. Thus the place of delivery was not the place of physical delivery to the buyer at destination. Accordingly, the appeal would be dismissed.

Scottish and Newcastle International Ltd v Othon Ghalanos Ltd [2006] EWCA Civ 1750, [2006] All ER (D) 324 (Dec) (Court of Appeal: Waller and Rix LJJ).

599   Jurisdiction—Convention jurisdiction—proceedings commenced in different contracting states—court first seised—use of domestic rule to correct error in service

See *Phillips v Nussberger*, para 2284.

600   Jurisdiction—Convention jurisdiction—tenancies of immovable property—nuisance

The claimant brought proceedings in the Austrian court pursuant to the Austrian Civil Code seeking an order against the defendant, a Czech company, requiring the defendant to put an end to the influences on the claimant's land caused by ionising radiation emitted from a power plant situated in the Czech Republic. The defendant disputed the jurisdiction of the Austrian court arguing that the Brussels Convention on Jurisdiction and the Enforcement of Judgments in Civil and Commercial Matters 1968 art 16(1)(a) was not applicable to an action for prevention of a nuisance. Article 16(1)(a) provided that in proceedings which had as their object rights in rem in immovable property or tenancies of immovable property, the courts of the contracting state in which the property was situated would have jurisdiction. A preliminary ruling was sought from the European

Court of Justice as to whether art 16(1)(a) was applicable. *Held,* art 16(1)(a) was by way of derogation to the general principle that if a defendant was not domiciled in a contracting state, each contracting state was to apply its own rules of international jurisdiction. Further, the provisions of art 16 had the effect of depriving parties of the choice of forum which would otherwise be theirs. The reason for exclusive jurisdiction under art 16(1)(a) was that the courts of the contracting state where the property was situated were best placed to deal with matters relating to rights in rem in, and tenancies of, immovable property. The exclusive jurisdiction of the courts of the contracting state in which the property was situated did not encompass all actions concerning rights in rem in immovable property, but only those which both came within the scope of the Brussels Convention and were actions which sought to determine the ownership or possession of immovable property and to provide the holders of those rights with protection for the powers which attached to their interest. An action for cessation of a nuisance, such as that brought in the present proceedings, did not fall within that category of actions, since it did not have as its object rights in rem in immovable property. It followed that such an action did not fall within the provisions of art 16(1)(a).

Case C-343/04 *Land Oberösterreich v CEZ* [2006] 2 All ER (Comm) 665 (ECJ: First Chamber).

601   Jurisdiction—exclusive jurisdiction clause—existence—insurance policy

The first defendant, an insurance company domiciled in Mauritius, underwrote bankers' blanket insurance for the second defendant, a commercial bank incorporated in Mauritius, in the form of three policies, each of which it reinsured in full back to back in the London market. The excess policies provided for increased cover for infidelity and premises and transit respectively. Each of those policies was expressly subject to Mauritius law and jurisdiction. The excess premises and transit policy was also reinsured by the claimants and covered loss of or damage to high value contents held by banks and similar institutions (the excess reinsurance contract). The conditions set out in that policy referred to a jurisdiction clause, but it was common ground that there had been no further discussion about a jurisdiction clause. The second defendant subsequently commenced proceedings in Mauritius against various defendants for fraud and proceedings against the first defendant in respect of its claim for direct insurance. The claimants responded by avoiding the reinsurance policies for misrepresentation and non-disclosure on the basis that the losses claimed were not attributable to premises or transit risks. An issue arose as to whether England was the appropriate forum for the just resolution of those disputes. The defendant argued that the general words of incorporation of the primary policy embraced a jurisdiction clause incorporating the Mauritius jurisdiction clause. The judge decided that the first defendant had failed to establish that there was a good arguable case that there was a Mauritius jurisdiction clause in the excess reinsurance contract, which meant that English law was its proper law and England was the appropriate forum for the resolution of the disputes. The defendants appealed. *Held,* on the evidence, the most one could say was that the parties intended to agree a jurisdiction clause but in the event had never done so. It followed that the claimants had a good arguable case that the reinsurance had not been subject to a Mauritius jurisdiction clause, and that it had not been shown that there were any grounds for interfering with the judge's conclusion. Accordingly, the appeal would be dismissed.

Dornoch Ltd v Mauritius Union Assurance Co Ltd [2006] EWCA Civ 389, [2006] 2 All ER (Comm) 385 (Court of Appeal: Sir Mark Potter P, May and Tuckey LJJ).

602   Jurisdiction—exclusive jurisdiction clause—parallel proceedings in English and foreign court—power to stay proceedings

The claimant, a mining company incorporated in Zambia, was insured by insurers in Zambia on a direct basis. The claimant was also insured by the first defendant, a company incorporated in Bermuda, though whether the insurance was direct or by way of reinsurance of the Zambian insurers was disputed. Additionally, the first defendant's insurance was reinsured by a group of European underwriters ('the reinsurers'). An avalanche caused substantial damage to a mine owned by the claimant, and the claimant brought proceedings directed at recovering an indemnity for their loss under their insurance arrangements. The claimant's original claim was in the English court against the Zambian insurers and the first defendant. However, the claimant and the Zambian insurers agreed that their dispute would be heard in Zambia under Zambian law, leaving the claim against the first defendant outstanding. The first defendant then brought Pt 20 proceedings against the reinsurers. The reinsurers sought to have the proceedings stayed on the basis that a Zambian law and jurisdiction clause applied, while the first defendant sought to rely on an English law and jurisdiction clause in its global policy. The judge refused to stay the Pt 20 proceedings and the reinsurers appealed. *Held,* there was no basis for interfering with the exercise of the judge's discretion not to enforce a Zambian jurisdiction clause, even on the hypothesis that the reinsurers had established a much stronger argument in favour of the applicability of such a clause. The critical factor was that the claimant had established its claim in England as a claim in good standing, based on an alleged insurance contract containing an English law and jurisdiction clause. The potential bifurcation of the claimant's claims in two separate jurisdictions with its attendant dangers was a given. The problem for the English court was how best to overcome or minimise those dangers. In the circumstances, the judge had been entitled to conclude that England was the jurisdiction in which the parties might find a solution to their problem as a whole. Accordingly, the appeal would be dismissed.

Konkola Copper Mines plc v Coromin [2006] EWCA Civ 5, [2006] 1 All ER (Comm) 437 (Court of Appeal: Sir Anthony Clarke MR, Rix and Richards LJJ). Decision of Colman J (2005 Abr para 698) affirmed.

603   Jurisdiction—family proceedings—orders relating to children—wardship jurisdiction—habitual residence

The parents of a child were originally from Kurdistan. The father had been given indefinite leave to remain in the United Kingdom. The mother gave birth to the child in the United Kingdom and, when the child was 19 months old, the father took the family to Kurdistan where the parents divorced. The mother signed an agreement granting custody of the child to the father. This was approved by the Kurdistan court. The mother saw the child once a week for a year before the father told her that she could no longer do so. The mother returned to the United Kingdom and issued wardship proceedings in respect of the child. It fell to be determined whether the child was habitually resident in the United Kingdom. *Held*, the question of habitual residence of a child was not always determinable by reference to the combined intention of the parties. It ultimately depended on whether, in all circumstances, it could properly and realistically be said that the child was habitually resident in England and Wales. It was impossible to hold that, at the commencement of proceedings, the child was habitually resident in the jurisdiction. There had been a common parental intention in that the state of intention on the part of the father that the child remain in Kurdistan had been accepted by the mother. This situation prevailed until the mother returned to the United Kingdom and commenced proceedings. The legal focus in such cases was on the factual situation, and here the child remained in Kurdistan in the custody of his father. It was not the function of the court to make declarations of unlawful detention abroad based on the nationality or domicile of the child concerned, or on the removal or retention of a child from the custody of a carer who was within the jurisdiction. Accordingly, the application would be dismissed.

Re A (A Child) (Wardship: Habitual Residence) [2006] EWHC 3338 (Fam), [2007] 1 FCR 390 (Family Division: Sir Mark Potter P). *Al-Habtoor v Fotheringham* [2001] EWCA Civ 186, [2001] 1 FCR 385 (2001 Abr para 613) applied.

604   Jurisdiction—family proceedings—parental responsibility—deemed acceptance of jurisdiction

EC Council Regulation 2201/2003 art 12(1) provides that the courts of a member state exercising jurisdiction on an application for divorce have jurisdiction in any matter relating to parental responsibility connected with that application where (1) at least one of the spouses has parental responsibility in relation to the child; (2) the jurisdiction of the courts has been accepted expressly or otherwise in an unequivocal manner by the spouses and by the holders of parental responsibility at the time the court is seised; and (3) acceptance of jurisdiction is in the superior interests of the child.

The parents of two children separated and a dispute over contact ensued. The mother, who alleged that the father had sexually abused the children, obtained permission from a county court to relocate permanently to Spain with the children. The order made provision for contact with the father and directed the mother to return to the jurisdiction if so ordered. After moving to Spain, the mother lodged a petition for divorce and obtained a decree absolute. The dispute over contact and allegations of sexual abuse continued. The father made applications for further consideration by the court, and a hearing in respect of the applications was fixed in the county court. The mother then obtained a without notice order by way of injunction from a Spanish court. She contacted the county court by fax, informing it of the Spanish order and declining to attend the final county court hearing. The father sought a declaration that the English courts had jurisdiction, a request to the Spanish court to decline jurisdiction, and an order remitting the case to the county court. The mother sought a declaration that the Spanish courts had jurisdiction and contended that the English courts should stay the proceedings in respect of parental responsibility. It fell to be determined whether, pursuant to Regulation 2201/2003, jurisdiction should be exercised by the courts of England or Spain. It was accepted that under art 8, the Spanish court would ordinarily exercise jurisdiction over the children unless the English court had jurisdiction by virtue of art 12. *Held*, if a party succeeded in establishing all three limbs of art 12(1), the court had to accept jurisdiction; otherwise, art 8 prevailed and the court had to decline jurisdiction. What was required was essentially not a discretionary exercise, save in relation to the children's superior interests, but a fact-finding exercise as to whether the mother by her conduct had accepted the jurisdiction of the English court in an unequivocal manner. The court had to take an objective approach, and consider what inference was to be drawn from the mother's conduct. The evidence demonstrated an unequivocal participation in the proceedings and thus an acceptance of the jurisdiction. It was then for the father to satisfy the superior interests test, but only on the balance of interests, and he had succeeded in so doing. The English court should exercise jurisdiction in relation to the father's applications for residence and contact and the Spanish court would be invited to decline jurisdiction. Judgment would be given accordingly.

C v C [2006] EWHC 3247 (Fam), [2006] All ER (D) 278 (Dec) (Family Division: Hedley J).

605   Jurisdiction—insolvency proceedings—reorganisation plan—order—nature of order

The appellant owned an insolvent shipping business, which was part of a group of companies that included various Isle of Man companies. A court in New York ordered a reorganisation plan to take effect in relation to the group, with the order recording the intention of the court to send a letter of request to the High Court of Justice of the Isle of Man asking for assistance in giving effect to the plan. The respondent, the creditors' committee, applied to the English court for an order vesting the shares in its representative. The appellant cross-claimed, asking the court not to recognise or enforce the terms of the plan on the ground that it had never submitted to the jurisdiction of the New York court and that an order of that court could, therefore, not affect its rights of property in shares in the Isle of Man. The appellant's claim was accepted, but the appellate court reversed that decision, deciding that the New York order was a judgment in personam with the effect that the business had submitted to the jurisdiction of the New York court. On the appellant's appeal, *held*, bankruptcy proceedings did not fall into either the category of judgments in rem or in personam. Judgments in rem and in personam were judicial determinations of the existence of rights. The purpose of bankruptcy proceedings, on the other hand, was not to determine or establish the existence of rights, but to provide a mechanism of collective execution against the property of the debtor by creditors whose rights were admitted or established. There should be a single bankruptcy in which all creditors were entitled and required to prove and no one should have an advantage because he happened to live in a jurisdiction where more of the assets or fewer of the creditors were situated. Although the underdeveloped state of the common law meant that unifying principles which applied to both personal and corporate insolvency had not been fully worked out, the underlying principle of universality was of equal application and in corporate insolvency was given effect by recognising the person who was empowered under the foreign bankruptcy law to act on behalf of the insolvent company as entitled to do so in England. The application of those principles was sufficient to confer on the Manx court jurisdiction to assist the creditors' committee to give effect to the plan. As there was no suggestion of prejudice to any creditor in the Isle of Man or local law which might be infringed, there could be no discretionary reason for withholding such assistance. The appellate court was right to order implementation of the plan. Accordingly, the appeal would be dismissed.

Cambridge Gas Transport Corp v Official Committee of Unsecured Creditors of Navigator Holdings plc [2006] UKPC 26, [2006] 3 All ER 830 (Privy Council: Lords Bingham of Cornhill, Hoffmann, Hutton, Rodger of Earlsferry and Carswell).

606   Jurisdiction—interim relief in support of foreign proceedings—freezing order

See *Dadourian Group International Inc v Simms*, para 1705.

607   Jurisdiction—related proceedings in different states—court first seised of proceedings—missing claim form

The claimant, the administrator of the estate of a third party, issued a claim form out of the High Court in London. The proceedings had their origin in a partnership between the third party and his partner that dealt in antiquities. The claim against the defendant, who resided in Switzerland, was for a declaration relating to a statue. A package was served on the defendant containing all the documents which the third party and the partner had intended to serve on the defendant, save the copy claim form. The claimant was unaware that the copy claim form was missing. Subsequently, the defendant instituted proceedings in Switzerland seeking declaratory relief which mirrored the relief sought in the English proceedings. The claimant applied for an order under CPR 6.9 to have the court's sanction for dispensing with service of the copy of the claim on the defendant, on the basis that that would enable those proceedings to obtain priority over the Swiss proceedings pursuant to the Lugano Convention on Jurisdiction and the Enforcement of Judgments in Civil and Commercial Matters 1988 art 21. The judge held that the High Court could entertain the English proceedings, despite the existence of the Swiss proceedings. The defendant appealed. *Held*, although the court would have granted the claimant relief under CPR 6.9 if it were a domestic case, it was not right to do so in a case where the sole purpose of the relief was to enable the inadequately served English proceedings to achieve priority, under the Lugano Convention art 21, over Swiss proceedings which had already obtained priority. The only reason for the judge's order dispensing with service of the copy claim form on the defendant under CPR 6.9 was to enable those proceedings to gain priority, under the Lugano Convention art 21, over the Swiss proceedings. Even if the order had been effective, it would have been inappropriate to make it for that reason. The Swiss proceedings had priority under art 21 and it was not possible for the court to invoke its discretionary jurisdiction under a domestic rule of procedure, such as CPR 6.9, to enable those proceedings to snatch back priority. Accordingly, the appeal would be allowed.

Phillips v Nussberger [2006] EWCA Civ 654, [2006] 3 All ER 838 (Court of Appeal: Pill, Neuberger and Wilson LJJ).

608   Jurisdiction—tort—damage sustained within the jurisdiction—determination of where damage sustained

CPR 6.20(8), which relates to service out of the jurisdiction, provides that a claim is made in tort where (a) damage was sustained within the jurisdiction; or (b) the damage sustained resulted from an act committed within the jurisdiction.

The claimants, a group of companies based in Bermuda, entered into a contract with the defendant, who was the president of a company based in the Seychelles, relating to the use of two satellite networks. The claimants had sent the draft agreement to their lawyers in London and decisions to enter into the contract were made there. The claimants made allegations of fraudulent misrepresentation and obtained permission to serve the defendant outside the jurisdiction pursuant to CPR 6.20(8)(a) and (b). The defendant sought an order setting aside the grant of permission to serve out of the jurisdiction on the basis that the claimants had not demonstrated a good arguable case that the claim fell within either CPR 6.20(8)(a) or (b). *Held*, the claimants had no good arguable case that substantial and efficacious acts committed within the jurisdiction by the defendant had given rise to the damages sustained. The only significant head of damage alleged to have been sustained within the jurisdiction was the claimants' liability towards the solicitors retained to prepare the draft agreement. The fact that a decision in regard to the engagement of the solicitors was made within the jurisdiction did not provide the necessary connecting factors and the court was not persuaded that any direct monetary damage was suffered within the jurisdiction. Accordingly, the application would be allowed.

Newsat Holdings Ltd v Zani [2006] EWHC 342 (Comm), [2006] 1 All ER (Comm) 607 (Queen's Bench Division: Steel J). *Domicrest Ltd v Swiss Bank Corpn* [1999] QB 548 (1998 Abr para 575); *Alfred Dunhill Ltd v Diffusion Internationale de Maroquinerie de Prestige SARL* [2002] 1 All ER (Comm) 950 (2002 Abr para 617); and *ABCI (formerly Arab Business Consortium International Finance and Investment Co) v Banque Franco-Tunisienne* [2003] EWCA Civ 205, [2003] 2 Lloyd's Rep 146 considered.

609   Jurisdiction—tort—defendant domiciled in another state—claim for negligent misstatement

The defendant Portuguese company issued a certificate for a helicopter engine in Portugal. The certificate related to the defendant's sale of the engine to an English buyer. The engine was sold on a number of occasions, each time accompanied by the certificate. The claimant had purchased the engine and subsequently sold it to another party, who had raised an action for breach of contract against the claimant in relation to the sale. Consequently the claimant brought proceedings against the defendant in the English courts seeking to recover damages for negligent misstatement in respect of statements alleged to have been contained in the certificate. The defendant applied for an order setting aside the claim, on the basis that the English court lacked jurisdiction. It was common ground that EC Council Regulation 44/2001 art 5(3) applied. However, the defendant contended that the tort of negligent misstatement was a claim under English law, which was not applicable in the circumstances, as England was neither the place where the damage or the event giving rise to the damage occurred. The claimant argued that England was the place where the damage had occurred since England was the only place in which the claimant had suffered loss. *Held*, in principle, the application of the test of where the damage had occurred should yield the same jurisdictional result wherever the claim was made. Consequently, the domestic court would not necessarily be assisted by a detailed analysis of the particular cause of action under the national law relied on. It was necessary to see where the event giving rise to the damage had produced its immediate or physical harmful effect. The initial and direct damage had occurred when the certificate was received by the claimant in England. Further, the claimant had acquired the engine in England when it would not otherwise have done so, and had sustained loss in England when it was sued in respect of the engine. Since England was the place where significant damage had been done to the immediate victim of the harmful act, it was therefore the place where the damage had occurred for the purposes of art 5(3). Therefore, England was the place where the event giving rise to liability had directly produced its harmful effect on the person who was the victim of the event and accordingly, the application would be refused.

London Helicopters Ltd v Heliportugal LDA-INAC [2006] EWHC 108 (QB), [2006] 1 All ER (Comm) 595 (Queen's Bench Division: Simon J).

610   Jurisdiction—tort—place where tort occurred—computer hacked from foreign country

See *Ashton Investments Ltd v OJSC Russian Aluminium (RUSAL)*, para 2332.

CONSTITUTIONAL LAW

Halsbury's Laws of England (4th edn) vol 8(2) (Reissue) paras 1–961

Articles

For articles relating to this title please refer to the Table of Articles at the beginning of the Abridgment.

611   Constitutional reform—supplementary provisions

The Constitutional Reform Act 2005 (Supplementary Provisions) Order 2006, SI 2006/1693 (in force on 28 June 2006), makes supplementary, transitory and transitional provision with respect to the Local Land Charges Act 1975 s 13A, to provide that from 3 April 2006 until 31 March 2007 the fees specified by registering authorities are those that were applicable immediately prior to 3 April 2006, as set out in the Local Land Charges Rules 1977, SI 1977/985, Sch 3.

612   Constitutional reform—temporary modifications

The Constitutional Reform Act 2005 (Temporary Modifications) Order 2006, SI 2006/227 (in force on 27 February 2006), directs that, until the commencement of the Constitutional Reform Act 2005 s 23, the senior Lord of Appeal in Ordinary may exercise the functions of the President of the Supreme Court under ss 45, 46.

613   Constitutional Reform Act 2005—commencement

The Constitutional Reform Act 2005 (Commencement No 4) Order 2006, SI 2006/228, brings ss 45 and 46 into force on 27 February 2006.

The Constitutional Reform Act 2005 (Commencement No 5) Order 2006, SI 2006/1014, brings into force (1) on 3 April 2006, ss 1–3, 5(1), (2), (5), 7, 9, 12, 13, 14 (in part), 15 (in part), 16, 17, 61 (so far as not already in force), 62–64, 65(4), 85 (except s 85(1)(a)), 86–96, 98–114, 115–118 (so far as not already in force), 119, 122, 139, 145 (in part), 146 (in part), Schs 1, 2, Sch 3 (except, for certain purposes, Sch 3 para 3(2), (3), (5)), Sch 4 paras 1–6, 13, 15–17, 19–41, 43–114, 115 (so far as not already in force), 116, 117 (so far as not already in force), 118 (so far as not already in force), 119, 120 (so far as not already in force), 121, 122 (so far as not already in force), 123 (so far as not already in force), 124, 126–141, 143–158, 160–211, 212 (so far as not already in force), 213–215, 217–228, 230–279, 280 (so far as not already in force), 281–308, 310–330, 331 (except Sch 4 para 331(2)(b)(iii), (vi)), 332–344, 346–350, 352–407, Sch 12 (so far as not already in force), Sch 13, Sch 14 (with exceptions), Sch 17 paras 1–6, and certain repeals in Sch 18; (2) on 2 October 2006, ss 67–84; and (3) on 2 April 2007, s 85(1)(a).

For a summary of the Act, see 2005 Abr para 711. See also the commencement table in the title STATUTES.

614   Gender recognition—application fees

The Gender Recognition (Application Fees) Order 2006, SI 2006/758 (in force on 6 April 2006), replaces the 2005 Order, SI 2005/638, and prescribes the level of fees payable in relation to applications to a Gender Recognition Panel under the Gender Recognition Act 2004. The order prescribes a fee of £140 for applicants whose relevant income is greater than £23,185, and a fee of £30 for applicants whose relevant income is greater than £15,460 but not greater than £23,185, and provides that no fee is payable (1) in circumstances where an applicant's relevant income is £15,460 or less, or where an applicant is in receipt of a qualifying benefit; (2) if the application is made under s 1(1) and the applicant has previously received an interim gender recognition certificate; (3) in relation to an application for a full gender recognition certificate following the grant of an interim gender recognition certificate where the applicant has been married; (4) in relation to an application for a full gender recognition certificate following the grant of an interim gender certificate where the applicant has been a civil partner; and (5) in relation to an application for a corrected certificate where the original contains an error.

615   Government of Wales Act 2006

The Government of Wales Act 2006 makes provision about the government of Wales. The Act received the royal assent on 25 July 2006 and certain provisions came into force on that day and on 1 April 2007. Specified provisions come into force on a date to be appointed, and the remaining provisions come into force immediately after the ordinary election under the Government of Wales Act 1998 s 3 held in 2007, or otherwise immediately after the first appointment is made under the 2006 Act s 46. For details of commencement see the commencement table in the title STATUTES.

Part 1 (ss 1–44) National Assembly for Wales
Section 1 provides for establishment of the legislative body called the National Assembly for Wales ('the Assembly'), which is to consist of Assembly constituency members and Assembly regional members. Section 2, Sch 1 provide for the Assembly constituencies, which are the parliamentary constituencies for which members of the United Kingdom Parliament are returned, and for the five Assembly electoral regions, and for alterations in those regions and in the allocation of seats to them. Subject to the Secretary of State's power to change the date of an ordinary general election under s 4, Assembly ordinary general elections are to take place every four years on the first Thursday in May: s 3. If the Assembly resolves that it should be dissolved with at least two-thirds of Assembly members voting in favour of the resolution, or if the Assembly fails to nominate an Assembly member to be the First Minister within the specified period, the Secretary of State must propose a

date for the holding of an extraordinary general election: s 5. Section 6 provides that each elector voting at an Assembly general election has two votes, the first for a candidate to be an Assembly constituency member and the second for a registered political party which has submitted a list of candidates for the Assembly electoral region in which the constituency is situated or for an individual who is a candidate for that region. Section 7 makes provision in relation to candidature for Assembly constituencies and electoral regions, and prevents a person from being a candidate for both a constituency and a region, for more than one constituency or for more than one region. Sections 8 and 9 provide for the calculation of electoral region figures and the allocation of seats to electoral region members. Section 10 deals with the filling of vacancies in seats for Assembly constituencies, and s 11 deals with the filling of vacancies in seats for Assembly electoral regions. Every person entitled to vote in a local government election in Wales is entitled to vote in an election to the Assembly: s 12. The Secretary of State may by order make provision for the conduct of elections and related matters: s 13. Section 14 sets out the term of office of Assembly members, and s 15 allows Assembly members to resign. Sections 16–18 set out the grounds of disqualification from being an Assembly member, the exceptions from disqualification and the effect of the return to the Assembly of a disqualified person. Legal proceedings may be brought by any person to determine whether a person is disqualified: s 19. Section 20 deals with members' salaries and allowances and provides for the payment of pensions, allowances and gratuities to former Assembly members. The Assembly must reduce the salary of any Assembly member who also receives a salary as a member of Parliament or a member of the European Parliament: s 21. The Assembly must publish annual information relating to payments made under ss 20 and 21: s 22. Section 23 requires every Assembly member to take an oath or affirmation of allegiance. Under s 24, the Assembly Commission must make payments to or in respect of political groups, where the Assembly has so determined, in order to assist Assembly members belonging to those groups to perform their functions as Assembly members. At its first meeting after a general election, the Assembly must elect a presiding officer and a deputy presiding officer (s 25) and must appoint a person to be the Clerk of the Assembly (s 26). Section 27, Sch 2 provide for the establishment, membership and functions of the National Assembly for Wales Commission which is to provide the Assembly with staff, property and services. Detailed provision relating to the Commission is set out in Sch 2. Section 28 provides for Assembly committees and sub-committees, and s 29 makes provision as to the composition of committees. Section 30 requires the Assembly to have an Audit Committee. Assembly proceedings are to be regulated by standing orders: s 31. By virtue of s 32, the Secretary of State for Wales may participate, but not vote, in proceedings of the Assembly, and is entitled to have access to documents relevant to those proceedings. Section 33 requires the Secretary of State for Wales, after the beginning of each parliamentary session, to consult the Assembly about the United Kingdom government's legislative programme, unless consultation on a particular Bill is inappropriate. Provision is made by s 34 about the participation in Assembly proceedings of the Counsel General to the Welsh Assembly Government. In the conduct of its proceedings, the Assembly must, so far as is both appropriate in the circumstances and reasonably practicable, give effect to the principle that the English and Welsh languages should be treated on a basis of equality: s 35. Section 36 requires standing orders to make various kinds of provision to safeguard standards of integrity in relation to Assembly proceedings, in particular the registration of Assembly members' interests and making of declarations of their interest in matters to which Assembly proceedings relate. Section 37 empowers the Assembly to require witnesses to appear to give evidence before, or to produce documents to it, its committees or their sub-committees, and s 38 requires the Clerk to give written notice to a person so called to give evidence or produce documents. Section 39 makes it a criminal offence for a person to refuse or fail so to give evidence or produce documents, and s 40 enables the presiding officer, or any other person authorised by standing orders, to require anyone giving evidence in Assembly proceedings to take an oath or make an affirmation. Section 41 makes provision in relation to legal proceedings by and against the Assembly. Statements made in proceedings in the Assembly, and statements published by or on behalf of the Assembly attract absolute privilege for the purposes of the law of defamation: s 42. Section 43 makes provision relating to the law of contempt and its effect on published accounts of Assembly proceedings. The Assembly is a public body for the purposes of the Prevention of Corruption Acts 1889–1916: 2006 Act s 44.

Part 2 (ss 45–92) Welsh Assembly Government
Section 45 provides for the establishment of the legislative body called the Welsh Assembly Government, which comprises the First Minister, the Welsh ministers, the Counsel General to the Welsh Assembly Government and the deputy Welsh ministers. Section 46 makes provision as to the appointment, office and functions of the First Minister, and s 47 deals with how the First Minister is chosen. Section 48 allows the First Minister to appoint Welsh ministers from among members of the Assembly and to remove them from office. Provision is made by s 49 for there to be a Counsel General who is legal adviser to and representative in the courts of the Welsh Assembly Government. Section 50 provides for the appointment and removal of deputy Welsh ministers by the First Minister, from among members of the Assembly. There may not be more than 12 persons who are either Welsh ministers or deputy Welsh ministers: s 51. Section 52 makes provision as respects persons appointed by the Welsh ministers to be members of the staff of the Welsh Assembly

Government, and provides that staff so appointed are members of the Home Civil Service. Section 53 requires the Assembly to make provision for the payment of salaries to the First Minister, the Welsh ministers, the deputy Welsh ministers and the Counsel General, and allows the Assembly to make provision for the payment of allowances, pensions and gratuities to them. Further provision as to remuneration and publication of amounts paid is made by s 54. Section 55 requires the First Minister, Welsh ministers and the Counsel General to take an official oath on their appointment, and requires all members of the Welsh Assembly Government to take the oath of allegiance unless they have already taken it as a member of the Assembly. Section 56 provides that the Welsh ministers, the First Minister and the Counsel General are to have those functions which are conferred or imposed on them by or under the Act or by any other enactment or prerogative instrument. Provision is made by s 57 as to the exercise of their functions by the Welsh ministers. Section 58, Sch 3 deal with the transfer of ministerial functions in relation to Wales to the Welsh ministers, or to the First Minister or the Counsel General. Section 59 enables the Welsh ministers to be designated for the purposes of enabling them to implement Community obligations. The Welsh ministers may do anything which they consider to be appropriate to achieve the promotion of the economic, social or environmental well-being of Wales (s 60) or to support specified cultural matters (s 61). The Welsh ministers, the First Minister and the Counsel General may make appropriate representations about any matter affecting Wales: s 62. Section 63 requires any minister of the Crown who exercises certain functions in relation to relevant cross-border bodies to consult the Welsh ministers before exercising such functions. The Welsh ministers may hold a poll in the whole or in any part of Wales for the purpose of ascertaining the views of those polled as to whether or how they should exercise their functions: s 64. Section 65 enables the Welsh ministers to promote or oppose any private Bill in Parliament. The Treasury may require the Welsh ministers to provide it with information which is in their possession or under their control and which is required for the exercise of any Treasury functions: s 66. Under s 67, the Counsel General, as the representative of the Welsh ministers in the courts, may institute, defend or appear in any legal proceedings relating to matters with respect to which any functions of the Welsh ministers, the First Minister or the Counsel General are exercisable. Section 68 allows the Secretary of State to make an order applying, subject to any appropriate modifications, the Local Government (Contracts) Act 1997 to contracts entered into by the Welsh ministers, the First Minister or the Counsel General. The Welsh ministers may charge for supplying copies of any document or any part of a document which they publish or make available for public inspection: 2006 Act s 69. The First Minister, the Welsh ministers and the Counsel General may give financial assistance to any person engaged in any activity which the Welsh ministers consider will secure, or help to secure, the attainment of any objective which they aim to achieve in the exercise of their functions (s 70) and may do anything which is calculated to facilitate or is conducive or incidental to the exercise of any of their functions (s 71). Under s 72, the Welsh ministers must establish a Partnership Council for Wales whose members, to be appointed by the Welsh ministers, are to comprise Welsh ministers or deputy Welsh ministers and members of Welsh local authorities. The Welsh ministers must make, keep under review, and from time to time remake or revise (1) a local government scheme setting out how they propose, in the exercise of their functions, to sustain and promote local government in Wales (s 73); (2) a voluntary sector scheme, setting out how they propose, in the exercise of their functions, to promote the interests of relevant voluntary organisations (s 74); (3) a business scheme setting out how they propose to take account of the interests of business in exercising their functions (s 75); (4) a regulatory impact assessment code, setting out their policy on the carrying out of regulatory impact assessments in relation to Welsh subordinate legislation and on the carrying out of consultation in connection with regulatory impact assessments (s 76); and (5) a sustainable development scheme, setting out how they propose, in the exercise of their functions, to promote sustainable development (s 79). Section 77 requires the Welsh ministers to make arrangements with a view to securing that their functions are exercised with due regard to the principle that there should be equality of opportunity for all people. The Welsh ministers are required to adopt a Welsh language strategy which sets out their proposals for promoting and facilitating the use of the Welsh language: s 78. A European Community obligation of the United Kingdom is also an obligation of the Welsh ministers, the First Minister or the Counsel General if and so far as the obligation could be implemented or complied with by the exercise by them of their functions: s 80. Section 81 provides that the Welsh ministers, First Minister and the Counsel General have no power to make subordinate legislation, or to do any other act, if the subordinate legislation or act is incompatible with the European Convention on Human Rights. Section 82 makes provision concerning international obligations of the United Kingdom which impinge on functions of the Welsh ministers, the First Minister or the Counsel General. Arrangements may be made between the Welsh ministers, the First Minister or the Counsel General and any minister of the Crown, government department, public authority or holder of a public office in England and Wales under which each exercises functions of the other: s 83. Section 84 makes supplemental provision relating to the exercise of functions by the Welsh ministers, the First Minister or the Counsel General, and s 85 provides that references in existing enactments to ministers of the Crown or government departments should be construed where necessary as including, as appropriate references to the Welsh ministers, the First Minister or the Counsel

General. Section 86 provides for certain reports and statements to be laid before the Assembly, rather than before Parliament. Section 87 deals with the holding of property, rights and liabilities of the Welsh Assembly Government. Section 88, Sch 4 deal with transfers of property rights and liabilities of ministers of the Crown to the Welsh ministers. Section 89 provides for the Crown in right of the United Kingdom Government in the United Kingdom and in right of the Welsh Assembly Government to be treated as having separate legal personality. Section 90 provides for the execution and authentication of legal documents by or on behalf of the First Minister, the Welsh ministers or the Counsel General and s 91 ensures the validity of the acts of a person as the First Minister and the Counsel General. The First Minister, the Welsh ministers, the Counsel General and the deputy Welsh ministers are Crown servants for the purposes of the Official Secrets Act 1989: 2006 Act s 92.

Part 3 (ss 93–102) Assembly Measures
Section 93 confers on the Assembly power to pass a type of subordinate legislation in relation to Wales called Measures of the National Assembly for Wales. Sections 94 and 95 make provision for the legislative competence of the Assembly, which is limited to the matters and subject to the restrictions set out in Sch 5. Where there is a proposal to add to the matters to which the Assembly has legislative competence, the Counsel General or the Attorney General may refer the proposal to the Supreme Court (or, until the commencement of the Constitutional Reform Act 2005 s 23(1), the Judicial Committee of the Privy Council) for a decision as to whether the matter relates to a field listed in the 2006 Act Sch 5 Pt 1: s 96. Sections 97, 98 make provision about Assembly proceedings in relation to proposed Assembly Measures. Section 99 enables the Counsel General or the Attorney General to refer to the Supreme Court (see supra) the question whether a proposed Assembly Measure would be within the Assembly's legislative competence. Section 100 allows the Assembly to reconsider a proposed Measure which the Counsel General or the Attorney General has referred to the Supreme Court where the Supreme Court has referred a question in connection with the matter to the European Court of Justice for a preliminary ruling. In specified circumstances, the Secretary of State may intervene and prohibit the Clerk of the Assembly from submitting a proposed Measure for approval by Her Majesty in Council: s 101. When a proposed Measure has been passed by the Assembly, it is for the Clerk to submit it for approval by Her Majesty in Council: s 102.

Part 4 (ss 103–116) Acts of the Assembly
Section 103, Sch 6 contain provision as to the holding of a referendum on the whether ss 107, 108, and ss 110–115 ('the Assembly Act provisions') should come into force, which would give the Assembly enhanced legislative competence. Section 104 provides the mechanism under which the First Minister or a Welsh Minister can initiate a proposal that a referendum be held on bringing the Assembly Act provisions into force and s 105 empowers the Welsh ministers to bring into force the Assembly Act provisions following indorsement in a referendum. As soon as the Assembly Act provisions have come into force Pt 3 ceases to have effect: s 106. Section 107 confers on the Assembly power to pass legislation, called Acts of the National Assembly for Wales, in relation to Wales. Sections 108 and 109 make provision for the legislative competence of the Assembly, limited to the subjects and subject to the restrictions set out in Sch 7, to pass Acts. Sections 110, 111 make provision about Assembly proceedings in relation to proposed Assembly Bills. Section 112 allows the Counsel General or the Attorney General to refer competence to the Supreme Court (see supra) the question whether a proposed Assembly Bill would be within the Assembly's legislative comptence. Section 113 allows the Assembly to reconsider a proposed Bill which the Counsel General or the Attorney General has referred to the Supreme Court where the Supreme Court has referred a question in connection with the matter to the European Court of Justice for a preliminary ruling. In specified circumstances, the Secretary of State may intervene and prohibit the Clerk of the Assembly from submitting a proposed Bill for royal assent: s 114. When a proposed Bill has been passed by the Assembly, it is for the Clerk to submit it for royal assent: s 115. Section 116 establishes a Welsh Seal and designates the First Minister as its keeper, and allows provision to be made about the preparation and publication of the letters patent that signify that royal assent has been given to an Act of the Assembly.

Part 5 (ss 117–145) Finance
Section 117 establishes a Welsh Consolidated Fund, which is to be held with the Paymaster General. The Secretary of State may make payments into the Fund out of money provided by Parliament, and any minister of the Crown and any government department may make payments to the Welsh ministers, the First Minister or the Counsel General: s 118. Under s 119, the Secretary of State must lay a written statement before the Assembly at least four months before the beginning of each financial year estimating the total payments that he will pay into the Fund and the amounts which will be paid to the Welsh ministers, the First Minister and the Counsel General in that financial year. Section 120 deals with the determination of sums which are to be paid into the Fund. The Welsh ministers may borrow from the Secretary of State amounts up to a total of £500m required either to cover a short term deficit in the Fund or to provide a working balance within it: s 121. Sums received by the Secretary of State by way of repayment must be paid into the National Loans Fund: s 122. Under s 123, the Secretary of State is required to prepare and send to the Comptroller and Auditor General for Wales accounts for each financial year in respect of any such loans and

repayments. A sum may only be paid out of the Fund in the prescribed circumstances: s 124. Sections 125, 126 set out the process of Budget resolutions, s 127 provides for deemed authorisations where no Budget resolution has been adopted by the Assembly before the beginning of the financial year, and s 128 allows unauthorised expenditure which is considered to be necessary in the public interest where, for reasons of urgency, it is not reasonably practicable for the expenditure to be authorised. Where a proposed payment would comply with s 124, the Auditor General for Wales must, at the request of the Welsh Ministers, grant approvals to draw payments out of the Fund: s 129. Where a sum is mistakenly paid into the Fund, s 130 allows the Auditor General for Wales to grant an approval to draw a payment equal to the amount of that sum out of the Fund. The Welsh ministers must, in accordance with directions given to them by the Treasury, prepare accounts for each financial year (s 131), and prepare an account of all receipts into and payments out of the Fund in any financial year (s 132). Section 133 sets out the functions of the principal accounting officer for the Welsh ministers. When examining any accounts of the Welsh ministers, the Auditor General for Wales has a right of access to documents and information relating to the accounts of any subsidiary of the Welsh ministers: s 134. Section 135 empowers the Auditor General for Wales to carry out examinations into the economy, efficiency and effectiveness with which the Welsh ministers and the Counsel General have used their resources in discharging their functions. Under s 136, the Comptroller and Auditor General may carry out examinations into payments into and out of the Fund. By s 137, the Assembly Commission must prepare accounts for each financial year in a form directed by the Treasury. Section 138 designates the Clerk of the Assembly as the principal accounting officer for the Assembly Commission, and makes provision for the temporary replacement if the clerk is incapable of acting as principal accounting officer or if the office of clerk is vacant. When examining any accounts of the Commission, the Auditor General for Wales has a right of access to documents and information relating to the accounts of any subsidiary of the Commission: s 139. The Auditor General for Wales may carry out examinations into the economy, efficiency and effectiveness with which the Commission has used its resources in discharging its functions: s 140. Where the Treasury has designated bodies which exercise functions of a public nature or are entirely or substantially funded from public money, so as to require them to provide information to the Welsh ministers, s 141 requires the Welsh ministers to prepare a set of accounts relating to all of those bodies, and s 142 requires the Auditor General for Wales to examine the accuracy of those accounts. Section 143 allows the Audit Committee of the Assembly to consider and report to the Assembly on any accounts, statement of accounts or report laid before the Assembly by the Auditor General for Wales. The Assembly must publish accounts, statement of accounts or reports laid before it by the Auditor General for Wales and any report laid before it by the Audit Committee under s 143: s 144. Section 145, Sch 8 provide for the establishment of the office of Auditor General for Wales.

Part 6 (ss 146–166) Miscellaneous and supplementary
Sections 146–148 define and make provision in relation to Welsh public records. Section 149, Sch 9 make provision about the resolution of devolution issues by way of legal proceedings. Section 150 enables the United Kingdom government to make subordinate legislation to deal with the consequences of any provision made by or under Welsh legislation. Section 151 enables Her Majesty by Order in Council to remedy ultra vires acts. The Secretary of State may intervene where the exercise of devolved functions by the First Minister, the Welsh ministers or the Counsel General might have a serious adverse impact on water resources, supply or quality in England: s 152. Where a court or tribunal decides that an Assembly Measure or Act or a provision of it is outside the Assembly's competence, s 153 allows that court or tribunal to remove or limit any retrospective effect of its decision, or to suspend for a specified period the effect of the decision. Where necessary and as far as is possible, Assembly legislation and proposed Assembly legislation must be read in such a way that it remains within the competence of the Assembly: s 154. Under s 155, Her Majesty may by Order in Council specify functions which are treated as being, or not being, functions exercisable by the First Minister, the Welsh ministers or the Counsel General; or exercisable in relation to Wales. English and Welsh texts of any type of Assembly legislation are to be treated as being of equal standing: s 156. Section 157 provides for the making of subordinate legislation, and ss 158, 159 deal with interpretation. Section 160, Sch 10 provide for minor and consequential amendments. Section 161 deals with commencement, and s 162, Sch 11 make transitional and transitory provisions and savings. Section 163, Sch 12 deal with repeals and revocations, and s 164 makes financial provision. Section 165 deals with extent and s 166 deals with short title.

Amendments, repeals and revocations
The list below mentions repeals and amendments which are or will be effective when the Act is fully in force. The list is not exhaustive.

Specific provisions of a number of Acts are amended or repealed. These include: Statutory Instruments Act 1946 ss 1, 11A; Laying of Documents before Parliament (Interpretation) Act 1948 s 1; Interpretation Act 1978 s 23B; National Audit Act 1983 ss 6, 8, 9; Copyright, Designs and Patents Act 1988 ss 163, 164, 166C, 166D; Government of Wales Act 1998 ss 1–124, 144, 145, 145A, 145C, 146A, 147, 154–156, Schs 1–3, 5, 7, 8, 11, 12; Human Rights Act 1998 s 21; Political Parties, Elections and Referendums Act 2000 ss 8, 10, 13, Schs 3, 21; Finance Act 2003 ss 61, 66,

107; Public Audit (Wales) Act 2004 ss 2, 6–11, 65, Sch 2; Constitutional Reform Act 2005 Sch 9; Public Services Ombudsman (Wales) Act 2005 ss 7–10, 12, 16, 21, 23–25, 28–30, 40–44, Schs 1–3, 6; and Inquiries Act 2005 ss 1, 27–30, 41, 43, 51.

616 Government trading funds—Driving Standards Agency—maximum borrowing

The Driving Standards Agency Trading Fund (Maximum Borrowing) Order 2006, SI 2006/623 (in force on 1 April 2006), increases from £30m to £70m the maximum that the Driving Standards Agency Trading Fund may borrow.

617 Government trading funds—Ordnance Survey Trading Fund—maximum borrowing

The Ordnance Survey Trading Fund (Maximum Borrowing) Order 2006, SI 2006/2835 (in force on 15 December 2006), amends the 1999 Regulations, SI 1999/965, by increasing from £30m to £40m the maximum that the Ordnance Survey Trading Fund may borrow.

618 Human rights

See HUMAN RIGHTS.

619 Identity Cards Act 2006

The Identity Cards Act 2006 makes provision for a national scheme of registration of individuals and for the issue of cards capable of being used for identifying registered individuals, and makes it an offence for a person to be in possession or control of an identity document to which he is not entitled, or of apparatus, articles or materials for making false identity documents. The Act also amends the Consular Fees Act 1980 and makes provision facilitating the verification of information provided with an application for a passport. The 2006 Act received the royal assent on 30 March 2006 and came into force in part on that day. Further provisions came into force on and between 30 May 2006 and 30 September 2006: SI 2006/1439, 2602. The remaining provisions come into force on a day or days to be appointed. For details of commencement, see the commencement table in the title STATUTES.

Section 1 requires the Secretary of State to establish and maintain a register of individuals, to be known as the National Identity Register, and sets out the statutory purposes of the register. Individuals entitled to be entered on the register are identified by s 2, and the information that may be recorded in the register is set out in s 3, Sch 1. Section 4 empowers the Secretary of State by order to designate documents for the purposes of registration. Provision is made for applications for entry to the register by s 5. Section 6 sets out the procedure for issuing cards capable of being used for identifying registered individuals ('ID cards'). Section 7 provides for the issue to and renewal of ID cards for individuals required to be entered in the register in accordance with a statutory obligation. The functions of persons issuing designated documents, namely designated documents authorities, in relation to the register and ID cards are dealt with in s 8. In order to maintain the accuracy of the register, s 9 empowers the Secretary of State or a designated documents authority to require the provision of information for the purpose of validating the register, and s 10 requires a person to whom an ID card has been issued to notify the Secretary of State about prescribed changes in circumstances affecting the information recorded about him in the register, and errors in that information of which he is aware. Provision is by s 11 made for invalidity and the surrender of ID cards in specified circumstances. Under s 12 the Secretary of State may provide a person with certain information recorded in an individual's entry in the register, with the consent of the individual, for identity verification purposes. Regulations may be made allowing or requiring public services to make it a condition of providing a service to an individual that the individual produces an ID card, other evidence of registrable facts about himself, or both, by virtue of s 13, and the procedure for making such regulations is set out in s 14. Section 15 permits the Secretary of State to make regulations authorising checks to be made of information recorded in the register by a person providing a public service in specified circumstances. It is unlawful to make it a condition of doing anything in relation to an individual that the individual must produce an ID card or information from his entry in the register by virtue of s 16. A power to provide information held on the register to certain persons for specified purposes without the consent of the registered person is provided for by s 17, and by s 18, which is concerned with the prevention and detection of crime. Section 19 makes provision for the correction of information provided for entry in the register which appears to be inaccurate or incomplete. The Secretary of State is empowered, by s 20, to authorise the provision of information recorded in the register to a public authority without an individual's consent in the absence of any authorisation for the provision of such information under ss 17–19, if there is compliance with requirements imposed by or under s 21. Section 22 establishes a National Identity Scheme Commissioner and sets out his functions. The Commissioner is required to report to the Secretary of State about the carrying out of his functions after the end of each calendar year: s 23. Section 24 amends the Regulation of Investigatory Powers Act 2000 so as to extend the jurisdiction of the Intelligence Services Commissioner and the Investigatory Powers Tribunal. Criminal offences relating to the possession of false identity documents are created by the 2006 Act s 25, and s 26 defines 'identity document' for the purposes of s 25. Section 27 creates an offence of unauthorised disclosure of information held on the register, s 28 creates an offence of providing false information for purposes connected with securing an entry or modification of an entry on the register or obtaining an ID card, and s 29 creates an offence of tampering with the register. Section 30 deals with consequential amendments relating to the new offences. Provision is made by s 31 for the imposition of civil penalties, s 32 establishes a procedure for objecting to the imposition of a civil penalty, and s 33 sets out the appeal procedure. Under s 34 the Secretary of State is required to issue a code of practice setting out the matters that must be considered when determining whether a civil penalty should be imposed, and the amount of such a penalty. Fees in respect of functions carried out under the Act are dealt with in s 35, and s 36 amends the Consular Fees Act 1980 so as to allow flexibility in the setting of fees for the carrying out of consular functions, including the setting of passport fees. The Secretary of State is required by the 2006 Act s 37 to report to Parliament on the likely costs of the ID cards scheme. Section 38 makes provision relating to the verification of information provided to the Secretary of State in connection with a passport application, and various amendments to legislation are made by s 39 in order to facilitate the use of ID cards in circumstances where a passport may currently be required. Section 40 deals with the making of orders and regulations under the Act, s 41 with expenses, and s 42 with interpretation. Section 43 relates to Scotland, and s 44, Sch 2 deal with short title, repeals, commencement, transitory provision and extent.

Amendments, repeals and revocations
The list below, which is not exhaustive, mention repeals and amendments which are or will be effective when the Act is fully in force.

Specific provisions of a number of Acts are amended or repealed. These include: Consular Fees Act 1980 s 1; Forgery and Counterfeiting Act 1981 s 5; Football Spectators Act 1989 ss 14E, 19, 21B, 21C, 22A; Criminal Justice Act 1993 s 1; Immigration and Asylum Act 1999 s 31; Regulation of Investigatory Powers Act 2000 ss 59, 65; Criminal Justice and Police Act 2001 ss 33, 35, 36; Asylum and Immigration (Treatment of Claimants, etc) Act 2004 ss 3, 14.

620   Identity cards—legislation—replacement of existing legislation—implementation

See *R (on the application of the Crown Prosecution Service) v Bow Street Magistrates' Court (James and others, interested parties)*, para 2733.

621   Judicial appointments—discipline—modification of offices

The Judicial Appointments and Discipline (Modification of Offices) Order 2006, SI 2006/678 (in force on 3 April 2006), amends the Constitutional Reform Act 2005 Sch 14 Pt 3, by adding a number of offices to which appointments or nominations are made by the Lord Chancellor to the list of relevant offices which will allow discipline of those office holders to be carried out in accordance with the Act.

The Judicial Appointments and Discipline (Modification of Offices) (No 2) Order 2006, SI 2006/1551 (in force on 10 July 2006), amends the 2005 Act supra by adding two offices to which appointments are made by the Lord Chancellor to the list of relevant offices in the Act.

622   Judicial discipline—procedures

The Judicial Discipline (Prescribed Procedures) Regulations 2006, SI 2006/676 (in force on 3 April 2006), provide for the procedures to be followed in the investigation and determination of allegations of misconduct by judicial office holders under the Constitutional Reform Act 2005 Pt 4 Ch 3 (ss 108–121). The regulations, in particular, (1) make provision for the designation by the Lord Chancellor of officials in an Office for Judicial Complaints ('OJC') to support the Lord Chancellor and the Chief Justices in the investigation and determination of allegations, and for the time limits within which a complaint must be made and for the extension of time limits; (2) make provision in relation to complaints and referrals, providing for the making of rules by the Lord Chief Justice (with the agreement of the Lord Chancellor) to govern the investigation of complaints: (a) against magistrates by local advisory committees; and (b) against members of specified tribunals by their President or other designated senior judicial officer, also provides for complaints to be withdrawn, and for either the Lord Chancellor or the Lord Chief Justice to refer complaints for further investigation; (3) make provision for the consideration of complaints by the OJC and allows the OJC to make inquiries, and to dismiss a complaint to the extent that it falls within criteria set out in the regulations and provides for the appointment of nominated judges to advise the Lord Chancellor and the Lord Chief Justice on the action to be taken in cases not dismissed by the OJC; (4) deal with the decisions which the Lord Chancellor and the Lord Chief Justice may take after a case has been investigated by the OJC and nominated judges, advisory committees or tribunal Presidents; (5) make provision for the referral of cases by the Lord Chancellor or Lord Chief Justice for investigation and also allows for the appointment of investigating judges and the procedures to be followed by them; (6) allow the Lord Chancellor and the Lord Chief Justice to dismiss cases, or to determine what disciplinary action they propose should be taken; (7) make provision for the establishment of review bodies and for their functions and procedures; and (8) contain miscellaneous provisions, including deferrals of cases, disclosure of information and procedural requirements in respect of reviews by the Ombudsman.

623 Lord Chancellor—functions—transfer, modification and abolition

The Lord Chancellor (Transfer of Functions and Supplementary Provisions) Order 2006, SI 2006/680 (in force on 3 April 2006), transfers, modifies and abolishes certain functions of the Lord Chancellor contained in secondary legislation.

The Lord Chancellor (Transfer of Functions and Supplementary Provisions) (No 2) Order 2006, SI 2006/1016 (in force on 3 April 2006), transfers certain of the Lord Chancellor's functions to the Lord Chief Justice. The order also modifies certain of the Lord Chancellor's functions and abolishes other functions, including his functions as a Lord of Appeal.

The Lord Chancellor (Transfer of Functions and Supplementary Provisions) (No 3) Order 2006, SI 2006/1640 (in force in part on the day after the day on which the Lord Chancellor ceases to hold office of Speaker of the House of Lords, and in part on 21 June 2006), transfers certain of the Lord Chancellor's functions in respect of the House of Lords to the Speaker of the House of Lords. The order also makes provision supplementary to specified transfers in respect of pay, pension, grants to persons ceasing to hold office, and allowances for the office of Speaker of the House of Lords, and amends the pension provision for the Lord Chancellor consequential on the provision made for the Speaker of the House of Lords.

624 Ministers—designation

The European Communities (Designation) Order 2006, SI 2006/608 (in force on 30 March 2006), designates, as the authority which may exercise the power to make regulations, conferred by the European Communities Act 1972 s 2(2), (1) the Secretary of State, in relation to (a) persistent organic pollutants, dangerous substances, preparations and chemicals; (b) the ecodesign of energy-using products; and (c) intellectual property rights; and (2) the Treasury, in relation to European cooperative societies. The order also revokes designations which are superseded.

The European Communities (Designation) (No 2) Order 2006, SI 2006/1461 (in force on 29 June 2006), designates, as the authority which may exercise the power to make regulations, conferred by the 1972 Act s 2(2) supra (1) the Secretary of State, in relation to (a) measures relating to the interoperability of electronic road user charging and road tolling systems; (b) measures relating to disclosure requirements in respect of companies, registration and publication of documents and particulars disclosed and languages in which disclosures are authorised or required to be made; and (c) matters relating to trade in certain goods, including technical assistance, which could be used for capital punishment, torture or other cruel, inhuman or degrading treatment or punishment; and (2) the Secretary of State and the Treasury, in relation to rights in respect of state pensions and benefits of members of the pension scheme provided for officials and servants of the Communities.

The European Communities (Designation) (Amendment) Order 2006, SI 2006/3329 (in force on 11 January 2007), amends SI 2000/2812, 2002/248, 2004/706, 2005/850 and 2766, which designate the National Assembly for Wales in relation to certain matters as the authority which may exercise the power to make regulations conferred by the 1972 Act s 2(2) supra, so as to clarify that the territorial scope of the designations includes the sea adjacent to Wales.

625 Ministers—transfer of functions—statutory instruments

The Transfer of Functions (Statutory Instruments) Order 2006, SI 2006/1927 (in force on 31 October 2006), transfers functions from the Minister for the Civil Service to the Secretary of State. In particular, the functions transferred are (1) the power conferred under the Statutory Instruments Act 1946 s 8 to make regulations for the purposes of the Act; and (2) the requirement under the Statutory Instruments Regulations 1947, SI 1948/1 that the Minister for the Civil Service must cause to be prepared an edition of statutory instruments known as the 'annual edition'.

626 Ministers—transfer of functions—third sector, communities and equality

The Transfer of Functions (Third Sector, Communities and Equality) Order 2006, SI 2006/2951 (in force on 13 December 2006), makes provision in connection with the establishment of the Office of the Third Sector in the Cabinet Office and of the Department for Communities and local government. The order (1) provides for a specified function of the Secretary of State to be exercisable concurrently with the minister for the Cabinet Office; (2) provides for the functions of the Secretary of State under specified enactments to be transferred to the minister for the Cabinet Office; (3) makes supplemental provision in relation to the entrusting to the Minister for the Cabinet Office of other functions formerly entrusted to the Home Secretary, including functions which relate to the voluntary and community sector, otherwise known as the third sector; and (4) makes supplemental provision in relation to the entrusting to the Secretary of State for Communities and local government of functions previously entrusted to the Home Secretary, including functions in relation to race relations, sponsorship of the Commission for Racial Equality, inter-faith matters, the promotion of civil renewal and community cohesion. The order also makes consequential amendments to primary legislation.

627   Northern Ireland

See NORTHERN IRELAND.

628   Public service pensions—compensatory service—early retirement

See *Chapman v South Holland DC*, para 1845.

629   Restrictive measures

See FOREIGN RELATIONS LAW.

630   Transfer of functions—Paymaster General

The Transfer of Functions (Office of Her Majesty's Paymaster General) Order 2006, SI 2006/607 (in force on 3 April 2006), transfers to the Commissioners for Her Majesty's Revenue and Customs the functions of the Paymaster General relating to the administration and oversight of the office of Her Majesty's Paymaster General and her powers to authorise or require action by or in relation to that office, for the purpose of discharging a duty or liability of the paymaster general or for any other purpose.

631   Transfer of functions—Secretary of State for Communities and Local Government

The Secretary of State for Communities and Local Government Order 2006, SI 2006/1926 (in force on 21 August 2006), makes provision in connection with the office of Secretary of State for Communities and Local Government and for transferring functions, property, rights and liabilities in consequence of ministerial changes. In particular, the order (1) incorporates the Secretary of State for Communities and Local Government as a corporation sole; it also provides for authentication of the corporate seal, the making of instruments by that Secretary of State and related matters; (2) transfers functions of the First Secretary of State to the Secretary of State for Communities and Local Government; (3) provides for the transfer of immovable property of the First Secretary of State, with associated rights and liabilities, and of other property rights and liabilities connected with the transferred functions or functions which have been entrusted to the Secretary of State for Communities and Local Government; (4) makes supplementary provision for continuity in relation to functions, property, rights or liabilities referred to in articles; and (5) makes consequential amendment.

632   United Nations

See FOREIGN RELATIONS LAW.

633   Wales—National Assembly for Wales—Community law—implementation—structural funds

The Structural Funds (National Assembly for Wales) Regulations 2006, SI 2006/3282 (in force on 1 January 2007), (1) enable the National Assembly for Wales to exercise certain specified functions under EC Council Regulation 1083/2006, which lays down general provisions on the European Regional Development Fund, the European Social Fund and the Cohesion Fund; (2) designate the Assembly as a managing authority, a certifying authority and an audit authority under the Council Regulation; (3) empower the Assembly to designate others to carry out managing or certifying authority functions; (4) empower the Assembly to exercise certain functions under EC Parliament and Council Regulation 1080/2006 in relation to the European Regional Development Fund; and (5) make provision in relation to the transfer of property, rights and liabilities from the Secretary of State to the Assembly.

634   Wales—National Assembly for Wales—disqualification

The National Assembly for Wales (Disqualification) Order 2006, SI 2006/3335 (in force on 10 January 2007), designates those offices disqualifying holders from membership of the National Assembly for Wales. SI 2003/437 is revoked.

635   Wales—National Assembly for Wales—electoral regions

See para 1193.

636   Wales—National Assembly for Wales—representation of the people

The National Assembly for Wales (Representation of the People) (Amendment) Order 2006, SI 2006/884 (in force on 23 March 2006), amends the 2003 Order, SI 2003/284, in relation to voting at the National Assembly for Wales elections. In particular, the order (1) removes the requirement to provide an address in the United Kingdom to which postal ballot papers should be sent; (2) allows voters to apply for a postal vote when they apply to be registered to vote; (3) provides that a registration officer may be satisfied that an application for an absent vote has been signed by an applicant by referring to any signature which the applicant has provided previously to the registration officer or the retuning officer; (4) requires that an application by a person for his ballot paper to be sent to a different address from that shown in the record should set out the reason for it; (5) specifies additional requirements where an application to vote by proxy at a particular National Assembly for Wales election is made on the grounds of the applicant's physical incapacity; (6) specifies the closing dates for applications to vote by post or proxy or for the appointment of a proxy; (7) sets out the requirements for the registration officer to notify the applicant of his decision to grant an application to vote by post or by proxy or for the appointment of a proxy; and (8) specifies the procedure in relation to the issue and receipt of ballot papers.

637   Wales—National Assembly for Wales—transfer of functions

The National Assembly for Wales (Transfer of Functions) Order 2006, SI 2006/1458 (in force on 8 June 2006), provides for the transfer of certain functions of the Secretary of State under the Education (Fees and Awards) Act 1983 and the Regulatory Reform (Fire Safety) Order 2005, SI 2005/1541, in so far as they are exercisable in relation to Wales, to the National Assembly for Wales.

The National Assembly for Wales (Transfer of Functions) (No 2) Order 2006, SI 2006/3334 (in force on 15 December 2006), varies the 1999 Order, SI 1999/672, and provides for certain functions under the Census Act 1920 to be transferred to the National Assembly for Wales. In particular, the order (1) varies the entry relating to the Environmental Protection Act 1990 so that the Assembly can exercise functions under s 156 in relation to waste disposal; (2) varies the entry relating to the Water Industry Act 1991 so that the functions of prescribing requirements relating to water fittings by reference to regulations made under the Water Industry Act 1991 s 74, will be transferred to the National Assembly in relation to any water or sewerage undertaker whose area is wholly or mainly in Wales, but not in relation to any licensed water suppliers; (3) transfers the regulation-making functions of the Chancellor of the Exchequer under the Census Act 1920, so far as exercisable in relation to Wales, to the National Assembly; (4) directs that no recommendation may be made to Her Majesty in Council to make an Order in Council under the Census Act 1920 s 1, directing that a census be taken for Wales, or any part of Wales, whether or not it is also recommended that a census be taken for any other part of Great Britain, unless the Assembly has been consulted about the making of that recommendation; and (5) prevents the transfer to the Assembly, of documentary or electronic records connected with functions included in the order, which would otherwise take place by operation of the Government of Wales Act 1998 s 23.

CONSUMER CREDIT

Halsbury's Laws of England (4th edn) vol 9(1) (Reissue) paras 1–400

Articles

For articles relating to this title please refer to the Table of Articles at the beginning of the Abridgment.

638   Consumer Credit Act 2006

The Consumer Credit Act 2006 amends the Consumer Credit Act 1974, extends the ombudsman scheme under the Financial Services and Markets Act 2000 to cover licensees under the 1974 Act. The Act received the royal assent on 30 March 2006 and came into force in part on that day. Further provisions came into force on 16 June and 1 October 2006: SI 2006/1508. The remaining provisions come into force on a day or days to be appointed. For details of commencement see the commencement table in the title STATUTES.

Section 1 provides a new definition of 'individual' which restricts the partnerships that are to be regarded as individuals to those consisting of two or three partners, not all of whom are bodies corporate. The financial limit for the regulation of consumer credit and consumer hire agreements under the 1974 Act is removed and the application of the provisions regulating credit advertisements to advertisements offering credit regardless of the sum involved and regardless of whether the creditor requires security is extended: s 2. By virtue of s 3, the Secretary of State is given the power to provide by order for the exemption of consumer credit agreements or consumer hire agreements from regulation where the debtor or hirer has a high net worth. Consumer credit and hire agreements entered into wholly or predominantly for the debtor's or hirer's business purposes where the credit provided or hire payments to be made exceed £25,000 are exempted from regulation: s 4. The Secretary of State, under s 5, has the power to alter the amount of £25,000 by order, subject to the affirmative resolution procedure. Section 6 requires creditors in regulated fixed-sum credit agreements to provide debtors with annual statements in the specified form, the first of which is required within one year of the day after the date on which the agreement was made. Section 7 requires creditors to issue statements to debtors setting out specified information in respect of running account credit agreements at intervals of no more than 12 months, and provides that where there are two or more debtors, a debtor may provide a dispensing notice to the creditor so as the creditor is not obliged to provide a statement to that debtor. The Office of Fair Trading ('OFT') is required to prepare and publish information sheets for debtors and hirers about arrears and default, and a creditor or owner must give a debtor or hirer an arrears information sheet at the same time as a notice of sums in arrears and a default information sheet at the same time as a default notice: s 8. Section 9 provides that creditors and owners must give to debtors and hirers notices of sums in arrears in respect of regulated agreements that are fixed sum credit agreements or hire agreements. Under s 10, a creditor must give to the debtor notices of sums in arrears in respect of regulated agreements that are running account agreements. Consequences are set out under s 11 for a creditor or owner if he fails to give a notice as required. Provision is made for where a debtor or hirer under a regulated agreement incurs a default sum: s 12. A creditor or owner, under s 13, may only require simple interest to be paid in respect of default sums payable by the debtor or hirer, including sums payable under non-commercial or small agreements. Section 14 extends from 7 to 14 days, the minimum period after which a creditor or owner may take action in respect of the agreement after having issued a default notice. A court has the power to determine in its discretion whether agreements are enforceable in accordance with specified provisions, regardless of the breach in question: s 15. Section 16 sets out the circumstances in which a debtor or hirer may apply for, and a court may grant, a time order in respect of a regulated agreement. Requirements are provided by s 17 to be imposed on a creditor or owner to notify and give information to debtors and hirers in the specified form about interest applying to a judgment debt by virtue of a term of the agreement enabling interest to accrue after judgment until payment. 'Default sum' means a sum payable by a debtor or hirer in connection with his breach of a regulated agreement, but does not include interest or sums that, as a consequence of a breach of the agreement, become payable earlier than they otherwise would have done: s 18.

Sections 19–22 enable a court to consider whether the relationship between the creditor and debtor arising out of that agreement is unfair to the debtor because of the terms of the agreement, the way in which the agreement is operated by the creditor, or any other thing done or not done by or on behalf of the creditor before or after the agreement was made. Under s 23, it is clarified that 'consumer credit business', and 'consumer hire business' include being, respectively, a creditor or an owner under regulated agreements. 'Debt administration', which means the taking of steps to perform duties under a consumer credit or consumer hire agreement on behalf of the creditor or owner, or to exercise or enforce rights under such an agreement on behalf of the creditor or owner, so far as these steps do not constitute debt collecting, is included as a type of ancillary credit business: s 24. Under s 25, the provision of 'Credit information services', which covers those businesses that help individuals to locate and correct records relating to their financial standing held by credit reference agencies and others in the credit and hire industries, is included as a type of ancillary credit business. Section 26 provides that a regulated consumer credit or hire agreement is unenforceable by a person acting in the course of a consumer credit or hire business who is not licensed to carry on a consumer credit or a consumer hire business of a description which covers the enforcement of the agreement, and ensures that a person who is not required to have a licence to carry out specified acts is not caught by these provisions. Applicants for licences, or for licence renewal are required to pay to the OFT such charge as the OFT specifies by general notice towards the OFT's costs of carrying out its functions: s 27. The OFT is given power, under s 28, to manage the application process in a more efficient way by requiring people to specify in applications for licences what businesses they want the licence to cover. Section 29 requires the OFT, in determining fitness, to have regard to the skills, knowledge and experience in relation to consumer credit, consumer hire or ancillary credit business, of the applicant and anyone who will work for him under that licence, and the practices and procedures that will be implemented in connection with the business, in addition to other matters. The OFT is required to prepare and publish guidance as to the way it determines the fitness of a person to hold a licence, and may revise any guidance on fitness: s 30. Section 31 makes consequential amendment. If the OFT determines to renew a licence on different terms to the application, to vary it compulsorily, or to revoke or suspend a licence, the OFT may, as part of that determination, authorise the licensee to carry on specified activities, for a specified period during which the OFT may specify requirements which the licensee must comply with, which it would otherwise no longer be licensed to carry on, for the purpose of winding up or transferring its business: s 32. Section 33 makes consequential amendment. The OFT is enabled to issue indefinite standard licences as the norm and to issue licences either indefinitely or for a specified period, provided definite licences do not exceed a period prescribed by the Secretary of State, and to vary the duration of licences in certain circumstances: s 34. Sections 35–37 make provision in relation to periodic payments for indefinite licences.

The OFT is provided with an intermediate power to impose requirements on licensees and may impose a requirement in relation to a business carried on, or proposed to be carried on, under the licence where it is dissatisfied with any matter in connection with specified matters and may, by notice, require the licensee to do or not to do, or cease to do: s 38. Section 39 provides for power of the OFT to impose requirements on the responsible person in relation to a group licence where the OFT is dissatisfied with the manner in which that person is regulating or otherwise supervising, or proposes to regulate or supervise, licensees under that licence. A person cannot be required to compensate or otherwise make amends to another person, and the OFT is given the power to vary or revoke requirements on its own motion or to do so on application by the person on whom the requirement has been imposed: s 40. The procedure the OFT must follow when imposing requirements is set out by s 41. Section 42 requires the OFT to issue guidance as to how it exercises, or how it proposes to exercise, its powers in relation to the imposition, variation or revocation of requirements, and the OFT must have regard to this guidance in exercising its powers in relation to requirements. A right of appeal is provided for persons on whom a requirement is imposed and affected persons against imposition, variation or revocation of a requirement by the OFT or refusal by the OFT of an application by the appellant for variation or revocation of a requirement: s 43. Section 44 provides for the information applicants under the 1974 Act may be required to provide in connection with their application. Provision is made under s 45 in relation to the duty on licensees to notify the OFT of certain changes to their circumstances or any errors or omissions in any information or document which they have provided. Section 46 allows the OFT, on giving notice, to require a person to provide specified information and documents. Under s 47 the OFT can issue a notice requiring a licensee under a standard licence, or the original applicant for a group licence, to ensure that an officer of an enforcement authority may enter the specified premises on reasonable notice and at reasonable times for the purposes of observing the licensee's or applicant's carrying on of his business, and to inspect relevant specified documents relating to the licensee's or applicant's business kept at those premises, where it is reasonably required for purposes connected with the OFT's functions; the licensee must give such access on such days and at such hours as the OFT reasonably requires, but is not required to secure access to premises if the OFT has not given reasonable notice or the access is sought in respect of premises used solely as a dwelling. The OFT can obtain a warrant from a justice of the peace if he is satisfied that there are reasonable grounds for believing that there is on the premises information or documents in relation to which the OFT could impose a requirement and that, if such a requirement were to be imposed, it would either not be complied with or the information or documents would be tampered with, and an officer of an enforcement authority may be authorised to enter and search the specified premises, to seize and detain any information of a description specified in the warrant and take such steps as are reasonably necessary to secure the protection of such documents or information, take such persons and equipment with him as he thinks necessary and use such force as reasonably necessary: s 48. Section 49 provides for the consequences of failing to comply with an information requirement. Anything done or not done by an officer of an enforcement authority, other than the OFT, will be treated as if done or not done by an officer of the OFT, other than in respect of any criminal proceedings brought against that officer, his enforcement authority or the OFT in respect of anything done or not done by that officer, and such an officer may not disclose any information that he obtains other than to the OFT unless he has the OFT's approval or is under a duty to make the disclosure: s 50. Section 51 makes consequential amendments.

Under s 52, the OFT has the power to impose civil penalties in the form of a penalty notice up to £50,000, on persons who do not comply with a requirement imposed by the OFT. Before determining to impose a penalty on a person, the OFT must give a notice to that person which informs him that it is minded to impose a penalty on him, and in relation to a group licence give a general notice of the imposition of a penalty on a person who is a responsible person: s 53. The OFT is required, under s 54, to prepare and publish a statement of policy as regards the exercise of its powers in relation to civil penalties. Sections 55–58, Sch 1, establish the Consumer Credit Appeal Tribunal which will deal with appeals in respect of decisions by the OFT, and deals with appeals to and from the Tribunal. Sections 59–61 extend the jurisdiction of the Financial Ombudsman Service ('FOS') to hear complaints involving licensed persons under the 1974 Act; the detailed operation of the new consumer credit jurisdiction is to be determined largely by rules made by FOS on which it is required to consult in accordance with the requirements of the 2006 Act Sch 2. Section 62 imposes a general duty on the OFT to monitor businesses being carried on under licences issued under the 1974 Act. The OFT may by general notice, only if it appears to the OFT that it is in the interests of hirers to do so, direct that the provision that the hirer, under a regulated consumer hire agreement, has a power to terminate the agreement by giving notice, does not apply to any consumer hire agreement falling within a specified description subject to such conditions as it may specify: s 63. The OFT can, by virtue of s 64, vary or revoke any determination made, or direction given by it, under the 1974 Act, except in relation to specified matters. Section 65 makes consequential amendment. Financial provision (s 66), interpretation (s 67), consequential amendments (s 68), transitional provision and savings (s 69), repeals (s 70), short title, commencement and extent (s 71) are provided for.

639   Credit agreement—compliance with statutory requirements—cancellation notice

A company marketed a claims management scheme, under which it would nominate a solicitor with whom a client would enter into a conditional fee agreement. A third party funded the investigation of the claim, the premium payable under a legal expenses insurance policy and the expected disbursements in accordance with a credit agreement regulated by the Consumer Credit Act 1974. In the event of a claim being unsuccessful, the policy provided for the payment of the amount advanced by the third party under the credit agreement. The benefit of the policy was assigned to the third party with the intention of giving it a direct claim against the insurer. The claimant was one of the insurers under the scheme and the defendant was a third party which funded investigations into claims. The company became insolvent and a large number of claims brought by its clients were dismissed or had to be discontinued. The claimant sought a declaration that the defendant had no direct claim against it on the ground that the credit agreement was unenforceable for failure to comply with the strict requirements of the 1974 Act concerning the client's right of cancellation. A cancellation notice in the prescribed form had to be included in every copy of the agreement given to the debtor. The words 'Your notice of cancellation will not affect your contract for insurance' appeared on the applicable prescribed forms, and the footnote required those words to be omitted where not applicable. It fell to be determined whether a notice of cancellation would affect the contract for insurance. *Held*, under s 69(1)(i), service of a cancellation notice cancelled any linked transaction as well as the agreement itself. However, contracts of insurance were excluded from s 69(1)(i) by the Consumer Credit (Linked Transactions) (Exemptions) Regulations 1983, SI 1983/1560. The purpose of the statement that a notice of cancellation would not affect the insurance contract was to communicate to the debtor in relatively straightforward terms the exclusion of contracts of insurance from the 1974 Act s 69(1)(i) by the 1983 Regulations. Therefore, in deciding whether the footnote requiring that statement to be omitted was applicable, the creditor had only to consider whether a transaction was a linked transaction in relation to the credit agreement and, if it was, whether the 1983 Regulations excluded it from the 1974 Act s 69(1)(i). In the case of the insurance policies it was clear that they were linked but exempt agreements not affected by s 69(1)(i). Therefore the defendant had been correct to have retained in the credit agreement the statement that a notice of cancellation would not 'affect' the insurance policy because, as a result of the 1983 Regulations, the policy itself would not be cancelled by virtue of the legislative provisions concerning cancellation. Accordingly, the application would be dismissed.

Goshawk Dedicated (No 2) Ltd v Governor and Company of the Bank of Scotland [2005] EWHC 2906 (Ch), [2006] 2 All ER 610 (Chancery Division: Sir Francis Ferris).

640   Credit agreement—debtor-creditor-supplier agreement—liability of creditor for breach by supplier—foreign transaction

The Consumer Credit Act 1974 s 75 provides that, if the debtor under a debtor-creditor-supplier agreement falling within s 12(b) or (c) has, in relation to a transaction financed by the agreement, any claim against the supplier in respect of a misrepresentation or breach of contract, he has a like claim against the creditor.

The defendants were sued as representatives of United Kingdom credit institutions licensed under the 1974 Act to carry on consumer credit business and who issued credit cards under regulated credit agreements with consumers. The credit card transactions commonly involved four parties: the card issuer or creditor, the customer or debtor, the supplier or merchant who accepted credit cards in payment for goods or services supplied to the customer, and the merchant acquirer, who recruited suppliers to the scheme, paid them and obtained reimbursement through the card network clearing system. In a three-party transaction, the role of the merchant acquirer would be carried out by the card issuer itself. The development of the four-party structure, where there was no direct contractual link between the card issuer and the supplier, together with the increasing ability to use credit cards abroad and the creation of large international credit card operating networks, led to the proceedings. Issues arose as to whether connected lender liability under s 75(1) attached to transactions entered into by means of credit cards where a four-party structure existed, and to transactions entered into outside the United Kingdom by cardholders using credit cards issued under credit agreements to which the 1974 Act applied, whether a three- or four-party structure was involved. *Held*, an agreement under which a card issuer made credit available to the cardholder for use in connection with transactions occurring under a four-party structure fell within s 12(b), with the result that connected lender liability attached to transactions entered into by the cardholder pursuant to it. Also, s 75(1) did apply in cases where the supply transaction was entered into abroad. The primary purpose of s 75 was to provide additional protection for debtors under credit agreements of the kinds to which it related. There was nothing in s 75(1) or (2) that provided for a distinction to be drawn between transactions entered into in the United Kingdom and those entered into abroad, to say nothing of transactions concluded on the Internet, the place of which might be quite difficult to determine. Judgment would be given accordingly.

Office of Fair Trading v Lloyds TSB Bank plc [2006] EWCA Civ 268, [2007] QB 1 (Court of Appeal: Waller, Smith and Moore-Bick LJJ).

641   Credit agreement—exempt agreements

The Consumer Credit (Exempt Agreements) (Amendment) Order 2006, SI 2006/1273 (in force on 1 June 2006), further amends the 1989 Order, SI 1989/869, so as to provide that the Consumer

Credit Act 1974 does not regulate debtor-creditor agreements where the creditor is a credit union and the rate of the total charge for credit does not exceed 26·9 per cent.

642   Enforcement—default notices—time limits

The Consumer Credit (Enforcement, Default and Termination Notices) (Amendment) Regulations 2006, SI 2006/3094 (in force on 19 December 2006), further amend the 1983 Regulations, SI 1983/1561 so as to provide that default notices served under the Consumer Credit Act 1974 s 87 must specify (1) that where action is required to be taken by the debtor or hirer to remedy the breach or pay compensation, this action must be taken within not more than 14 days after the service of the notice; and (2) where no such action is required to be taken, the date on or after which the creditor or owner intends to take action, must not be less than 14 days from the date of the notice.

CONTEMPT OF COURT

Halsbury's Laws of England (4th edn) vol 9(1) (Reissue) paras 401–527

643   Breach of court order—committal—appeal—permission to appeal

See *Wood v Collins*, para 2272.

644   Breach of court order—committal for contempt—immediate custodial sentence—mitigation

See *Goldsmith v Goldsmith*, para 2539.

645   Civil contempt—interference with administration of justice—reports of judicial proceedings—publication of outcome of case before judgment officially pronounced

The outcome of a case was published on the website of a legal journal before the court had handed down the official approved judgment. The entry was removed when the publisher of the journal became aware of the embargo on prior publication of the judgment. The court accepted an apology and explanation, and acknowledged that the damage done was not of any significance. However, it made the following statement.

Journalists should be familiar with the terms on which draft judgments are released to the parties prior to being pronounced and that journalists' legitimate interest in publishing matters should not collide with clear legal principles. Parties in an action are allowed to obtain copies of the draft judgment before the day on which the judgment is officially pronounced on condition that it is kept confidential. Any breach of that confidentiality will be a contempt of court. It follows that, in the absence of a special order stating that such draft judgments are public, all such judgments are subject to an embargo and cannot be published until they are officially pronounced.

Baigent v Random House; Re The Lawyer [2006] All ER (D) 26 (May) (Chancery Division: Peter Smith J). For related proceedings see *Baigent v Random House Group Ltd* [2006] EWHC 719 (Ch), [2006] All ER (D) 113 (Apr) (para 674).

646   Criminal contempt—interference with administration of justice—restrictions on reporting sentencing hearing—risk of prejudice to subsequent proceedings

See *Re B*, para 2351.

647   Committal for contempt—threatening behaviour towards jury—summary detention in a young offender's institution

The defendant made an emotional outburst in the presence of the jury when his mother was convicted for the importation of cocaine and sentenced to 12 years' imprisonment. The judge ordered that he be detained and Counsel instructed to act on his behalf, who conveyed his apologies to the court. The judge stated that he would not allow the jury to be shouted at in a threatening manner and that immediate and firm action was required. He found that the defendant, aged 19, had committed a contempt of court and ordered him to be detained in a young offender institution. The defendant appealed. *Held*, there was no authority or support for the proposition that in order to prove a contempt of court an intention to disrupt proceedings had to be proved. The power of summary punishment was a necessary power in order to protect the criminal justice process and, in particular, witnesses, participants in the trial and jurors. The summary procedure should only be used in exceptional cases and the decision to imprison a person for contempt should never be taken too quickly and there should always be time for reflection as to what was the best course to take. The judge had erred procedurally in permitting only ten minutes for the defendant to be seen by a representative. However the defendant had been in contempt of court as he had spoken words in a threatening manner to the jury, who, even after the verdict had been taken, were entitled to the court's protection. However it by no means followed from a finding of contempt that an immediate custodial sentence was necessary even where a contempt of court had taken place. The judge had also erred substantively in committing the defendant to custody at all. Accordingly, the appeal would be allowed and the committal to custody would be quashed.

R v Huggins [2007] All ER (D) 97 (Jan) (Court of Appeal: Moses LJ, Nelson J and Sir Charles Mantell). *Balogh v Crown Court at St Albans* [1975] QB 73, CA, and *R v Moran* (1985) 81 Cr App Rep 51, CA (1985 Abr para 426), considered.

648   Reports of judicial proceedings—reporting restrictions

See PRESS, PRINTING AND PUBLISHING.

CONTRACT

Halsbury's Laws of England (4th edn) vol 9(1) (Reissue) paras 601–1091, 1170–1184

Articles

For articles relating to this title please refer to the Table of Articles at the beginning of the Abridgment.

649   Applicable law

See CONFLICT OF LAWS.

650   Building contracts

See BUILDING CONTRACTS, ARCHITECTS, ENGINEERS, VALUERS AND SURVEYORS.

651   Collateral contract—lease—representations made by predecessor in title—covenant to repair

The Church Commissioners granted a lease of premises to a firm for a term of 25 years. Subsequently, the claimant, who was by then the landlord, wished to recover possession of the premises for development work and made proposals for the surrender of the lease. The firm's interest in the lease was eventually transferred to the defendant tenant. Negotiations for surrender of the lease continued with the defendant and were expressed to be 'subject to contract'. The parties later started discussions in respect of a new lease, and they exchanged various emails expressly marked 'subject to contract'. Those emails were followed by letters which discussed the terms of a draft lease that had been sent to the defendant's solicitors. In exchange for a surrender of the lease it was agreed that the defendant would not face a terminal schedule of dilapidations at the end of the new term of years. The tenant received written assurances it would not be served with terminal schedules of dilapidations. An amendment was subsequently made to the lease that entitled the landlord to enter and carry out repairs if a tenant failed to so do, provided any such action did not result in service of a schedule of dilapidations on the tenant. The owner of the premises then sold them to the claimant. Following the defendant's denial of liability for dilapidations to the leased premises, the claimant issued proceedings against the defendant. The defendant denied liability for the repairing obligations in reliance on the existence of a collateral contract and estoppel. *Held*, the assurances given and accepted by the parties were continuing assurances. The assurances by the claimant, or at least recorded in the relevant letter, were not intended to be overridden by the amendment made to the lease. Accordingly, the claim would be dismissed.

Business Environment Bow Lane Ltd v Deanwater Estates Ltd [2006] All ER (D) 61 (Dec) (Chancery Division: Briggs J).

652   Contractual term—construction—notification of claim—time limit—requirement for particulars of claim

By way of two agreements with the defendants, the claimants, an investment syndicate, subscribed for shares in a company. Both agreements contained certain warranties as to the accuracy of the management accounts. The agreements contained a clause ('the first clause') which provided that any claim by subscribers should be notified in writing to the company on or before the third anniversary of the completion date. A further clause ('the second clause') provided that, without prejudice to the provisions of the first clause, the subscribers would notify the company and the warrantors in writing as soon as reasonably practicable after the date on which they became aware of a claim against the warrantors, such notification to be of sufficient detail to enable the company and the warrantors to identify the claim and to respond to it. In subsequent proceedings between the parties, issues arose as to whether the second clause governed the first clause and, if not, what degree of specificity was required by the first clause. *Held*, the two clauses were separate, apart and independent from each other. Whatever was required for the second clause did not affect the first clause. On a proper construction of the first clause, a bald notification of the claim was sufficient and no particulars needed to be given, according to the natural and ordinary meaning of the words. It was impossible to identify from the background of the case and the business common sense of the transactions any purpose of the clause to promote certainty by requiring the giving of as much information about the claim as would be required for properly pleaded particulars of claim, supplemented if necessary by the particulars given under a request for further information. Judgment would be given accordingly.

Forrest v Glasser [2006] EWCA Civ 1086, [2006] All ER (D) 455 (Jul) (Court of Appeal: Ward, Laws and Longmore LJJ).

653 Contractual term—enforceability—refund conditional on timely payment of invoice—rule against penalties

The claimant employment agency's terms of business for the introduction to clients of permanent contract staff provided for the payment of a fee to the client for an introduction resulting in an 'engagement'. The contract provided for a refund of fees in a case where the engagement terminated before the expiry of 12 weeks, with a partial refund payable in certain cases. In a subsequent dispute between the claimant and the defendant client, an issue arose as to whether a clause in the contract which stipulated that a refund could only be payable where the invoice had been paid within seven days was a penalty clause and therefore unenforceable, or merely a simple condition precedent to any right to a refund. The district judge decided that the clause was a disguised penalty clause, and the claimant appealed. *Held*, the rule against penalties was an exception to the general principle of English law that a contract should be enforced in accordance with its terms. It was settled law that a penalty was a sum which, by the terms of the contract, a promisor agreed to pay to the promisee in the event of non-performance by the promisor of one or more of the obligations and which was in excess of the damage caused by such non-performance. The rule against penalties had no wider reach than that. In all the circumstances, the clause in question was no more than a condition precedent. It imposed no obligation on the client, and required no payment of money. The link between the condition precedent and the obligation imposed to pay the invoice within seven days did not bring the condition precedent within the rule against penalties. Moreover, the provisions of the terms of business had met a commercial need which arose directly out of the fact that the parties had decided to make provision for some entitlement to refund. That need was independent of any wish which the claimant might otherwise have had to ensure that payment obligations were met promptly, and would arise irrespective of whether the seven-day payment deadline was imposed. In any event, the dominant contractual purpose underlying the condition precedent had not been deterrence. It followed that the clause was effective and, accordingly, the appeal would be allowed.

Euro London Appointments Ltd v Claessens International Ltd [2006] EWCA Civ 385, [2006] 2 Lloyd's Rep 436 (Court of Appeal: Chadwick and Moore-Bick LJJ and Lawrence Collins J).

654 Contractual term—exclusion clause—incorporation—arbitration agreement

See *Sukuman Ltd v Commonwealth Secretariat*, para 230.

655 Contractual term—implied term—contract of compromise—implied withdrawal of offer to settle proceedings after hearing had ended

See *Hawley v Luminar Leisure plc*, para 2335.

656 Contractual term—implied term—insurance contract—disclosure of documents to underwriter—business efficacy

See *Goshawk Dedicated Ltd v Tyser & Co Ltd*, para 1716.

657 Contractual term—implied term—licence agreement—grant of sub-licence—requirement of licensor's consent—exercise of consent—scope of discretion

The defendant held a licence allowing him to berth a boat in the claimant's marina, initially for a period of 98 years, and wished to grant successive sub-licences to his brothers. The licence contained a power for the defendant to grant a sub-licence to a third party 'provided always' that any such third party was first approved by the claimant. The defendant requested the claimant's consent to the grant of the successive sub-licences. The claimant refused consent, believing that successive sub-licences of the type envisaged were outside the scope of the licence agreement, and sought declarations as to the scope of its powers to refuse consent. It argued that the proviso in the power contained in the licence gave it an absolute right to refuse to grant a sub-licence. The defendant contended that the claimant's discretion was qualified in that it could not be exercised in an arbitrary or capricious way. *Held*, where a contract required the consent of one party to be obtained from the other, such power was to be exercised honestly and in good faith, and not arbitrarily, capriciously or unreasonably. It could not have been the intention of the parties that the claimant, having granted the licence for a term of 98 years, should be able to frustrate its transfer by assignment or sub-licence on grounds unconnected with the proper operation of the licence agreement or the future conduct of the assignee or sub-licensee. If the grounds for the claimant's refusal to grant consent had nothing to do with the suitability of the sub-licensee to exercise the rights granted by the licence, then they were irrelevant and the refusal was unlawful. The claimant's refusal did not relate to the proposed sub-licensees but was based on a mistaken belief as to the power contained in the licence to grant successive sub-licences to them. It was therefore outside the scope of the claimant's discretion and questions of reasonableness did not arise. The claimant was not entitled to refuse its approval of the sub-licensees for the reasons which it had given. Judgment would be given accordingly.

Lymington Marina Ltd v Macnamara [2006] EWHC 704 (Ch), [2006] 2 All ER (Comm) 200 (Chancery Division: Patten J). *Associated Provincial Picture Houses Ltd v Wednesbury Corpn* [1948] 1 KB 223, CA; *Abu Dhabi National Tanker Co v Product Star Shipping Ltd, The Product Star (No 2)* [1993] 1 Lloyd's Rep, CA; *Gan Insurance Co Ltd v Tai Ping Insurance Co Ltd (No 2)* [2001] EWCA Civ 1047, [2001] 2 All ER (Comm) 299; and *Paragon Finance plc v Nash; Paragon Finance plc v Staunton* [2001] EWCA Civ 1466, [2002] 2 All ER 248 (2001 Abr para 641) considered.

658   Contractual term—standard term—construction

Claims by shareholders against the insured were settled following a court ordered mediation which led to a memorandum of understanding being agreed. The claimant insurer paid the insured's claim in full and sought to recover from the defendant reinsurers. The defendant contended that the claimant was in breach of the notification of loss/claims co-operation clause, a commonly used clause, in the reinsurance contract that provided that the reinsured would, on knowledge of any loss or losses which might give rise to a claim, advise the reinsurers as soon as was reasonably practicable and, in any event, within 30 days. The defendant alleged that the losses had been notified too late. *Held*, a claimant did not suffer a loss unless an actual loss was a 'proved fact'. No loss was known to the claimant until the memorandum of understanding had been agreed. Formal notification had been given to the defendant within 30 days of the memorandum, at which stage a 'might be' loss was turned into an actual quantifiable loss for the purposes of the reinsurance. Had there been no settlement, the claimant would have had no knowledge of any loss. Judgment would be given for the claimant.

AIG Europe (Ireland) Ltd v Faraday Capital Ltd [2006] EWHC 2707 (Comm), [2006] All ER (D) 373 (Oct) (Queen's Bench Division: Morison J).

659   Contractual term—transfer agreement—rights of third parties—enforcement of contractual term

The claimants had refurbishment work carried out. They were dissatisfied with the work and brought proceedings against the two defendants, seeking to hold them personally liable. The judge found that, although the contract for the works had been with a limited liability company, the assets and liabilities of the company had been transferred to the defendants as the members of a partnership. The transfer agreement provided that the purchasers undertook to complete outstanding customer orders and to pay in the normal course of time any liabilities properly incurred by the company. The judge held that the Contracts (Rights of Third Parties) Act 1999 applied since the claimants were third parties on whom the transfer agreement had purported to confer a benefit. On appeal by the defendants, an issue arose as to whether the 1999 Act applied having regard to the requirement in s 1(3) for the third party to be expressly identified in the contract by name, as a member of a class or as answering a particular description. *Held*, the term 'express' in s 1(3) was concerned with the benefit conferred on a third party, and with the identification of that person. It did not allow a process of construction or implication. There was nothing to limit the term 'liabilities properly incurred' to liabilities to customers. The transfer agreement did not identify any third party or class of third parties. Accordingly, the appeal would be allowed.

Avraamides v Colwill [2006] EWCA Civ 1533, [2006] All ER (D) 167 (Nov) (Court of Appeal: Waller and Leveson LJJ).

660   Contractual term—unfairness—discretionary bonus scheme for employees

See *Keen v Commerzbank AG*, para 1209.

661   Contractual term—unfairness—implied terms

See *Baybut v Eccle Riggs Country Park Ltd*, para 2503.

662   Illegality—enforceability—money laundering—suspicions of money laundering— refusal by bank to honour instructions

See *K Ltd v National Westminster Bank plc*, para 867.

663   Merger—merger in judgment—consequence—loss of cause of action

See *Messer Griesheim GmbH v Goyal MG Gases PVT Ltd*, para 2310.

664   Misrepresentation

See MISREPRESENTATION AND FRAUD.

665   Rescission—restitutio in integrum—impossibility of counter restitution

The parties were members of an orthodox Jewish family. The claimant and the defendants were siblings. Their parents had executed a Jewish will. The defendants were the executors. A dispute arose concerning the inheritance between the claimant and the defendants. It was incumbent on the parties to resolve the dispute in accordance with Jewish law. It was agreed that the matter be determined by a Beth Din which was to take place in Switzerland and under the Arbitration Act 1996. Subsequently, the matter was compromised. However, the first defendant indicated that he thought the compromise agreement null and void. The claimant issued proceedings for damages for repudiation of the agreement. The claimant applied for summary judgment and successfully struck out parts of the defence. One remaining defence was that the agreement was procured by duress. The agreement provided that all documents relating to it be destroyed. The judge held that this prejudiced the claimants and ordered the hearing of a preliminary issue as to whether a party could avoid a contract procured by duress where he could not offer the other party restitutio in integrum. *Held*, the common law remedy of rescission on the ground of duress required an ability to give counter restitution. Therefore, a party could not avoid a contract procured by duress in circumstances where he could not offer the other party substantial restitutio in integrum. Rescission at common law on the ground of fraudulent misrepresentation required an ability to give counter restitution. Rescission was meant to put parties back into the position they would have been had there been no contract. That logic required an ability to give counter restitution. There was no reason why the nature of the remedy of rescission or the circumstances in which it was available should differ depending on whether the ground of rescission was fraud or duress. Judgment would be given accordingly.

Halpern v Halpern (*No 2*) [2006] EWHC 1728 (Comm), [2006] 3 All ER 1139 (Queen's Bench Division: Nigel Teare QC).

666   Restitution

See RESTITUTION.

667   Sale of goods

See SALE OF GOODS AND SUPPLY OF SERVICES.

668   Sale of land

See CONVEYANCING.

CONVEYANCING

Halsbury's Laws of England (4th edn) vol 39(2) (Reissue) paras 1–300, vol 42 (Reissue) paras 1–400

Articles

For articles relating to this title please refer to the Table of Articles at the beginning of the Abridgment.

669   Contract of sale—completion—delay—failure to respond to request to delay completion—belief that silence constituted agreement to delay

See *Northstar Land Ltd v Brooks*, para 1290.

670   Conveyance of property—divorce proceedings—adult lacking in capacity—guidance

See para 1886.

671   Home information packs—prescribed documents

The Home Information Pack Regulations 2006, SI 2006/1503 (in force in part on 6 July 2006 and in part on 1 June 2007), prescribe the documents to be included in home information packs and the circumstances in which such documents are included. In particular, the regulations (1) distinguish between 'required' documents, which must be included in home information packs, and 'authorised' documents, which may be so included; (2) prohibit a home information pack from including any documents which are not required or authorised documents; (3) require a home information pack to be composed of original documents or true copies of them; (4) specify the required documents, which include an index, a sale statement, title information, additional information for commonhold and leasehold properties, information about the physical condition and energy efficiency of a property and property searches; (5) specify the authorised documents, which include translations, Braille versions, summaries or explanations of home information pack documents, additional title information or information relating to commonhold and leasehold properties, additional information relating to a property's physical condition, further property searches and searches relating to other premises; (6) provide that required documents must be included in home information packs at the first point of marketing; (7) require certain title information, home condition reports and required property searches to be no older than three months at the first point of marketing; (8) make provision in respect of required documents which are unavailable or unobtainable at the first point of marketing; (9) provide for the circumstances in which a home information pack or documents in it must or may be updated; (10) provide for exceptions in respect of seasonal accommodation, sales mixed with sales of non-residential premises, portfolios of residential properties, unsafe properties and properties which are to be demolished; (11) set at £200 the level of penalty charge for breach of a home information pack duty; (12) provide that a penalty charge notice does not apply where the content of certain home information pack documents fails to comply with the regulations, but a responsible person believes on reasonable grounds that it does; and (13) require home condition reports to be made by members of a certification scheme approved by the Secretary of State, and provide for the approval mechanism of such schemes.

672   Restrictive covenant

See EQUITY.

COPYRIGHT, DESIGN RIGHT AND RELATED RIGHTS

Halsbury's Laws of England (4th edn) vol 9(2) (2006 Reissue) paras 1–900

Articles

For articles relating to this title please refer to the Table of Articles at the beginning of the Abridgment.

673   Copyright—application to other countries

The Copyright and Performances (Application to Other Countries) Order 2006, SI 2006/316 (in force on 6 April 2006), replaces the 2005 Order, SI 2005/852, and applies the Copyright, Designs and Patents Act 1988 so as to confer copyright on creators of certain works originating from other countries and confer reciprocal protection on certain countries. The order qualifies literary, dramatic, musical and artistic works, films and typographical arrangements of published editions, sound recordings, wireless broadcasts, broadcasts, other than wireless broadcasts, for copyright protection where they are connected to the countries specified in the order. The order also qualifies certain performances and persons having recording protection where they are connected to the countries specified in the order, so that reciprocal protection is afforded to certain countries in respect of their performers and persons having recording rights and to certain countries for the making available of a performance.

674   Copyright—infringement—non-textual infringement—literary work

The claimant author alleged that his copyright in a book of his had been infringed by a subsequent novel and commenced proceedings against the defendant publishing house, which was responsible for the publication of the novel. The claimant sought relief for copyright infringement on the basis that the defendant had reproduced or authorised the reproduction of a substantial part of the copyright of his book. The claimant acknowledged that there was a significant amount of material which had not been derived from his book but alleged that the central theme of the novel had been copied by the novel's author. He claimed that this and other concepts had been copied by the novel's author and that, in so doing, the author had utilised the skill and labour expended by the claimant in creating his book. The defendant argued that the author had used the claimant's book as one of a number of sources and had used it only at a later stage in the composition of the novel. It contended that the synopsis for the novel had been written before the author had read the claimant's book. *Held*, copyright protection was not confined to the literal text in literary work. Changing a few immaterial words in a work that was otherwise the same would not escape liability. However, copyright should not protect against the borrowing of an idea contained in a work. The line to be drawn was to enable a fair balance to be struck between protecting the rights of the author and allowing literary development. Where a book was intended to be read as a factual account of historical events and a defendant accepted it as fact and did no more than repeat certain of those facts, a claimant could not claim a monopoly in those historical facts. Although facts, themes and ideas could not be protected, the way in which those facts, themes and ideas were put together could be protected. It followed that, to establish infringement, the claimant had to show that there was a putting together of facts, themes and ideas by him as a result of his efforts and that that putting together had been copied. In the present case, the author did not use the claimant's book when he wrote the synopsis. Moreover, the alleged central theme was not genuinely the central theme of the claimant's book. Accordingly, the claim would be dismissed.

Baigent v Random House Group Ltd [2006] EWHC 719 (Ch), [2007] IP & T 90 (Chancery Division: Peter Smith J).

675   Copyright—intellectual property—enforcement rights

See para 2120.

676   Copyright—performance rights—performer's moral and other rights

The Performances (Moral Rights, etc) Regulations 2006, SI 2006/18 (in force on 1 February 2006), make necessary amendments to the Copyright, Designs and Patents Act 1988 to enable the United Kingdom to ratify the World Intellectual Property Organisation Performers and Phonograms Treaty (Cm 3728). The regulations create two new moral rights for performers of qualifying performances. The first right (granted by s 205C) is the right to be identified as the performer, the second right (granted by s 205F) is the right to object to derogatory treatment. Exceptions to these rights are set out in ss 205E and 205G. The regulations also create a number of supplementary rights and make minor amendments.

677   Copyright—recording of broadcasts and cable programmes—educational
         establishments—certification of licensing schemes

The Copyright (Certification of Licensing Scheme for Educational Recording of Broadcasts and Cable Programmes) (Educational Recording Agency Limited) (Revocation) Order 2006, SI 2006/35 (in force on 9 January 2006), revokes the 1990 Order, SI 1990/879, which set out the licensing scheme certified by the Secretary of State.

678   Design right—intellectual property—enforcement rights

See para 2120.

679   Design right—infringement—method or principle of construction

The Copyright, Designs and Patents Act 1988 s 213(3)(a) provides that design right does not subsist in a method of principle or construction.

    The claimant company designed an expander section to a rigid or shell suitcase. Suitcases incorporating the expander design had been successfully marketed and sold, at the instigation or with the consent of the claimant. The claimant became aware that the defendant company had imported and sold expander suitcases which it alleged infringed its design rights in the expander design. The claimant's action to protect its design rights succeeded and the defendant appealed. *Held*, the 1988 Act s 213(3)(a) should be narrowly construed, and did not apply merely because a design served a functional purpose, it would not apply unless it could be shown that such purpose could not be achieved by any other means. Accordingly, the appeal would be dismissed.

    Landor & Hawa International Ltd v Azure Designs Ltd [2006] EWCA Civ 1285, [2007] FSR 181 (Court of Appeal: May, Neuberger and Wilson LJJ).

680   Design right—semiconductor topographies

The Design Right (Semiconductor Topographies) (Amendment) Regulations 2006, SI 2006/1833 (in force on 1 August 2006), amend the 1989 Regulations, SI 1989/1100, so as to give effect to EC Council Decision 94/824 on the extension of the legal protection of topographies of semiconductor products to persons from a member of the World Trade Organisation. In particular, the regulations provide for a modified version of the Copyright, Designs and Patents Act 1988 s 217(3) and include a list of qualifying countries, other than member states of the European Community which are parties to the Agreement establishing the World Trade Organisation. SI 1989/2147, 1990/1003, 1991/2237, 1992/400, 1993/2497, are revoked.

681   Resale right—artists

The Artist's Resale Right Regulations 2006, SI 2006/346 (in force on 14 February 2006), implement European Parliament and EC Council Directive 2001/84 on the resale right for the benefit of the author of an original work of art. The regulations, in particular, (1) create a new intellectual property right, known as resale right, which is to be enjoyed by the creator of a work of art, and that artist's successors in title, for as long as copyright continues to subsist in the work; (2) provide that the right consists in the entitlement to claim a royalty on the resale of the work following its first transfer by the artist; (3) specify that the royalty is to be based on the sale price, and set out how that amount is to be calculated; (4) define the works of art which are covered by the right, and detail the conditions under which a copy of a work is to be regarded as a work covered; (5) make provision for works which are the joint product of two or more artists; (6) impose a rebuttable presumption that a signatory of the work is its creator; (7) ensure that resale right may not be assigned or charged, but may be transmitted from one qualifying charitable body to another; (8) prohibit resale right from being waived; (9) preclude any agreement for the sharing or repayment of resale royalties, except in relation to the collection of resale right by a collecting society on the holder's behalf in return for a percentage of the royalty; (10) enable a resale right to be transmitted, on the death of its holder, to a natural person or to a qualifying charitable body, and make it clear that, in the absence of any heirs, it may pass to the Crown as bona vacantia; (11) restrict the exercise and transmission of resale right to qualifying charitable bodies and individuals who are EEA nationals or nationals of another specified country; (12) enable any person to hold and to exercise resale right in the capacity of a trustee for a person entitled to the right, and enable legal title to the right to be transferred to such a trustee or to the beneficiary; (13) define when a sale is to be regarded as a resale; (14) provide that a sale may be a resale even though the initial transfer of ownership in the work was not itself a sale; (15) require an art-market professional to be involved in the sale, either as principal or agent, for it to be a qualifying sale, and impose a minimum price threshold of 1,000 euro; (16) exempt certain sales where the work was recently acquired from the artist; (17) provide for the joint and several liability of art-market professionals and other agents; (18) enable resale right to be exercised only through an artists' collecting society; and (19) entitle holders of a resale right to request information about the sale from any art-market professional involved in the sale, and to apply to the court if such information is not provided within 90 days.

CORONERS

Halsbury's Laws of England (4th edn) vol 9(2) (2006 Reissue) paras 901–1100

Articles

For articles relating to this title please refer to the Table of Articles at the beginning of the Abridgment.

682   Discipline—designation

The Discipline of Coroners (Designation) Order 2006, SI 2006/677 (in force on 3 April 2006), designates coroners appointed under the Coroners Act 1998 s 1 and the Coroner of the Queen's Household appointed under s 29(1) as subject to the discipline regime set out in the Constitutional Reform Act 2005.

COSTS

Halsbury's Laws of England (4th edn) vol 10 (Reissue) paras 1–300

Articles

For articles relating to this title please refer to the Table of Articles at the beginning of the Abridgment.

683   Assessment of costs—conditional fee agreement—indemnity principle

The claimant entered into a conditional fee agreement ('CFA') with his solicitor in respect of a claim against the defendant for damages following a motor accident caused by the defendant. The claim was settled before proceedings began. However, the parties could not agree on costs, so proceedings for their determination were brought in the Supreme Court Costs Office. It came to light that the defendant's insurers were concerned that the CFA did not comply with the Conditional Fee Agreements Regulations 2000, SI 2000/692. The master took the view that the entitlement to fixed recoverable costs pursuant to CPR 45.9 and success fees pursuant to CPR 45.11 did not depend on the existence of a valid and enforceable CFA. The defendant appealed. *Held*, the clear intention underlying CPR 45.7–45.14 was to provide an agreed scheme of recovery which was certain and easily calculated. That was done by providing fixed levels of remuneration which might over-reward in some cases and under-reward in others, but which were regarded as fair when taken as a whole. It was clear that the draftsman of the CPR intended that the indemnity principle should not apply to the figures which were recoverable. The overriding objective of the CPR included saving expense and dealing with the cases in ways which were proportionate to the amount of money involved. The whole idea underlying CPR 45.7–45.14 was that it should be possible to ascertain the appropriate costs payable without the need for further recourse to the court. There was not an overriding need to enable the paying party to satisfy themselves that the CFA was compliant with the 2000 Regulations. Further, in cases falling under CPR 45.7–45.14 the receiving party did not have to demonstrate that there was a valid retainer between the solicitor and client, merely that the conditions laid down under the CPR had been complied with. Accordingly, the appeal would be dismissed.

Nizami v Butt; Kamaluden v Butt [2006] EWHC 159 (QB), [2006] 2 All ER 140 (Queen's Bench Division: Simon J).

684 Assessment of costs—conduct of parties—compulsory acquisition of land—discretion

Montserrat

Land belonging to the appellant company had been included in a compulsory land acquisition programme following a volcanic eruption which had devastated the island of Montserrat. The appellant considered that the value of the land was significantly higher than the government's initial offer. The appeal court determined that the land was worth only slightly more than the government had initially offered, and ordered each party to pay its own costs. On appeal, the issue arose whether a claimant who had been awarded compensation for the compulsory purchase of his land should be entitled to his own costs. *Held*, a claimant should be entitled to his costs of preparing and presenting his claim in full, and any reduction of the award should be exercised judicially. Where the claim was grossly excessive, it would be necessary to inquire whether the exaggeration gave rise to an obvious and substantial escalation in the costs. If it did, then the claimant could be deprived of part of his costs, and any such reduction should be proportionate to the amount of wasted time and costs properly attributable to the claimant's acts or omissions. Judgment would be given accordingly.

Blakes Estates Ltd v Government of Montserrat [2005] UKPC 46, [2006] 1 WLR 297 (Privy Council: Lords Nicholls of Birkenhead, Hoffmann, Rodger of Earlesferry, Walker of Gestingthorpe and Carswell). *Purfleet Farms Ltd v Secretary of State for Transport, Local Government and the Regions* [2002] EWCA Civ 1430, [2003] 1 P & CR 324 (2002 Abr para 573) applied.

685 Assessment of costs—conduct of parties—dishonest conduct of successful party—reduction in order for costs

In patent proceedings, the judge ruled in the defendants' favour despite finding them guilty of serious dishonesty. In awarding costs, the judge took the view that the claimant's expenditure on establishing dishonest conduct was disproportionate. On the claimant's appeal, an issue arose as to whether the effect of the judge's order was to allow certain of the defendants to recover costs of seeking to maintain a dishonest case. *Held*, consideration of a party's conduct should normally take place both at the stage when the judge was considering what order for costs he should make, and then during assessment. The court would want to ensure that dishonesty was penalised but that the party was not placed in double jeopardy. Where dishonest conduct was being reflected in an order, it was wise for a judge to make clear whether he was making the order on the basis that the paying party would still be entitled to raise the dishonesty in arguing that costs incurred in supporting the particular dishonesty were unreasonably incurred. There was no general rule that a losing party who could establish dishonesty had to receive all his costs of establishing that dishonesty, however disproportionate those costs might be. The natural construction where a judge ordered a percentage reduction was that the party guilty of dishonesty should not be entitled on assessment to say that the costs incurred in seeking to make a dishonest case could be taken as reasonably incurred because the judge had made a reduction. Further, there was no general rule that a losing party who could establish dishonesty had to receive all his costs of establishing that dishonesty. Proportionality and the conduct of the paying party in attacking that dishonesty was clearly something to which a trial judge was entitled to have regard. The judge had acted well within his discretion and had not misdirected himself in any way. Accordingly, the appeal would be dismissed.

Ultraframe (UK) Ltd v Fielding [2006] EWCA Civ 1660, [2006] All ER (D) 81 (Dec) (Court of Appeal: Waller and Jacob LJJ). *Aaron v Shelton* [2004] EWHC 1162 (QB), [2004] 3 All ER 561 (2004 Abr para 631) considered. For substantive proceedings see *Ultraframe (UK) Ltd v Fielding (No 2)* [2005] EWHC 1638 (Ch), [2006] FSR 293.

686 Assessment of costs—settlement of action—costs order in relation to action which has not been tried

When the parties to an action were unable to resolve the issue of costs they asked the judge to determine the issue. The judge made an order, but subsequently ordered a fresh hearing after the Court of Appeal's decision in *BCT Software Solutions v C Brewer & Sons Ltd* was brought to his attention. After the second hearing the judge, having considered the *BCT Software Solutions v C Brewer & Sons Ltd* decision, made no order as to costs. The claimant appealed, submitting that the *BCT Software Solutions v C Brewer & Sons Ltd* decision was distinguishable from the present case. *Held*, the judge had been correct to take into account the guidance given in *BCT Software Solutions v C Brewer & Sons Ltd*, which was an authority of general applicability to cases which had been settled or resolved without a judgment having been delivered and the judge was asked to adjudicate on the issue of costs. His decision to make no order for costs was not manifestly unjust. Accordingly, the appeal would be dismissed.

Promar International Ltd v Clarke [2006] EWCA Civ 332, [2006] All ER (D) 35 (Apr) (Court of Appeal: Hallett LJ and Bennett J). *BCT Software Solutions Ltd v C Brewer & Sons Ltd* [2003] EWCA Civ 939, [2004] FSR 150 (2004 Abr para 634) applied.

687   Association of Law Costs Draftsmen—investigation of complaints—Legal Services Ombudsman—jurisdiction

See para 2720.

688   Conditional fee agreement—after the event insurance premium—small personal injury case—proportionality

On a second appeal against a costs order made by a deputy district judge, the court considered (1) the proper approach to proportionality in a small personal injury case where the after the event insurance premium might appear large in comparison with the amount of damages reasonably claimed; (2) the proper approach to evidence of reasonableness of the choice and of the amount of the after the event premium in such cases; and (3) whether both staged or stepped premiums and single premiums for after the event insurance were legitimate for the purposes of the recoverability of a premium by a successful claimant, and whether it was reasonable that such premiums should be wholly or partially block-rated. *Held*, (1) if the court concluded that it was necessary to incur a staged premium, it should be judged a proportionate expense. However, necessity was not some absolute litmus test and might be demonstrated by the application of strategic considerations. Thus it might include, as the court was persuaded it did, the unavoidable characteristics of the market in after the event insurance. It did so because that very market was integral to the means of providing access to justice in civil disputes in what might be called the post-legal aid world. It was important to recognise that that conclusion ran with, not across, the grain of the procedural reforms expressed in the CPR. The very recognition that justice required a use of resources that was proportionate to what was at stake implied the correctness of a strategic approach. (2) There was in principle no difference between a two-staged success fee and a staged after the event premium. The financial risk to which the after the event provider was exposed inevitably rose as a case proceeded towards trial. While defendants might be liable to pay a higher premium if they took a case to trial and lost, the situation was no different from that facing them in relation to their liability to pay a higher success fee when claims were resolved against them 14 days or less before the date fixed for the commencement of a trial in the cases covered by the new arrangements for fixed recoverable success fees in CPR Pt 45. Exposure to that greater liability required a defendant to think very seriously about the merits of his position before a trial took place. That obligation too ran with the grain of the philosophy of the CPR. (3) It was not legitimate to compare the total premium payable at the third stage of a three-stage premium model with the single premium under a single premium model that was payable throughout the progress of a claim to trial. Accordingly, the appeal would be allowed.

The court added that a party who had an after the event insurance policy incorporating two or more staged premiums should inform its opponent that the policy was staged, and should set out accurately the trigger moments at which the second or later stages would be reached.

Rogers v Merthyr Tydfil CBC [2006] EWCA Civ 1134, [2007] 1 All ER 354 (Court of Appeal: Brooke, Laws and Smith LJJ). *Callery v Gray* [2001] EWCA Civ 1117, [2001] 3 All ER 833 (2001 Abr para 2969); *Callery v Gray (No 2)* [2001] EWCA Civ 1246, [2001] 4 All ER 1 (2001 Abr para 709) considered.

689   Conditional fee agreement—assignment

The claimant entered into a conditional fee agreement with a firm of solicitors. The solicitor who acted on the claimant's behalf moved to a second, and then to a third, firm. On each occasion the conditional fee agreement was purportedly assigned to the new firm. In costs assessment proceedings, the defendant contended that since the burden of a contract generally could not be assigned, where a solicitor took a client to a new firm on a conditional fee agreement that agreement could not be lawfully assigned to the new firm and the client would be obliged to enter into a new agreement. The master awarded the claimant his costs and the defendant appealed. *Held*, an exception to the general rule that only the benefit of a contract could be assigned was where the burden was conditional on the benefit. Where the events underlying the assignment were the trust and confidence a client had in his solicitor, a conditional fee agreement could be assigned by a firm of solicitors. The first firm had been obliged to act in the claimant's best interests and to secure for him the best possible outcome, and had been entitled to the benefit of payment for work done only if the claim was successful. It followed that the benefit of being paid was conditional on and inextricably linked to the meeting by that firm of its burden of ensuring to the best of its ability that the claimant's claim was successful. The benefit and burden of the conditional fee agreement therefore fell within the exception to the general rule and so could be assigned. Accordingly, the appeal would be dismissed.

Jenkins v Young Brothers Transport Ltd [2006] EWHC 151 (QB), [2006] 2 All ER 798 (Queen's Bench Division: Rafferty J). *Rhone v Stephens* [1994] 2 AC 310, HL (1994 Abr para 1308); and *Halsall v Brizell* [1957] Ch 169 considered.

690   Conditional fee agreement—enforceability—test of materiality—necessity for client to have suffered loss

In two separate cases an issue arose concerning the test of materiality in connection with a failure to comply with requirements, contained in the Courts and Legal Services Act 1990 s 58 and the Conditional Fee Agreements Regulations 2000, SI 2000/692, relating to conditional fee agreements. The issue in question was whether, in order to demonstrate that there had been a materially adverse effect either on the protection afforded to the client or on the proper administration of justice, the client had to have suffered actual prejudice. A further issue arose as to whether the enforceability of a conditional fee agreement was to be judged by reference to the circumstances existing at the time it was entered into, or by reference to the circumstances known to exist at the time when the question arose for decision. *Held*, there was no basis for interpreting the statutory provisions as requiring a court to hold that, however egregious a breach of the statutory requirements, it was not material if it had not in fact caused the client to suffer any loss. The primary purpose of the requirements was to provide protection to claimants. Difficulties of causation and loss were inherent in the common law, but there was no warrant for importing those difficulties into a statutory scheme which stated that breaches of its requirements rendered a conditional fee agreement unenforceable. In some cases, it might be helpful to have regard to what had actually happened, because that might shed light on the potential consequences of a breach (if the matter was judged at the date of the agreement) and therefore on the extent to which the breach had had a material adverse effect on the protection afforded to the client. In most cases, however, the court should focus its attention principally on the terms of the agreement and the advice and information given by the solicitor and other relevant circumstances which existed at the date of the agreement, and make a judgment as to whether, in the light of that material, the departure from the requirement in question had had a material adverse effect on the protection afforded to the client. With regard to the second issue, the enforceability of a conditional fee agreement, like any other contract, should as a matter of principle be capable of being determined as at the date that it was made. Its enforceability might otherwise change during the lifetime of the contract, thus making the contractual position between solicitor and client uncertain from day to day according to whether, at the point when the issue was being considered, it could be shown that the client had or had not suffered detriment as a result of the breach. Judgment would be given accordingly.

   Garrett v Halton BC; Myatt v National Coal Board [2006] EWCA Civ 1017, [2007] 1 All ER 147 (Court of Appeal: Brooke, Dyson and Lloyd LJJ). *Sharratt v London Central Bus Co Ltd* (*The Accident Group Test Cases*); *Hollins v Russell* [2003] EWCA Civ 718, [2003] 4 All ER 590 considered.
   SI 2000/692 revoked by SI 2005/2305.

691   Conditional fee agreement—excessive expenditure—costs-capping order

In the course of proceedings for passing off, the defendants applied for a costs-capping order against the claimant who had instructed lawyers under a conditional fee agreement which provided for a 100 per cent mark up without after the event insurance cover. The defendants submitted that the existence of a conditional fee agreement-assisted party without after the event insurance cover was sufficient to create risks to the other party so that a costs-capping order would be justified. *Held*, a conditional fee agreement with a large mark up and with no after the event insurance cover was not enough, by itself, to justify costs-capping at that stage. Instead, it was necessary to establish that the risk of excessive or extravagant expenditure and that such risk of expenditure could not be controlled by case management techniques or post-trial detailed assessments. In the present case, there were clear enough suggestions of potentially extravagant costs expenditure in two heads of expenditure. Case management was not capable of dealing with such risk. However, the two specific risk areas that had been identified were likely to be dealt with satisfactorily by the review that would be conducted by the costs judge on an after-trial costs assessment. The court was not satisfied that any other excessive expenditure could not be dealt with adequately by detailed costs assessments in due course. It had not been sufficiently proved that the risk of danger to the defendants was such that a costs-capping order should be made on the basis of the present evidence. Accordingly, the application would be dismissed.

   Knight v Beyond Properties PTY Ltd [2006] EWHC 1242 (Ch), [2007] FSR 157 (Chancery Division: Mann J). *Smart v East Cheshire NHS Trust* [2003] EWHC 2806, (2003) 80 BMLR 175 followed. *King v Telegraph Group Ltd* [2004] EWCA Civ 613, [2005] 1 WLR 2282 (2004 Abr para 644); and *Campbell v MGN Ltd* (*No 2*) [2005] UKHL 61, [2005] 4 All ER 793 (2005 Abr para 782) considered.

692   Conditional fee agreement—meaning—provision of litigation services—services provided before decision taken to pursue claim

The Courts and Legal Services Act 1990 s 58(2) defines a conditional fee agreement as an agreement with a person providing advocacy or litigation services which provides for his fees and expenses, or any part of them, to be payable only in specified circumstances. 'Litigation services' means any services which it would be reasonable to expect a person who is exercising, or contemplating exercising, a right to conduct litigation in relation to any proceedings, or contemplated proceedings, to provide: s 119(1).

The claimant was injured while travelling on a bus operated by the defendant. She consulted a firm of solicitors, who sent her a retainer letter which stated that, in the event the claim was disputed and she decided not to continue with the action, she would not be charged for the work done by the firm to that point. The defendant admitted liability, and in subsequent proceedings a consent order was made providing that the defendant was to pay the claimant's costs. The parties could not agree on costs, and at a detailed assessment an issue arose as to whether the retainer letter constituted a conditional fee agreement within the meaning of the 1990 Act s 58(2). The master decided that the letter was not a conditional fee agreement, but the defendant successfully appealed against that ruling. On the claimant's appeal, held, work done by a solicitor before a decision was made by a client not to pursue a claim did not amount to the provision of litigation services. 'Contemplated proceedings' within the meaning of s 119(1) were proceedings of which it could be said that there was at least a real likelihood that they would be issued. Until the potential defendant disputed the claim, it was not possible to say that proceedings were contemplated. Advising a client as to whether he had a good prima facie case and writing a letter of claim were not enough to amount to litigation services. That approach to the meaning of 'litigation services' was consistent with the statutory purpose of protecting clients. A client who, having received limited pre-litigation services, decided not to pursue a claim by litigation had no need for the panoply of protection afforded by the conditions stated in s 58(3). It was not intended by Parliament that the statutory regime should apply to agreements to provide such limited services. Accordingly, the appeal would be dismissed.

Gaynor v Central West London Buses Ltd [2006] EWCA Civ 1120, [2006] All ER (D) 453 (Jul) (Court of Appeal: Auld and Dyson LJJ and Sir Martin Nourse).

693   Costs—criminal cases

See CRIMINAL EVIDENCE AND PROCEDURE.

694   Costs—divorce proceedings

See MATRIMONIAL LAW.

695   Order for costs—cost capping order—application—conditional fee agreement—applicable principles

The claimant claimed damages for libel against the defendant in respect of allegations made about her in a national newspaper. The claimant's solicitors were acting under a conditional fee arrangement. In due course, the costs judge made a costs capping order, but that restriction was made on the claimant only. The claimant appealed in respect of certain details of the order, and issues arose relating to the principles to be applied in making the relevant assessment for a capping order. Held, it was inherent in the task of prospective costs capping that a good deal of informed guesswork would come into play. That was, if anything, more difficult in a libel action than in a 'standard' personal injury case. The costs of the capping exercise itself should not have any impact on the capped figure but should be treated separately, otherwise there might not be enough for the substantive litigation. However, it was easy for an unscrupulous and wealthy opponent, or even one who was unduly zealous or enthusiastic, to engage the capped party in correspondence or applications which would cause the budget to be used up in responding to them. In libel actions particularly, cases could change shape as they made their way towards trial, and thus a need would arise for money to be spent that could not have been foretold at the time of the capping. It might seem easy to appeal, or to come back and apply for an increase in the budget because of changed circumstances, but such procedural steps were in themselves risky and would inevitably incur extra costs. Also, it was important to try to ensure, so far as possible, 'equality of arms' and thus not to apply two different standards of what was 'reasonable' expenditure. What was reasonable for one side could hardly be unreasonable for the other. There was therefore a temptation to consider mutual costs capping, albeit not necessarily by reference to the same figures, since each side would inevitably have different tasks to perform. It was to be borne in mind that a costs capping order did not limit the expenditure of the capped party; it merely limited what could be recovered fro the other side in the event of success. Nevertheless, it was important always to have regard to the court's case management powers and, in particular, the power to obtain estimates on both sides and to limit costs as to what was proportionate. Judgment would be given accordingly.

Tierney v News Group Newspapers Ltd [2006] EWHC 3275 (QB), [2006] All ER (D) 321 (Dec) (Queen's Bench Division: Eady J).

696   Order for costs—discretion of court—disallowance of costs—failure to comply with time limit

The claimants were ordered to pay the defendants' costs of the appeal, 75 per cent of the defendants' costs in the court below and 20 per cent of the defendants' costs of his cross-appeal. There was then a five-year delay before detailed assessment took place. The claimants' solicitors therefore applied pursuant to CPR 44.14 for relief by way of disallowance of interest and a proportion of the defendants' costs. CPR 44.14 provided that, in certain circumstances, the court might disallow all or part of the costs that were being assessed. The costs judge dismissed the disallowance application save to the extent that the defendants' solicitors had conceded the disallowance of interest on the costs. The judge concluded that there were no sufficient reasons for disallowing costs as well as interest, and dismissed the claimants' appeal. On the claimants' further appeal, an issue arose as to the inter-relationship between CPR 44.14 and CPR 47.8. CPR Pt 47 provided for detailed assessment proceedings to be begun within three months of the judgment by which such costs were ordered to be assessed and provided that, if the receiving party did not do so, the court might disallow all or part of the interest otherwise payable to the receiving party but must not impose any other sanction except in accordance with CPR 44.14. *Held*, while non-compliance with a rule, practice direction or court order was the only jurisdictional requirement for the exercise of the power contained in CPR 44.14, it would usually be appropriate as a matter of discretion to consider the extent of any misconduct that had occurred in the course of such non-compliance. It would only be in the event of a breach of the rule which could properly be categorised as misconduct that it would usually be appropriate to use the power to disallow costs. The court should be hesitant to exercise further powers to impose further penalties by way of reducing otherwise allowable costs where the relevant rule not only gave to the party at the receiving end of the delay the option of preventing further delay by himself taking the initiative but also spelt out the normal sanction for penalising such delay, as CPR 47.8 did. In the present case there was no error in the exercise of his discretion by the judge. He pointed out correctly that the defendants' delay was not such as to be wilful, deliberate or contumelious and described the claimant as not being a model of co-operative expedition and said that that fact underlined his view that further sanction would be disproportionate and unnecessary. Accordingly, the appeal would be dismissed.

Haji-Ioannou v Frangos [2006] EWCA Civ 1663, [2006] All ER (D) 72 (Dec) (Court of Appeal: Sir Andrew Morritt C, Arden and Longmore LJJ). Decision of Lindsay J [2006] EWHC 279 (Ch), [2006] All ER (D) 375 (Feb) affirmed.

697   Order for costs—discretion of court—scheme of arrangement—objector

The court sanctioned two schemes of arrangement proposed by a company (the 'scheme company'), in respect of which objections had been put forward by an American company. As a result of the schemes, the scheme company was acquired by another company. The purchasing company and the American company subsequently applied to the court for a determination of the manner in which their costs should be paid. *Held*, the courts did not, as a rule, make costs orders against objecting shareholders or creditors when their objections were not frivolous and had been of assistance to the court. Sometimes no order for costs was made, and sometimes an order was made in favour of the objector. There was no established principle that that treatment, which differed from the ordinary rule in litigation that costs usually followed the event, applied to other objectors. The matter remained in all cases at the court's discretion. Regardless of whether a costs order was made pursuant to rules of court as between parties or directly pursuant to the Supreme Court Act 1981 s 51, costs only included the costs of or incidental to the litigation. The fair conclusion was for the American company to pay any additional costs incurred by the scheme company as a result of the objections being made. The scheme company sought only a proportion of counsel's fees, and the order would therefore be limited in that way. There would be no additional order as to costs. Judgment would be given accordingly.

Re Peninsular & Oriental Steam Navigation Co [2006] All ER (D) 82 (Oct) (Chancery Division: Warren J).

698   Order for costs—order against local authority—authority acting properly

The respondent applied to the appellant licensing authority for various extensions of the licensing hours of a public house it owned. The appellant rejected certain parts of the application, and the respondent appealed to the magistrates' court under the Licensing Act 2003 s 181. The justices allowed the appeal in part and, in deciding the issue of costs, considered that, although the appellant had carried out its duties in a conscientious and proper manner, the court had reached a different conclusion. It therefore ordered the appellant to pay the respondent 50 per cent of the costs. The appellant appealed against the costs order, submitting that it should not be required to pay costs where it had carried out its duties properly. *Held*, although justices did not have to refuse an award of costs where a licensing authority had acted reasonably and in good faith, that was an important factor. In the instant case, the appellant's criticisms were well founded, and the justices could not properly have awarded costs against the authority. Accordingly, the appeal would be allowed.

Cambridge CC v Alex Nesting Ltd [2006] All ER (D) 252 (May) (Queen's Bench Division: Richards LJ and Toulson J). *Bradford City MDC v Booth* (2000) 164 JP 485, DC (2000 Abr para 2569), applied.

699   Order for costs—order against non-party—company secretary and shareholder

The claimant, a debt recovery company, was owned by a solicitor, the defendant, and his wife. They sold their shares in the claimant and resigned as directors, but the solicitor remained as company secretary and solicitor. The claimant issued a statutory demand for debt against the defendant. The judge dismissed the claim, and was harshly critical of the defendant's behaviour and methods, and made an order under the Supreme Court Act 1981 s 51(3) that the defendant pay all costs of the action on an indemnity basis. The defendant appealed. *Held*, the costs could be awarded under s 51(3) against a director or shareholder who controlled and supported an action brought by the company in which he was interested if he was the real party for whose benefit the litigation was brought, even where he had acted without bad faith or impropriety. The question was whether any of the costs of the litigation brought by the claimant would have been incurred but for the involvement of the third party. The award against the defendant was justified, since he was the real party for whom the claimant's action had been brought and, irrespective of whether he had any real belief in the claim, the whole of the costs had been caused by his dishonesty, impropriety and exceptional conduct. Accordingly, the appeal would be dismissed.

Goodwood Recoveries Ltd v Breen [2005] EWCA Civ 414, [2006] 2 All ER 533 (Court of Appeal: May and Rix LJJ). *Dymocks Franchise Systems (NSW) Pty Ltd v Todd* [2004] UKPC 39, [2005] 4 All ER 195 (2005 Abr para 807) applied.

700   Order for costs—order against non-party—funder of litigation

The applicants successfully sought judgment and an order of costs against the first defendant, but failed to obtain judgment or an order of costs against the second defendant. They sought a variation of the costs order made in their favour against the first defendant so that it should be paid by the second defendant on the ground that he was the funder of the first defendant. *Held*, as there had been a material change of circumstances and a misrepresentation as to the correct factual situation, there was no reason in principle why the order sought should not be made. The applicants would have made the application at the time the judgment was given had the true financial position of the first defendant been known to them. The second defendant was in de facto control of the first defendant although he did not have a financial interest in the outcome of the litigation. The benefit did not need to be purely financial in circumstances where the litigation centred on a personal battle between one of the applicants and the second defendant and there was sufficient personal benefit to constitute a personal interest in the litigation. It was just to make the order in the terms sought. Accordingly, the application would be allowed.

Latimer Management Consultants Ltd v Ellingham Investments Ltd [2006] All ER (D) 357 (Oct) (Chancery Division: Livesey QC). *Lloyds Investment (Scandinavia) v Ager-Hanssen* [2003] EWHC 1740 (Ch), [2003] All ER (D) 258 (Jul); *Dymocks Franchise Systems (NSW) Pty Ltd v Todd* [2004] UKPC 39, [2005] 4 All ER 195 (2005 Abr para 807); and *Collier v Williams* [2006] EWCA Civ 20, [2006] 1 WLR 1945 (para 2282) applied.

701   Order for costs—order sanctioning business transfer scheme—opposition to scheme

See *Re Alliance Assurance Co Ltd; Re British Engine Insurance Ltd*, para 1332.

702   Order for costs—party with legal aid—cost protection—jurisdiction to award costs

The Access to Justice Act 1999 s 11(1) provides that, except in prescribed circumstances, costs ordered against an individual in relation to any proceedings or part of proceedings funded for him must not exceed the amount (if any) which is a reasonable one for him to pay having regard to all the circumstances including (1) the financial resources of all the parties to the proceedings; and (2) their conduct in connection with the dispute to which the proceedings relate; and for this purpose proceedings, or a part of proceedings, are funded for an individual if services relating to the proceedings or part are funded for him by the Legal Services Commission.

Various declarations had been made by the court in relation to the medical treatment of the defendants' child by the claimant health service trust. An application for permission to appeal and a substantive appeal brought by the defendants against the declarations were subsequently dismissed. The claimant sought an order for costs against the defendants pursuant to the 1999 Act s 11(1), as a necessary prerequisite for an application which the claimant wished to make to require the Legal Services Commission, which was funding the defendants in the litigation, to pay the claimant's costs of the defendants' unsuccessful permission application and appeal. Issues arose as to whether the s 11(1) order should be made and, if so, whether the amount to be paid by the defendants pursuant to that order should be specified. *Held*, where the court was considering whether to make a s 11(1) order, it should consider whether, but for cost protection, it would have made a costs order against the unsuccessful party. In the instant case, the answer to that question was clearly yes, as a matter of the proper exercise of judicial discretion to make orders for costs following the outcome of proceedings in the Court of Appeal. Moreover, in the circumstances, there was sufficient information to decide what amount the defendants should pay pursuant to that order, namely nothing at all. Judgment would be given accordingly.

Re Wyatt (A Child) (Medical Treatment: Continuation of Order) (Costs) [2006] EWCA Civ 529, [2006] All ER (D) 27 (May) (Court of Appeal: Laws, Wall and Lloyd LJJ).

703   Payment into court

See PRACTICE AND PROCEDURE.

704   Protected costs order—discretion of court—issues of general public importance

A marriage celebrated after 31 July 1971 is void on the grounds that the parties are not respectively male and female: Matrimonial Causes Act 1973 s 11(c).

The claimant, who was domiciled in England, went through a form of marriage that was lawful and valid by the law of British Columbia, which recognised as valid marriages between persons of the same sex. Since the coming into force of the Civil Partnership Act 2004, the petitioner and her partner were to be treated as having formed a civil partnership and not as being married. The petitioner sought a declaration, pursuant to the Family Law Act 1986 s 55, that her marriage was a valid marriage and a declaration of incompatibility, under the Human Rights Act 1998 s 4, in relation to the 1973 Act s 11(c). The Lord Chancellor intervened to make representations on behalf of the Crown. The petitioner sought a protected costs order that each party should bear its own costs and that there should be no further order as to costs. It was agreed that the nature of the proceedings were essentially 'quasi-public'. The petitioner submitted that her case, as pleaded, disclosed a real prospect of success and that it was in the public interest to make a declaration of incompatibility. *Held*, the court's discretion as to costs was at large under the Supreme Court Act 1981 s 51, CPR 44.3(1) and under CPR 3.1(2), which gave the court power to make any order for the purpose of managing the case and furthering the overriding objective. The petitioner's case was not unarguable in the light of modern developments within and outside Europe, but her case depended on establishing propositions that extended well beyond the current bounds of English and European jurisprudence. While the issues were of public interest and importance, they related to a measure carefully and recently considered and passed by Parliament with a view to producing equivalence, in a context in which the European Court of Human Rights clearly recognised the margin of appreciation and permitted it to operate. Further, there was scant evidence that a substantial number of same-sex couples were in the same position, or considered that the status, rights, and responsibilities accorded to them under the 2004 Act disadvantaged or demeaned them in any way in comparison to married couples. In the circumstances, the issues raised did not require resolution as a matter of general public importance. The present case was not one where it was appropriate to make the order sought. Accordingly, the application would be dismissed.

Wilkinson v Kitzinger [2006] EWHC 835 (Fam), [2006] 2 FCR 537 (Family Division: Sir Mark Potter P). *Bellinger v Bellinger* [2003] UKHL 21, [2003] 2 AC 430 (2003 Abr para 1819); and *R (on the application of Corner House Research) v Secretary of State for Trade and Industry* [2005] EWCA Civ 192, [2005] 4 All ER 1 (2005 Abr para 813) considered.

705   Security for costs—order—affordability—determination—claimant resident abroad

In libel proceedings, the claimants, who were resident in Sudan, were ordered by the judge to put up a sum for security for the costs of the defendants. The claimants appealed. *Held*, the principles governing security for costs under CPR 25.13 were that a claimant would not be required to lodge security for the defendant's costs where the claimant was a resident abroad whose case, at the moment of the interlocutory decision, appeared highly likely to succeed at trial. In most cases, a requirement for security for costs on the mere fact that the claimant resided abroad would amount to discrimination on the ground of national origin. What an order for security required was an established difficulty of enforcement in the country of residence. The requirement of a fair trial under the European Convention on Human Rights art 6 was met by the principle that the court could not fix security in what it knew was an unaffordable amount. A claimant who was resident abroad had to be full and candid in setting out what his means were to ensure that any security he was required to put up was within his means. Once satisfied that the case was one in which the claimant should put up security, the court either would be satisfied that it probably had a full account of the claimant's available resources, in which case it could calculate with reasonable confidence how much the claimant could afford to put up, or it would not be satisfied that it had a full account and so could not make the calculation. In the latter case, the court had a discretion to set an amount which represented its best estimate of what the claimant could afford. On the evidence, the judge had been entitled to make the order for security which he had made, Accordingly, the appeal would be dismissed.

Al-Koronky v Time-Life Entertainment Group Ltd [2006] EWCA Civ 1123, [2006] All ER (D) 447 (Jul) (Court of Appeal: Sedley, Keene and Longmore LJJ). *Keary Developments Ltd v Tarmac Constructions Ltd* [1995] 3 All ER 534, CA (1995 Abr para 521); and *Nasser v United Bank of Kuwait* [2001] EWCA Civ 556, [2002] 1 All ER 401 considered.

706   Security for costs—order—appropriateness of making 'unless' order

The claimant, a Romanian citizen, brought a libel action against the defendants, who were magazine publishers. As the claimant resided outside the jurisdiction, the defendants applied for security for costs. The claimant disputed that there would be additional costs in enforcing any judgment in

Romania, and also maintained that, since Romania was likely to be a member of the European Union by the time of any judgment in the defendants' favour, any order was inappropriate. He further maintained that an order would stifle the action. The senior master rejected those contentions and made an order for security which was in the form of an unless order. The claimant appealed, although there was no stay of the order pending the appeal. The vacation judge would not grant a stay on appeal either, and judgment was therefore entered against the claimant. The claimant later alleged to be able to provide the sum, but the defendant rejected an offer to resurrect the action and, at the hearing of the appeal, the judge decided that the claimant should have applied for permission to appeal the vacation judgment, and/or to serve a fresh claim form to avoid the limitation period. Not having taken any of those steps, he could not circumvent the effect of the vacation judgment. He therefore dismissed the appeal, and the claimant appealed. *Held*, the making of an order for security was not intended to be a weapon by which a defendant could obtain a speedy summary judgment without a trial. The obtaining of an order was intended to give a claimant a choice whether to put up security or to discontinue the claim. It was supposed to be a proper choice. If a court had made an unless order, and even if judgment had been entered pursuant to the security not being paid, and a claimant within a short period of time had come to the court with the right sum, the court should be willing to consider granting relief and setting the judgment aside. Each case would depend on its own facts, but in the case of security for costs a judgment following an unless order did not have the character of judgments given on the merits after a trial. Nor should the attitude of the court to staying such a judgment be the same as a judgment on the merits following a trial. The claimant had not deliberately flouted the order and there had not been a suggestion that he personally had had the money. Accordingly, the appeal would be allowed.

Radu v Houston [2006] EWCA Civ 1575, [2006] All ER (D) 295 (Nov) (Court of Appeal: Waller, Keene and Carnwarth LJJ).

707   Security for costs—steps taken in relation to assets rendering enforcement difficult—intent

The claimant brought proceedings against the defendant for a share in the profit of a property transaction. The defendant obtained an order for security for costs pursuant to CPR 25.13(2)(g), which gave the court jurisdiction to make such an order where a claimant had taken steps in relation to his assets that would make it difficult to enforce an order for costs against him. The order required that the claimant provide security for the defendant's costs for a specified sum and before a prescribed time, otherwise judgment would be entered for the defendant with costs payable by the claimant. The claimant did not provide the security within the time allotted and applied to extend the time limit. The application was refused and the claimant appealed, contending that the condition required in CPR 25.13(2)(g) was not satisfied, and that the provision should be construed narrowly, taking into consideration temporal limitations on previous steps taken in relation to assets by a claimant and a claimant's intention. The claimant also argued that the refusal to extend the time limit was contrary to the overriding objective and fettered the right to apply for permission to appeal and, if granted, the right to appeal. *Held*, the condition contained in CPR 25.13(2)(g) was objective and unconcerned with the claimant's motivation. While CPR 25.13(2)(d) contained the words 'with a view to', they had been omitted in CPR 25.13(2)(g), and it was thus impossible to avoid the inference that the omission had been deliberate in order to exclude the element of intent. Moreover, there was no temporal limitation in CPR 25.13(2)(g), since it would render imprecise the precise language of the provision and would entail inserting into it words that had been absent. Its existence would in any case be an unnecessary exercise as an order for security for costs could not be made unless the court was satisfied that it was just to do so, meaning that the court's discretion provided sufficient protection to a claimant. On the evidence, steps had been taken by the claimant in relation to his assets which brought the case within CPR 25.13(2)(g). Accordingly, the appeal would be dismissed.

Harris v Wallis [2006] All ER (D) 158 (Mar) (Chancery Division: Sir Francis Ferris). *Aoun v Bahri* [2002] EWCA Civ 1141, [2002] 3 All ER 182 (2002 Abr para 729) followed. *Chandler v Brown* [2001] All ER (D) 302 (Jul); and *Compagnie Noga D'Importation et D'Exportation SA v Abacha (as personal representatives of Sani Abacha (deceased)) (No 4)* [2004] EWHC 2601 (Comm), [2004] All ER (D) 292 (Nov) considered.

708   Wasted costs order—personal liability of solicitor—oral application—approach of judge

The second and third claimants, who were the directors and the shareholders of the first claimant company, brought negligence proceedings against the first defendant, which had originally been the claimants' solicitors, and the second defendant, which had taken over the practice of the first defendant. Solicitors acting for the second defendant ('the solicitors') acknowledged service of the claim form on behalf of both the first defendant and the second defendant. However, as the first defendant was an undischarged bankrupt at the time, it could not be served with the claim form without the prospective or retrospective leave of the court. The first defendant contacted the solicitors in order to object to the acknowledgment of service on its behalf, and to deny it the authority to act on its behalf. Ignoring that instruction, the solicitors filed a defence and a re-amended defence on behalf of both defendants. The first defendant subsequently successfully applied to strike out the claim, and the first defendant and the claimants then made an oral application for a wasted costs order against the solicitors claiming that, pursuant to the *Practice Direction* about Costs PD 43–48 para 53.4, the solicitor had acted improperly, unreasonably or negligently, causing them to incur unnecessary costs. The judge decided that there was evidence or other material which, if unanswered, would be likely to lead to a wasted costs order being made, and that the wasted costs proceedings were justified notwithstanding the likely costs involved. He therefore ordered a hearing into whether it was appropriate to make a wasted costs order. The solicitors appealed, contending that there was no material on which it could be concluded that it had acted improperly, unreasonably or negligently, and that it was improper to hold a further hearing in view of the costs. *Held*, the judge's approach had been wrong and outside his wide discretion. Forming a view that the matter ought to be investigated was different from forming a prima facie view that the solicitors had acted improperly, unreasonably or negligently. The solicitor in question, in acknowledging service on behalf of the first defendant, had not been an officious inter-meddler, and it had not been plain that he had acted improperly, unreasonably or negligently. Further, there had not been sufficient material as to whether the claimants and the first defendant had incurred unnecessary costs because of the solicitor's conduct and whether it would be proportionate to consider the second stage. Moreover, an oral application for a wasted costs order should only be heard if the basis of the costs sought to be recovered was narrow and clear. In other situations, the parties should apply pursuant to CPR Pt 23. Accordingly, the appeal would be allowed.

Regent Leisuretime Ltd v Skerrett [2006] All ER (D) 34 (Jul) (Court of Appeal: Mummery and Lloyd LJJ).

709 Wasted costs order—personal liability of solicitor—proceedings brought to delay payment of tax

The taxpayers were United Kingdom nationals who had sold their shares in a company. In their tax returns for the relevant year, they claimed that they had not been resident or ordinarily resident in the United Kingdom in that year. As they did not provide information supporting their claim, the Inland Revenue began an investigation into their liability to capital gains tax. Over the course of the investigation, the taxpayers did not provide information requested, failed to comply with notices issued pursuant to the Taxes Management Act 1970, concealed their change of address, and failed to pay penalties and costs orders made against them. The Revenue sought a wasted costs order against the taxpayers' solicitors in relation to an appeal against a decision of the Special Commissioners dismissing appeals against certain penalties. The solicitors contended that it had been open to the Revenue to take steps to enforce the costs orders and penalties, that they had acted on the taxpayers' instructions, and that the taxpayers would not waive privilege. *Held*, the appeal had been hopeless and had been prosecuted for reasons unconnected with success on the appeal. It was the last of a continuing series of actions and omissions on the part of the taxpayers and their solicitors designed to evade or delay liability for, and payment of, capital gains tax. The solicitors were prepared to be a party to any scheme or tactic of the taxpayers which was designed to achieve the taxpayers' objective. As competent solicitors, they should have been aware that the appeal was an abuse of process brought for an illegitimate collateral purpose and that their own actions were calculated to further, and did further, their clients' inadmissible objectives. The solicitors' conduct had occasioned the waste of the Revenue's costs, which the taxpayers would not discharge. It was just to make a wasted costs order against the solicitors. Accordingly, the application would be allowed.

Morris v Roberts (Inspector of Taxes) [2005] EWHC 1040 (Ch), [2006] STC 135 (May) (Chancery Division: Lightman J). *Medcalf v Mardell* [2003] 1 AC 120 applied. *Ridehalgh v Horsefield* [1994] Ch 205, CA (1994 Abr para 2188); *Tolstoy-Miloslavsky v Lord Aldington* [1996] 1 WLR 736, CA (1995 Abr para 2334); and *Fletamentos Maritimos SA v Effijohn International BV* [2003] Lloyd's Rep PN 26 considered.

COURTS

Halsbury's Laws of England (4th edn) vol 10 (Reissue) paras 301–900

Articles

For articles relating to this title please refer to the Table of Articles at the beginning of the Abridgment.

710 Civil proceedings—fees

The Civil Proceedings Fees (Amendment) Order 2006, SI 2006/719 (in force on 6 April 2006), further amends the 2004 Order, SI 2004/3121, so as to (1) impose a new fee for a request for the issue of a certificate of satisfaction in relation to an entry in the register of judgments, in place of the fee for a request for the issue of a certificate of satisfaction in relation to an entry in the registry of county court judgments; and (2) increase, from £15,050 to £15,460, the maximum gross annual income above which working tax credit is not a qualifying benefit for the purposes of exemption from court fees.

711 County court—districts

The Civil Courts (Amendment) Order 2006, SI 2006/1542 (in force on 6 July 2006), further amends the 1983 Order, SI 1983/713, by closing the Shoreditch and Clerkenwell county courts and replacing them with the Clerkenwell & Shoreditch county court.

712 County court—register of judgments

The Courts Act 2003 (Consequential Amendment) Order 2006, SI 2006/1001 (in force on 6 April 2006), amends the Child Support Act 1991 s 33(5), by replacing the reference to the register of judgments held in accordance with the County Courts Act 1984 with a reference to the register held in accordance with the Courts Act 2003.

713 Court of Appeal—proceedings involving asylum-seekers—anonymisation

Sir Anthony Clarke MR, has issued the following *Practice Note (Court of Appeal: Asylum-seeker Anonymisation)* (2006) Times, 24 August on 31 July 2006.

1. The Master of the Rolls said the Court of Appeal had decided to follow the universal practice observed by other European jurisdictions and to anonymise its judgments in cases involving asylum-seekers.

2. It was satisfied that the publication of the names of appellants might create avoidable risks for them in the countries from which they had come.

3. It would be impractical to introduce internal arrangements within the Civil Appeals Office which made any distinction between asylum-seekers and those seeking other relief under the immigration laws when those cases were received in the office from the Asylum and Immigration Tribunal or from the Administrative Court.

4. All applications and appeals raising asylum and immigration issues lodged on or after 2 October 2006 therefore are to be anonymised in the court's internal records by assigning two initials and the country of origin, AB (Turkey) for example, unless a judge gives a specific direction to contrary effect.

5. Such cases are then to be listed and referred to solely by reference to that name and the reference number allocated to them in the Civil Appeals Office, for example, *AB (Turkey)* Case No C5/2006/1234.

6. Hearings are to continue to take place in open court, unless the court directs otherwise.

7. If judgment is given in an asylum appeal, or a permission to appeal application, where the judgment is released from the usual restriction on citation, there will be a presumption that the asylum-seeker's anonymity will be preserved unless the court gives a direction to contrary effect.

8. On the other hand, there is to be a presumption that judgments in immigration appeals are to identify the name of the person seeking relief under the immigration laws unless the court gives a direction requiring anonymity.

9. If more than one judgment is issued by the Court of Appeal in a single year under the same name, the later judgments are to be numbered thus *AB (Turkey)* [2006] EWCA Civ 1; *AB (Turkey) (No 2)* [2006] EWCA Civ 1235; *AB (Turkey) (No 3)* [2006] EWCA 2045.

714 Court of Protection—rules

See para 1971.

715 Court of Session—jurisdiction—judicial review—decision-maker located in England

See *Tehrani v Secretary of State for the Home Department (Scotland)*, para 92.

716 Crown Court

See CRIMINAL EVIDENCE AND PROCEDURE.

717 European Court of Human Rights

See HUMAN RIGHTS.

718 European Court of Justice

See EUROPEAN COMMUNITIES.

719   Family Division—guidance—vacation business

See para 2300.

720   Family Division—proceedings—urgent and out of hours cases

See para 469.

721   High Court—jurisdiction—decision of Crown Court—judicial review—matter relating to trial on indictment

See *R (on the application of TH) v Crown Court at Wood Green*, para 752.

722   House of Lords—appellate jurisdiction—appeal on point of law of general public importance—change of circumstances

See *R (on the application of Bushell) v Newcastle upon Tyne Licensing Justices*, para 1732.

723   House of Lords—Lords of Appeal—removal of Lord Chancellor's membership

See para 623.

724   International Criminal Court

See FOREIGN RELATIONS LAW.

725   Judicial appointments—permitted persons—disclosure of information

The Permitted Persons (Designation) Order 2006, SI 2006/679 (in force on 3 April 2006), designates permitted persons for the purposes of the Constitutional Reform Act 2005 s 107, so as to allow them to disclose information to the Judicial Appointments Commission for the purposes of selection.

726   Judicial pensions—additional voluntary contributions

The Judicial Pensions (Additional Voluntary Contributions) (Amendment) Regulations 2006, SI 2006/747 (in force on 6 April 2006), further amend the 1995 Regulations, SI 1995/639, so as to (1) ensure compliance with the new tax regime set out in the Finance Act 2004; (2) extend the range of benefits payable by reference to what is permissible under the 2004 Act; (3) abolish free standing additional voluntary contributions schemes; and (4) provide for the closure of three additional voluntary contributions schemes, with provision to enable existing members to continue to contribute.

727   Judicial pensions—contributions

The Judicial Pensions (Contributions) (Amendment) Regulations 2006, SI 2006/749 (in force on 6 April 2006), amend the percentage of salary that is to form the rate of member contributions towards survivor benefits under the Judicial Pensions Act 1981 and the Judicial Pensions and Retirement Act 1993, so as to (1) allow members of schemes under those Acts to make additional contributions, up to the maximum of their total salary in any financial year, towards such benefits in respect of past service; (2) afford members of a scheme under the 1981 Act an additional opportunity to cease paying contributions from salary; and (3) revoke provisions relating to the taxation of refunded contributions.

728   Judicial pensions—qualifying judicial offices

The Judicial Pensions and Retirement Act 1993 (Addition of Qualifying Judicial Offices) Order 2006, SI 2006/391 (in force on 3 April 2006), amends the Judicial Pensions and Retirement Act 1993, so as to add coroner and deputy coroner to the list of qualifying judicial offices.

729   Judicial pensions—taxation—earnings cap

The Taxation of Judicial Pensions (Consequential Provisions) Order 2006, SI 2006/497 (in force on 6 April 2006), amends the Judicial Pensions and Retirement Act 1993, by replacing a reference to the earnings cap in the previous pension tax regime with a stand-alone provision having the same effect, and by removing a reference to the earnings cap in a provision for additional voluntary contributions. Corresponding amendments are made to the County Courts Act (Northern Ireland) 1959, the Resident Magistrates' Pensions Act (Northern Ireland) 1960 and the Judicial Pensions Act 1981. The 1993 Act s 18 is repealed, s 19 is amended.

730   Magistrates' courts

See MAGISTRATES.

731   Practice and procedure—practice directions—trial

See CRIMINAL EVIDENCE AND PROCEDURE; PRACTICE AND PROCEDURE.

732   Proceedings—publicity—restrictions on reporting—family proceedings—government consultation

See para 461.

733   Supreme Court—President—exercise of functions

See para 612.

CREMATION AND BURIAL

Halsbury's Laws of England (4th edn) vol 10 (Reissue) paras 901–1178

734   Burial—churchyard—closed churchyard

The petitioner sought a faculty for the burial of the ashes of her deceased father in a churchyard which had been closed by Order in Council. *Held*, to grant the faculty would be contrary to the policy of the parochial church council and the diocese. While it was proper to take into account pastoral considerations in reaching a decision, care had to be taken when considering whether the needs of one family should override the express policy of a parish and the diocese as a whole. An exception to burials contrary to diocesan and parish policy could only be made where there were powerful medical reasons to do so, the same principle as applied to exhumations. There was no evidence of any such reasons in this case and, accordingly, the petition would be dismissed.

Re St James the Great, Birstall (2006) Times, 14 August (Leicester Consistory Court: James Behrens Ch). Re Blagdon Cemetry [2002] Fam 299 (2002 Abr para 749) applied.

735   Burial—consecrated ground—restoration

See *Re Welford Road Cemetery, Leicester*, para 1091.

736   Burial—maintenance of graves—faculty for works—application

The petitioners applied on behalf of the council for a confirmatory faculty for the laying flat of over 100 gravestones because they were unsafe. The petition was opposed. *Held*, a previous inquiry had indicated that the council should meet the costs of re-erecting or re-stabilising memorials even where the person responsible for the memorial was known. Further, the need for a sensitive and sustainable approach had been recognised along with a need to review aspects of responding to threats to public safety. Subsequently, a debate in the House of Commons stated that any over-reaction to unsafe gravestones had the potential to cause great distress. These matters indicated that the court should not readily grant a faculty which would result in the laying down of significant numbers of memorials unless it was clearly shown to be necessary. If councils were unwilling to pay for the cost of repairs, more use should be made of the temporary protection afforded by a stake placed behind the memorial while efforts were made to contact the owner. Then, only as a last resort, might gravestones be laid flat. Therefore, the confirmatory faculty was refused and the council was required to reinstate and re-stabilise all the memorials in the cemetery. However, a faculty was granted for future work with conditions attached. Accordingly, the faculty would be refused.

Re Welford Road Cemetery, Leicester [2006] Fam 62 (Leicester Consistory Court: Behrens Ch).

737   Cremation—faculty for disinterment of cremated remains—presumption against exhumation—widow's wish for her ashes to be scattered with her husband's ashes

A husband's remains had been buried in consecrated ground. His widow made a will requesting that his ashes might be scattered with her own. Following the death of the widow, the executor of her will petitioned for a faculty for exhumation of the husband's remains, arguing that the request for exhumation was impliedly made in the widow's will. *Held*, the general principle was that exhumation would only be granted in exceptional circumstances, and such a request made in a will did not, in itself, amount to an exceptional circumstance. The petitioner had not shown any exceptional circumstances that could justify the grant of the faculty. Accordingly, the petition would be dismissed.

Re Robin Hood Cemetery, Solihull (2007) Times, 10 January (Birmingham Consistory Court: Cardinal Ch).

738   Cremation—incineration of body parts—scope of regulation

The Cremation (Amendment) Regulations 2006, SI 2006/92 (in force on 14 February 2006), further amend the Regulations as to Cremation 1930, SR & O 1930/1016, so as to (1) extend the definition of 'body parts' to all parts of bodies from deceased persons and parts of a stillborn child; (2) provide for the cremation of body parts removed during a post mortem and body parts of stillborn children; (3) authorise the incineration of body parts by establishments in possession of parts of a deceased body where the retention of that part of the body is no longer necessary and the families do not wish cremation or burial of the part; (4) allow coroners to deal with cases where a death has occurred outside the British Islands without the need for referral to the Secretary of State; and (5) require a medical referee to give reasons where he declines to allow a cremation.

739 Funeral payments—social fund payment—claim for funeral abroad

See *Esfandiari v Secretary of State for Work and Pensions*, para 2675.

CRIMINAL EVIDENCE AND PROCEDURE

Halsbury's Laws of England (4th edn) vol 11(1) (2006 Reissue) paras 1–620, vol 11(2) (2006 Reissue) paras 621–1049, vol 11(3) (2006 Reissue) paras 1050–1557 and vol 11(4) (2006 Reissue) paras 1558–2181

Articles

For articles relating to this title please refer to the Table of Articles at the beginning of the Abridgment.

740 Appeal—appeal by Crown—leave to appeal—charge dismissed before arraignment

The defendants were charged with conspiracy to cheat the public revenue, and were sent to the Crown Court for trial. However, before arraignment on the indictment, the defendants successfully applied pursuant to the Crime and Disorder Act 1998 Sch 3 para 2 for the charge to be dismissed on the basis that the evidence would not be sufficient for a jury properly to convict them. Pursuant to the Criminal Justice Act 2003 s 58 the prosecution applied for leave to appeal against that ruling, and an issue arose as to whether the judge's dismissal of the charge and quashing of the indictment amounted to a ruling from which an appeal might flow under s 58 so that the Court of Appeal had jurisdiction to hear the application. *Held*, despite the otherwise broad language of s 58, that provision and its ancillary provisions as a whole appeared to contemplate that an acquittal of the defendant was the necessary result of either the ruling itself or the prosecution's attempt, if unsuccessful, to appeal it. However, a successful application under the 1998 Act Sch 3 could not lead to an acquittal. Under Sch 3 para 2(6), the only remedy for the prosecution in the face of a dismissal of a charge or the quashing of an indictment was to seek the preferment of a voluntary bill of indictment. It could not be said that the 2003 Act had silently effected an implied amendment of the 1988 Act Sch 3 para 2(6)(a). It would be remarkable if the prosecution were able to add to its remedies a new right of appeal where it already had a remedy by way of the preferment of a voluntary bill of indictment. The Sch 3 dismissal procedure had not been put forward to Parliament as an example of a 'terminating ruling', despite the numerous examples discussed for that purpose in the Parliamentary debates. If it had been intended to include Sch 3 dismissal rulings within the 2003 Act s 58, it would have been expected that that important example would have been highlighted, and all the more so because the arguably closely analogous application of no case to answer made at half time during a trial was expressly contemplated in s 58(7)(a). It followed that there was no jurisdiction under s 58 to give leave to appeal against a ruling under the 1988 Act Sch 3 para 2 and, accordingly, the application would be refused.

R v Thompson (application under s 58 of the Criminal Justice Act 2003) [2006] EWCA Crim 2849, [2006] All ER (D) 301 (Nov) (Court of Appeal: Rix LJ, Dobbs J and Sir Charles Mantell).

741 Appeal—appeal to Court of Appeal—jurisdiction—constitution of Criminal Division—requirement for panel of three judges

The Supreme Court Act 1981 s 55(4)(a)(i) provides that a court of the Criminal Division of the Court of Appeal, if it consists of two judges, is duly constituted for every purpose except determining an appeal against conviction.

One of the judges was not present in court when the judgment was handed down. The appellants applied to make further submissions on the merits of their appeals against conviction. *Held*, an appeal was determined for the purposes of the 1981 Act s 55 when the decision was properly to be treated as binding on the judges themselves. An appeal against conviction was not necessarily determined when the judgment was delivered in open court but when all three judges approved the draft judgment and authorised its release to counsel. When the two judges handed down the judgment they had not determined the appeal, but had simply formally promulgated the judgment. Accordingly, the application was dismissed.

R v Steele; R v Corry; R v Whomes [2006] EWCA Crim 2000, [2007] 1 Cr App Rep 39 (Court of Appeal: Maurice Kay and Openshaw LJJ and Sir Charles Mantell). *R v Coates; R v Colman* [2004] EWCA Crim 2253, [2004] 4 All ER 1150 (2004 Abr para 665) considered.

742 Appeal—jurisdiction—appeal from preparatory hearing—application to quash indictment

The defendant was charged with procuring the execution of valuable securities by deception, contrary to the Theft Act 1968 s 20(2). The relevant counts in the indictment specified that the defendant had by deception, and with a view to gain, induced persons to sign bills of exchange, and thereby become liable under them, that were then dishonoured. In a preparatory hearing, purportedly held pursuant to the Criminal Procedure and Investigations Act 1996 s 29, the judge ruled that the signatures on the bills were indorsements, and amounted to 'execution' within the meaning of the 1968 Act s 20(2). The defendant sought permission to appeal against the ruling pursuant to the 1996 Act ss 35 and 36, which enabled a defendant to appeal against any ruling of a judge or court made at a preparatory hearing. *Held*, there was no jurisdiction to hear an appeal against the judge's ruling. The application had been to quash the indictment, notwithstanding the fact that the committal for trial had been entirely valid, and the indictment had been properly based on that committal. Such an application could not have been validly made. Preparatory hearings were concerned with facilitating the conduct of the trial, and it followed that, given that the trial process would be brought to an end were an application to quash the indictment successful, such an application was outside the scope of ss 35 and 36. Accordingly, the application would be dismissed.

R v T [2006] All ER (D) 142 (Feb) (Court of Appeal: Pill LJ, Swift J and Judge Radford). *R v Hedworth* [1997] 1 Cr App Rep 421, CA, applied. *R v Van Hoogstraten* [2003] EWCA Crim 3642, [2004] Crim LR 498 considered.

743   Appeal—leave to appeal—application—grounds

The defendant was convicted and sentenced to life imprisonment for the murder of a policeman, the attempted murder of two other policemen, possessing a firearm with intent to endanger life and possessing ammunition with intent to endanger life on the basis of evidence that linked him to the crime scene and the firearm. After refusal of his application to appeal, he renewed his application to appeal against conviction, submitting that the judge had wrongly refused to stay the indictment as an abuse of process on the ground of adverse press and media attention that made it impossible for him to receive a fair trial. Further, he claimed that there was unprecedented and highly visible security but no explanation had been given to the jury and that a television programme had been shown after his conviction about the shootings but that the television company had refused to provide details about how the programme had been put together. *Held*, when considering an application to appeal against conviction it was necessary to distinguish between two types of grounds of appeal. First, there were rare cases in which the grounds that were alleged were that there had been an abuse of process of such a nature that it justified quashing the conviction whether or not there were grounds to doubt the jury's verdict. The second type related to defects in procedure or summing up which did not fall within the first category, and which had no merit unless the jury might not have convicted had that defect not occurred. Since the grounds relied on by the defendant fell into the second category, the only consideration was whether any of the grounds were well-founded and could have had any effect on the guilty verdicts returned by the jury. The grounds did not seek to challenge evidence placed before the jury, but alleged defects in the procedure and summing up that amounted to no more than scratching at the periphery of the case and did not undermine the safety of the verdict. Since the evidence was overwhelming and the grounds raised no doubts as to the safety of the convictions, the convictions were not unsafe and accordingly, the appeal would be dismissed.

R v Bieber [2006] All ER (D) 276 (Oct) (Court of Appeal: Lord Phillips of Worth Matravers CJ, Pitchford and Calvert-Smith JJ).

744   Appeal—reference by Criminal Cases Review Commission—appropriateness of reference—safety of conviction

The defendant was convicted of conspiracy to contravene the Customs and Excise Management Act 1979 s 170(2). Following the conviction, material became available which the defendant argued cast doubt on the safety of his conviction. The defendant appealed against conviction and was granted bail pending appeal. He contended that, should the appeal be dismissed, he should not be returned to custody to serve the remainder of the sentence. The defendant submitted that, given that his application and renewed application for leave to appeal against sentence had previously been refused, the court was able to gain the jurisdiction to interfere with the sentence so as to prevent his return to custody by way of a reference by the Criminal Cases Review Commission pursuant to the Criminal Appeal Act 1995 s 9 prior to the judgment dismissing the conviction appeal being handed down. *Held*, on an examination of the new material against the background of the material available at trial, there was no doubt as to the safety of the verdict. In all the circumstances, there was no abuse of process entitling the court to intervene or to find the verdicts to be unsafe. Further, the device of seeking a reference from the Commission to enable the court to have the jurisdiction to interfere with a defendant's sentence was not intended by Parliament to be used routinely, although there would be circumstances in which it could be used to avoid injustice. However, that would have to be an exceptional case. The present case was not exceptional. Accordingly, the appeal would be dismissed.

R v Beardall [2006] EWCA Crim 577, [2006] All ER (D) 375 (Mar) (Court of Appeal: Pill LJ, Swift J and Judge Radford).

745 Appeal—reference by Criminal Cases Review Commission—duty to follow practice of Court of Appeal

Four persons were convicted of offences of conspiracy. In each case, after their appeals or applications for leave to appeal had been dismissed, a case committee of the Criminal Cases Review Commission, decided pursuant to the Criminal Appeal Act 1995 s 9(2) to refer the cases to the Court of Appeal. The claimant brought an application for judicial review of the decision to refer the cases, submitting that there should be symmetry of approach between the Commission and the Court of Appeal. *Held*, the independent Commission was under no obligation to have regard to, still less to implement, a practice of the Court of Appeal that operated at a stage with which the Commission was not concerned. The significant features of the Commission's statutory powers were, first, that, unlike the Court of Appeal, the Commission did not act within statutory time limits. Section 9(1)(a) expressly enabled it to refer a case 'at any time'. Secondly, the power to refer was not linked to consideration of whether there was a real possibility that the Court of Appeal would extend time or grant leave. Indeed, by virtue of s 9(2), once a reference was made, the need for the leave of the Court of Appeal was removed. Thirdly, the central test was in the form of a prediction of a real possibility that a conviction would not be upheld by the Court of Appeal, not of whether the continued existence of the conviction would be held to be a miscarriage of justice. Fourthly, the 1995 Act provided for a truly independent commission and clothed it with discretionary powers of the utmost width. Although it was empowered to seek the opinion of the Court of Appeal it was not bound to do so. Its obligation was to decide whether, on a substantive appeal, there would be a real possibility of the quashing of a conviction. Fifthly, in addressing that question, the Commission had to have regard to the way in which the Court of Appeal approached the unsafe test. Accordingly, the application would be dismissed.

R (on the application of Director of Revenue and Customs Prosecutions) v Criminal Cases Review Commission [2006] EWHC 3064 (Admin), [2006] All ER (D) 48 (Dec) (Queen's Bench Division: Maurice Kay LJ and Bean J). *R v Criminal Cases Review Commission, ex p Pearson* [1999] 3 All ER 498 (1999 Abr para 816) considered.

746 Appeal—unsafe conviction—rape—certificate of trial judge

The complainant had returned home from a public house. Later on the same day, the defendant visited the complainant's home. A week later, the complainant claimed that the defendant had raped her. At the defendant's trial, the defence argued that, while at the public house, the complainant had invited the defendant to her home and that consensual sexual intercourse had taken place. The defendant called a number of witnesses to testify to the previous sexual behaviour of the complainant and the events at the public house. The jury found the defendant guilty and, following the sentencing hearing, at which the defendant was sentenced to seven and a half years' imprisonment, the judge granted a certificate of fitness to appeal. He observed that the case was one in which counsel would have some difficulty in obtaining, on the conventional basis, the leave of the single judge to appeal, and that counsel had a better chance of obtaining a ruling by him as the trial judge that the case was fit for appeal. Further, he judged that there was a basis for finding that injustice might have been done considering that the trial had lasted for four and a half days, with a number of defence witnesses, while the jury had reached unanimous guilty verdicts within one hour and 17 minutes. The defendant appealed against his conviction. *Held,* it was well-established that there might be rare cases in which a defendant's appeal might be allowed on the basis that there was a lurking doubt as to the safety of the verdicts. The views of the trial judge as to the merits of a conviction were irrelevant to the task of the Court of Appeal. In the present case, the jury had to decide who they believed. They must have considered the case as they went along. It could not be said, in all the circumstances, that there was a substantial possibility that the case had not been properly considered by the jury so that the conviction should be held to be unsafe. Whether it could ever be the case that brevity of the jury's deliberations could afford a ground of appeal, therefore, did not arise. It was questionable whether the apprehension, of the type felt by the judge, about the case could form the proper basis for a trial judge's certificate. There was no lurking doubt as to the safety of the conviction. Accordingly, the appeal would be dismissed.

R v Webster [2006] All ER (D) 219 (Nov) (Court of Appeal: Laws LJ, Penry-Davey J and the Recorder of Chester).

747 Arrest—caution instead of arrest—compatibility with police policy

While investigating a burglary, two police officers mistakenly went to the claimant's flat to which they were admitted and where they found a cannabis cigarette, a grinder, one small cube of cannabis resin, and what they believed to be herbal cannabis. They arrested the claimant for allowing his premises to be used for the smoking of cannabis, contrary to the Misuse of Drugs Act 1971 s 8(d). At the police station, however, it was decided not to charge the claimant with the s 8(d) offence. Instead, the duty inspector administered a caution for possession of a Class C drug, on the basis that the claimant had been cautioned in the past for the same offence, and that police policy did not state that no arrests should be made for simple possession of cannabis or that, an arrest having been made, it was inappropriate to caution a person found in possession of cannabis. The claimant applied for judicial review of the decision to caution him, submitting that the inspector's decision had been in breach of police policy and standard operating procedures under which a person found in possession of cannabis for personal use was not to be arrested save in exceptional cases. *Held*, where it was argued that the caution was in breach of policy, the court would be reluctant to intervene save where the policy was clear and settled, and the breach was itself established. Any suggestion that a policy might limit the power to arrest conferred by statute on a constable had to be considered with regard to the statutory power conferred on each and every police constable. Moreover, although police forces across the country should aim for consistency, so various were the factual considerations and so wide the margin for judgment, that a public law challenge on the grounds of inconsistency was not to be contemplated. There was no clear and settled policy not to arrest or prosecute for simple possession of cannabis, and the policy did not state explicitly that there should be no cautions. The absence of any such clear and settled policy was fatal to the claimant's case. In any event, there had been no breach of the standard operating procedures, which did not deal with whether there should be any further prosecution or caution in express terms. Accordingly, the application would be dismissed.

R (*on the application of Mondelly*) *v Comr of Police for the Metropolis* [2006] EWHC 2370 (Admin), (2007) 171 JP 121 (Queen's Bench Division: Moses LJ, Ouseley and Walker JJ). *R v Metropolitan Police Comr, ex p Blackburn* [1968] 2 QB 118, CA; *R v Chief Constable of the Kent County Constabulary, ex p L* (*A Minor*) [1993] 1 All ER 756, DC (1991 Abr para 6); *R v Metropolitan Police Comr, ex p P* (1995) 160 JP 367, DC (1995 Abr para 755); and *R v Metropolitan Police Comr, ex p Thompson* [1997] 1 WLR 1519, DC (1999 Abr para 813) considered.

748   Arrest—European arrest warrant

See EXTRADITION.

749   Bail—application—refusal to hear application in public

See *R* (*on the application of Malik*) *v Central Criminal Court*, para 106.

750   Bail—exception to right to bail—failure by prosecution to act with due diligence—right to liberty

See *R* (*on the application of O*) *v Crown Court at Harrow; Re O* (*habeas corpus*), para 1583.

751   Bail—power to grant—right to liberty

See Application 543/03 *McKay v United Kingdom*, para 1582.

752   Bail—refusal of bail—judicial review—jurisdiction of High Court—matter relating to trial on indictment

The Supreme Court Act 1981 s 29(3) provides that, in relation to the jurisdiction of the Crown Court, other than its jurisdiction in matters relating to trial on indictment, the High Court has all such jurisdiction to make mandatory, prohibiting or quashing orders as the High Court possesses in relation to the jurisdiction of an inferior court.

The claimant, aged 17, was a prosecution witness in a trial involving ten defendants. He was arrested pursuant to a witness summons and was remanded into custody pursuant to the Criminal Procedure (Attendance of Witnesses) Act 1965 s 4(3). The Crown was granted permission to treat the claimant as a hostile witness. He gave evidence on several days, and was detained overnight and over the weekend. Four of the defendants did not cross-examine him. After the Crown had been given the opportunity to re-examine the claimant, he was remanded in custody for a further two weeks, as the judge was of the opinion that there was a real risk that either side might recall him to put further matters to him. The claimant was granted permission to seek judicial review of the judge's decision. The Secretary of State sought to challenge the claim on the basis that the judge's decision was a matter relating to trial on indictment so that, by virtue of the 1981 Act s 29(3), the court had no jurisdiction to entertain the claim. *Held*, a decision taken in the course of a trial by the trial judge to detain a witness pending receipt of further evidence was a matter relating to trial on indictment and therefore, in accordance with s 29(3), there was no jurisdiction to entertain the claim for judicial review. Firstly, the decision to detain the claimant as a witness was one which arose in the issue between the Crown and the defendant. It concerned his availability as a witness for the prosecution in circumstances where it was envisaged that there was a real possibility that he might have to be recalled in order to deal with matters which had not been canvassed with him by counsel for four defendants who had failed to cross-examine him. Secondly, the decision was made in the middle of the trial. Thirdly, the claimant was not deprived of remedies by virtue of the Divisional Court not having jurisdiction pursuant to s 29(3). Accordingly, the application would be dismissed.

R (*on the application of TH*) *v Crown Court at Wood Green* [2006] EWHC 2683 (Admin), [2006] All ER (D) 378 (Oct) (Queen's Bench Division: Auld LJ and Wilkie J). *DPP v Crown Court at Manchester and Huckfield* [1993] 4 All ER 928, HL (1993 Abr para 671); *R v Crown Court at Maidstone, ex p Clark; R v Governor of Elmley Prison, ex p Clark* [1995] 3 All ER 513, DC (1994 Abr para 738);

and *R (on the application of Shergill) v Crown Court at Harrow* [2005] EWHC 648 (Admin), [2005] All ER (D) 39 (Apr) (2005 Abr para 852) considered.

753 Costs—award out of central funds—refusal to make award—acquittal of defendant—intimation by judge that defendant guilty

See Application 8866/04 *Hussain v United Kingdom*, para 1574.

754 Costs—defence costs—discretion of court—successful litigant—reduction in costs

The claimant's appeal against a period of driving disqualification succeeded and the period was reduced. The Crown Court granted him an order for costs from central funds, pursuant to the Prosecution of Offences Act 1985 s 16(3). He claimed £650 plus value added tax in respect of expenses incurred in pursuing his appeal in which he had been represented by a solicitor advocate. The recorder allowed only £150 plus VAT, giving no reasons for his decision but maintaining that the order was within his discretion. The claimant sought judicial review of the decision. *Held*, there were no circumstances to justify the reduction of the £650 incurred by the claimant and no rational basis had been put forward justifying the sum of £150. There was no reason to assume that the sum claimed was inappropriate. Accordingly, the application would be allowed.

R (on the application of Galandauer) v Crown Court at Snaresbrook [2006] All ER (D) 306 (Jun) (Queen's Bench Division: Dyson LJ and Walker J).

755 Costs—defendant's costs order—application by defendant—entitlement to costs after claim for costs of defence attorney

The applicant received a notice, issued by the Serious Fraud Office, notifying him that it intended to prosecute him. The applicant entered into an agreement with his American attorney. The attorney undertook to act for him in the prosecution proceedings and the applicant agreed to pay for her services. She contacted solicitors in the United Kingdom who agreed to act for the applicant and to instruct counsel. The applicant was charged and stood trial. The judge directed the jury to return a verdict of not guilty and granted the applicant a defendant's cost order pursuant to the Prosecution of Offences Act 1985 s 16. The applicant subsequently applied for reimbursement of costs incurred as a result of the attorney's work on his case. A determining officer rejected that claim. The applicant appealed to a costs judge of the Supreme Court Costs Office, who stated that in light of the United Kingdom solicitors' bills a small sum would be allowed in respect of the attorney's work. The applicant made an application for judicial review of that decision. The issue to be decided was whether the decision of the costs judge had caused a real injustice. *Held*, in the circumstances, having admitted the claim in principle, the costs judge had erred in that he had not then carried out the task in the way that was required by the 1985 Act and the Costs in Criminal Cases (General) Regulations 1986, SI 1986/1335, namely by undertaking a detailed assessment of the work the attorney had done and, therefore, there had been a real injustice in awarding a figure which was not based on the task which ought to have been undertaken. Accordingly, the application would be allowed and the matter remitted for determination.

R (on the application of Brewer) v Supreme Court Costs Office [2006] EWHC 1955 (Admin), [2006] All ER (D) 401 (Jul) (Queen's Bench Division: Maurice Kay LJ and Mitting J).

756 Crime prevention orders—government consultation

The Home Secretary has presented to Parliament a consultation paper, *New Powers Against Organised Crime and Financial Crime* (Cm 6875), which deals with a possible modification to recent Law Commission proposals in relation to offences of assisting or encouraging the commission of crime so as to suggest extending the scope of the proposed offence to include occasions where the assistance or encouragement related not merely to occasions when it was believed that an offence would be committed but also to occasions when it was likely that an offence would be committed. The paper also suggests the introduction of serious crime prevention orders, which are not dissimilar to anti-social behaviour orders. These would be civil orders made by a court, probably the High Court, subject to an appeal to the Court of Appeal, on application by a specified prosecution agency. The grounds on which such an order might be made would be that an individual or an organisation had acted in a way which facilitated, or was likely to facilitate, the commission of serious crime, or that the terms of the order were necessary and proportionate to prevent such harm in the future. The restrictions which might be imposed could relate to the subject's financial dealings, for example requiring the use only of specified financial instruments (credit cards, bank accounts) and restrictions on the amount of cash he would be permitted to carry. In particular, views are sought on the nature of appropriate conditions. It is intended that such orders might be used, by way of example, when there was insufficient evidence to ground a prosecution, or the evidence available related to crimes committed outside the jurisdiction, or where the subject had been convicted of a serious crime overseas and, after release from custody, might be expected in the United Kingdom to be subject to strict licence conditions, or an order might be made in anticipation of a prosecution in the United Kingdom to limit potential harm while a case was being prepared, or as part of a deal with a person who was likely to turn Queen's evidence, or even as an alternative to prosecution in the case of individuals on the fringes of serious criminal activity. It is suggested that the standard of proof for orders should be the balance of probabilities.

757 Criminal investigation—power of court to discontinue

The defendant police service undertook an operation targeting persons suspected of downloading child pornography from the Internet. Records acquired during the investigation demonstrated that the claimant's credit card had been used to access two child pornography sites in the United States. The defendants obtained a warrant to search the claimant's house, and the claimant was arrested on suspicion of having downloaded indecent images of children. However, no indecent images were found on the computers seized by the defendants from the claimant's house. The claimant denied ever having accessed the relevant websites, alleging that he had been the victim of identity theft or that his son had used his credit card without his permission. He applied for judicial review of the defendants' decision to continue the investigation, submitting that the defendants should formally acknowledge that there was no case against him in order to alleviate the stress which it was causing to him and his family and the professional and employment difficulties which he was suffering. *Held*, although the court could intervene to close down an ongoing investigation on the basis that there was no prospect of a prosecution eventuating, it would only be appropriate in the most exceptional cases. Where there were unquestioning reasonable grounds to suspect a person under investigation, the court should be very slow to second-guess the police in deciding at what point he could be dismissed from the inquiry. Moreover, it was not clear what form of relief would be appropriate. The continuance of an investigation was a factual rather than a legal state of affairs. It had no formal status and, until proceedings were commenced by a charge, no public action would have been taken. Investigations might continue at various levels of intensity and might, for good reason, be put aside without prejudice to the possibility of being later revived in different circumstances. It would also be highly undesirable to put the police in the position where they had to issue public declarations of innocence. Innocent people sometimes became legitimately suspected of serious criminal offences. For such a person to have to endure an investigation, with all the stresses and problems to which that might give rise, was a great misfortune, but those consequences necessarily flowed from the fact that serious crimes had to be investigated. It could not be said that the refusal of the defendants formally to close their investigation of the claimant was so inexplicable as to be required to be characterised as irrational. Accordingly, the application would be dismissed.

R (on the application of C) v Chief Constable of 'A' Police [2006] EWHC 2352 (Admin), [2006] All ER (D) 124 (Sep) (Queen's Bench Division: Underhill J).

758 Criminal Justice Act 2003—commencement

The Criminal Justice Act 2003 (Commencement No 12) Order 2006, SI 2006/751, brings into force, on 6 April 2005, ss 328 (in part), 332 (in part), Sch 35 paras 5 (so far as not already in force), 6, 8, 9, 12 and certain repeals in Sch 37 Pt 11.

The Criminal Justice Act 2003 (Commencement No 13 and Transitional Provision) Order 2006, SI 2006/1835, brings into force on 24 July 2006 ss 33(1) (in part), 44–48, 331 (in part) and Sch 36 Pt 4 (paras 40–78). Transitional provision is also made.

The Criminal Justice Act 2003 (Commencement No 14 and Transitional Provision) Order 2006, SI 2006/3217, brings into force, on 1 January 2007, Sch 36 para 3 and, for certain purposes, ss 14, 15(1), (2). Transitional provision is also made.

For a summary of the Act, see 2003 Abr para 642. See also the commencement table in the title STATUTEs.

759 Criminal law

See CRIMINAL LAW.

760 Criminal Procedure Rules

The Criminal Procedure (Amendment) Rules 2006, SI 2006/353 (in force on 3 April 2006), amend the 2005 Rules, SI 2005/384, by (1) making new provision in relation to (a) applications for preparatory hearings where the prosecutor seeks an order that the trial be without a jury under the Criminal Justice Act 2003 s 43 or 44; (b) the rules on warrants; (c) appeals against refusals to excuse a person from jury service or to defer attendance; (d) external requests and orders, by applying certain rules to proceedings under the Proceeds of Crime Act 2002 (External Requests and Orders) Order 2005, SI 2005/3181; and (e) appeals against orders following the discharge of a jury because of jury tampering, applying certain rules to appeals under the 2003 Act s 47; and (2) revising the rules in relation to (a) hearsay evidence, by confining the application of the relevant provisions to cases where the evidence is admissible on the grounds that (i) it is in the interests of justice for it to be admissible; (ii) the witness is unavailable to attend; (iii) the evidence is contained in a business or other document; or (iv) the evidence is multiple hearsay; (b) evidence of a non-defendant's bad character, so that an application to introduce the previous convictions of a prosecution witness must be made within 14 days of the date when the prosecutor discloses those convictions; (c) the time limit for a defendant's application to exclude evidence of his own bad character, which is extended from 7 to 14 days; (d) appeals to the Court of Appeal against rulings adverse to the prosecution, to ensure that the registrar is not required to give or serve notice to a defendant or an interested party in a 'public interest ruling' case, unless a judge or the Court of Appeal directs otherwise; and (e) appeals to the Court of Appeal or House of Lords, to extend coverage to appeals made under the 2003 Act Sch 22 para 14.

The Criminal Procedure (Amendment No 2) Rules 2006, SI 2006/2636 (in force on 6 November 2006), further amend the CrimPR by adding new provisions (1) in relation to expert evidence, which set out the duty of an expert to the court and the content of an expert's report, and provide for when the new expert evidence rules are to apply; and (2) in relation to evidence about a complainant's sexual behaviour, which revise and simplify the rules about applications under the Youth Justice and Criminal Evidence Act 1999 s 41. The rules also amend the CrimPR so that they (a) govern the service of a requisition issued by a public prosecutor under the Criminal Justice Act 2003 s 29; (b) govern applications under the Domestic Violence, Crime and Victims Act 2004 s 17 for trial of some of the counts in an indictment without a jury; (c) govern the procedure on an appeal to the Court of Appeal under the Serious Organised Crime and Police Act 2005 s 74(8) against a sentence review decision; and (d) require that an expert whose findings are disclosed is made aware of that disclosure, which is relevant to the expert's duty to the court and require service on the court of a statement provided to another party.

761   Criminal proceedings—courts-martial proceedings

See ARMED FORCES.

762   Criminal record certificates—enhanced criminal record certificates—applications

The Police Act 1997 (Criminal Records) (Amendment) Regulations 2006, SI 2006/748 (in force on 6 April 2006), further amend the 2002 Regulations, SI 2002/233, so as to (1) increase the fees payable on application to the Secretary of State for a criminal record certificate from £29 to £31, and for an enhanced criminal record certificate from £34 to £36, and impose an additional fee of £6 in each case if the applicant seeks an urgent preliminary response from the Secretary of State as to his suitability for certain purposes; (2) add a list of the purposes in respect of which an application can be made for an enhanced criminal record certificate; (3) add the police forces specified to the list of police forces from which the Secretary of State can obtain information for the purposes of issuing a certificate; and (4) remove the reference to the Secretary of State paying a prescribed fee to the police for the information which they provide to him.

The Police Act 1997 (Criminal Records) (Amendment No 2) Regulations 2006, SI 2006/2181 (in force on 1 September 2006), further amend the 2002 Regulations supra so as to (1) add to the list of purposes for which an enhanced criminal record certificate can be issued, the purposes of considering a person's suitability for (a) a position concerned with providing care services, representative or advocacy services to vulnerable adults or; (b) a position as a member of a governing body of an educational institution; (2) make provision for a request for information as to whether a person is on a list of persons classified as unsuitable to work with vulnerable adults; (3) add the British Transport Police to the list of police forces which may be considered relevant for the purposes of obtaining information to be included in an enhanced criminal record certificate; and (4) provide an exception to the prohibition of disclosure of information beyond a registered body which has obtained such a certificate, namely a disclosure by an employment agency or business to an educational institution, or an institution in the further education sector, for the purpose of considering a person's suitability for a position at that institution.

763   Criminal record certificates—enhanced criminal record certificates—correction—accuracy of information

The Police Act 1997 s 117(1) provides that, where an applicant for a criminal records certificate believes that the information contained in the certificate is inaccurate, he may make an application in writing to the Secretary of State for a new certificate. The Secretary of State must consider any such application, and, where he is of the opinion that the information in the certificate is inaccurate, he must issue a new certificate: s 117(2).

The claimant and his employer made an application for an enhanced criminal record certificate, pursuant to the 1997 Act s 115. The certificate stated that the claimant had been arrested following an allegation that he had raped his daughter. That information was correct, but in the event no prosecution had been brought. The claimant sent to the Criminal Records Bureau a dispute confirmation form in which he set out the basis on which he sought the correction of the certificate by the defendant Secretary of State, in accordance with s 117, so as to delete any reference that he had engaged in sexual activity with his daughter. He alleged that the information in the disclosure was prejudicial and misleading. The Secretary of State refused to issue a corrected certificate, on the ground that he was satisfied that the information held was correct. The claimant applied for judicial review of that decision. *Held*, s 117(2) required the Secretary of State to determine only whether the fact that the allegations had been made against an individual had been accurately recorded. The Secretary of State was under no duty to consider whether the underlying allegations had any foundation. The wording of s 117(2) focused on whether the information in the certificate was accurate, not whether it was relevant or whether it was true. Moreover, the legislative policy was that information which might be true should be disclosed, that the decision whether to disclose was one for the chief officer of police, and that the ultimate decision as to what use to make of the information was one for the prospective employer. Accordingly, the application would be dismissed.

R (on the application of B) v Secretary of State for the Home Department [2006] EWHC 579 (Admin), [2006] All ER (D) 370 (Mar) (Queen's Bench Division: Munby J). *R (on the application of X) v Chief Constable of the West Midlands Police* [2004] EWCA Civ 1068, [2005] 1 All ER 610 (2004 Abr para 703) considered.

764   Criminal record certificates—enhanced criminal record certificates—suitability

See para 762.

765   Criminal records—registration

See para 2238.

766   Crown Court—disclosure—unused material—control and management

Lord Phillips of Worth Matravers CJ, has issued the following *Protocol (Disclosure: Control and Management of Unused Material in the Crown Court)*.

Introduction

1. Disclosure is one of the most important, as well as one of the most abused, of the procedures relating to criminal trials. There needs to be a sea-change in the approach of both judges and the parties to all aspects of the handling of the material, which the prosecution do not intend to use in support of their case. For too long, a wide range of serious misunderstandings has existed, both as to the exact ambit of the unused material to which the defence is entitled, and the role to be played by the judge in ensuring that the law is properly applied. All too frequently applications by the parties and decisions by the judges in this area have been made based either on misconceptions as to the true nature of the law or a general laxity of approach (however well-intentioned). This failure properly to apply the binding provisions as regards disclosure has proved extremely and unnecessarily costly and has obstructed justice. It is, therefore, essential that disclosure obligations are properly discharged, by both the prosecution and the defence, in all criminal proceedings, and the court's careful oversight of this process is an important safeguard against the possibility of miscarriages of justice.

2. The House of Lords stated in *R v H; R v C* [2004] UKHL 3, [2004] 2 AC 134 (2004 Abr para 736), at 147:

'Fairness ordinarily requires that any material held by the prosecution which weakens its case or strengthens that of the defendant, if not relied on as part of its formal case against the defendant, should be disclosed to the defence. Bitter experience has shown that miscarriages of justice may occur where such material is withheld from disclosure. The golden rule is that full disclosure of such material should be made.'

3. However, it is also essential that the trial process is not overburdened or diverted by erroneous and inappropriate disclosure of unused prosecution material, or by misconceived applications in relation to such material.

4. The overarching principle is therefore that unused prosecution material will fall to be disclosed if, and only if, it satisfies the test for disclosure applicable to the proceedings in question, subject to any overriding public interest considerations. The relevant test for disclosure will depend on the date the criminal investigation in question commenced (see heads 9–12, below), as this will determine whether the common law disclosure regime applies, or either of the two disclosure regimes under the Criminal Procedure and Investigations Act 1996.

5. There is very clear evidence that, without active judicial oversight and management, the handling of disclosure issues in general, and the disclosure of unused prosecution material in particular, can cause delays and adjournments.

6. The failure to comply fully with disclosure obligations, whether by the prosecution or the defence, may disrupt and in some cases even frustrate the course of justice.

7. Consideration of irrelevant unused material may consume wholly unjustifiable and disproportionate amounts of time and public resources, undermining the overall performance and efficiency of the criminal justice system. The aim of this *Protocol* is therefore to assist and encourage judges when dealing with all disclosure issues, in the light of the overarching principle set out in head 4, above. This guidance is intended to cover all Crown Court cases (including cases where

relevant case management directions are made at the Magistrates' Court). It is not, therefore, confined to a very few high profile and high cost cases.

8. Unused material which has been gathered during the course of a criminal investigation and disclosed by the prosecution pursuant to their duties is received by the defence subject to a prohibition not to use or disclose the material for any purpose which is not connected with the proceedings for whose purposes they were given it (s 17). The common law, which applies to all disclosure not made under the 1996 Act, achieves the same result by the creation of an implied undertaking not to use the material for any purposes other than the proper conduct of the particular case (see *Taylor v Serious Fraud Office* [1998] 4 All ER 801, HL (1998 Abr para 2056)). A breach of that undertaking would constitute a contempt of court. These provisions are designed to ensure that the privacy and confidentiality of those who provided the material to the investigation (as well as those who are mentioned in the material) is protected and is not invaded any more than is absolutely necessary. However, neither statute nor the common law prevents any one from using or disclosing such material if it has been displayed or communicated to the public in open court (unless the evidence is subject to continuing reporting restriction), and moreover, an application can be made to the court for permission to use or disclose the object or information.

Sources

9. It is not the purpose of this *Protocol* to rehearse the law in detail; however, some of the principal sources are set out here.

10. The correct test for disclosure will depend on the date the relevant criminal investigation commenced:

(a) In relation to offences in respect of which the criminal investigation began prior to 1 April 1997, the common law will apply, and the test for disclosure is that set out in *R v Keane* [1994] 2 All ER 478, CA (1994 Abr para 759).

(b) If the criminal investigation commenced on or after 1 April 1997, but before 4 April 2005, then the 1996 Act in its original form will apply, with separate tests for disclosure of unused prosecution material at the primary and secondary disclosure stages (the latter following service of a defence statement by the accused). The disclosure provisions of the 1996 Act are supported by the Criminal Procedure and Investigations Act 1996 (Code of Practice) (No 2) Order 1997, SI 1997/1033, issued under the 1996 Act s 23(1).

(c) Where the criminal investigation has commenced on or after 4 April 2005, the law is set out in the 1996 Act as amended by the Criminal Justice Act 2003 Pt V. There is then a single test for disclosure of unused prosecution material and the Criminal Procedure and Investigations Act 1996 (Code of Practice) Order 2005, SI 1995/985, issued under the 1996 Act s 23(1) will apply.

The 1996 Act also identifies the stage at which the prosecution is required to disclose material, and the formalities relating to defence statements. The default time limit for prosecution disclosure is set out in s 13 (see further at head 14, below). The time limits applicable to defence disclosure are set out in the Criminal Procedure and Investigations Act 1996 (Defence Disclosure Regulations) 1997, SI 1997/684.

11. Regard must be had to the Attorney General's Guidelines on Disclosure (April 2005). Although these do not have the force of law (*R v Brown (Winston)* [1994] 1 WLR 1599 (1994 Abr para 757)) they should be given due weight.

12. The Criminal Procedure Rules 2005, SI 2005/384, Pt 25 sets out the procedures to be followed for applications to the court concerning both sensitive and non-sensitive unused material. Part 3 is also relevant in respect of the court's general case management powers, and parties should also have regard to the *Consolidated Criminal Practice Direction* [2002] 3 All ER 904 (2002 Abr para 830).

13. SI 2005/384 Pts 22, 23 are set aside to make provision for other rules concerning disclosure by the prosecution and the defence, although at the date of this *Protocol* there are no rules under them.

The Duty to Gather and Record Unused Material

14. For the statutory scheme to work properly, investigators and disclosure officers responsible for the gathering, inspection, retention and recording of relevant unused prosecution material must perform their tasks thoroughly, scrupulously and fairly. In this, they must adhere to the appropriate provisions of the 2005 Order SI 2005/985.

15. It is crucial that the police (and indeed all investigative bodies) implement appropriate training regimes and appoint competent disclosure officers, who have sufficient knowledge of the issues in the case. This will enable them to make a proper assessment of the unused prosecution material in the light of the test for relevance under the 2005 Order, SI 2005/985, para 2(1), with a view to preparing full and accurate schedules of the retained material. In any criminal investigation, the disclosure officer must retain material that may be relevant to an investigation. This material must be listed on a schedule. Each item listed on the schedule should contain sufficient detail to enable the prosecutor to decide whether or not the material falls to be disclosed. The schedules must be sent to the prosecutor. Wherever possible this should be at the same time as the file containing the material

for the prosecution case but the duty to disclose does not end at this point and must continue while relevant material is received even after conviction.

16. Furthermore, the scheduling of the relevant material must be completed expeditiously, so as to enable the prosecution to comply promptly with the duty to provide primary (or, when the amended 1996 Act regime applies) initial disclosure as soon as practicable after:

(a) the case has been committed for trial under the Magistrates' Courts Act 1980 s 6(1) or 6(2); or

(b) the case has been transferred to the Crown Court under the Criminal Justice Act 1987 s 4, or the Criminal Justice Act 1991 s 53; or

(c) copies of documents containing the evidence are served on the accused in accordance with the Crime and Disorder Act 1998 (Service of Prosecution Evidence) Regulations 2005, SI 2005/902, where the matter has been sent to the Crown Court pursuant to the Crime and Disorder Act 1998 s 51 or 51A ; or

(d) a matter has been added to an indictment in accordance with the Criminal Justice Act 1988 s 40; or

(e) a bill of indictment has been preferred under the Administration of Justice (Miscellaneous Provisions) Act 1933 s 2(2)(b) or the Prosecution of Offences Act 1985 s 22B(3)(a).

17. Investigators, disclosure officers and prosecutors must promptly and properly discharge their responsibilities under the 1996 Act and statutory code, in order to ensure that justice is not delayed, denied or frustrated. In this context, under the 2005 Order, SI 2005/985, para 3(5), it is provided 'an investigator should pursue all reasonable lines of inquiry, whether these point towards or away from the suspect'.

18. Crown Prosecution Service lawyers advising the police pre-charge at police stations should consider conducting a preliminary review of the unused material generated by the investigation, where this is practicable, so as to give early advice on disclosure issues. Otherwise, prosecutors should conduct a preliminary review of disclosure at the same time as the initial review of the evidence. It is critical that the important distinction between the evidence in the case, on the one hand, and any unused material, on the other, is not blurred. Items such as exhibits should be treated as such and the obligation to serve them is not affected by the disclosure regime.

19. Where the single test for disclosure applies under the amended 1996 Act disclosure regime, the prosecutor is under a duty to consider, at an early stage of proceedings, whether there is any unused prosecution material which is reasonably capable of assisting the case for the accused. What a defendant has said by way of defence or explanation either in interview or by way of a prepared statement can be a useful guide to making an objective assessment of the material which would satisfy this test.

20. There may be some occasions when the prosecution, pursuant to surviving common law rules of disclosure, ought to disclose an item or items of unused prosecution material, even in advance of primary or initial disclosure under the 1996 Act s 3. This may apply, for instance, where there is information which might affect a decision as to bail; where an abuse of process is alleged; where there is material which might assist the defence to make submissions as to the particular charge or charges, if any, the defendant should face at the Crown Court; and when it is necessary to enable particular preparation to be undertaken at an early stage by the defence. Guidance as to occasions where such disclosure may be appropriate is provided in *R v DPP ex p Lee* [1999] 2 All ER 737 (1999 Abr para 847). However, once the 1996 Act is triggered (for instance, by committal, or service of case papers following a 1998 Act s 51 sending) it is the 1996 Act which determines what material should be disclosed.

The Judge's Duty to Enforce the Statutory Scheme

21. When cases are sent to the Crown Court under the 1998 Act s 51, the 2005 Regulations SI 2005/902 allow the prosecution 70 days from the date the matter was sent (50 days, where the accused is in custody) within which to serve on the defence and the court copies of the documents containing the evidence on which the charge or charges are based (in effect, sufficient evidence to amount to a prima facie case). These time limits may be extended and varied at the court's direction. Directions for service of these case papers may be given at the Magistrates' Court.

22. While it is important to note that this time limit applies to the service of evidence, rather than unused prosecution material, the court will need to consider at the Magistrates' Court or preliminary hearing whether it is practicable for the prosecution to comply with primary or initial disclosure at the same time as service of such papers, or whether disclosure ought to take place after a certain interval, but before the matter is listed for a PCMH.

23. If the nature of the case does not allow service of the evidence and initial or primary disclosure within the 70, or if applicable 50, days (or such other period as directed by the Magistrates' Court), the investigator should ensure that the prosecution advocate at the Magistrates' Court, preliminary Crown Court hearing, or further hearing prior to the PCMH, is aware of the problems, knows why and how the position has arisen and can assist the court as to what revised time limits are realistic.

24. It would be helpful if the prosecution advocate could make any foreseeable difficulties clear as soon as possible, whether this is at the Magistrates' Court or in the Crown Court at the preliminary hearing (where there is one).

25. Failing this, where such difficulties arise or have come to light after directions for service of case papers and disclosure have been made, the prosecution should notify the court and the defence promptly. This should be done in advance of the PCMH date, and prior to the date set by the court for the service of this material.

26. It is important that this is done in order that the listing for the PCMH is an effective one, as the defence must have a proper opportunity to read the case papers and to consider the initial or primary disclosure, with a view to timely drafting of a defence case statement (where the matter is to be contested), prior to the PCMH.

27. In order to ensure that the listing of the PCMH is appropriate, judges should not impose time limits for service of case papers or initial/primary disclosure unless and until they are confident that the prosecution advocate has taken the requisite instructions from those who are actually going to do the work specified. It is better to impose a realistic timetable from the outset than to set unachievable limits. Reference should be made to the 2005 Rules, SI 2005/384, Pt 3 and the *Consolidated Criminal Practice Direction* in this respect.

28. This is likewise appropriate where directions, or further directions, are made in relation to prosecution or defence disclosure at the PCMH. Failure to consider whether the timetable is practicable may dislocate the court timetable and can even imperil trial dates. At the PCMH, therefore, all the advocates—prosecution and defence—must be fully instructed about any difficulties the parties may have in complying with their respective disclosure obligations, and must be in a position to put forward a reasonable timetable for resolution of them.

29. Where directions are given by the court in the light of such inquiry, extensions of time should not be given lightly or as a matter of course. If extensions are sought, then an appropriately detailed explanation must be given. For the avoidance of doubt, it is not sufficient merely for the Crown Prosecution Service (or other prosecutor) to say that the papers have been delivered late by the police (or other investigator): the court will need to know why they have been delivered late. Likewise, where the accused has been dilatory in serving a defence statement (where the prosecution has complied with the duty to make primary or initial disclosure of unused material, or has purported to do so), it is not sufficient for the defence to say that insufficient instructions have been taken for service of this within the 14-day time limit: the court will need to know why sufficient instructions have not been taken, and what arrangements have been made for the taking of such instructions.

30. Delays and failures by the defence are as damaging to the timely, fair and efficient hearing of the case as delays and failures by the prosecution, and judges should identify and deal with all such failures firmly and fairly.

31. Judges should not allow the prosecution to abdicate their statutory responsibility for reviewing the unused material by the expedient of allowing the defence to inspect (or providing the defence with copies of) everything on the schedules of non-sensitive unused prosecution material, irrespective of whether that material, or all of that material, satisfies the relevant test for disclosure. Where that test is satisfied it is for the prosecutor to decide the form in which disclosure is made. Disclosure need not be in the same form as that in which the information was recorded. Guidance on case management issues relating to this point was given by Rose LJ in *R v CPS* (*Interlocutory Application under the Criminal Procedure and Investigations Act 1996 ss 35, 36*) [2005] EWCA Crim 2342.

32. Indeed, the larger and more complex the case, the more important it is for the prosecution to adhere to the overarching principle in head 4, above, and ensure that sufficient prosecution resources are allocated to the task. Handing the defence the 'keys to the warehouse' has been the cause of many gross abuses in the past, resulting in huge sums being run up by the defence without any proportionate benefit to the course of justice. These abuses must end.

The Defence Case Statement

33. Reference has been made above to defence disclosure obligations. After the provision of primary or initial disclosure by the prosecution, the next really critical step in the preparation for trial is the service of the defence statement. It is a mandatory requirement for a defence statement to be served, where the 1996 Act s 5(5) applies to the proceedings. This is due within 14 days of the date on which the prosecution has complied with, or purported to comply with, the duty of primary or initial disclosure. Service of the defence statement is a critical stage in the disclosure process, and timely service of the statement will allow for the proper consideration of disclosure issues well in advance of the trial date.

34. There may be some cases where it is simply not possible to serve a proper defence case statement within the 14-day time limit; well founded defence applications for an extension of time under the

1997 Regulations, SI 1997/684, reg 3 para 2 may therefore be granted. In a proper case, it may be appropriate to put the PCMH back by a week or so, to enable a sufficient defence case statement to be filed and considered by the prosecution.

35. In the past, the prosecution and the court have too often been faced with a defence case statement that is little more than an assertion that the defendant is not guilty. As was stated by the Court of Appeal in *R v Bryant* [2005] EWCA Crim 2079, [2005] All ER (D) 210 (Oct) (2005 Abr para 947) (per Judge LJ at [12]), such a reiteration of the defendant's plea is not the purpose of a defence statement. Defence statements must comply with the requisite formalities set out in the 1996 Act s 5(6), (7), or 6A, as applicable.

36. Where the enhanced requirements for defence disclosure apply under s 6A (namely, where the case involves a criminal investigation commencing on or after 4 April 2005) the defence statement must spell out, in detail, the nature of the defence, and particular defences relied on; it must identify the matters of fact on which the accused takes issue with the prosecution, and the reason why, in relation to each disputed matter of fact. It must further identify any point of law (including points as to the admissibility of evidence, or abuse of process) which the accused proposes to take, and identify authorities relied on in relation to each point of law. Where an alibi defence is relied on, the particulars given must comply with s 6(2)(a), (b). Judges will expect to see defence case statements that contain a clear and detailed exposition of the issues of fact and law in the case.

37. Where the pre 4 April 2005 1996 Act disclosure regime applies, the accused must, in the defence statement, set out the nature of the defence in general terms, indicate the matters on which the defendant takes issue with the prosecution and set out (in relation to each such matter) why issue is taken. Any alibi defence relied on should comply with the formalities in s 5(7)(a), (b).

38. There must be a complete change in the culture. The defence must serve the defence case statement by the due date. Judges should then examine the defence case statement with care to ensure that it complies with the formalities required by the 1996 Act. As was stated in at [35] of *R v H; R v C*:

'If material does not weaken the prosecution case or strengthen that of the defendant, there is no requirement to disclose it. For this purpose the parties' respective cases should not be restrictively analysed. But they must be carefully analysed, to ascertain the specific facts the prosecution seek to establish and the specific grounds on which the charges are resisted. The trial process is not well served if the defence are permitted to make general and unspecified allegations and then seek far-reaching disclosure in the hope that material may turn up to make them good. Neutral material or material damaging to the defendant need not be disclosed and should not be brought to the attention of the court.'

39. If no defence case statement—or no sufficient case statement—has been served by the PCMH, the judge should make a full investigation of the reasons for this failure to comply with the mandatory obligation of the accused, under the 1996 Act s 5(5).

40. If there is no—or no sufficient—defence statement by the date of PCMH, or any pre-trial hearing where the matter falls to be considered, the judge must consider whether the defence should be warned, pursuant to s 6E(2), that an adverse inference may be drawn at the trial. In the usual case, where s 6E(2) applies and there is no justification for the deficiency, such a warning should be given.

41. Judges must, of course, be alert to ensure that defendants do not suffer because of the faults and failings of their lawyers, but there must be a clear indication to the professions that if justice is to be done, and if disclosure to be dealt with fairly in accordance with the law, a full and careful defence case statement is essential.

42. Where there are failings by either the defence or the prosecution, judges should, in exercising appropriate oversight of disclosure, pose searching questions to the parties and, having done this and explored the reasons for default, give clear directions to ensure that such failings are addressed and remedied well in advance of the trial date.

43. The ultimate sanction for a failure in disclosure by the accused is the drawing of an inference under s 11. Where the amended 1996 Act regime applies, the strict legal position allows the prosecution to comment on any failure of defence disclosure, with a view to seeking such an inference (except where the failure relates to identifying a point of law), without leave of the court, but often it will be helpful to canvass the matter with the judge beforehand. In suitable cases, the prosecution should consider commenting on failures in defence disclosure, with a view to such an inference, more readily than has been the practice under the old 1996 Act regime, subject to any views expressed by the judge.

44. It is vital to a fair trial that the prosecution are mindful of their continuing duty of disclosure, and they must particularly review disclosure in the light of the issues identified in the defence case statement. As part of the timetabling exercise, the judge should set a date by which any application under s 8 (if there is to be one) should be made. While the defence may indicate, in advance of the cut-off date, what items of unused material they are interested in and why, such requests must relate to matters raised in the accused's defence statement. The prosecution should only disclose material in

response to such requests if the material meets the appropriate test for disclosure, and the matter must proceed to a formal s 8 hearing in the event that the prosecution declines to make disclosure of the items in question. The Lord Chief Justice's March 2005 *Protocol for the Control and Management of Heavy Fraud and Other Complex Criminal Cases* para 4(iv)–(vi)(a) should be construed accordingly.

45. If, after the prosecution have complied with, or purported to comply with, primary or initial disclosure, and after the service of the defence case statement and any further prosecution disclosure flowing there from, the defence have a reasonable basis to claim disclosure has been inadequate, they must make an application to the court under the 1996 Act s 8. The procedure for the making of such an application is set out in the 2005 Rules, SI 2005/384, Pt 25 r 25.6. This requires written notice to the prosecution in the form prescribed by r 25.6(2). The prosecution is then entitled (r 25.6(5)) to 14 days within which to agree to provide the specific disclosure requested or to request a hearing in order to make representations in relation to the defence application. As part of the timetabling exercise, the judge should set a date by which any applications under the 1996 Act s 8 are to be made and should require the defence to indicate in advance of the cut-off date for specific disclosure applications what documents they are interested in and from what source; in appropriate cases, the judge should require justification of such requests.

46. The consideration of detailed defence requests for specific disclosure (so-called 'shopping lists') otherwise than in accordance with the 2005 Rules, SI 2005/384, r 25.6, is wholly improper. Likewise, defence requests for specific disclosure of unused prosecution material in purported pursuance of the 1996 Act s 8 and the 2005 Rules, SI 2005/384, r 25.6, which are not referable to any issue in the case identified by the defence case statement, should be rejected. Judges should require an application to be made under the 1996 Act s 8 and in compliance with the 2005 Rules, SI 2005/384, r 25.6 before considering any order for further disclosure.

47. It follows that the practice of making blanket orders for disclosure in all cases should cease, since such orders are inconsistent with the statutory framework of disclosure laid down by the 1996 Act, and which was endorsed by the House of Lords in *R v H; R v C.*

Listing

48. It will be clear that the conscientious discharge of a judge's duty at the PCMH requires a good deal more time than under the old PDH regime; furthermore a good deal more work is required of the advocate. The listing of PCMHs must take this into account. Unless the court can sit at 10am and finish the PCMH by 10.30am, it will not therefore usually be desirable for a judge who is part-heard on a trial to do a PCMH.

49. It follows that any case which raises difficult issues of disclosure should be referred to the resident judge for directions. Cases of real complexity should, if possible, be allocated to a specific trial judge at a very early stage, and usually before the PCMH.

50. Although this *Protocol* is addressed to the issues of disclosure, it cannot be seen in isolation; it must be seen in the context of general case management.

Public Interest Immunity

51. Recent authoritative guidance as to the proper approach to PII is provided by the House of Lords in *R v H; R v C.* It is clearly appropriate for PII applications to be considered by the trial judge. No judge should embark on a PII application without considering that case and addressing the questions set out at [36], which for ease of reference we reproduce here:

'[36] When any issue of derogation from the golden rule of full disclosure comes before it, the court must address a series of questions:

(1) What is the material which the prosecution seek to withhold? This must be considered by the court in detail.

(2) Is the material such as may weaken the prosecution case or strengthen that of the defence? If no, disclosure should not be ordered. If yes, full disclosure should (subject to (3), (4) and (5) below) be ordered.

(3) Is there a real risk of serious prejudice to an important public interest (and, if so, what) if full disclosure of the material is ordered? If no, full disclosure should be ordered.

(4) If the answer to (2) and (3) is yes, can the defendant's interest be protected without disclosure or disclosure be ordered to an extent or in a way which will give adequate protection to the public interest in question and also afford adequate protection to the interests of the defence?

This question requires the court to consider, with specific reference to the material which the prosecution seek to withhold and the facts of the case and the defence as disclosed, whether the prosecution should formally admit what the defence seek to establish or whether disclosure short of full disclosure may be ordered. This may be done in appropriate cases by the preparation of summaries or extracts of evidence, or the provision of documents in an edited or anonymised form, provided the documents supplied are in each instance approved by the judge. In appropriate cases the appointment of special counsel may be a necessary step to ensure that the contentions of the prosecution are tested and the interests of the defendant protected (see head 23, above). In cases of exceptional difficulty the court may require the appointment of special counsel to ensure a correct answer to questions (2) and (3) as well as (4).

(5) Do the measures proposed in answer to (4) represent the minimum derogation necessary to protect the public interest in question? If no, the court should order such greater disclosure as will represent the minimum derogation from the golden rule of full disclosure.

(6) If limited disclosure is ordered pursuant to (4) or (5), may the effect be to render the trial process, viewed as a whole, unfair to the defendant? If yes, then fuller disclosure should be ordered even if this leads or may lead the prosecution to discontinue the proceedings so as to avoid having to make disclosure.

(7) If the answer to (6) when first given is no, does that remain the correct answer as the trial unfolds, evidence is adduced and the defence advanced?

It is important that the answer to (6) should not be treated as a final, once-and-for-all, answer but as a provisional answer which the court must keep under review.'

52. In this context, the following matters are emphasised:

(a) the procedure for making applications to the court is as set out in the 2005 Rules, SI 2005/384, Pt 25, r 25(1)–(5);

(b) where the PII application is a type 1 or type 2 application, proper notice to the defence is necessary to allow them to make focused submissions to the court before hearing an application to withhold material; the notice should be as specific as the nature of the material allows. It is appreciated that in some cases only the generic nature of the material can properly be identified. In some wholly exceptional cases (type 3 cases) it may even be justified to give no notice at all. The judge should always ask the prosecution to justify the form of notice given (or the decision to give no notice at all);

(c) the prosecution should be alert to the possibility of disclosing a statement in redacted form by, for example simply removing personal details. This may obviate the need for a PII application, unless the redacted material in itself would also satisfy the test for disclosure;

(d) except where the material is very short (say a few sheets only), or where the material is of such sensitivity that to do so would be inappropriate, the prosecution should have supplied securely sealed copies to the judge beforehand, together with a short statement of the reasons why each document is said to be relevant and fulfils the disclosure test and why it is said that its disclosure would cause a real risk of serious prejudice to an important public interest; in undertaking this task, the use of merely formulaic expressions is to be discouraged. In any case of complexity a schedule of the material should be provided showing the specific objection to disclosure in relation to each item, leaving a space for the decision;

(e) the application, even if held in private or in secret, should be recorded. The judge should give some short statement of reasons; this is often best done by document as the hearing proceeds;

(f) the tape, copies of the judge's orders (and any copies of the material retained by the court) should be clearly identified, securely sealed and kept in the court building in a safe or stout lockable cabinet consistent with its security classification, and there should be a proper register of all such material kept. Some arrangement should be made between the court and the prosecution authority for the periodic removal of such material once the case is concluded and the time for an appeal has passed.'

Third Part Disclosure

53. The disclosure of unused material that has been gathered or generated by a third party is an area of the law that has caused some difficulties: indeed, a Home Office Working Party has been asked to report on it. This is because there is no specific procedure for the disclosure of material held by third parties in criminal proceedings, although the procedure under the Criminal Procedure (Attendance of Witnesses) Act 1965 s 2 or the Magistrates' Courts Act 1980 s 97 is often used in order to effect such disclosure. It should, however, be noted that the test applied under both the 1965 Act and the 1980 Act is not the test to be applied under the 1996 Act, whether in the amended or unamended form. These two provisions require that the material in question is material evidence, that is, immediately admissible in evidence in the proceedings (see in this respect *R v Reading Justices, ex p Berkshire CC* [1996] 1 Cr App Rep 239 (1996 Abr para 855); *R v Derby Magistrates' Court, ex p B* [1995] 4 All ER 526 (1995 Abr para 826); and *R v Alibhai* [2004] EWCA Crim 681).

54. Material held by other government departments or other Crown agencies will not be prosecution material for the purposes of the 1996 Act s 3(2) or 8(4), if it has not been inspected, recorded and retained during the course of the relevant criminal investigation. The Attorney General's Guidelines on Disclosure, however, impose a duty on the investigators and the prosecution to consider whether such departments or bodies have material which may satisfy the test for disclosure under the 1996 Act. Where this is the case, they must seek appropriate disclosure from such bodies, who should themselves have an identified point for such inquiries (see the Attorney General's Guidelines on Disclosure paras 47–51).

55. Where material is held by a third party such as a local authority, a social services department, hospital or business, the investigators and the prosecution may seek to make arrangements to inspect the material with a view to applying the relevant test for disclosure to it and determining whether any or all of the material should be retained, recorded and, in due course, disclosed to the accused. In considering the latter, the investigators and the prosecution will establish whether the holder of the material wishes to raise PII issues, as a result of which the material may have to be placed before the court. The 1996 Act s 16 gives such a party a right to make representations to the court.

56. Where the third party in question declines to allow inspection of the material, or requires the prosecution to obtain an order before handing over copies of the material, the prosecutor will need to consider whether it is appropriate to obtain a witness summons under either the Criminal Procedure (Attendance of Witnesses) Act 1965 s 2 or the Magistrates' Court Act 1980 s 97. However, as stated above, this is only appropriate where the statutory requirements are satisfied, and where the prosecutor considers that the material may satisfy the test for disclosure. *R v Alibhai* supra makes it clear that the prosecutor has a 'margin of consideration' in this regard.

57. It should be understood that the third party may have a duty to assert confidentiality, or the right to privacy under the European Convention on Human Rights art 8, where requests for disclosure are made by the prosecution, or anyone else. Where issues are raised in relation to allegedly relevant third party material, the judge must ascertain whether inquiries with the third party are likely to be appropriate, and, if so, identify who is going to make the request, what material is to be sought, from whom is the material to be sought and within what time scale must the matter be resolved.

58. The judge should consider what action would be appropriate in the light of the third party failing or refusing to comply with a request, including inviting the defence to make the request on its own behalf and, if necessary, to make an application for a witness summons. Any directions made (for instance, the date by which an application for a witness summons with supporting affidavit under the 1965 Act s 2 should be served) should be put into writing at the time. Any failure to comply with the timetable must immediately be referred back to the court for further directions, although a hearing will not always be necessary.

59. Where the prosecution do not consider it appropriate to seek such a summons, the defence should consider doing so, where they are of the view (notwithstanding the prosecution assessment) that the third party may hold material which might undermine the prosecution case or assist that for the defendant, and the material would be likely to be 'material evidence' for the purposes of the 1965 Act. The defence must not sit back and expect the prosecution to make the running. The judge at the PCMH should specifically inquire whether any such application is to be made by the defence and set out a clear timetable. The objectionable practice of defence applications being made in the few days before trial must end.

60. It should be made clear, though, that 'fishing' expeditions in relation to third party material—whether by the prosecution or the defence—must be discouraged, and that, in appropriate cases, the court will consider making an order for wasted costs where the application is clearly unmeritorious and ill-conceived.

61. Judges should recognise that a summons can only be issued where the document(s) sought would be admissible in evidence. While it may be that the material in question may be admissible in evidence as a result of the hearsay provisions of the Criminal Justice Act 1991 ss 114–120, it is this that determines whether an order for production of the material is appropriate, rather than the wider considerations applicable to disclosure in criminal proceedings: see *R v Reading Justices, ex p Berkshire CC* (supra), upheld by the House of Lords in *R v Derby Magistrates' Court, ex p B* (supra).

62. A number of Crown Court centres have developed local protocols, usually in respect of sexual offences and material held by social services and health and education authorities. Where these protocols exist they often provide an excellent and sensible way to identify relevant material that might assist the defence or undermine the prosecution.

63. Any application for third party disclosure must identify what documents are sought and why they are said to be material evidence. This is particularly relevant where attempts are made to access the medical reports of those who allege that they are victims of crime. Victims do not waive the confidentiality of their medical records, or their right to privacy under the Convention art 8, by the mere fact of making a complaint against the accused. Judges should be alert to balance the rights of victims against the real and proven needs of the defence. The court, as a public authority, must ensure that any interference with the art 8 rights of those entitled to privacy is in accordance with the law and necessary in pursuit of a legitimate public interest. General and unspecified requests to trawl through such records should be refused. If material is held by any person in relation to family proceedings (for example, where there have been care proceedings in relation to a child, who has also complained to the police of sexual or other abuse) then an application has to be made by that person to the family court for leave to disclose that material to a third party, unless the third party, and the purpose for which disclosure is made, is approved by the Family Proceedings Rules 1991, SI 1991/1247, r 10.20A(3). This would permit, for instance, a local authority, in receipt of such

material, to disclose it to the police for the purpose of a criminal investigation, or to the Crown Prosecution Service, in order for the latter to discharge any obligations under the 1996 Act.

Conclusion

64. The public rightly expects that the delays and failures which have been present in some cases in the past where there has been scant adherence to sound disclosure principles will be eradicated by observation of this *Protocol*. The new regime under the Criminal Justice Act 2003 and the Criminal Procedure Rules 2005, SI 2005/384, gives judges the power to change the culture in which such cases are tried. It is now the duty of every judge actively to manage disclosure issues in every case. The judge must seize the initiative and drive the case along towards an efficient, effective and timely resolution, having regard to the overriding objective of the Criminal Procedure Rules 2005, SI 2005/384, Pt 1. In this way the interests of justice will be better served and public confidence in the criminal justice system will be increased.

767 Custody—time limits—extension—due diligence requirement

The Prosecution of Offences Act 1985 s 22(3)(b) provides that the court may, at any time before the expiry of a time limit, extend that limit if satisfied that the prosecution has acted with all due diligence and expedition.

The earliest date that could be fixed for the defendants' trial was outside of the custody time limits, and the prosecution obtained an extension to custody time limits under the 1985 Act s 22, without opposition. An independent contractor which was to supply certain telephone evidence was unable to supply that evidence within the new time limit and the prosecution made a further application to extend custody time limits. The defendants opposed the further extension on the ground that the prosecution had not acted with all due diligence and expedition for the purposes of s 22(3)(b), relying on a detailed chronology which disclosed evidence of significant periods of inactivity prior to the initial application. The trial judge disagreed and the defendants applied for judicial review. *Held*, in relation to a case involving a further extension of custody time limits, s 22(3)(b) focussed on those matters that had given rise to the need for the extension of time under consideration. Where a defendant asserted a lack of expedition or due diligence, and it appeared that that was the root cause of the application for the earlier extension of time, then those matters were properly a matter for the earlier application. A delay prior to the earlier application could be relied on in a later application only if it was the root cause of that later application. If a legal error had been made on an earlier application for an extension then that was a matter for appeal. It would be wrong and contrary to the principle of legal certainty to countenance an approach where a party on a later application could seek to impugn as legally flawed a decision on the earlier application. The root cause of the earlier extension was the court's inability to provide an earlier trial date and not any delay in obtaining the telephone evidence. Accordingly, the applications would be dismissed.

R (on the application of Thomas) v Central Criminal Court; R (on the application of Stubbs) v Central Criminal Court [2006] EWHC 2138 (Admin), [2006] 1 WLR 3278 (Queen's Bench Division: Laws LJ and Walker J). *R (on the application of Gibson) v Crown Court at Winchester* [2004] EWHC 699 (Admin), [2004] 3 All ER 475 (2004 Abr para 708) applied.

768 Disclosure of information—prosecution material—material in possession of manufacturer of breath-testing devices

The defendants, who had been charged with drink-driving, sought disclosure of material concerning the intoximeters which had measured the alcohol on their breath under the Criminal Procedure and Investigations Act 1996 s 8. It was alleged that the intoximeters were originally of an approved type, but had been altered in such a way as to take them out of type approval. The material sought was in the possession of the manufacturer of the intoximeters, which had supplied them to the police and serviced them under a contractual arrangement. The court ordered disclosure and stayed proceedings as an abuse of process when the prosecution failed to comply. On appeal, the prosecution submitted that the material in question could not be relevant to the defence because it went to the type approval, rather than the reliability, of the device. *Held*, the lawfulness of type approval was not a matter which could be raised as a defence to a charge of driving with excess alcohol in the criminal courts. The court required more than the asserted fact of unapproved modification to justify disclosure. There would have to be some material which explained how the alteration could go to loss of type approval and how disclosure could advance that point. There was no indication that the disclosure orders were justified when measured against the defences advanced and the stringent test required to show loss of type approval. Further, the relevant material was in the possession of the manufacturer of the breath-testing devices. Section 8 provided for the disclosure of prosecution material and the manufacturer did not become part of the prosecution on the ground that it had supplied the intoximeters to the police force and was under a contract to do so. Accordingly, the stay of proceedings in each case had been unjustified and the cases would be remitted to the magistrates' court for rehearing.

DPP v Wood; DPP v McGillicuddy [2005] EWHC 2986 (Admin), (2006) 170 JP 177 (Queen's Bench Division: Laws LJ and Ouseley J).

The defendant was stopped by police while driving his car. He provided a positive specimen of breath at the roadside, and was arrested and taken to a police station where two further specimens of breath were analysed. In the course of preliminary hearings, orders were made against the prosecution for secondary disclosure. The defence served a statement 18 months after primary disclosure by the prosecution and argued that changes in software used had taken the intoximeter outside of the approved type. At the start of the trial, more than four years after his arrest, the defendant sought a stay on the basis of the delay and contended that the prosecution was in contempt of court by failing to comply with the orders for disclosure. The judge refused to stay the hearing, finding that the defence statement had been served out of time so that in accordance with the Criminal Procedure and Investigations Act 1996 ss 5(5), 12, the defendant was not entitled to secondary disclosure. He also found that the Road Traffic Offenders Act 1988 s 15(2) did not compel the prosecution to adduce the quantitative result of the analysis carried out by the roadside device that had been stored in the memory of that device. The defendant was convicted and appealed. *Held*, a defendant was not entitled to secondary disclosure only if he had served his defence case statement in time. It could not have been Parliament's intention that a defendant should lose his right to discovery of material in the possession of the prosecution that might assist his case by reason of what might be a short delay in providing the defence statement. However, the judge had been bound to refuse to stay the proceedings since the issues raised by the defence statement relied on the defendant's truthfulness and technical evidence and not on the memory of witnesses. Evidence of the proportion of alcohol in a specimen for the purposes of s 15(2) was evidence that had actually been placed before the court. It followed that evidence of the proportion of alcohol stored in the memory of a roadside device was admissible if it had been obtained from the manufacturer. To hold otherwise would mean that in every case, the prosecution would have to obtain from the manufacturer of the roadside device an analysis of the proportion of alcohol in the relevant specimen and then put that analysis in evidence. Accordingly, the appeal would be dismissed.

Murphy v DPP [2006] All ER (D) 210 (Jun) (Queen's Bench Division: Maurice Kay LJ and Mitting J).

769   Domestic Violence, Crime and Victims Act 2004—commencement

The Domestic Violence, Crime and Victims Act 2004 (Commencement No 6) Order 2006, SI 2006/2662, brings s 55 into force on 4 October 2006. For a summary of the Act, see 2004 Abr para 713. See also the commencement table in the title STATUTES.

The Domestic Violence, Crime and Victims Act 2004 (Commencement No 7 and Transitional Provision) Order 2006, SI 2006/3423, brings into force, on 8 January 2007, ss 17–20, 30, 56, 58(1) (in part) and Sch 10 para 62. Transitional provision is also made.

For a summary of the Act, see 2004 Abr para 713. See also the commencement table in the title STATUTES.

770   Evidence—admissibility—competence of witness—very young child

The appellant was convicted of indecent assault on the complainant, a three-and-a-half-year-old girl. The complainant was interviewed nine weeks after the alleged incident, and the trial took place seven months later. On appeal, *held*, the Youth Justice and Criminal Evidence Act 1999 s 53 made it clear that the age of a witness did not determine whether he was competent to give evidence. In this instance, the judge should have reconsidered her decision as to the complainant's competence following her evidence, as she would have, or should have concluded that the complainant was not competent, as the complainant's answers in cross-examination were not intelligible in the context of the case. Had the complainant been interviewed appropriately and promptly, the age of the child would not have been an insurmountable obstacle for the prosecution. Special efforts had to be made to fast-track such cases and it was not an option to wait weeks for forensic evidence. Accordingly, the appeal would be allowed.

R v Powell (2006) Times, 17 January (Court of Appeal: Scott Baker LJ, Ramsey J and Judge Griffith Williams QC).

771   Evidence—admissibility—confession—relevant procedural standards

The defendant, who was aged 19 and illiterate, was interviewed by the police in connection with a murder. The first set of interviews took place in a detention centre, and lasted approximately two hours without a solicitor being present. The defendant was later arrested and taken to a police station, where he was interviewed a further four times, lasting a total of three hours, again without the benefit of legal representation. He initially denied any knowledge of the murder, but later admitted having a vague recollection of certain details, which were recorded in a statement and signed by the defendant. The following day he was again interviewed four times, lasting over three hours, but he denied having committed the offence. None of the interviews were recorded, and the notes taken by the police were incomplete and had not been signed by the defendant. At the defendant's trial, the only evidence against him was his 'confession', which the defendant unsuccessfully applied to exclude. In evidence he accepted that he had made the admissions, but stated that he had been lying in an attempt to prevent the police from persecuting him further. He said that the officers had abused and hit him, and that his requests for a solicitor were refused or ignored. He was convicted and his appeal against conviction was dismissed. More than 20 years after his conviction, the defendant's case was referred back to the Court of Appeal pursuant to the Criminal Appeal Act 1995 s 9 on the basis of fresh evidence about the defendant's mental state and likelihood of his having made a false confession. *Held*, the courts were more aware in modern times of the risk of false confessions. The procedural requirements in the Police and Criminal Evidence Act 1984 were designed to protect the vulnerable. Expert evidence was often needed to assess an accused's vulnerability and the reliability of a confession. On his arrival at a police station, a person was entitled to speak to a solicitor and to receive free legal advice in interview. The interview should be fully recorded. It followed that, when considering the safety of the present conviction, consideration would be given to those modern standards. Even judged by the standards prevailing at the time of the conviction, the case was worrying. The proof of murder depended almost entirely on the confession in 11 hours of interview by a 19-year-old illiterate defendant who did not have the benefit of a solicitor. The interview had not been fully recorded and the defendant had, more than once, retracted his confession. In the light of the expert evidence and modern standards, there could be no hesitation in concluding that the conviction was unsafe. Accordingly, the appeal would be allowed.

R v Nolan [2006] All ER (D) 98 (Nov) (Court of Appeal: Tuckey LJ, Holman and Hodge JJ).

772 Evidence—admissibility—declaration made in furtherance of conspiracy

The defendant and his co-defendants were charged with conspiracy to supply a Class A drug. A number of the co-defendants were also charged with conspiracy to supply cannabis. The prosecution case was that the defendant was working at a transporting company as an insider. The prosecution relied on recordings of conversations between co-conspirators which purportedly demonstrated that the defendant had allowed the company to transport a consignment of cocaine. The shipment had false consignee details and a false address, and it was common ground that the defendant had tracked the consignment for a co-conspirator. No point was taken at trial as to the admissibility of the recordings so far as the defendant was concerned. The defendant was convicted and, on his appeal, issues arose as to the admissibility of the recorded conversations, the nature of declarations made in furtherance of the conspiracy and the status of 'mere narrative'. *Held*, it was a matter for the trial judge as to whether any act or declaration by one conspirator was admissible to prove the participation of another. In particular, the judge had to be satisfied that the act or declaration was made by a conspirator and could reasonably be interpreted as having been made in furtherance of the alleged agreement, and that there was some further evidence beyond the document or utterance to prove that the other party had been a party to the agreement. The exclusion of 'mere narratives' as being admissible against anyone other than the maker of the declaration applied only to narrative at the conclusion of the conspiracy. Statements made during the conspiracy and as part of the conspiracy would be admissible because they were part of the natural process of making the arrangements to carry out the conspiracy. Evidence was admissible when it could be said of it that 'this is the enterprise in operation'. Moreover, evidence was admissible not just as to the nature and extent of the conspiracy but also as to the participation in it of persons absent at the time of the declaration. The evidence was not mere narrative, and certain 'eavesdrop' evidence relied on by the prosecution as showing that the defendant was a party to the conspiracy was, subject to one exception, admissible and compelling. Accordingly, the appeal would be dismissed.

R v Platten [2006] EWCA Crim 140, [2006] All ER (D) 194 (Feb) (Court of Appeal: Walker LJ, Gray and Cox JJ). *R v Barham* [1997] 2 Cr App Rep 119, CA; and *R v Smart* [2002] EWCA Crim 772, [2002] All ER (D) 446 (Mar) considered.

773 Evidence—admissibility—expert evidence—memories from early childhood— childhood amnesia

In two applications for permission to appeal against conviction of sexual offences against a child, the question of the admissibility of fresh expert evidence on the topic of childhood amnesia arose. The expert suggested that adults did not remember events of their early childhood in such a way that they could give a coherent narrative account of those events. The expert was particularly concerned at the production of a 'rather polished narrative' and as to how the complainants' witness statements seemed to him to reflect a kind of joint effort between the interviewing officer and the complainants. *Held*, where an adult was speaking of events which had occurred in his childhood, save where there was evidence of mental disability or learning difficulties, attempts to persuade the court to admit evidence on childhood amnesia should be carefully scrutinised. It was elementary that any witness statement should accurately reflect the most precise recollection which the witness had. However, the English legal process recognised that many witnesses describing events of which they had a clear memory did not immediately provide a completely coherent account. Sometimes the words used by the witness might convey a slightly inexact account of what the witness was saying. The expert had been unaware that police officers taking a statement would ask a series of questions and, having taken notes in relation to the answers, draft a statement for the witness to read and sign.

Further, the fact that a childhood experience was being described did not require the witness to confirm the accuracy of his memory by reverting to childishness or childish names. The issue to be decided by the jury was whether any witness, and in particular the complainant, was truthful and accurate. Accordingly, the applications would be refused.

R v S; R v W [2006] EWCA Crim 1404, [2006] All ER (D) 214 (Jun) (Court of Appeal: Sir Igor Judge P, Rafferty and Openshaw JJ).

774   Evidence—admissibility—expert evidence—report criticising value of hypnosis as memory aid

The defendant was charged with sexual offences allegedly committed against his daughter and her friend when they were young girls. At the time of the trial, the complainants were aged 33 and 34. The second complainant had not told anyone about the alleged abuse until she was an adult, and the first complaint she had made was during sessions of hypnotherapy. The prosecution served, as unused material, a statement from a therapist who had seen the second complainant, to the effect that she had revealed details of sexual abuse in her childhood. A defence expert prepared a report criticising the methods and techniques used by the therapist. The expert's report stated that hypnosis was not a reliable means of recalling past events, and that hypnotherapy merely facilitated the process of imagination and suggestibility, inducing susceptible people to accept events imagined during a session as memories of real past events. On an application to adduce the expert's report, the defence submitted that the second complainant's recall might have been a product of the therapy, and that there was a common public misconception that a person speaking while under hypnosis was unable to tell a lie. The judge refused permission to adduce the expert's evidence. The defendant was convicted of rape and indecent assault. He appealed, submitting that the refusal to allow the evidence to be admitted rendered the conviction unsafe. *Held*, there were passages in the report which were admissible as being outside the knowledge and experience of the ordinary juror. Had the false memory been engendered during the therapy session, there was a risk that the complainant could have regarded her 'memory' as genuine and real. It was clear that the expert was very experienced in the field. The criticisms he had made of the therapist and her techniques (she was less experienced and had fewer qualifications), were a matter for the jury to assess. The jury might well have accepted the expert's evidence and have reached different verdicts in the light of it. The judge had therefore erred in refusing the relevant parts of the expert's evidence to be admitted, and it followed that it could not be said that the convictions in relation to the second complainant were safe. Accordingly, the appeal would be allowed.

R v C [2006] All ER (D) 36 (Feb) (Court of Appeal: Gage LJ, Nelson J and Sir John Alliott). *R v Turner* [1975] QB 834, CA, applied.

775   Evidence—admissibility—hearsay—multiple hearsay—interests of justice

The appellant drove into a stationary car at a car park. A witness to the incident left a note of the appellant's registration number on the windscreen of the damaged car, and that number was subsequently passed on to the police by the girlfriend of the driver of the damaged car. The police recorded the number in the Police Incident Log. By the time the appellant was tried for careless driving and for failing to stop and report an accident, the original note had been lost. The justices decided to admit the Police Incident Log in evidence as a business or other document pursuant to the Criminal Justice Act 2003 s 117 in order to determine which car had been involved in the collision. The appellant was convicted and, on his appeal, he argued that the evidence of the Police Incident Log was inadmissible hearsay. *Held*, although the note constituted hearsay evidence within the meaning of ss 114 and 115, it was not properly admissible as a business or other document since the information was not received by the driver's girlfriend in the course of a trade, business or profession as required by s 117(2). Nevertheless, the evidence could have been properly admitted as multiple hearsay under s 121(1)(c), which permitted the court to admit such evidence where the interests of justice demanded it. The justices must have assumed the evidence in question to be reliable. As the registration number matched exactly that of the appellant's car, it was inconceivable that there had been an error in transmission. The justices, having concluded that it was in the interests of justice to have admitted this evidence under s 117, would inevitably have come to the same conclusion had they applied their minds specifically to s 114(2) or 121(1)(c). Accordingly, the appeal would be dismissed.

Maher v DPP [2006] EWHC 1271 (Admin), (2006) 170 JP 441 (Queen's Bench Division: Scott Baker LJ and Leveson J).

776   Evidence—admissibility—video recording—surveillance

See *R v Rosenberg*, para 2263.

777   Evidence—burden of proof—causing death by dangerous driving—aiding and abetting

See *R v Webster*, para 2472.

778   Evidence—burden of proof—reverse burden of proof—failure of child to attend school—prosecution of parent for knowledge of failure to attend

See *R (on the application of P) v Liverpool City Magistrates*, para 1140.

779   Evidence—character of accused—bad character—attacks on another person's character—attack made in defendant's interview

The victim visited the defendant's neighbour. During his visit, an incident occurred which culminated in the defendant coming from his flat with a machete, swinging it around and directing it towards the victim. When the police arrived, they stated that the defendant appeared to have consumed alcohol, was seen to be holding a cannabis cigarette and that his flat smelled of cannabis. In the defendant's interview, he stated that his neighbour, who did not, in the event, give evidence at trial, was a user of Class A drugs and that he was a liar. The defendant's case at his trial for affray and assault occasioning actual bodily harm was that his neighbour and the victim had effectively conspired to fabricate the allegations, and the victim was cross-examined on that basis. The defence unsuccessfully opposed the admission in evidence of the defendant's comments in interview as to the neighbour's untruthfulness and drug taking being adduced in evidence on the ground that the evidence was irrelevant to the issues in the case. Moreover, the prosecution successfully applied for evidence of the defendant's previous convictions for drug offences to be admitted, pursuant to the Criminal Justice Act 2003 s 101(1)(g), on the ground that the defendant had made an attack on another person's character. The defendant was convicted of affray but acquitted of assault occasioning actual bodily harm. He appealed against his conviction, contending that the judge had erred in allowing into evidence his previous convictions as they had no probative value and had only prejudicial effect. *Held*, s 101(1)(g) was not confined to situations as had arisen under the old law where a defendant personally or through his advocate attacked the character of a prosecution witness, the prosecutor or a deceased victim. The 2003 Act extended to attacks made on the character of a non-witness and it had to be taken that Parliament had intended to widen the gateway to include other persons irrespective of whether they were a witness in the trial. However, it was to be borne in mind that a trial judge nevertheless retained a discretion under the Police and Criminal Evidence Act 1984 s 78 and the 2003 Act s 101(3) as to whether the jury would hear of the defendant's bad character when the attack was merely made on the character of a non-witness. How a trial judge exercised his discretion was a matter for him; however, it would be unusual for evidence of a defendant's bad character to be admitted when the only basis of that application was an attack on the character of a non-witness who was also a non-victim. The fairness of the proceedings would normally be damaged by the admission of bad character evidence in such circumstances. While, if the accusations made against the neighbour had properly gone before the jury, the instant case might have been one of those rare cases in which s 101(1)(g) was satisfied in respect of a non-witness who was not a victim, in the circumstances, it was difficult to see what relevance the defendant's comment in interview had to the issues in the case. Accordingly, the appeal would be dismissed.

R v Nelson [2006] All ER (D) 290 (Dec) (Court of Appeal: Keene LJ, Cox and Bean JJ).

780   Evidence—character of accused—bad character—contamination of evidence

If on a defendant's trial before a judge and jury for an offence evidence of the defendant's bad character has been admitted under any of the Criminal Justice Act 2003 s 101(1)(c)–(g), and the court is satisfied at any time after the close of the case for the prosecution that the evidence is contaminated, and the contamination is such that, considering the importance of the evidence to the case against the defendant, his conviction of the offence would be unsafe, the court must either direct the jury to acquit the defendant of the offence or, if it considers that there ought to be a retrial, discharge the jury: s 107(1).

On an appeal against a conviction of sexual assault on a child, the Court of Appeal has given the following guidance as to the application of the 2003 Act s 107 where there is a possibility that evidence is contaminated. (1) Contamination may result from deliberate collusion, or the exercise of improper pressure, but it may equally arise innocently or through inadvertence. Moreover, 'contamination issues' extend to evidence of bad character in the broad sense as well as to unequivocal evidence of bad character arising from unchallenged, and usually unchallengeable, evidence of previous convictions. The direct concern of s 107 is not the admissibility of bad character evidence, but rather the consequences of its admission. The unusual feature of s 107 is that, after the admission of evidence, a duty is imposed on the judge to make what is, in truth, a finding of fact. Plainly, where the case goes to the jury, issues such as contamination and collusion will be left to them in the familiar way, with appropriate directions and warnings. However, the decision at the end of the prosecution case, or indeed at any later stage in the trial, whether the evidence of a witness is false, or misleading, or different from what it would have been had it not been contaminated, requires that the judge should form his own assessment, or judgment, of matters traditionally regarded as questions of fact for the exclusive decision of the jury. In enacting Pt 11 (ss 98–141), Parliament's purpose is to assist in the evidential based conviction of the guilty without putting those who are not guilty at risk of conviction by prejudice. The effect of s 107 is to reduce the risk of a conviction based on over-reliance on evidence of previous misconduct and to acknowledge the potential danger that, where the evidence is contaminated, the evidence of bad character might have a disproportionate impact on the evaluation of the case by the jury. (2) The duty under s 107 does not arise unless the judge is satisfied that there has been an important contamination of the evidence. Where he is so satisfied, what then follows is not a matter of discretion. The consequences are prescribed by statute. Regardless of whether there would, on the conventional approach, be a case to answer, the trial should be stopped. The jury has either to acquit the defendant in accordance with a judicial direction or, where the judge considers that the case should proceed to a retrial, the jury will be discharged from returning a verdict, and a retrial will be ordered. The order for a retrial will, in those circumstances, not normally be susceptible to a subsequent application based on an asserted abuse of process. Unless something fresh emerges, that will amount, in effect, to an appeal from the decision of the judge who, with all the relevant considerations in mind, has ordered a retrial. (3) When, in answer to a submission by the prosecution at the start of the trial that the defendant's previous bad character should be admitted before the jury, counsel for the defendant makes a responsible submission that there is material in the prosecution case itself to suggest that there has or may have been witness contamination, it will normally be sensible for the judge to postpone a decision until the suggested contaminated evidence has been examined at trial. If the decision to admit bad character evidence is postponed until the evidence of the complainants, and any other witnesses, is concluded. The judge, when deciding whether to admit the evidence of bad character, will have well in mind the precise details of the evidence actually given, with such weaknesses and problems as may have emerged. He will not then be acting on his judgment about anticipated evidence, but will be making a decision based on the evidence itself.

R v Card [2006] EWCA Crim 1079, [2006] 3 All ER 689 (Court of Appeal: Sir Igor Judge P, Mackay and Gross JJ).

781 Evidence—character of accused—bad character—fairness

The defendant had offered a plea to a charge of possession of a Class A drug but the trial had proceeded on a charge of possession with intent to supply. The defendant had two previous convictions for possession of heroin with intent to supply, to each of which he had pleaded guilty. Evidence of his previous convictions was not put before the jury and he was convicted. His appeal against that conviction was not heard until over a year later. The appeal was allowed on the ground that the recorder's summing up had been deficient and a retrial was ordered. Between the time of the trial and the time of the retrial, the Criminal Justice Act 2003 ss 99–110 had come into force allowing evidence of a defendant's bad character to be admitted. Therefore, at the retrial, the prosecution made an application to adduce evidence of the defendant's two previous convictions. The judge allowed the application and the defendant was convicted. The defendant contended that if the first trial had been conducted correctly or if the appeal and second trial had been heard promptly, he would have been tried in circumstances where his previous convictions could not have been put in evidence. The defendant argued that the judge should have excluded the evidence of the previous convictions in the interests of fairness and he made a renewed application for permission to appeal against his conviction. *Held,* no merit could be seen in that ground of appeal. The relevant provisions of the 2003 Act altered the criminal law by restricting the circumstances in which the prosecution was prevented from placing before the jury prejudicial material which was relevant to the jury's task. It was not alleged that there was anything unfair in that change in the law in itself, it having been a matter of chance whether defendants were brought to trial before or after that change came into effect. Further, the delay in hearing the defendant's appeal had not been so long as to render it an abuse of process to direct a retrial. Accordingly, the application would be dismissed.

R v Campbell (2006) Times, 30 May (Court of Appeal: Lord Phillips of Worth Matravers CJ, Henriques and Gross JJ).

782 Evidence—character of accused—bad character—multiple complainants— cross-admissibility

The Criminal Justice Act 2003 s 101(1)(d) provides that evidence of the defendant's bad character is admissible if it is relevant to an important matter in issue between the defendant and the prosecution.

The defendant, a dentist, was tried on an indictment alleging that he had indecently assaulted three teenage patients. The judge ruled that the evidence of any one complainant could be treated by the jury as admissible to support the evidence of another, provided that the possibility of collusion or contamination was excluded. The defendant was convicted in relation to two of the complainants and he appealed, submitting that the evidence of the complainants was not cross-admissible for the purposes of the 2003 Act s 101(1)(d). *Held,* where propensity to commit a particular offence was advanced by way of multiple complaints, none of which had yet been proved (and whether they were proved was the question which the jury had to answer), that was a different case from that in which propensity was advanced through proof of a previous conviction. However, the 2003 Act governed all evidence of bad character, not only conclusive or undisputable evidence. In a case of the present kind, the critical question for the judge was whether the evidence of one complainant was relevant as going, or being capable of going, to establish propensity to commit offences of the kind charged. Not all evidence of other alleged offending was necessarily admissible under s 101(1)(d). Rather, there had in each case to be an examination of whether the evidence really did tend to establish the relevant propensity. There would have to be sufficient similarity to make it more likely that each allegation was true. The likelihood or unlikelihood of innocent coincidence would continue to be a relevant and sometimes critical test. However, there was a myriad of possible situations that might arise. On the evidence in the present case, if the complainants' evidence was accepted, that evidence did tend to establish a propensity occasionally to molest young female patients in the course of examination. There was a sufficient connection and similarity between the allegations to make them cross-admissible. Accordingly, the appeal would be dismissed.

R v Chopra [2006] EWCA Crim 2133, [2006] All ER (D) 44 (Dec) (Court of Appeal: Hughes LJ, Mackay and Treacy JJ). *R v Weir* [2005] EWCA Crim 2866, [2006] 2 All ER 570 (2005 Abr para 880); *R v Cowie* [2003] EWCA Crim 3522, [2003] All ER (D) 354 (Nov); and *R v Hanson; R v Gilmore; R v Pickstone* [2005] EWCA Crim 824, [2005] 1 WLR 3169 (2005 Abr para 882) considered.

783   Evidence—character of accused—bad character—previous convictions

The defendant had concealed for 21 years the fact that he had been in the deceased's house before the deceased was kidnapped and killed. The defendant had been interviewed at the time and had been asked about his whereabouts at the time of the killing. A DNA link between the defendant and the deceased's property was subsequently produced and the defendant contended that he had committed a burglary in the property with his brother who had kidnapped and killed the deceased. The defendant's previous convictions were admitted pursuant to the Criminal Justice Act 2003. In his directions to the jury, the judge stated that the defendant's previous convictions could be taken into account and that they demonstrated a ruthless disregard for humanity. The defendant was convicted of murder and kidnapping and was sentenced to life imprisonment. On his appeal against conviction, he contended that the judge had failed to distinguish between dishonesty and credibility, contrary to the guidance given in *R v Hanson*. *Held*, where bad character evidence was admitted pursuant to s 101(1)(g), the defendant having attacked another person's character, the jury were entitled to take that evidence into account when considering whether the defendant had been truthful. It was clear that the provision under consideration in *R v Hanson* had not been s 101(1)(g) but rather s 101(1)(d), under which evidence was admissible where it related to an important matter in issue. It followed that the judge had been correct in his summing up. The conviction was not unsafe and, accordingly, the appeal would be dismissed.

R v George [2006] All ER (D) 71 (Jun) (Court of Appeal: Moses LJ, Beatson J and Judge Gordon). *R v Hanson; R v Pickstone; R v Gilmore* [2005] EWCA Civ 824, [2005] 1 WLR 3169 (2005 Abr para 882) considered.

784   Evidence—character of accused—bad character—previous convictions—foreign convictions

The Criminal Justice Act 2003 s 99(1) provides that the common law rules governing the admissibility of evidence of bad character in criminal proceedings are abolished. Section 99(1) is subject to s 118(1) in so far as it preserves the rule under which in criminal proceedings a person's reputation is admissible for the purposes of proving his bad character: s 99(2).

The defendant, a Polish national, was alleged to have raped, assaulted and falsely imprisoned the complainant. Pursuant to the 2003 Act s 101(1)(d), (g) the prosecution applied to adduce evidence of the defendant's previous convictions in Poland for offences which would, under domestic law, have amounted to rape and false imprisonment, on the ground that they demonstrated a propensity on the defendant's part to commit offences of the kind with which he was charged. The defendant submitted that the evidence should not be admitted by virtue of s 103, as it would have an adverse effect on the fairness of the proceedings. The defendant eventually agreed to the jury being presented with a short summary of the offences of which he had been convicted. He was convicted of rape, false imprisonment and assault by penetration. On his appeal, he argued that, in line with the rule in *Hollington v Hewthorn*, foreign convictions were not admissible as evidence of a person's character. *Held*, it was necessary to distinguish between admissibility of evidence and how admissible evidence was to be proved. The rule in *Hollington v Hewthorn* as to the inadmissibility of convictions had been abolished in criminal cases, in so far as it had ever applied or had survived the Police and Criminal Evidence Act s 73, by the 2003 Act s 99(1). It followed that foreign convictions were admissible pursuant and subject to s 101. Such convictions were provable under the Evidence Act 1851 s 7 where the necessary formalities were complied with, as they were in the present case. In accordance with the authorities, a sensible short version had been agreed and put before the jury. The safeguards in the 2003 Act s 103 as to fairness had been available and had been relied on by the defendant. The evidence had therefore not been wrongly admitted and, accordingly, the appeal would be dismissed.

R v Kordasinski (2006) Times, 16 November (Court of Appeal: May LJ, Clarke and Teare JJ). *Hollington v F Hewthorn & Co Ltd* [1943] KB 587, CA, considered.

785 Evidence—character of accused—bad character—previous convictions—proof

At the defendant's trial for burglary, the prosecution sought to admit evidence of the defendant's previous convictions, pursuant to the Criminal Justice Act 2003 s 101. The judge granted the application, and the prosecution adduced memoranda of conviction in which the name and date of birth corresponded with those of the defendant. The judge ruled that that was sufficient proof that the convictions recorded on the memoranda of conviction related to the defendant. The defendant was convicted. He appealed, contending that the judge had been wrong to admit the memoranda of conviction as prima facie evidence that the defendant was the person named in the memoranda when only the name and date of birth were proved to be the same. *Held*, the question of what was capable of giving rise to prima facie evidence of identification in the present context could not be regarded as a matter of law. Where a defendant had an extremely common name, and the date of birth on the memoranda was not precisely the same as that of the defendant, it might well be that the date of birth and name would not be properly admissible as giving rise, prima facie, to proof of identification. On the other hand, where a defendant had a highly unusual name, with different component parts, it might or might not be necessary to have recourse to the date of birth. Everything depended on the particular circumstances of the case. The judge had been correct to rule that the similarity between the defendant's name and the identical date of birth in the memoranda corresponded to the defendant, and was capable of proving that the defendant was the person to whom the memoranda related. However, although that matter should therefore have been left to the jury, the conviction was not unsafe in the circumstances of the case. Accordingly, the appeal would be dismissed.

R v Burns [2006] EWCA Crim 617, [2006] 1 WLR 1273 (Court of Appeal: Rose LJ, Stanley Burnton and Hedley JJ). *Pattison v DPP* [2005] EWHC 2938 (Admin), [2005] All ER (D) 237 (Dec) considered.

786 Evidence—character of person other than accused—previous convictions—probative value

The Criminal Justice Act 2003 s 100(1) provides that evidence of the bad character of a person other than the defendant is admissible if and only if (1) it is important explanatory evidence; (2) it has substantial probative value in relation to a matter which (a) is a matter in issue in the proceedings; and (b) is of substantial importance in the context of the case as a whole; or (3) all parties to the proceedings agree to the evidence being admissible.

The defendant was charged with indecent assault. The complainant, who was a prostitute and heroin addict, alleged that the defendant approached her, pushed her to ground, and indecently assaulted her. The defendant contended that the complainant had provided services to him for money, but that she had then demanded more money, had threatened to accuse him of rape, and attempted to grab a chain he was wearing. The issue at trial was credibility. The defendant had no previous convictions. The complainant had previous convictions for burglary, theft and going equipped to steal, to which she had pleaded guilty. The defendant applied for permission to cross-examine the complainant in relation to her previous convictions, on the ground that the matters went to her credibility, pursuant to the 2003 Act s 100. The judge refused the application. The defendant was convicted, and he appealed, arguing that the complainant's previous convictions were relevant to her propensity to behave in the manner alleged by the defendant for the purposes of s 100. *Held*, while, in the case of a defendant's bad character, propensity to commit offences of the kind with which he was charged was, under s 103(1)(a), included in matters in issue, there was no analogue to s 103(1)(a) in s 100. It could hardly be doubted that a complainant's propensity to act in the way the defendant had asserted the complainant had acted should otherwise be regarded as a matter in issue. Although the judge had been right to refuse the application on the basis on which it had been made, there was a significant basis on which it might be said that the previous convictions had substantial probative value in relation to a matter in issue, namely to support the argument that the complainant was liable to behave, or had a propensity to act, dishonestly. The defendant's case was essentially that the complainant had demanded money with menace. In those circumstances, the complainant's persistent record for dishonesty might very well have possessed substantial probative value on that issue, namely, propensity to dishonesty. Had the judge heard an application on that basis, it would have been proper for him to accede to it. Accordingly, the appeal would be allowed.

R v S [2006] All ER (D) 273 (Apr) (Court of Appeal: Laws LJ, Bodey J and Judge Radford). *R v Hanson* [2005] EWCA Crim 824, [2005] 1 WLR 3169 (2005 Abr para 882) considered.

787 Evidence—codes of practice

The Police and Criminal Evidence Act 1984 (Code of Practice C and Code of Practice H) Order 2006, SI 2006/1938 (in force on 25 July 2006), appoints 25 July 2006 for the coming into operation of (1) a new code of practice which makes specific provision for the detention, treatment and questioning by police officers of persons arrested under the Terrorism Act 2000 s 41; and (2) a revised code of practice covering those persons who have not been arrested under s 41.

The Police and Criminal Evidence Act 1984 (Codes of Practice) (Revisions to Code A) Order 2006, SI 2006/2165 (in force on 31 August 2006), gives effect to revisions of the Police and Criminal Evidence Act 1984 Code A, with the effect that constables of the British Transport Police operating from certain specified locations and exercising their powers throughout England and Wales are able to provide an electronic receipt rather than a full record when they undertake a stop or a stop and search, a full record then being made available to the person at a later time.

788 Evidence—defendant—decision not to give evidence—counsel's duty to record defendant's instruction

Cayman Islands
The appellant had been convicted of murder. He contended, on appeal to the Privy Council, that he had been denied a fair trial by the conduct of his counsel at trial, who had failed to call the appellant to give evidence in his defence, and had also failed to cross-examine two witnesses to the effect that they had fabricated the statement the appellant was alleged to have made. *Held*, Lord Steyn and Sir Swinton Thomas dissenting in part, the decision not to give evidence was one of such importance that it had long been recognised that it should be ordered in writing and, where possible, indorsed by the defendant. Although counsel culpably failed to have the matter recorded, there was acceptable affidavit evidence of the appellant's counsel and attorney that they had been following his instructions in not calling him to give evidence. As to the appellant's second contention, the position of his counsel and attorney was not that it would have been improper to advance the allegation against the witnesses, but that the appellant had instructed them not to advance it. The verdict of the trial court was safe and, accordingly, the appeal would be dismissed.
Ebanks v R [2006] UKPC 16, [2006] 1 WLR 1827 (Privy Council: Lords Rodger of Earlsferry, Steyn, Carswell and Mance and Sir Swinton Thomas).

789 Evidence—expert evidence—expert's report—guidance

Guidance has been given on the provision of expert evidence in criminal trials. The following information was necessary for inclusion in an expert's report: (1) details of the expert's academic and professional qualifications, experience and accreditation relevant to the opinions expressed in the report and the range and extent of the expertise, together with any limitations on it; (2) a statement setting out (a) the substance of all the written or oral instructions received; (b) questions on which an opinion was sought; (c) the materials provided and considered; and (d) the documents, statements, evidence, information or assumptions which were material to the opinions expressed or on which those opinions were based; (3) information relating to who had carried out, for example, measurements, examinations and tests, and the methodology used, and whether such measurements, examinations and tests were carried out under the expert's supervision; (4) where there was a range of opinion in the matters dealt with in the report, a summary of the range of opinion and the reasons for the opinion given, including any material facts or matters which detracted from the expert's opinions and any points which should fairly have been made against any opinions expressed; (5) relevant extracts of literature or any other material which might assist the court; and (6) a statement to the effect that the expert had complied with his duty to the court to provide independent assistance by way of objective unbiased opinion in relation to matters within his expertise, and an acknowledgment that the expert would inform all parties and, where appropriate, the court in the event of a change of opinion on any material issues. The guidance should also have been complied with in the event of any matters arising, after the exchange of experts' reports, which required a further or supplemental report.
R v Bowman [2006] EWCA Crim 417, (2006) Times, 24 March (Court of Appeal: Gage LJ, Cresswell and Field JJ).

790 Evidence—hearsay—admissibility—previous statement

The defendant was charged with sexual offences committed against his stepdaughter. The prosecution relied on complaints made by the complainant to her friend and, at a later stage, to her brother. An application was made to adduce the evidence from the friend and brother, pursuant to the Criminal Justice Act 2003 s 120. The judge decided that s 120 imposed no limitation on the admission of more than one hearsay statement as to a complaint by the alleged victim of crime, and that there was sufficient difference between the circumstances surrounding the two statements to justify the admission of the complaint to the brother. The defendant was convicted and he appealed, contending that the complaint to the brother was inadmissible. *Held*, there was no limitation in the 2003 Act on the admission of more than one hearsay statement as to a complaint made by an alleged victim. A statement admitted under the new statutory provisions was admissible to prove the truth of the matter stated and not merely to demonstrate consistency of the complainant's account as was the case under the old law. There was obviously a need to restrict evidence of complaint on complaint which might merely be self-serving. However, the judge had rightly ruled that the evidence of the complaint to the brother had relevance over and above that of the complaint to the friend some months earlier. The judge had proceeded expressly on the basis that the common law rules had gone and that there was no longer any question of considering whether a complaint had been made at the first reasonable opportunity as the old law required. The statutory test was differently expressed. The timing of the second complaint was, in all the circumstances, made as soon as reasonably could be expected after the alleged conduct in accordance with s 120(7)(d). Accordingly, the appeal would be dismissed.

R v O [2006] EWCA Crim 556, [2006] All ER (D) 177 (Jun) (Court of Appeal: Rose LJ, McCombe J and Sir Douglas Brown).

791 Evidence—hearsay—committal proceedings—magistrates' courts—subsequent repeal of legislation

See *R (on the application of the Crown Prosecution Service) v City of London Magistrates' Court*, para 1877.

792 Evidence—hearsay—common law rules

The Criminal Justice Act 2003 s 114(1)(b) provides that in criminal proceedings a statement not made in oral evidence in the proceedings is admissible as evidence of any matter stated if any rule of law preserved by s 118 makes it admissible. Section 115(3) provides that a matter stated is one which if the purpose, or one of the purposes, of the person making the statement appears to the court to have been to cause another person to believe the matter.

The defendant had been convicted of conspiracy to kidnap. The evidence against him included evidence that he was the user of particular telephone numbers on and around the date of the kidnapping. At the trial, the judge had held that the entries of the mobile phones of other conspirators was admissible to show that the defendant was party to the conspiracy. The defendant appealed. *Held*, the 2003 Act ss 114 and 118, when read together, abolished the common law hearsay rules, except where expressly reserved, and created a new rule against hearsay which did not extend to implied assertions. The telephone entries were not a matter stated within s 115 and were implied assertions which were admissible as they were no longer hearsay. Further statements by an admitted co-conspirator against another party to the enterprise would also be admissible as a reserved rule of common law under s 118(1). Accordingly, the appeal would be dismissed.

R v Singh [2006] EWCA Crim 660, [2006] 1 WLR 1564 (Court of Appeal: Rose LJ, Rafferty J and Sir Douglas Brown).

793 Evidence—hearsay—statement not made in oral evidence

In a case against the defendant, in which he was alleged to have been involved in an assault on the victim, the prosecution sought to rely on the evidence of two witnesses who stated that they had seen the defendant assaulting the victim. They had each been told the name of the defendant by another person. The defendant sought to exclude references to his name from the witnesses' evidence on the basis that it was inadmissible hearsay. The judge ruled that he had considered the nine factors in the Criminal Justice Act 2003 s 114 as to the admissibility of evidence and that although he was unable to form a clear view in relation to some of the factors, it was in the interests of justice for the evidence to be admitted. The defendant was convicted of wounding with intent. He applied for leave to appeal against his conviction. It fell to be considered what was meant in s 114(2) by 'the court must have regard to the following factors'. *Held*, if 'the court must have regard to the following factors' were to oblige a judge to carry out an investigation, it might result in a lengthy hearing of evidence into each of the nine factors in s 114(2). Rather, what was required was an exercise of judgment in the light of any particular factor identified in s 114, and for the judge to give consideration to those factors. There was nothing in the wording of the statute that required the judge to reach a specific conclusion in relation to each factor. Accordingly, the application would be refused.

R v T [2006] EWCA Crim 260, (2006) 170 JP Jo 353 (Court of Appeal: Rose LJ, Rafferty J and Sir Douglas Brown).

794 Evidence—identification—weak identification evidence—supporting evidence—direction to jury

The appellant was convicted of aggravated burglary on the basis of identification evidence given by the daughter of the property's occupants. The daughter had recognised the appellant as someone she had known for a long time, and had recognised the wig he had been wearing as one belonging to his sister. The judge had found that although the daughter's glance of the appellant was a fleeting one, the case was fit for a jury to answer in view of other supporting evidence. On appeal, it fell to be considered whether, where a judge had decided that identification evidence in a case was of such poor quality that he would not have left the case to the jury in the absence of supporting evidence, the jury should be directed that they should not convict on the basis of the evidence of identification alone in the absence of the supporting evidence. *Held*, no direction of the kind sought was required as a matter of principle. It was always open to a judge to warn the jury as to the dangers in respect of any particular aspect of the evidence, and any summing up had to be tailored to the circumstances of the case. Identification cases always required a careful direction from the judge drawing attention to the dangers of honest but mistaken identification. There were two distinct exercises for the judge. Firstly, he had to decide, in a case depending on identification evidence alone, whether that evidence crossed the quality threshold so that it would be safe for the case to be left for the jury to determine. Secondly, when summing up the case, he had to give the jury an appropriate Turnbull direction tailored to the facts of the case. Although there might be cases where, in the light of evidence that had unfolded, the jury should be directed not to convict on the evidence of an identifying witness alone, there was no general rule of principle of the kind submitted for by the appellant. It would have been inappropriate and unhelpful for the jury to have been directed not to convict on the identification evidence submitted unless they found that it was supported by one or more of the supporting pieces of evidence. The judge had given a classic Turnbull direction and had drawn attention to the various weaknesses in the identification evidence. The jury could have been in no doubt about the special need for caution as to that evidence. The conviction was not unsafe and, accordingly, the appeal would be dismissed.

R v Ley [2006] EWCA Crim 3063, [2006] All ER (D) 104 (Dec) (Court of Appeal: Scott Baker LJ, Penry-Davey J and Judge Loraine-Smith). *R v Turnbull* [1977] QB 224, CA (1977 Abr para 697); *R v Akaidere* [1990] Crim LR 808, CA; *Daley v R* [1994] AC 117, PC (1993 Abr para 738); and *R v Fergus* (1993) 98 Cr App Rep 313, CA (1993 Abr para 707), considered.

795   Evidence—memorandum of conviction—probative value

The Police and Criminal Evidence Act 1984 s 74(2) provides that, in any proceedings in which by virtue s 74 a person other than the accused is proved to have been convicted of an offence, he is to be taken to have committed that offence unless the contrary is proved.

The defendant was a passenger in a vehicle which was involved in a collision with a parked car. When interviewed, the defendant told the police that he was aware that the driver of the car was under age, but that the driver had only told him that the vehicle was stolen after the incident. The defendant was charged with allowing himself to be carried in a motor vehicle taken without consent, contrary to the Theft Act 1988 s 12. At trial, there was no statement from the owner of the vehicle, the prosecution relying on the driver's memorandum of conviction of theft of the vehicle. At the close of the prosecution case, the defendant submitted that there was no case to answer, arguing that, in the absence of a statement from the owner of the vehicle, there was no evidence that the vehicle in which the defendant had been travelling had been taken without consent. The justices accepted that submission. On the prosecution's appeal, *held*, the 1984 Act s 74(2) specifically provided for admission of a memorandum of conviction in the instant circumstances. As the issue before the justices was the effect of the driver's conviction, it was beyond doubt that there was sufficient evidence of a prima facie case against the defendant and that the burden of proof shifted to him. The absence of other evidence from the owner that the vehicle had been taken without his consent was irrelevant. Accordingly, the appeal would be allowed.

DPP v Parker [2006] All ER (D) 201 (May) (Queen's Bench Division: Scott Baker LJ and Leveson J).

796   Evidence—previous conviction—certificate of disqualification—proof of identity

The defendant was charged with driving a motor vehicle while disqualified. He was interviewed by police and was asked on two separate occasions whether he was a disqualified driver, but made no reply. The prosecution sought to prove the conviction by producing a certificate of conviction which stated the name, date of birth and address of the person convicted, and showed that that person had been disqualified from driving. The defendant gave no evidence. Under the Police and Criminal Evidence Act 1984 s 73(1) the fact of a person's conviction could be proved by producing a certificate of conviction and proving that the person named in the certificate was the person whose conviction was to be proved. The justices found that the defendant was the person to whom the certificate related because of the uniqueness of the name, the date of birth and the address. The defendant was convicted and he appealed. *Held*, the general principles relating to proof of disqualification by producing a certificate of conviction to the court were (1) that as with any other essential element of an offence, the prosecution had to prove to the criminal standard that the person accused was a disqualified driver; (2) that it could be proved by any admissible means such as an admission, even a non-formal one, by the accused; (3) that if a certificate of conviction was relied on pursuant to s 73, then it was an essential element of the prosecution case that the accused was proved to the criminal standard to be the person named on that certificate; (4) that three clear ways of such proof were (a) proof by an admission by or on behalf of the accused, (b) proof by the evidence of finger prints, and (c) proof by someone who was present in court at the time the person was convicted and disqualified being present to give evidence; (5) that there was no prescribed way that the accused had to be proved to be the person named on the certificate; (6) that an example of such means was a match between the personal details of the accused and those recorded on the certificate of conviction; (7) that even where the personal details such as the name of the accused were not uncommon, a match would be sufficient for a prima facie case and, in the absence of any evidence contradicting that prima facie case, the evidence would be sufficient for the court to convict; and (8) that the failure of the accused to give any contradictory evidence in rebuttal would be a matter to take into account if it were proper to do so and a warning had been given. The memorandum of conviction had been adduced in admissible form, the defendant had been confronted with the allegation that he was a disqualified driver and had ample opportunity to contradict that, but chose not to do so. It followed that the justices had been entitled to conclude that there was a prima facie case that the person referred to in the memorandum of conviction was the defendant and, in the absence of evidence from the defendant, that identity had been proved to the criminal standard. Accordingly, the appeal would be dismissed.

Pattison v DPP [2005] EWHC 2938 (Admin), [2006] 2 All ER 317 (Queen's Bench Division: Newman J).

797   Evidence—prosecution evidence—events occurring many years beforehand—inconsistencies—direction to jury

The defendants were convicted of several counts of cruelty, contrary to the Children and Young Persons Act 1933 s 1(1), which were found to have taken place between 20 and 30 years ago, when the defendants had worked at a boarding school for children with special needs. One of the findings against the second and third defendants was that they had, on three occasions, orchestrated and witnessed acts of violence perpetrated against three pupils by the rest of the school. Only one of the alleged victims had given evidence as to the incidents. The second had not been called and the third had said nothing about the incidents in evidence. Further, the evidence was unclear as to which of the defendants had instigated the attacks. The defendants appealed against their convictions. *Held*, cases concerning events alleged to have occurred a long time ago naturally gave rise to great concern. They required special consideration, not only as to whether they should be stayed on the ground that a fair trial would be impossible but also, if they were not stayed, as to whether any verdicts based on so distant a recollection were unsafe. The dangers inherent in such cases required a judge to scrutinise the evidence carefully so as to see whether it was safe to leave the case to the jury. That scrutiny required the judge to consider not only the nature and quality of the evidence but also any inconsistencies. It was not sufficient for a judge to remark that inconsistencies were a matter for the jury. Where the complaints were of events alleged to have occurred many years in the past, it was the responsibility of the judge to consider whether the inconsistencies were such that no jury, even when properly directed as to the significance of such inconsistencies, could safely convict. In the present appeals, there were issues as to whether the alleged events had taken place and as to which, if any, of the defendants had been responsible for instigating them and had been present when they had occurred. There was a paucity of clear evidence identifying who had been responsible for the attacks. The convictions were unsafe, and accordingly, the appeal would be allowed in part.

R v R [2006] EWCA Crim 2754, [2006] All ER (D) 339 (Dec) (Court of Appeal: Moses LJ, McCombe J and Judge Stephens QC). *R v Smolinski* [2004] All ER (D) 16 (May), CA, considered.

798   Evidence—request for evidence by overseas authority—nomination of court—availability of judicial review

The statutory body responsible for monitoring and enforcing corporate law, the stock exchange and securities trading in Australia carried out an investigation involving three men who were alleged to have used two Swiss financial institutions to conceal their own beneficial ownership of shares in an Australian company. The body asked the Secretary of State to exercise his powers under the Crime (International Co-operation) Act 2003 ss 13–15, as the body was seeking information from various people who were working in London. The Secretary of State nominated a court under s 15(1) as the one which was to receive evidence in relation to the request. The claimants, who were the legal representatives of persons mentioned in the requested documents, contended that the Secretary of State had acted unlawfully in the exercise of his discretion in the nomination of a court on the basis that the proceedings in England were duplicative. They also asked to be provided with a copy of the request from the Australian body. The Secretary of State refused to disclose the letter of request as it contained operationally sensitive material. The claimants applied for judicial review, and an issue arose as to whether the decisions of the Secretary of State were susceptible to judicial review. *Held*, the exercise of the Secretary of State's discretion under ss 13–15 was, in principle, susceptible to judicial review. Further, when the Secretary of State agreed to consider representations on behalf of the claimants, his consideration of those representations was also susceptible to judicial review. Such a review embraced general public law grounds as well as rights under the Human Rights Act 1998. Essentially, what the Secretary of State was empowered to do was to make arrangements by nominating a magistrates' court. What was envisaged was that the ministerial and procedural stage would give way to judicial proceedings in the magistrates' court. In the instant case, no one could know about the existence or extent of duplication until the documents were produced. That would only occur in the course of the proceedings in the magistrates' court. It followed that the Secretary of State was amply justified in rejecting the duplication argument, since that was a matter for the district judge. The application for judicial review was an attempt at a pre-emptive strike against the implementation of the request and the judicial proceedings before the district judge. If the claimants had any complaints they had to raise them before the district judge. Accordingly, the application would be dismissed.

R (on the application of Hafner) v Secretary of State for the Home Department [2006] EWHC 1259 (Admin), [2006] All ER (D) 378 (May) (Queen's Bench Division: Maurice Kay LJ and Keith J).

799   Evidence—retention of evidence—DNA sample—paternity test

See *Lambeth LBC v S*, para 422.

800   Evidence—witness—child witness—competence

The Youth Justice and Criminal Evidence Act 1999 s 53(3) provides that a person is not competent to give evidence in criminal proceedings if it appears to the court that he is not a person who is able to (1) understand questions put to him as a witness; and (2) give answers to them which can be understood.

The defendant was charged with indecently assaulting the complainant, who was aged six-and-a-half at appeal. Very shortly after the alleged offence, the complainant stated that the defendant had licked her genitals. A number of hours later, she was interviewed by the police in a video-recorded interview, where she repeated the allegation. At his trial, the defendant contended that the complainant was not a competent witness within the meaning of the 1999 Act s 53. The judge rejected that submission, stating that it was clear that she was capable of understanding questions put to her and that she was capable of offering answers to those questions in an intelligible way. The defendant was convicted of indecent assault, and he appealed. *Held*, the judge had set himself the correct test and had reached the correct decision on the evidence. The issue raised by s 53(1) was that of understanding, namely, whether the witness could understand what was being asked and whether the jury could understand the witness's answers. That was precisely the test which the judge had set himself. The words 'put to him as a witness' in s 53 meant the equivalent of being 'asked of him in court'. Therefore, an infant who could only communicate in baby language with its mother would not ordinarily be competent. However, a young child such as the complainant in the instant case, who could speak and understand basic English with strangers, would be competent. Moreover, there was no requirement in the 1999 Act that the witness in question should be aware of his status as a witness. Questions of credibility and reliability were not relevant to competence. Rather, those matters went to the weight of the evidence, and might be considered, if appropriate, at the end of the prosecution case by way of a submission of no case to answer. A child should not be found incompetent on the basis of age alone. Accordingly, the appeal would be dismissed.

R v MacPherson [2005] EWCA Crim 3065, [2006] All ER (D) 104 (Feb) (Court of Appeal: Rose LJ, Forbes and Calvert-Smith JJ).

801   Evidence—witness—child witness—video recording

The defendant was charged with two counts of indecent assault on the complainant, his seven-year-old daughter. At trial, the complainant gave evidence-in-chief via three video-recorded interviews, pursuant to the Youth Justice and Criminal Evidence Act 1999 s 27. In the third interview, she alleged that the defendant had touched her vagina. That statement was made only after the intervention of the complainant's mother, who had been present at the interview in contravention of the relevant guidelines. The judge decided that the third recorded interview was admissible, on the basis that it had been corroborated by medical evidence of injury to the complainant's vagina, consistent with penetration by a finger or an object. The defendant was convicted. Subsequently, another girl claimed that, during the material time, she and the complainant had played games involving the insertion of objects into the complainant's vagina. The defendant appealed against conviction, seeking to admit the other girl's evidence under the Criminal Appeal Act 1968 23, and arguing additionally that the third interview given by his daughter was inadmissible. *Held*, in relation to the video-recorded evidence, the test for admissibility was whether a reasonable jury properly directed could be sure that the witness had given a credible and accurate account on the videotape, notwithstanding any breaches of the guidelines. The reliability of the evidence would normally be assessed by reference to the interview itself, the conditions under which it had been held, the age of the child, and the nature and extent of any breach of the guidelines. There might be cases in which other evidence demonstrated that the breaches had not had the effect of undermining the credibility or accuracy of the video interview. Although the judge had not specifically identified the appropriate test, he had in practice adopted it, and if he had specifically identified the test, then the decision reached would have been open to him. Although the possibility that a different conclusion might have been reached applying the 1999 Act s 27(2) could not be excluded, it was difficult to imagine the circumstances in which that would be so. The defendant's claims relating to the admissibility of the video-recorded evidence therefore failed, but the appeal would be allowed on the basis of the fresh evidence.

R v K [2006] EWCA Crim 472, [2006] All ER (D) 144 (Mar) (Court of Appeal: Hooper LJ, Langstaff J and Sir John Blofield). *G v DPP* [1998] QB 919, DC (1997 Abr para 923), applied.

802   Evidence—witness—special measures directions—witness anonymity—right to a fair trial

The defendants had been convicted on various counts of murder and attempted murder. The witnesses had been given anonymity, voice modulation, screening and other special measures as they were in fear of their lives if they gave evidence against the defendants. The defendants appealed, and the issue of the anonymity of the witnesses in relation to the right to a fair trial arose. *Held*, the concealment of witnesses' identities was consistent with the right to a fair trial, provided that the need for anonymity was clearly established, that cross-examination of the witness by an advocate for the defendant was permitted, and that the trial was fair. A trial would not inevitably be considered unfair and the conviction unsafe because the evidence of anonymous witnesses, whose testimony could be tested in the adversarial process, might be decisive of the outcome. The discretion to permit evidence to be given by anonymous witnesses was beyond question. Accordingly, the appeals would be dismissed.

R v Davis; R v Ellis; R v Gregory; R v Simms; R v Martin [2006] EWCA Crim 1155, (2006) Times, 1 June (Court of Appeal: Sir Igor Judge P, Mitting and Fulford JJ). Application 51277/99 *Krasniki v Czech Republic*, ECtHR; *R v Sellick* [2005] EWCA Crim 651, [2005] 1 WLR 3257 (2005 Abr para 914); *Re Al-Fawwaz* [2001] UKHL 69, [2002] 1 AC 556 (2001 Abr para 1443); and *R (on the application of D) v Camberwell Green Youth Court* [2005] UKHL 4, [2005] 1 WLR 393 (2005 Abr para 885) considered.

803   Evidence—written statement—fear of giving oral evidence

The defendant stabbed the victim with a knife in the presence of two witnesses whom the defendant also threatened. At the defendant's trial for assault occasioning actual bodily harm and possession of an offensive weapon, the judge considered an application that the victim and the two witnesses should have their evidence read pursuant to the Criminal Justice Act 2003 s 116(2)(e). The victim and witnesses stated that they wished to have no further involvement because they feared repercussions. The application was allowed and the defendant was convicted of both charges. On the defendant's appeal against conviction, issues arose as to whether the judge had erred in permitting the victim and the two witnesses to have their evidence read pursuant to s 116. *Held*, the judge had been entitled to reach a conclusion as to the genuineness of the witnesses' fear on the basis of the evidence. There was ample evidence to justify the course taken by the judge. Courts would be ill-advised to seek to test the basis of fear by calling witnesses since that might undermine the very thing that s 116 was designed to avoid. Judges should be astute not to skew a fair trial by being too willing to accept assertions of fear since it was all too easy for witnesses to avoid the inconvenience and anxiety of a trial by saying that they did not wish to attend. Normally, a judge would have a much better feel than the Court of Appeal of the truth or otherwise of the assertions of fear. It was accepted that the judge had made his ruling at the outset and that, in those circumstances, had based it purely on the written assertions of the witnesses. Had the judge's ruling been plainly wrong, there would have been merit in the appeal. However, he had been right and, accordingly, the appeal would be dismissed.

R v Davies [2006] EWCA Crim 2643, [2006] All ER (D) 78 (Dec) (Court of Appeal: Moses LJ, Gibbs and Cooke JJ). *R v H; R v W; R v M* [2001] Crim LR 815, CA (2001 Abr para 810), not followed.

804   Indictment—bill of indictment—validity

At different stages, following the defendant being committed for trial, bills of indictment were preferred, leave having been given by different judges. An amended bill of indictment was signed, because an alternative count had been added. After his conviction, the defendant's application for permission to appeal was refused. When the Criminal Cases Review Commission investigated the indictment on which the defendant had been convicted, they found that there was evidence to suggest that the indictment had not been signed. They referred the case back to the Court of Appeal. The defendant contended that the Administration of Justice (Miscellaneous Provisions) Act 1933 s 2 provided that it was only on a signature by the proper officer of the court that the document would become an indictment. Further, he relied on the principle that it was not merely a comparatively meaningless formality that the proper officer's signature should be appended, but that it was a necessary condition to the existence of a proper indictment. *Held*, the proceedings had not been rendered automatically invalid by reason of the indictment not being signed. Under the new approach, absent a clear indication that Parliament had intended jurisdiction automatically to be removed following procedural failure, the decision of the court on an appeal such as that in the present case should be based on a wide assessment of the interests of justice, with particular focus on whether there was a real possibility that the prosecution or defendant might suffer prejudice. *R v Soneji* had weakened the distinction between mandatory and direct requirements, consideration of which was at the heart of *R v Morais*. In the present case, the decision in *R v Ashton*, based on *R v Soneji*, was binding. The bill of indictment had been lawfully preferred with the consent of a High Court judge, who had initialled the bill. However, the bill had simply not been signed by the officer of the court. The absence of that signature was a situation specifically contemplated by *R v Ashton*. Further, the signature, in the course of the trial, on an amended indictment by the proper officer of the court, was material. It was on an indictment signed, and properly so-called, that the conviction had been entered. Therefore, the proceedings had been validated. Accordingly, the appeal would be dismissed.

R v Clarke [2006] EWCA Crim 1196, [2006] All ER (D) 358 (May) (Court of Appeal: Pill LJ, Dobbs and Underhill JJ). *R v Soneji* [2005] UKHL 49, [2005] 4 All ER 321 (2005 Abr para 2738) applied. *R v Morais* [1988] 3 All ER 161, CA (1988 Abr para 551) not followed.

805   Legal aid

See LEGAL AID.

806   Plea of guilty—withdrawal—right to fair trial

An elderly lady was walking her dog when the three defendants approached her on motorcycles. Two of the motorcycles then collided and one appeared to fall on the dog. The lady died later that day from a heart condition, though it was not suggested that the defendants were legally responsible for her death. The defendants were charged with dangerous driving, driving otherwise than in accordance with a licence, using a motor vehicle without insurance, and using a motor vehicle without a valid test certificate. They pleaded guilty to all charges, but applications were made later on the same day to withdraw the guilty pleas in respect of the dangerous driving charge. The applications were refused and the defendants appealed, submitting that the refusal to accept the attempted withdrawals was wrong in practice and incompatible with the right to a fair hearing guaranteed by the European Convention on Human Rights art 6. *Held*, where a defendant made an unequivocal plea of guilty, which the court accepted, he was at that point proved guilty according to law within the meaning of art 6(2). The presumption of innocence ceased to apply and he could be sentenced on the basis that he had been proved guilty. A guilty plea could only found a conviction and bring to an end the presumption of innocence where it was unequivocal. If it was equivocal, it had to be treated as a plea of not guilty. If after a guilty plea had been made, it became apparent that the defendant did not appreciate the elements of the offence, then it was likely to be appropriate to allow withdrawal of the plea. That would also be so if it became apparent that the facts alleged by the prosecution did not add up to the offence charged. In the instant case, the court had taken all reasonable steps at the time of the pleas being entered. Accordingly, the appeal would be dismissed.

DPP v Revitt [2006] EWHC 2266 (Admin), [2006] 1 WLR 3172 (Queen's Bench Division: Lord Phillips of Worth Matravers CJ and Bean J).

807   Police and Justice Act 2006

See para 2245.

808   Probation—local probation boards—appointments

The Local Probation Boards (Appointment and Miscellaneous Provisions) (Amendment) Regulations 2006, SI 2006/2664 (in force on 1 November 2006), further amends the Local Probations Boards (Appointment) Regulations 2000, SI 2000/3342, (1) by removing the provision which provided that where practicable four of the persons appointed to a local probation board should be justices of the peace within the area of the board and two of the persons appointed should be members of a local authority for a local government area which falls within the area of the board; and (2) so that members of a local probation board other than the chief officer can be appointed for a term not exceeding three years The regulations also amend the 2001 Regulations, SI 2001/786, by reducing the number of members of a local probation board who must be present at a meeting for it to be a quorate to five.

809   Procedure—appeal—presentation of appeal by solicitors and counsel

The Court of Appeal emphasised that the overriding objective of the Criminal Procedure Rules, that all trials be dealt with efficiently and expeditiously, applied equally to appeals. The problem caused by bundles of unpaginated documents went further than merely wasting time and could have resulted in an adverse effect on the appellants' chances of success. There had been a clear breach of CrimPR 1.2(1)(a), which required each participant in the conduct of each case to prepare and conduct the case in accordance with the overriding objective, for which both solicitors and counsel had to accept some responsibility. It was quite wrong that any reference by the Criminal Cases Review Commissioners should be placed before the court more than six months after the date of its referral without good reason sanctioned by the court. The court suggested the following timetable: (1) within six weeks of the date of referral, the appellant's solicitors should cause all relevant papers to be bundled into files and paginated; (2) counsel should lodge a skeleton argument referring to the documents as paginated and apply to the Criminal Appeal Office for a date, giving estimated length of the hearing, and any other directions considered necessary; (3) within four weeks after, the prosecution should propose the inclusion of any further documentation which it required; (4) any response skeleton argument be lodged within two further weeks after; and (5) consideration be given to the question of whether a core bundle should be provided for the hearing. Any material breach of the requirements would run the risk of the appeal being stood out from the list at the risk of a wasted costs order being made.

R v Siddall; R v Brooke [2006] EWCA Crim 1353, (2006) Times, 26 July (Court of Appeal: Longmore LJ, Gloster and Openshaw JJ).

810 Procedure—consolidation—amendments—forms for use in criminal proceedings

Lord Phillips of Worth Matravers CJ, has issued the following *Practice Direction (Forms for Use in Criminal Proceedings)* [2006] All ER (D) 116 (Apr).

This *Practice Direction* further amends the *Consolidated Criminal Practice Direction* Annex D previously handed down by the Lord Woolf CJ reported at [2002] 3 All ER 904 (2002 Abr para 830). It sets out forms for use in connection with the criminal procedure rules that are amended by the Criminal Procedure (Amendment) Rules 2006, SI 2006/353. It takes effect on 3 April 2006 when the 2006 Rules come into force. The forms attached to this Practice Direction for use in connection with rr 15.1(1), 15.2(3) (application for preparatory hearing/extension of time); r 15.4(3) (order for preparatory hearing); and rr 34.2, 68.20(1) (notice of intention to introduce hearsay evidence) are substituted for the corresponding forms in the *Consolidated Criminal Practice Direction* Annex D. The form attached to this *Practice Direction* for use in connection with the 2006 Rules rr 68.3(1A), (2) is added to the forms set out in *Consolidated Criminal Practice Direction* Annex D. The table at the beginning of Annex D is amended by the corresponding substitutions and addition attached to this *Practice Direction*.

[Editor's note: Annex D and forms not reproduced in this summary.]

811 Procedure—preliminary hearing—relevant submissions

It has been held that, when dealing with matters preliminary to a trial, if the judge thinks it right to do so, his new case management powers permit him to deal with the issues exclusively by reference to written submissions and, if he sees fit, submissions limited to a length specified by him. He is not bound to allow oral submissions, and he is entitled to put a time limit on them. The necessary public element of any hearing is sufficiently achieved if the defendants themselves are supplied with copies of written submissions, if they wish to see them, and the representatives of the media present at court for any hearing are similarly supplied.

R v K [2006] EWCA Crim 724, [2006] All ER (D) 28 (Apr) (Court of Appeal: Sir Igor Judge P, Mitting and Fulford JJ).

812 Proceeds of crime—civil recovery—confiscation order—re-seizure of money

The police searched the claimants' home, and seized a quantity of cannabis and £6,756, pursuant to the Police and Criminal Evidence Act 1984 s 19. At that time, the minimum amount that could be seized under the Proceeds of Crime Act 2002 was £10,000. One of the claimants subsequently pleaded guilty to possession in relation to the drugs that had been found, but no order of forfeiture or deprivation was made in respect of the money. The other claimant demanded the return of the seized cash on the basis that the power of the police to retain it under the 1984 Act s 22 had lapsed with the guilty plea. The police issued two cheques, one in favour of each applicant, but immediately purported to seize them under the 2002 Act s 294. By that time, the minimum amount that could be seized under the 2002 Act had been reduced to £5,000. The district judge found as a preliminary issue that the 2002 Act did not apply to the instant case, and the defendant chief constable appealed. *Held*, money originally seized under the 1984 Act s 19 could be re-seized under the 2002 Act s 294 provided that the amount re-seized was greater than the minimum amount in force at the time of re-seizure. Seizure under s 294 could occur at any time. There was no time limit in ss 294 and 295 on the exercise of that power, and no sensible reason why there should be. Similarly, there was no reason in principle why there should be a special limitation on the exercise of s 294 because a different statutory power had been exercised over the same property. Each statute provided a different procedure to achieve the same result. Furthermore, just as seizures under the 1984 Act s 19 took place in a police station after the arrest and search of a suspect, cash already in the possession of the police could be seized. Accordingly, the appeal would be allowed.

Chief Constable of Merseyside Police v Hickman [2006] All ER (D) 04 (Mar) (Queen's Bench Division: Mitting J).

813 Proceeds of crime—confiscation order—risk of serious injustice

The Proceeds of Crime Act 2002 s 10(6) provides that where the court decides under s 6 that the defendant has a criminal lifestyle, the court does not need to make required assumptions in relation to particular property or expenditure if the assumption is shown to be incorrect, or there would be a serious risk of injustice if the assumption were made.

The defendants were convicted of various offences contrary to the Misuse of Drugs Act 1971 and the Criminal Law Act 1977. A financial investigation found that they had benefited from their offences but that the recoverable amount was nil. The prosecution sought confiscation orders against the defendants but the judge refused to grant the orders on the ground that there would be a serious risk of injustice. The prosecution appealed. *Held*, the court was required to determine whether the defendant had benefited from his criminal conduct and if he had, the court had to determine the amount of benefit and make a confiscation order for that amount. It was clear that Parliament had intended that, where a court found that there was a benefit, it had to make a confiscation order. The purpose of the 2002 Act s 10(6) was to ensure a sensible calculation of the benefit and that the assumptions were not so unreasonable or unjust in respect of that particular defendant that they should not be made; it was not to provide for the exercise discretion by the judge to determine whether it was fair to make the order against a particular defendant. It followed that the phrase 'serious risk of injustice' in s 10(6) could not mean hardship to the defendant by virtue of the order. Accordingly, the appeal would be allowed.

R v Jones (2006) Times, 8 August (Court of Appeal: Latham LJ, Forbes and Simon JJ).

814   Proceeds of crime—excluded activities—business in the regulated sector

The Proceeds of Crime Act 2002 (Business in the Regulated Sector) Order 2006, SI 2006/2385 (in force on 6 April 2007), further amends the Proceeds of Crime Act 2002 to add to the list of excluded activities the regulated activities of arranging deals in investments or advising on investments, in so far as the investment consists of rights under a regulated home reversion plan or a regulated home purchase plan, with the effect that a business will not be in the regulated sector to the extent that it conducts such activities.

815   Proceeds of crime—references to financial investigators

The Proceeds of Crime Act 2002 (References to Financial Investigators) (Amendment) Order 2006, SI 2006/57 (in force on 1 March 2006), further amends the 2003 Order, SI 2003/172, so as to add members of staff of the Serious Organised Crime Agency, Royal Mail and the Home Office to the list of accredited financial investigators under the Proceeds of Crime Act 2002.

816   Proceeds of crime—restraint order—non-appearance of applicant—re-instatement of proceedings

Bahamas

The applicants were subject to a restraint order, made by the second respondent pursuant to the Proceeds of Crime (Bahamas) Act 2000 s 26, in respect of moneys which had been credited to their joint account. The applicants made an application to discharge the order, which had been made ex parte, but their application was dismissed. The applicants appealed but the appeal was struck out due to the applicants' non-appearance pursuant to the Court of Appeal (Bahamas) Rules 1965 r 37(1). The applicants made an application for an order directing that the struck-out appeal be re-entered for hearing, pursuant to r 37(2), but the application was dismissed. The court held that the applicants had had sufficient notice of the appeal hearing as the hearing date had been published on the notice board outside the court, despite the fact that their legal representatives had been informed by the deputy registrar of the Court of Appeal that the appeal would not be listed during the month that it came on for hearing and had not been issued with a written notice of the hearing under r 31(2). The applicants appealed to the Privy Council against the Court of Appeal's refusal to reinstate the appeal. *Held*, it was rare that an application by a blameless absent litigant for re-instatement of proceedings which had been struck out as a result of his absence would be refused on account of the hopelessness of his case. The burden of establishing that the proceedings were hopeless rested with the person resisting re-instatement of the proceedings on the ground of that non-appearance. On the evidence, the non-appearance of anyone to prosecute the appeal was not attributable to any fault of the applicants or their legal representatives. Having regard to the considerations which were, on established authority, to be taken into account by a judge exercising a discretion whether or not to re-instate struck-out proceedings, it was appropriate that the applicants' appeal be re-instated. Accordingly, the appeal would be allowed.

Gaydamak v UBS Bahamas Ltd [2006] UKPC 8, [2006] 1 WLR 1097 (Privy Council: Lords Bingham of Cornhill, Hutton, Scott of Foscote, Walker of Gestingthorpe and Brown of Eaton-under-Heywood).

817   Prosecution of offences—private prosecution—caution administered—abuse of process

The appellant admitted assaulting and injuring the respondent. The police decided that the appellant should be cautioned rather than prosecuted, and the appellant was notified of that decision in a standard form. The form stated that a record would be kept of the incident, and that, if the appellant appeared before a court and was found guilty of another offence, details of the caution might be given to the court. The respondent subsequently instigated a private prosecution against the appellant. When the matter came before a magistrates' court, the appellant argued that his acceptance of a police caution on the indication that, if he accepted it, he would not face any further criminal proceedings, precluded a private prosecution. The justices were satisfied that allowing the prosecution to proceed would be an abuse of the process of the magistrates' court, and stayed the proceedings. On the respondent's appeal against that decision, the court ruled that the administration and acceptance of a caution were not sufficient to render the exercise of the right of private prosecution an abuse of process. The appellant appealed. *Held*, if the respondent had legal grounds for attacking the police decision to caution the appellant, he could apply for judicial review to quash that decision. If successful, the slate would be clean. There would be no citable caution on the appellant's record and he would be free to prosecute, but so long as that formal caution stood, induced by a representation that he would not be prosecuted, the private prosecution of the appellant did amount to an abuse. The abuse complained of was not abuse impairing the fairness of the trial, since evidence of the admission and caution could be excluded. Rather the abuse complained of went to the fairness of trying the appellant at all in the circumstances. Accordingly, the appeal would be allowed.

Jones v Whalley [2006] UKHL 41, [2006] 4 All ER 113 (House of Lords: Lords Bingham of Cornhill, Rodger of Earlsferry, Carswell, Brown of Eaton-under-Heywood and Mance). *R v Horseferry Road Magistrates' Court, ex p Bennett* [1994] 1 AC 42, HL (1993 Abr para 38), considered. Decision of Queen's Bench Divisional Court [2005] EWHC 931 (Admin), [2006] Crim LR 67 reversed.

818 Rehabilitation of offenders—spent convictions—exceptions

The Rehabilitation of Offenders Act 1974 (Exceptions) (Amendment) (England and Wales) Order 2006, SI 2006/2143 (in force on 26 July 2006), further amends the 1975 Order, SI 1975/1023, so as to (1) provide that questions may be asked relating to spent convictions to assess a person's suitability to undertake certain activities as a football steward; (2) provide an exception to the statutory requirement that spent convictions are not a proper ground for dismissal or for prejudicing a person in any occupation or employment relating to decisions to refuse approval for a person to undertake certain activities as a football steward; (3) make substitutions to the 1975 Order in relation to those who work with vulnerable adults and to reflect the new arrangements in relation to Her Majesty's Revenue and Customs and the Revenue and Customs Prosecution Office; and (4) add new proceedings in which spent convictions may be used.

The Rehabilitation of Offenders Act 1974 (Exceptions) (Amendment No 2) (England and Wales) Order 2006, SI 2006/3290 (in force on 7 December 2006), further amends the 1975 Order supra by extending the exceptions to the Rehabilitation of Offenders Act 1974, relating to the suitability of a person able to undertake certain activities as a football steward without a licence issued by the Security Industry Authority, to cover activities of the Football League as well as the Football Association and the Football Association Premier League.

819 Reporting restrictions—risk of prejudice to future proceedings—co-conspirator in terrorist plot

See *Re B*, para 2351.

820 Sentencing

See SENTENCING.

821 Serious organised crime and police—delegation of power to designate

The Serious Organised Crime and Police Act 2005 (Delegation under section 43) Order 2006, SI 2006/100 (in force on 1 March 2006), prescribes the grade of Deputy Director of the Serious Organised Crime Agency as the prescribed level for the purposes of the Serious Organised Crime and Police Act 2005 s 44(1).

822 Serious organised crime and police—designated staff—powers

The Serious Organised Crime and Police Act 2005 (Application and Modification of Certain Enactments to Designated Staff of SOCA) Order 2006, SI 2006/987 (in force on 1 April 2006), (1) modifies the Police and Criminal Evidence Act 1984 and the Anti-social Behaviour Act 2003, in relation to persons designated with the powers of a constable; and (2) modifies the Immigration Act 1971 and the Immigration and Asylum Act 1999, in relation to persons designated with the powers of an immigration officer.

823 Serious organised crime and police—offences—investigations

The Serious Organised Crime and Police Act 2005 (Amendment of Section 61(1)) Order 2006, SI 2006/1629 (in force on 20 June 2006), amends the Serious Organised Crime and Police Act 2005 s 61(1) by adding to the list of offences to which Pt 2 Ch 1 (ss 60–70) (investigatory powers of Director of Public Prosecutions etc) applies.

824 Serious organised crime and police—offender assisting investigation—review of sentence—appeal

The Serious Organised Crime and Police Act 2005 (Appeals under Section 74) Order 2006, SI 2006/2135 (in force on 28 August 2006), (1) makes provision for appeals to the Court of Appeal and the House of Lords under s 74(8); (2) makes provision for the powers of the Court of Appeal on appeal so that, if the Court of Appeal determines to allow an appeal and if it thinks fit, it may vary the sentence imposed by the Crown Court; (3) provides that certain powers of the Court of Appeal may be exercised by a single judge or the registrar of criminal appeals; and (4) provides that the House of Lords may exercise any powers of the Court of Appeal or may remit a case to that court.

825   Serious Organised Crime and Police Act 2005—commencement

The Serious Organised Crime and Police Act 2005 (Commencement No 5 and Transitional and Transitory Provisions and Savings) Order 2006, SI 2006/378, brings into force (1) on 1 March 2006, ss 6, 43, 44(1), 55(1) (in part), (2), Sch 2 para 8 and, for certain purposes, s 1(1), (2), Sch 1 paras 1–8, 9(1)–(3), 10, 11, 14, 15(1)–(4), 16–21; (2) on 1 April 2006, ss 1(1) (so far as not already in force), (2) (so far as not already in force), 2–5, 7, 11–16, 19–26, 28–38, 40, 41, 45–51, 53, 55 (so far as not already in force), 56, 57, 59, 71–81, 174(2) (in part), Sch 1 paras 1–8 (so far as not already in force), 9(1)–(3) (so far as not already in force), (4), 10 (so far as not already in force), 11 (so far as not already in force), 12, 13, 14 (so far as not already in force), 15(1)–(4) (so far as not already in force), (5), 16–21 (so far as not already in force), Sch 4 paras 1–11, 17–20, 22–24, 28–35, 41, 43–87, 93–106, 111, 112, 122–169, 173–200, and certain repeals in Sch 17 Pt 2; and (3) on 6 April 2006, ss 163(1)–(3) (in part), 165 (so far as not already in force), 174(2) (in part), Sch 14 paras 1–4, 6(b), (c), 7, 8, 10–12, 14, and certain repeals in Sch 17 Pt 2. Transitional, transitory and savings provisions are also made.

The Serious Organised Crime and Police Act 2005 (Commencement No 6 and Appointed Day) Order 2006, SI 2006/1085, brings into force (1) on 8 May 2006, ss 161(1), (5) (so far as not already in force), 174(2) (in part), Sch 13 paras 9, 10, 12, and certain repeals in Sch 17 Pt 2; (2) on 15 May 2006, s 102. The day appointed for the purposes of s 161(2) (relevant persons ceasing to be constable of Royal Parks Constabulary on appointed day) is 8 May 2006.

The Serious Organised Crime and Police Act 2005 (Commencement) (No 7) Order 2006, SI 2006/1871, brings s 144, Sch 10 into force on 20 July 2006 in specified areas.

The Serious Organised Crime and Police Act 2005 (Commencement No 9 and Amendment) Order 2006, SI 2006/2182, brings s 163(2) into force on 25 September 2006 and amends the Serious Organised Crime and Police Act 2005 (Commencement) (No 7) Order 2006, SI 2006/1871, supra so as to renumber it (No 8) in order to take account of the previous Serious Organised Crime and Police Act 2005 (Commencement No 7) Order 2006, SSI 2006/381, which applies to Scotland.

For a summary of the Act, see 2005 Abr para 938. See also the commencement table in the title STATUTES.

826   Terrorism Act 2006

See para 902.

827   Trial—closing speeches—order of speeches—fairness

See *Ramdhanie v State of Trinidad and Tobago*, para 519.

828   Trial—direction to jury—inciting a child under 13 to engage in sexual activity—intention that activity be carried out

A group of children were in an area by a telephone box. The telephone rang, and a male person asked the complainant, aged 11, to show him her 'fanny'. The defendant was arrested and his mobile telephone records examined. He was subsequently charged with intentionally causing or inciting a child under 13 to engage in sexual activity, contrary to the Sexual Offences Act 2003 s 8. In his directions to the jury, the judge stated that the prosecution had to prove that the person was under 13, that the defendant had incited that person, that the incitement had been intentional, that the activity incited was sexual, and that the defendant had intended that the incited activity should be carried out. The defendant was convicted. He appealed on the ground that the judge's directions in relation to the ingredients of the offences were confusing and insufficient. *Held*, s 8 created two offences, namely intentionally causing and intentionally inciting a person under 13 to engage in sexual activity. The essence of the offence of incitement was the encouragement of a person under 13 to engage in such activity. That had to be intentional and the defendant had to know what he was doing. However, given that the essence of the offence was incitement, it was not a necessary ingredient for incitement of sexual activity that the defendant intended that the incited activity should take place. While the judge had incorrectly directed the jury that the defendant had to intend that the incited activity should be carried out, that direction was, if anything, too favourable to the defendant. Accordingly, the appeal would be dismissed.

R v Walker [2006] All ER (D) 08 (Jun) (Court of Appeal: Keene LJ, Aikens and Goldring JJ).

829   Trial—fairness—delay—duty of court to expedite proceedings

Mauritius

The appellant, a Mauritian barrister, was charged with swindling. A trial date was set, but, owing to a series of adjournments, it was more than three years after that date before evidence was first taken. Further evidence was taken the following year and, a year after that, the prosecution entered a nolle prosequi. On the same day, a new charge of swindling was filed against the appellant. In relation to the second charge, it took more than two years before evidence was first heard and, more than a year later, the prosecution closed its case. The appellant made an unsuccessful application of no case to answer, and unsuccessfully sought to challenge the validity of the trial. Evidence was then given by and on behalf of the appellant. This took a further two years. More than five years after the filing of the second charges, after another series of lengthy adjournments, the appellant was convicted of swindling and sentenced to six months' imprisonment. His appeal on the ground of delay was rejected. He appealed further, seeking to rely on the Constitution of Mauritius 1968, which guaranteed a right to a fair hearing within a reasonable time. *Held*, the failure to complete a criminal prosecution within a reasonable time could amount to a breach of the 1968 Constitution irrespective of whether the defendant had been prejudiced by the delay. However, the hearing should not be stayed or a conviction quashed on account of delay alone unless the hearing was unfair or it was unfair to try the defendant at all. The time taken in the present case gave grounds for real concern and was prima facie unreasonable. There was nothing to suggest that the case had been unusually complex for a case of its type. Moreover, although the appellant had been intent on prolonging the trial, it had been incumbent on the court to take such steps as it could to expedite matters and to reach a conclusion. That should have led to the injection of an element of urgency after the nolle prosequi was entered and the trial had begun afresh. Much more could have been done to have hastened matters between the commencement of the second trial and its completion. It followed that the trial had not been completed within a reasonable time and, accordingly, the appeal would be allowed.

   Boolell v The State [2006] UKPC 46, [2006] All ER (D) 169 (Oct) (Privy Council: Lords Nicholls of Birkenhead, Rodger of Earlsferry, Walker of Gestingthorpe, Carswell and Brown of Eaton-under-Heywood). *A-G's Reference (No 2 of 2001)* [2003] UKHL 68, [2004] 2 AC 72 (2003 Abr para 703) considered.

830   Trial—fairness—substitution of judge—new judge unable to reply to material question put by jury

The defendant was charged with possession of Class A and B drugs with intent to supply. During the course of the jury's deliberations the judge became ill. A second judge took control of the case. Neither counsel applied for the jury to be discharged. In due course, the jury asked a question of the judge regarding evidence given by a police officer. It became apparent that there were potential difficulties which required time to analyse the question. When no solution could be found and, despite best attempts by counsel, no agreed answer could be formulated, the second judge stated that it was not a question that could be answered. The defendant was convicted and appealed. The court considered whether, in the circumstances of the second judge assuming conduct of the trial and his answer to the jury's question, the conviction was unsafe. *Held*, it was established that a judge should not normally be changed in the course of a trial. There was no power, until the moment when the jury returned to give their verdict, to change a judge, although it would be permissible in the event of illness for another judge to take over taking the verdict. The mere taking of a verdict could not be affected by the change of judge. In the present case, there was no doubt that the second judge had taken the right and obvious course in making a serious attempt to save the trial. Discharging the jury at the stage at which he entered the trial would have been premature. However, the fact that, despite the efforts made, the jury had not been provided with an answer to the given question was a matter for concern. The question had related to an issue that had been canvassed at trial. Moreover, had the answer been given, as was subsequently known, it would have tended to or provided some support for the defendant's case in argument to the jury. Despite the second judge and counsels' best efforts, the absence of the original judge at that late stage might have had a significant adverse effect on the outcome of the trial. Therefore, the conviction would be quashed and a retrial ordered. Accordingly, the appeal would be allowed.

   R v El-Ghaidouni [2006] All ER (D) 33 (Apr) (Court of Appeal: Sir Igor Judge P, Mackay and Gross JJ).

831   Trial—fairness—witness in receipt of payment from media

The defendants were charged with three murders. The prosecution alleged that a dispute between two groups of individuals, who were involved in the importation of cannabis, had given rise to the murders. The principal witness for the prosecution had been party to the conspiracy to import cannabis. The defence alleged that the witness had falsified his story in order to minimise his own criminality in order to receive a lenient sentence. The defendants were convicted and their application for leave to appeal against conviction was refused. It subsequently came to light that the witness, prior to giving evidence, had been involved in book and television collaborations about the murders. He had negotiated a deal with a journalist and a television company and had benefited financially from these collaborations. The Criminal Cases Review Commission referred the convictions to the Court of Appeal. *Held,* it was obvious that contacts and contracts between a witness and the media before a trial had the potential to create injustice. Each case had to be considered in the light of its own circumstances. It was apparent from the evidence that the journalist and the television producer had genuinely thought that their involvement with the witness was not inappropriate. They had considered that, so long as no prejudicial publication appeared before the conclusion of the trial, there was no harm in contracting with a witness. The contact made by the witness did not undermine the safety of the convictions. All the essentials of the witness's account had been imparted to police officers in interviews and reduced to witness statements before the witness had any dealings with the media. The material regarding dishonesty and criminal history which had been at the disposal of the defence had enabled them to cross-examine the witness. Had the jury known about the media contacts it was difficult to see how they could have added significantly to the cross-examination armoury in the circumstances. Accordingly, the appeals would be dismissed.

R v Steele [2006] EWCA Crim 195, [2006] All ER (D) 308 (Feb) (Court of Appeal: Kay LJ, Openshaw J and Sir Charles Mantel). *R v Pendleton* [2001] UKHL 66, [2002] 1 All ER 524 (2001 Abr para 808); *R v Austin* (unreported, 17 May 1996); *R v West* [1996] 2 Cr App Rep 374, CA (1996 Abr para 876), considered.

832 Trial—legal representation—appropriate number of counsel—budgetary considerations

It has been held that, in a criminal trial with multiple defendants, all of whom are in receipt of legal aid, consideration must be given to how many counsel should be instructed and, in particular, whether it is appropriate for there to be a junior counsel for each defendant.

R v Azam [2006] EWCA Crim 161, [2006] All ER (D) 340 (Feb) (Court of Appeal: Sir Igor Judge P, Dobbs J and Sir Douglas Brown).

833 Trial—open court—proceedings held in camera—right to oral hearing

The defendant was charged with conspiracy to cause explosions in the United Kingdom. During the course of pre-trial proceedings, the prosecution applied for certain evidence which related to the events concerning the defendant's treatment outside the jurisdiction to be given in camera, although it was not intended that any order should prohibit publication of, or public access to, any part of the trial or pre-trial process in which only his account of his treatment was given in evidence. The judge ordered that, for reasons of national security and the avoidance of harm to the due administration of justice, the court would sit in camera for those parts of the trial and the pre-trial process during which there was any evidence given or any reference made to evidence, information or argument which related to the material disclosed by the prosecution on notice. The defendant appealed against that ruling, and was supported by media interests, pursuant to the Criminal Justice Act 1988 s 159. The court considered the nature and proper method of conducting the application to appeal against the ruling and any subsequent appeal, particularly whether there was discretion within the Criminal Procedure Rules 2005, SI 2005/384, r 67.2(7) to determine the appeal with an oral hearing. *Held,* there was no discretion under r 67.2 to order an oral hearing. When deciding whether the process in the present case was fair, the starting point was the judge's conclusion that part of the trial should take place in camera. The absence of discretion was not incompatible with the European Convention on Human Rights and the express requirement that the determination of the appeal should take place without a hearing could not be ignored. The seriousness of the issues raised in the case did not create a jurisdiction to order a hearing of the appeal in open court. The logic behind r 67.2 was plain. The court would be considering an appeal against an order that public access to the whole or part of the trial should be restricted. A hearing in open court would normally involve disclosure to all parties of the material deployed before the judge. Pre-appeal disclosure to media interests of that material would render the order useless and the purpose of an in-camera hearing defeated. Accordingly, the appeal would be refused.

Re A [2006] EWCA Crim 4, [2006] 1 WLR 1361 (Court of Appeal: Sir Igor Judge P and Openshaw J and Sir Paul Kennedy). *Ex parte Guardian Newspapers Ltd* (1993) Times, 26 October (1993 Abr para 768); *R (on the application of Hammond) v Secretary of State for the Home Department* [2005] UKHL 69, [2005] All ER (D) 02 (Dec) (para 06/196); *Ekbatani v Sweden* (1988) 13 EHRR 504; *R v Beck; ex p Daily Telegraph* [1993] 2 All ER 177 (1992 Abr para 2042); *Ex parte Telegraph plc* [1993] 2 All ER 971 (1993 Abr para 2071); *Ex parte The Telegraph Group plc* [2001] EWCA Crim 1075, [2001] 1 WLR 1983 (2001 Abr para 2607) considered.

834 Trial—preparatory hearing—disclosure—application—jurisdiction of court—purpose of hearing

Following the dismissal of the defendants' application for leave to appeal against a ruling made in the course of a preparatory hearing under the Criminal Justice Act 1987 s 9(11), the court refused leave to appeal to the House of Lords, but certified that the following questions of law of general public importance were involved in the decision: (1) whether, for an appeal to lie to the Court of Appeal under s 9(11) from an order or ruling during the course of a preparatory hearing held under s 7, the order or ruling itself had to be for one of the purposes set out in s 7; (2) if so, whether an order or ruling in determination of an application for disclosure under the Criminal Procedure and Investigations Act 1996 s 8 fell within one of those purposes; and (3) in any event, whether an order or ruling in determination of an application for disclosure under s 8 could be the subject of an application under the provisions of the 1987 Act s 9(11).

R v H [2006] All ER (D) 319 (Jul) (Court of Appeal: Maurice Kay LJ, Crane and Dobbs JJ). For earlier related proceedings, see *R v H*, para 835.

835 Trial—preparatory hearing—disclosure—application—purpose of preparatory hearing

The Criminal Justice Act 1987 s 7(1) empowers a judge in a complex fraud trial to hold a preparatory hearing for the purposes of (1) identifying issues which are likely to be material to the verdict of the jury; (2) assisting the jury's comprehension of any such issues; (3) expediting the proceedings before the jury; or (4) assisting the judge's management of the trial. At the preparatory hearing, the judge may determine any question as to the admissibility of evidence and any other question of law relating to the case: s 9(1), (3).

At the defendant's trial for fraud and corruption, the judge decided to hold a preparatory hearing pursuant to the 1987 Act s 7. During the course of that hearing, the defendant made an application under the Criminal Procedure and Investigations Act 1996 for the disclosure of certain documents. The application was refused, and the defendant applied for leave to appeal against the decision, purportedly pursuant to the 1987 Act s 9(11). An issue arose as to whether the court had the jurisdiction to hear such an appeal, and in particular whether the application for disclosure was a matter falling within s 7(1). *Held*, in the present circumstances, the court had to look not at the possible consequences of an order made in the course of a preparatory hearing, but to the purpose of the order. An application concerning disclosure was not one of the purposes of a preparatory hearing within the meaning of s 7(1). The authorities regarding the interplay between ss 7 and 9 demonstrated the strict approach to be taken to the questions of what fell within the ambit of a preparatory hearing and what could be said to give rise to an interlocutory application pursuant to s 9 or the 1986 Act. The authorities illustrated that not every ruling applied for within a preparatory hearing would technically form part of such a hearing for the purposes of the 1987 Act. While there had been a culture change in relation to disclosure, that had not brought about any relabelling of what was part of a preparatory hearing. It had been established beyond doubt that there was no jurisdiction to hear the proposed appeal because the decision sought to be appealed did not form part of the preparatory hearing as construed. Accordingly, the application would be dismissed.

R v H [2006] EWCA Crim 1975, [2006] All ER (D) 92 (Jul) (Court of Appeal: Maurice Kay LJ, Crane and Dobbs JJ).

This decision has been affirmed on appeal: [2007] UKHL 7, [2007] All ER (D) 377 (Feb).

836 Trial—presence of accused—voluntary absence—withdrawal of representation—fairness

The defendant was charged with robbery and was remanded in custody. He was subsequently granted bail with conditions. He pleaded not guilty at the plea and directions hearing. On the first day of the warned list in which the trial had been placed, the court received a letter from his solicitors indicating that the defendant had failed to attend numerous appointments. The trial was relisted, but the defendant also failed to attend the relisted trial and, in due course, the matter came before the resident judge for consideration of whether the defendant should be tried in his absence. He ruled that the trial should proceed, even if the defendant failed to attend. On the eve of the trial, the defence team sought to reopen the ruling. On refusal of that application, the defendant's solicitor withdrew on the ground that she was unable to obtain clear instructions from her client. Counsel also withdrew on the basis that his instructing solicitors were withdrawing in the light of insufficient instructions. The defendant was convicted in his absence, and he appealed. *Held*, in all the circumstances, the proceedings, taken as a whole, were entirely fair and in compliance with the defendant's right to a fair trial. The judge had exercised correctly his discretion to proceed with the trial. On the basis of the information before him, he had rightly concluded that the defendant had voluntarily absented himself. The defendant had appreciated that, by absconding, the trial was likely to proceed in his absence. Given that he had made no attempt to contact his solicitor, he had appreciated that his solicitor would be unable to put forward a case on his behalf at trial and arrange representation for him. The fact that his defence was not before the jury was a consequence of a deliberate decision to abscond. Moreover, the case against the defendant was strong. Accordingly, the appeal would be dismissed.

R v O'Hare [2006] EWCA Crim 471, [2006] All ER (D) 155 (Mar) (Court of Appeal: Thomas LJ, McCombe J and Judge Stewart QC). *R v Jones* [2002] UKHL 5, [2002] 2 All ER 113 (2002 Abr para 211) considered.

837   Trial—retrial—application to quash acquittal and order retrial—murder

The defendant was retried for murder when the jury at trial failed to agree a verdict and, once again, the jury failed to reach a verdict. The prosecution formally offered no evidence and a verdict of not guilty was entered. Following the verdict, the defendant admitted on several occasions that he had murdered the victim and he pleaded guilty to charges of perjury. The prosecution then sought to have his acquittal quashed and for him to be retried under the Criminal Justice Act 2003 Pt 10 (ss 75–97). *Held,* for the court to quash an acquittal and order a retrial, there must be new and compelling evidence against the defendant in relation to the qualifying offence and it must be in the interests of justice for the court to make the order. The defendant had argued that it would not be fair for him to be prejudiced by his confessions and his plea of guilty to perjury that were made as a result of representations, or in reliance of a belief, that he could not and would not be retried for murder. It could not be said that the defendant was induced to confess and plead guilty to perjury as he had been told he could not be retried. At best, it could be said that had he known it was possible he could be retried he might not have repeatedly confessed his guilt and pleaded guilty to perjury. It was right to approach the case on the footing that he might not have provided the new and compelling evidence on which the prosecution's application was founded. The defendant had provided overwhelming evidence that could not be rebutted on reliance of the belief that he was immune from retrial. The issue was not whether it was fair that he should be exposed to the jeopardy of another trial but whether it was fair he should be exposed to the further punishment for murder of a mandatory life sentence, considering he had set out to put the record straight and paid the considerable penalty for perjury. The public would be outraged if the exception to the double jeopardy rule was not applied to the defendant on the basis that he would not have confessed had he appreciated he might be retried. There was no injustice in allowing a retrial. The sentence for perjury was imposed as punishment for lying under oath and it might be that the sentence reflected the consequences of the perjury which was the acquittal of the defendant of murder. For that reason it should be taken into account when determining the minimum term to be served should he be convicted of the crime. Accordingly, the application would be allowed.

R v Dunlop [2006] EWCA Crim 1354, [2007] 1 All ER 593 (Court of Appeal: Lord Phillips of Worth Matravers CJ, Sir Igor Judge P, Silber, Rafferty and Openshaw JJ).

838   Trial—retrial—application to quash acquittal and order retrial—reporting restrictions

The Court of Appeal has issued the following guidance in relation to the restriction under the Criminal Justice Act 2003 s 82 on the publication of matters which would prejudice a trial, in the context of an application under s 76 to quash an acquittal and order the retrial of an acquitted person. (1) Section 82(1), (3) addressed wider considerations than existed in relation to the Contempt of Court Act 1981, and acknowledged the inevitably detailed nature of the process which would take place before the retrial might be ordered. The court would have to examine the material in open court and satisfy itself that the evidence was not only 'new', but was 'compelling' evidence of the acquitted person's guilt. That evidence would have to be analysed, and subjected to argument on both sides, normally in close detail, with comment by the court as appropriate. That would take place in the context of evidence heard in the earlier trial or trials, which had not been sufficient to give rise to a conviction. Some cases were likely to attract huge national publicity, and others were likely to generate considerable interest in the locality, and attract significant local publicity. The venue of a retrial was a matter for decision at a later stage in the proceedings; however, it might well take into account the nature of the case and the publicity already attracted. (2) Where a retrial was ordered, it should not be delayed. The 2003 Act s 79(2) required that the court, when considering the interests of justice, should consider, amongst other things, the time that had elapsed since the offence and the statutory timetable for re-arraignment. (3) There were normally significant pre-trial limitations on the details of the evidence supporting the allegation against the defendant that might be reported. The media would normally wait for the prosecution opening speech, when the jury would first hear the detail. Section 82(1), (3) were plainly intended, so far as practical, to ensure that the same fairness of process would apply to any retrial. (4) Without restrictions, publicity could be given to all of the evidence considered by the court, including that which was considered new and compelling. In some cases that would give rise to a substantial risk to the administration of justice at the trial. While it would not always do so, the court would be concerned with the prejudice which might arise in any specific and individual case. The court had to consider whether the order sought by the Director of Public Prosecutions ('DPP') was too widely drawn, and had to examine each application and make an order only if satisfied that the interests of justice required the imposition of restrictions. In making the decision, the court should address the principles of open justice, in the sense of open proceedings, and the responsibility of the media for reporting legal proceedings. The court should remind itself, without the necessity for citation of authority, that juries were, and were to be treated as though they were, robust and independent minded, capable of evaluating the evidence called before them, and distinguishing it from pre-trial gossip and irrelevant comment. (5) It would be helpful for the court to remind itself of the principles relating to the 1981 Act. While those principles were in a different context to the 2003 Act, two distinct lines of jurisprudence would be unhelpful. (6) It was unlikely that any form of press release would be appropriate. At the very least, that would itself suggest that the DPP personally concluded (and the decision was required to be made by the DPP personally) that there was compelling new evidence sufficient to expose the acquitted person to the risk of double jeopardy. Moreover, in a case where the original trial had attracted significant public interest, the press release itself would create publicity, if only by way of reminder of the more notorious features of the case. No advantage from permitting press releases to be made in subsequent cases could be discerned. (7) The arrangements for giving notice of the application to quash an acquittal were prescribed by s 80. An application to prohibit publication might be made under s 82(6) by the DPP, and the application should not be made unless and until and investigation had been restarted after the original acquittal. After notice was given, the court might make an order restricting publication either of its own motion or on the application of the DPP. (8) Neither the acquitted person nor the media were entitled to set the process in motion; however, where the DPP had failed to make such an application, and the court became aware of possible prejudice to a subsequent retrial, the court would immediately act of its own motion. Generally speaking, the DPP should make an application to restrict publication of potentially prejudicial material as soon as any such risk became apparent. While the provision was new, it was anticipated that such applications would normally be made, albeit not inevitably granted. (9) The acquitted person should be notified of the intention to make an application pursuant to s 82. The court should be fully informed of his attitude to publicity. Arrangements should also be made for representatives of the media to be informed of the proposed application. 14 days' notice might be given. Media representatives might attend and submissions advanced on their behalf. In order to enable the business of the court to be conducted with sensible efficiency, representatives of the media should notify the court and the DPP not later than 48 hours before the hearing of the application of their intention to attend, and, if possible, the nature of the submissions to be made. Where nothing was heard by that date, the court would assume that there would be no such submission, and would proceed accordingly. If nothing was heard from media representatives, and the DPP and the acquitted person had agreed the terms of the order, the court might proceed on a consideration of the papers, and would only require the attendance of counsel if and when an indication to that effect had been given. The order itself would be pronounced in open court. Any such order would inevitably cease to have effect where the application to quash the acquittal was dismissed, where a retrial was ordered at the end of the retrial, or by order of the court. Only in exceptional circumstances would an order made pursuant to s 82 act as a permanent and indeterminate restriction on publication.

Re D (Acquitted Person: Retrial) [2006] EWCA Crim 733, [2006] 1 WLR 1998 (Court of Appeal: Sir Igor Judge P, David Steel and Hedley JJ).

839 Trial—sending to Crown Court for trial—notice of sending—form of notice

The Crime and Disorder Act 1998 s 51(1) provides that where an adult appears or is brought before a magistrates' court charged with an offence triable only on indictment, the court must send him forthwith to the Crown Court for trial (1) for that offence, and (2) for any either-way or summary offence with which he is charged which fulfils the requisite conditions set out in s 51(11). The court must specify in a notice the offence or offences for which a person is sent for trial under s 51 and the place at which he is to be tried; and a copy of the notice must be served on the accused and given to the Crown Court sitting at that place: s 51(7).

The claimant, who had been charged with conspiracy to supply drugs and the supply of Class A and B drugs, was sent by the magistrates' court for trial to the Crown Court pursuant to the 1998 Act s 51(1) and subsequently remanded in custody. The notice given by the justices, pursuant to s 51(7), stated that the claimant had committed offences of conspiracy and supply of drugs. The notice, charge sheet and the memorandum of an entry in the register of the magistrates' court were sent to the Crown Court detailing the offences but there was no express cross-reference between the notice, the charge sheet and the memorandum. The claimant subsequently gave notice of his intention to apply for dismissal of the charges for which he had been purportedly sent for trial. At the hearing of the application before the Crown Court, the claimant argued that the notice had failed to comply with the requirements of s 51(7) and had not contained offences known to law. The judge accepted the prosecution's submission that the committal had been invalid and that he lacked jurisdiction to dismiss the charges. The matter was sent back to the magistrates' court where the justices ruled that they had the necessary jurisdiction to send the claimant to the Crown Court. The notice purportedly given under s 51(7) on that occasion was substantially amended to include further details of the offences. On the claimant's application for a writ of habeas corpus, it fell to be determined whether the claimant had been effectively sent by the magistrates' court to the Crown Court pursuant to s 51(7). *Held*, considering the legislative framework of the 1998 Act, it would be curious if the defects in the notice had served to invalidate an otherwise effective committal. The decision of substance was that of the justices under s 51(1) to send the claimant to the Crown Court for trial. Only thereafter, and by way of an administrative act, was the notice prepared. No particular form had been prescribed for the s 51(7) notice nor were there any provisions dealing with the consequences of a defective notice. Moreover, there was no support in case law for the proposition that a defective s 51(7) notice rendered ineffective an otherwise unexceptionable committal under s 51(1). Further, it would have been absurd that charges were to be dismissed because of some technical deficiency in the s 51(7) notice, regardless of an otherwise proper committal and ample supporting material available to the judge in the Crown Court before whom the application had come. It would not be unduly burdensome to require a s 51(7) notice, as a matter of good practice, either to summarise the offence in a more careful form than was here the case or to cross-refer to documents, such as the charge sheet if unamended or, perhaps preferably, the memorandum of an entry in the register of the magistrates' court, to be sent to the Crown Court. Since the claimant had been effectively sent by the justices to the Crown Court and the judge's ruling to the contrary had been in error, the subsequent remand of the claimant in custody following that decision had been unsustainable and the claimant was, therefore, entitled to the relief sought. Accordingly, the application would be allowed.

R (on the application of Bentham) v Governor of HM Prison Wandsworth [2006] EWHC 121 (Admin), [2006] All ER (D) 80 (Feb) (Queen's Bench Division: Hooper LJ and Gross J).

840   Trial—stay of proceedings—abuse of process—charge founded on same facts as concluded prosecution—foreign jurisdiction

The defendant, a British citizen resident in Guyana, shot at a robber who was escaping from the scene of the crime. The robber later died as a result of his injuries. The defendant was convicted of unlawful possession of a firearm, but no other offence. More than 20 years later, the defendant settled in the United Kingdom, where he was charged with murder in relation to the shooting in Guyana. The defendant applied for the proceedings to be stayed as an abuse of process, submitting that the Crown could not bring a second set of proceedings arising from the same or substantially the same facts as proceedings that had already been concluded. The judge rejected the submission, and the jury convicted the defendant of manslaughter. The defendant appealed, arguing that the judge had erred in failing to stay the proceedings and that it had been unfair to try him in England as the procedural rules there were more favourable to the prosecution than those in Guyana. *Held*, the principle that the Crown was not permitted to bring a second set of proceedings arising from the same or substantially the same facts as proceedings that had already been concluded save in special circumstances did not apply where the first set of proceedings had been brought by foreign prosecutors, in a foreign jurisdiction. The principle was founded on an analogy with principles of civil law, and the fact that the Crown's domestic jurisdiction was indivisible. Different prosecuting authorities within the jurisdiction could be expected to co-operate and consult with each other. Foreign prosecutors were, however, wholly separate from the Crown, and consultation and co-operation with them was not always possible. Moreover, it had not been improper, unlawful, or an abuse of executive power to try the defendant in England, even if, or even because, the procedural rules would be more favourable to the prosecution. As a British citizen, the defendant had always been subject to trial in England, and subject therefore to English procedural rules. The defendant had been fairly tried, despite the lapse in time and the fact that the offence had occurred in a foreign country. The essential facts had not been in dispute. The issues had been whether the act performed had been unlawful, and what the defendant had intended at the time, which could be fairly decided on the basis of the facts admitted by the defendant, and the evidence he could give at trial. Accordingly, the appeal would be dismissed.

R v Cheong [2006] All ER (D) 385 (Feb) (Court of Appeal: Waller LJ, Mitting and Underhill JJ). *R v Beedie* [1998] QB 356, CA (1997 Abr para 809), distinguished. *R v Beckford* [1996] 1 Cr App Rep 94, CA (1995 Abr para 849), applied.

841   Trial—stay of proceedings—abuse of process—delay—factors to be considered

Where there had been a delay in a prosecution, the decision as to whether the proceedings should be stayed as an abuse of process was an exercise in judicial assessment dependent on judgment, rather than on any conclusion as to fact based on evidence. It therefore could be misleading to use the language of burden and standard of proof, which was more apt to an evidence-based fact-finding process. In essence, on an application for a stay for abuse of process on the ground of delay the judge should consider whether in all the circumstances a fair trial was possible notwithstanding the delay. In considering whether to grant a stay, the judge should bear in mind the following principles: (1) even where delay was unjustifiable, a permanent stay should be the exception rather than the rule; (2) where there was no fault on the part of the complainant or the prosecution, it would be very rare for a stay to be granted; (3) no stay should be granted in the absence of serious prejudice to the defence so that no fair trial could be held; (4) when assessing possible serious prejudice, the judge should bear in mind his power to regulate the admissibility of evidence, and that the trial process itself should ensure that all the relevant factual issues which arose from delay would be placed before the jury; and (5) if, after considering all those factors, the judge concluded that a fair trial would be possible, a stay should not be granted.

R v S [2006] EWCA Crim 756, (2006) 170 JP 434 (Court of Appeal: Rose LJ, Stanley Burnton and Hedley JJ). *Attorney General's Reference (No 1 of 1990)* [1992] 1 QB 630, CA (1992 Abr para 717), considered.

842   Trial—stay of proceedings—abuse of process—homicide—prior civil action—finding that cause of death uncertain

The defendant was charged with murdering his son. The mother of the victim had another son, in respect of whom care proceedings were subsequently commenced in view of the perceived risks to his wellbeing. The care proceedings came before a High Court judge approximately one year before the criminal trial took place. The family judge ruled that the evidence would not allow the court to determine which of the parents had inflicted all or any of the injuries to the victim, that he was unable to say on the evidence whether one parent was more likely to have inflicted the injuries than the other, and that it was not even possible to be sure that the victim's death had resulted from homicide. At the defendant's trial, the jury was unaware of any of the findings made by the judge in the family proceedings, and it was unsuccessfully submitted to the trial judge that the indictment should be stayed as an abuse of process. In the event, the defendant was convicted of manslaughter, attempting to choke, suffocate or strangle with intent to cause grievous bodily harm and causing grievous bodily harm. He appealed against conviction, arguing that the judge had erred in refusing to stay the proceedings in the light of the family judge's findings. *Held*, the purpose of the care proceedings, and the questions with which they were ultimately concerned, was to establish where and with whom the child should live and the arrangements required for his future upbringing and welfare. The proceedings brought and conducted by the local authority were not criminal proceedings in which the ultimate question for decision was whether the defendant had killed the victim. For that purpose, the court responsible for the care proceedings had been bereft of jurisdiction in that it was not competent to decide criminal proceedings. The decision in the care proceedings was not, and could not have been, a final determination of the criminal proceedings. No question of autrefois acquit, or issue estoppel, or double jeopardy could have arisen. Accordingly, the appeal would be dismissed.

R v L [2006] EWCA Crim 1902, [2006] All ER (D) 408 (Jul) (Court of Appeal: Sir Igor Judge P, Sir Mark Potter P and Crane J).

843   Trial—summing up—direction to jury—direction to convict—safety of conviction

The defendant in the first appeal had been charged with assault occasioning actual bodily harm. He had represented himself at trial. He admitted that he had deliberately punched the victim and that it had not been self-defence, but stated that he did not wish the jury to convict him because he believed that he had been justified in assaulting the victim. The judge stated that the defendant's justification for his admitted conduct did not constitute a defence in law, that he was taking the matter out of the hands of the jury and directed them to return a verdict of guilty. A jury member duly delivered a guilty verdict without any deliberation. In the second appeal, the defendant had climbed the roof of a town hall and damaged it in the course of a protest. He represented himself at his trial for criminal damage and contended that he had a defence of lawful excuse in view of the reasons for his protest. The judge informed the jury that the defendant had admitted damaging the property and that, as a matter of law, causing damage to property in order to secure an inquiry could not amount to a lawful excuse. In accordance with the direction of the judge, the jury found the defendant guilty. The Criminal Cases Review Commission referred the convictions to the Court of Appeal in view of a House of Lords ruling which stated that a judge could never direct the jury to return a guilty verdict. *Held*, although there were no circumstances in which a judge was entitled to direct a jury to return a verdict of guilty, it did not follow that, in every case where a judge had given a direction to convict, the conviction had to be considered unsafe. The course taken by the judges in completely taking away from the jury the decision as to guilt amounted to a significant legal misdirection or material irregularity despite the fact that the evidence had been clear, and the fact that the defendants had had no defence in law. The appeals were distinguishable from circumstances in which a judge might direct the jury that the defendant had no defence in law and that the only real verdict was a guilty one, at which point the jury were nevertheless sent out to deliberate and returned a guilty verdict. In each case, the judge had said that he was taking the decision away from the jury. It followed the verdicts had not in reality been of the jury at all but had been the verdict of the judge. Accordingly, the appeals would be allowed.

R v Caley-Knowles; R v Jones [2006] EWCA Crim 1611, [2006] 1 WLR 3181 (Court of Appeal: Tuckey LJ, Leveson and Irwin JJ). *R v Wang* [2005] UKHL 9, [2005] 1 All ER 782 (2005 Abr para 950) explained.

844   Verdict—murder—alternative verdict of manslaughter—direction to jury

The defendant had been charged with murdering a woman by asphyxiation. At his trial, the defendant contended that the death had occurred accidentally in the course of consensual asphyxial sex. The judge accepted the prosecution's suggestion that it would be wrong to leave an alternative verdict of manslaughter to the jury. The defendant was convicted and his appeal was dismissed and he appealed further. *Held*, the interests of justice were not served if a defendant who had committed a lesser offence was either convicted of a greater offence or was completely acquitted. The public interest in the administration of justice was best served if in any trial on indictment the judge left to the jury any obvious alternative offence supported by evidence, subject to any appropriate caution or warning but irrespective of the wishes of counsel. The duty should not be used to infringe a defendant's right to a fair trial. The judge's failure to offer the jury a manslaughter verdict, although understandable in the circumstances, was a material irregularity. No appellate court could be sure that a fully directed jury would not have convicted the defendant of manslaughter. Accordingly, the appeal would be allowed.

R v Coutts [2006] UKHL 39, [2006] 4 All ER 353 (House of Lords: Lords Bingham of Cornhill, Nicholls of Birkenhead, Hutton, Rodger of Earlsferry and Mance). Von Starck v R [2000] 1 WLR 1370, PC (2000 Abr para 910), considered. Decision of Court of Appeal [2005] EWCA Crim 52, [2005] 1 WLR 1605 (2005 Abr para 956) reversed.

845   Victims—code of practice—provision of services to victims

The Domestic Violence, Crime and Victims Act 2004 (Victims' Code of Practice) Order 2006, SI 2006/629 (in force on 3 April 2006), brings into operation, on 3 April 2006, the Code of Practice for Victims of Crime made pursuant to the Domestic Violence, Crime and Victims Act 2004 s 32, making provision as to the services to be provided to a victim of criminal conduct by persons which have functions relating to victims of criminal conduct or any aspect of the criminal justice system.

846   Youth Justice and Criminal Evidence Act 1999—commencement

The Youth Justice and Criminal Evidence Act 1999 (Commencement No 12) Order 2006, SI 2006/2885, brings into force, on 6 December 2006, s 61(2) (in part) and certain repeals in Sch 6. For a summary of the Act, see 1999 Abr para 925. See also the commencement table in the title STATUTES.

CRIMINAL LAW

Halsbury's Laws of England (4th edn) vol 11(1) (2006 Reissue) paras 1–620, vol 11(2) (2006 Reissue) paras 621–1049, vol 11(3) (2006 Reissue) paras 1050–1557 and vol 11(4) (2006 Reissue) paras 1558–2181

Articles

For articles relating to this title please refer to the Table of Articles at the beginning of the Abridgment.

847   Causing or allowing death of child or vulnerable adult—abuse of deceased—failure to obtain medical treatment

See R v Liu, para 2538.

848   Conspiracy—mental element—knowledge or intention—money laundering

The Criminal Law Act 1977 s 1(2) provides that where liability for any offence may be incurred without knowledge on the part of the person committing it of any particular fact or circumstance necessary for the commission of the offence, a person will not be guilty of conspiracy to commit that offence unless he and at least one other party to the agreement intend or know that that fact or circumstances will exist at the time when conduct constituting the offence is to take place.

The defendant operated a currency exchange office, and pleaded guilty to the charge of conspiracy to convert the proceeds of drug trafficking or criminal conduct contrary to the 1977 Act s 1(1), on the basis of laundering money which he suspected, but did not know, was the proceeds of crime. His appeal on the ground that the conviction was unsafe as a matter of law was unsuccessful, and he appealed to the House of Lords. Held, Baroness Hale of Richmond dissenting, the phrase 'intend or know' under s 1(2) was a provision of general application to all conspiracies and the word 'know' should be interpreted strictly, meaning true belief. In relation to the offence of converting another's proceeds of crime under the Criminal Justice Act 1988 s 93C(2) this meant that a conspirator had to be aware the property was the proceeds of crime. There was no incompatibility between the objective requirement that a defendant could be convicted of an offence under s 93C(2) if he had reasonable grounds to suspect that the property converted was the proceeds of crime, without having actual knowledge or suspicion, and the subjective requirement that the activity of the defendant had to be for the specified purpose of assisting another to avoid prosecution for a criminal offence or avoiding the making or enforcement of a confiscation order. The first requirement had both a subjective part, that the person suspected, and an objective part, that there were reasonable grounds for the suspicion. The essence of the mens rea was contained in the second requirement, what the purpose was. The defendant's purpose had to be proved to be to launder the proceeds of another person's criminal conduct. Where he knew the criminal origin of the property, his knowledge was linked to his purpose in engaging the activity if he had reasonable grounds to suspect that it had a criminal origin, his suspicion was linked to his purpose in the same way. Accordingly, the appeal would be allowed.

R v Saik [2006] UKHL 18, [2006] 4 All ER 866 (House of Lords: Lords Nicholls of Bikenhead, Steyn and Hope of Craighead, Baroness Hale of Richmond and Lord Brown of Eaton-under-Heywood). Decision of Court of Appeal [2004] EWCA Crim 2936, [2004] All ER (D) 383 (Nov) (2004 Abr para 752) reversed.

A number of appeals were heard together as they raised common issues concerning conspiracy to commit money laundering offences contrary to the Drug Trafficking Act 1994 s 49(2) and the Criminal Justice Act 1988 s 93C(2). The defendants were convicted of the offences before the decision of the House of Lords in *R v Saik*, in which it was held that, where conspiracy to launder money was charged, it had to be proved that the defendant had known of its illicit origins or, where no money was yet identified, that he intended that the money should be of illicit origin. In the instant cases, the judges had directed the juries that suspicion as to the money's origins was sufficient. Issues arose as to whether the law had been misapplied in treating proof of suspicion as being sufficient mens rea for the offence of conspiracy to launder money, and whether the convictions were nevertheless safe because the juries had been directed that it had been proved that the defendant had to have had the 'purpose' of assisting another to avoid prosecution or confiscation, and had to have found that he had, or the defendant's pleading guilty had necessarily admitted by his plea that he had had such a purpose. *Held*, following *R v Saik*, it was a misdirection in a case where conspiracy was charged to tell the jury that it was sufficient if the defendant suspected illicit origin. Moreover, it could not be said that proof of 'purpose' necessarily carried the necessary inference of intention as a matter of law, rather the jury might infer intention from the same evidence as that relating to the purpose. *R v Saik* did not stand for the proposition that proof of the purpose to assist another to avoid prosecution or confiscation could be said necessarily to amount to proof of intention, albeit not of knowledge. Judgment would be given accordingly.

R v Ramzan; R v Israel; R v Vaikilipour [2006] All ER (D) 318 (Jul) (Court of Appeal: Hughes LJ, Field J and Sir Richard Curtis). *R v Saik* [2006] UKHL 18, [2006] 2 WLR 993 (para 848) applied.

1998 Act s 93 replaced by Proceeds of Crime Act 2002 s 327. 1994 Act s 49(2) repealed: 2002 Act Sch 11 para 25 (2)(a), Sch 12.

849 Controlled drugs—use on premises—closure order—standard of proof

The Anti-social Behaviour Act 2003 s 2(3) empowers a magistrates' court to make a closure order only if it is satisfied that the premises in respect of which the closure notice was issued have been used in connection with the unlawful use, production or supply of a Class A controlled drug, and the use of the premises is associated with the occurrence of disorder or serious nuisance to members of the public.

In an appeal by way of case stated on a preliminary issue, a question arose as to the standard of proof to be applied by magistrates' courts when considering the making of a closure order under the 2003 Act s 2(3). The respondent contended that the criminal standard of proof was appropriate, as that was the standard used in relation to anti-social behaviour orders. The appellant chief constable submitted that there were relevant differences between a closure order and an anti-social behaviour order in that a closure order did not contain any allegation or finding against a named individual, a closure order was of far shorter duration, and the penalty for breach of a closure order was far less serious than that for breach of an anti-social behaviour order. *Held*, the civil standard of proof, namely the balance of probabilities, was the appropriate standard of proof to be applied to s 2(3). Notwithstanding the superficial similarity between a closure order and an anti-social behaviour order, they involved different concepts. There was a greater allegation on an individual under an anti-social behaviour order, and such an order could restrict the liberty of an individual in a far more direct manner than a closure order. Moreover, the penalty for breaching the orders were different. Accordingly, the appeal would be allowed.

Chief Constable of Merseyside Police v Harrison [2006] EWHC 1106 (Admin), [2007] QB 79 (Queen's Bench Division: Maurice Kay LJ and Tugendhat J). *R (on the application of McCann) v Crown Court at Manchester; Clingham v Kensington and Chelsea RLBC* [2002] UKHL 39, [2003] 1 AC 787 (2002 Abr para 2616) distinguished. *R (on the application of AN) v Mental Health Review Tribunal (Northern Region)* [2005] EWCA Civ 1605, [2006] 2 WLR 850 (2005 Abr para 2175) considered.

850 Crime (International Co-operation) Act 2003—commencement

The Crime (International Co-operation) Act 2003 (Commencement No 3) Order 2006, SI 2006/2811, brings ss 32–36, 42–46 into force on 1 November 2006. For a summary of the Act, see 2003 Abr para 724. See also the commencement table in the title STATUTES.

851 Criminal injuries—compensation—assault by foster parent—victim and offender living together

The claimant was received into care by a local authority and placed with foster parents. He was subjected to severe, non-accidental injuries and applied to the Criminal Injuries Compensation Appeals Panel for compensation. The Criminal Injuries Compensation Authority rejected his claim on the basis that the injuries must have been inflicted by one of the his foster parents and that under the Criminal Injuries Compensation Scheme 1969 no compensation was payable to persons living together as members of the same family. The claimant's application for judicial review was dismissed and he sought permission to appeal. *Held*, the claimant had been boarded out under the Boarding Out of Children Regulations 1955, SI 1955/1377. It was clear that the intention of placing a child with foster parents under the 1955 Regulations was that he should live with them in their dwelling as a member of their family. No blood relationship between the offender and victim was required for the exclusion in the 1969 Scheme to apply. It followed that the argument that the claimant and his foster parents were not living together as members of the same family had no prospect of succeeding. Accordingly, permission to appeal would be refused.

R (on the application of M) v Criminal Injuries Compensation Appeals Panel [2005] EWCA Civ 566, [2006] PIQR P75 (Court of Appeal: Buxton and Arden LJJ). Decision of Newman J [2004] EWHC 1701 (QB), [2005] PIQR P51 (2004 Abr para 787) affirmed.

852   Defence—necessity—use of drugs for medicinal purpose—availability of defence

The defendant had been in a car accident some years earlier in which he had sustained serious injuries. Subsequently, he had tried a number of pain-relief strategies. However, the treatments he tried proved ineffective or produced side effects. Before his arrest, he informed his doctor that he had found that cannabis provided pain relief. He was arrested and charged with possession of a Class B drug. He submitted that a defence of necessity was available to him on the basis that he was suffering from serious physical harm. The judge ruled that the defence of necessity was not available and the defendant pleaded guilty to possession of a Class B drug. On the defendant's plea against conviction, he contended that where the state provided that the only way in which a person could avoid severe medical problems was by breaking the criminal law and risking punishment, the state was subjecting that person to inhuman or degrading treatment. Therefore, he submitted that there was a conflict with the European Convention on Human Rights art 3, which could only be avoided by reading the Misuse of Drugs Act 1971 as subject to the defence of medical necessity. *Held,* the Convention art 3 did not assist the defendant. The defendant's submission attempted to elevate the state's obligation under art 3 to something well beyond an obligation not to subject an individual to inhuman or degrading treatment. Further, a defence of necessity on an individual basis as advocated by the defendant was in conflict with the purpose and effect of the legislative scheme of the 1971 Act. The state had done nothing to subject the defendant to either inhuman or degrading treatment. The state could not be regarded as responsible for the harm inflicted on the defendant, nor would art 3 require the state to take any steps to alleviate his condition. Accordingly, the appeal would be dismissed.

R v Altham [2006] EWCA Crim 7, [2006] 1 WLR 3287 (Court of Appeal: Scott Baker LJ, Ramsey J and the Recorder of Cardiff).

853   Defence—prevention of crime—crime under customary international law—disruption of activities at military bases

The Criminal Law Act 1967 s 3(1) provides that a person may use such force as is reasonable in the circumstances in the prevention of crime.

The defendants were war protesters who had disrupted activities at various military bases. They were convicted of conspiracy to cause criminal damage, having articles with intent to destroy or damage property, attempted arson and aggravated trespass in respect of their activities. The defendants appealed, claiming that they were entitled to rely on the defence of the use of reasonable force in the prevention of crime under the 1967 Act s 3(1). *Held*, in s 3 the word 'crime' referred to a crime in domestic law that had previously been either a felony or a misdemeanour, and had no application to crimes under international law. This construction was confirmed by the long title, which stated that the 1967 Act abolished the division of crimes into felonies and misdemeanours. A crime recognised in customary international law could be assimilated into the domestic criminal law, but that result would not follow automatically. While international law could establish a legal justification for Parliament to legislate, it could not create a crime triable directly in an English court. In the absence of statutory authority, the prosecution of the crime of aggression would be inconsistent with the fundamental principle of the constitution that the principal was always the state itself with the liability of individuals secondary. Indeed, it would be difficult for the courts, as the judicial branch of the state, to hold that the state itself had acted unlawfully. Furthermore, the courts would not inquire into the discretionary power of the Crown to make war, which fell squarely within the discretionary powers of the Crown to defend the realm and conduct its foreign affairs. Accordingly, the appeals would be dismissed.

R v Jones; Ayliffe v DPP; Swain v DPP [2006] UKHL 16, [2006] 2 All ER 741 (House of Lords: Lords Bingham of Cornhill, Hoffmann, Rodger of Earlsferry, Carswell and Mance). Decision of Court of Appeal [2004] EWCA Crim 1981, [2005] QB 259 affirmed.

854   Drug offence—closure of premises where drug used unlawfully—closure order— evidence and disclosure

In a case concerning the power of magistrates' courts to make closure orders, pursuant to the Anti-social Behaviour Act 2003 s 2, against premises where drugs were used unlawfully, issues arose as to the correct procedure for the service of evidence, in particular hearsay evidence, and the disclosure of documents in the possession of the police. *Held*, if the evidence which the police proposed to adduce was not served by the time of the first hearing of the closure order application, or if it was not fully served, fairness required that it should be served well in advance of an adjourned hearing. Generally, seven days before the adjourned hearing was likely to be the minimum period of time bearing in mind that the police could not suppose that the first hearing would always be adjourned and should have served their evidence by then. Also, if the police intended to rely on hearsay evidence, they would have to make an application for a direction under the Magistrates' Courts (Hearsay Evidence in Civil Proceedings) Rules 1999, SI 1999/681, r 3(2) to reduce the 21-day period required to serve a hearsay notice. That application would probably be made at the first hearing and the police therefore might need to serve an application to that end with the closure notice. If the court acceded to the application, the stipulated period for serving the hearsay notice would need to be sufficiently in advance of the adjourned hearing to enable the defendant fairly to deal with it. Moreover, the police should disclose documents which clearly and materially affected their case adversely or supported the defendant's case. Judgment would be given accordingly.

R (on the application of Cleary) v Highbury Corner Magistrates' Court [2006] EWHC 1869 (Admin), [2006] All ER (D) 376 (Jul) (Queen's Bench Division: May LJ and Langstaff J).

855 False imprisonment—detention following execution of search warrant—police officers searching for firearms

The police were granted a search warrant of the second claimant's house under the Firearms Act 1968 s 46. They had information that firearms used in violent incidents between two gangs were hidden in the house. The warrant authorised the police to enter, if necessary by force, and to search the premises and anyone found there. Armed officers surrounded the property and told the occupants to leave by the front door. The second claimant, who was the sister of a man whom the police believed was an important member of one of the gangs, left by the back door, and being unco-operative, was handcuffed and taken to wait in a police vehicle while the search was carried out. The first claimant, who was also linked to the gang and who had a number of convictions for assault, was escorted from the house and detained in a police car. When the search was completed and no weapons found the claimants were told that they were free to return to the house. The claimants brought an action seeking damages for trespass, assault, unlawful imprisonment and breach of their human rights. The judge decided that the police had reasonable cause to suspect that there were firearms on the property when seeking the warrant. The jury found that the police had acted reasonably, and the judge dismissed the claim. The claimants appealed. *Held*, although there was no provision in the 1964 Act specifically authorising the use of reasonable force in the execution of a warrant, the police had power to restrain or detain, even in very limited circumstances, those who might otherwise put lives in danger or themselves be put in danger. What was necessary and, therefore, to be implied, would all be a matter of fact and degree. Having regard to the authorities, there was an implied power to restrain persons if it was necessary to ensure the safe and effective exercise of an express or necessary power to search premises. In the present case, there were, on any objective view, good grounds for suspecting there were firearms at the property and possibly a criminal prepared to use them. If there was a danger to the public there was also a danger to the occupants of the house. It was, therefore, in the interests of the claimants, as well as those searching the house, for them to be kept out of harm's way. It followed that it had been open to the judge to find as he did. If there was any detention of any of the claimants, it was necessary and proportionate and in accordance with a procedure prescribed by law to secure the fulfilment of an important obligation, namely compliance with a court order. Accordingly, the appeal would be dismissed.

Connor v Chief Constable of Merseyside Police [2006] All ER (D) 293 (Nov) (Court of Appeal: Waller, Hallett and Leveson LJJ).

856 Fraud Act 2006

The Fraud Act 2006 makes provision for, and in connection with, criminal liability for fraud and obtaining services dishonestly. The Act received the royal assent on 8 November 2006 and came into force in part on that day. The remaining provisions came into force on 15 January 2007: SI 2006/3200. For details of commencement see the commencement table in the title STATUTES.

Section 1 creates a new general offence of fraud and sets out the penalties for committing it. The offence under s 1 is committed where a person (1) dishonestly makes a false representation, and intends, by making the representation to make a gain for himself or another or to cause loss to another or to expose another to a risk of loss (s 2); (2) dishonestly fails to disclose to another person information which he is under a legal duty to disclose, and intends, by failing to disclose the information, to make a gain for himself or another or to cause loss to another or to expose another to a risk of loss (s 3); or (3) dishonestly abuses a position in which he is expected to safeguard, or not to act against, the financial interests of another person, in order to make a gain for himself or another or to cause loss to another or to expose another to a risk of loss (s 4). 'Gain' and 'loss' are defined for the purposes of ss 2–4 in s 5. By virtue of s 6, a person is guilty of an offence if he has in his possession or under his control any article for use in the course of or in connection with any fraud.

Section 7 makes it an offence to make, adapt, supply or offer to supply any article knowing that it is designed or adapted for use in the course of or in connection with fraud, or intending it to be used to commit, or assist in the commission of, fraud. For the purposes of ss 6 and 7 'article' includes any program or data held in electronic form: s 8. Under s 9, a person is guilty of an offence if he is knowingly a party to the carrying on of a relevant business. The Companies Act 1985 Sch 24 is amended by the 2006 Act s 10 with the effect that the maximum custodial sentence for fraudulent trading under the companies legislation is increased to ten years. Section 11 makes it an offence for any person, by any dishonest act, to obtain services for which payment is required, with intent to avoid payment. By virtue of s 12, persons with a specified corporate role who are party to the commission of an offence under the 2006 Act by their body corporate are liable to be charged for the offence as well as the corporation. Under s 13, a person is protected from incriminating himself or his spouse or civil partner for the purposes of offences under the 2006 Act. Section 14 introduces Sch 1, which makes various consequential amendments, Sch 2, which makes transitional provision, and Sch 3, which makes various repeals and revocations. Section 15 deals with commencement and extent, and s 16 specifies the short title.

Amendments, repeals and revocations
Specific provisions of a number of Acts are amended or repealed. These include: Theft Act 1968 ss 15, 15A, 15B, 16, 20(2), 24A(3), (4); Theft Act 1978 ss 1, 2, 4(2), 5(1); Companies Act 1985 Sch 24; and Criminal Justice Act 1993 s 1(2).

857 Homicide—murder and related offences—Law Commission recommendations

The Law Commission has published its recommendations for legislation to replace the Homicide Act 1957, *Murder, Manslaughter and Infanticide* (HC 30; Law Com No 304). The existing offences of murder and manslaughter would be replaced by a three-tier structure of general offences, although the terms 'murder' and 'manslaughter' would continue to be used: 'first degree murder', 'second degree murder' and 'manslaughter'. First degree murder would encompass intentional killings and killings with intent to cause serious injury where the killer was aware that his conduct involved a serious risk of causing death (awareness of a risk being understood to involve consciously adverting to the risk). Second degree murder would encompass killings intended to cause serious injury; killings intended to cause injury, or fear or risk of injury, where the killer was aware that his conduct involved a serious risk (that is, the risk was more than insignificant or remote) of causing death; and killings intended to kill or to cause serious injury where the killer was aware that his conduct involved a serious risk of causing death, but established provocation, diminished responsibility, or that he killed in pursuance of a suicide pact. The Commission recommends that the offence of second degree murder should attract a maximum sentence of life imprisonment but that guidelines should be issued as to appropriate periods in custody for different categories of the offence. Under the proposed legislation, the offence of manslaughter would encompass killing another person through gross negligence (that is, where a person by his conduct caused the death of another, the risk that the conduct would cause death would have been obvious to a reasonable person in his position, he was capable of appreciating that risk at the material time, and the conduct fell far below what could reasonably have been expected of him in the circumstances); and killing another person through the commission of a criminal act intended by the defendant to cause injury, or through the commission of a criminal act that the defendant was aware involved a serious risk of causing some injury. Under the proposed legislation, a person would be taken to intend a result if he acted in order to bring it about; and, where a trial judge deemed it appropriate in the interests of justice, the jury should be directed that an intention to bring about a result might be found if it was shown that the defendant thought that the result was a virtually certain consequence of his action. Under the proposed legislation, A would be liable to be convicted of B's offence of murder (first or second degree) if A intended to assist or encourage B to commit the offence, or if A was engaged in a joint criminal venture with B and realised that B, or another party to the joint venture, might commit murder; but A would be liable for manslaughter if it were established that A and B had been parties to a joint venture to commit an offence, B committed murder in fulfilment of that venture, A intended or foresaw that non-serious harm, or the fear of harm, might be caused by a party to the venture, and a reasonable person in A's position (with A's knowledge of the relevant facts) would have foreseen an obvious risk of death or serious injury being caused by a party to the venture.

The Commission recommends that provocation, except where it was incited by the defendant so as to provide an excuse for violence and except where the defendant acted in considered desire for revenge, should be a partial defence, so that unlawful homicide which would otherwise be first degree murder should be second degree murder if the defendant acted in response to gross provocation (that is, words and/or conduct) which caused that person to have a justifiable sense of being seriously wronged, and/or to a fear of serious violence towards that person, or some other person, and if a person of the defendant's age and of ordinary temperament in the circumstances of the defendant might have reacted in the same or a similar way, having regard to all the circumstances of the defendant, other than matters bearing simply on his general capacity for self-control. A trial judge would not be required to leave the defence of provocation to the jury except where there was evidence on which a reasonable jury, properly directed, could conclude that it might apply.

The Commission also recommends that the proposed legislation should specify that a person who would otherwise be guilty of first degree murder should be guilty of second degree murder if, at the time he played his part in the killing, his capacity to understand the nature of his conduct, or to form a rational judgment, or to control himself, was substantially impaired by an abnormality of mental functioning arising from a recognised medical condition and/or developmental immaturity (in a person under the age of 18 years); and the abnormality, the developmental immaturity, or the combination of both provided an explanation for the defendant's conduct in carrying out, or taking part in, the killing.

The Commission recommends that duress should provide a full defence to first degree murder, second degree murder and attempted murder, provided that the threat was of death or life-threatening harm. The burden of proof of duress, on a balance of probabilities, should fall on the defendant.

The Commission calls for a public consultation on whether and, if so, to what extent, the law should recognise either an offence of 'mercy killing' or a partial defence of 'mercy killing'. Pending the outcome of such consultation, the Homicide Act 1957 s 4 should be retained. Further, it is recommended that the offence/defence of infanticide be retained without substantive amendment; and, where infanticide is not raised as an issue at a trial, the judge should be empowered, following a conviction for murder and before sentence is passed, to order a medical examination of the defendant with a view to establishing whether the requisite elements of infanticide were present, and that the resultant medical evidence should be available on any appeal to the Court of Appeal. The Commission has not addressed certain issues such as necessity and self-defence as justifications for killings, or the defences of insanity and intoxication. The recommendations are the first stage of the current review of the law of homicide. The Home Office is to undertake the second stage which will involve public consultation on broader areas of policy.

858   Incitement—incitement to commit offences abroad

The defendant was charged with the offence of inciting the distribution or showing of indecent photographs of children outside England and Wales. The court ruled that it had no jurisdiction to try the offence as the location of the act that was incited determined where a case should be prosecuted. The prosecution appealed. *Held*, the defendant had conceded that the court possessed jurisdiction over an allegation of incitement to distribute indecent photographs of children contrary to common law, even where the person incited was abroad, provided that the distribution of the photographs occurred at least in part in England and Wales. The ruling was wrong in law and, accordingly, the appeal would be allowed.

R v Tompkins (2006) Times, 17 August (Court of Appeal: Richards LJ, Simon and Wilkie JJ).

859   Incitement—replacement of common law offence—Law Commission recommendation

The Law Commission has published a report, *Inchoate Liability for Assisting and Encouraging Crime* (Cm 6878; Law Com No 300), in which it recommends the replacement of the common law offence of incitement by new statutory offences. The first of the proposed offences (that is, intentionally encouraging or assisting a criminal act) will be committed if a person who does an act capable of encouraging or assisting the doing of a criminal act in relation to an offence also intends to encourage or assist the doing of that criminal act (known as a 'cl 1 offence', by reference to the provisions of the draft Bill appended to the report). The nature of the intention required for a cl 1 offence is specified separately. The second and third proposed offences amount to encouraging or assisting criminal acts believing that one or more of them will be done. The second offence will be committed if a person who does an act capable of encouraging or assisting the doing of a criminal act also believes that the criminal act will be done and that his act will encourage or assist the doing of the criminal act (a 'cl 2(1) offence'). The third offence will be committed in the same way as the second offence, except that it will be committed in relation to one or more of a number of criminal acts (a 'cl 2(2) offence'). Special provisions elaborate on the meaning of the terms 'doing an act that is capable of encouraging the doing of a criminal act' and 'doing an act that is capable of encouraging or assisting the doing of a criminal act'. Separate provision is made also where the principal offence requires proof of fault or where particular circumstances and/or consequences must be proved for a conviction of the principal offence. The Commission recommends that explicit provision be made to the effect that the proposed offences may be committed regardless of whether the principal offence is committed; but neither the cl 2(1) nor the cl 2(2) offence will apply if the principal offence is under the proposed legislation or is listed in a Schedule to it.

It will be a defence to any of the proposed offences for a person to prove that he has acted for the purpose of preventing the commission of an offence, or for the purpose of preventing or limiting the occurrence of harm, if he can further prove that it was reasonable for him so to act. It will also be a defence to a cl 2(1) offence or a cl 2(2) offence for a person to prove that certain circumstances existed and that, in those circumstances, it was reasonable for him to act as he did or, if he merely believed that certain circumstances existed, if his belief was reasonable and it was reasonable for him so to act in the circumstances as he believed them to be. It will also be a defence to any proposed offence for a person to show that he was the prospective victim of a principal offence that existed for the protection of a particular category of persons, into which category he fell.

The Commission recommends a degree of extra-territorial jurisdiction for the proposed offences such that, if a person knows or believes that what he 'anticipates', as defined in this context, might take place in England or Wales, he may be guilty of an offence no matter where he was at any relevant time and, in the absence of proof of knowledge or belief, he may nevertheless be guilty of an offence in limited circumstances, but in such circumstances the consent of the Attorney General would be necessary for any prosecution. The mode of trial of the proposed offences will be that appropriate to the relevant principal offence. If the principal offence is murder, anyone guilty of one of the proposed offences will be liable to imprisonment for life. If the principal offence is not murder, the penalty will be the same as for the principal offence.

The Commission expects to publish a second report in due course on the law of complicity and innocent agency. Although the subject matter is akin to that of incitement, the Commission wishes to consider further the approach to the drafting of new offences to replace the existing law on secondary liability before publishing its recommendations on that subject.

860   Indecent photographs of children—importation—prohibition—notification requirements—sexual offenders register

See *Forbes v Secretary of State for the Home Department*, para 1602.

861   Indecent photographs of children—possession—images on hard drive of computer—control of images—lack of skill or specialist software to retrieve images

The defendant was charged with possessing indecent photographs of children contrary to the Criminal Justice Act 1988 s 160(1). Police officers had seized computers from the defendant's home and had found a number of images on the hard drives. However, a large number of the images had been deleted and could be retrieved only by using specialist software which the defendant did not have. The judge rejected the defendant's submission of no case to answer on the basis that he possessed the images if they remained on his computer's hard drive. The defendant was convicted and he appealed. *Held*, in the special case of deleted computer images, where a person could not retrieve or gain access to an image, he would no longer have custody or control of it. An image would therefore not be 'in his possession' for the purposes of s 160(1) by reason of his possession of the hard disk drive itself. It would be for the jury to decide whether images on a hard disk drive were in the control of the defendant and, therefore, in his possession, having regard to all the circumstances, including his knowledge. A person would not be in possession of an image unless he had the skill and specialist software to produce it on his screen, to make a copy of it, or to send it to another. Accordingly, the appeal would be allowed.

R v Porter [2006] EWCA Crim 560, [2006] All ER (D) 236 (Mar) (Court of Appeal: Dyson LJ, Grigson and Walker JJ). *DPP v Brooks* [1974] 2 All ER 840, PC (1974 Abr para 614); *R v Boyesen* [1982] 2 All ER 161, HL (1982 Abr para 673), considered.

862   Interception of communications—person with right to control communication system—meaning of control

The Regulation of Investigatory Powers Act 2000 s 1(2) provides that it is an offence for a person intentionally and without lawful authority to intercept any communication in the course of its transmission by means of a private telecommunication system. A person's conduct is excluded from criminal liability if he is a person with a right to control the operation or the use of the system: s 1(2)(b), (6)(a).

The defendant had been deputy chairman of a company. After he left the company, evidence that he had intercepted e-mail communications was discovered, and he was charged with the unlawful and unauthorised interception of e-mail communication to a public company, contrary to the 2000 Act s 1(2). The prosecution case was that the defendant had been responsible for the setting up of a rule which ensured that e-mails sent from certain individuals' accounts were also sent to another account. The defendant's case was that he had induced an employee to set up the rule, and that because that employee had been allowed to use the username and password of an administrator, the employee was excluded from criminal liability under s 1(2)(b), (6). The judge found that the right to control within the meaning of s 1(6) meant the right to authorise or to forbid the operation or use of the system. The defendant pleaded guilty, was sentenced to six months' imprisonment suspended for two years, and was fined £20,000. He sought permission to appeal against his conviction and sentence. *Held*, the meaning of to 'control' in the context of s 1(6) was to 'authorise and forbid'. It did not mean the unrestricted ability physically to use and operate the system. The concept of control extended to the control of how the system was used and operated by others. This was underlined by s 1(6)(b), which extended protection to a person who had the consent of the person with the right to control to make the interception. The objective of protecting the privacy of private communications would be undermined if anyone with unrestricted ability to operate and use a telecommunications system were exempt from criminal liability for intercepting communications.

There was an obvious gap between intercepting a personal message which had no financial implications, and intercepting confidential material of financial significance with the object of using it for commercial gain. When the defendant had planned the interception, he had wanted to use the material to gain control of the company, and high financial stakes had been involved. In these circumstances, the custody threshold had been passed and there was nothing wrong in principle with the suspended sentence being combined with a fine. Accordingly, permission to appeal would be refused.

R v Stanford [2006] EWCA Crim 258, [2006] 1 WLR 1554 (Court of Appeal: Lord Phillips of Worth Matravers CJ, Cresswell and Openshaw JJ). *R v Bow Street Metropolitan Stipendiary Magistrate, ex p Government of the United States of America* [1999] 4 All ER 1, HL (1999 Abr para 1658), considered.

863 Manslaughter—unlawful act—affray—deceased suffering from undiagnosed heart condition

The defendants were charged with manslaughter and affray after they assaulted a group of individuals, one of whom ran away, collapsed and later died. The deceased had heart disease, which had been undiagnosed before her death. It was agreed that the event most proximate to the collapse, and therefore most likely to have been the precipitating factor leading to her death, was her running away from the incident. The judge accepted that, when determining whether the affray had subjected the deceased to the risk of at least some physical harm, it was legitimate to aggregate the violence by the other defendants in order to decide whether that aggregated violence had been a cause of death. The defendants were convicted and the judge granted a certificate of fitness for appeal pursuant to the Criminal Appeal Act 1968 s 11(1A). *Held*, it was settled law that a person who inflicted quite a slight injury which unforeseeably led to the death of the victim was guilty of the offence of manslaughter and was criminally liable for the death. However, to hold the defendants liable for the death of the deceased, in the present circumstances, would involve an unwarranted extension of the law. The only dangerous act had been the assault by the second defendant and the deceased's death had not been caused by injuries that were a foreseeable result of the assault. Whether there was a liability under the Public Order Act 1986 s 3(2) for the acts or threats of violence by others depended on the application of the common law principles of liability of secondary parties for the consequences of acts carried out by a principal. A person was liable as a principal for his intended acts or threats of violence or where he was aware that his conduct might be violent or threaten violence. It followed that the 'aggregation' permitted by s 3(2) was not for the purposes of making an individual participant liable for the acts and threats of other participants, but it was for the different purposes of determining whether a person of reasonable firmness present at the scene would be in fear for his personal safety. The conviction for manslaughter would be quashed. The conviction for affray was not unsafe. Accordingly, the appeal would be allowed in part.

R v Carey [2006] EWCA Crim 17, [2006] All ER (D) 189 (Jan) (Court of Appeal: Dyson LJ, Tomlinson and Smith JJ). *R v Church* [1965] 2 All ER 72 followed. *DPP v Newbury* [1977] AC 500, HL; *R v Larkin* [1943] KB 174, CCA; *R v Roberts* (1971) 56 Cr App Rep 95, CA; *R v Dawson* (1985) 81 Cr App Rep 150, CA (1985 Abr para 553); and *R v Watson* [1989] 2 All ER 865, CA (1989 Abr para 464), considered.

864 Manslaughter—victim committing suicide after abuse—psychological injury

The defendant was charged with manslaughter and wounding, contrary to the Offences against the Person Act 1861 s 20. The deceased, the defendant's wife, had committed suicide. After her death, evidence emerged which suggested that she had been subjected to various forms of physical and psychological abuse from her husband. The prosecution case was that the final assault on her, on the evening on which she committed suicide, had triggered the suicide. On the basis of the evidence on which it relied, the prosecution conceded that no reasonable jury could be satisfied to the criminal standard that the deceased had suffered from any recognised psychiatric illness. Accordingly, the prosecution case depended on the submission that psychological injury without any recognised psychiatric illness was capable of constituting 'bodily harm' within the meaning of ss 18, 20 and 47. The judge ruled that there was no basis on which a reasonable jury, properly directed, could convict the defendant of either manslaughter or unlawful wounding. The prosecution applied for leave to appeal against the judge's ruling under the Criminal Justice Act 2003 s 58. The court considered whether the condition described by experts, expressly said not to amount to a recognisable or identifiable psychiatric illness, was capable of amounting to actual or grievous bodily harm for the purposes of the 1861 Act. *Held*, it was established law that psychiatric illness could amount to grievous or actual bodily harm. As to manslaughter, as a matter of law, the prosecution of a spouse, partner, or indeed any other individual whose unlawful conduct caused a recognisable psychiatric illness such as, for example, post-traumatic stress disorder, or reactive depression, with resulting suicide, subject always to the issues of causation, was not excluded from the ambit of the offence. However, it was settled and clear law that the phrase actual bodily harm was capable of including psychiatric injury, but it did not include mere emotions, nor did it include, as such, states of mind that were not themselves evidence of some identifiable clinical condition. The line identified in the authorities had been consistently applied. The logical conclusion of the prosecution's argument was that a blurring of that line should be permitted, but to do so would go beyond the well-understood principles by which the common law had developed incrementally and logically. In any event, the extension sought by the prosecution would introduce a significant element of uncertainty about the true ambit of the relevant legal principles to which the concept of 'bodily harm' in the 1861 Act applied, which would be compounded by the inevitable problems of conflating medical opinion in such a consistently developing area of expertise. It followed that by adhering to the principle of recognisable psychiatric illness, while some medical experts might be concerned with the way in which the definitions were arrived at, the issue which was required to be addressed could be clearly understood and those responsible for advising the prosecution and defence could approach their cases with an appropriate degree of certainty. Accordingly, the judge's ruling would be confirmed and the defendant acquitted.

R v Dhaliwal (appeal under s 58 of the Criminal Justice Act 2003) [2006] EWCA Crim 1139, [2006] All ER (D) 236 (May) (Court of Appeal: Sir Igor Judge P, Henriques and Fulford JJ). *McLoughlin v O'Brian* [1983] 1 AC 410, HL (1982 Abr para 2132); *R v Ireland; R v Burstow* [1998] AC 147, HL (1997 Abr para 929); and *R v Chan-Fook* [1994] 2 All ER 552, CA (1993 Abr para 834), considered.

865   Money laundering—exceptions—overseas conduct defence

The Proceeds of Crime Act 2002 (Money Laundering: Exceptions to Overseas Conduct Defence) Order 2006, SI 2006/1070 (in force on 15 May 2006), sets out exceptions to the defences in the Proceeds of Crime Act 2002 ss 327(2A), 328(3), 329(2A), and prescribes conduct which would be an offence punishable by imprisonment for a maximum term in excess of 12 months in any part of the United kingdom, subject to the specified exceptions.

866   Money laundering—failure to disclose—defence—extension

The Proceeds of Crime Act 2002 and Money Laundering Regulations 2003 (Amendment) Order 2006, SI 2006/308 (in force on 21 February 2006), amends the Proceeds of Crime Act 2002 s 330 and the Money Laundering Regulations 2003, SI 2003/3075, by extending the range of persons to whom the defence to a charge of failing to make a relevant disclosure applies so that it includes relevant professional advisers and providing a defence for a person who is employed by, or in partnership with, a professional legal advisor or other relevant professional advisor to provide assistance or support.

867   Money laundering—offences—disclosure—suspicion of engagement in money laundering

The applicant company had given instructions to the defendant bank to transfer money from its account. The defendant refused to follow the instructions on the ground that it would become concerned in an arrangement which it suspected would facilitate the use of criminal property by the applicant and made an authorised disclosure to the customs authorities under the Proceeds of Crime Act 2002 s 338. Its application for an injunction was unsuccessful, and it appealed. *Held*, it was not a breach of contract for the defendant to refuse to honour its mandate where to do so would be a criminal offence, and there could be no invasion, or threat of an invasion, of a legal right on the part of the defendant as was required before the applicant could apply for an injunction. In such a case, there was no issue that could be tried in any later legal proceedings and any application for an interlocutory mandatory injunction had to be refused. In civil cases, the definition of suspicion in criminal cases, that the person suspecting had to think that there was a possibility which was more than fanciful that the relevant facts existed, should also apply. While interfering in the performance of the contract of mandate between a bank and its customer was a serious matter, Parliament had considered that a limited interference was to be tolerated in preference to allowing money laundering. Accordingly, the appeal would be dismissed.

K Ltd v National Westminster Bank plc [2006] EWCA Civ 1039, [2006] 4 All ER 907 (Court of Appeal: Ward, Laws and Longmore LJJ).

868   Murder—defence—provocation—question for jury

See *R v James; R v Karimi*, para 2323.

869   Murder—defence—self-defence—test—compatibility with human rights

Armed police officers shot and killed a man after he appeared to be about to shoot at them with a gun. The gun was later found to be a cigarette lighter in the shape of a gun. The Crown Prosecution Service decided not to prosecute the officers. At a subsequent inquest into the death, the coroner decided that the evidence could not reasonably support a verdict of unlawful killing. He therefore directed the jury that it could reach either an open verdict or a verdict of lawful killing. He stated what the jury needed to decide in order to reach either verdict, which included a direction that, in order for the jury to bring in a verdict of lawful killing, it had to decide that the officers honestly believed that they were using such force as was reasonably necessary in all the circumstances. The jury returned a verdict of lawful killing. The claimant applied for judicial review of that decision, arguing that, in order to comply with the right to life guaranteed by the European Convention on Human Rights art 2(2), the common law test for self-defence required modification when applied to state agents such that the defence would be made out only where the use of force was no more than absolutely necessary. *Held*, the reasonableness test directed by the defendant was not in practice any different from the test as applied by the European Court of Human Rights to determine whether there had been a violation of art 2. To apply a different test when considering the actions of state agents would inappropriately fetter their actions to the detriment of their own safety and that of the public. In the circumstances, the defendant's direction to the jury had been appropriate. Accordingly, the application would be dismissed.

R (on the application of Bennett) v Inner South London Coroner [2006] EWHC 196 (Admin), (2006) 170 JP Jo 109 (Queen's Bench Division: Collins J). Application 18984/91 *McCann v United Kingdom* (1995) 21 EHRR 97, ECtHR (1995 Abr para 1589), considered.

870 Murder—diminished responsibility—abnormality of mind—consumption of alcohol

The defendant was charged with murder. At his trial the defendant raised the defence of diminished responsibility pursuant to the Homicide Act 1957 s 2(1). The judge had issued two questions for the jury to answer. The first concerned whether the defence had satisfied them that it was more likely than not that if the defendant had not taken drink he would not have killed. If the answer to that question was 'yes', the second question was whether the defence had satisfied the jury that it was more likely than not that if the defendant had not taken drink he would have been under diminished responsibility when he killed. If the answer to the first question was 'no', the verdict would be guilty. If the answer to the second question was 'no', the verdict would also be guilty, but if it was 'yes', the verdict would be not guilty of murder, but guilty of manslaughter by reason of diminished responsibility. The defendant was convicted and sentenced, with a tariff set at ten years' imprisonment. Subsequently, the defendant was granted leave to appeal against his conviction and sentence. The defendant submitted that the judge had incorrectly directed the jury as to the effect of alcohol as a factor for consideration in the defence of diminished responsibility. *Held,* in *R v Dietschmann*, the House of Lords had stated that s 2(1) meant that, if a defendant satisfied the jury that, notwithstanding the alcohol he had consumed and its effect on him, his abnormality of mind substantially impaired his mental responsibility for his acts in doing the killing, the jury should find him not guilty of murder but guilty of manslaughter. Since the law on the issue at the time of trial was as explained in *R v Dietschmann*, the misdirection by the judge rendered the verdict of murder unsafe. Therefore, since the court in *R v Dietschmann* had not stated any new principle of law and had only restated what the law was before the Court of Appeal had incorrectly approved the two questions raised following the judgment in *R v Gittens*, the defendant's conviction for murder would be quashed and a conviction for manslaughter substituted. Accordingly, the appeal would be allowed.

R v Hendy [2006] EWCA Crim 819, [2006] All ER (D) 194 (Apr) (Court of Appeal: Gage LJ, Forbes J and Dame Heather Steel). *R v Dietschmann* [2003] UKHL 10, [2003] 1 All ER 897(2003 Abr para 748); and *R v Gittens* [1984] 3 All ER 252 (1984 Abr para 564) considered.

871 Murder—soliciting murder—soliciting outside the jurisdiction—person solicited not a British national

The Offences against the Person Act 1861 s 4 provides that any person who solicits, encourages, persuades, or endeavours to persuade, or proposes to any person, to murder any other person, whether he be a subject of Her Majesty or not, and whether he be within the Queen's dominions or not, is guilty of a misdemeanour.

The defendant was an Imam of a mosque in London. Between 1997 and 2000 he made a number of speeches at the mosque, tape recordings of which were found in the defendant's possession, and he was found to be in possession of the 'Afghani Jihad Encyclopaedia'. The defendant was charged with soliciting to murder. At trial, the defendant submitted that no offence could be committed under the 1861 Act s 4 in respect of soliciting murder outside the jurisdiction unless the person solicited was a British national. That contention was rejected and the defendant was convicted. On his appeal, *held*, s 4 created inchoate offences in relation to murder that had proved to be an exception to that which was recognised to be the general position at common law, namely, that an inchoate offence was not committed unless the conduct planned or incited could, if carried out, be indictable in England. It followed that an offence would be committed contrary to s 4 in respect of soliciting murder outside the jurisdiction where the person solicited was not a British national. Accordingly, the appeal would be dismissed.

R v Hamza [2006] EWCA Crim 2918, [2006] All ER (D) 390 (Nov) (Court of Appeal: Lord Phillips of Worth Matravers CJ, Penry-Davey and Pitchford JJ). *R v Bernard* (1858) 22 JP 257; *Board of Trade v Owen* [1957] AC 602, HL; and *Treacy v DPP* [1971] AC 537, HL, considered.

872 Offences against the person—actual bodily harm—psychiatric injury

The defendant cut off the victim's pony tail without her consent. He was charged with assault thereby occasioning her actual bodily harm, contrary to the Offences against the Person Act 1861 s 47. The justices found that the cutting of the victim's hair did constitute an assault, but that there was no actual bodily harm as there was no bruising, bleeding or cutting of the skin and no expert evidence regarding psychological or psychiatric harm. They accordingly ruled that an essential element of the offence was missing and that there was no case to answer. The prosecution appealed by way of case stated. *Held*, actual bodily harm was not limited to injury but also extended to hurt and damage. 'Actual' meant that bodily harm should not be so trivial as to be without significance. It was not limited to harm to the skin, flesh and bones but it applied to all parts of the body. Hair was part of the body and intrinsic to each individual. An individual's hair was relevant to his or her autonomy. Even if it was scientifically and medically treated as dead tissue, the part of the hair which was attached to the scalp fell within the meaning of bodily in the term 'actual bodily harm'. The cutting of the victim's hair without consent constituted actual bodily harm for the purposes of s 47 and the case would be remitted to the justices with a direction to continue the hearing. Accordingly, the appeal would be allowed.

DPP v Smith [2006] EWHC 94 (Admin), [2006] 1 WLR 1571 (Queen's Bench Division: Sir Igor Judge P and Cresswell J). *R v Donovan* [1934] 2 KB 498; *R v Chan-Fook* [1994] 2 All ER 552 (1993 Abr para 834); *T v DPP* [2003] EWHC 266 (Admin), [2003] Crim LR 622 considered.

873   Offence of strict liability—statutory offence—low flying

See *R v Jackson*, para 251.

874   Public order—anti-social behaviour—removal of child from dispersal area—use of force

The Anti-social Behaviour Act 2003 s 30(6) provides that if, between the hours of 9 pm and 6 am, a constable in uniform finds a person in any public place in the relevant locality who he has reasonable grounds for believing is under the age of 16 and is not under the effective control of a parent or a responsible person aged 18 or over, he may remove the person to the person's place of residence.

The claimant sought judicial review of the defendant police commissioner's decision to authorise police officers to remove by force persons under the age of 16 from certain dispersal areas. The application was allowed on the basis that the 2003 Act s 30(6) authorised a constable to use police resources to take a person under 16 home if he was willing to be taken home, but did not entitle a constable to use force. The defendant appealed. *Held*, the word 'remove' naturally and compellingly meant 'take away using reasonable force if necessary'. This was not a matter of implication, but of meaning. If the word did not have that meaning, the power would, in the context, be pointless. The police did not need an express power merely to use their resources to take a child or young person home if he was willing to be taken home in the circumstances contemplated by s 30(6). In the context of a power given to constables, the word 'remove' connoted the use of reasonable coercion, if necessary. Section 30(6) did not have a curfew effect as it did not empower a constable to remove children arbitrarily simply because they were in a designated dispersal area at night. The constable was only entitled to act for a purpose for which the power was conferred, which was to protect children under the age of 16 within a designated dispersal area at night from the physical and social risks of anti-social behaviour by others, and to prevent children from themselves participating in anti-social behaviour within a designated dispersal area at night. Further, the discretionary power could only be used if, in the light of its purpose, it was reasonable to do so. Accordingly, the appeal would be allowed.

R (on the application of W) v Metropolitan Police Comr [2006] EWCA Civ 458, [2006] 3 All ER 458 (Court of Appeal: Sir Igor Judge P, May and Wall LJJ). Decision of Queen's Bench Divisional Court [2005] 3 All ER 749 (2005 Abr para 994) reversed.

875   Public order—anti-social behaviour in public place—direction to disperse—protest

Various members of a local Sikh community decided to organise protests against the performance of a certain play at a nearby theatre, as they believed the production to be offensive to their religion. Initially these were peaceful protests outside the theatre, but on one occasion more than 20 protesters made an attempt to enter the theatre. In reliance on two anti-social behaviour authorisation notices which were already in force in relation to the area, the police issued a verbal dispersal notice under the Anti-social Behaviour Act 2003 s 30(4) to the protesters. The claimant refused to comply with the notice, and he was arrested and subsequently cautioned. He sought judicial review of the police decision to issue the dispersal notice, contending that it was outside the power granted by the two authorisation notices. One of those notices was aimed at seasonal travellers rather than protesters, and the other was aimed at skateboarders. The application was dismissed, and the claimant appealed. *Held*, it was compellingly clear that Parliament intended that the dispersal regime under s 30 should apply to protests. It was only when the behaviour of a group of people moved beyond legitimate protest and into the realms of behaviour that caused actual or likely intimidation, harassment, alarm and distress that an officer could use an authorisation to direct the group to disperse. Any validly made authorisation could be used to empower police officers to issue dispersal directions to a group of people acting in an anti-social manner of a kind not contemplated at the time the authorisation was made. It simply could not be the case that police officers, faced with a volatile and threatening situation, were entitled to disperse drunken revellers who behaved in an anti-social fashion but not that group of protesters who were behaving in a potentially more alarming anti-social fashion. Accordingly, the appeal would be dismissed.

R (on the application of Singh) v Chief Constable of West Midlands Police [2006] EWCA Civ 1118, [2006] All ER (D) 449 (Jul) (Court of Appeal: Wall, Wilson and Hallett LJJ).

876 Public order—anti-social behaviour in public place—direction to disperse—validity

The Anti-social Behaviour Act 2003 s 30(1), (2) provides that where a relevant officer has reasonable grounds for believing that any members of the public have been intimidated, harassed, alarmed or distressed as a result of the presence or behaviour of groups in public places and that anti-social behaviour is a significant and persistent problem, he may give an authorisation that certain powers, conferred on a constable in uniform, are to be exercisable. The powers so conferred include the power to give a direction requiring the persons in the group to disperse: s 30(4)(a). An authorisation must specify the grounds on which it is given: s 31(1)(c)(ii).

A police superintendent issued an authorisation under the 2003 Act s 30(2), which stated that he had reasonable grounds to believe that members of the public had been intimidated, harassed, alarmed or distressed as a result of the presence or behaviour of groups in a specified area. Police officers encountered a large group of young people who were shouting, drinking alcohol and chasing each other about. An officer decided that he had reason to believe that the presence of the group was likely to intimidate, harass, alarm or distress members of the public and directed them to disperse. Some members of the group, including the claimant, failed to disperse and consequently she was arrested. At her trial the claimant submitted that the authorisation was invalid because it failed to state on its face the grounds on which it had been made. The claimant was convicted and she appealed by way of case stated. The question for the High Court was whether s 31(1)(c)(ii) required that the grounds on which an authorisation was given had to appear in the body of the instrument of authorisation. *Held*, the words 'must specify' in s 31(1)(c)(ii) was a mandatory requirement and required the officer who gave the authorisation to specify the grounds on which it was made in the authorisation itself. It was not sufficient for the authorisation simply to state the officer's belief; it had to state the grounds of belief. The purpose of the provision was to ensure that there was a properly thought out basis for making the authorisation and that that basis was expressed in a written form, which could later be examined and challenged. Accordingly, the appeal would be allowed.

Sierny v DPP [2006] EWHC 716 (Admin), (2006) 170 JP 697 (Queen's Bench Division: Hallett LJ and Nelson J).

877 Public order—causing harassment, alarm or distress—need for conduct to have been seen or heard

The defendant was charged with offences of disorderly conduct, contrary to the Public Order Act 1986 s 5(1)(a), and the racially aggravated version of that offence, contrary to the Crime and Disorder Act 1998 s 31(1)(c). It was alleged that, when two police officers had attended premises in the middle of the night, the defendant had used derogatory language about a particular black woman. The defendant had shouted and swore while being removed from the premises and after she had been taken outside into the street. The district judge found that the two police officers, ambulance crew, the householder and several neighbours were near enough to hear the racially abusive language, and that anybody hearing such language, black or white, was likely to be caused distress by it. He found the defendant guilty of racially aggravated conduct. She appealed against that decision, contending that, for an offence under the 1986 Act s 5(1)(a) to be proved, the words had actually to have been heard, and that the requirement under the 1998 Act s 28(1)(b) that an offence was racially aggravated where it was motivated by hostility to a member of a particular group was not satisfied. *Held*, for an offence under the 1986 Act s 5(1)(a) to be proved, there had to be evidence that someone was able to see or hear the conduct complained of, not that the conduct had actually been heard or seen. In the light of the judge's finding that the two police officers, the householder and neighbours had been able to hear the defendant's abusive language, her conduct fell within s 5(1)(a). Moreover, given the defendant's use of the words 'fucking nigger' and 'fucking coon bitch', there could be no doubt that her conduct had been motivated by hostility to at least one member of a racial group, sufficient to amount to racial aggravation under the 1988 Act s 28(1)(b). Accordingly, the appeal would be dismissed.

Taylor v DPP [2006] EWHC 1202, (2006) 170 JP Jo 485 (Queen's Bench Division: Keene LJ and Jack J).

878 Public order—demonstration in the vicinity of Parliament—demonstration starting before commencement of legislation

The Serious Organised Crime and Police Act 2005 s 132(1) provides that any person who organises, takes part in or carries on a demonstration in a public place in the designated area is guilty of an offence if, when the demonstration starts, authorisation for the demonstration has not been given under s 134(2). The Public Order Act 1986 s 14 does not apply in relation to a public assembly which is also a demonstration in a public place in the designated area: 2005 Act s 132(6).

The claimant had for several years been demonstrating in Parliament Square against the government's foreign policy towards Iraq. The local council unsuccessfully sought an injunction to remove him on the basis that he was obstructing the highway. The 2005 Act was subsequently enacted, which, by virtue of ss 132–138, made it a criminal offence to demonstrate in the area without proper authorisation. The claimant sought a declaration that the regime set out in ss 132–138 did not apply to him so that he did not need to seek authorisation for continuing his protest. The court made the declaration and the defendant appealed, contending that, on the true construction of s 132(1), the regime applied to the claimant. *Held*, construing the 2005 Act in its context and having regard to the plain intention of Parliament as deduced from the Parliamentary language, including the disapplication of the 1986 Act s 14, the 2005 Act s 132(1) extended to demonstrations actually starting before the commencement of the 2005 Act as surely as to those starting after. Those starting before, like the claimant's, were deemed to start at commencement; and in such cases the words 'when the demonstration starts' in s 132(1) referred to the time of commencement. The 1986 Act s 14 gave the police power to impose conditions in relation to demonstrations generally, provided that they consisted of two or more people. The purpose of the 2005 Act s 132(6) was to replace the 1986 Act s 14 with the provisions of the 2005 Act ss 132–138 in the case of demonstrations in the designated area, whenever they started. It was inconceivable that Parliament would have repealed the 1986 Act s 14 with respect to demonstrations which had already started, if it did not intend to apply the new provisions to such demonstrations. Accordingly, the appeal would be allowed.

R (on the application of Haw) v Secretary of State for the Home Department [2006] EWCA Civ 532, [2006] All ER (D) 94 (May) (Court of Appeal: Sir Anthony Clarke MR, Laws and Hallett LJJ). Decision of Queen's Bench Divisional Court [2005] EWHC 2061 (Admin), [2006] QB 359 (2005 Abr para 2960) reversed.

879   Public order—outraging public decency—need for multiple witnesses—conduct captured on closed-circuit television

The defendant was charged with the common law offence of outraging public decency by performing an act of a lewd, obscene and disgusting nature in the early hours of the morning in a bank foyer. The public had access to the foyer by way of a swipe card in order to access cash machines after the bank had closed, and passers-by could see in. The prosecution relied on the fact that the bank manager, when she reviewed the overnight closed-circuit television footage from the foyer, saw the defendant engaged in an act of oral sex with an unidentified woman. The prosecution conceded that no member of the public had actually witnessed the act when it was being committed, but submitted that the witnessing of the event on the video was sufficient to satisfy the requirements of the offence. The defendant was convicted and, on his appeal, *held*, for the common law offence of outraging public decency to be made out, the act had to be witnessed by more than one person. In the instant case, there had been no passers-by, meaning the only person to see the incident was the bank manager, by means of the closed-circuit footage. It followed that there were insufficient witnesses to satisfy the requirements of the common law offence and, accordingly, the appeal would be allowed.

Rose v DPP [2006] EWHC 852 (Admin), (2007) 171 JP Jo 57 (Queen's Bench Division: Stanley Burnton J).

880   Public order—public procession—requirement to give notification—monthly bicycle ride without fixed route

The Public Order Act 1986 s 11(1) provides that written notice must be given of any proposal to hold a public procession intended (1) to demonstrate support for, or opposition to, the views or actions of any person or body of persons, (2) to publicise a cause or campaign, or (3) to mark or commemorate an event, unless it is not reasonably practicable to give any advance notice of the procession. Section 11(1) does not apply where the procession is one commonly or customarily held in the police area (or areas) in which it is proposed to be held.

For several years monthly protests in the form of bicycle rides took place in London. The rides had no fixed route, but always started from the same location. The defendant wrote to the participants informing them that their 'cycle protests' were not lawful because no organiser had provided the police with the necessary notification pursuant to the 1986 Act s 11. Proceedings were then brought by the claimant as nominal party to clarify whether notice of future rides was in fact required. *Held*, a procession with no planned route and no organiser could be subject to a requirement to give notice. The prior existence of a planned route or an organiser was not a condition for the giving of notice. Similarly, its absence did not render the giving of notice 'not reasonably practicable' within the meaning of s 11(1). That provision concerned the practicalities of timing rather than the feasibility of giving the required details. Parliament had assumed the existence of a route and an organiser and, for better or for worse, there were requirements consequent on that assumption in the legislation. For the purposes of s 11(2), the single question was whether the event, defined by its collective intention, was commonly or customarily held in the material police area; the absence of a planned route had no legal consequences if notice of the procession was not required. Either the denial of a collective intention falling within s 11(1) or the continuity of a qualifying intention needed to attract the protection of s 11(2) would afford a defence to an offence under s 11, but it was hard to see how both could do so at the same time. Moreover, it was not open to the defendant or to the courts to treat the earlier rides as having themselves been unlawful, with the result that the procession in question should not be regarded as commonly or customarily held for the purposes of s 11(2). Judgment would be given accordingly.

Kay v Metropolitan Police Comr [2006] EWHC 1536 (Admin), [2006] RTR 469 (Queen's Bench Division: Sedley LJ and Gray J).

881 Proceeds of crime—assisting another to retain the benefit of criminal conduct—direction to jury—meaning of suspicion

The defendant was charged with assisting another person to retain the benefit of criminal conduct, knowing or suspecting that the other person was or had been engaged in criminal conduct, contrary to the Criminal Justice Act 1988 s 93A(1)(a). In his summing-up, the judge directed the jury as to whether the prosecution had proved that the defendant had suspected that her husband was engaged in criminal conduct or had benefited from it, dwelling in particular on the difference between 'suspecting' and 'knowing'. The defendant was convicted and, appealing against her conviction, argued that the judge had misdirected the jury. *Held*, in the context of the 1988 Act, the essential element in the word 'suspect' was that the defendant had to think that there was a possibility, which was more than fanciful, that the relevant facts existed. A vague feeling of unease would not suffice, but the statute did not require the suspicion to be targeted on specific facts, or based on reasonable grounds. Therefore, for the purpose of s 93A(1)(a), the prosecution had to prove that the defendant's acts of facilitating another person's retention of the proceeds of criminal conduct had been done by a defendant who had thought that there was a possibility, which was more than fanciful, that the other person had been engaged in or had benefited from criminal conduct. Where a judge considered it appropriate to assist the jury with the word 'suspecting', a direction along such lines would be accurate. The only possible qualification would be where a defendant had entertained a suspicion but, on further thought, had honestly dismissed it from his mind as being unworthy or as being outweighed by other considerations. In such a case a careful direction to the jury might be required, however, before such a direction was necessary there would have to be some reason to suppose that the defendant had gone through some such thought process. In the present case, the judge had technically misdirected the jury. However, the misdirection was not such as to render the conviction unsafe, and accordingly, the appeal would be dismissed.

R v Da Silva [2006] EWCA Crim 1654, [2006] 4 All ER 900 (Court of Appeal: Longmore LJ, Gloster J and Judge Diehl QC).

1988 Act s 93A replaced by Proceeds of Crime Act 2002 s 328.

882 Public order—racially aggravated offence—defence—police cell not a home or other living accommodation

The Public Order Act 1986 s 8 defines a dwelling as any structure or part of a structure occupied as a person's home or as other living accommodation.

The defendant was charged with intending to cause racially aggravated harassment, alarm or distress, contrary to the Crime and Disorder Act 1998 s 31(1)(b). The judge ruled that a police cell could be a dwelling, as defined by the Public Order Act 1986 s 8, for the purposes of s 4A, and consequently the 1998 Act s 31(1)(b), and found that the offence was not therefore made out. The prosecution appealed under the Criminal Justice Act 2003 s 58. *Held*, the 1998 Act s 31 made particular reference to the 1986 Act s 4A so that the issue to be decided was whether an offence under s 4A could be committed in a prison cell. An offence under s 4A could not be committed where the relevant words were used by a person inside a dwelling. It was argued that a police cell came within the meaning of 'other living accommodation' in s 8 because there were features of a person's accommodation in such a cell which were similar to a place where someone lived. However, a police cell was not a home, nor was it living accommodation where a person lived. It followed that a person detained in custody did not occupy a police cell as living accommodation and the judge had erred in this regard. Accordingly, the appeal would be allowed.

R v Francis (2007) Times, 17 January (Court of Appeal: Moses LJ, Goldring J and Judge Martin Stephens).

883 Putting a person in fear of violence—no case to answer—alternative charge of harassment

The defendant was charged with putting a person in fear of violence, contrary to the Protection from Harassment Act 1997 s 4. The judge ruled that there was no case to answer in respect of the charge, but decided that there was a case to answer in respect of the statutory alternative of harassment under s 2, which was a summary offence. It was common ground that it had not been permissible to add a count to the indictment alleging harassment contrary to s 2, as that offence was not one which could, by virtue of the Criminal Justice Act 1988 s 40, be added to the indictment as an alternative. However, by virtue of the 1997 Act s 4(5), the jury would have been permitted to return a verdict of not guilty of the offence under s 4 but guilty of the s 2 offence. The judge did not immediately invite the jury to find the defendant not guilty of the s 4 offence, but he informed them that, as a matter of law, they could not convict the defendant of that charge. He also directed them that it was open to them to convict the defendant of the statutory alternative. The defence case was heard and, in due course, the jury acquitted the defendant of blackmail and, on the judge's direction, of the s 4 offence. However, the jury convicted the defendant of the s 2 offence. The defendant appealed, submitting that the judge had not been permitted to take the course that he had in permitting the jury to return the verdict of guilty of the statutory alternative. *Held*, where a judge upheld a submission of no case to answer in respect of a count charging an offence contrary to s 4 but declined immediately to direct the jury to enter a not guilty verdict or to take a verdict in respect of that count, it was permissible for the case to continue with the jury, once in retirement, to deliberate as to the alternative offence of harassment and to return a not guilty verdict on the judge's direction in respect of the s 4 offence and to convict the defendant in relation to the s 2 offence. A verdict by the jury was no less a true verdict where it was returned on the proper direction of the judge rather than following deliberation on the evidence in retirement. Moreover, there was nothing in the authorities to support the proposition that, once a judge had found no case to answer on a count on an indictment, he was obliged immediately to stop the case and was prevented from permitting the jury to consider the alternative offence. By s 4(5), Parliament had given the jury the power to return a verdict of guilty on an alternative offence. It could not be said that the correct procedure in such circumstances would be for the judge to withdraw the count in its entirety and to leave the prosecution to start the prosecution all over again in relation to the summary only matter. Accordingly, the appeal would be dismissed.

R v Livesey [2006] All ER (D) 241 (Dec) (Court of Appeal: Hallett LJ, Mackay J and the Recorder of Birmingham). *R v Carson* (1990) 92 Cr App Rep 236, CA, applied. *R v Plain* [1967] 1 All ER 614, CA, distinguished. *R v Galbraith* [1981] 2 All ER 1060, CA (1981 Abr para 766), explained.

884   Racial and Religious Hatred Act 2006

The Racial and Religious Hatred Act 2006 makes provision about offences involving stirring up hatred against persons on racial or religious grounds. The Act received the royal assent on 16 February 2006 and comes into force on a day to be appointed.

Section 1, Schedule add provisions to the Public Order Act 1986 so as to (1) create new offences of stirring up religious hatred which involve the use of words or behaviour or display of written material, publishing or distributing written material, the public performance of a play, distributing, showing or playing a recording and broadcasting or including a programme in a programme service; (2) create a new offence of possession of threatening material with a view to using it in a way that is intended to stir up religious hatred; (3) provide that the offences of stirring up religious hatred are not intended to limit discussion, criticism or expressions of antipathy, dislike, ridicule or insult or abuse of particular religions or belief systems or lack of religion or of beliefs and practices of those who hold such beliefs or to apply to proselytisation, evangelism or the seeking to convert people to a particular belief or to cease holding a belief; (4) make it clear that the Act does not apply to fair and accurate reports of anything done in the United Kingdom or Scottish Parliaments or the fair and accurate contemporaneous reports of judicial proceedings; (5) provide that no prosecution for the offences of stirring up religious hatred will proceed without the consent of the Attorney General; and (6) provide that the maximum penalty for conviction for an offence of stirring up religious hatred is seven years' imprisonment. The Police and Criminal Evidence Act 1984 s 24A is amended so as to exempt the offences of stirring up racial or religious hatred from the power of citizens' arrest: 2006 Act s 2. Section 3 deals with commencement, short title and extent.

885   Regulation of investigatory powers—communications data—acquisition and disclosure—additional functions

The Regulation of Investigatory Powers (Communications Data) (Additional Functions and Amendment) Order 2006, SI 2006/1878 (in force on 26 July 2006), specifies additional purposes as purposes falling within the Regulation of Investigatory Powers Act 2000 s 22(2) so as to enable a designated person who believes that it is necessary on the grounds specified to obtain communications data to authorise the acquisition of and require the disclosure of that data. The order also makes consequential amendments to the Regulation of Investigatory Powers (Communications Data) Order 2003, SI 2003/3172.

886   Regulation of investigatory powers—directed surveillance—covert human intelligence sources

The Regulation of Investigatory Powers (Directed Surveillance and Covert Human Intelligence Sources) (Amendment) Order 2006, SI 2006/1874 (in force on 26 July 2006), amends the Regulation of Investigatory Powers Act 2000 Sch 1, which specifies public authorities which have the power to grant authorisations for the carrying out of directed surveillance and authorisations for the conduct or use of a covert human intelligence source. The order also amends the 2003 Order, SI 2003/3171, by adding and removing entries relating to individuals holding certain specified offices, ranks or positions in relevant public authorities who are entitled to authorise directed surveillance and authorise the use and conduct of covert human intelligence sources.

887 Road traffic offences

See ROAD TRAFFIC.

888 Sexual offence—causing a child to watch a sexual act—sexual gratification—temporal element

The Sexual Offences Act 2003 s 12(1) provides that a person commits an offence if, for the purpose of obtaining sexual gratification, he intentionally causes a person he believes to be under the age of 16 to watch a third person engaging in sexual activity, or to look at an image of any person engaging in sexual activity.

While the complainant, aged 13, was at his friend's house, the defendant, who was in his 30s and who also lived at the house, gave him alcohol and cannabis and showed him a pornographic film. When the complainant and the defendant were subsequently alone, the defendant touched the complainant's penis. At his trial for causing a child to watch sexual activity, contrary to the 2003 Act s 12, and sexual activity with a child, contrary to s 9, the judge directed the jury in relation to the s 12 offence that it would have to be satisfied that the defendant had showed the images for the purpose of obtaining sexual gratification, either by enjoying seeing the complainant looking at the images, or with a view to putting the complainant in the mood to provide sexual gratification to the defendant later. The defendant was convicted and, on his appeal, he contended that the judge's direction had been unlawful in so far as he had stated that conduct designed to secure future sexual gratification was relevant to the s 12 offence, whereas in fact such behaviour was properly the province of s 14. *Held*, on the proper construction of s 12, there was no temporal criterion for the obtaining by the defendant of sexual gratification from causing a child to watch a sexual act or to view sexual images. There was nothing in the language of s 12 which stated that the offence could only be committed where the display of the relevant material or act was contemporaneous or simultaneous to the sexual gratification. Moreover, the form which sexual gratification could take was not defined and, provided that the purpose was indeed sexual gratification, that might take any of the myriad forms which sexual gratification could take. There was nothing in s 12 which required that the sexual gratification had to be immediate or could not extend to a longer plan in obtaining further gratification in the event of the obtaining a sexual act with the child. In the instant case, where the showing of the pornography and the plying of the complainant with alcohol was the precursor to sexual activity with the complainant, the conclusion that the defendant had shown the pornography with the purpose of obtaining sexual gratification was inevitable. Accordingly, the appeal would be dismissed.

R v Abdullahi [2006] All ER (D) 334 (Jul) (Court of Appeal: Sir Igor Judge P, Gray and McCombe JJ).

889 Sexual offence—rape—consent—deception—HIV status

The Sexual Offences Act 2003 s 74 provides that, for the purposes of the offence of rape, a person consents if he agrees by choice, and has the freedom and capacity to make that choice. Where the defendant did the relevant act and intentionally deceived the complainant as to the nature or purpose of that act, it is to be conclusively presumed that the complainant did not consent to the relevant act and that the defendant did not believe that the complainant consented to the relevant act: s 76.

The complainant alleged that defendant had raped her. Following his arrest, the defendant informed the police that he had previously been diagnosed as being HIV positive, and admitted that he had not informed the complainant of his HIV status. At his trial, the judge allowed the prosecution to adduce evidence of the defendant's HIV status, ruling that, when considering whether the complainant had consented or whether the defendant had reasonably believed her to be consenting, the jury would have to be told of the statutory definition of rape in the 2003 Act s 74. He held that the fact that the defendant had not informed the complainant of his HIV status was a matter which the jury was entitled to take into account when deciding whether the complainant had consented or whether the defendant had reasonably believed her to be consenting. The defendant was convicted and, on his appeal, he contended that the judge had erred in allowing the prosecution to adduce the evidence of his HIV status, because such evidence was irrelevant to the issues before the jury and its admission was wrong in law. *Held*, the fact that a defendant who was HIV positive might not have disclosed his HIV status to a person with whom he had had sexual intercourse was not, in law, a matter which could in any way be relevant to the issue of consent to sexual activity within the meaning of s 74. The 2003 Act did not expressly concern itself with the full range of deceptions other than those identified in s 76, let alone any implied deception arising from the failure to disclose HIV status. While there might be good reasons for considering the extent to which it was right to criminalise sexual activity between those with sexually transmissible diseases who did not disclose that fact to their partners, the question of whether such activity should give rise to charges of rape or indecent assault rather than some tailor-made charges in relation to such activity was a matter for public debate. It followed that the admission of the defendant's HIV status was so prejudicial that it should not have gone before the jury. Accordingly, the appeal would be allowed.

R v B [2006] All ER (D) 173 (Oct) (Court of Appeal: Latham LJ, Henriques and Gloster JJ). *R v Dica* [2004] EWCA Crim 1103, [2004] QB 1257 (2004 Abr para 792) followed.

890 Sexual offence—rape of child under thirteen—genuine belief that child over fourteen—offence of strict liability

The defendant, aged 15, was charged with rape of a child under 13, contrary to the Sexual Offences Act 2003 s 5. He pleaded guilty on the basis that the complainant had willingly agreed to have sexual intercourse and that he had believed her to be aged 15. He had been advised that, by reason of the fact that the complainant was under 13 at the relevant time, the offence was committed irrespective of consent, reasonable belief in consent, and a reasonable belief as to age. The defendant was sentenced to a 12-month detention and training order and was made subject to the notification requirements for a period of five years. He appealed against conviction and sentence. He contended that s 5 was incompatible with the right to a fair trial enshrined in the European Convention on Human Rights art 6. He also submitted that the effect of the prosecution, conviction and sentence constituted a disproportionate interference with his right to respect for private life, which breached art 8. *Held*, the 2003 Act s 5 was not incompatible with the Convention art 6. The content and interpretation of domestic substantive law was not engaged by art 6 and there was no requirement to read it down. A considerable weight of jurisprudence supported the submission that the Convention art 6(2) imposed no fetter on the right of a state to enact and enforce a crime of strict liability and that art 6(2) was concerned with the procedural fairness of a trial rather than with the substantive law that fell to be applied at trial. Legislation creating an absolute offence would not render the trial under which it was enforced unfair, let alone infringe the prescription of innocence under art 6(2). A judge should normally be able to ensure that there was no interference with the defendant's right under art 8. In the present case, the judge had not infringed the defendant's art 8 rights by proceeding to sentence him for his conviction under the 2003 Act s 5 and the appropriate course was to quash the detention and training order and to substitute a 12-month conditional discharge. Accordingly, the appeal against conviction would be dismissed and the appeal against sentence would be allowed.

R v G (*Secretary of State for the Home Department intervening*) [2006] EWCA Crim 821, [2006] 1 WLR 2052 (Court of Appeal: Lord Phillips of Worth Matravers CJ, Andrew Smith and Wilkie JJ). *B* (*A Minor*) *v DPP* [2000] 2 AC 428, HL (2000 Abr para 942), considered.

891 Sexual offence—sexual assault—consent—reasonable belief in consent—mistaken identity

See *A-G's Reference* (*No 79 of 2006*); *R v Whitta*, para 2576.

892 Terrorism—counter-terrorism powers—power randomly to stop and search— authorisation of power

The Terrorism Act 2000 s 44(2) provides that an authorisation authorises any constable in uniform to stop a pedestrian in a specified area or place and to search him, and s 44(3) provides that authorisation may only be given if the person giving it considers it expedient for the prevention of acts of terrorism.

The claimants had been stopped and searched by police under the 2000 Act s 44 while at a protest against an arms fair. They sought judicial review of the defendant, the Metropolitan Police Commissioner's decision to give an authorisation under s 44 and the Secretary of State's confirmation, contending that ss 44–47 breached the European Convention on Human Rights arts 5, 8, 10 and 11. The application was dismissed, and the claimants appealed following the dismissal of their appeal to the Court of Appeal. *Held*, the interpretation that the 2000 Act s 44(3) should only permit an authorisation where the decision-maker had reasonable grounds for considering that the powers were necessary and suitable for the prevention of terrorism was invalid as Parliament's intention was clear. 'Expedient' had a meaning quite different from 'necessary'. Parliament had set in place a series of constraints on this power, including the requirement for authorisations, which, through a succession of such authorisations and confirmations, covered the whole of the Metropolitan police district. While the argument that this seemed excessive was attractive, the defendants had presented informed evaluations of the terrorist threat that showed its requirement. The defence also showed that the authorisations and extensions were the subject of informed consideration, and not just a routine bureaucratic exercise. There was no evidence that the authorisations or confirmations were unlawful. In the absence of special circumstances, there was no deprivation of liberty in violation of the Convention art 5, as being stopped and searched could not be regarded as being detained in the sense of being confined or kept in custody. As to respect for privacy under art 8, passengers regularly submitted to the searching of persons and opening of bags at airports, and such an ordinary superficial search could not be said to reach the level of seriousness required to engage the Convention. It was hard to see how the power to stop and search could be held to restrict the rights of free expression and free assembly so as to infringe art 10 or 11. The 2000 Act informed the public of the powers, if duly authorised and confirmed, and public documentation described the procedure in detail. There was no requirement for the existence of the authorisations to be publicised. The power to stop and search met the test of lawfulness and, accordingly, the appeal would be dismissed.

R (on the application of Gillan) v Metropolitan Police Comr [2006] UKHL 12, (2006) Times, 9 March (House of Lords: Lords Bingham of Cornhill, Hope of Craighead, Scott of Foscote, Walker of Gestingthorpe and Brown of Eaton-under-Heywood). Decision of Court of Appeal [2004] EWCA Civ 1067, [2005] 1 All ER 970 (2004 Abr para 827) affirmed.

893 Terrorism—excluded activities—business in the regulated sector

The Terrorism Act 2000 (Business in the Regulated Sector) Order 2006, SI 2006/2384 (in force on 6 April 2007), further amends the Terrorism Act 2000 to add to the list of excluded activities the regulated activities of arranging deals in investments or advising on investments, in so far as the investment consists of rights under a regulated home reversion plan or a regulated home purchase plan, with the effect that a business will not be in the regulated sector to the extent that it conducts such activities.

894 Terrorism—prevention—control order—continuance in force

The Prevention of Terrorism Act 2005 (Continuance in force of sections 1 to 9) Order 2006, SI 2006/512 (in force on 11 March 2006), continues in force until 10 March 2007, the Prevention of Terrorism Act 2005 ss 1–9 so as to retain the power of the Secretary of State to make a control order against an individual where he has reasonable grounds for suspecting the individual is or has been involved in terrorism-related activity and believes that it is necessary to impose obligations on the individual for purposes connected with protecting members of the public from a risk of terrorism.

895 Terrorism—prevention—control order—non-derogating order—power to quash—deprivation of liberty

The Secretary of State imposed control orders on the defendants pursuant to the Prevention of Terrorism Act 2005 s 2. Under the control orders each defendant was required to remain in his one bedroom residence at all times, save for a specified six-hour period during which he was confined to a specified urban area. Visitors had to be authorised by the Home Office, to which name, address, date of birth and photographic identity had to be supplied. The defendants' residences were subject to spot searches by the police. The court ruled that the obligations imposed by the control orders were so severe that they amounted to a deprivation of liberty contrary to the European Convention on Human Rights art 5. It followed that the Secretary of State had no power to make the orders and the court quashed them pursuant to the 2005 Act s 3(12). The Secretary of State appealed. *Held*, in order to determine whether someone had been 'deprived of his liberty' within the meaning of the Convention art 5, the starting point had to be his concrete situation and account should be taken of a whole range of criteria such as the type, duration, effects and manner of implementation of the measure in question. The judge had been required to make a value judgment as to whether the control orders had effected a deprivation of liberty, and it was clear that those orders had done so. Although it was questionable whether the 2005 Act s 3(12) applied to a control order which was ultra vires the Convention art 5, the judge had been correct in concluding that he had jurisdiction to quash the orders and the reasons he gave for doing so were compelling. Accordingly, the appeal would be dismissed.

Secretary of State for the Home Department v JJ [2006] EWCA Civ 1141, [2006] 3 WLR 866 (Court of Appeal: Lord Phillips of Worth Matravers CJ, Sir Anthony Clarke MR and Sir Igor Judge P).

896 Terrorism—prevention—control order—non-derogating order—review by court—right to fair hearing

The Prevention of Terrorism Act 2005 s 3(10) provides that, on a hearing in pursuance of directions under s 3(2)(c) or (6)(b) or (c), the function of the court is to determine whether any of the following decisions of the Secretary of State was flawed: (1) his decision that the requirements of s 2(1)(a) and (b) were satisfied for the making of the order; and (2) his decisions on the imposition of each of the obligations imposed by the order.

Pursuant to the 2005 Act s 2, the Secretary of State made a non-derogating control order against the defendant on the ground that he believed that the defendant intended to travel to Iraq to fight against coalition forces, which included United Kingdom forces. Under s 3, the High Court held a hearing to determine whether the Secretary of State's decisions in relation to the order were flawed. An issue arose as to whether the procedures in s 3 relating to the supervision by the court of non-derogating control orders made by the Secretary of State under s 2 were incompatible with the defendant's right to a fair hearing, guaranteed by the European Convention on Human Rights art 6(1). The judge decided that the procedures under the 2005 Act, under which the court merely reviewed the lawfulness of the Secretary of State's decision to make the order on the basis of the material available to him at that earlier stage, were conspicuously unfair and incompatible with the defendant's right to a fair hearing. On the Secretary of State's appeal, *held*, the provisions complied with the requirements of the Convention art 6(1). Firstly, the 2005 Act s 3(10) required the court to consider whether the decision of the Secretary of State in relation to the control order was flawed as at the time of the court's determination. Secondly, the terms of s 3(10), when read in the light of s 11(2) which had been overlooked by both the judge and counsel at first instance, had not restricted the court to a standard of review that fell short of that required to satisfy the Convention art 6. Thirdly, in reviewing the decision of the Secretary of State, the issue that had to be scrutinised by the court was whether there were reasonable grounds for the Secretary of State's suspicion. That exercise involved a consideration of a matrix of alleged facts, some of which were clear beyond reasonable doubt, some of which could be established on a balance of probability and some of which were based on no more than circumstances giving rise to suspicion. That exercise of consideration was different from that of deciding whether a fact had been established according to a specified standard of proof. It was the procedure for determining whether reasonable grounds for suspicion existed that had to be fair if art 6 was to be satisfied. Finally, art 6 had not automatically required disclosure of the evidence of the grounds for suspicion as there were circumstances, accepted in European and domestic case law, where the use of closed material was permissible provided that appropriate safeguards were in place, which were present under the 2005 Act. Accordingly, the appeal would be allowed.

Secretary of State for the Home Department v MB [2006] EWCA Civ 1140, [2006] All ER (D) 09 (Aug) (Court of Appeal: Lord Phillips of Worth Matravers CJ, Sir Anthony Clarke MR and Sir Igor Judge P). Decision of Sullivan J [2006] EWHC 1000 (Admin), [2006] All ER (D) 201 (Apr) reversed.

897   Terrorism—proscribed organisations—application for deproscription

The Proscribed Organisations (Applications for Deproscription etc) Regulations 2006, SI 2006/2299 (in force on 20 September 2006), replace the 2001 Regulations, SI 2001/107, and prescribe the procedure for an application to the Secretary of State for the exercise of his power by order either to remove an organisation from the list of proscribed organisations in the Terrorism Act 2000 Sch 2, or to provide for a name to cease to be treated as another name for an organisation so listed.

898   Terrorism—proscribed organisations—listed organisations

The Terrorism Act 2000 (Proscribed Organisations) (Amendment) Order 2006, SI 2006/2016 (in force on 26 July 2006), amends the Terrorism Act 2000 by adding Al-Ghurabaa, the Saved Sect, Baluchistan Liberation Army and Teyrebaz Azadiye Kurdistan to the list of proscribed organisations.

899   Terrorism—proscribed organisations—name changes

The Proscribed Organisations (Name Changes) Order 2006, SI 2006/1919 (in force on 14 August 2006), exercises the power conferred under the Terrorism Act 2006 s 3(6), which enables an order to provide that a name not specified is to be treated as another name for an organisation that is listed, with the effect that Kongra Gele Kurdistan and KADEK are to be treated as another name for the organisation listed as the Kurdistan Workers' Party.

900   Terrorism—terrorism cases—management of cases

Sir Igor Judge, President of the Queen's Bench Division, has issued the following *Protocol (Management of Terrorism Cases)* on 18 January 2006.

Terrorism Cases

1. This Protocol applies to 'terrorism cases' which are indictable only and will be sent to the Crown Court under the Crime and Disorder Act 1998 s 51 or are indictable offences which will be transferred to the Crown Court under the Criminal Justice Act 1987 s 4 (cases involving serious fraud). For the purposes of this Protocol a case is a 'terrorism case' where:

(a) One of the offences charged against any of the defendants is indictable only and it is alleged by the prosecution that there is evidence that it took place during an act of terrorism or for the purposes of terrorism as defined in the Terrorist Act 2000 s1. This may include, but is not limited to:

(i) murder;

(ii) manslaughter;

(iii) an offence under the Offences against the Person Act 1861 s 18 (wounding with intent);

(iv) an offence under s 23 or 24 (administering poison etc);

(v) an offence under s 28 or 29 (explosives);

(vi) an offence under the Explosive Substances Act 1883 s 2, 3 or 5 (causing explosions);

(vii) an offence under the Criminal Damage Act 1971 s 1(2) (endangering life by damaging property);

(viii) an offence under the Biological Weapons Act 1974 s 1 (biological weapons);

(ix) an offence under the Chemical Weapons Act 1996 s 2 (chemical weapons);

(x) an offence under the Terrorism Act 2000 s 56 (directing a terrorist organisation);

(xi) an offence under s 59 (inciting terrorism overseas);

(xii) offences under heads (v), (vii) and (viii), above, given jurisdiction by virtue of s 62 (terrorist bombing overseas);

(b) One of the offences so charged includes an allegation by the prosecution of serious fraud that took place during an act of terrorism or for the purposes of terrorism as defined in the Terrorist Act 2000 s1 and meets the test to be transferred to the Crown Court under the Criminal Justice Act 1987 s 4.

(c) One of the offences so charged includes an allegation that a defendant conspired, incited or attempted to commit an offence under head (1)(a) or (b), above.

The Terrorism Cases List

2. (a) All terrorism cases, wherever they originate in England and Wales, will be managed in a list known as the 'terrorism cases list' by the presiding judges of the South Eastern Circuit and such other judges of the High Court as are nominated by the President of the Queen's Bench Division.

(b) Such cases will be tried, unless otherwise directed by the President of the Queen's Bench Division, by a judge of the High Court as nominated by the President of the Queen's Bench Division.

3. The judges managing the terrorism cases referred to in head 2, above, will be supported by the London and SE Regional Co-ordinator's Office (the Regional Co-ordinator's Office). An official of that office or nominated by that office will act as the case progression officer for cases in that list for the purposes of the Criminal Procedure Rules 2005, SI 2005/384, Pt 3.4.

Procedure After Charge

4. Immediately after a person has been charged in a terrorism case, anywhere in England and Wales, a representative of the Crown Prosecution Service will notify the person on the 24 hour rota for special jurisdiction matters at Bow Street Magistrates' Court of the following information:

(a) The full name of each defendant and the name of his solicitor of other legal representative, if known;

(b) The charges laid;

(c) The name and contact details of the crown prosecutor with responsibility for the case, if known;

(d) Confirmation that the case is a terrorism case.

5. The person on the 24-hour rota will then ensure that all terrorism cases wherever they are charged in England and Wales are listed before the chief magistrate or other district judge designated under the Terrorism Act 2000. Unless the chief magistrate or other district judge designated under the 2000 Act directs otherwise, the first appearance of all defendants accused of terrorism offences will be listed at Bow Street Magistrates' Court.

6. In order to comply with the Police and Criminal Evidence Act 1984 s 46, if a defendant in a terrorism case is charged at a police station within the local justice area in which Bow Street Magistrates' Court is situated the defendant must be brought before Bow Street Magistrates' Court as soon as is practicable and in any event not later than the first sitting after he is charged with the offence. If a defendant in a terrorism case is charged in a police station outside the local justice area in which Bow Street Magistrates' Court is situated, unless the chief magistrate or other designated judge directs otherwise, the defendant must be removed to that area as soon as is practicable. He must then be brought before Bow Street Magistrates' Court as soon as is practicable after his arrival in the area and in any event not later than the first sitting of Bow Street Magistrates' Court after his arrival in that area.

7. As soon as is practicable after charge a representative of the Crown Prosecution Service will also provide the Regional Listing Co-ordinator's Office with the information listed in head 4, above.

8. The Regional Co-ordinator's Office will then ensure that the chief magistrate and the Legal Services Commission have the same information.

9. To allow for chief magistrate sitting in future at a different Magistrates' Court, all references to Bow Street Magistrates' Court in this protocol may be read as the Magistrates' Court where the chief magistrate regularly sits.

Cases to be sent to the Crown Court under the Crime and Disorder Act 1998 s 51

10. A preliminary hearing should normally be ordered by the Magistrates' Court in a terrorism case. The court should ordinarily direct that the preliminary hearing should take place about 14 days after charge.

11. The sending Magistrates' Court should contact the Regional Listing Co-ordinator's Office who will be responsible for notifying the Magistrates' Court as to the relevant Crown Court to which to send the case.

12. In all terrorism cases, the Magistrates' Court case progression form for cases sent to the Crown Court under the Crime and Disorder Act 1998 s 51 should not be used. Instead of the automatic directions set out in that form, the Magistrates' Court must make the following directions to facilitate the preliminary hearing at the Crown Court:

(a) Three days prior to the preliminary hearing in the terrorism cases list, the prosecution must serve on each defendant and the Regional Listing co-ordinator:

(i) a preliminary summary of the case;

(ii) the names of those who are to represent the prosecution, if known;

(iii) an estimate of the length of the trial;

(iv) a suggested provisional timetable which should generally include:

(A) the general nature of further inquiries being made by the prosecution;

(B) the time needed for the completion of such inquiries;

(C) the time required by the prosecution to review the case;

(D) a timetable for the phased service of the evidence;

(E) the time for the provision by the Attorney General for his consent if necessary;

(F) the time for service of the detailed defence case statement;

(G) the date for the case management hearing; and

(H) estimated trial date;

(v) A preliminary statement of the possible disclosure issues setting out the nature and scale of the problem including the amount of unused material, the manner in which the prosecution seeks to deal with these matters and a suggested timetable for discharging their statutory duty; and

(vi) Any information relating to bail and custody time limits.

(b) One day prior to the preliminary hearing in the terrorist cases list, each defendant must serve in writing on the Regional Listing Co-ordinator and the prosecution:

(i) the proposed representation;

(ii) observations on the timetable;

(iii) an indication of plea and the general nature of the defence.

Cases to be transferred to the Crown Court under the Criminal Justice Act 1987 s 4(1)

13. If a terrorism case is to be transferred to the Crown Court, the Magistrates' Court should proceed as if it is being sent to the Crown Court, as in heads 10–12, above.

14. When a terrorism case is so sent or transferred the case will go into the terrorism list and be managed by a judge as described in head 2, above.

The preliminary hearing at the Crown Court

15. At the preliminary hearing, the judge will determine whether the case is one to remain in the terrorism list and if so give directions setting the provisional timetable.

16. The Legal Services Commission must attend the hearing by an authorised officer to assist the court.

Use of Video Link

17. Unless a judge otherwise directs, all Crown court hearings prior to the trial will be conducted by video link for all defendants in custody.

Security

18. The police service and the prison service will provide the Regional Listing Co-ordinator's Office with an initial joint assessment of the security risks associated with any court appearance by the defendants within 14 days of charge. Any subsequent changes in circumstances or the assessment of risk which have the potential to impact on the choice of trial venue will be notified to the Regional Listing Co-ordinator's Office immediately.

901   Terrorism—United Nations measures

The Terrorism (United Nations Measures) Order 2006, SI 2006/2657 (in force on 12 October 2006), replaces, with savings, the 2001 Order, SI 2001/3365, and gives effect in the United

Kingdom to United Nations Security Council Resolution 1373 of 28 September 2001, relating to terrorism and United Nations Security Council Resolution 1453 of 20 December 2002, and humanitarian exemptions. The order also provides for enforcement of EC Regulation 2580/2001 on specific measures directed at certain persons and entities with a view to combating terrorism. In particular, the order (1) provides that designated persons are persons named in EC Council Decision 2006/379, and those identified in a direction given by the Treasury; (2) confers a power on the Treasury to give a direction to designate a person for the purposes of the order if one of a number of specified conditions is fulfilled in respect of the person, such conditions being that the Treasury have reasonable grounds to suspect that the person is or may be (a) a person who commits, attempts to commit, participates in or facilitates the commission of acts of terrorism; (b) a person named in the Council Decision; (c) a person owned or controlled, directly or indirectly, by a designated person; or (d) a person acting on behalf of or at the direction of a designated person; (3) requires the Treasury to take the steps that it considers appropriate, to publicise the direction or to inform only certain persons and to notify the person identified in the direction, and includes provision about the manner in which a direction has effect and appeals; (4) confers a power on the Treasury to specify that information contained in the direction is to be treated as confidential, and imposes a prohibition on disclosing such information except with lawful authority, which will lead to a criminal offence if contravened, and provides that the court may grant an injunction to prevent a breach; (5) prohibits any dealing with funds, financial assets and economic resources of anyone who commits, attempts to commit, participates in or facilitates the commission of acts of terrorism, including designated persons; anyone owned or controlled by them or anyone acting on their behalf of or at their direction, and makes it a criminal offence to contravene this prohibition; (6) prohibits making funds, financial assets, economic resources or financial services available to anyone in respect of anyone above, and makes it a criminal offence to contravene this prohibition; (7) makes it a criminal offence to circumvent the prohibitions or to facilitate the commission of an offence relating to a prohibition; (8) provides a licensing procedure to enable, for humanitarian and other purposes, certain acts to be exempted from the prohibitions; (9) confers a power on the Treasury to delegate its functions under this order; and (10) confirms that the provisions of this order apply to the Crown but, in the event of a contravention, the Crown is not criminally liable. SI 2003/1297, 2005/1525 are revoked. SI 2001/3801, 2002/111, 2005/3389 are amended.

902 Terrorism Act 2006

The Terrorism Act 2006 makes provision for and about offences relating to conduct carried out, or capable of being carried out, for purposes connected with terrorism, amends enactments relating to terrorism, and amends the Intelligence Services Act 1994 and the Regulation of Investigatory Powers Act 2000. The 2006 Act received the royal assent on 30 March 2006 and came into force in part on that day. The remaining provisions came into force on 13 April and 25 July 2006: SI 2006/1013, 1936. For details of commencement, see the commencement table in the title STATUTES.

Part 1 (ss 1–20) Offences
The 2006 Act s 1 creates an offence of encouragement of acts of terrorism or Convention offences (listed in Sch 1), and s 2 creates offences relating to the dissemination of terrorist publications. Under s 3, which deals with the application of ss 1, 2 to internet activity, a person providing or using an electronic service is deemed to have indorsed a statement if he has received a notice under s 3 and has failed to comply with it. The procedure for the giving of notices under s 3 is set out by s 4. Section 5 creates an offence of the preparation of terrorist acts, and s 6 provides that training for terrorism is an offence. Section 7 deals with powers of forfeiture in respect of offences under s 6. By virtue of s 8, attendance at a place used for terrorist training is also an offence. It is an offence, under s 9, to make or possess a radioactive device or to possess radioactive material with the intention of using the device or material in the course of, or in connection with, the commission or preparation of an act of terrorism, or for the purposes of terrorism. Section 10 creates a further offence of using a radioactive device, or radioactive material, in the course of, or in connection with, the commission of an act of terrorism or for the purposes of terrorism, and s 11 makes it an offence, in the course of, or in connection with, the commission of an act of terrorism, or for the purposes of terrorism, to demand the supply of a radioactive device or of radioactive material, or that a nuclear facility or access to a nuclear facility is made available, where this demand is supported with a threat to take action if the demand is not met. Section 12 amends the Serious Organised Crime and Police Act 2005 ss 128, 129, so as to create an offence of trespassing on nuclear sites. The 2006 Act ss 13–15 increase the maximum penalties for possession for terrorist purposes, for certain offences involving preparatory acts and threats relating to nuclear material, and for contravening notices requiring the disclosure of encrypted information. Section 16 amends the Criminal Procedure and Investigations Act 1996 s 29 so as to make preparatory hearings mandatory in terrorism cases. Provision is made by the 2006 Act s 17 in relation to the commission of certain offences abroad and the extra-territorial jurisdiction of the courts in the United Kingdom. Section 18 deals with the liability of company directors for certain offences under the Act, and s 19 requires the consent of the Director of Public Prosecutions before prosecutions for these offences are instituted. Section 20 is interpretational.

Part 2 (ss 21–35) Miscellaneous provisions
Sections 21–30 amend the Terrorism Act 2000. The 2006 Act s 21 widens the grounds of proscription of terrorist organisations, and s 22 deals with the situation in which a proscribed organisation may be identified by another name. The maximum period of detention of a terrorist suspect prior to his being charged with an offence is extended by s 23. Section 24 amends the grounds on which such detention may be authorised. Amendments made by s 23, extending the maximum detention period, cease to have effect one year after their commencement unless continued in force by the Secretary of State: s 25. By virtue of s 26, all premises warrants, which do not specify the set of premises to which they relate, may now be issued to enter and search premises for the purposes of a terrorist investigation and to enter and search premises for excluded or special procedure material. Similar provision is made in relation to Scotland: s 27. Powers of search, seizure and forfeiture of terrorist publications are created by s 28, and Sch 2 sets out the procedure for the forfeiture of such publications. Section 29 extends existing powers of search for ascertaining involvement with terrorism, so that an examining officer may search a vehicle at a port which is on a ship or aircraft, or which he reasonably believes has been or is about to be, on a ship or aircraft. Under s 30, authorisations for stop and search are extended to internal waters. Provision is made, amending the Intelligence Services Act 1994 s 6, in relation to the powers of the security and intelligence services with respect to warrants to carry out acts both overseas and in the United Kingdom: 2006 Act s 31. Section 32 deals with the duration and modification of, and safeguards attached to, interception warrants and amends the Regulation of Investigatory Powers Act 2000 ss 9, 16. The 2006 Act s 33 extends the regime governing disclosure notices issued for the purposes of terrorist investigations contained in the Serious Organised Crime and Police Act 2005. Statutory definitions of 'terrorism' are amended by the 2006 Act s 34. Section 35 amends the Anti-terrorism, Crime and Security Act 2001 Sch 1 so as to make provision in connection with applications for the extended detention of seized terrorist cash.

Part 3 (ss 36–39) Supplemental provisions
The operation of the Terrorism Act 2000, and of the 2006 Act Pt 1 is to be reviewed: s 36. Section 37, Sch 3 make consequential amendments and repeals, s 38 deals with expenses, and s 39 with short title, commencement and extent.

Amendments, repeals and revocations
The list below, which is not exhaustive, mention repeals and amendments which are or will be effective when the Act is fully in force.
   Specific provisions of a number of Acts are amended or repealed. These include: Explosive Substances Act 1883 s 3; Nuclear Material (Offences) Act 1983 s 2; Intelligence Services Act 1994 s 6; Criminal Procedure and Investigations Act 1996 s 29; Regulation of Investigatory Powers Act 2000 ss 9, 16, 53; Terrorism Act 2000 ss 1, 3, 5, 7, 9, 44, 45, 57, 63A, 123, 126, Schs 3, 5, 7, 8; Anti-terrorism, Crime and Security Act 2001 s 113, Sch 1; Criminal Justice Act 2003 ss 45(8), 306(2), (3); Serious Organised Crime and Police Act 2005 ss 60, 62, 70, 128, 129.

903   Theft—dishonest appropriation—loss sustained by victim

British Virgin Islands
While in the employ of the government, the first defendant awarded construction contracts to the second defendant, in whose companies the first defendant had a personal interest. The defendants were charged with theft. A magistrate found that the construction work had been done at a reasonable price so that the defendants' dishonest acts had not caused a loss to the government. The defendants were acquitted of the theft charges. The prosecution's appeal succeeded, and the defendants appealed. *Held*, in most cases of theft, there would be an original owner who suffered a loss due to a defendant's conduct. The defendants had conceded that they had appropriated property belonging to the government. By virtue of a provision corresponding to the Theft Act 1968 s 2(2), an appropriation might be dishonest even where there was a willingness to pay. That showed that the prospect of loss was not determinative of the dishonesty necessary to establish the offence. Accordingly, the appeal would be dismissed.
   Wheatley v Comr of Police of the British Virgin Islands [2006] UKPC 24, [2006] 1 WLR 1683 (Privy Council: Lords Bingham of Cornhill, Steyn, Clyde, Carswell and Mance). *R v Hinks* [2001] 2 AC 241, HL (2000 Abr para 979), considered.

**904   Theft—obtaining services by deception—asylum-seeker—purchase of flight ticket
        under false name**

See *R v Asfaw*, para 332.

905   Violent Crime Reduction Act 2006

The Violent Crime Reduction Act 2006 makes provision in relation to (1) reducing and dealing with the abuse of alcohol; (2) real and imitation firearms; (3) ammunition; and (4) knives and other weapons. The Act received the royal assent on 8 November 2006 and certain provisions came into force on that date. The remaining provisions come into force on a day or days to be appointed. For details of commencement, see the commencement table in the title STATUTES.

Part 1 (ss 1–27) Alcohol-related violence and disorder
Chapter 1 (ss 1–14) Drinking banning orders
Section 1 provides that a drinking banning order may impose prohibitions on an individual that are necessary for the purpose of protecting other persons from criminal or disorderly conduct by that individual while he is under the influence of alcohol. The period for which such an order may be in force must be not less than two months and not more than two years: s 2. The conditions for applying to a magistrates' court for an order are specified in s 3, and the right to apply for an order in county court proceedings is provided by s 4. Section 5 makes provision for the variation or discharge of orders under s 3 or 4. Under s 6, a criminal court may make a drinking banning order in relation to an individual where appropriate. Supplementary provision with regard to orders under s 6 is made by s 7, and provision for the variation or discharge of orders under s 6 is made by s 8. The court may make an interim drinking banning order while it is considering pursuant to s 6 whether the conditions for making a drinking banning order are satisfied: s 9. Section 10 entitles a person to appeal against an order made under s 3 or 6. By virtue of s 11, it is an offence to do anything prohibited by a drinking banning order. Provision may only be made for an order to cease to have effect on the completion by the subject of an approved course where the Secretary of State has approved the course: s 12. Under s 13, such a course is only to be regarded as completed if an appropriate certificate has been issued. Section 14 deals with interpretation.

Chapter 2 (ss 15–20) Alcohol disorder zones
Section 15 empowers local authorities to impose charges on holders of premises licences allowing the sale by retail of alcohol. Local authorities are also entitled to designate, with the consent of the police, a locality as an alcohol disorder zone where there is a problem with alcohol-related nuisance and disorder in that area: s 16. The procedure for the designation of such a zone is prescribed by s 17. Section 18 specifies the functions of the local chief officer of police in relation to the designation of zones. Under s 19, the Secretary of State is required to issue guidance about the manner in which local authorities, police authorities and chief officers of police are to exercise and perform their powers and duties in relation to alcohol disorder zones. Section 20 deals with interpretation.

Chapter 3 (ss 21–27) Other provisions
Under ss 21 and 22, provision is made for an accelerated review of licensed premises by a licensing authority, and for the attaching of temporary conditions to a premises licence pending the full review of the licence. Section 23 creates a new offence of unlawfully selling alcohol to a person aged under 18 on three or more different occasions in a period of three consecutive months. A senior police officer or an inspector of weights and measures may make a closure notice where there is evidence that a person has committed such an offence: s 24. Where a premises licence requires persons to be present to undertake manned guarding activities, by virtue of s 25 the licence must only contain a mandatory condition that they be licensed by the Security Industry Authority if they are required to be licensed under the Private Security Industry Act 2001. The 2006 Act s 26 limits the circumstances in which premises licensed by local authorities cannot be designated public places where restrictions on public drinking will apply. Under s 27, a police constable may issue an individual with a direction to leave a locality for up to 48 hours if the individual is likely to cause or contribute to the occurrence, repetition or continuance of alcohol-related crime or disorder in that locality and the direction is necessary to remove or reduce that likelihood.

Part 2 (ss 28–51) Weapons
Section 28 creates a new offence of using another person to look after, hide or transport a dangerous weapon, and s 29 prescribes the penalties for committing such an offence. By virtue of s 30, the minimum sentences for unlawful possession of certain prohibited weapons also apply to other serious offences involving the possession and criminal use of such weapons. Anyone who wishes to sell air weapons by way of trade or business is required to register with the police as a firearms dealer (s 31); such sales must be made face to face (s 32). The minimum age for acquiring or possessing an air weapon is increased by s 33 from 17 to 18 years. By virtue of s 34, it is an offence to fire an air weapon beyond the boundary of any premise. It is also an offence to purchase or sell primers for ammunition unless the purchaser has a valid firearm certificate or otherwise has lawful authority (s 35), and to manufacture, import or sell realistic imitation firearms (s 36). Defences to a charge of an offence under s 36 are prescribed by s 37, and s 38 defines 'realistic imitation firearm' for the purposes of ss 36 and 37. Under s 39, it is an offence to manufacture, modify or import an imitation firearm which does not conform to specifications set out in regulations made by the Secretary of State. Section 40 makes it an offence to sell an imitation firearm to a person aged under 18, and for a person aged under 18 to purchase an imitation firearm. The maximum custodial sentence for carrying an imitation firearm in a public place without lawful authority or reasonable excuse is increased by s 41 from six months to twelve months. The maximum term of imprisonment for the offences of having an article with a blade or point in a public place, or of having such an article or another offensive weapon on school premises is increased by s 42 from two to four years. The offence of selling a knife or an article with a blade or point to a person aged under 16 is extended by s 43 to

persons aged under 18. By virtue of s 44, the age at which a person may be sold or hired a crossbow, and at which a person may buy, hire or possess a crossbow, is increased from 17 to 18 years. A head teacher is enabled by s 45 to search or authorise the search of a pupil and his possessions where there is reason to suspect that he is carrying a knife or other offensive weapon. Equivalent provision is made by s 46 in relation to students of institutions in the further education sector, and by s 47 in relation to persons in attendance centres. Section 48 enables a constable to exercise his powers of entry and search of a school and persons on school premises for weapons where he has reasonable grounds for suspecting a relevant offence has been or is being committed. Section 49, Sch 1 make consequential amendments relating to minimum sentences. Supplementary provision in connection with Pt 2 is made by s 50, and s 51, Sch 2 deal with Northern Ireland.

Part 3 (ss 52–63) Miscellaneous
Section 52, Sch 3 make various amendments to the Football (Disorder) Act 2000 and the Football Spectators Act 1989. The 2006 Act s 53 extends provisions on the sale and disposal of football match tickets by unauthorised persons to cover ticket touting on the internet and other practices associated with the unauthorised sale and distribution of tickets. Section 54, Sch 4 enable the court, when a person is convicted on indictment of trafficking a person for sexual exploitation, to order the forfeiture of a vehicle, ship or aircraft used or intended to be used in connection with the offence. Provision is made by s 55 to ensure the continuity of sexual offences law. Persons who have been or become subject to notification requirements in Scotland as a result of being convicted of a particular sexual offence involving a child are also to be subject to the notification requirements in England and Wales: s 56. By virtue of s 57, persons aged 18 or over who receive a sentence of imprisonment for public protection are required to notify the police of certain personal details for an indefinite period. Section 58 enables a magistrate to authorise the entry and search of the home of a person subject to notification requirements for the purposes of assessing the risks that he may pose to the community. The limitation period for anti-social behaviour orders is amended (s 59) and the power of the court to make a parenting order and a sexual offences prevention order in the same proceedings is also amended (s 60). Section 61 expands certain references to committing for trial to include sending for trial. By virtue of s 62, the offence of changing the unique International Mobile Equipment Identity number on a mobile telephone handset may be committed by offering or agreeing to change or interfere with the number or other unique device identifier. Section 63 exempts certain persons from the licensing requirement in the Private Security Industry Act 2001. The 2006 Act s 64 deals with expenses, s 65, Sch 5 make various repeals, and s 66 deals with the short title, commencement and extent.

Amendments, repeals and revocations
The lists below, which are not exhaustive, mention repeals and amendments which are or will be effective when the Act is fully in force.

The following Acts are repealed in full: Licensed Premises (Exclusion of Certain Persons) Act 1980; and Football (Disorder) (Amendment) Act 2002.

Specific provisions of a number of Acts are amended or repealed. These include: Firearms Act 1968 ss 3, 22–24, 51A, Sch 6; Crossbows Act 1987 ss 1–3; Criminal Justice Act 1988 ss 139, 139A, 141, 141A; Football Spectators Act 1989 ss 2–7; Criminal Justice and Public Order Act 1994 s 166; Football (Disorder) Act 2000 s 5(2); Criminal Justice and Police Act 2001 s 21; Licensing Act 2003 s 21; and Sexual Offences Act 2003 ss 82, 128, 129.

CROWN PROCEEDINGS AND CROWN PRACTICE

Halsbury's Laws of England (4th edn) vol 12(1) (Reissue) paras 101–137

906   Prosecution—decision not to prosecute—obligation of Director of Public Prosecutions to consider prosecution

The deceased, the claimant's son, was aged 17 when he started work as a labourer. He fell to his death through a skylight while working for a sub-contractor firm. The inquest jury returned a verdict of unlawful killing. The Crown Prosecution Service considered a prosecution against the sub-contractor for manslaughter, but refused to prosecute such a case on the basis that it failed to satisfy the Code for Crown Prosecutors. In particular, although the solicitor dealing with the case was satisfied that the proposed defendants owed a duty of care to the deceased and were in varying degrees in breach of that duty, he was not satisfied that the degree of negligence displayed was so severe that it would amount to criminal negligence. The claimant sought judicial review of the decision not to prosecute. Held, if it could be demonstrated on an objective appraisal of the case that a serious point or points, supporting a prosecution had not been considered, that would give a ground for ordering reconsideration of the decision. Where it could be demonstrated that in a significant area a conclusion as to what the evidence to support a prosecution was irrational, that would provide a ground for ordering reconsideration. The points had to be such as to make it seriously arguable that the decision would otherwise be different; however the decision was one for the prosecutor and not for the court. Also, where an inquest jury had found unlawful killing, the reasons why a prosecution should not follow needed to be clearly expressed. The CPS solicitor dealing with the case had not dealt with the real thrust of any case that might be brought against the sub-contractor. It could not be said that he had given clear reasons as to why the inquest jury's verdict should not have led to a prosecution. Those failures provided a basis on which it was right to refer the matter back to the CPS. It was seriously arguable that a different decision might be reached once account was taken of those matters. Accordingly, the application would be allowed.

R (on the application of Dennis) v DPP [2006] EWHC 3211 (Admin), [2007] All ER (D) 43 (Jan) (Queen's Bench Division: Waller LJ and Lloyd Jones J). *R v DPP, ex p C* [1995] 1 Cr App Rep 136; *R v DPP, ex p Treadaway* (31 July 1997, unreported), *R v DPP, ex p Jones* [2000] IRLR 373, DC (2000 Abr para 952); and *R v DPP, ex p Manning* [2001] QB 330, DC (2000 Abr para 883), considered.

CUSTOM AND USAGE

Halsbury's Laws of England (4th edn) vol 12(1) (Reissue) paras 601–800

907   Finance Act 2006

See para 2465.

908   Imports—prohibited goods—fraudulent evasion of prohibition—indecent photographs of children

See *Forbes v Secretary of State for the Home Department*, para 1602.

909   Usage—insurance business—Lloyd's of London—underwriter's right to inspect documents held by brokers

See *Goshawk Dedicated Ltd v Tyser & Co Ltd*, para 1716.

910   Value added tax

See VALUE ADDED TAX.

CUSTOMS AND EXCISE

Halsbury's Laws of England (4th edn) vol 12(2) (2007 Reissue) paras 1–619, vol 12(3) (2007 Reissue) paras 620–1288

Articles

For articles relating to this title please refer to the Table of Articles at the beginning of the Abridgment.

911   Customs duty—customs valuation—transaction value—contact lenses supplied from overseas and associated services supplied in United Kingdom

EC Council Regulation 2913/92 art 29(1) provides that the customs value of the goods is the transaction value, that is, the price actually paid or payable for the goods when sold for export to the customs territory of the Community. The price actually paid or payable includes all payments made or to be made as a condition of sale of the imported goods by the buyer to the seller to satisfy an obligation of the seller: art 29(3)(a).

The taxpayer, a firm of opticians with branches throughout the United Kingdom, operated an offer for the supply of contact lenses by post through a sister company. The lenses would be posted in the form of a subscription from Jersey, which was a third territory for customs purposes. Customers in the United Kingdom would pay a fixed monthly amount for the lenses and, in addition to the lenses, received an initial examination or consultation, an annual check and other aftercare relating to use of the lenses from their local branch. The taxation authorities considered that the relevant valuation of the imported consignment was the total price paid by the customer, while the taxpayer contended that the relevant valuation was the price of the goods only. Proceedings were brought before a VAT and duties tribunal, which referred the matter to the European Court of Justice. *Held*, in order to determine the 'transaction value' for the purposes of EC Council Regulation 2913/92 art 29, the calculation had to be made on the basis of conditions on which the individual sale was made. Relevant conditions of the offer were that it included all of the associated services in addition to the goods, the services were those required by national law, no provision was made for additional options, the offer was paid for by a single payment which did not distinguish between the goods and services, and all of the services were provided by the taxpayer and its franchisees. In these circumstances, the offer was a global one in respect of which a single payment was made. Therefore, the supply of services had to be regarded as part of the payments made as a condition of sale by the buyer to the seller to satisfy an obligation of the seller within the terms of art 29(3)(a), and so was an integral part of the customs value. Accordingly, payment for the supply of those services and together with the goods as a whole constituted the transaction value within the meaning of art 29 and, therefore, was subject to customs duty.

Case C-491/04 *Dollond & Aitchison Ltd v Customs and Excise Comrs* [2006] 2 CMLR 1334 (ECJ: Second Chamber).

912   Excise duty—alcoholic beverages

The Beer, Cider and Perry, Spirits, and Wine and Made-wine (Amendment) Regulations 2006, SI 2006/1058 (in force on 1 May 2006), further amend (1) the Beer Regulations 1993, SI 1993/1228, so as to (a) relax the prohibition on mixing beers that are subject to different rates of excise duty by making the product of such mixing chargeable at the standard rate of excise duty; (b) remove the prohibition on the addition of other substances to beer and replace it with a restriction on the addition of water; and (c) remove provisions relating to the keeping of stock records; (2) the Cider and Perry Regulations 1989, SI 1989/1355, so as to (a) remove provisions relating to the examination and gauging of vessel, the keeping of books, records and accounts and stocktaking; and (b) provide for the collection of excise duty on cider and perry that is made in unregistered premises; (3) further amend the Spirits Regulations 1991, SI 1991/2564, so as to (a) remove in their entirety the provisions relating to entry of premises, examination of plant, general provisions as to plant, special conditions and requirements, sugar, gravity of wort or wash, ascertainment of original gravity after fermentation has commenced, taking account, entry books, notice of commencement of process, preservation and production of records, requirements in respect of distillation periods and the table for determining original gravity; (b) in relation to the provision covering approval of plant and process, require less detail from the distiller and allow application to be made by electronic communication; and (c) revise the provision covering warehouse to reflect the abolition of entry books and the requirement to take account; (4) the Spirits (Rectifying, Compounding and Drawback) Regulations 1998, SI 1988/1760, so as to remove the requirement for a rectifier or compounder who is authorised to receive duty-free spirits to make entry of his premises; (5) the Wine and Made-wine Regulations 1989, SI 1989/1356, so as to (a) remove the provisions relating to the examination and gauging of vessels, the keeping of entry books, records and accounts and stocktaking; and (b) provide for the collection of excise duty on wine and made-wine that is produced in unlicensed premises. SI 1978/1786, 1979/1146, 1989/916, and 1992/3157 are revoked.

913   Excise duty—alcoholic liquor—duty stamps

The Duty Stamps (Amendment of paragraph 1(3) of Schedule 2A to the Alcoholic Liquor Duties Act 1979) Order 2006, SI 2006/144 (in force on 1 February 2006), reduces the range of products that are required to bear duty stamps by amending the Alcoholic Liquor Duties Act 1979 Sch 2A para 1(3), so that it only applies to spirits, wine and made-wine of a strength of 30 per cent alcohol by volume or more.

The Duty Stamps Regulations 2006, SI 2006/202 (in force on 22 February 2006), make provision as to the administration of duty stamps on alcoholic liquors that are intended for consumption in the United Kingdom and amend the Excise Warehousing (etc) Regulations 1988, SI 1988/809. In particular, the regulations (1) provide for the circumstances in which alcoholic liquors are required to a carry duty stamp and the form that it must take, and provide circumstances in which goods that are relieved from excise duty are not required to bear a duty stamp; (2) regulate the design and appearance of duty stamps; and (3) make provision as to registration, records, ordering and obtaining duty stamps, and the affixing and positioning of duty stamps.

914   Excise duty—biogas—pilot projects—relief

The Fuel-testing Pilot Projects (Biogas Project) Regulations 2006, SI 2006/1348 (in force on 10 June 2006), provide that biogas used for the purposes of a specified project for an experimental period from 10 June 2006 until 28 February 2011 is to be wholly relieved from excise duty.

915   Excise duty—goods for personal and other private individual use—excise duty point

The Dutch applicant formed a wine group with 70 other private individuals, and ordered wine from France for his own use and that of the members of his group. A Dutch transport company transported the wine to the applicant's home and he then distributed the wine to the members of the group. The applicant did not engage in the activity on a commercial basis or with a view to making a profit. The Dutch authorities levied excise duty on a quantity of wine that the applicant received. The applicant disputed liability on the basis of EEC Council Directive 92/12, which provided that where products were acquired by private individuals for their own use and transported by them, the excise duty should be charged in the member state where the products were acquired. The Dutch court referred to the European Court of Justice the question whether a private individual, who was not operating commercially or with a view to making a profit, purchased products subject to excise duty in one member state, for his own requirements and for those of other individuals, and arranged for the products to be transported on his behalf by a transport company established in his home member state, had to pay excise duty levied in his home state. *Held*, where a private individual, who was not operating commercially or with a view to making a profit, acquired products subject to excise duty in another member state, for his own personal requirements and those of other private individuals, and arranged for them to be transported to his member state on his behalf by a transport company established in his member state, then excise duty would be levied in his member state as well, and the duty paid in the other member state would be refunded. The Directive required that for products to be exempt from the excise duty they had to be intended for the personal use of the private individual who acquired them and therefore excluded products acquired by a private individual for the use of other private individuals. The products could not be considered to be held for strictly personal purposes by the private individual who had required them. Also, in order to not be liable for excise duty in the private individual's member state, the products should have been transported personally by the private individual who purchased them. The fact that the products were transported to another member state by a transport company was sufficient to show that they were not held for strictly personal purposes, as required, as it facilitated the transport of quantities of products significantly exceeding those required for his own use. If the excise duty was payable only in the member state where products were purchased and transport was not carried out personally by the private individual, there would be an increased risk of fraud as such products covered by the exemption required no documentation.

Case C-5/05 *Staatssecretaris van Financien v Joustra* [2006] All ER (D) 311 (Nov) (ECJ: Third Chamber). Case C-296/95 *R v Customs and Excise Comrs, ex p EMU Tabac Sárl (Imperial Tobacco Ltd intervener)* [1998] All ER (EC) 402, ECJ (1998 Abr para 965), considered.

916   Excise duty—hydrocarbon oil—relief for sulphur-free diesel

The Hydrocarbon Oil Duties (Sulphur–free Diesel) (Hydrogenation of Biomass) (Reliefs) Regulations 2006, SI 2006/3426 (in force on 12 January 2007), provide for a partial relief from excise duty charged on sulphur-free diesel which is partly produced from the hydrogenation of biomass. In particular, the regulations, which will cease to have effect on 12 January 2009, (1) set out the scope of the relief; (2) provide that the relief is to be in the form of a remission of duty; (3) set out how the amount of duty remitted is calculated; (4) permit the Commissioners to impose conditions on the person claiming the relief; (5) provide for the cancellation and recovery of the relief in cases where there is a contravention of, or failure to comply with, any condition imposed by the Commissioners.

917   Excise duty—legacies imported from third countries—relief

The Relief for Legacies Imported from Third Countries (Application) Order 2006, SI 2006/3158 (in force on 1 January 2007), updates a reference to EEC Council Directive 77/388 in the Customs and Excise Duties (Personal Reliefs for Goods Permanently Imported) Order 1992, SI 1992/3193, which provides relief from duty and value added tax for legacies imported from a third country, so that Directive 77/388 will apply to the Republic of Bulgaria and to Romania.

918   Excise duty—surcharges or rebates—hydrocarbon oils etc

The Excise Duties (Surcharges or Rebates) (Hydrocarbon Oils etc) (Revocation) Order 2006, SI 2006/3235 (in force on 7 December 2006), revokes SI 2006/1979 with the effect that the adjustments made to liabilities to excise duty are cancelled in relation to products that are charged with duty on or after 7 December 2006, and the amount a person is liable to pay is increased to the amount specified in the Hydrocarbon Oil Duties Act 1979, as amended by the Finance Act 2006 s 7.

919   Excise duty—tobacco products—excise duty point—new member states

The Excise Duty Points (Etc) (New Member States) (Amendment) Regulations 2006, SI 2006/3159 (in force on 1 January 2007), amend the 2004 Regulations, SI 2004/1003, so as to give effect to derogations contained in the Act concerning the Accession of the Republic of Bulgaria and Romania to the European Union. In particular, the regulations (1) insert a new provison, which updates references to EEC Council Directive 92/12; and (2) make provision so that the excise duty point, for cigarettes acquired by a person in the new member states for his own use and transported by him to the United Kingdom, is the time when the tobacco products are charged with duty.

920   Excise duty—tobacco products—tobacco manufacturers

The Tobacco Products (Amendment) Regulations 2006, SI 2006/2368 (in force on 1 October 2006), further amend the 2001 Regulations, SI 2001/1712, by (1) changing the definition of a tobacco manufacturer; (2) imposing a requirement on the Commissioners for Her Majesty's Revenue and Customs to provide tobacco manufacturers with written notification of cigarettes and hand rolling tobacco seized under the Customs and Excise Management Act 1979 s 139; (3) requiring the Commissioners to provide to the manufacturer a sample of the seized products; (4) providing that the manufacturer may inspect the entire seizure at any reasonable time for a period of one month beginning with the day on which written notification was given; (5) requiring the manufacturer to provide the information specified within one month of the day on which notification was given, or, subject to agreement with the Commissioners, a later time; (6) enabling the Commissioners to dispense with the requirement to provide any of the information specified where they are satisfied that a manufacturer is unable to provide that information despite taking reasonable steps to do so; and (7) specifying the information to be provided by the manufacturer.

The Tobacco Products and Excise Goods (Amendment) Regulations 2006, SI 2006/1787 (in force on 1 August 2006), further amend (1) the Excise Goods (Holding, Movement, Warehousing and REDS) Regulations 1992, SI 1992/3135, by removing the definition of 'chewing tobacco'; and (2) the 2001 Regulations supra so as to (a) prevent registered tobacco factories and registered tobacco stores from being occupied by more than one manufacturer of tobacco products; (b) remove the prohibition on removal of tobacco products from a registered factory to a registered store that is not occupied by the manufacturer of those products; (c) for the purpose of determining the excise duty point for tobacco products, include the sale of such products to a person who is not a manufacturer within the concept of failure to comply with duty suspension arrangements; (d) enable a traveller from countries outside the European Union to import unmarked tobacco products in excess of his duty-free allowance, if he pays the excise duty on those products; (e) permit duty paid, but unmarked, tobacco products to be used for testing quality or testing products being developed; and (f) make provision for the remission of excise duty on tobacco products which are used for testing quality and on tobacco products which are being developed, provided they are not smoked by human beings.

921   Excise duty—travellers' allowances and personal reliefs—new member states

The Customs and Excise Duties (Travellers' Allowances and Personal Reliefs) (New Member States) (Amendment) Order 2006, SI 2006/3157 (in force on 1 January 2007), amends the 2004 Order, SI 2004/1002, so as to give effect to derogations contained in the Act concerning the Accession of the Republic of Bulgaria and Romania to the European Union which relate to quantitative limits on the amount of cigarettes which may, without further excise duty payment, be brought into certain existing member states from those new member states.

922   Excise goods—intra-Community trade

See para 920.

923   Finance Act 2006

See para 2465.

924   Free movement of goods—quantitative restrictions and equivalent measures—prohibition of doorstop selling

A woman operated a business, based in Germany, which involved visiting the private homes of individuals in other member states in order to sell jewellery. She also organised private parties at which she promoted and sold her products. A competitor brought a complaint against the woman on the basis that the woman's activities included doorstop selling and the holding of parties in Austria, where such practices were prohibited by statute. It fell to be determined whether the Austrian law was contrary to the right to the free movement of goods enshrined in the EC Treaty arts 28 and 30. *Held*, the prohibition on the selling of jewellery by way of visits to private homes was not precluded by art 28 provided the restriction affected, in law and in fact, the marketing of products from other member states in the same way as it affected domestic products. It was for the national court to determine whether the prohibition was liable to restrict the access to the market of products from other member states in comparison with domestic products, and whether the prohibition could be justified by an objective in the general interest for the purposes of art 30.

Case C-441/04 *A-Punkt Schmuckhandels GmbH v Schmidt* [2006] All ER (EC) 1118 (ECJ: Third Chamber).

925   Free movement of goods—quantitative restrictions and equivalent measures—prohibition of transport—proportionality

A local authority in Austria imposed a prohibition, in respect of a specified section of a major motorway, on the transportation of certain goods at night by lorries weighing over 7·5 tonnes. Austria claimed that the prohibition was necessary in order to comply with EC Council Directive 99/30, which set limit values for nitrogen dioxide in ambient air. The European Commission sought a declaration that Austria had failed to fulfil its obligations under the EC Treaty arts 28–30, on the ground that the prohibition mainly affected the international transit of goods and was therefore, at least indirectly, discriminatory. The Commission contended that the measure could not be justified on environmental grounds because it was discriminatory in its application, and that it did not comply with the principle of proportionality. *Held*, by prohibiting vehicles weighing over 7·5 tonnes from carrying certain categories of goods from travelling along a main route of communication between southern Germany and northern Italy, the Austrian authority had obstructed the free movement of goods and, in particular, their free transit. While the protection of the environment might justify the existence of national measures capable of obstructing intra-Community trade, the prohibition was not proportionate. The Austrian authorities were under a duty to examine carefully the possibility of using measures which were less restrictive of the freedom of movement and to discount them only if their inadequacy, in relation to the objective pursued, was clearly established. The measure adopted infringed the principle of proportionality and could not therefore be justified by reasons concerning the protection of air quality.

Case C-320/03 *EC Commission v Austria* [2006] All ER (EC) 513 (ECJ: Grand Chamber).

926 Free movement of goods—quantitative restrictions and equivalent measures—tax charged on goods delivered abroad

The applicant was an operator which had landed during the relevant financial year a large quantity of shrimp part of which was sold at auction in the Netherlands and part of which was delivered directly to Denmark to be marketed there. The respondent, a Dutch fish marketing board, levied a charge on the applicant in respect of the shrimp delivered to Denmark. The applicant's appeal against the decision was refused and, on its further appeal, a reference was made to the European Court of Justice for a preliminary ruling as to whether a charge such as the one imposed by the respondent constituted a charge having an effect equivalent to customs duties within the meaning of the EC Treaty art 25 or was discriminatory internal taxation prohibited by art 90. *Held*, a charge levied by an association governed by public law on the basis of criteria which were identical in the case of both national products intended for the national market and products for export to other member states constituted a charge having an effect equivalent to an export duty, prohibited by arts 23, 25, if the revenue from that charge was used to finance activities which benefited only the national products intended for the national market and the advantages stemming from the use of the revenue from that charge fully offset the burden borne by those products. On the other hand, if the advantages accruing to the national products processed or marketed on the national market from the use of the revenue generated by that charge offset only partially the burden borne by those products, such a charge would constitute a breach of the prohibition on discrimination laid down by art 90.

Case C-517/04 *Visserijbedrijf DJ Koornstra & Zn vof v Productschap Vis* [2006] 3 CMLR 565 (ECJ: Second Chamber).

927 Forfeiture—seizure of goods—confiscation of motor vehicle—appeal—amount within guidelines

During a week on holiday, the appellant travelled several times to the continent in his car. A customs officer stopped him to discuss his trips abroad and the goods he had brought back. The customs officer requested an interview, during which the appellant admitted that he had purchased an amount of cigarettes, tobacco, whiskey and wine, which, although substantial, was within the recommended guidelines, and which he maintained was for his own use. However, the Commissioners for Her Majesty's Revenue and Customs concluded that the goods were being held for a commercial purpose and that the appellant's goods and vehicle should be seized. The appellant appealed against the seizure of the vehicle. The Commissioners refused the request on the ground that the vehicle had been used for the improper importation of excise goods, and further, that it was not a first occurrence. The appellant made a further appeal to a VAT and duties tribunal. The tribunal dismissed the appeal and the appellant appealed further, disputing the transcript of the interview. *Held*, the tribunal's conclusion that the transcript was accurate was justified on the facts, in particular, the unchallenged evidence of the officer that the appellant signed it as a correct record. The fact that the quantity of the goods did not exceed the figure in the guidelines was not decisive as to whether the goods were held for commercial purposes or for private use. It was merely one of the relevant factors. In the present case, there were ample circumstances justifying the tribunal's conclusion. Accordingly, the appeal would be dismissed.

Harrison v Revenue and Customs Comrs [2006] EWHC 2844 (Ch), [2007] RTR 157 (Chancery Division: Lightman J).

928 Statistics of trade

The Statistics of Trade (Customs and Excise) (Amendment) Regulations 2006, SI 2006/3216 (in force on 1 January 2007), further amend the 1992 Regulations, SI 1992/2790, so as to (1) increase, from £225,000 to £260,000, the threshold, expressed in terms of annual value of intra-Community trade, above which a business is required to provide a supplementary declaration for Intrastat; the threshold applies separately for goods dispatched and goods received; (2) align the 1992 Regulations with EC Council and European Parliament Regulation 638/2004; (3) increase, from £14,000,000 to £14,500,000, the threshold, expressed in terms of annual value of intra-Community trade, above which 'delivery terms' information must be provided in the supplementary declaration; (4) enable the Commissioners for Her Majesty's Revenue and Customs to give directions specifying the format for the supplementary declaration where the declaration is delivered by electronic means; and (5) make necessary and appropriate textual changes.

929   Value added tax

See VALUE ADDED TAX.

930   Warehousekeepers and owners of warehoused goods

The Warehousekeepers and Owners of Warehoused Goods (Amendment) Regulations 2006, SI 2006/577 (in force on 1 April 2006), amend the 1999 Regulations, SI 1999/1278, so as to make provision for an authorised warehousekeeper to be relieved from liability to pay excise duty by abandoning goods to the Commissioners of Her Majesty's Revenue and Customs when a registered owner or duty representative either fails to provide the authorised warehousekeeper with his certificate of registration or fails to give notice to the authorised warehousekeeper that his registration has been revoked.

DAMAGES AND COMPENSATION

Halsbury's Laws of England (4th edn) vol 12(1) (Reissue) paras 801–1164

Articles

For articles relating to this title please refer to the Table of Articles at the beginning of the Abridgment.

Contributors

Our thanks to the following, who have contributed items to this title
Richard Adkinson, Counsel
Andrew Arentsen, Counsel
Leila Benyounes, Counsel
Sarah Boyd, Counsel
Nigel Brockley, Counsel
Richard Case, Counsel
CMHT, Solicitors
Richard Cole, Counsel
James Counsell, Counsel
Corinna Ferguson, Pupil Barrister
Dyer Burdett & Co, Solicitors
Stephen Garner, Counsel
Titus Gibson, Counsel
Peter Goodbody, Counsel
Andrew Granville Stafford, Counsel
Joanna Kerr, Counsel
David McHugh, Counsel
Colin Mendoza, Counsel
Chris Middleton, Counsel
Tom Nossiter, Counsel
Colm Nugent, Counsel
Andrew Granville Stafford, Counsel
Gurion Taussig, Counsel
Rebecca Tuck, Counsel
Jonathan Thompson, Counsel
Justyn Turner, Counsel
Anthony Verduyn, Counsel
Adam Walker, Counsel
Stuart Yeung, Counsel

931   Assessment of damages—equitable damages—damages in lieu of injunction—date of assessment

See *Liverpool and Lancashire Properties Ltd v Lunn Poly Ltd*, para 1703.

932   Assessment of damages—interest—interest on debt—ancillary proceedings

The Supreme Court Act 1981 s 35A(3) provides that, where there are proceedings (whenever instituted) before the High Court for the recovery of a debt, and the defendant pays the whole debt to the plaintiff (otherwise than in pursuance of a judgment in the proceedings), the defendant is liable to pay the plaintiff simple interest at such rate as the court thinks fit or as rules of court may provide on all or any part of the debt for all or any part of the period between the date when the cause of action arose and the date of the payment.

The claimant, who suffered from senile dementia of an Alzheimer's type, resided at a nursing home for which the defendant health board had responsibility. The claimant paid the entirety of the charges levied by the local authority in respect of his accommodation. The claimant subsequently sought to challenge the decision that he was not entitled to NHS funding, but his claim was refused by a special review panel. He applied for judicial review of that decision. Before permission to apply for judicial review had been granted, two further panels convened and found that the claimant had been eligible for continuing NHS funding for the entire period, that he should receive full reimbursement, and that the relevant NHS body should be responsible for the continuing cost of his placement at the nursing home. At the judicial review proceedings, an issue arose as to whether the court had jurisdiction pursuant to the 1981 Act s 35A to award interest on the sum to be repaid. Held, the term 'debt' in s 35A extended to sums of money subject to an obligation, however arising, to repay them. The principal sum to be repaid to the claimant could therefore properly be classed as a debt. To restrict the scope of debts to those arising under a contract would be unduly narrow. The essential ingredient was an obligation to pay over the money. Also, the phrase 'proceedings (whenever instituted)' in s 35A disclosed only one trigger point for the potential application of the provision, namely the institution of proceedings. It followed that s 35A applied to a claim which had been made ancillary to judicial review where the judicial review proceedings had not reached the permission stage. Irrespective of whether a claim on administrative law grounds was permitted to proceed beyond the permission stage, the proceedings allied to it for the recovery of debt or damages and, as in the present case, restitution had to be capable of trial as if they were common law proceedings. Furthermore, for the purpose of an award of interest, it was not necessary to consider the chances of success if the claim had proceeded to trial where the sum was paid before judgment. Judgment would be given accordingly.

R (on the application of Kemp) v Denbighshire Local Health Board [2006] EWHC 181 (Admin), [2006] All ER (D) 230 (Feb) (Queen's Bench Division: Langstaff J). *R v Kensington and Chelsea RLBC, ex p Ghebregiogis* (1994) 27 HLR 602 applied.

933 Assessment of damages—loss of opportunity—assessment at notional trial date—information available but not presented at notional trial date

The claimant was injured in a road traffic accident and was diagnosed as having sustained a false traumatic aneurysm of the left carotid artery, which prevented him from working. The other driver admitted liability, but damages proceedings were struck out for want of prosecution several years later. The claimant then brought a negligence claim against the defendants, his former solicitors, for the amount of damages he would have received from the other driver but for the defendants' incompetence. By the time of trial, it became apparent that the claimant did not have a false aneurysm, he did not need an operation and could work in precisely the same way as he had worked before. The claimant contended that that information was relevant to the proceedings against the defendants, as it revealed he had not acted unreasonably in refusing the operation and that there should therefore be no notional discount of the loss of earnings he had incurred. The defendants claimed that the damages should be reduced in the light of the claimant's failure to mitigate his loss, and that the fact that the diagnoses had later proven to be incorrect was irrelevant. The judge decided that the damages for loss of earnings should be discounted, and the claimant appealed. *Held*, there was authority for the proposition that, if the further evidence which became available should, if the solicitors had not been negligent, have been available at the trial to assist the claimant's case, it could be taken into account to the advantage of the claimant. The later scan and opinion, which would probably have been available at the date of the notional trial, had had a material influence on the question whether the claimant stood a good or a bad chance of convincing a trial judge at the earlier time that he was acting reasonably. Once that evidence had been introduced to the benefit of the claimant as in assessing the likelihood of what a notional judge would be likely to have done, it had to be evidence for all purposes. The defendant had also to be entitled to rely on it if it assisted in reaching a more accurate result as to what the claimant had in fact lost. Even if the claimant had not relied himself on the evidence, it ought to be admissible on the basis that it was better not to speculate or hazard guesses where hindsight could lead to a more accurate assessment of what a claimant had lost. Accordingly, the appeal would be allowed.

Dudarec v Andrews [2006] EWCA Civ 256, [2006] 2 All ER 856 (Court of Appeal: Waller, Sedley and Smith LJJ).

934 Assessment of damages—method—negligence—cost of cure

The buyer of a football club used the claimant company as the commercial vehicle to effect the transaction. The defendant firm of solicitors was hired by the buyer to provide legal advice in connection with the transaction. Under the sale agreement, the vendors were to take 25 per cent of the shares in a new company controlling the club, with the claimant taking the remaining 75 per cent. A new shareholders' agreement gave the vendors certain protections as minority shareholders, including provisions which operated to prevent their shareholdings being diluted without their consent or participation. It was intended that there would be a clause in that agreement providing for the buyer to be able to override the vendors' protection once it had invested a specified sum. However, that clause was removed by the defendants' partner acting in the transaction shortly before completion. The claimant brought an action for negligence against the defendants, contending that, owing to the absence of the clause, the claimant was not in a position to be able to dilute the vendors' shareholding as had originally been envisaged. The claimant subsequently bought out the vendors and claimed the cost of doing so from the defendants on the basis that that was what it cost to put itself in the position it should have been from the outset. An issue arose in damages as to whether the cost of cure relied on was the real and proper measure of the claimant's loss. *Held*, there was no reason in principle why the cost of cure should not be allowed in solicitor's negligence cases. Since the object of an award of damages was compensatory, and since that principle, and not the mechanism, was paramount, it would be surprising if any particular way of calculating loss would be allowed in certain types of case but not in others, merely because of their categorisation. It might be that certain types lent themselves naturally to certain ways of measuring loss, but that did not mean that in some instances another measure would be inappropriate. In the circumstances, the claimant had not established a cost of cure sufficiently clearly to enable the court to conclude that it was an appropriate measure of its loss. The amount claimed was not a reasonable sum to pay to cure the negligence. The claimant succeeded on liability but had failed to establish most of the loss relied on. Judgment would be given accordingly.

Fulham Leisure Holdings Ltd v Nicholson Graham & Jones (a firm) [2006] EWHC 2017 (Ch), [2006] All ER (D) 461 (Jul) (Chancery Division: Mann J).

935   Assessment of damages—personal injury—future pecuniary loss—settlement—continuity of payment reasonably secure

Clinical negligence claims were made against a defendant NHS Foundation Trust and a defendant NHS Trust which had applied for NHS Foundation Trust status. Both defendants were members of the Clinical Negligence Scheme for Trusts ('CNST'), a scheme covering liability for alleged clinical negligence. The scheme was administered by the NHS Litigation Authority ('NHSLA'). Orders were made by the Secretary of State in accordance with terms agreed by the parties in settlement of the claims. Each order included provision for appropriate periodical payments to be made to the claimant in respect of future pecuniary loss, pursuant to the Damages Act 1996 s 2(1)(a). Under the National Health Service Residual Liabilities Act 1996 s 1, if an NHS Trust ceased to exist the Secretary of State had to exercise his statutory powers to transfer property, rights and liabilities of the body so as to secure that all of its liabilities were dealt with. However, under the Health and Social Care (Community Health and Standards) Act 2003, the Secretary of State, in the event of an NHS Foundation Trust ceasing to exist, had a discretion as to whether to order the transfer of liabilities. The issue to be decided was whether the continuity of payment under each of the proposed orders was reasonably secure as required by the Damages Act 1996 s 2(3). *Held*, the various arrangements and agreements concluded between the NHSLA and the parties and between the NHSLA and the Secretary of State had overcome the essential difficulty and dealt satisfactorily with the perceived lacuna because they had ensured that the NHSLA was the effective source of the periodical payments made under each of the orders and that, if necessary, each order could be directly enforced against the NHSLA. The continuity of the payments was reasonably secure as required by s 2(3). Judgment would be given accordingly.

YM v Gloucestershire Hospitals NHS Foundation; Kanu v King's College Hospital Trust [2006] EWHC 821 (QB), [2006] All ER (D) 187 (Apr) (Queen's Bench Division: Forbes J).

936   Bereavement damages—restriction on class of entitled persons—compatibility with right to life

See *Cameron v Network Rail Infrastructure Ltd*, para 1533.

937   Breach of contract—breach of restrictions imposed by settlement agreement—entitlement to payment as quid pro quo for relaxation of settlement terms

The parties became involved in a trade mark dispute concerning the use of the initials of their names which were identical. They reached an agreement which placed substantial restrictions on the defendant's right to use the initials. An inquiry into whether the claimants had sustained damages by reason of the defendant's breaches of the agreement was ordered. At the trial of a preliminary issue, the court was asked to decide whether the claimants were entitled to claim damages in the form of a reasonable payment as a quid pro quo for relaxing their rights under the agreement. The claimants contended that, where there was a breach of contract, the innocent party was entitled to claim as damages a reasonable payment in respect of the hypothetical release of the breach of contract. The defendant argued that the profits which were sought to be attacked had to be demonstrated to be derived from the actual breach of contract. *Held*, in a case of this kind, the court had to consider the sum that would have been arrived at in negotiations between the parties had each been making reasonable use of their respective bargaining positions without holding out for unreasonable amounts. It was possible that the damages could reflect harm caused to the claimant's reputation and a reasonable price representing that, or a reasonable sum for the relaxation of the covenant or a negotiation of a reasonable sum that the parties would have agreed as being payable for the breach of the covenant by reference to the subsequent profits in percentage terms (or a combination of all three). The court could take into account the factors relating to the potential for earning profits without committing a breach of contract and the cost of making such profits. The overriding principle was that the damages were compensatory and not to be punitive. They should reflect the nature of the negotiations that took place hypothetically. Ordinarily, where a claim was based on subsequent profits, the claimants had to show that there was a reasonable prospect of there being a connection between the breach of contract and the subsequent profits. The claimants were entitled in the inquiry to seek damages in the form of a reasonable payment as a quid pro quo on the basis of their claim as presently formulated. Judgment would be given accordingly.

WWF-World Wide Fund for Nature (formerly World Wildlife Fund) v World Wrestling Federation Entertainment Inc [2006] EWHC 184 (Ch), [2006] All ER (D) 212 (Feb) (Chancery Division: Peter Smith J). *Wrotham Park Estate Co Ltd v Parkside Homes Ltd* [1974] 2 All ER 321 (1974 Abr para 1281) considered.

938 Breach of contract—measure of damages—date of assessment—multiple breaches—acceptance of breach

The claimant, a coal importer, concluded an agreement with the defendant, a coal trader, for the sale and delivery of five large shipments of coal by an agreed date. The sale contract also contained options, which the claimant duly exercised, for the purchase of two additional shipments of coal, that were to be delivered by a later date. Following the failure of the defendant to make delivery on time of any of the shipments, the claimant wrote to the defendant informing it that it would extend the available delivery time but that failure to comply in that time would be deemed a repudiatory breach of contract. The defendant contended that there was no formal contract, and the claimant responded by stating that it was treating the contract as being at an end. Judgment in default was eventually entered in favour of the claimant, and an issue arose as to the relevant date for determining damages. The claimant submitted that the appropriate date was the point at which it communicated to the defendant that the contract had been terminated, so that it was entitled to the difference in the contract price and the market value of the coal at that point. The defendant argued that damages should be assessed as at the earlier point when it had failed to make delivery within the terms of the agreement as originally made. *Held*, the claimant was entitled to base its claim on the wrongful failure of the defendant to deliver the optional shipments. Any earlier breaches by the defendant were certainly of a repudiatory nature, but the breaches were never accepted by the claimant as bringing the contract to an end. When the defendant failed to deliver within the period stipulated at the outset, its obligation was not terminated or cancelled; it remained obliged to deliver the shipments until it had actually done so. The claimant had acted reasonably from that point on in keeping open the contracts for the two optional shipments. The sale contract itself gave it the right to continue to demand performance, and it was plain on the facts that the claimant was pressing the defendant to perform and deliver the two optional shipments. The claimant was therefore entitled to the sum claimed. Judgment would be given accordingly.

Carbopego-Abastecimento de Combustiveis SA v Amci Export Corpn [2006] EWHC 72 (Comm), [2006] 1 Lloyd's Rep 736 (Queen's Bench Division: Aikens J).

939 Compensation Act 2006

See para 2771.

940 Consumer protection—compensation—claims management services

The Compensation (Claims Management Services) Regulations 2006, SI 2006/3322 (in force on 12 December 2006), (1) make provision about waiver, by the regulator appointed under the Compensation Act 2006, of the requirement for a person who provides regulated claims management services to be authorised; such a waiver will be granted to a person only if the regulator is satisfied that the Secretary of State intends to exempt the person from that requirement and only for a maximum period of six months; a waiver cannot be renewed; (2) provide that members of certain professions whose professional conduct is already regulated, in particular, barristers, solicitors and legal executives, and certain other classes of person that are regulated in other ways, will be exempted from the 2006 Act Pt 2 by order by the Secretary of State; certain persons or bodies that provide regulated claims management services on a not-for-profit basis will also be exempted; (3) deal with applications for authorisation to provide regulated claims management services; (4) authorise the regulator to prescribe fees for application for and grant of authorisations and the renewal of authorisations; the fees must be approved by the Secretary of State; (5) set out the requirements for the rules and codes of practice, with which authorised persons must comply; (6) set out the scheme for review by the regulator of an authorised person's handling of complaints; the regulator may review the authorised person's records and may give the authorised person directions about the future handling of the complaint or of complaints generally; (7) provide for the regulator to audit an authorised person's records, at a reasonable time and on reasonable notice; the authorised person is however not obliged to show the regulator anything that is an item subject to legal privilege, as defined in the Police and Criminal Evidence Act 1984; (8) provide for enforcement; the regulations deal with the investigation of allegations or suspicion that a person has breached the 2006 Act; (9) deal with the investigation of allegations or suspicion that authorised persons have failed to comply with conditions of authorisation; the regulations also provide for circumstances in which the regulator may apply to a judge of the High Court, circuit judge or justice of the peace for a search warrant; (10) deal with search warrants generally; and (11) deal with suspension and cancellation of an authorisation; an authorised person whose authorisation is cancelled, suspended or varied has the right of appeal to the Claims Management Services Tribunal and to the Court of Appeal.

941   Consumer protection—compensation—regulated claims management services

The Compensation (Regulated Claims Management Services) Order 2006, SI 2006/3319 (in force on 13 December 2006), prescribes specified services when provided in connection with certain kinds of claim; the services include advertising for claimants, referral of claimants to legal practitioners, advice in relation to claims and investigation of claims, and the kinds of claim include personal injury claims and criminal injuries compensation claims, employment-related claims such as claims for wages, unfair dismissal and discrimination, claims for housing disrepair, claims relating to financial products or services and industrial injuries disability benefits.

942   Consumer protection—compensation—specification of benefits

The Compensation (Specification of Benefits) Order 2006, SI 2006/3321 (in force on 13 December 2006), provides that a claim for industrial injuries benefit is to be treated as a claim for the purposes of the Compensation Act 2006 Pt 2.

943   Contribution—joint and several liability—discrimination damages

See *Miles v Gilbank*, para 1075.

944   Contribution—several tortfeasors—apportionment of liability—personal injury— asbestos related claims

See *Barker v Corus (UK) Ltd; Murray v British Shipbuilders (Hydrodynamics) Ltd; Patterson v Smiths Dock Ltd*, para 2075.

945   Contribution—third party proceedings—claim in respect of same damage—knowing receipt

The Civil Liability (Contribution) Act 1978 s 1(1) provides that any person liable in respect of any damage suffered by another person may recover contribution from any other person liable in respect of the same damage. A person is liable in respect of any damage for these purposes if the person who suffered it is entitled to recover compensation from him in respect of that damage: s 6(1).

The second claimant company was a subsidiary of the first claimant, the holding company of a multinational group of engineering companies. The defendant carried on the business of spread betting, primarily in relation to financial markets. An employee of another of the first claimant's subsidiaries arranged for the transfer of large sums of money into the defendant's account in order to finance his personal spread betting transactions with the defendant. The claimants' action against the defendant for the recovery of the money was settled on terms that the defendant pay the claimants a certain sum. The defendant brought Pt 20 proceedings against some of the past and present directors of the claimants and the group auditors (the Pt 20 defendants) claiming contribution or indemnity under the 1978 Act in relation to the sum repaid by the employee. The Pt 20 defendants applied for orders striking out the Pt 20 claim or summarily dismissing it, contending that the defendant's liability to restore the money was neither 'in respect of damage' nor to make 'compensation in respect of that damage' within the meaning of ss 1(1) and 6(1). *Held*, a claim for knowing receipt was a claim for compensation for damage sustained in consequence of a breach of trust notwithstanding that it might also be described as restitutionary. A claim for knowing receipt could not exist in the absence of the breach of trust from which the receipt originated. If the recipient had the relevant knowledge then he too was accountable to the trust or beneficiary and was liable to make good the loss or damage to the extent of what he had received. If the basis of his liability was not within the express reference to 'breach of trust' in s 6(1) then it appeared to be clearly comprehended by the following words 'or otherwise'. If that was not the case then the 1978 Act did not enable the court to order the defaulting trustee to contribute to the liability of or to indemnify the knowing recipient or vice versa. It followed that a disposition in breach of trust gave rise to damage, loss or harm to the trust and the beneficiaries and a liability on the part of both the defaulting trustee and a knowing recipient based on that breach of trust and the requisite knowledge to compensate for that damage, loss or harm by restoring to the trust or beneficiary the equivalent of that which it had lost. It followed that the defendant's Pt 20 claim satisfied the requirements of ss 1 and 6, and, accordingly, the application would be dismissed.

Charter plc v City Index Ltd [2006] EWHC 2508 (Ch), (2006) 9 ITELR 276 (Chancery Division: Sir Andrew Morritt C). *Friends' Provident Life Office v Hillier, May & Rowden* [1997] QB 85, CA (1995 Abr para 2839), applied.

946   Defamation—measure of damages—offer of amends—mitigation

See *Turner v News Group Newspapers Ltd*, para 1792.

947   Fatal accident—dependency claim—assessment of damages

The claimant, the deceased's widow, brought proceedings for damages on behalf of the deceased's estate and dependants. At the time of his death, the deceased and the claimant had been running a garage business in a partnership in which the claimant had played no active role. After the deceased's death, the claimant and her family had run the business. It fell to be determined whether, in assessing the dependency, any potential benefit to the claimant to be derived from the business was to be disregarded as an exception to the general rule that, where a wife was working before her husband's death, so that her earnings were contributing to the family pool, and she continued to work after his death, her earnings fell to be taken into account. *Held*, in assessing a dependency claim in a fatal accidents case, the task of the court was to assess whether and, if so, to what extent and for what duration, those on whose behalf the claim to a dependency was brought would have been financially dependent on the deceased. In the case of a claim brought on behalf of a widow, it would be necessary to consider whether she would have worked after the death of her husband, although she might not have been working at the time of his death. If the court was satisfied on the evidence that a widow would have returned to work if her husband had survived, and that her earnings would have contributed to the family pool, her prospective earnings would be taken into account in assessing the dependency. Had the deceased survived, the claimant would have continued to be supported by him from the profits generated by the business but the claimant would not have played any active role. Her position was quite different from that of a widow who would have continued working, or at some future date returned to work, and contributed to the family pool. If the claimant was obliged to give credit for future financial benefits from the business, she would not have been compensated for the loss of her dependency on the deceased.

Wolfe v Del Innocenti [2006] EWHC 2694 (QB), [2006] All ER (D) 359 (Oct) (Queen's Bench Division: Owen J). *Howitt v Heads* [1973] QB 64 not followed; *Cookson v Knowles* [1977] 2 All ER 820, CA (1977 Abr para 838) (affirmed [1979] AC 556, HL (1979 Abr para 863)), considered.

948   Measure of damages—future losses—prospective events—determination

See *Seafield Holdings (t/a Seafield Logistics) v Drewett*, para 1266.

949   Personal injury—assessment of damages—fatal accident—benefit accruing before death—double recovery

The Fatal Accidents Act 1976 s 4 provides that, in assessing damages in respect of a person's death in an action, benefits which have accrued or will or may accrue to any person from his estate or otherwise as a result of his death are to be disregarded.

The claimant's husband worked for the defendant company in Libya. He was a member of the defendant's provident fund scheme, under which an employee was entitled in appropriate circumstances to a permanent disability payment from the defendant of half of the amount of his accrued savings. On retirement, a member also received an end of service gratuity required under Libyan labour law. The husband was diagnosed with malignant mesothelioma resulting from tortious exposure to asbestos while in the employment of the defendant. He chose not to return to Libya and the defendant terminated his employment. The permanent disability payment accrued to the husband and passed into his estate, of which the claimant was the sole beneficiary, when he died some time later. The claimant sought damages under the 1976 Act. The only item of damages that was in dispute concerned the end of service payment, which the defendant argued was unrecoverable in view of the fact that the claimant had already received the permanent disability payment and should not be permitted double recovery. The claimant sought to rely on s 4. The judge ruled in her favour and the defendant appealed. *Held*, it was no objection in itself in a s 4 case that double recovery resulted. That possibility was inherent in the statute itself, because the issue of disregard of a sum could not arise unless that sum would in a proper computation and without disregard have to be taken into account as reducing the damages. The strong balance of probabilities was that the husband was on course to retire several years later, at which point the end of service benefits would have accrued. It was that benefit that he and the claimant had lost by his premature death. Section 4 did not come into operation as the disability payment which occurred was not a payment to the claimant but a payment to the deceased. What the claimant had in the event obtained was not that payment but the amount by which the estate was enhanced by having the payment made into it. That payment, however, only benefited the claimant because it formed part of the deceased's estate: the very item that s 4 said should not be brought into the account and for which credit did not have to be given. Accordingly, the appeal would be dismissed.

McIntyre v Harland & Wolff plc [2006] EWCA Civ 287, [2006] ICR 1222 (Court of Appeal: Buxton, Lloyd and Richards LJJ). *Auty v National Coal Board* [1985] 1 All ER 930, CA (1984 Abr para 769), distinguished.

950   Personal injury—assessment of damages—future pecuniary loss—periodical payments—variation in payments

The Damages Act 1996 s 2(8) provides that an order for periodical payments must be treated as providing for the amount of payments to vary by reference to the retail prices index at such times, and in such manner, as may be determined by or in accordance with the Civil Procedure Rules. An order for periodical payments may include provision disapplying or modifying the effect of the 1996 Act s 2(8): s 2(9).

The claimant had a serious accident at work. The defendant admitted liability, and an issue arose in damages concerning the approach the court should take when making an order for periodical payments. The claimant argued that a wage-related index such as the average earnings index was more suitable than the retail prices index as the mechanism for varying the sums payable under the periodical payments order. The defendant applied to strike out that contention from the claimant's statement of case, contending that the 1996 Act s 2(9), which authorised the court to impose a non-standard method for varying the payments, could only be triggered in exceptional circumstances. The application was dismissed and the defendant appealed. *Held*, there was nothing in the language of s 2(8), (9) to suggest that the power to make provision such as identified in s 2(9) might only be triggered in an exceptional case. There was no indication in s 2 that Parliament had intended to depart from the well-known principle that the object of the award was to place the injured party as nearly as possible in the same financial position as he would have been in but for the accident nor was there anything in the statute to indicate that, in implementing s 2, Parliament had intended the courts to depart from the principle that a victim of a tort was entitled to be compensated as nearly as possible in full for all pecuniary losses. The claimant should be allowed to advance his statement of case and adduce the evidence of an appropriate expert witness at the trial of the action. It would then be for the trial judge to decide whether it was appropriate to use the powers given to him in s 2(9), without being obliged to detect exceptional circumstances before he was at liberty to depart from the use of the retail prices index. Accordingly, the appeal would be dismissed.

Flora v Wakom [2006] EWCA Civ 1103, [2006] 4 All ER 982 (Court of Appeal: Sir Mark Potter P, Brooke and Moore-Bick LJJ).

951   Personal injury—assessment of damages—road traffic accident—causation—expert evidence

See *Casey v Cartwright*, para 2278.

952   Personal injury—assessment of damages—special damages—deductions—injury benefits

The claimant was seriously injured in a road traffic accident for which the defendant accepted liability. Her life expectancy was assessed for the purposes of the damages award at a further 33 years. A dispute arose concerning whether there should be a deduction from the claimant's compensation in respect of future direct payments for domiciliary care received from a local authority pursuant to the National Assistance Act 1948 s 29 and the Health and Social Care Act 2001 s 57. Recoupment of such direct payments was provided for in guidance issued by the Department of Health. *Held*, there was simply no principled basis on which the court could estimate what funding the claimant could reliably expect to receive from the authority over the rest of her life, and it could not be appropriate to impose on the claimant the unnecessary risk that funding from an alternative source might cease or be reduced rather than simply to order the provision in its entirety of a fund to meet the claimant's needs for the rest of her life. It was entirely reasonable for the claimant to decline to place reliance on state funding for any part of her care. Recoupment under the 1948 Act s 29 was a matter of discretion, informed only by ministerial guidance, which guidance was, in any event, inconclusive as to the thresholds at which a contribution might be sought, and silent as to the maximum amount of any such contribution. Ministerial guidance was essentially ephemeral in nature, subject to change without any form of legislative process. The possibility of a reduction in the level of publicly funded services was obvious to any moderately well-informed person, and, in the instant case, the court was invited, at the very least, to find that there was a substantial prospect that, for a significant proportion of the next 33 years, the claimant would continue to receive a sizeable contribution to her care costs. Moreover, the defendant had offered the claimant no indemnity in case her current funding from the authority should in the future be withdrawn or reduced, and it was entirely reasonable for the claimant to adopt a course of conduct that gave her an element of unfettered flexibility as to where she lived, however unlikely it might seem that she would wish to leave her home county. Judgment would be given accordingly.

Freeman v Lockett [2006] EWHC 102 (QB), [2006] PIQR P340 (Queen's Bench Division: Tomlinson J). *Godbold v Mahmood* [2005] EWHC 1002 (QB), [2005] All ER (D) 251 (Apr) considered. *Hodgson v Trapp* [1989] AC 807, HL (1988 Abr para 264); and *Sowden v Lodge; Crookdale v Drury* [2004] EWCA Civ 1370, [2005] 1 All ER 581 distinguished.

953   Personal injury—fatal accident claim—suicide following industrial accident

See *Corr v IBC Vehicles*, para 2077.

954   Personal injury—limitation periods

See LIMITATION OF ACTIONS.

955   Personal injury—pain and suffering—formation of pleural plaques resulting from exposure to asbestos—cause of action not founded by aggregating heads of claim

The defendant employers admitted negligently exposing the claimant employees to asbestos. The defendants denied, however, that the negligent exposure occasioned any injury on which a claim in damages could have been based. Each of the claimants had been diagnosed with pleural plaques, which did not normally occasion any symptoms. The pleural plaques did not in themselves lead to other, more serious, asbestos-induced conditions. However, the judge allowed the claims. On the defendants' appeals an issue was raised on which there was no direct authority at appellate level. The issue to be decided was whether, by aggregating with pleural plaques the risk of developing a more long-term asbestos-related disease or the anxiety at the prospect of suffering such a disease, sufficient damage could be demonstrated to found a cause of action. *Held,* Smith LJ dissenting, there was no legal precedent beyond first instance decisions, for aggregating three heads of claim which, individually, could not found a cause of action, so as to constitute sufficient damage to give rise to a legal claim. There was no logical basis for such an approach, nor was there any justification for departing from logic or legal principle in the case of asbestos-induced pleural plaques. If pleural plaques gave rise to a cause of action, on discovery of the existence of pleural plaques, a claimant would be advised that he should bring a claim in order to protect his position, even if he would not otherwise wish to do so unless and until he had developed symptomatic disease. There was a danger that those who made a business out of litigation, would encourage workers who had been exposed to asbestos to have CT scans in order to see whether they had pleural plaques for the sole purpose of bringing claims. Some claimants would be tempted to claim a final award, gambling, in effect, to the possible prejudice of themselves and their families, that they would not contract an asbestos-related disease. Accordingly, the appeals would be allowed.

Rothwell v Chemical & Insulating Co Ltd [2006] EWCA Civ 27, [2006] 4 All ER 1161 (Court of Appeal: Lord Phillips of Worth Matravers CJ, Longmore and Smith LJJ). Decision of Holland J [2005] EWHC 88 (QB), [2005] All ER (D) 219 (Feb) (para 05/810) reversed.

Personal injury—quantum of damages

Examples of awards of damages in personal injury or fatal accident cases are arranged in the following order. Cases involving more than one injury are classified according to the major injury suffered.

Brain damage	Burns	Arm and hand
Multiple injuries	Scarring	Leg and foot
Psychological damage	Head	Minor injuries
PTSD	Neck and shoulder	
Medical negligence	Back, chest and abdomen	
Food poisoning		

956   Brain damage

PSLA: £170,000
Total damages: £3,150,000
Sex: Male
Age at accident/infant settlement approval hearing: 10/17
Date of accident/infant settlement approval hearing: 4 September 1998/25 November 2005
Judge/Court: HHJ Hickinbottom/Queen's Bench Division

The claimant suffered **catastrophic head injuries** in a road traffic accident. The **primary injury was to the brain**. Scans demonstrated **haemorrhages and extensive contusions** within the **left temporal lobe** as well as within the **right frontal, temporal and parietal regions**. The claimant also sustained **orthopaedic injuries** including **fractures to the leg and hip**. He was **in hospital for nearly one year** before returning to the care of his family. He was diagnosed with **right sided hemi-pariaesis with gross neurological dysfunction**. He had **extreme physical and mental disability**. He was **unable to stand without support** and had **no active use of his dominant right hand**. His **speech and linguistic skills were compromised** and his **cognitive abilities reduced**. His **concentration and memory** were **markedly impaired**. He required **24-hour care**. The clear prognosis was that he was **unlikely to improve to any appreciable degree**. He would probably be **incapable of obtaining or retaining remunerative employment** and would certainly **require ongoing treatment** in the form of **physiotherapy, speech therapy and**

occupational therapy, as well as **possible orthopaedic surgery**. A **specialist brain injury case manager would be essential** for the claimant to enjoy some partial quality of life.

J (A Child) v Jones (deceased) (25 November 2005, unreported) (Nicholas Cooke QC and Andrew Arentsen, Counsel, for the claimant; Simon Browne, Counsel, for the defendant) (Kindly submitted for publication by Andrew Arentsen, Counsel).

957   Brain damage

PSLA: £40,000
Total damages: £299,969 (subject to 25 per cent reduction for contributory negligence)
Sex: Male
Age at accident: 18
Date of accident/trial: 10 August 2001/2 May 2006
Judge/Court: HHJ Vincent/Bodmin County Court

The claimant was involved in a road traffic accident when the car in which he was a rear seat passenger left the road. He was **struck on the head by the rear parcel shelf** of the car. Scans of his brain and skull showed a **small area of bleeding** in the **right parietal region**, which **had not caused any mass effect**. There was also a **small haemorrhage** noted in the **left frontal lobe**. The claimant suffered from **post-traumatic amnesia** for **four to five days** and had a **low Glasgow Coma Score**. He remained **in hospital for ten days**. On returning home, he **locked himself in his bedroom for three weeks** and was **depressed**. He had **reduced insight, attention and concentration**. He felt that his **personality had changed** and that he was **not as good at social interaction** as he had been beforehand. It was established at **13–16 months post-accident** that he had **continuing memory problems**. He **confused routes when driving**. His main complaint was of **difficulty in controlling his temper**. His anger was directed particularly at his family. **No significant deterioration of intellectual functioning** was found at that time but there were **cognitive defects consistent with closed head injury**. In particular, the claimant showed a **slowing of information processing**, and visual and memory tests confirmed a pattern of **executive memory dysfunction** which led to **problems with attending to, organising and consolidating more complex information**. Four years after the accident, a **neuropsychological report** confirmed that the claimant had suffered a **brain injury**. He was reporting a **narrow range of cognitive problems**, but tests highlighted that he had **significant difficulties with verbal memory** and **poor processing speed**, which were typical of a brain-injured patient. He suffered from **lapses in memory and concentration** as a result. Prior to the accident, his **intellectual ability** had been assessed to be in the **normal range**. After the accident, however, poor memory caused him to **forget names, conversations, words he wanted to use and appointments**. **Directions were also a problem** for him. It was likely that he would **continue to be affected by symptoms** from his brain injury but that they **would not deteriorate**. Any **improvement would be in terms of adaptation and adjustment**, which would take place **slowly over a number of years**. There was a **very small increased risk of epilepsy**. The claimant was also showing **anxiety and symptoms of post-traumatic stress disorder**, although it was not clear that the full diagnostic criteria for the disorder were met. **Following the accident** he had been affected by **anxiety and avoidance of stressful situations**, **diminished interest** in previously valued activities and social interactions, and **loss of confidence with panicking** in social gatherings. He still had **recurring problems with controlling anger and losing his temper** for no reason. All of these factors changed his character and he **would find it very difficult to engage in a long-term relationship**. He underwent **16 sessions of cognitive behaviour therapy** at around 50 months post-accident. This **helped to reduce his social phobia**, helped him to **control his panic attacks** in social situations and **reduced his self-consciousness**. It also helped to **increase his confidence and lift his low mood**. As a result, he was **able to recommence some limited socialising** and to travel in to his local town on his own, but it was still a **great effort to manage everyday situations** and **fatigue was a problem**. Due to the claimant's cognitive impairment, a **need was identified for a support worker** to assist him with adapting to live independently by establishing ways of coping with normal daily activities such as shopping, paying bills, managing his home and developing independent living skills. The support worker would also **facilitate involvement in social activities** and, eventually, **accompany the claimant during his return to work**. The claimant **had returned to his part-time job** on a market stall **ten weeks after the accident**, thanks to familiarity with the environment and a sympathetic employer. He had been **unable to remain in other work or resume a college course**, but the expectation was that he would **eventually be able to return to the same type of semi-skilled work** in which he would have been **if the accident had not occurred**. Such a return to work **would only be achieved with support** and the encouragement of an understanding employer. The cognitive impairment would **prevent him reaching the fullest extent of his work potential**. The judge made an award of **£35,000 for the head and brain injury and related problems**, having concluded that the injury came **within the moderate bracket of the JSB Guidelines** but was **well away from the top end**. The claimant also sustained an **injury to his left shoulder** in the accident. After the accident, the shoulder felt **sore**, but there was **not much bruising or swelling**. However, the claimant became aware of **instability and clicking** in the shoulder **a few days after returning home** from hospital. There were **no difficulties with grip or loss of sensation** in the arm, but the claimant found it **difficult to elevate the shoulder or hold up heavy objects**. There was **little change** in this situation. The claimant took some **painkillers** in the months after the accident. At **30 months post-accident**, there was a **feeling of instability** in the shoulder, as if it was **clicking out of joint and then returning spontaneously** to the normal position. This was accompanied by **intermittent discomfort** when the shoulder was **moved into certain positions**. The **main difficulty** was in working with the arm at **shoulder level or above**. Working with the arm **below shoulder level was not a problem** and the **instability did not affect social or domestic pursuits**. The claimant was able to put the shoulder into a position in which it appeared to **glide slightly out of joint with a clunking sensation**. There was **no sign of weakness or wasting** in the shoulder and there was otherwise a **full range of movement**. There was **occasional aching** in the shoulder and **increased pain after the occurrence of clicking**. Further examination confirmed that the **scapula showed a tendency towards coming away from the chest wall on forward flexion**. An MRI scan confirmed that there was probably **damage to the long thoracic nerve** due to a **traumatic injury suffered in the accident**. The **symptoms would be permanent** but ongoing functional difficulties would cause **little functional impairment in day-to-day life**. The judge expressed the view that the **shoulder injury on its own** would probably have attracted an award of £6,000–£7,000 but, in the circumstances, the **main award for the head and brain injury was raised by £4,000** to reflect the **additional hindrance from the shoulder symptoms**. The whole award was then **rounded up by a further £1,000** to reflect some **additional very short-term problems** with **cuts, grazes and neck and back symptoms**.

Madden v Ross (2 May 2006, unreported) (Gerwyn Samuel, Counsel, instructed by Preston Goldburn, Solicitors, for the claimant; Adrian Posta, Counsel, instructed by Ashfords, Solicitors, for the defendant) (Kindly submitted for publication by Adrian Posta, Counsel).

958   Brain damage

PSLA: £30,000
Total damages: £48,000
Sex: Male
Age at accident/trial: 38/43
Date of accident/trial: 9 May 2001/6 January 2006
Judge/Court: DJ Chrispin/Romford County Court

The claimant **sustained a head injury** when he was knocked off his bicycle by the defendant's car and **briefly rendered unconscious**. He was **taken by ambulance to hospital**, where a **fracture of the left parietal bone**, a **laceration along the right eyebrow** and **several facial abrasions** were noted, together with **bruising over both legs, the right flank and the lower back**. A **CT scan** taken the next day revealed **mild soft tissue swelling in the left temporo-parietal region** and a **small quantity of blood in the left temporal area**. The claimant's **eyebrow laceration was sutured**. He suffered **brief retrograde amnesia** and around **48 hours of post-traumatic amnesia**. He was **allowed home after five days**, but was **readmitted one day later** complaining of **headaches, dizziness and vomiting**. He was **discharged after a further two days**. He continued to **suffer headaches** and experienced **episodes of aggression**. He also **had nightmares** and was **reluctant to cross the road at the site of the accident**. His **cuts and bruises settled** within **two to three weeks**. Around **a month after** the accident, and apparently as a result of the claimant's **changed personality and tendency towards violence**, his partner of 12 years, with whom he had had three children, left him. Over the following months he was **admitted to psychiatric hospital on three separate occasions** following a number of **threatened and attempted suicides**. **Four months after** the accident he locked his partner in their house and **threatened to kill her**. When the police arrived he assaulted one of the officers and **spent several months in prison** as a result. **Eighteen months after** the accident he was still suffering **frequent mood swings** and was **easily angered**, but had managed to stay out of trouble for some months. He continued to suffer **frequent headaches** and felt that his **memory and concentration had deteriorated**. He also felt that his **balance was poor**. He complained of **low mood** and took **anti-depressant medication**. He suffered **phobic anxiety**, especially when **going out and taking public transport**. A **neurological expert** found that the claimant had sustained a **moderately serious head injury**, although he was of the opinion that many of the claimant's complaints, such as **altered personality, impaired memory and concentration, poor balance and vertigo**, were **related to post-concussional syndrome** and **would improve** over time. The neurologist found it **difficult to attribute the violent incidents to the accident**. At **three years post-accident** the claimant felt that his **headaches, vertigo and irritability** were **70 per cent improved**. However, he continued to complain of **low mood** and **difficulties with his memory and concentration**. An **MRI scan** showed evidence of a **mature brain injury involving both temporal lobes**. At **four years post-accident** the claimant felt that he was **80 per cent recovered**. He had **weaned himself off his anti-depressant medication** and his main complaints were of **residual agoraphobia and travel anxiety. Cognitive behavioural therapy was recommended** to address these complaints. He was **considering returning to work**. A **neuropsychological assessment** suggested that the claimant's **pre-accident intellectual ability had been limited**. There was **no clear evidence that the accident had caused intellectual deterioration**, although tests suggested that it had caused a **mild impairment in attention and some aspects of memory**, with some **slowness in mental processing. No further improvement** was expected, except for a **probable improvement in the agoraphobia and travel anxiety** following CBT. At the time of the trial, the claimant also experienced an **ongoing occasional mild ache in the lower back**, although it **did not restrict his activities**. He was left with a **faint 2 cm V-shaped scar over the right eyebrow**, which was visible only on close inspection, and a **1 cm scar to the back of the head**, which was hidden by his hair. As a result of the head injury he was also left with a **nine per cent residual risk of epilepsy over 20 years** from the date of the accident.

S (A Patient) v Hopal (6 January 2006, unreported) (Joanna Kerr, Counsel, instructed by Silverbeck Rymer, Solicitors, for the claimant; Romilly Cummerson, Counsel, instructed by Davies Lavery, Solicitors, for the defendant) (Kindly submitted for publication by Richard Menzies, Counsel).

959 Multiple injuries

PSLA: £10,000
Total damages: £11,171
Sex: Female
Age at accident/trial: 32/35
Date of accident/trial: 21 July 2002/6 March 2006
Judge/Court: Recorder Brown/Northampton County Court

The claimant was involved in a rear-end shunt road traffic accident in which she sustained a number of injuries. Following the accident, she **suffered headaches**, which appeared to be **random in nature**, in the **right side of her head on most days**. The medical evidence was that they were **tension headaches caused by underlying neck problems**, and that any **headaches occurring after 12 months** post-accident were **constitutional** in nature. The claimant also suffered an **aggravation of problems in her neck**, which had been **asymptomatic at the time of the accident**. Some of the **pain was referred into the arms and hands as pins and needles**. It was found that the accident **aggravated the pre-existing condition for 12 to 18 months**, and that **any symptoms beyond that time** were **not attributable** to the accident. She suffered a **whiplash injury to her left shoulder** which meant that she **could not lift her arm above head height** or place it behind her back for **21 to 24 months**. The injury **prevented her from sleeping on her side**. The medical expert **recommended a cortisone injection**, but the claimant **did not receive one** on the advice of her doctor. However, this **did not affect her recovery**. She also suffered an **injury to the lower back**, with **pain referring into the right leg**. It was found that she had been **suffering from asymptomatic degenerative changes in the lower back before the accident**, which had **brought forward these degenerative changes by three years**. The claimant also **suffered anxiety** as a result of the accident in the form of **nightmares and flashbacks**. The accident had a **significant impact on the claimant's domestic routines**. She was **unable to manage the pain**, and **had to sleep separately from her husband** because she **could not make herself comfortable** in bed with him. She had been attending college before the accident but **had to give up her studies** as she was **unable to concentrate in lectures**. At the time of the trial, she **had not yet been able to resume household chores or recommence her studies**, and she **still suffered from sleep disturbance**.

Porter v Mangham (6 March 2006, unreported) (Richard Adkinson, Counsel, for the claimant; Ruth Manning, Counsel, for the defendant) (Kindly submitted for publication by Richard Adkinson, Counsel).

960 Multiple injuries

PSLA: £6,500
Total damages: £20,046
Sex: Female
Age at accident/trial: 22/26
Date of accident/trial: 22 February 2003/7 September 2006
Judge/Court: HHJ Hawkesworth QC/Bradford County Court

The claimant, a **final year medical student**, suffered **multiple soft tissue injuries** in a road traffic accident. Symptoms included **bruising down the left side of her body and leg, cuts to her right hand**, a **bump to her head** resulting in **headaches** for a period and **soft tissue injuries to her cervical and lumbar spine**. She **attended her doctor six times** in the **three months** following the accident and then had **five sessions of physiotherapy**. She went home to recuperate. She had to **postpone her final exams for six months** which was a major upset for her. When she returned to her studies, she had **problems with her balance and unsteadiness** which was attributed to the effects of the accident. The **expert opinion** was that the **bruising settled in three months** and the **neck and back injuries** should settle in **21 months**. The **spinal symptoms** lasted for about **two and a half years** and **balance problems** for a **similar period**.

Hussain v Rider Holdings Ltd (7 September 2006, unreported) (Andrew Granville Stafford, Counsel, instructed by Irwin Mitchell, Solicitors, for the claimant) (Kindly submitted for publication by Andrew Granville Stafford, Counsel).

961   Multiple injuries

PSLA: £5,500
Total damages: £5,500
Sex: Male
Age at accident/trial: 35/39
Date of accident/trial: 15 June 2002/27 January 2006
Judge/Court: DJ Ilsley/Stoke-on-Trent County Court

The claimant was involved in a side-impact road traffic accident in which he sustained a **whiplash injury to the neck** with **referred pain into the right shoulder and back** and **neurological symptoms in the fingers of the dominant right hand. Immediately after** the accident, he became aware of **pain in the neck radiating into the right shoulder** and into the **lower back**. He also suffered an **injury to the right upper arm**, where he experienced **some bruising and aches and pains**. There was also a **tingling sensation in the fingers of his right hand**. He **attended his doctor on several occasions**, complaining of **continuing pain in his neck** and **tingling in his right fingers**. He was prescribed painkilling medication. He was **absent from work for one week** but had to return for financial reasons, even though his **symptoms were still intrusive**. His **neck and neurological symptoms** were **at their most acute for the first six months** post-accident. During this time, the **symptoms substantially inhibited the claimant's leisure pursuits**. He could not lift heavy objects, perform do-it-yourself activities or undertake heavy gardening. **Following physiotherapy** his **ongoing symptoms began to improve** gradually. However, on examination at **21 months post-accident**, the claimant still suffered from **continuing neck discomfort** and **crepitus** with **restricted neck rotation**. He also still had **ongoing symptoms in his right fingers**, which were diagnosed as an **acceleration of pre-existing right ulnar neuritis**. Medical opinion was that the accident had **accelerated pre-existing cervical spondylosis** in the neck and **pre-existing ulnar nerve neuropathy** by a period of **two years**.

James v Border Counties Electronics (27 January 2006, unreported) (Stephen Garner, Counsel, instructed by Blakemores, Solicitors, for the claimant; William Tyler, Counsel, instructed by DLA, Solicitors, for the defendant) (Kindly submitted for publication by Stephen Garner, Counsel).

962   Multiple injuries

PSLA: £5,000
Total damages: £5,695 (including interest)
Sex: Female
Age at accident: 60
Date of accident/trial: 20 November 2001/7 March 2005
Judge/Court: HHJ Edwards QC/Warrington County Court

The claimant **sustained multiple injuries** when she **tripped on uneven paving**. She sustained a **neck injury**, which **aggravated** for two years **symptoms of a pre-existing degenerative disease** of the cervical spine. There was an **injury to her left shoulder**, which probably involved a **minor chip to the bone**, although **symptoms resolved relatively swiftly**. The claimant also experienced **pain in her ribcage** for **six to eight weeks** as a result of a **soft tissue injury**, and suffered **intermittent headaches for six months**. She also had **minor abrasions**. After the accident, she exhibited a **degree of nervousness** when walking in snowy or icy conditions, which the judge accepted as a **minor psychological injury**.

Thomason v The Village Café (7 March 2005, unreported) (Kathrine Mallory, Counsel, for the claimant; Philip Holmes, Counsel, instructed by Mutual Law, Solicitors, for the defendant) (Kindly submitted for publication by Philip Holmes, Counsel).

963   Multiple injuries

PSLA: £4,500
Total damages: £4,926 (including interest)
Sex: Male
Age at accident: 30
Date of accident/trial: 25 February 2001/18 January 2005
Judge/Court: DJ Rank/Stoke-on-Trent County Court

The claimant was involved in a road traffic accident in which he sustained **soft tissue injuries and lacerations** to the **left ankle**, the **non-dominant left elbow** and the **left knee**. The **most serious injury** was to the **ankle**, in which the claimant was still suffering **some pain and stiffness at trial**. However, the judge found that the claimant had **neglected to undergo physiotherapy in accordance with the medical advice** given to him, and that if he had received therapy at the appropriate time, his **ankle symptoms would have resolved by around 20 months post-accident**. His **left elbow symptoms resolved within 12 to 14 months** of the accident. The **multiple lacerations** he had received **healed within six to eight weeks**, leaving **permanent scars**. Scarring to the knee was negligible, but **obvious red scars** remained on the claimant's **elbow and ankle**, and were considered by the judge to constitute a **significant feature of the case**.

Talbot v Guest (18 January 2005, unreported) (Philip Holmes, Counsel, instructed by McHugh, Solicitors, for the claimant; MDG Brunning, Counsel, for the defendant) (Kindly submitted for publication by Philip Holmes, Counsel).

964   Multiple injuries

PSLA: £4,250
Total damages: £5,118
Sex: Male
Age at accident/trial: 56/56
Date of trial: 16 March 2006
Judge/Court: DJ Simpson/Oldham County Court

The claimant sustained **multiple injuries** when he was **knocked off his bicycle by a car**, causing him to be **thrown over the roof** of the car and **land on the road**. The **most serious injury** was a **deep laceration to the right shin**, which left a **faded but permanent 10 cm transverse scar**. The scar was later found by the judge to be **'significantly noticeable' but not 'disfiguring'**. The laceration, which was initially stitched, **became infected** and **took several weeks to clear**, requiring **drainage, dressing and two courses of antibiotics**. The claimant also suffered **bony bruising to the coccyx, bruising to the right side of his chest and abdomen, bruising to his right knee** and abrasions, mainly to his **elbows and right hip**. The **pain in the coccyx was quite severe**, and **made lying down and driving difficult**. The abrasions were **also painful**, and made it **difficult for the claimant to get into a comfortable position in bed** at night. His **sleep was disturbed initially** and he was **sweating continuously for ten days**. Although he only took **one day off work**, he was **unable to do his job properly for three weeks**. He was a **very keen runner and cyclist before the accident**, but was **unable to cycle for six weeks** afterwards and **only returned to running several weeks later**. He stated that before the accident he **had been able to run about 35 miles each week**, but at **ten months post-accident** he could only manage a **slow ten-mile run twice a week** and suffered **severe discomfort if he attempted to run on a hard surface**. He was **concerned** as to whether he would ever regain **his pre-accident levels of fitness**. The prognosis was for a **recovery from the residual pain in the knee, coccyx and right elbow within about five months** of the accident. Afterwards, the claimant was left with a **3 cm mark from a healed abrasion** on the **point of the elbow**.

Stoor v Dean (16 March 2006, unreported) (Jonathan Thompson, Counsel, for the claimant) (Kindly submitted for publication by Jonathan Thompson, Counsel).

965   Psychological damage

PSLA: £14,000
Total damages: £140,119
Sex: Female
Age at accident: 49
Date of accident/trial: June 2002/7 April 2006
Judge/Court: Henriques J/Queen's Bench Division

The claimant suffered **depressive illness caused by work-related stress** due to having to cover for a colleague who was often absent from work. She was **absent from her work as a health visitor for six months** before returning on a phased return to work programme. However, **six months later another colleague left** without being replaced and the **claimant suffered a relapse** of her depressive illness. She was **off work for a further six weeks**. **Two months after the claimant's return to work** through another phased programme, another of her colleagues **took maternity leave** and was **not replaced**. **Four months later**, the claimant suffered a **second relapse of her depressive illness** and **did not return to work**. The defendant was found to be **liable for both relapses** of the claimant's depressive illness. Although it was found that the claimant would **never be able to work as a health visitor again**, it was expected that she would be able to resume **some form of employment within two years** of the trial.

Garrod v North Devon NHS Primary Care Trust (7 April 2006, unreported) (Charles Pugh, Counsel, and Hannah Sampson, Pupil Barrister, instructed by Douglas Mann & Co, Solicitors, for the claimant; Andrew Hogarth QC, instructed by Veitch Penny, Solicitors, for the defendant) (Kindly submitted for publication by Hannah Sampson, Pupil Barrister).

966 Psychological damage

PSLA: £2,500
Total damages: £2,500
Sex: Female
Age at accident/infant settlement approval hearing: 1/5
Date of infant settlement approval hearing: 4 January 2006
Judge/Court: HHJ McDuff QC/Birmingham County Court

The claimant was involved in a high speed rear-end shunt road traffic accident, after which she became **extremely distressed and frightened**. She was **hysterical and inconsolable**. After the accident she developed an **acute separation anxiety towards her mother**. She **became clingy** and was described as being **'like superglue'**. She suffered **constant disturbed sleep with intense nightmares** and would **only sleep in her mother's bed**. She suffered a **loss of confidence** when in the company of other children, and her **play sometimes became aggressive and rough**. She also developed a **significant travel phobia**, and had an **acute fear of travelling as a passenger** in a motor vehicle. Sometimes she would **try to get out of the car**, and she would also **adjust her seatbelt, cry hysterically** and **criticise her mother's driving**, urging her to slow down. **Psychological symptoms were acute** for a period of **eight months**, and began to **lessen gradually thereafter**. The psychological expert advised that the claimant had experienced symptoms of **child post-traumatic stress disorder during the initial eight months** when symptoms were at their worst. The prognosis was for **residual psychological symptoms to settle by 27 months post-accident**, and **recovery occurred in line with this prognosis**.

S (A Child) v Begum (4 January 2006, unreported) (Stephen Garner, Counsel, instructed by Colemans, Solicitors, for the claimant; DLA, Solicitors, for the defendant) (Kindly submitted for publication by Stephen Garner, Counsel).

967 Psychological damage

PSLA: £2,250
Total damages: £2,250
Sex: Male
Age at accident/infant settlement approval hearing: 10/13
Date of accident/infant settlement approval hearing: 10 May 2003/19 June 2006
Judge/Court: DJ Savage/Birmingham County Court

The claimant was injured when he was **pricked in the right thumb by a discarded needle sharp** left in a toy box. The needle **penetrated the skin but did not draw blood**. Immediately after the accident the claimant was **shocked and tearful** and was **taken to hospital**. Some of his **blood was taken for storage** and he was given the first of **three vaccinations against Hepatitis B**. **No tests for HIV were undertaken** as the risks were thought to be infinitesimal. A post-vaccination blood test confirmed that the claimant had **full immunity from Hepatitis B**. After the accident the claimant experienced **pain in the thumb for about a day**. He also **became upset whenever he had to undergo a further vaccination**. Even after it had been **confirmed that he had not suffered any infection** as a result of the accident he became **fearful of needles**, especially **when he had to have vaccinations** at school. However, due to his young age, other than a **short-lived fear of needles and the administration of vaccinations**, the claimant **did not really suffer any further psychological trauma** as he was **too young to understand the potential implications** of being pricked by a discarded needle.

K (A Child) v Arboretum Nursing Home (19 June 2006, unreported) (Stephen Garner, Counsel, instructed by AEW Litigation, Solicitors, for the claimant; Everatt & Co, Solicitors, for the defendant) (Kindly submitted for publication by Stephen Garner, Counsel).

968 Psychological damage

PSLA: £1,800
Total damages: £1,800
Sex: Female
Age at accident/infant settlement approval hearing: 14/16
Date of accident/infant settlement approval hearing: 29 October 2003/9 January 2006
Judge/Court: DJ Atkinson/Leicester County Court

The claimant was involved in a rear-end shunt road traffic accident. She was **shocked, shaken and emotional** immediately after the accident, and became **preoccupied with thoughts of what might have happened** had the accident been more serious. The **next morning** she felt the onset of **pain and stiffness in her neck and across her shoulders**, particularly the **left shoulder**. She also experienced **difficulty in turning her head**. She **attended her doctor later that day** and was diagnosed as having sustained a **whiplash injury to the neck** with **referred pain to the left shoulder**. The neck and shoulder **symptoms were at their most acute for four to five days**, during which the claimant **took painkillers** and was **absent from school**. Her **whiplash injury steadily improved** until she was **symptom-free**, at around **eight weeks post-accident**. She was **unable to play golf** for those **eight weeks**, and **did not feel like socialising** with friends for **six weeks**. Her **most significant and intrusive injuries were psychological**. She began to **relive the accident at night**, and was **kept awake** by such intrusive thoughts for **eight weeks**. She was also **quiet, withdrawn and clingy towards her mother** for **eight weeks**. She developed **acute travel phobia symptoms**. She became a **very reluctant and apprehensive passenger** and **refused to sit in the same place she had been seated at the time of the accident** when travelling in the vehicle involved. The diagnosis was that the claimant's **psychological symptoms were not clinically significant**, although they were **very upsetting** for her. The prognosis was for her **residual travel phobia to settle within 22 months** of the accident, and it was confirmed at the hearing that she had **recovered in line with this prognosis**.

C (A Child) v Dobbyn (9 January 2006, unreported) (Stephen Garner, Counsel, instructed by Colemans, Solicitors, for the claimant; Cogent, Solicitors, for the defendant) (Kindly submitted for publication by Stephen Garner, Counsel).

969   Psychological damage

PSLA: £1,640
Total damages: £1,640
Sex: Male
Age at accident/infant settlement approval hearing: 3/6
Date of accident/infant settlement approval hearing: 4 February 2003/16 February 2006
Judge/Court: DJ Dickinson/Worcester County Court

The claimant was involved in a rear-end shunt road traffic accident. After the accident he was **extremely frightened**, and was **distressed and crying**. He experienced **pain in the lower abdomen** due to the **restraining forces imposed by the seatbelt**, and he started to **develop bruising across the abdomen area**. He was **taken to see his doctor**, who diagnosed a **seatbelt injury to the lower abdomen**. The **bruising began to settle after two weeks**, during which the claimant was **absent from play school** on account of his injuries, although he **continued to experience some localised pain** across his abdomen. The **abdominal symptoms settled by six weeks** post-accident. The claimant also began to suffer from **enuresis during the day and night**. Prior to the accident he had been continent, but afterwards he exhibited **daytime enuresis on five occasions over a six-week period**. He also **wet the bed at night on several occasions**. **Enuresis symptoms** lasted for **about six weeks**. The claimant also became **more apprehensive about travelling by car**. He **refused to travel by car for one month** post-accident, and was a **reluctant and wary traveller** after that time. He became **more clingy and attention-seeking towards his mother** during the day. During the night, he experienced **difficulty in getting to sleep** because he had **intrusive thoughts** and **nightmares about car crashes**. He would often **sleep only in his mother's bed**. He also became **more aggressive towards other children**. The symptoms of **travel anxiety, clinginess and sleep disturbance** were **most acute** during the **month which followed the accident**. Thereafter they **began gradually to improve**. A child psychologist diagnosed **separation anxiety disorder** with **accident-related and clinically significant symptoms** which lasted for a period of **eight months**.

J (A Child) v O'Connor (16 February 2006, unreported) (Stephen Garner, Counsel, instructed by Blakemores, Solicitors, for the claimant; Beachcroft Wansbroughs, Solicitors, for the defendant) (Kindly submitted for publication by Stephen Garner, Counsel).

970   Psychological damage

PSLA: £1,250
Total damages: £1,984
Sex: Female
Age at accident/trial: 47/49
Date of accident/trial: 19 November 2004/5 May 2006
Judge/Court: HHJ Hollis/Hastings County Court

The claimant was involved in a high speed road traffic accident with the defendant's lorry. She was **initially very shocked**. The **next day** her **hip and neck began to hurt**. However, she **did not consult her doctor** and **took ibuprofen** for the pain, which **resolved within one to two weeks**. About **a week after** the accident, the claimant began to suffer from **flashbacks, anxiety, tearfulness and low mood**. She displayed a **lack of interest in her normal activities** and **had trouble sleeping**. She **attended her doctor**, who diagnosed **mild depression** and **prescribed a sedative** to help with the anxiety and insomnia. A medical report produced at approximately **six weeks post-accident** confirmed that the **depression was related to the accident** and was well-controlled by the prescribed medication. It also stated that the claimant's **symptoms were improving** and were expected to **fully resolve within a further six months**. The claimant **took the medication for a further four months** and all **psychological symptoms resolved as predicted**.

Cobby v Griffiths (5 May 2006, unreported) (Jane Clifton, Counsel, for the claimant) (Kindly submitted for publication by Jane Clifton, Counsel).

971 Psychological damage

See para 1011.

972 Post-traumatic stress disorder

PSLA: £4,000
Total damages: £5,256 (including interest)
Sex: Female
Age at accident: 36
Date of accident/trial: 3 October 2003/19 April 2006
Judge/Court: DJ Smedley/Liverpool County Court

The claimant was involved in a **frightening road traffic accident** in which her **car burst into flames**. She sustained **jarring injuries to her neck, lower back and right knee**, together with **post-traumatic stress disorder**. She **visited her doctor on three occasions** after the accident and was **absent from work for three weeks**. Her **physical injuries** had **resolved by seven and a half months** post-accident. Her **PTSD had also resolved** by that time, but she suffered **anxiety for a further nine months**. The judge awarded **£2,200 in respect of psychological injuries** and **£2,000 in respect of physical injuries**, with a discount for overlap.

King v Hindley (19 April 2006, unreported) (Titus Gibson, Counsel, for the claimant; Catherine Titchmarsh, Counsel, for the defendant) (Kindly submitted for publication by Titus Gibson, Counsel).

973 Post-traumatic stress disorder

See para 1002.

974 Medical negligence

PSLA: £4,000
Total damages: £6,500
Sex: Female
Age at accident/infant settlement approval hearing: 4/7
Date of accident/infant settlement approval hearing: 4 May 2003/2 May 2006
Judge/Court: DJ Middleton/Birmingham County Court

The claimant was examined by the defendant after complaining of **pain in the region of her left heel and ankle**. The defendant noted **slight swelling** in the **left heel area** and **discharged the claimant with Calpol**. The claimant went to school the following day, but the **pain persisted**. She **could weight bear**, but with a **slight limp**. She was again taken to the defendant, who noted **tenderness on the outside of the left ankle** and x-rayed the claimant, but **recorded no abnormalities**. The defendant **discharged her again** and advised her parents to give her **analgesics**. The **pain in the left ankle and heel persisted**, and the claimant was **taken to the defendant a third time**. On this occasion she was diagnosed as suffering a **medial ligament injury** in the **left ankle**. She was **put in a plaster cast** and **advised not to weight bear**. **Three weeks** later, the plaster cast was removed, revealing a **substantial loss of skin** over the **medial heel and ankle region**. The **area had become infected** with what a laboratory culture subsequently revealed to be **staphylococcus aureus**. A **further x-ray** taken by the defendant revealed **bone changes consistent with acute osteomyelitis**. The **claimant was admitted to hospital immediately** and underwent a **debridement of the damaged bone** in the left heel under general anaesthetic. Following the procedure she was given **large doses of antibiotics** and allowed to go home. She was **confined to a wheelchair for two weeks** while the antibiotics took effect, after which she was **allowed to weight bear a little**. She **took the antibiotics for a further four weeks**, by which time she was **able to weight bear fully**. By this time she had **missed most of the summer term** on account of her symptoms. The **area of the left heel healed**, leaving a **small, dimpled scar** in the left heel bone. The scar was **barely visible**, but the **skin was tethered to the heel bone**. **Consultant opinion** was that a **diagnosis of osteomyelitis should have been made four weeks earlier** than had been the case, and that the **failure to diagnose resulted in the need for the debridement**. Consultant opinion was also that there was a **five per cent risk** that the claimant's **heel bone could enlarge following growth spurts** in her teenage years, and that this could cause a **loss of mobility in the ankle** as the scar tissue was tethered to the heel bone. Such an occurrence **would necessitate surgical intervention**. Damages were awarded on the basis that the claimant had been subject to a **delay of**

four weeks before antibiotics had been prescribed, and consequently had **experienced pain and suffering** and had **had to undergo an unnecessary debridement**.

L (A Child) v The Royal Wolverhampton NHS Trust (2 May 2006, unreported) (Stephen Garner, Counsel, instructed by AEW Litigation, Solicitors, for the claimant; Browne Jacobson, Solicitors, for the defendant) (Kindly submitted for publication by Stephen Garner, Counsel).

975 Food poisoning

PSLA: £13,000
Total damages: £13,000
Sex: Male
Age at accident/trial: 24/27
Date of accident/trial: 1 August 2002/18 April 2006
Judge/Court: DJ Middleton/Walsall County Court

The claimant suffered an **acute gastrointestinal infection** by an unidentified pathogen while on a package holiday. He initially suffered from **diarrhoea, stomach cramps to the lower abdomen, sweating and shivering**. He **retched** but was **unable to vomit**. The **acute phase** of infection lasted for **three weeks**, and for a **further two months** the claimant was **exhausted** and suffering from **continuing pronounced symptoms**. He **took one week off work** on returning from his holiday and underwent a **short phase of working part-time** afterwards. He went on to suffer from **post-infective irritable bowel syndrome**. He suffered **recurring bouts of diarrhoea every few weeks**, which would last **from a few days to a week** at a time. This **alternated with constipation** lasting for **two to four days** and **resulting in diarrhoea**. There was **urgency of defecation**. The claimant suffered from **lower abdominal cramps** which were improved on bowel evacuation, but left him with a **sense of incomplete evacuation**. He **had to modify his lifestyle** by avoiding certain types of food, particularly in order to **alleviate symptoms of bloating, belching and indigestion**. His **social life had to be scaled back** as a result of **tiredness** and because his **condition would curtail his enjoyment of socialising**. The prognosis was for the **irritable bowel syndrome to continue indefinitely**, but to continue to **improve gradually over time**. The case was judged to fall between the **JSB Guidelines for injuries to internal organs** categories (b)(i) and (b)(ii).

Willey v My Travel UK Ltd (18 April 2006, unreported) (Anthony Verduyn, Counsel, instructed by Irwin Mitchell, Solicitors, for the claimant; Alan Saggerson, Counsel, for the defendant) (Kindly submitted for publication by Anthony Verduyn, Counsel).

976 Burns

PSLA: £1,215
Total damages: £1,215
Sex: Male
Age at accident/infant settlement approval hearing: 14/17
Date of accident/infant settlement approval hearing: 10 September 2003/9 February 2006
Judge/Court: DJ Morton/Dudley County Court

The claimant was involved in a heavy side-impact road traffic accident. At the moment of impact, he was **thrown about** and felt an **immediate pain across the left side of his neck**. He was **taken to hospital**, where it was discovered that he had sustained an **intense seatbelt burn**, which was **linear and 10 cm in length**, to the left side of the neck. The **burn became raised and red**. The claimant was **advised to take analgesics** for pain relief and to **apply cream** to soothe the burn. He **took two days off school** on account of his injury. He experienced **no specific limitation of movement** in the neck apart from a **slight restriction due to an increase in pain** caused by his **skin being stretched at the area of the burn**. He continued to apply the cream, which **brought some relief**. Within **seven days** of the accident, the **burn had started to settle**, but was **still sore and red**. The claimant was **unable to button up his school shirt properly** because of the burn. The **burn steadily improved** and **lessened in size**, and had **healed by two weeks post-accident**, although the claimant still felt **some discomfort and soreness** on certain movements of the head and neck. All **symptoms completely resolved within four weeks** of the accident. The claimant was **unable to participate in physical education lessons for three weeks** because flexing his neck caused pain. He was also **unable to play the trumpet and piano for three weeks** because he experienced pain when moving his head forwards.

Z (A Child) v Attridge (9 February 2006, unreported) (Stephen Garner, Counsel, instructed by Blakemores, Solicitors, for the claimant; Cogent, Solicitors, for the defendant) (Kindly submitted for publication by Stephen Garner, Counsel).

977 Scarring

PSLA: £5,500
Total damages: £5,276
Sex: Male

Age at accident/trial: 31/35
Date of trial: 14 November 2006
Judge/Court: DJ Cooke/Birmingham County Court

The claimant, a heavy goods vehicle driver, **suffered personal injury to the face** when he was **struck above the right eyebrow by a metal bar** that sprang loose on a lorry trailer. **Immediately after** the accident **he had a cut above the right eyebrow**, which was **bleeding profusely**. **He attended hospital** where the **laceration was cleaned and eight stitches applied**. **For three to four months following the injury**, the claimant had **shooting pains passing across his scalp and longitudinally**, along with **a feeling of altered sensation over the top of the scalp**. The **shooting pains and the altered sensation of the scalp disappeared of their own accord**. The **wound above the right eye healed within a few weeks leaving an L-shaped scar**. The **vertical component** was **1·5 cm in length** and **passed directly up through the centre of the right eyebrow, stretched in a transverse direction by 3 mm**. The **longer limb** of the L was **2·5 cm in length** and **passed longitudinally just under the lower border of the right eyebrow**. The **scar was permanent** and left **an obvious defect in the right eyebrow** as there was a gap in the hair. The **scar was noticeable at conversational distances**. Immediately adjacent to the vertical limb of the L-shaped scar, **just above the eyebrow, approximately 1 cm in either direction was an area of decreased sensation to light touch**. The **area of altered sensation** was also thought to be **permanent but did not trouble him on a daily basis**. The claimant conveyed his concerns that as he was tall, bald and Scottish, he felt **genuinely stigmatised by the scar**. He felt concerned that members of the public would **perceive him as a troublemaker**.

Hamilton v Malcolm Group Ltd (17 November 2006, unreported) (Stephen Garner, Counsel, instructed by AEW Litigation, Solicitors for the claimant) (Kindly submitted for publication by Stephen Garner, Counsel).

978   Head

PSLA: £4,300
Total damages: £4,300
Sex: Male
Age at accident/trial: 26/27
Date of accident/trial: 19 June 2006/19 September 2006
Judge/Court: DJ Pearl/Cambridge County Court

The claimant, a self-employed builder, was injured in a significant side impact road traffic accident. Immediately after the accident, the claimant developed **pain in his neck, across his chest and in the area of his mid-back**. He was thrown forcibly about inside the motor vehicle on impact and **struck the back of his head** on the interior of the car and suffered **a deep laceration which began to bleed profusely**. He went to hospital after the accident and the laceration to the back of the head required **six stitches**. The **soft tissue symptoms in the neck, across the chest and back were particularly acute for the first two weeks** post-accident. The symptoms then **began to improve**. The claimant was **absent from work for a period of six weeks** and during his absence he underwent **six sessions of osteopathic treatment to his neck and mid-back**. The osteopathy assisted, although the claimant was **not able to pursue his hobby of golf for several months** after the event due to his **neck symptoms preventing him swinging a golf club**. On examination by the medical expert **four months** after the accident, the claimant was still **suffering from residual symptoms in his neck, chest and mid-back area** but they **had improved**. The prognosis was for the **soft tissue injuries to settle** within **ten months** of the accident. The **laceration to the back of the claimant's head healed within a few weeks** of the accident. A **noticeable scar measuring three inches** in length remained. The claimant was **embarrassed about the appearance of the scarring** and so grew his hair long for a few weeks post-accident in order to cover up the cosmetic deficit. He also suffered **flashbacks** for **a few weeks** and suffered **symptoms of travel anxiety** for **several months**.

Trow v Haydes (19 September 2006, unreported) (Stephen Garner, Counsel, instructed by Colemans-ctts, Solicitors, for the claimant; Fatim Kirji, Counsel, instructed by Lyons Davidson, Solicitors, for the defendant) (Kindly submitted for publication by Stephen Garner, Counsel).

979   Head

PSLA: £1,000
Total damages: £1,000
Sex: Male
Age at accident/trial: 06/8
Date of accident/trial: 8 February 2004/20 September 2006
Judge/Court: DJ Sanghera/Coventry County Court

The claimant, a schoolboy, was injured when part of a metal ball dispenser fell and **struck him on the back of the head**. Immediately after the accident, he was **shocked, tearful and physically**

sick. He rapidly developed **a large bump on the right side of his head** towards the back and was taken to hospital. He **did not lose consciousness** but it was noted that **he was dazed**. **No neurological deficit was recorded** and he was **diagnosed as having suffered a minor head injury**. He was **nauseous and suffered from headaches for about a week** after the accident and **suffered from low mood** and **would not go outside or play games** during the same period. **He was given Calpol** and **did not attend school due to his symptoms for a week**. The lump on the side and back of the claimant's head was **very noticeable for a week and was very sore, swollen and tender** to the touch for approximately **two weeks**. He had **fully recovered** from the accident within **two weeks**.

M (*A Child*) *v JJB Sports* (20 September 2006, unreported) (Stephen Garner, Counsel, instructed by Ward & Rider, Solicitors, for the claimant; Praxis Partners, Solicitors, for the defendant) (Kindly submitted for publication by Stephen Garner, Counsel).

980   Neck

PSLA: £7,800
Total damages: £7,800
Sex: Female
Age at accident/infant settlement approval hearing: 12/17
Date of accident/infant settlement approval hearing: 13 May 2001/16 May 2006
Judge/Court: DJ Cernik/Northampton County Court

The claimant was involved in a heavy impact rear-end shunt road traffic accident. She was **shocked and tearful** immediately afterwards and began to develop **pain over the left side of her neck**. She also noticed some **tenderness in her chest and abdomen** as a result of **seatbelt pressure**. She was **taken to hospital**, where she was diagnosed as having sustained a **whiplash injury to the neck** and **seatbelt bruising**. The **bruising settled within about a month**. The claimant was **absent from school for two weeks** on account of her injuries, and was **unable to participate in physical education classes for four weeks** after her return to school. She also experienced, for **two to three months** post-accident, **psychological symptoms**, including **flashbacks, nightmares and travel anxiety**. The claimant's **neck injury was the most significant**. Her **symptoms were acute**, and she wore a **soft collar for six weeks**. On removal of the collar, she still experienced **some diffuse pain** in the **back of the neck on the left side**. She sometimes experienced **symptoms radiating between the shoulder blades**. She found on **most mornings** that her **neck was stiff on waking**. It became **painful if she stood in the same position for too long** and would sometimes **hurt if she remained seated** in the same position for **prolonged periods**, such as when she was reading or writing. She had been a **keen swimmer** but found after the accident that **sometimes her neck locked** while she was swimming and she would have to stop. She also **experienced neck pain while running**. **Orthopaedic opinion** was that she would suffer **daily residual neck symptoms on a permanent basis**. The symptoms, which were classified as being **slightly above nuisance-level**, would continue to **affect her everyday life and leisure pursuits**.

J (*A Child*) *v Kilroy* (16 May 2006, unreported) (Stephen Garner, Counsel, instructed by Ward and Rider, Solicitors, for the claimant; Keoghs, Solicitors, for the defendant) (Kindly submitted for publication by Stephen Garner, Counsel).

981   Neck

PSLA: (1) £2,800 (2) £3,250
Total damages: £6,050
Sex: (1) Male (2) Female
Date of trial: 23 October 2002/3 May 2005
Judge/Court: DJ Chandler/Southend County Court

The first claimant was driving and the second claimant was a passenger in the vehicle which was struck forcibly from the rear while stationary at a T-junction. **The first claimant**, a software developer, **sustained a bruising trauma to the left arm, a bruising trauma to the head and a whiplash injury to the neck**. He **attended his doctor** with **symptoms on two occasions** and was **advised to take anti-inflammatory medication**. He **developed stiffness in the left wrist two to three weeks post-accident** which was considered attributable to the accident. As a result to **a direct blow to the forehead he developed headaches which lasted for three days and localised bruising which settled within a week**. The most **significant injuries were to the arm and neck**. The **neck injury manifested itself around three days post-accident** and was at its **most significant for three weeks**. On examination **five months post-accident he continued to experience ongoing stiffness in the neck, disturbed sleep and left elbow stiffness**, the prognosis of which was that **the symptoms would resolve in around seven months post-accident**. His evidence was that **he continued to experience ongoing residual neck symptoms at 14 months post-accident around twice a week**, which had **almost settled by 19 months post-accident**.

The second claimant, a nurse, **sustained an exacerbation of pre-existing back symptoms and a whiplash injury to the neck**. The medical evidence was that **any symptoms beyond 6 months of the accident were probably due to her pre-existing back condition** and the prognosis in relation to her neck injuries was that they ought to **resolve in the same period**. She claimed that she **continued to experience occasional neck symptoms**, in particular when **turning her head to the right while driving at 19 months post-accident**.

Berry v Rustman (10 October 2005, unreported) (Adam Walker, Counsel, instructed by Silverbeck Rymer, Solicitors, for the claimants; Lucinda Harris, Counsel, instructed by Ricksons, Solicitors, for the defendant) (Kindly submitted for publication by Adam Walker, Counsel).

982   Neck

PSLA: £4,250
Total damages: £4,250
Sex: Male
Age at accident/trial: 80/85
Date of trial: 21 February 2006
Judge/Court: Recorder Million/Luton County Court

The claimant sustained a neck injury when he **lost his balance and fell into a ditch** while walking on a footpath. He initially **believed that he had broken his neck** and **required assistance getting out** of the ditch. He was **admitted to hospital** with **soft tissue injuries to the neck and low back**. However, **no fracture was identified** and he was **discharged to the care of his daughter**. He was **re-admitted** to hospital **three days later**, suffering from **pain which was preventing him from sleeping**. His doctor believed that the pain, which was **radiating into the claimant's left arm**, may have been caused by **ischaemic heart inertia**. After **two weeks of investigations** the claimant was again **discharged from hospital** and **took analgesics and anti-inflammatories**. Although at trial the claimant claimed to be **experiencing some neck pain**, the medical evidence suggested that the accident aggravated an **underlying pre-existing condition** of **degenerative and diffuse spondylosis** for a period of **12 to 18 months**. The claimant also suffered from **headaches and chest symptoms** after the accident, but **without any long term consequences**. Although he was **shaken by the accident** and **believed that he was going to die**, there were **no flashbacks or re-experiencing phenomena** that could suggest that he was suffering from post-traumatic stress disorder. The claimant's **interest in walking and ornithology subsided** following the accident, although he was **still able to enjoy reading**. He also **required domestic assistance from his daughter for some months** after the accident. Although the claimant **failed to establish liability** on the part of the defendant, the Recorder indicated that the nature of his injuries was such that they **would have fallen within band b(ii) of the JSB Guidelines for neck injuries**, and that a sum of £4,250 would have been appropriate.

Carter v Hertfordshire CC (21 February 2006, unreported) (Nigel Brockley, Counsel, instructed by Duffield Harrison LLP, Solicitors, for the defendant) (Kindly submitted for publication by Nigel Brockley, Counsel).

983   Neck

PSLA: £3,600
Total damages: £3,600
Sex: Male
Age at accident/trial: 29/32
Date of accident/trial: 14 January 2004/31 July 2006
Judge/Court: Recorder Mainds/Coventry County Court

The claimant was involved in a rear-end shunt road traffic accident. **Immediately after** the accident, he was **shocked and shaken** and started to experience **painful stiffness** over the **whole of the neck**. He **attended hospital**, where he was diagnosed as having sustained a **whiplash injury** to the neck. Symptoms were at their **most acute for the first two weeks** post-accident, during which time the claimant was **unable to go to work**. He suffered **sleep disturbance**, was **unable to drive** and required **assistance with domestic tasks**. After **two weeks** and a **short course of physiotherapy** treatment, the neck **symptoms began to improve steadily**. On **examination at seven months** post-accident, the claimant reported that he still had an **intermittent ache at the base of the neck**, particularly **after long periods of sitting**, but that **symptoms had improved by 60 per cent**. His **residual neck symptoms began to improve** gradually and, by the time of a second **examination at 15 months** post-accident, overall **symptoms had improved by 90 per cent**. The claimant still experienced, **very occasionally**, an **aching sensation across the back of the neck**, particularly if he had been **sitting in one position for too long** or **driving for a long distance**. The prognosis was for these **residual neck symptoms to resolve within 18 to 19 months** of the accident and damages were assessed on that basis.

Bunce v Lovatt (31 July 2006, unreported) (Stephen Garner, Counsel, instructed by Ward and Rider, Solicitors, for the claimant; Angela Frost, Counsel, instructed by Cogent, Solicitors, for the defendant) (Kindly submitted for publication by Stephen Garner, Counsel).

984 Neck

PSLA: £3,500
Total damages: £3,799 (including interest)
Sex: Female
Age at accident: 50
Date of accident/trial: 7 February 2002/13 May 2005
Judge/Court: DDJ Smith/Manchester County Court

The claimant was involved in a road traffic accident in which her **right shoulder and the right side of her head** were **thrown against the interior** of her car. She sustained a **whiplash injury to her neck** and experienced **severe pain** in her **right ear** and in the **right side of the neck**, together with **headaches, panic attacks and nausea**. Symptoms were **severe for two weeks** before starting to **improve gradually**. **No long-term consequences** were anticipated. The claimant also sustained a **modest psychological injury** which resulted in a **loss of confidence with regard to driving**. She also complained at trial of **continuing right shoulder pain**, but this was held **not to be attributable to the accident**.

Jennings v Rehman (13 May 2005, unreported) (Philip Holmes, Counsel, instructed by Neil Millar & Co, Solicitors, for the claimant; John Ratledge, Counsel, for the defendant) (Kindly submitted for publication by Philip Holmes, Counsel).

985 Neck

PSLA: £2,500
Total damages: £2,500
Sex: Female
Age at accident/infant settlement approval hearing: 8/12
Date of infant settlement approval hearing: 24 January 2006
Judge/Court: DJ Cohen/Edmonton County Court

The claimant was involved in a road traffic accident following which she **immediately felt pain, stiffness and restriction of movement**. She was **taken to hospital**. She experienced **continuous pain for ten days**, although she **only missed one week of school**. Her **sleep was disturbed for two weeks** on account of her symptoms. She was **unable to participate in physical activities** such as tennis and football **for one month** after the accident. Following this time the **pain diminished**, but on examination at **nine months post-accident** the claimant was still experiencing **ongoing symptoms of discomfort** when **running or lifting heavy items**. **Movement on extension was slightly decreased** from normal and there was some evidence of **tenderness on palpation of the neck**. The claimant made a full recovery within 18 months of the accident.

G (A Child) v Bleasdell (24 January 2006, unreported) (Saiful Islam, Counsel, instructed by Robinson King, Solicitors, for the claimant; Joanna Kerr, Counsel, instructed by Davies Wallis Foyster, Solicitors, for the defendant) (Kindly submitted for publication by Joanna Kerr, Counsel).

986 Neck

PSLA: £2,250
Total damages: £4,830
Sex: Female
Age at accident/trial: 38/39
Date of accident/trial: 24 December 2004/14 March 2006
Judge/Court: HHJ Head/Mansfield County Court

The claimant was involved in a road traffic accident, following which she was **in shock for a few hours**. By the next morning **stiffness had developed in her neck**, and her neck **condition deteriorated over the next two to three days**, before remaining **stiff for two to three weeks**. The claimant was **absent from her work** as a county court administrator for **four weeks**, and when she returned she was unable to lift heavy files and was **placed on light duties**. She was also **too frightened to drive for two weeks** and **unable to do housework for four weeks**. Although she had had **pre-existing neck problems for 21 years** prior to the accident, she had **received acupuncture** and found it to be very beneficial. The effect of the acupuncture was to cure the pain so that **at the time of the accident the claimant was effectively asymptomatic**, provided she took care in her activities. Although she was recommended physiotherapy, she **underwent a further course of acupuncture** following the accident and **found it to be helpful**. On examination at **six months post-accident** her **neck was still stiff**. The **prognosis** was that **symptoms would resolve by ten months post-accident**, and the claimant **recovered in line with this prognosis**.

Mistry v Rajani (14 March 2006, unreported) (Richard Adkinson, Counsel, instructed by McKeowns, Solicitors, for the claimant) (Kindly submitted for publication by Richard Adkinson, Counsel).

987 Neck

PSLA: £1,900
Total damages: £1,900
Sex: Female
Age at accident/infant settlement approval hearing: 30/31
Date of accident/infant settlement approval hearing: 5 October 2005/12 October 2006
Judge/Court: DJ Lettall/Stockport County Court

The claimant, a print-room operative, was driving a motor vehicle and was struck from behind while stationary by the defendant's car. She **felt the onset of neck pain about 20 minutes after the accident**, which became **much worse and her neck was very stiff**. The symptoms made it difficult for her to move around the house during the first few days post-accident and she did not leave the house as a result of them until 2 weeks after the accident, apart from attending medical appointments. The **acute phase of her symptoms lasted for six weeks after the accident**. When she was examined by the medico-legal expert **5 months post-accident, she experienced neck pain once a week or less** which was usually **exacerbated by going to the gym**, but displayed **no clinical signs of injury**. She was taken to **hospital on the day of the accident** and was **advised to take painkillers**, which **she did for 3 weeks**. She **attended her doctor the day after the accident** due to her neck feeling much worse and again **1 week post-accident. Five months after** the accident she was **no longer regularly taking analgesia**. Her **doctor signed her off for 2 weeks**, and when she returned to work **she was on light duties**. She was **unable to attend the gym as frequently** as she had been before the accident and **received assistance with domestic tasks** from a friend **for 4 weeks** after the accident. The medico-legal expert **diagnosed a cervical flexion hyperextension sprain** and gave **prognosis that the claimant would recover between 8 to 11 months post-accident**.

Kemp v Barton (12 October 2006, unreported) (David Calvert, Counsel, instructed by Leech & Co, Solicitors, for the claimant; Chris Middleton, Counsel, instructed by Greenwoods, Solicitors, for the defendant) (Kindly submitted for publication by Chris Middleton, Counsel).

988 Neck

PSLA: £1,150
Total damages: £1,150
Sex: Male
Age at accident/trial: 35/36
Date of accident/trial: 8 December 2004/23 May 2006
Judge/Court: DJ Harrison/Liverpool County Court

The claimant was involved in a side-impact road traffic accident. He was **distressed, shaking and nauseous** immediately after the accident. He developed **pain and stiffness** in the **back of the lower neck** the **following day**. He **attended his doctor** who diagnosed **whiplash injuries** and prescribed a **strong painkiller**, which the claimant found very effective and **took for about a month**. The **pain radiated into his shoulders and upper thoracic spine** and became **constant and severe** over the next 24 hours. It was **exacerbated** by any **movement of the head** or **bending of the neck. Symptoms remained at the same level for one week** before beginning to settle. During that week, the claimant was also **acutely aware of other road users** and for a **few weeks** afterwards he was **more cautious than usual when driving**. He was also **absent from his work** as a social worker for **one week**. He returned because his symptoms had improved, but none the less **described himself as 'soldiering on'**. Aspects of his work exacerbated his **symptoms for several weeks**, particularly driving on his frequent home visits. He had **difficulty with heavy housework, shopping and vacuum cleaning** for **six weeks** as a result of the pain in his back and neck. He **required one hour of assistance from his mother** in each of those weeks. He was also **unable**, for six weeks, **to go jogging or exercise at home**, which he had previously done three times each week. He was **unable to socialise** for the same amount of time and his **enjoyment of Christmas was marred** by his injuries. On examination at around **14 weeks post-accident**, the claimant was experiencing **no residual symptoms**. The medico-legal expert diagnosed a **forced flexion injury to the cervical and upper thoracic spine** that had **resolved within six weeks** of the accident. The expert also noted that the claimant's **psychological injuries had resolved within seven days**. In assessing damages, the judge took account of the **length and severity of the injuries**, as well as the **time of year** at which they had occurred.

Nolan v Pearson (23 May 2006, unreported) (Chris Middleton, Counsel, instructed by Irwin Mitchell, Solicitors, for the claimant; Matthew Cottrell, Counsel, instructed by Putsmans, Solicitors, for the defendant) (Kindly submitted for publication by Chris Middleton, Counsel).

989   Neck

PSLA: £600
Total damages: £600
Sex: Male
Age at accident/infant settlement approval hearing: 14/15
Date of accident/infant settlement approval hearing: 15 June 2005/2 February 2006
Judge/Court: DJ Jack/Telford County Court

The claimant was involved in a rear-end shunt road traffic accident following which he was **shocked and shaken** but experienced **no immediate pain**. **Two days later**, on waking, he was **aware of aching** in the **back of the neck** and in the **upper shoulder region**, and was **taken to his doctor**. He was informed that he had sustained a **whiplash injury to the neck** and was **advised to take painkillers** as necessary. The claimant was **absent from school for the rest of the day**. After a **further three days**, he began to notice **some easing of his neck symptoms**, which **resolved completely within two weeks** of the accident. He experienced **no significant restrictions of his social or domestic activities**.

C (A Child) v Western (2 February 2006, unreported) (Stephen Garner, Counsel, instructed by McKays, Solicitors, for the claimant; Jaggards, Solicitors, for the defendant) (Kindly submitted for publication by Stephen Garner, Counsel).

990   Neck

See para 978.

991   Neck and back

PSLA: £6,500
Total damages: £6,500
Sex: Male
Age at accident: 25
Date of accident/trial: 22 August 2002/2 August 2006
Judge/Court: DJ Asplin/Blackwood County Court

The claimant was involved in a rear-end shunt road traffic accident. One year earlier, he **had been involved in a similar accident** which had caused **whiplash injuries to his neck and back** and, most seriously, to his **shoulder**. At the **time of the second accident** his **neck and back pain had nearly resolved**, although his **shoulder pain continued to prevent him** from playing **badminton** and doing **weight and circuit training**. After the second accident the claimant was **absent from his work** as an education department surveyor for **one week**, following which he was **confined to desk work for a further two weeks** before returning to on-site duties, which involved some physical activity. His **neck and back symptoms had virtually resolved by six months** post-accident, although **some nuisance symptoms remained**. The medical evidence was that **neck and back symptoms attributable to the accident** were limited to a period of **three years**, as the claimant was involved in a further road traffic accident at that point. The claimant's view was that the **most serious injury was to his shoulder**, as it **prevented him from carrying out household chores** for **two to three weeks**. In the **longer term** his **leisure pursuits** of training, weightlifting, badminton and, to a lesser extent, golf were **adversely affected**. The claimant underwent an **operation on the right shoulder at three years** post-accident, but this was held to be **unrelated to the accident** in the light of the medical evidence. The claimant also **suffered from anxiety while driving** following the accident. He **drove a different route to work** and at the time of the trial had still **not returned to the site of the accident**. He **attended some counselling sessions** for his anxiety. The judge formed the view that the **shoulder injury was more of an exacerbation injury** than the neck and back symptoms, and awarded a total of £6,500, comprising **£3,500 for the neck and back injury**, **£2,500 for the shoulder injury** and **£500 for the anxiety**, with such figures reflecting an **overlap of symptoms**.

Gapper v Taviner (2 August 2006, unreported) (Richard Cole, Counsel, instructed by Shoosmiths, Solicitors, for the claimant; Joanne Williams, Counsel, instructed by Horwich Farrelly, Solicitors, for the defendant) (Kindly submitted for publication by Richard Cole, Counsel).

992   Neck and back

PSLA: £5,000
Total damages: £5,000
Sex: Male
Age at accident/trial: 34/35
Date of accident/trial: 13 January 2005/09 October 2004
Judge/Court: DJ McCullock/Slough County Court

The claimant **sustained a whiplash injury to the cervical and thoracic spine** in a road accident as well as **bruising to his knee**. He **attended his doctor and was signed off work for 3 weeks**. The **knee pain resolved within 1 week**. The **pain in his neck and upper back were severe for 4 to 5 weeks**. After **3 weeks he returned to work but only worked for 2 hours per day for a further 3 weeks**. At **4 and a half months post-accident movement in his neck was limited to between 15 and 50 per cent of normal** but **pain was intermittent in his neck and upper back**. He underwent **10 sessions of physiotherapy** and there was a **full resolution of physical symptoms within 22 months post-accident**. He **suffered depression for 5 to 6 weeks** and **travel anxiety for about 16 months**. He also underwent **3 sessions of cognitive behavioural therapy**.

Kalhar v Galatola (09 October 2006, unreported) (Richard Case, Counsel, instructed by Leech & Co, Solicitors, for the claimant) (Kindly submitted for publication by Richard Case, Counsel).

993 Neck and back

PSLA: £2,500
Total damages: £2,500
Sex: Male
Age at accident/trial: 46/47
Date of accident/trial: 26 September 2004/25 January 2006
Judge/Court: DJ Clark/Birkenhead County Court

The claimant was involved in a rear-end shunt road traffic accident. He was **shocked afterwards**, and the **following day** he began to experience **pain and stiffness** in his **neck and upper back**, **tension in his neck muscles**, and **headaches**. During the course of that day, his **neck symptoms worsened**, spreading **across his upper back** and becoming **more constant and intense**. His **headaches also became worse**. He **attended his doctor** and was prescribed painkillers. His **sleep was disturbed** that night. On his doctor's advice, he **took one week off from his work** as a lorry driver, since his duties included heavy lifting and driving for long periods. He **experienced difficulty on his return to work** with **turning his head to check mirrors**, as well as with **climbing into and out of his lorry**. For the first **seven weeks** after the accident, he **could not move his neck without experiencing pain**, and he also suffered **sharp back pain**. On **examination by a medico-legal expert** at **eight weeks post-accident**, the claimant was of the opinion that his **neck symptoms had resolved completely**. However, he assessed **improvement of his upper back symptoms** as being **below 50 per cent**. He still suffered from **intermittent pain in the upper back**, which was worse at the end of busy days. The expert recorded **tenderness in the para-vertebral muscles** on **both sides of the dorsal spine**, and diagnosed a **whiplash-type injury to the neck and upper back**. The expert assessed the claimant's **symptoms as mild but persistent**, and estimated that his **injuries increased** by about 15 per cent **his chance of suffering osteo-arthritis in the upper spine**. The expert predicted that the claimant would be able to perform his professional duties within a few months of the examination as well as he had done previously, but **suggested that the claimant should avoid lifting heavy objects** until his symptoms had resolved. This, in the expert's estimation, would be **between 11 and 14 months post-accident**. The claimant underwent **ten sessions of physiotherapy** in the **first four to five months following the accident**, which he found **improved his symptoms**. At **15 months post-accident**, he continued to experience **pain at the extremities of shoulder movement**. However, he was able to **ease his symptoms with painkillers** and by **undertaking exercises recommended by his physiotherapist**. His symptoms had **prevented him from playing golf**, and he was **still unable to play 15 months after** the accident. The judge assessed damages on the basis that the claimant suffered **symptoms until 14 months post-accident**. He **rejected** the claimant's contention that **headaches were a significant aggravating factor** because there was **no evidence as to how long headaches had lasted** and because **headaches were a common component of whiplash injuries**.

Allen v Naeem (25 January 2006, unreported) (Nigel Lawrence, Counsel, instructed by Michael W Halsall & Co, Solicitors, for the claimant; Chris Middleton, Counsel, instructed by Silverbeck Rymer, Solicitors, for the defendant) (Kindly submitted for publication by Chris Middleton, Counsel).

994 Neck and back

PSLA: £2,500
Total damages: £2,500
Sex: Female
Age at accident/infant settlement approval hearing: 14/15
Date of infant settlement approval hearing: 26 May 2006
Judge/Court: DDJ Muskath/Edmonton County Court

The claimant was involved in a rear-end shunt road traffic accident. **Immediately after** the accident she **attended Accident & Emergency** where she was **examined and discharged** with analgesia, advice and a soft cervical collar. She attended her doctor on four further occasions, and was referred for a course of physiotherapy. The claimant's physical symptoms caused six nights each week of sleep disturbance for at least five months. She also missed 30 days of school on account of her injuries, and refrained from participating in sporting activities for at least five months after her return. On examination at five months post-accident the expert diagnosed soft tissue injuries to the cervical and lumbar spine associated with discomfort in the claimant's spinal girdle musculature with pain on movement. The expert found that there was a full range of movement, but recommended a further course of eight to ten sessions of physiotherapy in addition to the 17 sessions which the claimant had already undergone. He concluded that the claimant would recover completely from her physical symptoms within 9 to 11 months of the accident. The claimant also suffered from psychological symptoms as a result of the accident. She experienced flashbacks for at least five months and was very anxious when confronted with circumstances similar to those of the accident, becoming tearful on occasions. She avoided travelling by car for one month after the accident. At the time of the examination it was reported that her symptoms were lessening gradually and on balance, the expert felt that she would recover completely from all psychological symptoms within 12 to 18 months of the accident without treatment. At the hearing it was confirmed that the claimant had recovered from all physical and psychological symptoms in accordance with the prognoses.

A (A Child) v Humphreys (26 May 2006, unreported) (Dalgarno, Solicitors, for the claimant; Joanna Kerr, Counsel, instructed by Davies Wallis Foyster, Solicitors, for the defendant) (Kindly submitted for publication by Joanna Kerr, Counsel).

995   Neck and back

PSLA: £2,500
Total damages: £2,500
Sex: Male
Age at accident/trial: 36/37
Date of accident/trial: 26 August 2004/8 June 2006
Judge/Court: HHJ Tetlow/Oldham County Court

The claimant was involved in a rear-end shunt road traffic accident in which he sustained whiplash injuries to his neck and back. Although pain was severe for a period of five weeks, he took no time off from his work as a managing director. However, he underwent five or six sessions of physiotherapy during the same period, which brought about an improvement in his symptoms. He was unable to play five-a-side football for several months as a result of his symptoms. On examination at five months post-accident he was still experiencing intermittent mild neck and lower back pain throughout each day. The pain was exacerbated by long car journeys. The medical expert advised the claimant to undergo further physiotherapy, and was of the opinion that a full recovery would take place within 11 months of the accident with such treatment. Damages were assessed on this basis.

Towns v Morley (8 June 2006, unreported) (Tom Nossiter, Counsel, instructed by Irwin Mitchell, Solicitors, for the claimant; Cogent, Solicitors, for the defendant) (Kindly submitted for publication by Tom Nossiter, Counsel).

996   Neck and back

PSLA: £1,650
Total damages: £1,650
Sex: Male
Age at accident/infant settlement approval hearing: 12/13
Date of infant settlement approval hearing: 6 June 2006
Judge/Court: DJ Diamond/Medway County Court

The claimant was involved in a rear-end shunt road traffic accident. He immediately felt pain and stiffness in his neck and developed a headache. He was taken to Accident and Emergency where he was examined and diagnosed as having sustained a soft tissue injury to the neck and back. He was advised to take analgesics and rest. He took one week off school, and attended his doctor after six days, complaining that the pain in his neck and back had worsened. He was advised to continue taking analgesics. The claimant's hobbies of football, cycling and swimming were affected for just over three months. His neck injury had more or less resolved by ten weeks post-accident, but his back pain persisted. On examination at three months post-accident he was still suffering from constant pain in the lower back and occasional discomfort in the neck after PE or games at school. Tenderness was evident in the lower back on palpation. The expert gave a prognosis for a full recovery from all symptoms within six to seven months of the accident, and at the hearing it was confirmed that recovery had been in line with this prognosis.

J (A Child) v Liu (6 June 2006, unreported) (Joanna Kerr, Counsel, instructed by Silverbeck Rymer, Solicitors, for the claimant) (Kindly submitted for publication by Joanna Kerr, Counsel).

997   Neck and back

PSLA: £1,500
Total damages: £1,534
Sex: Female
Age at accident/trial: 41/45
Date of accident/trial: 3 December 2002/5 October 2005
Judge/Court: DJ Kemp/Ilford County Court

The claimant was involved in a rear-end shunt of her stationary motor vehicle that **caused her to suffer a whiplash injury to her neck and lower back and to bang her head** against the seat's head-restraint. **She consulted her doctor the following day** and **attended one session of physiotherapy followed after by home exercises**. She **took analgesics for two weeks**. She **suffered some tenderness to the back of her head with headaches for two to three days**. The **symptoms in the neck settled over two weeks** with the claimant reporting that **symptoms in her lower back were about 80 per cent better at about four weeks post-accident**. The claimant continued to **suffer intermittent symptoms in her lower back**, however the medical evidence was that **these were due to constitutional changes arising from the claimant's age and the fact that she had previously suffered whiplash injuries** in 1989 and 2000. The medical evidence was that the accident had caused **symptoms in the lower back for a maximum period of six to eight weeks**.

Keyte v Wheeler (5 October 2006, unreported) (David McHugh, Counsel, instructed by Colemans CTTS, Soclitiors, for the claimant) (Kindly submitted for publication by David McHugh, Counsel).

998   Shoulder

PSLA: £3,000
Total damages: £3,500
Sex: Female
Age at accident/infant settlement approval hearing: 7/10
Date of infant settlement approval hearing: 3 March 2006
Judge/Court: DDJ Carter/Staines County Court

The claimant was involved in a head-on road traffic accident. She was **taken to Accident & Emergency immediately** afterwards, where a chest x-ray revealed a **fracture of the right clavicle**. **Neck pain**, **seatbelt marks** over the **lower abdominal wall** and a **head injury** were also noted, but CT scans of the head and abdomen disclosed **no abnormalities**. The claimant was **kept in hospital for two nights** before she was **discharged with her arm in a sling**. At home she found her **shoulder movement was restricted** and her **sleep was disturbed**, not only because of **nightmares** she suffered on her first few nights back home, but also because she was **unable to roll onto her injured right side**. She was **absent from school** on account of her injuries for **two weeks**, during which she was **unable to participate in her hobbies** of drawing, polishing and gardening, before returning, initially for **only a few hours each morning**. Within **four to six weeks** of the accident, a **full range of movement had returned** and the claimant had **returned to school full-time**, although she **could not participate in games or PE**. She **missed three school trips** during her absence, and was **refused permission by the school to take part in a fourth** as a result of her injuries. On examination at **seven months post-accident** the fracture was found to have **united completely without anatomical displacement**, and the claimant's **activity level was generally back to normal**. However, she **still suffered from aching in the right shoulder approximately twice each week**, and occasionally this would **restrict her activities**. The expert was of the opinion that all **remaining symptoms would resolve by ten months** post-accident, and at the hearing it was confirmed that a **full recovery had taken place in line with the expert's prognosis**.

D (A Child) v Lavers (3 March 2006, unreported) (Fancy and Jackson, Solicitors, for the claimant; Joanna Kerr, Counsel, instructed by Davies Wallis Foyster, Solicitors, for the defendant) (Kindly submitted for publication by Joanna Kerr, Counsel).

999   Shoulder

See paras 957, 991.

1000   Back

PSLA: £14,500
Total damages: £17,177
Sex: Female
Age at accident/trial: 25/29
Date of accident/trial: 27 March 2002/6 June 2006

Judge/Court: DJ Hickman/Milton Keynes County Court

The claimant sustained a **soft tissue injury to the lumbar spine** when she **lifted a box of heavy files** in the course of her employment as an office worker. She underwent **physiotherapy and acupuncture**, but was **still experiencing discomfort on a daily basis** in her back **four years after** the accident. However, she **continued to work with the aid of painkillers**. As there was a **history of degenerative changes to the spine** in the claimant's family, the agreed medical evidence was that her **symptoms probably would have presented in any event within 15 to 20 years** of the date of the accident. The prognosis was that **symptoms would be permanent**, so it followed that there had been an **acceleration of some 15 to 20 years**. There was estimated to be a **50 to 60 per cent chance** that the **symptoms would deteriorate** such that the claimant would **require a spinal fusion**, which would have a **60 to 70 per cent chance of a satisfactory outcome**. The **likelihood of surgical intervention** had been **accelerated by ten years** so that the claimant would probably **have to undergo the procedure** at a time when she was **likely to have young children**. The judge found that the claimant suffered a **constant nagging discomfort with flare-ups** and indicated that her symptoms fell at the **top end of the moderate (b)(ii) bracket of the JSB Guidelines**. The injury was found to be **aggravated** by the fact that the claimant was a **young woman who had been leading an active life** before the accident and had been **robbed of her youth by a significant acceleration of symptoms**.

Lane v Laing Construction Ltd (6 June 2006, unreported) (David McHugh, Counsel, instructed by HilliersHRW, Solicitors, for the claimant) (Kindly submitted for publication by David McHugh, Counsel).

1001   Back

PSLA: £11,000
Total damages: £15,129 (including interest)
Sex: Female
Age at accident/trial: 36/41
Date of accident/trial: 11 December 2000/15 December 2005
Judge/Court: McKinnon J/Birmingham County Court

The claimant was injured **when a bus drove into her parked car** while she was leaning into it. She **banged her head on the interior roof** and felt a **sharp pain in her back**. She **visited her doctor the next day**, and was prescribed **ibuprofen and rest**. She was **off work for three days**, during which she **required help from her family** with domestic chores. She suffered from **pain in her back, neck and shoulders** for **six months**, during which she **visited her doctor regularly** and underwent **physiotherapy**. Although there was **some improvement** in her symptoms, the claimant was still experiencing **pain in her back and neck at trial, five years post-accident**. The issue at trial was **whether her ongoing symptoms were related to the accident**. She had a **history of minor back problems** preceding the accident, and in the opinion of her medical expert had experienced an **augmentation of these previously minor problems**, with the result that her **back was more troublesome** than before. She was left with a **minor disability to her lower back** which was **attributable to the accident**. However, it was held that **any further deterioration would not be attributable** to it. The judge found that the **appropriate award for damages** fell around the **middle of category 6(B)(b)(ii)** of the JSB Guidelines.

Shaw v Travel West Midlands (15 December 2005, unreported) (Andrew Granville Stafford, Counsel, instructed by Irwin Mitchell, Solicitors, for the claimant; Mark Radburn, Counsel, instructed by DLA Piper Rudnick Gray Cary, Solicitors, for the defendant) (Kindly submitted for publication by Andrew Granville Stafford, Counsel).

1002   Back

PSLA: £10,000
Total damages: £10,000
Sex: Female
Age at accident/trial: 33/37
Date of accident/trial: 21 October 2002/18 May 2006
Judge/Court: HHJ MacIntyre/Oxford County Court

The claimant was involved in a heavy impact rear-end shunt road traffic accident. She was **shocked and shaken immediately afterwards** and **began to develop pain** in the **neck**, across the **shoulders** and in the **lower back**. She **attended hospital** where she was diagnosed as having sustained a **whiplash injury** and **was prescribed painkillers and then discharged**. **Within a week** of the accident her **lower back pain became acute**, although her **neck symptoms began to improve** and had **resolved within a month** of the accident. The claimant **had undergone a discectomy** after suffering **pre-existing back symptoms** prior to the accident and had a **vulnerable back** as a result. **Orthopaedic opinion** was that the **accident had accelerated back symptoms by two to five years**. The judge assessed damages based on an **acceleration of three**

and a half years. The claimant also suffered **psychological symptoms** after the accident. She suffered from **low mood, frequent daytime flashbacks, frequent nightmares and intrusive thoughts**. She also experienced **acute symptoms of travel anxiety** and was **reluctant to travel by car** except on essential journeys. She tended to **avoid travelling as a passenger**. Expert opinion was that she had suffered **mild post-traumatic stress disorder** with accompanying symptoms of **specific driving phobia**. She was advised to undergo a course of **cognitive behavioural therapy** and expected, with treatment, to **recover from her post-traumatic stress disorder and specific phobia symptoms by four years post-accident**.

Sheath v GE Capital Fleet Services (18 May 2006, unreported) (Stephen Garner, Counsel, instructed by Colemans, Solicitors, for the claimant; Karim Ghaly, Counsel, instructed by Eversheds, Solicitors, for the defendant) (Kindly submitted for publication by Stephen Garner, Counsel).

1003   Back

PSLA: £3,000
Total damages: £3,000
Sex: Female
Age at accident/infant settlement approval hearing: 12/14
Date of accident/infant settlement approval hearing: 5 June 2004/7 July 2006
Judge/Court: DJ Sheldrake/Birmingham County Court

The claimant suffered personal injury in a rear-end shunt road traffic accident. Immediately after the accident, she was **shocked and tearful** and developed **pain and discomfort** in her **neck and low back**. She was taken to hospital, where she was diagnosed as having sustained a **soft tissue whiplash injury to the neck** and a **soft tissue injury to the low back**. She was **absent from school for one week**. The **neck symptoms** were generally **modest and short-lived**. They **steadily improved** and **settled completely within four weeks**. The **low back injury was more significant**. Symptoms were **acute for two weeks** before starting to improve. The claimant **took analgesics on a daily basis** throughout this two-week period to help alleviate the pain. She was **unable to pursue her hobby of dancing** during the same period. When travelling as a passenger in motor vehicles, she suffered symptoms of **generalised travel anxiety** that **resolved within six months** of the accident. On examination at one year post-accident she was still suffering **occasional episodes of low back pain** that would occur after she had been sitting for a few hours or after physical exertion, such as physical education or dancing. The claimant's symptoms had settled by 16 to 17 months of the accident.

M (A Child) v Rhoden (7 July 2006, unreported) (Stephen Garner, Counsel, instructed by Michael Taylor and Associates, Solicitors, for the claimant; Cogent, Solicitors, for the defendant) (Kindly submitted for publication by Stephen Garner, Counsel).

1004   Back

PSLA: £2,650
Total damages: £2,650
Sex: Female
Age at accident/trial: 32/34
Date of accident/trial: 3 May 2004/31 January 2006
Judge/Court: HHJ Langan QC/Leeds County Court

The claimant was involved in a road traffic accident in which she sustained a **soft tissue strain to her back** and **soft tissue contusions to the chest**. She experienced **chest symptoms for six to eight weeks**, during which time she **took painkillers**. She took **three days off from her work** as a children's nursery manageress but, **on returning** to work, she found that the **job precipitated back pain**. For **four weeks** she **required care and assistance with household chores and childcare**. On examination at **ten weeks post-accident**, her **back discomfort was intermittent**, occurring at the **end of each working day**. At **eight and a half months** post-accident, she was **still suffering lower back pain each evening**. She experienced **pain in her back when lifting children at work**, and had **had to give up walking her dog** as this also caused back pain. The claimant underwent **three sessions of physiotherapy**, which **brought about an improvement** in her symptoms such that they had **fully resolved by 15 months post-accident**.

Jacobs v Hodgson (31 January 2006, unreported) (Tom Nossiter, Counsel, instructed by Morrish & Co, Solicitors, for the claimant; Simon Ross, Counsel, instructed by Cogent, Solicitors, for the defendant) (Kindly submitted for publication by Tom Nossiter, Counsel).

1005   Back

PSLA: £2,250
Total damages: £2,250
Sex: Male
Age at accident/trial: 41/44

Date of accident/trial: August 2003/3 April 2006
Judge/Court: DDJ Reed/Birmingham County Court

The claimant sustained personal injury when a **piece of wooden fascia board fell** from the exterior of his council-owned property and **struck him on the head**. He **fell backwards to the ground, injuring his back and shoulder** as he did so. He **attended his doctor within a few days** of the accident and was found to have sustained a **minor head injury** and a **back injury**. The **head injury resolved completely** within **two weeks**. The **back injury warranted physiotherapy at six months** post-accident. At the **time of the trial** there were **minor ongoing symptoms**, but the medical evidence was that **any symptoms beyond 12 months** post-accident were **attributable to a pre-existing back condition** rather than to the accident. The judge **did not consider that the head injury should be considered separately** from the back and shoulder injury, as the **head symptoms had been very short-lived**, and awarded general damages of £2,250.

White v Birmingham City C (3 April 2006, unreported) (Adam Walker, Counsel, instructed by Wixted & Co, Solicitors, for the claimant) (Kindly submitted for publication by Adam Walker, Counsel).

1006   Back

PSLA: £2,000
Total damages: £2,000
Sex: Male
Age at accident/infant settlement approval hearing: 13/15
Date of accident/infant settlement approval hearing: 5 September 2004/24 May 2006
Judge/Court: DDJ Rose/Coventry County Court

The claimant was involved in a rear-end shunt road traffic accident. **Immediately after** the accident, he began to develop **low back pain** and **pain across his chest and abdomen**. He was also **shocked and shaken** by the impact. He **attended hospital**, where he was diagnosed as having sustained a **soft tissue injury to the low back** and **seatbelt bruising to the chest and abdomen**. The **low back pain was so acute** on the **day after the accident** that the claimant was **unable to walk properly**. Shortly after the accident, he **visited a chiropractor** and underwent **14 sessions of treatment** before his **symptoms steadily settled**. Symptoms were **acute for two weeks**, during which the claimant was **absent from school**, before **gradually resolving over the next six months**. The **seatbelt contusions settled within two weeks** of the accident, although there was **residual tenderness** over the **chest and abdomen** for **two months**. The claimant was **unable to pursue his hobbies** of rugby and modern dance during this time. He also suffered symptoms of **psychological travel anxiety** after the accident. He **became hypervigilant** when travelling by car and **would often criticise the driver**. These symptoms also **settled within six months** of the accident.

B (A Child) v Heath (24 May 2006, unreported) (Stephen Garner, Counsel, instructed by Colemans, Solicitors, for the claimant; Beachcroft Wansbroughs, Solicitors, for the defendant) (Kindly submitted for publication by Stephen Garner, Counsel).

1007   Back

PSLA: £1,600
Total damages: £1,600
Sex: Male
Age at accident/trial: 38/39
Date of accident/trial: 6 December 2004/6 April 2006
Judge/Court: DJ Swindley/Bolton County Court

The claimant was involved in a rear-end shunt road traffic accident in which his **lower spine was jolted**. He **started to feel pain** in the spine about an **hour and a half after** the accident. He **attended his doctor three days later** and was advised to take **painkillers and exercise**. During the **first week** after the accident the claimant **continued his work as a taxi driver intermittently**, stopping work before his shifts ended and coming home to rest. The nature of his **work aggravated his symptoms**, which were **severe for three to four weeks**. On examination at **three months post-accident** the claimant was experiencing **intermittent lower back pain**, which occurred when **driving, bending, lifting and sitting for prolonged periods**. He displayed **tenderness on palpation** of the **right and left perivertebral muscles**, and **pain on extremes of forward flexion**. His **sleep was disturbed** by his symptoms. The medico-legal expert diagnosed a **soft tissue sprain to the lower back**, and predicted a **full recovery within six to nine months** of the accident. **Recovery was in line with this prognosis**, and the judge assessed damages on the basis of a **full recovery by six months** post-accident. The judge found **bracket 6(A)(c)(ii) of the JSB Guidelines** to be of assistance, despite the fact that the claimant had suffered exclusively from back symptoms.

Lukhat v Grote (6 April 2006, unreported) (Angela Geourgiou, Counsel, instructed by MRH LLP, Solicitors, for the claimant; Chris Middleton, Counsel, instructed by Silverbeck Rymer, Solicitors, for the defendant) (Kindly submitted for publication by Chris Middleton, Counsel).

1008   Back

PSLA: £1,250
Total damages: £1,250
Sex: Female
Age at accident/trial: 5/6
Date of accident/trial: 24 March 2005/7 September 2006
Judge/Court: DDJ Vaughan/Skipton County Court

The claimant was a rear near side passenger in a child safety seat in a vehicle when a heavy goods vehicle collided with the rear of the claimant's vehicle, pushing it across the road where it sustained a further frontal impact from another vehicle. The claimant sustained a **jarring injury to her back** which caused **pain to the middle area of her back with radiation to both sides within an hour** of the accident. The **pain to the back resolved** within **a few days**. She also sustained a **bruise over the mid line of the lumbar spine**, which again **resolved** fully **over several days**. On the night of the accident she suffered **restlessness and sleep loss** due to **anxiety and pain to the back** and she **wet the bed on two occasions** during the week following the accident. The claimant **attended her doctor** two days after the accident and was **prescribed pain relief**. She also experienced **vehicle anxiety and nervousness** which resolved fully **nine months** post-accident. The claimant was on her Easter holiday from school at the time of the accident and **did not require any further time off** and was able to **resume her physical education activities** on her return to school.

L (A Child) v Woodburn (7 September 2006, unreported) (Leila Benyounces, Counsel, instructed by Irwin Mitchell, Solicitors, for the claimant; Horwich Farrelly, Solicitors, for the defendant) (Kindly submitted for publication by Leila Benyounces, Counsel).

1009   Back

PSLA: £1,250
Total damages: £1,250
Sex: Female
Age at accident/infant settlement approval hearing: 15/16
Date of accident/infant settlement approval hearing: 15 August 2004/17 January 2006
Judge/Court: DJ Price/Wolverhampton County Court

The claimant was involved in a rear-end shunt road traffic accident. Immediately after the accident she **developed pain in her low back**. She **attended hospital** where a **low back strain** was diagnosed. She was **prescribed painkillers**, which she **took for one week**. The back pain was **acute and constant** for a period of **two weeks**, and became **more severe at night**. It subsequently **began to settle, resolving completely by six weeks post-accident**. The claimant took no time off school because the accident occurred during the school holidays, but her **social life was inhibited during the week after** the accident.

G (A Child) v Kahzaei (17 January 2006, unreported) (Stephen Garner, Counsel, instructed by Colemans, Solicitors, for the claimant; Cogent, Solicitors, for the defendant) (Kindly submitted for publication by Stephen Garner, Counsel).

1010   Chest

PSLA: £3,100
Total damages: £3,100
Sex: Female
Age at accident/trial: 36/38
Date of accident/trial: 10 February 2004/23 March 2006
Judge/Court: DDJ Rowley/Birmingham County Court

The claimant was involved in a side-impact road traffic accident in which she sustained a **soft tissue injury** to the **chest and rib cage** and **bruising across the right breast**. **Immediately after** the accident she began to develop **pain in the front of her chest around the sternum**. There was also **bruising and aching over the right breast**, extending along the **left side of the neck**. The claimant was **taken to hospital**. It was initially suspected that she had **fractured her sternum and ribs**, but x-rays revealed **no such fractures**. In the **three weeks** which followed the accident, the claimant suffered **acute and constant pain** in the **front of her chest** around the **rib cage and sternum**. She was **unable to sleep** and her chest **symptoms were aggravated by coughing or sneezing**. She also experienced **flashbacks and panic attacks** for **about a week**, and subsequently suffered from **travel anxiety**, especially when travelling the route on which the accident had occurred. Activities which entailed **bending and lifting were problematic** for **about a month** as they **aggravated the claimant's chest symptoms**. Her **domestic activities** were also restricted during this time. Afterwards, however, her chest and rib **symptoms became intermittent** and the **bruising** to the breast and neck **resolved**. She was **absent from her work** as an auxiliary nurse on account of her injuries for **six weeks**. On examination at **five months post-accident**, she reported only **occasional twinges in the chest** and said that she felt **80 per cent better**. However, she **still felt pain** if she **tried to lift heavy items**, especially at work, or if she **leant against her chest**. The prognosis was for the **residual chest symptoms to resolve within 14 to 17 months** of the accident, and **recovery was in line with this prognosis**.

Carr v Midlands Counties Heating Services Ltd (23 March 2006, unreported) (Stephen Garner, Counsel, instructed by Blakemores, Solicitors, for the claimant; Kate Thomas, Counsel, instructed by Mutual Law, Solicitors, for the defendant) (Kindly submitted for publication by Stephen Garner, Counsel).

1011   Arm

PSLA: £15,250
Total damages: £71,180
Sex: Male
Age at accident/trial: 31/37
Date of accident/trial: 9 March 2002/29 August 2006
Judge/Court: HHJ Harris QC/Oxford County Court

The claimant was injured when **he tripped over a defective manhole cover** in the course of his **employment** as an HGV driver. He sustained a **probable undisplaced fracture of the radial neck of his dominant right arm** together with **associated soft tissue injuries**. He attended the local hospital where he was given **a sling and supplied with painkillers** and he underwent **six months of physiotherapy**. He was **unable to work for about eight months** and suffered **symptoms of pain and a restriction of movement**. It was agreed that this injury caused **symptoms for 12 months** and **damages** for pain, suffering and loss of amenity were agreed at £6,250. The claimant also developed **ulnar nerve entrapment in the right elbow** the **first symptoms** of which became apparent at about **two years post-accident** with **pain in the elbow and pins and needles in the right hand**. He underwent **surgical decompression and transposition of the nerve** with a **full recovery thereafter**. The court assessed **damages** for this injury at £4,000. The **pain in the arm** and the **inability to return to work** caused the development of **moderately severe depression** ICD-10 criteria. His **long term partner left him** as a result of his **moodiness and impatience** at about **six months post-accident**. He underwent **counselling** for **six months**. At **three years post-accident** the symptoms amounted to **general low mood** and at **four years post-accident** there was reported **tearfulness and low mood with sleep disturbance and inability to concentrate. Cognitive behaviour therapy** was recommended with **improvement likely**. The court assessed **damages** for this injury at £5,000.

Hirons v Kraft Foods plc (29 August 2006, unreported) (Richard Case, Counsel, for the claimant) (Kindly submitted for publication by Richard Case, Counsel).

1012   Arm

PSLA: £3,500
Total damages: £5,378
Sex: Male
Age at accident/trial: 22/26
Date of trial: 2 December 2005
Judge/Court: DJ Jenkins/Bridgend County Court

The claimant suffered an **injury to his non-dominant left arm** when he **tripped and fell** down a defective step. He was **taken to hospital** where he was diagnosed as having sustained a **fracture to the pisiform bone in the left wrist** and a **laceration to the left elbow**. A **plaster cast was fitted** and the **wound was sutured**. The claimant **wore the cast for six weeks**, and was **absent from his job** as a factory worker for **nine weeks**. He developed a **scar measuring 4 cm by 1 cm** on his **left elbow**. By around **eight months post-accident**, he had made an **80 per cent recovery**. On examination at **15 months post-accident**, he complained of **some discomfort in the left hand**, which occurred **when he placed weight on it. Discomfort was intermittent**, occurring **four to five times each week**. It was **worse in cold weather**. There was **no functional loss**. The claimant's **mild intermittent symptoms** were predicted to **resolve completely by up to two years post-accident**.

Sutton v Bridgend CBC (2 December 2005, unreported) (Andrew Arentsen, Counsel, for the claimant) (Kindly submitted for publication by Andrew Arentsen, Counsel).

1013   Arm

PSLA: £2,150
Total damages: £2,150
Sex: Female
Age at accident: 11 months
Date of trial: 17 October 2006
Judge/Court: DJ Latham/Tunbridge Wells County Court

The claimant attended hospital with her parents to undergo tests as a result of her failure to thrive that was noted at an earlier check, and **underwent a sweat test for coeliac disease and cystic fibrosis**. This involved the application of metal electrodes to the claimant's forearm which were applied incorrectly, without a protective rubber pad, and **the claimant sustained burns to her right forearm** in the shape of two small circles. **Initially the burns had the appearance of blisters** and **were diagnosed as burns the following day** when she was **taken by her parents to her doctor**. **The burnt skin wept for approximately two weeks** before **forming a dry scab and eventually healing**. The medical evidence confirmed that **she had sustained partial thickness burns** and noted that **she had been left with two scars**. One of which was **positioned on the radial volar aspect of the right forearm** and **was a pale, slightly raised circular dermal scar, 0.5 cm in diameter** and was **visible at conversational distance**. The **second scar was less conspicuous, paler and measured 0.2 cm in diameter** but was **visible on closer inspection**. The **scars were considered to be permanent** but they were expected to **become less conspicuous as the claimant grew older**. The **scarring had a similar appearance to those of cigarette burns** and this had **caused the claimant's parents some upset** when specific comment had been made about them in a social setting.

B (A Child) v Maidstone & Tunbridge Wells NHS Trust (17 October 2006, unreported) (Adam Walker, Counsel, instructed by Keeble Hawson, Solicitors, for the claimant) (Kindly submitted for publication by Adam Walker, Counsel).

1014   Elbow

PSLA: £3,650
Total damages: £3,650
Sex: Male
Age at accident: 6
Date of infant settlement approval hearing: 14 March 2006
Judge/Court: DJ Wilson/Portsmouth County Court

The claimant was injured when he **fell off his bicycle after skidding on debris** left on the road by the defendant. He sustained a **moderate displaced fracture of the left elbow**. Following treatment he had to **wear a plaster cast for five weeks**. He made a **full recovery by two and a half years** post-accident. He was left with a **bump on the lateral aspect** of the elbow, but there were **no other residual abnormalities**.

R (A Child) v Barratt Developments plc (14 March 2006, unreported) (Dyer Burdett & Co, Solicitors, for the claimant) (Kindly submitted for publication by Dyer Burdett & Co, Solicitors).

1015   Elbow

See para 1011.

1016   Hand

PSLA: £4,000
Total damages: £4,050
Sex: Male
Age at trial: 57
Date of trial: 18 December 2006
Judge/Court: HHJ Graham Jones/Cardiff County Court

The claimant, a steel worker, **brought proceedings for Hand Arm Vibration Syndrome** ('HAVS') **caused by exposure to vibrating tools while employed** by the defendant. The claimant **did not complain of or suffer from the strict vascular effects of HAVS** but **did complain of sensori-neural symptoms**. The claimant **began to suffer symptoms** in the early 1990's. The **numbness and impaired dexterity became a constant feature. Symptoms were worse in cold weather and affected his grip strength as well as his fine dexterity**. He **fumbled small objects** such as buttons, glasses and coins and **had to use an elastic band to retain purchase on pens and pencils**. The claimant had **given up fishing and darts** and **struggled with jigsaw puzzles**. The claimant also **suffered pain when he cut his garden hedge** with an electric trimmer. His **dexterity was better in the warm but always remained impaired**. He was **graded SN 2 on the Stockholm scale**.

Slade v Corus (UK) Ltd (18 December 2006, unreported) (Andrew Arentsen, Counsel, for the claimant) (Kindly submitted for publication by Andrew Arentsen, Counsel).

1017　Hand

PSLA: £3,000
Total damages: £3,030
Sex: Male
Age at trial: 52
Date of trial: 14 December 2006
Judge/Court: HHJ Graham Jones/Cardiff County Court

The claimant, a steel worker, brought proceedings for **Hand Arm Vibration Syndrome** (**'HAVS'**) caused by **exposure to vibrating tools** while employed by the defendant. The claimant did not establish that he suffered from the vascular component of HAVS but **did establish the existence of sensori–neural deficit**. The claimant began to suffer **symptoms of tingling and numbness in the fingers** sometime in 1982. Initially it **directly followed the use of the vibrating tools** but over time the **numbness and impaired dexterity** became a constant feature. The claimant felt as if he were wearing oversize gloves. He dropped small objects such as cutlery. He had problems with small buttons and gave up playing darts. His dexterity was better in the warm but always remained impaired. The claimant's major problem was **constitutional arthritis of the hands which caused pain and cramps at the base of both thumbs**. It was **unrelated to vibration exposure**. The claimant was graded SN 1 on the Stockholm scale.

Dent v Corus (UK) Ltd (18 December 2006, unreported) (Andrew Arentsen, Counsel, for the claimant) (Kindly submitted for publication by Andrew Arentsen, Counsel).

1018　Hand

PSLA: £1,500
Total damages: £1,500
Sex: Male
Age at accident/trial: 55/59
Date of accident/Date of trial: 31 February 2003/23 November 2006
Judge/Court: DJ Saffman/Leeds County Court

The claimant, a yardman, picked up some rags in the defendant's yard that were **covered in solvent** that went through the claimant's gloves and came into contact with the skin on his hands. **Within about 30 minutes** he had developed **a burning sensation and redness on the backs of both hands and between his fingers**. He **sought first aid** and was **advised to apply E45 cream**. He saw his doctor's nurse when the **symptoms did not ease** and was **advised to continue with the E45 cream**. During the **first three weeks post-accident**, the claimant's **hands were painful and sore**. The **backs of the hands and the areas between the fingers were affected and red**, and there was **blistering**. If the hands came into **contact with hot water**, the claimant **felt a burning sensation**. The **discomfort disturbed his sleep** and **at work** he was **given light duties** as he did not want to stay at home. **After three weeks the skin on the back of his hands began to peel off** and the **blisters began to ease**. The damages were assessed on the basis that the **most serious consequences of the dermatitis resolved within the first three weeks**. The **medical expert** put the **recovery from the dermatitis** due to the exposure at work at **three months post-accident**. The claimant was also **unable to go swimming for three months**, he had previously gone about twice per month, and **could not cook meals** due to the state of his hands. His **intimate relationship** with his wife was also **adversely affected**.

Rigby v MFI UK Ltd (23 November 2006, unreported) (Tom Nossiter, Counsel, instructed by Morrish & Co, Solicitors for the claimant; Jonathan Godfrey, Counsel for the defendant) (Kindly submitted for publication by Tom Nossiter, Counsel).

1019　Thumb

PSLA: £10,500
Total damages: £17,276
Sex: Female
Age at accident/trial: 26/30
Date of accident/Date of trial: 22 September 2006/14 November 2006
Judge/Court: HHJ Finnerty/Bradford County Court

The claimant, a **keen horse woman**, was **injured in a road traffic accident** in which she was a seat-belted front seat passenger. The car overturned when it was driven around a bend too quickly and the defendant admitted liability. The claimant **suffered multiple injuries**, including **a fractured sternum, a minor head injury, an injury to her foot**, as well as **cuts and bruising**. The **major injury** was **a fracture of her right, dominant, thumb**. She **largely recovered** from the **effects of the injuries, except for the thumb, within a few months. Five months post-accident** she underwent **a fusion operation for her thumb**. She was **left with limited** movement and **some loss of strength. A plate was fixed over the top of the thumb** and it was **painful when knocked,** and would **shake and ache with use.** She felt she had **limited use of the joint** as **the tendons would stick to the plate** and she **could not make a 'thumb up' gesture.** She suffered what was described as **a significant soft tissue injury and fracture,** and although there had been **some improvement,** she would **always be left with symptoms.** She also had **three scars to the knee, hip and thumb, none** of which **were of any major cosmetic significance.** She was **off work for four weeks,** and had **lost a substantial amount of weight** which **she struggled to regain,** which **troubled her.** She **panicked and was more wary** when in a car than before the accident, however there was **no psychological evidence presented.** Her **hobbies of playing the guitar, saxophone and flute were substantially affected for a number of years,** as was **her ability to ride a horse. By trial she was working part time** and **undertaking a course to improve her horse riding skills** as she aspired to work in some unspecified capacity in the equine industry. The court awarded her a sum to **bring her horse riding skills up to the level,** and recognised that **her injury had affected her enjoyment of her work and hobby** in the equine field. While there was **no specific award for loss of congenial employment,** such sum should be viewed as part of the damages awarded for pain, suffering and loss of amenity.

Shaw v Barber (14 November 2006, unreported) (Richard Nall-Cain, Counsel, instructed by Tollers, Solcitiors for the claimant; Stuart Yeung, Counsel, instructed by Keoghs, Solicitors for the defendant) (Kindly submitted for publication by Stuart Yeung, Counsel).

1020 Thumb

PSLA: £4,500
Total damages: £4,500
Sex: Female
Age at accident/trial: 42/46
Date of accident/trial: 1 December 2002/7 March 2006
Judge/Court: DDJ Anthony/Birmingham County Court

The claimant sustained a **dislocation of the middle joint in her dominant right thumb** in a slipping accident. She experienced **pain in the thumb** immediately after the accident, and was **bleeding profusely from a laceration** in the underside of the thumb. The **end of the thumb** was also **bent at an abnormal angle.** The claimant **attended hospital** and underwent an x-ray, which showed that she had suffered a **dislocation of the joint in the centre of the thumb.** The dislocation was **reduced under local anaesthetic,** and the **wound on the underside of the thumb was closed** using steri-strips. The claimant's **right hand was placed in a plaster cast** to prevent movement, and she was **prescribed antibiotics.** The next day she had **throbbing pain** in the thumb and only **very limited use of her right hand. Ten days** after the accident, the **plaster case was replaced by a firm splint.** The claimant was **unable to drive for a month** after the accident, and was **absent from her work** as a school teacher for the **same amount of time.** She underwent **four sessions of physiotherapy,** but this **did not assist improve mobility** in the thumb. She was left with **constant stiffness** in the thumb, which **ached after prolonged use** in activities such as marking books or writing. She also suffered a **loss of grip strength** and of **50 per cent flexion in the interphalangeal joint.** She was left with a **transverse pale scar,** which measured about **13 mm in length,** on the **underside of the thumb.** The scar was **not tender** and was **only visible on close inspection,** but it was **permanent** and a **constant reminder** of the accident. On examination the prognosis was that the **ongoing thumb symptoms,** including the loss of mobility and grip strength, **would be permanent,** and that the claimant had also suffered the **onset of minor arthritis.**

Pearson v Snax 24 Ltd (7 March 2006, unreported) (Nageena Khalique, Counsel, instructed by Thompsons, Solicitors, for the claimant; Stephen Garner, Counsel, instructed by Mutual Law, Solicitors, for the defendant) (Kindly submitted for publication by Stephen Garner, Counsel).

1021 Leg

PSLA: £70,000
Total damages: £750,000
Sex: Male
Age at accident/settlement: 16/21
Date of accident/settlement: 5 October 2000/22 February 2006

The claimant sustained **severe injuries to his right leg and foot** when he was hit by the defendant's motor car while riding his motorcycle. The **right knee and thigh were degloved** and the **extensor mechanism of the knee and patella was split,** with **loss of approximately half of the lateral condoyle of the femur.** There was also a **displaced fracture of the lateral tibial plateau,** a **soft tissue injury down the tibia,** a **partial degloving** injury to the **right foot** and **underlying subluxation of the calcaneocuboid joint** with a **fracture of the third metatarsal.** The claimant underwent **in-patient treatment in hospital for 21 days.** Treatment included a **blood transfusion, catheterisation, debridement of the wounds** and **excision of dead tissue, reduction and plating** of the **fractured patella and tibial plateau, soft tissue repair, wiring of the right foot** and **skin grafts. Two years** after the accident, the claimant **slipped and suffered a further fracture to the femur** as a result of **continuing instability in the right leg**. There remained a **significant risk of future re-occurrence**. The claimant also underwent a **knee arthroplasty**, but **would require a further arthroplasty before the age of 25** as the initial arthroplasty was failing. Due to the claimant's injuries, there was **no guarantee that any future arthroplasty would be successful**. It was estimated that, in any event, any **future arthroplasty would have failed by the time the claimant was 50** and that he would then require an **above-knee amputation**. At the time of the settlement, the claimant suffered from a **significant reduction in mobility**. He relied on a **crutch for walking** and wore a **support brace**. He was **unable to bend his knee past 90 degrees**. He was **unable to use stairs** and had to be **accommodated on a single floor**. He was expected to **require aids, adaptations and eventually prosthetics throughout his life**, and a **modest amount of care** from his family. His **pain, stability and movement** were **expected to improve after an arthroplasty**, but to **deteriorate again** once the arthroplasty began to fail. The claimant's **lack of mobility affected his employment prospects** as well as his **leisure, sporting and social activities**. At the time of the accident, he had been training to become a precision engineer, but was **unable to complete his training** on account of his injuries. He would be **capable of full-time sedentary work until the arthroplasty began to fail**, at which point he would only be capable of undertaking **part-time sedentary work**. A **settlement** was reached comprising a lump sum of £237,479 plus £10,000 net per year for life.

Pimm v Paull (22 February 2006, unreported) (Bond Pearce LLP, Solicitors, for the claimant; Tayntons, Solicitors, for the defendant) (Kindly submitted for publication by Bond Pearce LLP, Solicitors).

1022   Leg

PSLA: £15,000
Total damages: £15,000
Sex: Male
Age at accident/trial: 06/14
Date of accident/trial: 19 August 1998/18 October 2006
Judge/Court: HHJ MacDuff QC/Birmingham County Court

The claimant, **a schoolboy**, was knocked down by a motor vehicle when crossing a pedestrian crossing. Immediately after the accident he was **in extreme pain in the right leg** and was **bleeding from a wound over the right leg**. He was unable to get up off the road and he **could not weight bear**. At hospital he was **diagnosed as having suffered an open compound fracture of the right tibia and fibula** and was **taken to theatre** where **the wound was cleaned** and **the fracture reduced**. The **leg was put into plaster**. After a couple of days the claimant developed **compartment syndrome** and underwent an **extensive fasciotomy**. After a few days the claimant was **taken back to theatre** and **the fracture was stabilised** using **Nancy nails. The fasciotomy area was cleaned** and **skin grafted using donor skin taken from the contra lateral thigh** and **his leg was put into a splint**. In total the claimant was **in hospital for a period of 8 days**. After discharge, he was **unable to weight bear for a period of 6 months**, after which he was able to **weight bear using crutches**. He needed **intense care and assistance** from his family **for a period of approximately 18 months** following the accident. During this period **he attended the hospital and physiotherapy on a regular basis**. He was **able to fully weight bear after 18 months**. He was **not able to run** and was **only able to walk for a few hundred yards**. He was **unable to participate in PE** at school. He **had to undergo further extensive physiotherapy for his right leg over a period of nearly seven years after the accident** before his leg felt normal again, such that that he was **able to run and walk long distances**. On final examination **nearly 7 years post-accident** the claimant's **right leg injury had settled**, other than **some symptoms of pain and aching during cold weather** which were **expected to settle within 6 months** of the final examination. **Seven years and 2 months following the accident his injuries had generally settled**. He had **extensive scarring on the right and left leg** following the **fasciotomy and stabilisation operation**. There was a **split skin graft donor site on the right leg measuring 10 by 12 cms** and a **scar on the lateral aspect of the left leg measuring 31 cms in length**. The **scars were expected to improve** over time but they **would always be permanent**. The claimant was **unhappy about the appearance of the scarring** although **the scars did not prevent him from doing anything**. He also **suffered a psychological phobia** of crossing roads with **associated nightmares and intrusive thoughts which persisted for 12 months post-accident**.

M (A Child) v Brown (18 October 2006, unreported) (Tony Watkin, Counsel, instructed by Rowe Cohen, Solicitors; Stephen Garner, Counsel, instructed by McGrath & Co, Solicitors, for the defendant) (Kindly submitted for publication by Stephen Garner, Counsel).

1023   Leg

PSLA: £4,000
Total damages: £4,000
Sex: Female
Age at accident: 1
Date of infant settlement approval hearing: 14 July 2005
Judge/Court: DJ Sparrow/Portsmouth County Court

The claimant sustained an **undisplaced fracture of the left tibia** when her mother, who was carrying her at the time, **slipped on spilt water on a flight of stairs** and fell. After the injury had been treated the claimant had to wear a **protective cast for two weeks**. She made a **full recovery** with **no complications** within **three to four weeks**.

B (A Child) v Connaught Cleaning Services (14 July 2005, unreported) (Dyer Burdett & Co, Solicitors, for the claimant) (Kindly submitted for publication by Dyer Burdett & Co, Solicitors).

1024   Knee

PSLA: £42,000
Total damages: £62,300
Sex: Female
Age at accident/trial: 25/30
Date of trial: 14 December 2006
Judge/Court: Recorder Paul Hartley Davies/Cardiff County Court

The claimant suffered **significant injuries in the course of a road traffic accident** in Switzerland. The **primary injury was to the right leg and included a fracture to the right femur, soft tissue damage to the right knee and a fracture of the right heel**. She also **suffered a fracture of the right third metacarpal and a closed concussional head injury with amnesia**. The claimant was **detained in hospital for a period of 17 days**. The **fracture to the femur was secured with an intra-meduallry nail and the metacarpal fracture treated with a plaster cast**. On discharge, **the claimant mobilised with a frame** and it was some **4 months before she commenced part time employment** at a local veterinary surgery. Subsequent **arthroscopic investigations revealed a partial tear of the anterior cruciate ligament and a medical mensical tear**. When examined **at 11 months post accident** for the purposes of the medico-legal report, the claimant **complained largely of ongoing knee discomfort**. She was also **troubled by intermittent aching in the thigh and of the hand**. The **pain in the heel had largely resolved**. She was **able to walk short distances but at a modest pace**. There was **a 20 cm scar on the thigh** that was **cosmetically unpleasant**. However, the **functional prognosis at that stage was positive**. The claimant **remained troubled by ongoing symptoms in the right knee**. She **underwent further surgery to remove the nail in the femur and two separate arthroscopies of the knee** to address **defects in the medial femoral condyle**. When examined **3 and 3/4 years post accident** for the second medico-legal report, she **reported significant ongoing problems**. Her **walking distance was limited and she would limp after extended time on her feet**. If she **walked fast the knee was painful** and she **could not kneel**. She **had commenced work** as a pet psychologist which she **had managed thus far without incident**. She **complained of occasional aching at the site of the femur fracture and in the right metacarpal**. The assessment was that the claimant had **articular cartilage degeneration in the main weight bearing area of the knee**. This would continue to **deteriorate and would probably result in significant arthritis**. There was **at least a 50 per cent chance that the claimant would require uni-compartmental arthroplasty in 20 years** and then **a full knee replacement 15 years thereafter**. The claimant was awarded the cost of surgery discounted by 50 per cent and for accelerated receipt and awarded a similarly discounted sum for a three month loss of earnings following surgery.

Sale v Sale (14 December 2006, unreported) (Andrew Arentsen, Counsel, for the defendant) (Kindly submitted for publication by Andrew Arentsen, Counsel).

1025   Knee

PSLA: £8,000
Total damages: £8,000
Sex: Male
Age at accident: 50
Date of accident/trial: 28 July 2002/21 August 2006
Judge/Court: HHJ Neil Bidder QC/Swansea County Court

The claimant **sustained a knee injury** while working as a freelance photographer at the defendant's theme park when he was **struck by a wave of water** produced by one of the rides and **slipped, collapsing on top of his left leg**. After a number of **visits to his doctor and his local hospital**, the claimant was eventually diagnosed as having **ruptured the quadriceps tendon of the left knee**. The claimant **underwent aspiration of the knee** under local anaesthetic. **One**

month after the accident, he underwent an **operation to repair the tendon** under **general anaesthetic**. The surgery left a **15 cm scar**, but this **did not cause significant cosmetic embarrassment**. The claimant **missed one week of photography work after the accident** and a **further three weeks after the operation**, but was later described by the judge as a stoic who was keen to get on with things. The claimant attended **three physiotherapy sessions every week for four months** following the operation. He was **unable to drive for a number of weeks** and **could not climb ladders or steps**, which was an **integral part of his job**. On examination at **16 months** post-accident, it was found that he had **made a good recovery**. However, he **still had problems with steps, ladders and steep banks**, and **had difficulty squatting and kneeling**. His **knee ached** if he spent **long periods of time on his feet** or **drove significant distances**. The consultant surgeon was of the opinion that the **knee had returned to 75 per cent of its pre-accident state** and that there was **unlikely to be any significant improvement** from that position. At trial, the claimant gave evidence that there had been **further improvement** and that he **considered the knee to be at 85 per cent of its pre-accident state**. He only encountered **significant difficulties** when undertaking his hobby of **long-distance walking**, for which he **required a walking pole**. He also had to **restrict his walks to distances of three to five miles**.

Cavaney v Oakwood Leisure Ltd (21 August 2006, unreported) (Richard Cole, Counsel, instructed by Pannone, Solicitors, for the claimant; Richard Viney, Counsel, instructed by Leo Abse and Cohen, Solicitors, for the defendant) (Kindly submitted for publication by Richard Cole, Counsel).

1026　Knee

PSLA: £5,750
Total damages: £5,750
Sex: Male
Age at accident/trial: 46/51
Date of accident/trial: 31 January 2002/26 April 2006
Judge/Court: DDJ Lang/Birmingham County Court

The claimant was **knocked down by a motor vehicle** on a pedestrian crossing. He was **struck below the knees** and went over the bonnet of the vehicle, **landing face down on the road**. He was **unable to stand** after the accident. At hospital, he was diagnosed as having sustained **soft tissue injuries to both knees** and to the **right lateral side of the lower calf muscle of the right leg**. His **knee symptoms** were particularly **acute for five weeks** before starting to stabilise. He underwent an **MRI scan and two arthroscopies** which revealed that he was suffering from **degenerative changes in both knees**. Medical opinion was that the **accident had accelerated by two and a half years pre-existing symptoms** in both knees. The **right calf injury settled within one year** of the accident. The claimant **attempted to return to his work** as a teacher **two weeks after** the accident but he was **unable to climb stairs** and **found standing difficult**, so was forced to take an **extra week off work**. He also experienced **difficulty in driving** as a result of his symptoms and **had to be driven to work** by his wife for **three months**. Damages were assessed on the basis that there was an **overlap between the two knee injuries** and that any **increase for the second knee injury** should be at an increment of **25 per cent**.

Tinkler v Siemens plc (26 April 2006, unreported) (Stephen Garner, Counsel, instructed by Cotterhill Hitchman, Solicitors, for the claimant; Rebecca Taylor, Counsel, instructed by Gorman Hamilton, Solicitors, for the defendant) (Kindly submitted for publication by Stephen Garner, Counsel).

1027　Foot

PSLA: £2,000
Total damages: £2,000
Sex: Male
Age at accident: 40
Date of accident/trial: 12 February 2002/24 February 2006
Judge/Court: Recorder Thom QC/Neath County Court

The claimant fell heavily when he **caught his right foot in a pothole** on a carriageway. He was in **marked pain** and had **difficulty bearing weight**, but thought he had only sprained his ankle. He **attended casualty one week after** the accident, and was diagnosed as having sustained a **twisting injury to the right foot** with a **fracture of the base of the fifth metatarsal**. He was subsequently **immobilised in a below-knee plaster**, which was **removed one month later**. He was **unable to work as a taxi driver for six weeks**. The orthopaedic evidence was that the claimant endured **three months of pain and suffering** as a result of his injury.

O'Gorman v Bridgend CC (24 February 2006, unreported) (Richard Cole, Counsel, for the claimant) (Kindly submitted for publication by Richard Cole, Counsel).

1028 Foot

See para 974.

1029 Ankle

PSLA: £5,750
Total damages: £6,500
Sex: Male
Age at accident/trial: 34/37
Date of accident/trial: 30 November 2002/13 October 2006
Judge/Court:DJ Asplin/Blackwood County Court

The claimant fell when he slipped on a drain 'fall' in a car park owned and occupied by the defendants. He was **assisted at the scene by a first aider** employed by the defendants and **attended hospital the next day**. He **suffered a minimally displaced fracture of the distal fibular** and was **placed in plaster and underwent regular review at the fracture clinic**. He **was in plaster for eight weeks** and **needed assistance with his day to day care including washing and cooking**, which he usually undertook, from his wife. **On release from plaster his ankle was markedly stiff** and **he was referred to physiotherapy. His Christmas was disrupted** as a result of the accident and he was **unable to return to work as a sales director for a forklift truck company until three months post-accident** and **was confined to his office for a further two months**. At examination **three years post-accident he retained some modest symptoms provoked by prolonged walking and by cold weather**. His **symptoms eased with rest**. His **range of movement was normal but at the extreme of plantar flexion he experienced sharp discomfort posterior to the distal fibular**. The expert concluded that **the residual aching would be permanent but it would not be disabling** and would be **unlikely to be the cause of any future deteriorating function**. The claimant also complained of **occasional problems when the ankle would give way**.

Creed v Somerfield Stores Ltd (13 October 2006, unreported) (Robert Smith, Counsel, for the claimant; Richard Cole, Counsel, for the defendant) (Kindly submitted for publication by Richard Cole, Counsel).

1030 Ankle

PSLA: £3,500
Total damages: £3,500
Sex: Female
Age at accident/infant settlement approval hearing: 10/13
Date of accident/infant settlement approval hearing: 21 March 2003/10 February 2006
Judge/Court: DDJ Mian/Birmingham County Court

The claimant was injured when her **left foot went into a pothole and turned over**. **Immediately after** the accident, she experienced **pain in her left foot**. She had to be **helped off the ground** and **had difficulty bearing weight on her left leg**. She was **taken to hospital**, where her **left foot was x-rayed**. The x-rays revealed **some fragmentation of the epiphysis** at the **base of the fifth metatarsal bone**, but **no convincing fracture**. The claimant's **leg was put into plaster**, which she **wore for three weeks**. She was **unable to participate in sports or physical education lessons** at school for **ten weeks**, following which her **symptoms gradually improved**. On examination at around **eight months post-accident**, she was diagnosed as having suffered a **significant soft tissue inversion injury to the left ankle** with a **sprain to the peroneus longus muscle** attached to the **base of the fifth metatarsal**. By **12 months post-accident**, her **symptoms had generally settled**, with the exception of some **mild tenderness on exertion**, particularly after physical education lessons at school. This was **also the case** at the time of a **further examination four months later. Residual symptoms finally resolved within 22 months** of the accident.

L (A Child) v Walsall MBC (10 February 2006, unreported) (Stephen Garner, Counsel, instructed by Ward and Rider, Solicitors, for the claimant; Browne Jacobson, Solicitors, for the defendant) (Kindly submitted for publication by Stephen Garner, Counsel).

1031 Ankle

PSLA: £3,250
Total damages: £3,250
Sex: Male
Age at accident/trial: 41/44
Date of accident/trial: 31 January 2003/10 July 2006
Judge/Court: HHJ Hamilton/Birmingham County Court

The claimant was injured when the taxi in which he was travelling skidded on ice and struck a tree. The impact drove the passenger door inwards and directly onto the claimant's left **ankle**, which began to **swell and ache**. The claimant also sustained **bruising to his toes** and **whiplash symptoms to the neck**. He attended hospital, where he was diagnosed with a **whiplash neck injury** and an **acute moderate sprain to the left ankle**, which was placed in a Tubigrip support. The claimant's **whiplash symptoms resolved within two weeks**. However, **ankle symptoms** were **acute for two to three weeks**. The claimant **had difficulty weight bearing** during this time and sometimes **had to mobilise with the aid of a stick** for support. He also **took painkillers regularly**. After two to three weeks his ankle **symptoms began steadily to improve**. However, he **continued to experience intermittent symptoms** until the time of a medical examination at **two years post-accident**. He experienced **intermittent aching**, especially if he had been on his feet for several hours, which was **more pronounced in cold weather**. The expert prognosis was that the claimant's **ongoing ankle symptoms were of nuisance value only** and did not affect his daily life or restrict his activities. It was found that a maximum of two years' worth of left ankle symptoms were related to the accident, and that any residual symptoms occurring after two years post-accident were unrelated.

Kenyon v Masters (10 July 2006, unreported) (Stephen Garner, Counsel, instructed by Blakemores, Solicitors, for the claimant; Colin Baron, Counsel, instructed by Hugh James, Solicitors, for the defendant) (Kindly submitted for publication by Stephen Garner, Counsel).

1032   Ankle

PSLA: £2,500
Total damages: £3,708
Sex: Female
Age at accident/trial: 31/33
Date of trial: 2 December 2005
Judge/Court: HHJ Gaskell/Cardiff County Court

The claimant sustained injuries when she was **struck by a reversing pallet truck**. She was **taken to hospital** and diagnosed as having sustained **soft tissue injuries to the left ankle, left knee and low back**. She was **absent from her job** as a factory worker for **three months**, during which time she underwent **eight sessions of physiotherapy**. By the time she returned to work she had **fully recovered from her back and knee injuries**, but was left with **residual pain in the ankle**. She was **unable to return to her hobby of dancing for six months**. On examination at **ten months post-accident**, it was found that she had made a **substantial improvement**. She complained of **discomfort in the left ankle in the mornings and in cold weather**. Wearing **high-heeled shoes** was sometimes **uncomfortable**. The **ankle would swell at the end of a long day** at work, but the claimant complained of **no functional restrictions**, and a **clinical examination** revealed a **full range of ankle and foot movement**. The **mild intermittent symptoms** were predicted to **resolve completely within a year** of the accident. At trial, the claimant **continued to complain of minor symptoms** which the court **attributed to the accident**.

Layland v Creative Print and Design Ltd (2 December 2005, unreported) (Andrew Arentsen, Counsel, for the claimant) (Kindly submitted for publication by Andrew Arentsen, Counsel).

1033   Toe

PSLA: £6,000
Total damages: £6,000
Sex: Female
Age at accident/trial: 30/34
Date of accident/trial: 2 September 2003/20 January 2006
Judge/Court: DDJ Beevers/Doncaster County Court

The claimant suffered personal injury when her **left foot became trapped** between a van and its moving tail-lift. She sustained a **crush injury to the left big toe**, which caused a **comminuted fracture of the distal phalanx** of the toe and an **avulsion of the nail**. She **attended hospital on the day** of the accident, where the **nail was glued on** and the **wound treated with butterfly sutures**. X-rays revealed the fracture. The **foot was bandaged**. The claimant **used crutches for one day**, but was **able to bear weight on her heel afterwards**. She used **ibuprofen and painkillers**. She **reattended hospital on a number of occasions** for reviews and changes of dressings, until she was **discharged from further hospital treatment at five weeks post-accident**. Her **mobility problems** meant that she required **care and assistance from her parents** for about **six weeks**. She was also **unable to start a new job for two months**. On examination at **14 months post-accident**, the claimant had **continuing problems** with the toe. She had **lost the avulsed nail** and a **new nail had regrown** which was **thicker and narrower** than the original nail, with the result that there was a **mild cosmetic defect**. She **could no longer wear pointed shoes**, as they **put pressure on the nail, which caused pain**. She experienced **aching pain in the toe in cold weather** and found that the **underfloor heating** at her workplace **caused the toe to throb**. She **could not run on a treadmill** at the gym **for** more than ten minutes and experienced **pain in the toe when dancing**. The medical expert found that there was a **tendency for the nail to ingrow at its medial border**. There was also a **ten per cent risk of infection** from the **abnormal ingrowth** of the nail, with the result that there was a **ten per cent chance** that the claimant would **require wedge resection surgery under local anaesthetic**. The claimant was left with **discomfort in the toe**, which would **persist along with the cosmetic defect**. At trial, **28 months post-accident**, she indicated that she **suffered on most evenings from throbbing in the toe**. She had to **remove her shoes** at work on most days to **ease her discomfort**. She experienced **numbness and throbbing** in the toe **in cold weather**, about **twice per week on average**. She also **had to trim the nail regularly to prevent it from ingrowing**.

Evans v Turner (t/a Able Van Hire) (20 January 2006, unreported) (Nick Blake, Counsel, instructed by Malcolm C Foy & Co, Solicitors, for the claimant; Tom Nossiter, Counsel, instructed by Beachcroft Wansbroughs, Solicitors, for the defendant) (Kindly submitted for publication by Tom Nossiter, Counsel).

1034   Minor injuries

PSLA: (1) £1,800 (2) £1,500 (3) £1,200
Total damages: (1) £1,800 (2) £1,500 (3) £1,200
Sex: (1) Female (2) Male (3) Male
Age at accident/infant settlement approval hearing: (1) 8/10 (2) 6/8 (3) 2/4
Date of accident/infant settlement approval hearing: 7 March 2004/20 June 2006
Judge/Court: DJ Woodhead/Huddersfield County Court

The claimants were passengers in a car which was involved in a road traffic accident in which they sustained **minor whiplash injuries**. The **first claimant** suffered **immediate pain** in the **head and right shoulder**, which resulted in **soft tissue injuries** requiring treatment with **painkillers**. The **head pain settled within a few days** but the first claimant experienced **ongoing pain and discomfort in the shoulder**, which had **resolved fully by 12 months post-accident**. She also experienced **sleep disturbance for one to two weeks** and **travel anxiety for around 18 months**.

The **second claimant** sustained **whiplash injuries to the left shoulder and neck** and a **soft tissue injury to his left thumb** after hitting his hand against the dashboard. He suffered from **pain, swelling and bruising to the thumb**, which **resolved in three to four weeks**. **Pain to the left shoulder and neck resolved within two months**, during which time the second claimant **did not take part in PE classes** at school. He also experienced **two nights of sleep disturbance** and **two months of travel anxiety**.

The **third claimant** sustained **whiplash injuries to the neck and forehead** after **banging his head** against the head restraint on the front seat. He suffered from **headaches for two weeks**. The **neck injury resolved within two months**, and associated **travel anxiety** had **resolved by six to seven months post-accident**.

I (A Child) v Richardson (20 June 2006, unreported) (Leila Benyounes, Counsel, instructed by Irwin Mitchell, Solicitors, for the claimant; Charles Crow, Counsel, instructed by Morris Orman Hearle, Solicitors, for the defendant) (Kindly submitted for publication by Leila Benyounes, Counsel).

1035   Minor injuries

PSLA: £2,700
Total damages: £2,700
Sex: Female
Age at accident/infant settlement approval hearing: 9/12
Date of accident/infant settlement approval hearing: 14 March 2004/20 July 2006
Judge/Court: DJ Rogers/Doncaster County Court

The claimant was involved in a road traffic accident in which she was jolted forwards and hit her head on the front seat restraint. She sustained **multiple soft tissue injuries** to the **head, chest and right arm**. The **blow to the head resulted in a lump** and caused the claimant to **suffer from headaches several times a week** for a **number of months**. She **took painkillers daily** for **six weeks**. She was **unable to pursue her hobby of dancing** for **four weeks**. She also experienced **pain in her chest** a few hours after the accident. This improved in the following weeks and became intermittent over the next few months. **Aching and stiffness** in the **right arm**, experienced within a few days of the accident, **gradually improved** over the following months. The claimant also suffered **travel anxiety, flashbacks, intrusive thoughts and nightmares** over a period of several months. All physical symptoms resolved within seven to ten months post-accident, and all psychological symptoms within 16 to 22 months.

V (A Child) v Ward (20 July 2006, unreported) (Leila Benyounes, Counsel, instructed by Oliver & Co, Solicitors, for the claimant) (Kindly submitted for publication by Leila Benyounes, Counsel).

1036   Minor injuries

PSLA: £2,500
Total damages: £2,500
Sex: Male
Age at accident/trial: 41/42
Date of accident/trial: 19 November 2004/2 March 2006
Judge/Court: DJ Khan/Manchester County Court

The claimant was involved in a rear-end shunt road traffic accident in which he sustained a **whiplash injury to the neck**, a **soft tissue injury to the right hip and low back**, a **torn ligament in the groin** and **travel anxiety**. He was **very shocked and shaken** following the accident. Shortly afterwards his **neck began to stiffen up** and **became sore**. He also began to develop **pain in the low back, right hip and groin**. He **attended his doctor**, who diagnosed **soft tissue injuries** and a **torn ligament in the right thigh**. The claimant was **advised to take analgesics** for pain relief, but his **symptoms persisted** and he visited his doctor again. On advice, he underwent **ten sessions of physiotherapy**, which **assisted his symptoms**. He took **no time off work**, as his job was sedentary in nature. However, for **four months** he had to **walk around after sitting for more than 15 minutes** as a result of his **low back pain**. His **neck symptoms settled within one month** of the accident. His **low back, right hip and groin pain** were **constant for five months** but were subsequently **eased by physiotherapy**. The **hip and groin pain settled at around six months** post-accident. On examination **four months later**, the claimant's **back pain was continuing on an intermittent basis**, and he was **experiencing pain once or twice per week**, for a **couple of hours** on each occasion. His ongoing **back pain adversely affected his hobby of squash**. The prognosis was for his **remaining physical symptoms to settle by around 14 to 16 months** post-accident. The claimant also **suffered travel anxiety** following the accident. He **became hypervigilant** and had a tendency to **overuse his rear view mirror**. The prognosis was for his **psychological symptoms to settle at around 12 to 13 months** post-accident. At trial the claimant confirmed that recovery of physical and psychological symptoms had been **in line with the prognoses**.

Wakefield v Centrica plc (2 March 2006, unreported) (Stephen Garner, Counsel, instructed by CS2, Solicitors, for the claimant; Daniel Paul, Counsel, instructed by Eversheds, Solicitors, for the defendant) (Kindly submitted for publication by Stephen Garner, Counsel).

1037   Minor injuries

PSLA: £2,500
Total damages: £2,500
Sex: Male
Age at accident/trial: 46/48
Date of accident/trial: 12 March 2004/20 June 2006
Judge/Court: HHJ Hawkesworth QC/Bradford County Court

The claimant was involved in a road traffic accident in which he sustained a **whiplash injury to his neck**, and **soft tissue injuries** to his **lower back, dominant right elbow and both wrists**. All **symptoms were acute for approximately four weeks**, although the claimant **took no time off from his work** as a training officer. He found that **sitting and standing for long periods** while at work **aggravated his symptoms**. He experienced **sleep disturbance** as a result of his discomfort. He took **painkillers**. The **elbow and right wrist injuries resolved after four weeks**, and his **neck, back and left wrist symptoms became intermittent**. He underwent a course of **physiotherapy for the neck and back symptoms**, which was of benefit. He was **unable to play cricket for two to three months**. The medical expert stated that any **neck symptoms continuing beyond three months** post-accident and any **back symptoms continuing beyond six months** post-accident were **constitutional in nature** and **unrelated to the accident**. The claimant's **left wrist symptoms resolved at five months** post-accident.

Jones v Fletcher (20 June 2006, unreported) (Tom Nossiter, Counsel, instructed by Irwin Mitchell, Solicitors, for the claimant; George Branchflower, Counsel, instructed by Cogent, Solicitors, for the defendant) (Kindly submitted for publication by Tom Nossiter, Counsel).

1038   Minor injuries

PSLA: £2,250
Total damages: £2,250
Sex: Female
Age at accident/infant settlement approval hearing: 13/15
Date of infant settlement approval hearing: 26 May 2006
Judge/Court: DDJ Muskath/Edmonton County Court

The claimant was involved in a rear-end shunt road traffic accident. **Immediately after** the accident she felt **shaken** and had **pain in her ankles, feet and dominant right wrist and thumb**. The **next day** she developed **neck pain**. **Two days after** the accident she **visited her doctor's** surgery, where an examination revealed **tenderness of the cervical and thoracic spine** with **pain on movement**. A **whiplash injury was diagnosed** and **analgesics** dispensed. Approximately **two weeks later**, the claimant **visited her doctor again**, complaining of **pain in her hands and neck**. She experienced **moderate pain in her neck for one month** after the accident, after which there was **gradual improvement**. During the **first two weeks** post-accident she also suffered from **associated migraines** and **vomited on two occasions**. A **pre-existing right wrist injury was aggravated** by the accident **substantially for two weeks**, then **intermittently**. **Moderate pain in the ankles and feet** lasted for **one month**, after which **discomfort was apparent** for a further **few weeks**, particularly **when the claimant was immobile**. All **foot and ankle symptoms settled within six weeks** of the accident. The claimant was **absent from school for a few days**, but was **sent home regularly** in the weeks after returning as she **tended to develop headaches and neck pain** when working at school and **ankle pain when climbing stairs** there. She **did not participate in PE for one month** after returning to school, and her **hobbies of tennis, horse riding and swimming were affected** for approximately **five to six months**. On **examination shortly after six months** post-accident the claimant reported that the **majority of her neck symptoms had settled**, although she continued to notice an **occasional mild aching discomfort** when undertaking sporting activities. The expert felt that the claimant would **recover from her remaining neck and wrist symptoms within eight or nine months** of the accident. At the hearing it was confirmed that **recovery had taken place in line with the prognosis**.

M (A Child) v Savill (26 May 2006, unreported) (Ian Mann, Counsel, instructed by Proddow Mackay, Solicitors, for the claimant; Joanna Kerr, Counsel, instructed by Davies Wallis Foyster, Solicitors, for the defendant) (Kindly submitted for publication by Joanna Kerr, Counsel).

1039 Minor injuries

PSLA: £1,700
Total damages: £3,794 (including interest)
Sex: Female
Age at accident/trial: 35/38
Date of accident/trial: 13 May 2002/13 May 2005
Judge/Court: DDJ Smith/Manchester County Court

The claimant was involved in a road traffic accident in which she sustained a **number of injuries**. An **injury to her neck** resulted in **pain and stiffness** with **limitation of movement**. Symptoms, which were **acute for one month, settled after three months**. She also sustained **injuries to her knees** and the **anterior chest wall**, both of which were **painful for one month** after the accident. A **back injury** caused by the accident **aggravated symptoms from a pre-existing low back condition** for **six to eight months**. The claimant also suffered psychological symptoms of **depression and situational anxiety**, which **resolved within eight months** of the accident.

Gagliardi v Makolli (13 May 2005, unreported) (Philip Holmes, Counsel, instructed by Neil Millar & Co, Solicitors, for the claimant) (Kindly submitted for publication by Philip Holmes, Counsel).

1040 Minor injuries

PSLA: £1,500
Total damages: £1,500
Sex: Male
Age at accident/infant settlement approval hearing: 4/5
Date of infant settlement approval hearing: 24 February 2006
Judge/Court: DDJ Perry/Cambridge County Court

The claimant was involved in a side-impact road traffic accident. On impact he was **tipped out of the seatbelt** he was wearing and **hit the right side of his head on a car window**. He **did not lose consciousness** but **vomited twice** after the impact. **Bruising developed** on the **right side of the head**, resolving **within three weeks** of the accident. The claimant also had **seatbelt bruising over the right hip and upper thigh**, which **settled within two to three weeks**. He **became very anxious** as a result of the accident, and **woke with nightmares every night** for the first **three or four nights** afterwards. On examination at **seven months post-accident** he was being **woken by nightmares** about the accident approximately **once per week**. **Sounds of ambulances** from the ambulance station close to his home **caused him to relive the accident**. The expert felt that the claimant was **recovering slowly** from his anxiety symptoms, but that he would **recover from all psychological symptoms within 13 to 15 months** of the accident. Recovery occurred **in line with this prognosis**.

B (A Child) v Martin (24 February 2006, unreported) (Paul Gosling, Counsel, instructed by Alexander Samuel & Co, Solicitors, for the claimant; Joanna Kerr, Counsel, instructed by Davies Wallis Foyster, Solicitors, for the defendant) (Kindly submitted for publication by Joanna Kerr, Counsel).

1041   Minor injuries

PSLA: £1,300
Total damages: £1,300
Sex: Female
Age at accident/infant settlement approval hearing: 10/12
Date of infant settlement approval hearing: 27 February 2006
Judge/Court: DJ Silverman/Edmonton County Court

The claimant was involved in a side-impact road traffic accident in which she was **jarred and knocked sideways** towards the driver before swinging back and **hitting her head on the passenger door window**. She **immediately felt pain** in her **neck and head**. **Swelling and bruising** developed **on her forehead** but **faded completely within five days** of the accident. The claimant suffered from **neck pain for two to three months** afterwards. On examination at **one year post-accident** she was diagnosed as having sustained a **whiplash injury to the neck**. She was **wary about travelling by car** following the accident, but all such **anxiety had resolved by the time of the examination**.

S (*A Child*) *v Blaney* (27 February 2006, unreported) (Joanna Kerr, Counsel, instructed by Silverbeck Rymer, Solicitors, for the claimant) (Kindly submitted for publication by Joanna Kerr, Counsel).

1042   Minor injuries

PSLA: £1,300
Total damages: £1,300
Sex: Female
Age at accident/trial: 43/47
Date of accident/trial: 19 August 2002/6 April 2006
Judge/Court: HHJ Behrens/Newcastle County Court

The claimant was injured when she **tripped on an uneven step** at a railway station en route to her honeymoon. She **fell forwards**, landing on her **knees and left hand** and **jerking her neck** as she fell. She experienced **pain and discomfort** in her **left hand, left wrist and neck** for **two days** before these **symptoms resolved**. She also sustained **grazing and bruising to her knees**. She **did not seek medical treatment** and was **able to clean up her grazes** with a first aid kit. The medical expert concluded that the claimant had **minor superficial abrasions and bruising** with **pain in her knees** for a total of **four weeks**. The claimant's evidence was that she had been **self-conscious of the appearance of her knees during her two-week honeymoon**, during which she had been **reluctant to wear a bikini** at the hotel pool and beach. She **had worn shorts** while walking around but **people had commented** on her knee abrasions and bruises, which had caused her to be **self-conscious about her appearance**. To an extent her **injuries had spoiled her honeymoon**, although she had still been **able to do almost everything she would have done otherwise**. General damages of £1,300 were awarded, including **£400 in respect of the special loss of amenity** suffered by the claimant as a result of her enjoyment of her honeymoon having been adversely affected.

Hillary v Arriva Trains Northern Ltd (6 April 2006, unreported) (Tom Nossiter, Counsel, instructed by Morrish & Co, Solicitors, for the claimant; Alan Weir, Counsel, instructed by Kershaw Abbott, Solicitors, for the defendant) (Kindly submitted for publication by Tom Nossiter, Counsel).

1043   Minor injuries

PSLA: £1,100
Total damages: £1,100
Sex: Male
Age at accident/infant settlement approval hearing: 10/12
Date of accident/infant settlement approval hearing: 12 April 2005/25 July 2006
Judge/Court: DJ Harrison/Birkenhead County Court

The claimant was involved in a rear-end shunt road traffic accident in which he sustained **injuries to the cervical and lumbar spine** and **bruising to the forehead**. He was **emotionally shaken, distraught, pale and nauseous** for a **few hours** afterwards but **did not attend hospital**. He suffered a further injury to his forehead the following day, but it was estimated that **bruising** as a result of the original accident would have **lasted for ten days**. The claimant **suffered headaches for three of those days**. He **took Calpol** and **refrained from his usual sporting activities** for **seven days**. He **did not miss any school** because the accident occurred **during the school holidays**. His **spinal injuries had resolved** by around **four weeks post-accident**. The claimant suffered **travel anxiety** as a result of the accident and, on **examination at nine and a half months** post-accident, he remained **too anxious to travel in his mother's car**. The medical expert predicted that these **symptoms would resolve within 12 to 13 months** of the accident, and damages were awarded on the basis of a **recovery in line with that prognosis**.

L (A Child) v Murt (25 July 2006, unreported) (Stephen Seed, Counsel, instructed by Brian Camp & Co, Solicitors, for the claimant; Chris Middleton, Counsel, instructed by Irwin Mitchell, Solicitors, for the defendant) (Kindly submitted for publication by Chris Middleton, Counsel).

1044   Minor injuries

PSLA: £1,000
Total damages: £1,245
Sex: Male
Age at accident: 39
Date of accident/trial: 22 July 2003/23 June 2005
Judge/Court: DJ Smith/Manchester County Court

The claimant was involved in a road traffic accident in which he sustained **soft tissue injuries** to the **cervical spine and head**, with **mild concussion**. Following the accident, he suffered from **headaches, nausea, recurring dizziness and loss of co-ordination**. His **headaches persisted for five days**. He also experienced **pain and stiffness** in his **neck and between his shoulder blades**, which continued for **two weeks**, giving rise to **sleep disturbance**. All **symptoms had resolved by two weeks post-accident**.

Hardy v Johnson (23 June 2005, unreported) (Philip Holmes, Counsel, instructed by Neil Millar & Co, Solicitors, for the claimant) (Kindly submitted for publication by Philip Holmes, Counsel).

1045   Minor injuries

PSLA: £1,000
Total damages: £1,000
Sex: Female
Age at accident/infant settlement approval hearing: 5/6
Date of accident/infant settlement approval hearing: 10 April 2005/10 January 2006
Judge/Court: DJ Middleton/Walsall County Court

The claimant suffered personal injury when a **heavy hotel door fell on top of her and knocked her to the ground**. The door **struck the claimant on the face**, close to her **left eye**, and also on **top of the left shoulder**. The claimant also **hit her left knee on the ground** when she was knocked down. She was **very distressed** after the accident. She sustained **significant bruising and redness around the left orbit**, and developed a **circular area of bruising** approximately **5 cm in diameter lateral to the left eye**. The eye also became **bloodshot and swollen**. The **bruising and pain settled within four weeks** of the accident. As a result of the impact from the door on the **tip of her left shoulder**, the claimant developed **bruising approximately 2·5 cm in diameter** and was **troubled by some localised pain** in the area. The **bruising and pain resolved within two weeks**. There was also **bruising of similar proportions to the left knee**. All **bruising, pain and associated discomfort settled within two weeks**. The claimant **missed two days of school** on account of her injuries. She also suffered **psychological upset**. Her **sleep was disturbed** on the night following the accident, and she was **very tearful and distressed**. She **returned to normal within about a week** of the accident.

D (A Child) v Wicksteed Park Ltd (10 January 2006, unreported) (Stephen Garner, Counsel, instructed by Fentons, Solicitors, for the claimant; Mills & Reeve, Solicitors, for the defendant) (Kindly submitted for publication by Stephen Garner, Counsel).

1046   Minor injuries

PSLA: £800
Total damages: £800
Sex: Male
Age at accident/infant settlement approval hearing: 4/6
Date of accident/infant settlement approval hearing: 26 July 2004/12 May 2006
Judge/Court: DJ Anson/Walsall County Court

The claimant was involved in a heavy-impact road traffic accident in which he **struck his head and left collar bone** on the car door. **Immediately after** the accident he was **shocked and tearful**. He was **taken to hospital**, where it was recorded that he had sustained **bruising injuries** to the **left side of his forehead** and to the **left collar bone**. The **bruising was tender for three days** before generally **resolving within a week** of the accident. The claimant's **most significant injury was psychological**. Following the accident he became **nervous when travelling by car**, and would **continually ask the driver if the airbag was going to deploy**, as it had in the accident. He would also **persistently ask the driver to slow down**. Although **able to travel by car**, he was **visibly upset** when doing so for **around a month**. All **residual travel anxiety had settled by three months post-accident**.

W (A Child) v Hinton (12 May 2006, unreported) (Stephen Garner, Counsel, instructed by Colemans, Solicitors, for the claimant; Horwich Farrelly, Solicitors, for the defendant) (Kindly submitted for publication by Stephen Garner, Counsel).

DEEDS AND OTHER INSTRUMENTS

Halsbury's Laws of England (4th edn) vol 13 (2007 Reissue) paras 1–300

1047   Deed—deed of trust—instrument under hand—amendment

Under the rules of a company pension scheme which had been constituted by a deed of trust, the normal retirement age for men was 65 and that for women was 60. Following a European Court of Justice ruling that discrimination between men and women in relation to pension benefits was unlawful, the trustees of the scheme issued a memorandum to the scheme members stating that pension benefits would be based on retirement at the same age for both men and women. The company's board then made an announcement that women's normal retirement age would be increased to 65. Neither the memorandum nor the announcement had been signed by the trustees. They sought declaratory relief from the court. *Held*, an instrument under hand only was a document in writing which either created or affected legal or equitable rights or liabilities, and which was authenticated by the signature of the author, but was not executed by him as a deed. As the court had no power to authorise a departure from the scheme's rules, or to waive one of their requirements, it followed that the purported amendment to the scheme was not valid. Further, no group estoppel applied so as to preclude those members who would have benefited from a reduced retirement age from alleging the contrary. Judgment would be given accordingly.

Trustee Solutions Ltd v Dubery [2006] EWHC 1426 (Ch), [2007] 1 All ER 308 (Chancery Division: Lewison J). Case C-262/88 *Barber v Guardian Royal Exchange Assurance Group* [1991] 1 QB 344, ECJ (1990 Abr para 2706), considered.

DISCRIMINATION

Halsbury's Laws of England (4th edn) vol 13 (2007 Reissue) paras 301–900

Articles

For articles relating to this title please refer to the Table of Articles at the beginning of the Abridgment.

1048   Age discrimination—employment—equal treatment

The Employment Equality (Age) Regulations 2006, SI 2006/1031 (in force on 1 October 2006), implement EC Council Directive 2000/78, so far as it relates to discrimination on grounds of age. In particular, the regulations (1) define direct discrimination, indirect discrimination, victimisation, instructions to discriminate and harassment which is, in each case, on the grounds of age; (2) prohibit discrimination, victimisation and harassment in the fields of employment and vocational training in respect of applicants, employees, contract workers, office-holders, police, persons seconded to the Serious Organised Crime Agency, barristers and partners in firms; (3) prohibit any such discrimination, victimisation and harassment by employers, trustees and managers of occupational pension schemes, trade organisations, qualifications bodies, vocational training providers, employment agencies and further and higher education institutions; (4) provide that any discrimination, victimisation or harassment occurring after a relevant relationship has ended is unlawful if it arises out of, and is closely connected to, that relationship; (5) provide for an exception where possessing a characteristic related to age is a genuine and determining occupational requirement for a post and it is proportionate to apply such a requirement; (6) make provision in relation to the vicarious liability of employers and principals and in relation to aiding unlawful acts; (7) provide for further exceptions in relation to (a) acts done in order to comply with a statutory provision; (b) acts related to national security; (c) positive action; (d) retirement; (e) the national minimum wage; (f) the provision of certain employment benefits based on length of service; (g) the provision of enhanced redundancy payments; (h) the provision of life assurance cover to workers who have had to retire early on grounds of ill health; and (i) various rules, practices, actions and decisions relating to occupational pension schemes; (8) make provision for enforcement and for remedies for individuals, including compensation, by way of proceedings in employment tribunals and in the county courts; (9) transfer the burden of proof to a respondent once a complainant has established facts from which a court or tribunal could conclude, in the absence of an adequate explanation, that an act of discrimination or harassment has been committed by the respondent; (10) establish a questionnaire procedure so as to assist complainants in obtaining information from respondents; (11) impose limitation periods of three months in respect of employment tribunals and six months in respect of county courts; (12) address the validity of discriminatory terms in contracts and collective agreements; (13) provide for their application to Crown servants and Parliamentary staff; and (14) impose a duty on employers to consider requests by employees to continue working beyond retirement.

The Employment Equality (Age) (Amendment) Regulations 2006, SI 2006/2408 (in force on 30 September 2006), amend SI 2006/1031 supra by postponing, until 1 December 2006, the coming into force of provisions relating to applicants and employees, relations which have come to an end, and pension schemes.

The Employment Equality (Age) (Amendment No 2) Regulations 2006, SI 2006/2931 (in force on 1 December 2006), further amend SI 2006/1031 so as to (1) provide that the pension schemes provision applies to both employers and trustees or managers in relation to occupational pension schemes and refers to 'pensionable service' rather than 'service'; (2) enable trustees or managers and an employer, subject to certain criteria, to avail themselves of a length of service related exemption for the award of benefits by an employer; (3) allow for a minimum level of pensionable pay before a worker may be admitted to a scheme and provide for the calculation of benefits from a scheme; (4) provide for schemes which are not contracted-out of the second state pension; (5) exempt different age-related rates of contributions to schemes provided that the aim is to make resulting benefits equal or more nearly equal; (6) exempt employer and member contributions which are limited by reference to a maximum level of pensionable pay; (7) exempt an employer's or member's contributions to a defined benefit arrangement that are limited by reference to a maximum level of pensionable pay; (8) allow schemes to set a minimum age from when an age related benefit is paid, and make it clear that there may be different minimum ages for different groups or categories of members and that the minimum age may be subject to the consent of the employer or the trustees or managers; (9) allow active or prospective members of a scheme to retain an entitlement to a minimum age for payment of age-related benefit; (10) subject to certain conditions, allow members who have a right to payment of enhanced early retirement benefits to retain that right when they become members of subsequent schemes; (11) allow schemes to set a minimum age from when an age related benefit is paid in the event of retirement on the grounds of redundancy or ill health; (12) provide for deferred members to have a different early retirement pivot age and late retirement pivot age from active members; (13) allow schemes to calculate any death benefits by reference to prospective service which the member could be treated as having completed if he had not died; (14) exempt payment of benefits to dependants where they are paid when the member dies while in receipt of a pension guaranteed for a particular period and exempt payment of different death benefits to deferred members who die before and after normal pension age; (15) provide an exemption where a scheme pays an additional pension to reflect that a member is not yet in receipt of his state retirement pension and an exemption for cessation of payment of such a pension when the person reaches his or her state pension age; (16) make it clear that, when a pension is paid to a dependant of a deceased member and is reduced to reflect that the dependant is younger than the member, the reduction must be an actuarial reduction; (17) restrict life assurance cover to pensioner members who have retired from a scheme on ill-health grounds; (18) allow different accrual rates or different death benefits for active or prospective members who are in comparable situations, where the aim is that they will on retirement have the same fraction, proportion or multiple of pensionable pay as an age-related benefit or death benefit; (19) enable any age-related benefit or death benefit to be limited by reference to a maximum number of years of pensionable service and/or by reference to a fraction, proportion or multiple of pensionable pay; (20) exempt payment of an age-related benefit or death benefit where the requirement to provide short service benefit under the Pensions Schemes Act 1993 s 71 applies; (21) exempt limits on any age-related benefit or death benefit where those benefits may only be calculated by reference to a maximum level of pensionable pay and provide for this limit to apply to all members or certain groups or categories of members; (22) exempt closure of any section of a scheme to workers who have not joined the section; (23) revise certain conditions of tax relief; (24) allow employers to limit, by reference to a maximum level of remuneration, contributions to personal pension schemes; (25) allow employers to set a minimum age for commencement of payment of contributions to a personal pension scheme or different minimum ages for different groups or categories of workers; and (26) allow employers to make equal contributions to personal pension schemes in respect of workers.

1049   Disability discrimination—code of practice—goods, facilities, services and premises

The Disability Discrimination Code of Practice (Goods, Facilities, Services and Premises) (Revocation) Order 2006, SI 2006/1966 (in force on 4 December 2006), revokes the Disability Discrimination Act 1995 Code of Practice on Rights of Access Goods, Facilities, Services and Premises, but provides, for the purposes of the Disability Discrimination Act 1995 s 53A(8A), for the Code to continue to have effect in the case of proceedings relating to an alleged act of unlawful discrimination which took place before 4 December 2006.

1050   Disability discrimination—code of practice—provision and use of transport vehicles

The Disability Discrimination Code of Practice (Supplement to Part 3 Code of Practice) (Provision and Use of Transport Vehicles) (Appointed Day) Order 2006, SI 2006/1094 (in force on 12 April 2006), appoints 18 April 2006 for the coming into effect of the supplement to the Code of Practice on the duties under the Disability Discrimination Act 1995 Pt 3 entitled 'Provision and Use of Transport Vehicles'.

1051   Disability discrimination—code of practice—services, public functions, private clubs and premises

The Disability Discrimination Code of Practice (Services, Public Functions, Private Clubs and Premises) (Appointed Day) Order 2006, SI 2006/1967 (in force on 20 July 2006), appoints 4 December 2006 for the coming into effect of the Disability Discrimination Act 1995 Code of Practice on Rights of Access: services to the public, public authority functions, private clubs and premises.

1052   Disability discrimination—definition of disability—guidance—appointed day

The Disability Discrimination (Guidance on the Definition of Disability) Appointed Day Order 2006, SI 2006/1005 (made on 30 March 2006), appoints 1 May 2006 as the day for the coming into force of the guidance on matters to be taken into account in determining questions relating to the definition of disability issued by the Secretary of State under the Disability Discrimination Act 1995 s 3(8).

1053   Disability discrimination—definition of disability—guidance—revocation

The Disability Discrimination (Guidance on the Definition of Disability) Revocation Order 2006, SI 2006/1007 (in force on 1 May 2006), revokes the guidance on matters to be taken into account in determining questions relating to the definition of disability referred to in the Disability Discrimination (Guidance and Code of Practice) (Appointed Day) Order 1996, SI 1996/1996.

1054   Disability discrimination—education—less favourable treatment—excluded pupil

The Disability Discrimination Act 1995 s 28B(4) provides that taking of a particular step by a responsible body in relation to a person does not amount to less favourable treatment if it shows that at the time in question it did not know, and could not reasonably have been expected to know, that he was disabled. Less favourable treatment, or a failure to comply with s 28C, is justified only if the reason for it is both material to the circumstances of the particular case and substantial: s 28B(7). If the responsible body is (a) under a duty imposed by s 28C in relation to the disabled person, but (b) it fails without justification to comply with that duty, its treatment of that person cannot be justified under s 28B(7) unless that treatment would have been justified even if it had complied with that duty: s 28B(8).

The respondents' son was excluded from school for repeated disruptive behaviour and abusive behaviour towards staff. The Special Educational Needs and Disability Tribunal stated that there had been sufficient information to lead to a conclusion that he was disabled and that he had been unlawfully discriminated against in that the school had failed to take reasonable steps required by the 1995 Act s 28C and therefore had failed to justify the unfavourable treatment in contravention of s 28B(8). The school appealed and an issue arose as to the school's knowledge of the disability. *Held*, the school was not only disputing that the pupil was disabled at the material time, but also that it did not know and could not reasonably have been expected to know that he was disabled. The tribunal's decision was defective in law as it had failed to say that the school had failed to prove what was required under s 28B(4). A balancing exercise was required under s 28B(1)(b) in that the responsible body had to show that the less favourable treatment was justified in all the circumstances, including the interests of the school and of the disabled pupil. The exclusion of a disabled pupil would amount to a contravention of s 28C(1) in that it would put him at a substantial disadvantage in comparison to a pupil who was not disabled. The tribunal did not make a finding under s 28B(7) that the reason for the exclusion was material and substantial. While the tribunal had considered whether the school had taken reasonable steps to ensure that the pupil was not put at a substantial disadvantage in accordance with s 28B(8), it had failed to consider the final words of s 28B(8). Accordingly, the appeal would be allowed.

Governing Body of O Comprehensive School v E [2006] EWHC 1468 (Admin), [2006] All ER (D) 247 (Jun) (Queen's Bench Division: Crane J).

1055   Disability discrimination—employment—associative discrimination

The claimant, who was not herself disabled within the meaning of the Disability Discrimination Act 1995, but was the carer for her disabled son, sought to bring a claim of disability discrimination against the defendants. The question arose as to whether she was entitled to bring the claim based on the concept of associative discrimination, on account of her son's disability. An employment tribunal decided that the question of whether associative discrimination was prohibited by EC Council Directive 2000/78 should be referred to the European Court of Justice for a preliminary hearing. The defendants appealed, contending that it was not possible to construe the 1995 Act in such a way as to include protection for associative discrimination and that, therefore, the reference sought was academic. *Held*, the 1995 Act was capable of interpretation, consistent with an interpretation of Directive 2000/78 which was favourable to the claimant, so as to include associative discrimination without distorting the words of the 1995 Act. The tribunal had been entitled to conclude that in order to determine the preliminary issue it was necessary to obtain the opinion of the European Court of Justice as to the proper interpretation of Directive 2000/78. Judgment would be given accordingly.

Coleman v Attridge Law (a firm) [2006] All ER (D) 326 (Dec) (Employment Appeal Tribunal: Judge Peter Clark presiding).

1056   Disability discrimination—employment—depressive disorder

See *Jones v Department for Constitutional Affair*, para 1224.

1057   Disability discrimination—employment—sickness—equivalence to disability

The claimant brought proceedings alleging disability discrimination under EC Council Directive 2000/78 after she was dismissed by her employer for spending eight months away from work by reason of sickness. The court referred the question whether sickness amounted to a disability to the European Court of Justice. *Held*, a person who had been dismissed by his employer solely on account of sickness would not fall within the prohibition of discrimination on the ground of disability. No provision of the EC Treaty prohibited discrimination on the ground of sickness. The legislature had, by using the term 'disability', deliberately chosen a term which was different from 'sickness'. Disability had to do with physical, mental or psychological impairments which hindered the participation of the person concerned in professional life over a long-term period.

Case C-13/05 *Chacón Navas v Eurest Colectividades SA* [2007] All ER (EC) 59 (ECJ: Grand Chamber).

1058   Disability discrimination—employment—sickness amounting to disability—justification of decision to dismiss

An employee was dismissed on account of her sickness absence record. By the time the employer had reached the last stage in its four-stage sickness absence procedure, the employee had lost 38 per cent of her working time due to sickness absence. At the hearing prior to her dismissal, the employee claimed that some of her absences were due to migraines caused by gynaecological problems, and that these would not recur because her medication had changed. After her dismissal, the employee brought a claim for unfair dismissal to an employment tribunal. The tribunal found that the employee had been discriminated against for a reason related to disability and unfairly dismissed, it being found that the employee's gynaecological problems amounted to a disability for the purposes of the Disability Discrimination Act 1995. The employer appealed, submitting that the question of whether the decision to dismiss the employee was justified had not been properly considered by the tribunal. *Held,* the tribunal had erred in finding that the decision to dismiss the employee on grounds of her sickness absence was not for a reason which was material and substantial within the meaning of the 1995 Act, because, but for the disability-related absences, the employee would not have been at risk of dismissal. The 1995 Act did not impose an absolute obligation on an employer to refrain from dismissing an employee who was absent wholly or in part on grounds of ill health due to disability. Whether, by taking disability-related absences into account, an employer acted unlawfully would generally depend on whether or not the employer was justified. In the present case, the tribunal failed to consider the question of justification. A tribunal should not answer the question whether a dismissal was justified merely by saying that it was because the employee was absent on grounds of disability. Therefore, the claim would be remitted to a freshly-constituted tribunal. Accordingly, the appeal would be allowed.

Royal Liverpool Children's NHS Trust v Dunsby [2006] IRLR 351 (Employment Appeal Tribunal: Judge Richardson presiding).

1059   Disability discrimination—employment—unfair dismissal—disability-related reason present in employer's mind

See *Taylor v OCS Group Ltd*, para 1268.

1060   Disability discrimination—further and higher education

The Disability Discrimination Act 1995 (Amendment) (Further and Higher Education) Regulations 2006, SI 2006/1721 (in force in part on 30 June 2006 and in part on 1 September 2006), amend the Disability Discrimination Act 1995 so as to implement further EC Council Directive 2000/78, establishing a general framework for equal treatment in employment and occupation so far as it relates to disability discrimination. In particular, the regulations (1) prohibit discrimination as regards the conferment of qualifications by educational institutions or the arrangements made for the purpose of conferring such qualifications; (2) prohibit harassment by relevant institutions and define what harassment means; (3) impose a duty on responsible bodies to make reasonable adjustments; (4) amend the definition of 'discrimination' and set out the ambit of the justification defence for an act which constitutes discrimination; (5) prohibit direct discrimination and define what the term means; (6) prohibit discrimination and harassment, and impose duties to make reasonable adjustments, in relationships which have come to an end;

(7) prohibit instructions and pressure to discriminate; (8) prohibit the publication of discriminatory advertisements; (9) make provision in relation to the burden of proof in certain disability discrimination proceedings; and (10) implement the directive's obligations with respect to further and higher education provided by local education authorities.

1061   Disability discrimination—premises

The Disability Discrimination (Premises) Regulations 2006, SI 2006/887 (in force on 4 December 2006), support the implementation of the Disability Discrimination Act 1995 ss 22–24M, which make provision about discrimination in relation to the disposal of premises. In particular, the regulations (1) provide that the mental incapacity justification, set out in the Disability Discrimination Act 1995 s 24 to a claim of discrimination in relation to the disposal of premises, will not apply where another person is acting for a disabled person in the circumstances specified; (2) prescribe that which is to be treated as a physical feature, and that which is not to be treated as an alteration of a physical feature for the purposes of the 1995 Act ss 24E(1) and 24J(5); (3) specify the objects that are to be treated as auxiliary aids or services; and (4) make provision (a) concerning the steps which it is reasonable for a controller of let premises to have to take where it is necessary to obtain the consent of any person to change a term of a letting; (b) with regard to the steps which it is reasonable for a controller of a let premises to have to take in prescribed circumstances where a term of the letting of a dwelling house prohibits the making of alterations or improvements to the premises, and the person to whom the premises are let has requested permission to make a disability related improvement; (c) in relation to commonholds, providing that the commonhold association is to be treated as a person managing any commonhold premises, thereby ensuring that provision made in the 1995 Act, providing that discrimination by a person managing any premises is unlawful, is applicable; and (d) with regard to discrimination in the disposal of an interest in a commonhold unit. SI 1996/1836 (as amended) is revoked.

1062   Disability discrimination—private hire vehicles—carriage of guide dogs

The Disability Discrimination Act 1995 (Private Hire Vehicles) (Carriage of Guide Dogs etc) (England and Wales) (Amendment) Regulations 2006, SI 2006/1617,(in force on 17 July 2006), amend the 2003 Regulations, SI 2003/3122, by providing that the exemption notice required to be displayed by an exempted private hire vehicle driver is no longer permitted to be displayed on the dashboard, and instead must be displayed on the windscreen facing outwards so that its front is clearly visible from the outside of the private hire vehicle.

1063   Disability discrimination—taxis—carrying of guide dogs

The Disability Discrimination Act 1995 (Taxis) (Carrying of Guide Dogs etc) (England and Wales) (Amendment) Regulations 2006, SI 2006/1616 (in force on 17 July 2006), amend the 2000 Regulations, SI 2000/2990, by providing that the exemption notice required to be displayed by an exempted taxi driver is no longer permitted to be displayed on the dashboard, and instead must be displayed on the nearside of and immediately behind the windscreen of the taxi, facing outwards so that its front is clearly visible from the outside of the taxi and its back clearly visible from the driver's seat.

1064   Disability discrimination—tenant—adjustment of common parts

The Disability Discrimination Act 1995 s 22(3) provides that it is unlawful for a person managing any premises to discriminate against a disabled person occupying those premises in the way he permits the disabled person to make use of any benefits or facilities, by refusing or deliberately omitting to permit the disabled person to make use of any benefits or facilities, or by evicting the disabled person, or subjecting him to any other detriment.

The claimant was elderly and had mobility problems which required the installation of a stair-lift in the flat which she leased under an underlease granted by the landlord. The lease granted the claimant an easement to use the communal staircase for egress but contained a covenant prohibiting structural alterations without the consent of the relevant leasor. The landlord refused consent for the installation, and the claimant brought proceedings under the 1995 Act s 22(3), alleging that the refusal was discriminatory. The court held that the refusal was discriminatory, as it was a decision relating to whether the claimant should be permitted to use a facility in a particular way, that it was detrimental to her, and that it would not be detrimental to a leasee without the claimant's disability, that therefore the landlord had treated the claimant less favourably than it would treat others who did not have the claimant's disabilities. The landlord appealed. *Held*, the judge had erroneously not first looked to see why the claimant had been treated in the way she had been treated. The judge should have carried out a two-stage process, first identifying the relevant act or omission on the part of the landlord, and second, identifying the relevant act or omission, if any, toward the relevant comparators. The judge had carried out the first stage only, and had not identified what, if any, acts or omissions the landlord had undertaken that constituted more favourable treatment towards the comparators. The complaint was that the landlord had failed to put the claimant in a better position than that to which she was entitled by the underlease, in effect, that the landlord had failed to take positive action. It had not treated her less favourably than it had treated or would treat anybody else. It was of critical significance that the managers of premises were not under any positive obligation to make adjustments or to agree to tenants making adjustments to common parts of the premises so as to make them more suitable for disabled people. This was in sharp distinction to other provisions of the 1995 Act which provided for positive obligations to be imposed. Accordingly, the appeal would be allowed.

Williams v Richmond Court (Swansea) Ltd [2006] EWCA Civ 1719, [2006] All ER (D) 218 (Dec) (Court of Appeal: Auld, Scott Baker and Richards LJJ).

1065   Disability Rights Commission Act 1999—commencement

The Disability Rights Commission Act 1999 (Commencement No 3) Order 2006, SI 2006/3189, brings the Act into force, so far as it is not already in force, on 4 December 2006. For a summary of the Act, see 1999 Abr para 1207. See also the commencement table in the title STATUTES.

1066   Equality Act 2006

The Equality Act 2006 makes provision for the establishment of the Commission for Equality and Human Rights and the dissolution of the Equal Opportunities Commission, the Commission for Racial Equality and the Disability Rights Commission and about discrimination on grounds of religion or belief. The Act also enables provision to be made about discrimination on grounds of sexual orientation, and imposes duties relating to sex discrimination on persons performing public functions. The Act received the royal assent on 16 February 2006 and came into force in part on that day. Further provisions came into force on and between 18 April 2006 and 6 April 2007: SI 2006/1082. The remaining provisions come into force on a day or days to be appointed. For details of commencement, see the commencement table in the title STATUTES.

Part 1 (ss 1–43) The Commission for Equality and Human Rights
Section 1 establishes the Commission for Equality and Human Rights, and s 2, Sch 1 set out provisions relating to the constitution of the Commission. The Commission is required to exercise its functions with a view to encouraging and supporting the development of equality, human rights, dignity of individuals and good relations between different groups in society: s 3. Section 4 requires the Commission to prepare, publish and review periodically a strategic plan setting out the details of activities or classes of activity which it intends to undertake, and the timetable and priorities for these activities. Before it prepares or reviews such a plan, the Commission must consult with those who have knowledge or experience relevant to its functions and others it considers appropriate: s 5. The unauthorised disclosure of certain information relating to the Commission's functions is an offence: s 6. Section 7 applies to Scotland. Section 8 requires the Commission to promote understanding of the importance of equality and diversity, encourage good practice in relation to equality and diversity, promote equality of opportunity, promote awareness and understanding of rights under the equality enactments and work towards the elimination of unlawful discrimination and harassment. Under s 9, the Commission is required to promote understanding of the importance of human rights, encourage good practice in relation to human rights, and promote awareness, understanding and protection of human rights. Section 10 sets out the Commission's duties concerning good relations between and within groups, and between groups and wider society, and requires the Commission to work towards eliminating prejudice against members of groups and enabling those members to participate in society. The Commission must monitor the effectiveness of the equality and human rights enactments: s 11. Under s 12, the Commission is required to publish reports on progress concerning the development of equality, human rights, dignity of individuals and good relations between different groups in society. In pursuance of its duties, the Commission may publish or otherwise disseminate ideas and information, undertake research, provide education or training, and give advice and guidance: s 13. Section 14 enables the Commission to issue a code of practice in respect of specified areas of discrimination legislation, to assist in compliance with the legislation and to promote equality of opportunity, or on specified provisions of landlord and tenant and housing legislation, and s 15 provides for the revision of the codes of practice. The Commission may conduct inquiries into a matter relating to its duties in respect of equality and diversity, human rights and groups: s 16, Sch 2. Section 17 empowers the Commission to make grants in pursuance of its duties relating to equality and diversity, human rights and groups. By virtue of s 18, the Commission may co-operate with other people or organisations when undertaking its human rights duties. The Commission may monitor crimes affecting members of certain groups, undertake activities to reduce crime within or affecting members of those groups and arrange social, recreational, sporting, civic, educational or other activities designed to involve members of groups: s 19. Section 20 empowers the Commission to conduct an investigation into whether a person has committed an unlawful act, has complied with an unlawful act notice, or has complied with an undertaking under s 23, and Sch 3 makes supplemental provision about investigations. Where the Commission is satisfied that a person who has been the subject of an investigation has committed an unlawful act, it may give him an unlawful act notice: s 21. Where such a notice requires the recipient to prepare an action plan, s 22 sets out the arrangements relating to the plan. Where the Commission thinks that a person has

committed an unlawful act, it may enter into an agreement with him under which he undertakes not to commit a specified unlawful act and to take or refrain from taking specified action, and the Commission undertakes not to proceed with an investigation or to issue an unlawful act notice: s 23. Section 24 empowers the Commission to apply for an injunction against a person who it believes is likely to commit an unlawful act, and an order requiring a party to an agreement made under s 23 to comply with an undertaking under the agreement. The Commission's powers to bring legal proceedings in respect of unlawful discriminatory advertisements, instructions to discriminate unlawfully or to cause another person to discriminate unlawfully are set out in s 25, and the procedural rules governing the exercise of those powers are set out in s 26. Provision is made by s 27 for the Commission to make arrangements for the provision of conciliation services. Under s 28, the Commission may give assistance to an individual who alleges that he is a victim of behaviour contrary to the equality enactments and who is or may become a party to legal proceedings relating to that alleged breach. Section 29 entitles the Commission to recover its expenses out of costs awarded or paid by agreement when a person whom it has assisted becomes entitled to have his costs or expenses repaid to him by another party. The Commission may institute or intervene in legal proceedings that are relevant to any of its functions: s 30. Provision is made by s 31, Sch 2 for the Commission to assess a public authority's compliance with the public sector duties for gender, race and disability. Where the Commission thinks that a person has failed to comply with any of those duties, it may give him a notice requiring compliance: s 32. Sections 33–35 provide for interpretation. Section 36 empowers the Secretary of State to remove specified functions from the Equal Opportunities Commission, the Commission for Racial Equality and the Disability Rights Commission and requires him, not later than 31 March 2009, to dissolve those Commissions. Provision is made by ss 37, 38 for the transfer of specified property, rights and liabilities from the three former Commissions to the Commission for Equality and Human Rights. Section 39 makes provision in relation to subordinate legislation and s 40, Sch 3 deal with consequential amendments. Transitional provision is made by ss 41–43.

Part 2 (ss 44–80) Discrimination on grounds of religion or belief
Section 44 defines 'religion' as any religion or lack of religion and defines 'belief' as any belief or lack of belief, and s 45 defines discrimination and victimisation. Subject to specified exceptions, it is unlawful for a person or body to discriminate against a person on the grounds of religion or belief in the provision of goods, facilities and services (s 46), in the disposal and management of premises in Great Britain (ss 47, 48), in the provision of education and associated benefits by a school maintained by a local education authority, an independent school or a special school (ss 49, 50). Subject to specified exceptions, it is unlawful for public authorities exercising any function and local education authorities in the exercise of their functions to discriminate against a person on the grounds of religion or belief: ss 51, 52. It is unlawful to operate a practice which is likely to result in unlawful discrimination if applied to persons of any religion or belief (s 53), and it is unlawful to publish or cause to be published an advertisement which indicates an intention to discriminate on grounds of religion or belief (s 54). Section 55 makes it unlawful to instruct, cause or induce, or attempt to cause or induce, another person to discriminate unlawfully on grounds of religion or belief. There are exceptions from the prohibition of unlawful discrimination on grounds of religion or belief in relation to anything done for the purpose of complying with domestic legislation (s 56), organisations and charities relating to religion or belief (ss 57, 58), faith schools (s 59), a requirement by a charity for members or prospective members to make a statement asserting their acceptance of a religion or belief (s 60), anything done to meet the special needs of people of particular religions or beliefs in relation to their education, training or welfare (s 61), care within family (s 62), anything done for the purpose of safeguarding national security, providing that the national security requirement justifies the action in question (s 63). The Secretary of State may, after consulting with the Commission, create a new exception to the prohibition of discrimination by public authorities or vary an existing exception: s 64. Section 65 provides that proceedings in respect of an act which is unlawful under Pt 2 can only be brought in accordance with the provisions in the Act. The claim in respect of an act of unlawful discrimination is to be brought in a county court by way of proceedings in tort for breach of statutory duty: s 66. Section 67 provides that such proceedings may not be brought in a county court in respect of an act of a public authority if the lawfulness of the act could be raised in immigration proceedings. Section 68 sets out the remedies which are available in an action for breach of statutory duty under s 66. Except with the permission of the court, proceedings under s 66 must be brought within six months of the alleged unlawful act: s 69. Section 70 indicates the way that information can be obtained by a claimant or potential claimant from the respondent or potential respondent to assist in his decision about whether to take proceedings. By virtue of s 71, rules of court may make provision permitting a court to take various forms of action which are considered expedient in the interests of national security. Contractual terms which provide for the doing of acts of unlawful discrimination or excluding or limiting liability for unlawful discrimination are unenforceable: s 72. A person who knowingly or recklessly helps another to do an act which is unlawful under Pt 2 is guilty of an offence: s 73. Anything done by a person in the course of his employment or as an agent is, by virtue of s 74, to be treated as also done by his employer or principal. However, it is a defence for the employer to prove that he took

all reasonable steps to ensure that the employee could not perform the discriminatory act: s 74. For the purpose of Pt 2, police officers are to be treated as if they were employees of their chief officer of police: s 75. A person with the power to facilitate access to a service, facility or benefit of any kind is subject to the same prohibition of discrimination as the actual provider: s 76. Section 77 amends the Employment Equality (Religion or Belief) Regulations 2003, SI 2003/1660, so that the definition of 'religion or belief' in the 2003 Regulations is the same as in the 2006 Act. Section 78 provides that Pt 2 applies to acts done on behalf of the Crown as they apply to acts done by a private person, but that proceedings cannot be brought against the Queen acting in her personal or private capacity. Section 79 deals with interpretation. By virtue of s 80, the prohibition of discrimination on the grounds of religion or belief generally applies only in Great Britain and in relation to British ships, hovercraft and aircraft.

Part 3 (ss 81, 82) Discrimination on grounds of sexual orientation
Section 81 empowers the Secretary of State to make regulations that prohibit sexual orientation discrimination, in terms similar to the provisions of Pt 2. Section 82 applies to Northern Ireland.

Part 4 (ss 83–90) Public Functions
Section 83 makes it unlawful for a public authority to discriminate or commit acts of harassment on grounds of sex when carrying out its functions, and sets out exceptions to the prohibition. Section 84 imposes on public authorities the duty of eliminating unlawful discrimination and harassment and of promoting equality of opportunity between men and women, and s 85 empowers the Secretary of State to impose specific duties on public authorities that he thinks will ensure better performance by them of that duty. The Commission for Equality and Human Rights may issue a code of practice about performance of these duties: s 86. Where a claim is brought concerning unlawful sex discrimination or harassment other than in the employment field, or unlawful disability discrimination, county court rules may make provision enabling the court to take various forms of action which are considered expedient in the interests of national security: ss 87, 89. Sections 88 and 90 make minor amendments.

Part 5 (ss 91–95) General
Section 91, Sch 4 deal with repeals. Ministers of the Crown, government departments and other agents of the Crown are bound by the Act: s 92. Section 93 deals with commencement, s 94 with extent and s 95 with short title.

Amendments, repeals and revocations
The lists below, which are not exhaustive, mention repeals and amendments which are or will be effective when the Act is fully in force.

The following Act is repealed in full: Disability Rights Commission Act 1999. Specific provisions of a number of Acts are amended or repealed. These include the Sex Discrimination Act 1975 ss 38–40, 53–61, 67–73, 75, 76, 76D, 76E, Sch 3; Race Relations Act 1976 ss 29–31, 43–52, 58–64, 66, 68, 71C–71E, 74(5), Schs 1, 4; County Courts Act 1984 Sch 2; Legal Aid Act 1988 Sch 5; Housing Act 1988 s 137; Employment Act 1989 Sch 6; Local Government and Housing Act 1989 s 180; Trade Union Reform and Employment Rights Act 1993 Sch 7; Disability Discrimination Act ss 16B, 16C, 17B, 28, 31B, 49E, 49F, 49H, 49I, 53A; Employment Tribunals Act 1996 Sch 1; Access to Justice Act 1999 Sch 4; Race Relations (Amendment) Act 2000 Sch 2; Special Educational Needs and Disabilities Act 2001 ss 35–37, Sch 7; Anti-terrorism, Crime and Security Act 2001, Sch 4; Nationality, Immigration and Asylum Act 2002 Sch 7; Disability Discrimination Act 2003 s 16(2), (3), Sch 1; Equality Act 2006 s 86.

1067 Racial discrimination—code of practice—employment

The Race Relations Code of Practice relating to Employment (Appointed Day) Order 2006, SI 2006/630 (in force on 6 April 2006), appoints 6 April 2006 as the day on which the revised Code of Practice on racial equality in employment comes into effect. SI 1983/1081 is revoked.

1068 Racial discrimination—code of practice—housing

The Race Relations Code of Practice (Housing) (Appointed Day) Order 2006, SI 2006/2239 (in force on 1 October 2006), replaces the Code or Practice in Rented Housing which was brought into effect by the Race Relations Code of Practice (Rented Housing) Order 1991, SI 1991/227 and the Code of Practice in Non-Rented (Owner Occupied) Housing which was brought into effect by the Race Relations Code of Practice (Non-Rented Housing) Order 1992, SI 1992/619, and appoints 1 October 2006 for the coming into effect of the revised Code of Practice on Racial Equality in Housing.

1069 Racial discrimination—employment—burden of proof

Scotland
An employee of Indian origin applied for a promotion but was unsuccessful. He complained to an employment tribunal that he had been unlawfully discriminated against, contrary to the Race Relations Act 1976. The tribunal sustained that complaint and awarded compensation to the

employee. However, that decision was reversed on appeal to the Employment Appeal Tribunal, which held that the tribunal had erred by drawing an inference of racial discrimination on the basis of evidence which showed merely that there had been unfair treatment and that the applicant was Indian. The employee appealed, submitting that, where it was found that an employer had treated an employee less favourably than it would have treated other persons, the employment tribunal was entitled to find that that treatment was on racial grounds. *Held*, the appellate tribunal had erred in principle. The employment tribunal had been entitled to treat the successful candidate for the promotion as a valid comparator for the purposes of its determination as to whether there had been less favourable treatment. Having found that there had been unfair treatment, it was clear that, even if, on the evidence, there had been an alternative tenable reason for the less favourable treatment given to the employee, the tribunal could conclude that that treatment was on racial grounds. As the employer had failed to negative that reason, the employee was bound to succeed. Accordingly, the appeal would be allowed.

Dhesi v Glasgow CC [2005] CSIH 86, 2006 SLT 128 (Inner House). *Wong v Igen Ltd* [2005] EWCA Civ 142, [2005] 3 All ER 812 applied.

1070 Racial discrimination—employment—dismissal—employee's political views— influence on dismissal

An employee, who was white, was employed as a bus driver. The majority of the employer's customers were Asian, and the employer's workforce was 35 per cent Asian. The employee, who was regarded as a satisfactory employee, was a member of a right-wing political party which had an overt racist and fascist agenda. The employee decided to stand as a candidate for the local council. Trade unions representing other members of the employer's workforce made representations to the employer requesting that it take action against the employee. The employee was elected as a local councillor, and was then summarily dismissed from his employment. The employer had received legal advice to the effect that the employee's continued employment would present a risk to the health and safety of its employees and passengers, and would potentially jeopardise the employer's reputation and ability to retain customers. The employee brought a complaint of race discrimination to an employment tribunal, alleging that the employer had treated him less favourably within the meaning of the Race Relations Act s 1(1)(a) by dismissing him on the ground of the Asian race and ethnic origin of the employer's customers. The complaint was dismissed, but the employee's appeal to the Employment Appeal Tribunal was allowed. On the employer's appeal, the employee submitted that the expression 'on racial grounds' in the 1976 Act covered any case in which the discriminator's less favourable act was referable to race, even if the race was that of a third party. *Held*, the proposition advanced by the employee was wrong in principle, inconsistent with the purposes of the legislation and unsupported by authority. Taken to its logical conclusion, his interpretation of the 1976 Act would mean that it could be an act of direct race discrimination for an employer, who was trying to improve race relations in the workplace, to dismiss an employee discovered to have committed an act of race discrimination, such as racist abuse, against a fellow employee or against a customer of the employer. That was not the kind of case for which the anti-discrimination legislation was designed. The grounds for the employee's dismissal did not become racial grounds merely because the employer had dismissed him in circumstances in which it wished to avoid the perceived detrimental effects of the employee's membership of, and election to office representing, the political party in question, which propagated racially discriminatory policies concerning non-white races who formed part of the employer's workforce and customer base. Accordingly, the appeal would be allowed.

Redfearn v Serco Ltd (t/a West Yorkshire Transport Service) [2006] EWCA Civ 659, [2006] ICR 1367 (Court of Appeal: Mummery and Dyson LJJ and Sir Martin Nourse). *Showboat Entertainment Centre Ltd v Owens* [1984] 1 All ER 836, EAT (1983 Abr para 2692), considered. Decision of Employment Appeal Tribunal [2005] IRLR 744 (2005 Abr para 1217) reversed.

1071 Racial discrimination—employment—equal pay and treatment—burden of proof

An employee, who had a strong Indian accent, worked on an evening shift where his duties included answering the telephone. When complaints were made that he was not easily understood, he was given five days' notice of being moved to the morning shift where he would not be required to answer the telephone. As a consequence of his transfer, his working hours were reduced and he was paid less. He complained to an employment tribunal that his transfer amounted to discrimination. He also argued that he was entitled to reasonable notice of any reduction in hours and that any deduction from his wages after only five days' notice was unlawful. The tribunal asked whether, for the purposes of the Race Relations Act 1976 s 54A, the employee had proved, on the balance of probabilities, facts from which it could conclude that the employer had committed an act of discrimination. It concluded that the employee had done so, and that the burden of proof passed to the employer. The tribunal stated that the transfer had been motivated by the need for whoever was answering the telephone to communicate effectively and that, while the employer's failure to speak to the employee about the problem might have been unreasonable, it was not discriminatory behaviour. The tribunal dismissed the employee's wage deduction claim and he appealed. *Held*, the guidelines in *Barton v Investec Henderson Crosthwaite Securities Ltd* were only guidelines, and not a substitute for the statutory language of the 1976 Act s 54A. No error of law was committed by a tribunal failing to set out the *Barton* guidelines or by failing to go through them in detail. In all the circumstances, the tribunal had found that the burden of proof, including the explanation for the absence of any warning, had been discharged by the employer. Although the tribunal had not specifically stated that the employer had discharged the burden of proving an adequate explanation in relation to the failure to warn, it was clear, reading the decision as a whole, that the tribunal had properly applied the law. However, on the true construction of the contract of employment, the requirement to give reasonable notice applied to the employer's power to reduce the employee's regular hours of work. The tribunal had erred in that regard. Accordingly, the appeal would be allowed in part.

Hundal v Initial Security Ltd [2006] All ER (D) 74 (Aug) (Employment Appeal Tribunal: Judge Altman presiding). *Barton v Investec Henderson Crosthwaite Securities Ltd* [2003] ICR 1205, EAT (2003 Abr para 955); *Wong v Igen Ltd* (*Equal Opportunities Commission intervening*); *Emokpae v Chamberlin Solicitors* (*Equal Opportunities Commission intervening*); *Webster v Brunel University* (*Equal Opportunities Commission intervening*) [2005] EWCA Civ 142, [2005] 3 All ER 812 (2005 Abr para 1194) applied. *King v The Great Britain-China Centre* [1991] ICR 516, CA, considered.

1072   Racial discrimination—employment—time limit—act extending over period of time

An employment tribunal must not consider a complaint of racial discrimination unless it is presented to the tribunal before the end of the period of three months beginning when the act complained of was done: Race Relations Act 1976 s 68(7)

An employee complained of racial discrimination by her employer, alleging 17 instances of racial discrimination some of which had occurred more than three months before the complaint was made. The employer contended that the complaint had been presented out of time. The employee claimed that the incidents of discrimination constituted an act extending over a period, for the purposes of the 1976 Act s 68(7)(b) and that, as a result, they were all in time, since the latest incident fell within the limitation period. The Employment Appeal Tribunal upheld a decision that the alleged incidents did not constitute a single act extending over a period and that 12 of the 17 claims were out of time. The employee appealed, submitting that all she had to show at the preliminary hearing stage was that her complaints were capable of being part of an act extending over a period. *Held*, an employee had to show a prima facie case that a complaint was part of an act extending over a period. There was no meaningful difference between that test and the test of whether complaints were capable of being part of an act extending over a period. Accordingly, the appeal would be dismissed.

Lyfar v Brighton & Sussex University Hospitals Trust [2006] EWCA Civ 1548, [2006] All ER (D) 182 (Nov) (Court of Appeal: Thorpe, Hooper and Hughes LJJ). *Hendricks v Metropolitan Police Comr* [2002] EWCA Civ 1686, [2003] 1 All ER 654 (2002 Abr para 1118) applied. *Robertson v Bexley Community Centre (t/a Leisure Link)* [2003] EWCA Civ 576, [2003] IRLR 434 considered. Decision of Employment Appeal Tribunal [2006] All ER (D) 285 (Mar) affirmed.

1073   Racial discrimination—prisoner of war—compensation scheme—eligibility criteria—country of birth

See *R (on the application of Elias) v Secretary of State for Defence*, para 2947.

1074   Racial discrimination—statutory duties

The Race Relations Act 1976 (General Statutory Duty) Order 2006, SI 2006/2470 (in force on 3 October 2006), further amends the Race Relations Act 1976 Sch 1A by omitting the entries for Scottish Homes, the Royal Fine Art Commission for Scotland, the Pensions Compensation Board and Bòrd na Gàidhlig (Alba), and by specifying other persons and bodies to which the general duty to have due regard to the need to eliminate unlawful racial discrimination and to promote equality of opportunity and good relations between persons of different racial groups applies.

The Race Relations Act 1976 (Statutory Duties) Order 2006, SI 2006/2471 (in force on 3 October 2006), imposes certain specific duties on bodies who are subject to the general duty under the Race Relations Act 1976 s 71(1) to have due regard, when exercising their functions, to the need to eliminate unlawful racial discrimination and to promote equality of opportunity and good relations between persons of different racial groups. Specifically, the order imposes on specified bodies and other persons a duty to (1) publish, by 2 March 2007, a scheme showing how it intends to fulfil the general duty and its duties; (2) have in place, by 2 March 2007, arrangements for fulfilling duties to monitor, by reference to racial groups, the number of staff in post and the number of applicants for employment, training and promotion, and provide that additional requirements apply where the person has at least 150 full-time equivalent staff. The order also amends the 2003 Order, SI 2003/3006, by removing the Pensions Compensation Board from the list of bodies excepted from the employment monitoring duties.

1075   Sex discrimination—employment—compensation—injury to feelings—joint and several liability

The Sex Discrimination Act 1975 s 42 provides that a person who knowingly aids another person to carry out an unlawful act of sex discrimination is to be treated as himself doing an unlawful act of the like description (s 42(1)) and an employee for whose act the employer is liable is deemed to aid the doing of the act by the employer (s 42(2)).

An employee brought a claim for sex discrimination against her employer on the ground that she had been discriminated against after becoming pregnant. An employment tribunal concluded that the defendant, who had been the employee's manager, had consciously fostered and encouraged a discriminatory culture at work. The tribunal made an award for injury to feelings jointly and severally against the employer and the defendant, on the ground that the defendant had aided the employer's act within the meaning of the 1975 Act s 42. The employer company was dissolved and could not pay compensation, and the defendant appealed on the ground that the award should not have been joint and several. The Employment Appeal Tribunal upheld the tribunal's decision and the defendant appealed further. *Held*, an employer who knowingly fostered and encouraged a sustained campaign of bullying and discrimination against a woman did an act which was unlawful by virtue of s 6(2). In accordance with s 41, when such acts were carried out by an employee they were to be treated as acts done by the employer as well as the employee. Under s 42(2), the defendant was deemed to have aided the employer in the doing of those acts and therefore, in accordance with s 42(1), she was herself to be treated as having acted unlawfully in doing those acts. Accordingly, the appeal would be dismissed.

Miles v Gilbank [2006] EWCA Civ 543, [2006] ICR 1297 (Court of Appeal: Chadwick, Sedley and Arden LJJ). Decision of Employment Appeal Tribunal [2005] All ER (D) 355 (Oct) (2005 Abr para 1240) affirmed.

1076   Sex discrimination—employment—equal pay and treatment—choice of comparator

The claimants, who were all female, worked as domestics at two of the defendant's hospitals. They successfully brought an action for indirect sex discrimination on the ground that porters at the hospitals, who were predominantly male, had received bonuses for work which was claimed to be of equal value to that of the claimants, whereas the predominantly female domestics had not. Caterers at the hospitals, a higher proportion of whom were female, had also received bonuses, but the claimants had not included them in the comparator group. The employer appealed. *Held*, logic demanded that the claimants compared themselves with the entire pool of workers who were obtaining the advantage denied to the claimants, rather than arbitrarily excluding a section of the advantaged group. A comparison between the claimant group and a larger comparator group was likely to be more statistically reliable. The correct comparator was the porters and the caterers taken together. However, since 65 per cent of that group was male, there was still a prima facie case of indirect sex discrimination and accordingly, the appeal would be dismissed.

Cheshire and Wirral Partnership NHS Trust v Abbott [2006] EWCA Civ 523, [2006] ICR 1267 (Court of Appeal: Auld and Keene LJJ and Sir Christopher Staughton). Case C-127/92 *Enderby v Frenchay Health Authority* [1994] 1 All ER 495, ECJ (1993 Abr para 2752), applied.

1077   Sex discrimination—employment—equal pay and treatment—determinant of pay— length of service

On an employee's complaint against her employer under the Equal Pay Act 1970 that she was being paid less than male colleagues doing the same job but with longer service, it fell to be determined whether, where the use by an employer of the criterion of length of service as a determinant of pay had a disparate impact as between relevant male and female employees, the EC Treaty art 141 required the employer to provide special justification for recourse to that criterion. Questions also arose as to whether, if the answer depended on the circumstances, what those circumstances were and whether the answer would be different if the employer applied to employees on an individual basis the criterion of length of service. *Held*, as a general rule, recourse to the criterion of length of service was appropriate to attain the legitimate objective of rewarding experience acquired which enabled a worker better to perform his duties. The employer did not have to establish that recourse to that criterion was appropriate to attain that objective unless the worker provided evidence capable of raising serious doubts. Where a job classification system based on an evaluation of the work to be carried out was used in determining pay, there was no need to show that an individual worker had acquired experience during the relevant period that had enabled him better to perform his duties. There might be situations in which recourse to the criterion of length of service had to be justified in detail by the employer. The employer was therefore free to reward length of service without having to establish the importance it had in the performance of specific tasks entrusted to the employee.

Case C-17/05 *Cadman v Health and Safety Executive* [2007] All ER (EC) 1 (ECJ: Full Court). Case C-109/88 *Handels-og Kontorfunktionaerernes Forbund i Danmark v Dansk Arbejdsgiverforening, acting on behalf of Danfoss* [1991] ICR 74, ECJ (1989 Abr para 2597), considered. For English proceedings see *Health and Safety Executive v Cadman* [2004] EWCA Civ 1317, [2005] ICR 1546.

1078   Sex discrimination—employment—equal pay and treatment—time limits for claims— transfer of undertakings

The Equal Pay Act 1970 s 2(4) provides that no claim in respect of the operation of an equality clause relating to a woman's employment may be referred to an employment tribunal if she has not been employed in the employment within the six months preceding the date of the reference.

The claimants had been denied access to an occupational pension scheme because they only worked part-time. They were subsequently transferred to new employers under the Transfer of Undertakings (Protection of Employment) Regulations 1981, SI 1981/1794. They made their claims, under the 1970 Act s 2(4), against their former employers more than six months after the transfers, but contended that the six-month time limit ran from the date on which employment with the transferee, rather than the transferor, ended. *Held*, where employment was transferred from one employer to another, any claim against the transferor in respect of the operation of an equality clause had to be brought within six months of the date when employment with the transferor ended. The plain and natural meaning of the 1970 Act s 2(4) was that the claim had to be brought within six months of the end of the employment to which the claim related. Where the claim related to the operation of an equality clause relating to an occupational pension scheme before the date of the transfer, it related to the woman's employment with the transferor. The effect of the claimants' argument was that a transferor would be exposed to claims relating to occupational pension schemes indefinitely, and that there would be a consequential lack of legal certainty. Accordingly, the appeal would be dismissed.

Preston v Wolverhampton Healthcare NHS Trust (No 3) [2006] UKHL 13, [2006] 3 All ER 193 (House of Lords: Lords Hope of Craighead, Scott of Foscote, Rodger of Earlsferry, Carswell and Brown of Eaton-under-Heywood). Decision of Court of Appeal [2004] EWCA Civ 1281, [2005] ICR 222 (2004 Abr para 1012) affirmed. For earlier related proceedings, see [2001] UKHL 5, [2001] 3 All ER 947 (2001 Abr para 1140).

1981 Regulations replaced by Transfer of Undertakings (Protection of Employment) Regulations 2006, SI 2006/246.

1079   Sex discrimination—employment—equal pay and treatment—unfair dismissal—upper age limit for bringing claim

Two employees were each dismissed by their respective employers. As they were both over the age of 65 at the time of dismissal, they were disqualified by virtue of the Employment Rights Act 1996 ss 109(1)(b) and 156(1)(b) from commencing proceedings for unfair dismissal and for obtaining redundancy payments. The employees brought a claim against their employers under the EC Treaty art 141, which set out the principle of equal pay between men and women. They contended that the statutory bar to bringing claims constituted indirect discrimination against them on the ground of their sex and was therefore unlawful. They pointed to statistics showing that relatively more women than men left employment under the age of 65 and, consequently, that relatively more men than women over the age of 65 were still in employment. That showed, they submitted, that relatively more men than women were prevented by the statutory bar from making unfair dismissal or redundancy claims and that that disparate effect constituted indirect discrimination. An employment tribunal ruled that the employees' contention was correct and that they had jurisdiction to hear their claims. The Employment Appeal Tribunal allowed the Secretary of State's appeal and that decision was affirmed on appeal. The employees appealed. *Held*, statistics were never more than a tool and the statistics deployed in the lower courts were not an apt tool for identifying indirect discrimination on the facts of the instant case. The disadvantage of which complaint was made was a result of discrimination on the ground of age but the age discrimination could not be passed off as sex discrimination on the ground that statistics showed that relatively more men than women continued in employment after the age of 65. The statistics did not point to indirect discrimination. To be relevant to that issue they would have had to deal with the position among men and women over 65 who worked and who therefore wished to receive equal pay for equal work. In order to raise an issue of indirect discrimination, they would have had to show that a substantially higher proportion of the men over 65 who worked than of the women over 65 who worked received merely the reduced pay package. In fact the statistics showed no such thing since, subject to the 1996 Act s 156(1)(a), 100 per cent of both groups received it. The EC Treaty art 141 did not guarantee equal pay over working lives which ended at different ages. It had the more straightforward aim of ensuring that men and women who were in the same position, doing equal work, received equal pay. The employees had not tried to show any respect in which, while they worked on after 65, they were receiving less by way of pay than any women over 65 received or would have received for equal work. In particular the employees neither had, nor could have, shown that any woman over 65 had or would have had those rights which the Act denied them. Accordingly, the appeals would be dismissed.

Rutherford v Secretary of State for Trade and Industry [2006] UKHL 19, [2006] All ER (D) 30 (May) (House of Lords: Lords Nicholls of Birkenhead, Scott of Foscote, Rodger of Earlsferry and Walker of Gestingthorpe and Baroness Hale of Richmond). Decision of Court of Appeal [2004] EWCA Civ 1186, [2004] 3 CMLR 1158 (2004 Abr para 1242) affirmed.

1080   Sex discrimination—employment—pregnant employee—demotion consequent to risk assessment

See *New Southern Railway Ltd v Quinn*, para 1457.

1081   Sex discrimination—employment—vocational training—detriment

A male student nurse had been undertaking certain clinical placements at the employer hospital where he claimed that he was treated differently from the way in which a female student would have been treated in that he was chaperoned while providing certain treatment to female patients. He commenced proceedings against the employer, identifying five specific incidents. In respect of one of the incidents, an employment tribunal decided that there had been a difference in treatment, but concluded that the applicant had not suffered a detriment. It unanimously dismissed all the applicant's complaints. On appeal by the employee, *held*, in order for there to be a detriment, the court or tribunal should find that, by reason of the act or acts complained of, a reasonable worker would or might take the view that he had thereby been disadvantaged in the circumstances in which he had to work. The test was whether the treatment was of such a kind that a reasonable worker would or might take the view that in all the circumstances it was to his detriment. The tribunal appeared to have approached the issue of detriment by assuming that, if the reason for the discriminatory policy was cogent and rational, it could not be justified to object to it. That approach had the effect of reintroducing justification under the guise of detriment. However unjustified the policy, it could not be said to be unreasonable for a male nurse to feel that it was demeaning and irritating to have to be chaperoned. Presumably, chaperones were not always readily available, in which case it might mean that the male student nurse could not carry out the procedure on that occasion at all. Accordingly, the appeal would be allowed.

Moyhing v Barts and London NHS Trust [2006] IRLR 860 (Employment Appeal Tribunal: Elias J presiding). *Khan v Chief Constable of West Yorkshire Police* [2001] UKHL 48, [2001] 4 All ER 834 (2001 Abr para 1131); and *Shamoon v Chief Constable of Royal Ulster Constabulary* [2003] UKHL 11, [2003] 2 All ER 26 (2003 Abr para 959) applied.

1082   Sex discrimination—pension—eligibility—age difference between men and women

The court heard three complaints that the United Kingdom had breached the prohibition of discrimination under the European Convention of Human Rights art 14 by delaying the equalisation of the pension age for men and women until 2020. The first applicant was a woman who complained that her invalidity benefit stopped when she became 60 where a man would receive the benefit until he was 65. The second and third applicants were men who complained that women were entitled to the state pension at 60 and were exempt from paying National Insurance contributions from that age. *Held*, a difference in treatment was discriminatory for the purposes of art 14 if it had no objective and reasonable justification, if it did not pursue a legitimate aim or of there was not a reasonable relationship of proportionality between the means employed and the aim sought to be realised. The court would only regard a difference in treatment based exclusively on the ground of sex as compatible with the European Convention of Human Rights where there were weighty reasons to do so. Contracting states enjoyed a wide margin of appreciation in relation to assessing to what extent differences in otherwise similar situations justified different treatment in order to implement social and economic policies. That also applied to systems of taxation or contributions which inevitably had to differentiate between groups of taxpayers and the implementation of which created marginal situations. A government often had to balance the need to raise revenue and reflect other social objectives in taxation policies. Governments were in a better position to assess those needs and requirements which could involve complex concerns about the financing of pensions and benefits which have an impact on the community than the court. Unless the government's policy in such an area was manifestly unreasonable, the court would generally respect the government's position. The original justification for the disparity had been to correct the financial inequality between the sexes as the change in women's working lives had evolved slowly and there was no common standard between European states. In the light of these factors and the far reaching implications for women and for the economy as a whole, the United Kingdom could not be criticised for not starting to move towards a single pensionable age earlier or for slowly introducing reforms in stages. Accordingly, there had been no violation of art 14.

Application 42735/02 *Barrow v United Kingdom*; Application 8374/03 *Pearson v United Kingdom*; Application 7212/02 *Walker v United Kingdom* [2006] All ER (D) 104 (Aug) (European Court of Human Rights).

1083   Sex discrimination—pension—transsexual

The claimant's birth certificate registered her gender as male. The Births and Deaths Registration Act 1953 s 29(1), (3) prohibited any alteration to the register of births, except in cases of clerical or factual error. Having been diagnosed as suffering from gender dysphoria, the claimant underwent gender reassignment surgery. Her application for a retirement pension to be paid when she reached the age of 60, the retirement age for women in the United Kingdom, was refused on the ground that the claim had been made before she reached the age of 65, the retirement age for men. A question arose as to whether EC Council Directive 79/7 on the progressive implementation of the principle of equal treatment for men and women in matters of social security, prohibited the refusal of a retirement pension to a male to female transsexual until she reached the age of 65 and who would have been entitled to such a pension at the age of 60 had she been held to be a woman as a matter of national law. *Held*, art 4(1) precluded legislation which denied a person who had undergone male to female gender reassignment entitlement to a retirement pension on the ground that she had not reached the age of 65, when she would have been entitled to such a pension at the age of 60 had she been held to be a woman as a matter of national law. National legislation which precluded a transsexual, in the absence of recognition of his new gender, from fulfilling a requirement which had to be met in order to be entitled to a right protected by Community law had to be regarded as being, in principle, incompatible with the requirements of Community law. That law did not affect the power of the member states to organise their social security systems and, in the absence of harmonisation at Community level, it was therefore for each member state to determine the conditions governing the right or duty to be insured with a social security scheme and the conditions for entitlement to benefits. Nevertheless, the member states had to comply with Community law when exercising that power.

Case C-423/04 *Richards v Secretary of State for Work and Pensions* [2006] ICR 1181 (ECJ: First Chamber). Case C-117/01 *KB v National Health Service Pensions Agency* [2004] All ER (EC) 1089, ECJ (2004 Abr para 1017), considered.

1084   Sex discrimination—statutory duties—public authorities

The Sex Discrimination Act 1975 (Public Authorities) (Statutory Duties) Order 2006, SI 2006/2930 (in force on 6 April 2007), imposes specific duties on the public authorities listed in the order. The purpose of the specific duties is to ensure better performance by listed authorities of their duty to have due regard to the need to eliminate unlawful discrimination and harassment and to promote equality of opportunity between men and women in carrying out their functions under the Sex Discrimination Act 1975 s 76A(1). In particular, the order (1) requires listed authorities to prepare and publish a Gender Equality Scheme by 30 April 2007; (2) requires listed authorities to implement certain components of each such scheme within three years beginning with the date on which they published the relevant scheme; (3) requires listed authorities to prepare and publish a revised scheme within three years after the publication of their first scheme at the latest, and to continue to publish a revised scheme every three years thereafter; (4) provides that a listed authority's scheme can be published as part of one or more other documents; and (5) requires listed authorities to take such steps as are reasonably practicable to report annually on the actions taken to meet the overall objectives in its scheme.

DISTRESS

Halsbury's Laws of England (4th edn) vol 13 (2007 Reissue) paras 901–1147

Articles

For articles relating to this title please refer to the Table of Articles at the beginning of the Abridgment.

EASEMENTS AND PROFITS À PRENDRE

Halsbury's Laws of England (4th edn) vol 14 paras 1–300; vol 16(2) (Reissue) paras 1–400

Articles

For articles relating to this title please refer to the Table of Articles at the beginning of the Abridgment.

1085   Easement—extinguishment—right of access

The claimant was the tenant of a flat in multiple occupation. The lease expressly granted rights in the nature of easements for the tenant to use the communal refuse bins in the area at the rear of the building, coupled with a right of access to the rear area for that purpose via the common parts of the building. The defendant's predecessor had erected a wall across the passage on the ground floor of the building leading to the rear area, thereby blocking off all access by the residents of the flats in the building. The wall had been erected to comply with the statutory duty on owners of houses in multiple occupation to ensure such houses had adequate fire precautions. In county court proceedings brought by the claimant, the judge held that the easement of access to the rear area had been extinguished once and for all with the erection of the wall pursuant to the statutory notice. The claimant appealed, arguing that the easement had not been extinguished. *Held*, the test for extinguishment of an easement was first, whether on the true construction of the relevant statutory regime, the effect of doing the act that Parliament had authorised was to expropriate property rights which were inconsistent with the doing of the act. If the answer to that was yes, that was the end of the matter. The right was expropriated if the answer was no, after which practical considerations might come into play. As the statutory regime in question did not, on its true construction, authorise the once and for all extinguishment of rights which were rendered unexercisable by the carrying out of works in compliance with the notice, there was a practicable possibility of the lessee's rights reviving at some time during the remainder of the term of the lease. In the present case, however, it was clear that in carrying out the works the defendant's predecessor had committed no actionable wrong with regard to the claimant. The fact that in erecting the wall the lessor was discharging a statutory obligation was a complete defence to any claim in nuisance at the suit of the lessee. Accordingly, the appeal would be dismissed.

Jones v Cleanthi [2006] EWCA Civ 1712, [2006] All ER (D) 146 (Dec) (Court of Appeal: Pill and Jonathan Parker LJJ and Sir Peter Gibson). Decision of Bell J [2005] EWHC 2646 (QB), [2006] 1 All ER 1029 (2005 Abr para 1245) affirmed.

1086   Easement—right of way—knowledge of servient owner—use of track over local authority land

The claimants owned a freehold property adjacent to land owned by a local authority on whose land was a boathouse. A track, the primary route, led across the authority's land to the boathouse. The land on which the boathouse stood had been let to a third party. The first claimant took over the third party's business and became the authority's tenant. There was also an alternative access way, the secondary route, to the use of which the authority had never made any objection. Subsequently, the authority granted the first claimant a new lease in respect of the boathouse. The authority then sold its land to the defendant company, which intended to develop the land by erecting houses on it. The first claimant agreed to give up his tenancy of the boathouse, but the claimants commenced proceedings seeking a declaration that they were entitled to rights of way to their land over both the primary and secondary routes. The judge dismissed their claims. On the claimants' appeal, *held*, where the grant of the tenancy of the servient land predated the user by the owner of the dominant land, it was necessary to ask whether, notwithstanding the tenancy, the freehold owner of the servient land could take steps to prevent the user during the tenancy. If the owner of the servient land could take steps to prevent the user, then it was necessary to ask whether the freehold owner had actual or implied knowledge of that user by the owner of the dominant land. If the owner of the servient land did have knowledge of the user and could take steps to prevent that user then acquiescence would be established. Where user of the servient land began before the grant of the tenancy, it was necessary to ask whether the freehold owner of the servient land had knowledge at or before the date of the grant. If so, then it was likely to be immaterial whether the terms of the tenancy were such that the owner of the servient land could take steps to prevent that user. If the owner of the servient land had not had knowledge of the user at the date of the grant, then the position was the same as it would have been had the grant pre-dated the user. In the present case, there was no doubt that the authority could have prevented the user of the track, and, having the requisite knowledge, had acquiesced in the user. Accordingly, the appeal would be allowed.

Williams v Sandy Lane (Chester) Ltd [2006] EWCA Civ 1738, [2006] All ER (D) 245 (Dec) (Court of Appeal: Chadwick and Wilson LJJ and Lindsay J).

ECCLESIASTICAL LAW

Halsbury's Laws of England (4th edn) vol 14 paras 301–1435

1087   Care of cathedrals—rules

The Care of Cathedrals Rules 2006, SI 2006/1941 (in force on a date to be appointed), replace the 1990 Rules, SI 1990/2335. In particular, the rules (1) prescribe the procedure for preliminary determinations under the Care of Cathedrals Measure 1990; (2) deal with applications for approval of proposals made by a cathedral chapter to a fabric advisory committee ('FAC'); (3) deal with applications for approval of proposals made by a cathedral chapter to the Cathedrals Fabric Commission for England ('CFCE'); (4) deal with appeals to the CFCE from decisions of an FAC or failure by a FAC to determine an application within the time limit under the 1990 Measure; (5) provide for proposals affecting cathedral clergy housing; (6) provide for the giving of notice to the CFCE of applications by a cathedral chapter for listed building or scheduled monument consent in respect of a building or monument within the cathedral precinct; (7) deal with applications for approval of proposals relating to objects of architectural, archaeological, artistic or historic interest; (8) implement the provisions relating to 'treasure' in the amended 1990 Measure; (9) provide a detailed procedure for reporting the finding of a potential treasure object and whether it is one which is within the Treasure Act 1996; (10) deal with requests for a review by a commission of review of a decision, including a decision on appeal by the CFCE or for determination by a commission in the event of non-determination by the CFCE within the statutory time-limit; (11) contain general provisions regarding procedure and evidence for the proceedings of FACs, the CFCE and any commission of review; (12) deal with registers of applications for approval made to

FACs and the CFCE; (13) deal with cathedral inventories and with records of cathedral works; and (14) contain general provisions regarding the sending and delivery of documents, copies of documents and the date of compliance with time limits and enables irregularities and procedural errors to be dealt with.

1088   Church of England—legal aid

The Church of England (Legal Aid) (Amendment) Rules 2006, SI 2006/1939 (in force on 1 August 2006), amend the 1995 Rules, SI 1995/2034, so as to (1) enable the deputy, if any, of the Secretary to the Legal Aid Commission ('the Commission') to issue interim certificates of legal aid on behalf of the Commission; and (2) provide for a statement of reasons to be given, for the Commission's decision on an application for legal aid and for a decision to discharge or revoke a legal aid certificate, to the applicant or assisted person, unless, in the case of an assisted person the certificate has been discharged as a result of that person's death, and to the solicitor of the applicant or assisted person.

1089   Church of England (Miscellaneous Provisions) Measure 2006

The Church of England (Miscellaneous Provisions) Measure 2006 makes provision for a number of matters affecting the Church of England. The Measure received the royal assent on 11 July 2006. Most of its provisions came into force on 1 October 2006 and the remaining provisions come into force on a day or days to be appointed. For details of commencement, see the commencement table in the title STATUTES.

Section 1, Sch 1 require the Board of Governors to apply any money arising from any sale or exchange of any part of the property of a benefice for specified purposes. Provision is made by s 2, Sch 2 in relation to the sealing and execution of documents by the Church Commissioners. The money standing to the credit of the capital account of a diocesan stipends fund may be applied, at the discretion of the Diocesan Board of Finance, with the concurrence of the bishop, for the acquisition of any land to be held as diocesan glebe land: s 3. Provision is made by s 4 in relation to the corporate funds of the Archbishops' Council. By virtue of s 5, the bishop must not give his consent in relation to powers exercised over land no longer required for the purpose of which it was acquired, unless he is satisfied that the land is no longer required for the purpose for which it was granted. Farnham Castle is to be held by the Church Commissioners as part of their corporate property: s 6. A chancellor, with the consent of the bishop of the diocese, must appoint a fit and proper person to act as deputy chancellor of the diocese: s 7. The Presidents, after consultation with the Appointments Committee of the Church of England, must appoint from among the members of any House of the Synod a panel of such number of persons as the Presidents may determine: s 8. Consequential amendment is made by s 9. A subsidiary of the Diocesan Board of Finance has, with respect to the holding, managing and dealing with diocesan glebe land specified by a scheme, the same powers and duties as the Board with respect to diocesan land held by it: s 10, Sch 3. Under s 11, any ecclesiastical property which is vested in the incumbent of a benefice which is vacant must be treated for the purposes of a compulsory acquisition of the property as being vested in the Board for the diocese in which the land is situated. Where a redundancy scheme or pastoral scheme provides for land annexed or belonging to a redundant building, or the whole of part of the site of a demolished building, or land annexed or belonging to the parish, the land or site vests in the Board to be held on trust for specified purposes: s 12, Sch 4. By virtue of s 13, a member of the Archbishops' Council who is not a member of General Synod, but is an ex-officio member, in the case of a lay person of the House of Laity, must be an actual communicant. Section 14, Sch 5 make miscellaneous amendments in relation to functions of Church Commissioners in connection with transactions affecting certain ecclesiastical property. Section 15, Sch 6 deal with repeals, and s 16 with citation, commencement and extent.

1090   Churches Conservation Trust—grants

The Grants to the Churches Conservation Trust Order 2006, SI 2006/1008 (in force on 1 April 2006), specifies the period 1 April 2006–31 March 2009 for the purposes of the Redundant Churches and other Religious Buildings Act 1969 s 1, enabling the Secretary of State, with the approval of the Treasury, to make grants to the Churches Conservation Trust during that period, up to a maximum aggregate amount of £9m. SI 2000/402 and 2003/829 are revoked.

1091   Faculty—cemetery—consecrated ground—restoration

The Care of Churches and Ecclesiastical Jurisdiction Measure 1991 (No 1) s 13(5) provides that, where at any time it appears to the consistory court of a diocese that a person has committed, or caused or permitted the commission of, any act in relation to a church or churchyard in the diocese or any article appertaining to a church in the diocese which was unlawful under ecclesiastical law, the court may make an order requiring that person to take such steps as the court may consider necessary, within such time as the court may specify, for the purpose of restoring the position so far as possible to that which existed immediately before the act was committed.

A consecrated part of a cemetery contained a large number of memorials of which a sizeable number had been laid flat after being tested for stability by, or on behalf of, the local authority. The rural dean and the bereavement services manager sought on behalf of the authority a confirmatory faculty to carry out memorial safety assessments to all memorials in the cemetery. The chancellor refused to grant the faculty sought in respect of work already carried out and ordered the authority to reinstate and repair to a safe condition all memorials which had been laid flat. The authority appealed against that decision, and an issue arose as to whether the 1991 Measure s 13(5) applied to the consecrated part of a cemetery. *Held*, on its true construction, s 13(5), which conferred on the chancellor an enforcement power in relation to churches and churchyards similar to that available to local planning authorities in respect of listed buildings, was not applicable to the consecrated part of a cemetery. In an appropriate case it was a useful power, but one which had always to be exercised with care and in accordance with the Faculty Jurisdiction (Injunctions and Restoration Orders) Rules 1992, SI 1992/2884, in order to achieve procedural fairness, particularly when an order was to be made of the court's own motion. Accordingly, the appeal would be allowed.

Re Welford Road Cemetery, Leicester [2006] All ER (D) 244 (Oct) (Arches Court of Canterbury). *Re West Norwood Cemetery* [1994] Fam 210 (1994 Abr para 1082) not followed.

1092   Faculty—churchyard—burial—closed churchyard
See *Re St James the Great, Birstall*, para 734.

1093   Faculty—sale of church silverware—good and sufficient ground
The petitioner sought a faculty to sell four items of silverware on the ground that they were redundant and that the church required the money that would be acquired from the sale for repairs. *Held,* when considering whether a good and sufficient ground had been established by a vicar for the sale of such items, there was a duty to weigh up all the circumstances and to bear in mind the whole picture of maintaining the viability of the church so that it could fulfil its calling for as long as possible while at the same time discharging its overall responsibility for what had been entrusted to it in the past. It was necessary for a chancellor not to allow anything to fetter his discretion in striking a proper balance. The exercise of the discretion involved a more complex balancing exercise than merely inquiring whether there was a sufficiently dire financial emergency to justify the sale of a historic asset. Accordingly, the faculty would be granted.

Re St John the Baptist, Stainton by Langworth (2006) Times, 26 May (Lincoln Consistory Court: Peter Collier QC, Ch).

1094   Fees—ecclesiastical judges and other officers
The Ecclesiastical Judges, Legal Officers and Others (Fees) Order 2006, SI 2006/1943 (in force on 1 January 2007), replaces the 2005 Order, SI 2005/2020, so as to increase fees in relation to (1) faculty proceedings; (2) proceedings, including appeals, for an injunction or a restoration order; (3) proceedings, including appeals, under the Care of Cathedrals (Supplementary Provisions) Measure 1994 s 4; (4) proceedings in respect of ecclesiastical offences under the Ecclesiastical Jurisdiction Measure 1963, including provision for all cases where proceedings have been instituted under the 1963 Measure or where a person has been authorised to lay a complaint under the 1963 Measure, and appeals; and (5) proceedings under the Clergy Discipline Measure 2003. The order also increases fees for appeals and for the taxation of costs, as well as the fees payable to the provincial registrars and the annual fees payable to the Vicars-General and the President and Deputy President of Tribunals.

The Legal Officers (Annual Fees) Order 2006, SI 2006/1940 (in force on 1 January 2007), replaces the 2005 Order, SI 2005/2018, and (1) increases the total of annual fees for diocesan registrars; (2) fixes new annual fees for the provincial registrars; and (3) makes provision in relation to the calculation of fees for duties and professional services undertaken by registrars and provincial registrars in connection with the Clergy Discipline Measure 2003.

1095   Fees—parochial fees
The Parochial Fees Order 2006, SI 2006/1942 (in force on 1 January 2007), replaces the 2005 Order, SI 2005/2016, and establishes a new table of fees payable for certain matters in connection with baptisms, marriages and burials, the erection of monuments in churchyards and other miscellaneous matters.

1096   Pastoral (Amendment) Measure 2006
The Pastoral (Amendment) Measure 2006 enables leases to be granted of parts of churches and of land belonging or annexed to a church. The measure received the royal assent on 11 July 2006 and comes into force on a day or days to be appointed. For details of commencement, see the commencement table in the title STATUTES.

Under s 1, a court may grant a faculty for a lease of a church on an application by the incumbent of the benefice comprising or including the parish in which the church is situated or, where the benefice is vacant, the bishop in the name and on behalf of the incumbent in the corporate capacity of the incumbent, provided that the court ensures that the premises remaining unlet, together with the premises let under any lease or leases are, taken as a whole, used primarily as a place of worship. Provision is made by s 2 for citation, commencement and extent.

EDUCATION

Halsbury's Laws of England (4th edn) vol 15(1) (2006 Reissue) paras 1–578, vol 15(2) (2006 Reissue) paras 579–1437

Articles

For articles relating to this title please refer to the Table of Articles at the beginning of the Abridgment.

1097   Careers services—inspection—Wales

The Inspection of the Careers and Related Services (Wales) Regulations 2006, SI 2006/3103 (in force on 1 April 2007), which apply in relation to Wales only, prescribe the details of the framework provided by the Education Act 2005 ss 55–57, for the inspection of the careers and related services in Wales by the Chief Inspector for Education and Training in Wales. In particular, the regulations (1) provide that a provider of careers or associated services which has not previously been inspected must be inspected within the period of six years from the date when it first became a provider; (2) provide that existing providers are to be inspected at six-year intervals; (3) require an inspection report to be prepared within 70 working days from completion of the inspection; (4) require an action plan to be prepared following an inspection; (5) require the action plan to be prepared within the period of fifty working days from the date on which the provider received a copy of the inspection report; and (6) provide for copies of reports and action plans to be sent to specified persons, and for their publication at the offices of the provider and on the internet.

1098   Chief Inspector of Schools—appointment—England

The Education (Chief Inspector of Schools in England) Order 2006, SI 2006/1460 (in force on 8 June 2006), reappoints Maurice John Smith to be Her Majesty's Chief Inspector of Schools in England from 8 June 2006 to 30 September 2006 and appoints Christine Bridget Gilbert to that post from 1 October 2006 until 30 September 2011. SI 2005/3505 is revoked.

1099   Childcare Act 2006

See para 448.

1100   Education Act 2002—commencement

The Education Act 2002 (Commencement No 8) (Wales) Order 2006, SI 2006/172, brings into force, in relation to Wales, (1) on 1 February 2006, ss 47, 48, 51 (so far as not already in force), 215(2) (in part), Sch 4 paras 3(6), 5–7, 12(2), (6), 13, 14, and certain repeals in Sch 22 Pt 3; and (2) on 1 September 2006, s 175.

The Education Act 2002 (Commencement No 9 and Transitional Provisions) (Wales) Order 2006, SI 2006/879, brings into force in relation to Wales, on 1 April 2006, ss 35–37, 40 (so far as not already in force), 215 (in part), Sch 2, Sch 3 (so far as not already in force), Sch 21 paras 30, 107, 110(3)(b) (in part), (c) (in part), and certain repeals in Sch 22 Pt 3. Transitional provision is also made.

The Education Act 2002 (Commencement No 10 and Transitional Provisions) (Wales) Order 2006, SI 2006/1336, brings into force, in relation to Wales, s 148 (in part), Sch 12 paras 3(1), (5) (in part), 4(2), 5. Transitional provision is also made.

The Education Act 2002 (Commencement No 9 and Savings) Order 2006, SI 2006/2895, brings into force, in relation to England, on 6 November 2006, ss 18 (so far as not already in force), 134 (so far as not already in force), 136–138, 140, 146 (so far as not already in force), 148 (so far as not already in force), 154(3), 158(3), 178 (so far as not already in force), 215 (in part), Sch 12 (so far as not already in force), Sch 21 paras 5, 6, 10, 15, 55, 79, 125, and certain repeals in Sch 22. Savings are also made.

For a summary of the Act, see 2002 Abr para 1164. See also the commencement table in the title STATUTES.

1101   Education Act 2005—commencement

The Education Act 2005 (Commencement No 1 and Transitional Provisions) (Wales) Order 2006, SI 2006/1338, brings into force (1) in relation to Wales, on 1 September 2006, ss 44–47, 51, 53 (in part), 54, 58–60, 61 (in part), 71, 105, 106, 115, 116, 117 (in part), 118, 123 (in part), Sch 5, Sch 7 paras 6–24, Sch 8, Sch 9 paras 8–21, 28–30, Sch 18 paras 1, 6, 15, and certain repeals in Sch 19 Pt 1; and (2) in relation to England and Wales, (a) on 1 September 2006, ss 19–43, 50, 52, 53 (in part), 61 (in part), 123 (in part), Schs 2–4, 6, Sch 7 para 5, Sch 9 paras 6, 7, 22, 24, 25, 27 and a repeal in Sch 19 Pt 1; and (b) on 1 April 2007, ss 55–57, 123 (in part), and certain repeals in Sch 19 Pt 1. Transitional and saving provisions are also made.

The Education Act 2005 (Commencement No 2 and Transitional Provisions and Savings) Order 2006, SI 2006/2129, brings into force (1) in relation to England and Wales, (a) on 1 August 2006, ss 65 (in part), 66(6), (10), (13), Sch 10 paras 4(4), 8; and (b) on 1 September 2006, ss 64, 65 (so far as not already in force), 66 (so far as not already in force), 67–69, 72 (in part), 73, Sch 10 paras 1–3, 4(1)–(3), (5)–(7), 5–7, 9–15, Sch 11, Sch 12 paras 1–8, 10–13, 14 (in part), 15, 16; and (2) in relation to England only, on 1 September 2006, ss 70, 71, 72 (in part), and Sch 12 para 9. Transitional provisions and savings are also made.

For a summary of the Act, see 2005 Abr para 1270. See also the commencement table in the title STATUTES.

1102   Education and Inspections Act 2006

The Education and Inspections Act 2006 makes provision in relation to primary, secondary and further education and training, and food or drink provided on school premises or in connection with the provision of education or childcare; provides for the establishment of an Office for Standards in Education, Children's Services and Skills and the appointment of Her Majesty's Chief Inspector of Education, Children's Services and Skills; makes provision for the functions of the Office and Chief Inspector; and amends the Leasehold Reform Act 1967 s 29 in relation to university bodies. The Act received the royal assent on 8 November 2006 and came into force in part on that day. Further provisions came into force on and between 12 December 2006 and 27 February 2007: SI 2006/2990, 3400. The remaining provisions come into force on a day or days to be appointed. For details of commencement see the commencement table in the title STATUTES.

Part 1 (ss 1–6) Education functions of local authorities
Section 1 imposes a general duty on local education authorities to promote high standards and requires them to exercise their functions with a view to promoting the fulfilment by every child of his educational potential. Local education authorities are required to exercise their functions on the provision of schools in their area with a view to securing diversity and increasing opportunities for parental choice: s 2. Local education authorities in England are required, under s 3, to respond to parental representations in relation to the exercise of the provision of primary and secondary schools. Section 4 requires all local education authorities to make arrangements to enable them to establish, so far as it is possible, the identities of children in their area who are not receiving a suitable education, with regard to statutory guidance. Local education authorities in England are required under s 5 to appoint school improvement partners to each of the maintained schools, excluding maintained nursery schools, in their area, who will act on behalf of the local education authority, providing challenge and support to a school in order to help improve the attainment and outcomes of pupils. Local education authorities have a duty to promote the well-being of persons aged 13–19, and of persons aged up to 25 with learning difficulties, by securing access for them to sufficient educational and recreational leisure-time activities and facilities, so far as is reasonably practicable, by providing activities and facilities, assisting others to do so, or by making other arrangements to facilitate access, which can include the provision of transport, financial assistance or information, and must supply and keep up to date information regarding those leisure-time activities and facilities that are available locally: s 6, Sch 1.

Part 2 (ss 7–32) Establishment, discontinuance or alteration of schools
Section 7 provides that a local education authority in England may publish a notice inviting proposals, other than from local education authorities, for the establishment of a new foundation, voluntary, or foundation special school, or Academy. Provision is made in relation to such proposals: Sch 2. The circumstances in which local education authorities are permitted to publish proposals for a community school or community special school are set out in s 8, and in general such proposals may be published only where prescribed conditions are met and only, subject to certain conditions, with the consent of the Secretary of State. Before publishing a notice local education authorities in England must consult such persons as they consider appropriate, and in discharging this duty they must have regard to any guidance given by the Secretary of State and regulations may require local education authorities to take further steps to promote public awareness of the proposals brought forward: s 9. Section 10 provides for the publishing of proposals with the consent of the Secretary of State for a new community, foundation, community special or foundation special school by local education authorities in England and other persons ('proposers'). Provision is made for local education authorities to publish proposals to establish a new maintained nursery school or a new 16–19 foundation school or foundation special school and for proposers to publish proposals to establish a new foundation school, voluntary school or foundation special school which is a 16–19 school, or is to replace an independent school, and for a new foundation special school to replace a non-maintained special school: s 11. Under s 12 a new maintained school may be a member of a

federation from the outset. Regulations may be made where a school is proposed to be situated in an area different from that of the local education authority who published a notice or, if the proposals are published outside a competition, different from that of the local education authority who it is proposed should maintain the school: s 13. By virtue of s 14, the power of a local education authority to establish and maintain a school within the area of another local education authority does not apply if the other local education authority is situated in Wales. Provision is made for the publication of statutory proposals where a local education authority or school governing body wish to close a maintained school in England, including maintained mainstream schools, special schools and nursery schools: s 15, Sch 2. Consultation is provided for under s 16 where the local education authority or the governing body propose to close a rural primary school or special school. Section 17 provides for the Secretary of State to direct a local education authority to discontinue a community or foundation special school on a date specified in the direction if he considers it expedient to do so in the interests of the health, safety or welfare of pupils at a school, and requires a local education authority to discontinue a school on the specific date given and provides that there is no requirement to publish statutory proposals for the school's closure. Provision is made under ss 18, 19 that where a local education authority or the governing body of a maintained school propose to make a prescribed alteration to a maintained school, and the proposals are ones that these bodies respectively may make, they must publish statutory proposals to do so, and that regulations may prescribe the alterations to maintained schools that require the publication of statutory proposals. Section 20 provides that certain schools may only publish certain proposals with the consent of the school's existing trustees, and of anyone by whom the foundation governors are appointed. Regulations may make provision about the publication and determination of such proposals: s 21. Such regulations in relation to proposals by a governing body of a community or voluntary controlled school to change category to a foundation school, must provide, under s 22, for the proposals to be determined by the governing body, and not be referred to the adjudicator, subject to certain conditions, and similar provision is made in respect of proposals for a change of category from community special school to foundation special school. Regulations made in relation to the publication and determination of proposals must make provision in connection with the referral of certain proposals to the adjudicator in certain circumstances: s 23. Regulations may, under s 24, make provision in connection with the implementation of approved proposals for the alteration of schools, including arrangements under which the duty to implement the proposals may be removed, or the proposals modified. Section 25 provides for the governing bodies of certain foundation schools with foundations to publish proposals to remove the foundation or to reduce the proportion of governors appointed by the foundation, while s 26 provides for procedure, and s 27 for implementation of such proposals. The opening or closing of maintained schools, or the making of prescribed alterations to them is prohibited without the publication and determination of statutory proposals: s 28. Under s 29, school organisation committees are abolished. Section 30 introduces Sch 3, which provides for amendments to legislation and reflects the replacement of the school organisation committee as decision maker by the local education authority, while s 31 provides for transitional provision and s 32 for interpretation.

Part 3 (ss 33–58) Further provisions about maintained schools
Section 33 provides for the foundations of certain foundation and foundation special schools, and the charity trustees of those foundations, to have specified characteristics and gives the Secretary of State the power in certain circumstances to remove and appoints charity trustees. Provision is made under s 34 for the requirement of the governing body of foundation schools in England with a foundation which appoint the majority of governors to the school's governing body to establish a parent council. The definition of 'capital expenditure' is modified to ensure that it reflects modern accounting practice and that optimal procurement arrangements are available to voluntary aided schools. Section 36 introduces Sch 4 which makes provision in relation to the disposal and change of use of land by maintained schools. Head teachers at foundation and voluntary controlled schools with a religious character are enabled to be teachers who are appointed specifically to teach religious education in accordance with the tenets of the school's designated religion: s 37. By virtue of s 38, the governing body of a maintained school has the duty to (1) promote the well-being of pupils at the school when discharging their functions relating to the conduct of the school; (2) promote community cohesion when discharging their functions relating to the conduct of the school; (3) have regard to any relevant Children and Young People's Plan in exercising their functions in relation to the conduct of the school; and (4) in relation to England, have regard to any views expressed by parents of registered pupils. Section 39 provides for the prohibition on selection on the basis of a pupil's ability in any maintained school, subject to certain exceptions. The status of school admissions code of practice is strengthened under s 40. In relation to England, the functions and role of admission forums are extended: s 41. Local education authorities, in relation to England, are required under s 42 to provide advice and assistance to parents of children living in the area of the authority to help them in the formulation of their preference on a school for their child. Section 43 makes provision in relation to the duty of community and voluntary controlled schools in England to comply with any decision made by their local authority to admit a child, if it is the school's admission authority. Interviewing as part of the admission process, subject to certain conditions, is

prohibited in any maintained school: s 44. By virtue of s 45, foundation and voluntary aided schools, designated by order as having a religious character, are required to consult a named body or person, to be prescribed by regulations, about their proposed admission arrangements. Section 46 makes provision in relation to the restriction of the alteration of admission arrangements in maintained schools in England. Provision is made in relation to objections to admission arrangements for maintained schools to be referred to the relevant authority: s 47. Local education authorities are required under s 48 to notify the governing body of a community or voluntary controlled school that a decision has been made to admit a looked after child who has been permanently excluded from two or more schools, and on receipt the governing body has seven days to refer the matter to the adjudicator where the admission of the child would cause serious prejudice to the provision of efficient education, or the efficient use of resources. Section 49 provides that, in relation to England, where a local authority directs a governing body for which they are not the admission authority to admit a child, where the child has been refused admission to or excluded from every school within a reasonable travelling distance, the governing body can refer the matter to the adjudicator. Provision is made in relation England for local authorities to direct an admission authority to admit a looked after child to a specified school: ss 50, 51. By virtue of s 52, the National Assembly for Wales has the power to make regulations about the admission of children looked after by local authorities in Wales to maintained schools in Wales. Section 53 provides that where a school with partially selective admission arrangements, which it would not now be lawful to introduce, has reduced the proportion of intake selected, it may not subsequently increase that proportion. Provision is made under s 54 for additional forms of banding to assess children's ability when applying for a place at school. Section 55 provides for a sixth-form pupil attending a maintained school to be able to withdraw himself from collective worship and, in the case of a non sixth-form pupil, that a parent may request that the pupil be excused. Regulations may prescribe the circumstances under which charges can be made for singing and musical instrument tuition: s 56. Section 57 introduces Sch 5, which contains provisions relating to the duties and powers of local education authorities in relation to the financing of maintained schools and the role of schools forums. In relation to England, the requirement for the Secretary of State to issue a code of practice on relationships between local education authorities and schools maintained by them is removed: s 58.

Part 4 (ss 59–73) Schools causing concern: England
Section 59 provides for definitions of 'maintained school' and 'eligible for intervention'. Provision is made under s 60 as to the legal procedure where local education authorities may issue formal warning notices to schools. A maintained school is eligible for intervention if, following an inspection Her Majesty's Chief Inspector of Education, Children's Services and Skills has given a notice that the school requires significant improvement and, where there is a further inspection, a school is only eligible for intervention if, following the inspection, the notice to the Secretary of State has not been superseded by either a report that the school no longer requires significant improvement or an additional notice to the Secretary of State that the school requires special measures: s 61. Under s 62, a maintained school is eligible for intervention if, following an inspection the Chief Inspector has given a notice that the school requires special measures and, where there is a further inspection, a school is only eligible for intervention if, following the inspection, the notice to the Secretary of State has not been superseded by either a report that the school no longer requires special measures. Sections 63–66 provide for local education authorities' powers in relation to maintained schools subject to intervention or special measures and ss 67–69 provide for the powers of the Secretary of State in relation to maintained schools subject to intervention or special measures. Section 70 introduces Sch 6, which provides for various matters relating to Interim Executive Boards appointed by the local education authority or the Secretary of State, and s 71 introduces Sch 7, which makes provision in relation to measures that need to be taken by a local education authority following the receipt of an inspection report stating that a school requires special measures or significant improvement. Local education authorities are required to have regard to guidance issued by the Secretary of State in relation to their discretionary powers: s 72. Section 73 provides for interpretation.

Part 5 (ss 74–75) Curriculum and entitlements
Section 74 provides for two new entitlements to the key stage 4 curriculum for pupils aged between 14 and 16 and s 75 provides for two new entitlements for young people who are over compulsory school age but who are not yet 19 years old.

Part 6 (ss 76–87) School travel and school food
Section 76 places a general duty on local education authorities in England to assess the school travel needs of their area, and to promote the use of sustainable modes of travel. Provision is made under s 77 and Sch 8 in relation to local education authorities in England's duty relating to travel arrangements for children. Section 78, Sch 9 make provision in relation to school travel schemes made by local education authorities in England covering home to school travel arrangements for pupils of compulsory school age or below. Such schemes must be piloted in accordance with regulations made by the Secretary of State: s 79. Under s 80 the Secretary of State is required to prepare and publish an evaluation of schemes before 1 January 2012 and he has the power to provide

by order that the new provisions will cease to have effect. Provision is made in relation to adults who benefit from transport arrangements made by local education authorities: s 81. Section 82 clarifies the defences available to parents facing a prosecution by a local education authority for their child's non-attendance at school. Greater responsibility is transferred from the Secretary of State to the Learning and Skills Council for England in relation to the provision of transport by local education authorities and their partners for 16–19 year olds: s 83. Under s 84 local education authorities are required to have regard to the religion or belief of parents in exercising their travel functions. Section 85 and Sch 10 make provision for consequential amendments. The powers to make regulations in connection with nutritional standards for school lunches are extended to cover all food and drink provided on the premises of maintained schools, and apply to food or drink provided by a local education authority or governing body of a school to registered pupils at any place other than the school: s 86. Under s 87, local education authorities and governing bodies no longer have a duty to charge for food and drink provided by them.

Part 7 (ss 88–111) Discipline, behaviour and exclusion

Chapter 1 (ss 88–96) School Discipline
Section 88 defines the responsibilities of the governing body for establishing the principles shaping a school's behaviour policy and s 89 defines the responsibilities of the head teacher for establishing and maintaining a behaviour policy for the school that promotes self-discipline, respect for others and proper regard for authority. 'Disciplinary penalty' is defined as a penalty imposed on a pupil by any school at which education is provided for him, where his conduct falls below the standard which could reasonably be expected of him: s 90. Provision is made under s 91 for the conditions that make lawful the imposition of a disciplinary penalty on a pupil at any school at which education is provided for him. Section 92 specifies the conditions that make the detention of a pupil outside school sessions lawful. A member of staff is enabled to use reasonable force to prevent a pupil from committing an offence, causing personal injury, damaging property or doing something that prejudices discipline at the school: s 93. By virtue of s 94, staff are protected against civil or criminal liability where a lawfully confiscated item is retained or disposed of. Section 95 provides for interpretation, and s 96 for consequential amendment.

Chapter 2 (ss 97–111) Parental responsibility and excluded pupils
Section 97 provides for voluntary parenting contracts between schools and local education authorities and parents to be used in cases of misbehaviour where the pupil has not been excluded. Parenting orders can be applied for by schools and in cases where a pupil has seriously misbehaved but not been excluded: s 98. Further provision is made under s 99 in relation to parenting contracts and parenting orders. Section 100 imposes a duty for schools to provide suitable full-time education to temporarily excluded pupils. Local education authorities are required to provide permanently excluded pupils with suitable full-time education: s 101. Under s 102 the Secretary of State, and the National Assembly may make regulations specifying the circumstances in which maintained schools, Academies, city technology colleges and city colleges for the technology of the arts must arrange reintegration interviews with the parents of temporarily excluded pupils, and the procedures and time limits connected with such an interview. Section 103 provides that it is an offence for a parent to fail to ensure that when their child is excluded, that the excluded pupil is not present in a public place during normal school hours on a day which is one of the first five school days to which the exclusion relates and is specified. Provision is made as to the notice the parent will receive from the school when their child is excluded: s 104. By virtue of s 105, a penalty notice may be given to a parent who appears to be guilty of an offence of failing to ensure their excluded child is not present in a public place. Section 106 provides for the Secretary of State to make regulations about the administration of penalty notices. Police Community Support Officers will be able to issue fixed penalty notices to parents of excluded pupils found in a public place during the first five days of exclusion: s 107. By virtue of s 108 police can remove excluded pupils from a public place to a designated place. Section 109 makes provision in relation to defences to offences that may be committed by a parent whose child fails to regularly attend a school at which he is a registered pupil. Local education authorities may use receipts from penalty notices for any of their functions specified in regulations, but any sums not so used must be paid to the Secretary of State. Definitions are provided for under s 111.

Part 8 (ss 112–159) Inspection and review of local authorities in England

Chapter 1 (ss 112–121) The Office and the Chief Inspector
Sections 112–121, Schs 11, 12 provide for the establishment and functions of the Office for Standards in Education, Children's Services and Skills and a new office of the Chief Inspector of Education, Children Services and Skills, Her Majesty's Inspectors of Education, Children's Services and Skills, the Children's Rights Director, and an annual report by the Chief Inspector to be provided for the Secretary of State.

Chapter 2 (ss 122) General Transfer of Functions
Section 122 provides for the general transfer to the Chief Inspector all functions of the existing Her Majesty's Chief Inspector of Schools in England, including inspections of schools, the inspection and regulation of child minding, day care and nursery education, inspection of independent schools and inspection of teacher training provision.

Chapter 3 (ss 123–134) Inspection of further education and training etc
Sections 123–133 provide for the inspection of further education colleges and other education and training providers, and for area inspections, which are concerned with the provision of education or training, in a specified area in England, for persons who are aged 15 or over but under 19. The Adult Learning Inspectorate is abolished as all of its inspection functions will in future be performed by the Chief Inspector: s 134.

Chapter 4 (ss 135–142) Inspection and review of local authorities in England
Sections 135–142 make provision for the Chief Inspector to undertake inspections and annual reviews of the performance of local authorities' functions, and sets out which of those functions are within the Chief Inspector's remit for these purposes.

Chapter 5 (ss 143–145) Inspection of CAFCASS functions
Sections 143–145 provide for powers of the Chief Inspector and that it is a duty for the Chief Inspector to inspect the performance of the Children and Family Court Advisory and Support Service ('CAFCASS') and is required to produce a written report of any inspection and send copies to the Secretary of State and CAFCASS.

Chapter 6 (ss 146–153) Further provision relating to the functions of Chief Inspector
Section 146 makes provision for the Secretary of State and the Chief Inspector to make arrangements for the inspection of secure training centres. The Secretary of State has the power to make regulations requiring the Chief Inspector to inspect adoption and fostering functions of a local authority on such occasions or at such intervals as the regulations specify: s 147. Functions of the Commission for Social Care Inspection as to the registration of children's homes, residential family centres, fostering agencies, voluntary adoption agencies, and adoption support agencies, are to be transferred, under s 148, to the Chief Inspector. Section 149, Sch 13 provide for the interaction between the Chief Inspector and other authorities. Any person who is authorised to exercise a power of entry or inspection on behalf of the Chief Inspector must, if required to do so, produce evidence of his authority to exercise the power: s 150. For the purposes of the law of defamation, under s 151, a report made by the Chief Inspector is privileged unless shown to have been made with malice. By virtue of s 152, the Chief Inspector may combine the reports of inspections carried out under two or more of his inspection functions, and to produce them as a combined report. Section 153 enables information obtained in connection with one of the Chief Inspector's functions to be used in connection with any other of his functions.

Chapter 7 (ss 154–159) Miscellaneous and supplementary
Section 154 provides new elements covering community cohesion which must be covered by inspection reports for schools. The Secretary of State may make regulations requiring a local authority in England to pay a fee to the Office in respect of its relevant functions and the Chief Inspector may make a scheme setting the fee level for periods when no regulations made by the Secretary of State are in force: s 155. Under s 156, the Chief Inspector no longer has the duty to inspect and report on the carrying out of the functions of the National Assembly in respect of family proceedings. Section 157 introduces Sch 14 which provides for minor and consequential amendments, and s 158 introduces Sch 15 which provides for transitional provision, while s 159 provides for interpretation.

Part 9 (ss 160–177) Miscellaneous
Section 160 makes provision in relation to the Chief Inspector's power to investigate complaints made by parents about schools. Provision is made in relation to innovation orders made by the Secretary of State or the National Assembly: s 161, Sch 16. Under s 162 the Secretary of State and the National Assembly, subject to specified conditions, have the power to repeal references in primary and secondary legislation to the terms 'local education authority' and 'children's services authority'. Section 163 makes provision in relation to the advice on such matters relating to the admission of pupils to relevant schools that an adjudicator is required to provide on request by the Secretary of State. The Department for Education and Skills is enabled to collect individual information about children receiving education funded by the local education authority otherwise than at a school: s 164. Members of staff, under s 165, have the power to use reasonable force in order to prevent a student at the institution from committing an offence, causing personal injury, damaging property or doing something that prejudices discipline at the institution. Section 166 provides for regulations that enable the governing bodies of maintained schools to make collaboration arrangements with further education bodies, and further education bodies to make collaboration arrangements with schools and with other further education bodies. Local authorities and governing bodies of maintained nursery schools must have regard to guidance issued by the Secretary of State about consultation with pupils on decisions affecting them: s167. Under s 168, the

Secretary of State or the National Assembly may issue a direction or make an order if the governing bodies of maintained nursery schools are unreasonably exercising, or are in default with regard to, their functions. Sections 169–171 make provision in relation to the prohibition or restriction of unsuitable persons from taking part in the management of independent schools. Provision is made in relation to offences committed in connection with independent schools: s 172. By virtue of s 173, the governing bodies of community, foundation or voluntary schools, as well as maintained nursery schools, have a duty to designate a member of the school staff as the person responsible for co-ordinating provision for children with special educational needs at the school, and the Secretary of State has the power to make regulations requiring governing bodies to ensure the special educational needs co-ordinators have certain experience or qualifications or both, and to confer other functions on these governing bodies relating to special educational needs co-ordinators. Section 174 makes further provision about the circumstances in which regulations may prescribe time-limits within which local education authorities must take certain steps in connection with assessments and statements of special educational needs. Provision is made for minor amendments relating to schools in Wales: s 175, Sch 17. The Learning and Skills Council, under s 175, has a power to manage and fund particular types of support for learners aged between 10 and 15, for the purpose of encouraging them to undergo education and training. Section 177 enables university bodies who are landlords, on the acquisition of the freehold by, or the granting of an extended lease to, a tenant, to impose with the consent of the Secretary of State or the National Assembly, restrictive covenants on tenants for the purpose of reserving the relevant land for possible development by that body or a related university body.

Part 10 (ss 178–191) General
Sections 178–180 makes provision in relation to the powers and functions of the National Assembly. General provision is made under s 181 for orders and regulations, under s182 for Parliamentary control of orders and regulations, under s 183 for consequential and transitional provisions, s 184 and Sch 18 for repeals, s 185 for financial provisions, s 186 for abbreviations of Acts, s 187 for interpretation, ss 188, 189 for commencement, s 190 for extent, and s 191 for short title.

Amendments, repeals and revocations
The list below, which is not exhaustive, mentions repeals and amendments which are or will be effective when the Act is fully in force.
Specific provisions of a number of Acts are amended or repealed. These include: Local Government Act 1972, s 177(1A)(b); Local Government Act 1974, s 25(5)(a); Children Act 1989 ss 26ZA, 79R(4); Employment Act 1989, s 26; Higher Education Act 1992 s 85C; Education Act 1996 ss 13A, 14(3A), 14A, 436A, 507A, 507B, 508A–508F, 509AD, 537B, 550A, 550B, 444; Education Act 1997 ss 4, 5; School Standards and Framework Act 1998 ss 15(7), 23A, 23B, 24, 27, 28, 28A, 31, 47A(6), 58(4), 61, 88A, 89D, 90(6), (7), (10), 90A, 95A–97D, 99(1), 114A, 127(5), (6), Sch 4; Care Standards Act 2000 s 45(4); Learning and Skills Act 2000 ss 3A–3D, 11A, 52–72, 90, 151(2), Schs 6, 10 Pt 3; Education Act 2002 s 2(7), (8), 85, 85A, 159(3), 162A(4), 162B(8), 167A–167D, 168A–168C, 178(3); Anti-social Behaviour Act 2003 s 21(4), 22A; Courts Act 2003 s 58(6); Health and Social Care (Community Health and Standards) Act 2003 ss 77(3), 79(7), 80(5), 110, 112, 116(1); Children Act 2004 ss 24, 38; Education Act 2005 ss 1–4, 11A–11C, 64–67, 69(a), 73, Schs 1, 10, 11; Childcare Act 2006 ss 14, 31, 50(4), 61(4), 80, 81.

1103   Further education—awards—mandatory awards

The Education (Mandatory Awards) (Amendment) Regulations 2006, SI 2006/930 (in force in part on 30 April 2006, and in part on 1 September 2006), further amend the 2003 Regulations, SI 2003/1994 and amend the 2005 Regulations, SI 2005/2083, so as to (1) provide that (a) the prescribed new payment rates will only apply in relation to an academic term which commences on or after 1 September 2006; and (b) where an academic year starts before 1 September 2005, but ends after 1 September 2006, the old payment and new payment rates shall be applied proportionally; (2) specify increases in the rates of fee awards in relation to courses at the University of Buckingham, the Guildhall School of Music and Heythrop College; (3) provide for increases in relation to other fee awards and grants; and (4) implement European Parliament and EC Council Directive 2004/38 by setting out all of the categories of person who are potentially eligible for a mandatory award.

1104   Further education—designated institutions—Workers' Educational Association

The Education (Designated Institutions in Further Education) (Amendment) Order 2006, SI 2006/408 (in force on 31 March 2006), amends the 1993 Order, SI 1993/435, so as to remove the Workers' Educational Association from the scope of the 1993 Order.

The Workers' Educational Association (Designated Institution in Further Education) Order 2006, SI 2006/409 (in force on 31 March 2006), redesignates the Workers' Educational Association, London EC2 for the purposes of the Further and Higher Education Act 1992 s 28.

1105   Further education—further education corporations—Wales

The Government of Further Education Corporations (Revocation) (Wales) Regulations 2006, SI 2006/621 (in force on 6 April 2006), revoke prescribed initial instruments and articles of government for further education corporations. SI 1992/1957 and 1992/1963 are revoked, in relation to Wales. SI 1994/1450 is revoked.

1106   Further education—providers of education—England

The Further Education (Providers of Education) (England) Regulations 2006, SI 2006/3199 (in force on 1 January 2007), require certain conditions to be complied with in respect of persons providing education at further education institutions in England. In particular, the regulations (1) provide that where a person will be regularly caring for, training, supervising or being solely in charge of persons under 18, there is a requirement for an enhanced criminal record check; in addition, if it is considered that by reason of the person having lived outside the United Kingdom, an enhanced criminal record check is not sufficient for the purposes of considering his suitability for a position working with under 18s, further checks, as may be considered appropriate, must be carried out, having regard to guidance issued by the Secretary of State; (2) provide that a person is exempt from the requirement to have an enhanced criminal record check and, where applicable, further checks outside the United Kingdom, where he has worked with under 18s in a school or further education institution in England within the preceding three-month period; (3) provide that where a person is to be appointed by the governing body of the institution, the governing body is required to carry out the checks; (4) provide that where a person is supplied by an employment business, including a local authority, to provide education at an institution, the governing body must not accept that person to work at the institution until written confirmation has been received from the employment business that all the relevant checks have been carried out; (5) provide that the governing body must also ensure that its contract or other arrangements with the employment business include provisions requiring the employment business to carry out the checks; and (6) provide that the governing body of an institution must also maintain a register of all persons providing education at the institution; the register must show whether the listed checks have been carried out or the relevant written confirmations received in respect of each person providing education and the dates that the checks were completed or confirmations received.

1107   Further education—student loans—repayment

The Education (Student Loans) (Repayment) (Amendment) Regulations 2006, SI 2006/2009 (in force on 1 September 2006), amend the 2000 Regulations, SI 2000/944, so as to (1) provide that, in relation to England only, certain categories of borrowers will have their students loans written off 25 years after they became liable to repay; (2) provide that the Secretary of State may impose penalties on borrowers who fail to comply with requests for information; (3) provide that where a borrower fails to provide information or to comply with a penalty notice, the Secretary of State may require him to repay his loan in full; and (4) provide for, in relation to England only, the repayment of student loans by borrowers who move overseas following their courses of higher education.

1108   Further education—student support—European institutions—England

The Assembly Learning Grants (European Institutions) Regulations 2006, SI 2006/3156 (in force on 31 December 2006), replace, in relation to England, SI 2000/2197, and make provision for the grant of support to students in connection with their attendance at a qualifying course at the College of Europe, the European University Institute or the Bologna Centre. SI 2006/953 and 1785 are revoked.

1109   Further education—student support—European institutions—Wales

The Assembly Learning Grants (European Institutions) (Wales) Regulations 2006, SI 2006/1794 (in force on 7 July 2006), replace, in relation to Wales, SI 2000/2197, and make provision for the grant of support to students in connection with their attendance at a qualifying course at the College of Europe, the European University Institute or the Bologna Centre.

1110   General Teaching Council for Wales—functions

The General Teaching Council for Wales (Additional Functions) (Amendment) Order 2006, SI 2006/1341 (in force on 31 May 2006), further amends the 2000 Order, SI 2000/1941, so as to (1) add persons ineligible for registration because the General Teaching Council for Wales is not satisfied as to their suitability to be teachers to the categories of persons in respect of which the Council must maintain records; and (2) require the Council to include in its records particulars of the grounds on which it is decided that a person is not suitable to be a teacher.

The General Teaching Council for Wales (Functions) (Amendment) Regulations 2006, SI 2006/1343 (in force on 31 May 2006), further amend the 2000 Regulations, SI 2000/1979, so as to (1) make provision for the application by the General Teaching Council for Wales ('the Council') of decisions made by the General Teaching Council for England in relation to a person's suitability to be a teacher; (2) require the Council to send a notice to all applicants for registration with its decision as to whether to register an applicant and provide that, where the Council refuses to register an applicant, the notice must explain the grounds for the decision and the right of appeal; (3) confer a right of appeal to the High Court on any person who has been refused registration on the grounds of suitability; and (4) provide for information as to suitability decisions to be provided to employers and to the General Teaching Councils for Scotland and Northern Ireland, and require such information to include details as to (a) where the person is registered, the date of registration on which the Council decided that the person was suitable to be a teacher; (b) where the Council decide that the person was not suitable, that fact; and (c) where the information is provided to the Scottish or Northern Ireland General Teaching Council, particulars of the grounds on which that decision was based.

1111   Grants and loans—assembly learning grants and loans—higher education—Wales

The Assembly Learning Grants and Loans (Higher Education) (Wales) Regulations 2006, SI 2006/126 (in force on 1 March 2006), provide for financial support for students who are ordinarily resident in Wales taking designated higher education courses. In particular, the regulations (1) introduce a distinction between old system eligible students and new system eligible students in relation to financial support to students for full-time courses; (2) provide that, to qualify for financial support, a student must fall within one of the listed categories and the specified eligibility provisions; (3) provide that support is only available under the regulations in respect of designated courses; (4) introduce new rules on previous study; the number of years of support available is reduced by the number of years of previously supported higher education; the National Assembly for Wales will be able to extend eligibility where there are compelling personal reasons for doing so in respect of the student concerned; (5) provide that students who have an honours degree qualification from a higher education institution in the United Kingdom will not be eligible for support under the regulations, but students undertaking a second degree course which leads to professional qualification as a social worker, medical doctor, dentist, veterinary doctor, architect, landscape architect, landscape designer, town planner or town and country planner will still be eligible for a maintenance loan; (6) amend the definition of 'end-on course' so that students going end-on from a foundation degree which started prior to 1 September 2006 to an honours degree will be treated as old system eligible students; (7) make provision for applications for support and time limits for applications, and specify the information that must be provided by applicants; (8) make provision for the grant for fees available to old system eligible students; (9) make new provision for loans for fees; (10) make provision for grants for living costs; (10) make provision for a special support grant for new system eligible students who are also eligible for income support and other means tested benefits such as housing benefit; (11) make provision for loans for living costs; (12) make provision for financial assessment of students for the calculation of the eligible student's contribution; (13) make provision for payment of grants and loans; (14) make provision for support for part-time courses; and (15) make provision for postgraduate students with disabilities. SI 2005/52 is revoked in relation to Wales.

The Assembly Learning Grants and Loans (Higher Education) (Wales) (Amendment) Regulations 2006, SI 2006/1863 (in force on 14 July 2006), amend the principal 2006 Regulations supra and implement EC European Parliament and Council Directive 2004/38 on the rights of European Community nationals and their families to move and reside in other member states. In particular, the regulations (1) introduce new categories of students who may potentially be eligible for support towards their tuition fees and/or maintenance support, which include (a) European Community nationals and their family members who acquire the right of permanent residence in the United Kingdom after a continuous period of five years residence in the United Kingdom; (b) family members of economically inactive European Community nationals who have yet to acquire the right of permanent residence; (c) European Economic Area or Swiss self-employed persons and their family members; (d) dependent direct relatives in the ascending line of the European Economic Area or Swiss migrant workers; (e) frontier workers and frontier self-employed persons; and (f) children of Swiss nationals, their spouses or their civil partners; (2) introduce a new form of support namely a loan in respect of the college fees payable by a qualifying student to a college or permanent private hall of the University of Oxford or to a college of the University of Cambridge in connection with his or her attendance on a qualifying course; (3) clarify that references in the principal 2006 Regulations to the Secretary of State are to be read as, or as including, references to the National Assembly for Wales; (4) amend the duration of period of eligibility in relation to certain categories of eligible students; (5) change the study rules; (6) provide that a grant or loan for fees may not exceed the fees payable by the student and that to receive a loan the student must enter into a contract with the National Assembly; (7) amend the rules in relation to eligibility for a special support grant; (8) amend the rules in relation to eligibility of part-time students so that the National Assembly now has a reserve power to confer eligibility in a case not otherwise expressly covered, bringing the rules in line with those for full-time students; (9) amend the amounts to be deducted when calculating support for part-time courses; and (10) amend the rules governing financial assessment of students' contributions to financial support.

1112   Higher education—fees and awards—England

The Education (Fees and Awards) (Amendment) Regulations 2006, SI 2006/483 (in force on 31 March 2006), further amend the 1997 Regulations, SI 1997/1972, so as to ensure that certain categories of person who were not formerly entitled to equal treatment with nationals of the United Kingdom with regards to tuition fees and maintenance support are so entitled to equal treatment.

1113   Higher education—fees and awards—Wales

The Education (Fees and Awards) (Amendment) (Wales) Regulations 2006, SI 2006/1795 (in force on 7 July 2006), further amend the 1997 Regulations, SI 1997/1972, so as to ensure that certain categories of person who were not formerly entitled to equal treatment with nationals of the United Kingdom with regards to tuition fees and maintenance support are so entitled to equal treatment.

1114   Higher education—student fees—amounts—England

The Student Fees (Amounts) (England) (Amendment) Regulation 2006, SI 2006/2382, (in force on 1 September 2007), amend the 2004 Regulations, SI 2004/1932, by increasing the basic and higher amounts which ordinarily apply and the lower basic and higher amounts that apply to specified courses.

1115   Higher education—student fees—qualifying course and persons—England

Student Fees (Qualifying Courses and Persons) Regulations 2006, SI 2006/482 (in force on 31 March 2006), designate the qualifying courses and qualifying persons who cannot be charged fees that exceed the basic or higher fee amounts applicable to the course set by the Student Fees (Amounts) (England) Regulations 2004, SI 2004/1932.

1116   Higher education—student support—maintenance

The Education (Student Support) Regulations 2006, SI 2006/119 (in force on 1 March 2006), (1) provide to eligible students taking designated full-time courses (a) fee support, with the effect that new system students are eligible for a fee loan and old system students are eligible for a grant for fees and a fee contribution loan; and (b) grants for living and other costs in the form of a maintenance or a special support grant where the student is eligible for certain social security benefits; (2) raise the age limit for qualifying for a loan for living costs to 60; (3) provide (a) for payment of support and recovery of overpayments, including for the Secretary of State to be able to request information from an applicant that is needed to assist with the recovery of a loan and can withhold payment of the loan until that information is supplied, an institution being required to send to the Secretary of State an attendance confirmation in respect of an eligible student; (b) that disabled students who are undertaking a designated full-time course but who are unable to attend for a reason relating to their disability are eligible for fee support, the loan for living costs, the grant for dependents, the higher education grant or the maintenance grant or special support grant; and (c) that the Secretary of State is able to make fee support available to eligible part time students. Provision is made for a new procedure to apply for support for part-time courses, requiring the institution to provide a declaration to accompany a student's application providing details about the course and confirming that the student has undertaken at least two weeks or has enrolled to undertake the course. The regulations also (i) set out the method for calculating the household income of a student taking a designated full-time course to find the contribution to be made, which can then be applied to reduce some types of support available; and (ii) revise the definition of 'independent' to include a student who has the care of a child on the first day of the academic year. SI 2005/5, as amended, is revoked.

The Education (Student Support) (Amendment) Regulations 2006, SI 2006/955 (in force on 30 April 2006), amend the 2005 Regulations, SI 2005/52, and SI 2006/119 supra, implement European Parliament and EC Council Directive 2004/38 on the rights of citizens of the European Union and their family members to move and reside freely in the territory of member states so far as the Directive relates to student support. In particular, the regulations (1) allow certain categories of person who were not formerly eligible for student support, to be eligible; (2) take into account the circumstances of students who are settled in the United Kingdom and who have exercised a right of residence within the territory comprising the European Economic Area and Switzerland; (3) remove transitional provisions relating to the introduction of civil partnerships that are now redundant; (4) provide that a student cannot qualify for an adult dependants' grant in respect of an adult dependant or his partner if that adult dependant or partner is an eligible student in his own right or holds a statutory award; (5) provide that a student cannot qualify for a parents' learning allowance in respect of his dependent child if that child is an eligible student in his own right or holds a statutory award; (6) introduce a new form of support in the form of a loan in respect of college fees payable by a qualifying student to a college or permanent private hall of the University of Oxford or to a college of the University of Cambridge in connection with his attendance on a qualifying course; and (7) amend one of the grounds on which a student is treated as an independent student for the purposes of the financial assessment.

The Education (Student Support) (Amendment) (No 2) Regulations 2006, SI 2006/1745 (in force on 1 August 2006), further amend SI 2006/119 in relation to England, to take account of the fact that the Guildhall School of Music and Drama will cease to be a private institution as a result of being designated under the Education Reform Act 1988 s 129 as an institution eligible to receive support from funds administered by the Higher Education Funding Council for England.

1117 Higher education—student support—supply of information—general provisions

The Education (Supply of Student Support Information to Governing Bodies) Regulations 2006, SI 2006/141 (in force on 1 March 2006), (1) enable the Secretary of State, the Student Loans Company and local authorities to whom student support functions have been transferred to supply information in connection with an application for student support by a student or his sponsors to governing bodies of institutions providing courses which are designated for the purposes of the student support scheme; (2) enable those authorities to supply to governing bodies information which is derived from such an application, such as whether a student is an eligible student within the meaning of the student support scheme or the amount of student support payable to a student under that scheme; (3) provide that such information may only be supplied for the purpose of assisting governing bodies to determine whether a student who has applied for student support is eligible for a bursary or other form of financial assistance offered by the relevant institution and the amount of the bursary or other financial assistance payable to that student and also, if relevant, to make a necessary payment to a student; and (4) provide that no information may be supplied without (a) in the case of information provided by an applicant or derived from an application, the applicant's consent; and (b) in the case of information provided by a sponsor, the sponsor's consent.

1118 Higher education—student support—supply of information—Wales

The Supply of Student Support Information to Governing Bodies (Wales) Regulations 2006, SI 2006/2828 (in force on 27 October 2006), (1) enable a student support authority to supply information in relation to an application for student support by either the student concerned or his or her sponsors to governing bodies of institutions which provide courses designated for the purposes of the student support scheme; (2) provide that such information may only be supplied for the purpose of assisting governing bodies to determine whether a student who has applied for student support is eligible for a bursary or other financial support; and (3) provide that no such information may be supplied without, in the case of information provided by the applicant or derived from the application, the applicant's consent or, in the case of information provided by the sponsor, the sponsor's consent.

1119 Higher Education Act 2004—commencement

The Higher Education Act 2004 (Commencement No 4) Order 2006, SI 2006/51, brings into force, on 14 January 2006, ss 23, 24 (so far as not already in force), 25, 43, 45, 50 (in part), certain repeals in Sch 7 and, in relation to England only, s 49 (in part), Sch 6 paras 7–9.

The Higher Education Act 2004 (Commencement No 2 and Transitional Provision) (Wales) (Amendment) Order 2006, SI 2006/1660, amends the Higher Education Act 2004 (Commencement No 2 and Transitional Provision) (Wales) Order 2005, SI 2005/1833, so that s 44(4) comes into force on 23 June 2006 instead of on 1 September 2006.

For a summary of the Act, see 2004 Abr para 1054. See also the commencement table in the title STATUTES.

1120 Independent schools—assisted places scheme—incidental expenses—England

The Education (Assisted Places) (Incidental Expenses) (Amendment) (England) Regulations 2006, SI 2006/1813 (in force on 1 September 2006), further amend the 1997 Regulations, SI 1997/1969, in relation to England, by revising the means test for determining eligibility to a uniform grant and increasing the amount of such grant in respect of clothing expenditure. Where the relevant income does not exceed £12,470, £83 is payable and where the relevant income exceeds that figure but does not exceed £13,431, £43 is payable. The 2006 Regulations also amend the means test for determining eligibility to a travel grant and increase the amount of grant payable in respect of school travel expenditure. Where the relevant income does not exceed £12,483, the travel grant will be of an amount equal to the school travel expenditure to which it relates. Where the relevant income exceeds that sum, the travel grant will be the amount, if any, by which the school travel expenditure to which it relates exceeds an amount, rounded down to the nearest multiple of £3, equal to one-twelfth of that part of the relevant income which exceeds £12,304.

1121 Independent schools—assisted places scheme—incidental expenses—Wales

The Education (Assisted Places) (Incidental Expenses) (Amendment) (Wales) Regulations 2006, SI 2006/3098 (in force on 23 November 2006), further amend the 1997 Regulations, SI 1997/1969, in relation to Wales, by revising the means test for determining eligibility to uniform grant and increasing the amount of such grant payable in respect of clothing expenditure. Where the relevant income does not exceed £12,470, £83 is payable and where the relevant income exceeds that figure but does not exceed £13,431, £43 is payable. The regulations also amend the means test for determining eligibility to travel grant, and increase the amount of grant payable in respect of school travel expenditure. Where the relevant income does not exceed £12,483, any travel grant will be an amount equal to the school travel expenditure to which it relates. Where the relevant income exceeds that sum, the travel grant will be the amount, if any, by which the school travel expenditure to which it relates exceeds an amount, rounded down to the nearest multiple of £3, equal to one-twelfth of that part of the relevant income which exceeds £12,304.

1122 Independent schools—assisted places scheme—relevant income—England

The Education (Assisted Places) (Amendment) (England) Regulations 2006, SI 2006/1812 (in force on 1 September 2006), further amend the 1997 Regulations, SI 1997/1968, in respect of the school year beginning on or after 1 September 2006, with the effect that (1) the deduction to be made to relevant income in respect of dependent relatives is increased from £1,575 to £1,625; and (2) the level of income at or below which fees are to be wholly remitted is increased from £12,182 to £12,470, with corresponding increases being made in the extent of remission where relevant income exceeds that sum.

1123 Independent schools—assisted places scheme—relevant income—Wales

The Education (Assisted Places) (Amendment) (Wales) Regulations 2006, SI 2006/3097 (in force on 23 November 2006), further amend the 1997 Regulations, SI 1997/1968, in relation to a school year beginning on or after 1 September 2006, by increasing (1) from £1,575 to £1,625 the deduction to be made in relevant income in respect of dependent relatives; and (2) from £12,182 to £12,470 the level at which, or below which, fees are to be wholly remitted, with corresponding increases in the extent of the remission where relevant income exceeds that sum.

1124 Inspectors of schools—England

The Education (Inspectors of Schools in England) (No 4) Order 2006, SI 2006/2658 (in force on 1 November 2006), appoints as Her Majesty's Inspectors of Schools in England the persons named in the order.

1125 Local education authority—action concerning matters in school—investigation of complaint

See *R (on the application of M) v Comr for Local Administration in England*, para 1856.

1126 Local education authority—budget statements—England

The Education (Budget Statements) (England) Regulations 2006, SI 2006/511 (in force on 27 March 2006), prescribe the form and content of the budget statement of a local education authority in England for the financial years 2006–07 and 2007–08 and for the earlier funding period comprising the financial year 2005–06.

1127 Local education authority—outturn statements—England

The Education (Outturn Statements) (England) Regulations 2006, SI 2006/1760 (in force on 28 July 2006), prescribe the form and contents of the outturn statement of a local education authority in England under the School Standards and Framework Act 1998 s 52(2), for the financial year beginning on 1 April 2005. The statement gives details of expenditure by the local education authority, and of other resources allocated by them to schools which they maintain. SI 2005/1386 is revoked.

1128 Local education authority—performance targets—England

The Education (Local Education Authority Performance Targets) (England) (Amendment) Regulations 2006, SI 2006/3150 (in force on 28 December 2006), amend the 2005 Regulations, SI 2005/2450, so as to (1) require targets to be set for the proportion of pupils aged 15 to achieve the level 2 threshold in approved external qualifications; and (2) require separate targets to be set in connection with (a) those pupils aged 15 who will have been looked after by the local authority for a continual period of 12 months by the end of the relevant school year; and (b) those pupils within an ethnic group where there are more than 30 pupils within the relevant group.

1129 Local education authority—proposals to re-organise school structure—consultation requirements

The defendant council wished to change the system of state education in its area from a three-tier system to a two-tier system. A number of parents who opposed the closure of middle schools formed the applicant association, which was involved in the statutory consultation process. The initial stages of the consultation process involved county-wide consultation of the general principle of whether a two-tier system should be adopted, with no consultation on the implications for specific schools.

The final stage focussed on specific schools, but the consultation was confined to the consideration of different two-tier models. The applicant sought judicial review of the consultation process on the ground that it precluded proper consultation on the alteration or closure of individual schools. *Held*, in order to comply with the consultation requirements of the School Standards and Framework Act 1998 ss 28 and 29, consultation had to be undertaken when the proposals in question were still at a formative stage. Under the defendant's consultation process, there was no consultation on the implications of the proposals during the initial stages for specific schools. During the final stage, the proposals were no longer at a formative stage because the defendant had precluded any public discussion of anything other than two-tier models. It followed that the consultees had been denied any opportunity to express their views as to whether a specific school should be part of a two-tier system or remain as part of the three-tier system. The effect was that the objectors had not been afforded any opportunity to present their case against closure of particular middle schools. Further, irrespective of the statutory consultation requirements, fairness required a consultation process in which those consulted should be permitted to express their views on whether specific schools should form part of a two-tier or three-tier system. Accordingly, the application would be allowed.

R (on the application of Parents for Legal Action Ltd) v Northumberland CC [2006] EWHC 1081 (Admin), [2006] LGR 646 (Queen's Bench Division: Mumby J).

1130   Maintained schools—change of category—England

The Education (Change of Category of Maintained Schools) (Amendment) (England) Regulations 2006, SI 2006/1164 (in force on 31 May 2006), further amend the 2000 Regulations, SI 2000/2195, for the purpose of adding Sch 2B of the regulations into the 2000 Regulations so as to rectify the fact that the 2005 Regulations, SI 2005/1731 failed to give effect to it.

The Education (Change of Category of Maintained Schools) (Amendment) (No 2) (England) Regulations 2006, SI 2006/1507 (in force on 1 August 2006), further amend the 2000 Regulations supra with the effect that the statutory provisions dealing with proposals for a school to change category now apply to primary community and voluntary controlled schools as well as secondary schools.

1131   Maintained schools—staffing—England

The School Staffing (England) (Amendment) Regulations 2006, SI 2006/1067 (in force on 12 May 2006), further amend the 2003 Regulations, SI 2003/1963, so as to require that, subject to exceptions, supply teachers employed by local education authorities or a person appointed to be a teacher or member of the support staff must, prior to or as soon as practicable after, his appointment be subject to an enhanced Criminal Records Bureau check made under the Police Act 1997.

The School Staffing (England) (Amendment) (No 2) Regulations 2006, SI 2006/3197 (in force on 1 January 2007), further amend the 2003 Regulations supra so as to require (1) the checking of a person's identity and right to work in the United Kingdom; (2) the keeping by schools of a register of such checks in respect of their own staff and supply staff; (3) the carrying out by local education authorities of the same checks on supply and school meals staff whom they appoint; (4) schools, in their arrangements with agencies, to place a teacher or member of support staff supplied by an agency under an obligation to provide confirmation that checks have been carried out on such workers so as to allow them to work at a school; and (5) that a person be subject to an enhanced Criminal Records Bureau check if he moves from a post which did not bring him regularly into contact with children or young persons to one which does bring him into such contact at the same school.

1132   Maintained schools—staffing—Wales

The Staffing of Maintained Schools (Wales) Regulations 2006, SI 2006/873 (in force in part on 1 April 2006 and in part on 1 September 2006), which make provision for the staffing of maintained schools, (1) cover general matters and in particular the delegation of authority, the performance of the head teacher, the conduct and discipline of staff, the capability of teachers and the provision of staff for community facilities and services; (2) deal with the appointment, suspension and dismissal of staff, a local education authority's entitlement to offer advice and the appointment of school meals staff, in relation to community, voluntary controlled, community special and maintained nursery schools; (3) deal with the appointment, suspension and dismissal of staff, the entitlement of a local education authority and appropriate diocesan authorities to offer advice and the appointment of head teachers for schools of Roman Catholic religious orders, in relation to foundation, voluntary aided and foundation special schools; and (4) relate to the staffing of new schools either with or without delegated budgets.

1133   Maintained schools—transition from primary to secondary schools—Wales

The Transition from Primary to Secondary School (Wales) Regulations 2006, SI 2006/520 (in force on 1 September 2006), make provision in relation to schools for which transition plans are required. In particular, the regulations (1) provide that in determining whether a primary school is a feeder school, regard is to be had to guidance issued by the National Assembly for Wales; (2) make provision for the determination of disputes by the National Assembly; (3) provide for the form, content and publication of transition plans; (4) make provision as to when the first plans must be drawn up and published and as to the first cohort of pupils to be covered; (5) provide for the review of plans and, where necessary or desirable; and (6) make provision as to the manner in which plans are to be published; and (7) require copies of plans to be sent to the local education authority or authorities by which the schools are maintained and to anyone who requests a copy.

1134   National Curriculum—disapplication of science—key stage 4—Wales

The Education (National Curriculum for Wales) (Disapplication of Science at Key Stage 4) Regulations 2006, SI 2006/1335 (in force on 1 August 2006), provide that the requirement that key stage 4 of the National Curriculum for Wales is to comprise science and is to specify attainment targets, programmes of study and assessment arrangements for that subject, is not to apply to a pupil at a maintained school where the head teacher of the school is satisfied that the pupil is pursuing a course leading to the award of an approved external qualification in science from the National Qualifications Framework at entry level one or two.

1135   National Curriculum—exceptions—key stage 4—England

The Education (National Curriculum) (Exceptions at Key Stage 4) (Revocation and Savings) (England) Regulations 2006, SI 2006/2495 (in force on 9 October 2006), revoke the 2003 Regulations, SI 2003/252, as amended, in relation to England, with the effect that the National Curriculum relating to science is no longer disapplied at key stage 4 where a pupil is participating in an extended work-related learning programme.

1136   Pupil—exclusion of pupil—appeal against exclusions—England

The Education (Pupil Exclusions and Appeals) (Miscellaneous Amendments) (England) Regulations 2006, SI 2006/2189 (in force on 6 September 2006), in relation to England, (1) further amend the Education (Pupils Exclusions and Appeals) (Maintained Schools) (England) Regulations 2002, SI 2002/3178, and the Education (Pupil Exclusions and Appeals) (Pupil Referral Units) (England) Regulations 2002, SI 2002/3179, so as to (a) provide that the head teacher of a school which has more than three terms per year must report exclusions which he is not already required to report broadly as often as head teachers of schools with three terms per year, who must report these exclusions at least every term; and (b) make provision for the disqualification of a person from being a member of an appeal panel if he does not satisfy training requirements; (c) provide that in relation to the procedure on appeal (i) the claimant and head teacher may make written representations, appear and make oral representations and be represented or accompanied by a friend; and (ii) the governing body and local education authority may make written representations, appear and make oral representations and be represented; and (2) further amend SI 2002/3178 so as to (a) provide that an appeal panel may appoint a clerk to the appeal panel who meets the training requirements; (b) specify the training requirements to be met by clerks, which are the same as for members of appeal panels; and (c) make provision for a clerk or member of an appeal panel who has acted in that capacity within the year preceding the 6 September 2006 to continue to act in that capacity but he must meet the training requirements if he is to continue acting after two years of that date.

1137   Pupil—exclusion of pupil—parenting orders—Wales

The Education (Parenting Orders) (Wales) Regulations 2006, SI 2006/1277 (in force on 11 May 2006), prescribe the conditions to be met before a local education authority may apply to a magistrates' court for a parenting order under the Anti-social Behaviour Act 2003 s 20. The conditions are that an application must not be made more than six months after the last occasion on which a pupil was excluded and must be made within the relevant period and, in the case of a pupil excluded for a fixed term, he must have been excluded at least twice in a 12-month period.

1138   Pupil—exclusion of pupil—refusal to wear school uniform—religious belief

See *R (on the application of Begum) v Headteacher and Governors of Denbigh High School*, para 1547.

1139   Pupil—exclusion of pupil—right to education

See *A v Head Teacher and Governors of Lord Grey School*, para 1553.

1140   Pupil—failure to attend school—prosecution of parent—knowledge of parent—burden of proof

The Education Act 1996 s 444(1A) provides that where a parent of a registered pupil at a school who is failing to attend regularly at that school knows that his child is failing to attend regularly at that school and fails without reasonable justification to cause him to do so, he is guilty of an offence.

The defendant's son was absent without authorisation from the school at which he was a registered pupil on 99 occasions out of a possible 122. The defendant was aware that her son was not attending school and had initiated several meetings with the school education welfare department, as well as contacting social services. The defendant's son made it clear that he would not attend school. On one occasion she had tried to physically drag him there, but he was much larger than the defendant and had fought her off. The view of the head of the year was that there was little more that the defendant could do that she had not already done in order to secure her son's attendance at school. The justices were of the opinion that the duty of a parent to ensure regular school attendance was almost a matter of strict liability and that it was for the defence to show, on the balance of probabilities, that the defendant had taken all reasonable steps and explored all possible avenues to ensure that her son was receiving regular schooling. The defendant was convicted of an offence under the 1996 Act s 444(1A). She sought judicial review of the decision on the basis that the court had misdirected itself in deciding that there was a burden of proof imposed on the defendant to establish a reasonable justification for her failure to secure her son's attendance at school. *Held*, if Parliament wished to make it plain that there was to be a legal burden of proof on a defendant, it would have said so in clear terms. There was no such wording in s 444(1A), which created an evidential burden. Once material was placed before the justices which could constitute a reasonable justification, the justices had to consider that material and could only convict if they were satisfied to the criminal standard of proof that there was no reasonable justification. The justices had been wrong to decide that the legal burden of proof rested with the defence. If they had applied their minds to the matter in a proper fashion and concluded that the burden of proof remained on the prosecution once the defendant had raised matters in evidence that were put before them, they would have been bound to reach a conclusion that she was not guilty of the offence under s 444(1A). Accordingly, the application would be granted and the conviction quashed.

R (on the application of P) v Liverpool City Magistrates [2006] EWHC 887 (Admin), [2006] ELR 386 (Queen's Bench Division: Collins J).

1141   Pupil—failure to attend school—prosecution of parent—reasons for absence

The appellant local education authority alleged that the respondent had failed to secure the regular attendance of her three children at primary school, contrary to the Education Act 1996 s 444(1). At trial, evidence was given which showed that the children had attended between 72 and 78 days out of a possible 114 days' attendance. The respondent had taken the children away from school for two holidays, for which leave had not been granted, which accounted for 18 days. The court decided that the respondent ought to have exercised more care regarding the absences for holidays during term time, but that those absences were justified and that the respondent had provided good and cogent reasons for the other absences. The respondent was acquitted, and the appellant appealed. *Held*, as the offence under s 444(1) was absolute, the justices were required to decide merely whether the children had failed, as a matter of fact, to attend school regularly. The reasons for those absences were irrelevant except for the purposes of computing the period to be considered, which was a question of fact and degree for the justices. Moreover, it was not for the justices to consider whether leave might have been justified, since s 444(3) made it plain that leave meant leave granted by the school. It followed that the justices had been wrong to consider whether the holidays, which were not authorised, were justified. The only reasonable conclusion on the facts was that the children had not attended school regularly. Accordingly, the appeal would be allowed.

Bromley LBC v C [2006] All ER (D) 80 (Mar) (Queen's Bench Division: Auld LJ and Sullivan J).

1142   Pupil—individual pupil information—England

The Education (Information About Individual Pupils) (England) Regulations 2006, SI 2006/2601 (in force on 31 October 2006), replace the 2001 Regulations, SI 2001/4020, and provide that (1) individual pupil information of a maintained school is to be provided by reference to a pupil's learning aims; (2) such information to be provided are: the qualification accreditation number, the start date, the planned end date, the actual end date, information of the pupil's progress or status in respect of the learning aim, and information identifying the syllabus, subject and the awarding body; (3) the information relating to a pupil's usual mode of travel to school must be provided for on the school register; (4) the information relating to a pupil's authorised and unauthorised absences must include reasons, if known, for such absences; and (5) information as to whether a pupil has been a child looked after by a local authority while he was on the school's register must be provided in relation to permanently excluded pupils. The regulations also provide for the collection of information on permanent exclusions in respect of primary, middle deemed primary, and special schools. SI 2002/3112, 2003/3277, 2005/3101 are revoked. SI 2003/689 is revoked, in part.

1143   Pupil—individual pupil information—Wales

The Education (Information About Individual Pupils) (Wales) (Amendment) Regulations 2006, SI 2006/30 (in force on 11 January 2006), amends the 2003 Regulations, SI 2003/3237, so as to (1) no longer require the governing body of a school to specify with whom a pupil speaks Welsh at home; (2) allow information about pupils who have left the school during the course of the school year to be included in the information that the governing body may be required to supply about sixth form pupils; and (3) provide that the information which may be required about pupils' basic skills needs for literacy and numeracy will now include pupils' needs at the end, as well as at the beginning, of their learning activities programme.

1144   Pupil—referral units—applicable enactments—England

The Education (Pupil Referral Units) (Application of Enactments) (England) (Amendment) Regulations 2006, SI 2006/1068 (in force on 12 May 2006), amend the 2005 Regulations, SI 2005/2039, by requiring teachers and support staff appointed by a local education authority to work in a pupil referral unit to be subject to an enhanced Criminal Records Bureau check prior to or as soon as possible after their appointment.

1145   Pupil—registration—England

The Education (Pupil Registration) (England) Regulations 2006, SI 2006/1751 (in force on 1 September 2006), replace the 1995 Regulations, SI 1995/2089, and provide that (1) the name of a pupil must be included in the admissions register from the beginning of the first day on which the school has agreed, or has been notified, that the pupil will attend the school; (2) a pupil may be marked in the attendance register as unable to attend due to exceptional circumstances where the school site, or part of it, is closed or where transport normally provided for that pupil by the school or the local education authority is unavailable; (3) where a pupil is attending another school at which he is a registered pupil he must be marked in the attendance register as attending an approved educational activity; (4) where a pupil is registered at more than one school his name may only be deleted from the admission register of a school which he has ceased to attend where the proprietor of any or every other school at which the pupil is registered gives his consent, except where the pupil has died, been permanently excluded or is of no fixed abode; (5) before deleting a pupil's name from the admission register on the ground that he has not returned from a leave of absence exceeding ten days, both the proprietor and the local education authority must have failed, after reasonable inquiry, to ascertain where the pupil is; (6) the period after which a pupil's name may be deleted from the admission register on the ground that the pupil has been continuously absent without authorisation has been changed to 20 school days and additionally, the proprietor must not have reasonable grounds to believe that the pupil is unable to attend the school by reason of sickness or unavoidable cause; (7) the name of a pupil who is detained in pursuance of a final court order or order of recall may only be deleted from the register where that order is for a period of not less than four months and where the proprietor does not have reasonable grounds to believe that the pupil will return to school at the end of that period; (8) the requirement to make a return to the local education authority where a pupil's name is deleted on certain grounds is extended; and (9) where a register is kept by means of a computer, that register must be backed-up in the form of an electronic, micro-fiche or printed copy not at least once a month. SI 1997/2624, in relation to England and 2001/2802 are revoked.

1146   Schools—admission arrangements—determination of admissions—Wales

The Education (Determination of Admission Arrangements) (Wales) Regulations 2006, SI 2006/174 (in force on 1 February 2006), replace the 1999 Regulations, SI 1999/126, in relation to Wales, so as to take into account the amendments made to the School Standards and Framework Act 1998 in relation to school admission arrangements by the Education Act 2002. The regulations set out the procedure which admission authorities must follow when determining their admission arrangements, including the consultation and notification process. In particular, the regulations (1) require all admission authorities to complete the consultation required by the 1998 Act s 89 before 1 March in the determination year (that is, the school year beginning two years before the school year in which the pupils will be admitted); there is a new duty to have regard to the indicated admission number for each relevant age group when determining the number of pupils to be admitted in any school year in any relevant age group; (2) provide that, where the admission arrangements are for a primary school, the duty under the 1998 Act s 89(2)(b) to consult other admission authorities in the 'relevant area' only applies to the authorities for other primary schools; (3) specify the additional consultation required by virtue of s 89(2)(d); an admission authority which is a local education authority must consult every neighbouring local education authority; (4) confer a new power on a governing body which is an admission authority to suspend consultation requirements in certain circumstances; the requirements are disapplied if the governing body consulted on its proposed arrangements within the previous two determination years, those arrangements are unchanged, and no objection has been made to the National Assembly for Wales about the admission arrangements in the preceding five years; (5) require the consultation to relate to all of the proposed admission arrangements, except any 'exempt arrangements', that is arrangements which cannot be introduced or altered except by means of statutory proposals; (6) require the admission authority to send a written copy of its proposed admission arrangements to each admission authority which it is required to consult, and invite its comments; any exempt arrangements must be included in this written consultation document for information purposes; (7) set out the requirements for notifying other admission authorities of the arrangements that are finally determined; this must be done in writing within 14 days from the date of the determination; there is a new requirement to notify all appropriate bodies who were entitled to be consulted even if they were not actually consulted because the consultation requirements have been suspended in accordance with head (4) supra; (8) additionally require details about admission arrangements which provide for selection of pupils by ability, to be published in a local newspaper; they also contain a new requirement for additional publication where the admission authority has determined an admission number for a relevant age group which is lower than the current indicated admission number for that age group; and (9) require an admission authority which must publish additional information under head (8) supra, to provide, on request, further details relating to their admission arrangements and to the parents' right of objection.

1147   Schools—admission arrangements—looked after children—England

The Education (Admission of Looked After Children) (England) Regulations 2006, SI 2006/128 (in force on 21 February 2006), prescribe the actions to be taken and the circumstances in which an admission authority for a maintained school must give priority in their admission arrangements to a 'relevant looked after child', that is, a child who is looked after by a local authority within the meaning of the Children Act 1989 s 22 at the time of their application and who will still be so looked after at the time when he is admitted to school. In particular, the regulations (1) require admission authorities to give priority in their oversubscription criteria to relevant looked after children, subject to the exceptions below; (2) specify that only those grammar schools which select pupils who have reached a pre-set standard of the school need give priority in their oversubscription criteria to relevant looked after children; grammar schools which select pupils on the basis of highest ranked results need not give priority to relevant looked after children; (3) allow admission authorities for schools designated as having a religious character to give first priority in their oversubscription criteria to all relevant looked after children, regardless of their faith; (4) require admission authorities for schools which have made provision in their admission arrangements for selection by ability or aptitude since the beginning of the 1997–1998 school year to give priority to relevant looked after children who have been selected by ability or aptitude over other children who have been selected by ability or aptitude; relevant looked after children who have not been allocated a place on the basis of ability or aptitude must be given priority over other children who have not been allocated a place on that basis; and (5) require admission authorities for schools which make provision for selection by banding to give priority to relevant looked after children within each band.

1148   Schools—admission arrangements—objections—Wales

The Education (Objections to Admission Arrangements) (Wales) Regulations 2006, SI 2006/176 (in force on 1 February 2006), contain provisions relating to the conditions under which objections about admission arrangements for maintained schools may be made and decided, and the implementation of any decisions. In particular, the regulations (1) limit the right of governing bodies to object; they cannot object to the admission arrangements for any other community or voluntary controlled school in the relevant area, nor can they object to admission arrangements for their own school unless the objection relates to the determination of the admission number for the school; (2) provide that an objection may not be made under the School Standards and Framework Act 1998 s 90(1) if the substance of the objection is to seek an alteration to the admission arrangements which can only be made by way of publishing statutory proposals, for example, the introduction of pupil banding or single sex admissions; (3) specify the time limits within which any objection must be made; these are six weeks after the notification that the arrangements have been determined or, where the objection is by a parent, six weeks following the publication of relevant details in a local newspaper; (4) define the parents who are eligible to make an objection; (5) deal with the type of objections a parent may make; (6) add a condition that a parental objection may only be determined by the National Assembly for Wales if five or more parents make the same or substantially the same objection to the same admission arrangements; (7) prescribe the way National Assembly decisions on objections are to be published; (8) provide that, when an objection to a school's admission arrangements has been decided, no further objection to the school's arrangements for that school year or the following year may be made on the same issue except where, in the following year the admission authority seeks to reintroduce arrangements to which an objection had previously been upheld; and (9) in a case where an objection has been upheld against the admission arrangements of an admission authority, enable another relevant admission authority to revise their admission arrangements to achieve consistency with the decision upholding the objection. SI 1999/125 is revoked.

1149   Schools—admission arrangements—selective admissions—aptitude for particular subjects—prescribed subjects—England

The Education (Aptitude for Particular Subjects) (Amendment) (England) Regulations 2006, SI 2006/3408 (in force on 27 February 2007), amend the 1999 Regulations, SI 1999/258, so as to provide that the subjects of design and technology, and information technology, are not prescribed for the purposes of the School Standards and Framework Act 1998 s 102(1) in relation to admission to maintained schools in England with effect for the school year 2008–09 and subsequent years, unless they were included in a school's admission arrangements in relation to the school year 2007–08.

1150   Schools—admission arrangements—transitional provisions—Wales

The Education Act 2002 (Transitional Provisions and Consequential Amendments) (Wales) Regulations 2006, SI 2006/173 (in force on 1 February 2006), which apply in relation to Wales only, (1) make transitional provision in connection with the bringing into force of provisions of the Education Act 2002 by the Education Act 2002 (Commencement No 8) (Wales) Order 2006, SI 2006/172, providing that the amended provisions do not apply until the school admissions year 2008–09; (2) amend the School Standards and Framework Act 1998 s 98 on provisions concerning admission for nursery education or to nursery or special schools so as to refer instead to provisions concerning publication of information about admissions, and provide that any regulations made under s 92 before 1 February 2006 are to have effect as if they had been made under the 1998 Act s 92 as amended; and (3) further amend the Education (School Organisation Proposals) (Wales) Regulations 1999, SI 1999/1671, the Change of Category of Maintained Schools (Wales) Regulations 2001, SI 2001/2678 and the School Organisation Proposals by the National Council for Education and Training for Wales Regulations 2004, SI 2004/1576, consequential to the repeal of the provisions of the 1998 Act relating to standard numbers, and the introduction by the National Assembly for Wales of a new method of assessing the capacity of a school for the purpose of the new provisions on determining admissions arrangements introduced by the Education Act 2002. SI 1999/1064 is revoked.

1151   Schools—admission arrangements—variation—Wales

The Education (Variation of Admission Arrangements) (Wales) Regulations 2006, SI 2006/177 (in force on 1 February 2006), prescribe the circumstances in which an admission authority may vary the admission arrangements it has determined for a particular school year. In particular, the regulations provide that an admission authority may vary the admission number it had determined for any relevant age group where necessary to implement approved statutory proposals, and a variation of the admission number is necessary to implement those proposals.

1152   Schools—consistent financial reporting—England

The Consistent Financial Reporting (England) (Amendment) Regulations 2006, SI 2006/437 (in force on 1 April 2006), amend the 2003 Regulations, SI 2003/373, so as to prescribe the date by which the local education authority must provide the Secretary of State with its governing bodies' financial statements.

1153   Schools—finance—England

The School Finance (England) Regulations 2006, SI 2006/468 (in force on 25 February 2006), make provision for the financial arrangements of local education authorities in relation to the funding of schools over the financial years 2006–07 and 2007–08. In particular, the regulations (1) define the LEA budget, the schools budget, central expenditure, and the individual schools budget, and set out the basis on which a local education authority may determine schools budget shares; (2) require each local education authority to set out, in a scheme, specified matters connected with the financing of schools which it maintains; (3) oblige local education authorities to notify the governing bodies of maintained schools of the schools budgets and their budget shares by no later than 31 March 2006 for the financial years specified; (4) impose limits on the deduction of certain expenditure from the schools budgets and introduce new powers for schools forums to vary those limits so as to authorise a deduction of particular amounts; (5) allow schools forums to approve changes to a local education authority's formula in specified circumstances, subject to specified conditions; (6) allow a local education authority to apply to the Secretary of State where a schools forum does not vary any limit or approve changes to the formula; (7) confer a new power on the Secretary of State to authorise deductions from, and vary limits on deductions from, the schools budget; and (8) retain the Secretary of State's power to approve any redetermination of budget shares to such extent as may be specified. SI 2003/3247, 2004/3131, 2005/526 are revoked.

1154   Schools—financial management—enactments relating to employment—modification—Wales

The Education (Modification of Enactments Relating to Employment) (Wales) Order 2006, SI 2006/1073 (in force on 12 May 2006), replaces, in relation to Wales, the 1999 Order, SI 1999/2256, and modifies various statutory provisions relating to employment to take account of the provisions contained in the Education Act 2002 ss 35, 36 and the Staffing of Maintained Schools (Wales) Regulations 2006, SI 2006/873.

1155 Schools—governance—disqualification from office and membership—bankruptcy and mental health—England

The Education (Disqualification Provisions: Bankruptcy and Mental Health) (England) Regulations 2006, SI 2006/2198 (in force on 8 September 2006), amend SI 2000/2872, 2002/2978, 3177 so that a person detained under the Mental Health Act 1983 cannot hold office as a member of a foundation body and cannot be a member of a school company. The regulations also update the bankruptcy related disqualification provisions in SI 2002/2978, 3177, 2003/348, 1558, which deal with disqualification from membership of school companies, school governorship and new school temporary governorship.

1156 Schools—infant class sizes—England

The Education (Infant Class Sizes) (England) (Amendment) Regulations 2006, SI 2006/3409 (in force on 27 February 2007), amend the 1998 Regulations, SI 1998/1973, so as to amend the categories of excepted pupils in relation to an infant class at a school. In particular, the regulations (1) add a new category for looked after children who are admitted to schools outside a normal admission round; and (2) amend the category which includes those for whom there are no other suitable schools within a reasonable distance from their home, by providing that a pupil cannot be treated as falling within this category unless the relevant Local Education Authority confirms that he does.

1157 Schools—information—education provision—England

The Education (Information as to Provision of Education) (England) (Amendment) Regulations 2006, SI 2006/1033 (in force on 30 April 2006), further amend the 1999 Regulations, SI 1999/1066, so as to change from a four year to a five year period for which local authorities must provide the forecasted figures of the number of pupils enrolled in primary schools; and require that local authorities divided into districts to provide forecasted figures every year of the number of pupils per district for the following school year, the fifth year of the period and the sixth year of the period for key stages three and four only.

1158 Schools—information—individual pupil information—prescribed persons—England

The Education (Individual Pupil Information) (Prescribed Persons) (Amendment) Regulations 2006, SI 2006/1505 (in force on 10 July 2006), further amend the 1999 Regulations, SI 1999/903, in relation to England, so as to (1) enable information collators to additionally provide, at such times as the Secretary of State may determine, any prescribed person or any person falling within a prescribed category, with (a) any of the information about individual pupils specified in the Education (Information about Individual Pupils) (England) Regulations 2001, SI 2001/4020, Schedule; and (b) any information about the educational achievements of pupils in external qualifications approved under the Learning and Skills Act 2000 s 98; (2) incorporate a number of additional persons to the list of prescribed persons; and (3) incorporate a number of additional prescribed categories.

1159 Schools—inspections—Chief Inspector of Education, Children's Services and Skills—England

The Office for Standards in Education, Children's Services and Skills (Transitional Provisions) Regulations 2006, SI 2006/2991 (in force on 12 December 2006), modify the Education and Inspections Act 2006 so as to make transitional provision for the preparation for the exercise of functions by the Chief Inspector of Education, Children's Services and Skills.

1160 Schools—inspections—Wales

The Education (School Inspection) (Wales) Regulations 2006, SI 2006/1714 (in force on 1 September 2006), replace the 1998 Regulations, SI 1998/1866. In particular, the regulations (1) in relation to school inspections (a) prescribe a fee of £150 for registration as a registered inspector; (b) provide for inspections to take place at intervals of six years from when the school was last inspected or, where there has been no previous inspection, from when it first admitted pupils; (c) specify those persons who must be notified by the appropriate authority of the time when the inspection is to take place; (d) make provision for the arrangements to be made by the appropriate authority for a meeting of parents prior to an inspection, and provides that only those persons listed may attend the meeting; (e) provide for the inspector conducting the inspection to have control of a meeting of parents; (f) make provision for an inspection to be completed within two weeks and that a report of the inspection is to be completed within 35 working days of the date on which the inspection was completed; (g) require the appropriate authority or proprietor to take reasonably practicable steps to ensure that a summary of the report is received by parents within ten working days from the receipt of the report by the authority or proprietor; (h) require the appropriate authority or proprietor to prepare an action plan within the period of 45 working days from the date on which they receive the report, and to send copies to those persons and bodies entitled to receive copies within a specified period; (i) provide that heads (g) and (h) supra do not apply to independent schools; (j) provide that a local education authority is required to prepare the statement they are required to prepare under the Education Act 2005 s 40(3)(a) within a specified period; and (k) allow fees, not exceeding the cost of supply, to be charged for inspection reports, summaries and action plans in specified cases; (2) in relation to denominational education (a) provide for inspections to take place at intervals of six years from when the school was last inspected or, where there has been no previous inspection of the provision, from when the school first admitted pupils; (b) provide for consultation with the appropriate diocesan authority on the choice of inspector; (c) prescribe periods within which such inspections are to be carried out, an inspection report and action plan are to be prepared, and an action plan is to be sent to those entitled to receive a copy of it; and (d) specify cases in which a fee, not exceeding the cost of supply, may be charged for a copy of an inspection report, summary or action plan; and (3) in relation to local education authority school inspection services requires an authority to keep accounts in respect of such a service.

1161   Schools—length of day and year—Wales

The Education (School Day and School Year) (Wales) (Amendment) Regulations 2006, SI 2006/1262 (in force on 1 August 2006), amend the 2003 Regulations, SI 2003/3231, so as to (1) provide for up to four sessions in each of the 2006–07 and 2007–08 school years to count as sessions on which the school met if they were devoted to the provision of certain forms of training; and (2) provide for such forms of training to be (a) the preparation and implementation of plans aimed at facilitating the transition of pupils between key stages and between primary school and secondary school; (b) forthcoming changes in the National Curriculum; and (c) the Assembly's plans for extending learning options for 14–19 year olds.

1162   Schools—lunches—nutritional standards—England

The Education (Nutritional Standards for School Lunches) (England) Regulations 2006, SI 2006/2381 (in force on 11 September 2006), amend the 2000 Regulations, SI 2000/1777, with new nutritional standards for school lunches in maintained schools and pupil referral units, except for nursery schools and nursery units within primary schools. In particular, the regulations (1) divide food into six groups and set out the requirements for school lunches to include food from the groups; (2) provide that drinks served as part of a school lunch must be within the specified list; (3) permit deep-fried food to be served only twice in a week; (4) limit confectionery and savoury snacks to healthier items without sugar, salt or fat; and (5) prevent the addition of salt after food is cooked and place limits on other condiments.

1163   Schools—new schools—admissions—Wales

The New School (Admissions) (Wales) Regulations 2006, SI 2006/175 (in force on 1 February 2006), make provision in relation to the determination of the initial admission arrangements for admission to new schools. In particular, the regulations (1) specify who is to be the admission authority for a new school in relation to its initial year, that is to say the body responsible for the determination of the arrangements for admission of pupils to the school for the school year in which it will first admit pupils; (2) require an admission authority for a new school to determine the initial admission arrangements not less than six months before the school opening date; an admission authority is under a duty to consult on the initial admission arrangements before they are so determined; (3) require an admission authority to determine, as part of the initial admission arrangements, an admission number for each relevant age group, that is to say the number of pupils in any relevant age group which it intends to admit to the school; where the initial admission arrangements have been determined before the relevant statutory proposals have been approved, the admission number will be that stated in the statutory proposal notice; (4) make provision, after the initial admission arrangements have been determined, for admission authorities and governing bodies of community and voluntary controlled schools who were required to be consulted under head (2) supra, to refer objections to the National Assembly for Wales; (5) provide for the initial admission arrangements to be varied either in view of a major change of circumstance, or where a variation is necessary to implement statutory proposals published under the School Standards and Framework Act 1998 s 28; where a proposed variation is because of a major change of circumstance, it must be referred to the National Assembly; and (6) provide for certain provisions of the Education Act 1996, the 1998 Act and the Education (School Information) (Wales) Regulations 1999, SI 1999/1812, to apply with modifications to new schools. SI 1999/2800 is revoked.

1164   Schools—school performance—information—England

The Education (School Performance Information) (England) (Amendment) Regulations 2006, SI 2006/2896 (in force on 30 November 2006), further amend the 2001 Regulations, SI 2001/3446, so as to (1) add definitions explaining the meaning of 'looked after children', 'school action', 'school action plus', and of the Special Educational Needs Code of Practice; (2) remove requirements for the provision of information to the local education authority about excluded pupils and the provision of information to the Secretary of State about permanently excluded pupils; (3) extend to the proprietors of Academies who provide primary education a requirement to provide to the Secretary of State, on request, general information about those primary schools; (4) extend to Academies a requirement to provide to the National Data Collection Agency information about second key stage assessment results; (5) require the provision of information to the Secretary of State about all fourth key stage pupils; (6) remove certain provisions relating to pupils who had taken particular courses at age 16, 17 and 18; and (7) cause information about pupils with special educational needs and who are either supported by school action plus or the subject of a statement of special educational needs to be provided to the Secretary of State as one category; information will be provided to the Secretary of State about the category of pupils who have special educational needs and are supported by school action but in respect of whom a statement of special educational needs has not been made.

1165   Schools—school performance—targets—England

The Education (School Performance Targets) (England) (Amendment) Regulations 2006, SI 2006/3151 (in force on 28 December 2006), further amend the 2004 Regulations, SI 2004/2858, so that a governing body is required to set targets for the proportion of pupils aged 15 to achieve the level 2 threshold in approved external qualifications including grades A*–C in GCSE English and mathematics.

1166   Schools—secondary schools—proposals—England

The Education (New Secondary School Proposals) (England) Regulations 2006, SI 2006/2139 (in force on 1 September 2006), prescribe matters relating to proposals for the establishment of new secondary schools pursuant to the competition regime set out in the Education Act 2005. In particular, the regulations (1) prescribe the information to be contained in a notice published by a local education authority inviting proposals for the establishment of a new secondary school; (2) prescribe the interval after which the proposals in response to a published notice must be sent to a local education authority; (3) specify persons whom a local education authority must consult prior to publishing a notice and set out a requirement for a public meeting and notification to the Secretary of State; (4) prescribe the information that has to be contained in (a) proposals for the establishment of a new secondary school made pursuant to a notice inviting proposals; and (b) proposals made by a local education authority; (5) prescribe the time within which such proposals must be published by a local education authority and specify the manner in which details of proposals received or made are to be published; (6) require a local education authority to make copies of proposals available for inspection and provide details of the bodies to whom copies of proposals are to be sent; (7) prescribe the steps to be taken by a local education authority for the purpose of promoting public awareness of any proposals published; (8) provide for the submission of published proposals, objections and comments received, to a school organisation committee within a specified timescale; (9) prescribe the persons or bodies whom a school organisation committee must consult before approving proposals with modifications; (10) provide for the events which can be specified in a conditional approval; (11) specify the only circumstances in which a school organisation committee must or may refer proposals or matters to the adjudicator; (12) prescribe the manner in which a school organisation committee must consult the Secretary of State when the proposals consist of or include a proposal to establish an academy; (13) provide for the information which must be provided by a school organisation committee or adjudicator to specified persons in connection with published proposals; (14) specify the manner in which a school organisation committee must vote; (15) provide that a local education authority may refer proposals to a school organisation committee if proposals which the authority could otherwise have determined require a conditional approval; (16) prescribe the process of publication of proposals where a local education authority or promoters wish to be relieved from the duty of implementing proposals where such implementation would be unreasonably difficult, or where circumstances have so altered since the publication of proposals that implementation would be unreasonably difficult; (17) specify the persons who may request (a) that the Secretary of State modify approved proposals; and (b) a later date by which an event specified in a conditional approval must occur, and prescribe the persons whom a school organisation committee must consult before modifying proposals; and (18) set out how certain provisions of the 2005 Act must be applied and modified in cases where proposals relate to a school which is proposed to be situated in an area other than that of the local education authority which published the notice. SI 1999/2213 is further amended. SI 2003/1200 and 1421 are revoked.

1167   Schools—secondary schools—proposals—England

The Education (New Secondary School Proposals) (England) Regulations 2006, SI 2006/2139 (in force on 1 September 2006), prescribe matters relating to proposals for the establishment of new secondary schools pursuant to the competition regime set out in the Education Act 2005. In particular, the regulations (1) prescribe the information to be contained in a notice published by a local education authority inviting proposals for the establishment of a new secondary school;

(2) prescribe the interval after which the proposals in response to a published notice must be sent to a local education authority; (3) specify persons whom a local education authority must consult prior to publishing a notice and set out a requirement for a public meeting and notification to the Secretary of State; (4) prescribe the information that has to be contained in (a) proposals for the establishment of a new secondary school made pursuant to a notice inviting proposals; and (b) proposals made by a local education authority; (5) prescribe the time within which such proposals must be published by a local education authority and specify the manner in which details of proposals received or made are to be published; (6) require a local education authority to make copies of proposals available for inspection and provide details of the bodies to whom copies of proposals are to be sent; (7) prescribe the steps to be taken by a local education authority for the purpose of promoting public awareness of any proposals published; (8) provide for the submission of published proposals, objections and comments received, to a school organisation committee within a specified timescale; (9) prescribe the persons or bodies whom a school organisation committee must consult before approving proposals with modifications; (10) provide for the events which can be specified in a conditional approval; (11) specify the only circumstances in which a school organisation committee must or may refer proposals or matters to the adjudicator; (12) prescribe the manner in which a school organisation committee must consult the Secretary of State when the proposals consist of or include a proposal to establish an academy; (13) provide for the information which must be provided by a school organisation committee or adjudicator to specified persons in connection with published proposals; (14) specify the manner in which a school organisation committee must vote; (15) provide that a local education authority may refer proposals to a school organisation committee if proposals which the authority could otherwise have determined require a conditional approval; (16) prescribe the process of publication of proposals where a local education authority or promoters wish to be relieved from the duty of implementing proposals where such implementation would be unreasonably difficult, or where circumstances have so altered since the publication of proposals that implementation would be unreasonably difficult; (17) specify the persons who may request (a) that the Secretary of State modify approved proposals; and (b) a later date by which an event specified in a conditional approval must occur, and prescribe the persons whom a school organisation committee must consult before modifying proposals; and (18) set out how certain provisions of the 2005 Act must be applied and modified in cases where proposals relate to a school which is proposed to be situated in an area other than that of the local education authority which published the notice. SI 1999/2213 is further amended. SI 2003/1200, 1421 are revoked.

1168   Schools—unauthorised absence—targets—Wales

The Education (School Performance and Unauthorised Absence Targets) (Wales) (Amendment) Regulations 2006, SI 2006/125 (in force on 1 February 2006), amend the 1999 Regulations, SI 1999/1811, so as to require all maintained schools, except special schools established in hospitals, to set absence targets.

1169   Single education plan—Wales

The Single Education Plan (Wales) Regulations 2006, SI 2006/877 (in force on 1 April 2006), (1) require a local education authority to prepare and publish a single education plan; (2) specify the content and duration of such a plan; (3) prescribe the persons and bodies whom a local education authority is required to consult when preparing a single education plan and the manner in which the consultation is to be carried out; (4) provide for the date on which a local education authority is required to adopt and publish a single education plan; (5) provide for the manner in which a local education authority is required to publish documents; (6) prescribe the persons to whom a local education authority is required to provide copies of a single education plan; and (7) revise the specified supporting information and the targets for attainment, attendance and exclusion. SI 2003/893 is amended and SI 1998/644, 2001/606, 2002/1187, 2003/1732 and 2005/434 are revoked.

1170   Special educational needs—England

The Education (Special Educational Needs) (England) (Consolidation) (Amendment) Regulations 2006, SI 2006/3346 (in force on 1 March 2007), further amend the 2001 Regulations, SI 2001/3455, in relation to England, so as to (1) update definitions to reflect the changes in legislation to which they refer and to define the expressions infant school, junior school and maintained special school for the purposes of provisions added by the regulations; (2) provide that a pupil attending a maintained special school will attend daily collective worship and receive religious education but may be withdrawn from either in accordance with the wishes of his parent; (3) clarify the circumstances when a copy of certain notices must be sent where the local education authority have decided to make an assessment under the Education Act 1996 s 323 or at the request of a responsible body under s 329A; (4) make it clearer that advice must be sought by an authority making an assessment of a child from a person responsible for his educational provision if advice cannot be obtained from a head teacher or person with general special educational needs experience or knowledge; (5) assist the reader by reminding him of the statutory time limit for serving statutory notices served under the 1996 Act ss 323(1), 329A; (6) provide for the circumstances when a child without a statement of special educational needs may be admitted to a maintained special school; (7) provide that where a child with a statement is within twelve calendar months of moving between infant school and junior school, the authority responsible for his statement must ensure that, before 15 February in the year of the transfer, his statement names the school or other institution he will be attending following the transfer; (8) impose a 15 working day time limit on transferring statements where a child has moved from the area of one authority to another beginning with the day on which the authority, from whose area the child has moved, is informed of the move; (9) update references to school inspectors and add a provision allowing statements to be shared with Secure Training Centres for the purpose of carrying out their educational functions; (10) make it clear that, where the Special Educational Needs and Disability Tribunal orders that the authority must make an assessment under the 1988 Act s 323(4) or 329A(7), the notice informing the parent that an assessment is to be made must be served within four weeks; (11) provide that where the Tribunal orders the authority to make and maintain a statement, the time limit is now five weeks to issue a proposed statement rather than to make a statement; (12) provide that where an authority is ordered by the Tribunal to amend a statement or to continue to maintain and amend a statement the authority must, in either case, amend the statement within five weeks rather than issue an amendment notice within five weeks; (13) provide that the date from which the periods for compliance referred to in the 2001 Regulations reg 25 is the date on which the order is made; (14) require an authority to serve a proposed statement within five weeks rather than to make a statement within five weeks where an appeal has been conceded against a decision not to make a statement; (15) make it clear that where an authority concedes an appeal under the 1988 Act ss 328, 329 and 329A the notice informing the parent that the assessment is to be made must be served within four weeks; (16) amend the date from which the periods for compliance referred to in the 2001 Regulations reg 26 commence to the date on which the authority concedes the appeal; (17) substitute the form of notice to accompany a copy of a proposed statement or a proposed amended statement (a) to specify more precisely what maintained schools are described in the list to be attached to it; (b) to allow for the Secretary of State to indicate what list must be provided to parents of non-maintained special schools and independent schools; and (c) to allow reference to a list indicated by the National Assembly for Wales; (18) substitute the form of notice to accompany an amendment notice; (19) specify what information and advice must be appended to a statement of special educational needs and make consequential amendments to the form of statement of special educational needs; (20) make transitional provisions; and (21) set out modifications to the 2001 Regulations which apply while the Childcare Act 2006 Sch 2 para 23 is not in force in England.

1171   Students—income-related benefits

See para 2625.

1172   Students—student fees—inflation index—England

The Student Fees (Inflation Index) Regulations 2006, SI 2006/507 (in force on 31 March 2006), sets out the index of prices to which the Secretary of State is required, by the Higher Education Act 2004 s 26(3), to have regard in deciding whether any increase in the basic and higher tuition fee amounts is no greater than required to maintain the value of the amounts in real terms.

1173   Students—student loans

The Education (Student Loans) (Amendment) (England and Wales) Regulations 2006, SI 2006/929 (in force in part on 30 April 2006, and in part on 1 August 2006), further amend the 1998 Regulations, SI 1998/211, by (1) implementing EC European Parliament and Council Directive 2004/38 on the rights of citizens of the Union and their family members to move and reside freely in the territory of member states so far as the Directive relates to student loans; (2) increasing, in line with inflation, the maximum amounts that may be lent to students in relation to an academic year commencing on or after 1 August 2006; (3) setting out the criteria that certain categories of students who were not previously eligible for a loan must satisfy in order to be eligible for a loan in connection with an academic year beginning on or after 1 August 2005 but before 1 July 2006, and sets out the time limits for applying for such loans; and (4) amending the terms of loans taken out on or after 30 April 2006. SI 2005/1718 is revoked, and 2005/2119 is amended.

1174   Teachers—pay and conditions

The Education (School Teachers' Pay and Conditions) (No 2) Order 2006, SI 2006/2133 (in force on 1 September 2006), brings into force the School Teachers' Pay and Conditions Document 2006 and Guidance on School Teachers' Pay, replacing the School Teachers' Pay and Conditions Document 2005. SI 2005/2212, 3479, and SI 2006/1274 are revoked.

The Education (School Teachers' Pay and Conditions) (No 2) (Amendment) Order 2006, SI 2006/3171 (in force on 1 January 2007), amends the 2006 Order supra, and the document which was given legal effect by the 2006 Order, in order to replace several incorrect entries in the pay spine for members of the leadership group and the pay scale for unqualified teachers. The order also inserts two definitions which appeared in the 2005 Document and were mistakenly omitted from the 2006 Document and inserts a reference to a teacher who takes up an excellent teacher post and a reference to excellent teachers, both of which should have been in the 2006 Document.

1175   Teachers—pensions

The Teachers' Pensions (Miscellaneous Amendments) Regulations 2006, SI 2006/736 (in force on 6 April 2006), further amend the Teachers' Superannuation (Additional Voluntary Contributions) Regulations 1994, SI 1994/2924, so as to (1) remove the constraints on accepting an election relating to the level of contributions and benefits; (2) provide that a transfer value which can only be paid if one is also payable under the Teachers' Pensions Regulations 1997, SI 1997/3001, only applies to a person who has ceased to be a contributor before 6 April 2006; and (3) provide that a person can elect to take part of his benefit as a lump sum if it is a pension commencement lump sum. The regulations also amend the 1997 Regulations so as to (a) increase the age at which a person can retire early on the basis of redundancy or in the interests of the efficient discharge of his employer's functions, from 50 to 55 years of age where the person is a post-5th April 2006 entrant; and (b) change the meaning of 'child'. The regulations also enable persons to elect that the amendments made do not apply if the effect is that the person is placed in a worse position.

The Teachers' Pensions (Miscellaneous Amendments) (No 2) Regulations 2006, SI 2006/2214 (in force on 1 October 2006), further amend the 1994 Regulations supra to extend the circumstances under which an outward transfer value may be made. The regulations also further amend the 1997 Regulations supra so as to (1) provide that, where a person has given up the right to receive part of his salary under a salary sacrifice arrangement, the amount given up counts as contributable salary; (2) provide that the Secretary of State can determine that, in exceptional circumstances, a person in respect of whom a direction has been given under the Education Act 2002 s 142 on the basis that the person is unsuitable to work with children can still be entitled to a pension under Case C (incapacity); (3) provide that, where a pension is commuted in exceptional circumstances of serious ill health, the whole pension, rather than so much of it as exceeds the person's guaranteed minimum, is commuted; and (4) provide that certain types of employment make up 'qualifying periods' in circumstances where an inward transfer of past service pension rights could have been made but the person has decided not to transfer those rights.

The Teachers Pensions etc (Reform Amendments) Regulations 2006, SI 2006/3122 (in force on 1 January 2007), further amend the Teachers' Pensions Regulations 1997, SI 1997/3001, so as to (1) provide for circumstances where an employment is pensionable; (2) increase, from 70 to 75 years of age, the maximum age at which a person can be in pensionable employment; (3) provide that members may acquire additional pension benefits; (4) enable persons to elect to pay additional contributions, either as a lump sum or in monthly payments, and in return receive an increased pension with or without increased benefits for dependants; (5) provide for entitlement to benefits under the provision relating to redundancy or efficient discharge of employer's functions; (6) amend the definition of 'normal pension age' and related terms; (7) introduce phased retirement benefits which allow a person to elect to receive some of his pension benefits without having to retire; (8) provide that the pension of a person who has a normal pension age of 65 and accrues reckonable service after reaching that age is actuarially enhanced; (9) enable a person to elect to receive a further lump sum in place of part of his pension; (10) provide for persons who retire on ill-health grounds and require an application for ill-health retirement pension to be signed by the person's employer and be accompanied by necessary medical evidence; (11) provide that, where death occurs on or after 1 January 2007, the death grant is three times the average salary; (12) provide for benefits to be paid to the surviving nominated partner of a member, such nominee being neither his surviving spouse or surviving civil partner; (13) require any death grant or supplementary death grant to be paid, in the absence of another nominee, to a surviving nominated partner and provide for short and long-term pensions to be paid to the surviving nominated partner; (14) enable a member to pay family benefit contributions to make periods of his service count for the purpose of calculating such a pension; (15) provide for the calculation of long-term pensions payable to children where a pension is payable to a surviving nominated partner; (16) provide for changes to the nomination of partner and nomination of other beneficiaries provisions; (17) provide that a pension payable to a survivor is payable for life if the member was in pensionable employment after 31 December 2006 or was paying or had paid additional contributions under specified previous provisions in respect of that period; (18) make new provisions for determining a person's average salary on which benefits are calculated; (19) provide that there is no longer a restriction on reckonable service including service in excess of 40 years before reaching 60; (20) provide for changes where a person is employed at a reduced salary; (21) enable the Secretary of State, before paying a lump sum, to require a declaration to be made relating to the recycling of the lump sum by the person to whom the payment is to be made; and (22) revise the definition of 'appropriate factor' so that it is determined from time to time by the Secretary of State after taking advice from the Government Actuary.

The regulations also further amend the Teachers' Superannuation (Additional Voluntary Contributions) Regulations 1994, SI 1994/2924, so that (a) 'dependant' includes a person in whose favour a nomination made under the nomination of partner provision of the 1997 Regulations has effect; (b) benefits may be provided from the age of 55; and (c) the options available if the participator dies within five years after the retirement commences are changed. The regulations also further amend the Teachers (Compensation for Redundancy and Premature Retirement) Regulations 1997, SI 1997/311, so that (i) employment at certain institutions within the higher education sector is no longer relevant employment; and (ii) long-term compensation payable to a survivor is payable for life if the teacher was in pensionable employment after 31 December 2006.

1176   Teachers—performance management—England

The Education (School Teacher Performance Management) (England) Regulations 2006, SI 2006/2661 (in force on 1 September 2007), replace the Education (School Teacher Appraisal) (England) Regulations 2001, SI 2001/2855, and apply to teachers whose pay and conditions are determined by order of the Secretary of State under the Education Act 2002 s 122, who are employed for one term or more, other than those who are undergoing an induction period or who are the subject of capability procedures. In particular, the regulations (1) require governing bodies, in the case of teachers employed at schools, and local education authorities, in the case of unattached teachers, to establish and implement a performance management policy for teachers; (2) provide for the appointment of reviewers and specify the procedure that must be followed when preparing and revising teachers' plans and reviewing their performance in the light of those plans in the teachers' planning and review statements; (3) allow head teachers and local education authorities to delegate their reviewer's duties to the teacher's line manager so as to enable head teachers and local education authorities to moderate the plans drawn up by line managers; (4) provide that teachers may appeal against any of the entries recorded in their statements; and (5) allow governing bodies and local education authorities to have regard to the results of their teachers' reviews when exercising any discretion in relation to their pay. SI 2000/2122 is amended.

1177   Teachers—redundancy and premature retirement—compensation

The Teachers (Compensation for Redundancy and Premature Retirement) (Amendment) Regulations 2006, SI 2006/2216 (in force on 1 October 2006), further amend the 1997 Order, SI 1997/311, by removing the requirement that discretionary compensation on the termination of employment may only be paid to persons who are not entitled to retirement benefits under the Teachers' Pensions Regulations 1997, SI 1997/3001, and by specifying the maximum compensation which can be paid as 104 weeks' pay, less the aggregate of any redundancy payments to which the person is entitled and any discretionary compensation for redundancy.

1178   Youth and community work—education and training—Wales

The Youth and Community Work Education and Training (Inspection) (Wales) Regulations 2006, SI 2006/2804 (in force on 23 October 2006), prescribe education and training provided by, or on behalf of, an institution within the higher education sector in Wales for the purpose of enabling persons to become youth and community workers, or as further training for persons who are youth and community workers, with the effect that the education and training is brought within the remit of the Chief Inspector under the Learning and Skills Act 2000 s 75.

ELECTIONS AND REFERENDUMS

Halsbury's Laws of England (4th edn) vol 15(3) (2007 Reissue) paras 1–343, vol 15(4) (2007 Reissue) paras 344–907

1179   Absent voting—transitional provisions

The Absent Voting (Transitional Provisions) (England and Wales) Regulations 2006, SI 2006/2973 (in force on 1 January 2007), (1) introduce a requirement for applicants for proxy or postal voting to provide personal identifiers, a signature and date of birth, and also enable transitional regulations to be made to provide for the capture of the personal identifiers of those who are existing absent voters; (2) require a registration officer to send a written notice to all existing absent voters who are entitled to an absent vote at an election occurring on or after 3 May 2007, requiring that they supply him with the required personal identifiers; an absent voter will have a period of six weeks within which to respond; where no response is received within the first three weeks, the registration officer is required to send a copy of the notice to the absent voter; (3) specify the information that must be included in the notice sent to existing absent voters together with the information that must be included with the notice or copy of the notice; (4) require a registration officer to determine whether an absent voter has failed or refused to provide the required personal identifiers; and (5) specify the consequences of a refusal or failure to provide the required personal identifiers; an existing absent voter will cease to be entitled to vote by post, by proxy or by post as proxy and any entry relating to him in the absent voting records must be removed; the registration officer must notify the absent voter and provide him with certain information.

1180 Annual canvass—form

The Representation of the People (Form of Canvass) (England and Wales) Regulations 2006, SI 2006/1694 (in force on 11 July 2006), replace the 2004 Order, SI 2004/1848, and specify a new form of words for use on the registration form provided by registration officers for those who register at times other than during the annual canvass period. SI 2001/341 is further amended.

1181 Electoral Administration Act 2006

The Electoral Administration Act 2006 makes provision in relation to the registration of electors and the keeping of electoral registration information, standing for election, the administration and conduct of elections and referendums and the regulation of political parties. The Act received the royal assent on 11 July 2006 and came into force in part on that day. Further provisions come into force on and between 11 September 2006 and 31 January 2007: SI 2006/1972, 2268, 3412. The remaining provisions come into force on a day or days to be appointed. For details of commencement, see the commencement table in the title STATUTES.

Part 1 (ss 1–8) Co-ordinated on-line record of electors
Section 1 confers a power on the Secretary of State to establish by order Co-ordinated On-line Record of Electors ('CORE') schemes for the keeping, and use, of specified electoral registration information. The uses to which information supplied to CORE may be put are defined by s 2. By virtue of s 3, the Secretary of State may make the necessary finances for the running of a CORE scheme available to the keeper under the scheme. Section 4 allows the Electoral Commission to be appointed as the keeper of a CORE scheme by the Secretary of State under s 1. Section 5 makes supplemental provisions in relation to CORE schemes. Before making an order to establish or vary a scheme, the Secretary of State must consult the Commission, the Information Commissioner and the local electoral registration officers who would be affected: s 6. Section 7 provides that a CORE keeper is liable in criminal law for a breach of his official duties, the penalty being a fine not exceeding £5,000. Section 8 deals with interpretation.

Part 2 (ss 9–13) Registration of electors
By virtue of s 9, the statement of registration officers' duties in relation to the maintenance of the registers for which they are responsible is expanded. Section 10 provides the possibility of anonymous registration of electors in certain circumstances and for the removal of an anonymous entry after 12 months, and Sch 1 Pt 1 makes further provision in connection with anonymous registration. Section 11, Sch 1 Pt 2 moves the deadline for applying for registration for an election closer to the day of poll. An electoral registration officer may remove an elector's name from the local register if it becomes apparent, after the process of registration has been completed, that the elector should not have been registered: s 12. Section 13 makes further provision to enable service personnel to register to vote.

Part 3 (ss 14, 15) Anti-fraud measures
Provision is made by s 14 for the collection of personal identifiers from persons applying to vote by post or proxy. Section 15 extends to the whole of the United Kingdom offences relating to the provision of false registration information.

Part 4 (s 16) Review of polling places
The duties and powers of local authorities, the Commission and returning officers are clarified by s 16.

Part 5 (ss 17–19) Standing for election
Section 17 reduces from 21 to 18 the age of qualification for election as a member of the House of Commons or a local authority, or election as mayor, Mayor of London or Assembly member of the Greater London Authority. Section 18, Sch 1 Pt 3 limit the right of Commonwealth citizens to stand for election for membership of the House of Commons to those with a right of abode or with indefinite leave to remain in the United Kingdom. By virtue of s 19, parliamentary election rules are amended.

Part 6 (ss 20–47) Conduct of elections etc
Maundy Thursday is removed from the list of days that are to be disregarded for the purposes of the electoral timetable: s 20, Sch 1 Pt 4. Section 21 enables candidates to use the name which they commonly use on the ballot paper. A candidate must state on the consent form that he is only standing in one constituency at a United Kingdom parliamentary election (s 22) and a person is guilty of a corrupt practice if he authorises a candidate to use a description knowing that that person will be standing in more than one constituency where the poll is to be held on the same day (s 23). The delay in rescheduling the date of poll as a result of the death of a candidate is reduced so that a registered political party may name an alternative candidate if its candidate dies and the original election timetable may continue uninterrupted should the deceased be an independent candidate: s 24. No expenses may be incurred, with a view to promoting or procuring the election of a

candidate at an election by any person other than the candidate, his election agent and persons authorised in writing by the election agent on account of (1) holding public meetings or organising any public display; (2) issuing advertisements, circulars or publication; (3) otherwise presenting to the electors the candidate or his views, or the extent or nature of his backing, or disparaging another candidate; or (4) in the case of an election of the London members of the London Assembly at an ordinary election, otherwise presenting to the electors the candidate's registered political party or the views of that party, or the extent or nature of that party's backing, or disparaging any other registered political party: s 25. Section 26 allows the Commission greater flexibility in prescribing the form in which the information required should be presented, without reducing the amount of information that must be included in the return. 'Election expenses' are defined by s 27 in relation to a candidate at an election as meaning any expenses incurred at any time in respect of any specified matter which is used for the purposes of the candidate's election after the date when he becomes a candidate at the election.

By virtue of s 28, the Commission may prepare a report on parliamentary by-elections and elections to the Scottish Parliament and the National Assembly for Wales. Under s 29, (a) representatives of the Commission have the right to attend electoral or referendum proceedings in order to observe and subsequently report on them and also have the right to observe the working practices of electoral registration officers, returning officers and counting officers; (b) other observers, whether individuals or organisations, may be accredited by the Commission so that they or their members may attend and observe certain proceedings at an election or a referendum; and (c) the Commission may produce a code of practice to regulate the attendance of all observers at such proceedings. Power is conferred on the Secretary of State by s 30 to prescribe a different form of ballot paper from that which is currently prescribed and to amend the directions to printers of ballot papers and those for the guidance of voters in voting. By s 31, ballot papers will no longer be attached by a perforation to counterfoils. The Secretary of State has power under s 32 to make an order applying to specified local elections in England and Wales to enable the inclusion of photographs of candidates on ballot papers to be piloted at those elections. The Commission is required by s 33 to prepare a report containing an assessment of the operation of every pilot order after the elections specified in such an order have taken place. Under s 34, the Secretary of State may make an order applying, on a general and permanent basis, similar provision to that found in a pilot order made under s 31. Section 35 removes the provision in electoral law that stipulates that mental health patients detained under civil powers must vote at elections by either post or proxy. Section 36 provides that a person who is required or authorised to give or display specified documents must, as he thinks appropriate, make such documents available in Braille and translate them into languages other than English. The materials that should be issued by the returning officer to those entitled to vote by post are specified by s 37. New circumstances where a tendered ballot paper may be issued to a voter are outlined in s 38.

Attempts by persons to exert undue influence that do not prove to be successful may amount, by virtue of s 39, to the corrupt practice of undue influence. It will be both a corrupt practice and criminal offence to apply for a postal or proxy vote with the intention of stealing another person's vote or gaining a vote to which the applicant is not entitled: s 40. The responsibility for storing electoral documents after an election is transferred by s 41 from the Clerk of the Crown to local electoral registration officers. Section 42 provides for access to election documents for elections other than parliamentary elections in a similar way to that provided for parliamentary elections, s 43 creates an offence of contravening regulations governing access to post-election documentation, and s 44 defines some of the terms used in s 42, in particular, 'electoral area'. The returning officer is required by s 45 to make the relevant list when a postal voter has returned a postal vote or a postal proxy vote. Returning officers are enabled by s 46 to correct errors or omissions that arise during the preparation for, and conduct of, elections. Section 47, Sch 1 Pt 5 amend provisions relating to the conduct of elections.

Part 7 (ss 48–66) Regulation of parties
Under s 48, the Commission may refuse to register a political party where the party proposes a name which, if it were to appear on a ballot paper, would be likely to mislead an elector as to the effect of his vote or adversely affect an elector's understanding of any directions given on the ballot paper or elsewhere that are provided for his guidance in voting. New provision is made by s 49 regarding the descriptions that candidates standing on behalf of political parties may use, and the process by which they may be registered with the Commission. Section 50 sets a new period within which a party must submit to the Commission confirmation of the party's registered particulars. The Commission has power under s 51 to remove parties from the register of political parties where they fail to confirm their registered particulars by the specified day. The requirement that parties must be registered by the last date for publication of the notice of election in order to use a description is removed by s 52. The number of accounting bands is increased to four by s 53 which enables the Secretary of State to vary by order the number of accounting bands in order to give effect to a recommendation of the Commission. The time within which a registered political party is required to submit unaudited accounts to the Commission is extended by s 54 from three to four months.

By virtue of s 55, the receipt of a policy development grant is treated as a donation that will need to be declared when a party submits its accounts to the Commission. Section 56 makes the requirement for the treasurer of a registered party to submit quarterly donation reports in respect of any recordable donation less burdensome for smaller political parties, such as residents associations. Section 57 removes the requirement to report multiple small donations. The register of donations must specify when a donation takes the form of sponsorship: s 58. By virtue of s 59, the requirement for holders of relevant elective office to report donations to the Commission, with one exception, is removed. Section 60 applies to Northern Ireland. Section 61, Sch 1 Pt 6, make provision for the regulation of loans and related transactions to political parties. The Secretary of State is empowered by s 62 to extend the loans regime to candidates, third parties and referendums. Section 63 applies to Northern Ireland. Section 64 imposes limits on campaign expenditure for constituency elections to the Scottish Parliament and the National Assembly for Wales and elections to the Northern Ireland Assembly. Section 65 increases the time limits for claims in respect of campaign expenditure. Section 66 provides that, in a referendum, material such as ballot papers and other material which may be prescribed under a conduct of referendums order, does not require imprints and that specified election material is not to be regarded as being published on behalf of a candidate merely because the material can be reasonably regarded as promoting, procuring or enhancing the candidate's electoral success or standing.

Part 8 (ss 67–73) Miscellaneous
Section 67 relates to the setting of performance standards, returns and reports on performance standards and the provision of information about expenditure on elections. Section 68 enables the Secretary of State to specify in an order a total overall amount a returning officer may recover for expenses incurred in connection with the services which he renders. Electoral registration officers and returning officers are required by s 69 to take such steps as they think appropriate to encourage the participation of electors in the electoral process. Under s 70, magistrates' courts may extend from 12 months to no more than 24 months the time for commencing proceedings. Section 71 maintains the current position that the power of arrest inside a polling station without warrant of a person suspected of committing personation rests with a police constable only. Section 72 supports any future consolidation of the main legislation from 1983 onwards relating to United Kingdom parliamentary elections and local government elections in England and Wales. Any common law rule which renders persons unable to vote on the basis of mental incapacity is abolished: s 73.

Part 9 (ss 74–79) General
Section 74, Sch 1 Pt 7 and Sch 2 deal with amendments and repeals, s 75 with financial provision, and s 76 with interpretation. Section 77 provides for commencement, s 78 deals with extent and s 79 with short title.

Amendments, repeals and revocations
The list below, which is not exhaustive, mentions repeals and amendments which are or will be effective when the Act is fully in force.

Specific provisions of a number of Acts are amended, added or repealed. These include: Representation of the People Act 1983 ss 7, 7A, 7C, 9, 9A–9C, 10A, 13B, 13D, 15, 18, 18A–18E, 56, 59, 61, 62A, 63, 65A, 75, 81, 90ZA, 115, 199B, Sch 1; Representation of the People Act 1985 s 2; Political Parties, Elections and Referendums Act 2000 ss 5, 6A–6F, 22, 28, 32, 33, 42, 45, 52, 62A, 68, 69, 71F–71W, 77, 92, 115, 126, 143, Schs 6A, 7, 9; Representation of the People Act 2000 Sch 4.

1182   Electoral Commission—policy development grants
The Elections (Policy Development Grants Scheme) Order 2006, SI 2006/602 (in force on 1 April 2006), replaces the 2002 Regulations, SI 2002/224, and (1) makes provision for a revised scheme, set out in the Schedule to the order, for the making, by the Electoral Commission, of grants to political parties to assist with the development of policies for inclusion in their manifestos for parliamentary elections, elections to the European Parliament, the Scottish Parliament, the National Assembly for Wales, and the Northern Ireland Assembly, local government elections and local elections in Northern Ireland; (2) removes the Ulster Unionist Party from the scheme because it no longer satisfies the eligibility requirement of having two Members of Parliament who have taken an oath; (3) allocates £2m annually by way of grant under the scheme, which is to be divided between eligible parties and will comprise a fixed amount, determined by dividing £1m by the number of eligible parties for the year, and a variable amount, determined by reference to each party's share of the vote, weighted by turn-out.

1183   Election petition—service of documents—validity of petition
The Election Petition Rules 1960, SI 1960/543, r 6(1) requires a petitioner, within five days of giving security, to serve on the respondent and on the Director of Public Prosecutions a notice of the presentation of the petition and of the nature and amount of the security which he has given, together with a copy of the petition. Service must be effected in the manner in which a claim form is served: r 6(2).

in relation to the rules of conduct that apply when an election of councillors of a principal area is not taken together with the poll at another election, (a) changes made to the nomination procedures with the effect that (i) candidates may use their common names on nomination forms and ballot papers; (ii) the minimum age for a candidate is reduced from 21 to 18 years; (iii) the rules on the use of authorised descriptions by candidates standing on behalf of registered political parties are revised to reflect amendments made to the Political Parties, Elections and Referendums Act 2000 ss 28A and 28B; and (iv) returning officers will be able to correct minor errors on nomination papers; (b) new security measures requiring that (i) security markings and unique identification marks are provided on ballot papers; (ii) counterfoils on ballot papers are replaced by corresponding number lists; and (iii) postal voters and postal proxies provide both their signature and date of birth when returning postal ballot papers; (c) the introduction of new requirements as to the information and accessibility of information to be provided by returning officers to electors; (d) changes made to the rules regarding (i) the persons who may be admitted to a polling station and the count to observe elections; and (ii) the retention and inspection of election documents after the poll; and (e) provision made regarding the transmission of information to a presiding officer of alterations to the electoral register taking effect on the day of the poll; (2) the corresponding rules of conduct which apply when the poll of a principal area election is taken together with the poll at a parliamentary election, a European Parliamentary election, another local government election, or a referendum or election of a elected mayor; and (3) modifications to the parliamentary elections rules made by the Combination of Polls (England and Wales) Regulations 2004, SI 2004/294.

1190   National Assembly for Wales—representation of the people

See para 636.

1191   National Assembly for Wales—returning officers—charges

The National Assembly for Wales (Returning Officers' Charges) Order 2006, SI 2006/3268 (in force on 8 December 2006), specifies services and expenses in respect of which a returning officer at an election to the National Assembly may recover charges. SI 2002/3053, 2003/3117 are revoked.

1192   Northern Ireland (Miscellaneous Provisions) Act 2006

See para 2096.

1193   Parliamentary constituencies—division—Wales

The Parliamentary Constituencies and Assembly Electoral Regions (Wales) Order 2006, SI 2006/1041 (in force on 25 April 2006), (1) sets out and describes the parliamentary constituencies into which Wales is to be divided; (2) sets out and describes the altered electoral regions of the National Assembly for Wales; and (3) requires electoral registration officers to amend the registers of parliamentary electors and the registers of local government electors so as to give effect to the order. SI 1995/1036 is revoked.

1194   Parliamentary elections—polling districts—polling places—review

The Review of Polling Districts and Polling Places (Parliamentary Elections) Regulations 2006, SI 2006/2965 (in force on 1 January 2007), specify the manner in which representations made by a returning officer in connection with a review are to be published by a relevant authority and specify the information that a relevant authority must publish on the completion of a review.

1195   Political donations—regulated transactions—anonymous electors

The Political Donations and Regulated Transactions (Anonymous Electors) (England and Wales) Regulations 2006, SI 2006/2974 (in force on 1 January 2007), prescribe the form of evidence required to establish that a donor who has an anonymous entry in an electoral register is indeed a registered elector. The regulations also state that the prescribed from of evidence is a certificate of anonymous registration issued pursuant to the Representation of the People (England and Wales) Regulations 2001, SI 2001/341, reg 45E.

1196   Political Parties, Elections and Referendums Act 2000—commencement

The Political Parties, Elections and Referendums Act 2000 (Commencement No 3 and Transitional Provisions) Order 2006, SI 2006/3416, brings into force, on 1 January 2007, s 143, Sch 18 para 14. Transitional provisions are also made. For a summary of the Act, see 2000 Abr para 1423. See also the commencement table in the title STATUTES.

1197   Political parties—registration—prohibited words and expressions

The Registration of Political Parties (Prohibited Words and Expressions) (Amendment) Order 2006, SI 2006/3252 (in force on 1 January 2007), amends the 2001 Order, SI 2001/3252, so as to apply the 2001 Order to party descriptions and to ensure that words and expressions that are prohibited in relation to a party name are also prohibited in relation to a registered description.

1198   Polls—combination

The Representation of the People (Combination of Polls) (England and Wales) (Amendment) Regulations 2006, SI 2006/3278 (in force on 1 January 2007 in relation to elections or referenda with a polling date of 3 May 2007 or later), amend the 2004 Regulations, SI 2004/294, so as to (1) remove obsolete provisions relating to conduct of the 2004 European parliamentary elections and the joint issue and receipt of postal ballots; (2) add references to three new functions of a returning officer which have been introduced by the Electoral Administration Act 2006; (3) make minor changes consequential on the coming into force of the 2006 Act; and (4) clarify directions for the guidance of voters at combined polls.

1199   Representation of the people—general provisions

The Representation of the People (England and Wales) (Amendment) Regulations 2006, SI 2006/752 (in force on 23 March 2006), further amend the 2001 Regulations, SI 2001/341, so as to (1) require an application for registration as an elector to include a statement as to the applicant's nationality; (2) remove the requirement for an applicant who will attain the age of 70 years in the period of twelve months beginning with the date of his application to state the date on which he will attain the age of 70 years; (3) allow voters to apply for a postal vote at the same time they apply to be registered to vote; (4) provide that a registration officer may satisfy himself that an application for an absent vote has been signed by the applicant by referring to any signature previously provided by the applicant to the registration officer or the returning officer; (5) require that where a person wishes his ballot paper to be sent to an address different from that shown in the record for the purposes of a particular election, he must specify the reasons as to why this is the case; (6) set out additional requirements relating to the applicant's physical incapacity, regarding applications for a proxy vote in respect of a particular election; (7) require that where a registration officer grants an application for a postal vote, he must notify the applicant of his decision; (8) allow applications for replacement ballot papers in the case of spoilt declarations of identity; (9) allow applications for replacement ballot papers, the declaration of identity or the envelopes supplied for their return where the voter claims to have lost or not received his ballot paper; (10) require the returning officer at both parliamentary and local government elections to send a copy of the completed statement to the Secretary of State and the Electoral Commission ten to 15 working days following the date of the poll; (11) confirm that the register will not be used for direct marketing purposes; (12) require that a data copy of the full register be provided, fee of charge, to the British Library and the National Library of Wales; (13) provide that a copy of the register may be supplied to any local authority in addition to the local authority by which the electoral registration officer was appointed; (14) extend the use that may be made of the full register by such local authorities to include use for the purposes of a local poll; (15) provide that a copy of the full register may be supplied to the Security Service, Government Communications Headquarters and the Secret Intelligence Service for use in respect of their statutory functions; (16) provide that police forces and organisations may use the register for the purpose of the vetting of constables, officers and employees for the purposes of safeguarding national security; (17) provide that a copy of the full register may be supplied to a library maintained by a library authority or to an archives service established by a local authority; (18) specify that, in addition to the authorised sale of a copy of the full register to government departments, it may also be sold to the Environment Agency and the Financial Services Authority subject to restrictions; and (19) relax such restrictions to a limited extent to allow the use of the register for the vetting of persons for the purposes of safeguarding national security. The regulations also further amend (a) the Local Authorities (Conduct of Referendums) (England) Regulations 2001, SI 2001/1298, so as to change the hours of polling on the day of a referendum from 8 am to 9 pm to 7 am to 10 pm; and (b) the Local Authorities (Mayoral Elections) (England and Wales) Regulations 2002, SI 2002/185, so as to change the hours for a mayoral election from 8 am to 9 pm to 7 am to 10 pm.

The Representation of the People (England and Wales) (Amendment) (No 2) Regulations 2006, SI 2006/2910 (in force on 1 January 2007), further amend the 2001 Regulations supra so as to (1) remove the offence of providing false information in pursuance of a requisition of information by a registration officer in consequence to the creation of a broader offence of providing false information to registration officers by the Electoral Administration Act 2006; (2) provide (a) for a reminder to be sent in each year to persons who have an anonymous entry, as the entitlement to registration terminates after 12 months unless a fresh application is made; and (b) that applications for registration accompanied by an application for an anonymous entry will not be available for public inspection; (3) revise the procedure for (a) making objections to registration; and (b) determining applications for registration and objections without a hearing; (4) set out the procedure (a) to be followed by registration officers when reviewing entitlement to registration, and providing the circumstances in which the procedure does not apply; and (b) for applying for an anonymous entry; (5) require the registration officer to (a) allow an application for an anonymous entry where the application is properly made and he is satisfied that evidence of the prescribed nature, an order or injunction of a court protecting the applicant or another person of his household from harassment or molestation, or an attestation made by a qualifying officer that the safety of the applicant or another of his household is at risk, has been provided; and (b) maintain a record of anonymous entries, to be used only for the purposes of registration, elections, referendums, the summoning of juries, of the police, security and intelligence services and related organisations, preventing disclosure except where this is ordered by a court; (6) provide that where a notice of alteration to the electoral register is issued by a registration officer on a polling day as a result of a court ruling or to correct a clerical error, the registration officer must communicate the contents of the notice to the presiding officer and a written record of the contents must be made; (7) make revisions to (a) reflect the requirement that persons wishing to vote by post, by proxy or by postal proxy must provide their signature and date of birth when applying; and (b) update the lists of health care professionals and others who may attest applications for proxy votes so that it also includes persons who may be caring for or treating persons with disabilities of a non-physical nature; and (8) set out the procedure by which a cancelled postal ballot should be retrieved from a ballot box.

EMPLOYMENT

Halsbury's Laws of England (4th edn) vol 16(1A) (Reissue) paras 1–558 and 16(1B) (Reissue) paras 559–952

Articles

For articles relating to this title please refer to the Table of Articles at the beginning of the Abridgment.

1200   Contract of employment—apprenticeship—tripartite training agreement

Nine months after an employee started work with his employer, the employee entered into a tripartite individual learning plan with the employer and a training provider. The plan stated that it was to be carried out under advanced modern apprenticeship arrangements. The employee was subsequently dismissed without notice. He complained that he had been unfairly dismissed or that his contract of employment had been breached. An employment tribunal held that there was neither a contract of employment nor a contract of apprenticeship between the employer and the employee. On appeal by the employee, the Employment Appeal Tribunal found that the employee was employed under a contract of employment but not under a contract of apprenticeship, so that he was entitled to damages of one week's wages on the basis that he was an ordinary employee but not damages for breach of a contract of apprenticeship. The employee appealed. *Held*, the contract of employment had to be treated as varied or overlaid by the tripartite trainee arrangements, and that variation gave rise to additional obligations on the employer. Subject to certain provisions in the plan, the employer was bound for the training period specified in the plan. The arrangement had the essential features of an apprenticeship. The fact that some training was provided by a party other than the employer did not deprive the relationship between employer and apprentice of a long-term character that persisted until completion of the training period. Accordingly, the appeal would be allowed.

Flett v Matheson [2006] EWCA Civ 53, [2006] ICR 742 (Court of Appeal: Pill, Wall and Lloyd LJJ). *Dunk v George Waller & Sons Ltd* [1970] 2 All ER 630, CA, applied. *Thorpe v Dul* [2003] All ER (D) 14 (Jul), EAT, considered. Decision of Employment Appeal Tribunal [2005] ICR 1134 (2005 Abr para 1362) reversed.

1201   Contract of employment—breach of contract—repudiatory breach—unauthorised deductions from wages—waiver or affirmation

See *New Southern Railway Ltd v Quinn*, para 1457.

1202   Contract of employment—duty of trust and confidence—establishment of competing business

See *Shepherds Investments Ltd v Walters*, para 529.

1203   Contract of employment—duty of trust and confidence—statutory grievance procedure—unfair dismissal

After becoming responsible for the care of her grandchild, an employee found difficulty in managing the hours of her full-time job and made an informal request to her manager that she be allowed to work a three-day week. The request was refused and the employee made a formal application under the Employment Rights Act 1996 s 80F. The employer refused the application and the employee resigned. Subsequently, she brought proceedings to an employment tribunal alleging indirect sex discrimination, unfair constructive dismissal and breach of the right to request flexible working. The claim succeeded on the basis that the employer had not made out a reason for its refusal, which fell within s 80G(1)(b). In particular, it found that the manner in which the employer had dealt with the request for flexible working amounted to a breach of the implied duty of trust and confidence, which entitled the employee to terminate her employment. The tribunal rejected the employer's contention that her claim of unfair constructive dismissal should be rejected on the grounds that she had not raised a grievance before instituting tribunal proceedings under the Employment Act 2002 s 32. On the employer's appeal, *held,* the tribunal had not erred in finding that the claimant's application to her employer requesting flexible working under the 1996 Act s 80F was also the presentation of a grievance for the purposes of the 2002 Act s 32. An employee was not obliged to go through both procedures separately. It was clear that the document which contained the presentation of a grievance could also fulfil another function about the same or about a different matter. Whether a document did constitute the presentation of a grievance was a question of fact. The employment tribunal was entitled to find that there had been the presentation of a grievance by the presentation to the employer of an application for flexible working. It could not be accepted that, at the time she made that application, the claimant did not have anything to be aggrieved about because the procedures under the flexible working provisions had not been exhausted. Accordingly, the appeal would be dismissed.

Commotion Ltd v Rutty [2006] ICR 290 (Employment Appeal Tribunal: Judge Burke QC presiding).

1204   Contract of employment—fixed-term contract—successive contracts—conversion into indefinite contract—Community law

The applicant was employed as a cook by a hospital under two successive fixed-term contracts. His second contract was not renewed by the hospital when it expired and the hospital formally dismissed him when he arrived at his workplace on the date of expiry of his contract. The applicant challenged the decision to dismiss him before a tribunal. He sought to rely on national legislation implementing EC Council Directive 1999/70, which gave legal force to the Framework Agreement on Fixed-term Work. Clause 5 required member states to introduce measures regarding objective reasons justifying the renewal of such contracts or relationships, the maximum total duration of successive fixed-term employment contracts or relationships, and/or the number of renewals of such contracts or relationships. The applicant submitted that his fixed-term contracts with the hospital should be deemed to be contracts of indefinite duration. The tribunal stayed proceedings and sought a preliminary ruling from the European Court of Justice as to whether the Framework Agreement precluded national legislation which, where abuse arose from a public sector employer's use of successive fixed-term contracts or working relationships, prevented the latter from being converted into indefinite contracts or working relationships, even where such conversion applied to contracts and working relationships concluded with a private sector employer. *Held*, the Framework Agreement should be interpreted as not, in principle, precluding such legislation where that legislation included another effective measure to prevent and, where relevant, punish the abuse of successive fixed-term contracts by a public sector employer. Although Directive 1999/70 and the Framework Agreement could also apply to fixed-term employment contracts and relationships concluded with public authorities and other public sector bodies, cl 5 did not preclude a member state from treating abuse of successive fixed-term employment contracts or relationships differently, according to whether those contracts or relationships were entered into with a private sector or public sector employer. However, cl 5 did place on a member state the mandatory requirement of effective adoption of at least one of the measures listed in that provision intended to prevent the abusive use of successive fixed-term employment contracts or relationships, where domestic law did not already included equivalent measures.

Case C-180/04 *Vassallo v Azienda Ospedaliera Ospedale San Martino di Genova e Cliniche Universitarie Convenzionate* [2006] All ER (D) 45 (Sep) (ECJ: Second Chamber). Case C-53/04 *Marrousu v Azienda Ospedaliera Ospedale San Martino di Genova e Cliniche Universitarie Convenzionate* [2006] All ER (D) 36 (Sep), ECJ (para 1206), applied.

1205   Contract of employment—fixed-term contract—successive contracts—objective reason

The Framework Agreement on Fixed-term Work (annexed to EC Council Directive 1999/70) cl 5(1)(a) provides that to prevent abuse arising from the use of successive fixed-term employment contracts, member states must introduce objective reasons justifying the renewal of such contracts. Member states must determine under what conditions fixed-term employment contracts are to be regarded as 'successive' and are deemed to be contracts of indefinite duration: cl 5(2).

A number of employees made a number of successive fixed-term employment contracts with their employer which was established in Greece. Each of the contracts was concluded for a period of eight months and was separated by a period of time ranging from a minimum of 22 days to a maximum of almost 11 months. On each occasion, the employees were reappointed to the same post as that in respect of which the initial contract had been concluded, though they were now either unemployed or employed by the employer on a provisional basis. Greek law provided that the unlimited renewal of fixed-term employment contracts was permitted if justified by an objective reason, and that there was an objective reason if a fixed-term contract was required by legislation. The employees sought a declaration that their fixed-term contracts had to be regarded as employment contracts of indefinite duration, in accordance with the Framework Agreement. The court referred to the European Court of Justice the question whether the fact solely that the conclusion of a fixed-term contract was required by a statutory provision could constitute an objective reason for the continual conclusion of successive fixed-term contracts. *Held*, cl 5(1)(a) precluded the use of successive fixed-term employment contracts where the justification advanced for their use was solely that it was provided for by a general provision of legislation of a member state. The concept of objective reasons required recourse to the particular type of employment relationship, as provided for by national legislation, to be justified by the presence of specific factors relating in particular to the activity in question and the conditions under which it was carried out. Clause 5 was to be interpreted as precluding a national rule under which only fixed-term employment contracts that were not separated from one another by a period of time longer than 20 working days were to be regarded as 'successive'. A succession of fixed-term contracts that, in fact, had been intended to cover fixed and permanent needs of the employer constituted an abuse. Therefore, the Framework Agreement precluded the application of national legislation which prohibited the conversion such contracts into an employment contract of indefinite duration.

Case C-212/04 *Adeneler v Ellinikos Organismos Galaktos* [2007] All ER (EC) 82 (ECJ: Grand Chamber).

1206 Contract of employment—fixed-term contract—successive contracts—public sector employer

The claimants had been employed by the defendant, an Italian public hospital, under a series of fixed-term contracts. The hospital decided not to renew the contracts and, on their expiry, formally dismissed the claimants when they arrived at their workplace. The claimants challenged their dismissal on the ground that the application of Italian legislation meant that the contracts should be deemed to be of indefinite duration. It fell to be determined whether the Framework Agreement on Fixed-Term Work, annexed to EC Council Directive 99/70, precluded national legislation which, where abuses arose from a public sector employer's use of successive fixed-term contracts or working relationships, prevented those fixed-term contracts from being converted into indefinite contracts or working relationships, even where such conversion applied to contracts and working relationships concluded with a private sector employer. *Held*, there was nothing in the Framework Agreement to suggest that it was limited to contracts for private sector workers. On its proper construction, the agreement did not preclude national legislation which, where there was abuse arising from the use of successive fixed-term employment contracts or relationships by a public sector employer, precluded their being converted into contracts of indeterminate duration, even though such conversion was provided for in respect of employment contracts and relationships with a private sector employer, where the legislation included another effective measure to prevent and, where relevant, punish the abuse of successive fixed-term contracts by a public sector employer.

Case C-53/04 *Marrousu v Azienda Ospedaliera Ospedale San Martino di Genova e Cliniche Universitarie Convenzionate* [2006] All ER (D) 36 (Sep) (ECJ: Second Chamber).

1207 Contract of employment—implied contract—agency worker

The claimant was supplied by an agency to carry out work for a local authority. After her engagement came to an end, the claimant commenced proceedings for unfair dismissal against the authority, even though she had no express contract of employment with it. She contended that there was an implied contract, since she had worked for the authority for five years and it was necessary to imply a contract to give business efficacy to the relationship. An employment tribunal found that there was an absence of the required mutuality of obligation necessary to support the existence of a contract between the claimant and the authority. On appeal by the claimant, *held*, the issue was whether the way in which the contract had been performed was consistent with an agency arrangement, or whether it was only consistent with an implied contract between the worker and the end-user. When the arrangements were genuine and accurately represented the relationship between the parties, as was likely to be the case where there was no pre-existing contract between the worker and the end-user, it would be a rare case where there would be evidence entitling a tribunal to imply a contract between the worker and the end-user. If any such contract was to be inferred, there should be some words or conduct which entitled the tribunal to conclude that the agency arrangements no longer dictated or adequately reflected how the work was being performed, and that the reality of the relationship was only consistent with the implication of the contract. Typically, the mere passage of time did not justify any such implication as a matter of necessity. The employment tribunal had been fully entitled to find that the circumstances did not exist which would justify the inference of an implied contract. It had done so by focusing on mutuality of obligations, although it might have more pertinently said simply that there had been no necessity to imply a contract. Accordingly, the appeal would be dismissed.

James v Greenwich LBC [2007] IRLR 168 (Employment Appeal Tribunal: Elias J presiding).

The claimant was engaged as a contractor by the employer, a telecommunications company. The claimant continued to submit invoices to the employer but they were not paid. He was told that the employer did not deal directly with contractors and that the claimant ought to deal with the employer through an agency. The claimant entered into a contract for services with an agency, after which the agency paid the employee's monthly invoices. When the employer informed the employee that it no longer required his services, he presented a complaint of unfair dismissal to an employment tribunal. The employer contended that the claimant was not an employee, and the tribunal dealt with that as a preliminary issue. It adjourned the issue until after the Court of Appeal had given its decision in *Dacas v Brook Street Bureau (UK) Ltd*. Applying the guidance in that case, the tribunal decided that the claimant had had an implied contract of employment with the employer. The Employment Appeal Tribunal upheld the decision and the employer appealed further. *Held*, the view of the majority in *Dacas* was correct. The essentials of a contract of employment were the obligation to provide work for remuneration and the obligation to perform it, coupled with control. It did not matter whether the arrangements for payment were made directly or indirectly. The guidance provided for employment tribunals was unimpeachable. While it was not strictly binding according to the rules of precedent, it was plainly right for employment tribunals to heed it. The guidance did not direct employment tribunals to reach any particular conclusion, only to consider the possibility that an implied contract might exist. Accordingly, the appeal would be dismissed.

Muscat v Cable & Wireless plc [2006] EWCA Civ 220, [2006] ICR 975 (Court of Appeal: Sir Anthony Clarke MR, Smith and Maurice Kay LJJ). *Dacas v Brook Street Bureau (UK) Ltd* [2004] EWCA Civ 217, [2004] ICR 1437 (2004 Abr para 1160) applied.

An employee's services had been provided by an agency which employed her under a contract of service. While working for the employer, a dispute arose as to whether the employee had falsified her timesheets. It was decided that she had not done so, but the employer refused to continue to employ the employee, and the agency also eventually terminated the contract of service after unsuccessfully attempting to relocate her. The employee brought a claim of unfair dismissal against the employer. At the hearing, the primary issue was whether the employee had been employed by the employer under a contract of employment. The tribunal concluded that, but for the existence of the contract of employment between the employee and the agency, it would have accepted the need to imply a contract between the employee and the employer. Notwithstanding that conclusion, the tribunal refused to find such an implied contract in the instant case on the grounds that there was no authority to support the proposition that such a contract could be implied between an employee and end-user where there existed a contract of employment between the employee and the agency, and that the agreed test of necessity for the implication of a contract of employment between the employee and the employer had not been made out. The employee's claim was therefore dismissed. On her appeal, *held*, where the contract between the employee and the agency was one for services, it might be possible to imply a contract of service between the employee and the end-user in order to afford the employee protection under the Employment Rights Act 1996. Where, however, the employee was employed by the agency, and, therefore, protected by the 1996 Act, there existed no policy considerations capable of justifying the extension of that protection to a second and parallel employer. The employee had been engaged by the agency under a contract of service, and her arguments in support of the implication of a contract between herself and the employer appeared to be solely founded on the assertion that her claim for unfair dismissal would have had a greater prospect of success as against the employer. In those circumstances, the tribunal had correctly refused to find an implied contract of employment between the employee and the employer. Accordingly, the appeal would be dismissed.

Cairns v Visteon UK Ltd [2007] All ER (D) 39 (Jan) (Employment Appeal Tribunal: Judge Peter Clark presiding).

1208   Contract of employment—mutuality of obligation—succession of individual engagements—continuity of employment

The Employment Rights Act 1996 s 212(1) provides that any week during the whole or part of which an employee's relations with his employer are governed by a contract of employment counts in computing the employee's period of employment. Any week not within s 212(1) during the whole or part of which an employee is absent from work on account of a temporary cessation of work counts in computing the employee's period of employment: s 212(3)(b).

The claimant was engaged by the defendant local education authority as a home tutor to teach children who were unable for various reasons to attend school. The defendant was under no contractual obligation to offer pupils to the claimant, and she was under no contractual obligation to accept the pupils whom the defendant asked the claimant to take on. However, once the claimant had agreed to take on the work, she was obliged to fulfil her commitment to the particular pupil and the defendant was obliged to continue to provide the work until the particular engagement had ceased. The claimant brought proceedings before an employment tribunal, claiming a declaration of written particulars of employment in respect of a certain ten-year period. It was common ground that there was no single contract of service of a global, umbrella or overarching character spreading over that period. The claimant relied on the succession of numerous individual teaching contracts during the period and on the application of the continuity provisions of the 1996 Act s 212 to bridge the gaps between the individual contracts. The defendant submitted that the claimant had had a series of short, fixed-term, discrete, individual teaching engagements, none of which was a contract of service, as they were lacking in the requisite 'irreducible minimum' of continuing mutual obligations. The tribunal found that the claimant had been an employee of the defendant during the relevant period, and that there was mutuality of obligation between the parties while the individual contracts were in force. The employment tribunal also ruled that the gaps between the individual contracts when the claimant was undertaking no work for the defendant were bridged by s 212. The defendant's appeal to the Employment Appeal Tribunal was dismissed, and, on its further appeal, *held*, once a contract for home tuition had been entered into and while the contract continued, the claimant was under an obligation to teach the pupil and the defendant was under an obligation to pay her for teaching the pupil made available to her by the defendant under the contract. That was all that was legally necessary to support the finding that each individual teaching engagement was a contract of service. Section 212 took care of the gaps between the individual contracts and secured continuity of employment for the purposes of the 1996 Act. Accordingly, the appeal would be dismissed.

Prater v Cornwall CC [2006] EWCA Civ 102, [2006] 2 All ER 1013 (Court of Appeal: Mummery, Longmore and Lewison LJJ).

1209 Contract of employment—terms of employment—entitlement to bonus—discretion of employer

An employee was employed by a bank for more than two years before being made redundant. Under his employment contract, he was eligible to participate in the employer's discretionary bonus scheme on specified written terms. Those terms stipulated that the amount and timing of the bonus were entirely at the discretion of the employer which, when deciding on the amount of any bonus, was entitled to take into account the performance of the individual and his business unit, as well as whether the employee was remaining in his present employment. The employee commenced proceedings against his employer for breach of contract by under-payment of discretionary bonuses for two years and by non-payment of a bonus for that part of the final year of his employment before he was made redundant. The employee submitted that the employer, in breach of an implied term of the employee's employment contract that the employer would not exercise irrationally or perversely any discretion it had in relation to the employee's bonus award, had paid him a bonus that was less than had been recommended by his manager. He also alleged that the employer's requirement that a person had to be employed in March of a particular year to be able to qualify for a bonus in that year was contrary to the Unfair Contract Terms Act 1977 s 3. *Held*, the employer had a very wide contractual discretion and it could not be said that its decisions on the employee's bonuses in respect of the two full years of his employment were irrational on their face. The burden of establishing that no rational bank in the City would have paid the employee a bonus of less than his manager recommended was a very high one. It would require an overwhelming case to persuade the court to find that the level of a discretionary bonus payment was irrational or perverse in an area where so much had to depend on the discretionary judgment of the bank in fluctuating market and labour conditions. Moreover, the employer was not precluded by s 3 from refusing to treat the employee as ineligible for a discretionary bonus for the final period of his employment. The regulation by s 3 of fairness of contract terms was not primarily directed at personal work or employment contracts and was not particularly appropriate to them. Accordingly, the application would be dismissed.

Keen v Commerzbank AG [2006] EWCA Civ 1536, [2007] IRLR 132 (Court of Appeal: Mummery, Jacob and Moses LJJ). *Brigden v American Express Bank Ltd* [2000] IRLR 94 (2000 Abr para 1429) considered.

1210 Contract of employment—terms of employment—holiday pay—incorporation of holiday pay into hourly pay

EC Council Directive 93/104 art 7(1) provides that member states must take the measures necessary to ensure that every worker is entitled to paid annual leave of at least four weeks. The minimum period of paid annual leave may not be replaced by an allowance in lieu, except where the employment relationship is terminated: art 7(2).

Employees worked under contracts which provided for the incorporation of holiday pay into hourly rates of pay. They complained to an employment tribunal that that they had not received holiday pay to which they were entitled under the Working Time Regulations 1998, SI 1998/1833, which implemented Directive 93/104. It fell to be determined whether contractual arrangements such as those in issue violated the employees' rights under art 7. *Held*, the holiday pay required by art 7(1) was intended to enable workers actually to take the leave to which they were entitled, and 'paid annual leave' in that provision meant that remuneration had to be maintained for the duration of annual leave, so that workers had to receive their normal remuneration for that period of rest. Article 7(2) was intended to ensure that a worker was normally entitled to actual rest, with a view to ensuring effective protection of his health and safety. It followed that an allowance in lieu of holiday, as imposed by the employees' contracts of employment, was contrary to art 7(2).

Cases C-131/04, C-257/04 *Robinson-Steele v RD Retail Services Ltd; Clarke v Frank Staddon Ltd; Caulfield v Hanson Clay Products Ltd* [2006] All ER (EC) 749 (ECJ: First Chamber). For earlier related proceedings see *Marshalls Clay Products Ltd v Caulfield; Clarke v Frank Staddon Ltd* [2004] EWCA Civ 422, [2004] ICR 1502 (2004 Abr para 1162).

1211   Contract of employment—terms of employment—implied term—conduct of work outside express terms of contact

An employee had been employed as a teacher at a unique assessment centre. Under the terms of her contract, she was required to work at the centre for nearly 13 hours per week. Subsequently, she entered into a separate contract of engagement with the local authority governing the terms of her appointment at a different unit. Problems arose between the employee and her employer and the employee went off sick, alleging that she had been the victim of bullying and harassment at the centre. The local authority commissioned an investigator to examine the employee's complaints, all but one of which were dismissed. The employee was willing to take part in a return to work plan suggested by the investigator, but did not accept his conclusions. The local authority suggested alternative proposals which involved the employee working at other sites. However, the employee insisted on returning to the centre. The employee had continued to receive remuneration but finally, the local authority ceased payment of her wages. The employee brought a complaint to an employment tribunal. The tribunal dismissed the claim. On the employee's appeal, the issue to be decided was whether the local authority had been contractually entitled to require the employee to work otherwise than at the centre. *Held,* where a written contract clearly defined an employee's contractual duties, he ought to be entitled to proceed on the basis that he was not obliged to undertake different duties. In such cases, the finding of an implied obligation to undertake work outside the express terms of the contract would only have been permissible in exceptional circumstances, and where the work was suitable and the employee suffered no detriment in terms of contractual benefits or status on account of the change of duties on a temporary basis. In the present case, the stance adopted by the employee had given rise to exceptional circumstances. The tribunal had properly considered the relevant factors and had been entitled to make the finding that the contract of employment with regard to the centre contained an implied term entitling the local authority to require the employee to work outside the scope of the express terms of the contract. Accordingly, the appeal would be dismissed.

Luke v Stoke-on-Trent City Council [2006] All ER (D) 232 (Dec) (Employment Appeal Tribunal: Underhill J presiding).

1212   Contract of employment—terms of employment—restriction on disclosing information

See *Freshtime UK Ltd v Wayne*, para 585.

1213   Contract of employment—terms of employment—restriction on practising as solicitor—protection of legitimate interests—reasonableness

The claimant, a firm of solicitors, employed the defendant, an assistant solicitor. Her contract of employment contained restrictive covenants, which included post-employment restrictions of limited duration. One of those purported not to allow the defendant to do the work of a solicitor at any place within a radius of six miles of the claimant's office for a period of one year. The defendant resigned and, the following week, she sent e-mails, soliciting work, to a number of established clients of the claimant. It sought injunctive relief against the defendant for breach of covenant. It fell to be determined whether the restriction was reasonable for the protection of the legitimate interests of the claimant. *Held,* the fact that the restriction was not limited to those clients with whom the defendant had had personal contact in the period of one year prior to termination was an important consideration. The emphasis on the statistics of personal client dealings in the last year of employment was superficially attractive but fundamentally misconceived for the reason that it neglected the importance of judging the reasonableness of the restriction as at the date when the contract was made and not the date when it came to an end. The non-dealing clause had the advantage of being certain as to its area of application and the protection which it provided was reasonable both as regards the restriction and the limited period of time for which the restriction was to operate. An area clause, which was not limited to the clients of the claimant, was wider than necessary to protect the claimant's legitimate interests. Having regard to the size of the population within a radius of six miles of the claimant's office, a radial restriction would serve mainly to protect the claimant from competition for the business of a very large number of commercial entities which were not clients of the firm. The claimant was not entitled to that sort of protection.

Allan Janes LLP v Johal [2006] EWHC 286 (Ch), [2006] ICR 742 (Chancery Division: Bernard Livesey QC).

1214   Contract of employment—working time—normal working hours—fixed number of hours—genuine pre-estimate

The Employment Rights Act 1996 s 234(1) provides that, where an employee is entitled to overtime pay when employed for more than a fixed number of hours in a week or other period, there are for the purposes of the 1996 Act normal working hours in his case.

Employee drivers were employed pursuant to a standard hours contract which stipulated a basic 40-hour week. The terms and conditions set out the basis on which drivers would receive enhanced pay after working 40 hours. The employees' pay was made up of two elements, a productivity amount calculated by reference to distance travelled rather than time taken, and a 'terminal loading times' amount, which was calculated by reference to a pre-determined loading and unloading period for each product transported. In subsequent proceedings before an employment tribunal, an issue arose as to whether the employees worked 'normal working hours' for the purposes of the 1996 Act ss 221–224. The employees maintained that normal working hours meant fixed actual hours, while the employer contended that they could also mean genuine pre-estimates of the actual hours worked. The tribunal decided that the employees did have normal working hours, and the employees appealed. *Held*, the phrase 'fixed number of hours' in s 234(1) meant actual fixed hours, not a notional number of hours even if it was a genuine pre-estimate. An employee had to be employed for a definite number of hours if he was to have 'normal working hours'. If the draftsman of s 234(1) had wished to ensure that the provision related only to actual hours worked and not any form of notional or pre-estimated hours, he was likely to have considered that the words 'fixed hours' would be appropriate. It would be necessary to redraft s 234(1) to add the words 'or for any other period which is a genuine pre-estimate of the number of hours he actually works' to achieve the result for which the employer contended. Accordingly, the appeal would be allowed.

Sanderson v Exel Management Services Ltd [2006] ICR 1337 (Employment Appeal Tribunal: Silber J presiding).

1215 Contract of employment—working time—time spent on call—employee required to be at place of employment

The Working Time Regulations 1998, SI 1998/1833, reg 10(1) provides that a worker is entitled to a rest period of not less than 11 consecutive hours in each 24-hour period. 'Rest period' means a period which is not working time, other than a rest break or leave to which the worker is entitled under the 1998 Regulations; and 'working time' means any period during which a worker is working, at his employer's disposal and carrying out his activity or duties: reg 2(1).

An employee, the manager of a care home, was provided with rent-free accommodation on site. An important part of her duties was to respond to emergencies. As a result she was on call for 24 hours a day for four days in every week, during which she was required to be on site or within three minutes of it. She claimed that she had been refused the daily rest periods and rest breaks to which she was entitled under the 1998 Regulations. An employment tribunal dismissed the claim and the employee appealed. *Held*, the whole period during which the employee was on call constituted working time. A worker who was provided with accommodation at her workplace and was required to be on site to answer calls throughout a period of 24 hours, but otherwise could sleep during the night or take recreation in her home, was working for the whole 24 hours for the purposes of the 1998 Regulations. The employee was required to remain at, or within a very short distance of, her home, which was located at her place of work, and was never off duty since she was always liable to answer calls directly from residents. She had to remain at the place determined by her employer with a view to performing services if need be or when requested to intervene. The whole period during which the employee was on call constituted working time so that she was entitled to daily rest periods in accordance with reg 10(1). Accordingly, the appeal would be allowed.

MacCartney v Oversley House Management [2006] IRLR 514 (Employment Appeal Tribunal: Richardson J presiding). Case C-151/02 *Landeshauptstadt Kiel v Jaeger* [2004] All ER (EC) 604, ECJ (2003 Abr para 1140); and Case C-303/98 *Sindicato de Médicos de Asistencia Pública (SIMAP) v Conselleria de Sanidad y Consumo de la Generalidad Valenciana* [2001] All ER (EC) 609, ECJ (2000 Abr para 1508), applied.

1216 Disability discrimination

See DISCRIMINATION.

1217 Employee—part-time employee—less favourable treatment—same or broadly similar work—retained firefighter

The Part-time Workers (Prevention of Less Favourable Treatment) Regulations 2000, SI 2000/1551, reg 2(4)(a) provides that a full-time worker is a comparable full-time worker in relation to a part-time worker if, at the time when the treatment that is alleged to be less favourable to the part-time worker takes place, both workers are employed by the same employer under the same type of contract and are engaged in the same or broadly similar work.

The appellants, who were retained firefighters, claimed that they had been treated less favourably than comparable full-time firefighters, in contravention of the 2000 Regulations. It fell to be determined whether full-time firefighters were comparable full-time workers within the meaning of reg 2(4)(a). The Court of Appeal found that, while the appellants were employed under the same type of contract as full-time firefighters, they were not engaged in the same or broadly similar work. The appellants appealed. *Held*, Lords Carswell and Mance dissenting, in deciding whether retained firefighters and full-time firefighters were engaged in the same or broadly similar work, the question was not whether the work was different but whether it was the same or broadly similar. Particular weight should be given to the extent to which the work was the same and to the importance of that work to the enterprise as a whole. Otherwise too much weight could be given to the differences in the work, which were the almost inevitable consequences of working less than full-time rather than working full-time. The appellants were comparable with full-time firefighters and, accordingly, the appeal would be allowed.

Matthews v Kent & Medway Towns Fire Authority [2006] UKHL 8, [2006] 2 All ER 171 (House of Lords: Lords Nicholls of Birkenhead and Hope of Craighead, Baroness Hale of Richmond, Lords Carswell and Mance). Decision of Court of Appeal [2004] EWCA Civ 844, [2004] 3 All ER 620 (2004 Abr para 1171) reversed in part.

1218   Employee—rights—compensation—increase of limits

The Employment Rights (Increase of Limits) Order 2006, SI 2006/3045 (in force on 1 February 2007) increases, from 1 February 2007, the limits applying to certain awards of employment tribunals, and other specified amounts payable under employment legislation. The increases apply where the event giving rise to the entitlement to compensation or other payments occurred on or after 1 February 2007. SI 2005/3352 is revoked.

1219   Employer—duty of care—duty to employee—nurse in special hospital—assault by violent patient

The six claimants were nurses employed by the defendant at a special hospital. One of the long-term patients at the hospital had a history of very violent and unpredictable behaviour, and had been diagnosed as having a psychopathic disorder. She had assaulted members of staff on a number of occasions, and had threatened to kill staff, or to harm fellow patients or staff. One night, the patient asked for painkillers for a self-inflicted wound. She appeared to be calm, but then without warning she launched a violent attack on the fifth claimant. The other claimants intervened and a violent struggle ensued. All six claimants were injured during the incident in various degrees of seriousness. The claimants issued proceedings for damages in negligence, arguing that the patient should, before the incident and because of her history, have been confined to her room at night, and that the defendant had failed in its duty to carry out a risk assessment in relation to the patient. The claim was allowed, and the defendant appealed. *Held*, the duty that the defendant owed to the patient was of relevance in considering the duty that the defendant owed to its employees, but it did not follow that the duty owed to employees could be tested simply by the question of whether what had occurred amounted to a breach of duty to the patient. If the defendant could take precautions so as not to expose its employees to needless risks and still not be in breach of its duty to its patient, then it might well be in breach of duty if it failed to take those precautions. The question whether it was in breach of duty would be tested by reference to the principles applicable as between employer and employee, not as between doctor and patient. There were methods whereby the defendant could protect other patients and staff from needless risks where high-risk patients were concerned without being in breach of duty to the patient. In concluding that there should have been an assessment, and that following such an assessment the defendant should have had a policy of confining the patient in her room at night, the judge had imposed the appropriate standard of care on the defendant in respect of its employees. Accordingly, the appeal would be dismissed.

Buck v Nottinghamshire Healthcare NHS Trust [2006] EWCA Civ 1576, [2006] All ER (D) 310 (Nov) (Court of Appeal: Waller, Carnwath and Maurice Kay LJJ). *King v Sussex Ambulance NHS Trust* [2002] EWCA Civ 953, [2002] ICR 1413 (2002 Abr para 1546); and *Cook v Bradford Community Health NHS Trust* [2002] All ER (D) 329 (Oct), CA, considered.

1220   Employer—vicarious liability—act within course of employment—protection of employee from harassment

See *Majrowski v Guy's and St Thomas's NHS Trust*, para 2773.

1221   Employer—vicarious liability—bullying at work—connection between employment and tort

See *Green v DB Group Services (UK) Ltd*, para 2781.

1222   Employment Appeal Tribunal—appeal—jurisdiction of Court of Appeal—appeal on point of law

An employment tribunal decided that a number of employees had been unfairly dismissed. Their appeal as to the appropriate level of compensation was dismissed by the Employment Appeal Tribunal and they appealed further. *Held*, the Court of Appeal's jurisdiction to hear the appeal, which was from a statutory tribunal, derived from the Employment Tribunals Act 1996 s 37(1), which provided for an appeal from the appeal tribunal on a point of law only. In no realistic sense could the Court of Appeal be hearing an appeal from the appeal tribunal if it was only concerned with whether the employment tribunal had come to the correct conclusion. Accordingly, the appeal would be dismissed.

Gover v Propertycare Ltd [2006] EWCA Civ 286, [2006] 4 All ER 69 (Court of Appeal: Buxton, Lloyd and Richards LJJ).

1223 Employment Appeal Tribunal—appeal—power to request further reasons

An employment tribunal upheld an employee's complaints of unlawful racial discrimination, victimisation, racial harassment and constructive unfair dismissal against her employer. The employer appealed, contending that the tribunal had failed to identify the relevant comparator for the purpose of the comparative exercise required to uphold the employee's complaints and that the tribunal's reasons were inadequate. An issue arose as to whether the Employment Appeal Tribunal was permitted to request an additional set of reasons from an employment tribunal. *Held*, the appeal tribunal was not prohibited from requesting further written reasons from a tribunal when it had already provided some. When exercising the discretion to refer the matter back to a tribunal, the appeal tribunal had to balance the desirability of obtaining the tribunal's unexpressed reasoning against the risk that a referral would simply permit the tribunal a second chance to construct a properly reasoned decision that arrived at the same conclusion as it had originally reached. The tribunal had failed to identify the relevant comparators in clear terms and to carry out the comparative exercise necessary for the claims of direct discrimination and victimisation. The tribunal also gave no explanation for its conclusion that the harassment claim was made out. Having made the necessary primary findings of fact and having set out the law to be applied, the real criticism of the tribunal in the instant case was that it had failed to explain how the application of the law to the facts it found led it to the conclusions it reached. The judgment by the tribunal was not so inadequate that a complete rehearing was necessary, but it was appropriate to refer the matter back to the tribunal to amplify its earlier reasoning. Judgment would be given accordingly.

Obonyo v Wandsworth NHS Primary Care Trust [2006] All ER (D) 94 (Feb) (Employment Appeal Tribunal: Judge Peter Clark presiding). *Barke v SEETEC Business Technology Centre Ltd* [2005] EWCA Civ 578, [2005] ICR 1373 (para 05/1610) applied. *Meek v City of Birmingham DC* [1987] IRLR 250, CA (1987 Abr para 916), considered.

1224 Employment tribunal—complaint—time limit—extension of time

An employer effected a unilateral reduction in the remuneration of one of his employees, causing the employee to hand in notice of his resignation with effect from a specified date. In his resignation letter he did not allude to the reasons for his resignation, but, on a later date, and still before the notice period had elapsed, he lodged a formal grievance about the reduction in his remuneration. The employer replied, acknowledging that the grievance was valid, and the employee therefore subsequently presented a claim in the employment tribunal of constructive unfair dismissal, unauthorised deductions from wages and breach of contract. At a pre-hearing review, the employer submitted that, as the claims were presented nearly six months after the termination of employment, they had been brought out of time. The employee argued that the lodging of the grievance entitled him to a three-month time extension pursuant to the Employment Act 2002 (Dispute Resolution) Regulations 2004, SI 2004/752, reg 15, which provided for such an extension of the normal time limit in circumstances in which the statutory dismissal or grievance procedure applied. The tribunal chairman decided that the claims were brought in time and, on the employer's appeal, an issue arose as to whether the time extension was available where the grievance was raised at a date prior to that on which the time for bringing the proceedings started to run. *Held*, when reg 15 referred to a grievance being lodged 'within' the normal time limit for the jurisdiction or to 'the period within which a complaint under the relevant jurisdiction must be presented' the only limit being referred to was the end of the period in question. While as a matter of language the words of the provision could be read as referring both to the beginning and the end of the period, they did not necessarily do so and that was not the natural reading in the context. The various statutory 'time limits' to which reg 15 referred were provisions concerned with setting a date after which proceedings might not be brought: they were not as such concerned with prescribing a start date. In every case there was a date before which the proceedings could not be brought, namely the date at which the cause of action accrued, and any proceedings brought before that date would be liable to be struck out as premature. However. that was an inherent consequence of the fact that the tribunal would have no jurisdiction unless a relevant act or omission was said to have occurred; it did not derive from the terms of the limitation provision. It followed that, on the true construction of reg 15, an employee's grievance was to be treated as lodged 'within the normal time limit' even if it was lodged before the effective date of termination or other date from which time started to run. Accordingly, the appeal would be dismissed.

HM Prison Service v Barua [2007] IRLR 4 (Employment Appeal Tribunal: Underhill J presiding).

An employee was suspended on suspicion of serious misconduct and, in response, put in a grievance against the allegations. The employee was badly affected by the allegations, and began to suffer from a major depressive disorder. Grievance and disciplinary proceedings were arranged, but were postponed on account of the employee's ill-health. Subsequently, a medical report advised the employer that the employee was not fit to participate in the hearings, and the employer was warned not to discriminate against the employee. Notwithstanding this, the employer proceeded to conduct the hearings in the employee's absence. The grievances were largely rejected and the employee was summarily dismissed for gross misconduct. An appeal hearing was dismissed and the employee presented a claim to an employment tribunal, alleging that the employer's conduct of the investigation had been discriminatory. The tribunal held that although the claim was out of time, in the present case, it was just and equitable to extend the time limit to allow the employee's claim to proceed. The employer appealed and the employee cross-appealed, submitting that he had initiated an applicable grievance procedure under the Employment Act 2002 (Dispute Resolution) Regulations 2004, SI 2004/752, reg 6(1), and that reg 6(5) had not disapplied that procedure because the grievance was not that the employer had dismissed or contemplated dismissal, but related to the manner in which the various steps were carried out. *Held,* for the purposes of reg 6(5), a grievance that the employer had dismissed or had contemplated dismissal included a complaint about the manner in which the employer was contemplating dismissal. Further, a grievance that an employer had dismissed an employee included a grievance about the manner in which the employer had dealt with an appeal against dismissal. In those circumstances, the tribunal had been right to conclude that the time extension had not applied to the employer by virtue of reg 6(5). In the present case, the decision that it had been just and equitable to allow the employee's claim to continue out of time had been open to it on the facts. The tribunal had given due weight to the matters before it and therefore had not erred in law. Accordingly, the appeal and the cross-appeal would be dismissed.

Jones v Department for Constitutional Affairs [2006] All ER (D) 345 (Nov) (Employment Appeal Tribunal: Judge Richardson presiding).

1225   Employment tribunal—grievance procedure—presentation of complaint—time limit

The Employment Act 2002 s 32(4) provides that an employee must not present a complaint to an employment tribunal under specified jurisdictions if it concerns a matter in relation to which the requirement to set out the grievance and send a copy to the employer has been complied with more than one month after the end of the original time limit for making the complaint.

A complaint had been made under the Disability Discrimination Act 1995, and the employment tribunal had extended the time limit for compliance with the statutory grievance procedure on the ground that it was just and equitable to do so. On appeal, the question arose as to whether the expression 'original time limit' in the 2002 Act s 32(4) referred to the primary three-month limitation period or to the primary period as extended by the tribunal. *Held*, the original time limit for making the complaint was the time limit provided for in the relevant legislation, and the period of that time limit included any extension made to the primary time limit under that legislation. It followed that the complaint's claim was not time-barred. Judgment would be given accordingly.

BUPA Care Homes (BNH) Ltd v Cann; Spillett v Tesco Stores Ltd [2006] ICR 643 (Employment Appeal Tribunal: Judge Peter Clark presiding).

1226   Employment tribunal—jurisdiction—challenge to compatibility of domestic law

An employee was a major in the Territorial Army. He brought a claim in an employment tribunal asserting that the denial of his right to a pension in respect of his service in the Territorial Army infringed the Part-time Workers (Prevention of Less Favourable Treatment) Regulations 2000, SI 2000/1551, reg 5. The employer contended that the employee's service was excluded by reg 13(2). The employee appealed to the Employment Appeal Tribunal, which upheld the tribunal's decision. Meanwhile, the employee made an application for judicial review on the ground that reg 13(2) was incompatible with EC Council Directive 97/81, and that the employment tribunal had no jurisdiction to determine that issue. The judge dismissed the application, having found that, as the employee was seeking to assert a private law claim against his employer, the Administrative Court had no jurisdiction to hear his claim. On the employee's further appeal, he contended that the tribunal had no jurisdiction to consider whether the 2000 Regulations could be disapplied because of a conflict with Community law. *Held,* the tribunal was not entitled to close its eyes to Community law and have regard only to domestic legislation. Therefore, it had jurisdiction to disapply a restriction in domestic law if that restriction was incompatible with Community law. Under the 2000 Regulations reg 8(1), the tribunal had jurisdiction to determine whether a part-time worker's rights had been infringed compared to those of a full-time worker. It clearly had jurisdiction to consider whether a worker fell within the exception under reg 13(2) and therefore, to decide that reg 13(2) was to be disapplied. Accordingly, the appeal would be dismissed.

R (on the application of Manson) v Ministry of Defence [2005] EWCA Civ 1678, [2006] ICR 355 (Court of Appeal: Keene, Scott Baker and Richards LJJ).

1227   Employment tribunal—jurisdiction—failure to follow statutory procedure

An employee had been dismissed before he had served one year with his employer. The employer had failed to operate the statutory grievance and disciplinary procedures, and had not provided the employee with written particulars of contract. The employee sought to bring a complaint of unfair dismissal before an employment tribunal, arguing that, had he been allowed access to the proper procedures and been given written particulars of his contract, he might not have been dismissed, and that the denial of access to those procedures and that information had been inherently unfair. The tribunal refused to accept the employee's claim on the basis that it had no jurisdiction to hear free-standing complaints of failure to follow statutory procedures. On appeal by the employee, it fell to be determined whether, in light of the fact that a claim for unfair dismissal by the employee had been excluded by the Employment Rights Act 1996 s 108(1), the tribunal had jurisdiction to hear the employee's claims of unfairness in relation to the failure to follow the statutory procedures. *Held*, on a proper construction of the statutory regime, contained in the 1996 Act, the Employment Act 2002, and the Employment Act 2002 (Dispute Resolution) Regulations 2004, SI 2004/752, a tribunal had no jurisdiction to hear a free-standing complaint of failure to follow the statutory procedures. While remedies were available for such failures, those remedies were dependent on there having been a valid cause of action under the legislative scheme. Since no such cause of action was open to the employee, the tribunal had been right to refuse to accept his claim form. Accordingly, the appeal would be dismissed.

Scott-Davies v Redgate Medical Services [2006] All ER (D) 29 (Dec) (Employment Appeal Tribunal: Judge McMullen QC presiding).

1228 Employment tribunal—jurisdiction—racial discrimination—burden of proof

See *Dhesi v Glasgow CC*, para 1069.

1229 Employment tribunal—jurisdiction—unfair dismissal—employment overseas

The first employee worked for a private firm at a Royal Air Force base in Ascension and the second employee worked for the Ministry of Defence at a military base in Germany. The third employee was an international airline pilot who was resident in Great Britain. His employer was based abroad. The employees claimed that they had been unfairly dismissed, contrary to the Employment Rights Act 1996 s 94(1). It fell to be determined whether s 94(1) was applicable. *Held*, s 94(1) did not have global effect, and the court had to give effect to its implied territorial limitations. For peripatetic employees and airline pilots, jurisdiction would be determined by where they were based. Although it would be unusual for an employee who worked and was based abroad to come within the scope of s 94(1), there were some who did. It was very unlikely that s 94(1) would be applicable in a case where the employer was not based in Great Britain, but mere British ownership would be insufficient. British citizenship or the fact that an employee was recruited in Britain would not be sufficient. The additional requisite element could be that the employee was posted abroad by a British employer for the purposes of a business carried out in Britain. Examples included a foreign correspondent of a British newspaper and an expatriate employee of a British employer who operated in an area which amounted to an extra-territorial British enclave in a foreign country.

Lawson v Serco; Botham v Ministry of Defence; Crofts v Veta [2006] UKHL 3, [2006] 1 All ER 823 (House of Lords: Lords Hoffmann, Woolf, Rodger of Earlsferry and Walker of Gestingthorpe and Baroness Hale of Richmond). *Todd v British Midland Airways Ltd* [1978] ICR 959, EAT (1978 Abr para 2977), considered. Decision of Court of Appeal in *Lawson v Serco* [2004] EWCA Civ 12, [2004] 2 All ER 200 (2004 Abr para 1197) reversed. Decision of Employment Appeal Tribunal in *Botham v Ministry of Defence* [2004] All ER (D) 210 (Nov) reversed. Decision of Court of Appeal in *Crofts v Cathay Pacific Airways Ltd* [2005] EWCA Civ 599, [2005] ICR 1436 (2005 Abr para 1390) affirmed.

1230 Employment tribunal—procedure—case management—order

An employee, a black police officer, applied for the position of field intelligence officer in a new department. The job was given to a white officer. The employee later alleged that she had never received an explanation for the decision, and brought a complaint of race discrimination against the police as her employer. At the hearing, the employer claimed that it had informed the employee that her application had been rejected on the basis of a vetting check and that she would not have been given the job even if there been no other applicants. The employer contended that it was prohibited by law from disclosing the reason why the employee had failed the vetting check. At a case management discussion, the employer was informed that its statement would be struck out unless it made full disclosure of its reasons for rejecting the employee's application. The employer appealed against that decision to the Employment Appeal Tribunal, and a hearing before a judge was held pursuant to the Regulation of Investigatory Powers Act 2000 s 18(7). The appeal tribunal judge ruled that he was satisfied that the employer was prohibited by law from revealing either the nature of the reasons for the employee's negative vetting or the legal provisions under which that refusal was made, and remitted the matter for a hearing on the merits without the disclosure requested. The employee appealed. *Held*, ordinarily, case management orders made in the exercise of an employment tribunal's wide discretion would not be disturbed on an appeal, which was confined to questions of law. In the instant case, however, it was wrong in law to make an 'unless order' with which the employer could not, on its case, comply without breaking the law, which it understood prohibited either disclosure of the information or of the legal basis for the prohibition on disclosure. The unless order had unjustifiably prevented the employer from defending the discrimination claim in the normal way, that is by adducing evidence in its defence at the substantive hearing. The appeal tribunal had therefore been right to allow the appeal on that point. Accordingly, the appeal would be dismissed.

Barracks v Coles [2006] EWCA Civ 1041, [2006] IRLR 73 (Court of Appeal: Sir Anthony Clarke MR, Mummery and Wall LJJ).

1231   Employment tribunal—procedure—case management—review of decision

The claimant brought claims of race and sex discrimination to an employment tribunal. He stated in the claims that he felt he had been selected for redundancy because of his trade union activities. At a case management discussion he applied to add claims of unfair dismissal. A first chairman decided that those claims should be treated as fresh claims and that issues as to whether they had been made in time should be the subject of a pre-hearing review. The claimant requested a review of that decision under the Employment Tribunals (Constitution and Rules of Procedure) Regulations 2004, SI 2004/1861, Sch 1 r 34(3)(e), on the ground that the interests of justice required such a review. A second chairman claimed to have no jurisdiction to review the decision and refused the application. At a pre-hearing review the unfair dismissal claims were adjudicated as being separate from the discrimination claims and rejected as out of time. The claimant appealed, contending that both chairmen had had the power to review the case management decision and should have found that the unfair dismissal claims were part of the original claim. *Held*, the first chairman's decision was not a decision falling within Sch 1 r 34(1), as it was not a refusal to accept the claimant's claim but a decision that the unfair dismissal claims were not part of the original claim. Neither chairman had the power to review that decision under Sch 1 r 34, but that did not prevent the reconsideration of the decision pursuant to the general powers conferred by Sch 1 r 10 to manage proceedings. In Sch 1 r 10, 'order' was to be construed as including all decisions taken by a tribunal in the proper exercise of its case management powers, except where such decisions were subject to the review procedure contained in Sch 1 rr 33 and 34. The decision was one which could properly be treated as an aspect of case management and could in principle be revisited. Had the matter been reconsidered in such a way, the claim should have been permitted to proceed. Accordingly, the appeal would be allowed.

Hart v English Heritage (Historic Buildings and Monuments Commission for England) [2006] ICR 655 (Employment Appeal Tribunal: Elias J presiding). *Onwuka v Spherion Technology UK Ltd* [2005] ICR 567, EAT, considered.

1232   Employment tribunal—procedure—evidence—secret recordings—admissibility

An employee had been a teaching assistant and midday meals supervisor at a school. She had been accused of misconduct and consequently faced an investigation into her conduct and disciplinary proceedings. The hearings during the proceedings were held in private and resulted in the employee's dismissal, which was upheld by the employer's appeal board. The employee had covertly recorded the proceedings and deliberations, and brought proceedings before an employment tribunal for unfair dismissal. The tribunal directed that the recordings were admissible and the employer appealed. *Held*, where an employee brought a claim for unfair dismissal and the claim raised issues relating to the reasonableness and conduct of the procedures leading to her dismissal, and confirmation of dismissal, the employee was prevented from relying on the recordings of the decision makers' private deliberations where she had agreed to withdraw while the panel deliberated in private, and the panel had given full reasons for its decision. The parties had all agreed prior to the meeting to withdraw so the panel could deliberate in private and that there would be no record of what had been said in their absence. Those participating in the deliberations had done so on the premise that none of them would have disclosed or published what had been said in private deliberations. That was an important ground rule on which the proceedings had been based and there was an important public interest in ensuring that the parties to proceedings followed those rules. The tribunal had erred in directing that the recordings on private deliberations were admissible. Accordingly, the appeal would be allowed.

Chairman and Governors of Amwell View School v Dogherty [2007] IRLR 198 (Employment Appeal Tribunal: Recorder Luba QC presiding). *BNP Parisbas v Mezzotero* [2004] IRLR 508, EAT; and *Heath v Metropolitan Police Comr* [2004] EWCA Civ 943, [2005] ICR 329 (2004 Abr para 2174) considered.

1233   Employment tribunal—procedure—evidence—'without prejudice' discussions

See *Vaseghi v Brunel University*, para 1295.

1234   Employment tribunal—procedure—notice of withdrawal of proceedings—set aside notice

The applicant applied to an employment tribunal to set aside his notice of withdrawal of discrimination proceedings against the defendant, given under the Employment Tribunals (Constitution and Rules of Procedure) Regulations 2004, SI 2004/1861, r 25(2). The application was refused and the Employment Appeal Tribunal dismissed the applicant's appeal. On his further appeal, *held*, there was ambiguity within r 25 and no authority on the point. However, employment tribunals did not have jurisdiction to set aside a notice of withdrawal of a claim which had been given. Accordingly, the appeal would be dismissed.

Khan v Heywood and Middleton Primary Care Trust [2006] EWCA Civ 1087, [2006] IRLR 793 (Court of Appeal: Brooke, Smith and Wall LJJ).

1235   Employment tribunal—procedure—point at which employer contemplating dismissing or taking action against employee—subjective or objective test

It fell to be determined at what point an employer first contemplated dismissing or taking action against an employee under the Employment Act 2002 (Dispute Resolution) Regulations 2004, SI 2004/752, reg 18(a). *Held*, what was contemplated by the employer was what was in his mind. No element of communication to the employee, whether actual or constructive, was to be imported into the wording of reg 18(a). The relevant date was not the date on which the employee had had actual knowledge that the employer was contemplating dismissal or the date when a reasonable employee would have concluded that the employer had first contemplated dismissal. Judgment would be given accordingly.

Madhewoo v NHS Direct [2006] All ER (D) 36 (Apr) (Employment Appeal Tribunal: Peter Clark J)

1236   Employment tribunal—procedure—respondent barred from proceedings—default judgment given without reasons—request for reasons

The Employment Tribunals (Constitution and Rules of Procedure) Regulations 2004, SI 2004/1861, Sch 1 r 9(b) provides that a respondent who has not presented a response to a claim or whose response has not been accepted is not entitled to take any part in the proceedings except, amongst other things, to make an application under Sch 1 r 33 for the review of a default judgment.

An employer failed to lodge its response to an employee's claim for unfair dismissal within the statutory time limit. An employment tribunal informed the employer that the response could not be accepted, and that it could take no part in the proceedings in accordance with the 2004 Regulations Sch 1 r 9. The employer made a review application stating that the response had originally been sent by first class post well in time and that there had been problems with the sorting office. The review application was refused without any consideration of the merits of the response. The employer subsequently received the tribunal's judgment, which stated that the employee had been unfairly dismissed and set out what the employer was required to pay in damages. No reasons were given as there was no requirement for reasons to be given in writing unless they were requested in accordance with Sch 1 r 30. The employer then asked for written reasons. The tribunal responded that the chairman would not deal with the request because the employer was not entitled to take any part in the proceedings. The employer appealed. *Held*, a request for reasons by a respondent who had not presented a response to a claim and who had been debarred from the proceedings, and who had positively indicated that those reasons were required for the purposes of consideration of the making of a review application under Sch 1 r 9(b), or as stimulated by a letter by the tribunal raising such a question with a view to the making of an application under Sch 1 r 35, would be within the ambit of Sch 1 r 9(b). A request for reasons with a view to an appeal, however, did not find its way into a broad construction of Sch 1 r 9. In such circumstances, written reasons could be provided in relation to any judgment or order if requested by the Employment Appeal Tribunal under Sch 1 r 30(3)(b). The debarring applied only to the steps in the employment tribunal and not the Employment Appeal Tribunal. Judgment would be given accordingly.

Leefe v NSM Music Ltd [2006] ICR 450 (Employment Appeal Tribunal: Burton J presiding).

1237   Employment tribunal—procedure—response to claim—time limit

An employee brought an action against his employer for constructive and unfair dismissal. An employment tribunal acknowledged receipt and acceptance of the claim by letter to the employee's solicitor, stating that a copy of the claim had been sent to the employer and the Advisory, Conciliation and Arbitration Service ('ACAS'). A conversation took place between ACAS and the employer's managing director who telephoned the employee. The employee alleged that it could be inferred from the conversation that the employer had received the papers. The employer wrote to the tribunal, stating that it had not received the papers. They were duly sent to the employer which provided a response within four weeks of having actually received them. The employee applied for a default judgment on the ground that the employer had been required to respond to the claim within 28 days of the date on which a copy was sent to it or, within that time, to seek an extension of time for presentation of its response, as required by the Employment Tribunals (Constitution and Rules of Procedure) Regulations 2004, SI 2004/1861, Sch 1 r 4(1). The application was refused on the ground that the claim had not been received by the employer until its re-service. The time for presentation of the response did not begin to run until the employer had received a copy of the claim so that the response had been validly presented within 28 days of the re-service of the claim. The employee appealed on the ground that the employer was required to present a response within 28 days of the date of sending, regardless of whether the papers were received. *Held*, Sch 1 r 4(1) stated that the time to present a response ran from the sending of the relevant documents and not from their receipt. It was not possible to construe the words 'was sent' as meaning 'was received' despite the obvious contrast with the wording of the previous legislation, Employment Tribunals (Constitution and Rules of Procedure) Regulations 2001, SI 2001/1171, Sch 1 r 3(1), which expressly provided that time for the presentation of a response should begin to run from receipt of the originating application. Time to present a response pursuant to the 2004 Regulations Sch 1 r 4(1) ran from the sending of the relevant documents to the employer rather than from receipt of them. The tribunal had erred in its construction of Sch 1 r 4(1) and, accordingly, the appeal would be allowed.

Bone v Fabcon Projects Ltd [2006] ICR 1421 (Employment Appeal Tribunal: Judge Burke QC presiding).

1238   Employment tribunal—procedure—substituted judgment—appeal—time from which period runs

An employee pursued before an employment tribunal two applications both of which had individual case numbers. However, the judgment as promulgated was headed, wrongly, as being in both cases. The employee brought the error to the attention of the tribunal office which issued a certificate of correction. Attached to that certificate was the entirety of the old judgment; the only amendment being the removal of the second case number from the top left hand corner. The employee lodged a notice of appeal, but this was deemed to have been lodged out of time on the basis that time began to run from the date when the judgment was originally issued. The employee appealed. *Held*, the positive deletion of the entirety of the tribunal's reasons and the substitution of an entirely fresh judgment meant that there was a complete substitution of a fresh judgment and that the time limit for lodging a notice of appeal ran from the date of the promulgation of the new reasons. For this reason, in the event of there being a need for a minor correction which would not constitute a review, the tribunal should have sent out the corrected page or pages under cover of a certificate of correction rather than sending out a certificate of correction which purported to delete the entirety of the reasons and to substitute corrected reasons. For the avoidance of any doubt, a statement that the date of promulgation remains unaltered could accompany the certificate. However, as this course had not been taken by the tribunal the employee's notice of appeal had been in time. Accordingly, the appeal would be allowed.

Aziz-Mir v Sainsbury's Supermarket plc [2007] All ER (D) 07 (Jan) (Employment Appeal Tribunal: Burton J presiding).

1239   Flexible working—eligibility, complaints and remedies

The Flexible Working (Eligibility, Complaints and Remedies) (Amendment) Regulations 2006, SI 2006/3314 (in force on 6 April 2007), further amend the 2002 Regulations, SI 2002/3236, so as to widen the scope of the statutory right for employees to request a contract variation, which previously applied to carers of children under six or disabled children under 18, to cover employees who care for certain adults. In particular, the regulations (1) amend the definitions of 'partner', 'relative' and 'special guardian'; (2) insert special guardian into the list of those eligible to make a request to care for a child; (3) provide that an employee making a request to care for a child needs to do so before the child is six or, where the child is disabled, 18; and (4) provide that the eligibility criteria to enable an employee to make a request to care for an adult are that the employee must have 26 weeks' qualifying service, and that the adult is in need of care and is married to, the partner or civil partner or a relative of the employee or is living at the same address as the employee.

1240   Gangmasters licensing—exclusions

See para 141.

1241   Health and safety at work

See HEALTH AND SAFETY AT WORK.

1242   Industrial training boards—levy—construction industry

The Industrial Training Levy (Construction Board) Order 2006, SI 2006/334 (in force on 19 February 2006), replaces the 2005 Order, SI 2005/546, and imposes a levy on employers in the construction industry for the purpose of raising money towards meeting the expenses of the Construction Industry Training Board. The levy (1) is to be limited to 0·5 per cent of payroll in respect of employees employed by such employers under contracts of service or apprenticeship and 1·5 per cent of payments made by the employers to persons under labour-only agreements; (2) is in respect of the levy period commencing on 19 February 2006 and ending on 31 March 2006; and (3) is to be assessed by the Board, and a person assessed to the levy may appeal to an employment tribunal against an assessment.

1243   Industrial training boards—levy—engineering construction

The Industrial Training Levy (Engineering Construction Board) Order 2006, SI 2006/335 (in force on 19 February 2006), replaces the 2005 Order, SI 2005/2089, and imposes a levy on employers in the engineering construction industry for the purpose of raising money towards meeting the expenses of the Engineering Construction Industry Training Board. The order also imposes a levy on employers who are not mainly engaged in engineering construction activities but are engaged in any related or administrative activities of a specified kind, and for those employers the levy is imposed only in respect of such related or administrative activities. The levy (1) is in respect of the levy period commencing on 19 February 2006 and ending on 31 December 2006; and (2) is to be assessed by the Board, and there is a right of appeal to an employment tribunal against an assessment.

1244 Maternity and parental leave—employees' rights and obligations

The Maternity and Parental Leave etc and the Paternity and Adoption Leave (Amendment) Regulations 2006, SI 2006/2014 (in force on 1 October 2006), further amend the Maternity and Parental Leave etc Regulations 1999, SI 1999/3312, and the Paternity and Adoption Leave Regulations 2002, SI 2002/2788, by (1) removing the additional length of service qualifying condition for additional maternity leave; (2) extending from 28 days to 8 weeks the period of notice which an employee is required to give to the employer of his or her intention to return to work earlier than the end of the additional maternity leave or additional adoption leave; (3) setting out notification requirements where the employee changes his or her mind more than once as to the intended return date; (4) enabling an employee on maternity leave or adoption leave to agree with the employer to work for up to ten days during the statutory maternity or adoption leave period without thereby bringing that period to an end or extending the maternity or adoption leave period; (5) adding the undertaking, considering undertaking and not undertaking any such work to the list of reasons for which an employee (a) is entitled to protection from being subjected to a detriment; and (b) if dismissed for such a reason, is unfairly dismissed; and (6) removing the small employers' exemption so that the employee has a right to return to the same or a similar job regardless of the size of the organisation for which he or she works.

1245 National minimum wage—deductions—living allowance

An employer provided its seasonal workers with accommodation. Under the accommodation agreement, the workers were charged a fixed sum every fortnight for gas and electricity. The Commissioners of Revenue and Customs issued enforcement notices against the employer, alleging that the workers were being paid lower than the minimum wage as a result of the deduction. The commissioners appealed following a decision by an employment tribunal to rescind the enforcement notices. *Held*, it was unlawful to cause workers' hourly rate of pay to fall below the statutory minimum by deducting a sum for gas and electricity from wages. It was agreed that the employer had taken full advantage of the amount it was permitted to take into account in relation to the provision of living accommodation, without adversely affecting the calculation of the minimum wage. The employer would have to subtract the excess from the total remuneration. Where a worker was under an obligation to pay a particular sum of money in order to make use of the accommodation on offer, the sum should properly be described as being in respect of the provision of living accommodation. Alternately, the deduction was made by the employer for its own benefit, as it and not the workers was liable to the utility companies. As such it was a payment which fell to be deducted from the workers' total remuneration under the National Minimum Wage Regulations 1999, SI 1999/584, reg 32(1)(b) or 34(1)(c). Accordingly, the appeal would be allowed.

Revenue and Customs Comrs v Leisure Employment Services Ltd [2006] ICR 1094 (Employment Appeal Tribunal: Elias J presiding).

1246 National minimum wage—hourly rate—increase

The National Minimum Wage Regulations 1999 (Amendment) Regulations 2006, SI 2006/2001 (in force on 1 October 2006), further amend the 1999 Regulations, SI 1999/584, so as to increase (1) from £5·05 to £5·35, the hourly rate of the national minimum wage; (2) from £4·25 to £4·45, the rate to be paid to workers aged between 18 and 21; (3) from £3 to £3·30 per hour, the rate to be paid to workers aged below 18 who have ceased to be of compulsory school age; and (4) from £3·90 to £4·15, in cases where the employer provides a worker with accommodation, the fixed amount per day value of accommodation. SI 2005/2019 is amended.

1247 Paternity leave and adoption leave—employees' rights and obligations

See para 1244.

1248 Protected disclosure—detriment—post-employment detriment

An employee's complaint of sex discrimination was settled without admission of liability. She subsequently made a further application to an employment tribunal complaining of victimisation. The details of her complaint related largely to allegations of sex discrimination, but she contended that it included a claim under the Employment Rights Act 1996 s 47B that she had been subjected by the employer to a detriment on the ground that she had made a protected disclosure. The detriment to which she said she had been subjected had arisen long after her employment had terminated, consisting of the employer's failure to provide a job reference and the employee's failure to progress with job applications. The tribunal decided as a preliminary issue that it had no jurisdiction to hear the protected disclosure claim because the acts of which complaint was made had all taken place after the employee's employment had come to an end. The Employment Appeal

Tribunal dismissed the employee's appeal and, on the employee's further appeal, *held*, Parliament could not seriously have intended to afford the whistle-blower protection only in respect of acts done in retaliation while the contract of employment subsisted and not to protect him from detriment suffered after his employment had terminated. The public interest, which led to the demand for the 1996 Act to protect individuals who made certain disclosures of information in the public interest and to give them an action in respect of that victimisation, would surely be sold short by allowing the former employer to victimise his former employee with impunity. It simply made no sense at all to protect the current employee but not the former employee, especially since the frequent response of the embittered exposed employer might well be dismissal and a determination to make life impossible for the employee for as long thereafter as he could. Accordingly, the appeal would be allowed.

Woodward v Abbey National plc [2006] EWCA Civ 822, [2006] 4 All ER 1209 (Court of Appeal: Ward, Maurice Kay and Wilson LJJ). *Relaxion Group plc v Rhys-Harper; D'Souza v Lambeth LBC; Jones v 3M Healthcare Ltd* [2003] UKHL 33, [2003] 4 All ER 1113 (2003 Abr para 963) applied. *Fadipe v Reed Nursing Personnel* [2001] EWCA Civ 1885, [2005] ICR 1760 not followed.

1249 Racial discrimination

See DISCRIMINATION.

1250 Redundancy—collective redundancies

The Collective Redundancies (Amendment) Regulations 2006, SI 2006/2387 (in force on 1 October 2006), further amend the Trade Union and Labour Relations (Consolidation) Act 1992 s 193 to provide that an employer proposing collective redundancies must notify the Secretary of State of his proposal before he gives notice to an employee to terminate an employee's contract of employment in respect of any of those dismissals.

1251 Sex discrimination

See DISCRIMINATION.

1252 Statutory adoption pay—entitlement—member of couple

The Adoption and Children Act 2002 (Consequential Amendment to Statutory Adoption Pay) Order 2006, SI 2006/2012 (in force on 1 October 2006), amends the Social Security and Benefits Act 1992 s 171ZL to provide that a person may not elect to receive statutory adoption pay where a child is placed or about to be placed with him as a member of a couple and his partner satisfies the entitlement conditions for statutory adoption pay and has elected to receive it.

1253 Statutory maternity pay—maternity allowance—overlapping benefits

The Statutory Maternity Pay, Social Security (Maternity Allowance) and Social Security (Overlapping Benefits) (Amendment) Regulations 2006, SI 2006/2379 (in force on 1 October 2006), further amend the Social Security (Overlapping Benefits) Regulations 1979, SI 1979/597, by providing for adjustments of all benefits at a rate equal to one-seventh of the appropriate weekly rate for each day of the week. The regulations also further amend the Statutory Maternity Pay (General) Regulations 1986, SI 1986/1960, by (1) providing that a woman's maternity pay period will begin in accordance with a notice to her employer indicating the day on which she expects his liability to pay statutory maternity pay ('SMP') to begin, such a day being 11 weeks or less before her expected week of confinement ('EWC') and not later than the day after she gives birth; (2) establishing that the maternity pay period is 39 consecutive weeks; (3) providing that a woman's maternity pay period will begin the day after she gives birth if that day is before the eleventh week before her EWC or, if it is after the twelfth week before her EWC, and she gives birth before the day specified in a notice to her employer indicating the day on which she expects his liability to pay her SMP to begin; (4) providing that a woman's maternity pay period will begin the day after her absence from work where she is absent because of pregnancy or confinement on a day four weeks or less before her EWC and, if earlier, before her actual confinement; (5) providing that a woman's maternity pay period will begin the day after she leaves her employment where she leaves 11 weeks or less before her EWC, before the start of the maternity pay period and, if earlier, before her actual confinement; (6) providing that SMP will be paid where a woman works for her employer for not more than ten days within her maternity pay period; and (7) allowing payments of SMP for a week or part of a week to be rounded up to the next penny. The regulations also further amend the Social Security (Maternity Allowance) Regulations 1987, SI 1987/416, by (a) providing that a woman will be subject to disqualification from maternity allowance if she works as an employed or self-employed earner for more than ten days during the maternity allowance period; and (b) extending the maternity allowance period to 39 weeks and allowing the maternity allowance period to commence no earlier than the day a woman becomes entitled to maternity allowance and no later than the day after which she is confined in specified circumstances.

1254   Statutory paternity pay and statutory adoption pay—general

The Statutory Paternity Pay and Statutory Adoption Pay (General) and the Statutory Paternity Pay and Statutory Adoption Pay (Weekly Rates) (Amendment) Regulations 2006, SI 2006/2236 (in force on 1 October 2006), amend (1) the Statutory Paternity Pay and Statutory Adoption Pay (General) Regulations 2002, SI 2002/2822, so as to (a) establish that the adoption pay period is 39 consecutive weeks; and (b) provide that statutory adoption pay must continue to be paid where an employee works for his employer for not more than ten days within the adoption pay period; and (2) the Statutory Paternity Pay and Statutory Adoption Pay (Weekly Rates) Regulations 2002, SI 2002/2818, so as to allow for payments of statutory adoption pay and statutory paternity pay for a week or part of a week to be rounded up to the next penny.

1255   Statutory paternity pay and statutory adoption pay—weekly rates

See para 1254.

1256   Statutory sick pay—general

See para 2680.

1257   Trade unions

See TRADE, INDUSTRY AND INDUSTRIAL RELATIONS.

1258   Transfer of undertaking—consultation—failure to consult—compensation

Scotland
An employee was a clerk in a bookmaking business. She occasionally performed deputy manager duties. The business was transferred to the employer in a transfer subject to the Transfer of Undertakings (Protection of Employment) Regulations 1981, SI 1981/1794. The employer stated that it intended to appoint another clerk to the role of deputy manager. The employee resigned and sought compensation for unfair constructive dismissal and failure to consult prior to the transfer contrary to reg 10. An employment tribunal found that, while there had been no constructive dismissal, there had been a serious and gross failure to consult for which the employee should be compensated, pursuant to reg 11. The compensation was fixed at six weeks' pay. On the employee's appeal, it fell to be determined whether the tribunal had erred in its assessment of compensation in respect of the failure to consult. *Held*, the tribunal should have adopted the same approach when assessing compensation for failure to consult under the 1981 Regulations as that adopted when assessing compensation for failure to consult under the Trade Union and Labour Relations (Consolidation) Act 1992 s 188. In other words, the tribunal should have awarded 13 weeks' pay as compensation for the failure to consult. In the circumstances, the failure had been serious and gross and there were no mitigating circumstances to justify a departure from that level of compensation. The wording of the compensation provisions in the 1981 Regulations and the 1992 Act reflected each other and underlined the importance of compliance with the duty to consult. Parliament had clearly intended that the awards in each case were to be penal, rather than solely compensatory, in nature. Accordingly, the appeal would be allowed in part. An order would be substituted that a sum equivalent to 13 weeks' pay was appropriate compensation for the failure to consult.
   Sweetin v Coral Racing [2006] IRLR 252 (Employment Appeal Tribunal: Smith LJ presiding). *GMB v Susie Radin Ltd* [2004] 2 All ER 279, EAT (2004 Abr para 2793), applied.

1259   Transfer of undertaking—contract of employment—collective agreement—wages

EC Council Directive 77/187 art 3 provides that on the transfer of an undertaking, the transferor's obligations arising from a contract of employment are to be transferred to the transferee, which must continue to observe the terms and conditions agreed in any collective agreement.
   The applicant's employment contract with his employer referred to and was governed by an industry-wide collective agreement. The employer transferred part of its business, along with the applicant, to the respondent company. The respondent was not a party to the collective agreement, and eventually increased the applicant's wages under a work agreement. Subsequently, a new collective agreement raised general wage rates, and the applicant's claim that the collective agreement applied to him was dismissed. On his appeal, it fell to be determined whether Directive 77/187 art 3 meant that the respondent would be bound by collective agreements made subsequent to the transfer of undertaking. *Held*, Directive 77/187 was mandatory and could not be derogated from in a manner unfavourable to employees. Existing employment contracts and relationships would automatically be transferred by the transfer of the business. Directive 77/187 did not indicate that it was intended to bind the transferee to collective agreements other than the one in force at the time of the transfer, or that the terms and conditions could be amended by a new collective agreement concluded after the transfer. The objective of Directive 77/187 was only to safeguard the rights and obligations of an employee on the day of the transfer.
   Case C-499/04 *Werhof v Freeway Traffic Systems GmbH & Co KG* [2006] 2 CMLR 1115 (ECJ: Third Chamber).

1260   Transfer of undertaking—protection of employment

The Transfer of Undertakings (Protection of Employment) Regulations 2006, SI 2006/246 (in force on 6 April 2006), implement EC Council Directive 2001/23 on the approximation of the law relating to business transfers, so as to make provision for the treatment of employees, and related matters, on the transfer of an undertaking or business or a service provision change. In particular, the regulations (1) define a transfer to which the regulations apply, which is described as a relevant transfer; the two categories of relevant transfer, which are not mutually exclusive, are the transfer of an undertaking or business to another person and a service provision change; (2) provide that a relevant transfer must not operate to terminate the contract of employment of a person employed by the transferor and assigned to the organised grouping of resources or employees subject to a relevant transfer but that any such contract is to have effect after the transfer as if originally made between the person so employed and the transferee; (3) provide that a collective agreement made by a transferor with a recognised trade union must, after the transfer, have effect as if made by the transferee with that trade union and provide for the transfer of recognition of an independent trade union; (4) provide that the dismissal of an employee by reason of the transfer is unlawful but that a dismissal for a reason connected with the transfer that is an economic technical or organisational reason entailing changes in the workforce is potentially lawful; (5) apply where, at the time of the transfer, the transferor is subject to relevant insolvency proceedings; (6) provide greater scope for the transferee to vary, subject to certain requirements, the terms and conditions of employment of transferring employees in circumstances where the transferor is subject to relevant insolvency proceedings; (7) provide that heads (2), (3), above, are not to apply to so much of a contract of employment or collective agreement as relates to any provision of an occupational pension scheme relating to old age, survivors or invalidity benefits; (8) provide that the transferor must provide employee liability information in respect of employees assigned to the organised grouping of resources or employees that is subject to a relevant transfer to the transferee in advance of a relevant transfer; (9) provide a remedy to a transferee for the failure of a transferor to comply with head (8), above; and (10) impose a duty on an employer to provide information to appropriate representatives of affected employees about a relevant transfer and measures he envisages taking in respect of it, long enough before a relevant transfer to enable the employer to consult those representatives with a view to seeking their agreement to the intended measures, and make provision for the election of employee representatives where there is no recognised independent trade union. SI 1981/1794 is revoked.

The Transfer of Undertakings (Protection of Employment) (Consequential Amendments) Regulations 2006, SI 2006/2405 (in force on 1 October 2006), make amendments consequential to the coming into force of SI 2006/246 supra by replacing references to the Transfer of Undertakings (Protection of Employment) Regulations 1981, SI 1981/1794, with appropriate references to SI 2006/246 in the Information and Consultation of Employees Regulations 2004, SI 2004/3426, the Employment Tribunals (Constitution and Rules of Procedure) Regulations 2004, SI 2004/1861, and the ACAS Arbitration Scheme (Great Britain) Order 2004, SI 2004/753.

1261   Transfer of undertaking—relevant transfer—continuity of employment—transfer of assets

Employees brought proceedings against the second defendant, a company under contract to carry out security checks at an airport and their former employer, the company tasked previously with the same services under a contract which had been terminated. At the employment tribunal, the employees sought a declaration that the employment relationship existing between them and the former employer continued with the second defendant on the basis of the German civil code which implemented EC Council Directive 2001/23. The tribunal stayed proceedings and referred the case to the European Court of Justice for a preliminary ruling on the question whether, in the context of an assessment as to whether there was a transfer of a business within the meaning of art 1, a finding that there was a transfer of assets from the original contractor to the new contractor presupposed their transfer for independent commercial use by the transferee. *Held,* art 1 had to be interpreted as meaning that in examining whether there was a transfer of an undertaking or business within the meaning of art 1, in the context of a fresh award of a contract and having regard to all the facts, the transfer of the assets for independent commercial use was not an essential criterion for a finding that there was a transfer of those assets from the original contractor to the new contractor. The transfer of assets was only a single factor in the overall assessment that had to be made by a national court when examining whether there had been a transfer of an undertaking or business within the meaning of art 1.

Cases C-232/04 and C-233/04 *Güney-Görres v Securicor Aviation (Germany) Ltd* [2006] 2 CMLR 173 (ECJ: Third Chamber).

1262   Transfer of undertaking—relevant transfer—date of transfer—continuity of period of employment

The United Kingdom transferred various vocational training responsibilities to private Training and Enterprise Councils ('TECs'). A number of civil servants undertook secondments with the TECs, retaining their status as government employees. Several employees eventually took up permanent positions with the TECs. Three such employees subsequently brought proceedings to determine the length of their continuity of employment. They relied on EC Council Directive 77/187 art 3(1), under which the transferor's rights and obligations arising from a contract of employment existing on the date of a transfer were, by reason of the transfer, transferred to the transferee. An employment tribunal decided that the employees had continuous employment from the start of their employment with the civil service. The Employment Appeal Tribunal reversed that decision, deeming that the transfer of the undertaking in question was completed before the employees took up employment with the TECs. However, that ruling was quashed by the Court of Appeal, which held that Directive 77/388 was sufficiently wide to embrace a transfer of a business which took place over a period of time. A subsequent referral to the European Court of Justice was made, which decided that art 3(1) had to be interpreted as meaning that the date of a transfer was the date on which responsibility as employer for carrying on the business of the unit transferred moved from the transferor to the transferee, and that, for the purposes of applying that provision, contracts of employment or employment relationships existing on the date of the transfer were deemed to be handed over on that date from the transferor to the transferee on that date, regardless of what had been agreed between the parties in that respect. The appeal came before the House of Lords. *Held*, it was clear from Community jurisprudence that the general rule was that the contracts of employment of workers assigned to the undertaking transferred were automatically transferred from the transferor to the transferee on the date of transfer, and that it was not possible for that rule to be derogated from in a manner unfavourable to employees. The rights conferred on them by Directive 77/388 could not be made subject to the consent either of the transferor or transferee nor the consent of the employee's representatives or the employees themselves. The employees had continuous employment with the TECs from the start of their employment with the civil service by virtue of Directive 77/388. On the other hand, it was a fundamental right of the employee to be free to choose his employer. He could not be obliged to work for an employer whom he had not freely chosen. The employees were in a position on or after the date of the transfer to choose of their own free will not to work for the TEC. They did not make that choice, with the result that their contracts of employment were transferred automatically to the TEC with continuity of employment on the date of transfer. Accordingly, the appeal would be dismissed.

Astley v North Wales Training and Enterprise Council Ltd (t/a Celtec Ltd) [2006] UKHL 29, [2006] 4 All ER 27 (House of Lords: Lords Bingham of Cornhill, Hope of Craighead, Rodger of Earlsferry, Carswell and Mance). Decision of Court of Appeal [2002] EWCA Civ 1035, [2002] 3 CMLR 366 affirmed.

1263 Unfair dismissal—compensation—calculation of award—dismissal without notice—failure to respect good industrial relations practice

An employee had a written contract of employment which provided for eight weeks' notice of termination and that during periods of sickness her employers would pay sickness benefit in accordance with government statutory sick pay legislation. The employee was injured in an accident and was unfit for work. Her employers told her that they would not require her to work out her notice. She brought complaints of wrongful and unfair dismissal before an employment tribunal. The claims succeeded, and the tribunal assessed damages for wrongful dismissal on the basis of eight weeks' pay at the normal weekly wage. In relation to unfair dismissal, it made a basic award and a compensatory award, no part of which related to the period of notice because that had been covered in the award from wrongful dismissal. The employers appealed, contending that damages for wrongful dismissal should have been based on the statutory sick pay legislation and the employee cross-appealed, contending that she was entitled to receive compensation for the eight-week notice period at the normal weekly wage for unfair dismissal. The appeal was allowed and the cross-appeal was dismissed. The employee appealed. *Held*, although there was authority for the precept that good industrial practice required an employer who dismissed an employee without notice to make a payment in lieu of notice at the normal rate of pay, it was uncertain whether an employer should be required to pay wages at the full rate to an employee who was unfit through sickness. However, even if it were accepted, that precept could not be applied to the assessment of compensation under the Employment Rights Act 1996 s 123 if the result would be an award greater than the loss caused to the employee as a consequence of the dismissal. If the employee had not been dismissed, she would have received remuneration equivalent to statutory sick pay during her period of absence, and so that was the correct measure of her weekly loss during the notice period. Accordingly, the appeal would be dismissed.

Burlo v Langley [2006] EWCA Civ 1778, [2007] IRLR 145 (Court of Appeal: Mummery, Smith and Leveson LJJ). *Norton Tool Co Ltd v Tewson* [1973] 1 All ER 183, NIRC, doubted.

1264 Unfair dismissal—compensation—calculation of award—speculation as to future earnings

An employee was employed as an engineer, and was suspended and dismissed following disciplinary procedures for bullying and harassing one of her colleagues. An employment tribunal found that while the dismissal was unfair, the employee had contributed 25 per cent to her dismissal by her own blameworthy conduct. The tribunal capped the employee's future losses at six months as in view of the circumstances, she would have been dismissed after six months and that due to the changes in the operation of the workplace she would have been made redundant within a few months. She successfully appealed and the Employment Appeal Tribunal found that the tribunal should have accepted that it could not sensibly reconstruct the situation and should not have reduced the losses. The employer appealed. *Held*, the tribunal's task, when deciding what compensation was just and equitable for future loss of earnings would almost inevitably involve a consideration of uncertainties. Any assessment of a future loss, including one that the employment would continue indefinitely, was a prediction that inevitably contained a speculative element. Tribunals could not be expected or allowed to opt out of their statutory duty to make such predictions because their task was a difficult one and might involve making speculations. Where evidence to the contrary was sparse, the tribunal should approach the question on the basis that loss of earnings in the employment would have continued indefinitely, but where there was evidence that this may not have been the case, that should be taken into account. When a conclusion was reached as to what was likely to have happened had the employment been allowed to continue, the reasons for that conclusion and the factors relied on should be sufficiently stated. The tribunal had evidence that the employment would not have continued indefinitely, that, at its lowest level, created a risk which a fact-finding tribunal could not ignore. While there had been material before the tribunal that might have justified the six-month limit, the reasons for the tribunal's decision did not emerge with sufficient clarity to be upheld. The matter had to be remitted back to the tribunal, but six months should be treated as a starting point above which the determination had to be made. Accordingly, the appeal would be allowed.

Thornett v Scope [2006] EWCA Civ 1600, [2007] IRLR 155 (Court of Appeal: Pill, Laws and Gage LJJ). *Gover v Propertycare Ltd* [2006] EWCA Civ 286, [2006] 4 All ER 69 (para 1222) applied.

1265   Unfair dismissal—compensation—deductions—pension payments

A final salary pension scheme operated by an employer included life insurance cover. On their dismissal, employee members of the scheme took early pension payments, which the scheme allowed without affecting their total pension entitlement, but did not purchase any replacement life assurance cover. An employment tribunal upheld the employees' complaints of unfair dismissal and set off the pension payments from the compensatory award. The tribunal awarded compensation for the future cost of buying life insurance cover but made no award for the cost of a replacement period between the dismissal and the date of the hearing. The employees appealed. *Held*, a pension was a form of deferred wages to which the employees had contributed during the term of their employment. As such, it was analogous to payments under a contract of insurance, which were not deductible from a compensatory award, rather than to a benefit, such as incapacity or sickness benefit receivable from the government, which was deductible. However, the employees were not entitled to compensation for the period during which they had no life assurance cover, as they had not suffered any financial loss from this and any sum paid would be a windfall. Accordingly, the appeal would be allowed in part.

Knapton v ECC Card Clothing Ltd [2006] ICR 1084 (Employment Appeal Tribunal: Judge McMullen presiding). *Parry v Cleaver* [1970] AC 1, HL, applied; *Morgans v Alpha Plus Security Ltd* [2005] 4 All ER 655, EAT (2005 Abr para 1424), distinguished.

1266   Unfair dismissal—compensation—determination—future losses

An employment tribunal decided that an employee had been unfairly and constructively dismissed. At the time of her dismissal, the employee had a long-standing underlying medical condition caused by matrimonial and domestic difficulties. Her pre-existing medical condition had been exacerbated by the employer's treatment of her. The tribunal considered that it had to decide, within the context of assessing the employee's right to compensation pursuant to the Employment Rights Act 1996 s 123, to what extent it might be said that the employee's continued incapacity to work was attributable to the acts or omissions of the employer. It concluded that it was satisfied that the cause of the employee's incapacity at that time was the treatment of her by the employer which had culminated in the employee's dismissal. The employee appealed against the tribunal's award of compensation on the grounds that it had wrongly applied a 'but for' test rather than following the guidance set out in established authority, which was to assess the percentage chance that extrinsic factors might have resulted in the employee's inability to work, and that the tribunal's finding that there was no material evidence to suggest that extrinsic factors might have resulted in an inability on the part of the employee to work was perverse in the light of the evidence that was before it in the form of the employee's medical records. *Held*, questions of quantification of a claimant's loss might depend on future uncertain events. Those questions were not decided on a balance of probability, but rather on the court's assessment of the risk eventuating or the prospect of promotion, which depended in part at least on the hypothetical acts of the claimant's employer. The tribunal had been correct to apply the 'but for' test to the employee's past losses. However, so far as future losses were concerned, the tribunal had been wrong to apply the 'but for' test and instead should have assessed the prospect of the employee having been unable to work because of her underlying illness, which had not been caused by the employer. Further, on the evidence, it had been the employer's treatment of the employee that had, on the balance of probabilities, been the cause of her problems at the time of the hearing. The tribunal's conclusion that there was no material evidence to the contrary in respect of its finding that the cause of the employee's incapacity had been the employer's conduct had not been perverse. It followed that the appeal on the perversity issue failed. Accordingly, the appeal would be allowed and the matter remitted to the same tribunal to determine the employee's losses on the basis of the prospect of her having suffered from her pre-existing illness after the remedies hearing.

Seafield Holdings (t/a Seafield Logistics) v Drewett [2006] ICR 1413. *Mallett v McMonagle* [1969] 2 All ER 178, HL; and *Allied Maples Group Ltd v Simmons & Simmons (a firm)* [1995] 4 All ER 907, CA (1995 Abr para 2782), applied. *Barber v Somerset CC* [2004] UKHL 13, [2004] 2 All ER 385 (2004 Abr para 1177) considered.

1267 Unfair dismissal—compensation—notice period

An employee worked as a nanny. Shortly before the termination of her contract of employment, she was involved in a car accident and, due to the injuries sustained, she was unable to work out her notice period. She was dismissed and her claim for unfair dismissal and wrongful dismissal was upheld by an employment tribunal which held that the employee was entitled to full pay for the notice period. The employer appealed contending that the terms of the contract were that the employee should receive statutory sick pay if absent ill. The employee relied on the Employment Rights Act 1996 s 88 and contended that, even if the employers were correct on that point, the case law established that an employee should be awarded full pay for the notice period. *Held*, there was no basis for the tribunal's conclusion that, under the contract, the employee would have been entitled to full pay for the period when she was absent for sickness. The contractual term was clear and there was no justification for saying that it was inapplicable to the notice period. Where the notice that the employer was required to give exceeded the statutory notice period by one week or more, the rights conferred by s 88 had no application. There was no longer any room for the proposition that good industrial relations practice could be relied on to increase the amount of compensation so as to award more than the true loss actually incurred as a consequence of the dismissal itself. Having regard to recent House of Lords authority, the previous Court of Appeal authority supporting the old practice could no longer be regarded as binding. Accordingly, the appeal would be allowed.

Burlo v Carter [2006] All ER (D) 54 (Mar) (Employment Appeal Tribunal: Elias J presiding). *Dunnachie v Kingston-upon-Hull City Council* [2004] UKHL 36, [2004] 3 All ER 1011 (2004 Abr para 1233) followed. *Norton Tool Co Ltd v Tewson* [1973] 1 All ER 183, NIRC, not followed.

1268 Unfair dismissal—misconduct—disciplinary hearing—procedural fairness—review or rehearing to cure earlier defects

An employee's claim against his employer for unfair dismissal succeeded. On the employer's appeal, it was argued that the employment tribunal had wrongly understood *Whitbread & Co plc v Mills* as authority for the proposition that an appeal hearing could cure the procedural defects of a first hearing only if it was a rehearing, the tribunal having found that the appeal hearing was merely a review. With regard to disability discrimination, the employer further argued that the tribunal, unlike the Employment Appeal Tribunal, had correctly dismissed the employee's claim under the Disability Discrimination Act 1995 s 5(1) because the material reason for dismissal was the employee's misconduct and was not related to his disability where the employer had not had a disability-related reason in his mind at the time of dismissal. *Held*, in *Whitbread*, the Employment Appeal Tribunal had used 'review' and 'rehearing' to illustrate the kind of hearing that would be thorough enough to remedy previous defects and the kind which would not. However, the illustration had been erroneously interpreted as propounding a rule of law that only a rehearing could cure earlier defects and that a mere review never could. The tribunal had fallen into that trap and the unfair dismissal question would have to be remitted. As to disability discrimination, it was wrong to argue that, in order to demonstrate that the employee had been dismissed for a reason which related to his disability, it was unnecessary to show that the reason relating to disability was present in the employer's mind. Accordingly, the appeal would be allowed.

Taylor v OCS Group Ltd [2006] ICR 1602 (Court of Appeal: Brooke, Dyson and Smith LJJ). *Whitbread & Co plc v Mills* [1988] ICR 776, EAT, considered.

1269 Unfair dismissal—protected disclosure—qualifying disclosure—failure to comply with legal obligation—action taken to confirm belief

The Employment Rights Act 1996 s 43B(1)(b) provides that a 'qualifying disclosure' in relation to unfair dismissal means any disclosure of information which, in the reasonable belief of the worker making the disclosure, tends to show that a person has failed, is failing or is likely to fail to comply with any legal obligation to which he is subject.

The claimant teacher hacked into the computer system of the defendant, the school at which he worked, in order to expose what he perceived to be its security failings. The head teacher accepted that the claimant was acting in good faith, but decided that the conduct was unacceptable and that he should be reprimanded. The claimant decided to resign, believing that his position had become untenable. He then brought proceedings for unfair dismissal against the defendant, contending that he had been disciplined for drawing its attention to breaches of the Data Protection Act 1998, which he argued was a qualifying disclosure within the meaning of the 1996 Act s 43B(1). An employment tribunal accepted that contention, and the defendant appealed. *Held*, the tribunal was fully justified in concluding that the claimant reasonably believed that disclosing the fact that he had hacked into the system tended to show that a principle under the 1998 Act would be likely to be infringed. The claimant had not been subject to any discipline proceedings when he had earlier forcibly expressed his view about the security system that should be adopted, nor was there any reason to suppose that he would have been disciplined if he had simply informed the defendant that someone else had hacked into the system. The defendant acted because of its belief that it was irresponsible for the claiamant to have done so even if the purpose was to demonstrate the force of his concerns. The tribunal's finding that the claimant had authority for testing the system did not bring him within the protected category. The law protected disclosure of information which the employee reasonably believed tended to demonstrate the kind of wrongdoing, or anticipated wrongdoing, which was covered by the 1996 Act s 43B. It did not protect the actions of the employee which were directed to establishing or confirming the reasonableness of that belief. It followed that the finding of automatic unfair dismissal could not stand, nor could the conclusion that the claimant had suffered a detriment by reason of making a protected disclosure. Accordingly, the appeal would be allowed.

Evans v Bolton School [2006] All ER (D) 384 (Mar) (Employment Appeal Tribunal: Elias J presiding).

This decision has been affirmed on appeal: [2006] EWCA Civ 1735, [2007] IRLR 126.

1270   Unfair dismissal—reason for dismissal—redundancy—dismissal procedures—failure to consult

An employee was a manager at a learning centre. Her employer decided to close the centre and dismissed the employee for reasons of redundancy, without consulting either her or her trade union. The employee instigated proceedings for unfair dismissal. An employment tribunal found that, although the employer had failed to follow a fair procedure, there were no suitable alternative jobs so that the outcome would not have been different even if formal consultation had taken place. The tribunal decided that the Employment Rights Act 1996 s 98A(2) applied and that the dismissal was fair. On her appeal, the employee submitted that the tribunal should not have considered s 98A(2) because it was not in force at the date of her dismissal. She also contended that if it was correct to apply *Polkey v AE Dayton Services Ltd* and even if there was a 100 per cent likelihood that she would have been dismissed if a fair procedure had been followed, the tribunal had erred in failing to set down the date on which that would have occurred, that is, a date later than the actual dismissal. *Held*, the tribunal had erred in holding that s 98A(2) applied to render the employee's dismissal fair, notwithstanding that the employer had failed to consult. Section 98A(2) applied where there was a procedure contained in an agreement or policy which related to dismissal of employees and which had not been followed. Section 98A(2) did not apply to breaches of the statutory dismissal procedure. The effect of s 98A(1) was to make automatically unfair a dismissal in breach of the minimum statutory requirements. It was not open to an employer to contend that dismissal would have occurred notwithstanding breach of those requirements. No specific procedure was identified by the employer or the tribunal. In any event, s 98A(2) applied only to dismissals taking effect on or after 1 October 2004. The tribunal had been entitled to conclude that, applying traditional principles, the claimant's compensatory ward fell to be reduced by 100 per cent but it should have determined the date on which the claimant would have been dismissed fairly had she been consulted. Accordingly, the appeal would be allowed in part. A finding of unfair dismissal substituted and the case would be remitted to the tribunal to determine the matter of compensation.

Mason v Governing Body of Ward End Primary School [2006] ICR 1128 (Employment Appeal Tribunal: Judge McMullen QC presiding). *Polkey v AE Dayton Services Ltd* [1988] AC 344, HL (1985 Abr para 2874), considered.

1271   Unfair dismissal—reason for dismissal—refusal to sign new contract of employment—restraint of trade clause

The claimants were dismissed for refusing to accept variations of their contracts of employment that imposed new and more demanding post-employment covenants. They complained to an employment tribunal, which decided that the covenants had been so unreasonable that the refusal to accept them could not be a 'reason of a kind such as to justify dismissal' under the Employment Rights Act 1996 s 98(1)(b), so that the dismissal could not be fair. The tribunal also ruled that the employer had acted unreasonably in treating the failure to accept the covenants as a sufficient reason for the dismissal, which was therefore also unfair under s 98(4). On the employer's appeal, the Employment Appeal Tribunal ruled that the employer's reason for dismissal fell within s 98(1) but that the tribunal had been entitled to find the dismissal unfair on the s 98(4) point. The employer appealed. *Held*, the refusal to accept an unreasonable covenant was not disqualified from counting as a reason that came within the terms of s 98(1). The question asked by s 98(1) was whether the employer's reason was of a kind such as to justify the dismissal, and the language used clearly indicated that the question was whether the reason fell within a category that was not excluded by law as a ground for dismissal or was a substantial other reason. It followed that, if the reason was whimsical or capricious or dishonest, or was based on an inadmissible ground such as race or sex, then it would be excluded by s 98(1). If, as in the instant case, the category into which the reason fell was one that could in law form a ground for dismissal, then it was necessary to proceed to the second stage of considering whether the employer had, under s 98(4)(a), acted reasonably or unreasonably in treating that reason as a sufficient reason for dismissing the employee. Fairness to both parties was best achieved by looking at the terms of the proposed contract in all the circumstances of the dismissal, as s 98(4) provided and required. It followed that the appeal tribunal's conclusion that the employment tribunal's first reason for finding in favour of the employees was not open to it was correct. It was also right to hold that the tribunal had correctly addressed s 98(4) and was entitled to come to the conclusion that the dismissal was unfair for some other substantial reason. Accordingly, the appeal would be dismissed.

Silverwood v Willow Oak Developments Ltd (t/a Windsor Recruitment) [2006] EWCA Civ 660, [2006] All ER (D) 351 (May) (Court of Appeal: Buxton and Neuberger JJ and Sir Martin Nourse). *Harper v National Coal Board* [1980] IRLR 260, EAT, considered. *Forshaw v Archcraft* [2005] IRLR 600, EAT (2005 Abr para 1431), overruled. Decision of Employment Appeal Tribunal [2006] IRLR 28 (2005 Abr para 1431) affirmed.

1272   Unfair dismissal—redundancy—information to be provided to employee prior to redundancy—requirement to give employee reasonable opportunity to consider his response

The Employment Act 2002 Sch 2 para 1 provides that the employer must set out in writing the employee's alleged conduct or characteristics, or other circumstances, which lead him to contemplate dismissing him, and must send the statement to the employee and invite him to attend a meeting to discuss the matter. The meeting must take place before action is taken, and must not take place unless (1) the employer has informed the employee what the basis was for including in the statement the grounds given in it, and (2) the employee has had a reasonable opportunity to consider his response to that information: Sch 2 para 2(1), (2).

An employer decided that its welding teams should be reorganised and that ten redundancies would have to be made. Meetings were arranged for the workforce and it was made clear that a process would take place for selecting the workers to be made redundant and that a further meeting would be arranged with those individuals who were going to be selected so that they could be informed of the position. The appellant employees received letters informing them that their positions were at risk and inviting them to a meeting. At the meeting the employees were informed of the selection criteria but not the detailed guidelines. At a further meeting the employees were informed that they had been selected for redundancy. They were not at any stage given an opportunity to comment on how their own particular performance had been assessed under the various criteria. They were given a document identifying the scores relevant to each criterion at the end of the meeting but without any opportunity to comment on the assessment. The employees brought proceedings in an employment tribunal. The tribunal held that the employees had failed to establish that their dismissal should be regarded as automatically unfair pursuant to the Employment Rights Act 1996 s 98A(1) because of a failure to comply with the statutory procedures. On appeal, the issue arose as to what information ought to be provided in compliance with the 2002 Act Sch 2 paras 1, 2. *Held*, when determining whether there had been compliance with the statutory procedure, the tribunal was not concerned with the reasonableness of the employer's selection criteria. The duty on the employer was to provide the ground for dismissal and the reasons why he was relying on that ground. At the first step the employer merely had to set out in writing the grounds which had led him to contemplate dismissing the employee, together with an invitation to attend a meeting. At that stage the statement need do no more than state the issue in broad terms. At the second step the employer had to inform the employee of the basis for the grounds given in the statement, which were simply the matters which had led the employer to contemplate dismissing the employee on the stated grounds. It was the contemplated dismissal of the specific employee which was in issue and might lead to tribunal proceedings, not just the decision that certain jobs would have to go. Further, in order to comply with the statutory provisions an employer should provide to the employee not only the basic selection criteria which had been used, but also the employee's own assessment. The employer had failed to give an individual assessment to each of the employees until they were leaving the meeting, when it had already decided that they should be made redundant. That was too late to amount to compliance with Sch 2 para 2 and left the employees with no opportunity to respond to that essential information at the meeting itself. Accordingly, the appeal would be allowed.

Alexander v Brigden Enterprises Ltd [2006] ICR 1277 (Employment Appeal Tribunal: Elias J presiding).

1273　Unfair dismissal—retirement age—normal retirement age

Employees employed as flying crew by the transferor company were entitled to work until aged 60, when they could retire on full pension. When the transferor was taken over by the transferee company, the employees continued to work as flying crew for the transferee which required its flying crew to retire at the age of 55. Many years after the transfer, the transferee required the employees to retire at 55. In unfair dismissal proceedings, the employees challenged the requirement. It fell to be determined whether the statutory normal retiring age set by the Employment Rights Act 1996 s 109, excluding the right given by s 94 not to be unfairly dismissed, was transferable under the Transfer of Undertakings (Protection of Employment) Regulations 1981, SI 1981/1794. *Held*, the statutory normal retiring age set by the 1996 Act s 109 was not transferable under the 1981 Regulations. The normal retiring age at any given time, although often heavily influenced by the contractual provision for retirement in force at the time, was, like the contractual term itself, subject to change, both before and after transfer. It was not something that was capable in terms of the 1996 Act s 109 of being frozen in perpetuity as at the moment of transfer. It was the normal retiring age for those in the position of an employee at the time of his dismissal that mattered, for it was that which, by s 109, determined whether, at that time, he had a right under s 94 not to be unfairly dismissed. However well disposed the courts should be to preserving pre-transfer contractual rights of employees corresponding, as provided by the 1981 Regulations reg 5(2)(a), to the 'powers, duties and liabilities' of the transferring employer 'under or in connection with any such contract', if the concept of normal retiring age might vary and, for that purpose was that applicable at the time of dismissal, there was nothing there to transfer or to preserve as at the time of transfer. All that was transferred was a general law right not to be unfairly dismissed before reaching normal retirement age, whatever that might be at the time of dismissal. Accordingly, the appeal would be dismissed.

Cross v British Airways plc [2006] EWCA Civ 549, [2006] ICR 1239 (Court of Appeal: Auld, Laws and Richards LJJ). Decision of Employment Appeal Tribunal [2005] IRLR 423 (2005 Abr para 1435) affirmed.

1996 Act s 109 repealed: SI 2006/1031.

1274　Unfair dismissal—upper age limit—compatibility with Community law

See *Rutherford v Secretary of State for Trade and Industry*, para 1079.

1275　Work and Families Act 2006

The Work and Families Act 2006 amends the Social Security Contributions and Benefits Act 1992 and the Employment Rights Act 1996 in order to (1) make provision about statutory rights to leave and pay in connection with the birth or adoption of children; (2) make provision about workers' entitlement to annual leave; and (3) provide for an increase in the maximum sums payable to employees on the insolvency of an employer. The 2006 Act received the royal assent on 21 June 2006 and came into force in part on that day. Further provisions came into force on and between 27 June 2006 and 6 April 2007: SI 2006/1682, 2232. The remaining provisions come into force on a day or days to be appointed. For details of commencement, see the table in the title STATUTES.

The 2006 Act s 1 increases, from 26 weeks to 52 weeks, the maximum period that statutory maternity pay and maternity allowance may be paid. An equivalent extension in relation to the payment of statutory adoption pay is made by s 2. New statutory rights to additional paternity leave for employees following the birth of a child or the placement of a child for adoption are created by the 2006 Act ss 3 and 4. Section 5 authorises the making of regulations which ensure that a person on additional paternity leave is entitled to the benefit of the terms and conditions of employment which would have applied had he not been absent. By virtue of s 6, the Secretary of State may make regulations entitling employees who satisfy certain conditions to additional statutory paternity pay following the birth of a child. The Secretary of State may also make regulations entitling employees who satisfy certain conditions to additional statutory paternity pay following the placement of a child for adoption: s 7. Under s 8, an employee must inform his employer of the date from which he expects liability for payment of additional statutory paternity pay to commence and the date on which he expects it to end. Provision concerning liability to pay additional statutory paternity pay, in relation to both birth and adoption, is made by s 9. Section 10 specifies the rate at which and the period for which additional statutory paternity pay is payable. Schedule 1, which makes various consequential amendments to enactments dealing with statutory leave and pay, is introduced by s 11. A qualifying employee is entitled, by virtue of s 12, to apply to his employer for a change in his terms and conditions of employment to facilitate care responsibilities he has for an adult. The Secretary of State is given a new free-standing power by s 13 to make provision concerning entitlement to annual leave. Under s 14, the Secretary of State may by order increase the weekly earnings limit used to calculate redundancy payments and the basic award for unfair dismissal. Section 15 gives effect to Sch 2, which makes various repeals. Section 16 deals with interpretation and s 17 with Northern Ireland. Financial provision is made by s 18. Section 19 deals with commencement and s 20 with the short title and extent.

Amendments, repeals and revocations

The list below, which is not exhaustive, mentions repeals and amendments which are or will be effective when the Act is fully in force.

Specific provisions of a number of Acts are amended or repealed. These include: Social Security Contributions and Benefits Act 1992 ss 165(1), 171ZEA–171ZEE, 171ZN(2); Employment Rights Act 1996 ss 80AA, 80BB, 80C, 80F; and Employment Act 2002 ss 6(2), 18, Sch 7 paras 3, 26(3), 33(3), 48(2), 49.

1276   Working time—general provisions

The Working Time (Amendment) Regulations 2006, SI 2006/99 (in force on 6 April 2006), further amend the 1998 Regulations, SI 1998/1833, by removing the exemption from limits on maximum weekly working time and night work where such working time is partly unmeasured or determined by the worker himself.

The Working Time (Amendment) (No 2) Regulations 2006, SI 2006/2389 (in force on 1 October 2006), further amend the 1998 Regulations supra by confirming that the definition of offshore work includes work performed in the British sector of the continental shelf (except in an area or part of an area in which the law of Northern Ireland applies) as designated under the Continental Shelf Act 1964 s 1(7), and work performed within the territorial waters of the United Kingdom adjacent to Great Britain.

1277   Working time—paid annual leave—minimum period of leave—financial allowance for days not taken

EC Parliament and Council Directive 93/104 art 7(2) provides that the minimum period of paid annual leave may not be replaced by an allowance in lieu.

Under Dutch legislation, an employee who had not made full use of his minimum annual leave entitlement could receive financial compensation in respect of that unused entitlement. The applicant federation of trade unions sought a declaration that the Netherlands had contravened Directive 93/104 art 7(2) by allowing an employee to exchange unused days of leave for financial compensation. A question relating to the interpretation of art 7 was referred to the European Court of Justice. *Held*, harmonisation at a Community level in relation to the organisation of working time was intended to guarantee better protection of the safety and health of workers by ensuring that they were entitled to minimum rest periods, in particular paid annual leave and adequate breaks. The entitlement of every worker to paid annual leave had to be regarded as a particularly important principle of Community social law from which there could be no derogations. The possibility of financial compensation in respect of the minimum period of annual leave carried over could create an incentive, incompatible with the objectives of the directive, not to take leave or to encourage employees not to do so. Consequently, art 7(2) precluded a national provision which permitted days of annual leave which were not taken during the course of a year to be replaced by an allowance in lieu in the course of a subsequent year.

Case C-124/05 *Federatie Nederlandse Vakbeweging v Netherlands* [2006] All ER (EC) 913 (ECJ: First Chamber).

1278   Working time—rest breaks—failure to implement Community legislation

The European Commission sought a declaration that the United Kingdom had failed to fulfil its obligations under EC Council Directive 93/104 in relation to certain aspects of the organisation of working time, which had been implemented by the Working Time Regulations 1998, SI 1998/1833. Part of the guidelines issued in relation to the 1998 Regulations stated that employers had to make sure that workers could take their rest breaks but were not required to make sure that they did so. The Commission argued that this indorsed and encouraged a practice of non-compliance as employers were instructed merely that those who wished to claim such rest periods were not prevented from doing so. *Held*, workers had actually to benefit from the daily and weekly periods of rest provided for. Member states were under an obligation to guarantee that each of the minimum requirements laid down by Directive 93/104 was observed in order to ensure that the rights conferred on workers were fully effective. Where a member state implemented the directive and provided that the workers were entitled to certain rights to rest but indicated in guidelines that employers were not required to ensure that workers exercised those rights, the member state did not guarantee compliance with the minimum requirements of the directive or its essential objective of protecting the safety and health of workers. In general, the directive's obligations would not require an employer to force his workers to claim the rest periods due to them. However, the guidelines were clearly liable to render the rights enshrined in the directive meaningless and were incompatible with its objective as they let it be understood that, while employers could not prevent rest periods from being taken, they were under no obligation to ensure that workers exercised such a right. The United Kingdom had therefore failed to fulfil its obligation under Directive 93/104 to adopt measures necessary to implement the rights of workers to daily and weekly rest.

Case C–484/04 *EC Commission v United Kingdom* [2006] IRLR 888 (ECJ: Third Chamber).

1279   Working time—road tanker drivers—hours and working time—temporary exception

The Community Drivers' Hours and Working Time (Road Tankers) (Temporary Exception) Regulations 2006, SI 2006/17 (in force on 12 January 2006), grant a temporary exception in relation to the operation of road tankers which transport petroleum products in the exceptional circumstances arising from the fire at Buncefield fuel depot, so that, until the end of 10 February 2006, time spent driving a road tanker to meet the exceptional circumstances is not subject to the fortnightly maximum driving period prescribed by EEC Council Direction 3820/85, the daily driving period, furthermore, prescribed by Direction 3820/85, is increased to ten hours and the minimum weekly rest period is reduced to 24 hours. The regulations also revise, in relation to road tankers, the Road Transport (Working Time) Regulations 2005, SI 2005/639, with the effect that the maximum working time in a week is increased to 66 hours, and up to six extra hours can be worked without affecting the average weekly working time.

The Community Drivers' Hours and Working Time (Road Tankers) (Temporary Exception) (Amendment) Regulations 2006, SI 2006/244 (in force on 11 February 2006), amend SI 2006/17 supra so as to extend, until 12 March 2006, its period of operation.

1280   Wrongful dismissal—reservation of right to bring High Court claim—failure to withdraw tribunal application—jurisdiction of High Court

An employee presented a complaint of unfair and wrongful dismissal to an employment tribunal. He stated that, in so far as his claim for damages for wrongful dismissal exceeded the statutory limit on awards for wrongful dismissal by an employment tribunal, he expressly reserved the right to pursue an action in the High Court. Subsequently, his legal advisers took the precaution of starting an action for wrongful dismissal in the High Court with a view to recovering the excess of any award he received in the employment tribunal. They did not, however, take the additional precaution of withdrawing his wrongful dismissal claim from the employment tribunal proceedings. The tribunal found that the employee had been unfairly and wrongfully dismissed, but limited its award to the capped amount of damages plus a compensatory award, leaving a shortfall in the damages. The employer applied to strike out the High Court action on the grounds of res judicata and abuse of process, contending that the wrongful dismissal claim had already been litigated in the employment tribunal and that the employee could not litigate the matter further in the ordinary courts. The claim was duly struck out and the employee appealed. The employer sought to rely on the doctrine of merger of causes of action, submitting that the employee's cause of action for wrongful dismissal had been transmuted into the judgment of the employment tribunal and had thereafter ceased to exist independently of the judgment. *Held*, where an employee expressly reserved the right, in a claim before an employment tribunal for wrongful dismissal, to bring proceedings for wrongful dismissal arising from the same facts in the High Court, the findings of the employment tribunal constituted issue estoppel or res judicata in the High Court proceedings. If the unfair dismissal claim was litigated first in the employment tribunal, it was neither necessary nor permissible to relitigate in High Court proceedings for wrongful dismissal the factual issues common to both causes of action. Moreover, the employee's cause of action for wrongful dismissal had clearly merged in the final judgment of the tribunal on the claim for wrongful dismissal as between the same parties as in the High Court proceedings. Merger was not prevented from taking place by the express statement that the employee expressly reserved his rights to bring High Court proceedings for the excess. The merger arose from the fact that the cause of action had been the subject of a final judgment of the tribunal. The claim for the excess was not a separate cause of action. Accordingly, the appeal would be dismissed.

Fraser v HLMAD Ltd [2006] EWCA Civ 738, [2007] 1 All ER 383 (Court of Appeal: Mummery and Moore-Bick LJJ).

ENFORCEMENT

Halsbury's Laws of England (4th edn) vol 17(1) (Reissue) paras 1–400

1281   Third party debt order—application to set aside—exceptional circumstances

The Republic of Congo was the judgment debtor of both the applicant and a third party. The third party had obtained an interim third party debt order and, before the order was made final, the applicant also sought a third party debt order. The interim order was made final before the application was heard, which meant that the applicant could obtain pari passu payment of its judgment debt only if the first order was set aside. In support of its claim, the applicant contended that the debtor was insolvent in the sense that it had insufficient assets to pay its English judgment creditors. *Held*, an interim third party debt order was a defeasible equitable charge that could be discharged on the application for the final order. However, when it was made final, it had priority over any subsequent order, and would be set aside only in exceptional circumstances, in the interests of justice. Although an interim order could be discharged where it conflicted with the operation of a mandatory insolvency regime in the case of an individual, estate or company, that had no application in the case of the judgment debtor. It followed that there was no special or exceptional reason to reopen the order. Accordingly, the application would be dismissed.

FG Hemisphere Associates LLC v Republic of Congo (2006) Times, 27 February (Queen's Bench Division: Cooke J).

1282   Third party debt order—interim order—application—evidence that third party owed money to judgment debtor—bank

The claimant judgment creditors applied under CPR 72.4 for an interim third party debt order against a bank. For the purposes of such an application, the applicant had to submit a form verifying that the third party in question owed money to, or held money to the credit of, the judgment debtor. On their application, the judgment creditors were able to establish that the judgment debtor had previously had an account which was in credit with the bank because he had earlier drawn, on the account named in the application, a cheque in their favour which had been honoured on presentation. They could not, however, establish that the bank was in debt to the judgment debtor at the time of the application. The master dismissed the application, holding that it could not be inferred merely from the previous existence of the bank account in credit that it still existed and was still in credit. The judgment creditors appealed. *Held*, in the absence of any contrary indication, the court could and should accept, as sufficient for the purposes of an interim third party debt order under CPR 72.4, evidence in which the judgment creditor was able to say no more than that the judgment debtor had previously had an account with the third party bank and that it had previously been in credit. The question was not only one of construction, and there were powerful considerations against a strict construction. In very many cases, the judgment creditor would not have knowledge in any detailed way of who owed what sums to the judgment debtor. Moreover, given the speed at which bank accounts could be closed or merged or have the credits therein transferred or reduced, a good number of applications would be prevented by insisting on cogent evidence of the judgment debtor's account being in credit as at the very day of the application or any later day—a level of proof to which remarkably few judgment creditors could aspire. Nor would the floodgates be opened by adopting a relaxed view as to what evidence was sufficient. Furthermore, it could be said that the whole point of the interim stage was to establish whether there was, indeed, a present debt from the third party to the judgment debtor and to establish its amount while then procuring, if it were found to exist, that it was preserved. Accordingly, the appeal would be allowed.

Alawiye v Mahmood (t/a Amsons) [2005] EWHC 277 (Ch), [2006] 3 All ER 668 (Chancery Division: Lindsay J).

EQUITY

Halsbury's Laws of England (4th edn) vol 16(2) (Reissue) paras 401–950

Articles

For articles relating to this title please refer to the Table of Articles at the beginning of the Abridgment.

1283   Equitable remedies—relief against forfeiture—option—option to purchase—clog on equity of redemption

The claimant owned the headlease of a commercial property. A contract was concluded to sell the remaining term to the defendant. On completion, the purchase price was left outstanding, secured by a charge on the property. The charge provided for repayment by monthly instalments of principal and interest. On the same day as it granted the charge, the defendant also granted the claimant an option to repurchase the property. The option was exercisable only if a principal sum was outstanding and if payments under the charge were in arrears. The defendant fell into arrears and the claimant sought to exercise the option. The defendant contended that the option was a clog on the equity of redemption and that it was in the nature of a penalty or provision for forfeiture and that the court should grant relief from forfeiture. Summary judgment was given to the defendant on the first ground. On appeal, the court expressed a provisional view that the application of the rule against 'clogs' depended not on whether there was a simultaneous grant of a mortgage and an option to purchase in favour of the mortgagee but, instead, on the substance of the transaction, which, in the present case, was one of sale and purchase rather than one of mortgage. *Held*, the substance of the transaction was that of a sale and purchase. The option formed part of the sale package, was a term of the contract of sale and purchase and was not referable wholly or mainly to the provision of the charge. Provisions of the type contained in the option could operate as a means of forfeiture, in the limited sense that the defendant's interest in the property was to be transferred to the claimant on the option being exercised. However, there were no grounds for relief from forfeiture in the present case. In particular, it could not be said that the object of the option was to secure the payment of money.

The option was a condition of the sale and purchase, with the object, in the event of the conditions for exercise being satisfied, of restoring the property to the claimant to deal with as owner. That purpose was not one that could be achieved by way of the court granting relief from forfeiture nor did the option have the features of a penalty clause. On its exercise, the defendant would recover the price it had paid. Accordingly, the claim would be allowed.

Warnborough Ltd v Garmite Ltd [2006] EWHC 10 (Ch), [2007] 1 P & CR 34 (Chancery Division: Richard Sheldon QC).

1284   Positive covenant—assignment—assignment of burden—benefit and burden linked

See *Jenkins v Young Brothers Transport Ltd*, para 689.

1285   Restrictive covenant—annexation—express contrary intention

The Law of Property Act 1925 s 63(1) provides that every conveyance is effectual to pass all the estate, right, title, interest, claim, and demand which the conveying parties respectively have, in, to, or on the property conveyed, or expressed or intended so to be, or which they respectively have power to convey in, to, or on the same. This applies only if and as far as a contrary intention is not expressed in the conveyance, and has effect subject to the terms of the conveyance: s 63(2).

The claimant was the successor in title to the vendor, the previous owner of a large cottage with a large garden and orchard parts of which the previous owner had sold. The conveyances contained a covenant by the purchaser not to erect any building on the land except a detached private dwelling house in accordance with plans approved by the vendor. The claimant proposed to demolish the cottage and replace it with eight self-contained apartments. The claimant sought a declaration that the defendants could not benefit from the covenant as the benefit of the covenant would not pass unless expressly assigned. *Held*, in a conveyance where the benefit of the covenant was said to benefit the land that remained unsold from time to time of a vendor, the effect was to annex the covenant to that land for the period in which the land remained unsold. The covenant was not annexed on the sale of the land and would only pass if there was an express assignment. The covenant was plainly intended to enable the vendor to control so long as she was the owner from time to time of the land unsold. Where she ceased to own a piece of the land by sale, the benefit of the covenant would cease to be annexed to that land on sale, unless it had been expressly assigned, when the benefit became enforceable by virtue of the assignment. The wording of the conveyance showed that the covenant touched and concerned the land for the time being that belonged to the vendor that was unsold, and thereafter, if the benefit had been expressly assigned. If, on the occasion of the next sale, there was no assignment, there was nothing on which s 63 could bite as there was no interest in land that was capable of being passed at that stage, as the vendor had plainly made a decision not to pass that benefit on. The plain wording of the conveyance was a sufficient contrary intention and it was unclear how s 63 could be used to counter the express wording of the covenant. Accordingly, the application would be allowed and the declaration granted.

Sugarman v Porter [2006] EWHC 331 (Ch), [2006] 2 P & CR 274 (Chancery Division: Peter Smith J). *Crest Nicholson Residential (South) Ltd v McAllister* [2004] EWCA Civ 410, [2004] 2 All ER 991 (2004 Abr para 1252); and *Harbour Estates Ltd v HSBC Bank plc* [2004] EWHC 1714 (Ch), [2005] Ch 194 (2004 Abr para 1711) applied.

1286   Restrictive covenant—breach—damages in lieu of injunction

The claimant sold land to defendant subject to a restrictive covenant which prohibited the defendant from erecting any buildings on it. The defendant obtained planning permission some years later, and erected a two-story garage and studio on the land. The claimant sought damages for breach of covenant as he would have reasonably demanded for relaxing the covenant. The judge held that the claimant had not acquiesced to the breach and awarded damages. The defendant appealed. *Held*, the court was entitled to issue damages in lieu of an injunction provided it had the jurisdiction to grant an injunction, whether or not it would have been prepared to do so on the facts. The claimant was required to establish a case for equitable relief by proving his legal right and an actual or threatened infringement by the defendant, as well as by overcoming all equitable defences such as laches, acquiescence or estoppel. The relevant test was whether it was unconscionable in all the circumstances for a party to continue to seek to enforce rights which he had at the date of the breach. It was not unconscionable for the claimant to seek to enforce his rights under the covenant. The covenant did not require submission or approval of plans but was a covenant not to erect any buildings. There was a clear distinction between a case where a beneficiary of a covenant knew he could prevent building works from commencing by the withholding of the approval of plans, and a case where the beneficiary was only aware there has been a breach when the building reached the first floor level. In the latter case it was much harder to see what a person could do to enforce the covenant. An action for damages would likely be the only remedy available, as it may well have been unrealistic to expect the court to order the demolishment of buildings or order that they not be completed. Accordingly, the claim would be allowed.

Harris v Williams-Wynne [2006] EWCA Civ 104, [2006] 2 P & CR 595 (Court of Appeal: Sir Andrew Morritt, Chadwick LJ and Sir Paul Kennedy). *Gafford v Graham* (1998) 71 P & CR 73, CA (1998 Abr para 1557), distinguished.

1287 Subrogation—unjust enrichment—insurers providing hire car to claimant

The defendant's car collided with the claimant's car while the latter was stationary. The claimant's car required repairs and during the time he was without his car he was provided with another by his insurers. The defendant admitted liability. The claimant's insurers brought proceedings seeking to recover costs from the defendant's insurers. The dispute centred on the cost of the hire car. It was argued that as the claimant's insurers had provided the replacement through a third party hire company the claimant's insurers ought to give credit for the introduction fee which that company might have paid to the claimant's insurers. The defendant submitted that damages should be limited to the reasonable cost of providing hire cars, arguing that an insurer could not recover by way of subrogation more than its true outlay, and invoking the rule that collateral benefits should be taken into account in assessing damages. The claimant submitted that the total cost was the sum paid to the hire company and that any payment by it to the claimant's insurers was incapable in law of impacting on the claim which was for the claimant's loss. *Held*, the claimant's insurers were entitled to recover the full cost of a hire vehicle from the defendant's insurers, notwithstanding that they had negotiated an undisclosed discount from the hire company. The claimant was under a liability to pay the hire charges and the hire company would have been entitled to recover them from him had the occasion arisen. The defendant's argument confused contractual subrogation, of the sort found in insurance cases, and subrogation as a remedy to prevent unjust enrichment. There was no reason in law why any profit of the claimant's insurers should be transferred to the tortfeasor or his insurers. Further, the claimant was placed in a worse position by having to accept the hire car, by virtue of assuming responsibility for returning the car in the same state as he received it rather than having the option to treat it as he wished. Therefore, the claimant was entitled to recover the full cost of the hire. Judgment would be given accordingly.

Bee v Jenson [2006] EWHC 3359 (Comm), [2007] RTR 115 (Queen's Bench Division: Morison J).

ESTOPPEL

Halsbury's Laws of England (4th edn) vol 16(2) (Reissue) paras 951–1094

Articles

For articles relating to this title please refer to the Table of Articles at the beginning of the Abridgment.

1288 Estoppel by representation—reliance on representation—grant of legal aid

See *Legal Services Commission v Marchioness*, para 1779.

1289 Estoppel by representation—requirements of estoppel—reliance on statements made—establishment of detriment

The claimant became a member of a company's final salary occupational pension scheme for senior employees. He received a letter which outlined his entitlement, after 20 years' pensionable service. Provided that certain circumstances were satisfied, he was to take pension benefits from the age of 62, rather than the scheme's normal retirement date of 65, without any actuarial reduction. He also received a booklet which contained information about the scheme, and which stated that the scheme's normal retirement date was 65. An information notice in the booklet stated that the claimant had the right to inspect the legal trust deed and rules governing the plan, and that the trust deed and the rules were to prevail. The defendant acquired some of the company's undertakings and became the claimant's principal employer for the purposes of the pension scheme. Following the receipt of a letter from the pensions officer stating that his normal retirement date for the purposes of an unreduced rate was 65, and not 62, the claimant appealed to the Pensions Ombudsman. The ombudsman held that a number of clear and unambiguous representations had been made to the claimant indicating that, on the completion of 20 years' pensionable service, his normal retirement date would be at the age of 62. He held that the claimant had relied on those representations and that it would be unjust to permit the trustees to go back on them. On the trustees' appeal against the ombudsman's decision, it fell to be determined whether those representations had in fact been made, whether the information notice in the booklet had made it impossible for the claimant to establish reliance on the statements in the booklet and letter and whether the claimant had incurred any detriment. *Held*, neither the letter nor the booklet had made the alleged representation or promise. Further, the warning that the interpretation of the booklet had to be read subject to the trust deed and rules made it impossible for the claimant to establish reliance on the statements in the booklet and the letter. Moreover, the claimant had not established detriment either to satisfy the requirements of estoppel by representation or as a relevant factor in determining whether it was inequitable or unconscionable to deny his entitlement to early retirement on a full pension. It followed that he had not established that the requirements of estoppel by representation or promissory estoppel had been satisfied so as to justify the ombudsman's decision. Accordingly, the appeal would be allowed.

Hutchinson v Steria Ltd [2006] EWCA Civ 1551, [2006] All ER (D) 349 (Nov) (Court of Appeal: Mummery, Jacob and Neuberger LJJ). *Greasley v Cooke* [1980] 3 All ER 710, CA, considered. *Tai Hing Cotton Mill Ltd v Liu Chong Hing Bank Ltd* [1985] 2 All ER 947, PC (1985 Abr para 165); and *Hearn v Younger* [2002] EWHC 963 (Ch), [2003] OPLR 45 applied. Decision of Peter Smith J [2005] EWHC 2993 (Ch), [2005] All ER (D) 352 (Dec) reversed.

1290   Estoppel by representation—silence—sale of land—completion date—request to delay date—failure to respond to request

A company sold a property to the defendants and reserved to itself an option to repurchase the property. The company then assigned the benefit of the option to the claimant which in turn exercised the option. On the afternoon of the date of completion, the claimant's solicitor asked the defendants' solicitor whether time for completion could be extended for a week. The defendants' solicitor said that he would take his clients' instructions and revert back to her, but instead, with the defendants, made a conscious decision not to respond. Six days later, they rescinded the contract for failure to complete and the claimant sought specific performance. The claim was dismissed and the claimant appealed. *Held*, no reasonably competent solicitor having conduct of an important completion would have understood from the silence of the other side that the defendants were agreeing to postpone completion. There was no justification for the claimant's solicitor believing that the defendants' manifest readiness to complete had been replaced by a willingness to postpone completion for a week. The judge was plainly right to find that the defendants' solicitor's failure to revert back to the claimant's solicitor could not possibly have amounted to a promise or assurance not to require completion on the agreed date. Accordingly, the appeal would be dismissed.

Northstar Land Ltd v Brooks [2006] EWCA Civ 756, [2006] 32 EG 80 (Court of Appeal: Ward and Smith LJJ and Cresswell J).

1291   Issue estoppel—res judicata—application to appeal before immigration tribunal

See *Ocampo v Secretary of State for the Home Department*, para 356.

1292   Issue estoppel—res judicata—wrongful dismissal—separate employment tribunal and High Court claims

See *Fraser v HLMAD Ltd*, para 1280.

1293   Promissory estoppel—statement or representation—reliance on statement

See *Tonkin v UK Insurance Ltd*, para 1721.

EVIDENCE [CIVIL]

Halsbury's Laws of England (4th edn) vol 17(1) (Reissue) paras 401–1059

Articles

For articles relating to this title please refer to the Table of Articles at the beginning of the Abridgment.

1294   Admissibility—hearsay evidence—anti-social behaviour order

See *R v W*, para 2527.

1295   Admissibility—'without prejudice' discussions—public interest

A number of employees had made complaints of racial discrimination against their employer, and unsuccessful settlement discussions had taken place prior to the proceedings in an employment tribunal. The employer circulated quarterly reports which referred to the amount of money which it had spent on defending the tribunal proceedings and criticised the employees and the trade union for pursuing unfounded allegations and making unwarranted demands for money. The employees lodged a complaint with the grievance committee which heard oral evidence about the discussions which had occurred between the parties but concluded that the grounds for grievance had not been established. The employees brought proceedings before an employment tribunal and the employer challenged the admissibility of the evidence of the settlement negotiations as they were protected by the 'without prejudice' privilege. The tribunal ruled that the previous proceedings were not admissible but that the report of the committee that contained references to the discussions was admissible. The employer appealed and the employees cross-appealed. *Held*, in discrimination cases, the necessity of revealing the truth of what had occurred and the public interest in the eradication of the evils of discrimination tipped the scales as against the necessity of protecting the 'without prejudice' privilege. The employees' case would have been severely hampered if they had not been permitted to refer to what had occurred in the discussions to support their case that they had not made unwarranted demands for money. The employer had placed those matters in the public arena through the publication of quarterly reports and should not be entitled to hide behind the cloak of privilege when attempting to justify its position before the committee. It would have been a clear abuse of a privileged occasion. Accordingly, the appeal would be dismissed and the cross-appeal would be allowed.

Vaseghi v Brunel University [2006] All ER (D) 163 (Oct) (Employment Appeal Tribunal: Judge Ansell presiding). *Savings and Investment Bank Ltd v Fincken* [2003] EWCA Civ 1630, [2003] All ER (D) 197 (Nov) (2003 Abr para 1214); and *BNP Paribas v Mezzotero* [2004] IRLR 508, EAT, considered.

1296   Criminal cases

See CRIMINAL EVIDENCE AND PROCEDURE.

1297   Expert evidence—expert witness—discussion between experts—leave to adduce evidence from new expert

The claimant suffered injury in two road traffic accidents. She issued proceedings for personal injury. Both the claimant and the defendants instructed an orthopaedic surgeon to provide expert evidence. Following each expert's report, the experts met with the consent of the parties and pursuant to an order of the court. Discussion between experts was governed by the CPR 35.12. The claimant's expert changed his opinion with the effect that the claimant's prospects of recovering substantial damages at trial for loss of future earnings were reduced. The claimant decided to consult another orthopaedic surgeon and sought permission at a case management conference to adduce expert evidence from that surgeon. The judge refused the application and the claimant appealed. *Held,* the scheme of CPR Pt 35 concerning experts' discussions did not rule out the granting of permission to call a further expert following an experts' discussion. However, it would be rare that that would appropriate. Where a court was asked for permission to adduce expert evidence from a new expert in circumstances where the applicant was dissatisfied with the opinion of his own expert following the experts' discussion, it would do so only where there was good reason to suppose that the applicant's first expert had agreed with the expert instructed by the other side or had modified his opinion for reasons which could not properly or fairly support his revised opinion. Where good reason was shown the court would have to consider whether it could properly be said that further expert evidence was reasonably required to resolve the proceedings. In the present case, the judge had not had regard to all the relevant matters and the claimant's application should be considered afresh. If the claimant was not permitted to rely on the evidence of the new expert and the court accepted the evidence of the original expert, the claimant would have a justifiable sense of grievance. Therefore, the claimant would be permitted to rely on the evidence of the new expert. Accordingly, the appeal would be allowed.

Stallwood v David [2006] EWHC 2600 (QB), [2007] 1 All ER 206 (Queen's Bench Division: Teare J).

1298   Expert evidence—expert witness—duties—conflict of interest

The claimant sought damages for nervous shock and psychiatric injury which he alleged had been caused by the negligent treatment of his son by the defendant, a medical practitioner. The claim was dismissed and the claimant appealed on the ground that the defendant's expert witness had not disclosed a conflict of interest. *Held,* a conflict of interest did not automatically disqualify an expert. The key question was whether the expert's opinion was independent. The need for the expert to give an independent opinion flowed from the overriding duty imposed on an expert witness, set out by CPR 35.3, to assist the court in relation to matters falling within the expert's expertise. This overrode any duty which the expert owed to his client. An independent opinion was a necessary quality of expert evidence but it did not always follow that it was a sufficient condition in itself. Where an expert had a material or significant conflict of interest, the court was likely to decline to act on his evidence or to give permission for his evidence to be adduced. Guidance issued to the courts as to the protocol for the instruction of experts to give evidence in civil claims did not refer to the need for disclosure by an expert of a conflict or potential conflict of interest. Accordingly, the appeal would be dismissed.

The court added that the Civil Procedure Rules Committee should give consideration to requiring an expert to make a statement following his report stating that (1) he had no conflict of interest of any kind other than any which he had disclosed in his report; (2) he did not consider that any interest which he had disclosed affected his suitability as an expert witness on any issue on which he had given evidence; (3) he would advise the party by whom he was instructed if, between the date of his report and the trial, there was any change in circumstances which affected his answers to (1) or (2) above.

Toth v Jarman [2006] EWCA Civ 1520, [2006] 4 All ER 1276 (Court of Appeal: Sir Mark Potter P, Arden and Wall LJJ). *National Justice Compañia Naviera SA v Prudential Assurance Co Ltd (The Ikarian Reefer)* [1992] 2 Lloyd's Rep 68 (1993 Abr para 1239) considered.

1299   Expert evidence—expert witness—immunity from suit—disciplinary proceedings

The appellant, a paediatrician, gave evidence in the successful prosecution of a woman for the murder of her two sons by refuting the proposition that the children might have died from sudden infant death syndrome. The woman's second appeal was allowed, and the court indicated that, while the appellant's evidence had not been subject to full argument, if it had been so subject, the appeal would have been successful on that ground also. The woman's father complained to the General Medical Council alleging serious professional misconduct on the part of the appellant. A fitness to practise panel of the Council heard the complaint and concluded that the appellant was guilty of serious professional misconduct. The appellant's appeal against the panel's decision succeeded and the Council appealed. *Held*, Sir Anthony Clarke MR dissenting, the two issues which arose were whether an expert witness should be entitled to immunity from disciplinary, regulatory or fitness to practise proceedings in relation to statements made or evidence given by him in or for the purpose of legal proceedings, and whether the panel was correct to find the appellant guilty of serious professional misconduct. It would be wrong in principle for the court to cut across or impliedly limit the powers of a panel by extending immunity from civil suit to fitness to practise proceedings. The purpose of such proceedings, which was to ensure, so far as reasonably possible, that those who were not fit to practise did not do so, was distinct from the purpose of civil proceedings. The panel should be entitled, and might be bound, to investigate where the conduct or evidence of an expert witness at or in connection with a trial, whether civil or criminal, raised the question whether the expert was fit to practise in his particular field. The threat of fitness to practise proceedings was in the public interest as it helped to deter those who might be tempted to give partisan evidence and not to discharge their obligation to assist the court by giving conscientious and objective evidence. It also helped to preserve the integrity of the trial process and public confidence both in the trial process and in the standards of the professions from which expert witnesses came. For most classes of case, the duties of a regulatory authority would have been laid down by statute or by royal charter or by the exercise of the royal prerogative and very often in mandatory terms. It was not appropriate for the common law to introduce a qualification on those duties. That was a matter for Parliament or the relevant authorities. Where an expert was called to give evidence he had an overriding duty to the court to assist it objectively, but he was also bound both by the ethical code and generally accepted standards of his profession. Where the conduct of an expert alleged to amount to a professional offence under scrutiny by his professional disciplinary body arose out of evidence he had given to a court or other tribunal, it was important that that body should fully understand and assess his conduct in the forensic context in which it had arisen. In the case of expert evidence involving opinion evidence as to causation, it was critical that the legal representatives of the party proposing to rely on such evidence should ensure that the witness's written and oral statements were confined to his expertise and were relevant and admissible to the important issues in the case. The medical expert should know his limits, and so was not absolved from responsibility from professional or forensic impropriety in the presentation and form of his evidence. While the respondent had been guilty of some professional misconduct, he had not intended to mislead the trial court and had honestly believed in the validity of his evidence when he presented it. While he had been properly criticised for not disclosing his lack of expertise, a finding of serious professional conduct was not justified. Accordingly, the appeal would be allowed in part.

Meadow v General Medical Council [2006] EWCA Civ 1390, [2006] 3 FCR 447 (Court of Appeal: Sir Anthony Clarke MR, Auld and Thompson LJJ). Decision of Collins J [2006] EWHC 146 (Admin), [2006] 2 All ER 329 reversed in part.

1300   Mode of giving evidence—use of video link—discretion of court

The claimant, who was resident abroad, was involved in an action against the defendants, a number of parties who, he claimed, were responsible for extensive defects in a house which the claimant had had built. He sought an order, pursuant to CPR 32.3, allowing him to give evidence by video link rather than in person. He contended that, if he came to the United Kingdom to give evidence, there was a risk that he would be liable to pay about £50m in capital gains tax following the sale of a substantial shareholding. The defendants resisted the application, contending that there was no evidence to support the claimant's assertions and that they would suffer prejudice if the order was made because the claimant would not be subject to the pressures of the witness box. *Held*, the court had a wide discretion under CPR 32.3 to allow the use of a video link. Although hearing evidence in such a manner was not ideal, it could be a convenient way of dealing with any part of the proceedings and could result in time and cost savings. The application was inherently unattractive, based as it was on the claimant's apparent wish to use the United Kingdom's justice system without contributing towards the cost of it, and on his wish to ensure that his status, as someone who paid no taxes in the United Kingdom, was not put in jeopardy by his desire to give evidence at the trial which he had instigated. However, there was nothing to suggest that the claimant had done anything unlawful. His evidence was also of critical importance in the trial. Further, it could not be said that the making of a video link order would cause prejudice to the defendants, as they would still be able to cross-examine the claimant by video link. The court could take into account, when assessing the evidence in the case, the fact that giving evidence from a video suite would be less stressful for the claimant than appearing in the witness box. There was also a genuine risk that the claimant would be made liable to a substantial sum by way of capital gains tax if he gave evidence in person, and he would therefore be prejudiced if the order was not made. Accordingly, the application would be allowed.

McGlinn v Waltham Contractors Ltd (No 2) [2006] EWHC 2322 (TCC), (2006) 108 Con LR 43 (Queen's Bench Division: Judge Peter Coulson QC). *Polanski v Conde Nast Publications Ltd* [2005] UKHL 10, [2005] 1 All ER 945 (2005 Abr para 1473) considered.

1301   Privilege—'without prejudice' communications—scope of rule

See *Bradford & Bingley plc v Rashid*, para 1815.

EXECUTORS AND ADMINISTRATORS

Halsbury's Laws of England (4th edn) vol 17(2) (Reissue) paras 1–900

Articles

For articles relating to this title please refer to the Table of Articles at the beginning of the Abridgment.

1302   Executor—appointment—partner in firm of solicitors—firm converting status to limited liability partnership—construction of will

By the terms of her will, a testatrix appointed as the executors and trustees of her will the partners at the date of her death of a specified firm of solicitors, or the firm which had at that point succeeded and carried on the practice of that firm. The firm subsequently merged with another firm, and eventually the merged firm converted its status to a limited liability partnership ('LLP'), in which all of the partners of the firm became members. When the testatrix died, the probate registry refused to grant probate of the will to members of the LLP. It accepted that the LLP had succeeded to the practice of the firm with which the testatrix had originally dealt, but took the view that it was not a 'firm' and that the members of the LLP were not 'partners' within the meaning of the will. The applicants sought a declaration that the registry's decision was erroneous, contending that the intention of the testatrix to appoint as executors the solicitors conducting the practice carried on by the firm at the date of the will was not frustrated by the exercise of the option available to those solicitors to alter the legal character of the vehicle through which they carried on that practice. *Held,* the court could and should take a practical and common sense view in eliciting and giving effect to the intention manifested by the testatrix. The testatrix had focused on the persons associated in carrying on for profit the practice carried on by the firm at the date of the will. The terms of the will were deliberately formulated so that changes in the vehicle by which the practice was carried on was very much of secondary importance. In the circumstances, with the LLP being substituted as that vehicle for the earlier partnership, the terms of the will could embrace the profit- sharing members of the LLP, who were the equivalent of partners in the previous partnership. However, even as the 'partner in the partnership' meant in the case of a partnership a profit-sharing partner and not merely a salaried partner or a person merely held out, but not in fact, a partner, so when transposed to a limited liability partnership the member had to mean a profit-sharing member. It followed that, on the true construction of the will, probate should be granted to applicants who were profit- sharing members of the LLP. Accordingly, the application would be allowed.

Re Rogers (deceased) [2006] EWHC 753 (Ch), [2006] 2 All ER 792 (Chancery Division: Lightman J).

1303   Family provision—application by fiancée—domicile of testator

The deceased, who was born in Cyprus but had lived in London most of his life, made a will which included a legacy to the claimant, with whom he had had a ten year relationship, and to whom he had become engaged four years before his death. After his death, the claimant brought proceedings against the deceased's estate for further financial provision under the Inheritance (Provision for Family and Dependants) Act 1975 s 2, and a preliminary issue arose as to whether the deceased had been domiciled in England at the date of his death. The judge held that he had been domiciled in England and that the court had jurisdiction to entertain the proceedings. The executors appealed. *Held,* the deceased had had a domicile of origin in Cyprus until it was proved that he had intended to reside permanently or indefinitely in England. Although the judge had correctly summarised the legal principles, his inference that the deceased had had a change of intention regarding his permanent home in the last eight years of his life, based on the development of his relationship with the claimant, was wrong. If the deceased had not acquired a domicile of choice in England, because he did not intend to live in England permanently, it could not reasonably be inferred that from what had happened in the last eight years of his life he had formed a different intention about his permanent home before he died. Accordingly, the appeal would be allowed.

Cyganik v Agulian [2006] EWCA Civ 129, [2006] 1 FCR 406 (Court of Appeal: Mummery and Longmore LJJ and Lewison J).

1304   Family provision—application by person living in same household as deceased—maintenance by deceased

The defendant, the son of the deceased, was solely entitled to the deceased's estate under the intestacy rules. The deceased and the claimant, a Polish national who had entered the United Kingdom on a six-month tourist visa, had lived together as husband and wife, and the deceased had made several cash transfers to the claimant's Polish bank account. During the time of their cohabitation, the claimant went to Poland for short periods and, on her return to the United Kingdom, re-entered on a six-month tourist visa. The claimant brought proceedings, under the Inheritance (Provision for Family and Dependants) Act 1975, seeking maintenance from the deceased's estate. The judge found that she was entitled to relief under s 1(1)(e) and assessed £50 per week as a reasonable financial provision for her to be sufficiently maintained in Poland. The claimant appealed and the defendant cross-appealed. The claimant submitted that the judge had failed to have regard to s 3(5) which required a court, in reaching its conclusion, to take into account the facts known to it at the date of the hearing and that the judge had infringed the EC Treaty art 12 by forcing the claimant to return to Poland. The defendant submitted that the judge had erred in finding the claimant eligible for relief. *Held*, the judge had not failed to take into account the events which had transpired after the death of the deceased. Rather, the judge had made numerous references to facts and matters which had occurred after the death. Further, art 12 was expressly stated only to apply within the scope of application of the treaty. The treaty had no application to the substantive law of succession to a deceased party's estate. The claimant's appeal on the basis that she had been discriminated against on the ground of nationality failed. She had still been an illegal overstayer and it was clear that the deceased had expected her to return to Poland after his death. There was no requirement under the 1975 Act that the claimant's ability to claim depended on her being legally resident in the United Kingdom and no such requirement should be read into the 1975 Act. There had been no requirement to consider the legality of the claimant's status. Accordingly, the appeal and cross-appeal would be dismissed.

Witkowska v Kaminski [2006] EWHC 1940 (Ch), [2006] 3 FCR 250 (Chancery Division: Blackburne J). *Re Dix (deceased)* [2004] EWCA Civ 139, [2004] 1 WLR 1399 (2004 Abr para 1272) applied.

1305   Family provision—reasonable financial provision—property held on joint tenancy

The deceased, who died intestate, had been the husband of the claimant and the father of the defendant. The deceased and the defendant had jointly owned a house as beneficial joint tenants. The deceased and the claimant had lived there, with their children, but the defendant became the sole owner of the house by right of survivorship. The defendant subsequently obtained a possession order against the claimant and the claimant commenced proceedings against the defendant pursuant to the Inheritance (Provision for Family and Dependants) Act 1975, on the basis that the disposition of the deceased's estate did not make reasonable financial provision for her. The judge held that the terms of s 9, that the deceased's severable share of the property, at its value immediately before his death, be treated as part of the net estate, precluded him from awarding the claimant more than half the value of the house as at the date of death. On the claimant's appeal, *held*, s 9 required a judge to take the proportionate share of the property which would have belonged to the deceased if there had been severance of joint ownership and treat that proportion of the property as the share of the property which he was empowered to treat as part of the estate. The words 'at the value thereof immediately before his death' in s 9 did not alter the notion of that property right so as to convert it from a certain share in a certain property, to a fluctuating share in that property, changing its index value as property prices moved up or down. To treat the value immediately before death as creating a cap on what could be awarded was to give the element of value an importance it did not seem to deserve. In the present case, the judge had been empowered to transfer one half of the property to the claimant. Judgment would be given accordingly.

Dingmar v Dingmar [2006] EWCA Civ 942, [2006] 3 WLR 1183 (Court of Appeal: Ward, Jacob and Lloyd LJJ).

1306   Probate—claim—discontinuance

CPR 57.11(2) provides that, at any stage of a probate claim, the court, on the application of the claimant or of any defendant who has acknowledged service, may order that the claim be discontinued or dismissed on such terms as to costs or otherwise as it thinks just.

The deceased, a widow, had been married twice. The defendant was one of the children of her first marriage. The claimant was of one of her second husband's children by a previous marriage. The deceased made a will naming the claimant and defendant as executors, and leaving her assets to her second husband and then to her grandchildren. Several years later, she made a further will, under which her second husband's family did not benefit. The second will bore an attestation clause and signatures indicating that it had been signed by the deceased in the presence of the defendant's mother-in-law. The claimant alleged that the second will had been made without the deceased's knowledge and approval. However, the claimant subsequently applied pursuant to CPR 57.11 to discontinue the proceedings, contending that the proceedings raised no serious issue, but that he had acted reasonably in bringing the proceedings and should not be required to pay costs. *Held*, in considering whether to grant permission to discontinue probate proceedings pursuant to CPR 57.11, the relevant question was whether, viewed objectively, there was at the time of the discontinuance a serious issue to be resolved in relation to the will. Costs would not be ordered against the discontinuing party unless there had been no reasonable grounds for opposing the will. In that regard, a reasonable but nevertheless ultimately mistaken belief in a state of affairs that if not mistaken would lead to a will being pronounced against did amount to a reasonable ground for opposing a will. In the instant case, the proceedings raised no serious issue in relation to the second will. The claimant had, however, acted reasonably in starting the proceedings, since he had reasonable cause for concern concerning the circumstances in which it had been made. Accordingly, the application would be allowed.

Wylde v Culver [2006] EWHC 1313 (Ch), [2006] 4 All ER 345 (Chancery Division: George Bompas QC). *Green v Briscoe* [2005] All ER (D) 96 (May) considered.

1307 Probate—lost will—copy of will—disputed authenticity

The claimant was the son of the deceased and the first and second defendants were the claimant's brother and sister. The claimant had a close relationship with the deceased and lived with him until his death. The defendants did not share a close relationship with the deceased. Following the deceased's death, the claimant and the first defendant searched unsuccessfully for a final will and testament. The defendants obtained a grant of administration on the basis of an assumed intestacy and possession proceedings were issued against the claimant, who resided in the family home. The claimant then found a copy of the deceased's will in the family home which bequeathed the residue of the estate, including the family home, to him, which tallied with the testamentary intention that the deceased had expressed. The claimant sought the revocation of the grant of administration and a pronouncement in favour of the will. The defendants disputed the authenticity of the will. *Held*, the witnesses to the will had given evidence that the copy found by the claimant was a genuine copy of the will which had been executed by the deceased. The claimant had rebutted the presumption that the will had been revoked by the deceased. Evidence from the claimant and others had shown a clear intention on the part of the deceased, consistent with the terms of the will, that the claimant should inherit the bulk of his estate. That intention had remained until the death of the deceased and therefore the original will had, in unexplained circumstances, been destroyed or lost by accident. Accordingly, the claim would be allowed.

Wren v Wren [2006] EWHC 2243 (Ch), [2006] 3 FCR 18 (Chancery Division: Rimer J).

1308 Probate—non-contentious probate—grant of administration—requirement for notice

The deceased left a sizeable estate with assets in various countries. The claimants were his sons by his first marriage. The third defendant was his daughter by the same marriage. A grant of administration ad colligenda bona of the deceased's estate was made in favour of the first and second defendants at a time when they were also acting as solicitors to the third defendant. The claimants issued proceedings seeking revocation of the grant to the first two defendants, on the grounds that the first defendant's affidavit in support of the application for the grant of administration had materially misrepresented the position and that no notice was given either of the application or of the issue of the grant. The grant was revoked by consent. The claimants applied for an order that the costs of the application to revoke the grant be paid by the defendants. The claimants contended that the application for the grant was an abuse of the without notice procedure, involving a serious breach of the obligation to make full and frank disclosure to the court. The first and second defendants contended that there was no requirement under the Non-Contentious Probate Rules 1987, SI 1987/2024, for notice to be given either of the application for a grant or of the grant itself, and that the first defendant's affidavit in support of the application fell far short of a material misrepresentation. *Held*, there was no requirement that the application, still less the grant, be made without notice. The 1987 Rules made provision for notice to be given in an appropriate case. Rule 61(1) permitted a registrar to be able to require any application to be made by summons, and r 66(1) allowed him to direct service of the summons on appropriate persons. Further, the registrar was given power by r 61(1) to require the application to be made to a judge and r 7(1)(b) provided that no grant was to be made by a registrar in any case in which it appeared to him that a grant ought not to be made without the directions of a judge or a district judge. Either of those procedures was appropriate to the instant case, and, if the claimants had been able to respond to the first defendant's affidavit, it would certainly have been suitable for a hearing by a judge or district judge. The grant of letters of administration should not have been made without notice to the claimants. The matter was highly contentious, the first defendant was making very serious allegations of dishonesty and misappropriation, and the urgency was not such as to preclude notice. Accordingly, the application would be allowed.

Ghafoor v Cliff [2006] EWHC 825 (Ch), [2006] 2 All ER 1079 (Chancery Division: David Richards J).

EXTRADITION

Halsbury's Laws of England (4th edn) vol 17(2) (Reissue) paras 1101–1305

Articles

For articles relating to this title please refer to the Table of Articles at the beginning of the Abridgment.

1309   Designated territories

The Extradition Act 2003 (Amendment to Designations) Order 2006, SI 2006/3451 (in force in part on 22 December 2006 and in part on 1 January 2007), amends (1) the Extradition Act 2003 (Designation of Part 2 Territories) Order 2003, SI 2003/3334, by (a) designating Serbia and Montenegro as separate territories consequent to the division of the two countries; (b) designating Bosnia and Herzegovina for additional purposes; and (c) removing the designation of Bulgaria and Romania as category 2 territories; and (2) the Extradition Act 2003 (Designation of Part 1 Territories) Order 2003, SI 2003/3333, by designating Bulgaria and Romania as category 1 territories.

1310   European arrest warrant—certification requirements—certification within warrant

The appellant was arrested pursuant to a European arrest warrant issued by a Spanish court. He claimed that the warrant was not valid because the Spanish court had failed to issue a certificate in relation to his alleged conduct as was required by the Extradition Act 2003 s 64(2)(b) and (c). His challenge was dismissed and he appealed. *Held*, s 64(2)(b) and (c) did not require the certificate to be separate from the warrant, and there was no reason why the material required by those provisions should not be set out in the warrant itself. To require separate documentation would add nothing to the protection of the person in respect of whom the warrant was issued. The warrant for the appellant's arrest contained the relevant information and so satisfied the requirements of s 64(2). Accordingly, the appeal would be dismissed.

Dabas v High Court of Justice, Madrid, Spain [2006] EWHC 971 (Admin), [2007] 1 WLR 145 (Queen's Bench Division: Latham LJ and Jack J).

This decision has been affirmed on appeal: [2007] UKHL 6, [2007] All ER (D) 373 (Feb).

1311   European arrest warrant—designation of territory—reciprocity between member states

A German court decided that German legislation relating to the treatment of European arrest warrants received from other member states was invalid. The German authorities subsequently issued a European arrest warrant in respect of the claimant. He was arrested in the United Kingdom and made representations to the defendant Secretary of State concerning the want of reciprocity in the United Kingdom which continued to accept European arrest warrants from Germany while Germany would not entertain European arrest warrants from the United Kingdom. The claimant argued that this was contrary to the principles of the Framework Decision on European Arrest Warrants and Surrender Procedures between Member States of the European Union and the German legislation which had implemented the Framework Decision. The claimant invited the defendant to redesignate Germany as a category 2 territory for the purposes of the German legislation. The defendant refused, having regard to the facts that amended legislation was before the German Parliament and that there was no reason why a territory not operating the European arrest warrant could not be designated a category 1 territory. The claimant sought judicial review of the defendant's decision. *Held*, having regard to the preamble to the Framework Decision, the spirit or philosophy underlying the principle of mutual recognition in the context of the European arrest warrant regime was not to promote retaliatory responses but to keep the regime in being and respond to lapses or legal difficulties in fellow member states by co-operative discussions. There might come a point when, all else having failed, a member state's lawful response to another's repudiation of the European arrest warrant system would be to withdraw co-operation but an overwhelming case would be required in order for the domestic court to conclude that such a point had been reached. The nature of the United Kingdom's response was a matter for the judgment of the defendant. The language in the German legislation of the power to designate was clearly not on its face limited to the purpose of implementing the Framework Decision. The true question was what room the law made for negotiation and persuasion in the achievement of the goals of the Framework Decision. It was one thing to designate a member state in category 1 as and when the

European arrest warrant regime was adopted there. It was quite another to respond to the other state's partial withdrawal with a similar approach. In the exercise of his judgment, the defendant's decision not to redesignate could not be faulted for the reasons he had given. Amending legislation remained under consideration in Germany so that it could not begin to be said that there was an overwhelming case for redesignation. Accordingly, the application would be dismissed.

R (on the application of Oliver) v Secretary of State for the Home Department [2006] EWHC 1847 (Admin), [2006] All ER (D) 459 (Jul) (Queen's Bench Division: Laws LJ and Walker J).

1312   European arrest warrant—validity—particulars of offence

The Extradition Act 2003 s 2(4)(c) provides that a Part 1 (European) arrest warrant must contain the particulars of the circumstances in which the person is alleged to have committed the offence, including the conduct alleged to constitute the offence, the time and place at which he is alleged to have committed the offence and any provision of the law of the category 1 territory under which the conduct is alleged to constitute an offence.

The claimant, a German national, lawfully entered the United Kingdom. A European arrest warrant was subsequently issued in respect of the claimant by the defendant Austrian judicial authority. The warrant was certified by the National Criminal Intelligence Service and the claimant was arrested. The offences in respect of which the warrant was issued were offences of fraud in connection with the marketing, sale and construction of environmentally sound houses. A district judge ordered that the claimant should be extradited to Austria. The claimant appealed, arguing that the requirements of the 2003 Act s 2(4)(c) had not been satisfied. He submitted that no particulars of the conduct alleged to constitute the offences had been provided, including the advance payments alleged to have been received, from whom, or why or how it was alleged that the claimant had pretended to sell houses. *Held*, in the circumstances, the particulars contained within the warrant were too vague and obscure to satisfy the requirements of s 2(4)(c). Accordingly, the appeal would be allowed.

Von der Pahlen v Leoben High Court [2006] All ER (D) 310 (Jun) (Queen's Bench Division: Dyson LJ and Walker J).

1313   Extradition order—appeal—notice of appeal—permitted period for lodging notice

The hearing in a magistrates' court of the application for the claimant's extradition ended at about 6.15 pm on a Friday evening, and the district judge ordered the claimant's extradition. The Extradition Act 2003 s 26(4) provided that notice of an appeal had to be given before the end of the permitted period, which was seven days starting with the day on which the order was made. The claimant lodged a notice of appeal on the Monday ten days after the order had been made, and the court office rejected it on the grounds that it was out of time. The claimant sought judicial review of the decision. He submitted that, because the magistrates' court had concluded its hearing after business hours on the Friday, the order should have been treated as having been made on the next business day, which was the following Monday, and hence his notice of appeal had been given before the end of the permitted period. *Held*, the day on which an extradition order was made was the actual day on which the district judge pronounced that the order for extradition was being made. The extension of a court's sitting hours beyond normal business hours for the court's offices did not alter the day on which the court made its order. There was nothing in any statute or procedural provisions to displace the normal meaning of 'day'. It followed that the claimant's notice of appeal had been lodged out of time and, accordingly, the application would be dismissed.

R (on the application of Amoako) v DPP [2006] EWHC 1572 (Admin), [2006] 4 All ER 230 (Queen's Bench Division: Ouseley J).

1314   Extradition proceedings—appeal—evidence—fresh evidence

The Extradition Act 2003 s 27(1), (4) provides that the court may allow the appeal against the making of an extradition order if evidence is available that was not available at the extradition hearing.

The appellant, a Lithuanian national, was convicted of a drugs offence while in Lithuania and sentenced to a term of imprisonment. Following his release, he continued to sell drugs and was arrested. He chose to become a police informer and, as a result, several of his former criminal associates were arrested. He came to the United Kingdom following an attack on him, and the respondent requested the appellant's extradition to face charges of theft and burglary. The request was granted and the appellant appealed, contending that his extradition would infringe his right, under the European Convention on Human Rights art 3, not to be subjected to torture, inhuman or degrading treatment. At the appeal hearing, the appellant adduced evidence as to the treatment of offenders in Lithuania that he contended could not have been obtained in time for the hearing before the district judge. It was submitted that, had the district judge seen that evidence, he would have come to a different decision and therefore the matter could be considered pursuant to the 2003 Act s 27. *Held*, the word 'available' in s 27 made it plain that the court would require to be persuaded that there was some good reason for the material not having been made available to the district judge. Furthermore, where there could be any suggestion of the appellant 'keeping his powder dry', he had to expect the court to view any application to rely on such evidence with some scepticism. Additional evidence of police brutality in Lithuania could not have been obtained in time for the hearing before the district judge. That material undoubtedly gave rise to concern about the way the police had behaved and the ability of the authorities to control that behaviour, but it did not go anywhere near establishing that the appellant would be at real risk of torture or other inhuman or degrading treatment. It followed that, if the district judge had seen that evidence, there would have been no sufficient basis on which he could have concluded that the appellant's life would be at risk of ill-treatment if he were to be returned. Accordingly, the appeal would be dismissed.

Miklis v Deputy Prosecutor General of Lithuania [2006] EWHC 1032 (Admin), [2006] 4 All ER 808 (Queen's Bench Division: Latham LJ and Tugendhat J). *Ladd v Marshall* [1954] 3 All ER 745, CA, considered.

1315   Extradition proceedings—bar to extradition—category 2 territory—suspected terrorist—trial in military tribunal—infringement of human rights—assurance given in diplomatic notes

The United States sought the extradition of the appellants on charges relating to terrorism. For the purposes of the Extradition Act 2003, the United States was designated a category 2 territory. Diplomatic notes were issued by the United States giving assurances that the appellants would be prosecuted before a federal court with the full panoply of rights and protections and that they would not be prosecuted before a military commission. Pursuant to a President's Military Order, military tribunals in the United States were authorised to try international terrorists and principles of law and rules of evidence generally recognised in the trial of criminal cases in domestic courts were not applicable. At the extradition hearings the appellants argued that, if they were to be extradited, there was a real prospect that they would be made subject to the order and detained indefinitely and/or put on trial before a military commission, which could lead to violations of their human rights. The district judge found that, if the appellants were designated under the order they would be deprived of their rights under the European Convention on Human Rights and exposed to the death penalty. He was satisfied, however, that their Convention rights would not be violated on extradition because of the assurances given in the diplomatic notes. He therefore decided that there were no bars to extradition. The appellants appealed. *Held*, diplomatic notes should be treated as being effective to refute, for the purposes of the 2003 Act, the claims of potential violation of Convention rights and associated bars to extradition. In the eyes of international law, such a note was regarded as binding on the state that issued it. There was also a fundamental assumption that the requesting state was acting in good faith. In the present case, the assurances in the notes were given by a mature democracy and over a period of more than 150 years there had been no instance of any assurance given by the United States in extradition proceedings having been dishonoured. Moreover, the United States would appreciate that its requests for the appellants' extradition had been acceded to expressly on the faith of the notes. It followed that the court should not conclude that the notes would not be fully honoured and the district judge had been correct to place confidence in them. Accordingly, the appeals would be dismissed.

Ahmad v Government of the United States of America [2006] EWHC 2927 (Admin), [2006] All ER (D) 418 (Nov) (Queen's Bench Division: Laws LJ and Walker J). *Re Serbeh* [2002] EWHC 2356 (Admin), [2002] All ER (D) 468 (Oct), DC; *R (on the application of Bermingham) v Director of the Serious Fraud Office; Bermingham v Government of the United States of America* [2006] EWHC 200 (Admin), [2006] 3 All ER 239, DC (para 1321); and *Welsh v Secretary of State for the Home Department* [2006] EWHC 156 (Admin), [2006] 3 All ER 204, DC (para 1325), applied.

1316   Extradition proceedings—bar to extradition—passage of time since commission of offence—unjustness or oppressiveness of extradition

The claimant, a Polish national, had lawfully entered the United Kingdom. Subsequently, the defendant, the appropriate Polish judicial authority, issued a European arrest warrant for the claimant. The Polish request was governed by the Extradition Act 2003 Pt I (ss 1–68), which had been enacted in order to transpose into national law the obligations imposed on it by the European Council Framework Decision on the European arrest warrant and the surrender procedures between member states. The warrant was issued in respect of offences of attempted robbery and robbery alleged to have been committed in Poland. The warrant was executed and the judge ordered that the claimant should be extradited. The claimant appealed. *Held,* the burden of proof was on the accused to show, on the balance of probabilities, that it would be unjust or oppressive to extradite him by reason of the passage of time since the commission of the alleged offence. The court had to proceed as if the accused were being prosecuted before an English court with the extraditing state as the prosecutor. However, in the present case, it was not for the claimant to have to show that there were no good reasons for the delay where the Polish authorities had given no reasons as to why the warrant had been served so late. In the absence of any explanation, the claimant was entitled to assert that there was a prima facie case calling for an answer. The effect of s 11(1)(c) was that if it appeared to the court that it would be unjust or oppressive to extradite a person by reason of the passage of time since he was alleged to have committed the offences, extradition was barred and his discharge had to be ordered. In the present circumstances, by reason of the passage of time, it was unjust to extradite the claimant. Accordingly, the appeal would be allowed.

Kociukow v District Court of Bialystok III Penal Division [2006] EWHC 56 (Admin), [2006] 2 All ER 451 (Queen's Bench Division: Hallett LJ and Jack J).

1317 Extradition proceedings—category 1 territory—person serving prison sentence in United Kingdom

The Extradition Act 2003 s 11(1)(c) provides that in extradition proceedings, the judge must decide whether the person's extradition to the category 1 territory is barred by reason of the passage of time. The judge must decide whether the person's extradition would be compatible with the rights under the European Convention on Human Rights, within the meaning of the Human Rights Act 1998, and if the judge decides that question in the affirmative he must order the person to be extradited to the category 1 territory in which the warrant was issued: 2003 Act s 21(1), (3). If at any time in the extradition hearing the judge is informed that the person in respect of whom the warrant is issued is serving a sentence of imprisonment or another form of detention in the United Kingdom, the judge may adjourn the extradition hearing until the sentence has been served: s 23.

The claimant was serving a nine-year prison sentence in the United Kingdom when a warrant for his extradition was executed on behalf of the High Court of Dublin. An application was made to the district judge that the extradition hearing be postponed to a date closer to the release date of the sentence being heard, which he rejected. The potential release date of the claimant was three years after the date of the application. The judge then granted the extradition order, after considering the 2003 Act ss 11 and 21. The claimant appealed against the order. *Held*, the point at which ss 11 and 21 should be considered was a matter of degree. However, it was irrational not to exercise the power under s 23 and to consider ss 11 and 21 where the offender would not be released for at least three years. The extradition order would be quashed. Accordingly, the appeal would be allowed.

R (on the application of Slator) v Bow Street Magistrates' Court (2006) Times, 25 October (Queen's Bench Division: Auld LJ and Wilkie J).

1318 Extradition proceedings—committal proceedings—arrest warrant—statement that person unlawfully at large—inference

The appellant's arrest was requested by the respondent by means of a European arrest warrant. The warrant alleged that the appellant had committed a serious assault. He was acquitted by the county court, but later convicted by the Court of Appeal. He was present at both hearings. A sentence of two-and-a-half years' imprisonment was imposed. He was required to attend to commence serving his sentence but absconded. The district judge, rejecting the appellant's contention that the warrant did not make it clear that the appellant was unlawfully at large, ordered the appellant's extradition. The appellant appealed, arguing that the district judge had not been entitled to conclude that the requirement of the Extradition Act 2003 s 2(5) for a statement that the person named in the warrant was unlawfully at large had been satisfied. *Held*, in order to satisfy the requirements of s 2(5), the warrant did not need to say in terms that the person was unlawfully at large; it was enough that that could be inferred from the statement as a whole. The district judge's conclusion that the appellant had been unlawfully at large was one which had been properly open to him on the basis of the material in the warrant. Accordingly, the appeal would be dismissed.

Kuprevicius v Vice Minister of Justice Ministry of Justice, Lithuania [2006] All ER (D) 265 (May) (Queen's Bench Division: Richards LJ and Toulson J).

1319 Extradition proceedings—committal proceedings—conviction obtained in absence of accused—interests of justice

The applicant was a fugitive offender, having been convicted in his absence of offences in Italy. The evidence against him consisted of statements by three of his co-accused that had been given in interview. However, two co-accused retracted their statements in giving evidence at the applicant's trial and the third co-accused could not be cross-examined as he refused to answer any questions. The government sought the applicant's extradition under the Extradition Act 1989 and he was committed to bail to await the decision of the Secretary of State. The applicant challenged his detention on bail. It fell to be determined whether it would be in the interests of justice for the purposes of s 6(2) to return the applicant to Italy. He submitted that it would not be in the interests of justice because his conviction violated his rights under the European Convention on Human Rights art 6 and would have done so even if he had been present. *Held,* the reliance on the truth of the content of the depositions of each of the co-accused at the applicant's trial violated art 6. There had been no adequate opportunity to challenge the evidence against the applicant from any of the co-accused. Therefore, in all the circumstances, it would not be in the interests of justice to return the applicant to Italy. Judgment would be given accordingly.

Re Migliorelli [2006] All ER (D) 365 (Feb) (Queen's Bench Division: Smith LJ and Cresswell J).

1320   Extradition proceedings—committal proceedings—extraditable offence—validity of warrant

The Government of Spain sought the extradition of the appellant in respect of offences related to terrorism. European arrest warrants were issued, which followed the pro forma warrant pursuant to the Framework Decision on the European Union Arrest Warrant. An order of commitment was annexed to the first warrant and treated as being annexed to the second one. The judge held under the Extradition Act 2003 s 10 that the conduct set out in the warrant amounted to framework offences and that those offences were extradition offences within s 64. On his appeal, the appellant submitted that the arrest warrant did not comply with the requirements of s 2(4)(c). He also argued that his mental condition was such that, under s 25, it would be unjust or oppressive to extradite him. *Held,* although s 27 permitted the court to allow an appeal only if it was satisfied that the judge ought to have decided a question before him at the extradition hearing differently, or would have decided it differently if he had considered the new evidence raised on appeal, the court could still examine the validity of the warrant. Section 2(4)(c) did not require the provision of the text of the law of the requesting state. It required only that the provisions of the foreign law should be identified and not that the provisions be set out in detail. The other issue to be decided was not whether the appellant was suffering from a psychiatric disorder, but whether by reason of his mental condition it would be unjust or oppressive to extradite him. Evidence showed that, if extradited, proper examination would be made to ascertain whether the appellant was fit to stand trial. Such examination would also establish whether he was a suicide risk and whether he was in need of psychiatric treatment. Even though it might turn out that the appellant was of low intelligence and might be unfit to stand trial, it was not unjust or oppressive to return him. Accordingly, the appeal would be dismissed.

Boudhiba v Central Examining Court No 5 of the National Court of Justice Madrid Spain [2006] EWHC 167 (Admin), [2006] 3 All ER 574 (Queen's Bench Division: Smith LJ and Newman J).

1321   Extradition proceedings—conduct comprising offence mainly committed in United Kingdom—human rights

The defendants, who were British citizens and resident in the United Kingdom, were employed by a British bank. Following a swap sub undertaken on behalf of an American client of the bank, the defendants were indicted in Texas on charges of wire fraud and aiding and abetting wire fraud. The United States government sought the extradition of the defendants, and warrants were issued for their arrest under the Extradition Act 2003. The district judge decided that the Texas indictment specified conduct which occurred in the United States, and that the fact that it was a United Kingdom company which had suffered the loss was irrelevant. The defendants argued that they should be charged, if at all, in the United Kingdom. The Director of the Serious Fraud Office decided not to open an investigation into the defendants under the Criminal Justice Act 1987 s 1(3) on the basis that part of the conduct occurred in the United States and the American authorities were dealing with it. At a resumed hearing, the district judge rejected a submission that the proceedings were an abuse of the process of the United Kingdom court, and also concluded that the extradition was not incompatible with the defendants' right to a private and family life under the European Convention on Human Rights art 8. In due course the Secretary of State authorised the defendants' extradition. They appealed against the decisions of the judge and the Secretary of State, and applied for judicial review of the decision of the Director of the Serious Fraud Office. *Held,* the 1987 Act s 1(3) did not invite the Director to constitute himself the judge of the proper forum for the defendants' trial or to do so as a means of protecting the defendant's Convention rights. The provision conferred merely a power to investigate, since otherwise the power of the district judge would be usurped. Also, where a proposed extradition was properly constituted according to the domestic law of the sending state and the relevant bilateral treaty, and its execution was resisted on human rights grounds, a wholly exceptional case would have to be shown to justify a finding that the extradition would on the particular facts be disproportionate to its legitimate aim. It would have been better if the district judge had not simply taken it as a given that the defendants were to be prosecuted in the United States and not in the United Kingdom. Nevertheless, an appeal could only be allowed if the court concluded that the judge, on a proper appreciation of the material before him, would or might have concluded that the defendants' extradition would be a disproportionate interference with their rights under the Convention art 8. There were very substantial connections with the United States and the case was perfectly properly triable there. Further, there was nothing exceptional about the personal circumstances of the defendants to make a case on the ground of proportionality. Accordingly, the application and the appeals would be dismissed.

R (on the application of Bermingham) v Director of the Serious Fraud Office; Bermingham v Government of the United States of America [2006] EWHC 200 (Admin), [2006] 3 All ER 239 (Queen's Bench Division: Laws LJ and Ouseley J).

1322   Extradition proceedings—disclosure—state or judicial authority

Two extradition cases heard together raised disclosure issues. In the first case, an attempt was made by the United States government to extradite two individuals. Several hearings took place and resulted in an order for disclosure of documents and consideration of issues as to whether there was power to order disclosure. The second case concerned European arrest warrants issued by the Spanish courts. The Spanish government argued that the court had no power to order disclosure in relation to an argument that proceedings under the Extradition Act 2003 amounted to an abuse of process. In each case, the judge held that an order for disclosure should be made. On appeal, *held*, neither the rules governing disclosure in a civil action nor those governing disclosure in a criminal trial could be applied to an extradition hearing. Those rules formed part of an adversarial process which differed from extradition proceedings. The appropriate course for the judge to take if he had reason to believe that an abuse of process might have occurred would be to call on the judicial authority which had issued the arrest warrant, or the state seeking extradition, for whatever information the judge required in order to determine whether an abuse of process had occurred. The information and evidence thereby obtained should be made available to the party contesting extradition. The standards required by the European Convention on Human Rights art 13 should apply to the extradition proceedings. Where an order for disclosure was made, it required one party to disclose documents to the other, not to the court, but where extradition was sought, the court was under a duty to satisfy itself that all the requirements for making the order were satisfied and that none of the bars to making the order existed. There might be occasions where a judicial authority or requesting state was content that the court should see evidence but, on reasonable grounds, was not prepared that it should be disclosed to the person whose extradition was sought. The judge would be capable of evaluating the material which was produced to him, whether favourable or unfavourable to the party resisting extradition. The issue would then be whether, if a decision was reached without allowing that person the chance to comment on the material, the procedure would fail to satisfy the requirement of fairness. If the judge concluded that a fair trial would be impossible without the material being shown, then the appropriate course would be for the judge to hold that fair process was impossible and to discharge the person whose extradition was sought. Judgment would be given accordingly.

R (on the application of the Government of the United States of America) v Bow Street Magistrates' Court; R (on the application of the Central Examining Court, Madrid) v Bow Street Magistrates' Court [2006] EWHC 2256 (Admin), [2006] All ER (D) 18 (Sep) (Queen's Bench Division: Lord Phillips CJ and Cresswell J).

1323 Extradition proceedings—extraditable offence—offences not constituting offences in United Kingdom

The German authorities sought the extradition of the appellant, a German national, on the ground that he had been involved in VAT fraud committed in Germany while operating in the United Kingdom. The extraditing court ruled that some of the offences on the request were extradition offences on which the Home Secretary made an extradition order. The appellant appealed. *Held*, some of the offences alleged in the request were not criminal in the United Kingdom. Under the European Convention on Extradition (Second Protocol) art 14(1)(b) a person who had been extradited would not be processed against for any offence other than that for which he was extradited. There was no basis for saying that the Republic of Germany would not comply with art 14(1)(b). All the English court had to do was honour its obligations under the extradition request. The extraditing court's certificate which stated that some of the offences charged were not offences in the United Kingdom was sufficient to safeguard his right not to face charges on those offences on his extradition to Germany.

Arian v Republic of Germany [2006] All ER (D) 208 (Mar) (Queen's Bench Division: Moses LJ and Stanley Burnton J).

1324 Extradition proceedings—extradition to category 2 territory—designation—lawfulness

The Extradition Act 2003 s 84(7) provides that where extradition is requested to a category 2 territory designated by the Secretary of State, the judge must not decide, under s 84(1), whether there is sufficient evidence to constitute a case to answer.

The Treaty on Extradition between the Government of the United States of America and the Government of the United Kingdom of Great Britain and Northern Ireland 2003 had been signed by both countries, but had only been ratified by the United Kingdom. It followed that a former treaty, which provided that extradition should be granted only if there was sufficient evidence according to the law of the requested party, remained in force. The claimant had been made the subject of an order for extradition to the United States, a category 2 territory designated by the Extradition Act 2003 (Designation of Part 2 Territories) Order 2003, SI 2003/3334, for the purposes of the 2003 Act s 84, and he sought judicial review of that decision. *Held*, where there was a conflict, the terms of an extradition treaty had to give way to the relevant legislation. Nothing in the 2003 Act suggested that designation as a category 2 territory was dependent on a bilateral treaty between the United Kingdom and the requesting country. It followed that the protective conditions of the former treaty could not obstruct, hinder or postpone the application of the 2003 Act. The 2003 Order had been made consistently with, and its authority had been derived from, current primary legislation, and it had not violated any continuing, enforceable, free-standing rights vested in the claimant. Therefore, there was no basis for concluding that its continuation in force represented a legally flawed or irrational decision. Accordingly, the application would be dismissed.

R (on the application of Norris) v Secretary of State for the Home Department [2006] EWHC 280 (Admin), [2006] 3 All ER 1011 (Queen's Bench Division: Sir Igor Judge P and Cresswell J).

1325   Extradition proceedings—extradition to category 2 territory—existence of speciality arrangements

The Extradition Act 2003 s 95(1) provides that the Secretary of State must not order a person's extradition to a category 2 territory if there are no speciality arrangements with that territory. Section 95(3) provides that there are speciality arrangements with a category 2 territory if, under the law of that territory or arrangements made between it and the United Kingdom, a person who is extradited to the territory from the United Kingdom may be dealt with in the territory for an offence committed before his extradition only if the offence is one falling within s 95(4) or he is first given an opportunity to leave the territory.

The Secretary of State ordered the appellants' extradition to the United States of America. The appellants submitted that the United States would breach the speciality rule in that its courts would permit the extradition offence to be proved by evidence relating to offences for which extradition had been expressly refused. The appellants also submitted that, if convicted in the United States, they would be dealt with for money laundering offences for which extradition had been refused, as the relevant United States sentencing guidelines would use the facts of those offences to increase the sentences which the appellants would receive for the extradition offences. *Held*, firstly, the speciality rule did not limit the evidence which could be admitted to prove the extradition offence, and would not be breached where the United States courts permitted the extradition offence to be proved by evidence relating to offences for which extradition had been expressly refused. Secondly, the effect of the 2003 Act s 95 was to impose a prohibition on extradition where the conditions it contained were not met. It required English courts to reach their own view as to whether the practice in the United States amounted to 'dealing with' someone, which included punishing him, in a way prohibited by s 95. However, it was not intended to require the imposition of peculiarly English or United Kingdom sentencing practices before extradition could occur, and could not have been intended to halt extraditions to the United States on the basis of a long-standing sentencing practice in that country. The absence of an arrangement which would prevent an extradited person from being punished for an extradition offence in the way he could be punished under United States sentencing guidelines did not show that no speciality arrangement was in place. Such a person was not being 'dealt with' within the scope of s 95(3) for an offence for which he had not been or could not have been extradited, but by reference to conduct which was relevant to the gravity of the way in which he committed the offence or to the offending behaviour revealed by it. Accordingly, the appeal would be dismissed.

Welsh v Secretary of State for the Home Department [2006] EWHC 156 (Admin), [2006] 3 All ER 204 (Queen's Bench Division: Laws LJ and Ouseley J).

1326   Extradition proceedings—initial hearing—identity of person arrested

A question arose as to whether a senior district judge had jurisdiction to review the finding of identity of the appellant, a person in respect of whom a European arrest warrant had been issued, where the identification had been made initially at a previous hearing. *Held*, it was doubtful whether a district judge had jurisdiction to review the finding of identity previously made at an earlier hearing. In the absence of such jurisdiction, the appropriate route for challenging the original decision would be by way of judicial review. Under the Extradition Act 2003, the question of identity fell to be resolved at an initial hearing. There was no right of appeal by the appellant against a decision under s 7(2). The district judge was plainly entitled to reach the decision which he had and, considering the whole of the arrest warrant, it contained sufficient evidence to establish that the appellant, who admittedly identified himself in court, was the person referred to in the warrant. Accordingly, the appeal would be dismissed.

Hilali v Central Court of Criminal Proceedings No 5 of the National Court, [2006] EWHC 1239 (Admin), [2006] 4 All ER 435 (Queen's Bench Division: Scott Baker LJ and Openshaw J). *Nikonovs v Governor of Brixton Prison* [2005] EWHC 2405 (Admin), [2006] I All ER 927 (2005 Abr para 1487) considered.

1327   Extradition proceedings—person convicted in his absence—entitlement to retrial on return—ratification by territory of European Convention on Human Rights

The Romanian government sought to extradite the appellant, a Chinese national, on the basis that he had been convicted of murder in his absence. The appellant denied committing the offences and having any knowledge of the proceedings until he was arrested in the United Kingdom pursuant to the Extradition Act 2003 s 73. As the appellant had been convicted in his absence, the court had to proceed under s 85, with the result that issues arose as to whether, if extradited, he would be entitled to a retrial on his return to Romania and whether that retrial would comply with the requirements under s 85(8) that he would receive free legal assistance and have the right to examine witnesses. There was evidence before the court that Romania had ratified the European Convention on Human Rights and that, in any event, the Romanian Code of Penal Procedure provided that a person who had been extradited to Romania following a conviction in his absence had a right to a retrial. The district judge decided that the appellant would receive a fair retrial once he returned to Romania, and remitted the case to the Secretary of State for the Home Department. The appellant appealed against that decision. *Held*, it was neither necessary nor right to examine what a requesting state did in practice, provided that that state's constitution provided unequivocally that the European Convention on Human Rights was part of its law and that the terms of art 6 overrode the state's criminal code. The requirements of art 6 were clearly that there had to be a retrial to which the rights to a fair hearing applied. As there was no ambiguity about the rights that the Romanian Constitution provided, the district judge had been correct in finding that the appellant would receive a fair retrial once he returned to Romania. However, as the 2003 Act s 85(5) required a district judge to discharge a person unless he was satisfied that the passage of time since the events would not have any impact on the retrial, the district judge had failed to ask the correct question in relation to the passage of time before the retrial. Whether the defendant had fled Romania and hid was not precisely the same question as whether he had voluntarily absented himself from the trial. The judge should have considered whether it would be possible for the appellant to find witnesses to establish his alibi. Accordingly, the appeal would be allowed in part.

An Chen v Government of Romania [2006] All ER (D) 265 (Jun) (Queen's Bench Division: Maurice Kay LJ and Mitting J). *Government of Albania v Bleta* [2005] EWHC 475 (Admin), [2005] 3 All ER 351, DC (2005 Abr para 1484), distinguished. *Kakis v Government of the Republic of Cyprus* [1978] 2 All ER 634, HL (1978 Abr para 1309), applied.

1328 Extradition proceedings—physical or mental condition of defendant—unjustness or oppressiveness of extradition

The respondent government requested the extradition of the appellant on charges relating to indecent photographs of a child. According to medical evidence, the appellant was morbidly obese and suffered from chronic obstructive pulmonary disease. The appellant contended that his life would be in danger if he had to take a long air trip to the United States of America and that his removal would be contrary to the Extradition Act 2003 s 91 or a breach of his right to life guaranteed by the European Convention on Human Rights art 3. A district judge considered that, as the appellant's condition had not worsened since the time when he was medically examined prior to absconding from the United States by aeroplane, he could return there. The judge stated that he was satisfied that the risk that such a journey could entail would be sufficiently met by the assurances from the respondent that the appellant would only be put on a flight if a medical examination showed that it was safe for the appellant and that medical provision would be available to him during the flight. The appellant appealed. *Held*, the presence of the risk to health did not mean that no risk could be taken. Each case had to involve a careful assessment of the risk and the danger the exercise would involve. There was sufficient material before the judge for him to reach the conclusion to which he came. The medical report adopted the findings of the report compiled at the time the appellant had fled and there was nothing in the later report which suggested that the appellant's condition had deteriorated. Furthermore, it had been proper for the judge to take into account the assurances from the respondent that it would assess the appellant's condition before putting him on a flight. It followed that the extradition would not be unjust or oppressive. Accordingly, the appeal would be dismissed.

McCaughey v Government of the United States of America [2006] All ER (D) 128 (Jan) (Queen's Bench Division: Smith LJ and Newman J).

FINANCIAL SERVICES

Halsbury's Laws of England (4th edn) vol 18(1) (Reissue) paras 1–628

Articles

For articles relating to this title please refer to the Table of Articles at the beginning of the Abridgment.

1329 Financial markets and insolvency—settlement finality

The Financial Markets and Insolvency (Settlement Finality) (Amendment) Regulations 2006, SI 2006/50 (in force on 2 February 2006), further amend the 1999 Regulations, SI 1999/2979, by extending them to Northern Ireland.

1330 Financial services and markets—appointed representatives

The Financial Services and Markets Act 2000 (Appointed Representatives) (Amendment) Regulations 2006, SI 2006/3414 (in force on 1 November 2007), further amend the 2001

Regulations, SI 2001/1217, and implement in part European Parliament and Council Directive 2004/39 on markets in financial instruments. The regulations, in particular, add a new requirement that the contract between an authorised person who is an investment firm or credit institution, other than a firm or institution based in another EEA state, and an appointed representative must contain a provision requiring the representative to be entered on the register that is applicable to the representative under the Financial Services and Markets Act 2000 s 39.

1331   Financial services and markets—capital requirements

The Capital Requirements Regulations 2006, SI 2006/3221 (in force on 1 January 2007), implement, in part, EC European Parliament and Council Directive 2006/48 relating to the taking up and pursuit of the business of credit institutions and EC European Parliament and Council Directive 2006/49 on the capital adequacy of investment firms and credit institutions. The regulations impose obligations on the Financial Services Authority, the competent authority for the United Kingdom, for the purpose of implementing procedural requirements for the prudential supervision of pan-European groups, co-operation between competent authorities and the recognition of external credit assessment institutions by the competent authorities so that their credit assessments may be used to calculate capital requirements. In particular, the regulations (1) make provision in relation to applications by pan-European groups for permission to calculate their capital requirements in accordance with one of the advanced methods allowed by Directive 2006/48; (2) make provision for co-operation between competent authorities; (3) make provision for the Financial Services Authority to recognise External Credit Assessment Institutions as eligible, so that their credit assessments may be used by credit institutions and certain defined investment firms; (4) contain miscellaneous provisions relating to restrictions on disclosure required by Directive 2006/48 art 136, functions of the Financial Services Authority and the service of notices; and (5) contain provisions relating to the recognition of External Credit Assessment Institutions.

1332   Financial services and markets—control of business transfers—insurance business transfer scheme—order sanctioning scheme

The court had before it an application for an order under the Financial Services and Markets Act 2000 Pt VII (ss 104–117) sanctioning a scheme for a transfer of general insurance and reinsurance business. The various jurisdictional and procedural pre-conditions to the court sanctioning the scheme had been satisfied. In accordance with s 109, the Financial Services Authority approved the appointment of the independent expert and the form of his scheme report. However, an objector, a reinsurer who questioned the adequacy of the Authority's powers on a proposed change of control, wrote to the applicant stating its concerns and giving notice that it intended to appear at the hearing in order to object to the proposed transfer. Shortly before the hearing, a first letter, sent by the Authority to the independent expert nine months earlier, was disclosed to the objector. The applicant did not oppose the objector's application for an adjournment in order to consider the contents of the letter and the hearing was rescheduled. Over the adjournment, the objector concluded that provided the Authority confirmed that its position was as set out in its first letter, the objector would not oppose the application to sanction the transfer. The Authority confirmed its position in a second letter. At the rescheduled hearing, the objector applied for an order for payment of its costs by the applicant. The applicant did not seek an order for costs against the objector but submitted that the right order would be no order as to costs. *Held*, in ordinary contested litigation, it would require very unusual circumstances for a party who had withdrawn his opposition to be awarded his costs. Ordinarily, such a party could expect to pay the other party's costs, incurred as a result of its opposition. However, there were a significant number of authorities on applications for sanction of schemes of arrangement and reduction of capital under the Companies Acts that indicated that the usual approach in ordinary litigation did not apply to such applications. Those authorities were in point to applications made under the 2000 Act Pt VII. There were significant similarities between applications that distinguished them from ordinary litigation and that called for a different approach. In ordinary litigation, a claimant sought a remedy against a defendant in respect of a past or threatened act alleged to be in breach of the claimant's enforceable rights. In the case of the relevant applications under the Companies Acts or the 2000 Act, it was the applicant who invoked a statutory procedure which would, in the case of a scheme of arrangement or business transfer, generally involve a change in the legal rights of members and/or creditors of the applicant. The production of the Authority's first letter and the confirmation of its contents by the second letter had satisfied the objector. That sequence of events did not entitle the objector to an order for costs in its favour. Accordingly, no order would be made.

Re Alliance Assurance Co Ltd; Re British Engine Insurance Ltd [2006] All ER (D) 196 (Oct) (Chancery Division: Richards J). *Re Peninsular & Oriental Steam Navigation Co* [2006] All ER (D) 82 (Oct) (para 697) considered.

1333   Financial services and markets—designated professional bodies—Royal Institute of Chartered Surveyors

The Financial Services and Markets Act 2000 (Designated Professional Bodies) (Amendment) Order 2006, SI 2006/58 (in force on 10 February 2006), makes the Royal Institute of Chartered

Surveyors ('the Institution') a designated professional body for the purposes of the Financial Services and Markets Act 2000 Pt 20, so as to enable members of the Institution to be exempt from the requirement to obtain permission from the Financial Services Authority in order to carry out certain regulated activities.

1334   Financial services and markets—disclosure of confidential information

The Financial Services and Markets Act 2000 (Disclosure of Confidential Information) (Amendment) Regulations 2006, SI 2006/3413 (in force in part on 20 January 2007 and in part on 1 November 2007), further amend the 2001 Regulations, SI 2001/2188, by (1) removing references to the listings directive and adding a definition of 'markets in financial instruments directive information'; (2) providing that (a) the provision in relation to the disclosure of single market and directive information applies to markets in financial instruments directive information where confidential information has been received by the Financial Services Authority from a European Economic Area competent authority or a non-European Economic Area regulatory authority; and (b) where information obtained from a European Economic Area competent authority or a non-European Economic Area regulatory authority has been made subject by that authority to a requirement not to disclose, that information can only be disclosed in accordance with that requirement unless that authority consents to other uses, the requirement however not applying to disclosure to the Bank of England, the European Central Bank, the central bank of any country or territory outside the United Kingdom, or a body (other than a central bank) in a country or territory outside the United Kingdom having functions as a monetary authority or responsibility for payment systems; (3) removing the restrictions from disclosure of information received by the Financial Services Authority under the listings directive, and providing that the provision concerning disclosure of confidential information not subject to directive restrictions is to apply to markets in financial instruments directive information, except where that information has been received from a European Economic Area competent authority or a non-European Economic Area regulatory authority, and that authority has not given its express consent for disclosure; (4) providing a list of bodies to which confidential information subject to directive restrictions can be disclosed and the uses to which that information may be put; (5) extending the uses to which the Office of Fair Trading and the Competition Commission may put the information, and adding any body carrying on activities concerned with any of the matters set out in the Companies (Audit, Investigations and Community Enterprise) Act 2004 ss 14 and 16(2), and the Financial Reporting Council and its operating bodies, and the uses to which these bodies may put that information; and (6) specifying a list of bodies to which confidential information not subject to directive restrictions may be disclosed and the uses to which that information may be put, and revising the list to include the Gambling Commission and its functions.

1335   Financial services and markets—European Economic Area passport rights

The Financial Services and Markets Act 2000 (EEA Passport Rights) (Amendment) Order 2006, SI 2006/3385 (in force in part on 1 April 2007 and in part on 1 November 2007), amend the 2001 Regulations, SI 2001/2511, by (1) supplementing the prescribed information which the home state regulator must provide to the Financial Services Authority in relation to an EEA investment firm seeking to provide services in the United Kingdom or to establish a branch in the United Kingdom; (2) setting out the requirements to be complied with before an EEA investment firm which is providing services in the United Kingdom or which has established a branch in the United Kingdom can make certain significant changes to its operations in the United Kingdom; and (3) prescribing the requirements to be complied with before a United Kingdom investment firm which is providing services in another EEA state or which has established a branch in another EEA state can make certain significant changes to its operations in that state.

1336   Financial services and markets—Gibraltar

The Financial Services and Markets Act 2000 (Gibraltar) (Amendment) Order 2006, SI 2006/1805 (in force on 31 July 2006), further amends the 2001 Order, SI 2001/3084, so as to enable investment firms based in Gibraltar to exercise certain rights to establish branches and provide services in the United Kingdom.

1337   Financial services and markets—investment exchanges and clearing houses—recognition requirements

The Financial Services and Markets Act 2000 (Recognition Requirements for Investment Exchanges and Clearing Houses) (Amendment) Regulations 2006, SI 2006/3386 (in force on 1 November 2007), amend the 2001 Regulations, SI 2001/995, by (1) adding requirements (a) concerning the suitability of the persons who effectively direct the business and operations of an exchange, and persons who are in a position to exercise significant influence over the management of an exchange; and (b) for exchanges to make available to the public on reasonable commercial terms information about transactions in shares, and enabling the Financial Services Authority to waiver or defer the publication requirements in specified circumstances; (2) specifying requirements in relation to

(a) exchanges' rules governing admission of financial instruments to trading, and requirements for exchanges relating to information disclosure obligations; (b) exchanges' rules concerning access to, or membership of, their facilities; and (c) exchanges and clearing houses providing central counterparty, clearing or settlement services, it being provided that (i) the exchanges and clearing houses must secure that investment firms and credit institutions established in other European Economic Area states have access to the facilities on equal terms to United Kingdom firms and institutions for the purpose of finalising or arranging the finalisation of transactions in financial instruments; and (ii) the exchanges may refuse access to the facilities on legitimate commercial grounds; (3) requiring exchanges' rules to permit users and members to have a choice of settlement facilities; (4) restricting the power of exchanges to suspend or remove financial instruments from trading where to do so would be likely to cause significant damage to the interests of investors or the orderly functioning of the financial markets; and (5) providing that exchanges operating a multilateral trading facility must also operate a regulated market.

1338 Financial services and markets—markets in financial instruments—modification of powers

The Financial Services and Markets Act 2000 (Markets in Financial Instruments) (Modification of Powers) Regulations 2006, SI 2006/2975 (in force on 6 December 2006), further amend the 2000 Act so that (1) the Financial Services Authority is empowered to make rules applying to authorised persons who are investment firms (as defined) with respect to their provision of prescribed ancillary services which are not regulated activities for the purposes of the 2000 Act; (2) limitations on the Authority's power to make financial promotion rules are removed; (3) the Authority has a duty to give guidance on outsourcing by investment firms and credit institutions; (4) where regulations under s 286 require investment exchanges to make information available to the public, the regulations may authorise the Authority to waive or defer those publication requirements; and (5) provision in regulations under s 286 need not apply in the case of overseas investment exchanges or clearing houses.

1339 Financial services and markets—regulated activities

The Financial Services and Markets Act 2000 (Regulated Activities) (Amendment) Order 2006, SI 2006/1969 (in force in part on 1 October 2006 and in part on 6 April 2007), further amends the 2001 Order, SI 2001/544, so that (1) the establishment, operation or winding up of a personal pension scheme as well as the establishment etc of a stakeholder pension scheme is a regulated activity for the purposes of the Financial Services and Markets Act 2000; (2) rights under a personal pension scheme become investments falling within the scope of regulation under the Act; (3) where an existing permission allows the authorised person to establish, operate or wind up a stakeholder pension scheme, he is treated as having permission also for the activity of establishing, operating or winding up a personal pension scheme; (4) where the authorised person has permission to carry on certain activities in relation to the specified investment of rights under a stakeholder pension scheme, he is to be treated as having permission to carry on those activities in relation to the new specified investment of rights under a personal pension scheme; (5) an interim permission is conferred on certain applicants who have applied to the Financial Services Authority for permission relating to the activity of establishing, operating or winding up a personal pension scheme or which relate to the specified investment of rights under a personal pension scheme and whose application is pending on the date when those activities become regulated; (6) interim approval is conferred in similar terms to those in head (5) supra on individuals working for a person who benefits from an interim permission and who would need approval; (7) the Authority may modify, amongst other things, its rules in their application to persons with an interim permission or an interim approval; and (8) provisions in, or made under, the Act are applied to certain persons with an interim permission or an interim approval.

The Financial Services and Markets Act 2000 (Regulated Activities) (Amendment) (No 2) Order 2006, SI 2006/2383 (in force in part on 6 November 2006 and in part on 6 April 2007), further amends the 2001 Order supra so as to specify, for the purposes of the Financial Services and Markets Act 2000, the kinds of activities which involve entering into, administering, arranging and advising on regulated home reversion plans and regulated home purchase plans as being regulated activities. In particular, the order (1) revises the definitions of 'overseas person' and 'high net worth company'; (2) provides for exclusions to (a) home reversion and home purchase arranging; (b) home reversion and home purchasing advising which relate to advice given in the media and advice given in the course of administration by an authorised person; and (c) the entering into and administering of regulated home reversion and purchase plans which relate to arranging administration by an authorised person and administration pursuant to an agreement with an authorised person; (3) provides that products which have the features of both a regulated home purchase plan and a regulated mortgage contract will not be considered a regulated mortgage contract; (4) specifies rights under regulated home reversion plans and rights under regulated home purchase plans as specified investments; (5) confers an interim permission on certain applicants who have applied for permission under the 2000 Act Pt 4 (ss 40–55) to enter into, administer, arrange or advise on regulated home reversion plans or regulated home purchase plans and whose application is pending on the date when those activities become regulated activities; (6) confers interim approval on people who are working for a person who has applied for permission under Pt 4 and who would need approval under Pt 5 (ss 56–71); and (7) enables the Financial Services Authority to modify its rules in their application to persons with an interim permission or interim approval.

The Financial Services and Markets Act 2000 (Regulated Activities) (Amendment No 3) Order 2006, SI 2006/3384 (in force in part on 1 April 2007 and in part on 1 November 2007), further amends the 2001 Order so that (1) in respect of any regulated activity that falls within the scope of European Parliament and EC Council Directive 2004/39, the exclusions applicable to that activity are to be disregarded if they are incompatible with Directive 2004/39; (2) operating a multilateral trading facility is a separate regulated activity for the purposes of the 2000 Act; (3) provision in relation to options, futures and contracts for differences applies to specified additional financial instruments, to the extent that an investment firm, credit institution or, in some circumstances, a management company or a market operator carries on an investment service or activity in relation to the investment; and (3) definitions of 'investment firm', 'credit institution', 'market operator', 'multilateral trading facility' and 'investment services and activities' are added.

1340 Investment Exchanges and Clearing Houses Act 2006

The Investment Exchanges and Clearing Houses Act 2006 confers power on the Financial Services Authority to disallow excessive regulatory provision by recognised investment exchanges and clearing houses. The Act received the royal assent on 19 December 2006 and came into force on 20 December 2006.

Section 1 confers power on the Authority to disallow excessive regulatory provision by recognised bodies and provides that any regulatory provision made by a recognised body in contravention of a direction by the Authority is of no effect. Procedural and other supplementary provisions under s 2 (1) impose a duty on recognised bodies to notify the Authority of proposed changes to their regulatory provision and extend the Authority's existing power to make rules requiring recognised bodies to notify it of certain events and information to include a power to specify types of proposed new regulatory provision or circumstances in which proposed new regulatory provision does not need to be notified, and to make procedural provision in relation to the notification of proposed new regulatory provision; (2) provide for an initial period in which the Authority may consider whether to call in a proposal for further scrutiny; (3) describe what is to happen if the Authority calls in a proposed change to regulatory provision for examination. Section 3 confers power on the Authority, for 12 months following royal assent, to give directions about notification. The restriction on disproportionate regulatory provision is included by s 4 in the grounds for refusing an application for recognition as an investment exchange or clearing house. Section 5 deals with short title and commencement.

FIRE SERVICES

Halsbury's Laws of England (4th edn) vol 18(2) (Reissue) paras 1–200

Articles

For articles relating to this title please refer to the Table of Articles at the beginning of the Abridgment.

1341 Emergency Workers (Obstruction) Act 2006

The Emergency Workers (Obstruction) Act 2006 makes it an offence to obstruct or hinder persons who provide emergency services. The Act received the royal assent on 8 November 2006 and certain provisions came into force on that day. The remaining provisions come into force on a day or days to be appointed. For details of commencement, see the commencement table in the title STATUTES.

Section 1 provides that it is an offence for a person without reasonable excuse to obstruct or hinder another while that other person is employed in a specified capacity and responding to emergency circumstances. It is an offence to obstruct or hinder another without reasonable excuse where the person being obstructed or hindered is assisting a person who is responding to emergency circumstances in a specified capacity: s 2. A person may, under s 3, be convicted of such offences, notwithstanding that it is effected by means other than physical means or effected by action directed only at any vehicle, vessel, apparatus, equipment or other thing or any animal used or to be used by a person. Section 4 provides that a person guilty of an offence is liable on summary conviction to a fine not exceeding level 5 on the standard scale. The Secretary of State may by order add or remove a person or description of person to or from s 1(2) and may make such provision connected with such modification as he thinks fit: s 5. Section 6 provides for repeals, and s 7 provides for short title, commencement and extent.

1342   Fire and rescue services—charging—Wales

The Fire and Rescue Services (Charging) (Wales) Order 2006, SI 2006/1852 (in force on 13 July 2006), specifies the actions for which a fire and rescue authority may make a charge and specifies the persons who may be subject to the charge.

1343   Fire and rescue services—Fire and Rescue National Framework—England

The Fire and Rescue Services (National Framework) (England) Order 2006, SI 2006/1084 (in force on 10 May 2006), replaces, for the purposes of the Fire and Rescue Services Act 2004 s 21, the Fire and Rescue National Framework 2006/06 with the 2006/08 Framework.

1344   Firefighters—compensation scheme—England

The Firefighters' Compensation Scheme (England) Order 2006, SI 2006/1811 (in force on 7 August 2006 but having retrospective effect), provides for a new compensation scheme for firefighters which consists primarily of provisions relating to ill health and injury awards in respect of firefighters, their spouses, civil partners, children and other dependants, that are similar to those contained in, but to be removed from, the Firemen's Pension Scheme Order 1992, SI 1992/129. The new scheme also includes provisions which relate to the payment of compensation in respect of firefighters who die or sustain seriously disabling injuries while on duty, and which provide, where a firefighter dies while on duty, for the payment to his dependants of a lump sum equivalent to the amount which a person employed in the role of firefighter by the same fire and rescue authority would receive as five years' pensionable pay after four years' service, at the rate applying at the date of the incident, or, if he has no dependants, for a flat-rate payment of £950 to his estate, with such amounts subject to abatement depending on the amount of any damages or compensation received by the firefighter or his dependants and any gratuities paid. The order also enables a person whose position under the new scheme would be less favourable than under the pension scheme set out in the 1992 Order to elect to retain benefits under that scheme provided that notice of election is given to the fire and rescue authority before 30 September 2006. The order has retrospective effect by virtue of the Superannuation Act 1972 s 12.

The Firefighters' Compensation Scheme (England) (Amendment) Order 2006, SI 2006/3434 (in force on 25 January 2007), amends provisions of the Firefighters' Compensation Scheme set out in the principal 2006 Regulations supra. The main effects of the amendments, which have effect from 6 April 2006, are that (1) the former distinction between regular firefighters and retained and volunteer firefighters is removed; and (2) the insertion of references to relevant provisions of the new pension scheme ensures that the provisions of the compensation scheme apply to members of both pension schemes.

1345   Firefighters—pension scheme—England

The Firefighters' Pension Scheme (Amendment) (England) Order 2006, SI 2006/1810 (in force on 7 August 2006 but having retrospective effect), further amends the Firefighters' Pension Scheme, as set out in the 1992 Order, SI 1992/129. In particular, the order (1) provides for a lower tier ill health pension for firefighters who are found by an independent qualified medical practitioner, to be capable of undertaking employment outside the fire and rescue service for not less than 30 hours a week on average over a 12-month period, whether they in fact take up any employment; (2) provides for a lower tier ill health pension and a higher tier ill health pension to be made available to those who are found to be incapable of undertaking such employment; (3) prescribes a new method of calculating certain lower tier ill health pensions with the effect that a pensioner who has five or more years' pensionable service will be entitled to immediate payment of an amount calculated as if he had been entitled to immediate payment of a deferred pension; (4) allows a fire and rescue authority to (a) terminate a higher tier ill health pension where, on a review of the pensioner's condition, it is established that he is capable of undertaking employment for not less than 30 hours a week on average over a 12-month period; and (b) terminate a pensioner's lower tier ill health pension where, on a review of his condition, it is established that he is capable of performing the duties of the role from which he retired and he accepts or declines an authority's offer to take up employment in that role, with the effect that if he declines such an offer, he becomes entitled to a deferred pension and his entitlement to a lower tier ill health pension is terminated; (5) requires each authority to establish and maintain a Firefighters' Pension Fund for the purposes of the Scheme whereby pension contributions made by firefighters and their employing authorities will be paid into the Fund and pension and related payments will be made out of it; (6) empowers the Secretary of State to make payments into the Fund to meet any deficits which result from more being paid out in pensions and related payments than has been paid in through contributions, and to request the repayment of any surpluses in the Fund which result from more being paid in through contributions than is paid out in pensions and related payments; (7) provides that such payments will, in the first instance, be made on the basis of estimates and that any adjustments for any remaining deficit or surplus will be made following the submission by an authority of its audited and unaudited accounts; (8) removes from the Scheme provisions relating to non-contributory compensation for death and injury; (9) lists the provisions of the Scheme which cease to have effect, having been superseded by corresponding provisions of the Firefighters' Compensation Scheme (England) Order 2006, SI 2006/1811; (10) provides that a person who withdraws his appeal to a board of medical referees within 21 days of the date appointed for the interview or medical examination may be required to pay an authority an amount not exceeding that payable by the authority in respect of the board's fees and allowances; (11) provides for the Scheme to cease to have effect on the day on which a new scheme, under the Fire and Rescue Services Act 2004 s 34, is brought into operation as respects (a) persons who take up employment with an authority as regular firefighters on or after 6 April 2006; (b) persons who, having made an election not to pay pension contributions, cancel that election on or after that date; and (c) the spouses, civil partners and dependants of those two classes of person; and (12) requires persons who take up employment with an authority as firefighters on or after 6 April 2006 to make pension contributions at a lower rate than is required of firefighters whose employment has begun before that date. The order has retrospective effect by virtue of the Superannuation Act 1972 s 12.

The Firefighters' Pension Scheme (England) Order 2006, SI 2006/3432 (in force on 25 January 2007 but having effect from 6 April 2006), makes provision for a new pension scheme for and in respect of firefighters (including retained and volunteer firefighters) employed by fire and rescue authorities in England. The normal retirement age under the scheme is 60 and the age at which deferred pensions will normally be paid will be 65. The scheme (1) makes provision for the payment of pensions to firefighter members; (2) provides for pensions for surviving spouses, civil partners, nominated partners and for children; (3) provides for the payment of death grants and post-retirement death grants; (4) deals with pension-sharing on divorce; (5) makes provision in relation to firefighters who serve in the reserve forces; (6) provides for the determination of questions and appeals arising under the scheme; (7) deals with the review, withdrawal and forfeiture of awards; (8) contains provisions about qualifying service and pensionable service; (9) deals with pensionable pay, pension contributions and the purchase of additional service; (10) provides for transfers into and out of the scheme; (11) deals with the accounting aspects of the scheme; and (12) provides for the payment of awards.

The Firefighters' Pension Scheme (Amendment) (No 2) (England) Order 2006, SI 2006/3433 (in force on 25 January 2007), further amends the Firemens' Pension Scheme, as set out in the 1992 Order, SI 1992/129, so as to ensure consistency with the new pension scheme introduced by the principal 2006 Order supra. The order also updates and replaces a number of definitions.

1346 Firefighters—pension scheme—Wales

The Firefighters' Pension (Wales) Scheme (Amendment) Order 2006, SI 2006/1672 (in force on 23 June 2006 but having retrospective effect), provides for the Firefighters' Pension Scheme, set out in the Firemen's Pension Scheme Order 1992, SI 1992/129, Sch 2, to continue in force subject to the modifications specified in the order. In particular, the order (1) makes amendments which are consequential on the revocation of the Fire Services Act 1947 and its replacement by the Fire and Rescue Services Act 2004; for example, references to fire authorities have been amended to references to fire and rescue authorities and references to brigades have been amended to references to fire and rescue services or, depending on the particular context, to fire and rescue authorities; (2) replaces a rule which provided for compulsory retirement at 55 for those of Station Officer or lower rank, and at 60 for those of Assistant Divisional Officer rank or higher rank, with a rule providing for a normal pension age of 55, whatever the individual's role; (3) corrects an anomaly, which allowed an individual who was found to be unfit for fire-fighting, but able to carry out other duties, to leave with a deferred pension prior to re-deployment, and immediately request early payment of that pension on the ground that he was permanently unfit for fire-fighting; (4) substitutes certain rules to reflect the fact that the surviving spouse of a deceased firefighter may be either a widow or a widower; the opportunity has been taken to correct an error, which limited, by reference to the date of the marriage, awards payable to widows; (5) substitutes a rule, which relates to the payment to a surviving spouse of a gratuity instead of a pension; (6) amends a rule, which relates to the way in which firefighters' pensions are calculated, so as to enable fire and rescue authorities which have introduced 'salary sacrifice' schemes to collect pension contributions based on the amount of pay before reduction for the sacrifice; (7) amends a rule, which prevents the duplication of certain injury awards; the main change of substance is to prevent duplicate injury awards in cases where the individual is employed both as a regular firefighter and as a retained firefighter, whether by the same fire and rescue authority or by different fire and rescue authorities; (8) amends the definition of 'independent qualified medical practitioner' to reflect a change in the meaning of 'a competent authority' brought about by the General and Specialist Medical Practice (Education, Training and Qualifications) Order 2003, SI 2003/1250; and (9) makes amendments which are consequential on the Civil Partnership Act 2004, so as to enable civil partners to qualify for survivor benefits under the Scheme on the same basis as spouses. The order has retrospective effect by virtue of the Superannuation Act 1972 s 12.

FISHERIES

Halsbury's Laws of England (4th edn) vol 18 paras 601–1000

Articles

For articles relating to this title please refer to the Table of Articles at the beginning of the Abridgment.

1347 Fishery products—official controls—charges—England

See para 1364.

1348 Fishery products—official controls—charges—Wales

See para 1365.

1349 Fishing boats—licence conditions—quotas—compatibility with Community law

The defendants were commercial fishermen who each owned and operated a fishing vessel which fell within the 'under ten metre' fleet. Under EEC Council Regulation 2847/93, vessels over ten metres were required to keep a log book of their fishing operations, including the quantities of each species of fish caught, and to comply with other monitoring obligations relevant to member states' annual fish quota. Under ten metre boats were exempt from the requirements. The Sea Fish (Conservation) Act 1967 provided for the licensing of fishing, and under s 4(6) it was a criminal offence if the licence condition was broken. The Department for the Environment, Food and Rural Affairs decided to impose individual monthly quotas in respect of each under ten metre boat and the defendants' licences were modified so as to limit their monthly catch of cod. The defendants exceeded the limit, and were charged with breaching a condition of their licence. They pleaded guilty and were fined. They appealed. *Held*, the imposition of monthly catch limits as a condition of the defendants' fishing licences was not incompatible with the exemption of their vessels from the detailed record keeping and reporting obligations required of over ten metre vessels under Regulation 2847/93. The imposition of monthly catch limits as a condition of the fishing licences did not impose on them the obligations required of over ten metre vessels. There was no legal requirement to maintain a log book or complete a landing declaration as a condition of the licences and no administrative requirement to do so. There was no practical requirement, for enforcement purposes, for the defendants to keep a log book rather than a rough and ready record of catches in order to enable them to keep a tally and comply with the relevant monthly limits. The exemption for under ten metre vessels from the record keeping and reporting obligations did not prohibit other measures of control adopted by the member state. There was no legal or evidential ground for suggesting that it would be disproportionate to require the under ten metre fleet to keep some record of the quantity of fish caught and sold. It was also well established that the Common Fisheries Policy did not allow fishermen or member states to avoid quota restrictions by arguing that it would be contrary to Community law to discard fish once caught. The system of enforcement was not unworkable without the obligation to complete landing declarations. Accordingly, the appeal would be dismissed.

R v Bossom [2006] EWCA Crim 1489, [2006] 4 All ER 995 (Court of Appeal: Gage LJ, Forbes and Cox JJ).

1350 Fishing vessels—satellite tracking devices—Wales

The Fishing Boats (Satellite-Tracking Devices) (Wales) Scheme 2006, SI 2006/2799 (in force on 20 October 2006), makes provision for funding satellite-tracking devices on fishing boats which are administered in Wales and which are required on board fishing boats over 15 metres as a result of EC Commission Regulation 2244/2003 laying down detailed provisions regarding satellite-based vessel monitoring systems. In particular, the scheme (1) sets out the eligibility criteria and gives details of the method of applying for funding under the scheme; (2) deals with the approval of such applications; (3) makes provision for payment under the scheme and sets out the circumstances in which payments will not be made to successful applicants; (4) sets out the powers of an authorised officer; (5) requires any applicant or any employee of any applicant to assist an authorised officer; (6) makes provision regarding the revocation of approval of an application and the conditions and consequences of revocation; and (7) makes provision for rates of interest where sums are recovered.

1351 Sea fishing—Community provisions—quotas—enforcement—England

The Sea Fishing (Enforcement of Annual Community and Third Country Fishing Measures) (England) Order 2006, SI 2006/1970 (in force on 15 August 2006), makes provision for the enforcement of certain restriction and obligations relation to sea fishing by Community vessels and third country vessels which are contained in EC Council Regulation 51/2006.

1352   Sea fishing—Community satellite monitoring measures—enforcement—Wales

The Sea Fishing (Enforcement of Community Satellite Monitoring Measures) (Wales) Order 2006, SI 2006/2798 (in force on 20 October 2006), provides for the enforcement of EC Commission Regulation 2244/2003 laying down detailed provisions regarding satellite-based vessel monitoring systems, and replaces the 2000 Order, SI 2000/1078. In particular, the order (1) applies to British and European Community fishing boats within Wales and create offences for contravening requirements relating to (a) the installation of a satellite-tracking device; (b) the information to be transmitted by the satellite-tracking device; (c) the responsibilities relating to a satellite-tracking device; (d) the technical failure or non-functioning of the satellite tracking-device; and (e) the switching off of a satellite-tracking device in port without prior notification; (2) applies to third country fishing boats within Wales and create offences for contravening requirements relating to heads (1)(a)–(d) above; (3) confers certain powers on British sea-fishery officers for the purposes of enforcing Regulation 2244/2003; (4) provides for protection of such officers from liability; (5) provides for an offence of failing to comply with requirements imposed by officers or obstructing them in the exercise of their powers; and (6) deals with corporate and equivalent offences and admissibility of documents in evidence. SI 2002/677 is revoked.

1353   Sea fishing—landing and sale of fish—buyers and sellers—registration—Wales

The Registration of Fish Buyers and Sellers and Designation of Fish Auction Sites (Wales) Regulations 2006, SI 2006/1495 (in force on 9 June 2006), provide, in relation to Wales, for (1) the registration by the National Assembly for Wales of sellers of first fish sales; (2) the designation of fish auction sites; and (3) the registration of buyers of first sale fish. The regulations (a) require (i) registered fish sellers to maintain records of their sales of first fish sales; (ii) buyers of first sale fish to maintain records of their purchases of first sale fish; and (b) provide an offence to (i) sell first sale fish at a designated auction site unless registered as a fish seller; (ii) buy first sale fish unless registered or bought for private consumption; (iii) sell first sale fish landed otherwise than by a licensed fishing vessel; and (iv) buy first sale fish unless the fish has been landed by a licensed fishing vessel. Penalties for these offences are, on summary conviction, a fine not exceeding the statutory maximum, and on conviction on indictment, a fine. Where a person is convicted of an offence a court may revoke the registration or designation concerned and may order that the person convicted is disqualified from applying for registration or designation for a specified period. The regulations also confer powers of enforcement on British sea fishery officers, which may be exercised in relation to premises and any fishing boat within Wales, and make provision for their protection by providing offences and penalties for their obstruction.

1354   Sea fishing—northern hake stock—Wales

The Sea Fishing (Northern Hake Stock) (Wales) Order 2006, SI 2006/1796 (in force on 7 July 2006), provides for the administration and enforcement of the monitoring, inspection and surveillance provisions of EC Council Regulation 811/2004. In particular, the order (1) creates offences in respect of a contravention, by a person or specified individuals, in charge of a fishing boat in relation to (a) failing to record and account for time in a log book, (b) failing to provide information and/or follow directions of a British sea-fishery officer when landing at a designated port, (c) failing to land in a designated port where more than two tonnes of northern hake are to be landed, (d) failing to comply with the 8 per cent tolerance for log book records relating to catches of fish, and (e) the mixing of species and transporting of northern hake in an inconsistent manner with Regulation 811/2004; (2) provides for the recovery of fines imposed, or treated as imposed, by a magistrates' court; (3) confers powers on British sea-fishery officers to enter premises, to go on board fishing boats, stop and search vehicles transporting fish, examine fish, require the production of documents, take a boat to the nearest convenient port and seize fish and fishing gear; and (4) makes provision for offences.

1355   Sea fishing—passive fishing gear and beam trawls—marking and identification—England

The Sea Fishing (Marking and Identification of Passive Fishing Gear and Beam Trawls) (England) Order 2006, SI 2006/1549 (in force on 10 July 2006), (1) specifies that contravention of the requirements as to the deployment, marking and identification of passive fishing gear, buoys and beam trawls constitutes an offence; (2) confers powers of enforcement on British sea fishery officers; (3) provides for the protection of British sea fishery officers and their assistants from civil or criminal proceedings where anything done or omitted to be done was in good faith, on reasonable grounds and in the exercise of reasonable care and skill; (4) specifies offences and provides for penalties applicable in situations where the British sea fishery officers are obstructed in their investigations; (5) makes provision in respect of offences by bodies corporate, partnerships and unincorporated associations; and (6) allows for the admissibility in evidence of logbooks and other documents.

1356   Sea fishing—restriction on days at sea

The Sea Fishing (Restriction on Days at Sea) (Monitoring, Inspection and Surveillance) Order 2006, SI 2006/1327 (in force on 1 June 2006), provides (1) for the establishment of a management system for days at sea based on monthly entitlement and linked to management periods, (2) for offences in relation to management periods; (3) for the calculation of the allocation of days (a) for fishing in the Cod Recovery and Sole Recovery Zones; and (b) when a fishing boat is involved in pair trawling; (4) for the adjustment of allocations of days by the Secretary of State; (5) for offences in relation to allocations of days and other restrictions on presence in the Cod Recovery Zone and the Sole Recovery Zone; (6) for the transfer of days, wherein unused days within an allocation of days may be transferred from an allocation relating to one English fishing boat to an allocation relating to another British fishing boat, and for an offence of giving false information in a notification made for the purpose of transfer; (7) for an offence in relation to (a) the carriage and operation of fishing gears and the combined use of regulated and unregulated gears; and (b) the maintenance of log-books; (8) for monitoring, inspection and surveillance in respect of fishing in the Sole Recovery Zone; and (9) for enforcement, including in relation to (i) penalties; (ii) the recovery of fines; (iii) powers for British sea-fishery officers, including the power to enter premises, to go on board fishing boats and to stop and search vehicles transporting fish; and (iv) the protection of officers in the exercise of the powers conferred.

FOOD

Halsbury's Laws of England (4th edn) vol 18(2) (Reissue) paras 201–600

Articles

For articles relating to this title please refer to the Table of Articles at the beginning of the Abridgment.

1357   Contaminants in food—charges for residues—surveillance

The Charges for Residues Surveillance Regulations 2006, SI 2006/2285 (in force on 1 October 2006), (1) require fees to be paid for the Secretary of State's surveillance of animals and animal products for residues of veterinary medicinal products and other substances; (2) lay down provisions relating to the liability for and recovery of fees; (3) enable the Secretary of State to require information and supporting evidence to be supplied to him for the purpose of enabling him to calculate fees; (4) create offences of failing to comply with a demand to supply information and supplying false or misleading information; (5) make changes to fees ranging approximately from decreases of 25 per cent to increases of 45 per cent; (6) require the Secretary of State to publicise the appointment of fish feed manufacturers as his agent for the collection of the charge for the inspection and control of brown trout and rainbow trout; (7) make it an offence knowingly to supply false or misleading information to the Secretary of State for the purpose of calculating charges payable under the regulations, whether or not it is requested by the Secretary of State; (8) give effect, until 1 January 2007, to EC Council Directive 85/73 art 2 on the financing of veterinary inspections and controls; and (9) from 1 January 2007 give effect, except for honey, to art 27. SI 1997/2893 is revoked.

1358   Contaminants in food—general provisions—England

The Contaminants in Food (England) Regulations 2006, SI 2006/1464 (in force on 1 July 2006), make provision for the execution and enforcement of EC Commission Regulation 466/2001 setting maximum levels for contaminants in foodstuffs. In particular, the regulations (1) provide that it is an offence, except in certain cases relating to food placed on the market before a date given in specified Community legislation (a) to place on the market certain foods if they contain contaminants of any kind specified in Regulation 466/2001 at levels exceeding those specified; (b) to use food containing such contaminants at such levels as ingredients in the production of certain foods; (c) to mix foods that do not comply with the maximum levels referred to above with foods which do comply; (d) to mix foods to which Regulation 466/2001 relates and which are intended for direct consumption with foods to which Regulation 466/2001 relates and which are intended to be sorted or otherwise treated prior to consumption; or (e) to detoxify by chemical treatment food not complying with the limits specified in Regulation 466/2001; (2) specify the enforcement authorities; and (3) provide for the application of specified provisions of the Food Safety Act 1990 for the purposes of the regulations. The regulations also make a consequential amendment to the Food Safety (Sampling and Qualifications) Regulations 1990, SI 1990/2463, the effect being to disapply the sampling and analysis provisions of the 1990 Regulations only to the extent that those matters are regulated by the specified Community instruments. SI 2005/3251 is revoked.

1359   Contaminants in Food—general provisions—Wales

The Contaminants in Food (Wales) (No 2) Regulations 2006, SI 2006/1850 (in force on 13 July 2006), replace the 2006 Regulations, SI 2006/485, which replaced the 2002 Regulations, SI 2002/364, and make provision for the execution and enforcement of EC Commission Regulation 466/2001 setting maximum levels for contaminants in foodstuffs. In particular, the regulations (1) provide that it is an offence, except in certain cases relating to food placed on the market before a date given in specified Community legislation (a) to place on the market certain foods if they contain contaminants of any kind specified in Regulation 466/2001 at levels exceeding those specified, subject to a derogation applicable to certain types of lettuce and to fresh spinach; (b) to use food containing such contaminants at such levels as ingredients in the production of certain foods; (c) to mix foods that do not comply with the maximum levels referred to above with foods which do; (d) to mix foods to which Regulation 466/2001 relates and which are intended for direct consumption with foods to which Regulation 466/2001 relates and which are intended to be sorted or otherwise treated prior to consumption; or (e) to detoxify by chemical treatment food not complying with the limits specified in Regulation 466/2001; (2) specify the enforcement authorities; (3) provide for the application of specified provisions of the Food Safety Act 1990 for the purposes of the regulations; and (4) amend the Food Safety (Sampling and Qualifications) Regulations 1990, SI 1990/2463, the effect being to disapply the sampling and analysis provisions only to the extent that those matters are regulated by EC Commission Directives 2001/22, 2002/63, 2002/69, 2004/16, 2005/10, and EC Commission Regulation 401/2006.

1360   Curd cheese—market restriction—England

The Curd Cheese (Restriction on Placing on the Market) (England) Regulations 2006, SI 2006/2787 (in force on 18 October 2006), implement EC Commission Decision 2006/694 prohibiting the placing on the market of curd cheese manufactured in a dairy establishment in the United Kingdom. In particular, the regulations (1) prohibit the placing on the market of any curd cheese manufactured by Bowland Dairy Products Limited, located at Fulshaw Head Farm, Barrowford, Lancashire BB9 6RA and approved under the number UK PE 23; (2) apply with modifications certain provisions of the Food Safety Act 1990; (3) provide for the inspection and seizure of products that are suspected of having been placed on the market in contravention of the specified prohibition; (4) create offences and penalties; and (5) make provision for the enforcement of the regulations.

1361   Curd cheese—market restriction—Wales

The Curd Cheese (Restriction on Placing on the Market) (Wales) Regulations 2006, SI 2006/2792 (in force on 18 October 2006), implement EC Wales Commission Decision 2006/694 prohibiting the placing on the market of curd cheese manufactured in a dairy establishment in the United Kingdom. In particular, the regulations (1) prohibit the placing on the market of all curd cheese manufactured by a specified Dairy company; (2) apply with modifications certain provisions of the Food Safety Act 1990; (3) provide for the inspection and seizure of products that are suspected of having been placed on the market in contravention of the specified prohibition; (4) create offences and penalties; and (5) make provision for the enforcement of the regulations.

1362   Fish—labelling—England

The Fish Labelling (Amendment) (England) Regulations 2006, SI 2006/506 (in force on 6 April 2006), amend the 2003 Regulations, SI 2003/461, by providing that commercial designations accepted in other member states are names prescribed by law, and replacing the 2003 Regulations Schedule, which provides for a list of commercial designations for the species of sea fish, salmon and freshwater fish and shellfish.

1363   Fish—labelling—Wales

The Fish Labelling (Wales) (Amendment) Regulations 2006, SI 2006/1339 (in force on 24 May 2006), amend the 2003 Regulations, SI 2003/1365, by providing that commercial designations accepted in other member states are names prescribed by law, and replacing the 2003 Regulations Schedule, which provides for a list of commercial designations for the species of sea fish, salmon and freshwater fish and shellfish.

1364   Fishery products—official controls—charges—England

The Fishery Products (Official Controls Charges) (England) Regulations 2006, SI 2006/2904 (in force on 1 January 2007), replace the 2005 Regulations, SI 2005/2991, and provide for the execution and enforcement of EC European Parliament and Council Regulation 882/2004, in relation to charges for carrying out official controls performed on fishery products. In particular, the regulations (1) set out the types of costs which may be incurred in exercising the official controls required; (2) specify rates for the calculation of the sterling equivalent of any sums specified in euros; (3) prescribe how the length of an account period is to be determined; (4) provide that where charges are imposed on more than one person, they may be enforced jointly or separately; (5) require authorities to which charges are payable to calculate those charges, recalculate them in the event of an error and give notice of amounts due to those liable to pay such charges; (6) provide for appeals against the decisions of authorities imposing charges; (7) provide for the payment of charges by one food authority to another; (8) require payment of a specified amount to the relevant food authority by vendors of relevant fishery products or relevant landed fishery products in relation to the first placing on the market or first sale in a fish market of such products; (9) require those vendors to supply the relevant food authority with returns in respect of the aggregate of transactions for which charges are payable and require them to keep records; (10) require payment of a specified amount to the relevant food authority by proprietors or operators of processing establishments in relation to fishery products entering the establishment concerned; and (11) require those proprietors and operators of processing establishments to supply the relevant food authority with returns in respect of fishery products for which charges are payable and require them to keep records.

1365   Fishery products—official controls—charges—Wales

The Fishery Products (Official Controls Charges) (Wales) Regulations 2006, SI 2006/3344 (in force on 1 January 2007), replace the 2005 Regulations, SI 2005/3297, and provide for the execution and enforcement of EC European Parliament and Council Regulation 882/2004, in relation to charges for carrying out official controls performed on fishery products. In particular, the regulations (1) set out the types of costs which may be incurred in exercising the official controls required; (2) specify rates for the calculation of the sterling equivalent of any sums specified in euros; (3) prescribe how the length of an account period is to be determined; (4) provide that where charges are imposed on more than one person, they may be enforced jointly or separately; (5) require authorities to which charges are payable to calculate those charges, recalculate them in the event of an error and give notice of amounts due to those liable to pay such charges; (6) provide for appeals against the decisions of authorities imposing charges; (7) provide for the payment of charges by one food authority to another; (8) require payment of a specified amount to the relevant food authority by vendors of relevant fishery products or relevant landed fishery products in relation to the first placing on the market or first sale in a fish market of such products; (9) require those vendors to supply the relevant food authority with returns in respect of the aggregate of transactions for which charges are payable and require them to keep records; (10) require payment of a specified amount to the relevant food authority by proprietors or operators of processing establishments in relation to fishery products entering the establishment concerned; and (11) require those proprietors and operators of processing establishments to supply the relevant food authority with returns in respect of fishery products for which charges are payable and require them to keep records.

1366   Food for particular nutritional uses—substances for specific nutritional purposes—England

The Food for Particular Nutritional Uses (Addition of Substances for Specific Nutritional Purposes) (England) (Amendment) Regulations 2006, SI 2006/3116 (in force on 31 December 2006), further amend the 2002 Regulations, SI 2002/1817, in implementation of EC Commission Directive 2006/34, which amends EC Commission Directive 2001/15. In particular, the regulations (1) add certain substances to the list of vitamins and minerals categories which may be added for specific nutritional purposes in designated foods for particular nutritional uses; (2) add a substance in the minerals category to the list of substances which may be added for specific nutritional purposes in foods for special medical purposes; and (3) update the definition of 'Directive 2001/15'. SI 2002/333 amended.

1367   Food safety—animal products—veterinary residues

The Animals and Animal Products (Examination for Residues and Maximum Residue Limits) (Amendment) Regulations 2006, SI 2006/755 (in force on 6 April 2006), further amend the 1997 Regulations, SI 1997/1729, so as to transpose EC European Parliament and Council Directive 2003/74 and EC Commission Decision 2002/657.

1368   Food safety—ceramic articles—England

The Ceramic Articles in Contact with Food (England) Regulations 2006, SI 2006/1179 (in force on 30 June 2006), replace the Ceramic Ware (Safety) Regulations 1988, SI 1988/1647, and implement EEC Council Directive 84/500 on the approximation of the laws of member states relating to ceramic articles intended to come into contact with foodstuffs. In particular, the regulations (1) define ceramic article; (2) set a limit on the amount of lead and cadmium which may be transferred by a ceramic article; (3) set out the requirements for testing such an article; (4) require a written declaration of compliance to accompany a ceramic article or articles not yet in contact with food at all marketing stages up to the retail stage; (5) require a manufacturer or importer into the European Community to keep appropriate documentation to show that the materials used to make the articles did not come into contact with lead or cadmium; (6) provide for enforcement by food authorities and port health authorities in their respective areas or districts; and (7) set out the penalties for failure to comply with the regulations and the defences that are available.

1369 Food safety—ceramic articles—Wales

The Ceramic Articles in Contact with Food (Wales) Regulations 2006, SI 2006/1704 (in force on 30 June 2006), implement EEC Council Directive 84/500 on the approximation of the laws of member states relating to ceramic articles intended to come into contact with foodstuffs. In particular, the regulations (1) define 'ceramic article'; (2) set a limit on the amount of lead and cadmium which may be transferred by a ceramic article; (3) set out the requirements for testing such an article; (4) require a written declaration of compliance to accompany a ceramic article or articles not yet in contact with food at all marketing stages up to the retail stage; (5) require a manufacturer or importer into the European Community to keep appropriate documentation to show that the materials used to make the articles did not come into contact with lead or cadmium; (6) provide for enforcement by food authorities and port health authorities in their respective areas or districts; and (7) set out the penalties for failure to comply with the regulations and the defences that are available.

1370 Food safety—control orders—emergency control orders—nuts—England

The Food (Emergency Control) (Revocation) (England) Regulations 2006, SI 2006/2289 (in force on 1 October 2006), revoke, in relation to England, the Food (Peanuts from China) (Emergency Control) (England) (No 2) Regulations 2002, SI 2002/2350, the Food (Figs, Hazelnuts and Pistachios from Turkey) (Emergency Control) (England) (No 2) Regulations 2002, SI 2002/2351, the Food (Brazil Nuts) (Emergency Control) (England) Regulations 2003, SI 2003/1722, the Food (Pistachios from Iran) (Emergency Control) (England) Regulations 2003, SI 2003/1956, and the Food (Peanuts from Egypt) (Emergency Control) (England) Regulations 2003, SI 2003/2074.

1371 Food safety—control orders—emergency control orders—revocation—Wales

The Food (Emergency Control) (Revocation) (Wales) Regulations 2006, SI 2006/2830 (in force on 27 October 2006), revoke the Food (Peanuts from China) (Emergency Control) (Wales) (No 2) Regulations 2002, SI 2002/2295, the Food (Peanuts from China) (Emergency Control) (Amendment) (Wales) Regulations 2003, SI 2003/2299, the Food (Figs, Hazelnuts and Pistachios from Turkey) (Emergency Control) (Amendment) (Wales) Regulations 2002, SI 2002/1726, the Food (Figs, Hazelnuts and Pistachios from Turkey) (Emergency Control) (Wales) (No 2) Regulations 2002, SI 2002/2296, the Food (Figs, Hazelnuts and Pistachios from Turkey) (Emergency Control) (Wales) (Amendment) Regulations 2003, SI 2003/2292, the Food (Brazil Nuts) (Emergency Control) (Wales) Regulations 2003, SI 2003/2254, the Food (Pistachios from Iran) (Emergency Control) (Wales) (No 2) Regulations 2003, SI 2003/2288, the Food (Pistachios from Iran) (Emergency Control) (Wales) (No 2) (Amendment) Regulations 2005, SI 2005/257, and the Food (Peanuts from Egypt) (Emergency Control) (Wales) Regulations 2003, SI 2003/2910, which implemented Commission Decisions imposing conditions on the import of specific products that could be contaminated with excessive levels of aflatoxins.

1372 Food safety—control orders—Kava-kava—Wales

The Kava-kava in Food (Wales) Regulations 2006, SI 2006/1851 (in force on 14 July 2006), prohibit the sale, possession for sale, offer, exposure or advertisement for sale and the importation into Wales from outside the United Kingdom, of any food consisting of, or containing, Kava-kava. Any such food may be treated as being unfit for human consumption and be liable to be seized and destroyed.

1373 Food safety—food hygiene—England

The Food Hygiene (England) Regulations 2006, SI 2006/14 (in force on 11 January 2006), which replace the 2005 Regulations, SI 2005/2059, provide for the execution and enforcement of EC Parliament and Council Regulations 852/2004, 853/2004 and 854/2004 and EC Commission Regulations 2073/2005 and 2075/2005 ('the Community Regulations') and, in particular (1) create presumptions that, for the purposes of the regulations, specified food is intended for human consumption; (2) provide that the Food Standards Agency is the competent authority for the purposes of the Community Regulations except where it has delegated competences as provided for in the Community Regulations; (3) make provision for execution and enforcement; (4) make provision for the service on food business operators of hygiene improvement notices, hygiene prohibition notices and orders, hygiene emergency prohibition notices and orders, remedial action notices and detention notices; (5) provide that where the commission of an offence under the regulations is due to the act or default of some other person, that person is guilty of the offence; (6) supply a defence of due diligence; (7) provide for the procurement and analysis of samples; (8) confer powers of entry on authorised officers of an enforcement authority; (9) create an offence of obstructing such an officer; (10) impose a time limit for bringing prosecutions; (11) create an offence of failing to comply with specified Community Regulations provisions; (12) provide for penalties for offences; (13) provide that a person is to be considered not to have contravened or failed to comply with a specified provision of Regulation 852/2004 provided the specified requirements are complied with; (14) make provision in relation to offences by bodies corporate and Scottish partnerships; (15) provide a right of appeal in respect of (a) the service of a hygiene improvement notice or a remedial action notice; (b) an enforcement authority's refusal to issue a certificate under the specified provisions to the effect that the authority is satisfied that a food business operator has taken measures to secure that the health risk condition is no longer fulfilled with respect to the food business concerned; (c) the making of a hygiene prohibition order or a hygiene emergency prohibition order; (16) apply, with a modification, the Food Safety Act 1990; (17) provide for the issue of codes of recommended practice to food authorities by the Secretary of State; (18) make provision protecting officers acting in good faith; (19) provide for the revocation and suspension of designations and appointments; (20) require any food certified by an authorised officer of an enforcement authority as not having been produced, processed or distributed in compliance with the regulations and the Community Regulations to be treated, for the purposes of the 1990 Act s 9, as failing to comply with food safety requirements; (21) provide for the service of documents; (22) make further provision in relation to (a) bulk transport in seagoing vessels of liquid oils or fats and the bulk transport by sea of raw sugar; (b) temperature control requirements; (c) the direct supply by producers of small quantities of meat from poultry and lagomorphs slaughtered on their farms; and (d) restrictions on the sale of raw milk intended for direct human consumption; and (23) make consequential amendments to specified legislation.

1374   Food safety—food hygiene—Wales

The Food Hygiene (Wales) Regulations 2006, SI 2006/31 (in force on 11 January 2006), which replace the 2005 Regulations, SI 2005/3932, provide for the execution and enforcement of EC Parliament and Council Regulations 852/2004, 853/2004 and 854/2004 and EC Commission Regulations 2073/2005 and 2075/2005 ('the Community Regulations') and, in particular (1) create presumptions that, for the purposes of the regulations, specified food is intended for human consumption; (2) provide that the Food Standards Agency is the competent authority for the purposes of the Community Regulations except where it has delegated competences as provided for in the Community Regulations; (3) make provision for execution and enforcement; (4) make provision for the service on food business operators of hygiene improvement notices, hygiene prohibition notices and orders, hygiene emergency prohibition notices and orders, remedial action notices and detention notices; (5) provide that where the commission of an offence under the regulations is due to the act or default of some other person, that person is guilty of the offence; (6) supply a defence of due diligence; (7) provide for the procurement and analysis of samples; (8) confer powers of entry on authorised officers of an enforcement authority; (9) create an offence of obstructing such an officer; (10) impose a time limit for bringing prosecutions; (11) create an offence of failing to comply with specified provisions of Regulations 852/2004 and 853/2004; (12) provide for penalties for offences; (13) provide that a person is to be considered not to have contravened or failed to comply with a specified provision of Regulation 852/2004 provided the specified requirements are complied with; (14) make provision in relation to offences by bodies corporate and Scottish partnerships; (15) provide a right of appeal in respect of (a) the service of a hygiene improvement notice or a remedial action notice; (b) an enforcement authority's refusal to issue a certificate under the specified provisions to the effect that the authority is satisfied that a food business operator has taken measures to secure that the health risk condition is no longer fulfilled with respect to the food business concerned; (c) the making of a hygiene prohibition order or a hygiene emergency prohibition order; (16) apply, with a modification, the Food Safety Act 1990; (17) provide for the issue of codes of recommended practice to food authorities by the National Assembly for Wales; (18) make provision protecting officers acting in good faith; (19) provide for the revocation and suspension of designations and appointments; (20) require any food certified by an authorised officer of an enforcement authority as not having been produced, processed or distributed in compliance with the regulations and the Community Regulations to be treated, for the purposes of the 1990 Act s 9, as failing to comply with food safety requirements; (21) provide for the service of documents; (22) make further provision in relation to (a) bulk transport in seagoing vessels of liquid oils or fats and the bulk transport by sea of raw sugar; (b) temperature control requirements; (c) the direct supply by producers of small quantities of meat from poultry and lagomorphs slaughtered on their farms; and (d) restrictions on the sale of raw milk intended for direct human consumption; and (23) make consequential amendments to specified legislation.

The Food Hygiene (Wales) (Amendment) Regulations 2006, SI 2006/1534 (in force on 15 June 2006), make a minor drafting correction to the principal 2006 Regulations, SI 2006/31, supra.

1375   Food safety—materials in contact with food—England

The Plastic Materials and Articles in Contact with Food (England) Regulations 2006, SI 2006/1401 (in force on 30 June 2006), replace, in relation to England, the 1998 Regulations, SI 1998/1376, and provide for the execution and enforcement of EC Commission Regulation 1895/2005 on the restriction of use of certain epoxy derivatives in materials and articles intended to come into contact with food. The regulations (1) prohibit specified activities in relation to any plastic material or article which fails to meet the appropriate required standards; (2) prohibit the use of monomers and additives in the manufacture of plastic materials and articles other than in accordance with specified conditions; (3) specify the required standards relating to (a) the capability of a monomer or an additive to confer its constituents to foods; (b) products obtained by bacterial fermentation; (c) the overall migration limits from plastic materials or articles to food; and (d) the migration of primary aromatic amines from plastic materials or articles to food; (4) specify the methods for determining the capability of a plastic material or article to transfer its constituents to food and for detecting the presence of any such constituents in food; (5) provide that prior to the retail stage plastic materials and articles must be accompanied by certain specified written information, including a declaration of legislative compliance; (6) designate food authorities and port health authorities as enforcement authorities in their respective areas or districts; (7) specify the procedure to be followed when sending a sample for analysis; (8) provide for a reference sample to be analysed by the Laboratory for the Government Chemist; (9) provide for the procedure to be followed and the time limit to be observed where a person wishes to apply to the European Food Safety Authority for authorisation of a new additive; and (10) provide for offences, defences and penalties.

The Plastic Materials and Articles in Contact with Food (England) (No 2) Regulations 2006, SI 2006/2687 (in force on 19 November 2006), implement EEC Council Directives 82/711 and 85/572 and EC Commission Directive 2002/72, so as to (1) revise the definition of 'the Directive' to include the amendments made to Directive 2002/72 by EC Commission Directive 2005/79, which introduces new provisions relating to PVC gaskets containing epoxidised soybean oil and makes revisions to the lists of authorised monomers (including other starting substances) and additives, and their conditions of use in the manufacture of food contact plastics; and (2) make provision for a transitional defence in relation to the sale of jars of foods for infants and young children sealed with PVC gaskets containing epoxidised soybean oil. SI 2006/1401 is revoked.

1376   Food safety—materials in contact with food—Wales

The Plastic Materials and Articles in Contact with Food (Wales) Regulations 2006, SI 2006/2982 (in force on 19 November 2006), replace with amendments the 1998 Regulations, SI 1998/1376, in so far as they apply in relation to Wales, and provide for the execution and enforcement of EC Commission Regulation 1895/2005 on the restriction of use of certain epoxy derivatives in materials and articles intended to come into contact with food. In particular, the regulations (1) prohibit specified activities in relation to any plastic material or article which fails to meet the appropriate required standards; (2) prohibit the use of monomers and additives in the manufacture of plastic materials and articles other than in accordance with specified conditions; (3) specify the required standards relating to the capability of a monomer or an additive to confer its constituents to food; (4) specify the required standard for products obtained by bacterial fermentation; (5) specify the required standard relating to overall migration limits from plastic materials or articles to food; (6) specify the required standards relating to the migration of primary aromatic amines from plastic materials or articles to food; (7) specify the methods for determining the capability of a plastic material or article to transfer its constituents to food, and for detecting the presence of any such constituents in food; (8) provide that prior to the retail stage plastic materials and articles must be accompanied by certain specified written information, including a declaration of legislative compliance; (9) designate food authorities and port health authorities as the enforcement authorities in their respective areas or districts; (10) specify the offences that may be committed under these regulations and set out the maximum penalties on conviction; (11) provide for defences of a general nature, such as exercise of due diligence etc, to certain offences; (12) provide for a transitional defence relating to the sale of jars in foods for infants and young children sealed PVC gaskets containing epoxidised soybean oil; (13) provide for transitional defences in relation to certain plastic materials or articles that have already been manufactured or put into circulation in advance of a change in the law that would otherwise have made their manufacture or circulation unlawful; (14) specify the procedure to be followed when sending a sample for analysis; (15) make provision for a reference sample to be analysed by the Laboratory for the Government Chemist; and (16) set out the procedure to be followed and the time limit to be observed where a person wishes apply to the European Food Safety Authority for the authorisation of a new additive.

1377   Food safety—official feed and food controls—England

The Official Feed and Food Controls (England) Regulations 2006, SI 2006/15 (in force on 11 January 2006), which replace the 2005 Regulations, SI 2005/2626, provide for the execution and enforcement of EC Parliament and Council Regulation 882/2004 on official controls performed to ensure the verification of compliance with feed and food law, animal health and animal welfare rules and impose prohibitions on the introduction of certain feed and food into England in implementation of European Parliament and Council Regulation 178/2002, laying down the general principles and requirements of food law, establishing the European Food Safety Authority and laying down procedures in matters of food safety. In particular, the regulations (1) designate specified bodies as competent authorities for the purposes of Regulation 882/2004; (2) provide for the exchange and provision of information by competent authorities; (3) enable a competent authority to require a control body to provide information and make records available; (4) provide that a person who (a) fails to comply with a requirement to provide information or make records available; or (b) in purported compliance with such a requirement, furnishes false or misleading information, is guilty of an offence; (5) provide for the issue of codes of recommended practice to feed and food authorities by the Secretary of State (6) accord the Food Standards Agency the function of monitoring the performance of enforcement authorities in enforcing certain legislation; (7) confer powers on the Agency, for the purpose of monitoring such performance, to require information to be provided and records to be made available, and to authorise individuals, who may thereby exercise certain powers, including a power of entry; (8) define various terms; (9) provide that a person who (a) obstructs a person exercising powers to enter premises, take samples or inspect and copy records; (b) fails to comply with requirements to provide information, make available records or provide facilities, records, information or other assistance; or (c) in purported compliance with such a requirement, furnishes false or misleading evidence, is guilty of an offence; (10) provide a right of appeal in respect of a decision of the competent authority concerning the approval of certain establishments; (11) permit an authorised officer of a competent authority to take with him a member of staff of the competent authority of another member state for the purpose of conducting an administrative inquiry; (12) provide that, when an enforcing officer, as defined, enters premises for the purpose of executing and enforcing official controls, that officer may take with him a Commission expert to enable that expert to carry out relevant functions; (13) provide that a person who enters premises under the powers referred to above and discloses any information obtained on the premises with regard to any trade secret is guilty of an offence unless that person does so in the performance of his duty; (14) specify the authorities which are responsible for executing and enforcing the provisions relating to offences; (15) confer powers of entry on authorised officers of an enforcement authority; (16) create an offence of obstructing such an officer acting in the execution of his duties; (17) prescribe the penalties for offences; (18) specify the time limit for bringing prosecutions for offences; (19) provide that the Commissioners for Her Majesty's Revenue and Customs are to carry out the functions given to customs services under specified provisions of Regulation 882/2004; (20) make provision for the deferred enforcement and execution of the import provisions until a product reaches its destination; (21) prohibit the introduction into England of certain feed and food unless specified conditions are met; (22) provide for the checking of products introduced into England; (23) provide that an enforcement authority has the power to do anything that a competent authority may do under specified provisions of Regulation 882/2004, and is the competent authority for certain purposes; (24) provide for the service of notices when an authorised officer of an enforcement authority wishes to take certain measures or exercise certain powers; (25) provide a right of appeal in respect of the service of such a notice; (26) provide for the Secretary of State or the Agency, by written declaration, to suspend or impose conditions on the introduction into England of any product from a third country where either of them learns or reasonably suspects that any food or feed that has been or may be introduced into England from that third country is likely to constitute a serious risk to animal or public health; (27) provide for charges to be payable in relation to controls carried out on consignments; (28) provide for the procurement and analysis of samples of food for the purposes of the execution and enforcement of the import provisions; (29) confer powers of entry on authorised officers of a food authority in relation to the execution and enforcement of the import provisions; (30) create the offence of obstructing an officer acting in the execution of the import provisions; (31) create offences of contravening or failing to comply with specified regulations and failing to comply with a notice served under the import provisions, and provide for penalties for offences under those provisions; (32) prescribe the time limit for bringing prosecutions for such offences; (33) provide that, where the commission of an offence is due to the act or default of some other person, that person is guilty of the offence; (34) provide that, in proceedings for an offence, it is a defence for the accused to prove that he took all reasonable precautions and exercised all due diligence to avoid the commission of the offence; (35) make provision in relation to offences by bodies corporate and Scottish partnerships; (36) provide for the protection of officers acting in good faith; and (37) make provision for the service of documents. SI 2005/3280 is amended.

The Official Controls (Animals, Feed and Food) (England) Regulations 2006, SI 2006/3472 (in force on 16 February 2007), apply and enforce European Parliament and Council Regulation 882/2004 in England in relation to animal health and welfare rules, and feed and food law excluded from the Official Feed and Food Controls Regulations (England) 2006 supra (the '2006 Regulations'), which also apply and enforce Regulation 882/2004. The regulations provide for the designation of the Secretary of State and local authorities, including food authorities, as competent authorities for the purposes of Regulation 882/2004 art 4.1. The designations relate to: (1) animal health and welfare rules; (2) food law which concerns controls on animals; (3) feed law not listed in the 2006 Regulations Sch 3; and (4) food law concerning controls on food excluded from the designations in the 2006 Regulations, namely: (a) organic foods, including imported organic food products; (b) protected name food products and specific character food products; (c) veterinary medicines residues; (d) pesticides residues; (e) the import from third countries of, and intra-Community trade in, products of animal origin; and (f) beef labelling. The regulations also relate to transmissible spongiform Encephalopathies in relation to testing, including sampling, controls on bovine, ovine and caprine animals slaughtered for human consumption. The designations do not include medicated feedingstuffs and zootechnical additives, which are covered in the Veterinary Medicines Regulations 2006, SI 2006/2407, Sch 5. Specifically, the regulations (i) provide for the exchange of information between competent authorities in England and elsewhere in the United Kingdom, and in the European Union; (ii) create independent powers for a competent authority's auditors to conduct audits; (iii) make provision for the Secretary of State to call for information from a local authority about its audits; and for him to require an auditor to carry out an audit of that local authority's official controls as a competent authority; (iv) provide that where the Secretary of State arranges that the Food Standards Agency is to carry out an audit for purposes of Regulation 882/2004 of relevant legislation under the regulations, monitoring provisions of the 2006 Regulations apply together with the corresponding enforcement provisions from the 2006 Regulations; (v) supplement existing powers of inspectors so that they may bring Commission experts with them for purposes of the Commission's own audits; (vi) make provisions to facilitate assistance and co-operation between member states required under Regulation 882/2004, in particular to enable officials of the Commission and other member states to attend with an inspector who investigates suspected breaches under the relevant legislation;(vii) provide for the enforcement of the regulations; and (viii) amend the 2006 Regulations so as to amend the definition of 'relevant food law'.

1378   Food safety—official feed and food controls—Wales

The Official Feed and Food Controls (Wales) Regulations 2006, SI 2006/590 (in force on 8 March 2006), which replace the 2005 Regulations, SI 2005/3254, provide for the execution and enforcement of EC Parliament and Council Regulation 882/2004 on official controls performed to ensure the verification of compliance with feed and food law, animal health and animal welfare rules and impose prohibitions on the introduction of certain feed and food into Wales in implementation of European Parliament and Council Regulation 178/2002, laying down the general principles and requirements of food law, establishing the European Food Safety Authority and laying down procedures in matters of food safety. In particular, the regulations (1) designate specified bodies as competent authorities for the purposes of Regulation 882/2004; (2) provide for the exchange and provision of information by competent authorities; (3) enable a competent authority to require a control body to provide information and make records available; (4) provide that a person who (a) fails to comply with a requirement to provide information or make records available; or (b) in purported compliance with such a requirement, furnishes false or misleading information, is guilty of an offence; (5) provide for the issue of codes of recommended practice to feed and food authorities by the National Assembly for Wales (6) accord the Food Standards Agency the function of monitoring the performance of enforcement authorities in enforcing certain legislation; (7) confer powers on the Agency, for the purpose of monitoring such performance, to require information to be provided and records to be made available, and to authorise individuals, who may thereby exercise certain powers, including a power of entry; (8) define various terms; (9) provide that a person who (a) obstructs a person exercising powers to enter premises, take samples or inspect and copy records; (b) fails to comply with requirements to provide information, make available records or provide facilities, records, information or other assistance; or (c) in purported compliance with such a requirement, furnishes false or misleading evidence, is guilty of an offence; (10) provide a right of appeal in respect of a decision of the competent authority concerning the approval of certain establishments; (11) permit an authorised officer of a competent authority to take with him a member of staff of the competent authority of another member state for the purpose of conducting an administrative inquiry; (12) provide that, when an enforcing officer, as defined, enters premises for the purpose of executing and enforcing official controls, that officer may take with him a Commission expert to enable that expert to carry out relevant functions; (13) provide that a person who enters premises under the powers referred to above and discloses any information obtained on the premises with regard to any trade secret is guilty of an offence unless that person does so in the performance of his duty; (14) specify the authorities which are responsible for executing and enforcing the provisions relating to offences; (15) confer powers of entry on authorised officers of an enforcement authority; (16) create an offence of obstructing such an officer acting in the execution of his duties; (17) prescribe the penalties for offences; (18) specify the time limit for bringing prosecutions for offences; (19) provide that the Commissioners for Her Majesty's Revenue and Customs are to carry out the functions given to customs services under specified provisions of Regulation 882/2004; (20) make provision for the deferred enforcement and execution of the import provisions until a product reaches its destination; (21) prohibit the introduction into Wales of certain feed and food unless specified conditions are met; (22) provide for the checking of products introduced into Wales; (23) provide that an enforcement authority has the power to do anything that a competent authority may do under specified provisions of Regulation 882/2004, and is the competent authority for certain purposes; (24) provide for the service of notices when an authorised officer of an enforcement authority wishes to take certain measures or exercise certain powers; (25) provide a right of appeal in respect of the service of such a notice; (26) provide for the National

Assembly for Wales or the Agency, by written declaration, to suspend or impose conditions on the introduction into Wales of any product from a third country where either of them learns or reasonably suspects that any food or feed that has been or may be introduced into Wales from that third country is likely to constitute a serious risk to animal or public health; (27) provide for charges to be payable in relation to controls carried out on consignments; (28) provide for the procurement and analysis of samples of food for the purposes of the execution and enforcement of the import provisions; (29) confer powers of entry on authorised officers of a food authority in relation to the execution and enforcement of the import provisions; (30) create the offence of obstructing an officer acting in the execution of the import provisions; (31) create offences of contravening or failing to comply with specified regulations and failing to comply with a notice served under the import provisions, and provide for penalties for offences under those provisions; (32) prescribe the time limit for bringing prosecutions for such offences; (33) provide that, where the commission of an offence is due to the act or default of some other person, that person is guilty of the offence; (34) provide that, in proceedings for an offence, it is a defence for the accused to prove that he took all reasonable precautions and exercised all due diligence to avoid the commission of the offence; (35) make provision in relation to offences by bodies corporate and Scottish partnerships; (36) provide for the protection of officers acting in good faith; and (37) make provision for the service of documents. SI 2005/3368 is amended.

1379 Food safety—smoke flavourings—validity of EC legislation

See Case C-66/04 *United Kingdom v European Parliament*, para 2987.

1380 Meat—inspections and control for certain substances and residues—charges

The Charges for Inspections and Controls (Amendment) Regulations 2006, SI 2006/756 (in force on 6 April 2006), further amends the 1997 Regulations, SI 1997/2893, by clarifying provision concerning charges imposed in connection with a surveillance programme for residues of veterinary medicines and certain other substances.

1381 Meat—official controls on live animals and animal products—charges—England

The Meat (Official Controls Charges) (England) Regulations 2006, SI 2006/2705 (in force on 1 January 2007), (1) replace the 2005 Regulations, SI 2005/2983; (2) require the Agency to notify the operator of each slaughterhouse, game-handling establishment and cutting plant in which official controls have been exercised of the official controls charge that has arisen; (3) provide that any official controls charge notified to the operator is payable by the operator to the Agency on demand; (4) allow the Agency to refuse to exercise any further official controls at given premises where, despite a Court order requiring the operator of the premises to pay the official controls charge for which he is liable, he fails to comply with the order; (5) require persons to supply the Agency on demand with (i) such information as it may reasonably require for the purpose of calculating the official controls charge or notifying the operator of it; and (ii) such evidence as it may reasonably require to verify the information provided; (6) provide that a person is guilty of an offence where (a) in response to a demand for information or evidence, he knowingly or recklessly furnishes false or misleading information; or (b) without reasonable excuse, fails to comply within a reasonable time with a demand for information or evidence; and (7) set out how the official controls charge is to be calculated.

1382 Meat—official controls on live animals and animal products—charges—Wales

The Meat (Official Controls Charges) (Wales) Regulations 2006, SI 2006/3245 (in force on 1 January 2007), which replace the 2005 Regulations, SI 2005/3370, and provide for the execution and enforcement of EC Parliament and Council Regulation 882/2004 arts 26, 27. In particular, the regulations (1) require the Food Standards Agency to notify the operator of each slaughterhouse, game-handling establishment and cutting plant in which official controls have been exercised of the official controls charge that has arisen in relation to those official controls; (2) provide that any official controls charge so notified is payable by the operator to the Agency on demand; (3) allow the Agency to refuse to exercise any further official controls at given premises where, the operator of those premises refuses to comply with a court order requiring him to pay the official controls charge for which he is liable; (4) require persons to supply the Agency on demand with such (a) information as the Agency may reasonably require for the purpose of calculating the official controls charge or notifying an operator of it; and (b) evidence as the Agency may reasonably require to verify such information; (5) provide that a person who, in response to a demand for information or evidence, knowingly or recklessly furnishes false or misleading information, or without reasonable excuse fails to comply within a reasonable time with a demand for information or evidence, is guilty of an offence; and (6) set out how the official controls charge is to be calculated.

1383 Olive oil—marketing standards

The Olive Oil (Marketing Standards) (Amendment) Regulations 2006, SI 2006/3367 (in force on 10 January 2007), amend the 2003 Regulations, SI 2003/2577, by updating the reference in those regulations to EC Commission Regulation 1019/2002 so as to take account of an amendment by EC Commission Regulation 1044/2006 on marketing standards for olive oil.

1384 Rice products—market restriction—England

The Rice Products (Restriction on First Placing on the Market) (England) Regulations 2006, SI 2006/2921 (in force on 9 November 2006), implement, in relation to England, EC Commission Decision 2006/601, as amended, on emergency measures regarding the non-authorised genetically modified organism 'LL RICE 601' in rice products. The regulations (1) prohibit the first placing on the market of any rice product, except where (a) it is accompanied by an original analytical report satisfying specified requirements and confirming that the product does not contain the genetically modified rice, LL RICE 601; (b) official sampling and analysis carried out in accordance with specified methods and within a specified time limit shows that the product does not contain such rice; and (c) specified requirements for split consignments are complied with; (2) provide that a person who knowingly contravenes that prohibition is guilty of an offence and prescribe penalties for that offence; (3) provide for enforcement; and (4) apply, with modifications, certain provisions of the Food Safety Act 1990.

1385 Rice products—market restriction—Wales

The Rice Products (Restriction on First Placing on the Market) (Wales) Regulations 2006, SI 2006/2923 (in force on 9 November 2006), implement, in relation to Wales, EC Commission Decision 2006/601, as amended, on emergency measures regarding the non-authorised genetically modified organism 'LL RICE 601' in rice products. The regulations (1) prohibit the first placing on the market of any rice product, except where (a) it is accompanied by an original analytical report satisfying specified requirements and confirming that the product does not contain the genetically modified rice LL RICE 601; (b) official sampling and analysis carried out in accordance with specified methods and within a specified time limit shows that the product does not contain such rice; and (c) specified requirements for split consignments are complied with; (2) provide that a person who knowingly contravenes that prohibition is guilty of an offence and prescribe penalties for that offence; (3) provide for enforcement; and (4) apply, with modifications, certain provisions of the Food Safety Act 1990.

The Rice Products (Restriction on First Placing on the Market) (Wales) (Amendment) Regulations 2006, SI 2006/2969 (in force on 15 November 2006), make a minor amendment to the principal 2006 Regulations supra.

1386 Slaughterhouses—pig carcases—grading—England

The Pig Carcase (Grading) (Amendment) (England) Regulations 2006, SI 2006/2192 (in force on 5 September 2006), amend the 1994 Regulations, SI 1994/2155, and incorporate the amendments of EC Commission Decision 2004/374, which amend EC Commission Decision 2004/370, and remove certain rules for the grading of pig carcases in the United Kingdom. The regulations also (1) update the reference to the Commission Regulation so as to refer to EC Commission Regulation 3127/94 as amended; (2) provide for carcases to be weighed in an alternative way; (3) provide for carcases to be marked in an alternative way; and (4) provide for notices to be served by fax and other electronic communication. SI 2003/2949, and 2004/1505 are revoked.

FOREIGN RELATIONS LAW

Halsbury's Laws of England (4th edn) vol 18(2) (Reissue) paras 601–1046

Articles

For articles relating to this title please refer to the Table of Articles at the beginning of the Abridgment.

1387 Asylum

See BRITISH NATIONALITY, IMMIGRATION AND ASYLUM.

1388 Consular fees

The Consular Fees (Amendment) Order 2006, SI 2006/1912 (in force on 5 October 2006), amends the 2005 Order, SI 2005/1465, by increasing the fees for issuing passports in the United Kingdom, and providing that the fee for issuing a biometric passport in the United Kingdom is the same as the fee for issuing a non-biometric passport in the United Kingdom.

1389   Jurisdiction of English courts—act of foreign state—principle of non-justiciability—claim arising out of attempted coup

The first claimant, the President of the Republic of Equatorial Guinea, and the second claimant, the Republic of Equatorial Guinea, brought proceedings arising out of an alleged conspiracy to overthrow the government by means of a private coup, to seize control of the state and its valuable assets, to kill or injure the first claimant and to install the sixth defendant, who was an Equato-Guinean living in Spain, as the new President. The coup failed. The judge struck out the first claimant's claim for damages for assault, conspiracy and intentional infliction of harm by unlawful means against the defendants, but refused to strike out the claim for an injunction. The claimants appealed, and the defendants cross-appealed against the refusal to strike out the claim for an injunction. An issue arose as to whether the claims were justiciable or whether the court should decline to entertain them because they amounted to an exercise of sovereign power by Equatorial Guinea within the jurisdiction of the English courts. *Held*, the critical question on the issue of justiciability was whether, in bringing a claim, a claimant was doing an act which was of a sovereign character or which was done by virtue of sovereign authority, and whether the claim involved the exercise or assertion of a sovereign right. If so, then the court would not determine or enforce the claim. The claims by the second claimant were not justiciable, and the court would decline to entertain them because they amounted to an exercise of the sovereign power of Equatorial Guinea within the jurisdiction of the English courts. That applied both to the claim for special damages and to the claim for an injunction. Judgment would be given accordingly.

Mbasogo v Logo Ltd [2006] EWCA Civ 1370, [2006] All ER (D) 263 (Oct) (Court of Appeal: Sir Anthony Clarke MR, Dyson and Moses LJJ). *Austria (Emperor) v Day and Kossuth* (1861) 3 De GF & J 217, CA, considered.

1390   Jurisdiction of English courts—act of foreign state—principle of non-justiciability—refusal by Secretary of State to intervene

See *R (on the application of Al Rawi) v Secretary of State for Foreign and Commonwealth Affairs*, para 96.

1391   North Korea—United Nations measures—overseas territories

The North Korea (United Nations Measures) (Overseas Territories) Order 2006, SI 2006/3327 (in force on 16 December 2006), made under the United Nations Act 1946, gives effect in the listed territories to Resolution 1718(2006) adopted by the Security Council of the United Nations on 14 October 2006. In particular, the order (1) requires the governor of each territory to maintain a list of persons and entities designated by the Committee of the Security Council as subject to an asset freeze, and to publish the list in the official gazette of the territory, as well as a list of restricted goods and prohibited luxury goods as necessary; (2) makes it a criminal offence for any person to supply restricted or prohibited luxury goods without a licence; (3) prohibits the exportation of restricted or prohibited luxury goods and makes it a criminal offence to contravene this prohibition; (4) prohibits the provision of technical or financial assistance relating to restricted goods and makes it a criminal offence to contravene this prohibition; (5) prohibits the use of ships, aircraft and vehicles to carry restricted goods or prohibited luxury goods to North Korea, and makes it a criminal offence to contravene this prohibition; (6) prohibits the procurement of restricted goods from North Korea, and makes it a criminal offence to contravene this prohibition; (7) prohibits any dealing with funds, financial assets and economic resources of designated persons, and makes it a criminal offence to contravene this prohibition; (8) prohibits making funds, financial assets and economic resources available to designated persons, and makes it a criminal offence to contravene this prohibition; (9) makes it a criminal offence to circumvent the above prohibitions or to facilitate the commission of an offence relating to these prohibitions; (10) gives the governor power to direct that a person or entity suspected of being controlled or directed, or in the case of an entity, owned, controlled or directed, by a designated person, or of acting on behalf of or at the direction of a designated person is to be treated for the purposes of the prohibitions and offences as if he were a designated person; the order also creates an appeal process in respect of any such direction; (11) provides a licensing procedure to enable, for humanitarian purposes, certain dealings or activities to be exempted from the asset freeze prohibitions; (12) provides for penalties applying on conviction for offences under the order; (13) makes provision about information and evidence; and (14) contains the list of prohibited luxury goods.

1392   Outer space—legislation—extension to Bermuda

The Outer Space Act 1986 (Bermuda) Order 2006, SI 2006/2959 (in force on 14 December 2006), extends the Outer Space Act 1986 to Bermuda, subject to specified exceptions and modifications.

1393   Privileges and immunities—Commonwealth countries and Ireland

The Commonwealth Countries and Ireland (Immunities and Privileges) (Amendment) Order 2006, SI 2006/309 (in force on 1 April 2006), affords partial relief from general rates to the offices and residence of the Turks and Caicos Islands government representative in London.

1394   Privileges and immunities—European Organisation for Nuclear Research

The European Organisation for Nuclear Research (Privileges and Immunities) Order 2006, SI 2006/1922 (in force on a date to be notified in the London Gazette), confers the legal capacities of a body corporate on the European Organisation for Nuclear Research and confers privileges and immunities on representatives of its members attending meetings of the organisation, its director-general and officials.

1395   Privileges and immunities—International Criminal Court

The International Criminal Court (Immunities and Privileges) (No 1) Order 2006, SI 2006/1907 (in force on a date to be notified in the London Gazette), confers the legal capacities of a body corporate on the International Criminal Court and confers privileges and immunities on representatives of states participating in the proceedings of the court, its judges, prosecutor, deputy prosecutors, registrar, deputy registrar, staff of the office of the prosecutor, staff of the registry, other personnel recruited locally by the court, counsel and persons assisting defence counsel, witnesses, victims, experts and other persons required to be present at the seat of the court. SI 2002/793 is revoked.

The International Criminal Court (Immunities and Privileges) (No 2) Order 2006, SI 2006/1908 (in force on a date to be notified in the London Gazette), confers privileges and immunities on representatives of states participating in the Assembly of States Parties to the Rome Statute and its subsidiary organs, and representatives of states and intergovernmental organisations invited to Assembly meetings.

1396   Privileges and immunities—international organisations

The International Organisations (Immunities and Privileges) Miscellaneous Provisions Order 2006, SI 2006/1075 (in force on 12 April 2006), makes amendments to various orders consequential on the coming into force of the Civil Partnership Act 2004, so as to confer privileges and immunities on civil partners to the same extent, and in the same circumstances, as such privileges and immunities have been conferred on spouses of individuals specified in those orders.

1397   Privileges and immunities—state immunity—civil claim against foreign official— torture

The claimant in the first action issued proceedings against the Ministry of Interior of the Kingdom of Saudi Arabia ('the Kingdom'), and a servant or agent of the Kingdom, arising out of alleged false imprisonment and torture in the Kingdom. Permission was granted by the master without notice to serve the defendants out of the jurisdiction. The Kingdom applied to set aside service and to dismiss the claimant's claim on the ground of state immunity under the State Immunity Act 1978. The master set aside service of the proceedings and refused permission to serve the agent by an alternative method. The claimant appealed. In the second case, the claimants issued proceedings against four defendants who were also agents of the Kingdom, contending that they had been subjected to torture by the first two defendants, which the third and fourth defendants had caused or permitted or negligently failed to prevent. The master refused the claimants' without notice application to serve the proceedings out of the jurisdiction on the ground of state immunity under the 1978 Act, and the claimants appealed. The claimant's appeal in the first case was dismissed in relation to state immunity, but his appeal against refusal of permission to serve the agent out of the jurisdiction by an alternative method was allowed. The appeal of the other claimants against the refusal of permission to serve all four defendants out of the jurisdiction was allowed. On the appeal of the various parties against the adverse orders made, *held*, the court had been right to dismiss the claim against the Kingdom in the first case on the ground of state immunity. Moreover, an English court could not entertain torture claims against the individual defendants. A state could act only through its servants and agents; their official acts were the acts of the state, and the state's immunity in respect of them was fundamental to the principle of state immunity. The court's error in holding to the contrary had the effect that, while the Kingdom had been held to be immune, and the Ministry of the Interior, as a department of the government, had been held to be immune, the Minister of the Interior had not been. That had led the court to a second error: its conclusion that a civil claim against an individual torturer did not indirectly implead the state in any more objectionable respect than a criminal prosecution. A state was not criminally responsible in international or English law, and therefore could not be directly impleaded in criminal proceedings. It was, however, clear that a civil action against individual torturers based on acts of official torture did indirectly implead the state since their acts were attributable to it. Were those claims against the individual defendants to proceed and be upheld, the interests of the Kingdom would be obviously affected, even though it was not a named party. Judgment would be given accordingly.

Jones v Ministry of the Interior Al-Mamlaka Al-Arabiya as Sudiya; Mitchell v Al-Dali [2006] UKHL 26, [2007] 1 All ER 113 (House of Lords: Lords Bingham of Cornhill, Hoffmann, Rodger of Earlsferry, Walker of Gestingthorpe and Carswell). Decision of Court of Appeal [2004] EWCA Civ 1394, [2005] QB 699 (2004 Abr para 1255) reversed in part.

1398   Privileges and immunities—state immunity—jurisdiction—exceptions—submission to jurisdiction

The claimant, a Swedish company engaged in oil exploration and extraction, entered into a joint venture agreement with the first defendant state and the second defendant, a former state enterprise, to exploit various oil fields in Lithuania. The agreement contained an arbitration clause and also stated that both defendants waived their rights to sovereign immunity. A dispute arose between the parties, which was referred to arbitration. The arbitral panel made an award in favour of the claimant, and the claimant was given permission to enforce the award in England under the Arbitration Act 1996 s 101. The first defendant acknowledged service of the claim form seeking to enforce the award but applied to have it and the enforcement order set aside, arguing that the claim raised issues of state immunity. The claimant's application to have the first defendant's application struck out was dismissed. At the hearing of the first defendant's application, the claimant contended that the first defendant had waived its immunity in the agreement and that the State Immunity Act 1978 s 9, which provided that immunity did not apply in respect of proceedings in the courts of the United Kingdom where a state had agreed in writing to submit a dispute to arbitration, applied to enforcement proceedings, and in particular to proceedings which related to the enforcement of a foreign arbitral award. The judge accepted the claimants' contentions and the first defendant appealed. *Held*, the first defendant had agreed to submit disputes with the claimant to arbitration, and the first award had finally disposed of the issue as far as the parties were concerned. Under Lithuanian law an arbitration clause was regarded as an autonomous agreement, that is, an agreement which gave rise to rights and obligations which existed independently of the contract within which it was found, and an agreement to arbitrate under the rules conferred on the arbitrators jurisdiction to decide whether they had jurisdiction in any given case. By agreeing to independent arbitration, the parties had conferred on the arbitrators jurisdiction to determine that question and were therefore bound by their award. Moreover, the claimant's application for leave to enforce the second award fell within s 9(1), and the first defendant was therefore unable to claim immunity in respect of it. The first award established that the first defendant had agreed in writing to refer disputes to arbitration and was therefore sufficient to bring the case within s 9. There was no basis for construing s 9, particularly when viewed in the context of the provisions of s 13 dealing with execution, as excluding proceedings relating to the enforcement of a foreign arbitral award. Arbitration was a consensual procedure and the principle underlying s 9 was that, if a state had agreed to submit to arbitration, it had rendered itself amenable to such process as might be necessary to render the arbitration effective. Accordingly, the appeal would be dismissed.

Svenska Petroleum Exploration AB v Government of the Republic of Lithuania [2006] EWCA Civ 1529, [2006] All ER (D) 156 (Nov) (Court of Appeal: Sir Anthony Clarke MR, Scott Baker and Moore-Bick LJJ).

1399   Restrictive measures—Ivory Coast

The Ivory Coast (Restrictive Measures) (Overseas Territories) (Amendment) Order 2006, SI 2006/610 (in force on 10 March 2006), amends the 2005 Order, SI 2005/242, so as to give effect to the ban on the importation of rough diamonds from the Ivory Coast.

1400   Restrictive measures—Uzbekistan

The Uzbekistan (Restrictive Measures) (Overseas Territories) Order 2006, SI 2006/310 (in force on 16 February 2006), which applies to specific territories, gives effect to EC Common Position 2005/792 CFSP. In particular, the order prohibits (1) the delivery or supply of arms and related matériel to Uzbekistan, and the use of vessels, aircraft and vehicles for the carriage of such goods to Uzbekistan; (2) the provision of technical assistance, brokering services and other services related to military activities and to the provision, manufacture, maintenance and use of arms and related matériel to any person, entity or body in, or for use in Uzbekistan; and (3) the provision of financing or financial assistance related to military activities to any person, entity or body in, or for use in Uzbekistan. The order also makes provision as to inspections, investigations and enforcement.

1401   State responsibility—act of executive—invasion of foreign territory—lawfulness

See *R (on the application of Gentle) v Prime Minister*, para 1536.

1402   United Nations—international tribunals—Former Yugoslavia and Rwanda

The United Nations (International Tribunals) (Former Yugoslavia and Rwanda) (Amendment) Order 2006, SI 2006/1923 (in force on 22 August 2006), further amends the 1996 Order, SI 1996/716, so as to reflect the decisions of the Security Council of the United Nations in Resolutions 1411 (2002), 1431 (2002), 1481 (2003), 1597 (2005), and 1660 (2006). The order also further amends the 1996 Order, SI 1996/1296, so as to reflect the decisions of the Security Council of the United Nations in Resolutions 1411 (2002), 1503 (2003), and 1512 (2003). The order also makes provision to implement the decision of the Security Council of the United Nations in Resolution 1431 (2002) which established a pool of ad litem judges in the International Tribunal for Rwanda.

The United Nations (International Tribunals) (Former Yugoslavia and Rwanda) (Amendment) (No 2) Order 2006, SI 2006/3326 (in force on 22 January 2007), amends SI 2006/1923 supra so as to remedy a technical defect, which was the deletion of certain articles from the United Nations (International Tribunal) (Rwanda) Order 1996, SI 1996/1296, Schedule, which were not included in the Statute of the International Tribunal for Rwanda.

1403   United Nations—measures—Al-Qaida and Taliban

The Al-Qaida and Taliban (United Nations Measures) Order 2006, SI 2006/2952 (in force on 16 November 2006), amends the 2002 Order, SI 2002/111, and gives effect in the United Kingdom to the following Security Council resolutions adopted by the Security Council of the United Nations: 1267 (1999), 1333 (2000), 1363 (2001), 1390 (2002), 1452 (2002), 1455 (2003), 1453 (2004) and 1617 (2005). The order also provides for enforcement of EC Council Regulation 881/2002, as amended, on specific restrictive measures directed against certain person and entities associated with Usama bin Laden, the Al-Qaida network and the Taliban. The order (1) provides that Usama bin Laden, persons designated by the committee of the Security Council and those identified in a direction given by the Treasury are designated persons; (2) confers a power on the Treasury to give a direction to designate a person if one of a number of specified conditions is fulfilled and Treasury have reasonable grounds to suspect that the person is or may be (a) Usama bin Laden; (b) a designated person; (c) any person owned or controlled, directly or indirectly, by such a person; or (d) any person acting on behalf or at the direction of such a person; (3) makes provision about the Treasury's directions, including a requirement for the Treasury to take steps that it considers appropriate to publicise the direction or to inform only certain persons and to notify the person identified in the direction; (4) confers a power on the Treasury to specify that information contained in the direction is to be treated as confidential, imposes a prohibition on disclosing such information except with lawful authority and makes it a criminal offence to contravene this prohibition and provides that the Court may grant an injunction to prevent a breach; (5) prohibits any dealing with funds, financial assets and economic resources of designated persons, anyone owned or controlled by them or anyone acting on their behalf or at their direction; (6) prohibits making funds, financial assets or economic resources available to anyone in respect of whom the provision of freezing funds and economic resources of designated persons applies; (7) makes it a criminal offence to circumvent the prohibitions or to facilitate the commission of an offence relating to a prohibition; (8) provides a licensing procedure to enable, for humanitarian and other purposes, certain acts to be exempted from the prohibitions; (9) confers a power on the Treasury to delegate its functions under the order; and (10) confirms that the provisions of this order apply to the Crown but, in the event of a contravention, the Crown is not criminally liable. SI 2002/251 is revoked.

1404   United Nations—measures—Lebanon and Syria

The Lebanon and Syria (United Nations Measures) (Overseas Territories) Order 2006, SI 2006/311 (in force on 16 February 2006), gives effect to the territories listed in the United Nations Security Council Resolution 1636 Sch 1 of 31 October 2005, which requires certain measures to be taken against designated individuals suspected of an involvement in a specific terrorist bombing. The measures include the freezing of funds, financial assets and economic resources of the designated individuals to ensure that any funds, financial assets and economic resources are not made available to them.

1405   United Nations—measures—North Korea

The North Korea (United Nations Measures) Order 2006, SI 2006/2958 (in force on 16 November 2006), gives effect in the United Kingdom to Security Council of the United Nations resolution 1718(2006). The order (1) provides that the persons designated by the Security Council, a Security Council Committee or the Treasury are designated persons; (2) provides that the Treasury can give directions to designate persons if one of the specified conditions is fulfilled and that the Treasury have reasonable grounds to suspect that the person is or may be a person designated by the Security Council or the committee or a person acting on behalf of or at the direction of any such person; (3) makes provision about the Treasury's directions, including a requirement for the Treasury to take the steps it considers appropriate to publicise the direction; (4) prohibits any dealing with funds, financial assets and economic resources of designated persons; (5) prohibits making funds, financial assets or economic resources available to designated persons; (6) makes it a criminal offence to circumvent the prohibitions or to facilitate the commission of an offence relating to a prohibition; (7) provides a licensing procedure to enable, for humanitarian and other purposes, certain acts to be exempted from the prohibitions; (8) confers a power on the Treasury to delegate its functions under the order; (9) confirms that the provisions of this order apply to the Crown but, in the event of a contravention, the Crown is not criminally liable; and (10) makes provision about information and evidence.

1406　United Nations—measures—Sudan

The Sudan (United Nations Measures) Order 2006, SI 2006/1454 (in force on 9 June 2006), replaces the 2005 Order, SI 2005/1259, and gives effect in the United Kingdom to United Nations Security Council Resolution 1591(2005), and United Nations Security Council Resolution 1672(2006), and provides for the enforcement of EC Council Regulations 1184/2005 and 760/2006. In particular, the order (1) requires the Treasury to maintain a list of designated persons and to make the list publicly available; (2) prohibits any dealing with funds, financial assets and economic resources of designated persons; (3) prohibits making funds, financial assets and economic resources available to designated persons; (4) makes it a criminal offence to circumvent the prohibitions or to facilitate the commission of an offence relating to a prohibition; (5) confers a power on the Treasury to direct that a person suspected of being owned or controlled, directly or indirectly, by a designated person or of acting on behalf of or at the direction of a designated person is to be treated, for the purposes of the prohibitions and offences, as if he were a designated person; (6) provides a licensing procedure to enable, for humanitarian purposes, certain acts to be exempted from the prohibitions; and (7) makes provision about information and evidence.

1407　United Nations—measures—terrorism

See CRIMINAL LAW.

FORESTRY

Halsbury's Laws of England (4th edn) vol 19(1) (Reissue) paras 1–100

1408　Forest reproductive material—marketing

The Forest Reproductive Material (Great Britain) (Amendment) Regulations 2006, SI 2006/2530 (in force on 9 October 2006), amend the 2002 Regulations, SI 2002/3026, so as to implement EC Commission Decision 2005/942, authorising member states to take decisions under EC Council Directive 1999/105 on assurances afforded in respect of forest reproductive material produced in third countries, and EC Commission Regulations 69/2004, authorising derogations from certain provisions of Directive 1999/105 in respect of the marketing of forest reproductive material derived from certain basic material. The regulations also (1) amend the definitions of 'master certificate' so as to include an official certificate from a third country, and of 'official body' so as to include official bodies in third countries; (2) exempt, in the case of Pinus pinaster Ait, from a specified requirement; (3) make provisions for the conditions under which forest reproductive material from third countries may be marketed; (4) add the length of time in nursery to the information which a registered supplier must provide when dispatching forest reproductive material to a destination in another member state; (5) remove the prohibition on importing forest reproductive material in respect of certain material from certain third countries, providing that certain conditions are met; (6) add phytosanitary certificates and import notifications to the list of documents which must be retained by a registered supplier or other person who undertakes the collecting or production, storage, processing or transportation of forest reproductive material; and (7) insert new procedural provisions on the period for bringing a prosecution under the 2002 Regulations.

1409　Forestry Commissioners—regulatory reform

The Regulatory Reform (Forestry) Order 2006, SI 2006/780 (in force on 16 March 2006), amends the Forestry Act 1967 so as to (1) permit the Forestry Commissioners to delegate their power to charge for facilities provided on land placed at their disposal, in England, by the Secretary of State or, in Wales, by the National Assembly for Wales; (3) provide the Commissioners with incidental powers to form and, subject to Treasury approval, invest in bodies corporate, to make loans to establish charitable trusts and to act, and to appoint persons to act, as officers of bodies corporate or as trustees of charitable trusts for the purpose of their functions under the Act or under the 1968 Act so far as relating to land in England and Wales; (4) permit the Commissioners to exploit intellectual property arising from research carried out by the Commissioners or which they have aided in carrying out; (5) allow the Commissioners to serve a restocking notice on any person who appears to them to have committed an offence in England and Wales under the 1967 Act s 17; (6) provide that the same provisions that apply to an applicant for a felling licence apply to a person served with a restocking notice; (7) permit the Commissioners to delegate their power to charge and make any arrangements entered into between the Commissioners and another person in relation to the Commissioners to provide or arrange for or assist in the provision of facilities for tourism, recreation or sport on land placed at their disposal, in England, by the Secretary of State, and, in Wales, by the National Assembly for Wales, and to charge in connection with those facilities.

1410   Forestry projects—environmental impact assessment

The Environmental Impact Assessment (Forestry) (England and Wales) (Amendment) Regulations 2006, SI 2006/3106 (in force on 31 December 2006), amend the 1999 Regulations, SI 1999/2228, so as to implement amendments made to EC Council Directive 85/337 on the assessment of the effects of certain public and private projects on the environment by EC Council Directive 2003/35. In particular, the regulations (1) amend the definition of 'countryside bodies' to include any other body designated by statute as having specific environmental responsibilities; (2) require the Forestry Commissioners, in exercising their power to direct that a particular project is exempt from the environmental assessment requirements, to consider whether another form of assessment would be appropriate and to provide information obtained under that assessment to the public; (3) substitute for the reference to the Environmental Information Regulations 1992, SI 1992/3240, which are now revoked, a reference to provisions in the Environmental Information Regulations 2004, SI 2004/3391; (4) extend the current requirements for the supply of information by the applicant for consent; (5) require the applicant to notify the public of the nature of the decision the Forestry Commissioners may take in relation to the application for consent; and (6) require the Forestry Commissioners to include in a public register directions received from the appropriate authority.

FUEL AND ENERGY

Halsbury's Laws of England (4th edn) vol 19(1) (Reissue) paras 501–800, vol 19(2) (Reissue) paras 801–1922

Articles

For articles relating to this title please refer to the Table of Articles at the beginning of the Abridgment.

1411   Atomic energy—disclosure of information—radiological emergencies—repairs to nuclear submarine

The European Commission received a number of complaints concerning the repairs that were being carried out by the United Kingdom government to a nuclear submarine in Gibraltar. Under EC Council Directive 89/618 art 5(3), information concerning health protection measures had to be communicated to the public in the event of a radiological emergency. The Commission applied for a declaration that, in relation to the repairs, the United Kingdom government had failed to comply with its obligations under art 5(3). *Held*, applying settled principles, the use of nuclear energy for military purposes was outside the scope of all the provisions of Directive 89/618. Judgment would be given accordingly.

Case C-65/04 *European Commission v United Kingdom* [2006] All ER (D) 152 (Mar) (ECJ: First Chamber).

1412   Atomic energy—nuclear industries—security

The Nuclear Industries Security (Amendment) Regulations 2006, SI 2006/2815 (in force on 25 November 2006), amend the 2003 Regulations, SI 2003/403, so as to provide that any person who has possession or control of sensitive nuclear information and is involved in activities on a nuclear site or concerning uranium enrichment must maintain appropriate security standards to minimise risk of loss, theft or unauthorised disclosure of sensitive nuclear information or uranium enrichment equipment or software, and must ensure that each of their officers, employees, contractors and consultants is familiar with the relevant security standards. They are also required to comply with directions from the Secretary of State regarding the use or employment of an officer, employee, contractor or consultant and to report to the Secretary of State any matter which may affect the security of sensitive nuclear information or uranium enrichment equipment or software.

1413   Climate change agreements—eligible facilities

The Climate Change Agreements (Eligible Facilities) Regulations 2006, SI 2006/60 (in force on 21 January 2006), apply to installations covered by the Finance Act 2000 Sch 6 para 51 by virtue of the Climate Change Agreements (Energy-intensive Installations) Regulations 2006, SI 2006/59, and to sites on which there is such an installation or part of an installation. In particular, the regulations (1) provide that such an installation will be taken to be a facility eligible for inclusion in a climate change agreement where (a) the installation or site is an eligible facility under the 2001 Regulations, SI 2001/662; (b) the installation or site meets the energy intensity criteria or belongs to a business sector that meets the energy intensity criteria; and (c) the energy to be supplied to the installation or site will be used for the purpose of carrying out an eligible process; (2) set out when the energy intensity criteria will be met; and (3) define an 'eligible process' as being a process or activity or combination of processes or activities carried out at an installation or site which, when taken alone or together within the business sector to which the installation or site belongs, meets the energy intensity criteria.

The Climate Change Agreements (Eligible Facilities) (Amendment) Regulations 2006, SI 2006/1931 (in force on 15 August 2006), amend SI 2006/60 supra by adding new descriptions of relevant processes and activities carried out at an installation or a site on which there is an installation that are relevant for the purposes of determining whether such installation or site is to be taken to be a facility that is eligible for inclusion in a climate change agreement.

1414   Climate change agreements—energy-intensive installations

The Climate Change Agreements (Energy-intensive Installations) Regulations 2006, SI 2006/59 (in force on 21 January 2006), expand the types of installation that a facility, which is taken as being covered by a climate change agreement where a reduced rate of climate change levy on supplies of taxable commodities may apply, to include installations for (1) separating from air, and then compressing or liquefying nitrogen, oxygen or argon; (2) extracting and processing kaolinitic clay in combination with its accessory minerals; (3) processing calcium carbonate based minerals for use as filler or whitener; (4) heat-treating metals; (5) horticulture; (6) manufacturing textiles; and (7) producing plastic film.

1415   Climate Change and Sustainable Energy Act 2006

The Climate Change and Sustainable Energy Act 2006 makes provision about the reduction of emissions of greenhouse gases, the alleviation of fuel poverty, the promotion of microgeneration and the use of heat produced from renewable sources, compliance with building regulations relating to emissions of greenhouse gases and the use of fuel and power, the renewables obligation relating to the generation and supply of electricity and the adjustment of transmission charges for electricity. The Act received the royal assent on 21 June 2006 and came into force in part on that day. Further provisions came into force on 21 August 2006 and 1 January 2007. The remaining provisions come into force on a day or days to be appointed. For details of commencement, see the commencement table in the title STATUTES.

Section 1 defines the principal purpose of the 2006 Act as being to enhance the United Kingdom's contribution to combating climate change. The Secretary of State is required by s 2 to produce an annual report on greenhouse gas emissions, including steps taken by government to reduce such emissions. Under s 3, the Secretary of State must publish an energy measures report, to which every local authority must have regard when exercising its functions. A duty is imposed on the Secretary of State by s 4 to designate at least one target in respect of the number of microgeneration systems installed in England and Wales. Where a target is so designated, the annual sustainable energy report published by the Secretary of State must contain appropriate information about things done for the purpose of meeting the target: s 5. By virtue of s 6, each sustainable energy report must include appropriate information about things done for the purpose of implementing the strategy for the promotion of microgeneration published under the Energy Act 2004 s 82. For the purposes of increasing the amount of electricity generated by microgeneration, the Secretary of State is authorised to make relevant modifications to conditions of distribution or supply licences: 2006 Act s 7. Consultation requirements in relation to such modifications are imposed by s 8. The Gas and Electricity Markets Authority must keep under review activities connected with the generation of electricity by microgeneration or with the transmission and supply of electricity so generated: s 9. Under s 10, the Secretary of State is required to carry out a review of the effect of certain development orders in order to determine the provision such orders should make in relation to microgeneration. Building regulations may be made which provide for the production of heat or the generation of electricity by microgeneration: s 11. Section 12 provides that each sustainable energy report must also contain details of the progress made towards reaching targets for the energy efficiency of residential accommodation, emissions of carbon dioxide and the number of households in which one or more persons are living in fuel poverty. Time limits are provided by s 13 for prosecuting contraventions of building regulations relating to emissions and the use of fuel and power. The Secretary of State is under a duty to report on the steps taken to secure compliance with provisions of building regulations relating to the conservation of fuel and power or reducing emissions of greenhouse gases: s 14. Section 15 enables the Secretary of State to impose carbon emissions reduction targets on gas transporters and suppliers, including in relation to measures for increasing the amount of electricity generated, or heat produced, by microgeneration. Similar provision is made by s 16 in respect of electricity distributors and suppliers. Section 17 introduces the Schedule, which makes various consequential amendments. The Secretary of State is required to publish a report on the contribution that is capable of being made by dynamic demand technologies to reducing emissions of greenhouse gases (s 18), and to take such steps as he considers appropriate to promote community energy projects (s 19). Parish councils and community councils are entitled by virtue of s 20 to encourage or promote various local energy saving measures. Under s 21, the Secretary of State has a duty to take appropriate steps to promote the use of heat produced from renewable sources. Section 22 requires a sustainable energy report to contain information about steps taken to promote community energy projects and the use of renewable heat. The Gas and Electricity Markets Authority may issue a green certificate in relation to the generation by two or more generating stations of energy from renewable sources: s 23. Section 24 makes further provision in relation to green certificates, and s 25 provides for the adjustment of transmission charges for electricity. Section 26 deals with interpretation, s 27 with expenses, s 28 with commencement and s 29 with the short title and extent.

Amendments, repeals and revocations
The list below, which is not exhaustive, mentions repeals and amendments which are or will be effective when the Act is fully in force.

Specific provisions of a number of Acts are amended or repealed. These include: Building Act 1984 Sch 1 para 7; Gas Act 1986 s 33BC; Electricity Act 1989 ss 32, 32B, 41A, 47; Sustainable Energy Act 2003 s 1; and Energy Act 2004 s 185.

1416 Climate change levy—general provisions

The Climate Change Levy (General) (Amendment) Regulations 2006, SI 2006/954 (in force on 1 April 2006), further amend 2001 Regulations, SI 2001/838, by making consequential amendments to the rules about how exemptions from climate change levy are claimed and made available following the abolition after 31 March 2006 of the half-rate for supplies of electricity, gas and solid fuels to horticultural producers.

1417 Electricity—electromagnetic compatibility

The Electromagnetic Compatibility (Amendment) Regulations 2006, SI 2006/1449 (in force on 28 June 2006), amend the 2005 Regulations, SI 2005/281, so as to provide that only radio equipment and telecommunications terminal equipment covered by EC Directive 1995/5 on radio equipment and telecommunications terminal equipment and the mutual recognition of their conformity is excluded from the application of the 2005 Regulations.

The Electromagnetic Compatibility Regulations 2006, SI 2006/3418 (in force in part on 20 January 2007 and in part on 20 July 2007), implement European Parliament and Council Directive 2004/108 on the approximation of the laws of member states relating to electromagnetic compatibility and repealing EEC Directive 89/336. The regulations, which do not apply to a fixed installation put into service before 20 July 2007 unless it is modified after that date in a way that may affect its electromagnetic compatibility, replace the 2005 Regulations, SI 2005/281. In particular, the regulations (1) provide for the disapplication of certain regulations made under the Wireless Telegraphy Act 1949 s 10 to the extent that these regulations impose electromagnetic compatibility requirements, excluding radio frequency planning requirements, which must be complied with if apparatus to which the regulations apply is to be supplied or taken into service and used for the purpose for which it was intended; (2) impose essential requirements concerning the electromagnetic compatibility of equipment which must be complied with if such equipment is to be placed on the market or put into service, or both; (4) provide that apparatus may not be placed on the market unless the specified requirements have been complied with; (5) provide that apparatus may not be put into service unless the essential requirements are complied with when it is properly installed, maintained and used for its intended purpose; (6) provide that compliance can be demonstrated by the internal production control procedure or in addition through the appointment of a notified body; (7) set out provisions relating to the CE marking including the requirements for properly affixing the CE marking; (8) set out the provisions relating to the issue of an EC declaration of conformity; (9) provide for the retention of certain documents by the responsible person; (10) set out the provisions relating to the appointment and functions of United Kingdom notified bodies; (11) set out the general requirements relating to the putting into service of fixed installations, and provide for certain exemptions; (12) set out provisions relating to enforcement, including the appointment of enforcement authorities and their powers to make test purchases, search, seize and detain and require production of documents; (13) make provision for offences and provide for a defence of due diligence; (14) set out the powers of the court including power to require a matter to be remedied, power of forfeiture and recovery of costs of enforcement; and (15) make provision in respect of miscellaneous matters relating to service of documents, duty to inform the Secretary of State of certain actions and savings for certain privileges and actions taken under other enactments.

1418 Electricity—exemption—interconnector licence

The Electricity Act 1989 (Exemption from the Requirement for an Interconnector Licence) Order 2006, SI 2006/2002 (in force on 14 August 2006), grants exemption from the Electricity Act 1989 s 4(1)(d), which prohibits participation in the operation of an electricity interconnector without a licence, to five bodies, each of which participates in the operation of one of three electricity Interconnectors.

1419　Electricity—non-fossil fuel sources—arrangements

The Electricity from Non-Fossil Fuel Sources Arrangements (England and Wales) Order 2006, SI 2006/2388 (in force on 1 October 2006), modifies certain contracts between certain generators of electricity and the Non-Fossil Purchasing Agency Limited so that the intended financial incentive for generators to meet the requirements placed on them in relation to supplying heat is present.

1420　Electricity—offshore generating stations—applications for consent

The Electricity (Offshore Generating Stations) (Applications for Consent) Regulations 2006, SI 2006/2064 (in force on 1 October 2006), make provision in connection with applications under the Electricity Act 1989 s 36 for consent to construct, extend or operate an offshore generating station, and any application under s 36A for a declaration relating to public rights of navigation, where such an application is made with a s 36 application. Specifically, the regulations (1) identify the publications within which notice of an application for consent under the 1989 Act s 36 should be advertised; (2) provide that the notice must include a map showing the location of the generating station and indicate where such a map may be inspected; (3) identify the public consultation bodies on whom notice of an application under s 36 should be served; (4) make provision for service of notice of a s 36 application where no part of the place where the development is due to take place lies within the jurisdiction of a relevant planning authority; (5) provide that notices must be served on planning authorities likely to have an interest in the proposed development; (6) require an applicant when serving notice to state the time within which and the manner in which objections to a proposal should be notified to the Secretary of State; (7) require any objection by a relevant planning authority to be made within four months of service of notice of an application, where a development falls within the jurisdiction of that authority; (8) make provision for the publication of notice of any public inquiry to be held; (9) provide that such notice must state that a copy of the application, and of the map referred to in it, can be inspected at the same location or locations used to display the map pursuant to the requirement under head (2) above, or, if that is not possible, at a suitable alternative location as near as possible to it; (10) make provision for fees payable on applications for consent; and (11) disapply the Electricity (Applications for Consent) Regulations 1990, SI 1990/455, in relation to applications under the 1989 Act s 36 concerning offshore generating stations.

1421　Electricity—prepayment meter

The Electricity (Prepayment Meter) Regulations 2006, SI 2006/2010 (in force on 1 September 2006), enable an electricity supplier to collect sums through an electricity prepayment meter in prescribed circumstances. In particular, the regulations (1) allow an electricity prepayment meter to be used to collect sums relating to (a) the supply of electricity or the provision of an electricity meter at premises previously owned or occupied by the customer; and (b) the supply of gas or the provision of a gas meter, either at the premises where the prepayment meter is installed or at premises previously owned or occupied by the customer; (2) allow sums owing for such purposes to be consolidated with sums due for the supply of electricity or the provision of an electricity meter at the premises on which the prepayment meter is installed; (3) require the customer and supplier to enter into an agreement to use the prepayment meter for such purposes; and (4) specify written terms that must be included in such an agreement, where applicable.

1422　Electricity—renewables obligation

The Renewables Obligation Order 2006, SI 2006/1004 (in force on 1 April 2006), replaces the 2005 Order, SI 2005/926, and replaces the renewables obligation, which is imposed on all suppliers of electricity in England and Wales licensed under the Electricity Act 1989, to supply to customers in Great Britain specified amounts of electricity generated from renewable sources. In particular, the order (1) requires, through the imposition of the renewables obligation, an electricity supplier to produce evidence of the supply of electricity generated from renewable sources to the Gas and Electricity Markets Authority, in the form of certificates known as ROCs; (2) provides for the method by which the amount of an electricity supplier's renewables obligation is to be determined; (3) determines what types of electricity generated from renewable sources are eligible to satisfy an electricity supplier's renewables obligation; (4) relates to arrangements whereby electricity generated by a generating station is sold to an electricity supplier and then purchased back by the operator of the generating station; (5) enables an electricity supplier to discharge, in whole or in part, its renewables obligation by the alternative means of making a payment to the Authority or by producing certificates certifying specified matters; (6) provides for the Authority to issue ROCs and to maintain a ROC register; (7) provides for the revocation of ROCs in specified circumstances; (8) contains special arrangements enabling generating stations with a declared net capacity of 50 kilowatts or less to be able to claim ROCs on an annual rather than monthly basis; (9) deals with the allocation of payments made to the Authority between those electricity suppliers which are subject to renewables obligations; (10) provides for an electricity supplier to be treated as having discharged its renewables obligation by making a late payment if certain conditions are satisfied; (11) makes provision for mutualisation; (12) makes provision relating to the Authority's functions, and enables it to obtain information for the purposes of discharging those functions; and (13) provides for the preliminary accreditation and accreditation of generating stations.

1423 Electricity—supply—safety

The Electricity Safety, Quality and Continuity (Amendment) Regulations 2006, SI 2006/1521 (in force on 1 October 2006), amend the 2002 Regulations, SI 2002/2665, by (1) incorporating an amendment to the British Standard Requirements for Electrical Installations (BS7671) into the 2002 Regulations as to the requirement to harmonise cable core colours across the European Union; (2) ensuring that tramways, trolley vehicle systems and other forms of guided transport are afforded the same exceptions from the 2002 Regulations as is the case for railways; (3) augmenting the current duty for generators and distributors to maintain sufficient clearances between electricity lines and trees to avoid danger to the public by requiring further vegetation control in order to avoid, so far as is reasonably practicable, interference with or interruption of supply; (4) providing that such an augmentation is applicable from 31 January 2009; and (5) extending the scope of the 2002 Regulations to the UK Renewable Energy Zone and confirming their application to territorial waters adjacent to Great Britain.

1424 Energy—boilers—efficiency

The Boiler (Efficiency) (Amendment) Regulations 2006, SI 2006/170 (in force on 21 February 2006), further amend the 1993 Regulations, SI 1993/3083, so as to provide that those regulations do not apply to units that operate in cogeneration mode, where cogeneration means the simultaneous generation in one process of thermal energy and electrical and/or mechanical energy.

1425 Energy Act 2004—commencement

The Energy Act 2004 (Commencement No 7) Order 2006, SI 2006/1964, brings into force, on 14 August 2006, ss 145(2), (4), 147(5), 149(2), (4), (10), 151 and 153. For a summary of the Act, see 2004 Abr para 1372. See also the commencement table in the title STATUTES.

1426 Finance Act 2006

See para 2465.

1427 Gas—prepayment meter

The Gas (Prepayment Meter) Regulations 2006, SI 2006/2011 (in force on 1 September 2006), enable a gas supplier to collect sums through a gas prepayment meter in prescribed circumstances. In particular, the regulations (1) allow a gas prepayment meter to be used to collect sums relating to the supply of gas or the provision of a gas meter at premises previously owned or occupied by the customer; (2) allow sums owing for such purposes to be consolidated with sums due for the supply of gas and the provision of a gas meter at the premises on which the prepayment meter is installed; (3) require the customer and gas supplier to enter into an agreement to use the prepayment meter for such purposes; and (4) specify written terms that must be included in such an agreement, where applicable.

1428 Gas—supply—licence—exemption

The Gas Act 1986 (Exemption from the Requirement for an Interconnector Licence) Order 2006, SI 2006/2000 (in force on 14 August 2006), grants an exemption from the Gas Act 1986 s 5(1)(aa) to any person who participates in the operation of a gas interconnector that does not subsist wholly or partly to connect a gas transportation system in Great Britain to an equivalent system situated in another country or territory.

1429 Gas and Electricity Markets Authority—appeal—modification of time limits

The Electricity and Gas Appeals (Modification of Time Limits) Order 2006, SI 2006/1519 (in force on 27 July 2006), amends the Energy Act 2004 Sch 22 so as to extend, from five to twenty-eight days, the time limit within which costs incurred by the Competition Commission, or costs which the Competition Commission orders one party to pay to the other, in connection with the determination of appeals must be paid.

1430 Nuclear reactors—decommissioning—environmental impact assessment

The Nuclear Reactors (Environmental Impact Assessment for Decommissioning) (Amendment) Regulations 2006, SI 2006/657 (in force on 6 April 2006), amend the 1999 Regulations, SI 1999/2892, so as to implement EC Council Directive 2003/35 providing for participation in respect of the drawing up of certain plans and programmes relating to the environment. In particular, the regulations (1) provide for the licensee to stop the part of the project that is subject to change in addition to any other part, including the entire project, that the executive may direct; and (2) replace the reference to the Environmental Information Regulations 1992, SI 1992/3240, with a reference to the Environmental Information Regulations 2004, SI 2004/3391.

1431   Oil—taxation—market value

The Oil Taxation (Market Value of Oil) Regulations 2006, SI 2006/3313 (in force on 14 December 2006), make provision in relation to the categorisation of oils for the purposes of the Oil Taxation Act 1975 Sch 3 and the methods of valuing Category 1 and Category 2 oils which are held as part of a participator's stock, sold otherwise than at arm's length or are relevantly appropriated. The regulations (1) prescribe those oils which are Category 1 oils for the purposes of valuation; (2) define terms used in connection with the valuation of Category 1 oils; (3) describe the steps to be taken in determining the value of Category 1 oils; (4) set out the rules for determining the notional delivery day to be used in the calculation for a Category 1 oil; (5) set out the rules for determining the average reference value to be used in such a calculation; (6) specify the adjustment factors to be applied in such a calculation; (7) detail the process by which the market value of a quantity of Category 1 oil is arrived at; (8) prescribe two methods of valuing Category 2 oils; and (9) prescribe an alternative method in cases where the participator's contracts normally provide for the price to be determined (a) in the case of oil transported by ship from the place of extraction to a place in the United Kingdom or elsewhere, by reference to the actual date of the completion of the load, or completion of the discharge, of the cargo; or (b) in the case of oil transported by pipeline to a place in the United Kingdom and loaded on to a ship there, by reference to the date of the bill of lading.

1432   Petroleum—licensing—exploration and production—seaward and landward areas

The Petroleum Licensing (Exploration and Production) (Seaward and Landward Areas) (Amendment) Regulations 2006, SI 2006/784 (in force on 13 April 2006), amend the model clauses prescribed in the 2004 Regulations, SI 2004/352, for the purposes of the 24th and subsequent rounds of licensing in seaward areas and the 13th and subsequent rounds of licensing in landward areas. In particular, the regulations (1) make provision for a new model clause which applies to production and petroleum exploration and development licences and which provides that, where the Secretary of State revokes a licence, any well drilled by the licensee pursuant to that licence must be plugged and sealed as soon as possible or, if the Secretary of State so directs, left in good order and fit for further working; (2) amend an existing clause in production and petroleum exploration and development licences so as to provide that well casings and fixtures left in position at the expiry or determination of the licensee's rights, or at the completion of any works required of the licensee, are the property of the Secretary of State; and (3) provide that the insolvency events specified, wherever they occur, entitle the Secretary of State to revoke certain licences.

1433   Petroleum—offshore installations—safety zones

The Offshore Installations (Safety Zones) Order 2006, SI 2006/356 (in force on 8 March 2006), establishes safety zones having a radius of 500 metres from the specified point around each specified installation stationed in waters to which automatic establishment of safety zones under the Petroleum Act 1987 s 21(7) applies.

The Offshore Installations (Safety Zones) (No 2) Order 2006, SI 2006/952 (in force on 19 April 2006), establishes safety zones to which the Petroleum Act 1987 s 21(7) applies. In particular, such safety zones have a radius of 500 metres from the point around the specified installation which are stationed in waters.

1434   Petroleum revenue tax—attribution of blended crude oil

The Petroleum Revenue Tax (Attribution of Blended Crude Oil) Regulations 2006, SI 2006/3312 (in force on 14 December 2006), make provision in relation to the attribution of blended crude oil across the originating field interests of a participator or seller so that the allocation reflects the extent of the participator or seller's actual or projected production entitlements in an originating field for tax purposes. Specifically, the regulations (1) specify the formula and associated rules to be used in calculating the allocation of blended crude oil lifted; (2) provide a method of allocating blended oil, derived from more than one field and which is lifted under a period of entitlement contract or a term contract, to each of the fields from which it has been derived; (3) make special provision for balancing parcels where a participator's contract with a purchaser permits the purchaser to notify the participator of the volume of oil which is to be lifted under it in a particular period; (4) provide for the sale of field interests, including by specifying the formula and associated rules used to calculate the allocation of blended crude oil sold under month of entitlement or term contracts across the field interests of a seller on a monthly basis; and (5) detail the steps to be followed in calculating the amount of any nomination excess to allocate to a particular originating field where a participator makes a relevant delivery of blended crude oil.

1435 Petroleum revenue tax—nomination scheme for disposals and appropriations

The Petroleum Revenue Tax (Nomination Scheme for Disposals and Appropriations) (Amendment) Regulations 2006, SI 2006/3089 (in force on 12 December 2006), further amend the Petroleum Revenue Tax (Nomination Scheme for Disposals and Appropriations) Regulations 1987, SI 1987/1338, so that (1) proposed sales other than under a Brent-Forties-Oseberg Forward contract are excluded from the Finance Act 1987 s 61 and the nomination scheme; (2) the primary manner for making nominations is by e-mail, except in the case of disruption of e-mails, when telephone facsimile may be used; (3) the transaction base time for a proposed sale of oil is defined; and (4) the maximum volume tolerance is reduced from 5 per cent to 1 per cent.

1436 Public procurement—award of contracts—procedure

See para 396.

1437 Radioactive substances—testing instruments

The Radioactive Substances (Testing Instruments) (England and Wales) Exemption Order 2006, SI 2006/1500 (in force on 6 October 2006), replaces the 1985 Order, SI 1985/1049 and in addition, provides for references to the Radioactive Substances Act 1993. The order also provides that (1) a waste collection authority under this order means a local authority which is a waste collection authority within the meaning of the Environmental Protection Act 1990 s 30(3); (2) references to 'free from patent defect' is removed from certain definitions; (3) a person is not exempt from registration if a source is defective or damaged or leaks radioactive material; (4) a person is not exempt from registration under s 10 in respect of an electrodeposited source that consists of iron 55; and (5) a person is exempt from registration in respect of mobile radioactive apparatus that consists of a testing instrument or a source containing electrodeposited nickel 63.

GIFTS

Halsbury's Laws of England (4th edn) vol 20(1) (Reissue) paras 1–100

Articles

For articles relating to this title please refer to the Table of Articles at the beginning of the Abridgment.

GUARANTEE AND INDEMNITY

Halsbury's Laws of England (4th edn) vol 20(1) (Reissue) paras 101–400

Articles

For articles relating to this title please refer to the Table of Articles at the beginning of the Abridgment.

1438 Guarantee—agreement—enforceability—agreement to answer for debt of another—claimants not party to documentation

The claimants sold a company to the second defendant. Part of the purchase price was paid on completion but another part was left outstanding to be paid in instalments. The first defendant issued loan notes to the claimants in respect of the debt which provided that, if any instalment was not paid on time, the full outstanding balance became payable immediately. The first defendant failed to pay the first instalment. The company was placed in administration and its business and assets sold. The claimants believed that they had the benefit of a guarantee from the first defendant of the second defendant's debt and gave notice to the first defendant of a claim under the guarantee. The first defendant refused to pay and the claimants commenced proceedings seeking judgment against the first defendant. On the claimants' application for summary judgment, *held,* the intention of the parties when the guarantee was given was that it should be given by the first defendant to the claimants, and should be enforceable by them directly against the first defendant. The parties had not failed to achieve their intention because of the way in which the documents were structured. Under the law relating to promises made in deeds, the claimants were entitled to enforce the first defendant's promise to them that it had guaranteed payment of the second defendant's debt to them. In the circumstances of the transaction it did not matter that the claimants were not signatory parties to the loan note, guarantee instrument or guarantee deed. These documents were types of deeds which were intended not merely to create rights enforceable by non-parties such as the claimants, but which in law achieved the intention. Accordingly, the application would be granted.

Moody v Condor Insurance Ltd [2006] EWHC 100 (Ch), [2006] 1 All ER 934 (Chancery Division: Park J).

1439   Guarantee—agreement—enforceability—unsigned e-mail

The claimant supplied products to a company of which the defendant was a director. The company failed to pay for the products and the claimant presented a petition to wind up the company. The defendant asked a member of his staff to send an e-mail to the claimant's solicitors requesting an adjournment of the petition subject to a personal guarantee being given by him in favour of the claimant and an undertaking being given by him pending the signing of the personal guarantee. The e-mail was not signed by the defendant. On receipt of the e-mail, a clerk employed by the solicitors telephoned the defendant and agreed to adjourn the petition. Although an agreement to cover the personal guarantee was sent to the defendant, nothing further was heard from him. The claimant applied for summary judgment. The defendant asserted that the claimant had failed to produce any signed agreement or personal guarantee and that the only maintainable claim that the claimant had was against the company. The judge concluded that the e-mail was sufficient to satisfy the requirements of the Statute of Frauds (1677) s 4 and the defendant appealed. *Held,* where there was an offer in writing made by the party to be bound which contained the essential terms of what was offered and the party to be bound agreed that his offer had been accepted unconditionally, albeit orally, that was a sufficient note or memorandum to satisfy the requirements of s 4. The e-mail was capable of being a sufficient note or memorandum for the purpose of s 4 because it was in writing and the offer was accepted orally on behalf of the claimant. However, the automatic insertion of a person's e-mail address after the document had been transmitted by either the sending or receiving Internet service provider did not constitute a signature for the purposes of s 4. Therefore, the e-mail did not bear a signature sufficient to satisfy the requirements of s 4. Accordingly, the appeal would be allowed.

J Pereira Fernandes SA v Mehta [2006] EWHC 813 (Ch), [2006] 2 All ER 891 (Chancery Division: Judge Pelling QC). *Caton v Caton* (1867) LR 2 HL 129; and *Evans v Hoare* [1892] 1 QB 593 considered.

1440   Guarantee—performance bond—counter-indemnity—recovery of payment—fraud defence—test

A subsidiary of the defendant aircraft manufacturer entered into a service contract with the Saudi Ministry of Defence, under which the subsidiary was obliged to arrange a performance bond. The subsidiary duly opened an account with the claimant, a Saudi-based commercial bank, which granted a performance bond facility. The defendant then entered into a deed of guarantee and indemnity undertaking to pay the bank any due amounts which the subsidiary failed to pay. The Saudi Ministry of Defence subsequently demanded payment under the performance bond. The claimant paid the demand and claimed under the counter-indemnity it had from the subsidiary and the guarantee from the defendant. The defendant refused to pay, and the claimant applied for summary judgment. The defendant submitted that the payment by the claimant of the money and the subsequent claim by the Saudi Ministry of Defence was part of a scheme to defraud the defendant of the amount paid under the performance bond. The judge found that there was no basis for a defence of fraud on the material before the court. On the defendant's appeal, it argued that the appropriate test for the judge to apply was whether its defence had a real prospect of success, rather than the stricter test applicable where application for summary judgment had been brought against a bank which had refused to make payment under a performance bond. *Held,* in a bank's application for summary judgment under a counter-indemnity in respect of obligations under a performance bond, it was sufficient for a defendant to establish that a defence based on the fraud exception had a real prospect of success in order for the application to fail. Such a defence, however, created a high hurdle to meet at trial. The evidence of fraud should be clear, both as to the fact of the fraud and as to the bank's knowledge. In the instant case, although the judge had misdirected himself in applying the test, the defendant had not discharged the burden on it of showing that it had a real prospect of proving by clear evidence the fraud exception at trial. Accordingly, the appeal would be dismissed.

Banque Saudi Fransi v Lear Siegler Services Inc [2006] EWCA Civ 1130, [2007] 1 All ER (Comm) 67 (Court of Appeal: Pill, Arden and Scott Baker LJJ).

1441   Guarantee—surety—duty of creditor to obtain proper price for security—applicability to guarantor

The defendants provided personal guarantees to the claimant bank in respect of the indebtedness to the claimant of a certain company. The company's indebtedness was secured against its own property. The company subsequently went into administration and, after the realisation of the security and liquidation, its outstanding indebtedness to the claimant exceeded the value of the guarantee. The claimant therefore issued proceedings seeking to recover under the guarantee. The defendants contended in their defence that the claimant had failed in its duty to obtain a proper price for the property in that it had allowed the administrators to sell the property at an undervalue. An issue arose as to whether the claimant owed a duty to the defendants as guarantors to obtain a proper price for the property. *Held,* it was settled law that a creditor owed a duty of care to a surety as well as to the principal debtor to take reasonable care to ensure a proper price was obtained for any security. A guarantor of the principal debtor's liabilities was interested in the security in two respects. First, before realisation by the creditor, if he paid the amount owed by the principal debtor he would be entitled to the security by way of subrogation to the rights of the creditor. Secondly, his liability, like that of the principal debtor, fell to be extinguished or reduced by the amount realised by the creditor when he realised the security, assuming it to be sufficient. It was because of the second of those interests that the creditor owed the guarantor, as well as the principal debtor, a duty to obtain a proper price if he realised a security for the liabilities of the principal debtor. Judgment would be given accordingly.

Barclays Bank plc v Kingston [2006] EWHC 533 (QB), [2006] 2 Lloyd's Rep 59 (Queen's Bench Division: Stanley Burnton J). *Standard Chartered Bank Ltd v Walker* [1982] 3 All ER 938, CA (1982 Abr para 422); *American Express International Banking Corpn v Hurley* [1985] 3 All ER 564 (1985 Abr para 329); and *Skipton Building Society v Stott* [2001] QB 261, CA, applied. *Burgess v Auger; Burgess v Vanstock Ltd* [1998] 2 BCLC 478 distinguished.

1442 Indemnity—counter-indemnity—recovery of payment—fraud defence—test

See *Banque Saudi Fransi v Lear Siegler Services Inc*, para 1440.

1443 Indemnity—extent of liability—construction of contract

The claimant was the demise charterer of a purpose-built seismic survey vessel. While performing work pursuant to a contract made with the defendant, the vessel struck a wellhead marker buoy owned by an oil company. The claimant admitted negligence, and began a limitation action which resulted in the award of a decree limiting its liability to the defendant to a specified amount. The claimant also made an application under CPR Pt 8 concerning the proper construction of the contract, and specifically a clause under which the parties agreed that the claimant's liability would not exceed the aggregate amount of payments received by the claimant, and the defendant would indemnify the claimant for any amounts in excess of such amount. A further clause required the claimant to take out general third party insurance with specified levels of minimum property damage cover and protection and indemnity cover. The claimant contended that, on a proper construction of the clauses, the defendant was liable to indemnify the claimant for any amount of its liability to a third party, namely the oil company, which exceeded the amount of its remuneration under the contract. The defendant contended that, given that the claimant was not acting as the servant or agent of the defendant, the claimant should bear the consequences of its own negligence, as borne out by the inclusion of the clause relating to insurance. *Held*, on the proper construction of the contract, the claimant was not entitled to the indemnity sought. If it were otherwise, the claimant would obtain an indemnity in excess of what it received under the contract. A limitation of liability under the contract could only be effective to limit a liability owed to one contracting party to the other contracting party, not third parties such as the oil company. Judgment would be given accordingly.

Westerngeco Ltd v ATP Oil & Gas (UK) Ltd [2006] EWHC 1164 (Comm), [2006] 2 All ER (Comm) 637 (Queen's Bench Division: Aikens J).

HEALTH AND SAFETY AT WORK

Halsbury's Laws of England (4th edn) vol 20(1) (Reissue) paras 501–735, vol 20(2) (Reissue) paras 736–1070.

Articles

For articles relating to this title please refer to the Table of Articles at the beginning of the Abridgment.

1444 Breach of statutory duty—breach of health and safety regulations—meaning of 'health and safety regulations'

See *Polestar Jowetts v Komori UK Ltd; Vibixa v Komori UK Ltd*, para 2737.

1445 Compensation Act 2006

See para 2771.

1446 Dangerous substances—asbestos—control

The Control of Asbestos Regulations 2006, SI 2006/2739 (in force in part on 13 November 2006 and in part on 6 April 2006), implement EC Council Directives 76/769, 83/477, 90/394 and 98/24, and replace (1) the Asbestos (Licensing) Regulations 1983, SI 1983/1649, with the effect that licences granted to allow work with asbestos are made subject to a maximum duration of three years; (2) the Asbestos (Prohibitions) Regulations 1992, SI 1992/3067 (as amended), so as to make provision in relation to prohibitions on exposure to, importation of, supply, and use of, asbestos, and remove expired derogations; and (3) the Control of Asbestos at Work Regulations 2002, SI 2002/2675, so as to (a) introduce a new control limit common to all types of asbestos; (b) provide for the measurement of the control limit by the 1997 World Health Organisation ('WHO') recommended method; (c) apply duties to all work with asbestos, except in respect of licensing, notification, accident and emergency arrangements, asbestos areas and health surveillance in respect of sporadic and low intensity exposure; (d) disapply provisions concerning asbestos in respect of ships other than naval ships; (e) extend the list of topics on which information, instruction and training must be given to employees; and (f) provide (i) for the provision of respiratory protective equipment so far as is reasonably practicable to any employee who is exposed to asbestos; (ii) for a prohibition on exceeding the control limit and for the actions to be taken if this occurs; (iii) that only competent persons may enter respirator zones or supervise employees in respirator zones; and (iv) for accreditation of persons who are requested to assess premises for the issue of a site clearance certificate for reoccupation. SI 1992/2966, SI 2004/568, and SI 2004/3168 Art 63 are amended.

1447   Dangerous substances—ionising radiation—medical exposure

The Ionising Radiation (Medical Exposure) (Amendment) Regulations 2006, SI 2006/2523 (in force on 1 November 2006), further amend the 2000 Regulations, SI 2000/1059, so as to (1) substitute the Commission for Healthcare Audit and Inspection for the Secretary of State as the appropriate authority; (2) add a definition of 'ethics committee' and remove the definition of 'Local Research Ethics Committee'; (3) remove the terms 'registered medical practitioner' and 'dental practitioner' from the definitions of 'practitioner' and 'referrer', and substitute the term 'registered health care professional' for 'health professional'; (4) clarify that the word 'record' refers to the record of training undertaken, which the employer is required to keep and have available for inspection by the appropriate authority; and (5) make transitional provision in relation to incomplete investigations, proceedings, appeals and other matters, including notifications by employers of incidents of overexposure, providing, as regards England, that the Secretary of State will continue to be the appropriate authority in relation to such matters.

1448   Employer—breach of statutory duty—duty to maintain work equipment—meaning of 'work equipment'

The Provision and Use of Work Equipment Regulations 1998, SI 1998/2306, reg 3(2) provides that the duty to provide safe work equipment applies to such equipment provided for use or used by an employee of his at work. 'Work equipment' means any machinery, appliance, apparatus, tool or installation for use at work (whether exclusively or not): reg 2(1).

The claimant was employed by the defendant firm as a receptionist at their office, which was located in a suite on the second floor of a building. Access to the offices was by means of stairs and a lift, both of which opened into a lobby area on the ground floor. The lift, stairs and lobby area were common parts of the building. The claimant was injured while leaving the lift on the ground floor at the end of her working day. The safety mechanism on the lift failed to function, causing the lift door to close on one of her hands. The claimant brought proceedings pursuant to the 1998 Regulations. The defendants argued that the lift did not constitute 'work equipment' within the meaning of reg 2(1), as it had not been used by the claimant 'at work' for the purposes of reg 3(2), since the injury was sustained after the claimant had left their premises at the end of the day's work. They relied on the fact that the lift was outside their premises, outside their control, and not for their employees' exclusive use. The judge decided that the lift did constitute 'work equipment', and the defendants appealed against that decision. *Held*, whether the employee was acting in the course of his employment was certainly an important factor to be considered in deciding whether he was using equipment 'at work' at the material time. However, the expression 'at work' might import a spatial or geographical limitation on the places at which, and hence the equipment to which, the duty attached. The degree of control exercised over the equipment by the employer might also be a factor in deciding whether the equipment was being used at work within the meaning of the 1998 Regulations. For the present purposes, the line should not be drawn when the claimant left her office to enter the lift or when the lift left the second floor. Accordingly, the appeal would be dismissed.

Reid v PRP Architects [2006] EWCA Civ 1119, [2007] PIQR P44 (Court of Appeal: Pill, Smith and Neuberger LJJ). *Armstrong, Whitworth & Co Ltd v Redford* [1920] AC 757, HL; and *Stark v Post Office* [2000] ICR 1013, CA (2000 Abr para 1663), considered.

1449   Employer—breach of statutory duty—duty to maintain work equipment—stabilisation by clamping—movable suspended ladder

The Provision and Use of Work Equipment Regulations 1998, SI 1998/2306, reg 4(1) requires every employer to ensure that work equipment is so constructed or adapted as to be suitable for the purpose for which it is used or provided. Every employer must also ensure that work equipment or any part of work equipment is stabilised by clamping or otherwise where necessary for purposes of health or safety: reg 20.

The claimant was working at sea on board a semi-submersible production platform which was stationary while it was being fitted out. The accommodation provided for men working on the platform was equipped with two-tier bunks and with suspended ladders held in position by retaining bars which provided access to the top bunks. The claimant was injured after a suspended access ladder came detached as he was attempting to descend from a top bunk. The claimant brought personal injury proceedings alleging a breach by the defendant employer of the 1998 Regulations regs 4 and 20. The claim was dismissed and, on the claimant's appeal, the court decided that the defendant was 50 per cent to blame for the accident. On the claimant's appeal against that decision, *held*, there was no definition of what was meant by 'necessary' in reg 20. However, reg 4(4) provided that 'suitable' in reg 4 meant suitable in any respect which it was reasonably foreseeable would affect the health and safety of any person. The same test should be applied to what was 'necessary' for the purposes of reg 20. The obligation in both provisions was to anticipate situations which might give rise to accidents. The employer was not permitted to wait for that to happen. In the instant case, the accident was caused by the defendant's breaches of regs 4(1) and 20. It was plain from the findings of fact at first instance that movable suspended ladders were not suitable for the purpose for which they were provided because of the risk that workers would be injured if they were not replaced properly. To avoid the risk of injury it was necessary for them be clamped or otherwise fixed to the sides of the bunks to which they were to provide access. It followed that the claimant was entitled to damages. However, the appellate court was entitled to find that the blame for the accident should be shared equally. Accordingly, the appeal would be allowed in part.

Robb v Salamis (M&I) Ltd [2006] UKHL 56, 2006 SLT 158 (House of Lords: Lords Hope of Craighead, Clyde, Scott of Foscote, Rodger of Earlsferry and Carswell).

1450   Employer—breach of statutory duty—exposure to asbestos—formation of pleural plaques—cause of action not founded by aggregating heads of claim

See *Rothwell v Chemical & Insulating Co Ltd*, para 955.

1451   Employer—breach of statutory duty—factual issues in medical cases—guidance on trying issues

An employee was employed by the employer, a firm of solicitors, for 19 years. The employee brought an action seeking damages for personal injuries consisting of a work-related upper limb disorder incurred during the course of her employment. The employee claimed that her injuries had resulted from negligence by the employer and breach of statutory duty, including breach of the Health and Safety (Display Screen Equipment) Regulations 1992, SI 1992/2792, reg 6. The employee submitted that she had suffered intermittent pain in her wrists, for about ten years, and that the pain had eventually reached her neck. It was common ground that the employee's workload had increased substantially in the last year of her employment. The employer conceded that it had breached reg 6, but claimed that the breach had not caused the injuries. The employee's claim was allowed and the employer appealed. *Held,* the evidence that the employee's injuries were work-related was overwhelming. The employer was in breach of statutory duty and the judge was clearly right to find that the employee's injuries were caused by those breaches. To ensure that factual issues in medical cases were efficiently tried, certain guidelines should be followed. A party who sought to contradict a factually pleaded case on the basis of medical records should indicate that intention in advance, either by amendment of his pleadings or by informal notice. The opposite party should then indicate the extent to which they took objection to the accuracy of the records. When the area of dispute was identified, a decision would have to be taken as to whether the records needed to be formally proved. Therefore, not only would the ambit of the dispute be clarified but it would also be clear what interpretation was sought to be put on records. If those precautions were not taken, the judge might be reluctant to permit reference to reports of the patient's statements in the medical records for the purpose of contradicting her evidence. On the other hand, if there was unreasonable failure to admit that such statements were made, to the extent that it was necessary to call doctors to court simply to prove formally the statements, such failure of co-operation was likely to be penalised in costs. Accordingly, the appeal would be dismissed.

Fifield v Denton Hall Legal Services [2006] EWCA Civ 169, [2006] All ER (D) 104 (Mar) (Court of Appeal: Buxton, Jonathan Parker and Wall LJJ).

1452   Employer—breach of statutory duty—fine—level of fine

The appellant company was responsible for inspecting railway track which had disintegrated and resulted in the derailment of a train. Another company owned the infrastructure of the rail network and had overall responsibility for the safety of the track. The appellant pleaded guilty to failing to discharge its duty as an employer under the Health and Safety at Work etc Act 1974 s 3(1) to persons not in its employment in breach of s 33. It appealed against the amount of the fine of £10m. *Held,* s 3 required positive steps to be taken by all concerned in the operation of the business of a company to ensure that the company's activities involved the minimum risk to employees and to third parties. Knowledge that breach of the duty under s 3 would result in a fine of sufficient size to affect dividends or share price would be a powerful incentive for management to comply with the duty. The fine should reflect the degree of fault and the consequences so as to raise appropriate concern on the part of shareholders as to what had occurred but did not always have to be large enough to affect dividends or the share price. Where a breach of the duty imposed by s 3 might be the result of negligence or inadvertence on the part of an individual that reflected no fault on the part of the management, the system which it had put in place, or the training which it had provided, a deterrent sentence on the company was neither appropriate nor possible. The fine should reflect the seriousness of the consequences of an individual's shortcoming but it should be smaller by an order of magnitude than the fine for a breach of duty that consisted of a systemic failure. There had had been a serious systemic failure on the part of the appellant. It was a substantial company and, while the fine was severe, it was hard to say that it was wrong in principle. There was, however, disparity between the appellant's fine and that imposed on the other company which owned the rail network infrastructure. In the interest of proportionality, the appellant's fine should be reduced but not to a level at which it failed to give proper effect to the appropriate principles. Accordingly, the appeal would be allowed and the fine reduced to £7·5m.

R v Balfour Beatty Rail Infrastructure Services Ltd [2006] EWCA Crim 1586, (2006) Times, 18 July (Court of Appeal: Lord Phillips of Worth Matravers CJ, Nelson and Silber J).

1453   Employer—breach of statutory duty—safe place of work—construction industry— meaning of 'construction work'

Scotland
The claimant was employed as a painter and decorator by the defendant local authority. He was injured while working on a flat owned by the defendant, and brought a claim under the Construction (Health, Safety and Welfare) Regulations 1996, SI 1996/1592. By virtue of reg 3(1), the 1996 Regulations applied to construction work carried out by a person at work. Regulation 2(1)(a) specified that 'construction work' included redecoration. The judge dismissed the claim on the basis that the work being undertaken by the claimant did not amount to 'construction work' for the purposes of reg 3(1). The claimant appealed. *Held*, the judge's interpretation of reg 2(1)(a) was plainly erroneous, as the redecoration work being carried out by the claimant came expressly within the ambit of that provision and therefore constituted construction work for the purposes of reg 3(1). Accordingly, the appeal would be allowed.

Matthews v Glasgow CC [2006] CSIH 1, 2006 SLT 88 (Inner House).

1454   Employer—breach of statutory duty—safety of work equipment—safety mechanism switched off

See *A-G's Reference (No 89 of 2006); R v Shaw*, para 2579.

1455   Employer—duty of care—asbestos exposure—exposure by more than one employer—apportionment of damages

See *Barker v Corus (UK) Ltd; Murray v British Shipbuilders (Hydrodynamics) Ltd; Patterson v Smiths Dock Ltd*, para 2075.

1456   Employer—duty of care—fire safety—commencement of provisions

The Regulatory Reform (Fire Safety) Subordinate Provisions Order 2006, SI 2006/484 (in force on 31 March 2006), amends the Regulatory Reform (Fire Safety) Order 2005, SI 2005/1541, by changing its commencement date from 1 April 2006 to 1 October 2006.

1457   Employer—duty to undertake risk assessment—expectant mother—avoidance of risk

The Management of Health and Safety at Work Regulations 1999, SI 1999/3242, reg 16(3) provides that, in relation to risk assessment in respect of an expectant mother, where it is not reasonable to alter the working conditions or hours of work, or if it would not avoid such risk, the employer must suspend the employee from work for so long as is necessary to avoid such risk.

An employee had been promoted to the post of station manager on a three-month trial period, and had been told that a recommendation would be made to confirm her promotion. She then informed the employer that she was pregnant. The employer carried out a risk assessment in respect of her and concluded that the risks of the new post, including possible exposure to extreme heat or cold, the risk of slipping or falling and the risk of physical abuse, were too high. It therefore returned the employee to her previous post and previous salary. Six months later she resigned and complained to an employment tribunal of constructive dismissal and unlawful deductions from wages. The tribunal held that the word 'avoid' in the 1999 Regulations reg 16(2) did not impose an absolute obligation on the employer to avoid the risk altogether. It further held that the managers had jumped to the conclusion that the employee could not continue as station manager because of their personal feelings, rather than consequent to an appropriate analysis of the risk assessments. It therefore concluded that she had been discriminated against on the grounds of sex, and that her removal from her role and the consequent reduction in her salary had been because she was pregnant. The employer appealed, contending that the tribunal had misconstrued the phrase 'avoid the risk' and that the employee had affirmed her contract of employment or waived her right to treat the contract as discharged by reason of her demotion. *Held*, the tribunal had been entitled to find that the managers had jumped to the conclusion that the employee could not continue in her position because of their personal feelings. Further, an employer was only entitled to suspend a woman on maternity grounds where it could show that a risk could not be avoided. The term 'avoid the risk' could not mean the complete avoidance of all risks but rather to reduce them to their lowest acceptable level. The employer had failed to show that the risk could not have been avoided by altering her working conditions or hours of work. Further, consequent on its demotion of the employee, the employer had breached the contract of employment by making unlawful deductions from her salary, and that had continued from month to month. She was entitled to treat the contract of employment as having been repudiated for that reason alone without there being any waiver of her right to do so or affirmation of the contract. Accordingly, the appeal would be dismissed.

New Southern Railway Ltd v Quinn [2006] ICR 761 (Employment Appeal Tribunal: Judge Serota presiding).

1458   Fees

The Health and Safety (Fees) Regulations 2006, SI 2006/336 (in force on 6 April 2006), replace the 2005 Regulations, SI 2005/676, and fix or determine the fees payable (1) by an applicant to, in most cases, the Health and Safety Executive, in respect of an application made for (a) an approval under mines and quarries legislation; (b) an approval of plant or equipment under the Agriculture (Tractor Cabs) Regulations 1974, SI 1974/203; (c) an approval of a scheme or programme under the Freight Containers (Safety Convention) Regulations 1984, SI 1984/1890; (d) a licence under the Asbestos (Licensing) Regulations 1983, SI 1983/1649, and the amendment to, replacement of, and reassessment of an application to grant, such a licence; (e) an approval of dosimetry services for the purposes of the Ionising Radiations Regulations 1999, SI 1999/3232, or the Radiation (Emergency Preparedness and Public Information) Regulations 2001, SI 2001/2975; (f) a licence to manufacture or store explosives, or for registration for storing explosives, under the Manufacture and Storage of Explosives Regulations 2005, SI 2005/1082, for an acetylene importation licence under the Explosives Act 1875 s 40(9), for an approval under certain instruments made under the 1875 Act in relation to acetylene, for a licence under the Petroleum (Consolidation) Act 1928, for the transfer of a licence under the Petroleum (Transfer of Licences) Act 1936, for the approval of a classification of an explosive under the Classification and Labelling of Explosives Regulations 1983, SI 1983/1140, or for an explosive certificate under the Control of Explosives Regulations 1991, SI 1991/1531; (g) an explosives licence under the Dangerous Substances in Harbour Areas Regulations 1987, SI 1987/37; (h) an approval under the Health and Safety (First-Aid) Regulations 1981, SI 1981/917; and (i) an approval under the Offshore Installations and Pipeline Works (First-Aid) Regulations 1989, SI 1989/1671; (2) in respect of a notification or application under the Genetically Modified Organisms (Contained Use) Regulations 2000, SI 2000/2831, or the Notification of New Substances Regulations 1993, SI 1993/3050; (3) for medical examinations and surveillance by an employment medical adviser pursuant to specified statutory provisions; and (4) by specified persons in the offshore, rail and gas industries for the performance by the Executive of certain prescribed functions.

1459   Health Act 2006

See para 2028.

1460   Railways—Office of Rail Regulation—enforcement of health and safety law

See para 2423.

1461   Working time

See EMPLOYMENT.

1462   Workplace—health and safety—management

The Management of Health and Safety at Work (Amendment) Regulations 2006, SI 2006/438 (in force on 6 April 2006), further amend the 1999 Regulations, SI 1999/3242, so as to extend to an employee, protection against a claim made by a third party in circumstances where an employee may owe a duty to a third party.

HIGHWAYS, STREETS AND BRIDGES

Halsbury's Laws of England (4th edn) vol 21 (2004 Reissue) paras 1–947

Articles

For articles relating to this title please refer to the Table of Articles at the beginning of the Abridgment.

1463   Highway—crime prevention—designated areas

The Crime Prevention (Designated Areas) Order 2006, SI 2006/302 (in force on 17 March 2006), designates, under the Highways Act 1980 s 118B(1)(a), an area in the city of Leeds for the purposes of s 118B.

1464   Highway—gating order—England

The Highways Act 1980 (Gating Orders) (England) Regulations 2006, SI 2006/537 (in force on 1 April 2006), set out the procedures relating to gating orders made under the Highways Act 1980. In particular, the regulations (1) relate to the publicising of proposals to make a gating order; (2) oblige councils to consider representations as to the making of a gating order; (3) enable councils to hold a public inquiry in relation to a proposed gating order and require them to do so where the emergency services or a council object to the making of the gating order; (4) prevent councils from making a gating order until at least 28 days have been allowed for representations to be made and any public inquiry has been concluded; (5) set out the content of gating orders and require them to be publicised; (6) set out the procedure to be followed when it is proposed to vary or revoke a gating order; (7) make provision relating to conduct of public inquiries; and (8) provide that councils must keep a register of all gating orders.

1465   Highway—highway authority—duty to maintain highway—defence—tilting manhole cover

While walking along a public street of shops, the claimant stepped on a manhole cover which tilted and caused her foot to fall into the manhole, injuring her ankle. The claimant brought proceedings alleging that the defendant local authority had failed in it duty to maintain the highway in question. The defendant sought to rely on the Highways Act 1980 s 58(1), which provided that it was a defence to such a claim for an authority to show that it had taken reasonable care to secure that the highway was not dangerous for traffic. The defendant produced evidence of its system of monthly visual inspections, under which an inspector, who was on foot, looked for uneven pavement surfaces. The judge rejected the defence, deciding that a reasonable system of inspection required the defendant to check that the manhole covers were secure and not liable to tilt and that the defendant had not adduced any evidence to show that it was difficult or impractical to have a system whereby manhole covers were inspected to check that they were secure. The defendant appealed. *Held*, the standard of maintenance appropriate for a manhole cover in a shopping street was a standard which ensured, so far as was reasonable, that pedestrians were not at risk of falling into a hole which might be large and contain pipes, cables and other items. Manhole covers which were liable to tip if stood on by a pedestrian in a shopping street required urgent maintenance and repair because of the risk of serious injury. It followed that, when a highway authority was unable to prove the cause of such a defect, that inability was very likely to cause the authority difficulty in discharging the burden of proof laid on it by s 58. There was evidence that the defendant had given no consideration at all to the question of how to inspect manhole covers to ensure that they were secure. The defendant's system of inspection was designed to identify and avoid a different hazard, namely, uneven pavement surfaces which might cause a pedestrian to trip. Accordingly, the appeal would be dismissed.

Atkins v Ealing MBC [2006] EWHC 2515 (QB), [2006] All ER (D) 186 (Oct) (Queen's Bench Division: Teare J). *Mills v Barnsley MBC* [1992] PIQR 291, CA, applied.

1466   Highway—highway authority—duty to maintain highway—drainage systems

A highway authority had settled three consolidated cases arising from persons injured in road accidents caused by the presence of floodwater on a road resulting from a long-standing blockage of the drainage system. The authority sought to recover its outlay from its highway maintaining agents. The judge held that the drainage of the highway was not part of the maintenance. The authority appealed. *Held*, a highway authority's duty to maintain the highway was not confined to the surface of the road; the duty was to maintain the structure and fabric of the roadway, and the surface was simply part of that. The engineers had said that the flooding was due to poor drainage maintenance, which was the natural use of the term 'maintenance'. Accordingly, the appeal would be allowed.

Department of Transport, Environment and the Regions v Mott Macdonald Ltd [2006] EWCA Civ 1089, (2006) Times, 17 August (Court of Appeal: Sir Andrew Morritt C, Carnwath and Moses LJJ). *Burnside v Emerson* [1968] 3 All ER 741, CA, followed.

1467   Highway—restricted byways

The Restricted Byways (Application and Consequential Amendment of Provisions) Regulations 2006, SI 2006/1177 (in force on various dates), (1) provide that the provisions of Acts and subordinate legislation relating to highways, or highways of a particular description, will apply to restricted byways; and (2) amend the Highways Act 1980 s 47, under which a highway authority may apply to a magistrates' court for an order that a highway will cease to be maintainable at the public expense, so that such a provision will not to apply in relation to restricted byways.

1468 Public right of way—extinguishment order—refusal of confirmation—effect of related public path creation agreement

The Highways Act 1980 s 118(2) prohibits the Secretary of State from confirming a public path extinguishment order unless he is satisfied that it is expedient to do so having regard to the extent to which it appears to him that the path would, apart from the order, be likely to be used by the public.

A local highway authority entered into a public path creation agreement, pursuant to the 1980 Act s 25, with a group of landowners and tenants. The agreement provided that the owners and tenants would dedicate paths for public use, with such dedications becoming effective immediately before the extinguishment by order of certain specified paths. The authority then made four public path extinguishment orders under s 118(1) so as to extinguish a number of obsolete paths. An inspector appointed by the Secretary of State refused to confirm three of the orders on the ground that, as a matter of law, she was precluded from taking account of the public path creation agreements and therefore could not find that the paths to be extinguished were not likely to be used by the public. The decision was upheld in judicial review proceedings, and the authority appealed. *Held*, the phrase 'apart from the order' in s 118(2) should be given the natural meaning of the words it contained. The Secretary of State should consider what use the public were likely to make of a path, ignoring completely the fact that the authority had ordered its closure. The words therefore required the decision-maker to assume that the extinguishment order had not been made. On that assumption, the public path creation agreement did not come into effect, as it was contingent on the making of the extinguishment orders, and the new footpaths provided for under the agreement would not be created. It followed that the inspector had been right to exclude the creation agreement from her consideration, since, apart from the order, no new paths were created and the public were therefore bound to continue to use the paths which the authority had ordered to be extinguished. Accordingly, the appeal would be dismissed.

R (on the application of Hertfordshire CC) v Secretary of State for Environment, Food and Rural Affairs [2006] EWCA Civ 1718, [2006] All ER (D) 203 (Dec) (Court of Appeal: Ward, Wall and Richards LJJ). Decision of Sullivan J [2005] All ER (D) 157 (Oct) affirmed.

1469 Public right of way—registers—Wales

The Public Rights of Way (Registers) (Wales) Regulations 2006, SI 2006/42 (in force on 15 January 2006), prescribe the content of the information relating to public rights of way-related applications, declarations and associated documents which is to be kept, and the manner in which that information is to be kept, on registers established and maintained by local authorities in Wales.

1470 Street works—inspection fees—Wales

The Street Works (Inspection Fees) (Wales) Regulations 2006, SI 2006/1532 (in force on 2 October 2006), replace the 1992 Regulations, SI 1992/1688, in relation to Wales, so as to (1) define 'chargeable unit of inspection' as an inspection at random of less than ten per cent and not more than 10·5 per cent of each phase of works, and not more than 30 per cent of the total number of reckonable units of inspection in any year; (2) define 'unit of inspection', in the case of clusters of not more than five excavations, or not more than ten where the works relate to service pipes or line, so that the previous requirement in such cases, all the excavations are the subject of one notice of starting date, is replaced by two requirements; that all excavations are in the same street, and that they be part of the same works; (3) replace the five phases of work with three; (4) replace 'estimated numbers of units of inspection' for 'number of reckonable units of inspection', being the average number of units of inspection for that undertaker during the three preceeding years; and (5) make provision for new undertakers to estimate the number of units of inspection they expect to generate for the first three years. SI 2001/2681, 2002/3181, 2004/1809 are revoked.

1471 Street works—reinstatement of streets—Wales

The Street Works (Reinstatement) (Amendment) (Wales) Regulations 2006, SI 2006/2934 (in force on 24 January 2007), amend the 1992 Regulations, SI 1992/1689, so as to reflect the fact that paragraphs have been renumbered, and headings have been renamed, in the new Code of Practice, which prescribes requirements for the specification of materials to be used and the standard of workmanship to be observed by undertakers in reinstating streets. The regulations also follow the new Code by providing that the Code applies to all roads carrying up to 125 million standard axles.

1472 Street works—works affecting apparatus—compensation—guidance

The Court of Appeal has issued the following guidance in relation to the New Roads and Street Works Act 1991 s 82, which requires persons with apparatus in the street to be compensated in respect of any expense reasonably incurred in making good damage to that apparatus caused by the execution of street works or any other specified event: (1) The provisions of s 82 form a complete code, excluding the application of the common law, in respect of the execution of street works under the authority of statute or of a licence. Section 82(6) is directed at liability to third parties other than those listed as benefiting from the imposition of strict liability. The overall statutory scheme does not require the laying of ducting in the carriageway except where there is absolutely no alternative. (2) If the defendant causes damage or is required to rectify damage caused to the claimant's ducting in the course of street works, whoever it is that actually does the work that constitutes the damage, the defendant has to pay for the making good of that damage unless it can establish negligence or misconduct under s 82(4). The mere laying of ducting without giving a s 69 notice to the defendant will not count as such misconduct; the issue is where the ducting is and how it has been laid. If it obstructs access to the defendant's cables and has been laid outside the dimensions laid down in the guidance given by the National Joint Utilities Group in NJUG7, it will be assumed that the case is one of negligence or misconduct, unless the claimant can demonstrate circumstances preventing the application of the NJUG7 guidance. If the ducting has been laid by a contractor whose instructions permitted him to depart from NJUG7 without having to show good reason, it will be assumed that such departure has occurred. When contemplating interference with the claimant's ducting, irrespective of whether the case is one where a s 82(4) defence may be available, the defendant has to give the claimant, so far as reasonably practicable, the opportunity to monitor the execution of the works envisaged by s 69, and comply with any reasonable requirement (including that the claimant itself should undertake the works) that the claimant imposes. The effect of the defendant omitting to follow that course would be to expose it to claims by the claimant that the work had been unnecessary, or that the damage had been caused because of lack of skill or understanding on the part of the operatives. However, the defendant is not liable for the cost of the claimant attending on site if nothing that can be described as damage occurs. 'Damage' here has its ordinary meaning of interference with the physical structure of an object in a way that did not enhance its viability or value. If the claimant attends and merely moves the ducting, without interference with its structure as opposed to its position in the ground, then it would appear that, since nothing has occurred that could be described as damage, there is no basis in the 1991 Act for the claimant to be compensated for its work. (3) The parties should give full disclosure to the other of the location of their various apparatus. Firstly, although a failure to give a s 69 notice would not necessarily count as misconduct, as a scheme has been suggested that depends on notification, a failure to co-operate on the part of the claimant will count as misconduct. Secondly, when the defendant is contemplating pre-planned repair work it has to give notice to the claimant to enable it to consider how and under what conditions its ducting was laid. Thirdly, as soon as the defendant decides that ducting needs to be moved or otherwise interfered with, irrespective of whether it is working in a location in respect of which the claimant has not given notice and irrespective of whether it is in the course of pre-planned work, the defendant has to give immediate notice to the claimant since that at least will always be practicable even if the work has to start at once. Fourthly, the claimant has to make arrangements to attend promptly on site to enable it to determine what directions it needs to give to the defendant or whether it should undertake the work itself. It would plainly be a good idea if the claimant trained a number of the defendant's operatives so that it could sub-contract the work to one of them. If the claimant does not take the opportunity to give directions or undertake the work itself then it will forfeit any right to complain of excessive or incompetent work. (4) Recourse to any court has to be avoided in future. The parties should arrange to refer any dispute to a single engineer, agreed by them or in default appointed by the President of the Institute of Electrical Engineers, who will determine any dispute on the basis of short written submissions with photographs of the site. He will apply the principles set out in this judgment so far as they are relevant and because he will act as an expert, his decisions will not be subject to appeal. Should the parties reappear in court, and particularly in the Court of Appeal, in circumstances that have led them to litigation because of a failure to operate the suggested system, they are likely to receive short shrift and certainly to encounter an unsympathetic approach to costs.

Telewest Ltd v Yorkshire Electricity Distribution plc [2006] EWCA Civ 1418, [2006] All ER (D) 369 (Oct) (Court of Appeal: Buxton, Sedley and Dyson LJJ).

1473   Traffic Management Act 2004—commencement

The Traffic Management Act 2004 (Commencement No 1) (England) Order 2006, SI 2006/1736, brings s 94 into force in relation to England on 29 September 2006.

The Traffic Management Act 2004 (Commencement No 1) (Wales) Order 2006, SI 2006/2826, brings into force on 26 October 2006, in relation to Wales, ss 5(4), (5), 10, 16–31, 72–96, 98 (in part), and the repeals in Sch 12 Pt 2.

For a summary of the Act, see 2004 Abr para 1413. See also the commencement table in the title STATUTES.

HOUSING

Halsbury's Laws of England (4th edn) vol 22 (2006 Reissue) paras 1–741

Articles

For articles relating to this title please refer to the Table of Articles at the beginning of the Abridgment.

1474   Accommodation needs—assessment—gipsies and travellers—England

The Housing (Assessment of Accommodation Needs) (Meaning of Gipsies and Travellers) (England) Regulations 2006, SI 2006/3190 (in force on 2 January 2007), define 'gipsies and travellers' for the purposes of the duty of local housing authorities to carry out an assessment of the accommodation needs of gipsies and travellers residing in or resorting to their district.

1475   Clearance area—purchase of land—compulsory purchase order—properties demolished following designation of clearance area—exclusion from order

It has been held that, once it has been established that properties are unfit for habitation at the time of the designation of a clearance area, the Housing Act 1985 s 290(4) does not limit the Secretary of State's discretion to exclude from a compulsory purchase order those properties which were subsequently demolished and which did not fall within s 290(2). It is clear that, while s 290(4) alerts a housing authority to the fact that it may exercise its powers of purchase even where a building within a clearance area has been demolished, whether that demolished property should be included within a compulsory purchase order is a matter of discretion for the Secretary of State.

Rowe v First Secretary of State; Burnley BC v First Secretary of State [2006] All ER (D) 149 (Mar) (Queen's Bench Division: Beatson J).

1476   Empty dwelling management orders—prescribed exceptions and requirements—England

The Housing (Empty Dwelling Management Orders) (Prescribed Exceptions and Requirements) (England) Order 2006, SI 2006/367 (in force on 6 April 2006), provides, in relation to England, additional requirements that a local housing authority must comply with when making an application to a residential property tribunal for authorisation of an empty dwelling management order and prescribes the circumstances in which the residential property tribunal will not authorise the making of an interim order.

1477   Empty dwelling management orders—prescribed exceptions and requirements—Wales

The Housing (Empty Dwelling Management Orders) (Prescribed Exceptions and Requirements) (Wales) Order 2006, SI 2006/2823 (in force on 26 October 2006), prescribes exceptions for the purposes of a residential property tribunal's authorisation with regards to the making of a final empty dwelling management order ('EDMO') and prescribes the additional requirements that a local housing authority must comply with when making an application to a residential property tribunal for authorisation of an interim EDMO.

1478   Home energy—efficiency scheme—England

The Home Energy Efficiency Scheme (England) (Amendment) Regulations 2006, SI 2006/1953 (in force on 10 August 2006), amend, in relation to England, the 2005 Regulations, SI 2005/1530, so as to (1) increase, from £15,050 to £15,460, the qualifying cut-off point in relevant income for households in receipt of child tax credit or working tax credit; (2) extend the category of applicants who may apply for a grant to householders who have attained, or are living with a partner who has attained, the age of 60 and who do not otherwise qualify for a grant; and (3) provide that householders who qualify under the newly introduced category of applicants can receive a grant, limited to £300, for the purpose of the provision or replacement of, or improvements to, certain heating systems installed in the dwelling.

1479   Homeless persons—allocation of housing—eligibility—miscellaneous provisions—England

The Allocation of Housing and Homelessness (Eligibility) (England) Regulations 2006, SI 2006/1294 (in force on 1 June 2006), make provision for which persons from abroad will be ineligible or eligible for an allocation of housing accommodation under the Housing Act 1996 Pt 6 (ss 159–174) and for housing assistance under Pt 7 (ss 175–218), and take account of the implementation of EC European Parliament and Council Directive 2004/38. In particular, the regulations (1) prescribe the classes of person subject to immigration control who are eligible for an allocation of housing accommodation and for housing assistance respectively; (2) prescribe those classes of person who are not subject to immigration control but who are to be treated as persons from abroad who are ineligible for an allocation of housing accommodation and for housing assistance respectively; these classes relate principally to British nationals, and to those EU citizens and nationals of Norway, Iceland, Liechtenstein and Switzerland who are not subject to immigration control; (3) provide that such persons will be ineligible for an allocation of social housing or for homelessness assistance if (a) they are not habitually resident in the United Kingdom, Channel Islands, Isle of Man or Republic of Ireland, unless exempted from the requirement to be habitually resident; or (b) if their only right to reside in the United Kingdom, the Channel Islands, the Isle of Man or the Republic of Ireland is a right derived from the Treaty establishing the European

Community to reside in another member state either for an initial period of up to three months after arrival or as a jobseeker; and (4) make transitional provisions in relation to applications for an allocation of housing accommodation or housing assistance before 1 June 2006. SI 2000/701, 2004/1235, 2006/1093 are revoked, SI 2002/3264 amended.

The Allocation of Housing and Homelessness (Miscellaneous Provisions) (England) Regulations 2006, SI 2006/2527 (in force on 9 October 2006), make provision in relation to the allocation of housing accommodation under the Housing Act 1996 Pt 6 (ss 159–174) and to housing assistance under Pt 7 (ss 175–218). In particular, the regulations (1) amend the provisions of the Allocation of Housing and Homelessness (Eligibility) (England) Regulations 2006, SI 2006/1294, so as to substitute for old Class D a new class of persons who are eligible for an allocation and for housing assistance; and (2) make provision in relation to the conditions which must be met under the 1996 Act s 198(4) in order for a local housing authority to refer an application for housing assistance to another authority; the period of time in which the previous application must have been made is also prescribed.

The Allocation of Housing and Homelessness (Eligibility) (England) (Amendment) Regulations 2006, SI 2006/2007 (in force on 25 July 2006), amend the 2006 Regulations, SI 2006/1294 supra, so as to create an exemption, which has effect until 31 January 2007, that a person not subject to immigration control who is not habitually resident, and who left Lebanon on or after 12 July 2006 because of the armed conflict there, is not ineligible for an allocation for housing assistance.

The Allocation of Housing and Homelessness (Eligibility) (England) (Amendment) (No 2) Regulations 2006, SI 2006/3340 (in force on 1 January 2007), further amend the 2006 Regulations, SI 2006/1294, so as to insert a new category of persons who are exempt from the habitual residence test. The category applies to nationals of Bulgaria and Romania, countries which accede to the European Union on 1 January 2007. Those Bulgarian and Romanian nationals who are subject to the worker authorisation scheme established by the Accession (Immigration and Worker Authorisation) Regulations 2006, SI 2006/3317, are exempt from the habitual residence test when they are treated as workers pursuant to those regulations.

1480 Homeless persons—duty of local authority to provide accommodation—child in need—delay in making decision

The applicant was 17 when she was made homeless and sought assistance from her local housing authority. The authority delayed making a decision in relation to her application for 28 days, until she was 18-years-old, so she lost her priority status, and in the meantime tried to arrange mediation between the applicant and her mother. The applicant appealed against the authority's decision that she was not in priority need. *Held*, it was illegitimate to determine that a person was not in priority need as inquiries normally last 28 days and a person might be 18 before the end of that period. The authority was not entitled to postpone a decision in order to avoid a duty and it was not lawful for it to postpone a decision on the basis that by doing so the applicant would have reached the age of 18 before the decision was taken. A child who had been made homeless ought, if conceivably possible, be reconciled with the parent or whoever had been responsible for the decision to exclude the child, provided there was no danger to the child or others. The authority had the right to have the time to check whether a decision to exclude the child, and whether the reasons given by the child for being excluded were genuine. It could not be right, however, for an authority to persuade a family into mediation and use the time mediation would take to deprive an applicant of a right they would have had without mediation. Accordingly, the appeal would be allowed.

Robinson v Hammersmith and Fulham LBC [2006] EWCA Civ 1122, [2006] 1 WLR 3295 (Court of Appeal: Walker, Jonathan Parker and Jacob LJJ).

1481 Homeless persons—duty of local authority to provide accommodation—child in need—former relevant child

The claimant was asked by her mother to leave home when she was aged 17. She had never been in local authority care. Pursuant to the Housing Act 1996 and the Homelessness (Priority Need for Accommodation) (England) Regulations 2002, SI 2002/2051, the defendant local housing authority provided the claimant with temporary bed and breakfast accommodation. In judicial review proceedings, the claimant contended that the defendant should have identified her as a child in need under the Children Act 1989 s 17(1), (10) and should have provided her with accommodation under s 20. She submitted that the defendant's action in providing her with temporary accommodation under the 1996 Act was unlawful, and that as a consequence she had been deprived of the services which would have been available to her at the age of 18, had the provisions of the Children (Leaving Care) (England) Regulations 2001, SI 2001/2874, been applied to her, and had she, in particular, been treated as 'a former relevant child' within the meaning of the 1989 Act s 23C. *Held*, faced with a person in the claimant's position, the defendant had to act at once. Particularly in areas where a local authority's housing functions were separate from its social services functions, it would be absurd if a housing department had to turn away a homeless 17-year-old who had never been in care or looked after by a local authority on the ground that social services owed her a duty to accommodate her under s 20 as a child in need, and because, for that reason, she did not qualify as being in priority need for housing under the 1996 Act s 188. Section 188(1) required an authority merely to have reason to believe that the conditions were met. It was, therefore, dealing with apparent priority need, and was entitled to act accordingly. On the day on which the claimant had sought help from the defendant, she was not a relevant child within the terms of the 1989 Act s 23A(2). She could, however, have properly appeared to the defendant to be someone who might fall within the 2002 Regulations reg 3(1). It followed that, at that date, she fulfilled the criteria laid down in the 1996 Act s 188, and it was therefore lawful for the defendant to believe that she was a person in priority need. Accordingly, the application would be dismissed.

R (on the application of M) v Hammersmith and Fulham LBC [2006] EWCA Civ 917, [2006] 2 FCR 647 (Court of Appeal: Pill, Wall and Lloyd LJJ).

1482   Homeless persons—duty of local authority to provide accommodation—former asylum-seeker—local connection

The claimant was a successful asylum-seeker who had been provided with accommodation by the first local authority during his claim. Following his grant of indefinite leave to remain in the United Kingdom, the first authority offered him long-term accommodation under the Immigration and Asylum Act 1999 s 95. He rejected the offer and applied to the defendant local authority for accommodation, where his brothers had been settled for over a year, and his cousins had been living for more than ten years. The defendant referred his application back to the first authority on the grounds that he had no local connection, as he had no permanent job in the area, had not been living there for six of the past twelve months or three of the past five years, and did not have close family members there as his brothers had not lived there for five years and cousins did not constitute a family connection. Following a failed review, the claimant successfully appealed to the county court. The defendant appealed. *Held*, the question was whether the bond between the claimant and one or more of his extended family could be regarded as meeting the standard of 'near relatives' recognised in guidelines issued by the Secretary of State under the Housing Act 1996. The reviewing officer had addressed the question, and was entitled to decide that it did not meet that standard. Under s 199(6), (7) a former asylum-seeker was treated as having a local connection with the authority which provided him with accommodation under the 1999 Act s 95, regardless of whether it was an area he would choose to live in, and in which he had no support from friends and family. Parliament must have regarded this feature of its dispersal policy as acceptable. It was therefore impossible to criticise the defendant for taking the view that the lack of friends or family in the first authority's area was not a sufficient reason for referring his application back to the first authority. Accordingly, the appeal would be allowed.

Ozbek v Ipswich BC [2006] EWCA Civ 534, [2006] HLR 777 (Court of Appeal: Chadwick, Sedley, and Arden LJJ).

1483   Homeless persons—duty of local authority to provide accommodation—intentional homelessness—priority need—eviction

The Protection from Eviction Act 1977 s 3(1) provides that it is not lawful for the owner of any premises that have been let as a dwelling under a tenancy to enforce against the occupier, otherwise than by proceedings in the court, his right to recover possession of the premises. This applies in relation to premises occupied as a dwelling under a licence as it applies in relation to premises let under a tenancy: s 3(2B).

The claimant sought accommodation as a homeless person. The defendant local housing authority provided the claimant and her children with a self-contained flat pending its investigation of her case in accordance with the Housing Act 1996 s 188(1). The defendant found that the claimant was eligible for assistance, homeless and in priority need, but that she had made herself intentionally homeless and informed her that her accommodation would be cancelled. The claimant obtained an interim injunction restraining her eviction under the 1977 Act s 3, but her application for a permanent injunction was rejected and she appealed. *Held*, Lloyd LJ dissenting, s 3(2B) did not apply to a licence of accommodation secured by a local authority for a homeless person in discharge of its duty to provide accommodation while it considered his case under the 1996 Act s 188(1). The procedural safeguards of the 1977 Act did not need be followed in such a case due to the public law context of, and duties imposed on, local authorities by the 1996 Act Pt 7 (ss 175–218). The obligation under s 188(1) was to secure accommodation to meet a transient need. Accordingly, the appeal would be dismissed.

Desnousse v Newham LBC [2006] EWCA Civ 547, [2006] QB 831 (Court of Appeal: Pill, Tucky and Lloyd LJJ). *Mohamed v Manek* (1995) 94 LGR 211, CA (1995 Abr para 1812), applied.

1484   Homeless persons—duty of local authority to provide accommodation—intentional homelessness—priority need—relevant factors

The Housing Act 1996 s 190(1), (2)(a) provides that, where a local housing authority is satisfied that an applicant (1) is homeless and is eligible for assistance; (2) became homeless intentionally; and

(3) has a priority need, it must secure that accommodation is available for his occupation for such period as it considers will give him a reasonable opportunity of securing accommodation for his occupation.

The claimant applied to the defendant local housing authority for assistance with housing, and was provided with temporary accommodation pending an assessment. The authority subsequently informed the claimant that it was satisfied that she was homeless and had a priority need, but that she had become homeless intentionally and was therefore required to leave the temporary accommodation. The claimant had made genuine attempts to find accommodation, but had difficulty finding the money to finance a deposit. The claimant applied for judicial review, seeking mandatory relief against the authority, including an order requiring it to provide accommodation for her. The judge dismissed the application, deciding that the words 'reasonable opportunity of securing accommodation' in the 1996 Act s 190(2)(a) involved consideration by the authority both of the claimant's individual situation and that of the authority itself, including such things as the resources available to the authority, the demand for housing in the area, and the demand from those who were not intentionally homeless. The claimant appealed. *Held*, while the authority could decide, subject to the supervision of the court under ordinary principles, what amounted to a reasonable opportunity of securing accommodation, the expression did not permit it, in doing so, to have regard to considerations peculiar to it, such as the extent of its resources and other demands on it. It was what was reasonable from the claimant's standpoint, having regard to his circumstances and in the context of the accommodation potentially available. What amounted to a reasonable opportunity would depend on the particular circumstances, but it was an assessment the authority was capable of making without converting it into a duty to meet the claimant's needs. In the particular statutory context, a distinction was maintainable between giving a reasonable opportunity and giving such opportunity as would succeed in obtaining accommodation. The duty to provide a reasonable opportunity fell short of a duty to provide long-term accommodation. Accordingly, the appeal would be allowed.

R (on the application of Conville) v Richmond upon Thames LBC [2006] EWCA Civ 718, [2006] All ER (D) 37 (Jun) (Court of Appeal: Pill, Keene and Gage LJJ). Decision of Goldring J [2005] EWHC 1430 (Admin), [2006] HLR 1 reversed.

1485   Homeless persons—duty of local authority to provide accommodation—intentional homelessness—review of decision—appeal

It has been held that a local housing authority which is appealing to the Court of Appeal from a decision of a county court to quash a review of a decision that an applicant for housing assistance under the Housing Act 1996 Pt VII (ss 175–218) is intentionally homeless, should not be required, while the appeal or an application for permission to appeal is pending, to carry out a further review of the original decision. It is also unsatisfactory if the decision reached on the further review is itself made the subject of another appeal to the county court under s 204. There is no reason in principle why, in a case where an application for permission to appeal, or an appeal, from a review decision is pending in the Court of Appeal, the parties should not take the sensible and obvious course of agreeing that performance of the duty imposed on the authority by s 204(4) should await the outcome of the application or the appeal or, if the parties will not take that sensible and obvious course, why the authority should not invite the court on the application for permission to appeal to stay the effect of the order quashing the first review decision until after the application or the appeal has been determined.

William v Wandsworth LBC; Bellamy v Hounslow LBC [2006] EWCA Civ 535, [2006] HLR 809 (Court of Appeal: Chadwick, Sedley and Arden LJJ).

1486   Homeless persons—duty of local authority to provide accommodation—intentional homelessness—review of decision—good faith or wilful ignorance

The appellant had a council tenancy of a two-bedroom flat which was suitable accommodation for the purposes of the Housing Act 1996. She voluntarily gave up the tenancy of the flat and rented a larger private property, ignoring advice that, in doing so, she risked being intentionally homeless. She made an incomplete application for housing benefit and failed to respond to requests for further information. She did not, therefore, receive any housing benefit and eventually became homeless when a possession order was enforced against her. She applied to the respondent authority for assistance. The respondent declined to assist, being of the view that the appellant was intentionally homeless, so that it did not have a duty to house her. The appellant requested a review under s 202 and the respondent confirmed its original decision. On appeal by the appellant, she argued that the review decision had failed properly to consider the application of s 191(2), which provided that an act or omission in good faith on the part of a person who was unaware of any relevant fact should not be treated as deliberately making himself intentionally homeless for the purpose of s 191(1). *Held*, having regard to the authorities in conducting a review under s 202, a local housing authority was obliged to consider the effect of s 191(2), even if it had not been specifically invited to do so, if it was sensibly capable of arising on the facts. An applicant's appreciation of the prospects of future housing could be treated as awareness of a relevant fact for the purposes of s 191(2) provided that it was sufficiently specific and provided that it was based on some genuine investigation and not mere aspiration. If it was established that the applicant was unaware of a relevant fact, the question was not whether the ignorance was reasonable but whether it was in good faith. The statutory dividing line came not at the point where the applicant's ignorance of a relevant fact was due to his own unreasonable conduct but at the point where, for example, by shutting his eyes to the obvious he could be said not to have acted in good faith. Wilful ignorance, at least, had to fail the good faith test. If the applicant had no real prospect of future housing, it could not be said that an original decision maker or a review panel would fall into legal error by failing to invoke s 191(2) in favour of the applicant. The review decision did not accept the facts on which it was suggested that s 191(2) arose for consideration. The facts found showed at best that the appellant took the tenancy of the larger property not knowing whether housing benefit would cover the rent and not being bothered about the rent. Her conduct might be characterised as wilful ignorance or shutting her eyes to the obvious, thus failing the good faith test. It followed that the judge had reached the correct conclusion and, accordingly, the appeal would be dismissed.

F v Birmingham City Council [2006] EWCA Civ 1427, [2006] All ER (D) 20 (Nov) (Court of Appeal: May, Gage and Hallett LJJ).

1487   Homeless persons—duty of local authority to provide accommodation—intentional homelessness—priority need—review of decision—reasonably relevant factors

The claimant was provided with temporary bed and breakfast accommodation by the defendant local authority. The defendant subsequently informed the claimant, pursuant to the Housing Act 1996 s 190, that she was homeless, in priority need on account of her 11-year-old son, but that she had become homeless intentionally. The claimant was given notice to vacate in 28 days and details of private property to rent. The claimant asked for a review of the decision of intentional homelessness, claiming that she was unable to secure private rented accommodation because she did not have sufficient funds. The defendant contended that there was no basis to overturn the original decision that she was intentionally homeless. The claimant made an application for judicial review. The issue to be decided was whether the defendant had failed to secure accommodation for such period as it considered would give the claimant a reasonable opportunity of securing accommodation, contrary to its obligation under s 190(2)(a). *Held,* to give the claimant a reasonable opportunity of securing accommodation involved a consideration by the defendant both of the claimant's individual situation and that of the defendant itself. That would involve consideration of the claimant's financial difficulties, but not to the exclusion of everything else. Factors considered reasonably relevant had to include the resources available to the defendant, the demand for housing in the area and the demand from those who were not intentionally homeless. In the circumstances, the defendant had adequately discharged its duty under s 190(2)(a) and acted lawfully in refusing to provide the financial assistance requested. Accordingly, the application would be dismissed.

R (on the application of Conville) v Richmond Upon Thames LBC [2005] EWHC 1430 (Admin), [2006] HLR 1 (Queen's Bench Division: Goldring J).

1488   Homeless persons—duty of local authority to provide accommodation—offer of temporary accommodation—refusal of offer

The claimant was a secure tenant of the defendant local housing authority at premises where she lived with her five children. The property was among those transferred to a housing association, of which the claimant became an assured tenant. The association obtained an order for possession of the claimant's home because of the anti-social behaviour of two of her sons. She applied to the defendant for assistance as a homeless person under the Housing Act 1996 Pt VII (ss 175–218). The judge allowed her appeal under s 204, reversing the defendant's decision that she was intentionally homeless. The defendant accepted that it was obliged, under s 193(2), to secure suitable accommodation for her and her family. It offered an assured shorthold tenancy from a private landlord with an initial fixed term of six months. The claimant accepted the offer, but then refused to move in because she feared for her family's safety following the publicity her case had received. In a review decision, the defendant maintained that it no longer had a duty to the claimant under s 193. She appealed to the county court, and the judge held that the defendant's duty to the claimant under s 193(2) had ceased under s 193(5) because she had refused the offer of an assured shorthold tenancy of suitable accommodation from a private landlord. The claimant appealed, contending that the refusal by a homeless person of an offer, made by a private landlord, of an assured shorthold tenancy could never be sufficient to bring to an end the duty owed by a local housing authority under s 193(2). *Held,* s 193(5) was capable of applying to any offer of suitable accommodation, including an offer of an assured shorthold tenancy from a private landlord, apart from a qualifying offer under s 193(7B). Section 193(7B) was neutral as to whether an offer to which it applied was of temporary or permanent accommodation, but it was much more likely in practice to apply to an offer of accommodation that was or might become temporary. An assured shorthold tenancy from a private landlord might be technically insecure, but might in practice extend for a number of years. If the claimant accepted the offer and the accommodation subsequently ceased to be available, the defendant's duty would have to be performed again, assuming that the claimant's circumstances had not otherwise relevantly changed. The defendant's solution to the construction of the amended s 193 was correct, and the judge had reached the correct conclusion. Accordingly, the appeal would be dismissed.

Griffiths v St Helen's MBC [2006] EWCA Civ 160, [2006] 1 WLR 2233 (Court of Appeal: May and Rix LJJ and Coleridge J).

1489   Homeless person—duty of local authority to provide accommodation—person in need of care and attention

See *R (on the application of M) v Slough BC*, para 2699.

1490   Homeless persons—duty of local authority to provide accommodation—person subject to immigration control

The claimant, a Jamaican national, came to the United Kingdom with her five children. Several years later, when her leave to remain had expired, she made an application for support and accommodation. It was common ground that, as she did not have leave to remain, she was a person subject to immigration control within the meaning of the Immigration and Asylum Act 1999 s 115(9) and that she was ineligible for housing benefit under s 115(1)(j). Moreover, she was disqualified from having housing allocated to her under the Housing Act 1996 Pt VI (ss 159–174) or housing benefit under s 160A(3), (4). Moreover, under s 185(2), (2A), she was ineligible for housing under the homelessness provisions in Pt VII (ss 175–218). A report into the claimant's mental state concluded that she was suffering from severe anxiety relating to her children, four of whom were the subject of care proceedings. The claimant sought judicial review of the local authority's decision to refuse to provide her with support and accommodation. Issues arose as to whether the authority had the power to provide accommodation to the claimant under the Housing Act 1985 s 21 and whether the authority was obliged to provide support and accommodation to the claimant under the National Assistance Act 1948 s 21. *Held*, once it was accepted that an applicant for housing was not eligible for assistance under the 1996 Act Pt VII, any remaining power the authority had to pick and choose its tenants under the 1985 Act s 21 had to be exercised in conformity with the 1996 Act Pt VII. Section 183 was a clear indication that Parliament had intended that all cases in which the authority had reason to believe that a person was homeless or threatened with homelessness were to be funnelled through Pt VII. The terms of s 183 would be subverted were it to be open to such a person to circumvent the restriction by invoking the general power of management under the 1985 Act s 21. In relation to the second issue, the barrier in the 1948 Act s 21(1A) to providing accommodation under s 21 was not removed where the need for care and attention arose solely because of the physical effects of destitution. In principle, mental illness could come within the expression 'physical effects' of destitution. However, it had to be considered whether the need for care and attention had indeed arisen solely from destitution or its physical effects. Judgment would be given accordingly.

R (on the application of PB) v Haringey LBC [2006] EWHC 2255 (Admin), [2006] All ER (D) 82 (Sep) (Queen's Bench Division: Andrew Nichol QC).

1491   Homeless persons—duty of local authority to provide accommodation—priority need—refusal of accommodation

The claimant had applied for accommodation as a result of being in priority need and unintentionally homeless. The defendant local housing authority offered the claimant accommodation which she rejected on the grounds that accepting it would expose her to a risk from her violent and abusive former partner. Following a review of its decision, the defendant refused to offer alternative accommodation. The claimant obtained a declaration that it was not reasonable for her to accept the accommodation. The defendant appealed. *Held*, the defendant's review decision letter had not specifically dealt with the issue as to whether it was reasonable for the claimant to accept the accommodation. The Housing Act 1996 s 193(7F) required the defendant to be satisfied as to the suitability of the accommodation and the reasonableness of acceptance. The defendant's view that suitability and reasonableness could be considered together was unsustainable. Under this view, if accommodation was suitable, refusal to accept was unreasonable, which would render the second limb of s 193(7F) otiose. The language of s 193 did not permit the defendant's construction. The defendant had not considered the issue of reasonableness of acceptance and, accordingly, the appeal would be dismissed.

Slater v Lewisham LBC [2006] EWCA Civ 394, [2006] HLR 673 (Court of Appeal: Ward LJ, Sir Martin Nourse and Sir Charles Mantell).

1492   Homeless persons—duty of local authority to provide accommodation—priority need—vulnerable person

The 36-year-old claimant had grown up from the age of three in local authority care, and, from the age of 17, he had lived rough on the streets, with spells in short-term hostels and in prison. He was chronically depressed, suffered from mild asthma and hepatitis C, and had been addicted to hard drugs since the age of 13. The claimant applied to the defendant local housing authority as being in priority need of housing, on the basis that he was vulnerable for an 'other special reason' in terms of the Housing Act 1996 s 189(1)(c). The defendant refused his claim. On appeal, it was held that the claimant would be likely to be less able to look after his physical health than an ordinary homeless person, and that injury or detriment could result in the terms of increased drug addiction, infection, suicide or death from overdoses. The defendant appealed. *Held*, there were stark facts, or appraisals of fact, which pointed towards the conclusion that the claimant was vulnerable for a statutorily recognised reason. The reviewing officer had an obligation to acknowledge, take into account and evaluate these facts along with everything else. In that he had partly failed. It followed that the case would have to be reconsidered. In reconsidering the decision, the decision-maker would have to consider whether the fact that the claimant had been in care was also a cause of vulnerability. Although drug addiction could not necessarily be regarded as the sole cause of vulnerability, on the evidence there was a live question whether his introduction to hard drugs at the age of 13 was connected with his period in care and, if so, whether his present state was at least in part a continuing consequence of that. Accordingly, the appeal would be dismissed.

Crossley v Westminster CC [2006] EWCA Civ 140, [2006] All ER (D) 321 (Feb) (Court of Appeal: Sedley, Latham and Longmore LJJ). *R v Waveney DC, ex p Bowers* [1982] 3 All ER 727, CA (1982 Abr para 1526), considered.

1493 Homeless persons—immigration control—Wales

The Homelessness (Wales) Regulations 2006, SI 2006/2646 (in force on 9 October 2006), insert a new class of persons who are subject to immigration control, who are eligible for housing assistance and who have humanitarian protection. SI 2000/1079 is revoked.

1494 Houses in multiple occupation—excluded buildings—specified educational establishments—England

The Houses in Multiple Occupation (Specified Educational Establishments) (England) (No 2) Regulations 2006, SI 2006/2280 (in force on 1 October 2006), specify educational establishments so that the buildings used to accommodate full-time students do not constitute houses in multiple occupation. SI 2006/647 is revoked.

1495 Houses in multiple occupation—excluded buildings—specified educational establishments—Wales

The Houses in Multiple Occupation (Specified Educational Establishments) (Wales) Regulations 2006, SI 2006/1707 (in force on 7 July 2006), specify educational establishments so that the buildings used to accommodate full-time students do not constitute houses in multiple occupation.

1496 Houses in multiple occupation—licensing—prescribed descriptions—England

The Licensing of Houses in Multiple Occupation (Prescribed Descriptions) (England) Order 2006, SI 2006/371 (in force on 6 April 2006), prescribes a description of a house in multiple occupation ('HMO') to which the Housing Act 2004 Pt 2 applies. In particular, the order sets out the conditions HMOs must satisfy in order to be of a description prescribed and lists the storeys of an HMO that are to be taken into account when calculating whether the HMO or any part of it comprises three storeys or more.

1497 Houses in multiple occupation—licensing—prescribed descriptions—Wales

The Licensing of Houses in Multiple Occupation (Prescribed Descriptions) (Wales) Order 2006, SI 2006/1712 (in force on 30 June 2006), prescribes a description of a house in multiple occupation ('HMO') to which the Housing Act 2004 Pt 2 applies. In particular, the order (1) sets out the conditions HMOs must satisfy in order to be of a description prescribed; and (2) lists the storeys of an HMO that are to be taken into account when calculating whether the HMO or any part of it comprises three storeys or more.

1498 Houses in multiple occupation—licensing and management—England

The Licensing and Management of Houses in Multiple Occupation and Other Houses (Miscellaneous Provisions) (England) Regulations 2006, SI 2006/373 (in force on 6 April 2006), which apply in relation to England only, specify (1) the circumstances when persons are regarded as forming a single household for the purpose of deciding whether a building is a house in multiple occupation; (2) that migrant workers, seasonal workers and asylum-seekers are to be treated as occupying premises as their only or main residence where the occupation is in consideration of employment and the building provided by the employer, or where the accommodation is provided under the Immigration Act 1999 s 95 and funded by the National Asylum Support Service; (3) a description of buildings that are not houses in multiple occupation; (4) provisions concerning applications for licences, including the information that must be supplied with an application; (5) the standards to be applied when determining the suitability of a house for multiple occupation for licensing; (6); the manner in which designations of areas, and revocations of designations, must be published; and (7) the information, on licences granted, temporary exemption notices exempting a house from licensing and management orders, that must be contained in registers held by local housing authorities.

1499   Houses in multiple occupation—licensing and management—Wales

The Licensing and Management of Houses in Multiple Occupation and Other Houses (Miscellaneous Provisions) (Wales) Regulations 2006, SI 2006/1715 (in force on 30 June 2006), (1) specify the circumstances when persons are to be regarded as forming a single household for the purposes of deciding whether a building is a house in multiple occupation ('HMO'); (2) provide that migrant workers, seasonal workers and asylum-seekers are to be treated as occupying certain premises as their only or main residence; (3) specify a description of buildings that are not HMOs for the purposes of the Act; (4) make provision about applications for licences and the information that must be supplied with an application; (5) prescribe the standards to be applied when determining the suitability of a HMO for licensing; (6) specify the manner in which designations of areas and revocations of such designations must be published; and (7) specify the information that must be contained in registers held by local housing authorities of licences granted, temporary exemption notices that exempt a house from licensing and management orders.

1500   Houses in multiple occupation—management—England

The Management of Houses in Multiple Occupation (England) Regulations 2006, SI 2006/372 (in force on 6 April 2006), impose duties on a person managing a house in multiple occupation in respect of (1) providing information to occupiers; (2) taking safety measures, including fire safety measures; (3) maintaining the water supply and drainage; (4) supplying and maintaining gas and electricity, including having it regularly inspected; (5) maintaining common parts, fixtures, fittings and appliances; (6) maintaining living accommodation; and (7) providing waste disposal facilities. Duties are also imposed on occupiers of a house in multiple occupation for the purpose of ensuring that the person managing it can effectively carry out his duties. Any person who fails to comply with the requirements commits an offence punishable on summary conviction with a fine not exceeding level five on the standard scale.

1501   Houses in multiple occupation—management—Wales

The Management of Houses in Multiple Occupation (Wales) Regulations 2006, SI 2006/1713 (in force on 30 June 2006), impose duties on a person managing a house in multiple occupation ('HMO') in respect of (1) providing information to occupiers; (2) taking safety measures including fire safety measures; (3) maintaining the water supply and drainage; (4) supplying and maintaining gas and electricity including having it regularly inspected; (5) maintaining common parts, fixtures, fittings and appliances; (6) maintaining living accommodation; and (7) providing waste disposal facilities. Duties are also imposed on occupiers of a HMO so as to enable a person managing it to effectively carry out the duties imposed on him.

1502   Housing Act 2004—commencement

The Housing Act 2004 (Commencement No 5 and Transitional Provisions and Savings) (England) Order 2006, SI 2006/1060, brings into force (1) on 6 April 2006, ss 72(2), (3), (5)–(7), 95(2), (4), (6), 265(1) (in part), Sch 15 paras 2–6, 8–36, 38–44, and, in so far as they are not already in force, ss 1, 3–8, 10–52, 54, 55, 58–71, 75–78, 82–94, 98–133, 135–147, 232, 235, 236, 238–243, Schs 1–7; and (2) on 6 July 2006, ss 73, 96 and, in so far as they are not already in force, ss 72, 74, 95, 97, 134. Transitional provisions and savings are also made.

The Housing Act 2004 (Commencement No 6) (England) Order 2006, SI 2006/3191, brings into force, in relation to England, on 2 January 2007, ss 225 (so far as not already in force), 226, 265(1) (in part) and Sch 15 para 47.

The Housing Act 2004 (Commencement No 3 and Transitional Provisions and Savings) (Wales) Order 2006, SI 2006/1535, brings into force, in relation to Wales, on 16 June 2006, (1) in so far as they are not already in force, ss 1, 3, 5–8, 10–52, 54, 55, 58–78, 82–147, 229–232, 235, 236, 238–243, Schs 1–7, 13; and (2) ss 265(1) (in part), 266 (in part), Sch 15 paras 2–6, 9–36, 38–44 and certain repeals in Sch 16. Transitional provisions and savings are also made.

For a summary of the Act, see 2004 Abr para 1428. See also the commencement table in the title STATUTES.

1503   Housing benefit

See SOCIAL SECURITY.

1504   Housing Corporation (Delegation) etc Act 2006

The Housing Corporation (Delegation) etc Act 2006 makes provision about the delegation of functions by the Housing Corporation and Housing for Wales and about the validation of things done or evidenced by, and the authentication of the fixing of, their seals. The Act received the royal assent on 19 July 2006 and came into force on that day.

Section 1 adds a provision to the Housing Associations Act 1985 to authorise the Housing Corporation to delegate the exercise of any of its functions to any of its members, committees, sub-committees or employees and provides that the Corporation and Housing for Wales, before its abolition, are to be taken to have been so authorised. The 2006 Act s 2 deals with short title and extent.

1505   Housing renewal grants—form and particulars—Wales

The Housing Renewal Grants (Prescribed Form and Particulars) (Amendment) (Wales) Regulations 2006, SI 2006/2800 (in force on 20 October 2006), further amend the 1996 Regulations, SI 1996/2891, so as to (1) permit local housing authorities to use forms of their own design which have the same effect as the prescribed form for applications for a housing renewal grant; (2) replace references in the prescribed form to qualifying park homes with references to caravans; and (3) make changes relating to civil partnership.

1506   Housing renewal grants—means testing—Wales

The Housing Renewal Grants (Amendment) (Wales) Regulations 2006, SI 2006/2801 (in force on 20 October 2006), further amend the 1996 Regulations, SI 1996/2890, so that (1) the means test for determining the amount of grant which may be paid by local housing authorities no longer applies where an application for grant is made by the parent or guardian of a disabled child or young person; (2) modified provision applies in relation to relevant persons who have attained, or whose partners have attained, the qualifying age for state pension credit; (3) the applicable amount for the purpose of determining the amount of grant payable is increased; (4) the loan generation factors are uprated; (5) the income and capital of a child or young person are disregarded; (6) the maximum deduction which may be made, in cases meeting certain conditions, is increased in respect of average weekly relevant child care charges for the purpose of determining income on a weekly basis; (7) the amounts specified as sums to be excluded from a student's grant income where the student does not have a student loan is increased; (8) applicable amounts and premiums are uprated; (9) specified persons need to work fewer hours in order to qualify for an increase in the sums to be disregarded from their earnings; (10) the references to rules of court are updated; and (11) provision is made disregarding, from the calculation of capital, certain amounts received by victims of the London bombings on 7 July 2005. SI 2005/2605 is revoked.

1507   Housing standards—housing health and safety rating system—Wales

The Housing Health and Safety Rating System (Wales) Regulations 2006, SI 2006/1702 (in force on 30 June 2006), relate to the evidence-based system of the assessment of housing conditions. In particular, the regulations (1) prescribe descriptions of hazards in relation to residential premises with reference to the occurrence of matters or circumstances specified; (2) prescribe, for the purposes of the Housing Act 2004 s 10, a fire hazard as one where the risk of harm arises from exposure to uncontrolled fire and associated smoke; (3) provide for the manner in which, and the extent to which, premises are to be inspected under the housing health and safety rating system; (4) prescribe the method for calculating the seriousness of hazards to be expressed as a numerical score; (5) provide for the categorisation of a hazard as either a category one hazard or a category two hazard, according to its numerical score; and (6) describe each class of harm.

1508   Interim management orders—prescribed circumstances—England

The Housing (Interim Management Orders) (Prescribed Circumstances) (England) Order 2006, SI 2006/369 (in force on 6 April 2006), prescribes the category of circumstances that must be satisfied before a residential property tribunal can authorise a local housing authority to make an interim management order in respect of a house to which the Housing Act 2004 s 103 applies.

1509   Interim management orders—prescribed circumstances—Wales

The Housing (Interim Management Orders) (Prescribed Circumstances) (Wales) Order 2006, SI 2006/1706 (in force on 30 June 2006), prescribes the category of circumstances that must be satisfied before a residential property tribunal can authorise a local housing authority to make an interim management order in respect of a house to which the Housing Act 2004 s 103 applies.

1510   Local authority housing—allocation of housing—eligible persons—Wales

The Allocation of Housing (Wales) (Amendment) Regulations 2006, SI 2006/2645, (in force on 9 October 2006), amend the 2003 Regulations, SI 2003/239, in relation to Wales, by adding those who have been granted humanitarian protection under the Immigration Rules to the persons eligible for an allocation of housing accommodation.

1511   Local authority housing—introductory tenancies—trial period extension—review—England

The Introductory Tenancies (Review of Decisions to Extend a Trial Period) (England) Regulations 2006, SI 2006/1077 (in force on 3 May 2006), make provision in respect of procedures to be followed where a landlord wishes to extend an introductory tenancy. The regulations (1) provide that the tenant is entitled to request an oral hearing and set out how this right is to be exercised; (2) require the landlord to give the tenant notice of the review; (3) provide that the review must be carried out by a person who was not involved in the original decision; (4) provide that, if the person carrying out the review and the person who made the decision to extend the trial period are both officers of the landlord, the person carrying out the review must hold a position in the landlord's organisation senior to the person who made the original decision; (5) set out the requirements in relation to written representations at the review; and (6) set out the procedures to be followed during a review by way of an oral hearing.

1512   Local authority housing—introductory tenancies—trial period extension—review—Wales

The Introductory Tenancies (Review of Decisions to Extend a Trial Period) (Wales) Regulations 2006, SI 2006/2983 (in force on 17 November 2006), apply in relation to Wales, and make provision in respect of procedures to be followed where a landlord wishes to extend an introductory tenancy. The regulations (1) provide that the tenant is entitled to request an oral hearing and set out how this right is to be exercised; (2) require the landlord to give the tenant notice of the review; (3) provide that the review must be carried out by a person who was not involved in the original decision; (4) provide that, if the person carrying out the review and the person who made the decision to extend the trial period are both officers of the landlord, the person carrying out the review must hold a position in the landlord's organisation senior to the person who made the original decision; (5) set out the requirements in relation to written representations at the review; and (6) set out the procedures to be followed during a review by way of an oral hearing.

1513   Local authority housing—persons subject to immigration control—England

The Persons Subject to Immigration Control (Housing Authority Accommodation and Homelessness) (Amendment) Order 2006, SI 2006/2521 (in force on 9 October 2006), further amends the 2000 Order, SI 2000/706, by replacing in part class B of persons subject to immigration control for the purposes of the Immigration and Asylum Act 1999 s 118 to reflect changes to the process of and language used in the granting of leave outside immigration rules, and by adding a new class that covers persons who have humanitarian protection under the immigration rules.

1514   Local authority housing—secure tenancy—possession proceedings— subsequent bankruptcy order

The defendant occupied premises as a tenant of the claimant local authority. The tenancy was a secure tenancy and therefore could not be terminated except by a court order. The claimant commenced proceedings against the defendant when he failed to pay rent and the claimant obtained a possession order. The order was not to be enforced so long as the defendant paid the current rent plus a further weekly payment. Subsequently, a bankruptcy order was made against the defendant on his own petition. The defendant applied for the discharge of the possession order on the grounds that his liability for the arrears of rent and costs were debts provable in his bankruptcy and the order for possession was precluded by the Insolvency Act 1986 s 285(3)(a). The judge dismissed the application. The defendant's appeal was unsuccessful. On his further appeal, *held*, the secure tenancy had ended before the bankruptcy order was made. Therefore, the principal submission for the defendant that the maintenance of the possession order constituted a remedy against the property of the defendant in the form of the benefit of the secure tenancy precluded by s 285(3) had to be rejected. While it subsisted, the benefit of the secure tenancy was property of the defendant but it did not subsist at the time the bankruptcy order was made and was not subsisting at the present time. Further, the right to seek a postponement of the date for possession or to discharge it altogether arose and continued to subsist because of the existence of the possession order. The possession order was in no sense a remedy against that right in respect of the arrears of rent. Those consequences were entirely consistent with the purpose of s 285, namely to preserve the estate of the bankrupt for the benefit of his unsecured creditors. The benefit of a secure tenancy did not vest in the trustee in bankruptcy so there was no property to preserve in that respect. The court would fix the sum to be paid in respect of the arrears and current use and occupation in a sum the bankrupt could pay out of current income, which did not vest in the trustee either. Accordingly, the appeal would be dismissed.

Harlow DC v Hall [2006] EWCA Civ 156, [2006] 1 WLR 2116 (Court of Appeal: Sir Andrew Morritt C, Chadwick LJ and Sir Paul Kennedy).

1515   Local authority housing—suitability of accommodation—Wales

The Homelessness (Suitability of Accommodation) (Wales) Order 2006, SI 2006/650 (in force in part on 3 April 2006, in part on 2 April 2007 and in part on 7 April 2008), specifies the circumstances in which accommodation made available by a local housing authority under the Housing Act 1996 Pt VII (ss 175–218) for an applicant who is homeless or threatened with homelessness, will not be regarded as suitable. In particular, the order (1) applies to persons in priority need and specifies matters relating to the health needs of a person, any disability of a person and the proximity of social services and other support, which must be taken into account in determining whether accommodation is suitable for a person; (2) specifies that Bed and Breakfast accommodation ('B&B accommodation') may only be regarded as suitable if it complies with a basic standard requirement that all statutory requirements are met; (3) specifies minimum standards for B&B accommodation used for households containing or consisting of one or more minors aged 16 or 17 or a pregnant woman; (4) provides for exceptions relating to the length of time spent in B&B accommodation, the standard of the B&B accommodation and the choice of the homeless household; (5) extends the minimum standards to the types of shared accommodation specified; and (6) extends similar restrictions to all priority need households.

1516   Local authority housing—tenancies—creation, terms and termination—Law Commission proposals

See para 1778.

1517   Management orders—empty dwelling management orders—supplemental provisions—England

The Housing (Management Orders and Empty Dwelling Management Orders) (Supplemental Provisions) (England) Regulations 2006, SI 2006/368 (in force on 6 April 2006), require a local housing authority that is treated as the lessee under a lease of premises that are subject to an interim or final empty dwelling management order to (1) give notice to the immediate lessor that a management order or empty dwelling management order has been made and explain the consequences of the order; and (2) be liable for the payment of ground rent, service charges and other charges due as the lessee.

1518   Management orders—empty dwelling management orders—supplemental provisions—Wales

The Housing (Management Orders and Empty Dwelling Management Orders) (Supplemental Provisions) (Wales) Regulations 2006, SI 2006/2822 (in force on 26 October 2006), make supplementary provisions where a local housing authority is to be treated as the lessee under a lease of premises that is subject to an interim or final management order, or an interim or final empty dwelling management order ('EDMO') made under the Housing Act 2004. In particular, the regulations (1) provide that where a local housing authority is to be treated as lessee of premises instead of another person, the local housing authority is required to give notice to the immediate lessor of that relevant person that a management order or EDMO has been made and explain the consequences of the order; and (2) provide for the local authority to be liable for the payment of ground rent, service charges and other charges due as if it were the lessee, from date the order comes into force, but requires the relevant person to be sent copies of any notices served on the local housing authority.

1519   Residential property tribunal—fees—England

The Residential Property Tribunal (Fees) (England) Regulations 2006, SI 2006/830 (in force on 13 April 2006), require a fee of £150 to be paid when an appeal or application is made to a residential property tribunal relating to (1) the refusal of a local housing authority to (a) approve the use of premises where a prohibition order is in place in relation to those premises; (b) grant a temporary exemption notice in relation to a house in multiple occupation which is subject to compulsory licensing; or (c) grant a temporary exemption notice in relation to premises which are subject to selective licensing; (2) an authority's making of, or refusal to revoke or vary, an improvement notice or a prohibition order; (3) the level of expenses demanded by an authority in respect of works it has carried out where an improvement notice has not been complied with; (4) an authority's decision or refusal to grant a licence and its decision or refusal to revoke or vary such a licence; (5) an authority's grant of, or the terms of, an interim or final management order or a final empty dwelling management order, and its decision or refusal to revoke or vary either such order; (6) compensation payable to a third party where a management order is made; (7) the grant of a demolition order; and (8) an application to carry out works to unfit premises. The regulations also (a) provide that no fee is payable to the tribunal where the grounds for appeal against a management order include a failure to deal with payment in relation to specified matters; (b) provide for an appellant or applicant to be liable for payment of the fee and for the fee to be waived where he or his partner is in receipt of specified benefits; and (c) set out the circumstances in which the tribunal may order one party to an appeal or application to reimburse any fees incurred by another party.

1520   Residential property tribunal—fees—Wales

The Residential Property Tribunal (Fees) (Wales) Regulations 2006, SI 2006/1642 (in force on 23 June 2006), require a fee of £150 to be paid when an appeal or application is made to a tribunal relating to (1) the refusal of a local housing authority to (a) approve the use of premises where a prohibition order is in place in relation to those premises; (b) grant a temporary exemption notice in relation to a house in multiple occupation which is subject to compulsory licensing; and (c) grant a temporary exemption notice in relation to premises which are subject to selective licensing; (2) a local housing authority's making of, or refusal to revoke or vary (a) an improvement notice; or (b) a prohibition order; (3) the level of expenses demanded by a local housing authority in respect of works it has carried out where an improvement notice has not been complied with; (4) a local housing authority's grant or refusal to grant a licence and its decision (or refusal) to revoke or vary such a licence; (5) a local housing authority's grant of, or terms of (a) an interim or final management order, and its decision (or refusal) to revoke or vary such an order; (b) a final empty dwelling management order, and its decision (or refusal) to revoke or vary such an order; (6) compensation payable to a third party where a management order is made; (7) the grant of a demolition order; and (8) an application to carry out works to unfit premises. The regulations also provide (i) that a fee is not payable where the grounds for appeal against a management order include failure to deal with payment to deal with specified matters; (ii) for the appellant or applicant to be liable for payment of the fee and for the fee to be waived where the appellant or applicant or the partner of the appellant or applicant is in receipt of specified benefits; and (iii) for the circumstances in which the tribunal may order one party to an appeal or application to reimburse any fees incurred by another party.

1521   Residential property tribunal—procedure—England

The Residential Property Tribunal Procedure (England) Regulations 2006, SI 2006/831 (in force on 13 April 2006), regulate the procedure to be followed for applications and appeals made to a residential property tribunal ('RPT') under the Housing Act 2004 or the Housing Act 1985 Pt 9 (ss 264–323). In particular, the regulations (1) specify the proceedings to which they apply; (2) set out the overriding objective of dealing fairly and justly with applications; (3) make provision in connection with requests for extension of time to make an application in those cases where the RPT has the power to permit such an extension; (4) provide details of the information to be included with an application, and specify additional documents for particular applications; (5) make provision in respect of the RPT acknowledging an application and sending copy documents to the respondent and a notice specifying the date by which the respondent should reply to the RPT; (6) provide for the respondent's reply; (7) permit the RPT to hold an oral hearing at short notice where a local housing authority has applied for authorisation of an interim management order and where it appears to the RPT on the basis of information accompanying the application that specified exceptional circumstances exist; (8) make provision for applications to be joined as a party to the proceedings; (9) specify circumstances where two or more separate applications, or particular issues arising in separate applications, may be determined together; (10) provide that, where an application fee is unpaid for 14 days, the application will be treated as withdrawn unless there are reasonable grounds not to do so; (11) enable the duty to supply a document to be satisfied by supplying it to a party's or interested person's representative where this is requested in writing; (12) require the RPT to ensure that interested persons are notified of the application together with an explanation of the procedure for applying to be joined as a party; (13) provide for the distribution of relevant documents by the RPT; (14) make provision in relation to the RPT's powers to order the supply of information and documents and with failure to comply with such an order; (15) enable the RPT to determine an application without an oral hearing; (16) make provision for interim orders in certain cases; (17) make procedural provision in respect of directions under the RPT's general power; (18) make provision in relation to inspection of premises and the neighbourhood; (19) provide for adducing expert evidence to the RPT; (20) enable the RPT to hold a case management conference, including a pre-trial review, on not less than 14 days' notice to the parties, or a shorter period if agreed by the parties; (21) specify details of the RPT's remaining case management powers and allow it to extend the time for various steps in the action; (22) provide for the giving of notice appointing the date, time and place of a hearing; (23) make provision for the RPT to postpone a hearing; (24) set out the RPT's powers at a hearing; (25) make provision as to when a hearing may be held in private as an exception to the general rule that it should be held in public; (26) set out those who are entitled to be present at hearings held in private and at the RPT's deliberations to determine the application; (27) enable the RPT to proceed with a hearing in the absence of a party who fails to appear; (28) specify how and when the RPT will give and record decisions and reasons; (29) provide that the RPT must not award costs under its powers without giving the party concerned the opportunity to make representations and that costs awarded may not exceed £500; (30) specify how an application may be withdrawn in whole or part, and stipulate circumstances in which the permission of the RPT is required for withdrawal of an application; (31) provide for a decision of a RPT to be enforced in a county court with the court's permission; (32) make provision relating to requests to a RPT for permission to appeal to the Lands Tribunal; (33) require the RPT to make appropriate arrangements where any person taking part in the proceedings requires translation, interpretation, or other assistance to enable effective participation in the proceedings; (34) make provision about the requirements where a document or notice is required or authorised to be supplied, including the circumstances in which communication by fax or electronic communication, such as e-mail, or by a private delivery service will be acceptable; (35) provide that, if the specified time for doing any act expires on a weekend or public holiday, the act will be in time if done on the next working day; (36) enable the RPT, after giving notice of at least 21 days to the applicant, to dismiss in whole or in part any application considered to be frivolous, vexatious, or otherwise an abuse of process; (37) provide that irregularities by parties will not in themselves render the proceedings void; (38) allow mechanical or other reproduction of a signature, so long as the name of the person signing is added underneath in a way which enables him to be identified; and (39) specify applications which may be made to a RPT and in respect of each specify the additional documents which must be included with an application, and the persons who may be named as respondents to the application.

1522   Residential property tribunal—procedure—Wales

The Residential Property Tribunal Procedure (Wales) Regulations 2006, SI 2006/1641 (in force on 23 June 2006), regulate the procedure to be followed for applications and appeals made to a residential property tribunal ('RPT') under the Housing Act 2004 or the Housing Act 1985 Pt 9 (ss 264–323). In particular, the regulations (1) specify the proceedings to which they apply; (2) set out the overriding objective of dealing fairly and justly with applications; (3) make provision in connection with requests for extension of time to make an application in those cases where the RPT has the power to permit such an extension; (4) provide details of the information to be included with an application, and specify additional documents for particular applications; (5) make provision in respect of the RPT acknowledging an application and sending copy documents to the respondent and a notice specifying the date by which the respondent should reply to the RPT; (6) provide for the respondent's reply; (7) permit the RPT to hold an oral hearing at short notice where a local housing authority has applied for authorisation of an interim management order and where it appears to the RPT on the basis of information accompanying the application that specified exceptional circumstances exist; (8) make provision for applications to be joined as a party to the proceedings; (9) specify circumstances where two or more separate applications, or particular issues arising in separate applications, may be determined together; (10) provide that, where an application fee is unpaid for 14 days, the application will be treated as withdrawn unless there are reasonable grounds not to do so; (11) enable the duty to supply a document to be satisfied by supplying it to a party's or interested person's representative where this is requested in writing; (12) require the RPT to ensure that interested persons are notified of the application together with an explanation of the procedure for applying to be joined as a party; (13) provide for the distribution of relevant documents by the RPT; (14) make provision in relation to the RPT's powers to order the supply of information and documents and with failure to comply with such an order; (15) enable the RPT to determine an application without an oral hearing; (16) make provision for interim orders in certain cases; (17) make procedural provision in respect of directions under the RPT's general power; (18) make provision in relation to inspection of premises and the neighbourhood; (19) provide for adducing expert evidence to the RPT; (20) enable the RPT to hold a case management conference, including a pre-trial review, on not less than 14 days' notice to the parties, or a shorter period if agreed by the parties; (21) specify details of the RPT's remaining case management powers and allow it to extend the time for various steps in the action; (22) provide for the giving of notice appointing the date, time and place of a hearing; (23) make provision for the RPT to postpone a hearing; (24) set out the RPT's powers at a hearing; (25) make provision as to when a hearing may be held in private as an exception to the general rule that it should be held in public; (26) set out those who are entitled to be present at hearings held in private and at the RPT's deliberations to determine the application; (27) enable the RPT to proceed with a hearing in the absence of a party who fails to appear; (28) specify how and when the RPT will give and record decisions and reasons; (29) provide that the RPT must not award costs under its powers without giving the party concerned the opportunity to make representations and that costs awarded may not exceed £500; (30) specify how an application may be withdrawn in whole or part, and stipulate circumstances in which the permission of the RPT is required for withdrawal of an application; (31) provide for a decision of a RPT to be enforced in a county court with the court's permission; (32) make provision relating to requests to a RPT for permission to appeal to the Lands Tribunal; (33) require the RPT to make appropriate arrangements where any person taking part in the proceedings requires translation, interpretation, or other assistance to enable effective participation in the proceedings; (34) make provision about the requirements where a document or notice is required or authorised to be supplied, including the circumstances in which communication by fax or electronic communication, such as e-mail, or by a private delivery service will be acceptable; (35) provide that, if the specified time for doing any act expires on a weekend or public holiday, the act will be in time if done on the next working day; (36) enable the RPT, after giving notice of at least 21 days to the applicant, to dismiss in whole or in part any application considered to be frivolous, vexatious, or otherwise an abuse of process; (37) provide that irregularities by parties will not in themselves render the proceedings void; (38) allow mechanical or other reproduction of a signature, so long as the name of the person signing is added underneath in a way which enables him to be identified; and (39) specify applications which may be made to a RPT and in respect of each specify the additional documents which must be included with an application, and the persons who may be named as respondents to the application.

1523 Selective licensing of houses—additional conditions—Wales

The Selective Licensing of Houses (Additional Conditions) (Wales) Order 2006, SI 2006/2825 (in force on 26 October 2006), sets out additional conditions which must be met before a local housing authority designates an area of their district or an area in their district as subject to selective licensing.

1524 Selective licensing of houses—specified exemptions—England

The Selective Licensing of Houses (Specified Exemptions) (England) Order 2006, SI 2006/370 (in force on 6 April 2006), specifies, for the purposes of the Housing Act 2004 Pt 3, the descriptions of tenancies and licences of houses, or of dwellings contained in houses, that are exempt tenancies or licences.

1525 Selective licensing of houses—specified exemptions—Wales

The Selective Licensing of Houses (Specified Exemptions) (Wales) Order 2006, SI 2006/2824 (in force on 26 October 2006), specifies, for the purposes of the Housing Act 2004 Pt 3, the descriptions of tenancies and licences of houses, or of dwellings contained in houses, that are exempt tenancies or licences.

1526 Social housing—grants to bodies other than registered social landlords—additional purposes—England

The Social Housing (Grants to Bodies other than Registered Social Landlords) (Additional Purposes) (England) Order 2006, SI 2006/583 (in force on 6 April 2006), specifies the following additional purposes for which the Housing Corporation may give grant to persons other than registered social landlords: (1) managing public sector or former sector housing where those managing are the occupiers of that housing; (2) facilitating or encouraging improvements in, or providing services in connection with, the management of such housing; (3) providing educational or training courses in housing management to occupiers of such housing; (4) providing services for those providing such courses; and (5) providing financial assistance, or other assistance for those attending such courses.

1527 Social landlords—additional purposes—England

The Social Landlords (Permissible Additional Purposes) (England) Order 2006, SI 2006/1968 (in force on 24 August 2006), adds to the purposes or objects for the eligibility for registration as a social landlord under the Housing Act 1996 s 2, the provision, construction, improvement or management of caravan sites for gipsies and travellers, and the provision of services to those sites.

See para 2784.

1528 Social landlords—housing association—business

See *Riverside Housing Association Ltd v Revenue and Customs Comrs*, para 2942.

1529 Student accommodation—management of premises—codes of practice—England

See para 1748.

1530 Student accommodation—management of premises—codes of practice—Wales

See para 1749.

HUMAN RIGHTS

Halsbury's Laws of England (4th edn) vol 8(2) (Reissue) paras 101–200

Articles

For articles relating to this title please refer to the Table of Articles at the beginning of the Abridgment.

1531 Convention right—action incompatible with right—proceedings—Proscribed Organisations Appeal Commission

The Proscribed Organisations Appeal Commission (Human Rights Act 1998 Proceedings) Rules 2006, SI 2006/2290 (in force on 20 September 2006), provide that the Proscribed Organisations Appeal Commission is the appropriate tribunal for the purpose of the Human Rights

Act 1998 s 7, in relation to proceedings against the Secretary of State, in respect of a refusal by him to remove an organisation from the list of proscribed organisations, or a refusal to provide for a name to cease to be treated as a name for an organisation listed as a proscribed organisation. SI 2001/127 is revoked.

1532 Convention right—asylum application—qualified right

See *EM (Lebanon) v Secretary of State for the Home Department*, para 329.

1533 Convention right—breach—public authority—railway infrastructure company

The Human Rights Act 1998 s 6(1) provides that it is unlawful for a public authority to act in a way which is incompatible with a right under the European Convention on Human Rights. 'Public authority' includes any person certain of whose functions are functions of a public nature (1998 Act s 6(3)(b)), but a person is not a public authority by virtue only of s 6(3)(b) if the nature of a particular act is private (s 6(5)).

The deceased died as a result of injuries sustained in a railway accident. She was the mother of three of the claimants who, as they were not financially dependent on her, were not included in the class of persons entitled to bring proceedings for damages under the Fatal Accidents Act 1976 s 1A on behalf of her estate. They were only entitled to recover funeral expenses. They claimed that this was a breach of the right to life guaranteed by the Convention art 2, alleging that the defendant's failure to maintain defective points had caused the accident. The defendant had formerly had the national railway infrastructure vested in it as well as statutory powers to regulate safety on the railway network. In order to succeed in their claim, the claimants had to prove that the defendant, at the material time, was a public authority and acting as such. The defendant applied for summary judgment on the ground that the claim had no real prospect of success. *Held*, it was clear that, as originally set up by statute, the defendant had had functions which were of a public nature. However, as a result of the Railways (Safety Case) Regulations 2000, SI 2000/2688, the defendant was now exercising hybrid functions. The specific act of maintaining rail track was difficult to classify as a public function within the 1998 Act s 6, and the appropriate conclusion was that the defendant was not, and was not acting as, a public authority. The mere fact that relatives of the deceased had no claim other than in respect of funeral expenses arising from the death of the deceased did not involve the state in any breach of its obligations under the Convention art 2. Accordingly, the application would be granted.

Cameron v Network Rail Infrastructure Ltd [2006] EWHC 1133 (QB), [2006] PIQR P451 (Queen's Bench Division: Sir Michael Turner).

1534 Convention right—public authority—private person performing functions of a public nature—provision of accommodation

The claimants were all in the residential care of the defendant local authority by reason of age and infirmity and were provided with that care in accordance with the defendant's statutory obligations under the National Assistance Act 1948 s 21. The defendant decided to seek a private sector operator to accept transfer of, operate and expand two care homes. The claimants applied for judicial review of that decision, and issues arose as to whether (1) a private body, in providing accommodation to persons in need of care and assistance pursuant to arrangements made with a local authority in the exercise of that authority's functions under ss 21 and 26, itself exercised functions of a public nature within the meaning of the Human Rights Act 1998 s 6(3)(b) so that it fell to be treated, in the exercise of those functions, as a public authority for the purposes of s 6(1); and (2) if not, the transfer of such a home by a local authority to a private sector provider pursuant to the 1948 Act s 26 would be unlawful under the 1998 Act s 6(1) as constituting a breach of the rights of the residents of the home under the European Convention on Human Rights. *Held*, a private body was not exercising functions of a public nature in those circumstances. Moreover, a transfer from local authority to private sector accommodation did not, in principle, lead to the residents' Convention rights being either diminished or removed. In effect, the residents would continue to retain their Convention rights' protection under the 1998 Act in the same way and to the same extent as under the previous arrangement. Judgment would be given accordingly.

R (on the application of Johnson) v Havering LBC [2006] EWHC 1714 (Admin), [2006] All ER (D) 133 (Jul) (Queen's Bench Division: Forbes J). *R (on the application of Heather) v Leonard Cheshire Foundation* [2002] EWCA Civ 366, [2002] 2 All ER 936 (2002 Abr para 1751); and *Poplar Housing and Regeneration Community Association Ltd v Donoghue* [2001] EWCA Civ 595, [2002] QB 48 (2001 Abr para 1835) applied.

1535 Data protection

See CONFIDENCE AND DATA PROTECTION.

1536   European Convention on Human Rights—interpretation—application of international law

The two applicants, the mothers of soldiers who had died while serving in the armed forces in Iraq, sought an inquiry as to whether the government had taken reasonable steps to satisfy itself that the invasion of Iraq was lawful under the principles of public international law. The claimants argued that, by failing to do so, the government had breached the right to life, guaranteed by the European Convention on Human Rights art 2, in not safeguarding the lives of the members of the armed forces. The application for permission to seek judicial review of the government's decision to refuse to hold the inquiry was dismissed, but the Court of Appeal decided to hear the application. *Held*, the United Kingdom was not obliged by art 2 to set up an independent inquiry into the invasion. The principles of international law played a part in the construction of the Convention but they had not been imported wholesale into it as the Convention was only concerned with domestic rights. It respected the general principle of the separation of powers between the executive and the courts, including the principle that there remained some areas which were essentially matters for the executive and not the courts. Accordingly, the application would be dismissed.

   R (on the application of Gentle) v Prime Minister [2006] EWCA Civ 1690, [2006] All ER (D) 147 (Dec) (Court of Appeal: Sir Anthony Clarke MR, Sir Igor Judge P and Dyson LJ).

1537   European Court of Human Rights—application—admissibility—exhaustion of domestic remedy—declaration of incompatibility

The applicants were unmarried sisters, one of whom was aged 88 and the other aged 81. They had lived together all their lives, for the last 30 years in a house built on land inherited from their parents. The house was owned in their joint names and had a value which brought it within the scope of inheritance tax. Each sister, in addition to her joint share in the house, owned significant investments and other property. They submitted that the value of the house had increased to the point that each sister's one-half share was worth more than the current exemption threshold for inheritance tax, and that the survivor might have to sell the house in order to pay the tax. They brought a complaint that this constituted an infringement of their right to peaceful enjoyment of their possessions under the European Convention on Human Rights First Protocol art 1, taken in conjunction with their right under art 14 not to be discriminated against. The applicants argued that they could properly be regarded as being in a similar situation to a married or same-sex couple within the scope of the Civil Partnership Act 2004. The national authority submitted that the complaint was prospective and hypothetical because no liability to inheritance tax had yet accrued, and might never accrue so that the applicants could not claim, therefore, to be victims of any violation as required by the Convention art 34, and that, if the applicants had an arguable complaint under the Convention, they could and should have brought a claim for a declaration of incompatibility under the Human Rights Act 1998 s 4. *Held*, in order to claim to be a victim of violation, a person had to be directly affected by the impugned measure. Because of the ages of the applicants it was virtually certain that one of them would in the not too distant future be required to pay substantial inheritance tax on property inherited from her sister. It followed that they could claim to be directly affected. Moreover, the remedy under the 1998 Act allowing an applicant to seek a declaration from a domestic court that legislation was incompatible with the Convention was not sufficiently effective for the purposes of art 35. First, because a declaration was not binding on the parties to the proceedings in which it was made, and secondly, because a declaration provided the appropriate minister with a power, not a duty, to amend the offending legislation by order so as to make it compatible with the Convention. Moreover, the minister concerned could exercise that power only if he considered that there were compelling reasons for doing so. The applicants could not have been expected to exhaust, before bringing their human rights application, a remedy which was dependent on the discretion of the executive. Judgment would be given accordingly.

   Application 13378/05 *Burden v United Kingdom* [2007] 1 FCR 69 (European Court of Human Rights).

1538   European Court of Human Rights—decision—favourable judgment given after disqualification undertaking accepted—declaration that undertaking should not have been offered

See *Re Blackspur Group plc (No 4); Secretary of State for Trade and Industry v Davies*, para 527.

1539   European Court of Human Rights—decision—incompatibility with previous House of Lords ruling—approach of inferior court

In the first of two appeals, a housing trust let the appellant tenants into possession of residential properties owned by a local authority under a licence granted by the authority. The licence was replaced by leases to the trust that allowed the authority to terminate the leases. Subsequently, the authority terminated the leases. The appellants contended that the trust had granted the leases as agent for the authority and, therefore, that they were the authority's tenants and had security of tenure under the Housing Act 1985 Pt IV ss 79–117. Their claims were dismissed and they appealed unsuccessfully. In the second appeal, the appellants were gypsies who moved onto land owned by the local authority. The authority commenced successful possession proceedings and the appellants' appeal was dismissed. Both sets of appellants appealed further. *Held,* it was not necessary for a local authority to prove in every case that domestic law complied with the European Convention on Human Rights art 8. Courts should proceed on the assumption that domestic law struck a fair balance and was compatible with art 8. If the court was satisfied that the domestic law requirements for making a possession order had been met, the court should make a possession order unless the occupier showed that, highly exceptionally, he had a seriously arguable case that the law which required the court to make a possession order was incompatible with the Convention. Alternatively, the occupier had to show that the local authority's exercise of its power to seek a possession order was an unlawful act within the meaning of the Human Rights Act 1998 s 6. Where a court would ordinarily be bound to follow the decision of another court higher in the domestic hierarchy, but that decision appeared to be inconsistent with a later ruling of the European Court of Human Rights, the court should follow the binding precedent. It was by the decisions of national courts that the domestic standard had initially to be set, and to those decisions the ordinary rules of precedent should apply. In the first appeal, the appellants had no right to retain possession of their properties after the termination of their leases and had become trespassers with no right to remain. In the second appeal, it was plain that the eviction of the appellants was in accordance with domestic property law, which had the legitimate end of enabling public authorities to evict unlawful squatters from public land. Accordingly, the appeals would be dismissed.

Kay v Lambeth LBC; Leeds City Council v Price [2006] UKHL 10, [2006] 2 AC 465 (House of Lords: Lords Bingham of Cornhill, Nicholls of Birkenhead, Hope of Craighead, Scott of Foscote and Walker of Gestingthorpe, Baroness Hale of Richmond and Lord Brown of Eaton-under-Heywood). Decision of Court of Appeal *Lambeth LBC v Kay* [2004] EWCA Civ 926, [2004] HLR 1061 (2004 Abr para 1753); *Leeds CC v Price* [2005] EWCA Civ 289, [2005] 1 WLR 1825 affirmed.

1540   Freedom of assembly—demonstration—stop and search powers—authorisation

See *R (on the application of Gillan) v Metropolitan Police Comr*, para 892.

1541   Freedom of assembly—demonstration—suspected protesters—power to prevent access to site

See *R (on the application of Laporte) v Chief Constable of Gloucestershire Constabulary*, para 2255.

1542   Freedom of expression—disclosure of information—confidential information

See *CC v AB*, para 582.

1543   Freedom of expression—disclosure of information—consequential identification of children

See *British Broadcasting Corpn v Rochdale MBC*, para 484.

1544   Freedom of expression—harassment—surveillance by private individual

See *Howlett v Holding*, para 1708.

1545   Freedom of expression—interference—necessity in a democratic society—just satisfaction

The applicant, the publisher of a magazine, published a review of a political book. A politician, mentioned in the book and the review, filed a compensation claim against the applicant. The court found that the applicant had given the impression that the politician had played down the extent of crimes committed in concentration camps by using the term 'punishment camps', and ordered the applicant to pay compensation to the politician, publish the judgment and to forfeit the issue of the magazine. The applicant's appeal was dismissed and it lodged an application with the European Court of Human Rights, alleging that its right to freedom of expression had been violated. The issue to be decided was whether the interference with the applicant's right to freedom of expression was necessary in a democratic society. *Held,* in considering whether the European Convention on Human Rights art 10 had been violated, the court had to decide whether the reasons submitted by the domestic courts were relevant and sufficient and whether the interference was proportionate to the legitimate aim pursued. A distinction should be drawn between statements of fact and value judgments. Where a statement amounted to a value judgment, the proportionality of an interference might depend on whether there existed a sufficient factual basis for the statement. The limits of acceptable criticism were wider for a politician than for a private individual. The politician was a high-profile figure who had been known for his ambiguous statements about the National Socialist Regime for a long time. The use of the term 'punishment camp' which implied that persons were detained there for having committed punishable offences, might reasonably be criticised as a belittlement of the concentration camps, in particular where the phrase was used by a person whose ambiguity towards the Nazi era was well-known. Therefore, the applicant's statement had not been excessive in the circumstances. The reasons given by the domestic courts were not relevant and sufficient to justify the interference. Further, the forfeiture of the issue of the magazine was a severe and intrusive measure, so that the interference was also disproportionate. Therefore, the interference was not necessary in a democratic society. Accordingly, there had been a violation of art 10 and just satisfaction would be awarded.

Application 58547/00 *Wirtschafts-Trend Zeitschriften-Verlags GmbH v Austria* [2006] EMLR 152 (European Court of Human Rights).

1546   Freedom of expression—reporting restrictions—family proceedings—parents seeking publicity—previous media attention

See *Re Webster (A Child)*, para 467.

1547   Freedom of religion—refusal to wear school uniform—exclusion of pupil

The defendant school's uniform requirements for girls included a shalwar kameeze, which was seen as satisfying the religious requirements that Muslim girls should wear modest dress, and girls from other faith groups, such as Hindus and Sikhs, also wore it. The claimant pupil decided that the shalwar kameeze was not an appropriate form of dress for herself as a Muslim girl who had reached puberty. She therefore began to attend the school dressed in a jilbab, a form of dress which concealed the shape of her arms and legs. The defendant refused to allow the claimant to attend while she was wearing the jilbab. The claimant applied for judicial review of that decision, arguing that her exclusion from the school infringed her right to manifest her religion or beliefs, guaranteed by the European Convention on Human Rights art 9. The judge dismissed her application, but the Court of Appeal made a declaration that her rights under art 9 had been infringed. The defendant appealed. *Held*, art 9 did not require that one should be allowed to manifest one's religion at any time and place of one's own choosing. It was settled law that what constituted interference would depend on all the circumstances of the case, including the extent to which in the circumstances an individual could reasonably expect to be at liberty to manifest his beliefs in practice. Wearing a jilbab to a mixed school was, for the claimant, a manifestation of her religion. The fact that most other Muslims might not have thought it necessary was irrelevant. However, there was nothing to stop her from going to school where her religion did not require a jilbab or where she was allowed to wear one. Her family had chosen that school for her with knowledge of its uniform requirements. She could have sought the help of the school and the local education authority in solving the problem. They would no doubt have advised her that, if she was firm in her belief, she should change schools. It followed that there was no interference with the claimant's right to manifest her belief in practice or observance. Accordingly, the appeal would be dismissed.

R (on the application of Begum) v Headteacher and Governors of Denbigh High School [2006] UKHL 15, [2006] 2 All ER 487 (House of Lords: Lords Bingham of Cornhill, Nicholls of Birkenhead, Hoffmann and Scott of Foscote and Baroness Hale of Richmond). Decision of Court of Appeal [2005] EWCA Civ 199, [2005] 2 All ER 396 (2004 Abr para 1077) affirmed.

1548   Freedom of expression—restriction on political advertising on television and radio—unjust interference

The applicant sought a declaration under the Human Rights Act 1998 s 4 that the prohibition on political advertising on television and radio imposed by the Communications Act 2003 was incompatible with the European Convention on Human Rights art 10. *Held*, Parliament, in the context of the overall scheme of the 2003 Act for control of the content and nature of political broadcasting, had acted within the ambit of the discretionary judgment available to it in introducing and maintaining the prohibition on political advertising in ss 319(2)(g), 321(2), (3). The justification for the view embodied in the legislation had been clearly made out and there was no basis for granting the declaration sought. Accordingly, the application would be refused.

R (on the application of Animal Defenders International) v Secretary of State for Culture, Media and Sport [2006] EWHC 3069 (Admin), [2007] EMLR 158 (Queen's Bench Division: Auld LJ and Ouseley J).

1549   Gender recognition—application fees

The Gender Recognition (Application Fees) Order 2006, SI 2006/758 (in force on 6 April 2006), replaces the 2005 Order, SI 2005/638, and prescribes the level of fees payable in relation to applications to a Gender Recognition Panel under the Gender Recognition Act 2004. The order prescribes a fee of £140 for applicants whose relevant income is greater than £23,185, and a fee of £30 for applicants whose relevant income is greater than £15,460 but not greater than £23,185, and provides that no fee is payable (1) in circumstances where an applicant's relevant income is £15,460 or less, or where an applicant is in receipt of a qualifying benefit; (2) if the application is made under s 1(1) and the applicant has previously received an interim gender recognition certificate; (3) in relation to an application for a full gender recognition certificate following the grant of an interim gender recognition certificate where the applicant has been married; (4) in relation to an application for a full gender recognition certificate following the grant of an interim gender certificate where the applicant has been a civil partner; and (5) in relation to an application for a corrected certificate where the original contains an error.

1550 Prohibition of discrimination—bereavement allowance—widower's entitlement

The applicant was a widower whose wife had died at a time when widow's bereavement allowance was governed by the Income and Corporation Taxes Act 1988 and married couples were taxed as a single entity. A married man could claim the married man's allowance in respect of his wife's earnings in the year of his wife's death. Independent taxation of spouses was subsequently introduced and each partner was entitled to claim a personal allowance, although the husband retained the right to claim a married couple's allowance, which was the difference between the former married man's allowance and a single person's allowance. Subsequently, a married woman became entitled to share the married couple's allowance with her husband. Widow's bereavement allowance was abolished by the Finance Act 1999 s 34. The applicant made an application for widow's bereavement allowance after the coming into force of the Human Rights Act 1998. The claim was refused. The House of Lords examined whether a claimant who had been refused the allowance could have the decision overturned under the 1998 Act, and concluded that he could not. The applicant complained to the European Court of Human Rights. *Held*, the European Convention on Human Rights art 14 did not prohibit a member state from treating certain groups differently in order to correct 'factual inequalities' between them. In certain circumstances, a failure to correct inequality through different treatment might in itself give rise to a violation. A difference in treatment was, however, discriminatory if it had no objective and reasonable justification. Widow's bereavement allowance was intended to rectify the inequality occasioned by the fact that, when married couples were taxed as a single entity, a widowed man could continue to claim a married man's allowance in the year following his wife's death, whereas a widowed woman received only a single person's allowance. However, it became obsolete when independent taxation of spouses was introduced and spouses given the choice as to how to share the married couple's allowance. From then until its abolition, the difference in treatment between men and women in relation to the widow's bereavement allowance was not reasonably and objectively justified. Accordingly, there had been a violation of the applicant's rights.

Applications 63469/00, 63475/00, 63484/00, 63684/00 *Hobbs v United Kingdom* [2006] All ER (D) 178 (Nov) (European Court of Human Rights).

1551 Prohibition of discrimination—funeral expenses—payment out of social fund—claim for funeral abroad

See *Esfandiari v Secretary of State for Work and Pensions*, para 2675.

1552 Prohibition of discrimination—social security benefits—reduced earnings allowance—age limits for entitlement

See Applications 65731/01 and 65900/01 *Stec v United Kingdom*, para 2663.

1553 Right to education—exclusion of pupil—unlawful exclusion

The claimant, a child of compulsory school age, was charged with arson in connection with a fire at his school. He was temporarily excluded from school and his exclusion was extended several times. Self-assessed revision work was provided for the claimant to do at home, and he was permitted to sit examinations at the school. After the term of the claimant's exclusion had exceeded the legal maximum period for a fixed-term exclusion, the head teacher convened a meeting with the claimant's parents concerning the claimant's reintegration into the school. Neither the claimant nor his parents attended the meeting, and the head teacher removed the claimant from the school roll. Neither the exclusions nor the removal of the claimant from the school roll complied with the relevant statutory requirements. The claimant brought proceedings against the defendant head teacher and school governors, claiming that his right to education under the European Convention on Human Rights First Protocol art 2 had been infringed. The judge decided that the claimant's art 2 rights had not been infringed, but that decision was reversed on appeal. The claimant appealed. *Held*, the test under art 2 was whether the authorities of the state had acted so as to deny to a pupil effective access to such educational facilities as the state provided for pupils. Article 2 gave no right to education of a particular kind or quality, other than that prevailing in the member state. There was no Convention guarantee of compliance with domestic law, or of education at or by a particular institution. There was no Convention objection to the expulsion of a pupil from an educational institution on disciplinary grounds, unless (in the ordinary way) there was no alternative source of state education open to the pupil. The claimant and his parents had consistently rejected the efforts made by the school to assist him. The parents had failed to collect work for the pupil, had declined the offer of tuition from the Pupil Referral Unit, and had not attended the meeting at which the claimant's potential readmission had been discussed. It was a matter for regret when any pupil, not least an able pupil like the claimant, lost months of schooling. But that was not a result which could, in the instant case, be laid at the door of the school. It followed that art 2 had not been infringed and, accordingly, the appeal would be allowed.

A v Head Teacher and Governors of Lord Grey School [2006] UKHL 14, [2006] 2 AC 363 (House of Lords: Lords Bingham of Cornhill, Nicholls of Birkenhead, Hoffmann and Scott of Foscote and Baroness Hale of Richmond). Decision of Court of Appeal [2004] EWCA Civ 382, [2004] QB 1231 (2004 Abr para 1473) reversed.

1554   Right to fair and public hearing—arbitration proceedings—exclusion of right to appeal—exclusion clause incorporated by reference

See *Sukuman Ltd v Commonwealth Secretariat*, para 230.

1555   Right to fair and public hearing—civil proceedings—access to court—time limits— disavowal of paternity—admissibility of scientific evidence

See Application 26111/02 *Mizzi v Malta*, para 1608.

1556   Right to fair and public hearing—civil proceedings—access to court—vexatious litigant

See *R (on the application of Ewing) v Department for Constitutional Affairs*, para 2326.

1557   Right to fair and public hearing—civil proceedings—care proceedings—dispensing with parental agreement—undue delay

See *Dundee CC v K*, para 413.

1558   Right to fair and public hearing—civil proceedings—care proceedings—fairness

A final care order in respect of a child was made in favour of a local authority. The mother appealed on the ground that there had been departures from good practice by the authority when seeking the care order that breached her human rights. *Held*, actual infringement of parental human rights in the course of care proceedings had to be rooted out and exposed in court. However, the precepts of good practice should not be used to derail the proceedings from reaching prompt necessary conclusions referable to, and in the interests of the child. In this instance, the departure from good practice was insufficient to affect the fairness of the proceedings and, accordingly, the appeal would be dismissed.

Re J (Care: Assessment: Fair Trial) [2006] EWCA Civ 545, [2006] 2 FCR 107 (Court of Appeal: Wilson and Richard LJJ and Bennett J). *Re V (A Child) (Care: Pre-Birth Actions)* [2004] EWCA Civ 1575, [2006] 2 FCR 121 (2004 Abr para 1476); and *Re C (Care Proceedings: Disclosure of Local Authority's Decision-Making Process)* [2002] EWHC 1379 (Fam), [2002] 2 FCR 673 (2002 Abr para 1642) considered.

1559   Right to fair and public hearing—civil proceedings—independent and impartial tribunal—care worker—allegation of misconduct

See *R (on the application of Wright) v Secretary of State for Health*, para 2710.

1560   Right to fair and public hearing—civil proceedings—independent and impartial tribunal—housing benefit and council tax benefit review board

See Application 60860/00 *Tsfayo v United Kingdom*, para 2641.

1561   Right to fair and public hearing—civil proceedings—right to legal representation— competence of lay representative

The taxpayer was compulsorily assessed for value added tax and made subject to a civil evasion penalty. On his appeal to a VAT and duties tribunal, the taxpayer was represented by an accountant, rather than a lawyer. Although he was entitled to publicly funded legal representation, he had not been made aware of the fact. He appealed on the ground of incompetent representation. *Held*, the mere fact that the appellant was represented by an accountant, rather than a lawyer, was not enough in itself to put the tribunal on notice that the representation might not be competent or effective. It was common for taxpayers to be represented by accountants before a tribunal and, in most cases, there was no need for particular legal skills. The conduct of a case was essentially a matter between a party and his chosen representative and the tribunal should respect that choice. Although it was unfortunate that the taxpayer had not been made aware of the availability of legal aid, that was not issue. In the absence of any reason to doubt the competence of the taxpayer's accountant, the tribunal would have no reason to inquire into the reason for the taxpayer's choice of representative, or his knowledge of the availability of legal aid. Accordingly, the appeal would be dismissed.

Khan v Revenue and Customs Comrs [2006] EWCA Civ 89, [2006] STC 1167 (Court of Appeal: Buxton, Carnwath and Lloyd LJJ).

1562   Right to fair and public hearing—civil proceedings—tax assessment

See *Significant Ltd v Farrel (Inspector of Taxes)*, para 1630.

1563   Right to fair and public hearing—criminal proceedings—anonymous witness

See *R v Davis; R v Ellis; R v Gregory; R v Simms;* and *R v Martin*, para 802.

1564   Right to fair and public hearing—criminal proceedings—child—crime of strict liability

See *R v G (Secretary of State for the Home Department intervening)*, para 890.

1565   Right to fair and public hearing—criminal proceedings—confiscation order—delay in making order

The defendant was convicted of various counts of drugs supply. After his conviction, the prosecution brought confiscation proceedings pursuant to the Drug Trafficking Act 1994. An order made for disclosure of assets was not complied with and the judge directed that the case should be listed for hearing. The defendant was granted a postponement of the hearing until his appeals were resolved. Subsequently, the defendant's total sentence was reduced from nine to six years' imprisonment. The defendant failed to attend confiscation proceedings. The judge found that there were exceptional circumstances to justify a further postponement of the confiscation proceedings. The defendant's appeal against conviction on remaining grounds was later dismissed, and the Crown Court judge found further exceptional circumstances to justify a further postponement of the confiscation proceedings. Confiscation proceedings eventually began, and an order was made. The defendant appealed against the confiscation order. He contended that the delay in the confiscation proceedings, caused in part by the slow listing of his appeals, was excessive so that the right, guaranteed by the European Convention on Human Rights art 6, for his rights and liabilities to be resolved within a reasonable time had been contravened. *Held*, while some delay had been caused in the hearing of the appeal against conviction and the second substantive hearing, it was to be borne in mind that the 16-month period before the second hearing of the conviction appeal was a period in which the defendant was pursuing further grounds of appeal, which were eventually ruled to be unmeritorious. In all the circumstances, the delay was not such as to breach the reasonable time requirement. Accordingly, the appeal would be dismissed.

R v Norman [2006] EWCA Crim 1769, [2006] All ER (D) 75 (Sep) (Court of Appeal: Gage LJ, Bean J and the Recorder of Cardiff).

Confiscation proceedings are now under the Proceeds of Crime Act 2002 Pt 2 (ss 6–91).

1566   Right to fair and public hearing—criminal proceedings—extradition—conviction obtained in absence of accused—opportunity to challenge evidence

See *Re Migliorelli*, para 1319.

1567   Right to fair and public hearing—criminal proceedings—hearing within reasonable time—procedural delays

The applicant was a former member of the British Secret Intelligence Service who had signed the Official Secrets Act 1911. While a member of the service he became an agent for the Soviet Union and was later convicted of unlawfully communicating information contrary to the 1911 Act and imprisoned. He escaped from prison and fled to Moscow. He wrote his autobiography and signed a contract with a publisher to publish the book in the United Kingdom. He was paid an advance on royalties and a further advance royalty payment was due to him on publication. After the book was published, the Attorney General instituted proceedings seeking from the applicant any financial benefit from publication, arguing that in writing the book, the applicant had acted in breach of the duty of confidence he owed to the Crown. Proceedings were heard by the High Court, the Court of Appeal and the House of Lords. At each stage delays were incurred in relation to the applicant's legal representation and the release of royalties to pay for his representation. The applicant complained to the European Court of Human Rights that the length of the proceedings was incompatible with the right under the European Convention on Human Rights art 6(1) to trial within a reasonable time. *Held*, the reasonableness of the length of proceedings had to be assessed in the light of the circumstances of the case and with reference to the complexity of the case, the conduct of the applicant, the relevant authorities and what was at stake for the applicant in the dispute. A state was responsible for the manner in which it provided for mechanisms to comply with the reasonable time requirement. Where a state allowed proceedings to continue beyond the reasonable time prescribed by art 6 without doing anything to advance them, it would be responsible for the resultant delay. Since the proceedings were legally complex, the state could not be considered at fault for having raised novel questions of law. However, the proceedings were neither factually nor administratively difficult. While what was at stake for the applicant had some financial importance, its significance was not acute. The proceedings against the applicant had not been pursued with the diligence required by art 6(1) and the applicant's civil rights and obligations had not been determined within a reasonable time. Accordingly, there had been a violation of art 6 and damages would be awarded.

Application 68890/01 *Blake v United Kingdom* [2006] All ER (D) 126 (Sep) (European Court of Human Rights). For earlier related proceedings see *A-G v Blake (Jonathan Cape Ltd, third party)* [2001] 2 AC 68, HL (2000 Abr para 2746).

1568   Right to fair and public hearing—criminal proceedings—independent and impartial tribunal—court-martial—application of military law to civilians

See Application 40426/98 *Martin v United Kingdom*, para 245.

1569   Right to fair and public hearing—criminal proceedings—independent and impartial tribunal—life sentence—minimum term—review by same judge

See *R v Sampson*, para 2555.

1570   Right to fair and public hearing—criminal proceedings—independent and impartial tribunal—temporary judge

Scotland

Scottish law permitted the Secretary of State to appoint persons to act as temporary judges in the Court of Session. Such judges were not to be treated as judges of the court for the purposes of any other rule of law relating to the appointment, tenure of office, retirement, removal or disqualification of judges of the court. The appellant appeared on charges of assault before a temporary judge who had been appointed for a three-year period. He was sentenced to ten years' imprisonment and, on his appeal, he contended that he had not received a fair hearing to which he was entitled under the European Convention on Human Rights art 6(1). The appellant submitted that a temporary judge was not an independent and impartial tribunal for the purposes of art 6(1), as such a judge was not appointed pursuant to a proper legal framework and had no automatic right to reappointment or security of tenure, so that there was an absence of guarantees against outside pressures. The Solicitor General for Scotland resisted the appellant's contention, which was unanimously rejected by the High Court of Justiciary. On the appellant's further appeal, *held,* the act of the Lord Advocate in bringing criminal proceedings and seeking a conviction in the High Court of Justiciary before a person who was acting as a temporary judge was not incompatible with the defendant's right to a fair trial under art 6(1). In the circumstances there was no reason to doubt the independence or impartiality of temporary judges appointed from the Bar to act as judges in the High Court of Justiciary. The fair-minded and informed observer, would not have concluded that there was a real risk that the temporary judge was biased. The security of tenure which he had enjoyed during the period of his appointment, together with the fact that issues as to the work that he was to be employed to do and as to his reappointment at the expiry of that period were in the hands, not of the Lord Advocate, but of the Lord President, provided the guarantees that were needed to meet the requirements of independence and impartiality guaranteed by art 6(1). Accordingly, the appeal would be dismissed.

Kearney v HM Advocate [2006] UKPC D1, 2006 SLT 499 (Privy Council: Lords Bingham of Cornhill and Hope of Craighead, Baroness Hale of Richmond, Lords Carswell and Brown of Eaton-under-Heywood). Decision of High Court of Justiciary 2005 SLT 74 (2005 Abr para 1747) affirmed.

1571   Right to fair and public hearing—criminal proceedings—murder—alternative verdict of manslaughter

See *R v Coutts*, para 844.

1572   Right to fair and public hearing—criminal proceedings—penalty—tax return—failure to furnish information

A Revenue inspector issued a notice of inquiry into the taxpayer's tax return. The taxpayer failed to comply with a notice served under the Taxes Management Act 1970 s 19A, requiring him to produce specified documents and information. A penalty was issued to him, pursuant to s 97AA(1)(a), and he was notified that further daily penalties, imposed under s 97AA(1)(b) and (2), could be charged for his continued failure to provide the information. Subsequently, the Revenue appropriated a sum from a payment made by the taxpayer in satisfaction of the penalty. The taxpayer appealed. He contended that the inquiry, the imposition of the penalty and the threat of further penalties constituted criminal charges for the purpose of the European Convention on Human Rights art 6. He claimed that his right to a fair hearing under art 6 had been violated and that the threat of further penalties infringed his right against self-incrimination. *Held,* the penalty imposed by the 1970 Act s 97AA(1)(a), which had to be distinguished from penalties imposed under s 97AA(1)(b) and (2), was part of the civil law in domestic classification. However, the classification of the penalty in domestic law was no more than a starting point. For the determination of whether the charge was criminal in character the court also had to consider the nature of the offence and the nature and degree of severity of the penalty that could be imposed. Although there was an element of punishment in the modest penalty, its primary function was to secure documents for the Revenue. The penalty was not a criminal charge within the meaning of the Convention art 6, and so there was no scope for any complaint that the taxpayer's privilege against self-incrimination had been violated. Accordingly, the appeal would be dismissed.

Harvard Sharkey v Revenue and Customs Comrs [2006] EWHC (Ch) 300, (2006) 77 TC 484 (Chancery Division: Etherton J). *Han v Customs and Excise Comrs; Martins v Customs and Excise*

Comrs; Morris v Customs and Excise Comrs [2001] EWCA Civ 1040, [2001] 4 All ER 687 (2001 Abr para 1784); and *Engel v Netherlands* (1976) 1 EHRR 647, ECtHR, considered.

1573   Right to fair and public hearing—criminal proceedings—plea—guilty plea—withdrawal

See *DPP v Revitt*, para 806.

1574   Right to fair and public hearing—criminal proceedings—presumption of innocence—acquittal of defendant—intimation by judge that defendant guilty—refusal to make costs order

The applicant was arrested on suspicion of having intimidated witnesses. At an identity parade he was positively identified by one of two witnesses. The applicant was charged and pleaded not guilty to five counts of doing acts tending and intended to pervert the course of public justice. The witness who had identified the applicant did not attend and the trial had to be aborted. At the relisted trial, counsel for the Crown informed the court that the witness did not want to give evidence and that the prosecution did not feel that she ought to be compelled to give evidence. No evidence was offered, and the applicant was duly acquitted. He made an application for a defendant's costs order under the Prosecution of Offences Act 1985 s 16(2)(b). The judge stated that there was compelling evidence on the court papers and that he was not going to exercise his discretion to make an order for costs in favour of the applicant. The applicant complained to the European Court of Human Rights, alleging that the judge's comments on refusing a defendant's costs order were incompatible with art 6(2), under which a person charged with a criminal offence was to be presumed innocent until proved guilty. *Held*, the presumption of innocence enshrined in art 6(2) would be violated if a statement of a public official concerning a person charged with a criminal offence reflected an opinion that he was guilty unless he had been proved so according to law. It sufficed, even in the absence of any formal finding, that there was some reasoning to suggest that the official regarded that person as guilty. However, the Convention did not guarantee a defendant who had been acquitted the right to reimbursement of his costs. The prosecution failed in this case because a key witness declined to attend court, and in the circumstances, the prosecution preferred to drop the case rather than compel the witness. There was no question of any conduct by the applicant which could have brought him within the sort of cases in which a costs order might be refused, and no suggestion that he was in any way responsible for the non-attendance of the witness. The only natural interpretation which could be put on the judge's words was that he was refusing the order because he was of the view that, although the key witness had not given evidence and the applicant had been acquitted, the applicant was in fact guilty of the offence. That amounted to a reliance on suspicions as to the applicant's innocence after he had been acquitted and was incompatible with the presumption of innocence. Judgment would be given accordingly.

Application 8866/04 *Hussain v United Kingdom* [2006] All ER (D) 83 (Mar) (European Court of Human Rights).

1575   Right to fair and public hearing—criminal proceedings—reasonable time requirement—duty of court to expedite proceedings

See *Boolell v The State*, para 829.

1576   Right to fair and public hearing—criminal proceedings—terrorism—control order—review by court

See *Secretary of State for the Home Department v MB*, para 896.

1577   Right to fair and public hearing—mental patient—treatment without consent—medical necessity

See *R (on the application of B) v Haddock*, para 1982.

1578   Right to liberty—anti-terrorism legislation—control order

See *Secretary of State for the Home Department v JJ*, para 895.

1579   Right to liberty—discrimination—release on licence—long-term prisoners and prisoners liable to deportation—power to release vested in Secretary of State rather than Parole Board

See *R (on the application of Clift) v Secretary of State for the Home Department; R (on the application of Hindawi) v Secretary of State for the Home Department*, para 2357.

1580   Right to liberty—lawfulness of detention—asylum-seeker

The applicant, an Iraqi national, arrived in the United Kingdom and claimed asylum. Shortly after arriving he was detained at a reception centre, which was used for holding those who were deemed not likely to abscond and who could be dealt with by a fast-track procedure. Three days after the detention had begun, the applicant's legal representative was informed that the reason for the applicant being held was that he was an Iraqi who met the criteria to be detained at a centre. The applicant was released after one week, and applied for judicial review of the decision to detain him, alleging that his detention was inconsistent with his right to liberty, guaranteed by the European Convention on Human Rights art 5. He claimed that he did not come within art 5(1)(f), which provided an exception in relation to the lawful arrest or detention of a person for the purpose of preventing his effecting an unauthorised entry into the country. The court decided that the detention did not have to be 'necessary' to satisfy art 5(1)(f), and that the applicant's Convention rights had not been infringed. The applicant complained to the European Court of Human Rights that his detention had not been compatible with art 5(1)(f), and that he had not been informed of the reasons for his detention, contrary to art 5(2). *Held*, until a potential immigrant had been granted leave to remain in the country, he had not effected a lawful entry, and detention could reasonably be considered to be aimed at preventing unlawful entry for the purposes of art 5(1)(f). Furthermore, there was no requirement in art 5(1)(f) that the detention of a person to prevent his effecting an unauthorised entry should reasonably be considered to be necessary, for example to prevent his committing an offence or fleeing. All that was required was that the detention should be a genuine part of the process of determining whether the individual should be granted immigration clearance or asylum, and that it should not otherwise be arbitrary. It followed that the applicant's detention was to prevent his effecting an unlawful entry and was the result of a bona fide application of the policy on fast-track immigration decisions. The detention was for seven days, which, in all the circumstances, was not excessive. However, there had been a violation of art 5(2). General statements such as Parliamentary announcements could not replace the need for the individual to be informed of the reasons for his arrest or detention. Moreover, a failure to give reasons within the first three days of custody did not satisfy the requirement that the reasons be given promptly. Accordingly, the application would be allowed in part.

Application 13229/03 *Saadi v United Kingdom* [2006] All ER (D) 125 (Jul) (European Court of Human Rights). Application 12244/86 *Fox, Campbell and Hartley v United Kingdom* (1991) 14 EHRR 108, ECtHR; and Application 51564/99 *Conka v Belgium* (2002) 11 BHRC 555, ECtHR, considered.

1581   Right to liberty—lawfulness of detention—detention during war—supremacy of international law

The claimant, who held dual British and Iraqi nationality, was arrested in Iraq by British forces on suspicion of belonging to a terrorist group involved in weapons smuggling and explosive attacks in Iraq. He was not charged with any offence, and the Secretary of State acknowledged that, as matters stood, there was not enough admissible evidence against him to support the bringing of criminal charges in a court of law. The claimant brought judicial review proceedings, challenging the lawfulness of his continued detention and the refusal of the Secretary of State to return him to the United Kingdom. The application was dismissed, and he appealed, contending that his detention was in breach of his right to liberty under the European Convention on Human Rights art 5(1). The Secretary of State submitted that the claimant's detention was authorised by Resolutions 1511 and 1546 of the United Nations Security Council, which had the effect of qualifying the right under the Convention art 5. *Held*, while there was inevitably a conflict between a power to intern for imperative reasons of security during the course of an emergency, and a right to due process by a court in more settled times, the Charter of the United Nations art 103 gave Resolution 1546 precedence, in so far as there was a conflict. That was not to say that those whose task was to determine whether internment was necessary for imperative reasons of security did not have to approach their duties with all due seriousness, when the right to personal liberty was in question. In particular, they should ask themselves whether internment was a proportionate response to the threat to security posed by the internee. Accordingly, the appeal would be dismissed.

R (on the application of Al-Jedda) v Secretary of State for Defence [2006] EWCA Civ 327, [2006] All ER (D) 435 (Mar) (Court of Appeal: Brooke, May and Rix LJJ).

1582   Right to liberty—lawfulness of detention—detention pending trial—bail—power to grant

The applicant was arrested in Northern Ireland on suspicion of having carried out a robbery in that jurisdiction. The following day he was charged with the offence, and on the day after that he appeared before a magistrates' court, where an application for bail was made on his behalf. The resident magistrate refused the application on the basis that the offence was a scheduled offence so that, by virtue of the Terrorism Act 2000 s 67(2) and the Northern Ireland (Emergency Provisions) Act 1996 s 3(2), the power to grant bail was limited to the High Court, Court of Appeal and the trial judge. On the same day, an application was made to the High Court for bail. The application was heard and granted the next day. The applicant made an application for judicial review, contending that, by limiting the power of the magistrate to grant bail, the relevant provisions were contrary to his right to liberty under the European Convention on Human Rights art 5. The application and an appeal were dismissed, and the applicant appealed to the European Court of

Human Rights. *Held*, at the very early stages of pre-trial detention there had to exist an opportunity for judicial consideration of release pending trial. Although there was no express requirement of promptness in art 5, such consideration had to take place with due expedition in order to keep any unjustified deprivation of liberty to an acceptable minimum. It was desirable, in order to minimise delay, that the judicial officer who conducted the first automatic review of lawfulness and the existence of a ground for detention also had competence to consider release on bail. Such was, however, not a requirement of the Convention. There was no reason in principle why the issues could not be dealt with by two judicial officers within the requisite time-frame. In any event, it could not be necessary for the examination of bail to take place with any more speed than was demanded of the first automatic review, which had previously been identified in the court's jurisprudence as being a maximum of four days. In the instant case, the procedure had been conducted with due expedition, leading to the applicant's release three days after his arrest. It followed that there had been no violation of art 5 and, accordingly, the appeal would be dismissed.

Application 543/03 *McKay v United Kingdom* (2006) Times, 30 October (European Court of Human Rights).

1583 Right to liberty—lawfulness of detention—detention pending trial—bail—refusal—failure by prosecution to act with due diligence

The Criminal Justice and Public Order Act 1994 s 25(1) provides that a person who has been charged with or convicted of a specified offence, which includes rape, is to be granted bail only if the court considering the grant of bail is satisfied that there are exceptional circumstances which justify it.

The defendant, who had a previous conviction for rape, was charged with rape, false imprisonment and indecent assault. He was remanded in custody pursuant to the 1994 Act s 25(1) because the judge was not satisfied that there were exceptional circumstances which justified the granting of bail. The defendant's custody time limit expired and the prosecution's application for the extension of the time limit under the Prosecution of Offences Act 1985 s 22(3) was refused on the ground that the prosecution had not acted with all due diligence and expedition. The defendant was again refused bail on the grounds of a lack of exceptional circumstances. The defendant sought judicial review of the decision not to grant him bail, contending that the continued reliance on the 1994 Act s 25(1) after the expiry of the custody time limit contravened his right, under the European Convention on Human Rights art 5(3), to a trial within a reasonable time or to release pending trial. His application was refused and he appealed. *Held*, the 1994 Act s 25(1) placed an evidential burden on a defendant to adduce evidence to support the existence of exceptional circumstances which justified the grant of bail. However, in a case where the court was unsure as to whether the defendant should be released, the burden remained on the prosecution to satisfy the court that bail should not be granted. Section 25 should be read so as to make that plain. Even where the custody time limit had expired and an extension had been refused for lack of due diligence, the continued detention of the defendant would not automatically amount to a violation of the Convention art 5(3). The 1994 Act s 25 should be construed and applied essentially as a guide to the proper operation of the Bail Act 1976. Additionally, in those cases in which it operated it disapplied the ordinary requirement that bail should be granted automatically to any defendant whose custody time limit had expired. There had been no violation of the defendant's rights and, accordingly, the appeal would be dismissed.

R (on the application of O) v Crown Court at Harrow; Re O (habeas corpus) [2006] UKHL 42, [2006] 3 All ER 1157 (House of Lords: Lords Nicholls of Birkenhead and Hutton, Baroness Hale of Richmond, Lords Carswell and Brown of Eaton-under-Haywood). Decision of Queen's Bench Divisional Court [2003] EWHC 868 (Admin), [2003] 1 WLR 2756 (2003 Abr para 1484) affirmed.

1584 Right to liberty—lawfulness of detention—prisoner released on licence—recall to custody—reasons for recall

See *R (on the application of Hirst) v Secretary of State for the Home Department*, para 2359.

1585 Right to life—armed forces—deployment—safety

See *R (on the application of Gentle) v Prime Minister*, para 1536.

1586 Right to life—attempted suicide of prisoner—investigation—procedural requirements

The claimant attempted to hang himself while in custody. He survived, but was left with permanent and irreversible brain damage. A senior investigating officer in the prison service conducted an investigation into the incident. The defendant accepted that the investigation did not satisfy the obligations of the state under the European Convention on Human Rights art 2 (right to life), because the report had not been published and neither the claimant nor his representatives had played any part in it. The defendant proposed that the Prisons and Probation Ombudsman should carry out a further inquiry, which would be held in private and during which the claimant's representatives would be able to suggest questions to be put to witnesses, but would have no opportunity to cross-examine them. The claimant sought judicial review of the defendant's proposals. The judge declared that, in order to satisfy the requirements of art 2, the defendant had to conduct a full and effective investigation into the circumstances of the claimant's attempted suicide and that the investigation had to fulfil certain specified procedural criteria. The respondent appealed. *Held*, the judge was correct to hold that the investigation into the claimant's attempted suicide should be held in public in the sense that he had intended. The judge could not have meant that the whole process had to be in public. No inquiry was ever wholly in public. The judge had to have contemplated simply that the Ombudsman would make the evidence and any written submissions public and take oral evidence in public, subject to the proviso which he included in the order to the effect that there might be Convention compatible reasons for not holding the whole investigation in public. However, the judge had gone too far in concluding that the claimant's representatives had to be entitled to cross-examine witnesses. They had in general to be entitled to see the written evidence, to be present during oral evidence and to make appropriate submissions, including submissions as to what lines of inquiry should be adopted, what questions asked and, indeed, who should be permitted to ask witnesses questions about what. Accordingly, the appeal would be allowed in part.

R (on the application of D) v Secretary of State for the Home Department [2006] EWCA Civ 143, [2006] All ER (D) 403 (Feb) (Court of Appeal: Sir Anthony Clarke MR, Tuckey and Dyson LJJ). *R (on the application of Amin) v Secretary of State for the Home Department* [2003] UKHL 51, [2004] 1 AC 653 (2003 Abr para 1494); Application 46477/99 *Edwards v United Kingdom* (2002) 12 BHRC 190, ECtHR (2002 Abr para 1716); and Application 24746/94 *Jordan v United Kingdom* (2001) 37 EHRR 52, ECtHR (2001 Abr para 1814), applied. Decision of Munby J [2005] EWHC 728 (Admin), [2005] All ER (D) 406 (Apr) reversed in part.

1587   Right to life—death in custody—investigation into death—juvenile offender

The applicant's son, aged 16 years, hanged himself in a young offenders' institution where he was serving a two-year sentence for robbery. An inquest was held into his death and a verdict of accidental death was returned. The coroner recommended that a public inquiry into sentencing policy, including the pre-sentence exercise and the allocation process, should take place. The Secretary of State rejected the recommendation and concluded that the Sentencing Guidelines Council should review the sentencing issues raised by the case, and commissioned an independent review into other matters raised by the case. The applicant's application for judicial review of the Secretary of State's decision was dismissed and the applicant appealed. *Held,* the applicant had not established that the Secretary of State had breached the European Convention on Human Rights art 2 by failing to convene a public inquiry. Setting up a public inquiry was not the only way in which the obligation under art 2 could be discharged. It was not a case in which the Secretary of State had failed to confront the issues which had emerged or failed to give serious consideration to possible improvements. The combination of the inquest and the measures taken, including the deliberations of the Council, had achieved compliance with the art 2 obligations. It could not be said that the only appropriate action was for a judge to be given the task of resolving such issues, at or following a public inquiry. The bereaved family had been fully involved at the inquest and had been invited to make representations. It had been recognised that they could make an input into questions of policy but, because broad issues of public concern were involved, many other factors had to be taken into account. Accordingly, the appeal would be dismissed.

R (on the application of Scholes) v Secretary of State for the Home Department [2006] EWCA Civ 1343, (2007) 93 BMLR 136 (Court of Appeal: Pill and Arden LJJ). Decision of Bennett J [2006] EWHC 1 (Admin), (2006) 170 JP 243 affirmed.

1588   Right to life—extradition—risk to health

See *McCaughey v Government of the United States of America*, para 1328.

1589   Right to life—victim shot dead by state agent—common law test of self-defence

See *R (on the application of Bennett) v Inner South London Coroner*, para 869.

1590   Right to life—witness shot dead by person charged with offence—failure of police to protect witness

The deceased was required to give evidence at the theft trial of a former employee. The police were informed of threats directed towards the deceased but no action was taken. The deceased was murdered and the police officer involved faced disciplinary proceedings during which he conceded that he should have appreciated the risk to the deceased's life and the need to protect him. The claimant, the administrator of the deceased's estate, brought proceedings under the Human Rights Act 1998 s 7, claiming damages under s 8. *Held*, when considering the proper approach to a claim under s 7, it was necessary to take into account that the positive obligation to protect life under the European Convention on Human Rights art 2 was unqualified and self-evidently fundamental. However, art 2 was not to be interpreted so as to impose a disproportionate burden on the state authorities, although the state's positive obligation to protect life included a positive obligation in certain circumstances to take preventive measures to protect an identified individual whose life was at risk as a result of the criminal acts of a third party. The greater the failure to take such measures as were reasonably open to them to alleviate a risk to human life, the greater the likelihood that the authorities would be held to have failed to comply with their obligation under art 2. In the present case, the positive obligation in art 2 was engaged and was breached. The police officer had not exercised his judgment at all so far as protection was concerned and the risk to the deceased was an immediate one. A claimant who brought a claim under the 1998 Act s 7 did not have to show damage in order to seek a declaration that Convention rights had been violated. Judgment would be given accordingly.

Van Colle v Chief Constable of the Hertfordshire Police [2006] EWHC 360 (QB), [2006] 3 All ER 963 (Queen's Bench Division: Cox J). *Hill v Chief Constable of West Yorkshire* [1989] AC 53, HL (1988 Abr para 1718); *R v Lord Saville of Newdigate, ex p A* [1999] 4 All ER 860 (1999 Abr para 7); Case 87/1997/871/1083 *Osman v United Kingdom* [2000] 29 EHRR 245, ECtHR (1998 Abr para 1801); *Anufrijeva v Southwark LBC; R (on the application of N) v Secretary of State for the Home Department; R (on the application of M) v Secretary of State for the Home Department* [2003] EWCA Civ 1406, [2004] 1 All ER 833 (2003 Abr para 1505) considered.

1591 Right to marry—person subject to immigration control—certificate of approval to marry—denial of certificate

See *R (on the application of Baiai) v Secretary of State for the Home Department*, para 365.

1592 Right to marry—person subject to immigration control—non-Church of England marriage

See *R (on the application of Baiai) v Secretary of State for the Home Department*, para 379.

1593 Right to marry—same-sex parties—discrimination

See *Wilkinson v Kitzinger*, para 705.

1594 Right to peaceful enjoyment of possessions—inheritance taxation—cohabiting siblings—discrimination

See Application 13378/05 *Burden v United Kingdom*, para 1537.

1595 Right to peaceful enjoyment of possessions—land—compulsory purchase order

See *Pascoe v First Secretary of State*, para 2851.

1596 Right to peaceful enjoyment of possessions—reduced income—medical practitioner—suspension

The claimant, a doctor, was suspended from practising by the defendant primary care trust pursuant to the National Health Service (Performers List) Regulations 2004, SI 2004/585, reg 13. Following a further hearing at which the claimant did not appear due to illness, the defendant wrote to the claimant informing him that the suspension was to continue. The defendant later admitted that there were procedural irregularities in the making of these decisions in that the claimant was neither told of the allegations against him nor given any opportunity to deal with them so that the decisions were a nullity. Two months later, another hearing was held, at which the claimant again complained of procedural deficiencies on the ground that he had been denied legal representation and a witness who he sought to cross-examine had not attended. The claimant sought judicial review of a decision to suspend him for six months. The defendant offered a fresh hearing and stated that it would revoke the suspension imposed but did not do so. The claimant contended that the hearings were in breach of his right, under the European Convention on Human Rights art 6, to a fair hearing and his right, under the First Protocol art 1, to peaceful enjoyment of possessions. *Held*, the requirement that questioning of witnesses be channelled through the chair was not improper nor was the general bar on legal representation. Nevertheless, while speed and informality were important, there had to be fairness to the practitioner. In that context, it was known that suspension would be for a limited period and that the practitioner should not lose out financially while suspended. It followed that fairness would only require the more formal trappings of legal representation and cross examination in very exceptional cases, of which the present case was not one. However, there were serious flaws at the hearing that rendered it unfair and so unlawful. Moreover, inclusion on the performers list was akin to the possession of a licence and amounted to a possession for the purposes of the First Protocol art 1. If a suspension had been properly and lawfully imposed, interference with the right of peaceful enjoyment would be proportionate and so justified. Where, however, suspension was unlawful, and the claimant could establish that he had suffered recoverable damage, he might be entitled to sums to recompense him for such loss. While the goodwill of the practice was not marketable, the inclusion had an intrinsic value in that it enabled the claimant to practise. Since the amount of his remuneration would be affected by his patient numbers, suspension might well affect the economic value to him of his practice. Thus inclusion in the list had a present value apart from the right to future income. Accordingly, the application would be allowed.

R (on the application of Malik) v Waltham Forest Primary Care Trust [2006] EWHC 487 (Admin), [2006] 3 All ER 71 (Queen's Bench Division: Collins J). *R (on the application of Dr S) v Knowsley NHS Primary Care Trust; R (on the application of Ghosh) v Northumberland NHS Care Trust* [2006] EWHC 26 (Admin), [2006] All ER (D) 111 (Jan) distinguished.

1597   Right to privacy—invasion of personal privacy—prison visitor—search

An order was made that all of a prisoner's visitors be strip-searched before visits. The first applicant, the prisoner's mother, and the second applicant, the first applicant's son, were not made aware of the order and, on their first visit, they were informed that they would be strip-searched. They were taken to separate rooms where a visual examination of the first applicant's sexual organs and anus was conducted and the second applicant was touched on his penis and his foreskin was pulled back. The applicants' civil claims against the Home Office were dismissed on the basis that there had been no unlawful act save for the touching of the second applicant's penis, constituting an unlawful battery. The applicants brought an action before the European Court of Human Rights under the European Convention on Human Rights arts 3, 8, 13. *Held*, a search carried out in an appropriate manner with due respect for human dignity and for a legitimate purpose might be compatible with art 3 but a search which was carried out with debasing elements would significantly aggravate the inevitable humiliation caused by the procedure. Where a measure fell short of art 3, it might still be caught by art 8. The requirement to be strip-searched would generally constitute an interference under art 8(1) and would need to be justified under art 8(2). Where procedures were laid down for the proper conduct of searches on outsiders to a prison, it was incumbent on the prison authorities to comply with those safeguards. In the present case, although there was no direct evidence to connect the applicants with smuggling drugs, the prison authorities had suspected the applicants of bringing in drugs to the prison. The searching of visitors might be considered a legitimate measure to combat this, although the application of such an invasive procedure to persons who were not convicted prisoners or under reasonable suspicion of having committed a criminal offence had to be conducted with rigorous adherence to procedures and with respect to their human dignity. The searches had not been proportionate to the legitimate aim of combating drugs. While the treatment of the applicants had caused distress, it did not reach the minimum level of severity for art 3 but there had been a breach of art 8. In all circumstances of the case, the applicants did not have a means of obtaining redress for the breach of art 8. Accordingly, there had also been a violation of art 13.

Application 12350/04 *Wainwright v United Kingdom* [2006] All ER (D) 125 (Sep) (European Court of Human Rights). Application 89/1991/341/414 *Costello-Roberts v United Kingdom* [1994] 1 FCR 65, ECtHR (1993 Abr para 1416); *Wainwright v Home Office* [2003] UKHL 53, [2003] 4 All ER 969 (2003 Abr para 1503); and Application 39084/97 *Yankov v Bulgaria* (2004) 15 BHRC 592, ECtHR (2004 Abr para 1568) considered. For earlier proceedings, see *Wainwright v Home Office* [2003] UKHL 53, [2004] 2 AC 406 (2003 Abr para 1503).

1598   Right to privacy—publication of book—personal information—freedom of expression

See *McKennitt v Ash*, para 584.

1599   Right to private and family life—asylum-seeker—indefinite leave to remain as dependent relative

See *Mukarkar v Secretary of State for the Home Department*, para 323.

1600   Right to private and family life—asylum-seeker—removal to safe country—delay— appropriate time to make human rights complaint

The claimant, a citizen of Afghanistan, travelled to Austria and claimed asylum. Before the Austrian authorities had decided his claim he moved to the United Kingdom, where he also claimed asylum. Five months later, the United Kingdom asked the Austrian authorities to accept responsibility for dealing with the claimant's asylum claim, which they duly did the following day. The Secretary of State subsequently certified the claimant's United Kingdom asylum claim, but for the next two years nothing else happened either to progress the claimant's asylum claim in the United Kingdom or to return him to Austria. The claimant was then detained and served with a notice that directions had been given for his removal to Austria. The claimant was granted permission to apply for judicial review of that decision. The judge decided that it would be wholly unreasonable, after the lapse of more than two years, for the claimant to be transferred against his wishes to Austria, and that he was entitled to have his asylum claim heard in the United Kingdom. On the Secretary of State's appeal against that decision, the claimant submitted that the passage of time occasioned by the Secretary of State's delay had given rise to the basis of a claim under the European Convention on Human Rights art 8 in that he had developed connections and relationships in the United Kingdom, that he should not be removed to Austria without those matters being considered, and that, if he were to be removed without that having been done, he would be in no position to assert an art 8 claim in Austria based on the same facts. *Held*, any art 8 point should have been canvassed on its merits before the judge, but it had not been. In those circumstances it was not open to the claimant to urge art 8 issues in support of a submission that his removal to Austria for determination of his asylum claim would be perverse or unreasonable. If art 8 was taken out of the equation, there was nothing left in the perversity case. While the Secretary of State's delay was deplorable and unexplained, the court could not quash the removal directions in order to punish or discipline the Home Office. Accordingly, the appeal would be allowed.

R (on the application of AA) (Afghanistan) v Secretary of State for the Home Department [2006] EWCA Civ 1550, [2006] All ER (D) 302 (Nov) (Court of Appeal: May, Laws and Gage LJJ).

1601   Right to private and family life—confidential information—disclosure by newspaper

See *HRH Prince of Wales v Associated Newspapers Ltd*, para 583.

1602   Right to private and family life—criminal conviction—importation of indecent photographs of children—inclusion on sexual offenders register

The claimant imported indecent photographs of children. He was convicted of fraudulent evasion of the prohibition on the importation of goods, contrary to the Customs and Excise Management Act 1979 s 170(2)(b). He appealed against the dismissal of his claim for a declaration that the requirement that he be placed on the sexual offenders register under the Sexual Offences Act 2003 s 81 and Sch 3 para 14(a) was incompatible with the right to privacy, guaranteed by the European Convention on Human Rights art 8. *Held*, the objective of the notification requirement was to provide children, wherever they might live in the world, with such protection as the law in their country could offer them against exploitation for sexual purposes. The United Nations Convention on the Rights of a Child 1989 art 19 provided that all appropriate legislative and administrative measures should be taken to protect children from sexual abuse. Parliament had decided that the importation of indecent material involving children in contravention of the 1979 Act s 170(2)(b) should be included under the statutory scheme for notification among other forms of sexual offences. It was entirely appropriate for notification requirements to be imposed on those who have been convicted of offences which were directly connected with child exploitation. This also applied to those who decided to import prohibited goods, careless or heedless of the risk that the goods contained or included material such as child pornography. The statutory notification requirements were not a disproportionate interference with the rights of an individual for a person who was responsible for the importation of indecent material involving children. Accordingly, the appeal would be dismissed.

Forbes v Secretary of State for the Home Department [2006] EWCA Civ 962, [2006] 4 All ER 799 (Court of Appeal: Sir Igor Judge P, Scott Baker and Hallett LJJ).

1603   Right to private and family life—confidential information—disclosure by newspaper

See *HRH Prince of Wales v Associated Newspapers Ltd*, para 583.

1604   Right to private and family life—covert surveillance—authorisation

The applicant had been found guilty of conspiracy to import and supply class A drugs on the basis of recordings made by a covert listening device used as evidence. Although the chief constable had initially authorised the use of covert surveillance, the authorisation had lapsed and had not been renewed for part of the period of surveillance. He complained to the European Court of Human Rights that his rights under the European Convention on Human Rights had been violated. *Held*, the United Kingdom accepted that there had been a violation of the right to a private and family life under art 8. The recordings were not obtained in accordance with the law and, accordingly, the application would succeed.

Application 30034/04 *Elahi v United Kingdom* (2006) Times, 21 July (European Court of Human Rights).

1605   Right to private and family life—defendant in extradition proceedings—proportionality

See *R (on the application of Bermingham) v Director of the Serious Fraud Office; Bermingham v Government of the United States of America*, para 1321.

1606   Right to private and family life—deportation order—duty of court

See *R v Carmona*, para 2545.

1607   Right to private and family life—deportation order—removal of non-British mother

See *Nguyen v Secretary of State for the Home Department*, para 360.

1608   Right to private and family life—disavowal of paternity—admissibility of scientific evidence

The applicant's former wife had become pregnant when she and the applicant were cohabiting 40 years earlier. At that time, an action for disavowal of paternity was admissible only if the husband could prove both the adultery of his wife and the concealment of the birth. The applicant had been aware of the wife's pregnancy, and so would had been unable to challenge his paternity. The law was changed so that scientific evidence was admissible in support of an action to disavow paternity. The applicant sought a declaration that he had the right to proceed with an action of rejection of paternity, but his application was refused because such proceedings had to have been brought within six months of the birth. He complained that his rights under the European Convention on Human Rights arts 6 and 8 had been violated. *Held*, although the institution of time limits for an action for disavowal could serve the interests of legal certainty and the interests of the children, the application of the rules in question should not prevent a litigant from making use of a remedy. The practical impossibility of the applicant denying paternity from the day of the daughter's birth until the present time had impaired the essence of his right to a court under art 6(1). The potential interest of the daughter to enjoy having the applicant as her father could not outweigh his legitimate right to have at least one occasion to reject the paternity of a child who, according to scientific evidence, was not his own. Accordingly, there had also been a violation of art 8.

Application 26111/02 *Mizzi v Malta* [2006] 1 FCR 256 (European Court of Human Rights).

1609   **Right to private and family life—disclosure of medical records—child placed with foster parent infected with HIV—local authority's duty of disclosure to parents**

See *Brent LBC v N (Foster Carers)*, para 586.

1610   **Right to private and family life—establishment of family—access to artificial insemination facilities—prisoner**

The applicants met while serving sentences in prison. They subsequently married and applied for facilities for artificial insemination in order to increase their chances of having a child. The Secretary of State refused their application pursuant to the general government policy under which such requests were to be granted only in exceptional circumstances. The policy was said to reflect the need to maintain public confidence in the penal system and the welfare of any child conceived as a result of artificial insemination. The applicants were refused permission to seek judicial review of the decision or to appeal against the refusal. They brought proceedings alleging that the refusal of access to artificial insemination facilities breached their right, under the European Convention of Human Rights art 8, to respect for private and family life and their right, under art 12, to found a family. *Held*, the impugned restriction did not limit a general entitlement already in place in a prison environment, but rather concerned the state's refusal to take steps exceptionally to allow something (namely, the possibility of the begetting of children by prisoners) which was not already an existing general right or entitlement. The applicants' complaint was effectively that, in refusing them access to artificial insemination facilities, the state had failed to fulfil a positive obligation to secure respect for private or family life. The requirements of the notion of respect for family life were not clear cut, especially as far as the positive obligations inherent in that concept were concerned. The area was one in which there was little common ground between member states. It was, therefore, an area in which contracting states enjoyed a wide margin of appreciation. In setting his policy, the Secretary of State had been entitled to have regard to the maintenance of public confidence in the penal system and the interests of any child conceived. It was of importance that the policy did not impose a blanket restriction on a prisoner's access to artificial insemination, without any consideration of individual circumstances. Notwithstanding that artificial insemination remained the only realistic hope of the applicants having a child, the decision to refuse them access to such facilities had not fallen outside the state's margin of appreciation. It followed that there had been no violation of their Convention rights. Accordingly, the application would be dismissed.

Application 44362/04 *Dickson v United Kingdom* [2006] 2 FCR 1 (European Court of Human Rights). *R (on the application of Mellor) v Secretary of State for the Home Department* [2001] EWCA Civ 472, [2002] QB 13 (2001 Abr para 2614) considered.

1611   **Right to private and family life—family proceedings—ancillary relief proceedings—service of subpoena on co-respondent—matters to be taken into consideration**

See *M v M (Financial Misconduct; Subpoena Against Third Party)*, para 1884.

1612   **Right to private and family life—medical treatment—child—treatment without parental knowledge or consent—sexual matters**

See *R (on the application of Axon) v Secretary of State for Health*, para 1949.

1613   **Right to private and family life—medical treatment—fertilisation treatment—creation of embryos—withdrawal of partner's consent to use of embryo**

See Application 6339/05 *Evans v United Kingdom*, para 1925.

1614   **Right to private and family life—parent suspected of child abuse—misdiagnosis of abuse—duty of care**

See *Lawrence v Pembrokeshire CC*, para 2083.

1615   Right to private and family life—parties to adulterous relationship—restraint of publication of information

See *CC v AB*, para 582.

1616   Right to private and family life—paternity of child—determination

See *Lambeth LBC v S*, para 422.

1617   Right to private and family life—personal information—publication of book—freedom of expression

See *McKennitt v Ash*, para 584.

1618   Right to private and family life—respect for home—compulsory acquisition—urban regeneration

See *Pascoe v First Secretary of State*, para 2851.

1619   Right to private and family life—respect for home—police search of house—house no longer occupied by suspect—public protection defence

Police officers investigating armed robberies obtained a warrant to search a house at which the mother of a suspect had lived, and which the suspect had been known to give as his address, for cash stolen in the course of the robberies. The applicants, a family with four young children, had actually been living at the house for some months. Officers arrived at the house at 7 am and, unaware that the applicants were the only occupiers, began to use a metal ram to force open the reinforced door. The applicants awoke and were frightened. The officers realised that there had been a mistake and apologised. The premises were quickly searched to see if the suspect was there, and the officers then left, saying that the damage would be made good. The applicants commenced proceedings against the defendant for trespass, but the claim and an appeal were dismissed on the basis that they could not demonstrate the warrant was maliciously procured since the motive of the police was not improper. The applicants then complained to the European Court of Human Rights that the forcible entry by the police breached their right to respect for their home under the European Convention on Human Rights art 8, and that they had been denied an effective remedy under art 13. The defendant argued that any interference with art 8 rights was justified under art 8(2) as being necessary for the purposes of investigating crime. *Held*, the notion of necessity implied that the interference corresponded to a pressing social need and, in particular, that it was proportionate to the legitimate aim pursued. The exercise of powers to interfere with home and private life had to be confined within reasonable bounds to minimise the impact of such measures on the personal sphere of the individual. The fact that the police did not act maliciously was not decisive under the Convention, which was geared to protecting against abuse of power, however motivated or caused. As basic steps to verify the connection between the address and the offence under investigation had not been effectively carried out, the resulting police action, which had caused the applicants considerable fear and alarm, could not be regarded as proportionate. It followed that there had been a violation of art 8. In relation to art 13, the domestic courts had held that it was in effect irrelevant that there were no reasonable grounds for the police action as damages only lay where malice could be proved, and negligence did not qualify. The courts were unable to examine issues of proportionality or reasonableness and, as various judges in the domestic proceedings had noted, the balance was set in favour of protection of the police. In those circumstances, there had been a breach of art 13. Accordingly, the application would be allowed.

Application 28867/03 *Keegan v United Kingdom* [2006] All ER (D) 235 (Jul) (European Court of Human Rights). For earlier related proceedings see *Keegan v Chief Constable of Merseyside Police* [2003] EWCA Civ 936, [2003] 1 WLR 2187 (2003 Abr para 2610).

1620   Right to private and family life—respect for home—travellers—eviction from unauthorised encampments

The claimants, who were travellers, set up encampments in two unauthorised places in the respondent local authority's area, both of which were wholly unsuitable for camping on. After receiving complaints from local residents, and after considering 'Guidance on Managing Unauthorised Camping', issued by the Home Office and the Office of the Deputy Prime Minister, the authority issued possession proceedings in respect of both encampments. The authority had an absolute legal entitlement to the land concerned and was under no duty to supply caravan sites, and in any event had no such sites. The claimants had no legal entitlement to occupation and had not asserted that that the authority had any obligation to supply a site. However, the claimants sought judicial review of the authority's decision to issue possession proceedings on the ground that the authority's proposals to evict them from their encampments without offering an alternative 'non-bricks and mortar' solution on a temporary and eventually permanent basis was an interference with their right to respect for private and family life under the European Convention on Human Rights art 8. *Held*, the authority had looked at the appropriate guidance and taken into account all material considerations and had not therefore acted perversely, nor *Wednesbury* unreasonably, in reaching its decision to issue proceedings for possession. Although there was at least some interference with the claimants' art 8 rights it was very much at the lower end of the spectrum, given the powerful case for the entitlement of a local authority landowner to enforce its ownership rights and planning duties. Reasonable decisions of the authority fell within the exceptions provided for by art 8(2) and, accordingly, the application would be dismissed.

R (*on the application of Casey*) *v Crawley BC* [2006] EWHC 301 (Admin), [2006] LGR 239 (Queen's Bench Division: Burton J).

1621   Right to private and family life—social security benefits—entitlement—person with same-sex partner—discrimination

The respondent lived with her same-sex partner in a jointly-owned house with a mortgage for which they were both responsible. The respondent's two children lived mainly with their father, from whom the respondent was divorced. In the calculation of the respondent's payments under the Child Support Act 1991 and the Child Support (Maintenance Assessments and Special Cases) Regulations 1992, SI 1992/1815, her same-sex partner's contribution to their joint housing costs was treated by the appellant as reducing her deductible housing costs. If she had been living with a man, his contribution to the mortgage would have been treated as part of hers, and her weekly payment would have been significantly smaller. The respondent complained that this infringed her right to a family life under the European Convention on Human Rights art 8, when taken in conjunction with her right not to be discriminated against under art 14. An appeal tribunal accepted her claim, and that decision was affirmed by the Child Support Commissioner. The appellant appealed unsuccessfully to the Court of Appeal. The appellant then made a further appeal, by which time the Civil Partnership Act 2004 had come into force, with the effect that the respondent was put in the same position as she would have been had she been in a heterosexual relationship. The appellant contended that the maintenance formula contained in the 1992 Regulations did not fall within the scope of the Convention art 8 for the purposes of art 14. *Held*, there was no simple bright-line test for determining how close the link had to be between the alleged discrimination and the rights granted by the substantive article. The general guidance that could be derived from the European Court of Human Rights did not lead to the conclusion that even a tenuous link was sufficient, nor did it lead to the conclusion that precisely the same sort of approach was appropriate, whatever the substantive article was in point. When considering art 8, it had to be borne in mind that its unique feature was that it was concerned with the failure to accord respect for family life and the method of calculation of the respondent's maintenance assessment under the 1991 Act and the 1992 Regulations did not fall within the ambit of her right to respect for the family relationship between her and her two children by her marriage to her ex-husband. The respondent was of course entitled to respect for her continuing relationship with her children, but she was not complaining of being deprived of all contact with her children. On the contrary, they spent part of the time with her at her home. The complicated formulae employed by the legislation were intended to strike a fair balance between the competing demands of the children and the new household. To that extent the legislation was intended, in a general sort of way, to be a positive measure promoting family life, or limiting the damage inevitably caused by the breakdown of relationships between couples who have had children. It followed that the Convention art 8 was not engaged and, accordingly, the appeal would be allowed.

M v Secretary of State for Work and Pensions [2006] UKHL 11, [2006] 2 AC 91 (House of Lords: Lords Bingham of Cornhill, Nicholls of Birkenhead and Walker of Gestingthorpe, Baroness Hale of Richmond and Lord Mance). Decision of Court of Appeal [2004] EWCA Civ 1343, [2005] 2 WLR 740 (2004 Abr para 2586) reversed.

1622   Right to private and family life—surveillance by neighbour—video recording given to police

See *R v Rosenberg*, para 2263.

1623   Right to private and family life—travellers occupying site under licence agreement—application for possession order

See *Birmingham City Council v Doherty*, para 1763.

1624   Right to private and family life—witness—application for disclosure of medical records

The applicant was the complainant and main prosecution witness at the trial of the offender, who was charged with sexual offences. The applicant had been receiving psychiatric treatment from an NHS foundation trust. The offender sought a witness summons directed to the trust requiring the production of the applicant's medical records, which had to be made in accordance with the CrimPR. At a public interest immunity hearing, the trust argued that confidentiality between doctor and patient belonged to the patient and not the trust. The judge found that evidence from the applicant's medical notes was relevant to her credibility, and ordered disclosure. The applicant attended court without any representation and reluctantly agreed to disclosure. The applicant made an application for judicial review relying on the right to privacy contained in the European Convention on Human Rights art 8. *Held*, although the existing legislation and the CrimPR did not oblige the court to give notice of an application for a witness summons directed at an NHS trust to the patient whose records were sought, the overriding objective of the CrimPR required it. A patient also had a right of privacy under the Convention art 8 and procedural fairness required that a patient be given the opportunity to make representations before the order was made. Since the CrimPR did not require that of the person applying for the summons, the requirement was on the court as a public authority to do so. Further, despite the fact that the Convention art 8 contained no explicit procedural requirements, the court had to have regard to determine whether it had been conducted in a manner that was fair and afforded due respect to the interests protected by art 8. What had to be determined was whether the person had been involved in the decision-making process to a degree sufficient to provide them with the requisite protection of their interests. If they had not, there would be a failure to respect their privacy and the interference resulting from the decision would not be capable of being regarded as 'necessary' within the meaning of art 8. In the present case, the court had acted incompatibly with the claimant's rights under art 8. Accordingly, the application would be allowed.

R (on the application of B) v Stafford Combined Court [2006] EWHC 1645 (Admin), [2006] All ER (D) 22 (Jul) (Queen's Bench Division: May LJ and Forbes J).

1625   Torture or inhuman or degrading treatment or punishment—asylum-seeker—risk of persecution

See *AK v Secretary of State for the Home Department*, para 322.

1626   Torture or inhuman or degrading treatment or punishment—drug offence—use of drugs for medicinal purpose—defence

See *R v Altham*, para 853.

1627   Torture or inhuman or degrading treatment or punishment—medical treatment— refusal to fund treatment

See *R (on the application of Rogers) v Swindon NHS Primary Care Trust*, para 2051.

1628   Torture or inhuman or degrading treatment or punishment—mentally ill patient— medical treatment without consent

See *R (on the application of B) v S*, para 1981.

1629   Torture or inhuman or degrading treatment or punishment—offender—police brutality—evidence

See *Miklis v Deputy Prosecutor General of Lithuania*, para 1314.

INCOME TAXATION

Halsbury's Laws of England (4th edn) vol 23(1) (Reissue) paras 1–950, vol 23(2) (Reissue) paras 951–1836

Articles

For articles relating to this title please refer to the Table of Articles at the beginning of the Abridgment.

1630   Assessment—appeal—appeal by way of case stated—transmission to High Court— time limit

The General Commissioners (Jurisdiction and Procedure) Regulations 1994, SI 1994/1812, reg 24(1) provides that any irregularity resulting from any failure to comply with any provision of the regulations or with any direction given by a tribunal before the tribunal has reached its final determination does not of itself render the proceedings void. Where any such irregularity comes to the attention of a tribunal, the tribunal before reaching its final determination may, and if it considers that any person may have been prejudiced by that irregularity must, give such directions as it thinks just to cure or waive the irregularity: reg 24(2).

The taxpayer company filed a return which claimed a capital allowance of 100 per cent in respect of its expenditure on a printer. An inspector of taxes reduced the allowance to 40 per cent. Following the dismissal of its appeal, the taxpayer requested the General Commissioners to state and sign a case for the opinion of the High Court. The taxpayer failed to transmit the case to the High Court within 30 days of receiving it, as prescribed by the 1994 Regulations reg 22(4)(a). The taxpayer applied for an extension of time within which to bring its appeal by way of case stated and issued an appellant's notice seeking an appeal. It also claimed that the strict enforcement of reg 22(4)(a) was in breach of its right, under the European Convention on Human Rights art 6(1), to a fair trial The inspector of taxes sought to have the notice struck out. Held, the procedure of an appeal by way of case stated under the 1994 Regulations was not within the definition of 'proceedings' in reg 2, as it arose after the final determination of proceedings. The irregularity covered by reg 24 was one which arose in the course of, or before, the determination of proceedings. Regulation 24 was irrelevant to any non-compliance with the 1994 Regulations that occurred after the proceedings had been determined, such as where the non-compliance was the taxpayer's failure to transmit the case stated to the High Court within the 30-day period. Regulation 24 did not dispense with the requirements with which the taxpayer had not complied or override the consequences of such non-compliance. The only dispensing power was vested in the tribunal and, since the High Court did not come within the definition of 'tribunal', the taxpayer could not rely on reg 24 to cure the irregularity in this case. Further, the Convention art 6(1) did not apply to proceedings concerned with the assessment of tax, such as an appeal by way of case stated under the 1994 Regulations. Moreover, the purpose of art 6(1) was to ensure procedural fairness. The judicial process in the present case had been fair and it was the taxpayer's own failure to comply with the straightforward task of transmitting the case to the High Court within the time limit that had caused the problem. Accordingly, the application for an extension of time would be dismissed and the taxpayer's notice struck out.

Significant Ltd v Farrel (Inspector of Taxes) [2005] EWHC 3434 (Ch), [2006] STC 1626 (Chancery Division: Blackburne J). *New World Medical Ltd v Cormack (Inspector of Taxes)* [2002] EWHC (Ch) 1787, [2002] STC 1245 (2002 Abr para 1764) considered. Application 44759/98 *Ferrazzini v Italy* (2001) 34 EHRR 1068 (2001 Abr para 1759) applied.

1631   Basic rate limit and personal reliefs—indexation

The Income Tax (Indexation) Order 2006, SI 2006/872 (made on 22 March 2006), prescribes the basic rate limit and the personal reliefs for 2006–07, increased in accordance with the percentage increase in the retail prices index for September 2005 over that for September 2004. The basic rate limit will be £33,300. The starting rate limit will be £2,150. The amounts have effect unless Parliament determines otherwise.

The Income Tax (Indexation) (No 2) Order 2006, SI 2006/3241 (made on 6 December 2006), prescribes, for 2006–07, as the personal allowance, £5,225 for persons aged 65 and under, or £7,550 for persons aged 65–74, or £7,690 for persons aged 75 and over. The enhanced reliefs on account of age are reduced where a claimant's total income for the year of assessment exceeds £20,900. The married couple's allowance, in relation to pre-5 December marriages, is increased to £6,285 (for those aged 70–74 and born before 6 April 1935) or £6,365 (for those aged 75 and over). The minimum married couple's allowance is £2,440, and the enhanced reliefs on account of age are reduced where a claimant's total income for the year of assessment exceeds £20,900. The blind person's allowance is £1,730. The amounts are increased in accordance with the percentage increase in the retail prices index for September 2006 over that for September 2005 and have effect unless Parliament determines otherwise.

1632   Capital allowances—industrial buildings or structures—warehouse—trade consisting in storage of goods

The Capital Allowances Act 1990 s 18(1)(f)(i) provides that an industrial building or structure means a building or structure in use for the purposes of a trade which consists in the storage of goods or materials which are to be used in the manufacture of other goods or materials. This applies in relation to a part of a trade or undertaking as it applies in relation to a trade or undertaking except that where part only of a trade or undertaking complies with the condition, a building or structure is not by virtue of s 18(2) an industrial building or structure unless it is in use for the purposes of that part of that trade or undertaking: s 18(2)

The taxpayer company imported window and door fixtures and fittings which it promoted and sold in the United Kingdom. Large quantities of the imported goods were stored in warehouses for which the taxpayer claimed industrial buildings allowances. The Commissioners for Her Majesty's Revenue and Customs refused the claim on the basis that the taxpayer's use of the warehouses did not satisfy the conditions of the 1990 Act s 18(1)(f)(i). A Special Commissioner allowed the taxpayer's appeal against the Commissioners' decision and they appealed. *Held*, since the taxpayer's main business was that of the importation and the sale of goods and not the storage of goods, the warehouse did not qualify as a building in use for the purposes of a trade which consisted in the storage of goods. 'Consists in' did not mean 'involves'. The only way the warehouse expenditure could qualify for an industrial building allowance was under s 18(2). The primary purpose of s 18(2) was to deal with composite trades. The taxpayer's storage was not a separate part of a composite business as it was not a commercial activity in its own right, although it was carried out in a separate building. For an operation to be part of a trade within the meaning of s 18(2), it had itself to be an activity in the nature of a trade. A trade for those purposes was not limited to the selling of goods and could include both manufacturing and processing operations. Section 18(2) operated only to expand the definition contained in s 18(1), not to alter it. The decision of the Special Commissioner was based on a misdirection as to the correct interpretation of s 18(2) and had to be set aside. Accordingly, the appeal would be allowed.

Maco Door and Windows Hardware (UK) Ltd v Revenue and Customs Comrs [2006] EWHC 1832 (Ch), (2006) Times, 11 August (Chancery Division: Patten J). *IRC v Saxone, Lilley and Skinner (Holdings) Ltd* [1967] 1 All ER 756, HL; *Kilmarnock Equitable Co-operative Society Ltd v IRC* (1966) 42 TC 675, IH; and *Bestway (Holdings) Ltd v Luff (Inspector of Taxes)* [1998] STC 357 (1998 Abr para 1835) considered.

1990 Act s 18 now Capital Allowances Act 2001 s 274.

1633   Capital allowances—plant and machinery—energy-saving plant and machinery

The Capital Allowances (Energy-saving Plant and Machinery) (Amendment) Order 2006, SI 2006/2233 (in force on 7 September 2006), further amends the 2001 Order, SI 2001/2541, by revising the definitions of 'Energy Technology Criteria List' and 'Energy Technology Product List', and removing class (d) from the list of technology classes in the Energy Technology Product list.

1634   Capital allowances—plant and machinery—environmentally beneficial plant and machinery

The Capital Allowances (Environmentally Beneficial Plant and Machinery) (Amendment) Order 2006, SI 2006/2235 (in force on 7 September 2006), further amends the 2003 Regulations, SI 2003/2076, by revising the definitions of 'the Water Technology Criteria List' and 'the Water Technology Product list,' and adding the technology classes of efficient washing machines and small scale slurry and sludge dewatering equipment to the Water Technology Product list.

1635   Construction industry—sub-contractors—tax certificate—issue of certificate—delay

The taxpayer, a construction company, applied for a sub-contractor's tax certificate from the defendant Revenue. As a consequence of a delay in the issue of the certificate, the taxpayer claimed that it had suffered serious economic loss. There fell to be determined, as preliminary issues, whether a breach of the Income and Corporation Taxes Act 1988 s 561(2) would give rise to a cause of action for damages, and whether the defendant owed a common law duty of care to process with reasonable expedition the taxpayer's application for a certificate under s 561(1). Issues also arose as to whether the individual Construction Industry Scheme ('CIS') officer owed a duty of care, and whether the Revenue would be vicariously liable for any breach of that duty. *Held,* Parliament had not intended to confer a private law claim for damages on sub-contractors experiencing delay in the processing of their certificate applications. Rather, it had provided an express remedy in the case of refusals and cancellations. On appeal by a sub-contractor, the Commissioners could reverse the Revenue's decision to refuse or cancel a certificate, but could not award any form of compensation for losses incurred by reason of a wrongful refusal or cancellation. Parliament had not intended sub-contractors who had certificates refused or cancelled to have a claim for compensation. Nonetheless, the denial of a private claim would not reduce to pious aspiration the duties imposed on the Revenue by s 561(2). Sub-contractors experiencing undue delay would be able to enforce performance of the Revenue's duty by an application for judicial review. Further, it was wholly unrealistic to treat any part of Pt XII Ch IV (ss 477A–491) as having been enacted for the protection or benefit of sub-contractors. Those provisions were enacted to protect the Revenue against potential fraud by sub-contractors. The fact that s 561 created an exemption from the general scheme did not alter that fact. Furthermore, the relevant question was not whether it would have been appropriate or reasonable for Parliament to have provided a private law remedy but whether, as a matter of construction, it had actually intended to do so. The Revenue did not owe a direct duty of care to process with reasonable expedition a claimant's application for a tax certificate. It was part and parcel of the CIS that all sub-contractor applicants would have some personal contact with Revenue officers. However, that did not affect whether the Revenue owed a duty to process an application with reasonable expedition. Judgment would be given accordingly.

Neil Martin Ltd v Revenue and Customs Comrs [2006] All ER (D) 137 (Sep) (Chancery Division: Andrew Simmonds QC). *Cutler v Wandsworth Stadium Ltd* [1949] AC 398, HL; *Lonrho Ltd v Shell Petroleum Co Ltd (No 2)* [1982] AC 173, HL (1981 Abr para 2918); *Phelps v Hillingdon LBC* [2000] 4 All ER 504, HL (2000 Abr para 1324); *X (Minors) v Bedfordshire CC; M (A Minor) v Newham LBC; E (A Minor) v Dorset CC; Christmas v Hampshire CC; Keating v Bromley LBC* [1995] 2 AC 633, HL (1995 Abr para 2833); *Stovin v Wise (Norfolk CC, third party)* [1996] 3 All ER 801, HL (1996 Abr para 1518); *Gorringe v Calderdale MBC* [2004] UKHL 15, [2004] 2 All ER 326 (2004 Abr para 1399); *Carty v Croydon LBC* [2005] 2 All ER 517 (2005 Abr para 1339); *Customs and Excise Comrs v Barclays Bank plc* [2006] UKHL 28, [2006] 3 WLR 1 (para 2072); *Bolam v Friern Hospital Management Committee* [1957] 2 All ER 118; *R v Criminal Injuries Compensation Board, ex p Cummins* [1992] 1 PIQR Q81 (1992 Abr para 772) considered.

The requirement to obtain a sub-contractor's tax certificate is replaced, as from 6 April 2007, by a requirement to register: Finance Act 2004 s 63.

1636   Construction industry—sub-contractors—tax certificate—refusal of certificate—failure to comply with statutory obligations

The Revenue refused the taxpayer's application for a Construction Industry Scheme certificate under the Income and Corporation Taxes Act 1988 s 565. On appeal, the General Commissioners found the taxpayer's failure to comply with the requirements of s 565 to be minor and technical, and granted the certificate. The Revenue appealed. *Held*, the provisions of s 565 were rigorously prescriptive. A sub-contractor had to have had for the previous three years a satisfactory record of compliance with its own obligations, unless, by virtue of s 565(4) any failure to do so could be regarded as 'minor and technical'. If a failure was too serious to rank as such then the Revenue had no power in law to issue a certificate. The taxpayer accepted that it had, on 32 out of a possible 34 occasions, failed to submit PAYE and National Insurance payments to the Revenue on time. The regularity and frequency of those failures could not be regarded as 'minor and technical' and, accordingly, the appeal would be allowed.

Revenue and Customs Comrs v Facilities and Maintenance Engineering Ltd [2006] EWHC 689 (Ch), (2006) 77 TC 575 (Chancery Division: Park J).

The taxpayer had operated within the construction industry for more than three years and had been granted a construction industry scheme ('CIS') certificate pursuant to the Income and Corporation Taxes Act 1988 s 561. When the certificate was due for renewal, an Inland Revenue inspector determined that the taxpayer had been in breach of the conditions set out in s 565(3), in that it had failed to comply with its obligations to account for PAYE and national insurance contributions so that the CIS certificate should not be renewed. The General Commissioners allowed the taxpayer's appeal against the inspector's decision on the basis that the taxpayer's admitted failures to comply with its obligations had been 'minor and technical' within the meaning of s 565(4). The Revenue's appeal was successful and the taxpayer appealed. *Held*, the judge was right to reject the notion that the whole tax compliance record fell to be taken into account. The absence of any warning was irrelevant as was the fact that a certificate had been granted or renewed where it might have been refused. The first condition in s 565(4) looked to the past, and required a decision as to whether the failure relied on was 'minor and technical'. The second condition looked to the future. There was no justification for construing the first condition in such a way as to pre-empt the second. Further, the fact that corporation tax or individual income tax was paid on time could say nothing of the quality of the failure to pay PAYE and national insurance contributions relied on by the commissioners. In the present case, the only reasonable conclusion was that the failure relied on was other than minor and technical. Accordingly, the appeal would be dismissed.

Arnold (Inspector of Taxes) v G-Con Ltd [2006] EWCA Civ 829, [2006] STC 1516 (Court of Appeal: Jonathan Parker and Hughes LJJ and Sir Peter Gibson). Decision of Mann J [2005] EWHC 2456 (Ch), [2006] STC 693 (2005 Abr para 1800) affirmed.

The requirement to obtain a sub-contractor's tax certificate is replaced, as from 6 April 2007, by a requirement to register: Finance Act 2004 s 63.

1637   Construction industry—sub-contractors—tax certificate—refusal of certificate—review

The taxpayer applied for a construction industry certificate pursuant to the Income and Corporation Tax Act 1988 ss 559 and 565. The board responsible for issuing such certificates decided that two of three conditions for eligibility for a certificate were not satisfied in the taxpayer's case, and therefore denied the application. The taxpayer appealed against that decision, but prior to the appeal hearing the defendants wrote to the taxpayer stating that they were considering whether the taxpayer in fact satisfied the other condition ('the compliance test'), so that, if the taxpayer's appeal was successful, there could be a full determination of the application. A preliminary hearing was subsequently held in relation to whether it was open to the defendants to raise the issue of the compliance test. At the hearing, the Special Commissioner elected to decide for himself whether all three statutory tests were satisfied, saying that his function was to review the reasons that were given. Although he recognised that he had full jurisdiction to substitute his own view for that of the board, he considered that he could only do so in relation to the reasons actually given for the refusal. Since a failure to satisfy the compliance test was not a reason given and had not been expressly kept open by the commissioners at the time of the refusal, he did not consider it was his function to review the decision by reference to the compliance test. The defendants appealed. *Held*, if evidence emerged that any of the three statutory conditions were not satisfied, the taxpayer was not entitled to a certificate and the defendants could not grant such a certificate, subject to questions of abuse of power and frustration of legitimate expectations. In those circumstances, the Special Commissioner's identification of his task on the appeal and his statement that that did not involve putting himself in the shoes of the commissioners could not be accepted. That was precisely what he did have to do. The Special Commissioner was also wrong when he stated that he could take no account of the fact that he would indirectly be granting a certificate knowing that the compliance test had not been satisfied: it seemed that, to the contrary, it was a factor which he had to take into account and that it was, apart from questions of abuse of power and legitimate expectations, determinative. It was therefore open to the defendants to raise the issue of the compliance test, and, accordingly, the appeal would be allowed.

Revenue and Customs Comrs v Oriel Support Ltd [2006] EWHC 3217 (Ch), [2006] All ER (D) 223 (Dec) (Chancery Division: Warren J). *Hudson (Inspector of Taxes) v JDC Services Ltd* [2004] EWHC 602 (Ch), [2004] STC 834 (2004 Abr para 1583) applied.

The requirement to obtain a sub-contractor's tax certificate is replaced, as from 6 April 2007, by a requirement to register: Finance Act 2004 s 63.

1638   Corporation tax—advance corporation tax—exemption—dividends paid to parent company—requirement for parent company to be based in European Union

United Kingdom corporation tax legislation provided that advance corporation tax was to be paid when a company distributed dividends. The Income and Corporation Taxes Act 1988 s 247 allowed a subsidiary company which made a distribution to its parent company, which was also resident in the United kingdom, to make a group income election and avoid the advance corporation tax payment. The European Court of Justice had held that, in respect of parent companies resident in other member states of the European Union, s 247 was incompatible with the EC Treaty art 43. The taxpayers, subsidiaries of companies that were not based in other member states, brought an action in England claiming that it was unlawful that subsidiaries of holding companies not resident in a member state were not allowed to make a group income election. They contended that the rule infringed the non-discrimination articles of the double taxation agreements between the United Kingdom and the countries in which the holding companies were resident and that those articles were given effect in domestic law by the 1988 Act s 788. The judge held that the legislation was a breach of the relevant double taxation agreement, but that they were not part of United Kingdom law, so that that afforded no remedy. On the taxpayers' appeal, *held,* the advance corporation tax provisions, on their face, were inconsistent with the non-discrimination article. The United Kingdom subsidiary of a foreign company could not avoid having to pay advance corporation tax when it paid a dividend by entering into a group income election, unlike members of a United Kingdom group. However, the non-discrimination article had not been made part of United Kingdom law in so far as it related to advance corporation tax. The judge was right to conclude that not everything in a double taxation agreement was enacted by s 788. Given that the terms of s 788(3) were not designed necessarily to implement as part of United Kingdom law everything relating to corporation tax that might be covered in a double taxation agreement, there was no reason to give the words that did define what was to be implemented a wide meaning rather than what the court concluded was their natural meaning. Accordingly, the appeal would be dismissed.

NEC Semi-Conductors Ltd v Revenue and Customs Comrs [2006] EWCA Civ 25, [2006] STC 606 (Court of Appeal: Mummery, Sedley and Lloyd LJJ). Decision of Park J [2003] EWHC 2813 (Ch), [2004] STC 489 (2004 Abr para 1553) affirmed.

1639   Corporation tax—advance corporation tax—exemption—dividends paid to parent company—requirement for parent company to be based in United Kingdom

See *Pirelli Cable Holding NV v IRC*, para 3002.

1640   Corporation tax—advance corporation tax—interest—availability of set-off

The Taxes Management Act 1970 s 87(1) provides that any tax assessable in accordance with the provisions relating to income tax on company payments which are not distributions carries interest at the prescribed rate from the date when the tax becomes due and payable until payment. Where (1) a company pays an amount of advance corporation tax in respect of qualifying distributions actually made by it in the relevant period; (2) the amount, or part of it, is available to be dealt with under the Income and Corporation Taxes Act 1988 s 246N; and (3) there is as regards the company an amount of notional foreign source advance corporation tax for the relevant period, an amount of the advance corporation tax paid is to be repaid to the company, or set off, or partly repaid and partly set off: s 246N(2).

The taxpayer failed to pay its advance corporation tax liability by the due date, and interest therefore began to run on the outstanding sum pursuant to the 1970 Act s 87(1). The 1988 Act granted the company a right to elect, in appropriate circumstances, for a dividend which it paid to be treated as a foreign income dividend. The Revenue issued proceedings claiming the unpaid interest. The taxpayer argued that 'payment' within the meaning of the 1970 Act s 87(1) could extend to a set-off. The judge decided that it could not, and that set-off could not therefore be established. The taxpayer's appeal was dismissed and, on its further appeal, *held,* on the true construction of s 87 and the 1988 Act s 246N(2), 'payment' could extend to a set-off. A perpetual liability to pay interest, subject only to a discretionary, and possibly dubious, official power of remission would be so disproportionate a penalty as to raise real doubt whether Parliament could have intended the system to work like that. Section 246N(2) described the statutory machinery as it ought to operate. It was not concerned with the consequences of non-compliance. Moreover, the reference to tax being 'set off' looked forward to s 246Q(2), which referred to an amount being 'set off against the company's liability to corporation tax for the relevant period', a clear echo of the familiar process under s 239(1). It was not an ordinary set-off of cross-claims. It was treating a payment of advance corporation tax by a company to the Revenue as discharging in advance a liability to mainstream corporation tax. Further, there was a deterrent to non-payment in the interest charge under the 1970 Act s 87. If the Treasury considered that the deterrent was insufficiently severe it could provide a stiffer sanction, but the notion of a perpetual liability to pay interest, subject only to the possibility of administrative remission, could not be justified on grounds of policy. Also, set-off was a general principle founded in simple convenience and fairness. It should be taken to apply generally to all liquidated cross-claims unless excluded by statute or contract. Accordingly, the appeal would be allowed.

Mellham Ltd v Burton (Collector of Taxes) [2006] UKHL 6, (2006) 77 TC 608 (House of Lords: Lords Nicholls of Birkenhead, Hoffmann, Phillips of Worth Matravers, Walker of Gestingthorpe and Brown of Eaton-under-Heywood). Decision of Court of Appeal [2003] EWCA Civ 173, [2003] STC 441 (2003 Abr para 1554) reversed.

1988 Act ss 246N, 246Q repealed: Finance (No 2) Act 1997 Sch 6 para 3(1), Sch 8 Pt II(11).

1641   Corporation tax—authorised investment funds

The Authorised Investment Funds (Tax) Regulations 2006, SI 2006/964 (in force on 1 April 2006), make provision concerning the tax treatment of authorised investment funds. Specifically, the regulations (1) define an 'authorised investment fund' as an open-ended investment company or an authorised unit trust scheme, and define 'open-ended investment company' and 'authorised unit trust scheme' for that purpose; (2) provide that capital profits, gains or losses arising to an authorised investment fund must not be brought into account for the purposes of the Finance Act 1996 Pt 4 Ch 2 (ss 80–105) (loan relationships) or the Finance Act 2002 Sch 26 (derivative contracts); (3) make supplementary provision concerning the purposes of an authorised investment fund's loan relationships; (4) provide for the treatment of interest distributions; (5) prevent the carrying-back of deficits on loan relationships to earlier periods; (6) require amounts shown as available in distribution accounts to be shown as available for distribution as yearly interest or as dividends; (7) specify that, before an interest distribution may be made, an amount must satisfy the specified qualifying investments test; (8) make provision for dividend distributions; (9) provide for the revised treatment of amounts available for distribution which are de minimis; (10) relax the general obligation to deduct a sum representing tax when any yearly interest is paid ('the deduction obligation') in a number of specified cases; (11) provide that the deduction obligation does not apply to interest distributions; (12) provide for the unfranked part of the dividend distribution to be treated as an annual payment and not as a dividend distribution or an interest distribution; (13) specify how the unfranked part of the dividend distribution is to be calculated; (14) impose a charge to tax on substantial QIS holdings (as defined) in qualified investor schemes, and create various exceptions from the charge; (15) provide that the amount charged to tax is calculated by reference to the difference in value of the substantial QIS holding between two specified measuring dates; (16) provide that a participant must value his holding on the first measuring date, subject to various specified exceptions; (17) define how the first measuring date is to be calculated; (18) make provision for the disposals of holdings, including with respect to reorganisations, the disposal of part of a holding and disposals where no gain or loss arises; (19) modify the application of the Income and Corporation Taxes Act 1988 s 234A (information relating to distributions) to authorised investment funds; (20) require an authorised investment fund making interest distributions without deduction of tax to report this information to the Commissioners for Revenue and Customs; (21) empower the commissioners to require information to be given concerning interest distributions made without deduction of tax, and to inspect records; (22) restrict the circumstances in which such information may be used by the commissioners; (23) enable the commissioners to inspect residence declarations; (24) make provision for the cases in which an open-ended investment company issues shares of different denominations, and prohibit discrimination in respect of different classes of shares; (25) regulate the tax treatment of amalgamations of authorised unit trusts with, and the conversion of authorised unit trusts into, open-ended investment companies; and (26) make consequential amendments and modifications to various primary tax legislation.

The Authorised Investment Funds (Tax) (Amendment) Regulations 2006, SI 2006/3239 (in force on 7 December 2006), amend the 2006 Regulations supra so as to provide that in a specified case where an authorise investment fund is eligible for double taxation relief, an amount of tax equal to the participant's portion of the foreign tax is treated as foreign tax and not as United Kingdom tax for the purposes of the Income and Corporation Taxes Act 1988 s 798A and s 804C, to the extent that it applies to business of a company which is not a long-term business.

1642   Corporation tax—avoidance—anti-avoidance provisions—subsidiary established in another member state—right of establishment

The taxpayer was a parent company resident in the United Kingdom with a number of subsidiaries in various countries. Two of the subsidiaries carried on the business of raising finance and providing it to subsidiaries in the group from Ireland, where they were established in order to benefit from the favourable tax conditions. The profits of those subsidiaries were charged to tax in the United Kingdom under the Income and Corporation Taxes Act 1988 ss 747–756, Schs 24–26. The taxpayer maintained that the provisions of the 1988 Act contravened the principle of freedom of establishment under the EC Treaty art 43, and extended to companies under art 48. *Held*, arts 43, 48 precluded the inclusion in the tax base of a resident company established in a member state of profits made by a controlled foreign company in another member state, where those profits were subject in the second state to a lower level of taxation than that applicable in the first state, unless such inclusion related only to wholly artificial arrangements intended to escape the national tax normally payable. Such a tax measure could not be applied where it was proven on the basis of objective factors, which were ascertainable by third parties, that despite the existence of tax motives, the controlled company was actually established in the host member state and carried on genuine economic activities there.

Case C-196/04 *Cadbury Schweppes plc v IRC* [2007] Ch 30 (ECJ: Grand Chamber). Case C-446/03 *Marks & Spencer plc v Halsey (Inspector of Taxes)* [2006] Ch 184, ECJ (2005 Abr para 3231), considered.

1643 Corporation tax—avoidance—transfer of securities—variable interest rate

The taxpayers, a company and its subsidiary, adopted a merchant bank scheme under which, if they were to invest a sum in a bond carrying interest at a fixed rate and then dispose of it after 11 months before the date of the first interest payment, which would be an amount less than the interest which had accrued, the company would realise a capital gain which it could shelter by using capital losses within the group. Subsequently, an associate of the group issued loan notes to the company, with provision for early redemption. The notes provided that the principal was to carry interest at a fixed rate, without compounding, for the period from, and including, the issue date to, but excluding, the maturity date or the date of earlier redemption. The notes made provision for the payment of the interest at the specified rate in the event of early redemption up to the date of redemption, allowing for any interest payments which had already been made. Lloyds Bank offered to purchase the notes. The inspector of taxes took the view that the notes were variable rate securities under the Income and Corporation Taxes Act 1988 s 717. The taxpayers' appeals to the Special Commissioners and the High Court, claiming that the securities carried interest at a fixed rate which was the same throughout the period from issue to redemption, was dismissed. On the taxpayers' further appeal, *held,* Sir Peter Gibson dissenting, as a matter of construction the notes did not fall within s 717(2)(a) and fell within the variable interest rate regime. The existence of the two regimes for the taxation of accrued interest on the transfer of securities and the different way in which they dealt with how to apportion the consideration for the transfer of an accrued right to payment of interest in the future provided the context in which to consider the proper construction of s 717(2), because s 717(2), (4) determined which regime governed a security. The court was bound to consider which of the two regimes was the more appropriate for ascertaining the accrued amount on which to assess the transferor to tax. Under the variable interest regime the inspector was able to assess the accrued amount on the basis that the notes carried a certain rate of interest for the period from issue to redemption. The court did not accept the taxpayers' submission that the inspector's decision led to the performance of the wrong exercise in comparing amounts payable with rates of interest. Accordingly, the appeal would be dismissed.

Cadbury Schweppes plc v Williams (Inspector of Taxes) [2006] EWCA Civ 657, [2007] STC 106 (Court of Appeal: Sir Andrew Morritt C, Tuckey LJ and Sir Peter Gibson).

1644 Corporation tax—branch of company established in another member state— discrimination

The applicant company was based in Luxembourg but had a branch in Germany. The German tax authority fixed the taxable amount for corporation tax in respect of the applicant at a particular level. The applicant appealed against the decision, arguing that the tax rate was discriminatory and infringed its right to freedom of establishment under the EC Treaty art 43 read in conjunction with art 48. The appeal was dismissed and, on the applicant's further appeal, it fell to be determined whether arts 43 and 48 precluded a national law which, in the case of a branch of a company with its seat in another member state, laid down on the profits of that branch a tax rate which was higher than that on the profits of a subsidiary of such a company where the subsidiary distributed its profits in full to its parent company. *Held*, arts 43 and 48 precluded a national law of that type. It was for the national court to determine the tax rate which had to be applied to the profits made by a branch, by reference to the overall tax rate which would have been applicable if the profits of a subsidiary had been distributed to its parent company. The tax rate applicable to the profits of a branch of a parent company with its seat in another member state constituted unfavourable treatment in relation to the reduced tax rate applicable to the profits of a subsidiary of such a company. The refusal to apply the reduced tax rate to branches rendered it less attractive, for a company with its seat in another member state, to exercise the right to freedom of establishment through a branch. Such a national law restricted the freedom to choose the appropriate legal form in which to pursue activities in another member state. It was therefore necessary to examine whether that differential treatment had been objectively justified. In the circumstances, it would seem that German subsidiaries and branches of companies with their seat in Luxembourg were in an objectively comparable situation.

Case C-253/03 *CLT-UFA SA v Finanzamt Köln-West* [2006] 2 CMLR 743 (ECJ: Third Chamber).

1645   Corporation tax—deduction of costs relating to shareholdings—discrimination

The respondent, a company registered in Germany, was the sole shareholder in a second German company, which in turn owned all of the shares in an Austrian company. In two successive years, the Austrian company distributed to the second company dividends, which were received tax-free and passed on to the respondent. Under German law, the dividends thereby redistributed were not taken into account in the calculation of the basis of assessment for corporation tax to which the respondent was liable. The respondent deducted as operating expenditure the entire amount of the interest on the capital borrowed to acquire its shareholding in the second company, as well as the incidental administrative costs. The German tax authority refused to allow the deduction of those costs to the extent to which they corresponded proportionately to the tax-free dividends, in particular those derived from the Austrian company. It fell to be determined whether it was contrary to the EC Treaty art 52, taken in conjunction with arts 58 and 73b, for financing costs incurred by a corporation that had a direct economic link to profits, not subject to tax in its own state, and that derived from a holding in a capital company established in another member state, to be deducted as operating expenditure only in so far as no profits from that holding were distributed on a tax-free basis. *Held*, art 52 had to be interpreted as precluding legislation of a member state which excluded the possibility of deducting for tax purposes financing costs incurred by a parent company subject to unlimited tax liability in that state in order to acquire holdings in a subsidiary where those costs related to dividends which were exempt from tax because they were derived from an indirect subsidiary established in another member state, whereas such costs might be deducted where they related to dividends paid by an indirect subsidiary established in the same member state as that of the place of the registered office of the parent company and which, in reality, also benefited from a tax exemption. The freedom of establishment conferred by art 52 on Community nationals included, pursuant to art 58, the right of companies to pursue their activities in the member state concerned through a subsidiary, a branch or an agency. The tax position of the respondent was less favourable than it would have been had its indirect subsidiary been established in Germany. In the light of that difference in treatment, a parent company might be dissuaded from carrying on its activities through the intermediary of subsidiaries or indirect subsidiaries established in other member states, contrary to art 52.

Case C-471/04 *Finanzamt Offenbach am Main-Land v Keller Holding GmbH* [2006] 2 CMLR 774 (ECJ: First Chamber).

EC Treaty arts 52, 58, 73b now arts 43, 48, 56.

1646   Corporation tax—derivative contracts—profits and losses

The Finance Act 2002, Sch 26, (Parts 2 and 9) (Amendment) Order 2006, SI 2006/3269 (in force on 30 December 2006), (1) further amends the Finance Act 2002 Sch 26 so as to (a) provide for the new method of classifying derivative contracts; (b) makes provisions that apply to contracts which (i) become derivative contracts; and (ii) cease to be derivative contracts; and (2) amends references in the Taxation of Chargeable Gains Act 1992.

1647   Corporation tax—films and sound recordings—relief

The Finance Act 2006, Section 53(2) (Films and Sound Recordings: Power to alter Dates) Order 2006, SI 2006/3265 (in force on 29 December 2006), amends the Finance Act 2006 Pt 3 Ch 3 (ss 31–53) so as to provide that the new films tax relief will only apply to films that commenced principal photography on or after 1 January 2007; and that existing reliefs in the Finance (No 2) Act 1992 ss 40A–43 and the Income Tax (Trading and Other Income) Act 2005 Pt 2 Ch 9 (ss 130–144) are withdrawn from that date.

1648   Corporation tax—group relief—overseas losses—European Economic Area insurance companies

The Group Relief for Overseas Losses (Modification of the Corporation Tax Acts for Non-resident Insurance Companies) (No 2) Regulations 2006, SI 2006/3389 (in force on 8 January 2007), modify (1) the Income and Corporation Taxes Act 1988 and the Finance Act 1989 so that they apply to EEA life insurance companies; and (2) the General Insurance Reserves (Tax) Regulations 2001, SI 2001/1757, and the Insurance Companies (Reserves) (Tax) Regulations 1996, SI 1996/2991, so that they apply to EEA general insurers. The definitions of 'insurance business transfer scheme' and 'periodical return' are also modified so as to refer to their EEA equivalents and provide for an assumption that the trade of a non-resident company is taxed under Schedule D Case 1. SI 2006/3218, which contained a technical error, is revoked.

1649   Corporation tax—investment trusts—accounts
See para 1672.

1650   Corporation tax—Lloyd's underwriters—conversion to limited liability underwriting
The Lloyd's Underwriters (Conversion to Limited Liability Underwriting) (Tax) Regulations 2006, SI 2006/112 (in force on 14 February 2006), amend the definition of 'successor partnership' to include limited liability partnerships.

1651   Corporation tax—Lloyd's underwriters—Scottish limited partnerships—Lloyd's partnerships
The Lloyd's Underwriters (Scottish Limited Partnerships) (Tax) (Amendment) Regulations 2006, SI 2006/111 (in force on 14 February 2006), amend the 1997 Regulations, SI 1997/2681, so that 'Lloyd's partnerships' are defined as Scottish limited partnerships or limited liability partnerships.

1652   Corporation tax—real estate investment trusts—assessment and recovery of tax
The Real Estate Investment Trusts (Assessment and Recovery of Tax) Regulations 2006, SI 2006/2867 (in force on 1 January 2007), make provision for the assessment and recovery of tax arising on distributions made by real estate investment trusts. In particular, the regulations (1) set out the rules for the assessment and recovery of tax in the case of a real estate investment trust which is a company not forming part of a group to which the Finance Act 2006 Pt 4 (ss 103–145) applies; (2) set out the basic rule that, on making a relevant distribution the company must deduct a sum representing tax at the basic rate in force for the year in which it is made; (3) impose a duty to deliver returns and account for tax in respect of relevant distributions; (4) set out when tax is due; (5) provide for the supply of certificates of deduction of tax to be given by the company; (6) provide that the payments specified will not be subject to the deduction of tax; (7) provide for assessments by officers of Revenue and Customs; and (8) provide for the application of the Income Tax Acts in respect of payments and assessments of tax.

The Real Estate Investment Trusts (Assessment and Recovery of Tax) (Amendment) Regulations 2006, SI 2006/3222 (in force on 26 December 2006), make a minor drafting correction to SI 2006/2867 supra.

1653   Corporation tax—real estate investment trusts—breach of conditions
The Real Estate Investment Trusts (Breach of Conditions) Regulations 2006, SI 2006/2864 (in force on 1 January 2007), make provision about the consequences flowing from a breach of the conditions in the Finance Act 2006 Pt 4 (ss 103–115), or a breach of the profit: financing costs ratio in s 115(2), applying to a real estate investment trust. Specifically, the regulations (1) provide that, notwithstanding a breach of Conditions 3 and 4 in the 2006 Act s 106 in consequence of a company's becoming a member of a group or another group to which Pt 4 applies, Pt 4 is to continue to apply to the company; (2) provide that, notwithstanding a breach of Condition 4 in s 106 caused by someone other than the company, Pt 4 continues to apply provided that the breach is remedied no later than the end of the accounting period following that in which it began; (3) provide that, if a company breaches Condition 3 or Condition 4 in s 106 otherwise than in prescribed circumstances, Pt 4 is taken to have ceased to apply to the company at the end of the previous accounting period; (4) make provision for the consequences of breaching (a) the property-holding conditions or the distribution condition in s 107; (b) the balance of business conditions; and (c) multiple conditions in Pt 4; (5) prescribe information requirements in respect of breaches of the conditions in s 106(5) or (6), 107 or 108; (6) impose a charge to tax where there is a distribution to a person holding more than the maximum permitted shareholding in a company to which Pt 4 applies; (7) impose obligations about the furnishing of information about such a distribution; (8) impose a charge to tax where the ratio of profit to financing costs is less than 1·25; and (9) provide for the termination of the real estate investment trust régime under s 129(2)(b) where two notices under s 117 have been served within a ten-year period.

1654   Corporation tax—real estate investment trusts—financial statements of group real estate investment trusts
The Real Estate Investment Trusts (Financial Statements of Group Real Estate Investment Trusts) Regulations 2006, SI 2006/2865 (in force on 1 January 2007), make provision relating to the contents of the financial statements of group real estate investment trusts. Specifically, the regulations (1) provide that a member of a group has significant influence over another entity if the group member holds more than 20 per cent of the beneficial interest in that other entity, and that percentages of beneficial interest in an entity are to be determined by reference to profits available for distribution to equity holders; (2) require the principal company in the group to prepare, for each of its accounting periods, a financial statement for the group in so far as it carries on property rental business, and a financial statement for the group in so far as it carries on other business; (3) require the group to prepare a financial statement in relation to the group's property rental business in

respect of its United Kingdom business; (4) prescribe general matters that must be included in the statements; (5) specify how the amount of financing costs (external) to be shown in the property rental statement are to be determined; (6) make provision for the treatment of items which arise from events or transactions that are outside the ordinary transactions of the group, and which are not expected to recur regularly and frequently; (6) provide that, if a member of the group holds a percentage of the beneficial interest in another entity which is not a member of the group, the group member must account for income received on the basis that the beneficial interest is held as an investment, and must show that beneficial interest as an asset of the group member; (7) provide that a joint venture company in which a group member is a joint venturer, an open-ended investment company over which the group member has significant influence, and a non-corporate entity over which a group member has significant influence are to be treated, for accounting purposes, as members of the group; (8) make further provision relating to the content of the financial statement for the group's property rental business in respect of its United Kingdom business; and (9) specify the time by which the financial statements must be supplied.

1655 Corporation tax—real estate investment trusts—joint ventures

The Real Estate Investment Trusts (Joint Ventures) Regulations 2006, SI 2006/2866 (in force on 1 January 2007), provide details as to how the Real Estate Investment Trusts regime ('the UK-REIT regime'), which was introduced by the Finance Act 2006, apply to joint ventures. In particular, the regulations (1) provide details for a notice to be given by a single company ('the venturing company') which is carrying on a joint venture with another person and wishes for the UK-REIT regime to apply to that joint venture ('the joint venture company'); (2) set out the conditions that must be met by the venturing company and the joint venture company to join the UK-REIT regime; (3) provide for the financial statements that the venturing company must prepare in respect of the joint venture company; (4) set out certain requirements with which the venturing company must comply; (5) provide for the modification of certain tax charges and exemptions in respect of the venturing company and the joint venture company; (6) set out details of the notice that must be given by the principal company of the venturing group; (7) set out the conditions that must be met by the venturing group and joint venture company; (8) provide for the financial statements that the principal company of the venturing company must prepare in respect of the joint venture company; (9) provide for the application and modification of certain tax charges and exemptions in respect of the group venturing company and the joint venture company; (10) deal with situations where (a) a venturing company applies to join a joint venture; and (b) a joint venturing company becomes a member of a group joint venture; and (11) provide for the modification of entry charges in respect of non-resident joint venture companies and venturing groups.

1656 Corporation tax—return—inquiry—closure notice—application to require issue of notice—determination of point of law

The Revenue had made an inquiry into the taxpayer's company tax returns. The taxpayer applied to the Special Commissioners for a direction to the Revenue to issue a closure notice in accordance with the Finance Act 1998 Sch 18 para 33 to certify the completion of the inquiry. The Commissioners stayed the proceedings pending their referral of a number of questions to the European Court of Justice as to the compatibility with the EC Treaty of certain provisions of United Kingdom tax law relating to controlled foreign companies. The Revenue appealed against the Commissioners' decision. *Held*, there was no limitation in the 1998 Act Sch 18 para 33 which restricted the Commissioners' role to scrutinising the factual investigation performed by the Revenue. Schedule 18 para 33 would seem to confer on the Commissioners a power to do anything which they reasonably considered necessary so as to be satisfied as to matters required by it. There would need to be clear statutory language for the court to take the view that it was sufficient for the Revenue to hold a view of the law that was reasonable. It would be constitutionally anomalous if the Commissioners could not come to their own decision on a point of law and had to abide by the Revenue's view as part of the executive, even if the Revenue had to establish that the view was a reasonable one for it to hold. On its true construction, Sch 18 para 33 gave the Commissioners jurisdiction to determine incidental points of law that needed to be resolved on an application for closure. This enabled the Commissioners to make the references to the European Court of Justice and, accordingly, the appeal would be dismissed.

Revenue and Customs Comrs v Vodafone 2 [2006] EWCA Civ 1132, [2006] STC 1530 (Court of Appeal: Mummery, Arden and Moore-Bick LJJ). Decision of Park J [2005] EWHC 3040 (Ch), [2006] STC 483 (2005 Abr para 1807) affirmed.

1657 Corporation tax—securitisation companies

The Taxation of Securitisation Companies Regulations 2006, SI 2006/3296 (in force on 12 December 2006), make provision as to the application of the Corporation Tax Acts in relation to a securitisation company. In particular, the regulations (1) define 'securitisation company'; the five different types of securitisation company are a note-issuing company, an asset-holding company, an intermediate borrowing company, a warehouse company and a commercial paper-funded company, each of which must have a retained profit in order to constitute a securitisation company; (2) set out requirements for each type of securitisation company; (3) define retained profit; (4) provide that specified regulations do not apply to a securitisation company which does not meet, or has not met, the payments condition; this condition essentially requires that subject to the retention of amounts required to provide for losses, expenses, creditworthiness and retained profit, all amounts received by a securitisation company must be paid out; (4) provide that the specified regulations do not apply to a securitisation company which has, or has had, an unallowable purpose; (5) specify companies to which the regulations do not apply unless the company elects that they are to apply; (5) provide for the charge to corporation tax; (6) make provision for the application, modification and non-application of provisions of the Corporation Tax Acts 1988 by (a) making provision so that an accounting period ends when a company ceases to be a securitisation company; (b) making provision so that only dividend payments by a securitisation company constitute 'distributions' for the purposes of the 1988 Acts; (c) excluding group relief provisions in relation to securitisation companies; (d) disapplying certain provisions relating to transactions within groups in the Taxation of Chargeable Gains Act 1992; (e) disapplying provisions in the Finance Act 1996 Sch 9 regarding special computational provisions in relation to loan relationships; (f) disapplying provisions in the Finance Act 2002 Sch 26 regarding transactions within groups in relation to derivative contracts; and (g) disapplying the Finance Act 2005 s 83 regarding the application of accounting standards to securitisation companies.

1658 Corporation tax—small companies' relief—associated company—company carrying on trade or business

The taxpayer was one of four companies under the control of the same person. In 1966, one of the companies vacated its premises and let them on a tenant's repairing lease. In 1995, the taxpayer ceased trading and its sole income came from the rent received from the premises. A Special Commissioner determined that, for the purpose of entitlement to the small companies' rate of corporation tax under the Income and Corporation Taxes Act 1988 s 13, the taxpayer did not carry on any trade or business, so that the relevant profits of the defendant as an associated company, were not restricted under s 13(3), (4). The Revenue appealed. *Held*, the Commissioner was entitled to conclude that the rent received did not come from a source that amounted to business. The Commissioner had taken into account that the taxpayer had described its principal activity as property investment and, while rent might constitute investment from a source consisting of a business, he was entitled to take into account that the lettings took place in 1966 and, since it ceased trading, there had been no indication of any business. The taxpayer left its former trading premises and let it out with no active participation or management. There was no artificial arrangement to take advantage of the small companies' rate. Accordingly, the appeal would be dismissed.

Revenue and Customs Comrs v Salaried Persons Postal Loans Ltd [2006] EWHC 763 (Ch), [2006] STC 1315 (Chancery Division: Lawrence Collins J). *Edwards (Inspector of Taxes) v Bairstow* [1954] AC 14, HL, applied. *American Leaf Blending Co v Director-General of Inland Revenue* [1979] AC 676, PC (1978 Abr para 1623); and *Jowett (Inspector of Taxes) v O'Neill* [1998] STC 482 (1998 Abr para 1844) considered.

1659 Corporation tax—venture capital trusts—accounts

See para 1672.

1660 Double taxation relief—taxes on income—Botswana

The Double Taxation Relief (Taxes on Income) (Botswana) Order 2006, SI 2006/1925 (in force on 19 July 2006), sets out an agreement between the United Kingdom and Botswana dealing with the avoidance of double taxation and fiscal evasion.

1661 Double taxation relief—taxes on income—computation of credit relief

The taxpayer was an insurance company incorporated in England and Wales. A dispute arose between the taxpayer and the Revenue as to the calculation of the taxpayer's entitlement to double taxation relief in respect of insurance business carried on abroad. The double taxation treaty with France, which followed the standard form of the majority of double taxation treaties, was taken as a sample treaty. It provided that French tax had to be allowed as a credit against any United Kingdom tax computed by reference to the same profits, income or chargeable gains by reference to which the French tax was computed. The taxpayer claimed that it was entitled to credit against the amount of corporation tax payable on its profits from its pension business generally, tax deducted at source by the authorities in foreign countries, on the relevant parts of its income from investments sourced in those countries and held as part of its long-term insurance fund. However, the Revenue contended that the taxpayer's right to credit was limited to the extent of the corporation tax payable on such proportion of the overall profits of its pension business as the gross foreign income bore to the overall income. The Special Commissioners decided in favour of the taxpayer and the Revenue appealed. *Held*, while the relevant provision of the sample treaty was capable of being construed in the manner for which the Revenue contended, it was at least as apt to be construed in the sense contended for by the taxpayer, that the foreign income on which the foreign tax arose had to enter into the computation of the United Kingdom tax against which credit for the foreign tax was claimed. Construed in that way, the provision did not purport to impose a detailed restriction on the creditability of foreign tax but simply required a connection between the source of the foreign tax and the United Kingdom tax against which it was to be credited so that the former should be part of the computation of the latter. The taxpayer was, therefore, entitled to credit against the amount of corporation tax payable in respect of any year of assessment on its profits from its pension business generally, tax deducted at source by the authorities in foreign countries, on the relevant parts of its income from investments sourced in those countries and held as part of its long-term insurance fund. Accordingly, the appeal would be dismissed.

Legal & General Assurance Society Ltd v Revenue and Customs Comrs [2006] EWHC 1770 (Ch), [2006] STC 1763 (Chancery Division: Evans-Lombe J). *George Wimpey International Ltd v Rolfe (Inspector of Taxes)* (1989) 62 TC 597 (1989 Abr para 1207) considered.

1662   Double taxation relief—taxes on income—Japan

The Double Taxation Relief (Taxes on Income) (Japan) Order 2006, SI 2006/1924 (in force on 19 July 2006), sets out an agreement between the United Kingdom and Japan dealing with the avoidance of double taxation and fiscal evasion.

1663   Double taxation relief—taxes on income—Poland

The Double Taxation Relief (Taxes on Income) (Poland) Order 2006, SI 2006/3323 (in force on a date to be published in the London Gazette), sets out a Convention between the United Kingdom and Poland dealing with the avoidance of double taxation and fiscal evasion.

1664   Employment income—car for private use—motor home used as office

The taxpayer, the director of a pharmacy company, used a motor home purchased in the name of the company as a mobile office. The vehicle was assessed as a taxable emolument for income tax purposes. The taxpayer accepted that some measure of taxable benefit applied to him by reason of the motor home being available to him, but alleged that the benefit should not be calculated under the car benefits rules set out in the Income and Corporation Taxes Act 1988. A Special Commissioner ruled that the vehicle was a 'car' within the meaning of s 168(5), and was therefore taxable. The taxpayer appealed, contending that the special commissioner was wrong and that, if the car benefits rules did apply, there should be some form of apportionment to reflect the fact that he had made use of the motor home for only two weeks out of the tax year in question. *Held*, notwithstanding that the vehicle at issue was used mainly as an office, it clearly came within the statutory definition of 'car' in s 168(5), as that definition referred to any mechanically propelled vehicle, subject to various exceptions which did not apply to the taxpayer. Moreover, it was clear from the provisions of the 1988 Act that the tax liability imposed in the instant case was a full year's benefit and, in the absence of certain circumstances as set out in the statute, that period could not be scaled down to reflect the personal use of the motor home by the taxpayer. Accordingly, the appeal would be dismissed.

Morris v Revenue and Customs Comrs; County Pharmacy Ltd v Revenue and Customs Comrs [2006] EWHC 1560 (Ch), [2006] STC 1593 (Chancery Division: Park J).

1665   Exemptions—childcare vouchers and employer contracted childcare

The Income Tax (Exempt Amounts for Childcare Vouchers and for Employer Contracted Childcare) Order 2006, SI 2006/882 (in force on 6 April 2006), amends the Income Tax (Earnings and Pensions) Act 2003 s 270A so as to increase from £50 to £55 the exempt amounts for income tax purposes in respect of qualifying childcare vouchers provided for an employee and the provision by an employer for an employee for care for a child.

1666   Exemptions and reliefs—interest and royalty payments

The Exemption from Income Tax for Certain Interest and Royalty Payments (Amendment of Section 757(2) of the Income Tax (Trading and Other Income) Act 2005) Order 2006, SI 2006/3288 (in force on 1 January 2007), amends the Income Tax (Trading and Other Income) Act 2005 s 757(2) by adding a reference to EC Council Directive 2006/98, which amends EC Council Directive 2003/49 on a common system of taxation applicable to interest and royalty payments made between associated companies of different member states.

1667   Finance Act 2006

See para 2465.

1668   Individual savings accounts—building society bonus—exemption from tax

The Individual Savings Account (Amendment) Regulations 2006, SI 2006/3194 (in force on 1 January 2007), further amend the 1998 Regulations, SI 1998/1870, so that annual bonuses that are paid to building society members who hold an Individual Savings Account ('ISA') are exempt from income tax and capital gains tax in so far as the bonuses are calculated by reference to assets in the ISA, and bonuses paid directly into the ISA do not count against their annual subscription limits.

1669   Insurance companies—Corporation Tax Acts

The Insurance Companies (Corporation Tax Acts) (Amendment) Order 2006, SI 2006/1358 (in force on 9 June 2006), amends the Income and Corporation Taxes Act 1988 Pt 12 Ch 1 (ss 431–458A) in relation to the apportionment rules applying to companies carrying on life assurance business that attribute income and gains of such a company's inherited estate to categories of the company's business.

The Insurance Companies (Corporation Tax Acts) (Amendment No 2) Order 2006, SI 2006/3387 (in force on 8 January 2007), further amends the Income and Corporation Taxes Act 1988 and the Finance Act 1989 in consequence of a change to the rules contained in the Prudential Sourcebook for Insurers. The order allows an additional amount to be brought into account in computing an insurance company's closing liabilities, in the case of life assurance business, and long term business provision, in the case of long-term business which is not life assurance business, for the first period of account ending on or after 31 December 2006 and its opening liabilities and long term business provision for the next period of account, to mitigate the effects of a rule change in the Insurance Prudential Sourcebook.

1670   Insurance contract—premium trust fund

The Lloyd's Sourcebook (Finance Act 1993 and Finance Act 1994) (Amendment) Order 2006, SI 2006/3273 (in force on 31 December 2006), amends the Finance Act 1993 s 184(1) and the Finance Act 1994 s 230 so as to replace references to the Lloyd's Sourcebook with references to the Insurance Prudential Sourcebook. SI 2005/1538 is revoked.

1671   International matters—exchange of information between member states—mutual assistance provisions

The Mutual Assistance Provisions Order 2006, SI 2006/3283 (in force on 1 January 2007), updates the definition of the 'Mutual Assistance Directive' in the Finance Act 2003 s 197(4) so as to take account of amendments made to that Directive by EC Council Directives 2004/106 and 2006/98.

1672   Loan relationships—investment trusts—capital profits, gains or losses

The Investment Trusts and Venture Capital Trusts (Definition of Capital Profits, Gains or Losses) Order 2006, SI 2006/1182 (in force on 18 May 2006), defines the expression 'capital profits, gains or losses' in the cases of investment trusts and venture capital trusts that prepare accounts in accordance with international accounting standards.

1673   Loan relationships—venture capital trusts—capital profits, gains or losses

See para 1672.

1674   Loan relationships and derivative contracts—change of accounting practice

The Loan Relationships and Derivative Contracts (Change of Accounting Practice) (Amendment) Regulations 2006, SI 2006/3238 (in force on 27 December 2006), further amend the 2004 Regulations, SI 2004/3271, so as to (1) provide that prescribed debits and credits are brought into account in an accounting period commencing on or after 1 January 2006; (2) make provision for debts and credits in relation to dormant account transition amounts will not be brought into account until the first accounting period beginning on or after 1 January 2008; (3) provide that debits and credits in relation to specified derivative contracts and loan relationships are not brought into account; and (4) make provision in relation to certain debits and credits which are not prescribed for the purposes of the 2004 Regulations.

1675   Loan relationships and derivative contracts—profits and losses—disregard and bringing into account

The Loan Relationships and Derivative Contracts (Disregard and Bringing into Account of Profits and Losses) Regulations 2006, SI 2006/843 (in force on 22 March 2006), (1) provide that certain exchange losses are not to be brought into account where the obligations may be settled in more than one currency; and (2) provide that the amount of a loss arising on certain derivative contracts is not to be recognised in determining a company's profit or loss for any period.

The Loan Relationships and Derivative Contracts (Disregard and Bringing into Account of Profits and Losses) (Amendment) Regulations 2006, SI 2006/936 (in force on 29 March 2006), amend the 2006 Regulations, SI 2006/843, so as to provide that the amount of loss arising on certain derivative contracts is not to be recognised in determining a company's profit or loss for any period.

The Loan Relationships and Derivative Contracts (Disregard and Bringing into Account of Profits and Losses) (Amendment) Regulations 2006, SI 2006/3236 (in force on 27 December 2006), amend the 2004 Regulations, SI 2004/3256, so as to (1) make provision for companies to elect that specified regulations will not apply to a currency contract, a commodity contract, a debt contract, or an interest rate contract, as the case may be, but that instead a specified regulation must apply; (2) identify an accounting mismatch when fair value profits or losses are not brought into account on the hedged item in respect of the risk that is being hedged; (3) provide that credits and debits in respect of exchange gains and losses are disregarded in relation to loan relationships to which the Finance Act 1996 s 93 applied immediately before the start of the first accounting period of a company to begin on or after 1 January 2005; and (4) prescribe the amounts to be disregarded in cases where s 94A does not apply in the first accounting period of the company to begin on or after 1 January 2005.

1676   Loan relationships—unit trust schemes and offshore funds—non-qualifying investments test

The Unit Trust Schemes and Offshore Funds (Non-qualifying Investments Test) Order 2006, SI 2006/981 (in force on 20 April 2006), further amends the Finance Act 1996 Sch 10 para 8 so as to extend the descriptions of investments that are qualifying investments. In particular, the order (1) updates the list of qualifying investments so as to bring it into line with commercial practice and to include further investments which produce returns similar to interest-bearing investments; and (2) provides that the definition of the non-qualifying investments test will apply for the purposes of taxation of authorised investment funds.

1677   Non-resident—sportsman—payments connected with activities as sportsman

The Income and Corporation Taxes Act 1988 s 555(1) provides that where a person who is an entertainer or sportsman of a prescribed description performs an activity of a prescribed description in the United Kingdom ('a relevant activity'), Pt 8 Ch 3 (ss 555–558) applies if he is not resident in the United Kingdom in the year of assessment in which the relevant activity is performed. Where a payment is made (to whatever person) and it has a connection of a prescribed kind with the relevant activity, the person by whom it is made must on making it deduct out of it a sum representing income tax and must account to the Commissioners for Her Majesty's Revenue and Customs for the sum: s 555(2).

The taxpayer, a professional tennis player not resident in the United Kingdom, formed a company through which he entered into indorsement contracts with two manufacturers of sports clothing and equipment. Neither of the manufacturers had a tax presence in the United Kingdom. The taxpayer received from the manufacturers payments which derived, at least in part, from his participation in tournaments in the United Kingdom. It fell to be determined whether the 1988 Act s 555(2) had extra-territorial effect so that the taxpayer could be assessed to income tax under s 556 in respect of the payments. *Held*, Lord Walker of Gestingthorpe dissenting, that foreign entertainers and sportsmen who, or whose controlled companies, received payments in connection with their commercial activities in the United Kingdom should be subject to the charge to tax was the clear legislative intention of ss 555 and 556. The territorial principle could not be implied so as to limit the clear language of s 555(2). It could not have been Parliament's intention to allow the tax liability imposed by s 556 to be avoided simply by ensuring that the potentially taxable payments were made by foreign entities with no residence or trading presence in the United Kingdom, making payment of tax essentially voluntary. The purpose of ss 555–558 was to make foreign entertainers and sportsmen subject to a charge to tax on profits or gains obtained in connection with their activities in the United Kingdom. It would be impossible to imply a limitation by reference to the foreign status of the payer. One of the reasons that the collection regime was introduced was the difficulty of collecting the tax under s 556 on the profits and gains from the infrequent or sporadic commercial activities or presence in the United Kingdom of such taxpayers. Accordingly, the appeal would be allowed.

Agassi v Robinson (Inspector of Taxes) [2006] UKHL 23, (2006) 77 TC 686 (House of Lords: Lords Nicholls of Birkenhead, Hope of Craighead, Scott of Foscote, Walker of Gestingthorpe and Mance). Decision of Court of Appeal [2004] EWCA 1518, [2005] 1 WLR 1090 (2004 Abr para 1615) reversed.

1678   Overseas life insurance companies

The Overseas Life Insurance Companies Regulations 2006, SI 2006/3271 (in force on 31 December 2006), replace the Overseas Insurance Companies Regulations 2004, SI 2004/2200, and amend the Income and Corporation Taxes Act 1988, the Finance Act 1989, the Taxation of Chargeable Gains Act 1992, the Finance (No 2) Act 1992; the Finance Act 1995, the Finance Act 1996, the Capital Allowances Act 2001, the Finance Act 2002, and the Insurance Companies (Overseas Life Assurance Business) (Compliance) Regulations 1995, SI 1995/3237, so as to (1) set out all the modifications required so that provisions relating to UK companies carrying on life assurance business apply appropriately to overseas life insurance companies; and (2) provide for different provisions in some cases for EEA firms and EC Treaty firms.

1679 Pay As You Earn

The Income Tax (Pay As You Earn) (Amendment) Regulations 2006, SI 2006/243 (in force on 6 April 2006), further amend the 2003 Regulations, SI 2003/2682, in relation to a charge of income tax when a person becomes entitled to a social security pension lump sum ('a lump sum') provided for in the Finance (No 2) Act 2005, s 7. In particular, the regulations provide (1) that the 2003 Regulations Pts 2, 3 do not apply to a lump sum but that the remainder will apply as if a basic rate code had been issued in respect of the lump sum; (2) for the determination of the rate of income tax to be deducted from the payment of the lump sum which will either be the rate notified to the Department for Work and Pensions ('the Department') by the recipient of the lump sum, or in the absence of any such notification, the basic rate; (3) for the Department to issue a certificate containing certain details of the deduction; (4) that the Department may repay any overpayment of income tax in respect of the lump sum if the wrong amount has been deducted due to an administrative error by the Department; (5) for the maintenance of records by the Department and the notification of any payments to an officer of Revenue and Customs; and (6) that the application of the 2003 Regulations in respect of any other Pay As You Earn income of the recipient will not be affected.

The Income Tax (Pay As You Earn, etc), (Amendment) Regulations 2006, SI 2006/777 (in force on 6 April 2006), further amend (1) the 2003 Regulations supra by removing (a) working tax credit paid through payroll from an employer's calculation as to whether or not he is entitled to pay deductions of tax and national insurance contributions on a quarterly basis; (b) various definitions relating to working tax credits; (c) the condition that an employer is required to prepare or maintain a deduction working sheet in respect of an employee to whom he paid working tax credit; and (d) an amount deducted for working tax credit from the total amount of tax due for the year in question when calculating the amount of a surcharge; and (2) the Income Tax (Incentive Payments for Voluntary Electronic Communication of PAYE Returns) Regulations 2003, SI 2003/2495, by removing from the definition of a small employer a reference to working tax credit.

1680 Pension schemes—taxation

See para 2192.

1681 Property income—deduction—energy-saving items

The Energy-Saving Items Regulations 2006, SI 2006/912 (in force on 6 April 2006), specify, for the purposes of the Income Tax (Trading and Other Income) Act 2005 s 312(5)(c), hot water system insulation and draught proofing as items of an energy-saving nature.

1682 Relief—extra-statutory concession—bereavement allowance—widower

See Applications 63469/00, 63475/00, 63484/00, 63684/00 *Hobbs v United Kingdom*, para 1550.

1683 Relief—pension scheme—retirement benefit scheme—payment in connection with past service

See *Revenue and Customs Comrs v Barclays Bank plc*, para 2146.

1684 Return—failure to furnish information—penalty—right to fair hearing—civil or criminal proceedings

See *Harvard Sharkey v Revenue and Customs Comrs*, para 1572.

1685 Savings income—reporting of information

The Reporting of Savings Income Information Regulations 2006, SI 2006/3286 (in force on 1 January 2007), amend the 2003 Regulations, SI 2003/3297, by adding new entries to the list of public authorities by whom a further issue of negotiable debt securities will have the effect of treating the whole issue as a money debt for the purpose of reporting under EC Council Directive 2003/48 on the taxation of savings income in the form of interest payments.

1686 Special classes—Lloyd's underwriters—double taxation relief—corporate members

The Lloyd's Underwriters (Double Taxation Relief) (Corporate Members) Regulations 2006, SI 2006/3262 (in force on 31 December 2006), make provision for double taxation relief in respect of the profits or losses arising from the underwriting business carried on by a corporate member of Lloyd's. In particular, the regulations (1) state the principle that relief from United Kingdom corporation tax is to be given under the Income and Corporation Taxes Act 1988 in respect of the foreign tax payable by allowing the amount of the pool of adjusted sums of foreign tax for an accounting period as a credit against the United Kingdom corporation tax payable on the profits arising from the corporate member's underwriting business; (2) provide for certain sections of the Income and Corporation Taxes Act 1988 Ch 2 Pt 18 to apply for the purposes of the regulations; (3) determine how the amount of the pool of adjusted sums of foreign tax for an accounting period is ascertained by (a) providing that the amount of the pool of adjusted sums of foreign tax for an accounting period is calculated by reference to the foreign tax payable for the corresponding foreign period of accounting, and that an accounting period corresponds to a foreign period of accounting if the foreign period of accounting ends in the period of twelve months immediately preceding the beginning of the accounting period; (b) making further provisions that apply if an accounting period or a foreign period of accounting is not a period of twelve months; (c) providing for foreign amounts of tax to be adjusted in certain circumstances to determine the adjusted sums of foreign tax; (d) setting out how the calculation of the amount of the pool of adjusted sums of foreign tax is made; and (e) making provisions that apply if there is a refund of foreign tax; and (4) explain how the amount of the pool of adjusted sums of foreign tax for an accounting period is allowed as a credit against the United Kingdom corporation tax payable on the profits arising from the corporate member's underwriting business.

1687   Tax avoidance schemes—descriptions of arrangements

The Tax Avoidance Schemes (Prescribed Descriptions of Arrangements) Regulations 2006, SI 2006/1543 (in force on 1 August 2006), replace the 2004 Regulations 2004, SI 2004/1863, as amended, and provide for the disclosure of tax avoidance schemes in relation to income tax, corporation tax and capital gains tax in respect of prescribed arrangements falling within any description specified for the purposes of the Finance Act 2004 Pt 7 (ss 306–319). The prescribed arrangements are (1) arrangements which a promoter or, where he is obliged to report them, a user might wish to keep confidential from either Her Majesty's Revenue and Customs or other promoters; (2) arrangements for which a promoter might reasonably expect a premium fee; (3) arrangements (a) where the tax advantage arises, to more than an incidental degree, from the inclusion of a financial product; (b) where a promoter or a person connected with him becomes a party to the financial product; (c) where the price of the financial product differs significantly from what may reasonably be expected in the open market; (d) which involve the use of standardised tax products; (e) which are made available to more than one individual and are expected to generate losses to enable an individual to reduce his income tax or capital gains tax liability; (f) which include a plant or machinery lease.

1688   Tax avoidance schemes—information

The Tax Avoidance Schemes (Information) (Amendment) Regulations 2006, SI 2006/1544 (in force on 1 August 2006), further amend the 2004 Regulations, SI 2004/1864, by requiring prescribed arrangements in connection with tax avoidance schemes to be notified to the Commissioners for Her Majesty's Revenue and Customs, under the Finance Act 2004 s 310, 30 days from the date of the first transaction which forms part of the arrangements.

1689   Tax credit—relief—qualifying distribution—foreign company

The taxpayer was a Swiss bank with a branch in London that acted as a market maker on the London Stock Exchange. Agreed corporation tax computations disclosed that the taxpayer had accumulated substantial trading losses from the conduct of its banking business in London. During the same period, the surplus of United Kingdom dividends, and manufactured dividends, received by the taxpayer over manufactured dividends paid amounted to almost £250,000. Had the taxpayer been a person resident in the United Kingdom, that figure would have attracted tax credits, pursuant to the Income and Corporation Taxes Act 1988 s 231. The taxpayer's claim, under s 788(6), for relief to be given under s 788(3)(a) was refused and it appealed. *Held*, the tax credit to which the taxpayer was entitled under the express provisions of s 242(1)(c) and under an implied provision in s 243 was 'a tax credit under s 231' within the definition of 'tax credit' in s 832(1). It was clear that the reference in that definition was to the tax credit described in s 231(1), and not the particular tax credit payable in the particular circumstances specified in s 231(2) and (3). It followed that the reference to 'a tax credit under s 231' in s 788(3)(d) was also a reference to the tax credit specified in s 231(1), and was not confined to the particular tax credit payable in the particular circumstances specified in s 231(2) and (3), but extended to the tax credit payable pursuant to ss 242(1)(c) and 243. If s 788(3)(d) embraced s 231(3), it contemplated the payment of a tax credit to a foreign individual even where, were the individual a United Kingdom taxpayer, there would be no charge to income tax because, for example, the taxpayer's personal allowance and reliefs exceeded taxable income, including the dividends, and even though there had been no deduction or withholding of tax at source. If that anomalous financial benefit was extended to a foreign individual, there was no obvious reason to adopt a forced interpretation of s 788(3)(d) in order to prevent its extension to a foreign company. Accordingly, the appeal would be allowed.

UBS AG v Revenue and Customs Comrs [2006] EWHC 117 (Ch), [2006] STC 716 (Chancery Division: Etherton J). *Pirelli Cable Holdings NV v IRC* [2006] UKHL 4, (2006) 77 TC 409 (para 3002) considered.

1690 Tax Information Exchange Agreement—taxes on income—Gibraltar

The Tax Information Exchange Agreement (Taxes on Income) (Gibraltar) Order 2006, SI 2006/1453 (made on 7 June 2006), sets out the Tax Information Exchange Agreement between the United Kingdom and Gibraltar, which secures application in Gibraltar of the same measures as are contained in EC Council Directive 2003/48 on taxation of savings income in the form of interest payments and constitutes a reciprocal arrangement between the United Kingdom and Gibraltar for the exchange of information on savings income in the form of interest payments made cross-border from one party to individuals resident in the other contracting party.

1691 Tonnage tax—Community-flagging—exception of financial year 2006

The Tonnage Tax (Exception of Financial Year 2006) Order 2006, SI 2006/333 (in force on 1 April 2006), disapplies, for the financial year 2006, the Finance Act 2000 Sch 22 para 22A, which introduced, in order to comply with European Community guidelines on state aid to maritime transport, a general requirement that ships entering the tonnage tax regime in future should be Community-flagged.

1692 Tonnage tax—training requirement

The Tonnage Tax (Training Requirement) (Amendment) Regulations 2006, SI 2006/2229 (in force on 1 October 2006), further amend the 2000 Regulations, SI 2000/2129, by increasing the amount of the payments which fall to be made in lieu of training so that, in respect of a relevant four-month period commencing on or after 1 October 2006, the figure by which the number of months is to be multiplied is increased from £621 to £634 and, in the case of the higher rate payment where there has been a failure to meet the training commitment, the basic rate to be used in the calculation is increased from £565 to £577.

1693 Trading and other income—abolition of Schedule D—consequential amendments

The Income Tax (Trading and Other Income) Act 2005 (Consequential Amendments) Order 2006, SI 2006/959 (in force on 30 March 2006), amends the Income Tax (Trading and Other Income) Act 2005, with the purpose of clarifying the law following the abolition of Schedule D for income tax purposes, so as to ensure that the law continues to be unchanged after the 2005 Act came into force. In particular, the order provides that (1) the Finance (No 2) Act 1992 Sch 12 continues to apply to foreign companies for income tax purposes; (2) the Taxation of Chargeable Gains Act 1992 s 143(1) continues to apply in respect of futures and options, the profits and gains of which are exempt from income tax, as well as those exempt from corporation tax; (3) the Taxation of Chargeable Gains Act 1992 s 161 continues to apply to persons chargeable to income tax; and (4) where a person contracts out research and development in certain circumstances under the Finance Act 2002 Sch 12, the contractor's profits will continue to not be chargeable to income tax.

1694 Trading losses—partnerships—restrictions on contributions to a trade

The Partnerships (Restrictions on Contributions to a Trade) Regulations 2006, SI 2006/1639 (in force on 22 June 2006), supplement the Income and Corporation Taxes Act 1988 ss 117, 118ZB and 118ZE by virtue of which limited partners, members of a limited liability partnership and non-active partners are able to set off their share of a partnership's trading losses against their other income or gains. The regulations exclude amounts of a specified description when computing such an individual's capital contribution to the trade, in respect of a film-related loss where, on or after 20 December 2005, (1) a relevant partner has disposed of his rights which arise from the trade of the partnership; (2) the rights of the relevant partner to share in the subsequent profits of the partnership are reduced or extinguished, or his share of the losses arising from the trade is increased; (3) a new partner is admitted into the partnership; and (4) the new partner contributes capital to the partnership. Where these conditions are met, (a) the capital contributed by the new partner is apportioned between the relevant partners who were in the partnership immediately before the new partner was admitted to the partnership, according to the profit-sharing arrangements which were in place at that time; (b) the amount apportioned to the relevant partner is excluded when computing his contribution to the trade, but not to the extent that this gives rise to a contribution which is less than nil, at the time when the latest of the events referred to in heads (1)–(4) supra occurs; and (c) provision is made for the recalculation of the relevant partner's contribution to the trade for determining, at the time of that event, whether it is an exit event within the meaning of the Finance Act 2004 s 119(2)(b) or (c) and the amount chargeable for the purposes of s 119(5). Power to make the retrospective provision made by the regulations is conferred by s 122A(3)(a).

1695   Unit trust scheme—unauthorised scheme—pension fund pooling scheme

The Income Tax (Pension Funds Pooling Schemes) (Amendment) Regulations 2006, SI 2006/1162 (in force on 16 May 2006), further amend the 1996 Regulations, SI 1996/1585, by providing that a unit trust scheme does not cease to qualify as a pension funds pooling scheme if it no longer has the specified characteristics for such a scheme solely because it is wound up.

INDUSTRIAL AND PROVIDENT SOCIETIES

Halsbury's Laws of England (4th edn) vol 24 (Reissue) paras 1–200

1696   Audit exemption—increase of thresholds

The Friendly and Industrial and Provident Societies Act 1968 (Audit Exemption) (Amendment) Order 2006, SI 2006/265 (in force on 6 April 2006), amends the Friendly and Industrial and Provident Societies Act 1968 s 4A, which exempts smaller societies from the obligation to appoint qualified auditors to audit their accounts, by increasing the qualifying asset threshold to £2.8m and the qualifying turnover threshold to £5.6m.

1697   Community benefit societies—assets—restrictions on use

The Community Benefit Societies (Restriction on Use of Assets) Regulations 2006, SI 2006/264 (in force on 6 April 2006), enable community benefit societies to ensure, by means of a restriction on use rule, that their assets are only used for a purpose that is for the benefit of the community or for other limited purposes. In particular, the regulations (1) set out (a) the terms of a restriction on use and how it may be imposed; (b) the purposes for which a society's assets may be used once it has a restriction on use; (c) the kinds of community benefit society which may have a restriction on use; and (d) that a restriction on use is unalterable; (2) provide that the Financial Services Authority may enforce a restriction on use by (a) issuing an enforcement notification requiring the society to take the necessary steps to ensure that a breach of the restriction on use is brought to an end or is not repeated; and (b) requiring an officer of a society who has been knowingly concerned in a breach of the restriction on use, to make a payment to the society or directing that he be removed from his position; (3) make provision for warning notices and appeals; and (4) confer power on courts, on an application by the Financial Services Authority, to make an order restraining a breach of a restriction of use and directing an officer of the society to take steps to prevent a contravention or bring it to an end.

1698   Credit unions—maximum interest rate on loans

The Credit Unions (Maximum Interest Rate on Loans) Order 2006, SI 2006/1276 (in force on 1 June 2006), increases, from one to two per cent per month, the maximum rate of interest which a credit union may charge on loans made by it.

1699   Registered society—contract—transfer of engagements to another registered society

The Industrial and Provident Societies Act 1965 s 51(1) provides that any registered society may by special resolution transfer its engagements to any other registered society which may undertake to fulfil those engagements, and if that resolution approves the transfer of the whole or any part of the society's property to that other society, the whole or, as the case may be, that part of the society's property vests in that other society without any conveyance or assignment.

The claimant was a society registered under the 1965 Act. The defendant building company entered into a contract for the construction of a building with a company, which was registered under the 1965 Act. The contract provided that neither party would assign the contract without written consent. At a general meeting of the company, a special resolution was passed pursuant to s 51 to transfer the whole of its property, assets and engagements to the claimant. The defendant was not notified of the assignment of the contract. The claimant issued a notice of arbitration. The arbitrator took the view that the transfer effected by the resolution did not constitute an assignment of the company's interest in the building as envisaged by the building contract but that, even if there had been an assignment, s 51 overrode the restriction on assignment contained in the contract. The defendant's appeal against that decision succeeded and the claimant appealed further. *Held*, on its true construction, s 51(1) operated so as to vest the benefit of the building contract in the claimant, notwithstanding the prohibition against assignment and the absence of consent. The purpose of s 51(1) was to enable one registered society to transfer to another its engagements and property simply by passing a special resolution which would vest the transferor's property without the need for a conveyance or assignment. The force of the statutory language dispensed with the need for the consent of the defendant to the transfer to the claimant of the benefit of the building contract. Further, it would not be consistent with Parliament's intention if it was only lawful to transfer the benefits of contracts or engagements where that was contractually permissible. That would defeat the purpose of the beneficial statutory intervention. Accordingly, the appeal would be allowed.

Co-operative Group (CWS) Ltd v Stansell Ltd [2006] EWCA Civ 538, [2006] 1 WLR 1704 (Court of Appeal: Mummery, Longmore and Jacob LJJ).

1700   Registration—limited company—housing association—business

See *Riverside Housing Association Ltd v Revenue and Customs Comrs*, para 2942.

INHERITANCE TAXATION

Halsbury's Laws of England (4th edn) vol 24 (Reissue) paras 401–800

Articles

For articles relating to this title please refer to the Table of Articles at the beginning of the Abridgment.

1701   Delivery of accounts—excepted estates

The Inheritance Tax (Delivery of Accounts) (Excepted Estates) (Amendment) Regulations 2006, SI 2006/2141 (in force on 1 September 2006), amend the 2004 Regulations, SI 2004/2543, so as to (1) increase (a) the cash limit attributable to property which immediately before the person's death was (i) settled property, from £100,00 to £150,000; or (ii) situated outside the United Kingdom, from £75,000 to £100,000; (b) the maximum aggregate value of transfers from £100,000 to £150,000, and (c) the gross value of the person's estate situated in the United Kingdom wholly attributable to cash or quoted shares or securities from £100,000 to £150,000; and (2) provide that, if the Inheritance Tax Act 1984 ss 151A–151C, concerning alternatively secured pension funds, apply by reason of an individual's death, that individual's estate is not an excepted estate.

1702   Finance Act 2006

See para 2465.

INJUNCTIONS

Halsbury's Laws of England (4th edn) vol 24 (Reissue) paras 801–1100

Articles

For articles relating to this title please refer to the Table of Articles at the beginning of the Abridgment.

1703   Damages in lieu of injunction—date of assessment

It has been held that post-valuation events are normally irrelevant to the assessment of compensatory damages in lieu of an injunction under the Chancery Amendment Act 1858, but that, given the quasi-equitable nature of such damages, the judge can direct a departure from the norm where there are good reasons for doing so, either by selecting another valuation date or by directing a specific post-valuation event to be taken into account or a pre-valuation event to be disregarded. There is no absolute rule that damages cannot be assessed on the basis of events arising after an action in respect of which an injunction has been sought, or even following the refusal of such an injunction.

Liverpool and Lancashire Properties Ltd v Lunn Poly Ltd (2006) Times, 18 April (Court of Appeal: Auld, Scott Baker and Neuberger LJJ).

1704   Freezing order—application—information obtained from party subject to order— permission to use information—guidelines

The claimant brought an action against the defendants seeking damages for conspiracy and fraud. A worldwide freezing order was made against them. A subsequent order was made requiring the defendants to file affidavits and to attend for cross-examination on their affidavits. The claimant undertook not to use the evidence obtained pursuant to the order for the purpose of any committal proceedings or the trial of the action without the leave of the court. The cross examination took place. The claimant applied to be released from his undertaking before the trial of the action. The judge acceded to that application and the defendants appealed. *Held,* The court should provide significant protections for the subject of a freezing injunction who was cross-examined or who provided information under a freezing order. None the less the court should lend its weight to an application to use information obtained from such a person for the purpose of enforcing or policing the freezing order. The threat of contempt proceedings was more likely to motivate a person to give information frankly if the court was willing to give permission to use that information in contempt proceedings in exceptional circumstances. The court should not shrink from enabling a party who had obtained a freezing order to use the information obtained if that was necessary to protect that party's position. In a case such as the present one, it ought to be just and convenient for the information to be used for the purpose of enforcing or policing the freezing order. In general, the court would need to examine the basis on which it was said that the party had failed to comply with an order of the court, and to consider whether in all the circumstances it would be reasonable for committal proceedings to be brought. In contempt proceedings, permission to use information obtained pursuant to a freezing order should be granted where it was convenient for that information to be used for the purpose of establishing the contempt rather than for the purpose of enforcing or policing the freezing order as such. Accordingly, the appeal would be dismissed.

   Dadourian Group International Inc v Simms [2006] EWCA Civ 1745, [2006] All ER (D) 305 (Dec) (Court of Appeal: Sir Andrew Morritt C, Arden and Longmore LJJ).

1705 Freezing order—application—permission to enforce order in foreign jurisdiction—guidelines

The Court of Appeal has issued the following guidelines for courts to apply when dealing with an application for permission to enforce a worldwide freezing order in a foreign jurisdiction: (1) the principle applying to the grant of a permission to enforce a worldwide freezing order abroad is that the grant of the permission should be just and convenient for the purpose of ensuring the effectiveness of the order, and should not be oppressive to the parties to the English proceedings or to third parties who might be joined to the foreign proceedings; (2) all the relevant circumstances and options must be considered, with particular consideration to be given to granting relief subject to terms, to the proportionality of the steps proposed to be taken abroad and to the form of any order; (3) the interests of the applicant should be balanced against the interests of the other parties to the proceedings and any new party likely to be joined to the foreign proceedings; (4) permission should not normally be given in terms that would enable the applicant to obtain relief in the foreign proceedings which is superior to the relief given by the worldwide freezing order sought; (5) the evidence in support of the application for permission should contain all the information, so far as it can reasonably be obtained in the time available, necessary to enable the judge to reach an informed decision, including evidence as to (a) the applicable law and practice in the foreign court; (b) the nature of the proposed proceedings to be commenced; and (c) the assets believed to be located in the jurisdiction of the foreign court, with the names of the parties who hold those assets; (6) the applicant must show that there is a real prospect that assets which are intended to be subject to the worldwide freezing order are located within the jurisdiction of the foreign court; (7) there must be a risk of dissipation of the assets in question; and (8) although the application should normally be made on notice to the respondent, in cases of urgency and where it is just to do so, permission may be given without notice provided that the respondent is given the earliest practicable opportunity of having the matter reconsidered by the court at a hearing of which he is given notice.

   Dadourian Group International Inc v Simms [2006] EWCA Civ 399, [2006] 3 All ER 48 (Court of Appeal: Ward, Arden and Moore-Bick LJJ). Decision of Laddie J [2005] EWHC 268 (Ch), [2005] 2 All ER 651 (2005 Abr para 1856) affirmed.

1706 Freezing order—power to make—order against third party

The applicant presented a creditors' petition for the winding up of a company based on the large amount of value added tax the company had not paid. The applicant alleged that the company's VAT liability had arisen as a consequence of its participation in a large scale VAT missing trader and/or carousel fraud, and that each of the respondents was improperly implicated in the fraud, with the consequence that the company had substantial claims against each of the respondents that would have been pursued by the liquidator if the company were wound up. On that basis, the applicant obtained freezing orders against each of the respondents. The respondents applied to have the orders discharged, contending that the court did not have jurisdiction to grant and continue them. They sought to rely on the fact that the applicant had no cause of action for a monetary judgment against the respondents, and contended that the present case was not one where the respondents had been holding assets on behalf of the company so that the extended jurisdiction was not invoked, and that a further extension to that jurisdiction was not merited. *Held*, the jurisdiction to grant freezing orders against third parties was not rigidly restricted to those cases in which the third party was in control of the assets of the defendant to the action. Once that boundary line had been breached, there was no wider boundary, with sufficient clarity, that served as a workable condition to the exercise of that jurisdiction. In the present case, there had existed jurisdiction for the making and continuation of the freezing orders against the respondents. Also, where an application for a freezing order had been made by a petitioning creditor in advance of the hearing of a winding-up petition, exceptional circumstances needed to be shown before that course was to be preferred to the ordinary and well established alternative of appointing a provisional liquidator. In the present case, the proximity of the hearing of the winding-up petition, and the fact that the discharge of the freezing orders would have resulted in the immediate appointment of a provisional liquidator who would have sought to obtain identical freezing orders against the respondents resulted in the discretion being exercised in favour of the applicant. Accordingly, the application would be dismissed.

Revenue and Customs Comrs v Egleton [2006] EWHC 2313 (Ch), [2007] 1 All ER 606 (Chancery Division: Briggs J). *Aiglon Ltd v Gau Shan Co Ltd* [1993] 1 Lloyd's Rep 164 (2002 Abr para 1479); *Cardile v LED Builders PTY Ltd* (1999) 162 ALR 294, Aust HC; and *C Inc plc v L* [2001] 2 All ER (Comm) 446 (2001 Abr para 1917) considered.

1707 Injunction to prevent defendant from acting as arbitrator—breach of duty—potential bias

See *Weissfisch v Julius*, para 227.

1708 Injunction to prevent flying of aircraft with banners—freedom of expression—surveillance

The claimant, a local councillor, had spoken publicly about a planning application made by the defendant. In a campaign of harassment of the claimant, the defendant flew banners from his aircraft referring to the claimant in abusive and derogatory terms, dropping leaflets and, in an attempt to prove that the claimant was committing benefit fraud, placing her under secret surveillance. The claimant sought an injunction forbidding the defendant from flying aircraft with banners referring to the claimant and from putting her under any form of surveillance. *Held*, there had been a clear and consistent campaign of harassment by the defendant against the claimant. The defendant's assertion that an injunction would violate his freedom of expression, guaranteed by the European Convention on Human Rights art 10, did not have automatic precedence over the claimant's right under art 8 to her physical and psychological integrity. In some cases, together with the other necessary ingredients, one's right of free speech could fall within the concept of harassment. The claimant was entitled to the protection of an injunction against the flying of banners from aircraft since placing her in a situation where she could be the subject of surveillance at any time amounted to harassment under the Protection from Harassment Act 1997 s 1(1). Even where the surveillance was secret, the knowledge that surveillance could be taking place was sufficient. The defendant could not avail himself of the defence of pursuing a course of conduct to detect crime under s 1(3) because the defence existed for the benefit of law enforcement agencies. Moreover, even if the defence were available to private citizens, the defendant had not established a rational justification for his actions. Accordingly, the appeal would be dismissed.

Howlett v Holding [2006] EWHC 41 (QB), [2006] All ER (D) 162 (Jan) (Queen's Bench Division: Eady Reasons J). *Thomas v News Group Newspapers Ltd* [2001] EWCA Civ 1233, [2002] EMLR 78 (2001 Abr para 880) applied.

1709 Injunction to prevent obstruction of laboratory construction—interim injunction—continuation of injunction

See *Chancellor, Masters and Scholars of the University of Oxford v Broughton*, para 2318.

1710 Injunction to restrain publication—child involved in proceedings—continuation of injunction following conclusion of proceedings

See *Clayton v Clayton*, para 482.

1711 Injunction to restrain publication—details of adulterous relationship—privacy of parties

See *CC v AB*, para 582.

1712 Injunctive relief—without notice application—family proceedings—placement of elderly person—procedure—guidance

The applicant's husband had been admitted to a nursing home. However, when the home found that it was unable to care for him the respondent local authority made a without notice application for his placement in an elderly mentally infirm home. The application was granted and the husband was placed in the home. The applicant challenged the respondent's decision to bring a without notice application. *Held*, notwithstanding the applicant's criticisms of the authority's conduct, the authority's decision to seek without notice relief of the type that it had, the manner in which it had informed her of that relief and the way it had implemented it, constituted a reasonable and proportionate approach to promote the best interests of the husband. The court would endorse guidance in case authorities and did not seek to add to it save to emphasise that on a without notice application, good practice, fairness and common sense demanded that on any such application the applicant should provide the court with (1) a balanced, fair and particularised account of the events leading up to the application and, in many cases, a brief account of what the applicant thought the respondent's case was, or was likely to be; (2) where available and appropriate, independent evidence; (3) a clear and particularised explanation of the reasons why the application was made without notice and the reasons why the permission to apply to vary or discharge the injunction granted should be on notice, rather than immediately or forthwith as in the standard collection and location orders, and why the return date should not be within a short period of time; and (4) in many cases, an account of the steps the applicant proposed concerning service, the giving of an explanation of the order and the implementation of an order. This was likely to be of particular importance in cases where emotional issues were involved and family members of a person who lacked capacity were the subject of the injunctions and orders and would inform them of issues as to the need for, and the proportionality of, the relief sought and granted. Accordingly, the application would be refused.

B BC v S [2006] EWHC 2584 (Fam), [2007] 1 FCR 574 (Family Division: Charles J).

1713   Interim injunction—undertaking as to damages—discharge of injunction— amendment of undertaking

The claimant was the owner and exclusive licensee of a patent which claimed a process for making a pharmaceutical drug. The defendant wished to sell the drug in the United Kingdom. The drug would be imported by two Canadian companies. The claimant alleged infringement of its patent and applied for an interim injunction. The injunction was granted, subject to the claimant giving a cross-undertaking as to damages. The trial judge dismissed the action and revoked the patent but continued the injunction pending the final order, on the basis of a further cross-undertaking. The companies applied to be joined as defendants in order to obtain a ruling that such joinder would have retrospective effect, thus entitling them to claim on the cross-undertaking. The judge stayed an inquiry as to damages on the cross-undertaking, pending the determination of the companies' application. On appeal, the judge's revocation was reversed but it was held that the patent had not been infringed. The defendant sought to enforce the cross-undertaking in favour of the companies on the grounds that they were entitled to recover the losses sustained by virtue of a restitutionary cause of action and that the claimant was estopped by convention from denying that the companies were entitled to claim their own losses. The restitution claim was struck out but it was held that the estoppel issue was arguable and had to go to trial. The defendant appealed and the claimant cross-appealed. *Held*, there was no possible basis for a third party to have a claim in restitution in respect of benefits which accrued to a wrongful injunctor. When an injunction was granted, there were often non-parties who were affected. Others apart from the claimant would have benefited and that would include those of its customers who had gained from the higher price which resulted from the injunction. Likewise there were likely to be losers. The court could not put the clock back so as to undo all winnings and restore all losses caused to all who were affected by the wrong injunction. Under the guise of restitution, damages were really being claimed. Further, the basis of the plea for estoppel by convention and estoppel by representation was not sustainable. An inter-partes estoppel could not operate so as to expand or contract the effect of a court order. An estoppel could not be used as a key element of a claim and, in particular, it could not operate to create a legal relationship when there was none at the outset. Accordingly, the appeal would be dismissed and the cross appeal allowed.

Smithkline Beecham plc v Apotex Europe Ltd [2006] EWCA Civ 658, [2006] 3 WLR 1146 (Court of Appeal: Sir Andrew Morritt C, Jacob and Moore-Bick LJJ). Decision of Lewison J [2005] EWHC 1655 (Ch), [2005] FSR 930 (2005 Abr para 1880) reversed in part.

1714   Undertaking—court's power to modify—undertaking inappropriate from outset

The claimant appealed against a decision to modify an undertaking given by the defendant, which released the defendant from certain aspects of the undertaking and imposed a time limit for it to remain in force. *Held*, it could never be an appropriate exercise of a first instance judge's discretion to change the wording of a previous order given on a final basis unless that was justified by circumstances such as a change of relevant facts. Where a judge felt that an undertaking given by a party in earlier proceedings was inappropriate from the outset, the appropriate course was not to reconsider it at first instance, but to leave it for an appeal. Accordingly, the appeal would be allowed.

Mid Suffolk DC v Clarke [2006] EWCA Civ 71, (2006) Times, 10 March (Court of Appeal: Buxton, Gage and Lloyd LJJ).

INNS AND INNKEEPERS

Halsbury's Laws of England (4th edn) vol 24 (Reissue) paras 1101–1154

Articles

For articles relating to this title please refer to the Table of Articles at the beginning of the Abridgment.

INSURANCE

Halsbury's Laws of England (4th edn) vol 25 (2003 Reissue) paras 1–855

Articles

For articles relating to this title please refer to the Table of Articles at the beginning of the Abridgment.

1715   Insurance business—business transfer scheme—control

See *Re Alliance Assurance Co Ltd; Re British Engine Insurance Ltd*, para 1332.

1716   Insurance business—disclosure—disclosure by broker to underwriter—implied contract permitting inspection—business efficacy

The claimants were Lloyd's syndicates which sought access to placing, claims and premium accounting documents in the possession of the defendant Lloyd's brokers. There was a practice at Lloyd's whereby underwriters who had not retained such documents would obtain them, if needed, from the insured's broker. The terms of business agreement at Lloyd's made provision for the disclosure of documents, but also provided that nothing in the agreement overrode the broker's duty to place the interests of its client before all other considerations. The claimants argued, on grounds of business efficacy, that a term had to be implied in the insurance contracts between underwriters and their insureds obliging the insureds to permit inspection, through their brokers, of the documents in question. They further claimed that either by way of implied contract or under the terms of business agreement they had a right against the brokers to inspect documents in their hands. However, it was held that the defendants were not required to disclose the documents in question and the claimants appealed. *Held*, in the Lloyd's market there had at all relevant times been a term to be implied in insurance contracts between underwriters and insureds that placing and premium documents which had previously been shown to underwriters and premium accounting documents which were necessary to the operation of the contract, where retained by the brokers, should be available to underwriters in cases of reasonable necessity. The matter was to be seen against the practice at Lloyd's where placing and claims documentation was retained by brokers and not underwriters. In respect of placing documents, it was hard to see how an insurance contract could be operated unless such documents were in the hands of both parties. The placing and claims documents which the claimants sought disclosure of were merely those documents the insureds had originally disclosed to the underwriters, as a matter of good faith, in the making of a purportedly fair presentation. Further, it was both reasonable and necessary, on the grounds of business efficacy, for the documentation in question, to be available to underwriters and, in the insurance context, that implication was supported by the obligation of good faith. Necessity required that the term be implied into the insurance contract itself. In respect of the position between syndicates and brokers, there was no conflict with the broker's duty to the insured and the express agreement for the production of the relevant documents in the terms of business agreement because the insured and underwriter had agreed that the broker should disclose the documents in his possession to the underwriter. Accordingly, the appeal would be allowed.

Goshawk Dedicated Ltd v Tyser & Co Ltd [2006] EWCA Civ 54, [2006] 1 All ER (Comm) 501 (Court of Appeal: Sir Anthony Clarke MR, Rix and Richards LJJ). Decision of Christopher Clarke J [2005] EWHC 461 (Comm), [2005] 2 All ER (Comm) 115 (2005 Abr para 1883) reversed.

1717   Insurance policy—claim notification clause—insurer's right to reject claim

The defendant, an eleven-year-old boy, lit a fire which spread to a mill and caused extensive damage. The claimant brought proceedings against the defendant for stock destroyed in the fire. The defendant sought an indemnification from an insurer under a policy taken out by his mother that provided cover for liability arising from accidental damage to property. Liability arising from wilful acts was excluded under the policy, and the policy also contained a claims notification clause which stipulated that the insured had to inform the insurer immediately after any incident involving third party injury for which the insured might be held responsible. The insurer, which was joined as a party to the proceedings, rejected the claim on the grounds that the act in question was wilful and that it had not been informed of the incident until more than one year after it occurred. It contended that, although the claims notification clause did not amount to a condition precedent and was an innominate term, there had been a serious breach of that term which had serious consequences for the insurer so that it was entitled to reject the claim. The judge decided that the defendant was entitled to the indemnity and the insurer appealed. *Held*, in the context of a standard exclusion clause in a home insurance policy, the term 'wilful' meant 'reckless', that is, where a person performed an action knowing it was risky, or not caring whether it was risky. It did not require an intention to cause the damage of the kind caused, but nor was it wide enough to include all deliberate actions. A 'wilful act' was a deliberate act, which would take any other meaning from the context in which it was used. In the present case, it occurred in a clause excluding insurance cover for ' any wilful, malicious or criminal acts'. It was clear what the words 'malicious' and 'criminal' meant, and the term 'wilful' denoted a blameworthy state of mind that was more than simply a deliberate or intentional act. If it simply denoted a deliberate or intentional act, then much of the wide cover provided by the policy would be excluded since most actions, including negligent actions, were deliberate or intentional. While the defendant's conduct might be described as stupid, he had not been reckless. Therefore, the insurer was liable under the policy. Accordingly, the appeal would be dismissed.

Ronson International Ltd v Patrick (Royal London Mutual Insurance Society Ltd, Pt 20 defendant) [2006] EWCA Civ 421, [2006] 2 All ER (Comm) 344 (Court of Appeal: Tuckey, Thomas and Hallett LJJ). Decision of Judge Richard Seymour QC [2005] All ER (D) 62 (Jul) (2005 Abr para 1886) affirmed.

1718   Insurance policy—claim notification clause—waiver—insurer's repudiation of liability

Belize

The claimant's commercial premises, which had been insured by the defendant insurer against fire damage, were destroyed by fire. The insurance policy required the claimant to give written notice of the particulars of the claim to the defendant within 15 days of the loss of or damage. The claimant contacted the defendant and claimed that, at the subsequent meeting, the defendant's representative repudiated the defendant's liability under the policy. The claim under the policy was dismissed, the court accepting the argument that the notification requirement had not been fulfilled. The claimant's appeal against the decision was dismissed. He appealed further, arguing that the defendant had repudiated its liability under the policy so that the claimant had been released from any further procedural obligation. *Held*, there was no rule that repudiation by an insurer of liability, on a ground unconnected with compliance by the insured with the provisions of the policy regarding the delivery of a formal claim in writing and particulars of the loss or damage in question, relieved the insured of the obligation to comply with those provisions. However, it could be that the repudiatory words justified the inference of a waiver by the insurer of its right to insist on compliance by the insured with the contractual provisions in question. A waiver by an insurer of a procedural obligation on the insured, such as the delivery of particulars of loss or damage within a specified period, could be produced by conduct either before or after the insured was in breach of the obligation. There was no basis on the facts on which it could be said that the defendant's representative had elected to relieve the claimant of the contractual obligation to comply with the procedural requirements if he wanted to pursue a claim under the policy. Further, the defendant was not prevented from resisting the claim on an alternative basis where the claimant had been entitled on the facts to consider the representative's remark as a repudiation of the defendant's liability. Accordingly, the appeal would be dismissed.

Nasser Diab v Regent Insurance Co Ltd [2006] UKPC 29, [2006] 2 All ER (Comm) 704 (Privy Council: Lords Scott of Foscote and Walker of Gestingthorpe, Baroness Hale of Richmond, Lord Carswell and Sir Martin Nourse). *Super Chem Products Ltd v American Life and General Insurance Co Ltd* [2004] UKPC 2, [2004] 1 All ER (Comm) 713 (2004 Abr para 1661); and *Re Coleman's Depositories Ltd and Life and Health Assurance Association* [1907] 2 KB 798, CA, considered.

1719   Insurance policy—construction—duty to provide information in reasonable time

The first defendant's insurance policy with the second defendant insurer contained a claims co-operation condition. The insurer claimed that the first defendant had breached this condition by failing to provide information within a reasonable time, and consequently it was entitled to decline to indemnify the first defendant. It was held that there was no such breach and the insurer appealed. *Held*, the insurer was entitled to receive information in good time so as to take appropriate action which might include deciding to take control of the case. Much of the information was in existence and providing it more than two and a half years later was unreasonably late. There was no rule that a co-operation condition was not broken if it turned out that the insurer was not prejudiced by the failure to co-operate; the insurer was entitled to receive the information in good time whether it was prejudiced or not. Accordingly, the appeal would be allowed.

Shinedean Ltd v Alldown Demolition (London) Ltd (in liquidation) [2006] EWCA Civ 939, [2006] 2 All ER (Comm) 982 (Court of Appeal: Sir Anthony Clarke MR, May and Gage LJJ).

1720   Insurance policy—construction—exclusion clause—children's care home—deliberate act or omission of staff—sexual and physical abuse

The claimants, who were former residents of children's care homes, brought proceedings in negligence against the company which operated the homes, alleging that they had been sexually and/or physically abused by members of staff. The judge allowed the claim, deciding that the system of care operated by the company was neither adequate nor properly organised or supervised. The claimants then brought proceedings against the defendant, the insurer of the company, contending that the company had incurred liability to the claimants by the earlier judgment and that, as the company was now insolvent, they were entitled to claim directly against the defendant. The latter sought to rely on clauses in the relevant policies that excluded liability for loss resulting from any deliberate act or omission of the company or those who carried out a senior management role in it. The judge ruled in favour of the claimants, and the defendant appealed. *Held*, on the true construction of the policies, deliberate acts of sexual and physical abuse by staff members, and similar acts by principals of the various homes, all fell outside the company's cover so that the defendant was not obliged to meet the claims in respect of those acts. The defendant was, however, liable for the other acts of abuse complained about in the earlier proceedings against the company. Accordingly, the application would be allowed in part.

KR v Royal and Sun Alliance plc [2006] EWCA Civ 1454, [2006] All ER (D) 42 (Nov) (Court of Appeal: Sir Anthony Clarke MR, Longmore and Scott Baker LJJ). For earlier related proceedings see *KR v Bryn Alyn Community (Holdings) Ltd (in liquidation)* [2003] EWCA Civ 783, [2003] QB 1441 (2003 Abr para 611).

1721 Insurance policy—construction—reinstatement—proper approach to making claim

The claimants' home, two converted barns, was insured under a policy with the defendant insurance company. Most of the property was destroyed by fire. The defendant made a payment in respect of ground works but challenged a scheme, proposed by the claimants, for the reinstatement of the property on the ground that the scheme was not in fact one for reinstatement and was not properly documented. The claimants argued that the defendant was estopped from querying the scheme because the ground works for it were already in place and, if the floor area of the scheme could be shown to be almost the same as that of the destroyed property, then the scheme was one of reinstatement. The claimants sought damages for late payment of their claim in the light of the defendant's duty under the policy to act quickly. *Held*, an insured could not choose to make minor or significant changes to improve that which was there before and then try to persuade an insurer that the proposed scheme was in fact one of reinstatement, or sit back and wait for the insurer to spot the improvements. Any elements of improvement should be made plain to the insurer and a full set of drawings should be prepared for the scheme in question. A scheme producing the same floor area as the destroyed building was not necessarily a reinstatement scheme. An insured's attempt at making improvements without making them plain could amount to fraud, which would taint the whole claim. Even if what happened could not be said to be fraudulent, it would inevitably cause delay, suspicion and antagonism and would be a clear failure on the part of the insured to comply with his obligations under the policy. Furthermore, the same floor area could be achieved by buildings of different shapes and such an approach took no account of what various parts of the property were used for and their condition before the fire. The claimants and their advisers had deliberately misled the defendant and could, therefore, not rely on estoppel to prevent the defendant from challenging the proposed scheme. The claimants' scheme was not one for the reinstatement of the property and produced unreliable figures whereas the defendant's proposed scheme was one for reinstatement and did produce reliable figures. Furthermore, having regard to previous authority, it was difficult to conclude that there was another or separate breach of contract arising out of the general obligation at the end of the policy to act quickly so as to give rise to a claim for damages for failure to pay the claim. In those circumstances, the claimant was not entitled to claim for delay and consequential damages. Judgment would be given accordingly.

The court added that since estoppel was an equitable remedy, designed to prevent injustice, it was very difficult for a party to rely on such a remedy in any circumstances where, even passively, he had misled the party into making the relevant statement or representation.

Tonkin v UK Insurance Ltd [2006] EWHC 1120 (TCC), [2006] 2 All ER (Comm) 550 (May) (Queen's Bench Division: Judge Peter Coulson QC). *Sprung v Royal Insurance* [1999] Lloyd's Rep IR 111, CA, applied.

1722 Insurance policy—excess policy—jurisdiction clause—losses—appropriate jurisdiction for proceedings

See *Dornoch Ltd v Mauritius Union Assurance Co Ltd*, para 601.

1723 Insurance premium tax—application for registration

The Insurance Premium Tax (Amendment) Regulations 2006, SI 2006/2700 (in force on 1 December 2006), further amend the 1994 Regulations, SI 1994/1774, so as to substitute a new application form for registration.

1724 Liability insurance—indemnity basis of contract—asbestos claim—time of injury

The employee of an electrical contractor had inhaled asbestos dust while working on a site owned by the claimant local authority, and again while employed by another company. Nearly 30 years after working on the claimant's site, the employee developed breathing difficulties and was diagnosed as suffering from mesothelioma. He died ten months later and his widow brought proceedings against the claimant and the company. The proceedings were settled, and the claimant and the company each paid half of the compensation. The claimant sought to recover the amount it had paid from the defendant, its public liability insurer when the employee's mesothelioma had occurred. The defendant denied liability and suggested that the insurer at the time when the employee had inhaled the asbestos dust, or at the time of his first bodily reaction to such inhalation, was liable. The judge rejected the defendant's argument and held that, since the mesothelioma was an accidental bodily injury which had occurred during the currency of the defendant's cover, the defendant was liable to indemnify the claimant. The defendant appealed. *Held*, the contract between the parties was an agreement to indemnify against liability. The indemnity which the claimant was seeking was an indemnity against its liability for its share of the sum which was ultimately paid to the employee's widow. No such liability existed on the employee's initial exposure to the asbestos or his initial bodily reaction to such exposure because he was not suffering any injury at that time. As a matter of authority, it was well accepted in the general law that words such as 'injury' or 'damage' in indemnity agreements did not include injury or damage which would happen in the future. Accordingly, the appeal would be dismissed.

Bolton MBC v Municipal Mutual Insurance Ltd [2006] EWCA Civ 50, [2006] 1 WLR 1492 (Court of Appeal: Auld, Longmore and Hallett LJJ).

1725   Marine insurance—broker's lien on insurance policy—reinsurance broker's right to lien over loss proceeds

The Marine Insurance Act 1906 s 53(2) provides that unless otherwise agreed, the broker has, as against the assured, a lien on the policy for the amount of the premium in respect of effecting the policy.

The first defendant was an insurance broker which had placed insurance for a fleet of vessels with the second defendant, an insurance company, which in turn was reinsured. The claimant was the broker for the reinsurance. The claimant brought an action against the first defendant and, in the alternative, the second defendant to recover premiums. Subsequently, the second defendant counterclaimed for money collected by the claimant from reinsurers for a particular claim sustained by an insured vessel. The claimant served a defence to the counterclaim asserting a lien over the loss proceeds, under the 1906 Act s 53(2), for the premiums it was seeking to recover. Judgment was given against the first defendant. In relation to the outstanding claims between the claimant and the second defendant, it fell to be determined whether the claimant was entitled to a lien over the loss proceeds. *Held*, it was clear that a broker who had a lien over the policy had a commensurate right to retain claims proceeds collected under it in so far as necessary to satisfy the debt secured by the lien. It followed that the claimant had a lien over the proceeds of the policy both as against the second defendant and any other intermediary, irrespective of whether the second defendant was under a direct obligation to pay the premium. Accordingly, the claimant was entitled to the lien and the counterclaim would be stayed.

Heath Lambert Ltd v Sociedad de Corretaje de Seguros [2006] EWHC 1345 (Comm), [2006] 2 All ER (Comm) 543 (Queen's Bench Division: Judge Mackie QC). *Eide UK Ltd v Lowndes Lambert Group Ltd* [1998] 1 All ER 946, CA (1987 Abr para 1954), applied.

1726   Marine insurance—liability of insurer—required particulars of claim—non-disclosure

The claimant was the owner of a vessel insured on a total loss only basis by the defendant insurer under a war risks policy. The vessel was damaged by an explosion to such an extent as to be a constructive total loss. The defendant refused to pay on the ground that it was entitled to avoid the policy for non-disclosure. The judge found for the defendant and the claimant appealed. The issue to be decided was whether certain facts extant at the time of placing, which had not been disclosed to the defendant, were material circumstances. Those facts included the existence of criminal proceedings in Greece concerning allegations of fraud against the claimant. Those charges were subsequently dismissed but it was the existence of the allegations themselves which the defendant asserted was material. The claimant sought to draw a distinction between allegations which related to the insured risk and allegations which bore no relation to that risk. It submitted that the court ought somehow to limit the extent to which allegations which ultimately turned out to be false should be held to be material to that risk and disclosable. *Held*, what had to be disclosed could not be defined as a matter of law in the manner suggested by the claimant. It was a matter of evidence as to what was a material circumstance. A material circumstance was defined by authority as one which would have an effect on the mind of a prudent underwriter in estimating the risk, and it was not necessary that it should have a decisive effect on his acceptance of the risk or the amount of premium to be paid. Expert evidence had to be called as to what would influence the judgment of an underwriter. In the present case, the allegations of dishonesty which had been the subject of the proceedings in Greece had clearly been material, and should have been disclosed. Accordingly, the appeal would be dismissed.

North Star Shipping Ltd v Sphere Drake Insurance plc (No 2) [2006] EWCA Civ 378, [2006] 2 All ER (Comm) 65 (Court of Appeal: Waller, Longmore and Lloyd LJJ).

1727   Marine insurance—policy—construction—warranty that vessel fully crewed

By a contract of marine insurance, the claimant insured a vessel owned by the defendant. The contract provided for the vessel to be warranted 'fully crewed'. While the vessel was laid up alongside a berth in a marina in the United States of America, a fire started in the vessel, resulting in severe damage to it. No crew were on board at the time. In the ensuing dispute between the parties, an issue arose as to the construction of the phrase 'fully crewed'. The claimant contended that the warranty meant that the defendant was obliged to keep at least one crew member on board the vessel at all times. The defendant submitted that the warranty looked to the crew actually employed, not to their location at any particular time, or that the warranty went no further than requiring a sufficient crew to look after the vessel. *Held*, on its true construction, the warranty obliged the defendant to keep at least one crew member on board 24 hours a day, subject to emergencies rendering his departure necessary or necessary temporary departures for the purpose of performing his crewing duties or other related activities. Judgment would be given accordingly.

GE Frankona Reinsurance Ltd v CMM Trust No 1400, The Newfoundland Explorer [2006] EWHC 429 (Admlty), [2006] 1 All ER (Comm) 665 (Queen's Bench Division: Gross J). *Simmonds v Cockell* [1920] 1 KB 843; and *Brownsville Holdings Ltd v Adamjee Insurance Co Ltd* [2000] 2 All ER (Comm) 803 (2000 Abr para 1919) applied.

1728 Motor insurance—Motor Insurers' Bureau—uninsured driver—notice requirements

See *Richardson v Watson*, para 1814.

1729 Motor insurance—rights of third parties—direct action against insurer—excluded liability—relevant knowledge

The Road Traffic Act 1988 s 151(4) provides that, in s 151(2)(b), 'excluded liability' means a liability in respect of bodily or property damage to any person who was allowing himself to be carried in or on the vehicle and knew or had reason to believe that the vehicle had been stolen or unlawfully taken, not being a person who (1) did not know and had no reason to believe that the vehicle had been stolen or unlawfully taken until after the commencement of his journey; and (2) could not reasonably have been expected to have alighted from the vehicle.

The claimant was seriously injured in a road traffic accident. The vehicle involved in the accident was being driven by the first defendant, the claimant's 17-year-old brother, who did not have a driving licence. The vehicle belonged to the employer of a friend of the claimant, and was insured by the employer under a policy which extended cover to social, domestic and pleasure purposes where the vehicle was being driven by someone who had attained the age of 25, held a driving licence, and had been permitted by the owners to drive it. The claimant alleged that the accident was caused by the first defendant's negligence. The owners' insurers repudiated any liability to indemnify the first defendant for such damages as he might be ordered to pay for the claimant's injuries, since the first defendant had not had the owners' permission to drive the vehicle. The question of whether the insurers were entitled to repudiate liability was ordered to be tried as a preliminary issue in the claim for damages for personal injuries. The issue was whether the first defendant's liability to the claimant was an excluded liability under the 1988 Act s 151(2)(b), on the ground that the claimant knew or had reason to believe that the vehicle had been stolen or unlawfully taken within the meaning of s 151(4). *Held*, the insurers did not have to prove that the injured passenger actually believed that the vehicle had been stolen or unlawfully taken. What had to be proved was that the injured passenger had the information which would have afforded him good reasons for believing that the vehicle had been stolen or unlawfully taken had he applied his mind to the topic. The friend knew that only he had permission to drive the van and that the owners would not have permitted the first defendant to drive it. By allowing the first defendant to drive in those circumstances, the friend had appropriated the van to his own use in a manner which repudiated the owners' rights and assumed control of the vehicle for his own purposes. He had, therefore, to be regarded as having unlawfully taken the van within the meaning of s 151(4). The same was true for the first defendant. He had taken the vehicle by taking the keys and driving it. As for the claimant, while he could not be said to have known that the first defendant had not been permitted to drive the vehicle, he would have had every reason to believe that he had not been permitted to drive it and, therefore, every reason to believe that the vehicle had been unlawfully taken. Liability was therefore excluded by virtue of s 151(4). Judgment would be given accordingly.

McMinn v McMinn [2006] EWHC 827 (QB), [2006] 3 All ER 87 (Queen's Bench Division: Keith J). *White v White* [2001] UKHL 9, [2001] 2 All ER 43 (2001 Abr para 1952); *R v Phipps* [1970] RTR 209, CA; and *McKnight v Davies* [1974] RTR 4 considered.

1730 Reinsurance—contract of reinsurance—loss—actual loss

See *AIG Europe (Ireland) Ltd v Faraday Capital Ltd*, para 658.

1731 Reinsurance—contract of reinsurance—nature of contract—applicable law

See *CGU International Insurance plc v AstraZeneca Insurance Co Ltd*, para 592.

INTOXICATING LIQUOR

Halsbury's Laws of England (4th edn) vol 26 (2004 Reissue) paras 1–500

Articles

For articles relating to this title please refer to the Table of Articles at the beginning of the Abridgment.

1732   Licence—old on-licence—special removal—premises pulled down for public purpose—renewal of licence—grounds for objections

A city council acquired a public house for the purposes of redevelopment. The vendor of the public house applied to the licensing justices for a special removal of the on-licence to premises which it had acquired in the same licensing district. Under the Licensing Act 1964 s 15(1), the justices could only refuse the removal on the grounds that the vendor was not a fit and proper person or that the premises had been ill-conducted or were structurally deficient or unsuitable. The justices granted the application. Judicial review proceedings were brought by local residents. The judge held that the justices had no jurisdiction under s 15 because, at that time, the premises were not 'occupied' or about to be 'occupied' for a 'public purpose' within the meaning of s 15(1)(a). He therefore quashed the removal. His order was affirmed by the Court of Appeal. On appeal to the House of Lords, it fell to be determined whether the appeal should be entertained because, since the decision of the Court of Appeal, the 1964 Act had been repealed. *Held*, although the possibility that the House of Lords might in its discretion decide to revoke its permission to appeal if it appeared that subsequent events had made the prospective cost of the appeal disproportionate to the value or importance of the substantive question in dispute, the grant of permission to appeal would ordinarily entitle an appellant to bring before the House any genuine issue between the parties. There was no rule of law or practice that the House would not proceed with an appeal because there had been a change of circumstances as a result of which the questions which remained in issue between the parties were no longer of general public importance. Unless the House had expressly restricted its leave to the particular issue, the appellant was even at liberty to abandon the point of general public importance and argue any point which was otherwise open to him but which, taken by itself, would never have justified the grant of leave. As regards the present case, a public authority which obtained legal possession of licensed premises with a view to putting them to some future public use was in immediate occupation of those premises for the purposes of s 15. The possession of the authority was sufficient to exclude the licensee, who would be committing a trespass if he attempted to re-enter and carry on his business. Once one treated the council as having gone into occupation when it took possession, it was clear that its occupation had to have been for a public purpose, namely, for the implementation of the development scheme. It followed that the conditions for a special removal were satisfied and the justices had jurisdiction to grant it. Accordingly, the appeal would be allowed.

R (on the application of Bushell) v Newcastle upon Tyne Licensing Justices [2006] UKHL 7, [2006] 2 All ER 161 (House of Lords: Lords Hoffmann, Scott of Foscote, Rodger of Earlsferry, Walker of Gestingthorpe and Brown of Eaton-under-Heywood). *Sirius International Insurance Co (Publ) v FAI General Insurance Ltd* [2004] UKHL 54, [2005] 1 All ER 191 (2004 Abr para 215) considered. Decision of Court of Appeal [2004] EWCA Civ 767, [2004] 3 All ER 493 (2004 Abr para 1680) reversed.

1733   Licence—permitted hours—conditions imposed on operation of public house—costs

The respondents were the operators of a public house. They applied to the appellant local authority to extend the licensing conditions so as to conduct additional entertainment activities, and so as to serve alcohol until the early hours of the morning. The authority granted the changed conditions but decided that opening hours were to cease at midnight, on the ground that the hours sought by the respondents would create too high a risk of a substantial public nuisance in the form of noise. The respondents successfully appealed, with the judge imposing conditions broadly in line with those sought. Costs were awarded in favour of the respondents. The authority appealed. Prior to the conclusion of the hearing, a form of order stating the conditions was agreed by the parties. However, the issue of costs remained outstanding. The authority maintained that the reasons given for the award of costs had been inadequate. *Held*, there was no difference in the position of the judge under the Magistrates' Courts Act 1980 s 64(1) and the relevant provision in the present case, namely the Licensing Act 2003 s 81. Under both provisions the judge had a very wide discretion. It was unlikely that the old position which did not require reasons for decisions on costs to be given still applied. However, it was not necessary for a judge to give detailed reasons. It was sufficient if he made it clear that he appreciated the principle under which he was acting. It was undesirable for courts to encourage satellite litigation on issues such as costs. The critical reasons were not those as originally provided, but in the case stated. The judge had given sufficient reasons in the present case. There was no basis to interfere with his exercise of discretion. Accordingly, the appeal would be dismissed.

Crawley BC v Attenborough [2006] EWHC 1278 (Admin), (2006) 170 JP 593 (Queen's Bench Division: Scott Baker LJ and Openshaw J).

1734   Licence—premises licence—application for extension—rejection in part—order for costs

See *Cambridge CC v Alex Nesting Ltd*, para 698.

1735   Licensing authority—duties—promotion of licensing objectives

Under the Licensing Act 2003, licensing authorities are required to carry out their functions with a view to promoting the licensing objectives set out in s 4(2): s 4(1).

The Secretary of State issued guidance which dealt with the cumulative impact of a concentration of licensed premises in an area. The defendant licensing authority's licensing policy included a statement that the cumulative impact policy applied in an area where the applicant operated a large number of public houses. The applicant applied to the defendant under s 34 for a variation of the permitted hours of its public houses. The police objected to the application and the matter came before the defendant's licensing sub-committee. The applicant sought judicial review of the sub-committee's decision not to grant the extension. *Held,* there was nothing in the 2003 Act, the Secretary of State's guidance or the defendant's statement of licensing policy that precluded reliance on a cumulative impact policy. The statute did not directly preclude reliance on a cumulative impact policy in the case of an application to extend the permitted hours and it did not specifically mention the term 'cumulative impact'. Save where the guidance itself provided how conflicts and tensions were to be resolved, how that should be done was a matter for the local licensing authority. Both in formulating its statement of policy and in determining a particular application, the authority had to have regard to the guidance. Any tension between the policy elements favouring the lengthening of licensing hours and recognising the needs of an area in which there was a particular concentration of licensed premises was not resolved by the guidance. There was nothing in the guidance that expressly precluded or restricted the applicability of cumulative impact policies to variation which only sought to lengthen licensing hours and no limit should be applied. While it was true that the focus of the guidance was on new applications for licences, there were several references to material variations. The authority was entitled to have a policy provided it was prepared to consider that an exception to it should be made in a given case. The sub-committee had been entitled to conclude that the application to extend the terminal hours was directly relevant to the special cumulative impact policy and was thus a material variation of the licence. The defendant was entitled to conclude that its cumulative impact policy applied to the application and, accordingly, the application would be dismissed.

R (on the application of JD Wetherspoon plc) v Guildford BC [2006] EWHC 815 (Admin), [2007] 1 All ER 400 (Queen's Bench Division: Beatson J).

JURIES

Halsbury's Laws of England (4th edn) vol 26 (2004 Reissue) paras 501–600

Articles

For articles relating to this title please refer to the Table of Articles at the beginning of the Abridgment.

1736 Deliberations—confidentiality—interview of juror following trial—need for leave

It has been held that it is highly undesirable for any person to seek to interview a juror following a trial without first obtaining the leave of the Court of Appeal. There is a high risk that any such inquiry will cross the threshold into the forbidden territory of the jury's deliberations. The circumstances in which the court will need to hear evidence from a juror or jurors are likely to be rare and exceptional. Since the introduction of the requirement for judges to tell jurors that they should report any irregularities occurring in the course of the trial to the court, silence as to any such irregularity will almost certainly mean that the Court of Appeal will assume that none had occurred.

R v Adams [2007] EWCA Crim 1, [2007] All ER (D) 25 (Jan) (Court of Appeal: Gage LJ, Silber and Treacy JJ).

1737 Trial—libel—preliminary hearing—need for jury

The Supreme Court Act 1981 s 69(1) provides that a libel action is to be tried with a jury, unless the court is of the opinion that the trial requires any prolonged examination of documents or accounts or any scientific or local investigation which cannot conveniently be made with a jury. An action not falling within s 69(1) is to be tried without a jury unless the court in its discretion orders it to be tried with a jury: s 69(3). Section 69(1), (3) does not affect the power of the court to order that different questions of fact arising in any action be tried by different modes of trial; and where any such order is made, s 69(1) has effect only as respects questions relating to any such charge, claim, question or issue as is mentioned therein: s 69(4).

The claimant, an internationally renowned cyclist, sought damages for libel in respect of an article printed in the defendants' newspaper. The parties agreed that the issue of the meaning of the words would be decided as a preliminary issue. The defendants wanted the preliminary issue to be decided by a jury, the claimant by a judge alone. The claimant argued that, by virtue of the 1981 Act s 69(4), the court did not have jurisdiction to order the issue of meaning to be tried with a jury, where the rest of the action was to be decided by a judge alone. The judge decided that there was no significant countervailing advantage in favour of jury trial for the purposes of resolving the issue of meaning, so as to justify the unusual step of having two different modes of trial. He therefore ordered that the preliminary issue should be tried by a judge alone other than himself. On the defendants' appeal against that ruling, *held*, the first part of s 69(4) gave the court an open discretion within its terms that was not moderated by the second part of s 69(4). Syntactically, the second part of s 69(4) was not entirely straightforward, but its general import was that, when an order under s 69(4) was made, s 69(1) remained to be applied to the remainder of the action. The judge had been entitled to take account of the general advantage of having all issues tried by the same tribunal, and had been right, in the light of the opening words of s 69(4), not to start with any predisposition in favour of jury trial. Accordingly, the appeal would be dismissed.

Armstrong v Times Newspapers Ltd [2006] EWCA Civ 519, [2006] 1 WLR 2462 (Court of Appeal: Sir Anthony Clarke MR, May and Dyson LJJ).

LAND CHARGES

Halsbury's Laws of England (4th edn) vol 26 (2004 Reissue) paras 601–800

1738   Pending land action—registration—recovery of judgment debt—registration of unilateral notice

Various actions between the claimant and the fourth defendant resulted in the fourth defendant incurring substantial liabilities to the claimant. The claimant alleged that the fourth defendant was trying to prevent him from recovering his judgment debt by hiding assets and registered a unilateral notice against a property of which the fifth defendant was registered proprietor, on the basis that the fourth defendant beneficially owned the property. The fifth defendant applied for a vacation of the unilateral notice, contending that the action commenced by the claimant in respect of the property did not amount to a 'pending land action' within the meaning of the Land Charges Act 1972 s 17, which defined such an action as 'any action or proceeding pending in court relating to land or any interest in or charge on land'. The claimant contended that he needed to establish that the property belonged beneficially to the fourth defendant because the fourth defendant would not do so, in order to conceal the property from the claimant. It fell to be determined whether such an action was capable of being registered as a pending land action within the meaning of s 17. *Held*, the purpose of the phrase 'pending land action' was to put prospective purchasers on notice that there was a dispute which might affect the title to land. In order for an action to fall within that definition the claimant had to show a genuine interest in the outcome of the litigation. The claimant had a legitimate interest in asserting, on behalf of the fourth defendant, what the fourth defendant would normally be expected to assert. In those circumstances, it was difficult to see how such an action could not be a relevant action. It followed that the claimant's proceedings fell within s 17 and, accordingly, the application would be dismissed.

Godfrey v Torpey [2006] All ER (D) 77 (May) (Chancery Division: Peter Smith J). *Calgary and Edmonton Land Co Ltd v Dobinson* [1974] Ch 102 (1974 Abr para 1904); and *Selim Ltd v Bickenhall Engineering Ltd* [1981] 3 All ER 210 (1981 Abr para 1730) considered.

LAND REGISTRATION

Halsbury's Laws of England (4th edn) vol 26 (2004 Reissue) paras 801–1208

Articles

For articles relating to this title please refer to the Table of Articles at the beginning of the Abridgment.

1739   Fees

The Land Registration Fee Order 2006, SI 2006/1332 (in force on 7 August 2006), replaces the Land Registration Fee Order 2004, SI 2004/595, and makes changes to land registration fees. The principal effects of the order are that (1) the fee of £80 payable for each registered title affected on an application for the determination of the exact line of a boundary has been replaced with a single fee of £80; (2) the fees for inspection and for official copies of the register and of documents have been increased as follows: (a) the fees for inspection of an individual register or caution register, or a title or caution plan, or an individual register and title plan of a commonhold common parts title have been increased from £2 to £3, when from a remote terminal, and from £4 to £6 in other cases; (b) the fees for inspection of any or all documents referred to in an individual register or of any other document kept by the registrar which relates to an application to him, other than, in each case, leases, have been increased from £2 to £5, when from a remote terminal, and from £4 to £10 in other cases; there are now fees relating specifically to inspection of leases referred to in an individual register and these increase the fees that applied previously from £2 to £10, when from a remote terminal, and from £4 to £20 in other cases; (c) the fees for an official copy of an individual register or caution register, or a title or caution plan, or an individual register and title plan of a commonhold common parts title have been increased from £2 to £3, when requested in electronic form from a remote terminal, and from £4 to £6 when requested in paper form by any permitted means; (d) the fees for an official copy of any or all documents referred to in an individual register, other than leases, have been increased from £2 to £5, where a copy in electronic form is requested from a remote terminal, and from £4 to £10 when requested in paper form by any permitted means; (e) there are now fees relating specifically to an official copy of a lease referred to in an individual register and these increase the fees that applied previously from £2 to £10, where a copy of the lease is held in electronic form and the request for a copy in electronic form is from a remote terminal, and from £2 or £4 to £20, where a copy of the lease is not held in electronic form or where a copy in paper form is requested by any permitted means; (f) the fees for an official copy of any other document kept by the registrar which relates to an application to him have been increased from £2 to £5, where a copy of the document is held in electronic form and the request for a copy in electronic form is from a remote terminal, and from £4 to £10 where a copy of the document is not held in electronic form or where a copy in paper form is requested by any permitted means; and (3) the fees for official searches of the register, of pending first registration applications and of the index of relating franchises and manors have been increased from £2 to £3, when requested from a remote terminal, and from £4 to £6 in other cases; the fee for the issue of certificates of inspection of a title plan has also been increased from £4 to £6.

1740 Register—notice—unilateral notice—vacation—court's inherent jurisdiction

The claimants agreed to purchase property on a long lease from the defendant, but refused to complete the purchase, forfeiting their deposits, because they were unhappy about the defendant's design and workmanship. The claimants sought damages and a declaration that the defendant had been in repudiatory breach of contract, which had entitled the claimants to rescind the contract for sale. The defendant entered into dealings with a third party for the sale of the property, and the claimants asked the defendant to pay the net proceeds of sale into court or into an escrow account pending trial. The defendant refused, and the claimants applied for unilateral notices to be placed on the Land Registry against the property for the protection of alleged liens held by the claimants in respect of their deposits. The notices were registered at the Land Registry. The defendant, unable to proceed with the sale with the notices in place, applied to the court for an order vacating them. *Held*, although the claimants had a prima facie entitlement, under the Land Registration Act 2002 s 34(1), to register the notices, the court retained an inherent jurisdiction to vacate any such notice, with the balance of convenience being the primary consideration. The balance of convenience overwhelmingly favoured the discharge of the notices. Their registration was of no practical value to the claimants as a bank already had a first charge on the property. The late timing of the registration indicated that the intention had been to put commercial pressure on the defendant before the trial. The notices presented a major disadvantage to the defendant, as they would prevent the pending sale from going ahead. It would be disproportionate to allow them to remain and, accordingly, the application would be allowed.

Donnelly v Weybridge Construction Ltd [2006] EWHC 348 (TCC), [2006] BLR 158 (Queen's Bench Division: Judge Coulson QC).

LANDLORD AND TENANT

Halsbury's Laws of England (4th edn) vol 27(1) (2006 Reissue) paras 1–700, vol 27(2) (2006 Reissue) paras 701–1385, vol 27(3) (2006 Reissue) paras 1386–2000

Articles

For articles relating to this title please refer to the Table of Articles at the beginning of the Abridgment.

1741 Assured tenancy—possession proceedings—conduct causing nuisance or annoyance—ability to control nuisance-maker

The defendant was an assured tenant under the Housing Act 1988 of a house in which she lived with her son. The claimant housing trust brought an action for possession of the house pursuant to Sch 2 Pt II Ground 14, which referred to conduct on the part of the tenant, or a person residing with him, which caused a nuisance or annoyance. The defendant's son had criminal convictions, was subject to an anti-social behaviour order, and had other fetters on his conduct such as electronic tagging. Evidence was given that the defendant was unable to discipline or control the actions of her son and that she was not in a position to exclude him from the house. The judge decided that the ground for possession was satisfied and that it was reasonable to make an order for possession, but that the order should be suspended pursuant to s 9(3) on terms that no further acts of nuisance were to be committed. The defendant appealed, submitting that the judge should not have made an order for possession under s 9(3), on the ground that her son's behaviour was beyond her control and was already being effectively controlled by external agencies. *Held*, the fact that the defendant could not control the nuisance-maker was a factor which would normally assist her in resisting an order for possession in relation to past breaches, especially where she had done her best to stop the nuisance. However, unless the nuisance-maker had vacated, or would shortly vacate, the property, that was a factor which might often assist the landlord if he was asking the court to make an outright order for possession or to suspend the order for possession on terms which related to the behaviour of the nuisance-maker. In some cases, it might be that a judge would conclude that it was not open to him to impose a condition that there were no further acts of nuisance on a suspended order because it would cause exceptional hardship to the tenant or would be otherwise unreasonable. Nevertheless, in cases where serious and persistent nuisance had been caused, the only realistic alternative to making a suspended order subject to such a condition would be to make an outright order. On that basis it would be hard for the tenant to argue that a suspended order on such terms fell foul of s 9(3). Accordingly, the appeal would be dismissed.

Knowsley Housing Trust v McMullen [2006] EWCA Civ 539, [2006] HLR 843 (Court of Appeal: Auld, Rix and Neuberger LJJ).

1742   Assured shorthold tenancy—statutory notice—period of notice

The Housing Act 1988 s 5(2) provides that if an assured tenancy which is a fixed term tenancy comes to an end other than by virtue of an order of the court or a surrender or other action on the part of the tenant, then the tenant is entitled to remain in possession of the dwelling house let under the tenancy and his right to possession depends on a periodic tenancy arising under s 5. Such a periodic tenancy is one under which the periods of the tenancy are the same as those for which rent was last payable under the fixed term tenancy: s 5(3)(d).

A tenant had an assured shorthold tenancy for a period of a year less a day at an annual rent payable by equal quarterly payments. The landlord issued possession proceedings but the tenant successfully claimed that the tenancy was an annual one and the proceedings premature. The landlord appealed. *Held,* the court had to give the words of the 1988 Act s 5 their ordinary meaning, which compelled ascertainment of the amount of rent that was last payable under the terms of the tenancy. While the rent was annual, it was expressly payable quarterly in advance. Therefore, the period was a quarterly period and not an annual one. Accordingly, the appeal would be allowed.

Church Comrs for England v Meya [2006] EWCA Civ 821, [2007] HLR 38 (Court of Appeal: Ward and Smith LJJ and Creswell J).

1743   Covenant—covenant not to make alterations without consent—refusal of consent—disability discrimination

See *Williams v Richmond Court (Swansea) Ltd*, para 1064.

1744   Covenant—covenant to repair—construction—main structures of property

The claimant landlord let a two-storey maisonette in a block of residences to the defendants. The lease required the claimant to maintain the 'main structures' of the property. A defect subsequently became apparent in the joists between the two floors of the maisonette and the claimant brought proceedings to recover the cost of repair from the defendants. There was expert evidence that the joists provided a degree of lateral support to the party walls of neighbouring residences. The judge found that the joists were part of the 'main structures' of the property and so the claimant was liable for their repair. The claimant appealed. *Held,* although 'structure' and 'main structure' took their meaning from the particular lease and surrounding circumstances, a good working definition was that the structure of the dwelling house consisted of those elements of the overall dwelling house which gave it its essential appearance, stability and shape. The expression did not extend to the many and various ways in which the dwelling house would be fitted out, equipped, decorated and generally made to be habitable, nor should it be limited to those aspects of the dwelling house which were load bearing in a technical sense. 'Main structure' was more restrictive. As a matter of ordinary language, the joists in the maisonette were part of the structure of the building and they were part of the 'main structures' for the purposes of the lease. They played a significant part in keeping the structure of the building sound such that their repair would be to the benefit of a number of tenants. Furthermore, an ordinary person would regard them as an essential part of its structure and it was more likely in practical terms that the parties expected the maintenance of the floor joists to be the responsibility of the claimant. Accordingly, the appeal would be dismissed.

Marlborough Park Services Ltd v Rowe [2006] EWCA Civ 436, [2006] 23 EG 166 (Court of Appeal: Tuckey, Sedley and Neuberger LJJ).

1745   Covenant—covenant to repair—material compliance with covenant

A landlord demised to a tenant an office block for a specified term. The lease provided that the tenant might give not less than 13 months notice to the landlord of termination of the lease if the tenant had materially complied with all its obligations under the lease down to the date for which notice of termination had been given. The tenant gave notice terminating the lease, undertook a substantial repair programme in order to comply with the tenant's covenants and vacated the premises. The landlord claimed that the lease was still subsisting because the tenant had materially failed to comply with its repairing and other obligations under the lease and commenced proceedings seeking declarations to that effect. The judge declared that the lease had been terminated pursuant to the notice given by the tenant to the landlord. The landlord appealed, contending that the judge had misdirected himself as to the test of material compliance. *Held*, the test of material compliance was an objective one. Materiality had to be assessed by reference to the ability of the landlord to re-let or sell the property without delay or additional expenditure. Where the provision was absolute then any breach would preclude an exercise of the break clause. There was no justification for attributing to the parties an intention that the insertion of the word 'material', was intended to permit only breaches which were trivial or trifling. Nor was it of any assistance to consider whether the word 'material' permitted more or different breaches than the commonly used alternatives 'substantial or 'reasonable.' The words 'substantial' and 'material', depending on the context, were interchangeable. The word 'reasonable' connoted a different test. In the present case the judge had applied the wrong test. However, applying the right test to the facts as found by the judge, the tenant had still materially complied with its obligations. Accordingly, the appeal would be dismissed.

Fitzroy House Epworth Street (No 1) Ltd v The Financial Times Ltd [2006] EWCA Civ 329, [2006] 2 All ER 776 (Court of Appeal: Sir Andrew Morritt C, Jacob and Moore-Bick LJJ).

1746 Covenant—restrictive covenant

See EQUITY.

1747 Landlord—management of premises—codes of practice—residential property—Wales

The Approval of Codes of Management Practice (Residential Property) (Wales) Order 2006, SI 2006/178 (in force on 1 February 2006), provides that the National Assembly for Wales approves the code of practice called 'The Rent Only Management Code', which relates to the management of residential property by landlords and others who discharge the management function. The order also provides that the National Assembly withdraws the approval given in the 1996 Order, SI 1996/2839, for a code called 'The Rent Only Residential Management Code'.

1748 Landlord—management of premises—codes of practice—student accommodation—England

The Housing (Approval of Codes of Management Practice) (Student Accommodation) (England) Order 2006, SI 2006/646 (in force on 6 April 2006), approves three codes of practice laying down standards of conduct and practice to be followed with regard to the management of houses in multiple occupation and other buildings that are occupied solely or principally by full-time students.

1749 Landlord—management of premises—codes of practice—student accommodation—Wales

The Housing (Approval of Codes of Management Practice) (Student Accommodation) (Wales) Order 2006, SI 2006/1709 (in force on 7 July 2006), approves three codes of practice laying down standards of conduct and practice to be followed with regard to the management of houses in multiple occupation and other buildings that are occupied solely or principally by full-time students.

1750 Lease—assignment—obligation to pay rent—indemnity covenant for payment of rent

The Landlord and Tenant (Covenants) Act 1995 s 17(2) provides that a former tenant is not liable under the tenancy to pay any amount in respect of any fixed charge payable under the covenant, unless, within the period of six months beginning with the date when the charge becomes due, the landlord serves on the former tenant a notice informing him that the charge is now due and that, in respect of the charge, the landlord intends to recover from the former tenant such amount as is specified in the notice and (where payable) interest calculated on such basis as is so specified.

By two underleases, hotel premises were demised to the claimant. The claimant then assigned the underleases to the defendant. By virtue of the Land Registration Act 1925 s 24, the assignments contained a covenant by the defendant that he and his successors would pay the rent reserved by, and comply with the covenants and conditions contained in, the underleases and would indemnify the claimant in the event of breach. The underleases subsequently became vested in a company which defaulted on payment of rent. Its mortgagees then appointed administrative receivers. The reversioner to the underleases then served statutory demands on the claimant, which paid both the claimed sum and further rent which subsequently accrued under the leases. The claimant commenced proceedings against the defendant for those sums and declaratory relief as regards future liabilities. *Held*, the 1995 Act s 17(2) was designed to relieve the former tenant of liability in respect of any fixed charge unless the landlord had taken a purely formal step of notification to preserve the former tenant's liability. Such a construction seemed entirely consistent with Parliament's intention. Bearing in mind the policy behind s 17(2), the notice served by the reversioner specifying rent due under the original lease had not been effective to render the claimant liable, since it did not contain the relevant paragraph informing the claimant that there was a possibility that its liability in respect of the fixed charge would subsequently be determined for a greater amount. However, the claimant would not be debarred from recovering the rent which it had subsequently paid. The claimant had found itself in a position where, in order to stem the onslaught of future liabilities, it had to incur the expense of meeting the rent arrears irrespective of its strict liability to the reversioner to pay the same. If that was the correct analysis, the fact that the claimant had paid sums in respect of rent which had not been the subject of valid s 17 notices, and the fact that it had procured the service of s 17 notices which would not otherwise have been served, were irrelevant to the question of its being able to recover those sums from the defendant. Accordingly, judgment would be given for the claimant.

Scottish & Newcastle v Raguz [2006] EWHC 821 (Ch), [2006] 4 All ER 524 (Chancery Division: Hart J).

1751   Lease—forfeiture—reform of law—Law Commission proposals

The principal significance of the law of forfeiture now lies in the fields of tenancies of commercial premises and long residential leases, and its abolition is recommended by the Law Commission in its paper, *Termination of Tenancies for Tenant Default* (Cm 6946; Law Com No 303), which has been presented to Parliament by the Secretary of State for Constitutional Affairs and Lord Chancellor. The Commission recommends the replacement of the remedy of forfeiture by a new statutory scheme based on the concept of 'tenant default', that is a breach by the tenant, or any person guaranteeing the tenant's obligations under the tenancy, of a covenant in the tenancy, whether express, implied or imposed by law, other than an 'excepted covenant' (namely, in post-commencement tenancies, a covenant expressly excepted by the tenancy; a different definition would be applicable to pre-commencement tenancies). The need for tenancy agreements to contain express rights of re-entry or forfeiture clauses would be removed. Except where the court might dispense with such requirement, written notice would need to be given to the tenant before any termination action was taken by the landlord, and also to persons with interests deriving out of the tenancy (for example, mortgagees and subtenants) and such persons would be able to apply to the court for orders protecting their interests in the property. In the absence of a transfer order or new tenancy order made by the court, any qualifying interests deriving out of the tenancy would end when the tenancy came to an end. In consequence of a termination claim, the court might make an order requiring the tenant to take specified action to remedy the tenant default. Although the new statutory scheme would be predominantly a court-based system, provision would be made for an exchange of information at an early stage in the process which might result in negotiation and compromise, using, where appropriate, various means of dispute resolution. There would also be a summary termination procedure, entitling the landlord, in the absence of a discharge order, to termination of the tenancy within one month, available to a landlord in appropriate cases, for example, where the tenant had abandoned the premises or where the tenant had no reasonable prospect of defending a termination claim in court. The text of a draft Bill, the Landlord and Tenant (Termination of Tenancies) Bill, which would give effect to the Law Commission's recommendations, is appended to the report.

1752   Lease—licensed premises—tied house covenant—validity

See *Crehan v Inntrepreneur Pub Co*, para 2985.

1753   Lease—repudiation—vacation of premises and failure to pay rent—recovery of rent

The defendant solicitors leased an office from the claimant landlords on a five year lease. The defendants ceased practising as solicitors three years into the lease and had no further need for the office. Soon after they vacated the premises, they stopped paying the rent and water rates. Almost a year later, the landlords sued for the arrears due up to the date of their claim, seeking only a money judgment for the sums then due. The defendants argued that the landlords were fully aware of the plight of the defendants which had led to them ceasing to practise as solicitors, but had failed to forfeit the lease in order to mitigate their own loss, and had failed to attempt to re-let the premises. The judge held that a landlord was not required to mitigate his loss when seeking to recover arrears of rent. The second defendant appealed. *Held*, where one party had repudiated a contract, the innocent party was entitled to elect either to accept or reject the repudiation, except in a case where damages would be an adequate remedy and an election to keep the contract alive would be wholly unreasonable. If a landlord recovered possession from a tenant who had been in breach of the lease and then re-let the premises at a lower rent, it was clear that he would not be entitled to recover damages from the former tenant in respect of loss of future rent after termination. In those circumstances, either damages were not an adequate remedy for the landlord, or at least the landlord would be acting reasonably in taking the view that he should not terminate the lease because he might well not be able to recover such damages. Moreover, if the landlords had chosen to regard it as up to the tenants to propose an assignee or a new tenant, rather than take the initiative themselves, that was not unreasonable, still less wholly unreasonable. Accordingly, the appeal would be dismissed.

Reichman v Beveridge [2006] EWCA Civ 1659, [2006] All ER (D) 186 (Dec) (Court of Appeal: Auld, Rix and Lloyd LJJ). *White & Carter (Councils) Ltd v McGregor* [1962] AC 413, HL; *Clea Shipping Corpn v Bulk Oil International Ltd; The Alaskan Trader* [1984] 1 All ER 129 (1983 Abr para 3060); and *Gator Shipping Corpn v Trans-Asiatic Oil Ltd SA and Occidental Shipping Establishment, The Odenfeld* [1978] 2 Lloyd's Rep 357 considered.

1754   Lease—right to acquire new lease—counter-notice—redevelopment—premises in which tenant's flat contained

A landlord was the freehold owner of two blocks of flats. The contractual term of the lease of a tenant, the underlessee of one of the flats, expired and the tenant gave notice to the landlord, under the Leasehold Reform, Housing and Urban Development Act 1993 s 42, claiming the right to obtain a new lease. The landlord admitted the tenant's right to claim a new lease in a counter-notice under s 45 but stated that it intended to apply for an order under s 47 that the right should not be exercisable on the basis that the landlord intended to redevelop the premises in which the flat was contained. By virtue of s 47, the right to acquire a new lease was not exercisable by the tenant by reason of the landlord's intention to redevelop any premises in which the tenant's flat was contained, and on such an order becoming final the tenant's notice would cease to have effect. The landlord intended to create a single maisonette out of the tenant's flat and a vertically adjacent flat. The landlord sought a declaration that the tenant's right to acquire a new lease was not exercisable by reason of the landlord's intention to redevelop the premises. The judge preferred the tenant's argument that the expression 'any premises' in s 47, taken as a whole, was intended to refer to the building as a whole or a self-contained part of it. On the landlord's appeal, it fell to be determined whether the part of the block which comprised the tenant's flat constituted 'any premises in which the tenant's flat is contained' within the meaning of s 47. *Held*, May LJ dissenting, there was nothing in either the policy or the language of the Act that indicated that a part of the building that comprised two adjacent flats did not constitute premises in which each was contained, whether the two flats were vertically or horizontally contiguous. It was not possible to identify some irreducible minimum unit that constituted 'premises in which the tenant's flat is contained' for the purposes of ss 45 and 47. The creation of a single maisonette out of two vertically adjacent flats did not seem to run counter to the purposes of the statute and that part of the building that comprised the two flats could properly be described as premises containing the tenant's flat just as much as the floor of the building on which the flat was situated. Accordingly, the appeal would be allowed.

Majorstake v Curtis [2006] EWCA Civ 1171, [2006] 4 All ER 1326 (Court of Appeal: May, Neuberger and Moore-Bick LJJ).

1755   Lease—service charge—costs incurred—determination of liability to pay service charges

A landlord, the freeholder of a building, let the upper floors on a long lease, the headlease. The flats of which the upper floors consisted were separately sublet on 24 subleases. The tenant under the headlease was a non-profit making company owned by 15 of the subtenants. Under the headlease, the landlord was responsible for keeping the building, other than the upper floors, in good repair, and the company was obliged to pay the landlord a maintenance charge equal to 90 per cent of the costs incurred by the landlord in discharging its repairing obligations. The maintenance charge was effectively passed on by the subleases, each of which obliged each subtenant to pay to the company one twenty-fourth of the maintenance charge levied on the company by the landlord. The applicant, a subtenant who was not a member of the company, sought to challenge the amount of the maintenance charge levied by the landlord on the company on the ground that the amount was unreasonable. He applied to a leasehold valuation tribunal for a determination as to the amount which was properly payable. It fell to be determined whether the maintenance charge was a service charge within the meaning of the Landlord and Tenant Act 1985 and whether the applicant had the requisite status to challenge the amount of the maintenance charge given that the obligation to pay it lay on the company as tenant under the headlease. The tribunal decided both issues in the applicant's favour. The landlord's appeal was dismissed and it appealed further. *Held*, notwithstanding that a mesne landlord owned the entire building, the applicant was a tenant of part of a building occupied or intended to be occupied as a separate dwelling within the terms of s 38. Reading the definition as consisting of two parts, that is a building occupied or intended to be occupied as a separate dwelling and part of a building occupied or intended to be occupied as a separate dwelling, a tenant of a property which fell within the second part of the definition was not taken out of the definition by reason of the fact that he was not the tenant of a property which fell within the first part. Further, there was no justification for implying any general restriction. In most cases, the applicant for a determination under s 27A as to the proper amount of service charge payable would be the party who was liable to pay the service charge the subject of the challenge, and the respondent to the application would be the party seeking to levy it on the applicant but there was no reason why that should inevitably be the case. Accordingly, the appeal would be dismissed.

Ruddy v Oakfern Properties Ltd [2006] EWCA Civ 1389, [2007] 1 All ER 337 (Court of Appeal: Pill, Jonathan Parker and Moses LJJ).

1756   Leasehold enfranchisement—acquisition of freehold—relevant date for determining rateable value—two properties let with obligation to convert into single dwelling

The Leasehold Reform Act 1967 s 4A(1) provides for the right to leasehold enfranchisement where the amount of rent payable during the initial year did not exceed two-thirds of the rateable value of the property on the relevant date. 'The relevant date' means the date of the commencement of the tenancy or, if the property did not have a rateable value on that date, the date on which it first had a rateable value: s 4A(2)(b).

A lessee took a long tenancy of two self-contained semi-detached cottages under a lease which required the cottages to be converted into a single dwelling within a year. The current tenant took over the lease and sought a declaration that she was entitled to acquire the freehold pursuant to the 1967 Act s 4A. Section 4 provided for the rent limits and s 4A provided for alternative rent limits. The essential question was which date was the relevant date for determining the rateable value of the property. If the relevant date was the commencement of the lease, the tenant would not be entitled to acquire the freehold because the initial amount of rent payable on the two cottages exceeded two-thirds of their combined rateable value; if the relevant date was after the conversion she would be so entitled because the rent payable on the converted property was less than two-thirds of its rateable value. The judge decided that it was the landlord's intention that the property subject to the tenancy was a single dwelling house, and the dwelling house did not have a rateable value at the commencement of the tenancy because it did not exist. On this basis he held that the relevant date was the date when the current dwelling house appeared on the valuation list, and so the tenant was entitled to acquire the freehold. The landlord appealed. *Held*, the definition of 'the relevant date' in s 4A(2)(b) referred to the rateable value that was that of 'the property', in contrast to the definition of that term in s 4(1), which referred to the rateable value of 'the house'. This showed that that particular attention had been paid to differences in wording between the various statutory provisions. The purpose of s 4A was to counter increases in ground rent since the commencement of a tenancy. The statutory provisions did not distinguish between conversion works that a tenant was required to do and those which a tenant did voluntarily. On the trial judge's construction, a tenant would be able to procure entitlement to acquire the freehold by voluntarily undertaking a conversion so as to increase the rateable value of the property in relation to the initial year's rent. At the date of the commencement of the tenancy the property consisted of two hereditaments each of which had a separate rateable value, and so for the purpose of s 4A the rateable value of the property was the aggregate of those two hereditaments. As the rent payable exceeded two-thirds of that rateable value, the tenant was not entitled to acquire the freehold. Accordingly, the appeal would be allowed.

Neville v Cowdray Trust Ltd [2006] EWCA Civ 709, [2006] 1 WLR 2097 (Court of Appeal: May and Latham LJJ). *Dixon v Allgood* [1987] 3 All ER 1082, HL (1987 Abr para 1453), considered.

1757   Leasehold enfranchisement—dwelling house—meaning of 'house'—residential and commercial use

The Leasehold Reform Act 1967 s 2(1) provides that, for the purposes of Pt I (ss 1–37), 'house' includes any building designed or adapted for living in and reasonably so called, notwithstanding that the building is not structurally detached, or was or is not solely designed or adapted for living in.

The claimants in two conjoined cases were the lessors of properties which had been built in the eighteenth century as single houses. In the case of the first claimant, the property, in which the first defendant had a long leasehold estate, had been occupied as a residence until the 1950s, and thereafter, following substantial alterations and extensions, was used commercially for an antiques business. In the case of the second claimant, the property, which was owned by the second defendant and in respect of which the first defendant held a long leasehold, had been occupied as a residence until the 1940s, after which, while the upper floors remained in residential use, the lower floors were used commercially. After a while, however, the property was left unoccupied and it subsequently became dilapidated and incapable of occupation. The claimants gave the defendants notice of their desire to acquire the freehold of the properties, pursuant to the 1967 Act. The defendants disputed the claimants' rights to the freehold, arguing that each property was not a house within the meaning of s 2(1). At a hearing, the judge emphasised the importance of the physical state of the properties at the time notice had been given, and found that, in the first claimant's case, the property had been adapted for commercial rather than residential use, and that, in the second claimant's case, the property was too dilapidated for residential use. He therefore held that neither property was designed or adapted for living in within the meaning of s 2(1). The defendants appealed. *Held*, on the proper construction of s 2(1), the true test was whether premises, viewed as at the moment when notice was given, were designed or adapted for residential use. The essential issue was whether residential use was the premises' purpose. In the circumstances, as the first claimant's property had been adapted for commercial use, and the second claimant's property was in a state of grave dilapidation, the judge had applied the correct test and had been entitled to come to the conclusions he had. Accordingly, the appeals would be dismissed.

Mallett & Sons (Antiques) Ltd v Grosvenor West End Properties Ltd; Boss Holdings Ltd v Grosvenor West End Properties Ltd [2006] EWCA Civ 594, [2006] 1 WLR 2848 (Court of Appeal: Tuckey, Laws and Carnwath LJJ).

1758   Leasehold enfranchisement—neighbouring tenants sharing common owner— reciprocal rights over property—continuation after enfranchisement

The claimants owned property neighbouring that of the defendants. The two plots of land had been held under tenancies from a common owner prior to their enfranchisement under the Leasehold

Reform Act 1967. The boundary between the two properties ran down the middle of a path between them. The claimants obtained a declaration that they were entitled to a right of way over the half of the path owned by the defendants. On appeal, questions arose as to the application of the rule in *Wheeldon v Burrows*, that a person could not agree to grant land and at the same time deny to the grantee what was obviously necessary for the grantee's reasonable enjoyment, and that the grantor was entitled to only those rights over the land which he had expressly reserved in the grant. *Held*, the rule in *Wheeldon v Burrows* had no application to a conveyance executed to give effect to the obligation to enfranchise imposed by the 1967 Act s 8(1), and the question of which, if any, easements passed to the tenant on the conveyance of the freehold turned on the operation of the Law of Property Act 1925 s 62. The application of the second part of the rule was limited by the need to construe the conveyance executed so as to give effect to the common intention of the parties that the estate conveyed was an estate in fee simple subject to the tenant's encumbrances. Where two plots had been held under tenancies from a common owner, it might well be that the tenant of each plot had rights over the leasehold interest of the other. The position after the enfranchisement of both plots was that the former tenants of those plots would continue to enjoy the same rights over each other's plots as they had prior to the enfranchisement. If they were entitled to reciprocal easements under the former leases, those easements were in effect enfranchised, regardless of which plot had been enfranchised first. Accordingly, the appeal would be dismissed.

Kent v Kavanagh [2006] EWCA Civ 162, [2007] Ch 1 (Court of Appeal: Chadwick and Longmore LJJ and Lewison J).

1759 Leasehold valuation tribunals—appeal—application for permission to appeal

The Lands Tribunal (Amendment) Rules 2006, SI 2006/880 (in force in relation to England on 28 April 2006 and in relation to Wales on 16 June 2006), amends the 1996 Rules, SI 1996/1022, in relation to appeals from the leasehold valuation tribunal and residential property tribunals. In particular, the rules (1) amend the legislation dealing with applications for permission to appeal to the Lands Tribunal; (2) reduce the time limit for applying to the Tribunal for permission to appeal after a refusal of permission by the leasehold valuation tribunal or residential property tribunal from 28 days to 14 days; (2) provide that the Tribunal may make an urgency direction on application by one of the parties according to the normal interlocutory procedures, or by the Tribunal on its own initiative, having given the parties opportunity to make representations.

1760 Licence to occupy land—supplies to licensee incidental to licence—value added tax implications

See *Byrom (t/a Salon 24) v Revenue and Customs Comrs*, para 2902.

1761 Mobile homes—written statement of terms—form—England

The Mobile Homes (Written Statement) (England) Regulations 2006, SI 2006/2275 (in force on 1 October 2006), replace the 1983 Regulations, SI 1983/749, in relation to England, and provide that, before an agreement to which the Mobile Homes Act 1983 s 1 applies is entered into, the owner of a site must give to a proposed occupier of a mobile home a written statement to be in the form prescribed specified.

1762 Possession—order—breach of order—continued occupation by tenant—revival of tenancy

The Housing Act 1985 s 82(2) provides that, where the landlord obtains an order for the possession of the dwelling house, the tenancy ends on the date on which the tenant is to give up possession in pursuance of the order.

The landlord local authority sought possession of the flat of a secure tenant on the ground that the tenant was causing a nuisance to and harassing his neighbours. The judge imposed an order for possession after 28 days, to be suspended so long as the tenant complied with the terms of the tenancy agreement relating to his behaviour. The order was to remain in existence until a specified date, the landlord being granted permission to apply for an extension. The landlord subsequently took the view that the tenant had breached the terms of his tenancy and thereby broken the terms of the suspension of the order. It therefore sought to return to court for permission to issue a warrant for possession. The judge ordered that the suspended order for possession be extended for a further six months and that the warrant for possession be adjourned. The tenant argued that the judge's order had the effect of reviving the original tenancy, which in turn meant that the slate had been wiped clean in respect of his breaches up to that date so that the landlord could rely only on breaches subsequent to the order, and had to start fresh proceedings in order to do so since the order had been made in respect of a tenancy which had expired. The judge ruled in favour of the landlord on the ground that the judge who had made the second order had been concerned only with case management and that, in extending the order, had not been addressing the substantive rights of the parties. The tenant appealed, contending that, on the proper construction of the 1985 Act s 82(2), the extension of the currency of the order also postponed the date of possession. *Held*, if the period of suspension of a possession order was extended, that did not of itself change the date on which the tenant was to give up possession for the purposes of s 82(2) if that date had already arrived. The second order had not, therefore, relieved the tenant from the consequences of his breaches. That the judge had kept in place the application to enforce the sanction imposed for the original breaches of the tenancy showed quite clearly that the last thing he had seen himself as doing was relieving the tenant from the consequences of those breaches. Accordingly, the appeal would be dismissed.

Richmond v Kensington and Chelsea LBC [2006] EWCA Civ 68, [2006] 1 WLR 1693 (Court of Appeal: Buxton, Gage and Lloyd LJJ). *Burrows v Brent LBC* [1996] 4 All ER 577, HL (1996 Abr para 1840), applied.

1763   Possession—order—occupation of site under licence agreement—travellers—human rights

The defendants were a family of travellers who occupied a site as their home under a licence agreement with the local authority. The authority served notice to quit, and then, on the expiry of the notice, commenced possession proceedings in a county court. The authority argued that possession was required to carry out essential improvements, and that the site would then be managed as temporary accommodation for travellers coming to the city, as recommended by central government. It argued that the defendants' presence deterred other travellers from going there and that the site was severely underused, causing unauthorised encampments to be set up elsewhere in the city. The defendants argued that the authority's action was contrary to their rights under the European Convention on Human Rights art 8. Summary judgment was made in favour of the authority, and the defendants appealed. *Held*, the principle that the enforcement of a right to possession in accordance with the domestic law of property could never be incompatible with art 8 required modification in the light of recent authority of the European Court of Human Rights, but the exception should be narrowly defined. The ordinary presumption was that the property right of a public landowner supplied the justification required by art 8(2). In a normal case, there was no need for the authority to plead or prove individual justification. There were only two possible 'gateways' for a successful defence to summary judgment in such cases: firstly, if there was a seriously arguable challenge under art 8 to the law under which the possession was made, but only where it was possible, with the interpretative aids of the Human Rights Act 1998, to adapt the domestic law to make it more compliant, or secondly, if there was a seriously arguable challenge on conventional judicial review grounds to the authority's decision to recover possession. In the instant case, the authority's decision depended not on a factual allegation of nuisance or misconduct, or the bald ground that the family were trespassers, but on an administrative judgment about the appropriate use of its land in the public interest. That was well within the authority's margin of appreciation. It followed that the decision was open to challenge on conventional judicial review grounds, but not on the grounds that it was contrary to art 8. Accordingly, the appeal would be dismissed.

Birmingham City Council v Doherty [2006] EWCA Civ 1739, [2006] All ER (D) 348 (Dec) (Court of Appeal: Tuckey, Carnwath and Neuberger LJJ).

1764   Possession—order—postponement—conditions—fixing of date for possession

A landlord, a local housing authority, brought possession proceedings against the secure tenants of two properties owned by it on the ground that they were in arrears of rent. In each case, a possession order was granted in accordance with the applicable prescribed form, which fixed a date for possession but provided that the order would not be enforced so long as the tenant paid off the arrears at a defined weekly rate in addition to the current rent. On the tenants' appeals, the question arose as to whether it had been correct for the judges to fix a date for possession on the face of the orders. *Held*, the courts possessed more flexible powers for setting the terms of a postponed possession order than was generally appreciated, and a judge was not obliged to use the standard form in any given case. The Housing Act 1985 s 85(2) allowed the court to postpone the date for possession 'for such period or periods as the court thinks fit' and it followed that the court could make an order which set out a date for possession but provided that the date would be postponed and the tenancy would continue so long as the conditions set out in the order continued to be satisfied. The judges had fettered their discretion too narrowly and, accordingly, the appeals would be allowed.

Bristol City Council v Hassan; Bristol City Council v Glastonbury [2006] EWCA Civ 656, [2006] 4 All ER 420 (Court of Appeal: Brooke, Dyson and Jacob LJJ).

1765   Possession—order—postponement—trespassers

It has been held that the power under the Housing Act 1980 s 89 to postpone an order for the possession of land does not apply to trespassers, as that provision is not intended to grant squatters rights which they did not previously have.

Boyland and Son Ltd v Rand (2007) Times, 18 January (Court of Appeal: Ward and Neuberger LJJ).

1766   Possession—order—restrictions on right to possession—statutory protection

A tenant had been granted a tenancy of premises by the landlord's predecessors, which was protected by the Rent Act 1977. The tenant and the previous landlord then had a dispute about the state of the premises, which had become uninhabitable, and the tenant refused to pay rent. The current landlord subsequently became landlord by assignment and commenced an action for arrears of rent. The landlord contended that the statutory tenancy had terminated. The tenant asserted that the statutory tenancy continued. The proceedings were compromised and the terms embodied in a Tomlin order which provided that the landlord agreed to carry out items of work, on completion of which the tenant would become liable for rent. Subsequently, most of the works were carried out, but the tenant was not satisfied and still refused to pay rent. Finally, the landlord issued proceedings for arrears of rent and possession. The judge found that the statutory tenancy had been settled and stayed under the Tomlin order in the tenant's favour and therefore concluded that it would be an abuse of process for the landlord to contend that the tenant had lost his statutory protection earlier. The claim for possession failed and the landlord appealed. *Held,* in the circumstances, the landlord could have challenged the tenant's status as a statutory tenant in the earlier proceedings. In fact, the landlord had done so on the pleadings but had not taken the issue to trial. Instead, the issue had been abandoned and agreement had been reached on the basis that the tenant had, at that date, been a statutory tenant. It was clear that the agreement between the parties had settled the issue of the tenant's intention to return to actual occupation once the premises were habitable. Further, there was ample evidence from which the judge could infer that the claimant had that intention. In particular, the way in which he had acted in respect of the repairs had been consistent with an intention to move back in. Accordingly, the appeal would be dismissed.

The Carphone Warehouse UK Ltd v Malekout [2006] EWCA CIV 767, [2006] HLR 26 (Court of Appeal: Ward and Smith LJJ and Cresswell J).

1767   Possession—right of re-entry and forfeiture—enforcement—mixed residential and commercial premises

The Protection from Eviction Act 1977 s 2 provides that, where any premises are let as a dwelling on a lease which is subject to a right of re-entry or forfeiture, it is not lawful to enforce that right otherwise than by proceedings in the court while any person is lawfully residing in the premises or part of them.

A tenant took an assignment of a lease granted by the landlords of premises which consisted of a ground floor shop with a flat above. The tenant went into arrears, and the landlords purported to exercise their right of re-entry by causing bailiffs to change the locks of the shop. The tenant remained resident in the flat, which had a separate entrance. The landlords then issued a claim for an order for possession of the flat on the basis that, by virtue of their re-entry, the lease had been forfeited. In the possession proceedings, the tenant argued that the premises were 'let as a dwelling' within the meaning of the 1977 Act s 2 so that the lease had not been lawfully forfeited. The judge decided that the premises were not let as a dwelling and made an order for possession. The tenant appealed. *Held,* the phrase 'let as a dwelling' meant 'let wholly or partly as a dwelling' and therefore applied to premises which were let for mixed residential and business purposes. A tenant should not be at risk of returning home to discover that, unbeknown to him, he and his family had been locked out and were homeless. If they were to be evicted, the eviction should be conducted in an orderly fashion, on at least some prior notice, by officers subject to court direction. If there was to be an issue as to whether the landlord was entitled to forfeiture under the terms of the tenancy, it was preferable, particularly in relation to a home, for the court to determine it in advance of eviction rather than in proceedings brought by the tenant for an injunction and damages in the wake of it or in criminal proceedings against the landlord under s 1. There was no reason why those considerations should not apply to a tenant for whom the premises represented not only his home but also his place of business. Accordingly, the appeal would be allowed.

Pirabakaran v Patel [2006] EWCA Civ 685, [2006] 4 All ER 506 (Court of Appeal: Wilson LJ and Sir Peter Gibson). *National Trust for Places of Historic Interest or Natural Beauty v Knipe* [1997] 4 All ER 627, CA (1997 Abr para 74), distinguished.

1768   Rent—set-off against claims for rent—assignment of reversion—damages for defective construction

See *Edlington Properties Ltd v JH Fenner & Co Ltd*, para 2587.

1769   Residential property tribunal—fees—England

See para 1519.

1770   Secure tenancy—possession order—grant of tenancy induced by misrepresentation—assigned tenancy

The Housing Act 1985 Sch 2 Ground 5 provides that the tenant is the person to whom the tenancy was granted and the landlord was induced to grant the tenancy by a false statement made knowingly or recklessly by the tenant, or a person acting at the tenant's instigation.

A husband and wife applied to a local authority as homeless persons under the Housing Act 1996 Act Pt VII (ss 175–218). The authority accepted that it was under a duty to provide them with accommodation and granted a secure tenancy to the husband who assigned the tenancy to the wife.

The authority sought rescission of the tenancy on the ground of fraudulent misrepresentation and an order for possession as a result, or an order for possession under the 1985 Act Sch 2 Ground 5. The application was refused and the authority appealed. *Held*, the expression in Ground 5 'the tenant is' in the present tense could only refer to the person who was the tenant at the date of the hearing, rather than at the date of the grant of the tenancy. The inclusion of any predecessor in title would mean the expression would serve no purpose. Sections 82 and 84 provided that the landlord could only bring an end to a secure tenancy by obtaining an order for possession. It could not be brought about in some other way such as obtaining an order for rescission. The fact that an order for rescission operated retrospectively did not mean that, until the order was made, the contract did not exist. A voidable contract continued to have full effect until and unless it was brought to an end. Accordingly, the appeal would be dismissed.

Islington LBC v Uckac [2006] EWCA Civ 340, [2006] 1 WLR 1303 (Court of Appeal: Mummery and Dyson LJJ and Sir Charles Mantell).

1771   Secure tenancy—right of succession—entitlement

The Housing Act 1985 s 87 provides that a person is qualified to succeed a tenant under a secure tenancy if he occupies the dwelling house as his only or principal home at the time of the tenant's death and he is a member of the tenant's family and has resided with the tenant throughout the period of twelve months ending with the tenant's death unless the tenant was himself a successor. A tenant is himself a successor if he was a joint tenant and has become the sole tenant: s 88(1)(b).

The defendant lived with his parents who had been let a property by the local authority on a joint contractual tenancy. The father died and the mother became the sole contractual tenant and a secure tenant with the coming into force of the Housing Act 1980 s 47. The mother died and the authority was granted possession of the property. The defendant appealed. *Held*, under the 1985 Act ss 87 and 88, a person who had been a joint contractual tenant and became a sole contractual tenant by right of survivorship, and a secure tenant under the 1980 Act, was not a successor under the 1995 Act s 88. The mother had not been a successor to a secure tenancy, or any tenancy as, prior to the father's death, she had been a tenant jointly with him. On his death, she became the sole tenant of the tenancy interest due to survivorship. Accordingly, the appeal would be allowed.

Birmingham CC v Walker [2006] EWCA Civ 815, [2006] 2 FCR 623 (Court of Appeal: Mummery and Rix LJJ and Peter Smith J).

1772   Secure tenancy—right to buy—charges on dwelling houses—priority of charges— Wales

The Housing (Right to Buy) (Priority of Charges) (Wales) Order 2006, SI 2006/950 (in force on 31 March 2006), specifies Church House Trust plc as an approved lending institution for the purposes of the Housing Act 1985 s 156. The company also becomes an approved lending institution for the purposes of s 36 and the Housing Act 1996 s 12.

1773   Secure tenancy—right to buy—exercise of right—notice of intention to withdraw from purchase

The Housing Act 1985 s 122(1), (3) provides that, where a secure tenant claims to exercise the right to buy the property by giving written notice to that effect, the notice may be withdrawn at any time by notice in writing served on the landlord.

The claimant's mother was a secure tenant of a property owned by the local housing authority, in which they both lived. Pursuant to the 1985 Act s 122, the claimant's mother served on the authority a written notice claiming to exercise her right to buy the property. The authority served on them notices admitting their right to buy the property, and informed them that, if they wished to exercise their right to a mortgage, they should serve a written notice within three months. However, the claimant and his mother never claimed to exercise their right to a mortgage. An officer of the local authority subsequently circulated an internal memorandum stating that the claimant no longer intended to proceed with the purchase, and the freehold interest in the property was eventually transferred to the defendant housing association. Several years later, following the death of the claimant's mother, the claimant indicated to the defendant that he proposed to exercise the right to buy the property, pursuant to the earlier notice and at the price specified therein. The defendant denied that it remained open for him to do so. The claimant contended that he had not given written notice of an intention not to make the purchase, as required by s 122, with the effect that there had been no withdrawal. The judge ruled in favour of the defendant, on the basis that, in the circumstances, there had been an oral notification of the intention not to proceed, which sufficed to defeat the claim. The claimant appealed. *Held*, technically, a withdrawal within the meaning of s 122(3) had to be by notice in writing. What, however, Parliament had not sought to do was to exclude from the armoury of the court, when invited to enforce a right to buy under the 1985 Act, elementary principles of common law and equity relating to those who asserted rights which they had abandoned or waived or were estopped from asserting or which, in the light of their words or silences, actions or inactions, it would be inequitable for them to assert. There had been an express representation to the authority that the claimant and his mother did not intend to proceed with the purchase. Prima facie there was thus an express abandonment on their part of the right generated by the notice served under s 122. Accordingly, the appeal would be dismissed.

Martin v Medina Housing Association Ltd [2006] EWCA Civ 367, [2007] 1 All ER 813 (Court of Appeal: Ward and Wilson LJJ and Sir Martin Nourse).

1774 Secure tenancy—right to buy—local authority seeking possession—guidance

In an appeal brought by the claimant local housing authority, an issue arose as to how the court should proceed where a landlord applied for possession of a residential property pursuant to the Housing Act 1985 s 82 at the same time as a tenant sought to exercise his right to buy the same property pursuant to s 118. *Held*, the cases where it would not be right to hear both claims at the same time would be rare. Where each claim appeared to be well-founded, at least in the absence of the other, the court would have to carry out a balancing exercise which would involve comparing factors which were largely incommensurate with another. When considering the force of those factors in a particular case, it was necessary for the judge to look into the evidence with some care. The length of the period the tenant had occupied the property, whether it was and had been his only home for that period, the importance to the tenant of continuing to live, indeed of owning, the property which was and had been his home, and the inconvenience and disruption of moving, would depend very much on the facts of the particular case, as would the financial advantage, and indeed financial importance to the tenant, of acquiring the property at a discount. Equally, the importance to a local authority of having its housing stock fully occupied, and the efficiency with which the particular local authority deployed its housing stock, would differ from one authority to another, and would no doubt vary from time to time within a particular authority. While the depth and length of any judicial inquiry into such matters had, of course, to be limited by reference to proportionality, it would be impossible to carry out a sensible balancing exercise of the sort required in such a case without some sort of proper inquiry into such issues. Judgment would be given accordingly.

Basildon DC v Wahlen [2006] EWCA Civ 326, [2007] 1 All ER 734 (Court of Appeal: Neuberger and Moses LJJ). *Kensington and Chelsea LBC v Hislop* [2003] EWHC 2944 (Ch), [2004] 1 All ER 1036 (2004 Abr para 1751) considered.

1775 Secure tenancy—sub-tenancy—landlord and head-lessor both satisfying landlord condition—security of tenure against head-lessor

See *Kay v Lambeth LBC; Leeds City Council v Price*, para 1539.

1776 Secure tenancy—variation of terms—power to vary

A clause in a secure tenancy agreement of a local housing authority provided that the agreement could only be varied if a majority of the tenants' representatives agreed at a special meeting where 25 per cent of the representatives were present. The authority proposed unilaterally to remove the clause on the ground that it constituted an unlawful fetter on the authority's ability to vary a secure tenancy which it could only do under the Housing Act 1985 ss 102, 103. A tenant brought proceedings for judicial review of the authority's decision. *Held*, ss 102 and 103 provided for three specific ways in which a tenancy could be varied and not otherwise. A clause which purported to limit the authority's power to vary an agreement was an unlawful fetter of the authority's discretion. Such a clause was void from the outset and, therefore, could not give rise to a legitimate expectation on the part of the tenant that the authority would comply with the limitation. Accordingly, the application would be dismissed.

R (on the application of Kilby) v Basildon DC [2006] EWHC 1892 (QB), [2006] HLR 892 (Queen's Bench Division: McCombe J).

1777 Security of tenure—exceptions from secure tenancy—dwelling house leased to local housing authority—lessor's right obtain vacant possession

The Housing Act 1985 Sch 1 para 6 provides that a tenancy is not a secure tenancy if (a) the dwelling house has been leased to the landlord with vacant possession for use as temporary housing accommodation, and (b) the terms on which it has been leased include provision for the lessor to obtain vacant possession from the landlord on the expiry of a specified period or when required by the lessor.

A private landlord let a flat with vacant possession to the claimant local housing authority. The lease permitted the claimant to sublet the premises to persons requiring temporary accommodation on the understanding that any such tenancy would not benefit from the provisions relating to security in the 1985 Act by virtue of the exception in Sch 1 para 6. The lease contained provision which allowed the claimant to terminate the tenancy before the expiry of the term, but contained no corresponding provision allowing the landlord to determine the lease before the expiration of the term. The claimant granted a subtenancy to the defendant during the currency of the head lease and the subtenancy continued until after the head lease had been replaced by another on broadly the same terms as the original. Arrears of rent on the subtenancy mounted up and the claimant applied for a possession order. On the determination of the preliminary issue of whether Sch 1 para 6 applied, it was held that the defendant did not have a secure tenancy. The defendant appealed. *Held*, Sch 1 para 6(a) was concerned only with the position as between the landlord and the claimant, and it was clear that the premises had been leased to the claimant with vacant possession. The actual occupation of the defendant at any given time was immaterial. The requirement of Sch 1 para 6(b) was a single provision for the head lease to include provision for the landlord to obtain vacant possession either on the expiry of a specified period or when required by him. Since the head lease only included a provision for him to obtain vacant possession on the expiry of a specified period, that requirement had not been satisfied. Accordingly, the appeal would be allowed.

Haringey LBC v Hickey [2006] EWCA Civ 373, [2006] HLR 665 (Court of Appeal: Tuckey and Laws LJJ and Sir Martin Nourse).

1778 Tenancies—creation, terms and termination—Law Commission proposals

The Law Commission proposals, *Renting Homes: the final report* (Law Com 297), have been presented to Parliament by the Secretary of State for Constitutional Affairs and Lord Chancellor (Cm 6781). With the exception of contracts covered by other legislation (for example, business tenancies, tenancies protected by the Rent Act 1977, long tenancies and agricultural tenancies) and contracts excluded on social policy grounds (for example, tenancies and licences where no rent or other consideration is payable, holiday lets, accommodation in care institutions, accommodation in barracks, accommodation shared with a landlord), it is proposed that the scheme described in the Command Paper should apply to all contracts to occupy premises for residential purposes. There would be two types of occupation contract: (1) the 'secure contract' (modelled on the existing secure tenancy); and (2) the 'standard contract' (modelled on the existing assured shorthold tenancy). Community landlords (for example, local authorities, new town corporations, housing action trusts, urban development corporations and certain housing co-operatives) would be required in the main to enter into secure contracts. Existing tenancy agreements and licences would be converted into secure or standard contracts, except that such conversion would not be automatic in respect of agreements protected by the 1977 Act and protected agricultural occupancies would not be converted. The Commission has expressly excluded from its consideration the related issues of housing benefit and rent regulation. The position regarding Wales is unclear. If the Government of Wales Bill receives the royal assent, the subject of the Command Paper will fall within the legislative competence of the National Assembly for Wales but, nevertheless, the Commission recommends that its proposals should be implemented for both England and Wales in a single Act but that the National Assembly should be responsible for future legislative competence within the area.

Landlords would be required to provide occupiers (formally, 'contract-holders') with written statements of their contracts. Model contracts requiring the parties to complete only the front page would be prescribed and, provided that the terms relating to key matters were in plain, intelligible, language, the model contracts would not be subject to the Unfair Terms in Consumer Contracts Regulations 1999, SI 1999/2083. Use of the model forms would not be mandatory. The contracts would provide four classes of terms: (a) terms relating to key matters (for example, the address of the property, rent, effective date); (b) fundamental terms (that is, the provisions of the primary legislation which were incorporated into the contract, namely the essential rights and obligations of the parties); (c) supplementary terms (that is, provisions of delegated legislation that were incorporated into the contract, such as the obligation to pay rent and the obligation to look after the premises); and (d) additional terms (that is, specific issues which the parties chose to include in the contract, but as to which there would be no statutory provision). The parties would be able to modify most of the statutory fundamental provisions, but not those relating to prohibited conduct, to the consequences of securing the contract by deception, to survivorship, or to the effect of the death of the occupier), provided that the modification or omission enhanced the position of the occupier. The parties would also be able to modify the supplementary provisions, regardless of whether the position of the occupier would be enhanced, but any supplementary term as modified would have to comply with the 1999 Regulations. The fundamental terms of a contract would enable the parties to vary a contract after it had been agreed (for example, as to the amount of rent). Secure contracts would allow occupiers to take in lodgers. A party would be able to be added to the contract if the landlord so consented (consent not to be unreasonably withheld, but might be made subject to conditions). Consent would be deemed to have been given if a written request to add a party were not responded to in writing within a specified time. Occupiers would be permitted to provide for sub-occupation and to transfer their contracts. A joint occupier would be able to terminate his interest without ending the contract as a whole. Similarly, on the death of a joint occupier, the surviving joint occupiers would have all the rights and obligations under the contract. Where there was no joint contract, the surviving spouse or partner, on a death, would have a statutory right of succession, with priority over any other potential successor (a 'priority successor'). If there was no such person, a wider circle of people ('reserve successors') would acquire the right to succeed. It is recommended that, similarly to the current position in Scotland, certain classes of carer who have given up their own homes to look after the deceased should be included within the term 'reserve successor'.

The language of the repairing obligations of a landlord under the Landlord and Tenant Act 1985 s 11 would be modernised and the requirements adapted, regard being had also to the recommendations contained in the Law Commission report, *Landlord and Tenant: responsibility for state and condition of property* (1996, Law Com 238) (see 1996 Abr para 1854). The right to take action to enforce these provisions would be extended. No specific recommendations are made with regard to effecting improvements to property. The Law Commission recommends a new approach to prohibited behaviour. Occupiers should be prohibited from using, or threatening to use, violence against any person lawfully living in the premises, from doing anything which creates a risk of significant harm to such a person, from engaging in, or threatening to engage in, conduct capable of causing nuisance or annoyance to any person who either is living in the locality of the premises or is engaged in lawful activity in, or in the locality of, the premises, and from using, or threatening to use, the premises, or any common parts which they are entitled to use, for criminal purposes. This prohibition would be a fundamental term in all contracts. Breach of the term would be a ground for possession. The courts would also have jurisdiction to grant injunctions restraining such conduct. Community landlords and charity landlords would be able to apply to the court on this ground for an order demoting, for a trial period, a secure contract to a standard contract. Other fundamental terms of a contract would make it clear that, where a landlord was induced by deception to enter into the contract, the deception might lead to a loss of possession. In the absence of a special reason, a landlord would not be able to do anything which would interfere with the occupier's right to occupation; and the landlord's name and address would be provided as a fundamental term.

The Commission recommends the retention of the existing fundamental principles relating to terminating contracts for occupation of premises: a landlord must initiate proceedings for possession by issuing a notice (a 'possession notice') and this must be followed by appropriate court procedures. However, it is recommended that, if the possession notice is not followed by actual proceedings within six months, or four months where possession of the premises subject to a standard contract is sought on the notice-only ground, (i) the notice should lapse, (ii) proceedings should not normally be started until one month after the possession notice has been given, and (iii) landlords under standard contracts should give two months' no-fault possession notice, although it is recommended that the existing inability of a private landlord to obtain a possession order on the notice-only ground for the first six months of an assured shorthold tenancy should be abolished. The existing statutory grounds for possession should be replaced by two classes of grounds, that would become fundamental terms of the contract: (A) breach of the occupation contract; and (B) estate management grounds (for example, redevelopment, specially designed accommodation where no person in need of such is living, and under-occupied premises. In addition, landlords under standard contracts would be able to rely on the mandatory notice-only ground for possession and the mandatory serious rent arrears ground. The Commission also recommends that the exercise of discretion in possession cases should be structured in order to ensure that the court consciously balances the interests of those threatened with eviction against the interests of the landlord and also, perhaps, the interests of other occupiers who have paid rent on time. A new procedure is proposed to enable landlords to regain possession without court proceedings where premises have been abandoned.

A draft Bill which, if enacted, would implement the recommendations is appended to the report.

LEGAL AID

Halsbury's Laws of England (4th edn) vol 27(3) (Reissue) paras 2001–2223

Articles

For articles relating to this title please refer to the Table of Articles at the beginning of the Abridgment.

1779   Civil proceedings—costs—charge on property—estoppel

A discretionary trust provided for three classes of beneficiaries, one of which included the defendants, the settlor's two children, and a third party. Notwithstanding the definition in the trust deed of the class of beneficiaries, no person who was or would be an excepted person would be a beneficiary. The trustees appointed the defendants and the third party to be beneficiaries and reclassified the other two classes of beneficiaries so that they became 'excepted persons'. Seven years later, breach of trust proceedings were commenced against the trustees by the defendants, the third party and a company. The prayer for relief was on behalf of the trust and/or the company. No indication was given in the pleading that any other person or body was a beneficiary or likely beneficiary under the trust. During part of the proceedings, the defendants were recipients of legal aid from the claimant in excess of £700,000. A further seven years later, proceedings came to an end. By virtue of an agreement, a payment of £1·5m was to be made to the defendants' solicitors to hold to the order of new trustees on the terms of the trust subject to the payment of the claimant of any sums due under statutory charges in force in relation to the proceedings. The agreement stated that the defendants and the third party were beneficiaries under the trust and that, at the date of the agreement, there were no other beneficiaries. The claimant alleged that the sum of £1·5m had become subject to a statutory charge under the Legal Aid Act 1988 s 16(6) when it was paid to the defendants' solicitors, and that the representation that the defendants and the third party were the only beneficiaries under the trust estopped them from alleging that there were other beneficiaries or potential beneficiaries under the trust. *Held*, a person recovered property for himself for the purposes of s 16(6) if a sum of money was paid over either to him or another provided the payment was made by an opposing party to the litigation to benefit the legally assisted person. In making a judgment about whether the payment did benefit the legally assisted person, the court should look at the realities behind the judgment or agreement in question. In making that assessment, it should take into account the relevant factual circumstances, including the evidence and pleadings in the litigation for which legal aid was granted. The defendants had recovered property for themselves as a consequence of the payment to the trustees under the agreement and, consequently, the claimant could invoke s 16(6). The defendants had made a representation on which the claimant had relied. The ingredients for estoppel having thereby been established, the defendants were estopped from alleging that there were other beneficiaries or potential beneficiaries under the trust. Accordingly, the application would be allowed.

Legal Services Commission v Marchioness [2006] All ER (D) 124 (Dec) (Chancery Division: Judge Wyn Williams QC). *Hanlon v Law Society* [1981] AC 124, HL (1980 Abr para 1790); and *Manley v Law Society* [1981] 1 All ER 401, CA (1980 Abr para 1787), applied.

1988 Act s 16 replaced by Access to Justice Act 1999 s 10.

1780 Community Legal Service—financial—eligibility limits and thresholds

The Community Legal Service (Financial) (Amendment) Regulations 2006, SI 2006/713 (in force on 10 April 2006), further amend the 2000 Regulations, SI 2000/516, so as to (1) increase the financial eligibility limits for monthly and disposable income; (2) make provision for persons in receipt of specified benefits to be taken as automatically satisfying the financial eligibility requirements; and (3) increase the capital limit for asylum claims.

The Community Legal Service (Financial) (Amendment No 2) Regulations 2006, SI 2006/2363 (in force on 2 October 2006), further amend the 2000 Regulations supra so as to (1) include proceedings under the Civil Partnership Act 2004 in the definition of 'family proceedings'; (2) increase the range of legal help available to those in receipt of certain benefits provided under the Immigration and Asylum Act 1999; and (3) transfer (a) the power to disapply certain eligibility limits in relation to applications for funding of services at inquests to the Legal Services Commission in limited circumstances; and (b) the power to waive part or all of contributions that may be payable is transferred to the Lord Chancellor in limited circumstances.

1781 Community Legal Service—funding—counsel in family proceedings

The Community Legal Service (Funding) (Counsel in Family Proceedings) (Amendment) Order 2006, SI 2006/2364 (in force on 2 October 2006), further amends the 2001 Order, SI 2001/1077, by changing the references to those within the Legal Services Commission who are responsible for considering certain claims, applications and appeals.

1782 Community Legal Service—funding—exception

The Community Legal Service (Funding) (Amendment) Order 2006, SI 2006/2366 (in force on 2 October 2006), further amends the 2000 Order, SI 2000/627, by providing that contracts for Community Legal Advice Centres and Community Legal Advice Networks are an exception to the limitation on the powers of the Legal Services Commission to pay remuneration under contract for the provision of funded services

1783 Criminal Defence Service—financial eligibility

The Criminal Defence Service (Financial Eligibility) Regulations 2006, SI 2006/2492 (in force on 2 October 2006), set out the criteria relating to financial eligibility which must be satisfied before individuals involved in criminal proceedings in a magistrates' court may receive publicly funded representation. Specifically, the regulations provide that (1) an individual in receipt of certain benefits such as income support is automatically eligible, as are those under the age of 16 or under the age of 18 and in full-time education; (2) If the individual has a partner, the partner's resources are to be treated as those of the individual, unless the partner has a contrary interest in the proceedings; (3) an individual may be required to provide evidence in support of his application, and in failing to do so, the representation authority, the Legal Services Commission or its delegate, will withdraw a representation order if previously granted; (4) an individual is financially eligible for a representation order if his gross income, adjusted to take account of any partner or children living with him, is £11,590 or less, and ineligible if it is £20,740 or more;.(5) where an individual's gross income falls between such amounts, the individual is eligible if his annual disposable income does not exceed £3,156; (6) where there is a change in an individual's financial circumstances which might affect his eligibility for a representation order, he must notify the representation authority of the change if he has been granted a representation order, and he may make a renewed application if his previous application had been refused because he was financially ineligible; (7) an individual may apply to the representation authority for the review of a decision that he is financially ineligible, on the grounds that his income has been miscalculated and may also apply to the Commission, notwithstanding that he is financially ineligible, on the grounds that he can nevertheless not afford to pay for legal assistance; and (8) the Commission may refer a question arising on a review to the High Court for a decision.

1784 Criminal Defence Service—funding

The Criminal Defence Service (Funding) (Amendment) Order 2006, SI 2006/389 (in force on 13 March 2006), further amends the 2001 Order, SI 2001/855, so as to confer on solicitors a right to apply for the reclassification of certain offences when having their fees determined.

1785 Criminal Defence Service—representation

The Criminal Defence Service (General) (No 2) (Amendment) Regulations 2006, SI 2006/2490 (in force on 2 October 2006), further amend the 2001 Regulations, SI 2001/1437, so as to (1) take account of the transfer of responsibility for granting rights to representation in criminal proceedings in magistrates' court from the court to the Legal Services Commission; (2) remove the requirement that application for representation orders be made on a prescribed form; and (3) make provision that where a representation order is withdrawn and a new order granted, the same representative should usually be appointed.

1786 Criminal Defence Service—representation orders—appeals

The Criminal Defence Service (Representation Orders: Appeals etc) Regulations 2006, SI 2006/2494 (in force on 2 October 2006), provide for appeals or renewed applications where an individual involved in criminal proceedings has been refused publicly funded representation on the grounds that the interests of justice do not require him to be granted an order giving a right to such representation.

1787 Criminal Defence Service Act 2006

The Criminal Defence Service Act 2006 makes provision about representation funded as part of the Criminal Defence Service. The Act received the royal assent on 30 March 2006 and came into force in part on that day. The remaining provisions came into force on 2 October 2006: SI 2006/2491. For details of commencement, see the commencement table in the title STATUTES.

Section 1 deals with the grant of rights to representation, and enables regulations to be made to provide the Legal Services Commission with the powers to grant and withdraw rights to representation. Section 2 provides for rights to representation to be granted only where an individual satisfies financial eligibility criteria. Section 3 deals with the making of contribution orders against individuals who have been granted public funding. Section 4 makes consequential amendments, and s 5 deals with short title, commencement and extent.

Amendments, repeals and revocations

Specific provisions of the Access to Justice Act 1999 are added or amended: ss 17, 17A, 25, 26, Schs 1, 3.

1788 Criminal proceedings—legal representation—appropriate number of counsel— budgetary considerations

See *R v Azam*, para 832.

1789 Criminal proceedings—Legal Services Commission—publicly funded representations

The Criminal Defence Service (Representation Orders and Consequential Amendments) Regulations 2006, SI 2006/2493 (in force on 2 October 2006), (1) empower the Legal Services Commission, instead of the court, to grant a right to publicly funded representation in criminal proceedings in a magistrates' court where it does not already have the power; (2) provide for a representation order to extend to the Crown Court if the proceedings are to continue there; and (3) make amendments to legislation consequential on the transfer of responsibility for granting representation orders from the court to the Commission.

1790 Reform—government intentions

The Secretary of State for Constitutional Affairs and the Lord Chancellor has presented to Parliament the government's plans for reforming the current system of legal aid, *Legal Aid Reform: the way ahead* (Cm 6993). This follows a consultation paper and the review of legal aid procurement by Lord Carter of Coles. Although opposition has been expressed to the concept of fixed and graduated fees for legal aid, the government has stated the principles on which its approach to buying legal aid will be based: a focus on service to the client rather than simply on the hours worked; best value competition based on quality, price and capacity; fixed and graduated fees to manage the transitional period, both to prime the market and stabilise spending, subject to exceptional circumstances and particular local market conditions; and measures to ensure financial stability both in the transitional period and in the long term.

Fixed fees for legal aid work in police stations will be introduced from October 2007, prior to the introduction of competitive tendering on an area basis from October 2008. Revised standard fees (rolling up travel and waiting payments) will be introduced in magistrates' courts from April 2007, and competitive tendering will be introduced from October 2008. A revised graduated fees scheme, incorporating fees for many ancillary hearings in the revised fees, for advocates will be introduced from April 2007; the lead advocate will control the pre-trial phase, will be responsible for the conduct of the case advocacy and will manage any sub-contracted payment. A panel of 'very high cost cases' providers will be introduced and a litigators' graduated fees scheme will be introduced from October 2007 for all Crown Court cases not individually contracted out to such defence teams. This scheme will replace the present scheme in which fees are paid ex post facto in non-contracted cases. Further consultation is required as to the qualifications of the defence teams and the selection process to be followed. A single graduated fees scheme will be introduced by October 2008 that will combine fees for both litigators and advocates and commence competitive tendering.

The Legal Services Commission will consult on new proposals for a family private representation scheme with a view to implementing the scheme in April 2008. In anticipation of those proposals, in April 2007 the rates for solicitors in private family law cases in the county court and in the family proceedings court will be harmonised. Early in 2007, further consultations will be held on a revised graduated fees scheme for care proceedings and a revised scheme for family help—private. There will also be consultation on proposals for advocacy fees for solicitors and barristers in both care proceedings and private family law. The current tailored fixed fee scheme will continue to be applicable until October 2007 and current payments to 'not for profit' providers will continue until that date. On 1 October 2007, a replacement tailored fixed fee scheme applicable to solicitors and the 'not for profit' sector will take effect. Details of the replacement scheme are set out. Changes to the proposed schemes for immigration and asylum cases, and for mental health cases, are expected to be announced with a view to implementation in October 2007.

A new unified contract will take effect on 1 April 2007 for civil providers (solicitors and the 'not for profit' sector), and on 1 April 2008 for providers in criminal cases. The unified contract will contain revised standard terms, but the contract specifications will remain largely in their current form until the introduction, in October 2007, of the new fees schemes.

A detailed timetable for the proposed changes is set out.

LIBEL AND SLANDER

Halsbury's Laws of England (4th edn) vol 28 (Reissue) paras 1–400

Articles

For articles relating to this title please refer to the Table of Articles at the beginning of the Abridgment.

1791   Damages—award—offer of amends—effect of mitigation on amount of compensation

A newspaper, of which the first defendant was the owner and publisher, and the second defendant, the editor, published an article shortly after a bomb attack on the London Underground linking the claimant journalist to the attacks. After the claimant commenced libel proceedings, the newspaper printed an apology and the first defendant made an unqualified offer of amends. Neither the first nor the second defendant took part in the litigation and default judgment was entered against the second defendant. The issue to be decided was the assessment of compensation, due from the first defendant under the Defamation Act 1996 s 3 in accordance with the offer of amends procedure, and of damages against the second defendant. *Held,* there was a cap on the amount of compensation payable by a defendant who had the benefit of statutory protection, but there was room for the overall compensation in respect of the libel to be fixed at a higher figure. Special care was required to ensure that there was no double counting or other inconsistency in arriving at that total. It was clear that a defendant who had not made an offer of amends was not entitled to the benefits which flowed specifically from the statutory procedure. In the present case, the libel was exceptionally grave. The distress caused to the claimant would have been real, lasting and severe. Therefore, the appropriate starting point was £180,000. To the extent that the newspaper had published an apology, there was some mitigation. The delay and dismissive attitude of the defendants were, however, aggravating factors. In relation to the first defendant, the appropriate discount under the offer of amends procedure was one-third. With regard to the second defendant, damages would be assessed at £175,000. Therefore, the defendants were jointly and severally liable in the sum of £175,000. Judgment would be given accordingly.

Veliu v Mazrekaj [2006] EWHC 1710 (QB), [2006] All ER (D) 129 (Jul) (Queen's Bench Division: Eady J).

1792   Defamation—damages—offer of amends—mitigation

The claimant sought damages for libel from the first defendant, a newspaper publisher, and the second defendant, the claimant's former wife, in connection with an article published in the defendant's newspaper alleging that, by introducing the second defendant to certain individuals, the claimant had ruined his marriage to the second defendant. The defendant made an unqualified offer to make amends under the Defamation Act 1996 s 2, giving notice that, if agreement on compensation could not be reached and the issue had to be decided by the court, further matters would be relied on. A correction and apology were published but compensation was not agreed. The judge awarded compensation under s 3(5) and the claimant appealed. It fell to be determined whether the principle that evidence of specific acts of misconduct by the claimant could not be put in on the issue of damages applied. *Held*, the principle was based on concern about the risks of 'trials within a trial', a concern which the court was now better equipped to deal with than in the past because of its case management powers. The principle had never been absolute. One major exception was in respect of evidence of particular acts of misconduct put before the jury in support of a plea of justification or fair comment that had then failed. The basis for that exception lay in the direct relevance such evidence was likely to have to the subject matter of the defamatory words. It did not make sense for the jury to consider damages when a defence had been struck out before the calling of evidence, when directly relevant background evidence on damages was regularly allowed to be taken into account in cases where it related to a defence subsequently struck out by the judge or rejected by the jury. If evidence was to be admissible, it had to be evidence which was so clearly relevant to the subject matter of the libel or to the claimant's reputation or sensitivity in that part of his life that there would be a real risk of the jury assessing damages on a false basis if they were kept in ignorance of the facts to which the evidence related. As no defence had been offered, there would have been no opportunity for evidence of specific acts of misconduct on the part of the claimant to have been put before the court in support of a plea of justification or fair comment or to show lack of malice. The defendant would have been deprived of that opportunity. Moreover, in 'offer of amends' cases the claimant's reputation had been repaired to the full extent that was possible by means of a suitable correction and apology. Consequently, injury to feelings tended to play a more significant part in the assessment of statutory compensation than was normally the case in the determination of damages in litigation, particularly where the claimant was not well-known. In determining the extent of the injury to the claimant's feelings, evidence about his past conduct in that aspect of his life that was the subject matter of the libel might be particularly relevant. The judge had been entitled to admit in evidence the matters relied on in mitigation by the defendant. Accordingly, the appeal would be dismissed.

Turner v News Group Newspapers Ltd [2006] EWCA Civ 540, [2006] 4 All ER 613 (Court of Appeal: Pill, Keene and Moses LJJ). *Plato Films Ltd v Speidel* [1961] AC 1090, HL; *Burstein v Times Newspapers Ltd* [2002] EWCA Civ 1739, [2001] 1 WLR 579 (2002 Abr para 2818); and *Scott v Sampson* (1882) 8 QBD 491, DC, considered.

1793   Defence—fair comment—facts relied on—facts not referred to in defamatory statement—existence of facts at date of publication

The claimant brought proceedings in libel in respect of an article which appeared in a newspaper published by the defendant. The defendant claimed that the article amounted to fair comment on a matter of public interest. The claimant sought to strike out various parts of the defence, in particular complaining of the claimant's attempt to introduce a range of alleged facts which was not to referred to or indicated in the article. The question therefore arose whether a defendant could rely on facts, in support of a plea of fair comment, if they were not referred to or indicated in the words complained of themselves. A further issue arose as to how far a defendant had to show that the author of the words complained of was aware, at the time of publication, of the facts sought to be relied on in the defence to support the comment. *Held*, having regard to the right of freedom of expression, the right to comment freely on matters of public interest would be far too circumscribed if it were a necessary ingredient of the defence of fair comment that the commentator should be confined to pleading the facts stated in the words complained of. Facts pleaded to support fair comment had to have existed at the time of publication and had to have been known, at least in general terms, when the comment was made, although it was not necessary that they should all have been in the forefront of the commentator's mind. Further, a commentator could rely on a specific or a general fact even if he had forgotten it, because it might have contributed to the formation of his opinion. The purpose of the defence of fair comment was to protect honest expressions of opinion on, or inferences honestly drawn from, specific facts. The ultimate test was the objective one of whether someone could have expressed the commentator's defamatory opinion or drawn the inference on the facts known to the commentator, at least in general terms, on which he was purporting to comment. Applying those principles, a number of passages in the defendant's pleadings would be struck out. Judgment would be given accordingly.

Lowe v Associated Newspapers Ltd [2006] EWHC 320 (QB), [2006] 3 All ER 357 (Queen's Bench Division: Eady J). *Cohen v Daily Telegraph Ltd* [1968] 2 All ER 407, CA, considered.

1794   Defence—innocent dissemination—publisher—internet service provider

The claimant brought libel proceedings for statements hosted on websites which he claimed were the responsibility of the individual defendants since they published the words complained of via the services provided by the relevant internet service provider ('ISP'). The claimant also sought damages against the ISP defendants. The ISP defendants applied for orders that the claims against them be struck out or dismissed on a summary basis. It fell to be determined whether the provider of such services could be liable in respect of material which was simply communicated via the services which they provided. *Held*, an ISP which performed no more than a passive role in facilitating postings on the internet could not be deemed to be a publisher at common law and no liability for libel could attach to such a person. In order to impose legal responsibility on anyone under common law for the publication of words, it was essential to demonstrate a degree of awareness, or at least an assumption, of general responsibility. Although it was not always necessary to be aware of defamatory content to be liable for defamatory publication, for a person to be held responsible, there had to be knowing involvement in the process of publication of the relevant words. In the present case, the claimant had no realistic prospect of being able to establish that any of the ISP defendants had knowingly participated in the relevant publications. Judgment would be given accordingly.

Bunt v Tilley [2006] EWHC 407 (QB), [2006] 3 All ER 336 (Queen's Bench Division: Eady J). *Emmens v Pottle* (1885) 16 QBD 354, CA; and *McLeod v St Aubyn* [1899] AC 549, PC, considered; *Godfrey v Demon Internet Ltd* [1999] 4 All ER 342 (1999 Abr para 2137) distinguished.

1795   Defence—privilege—qualified privilege—allegations of feud—political party

The claimants, two brothers who were active members of the British National Party ('BNP'), made a complaint regarding a series of articles by the defendants which covered what was described as a feud between different factions of the BNP. The claimants alleged that the words used had the natural and ordinary meaning that the first claimant stole money collected at a BNP rally and did not return it until he was threatened with being reported to the police and that both claimants threatened to kneecap, torture and kill two other BNP members and their families, and might be subject to police investigation. The defendant raised a plea of justification and alternatively a plea of qualified privilege. *Held*, all who ventured into public life in a modern democracy had to expect to have their motives subject to scrutiny and discussion, and politicians had to accept robust criticism. Political commentators had a duty to cover the goings-on in political parties, including disputes fully and impartially. The public, especially those who had a vote, had a legitimate interest to have such information available. While there was no general category of privilege attached to political speech, it was obvious that an important factor in determining the merits of a privilege plea would be the political significance of a publication. While the reporting of both sides in a disinterested way was an important element in the doctrine of reportage, a journalist or publisher would not be deprived of the opportunity of such a defence merely by reason of having a particular personal or corporate stance. What was important was the way in which a particular dispute or controversy was reported, rather than the political stance of the defendant. The defendant was far from neutral as far as BNP and the readers of the words were concerned, but that did not mean that he was incapable of objective and disinterested reporting of what went on within the party and readers would be well aware that he was merely reporting the conflicting positions rather than taking sides. The reader would be interested in the allegations and cross-allegations of criminal offences and not necessarily their truth or falsity. The party had presented itself before the electorate of London and in that context the readers were entitled to know about the allegations. Accordingly, the complaint would be dismissed.

Roberts v Gable [2006] EWHC 1025 (QB), [2006] EMLR 692 (Queen's Bench Division: Eady J). *Al-Fagih v HH Saudi Research and Marketing (UK) Ltd* [2001] EWCA Civ 1634, [2002] EMLR 215 applied. *Reynolds v Times Newspapers Ltd* [2001] 2 AC 127, HL (1999 Abr para 2135), considered.

1796   Defence—privilege—qualified privilege—availability—statement at election

The claimant had been a candidate in a local government by-election. She brought proceedings for libel against the defendants, a rival candidate and his election agent, in respect of words contained in one of their party's leaflets. The defendants sought permission to amend their defence to add a plea of qualified privilege to the original pleas of justification and fair comment. The claimant contended that the defence was precluded by the Defamation Act 1952 s 10, which provided that a defamatory statement published by or on behalf of any candidate in any election to a local government authority or Parliament was not to be deemed to be published on a privileged occasion on the ground that it was material to a question in issue in the election. The court considered as a preliminary issue whether that was the effect of s 10, in light of the court's duty under the Human Rights Act 1998 s 3 to give effect to legislation, so far as it was possible, in a way that was compatible with the right to a fair hearing and to freedom of expression under the European Convention on Human Rights arts 6, 10. *Held*, the 1952 Act *s* 10 did not preclude an election candidate from relying on the defence of qualified privilege. A candidate could not claim a special privilege by virtue only of publishing words that were material to a question in issue in the election, but he might be able to establish a defence of qualified privilege if the ingredients recognised at common law were present on the facts of the case. The 1952 Act did not specify that a candidate should be confined to the defences of fair comment and justification. Therefore, there was no difficulty in interpreting s 10 in a way that was compatible with Convention rights. It followed that the pleaded defence of privilege was not barred. Judgment would be given accordingly.

Culnane v Morris [2005] EWHC 2438 (QB), [2006] 2 All ER 149 (Queen's Bench Division: Eady J). *Plummer v Charman* [1962] 3 All ER 823, CA, not followed.

1797   Defence—privilege—qualified privilege—duty of newspaper to publish

The defendant, a newspaper publisher, printed articles concerning the claimant member of Parliament's involvement with Iraq against the background of the invasion of that country by coalition forces. The articles were said to be based on papers found in government offices. The claimant sought damages in libel. The defendant did not seek to plead justification but raised the defences of qualified privilege and fair comment. The judge allowed the claim and awarded damages to the claimant. On the defendant's appeal, an issue arose as to whether the judge had erred in the amount of damages he had awarded. The defendant submitted that the newspaper would have been entitled to publish the contents of the papers as reportage, and that damages should only take account of any marginal damage to the claimant's reputation over and above that occasioned by the papers themselves, of which he did not complain. *Held,* the newspaper had not merely reported what the papers said but had adopted and embellished them. It had alleged that the claimant had taken money from the Iraqi oil-for-food programme. That was not a mere repeat of the papers. Whatever the precise line between fact and comment, the allegations which the judge had considered not to be protected by qualified privilege were allegations of fact and opinion. Further, while it could not be said that the issues, which had been complained of, did not contain comment or that some of that comment was not honest comment, that did not affect the validity of the judge's decision, which was based on his conclusion that the key allegations were allegations of fact. In those circumstances, the appeal could not succeed on the defence of fair comment once it had been held that qualified privilege failed. As to damages, it was the function of the judge to assess them on the basis of the damage to the claimant's reputation caused by the articles complained of and held to be defamatory. It was not his role to assess what damage might have been suffered to his reputation if the newspaper had published different articles which contained defamatory material, but in respect of which it had a good defence of qualified privilege. Accordingly, the appeal would be dismissed.

Galloway v Telegraph Group Ltd [2006] EWCA Civ 17, [2006] All ER (D) 178 (Jan) (Court of Appeal: Sir Anthony Clarke MR, Chadwick and Laws LJJ). Decision of Eady J (2004 Abr para 1777) [2004] EWHC 2786 (QB), [2004] All ER (D) 33 (Dec) affirmed.

1798   Defence—privilege—qualified privilege—public interest

The claimants, who were the owner and director of a Saudi Arabian company, instituted libel proceedings against the defendant newspaper. The claimants alleged that the defendant had published an article that implied the claimants had terrorist links. The jury found the article to be defamatory of the claimants, and the judge dismissed the defence of qualified privilege based on publication in the public interest. The defendant's appeal against that decision was dismissed and, on its further appeal, *held,* in deciding whether the defendant could rely on the public interest defence, the first question was whether the subject matter of the article was a matter of public interest, which was a question for the judge. In answering that question, it was not helpful to apply the classic test for the existence of a privileged occasion and ask whether there was a duty to communicate the information and an interest in receiving it. The defence was developed from the traditional form of privilege by a generalisation that, in matters of public interest, there could be said to be a professional duty on the part of journalists to impart the information and an interest in the public in receiving it. That generalisation having been made, it should be regarded as a proposition of law and not decided each time as a question of fact. If the publication was in the public interest, the duty and interest were taken to exist. If the article as a whole concerned a matter of public interest, the next question was whether the inclusion of the defamatory statement was justifiable. On that question, allowance had to be made for editorial judgment. The inquiry then shifted to whether the steps taken to gather and publish the information were responsible and fair. Although previous case law had established a non-exhaustive list of ten matters which should in suitable cases be taken into account in deciding the issue of responsible journalism, they were not tests which the publication had to pass. The standard of conduct required of the newspaper had to be applied in a practical and flexible manner. There was no basis for rejecting the public interest defence in the instant case, and, accordingly, the appeal would be allowed.

Jameel v Wall Street Journal Europe Sprl [2006] UKHL 44, [2006] 4 All ER 1279 (House of Lords: Lords Bingham of Cornhill, Hoffmann, Hope of Craighead and Scott of Foscote and Baroness Hale of Richmond). *Reynolds v Times Newspapers Ltd* [1999] 4 All ER 609 (1999 Abr para 2135) applied. Decision of Court of Appeal [2005] EWCA Civ 74, [2005] QB 904 (2005 Abr para 1994) reversed.

1799   Libel—publication—Internet publication—substantial publication within jurisdiction—rebuttable presumption

The claimant initiated libel proceedings against the defendants, a French national resident in Switzerland and a Swiss company, in respect of two reports on their website. The defendants denied

that there had been a publication on the website within the court's jurisdiction. The claimant applied
to strike out that part of the defence, or alternatively for summary judgment, and argued that he
could rely on a rebuttable presumption that substantial publication of the item had taken place
within the court's jurisdiction, as it had been published on an Internet site open to general access.
Held, in a case of Internet libel, the claimant was not entitled to rely on a presumption of law that
the publication had been to a substantial but unquantifiable number of people within the
jurisdiction. Rather, it was for the claimant to prove that the material in question had been accessed
and downloaded. It would not be right at the interim stage to conclude that it would be perverse for
a jury to draw any other inference than that there had been substantial publication within the
jurisdiction and, accordingly, the application would be dismissed.

Al Amoudi v Brisard [2006] EWHC 1062 (QB), [2006] 3 All ER 294 (Queen's Bench Division:
Gray J). *Loutchansky v Times Newspapers Ltd (No 2)* [2001] EWCA Civ 536, [2001] 4 All ER 115
(2001 Abr para 2044) applied. *Fullam v Newcastle Chronicle and Journal Ltd* [1977] 3 All ER 32, CA
(1977 Abr para 1716), distinguished.

1800   Malicious falsehood—slander of title—reasonableness of belief—reliance on legal advice

See *Assured Quality Construction Ltd v Thompson*, para 2884.

1801   Trial—preliminary hearing—need for jury—case requiring prolonged examination of documents

See *Armstrong v Times Newspapers Ltd*, para 1737.

LIBRARIES AND OTHER SCIENTIFIC AND CULTURAL INSTITUTIONS

Halsbury's Laws of England (4th edn) vol 28 (Reissue) paras 401–700

1802   Museums—Natural History Museum—authorised repositories

The Natural History Museum (Authorised Repositories) Order 2006, SI 2006/1547 (in force on
10 July 2006), amends the British Museum Act 1963 so as to alter the description of the Natural
History Museum's authorised repository in South Kensington.

1803   National Endowment for Science, Technology and the Arts—amount of endowment

The National Endowment for Science, Technology and the Arts (Increase of Endowment)
Order 2006, SI 2006/396 (in force on 17 February 2006), permits the Secretary of State to increase
the amount of the endowment of the National Endowment for Science, Technology and the Arts to
£75,000,000, payable out of the money held in the National Lottery Distribution Fund and
allocated for expenditure on or connected with health, education or the environment.

1804   National Lottery—distribution fund—allocation of funds—sport

See para 309.

1805   Public Lending Right Scheme—commencement of variation

The Public Lending Right Scheme 1982 (Commencement of Variation) Order 2006, SI 2006/3294
(in force on 2 January 2007), gives effect to a variation of the Public Lending Right Scheme 1982
which increases the rate per loan from 5·57p to 5·98p.

LICENSING

Halsbury's Laws of England (4th edn) vol 6 (2003 Reissue) paras 224–247, vol 26 (2004 Reissue)
paras 1–500

Articles

For articles relating to this title please refer to the Table of Articles at the beginning of the
Abridgment.

1806   Clubs—licence

See CLUBS.

1807   Gambling—licence

See BETTING, GAMING AND LOTTERIES.

1808   Intoxicating liquor—licence

See INTOXICATING LIQUOR.

1809   Public houses—licensing authority—duties—promotion of licensing objectives

See R (*on the application of JD Wetherspoon plc*) *v GBC*, para 1735.

1810   Public houses—sale of liquor—non-domestic rating—England

The Licensing Act 2003 (Consequential Amendment) (Non-Domestic Rating) (Public Houses in England) Order 2006, SI 2006/591 (in force on 31 March 2006), makes consequential amendments to the Non-Domestic Rating (Public Houses and Petrol Filling Stations) (England) Order 2001, SI 2001/1345, to take account of the commencement of the Licensing Act 2003. The order provides that the definition of a 'public house' is intended to include any premises in respect of which there is in force a premises licence under the 2003 Act authorising the retail sale of alcohol for consumption on the premises, or for consumption both on and off the premises, and excludes cases where the licence contains conditions restricting alcohol sales to customers in premises being used as a restaurant, hotel or boarding house.

LIEN

Halsbury's Laws of England (4th edn) vol 28 (Reissue) paras 701–800

1811   Insurance broker—lien over insurance policy

See *Heath Lambert Ltd v Sociedad de Corretaje de Seguros*, para 1725.

LIMITATION OF ACTIONS

Halsbury's Laws of England (4th edn) vol 28 (Reissue) paras 801–1136

Articles

For articles relating to this title please refer to the Table of Articles at the beginning of the Abridgment.

1812   Limitation period—expiry—addition of new claim—claim against one defendant based on facts advanced by another defendant

The Limitation Act 1980 s 35(4), (5) provides that rules of court may provide for allowing a new claim to be made where, in the case of a claim involving a new cause of action, the new cause of action arises out of the same facts or substantially the same facts as are already in issue on any claim previously made in the original action.

The claimant was the owner of a plot of land on which construction works were taking place. The first defendant was employed as piling contractor and the second defendant provided structural engineering services in relation to the works. A neighbouring building suffered damage on two occasions which was said to have been caused by the piling works. The claimant brought proceedings close to the expiry of the limitation period and, consequently, was unable to comply with the relevant pre-action protocol. In its particulars of claim, the claimant alleged that the first defendant was liable in negligence and breach of contract for the first incident and that the second defendant was similarly liable for the second incident. In its defence, the second defendant asserted that it was in fact the first defendant that was liable in negligence and breach of contract for the second incident. The claimant sought permission to amend its particulars of claim by adding those matters pleaded by the second defendant as a fresh claim against the first defendant after the expiry of the limitation period. The first defendant argued that, in view of the 1980 Act s 35(5), a claimant could not adopt the facts pleaded by one defendant by way of defence as a fresh claim against another defendant, after the expiry of the relevant limitation period. *Held*, s 35(5) gave the court a discretion, after the expiry of the limitation period, to allow a claimant to plead a new cause of action that arose out of substantially the same facts as had been put in issue by the defence of any defendant. It was not open to a court of first instance to put a gloss on the Court of Appeal's formulation or to read in words that would narrow its effect. Further, the rationale behind the exception in s 35(5) to the limitation principle was that, once particular facts were in issue and fell to be investigated, the claimant should be entitled to rely on any cause of action arising out of those facts. Such considerations were equally valid whether the facts had been put in issue by one or other or both defendants, and the need to protect defendants against fresh claims made after the expiry of the limitation period was much less when the court was bound to investigate the facts underlying those claims in any event. Finally, the court retained a discretion whether to grant the amendments sought, and would act to protect a defendant against any injustice by refusing permission to amend. Judgment would be given accordingly.

Charles Church Developments Ltd v Stent Foundations [2006] All ER (D) 54 (Dec) (Queen's Bench Division: Jackson J).

1813   Limitation period—expiry—discretion to disapply

The Limitation Act 1980 s 33(3)(a) provides that, in considering whether to exclude the time limit for actions in respect of personal injuries or death and to permit an action to proceed, the court must have regard to all the circumstances of the case, and in particular to the length of, and the reasons for, the delay on the plaintiff's part.

The claimant was injured when a vehicle driven by the defendant smashed into the rear of her car. The defendant's insurers wrote to the claimant's solicitors informing them that liability was not disputed and setting in train the obtaining of medical reports. The solicitor's clerk dealing with the claimant's case neglected, however, to issue the claim in the county court until after the primary three year limitation period provided by the 1980 Act s 11(4). The claimant was led to believe that all was proceeding smoothly, but at court her claim was struck out by the district judge of his own motion. The claimant then issued a second set of proceedings, which gave rise to the question of whether the court had the discretion to disapply the limitation period pursuant to s 33, or whether a claimant who had actually started an action before the expiry of the primary limitation period had not been prejudiced by s 11, and therefore could not bring himself within the provisions of s 33(3). The judge decided that the court did not have the discretion pursuant to s 33 to disapply s 11. On the claimant's appeal, *held*, the principle that the court had no discretion under s 33 if the claimant had begun an action between the same parties within the primary period of three years had to be confined to that narrow situation. In the instant case, that situation had not arisen, and it followed that the judge had erred in applying the rule. The court had, therefore, to exercise its own discretion as to whether it would be equitable to allow the claimant's action to proceed. In the circumstances, to refuse to allow the claim to proceed would give a totally unexpected windfall benefit for the defendant's insurers, which was not a satisfactory solution. Looking at the case in the round, justice and fairness dictated that it would be equitable that the claimant be permitted to proceed with her action because the prejudice to the defendant did not outweigh the prejudice to the claimant in having her claim struck out as time-barred. Accordingly, the appeal would be allowed.

Adams v Ali [2006] EWCA Civ 91, [2006] 1 WLR 1330 (Court of Appeal: Ward, Arden and Dyson LJJ). *Walkley v Precision Forgings Ltd* [1979] 2 All ER 548, HL (1979 Abr para 1761), distinguished.

1814   Limitation period—expiry—discretion to extend—personal injury or death—writ issued in time in first action—second action

The claimant was injured in a road traffic accident for which the first defendant, who was not insured, was responsible. The Motor Insurer's Bureau ('MIB') made an interim payment to the claimant. Two days before the expiry of the three-year limitation period for a personal injury action contained in the Limitation Act 1980 s 11, the claimant issued proceedings against the first defendant. However, the claimant failed to serve the requisite notice on the MIB. Having been joined as a party to the proceedings, the MIB denied liability, relying on the failure to comply with the notice condition, and counterclaimed for return of the interim payment. Subsequently, the claimant issued duplicate proceedings against the first defendant, this time giving the necessary notice to the MIB, which was also joined as a party to the second action. Its defence was that the action was statute-barred by s 11. The claimant sought an order under s 33 disapplying the ordinary three-year time limit. The judge ruled that he was precluded by a previous House of Lords decision from exercising the power conferred on the court by s 33. The claimant's appeal to the Court of Appeal was dismissed on account of that decision but permission to appeal to the House of Lords was granted. The MIB cross-appealed. *Held,* while the House of Lords had exercised sparingly its power to depart from its own precedent and it had never been thought enough to justify doing so that a later generation of law lords would have resolved an issue differently from their predecessors, too rigid an adherence to precedent might lead to injustice in a particular case and unduly restrict the development of the law. The present case was not one in which contracts or fiscal arrangements had been entered into on the faith of a settled rule. If the court departed from the previous authority, there would be no detriment to public administration. The previous authority should be departed from as it unfairly deprived claimants of a right Parliament had intended them to have and had driven the Court of Appeal to draw distinctions which were so fine as to reflect no credit on the present area of law. Therefore, the case would be remitted to the original court for the judge to resolve the application under s 33. Accordingly, the appeal would be allowed and the cross-appeal dismissed.

Horton v Sadler [2006] UKHL 27, [2006] 3 All ER 1177 (House of Lords: Lords Bingham of Cornhill, Hoffmann, Rodger of Earlsferry, Carswell and Brown of Eaton-under-Heywood). *Walkley v Precision Forgings Ltd* [1979] 2 All ER 548, HL (1979 Abr para 1761), overruled. Decision of Court of Appeal [2004] EWCA Civ 936, [2004] All ER (D) 322 (Jun) reversed.

The claimant's husband was killed when the car driven by him collided with a car driven by the first defendant, who was uninsured. The claimant brought a claim against the first defendant. It was a condition precedent of the Motor Insurers' Bureau ('MIB') that the claimant had to give timely notice to the MIB for it to meet any liability established against the first defendant. The claimant failed to do this. Subsequently, the claimant discontinued the claim and commenced a second action, outside the three-year limitation period, against the first defendant although on this occasion timely notice was given to the MIB. The second action was struck out as an abuse of process. The claimant appealed. *Held*, the object of the notice provision was to ensure that the MIB was able to intervene in order to defend a claim and to prevent the entry of a default judgment, rather than to prevent stale claims. The past custom of the MIB was that it was common for a claimant, who failed to comply with the MIB's notice requirements, to discontinue an action and commence a second action. The MIB had previously made no objection to this procedure when the second action had been within the limitation period and had, on occasion, decided not to take any point on the lateness of notice, so as to save the claimant the trouble of commencing fresh proceedings. There was no objection in principle to the claimant discontinuing proceedings and commencing a fresh action, in which a timely notice was given to the MIB. Therefore, the action should not have been struck out on the ground of abuse of process. Accordingly, the appeal would be allowed.

Richardson v Watson [2006] EWCA Civ 1662, (2006) Times, 13 December (Court of Appeal: Lord Phillips of Worth Matravers CJ, Scott Baker and Leveson LJJ).

1815 Limitation period—expiry—mortgage debt—documents amounting to acknowledgments

The claimant was the mortgagee of a property under a mortgage created by the defendant to secure repayment of the sum advanced towards the purchase of the property. Payments under the mortgage fell into arrears. Ten months after the last payment had been made, following a possession order, the property was sold leaving a shortfall. Eleven years and nine months later, the claimant issued proceedings seeking recovery of the debt. The defendant argued that the claim was statute-barred by the Limitation Act 1980 since the 12-year period prescribed by s 20(1) for recovering the principal mortgage debt had started to run on the date of the last payment so that, but for any acknowledgment of the debt under s 29(5), time would have expired before the issue of the proceedings. The claimant relied on correspondence between the parties nearly two years before the issue of the proceedings as constituting an acknowledgment of the debt for the purposes of the 1980 Act. The judge held that although the final letter was written without prejudice and therefore inadmissible, the earlier letter was not and it followed that the claim was not statute-barred. The defendant appealed successfully. The claimant's appeal to the Court of Appeal was unsuccessful. On further appeal by the claimant, *held*, the without prejudice rule had no application to open communications designed to discuss the repayment of an admitted liability rather than to negotiate a disputed liability. It was impossible to regard the correspondence as constituting negotiations aimed at settlement. Nor did the underlying public policy justification for the rule appear to have any application in such circumstances. That justification rested on the desirability of preventing statements made in the course of negotiations for settlement being brought before the court as admissions on the question of liability. No statements had been made with a view to settling a dispute since the debt had been admitted. Some acknowledgments would attract without privilege protection but those would be cases where the extent of the liability was genuinely in dispute and the parties were attempting to settle that difference. Accordingly, the appeal would be allowed.

Bradford & Bingley plc v Rashid [2006] UKHL 37, [2006] 4 All ER 705 (House of Lords: Lords Hoffmann, Hope of Craighead, Walker of Gestingthorpe, Brown of Eaton-under-Heywood and Mance). Decision of Court of Appeal [2005] EWCA Civ 1080, [2005] All ER (D) 330 (Jul) reversed.

1816 Limitation period—expiry—new claim—substitution of party—mistake

The Limitation Act 1980 s 35(4), (5)(b) provides that a new claim involving a new party may be made if the addition or substitution of the new party is necessary for the determination of the original action. The addition or substitution of a new party is not necessary for the determination of the original action unless the new party is substituted for a party whose name was given in any claim made in the original action in mistake for the new party's name: s 35(6)(a).

The claimant suffered severe brain damage after receiving two doses of a vaccine. He commenced proceedings against the defendant, which he believed to be the manufacturer of the vaccine. In fact, the vaccine was manufactured by another company. The claimant therefore applied to substitute the actual manufacturer for the defendant in the claim. However, the application was made after the ten-year limitation period under the Consumer Protection Act 1987 had expired. The claimant submitted that the substitution was necessary for the determination of the original action so that the claim was effectively a new one for the purposes of the 1980 Act s 35(5). *Held*, the express words of s 35(6)(a) could not be interpreted as meaning that, notwithstanding that the name of the defendant was given in a claim made in the original action in mistake for the name of another person, the condition was nevertheless not satisfied where the claimant was not under any mistake about the identity of the party against whom it was intending to proceed at the time when the relevant limitation period expired. Moreover, the true construction of s 35(4)–(6) was that, where the new party was to be substituted for a party whose name had been given in a claim in the original action in mistake for the new party's name, substitution was to be regarded as necessary for the determination of the original action. On that basis, the conclusion that the defendant's name had been given in a claim made in the original action in mistake for the name of the actual manufacturer necessarily meant that the substitution was to be regarded as necessary for the determination of the original action. Accordingly, the application would be allowed.

O'Byrne v Aventis Pasteur MSD Ltd [2006] EWHC 2562 (QB), (2006) 92 BMLR 130 (Queen's Bench Division: Teare J). *Morgan Est (Scotland) Ltd v Hanson Concrete Products Ltd* [2005] EWCA Civ 134, [2005] 3 All ER 135 (2005 Abr para 2497) considered.

1817   Limitation period—expiry—trust property—fraudulent breach of trust—dishonest assistance claim

The deceased had appointed the first defendant, a solicitor, and his partners as the executors and trustees of his will. After the death of the deceased, the first defendant had duly undertaken the administration of the deceased's estate. Over a period of nine years, the first defendant misappropriated a substantial sum out of the assets of the estate. The claimants, who had been appointed trustees of the estate, commenced proceedings for damages arising from the first defendant's breaches of trust. A compromise was reached with all the defendants apart from the twelfth defendant, the first defendant's wife. The claimants commenced new proceedings against the twelfth defendant alone for damages arising from her knowing assistance in the fraudulent breaches of trust by the first defendant. Preliminary issues arose as to the scope of the Limitation Act 1980 s 21(1)(a), (3). It fell to be determined whether s 21(1)(a) applied to dishonest assistance claims with the consequence that there was no applicable period of limitation, and if the dishonest assistance claims were subject to the six-year primary limitation under s 21(3), whether time had begun to run given that there were beneficiaries entitled to a future interest in the trust property, which interest had not yet fallen into possession. *Held,* s 21(1)(a) only applied to claims against express trustees and category one trustees. The case against the twelfth defendant with regard to the dishonest assistance claims could not fall within category one since there was no pre-existing trust relationship on her part which had arisen before the transactions occurred. Therefore, s 21(1)(a) did not apply to the dishonest assistance claims and the normal primary period of limitation of six years from the date of the accrual of the cause of action applied. However, s 21(3) applied to the claim brought by the trustees. The claimants, as trustees, had no personal interest in the outcome. The real litigants were the beneficiaries. When s 21(3) referred to an action by beneficiaries, it included at least by analogy, actions brought exclusively on their behalf by trustees who did not have a personal interest in the outcome. It followed that s 21(3) applied to postpone the running of the primary period of limitation with regard to the beneficiaries with future interests so that the second proceedings were not time-barred. Judgment would be given accordingly.

Cattley v Pollard [2006] EWHC 3130 (Ch), [2006] All ER (D) 106 (Dec) (Chancery Division: Richard Sheldon QC).

1818   Limitation period—personal injuries—discretion to disapply time limit—proper exercise

The claimant, who had used vibrating equipment at work for more than 20 years, began to experience tingling and numbness in his fingers. No action was taken in connection with the condition, however, until approximately ten years later when a nurse conducting a routine health care assessment decided to refer the claimant's case to a doctor. The doctor wrote to the claimant telling him that he had some symptoms that might be attributable to exposure to vibration at work, and he examined the claimant shortly afterwards. The doctor then wrote to the claimant confirming that he was suffering from hand-arm vibration syndrome and that he would be reviewed again clinically in a year. The defendants, the claimant's employers, knew of the need for that review, but in the event the matter was not revisited until three years later. Almost a year after that, the claimant commenced legal proceedings against the defendants. At a preliminary hearing, the judge decided that the limitation period started to run, at the very latest, on receipt of the doctor's second letter, meaning that the limitation period had expired. However, the judge decided to exercise her discretion under the Limitation Act 1980 s 33 to disapply the primary provisions in relation to limitation so that the action could proceed. The defendants appealed, relying on Court of Appeal authority supporting the proposition that the discretion under s 33 should be exercised only if the case merited 'exceptional indulgence' to the claimant. *Held,* the words 'exceptional indulgence' meant no more than an indulgence that represented an exception to the general rule that a claim should be brought within the primary limitation period. Inevitably, that cast a burden on the claimant to demonstrate good reason to justify the exception, but that burden was itself not intended to suggest that it had necessarily become more difficult since it was first introduced. The discretion remained unfettered but its exercise required justification. The judge correctly identified the approach required by the 1980 Act and analysed the specific factors identified as relevant, particularly the fact that the occupational physician who had been engaged by the defendants had specifically raised the possibility of hand-arm vibration syndrome and suggested a review after one year, but that the defendants had not ensured that the claimant had such a review. Accordingly, the appeal would be dismissed.

Kew v Bettamix Ltd (formerly Tarmac Roadstone Southern Ltd) [2006] EWCA Civ 1535, [2006] All ER (D) 173 (Nov) (Court of Appeal: Waller and Leveson LJJ).

1819   Limitation period—time from which period runs—action on a specialty

See *Hill v Spread Trustee Co Ltd*, para 278.

1820   Limitation period—time from which period runs—action to recover contribution

The Limitation Act 1980 s 10(1) provides that, where under the Civil Liability (Contribution) Act 1978 any person becomes entitled to a right to recover contribution in respect of any damage from any other person, no action to recover contribution by virtue of that right may be brought after the expiration of two years from the date on which that right accrued. If the person in question is held liable in respect of that damage, the date on which a right to recover contribution in respect of any damage accrues to any person is the date on which the judgment is given, or the date of the award (as the case may be), and for this purpose no account is to be taken of any judgment or award given or made on appeal in so far as it varies the amount of damages awarded against the person in question: 1980 Act s 10(2), (3).

An employee of the claimant company was injured at work by a lift installed and maintained by the first and second defendant companies. The employee obtained judgment on liability against the claimant with damages to be assessed. It was not until more than two years later that damages were assessed. Four months after the date of assessment, the claimant brought a claim against the first and second defendants for contribution under the 1978 Act s 1. A preliminary issue arose whether the two-year period of limitation for contribution proceedings prescribed by the 1980 Act s 10 ran from the date of a judgment on liability with damages to be assessed or from the date of assessment of those damages. The judge decided that the two-year limitation period ran from the date of judgment on liability, and the claimant appealed. *Held*, the judgment or award referred to in s 10(3) as setting the relevant date for the running of time against a tortfeasor who sought contribution under the 1978 Act was a judgment or award which ascertained the quantum, and not merely the existence, of the tortfeasor's liability. The reference in the postscript to s 10(3) to a judgment or award varying the amount of damages was suggestive of the underlying assumption that the judgment or award already referred to earlier in s 10(3) was a judgment or award which ascertained damages. That pointer was underlined, but more strongly, by s 10(4). Where there was no judgment or award, but the victim's claim was dealt with simply by agreement, the relevant date was the earliest date on which the amount to be paid was agreed, and that was so whether liability was admitted or not. Accordingly, the appeal would be allowed.

Aer Lingus plc v Gildacroft Ltd [2006] EWCA Civ 4, [2006] 2 All ER 290 (Court of Appeal: Sir Anthony Clarke MR, Rix and Moore-Bick LJJ). Decision of Simon J [2005] EWHC 1556 (QB), [2005] All ER (D) 278 (Jun) (2005 Abr para 2013) reversed.

1821   Limitation period—time from which period runs—administration of estates

The Limitation Act 1980 s 22(a) provides that no action in respect of any claim to the personal estate of a deceased person or to any share or interest in any such estate, whether under a will or on intestacy, may be brought after the expiration of 12 years from the date on which the right to receive the share or interest accrued.

The deceased died intestate and the defendant was granted letters of administration the following year. Twelve years later, the claimants commenced proceedings for the removal of the defendant as personal representative, the appointment of an independent solicitor in her place and an account of administration. The judge decided that the proceedings were not time-barred under the 1980 Act s 22(a) as time did not start running until the end of the 'executor's year' provided for by the Administration of Estates Act 1925 under which the executor was not bound to distribute the estate of the deceased before the expiration of one year from death. The judge also held that, if he were wrong, the claim would fall within the 1980 Act s 21(1)(b), which provided that no limitation period in the 1980 Act applied to the recovery of trust property from the trustee. The defendant appealed. *Held*, proceedings to remove the personal representative of an intestate and appoint a substitute in his place did not fall within s 22(a). The primary remedy for a beneficiary who complained of an unjustified delay by an administrator in getting in the assets, paying the administration expenses and debts and distributing the residuary estate was an administration action. The power to remove and replace a personal representative was exercisable in circumstances where the beneficiary could have commenced an administration action. In a case where time would not run against the beneficiary in an administration action there was no reason why it should run if the only relief sought was the replacement of the personal representative. Parliament had not contemplated that s 22(a) would apply to claims against the personal representative of an intestate in relation to real estate which remained unsold or at a time when the estate remained unadministered. Where s 22(a) applied, the period would not begin to run until the administrator had paid the costs, funeral and testamentary and administration expenses, debts and other liabilities properly payable out of the assets in his hands and other liabilities properly payable out of the assets in his hands, and had provided for the payment of any pecuniary legacies, as until then he would not be in a position to distribute the residuary estate. Section 22(a) had no application to the claim to remove the defendant as administratix. The claims against the defendant to an account and payment were claims in relation to real and personal property which had come into her hands as administratix and fell within s 21(1)(b) so that no period of limitation prescribed by the 1980 Act applied. As they were claims within s 21(1)(b) they were not claims to which s 22 had any application. Accordingly, the appeal would be dismissed.

Re Loftus (deceased); Green v Gaul [2006] EWCA Civ 1124, (2006) 9 ITELR 107 (Court of Appeal: Chadwick, Thomas and Lloyd LJJ). *Re Pauling's Settlement Trusts, Younghusband v Coutts & Co* [1964] Ch 303, CA; and *Gwembe Valley Development Co Ltd v Koshy (No 3)* [2003] EWCA Civ 1048, [2004] 1 BCLC 131 (2003 Abr para 1726) considered. Decision of Lawrence Collins J [2005] EWHC 406 (Ch), [2005] 2 All ER 700 (2005 Abr para 2014) affirmed.

1822   Limitation period—time from which period runs—deliberate concealment of facts— validity of certificate of quality

The defendant issued a certificate of quality in respect of a cargo of gasoline. However, the defendant had applied the incorrect test when testing the fuel, and in fact the cargo did not meet the required specification. The claimant sold the cargo under a contract stating that the cargo met the specification. When it emerged that the defendant had applied the wrong test, a retest was taken which confirmed that the fuel did not meet the standard for certification. The claimant, who was aware only that the wrong test had been applied, contacted the defendant, but the defendant informed the claimant that it was standing by the certificate. On the basis of that statement, the claimant issued a claim under the tort of deceit against the defendant, alleging that it had implied that the certificate was valid, which had induced the claimant to rely on it in its dealings with the purchaser of the cargo. The judge decided that the defendant was reckless as to the truth of the implied representation so that it was liable for the claimant's financial losses. The defendant appealed, arguing that the judge had been wrong in making the finding of deceit, and that, as the claim had been brought more than six years after the representation had been made, the claim was time-barred in respect of any of its causes of action apart from deceit. The claimant contended that there had been deliberate concealment by the defendant within the meaning of the Limitation Act 1980 s 32, with the effect that the time limit did not apply. *Held*, the judge had not been entitled to come to the conclusion which he had in relation to deceit. The representation found had been imprecise and, in an action for deceit, unfairly so. The representation that the certificate was valid had not been expressly or even impliedly made, but had been derived as a matter of overall impression. The defendant had not made the representation which the judge had found him to have made, and in any event the judge had not found with sufficient clarity a representation of fact which was false in a sense which the claimant had sought to make the basis of its claim in deceit. However, the defendant had been under a duty to reveal to the claimant the existence and content of the retests. The accuracy of a certificate to buyers and sub-buyers was clearly important. Not only as a matter of law, but also commercially, it challenged reality to think that a certifier, armed with tests that suggested that the tests used to complete the certificate had or might have produced incorrect results, could nonetheless simply do nothing about it, and in particular could properly say nothing about those tests to those who had employed him to certify. It followed that, for the purposes of s 32, the judge had been entitled to find that the defendant had deliberately concealed the holding and results of the retests. Accordingly, the appeal would be allowed in part.

AIC Ltd v ITS Testing Services (UK) Ltd, The Kriti Palm [2006] EWCA Civ 1601, [2006] All ER (D) 381 (Nov) (Court of Appeal: Buxton and Rix LJJ and Sir Martin Nourse).

1823   Limitation period—time from which period runs—extension of time limit—meaning of original time limit

See *BUPA Care Homes (BNH) Ltd v Cann*, para 1225.

1824   Limitation period—time from which period runs—knowledge required for bringing action—knowledge of relevant damage

The Limitation Act 1980 s 14A(6)(a) provides that the knowledge required for bringing an action for damages in respect of the relevant damage means knowledge of the material facts about the damage in respect of which damages are claimed. The material facts about the damage are such facts as would lead a reasonable person who had suffered such damage to consider it sufficiently serious to justify his instituting proceedings: s 14A(7).

The defendant, a firm of solicitors, had advised the claimants in relation to a corporate restructure. The claimants had sought to defer to a later date their option as tenants to break a lease, and the landlord had agreed in principle. However, as a result of the restructure, the benefit of break clauses in a lease had been lost. One of the claimants' in-house solicitors had become aware of this on a date soon afterwards ('the relevant date'). The landlord subsequently resiled from the agreement in principle. A little over three years after the relevant date, the claimants brought proceedings in negligence and for breach of duty under the retainer against the defendant. The judge found that the claimants had had the knowledge required for bringing an action for damages in respect of the relevant damage, for the purposes of the 1980 Act s 14A(5), on the relevant date, such that their claim was out of time. The claimants appealed, arguing that the loss of the options to break the lease was not relevant damage because they had not been aware that the landlord would rely on that loss. They contended that it was not until they had become aware that the landlord intended to resile from the agreement in principle that they had knowledge of the damage sufficient to satisfy s 14A(7). *Held*, it was impossible to contend that the loss of the options was not relevant damage for the purpose of the knowledge required by s 14A(7), since the relevant damage in that context was the damage in respect of which damages were claimed. It was also impossible to contend that the landlord's agreement in principle to the deferment, at a time when it thought that the options were exercisable, could have been taken as any indication that it would be willing to affirm that agreement once it knew that the options were not exercisable. The claimants had had knowledge sufficient to satisfy s 14A(7) on the relevant date and, accordingly, the appeal would be dismissed.

3M United Kingdom plc v Linklaters & Paines [2006] EWCA Civ 530, [2006] 28 EG 106 (Court of Appeal: Chadwick, Wall and Moore-Bick LJJ). *Dobbie v Medway Health Authority* [1994] 4 All ER 450, CA (1994 Abr para 1830), applied.

1825 Limitation period—time from which period runs—knowledge required for bringing action—negligent advice

The Limitation Act 1980 s 14A(5) provides that the starting date for reckoning the period of limitation where the facts relevant to the cause of action are not known at the date of accrual of the cause of action is the earliest date on which the plaintiff first had both the knowledge required for bringing an action and a right to bring such an action. Such knowledge must be of both the material facts about the damage in respect of which damages are claimed, and of the other facts relevant to the current action mentioned in s 14A(8): s 14A(6). The other facts referred to in s 14A(6) are that the damage was attributable in whole or in part to the act or omission which is alleged to constitute negligence: s 14A(8).

The claimant acquired the controlling interest in an agricultural machinery company which he knew from the outset would require the injection of a large amount of additional capital before it turned to profitability. In the event, despite further substantial cash injections in the following four years, it failed. Throughout the whole course of the enterprise the claimant had been advised by the defendant firm of accountants. Three years before he issued proceedings against the defendant, which was the date at which the claimant's knowledge fell to be considered for the purposes of the 1980 Act s 14A, the claimant knew that the moneys injected had become lost to him and the company was hopelessly insolvent. He believed, however, that his losses were to be explained not by any deficiency in the advice he had received when making his investments, but rather by a variety of damaging economic factors. It was not until six months later that the claimant first began to question the soundness of the defendant's investment advice and only then did the investigations start which finally led to the issue of a negligence claim against the defendant. The defendant pleaded that any claims for breaches of contractual duty occurring, and any tortious claims for losses accruing, prior to the three years before the claim were statute-barred. In reply the claimant pleaded that the earliest date on which he had the knowledge referred to in s 14A(5) was the later date. The judge decided the issue in favour of the defendant, but that decision was reversed on the claimant's appeal. The defendant appealed. *Held*, in order for the defendant to be able to rely on s 14A(8), what the claimant had to know to set time running was the essence of the act or omission to which his damage was attributable, the substance of what ultimately came to be pleaded as his case in negligence. The language and intent of s 14A(8) were clear: in addition to having knowledge of the material facts about the damage, a claimant had to know that there was a real possibility the damage was caused by the acts or omissions alleged to have constituted negligence. The claimant's damage was alleged to have been caused by some flaw or inadequacy in his advisers' investment advice; that was the essence of the claimant's claim. There was nothing latent about the damage, or about the identity of the prospective defendant. Time started to run against the claimant when he knew enough for it to be reasonable for him to embark on preliminary investigations into that possibility. It had been reasonable for the claimant to do so long before the point at which the disparity between the defendant's advice and the company's disastrous losses became absolutely apparent. It followed that the claimant had failed to discharge the burden of proof resting on him. Accordingly, the appeal would be allowed.

Haward v Fawcetts [2006] UKHL 9, [2006] 3 All ER 497 (House of Lords: Lords Nicholls of Birkenhead, Scott of Foscote, Walker of Gestingthorpe, Brown of Eaton-under-Heywood and Mance).

1826 Limitation period—time from which period runs—mistake—payment of tax

See *Deutsche Morgan Grenfell Group plc v IRC*, para 2458.

1827   Limitation period—time from which period runs—mortgage—right to receive—charging order made over property

The Limitation Act 1980 s 20(1) provides that no action may be brought to recover (1) any principal sum of money secured by a mortgage or other charge on property; or (2) proceeds of the sale of land, after the expiration of 12 years from the date on which the right to receive the money accrued.

A bankrupt and his partner bought a property in their joint names with the assistance of a mortgage. A bankruptcy order was made against the bankrupt and a trustee in bankruptcy was appointed. The trustee applied for an order for possession of the property. Two years later, an order was made pursuant to the Insolvency Act 1986 s 313 imposing a charge on the bankrupt's property and removing it from the bankrupt's estate. More than 12 years after the making of that order, the trustee applied for orders of possession and sale of the property on the ground that, after repayment of the mortgage on the property, there was an equity available for the benefit of the bankrupt's creditors. The bankrupt contended that the application was time-barred pursuant to the 1980 Act s 20(1), as the order made under the 1986 Act s 313 amounted to an action for the purposes of the 1980 Act s 20(1). That argument was rejected by the registrar, but the bankrupt's appeal against that decision was allowed. The trustee appealed. *Held*, the right to receive under the 1986 Act s 313 had not accrued for the purposes of the 1980 Act s 20(1) and would not do so until an order for the sale of the property was made by the court. If s 20(1) was to apply, the 'right to receive' had to be a present rather than a deferred right, and it had to have accrued when the order for the charge was made. It was quite inconsistent with the purpose of the 1986 Act s 313 that there should be a right to receive any money at that stage. The only source of payment was the proceeds of sale of the property subject to the charge; but the whole object of s 313 was to defer the realisation of the property until the circumstances justified its sale. No interest was payable in the meantime because it was rolled up until sale. Since the true view was that a charge imposed by an order made under s 313 secured a future obligation, no right to receive the principal sum secured could accrue until the obligation became a present one. In the case of charges imposed by orders made under s 313, the right to receive could not predate an order for the sale of the property. It followed that time had not started to run under s 20(1) and, accordingly, the appeal would be dismissed.

Gotham v Doodes [2006] EWCA Civ 1080, [2007] 1 All ER 527 (Court of Appeal: Sir Andrew Morritt C, Carnwath and Moses LJJ).

1828   Limitation period—time from which period runs—negligence—damage—contingent liability

A solicitor misappropriated significant sums from his client account over a number of years. Throughout that time, the solicitor delivered to the claimant an annual accountant's report, prepared by the defendant firm of accountants, which certified that the solicitor's books and accounts had been examined and there had been compliance with the relevant regulations. Relying on those reports, the claimant made no investigation into the solicitor's practice. Over the course of the following months, several of the solicitor's clients brought complaints against the solicitor and sought to recover sums from the Solicitors' Compensation Fund. The claimant wrote to the defendant saying that it proposed to hold it liable for payments which had to be made out of the fund, which it said were attributable to the negligent reports. The claim form was eventually issued more than six years after the last act of misappropriation. The defendant therefore argued that the claims were statute-barred, and a preliminary issue was tried as to the date that the cause of action accrued. The judge decided that the limitation period had expired, but his decision was reversed on appeal. The defendant appealed, contending that the damage had occurred in its entirety at the time of misappropriation, notwithstanding that the claims were brought afterwards. *Held*, incurring a contingent liability was not, as such, actionable damage. Where there was a purely contingent obligation, no actual damage would be sustained until the contingency was fulfilled and the loss became actual and, until that happened, the loss was prospective and might never be incurred. The existence of a contingent liability might depress the value of other property or it might mean that a party to a bilateral transaction had received less than he should have done, or was worse off than if he had not entered into the transaction, according to what was the appropriate measure of damages in the circumstances. By virtue of the terms of the fund rules, the solicitor's misappropriations gave rise to the possibility of a liability to pay a grant out of the fund, contingent on the misappropriation not being otherwise made good and a claim in the proper form being made. Such a liability would be enforceable only in public law, by judicial review, but would still count as damage. Nevertheless, until a claim was actually made, no loss or damage was sustained by the fund. It followed that the cause of action in tort did not accrue in the claimant's favour against the defendant until it first received a claim on its fund from one of the solicitor's clients. Accordingly, the appeal would be dismissed.

Law Society v Sephton & Co (a firm) [2006] UKHL 22, [2006] 2 AC 543 (House of Lords: Lords Hoffmann, Scott of Foscote, Rodger of Earlsferry, Walker of Gestingthorpe and Mance). Decision of Court of Appeal [2004] EWCA Civ 1627, [2005] QB 1013 (2004 Abr para 1806) affirmed.

1829   Limitation period—time from which period runs—personal injury—actual and constructive knowledge—sexual abuse

The claimant had been resident at the first defendant's school, where he alleged that he had suffered physical and sexual abuse. He subsequently attended an institution run by the third defendant, where the claimant alleged that he suffered sexual abuse by an officer of the institution. After leaving the institution, the claimant led a normal life but, following a chance meeting with the officer who had abused him, the claimant suffered a breakdown. The police made inquiries into the conduct of certain individuals, the perpetrators of the abuses, although not as a result of any approach by the claimant. After the police had interviewed him, the claimant decided to seek justice by pursuing those individuals in the criminal courts. He was advised that he might have a civil claim but that he should await the outcome of the criminal trial. Those individuals were convicted on several counts of cruelty, buggery and indecent assault, some of which related to the claimant. The claimant issued proceedings relying on an expert report which said that the claimant was suffering from post-traumatic stress disorder. The claimant alleged that it was only after reading the report that he knew what had happened to him. It fell to be determined whether the action was time-barred under the Limitation Act 1980. The judge held that the claimant had first known that he had a significant injury when he spoke to the police so that the claim had been started within the three-year limitation period. He also ruled, however, that had it been necessary he would not have exercised his discretion under s 33 to extend time. The defendants appealed and the claimant cross-appealed against the s 33 decision. *Held*, the approach of authority to reasonableness indicated that, if a person who had suffered a particular type of injury would reasonably be inhibited by the injury itself from instituting proceedings, then that was a factor that should be taken into account in deciding whether he would have considered it sufficiently serious to justify proceedings. The standard that had to be applied was that of the reasonable behaviour of a victim of child abuse who had suffered the degree of injury suffered by the claimant in question and of which he had knowledge. It would be a question of fact in each case. It made no sense to say that, in deciding whether a claimant would reasonably consider an injury to be sufficiently serious to justify litigation, the court should take account of the intelligence and personal characteristics of the claimant. The claimant had obtained his knowledge within the months following the chance meeting more than six years before he commenced proceedings. Therefore, the judge had not erred in his exercise of discretion under s 33. Accordingly, the appeal would be allowed and the cross-appeal dismissed.

Young v South Tyneside MBC [2006] EWCA Civ 1534, [2007] 1 All ER 895 (Court of Appeal: Buxton and Dyson LJJ and Sir Peter Gibson).

1830   Limitation period—time from which period runs—sums recoverable by statute

See *Revenue and Customs Comrs v Hyde Industrial Holdings Ltd*, para 2637.

1831   Limitation period—trespass to the person—sexual assault

In each of three conjoined appeals the claimants sought damages for harm caused by incidents of sexual assault occurring several years earlier. The court in each case dismissed the claim on the basis of a decision of the House of Lords that an action based on an intentional sexual assault was subject to a non-extendable six-year limitation period, rather than the extendable three-year time limit prescribed by the Limitation Act s 11(1) in respect of actions for negligence, nuisance and breach of duty. The claimants appealed, contending that the decision was no longer valid as s 11(1) should be construed differently in the light of the Human Rights Act 1998 s 3, and because it could be distinguished on the basis that the claimant in that case could also rely on a breach or breaches of a duty of care that did not arise solely in connection with the deliberate act or acts of trespass to the person. *Held*, it was not open to the court to depart from the House of Lords' decision, at least absent the 1998 Act. In that respect, s 3 did not apply to the instant facts to enable a different interpretation of the 1980 Act s 11(1), since to give it that effect would interfere with the defendants' accrued right to say that the claim was time-barred under the 1980 Act s 2. The 1998 Act did not retrospectively confer on a claimant a cause of action which he would not otherwise have had, and the same applied to accrued defences. Moreover, the basis of the decision of the House of Lords was that the 1980 Act s 11(1) did not apply to the claim of deliberate sexual abuse because it did not give rise to an action for damages for negligence, nuisance, or breach of duty. Applying that test, each of the cases fell outside s 11(1). Accordingly, the appeals would be dismissed.

A v Hoare; H v Suffolk CC; X and Y v Wandsworth LBC [2006] EWCA Civ 395, [2006] 1 WLR 2320 (Court of Appeal: Sir Anthony Clarke MR, Brooke and Arden LJJ). *Stubbings v Webb* [1993] 1 All ER 322, HL (2002 Abr para 1629), applied. Decision of Jack J in *A v Hoare* [2005] EWHC 2161 (QB), [2005] All ER (D) 150 (Oct) (2005 Abr para 1720) affirmed.

LOCAL GOVERNMENT

Halsbury's Laws of England (4th edn) vol 29(1) (Reissue) paras 1–714

Articles

For articles relating to this title please refer to the Table of Articles at the beginning of the Abridgment.

1832   Council tax

See RATING AND COUNCIL TAX.

1833   Employment—early termination—discretionary compensation

The Local Government (Early Termination of Employment) (Discretionary Compensation) (England and Wales) Regulations 2006, SI 2006/2914 (in force on 29 November 2006), replace the 2000 Regulations, SI 2000/1410, and apply to those persons whose local government employment is terminated on or after 1 October 2006 by reason of redundancy, in the interests of the service or where a joint appointment comes to an end. In particular, the regulations (1) confer a power on an employing authority to increase a redundancy payment made under the Employment Rights Act 1996; (2) allow an employer to award compensation in the form of a lump sum of an amount that must not exceed 104 weeks' pay; (3) require each employing authority to have and publish a policy that they apply in the exercise of their discretionary powers; (4) provide that any payments made must not be met out of any local government pension scheme funds; and (5) provide for transitional provisions. SI 2002/769 is revoked.

1834   Finance—accounts and audit—England

The Accounts and Audit (Amendment) (England) Regulations 2006, SI 2006/564 (in force on 1 April 2006), further amend the 2003 Regulations, SI 2003/533, so as to (1) substitute new definitions of 'working day', 'relevant body', 'small relevant body' and 'responsible financial officer'; (2) provide that any reference to a relevant body is to be read, in relation to a parish meeting, as a reference to the chairman of that meeting; (3) require the findings of reviews of the system of internal control to be considered by a committee of the relevant body or by members of the body meeting as a whole; (4) change references to 'proper practices' to 'proper practices in relation to accounts' and 'proper practices in relation to internal control', as appropriate; (5) require bodies to review their system of internal audit once a year and require the findings of the review to be considered by a committee of the body or by the body as a whole, as part of the consideration of the system of internal control; (6) provide for the statement of accounts of passenger transport executives to be no less informative than statements prepared under the Companies Act 1985; (7) require passenger transport executives to charge retirement benefits to a revenue account; (8) require smaller relevant bodies to prepare statements of accounts for approval by June of each year, instead of September; (9) require the publication of a statement of accounts of a smaller relevant body to be by September rather than December, with the change to be phased in over three years; (10) alter the reference to the annual letter to local government bodies; and (11) make a minor change in relation to joint committees. SI 1983/1849 is revoked.

1835   Finance—calculation of budgetary requirements—England

The Local Authorities (Alteration of Requisite Calculations) (England) Regulations 2006, SI 2006/247 (in force on 8 February 2006), which apply to the financial year beginning on 1 April 2006, modify provisions in the Local Government Finance Act 1992 and the Greater London Authority Act 1999, which relate to the calculation of budgetary requirements, so as to (1) omit references to "relevant special grants" since no special grants are being defined as relevant special grants for the financial year; (2) alter, for authorities in England, the definition of 'police grant'; and (3) add, for authorities in England, definitions of sums payable in respect of redistributed non-domestic rates and revenue support grant to ensure that the amounts of redistributed non-domestic rates and revenue support grant excluded from the budget requirement calculation relate only to such amounts payable under the Local Government Finance Report (England) 2006/2007.

1836   Finance—calculation of budgetary requirements—Wales

The Local Authorities (Alteration of Requisite Calculations) (Wales) Regulations 2006, SI 2006/344 (in force on 15 February 2006), which apply to the financial year beginning on 1 April 2006, modify provisions in the Local Government Finance Act 1992, which relate to the calculation of budgetary requirements, so as to (1) omit references to "relevant special grants" since no special grants are being defined as relevant special grants for the financial year; (2) add, for billing authorities and major precepting authorities in Wales, definitions of sums payable in respect of redistributed non-domestic rates and revenue support grant to ensure that the amounts of redistributed non-domestic rates and revenue support grant excluded from the budget requirement calculation relate only to such amounts payable under the Local Government Finance Reports for the year 2006–2007; and (3) add a definition of 'floor funding' and provide that such major precepting authorities in Wales must take into account any floor funding received from the Secretary of State for the financial year 2006–2007 when making the required calculations for that year.

1837   Finance—capital finance and accounting—Wales

The Local Authorities (Capital Finance and Accounting) (Wales) (Amendment) Regulations 2006, SI 2006/944 (in force on 1 April 2006), further amend the 2003 Regulations SI 2003/3239, so as to (1) add a definition of 'small scale disposal' as a disposal by a local authority of an interest in housing land where the National Assembly for Wales has consented to the disposal subject to the local authority being satisfied that the majority of secure and introductory tenants are not opposed to it and where the aggregate number of dwelling-houses disposed of by the local authority in the five year period ending on the date of disposal does not exceed 499; (2) provide for small scale disposals to be excluded from the requirements to pool receipts from the disposals of housing land; (3) exclude small scale disposals for which notional capital receipts have to be determined under the 2003 Regulations; (4) treat a payment of a levy on a disposal under the Leasehold Reform, Housing and Urban Development Act 1993 as capital expenditure; (5) ensure that, in relation to the calculation of minimum revenue, any change in the housing capital finance requirement will not affect the council fund capital finance requirement calculation or the council fund minimum revenue provision calculation; and (6) provide that a local authority in Wales is only required to make pooling contributions to the National Assembly where that local authority's existing opening housing revenue account ('HRA') capital financing requirement, or that local authority's HRA subsidy capital financing requirement, is nil, or a negative amount.

1838   Finance—levies—joint waste disposal authorities—England

The Joint Waste Disposal Authorities (Levies) (England) Regulations 2006, SI 2006/248 (in force on 1 March 2006), which apply to England only, confer a power on joint waste disposal authorities established under the Waste Regulation and Disposal (Authorities) Order 1985, SI 1985/1884, to issue levies on their constituent councils for the purpose of meeting their expenses in respect of financial years beginning on or after 1 April 2006 where, but for the Local Government Finance Act 1988 s 117, they would have a power to require the councils to pay those expenses. The regulations make provision, in particular, as to (1) when levies are to be issued; (2) the apportionment of levies between authorities, including special provisions for the Greater Manchester Waste Disposal Authority; (3) interest on unpaid levies; (4) the anticipation of levies; and (5) transitional provisions providing for the Levying Bodies (General) Regulations 1992, SI 1992/2903, to cease to apply to levies issued or anticipated by joint waste disposal authorities in respect of any financial year commencing on or after 1 April 2006 except as specified.

1839   Local authority—access to information—variation

The Local Government (Access to Information) (Variation) Order 2006, SI 2006/88 (in force on 1 March 2006), amends the Local Government Act 1972 in relation to access to exempt information, by (1) replacing descriptions of information listed with simpler and clearer descriptions; (2) replacing some of the previous qualifications with a public interest test, with the effect that information will be exempt information if and so long as in all the circumstances of the case, the public interest in maintaining the exemption outweighs the public interest in disclosing the information; and (3) transferring to the National Assembly for Wales the relevant powers in so far as they are exercisable in relation to principal councils in Wales.

1840   Local authority—best value authority—performance indicators—England

The Local Government (Best Value) Performance Indicators and Performance Standards (Amendment) (England) Order 2006, SI 2006/553 (in force on 1 April 2006), amends the 2005 Order, SI 2005/598, so as to make alterations to the statutory performance indicators and standards for best value authorities, excluding police authorities, so as to include indicators requiring authorities to measure performance using user satisfaction surveys. In particular, the order amends the performance indicators for corporate health, education, housing and housing related services, housing and council tax benefit, waste and cleanliness, transport, planning, major, minor and other planning applications and culture and related services.

1841   Local authority—best value authority—performance indicators—police authorities

The Police Authorities (Best Value) Performance Indicators (Amendment) Order 2006, SI 2006/620 (in force on 1 April 2006), amends the 2005 Regulations, SI 2005/470, by making changes to the indicators by which a police authority's performance can be measured.

1842   Local authority—best value authority—power to trade—England

The Local Government (Best Value Authorities) (Power to Trade) (Amendment) (England) Order 2006, SI 2006/3102 (in force on 15 December 2006), further amends the 2004 Order, SI 2004/1705, so as to provide a power to trade to those local authorities whose performance has been categorised, by an order made under the Local Government Act 2003 s 99(4), as excellent, good or fair. The order extends the power to trade to those local authorities whose performance has been categorised by an order, made under s 99(4), as '4 stars', '3 stars', '2 stars' and '1 star'.

1843   Local authority—best value authority—power to trade—Wales

The Local Government (Best Value Authorities) (Power to Trade) (Wales) Order 2006, SI 2006/979, which applies to best value authorities which are county councils, county borough councils, national park authorities and fire and rescue authorities, authorises any such best value authority to trade in any of its ordinary functions subject to conditions requiring the prior preparation and approval of a business case, and the recovery of any costs incurred by an authority in anything it supplies, including accommodation, goods, services or staff, to a company through which the trading power is exercised.

1844   Local authority—contracting out—Transport for London—investment and highway functions

See para 1864.

1845   Local authority—employee—early retirement—compensation—policy of supplementing credited period—power to disapply

The respondent local authority had a published policy, in accordance with the Local Government (Early Termination of Employment) (Discretionary Compensation) (England and Wales) Regulations 2000, SI 2000/1410, reg 26(1), of awarding added years to pensionable service in the case of persons retiring early. The appellant employee was informed that, owing to restructuring, he was to be offered early retirement and, if he accepted, he would receive five years' added compensatory service, awarded at the respondent's discretion. The appellant applied for early retirement, which was duly accepted by the respondent. However, the respondent elected to set aside its existing policy and pay redundancy based on actual salary, statutory pension and lump sum but with no added years credited. The appellant complained to the Pensions Ombudsman that the respondent had acted unlawfully by failing to award him credited periods under reg 8. The Ombudsman decided that the authority had been entitled to review and alter its policy and that, although the premature implementation of the policy constituted an act of maladministration, that act had not caused injustice to the appellant and it would be inequitable for him to succeed in his claim. The appellant appealed, submitting that the respondent's failure to apply the existing policy was an unlawful exercise of power and not simply an act of maladministration. *Held*, it was well established that a local authority had the power to depart from stated policies where individual circumstances demanded it. It would be extraordinary, therefore, if Parliament had intended to cure the problems caused by over-generous applications of the reg 8 power by requiring local authorities not only to formulate and publish their policy on such matters, but also to apply that policy regardless of the circumstances of any particular case. Regulation 26 did not require the policy to be applied regardless of the circumstances, and left intact the ability of a local authority to exercise its discretion in some other way in appropriate cases, however limited. The considerations of workability, affordability and reasonableness which reg 26(4) required a local authority to be satisfied about when formulating and reviewing its policy were likely to inform any decision to depart from an existing policy in any particular case. It was difficult to see how any exercise of the discretion to add years could be carried out other than on the basis of the consideration of those criteria. The respondent's decision was taken, applying those criteria, and there had been no suggestion that that decision was in any sense flawed. Accordingly, the appeal would be dismissed.

Chapman v South Holland DC [2006] EWHC 27 (Ch), [2006] LGR 437 (Chancery Division: Patten J).

1846   Local authority—employee—remuneration—assistants for political groups—England

The Local Government (Assistants for Political Groups) (Remuneration) (England) Order 2006, SI 2006/1509 (in force on 4 July 2006), which applies in relation to England only, replaces the 1995 Order, SI 1995/2456, and increases to £34,986 the amount specified for the purposes of the Local Government and Housing Act 1989 s 9 as the highest amount of annual remuneration for persons holding appointments as assistants for political groups.

1847   Local authority—executive arrangements—access to information—England

The Local Authorities (Executive Arrangements) (Access to Information) (Amendment) (England) Regulations 2006, SI 2006/69 (in force on 1 March 2006), further amend the 2000 Regulations, SI 2000/3272, and are made as a result of changes made by the Local Government (Access to Information) (Variation) Order 2006, SI 2006/88, to the Local Government Act 1972 Pt 5A, relating to access to meetings and documents of certain authorities, committees and sub-committees, and Sch 12A, relating to access to information and exempt information. The regulations make provision for the application of Sch 12A in the 2000 Regulations in relation to rights of access for members of a local authority to documents in the possession, or under the control, of the executive of that authority.

1848 Local authority—functions and responsibilities—England

The Local Authorities (Functions and Responsibilities) (Amendment) (England) Regulations 2006, SI 2006/886 (in force on 21 April 2006), further amend the 2000 Regulations, SI 2000/2853, so as to (1) specify that the power to resolve not to issue a casino licence and the function of enforcing byelaws as functions are not to be the responsibility of the executive; (2) provide for functions relating to certain plans and strategies which are to be the shared responsibility of the authority and the executive; (3) provide that the power to resolve not to issue a casino premises licence under the Gambling Act 2005 s 166 and the power to enforce byelaws are not the responsibility of the executive; (4) replace the reference to a children's services plan to a reference to a children and young people's plan, and the reference to an early years development plan to a reference to a licensing authority policy statement; and (5) remove reference to a community care plan and an education development plan which local authorities are no longer required to prepare and publish.

1849 Local authority—improvement plans—Wales

The Local Government (Improvement Plans) (Wales) Order 2006, SI 2006/615 (in force on 1 April 2006), specifies the date by which an authority's improvement plan for a financial year must be published and the date by which copies of an auditor's report relating to the plan are to be sent to the authority, the Auditor General for Wales and, if required, the National Assembly for Wales. SI 2002/886 is revoked.

1850 Local authority—members—code of conduct—observation of code in performing functions—bringing office into disrepute

The Local Authorities (Model Code of Conduct) (England) Order 2001, SI 2001/3575, Sch 1 para 4 provides that a member of a local authority which is operating executive arrangements must not in his official capacity, or any other circumstance, conduct himself in a manner which could reasonably be regarded as bringing his office or authority into disrepute. The Local Government Act 2002 s 52 requires a member to give to the authority an undertaking or declaration that in performing his functions he will observe the authority's code of conduct.

The Mayor of London, who was subject to the model code of conduct set out in the 2001 Order Sch 1 para 4, was approached by a journalist as he was leaving a function and refused to offer a comment. An exchange followed in which the mayor stated that he disapproved of the journalist's newspaper and asked whether he was a German war criminal. The journalist replied that he was Jewish and that he was offended by the comment, at which the mayor compared the journalist to a concentration camp guard and said that his newspaper had supported fascism. A complaint was made by the Ethical Standards Officer and the respondent tribunal found that although the mayor had not been acting in his official capacity when he had made the remarks, he had failed to comply with the code of conduct and directed that the mayor should be suspended. He appealed. *Held*, the words 'performing his functions' in the 2002 Act s 52 had to have been intended to have some effect. The words did not necessarily cover the same conduct as 'in his official capacity', but could extend further. They covered activities which were apparently within the performance of a member's functions. The expression should be construed so as to apply to a member who was using his position in doing or saying whatever was said to amount to misconduct. It followed that conduct which was outside of a member's official capacity could be covered by the words in s 52 and so could properly be within the code of conduct. It followed that where a member was not acting in his official capacity he would still be covered by the code if he misused his position as a member. That link with his membership with the authority was required. If it were thought appropriate to subject a member of a local authority to a code which extended to conduct in his private life, Parliament should have spelled out what was to be covered. The mayor had not been in his official capacity when he had made the remarks in question, and so the 2001 Order Sch 1 para 4 did not apply to what he had said. Therefore, the tribunal's finding that there had been a failure to follow the provisions of the code could not stand. Further, although the tribunal had been entitled to conclude that what the mayor had said had brought him into disrepute, it was doubtful that whether it had brought his office into disrepute. The tribunal had applied a test which failed to recognise the real distinction between the man and the office. Accordingly, the appeal would be allowed.

Livingstone v Adjudication Panel for England [2006] EWHC 2533 (Admin), [2006] LGR 799 (Queen's Bench Division: Collins J).

1851 Local authority—members—indemnities—Wales

The Local Authorities (Indemnities for Members and Officers) (Wales) Order 2006, SI 2006/249 (in force on 8 February 2006), provides for circumstances in which a relevant authority may provide an indemnity to any of its members or officers or secure the provision to them of insurance. In particular, the order (1) makes it clear than an indemnity may be provided by means of a relevant authority securing the provision of an insurance policy for a member or officer; (2) sets out the cases in which indemnities, including those provided by insurance, may be provided; (3) prevents the provision of an indemnity, or securing of insurance, in relation to criminal offences, any other intentional wrongdoing, fraud, recklessness, or in relation to the bringing of, but not the defence of, any action in defamation; (4) confers a limited power to provide an indemnity, including any indemnity provided by insurance, where the action or inaction complained of is outside the powers of the relevant authority itself or where a member or officer makes a statement that certain steps have been taken or requirements fulfilled but it later becomes clear that this is not the case; and (5) gives a relevant authority the freedom to negotiate such terms for any indemnity or policy of insurance as it thinks appropriate, but requires that such terms include provision for repayment of sums expended by the relevant authority or the insurer in cases where a member has been found to be in breach of the code of conduct applicable to him as a member of the relevant authority, or where a member or officer is convicted of a criminal offence.

1852   Local authority—relevant authority—conduct of members—standards committees—general provisions

The Relevant Authorities (Standards Committee) (Amendment) Regulations 2006, SI 2006/87 (in force on 1 March 2006), further amend the 2001 Regulations, SI 2001/2812, and apply to relevant authorities in England, other than parish councils, and to police authorities in Wales. The regulations are made as a result of changes made by the Local Government (Access to Information) (Variation) Order 2006, SI 2006/88, to the Local Government Act 1972 Pt 5A (ss 100A–100K), relating to access to meetings and documents of certain authorities, committees and sub-committees, and Sch 12A, relating to access to information and exempt information, and make provision for the application of those provisions to the 2001 Regulations.

1853   Local authority—relevant authority—conduct of members—standards committees—Wales

The Standards Committees (Wales) (Amendment) Regulations 2006, SI 2006/1849 (in force on 14 July 2006), amend the 2001 Regulations, SI 2001/2283, so as to (1) add a new definition of 'sub-committee' and provide for the size of the sub-committee; (2) provide that the appointment of a community committee member to a standards committee of a local authority is to be made by that local authority who is obliged to consult the specified bodies; (3) make provision as to the term of office of a community committee member; (4) provide for the reappointment of an independent member of a standards committee; (5) make provision as to the reappointment of a community committee member; (6) confirm that an independent member of a standards committee who has been reappointed to a standards committee for a further consecutive term may be elected as a chairperson or a vice-chairperson of that committee; and (7) provide that the quorum for a meeting of a sub-committee is two members, including the chairperson.

1854   Local authority—standards investigations—Wales

The Public Services Ombudsman for Wales (Standards Investigations) Order 2006, SI 2006/949 (in force on 1 April 2006), (1) makes provision for the application of the Local Government Act 2000 ss 60–63 and the Public Services Ombudsman (Wales) Act 2005 ss 26, 32 to standards investigations under the 2000 Act s 69; and (2) extends absolute privilege for the purposes of the law of defamation to statements of members of the Ombudsman's staff, persons acting on the Ombudsman's behalf and persons assisting the Ombudsman in the exercise of specified functions. SI 2001/2286 is revoked.

1855   Local authority—standing orders—Wales

The Local Authorities (Standing Orders) (Wales) Regulations 2006, SI 2006/1275 (in force on 3 July 2006), require relevant authorities in Wales to make or modify standing orders so that they include the provisions set out in the regulations, or provisions to the like effect. In particular, the regulations (1) provide that a relevant authority which is operating executive arrangements must have standing orders relating to its staff which include the provisions set out in the regulations; (2) provide that the standing orders must be the appropriate ones for the particular form that the executive takes and, if that form changes, the standing orders must be varied accordingly; (3) provide that a relevant authority which is operating alternative arrangements must have standing orders relating to its staff which include the provisions set out in the regulations, or provisions to the like effect; (4) provide that a relevant authority must, in respect of disciplinary action against the head of the authority's paid service, its monitoring officer and its chief finance officer, make standing orders incorporating the provisions set out in the regulations, or provisions to the like effect; (5) provide that such standing orders must be made no later than the first ordinary meeting of the relevant authority falling after the day on which the regulations come into force; and (6) prescribe a procedure for investigation by an independent person, which is to be followed where there is alleged to have been misconduct by the head of the authority's paid service, its monitoring officer or its chief finance officer which the investigation committee, having considered the matter, consider should be further investigated. SI 1993/202 is revoked, in relation to Wales, but not in relation to a national park authority in Wales.

1856   Local commissioner—investigation of local government maladministration—limits of jurisdiction

The claimant, the father of a child who attended a school maintained by a local authority, was dissatisfied with investigations carried out by the school into allegations by the child of misconduct by a teacher. In a complaint to the authority, the claimant listed witnesses who should have been, or who should be, contacted in order to investigate the matter properly. The authority rejected the complaint and the claimant complained to the defendant commissioner, under the Local Government Act 1974 s 26, arguing that the authority's investigation had been inappropriate and inadequate. The defendant was originally of the opinion that he had no jurisdiction to deal with the complaint as the subject matter of the authority's investigation was outside his jurisdiction by virtue of s 26(8) and Sch 5 para 5(2), which prohibited him from investigating any action concerning conduct, curriculum, internal organisation, management or discipline, in any school or other educational establishment maintained by the authority. However, following correspondence from the claimant, the defendant determined that he did have jurisdiction but declined to exercise his discretion to conduct an investigation. The claimant sought judicial review of the defendant's decision. *Held*, on the true construction of s 26(8) and Sch 5 para 5(2), the defendant had no jurisdiction to consider complaints concerning an authority's complaints procedure when the subject matter of the procedure was outside his jurisdiction. The authority was taking 'action' to investigate matters that concerned conduct in the school. The purpose of Sch 5 para 5(2) was to preclude the defendant from looking into matters that went on in local authority schools. There would be difficulties in drawing the line between the investigation of a complaint concerning the manner of an investigation and the underlying subject matter and the possibility of an unfair result if the latter could not be considered. Accordingly, the application would be dismissed.

    R (on the application of M) v Comr for Local Administration in England [2006] All ER (D) 375 (Oct) (Queen's Bench Division: Collins J).

1857   Local Government Act 2003—commencement

The Local Government Act 2003 (Commencement No 1 and Savings) (Wales) Order 2006, SI 2006/3339, brings s 63 into force on 1 April 2007. For a summary of the Act, see 2003 Abr para 1773. See also the commencement table in the title STATUTES.

1858   Local Government Pension Scheme—general

The Local Government Pension Scheme (Amendment) Regulations 2006, SI 2006/966 (in force in part on 1 April 2006, in part on 6 April 2006 and in part on 1 October 2006), further amend the 1997 Regulations, SI 1997/1612, by (1) making further provision for the commutation of annual pension entitlement; (2) requiring an administrating authority which has considered whether to obtain a revised rate and adjustments certificate, and which has therefore determined an increased liability over the 2004 valuation of its pension fund, to spread that liability over the 2005 Funding Strategy Statement Period; (3) making revisions to address changes in the tax regime consequent on the Finance Act 2004; and (4) effecting the removal of the 85 year rule.

The Local Government Pension Scheme (Amendment) (No 2) Regulations 2006, SI 2006/2008 (in force on 1 October 2006), further amend the 1997 Regulations supra in order to (1) address changes in the tax regime consequent on the enactment of the Finance Act 2004; (2) require employers to have and publish a statement of their policy concerning the exercise of their discretionary functions in relation to the time of payment; and (3) provide for the commutation of the annual pension entitlement of councillors.

1859   Local Government Pension Scheme—ombudsman—Wales

The Public Services Ombudsman (Wales) Act 2005 (Consequential Amendments to the Local Government Pensions Scheme Regulations 1997 and Transitional Provisions) Order 2006, SI 2006/1011 (in force on 31 March 2006), amend the Local Government Pension Scheme Regulations 1997, SI 1997/1612, so as to make the Public Services Ombudsman for Wales a resolution body for the purposes of the 1997 Regulations. The effect of the order is that any person for the time being specified in a resolution made by the Ombudsman under the 1997 Regulations is not entitled to membership of the Principal Civil Service Pension Scheme unless specified circumstances apply.

1860   Public Services Ombudsman—Local Government Pension Scheme—Wales

See para 1859.

1861   Public Services Ombudsman—standards investigations—Wales

See para 1854.

1862   Revenue support grant—specified bodies—Wales

The Revenue Support Grant (Specified Bodies) (Wales) (Amendment) Regulations 2006, SI 2006/764 (in force on 20 March 2006), further amend the 2000 Regulations, SI 2000/718, so as to remove the Public Private Partnerships Programme Limited and Syniad from the list of specified bodies and add the Welsh Local Government Association.

LONDON GOVERNMENT

Halsbury's Laws of England (4th edn) vol 29(2) (Reissue) paras 1–500

1863   Greater London Authority—finance—council tax—calculation of precepts—allocation of grants

The Greater London Authority (Allocation of Grants for Precept Calculations) Regulations 2006, SI 2006/351 (in force on 16 February 2006), prescribe for the financial year beginning on 1 April 2006 the amounts of redistributed non-domestic rates and specified grants relating to the police and non-police expenditure of the Greater London Authority and functional bodies which the Greater London Authority must take into account when calculating the amounts of council tax for the City of London and the remainder of Greater London.

1864   Transport—Transport for London—contracting out—investment and highway functions

The Transport for London (Best Value) (Contracting Out of Investment and Highway Functions) Order 2006, SI 2006/91 (in force on 20 January 2006), enables Transport for London to contract out the investment and highway functions which local authorities are authorised to contract out by virtue of the Local Authorities (Contracting Out of Investment Functions) Order 1996, SI 1996/1883, the Local Authorities (Contracting Out of Highways Functions) Order 1999, SI 1999/2106, and the Local Authorities (Contracting Out of Highways Functions) (England) Order 2001, SI 2001/4061.

MAGISTRATES

Halsbury's Laws of England (4th edn) vol 29(2) (Reissue) paras 501–1000

Articles

For articles relating to this title please refer to the Table of Articles at the beginning of the Abridgment.

1865   Collection of fines—final scheme

The Collection of Fines (Final Scheme) Order 2006, SI 2006/1737 (in force on 3 July 2006), provides for a final scheme and gives effect to the final version of the Courts Act 2003 Sch 5 in all local justice areas and indefinitely. In particular, the order (1) amends the application of Sch 5 with the effect that the final scheme will apply to the collection of any sum imposed on conviction, such as fines, costs or sums required to be paid under a compensation order or a confiscation order, regardless of whether those sums are imposed together with a fine or on their own without a fine; (2) removes the definition of immediate payments and alters the scheme so that no difference is made between the treatment of cases where an offender is required to pay immediately or is given time to pay; (3) ensures that the provision for attachment of earning orders and applications for benefit deductions apply in every case where the relevant court is dealing with a person who is liable to pay a sum imposed on conviction other than where a court is hearing an appeal; (4) clarifies that an attachment of earnings order or an application for benefit deductions is made to secure the whole of the sum due rather than any single constituent part of that sum, such as a sum payable under a compensation order; (5) requires the court, where appropriate, to make either an attachment of earnings order or an application for benefit deductions in cases where a person is liable to pay a sum under a compensation order; (6) provides that such a duty is not dependent on any conclusion that the person is an existing defaulter, nor does it require the person's consent; (7) removes the provisions relating to the giving of discounts for early payments; (8) removes provisions relating to the imposition of automatic increases in fines; (9) specifies a further step available against defaulters which allows a fines officer to take enforcement proceedings in a county court or the High Court where a third party debt order or a charging order can be made to secure the payment of the sum due; (10) allows the court, on the referral of a case, to exercise any of its standard powers while keeping the collection order in place; (11) removes the reference to the fines collection regulations and the power to make provision in fines collection regulations for cases that were transferred from one area to another, which were only required for the purposes of piloting the provisions in Sch 5; and (12) provides that the standard powers in respect of persons liable to pay fines are those powers that the court would have had if a collection order had not been made, but the person had been liable to pay the sum due. The order also amends the Attachment of Earnings Act 1971 by removing the power of a magistrates' court to make an attachment of earnings order to secure the payment of a sum imposed on conviction and ensures that the only powers and obligations to make attachment of earnings orders in relation to those sums are the powers and obligations under the 2003 Act Sch 5. The order also amends the Magistrates' Courts Act 1980 so as to (a) allow the court to issue a warrant of arrest to secure a person's attendance, following the person's failure to appear in answer to a summons issued by a fines officer; (b) allow the fines officer to take proceedings in the High Court or a county court to recover a sum imposed on conviction; (c) ensure that the provisions relating to the transfer of fines from one area or jurisdiction to another apply to fines that are being enforced under the 2003 Act Sch 5; and (d) ensure that any warrant of distress issued by a court or a fines officer can be executed in the same way that a warrant of distress issued by a justice of peace is executed.

1866 Collection of fines—general provisions

The Fines Collection Regulations 2006, SI 2006/501 (in force on 27 March 2006), replace the 2004 Regulations, SI 2004/176, and (1) make provision for the amount by which a court must increase relevant fines; (2) set out the methods by which a further steps notice may be delivered to a person who is liable to pay a sum due; (3) allow a fines officer to issue a summons to secure such a person's attendance at court; (4) contain provision for calculating the deductions that an employer must make from a person's earnings under an attachment of earnings order; (5) make provision relating to the procedure for making a clamping order, the clamping, removal, storage and sale of clamped vehicles and the release of clamped vehicles on payment of the charges and sum due; (6) apply, with modifications, the Magistrates' Courts (Attachment of Earnings) Rules 1971, SI 1971/809 so as to ensure that (a) the rule relating to the service of attachment of earnings orders and the giving of a notice of cessation apply in relation to orders made by a fines officer or a court; (b) orders made by a court or a fines officer may be varied by the court or the fines officer on a change of employment; (c) a court or a fines officer may discharge an order if it appears that the person subject to the order is not employed by the employer named in the order; (d) a court or a fines officer may make a consolidated attachment order; and (e) a court or a fines officer, having the power to make an attachment of earnings order, may transfer the fine or other sum due to another local justice area with a view to the making of a consolidated attachment order; and (7) apply, with modifications, the Fines (Deduction from Income Support) Regulations 1992, SI 1992/2182 so as to (a) disapply, in certain circumstances, the regulation which allows applications for benefit deductions to be made; (b) provide that where an application for benefit deductions is made, the court or the fines officer making that application may require the person subject to the application to give the information necessary to complete it; (c) apply the regulation which prescribes the content of an application for benefit deductions to applications made by a court or a fines officer; (d) provide that the regulation concerning the deductions to be made from benefits pursuant to an application applies to applications made by a court or a fines officer and applies in relation to the collection of any sum specified; (e) apply the regulation concerning the circumstances, time of making and termination of deductions from benefits in relation to applications made by a court or a fines officer; and (f) ensure that a court or a fines officer may withdraw an application for deduction from benefit after making it. SI 2004/1407, 2005/484 are revoked.

1867 Collection of fines—pilot scheme

The Collection of Fines (Pilot Scheme) and Discharge of Fines by Unpaid Work (Pilot Schemes) (Amendment) Order 2006, SI 2006/502 (in force in part on 27 March 2006 and in part on 30 March 2006), (1) modifies the Courts Act 2003 Sch 5 so as to (a) provide that the final scheme for the collection of fines will apply to the collection of any sum imposed on conviction regardless of whether those sums are imposed together with a fine, or on their own without a fine; (b) remove the definition of immediate payments and alters the scheme so that no difference is made between the treatment of cases where an offender is required to pay immediately or is given time to pay; (c) ensure that the provisions of Pt 3 (ss 43–50) apply in every case where the relevant court is dealing with a person who is liable to pay a sum imposed on conviction; (d) other than where the court is hearing an appeal; (e) remove provision giving discounts for early payments and those imposing automatic increases in fines; (f) provide for a fines officer to take enforcement proceedings in a county court or the High Court, where a third party debt order or a charging order can be made to secure the payment of the sum due; (g) permit the court to increase a fine in cases where the person is in default on a collection order due to his wilful refusal or culpable neglect; (h) allow the court in certain cases to exercise any of its standard powers whilst keeping the collection order in place, if required; (i) remove the power to make provision in fines collection regulations for cases that are transferred from one area to another; and (k) provide that standard powers in respect of persons liable to pay fines will no longer be applied; (2) modifies Attachment of Earnings Act 1971, in relation to the purposes of the fines collection pilot scheme, so as to (a) remove the power of a court to make an attachment of earnings order ('AEO') to secure the payment of a sum imposed on conviction; (b) provide for the disapplication of the provisions about applications for AEOs in cases where the AEO is to be made under the 2003 Act Sch 3 which gives powers to, and imposes obligations on, the courts and fines officers to make AEOs of their own motion; (c) remove the powers to make attachment of earnings orders, without the need for an application, in relation to fines and compensation orders; and (d) provide that where an AEO is made under Sch 5, the deductions from earnings are calculated and made in accordance with fines collections regulations; (3) modifies the Magistrates' Courts Act 1980, only for the purposes of the fines collection pilot scheme, so as to (a) permit the court to issue a warrant of arrest to secure a person's attendance before it following his failure to appear in answer to a summons issued by a fines officer; (b) allow the fines officer to take proceedings in the High Court or county court to recover a sum imposed on conviction; (b) provide for the transfer of fines, from one area or jurisdiction to another and allows a fines officer to make the relevant order for transfer; and (c) ensure that any warrant of distress issued by a fines officer can be executed in the same way that a warrant of distress issued by a justice of peace is executed; and (4) amends the Discharge of Fines by Unpaid Work (Pilot Schemes) Order 2004, SI 2004/2198, so as to extend those schemes for a further year ending on 31 March 2007.

1868   Discharge of fines by unpaid work—pilot scheme

See para 1867.

1869   Family proceedings

See CHILDREN AND YOUNG PERSONS.

1870   Justices—jurisdiction—exercise of discretion

See *Bromley LBC v C*, para 1141.

1871   Justices—jurisdiction—issue of summons—private prosecution

The claimant's son was struck by a car and killed. The Crown Prosecution Service commenced criminal proceedings against the driver for driving without due care and attention, but subsequently discontinued the prosecution. The claimant laid an information before a magistrates' court seeking the issue of a summons for a private prosecution against the driver. The magistrate refused to issue the summons on the basis that there were no special circumstances applicable. The claimant laid another information before a different magistrates' court seeking the issue of a summons for a private prosecution. The second magistrates' court, which was not informed of the decision of the first magistrates' court, issued the summons. The summons was subsequently withdrawn on the basis that although the first decision was not binding, it was persuasive. The second magistrates' court advised the claimant to go back to the first magistrates' court. The claimant therefore sought to have the matter re-listed before the first magistrates' court but that request was refused. The claimant sought judicial review of all three decisions. *Held*, when a magistrate was considering whether to issue a summons for a private prosecution, where the Crown Prosecution Service had also brought and discontinued a prosecution arising from the same events, the magistrate should not require special circumstances before agreeing to issue the summons. The test applicable as to whether a Crown prosecutor should pursue a prosecution, that is, whether there was sufficient evidence and whether a prosecution would be in the public interest, did not apply to a private prosecution. The magistrate should take into account whether (1) the allegations were an offence known to the law and whether the ingredients of the offence were prima facie present; (2) the offence was time-barred; (3) the court had jurisdiction; (4) the informant had the authority to prosecute; and (5) there was any other relevant factor. The magistrate had applied the wrong test in the first decision by refusing to issue a summons. With regard to the second decision, although the magistrate had stated that the first decision was not binding, the first decision appeared to have been determinative and the second magistrates' court failed to take account of the requisite steps. Since the third decision had been made on the basis that the first decision was right and that more information was needed before the matter could be re-listed, the third decision was also flawed. Accordingly, the application would be allowed and all three decisions would be quashed.

R (on the application of Charlson) v Guildford Magistrates' Court [2006] EWHC 2318 (Admin), [2006] 1 WLR 3494 (Queen's Bench Division: Silber J).

1872   Justices—powers—committal to Crown Court for sentence—variation or discharge of restraining order—lawfulness

See *R (on the application of Lee) v Crown Court at Leeds*, para 2563.

1873   Justices—youth court—committal to Crown Court for trial—rape by 12-year-old child

The first defendant, a 16-year-old male, boarded a bus with two other youths and intimidated a 17-year-old male into handing over his wallet and other valuable items. No actual violence was used and no direct threats were issued. The second defendant, a 13-year-old girl, and two other girls approached other groups of girls and used intimidatory pushing and jostling to rob them. The second defendant was charged with robbery and attempted robbery. The third defendant used force to rape a 13-year-old girl in his home despite her explicit objections. He was charged with two offences of rape when he was 12 years old. The youth court in each case considered that the likely sentence on conviction would be in excess of two years' imprisonment and all the defendants were committed for trial at the Crown Court. They sought judicial review of the decisions to commit them. *Held*, having regard to the relevant guidelines for sentencing the perpetrators of street robberies, there was no realistic prospect that either the first or second defendant would receive a custodial sentence of over two years. However, there was a real possibility that the third defendant, if convicted, would be sentenced to more than two years' imprisonment. Although there was authority that a youth court should never accept jurisdiction for a charge of rape, that authority was established at a time when a child under the age of 14 years could not be charged with rape, and it was doubtful that such a hard and fast rule now applied in the case of a 12-year-old defendant. Accordingly, the applications of the first and second defendants would be allowed and the application of the third defendant would be dismissed.

R (on the application of W) v Brent Youth Court; R (on the application of S) v Enfield Youth Court; R (on the application of B) v Richmond-on-Thames Youth Court [2006] EWHC 95 (Admin), (2006) 170 JP 198 (Queen's Bench Division: Sir Anthony Clarke MR, Laws and Hallett LJJ). *R v Billam* [1986] 1 All ER 985, CA (1986 Abr para 123), doubted.

1874 Justices' clerks—assistants—qualifications

The Assistants to Justices' Clerks Regulations 2006, SI 2006/3405 (in force on 9 January 2007), replace the Justices' Clerks (Qualifications of Assistants) Rules 1979, SI 1979/570, and (1) prescribe the qualifications which must be held by assistants to justices' clerks; (2) enable the Lord Chancellor to designate otherwise non-qualified persons as assistants to justices' clerks for up to six months in certain circumstances; and (3) prescribe circumstances in which a person unqualified to act as an assistant clerk may be designated as such for the purposes of performing specified functions out of court. SI 1998/3107, 1999/2814 and 2001/2269 are revoked.

1875 Local justice areas—reorganisation

The Local Justice Areas (No 1) Order 2006, SI 2006/1839 (in force in part on 2 August 2006 and in part on 1 January 2007), creates (1) a new local justice area named Shrewsbury and North Shropshire, which replaces the local justice areas of Shrewsbury, Oswestry and Drayton; and (2) a new local justice area named Telford and South Shropshire, which replaces the local justice areas of Telford and Bridgnorth and South Shropshire.

The Local Justice Areas (No 2) Order 2006, SI 2006/2315 (in force in part on 22 September 2003 and in part on 1 January 2007), creates a new local justice area named Gwent, which replaces the local justice areas of North West Gwent and South East Gwent.

1876 Magistrates' courts—anti-social behaviour orders—composition of benches

Sir Igor Judge, President of the Queen's Bench Division, has issued the following *Practice Direction (Magistrates' Courts: Composition)* [2006] 1 WLR 636, with the agreement of the Master of the Rolls on 24 February 2006.

1. Where there is an application to a magistrates' court for an anti-social behaviour order under the Crime and Disorder Act 1998 s 1, or an application to a magistrates' court for an anti-social behaviour order to be varied or discharged under s 1(8), and the person against whom the order is sought is under 18, the justices constituting the court should normally be qualified to sit in the youth court.

2. Applications for interim orders under s 1D, including those made without notice, may be listed before justices who are not so qualified.

3. If it is not practicable to constitute a bench in accordance with head 1, above, in particular where to do so would result in a delayed hearing, this *Practice Direction* does not apply.

1877 Magistrates' courts—committal proceedings—failure to serve required notice—abuse of process

The claimant charged the interested party on an indictment that specified various property offences, intending to rely on hearsay evidence. At a committal hearing, the interested party was discharged on all charges on the basis that the claimant had failed to serve the relevant notice pursuant to the Magistrates' Court Act 1980 s 5D in relation to the hearsay evidence. Subsequently, the Criminal Justice Act 1988 ss 23, 24, the hearsay provisions, were repealed by the Criminal Justice Act 2003. The interested party appeared before the magistrates' court for a second time on proceeds of crime charges. The defendant argued that the claimant had not complied with the 1980 Act s 5D, raising a discussion as to whether the claimant was required to give notice of its intention to rely on evidence which might be admissible at trial pursuant to the 1988 Act ss 23, 24, when those sections had been repealed by the 2003 Act. The justices concluded that the 1980 Act took priority. They decided that there was insufficient evidence to put the interested party on trial on the ground that s 5D still applied and the claimant had failed to comply with it. Subsequently, the claimant contended that one of the original charges was not reliant on hearsay evidence and sought committal on that single charge. The defence sought to challenge that committal as an abuse of the court's process. The justices decided that as the interested party had previously been discharged on that charge, it constituted an abuse of process for the case to continue. The claimant sought judicial review of the decision. *Held*, hearsay evidence in criminal proceedings, including magistrates' courts proceedings was, since the repeal of the 1988 Act ss 23, 24, governed by the 2003 Act. The justices had fallen into error in dealing with the 1980 Act s 5D. Although s 5D had not been repealed, the reality was that it had ceased to have potency since the repeal of the 1988 Act ss 23, 24. It was therefore otiose to contemplate the service of a notice under the 1980 Act s 5D to the extent relied on. Further, while the magistrates' court had a jurisdiction to restrain abuses of its process, that power was one which ought only to be employed in exceptional circumstances. That jurisdiction was usually invoked either where the court concluded that the defendant could not receive a fair trial, or it concluded that it would be unfair for the defendant to be tried. The present case did not fall within those categories. The justices had erred in basing their decision on s 5D. Accordingly, the application would be allowed.

R (on the application of the Crown Prosecution Service) v City of London Magistrates' Court [2006] All ER (D) 37 (Apr) (Queen's Bench Division: Maurice Kay LJ and Tugendhat J).

1878   Magistrates' courts—fees

The Magistrates' Courts Fees (Amendment) Order 2006, SI 2006/715 (in force on 6 April 2006), amends the 2005 Order, SI 2005/3444, so as to (1) add a new fee of £20 which applies on an application to vary, extend or revoke an order made in family proceedings which is not otherwise charged under any other numbered fee; (2) change the reference to the register of fines so that it refers to the register of judgments, orders and fines; (3) ensure that the fee payable on a complaint or application and the issue of a summons is also payable on the issue of a warrant of arrest without issuing a summons; (4) provide that the fee payable on the issue of a warrant of arrest is now only payable applies on the issue of such a warrant if a summons is not obeyed; (5) provide that only one fee is chargeable if an application is made or permission sought (a) under or relating to provisions of the Children Act 1989 which are listed in two or more different numbered fees; (b) under or relating to two or more provisions of the 1989 Act which are listed in the same numbered fee; and (c) in respect of two or more children; (6) clarify that a separate fee is payable for each child in respect of which an application for a declaration of parentage is made; and (7) clarify that the fee payable on an application or request for permission under the Adoption and Children Act 2002 Pt 1 (ss1–110) is also payable in relation to applications to vary or revoke an order made under the 2002 Act.

1879   Magistrates' courts—procedure—decision—previous convictions

The applicant was convicted by justices of common assault. The clerk to the justices had made the justices aware of the applicant's previous offences after their decision had been formulated but before their decision as to conviction in open court. The applicant sought judicial review of the decision to convict him, on the ground that it was unjust for the previous offences to be known at the time of the justices' decision. *Held*, the question was whether it was appropriate to quash the decision on the perception of injustice. Advice about sentencing from clerks should not be given until after the justices had delivered their verdict, heard antecedents and heard from counsel. Legal advisers should only attend when called on and should not do or say anything regarding the convictions until a verdict was announced in open court. However, the decision to convict was not unjust and, accordingly, the application would be dismissed.

R (on the application of Murchison) v Southend Magistrates' Court [2006] All ER (D) 157 (Jan) (Queen's Bench Division: Hallet LJ and Jack J).

1880   Magistrates' courts—procedure—jurisdiction of court

See *Farley v Child Support Agency*, para 444.

1881   Magistrates' courts—recovery of cash—minimum amount—proceeds of crime

The Proceeds of Crime Act 2002 (Recovery of Cash in Summary Proceedings: Minimum Amount) Order 2006, SI 2006/1699 (in force on 31 July 2006), replaces the 2004 Order, SI 2004/420, and reduces, from £5,000 to £1,000, the minimum amount for the purposes of the Proceeds of Crime Act 2002 Pt 5 Ch 3 (ss 289–303), so that the power of customs officers and constables to search for and seize cash derived from, or intended for use in unlawful conduct is limited to cash which amounts to at least that amount.

MARKETS, FAIRS AND STREET TRADING

Halsbury's Laws of England (4th edn) vol 29(2) (Reissue) paras 1001–1160

1882 Market—rights of market—authorisation to sell meat and fish at horticultural market

The Covent Garden Market Act 1961 s 18(1)(f) provides that the Covent Garden Market Authority has power to carry on all such other activities as it may appear to the authority to be requisite, advantageous or convenient for it to carry on for or in connection with the discharge of its duties or with a view to making the best use of any of its assets. However, the authority may not by virtue of s 18(1)(f) carry on activities with a view to making the best use of any of its assets except with the consent of the minister: s 18(1).

New Covent Garden Market was a market for the sale of horticultural produce. The Covent Garden Market Authority sought consent under the 1961 Act s 18(1)(f) to authorise face-to-face trading in meat or fish at the market. The Secretary of State gave consent which allowed the authority to grant leases for the purpose of selling fish or meat on such parts of the site as it considered were surplus to its requirements, with the proviso that the consent should not be taken as granting any market rights. The Corporation of London, as the owner of nearby fish and meat markets, sought judicial review of the decision. The application was allowed by the Court of Appeal and the authority and the Secretary of State appealed. *Held*, the language of s 18(1)(f) was wide, and the words 'or with a view to making the best use of any of its assets' strongly suggested that the activities need not relate to authority's duties relating to horticultural produce. The Court of Appeal restrictive interpretation of that provision, that it could not authorise an activity at New Covent Garden Market that was in competition with either of the corporation's markets, could not be accepted. The proprietor of a market could not complain about competition unless, first, the competition constituted a rival market, second, the rival was trading within the area in which the proprietor was entitled to protection from competition and, third, the competition was sufficiently substantial to constitute in law a disturbance to the proprietor's market. The first and third requirements raised issues of degree and were dependant on the facts. If what the authority had done in purported reliance of the consent did constitute an interference with the corporation's market rights, then the corporation could obtain a remedy in tort. Accordingly, the appeal would be allowed.

R (on the application of Corpn of London) v Secretary of State for Environment, Food and Rural Affairs [2006] UKHL 30, [2006] 3 All ER 1130 (House of Lords: Lords Nicholls of Birkenhead, Hope of Craighead and Scott of Foscote, Baroness Hale of Richmond and Lord Mance). Decision of Court of Appeal [2005] 1 WLR 1286 (2004 Abr para 1897) reversed.

1883 Street trading—trading without licence—single vehicle advertised for sale

The London Local Authorities Act 1990 s 38(2) provides that, in any proceedings for an offence of unlicensed street trading, it is presumed that any article which is displayed in any street has been exposed or offered for sale unless it can be proved to the satisfaction of the court that it was brought into that street for some purpose other than street trading.

The appellant local authority alleged that the defendant had committed a street trading offence contrary to the 1990 Act s 38(1)(a). The defendant, who did not have a street trading licence, had fixed a notice to the window of his car indicating that it was for sale, and had parked the car on the street outside the surgery of his general practitioner with whom he had an appointment. The district judge concluded that one of the purposes for which the defendant had brought the vehicle into the street remained the offer for sale of the vehicle and that the statutory defence provided by s 38(2) was therefore not established as it had not been proved that the car was brought into the street for some purpose other than street trading. The authority subsequently brought another prosecution against the defendant in relation to a separate incident of unlicensed street trading. The allegation again related to the placing of an advertisement in the window of a private car. The vehicle in question had been loaned by the defendant to another person, the defendant having the expectation that it would be placed in a garage by that person and not parked in public. The judge decided that the defence under s 38(2) had been made out. On appeal by the defendant against the first ruling, and by the appellant against the second ruling, *held*, the question that had to be asked when deciding whether an article was brought into a street for some purpose other than street trading was why it was in that street and nowhere else at the material time. A person could rely on the defence under s 38(2) notwithstanding that there was a duality of purpose. In relation to the second alleged offence, there was nothing in the 1990 Act which deemed the registered keeper to be responsible for his car when it was in the possession and control of someone else. On the facts, the defendant should have been acquitted in both cases. Accordingly, the defendant's appeal would be allowed and the appellant's appeal would be dismissed.

Onasanya v Newham LBC; Newham LBC v Onasanya [2006] EWHC 1775 (Admin), [2006] 4 All ER 459 (Jul) (Queen's Bench Division: Maurice Kay LJ and Mitting J).

MATRIMONIAL LAW

Halsbury's Laws of England (4th edn) vol 29(3) (Reissue) paras 1–1102

Articles

For articles relating to this title please refer to the Table of Articles at the beginning of the Abridgment.

1884   Ancillary relief—financial provision—division of assets—conduct of parties—financial irresponsibility

The parties had jointly owned a company, the husband owning 85 per cent of the share capital and the wife 15 per cent. The husband borrowed substantial sums from the company and began to gamble heavily. The marriage broke down and the husband formed a relationship with the co-respondent. The wife petitioned for divorce and instigated ancillary relief proceedings, in the course of which the husband gave certain undertakings, including a promise not to gamble and an undertaking to provide financial details and records. The husband continued to gamble, failed to provide proper answers to questions and gave incomplete disclosure. The wife submitted that she should receive a 65 per cent share of the residual assets because of her husband's financial irresponsibility. The husband claimed that there should be an equal division. The wife also obtained permission to serve a subpoena duces tecum against the co-respondent, which required her to provide financial information which the husband had failed to supply. However, the co-respondent submitted that some of the information sought from her, including unredacted bank statements, separation documents relating to her former partner and estate accounts relating to her late father, was oppressive and infringed her right to respect for private and family life under the European Convention on Human Rights art 8, given that she was a stranger to the litigation and neither side intended to call her as a witness. *Held*, the husband had not been frank and open either in his approach to the proceedings or with the court, having chosen to ignore or disregard court orders where it had suited him to do so. This was conduct which it would be inequitable to disregard, under the Matrimonial Causes Act 1973 s 25(2)(g), in deciding how the available assets should be divided. A fair and just division of the residual assets, taking into account the husband's conduct and the parties' respective needs and resources, would be a division of 62·5 per cent to the wife and 37·5 per cent to the husband. As to the subpoena, it was well established that there was no power to require a third party to file an affidavit or sworn statement in ancillary relief proceedings. This included a co-respondent, who was not a party to such an application. Any court requirement of someone who was not a party to proceedings to disclose personal financial information was an interference with that person's right to respect for privacy and therefore had to be justified as necessary for the protection of the rights of the applicant. In determining an application for disclosure against a third party in ancillary relief proceedings, the court had to take account of (1) the importance of the information to the issues in the proceedings; (2) whether the applicant had taken appropriate but unsuccessful steps to obtain the information within the proceedings and to enforce orders for disclosure before applying for third party disclosure; (3) whether it would be sufficient instead for the court to draw inferences adverse to the respondent from the respondent's refusal to supply the required information and to comply with court orders; (4) the relationship between the respondent and the third party; and (5) if disclosure was necessary and proportionate, whether the documents contained private information which could be protected by editing. There had been a clear history of failure by the husband to provide information and a strong suspicion that he had not been frank about the transfer of funds to the co-respondent. The wife had taken all reasonable steps to elicit the relevant information from the husband within the proceedings and the matter could not have been adequately dealt with by drawing adverse inferences. Judgment would be given accordingly.

M v M (Financial Misconduct; Subpoena Against Third Party) [2006] 2 FCR 555 (Family Division: Peter Hughes QC).

1885   Ancillary relief—financial provision—division of assets—equality

The parties had no significant resources when they married 20 years before the present proceedings. On their separation, the husband moved to Bermuda and the wife remained in England. She issued a petition for divorce, that included an application for ancillary relief. The total of all resources held by the parties consisted of £131,323,000, of which £6,634,000 was in the wife's name, £56,564,000 was in the husband's name and £68,125,000 was in a trust fund. The wife argued that, during their long marriage, in which all the wealth had been generated from scratch, she had played her full part as wife and the mother of two sons, and fairness dictated that the fortune generated during the marriage should be split evenly. However, she was prepared to accept a 45/55 per cent split to recognise the husband's special contribution to the generation of the wealth if, despite her submissions, the court was to hold that that was a factor properly to be taken into account in the divisionary process. The issues between the parties fell to be resolved pursuant to the statutory balancing exercise found in the Matrimonial Causes Act 1973 s 25. *Held*, this was one of the very small category of cases where, wholly exceptionally, the wealth created was of extraordinary proportions from extraordinary talent and energy. Taking everything into account, the wife would be entitled to a total of about £48m, just under 37 per cent of the total of the assets. Judgment would be given accordingly.

Charman v Charman (No 2) [2006] EWHC 1879 (Fam), [2007] 1 FCR 33 (Family Division: Coleridge J). For earlier related proceedings see [2005] EWCA Civ 1606, [2006] 1 WLR 1053 (2005 Abr para 2079).

1886 Ancillary relief—financial provision—division of assets—property—adults lacking in capacity

Laurence Oates, Official Solicitor to the Supreme Court, has issued the following *Practice Note (Ancillary Relief Orders: Conveyancing for Mentally Incapacitated Adults)* [2006] 1 FLR 480.

1. This *Practice Note* is issued by the Official Solicitor to the Supreme Court. It gives his understanding of the law and practice applying to the implementation of property adjustment orders and orders for sale in ancillary relief proceedings under the Matrimonial Causes Act 1973 Pt II or the Civil Partnership Act 2004 s 72, Sch 5, where one of the parties is under mental incapacity. It has been seen in draft and approved by the Master of the Court of Protection and the Senior District Judge at the Principal Registry of the Family Division of the High Court.

2. A petitioner or respondent who lacks capacity to conduct matrimonial proceedings or civil partnership proceedings for himself or herself will require to be represented through a next friend or guardian ad litem. If he or she lacks capacity to conduct the proceedings, he or she is likely also to lack capacity to sign a contract for sale of a property, a transfer or other conveyance arising from an order made in those proceedings. Capacity is issue specific, so medical evidence establishing incapacity to conduct the litigation may have to be supplemented by specific evidence as to capacity to execute the conveyancing documents.

Powers of the family court

3. On or after granting a decree of divorce, nullity or judicial separation in matrimonial proceedings or, in civil partnership proceedings, making a dissolution, nullity or separation order, the court may make an order for the transfer of the family home or other property from one party to the other, or other orders for property adjustment, under the 1973 Act s 24 or the 2004 Act Sch 5 para 7 (as the case may be). Further, where the court makes such an order or makes an order for secured periodical payments or for the payment of a lump sum under the 1973 Act s 23 or the 2004 Act Sch 5 para 2, it may make an order for the sale of any property in which, or in the proceeds of which, either party has an interest. However, for any such order to be put into effect where one of the parties is under mental incapacity, it will be necessary to obtain either an authority of the Court of Protection or, where that party is a trustee of a jointly owned property, an order providing for a substitute trustee to be made (see the Law of Property Act 1925 s 22, which is explained in head 8, below).

4. Only the persons listed in the Mental Health Act 1983 s 94 may give any approval or make any order required for the management of property and affairs of a patient under Pt VII. These persons are the nominated judges of the Court of Protection (High Court judiciary of the Chancery and Family divisions), the Master of the Court of Protection and his nominated officers.

5. The Supreme Court Act 1981 s 39 (applied in County Courts by the County Courts Act 1984 s 38) authorises the (High or County) Court to order that a person (usually the District Judge) may sign the conveyance on behalf of a litigant, where that litigant 'neglects or refuses' to comply with an order. In the opinion of the Official Solicitor, a mentally incapacitated person who lacks capacity to sign a conveyance has neither neglected nor refused to comply with an order, hence this provision may not be used to avoid the need to obtain an authority of the Court of Protection or appoint a substitute trustee.

Where the patient is sole owner of the property

6. Where a receiver has been appointed, it is generally for the receiver to liaise with the Court of Protection and to obtain the necessary authority of that court to the sale (or any purchase). See *Court of Protection Practice Note*.

7. Where no receiver has been appointed, it is necessary to apply to the Court of Protection for a person to be authorised to carry the terms of the family court order into effect on behalf of the patient. The authority can be drafted to extend to ancillary documentation, such as surrender of an endowment policy. Where the Official Solicitor is acting as next friend or guardian ad litem, he can apply for authority and, once granted will be able to sign the documentation on behalf of the patient to enable the transaction to proceed. The costs of this application should be provided for in the family court order as these will not be paid by any CLS funding that is available to the patient. The application to the Court of Protection must be supported by medical evidence in form CP3.

Patient as joint owner of the property

8. If a patient is a co-owner of property with another then the 1925 Act s 22(2) prevents the disposition of the legal estate in land so long as one trustee is a patient. It will therefore be necessary to replace the patient as trustee before a sale can proceed (unless there is a registered Enduring Power of Attorney).

9. The appointment of a new trustee can be made by the family court under the Trustee Act 1925 ss 41, 44. Where the Official Solicitor is acting as next friend or guardian ad litem, his family litigation division can provide precedent documentation for the appointment of the Official Solicitor as new trustee in the patient's place.

10. The county court has jurisdiction under s 41 where the trust or estate or fund to be dealt with in the court does not exceed the county court limit, currently £30,000 (see the Trustee Act 1925 s 63A). This jurisdictional limit may be exceeded by agreement of the parties (1984 Act s 24).

11. Once the order appointing a substitute trustee has been made, the sale can proceed, the sellers being the co-owner and the new trustee (usually the Official Solicitor). No mention of the patient should appear on the contract nor on the transfer. A copy of the order providing for the new trustee will need to be produced to HM Land Registry with the transfer documentation. The costs of the new trustee should be provided for in the family court order and should generally be met from the gross proceeds of sale.

Property jointly owned to be jointly transferred to one party

12. If the family court orders the patient's share of jointly owned property to be transferred to the other joint owner it will usually be necessary for an application to be made to the Court of Protection for authority for the Official Solicitor (or some other party) to take all necessary steps in the name and on behalf of the patient to secure the transfer of all his/her legal and beneficial interest in the property. Similarly, where the share of the spouse with capacity is to be transferred to the patient, authority of the Court of Protection will be needed for any covenants to be executed on behalf of the patient as transferee. In either case, while awaiting the authority, the wording of the transfer should be agreed. The Official Solicitor has a form of transfer which may be used in such circumstances. Once the authority is received, the documentation can be completed. Provision will need to be made in the matrimonial court order for the costs of any application to the Court of Protection.

1887   Ancillary relief—financial provision—division of assets—substantial contribution

A husband and wife had been married for seven years and had two children. They divorced after the husband assaulted the wife and pleaded guilty to assault occasioning actual bodily harm. The wife claimed ancillary relief in the divorce proceedings. The husband had been a wealthy man at the time of the marriage and had been the breadwinner and provider, buying successive matrimonial homes. The wife had not been wealthy before the marriage and had not worked during it. The issue for the determination of the court concerned the split of the assets so as to effect a clean break, subject to an agreement that the husband would continue to pay annual maintenance and school fees for the children. The assets in issue included the husband's property portfolio, which consisted of properties acquired before the marriage for the purpose of obtaining income from rentals and capital appreciation, and his pension portfolio, which had substantially increased in value during the subsistence of the marriage. *Held*, there would be no allowance in favour of the wife in respect of either conduct or compensation. No separate consideration arose out of the duration of the marriage. Allowance would, however, be made for the substantial financial contribution the husband had made to the marriage, over and above the norm, after taking into account the wife's contribution as carer and homemaker. The husband's contribution was sufficient to justify an entitlement to 60 per cent of the matrimonial property, and he would retain the whole of the pre-matrimonial property. Judgment would be given accordingly.

S v S [2006] EWHC 2793 (Fam), [2006] All ER (D) 137 (Nov) (Family Division: Burton J). *White v White* [2001] 1 AC 596, HL (2000 Abr para 1264); and *Miller v Miller; McFarlane v McFarlane* [2006] UKHL 24, [2006] 2 AC 618 (para 2326) applied.

1888   Ancillary relief—financial provision—high value cases

See *Re S* (*A Child: Unmarried Parents: Financial Provision*), para 470.

1889   Ancillary relief—financial provision—matters to which court must have regard— fairness

In the first case, the parties had been married for less than three years and had no children. The marriage ended when the husband told the wife that the marriage was at an end. The wife was awarded a capital sum of £5m on the ground that it would be unfair to focus on the length of the marriage without considering the reason for which it had ended. The husband appealed. In the second case, the parties had been married for 16 years and had three children. The wife had given up a successful career to raise the children. The parties agreed that there was insufficient capital to achieve a clean break, and it was agreed that the wife was entitled to a maintenance award on a joint lives or further order basis. A periodical payments order of £250,000 a year, limited to five years after which the prospects of a clean break would be reassessed, was made in favour of the wife. *Held*, in most cases, fairness did not require consideration of the parties' conduct because it was not relevant to the basis on which financial ancillary relief was awarded. However, the Matrimonial Causes Act 1973 s 25(2)(g) permitted conduct to be taken into account where it would be inequitable to disregard it. In the second case, due to the way the parties had conducted their marriage, there would be significant future economic disparity sustained by the wife. The husband's high level of earnings was the result of the parties' joint endeavours at the earlier stages of his career. A deferred clean break was something that would merit careful consideration at a suitably early date. However, that did not mean that the joint lives order should be set aside in favour of an extendable five-year order. Accordingly, the appeal in the first case would be dismissed; the appeal in the second case would be allowed.

Miller v Miller; McFarlane v McFarlane [2006] UKHL 24, [2006] 2 AC 618 (House of Lords: Lords Nicholls of Birkenhead, Hoffmann, Hope of Craighead and Mance and Baroness Hale of Richmond). Decision of Court of Appeal in *Miller* [2005] EWCA Civ 984, [2005] 2 FCR 713 (2005 Abr para 2071) affirmed. Decision in *McFarlane* [2004] EWCA Civ 872, [2005] Fam 171 (2004 Abr para 1904) reversed in part.

1890 Ancillary relief—financial provision—matters to which court must have regard—post-nuptial agreement

A wife moved into her husband's family home before their marriage, and it was agreed that she would give up her employment, thereby becoming wholly dependant on the husband and his family for financial support. The husband received a substantial inheritance and they were married the same year, and had two children. The relationship began to deteriorate and the wife committed adultery with the husband's best friend. The husband was informed of the adultery and was extremely angry and suggested that he would only consider reconciliation were the wife to comply with his conditions, including that she signed a post-nuptial agreement. The husband continued to bully her with threats of that nature, ultimately stating that she was to leave the family home had she not signed it. In a state of distress, the wife contacted her solicitors, who had been chosen by the husband, and signed the agreement. The husband subsequently became aware that the wife had become involved with his best friend again and divorce proceedings were commenced. The wife applied for ancillary relief and an issue arose as to whether the post-nuptial agreement should be enforced. *Held*, it was established that an agreement entered into between husband and wife did not oust the jurisdiction of the court. Pre-nuptial 'contracts' had become increasingly common place and were, subject to the discretion of the court and the application of a test of fairness or manifest unfairness, much more likely to be accepted by the courts as governing what should occur between the parties when the prospective marriage came to an end. The agreements were not enforceable per se although they could be persuasive, or definitive, depending on the precise circumstances that led to their completion. Where it was clear that interdependence and mutual influence between the parties were the basis of the relationship, the court had to take special care when assessing the manner in which each party's conduct affected the other. If a wife had been accustomed to placing reliance on her husband's decisions she might be much more easily influenced than an individual in a commercial transaction. The wife's will had been overborne by her husband exercising undue pressure of influence over her that had affected her ability to make clear, calm or rational decisions, and therefore the terms of the agreement would not be implemented. The law would be applied in accordance with the Matrimonial Causes Act 1973 s 25. There should not be an equal division of assets as an equal division would not be appropriate and it would not be discriminatory to the wife if she were to receive less than half. While the wife had not suffered any economic disadvantage at all, she clearly had needs as a result of her dependency on the husband during the course of the marriage and the fact that she was going to care for the children until they reached adulthood. Accordingly, the application would be allowed in part.

A v A [2006] EWHC 2900 (Fam), [2007] All ER (D) 41 (Jan) (Family Division: Baron J). *Edgar v Edgar* [1980] 3 All ER 887, CA (1980 Abr para 958); *Royal Bank of Scotland v Etridge* (No 2) [2001] UKHL 44, [2001] 4 All ER 449 (2001 Abr para 2266); *White v White* [2001] 1 AC 596, UKHL (2001 Abr para 1952); and *Miller v Miller; McFarlane v McFarlane* [2006] UKHL 24, [2006] 3 All ER 1 (para 1889) considered

1891 Ancillary relief—financial provision—pension assets—appropriate treatment

The parties divorced and both applied for ancillary relief. An issue arose concerning the treatment of their respective pensions. The husband had retired on ill-health grounds and had a pension which was already in payment at the time of the proceedings. The wife had a pension which was also in payment, and which had a value of approximately one-tenth of the husband's. In the preparation of the ancillary relief applications, the wife emphasised that, at the date of the marriage, she was richer than the husband and, therefore, had brought in greater assets. The husband relied on the cash equivalent transfer value of the pension at the date of the marriage, at which point it had not been in payment. The husband argued that each party should retain the pension, while the wife sought a division in her favour. The judge ordered a split in the wife's favour, with each party's share to include his or her pension. The husband's appeal against the judge's treatment of the pension assets was dismissed and, on his further appeal, *held*, it might be possible in hypothetical cases to aggregate the value of pensions with that of other assets and distribute the resultant total value between the parties, such as where the parties had pensions in payment of approximately equal value, and/or where the value of the pensions was small in comparison with other assets. In the instant case, however, the husband's pension (if included as part of his assets) represented approximately 35 per cent of his assets. The value of the wife's pension (if included as part of her assets) represented approximately 3 per cent of her assets. Moreover, the husband's pension was approximately ten times more valuable than the wife's. In those circumstances, a failure to treat the pensions as different in kind from the other assets, without at any rate making a significant adjustment to reflect the difference, was bound to lead to unfairness. Pensions in payment did not sit comfortably in the category of 'property', for they were unrealisable and non-transferable. Nor did they sit comfortably in the category of 'income', since they did not derive from future endeavour but from past employment or contribution which would generally have been effected during the years of marriage. It was appropriate to share the husband's pension rights with the wife in such a way as to bring the value of her own and the approximate part of the husband's pension rights up to the appropriate proportion of the value of the totality of the two pension rights. Accordingly, the appeal would be allowed.

Martin-Dye v Martin-Dye [2006] EWCA Civ 681, [2006] 4 All ER 779 (Court of Appeal: Lord Phillips of Worth Matravers CJ, Thorpe and Dyson LJJ).

1892   Ancillary relief—financial provision—periodical payments—nominal order—variation

A husband and wife separated and a consensual order was made providing for the transfer of the wife's interest in the matrimonial home to the husband and for the husband to provide the wife with a sum to enable her to purchase a home. The order also contained a nominal order for periodical payments. Following the making of the order, the wife made no attempt to obtain paid employment, instead moving to an expensive area and undertaking a series of ill-advised investments. The husband's wealth increased, and the wife subsequently sought variation of the nominal order. The husband contended that the wife should receive no uplift and that the order should be discharged. The district judge ordered that the nominal order should be increased and capitalised in a certain sum pursuant to the Matrimonial Causes Act 1973 s 31(7B), thereby achieving a clean break. The husband appealed, submitting that the district judge had erred in law because the wife had failed to establish the condition precedent to the exercise of the discretion, namely that, despite her best endeavours, her attempts at self-help had failed. In the alternative, it was submitted that the district judge's conclusion in the exercise of his discretion had been plainly wrong, in light of factors including the wife's failure to satisfy that condition. *Held*, the establishment of a condition precedent could not be found in the statutory provisions or authorities relating to them and it followed that the district judge had not erred in law. Section 31(7) expressly referred to 'all the circumstances of the case' and 'to changes in the matters to which the court was to have regard when making the order'. The statutory language demonstrated that the court was to have regard to all the relevant circumstances and within them matters listed in the statute. That precluded the condition precedent or trigger approach because such an approach would isolate a relevant factor or factors and would demand that it, or they,were assessed in isolation and without any balancing with, or overview taking account of, all relevant factors, whereas the statutory provisions demanded such a balancing exercise and overview. The findings made by the district judge showed that the wife did not satisfy the condition or trigger of demonstrating that the present situation had arisen notwithstanding her best endeavours to help herself. There was a powerful case that the wife had been undeserving of an exercise of the statutory discretion to vary the nominal period payments. However, it could not be said that the district judge was plainly wrong and, accordingly, the appeal would be dismissed.

N v N [2006] EWHC 3269 (Fam), [2006] All ER (D) 292 (Dec) (Family Division: Charles J).

1893   Ancillary relief—financial provision—property and financial resources—assets of extended family

A couple separated after seven years of marriage. The husband worked for his family's shipping business, though he was not formally employed by it. The couple lived in a house which was registered in the name of the husband's brother. During the marriage the matrimonial home underwent extensive renovation, which was funded partly by the husband's family and partly by the wife's father. The couple's income came largely through payments made by an offshore company forming part of the shipping business. The wife claimed ancillary relief, contending that her husband was the beneficial owner of the house and of two of the offshore companies of the business. In the alternative, she contended that the court should include the parent's resources in its assessment of the husband's resources. *Held*, on the evidence, the husband was not the beneficial owner of the house or the companies. Moreover, the assets and income identified by the wife were not those which the husband was entitled to, either in law or as beneficiary under a trust. It would be wrong in principle to make an award which ranged outside assets and income which were the husband's as of right. It would also be wrong to appropriate the entirety of the husband's assets and income on the basis that his parents would provide for his support from their resources, as this would put improper pressure on them. Judgment would be given accordingly.

TL v ML (Ancillary Relief: Claim Against Assets of Extended Family) [2005] EWHC 2860 (Fam), [2006] 1 FCR 465 (Family Division: Nicholas Mostyn QC).

1894 Ancillary relief—financial provision—property division—confiscation order proceedings—conflicting rights of receiver

A husband was convicted in Holland of drug trafficking offences and was sentenced to a term of imprisonment. Confiscation proceedings remained outstanding in Holland. Meanwhile, the applicant, his wife, divorced him. In concurrent proceedings in the Queen's Bench Division and the Family Division, the judge dealt with an application for a restraint order under the Drug Trafficking Act 1994, which covered the whole of the husband's assets, and the applicant's claims for ancillary relief under the Matrimonial Causes Act 1973. He found that the husband was the main beneficial owner of certain properties, with the applicant having a 13.3 per cent beneficial interest, by reason of a gift, in the former matrimonial home. All the family assets apart from the gift were the proceeds of drug trafficking, which the applicant knew about. The judge ordered the sale of the properties, declared that the applicant was entitled to a sum equivalent to her beneficial interest and subjected the remaining assets to a restraint order, so as to satisfy any confiscation order made by the Dutch court. The prosecution appealed. *Held,* where assets were tainted and subject to confiscation they should ordinarily, as a matter of justice and public policy, not be distributed. In the present case, the judge had erred. Although he found all the assets were tainted as the proceeds of drug dealing, he had failed to give sufficient weight to the inevitable consequences of that finding. His error lay in thinking that in every case, all factors were relevant. In cases such as these, the knowledge of the applicant, throughout her married life, that the lifestyle and the assets she had enjoyed were derived from drug trafficking, was dispositive. Therefore, the order for the lump sum would be set aside and the restraint order varied. Accordingly, the appeal would be allowed.

Richards v Richards; Crown Prosecution Service v Richards [2006] EWCA Civ 849, [2006] 2 FCR 452 (Court of Appeal: Thorpe and Moses LJJ and Hedley J).

1895 Ancillary relief—financial provision—variation of interim order—costs allowance for less wealthy spouse

A wealthy wife applied for a clean break with her relatively impoverished husband in ancillary proceedings. The husband, in order to cover his costs in procuring the legal advice and representation which he needed in order to make an adequate response to his wife's application, applied for a variation to the periodical payments order that had been made in his favour. The husband already owed the wife £46,000 in costs. The judge found that there was no other way the husband could reasonably have procured legal advice and representation, he ordered the wife to increase the periodical payments until the end of the financial dispute resolution. The wife appealed. *Held,* the question was whether an applicant for a costs allowance could demonstrate that he could not reasonably procure legal advice and representation by any other means. The applicant had to demonstrate that he could not reasonably deploy his assets to fund legal services, either directly or as the means of raising a loan, or could not reasonably procure legal services by the offer of a charge on ultimate capital recovery. The court would also need to be satisfied that there was no public funding that would furnish the applicant with legal advice and representation at an apt level of expertise for the proceedings. It would not be reasonable for the court to exercise its discretion when making a costs order unless the applicant had made such demonstration. It would not always be a sufficient condition, but it was a necessary one as a matter of common sense. The applicant's demonstration would incline towards the making of an allowance, but at that stage other factors might come into play which would on occasion lead the court to decline to make the allowance despite the demonstration. The reasonableness of the applicant's position, as far as could be determined at such an early stage, and the subject matter of the proceedings would be relevant, as well as a variety of other factors, such as that the husband owed the wife £46,000 in costs already. The judge's approach to the application had been essentially correct. Accordingly, the appeal would be dismissed.

Currey v Currey [2006] EWCA Civ 1338, [2007] Fam Law 12 (Court of Appeal: Chadwick and Wilson LJJ and Lindsay J).

1896 Ancillary relief—procedure—costs

Sir Mark Potter, P, has issued the following *Practice Direction (Ancillary Relief: Costs)* [2006] 1 WLR 634 with the approval and concurrence of the Lord Chancellor on 20 February 2006.

1. The Family Proceedings (Amendment) Rules 2006, SI 2006/352, make significant changes to the court's power to make costs orders in ancillary relief proceedings. The new rules will come into force on 3 April 2006. They will apply to an application for ancillary relief contained in a petition or answer filed on or after 3 April 2006, or to such an application which has not been made in a petition or answer but is made in Form A on or after that date. The rules will also apply to an application under the Matrimonial Causes Act 1973 s 10(2) or under the Civil Partnership Act 2004

s 48(2) made in Form B on or after that date. They do not however apply to such applications if they are to be heard by the court with an application which was made before that date.

2. Under the new rules the court will only have power to make a costs order in ancillary relief proceedings when this is justified by the litigation conduct of one of the parties: see the Family Proceedings Rules 1991, SI 1991/1247, r 2.71. When determining whether and how to exercise this power the court will be required to take into account the list of factors set out in the rules. The court will no longer be able to take into account any offers to settle expressed to be 'without prejudice' or 'without prejudice save as to costs' in deciding what, if any, costs order to make.

3. The new rules require the completion of Forms H and H1: see r 2.61F. Form H is to be used at interim hearings so that the court has available to it a realistic estimate of the costs incurred to date. Form H1 is for use at a final hearing to provide the court with accurate details of the costs which each party has incurred, or expects to incur, in relation to the ancillary relief proceedings. The purpose of this form is to enable the court to take account of the impact of each party's costs liability on their financial situations. Parties should ensure that the information contained in these forms is as full and accurate as possible and that any sums already paid in respect of a party's ancillary relief costs are clearly set out. Where relevant, any liability arising from the costs of other proceedings between the parties should continue to be referred to in the appropriate section of a party's Form E; any such costs should not be included in Forms H or H1.

4. Parties who intend to seek a costs order against another party in proceedings to which r 2.71 applies should ordinarily make this plain in open correspondence or in skeleton arguments before the date of the hearing. In any case where summary assessment of costs awarded under r 2.71 would be appropriate parties are under an obligation to file a statement of costs in CPR Form N260: see *Practice Direction About Costs* (supplementing CPR Pts 43–48) (1999) PD 43, s 13, and head 6, below.

5. An order for maintenance pending suit which includes an element to allow a party to deal with legal fees (see *A v A* (*Maintenance Pending Suit: Payment of Legal Fees*) [2001] 1 WLR 605 (2000 Abr para 1259); *G v G* (*Maintenance Pending Suit: Legal Costs*) [2002] 3 FCR 339 (2002 Abr para 2047); *McFarlane v McFarlane* [2005] Fam 171; and *Moses-Taiga v Taiga* [2005] EWCA Civ 1013) is an order made pursuant to the Matrimonial Causes Act 1973 s 22, and is not a 'costs order' within the meaning of the 1991 Rules r 2.71.

6. The *President's Practice Direction* (*Family Proceedings: Allocation and Costs*) [1999] 3 All ER 192 dated 22 April 1999 (1999 Abr para 2715) (as supplemented by the *President's Practice Direction* (*Family Proceedings: Costs*) [2000] 4 All ER 1072 (2000 Abr para 485) dated 24 July 2000) makes provision in relation to the application of the *Practice Direction About Costs* (supplementing CPR Pts 43–48) to family proceedings to which the 1991 Rules apply. Those President's directions will apply to a costs order made under r 2.71 as though the reference to the *Practice Direction About Costs* supplementing CPR Pts 43–48 were a reference to that direction excluding s 6, paras 8.1–8.4, ss 15, 16.

1897   Civil partnership

See CIVIL PARTNERSHIP.

1898   Divorce—proceedings—jurisdiction—domicile

See *R v R* (*Divorce: Jurisdiction: Domicile*), para 595.

1899   Family proceedings—fees

The Family Proceedings Fees (Amendment) Order 2006, SI 2006/739 (in force on 6 April 2006), further amends the 2004 Order, SI 2004/3114, so as to increase, from £15,050 to £15,460, the maximum gross annual income taken into account for the purposes of working tax credit, above which working tax credit is not a qualifying benefit for the purposes of exemption from court fees.

1900   Family proceedings—gender recognition—procedure

Dame Elizabeth Butler-Sloss, P, has issued the following *President's Direction* (*Gender Recognition Act 2004: Procedure*) [2005] 2 FLR 122 with the approval and concurrence of the Lord Chancellor on 5 April 2005.

1. Introduction
The Gender Recognition Act 2004 provides transsexual people with the opportunity to obtain legal recognition in their acquired gender. Legal recognition follows from the issue of a full gender recognition certificate by a Gender Recognition Panel. Section 4 requires that where a Panel has granted an application to a married applicant, the gender recognition certificate that it must issue is to be an interim gender recognition certificate. The interim certificate may then be used by either party to the marriage as evidence in support of an application to annul the marriage under the Matrimonial Causes Act 1973 s 12(g), or Sch 1 para 11(1)(e) ('that an interim gender recognition certificate has, after the time of the marriage, been issued to either party to the marriage').

2. Application

2.1 This *Practice Direction* applies to proceedings for divorce, judicial separation and annulment of marriage commenced on or after 4 April 2005.

2.2 Where proceedings for divorce, judicial separation or annulment of marriage have been commenced prior to this date, heads 3.2–3.5, below will apply to those proceedings if, but only if, the court acquires protected information, as defined by the 2004 Act s 22, in respect of a party to those proceedings.

3. Title of the cause
3.1 When a party to a matrimonial cause has changed his or her name since marriage, by deed poll or otherwise, the name currently being used by the party should appear first on any petition, answer and statement of arrangements followed by 'formerly known as (married name)'.

3.2 Subject to head 3.3, below, when describing the parties in any decree, order, notice or other document issued by the court, the parties should be described by their full current names only.

3.3 When giving details of the parties in any court list, including a special procedure cause list, they should be described by the initials and surname of their current names only, for example, *AB Jones v CD Jones*.

3.4 For the sake of clarity, in any document or court list mentioned in heads 3.2, 3.3, above party titles, ie Mr, Mrs, Miss, etc, should be omitted.

3.5. The Practice Note of 2 May 1940 (Title of Cause) will cease to have effect.

4. Evidence at trial of cause
This part of the *Practice Direction* applies where the following conditions are met:

(a) proceedings for annulment of marriage are brought under the 1973 Act s 12(g) or Sch 1 para 11(1)(e) and under no other ground under the 2004 Act ss 11 or 12 or Sch 1 para 11; and

(b) the cause is an undefended cause.

4.1 Any party requesting directions for trial may, in addition to the requirements of FPR r 2.25(2), state in their request that they would wish to give their evidence at the trial of the cause in accordance with the provisions of this *Practice Direction*; and in that event, the request must be accompanied by an affidavit setting out the information required by the appendix to this *Practice Direction*.

4.2 Where directions for trial are given in accordance with FPR r 2.24(5) in respect of a request to which head 4.2, above applies, a direction may also be given under r 2.28(3) that the affidavit lodged with the request for directions will be treated as the evidence of that party at the trial of the cause, unless otherwise directed.

4.3 In the case of an undefended cause proceeding on the respondent's answer, this part of the *Practice Direction* and the contents of the appendix will apply with appropriate modifications.

4.4 The appendix sets out a form of affidavit that may be used for the purposes of head 4.2, above.

[Editor's note: Appendix, not reproduced in this summary, contains form of affidavit.]

1901 Family proceedings—matrimonial home—transfer of tenancy order—matters to which court must have regard—misconduct

The Family Law Act 1996 Sch 7 para 5 provides that, in determining whether to exercise its powers relating to the transfer of tenancies on divorce, the court must have regard to all the circumstances of the case including the matters mentioned in s 33(6)(a)–(c).
A husband admitted some of a number of allegations of misconduct made against him by his wife. The wife obtained an order under the 1996 Act Sch 7 para 5, transferring into her sole name a joint tenancy held with her husband, in part on the basis of the husband's admitted misconduct. The husband appealed, relying on the fact that Sch 7 para 5 specifically referred to the factors set out in s 33(6)(a), (b) and (c), which related to the housing and welfare needs and the financial resources of the parties, but did not refer to s 33(6)(d), which related to the conduct of the parties. *Held*, the court could have regard to a party's admitted misconduct in considering whether it should transfer a tenancy to one of the parties pursuant to Sch 7 para 5. If the absence of express reference to s 33(6)(d) were construed as placing such a fundamental limitation on the exercise of the court's discretion, all sorts of practical difficulties would arise as to whether something constituted conduct. If judges were to exercise what was often a difficult and finely balanced discretionary judgment under Sch 7, it was extremely important that they should look at the case in the round, and have regard to all relevant circumstances. It followed that the judge had been entitled to take account of the husband's admitted misconduct. Accordingly, the appeal would be dismissed.
Lake v Lake [2006] EWCA Civ 1250, [2006] All ER (D) 297 (Jul) (Court of Appeal: Thorpe and Wall LJJ). *Miller v Miller; McFarlane v McFarlane* [2006] UKHL 24, [2006] 3 All ER 1 (para 1889) distinguished.

1902   Family proceedings—publicity—restrictions on reporting—government consultation

See para 461.

1903   Family Proceedings Rules

The Family Proceedings (Amendment) Rules 2006, SI 2006/352 (in force on 3 April 2006), further amend the 1991 Rules, SI 1991/1247, so as to make provision about the costs of ancillary relief proceedings. In particular, the rules (1) omit the existing rules about costs in such proceedings and insert a new rule which provides that the court will not make a costs order in ancillary relief proceedings unless it is appropriate to do so because of the conduct of one of the parties in relation to them; the factors which the court must have regard to before making a costs order under the new rule are set out; (2) require the completion of a costs estimate at interim hearings (Form H) and the completion of a detailed statement of costs at any final ancillary relief hearing (Form H1); (3) make changes consequential to the other changes made by the rules; and (4) provide that the new rules about costs in ancillary relief proceedings only apply to proceedings commenced after the rules come into force.

The Family Proceedings (Amendment) (No 2) Rules 2006, SI 2006/2080 (in force on 21 August 2006), further amend the 1991 Rules supra, in particular the provision relating to which documents must be sent to the court when it is considering an application for a consent order which includes an order in relation to pension sharing. The rules also provide, where there is an application for ancillary relief which includes an application for a pension sharing order or a pension attachment order, for information to be given to the other party by the party with pension rights in certain circumstances.

1904   Marriage—nullity—consent—duress—forced marriage

The applicant was born and raised in the United Kingdom and, while on holiday with her parents in Pakistan at the age of 16, she went through a ceremony of marriage with the respondent, her first cousin. The parents had threatened to kill themselves unless the applicant went through the ceremony, and had told her that they would not permit her to return to the United Kingdom. The applicant went through with the ceremony but the marriage was not consummated. Seven months after the ceremony, the applicant persuaded her mother to let her return to the United Kingdom where she sought a nullity decree. *Held*, the applicant's will had been overborne by duress, destroying the reality of her consent. While there had been no direct physical violence, she had been the victim of emotional pressure and moral blackmail over many months. There was no requirement that the respondent be the source of the duress. Accordingly, the application would be granted.

   NS v MI [2006] EWHC 1646 (Fam), [2006] Fam Law 839 (Family Division: Munby J). *Hirani v Hirani* (1982) 4 FLR 232, CA (1983 Abr para 1008), considered.

1905   Marriage—party to a marriage—other party to the marriage

See *J v C*, para 477.

1906   Marriage—validity—illegal immigrant wishing to marry—certificate of approval to marry—denial of certificate

See *R (on the application of Baiai) v Secretary of State for the Home Department*, para 365.

1907   Marriage—validity—same-sex parties—ceremony carried out in Canada

See *Wilkinson v Kitzinger*, para 705.

1908   Matrimonial home—registration in joint names—husband declared bankrupt—constructive trust—beneficial interest—intention of parties

See *Supperstone v Hurst*, para 2882.

1909   Pensions—Pension Protection Fund—divorce

See para 2174.

1910   Unmarried parties—cohabitation—financial rights on breakdown of relationship—Law Commission consultation

Following concern expressed in the House of Lords during the passage of the Civil Partnership Bill through Parliament, the Parliamentary Secretary at the Department for Constitutional Affairs referred to the Law Commission for consideration the financial hardship suffered by cohabitants and their children on the termination of their relationships by breakdown or death. In response, the Commission has published a consultation paper (No 179), *Cohabitation: the financial consequences of relationship breakdown*. It has also published an 'overview' of the consultation paper. The Commission, recognising that, under existing law, when a cohabiting relationship of two or more years' duration is ended by death the surviving party has a specific claim for financial provision from the estate of the deceased party, focused its attention principally on the financial consequences of termination of the relationship by breakdown. Further, the Commission is at pains to point out that it is not making recommendations for the reform of the law but is asking specific questions and inviting views on a number of provisional proposals. No new status of 'cohabitant' conferring a broad range of rights and privileges is proposed, and the Commission provisionally rejects the view that new remedies providing financial relief on separation should attach to some new status into which cohabiting couples could 'opt in' by registration. The Commission does not consider that all cohabitating couples should have access to some remedy merely because of the breakdown of their relationship; it also considers that couples should be able to 'opt out' of any scheme devised to cover the financial consequences of such breakdown. Views are sought on the criteria, if any, for 'opt out' agreements to be valid, the consequences of an invalid purported agreement, and whether the court should be able to set aside an 'opt out' agreement.

The Commission provisionally proposes that a new statutory scheme should be introduced providing financial relief on separation to 'eligible cohabitants', unless the parties have specifically opted out of the scheme. For such purposes, those eligible for relief should be defined by reference to the sharing of a joint household, and a checklist should be drawn up of factors to be taken into account in determining whether the parties were cohabiting. The paper suggests that cohabitants who are the parents of a child born before, during or following their cohabitation should automatically be eligible to apply for financial remedies under the suggested scheme. Views are sought on the eligibility for financial relief of cohabitants with a child who is not the child of both parties and on whether cohabitants without a child should be eligible for financial relief simply by reference to cohabitation for a specified minimum period.

The Law Commission provisionally rejects the possibility of extending the Matrimonial Causes Act 1973 Pt II (ss 21–40A) to cohabitants on separation. It is provisionally proposed that the jurisdiction of the court, on the separation of parties to cohabitation, should be to make any of the following orders: periodical payments, lump sum payments, property adjustment, property settlement, orders for sale, pension sharing, and interim payments on account. It is provisionally suggested that the courts should not apply fixed rules for property division but should exercise a discretion structured by principles to determine the basis on which any financial relief should be granted. Views are sought on the principles which should justify and quantify awards of financial relief. The Commission suggests that the court should determine whether, and to what extent, either party's economic position following separation would be improved by the retention of economic benefits arising from contributions made by the other party during their relationship, or impaired by economic sacrifices made as a result of that party's contributions to the relationship, or as a result of continuing child care responsibilities following separation. Views are sought specifically on whether awards should only be made where it would be substantially/manifestly unfair not to do so; on whether the parties' conduct should only be relevant to financial relief where the conduct relates to litigation or financial misconduct; on whether particular regard should be paid to the needs of the parties and any children and/or the financial resources which each party has or is likely to have in the foreseeable future; and on the weight to be attached to the 'clean break' principle and how it might relate to the other principles to be applicable on separation. The Commission provisionally proposes that claims for financial relief should be brought within one year, that might be extended with the court's permission in exceptional circumstances, of the parties' separation.

Provisionally rejecting the suggestion that cohabitants should have an automatic right to a share of a deceased party's estate on an intestacy, the Commission provisionally suggests adjustments that should be made to the Inheritance (Provision for Family and Dependants) Act 1975 following the enactment of a statutory scheme for financial relief for cohabitants on separation to bring that Act into line with the new scheme; and that the court, on making an order under the new scheme, should be empowered to rule that neither cohabitant should be able to make a claim under the 1975 Act against the other's estate.

MEDICAL PROFESSIONS

Halsbury's Laws of England (4th edn) vol 30(1) (Reissue) paras 1–942

Articles

For articles relating to this title please refer to the Table of Articles at the beginning of the Abridgment.

1911 Dentistry—European qualifications—complementary professions

The European Qualifications (Professions Complementary to Dentistry) Regulations 2006, SI 2006/1718 (in force on 28 July 2006), further amend the European Communities (Recognition of Professional Qualifications) (Second General System) Regulations 2002, SI 2002/2934, so as to apply the requirements of EEC Council Directive 92/51 on a second general system for the regulation of professional education and training to the professions of clinical dental technician, dental nurse, dental technician and orthodontic therapist. The regulations also amend the Dentists

Act 1984 s 36C by adding references to such professions and further, by providing that a person with free movement rights in the European Economic Area or Switzerland may not be required to demonstrate proficiency in the English language as a condition of registration in the professional register.

1912   Dentistry—regulation of dentists and dental care professionals—transitional provisions

The Dentists Act 1984 (Amendment) Order 2005 Transitional Provisions Order of Council 2006, SI 2006/1671 (in force on 31 July 2006), makes transitional provisions relating to the new arrangements for the regulation of dentists and dental care professionals. In particular, the order (1) sets out the arrangements for dealing with fraud and error cases relating to registration in the dentists register which are ongoing when the new arrangements come into force; (2) ensures that determinations, directions and orders relating to suspension or erasure from, or conditional registration in, the dentists register under the old arrangements continue to have effect, with measures for moving old cases to the new system; (3) sets out measures for concluding the work of the General Dental Council's continuing professional development committee, which is being abolished; (4) deals with outstanding erasure or suspension cases relating to disqualification in another member state of the European Economic Area or Switzerland; (5) ensures that the restrictions on individuals carrying on the business of dentistry will continue to apply to individuals who are or were suspended or erased from the dentists register under the old arrangements; (6) makes provision relating to the new arrangements for the registration of dental care professionals; and (7) ensures that the Council for the Regulation of Health Care Professions will continue to be able to review the outstanding misconduct or crime cases before the professional conduct committee which are being disposed of under the old arrangements.

1913   General Chiropractic Council—professional conduct committee and health committee—procedure

The General Chiropractic Council (Professional Conduct Committee and Health Committee) Amendment Rules Order of Council 2006, SI 2006/1630 (in force on 30 June 2006), further amend the General Chiropractic Council (Professional Conduct Committee) Rules 2000, SI 2000/3290, and the General Chiropractic Council (Health Committee) Rules 2000, SI 2000/3291, by revising the manner of the proceedings concerning the submission of evidence to the committees, and by approving rules made by the General Chiropractic Council which provide for the procedure to be followed by the professional conduct committee and the health committee in considering allegations as to a chiropractor's conduct, competence or ability to practise due to a physical or mental condition.

1914   General Dental Council—appointments committee—committee members

The General Dental Council (Appointments Committee and Appointment of Members of Committees) Rules Order of Council 2006, SI 2006/1664 (in force on 31 July 2006), approves rules made by the General Dental Council providing for (1) the constitution of the appointments committee of the General Dental Council; and (2) the system of appointment of members to the health committee, the interim orders committee, the professional performance committee and the registration appeals committee of the General Dental Council. The order also provides for the appointment of a chairman to the committees and the quorum. Similar provision is made providing for the constitution of and appointment of members to the investigating committee of the General Dental Council. The General Dental Council (Appointment of Members of Committees) Rules 2003 and the General Dental Council (Appointments Committee) Rules 2003 are revoked.

1915   General Dental Council—constitution—members

The General Dental Council (Constitution) Order of Council 2006, SI 2006/1666 (in force on 31 July 2006), (1) specifies the numbers of each of the three categories of members of the Council; (2) provides for the appointment of lay members; and (3) makes provision as to members' tenure of office, termination of office and by-elections.

1916   General Dental Council—constitution of committees

The General Dental Council (Constitution of Committees) Order of Council 2006, SI 2006/1665 (in force on 31 July 2006), provides for the constitution of the health committee, the interim orders committee, the investigating committee, the professional conduct committee, the professional performance committee and the registration appeals committee, of the General Dental Council. Each is to consist of five natural persons, of good character, who are fit and proper persons to act as members of the committee of the Council, of which at least one must be (1) a natural person who is neither a registered dentist nor a registered dental care professional; (2) a registered dentist; and (3) in any case concerning a person's registration in the dental care professional register, a registered dental care professional. SI 2003/1081 (as amended) is revoked.

1917   General Dental Council—fitness to practise—committees—procedure

The General Dental Council (Fitness to Practise) Rules Order of Council 2006, SI 2006/1663 (in force on 31 July 2006), approves the General Dental Council (Fitness to Practise) Rules 2006, which set out the procedures to be followed by the Council's investigating committee, health committee, professional conduct committee, professional performance committee and interim orders committee in carrying out their functions. Those rules relate to proceedings against both dentists and members of professions complementary to dentistry, and cover proceedings relating to a practitioner's fitness to practise and proceedings relating to whether an entry in the dentists register or the dental care professionals register has been fraudulently procured.

1918   General Dental Council—professions complementary to dentistry

The General Dental Council (Professions Complementary to Dentistry) Regulations Order of Council 2006, SI 2006/1440 (in force on 31 July 2006), approve regulations made by the General Dental Council specifying professions complementary to dentistry and titles applying to each specified profession. In particular, the regulations (1) specify the professions pursued by dental nurses, dental technicians, clinical dental technicians and orthodontic therapists; (2) contain transitional provisions regarding the entitlement to registration of certain dental nurses and dental technicians; and (3) contain an exemption from the offence contained in the Dentists Act 1984 s 39 regarding the use of the titles specified in relation to the professions pursued by dental nurses or dental technicians.

The General Dental Council (Professions Complementary to Dentistry) (Business of Dentistry) Rules Order Council 2006, SI 2006/1670 (in force on 31 July 2006), approves rules made by the General Dental Council specifying classes of registered dental care professionals, with the effect that a member of such a class may carry on the business of dentistry as an individual under the Dentists Act 1984 s 41.

The General Dental Council (Professions Complementary to Dentistry) (Dental Hygienists and Dental Therapists) Regulations Order of Council 2006, SI 2006/1667 (in force on 31 July 2006), approves regulations made by the General Dental Council specifying the professions complementary to dentistry, with the effect that dental hygienists and dental therapists are brought within the system of regulation set out in the Dentists Act 1984 Pt 3A, (ss 36A–36Z2).

The General Dental Council (Professions Complementary to Dentistry) (Qualifications and Supervision of Dental Work) Rules Order of Council 2006, SI 2006/1669 (in force on 31 July 2006), approves rules made by the General Dental Council providing for the procedure in relation to, and the effect of, a decision to withdraw approval of qualifications in professions complementary to dentistry, and specify registered dental care professionals who are authorised to carry out direct personal supervision of certain kinds of dental work under the Dentists Act 1984 s 37.

1919   General Dental Council—registration appeals

The General Dental Council (Registration Appeals) Rules Order of Council 2006, SI 2006/1668 (in force on 31 July 2006), approves rules made by the General Dental Council providing for the procedure to be followed by the registration appeals committee of the General Dental Council, when determining an appeal by a person against a decision relating to the registration of dentists and dental care professionals. Provision is made in respect of the notice of appeal, further evidence and documents which may be sent or prepared in relation to the appeal, preliminary hearings and the conduct and procedure at an oral hearing.

1920   General Optical Council—continuing education and training

The General Optical Council (Continuing Education and Training) (Amendment No 2) Rules Order of Council 2006, SI 2006/2901 (in force on 1 January 2007), approves the General Optical Council (Continuing Education and Training) (Amendment No 2) Rules 2006, which change the period of calculation for the required continuing education and training points from one year to three years, increase from £35 to £45 the fee to be paid by those persons wishing to provide continuing education and training courses and set out the requirements imposed on an applicant for the restoration of his name to a register or for the restoration of an entry relating to a specialty.

1921   General Osteopathic Council—continuing professional development

The General Osteopathic Council (Continuing Professional Development) Rules Order of Council 2006, SI 2006/3511 (in force on 1 March 2007), which is made under the Osteopaths Act 1993, approves rules made by the General Osteopathic Council which set out the requirements in respect of post registration training which have to be met by registered osteopaths. In particular, the order provides for the circumstances in which an osteopath may be removed from the register for non-compliance with the requirements, and make provision regarding applications for restoration to the register following such removal.

1922   Health Act 2006

See para 2028.

1923   Health Professions Council—register—parts and entries

The Health Professions (Parts of and Entries in the Register) (Amendment) Order of Council 2006, SI 2006/1996 (in force on 21 August 2006), further amends the 2003 Order, SI 2003/1571, by providing that, in the case of chiropodists and podiatrists, physiotherapists and radiographers (diagnostic or therapeutic), registration may include an entry indicating that a registrant is qualified to order drugs, medicines and appliances as a supplementary provider, and by allowing for other qualifications or competencies in a particular field or level of practice to be entered.

1924   Health Professions Wales—abolition

The Health Professions Wales Abolition Order 2006, SI 2006/978 (in force on 1 April 2006), abolishes Health Professions Wales and makes provision for the transfer of its staff, property and records and for the winding up of its affairs. SI 2004/550, 551 are revoked.

1925   Human fertilisation and embryology—fertilisation treatment—creation of embryos—withdrawal of partner's consent to use of embryo

The applicant and her former partner had attended a clinic and the applicant had undergone IVF treatment. The former partner had signed consents in compliance with the Human Fertilisation and Embryology Act 1990 Sch 3 para 2(1)(a). Following the discovery that the claimant had a cancerous tumour in both ovaries, eggs were harvested from her and fertilised. Six embryos were created and stored. As a result of an operation to remove the tumours, unless the applicant could use the frozen embryos, she had no prospect of bearing a child which was genetically hers. Before an embryo transfer had been attempted, the relationship between the applicant and her former partner ended. The former partner withdrew his consent to the use of the embryos. The applicant sought an injunction requiring the second defendant to restore his consent and a declaration that s 12, Sch 3 were incompatible with her rights under the European Convention on Human Rights art 8. The judge dismissed the claim and the applicant's appeal was also dismissed. Permission to appeal to the House of Lords was refused and the applicant made an application to the European Court of Human Rights. *Held,* in adopting a clear rule, which was explained to the parties and was set out on the forms which they both signed, the United Kingdom had not exceeded the margin of appreciation afforded to it, or upset the fair balance required under the Convention art 8. Since the use of IVF treatment gave rise to sensitive moral and ethical issues against a background of fast-moving medical developments, the margin of appreciation afforded to the respondent state had to be a wide one. The state's wide margin of appreciation extended both to its decision to intervene in the area and to the detailed rule which it lay down in order to achieve a balance between the competing public and private interests. Although there was a clear difference between the involvement of the two parties in the process of IVF treatment, it did not follow that the art 8 rights of the male donor would necessarily be worth less than those of the female. The absence of a power in the 1990 Act to override a genetic parent's withdrawal of consent did not, even in the exceptional circumstances of the present case, upset the fair balance required by the Convention art 8. Judgment would be given accordingly.

Application 6339/05 *Evans v United Kingdom* [2006] 1 FCR 585 (European Court of Human Rights). For earlier proceedings, see *Evans v Amicus Healthcare Ltd* [2004] EWCA Civ 727, [2004] 3 All ER 1025 (2004 Abr para 1946) affirmed.

1926   Human tissue—ethical approval

The Human Tissue Act 2004 (Ethical Approval, Exceptions from Licensing and Supply of Information about Transplants) Regulations 2006, SI 2006/1260 (in force on 1 September 2006), (1) provide that ethical approval for the purposes of certain provisions of the Human Tissue Act 2004 is approval by a research ethics authority; (2) provide that licensing by the Human Tissue Authority is not required for storage of relevant material which has come from a human body where the relevant material has come from (a) a living person unless storage is for the purpose of transplantation, other than transplantation of an organ or part-organ or where the storage is for less than 48 hours; (b) a living person where storage is for the purpose of research for which ethical approval has been given or sought; (c) a human body where storage is for the purpose of transplantation of an organ or part of an organ or the storage period is for less than 48 hours; (d) a human body where storage is for the purpose of transplantation and either the material is an organ or part of an organ, or the storage period is for less than 48 hours; and (3) specify the information which must be provided to NHS Blood and Transplant in connection with transplants using certain material from a human body.

1927   Human tissue—Human Tissue Authority—licensing—exceptions

See para 1926.

1928 Human tissue—persons lacking capacity to consent—transplants

The Human Tissue Act 2004 (Persons who Lack Capacity to Consent and Transplants) Regulations 2006, SI 2006/1659 (in force on 1 September 2006), make provision as to the circumstances in which certain activities may be carried out in relation to material from the bodies of persons lacking capacity to consent for the purposes of certain provisions of the Human Tissue Act 2004, and in relation to restrictions on transplants involving a live donor. In particular, the regulations (1) provide that an adult who lacks capacity is deemed to consent to the storage or use of relevant material where those activities are in his best interests or carried out for the purpose of an authorised clinical trial or certain approved research; (2) prescribe the excepted purposes for which the results of DNA analysis may be used where the analysis is of DNA that has been manufactured by the body of an adult who lacks capacity to consent; (3) define 'transplantable material' for the purposes of ss 33, 34; (4) specify the circumstances in which transplants of such material from the body of a live donor may be carried out without contravening the specified restrictions, which are disapplied if the matter has been referred to the Human Tissue Authority ('the Authority') and if, after certain required interviews have taken place, the Authority is satisfied that certain specified conditions have been met; (5) provide that a panel of at least three members of the Authority must make the decision on whether a transplant involving a live donor is to be restricted in any case or organ donation (a) where a child is involved; (b) where the donor is an adult who lacks the capacity to consent; or (c) where the donor is an adult who has capacity to consent but where there are paired donations, pooled donations or an altruistic donation; (6) provide for a right of reconsideration of such a decision, which may be exercised by (a) the Authority, where it is satisfied that there has been a material change in the circumstances since the decision was made or that any information given to it was in a material respect false or misleading; (b) the donor; (c) the recipient; or (d) the registered medical practitioner who referred the matter to the Authority; and (7) make provision regarding the procedure to be followed in the event of a reconsideration.

1929 Human tissue—supply of information—powers of entry and search

The Human Tissue Act 2004 (Powers of Entry and Search: Supply of Information) Regulations 2006, SI 2006/538 (in force on 7 April 2006), prescribes the information that must be included in an appropriate statement that is given to an occupier when entering and searching premises in accordance with a warrant. The information provided must include a statement of authorisation, a statement of the duly authorised person's rights, powers and obligations and a statement that a person commits an offence if he fails without reasonable excuse to comply or intentionally obstructs the investigators, rights of entry and search.

1930 Human tissue—supply of information—transplants

See para 1926.

1931 Human Tissue Act 2004—commencement

The Human Tissue Act 2004 (Commencement No 4 and Transitional Provisions) Order 2006, SI 2006/404, brings into force (1) on 1 March 2006, for certain purposes, ss 16(1), (2)(e)(ii), 17–25, 37, 39, 41, 44, 48–54, 56, 58(1), (2), Schs 3, 5, Sch 6 para 5; and (2) on 7 April 2006, the provisions mentioned in head (1) supra, so far as they are not already in force.

The Human Tissue Act 2004 (Commencement No 5 and Transitional Provisions) Order 2006, SI 2006/1997, amended by SI 2006/2169, brings into force (1) on 31 July 2006, for certain purposes, so far as they are not already in force, ss 16–24, 37, 39–41, 44, 52–54, 58 and Sch 3; (2) on 1 September 2006, those provisions of the Act, except those mentioned in head (3) infra, that are not already in force; and (3) on 1 December 2006, ss 5 and 8. Transitional provision is also made.

For a summary of the Act, see 2004 Abr para 1949. See also the commencement table in the title STATUTES.

1932 Medical practitioner—consultant orthopaedic surgeon—duty of care

See *West Bromwich Albion Football Club Ltd v El-Safty*, para 2074.

1933 Medical practitioner—disciplinary proceedings—decisions capable of being referred to High Court—finding that proceedings constitute abuse of process

A doctor was deceived by an undercover journalist into handing over a medical certificate in return for money. The doctor was charged with serious professional misconduct, but the proceedings before a fitness to practise panel of the applicant, the General Medical Council, were stayed as an abuse of process on the basis of entrapment. On the applicant's appeal, issues arose as to whether the decision of the panel was a 'final decision' within the meaning of the National Health Service Reform and Health Care Professions Act s 29(2) and whether the imposition of the stay was unduly lenient or manifestly inappropriate. *Held*, the mischief at which s 29 was aimed occurred just as much where a disciplinary tribunal wrongly brought the case to an end on the grounds of abuse of process as where it wrongly concluded that the conduct did not amount to professional misconduct or where it imposed too lenient a penalty. It followed that a finding by the panel of an abuse of process did amount to a 'final decision' within the meaning of s 29(2)(a). However, to impose a stay was exceptional. The rationale of the doctrine of abuse of process, namely the court's repugnance in permitting its process to be used in the face of the executive's misuse of state powers by its agents, was absent in the case of misconduct by non-state agents. The abuse of process relied on had nothing to do with the state or the applicant as prosecuting body. The panel had therefore erred in imposing the stay. Judgment would be given accordingly.

Re Saluja (Reference of decision by General Medical Council in disciplinary proceedings); Council for the Regulation of Healthcare Professionals v General Medical Council [2006] EWHC 2784 (Admin), (2006) 92 BMLR 153 (Queen's Bench Division: Goldring J).

1934   Medical practitioner—disciplinary proceedings—professional misconduct—serious misconduct—expert evidence—immunity from disciplinary procedures

See *Meadow v General Medical Council*, para 1299.

1935   Medical practitioner—disciplinary proceedings—professional misconduct—unproven complaints—disclosure

The applicant had been acquitted of five accounts of indecent assault and the General Medical Council decided that there was no case to answer on complaints of a similar nature made against him. Following further allegations against him of sexual offences on incapacited patients who were unfit to give evidence in court, he was informed of the decision to issue an alert letter. His application for judicial review of the decision was refused and he appealed. *Held*, a health service circular laid down the provisions for alert letters, which was the way that all NHS bodies were made aware of a doctor whose conduct could place patients or staff at risk. It was unlawful to issue an alert letter in relation to a doctor's conduct where the conduct had been considered by a relevant disciplinary or other body such as the Crown Court and no adverse finding had been made. The 'pressing need' test, according to which disclosure should only be made when there was a pressing need for it, would be applied. The importance of the decision to the applicant required nothing less. It was inescapable that there was a more than fanciful possibility that the applicant represented a danger to women in his care, in particular possibly disturbed women, which was a powerful factor in demonstrating a pressing need. The alert letter was lawful as it made it clear that anyone making an inquiry should be told that no findings of sexual assault had ever been made against the applicant. There was a positive legal duty on those issuing alert letters to monitor cases. There should be regular reviews at reasonably short intervals at which substantive consideration was to be given as to whether the letter needed to be maintained. Accordingly the appeal would be dismissed.

R (on the application of Dr D) v Secretary of State for Health [2006] EWCA Civ 989, (2006) Times, 28 August (Court of Appeal: Ward, Laws and Longmore LJJ). *R v Chief Constable of North Wales Police, ex p Thorpe* [1999] QB 396, CA (1998 Abr para 2467); and *R (on the application of X) v Chief Constable of West Midlands Police* [2004] EWCA Civ 1068, [2005] 1 All ER 610 (2004 Abr para 703) considered.

1936   Medical practitioner—member of union—decision not to renew membership—no warning of termination—personal information unfairly processed

See *Johnson v Medical Defence Union Ltd*, para 588.

1937   Medical practitioner—negligence—duty of care—private laboratory engaged to perform tissue testing—proximity to patient

See *Farraj v King's Healthcare NHS Trust*, para 2084.

1938   Medical practitioner—postgraduate education and training—fees

The Postgraduate Medical Education and Training Board (Fees) Rules Order 2006, SI 2006/515 (in force on 1 April 2006), replaces the 2005 Order, SI 2005/1872, and approves the Postgraduate Medical Education and Training Board (Fees) Rules 2006, which prescribe the fees that are payable to the Postgraduate Medical Education and Training Board ('the Board') in respect of the exercise by the Board of certain of its functions. The functions in respect of which fees are payable include (1) issuing Certificates of Training for general practitioners and specialists; (2) applications to the Board to determine whether certain persons not holding Certificates of Completion of Training have met particular standards of equivalence; and (3) appeals against the Board's decisions.

1939   Medical practitioner—registration

The Medical Act 1983 (Amendment) and Miscellaneous Amendments Order 2006, SI 2006/1914 (in force in part on 19 July 2006, in part on 20 July 2006 and in part on dates to be notified in the London, Edinburgh and Belfast Gazettes), amends the Medical Act 1983, makes consequential changes to other legislation and makes unconnected amendments to the Opticians Act 1989 and the

Nursing and Midwifery Order 2001, SI 2002/253. In particular, the order (1) renames registration decisions panels as registration panels; (2) abolishes the register of medical practitioners with limited registration, thereby requiring the General Medical Council to keep only one register of medical practitioners; (3) provides that medical practitioners will no longer be able to apply for limited registration, but that those on the register of medical practitioners with limited registration prior to the abolition of that register will transfer to the Council's register, with exceptions, following an initial period of work in an approved practice setting; (4) provides for any outstanding applications for limited registration to be dealt with as applications for provisional or full registration; (5) requires medical practitioners with provisional registration who are in training in the United Kingdom to complete a programme for provisionally registered doctors ('the programme'), recognised by the education committee of the Council, before they can become fully registered medical practitioners; (6) provides that the education committee is to (a) determine the requirements of the programme; (b) be responsible for determining which bodies may be involved in the programme; and (c) be responsible for the arrangements for monitoring such bodies; (7) provides that the programme will be open to all provisionally registered doctors, including those who have qualified overseas; (8) confers powers on the Council to limit the length of time for which medical practitioners may be provisionally registered; (9) allows bodies other than universities to hold qualifying examinations; (10) provides that medical practitioners who have qualified outside the European Economic Area or Switzerland are to be given full registration provided that they have an acceptable overseas qualification and have demonstrated that they have the requisite knowledge, skills and experience; (11) requires the registrar to provisionally register a medical practitioner so as to enable him to participate in the programme or, transitionally, to be employed as a house doctor, where the registrar determines that the medical practitioner does not yet have the requisite knowledge, skills and experience to qualify for full registration, but has sufficient knowledge and skills to embark on the programme or, transitionally, to be employed as a house doctor; (12) creates a new category of temporary registration for overseas practitioners who are to be employed or engaged within the United Kingdom to provide particular medical services for persons who are not nationals of the United Kingdom; (13) provides that the registration of such overseas practitioners is conditional on their only providing particular medical services at particular establishments and only providing those services to patients who are not nationals of the United Kingdom, except in an emergency; (14) provides for separate registration arrangements for visiting eminent specialists; (15) makes the entitlement to registration conditional on the applicant's fitness to practise not being impaired; (16) confers extended powers on the registrar to obtain information about whether a medical practitioner's fitness to practise is, or was, impaired at the time of registration and, where this is the case, enables the registrar to remove the practitioner from the Council's register, subject to rights of appeal, if new information comes to light showing that his fitness to practise was impaired at the time of registration but that this was not disclosed at the time, or if a medical practitioner refuses to co-operate with the new information gathering arrangements; (17) allows a medical practitioner to appeal through the courts where his restoration to the register has been refused for a reason relating to his fitness to practise; (18) amends the fitness to practise procedures for medical practitioners after registration so as to (a) confer powers on the Council to apply to a court to require the production of documents from third parties relating to fitness to practise investigations where such documents have not been supplied within 14 days; (b) confer powers on the Council to disclose information relating to a medical practitioner's fitness to practise in specified circumstances; (c) provide for a list of decisions of panels and committees that are required to be published, although the Council may withhold, in the course of publication, information concerning a person's physical or mental health where it considers the information to be confidential; (d) make an allowance for the possibility that a medical practitioner will concede, during an investigation into his fitness to practise, that his fitness to practise is impaired and, in such circumstances, allow the Council to make rules in respect of the agreement of undertakings to be observed by the practitioner, and the procedure to be followed where such undertakings are breached; (e) provide that fitness to practise hearings are to be in public, except to the extent that rules made by the Council provide otherwise; and (f) make changes to the making of legal assessors rules; (19) provides that the provisions of the 1983 Act relating to voluntary erasure from the Council's register and those relating to fraudulent or incorrect entry are to apply if a person's registration has been suspended; (20) provides that the cases relating to fraudulent or incorrect entry are to be dealt with by the registrar rather than the Council, with rights of appeal to the registration appeals panels; (21) makes changes to ensure that revalidation of a medical practitioner's licence to practise can take place at any time, and to allow the Council to make regulations about requiring medical practitioners to supply information to assist licensing authorities in determining when and how to revalidate their licences; (22) requires licence to practise appeals to be held in public, except to the extent that rules provide otherwise; (23) requires all medical practitioners who hold a licence to practise to be covered by an adequate and appropriate indemnity agreement such as a policy of insurance; (24) confers information gathering powers relating to such a requirement, so that applicants for licences to practise who cannot demonstrate adequate cover may be refused a licence to practise; (25) provides that medical practitioners may face disciplinary proceedings or withdrawal of their licences to practise if they breach either the notification requirements relating to the new requirement or the requirement itself; (26) makes provision for appeals and in respect of restoration to the register of those who are subject to erasure; (27) requires all medical practitioners who are newly fully registered, newly restored to the register or transferred from the register of medical practitioners with limited registration, with exceptions, to work in an approved practice setting until the first revalidation of their fitness to practise by the Council; (28) provides for guidance from the Council on suitable practice settings for medical practitioners who are newly fully registered or newly restored and who are exempt from the previous requirement; (29) makes provision in relation to the time of payment of retention fees; (30) removes the requirement for the Privy Council to approve fees regulations; (31) amends the limitations on persons, other than registered medical practitioners, being entitled to recover charges through the courts for certain medical services so as not to prohibit recovery of charges by other specified providers of such services; (32) amends the 1989 Act so as to provide that the main objective of the General Optical Council, in exercising functions that affect the health and safety of members of the public, is to protect, promote and maintain the public's health and safety; and (33) further amends the 2001 Order so as to (a) provide that the Nursing and Midwifery Council no longer needs to prescribe criteria for assigning overseas electors to a particular national constituency as electors are required to make the selection themselves; and (b) provide that the terms of office of alternate members of the Nursing and Midwifery Council expire at the same time as those of their registrant counterparts. Various consequential amendments and revocations are made.

1940   Medical practitioner—specialist register—application—time limit

The system relating to the recognition of consultant doctors was changed by the European Specialist Medical Qualifications Order 1995, SI 1995/3208. Under the new rules, practitioners who wished to be appointed as consultants had to be awarded a certificate entitling them to be entered onto a specialist register maintained by the General Medical Council. Transitional provision was made by art 12, which enabled specialists who were already practising to apply to be on the register. By virtue of art 12(2A), the defendant training authority was required to determine by a certain date the applications of such practitioners who wished to be placed on the register. The claimant, a specialist in family planning and reproductive health care, applied for inclusion on the specialist register, but was advised by the defendant that her specialty did not qualify for inclusion. However, the Court of Appeal later ruled that that the defendant was wrong to exclude that specialty from recognition, and the claimant therefore made a fresh application. That application was rejected on the grounds that it was out of time, and her appeal to the Office of the Director of Appeal was dismissed. The claimant applied for judicial review of that decision. The central issue for determination was whether the date mentioned in art 12(2A) constituted a cut-off point precluding doctors from applying under art 12(2A) after the relevant date. *Held*, the wording of art 12(2A) showed that it was not intended that it should constitute an application time-bar obligation on doctors, which would have meant the defendant was not entitled to consider applications after the relevant date. Article 12(2A) did not impose any obligation on applicants but merely an obligation on the defendant to determine the applications of those who had applied by a certain date. It followed that the defendant was obliged to consider the claimant's application and, accordingly, the application would be allowed.

Malone v Specialist Training Authority of the Medical Royal Colleges [2005] EWHC 2470 (Admin), (2006) 87 BMLR 108 (Queen's Bench Division: Silber J).

1941   Medical practitioner—suspension—hearing—procedural requirements

See *R (on the application of Malik) v Waltham Forest Primary Care Trust*, para 1596.

1942   Nurses agencies—England

See para 2689.

1943   Nursing and Midwifery Council—practice committees—constitution—rules

The Nursing and Midwifery Council (Practice Committees) (Constitution) Rules Order of Council 2006, SI 2006/1199 (in force on 31 July 2006), approves the Nursing and Midwifery Council (Practice Committees) (Constitution) Rules 2006 made by the Nursing and Midwifery Council in respect of the constitution and procedure of the investigating committee, the conduct and competence committee and the health committee. SI 2003/1738 is revoked.

1944   Nursing and Midwifery Council—register—parts and entries

The Nurses and Midwives (Part of and Entries in the Register) Amendment Order of Council 2006, SI 2006/1015 (in force on 1 May 2006), further amends the 2004 Order, SI 2004/1765, by changing the recordable qualifications in the statutory register of nurses and midwives maintained by the Nursing and Midwifery Council, with the effect that (1) the former qualification to order drugs, medicines and appliances from the Extended Formulary has been changed to a qualification to order them as a nurse independent prescriber; (2) some nurse independent prescribers are qualified to act as supplementary prescribers; and (3) the former annotation for supplementary prescribers is revised to reflect the dual nature of their qualification.

1945 Nursing and Midwifery Council—transitional provisions

The Nursing and Midwifery Order 2001 (Transitional Provisions) (Amendment) Order of Council 2006, SI 2006/1441 (in force on 1 June 2006), amends the 2004 Order of Council, SI 2004/1762, so as to provide that, in relation to outstanding cases relating to the fitness to practise of nurse and midwives, it is no longer a requirement that a member of the Nursing and Midwifery Council should be a member of the preliminary proceedings committee, the professional conduct committee or the health committee.

1946 Patient—adult lacking capacity—medical and welfare decisions—role of Official Solicitor

Laurence Oates, Official Solicitor to the Supreme Court, has issued the following *Practice Note* (*Official Solicitor: Declaratory Proceedings: Medical and Welfare Decisions for Adults who Lack Capacity*) [2006] 2 FLR 373 issued on 28 July 2006.

Introduction

1. This *Practice Note* supersedes *Practice Note* [2001] 2 FCR 569 (2001 Abr para 2238). It deals only with cases concerning adults who lack capacity. It is subject to judicial decisions and applies pending the coming into force of the Mental Capacity Act 2005. It has been issued with the approval of the President of the Family Division.

Jurisdiction

2. The High Court, but not the county court, has inherent jurisdiction to make decisions about the lawfulness of proposed medical treatment, or withdrawal of medical treatment, or as to welfare issues such as where someone should live or with whom they should have contact in respect of adults who lack capacity to make such decisions for themselves. The jurisdiction is discretionary, and will be exercised whenever there is a serious justiciable issue requiring a decision by the court.

3. The proceedings in relation to adults are civil proceedings to which the CPR apply and should be brought in the Family Division.

The Need for Court Involvement

4. In *Re S (Hospital Patient Court's Jurisdiction)* [1996] Fam 1 (1995 Abr para 2025) Sir Thomas Bingham MR said:

'In cases of controversy and cases involving momentous and irrevocable decisions, the courts have treated as justiciable any genuine question as to what the best interests of a patient require or justify. In making these decisions the courts have recognised the desirability of informing those involved whether a proposed course of conduct will render them criminally or civilly liable; they have acknowledged their duty to act as a safeguard against malpractice, abuse and unjustified action; and they have recognised the desirability, in the last resort, of decisions being made by an impartial, independent tribunal.'

5. There are certain categories of medical treatment cases in which case law has established that a court application should be made:

(a) where it is proposed to withdraw artificial nutrition and hydration from a patient in the permanent vegetative state (see *Re Airedale NHS Trust v Bland* [1993] AC 789 (1992 Abr para 1770)); see the Official Solicitor's website www.officialsolicitor.gov.uk for further information on the practice and procedure in these cases;

(b) the sterilisation for contraceptive purposes of a person who cannot consent (see *S (Adult Patient: Sterilisation)* [2000] 3 WLR 1288 (2000 Abr para 2237)); see the Official Solicitor's website for further information); and

(c) certain termination of pregnancy cases (see *D v An NHS Trust (Medical Treatment: Consent: Termination)* [2003] EWHC 2793 (Fam), [2004] 1 FLR 1110 (2004 Abr para 1990)).

6. As a matter of good practice medical practitioners should seek a declaration, particularly in relation to withdrawal or withholding of life sustaining treatment, where the legality of so doing is in doubt (see *R (on the application of Burke) v GMC* [2005] EWCA 1003, [2005] 3 WLR 1132 (2005 Abr para 2142)). In general, any serious treatment decision where there is a disagreement between those involved and those close to the patient, where the treatment proposed may involve the use of force to restrain the patient or otherwise may be resisted by the patient or where there are doubts and difficulties over the assessment of either the patient's capacity or best interests should be referred to the court.

7. Welfare decisions may need to be referred to the court when there is disagreement between the patient's family or carers, and those with a duty of care toward the patient, commonly a local authority, over issues such as:

(a) place of residence, care arrangements or contact with family members or others (see *Re F (Adult: Court's Jurisdiction)* [2001] Fam 38 (2000 Abr para 2258) and *Re S (Adult's Lack of Capacity: Carer and Residence)* [2003] EWHC 1909 (Fam), [2003] 2 FLR 1235); or

(b) an adult's capacity to marry (see *Sheffield City Council v E* [2004] EWHC 2808 (Fam), [2005] Fam 326 (2004 Abr para 1919)).

The Proceedings

8. These applications are invariably brought in the Family Division under CPR Pt 8. The claimant should file all the evidence with the claim form. The relief sought should include declarations as to the patient's lack of capacity, and as to what the claimant asserts is lawful as being in the patient's best interests, for example to provide, or withdraw as the case may be, the relevant medical treatment, to provide the patient with residential care, or limit contact with a specified person or persons etc.

9. The evidence filed must deal with litigation capacity, decision making capacity and, in all but capacity to marry cases, best interests. The court has no jurisdiction to consider whether or not it is in a person's best interests to marry or to enter into a particular marriage, only whether or not that person has the capacity to marry (see *Sheffield City Council v E*).

10. The Official Solicitor may be consulted as to the drafting of the relief sought.

Capacity

11. There is a rebuttable resumption that an adult has capacity for all purposes. The test of capacity is issue specific (see *Masterman-Lister v Brutton and Co* [2002] EWCA Civ 1889, [2003] 1 WLR 1511 (2003 Abr para 2135)). A person may be detained under the Mental Health Act 1983 yet have capacity to make medical treatment or other decisions (see *Re C (Adult: Refusal of Medical Treatment)* [1994] 1 All ER 819).

12. The test of capacity to consent to or refuse medical treatment may be found in *Re MB (An Adult: Medical Treatment)* [1997] 2 FCR 541 (1997 Abr para 2310). A competent person may validly decide for religious or other reasons, including reasons which appear to others irrational, to refuse treatment knowing this may lead to death.

13. The test of capacity to marry may be found in *Estate of Park: Park v Park* [1953] 2 All ER 1411. See also *Sheffield City Council v E*.

14. Capacity to conduct litigation is a separate issue from capacity to make the decision which is the subject of the proceedings. In the opinion of the Official Solicitor, although in some circumstances an adult may have capacity to make a particular decision, but lack capacity to conduct litigation relating to that decision, it is difficult to envisage circumstances in which a person could lack decision making capacity but have capacity to conduct litigation in relation to that same issue.

15. Medical evidence as to capacity is required in every case, generally from a psychiatrist. Where a patient suffers from learning difficulties the evidence of a psychologist may suffice, although if the patient additionally suffers from mental illness, the evidence of a psychiatrist should be adduced. Experience suggests that it is necessary for instructions to the assessing practitioner to be carefully drafted and to outline the relevant test(s).

Advance Directives

16. A directive given by the patient refusing or otherwise making decisions about treatment, if made and not revoked at a time when the patient had capacity, and if directed to the situation which in fact arises, is as binding a decision as it would have been if made at the time the question arises. The court may be invited to consider evidence of capacity at the time the directive was made, to consider whether the terms of the directive are apt in relation to the situation where it falls to be implemented, and to consider whether there has been any express or implied revocation of the directive. However, where it is proposed to implement the terms of a directive in a manner which may lead to death or serious irreparable harm, the matter should be referred to the court (see *Re T (Adult: Refusal of Treatment)* [1993] Fam 95, *St George's Healthcare NHS Trust v S; R v Collins* [1999] Fam 26 (1998 Abr para 2207), *HE v A Hospital NHS Trust* [2003] EWHC 1017 (Fam), [2003] 2 FLR 408).

Best Interests

17. In medical treatment cases the claimant must adduce evidence from the responsible medical practitioner not only (a) that performing the particular operation would not be negligent but also (b) that it is necessary in the best interest of the patient (see *Re A (Male Sterilisation)* [2001] 1 FCR 193 (2000 Abr para 2239)).

18. The court's jurisdiction is to declare the best interest of the patient on the application of a welfare test analogous to that applied in wardship (see *Re S (Sterilisation: Patient's Best Interests)* [2000] 2 FLR

389). The judicial decision will incorporate broader ethical, social, moral and welfare considerations. Emotional, psychological and social benefit to the patient will be considered (see *Re Y (Mental Patient: Bone Marrow Transplant)* [1997] Fam 110). The court will wish to prepare a balance sheet listing the advantages and disadvantages for the patient. If potential advantages and disadvantages are to be relied on then the court will wish to assess in percentage terms the likelihood of them in fact occurring (see *Re A (Male Sterilisation)*).

Parties

19. The claimant should usually be the NHS trust or other body responsible for the patient's care, such as a local authority. Should they decline to bring proceedings, any properly interested person, such as a family member or other individual closely connected with the patient, may bring proceedings, in which case the body with clinical or caring responsibility should be made a party (see *Re S (Hospital Patient: Court's Jurisdiction)* [1996] Fam 1 (1995 Abr para 2025)). The patient must always be a party.

20. A person may not, without the permission of the court, make an application against a patient before proceedings have started, or take any step in proceedings except issuing and serving a claim form or applying for the appointment of a litigation friend until the patient has a litigation friend (see CPR 21.3). The Official Solicitor may be contacted out of hours in cases of emergency (see *Practice Note (Official Solicitor, CAFCASS and the National Assembly for Wales: Urgent and out of hours cases in the Family Division of the High Court)* [2006] 2 FLR 354 (para 469)).

21. The Official Solicitor should be invited to accept appointment in respect of an incapacitated adult. Where a litigation friend is required in respect of a child approaching the age of 18 who is likely to be under incapacity on attaining majority, the Official Solicitor and CAFCASS or CAFCASS Cymru will discuss between them which of them should accept appointment. Where the patient does not have a litigation friend, for example because he has, or may have, litigation capacity, the Official Solicitor may be invited to assist the court as advocate to the court.

The Directions Hearing

22. Unless the matter requires an urgent substantive hearing, the claimant should fix a directions hearing. The court should, if appropriate, be asked to hold the directions hearing in private to protect the interests of the patient (see CPR r 39.2(3)(d)). The court will use the directions hearing to:

(a) make orders where necessary to preserve the anonymity of the patient, family and other parties;

(b) set a timetable for the Official Solicitor to conduct inquiries, obtain expert evidence and file his statement or report;

(c) fix a further hearing, to serve either as a final hearing if the matter is unopposed or as a final directions hearing to fix a contested hearing.

Further Guidance on Certain Cases

23. Further guidance on particular aspects relating to permanent vegetative state, sterilisation, termination of pregnancy and welfare cases can be found on the Official Solicitor's website at www.officialsolicitor.gov.uk.

24. If a reporting restriction order is to be sought in relation to any case covered by this *Practice Note* the party seeking such an order should refer to the *President's Direction (Applications for Reporting Restriction Orders)* [2005] Fam Law 397 (2005 Abr para 499). In *Clayton v Clayton* [2006] EWCA Civ 878, [2006] Fam 83 (para 482) the Court of Appeal provided guidance, amongst other matters, on restrictions on publicity and disclosure in children's cases after the case has been concluded, and similar consideration as to whether a reporting restriction order should continue to apply after the conclusion of the case may need to be given in a case concerning the welfare of an adult.

Consultation with Official Solicitor

25. Members of the Official Solicitor's legal staff are prepared to discuss medical cases before proceedings are issued. Inquiries about adult medical and welfare cases should be addressed to a family and medical litigation lawyer at the Office of the Official Solicitor, 81, Chancery Lane, London, WC2A 1DD, telephone 020 7911 7127, fax number 020 7911 7105, email enquiries@offsol.gsi.gov.uk.

1947   Patient—capacity—management and administration of affairs and property—test of incapacity

The claimant suffered serious brain injuries when his motorcycle collided with a motor vehicle driven by the defendant. Quantum was in issue, but it was common ground that the claimant would never work again. Doubts arose to his capacity to deal with the litigation and the management of the sum which would be awarded. It fell to be determined as a preliminary issue whether the claimant was a patient within the meaning of the Mental Health Act 1983 Pt VII (ss 93–113). Evidence from the claimant's wife suggested that he was susceptible to the influence of others. An issue arose as to whether medical practitioners, in deciding whether a person lacked capacity, were entitled to have regard to vulnerability to exploitation. *Held*, psychiatrists and psychologists, when considering the question of capacity, including vulnerability to exploitation, would normally wish to take into account all aspects of the personality and behaviour of the persons in question. However, vulnerability to exploitation did not in itself lead to the conclusion that there was lack of capacity as many people who had full capacity were also vulnerable to exploitation. The issue was whether the person concerned had the ability to make a rational decision. The claimant was unable to deal with the advice which he was likely to receive or give reliably rational instructions based on that advice and, accordingly, was a patient.

Lindsay v Wood [2006] EWHC 2895 (QB), [2006] All ER (D) 204 (Nov) (Queen's Bench Division: Stanley Burnton J). *Masterman-Lister v Brutton & Co* [2002] EWCA Civ 1889, [2003] 3 All ER 162 (2003 Abr para 2135) considered.

1948   Patient—medical treatment—child—grave illness—declaration by court concerning treatment

A child was diagnosed as suffering from the most severe form of spinal muscular atrophy. By the time proceedings were issued, save for movement of his eyes and slight movement of his eyebrows, corners of his mouth, thumb and toes or feet, he could not move. His treating consultants stressed that the medical procedures to which he was exposed inevitably caused distress and pain. There was no evidence from MRI scans that indicated that the child suffered from any lack of cognition or brain damage. The claimant sought a declaration that it would be lawful and in the child's best interests for medical staff to withdraw all forms of ventilation from him to ensure he was given treatment by way of pain relief and sedation and nursing care as might be appropriate to ensure that he suffered the least distress and pain and retained the greatest dignity. *Held*, even taking into account predicted deterioration, it was not currently in the child's best interests to discontinue ventilation. It was totally unacceptable to proceed on any basis other than on the assumption that the child had normal, age appropriate cognition and power of thought. The court did not consider that from one day to the next all the routine discomfort, distress and pain that the doctors described outweighed the benefits of continued ventilatory support, so that the court could say that it was in his best interests that those benefits, and life itself, should end. Although the court's opinion was that it was in the child's best interests to continue with continuous pressure ventilation it would not make an order or declaration to that effect. There were, however, procedures that went beyond maintaining ventilation that required the positive infliction of pain, which, if necessary, meant that the child had moved naturally towards his death despite the ventilation. If that point were reached, it would then be in his best interests to withhold those procedures. The court would make a permissive declaration to that effect. Judgment would be given accordingly.

An NHS Trust v MB (A Child Represented by CAFCASS as Guardian ad Litem) [2006] EWHC 507 (Fam), [2006] 2 FLR 319 (Family Division: Holman J). *Re Wyatt* [2005] 3 FCR 263 (para 06/406), *Airedale NHS Trust v Bland* [1993] 1 All ER 821 (1992 Abr para 1770); and *Re J* [1990] 3 All ER 930 (1990 Abr para 264) considered.

1949   Patient—medical treatment—child—treatment without parental knowledge or consent—sexual matters

The Secretary of State published guidance which stated that a medical professional could provide advice and treatment on sexual matters to young people under the age of 16 without the knowledge or consent of their parents provided there was compliance with certain important and stringent conditions laid down by the House of Lords. The claimant, a parent, applied for judicial review of the guidance, submitting that a declaration should be made that a doctor was under no obligation to keep confidential advice and treatment which he proposed to provide to a young person under the age of 16 in respect of contraception, sexually transmitted infections and abortion, and therefore should not provide such advice and treatment without the parents' knowledge unless to do so would or might prejudice the child's physical or mental health so that it was in the child's best interest not to do so. The claimant also contended that the guidance violated parents' rights under the European Convention on Human Rights art 8 (right to respect for family life). *Held*, a health professional was entitled to provide medical advice and treatment on sexual matters without the parent's knowledge or consent provided he or she was satisfied that (1) the young person, although under 16 years of age, understood all aspects of the advice; (2) the medical professional could not persuade the young person to inform his parents or to allow the medical professional to inform the parents that their child was seeking advice and/or treatment on sexual matters; (3) the young person was very likely to begin or to continue having sexual intercourse with or without contraceptive treatment or treatment for a sexually transmissible illness; (4) unless the young person received advice and treatment on the relevant sexual matters, his physical or mental health or both were likely to suffer; and (5) the best interests of the young person required him to receive advice and treatment on sexual matters without parental consent or notification. As a matter of principle, a parent would not retain an art 8 right to parental authority relating to a medical decision where the young person concerned had understood the advice provided by the medical professional and its implications. Accordingly, the application would be dismissed.

R (on the application of Axon) v Secretary of State for Health [2006] EWHC 37 (Admin), [2006] QB 539 (Queen's Bench Division: Silber J). *Gillick v West Norfolk and Wisbech Area Health Authority* [1986] AC 112, HL (1985 Abr para 1758) applied.

1950   Patient—medical treatment—consent—absence of consent—best interests of patient

The patient, a delusional schizophrenic, was detained under the Mental Health Act 1983 s 3. She was diagnosed as suffering from an ovarian tumour, for which she persistently refused treatment. The applicant primary care trust applied to the court for a declaration that the patient lacked the capacity to make decisions about her medical treatment, that it was in her best interests to receive medical treatment, and that it was lawful for those administering that treatment to provide sedation and, if necessary, reasonable physical restraint. *Held*, no medical treatment could be given without the consent of an adult patient who was competent to make that decision. There was a presumption of competency in that respect. However, it was rebuttable. A person lacked capacity if some impairment of mental functioning rendered him or her unable to make a decision whether to consent or refuse treatment. Such inability occurred when either the patient was unable to comprehend and retain the material relevant to the decision, especially the likely consequences of having or not having the treatment in question, or where the patient was unable to use the information and weigh it in the balance as part of the process of arriving at a decision. In the present case, the court was satisfied that the patient lacked the capacity to make decisions about her medical treatment. Further, the positive, though not absolute, obligation imposed by the European Convention on Human Rights art 2 to give life-sustaining treatment where responsible medical treatment was in the patient's best interests had to be borne in mind. In the case of a patient who lacked the capacity to give consent, it was lawful to impose treatment despite the absence of consent and to use sedation and the reasonable use of restraint in order to administer treatment if it was in the patient's best interests. In the present case, if the patient's condition was to be alleviated, there was no feasible alternative to surgery. Without it her symptoms would worsen and were likely to end her life. Accordingly, the application would be granted.

Trust A v H (An Adult Patient) [2006] EWHC 1230 (Fam), [2006] 2 FLR 958 (Family Division: Sir Mark Potter P).

1951   Patient—medical treatment—withdrawal—persistent vegetative state—new evidence as to treatment

A patient had suffered brain damage and was in a vegetative state. The NHS trust responsible for the patient sought a declaration that it would be lawful to discontinue and withhold all life sustaining treatment and medical support. The trust relied on a report of a consultant physician, which stated that the patient was in a permanent form of the vegetative state and that there was no clinical reason why life sustaining medical treatment should not be discontinued. Subsequently, a research article was published that reported some improvements in three other patients who were also in a vegetative state after the administration of a drug. In comment on the research, the consultant physician stated that, although he considered that the chances of success were slim, there was no reason why the patient should not be given a trial. *Held*, it was well established that the existence of a patient in what was known as the persistent vegetative state with no prospect of recovery was of no benefit to the patient and that it was lawful to cease to give medical treatment and care to such a patient. The court would have made the declaration sought without hesitation in the absence of the recently published research article. However, in the light of that article, which a leading expert considered had an outside chance of success and was unlikely to involve any kind of suffering should consciousness be restored, it was in the patient's best interests for her to undergo a short trial. Judgment would be given accordingly.

NHS Trust v J [2006] All ER (D) 290 (Nov) (Queen's Bench Division: Potter J). *Airedale NHS Trust v Bland* [1993] 1 All ER 821, HL (1992 Abr para 1770), applied.

MEDICINAL PRODUCTS AND DRUGS

Halsbury's Laws of England (4th edn) vol 30(2) (Reissue) paras 1–400

Articles

For articles relating to this title please refer to the Table of Articles at the beginning of the Abridgment.

1952   Controlled drugs—list—reclassification

The Misuse of Drugs Act 1971 (Amendment) Order 2006, SI 2006/3331 (in force on 18 January 2007), further amends the Misuse of Drugs Act 1971 Sch 2 by reclassifying methylamphetamine, previously a Class B drug, as a Class A drug.

1953   Controlled drugs—management and use—supervision

The Controlled Drugs (Supervision of Management and Use) Regulations 2006, SI 2006/3148 (in force on 1 January 2007), contain measures relating to arrangements underpinning the safe management and use of controlled drugs in England and Scotland. In particular, the regulations (1) outline preliminary matters; (2) provide that accountable officers are given a number of functions relating to the safe management and use of controlled drugs; essentially, these require the establishment by the accountable officer of a number of sets of arrangements which relate to the safe management and use of controlled drugs; (3) provide that as well as the basic arrangements, these include safe disposal arrangements and auditing arrangements; (4) provide that as well as being given functions in relation to their own designated bodies, accountable officers are given functions in relation to health care professionals and others whose work involves the management and use of controlled drugs, for which their designated body is responsible; (5) provide that accountable officers for primary care trusts and health boards also have particular responsibilities for setting up local intelligence networks, relating to the management and use of controlled drugs, for their area; (6) contain arrangements in relation to periodic inspections of premises used for the management and use of controlled drugs, where these issues would not be dealt with as part of other health and social care inspections, and other measures in relation to powers of entry; (7) deal with co-operation between a number of listed health care bodies and other organisations, and in particular contain detailed arrangements with regard to the disclosure of information between the bodies that are required to co-operate with each other in connection with the identification of cases where action may need to be taken against individuals; and (8) provide record keeping requirements, and duties with regard to occurrence reports, which are quarterly statements that accountable officers must make about details of concerns that their designated body has; accountable officers have duties to take action with regard to concerns that they have, and persons acting in good faith under the arrangements for sharing information are protected from damages claims.

1954   Controlled drugs—misuse

The Misuse of Drugs (Amendment) Regulations 2006, SI 2006/986 (in force on 1 May 2006), further amend the 2001 Regulations, SI 2001/3998, so as to (1) replace references to 'extended formulary nurse prescribers' with references to 'nurse independent prescribers', so that nurse independent prescribers will be allowed to prescribe, supply, possess, administer and give directions for the administration of specified controlled drugs. In particular, the regulations allow nurse independent prescribers to prescribe and supply diazepam, lorazepam and midazolam for the treatment of tonic-clonic seizures.

The Misuse of Drugs (Amendment No 2) Regulations 2006, SI 2006/1450 (in force in part on 7 July 2006 and in part on 1 January 2007), further amend the 2001 Regulations supra so as to (1) provide that private prescriptions issued for human use containing controlled drugs must be written on a prescription form issued for the purposes of private prescribing by a Primary Care Trust in England or a Local Health Board in Wales and must specify the prescriber identification number of the person issuing it; (2) provides an exception to head (1) where the issuer of the prescription believes on reasonable grounds that a private prescription is to be supplied by a pharmacist in a hospital, in which case it does not need to be on the prescribed form; (3) increase from 13 to 28 days the maximum validity period for a prescription containing a specified controlled drug; (4) provide exceptions to the requirement that a person must not supply a specified drug n prescription unless the prescription complies with certain conditions; and (5) make provision relating to the identification of persons collecting prescriptions for controlled drugs and to the recording requirements and Controlled Drugs Register.

The Misuse of Drugs (Amendment No 3) Regulations 2006, SI 2006/2178 (in force on 11 August 2006), further amend the 2001 Regulations, SI 2001/3998, so as to (1) exclude veterinary prescriptions from the requirement that all private prescriptions containing specified controlled drugs must be issued on a standard form which includes the prescriber identification number of the person issuing it, and that all such prescriptions must be submitted to the relevant National Health agency after the drug has been supplied; and (2) remove from the requirements concerning the retention of private prescriptions, prescriptions, other than veterinary prescriptions, containing specified controlled drugs.

1955   Drugs Act 2005—commencement

The Drugs Act 2005 (Commencement No 4) Order 2006, SI 2006/2136, brings s 20 into force on 1 October 2006. For a summary of the Act, see 2005 Abr para 2148. See also the commencement table in the title STATUTES.

1956   Health Act 2006

See para 2028.

1957   Medicinal products—blood safety and quality

The Blood Safety and Quality (Amendment) Regulations 2006, SI 2006/2013 (in force on 31 August 2006), amend the 2005 Regulations, SI 2005/50, and implement EC Commission Directives 2005/61, 2005/62, which contain further technical requirements with regard to blood and blood components. In particular, the regulations (1) add further definitions and amend existing definitions; (2) provide that the import of blood or blood components from a country outside the European Community may only be undertaken by a blood establishment, a licensed manufacturer of medicines or a manufacturer of medical devices; (3) provide that the quality system maintained by blood establishments must comply with the requirements of Directive 2005/62 and require that blood establishments retain records of serious adverse events; (4) impose further requirements on blood establishments and hospital blood banks with regard to traceability; (5) provide that the quality system maintained by hospital blood banks must comply with the requirements of Directive 2005/62; (6) require facilities which receive blood to keep certain records; (7) require that facilities which undertake blood transfusions report adverse events and reactions to the blood establishment from which the blood involved in the adverse incident was received, and to the Secretary of State; (8) provide that any person who imports blood and blood components imported into the European Community must ensure that that blood and those blood components have been prepared to equivalent standards to those set out in Directive 2005/62; (9) extend the Secretary of State's obligations regarding inspection and record keeping to include facilities; (10) impose an obligation on the Secretary of State to notify details of serious adverse reactions and events to the competent authorities of other member states in appropriate cases; (11) confer a power of entry into a facility on the Secretary of State; (12) provide that breach of the obligations placed on facilities is a criminal offence; (13) provide that a fee is payable by a facility in respect of haemovigilance, except where a facility has made arrangements with a hospital blood bank that the blood bank will report adverse incidents on the facility's behalf and provide for an inspection; and (14) include certain technical requirements relating to haemovigilance.

1958   Medicinal products—homoeopathic products—registration

The Medicines (Advisory Board on the Registration of Homoeopathic Products) Amendment Order 2006, SI 2006/2386 (in force on 1 September 2006), further amends the 1995 Order, SI 1995/309, to extend the functions of the Advisory Board on the Registration of Homoeopathic Products to include the provision of advice on the safety, quality and efficacy of homoeopathic medicinal products which have a product licence of right, or national homoeopathic products which have a marketing authorisation, or in respect of which an application for such an authorisation is made.

1959   Medicinal products—medical devices—fees

See para 1963.

1960   Medicinal products—products for animal use—prohibition

See para 1367.

1961   Medicinal products—products for human use—administration and sale or supply

The Medicines for Human Use (Administration and Sale or Supply) (Miscellaneous Amendments) Order 2006, SI 2006/2807 (in force on 17 November 2006), further amends (1) the Prescription Only Medicines (Human Use) Order 1997, SI 1997/1830, so as to (a) revise the definition of 'medicinal product'; (b) create an exemption from the requirement that a prescription only medicine may only be administered by an appropriate practitioner or a person acting in accordance with his directions, by allowing persons who are operators under the Ionising Radiation (Medical Exposure) Regulations 2000, SI 2000/1059, to administer radioactive medicinal products or other prescription only medicines administered in connection with medical exposures, provided that the operator satisfies certain conditions, including the requirement that he acts under the authorisation of, or in accordance with the guidelines issued by, a person who is a practitioner under the 2000 Regulations supra, and the holder of a certificate under the Medicines (Administration of Radioactive Substances) Regulations 1978, SI 1978/1006; and (c) extend the list of prescription only medicines which may be sold or supplied or administered by chiropodists and podiatrists in the course of their professional practice; (2) the 1997 Regulations supra, and the Medicines (Pharmacy and General Sale–Exemption) Order 1980, SI 1980/1924, so as to provide an exemption from restrictions on supply for persons holding a certificate in first aid from the Mountain Rescue Council of England and Wales, to enable them to supply pharmacy and general sale list medicines or prescription only medicines for the treatment of sick or injured persons; and (3) the 1980 Regulations supra, by extending the list of medicines which may be sold or supplied by chiropodists and podiatrists in the course of their professional practice.

1962 Medicinal products—products for human use—clinical trials

The Medicines for Human Use (Clinical Trials) Amendment Regulations 2006, SI 2006/1928 (in force on 29 August 2006) further amend the 2004 Regulations, SI 2004/1031, so as to implement EC Commission Directive 2005/28 on good clinical practice as regards investigational medicinal products for human use and the requirements for authorisation of the manufacturing or importation of such products. In particular, the regulations (1) provide for the delegation of functions by a sponsor; (2) impose new requirements on sponsors and investigators in relation to the investigator's brochure and trial documentation; (3) provide that the functions of a member state and a competent authority under Directive 2005/28 are to be exercised by the licensing authority, unless they fall to be performed by the exercise of powers and duties conferred on another person or body under or by virtue of the 2004 Regulations; (4) make changes to the obligations of ethics committees; (5) make provision for the sharing of information between ethics committees and the licensing authority; (6) amend the provisions on the scope and procedure for manufacturing authorisations and the obligations of the holders of such authorisations; (7) revise the conditions and principles of good clinical practice which apply to all trials; (8) remove the requirement for the appropriate fee to accompany applications (a) for clinical trial authorisations; (b) to amend clinical trial authorisations; (c) for manufacturing authorisations; and (d) to amend manufacturing authorisations, where the applicant has made arrangements with the licensing authority for the payment of the fee at a different time; (9) require serious breaches of good clinical practice or trial protocol to be notified to the licensing authority; (10) extend the application of the infringement notices regime to (a) breaches of the sponsor's responsibilities for the investigator's brochure; (b) the requirement not to start or conduct a clinical trial without a clinical trial authorisation or a favourable opinion from an ethics committee; (c) the requirement of the sponsor to report serious breaches of good clinical practice or trial protocol; and (d) the requirements relating to the trial master file and archiving; (11) create criminal offences for (a) breach of the sponsor's responsibility for the investigator's brochure; (b) breach of the requirement of a sponsor to report serious breaches of good clinical practice or trial protocol; and (c) breach of the trial master file and archiving requirements; and (12) correct various errors in the 2004 Regulations.

The Medicines for Human Use (Clinical Trials) Amendment (No 2) Regulations 2006, SI 2006/2984 (in force on 12 December 2006), further amend the 2004 Regulations, SI 2004/1031, so as to create an exception to the general rule that an incapacitated adult cannot be included in a clinical trial unless specified conditions have been met, in particular that the adult's legal representative has given informed consent. The regulations also provide that the exception applies only when the following conditions are met: (1) treatment is required urgently; (2) the nature of the trial also requires urgent action; (3) it is not reasonably practicable to meet the specified conditions; and (4) an ethics committee has given approval to the procedure under which the action is taken.

1963 Medicinal products—products for human use—fees

The Medicines for Human Use and Medical Devices (Fees Amendments) Regulations 2006, SI 2006/494 (in force on 1 April 2006), further amend the Medicines (Homoeopathic Medicinal Products for Human Use) Regulations 1994, SI 1994/105, the Medical Devices (Consultation Requirements) (Fees) Regulations 1995, SI 1995/449, and the Medicines (Products for Human Use—Fees) Regulations 1995, SI 1995/1116, by increasing the various fees payable under those sets of regulations and by providing that the fee in SI 1995/1116 payable in respect of a manufacturer's licences relating solely to import of medicines from third countries are the same as for other manufacturers' licences.

The Medicines for Human Use (Fees Amendments) Regulations 2006, SI 2006/2125 (in force on 1 September 2006), further amend the Medicines (Products for Human Use-Fees) Regulations 1995, SI 1995/1116, so as to (1) provide for capital fees payable in connection with an application for a grant or variation of a marketing authorisation for a national homoeopathic medicinal product; and (2) provide for the periodic fee payable in connection with the holding of such an authorisation. The regulations also further amend the 1994 Regulations supra so as to (a) make provision for the capital fees payable for applications for the grant and variation of certificates of registration; (b) provide that reduced fees are payable in respect of applications for certificates of registration for products that have an identical formulation to, or are prepared from a homoeopathic stock identical to another homoeopathic stock used in the preparation of, a national homoeopathic product in respect of which a marketing authorisation has been granted.

1964 Medicinal products—products for human use—marketing authorisations— homoeopathic products

The Medicines for Human Use (National Rules for Homoeopathic Products) Regulations 2006, SI 2006/1952 (in force on 1 September 2006), further amend the Medicines for Human Use

(Marketing Authorisations Etc) Regulations 1994, SI 1994/3144, so as to (1) define 'national homoeopathic product'; (2) set out specific rules for applications for marketing authorisations for national homoeopathic products; and (3) provide for an offence where the holder of a marketing authorisation for such a product fails to update the data required or fails to supply information which might entail the amendment of that data.

1965 Medicinal products—products for human use—prescribing

The Medicines for Human Use (Prescribing) (Miscellaneous Amendments) Order 2006, SI 2006/915 (in force on 1 May 2006), further amends the Prescription Only Medicines (Human Use) Order 1997, SI 1997/1830, so as to (1) include nurse independent prescribers and pharmacist independent prescribers as appropriate practitioners who are able to prescribe prescription only medicines; (2) define the classes of prescription only medicines which may be prescribed by nurse independent prescribers and specify the conditions as to cases and circumstances in which nurse independent prescribers can prescribe, administer or give directions for administration for certain prescription only medicines containing controlled drugs; (3) specify controlled drugs which may be prescribed, administered or directed for administration by nurse independent prescribers and the conditions for such use; (4) change the title of certain nurses able to prescribe prescription only medicines from 'district nurse/health visitor prescribers' to 'community practitioner nurse prescribers'. The regulations also further amend the Medicines (Pharmacy and General Sale-Exemption) Order 1980, SI 1980/1924, so as to provide an exemption form the restrictions on sale and supply in hospitals and health centres where such sale or supply is in accordance with the written directions of a pharmacist independent prescriber, a community practitioner nurse prescriber, a nurse independent prescriber or a nurse independent/supplementary prescriber.

1966 Medicinal products—products for human use—traditional herbal medicinal products

The Medicines (Traditional Herbal Medicinal Products for Human Use) (Consequential Amendment) Regulations 2006, SI 2006/395 (in force on 1 April 2006), further amend the Medicines (Retail Sale or Supply of Herbal Remedies) Order 1977, SI 1977/2130, so as to renumber art 1A as art 1B.

1967 Medicinal products—radioactive substances—administration

The Medicines (Administration of Radioactive Substances) Amendment Regulations 2006, SI 2006/2806 (in force on 17 November 2006), amend the 1978 Regulations, SI 1978/181, so as to provide that radioactive medicinal products may be administered by a person who is not a certificate holder, in the absence of a doctor or a dentist's directions, in specified circumstances, where the administration involves a medical exposure under the Ionising Radiation (Medical Exposure) Regulations 2000, SI 2000/1059. In particular, the regulations make provision for persons who are operators under the 2000 Regulations to administer radioactive medicinal products; the operator must be acting in accordance with the relevant procedures and protocols under the 2000 Regulations, and, in addition, he must be acting under the authorisation of, or in accordance with guidelines issued by, a person who is a practitioner under the 2000 Regulations and also a certificate holder.

1968 Medicinal products—sale or supply—miscellaneous provisions

The Medicines (Sale or Supply) (Miscellaneous Amendments) Regulations 2006, SI 2006/914 (in force on 1 May 2006), (1) further amend the Medicines (Sale or Supply) (Miscellaneous Provisions) Regulations 1980, SI 1980/1923, (a) so that a 'health prescription' includes a prescription issued by a community practitioner nurse prescriber, a nurse independent prescriber or a pharmacist independent prescriber, under or by virtue of legislation relating to the National Health Service; (b) so as to reflect changes which have been made to the nurses' professional register and to the entries in that register indicating who is qualified to act as a prescriber; and (c) so that the particulars which must be included in pharmacy records must include certain particulars relating to such prescribers; (2) further amend the Medicines for Human Use (Marketing Authorisations etc) Regulations 1994, SI 1994/3144, so as to reflect changes which have been made to the nurses' professional register and to the entries in that register indicating who is qualified to act as a prescriber; (3) further amend the Medicines (Child Safety) Regulations 2003, SI 2003/2317, (a) so that the requirements relating to the packaging of certain medicinal products do not apply to the retail sale, or supply corresponding to retail sale, of a product by a pharmacy, where that sale or supply is in accordance with a prescription given by a pharmacist independent prescriber; and (b) so as to reflect changes which have been made to the nurses' professional register and to the entries in that register indicating who is qualified to act as a prescriber; and (4) amend the Medicines (Traditional Herbal Medicinal Products for Human Use) Regulations 2005, SI 2005/2750, so as to reflect changes which have been made to the nurses' professional register and to the entries in that register indicating who is qualified to act as a prescriber.

1969   Pharmacies—registration and fees—applications

The Medicines (Pharmacies) (Applications for Registration and Fees) Amendment Regulations 2006, SI 2006/3264 (in force on 1 January 2007), further amend the 1973 Regulations, SI 1973/1822, by increasing (1) from £474 to £492, the fees for registration of premises at which a retail pharmacy business is, or is to be, carried on; (2) from £150 to £156, retention fees; and (3) from £474 to £492, the penalty for failure to pay retention fees. SI 2005/3259 is revoked.

1970   Veterinary medicines

The Veterinary Medicines Regulations 2006, SI 2006/2407 (in force on 1 October 2006), replace the 2005 Regulations, SI 2005/2745, and make provision for the authorisation, manufacture, classification, distribution and administration of veterinary medicinal products, in implementation of EC Parliament and Council Directive 2001/82, as amended by EC Parliament and Council Directive 2004/28. In particular, the regulations (1) provide that a veterinary medicinal product must have a marketing authorisation granted by the Secretary of State or the European Medicines Agency before being placed on the market, and make provision for the grant of such an authorisation; (2) require a veterinary medicinal product to be manufactured by a person holding a manufacturing authorisation, and make provision for the grant of such an authorisation; (3) regulate the supply and possession of veterinary medicinal products; (4) introduce new classifications of veterinary medicinal products; (5) provide that a veterinary medicinal product may only be administered as specified in its marketing authorisation or, in the case of administration by a veterinary surgeon, in a prescribed manner outside the terms of the marketing authorisation; (6) make provision in relation to the importation and advertising of veterinary medicinal products; (7) create an offence of buying a veterinary medicinal product, other than in specified circumstances, without a wholesale dealer's authorisation; (8) impose controls on medicated feedingstuffs and feedingstuffs containing specified additives; (9) provide for exemptions and fees; (10) require records to be kept in relation to veterinary medicinal products; (11) create offences relating to the importation, possession and supply of unauthorised veterinary medicinal products; (12) make provision for the continuation of the Veterinary Products Committee, and provide for a representations procedure to the committee to apply in certain circumstances; and (13) make provision for enforcement and penalties.

MENTAL HEALTH

Halsbury's Laws of England (4th edn) vol 30(2) (Reissue) paras 401–773

Articles

For articles relating to this title please refer to the Table of Articles at the beginning of the Abridgment.

1971   Court of Protection—rules

The Court of Protection (Amendment) Rules 2006, SI 2006/653 (in force on 1 April 2006), further amend the 2001 Regulations, SI 2001/824, so as to (1) increase various fees; (2) change the point at which an annual administration fee becomes payable in relation to the making of a short order or a direction; and (3) change the point until which the winding up fee is payable.

1972   Court of Protection—statutory will—execution of will—management of patient's property

A patient lacked testamentary capacity as a result of senile dementia and was looked after by the appellant, her son. Before her illness, the patient had made a will appointing the appellant sole executor and dividing her estate equally between him, her other son and her daughter. A receiver was appointed despite the appellant maintaining that the patient would not wish to incur the costs of having a professional receiver. Disharmony between the children meant that problems in the administration of the estate might arise. The receiver applied to the Court of Protection to make a statutory will. The judge concluded that it was in the interests of the patient to make a new will and appointed the receiver's firm in the appellant's place. The dispositive provisions of the original will remained as before. The appellant's appeal was dismissed, the judge holding that the administration had the best chance of proceeding efficiently if it was in the hands of an independent party. After the determination of the receivership, the appellant and his sister were appointed as joint interim receivers but, since no working relationship was established between them, the interim receivership was discharged and an independent panel receiver appointed. On the appellant's appeal, *held,* on an application to make a statutory will, it was the patient who had to be considered, the function of the court being to do for the patient what the patient would do for herself, if she could act with the benefit of advice from a competent solicitor. A competent solicitor would point out any relevant change of circumstances since the making of the original will, including the discord existing among the patient's children, and would advise her about the difficulties in the administration of her estate that would follow if the appellant remained sole executor. A solicitor would also advise the patient of the practical advantages of having an executor connected with the receivership in order to keep continuity between the receivership and the executorship. It was also clear that the size and nature of the patient's estate was such that it would be difficult to administer without the involvement of professionals. Therefore, the judge had not been wrong to affirm the decision to make a statutory will appointing an independent professional executor in place of the appellant. Accordingly, the appeal would be dismissed.

G v Official Solicitor [2006] EWCA Civ 816, [2006] WTLR 1201 (Court of Appeal: Mummery, Arden and Moore-Bick LJJ).

1973   Mental capacity—appropriate body—England

The Mental Capacity Act 2005 (Appropriate Body) (England) Regulations 2006, SI 2006/2810 (in force in part on 1 February 2007 and in part on 1 April 2007), define 'appropriate body', for the purposes of the Mental Capacity Act 2005 ss 30–32, as a committee which is established to advise on, or on matters which include, the ethics of intrusive research in relation to people who lack capacity to consent to it and which is recognised for that purpose by the Secretary of State.

The Mental Capacity Act 2005 (Appropriate Body) (England) (Amendment) Regulations 2006, SI 2006/3474 (in force on 31 January 2007), amend the principal 2006 Regulations supra so as to revise the date on which the regulations are to come into force, providing that the regulations will now come into force on 1 July 2007 for the purpose of enabling applications for ethical approval to be made and determined, and on 1 October 2007 for all other purposes.

1974   Mental capacity—independent mental capacity advocates—England

The Mental Capacity Act 2005 (Independent Mental Capacity Advocates) (General) Regulations 2006, SI 2006/1832 (in force in part on 1 November 2006 and in part on 1 April 2007), (1) define 'NHS body' and 'serious medical treatment' for the purposes of specified provisions in the Mental Capacity Act 2005 which deal with independent mental capacity advocates ('IMCAs'); (2) provide that a person can only be appointed to act as an IMCA if he satisfies certain requirements as to the experience, training, good character and independence and has been approved by a local authority, or is a member of a class which has been so approved; (3) set out the steps an IMCA must take once he has been instructed to act in a particular case; (4) provide that an IMCA who is instructed to represent a person in relation to any matter may challenge a decision made in that matter in relation to that person, including any decision as to whether that person lacks capacity; and (5) provide that, for the purpose of making such a challenge, the IMCA is treated in the same way as any other person caring for that person or interested in his welfare.

1975   Mental capacity—independent mental capacity advocates—expansion of role

The Mental Capacity Act 2005 (Independent Mental Capacity Advocates) (Expansion of Role) Regulations 2006, SI 2006/2883 (in force in part on 1 November 2006 and in part on 1 April 2007), adjust the obligation to make arrangements as to the availability of independent mental capacity advocates ('IMCAs') that is imposed by the Mental Capacity Act 2005 s 35. The Secretary of State may also make arrangements to enable IMCAs to be available to represent a person who lacks capacity to agree to the outcome of an accommodation review or to protective measures taken in adult protection cases. In particular, the regulations (1) provide that arrangements under s 35 may extend to cover IMCAs who are instructed under specified circumstances; (2) specify circumstances where an NHS body or a local authority must review the arrangements made in relation to a person's accommodation and provide that such a person must not have capacity to participate in the review and there must be no one else who can be consulted as to matters affecting his best interests; (3) specify circumstances where it is alleged that a person is or has been abused or neglected by another person or that he is abusing or has abused another person; (4) provide that protective measures affecting such a person must have been taken, or be proposed, by an NHS body or local authority in accordance with any adult protection procedures which have been set up pursuant to certain statutory guidance; (5) provide that an NHS body or local authority may instruct an IMCA to represent a person if the NHS body considers, or the local authority consider, that it would be of particular benefit to the person; and (6) provide that the NHS body or local authority must take account of information provided by the IMCA and of any submissions made by him.

1976   Mental Capacity Act 2005—commencement

The Mental Capacity Act 2005 (Commencement No 1) Order 2006, SI 2006/2814, brings into force (1) on 1 November 2006, ss 35–41 (for certain purposes); (2) on 1 February 2007, ss 30–34 (for certain purposes); (3) on 1 April 2007, ss 35–41 (for remaining purposes); and (4) on 1 April 2008, ss 30–34 (for certain purposes).

The Mental Capacity Act 2005 (Commencement No 1) (Amendment) Order 2006, SI 2006/3473, amends SI 2006/2814 supra so that ss 30–34 now come into force for certain purposes on 1 July 2007 and for remaining purposes on 1 October 2008.

For a summary of the Act, see 2005 Abr para 2174. See also the commencement table in the title STATUTES.

1977 Mentally-ill offender—manslaughter—psychopathic disorder

See *R v Staines*, para 2557.

1978 Patient—detention—conditional discharge—recall by Secretary of State

The claimant, a paranoid schizophrenic, was convicted of an offence of unlawful wounding and he was ordered to be detained in a hospital as a restricted patient under the Mental Health Act 1983. The claimant was conditionally released by mental health review tribunals on numerous occasions but on two occasions the Secretary of State decided to recall the claimant to hospital using his powers under s 42. The claimant sought judicial review of those decisions. *Held*, if the Secretary of State had, on the basis of medical evidence and any other material that he had, reached the opinion that a patient's mental deterioration was likely to take place in the near future unless that patient was recalled, and such deterioration put the health and safety of himself and others at risk, he was entitled to order the patient's recall. He had not misapplied the relevant test on the construction of s 42 and his decisions could not be regarded as unlawful. There had been an abundance of medical evidence before the Secretary of State to support his decisions. The evidence demonstrated that the claimant was suffering from schizophrenia and that should his use of illicit drugs continue, there would be an imminent and inevitable danger posed to himself and the public, including his family. Accordingly, the application would be dismissed.

R (on the application of MM) v Secretary of State for the Home Department [2006] All ER (D) 332 (Nov) (Queen's Bench Division: Mitting J). *R (on the application of Von Brandenburg (aka Hanley)) v East London and City Mental Health Trust* [2003] UKHL 58, [2004] 2 AC 280 (2003 Abr para 1897) considered.

1979 Patient—detention—leave of absence—decision of responsible medical officer—duty of Secretary of State

The claimant, a paranoid schizophrenic, was detained at a high security hospital. His responsible medical officer recommended his transfer to a different private hospital on a medium secure ward by means of trial leave pursuant to the Mental Health Act 1983 s 17. The application was dismissed by the defendant National Health Service trust, and the claimant sought judicial review of the decision. In dismissing the application, the judge decided that it was for the responsible medical officer to decide on clinical grounds whether leave of absence should be granted pursuant to s 17, but it was for the defendant to decide whether resources could and should be expended in funding the recommended stay. The claimant appealed. *Held*, under the National Health Service Act 1977 s 3, the Secretary of State had a duty to provide hospital accommodation to the extent necessary to meet all reasonable requirements. The decision whether any particular services should be provided under s 3 was one for the Secretary of State, or his delegate. A responsible medical officer had no power to give directions as to how others were to discharge their functions, and the 1983 Act s 17 could not be construed as conferring such a power. Indeed, the Secretary of State was not bound to accept and act on the clinical judgment of the responsible medical officer, and could consider the opinions of others responsible for providing psychiatric services for those detained in such conditions as well as the opinion of the officer. No duty to facilitate decisions lawfully made under the 1983 Act could be derived from the mere fact that the responsible medical officer was in charge of the patient's treatment. The weight that a trust should give to the opinion of the responsible medical officer had to be a matter for the decision-maker having regard to all the relevant circumstances. They would include how long the responsible medical officer had been in charge of the treatment of the patient, the strength of conviction with which the officer's clinical judgment had been expressed, the weight of other clinical opinion and the reasons given by other medical practitioners for their disagreement with the opinion expressed by the officer. Accordingly, the appeal would be dismissed.

R (on the application of K) v West London Mental Health NHS Trust [2006] EWCA Civ 118, [2006] 3 All ER 141 (Court of Appeal: Waller, Arden and Dyson LJJ). *R v North and East Devon Health Authority, ex p Coughlan* [2001] QB 213, CA (1999 Abr para 2405); and *R (on the application of F) v Oxfordshire Mental Health NHS Trust* [2001] EWHC 535 (Admin), [2001] All ER (D) 19 (Jul) applied.

1980 Patient—litigation—capacity to litigate and compromise proceedings

See *Bailey (by his litigation friend Ashton) v Warren*, para 2314.

1981 Patient—medical treatment—consent to treatment—compulsory treatment—human rights

The claimant had been detained at a secure hospital under the Mental Health Act 1983 ss 37 and 41 following his conviction of rape. He had been diagnosed as suffering from bipolar affective disorder, but medication for that condition had been eventually discontinued. The claimant's responsible medical officer believed that the claimant's condition was deteriorating and wished to treat him with anti-psychotic medication, administered by injection, and a mood stabiliser. The claimant refused to consent to that treatment, and the responsible medical officer sought to medicate him by compulsion, arguing that he was entitled so to do pursuant to s 58. He obtained the certificate required under s 58 from the second opinion appointed doctor. The claimant applied for judicial review in order to challenge the legality of what was proposed. The application was dismissed, and on the claimant's appeal, the following issues arose: (1) whether the judge had erred in finding that the claimant lacked capacity; (2) if not, whether the appeal should be dismissed without consideration of the other issues, on the ground that they were academic; (3) if not, whether compulsory treatment of a patient with capacity would violate the European Convention on Human Rights arts 3, 8 and 14, unless it satisfied the threshold requirement; and (4) whether the judge was wrong to find that the proposed treatment constituted a medical or therapeutic necessity. *Held*, whatever the precise test for the capacity to consent to treatment, it was plain that a patient would lack that capacity if he was not able to appreciate the likely effects of having or not having the treatment. The judge had found that that was the position so far as the claimant was concerned in that he did not accept even the possibility that he might be mentally ill and thus in need of treatment. The claimant's appeal was largely founded on the premise, demonstrated to be false, that he had had capacity at the material time. That fact should not result in dismissal of the appeal without considering the issues that the claimant sought to raise. Also, in the light of the judge's findings that the purposes of giving medication were to alleviate the claimant's current symptoms and to produce a stability, to improve his chances of rehabilitation, to improve his level of insight into his illness so that he could come to co-operate in his treatment plan and also engage in other therapy designed to address his insight into his offending, to increase the chances of his proceeding to a lower security setting sooner (or indeed at all), to protect him against the chance of future relapse of his life-long condition (the prophylactic effect), and to reduce the risk of his suffering harm at the hands of others and to reduce the risk of his causing harm to others, the judge had been entitled to consider that the treatment was in the claimant's best interests and that it had been convincingly shown that it was a medical necessity. The imposition of the proposed anti-psychotic medication would therefore be lawful under English law and would not infringe the Convention. Accordingly, the appeal would be dismissed.

R (on the application of B) v S [2006] EWCA Civ 28, [2006] All ER (D) 200 (Jan) (Court of Appeal: Lord Phillips of Worth Matravers CJ, Thorpe and Rix LJJ).

1982   Patient—restricted patient—treatment without consent—medical necessity

The claimant was a person detained and subject to restrictions in a high security hospital pursuant to orders under the Mental Health Act 1983 ss 37 and 41. Initially, he had been classified as suffering from psychopathic disorder. However, a doctor formed the view that the claimant had begun to suffer from a mental illness as well as psychopathic disorder, and that a certain type of medication would alleviate that condition and also provide a gateway for the treatment of the psychopathic disorder. Following the claimant's refusal to consent to the proposed treatment, the doctor obtained authorisation for treatment without consent under s 58(3). The claimant challenged the lawfulness of the treatment by way of judicial review. The application was dismissed and the claimant appealed. *Held*, when forcible treatment was challenged the court had to be satisfied of the medical or therapeutic necessity of the treatment, but this did not mean that it had to be convinced of each of the individual matters going to the test of medical necessity. Further, it was not necessary to classify or to diagnose with certainty the precise form of mental disorder necessitating the treatment in issue. Where the question was whether proposed forcible treatment infringed the patient's human rights the court had to conduct a full hearing of the merits, rather than merely a review of the decision. The judge had conducted a merits review on a full consideration, analysis and assessment of the evidence. Accordingly, the appeal would be dismissed.

R (on the application of B) v Haddock [2006] EWCA Civ 961, (2006) 93 BMLR 52 (Court of Appeal: Auld, Scott Baker and Neuberger LJJ). Application 10533/83 *Herczegfalvy v Austria* (1992) 15 EHRR 437, ECtHR, considered; *R (on the application of Wilkinson) v Responsible Medical Officer Broadmoor Hospital* [2001] EWCA Civ 1545, [2002] 1 WLR 419 (2001 Abr para 2261) applied.

MISREPRESENTATION AND FRAUD

Halsbury's Laws of England (4th edn) vol 31 (2003 Reissue) paras 701–876

1983   Deceit—damages—representation—validity of certificate

See *AIC Ltd v ITS Testing Services (UK) Ltd, The Kriti Palm*, para 1822.

1984   Fraudulent misrepresentation—damages—duty to disclose—evidence—admissibility

The claimant was a partner and the defendant a senior partner in a firm of solicitors. When some of the partners decided to join another firm, a deed of dissolution was executed, whereby the firm would be dissolved and the claimant and the defendant would enter into a new partnership. The Law Society subsequently intervened on the grounds of suspected dishonesty on the part of the defendant. Disciplinary proceedings were commenced and the Solicitors Disciplinary Tribunal ('SDT') concluded that the defendant should be struck off. The parties had entered into an agreement to deal with the defendant's suspension from practice, and the defendant successfully sought specific performance of that agreement. The claimant brought proceedings against the defendant claiming damages for negligence and misrepresentation. He claimed that the defendant had owed a duty to disclose anything which might affect his status as a solicitor and his ability to enter into the agreement, and that he would not have entered into the agreement had such a disclosure been made. The defendant contended that the claimant had been fully aware of the facts which had resulted in the disciplinary proceedings and that the findings in the SDT proceedings were inadmissible. *Held*, prospective partners had a duty to disclose material matters. Where there was a duty to disclose, and the failure to disclose was fraudulent, there would be an action in deceit and damages would be an available remedy. The deliberate withholding of information which the person knew or believed to be material, if done dishonestly or recklessly, might amount to a fraudulent misrepresentation. Further, the court was not precluded by the decision in the first action from deciding the question of the admissibility of the findings of the SDT. The SDT's order was evidence of the fact that the defendant was struck off on the grounds of dishonesty. In the present case, it would be unfair to require the claimant to prove dishonesty in transactions to which he was not a party and in relation to which the only evidence available was that contained in the Law Society's complaint. Accordingly, the claim would be allowed.

Conlon v Simms [2006] EWHC 401 (Ch), [2006] 2 All ER 1024 (Chancery Division: Lawrence Collins J).

1985   Misrepresentation—grant of tenancy to husband—tenancy assigned by husband to wife—validity

See *Islington LBC v Uckac*, para 1770.

1986   Misrepresentation—representation by conduct—misapprehension by customer that trader connected with trade competitor—failure by trader to correct misapprehension

The claimants, who formed the Sky group of companies, alleged that the defendants had been passing off extended warranty contracts relating to the equipment on which the claimants' broadcasts were viewed as if those contracts had been made or approved by the claimants. They claimed that the defendants enjoyed substantial goodwill associated in particular with the word 'Sky', both on its own and as part of words and phrases such as 'Skycare', 'Sky Plan' and 'Sky Repair Protection Plan', and that the defendants had been passing off their extended warranty and repair services as if they and their businesses were either part of the Sky group and its businesses, or authorised, endorsed or approved by the Sky group as extended warranty providers. The claimants also complained about the use by the defendants of corporate names or related phrases which included 'Sky', the misleading form and content of written marketing material designed, produced and published by some of the defendants, and the misleading conduct of the large telephone sales force employed by two of the defendants. Their primary contention was that passing off was both the intended and achieved objective of the whole of the defendants' marketing campaign. *Held*, where the existence of a de facto monopoly in particular goods or services gave rise to the likelihood that the arrival on the market of a competing or related product would cause confusion in the mind of the relevant section of the public, there was an increased risk that the marketing method adopted by the competitor would cause or contribute to that confusion by an implied misrepresentation, albeit that the same method might not have done so in the absence of that monopoly. In such circumstances the competitor was not subjected to a free-standing duty to distinguish his product from any connection with the monopoly, but he was obliged to take such care as would prevent his chosen marketing method from conveying any misrepresentation to the effect that there was such a connection. The adequacy of the steps taken by the competitor to avoid any such implied misrepresentation would be a question of fact. When a trader who had made no misrepresentation to an intended customer realised from something the customer said or did that the customer was under a self-induced misapprehension that the trader was, or was connected with, his competitor, but the trader did nothing to correct that mistaken belief, that behaviour constituted misrepresentation by conduct. Selling a warranty to a customer who had made it clear that he thought he was being offered a warranty from, or officially approved by, the Sky group constituted misrepresentation by conduct if the warranty came from a wholly independent and non-approved source, and if the seller did nothing to correct the customer's mistaken belief. Judgment would be given accordingly.

British Sky Broadcasting Group plc v Sky Home Services Ltd [2006] EWHC 3165 (Ch), [2007] FSR 321 (Chancery Division: Briggs J). *Reckitt & Colman Products Ltd v Borden Inc* [1990] 1 All ER 873, HL (1990 Abr para 2478); and *Bovril Ltd v Bodega Co Ltd* (1916) 33 RPC 153 applied.

1987 Negligent misrepresentation—inducement to enter contract—inaccurate explanation of nature of investment product—investor failing to read terms of contract

The first claimant, a company used as an investment vehicle by its shareholders, which included the second claimant, began investing in emerging market instruments with the defendant bank. A regional manager of one of the defendant's subsidiaries met the second claimant to discuss potential investment in certain Russian Treasury issued bonds, which were known to carry a significant investment risk. The claimants decided to invest a large amount of money into the bonds, but no formal contract was made at that point. A document containing what were described as final terms and conditions relating to a hedged Russian Treasury bill was subsequently sent to the defendant as an attachment to an email. The document described the investment as a deposit and set out various terms relating to it, but did not set out the terms of a contract between the parties. The second claimant signed and returned the document and an accompanying risk disclosure statement without reading them. In the event the Russian government announced a moratorium on debt obligations arising under the bonds, and the claimants brought proceedings against the defendant under the Misrepresentation Act 1967 s 2(1). The judge decided that the second claimant's signature on the documents did not nullify the defendant's earlier misrepresentation because he had no reason to think that they would related to a fundamentally different product. The defendant appealed, submitting that anything stated in earlier conversations with the claimants was displaced by the signed document, irrespective of whether it had been read. *Held*, the starting point when considering any claim for misrepresentation had to be to determine whether the defendant did in fact make the statement on which the claimant relied. In the present case, the representation made by the defendants to the second claimant did not support a claim under s 2(1). The true position appeared clearly from the terms of the very contract which the claimants said they were induced to enter by the misrepresentation. Moreover, it was not buried in a mass of small print but appeared on the face of the documents as part of the description of the investment product to which the contract related. If the second claimant had read the terms of the document it would have been clear to him that the nature of the investment was fundamentally different from that which he had been given to understand. Accordingly, the appeal would be allowed.

Peekay Intermark Ltd v Australia and New Zealand Banking Group Ltd [2006] EWCA Civ 386, [2006] 2 Lloyd's Rep 511 (Court of Appeal: Chadwick and Moore-Bick LJJ and Lawrence Collins J). Decision of Richard Siberry QC [2005] All ER (D) 386 (May) (2005 Abr para 2193) reversed.

1988 Serious fraud

See CRIMINAL LAW.

MISTAKE

Halsbury's Laws of England (4th edn) vol 32 (2005 Reissue) paras 1–100

Articles

For articles relating to this title please refer to the Table of Articles at the beginning of the Abridgment.

1989 Mistake of law—payment of tax—discovery of mistake

See *Deutsche Morgan Grenfell Group plc v IRC*, para 2458.

MONEY

Halsbury's Laws of England (4th edn) vol 32 (2005 Reissue) paras 101–300

1990 African Development Fund—contribution

The African Development Bank (Tenth Replenishment of the African Development Fund) Order 2006, SI 2006/2327 (in force on 6 July 2006), approves the making of a payment on behalf of the United Kingdom government to the African Development Bank of sums not exceeding £206,191,098 as a further contribution to the African Development Fund in accordance with the arrangements made with the Fund pursuant to Resolution ADF/BD/IF/2005/83 adopted by the Board of Governors of the Bank on 4 May 2005. The order provides for the redemption of non-interest-bearing and non-negotiable notes issued by the Secretary of State in payment of the further contribution.

1991 International Development (Reporting and Transparency) Act 2006

The International Development (Reporting and Transparency) Act 2006 requires the Secretary of State to report annually on total expenditure on international aid and on the breakdown of such aid, and in particular on progress towards the target for expenditure on official development assistance to constitute 0·7 per cent of gross national income, and requires such reports to contain information about expenditure by country, about the proportion of expenditure in low income countries and about the effectiveness of aid expenditure and the transparency of international aid. The Act received the royal assent on 25 July 2006 and came into force in part on that day. The remaining provisions came into force on 25 October 2006. For details of commencement, see the commencement table in the title STATUTES.

Section 1 provides that the Secretary of State must lay a report about international aid before each House of Parliament each year and which may revise anything contained in a previous annual report. The information that each annual report must include is specified: s 2, Schedule. Under s 3, the Secretary of State must include in each annual report his assessment of the year in which he expects the target for expenditure on official development assistance to amount to 0·7 per cent of gross income will be met by the United Kingdom. Each annual report must include the Secretary of State's assessment of progress in relation to promoting untied aid and progress and effectiveness related to the Millennium Goals 1 to 7 as set out in the Annex to United Nations General Assembly document A/56/326 6 September 2001, entitled 'Road map towards the implementation of the United Nations Millennium Declaration: Report of the Secretary General': s 4. Section 5 provides that the Secretary of State must include in each annual report such general or specific observations, including the Millennium Development Goal 8, as he thinks appropriate on the effects of policies and programmes pursued by the government department on the promotion of sustainable development in countries outside the United Kingdom and the reduction of poverty in such countries. The Secretary of State must, under s 6, include in each annual report such observations as he thinks appropriate about the contribution by government departments to the promotion of transparency in the provision of aid and the use made of aid provided. Section 7 makes miscellaneous provision, s 8 provides for expenses and s 9 provides for short title and commencement.

1992   Multinational development banks—African Development Fund—contribution

The African Development Fund (Multilateral Debt Relief Initiative) Order 2006, SI 2006/2321 (in force on 6 July 2006), approves the making of payments on behalf of the United Kingdom government of sums not exceeding £79,190,000 as additional contributions to the African Development Fund between 2006 and 2015. The order also approves the redemption of non-interest-bearing and non-negotiable notes issued by the Secretary of State in payment of the further contribution.

1993   Multinational development banks—Asian Development Bank—contribution

The Asian Development Bank (Eighth Replenishment of the Asian Development Fund) Order 2006, SI 2006/2324 (in force on 6 July 2006), approves the making of a payment to the Asian Development Bank of a sum not exceeding £114,135,370 as the contribution of the United Kingdom government to the eighth replenishment of the resources of the bank. The order also provides for the redemption of non-interest-bearing and non-negotiable notes issued by the Secretary of State in respect of the payment.

1994   Multinational development banks—Caribbean Development Bank—contribution

The Caribbean Development Bank (Sixth Replenishment of the Unified Special Development Fund) Order 2006, SI 2006/2325 (in force on 6 July 2006), approves the making of a payment to the Caribbean Development Bank of a sum not exceeding £23,492,000 as the contribution of the United Kingdom government to the sixth replenishment of the resources of the bank. The order also provides for the redemption of non-interest-bearing and non-negotiable notes issued by the Secretary of State in respect of the payment.

1995   Multinational development banks—International Development Association—contribution

The International Development Association (Fourteenth Replenishment) Order 2006, SI 2006/1071 (in force on 15 March 2006), approves (1) the making of a payment on behalf of the government of the United Kingdom of a sum not exceeding £1,430,000,000 as a further contribution to the International Development Association, in accordance with the arrangements made with the Association pursuant to Resolution 209, which was adopted by the Board of Governors of the Association on 13 April 2005; and (2) the redemption of non-interest-bearing and non-negotiable notes issued by the Secretary of State in payment of the further contribution.

The International Development Association (Multilateral Debt Relief Initiative) Order 2006, SI 2006/2323 (in force on 14 June 2006), approves the making of payments on behalf of the United Kingdom government of sums not exceeding £591,570,000 as additional contributions to the International Development Association between 2006 and 2016. The order also approves the redemption of non-interest-bearing and non-negotiable notes issued by the Secretary of State in payment of the further contribution.

MORTGAGE

Halsbury's Laws of England (4th edn) vol 32 (2005 Reissue) paras 301–968

Articles

For articles relating to this title please refer to the Table of Articles at the beginning of the Abridgment.

1996   Mortgagee—power of sale—improper exercise—breach of contract

The claimants and the first two defendants were parties to agreements relating to a development of penthouses in a block that was owned by the second claimant. The first defendant was granted a development lease which was charged to the second defendant as mortgagee. The first defendant entered into covenants under which it agreed to pay commission to the claimants on the final sale of the penthouses and granted a leaseback option, which was exercisable should the development not be built on time. The first defendant ran into financial difficulties that jeopardised its ability to complete the development within a reasonable time. Therefore, the second defendant agreed to sell the lease as mortgagee to the fifth defendant, which would help to finance the development. In various proceedings, it was held that an application by the claimants for an injunction to prevent the assignment because it would breach the first defendant's covenants should be refused. Further, there was no reasonable ground for refusing consent to the assignment and that any right to forfeit the lease for failure to complete the development on time had been waived. The claimants brought further proceedings in which they challenged the legality of the sale and claimed damages for breaches of the first defendant's covenants. *Held*, the claimants were estopped from arguing that the second defendant had had no power of sale. The earlier ruling that there was no reasonable ground for refusing consent to the assignment, necessarily incorporated a finding that the application for consent had been valid. Had there been no power of sale, the second defendant would not have been entitled to apply for consent. However, it was not an abuse of process for the claimants to claim damages for breach of the first defendant's covenants. In exercising a power of sale, a mortgagee's equitable duties to subsequent encumbrancers were measured by the extent of their security. The second defendant owed no equitable duty to the second claimant, whose entitlement was an unsecured one as the holder of the equity of redemption in the leaseback option. Further, a mortgagee's equitable duty arose only when it exercised its power of sale, and did not curtail its right to act in its own interests when deciding whether to exercise the power. Accordingly, the claim would be allowed in part.

Meretz Investments NV v ACP Ltd [2006] EWHC 74 (Ch), [2006] 3 All ER 1029 (Chancery Division: Lewison J).

1997   Mortgagee—right to recover shortfall—limitation period

See *Bradford & Bingley plc v Rashid*, para 1815.

NATIONAL HEALTH SERVICE

Halsbury's Laws of England (4th edn) vol 33 (Reissue) paras 1–600

Articles

For articles relating to this title please refer to the Table of Articles at the beginning of the Abridgment.

1998   Appointments Commission—membership and functions

The Appointments Commission Regulations 2006, SI 2006/2380 (in force on 1 October 2006), make provision concerning the membership and functions of the Appointments Commission ('the Commission'). In particular, the regulations (1) prescribe the number of members of the Commission and of persons to be appointed to the Health and Social Care Appointments Committee of the Commission; (2) provide for the period of office of the chairman and non-executive members of the Commission and of persons appointed to the Health and Social Care Appointments Committee; (3) make provision for disqualification for appointment, termination of office and suspension from office; (4) provide for the Secretary of State to determine their remuneration and allowances; (5) confer functions on the Commission in relation to appointments to certain bodies and matters relating to such appointments; and (6) make provision for payments by the Secretary of State to the Commission.

1999   Benefits—injury benefits

See para 2043.

2000   Charges—dental services—England

The National Health Service (Dental Charges) Amendment Regulations 2006, SI 2006/1837 (in force on 10 August 2006), which apply in relation to England only, amend the 2005 Regulations, SI 2005/3477, by removing crowns in other materials from the list of appliances for which a Band 3 charge may be made and recovered.

2001   Charges—dental services—Wales

The National Health Service (Dental Charges) (Wales) Regulations 2006, SI 2006/491 (in force on 1 April 2006), replace the National Health Service (Dental Charges) Regulations 1989, SI 1989/394, in relation to Wales and provide for the making and recovery of charges for the provision of dental treatment and the supply of dental appliances under the National Health Service Act 1977, reflecting the revised dental charging powers in s 79, Sch 12ZA. The regulations (1) provide for charges for (a) the provision of dental treatment, including urgent treatment and orthodontic treatment, and the supply of dental and orthodontic appliances by a provider of relevant primary dental services; (b) the supply of dental appliances under the 1977 Act otherwise than by a provider of relevant primary dental services; and (c) the replacement, as part of relevant primary dental services, of a dental or orthodontic appliance lost or damaged by an act or omission of the patient; (2) set out various circumstances in which no charge may be made and recovered for the provision of dental treatment or the supply of dental appliances under the 1977 Act; (3) prescribe the applicable charges and the system for calculating those charges; (4) provide that only one charge for a course of treatment may be made and recovered even if provided by more than one provider; (5) detail the circumstances in which charges cannot be made and recovered for both treatment provided after a course of treatment is complete and for the repair or replacement of a restoration; (6) specify the conditions for statutory exemptions from charges; (7) prescribe the procedure for making and recovering charges; (8) make provision for the repayment of charges which have been paid where a person has the benefit of a statutory exemption but has not complied with certain conditions; (9) provide for a reduction in the remuneration of a provider of relevant primary dental services by the amount of the charges payable; and (10) require a dental practitioner remunerated by either a local heath board or NHS trust, which is providing relevant primary dental services itself, to account for, and pay to, the body by which he is remunerated the amount of the charges he has recovered from patients.

The National Health Service (Dental Charges) (Wales) (Amendment) Regulations 2006, SI 2006/3366 (in force on 15 December 2006), correct an error in SI 2006/491 supra by removing a reference in the list of appliances for which a particular charge may be made and recovered.

2002   Charges—drugs and appliances—England

The National Health Service (Charges for Drugs and Appliances) and (Travel Expenses and Remission of Charges) Amendment Regulations 2006, SI 2006/675 (in force on 1 April 2006), further amend the National Health Service (Charges for Drugs and Appliances) Regulations 2000, SI 2000/620, by increasing prescription and other charges payable. The regulations also amend the National Health Service (Travel Expenses and Remission of Charges) Regulations 2003, SI 2003/2382, by (1) providing that the calculation as to whether a person is entitled to payment in part of NHS travel expenses is made by reference to the travel expenses incurred in any week; and (2) increasing the amounts used as the basis for calculating entitlement to the payment of travel expenses and the remission of charges.

2003   Charges—drugs and appliances—Wales

The National Health Service (Charges for Drugs and Appliances) (Wales) (Amendment) Regulations 2006, SI 2006/943 (in force on 1 April 2006), further amend the 2001 Regulations, SI 2001/1358, by limiting the availability of the exemption from the charge of drugs and appliances to those persons who are under 25 years of age, or who present a Welsh prescription form or a batch issue relating to a Welsh repeatable prescription for dispensing in Wales.

The National Health Service (Charges for Drugs and Appliances) (Wales) (Amendment) (No 2) Regulations 2006, SI 2006/1792 (in force on 1 August 2006), further amend the 2001 Regulations supra so as to (1) make provision for the application of charges of pharmaceutical services that are provided by chemists in respect of Welsh prescriptions, to be applied to equivalent prescriptions presented by qualifying patients who also present a valid entitlement card; and (2) make provision for qualifying patients who are under the age of 25 years to claim an exemption from charge where they present an equivalent prescription form or equivalent batch issue relating to an equivalent repeatable prescription together with a valid entitlement card.

2004   Charges—optical services—England

The National Health Service (Optical Charges and Payments) Amendment Regulations 2006, SI 2006/479 (in force on 1 April 2006), further amend the 1997 Regulations, SI 1997/818, so as to increase (1) the redemption value of a voucher issued towards the cost of replacement of a single contact lens; (2) the maximum contribution by way of voucher to the cost of repair of a frame; (3) the value of vouchers issued towards the cost of the supply and replacement of glasses and contact lenses; (4) the additional values for vouchers for prisms, tints, photocromic lenses and special categories of appliances; and (5) the value of vouchers issued towards the cost of the repair and replacement of optical appliances.

The National Health Service (Optical Charges and Payments) Amendment (No 2) Regulations 2006, SI 2006/3123 (in force on 20 December 2006), further amend the 1997 Regulations, SI 1997/818, so as to make reference to an increase of 2·5 per cent in National Health Service sight fees.

2005   Charges—optical services—Wales

The National Health Service (Optical Charges and Payments) (Amendment) (Wales) Regulations 2006, SI 2006/1749 (in force on 5 July 2006), further amend the 1997 Regulations, SI 1997/818, by increasing (1) the redemption value of a voucher issued towards the cost of replacement of a single contact lens; (2) the maximum contribution by way of voucher to the cost of repair of a frame; (3) the value of vouchers issued towards the costs of the supply and replacement of glasses and contact lenses; (4) the additional values for vouchers for prisms, tints, photocromic lenses and special categories of appliances; and (5) the value of vouchers issued towards the cost of repair and replacement of optical appliances.

2006   Charges—overseas visitors

The National Health Service (Charges to Overseas Visitors) (Amendment) Regulations 2006, SI 2006/3306 (in force on 15 January 2007), further amend the 1989 Regulations, SI 1989/306, so as to (1) extend to an overseas visitor who is a missionary the exemption from charges to overseas visitors; (2) provide that the spouse, civil partner or child of certain overseas visitors is also exempt from charges; in all other remaining cases, it continues to be a requirement that the spouse, civil partner or child of an overseas visitor also lives on a permanent basis with the overseas visitor in the United Kingdom in order to be exempt from charges; and (3) omit certain countries from the list of countries or territories in respect of which the United Kingdom government has entered into a reciprocal agreement, such countries having now become part of the European Union.

2007   Charges—recovery of charges—personal injuries—reviews and appeals
See para 2010.

2008   Charges—recovery of charges—personal injuries—treatment for persons receiving compensation

The Personal Injuries (NHS Charges) (General) and Road Traffic (NHS Charges) (Amendment) Regulations 2006, SI 2006/3388 (in force on 29 January 2007), make provision in connection with a scheme for the recovery of charges, provided for by the Health and Social Care (Community Health and Standards) Act 2003 Pt 3 (ss 150–169), in cases where injured persons who have received compensation payments in respect of their injuries have received NHS hospital treatment or ambulance services. In particular, the regulations (1) specify the particulars to be included in applications for certificates of NHS charges and the period within which certain applications must be made; (2) prescribe circumstances in which the amount of NHS charges may be reduced where an injured person agrees to share liability for their injury; (3) prescribe the particulars which must be provided to a person on whom a certificate is served; (4) specify the classes of people who must provide information relating to an injured person to the Secretary of State and the timeframes within which such information must be provided; (5) prescribe the manner in which the Secretary of State must forward payments of NHS charges to hospitals and ambulance trusts, and the information which must accompany any such payments; (6) make provision as to how the scheme is to apply where there has been a structured settlement, interim payment or payment into court; (7) limit the liability of insurers in respect of compensation payments where the insured person's liability to pay in respect of the injury is greater that the amount provided for by that person's insurance policy; and (8) provide that payments made under the Criminal Injuries Compensation Act 1995 and the Vaccine Damage Payments Act 1979 are exempt from the scheme. SI 2005/475 is amended.

2009   Charges—road traffic accidents—casualties—recovery of charges—general provisions

The Road Traffic (NHS Charges) Amendment Regulations 2006, SI 2006/401 (in force on 1 April 2006), further amend the 1999 Regulations, SI 1999/785, by increasing, in respect of incidents occurring on or after 1 April 2006 (1) from £483 to £505, the charge for NHS treatment for a traffic casualty who is not admitted to hospital; (2) from £593 to £620, the daily charge for NHS in-patient treatment; and (3) from £35,500 to £37,100, the maximum charge for in-patient treatment. The regulations also make provision maintaining the current charges for incidents occurring before 1 April 2006.

2010   Charges—road traffic accidents—casualties—recovery of charges—reviews and appeals

The Personal Injuries (NHS Charges) (Reviews and Appeals) and Road Traffic (NHS Charges) (Reviews and Appeals) (Amendment) Regulations 2006, SI 2006/3398 (in force on 29 January 2007), make provision, in relation to a certificate of NHS charges issued by the Secretary of State under the Health and Social Care (Community Health and Standards) Act 2003, (1) for the circumstances and timing of reviews by the Secretary of State of certificates; (2) for the Secretary of State to inform a person to whom a certificate is issued of particulars relating to appeals against certificates; (3) as to the manner and timing of applying for a waiver of the requirement to pay the amount specified in the certificate before appealing against the certificate and for appealing a waiver decision; (4) as to the manner and timing of appealing against a certificate; (5) for general matters relating to appeals against waiver decisions or certificates; (6) as to the grounds on which, and manner by which, an application can be made for an extension of the time limits for making an appeal against a waiver decision or certificate; (7) for the application of certain provisions, modified appropriately, of the Social Security Regulations relating to procedural matters of the appeal tribunal to appeals against waiver decisions and certificates; and (8) for the consolidation of appeals against certificates relating to the same injury. The regulations also correct an error in the Road Traffic (NHS Charges) (Reviews and Appeals) Regulations 1999, SI 1999/786, by removing an incorrect cross reference.

2011   Clinical negligence scheme—liabilities under scheme—England

The National Health Service (Clinical Negligence Scheme) Amendment (No 2) Regulations 2006, SI 2006/3087 (in force on 22 November 2006), further amend the 1996 Regulations, SI 1996/251, so as to remake the provisions of the 2006 Regulations, SI 2006/2390, which amended the 1996 Regulations, which established a scheme whereby NHS trusts and certain other bodies providing NHS services may make provision for meeting liabilities to third parties in connection with personal injury arising out of negligence in the carrying out of their functions. In particular, the regulations (1) include as liabilities to which the scheme applies certain liabilities incurred by third parties whom a primary care trust has engaged to provide services under the National Health Service Act 1977 which, immediately before that engagement, it was providing itself; (2) provide that for the purposes of the scheme, such liabilities are to be treated as if they were liabilities of the primary care trust which has engaged the person; and (3) make consequential amendments to the 1996 Regulations relating to payments under the scheme to allow such payments to be made in cases relating to the liabilities to which the scheme is applied by the foregoing amendments. SI 2006/2390 is revoked.

2012   Commission for Patient and Public Involvement In Health—membership and procedure

The Commission for Patient and Public Involvement in Health (Membership and Procedure) (Amendment) Regulations 2006, SI 2006/486 (in force on 1 April 2006), further amend the 2002 Regulations, SI 2002/3038, so as to remove the modification of the Local Government Act 1972 Sch 12A in its application to the Commission for Patient and Public Involvement in Health so that it will apply to the Commission in unmodified form.

2013   Dental services—general dental services—abolition of Dental Practice Board—transitional provisions

The General Dental Services, Personal Dental Services and Abolition of the Dental Practice Board Transitional and Consequential Provisions Order 2006, SI 2006/562 (in force on 1 April 2006), makes (1) transitional provision in respect of general dental services provided before 1 April 2006; (2) transitional provision in respect of personal dental services provided before 1st April 2006; (3) transitional arrangements in relation to the National Health Service (Service Committees and Tribunals) Regulations 1992, SI 1992/664, which are also amended; (4) transitional provisions in relation to the abolition of the Dental Practice Board and the transfer of its functions to the NHS Business Services Authority; and (5) miscellaneous, minor and consequential amendments and revocations.

2014   Dental services—general dental services—contracts—England

The National Health Service (General Dental Services Contracts and Personal Dental Services Agreements) Amendment Regulations 2006, SI 2006/563 (in force on 1 April 2006), amend the National Health Service (General Dental Services Contracts) Regulations 2005, SI 2005/3361, so as to correct an error in respect of the units of orthodontic activity provided in respect of a patient aged 18 years or over in order to refer to 23 units of orthodontic activity. The regulations also amend the National Health Service (Personal Dental Services Agreements) Regulations 2005, SI 2005/3373, so as to correct a reference in order to refer to 'that body' and correct a reference in order to refer to 'dental services' in respect of the arrangements that fall outside normal surgery hours. In addition, the regulations amend SI 2005/3361 and SI 2005/3373, so as to amend the definition of family member by removing the reference to registered in relation to a patient as patients will no longer be registered with a dental practitioner.

2015   Dental services—general dental services—contracts—Wales

The National Health Service (General Dental Services Contracts) (Wales) Regulations 2006, SI 2006/490 (in force on 1 March 2006), set out, in relation to Wales, the framework for general dental services contracts under the National Health Service Act 1977 s 28K. In particular, the regulations (1) prescribe the conditions which, in accordance with s 28M, must be met by a contractor before the local health board may enter into a general dental services contract with it; (2) prescribe the procedure for pre-contract dispute resolution, in accordance with s 28P(1); (3) set out the procedures, in accordance with s 28P(3), by which the contractor may obtain health service body status; (4) prescribe the terms which, in accordance with ss 28O, 28P, must be included in a general dental services contract, in addition to those contained in the 1977 Act including terms relating to (a) the type and duration of the contract; (b) the services to be provided and the manner in which they are to be provided; (c) finance, fees and charges; (d) prescribing of drugs and appliances; (e) the conditions to be met by those who perform services or are employed or engaged by the contractor; (f) patient records, the provision of information and rights of entry and inspection; (g) complaints; (h) procedures for dispute resolution; (i) procedure for a mid-year review of activity under the contract; and (j) procedures for variation and termination of contracts; and (5) make transitional provision.

The National Health Service (General Dental Services Contracts and Personal Dental Services Agreements) (Amendment) (Wales) Regulations 2006, SI 2006/947 (in force on 1 April 2006), amend the National Health Service (Personal Dental Services Agreements) (Wales) Regulations 2006, SI 2006/489, and the National Health Service (General Dental Services Contracts) (Wales) Regulations 2006, SI 2006/490, so as to (1) change the definition of 'family member' by removing references to patients being registered, as patients will no longer be registered with a dental practitioner; (2) correct an error in SI 2006/490 in respect of the units of orthodontic activity provided for a patient aged 18 years or over; and (3) correct two references in SI 2006/489 so that they refer to the relevant body and to dental services in respect of the arrangements that fall outside normal surgery hours.

See para 2020.

2016   Dental services—general dental services—transitional provisions—Wales

The General Dental Services and Personal Dental Services Transitional Provisions Order 2006, SI 2006/488 (in force on 3 March 2006), makes transitory and transitional provisions relating to the new arrangements on 1 April 2006 for the provision of general dental services under the National Health Service Act 1977 s 28L in respect of general dental services contracts entered into under s 28K, and the abolition on 31 March 2006 of pilot schemes for personal dental services by the Health and Social Care (Community Health and Standards) Act 2003 s 178 and their replacement from 1 April 2006 with permanent arrangements for personal dental services under the 1977 Act s 28C. In relation to general dental services contracts, the order sets out the circumstances in which those currently providing general dental services and personal dental services will be entitled to enter into a general dental services contract. In particular, the order (1) provides a right of appeal to the National Assembly for Wales where a local health board refuses to enter into a general dental services contract because it is not satisfied that the criteria relating to suspended dental practitioners are met; (2) makes provision in relation to the duration of entitlement to a general dental services contract in the case of a suspended dental practitioner who has appealed under head (1), above, and of dental practitioners who are performing relevant service (certain service in the armed forces); (3) provides a right of appeal where a contract is not entered into because of a failure to act by a local health board; and (4) makes provision in relation to general dental services contracts entered into under heads (1)–(3), above. In relation to personal dental services agreements, the order sets out the circumstances in which those currently providing general dental services and personal dental services will be entitled to enter into a personal dental services agreement. In particular, the order (a) provides a right of appeal to the National Assembly where a local health board refuses to enter into a personal dental services agreement for the provision of orthodontic care and treatment because it is not satisfied that the criteria relating to suspended dental practitioners are met; (b) makes provision in relation to the duration of entitlement to a general dental services contract in the case of a suspended dental practitioner who has appealed under head (a), above, and of dental practitioners who are performing relevant service; (c) provides a right of appeal where an agreement is not entered into because of a failure to act by a local health board; and (d) makes provision in relation to personal dental services agreements entered into under heads (a)–(c), above. The order also includes transitory provisions relating to current arrangements for general dental services under the 1977 Act s 35 and pilot schemes, in particular with regard to treatment plans.

The General Dental Services and Personal Dental Services Transitional and Consequential Provisions (Wales) Order 2006, SI 2006/946 (in force on 1 April 2006), makes further transitional and consequential provision in relation to (1) new arrangements for the provision of general dental services in respect of general services contracts; (2) the abolition of pilot schemes for personal dental services and their replacement with permanent arrangements; and (3) the introduction of new arrangements for primary dental services and the transfer of functions to the NHS Business Services Authority.

2017   Dental services—performers lists—Wales

The National Health Service (Performers Lists) (Wales) (Amendment) Regulations 2006, SI 2006/945 (in force on 1 April 2006), further amend the 2004 Regulations, SI 2004/1020, in order to provide for lists of persons performing primary dental care to be kept by local health boards in accordance with the National Health Service Act 1977 s 28X. In particular, the regulations (1) add various definitions; (2) make provision for national disqualification; (3) provide that, subject to specified exceptions, no dentist may perform any primary dental services unless he is included in such a list; (4) specify the information that is to be included in the list; (5) require the list to be published; (5) provide for certain specified information to be given by dentists; (6) provide further grounds on which a local health board may or must refuse to admit a dentist to its list, and prescribe matters to which it must have regard; (7) provide additional grounds for the mandatory removal of a dentist from a list; and (8) prescribe an additional ground of appeal for a dentist. SI 2004/1020 Sch 1 is revoked.

2018   Dental services—personal dental services—abolition of Dental Practice Board—transitional provisions

See para 2013.

2019   Dental services—personal dental services—agreements—England

See para 2014.

2020   Dental services—personal dental services—agreements—Wales

The National Health Service (Personal Dental Services Agreements) (Wales) Regulations 2006, SI 2006/489 (in force on 1 March 2006), set out the framework for personal dental services agreements under the National Health Services Act 1977 s 28C. In particular, the regulations (1) prescribe the conditions which must be met by a contractor before a relevant body may enter into a personal dental services agreement with it; (2) prescribe the procedure for pre-agreement dispute resolution in cases where the contractor is not a health service body; (3) provide that a contractor is to be registered as a health service body for the purposes of the National Health Service and Community Care Act 1990 s 4, unless it objects by serving a notice on a relevant body before an agreement is made; (4) prescribe the terms which must be included in a personal dental services agreement, including terms relating to (a) whether the agreement is an NHS contract; (b) the services to be provided and the manner in which they are to be provided; (c) finance, fees and charges; (d) the prescription of drugs and appliances; (e) the conditions to be met by those performing services or who are employed or engaged under the agreement; (f) patient records, the provision of information and rights of entry and inspection; (g) complaints; (h) dispute resolution procedures; (i) the procedure for a mid-year review of activity under the agreement; and (j) the variation and termination of agreements; and (5) provide for a contractor to terminate its agreement and enter into a general dental services contract.

See para 2015.

2021   Dental services—personal dental services—transitional provisions—Wales

See para 2016.

2022   Dental services—primary dental services—exercise of functions—England

The Functions of Primary Care Trusts and Strategic Health Authorities and the NHS Business Services Authority (Awdurdod Gwasanaethau Busnes y GIG) (Primary Dental Services) (England) Regulations 2006, SI 2006/596 (in force on 1 April 2006), relate to the provision of dental services and provide for functions of primary care trusts to be exercised by the NHS Business Services Authority. In particular, the regulations (1) set out the functions, as well as ancillary, related or supplemental functions, which are to be exercised by the Authority in respect of the provisions specified; (2) limit the exercise of the function of a primary care trust in respect of making payments under directions made under the National Health Service Act 1977, except in a case where the Authority is unable to exercise the function; and (3) make provision in respect of obligations, rights or liabilities arising from a general dental services contract or a personal dental services agreement under which the functions specified are exercisable by the Authority.

2023   Dental services—primary dental services—exercise of functions—Wales

The Functions of Local Health Boards and the NHS Business Services Authority (Awdurdod Gwasanaethau Busnes y GIG) (Primary Dental Services) (Wales) Regulations 2006, SI 2006/941 (in force on 1 April 2006), relate to the provision of dental services and provide for functions of local health boards to be exercised by the NHS Business Services Authority. In particular, the regulations (1) set out the functions, as well as ancillary, related or supplemental functions, which are to be exercised by the Authority in respect of the provisions specified; (2) limit the exercise of the function of a local health board in respect of making payments under directions made under the National Health Service Act 1977, except in a case where the Authority is unable to exercise the function; and (3) make provision in respect of obligations, rights or liabilities arising from a general dental services contract or a personal dental services agreement under which the functions specified are exercisable by the Authority.

2024   General medical services—performers lists—England

The National Health Service (Performers Lists) Amendment Regulations 2006, SI 2006/1385 (in force on 3 July 2006), further amend the 2004 Regulations, SI 2004/585, so as to (1) clarify that a performer who is suspended from a list is still treated as being included in such a list in relation to any application he may make for inclusion in another list; and (2) permit a doctor, who is undertaking the post-resignation part of a foundation programme for newly qualified doctors, to perform primary medical services without being a general medical practitioner or on a list, but only in so far as the performance of primary medical services constitutes part of that programme.

2025   General medical services—transitional and consequential provisions—Wales

The General Medical Services Transitional and Consequential Provisions (Wales) (Amendment) Order 2006, SI 2006/360 (in force on 1 March 2006), amends General Medical Services Transitional and Consequential Provisions (Wales) (No.2) Order 2004, SI 2004/1016, so as to correct an error and disapply a requirement for the consent of the National Assembly for Wales for the employment of a GP Registrar for the purpose of being trained by a GP Trainer.

2026   General ophthalmic services—England

The National Health Service (General Ophthalmic Services etc) Amendment Regulations 2006, SI 2006/1550 (in force on 19 July 2006), further amend, in relation to England, the 1986 Regulations, SI 1986/975, and the National Health Service (General Ophthalmic Services Supplementary List) and (General Ophthalmic Services Amendment and Consequential Amendment) Regulations 2005, SI 2005/408, so as to (1) revise (a) provisions relating to payments to practitioners suspended from an ophthalmic list; (b) the terms of service with which contractors providing general ophthalmic services have to comply; and (c) the terms of service regarding a contractor's duty of co-operation with the investigation of complaints; and (2) ban the use of telephone services for the purposes of the provision of general ophthalmic services which make use of national rate numbers (starting with 087), premium rate numbers (starting with 090 or 091) or personal numbers (starting with 070).

2027   General ophthalmic services—supplementary list—Wales

The National Health Service (General Ophthalmic Services Supplementary List) and (General Ophthalmic Services) (Amendment and Consequential Amendment) (Wales) Regulations 2006, SI 2006/181 (in force in part on 1 February 2006 and in part on 1 August 2006), (1) provide that each local health board must prepare and publish a supplementary list and that no ophthalmic medical practitioner or optician; may assist in performing general ophthalmic services unless his or her name is included in such a list or an ophthalmic list; (2) set out how to apply to be included in the list and requires certain information to be given; (3) provides for the relaxation of requirements under head (2) for a practitioner who is included in the ophthalmic list of that local health board; (4) provision is made for a practitioner to be readmitted to the supplementary list on a successful appeal against conviction; (5) specify the grounds on which the local health board may or must refuse to admit a practitioner to the supplementary list, and the matters to which it must have regard; (6) set out the circumstances in which a local health board may defer consideration of an application to include a practitioner in the supplementary list and the procedure to be followed in that respect; (7) provide for a local health board to enter a practitioner's name in the supplementary list subject to conditions and provides that a practitioner's name to be included in that list, until any appeal against the conditions has been decided, provided that the practitioner agrees to be bound by the conditions until the appeal has been determined; (8) requires that a practitioner notify the local health board in writing, within seven days, if the practitioner, or a company of which he or she is a director, incurs any criminal convictions or other specified matters occur; (9) provide for the mandatory removal from its supplementary list by a local health board of any practitioner convicted of murder or of a criminal offence and sentenced to over six months imprisonment and for discretion to remove a practitioner on specified grounds; (10) set out the criteria for decisions on discretionary removals from the supplementary list; (11) provide for a local health board to (a) impose conditions on a practitioner whose name is included in the supplementary list and for the practitioner to be removed if he or she fails to comply with those conditions; and (b) suspend a practitioner from the supplementary list, if certain conditions are met, for the procedure to be followed and for payments to suspended practitioners; (12) make provision for review and the procedure to be followed by local health boards where the local health board decides to conditionally include, contingently remove, or suspend a practitioner from the supplementary list; (13) provide for appeals from specified decisions to be heard by the FHSAA; (14) require a local health board to notify specified persons of specified information relating to decisions to refuse to admit, impose conditions, remove (or contingently remove) or suspend a practitioner from the supplementary list; (15) provide for the circumstances in which a practitioner (a) may or may not withdraw from the supplementary list; or (b) may not withdraw from the supplementary list; (16) provide for changes to the statutory periods for review under the National Health Service Act 1977 s 49N, in specified circumstances; (17) make provision for the disclosure of information to specified persons; (18) provide for practitioners already assisting in the provision of general ophthalmic services before the in force date to continue to do so until not later than 1 August 2006 while their applications for inclusion in a supplementary list are determined; (19) further amend the National Health Service (General Ophthalmic Services) Regulations 1986, SI 1986/975 so as to (a) ensure like provision in relation to ophthalmic lists to that provided for supplementary lists; (b) provide for opticians which are corporate bodies practising as ophthalmic opticians and extend the categories of persons who may be included in an ophthalmic list; (c) clarify who may sign a claim for payment and provides when a counter-signature is also required; (d) provide for opticians to refer patients to a doctor within the hospital eye service, to so inform the patient's doctor and to give the patient a statement to that effect; and (e) require corporate opticians already included in an ophthalmic list to provide further information required by a certain date; (20) amend the National Health Service (Optical Charges and Payments) Regulations 1997, SI 1997/818, so as to make provision for the introduction of supplementary lists.

2028   Health Act 2006

The Health Act 2006 provides for the prohibition of smoking in certain premises, places and vehicles, makes provision in relation to the prevention and control of health care associated infections, makes provision in relation to the management and use of controlled drugs, makes provision in relation to the supervision of certain dealings with medicinal products and the running of pharmacy premises, and provides for the establishment and functions of the Appointments Commission. The Act received the royal assent on 19 July 2006 and came into force in part on that day. Further provisions came into force on and between 28 September 2006 and 28 February 2007: SI 2006/2603, 3125. The remaining provisions come into force on a day or days to be appointed. For details of commencement, see the commencement table in the title STATUTES.

Part 1 (ss 1–13) Smoking

Chapter 1 (ss 1–12) Smoke-free premises, places and vehicles
Section 1 introduces the prohibition of smoking in certain premises, places and vehicles and specifies what the word 'smoking' refers to. Section 2 provides that enclosed or substantially enclosed premises which are open to the public, and shared workplaces, must be smoke-free. However, regulations may be made exempting premises or areas from the requirement to be smoke-free: s 3. Section 4 enables regulations to be made that designate additional smoke-free places. In addition, s 5 allows regulations to provide for vehicles to be smoke-free. Section 6 imposes a duty on any person who occupies or is concerned with the management of smoke-free premises to display no-smoking signs, and allows regulations to impose a corresponding duty in relation to any premises or vehicle designated smoke-free. It is an offence to fail to comply with such a duty: s 6. Section 7 creates the offence of smoking in a smoke-free place, and s 8 makes it an offence for the person in control or concerned in the management of smoke-free premises to cause a person smoking there to stop smoking. An authorised officer who has reason to believe a person has committed an offence under s 6 or 7 may issue a penalty notice in respect of the offence, and if the person pays the penalty he will be discharged of any liability to conviction for the offence: s 9, Sch 1. Section 10 makes provision for regulations to designate bodies as enforcement authorities for the purposes of the smoke-free legislation, and provision about powers of entry is made by Sch 2. It is an offence to intentionally obstruct an authorised officer of an enforcement authority who is exercising his function in relation to the smoke-free legislation: s 11. Section 12 provides for interpretation and provides for the smoke-free legislation to have effect in relation to the territorial sea.

Chapter 2 (s 13) Age for sale of tobacco etc
Section 13 empowers the Secretary of State to change the minimum age for sale of tobacco products to an age which is not lower than 16 and not higher than 18.

Part 2 (ss 14–16) Prevention and control of health care associated infections
Section 14 empowers the Secretary of State to issue a code of practice on the prevention and control of health care associated infections, imposes a consultation requirement on him before he issues or substantially revises such a code and requires NHS bodies to observe the code in discharging their

duty to ensure quality in health care. The Commission for Healthcare Audit and Inspection must take the code into account when it conducts an annual review of health care and when it reviews health care provided by or for an English NHS body or cross-border special health authority: s 15. Section 16 empowers the Commission to serve improvement notices on an NHS body or cross-border special health authority where, following a review or investigation, it is of the view that any of the applicable provisions of the code are not being observed in any material respect in relation to the provision of health care, and provides for action to be taken by the Commission after it has served an improvement notice.

Part 3 (ss 17–33) Drugs, medicines and pharmacies

Chapter 1 (ss 17–25) Supervision of management and use of controlled drugs
Section 17 enables regulations to be made requiring designated bodies to appoint an accountable officer and provides for the responsibilities that may be imposed on accountable officers. Regulations may require designated bodies to co-operate, by sharing intelligence and co-ordinating action, in order to ensure the safe management of controlled drugs and to safeguard patients from harm: ss 18, 19. Section 20 empowers police constables and other authorised persons to enter the premises of healthcare providers and to inspect the arrangements for the safe management of controlled drugs and s 21 creates an offence of obstructing a person making an inspection or deliberately concealing material or information relevant to the inspection. The Secretary of State and the National Assembly for Wales may give guidance to designated bodies and responsible bodies about the appointment of the accountable officer, the accountable officer's functions and the duty to co-operate: s 22. The provisions of Pt 3 Ch 1 apply to the Crown and to people in the public service of the Crown: s 23. Section 24 provides that the Secretary of State is to exercise the functions conferred by Pt 3 Ch 1 in relation to England and the National Assembly for Wales is to exercise those functions in relation to Wales. Section 25 is interpretational.

Chapter 2 (ss 26–33) Medicines and pharmacies
In relation to exemptions for pharmacists from certain licensing requirements and in relation to the sale or supply of medicines not on the general sale list, the Secretary of State may prescribe conditions which must be complied with if the preparation, assembly, dispensation or supply of a medicine is to be considered as done under the supervision of a pharmacist. Sections 27 and 28 make provision in relation to the requirements for retail pharmacy businesses carried on by individuals or partnerships and for such businesses carried on by a body corporate. Where a pharmacist dies or is otherwise prevented from carrying on his business, the requirement that at each premises the retail pharmacy business is under the personal control of a pharmacist is replaced by s 29 with a requirement for there to be a responsible pharmacist. Section 30 makes provision in relation to duties and responsibilities of a responsible pharmacist and provides that failure to comply with any of those requirements may constitute misconduct. Section 31 makes provision in relation to enforcement. Certain of the Secretary of State's order-making powers relating to medicines are extended by ss 32 and 33.

Part 4 (ss 34–56) The National Health Service

Chapter 1 (ss 34–36) Pharmaceutical services
Section 34 empowers the Secretary of State and the National Assembly for Wales to enable charges to be levied in respect of an application to be included in the pharmaceutical list. Regulations may be made under s 35 authorising a primary care trust or the National Assembly to take account of any proposals in applications relating to the sale or supply of over the counter medicines and other healthcare products and advice related to the supply of such products. In relation to the supervision of transactions by pharmacists, s 36 clarifies that regulations may provide for exemptions from the requirement that a registered pharmacist, or the person lawfully conducting a retail pharmacy business, undertakes that medicines will be dispensed by or under the supervision of a pharmacist.

Chapter 2 (ss 37–43) Ophthalmic services
Section 37 sets out the duty of a primary care trust to provide or secure the provision of a sight testing service and other primary ophthalmic services. Section 38 allows primary care trusts to enter into general ophthalmic services contracts under which primary ophthalmic services are provided and makes provision in relation to those contracts. By virtue of s 39, only a person on the performers list of a primary care trust may perform primary ophthalmic services and the Secretary of State may prescribe the qualifications and experience which a medical practitioner who applies for inclusion in a primary ophthalmic services list must have. Section 40 enables primary care trusts to provide assistance or support to those providing or proposing to provide primary ophthalmic services. A primary care trust may recognise a local optical committee which is representative of those who have entered into a general ophthalmic services contract and those who are performing primary ophthalmic services in its area, and regulations may be made requiring a primary care trust, in the exercise of its functions relating to primary ophthalmic services, to consult such a committee: s 41. By virtue of s 42, regulations may be made enabling the Secretary of State to disqualify a provider of optical appliances from receiving payments in respect of optical appliances supplied in a specified area. Section 43 makes transitional provision.

Chapter 3 (ss 44–55) Protection of NHS from fraud and other unlawful activities
Section 44 sets out the general purpose of Pt 4 Ch 3, which is to confer power to require the production of documents in connection with the counter fraud functions of the appropriate national authority (ie the Secretary of State or the National Assembly for Wales) and the security management functions of the Secretary of State. For the purposes of Pt 4 Ch 3, 'NHS body' means a strategic health authority, a local health board, a special health authority, a primary care trust, an NHS trust or an NHS foundation trust: s 45. Section 46 sets out when the appropriate national authority may serve a notice requesting production of documents relevant to the exercise of its counter fraud functions and when the Secretary of State may serve a notice requesting production of documents relevant to the exercise of his security management functions. Where such a notice has been served, s 47 empowers the appropriate national authority to take away any documents produced under the notice, take copies of the whole or specific parts of those documents and ask the person producing those documents to explain them. The appropriate national authority may direct a special health authority to carry out its functions of serving and executing notices for the production of documents: s 48. The appropriate national authority may publish a code of practice relating to the exercise of delegated functions by a special health authority and to the procedures to be followed for the disclosure of information obtained through the use of these powers: s 49. By virtue of s 50, information which has been acquired under Pt 4 Ch 3 and is held by or on behalf of the appropriate national authority may be disclosed in specified circumstances, or when the person to whom the information relates consents to its disclosure. Section 51 provides for special protection of information obtained from personal records in compliance with a notice served under s 46. Sections 52 and 53 create offences of failing to comply with ss 46, 47 and 53. Provision is made by s 54 for the manner in which a notice may be served under s 46. Section 55 is interpretational.

Chapter 4 (s 56) Audit
Section 56 and Sch 3 make provision in relation to National Health Service accounts and audit.

Part 5 (ss 57–71) Appointments Commission
Section 57 establishes the Appointments Commission and provides for the abolition of the National Health Service Appointments Commission. Detailed provision as to the Appointments Commission's constitution, membership and proceedings is set out in Sch 4. The Secretary of State may direct the Commission to exercise all or part of his power to appoint members of specified health bodies, including strategic health authorities and special health authorities, and members and trustees of NHS trusts and primary care trusts: s 58, Sch 5. A requirement that the Secretary of State exercises his functions jointly or concurrently with a devolved authority or any other person who is not a minister of the Crown does not prevent the Secretary of State from giving a direction under s 58, but in such a case he must first consult that authority or other person: s 59. Section 60 requires the Appointments Commission to exercise so much of any function of the Privy Council relating to the appointment of members to the health regulatory bodies listed in Sch 6 as may be specified in a direction given by the Privy Council. Section 61 enables the National Assembly for Wales to direct the Appointments Commission to exercise its appointment functions relating to the appointment of members to the Healthcare Commission and the Health Protection Agency. Where directions are issued to the Appointments Commission by the Secretary of State, the Privy Council or the National Assembly in relation to their appointment functions, it may exercise the functions it is directed to perform in such manner as it thinks fit, subject to the relevant statutory provisions relating to the making of the appointments and anything contained in the directions: s 62. Section 63 enables the Appointments Commission to enter into an arrangement with the board of governors of an NHS foundation trust to assist it with its functions relating to the appointment of members of the board, and gives the Commission a similar power in relation to the appointment of members of other bodies. Provision is made by s 64 allowing the Appointments Commission to provide a range of additional services connected with appointments when it is directed to exercise appointment functions under s 58 or 60 or when it makes arrangements under s 63, including the giving of general advice, mentoring and other assistance and the provision of training to specified people. Under s 65, the Secretary of State may make regulations conferring additional functions on the Appointments Commissionrelating to appointments to bodies to which appointments may be made under s 58, 60 or 61 or to those to which assistance may be given as provided in s 63. Section 66 outlines the standards which the Appointments Commission must maintain in the exercise of its functions and contains provisions about other things it may do in connection with the exercise of its functions. Section 67 requires the Appointments Commission to prepare an annual report and sets out specific requirements which must be met. The Appointments Commission must provide the Secretary of State, the Privy Council, the Commissioner for Public Appointments or any government department with such information or reports in connection with its functions as they may request: s 68. Section 69, Sch 7 make provision for the transfer of the staff, property, rights and liabilities of the National Health Service Appointments Commission to the Appointments Commission. Directions given by the Secretary of State, the Privy Council or the National Assembly must be given in writing and may be varied or revoked by another direction: s 70. Section 71 provides for interpretation.

Part 6 (ss 72–75) Miscellaneous
Section 72 empowers the Secretary of State to direct a special health authority to carry out a function that relates to the training of social care workers. By virtue of s 73, contributory negligence may be taken into account in NHS cost recovery cases where the primary compensation claim is settled by mediation or by other specified means of alternative dispute resolution. Section 74 empowers the Secretary of State to transfer the criminal liabilities of any English NHS body on its abolition or dissolution to another specified English NHS body and empowers the National Assembly for Wales to transfer the criminal liabilities of a Welsh special health authority, a local health board and a Welsh NHS Trust on its abolition or dissolution to another specified Welsh NHS body. The Secretary of State or the National Assembly may make orders dealing with out-of-date references in legislation to health authorities: s 75.

Part 7 (ss 76–84) Final provisions
Section 76 provides that where an offence has been committed by a body corporate, a partnership or an unincorporated association with the consent or connivance of an officer of the company, a partner of the partnership or an officer or member of the unincorporated association, that individual is also guilty of the offence. Procedural provisions regarding certain matters where criminal proceedings are brought against partnerships or other unincorporated associations are contained in s 77. Section 78 contains certain transitional modifications in relation to penalties for offences under the Act. Section 79 provides for the making of orders and regulations. Section 80 and Schs 8 and 9 provide for amendments, repeals and revocations. Provision is made by s 81 for expenditure incurred under or attributable to the Act to be paid out of money provided by Parliament. Section 82 provides for interpretation, s 83 deals with commencement and s 84 deals with short title and extent.

Amendments, repeals and revocations
The list below, which is not exhaustive, mentions repeals and amendments which are or will be effective when the Act is fully in force.
Specific provisions of a number of Acts are amended or repealed. These include: Pharmacy Act 1954 s 15(3), (4), Sch 1 para 3A; Medicines Act 1968 ss 15, 18, 38. 39, 44, 45A, 49N, Sch 12; National Health Service Act 1977 ss 3, 15, 18A, 19, 26, 38, 39, 41, 43D, 44, 45A, 49F, 49H, 49N, 72, 103, 126, 128, Sch 9A; Health and Social Services and Social Services Adjudications Act 1983 Sch 5 para 3; Medical Act 1983 Sch 1 para 4ZA; Dentists Act 1984 Sch 1 paras 1, 2A; Opticians Act 1989 Sch 1 para 2A; National Health Service and Community Care Act 1990 ss 4A, 11(7), 20(2), Sch 2 para 24; Trade Union and Labour Relations (Consolidation) Act 1992 s 279(2); Osteopaths Act 1993 Sch 1 para 11A; Health Service Commissioners Act 1993 ss 2A(1), 6(5); Chiropractors Act 1994 Sch 1 para 11A; Health Authorities Act 1995 Sch 1 para 50; National Health Service (Residual Liabilities) Act 1996 s 1(1), (2); Employment Rights Act 1996 s 43K(1); Pharmacists (Fitness to Practise) Act 1997 Schedule para 5; Audit Commission Act 1998 ss 5, 53, Sch 2 paras 1, 1A, 1C; Government of Wales Act 1998 s 144(2); Health Act 1999 Sch 3 para 2, Sch 4 para 33; Government Resources and Accounts Act 2000 s 14(1), (3), (4); Freedom of Information Act 2000 Sch 1 para 43A; Health and Social Care Act 2001 Sch 1 para 11(a); National Health Service Reform and Health Care Professions Act 2002 s 17, Sch 6 para 6, Sch 7 para 5; Health and Social Care (Community Health and Standards) Act 2003 ss 7(5), 150(7), 187, 188, Sch 6 para 3, Sch 7 para 3; Health Protection Agency Act 2004 Sch 1 para 2; Health Protection Agency Act 2004 Sch 1 para 2, 38; and Public Audit (Wales) Act 2004 s 61(1), Sch 2 paras 2, 38.

2029 Health and Social Care Act 2001—commencement
The Health and Social Care Act 2001 (Commencement No 14) (England) Order 2006, SI 2006/481, brings into force, in relation to England (1) on 28 February 2006, for the purpose of making regulations, s 40, Sch 3; and (2) on 1 April 2006, ss 40 (so far as not already in force), 67 (in part), Sch 3 (so far as not already in force), Sch 5 paras 5(12)(a), 11(4), and the repeals in Sch 6 Pt 2. For a summary of the Act, see 2001 Abr para 2309. See also the commencement table in the title STATUTES.

2030 Health and Social Care (Community Health and Standards) Act 2003— commencement
The Health and Social Care (Community Health and Standards) Act 2003 Commencement (No 3 and No 8) (Amendment) Order 2006, SI 2006/836, amends (1) the Health and Social Care (Community Health and Standards) Act 2003 Commencement (No 3) Order 2004, SI 2004/759, so as to delay (a) until 1 April 2007, the date of the coming into force of s 50(1) in relation to special health authorities ('SHAs') performing functions only or mainly in respect of England, and (b) until 1 April 2008, that date in relation to cross-border SHAs; and (2) the Health and Social Care (Community Health and Standards) Act 2003 Commencement (No 8) Order 2005, SI 2005/2925, so as to revoke certain provisions relating to fees and transitional provision.

The Health and Social Care (Community Health and Standards) Act 2003 Commencement (No 9) Order 2006, SI 2006/1680, brings into force (1) in relation to England, (a) on 27 June 2006, s 105(1) (in part), (6) (for regulation-making purposes); (b) on 1 September 2006, so far as not already in force, ss 113(1), (3), (4), 114(1), (2), (5), (6), 115, 196 (in part), and a repeal in Sch 14; and (2) in relation to England and Wales, on 1 August 2006, s 105(3)–(5), (7) and, for all remaining purposes, s 105(1), (6). Transitional provision is also made.

The Health and Social Care (Community Health and Standards) Act 2003 (Commencement) (No 10) Order 2006, SI 2006/2817, brings s 185 (so far as not already in force) and a repeal in Sch 14 Pt 4 into force on 27 October 2006.

The Health and Social Care (Community Health and Standards) Act 2003 Commencement (Wales) (No 4) Order 2006, SI 2006/345, brings into force, in relation to Wales (1) on 15 February 2006, ss 170 (in part), 171(1) (in part), 172(1), 173 (so far as not already in force), 177(1)–(11) (in part), 179(1) (so far as not already in force), 180 (so far as not already in force), 182(2), 183 (for regulation-making purposes), 184 (in part), Sch 11 paras 7 (in part), 14 (in part), 15 (in part), 39 (so far as not already in force), and certain repeals in Sch 14; and (2) on 1 April 2006, ss 170 (so far as not already in force), 171(1) (in part), (2), 172(2), 177 (in part), 178 (in part), 183 (so far as not already in force) and, to the extent that they relate to dental services in so far as they are not already in force, Sch 11 paras 2, 3,11, 17–20, 21(1) (in part), (5) (in part), 22(1) (in part), (3)(b), 24(b), 28–31, 36(b), 45 (in part), 46(1), (2)(b), (3)(b), (c), 50, 66, 67(b), 68, 69 (in part), 72, and certain repeals in Sch 14 Pt 4. A transitional provision in the Health and Social Care (Community Health and Standards) Act 2003 (Commencement No 1) (Wales) Order 2004, SI 2004/480, is also amended.

The Health and Social Care (Community Health and Standards) Act 2003 (Commencement) (No 11) Order 2006, SI 2006/3397, brings into force, (1) on 15 January 2007, s 147 (in part), Sch 9 para 15; (2) on 28 January 2007, so far as it is not already in force, s 150(1)–(7), (10)–(14); and (3) on 29 January 2007, ss 151–164, 166–169, 196 (in part), Sch 10 and certain repeals in Sch 14 Pt 3. Savings are also made.

For a summary of the Act, see 2003 Abr para 1931. See also the commencement table in the title STATUTES.

2031   Health authorities—membership and procedure—England

The Health Authorities (Membership and Procedure) Amendment (England) Regulations 2006, SI 2006/1393 (in force on 1 July 2006), further amend the 1996 Regulations, SI 1996/707, in relation to England, by removing the requirement for one of the non-officer members of an authority to be a person who holds a post in an institution within the higher education sector which provides education leading to registration in certain health professions, and by removing the provision as to the termination of such a person's appointment as a member of the authority where the person ceases to hold such a post.

2032   Health professionals

See MEDICAL PROFESSIONS.

2033   Local health boards—establishment—Wales

The Local Health Boards (Establishment) (Wales) (Amendment) Order 2006, SI 2006/1790 (in force on 6 July 2006), amends the 2003 Order, SI 2003/148, so as to change the names of Caerphilly, Powys and Rhondda Cynon Taff local health boards to reflect their status as teaching local health boards.

2034   Local health boards—functions—dental public health—Wales

The Functions of Local Health Boards (Dental Public Health) (Wales) Regulations 2006, SI 2006/487 (in force on 1 March 2006), set out the functions to be exercised by local health boards in Wales in relation to oral health.

2035   Local health board—functions—exercise by NHS Business Services Authority—Wales

See para 2023.

2036   National Health Service Act 2006

The National Health Service Act 2006 consolidates certain enactments relating to the health service. The Act received the royal assent on 8 November 2006 and came into force, with certain exceptions, on 1 March 2007. For details of commencement, see the commencement table in the title STATUTES.

2037   National Health Service bodies—complaints—Healthcare Commission—England

The National Health Service (Complaints) Amendment Regulations 2006, SI 2006/2084 (in force on 1 September 2006), amend the 2004 Regulations, SI 2004/1768, so as to (1) provide for the transfer, to the appropriate local authority, of complaints made to NHS bodies that relate to matters that are functions of local authorities; (2) enable NHS bodies to designate as complaints managers, persons who are not employees of the NHS body and who may also be complaints managers for other NHS bodies; (3) exclude complaints that have already been investigated and complaints that relate to schemes established under the Superannuation Act 1972; (4) increase the time limit for an NHS body to respond to a complaint from 20 to 25 working days and provide for the complainant to be able to agree to a longer period; (5) increase the time limit within which a complainant may request the consideration of a complaint by the Healthcare Commission ('the Commission') and prevent the Commission from considering a complaint where it relates to the NHS Bursary Scheme; (6) broaden the remit of the Commission in respect of complaints relating to NHS foundation trusts and increase the time within which a complainant may request the consideration of such a complaint by the Commission; (7) require the Commission to consider any views given by the Independent Regulator of NHS Foundation Trusts in determining how to handle a complaint; (8) reduce the prescription of the management of independent panels used by the Commission to hear and consider complaints; and (9) require the Commission to send an investigation report of a complaint to the Independent Regulator where the it so requests.

2038 National Health Service (Consequential Provisions) Act 2006

The National Health Service (Consequential Provisions) Act 2006 makes provision for repeals, revocations, consequential amendments, transitional and transitory modifications and savings in connection with the consolidation of enactments in the National Health Service Act 2006 and the National Health Service (Wales) Act 2006. The Act received the royal assent on 8 November 2006 and comes into force, with certain exceptions, on 1 March 2007. For details of commencement, see the commencement table in the title STATUTES.

DESTINATION TABLE

1. This table shows how enactments repealed by the National Health Service (Consequential Provisions) Act 2006 (c 43) are dealt with by the National Health Service Act 2006 (c 41) ('NHSA') and the National Health Service (Wales) Act 2006 (c 42) ('NHSWA'). Provisions of the National Health Service Act 2006 are referred to by number only; provisions of the National Health Service (Wales) Act 2006 are preceded by a 'W'.

2. The following abbreviations are used in the table:

Acts of Parliament and Statutory Instrument

1977	National Health Service Act 1977 (c 49)
1990	National Health Service and Community Care Act 1990 (c 19)
1995	Health Authorities Act 1995 (c 17)
1997	National Health Service (Primary Care) Act 1997 (c 46)
1999	Health Act 1999 (c 8)
2001	Health and Social Care Act 2001 (c 15)
2002	National Health Service Reform and Health Care Professions Act 2002 (c 17)
2003	Health and Social Care (Community Health and Standards) Act 2003 (c 43)
2006	Health Act 2006 (c 28)
PCO 2006	National Health Service (Pre-consolidation Amendments) Order 2006 (SI 2006/1407)

3. See generally, as to functions exercisable in relation to Wales, the National Assembly for Wales (Transfer of Functions) Order 1999, SI 1999/672. This transferred, with some exceptions noted in Sch 1 to that order, functions of a Minister of the Crown under the National Health Service Act 1977, the National Health Service and Community Care Act 1990 and the Health Act 1999, so far as exercisable in relation to Wales, to the National Assembly for Wales.

National Health Service Act 1977 (c 49)

Existing provision	Rewritten provision	Remarks
Part 1 Services and Administration		
1 Secretary of State's duty as to health service		
(1)	1(1), (2); W 1(1), (2)	

Existing provision	Rewritten provision	Remarks
(2)	1(3); W 1(3)	
2 Secretary of State's general power as to services		
	2(1), (2); W 2(1), (2)	
3 Services generally		
(1)	3(1); W 3(1)	Amended 2006 Sch 8 para 7(2).
(1A)	6(1); W 6(1)	Inserted National Health Service Act 1977 and National Health Service and Community Care Act 1990 (Amendment) Regulations 2002 (SI 2002/2759), reg 3(1). Amended PCO 2006, Sch 1 Pt 1 para 2.
(2)	221; W 168	
(3)	2(2), 3(3); W 2(2), W 3(3)	Repealed in part 2003, Sch 14 Pt 4.
(4)	3(2); W 3(2)	Inserted 2003 Sch 11 para 8. Amended 2006 para 7(4).
4 High security psychiatric services		
		Substituted 1999 s 41(1).
(1)	4(1); W 4(1)	
(2)	4(2); W 4(2)	
(3)	4(3), (4); W 4(3), (4)	
5 Other services		
(1)(a)	Sch 1 para 1; W Sch 1 para 1	Repealed in part Health and Medicines Act 1988 (c 49) s 10(1), Sch 3; Repealed in part School Standards and Framework Act 1998 (c 31), Sch 31.
(1)(b)	Sch 1 para 8; W Sch 1 para 8	
(1B)	—	Unnecessary.
(2)(a)	Sch 1 para 9; W Sch 1 para 9	

Existing provision	Rewritten provision	Remarks
(2)(c)	Sch 1 para 12(1), (2); W Sch 1 para 12(1), (2)	Amended Public Health Laboratory Service Act 1979 (c 23) s 1(1).
(2)(d)	Sch 1 para 13(1), (2); W Sch 1 para 13(1), (2)	Repealed in part PCO 2006 Sch 2.
(2A)	Sch 1 para 12(3), (4); W Sch 1 para 12(3), (4)	Inserted Public Health Laboratory Service Act 1979 (c 23) s 1(2).
(2B)	6(2); W 6(2)	Inserted Health and Social Security Act 1984 (c 48) s 9(1).
6 Central Health Services Council, and standing advisory committees		
(3)	250(1), (4); W 189(1), (4)	Amended Health Services Act 1980 (c 53) s 8(3). Repealed in part Health Services Act 1980 (c 53) s 8(3), Sch 7.
(4)	250(2); W 189(2)	Substituted Health Services Act 1980 (c 53) s 8(3).
(5)	250(3); W 189(3)	Repealed in part Health Services Act 1980 (c 53) s 8(3), Sch 7.
8 Health Authorities and Strategic Health Authorities		
		Substituted 2002 s 1(2). Spent in relation to Health Authorities due to the abolition of all Health Authorities by the Health Authorities (Transfer of Functions, Staff, Property, Rights and Liabilities and Abolition) (Wales) Order 2003 (SI 2003/813) (W 98). No continuing duty to establish Health Authorities by virtue of the Government of Wales Act 1998 (c 38) s 27(7).
(1)	13(1), (10)	
(2)	13(2)	
(3)	13(3)	
(4)	13(2)	
(5)	13(4)	
(6)	13(5)	
(7)	13(6)	
(8)	13(7)	
(9)	13(8)	Inserted 2006, s 74(1).
(10)	13(9)	Inserted 2006, s 74(1).
11 Special Health Authorities		
(1)	28(1), (8); W 22(1), (8)	Substituted 1999, Sch 4 para 6.
(2)	28(2); W 22(2)	
(3)	28(3); W 22(3)	Amended 1995, Sch 1 para 2.

Existing provision	Rewritten provision	Remarks
(4)	28(4); W 22(4)	
(4A)	28(5); W 22(5)	Inserted 2006, s 74(2).
(4B)	28(6); W 22(6)	Inserted 2006, s 74(2).
(5)	28(7); W 22(7)	
12 Supplementary provisions for ss 8 and 11		
(2)	13(10), 28(8); W 22(8)	Amended 1995, Sch 1 para 3; 2002, Sch 1 para 2.
15 Duty of Family Practitioner Committees		
(1)	22; W 15	Amended Health and Social Security Act 1984 (c 48) s 5(2); 1990, s 12(1)(b); 1995, Sch 1 para 6(a); 2002, Sch 2 para 2(2); 2003, Sch 11 para 9; 2006, Sch 8 para 8; PCO 2006, Sch 1 Pt 1 para 3.
(1ZA)	16(1); W 14(1)	Inserted 1997, Sch 2 para 4(2). Amended 2002, Sch 3 para 11.
(1ZB)	16(2); W 14(2)	Inserted 1997, Sch 2 para 4(2).
16 Exercise of functions		Substituted 1999, Sch 4 para 9.
(1)	14(1)	Amended 2002, Sch 1 para 3(a). Repealed in part PCO 2006, Sch 1 Pt 1 para 4.
(2)	14(2), (3)	Amended 2002, Sch 1 para 3(b), Sch 5 para 5.
(3)	29(1); W 25(1)	
(4)	14(4), 29(2); W 25(2)	Amended 2002, Sch 1 para 3(c).
16A Primary Care Trusts		Inserted 1999, s 2(1).
(1)	18(1), (2)	Substituted 2002, s 2(2).
(1A)	18(3)	Inserted 2002, s 2(2).
(2)	18(2)	
(3)	18(2), (4)	Amended 2002, s 2(3).
(4)	18(5)	
(5)	18(6), (7)	
(6)	18(8)	
16B Exercise of functions by Primary Care Trusts		Inserted 1999, s 2(1).
(1)	19(1)	
(2)	19(2), (3)	Amended 2002, Sch 1 para 4(a), Sch 5 para 6.

Existing provision	Rewritten provision	Remarks
(3)	19(4), 29(2)	Amended 2002, Sch 1 para 4(b).
(4)	19(5), (6)	Inserted 2003, s 182(1).
16BA Local Health Boards		
		Inserted s 6(1).
(1)	w 11(1)	
(2)	w 11(2)	
(3)	w 11(3)	
(4)	w 11(4)	
(5)	w 11(5)	
(6)	w 11(6)	
16BB Local Health Boards: functions		
		Inserted 2002, s 6(1).
(1)	w 12(1)	
(2)	w 12(1)	
(3)	w 12(2)	
(4)	w 12(3)	Amended 2003, Sch 11 para 10.
(5)	w 204(3)	
16BC Exercise of functions by Local Health Boards		
		Inserted 2002, s 6(1)
(1)	w 13(1)	Amended PCO 2006, Sch 1 Pt 1 para 5.
(2)	w 13(2), (3)	
(3)	w 13(4)	
(4)	w 13(5), (6)	Inserted 2003, s 182(2).
16C Advice for Health Authorities and Primary Care Trusts		
		Inserted 1999, Sch 4 para 10
(1)	17, 23; W 16	Amended 2002, Sch 1 para 5(a).
(2)	23; W 16	Amended 2002, Sch 1 para 5(b), Sch 5 para 7.
16CA Primary dental services		
		Inserted 2003, s 170.
(1)	99(1); W 56(1)	
(2)	99(2); W 56(2)	
(3)	99(3); W 56(3)	
(4)	99(4); W 56(4)	
(5)	99(5); W 56(5)	
(6)	99(6); W 56(6)	

Existing provision	Rewritten provision	Remarks
16CB Dental Public Health		
		Inserted 2003, s 171(1).
(1)	111(1)	
(2), (3)	w 67(1), (2)	
(4)	111(2)	
(5)	w 67(3)	
16CC Primary medical services		
		Inserted 2003, s 174.
(1)	83(1); W 41(1)	
(2)	83(2); W 41(2)	
(3)	83(3); W 41(3)	
(4)	83(4); W 41(4)	
(5)	83(5); W 41(5)	
(6)	83(6); W 41(6)	
16CD Primary ophthalmic services		
		Inserted 2006, s 37.
(1)	115(1)	
(2)	115(2)	
(3)	115(3)	
(4)	115(4)	
(5)	115(5)	
(6)	115(6)	
(7)	115(7)	
(8)	115(8)	
(9)	115(9)	
(10)	115(10)	
16CE Regulations under section 16CD: supplementary		
		Inserted 2006, s 37.
(1)	116(1)	
(2)	116(2)	
(3)	116(3)	
16D Secretary of State's directions: distribution of functions		
		Inserted 1999, s 12(1).
(1)	7(1); W 24(1)	Amended 2002, s 3(2), Sch 1 para 6. Repealed in part PCO 2006, Sch 1 Pt 1 para 6.
(2)	7(2)	Amended 2002, Sch 1 para 6. Repealed in part PCO 2006, Sch 1 Pt 1 para 6.

Existing provision	Rewritten provision	Remarks
(3)	7(3); W 24(3)	
17 Directions as to exercise of functions		
		Substituted 1999, s 12(1).
(1)	8(1); W 19(1), 23(1)	Repealed in part PCO 2006, Sch 1 Pt 1 para 7.
(2)	8(2); W 19(1), W 23(1)	Amended 2002, Sch 1 para 7.
(3)	8(3); W 19(3), W 23(3)	Substituted 2001, Sch 5 para 5(3).
17A Strategic Health Authority's directions: distribution of functions		
		Inserted 1999, s 12(1). Substituted 2002, s 3(3).
(1)	15(1)	
(2)	15(2)	
(3)	15(3)	
(4)	15(4), (5)	
(5)	15(6)	
17B Health Authority's directions: exercise of functions		
		Inserted 1999, s 12(1).
(1)	20(1)	Amended 2002, Sch 1 para 8. Repealed 2002, s 3(4).
(2)	20(2)	
18 Directions and regulations under preceding provisions		
(1)	273(4); W 204(3)	Substituted 1999, s 12(3).
(1A)	273(4); W 204(3)	Inserted 1999, s 12(3). Amended and Repealed in part 2002, s 3(5). Repealed in part Health (Wales) Act 2003 (c 4) Sch 3 para 3.
(1B)	273(3)	Inserted 1999, s 12(3). Amended 2002, Sch 1 para 9.
(3)	73(1), (2), 273(1); W 31(1), (2), W 204(1)	Amended 1995, Sch 1 para 9; 1999, s 12(4). Repealed in part 1995, s 3(8). Repealed in part PCO 2006, Sch 1 Pt 1 para 8.
18A Provision of services etc		
		Inserted 1999, s 5.
(1)	21(1)	
(2)	21(2)	
(3)	21(3)	Amended 2003, Sch 11 para 12; 2006 para 9.
(4)	21(4)	
(5)	21(5)	

Existing provision	Rewritten provision	Remarks
(6)	21(6)	Amended 2003, Sch 4 para 24.
(7)	21(4), (5), (7)	
19 Advisory committees for Wales		
(1)	w 190(1), (2)	
(2)	w 190(3), (4)	
(4)	w 190(5)	
19A Independent advocacy services		
		Inserted 2001, s 12.
(1)	248(1); W 187(1)	
(2)	248(2); W 187(2)	Amended 2003, Sch 9 para 9; Public Services Ombudsman (Wales) Act 2005 (c 10) Sch 6 para 20(2).
(3)	248(3); W 187(3)	Substituted Public Services Ombudsman (Wales) Act 2005 (c 10) Sch 6 para 20(3).
(4)	248(4); W 187(4)	
(5)	248(5); W 187(5)	
(6)	248(6); W 187(6)	
(7)	248(7), (8)	Inserted 2002, s 16(5).
20A Community Health Councils in Wales		
		Inserted Health (Wales) Act 2003 (c 4) s 1(1).
(1)	w 182(1)	
(2)	w 182(2)	
(3)	w 182(3)	
(4)	w 182(4)	
21 Local social services authorities		
(1)	254(1); W 192(1)	Repealed in part Children Act 1989 (c 41) Sch 15.
(2)	254(2), (3); W 192(2), (3)	
(3)	254(4); W 192(4)	
(4)	254(2); W 192(2)	Inserted PCO 2006 Sch 1 Pt 1 para 9.
22 Co-operation between health authorities and local authorities		
(1)	82	Substituted 1999, s 27.
(1A)	82	Substituted 1999, s 27. Amended 2002, Sch 1 para 10, Sch 5 para 8; 2003, Sch 4 para 25.
23 Voluntary organisations and other bodies		

Existing provision	Rewritten provision	Remarks
(1)	12(1), (2); W 10(1), (2)	Repealed in part Health Services Act 1980 (c 53) Sch 7.
(2)	12(3), (4), 275(1); W 10(3), (4), W 206(1)	Amended 1995, Sch 1 para 13; 1999 (Supplementary, Consequential etc Provisions) Order 2000 (SI 2000/90) Sch 1 para 13(2); 2002, Sch 1 para 11, Sch 5 para 9.
(3)	12(5), (6); W 10(5), (6)	
(5)	12(7); W 10(7)	

25 Supplies not readily obtainable

	255(1); W 193(1)	Amended Health and Medicines Act 1988 (c 49) Sch 2 para 2.

26 Supply of goods and services by Secretary of State

(1)	80(1)–(4), 275(1); W 38(1)–(4), W 206(1)	Amended 1995, Sch 1 para 14; 1999, Sch 4 para 11; 2002, Sch 1 para 12, Sch 5 para 10.
(2)	80(5); W 38(5)	Substituted 1997, Sch 2 para 5(2). Amended 2006 para 11; PCO 2006, Sch 1 Pt 1 para 11. Repealed in part 2003, Sch 11 para 13.
(3)	80(6), 275(1); W 38(6), W 206(1)	Amended 1995, Sch 1 para 14; 1999, Sch 4 para 11; 2002, Sch 1 para 12; PCO 2006, Sch 1 Pt 1 para 11.
(4)	80(7); W 38(7)	Added Health Services Act 1980 (c 53) s 3(1). Amended 1995, Sch 1 para 14; 1997, Sch 2 para 5(3); 1999, Sch 4 para 11; 2002, Sch 1 para 12; 2003, Sch 11 para 13(3); 2006 para 11; PCO 2006, Sch 1 Pt 1 para 11.

27 Conditions of supply under s 26

(1)	81(1); W 39(1)	Amended 1995, Sch 1 para 15; 1999, Sch 4 para 12; 2002, Sch 1 para 13.
(2)	81(2); W 39(2)	
(3)	81(3); W 39(3)	Amended 1995, Sch 1 para 15(b); 1999, Sch 4 para 12; 2002, Sch 1 para 13, Sch 5 para 11.
(4)	81(4), (5); W 39(4), (5)	

Existing provision	Rewritten provision	Remarks
(6)	81(6); W 39(6)	
28 Supply of goods and services by local authorities		
(1)	74(1); W 32(1)	Amended 1995, Sch 1 para 16(a); 1999, Sch 4 para 13(a); 2002, Sch 1 para 14(a), Sch 5 para 12(a).
(2)	74(2); W 32(2)	
(3)	74(3), (4); W 32(3), (4)	Amended Act 1990, Sch 2 para 21; 1995, Sch 1 para 16(b); 1999, Sch 4 para 13(b); 2002, Sch 1 para 14(b), Sch 5 para 12(b); 2003, Sch 4 para 26.
28A Power to make payments towards expenditure on community services		
		Substituted Health and Social Services and Social Security Adjudications Act 1983 (c 41) s 1.
(1)	256(1); W 194(1)	Amended 1995, Sch 1 para 17(a); 1999, s 29(2); 2002, Sch 5 para 13(a).
(2)	256(1), (2); W 194(1), (2)	Amended Housing (Consequential Provisions) Act 1985 (c 71) Sch 2 para 38; Local Government (Wales) Act 1994 (c 19) Sch 10 para 11; Education Act 1996 (c 56), Sch 37 para 44; Housing Act 1996 (Consequential Provisions) Order 1996 (SI 1996/2325), Sch 2 para 9(2); 1999, Sch 4 para 14(2); Local Government Act 2000 (c 22) Sch 5 para 17. Repealed in part Government of Wales Act 1998 (c 38) Sch 18. Repealed in part PCO 2006, Sch 1 Pt 1 para 12.
(2A)	256(3); W 194(3)	Inserted 1999, s 29(3).
(2B)	256(4); W 194(4)	Inserted 1999, s 29(3). Amended 2002, Sch 1 para 15, Sch 5 para 13; 2003, Sch 4 para 27.
(3)	256(5); W 194(5)	
(5)	256(6); W 194(6)	
(6)	—	Unnecessary.
(7)	256(7); W 194(7)	Amended 1995, Sch 1 para 17.
(8)	256(8); W 194(8)	Repealed in part 1999, Sch 4 para 14.

Existing provision	Rewritten provision	Remarks
(9)	257(1)–(4); W 195(1)–(4)	Amended 1999, Sch 4 para 14.

28B Power of Secretary of State to make payments towards expenditure on community services in Wales

(1)	w 196(1), (2)	Repealed in part Government of Wales Act 1998 (c 38) Sch 18.
(2)	w 196(3)	
(3)	w 196(4)	
(4)	w 196(5)	
(5)	w 196(6)	

28BB Power of local authorities to make payments to NHS bodies

		Inserted 1999, s 30.
(1)	76(1); W 34(1)	
(2)	76(1); W 34(1)	Amended 2002, Sch 1 para 16, Sch 5 para 14.
(3)	76(2); W 34(2)	
(4)	76(3); W 34(3)	
(5)	—	Unnecessary.
(6)	76(4); W 34(4)	
(7)	76(5); W 34(5)	

28C Personal medical dental expenses

		Inserted 1997, s 21(1).
(1)	92(1), (2), 107(1), (2); W 50(1), (2), W 64(1), (2)	Amended 2002, Sch 3 para 7(2); 2003, Sch 11 para 14.
(2)	92(3)–(5), 107(3)–(5); W 50(3)–(5), W 64(3)–(5)	Amended 2001, Sch 5 para 11(4); 2003, Sch 11 para 14.
(4)	92(6), 107(6)	Amended 1999, Sch 4 para 15; 2003, Sch 11 para 14. See also National Health Service (Consequential Provisions) Act 2006 Sch 2 para 15(a), (b).
(5)	—	Spent.

Existing provision	Rewritten provision	Remarks
(6)	92(7), 107(7); W 50(6), W 64(6)	Amended 2002, Sch 3 para 7(2).
28D Persons with whom agreements may be made		
		Inserted 1997, s 21(1).
(1)	93(1), 108(1); W 51(1), W 65(1)	Amended 1999, Sch 4 para 16(a); 2002, Sch 3 para 7(3); Act 2003, s 177(2), Sch 11 para 15(2); Primary Medical Services (Scotland) Act 2004 (Consequential Modifications) Order 2004 (SI 2004/957), Schedule para 3.
(1A)	93(2), 108(2); W 51(2), W 65(2)	Inserted 2003, s 177(3).
(2)	93(3), 108(3); W 51(3), W 65(3)	Amended 1999, Sch 4 para 16(b); 2003, s 177(4), (5), (6), Sch 11 para 15(3), (4); PCO 2006, Sch 1 Pt 1 para 13. Repealed in part 2003, Sch 14 Pt 4.
28E Personal medical or dental services: regulations		
		Inserted 1997, s 22(1).
(1)	94(1), 109(1); W 52(1), W 66(1)	
(2)	94(2), 109(2); W 52(2), W 66(2)	Amended 2002, Sch 3 para 8(a). Repealed in part 2003, Sch 14 Pt 4.
(3)	94(3), 109(3); W 52(3), W 66(3)	Amended 2002, Sch 3 para 8(b); 2003, s 177(7). Repealed in part 2003, Sch 14 Pt 4.
(3A)	94(4), 109(4), 273(1), (4); W 52(4), W 66(4), W 204(1), (3)	Inserted 2003, s 177(8).
(3B)	94(5), 109(5); W 52(5), W 66(5)	Inserted 2003, s 177(8).

Existing provision	Rewritten provision	Remarks
(3C)	94(6), 109(6); W 52(6), W 66(6)	Inserted 2003, s 177(9).
(3D)	94(7), 109(7); W 52(7), W 66(7)	Inserted 2003, s 177(10).
(3E)	94(8), 109(8); W 52(8), W 66(8)	Inserted 2003, s 177(11).
(3F)	94(9), 109(9); W 52(9), W 66(9)	Inserted 2003, s 177(11).

28EE Delegation of Health Authority functions relating to s 28C arrangements

		Inserted 1999, s 6(2)
(2)	95(1), 110(1)	Amended 2002, Sch 3 para 14(b); 2003, Sch 11 para 16; PCO 2006, Sch 1 Pt 1 para 14.
(3)	95(2), 110(2)	

28I Use of accommodation

		Substituted PCO 2006, Sch 1 Pt 1 para 15.
(1)	98, 114, 168	
(2)	w 55, W 70	

28J Local pharmaceutical services schemes

	144; W 102	Inserted 2001, s 40(1). Amended 2002, Sch 2 para 78.

28K General dental services contracts: introductory

		Inserted 2003, s 172(1).
(1)	100(1); W 57(1)	
(2)	100(2); W 57(2)	
(3)	100(3); W 57(3)	
(4)	100(4); W 57(4)	

28L Requirement to provide certain primary dental services

		Inserted 2003, s 172(1).

Existing provision	Rewritten provision	Remarks
(1)	101(1); W 58(1)	
(2)	101(2); W 58(2)	
28M Persons eligible to enter into GDS contracts		
		Inserted 2003, s 172(1).
(1)	102(1); W 59(1)	
(2)	102(2); W 59(2)	
(3)	102(3); W 59(3)	
(4)	102(4); W 59(4)	Amended PCO 2006, Sch 1 Pt 1 para 16.
28N GDS contracts: payments		
		Inserted 2003, s 172(1).
(1)	103(1); W 60(1)	
(2)	103(2); W 60(2)	
(3)	103(3); W 60(3)	
(4)	103(4); W 60(4)	
(5)	273(1), (4); W 204(1), (3)	
(6)	103(5); W 60(5)	
(7)	—	Unnecessary.
28O GDS contracts: other required terms		
		Inserted 2003, s 172(1).
(1)	104(1); W 61(1)	
(2)	104(2); W 61(2)	

Existing provision	Rewritten provision	Remarks
(3)	104(3); W 61(3)	
(4)	104(4); W 61(4)	
28P GDS contracts: disputes and enforcement		
		Inserted 2003, s 172(1).
(1)	105(1); W 62(1)	
(2)	105(2); W 62(2)	
(3)	105(3); W 62(3)	
(4)	105(4); W 62(4)	
(5)	105(5); W 62(5)	
28Q General medical services: introductory		
		Inserted 2003, s 175(1).
(1)	84(1); W 42(1)	
(2)	84(2); W 42(2)	
(3)	84(3); W 42(3)	
(4)	84(4); W 42(4)	
(5)	84(5); W 42(5)	
28R Requirement to provide certain primary medical services		
		Inserted 2003, s 175(1).
(1)	85(1); W 43(1)	
(2)	85(2); W 43(2)	
28S Persons eligible to enter into GMS contracts		
		Inserted 2003, s 175(1).

Existing provision	Rewritten provision	Remarks
(1)	86(1); W 44(1)	
(2)	86(2); W 44(2)	
(3)	86(3); W 44(3)	
(4)	86(4); W 44(4)	
(5)	86(5); W 44(5)	
28T GMS contracts: payments		
		Inserted 2003, s 175(1).
(1)	87(1); W 45(1)	
(2)	87(2); W 45(2)	
(3)	87(3); W 45(3)	
(4)	87(4); W 45(4)	
(5)	273(1), (4); W 204(1), (3)	
(6)	87(5); W 45(5)	
(7)	—	Unnecessary.
28U GMS contracts: prescription of drug etc		
		Inserted 2003, s 175(1).
1)	88(1); W 46(1)	
(2)	88(2); W 46(2)	
(3)	88(3); W 46(3)	
(4)	273(1); W 204(1)	

Existing provision	Rewritten provision	Remarks
(5)	88(4); W 46(4)	

28V GMS contracts: other required terms

		Inserted 2003, s 175(1).
(1)	89(1); W 47(1)	
(2)	89(2); W 47(2)	
(3)	89(3); W 47(3)	
(4)	89(4); W 47(4)	
(5)	89(5); W 47(5)	
(6)	89(6); W 47(6)	

28W GMS contracts: disputes and enforcement

		Inserted 2003, s 175(1).
(1)	90(1); W 48(1)	
(2)	90(2); W 48(2)	
(3)	90(3); W 48(3)	
(4)	90(4); W 48(4)	
(5)	90(5); W 48(5)	

28WA General ophthalmic services contracts: introductory

		Inserted 2006, s 38.
(1)	117(1)	
(2)	117(2)	
(3)	117(3)	
(4)	117(4)	
(5)	117(5)	

28WB Persons eligible to enter into GOS contracts

		Inserted 2006, s 38.
(1)	118(1)	
(2)	118(2)	

Existing provision	Rewritten provision	Remarks
28WC Exclusion of contractors		
		Inserted 2006, s 38.
(1)	119(1)	
(2)	119(2)	
28WD GOS contracts: payments		
		Inserted 2006, s 38.
(1)	120(1)	
(2)	120(2)	
(3)	120(3)	
(4)	120(4)	
(5)	273(1), (4)	
(6)	120(5)	
28WE GOS contracts: other required terms		
		Inserted 2006, s 38.
(1)	121(1)	
(2)	121(2)	
(3)	121(3)	
(4)	121(4)	
(5)	121(5)	
28WF GOS contracts: disputes and enforcement		
		Inserted 2006, s 38.
(1)	122(1)	
(2)	122(2)	
(3)	122(3)	
(4)	122(4)	
(5)	122(5)	
28X Persons performing primary medical and dental services		
		Inserted 2003, s 179(1).
(1)	91(1); W 49(1)	
(1A)	146(1)	Inserted PCO 2006, Sch 1 Pt 1 para 17.
(2)	106(1); W 63(1)	
(2A)	123(1)	Inserted 2006.
(3)	91(2), 106(2), 123(2), 146(2); W 49(2), W 63(2)	Amended PCO 2006, Sch 1 Pt 1 para 17.
(4)	91(3), 106(3), 123(3), 146(3); W 49(3), W 63(3)	

Existing provision	Rewritten provision	Remarks
(5)	91(4), 106(4), 123(4), 146(4); W 49(4), W 63(4)	
(6)	91(5), 106(5), 123(5), 146(5); W 49(5), W 63(5)	
(6A)	123(6)	Inserted 2006, s 39(4).
(7)	91(6), 106(6), 123(7), 146(6); W 49(6), W 63(6)	
28Y Assistance and support		
		Inserted 2003, s 180.
(1)	96(1), 112(1), 124(1), 147(1); W 53(1), W 68(1)	Amended PCO 2006, Sch 1 Pt 1 para 18.
(2)	96(2), 112(2), 124(2), 147(2); W 53(2), W 68(2)	
(3)	96(3), 112(3), 124(3), 147(3); W 53(3), W 68(3)	
38 Arrangements for general ophthalmic services		
(1)	w 71(1), (2)	Amended Health and Social Security Act 1984 (c 48), s 1(3); Family Practitioner Committees (Consequential Modifications) Order 1985 (SI 1985/39) art 7(11); Amended Health and Medicines Act 1988 (c 49), s 13(1); Amended 1995, Sch 1 para 27; Repealed 2006 para 12.
(2)	w 71(3), (4)	Inserted Health and Medicines Act 1988 (c 49) s 13(1).
(3)	w 71(5)	Inserted Health and Medicines Act 1988 (c 49) s 13(1).
(4)	w 71(6)	Inserted Health and Medicines Act 1988 (c 49) s 13(1).

Existing provision	Rewritten provision	Remarks
(5)	w 71(7)	Inserted Health and Medicines Act 1988 (c 49) s 13(1).
(6)	w 71(8), (9)	Inserted Health and Medicines Act 1988 (c 49) s 13(1).
(7)	w 71(10)	Inserted Health and Medicines Act 1988 (c 49) s 13(1).

39 Regulation as to s 38

(1)	w 72(1), (2)	Amended Health Services Act 1980 (c 53) para 52; Health and Social Security Act 1984 (c 48), Sch 1 para 1. Renumbered and amended 2001, s 20(5). Amended 2006 para 13. Repealed in part Health and Social Security Act 1984 (c 48) s 1(4); 2006 para 13.
(2)	w 72(3)	Inserted 2001, s 20(5). Repealed in part 2006 para 13.
(3)	w 72(4)	Inserted 2001, s 20(5). Repealed in part 2006 para 13.
39(4)	w 72(5)	Inserted 2001, s 23(4).
39(5)	w 72(6)	Inserted 2001, s 23(4).

40 Medical practitioners with qualification prescribed under s 38

	w 73	

41 Arrangements for pharmaceutical services

		Substituted 2001, s 42(1).
(1)	126(1)–(3); W 80(1)–(3)	Amended 2002, Sch 2 para 13(2); 2003, Sch 11 para 18.
(2)	126(8); W 80(8)	
(3)	126(4); W 80(4)	Amended Health Professions Order 2001 (Consequential Amendments) Order 2003 (SI 2003/1590), Schedule para 3; Health Act 1999 (Consequential Amendments) (Nursing and Midwifery) Order 2004 (SI 2004/1771) para 8; Dentists Act 1984 (Amendment) Order 2005 (SI 2005/ 2011) Sch 6 para 1(3); 2006, Sch 8 para 14.
(4)	126(5); W 80(5)	
(5)	126(6); W 80(6)	Amended 2002, Sch 2 para 13(3).
(6)	126(7); W 80(7)	Amended 2002, Sch 2 para 13(3).
(7)	126(9); W 80(9)	

41A Arrangements for providing additional pharmaceutical services

		Inserted 1997, s 27(1).

Existing provision	Rewritten provision	Remarks
(1)	127(1); W 81(1)	Amended 2001, s 43(1); 2002, Sch 2 para 14.
(1A)	127(2); W 81(2)	Inserted 2001, s 43(1). Amended 2002, Sch 2 para 14.
(2)	—	Unnecessary.
(3)	127(3); W 81(3)	
(4)	127(4); W 81(4)	
41B Terms and conditions, etc		
		Inserted 1997, s 28(1).
(1)	128(1); W 82(1)	Amended 2002, Sch 2 para 15.
(2)	128(2); W 82(2)	
(3)	128(3); W 82(3)	
(4)	128(4); W 82(4)	Amended 2002, Sch 2 para 15.
(5)	128(5); W 82(5)	Amended 2002, Sch 2 para 15.
(6)	128(6); W 82(6)	Amended 2002, Sch 2 para 15.
42 Regulations as to pharmaceutical services		
		Substituted National Health Service (Amendment) Act 1986, s 3(1).
(1)	129(1); W 83(1)	Amended 1995, Sch 1 para 30; 2001, s 43(2); 2002, Sch 2 para 16(2).
(2)	129(2); W 83(2)	Amended 1995, Sch 1 para 30; 2001, s 43(3); 2002, Sch 2 para 16(3).
(2A)	129(3); W 83(3)	Inserted 2001, s 40(3).
(2B)	129(4); W 83(4)	Inserted 2006, s 35.
(2C)	129(5); W 83(5)	Inserted 2006, s 35.

Existing provision	Rewritten provision	Remarks
(3)	129(6); W 83(6)	Amended Pharmaceutical Qualifications (EEC Recognition) order 1987 (SI 1987/2202) art 4; 1990, s 12(3); 1995, Sch 1 para 30; 2001, s 20(6), s 23(5); 2002, Sch 2 para 16(4); National Health Service Reform and Health Care Professions Act 2002 (Supplementary, Consequential etc Provisions) Regulations 2002 (SI 2002/2469) Sch 1 para 30. Repealed in part 2001, s 20(6).
(3A)	129(7); W 83(7)	Inserted 2001, s 43(4).
(3B)	129(8), (9); W 83(8), (9)	Inserted 2001, s 43(4). Amended 2002, Sch 2 para 16(5).
(3C)	129(10); W 83(10)	Inserted 2001, s 23(5).
(4)	130(1); W 84(1)	
(4A)	130(2); W 84(2)	Inserted 2001, s 20(6).
(5)	130(3); W 84(3)	
42A Power to charge: England		
		Inserted 2006, s 34(1).
(1)	131(1)	
(2)	131(2)	
(3)	131(3)	
(4)	131(4)	
(5)	131(5)	
42B Power to charge: Wales		
		Inserted 2006, s 34(1).
(1)	—	See the National Health Service (Consequential Provisions) Act 2006 Sch 2 para 15(c).
(2)	—	See the National Health Service (Consequential Provisions) Act 2006 Sch 2 para 15(c).
(3)	—	See the National Health Service (Consequential Provisions) Act 2006 Sch 2 para 15(c).
(4)	w 85(1)	
(5)	w 85(2)	
(6)	w 85(3)	See, as to sub-s (6)(a), the National Health Service (Consequential Provisions) Act 2006 Sch 2 para 15(c).
(7)	w 85(4)	See, as to sub-s (6)(a), the National Health Service (Consequential Provisions) Act 2006 Sch 2 para 15(c).
(8)	w 85(5)	

43 Persons authorised to provide pharmaceutical services

Existing provision	Rewritten provision	Remarks
(1)	132(1); W 86(1)	Amended Health Services Act 1980 (c 53) s 21(2); 1995, Sch 1 para 31; 2002, Sch 2 para 17(2); 2003, Sch 11 para 19.
(2)	132(2); W 86(2)	Substituted 2006, s 36(1).
(2A)	132(3); W 86(3)	Substituted 2002, Sch 2 para 17(3).
(2B)	132(3); W 86(3)	Inserted 1997, s 29(1).
(2BA)	132(4); W 86(4)	Inserted 2001, s 20(7). Amended 2002, Sch 2 para 17(4).
(2BB)	132(5); W 86(5)	Inserted 2001, s 20(7). Amended 2002, Sch 2 para 17(5).
(2C)	132(6); W 86(6)	Inserted 1997, s 29(1).
(3)	132(7); W 86(7)	Inserted 1990, Sch 9 para 18(2). Amended 1997, Sch 2 para 14; 2001, s 42(2).
(4)	132(8); W 86(8)	Inserted Pharmacists (Fitness to Practise) Act 1997 (c 19) Schedule para 6.
(5)	132(9); W 86(9)	Inserted Pharmacists (Fitness to Practise) Act 1997 (c 19) Schedule para 6.

42ZA Conditional inclusion in medical, dental, ophthalmic and pharmaceutical lists

		Inserted 2001, s 21.
(1)	148(1); W 104(1)	Amended 2002, Sch 2 para 18(2).
(2)	148(2); W 104(2)	
(3)	148(1); W 104(1)	Repealed in part 2003, Sch 14 Pt 4.
(4)	148(3); W 104(3)	Amended 2002, Sch 2 para 18(3).
(5)	148(4); W 104(4)	Amended 2002, Sch 2 para 18(4).
(6)	148(5); W 104(5)	

Existing provision	Rewritten provision	Remarks
(7)	148(6); W 104(6)	Amended 2002, Sch 2 para 18(5).
43A Regulations as to remuneration		
		Substituted PCO 2006, Sch 1 Pt 1 para 19.
(1)	164(1), (2); W 76(1), (2), W 88(1), (2)	
(2)	164(3), (4); W 76(3), (4), W 88(3), (4)	
(3)	164(5); W 76(5), W 88(5)	
(4)	164(6); W 76(6), W 88(6)	
(5)	164(7), (8); W 76(7), (8), W 88(7), (8)	
(6)	164(9); W 76(9), W 88(9)	
(7)	164(10); W 76(10), W 88(10)	
43B Remuneration–supplementary		
		Substituted PCO 2006, Sch 1 Pt 1 para 19.
(1)	165(1); W 77(1), W 89(1)	
(2)	165(2); W 77(2), W 89(2)	

Existing provision	Rewritten provision	Remarks
(3)	165(3); W 77(3), W 89(3)	
(4)	165(4); W 77(4), W 89(4)	
(5)	165(5); W 77(5), W 89(5)	
(6)	165(6); W 77(6), W 89(6)	
(7)	165(7); W 77(7), W 89(7)	
(8)	165(8); W 77(8), W 89(8)	
(9)	165(9), (10); W 77(9), (10), W 89(9), (10)	
(10)	165(11); W 77(11), W 89(11)	
42C Indemnity cover		Inserted 1999, s 9(1).
(1)	166(1); W 120(1)	
(2)	166(2); W 120(2)	Amended 2002, Sch 2 para 19.
(3)	166(1)–(3); W 120(1)–(3)	Amended 2002, Sch 2 para 19 para 3. Repealed in part 2003, Sch 14 Pt 4.

Existing provision	Rewritten provision	Remarks
(4)	166(4); W 120(4)	
42D Supplementary lists		
		Inserted 2001, s 24(1).
(1)	149(1); W 105(1)	Amended 2002, Sch 2 para 20(2). Repealed in part 2003, Sch 14 Pt 4.
(2)	149(2); W 105(2)	
(3)	149(3); W 105(3)	Amended 2002, Sch 2 para 20(3).
(4)	149(4); W 105(4)	Amended 2002, Sch 2 para 20(4).
(5)	149(5); W 105(5)	
(6)	149(6); W 105(6)	
(7)	149(7); W 105(7)	Amended 2002, Sch 2 para 20(5).
(8)	149(8); W 105(8)	Amended 2002, Sch 2 para 20(6).
(9)	149(9); W 105(9)	Amended 2002, Sch 2 para 20(7).
(10)	150(1), (2); W 106(1), (2)	Amended 2002, Sch 2 para 20(8); 2003, Sch 11 para 20(b). Repealed in part 2003, Sch 11 para 20(a).
(11)	150(3); W 106(3)	Amended 2002, Sch 2 para 20(9).
44 Recognition of local representative committees		
(B2)	167(1)–(4)	Inserted 2002, s 5(4). Amended PCO 2006, Sch 1 Pt 1 para 20. Repealed in part 2006 para 16.
(1)	w 78(1), (2), W 90(1), (2)	Amended 1990, s 12(4); 1995, Sch 1 para 32; 2001, s 43(6); 2003, Sch 11 para 21(4). Repealed in part Health and Social Security Act 1984 (c 48) Sch 8; 1999, Sch 5.
(2)	167(5); W 78(3), W 90(3)	Amended 1990, s 12(4); 1995, Sch 1 para 21. Repealed in part 2002, s 5(5).

Existing provision	Rewritten provision	Remarks
(3)	167(2), (3)	Inserted 1999, s 11(4). Amended 2001, Sch 5 para 5(7); PCO 2006, Sch 1 Pt 1 para 20. Repealed in part 2003, Sch 11 para 21(5).
(3A)	167(2)	Inserted PCO 2006, Sch 1 Pt 1 para 20.
(4)	167(2), (3)	Inserted 1999, s 11(4). Amended 2002, s 5(7); PCO 2006, Sch 1 Pt 1 para 20.

45 Functions of local representative committees

Existing provision	Rewritten provision	Remarks
(1)	w 78(4), W 90(4)	Substituted 1999, s 11(6). Amended and Repealed in part 2003, Sch 11 para 22(3).
(1ZA)	167(6)	Substituted PCO 2006, Sch 1 Pt 1 para 21.
(1A)	167(7); W 78(5), W 90(5)	Substituted 1999, s 11(6). Amended 2002, s 5(10). Amended and Repealed in part 2003, Sch 11 para 22(5).
(1B)	167(8); W 78(6), W 90(6)	Substituted 1999, s 11(6).
(1C)	167(12)	Substituted 1999, s 11(6). Substituted in Pt 2003, Sch 11 para 22. Amended PCO 2006, Sch 1 Pt 1 para 21.
(2)	167(9); W 78(7), W 90(7)	Substituted 1999, s 11(6). Amended 2002, s 5(11). Substituted in Pt 2003, Sch 11 para 22(6).
(3)	167(10), (11); W 78(8), (9), W 90(8), (9)	Amended 1995, Sch 1 para 33; 2002, s 5(12); 2003, Sch 11 para 22(7). Repealed in part 1999, s 11(7).
(4)	167(13)	Amended 1995, Sch 1 para 33; 2002, s 5(12). Amended and Repealed in part 2003, Sch 11 para 22(8).
(5)	167(9), (14); W 78(10), W 90(10)	Inserted 1999, s 11(8). 2003, Sch 11 para 22(9).

45A Local Medical Committees

Existing provision	Rewritten provision	Remarks
		Inserted 2003, Sch 11 para 23.
(1)	97(1)	
(2)	w 54(1)	
(3)	97(2); W 54(2)	Amended 2006 para 17(2).
(4)	97(3); W 54(3)	Amended 2006 para 17(3).

Existing provision	Rewritten provision	Remarks
(5)	97(4); W 54(4)	
(6)	97(5); W 54(5)	
(7)	97(6); W 54(6)	
(8)	97(7)	
(9)	97(8); W 54(7)	
(10)	97(9); W 54(8)	
(11)	97(10); W 54(9)	
(12)	97(11); W 54(10)	
(13)	97(12); W 54(11)	
45B Local Dental Committees		
		Inserted 2003, Sch 11 para 23.
(1)	113(1)	
(2)	w 69(1)	
(3)	113(2); W 69(2)	
(4)	113(3); W 69(3)	
(5)	113(4); W 69(4)	
(6)	113(5); W 69(5)	
(7)	113(6); W 69(6)	
(8)	113(7)	
(9)	113(8); W 69(7)	
(10)	113(9); W 69(8)	

Existing provision	Rewritten provision	Remarks
(11)	113(10); W 69(9)	
(12)	113(11); W 69(10)	
(13)	113(12); W 69(11)	
45C Local Optical Committees		
		Inserted 2006, s 41.
(1)	125(1)	
(2)	125(2)	
(3)	125(3)	Amended 2006 para 17(2).
(4)	125(4)	Amended 2006 para 17(3).
(5)	125(5)	
(6)	125(6)	
(7)	125(7)	
(8)	125(8)	
(9)	125(9)	
(10)	125(10)	
(11)	125(11)	
49F Disqualification of practitioners		
		Inserted 2001, s 25.
(1)	151(1), (9); W 107(1), (9)	Amended 2002, Sch 2 para 21. Repealed in part 2003, Sch 14 Pt 4.
(2)	151(2); W 107(2)	
(3)	151(3); W 107(3)	
(4)	151(4); W 107(4)	
(5)	—	Unnecessary.
(6)	151(5); W 107(5)	Amended 2002, Sch 2 para 21.
(7)	151(6); W 107(6)	Amended 2002, Sch 2 para 21.
(8)	151(7); W 107(7)	
(9)	151(8); W 107(8)	
49G Contingent removal		
		Inserted 2001, s 25.

Existing provision	Rewritten provision	Remarks
(1)	152(1); W 108(1)	Amended 2002, Sch 2 para 21.
(2)	152(2); W 108(2)	
(3)	152(3); W 108(3)	Amended 2002, Sch 2 para 21.
(4)	152(4); W 108(4)	Amended 2002, Sch 2 para 21.

49H Fraud and unsuitability cases: supplementary

		Inserted 2001, s 25.
(1)	153(1); W 109(1)	Amended PCO 2006, Sch 1 Pt 1 para 22.
(2)	153(2); W 109(2)	

49I Suspension

		Inserted 2001, s 25.
(1)	154(1); W 110(1)	Amended 2002, Sch 2 para 21.
(2)	154(2); W 110(2)	
(3)	154(3); W 110(3)	Amended 2002, Sch 2 para 21.
(4)	154(4); W 110(4)	Amended 2002, Sch 2 para 21.
(5)	154(5); W 110(5)	
(6)	154(6); W 110(6)	Amended 2002, Sch 2 para 21.
(7)	154(7); W 110(7)	
(8)	154(8); W 110(8)	Amended 2002, Sch 2 para 21.
(9)	154(9); W 110(9)	

Existing provision	Rewritten provision	Remarks
(10)	154(10); W 110(10)	
49J Suspension pending appeal		
		Inserted 2001, s 25.
(1)	155(1); W 111(1)	Amended 2002, Sch 2 para 22.
(2)	155(2); W 111(2)	
(3)	155(3); W 111(3)	Amended 2002, Sch 2 para 22.
(4)	155(4); W 111(4)	
(5)	155(5); W 111(5)	Amended 2002, Sch 2 para 22.
(6)	155(6); W 111(6)	Amended 2002, Sch 2 para 22.
(7)	155(7); W 111(7)	
49K Effect of suspension		
		Inserted 2001, s 25.
	156; W 112	
49L Review of decisions		
		Inserted 2001, s 25.
(1)	157(1); W 113(1)	Amended 2002, Sch 2 para 23.
(2)	157(2); W 113(2)	Amended 2002, Sch 2 para 23.
(3)	157(3); W 113(3)	Amended 2002, Sch 2 para 23.
49M Appeals		
		Inserted 2001, s 25.
(1)	158(1); W 114(1)	Amended 2002, Sch 2 para 24.
(2)	158(2); W 114(2)	Amended 2002, Sch 2 para 24.

Existing provision	Rewritten provision	Remarks
(3)	158(3); W 114(3)	Amended 2002, Sch 2 para 24.
(4)	158(4); W 114(4)	Amended 2002, Sch 2 para 24.
(5)	158(5); W 114(5)	Amended 2002, Sch 2 para 24.
(6)	158(6); W 114(6)	Amended 2002, Sch 2 para 24.
(7)	158(7), (8); W 114(7), (8)	Amended 2002, Sch 2 para 24.
49N National disqualification		
		Inserted 2001, s 25.
(1)	159(1); W 115(1)	Amended 2002, Sch 2 para 25; 2003, Sch 11 para 24.
(2)	159(2); W 115(2)	
(3)	159(3); W 115(3)	Amended 2002, Sch 2 para 25.
(4)	159(4); W 115(4)	Amended 2002, Sch 2 para 25. Repealed in part 2006 para 20.
(5)	159(5); W 115(5)	
(6)	159(6); W 115(6)	Amended 2002, Sch 2 para 24.
(7)	159(7); W 115(7)	
(8)	159(8); W 115(8)	
(9)	159(9); W 115(9)	
49O Notification of decisions		
		Inserted 2001, s 25.
	160; W 116	Amended 2002, Sch 2 para 26.
49P Withdrawal from lists		
		Inserted 2001, s 25.

Existing provision	Rewritten provision	Remarks
	161; W 117	Amended 2002, Sch 2 para 27.
49Q Regulations		
		Inserted 2001, s 25.
(1)	162(1); W 118(1)	Amended 2002, Sch 2 para 28.
(2)	162(2); W 118(2)	Amended 2002, Sch 2 para 28.
(3)	162(3); W 118(3)	Amended 2002, Sch 2 para 28.
49R Corresponding provision in Scotland and Northern Ireland		
		Inserted 2001, s 25.
(1)	163(1); W 119(1)	
(2)	163(2); W 119(2)	
(3)	163(3); W 119(3)	
(4)	163(4); W 119(4)	
(5)	163(5); W 119(5)	
49S The Family Health Services Appeal Authority		
		Inserted 2001, s 27(1).
(1)	169(1)	
(2)	169(5)	
(3)	169(2)	
(4)	169(3)	
(5)	273(4)	
(6)	169(4)	
(7)	171(1)	
(8)	171(2)	Amended 2002, Sch 1 para 18.
50 Exercise of choice of practitioner in certain cases		
	w 74	Amended 1997, Sch 2 para 15.
51 University clinical teaching and research		
(1)	258(1); W 197(1)	Numbered as (1) and amended 1995, Sch 1 para 35.
(2)	258(2); W 197(2)	Inserted 1995, Sch 1 para 35. Amended 1999, Sch 4 para 23; 2002, Sch 1 para 19, Sch 5 para 15.

Existing provision	Rewritten provision	Remarks
(3)	258(2); W 197(2)	Inserted 1995, Sch 1 para 35. Amended 1999, Sch 4 para 23; 2002, Sch 1 para 19, Sch 5 para 15
52 Use of accommodation		
	168; W 79, W 91	Repealed in part 2003, Sch 14 Pt 4.
54 Sale of medical practices		
		Substituted 1997, s 34(1).
(1)	259(1)–(5)	Amended 2002, Sch 2 para 29; 2003, Sch 11 para 26(2).
(2)	259(5)	Amended 2002, Sch 2 para 29; 2003, Sch 11 para 26(3).
(3)	259(6)	
56 Inadequate services		
	133; W 75, W 87	Amended Health and Social Security Act 1984 (c 48) Sch 3 para 8; 1995, Sch 1 para 37; 2002, Sch 2 para 30. Repealed in part 2003, Sch 14 Pt 4.
57 Maximum price of medical supplies may be controlled		
(1)	260(1)	Repealed in part 1999, s 38(5).
(2)	260(2), (5)	
(3)	260(4), (5)	
62 Restriction of powers under ss 25, 58 and 61		
	255(2); W 193(2)	Repealed in part Health and Medicines Act 1988 (c 49) Sch 3.
63 Hospital accommodation on part payment		
(1)	189(1), (2); W 137(1), (2)	
(1C)	189(3); W 137(3)	
64 Expenses payable by remuneratively employed resident patients		
	190; W 138	
65 Accommodation and services for private patients		
		Substituted Health and Medicines Act 1988 (c 49) s 7(10).
(1)	Sch 2 para 15(1), (2), Sch 6 para 11(1), (2); W Sch 2 para 15(1), (2), W Sch 5 para 11(1), (2)	Amended 1990, s 25(2); 1995, Sch 1 para 38.

Existing provision	Rewritten provision	Remarks
(1A)	Sch 2 para 15(3), Sch 6 para 11(3); W Sch 2 para 15(3), W Sch 5 para 11(3)	Inserted 1990, s 25(3). Amended 1995, Sch 1 para 38.
(2)	Sch 2 para 15(4), Sch 6 para 11(4); W Sch 2 para 15(4), W Sch 5 para 11(4)	Amended 1990, s 25(4); 1995, Sch 1 para 38.
(4)	Sch 2 para 15(5), Sch 6 para 11(5); W Sch 2 para 15(5), W Sch 5 para 11(5)	Amended 1990, Sch 9 para 18(4) (part); 2003, Sch 4 para 29.

72 Permissions for use of facilities in private practice

Existing provision	Rewritten provision	Remarks
(1)	267(1); W 198(1)	
(2)	267(2); W 198(2)	
(3)	267(3); W 198(3)	
(4)	267(4); W 198(4)	
(5)	267(5); W 198(5)	Amended 2003, Sch 11 para 27; 2006 para 21. Repealed in part Health and Social Security Act 1984 (c 48) Sch 8; 2003, Sch 14 Pt 4.
(6)	267(6); W 198(6)	Amended 2003, Sch 11 para 27(3).

77 Charges for drugs, medicines or appliances, or pharmaceutical services

Existing provision	Rewritten provision	Remarks
(1)	172(1), (2); W 121(1), (2)	
(2)	174; W 123	
(3)	—	Unnecessary.
(4)	172(3); W 121(3)	Inserted 2003, Sch 11 para 28.

78 Charges for dental or optical appliances

Existing provision	Rewritten provision	Remarks
(1)	179(1), (2); W 128(1), (2)	Repealed in part Health and Medicines Act 1988 (c 49) Sch 3.

Existing provision	Rewritten provision	Remarks
(3)	—	Unnecessary. Amended 2003, Sch 11 para 29.
79 Charges for dental treatment		
(1)	176(1); W 125(1)	
(2)	176(2); W 125(2)	
(3)	176(3); W 125(3)	
(4)	—	Unnecessary.
(5)	176(4); W 125(4)	
(6)	176(5); W 125(5)	
80 Charges for designated facilities		
	187; W 135	
81 Charges for more expensive supplies		
	185; W 133	Amended Health Act 1999 (Supplementary Consequential etc Provisions) Order 2000 (SI 2000/90) Sch 1 para 13(3). Repealed in part 2003, Sch 14 Pt 4.
82 Charges for repairs and replacements in certain cases		
	186; W 134	Amended Health Act 1999 (Supplementary Consequential etc Provisions) Order 2000 (SI 2000/90) Sch 1 para 13(3). Repealed in part 2003, Sch 14 Pt 4.
83 Sums otherwise payable to those providing services		
	188; W 136	Amended Health Act 1999 (Supplementary Consequential etc Provisions) Order 2000 (SI 2000/90), Sch 1 para 13(4).
83A Remission and repayment of charges and payment of travelling expenses		
		Inserted Social Security Act 1988 (c 7) s 14(1).
(1)	182, 183; W 130, W 131	Amended Health Act 1999 (Supplementary Consequential etc Provisions) Order 2000 (SI 2000/90) Sch 1 para 13(5); PCO 2006, Sch 1 Pt 1 para 23.
(2)	180(5), 184(1); W 129(5), W 132(1)	

Existing provision	Rewritten provision	Remarks
(3)	180(4), 184(2); W 129(4), W 132(2)	
(4)	180(6), 184(3); W 129(6), W 132(3)	
84A Intervention orders		
		Inserted 2001, s 13(1).
(1)	66(2); W 26(2)	
(2)	66(1); W 26(1)	Amended 2002, Sch 1 para 21, Sch 5 para 16.
(3)	66(3); W 26(3)	
84B Intervention orders: effect		
		Inserted 2001, s 13(1).
(1)	67(1); W 27(1)	Amended 2002, Sch 1 para 22(a), Sch 5 para 17.
(2)	67(2); W 27(2)	
(3)	67(3); W 27(3)	
(4)	67(4); W 27(4)	
(5)	67(5); W 27(5)	
(6)	67(6); W 27(6)	Repealed in part PCO 2006, Sch 2.
(7)	67(7); W 27(7)	
(8)	67(8); W 27(8)	
(9)	67(9); W 27(9)	
85 Default powers		

Existing provision	Rewritten provision	Remarks
(1)	68(1), (2); W 28(1), (2)	Amended 1990, Sch 9 para 18(7); 1995, Sch 1 para 41; 1999, Sch 4 para 25; PCO 2006, Sch 1 Pt 1 para 24. Repealed in part 2001, Sch 5 para 5(9); 2003, Sch 11 para 32(b).
(2)	68(3); W 28(3)	Amended 1990, Sch 9 para 18(7).
(5)	68(4); W 28(4)	
86 Emergency powers		
	253; W 191	Amended 1990, Sch 9 para 18; PCO 2006, Sch 1 Pt 1 para 25.
87 Acquisition, use and maintenance of property		
(1)	211(1), (2); W 159(1), (2)	
(2)	211(3); W 159(3)	
(3)	211(4); W 159(4)	
(4)	211(5); W 159(5)	Substituted Acquisition of Land Act 1981 (c 67) Sch 4 para 28.
(5)	211(6); W 159(6)	
(6)	211(7); W 159(7)	Substituted Planning (Consequential Provisions) Act 1990 (c 11) Sch 2 para 40.
88 Transferred property free of trusts		
(1)	219(1)	
(2)	219(2); W 166	
90 Gifts on trust		
	Sch 2 para 12, Sch 6 para 8; W Sch 5 para 8	
91 Private trusts for hospitals		
(1)	218(1), (2)	
(2)	218(3)	
(3)	218(4)	Amended 1990, s 11(4); 1995, Sch 1 para 43; 1999, Sch 4 para 27; 2002, Sch 1 para 25; 2003, Sch 4 para 34. Modified 1999, s 13(11). Repealed in part 1990, Sch 10.
(4)	218(5)	Repealed in part 1999, Sch 4 para 27.
92 Further transfers of trust property		

Existing provision	Rewritten provision	Remarks
(1)	213(1); W 161(1)	Amended 1990, s 11(5); 1995, Sch 1 para 44; 2002, Sch 1 para 26, Sch 2 para 33.
(1A)	213(2); W 161(2)	Inserted 1995, Sch 1 para 44. Amended 1999, Sch 4 para 28; 2002, Sch 1 para 26, Sch 5 para 19; 2003, Sch 4 para 35.
(2)	214(1); W 162(1)	Amended 1990, s 11(5); 1995, Sch 1 para 44.
(3)	214(2); W 162(2)	Amended 1990, s 11(5); 1995, Sch 1 para 44.
(4)	213(3), 214(4); W 161(3), W 162(4)	Amended 1990, s 11(5); 1995, Sch 1 para 44.
(5)	213(4), 214(5); W 161(4), W 162(5)	
(6)	214(3); W 162(3)	Inserted 1990, s 11(5).
(7)	214(3); W 162(3)	Inserted 1999, Sch 4 para 28. Amended 2003, Sch 4 para 35.

93 Trust property previously held for general hospital purposes

(1)	220(1), (2); W 167(1), (2)	
(2)	220(3), (4); W 167(3), (4)	Repealed in part 1995, Sch 3.
(3)	220(5); W 167(5)	
(4)	220(6); W 167(6)	

94 Application of trust property: further provisions

(1)	216(1); W 164(1)	Applied 1995, Sch 2 para 5(3).
(2)	216(2); W 164(2)	
(3)	216(3); W 164(3)	Applied 1995, Sch 2 para 5(3).

Existing provision	Rewritten provision	Remarks
95 Special trustees for a university or teaching hospital		
(1)	212(1)–(3), (7); W 160(1)–(3), (7)	Amended Health Services Act 1980 (c 53) Sch 1 para 68.
(2)	212(5); W 160(5)	
(3)	212(4); W 160(4)	
(4)	212(6); W 160(6)	
96 Trusts: supplementary provisions		
(1)	217(1), (2); W 165(1), (2)	Amended 1999, Sch 4 para 29. Extended 1990, s 11(6); 2003, Sch 4 para 36.
(1A)	217(3), (4); W 165(3), (4)	Inserted 1990, s 11(6). Amended 1995, Sch 1 para 45; 2002, Sch 1 para 27.
(2)	217(5); W 165(5)	Amended Charities Act 1993 (c 10) Sch 6 para 30.
(3)	217(6), (7); W 165(6), (7)	Amended 1999, Sch 4 para 29. Extended 1990, s 11(6); 2003, Sch 4 para 36.
(4)	217(1); W 165(1)	Inserted PCO 2006, Sch 1 Pt 1 para 27.
96A Power of health authorities, etc to raise money, etc, by appeals, collections, etc		
		Inserted Health Services Act 1980 (c 53) s 5(1).
(1)	222(1), (2); W 169(1), (2)	Amended 1990, Sch 2 para 23(1); 1995, Sch 1 para 46; 2002, Sch 1 para 28, Sch 5 para 20.
(3)	222(3), (4), (5); W 169(3), (4), (5)	Amended 1990, Sch 2 para 23(2); 1995, Sch 1 para 46; 2002, Sch 1 para 28, Sch 5 para 20.
(4)	222(6); W 169(6)	Amended 1990, Sch 2 para 23(2); 1995, Sch 1 para 46; 2002, Sch 1 para 28, Sch 5 para 20.
(5)	215(1), (2); W 163(1), (2)	Amended 1990, Sch 2 para 23(3); 1995, Sch 1 para 46; 2002, Sch 1 para 28, Sch 2 para 34. Repealed in part 1999, Sch 4 para 30(2).
(5A)	215(3), (4); W 163(3), (4)	Inserted 1990, Sch 2 para 23(4).
(5B)	215(3), (4); W 163(3), (4)	Inserted 1999, Sch 4 para 30(3).

Existing provision	Rewritten provision	Remarks
(6)	215(5); W 163(5)	Amended 1990, Sch 2 para 23(5). Repealed in part 1995, Sch 1 para 46.
(7)	222(7); W 169(7)	Amended 1990, Sch 2 para 23(2); 1995, Sch 1 para 46; 2002, Sch 1 para 28, Sch 5 para 20.
(8)	222(8), (9), (10); W 169(8), (9), (10)	Amended 1990, Sch 2 para 23(2); 1995, Sch 1 para 46; 2002, Sch 1 para 28, Sch 5 para 20. Repealed in part 1995, Sch 1 para 46.
(9)	222(11); W 169(11)	Amended 1990, Sch 2 para 23(2); 1995, Sch 1 para 46; 2002, Sch 1 para 28, Sch 5 para 20.
(10)	222(12); W 169(12)	
(11)	222(1)	Inserted 1999, Sch 4 para 30(4).
(12)	215(2), (3), (4), 222(1)	Inserted 2003, Sch 4 para 37.

96B Trust-funds and trustees for Primary Care Trusts

		Inserted 1999, s 7.
(1)	Sch 3 para 12(1)	
(2)	Sch 3 para 12(1)	
(3)	Sch 3 para 12(2)	
(4)	Sch 3 para 12(3)	

96C Public-private partnerships

		Inserted 2001, s 4.
(1)	223(1); W 170(1)	
(2)	223(2); W 170(2)	
(3)	223(3); W 170(3)	
(4)	223(4), 275(1); W 170(4), W 206(1)	
(5)	223(5); W 170(5)	

97 Means of meeting expenditure of Health Authorities and Special Health Authorities out of public funds

		Substituted 1995, Sch 1 para 47.
(A1)	224(1)	Inserted 2002, s 7(2).
(1), (3)		Substituted 1997, s 36. Spent.
(3AA)		Inserted 2001, s 1(2). Spent.

Existing provision	Rewritten provision	Remarks
(3BB)	231; W 177	Substituted 1999, s 4(2). Amended 2002, s 10(2).
(3C)	224(2)	Inserted 1999, s 8(2). Substituted 2001, s 2(2). Amended 2002, s 7(3).
(3D)	224(3)	Inserted 1999, s 8(2). Amended 2001, s 2(3); 2002, s 7(4).
(3E)	224(4)	Inserted 1999, s 8(2).
(3F)	224(5), (6)	Inserted 1999, s 8(2). Amended 2002, s 7(5).
(4)	225(1); W 171(1)	
(5)	224(7), (8), 225(2), (3); W 171(2), (3)	Amended 1999, s 8(3); 2002, s 7(6).
(6)	224(9), 225(4); W 171(4)	Amended 1997, Sch 2 para 22; 1999, Sch 4 para 31(2). Amended and Repealed in part 2002, s 7(7).
(9)	224(10), 225(5); W 171(5)	Amended 1999, Sch 4 para 31(4); 2002, s 7(9).
97A Financial duties of Health Authorities and Special Health Authorities		
		Substituted 1995, Sch 1 para 48.
(1)	226(1)	Amended 1997, Sch 2 para 23; 2002 para 4(2).
(2)	226(2); W 172(1)	
(3)	226(3), 227(3); W 172(2), W 173(3)	Amended 2002 para 4(3).
(4)	—	Unnecessary.
(6)	226(4); W 172(3)	Repealed 1999, Sch 4 para 32.
(7)	226(5); W 172(4)	Amended 2002 para 4(3).
(8)	226(6); W 172(5)	Amended 2002 para 4(3).
(9)	226(7); W 172(6)	Amended 2002 para 4(3).
97AA Resource limits for Health Authorities and Special Health Authorities		
		Inserted Government Resources and Accounts Act 2000 (c 20) s 12(1).
(1)	227(1); W 173(1)	Amended 2002 Sch 8 para 5.

Existing provision	Rewritten provision	Remarks
(2)	—	Spent.
(2A)		Inserted 2001, s 1(3). Spent.
(3)	227(2); W 173(2)	Amended 2002, Sch 8 para 5.
(4)	227(4); W 173(4)	
(5)	227(3); W 173(3)	
(6)	227(5); W 173(5)	
(7)	227(6); W 173(6)	
97C Public funding of Primary Care Trusts		
		Substituted 2002, s 8.
(1)	228(1)	
(2)	228(2)	
(3)	228(3)	
(4)	228(4)	
(5)	228(5)	
(6)	228(6), (7)	
(7)	228(8), (9)	
(8)	228(10)	
(9)	228(11)	
97D Financial duties of Primary Care Trusts		
		Inserted 1999, s 3.
(1)	229(1)	Amended 2001, s 3(4). Repealed in part 2002, Sch 8 para 6.
(2)	229(2), 230(7)	
(3)	—	Unnecessary.
(4)	229(3)	
(5)	229(4)	
(6)	229(5)	
(7)	229(6)	
(8)	229(7)	
97E Resource limits for Primary Care Trusts		
		Inserted Government Resources and Accounts Act 2000 (c 20) s 13(1).
(1)	230(1)	Amended 2002, Sch 8 para 7(2).
(2)	230(2)	
(2A)	230(3)	Inserted 2001, s 1(5).
(3)	230(4)	
(4)	230(5)	
(5)	230(6)	
(6)	230(7)	
(7)	230(8)	
97F Public Funding of Local Health Boards		

Existing provision	Rewritten provision	Remarks
		Inserted 2002, s 9.
(1)	w 174(1)	
(2)	w 174(2)	
(3)	w 174(3)	
(4)	w 174(4)	
(5)	w 174(5)	
(6)	w 174(6), (7)	
(7)	w 174(8), (9)	
(8)	w 174(10)	
(9)	w 174(11)	
97G Financial duties of Local Health Boards		
		Inserted 2002, s 9.
(1)	w 175(1)	
(2)	w 175(2)	
(3)		Unnecessary.
(4)	w 175(3)	
(5)	w 175(4)	
(6)	w 175(5)	
(7)	w 175(6)	
(8)	w 175(7)	
97H Resource Limits for Local Health Boards		
		Inserted 2002, s 9.
(1)	w 176(1)	
(2)	w 176(2)	
(3)	w 176(3)	
(4)	w 176(4)	
(5)	w 176(5)	
(6)	w 176(6)	
(7)	w 176(7)	
(8)	w 176(8)	
98 Accounts and audit		
	232; W 178	Substituted 2006, s 56.
100 Other payments		
(1)	170(1), Sch 19 para 8; W Sch 13 para 8	Amended 2001, Sch 5 para 5(10); 2003, Sch 11 para 35. Repealed in part Health Services Act 1980 (c 53) Sch 7. Repealed in part 2001, Sch 5 para 5(10); 2003, Sch 11 para 35, Sch 14 Pt 4; PCO 2006, Sch 1 Pt 1 para 29.
(2)	170(3), Sch 19 para 10; W Sch 13 para 10	Amended PCO 2006, Sch 1 Pt 1 para 29. Repealed in part Health and Social Services and Social Security Adjudications Act 1983 (c 41) Sch 9 para 21.
101 Secretary of State's receipts		
	—	Spent.
102 Allowances and remuneration for members of certain bodies		
	—	Functions of the Minister for the Civil Service transferred to the Treasury by the Transfer of Functions (Minister for the Civil Service and Treasury) Order 1981 (SI 1981/1670).

Existing provision	Rewritten provision	Remarks
(1)	170(2), 233(1), Sch 19 para 9; W 179(1), W Sch 13 para 9	Amended 1997, Sch 2 para 24; 2001, s 27(2). Repealed in part Health Services Act 1980 (c 53) Sch 7; 2001, Sch 5 para 5(11); 2003, Sch 14 Pt 4; PCO 2006, Sch 1 Pt 1 para 30.
(2)	170(2)	Amended 1997, Sch 2 para 24; 2001, s 27(2). Repealed in part General and Specialist Medical Practice (Education, Training and Qualifications) Order 2003 (SI 2003/1250) Sch 9 para 2(b); 2001, Sch 5 para 5(11); 2003, Sch 14 Pt 4; PCO 2006, Sch 1 Pt 1 para 30. S 102(2)(e) spent.
(4)	170(3), 233(2), Sch 19 para 10; W 179(2), W Sch 13 para 10	Repealed in part PCO 2006, Sch 1 Pt 1 para 30.

103 Special arrangements as to payment of remuneration

Existing provision	Rewritten provision	Remarks
(1)	234(1), (2); W 180(1), (2)	Amended 2003, Sch 11 para 38; 2006 para 22; PCO 2006, Sch 1 Pt 1 para 31. Repealed in part 2003, Sch 11 para 36.
(2)	234(3); W 180(3)	
(3)	234(4); W 180(4)	Inserted 1990, Sch 9 para 18(9); 1999, s 4(3); 2001, Sch 5 para 5(12)(a); 2002, Sch 2 para 35.

104 Superannuation of officers of certain hospitals

Existing provision	Rewritten provision	Remarks
(1)	235(1)	Amended 2002 para 8.
(2)	235(2)	
(3)	235(3)	

105 Payments for certain medical examinations

Existing provision	Rewritten provision	Remarks
(1)	236(1); W 181(1)	Amended Mental Health (Amendment) Act 1982 (c 51) Sch 3 para 56; Mental Health Act 1983 (c 20) Sch 4 para 47(b).
(2)	236(2); W 181(2)	1995, Sch 1 para 54; 2002 para 9; 2003, Sch 4 para 39, Sch 11 para 37
(3)	236(3); W 181(3)	

121 Charges in respect of non-residents

Existing provision	Rewritten provision	Remarks
	175; W 124	Amended Health and Medicines Act 1988 (c 49) s 7(12), (14).

122 Recovery of charges

Existing provision	Rewritten provision	Remarks
(1)	191(1); W 139(1)	

Existing provision	Rewritten provision	Remarks
(2)	191(2); W 139(2)	Repealed in part 1999, Sch 4 para 36.

122A Recovery of other charges and payments

		Inserted 1999, s 39(1).
(1)	192(1); W 140(1)	
(2)	192(2); W 140(2)	
(3)	192(3); W 140(3)	
(4)	192(4); W 140(4)	
(5)	192(5); W 140(5)	
(6)	192(6); W 140(6)	
(7)	192(7); W 140(7)	

122B Penalties

		Inserted 1999, s 39(1).
(1)	193(1), (2); W 141(1), (2)	
(2)	193(3); W 141(3)	
(3)	193(4); W 141(4)	
(4)	193(5); W 141(5)	
(5)	193(6); W 141(6)	
(6)	193(7); W 141(7)	
(7)	193(8); W 141(8)	

Existing provision	Rewritten provision	Remarks
(8)	272(6); W 203(6)	
122C Offences		Inserted 1999, s 39(1).
(1)	194(1); W 142(1)	
(2)	194(2); W 142(2)	
(3)	194(3); W 142(3)	
(4)	194(4); W 142(4)	
(5)	194(5); W 142(5)	
(6)	194(6); W 142(6)	
(7)	194(7), (8); W 142(7), (8)	
(8)	194(9); W 142(9)	
123 Persons displaced by health service development		
(1)	268(1), (2), (3); W 199(1), (2), (3)	Amended New Towns Act 1981 (c 64) Sch 12 para 26; Housing (Consequential Provisions) Act 1985 (c 71) Sch 2 para 38(4).
(2)	268(4); W 199(4)	Repealed in part PCO 2006 Pt 1, Sch 1 para 32.
124 Special notices of births and deaths		
(1)	269(1); W 200(1)	
(2)	269(2); W 200(2)	Amended 1995, Sch 1 para 55(a); 2002, Sch 2 para 36.
(3)	269(3); W 200(3)	
(4)	269(4), (5); W 200(4), (5)	Amended 1995, Sch 1 para 55(b); 2002, Sch 2 para 36; PCO 2006, Sch 1 Pt 1 para 33.

Existing provision	Rewritten provision	Remarks
(5)	269(6), (7); W 200(6), (7)	Amended 1995, Sch 1 para 55(c); 2002, Sch 2 para 36.
(6)	269(8), (9); W 200(8), (9)	Amended by virtue of Criminal Law Act 1977 (c 45) s 31(6); by virtue of Criminal Justice Act 1982 (48) s 46; 1995, Sch 1 para 55(d); 2002, Sch 2 para 36.
(7)	269(10); W 200(10)	Amended 1995, Sch 1 para 55(e); 2002, Sch 2 para 36.
124A Provision of information by Registrar General		Inserted 1999, s 42.
(1)	270(1); W 201(1)	
(2)	270(2); W 201(2)	
(3)	270(3); W 201(3)	Amended and Repealed in part Adoption and Children Act 2002 (c 38) Sch 3 para 20.
(4)	270(4); W 201(4)	
125 Protection of members and officers of authorities		
	69(1), (2)	Amended 1990, Sch 2 para 25; 1995, Sch 1 para 56; Health Act 1999 (Supplementary Consequential etc Provisions) Order 2000 (SI 2000/90), Sch 1 para 13(7); 2002, Sch 1 para 31, Sch 5 para 23; 2003, Sch 4 para 41; PCO 2006, Sch 1 Pt 1 para 34. Repealed in part 2002, Sch 5 para 23; 2003, Sch 14 Pt 4.
126 Orders and regulations, and directions		
(1)	272(2)–(5); W 203(2)–(4)	
(1A)	—	Spent.
(2)	—	See National Health Service (Consequential Provisions) Act 2006 Sch 2 para 12. Amended 1990, s 65(2). Repealed in part SI 2003/1250, Sch 9 para 2(c).
(3)	273(1); W 204(1)	Amended 1990, s 65(2).
(3A)	273(3), (4); W 204(3)	Inserted 1995, Sch 1 para 57. Amended 1999, s 65(2).
(3B)	273(4); W 204(3)	Substituted 1995, Sch 1 para 57.
(3C)	—	Unnecessary.

Existing provision	Rewritten provision	Remarks
(4)	272(7), (8), (9); W 203(9), (10)	Amended 1990, s 65(2).2006, s 34(2); PCO 2006, Sch 1 Pt 1 para 35. Repealed in part 2003, Sch 14 Pt 4.
(5)	272(7); W 203(9)	
127 Supplementary regulatory powers		
	274; W 205	Repealed in part PCO 2006, Sch 1 Pt 1 para 37.
128 Interpretation and construction		
(1)	148(7), 192(8), 235(4), 254(5), 256(9), 260(5), 275(1), Sch 4 para 34; W 104(7), W 192(5), W 194(9), W 206(1), W Sch 3 para 34	Amended Health Services Act 1980 (c 53) Sch 1 para 77; Medical Act 1983 (54) Sch 5 para 16(b); Mental Health Act 1983 (c 20) Sch 4 para 47(d); Dentists Act 1984 (c 24) Sch 5 para 9; 1990, s 26(1), (2), (3); Local Government (Wales) Act 1994 (c 19) Sch 10 para 11(3); Education Act 1996 (c 56) Sch 37 para 45; 1997, Sch 2 para 28 (part); National Health Service (Private Finance) Act 1997 (c 56) s 1(5); 1999, Sch 4 para 38; 2001, s 27(3); 2003, Sch 4 para 42, Sch 11 para 39; 2006 para 24; Opticians Act 1989 (Amendment) Order 2005 (SI 2005/848), Sch 1 para 9; PCO 2006, Sch 1 Pt 1 para 38.
(1A)	275(3)	Inserted 1999, Sch 4 para 38. Amended 2002, Sch 1 para 33.
(2)	275(4); W 206(3)	
(3)	—	Unnecessary
129 Transitional provisions and savings, consequential amendments, and repeals		
	—	Spent.
130 Short title, extent and commencement		
(1)	—	Spent.
(2)	278(2); W 209(2)	
(3)	278(2); W 209(2)	
(4)	278(4); W 209(3)	
(5)	—	Spent.
Sch 1 Additional provisions as to the medical and dental inspection and treatment of pupils		
para 1	Sch 1 para 2; W Sch 1 para 2	Amended Education Act 1996 (c 56) Sch 37 para 46(a). Repealed in part 2003, Sch 14 Pt 4.
para 2	Sch 1 para, 3, 4; W Sch 1 para, 3,4	

Existing provision	Rewritten provision	Remarks
para 3	Sch 1 para 5; W Sch 1 para 5	Amended Health and Medicines Act 1988 (c 49) Sch 2 para 7(3); amended School Standards and Framework Act 1998 (c 31), Sch 30 para 8(a).
para 4	Sch 1 para 6; W Sch 1 para 6	Amended Health and Medicines Act 1988 (c 49) Sch 2 para 7(4); Education Act 1996 (c 56) Sch 37 para 46(b); School Standards and Framework Act 1998 (c 31) Sch 30 para 8(b).
Sch 2 Additional provisions as to vehicles for those suffering disability		
para 1	Sch 1 para 10(1), (2), (5); W Sch 1 para 10(1), (2), (5)	Amended Vehicle Excise and Registration Act 1994 (c 22) Sch 3 para 10.
para 2	Sch 1 para 10(3)–(5); W Sch 1 para 10(3)–(5)	
para 3	Sch 1 para 11; W Sch 1 para 11	
para 4	—	Unnecessary.
Sch 4 Central Health Services Council and Advisory Committees		
para 2	Sch 19 para 1; W Sch 13 para 1	Repealed in part Health Services Act 1980 (c 53) Sch 7.
para 3	Sch 19 para 2; W Sch 13 para 2	Repealed in part Health Services Act 1980 (c 53) Sch 7.
para 4	Sch 19 para, 3, 4; W Sch 13 para, 3,4	Repealed in part Health Services Act 1980 (c 53) Sch 7.
para 5	Sch 19 para, 5, 6; W Sch 13 para, 5,6	Repealed in part Health Services Act 1980 (c 53) Sch 7.
para 6	Sch 19 para 7; W Sch 13 para 7	Repealed in part Health Services Act 1980 (c 53) Sch 7.
Sch 5 Health Authorities and Special Health Authorities		
Part 1 Membership of Strategic Health Authorities and Health Authorities		Inserted 1995, Sch 1 para 59 (original Pt 1 repealed 1990, Sch 10). Amended 2002, Sch 1 para 34(2).
para 1	Sch 2 para 3	Inserted 1995, Sch 1 para 59; Amended 2002, Sch 1 para 34(2).
para 2	Sch 2 para 4	Inserted 1995, Sch 1 para 59; Amended 2002, Sch 1 para 34(2).
para 3	Sch 2 para 5	Inserted 1995, Sch 1 para 59; Amended 2002, Sch 1 para 34(2).
para 4	Sch 2 para 6	Inserted 1995, Sch 1 para 59; Amended 2002, Sch 1 para 34(2).
para 4A	—	Spent because of the abolition of Health Authorities. Inserted 2002, Sch 1 para 34(2).

Existing provision	Rewritten provision	Remarks
Part 3 Supplementary provisions		
para 8	Sch 2 para 1, Sch 6 para 1; W Sch 5 para 1	Amended 1995, Sch 1 para 60; 2002, Sch 1 para 34(3).
para 9(1)	Sch 2 para 2(1), Sch 6 para 2(1); W Sch 5 para 2(1)	Amended 1990, Sch 1 para 7; 1995, Sch 1 para 60. PCO 2006, Sch 1 Pt 1 para 39.
para 9(2)	Sch 2 para 2(2), Sch 6 para 2(2); W Sch 5 para 2(2)	
para 9(3)	Sch 2 para 2(3), Sch 6 para 2(3); W Sch 5 para 2(4)	
para 9(4)	Sch 2 para 2(4), Sch 6 para 2(4); W Sch 5 para 2(5)	Amended 1999, Sch 4 para 39(2).
para 9(5)	Sch 2 para 2(5), Sch 6 para 2(5); W Sch 5 para 2(6)	
para 9(6)	Sch 2 para 2(6), Sch 6 para 2(6); W Sch 5 para 2(7)	
para 10(1)	Sch 2 para 7(1), (2), (3), (4), Sch 6 para 3(1), (2), (3), (4); W Sch 5 para 3(1), (2), (3), (4)	Amended Health and Social Services and Social Security Adjudications Act 1983 (c 41) Sch 6 para 3(1); 1995, Sch 1 para 60; 2001, s 6(1). Repealed in part Health and Social Security Act 1984 (c 48) Sch 3 para 14.
para 10(1A)	Sch 2 para 7(5), (6), Sch 6 para 3(5), (6); W Sch 5 para 3(5), (6)	Inserted Health and Social Services and Social Security Adjudications Act 1983 (c 41) Sch 6 para 3(2). Amended 1990, Sch 1 para 8.
para 10(1B)	Sch 2 para 7(7), Sch 6 para 3(7); W Sch 5 para 3(7)	Inserted Health and Social Services and Social Security Adjudications Act 1983 (c 41) Sch 6 para 3(2).
para 10(2)	Sch 2 para 7(8), Sch 6 para 3(8); W Sch 5 para 3(8)	Repealed in part Family Practitioner Committees (Consequential Modifications) Order 1985 (SI 1985/39) art 7.

Existing provision	Rewritten provision	Remarks
para 10(2A)	Sch 2 para 7(9), Sch 6 para 3(9); W Sch 5 para 3(9)	Inserted Health and Social Services and Social Security Adjudications Act 1983 (c 41) s 15(b). Amended Dentists Act 1984 (c 24) Sch 5 para 10. Substituted Dentists Act 1984 (Amendment) Order 2005 (SI 2005/2011) Sch 6 para 1(4).
para 10(2B)	Sch 2 para 7(10), Sch 6 para 3(10); W Sch 5 para 3(10)	Inserted Dentists Act 1984 (Amendment) Order 2005 (SI 2005/2011) Sch 6 para 1(4).
para 10(2C)	Sch 2 para 7(11), Sch 6 para 3(11); W Sch 5 para 3(11)	Inserted Dentists Act 1984 (Amendment) Order 2005 (SI 2005/2011) Sch 6 para 1(4).
para 10(3)	Sch 2 para 7(12), Sch 6 para 3(12); W Sch 5 para 3(12)	Repealed in part Family Practitioner Committees (Consequential Modifications) Order 1985 (SI 1985/39) art 7. Repealed in part 1995, Sch 1 para 60. Repealed in part 1999, Sch 4 para 39(3).
para 10(4)	Sch 2 para 7(13), Sch 6 para 3(13); W Sch 5 para 3(13)	
para 11(1)	Sch 2 para 8(1), Sch 6 para 4(1); W Sch 5 para 4(1)	
para 11(2)	Sch 2 para 8(2), Sch 6 para 4(2); W Sch 5 para 4(2)	Amended 1995, Sch 1 para 60.
para 11(3)	Sch 2 para 8(3), Sch 6 para 4(3); W Sch 5 para 4(3)	Amended 1995, Sch 1 para 60.
para 12	Sch 2 para 9, Sch 6 para 5; W Sch 5 para 5	Amended Family Practitioner Committees (Consequential Modifications) Order 1985 (SI 1985/39) art 7(22). Amended 1990, Sch 1 para 9. Amended 1999, Sch 4 para 39(4). Repealed in part 1995, Sch 1 para 60.
para 12A	Sch 2 para 10, Sch 6 para 6; W Sch 5 para 6	Inserted 1990, Sch 1 para 10. Amended 1995, Sch 1 para 60.
para 12B(1)	Sch 2 para 13(1), Sch 6 para 9(1); W Sch 5 para 9(1)	Inserted PCO 2006, Sch 1 Pt 1 para 39.
para 12B(2)	Sch 2 para 13(2), Sch 6 para 9(2); W Sch 5 para 9(2)	Inserted PCO 2006, Sch 1 Pt 1 para 39.

Existing provision	Rewritten provision	Remarks
para 12B(3)	Sch 2 para 13(3), Sch 6 para 9(3); W Sch 5 para 9(3)	Inserted PCO 2006, Sch 1 Pt 1 para 39.
para 13	Sch 2 para 11, Sch 6 para 7; W Sch 5 para 7	
para 14	Sch 2 para 14, Sch 6 para 10; W Sch 5 para 10	
para 15(1)	Sch 2 para 16(1), Sch 6 para 12(1); W Sch 5 para 12(1)	Substituted 1999, Sch 4 para 39(5).
para 15(1A)	Sch 2 para 16(2), Sch 6 para 12(2); W Sch 5 para 12(2)	Substituted 1999, Sch 4 para 39(5).
para 16	Sch 2 para 17, Sch 6 para 13; W Sch 5 para 13	
Sch 5A Primary Care Trusts		
Part 1 PCT Orders		
		Inserted 1999, Sch 1
para 1(1)	Sch 3 para 13(1)	
para 1(2)	Sch 3 para 13(2)	
para 2(1)	Sch 3 para 14(1)	
para 2(2)	Sch 3 para 14(2)	
para 2(3)	Sch 3 para 14(3)	Amended 2002, s 2(4).
para 2(4)	Sch 3 para 14(4)	Amended 2002, s 2(4).
Part 2 Constitution and Membership		
para 3	Sch 3 para 1	
para 4	Sch 3 para 3	
para 5(1)	Sch 3 para 4(1)	
para 5(2)	Sch 3 para 4(2)	
para 5(3)	Sch 3 para 4(3)	
para 6	Sch 3 para 5	
para 7	Sch 3 para 6	
para 8(1)	Sch 3 para 7(1)	Substituted 2001, s 6(2).
para 8(2)	Sch 3 para 7(2)	Substituted 2001, s 6(2).
para 8(3)	Sch 3 para 7(3)	Substituted 2001, s 6(2).
para 8(4)	Sch 3 para 7(4)	Substituted 2001, s 6(2).
para 9(1)	Sch 3 para 8(1)	
para 9(2)	Sch 3 para 8(2)	
para 9(3)	Sch 3 para 8(3)	
para 10	Sch 3 para 9	Amended 2002, Sch 1 para 35(2).

Existing provision	Rewritten provision	Remarks
para 10A(1)	Sch 3 para 10(1)	Inserted 2002, Sch 2 para 37. Substituted Dentists Act 1984 (Amendment) Order 2005 (SI 2005/2011) Sch 6 para 1(5).
para 10A(2)	Sch 3 para 10(2)	Inserted 2002, Sch 2 para 37. Substituted Dentists Act 1984 (Amendment) Order 2005 (SI 2005/2011) Sch 6 para 1(5).
para 10A(3)	Sch 3 para 10(3)	Inserted 2002, Sch 2 para 37. Substituted Dentists Act 1984 (Amendment) Order 2005 (SI 2005/2011) Sch 6 para 1(5).
para 11(1)	Sch 3 para 11(1)	Cross-heading amended 2001, Sch 5 para 5(15).
para 11(2)	—	Repealed 2001, s 6(2).
para 11(3)	Sch 3 para 11(2)	
para 11(4)	Sch 3 para 11(3)	
para 11(5)	Sch 3 para 11(4)	
Part 3 Powers and Duties		
para 12(1)	Sch 3 para 15(1)	
para 12(2)	Sch 3 para 15(2)	
para 13(1)	Sch 3 para 16(1)	Amended National Health Service Reform and Health Care Professions Act 2002 (Supplementary, Consequential etc Provisions) Regulations 2003 (SI 2003/1937) Sch 1 para 1.
para 13(2)	Sch 3 para 16(2)	
para 14(1)	Sch 3 para 18(1)	
para 14(2)	Sch 3 para 18(2)	
para 15	Sch 3 para 19	
para 16(1)	Sch 3 para 20(1)	Amended 2002, s 2(4).
para 16(2)	Sch 3 para 20(2)	
para 16(3)	Sch 3 para 20(3)	Amended 2002, s 2(4).
para 17	Sch 3 para 21	
para 18	Sch 3 para 2(1)	
para 19(1)	Sch 3 para 22(1)	
para 19(2)	Sch 3 para 22(2)	
para 19(3)	Sch 3 para 22(3)	
para 20(1)	Sch 3 para 23(1)	Amended 2002, Sch 1 para 35(3). Amended 2003, Sch 4 para 43.
para 20(1A)	Sch 3 para 23(2)	Inserted 2006, s 74(3).
para 20(2)	Sch 3 para 23(3)	
para 20(3)	Sch 3 para 23	
Part 4 Transfer of Property		
para 21(1)	Sch 3 para 24(1)	
para 21(2)	Sch 3 para 24(2)	Amended 2002, Sch 1 para 34(4).
para 21(3)	Sch 3 para 24(3)	
para 21(4)	Sch 3 para 24(4)	
para 21(5)	Sch 3 para 24(5)	Amended 2002, Sch 1 para 34(4).
para 22(1)	Sch 3 para 25(1)	
para 22(2)	Sch 3 para 25(2)	
para 22(3)	Sch 3 para 25(3)	
para 22(4)	Sch 3 para 25(4), (5)	
para 22(5)	—	
para 22(6)	Sch 3 para 25(7)	

Existing provision	Rewritten provision	Remarks
Part 5 Transfer of Staff		
para 23(1)	Sch 3 para 26(1)	
para 23(2)	Sch 3 para 26(2)	Amended 2002, Sch 1 para 35(5).
para 23(3)	Sch 3 para 26(3)	
para 24(1)	Sch 3 para 27(1)	
para 24(2)	Sch 3 para 27(2)	
para 24(3)	Sch 3 para 27(3)	
para 24(4)	Sch 3 para 27(4)	
para 24(5)	Sch 3 para 27(5), (6)	
para 25(1)	Sch 3 para 28(1)	
para 25(2)	Sch 3 para 28(2)	
para 26	Sch 3 para 29	
Sch 5B Local Health Boards		
		Inserted 2002, Sch 4.
Part 1 LHB Orders		
para 1(1)	W Sch 2 para 11(1)	
para 1(2)	W Sch 2 para 11(2)	
para 2(1)	W Sch 2 para 12(1)	
para 2(2)	W Sch 2 para 12(2)	
para 2(3)–(5)	—	Spent because of the abolition of Health Authorities.
Part 2 Status, Constitution and Membership		
para 3	W Sch 2 para 2	
para 4	W Sch 2 para 1	
para 5	W Sch 2 para 3	
para 6(1)	W Sch 2 para 4(1)	
para 6(2)	W Sch 2 para 4(2)	
para 6(3)	W Sch 2 para 4(3)	
para 7	W Sch 2 para 5	
para 8	W Sch 2 para 6	
para 9(1)	W Sch 2 para 7(1)	
para 9(2)	W Sch 2 para 7(2)	
para 9(3)	W Sch 2 para 7(3)	
para 9(4)	W Sch 2 para 7(4)	
para 10(1)	W Sch 2 para 8(1), (2)	
para 10(2)	W Sch 2 para 8(3)	
para 10(3)	W Sch 2 para 8(4)	
para 11	W Sch 2 para 9	
para 12(1)	W Sch 2 para 10(1)	
para 12(2)	W Sch 2 para 10(2)	
para 12(3)	W Sch 2 para 10(3)	
para 12(4)	W Sch 2 para 10(4)	
Part 3 Other Matters		
para 13(1)	W Sch 2 para 13(1)	
para 13(2)	W Sch 2 para 13(2)	
para 13(3)	W Sch 2 para 13(3)	
para 14(1)	W Sch 2 para 14(1)	
para 14(2)	W Sch 2 para 14(2)	

Existing provision	Rewritten provision	Remarks
para 15(1)	W Sch 2 para 17(1)	
para 15(2)	W Sch 2 para 17(2)	
para 16	W Sch 2 para 18	
para 17	W Sch 2 para 19	
para 18(1)	W Sch 2 para 20(1)	
para 18(2)	W Sch 2 para 20(2)	
para 18(3)	W Sch 2 para 20(3)	
para 19(1)	W Sch 2 para 21(1)	
para 19(1A)	W Sch 2 para 21(2)	Inserted 2006, s 74(4).
para 19(2)	W Sch 2 para 21(3)	
para 19(3)	W Sch 2 para 21(4)	
para 20(1)	W Sch 2 para 22(1)	
para 20(2)	W Sch 2 para 22(2)	
para 20(3)	W Sch 2 para 22(3)	
para 20(4)	W Sch 2 para 22(4)	
para 20(5)	W Sch 2 para 22(5)	
para 21(1)	W Sch 2 para 23(1)	
para 21(2)	W Sch 2 para 23(2)	
para 21(3)	W Sch 2 para 23(3)	
para 21(4)	W Sch 2 para 23(4), (5)	
para 21(5)	W Sch 2 para 23(6)	
para 21(6)	W Sch 2 para 23(7)	
para 22(1)	W Sch 2 para 24(1)	
para 22(2)	W Sch 2 para 24(2)	
para 22(3)	W Sch 2 para 24(3)	
para 23(1)	W Sch 2 para 25(1)	
para 23(2)	W Sch 2 para 25(2)	
para 23(3)	W Sch 2 para 25(3)	
para 23(4)	W Sch 2 para 25(4)	
para 23(5)	W Sch 2 para 25(5), (6)	
para 24(1)	W Sch 2 para 26(1)	
para 24(2)	W Sch 2 para 26(2)	
para 25	W Sch 2 para 27	
para 26	W Sch 2 para 28	
Sch 6 Additional provisions as to advisory committees for Wales		
para 1(1)	W Sch 14 para 1(1), (2)	
para 1(2)	W Sch 14 para 1(3)	
para 2	W Sch 14 para 2	
para 3	W Sch 14 para 3	
para 5	W Sch 14 para 4	
Sch 7A Further provisions about Councils under s 20A		
para 1	W Sch 10 para 1	
para 2	W Sch 10 para 2	
para 3(1)	W Sch 10 para 3(1)	Amended and Repealed in part 2003, Sch 11 para 40.
para 3(2)	W Sch 10 para 3(2)	Amended 2003, Sch 11 para 40.
para 3(3)	W Sch 10 para 3(3)	
para 4	W Sch 10 para 4	

Existing provision	Rewritten provision	Remarks
para 5	W Sch 10 para 5	
Sch 8 Local Social Services Authorities		
para 1(1)	Sch 20 para 1; W Sch 15 para 1	Amended 1990, Sch 9 para 18. Repealed in part Children Act 1989 (c 41) Sch 15.
para 2(1)	Sch 20 para 2(1), (2), (3); W Sch 15 para 2(1), (2), (3)	Amended Mental Health Act 1983 (c 20) Sch 4 para 47. Repealed in part 1990, Sch 9 para 18.
para 2(2)	Sch 20 para 2(4), (5); W Sch 15 para 2(4), (5)	Repealed in part Mental Health Act 1983 (c 20) Sch 4 para 47; Children Act 1989 (c 41) Sch 15.
para 2(2A)	Sch 20 para 2(6); W Sch 15 para 2(6)	Inserted Immigration and Asylum Act 1999 (c 33) s 117(2).
para 2(2B)	Sch 20 para 2(7); W Sch 15 para 2(7)	Substituted Nationality, Immigration and Asylum Act 2002 (c 41) s 45(7).
para 2(3)	Sch 20 para 2(8), (9); W Sch 15 para 2(8), (9)	Amended Mental Health Act 1983 (c 20) Sch 4 para 47. Repealed in part 1990, Sch 10.
para 2(4A)	Sch 20 para 2(10); W Sch 15 para 2(10)	Inserted Children Act 1989 (c 41) Sch 12 para 34.
para 2(4AA)	Sch 20 para 2(11); W Sch 15 para 2(11)	Inserted 1990, Sch 9 para 18.
para 3(1)	Sch 20 para 3(1), (2)	Repealed in part Children Act 1989 (c 41) Sch 15.
para 4	Sch 20 para 4; W Sch 15 para 3	Inserted Health and Social Services and Social Security Adjudications Act 1983 (c 41) Sch 9 para 23.
Sch 8A Local Pharmaceutical Services Schemes		
		Inserted 2001, Sch 3.
para 1(1)	Sch 12 para 1(1); W Sch 7 para 1(1)	Amended 2002, Sch 2 para 81(2).
para 1(2)	Sch 12 para 1(2); W Sch 7 para 1(2)	Amended 2002, Sch 2 para 81(2).
para 1(3)	Sch 12 para 1(7), (8); W Sch 7 para 1(7), (8)	
para 1(4)	Sch 12 para 1(3); W Sch 7 para 1(3)	
para 1(5)	Sch 12 para 1(4); W Sch 7 para 1(4)	Amended 2003, Sch 11 para 41.

Existing provision	Rewritten provision	Remarks
para 1(6)	Sch 12 para 1(7); W Sch 7 para 1(7)	
para 1(7)	Sch 12 para 1(5); W Sch 7 para 1(5)	Amended 2002, Sch 2 para 81(2).
para 1(8)	Sch 12 para 1(6); W Sch 7 para 1(6)	Repealed in part 2002, Sch 2 para 81(2). Amended 2003, Sch 4 para 44.
para 1(9)	—	Spent because of the repeal of 1990, s 3.
para 2(1)	Sch 12 para 2(1); W Sch 7 para 2(1)	Amended 2002, Sch 2 para 81(2).
para 2(2)	Sch 12 para 2(2); W Sch 7 para 2(1)	Amended 2002, Sch 2 para 81(2).
para 2(3)	Sch 12 para 2(3); W Sch 7 para 2(3)	
para 3(1)	Sch 12 para 3(1); W Sch 7 para 3(1)	
para 3(2)	Sch 12 para 3(2); W Sch 7 para 3(2)	Amended 2002, Sch 2 para 81(2).
para 3(3)	Sch 12 para 3(3); W Sch 7 para 3(3)	Amended 2002, Sch 2 para 81(2).
para 4(1)	178(1); W 127(1)	
para 4(2)	178(2); W 127(2)	
para 4(3)	178(3); W 127(3)	

Sch 9A The Family Health Services Appeal Authority

		Inserted 2001, s 27(4).
para 1	Sch 13 para 1	
para 2	Sch 13 para 2	
para 3	Sch 13 para 3	
para 4	Sch 13 para 4	
para 5	Sch 13 para 5	Amended Constitutional Reform Act 2005 (c 4) Sch 4 para 95.
para 6	Sch 13 para 6	Amended 2003, Sch 11 para 42(2), (3); PCO 2006, Sch 1 Pt 1 para 40.
para 7	Sch 13 para 7	
para 8	Sch 13 para 8	
para 9	Sch 13 para 9	

Existing provision	Rewritten provision	Remarks
para 10	Sch 13 para 10	Amended 2003, Sch 11 para 42(4); PCO 2006, Sch 1 Pt 1 para 40.
para 11	Sch 13 para 11	
para 12	Sch 13 para 12	
para 13	Sch 13 para 13	
para 14	Sch 13 para 14	
para 15	Sch 13 para 15	
para 16	Sch 13 para 16	
para 17	Sch 13 para 17	Amended 2003, Sch 11 para 42(5).
para 18	Sch 13 para 18	
para 19(1)	Sch 13 para 19(1)	
para 19(2)	Sch 13 para 19(2)	
para 19(3)	Sch 13 para 19(3)	
para 20	Sch 13 para 20	
para 21	Sch 13 para 21	
Sch 10 Adittional provisions as to prohibition of sale of medical practices		
para 1(1)	Sch 21 para 1(1)	Repealed in part 1997, Sch 2 para 30(2).
para 1(2)	Sch 21 para 1(2)	Substituted 1997, Sch 2 para 30(3). Amended 2001, s 14(3)(a).
para 1(3)	Sch 21 para 1(3), (4)	Amended 2001, s 14(3).
para 1(4)	Sch 21 para 1(5)	Amended 2001, s 14(3).
para 1(5)	Sch 21 para 1(6)	
para 1(6)	Sch 21 para 1(7)	Amended 2001, s 14(3).
para 1(7)	Sch 21 para 1(8)	Amended 2001, s 14(3).
para 2(1)	Sch 21 para 2(1)	Substituted 1997, Sch 2 para 30(5).
para 2(1A)	Sch 21 para 2(2)	Substituted 1997, Sch 2 para 30(5).
para 2(1B)	Sch 21 para 2(3)	Substituted 1997, Sch 2 para 30(5).
para 2(2)	Sch 21 para 2(4), (5), (6)	Repealed in part 1997, Sch 2 para 30(6).
para 2(3)	Sch 21 para 2(7)	Substituted 1997, Sch 2 para 30(7).
para 2(3A)	Sch 21 para 2(8)	Substituted 1997, Sch 2 para 30(7).
para 2(4)	Sch 21 para 2(9), (10), (11)	Substituted 1997, Sch 2 para 30(8).
para 2(5)	Sch 21 para 2(12), (13)	Substituted 1997, Sch 2 para 30(8).
para 2(6)	Sch 21 para 3(1)	
para 2(7)	Sch 21 para, 3(2), 5	Substituted 1997, Sch 2 para 30(9).
para 3	Sch 21 para 4	Inserted 1997, Sch 2 para 30(1). Amended 2003, Sch 11 para 43.
Sch 11 Additional provisions as to the control of maximum prices for medical supplies		
para 1(1)	260(3)	
para 1(2)	Sch 22 para 1(1)	
para 1(3)	Sch 22 para 1(2)	
para 1(4)	—	Unnecessary.
para 2(1)	Sch 22 para 2(1)	
para 2(2)	Sch 22 para 2(2)	
para 2(3)	Sch 22 para 2(3)	
para 2(4)	Sch 22 para 2(4)	
para 3	Sch 22 para 3	Amended PCO 2006, Sch 1 Pt 1 para 41.
para 4(1)	Sch 22 para 4(1)	
para 4(2)	Sch 22 para 4(2)	

Existing provision	Rewritten provision	Remarks
para 5	Sch 22 para 5	
para 5A	Sch 22 para 6	Inserted Freedom of Information (Removal and Relaxation of Statutory Prohibitions on Disclosure of Information) Order 2004 (SI 2004/3363) art 7.
para 6	Sch 22 para 7	
para 7(1)	Sch 22 para 8(1), (2)	
para 7(2)	Sch 22 para 8(3)	Amended by virtue of Magistrates' Courts Act 1980 (c 43) s 32(2). Repealed in part by virtue of Criminal Law Act 1977 (c 45) s 32(1).
para 7(3)	—	Spent by virtue of Criminal Law Act 1977 (c 45) s 32(1).
para 8(1)	Sch 22 para 9(1)	
para 8(2)	Sch 22 para 9(2)	
para 8(3)	Sch 22 para 9(3), (5)	Amended by virtue of Criminal Justice Act 1982 (c 48) s 37. Repealed in part Criminal Justice Act 2003 (c 44) Sch 25 para 74.
para 9(1)	Sch 22 para 10(1), (2)	
para 9(2)	Sch 22 para 10(3)	
para 9(3)	Sch 22 para 10(4)	
para 9(4)	Sch 22 para 10(5)	Amended by virtue of Criminal Justice Act 1982 (c 48) s 37. Repealed in part Criminal Justice Act 2003 (c 44) Sch 25 para 74.
para 10(1)	—	Not repealed in relation to Scotland and Northern Ireland; not applicable in relation to England and Wales so not reproduced.
para 10(2)	—	Not repealed in relation to Scotland and Northern Ireland; not applicable in relation to England and Wales so not reproduced.
para 10(3)	—	Not repealed in relation to Scotland and Northern Ireland; not applicable in relation to England and Wales so not reproduced.
Sch 12 Additional provisions as to regulations for the making and recovery of charges		
para 1(1)	173(1); W 122(1)	Amended PCO 2006, Sch 1 Pt 1 para 42.
para 2(1)	179(1), (2), (5); W 128(1), (2), (5)	Substituted Health and Medicines Act 1988 (c 49) Sch 2 para 8(1). Amended PCO 2006, Sch 1 Part para 42.
para 2(2)	179(3), (5); W 128(3), (5)	Amended PCO 2006, Sch 1 Part para 42. Repealed in part Health and Medicines Act 1988 (c 49) Sch 3. Pt unnecessary.
para 2(8)	179(4); W 128(4)	Repealed in part 2003, Sch 14 Pt 4.
para 2A(1)	180(1), (2); W 129(1), (2)	Inserted Health and Social Security Act 1984 (c 48) Sch 1 para 3. Amended PCO 2006, Sch 1 Part para 42.

Existing provision	Rewritten provision	Remarks
para 2A(2)	180(7); W 129(7)	Inserted Health and Social Security Act 1984 (c 48) Sch 1 para 3.
para 2A(3)	180(3), (4); W 129(3), (4)	Inserted Health and Social Security Act 1984 (c 48) Sch 1 para 3. Substituted Health and Medicines Act 1988 (c 49) s 13(3). Amended PCO 2006, Sch 1 Part para 42.
para 2A(3A)	180(5); W 129(5)	Substituted Health and Medicines Act 1988 (c 49) s 13(3).
para 2A(3B)	180(6); W 129(6)	Substituted Health and Medicines Act 1988 (c 49) s 13(3).
para 2A(4)	180(10); W 129(10)	Inserted Health and Social Security Act 1984 (c 48) Sch 1 para 3.Amended PCO 2006, Sch 1 Part para 42.
para 2A(5)	180(11); W 129(11)	Inserted Health and Social Security Act 1984 (c 48) Sch 1 para 3.
para 2A(6)	180(12); W 129(12)	Added PCO 2006, Sch 1 Part para 42.
para 2B(1)	181(1)	Inserted 2006, s 42(3).
para 2B(2)	181(2)	Inserted 2006, s 42(3).
para 2B(3)	181(3)	Inserted 2006, s 42(3).
para 2B(4)	181(4)	Inserted 2006, s 42(3).
para 2B(5)	181(5)	Inserted 2006, s 42(3).
para 2B(6)	181(6)	Inserted 2006, s 42(3).
para 2B(7)	181(7)	Inserted 2006, s 42(3).
para 2B(8)	181(8)	Inserted 2006, s 42(3).
para 2B(9)	181(9)	Inserted PCO 2006, Sch 1 Pt 2 para 15.
para 4	Sch 1 para 7; W Sch 1 para 7	
para 7	173(2), (3), 180(8), (9); W 122(2), (3), W 129(8), (9)	
Sch 12ZA Dental charging: exemptions		
		Inserted 2003, s 183(2).
para 1(1)	177(1); W 126(1)	
para 1(2)	177(6); W 126(6)	
para 1(3)	177(7); W 126(7)	

Existing provision	Rewritten provision	Remarks
para 1(4)	177(8); W 126(8)	
para 1(5)	177(1); W 126(1)	
para 2(1)	177(2); W 126(2)	
para 2(2)	177(2); W 126(2)	
para 3	177(3); W 126(3)	
para 4	177(2); W 126(2)	
para 5	177(4); W 126(4)	
para 6	177(2); W 126(2)	
para 7	177(5); W 126(5)	
Sch 12A Expenditure of Health Authorities and Primary Care Trusts		
para 1	—	Amended 2003, Sch 11 para 45. Repealed in part 2003, Sch 14 Pt 4. Spent because of the abolition of Health Authorities.
para 2	—	Amended 2003, Sch 11 para 45. Repealed in part 2003, Sch 14 Pt 4. Spent because of the abolition of Health Authorities.
para 3	—	Amended 2002, s 10(4). Spent because of the abolition of Health Authorities.
para 4(1)	Sch 14 para 1(1)	Amended 2002, s 10(5) para 12; 2003, Sch 11 para 45. Repealed in part 2003, Sch 14 Pt 4.
para 4(2)	Sch 14 para 1(2)	Amended 2002, s 10(5) para 12; 2003, Sch 11 para 45. Repealed in part 2003, Sch 14 Pt 4.
para 5(1)	Sch 14 para 2(1)	Amended 2002, s 10(6), (7) para 12; 2003, Sch 11 para 45. Repealed in part 2003, Sch 14 Pt 4.
para 5(2)	Sch 14 para 2(2)	Amended 2002, s 10(6), (7) para 12; 2003, Sch 11 para 45. Repealed in part 2003, Sch 14 Pt 4.
para 6(1)	Sch 14 para 3(1)	Substituted 2002, s 10(8).
para 6(2)	Sch 14 para 3(2)	Substituted 2002, s 10(8).
para 6(3)	Sch 14 para 3(3)	Substituted 2002, s 10(8).
para 6(4)	Sch 14 para 3(4)	Substituted 2002, s 10(8).
para 6(5)	Sch 14 para 3(5)	Substituted 2002, s 10(8).
para 6A(1)	W Sch 8 para 1(1)	Inserted 2002, s 10(9).

Existing provision	Rewritten provision	Remarks
para 6A(2)	W Sch 8 para 1(2)	Inserted 2002, s 10(9). Amended 2003, Sch 11 para 45. Repealed in part 2003, Sch 14 Pt 4.
para 6B(1)	W Sch 8 para 2	Inserted 2002, s 10(9)
para 6B(2)	W Sch 8 para 2	Inserted 2002, s 10(9). Amended 2003, Sch 11 para 45. Repealed in part 2003, Sch 14 Pt 4.
para 6C(1)	W Sch 8 para 3(1)	Inserted 2002, s 10(9).
para 6C(2)	W Sch 8 para 3(2)	Inserted 2002, s 10(9).
para 6C(3)	W Sch 8 para 3(3)	Inserted 2002, s 10(9).
para 6C(4)	W Sch 8 para 3(4)	Inserted 2002, s 10(9).
para 6C(5)	W Sch 8 para 3(5)	Inserted 2002, s 10(9).
para 7(1)	Sch 14 para 4(1); W Sch 8 para 4(1)	Amended 2001, Sch 5 para 5(17); 2002, s 10(10).
para 7(2)	Sch 14 para 4(2); W Sch 8 para 4(2)	Amended 2001, Sch 5 para 5(17); 2002, s 10(10).
para 7(3)	Sch 14 para 4(3); W Sch 8 para 4(3)	Amended 2002, s 10(10); 2003, Sch 4 para 45.
para 7(4)		Inserted 2001, Sch 5 para 5(17). Unnecessary.

Sch 12B Accounts and audit

Existing provision	Rewritten provision	Remarks
		Inserted 2006, Sch 3.
para 1(1)	Sch 15 para 1(1)	
para 1(2)	Sch 15 para 1(1), (2)	
para 2	W Sch 9 para 1	
para 3(1)	Sch 15 para 2(1)	
para 3(2)	Sch 15 para 2(2)	
para 3(3)	W Sch 9 para 2(1)	
para 3(4)	W Sch 9 para 2(2)	
para 3(5)	Sch 15 para 2(3); W Sch 9 para 2(3)	
para 4(1)	Sch 15 para 3	
para 4(2)	W Sch 9 para 3	
para 5(1)	Sch 15 para 4(1)	
para 5(2)	Sch 15 para 4(2)	
para 5(3)	Sch 15 para 4(3)	
para 5(4)	Sch 15 para 4(4)	
para 6(1)	Sch 15 para 5(1)	
para 6(2)	Sch 15 para 5(2)	
para 6(3)	Sch 15 para 5(3)	
para 6(4)	Sch 15 para 5(4)	
para 6(5)	W Sch 9 para 4	
para 7(1)	Sch 15 para 6(1)	
para 7(2)	Sch 15 para 6(2)	
para 7(3)	Sch 15 para 6(3)	

Existing provision	Rewritten provision	Remarks
para 8(1)	Sch 15 para 7(1)	
para 8(2)	Sch 15 para 7(2), (3)	
para 8(3)	Sch 15 para 7(4)	
para 8(4)	Sch 15 para 7(5)	
para 8(5)	Sch 15 para 7(6)	
para 8(6)	Sch 15 para 7(7)	
para 9(1)	W Sch 9 para 5(1)	
para 9(2)	W Sch 9 para 5(2), (3)	
para 9(3)	W Sch 9 para 5(4)	
para 9(4)	W Sch 9 para 5(5)	
para 9(5)	W Sch 9 para 5(6)	
para 9(6)	W Sch 9 para 5(7)	
para 10(1)	Sch 15 para 8(1); W Sch 9 para 6(1)	
para 10(2)	Sch 15 para 8(2); W Sch 9 para 6(2)	
para 10(3)	Sch 15 para 8(3); W Sch 9 para 6(3)	
para 10(4)	—	Unnecessary.
para 11(1)	Sch 15 para 9(1); W Sch 9 para 7(1)	
para 11(2)	Sch 15 para 9(2); W Sch 9 para 7(2)	
para 11(3)	—	Unnecessary.
para 12	—	Unnecessary.
Sch 14 Transitional provisions and savings		
	—	See National Health Service (Consequential Provisions) Act 2006, Sch 2 for savings. Otherwise spent.
Sch 15 Consequential amendments		
	—	Spent.

Public Health Laboratory Service Act 1979 (c 23)

Existing provision	Rewritten provsion	Remarks
1 Extension of public health laboratory service		
(1)	Sch 1 para 12(1); W Sch 1 para 12(1)	Amends 1977, s 5(2)(c).

Existing provision	Rewritten provsion	Remarks
(2)	Sch 1 para 12(2)–(4); W Sch 1 para 12(2)–(4)	Inserts 1977, s 5(2A).
3 Short title and extent		
		Spent

Health Services Act 1980 (c 53)

Existing provsion	Rewritten provsion	Remarks
3 Extension of the powers to make services available to local authorities etc under s 26 of the 1977 Act and the Scottish Act 1978 s 15.		
(1)	80(7); W 38(7)	Inserts 1977, s 26(4).
5 Power of health authorities, etc to raise money, etc by appeals, collections etc		
(1)	215(1), (2), (5), 222; W 163(1), (2), (5), W 169	Inserts 1977, s 96A.
8 Dissolution of the Central Health Services Council		
(1)	—	Spent. Abolishes the Central Health Services Council under 1977, s 6(1).
(2)	—	Spent. Provides for the membership of standing advisory committees under 1977, s 6(3) after the abolition of the Central Health Services Council.
(3)	250(2), (4); W 189(2), (4)	Amends 1977, s 6(3). Substitutes 1977, s 6(4).
21 Regulation of right to provide pharmaceutical services		
(2)	132(1), (2); W 86(1), (2)	Amends 1977, s 43.
Sch 1 Amendments consequential on changes in the local administration of the Health Service		
para 52	W 72(2)	Amends 1977, s 39.
para 66	219; W 166	Amends 1977, s 88.
para 68	212(1); W 160(1)	Amends 1977, s 95(1).
para 77	275(1); W 206(1)	Amends 1977, s 128(1).
para 83	—	Spent. Amends 1977, Sch 15.
Sch 5 Amendments of the 1977 Act and the Scottish Act 1978 relating to exemptions from charges for certain services and appliances		
para 1	173(1); W 122(1)	Amends 1977, Sch 12 para 1.

Existing provsion	Rewritten provsion	Remarks
para 2(1)	—	Introductory.
para 2(5)	—	Spent.
para 4	173(2), (3), 180(8), (9); W 122(2), (3), W 129(8), (9)	Substitutes 1977, Sch 12 para 7 (mistakenly repealed 2003, Sch 14 Pt 4).

British Nationality Act 1981 (c 61)

Existing provision	Rewritten provision	Remarks
Sch 7 Consequential Amendments		
	Sch 22 para 3(2)	Amends 1977, Sch 11 para 3.

New Towns Act 1981 (c 64)

Existing provision	Rewritten provision	Remarks
Sch 12 Consequential Amendments		
para 26	268(3); W 199(3)	Amends 1977, s 123(1).

Acquisition of Land Act 1981 (c 67)

Existing provision	Rewritten provision	Remarks
Sch 4 Consequential Amendments		
para 28	211(5); W 159(5)	Substitutes 1977, s 87(4).

Mental Health (Amendment) Act 1982 (c 51)

Existing provision	Rewritten provision	Remarks
Sch 3 Consequential Amendments		
para 56	236(1); W 181(1)	Amends 1977, s 105(1).

Mental Health Act 1983 (c 20)

Existing provision	Rewritten provision	Remarks
Sch 4 Consequential Amendments		
para 47(a)	—	Spent. Amends 1977, s 4 (prior to its substitution by 1999, s 41(1)).
para 47(b)	236(1); W 181(1)	Amends 1977, s 105(1).
para 47(c)	—	Repeals in part 1977, s 105(3).
para 47(d)	275(1); W 206(1)	Amends 1977, s 128(1).

Existing provision	Rewritten provision	Remarks
para 47(e)	Sch 20 para 2(2), (8); W Sch 15 para 2(2), (8)	Amends 1977 para 2.

Health and Social Service and Social Security Adjudications Act 1983 (c 41)

Existing provision	Rewritten provision	Remarks
1 Joint financing of community services in England and Wales		
	256, 257; W 194, W 195	Inserts 1977 ss 28A, 28B.
13 Repeal of provisions about designation and membership of teaching authorities		
	—	Repeals 1977, s 9.
15 Dental practitioners whose registration is suspended–England and Wales		
(b)	—	Spent. Inserts 1977, Sch 5 para 10(2A) (subsequently substituted by the Dentists Act 1984 (Amendment) Order 2005 (Dentists Act 1984 (Amendment) Order 2005 (SI 2005/2011)) Sch 6 para 1(4)).
Sch 5 Amendments of National Health Service Act 1977		
para 1	—	Introductory.
para 2	—	Spent. Inserts 1977, s 22(3A), (6) (subsequently repealed 1999, s 32); amends 1977, s 22(4) (subsequently repealed 1999, s 32).
Sch 6 Medical Practitioners etc		
para 3(1)	Sch 2 para 7(1)–(4), Sch 6 para 3(1)–(4); W Sch 5 para 3(1)–(4)	Amends 1977, Sch 5 para 10(1).
para 3(2)	Sch 2 para 7(6), (7), Sch 6 para 3(6), (7); W Sch 5 para 3(6), (7)	Inserts 1977, Sch 5 para 10(1A), (1B).
Sch 9 Minor and consequential amendments		
para 21	—	Repeals in part 1977, s 100(2).
para 23	Sch 20 para 4; W Sch 15 para 3	Inserts 1977 para 4.

Medical Act 1983 (c 54)

Existing provision	Rewritten provision	Remarks
Sch 5 Consequential amendments of enactments		
para 16(b)	275(1); W 206(1)	Amends 1977, s 128(1).

Dentist Act 1984 (c 24)

Existing provision	Rewritten provision	Remarks
Sch 5 Consequential amendments		
para 9	275(1); W 206(1)	Amends 1977, s 128(1).
para 10	—	Spent. Amends 1977, Sch 5 para 10(2A) (subsequently substituted Dentists Act 1984 (Amendment) Order 2005 (Dentists Act 1984 (Amendment) Order 2005 (SI 2005/2011)) Sch 6 para 1(4)).

Health and Social Security Act 1984 (c 48)

Existing provision	Rewritten provision	Remarks
1 Supply etc of optical appliances		
(3)	W 71(1)	Amends 1977, s 38(1).
(4)	—	Repeals in part 1977, s 39(1).
(6)	—	Spent.
5 Family Practitioner Committees		
(2)	22; W 15	Amends 1977, s 15(1).
9 Holidays for patients, etc		
(1)	6(2); W 6(2)	Inserts 1977, s 5(2B)
Sch 1 Part 1 Amendments of the National Health Service Act 1977		
para 1	W 72(1)	Amends 1977, s 39.
para 3	180(1), (2), (7), (10), (11); W 129(1), (2), (7), (10), (11)	Inserts 1977, Sch 12 para 2A.
Sch 3 Family Practitioner Committees		
para 1	—	Introductory.
para 3(b)	—	Spent. Amends 1977, s 22(2) (subsequently repealed 1999, s 32).
para 8	133(2); W 87(2)	Amends 1977, s 56.

Housing (Consequential Provisions) Act 1985 (c 71)

Existing provision	Rewritten provision	Remarks
Schedule 2 Consequential Amendments		
para 38(1)	—	Introductory.
para 38(2)	256(1); W 194(1)	Substitutes 1977, s 28A(2)(d).

Existing provision	Rewritten provision	Remarks
para 38(4)	268(3); W 199(3)	Amends 1977, s 123(1).

National Health Service (Amendment) Act 1986 (c 66)

Existing provision	Rewritten provision	Remarks
3 Pharmaceutical services		
(1)	129(1), (2), (6), 130(1), (3); W 83(1), (2), (6), W 84(1), (3)	Substitutes 1977, s 42.

Social Security Act 1988 (c 7)

Existing provision	Rewritten provision	Remarks
14 Remission of Health Service charges and payment of travelling expenses		
(1)	182, 183, 184; W 130, 131, 132	Inserts 1977, s 83A.

Community Health Council provision (Access to Information) Act 1988 (c 24)

Existing provision	Rewritten provision	Remarks
1 Access to meetings and documents of Community Health Councils		
(6)	—	Spent, due to substitution of Local Government Act 1972 (c 70) Sch 12A.

Health and Medicines Act 1988 (c 49)

Existing	Rewritten	Remarks
7 Additional powers for financing health service		
(10)	Sch 2 para 15(1), (2), (4), (5), Sch 6 para 11(1), (2), (4), (5); W Sch 2 para 15(1), (2), (4), (5), W Sch 5 para 11(1), (2), (4), (5)	Substitutes 1977, s 65, s 66 with new s 65.
(12)	175(1); W 124(1)	Amends 1977, s 121.
10 Dental services		
(1)(a)	—	Repeals in part 1977, s 5(1)(a).
(1)(b)	—	Inserts 1977, s 5(1A) (now repealed), (1B) (unnecessary).
11 Charges for dental appliances and treatment		
(1)	—	Spent. Inserts 1977, s 78(1A) (now repealed).
(2)	—	Spent. Amends 1977, s 79(1) (now substituted).

Existing	Rewritten	Remarks
(3)	—	Spent. Inserts 1977, s 79A (now substituted).
13 General ophthalmic services and optical appliances		
(1)	W 71	Amends 1977, s 38.
(3)	180(3), (4), (5), (6); W 129(3), (4), (5), (6)	Substitutes 1977, Sch 12 para 2A(3).
Sch 2 Consequential amendments		
para 1	—	Introductory.
para 2	255(1); W 193(1)	Amends 1977, s 25.
para 7(1)	—	Introductory.
para 7(3)	Sch 1 para 5(2); W Sch 1 para 5(2)	Amends 1977, Sch 1 para 3.
para 7(4)	Sch 1 para, 5(3), 6; W Sch 1 para, 5(3), 6	Amends 1977, Sch 1 para 4.
para 8(1)	179(1), (5); W 128(1), (5)	Amends 1977, Sch 12 para 2.

Children Act 1989 (c 41)

Existing provision	Rewritten provision	Remarks
Sch 12 Minor amendments		
para 34	Sch 20 para 2(10); W Sch 15 para 2(10)	Inserts 1977 Sch 8 para 2(4A).

Planning (Consequential Provisions) Act 1990 (c 11)

Existing provision	Rewritten provision	Remarks
Sch 2 Consequential amendments		
para 40	211(7); W 159(7)	Substitutes 1977, s 87(6).

National Health Service and Community Care Act 1990 (c 19)

Existing provision	Rewritten provision	Remarks
1 Regional and District Health Authorities		
(3)	—	Spent.
4 NHS contracts		
(1)	9(1); W 7(1)	

Existing provision	Rewritten provision	Remarks
(2)	9(4); W 7(4)	Amended Health and Personal Social Services (Northern Ireland and Consequential Amendments) Order 1991 (SI 1991/195) art 7(3). Amended 1995, Sch 1 para 68. Amended 1999, Sch 4 para 76. Amended 2002, Sch 1 para 40, Sch 5 para 31. Amended Health (Wales) Act 2003 (c 4) Sch 3 para 6. Substituted in Pt Health and Social Care (Community Health and Standards) Act 2003 (Commission for Healthcare Audit and Inspection and Commission for Social Care Inspection) (Consequential Provisions) Oreder 2004 (SI 2004/2987), art 2(1)(c). Repealed in part 1995, Sch 1 para 68. Repealed in part 2003, Sch 13 para 6(a), Sch 14 Parts 4, 7.
(3)	9(5), (6); W 7(5), (6)	
(4)	9(7); W 7(7)	
(5)	9(8); W 7(8)	
(6)	9(10); W 7(10)	Repealed in part 1999, Sch 4 para 76.
(7)	9(11); W 7(11)	Repealed in part 1999, Sch 4 para 76.
(8)	9(12), (13); W 7(12), (13)	
(9)	—	Spent due to the abolition of NHS trusts in Scotland.
(10)	10; W 8	Inserted Health and Personal Social Services (Northern Ireland and Consequential Amendments) Order 1991 (SI 1991/195) art 7(5).

4A Provisions of certain services under NHS contracts

		Inserted 1997, s 31(1).
(1)	11(1), (2); W 9(1), (2)	Amended 2002, Sch 1 para 41, Sch 2 para 54; Smoking, Health and Social Care (Scotland) Act 2005 (Consequential Modifications) (England, Wales and Northern Ireland) Order 2006 (SI 2006/1056) Schedule para 5(a).
(2)	11(3); W 9(3)	

Existing provision	Rewritten provision	Remarks
(3)	11(4), (5), (7); W 9(4)	Amended 2001, Sch 5 para 8; Smoking, Health and Social Care (Scotland) Act 2005 (Consequential Modifications) (England, Wales and Northern Ireland) Order 2006 (SI 2006/1056) Schedule para 5(b).
(4)	11(6); W 9(5)	Inserted Smoking, Health and Social Care (Scotland) Act 2005 (Consequential Modifications) (England, Wales and Northern Ireland) Order 2006 (SI 2006/1056) Schedule para 5(c).
5 NHS trusts		
(1)	25(1); W 18(1)	Amended 1999, s 13(1)(a).
(2)	25(3); W 18(3)	Substituted 1995, Sch 1 para 69(b).
(5)	Sch 4 para 1, 3; W Sch 3 para s 1, 3	
(6)	Sch 4 para 5(2); W Sch 3 para 5(2)	Substituted 1999, s 13(1)(b).
(6A)	Sch 4 para 24; W Sch 3 para 24	Inserted 1997, Sch 2 para 65.
(7)	Sch 4 para 4; W Sch 3 para 4	Amended 1995, Sch 1 para 69(d).
(8)	25(4); W 18(4)	
(9)	44(7), Sch 4 para, 19(2), 20(2); W Sch 3 para 19(12), 20(2)	Substituted 1999, s 14.
(10)	Sch 4 para 22; W Sch 3 para 22	
6 Transfer of staff to NHS trusts		
(1)	Sch 4 para 8(1), (2); W Sch 3 para 8(1), (2)	Amended 1995, Sch 1 para 70. Amended 1999, Sch 4 para 77.
(2)	Sch 4 para 8(3); W Sch 3 para 8(3)	
(3)	Sch 4 para 8(4); W Sch 3 para 8(4)	Amended 1995, Sch 1 para 70. Amended 1999, Sch 4 para 77.
(4)	Sch 4 para 8(5); W Sch 3 para 8(5)	Amended 1995, Sch 1 para 70. Amended 1999, Sch 4 para 77.

Existing provision	Rewritten provision	Remarks
(5)	Sch 4 para 8(6); W Sch 3 para 8(6)	Amended 1995, Sch 1 para 70. Amended 1999, Sch 4 para 77.
(6)	Sch 4 para 8(7); W Sch 3 para 8(7)	
(7)	Sch 4 para 8(8); W Sch 3 para 8(8)	
7 Supplementary provisions as to transfer of staff		
(1)	Sch 4 para 8(9); W Sch 3 para 8(9)	Amended 1995, Sch 1 para 71. Amended 1999, Sch 4 para 78.
(2)	Sch 4 para 8(10); W Sch 3 para 8(10)	Repealed in part Employment Protection (Part-time Employees) Regulations 1995 (SI 1995/31) Schedule (those Regulations subsequently repealed by Employment Rights Act 1996 (c 18) Sch 3).
(3)	Sch 4 para 8(11); W Sch 3 para 8(11)	Amended Employment Rights Act 1996 (c 18) Sch 1 para 45(2).
8 Transfer of property, rights and liabilities to NHS trust		
(1)	Sch 4 para 9(1); W Sch 3 para 9(1)	Amended 1999, Sch 4 para 79. Amended 2002, Sch 1 para 42, Sch 5 para 32. Repealed in part 1999, Sch 4 para 79.
(2)	Sch 4 para 9(2); W Sch 3 para 9(2)	Amended 1999, Sch 4 para 79. Amended 2002, Sch 1 para 42, Sch 5 para 32.
(3)	Sch 4 para 9(3); W Sch 3 para 9(3)	Amended 1999, Sch 4 para 79. Amended 2002, Sch 1 para 42, Sch 5 para 32.
(4)	Sch 4 para 9(4); W Sch 3 para 9(4)	
(5)	Sch 4 para 9(5), (6); W Sch 3 para 9(5), (6)	Amended 1999, Sch 4 para 79. Amended 2002, Sch 1 para 42, Sch 5 para 32.
(6)	Sch 4 para 9(7); W Sch 3 para 9(7)	Substituted 1999, Sch 4 para 79. Amended 2002, Sch 1 para 42, Sch 5 para 32.
(7)	Sch 4 para 9(8), (9); W Sch 3 para 9(8), (9)	
(8)	Sch 4 para 9(10); W Sch 3 para 9(10)	
(9)	Sch 4 para 9(11), (12); W Sch 3 para 9(11), (12)	
9 Originating capital of, and other financial provisions relating to NHS trusts		

Existing provision	Rewritten provision	Remarks
(1)	Sch 5 para 1(1), (2), (8); W Sch 4 para 1(1), (2), (8)	Amended 1999, s 15(2).
(2)	Sch 5 para 1(3); W Sch 4 para 1(3)	Amended 1999, s 15(2).
(3)	Sch 5 para 1(4); W Sch 4 para 1(4)	Amended 1999, s 15(2).
(4)	Sch 5 para 1(5); W Sch 4 para 1(5)	Substituted 1999, s 15(3).
(7)	Sch 5 para 1(6); W Sch 4 para 1(6)	Amended 1999, s 15(5).
(8)	272(2), Sch 5 para 1(7); W 203(2), W Sch 4 para 1(7)	
(9)	27; W 21	Amended 2001, s 3(2).
10 Financial obligations of NHS trusts		
(1)	Sch 5 para 2(1); W Sch 4 para 2(1)	
(2)	Sch 5 para 2(2), (3); W Sch 4 para 2(2), (3)	
11 Trust funds and trustees for NHS trusts		
(1)	Sch 4 para 10(1); W Sch 3 para 10(1)	Amended 1999, s 13(6).
(2)	Sch 4 para 10(2); W Sch 3 para 10(2)	
(3)	Sch 4 para 10(3); W Sch 3 para 10(3)	
(4)	218(4)	Amends 1977, s 91.
(5)	213(1), 214(3); W 161(1), W 162(3)	Amends 1977, s 92.
(6)	217(1), (3); W 165(1), (3)	Amends and extends 1977, s 96.
12 Functions of Family Health Services Authorities		

Existing provision	Rewritten provision	Remarks
(1)	22; W 15	Amends 1977, s 15.
(3)	129(6); W 83(6)	Amends 1977, s 42(3).
(4)	W 78(1), W 90(1)	Amends 1977, s 44.

21 Schemes for meeting losses and liabilities etc of certain health service bodies

(1)	71(1); W 30(1)	
(2)	71(2); W 30(2)	Amended 1995, Sch 1 para 79; 1999, Sch 4 para 81(2); 2002, Sch 1 para 43, Sch 5 para 33; 2003, Sch 4 para 84; Health Protection Agency Act 2004 (c 17) Sch 3 para 11(3). Substituted in part Health and Social Care (Community Health Standards) Act 2003 (Commission for Healthcare Audit and Inspection and Commission for Social Care Inspection) (Consequential Provisions) Order 2004 (SI 2004/2987) art 2(1)(c). Repealed in part 2003, Sch 13 para 6(b).
(3)	71(3); W 30(3)	Amended 1995, Sch 1 para 79; 1999, Sch 4 para 81(3); 2002, Sch 1 para 43; 2003, Sch 4 para 84.
(4)	71(4)–(7); W 30(4)–(6)	Amended 1995, Sch 1 para 79; 1999, Sch 4 para 81(3); 2002, Sch 1 para 43; 2003, Sch 4 para 84.
(5)	71(8); W 30(7)	Substituted Financial Services and Markets Act 2000 (Consequential Amendments and Repeals) Order 2001 (SI 2001/3649) art 319. (Note purported amended 2002, Sch 1 para 43 and 2003, Sch 3 para 84).

25 Transfer to DHA of certain functions relating to private patients

(1)	—	Introductory.
(2)	Sch 2 para 15(1), (2), Sch 6 para 11(1), (2); W Sch 2 para 15(1), (2), W Sch 5 para 11(1), (2)	Amends 1977, s 65(1).
(3)	Sch 2 para 15(3), Sch 6 para 11(3); W Sch 2 para 15(3), W Sch 5 para 11(3)	Inserts 1977, s 65(1A).

Existing provision	Rewritten provision	Remarks
(4)	Sch 2 para 15(4), Sch 6 para 11(4); W Sch 2 para 15(4), W Sch 5 para 11(4)	Amends 1977, s 65(2).
(5)	—	Spent. Inserts 1977, s 65(3) (subsequently repealed).
26 Interpretation of Pt 1		
(1)	275(1); W 206(1)	
(2)	275(1), Sch 4 para 34; W 206(1), W Sch 3 para 34	
(3)	9(4), 275(1), Sch 4 para 34, Sch 5 para 5; W 7(4), W 206(1), W Sch 3 para 34, W Sch 4 para 5	
65 Regulations, orders and directions		
(2)	272(7), 273(1); W 203(9), W 204(1)	Amends 1977, s 126.
Sch 1 Health Authorities and Family Health Services Authorities		
para 7	Sch 2 para 2(1),Sch 6 para 2(1); W Sch 5 para 2(1)	Amends 1977, Sch 5 para 9(1).
para 8	Sch 2 para 7(5),Sch 6 para 3(5); W Sch 5 para 3(5)	Amends 1977, Sch 5 para 10(1A).
para 9	Sch 2 para 9, Sch 6 para 5; W Sch 5 para 5	Amends 1977, Sch 5 para 12.
para 10	Sch 2 para 10,Sch 6 para 6; W Sch 5 para 6	Inserts 1977, Sch 5 para 12A.

Existing provision	Rewritten provision	Remarks
Sch 2 National Health Service Trusts		
para 1(1)	25(2); W 18(2)	
para 1(2)	272(2); W 203(2)	
para 2	—	Unnecessary.
para 3(1)	Sch 4 para 5(1), (5); W Sch 3 para 5(1), (5)	Amended 1995, Sch 1 para 85. Amended 1999, Sch 4 para 83.
para 3(2)	Sch 4 para 5(3); W Sch 3 para 5(3)	Amended 1999, s 13(7).
para 3(3)	Sch 4 para 5(4); W Sch 3 para 5(4)	
para 3(4)	Sch 4 para 5(6); W Sch 3 para 5(6)	
para 4(1)	Sch 4 para 6(1); W Sch 3 para 6(1)	Amended 1995, Sch 1 para 85. Amended 1999, Sch 4 para 83. Amended 2002, Sch 1 para 46, Sch 5 para 36.
para 4(2)	Sch 4 para 6(2); W Sch 3 para 6(2)	Amended 1995, Sch 1 para 85. Amended 1999, Sch 4 para 83. Amended 2002, Sch 1 para 46, Sch 5 para 36.
para 5(1)	Sch 4 para 7(1); W Sch 3 para 7(1)	
para 5(2)	Sch 4 para 7(2); W Sch 3 para 7(2)	
para 5(3)	Sch 4 para 7(3); W Sch 3 para 7(3)	Amended 1995, Sch 1 para 85. Amended 2002, Sch 1 para 46.
para 6(1)	26; W 20	Repealed in part 1999, Sch 4 para 83.
para 7(1)	Sch 4 para 12(1); W Sch 3 para 12(1)	
para 7(2)	Sch 4 para 12(2); W Sch 3 para 12(2)	Amended Audit Commission Act 1998 (c 18) Sch 3 para 20.
para 7(3)	Sch 4 para 12(3); W Sch 3 para 12(3)	
para 8	Sch 4 para 13; W Sch 3 para 13	

Existing provision	Rewritten provision	Remarks
para 9(1)	Sch 4 para 11(1); W Sch 3 para 11(1)	
para 9(2)	Sch 4 para 11(2); W Sch 3 para 11(2), (3)	
para 9(3)	Sch 4 para 11(3); W Sch 3 para 11(4)	
para 10(1)	Sch 4 para 15(1); W Sch 3 para 15(1)	
para 10(2)	Sch 4 para 15(2); W Sch 3 para 15(2)	Inserted 1999, s 41(3).
para 10(3)	Sch 4 para 15(3); W Sch 3 para 15(3)	Inserted 1999, s 41(3).
para 11	Sch 4 para 16; W Sch 3 para 16	
para 12	Sch 4 para 17; W Sch 3 para 17	
para 13	Sch 4 para 18; W Sch 3 para 18	Amended 1995, Sch 1 para 85. Amended 1999, Sch 4 para 83. Amended 2002, Sch 1 para 46, Sch 5 para 36.
para 14	44(6), Sch 4 para 19(1); W Sch 3 para 19(1)	Applied 2003, Sch 4 para 85(a).
para 15	Sch 4 para 20(1); W Sch 3 para 20(1)	
para 15A	Sch 4 para 21; W Sch 3 para 21	Inserted National Health Service Act 1977 and National Health Service and Community Care Act 1990 (Amendment) Regulations 2002 (SI 2002/2759) reg 4.
para 16(1)	Sch 4 para 14(1), (2); W Sch 3 para 14(1), (2)	Repealed in part 2001, s 6(3), Sch 6, Pt 1.
para 16(2)	Sch 4 para 14(3); W Sch 3 para 14(3)	Amended 1999, s 13(8).
para 16(3)	Sch 4 para 25(1); W Sch 3 para 25(1)	Inserted 2001, s 6(3).
para 16(4)	Sch 4 para 25(2); W Sch 3 para 25(2)	Inserted 2001, s 6(3).

Existing provision	Rewritten provision	Remarks
para 16(5)	Sch 4 para 25(3); W Sch 3 para 25(3)	Inserted 2001, s 6(3).
para 16(6)	Sch 4 para 25(4); W Sch 3 para 25(4)	Inserted 2001, s 6(3).
para 17(1)	Sch 4 para 26(1), (2), (4); W Sch 3 para 26(1), (2), (4)	
para 17(2)	Sch 4 para 26(3); W Sch 3 para 26(3)	
para 18	Sch 4 para 2(1), (2); W Sch 3 para 2(1), (2)	
para 22	185(2), 186(2); W 133(2), W 134(2)	Amends 1977, s 81, 82.
para 23(1)	222(1); W 169(1)	Amends 1977, s 96A(1). Repealed in part 1995, Sch 3.
para 23(3)	215(1), (2); W 163(1), (2)	Amends 1977, s 96A(5).
para 23(4)	215(3), (4); W 163(3), (4)	Inserts 1977, s 96A(5A).
para 25	69(1)	Amends 1977, s 125. Repealed in part 1995, Sch 3. Repealed in part 2003, Sch 14 Pt 1.
para 26(1)	Sch 4 para 27(1); W Sch 3 para 27(1)	
para 26(2)	Sch 4 para 27(2); W Sch 3 para 27(2)	
para 26(3)	Sch 4 para 27(3); W Sch 3 para 27(3)	
para 27	Sch 4 para 32; W Sch 3 para 32	
para 28(1)	Sch 4 para 33(1); W Sch 3 para 33(1)	
para 28(2)	Sch 4 para 33(2); W Sch 3 para 33(2)	

Existing provision	Rewritten provision	Remarks
para 28(3)	Sch 4 para 33(3); W Sch 3 para 33(3)	
para 29(1)	Sch 4 para 28(1); W Sch 3 para 28(1)	
para 29(2)	Sch 4 para 28(2); W Sch 3 para 28(2)	
para 29(3)	Sch 4 para 28(3); W Sch 3 para 28(3)	
para 30(1)	Sch 4 para 29(1); W Sch 3 para 29(1)	Amended 1995, Sch 1 para 85. Amended 1999, Sch 4 para 83. Amended 2002, Sch 1 para 46, Sch 5 para 36. Amended 2003, Sch 4 para 85(b).
para 30(1A)	Sch 4 para 29(2); W Sch 3para.29(2)	Inserted 2006, s 74(5).
para 30(2)	Sch 4 para 29(3); W Sch 3 para 29(3)	Amended 1995, Sch 1 para 85. Amended 2002, Sch 1 para 46.
para 30(3)	Sch 4 para 29(4); W Sch 3 para 29(4)	
para 31	Sch 4 para 30(1), (2); W Sch 3 para 30(1), (2)	Amended 1995, Sch 1 para 85. Amended 2002, Sch 1 para 46, Sch 2 para 58.
para 32	Sch 4 para 31; W Sch 3 para 31	Amended 2003, Sch 4 para 85(c).
Sch 3 Financial provisions relating to NHS trusts		
para 1(1)	Sch 5 para 3(1), (2); W Sch 4 para 3(1), (2)	Amended 1999, s 17(2).
para 1(2)	Sch 5 para 3(3); W Sch 4 para 3(3)	
para 1(6)	Sch 5 para 3(4); W Sch 4 para 3(4)	Substituted 1999, s 17(4). Repealed in part 2003, Sch 14 Pt 6.
para 2(1)	Sch 5 para 4(1); W Sch 4 para 4(1)	
para 2(2)	Sch 5 para 4(2); W Sch 4 para 4(2)	
para 2(3)	Sch 5 para 4(3); W Sch 4 para 4(3)	

Existing provision	Rewritten provision	Remarks
para 2(4)	Sch 5 para 4(4); W Sch 4 para 4(4)	
para 3(1)	Sch 5 para 5	Amended 1999, s 13(9).
para 3(2)	W Sch 4 para 5	Amended 1999, s 13(9).
para 4	272(2), (4); W 203(2), (4)	
para 5(1)	Sch 5 para 6; W Sch 4 para 6	
para 5A(1)	Sch 5 para 7(1); W Sch 4 para 7(1)	Inserted 2001, s 3(1).
para 5A(2)	Sch 5 para 7(2); W Sch 4 para 7(2)	Inserted 2001, s 3(1).
para 6	Sch 5 para 8; W Sch 4 para 8	Amended 1999, Sch 4 para 84(2).
para 7	Sch 5 para 9; W Sch 4 para 9	Substituted 1999, Sch 4 para 84(3).
para 8	Sch 5 para 10; W Sch 4 para 10	Inserted 1999, Sch 4 para 84(4).

Sch 9 Minor and consequential amendments

Existing provision	Rewritten provision	Remarks
para 18(2)	132(7); W 86(7)	Inserts 1977, s 43(3).
para 18(3)	189(3); W 137(3)	Inserts 1977, s 63(1C).
para 18(4)	Sch 2 para 15(5), Sch 6 para 11(5); W Sch 2 para 15(5), W Sch 5 para 11(5)	Inserts 1977, s 65(4).
para 18(5)	183; W 131	Amends 1977, s 83A.
para 18(7)	68(1)–(3); W 28(1)–(3)	Amends 1977, s 85(1), (2). Repeals 1977, s 85(3), (4).
para 18(8)	253(1), (2); W 191(1), (2)	Amends 1977, s 86.

Existing provision	Rewritten provision	Remarks
para 18(9)	234(4); W 180(4)	Inserts 1977, s 103(3).
para 18(12)	191(1); W 139(1)	Amends 1977, s 122(1).
para 18(14)	Sch 20 para, 1, 2(11); W Sch 15 para, 1, 2(11)	Amends 1977, Sch 8 paras 1,2.

Local Government (Wales) Act 1994 (c 19)

Existing provision	Rewritten provision	Remarks
Sch 10 Social services		
para 11(1)	—	Introductory.
para 11(2)	256(1); W 194(1)	Amends 1977, s 28A.
para 11(3)	275(1); W 206(1)	Amends 1977, s 128(1).
para 11(4)	—	Spent (amends 1977, Sch 7, subsequently repealed Health (Wales) Act 2003 (c 4) s 1(4)).

Vehicle Excise and Registration Act 1994 (c 22)

Existing provision	Rewritten provision	Remarks
Sch 3 Consequential amendments		
para 10	Sch 1 para 10(2); W Sch 1 para 10(2)	Amends 1977, Sch 2 para 1(c).

Health Authorities Act 1995 (c 17)

Existing provision	Rewritten provision	Remarks
3 Preparations for reorganisation of authorities		
(8)	—	Repeals in part 1977, s 18(3).
Sch 1 Amendments		
para 1	—	Introductory.
para 2	28(3); W 22(3)	Amends 1977, s 11.
para 3	13(10), 28(8); W 22(8)	Amends 1977, s 12.
para 5	—	Repeals 1977, s 14.
para 6	22; W 15	Amends and partially repeals 1977, s 15.
para 7	—	Spent. Substitutes 1977, s 16 (subsequently substituted by 1999, Sch 4 para 9).

Existing provision	Rewritten provision	Remarks
para 8	—	Spent. Substitutes 1977, s 17 (subsequently substituted by 1999, s 12(1)).
para 9	—	Spent. Amends 1977, s 18 (subsequently substituted in Pt by 1999, s 12(3)).
para 10	W 190(4)	Amends and partially repeals 1977, s 19.
para 12	—	Amends 1977, s 22 (subsequently substituted and repealed 1999, ss 27, 32).
para 13	12(4); W 10(4)	Amends 1977, s 23(2).
para 14	80(3), (6), (7); W 38(3), (6), (7)	Amends 1977, s 26(1), (3), (4).
para 15	81(1), (3); W 39(1), (3)	Amends 1977, s 27(1), (3).
para 16	74(1); W 32(1)	Amends 1977, s 28(1), (3).
para 17	272(7); W 203(9)	Amends 1977, s 28A.
para 27	W 71(1)	Amends 1977, s 38.
para 28	W 72(2)	Amends 1977, s 39.
para 30	129(1), (2), (6); W 83(1), (2), (6)	Amends 1977, s 42.
para 31	W 86(1)	Amends 1977, s 43.
para 32	W 78(1), (2), W 90(1), (2)	Amends 1977, s 44.
para 33	167(9)	Amends 1977, s 45.
para 35	258(1), (2); W 197(1), (2)	Amends 1977, s 51.
para 37	133(1), (2); W 75(1), (2), W 87(1), (2)	Amends 1977, s 56.
para 38	Sch 2 para 15(1), Sch 6 para 11(1)–(4); W Sch 2 para 15(1)–(4), W Sch 5 para 11(1)–(4)	Amends 1977, s 65.
para 39	188(2); W 136(2)	Amends 1977, s 83.
para 40	183; W 131	Amends 1977, s 83A.

Existing provision	Rewritten provision	Remarks
para 41	68(1); W 28(1)	Amends 1977, s 85(1).
para 42	Sch 6 para 8; W Sch 5 para 8	Amends 1977, s 90.
para 43	218(4)	Amends 1977, s 91.
para 44	213(1)–(3), 214(1), (2), (4); W 161(1)–(3), W 162(1), (2), (4)	Amends 1977, s 92. Inserts 1977, s 92(1A).
para 45	217(3); W 165(3)	Amends 1977, s 96(1A).
para 46	222(1); W 169(1)	Amends 1977, s 96A.
para 47	224(7)–(10), 225; W 171	Substitutes 1977, s 97.
para 48	226; W 172	Substitutes 1977, s 97A.
para 49	—	Repeals 1977, s 97B.
para 52	—	Spent. Amends 1977, s 103 (further substituted).
para 54	236(2); W 181(2)	Amends 1977, s 105.
para 55	269(2), (4), (6); W 200(2), (4), (6), (9), (10)	Amends 1977, s 124.
para 56	69(1)	Amends 1977, s 125.
para 57	273(3), (4); W 204(3)	Amends 1977, s 126.
para 59	Sch 2 paras, 3, 4, 5, 6	Inserts 1977, Sch 5 Pt 1 (paras 1, 2, 3, 4).
para 60	Sch 2 paras 7(4), 8(2), (3), 10, Sch 6 para, 1, 2(1), 3(4), 4(2), (3), 6; W Sch 5 para, 1, 2(1), 3(4), 4(2), (3), 6	Amends 1977, Sch 5 paras 8, 9, 10, 11, 12, 12A. Repeals 1977, Sch 5 para 15(3).
para 61	W Sch 14 para 4	Amends 1977, Sch 6.
para 64	—	Spent. Amends 1977, Sch 14.
para 68	9(4); W 7(4)	Amends 1990, s 4(2).

Existing provision	Rewritten provision	Remarks
para 69(a)	—	Spent. Amends 1990, s 5(1) (subsequently further substituted by 1999, s 13(1)(a)).
para 69(b)	25(3); W 18(3)	Substitutes 1990, s 5(2), (3), (4).
para 69(c)	—	Spent. Amends 1990, s 5(6) (subsequently substituted by 1999, s 13(1)(b)).
para 69(d)	Sch 4 para 4(2); W Sch 3 para 4(2)	Amends 1990, s 5(7).
para 70	Sch 4 para 8(1), (4), (5), (6); W Sch 3 para 8(1), (4), (5), (6)	Amends 1990, s 6(1), (3), (4), (5).
para 71	Sch 4 para 8(9); W Sch 3 para 8(9)	Amends 1990, s 7(1).
para 72	Sch 4 para 9(1), (3), (6), (7); W Sch 3 para 9(1), (3), (6), (7)	Amends 1990, s 8.
para 78	—	Spent. Amends 1990, s 20 (subsequently repealed)
para 79	71(2), (3), (6); W 30(2), (3), (6)	Amends 1990, s 21.
para 85	Sch 4 paras 5(1), 6, 7(3), 18, 29(1), (3), 30(1); W Sch 3 paras 5(1), 6, 7(3), 18, 29(1), (3), 30(1)	Amends 1990, Sch 2 paras 3, 4, 5, 13, 30, 31.
para 119(4)(a)	—	Spent. Inserts definition of 'Health Authority' in Access to Health Records Act 1990 (c 23) s 11.

National Health Service (Residual Liabilities) Act 1996 (c 15)

Existing provision	Rewritten provision	Remarks
1 Transfer of residual liabilities: England and Wales		
(1)	70(1); W 29(1)	Amended National Health Service Reform and Health Care Professions Act 2002 (Supplementary, Consequential etc Provisions) Regulations 2002 (SI 2002/2469) Sch 1 para 21; 2006, Sch 8 para 36.
(2)	70(2); W 29(2)	Amended National Health Service Reform and Health Care Professions Act 2002 (Supplementary, Consequential etc Provisions) Regulations 2002 (SI 2002/2469) Sch 1 para 21; 2006, Sch 8 para 36.

Employment Rights Act 1996 (c 18)

Existing provision	Rewritten provision	Remarks
Sch 1 Consequential amendments		
para 45(1)	—	Introductory.
para 45(2)	Sch 4 para 8(11); W Sch 3 para 8(11)	Amends 1990, s 7(3).

Education Act 1996 (c 56)

Existing provision	Rewritten provision	Remarks
Sch 37 Consequential amendments		
para 44	256(1); W 194(1)	Amends 1977, s 28A(2)(c).
para 45	275(1); W 206(1)	Amends 1977, s 128(1).
para 46(a)	Sch 1 para 2(1); W Sch 1 para 2(1)	Amends 1977, Sch 1 para 1(a)(ii).
para 46(b)	Sch 1 para 6; W Sch 1 para 6	Amends 1977, Sch 1 para 4.

Pharmacists (Fitness to Practise) Act 1997 (c 19)

Existing provision	Rewritten provision	Remarks
Sch Fitness to practice of registered pharmaceutical chemists		
para 6	132(8), (9); W 86(8), (9)	Amends 1977, s 43.

National Health Service (Primary Care) Act 1997 (c 46)

Existing provision	Rewritten provision	Remarks
21 Provision of personal medical or dental services		
(1)	92, 93, 107, 108; W 50, W 51, W 64, W 65	Inserts 1977 ss 28C, 28D.
22 Supplementary regulations		
(1)	94, 109; W 52, W 66	Inserts 1977, s 28E.
26 Charges for dental treatment		

Existing provision	Rewritten provision	Remarks
(1)	—	Spent. Inserts 1977, s 78A (now substituted).
27 Provision of additional pharmaceutical services		
	—	Inserts 1977, s 41A.
(1)	127(1), (3), (4); W 81(1), (3), (4)	
28 Terms and conditions etc		
	—	Inserts 1977, s 41B
(1)	128; W 82	
29 Authorised provision of pharmaceutical services by medical practitioners		
	—	Amends 1977, s 43.
(1)	132(3), (6); W 86(3), (6)	
31 Provision of certain services under NHS contracts		
(1)	11; W 9	Inserts 1990, s 4A.
34 Sale of medical practices		
(1)	259	Substitutes 1977, s 54.
36 Expenditure of Health Authorities		
	—	Substitutes 1977, s 97 (1), (2), (3), (3A), (3B).
Sch 2 Amendments		
para 3	—	Introductory.
para 4(1)	—	Introductory.
para 4(2)	16(1), (2); W 14(1), (2)	Inserts 1977, s 15(1ZA), (1ZB).
para 5(1)	—	Introductory.
para 5(2)	80(5); W 38(5)	Substitutes 1977, s 26(2).
para 5(3)	80(7); W 38(7)	Amends 1977, s 26(4).
para 14	132(7); W 86(7)	
para 15	W 74	Amends 1977, s 50.
para 22	224(9), 225(4); W 171(4)	Amends 1977, s 97(6).
para 23	226(1)	Amends 1977, s 97A(1).
para 27	273(1); W 204(1)	Amends 1977, s 126(3).
para 28	21(7), 192(8), 275(1); W 206(1)	Amends 1977, s 128(1).

Existing provision	Rewritten provision	Remarks
para 30(1)	—	Introductory.
para 30(2)	—	Repeals in part 1977, Sch 10 para 1.
para 30(3)	Sch 21 para 1(2)	Substitutes 1977, Sch 10 para 1(2).
para 30(4)	—	Repeals 1977, Sch 10 para 1(8).
para 30(5)	Sch 21 para 2(1), (2), (3)	Substitutes 1977, Sch 10 para 2(1), (1A), (1B).
para 30(6)	—	Repeals in part 1977, Sch 10 para 2(2).
para 30(7)	Sch 21 para 2(7), (8)	Substitutes 1977, Sch 10 para 2(3), (3A).
para 30(8)	Sch 21 para 2(9), (10), (11), (12), (13)	Substitutes 1977, Sch 10 para 2(4), (5).
para 30(9)	Sch 21 para 3(2), 5	Substitutes 1977, Sch 10 para 2(7).
para 30(10)	Sch 21 para 4	Inserts 1977, Sch 10 para 3.
para 31	—	Spent. Amends 1977, Sch 12 para 1(1)(b) (subsequently substituted).
para 65(1)	—	Introductory.
para 65(2)	Sch 4 para 24; W Sch 3 para 24	Inserts 1990, s 5(6A).

National Health Service (Private Finance) Act 1997 (c 56)

Existing provision	Rewritten provision	Remarks
1 Powers of NHS trusts to enter into agreements		
	—	Applies to Primary Care Trusts as it applies to NHS trusts by virtue of 1999, Sch 4 para 89. Applies to Local Health Boards by virtue of 2002, s 6(4).
(1)	Sch 3 para 17(1), Sch 4 para 23(1); W Sch 2 para 16(1), W Sch 3 para 23(1)	
(2)	Sch 3 para 17(2), Sch 4 para 23(2); W Sch 2 para 16(2), W Sch 3 para 23(2)	
(3)	Sch 3 para 17(3), Sch 4 para 23(3); W Sch 2 para 16(3), W Sch 3 para 23(3)	
(4)	Sch 3 para 17(4), Sch 4 para 23(4); W Sch 2 para 16(4), W Sch 3 para 23(4)	

Existing provision	Rewritten provision	Remarks
(5)	Sch 3 para 17(3), (5), Sch 4 para 23(5); W Sch 2 para 16(5), W Sch 3 para 23(5)	
(6)	Sch 3 para 17(6), Sch 4 para 23(6); W Sch 2 para 16(6), W Sch 3 para 23(6)	

Audit Commission Act 1998 (c 18)

Existing provision	Rewritten provision	Remarks
Sch 3 Consequential amendments		
para 20	Sch 4 para 12(2); W Sch 3 para 12(2)	Amends 1990, Sch 2 para 7(2).

School Standard and Framework Act 1998 (c 31)

Existing provision	Rewritten provision	Remarks
Sch 30 Minor and consequential amendments		
para 8(a)	Sch 1 para 5(1), (2); W Sch 1 para 5(1), (2)	Amends 1977, Sch 1 para 3.
para 8(b)	Sch 1 para 6; W Sch 1 para 6	Amends 1977, Sch 1 para 4.

Government of Wales Act 1998 (c 38)

Existing provision	Rewritten provision	Remarks
27 Reform of Welsh Health Authorities		
(6)	—	Spent because of the abolition of Health Authorities.
(7)	—	Spent because of the abolition of Health Authorities.

Health Act 1999 (c 8)

Existing provision	Rewritten provision	Remarks
1 Repeal of law about fund-holding practices		
	—	Repeals 1990 ss 14–17.
2 Primary Care Trusts		
(1)	18, 19	Inserts 1977, ss 16A, 16B.
(2)	Sch 3	Inserts 1977, Sch 5A.
3 Primary Care Trusts: finance		
	229, 230(7)	Inserts 1977, ss 97C, 97D (s 97C subsequently substituted by 2002, s 8).

Existing provision	Rewritten provision	Remarks
4 Expenditure of Health Authorities and Primary Care Trusts		
(1)	Sch 14 para, 1(1), (2), 2(1), (2), 4(1), (2), (3); W para 4(1)–(3)	Inserts 1977, Sch 12A.
(2)	231; W 177	Repeals 1977, s 97(2) and substitutes s 97(3BB) thereof.
(3)	234(4); W 180(4)	Amends 1977, s 103(3).
(4)	—	Spent.
5 Primary Care Trusts: provision of services etc		
	— 21	Inserts 1977, s 18A.
6 Delegation of Health Authority functions relating to pilot schemes and s 28C arrangements		
(2)	95(1), (2), 110(1), (2)	Inserts 1977, s 28EE.
7 Primary Care Trusts: trust-funds and trustees		
	Sch 3 para 12	Inserts 1977, s 96B.
8 Payments relating to past performance		
(1)	—	Introductory words.
(2)	224(3), (4), (5), (6)	Inserts 1977, s 97(3C), (3D), (3E), (3F).
(3)	224(8)	Amends 1977, s 97(5).
9 Indemnity cover for Part II services		
(1)	166; W 120	Inserts 1977, s 43C.
(4)	W 72(2)	Amends 1977, s 39.
11 Local representative committees		
(1)	—	Introductory.
(3)	—	Repeals in part 1977, s 44(1).
(4)	167(2), (3)	Inserts 1977, s 44(3), (4), (5).
(5)	—	Introductory.
(6)	167(7), (8), (12); W 78(5), (6), W 90(5), (6)	Substitutes 1977, s 45(1), (1A), (1B), (1C).
(7)	—	Repeals in part 1977, s 45(2).
(8)	167(9), (13), (14); W 78(10), W 90	Inserts 1977, s 45(4), (5).
12 Directions		

Existing provision	Rewritten provision	Remarks
(1)	7(1), (2), (3), 8(1), (2), 20(1), (2); W 19(1), W 23(1), W 24(1), (3)	Inserts 1977, ss 16D, 17, 17A, 17B.
(2)	—	Spent.
(3)	273(1), (3), (4); W 204(1), (3)	Substitutes in part 1977, s 18 (by inserting new sub-ss (1), (1A), (1B)).
(4)	73(1); W 31(1)	Amends 1977, s 18(3).
(5)	—	Repeals 1977, s 13.
13 Establishment orders		
(1)(a)	25(1); W 18(1)	Amends 1990, s 5(1).
(1)(b)	Sch 4 para 5(2); W Sch 3 para 5(2)	Amends 1990, s 5(6).
(2)	Sch 4 para 34, Sch 5 para 5; W Sch 3 para 34, W Sch 4 para 5	Amends 1990, s 26(3).
(3)	—	Saved in National Health Service (Consequential Provisions) Act 2006, Sch 2 para 19.
(4)	—	Saved in National Health Service (Consequential Provisions) Act 2006, Sch 2 para 19.
(6)	Sch 4 para 10(1); W Sch 3 para 10(1)	Amends 1990, s 11(1).
(7)	Sch 4 para 5(3); W Sch 3 para 5(3)	Amends 1990, Sch 2 para 3(2).
(8)	Sch 4 para 14(3); W Sch 3 para 14(3)	Amends 1990, Sch 2 para 16(2).
(9)	Sch 5 para 5; W Sch 4 para 5	Amends 1990, Sch 3 para 3(1), (2).
(10)	—	Saved in National Health Service (Consequential Provisions) Act 2006, Sch 2 para 19.
(11)	—	Spent.
14 Exercise of powers		

Existing provision	Rewritten provision	Remarks
	44(7), Sch 4 para, 19(2), 20(2); W Sch 3 paras 19(2), 20(2)	Substitutes 1990, s 5(9).
15 Public dividend capital		
(1)	—	Introductory.
(2)	Sch 5 para 1(1), (2), (3), (4); W Sch 4 para 1(1), (2), (3), (4)	Amends 1990, s 9(1), (2), (3).
(3)	Sch 5 para 1(5); W Sch 4 para 1(5)	Substitutes 1990, s 9(4).
(4)	—	Repeals 1990, s 9(5), (6).
(5)	Sch 5 para 1(6); W Sch 4 para 1(6)	Amends 1990, s 9(7).
(6)	—	Repeals 1990, Sch 3 paras 3(3), 5(2).
17 Borrowing		
(1)	—	Introductory.
(2)	Sch 5 para 3(2); W Sch 4 para 3(2)	Amends 1990, Sch 3 para 1(1).
(3)	—	Repeals 1990, Sch 3 paras 1(3), (4), (5).
(4)	Sch 5 para 3(4); W Sch 4 para 3(4)	Substitutes 1990, Sch 3 para 1(6).
26 Co-operation between NHS bodies		
	72	Amended 2002, Sch 1 para 51.
27 Co-operation between NHS bodies and local authorities		
(1)	—	Introductory.
(2)	82	Substitutes 1977, s 22(1), (1A).
28 Plans for improving health etc		
(1)	24(1); W 17(1)	Amended Health, Social Care and Well-being Strategies (Wales) Regulations 2003 (SI 2003/154) Schedule para 6.
(2)	24(2); W 17(2)	Amended 2002, Sch 2 para 69(2). Amended Health, Social Care and Well-being Strategies (Wales) Regulations 2003 (SI 2003/154) Schedule para 7.
(3)	24(3); W 17(3)	Amended 2002, Sch 2 para 69(3). Amended Health, Social Care and Well-being Strategies (Wales) Regulations 2003 (SI 2003/154) Schedule para 8.
(4)	24(3); W 17(4)	Substituted 2002, Sch 2 para 69(4). Amended Health, Social Care and Well-being Strategies (Wales) Regulations 2003 (SI 2003/154) Schedule paras 9, 10.
(5)	24(4); W 17(5)	Amended 2002, Sch 2 para 69(5). Amended Health, Social Care and Well-being Strategies (Wales) Regulations 2003 (SI 2003/154) Schedule para 11.

Existing provision	Rewritten provision	Remarks
(6)	24(5); W 17(6)	Amended 2002, Sch 1 para 52, Sch 2 para 69(6). Amended Health, Social Care and Well-being Strategies (Wales) Regulations 2003 (SI 2003/154) Sch paras 12, 13, 14.
(7)	24(6); W 17(7)	Amended Health, Social Care and Well-being Strategies (Wales) Regulations 2003 (SI 2003/154) Schedule para 15. Substituted 2002, Sch 2 para 69(7).
(8)	24(7); W 17(8)	Amended 2002, Sch 2 para 69(8). Amended Health, Social Care and Well-being Strategies (Wales) Regulations 2003 (SI 2003/154) Sch paras 16, 17, 18.
(9)	—	Amended 2002, Sch 1 para 52. Amended Health, Social Care and Well-being Strategies (Wales) Regulations 2003 (SI 2003/154) Schedule para 19. Unnecessary
(10)	24(8); W 17(9)	Amended PCO 2006, Sch 1 Pt 2 para 5.
29 Payments by NHS bodies to local authorities		
(1)	—	Introductory.
(2)	256(1); W 194(1)	Amends 1977, s 28A(1).
(3)	256(3), (4); W 194(3), (4)	Inserts 1977, s 28A(2A), (2B).
30 Payments by local authorities to NHS bodies		
	76; W 34	Inserts 1977, s 28BB.
31 Arrangements between NHS bodies and local authorities		
(1)	75(1); W 33(1)	
(2)	75(2); W 33(2)	
(3)	75(3); W 33(3)	
(4)	75(4); W 33(4)	
(5)	75(5); W 33(5)	
(6)	75(6); W 33(6)	

Existing provision	Rewritten provision	Remarks
(7)	75(7); W 33(7)	
(8)	75(8); W 33(8)	Amended 2002, Sch 1 para 53, Sch 5 para 45; 2003, Sch 4, paras 108, 109.
(9)	75(9); W 33(9)	Inserted 2001, s 48(2).
32 Joint consultative committees		
	—	Repeals 1977, s 22(2)–(6).
33 Powers relating to voluntary schemes		
(1)	261(1)	
(2)	261(2)	
(3)	261(3)	
(4)	261(4)	
(5)	261(5)	
(6)	261(6)	
(7)	261(7)	
(8)	261(8)	
34 Power to control prices		
(1)	262(1)	
(2)	262(2)	
35 Statutory schemes		
(1)	263(1)	
(2)	263(2)	
(3)	263(3)	
(4)	263(4)	
(5)	263(5)	
(6)	263(6)	
(7)	263(7)	
36 Statutory schemes: supplementary		
(1)	264(1)	
(2)	264(2)	
(3)	264(3)	
37 Enforcement		
(1)	265(1)	
(2)	265(2)	
(3)	265(3)	
(4)	265(4)	
(5)	265(5)	
(6)	265(6)	
(7)	265(7)	
(8)	265(8)	
(9)	265(9)	
(10)	265(10)	
38 Controls: supplementary		
(1)	266(1), (2)	
(2)	—	Unnecessary.
(3)	266(3)	
(4)	266(4)	

Existing provision	Rewritten provision	Remarks
(5)	260(1), 266(5)	Repeals in part 1977, s 57.
(6)	266(6)	
(7)	266(6)	
(8)	266(6)	
39 Evasion of charges etc		
(1)	192, 193, 194, 272(6); W 140, W 141, W 142, W 203(6)	Inserts 1977, ss 122A, 122B, 122C.
41 High security psychiatric services		
(1)	4; W 4	Substitutes 1977, s 4.
(2)	—	Spent.
(3)	Sch 4 para 15(2), (3); W Sch 3 para 15(2), (3)	Inserts 1990, Sch 2 para 10(2), (3).
42 Provision of information be Registrar General		
	270; W 201	Inserts 1977, s 124A.
62 Regulations and orders		
(2)	273(4); W 204(3)	
(3)	273(1); W 204(1)	
(5)	—	Unnecessary. Modifies 1977, s 126(4).
(8)	272(6)	
68 Extent		
(1)(a)	—	Spent.
(4)	278(3)	
Sch 1 Primary Care Trusts		
	— Sch 3	Inserts 1977, Sch 5A.
Sch 2A Section 31 arrangements: transfer of staff		
		Inserted 2001, Sch 4.
para 1	Sch 18 para 1; W Sch 12 para 1	
para 2(1)	Sch 18 para 2(1); W Sch 12 para 2(1)	

Existing provision	Rewritten provision	Remarks
para 2(2)	Sch 18 para 2(2); W Sch 12 para 2(2)	
para 2(3)	—	Unnecessary.
para 3(1)	Sch 18 para 3(1); W Sch 12 para 3(1)	
para 3(2)	Sch 18 para 3(2); W Sch 12 para 3(2)	
para 3(3)	Sch 18 para 3(3); W Sch 12 para 3(3)	
para 3(4)	Sch 18 para 3(4); W Sch 12 para 3(4)	
para 3(5)	Sch 18 para 3(5); W Sch 12 para 3(5)	
para 4(1)	Sch 18 para 4(1); W Sch 12 para 4(1)	
para 4(2)	Sch 18 para 4(2); W Sch 12 para 4(2)	
para 4(3)	Sch 18 para 4(3); W Sch 12 para 4(3)	
para 4(4)	Sch 18 para 4(4); W Sch 12 para 4(4)	
para 5(1)	Sch 18 para 5(1); W Sch 12 para 5(1)	
para 5(2)	Sch 18 para 5(2); W Sch 12 para 5(2)	
Sch 4 Amendments of enactments		
para 4	—	Introductory.
para 6	28(1); W 22(1)	Substitutes 1977, s 11(1).
para 7	—	Repeals 1977, s 12(1).
para 8	—	Repeals 1977, s 15(1B), (1BA), (1C), (1D).
para 9	14, 29; W 25	Substitutes 1977, s 16.
para 10	17, 23; W 16	Inserts 1977, s 16C.

Existing provision	Rewritten provision	Remarks
para 11	80(3), (6), (7); W 38(3), (6), (7)	Amends 1977, s 26(1), (3), (4).
para 12	81(1), (3); W 39(1), (3)	Amends 1977, s 27(1), (3).
para 13	74(1), (3); W 32(1), (3)	Amends 1977, s 28(1), (3).
para 14	256(1), 257; W 194(1), W 195	Amends and repeals in part 1977, s 28A.
para 15	92(6), 107(6)	Amends 1977, s 28C(4). In relation to Wales, see National Health Service (Consequential Provisions) Act 2006, Sch 2 para 15.
para 16(a)	93(1), 108(1); W 51(1), W 65(1)	Amends 1977, s 28D(1).
para 16(b)	93(3), 108(3); W 51(3), W 65(3)	Amends 1977, s 28D(2).
para 23	258(2); W 197(2)	Amends 1977, s 51(2), (3).
para 24	—	Repeals 1977, s 65(3).
para 25	68(1); W 28(1)	Amends 1977, s 85(1).
para 26	—	Repeals in part 1977, s 85(1).
para 27	218(4)	Substitutes in part 1977, s 91(3). Repeals in part 1977, s 91(4).
para 28	213(2), 214(3); W 161(2), W 162(3)	Amends 1977, s 92(1A). Inserts 1977, s 92(7).
para 29	217(1); W 165(1)	Amends 1977, s 96(1), (3).
para 30(1)	—	Introductory.
para 30(2)	—	Repeals in part 1977, s 96A(5).
para 30(3)	215(3), (4)	Inserts 1977, s 96A(5B).
para 30(4)	222(1)	Inserts 1977, s 96A(11).
para 31(1)	—	Introductory.
para 31(3)	—	Repeals 1977, s 97(7).

Existing provision	Rewritten provision	Remarks
para 31(4)	224(10), 225(5); W 171(5)	Amends 1977, s 97(9).
para 32	—	Repeals 1977, s 97A(5).
para 36	—	Repeals in part 1977, s 122(2).
para 37	272(3), (5), (8), 273(3), (4); W 203(10)	Amends 1977, s 126.
para 38	275(1), (3); W 206(1)	Amends 1977, s 128.
para 39(1)	—	Introductory.
para 39(2)	Sch 2 para 2(4), Sch 6 para 2(4); W Sch 5 para 2(5)	Amends 1977, Sch 5 para 9(4).
para 39(3)	—	Repeals in part 1977, Sch 5 para 10(3).
para 39(4)	Sch 2 para 9, Sch 6 para 5; W Sch 5 para 5	Amends 1977, Sch 5 para 12.
para 39(5)	Sch 2 para 16(1), (2), Sch 6 para 12(1), (2); W Sch 5 para 12(1), (2)	Substitutes 1977, Sch 5 paras 15(1), (1A).
para 76	9(4); W 7(4)	Amends 1990, s 4(2), (6), (7).
para 77	Sch 4 para 8(1), (4), (5), (6); W Sch 3 para 8(1), (4), (5), (6)	Amends 1990, s 6(1), (3), (4), (5).
para 78	Sch 4 para 8(9); W Sch 3 para 8(9)	Amends 1990, s 7(1).
para 79	Sch 4 para 9(1), (3), (6), (7); W Sch 3 para 9(1), (3), (6), (7)	Amends 1990, s 8(1), (2), (3), (5). Substitutes 1990, s 8(6).
para 81	71(2), (3), (6)	Amends 1990, s 21.
para 83	Sch 4 paras 5(1), 6(1), (2), 18, 29(1); W Sch 3 paras 5(1), 6(1), (2), 18, 29(1)	Amends 1990, Sch 2, paras 3, 4, 13, 30. Repeals in part 1990, Sch 2 para 6. Repeals 1990, Sch 2 paras 19, 20.
para 84(1)	—	Introductory.
para 84(2)	Sch 5 para 8; W Sch 4 para 8	Amends 1990, Sch 3 para 6.
para 84(3)	Sch 5 para 9; W Sch 4 para 9	Substitutes 1990, Sch 3 para 7.

Existing provision	Rewritten provision	Remarks
para 84(4)	Sch 5 para 10; W Sch 4 para 10	Inserts 1990, Sch 3 para 8.
para 87	70(1), (2); W 29(2)	Amends National Health Service (Residual Liabilities) Act 1996 (c 15) s 1.
para 89	Sch 3 para 17	Applies National Health Service (Private Finance) Act 1997 (c 56) s 1 to Primary Care Trusts

Immigration and Asylum Act 1999 (c 33)

Existing provision	Rewritten provision	Remarks
117 Other restrictions on assistance: England and Wales		
(2)	Sch 20 para 2(6); W Sch 15 para 2(6)	Inserts 1977, Sch 8 para 2(2A), (2B).

Government Resources and Accounts Act 2000 (c 20)

Existing provision	Rewritten provision	Remarks
12 Health Authorities and Special Health Authorities		
(1)	227; W 173	Inserts 1977, s 97AA.
(2)	W 173	Modifies 1977, s 97AA in its application to Wales
13 Primary Care Trusts		
(1)	230	Inserts 1977, s 97E.
(2)	—	Modifies 1977, s 97E in its application to Wales. Not necessary because there are no Primary Care Trusts in Wales

Local Government Act 2000 (c 22)

Existing provision	Rewritten provision	Remarks
Sch 5 Minor and Consequential Amendments		
para 17	256(1); W 194(1)	Amends 1977, s 28A(2).

Health and Social Care Act 2001 (c 15)

Existing provision	Rewritten provision	Remarks
1 Determination of allotments to and resource limits for Health Authorities and Primary Care Trusts		
(1)	—	Introductory.
(2)	—	Inserts 1977, s 97(3AA). Spent because of the abolition of Health Authorities
(3)	—	Inserts 1977, s 97AA(2A). Spent because of the abolition of Health Authorities
2 Payments relating to past performance		

Existing provision	Rewritten provision	Remarks
(1)	—	Introductory.
(2)	224(2)	Substitutes 1977, s 97(3C).
(3)	—	Amends 1977, s 97(3D). Spent because of the abolition of Health Authorities.

3 Supplementary payments to NHS trusts and Primary Care Trusts

(1)	Sch 5 para 7(1), (2); W Sch 4 para 7(1), (2)	Inserts 1990, Sch 3 para 5A.
(2)	—	Amends 1990, s 9(9). Unnecessary.

4 Public-private partnerships

	223; W 170	Inserts 1977, s 96(C).

6 Terms and conditions of employment by health service bodies

(1)	Sch 2 para 7(1)–(4), Sch 6 para 3(1)–(4); W Sch 5 para 3(1)–(4)	Amends 1977, Sch 5 para 10(1).
(2)	Sch 3 para 7(1)–(4)	Substitutes 1977, Sch 5A para 8. Repeals in part 1977, Sch 5A para 11(2).
(3)	Sch 4 para 25(1)–(4); W Sch 3 para 25(1)–(4)	Inserts 1990, Sch 2 paras 16(3), (4), (5), (6). Repeals in part 1990, Sch 2 para 16(1).

7 Functions of overview and scrutiny committees

(2)	244(1); W 184(1)	
(3)	244(2); W 184(2)	Amended 2002, s 21; 2003, Sch 4 para 116.
(4)	244(3); W 184(3)	Amended 2002, Sch 1 para 55(2), Sch 5 para 50; 2003, Sch 4 para 116.
(5)	244(4); W 184(4)	

8 Joint overview and scrutiny committees etc

(1)	245(1); W 185(1)	
(2)	245(2); W 185(2)	
(3)	245(3); W 185(3)	
(4)	245(4); W 185(4)	

Existing provision	Rewritten provision	Remarks
(5)	245(5); W 185(5)	
(6)	245(6); W 185(6)	
(7)	245(7); W 185(7)	
(8)	245(8); W 185(8)	
(9)	245(9); W 185(9)	
9 Overview and scrutiny committees: exempt information		
(1)	246(1); W 186(1)	
(2)	246(2); W 186(2)	
(3)	246(2); W 186(2)	
(4)	246(3); W 186(3)	
(5)	246(4); W 186(4)	
(6)	246(5); W 186(5)	
10 Application to the City of London		
(1)	247(1)	
(2)	247(2)	
(3)	247(3)	
(4)	247(4)	
(5)	247(5)	
11 Public involvement and consultation		
(1)	242(2); W 183(1)	
(2)	242(1); W 183(1)	Inserted 2002, Sch 8 para 35; 2003, s 30. Repealed in part 2003, Sch 14 Pt 4.
(3)	242(3); W 183(2)	
(4)	242(4)	Inserted 2002, Sch 8 para 35.

Existing provision	Rewritten provision	Remarks
(5)	242(5)	Inserted 2002, Sch 8 para 35.
(6)		Inserted 2002, Sch 8 para 35. Unnecessary.
12 Independent advocacy services		
	248; W 187	Inserts 1977, s 19A.
13 Intervention orders		
(1)	66, 67; W 26, W 27	Inserts 1977, ss 84A, 84B.
(2)	272(3)	Amends 1977, s 126(1).
14 Abolition of Medical Practices Committee		
(1)	—	Abolishes Medical Practices Committee.
(3)	Sch 21 para 1(2), (3), (4), (5), (7), (8)	Amends 1977, Sch 10.
16 Abolition of NHS Tribunal		
	—	Abolishes the National Health Service Tribunal.
20 Medical, dental, ophthalmic and pharmaceutical etc lists		
(1)	—	Introductory.
(5)	W 72	Amends 1977, s 39.
(6)	129(6), 130(2); W 83(6), W 84(2)	
(7)	132(4), (5); W 86(4), (5)	
21 Conditional inclusion in medical, dental, ophthalmic and pharmaceutical lists		
	148; W 104	Inserts 1977, s 43ZA.
23 Declaration of financial interests, gifts, etc		
(1)	—	Introductory.
(4)	W 72(5), (6)	Inserts 1977, s 39(4), (5).
(5)	129(6), (10); W 83(6), (10)	Amends 1977, s 42(3). Inserts 1977, s 42(3C).
24 Supplementary lists		
	—	Inserts 1977, s 43D
	149, 150; W 105, W 106	
25 Suspension and disqualification of practitioners		
	—	Inserts 1977, ss 49F–49R.

Existing provision	Rewritten provision	Remarks
	151–163; W 107–119	
27 The Family Health Services Appeal Authorities		
(1)	169, 171	Inserts 1977, s 49S
(2)	170(2)	Amends 1977, s 102.
(3)	275(1); W 206(1)	Amends 1977, s 128(1).
(4)	Sch 13	Inserts 1977, Sch 9A.
28 Pilot Schemes		
(1)	134(1); W 92(1)	Amended 2002, Sch 2 para 73(2).
(2)	134(2); W 92(2)	Amended 2002, Sch 2 para 73(3).
(3)	134(3); W 92(3)	
(4)	134(4); W 92(4)	Amended 2003, Sch 11 para 71.
(5)	134(7); W 92(7)	
(6)	134(5); W 92(5)	Amended 2002, Sch 2 para 73(4).
(7)	134(6); W 92(6)	Amended 2003, Sch 4 para 117. Repealed in part 2002, Sch 2 para 73(5).
(8)	134(7); W 92(7)	
(9)	134(8); W 92(8)	
29 Making pilot schemes		
	135; W 93	
30 Designation of priority neighbourhoods or premises		
(1)	136(1); W 94(1)	
(2)	136(2); W 94(2)	

Existing provision	Rewritten provision	Remarks
(3)	136(3); W 94(3)	
(4)	—	Unnecessary.
31 Reviews of pilot schemes		
(1)	137(1); W 95(1)	
(2)	137(2); W 95(2)	
(3)	137(3); W 95(3)	
(4)	137(4); W 95(4)	
32 Variation and termination of pilot schemes		
(1)	138(1); W 96(1)	Amended 2002, Sch 2 para 76.
(2)	138(2); W 96(2)	Amended 2002, Sch 2 para 76.
(3)	138(3); W 96(3)	Amended 2002, Sch 2 para 76.
33 NHS contracts		
(1)	139(1); W 97(1)	Amended 2003, Sch 4 para 118.
(2)	139(2); W 97(2)	
(3)	139(3); W 97(3)	
(4)	139(4); W 97(4)	
(5)	139(5); W 97(5)	
(6)	139(6); W 97(6)	
(7)	139(7); W 97(7)	

Existing provision	Rewritten provision	Remarks
(8)	139(8); W 97(8)	
(9)	139(9); W 97(9)	
(10)	139(10); W 97(10)	
(11)	139(11); W 97(11)	
34 Funding of preparatory work		
(1)	140(1); W 98(1)	Amended 2002, Sch 2 para 77.
(2)	140(2); W 98(2)	
(3)	140(3); W 98(3)	Amended 2002, Sch 2 para 77.
35 Charges, recovery of payments and penalties		
(1)	178(1); W 127(1)	
(2)	178(2); 178(1); W 127(2)	
(3)	178(3); 178(1); W 127(3)	
36 Effect of 1977 Act		
(1)	W 24(2)	
(1A)	W 24(2)	Inserted 2002, s 4(2).
(2)	141; W 99	In relation to Wales, see National Health Service (Consequential Provisions) Act 2006, Sch 2 para 15.
(3)	—	Spent due to the repeal of 1990, s 3.
37 Premises from which piloted services may be provided		
	142; W 100	
38 Control of entry regulations		
	143; W 101	
40 Provision for LPS schemes		
(1)	144; W 102	Inserts 1977, s 28J. Amended 2002, Sch 2 para 78.

Existing provision	Rewritten provision	Remarks
(2)	Sch 12; W Sch 7	Inserts 1977, Sch 8A.
(3)	129(3); W 83(3)	Inserts 1977, s 42(2A).

41 Corresponding provision and application of enactments

Existing provision	Rewritten provision	Remarks
(1)	145(1); W 103(1)	Repealed in part 2003, Sch 14 Pt 4.
(2)	145(2); W 103(2)	
(2A)	145(3); W 103(3)	Inserted PCO 2006, Sch 1 Pt 2 para 7.
(3)	145(4); W 103(4)	

42 Variation and termination of pilot schemes

(1)	126; W 80	
(2)	132(7); W 86(7)	

43 Remote provision of pharmaceutical, etc services

(1)	127(1), (2); W 81(1), (2)	
(2)	129(1); W 83(1)	
(3)	129(2); W 83(2)	
(4)	129(7)–(9); W 83(7)–(9)	
(6)	W 90(1)	Amends 1977, s 44(1).

45 Care Trusts

(1)	77(1); W 35(1)	
(2)	77(2); W 35(2)	
(3)	77(3), (4); W 35(3), (4)	

Existing provision	Rewritten provision	Remarks
(4)	77(5); W 35(5)	
(5)	77(6); W 35(6)	
(6)	77(7); W 35(7)	
(7)	77(8); W 35(8)	
(8)	77(9); W 35(9)	
(9)	77(10); W 35(10)	
(10)	77(11); W 35(11)	
(11)	77(12); W 35(12)	

46 Directed partnership arrangements

(1)	78(1); W 36(1)	
(2)	78(2); W 36(2)	
(3)	78(3); W 36(3)	
(4)	78(4); W 36(4)	
(5)	78(3), (5); W 36(3), (5)	

47 Further provisions about directions in connection with directed partnership arrangements and Care Trusts

(1)	79(1); W 37(1)	
(2)	79(2); W 37(2)	
(3)	79(3); W 37(3)	

Existing provision	Rewritten provision	Remarks
(4)	79(4); W 37(4)	
(5)	273(1); W 204(1)	
(6)	—	Unnecessary.
(7)	79(5); W 37(5)	
(8)	79(6); W 37(6)	
48 Transfer of staff in connection with partnership arrangements		
(1)	—	Introductory.
(2)	75(9); W 33(9)	Inserts 1999, s 31(9).
(3)	272(3); W 203(3)	Amends 1999, s 62(1).
(4)	Sch 17; W Sch 11	Inserts 1999, Sch 2A.
60 Control of patient information		
(1)	251(1), (3)	
(2)	251(2)	
(3)	251(4)	
(4)	251(5)	
(5)	251(6)	
(6)	251(7), (8)	
(7)	251(9)	
(8)	251(10)	
(9)	251(11)	
(10)	251(12), (13)	
61 Patient Information Advisory Group		
(1)	252(1)	
(2)	252(2)	
(3)	252(3)	
(4)	252(4)	
(5)	252(5)	
(6)	252(6)	
64 Regulations and orders		
(3)	272(6)	
68 Powers of National Assembly for Wales under amended Acts		
(2)	—	Spent.
(3)	—	Spent.
Sch 1 Exempt information relating to health services		
para 1	Sch 17 para 1; W Sch 11 para 1	

Existing provision	Rewritten provision	Remarks
para 2	Sch 17 para 2 W Sch 11 para 2	
para 3	Sch 17 para 3: W Sch 11 para 3	
para 4	Sch 17 para 4; W Sch 11 para 4	
para 5	Sch 17 para 5; W Sch 11 para 5	
para 6	Sch 17 para 6; W Sch 11 para 6	
para 7	Sch 17 para 7; W Sch 11 para 7	
para 8	Sch 17 para 8; W Sch 11 para 8	
para 9	Sch 17 para 9; W Sch 11 para 9	
para 10	Sch 17 para, 10, 11; W Sch 11 para, 10, 11	Amended 2002, Sch 2 para 79.
para 11	Sch 17 para, 12, 13(1); W Sch 11 para, 12,13(1)	Substituted 2003, Sch 11 para 72. Amended 2006, Sch 8 para 45.
para 13	Sch 17 para 14; W Sch 11 para 14	Amended 2003, Sch 11 para 72.
para 14	Sch 17 para 15; W Sch 11 para 15	
para 15	Sch 17 para 16; W Sch 11 para 16	
para 16	Sch 17 para 17; W Sch 11 para 17	
para 17	Sch 17 para 18; W Sch 11 para 18	
para 18	Sch 17 para 19; W Sch 11 para 19	

Existing provision	Rewritten provision	Remarks
para 19	Sch 17 para 20; W Sch 11 para 20	
Sch 2 Pilot schemes		
para 1(1)	Sch 11 para 1(1); W Sch 6 para 1(1)	Amended 2002, Sch 2 para 80.
para 1(2)	Sch 11 para 1(2); W Sch 6 para 1(2)	
para 2(1)	Sch 11 para 2(1); W Sch 6 para 2(1)	Amended 2002, Sch 2 para 80.
para 2(2)	Sch 11 para 2(2); W Sch 6 para 2(2)	Amended 2002, Sch 2 para 80.
para 2(3)	Sch 11 para 2(3); W Sch 6 para 2(3)	Amended 2002, Sch 2 para 80.
para 2(4)	Sch 11 para 2(4); W Sch 6 para 2(4)	Amended 2002, Sch 2 para 80.
para 2(5)	Sch 11 para 2(5); W Sch 6 para 2(5)	Amended 2002, Sch 2 para 80.
para 2(6)	Sch 11 para 2(6); W Sch 6 para 2(6)	
para 3(1)	Sch 11 para 3(1); W Sch 6 para 3(1)	
para 3(2)	Sch 11 para 3(2) W Sch 6 para 3(2)	Amended 2002, Sch 2 para 80.
para 3(3)	Sch 11 para 3(3); W Sch 6 para 3(3)	Amended 2002, Sch 2 para 80.
para 4(1)	Sch 11 para 4(1) W Sch 6 para 4(1)	Amended 2002, Sch 2 para 80.
para 4(2)	Sch 11 para 4(2); W Sch 6 para 4(2)	Amended 2002, Sch 2 para 80.
para 4(3)	Sch 11 para 4(3); W Sch 6 para 4(3)	
para 4(4)	Sch 11 para 4(4); W Sch 6 para 4(4)	Amended 2002, Sch 2 para 80.

Existing provision	Rewritten provision	Remarks
para 4(5)	Sch 11 para 4(5); W Sch 6 para 4(5)	
para 4(6)	Sch 11 para 4(6); W Sch 6 para 4(6)	
para 5(1)	Sch 11 para 5(1); W Sch 6 para 5(1)	Amended 2002, Sch 2 para 80.
para 5(2)	Sch 11 para 5(2); W Sch 6 para 5(2)	Part substituted 2003, Sch 11 para 73.
para 5(3)	Sch 11 para 5(3) W Sch 6 para 5(3)	Amended 2002, Sch 2 para 80.
para 5(4)	Sch 11 para 5(4); W Sch 6 para 5(4)	Amended 2002, Sch 2 para 80.
para 6	Sch 11 para 6; W Sch 6 para 6	
para 7(1)	Sch 11 para 7(1); W Sch 6 para 7(1)	Amended 2002, Sch 2 para 80.
para 7(2)	Sch 11 para 7(2); W Sch 6 para 7(2)	Amended 2002, Sch 2 para 80.
para 7(3)	Sch 11 para 7(3); W Sch 6 para 7(3)	
para 7(4)	Sch 11 para 7(4); W Sch 6 para 7(4)	Amended 2002, Sch 2 para 80.
Sch 3 LPS Schemes		
	Sch 12; W Sch 7	Inserts 1977, Sch 8A. Amended 2002, Sch 2 para 81.
Sch 4 Partnership arrangements: transfer of staff		
	Sch 18; W Sch 12	Inserts 1999, Sch 2A.
Sch 5 Minor and consequential amendments		
para 5(1)	—	Introductory.
para 5(2)	—	Repeals 1977, s 7.
para 5(3)	8(3); W 19(3), W 23(3)	Substitutes 1977, s 17(3).
para 5(8)	—	Repeals 1977 s 46–49E.
para 5(9)	—	Repeals in part 1977, s 85(1).

Existing provision	Rewritten provision	Remarks
para 5(10)	170(1)	Amends 1977, s 100(1). Repeals 1977, s 100(1)(c).
para 5(11)	—	Repeals in part 1977, s 102(1), (2).
para 5(12)	234(4); W 180(4)	Amends 1977, s 103(3). Repealed in part PCO 2006, Sch 2.
para 5(13)	272(2), (7)	Amends 1977, s 126. Repealed in part PCO 2006, Sch 2.
para 5(14)	148(7); W 104(7)	Amends 1977, s 128.
para 5(15)	Sch 3 para 11(1)	Amends 1977, Sch 5A para 11, cross-heading.
para 5(16)	—	Repeals 1977, Sch 9.
para 5(17)	Sch 14 para 4(1), (2); W para 4(1), (2)	Amends 1977, Sch 12A para 7.
para 8	11(5); W 9(4)	Amends 1990, s 4A(3).
para 11(1)	—	Introductory.
para 11(4)	92(4), 107(4); W 50(4), W 64(4)	Amends 1977, s 28C(2)(a) (by amending 1997, s 21).
para 12(1)	—	Introductory.
para 12(3)	—	Repeals in part 1999, s 66(5).

National Health Service Reform and Health Care Professions Act 2002 (c 17)

Existing provision	Rewritten provision	Remarks
1 English Health Authorities: change of name		
(1)	—	Changes name of English Health Authorities to Strategic Health Authorities.
(2)	13	Substitutes 1977, s 8.
2 Primary Care Trusts		
(1)	—	Introductory.
(2)	18(1)–(3)	Substitutes 1977, s 16A(1), (1A).
(3)	18(2)	Amends 1977, s 16A(3).
(4)	Sch 3 para, 14(3), (4), 20(1), (3)	Amends 1977, Sch 5A, paras 2, 16.
3 Directions: distribution of functions		
(1)	—	Introductory.
(2)	7(1)	Amends 1977, s 16D(1).
(3)	15	Substitutes 1977, s 17A.
(4)	—	Repeals in part 1977, s 17B(1).
(5)	—	Amends and Repeals in part 1977, s 18(1A). (s 3(5)(a), (c) already repealed by the Health (Wales) Act 2003 (c 4) as provision made there supersedes provision made by this provision).

4 Personal medical services, personal dental services and local pharmaceutical services

Existing provision	Rewritten provision	Remarks
(2)	W 24(2)	Inserts 2001, s 36(1A).
5 Local Representative Committees		
(1)	—	Introductory.
(4)	167(1), (4)	
(5)	—	Repeals in part 1977, s 44(2).
(7)	167(2), (3)	Amends 1977, s 44(4).
(8)	—	Introductory.
(10)	167(7); W 78(5), W 90(5)	Amends 1977, s 45(1A).
(11)	—	Spent.
(12)	167(9), (10), (11)	Amends 1977, s 45(2), (3).
6 Local Health Boards		
(1)	W 11–13, W 204(3)	Inserts 1977, ss 16BA, 16BB, 16BC.
(3)	W 203(3)	Amends 1977, s 126.
(4)	W Sch 2 para 16	Applies National Health Service (Private Finance) Act 1997 (c 56) s 1 to Local Health Boards
7 Funding of Strategic Health Authorities and Health Authorities		
(1)	—	Introductory.
(2)	224(1)	Inserts 1977, s 97(A1).
(3)	224(2)	Inserts 1977, s 97(3C).
(4)	224(3)	Inserts 1977, s 97(3D).
(5)	224(5)	Inserts 1977, s 97(3F).
(6)	224(7)	Amends 1977, s 97(5).
(7)	224(9)	Amends and repeals in part 1977, s 97(6).
(8)	—	Repeals 1977, s 97(8).
(9)	224(10)	Amends 1977, s 97(9).
8 Funding of Primary Care Trusts		
	228	Substitutes 1977, s 97(C).
9 Funding of Local Health Boards		
(1)	W 174–176	Inserts 1977 ss 97F, 97G, 97H.
10 Expenditure of NHS bodies		
(1)	—	Introductory.
(2)	—	Amends 1977, s 97(3BB).
(3)	—	Introductory.
(4)	—	Amends 1977, Sch 12A para 3. Spent because of the abolition of Health Authorities.
(5)	Sch 14 para 1(2)	Amends 1977, Sch 12A para 4(2).
(6)	Sch 14 para 2(1)	Amends 1977, Sch 12A para 5(1).
(7)	Sch 14 para 2(2)	Amends 1977, Sch 12A para 5(2).
(8)	Sch 14 paras 3(1)–(5)	Substitutes 1977, Sch 12A para 6.
(9)	W Sch 8 paras 1–3	Inserts 1977, Sch 12A paras 6A–6C.
(10)	Sch 14 para 4; W Sch 8 para 4	Amends 1977, Sch 12A para 7.

Existing provision	Rewritten provision	Remarks
15 Establishment of Patients' Forums		
(1)	237(1)	Amended 2003, s 31(2). Repealed in part 2003, Sch 14 Pt 1.
(2)	237(2)	
(3)	237(3)	
(4)	237(4)	
(5)	237(5)	
(6)	237(6)	
(7)	237(7)	
(8)	237(8)	
(9)	237(9)	Amended 2003, s 31(2).
16 Additional functions of PCT Patients' Forums		
(1)	238(1)	
(2)	238(2)	
(3)	238(3)	
(4)	238(4)	
(5)	248(7), (8)	Inserts 1977, s 19A(7).
(6)	238(5)	
17 Entry and inspection of premises		
(1)	239(1)	Amended 2003, s 31(3), Sch 11 para 74(2); 2006 para 49. Repealed in part 2003, Sch 11 para 74(2).
(2)	239(2)	Amended 2003, Sch 11 para 74(3); 2006 para 49.
(3)	239(3)	
(4)	—	Unnecessary.
18 Annual reports		
(1)	240(1)	
(2)	240(2)	Amended 2003, s 31(4).
(3)	240(3)	
(4)	240(4)	
19 Supplementary		
(1)	241(1)	
(2)	241(2)	Amended 2003, s 31(5).
(3)	241(3)	
(4)	241(4)	Amended 2003, s 31(5).
(5)	241(5)	
20 The Commission for Patient and Public Involvement in Health		
(1)	243(1)	
(2)	243(2)	
(3)	243(3)	
(4)	243(4)	
(5)	243(5)	
(6)	243(6)	
(7)	243(7)	Substituted in part Health and Social Care (Community Health and Standards) Act 2003 (Commission for Healthcare Audit and Inspection and Commission for Social Care Inspection) (Consequential Provisions) Order 2004 (SI 2004/2987) art 2(1)(d).
(8)	243(8)	
(9)	243(9)	

Existing provision	Rewritten provision	Remarks
(10)	243(10)	Amended 2003, s 32(2).
(11)	243(11)	
(12)	243(12)	Amended 2003, s 32(3).
21 Overview and scrutiny committees		
	244(2); W 184(2)	Amends 2001, s 7(3).
23 Joint working with the prison service		
(1)	249(1)	
(2)	249(2); W 188(1)	
(3)	249(3); W 188(2)	
(4)	249(4); W 188(3)	
(5)	249(5); W 188(4)	
24 Health and well-being strategies in Wales		
(1)	W 40(1)	
(2)	W 40(2)	
(3)	W 40(3)	
(4)	W 40(4)	
(5)	W 40(5)	
(6)	W 40(6)	
(7)	W 40(7)	
(8)	W 40(8)	
(9)	W 40(9)	
36 Amendments of Health service legislation in connection with consolidation		
	—	Spent.
Sch 1 English Health Authorities: change of name		
para 1	—	Introductory.
para 2	13(10)	Amends 1977, s 12(2).
para 3	14(1), (2), (3), (4)	Amends 1977, s 16.
para 4	19(3), (4)	Amends 1977, s 16B.
para 5	17	Amends 1977, s 16C.
para 6	7(1), (2)	Amends 1977, s 16D.
para 7	8(2)	Amends 1977, s 17.
para 8	20(1)	Amends 1977, s 17B(1).
para 9	273(3)	Amends 1977, s 18(1B).
para 10	82	Amends 1977, s 22(1A).
para 11	12(4)	Amends 1977, s 23(2).
para 12	80(3), (6), (7)	Amends 1977, s 26.
para 13	81(1), (3)	Amends 1977, s 27.
para 14	74(1), (3); W 32(3)	Amends 1977, s 28.

Existing provision	Rewritten provision	Remarks
para 15	256(4); W 194(4)	Amends 1977, s 28A.
para 16	76(1); W 34(1)	Amends 1977, s 28BB.
para 18	171(2)	Amends 1977, s 49S(8).
para 19	258(2); W 197(2)	Amends 1977, s 51.
para 20	Sch 2 para 15;, Sch 6 para 11; W Sch 2 para 15, W Sch 5 para 11	Amends 1977, s 65.
para 21	66(1); W 26(1)	Amends 1977, s 84A(2).
para 22	67(1); W 27(1)	Amends 1977, s 84B(1).
para 23	68(1); W 28(1)	Amends 1977, s 85(1).
para 24	Sch 2 para 12	Amends 1977, s 90.
para 25	218(4)	Amends 1977, s 91(3).
para 26	213(1), (2); W 161(1), (2)	Amends 1977, s 92(1), (1A).
para 27	217(3); W 165(3)	Amends 1977, s 96(1A).
para 28	215(2), 222(1)	Amends 1977, s 96A.
para 31	69(1)	Amends 1977, s 125.
para 32	273(3)	Amends 1977, s 126.
para 33	275(3)	Amends 1977, s 128.
para 34(1)	—	Introductory.
para 34(2)	Sch 2 paras 3, 4, 5, 6	Amends 1977, Sch 5 Pt 1 (paras 1, 2, 3, 4). Inserts 1977, Sch 5 para 4A.
para 34(3)	Sch 2 para 1	Amends 1977, Sch 5 para 8.
para 35(1)	—	Introductory.
para 35(2)	Sch 3 para 9	Amends 1977, Sch 5A para 10.
para 35(3)	Sch 3 para 23(1)	Amends 1977, Sch 5A para 20.
para 35(4)	Sch 3 para 24(2), (5)	Amends 1977, Sch 5A para 21.
para 35(5)	Sch 3 para 26(2)	Amends 1977, Sch 5A para 23.
para 40	9(4); W 7(4)	Amends 1990, s 4(2).
para 41	11(1)	Amends 1990, s 4A(1).

Existing provision	Rewritten provision	Remarks
para 42	Sch 4 para 9(1), (3), (6), (7); W Sch 3 para 9(1), (3), (6), (7)	Amends 1990, s 8(1)–(3), (5), (6).
para 43	71(2), (3), (6)	Amends 1990, s 21.
para 46	Sch 4 para, 6(1), (2), 7, 18, 29(1), (3), 30(1); W Sch 3 para, 6(1), (2), 7, 18, 29(1), (3), 30(1)	Amends 1990, Sch 2 paras 4, 5, 13, 30, 31.
para 51	72	Amends 1999, s 26.
para 52	24(5); W 17(6)	Amends 1999, s 28(6), (9).
para 53	75(8); W 33(8)	Amends 1999, s 31.
para 55(1)	—	Introductory.
para 55(2)	244(3); W 184(3)	Amends 2001, s 7(4).
para 55(3)	78(3); W 36(3)	Amends 2001, s 46(5).
Sch 2 Reallocation of functions of Health Authorities to Primary Care Trusts		
para 1	—	Introductory.
para 2(1)	—	Introductory.
para 2(2)	22; W 15	Amends 1977, s 15(1).
para 12(1)	—	Introductory.
para 12(2)	W 72(1)	Amends 1977, s 39(1).
para 12(4)	W 72(4)	Amends 1977, s 39(3).
para 13(1)	—	Introductory.
para 13(2)	126(1)	Amends 1977, s 41(1).
para 13(3)	126(6), (7)	Amends 1977, s 41(5), (6).
para 14	127(1), (2)	Amends 1977, s 41A.
para 15	128(1), (4)–(6)	Amends 1977, s 41B.
para 16	129(1), (2), (6), (8), 130(2); W 83(2), (6), W 84(2)	Amends 1977, s 42.
para 17(1)	—	Introductory.
para 17(2)	132(1)	Amends 1977, s 43(1).
para 17(3)	132(3); W 86(3)	Substitutes 1977, s 43(2A).
para 17(4)	132(4)	Amends 1977, s 43(2BA).
para 17(5)	132(5)	Amends 1977, s 43(2BB).

Existing provision	Rewritten provision	Remarks
para 18(1)	—	Introductory.
para 18(2)	148(1)	Amends 1977, s 43ZA(1).
para 18(3)	148(3)	Amends 1977, s 43ZA(4).
para 18(4)	148(4)	Amends 1977, s 43ZA(5).
para 18(5)	148(6)	Amends 1977, s 43ZA(7).
para 19	166(2), (3)	Amends 1977, s 43C.
para 20(1)	—	Introductory.
para 20(2)	149(1)	Amends 1977, s 43D(1).
para 20(3)	149(3)	Amends 1977, s 43D(3).
para 20(4)	149(4)	Amends 1977, s 43D(4).
para 20(5)	149(7)	Amends 1977, s 43D(7).
para 20(6)	149(8)	Amends 1977, s 43D(8).
para 20(7)	149(9)	Amends 1977, s 43D(9).
para 20(8)	150(2)	Amends 1977, s 43D(10).
para 20(9)	150(3)	Amends 1977, s 43D(11).
para 21	151, 152, 154	Amends 1977, ss 49F, 49G, 49H.
para 22	155(1), (3), (5), (6)	Amends 1977, s 49J.
para 23	157(1), (2), (3)	Amends 1977, s 49L.
para 24	158(1)–(7)	Amends 1977, s 49M.
para 25(1)	—	Introductory.
para 25(2)	159(1)	Amends 1977, s 49N(1).
para 25(3)	159(3)	Amends 1977, s 49N(3).
para 25(4)	159(4)	Amends 1977, s 49N(4).
para 25(5)	159(6)	Amends 1977, s 49N(6).
para 26	160	Amends 1977, s 49O.
para 27	161	Amends 1977, s 49P.
para 28(1)	—	Introductory.
para 28(2)	162(1)	Amends 1977, s 49Q(1).
para 28(3)	162(2)	Amends 1977, s 49Q(2).
para 28(4)	162(3)	Amends 1977, s 49Q(3).
para 29	259(2), (5)	Amends 1977, s 54.
para 30	133(1), (2)	Amends 1977, s 56.
para 31	—	Spent due to substitution of reference to Primary Care Trust.
para 32	183; W 131	Amends 1977, s 83A.
para 33	213(1); W 161(1)	Amends 1977, s 92.
para 34	215(2)	Amends 1977, s 96A(5).
para 35	234(4); W 180(4)	Amends 1977, s 103(3).
para 36	269(2), (4), (6), (7), (9), (10); W 200(2), (6)	Amends 1977, s 124.

Existing provision	Rewritten provision	Remarks
para 37	—	Spent. Inserts 1977, Sch 5A para 10A (subsequently substituted by Dentists Act 1984 (Amendment) Order 2005 (SI 2005/2011) Sch 6 para 1(5)).
para 54	11(1)	Amends 1990, s 4A(1).
para 58	Sch 4 para 30(1); W Sch 3 para 30(1)	Amends 1990, Sch 2 para 31.
para 67	—	Introductory.
para 69(1)	—	Introductory.
para 69(2)	24(1), (2)	Amends 1999, s 28(1), (2).
para 69(3)	24(3)	Amends 1999, s 28(3).
para 69(4)	24(3); W 17(4)	Substitutes 1999, s 28(4).
para 69(5)	24(4)	Amends 1999, s 28(5).
para 69(6)	24(5); W 17(6)	Amends 1999, s 28(6).
para 69(7)	24(6); W 17(7)	Substitutes 1999, s 28(7).
para 69(8)	24(7)	Amends 1999, s 28(8).
para 73(1)	—	Introductory.
para 73(2)	134(1)	Amends 2001, s 28(1).
para 73(3)	134(2)	Amends 2001, s 28(2).
para 73(4)	134(5)	Amends 2001, s 28(6).
para 73(5)	—	Repeals in part 2001, s 28(7).
para 74	136(1), (2)	Amends 2001, s 30.
para 75	137(3)	Amends 2001, s 31.
para 76	138(1)–(3)	Amends 2001, s 32(1)–(3).
para 77	140(1), (3)	Amends 2001, s 34(1), (3).
para 78	144	Amends 2001, s 40(1).
para 79	Sch 17 para 10; W Sch 11 para 10	Amends 2001, Sch 1 para 10.
para 80	Sch 11 para, 2(5), 5(1)	Amends 2001, Sch 2.
para 81	—	Amends 1977, Sch 8A (by amending 2001, Sch 3).
para 82	—	Amends 2001, Sch 5 para 9.

Sch 3 Amendments relating to personal medical services and personal dental services

para 1	—	Introductory
para 7(1)	—	Introductory.
para 7(2)	92(1), (7), 107(1), (7)	Amends 1977, s 28C (by amending 1997, s 21(1)). (Note that para 7(2)(b) amends 1977, s 28C(3) which was repealed by 2003, Sch 14 Pt 4.)
para 7(3)	93(1), 108(1)	Amends 1977, s 28D (by amending 1997, s 21(1)).

Existing provision	Rewritten provision	Remarks
para 8	94(2), (3), 109(2), (3)	Amends 1977, s 28E (by amending 1997, s 22(1)). (Note that para 8(c) and (d) amend 1977, s 28E(7) and (8) respectively, which were repealed by 2003, Sch 14 Pt 4.)
para 11	16(1)	Amends 1977, s 15(1ZA).
para 14(a)	—	Repeals 1977, s 28EE(1) (by amending 1999, s 6(2) which inserts it).
para 14(b)	95(1), 110(1)	Amends 1977, s 28EE(2) (by amending 1999, s 6(2) which inserts it).
Sch 4 Local Health Boards		
	W	Inserts 1977, Sch 5B.
	Sch 2	
Sch 5 Amendments relating to Local Health Boards		
para 4	—	Introductory.
para 5	14(3)	Amends 1977, s 16(2).
para 6	19(3)	Amends 1977, s 16B(2).
para 7	W 16	Amends 1977, s 16C.
para 8	82	Amends 1977, s 22.
para 9	12(4); W 10(4)	Amends 1977, s 23(2).
para 10	80(3); W 38(3)	Amends 1977, s 26(1).
para 11	81(1), (3); W 39(1), (3)	Amends 1977, s 27(3).
para 12	74(3); W 32(1), (3)	Amends 1977, s 28(1), (3).
para 13	256(4); W 194(1), (3), (4)	Amends 1977, s 28A.
para 14	76(1); W 34(1)	Amends 1977, s 28BB(2).
para 15	258(2); W 197(2)	Amends 1977, s 51(2), (3).
para 16	66(1); W 26(1)	Amends 1977, s 84A(2).
para 17	67(1); W 27(1)	Amends 1977, s 84B(1).
para 18	68(1); W 28(1)	Amends 1977, s 85.
para 19	213(2); W 161(2)	Amends 1977, s 92.
para 20	W 169(1)	Amends 1977, s 96A.

Existing provision	Rewritten provision	Remarks
para 23	69(1)	Amends 1977, s 125.
para 31	9(4); W 7(4)	Amends 1990, s 4(2).
para 32	Sch 4 para 9(1), (3), (6), (7); W Sch 3 para 9(1), (3), (6), (7)	Amends 1990, s 8(1)–(3), (5), (6).
para 33	W 30(2)	Amends 1990, s 21(2).
para 36	Sch 4 para, 6(1), 18, 29(1); W Sch 3 paras 6(1), 18, 29(1)	Amends 1990, Sch 2 para, s 4, 13, 30.
para 43	—	Introductory.
para 45	75(8); W 33(8)	Amends 1999, s 31(8).
para 49	—	Introductory.
para 50	244(3); W 184(3)	Amends 2001, s 7(4).
para 51	78(3); W 36(3)	Amends 2001, s 46(5).

Sch 6 The Commission for Patient and Public Involvement in Health

Existing provision	Rewritten provision	Remarks
para 1	Sch 16 para 1	
para 2(1)	Sch 16 para 2(1)	
para 2(2)	Sch 16 para 2(2)	
para 3	Sch 16 para 3	
para 4(1)	Sch 16 para 4(1)	
para 4(2)	Sch 16 para 4(2)	
para 5	Sch 16 para 5	
para 6	—	Repealed 2006 para 50.
para 7(1)	Sch 16 para 6(1)	
para 7(2)	Sch 16 para 6(2)	
para 7(3)	Sch 16 para 6(3)	
para 7(4)	Sch 16 para 6(4)	
para 8(1)	Sch 16 para 7(1)	
para 8(2)	Sch 16 para 7(2)	
para 8(3)	—	Unnecessary.
para 8(4)	Sch 16 para 7(3)	
para 9	Sch 16 para 8	
para 10(1)	Sch 16 para 9(1)	
para 10(2)	Sch 16 para 9(2)	
para 11(1)	Sch 16 para 10(1)	
para 11(2)	Sch 16 para 10(2)	
para 11(3)	—	Repealed PCO 2006, Sch 1 Pt 2 para 11.
para 11(4)	Sch 16 para 10(3)	
para 12(1)	Sch 16 para 11(1)	
para 12(2)	Sch 16 para 11(2)	
para 12(3)	Sch 16 para 11(3)	

Existing provision	Rewritten provision	Remarks
para 12(4)	Sch 16 para 11(4)	
para 12(5)	—	Unnecessary.
para 13(1)	Sch 16 para 12(1)	
para 13(2)	Sch 16 para 12(2)	
para 13(3)	Sch 16 para 12(3)	
para 13(4)	—	Unnecessary.
para 14	Sch 16 para 13	
para 15	Sch 16 para 14	
Sch 8 Minor and consequential amendments		
para 1	—	Introductory.
para 3	166(1); W 120(1)	Amends 1977, s 43C(3).
para 4(1)	—	Introductory.
para 4(2)	226(1)	Amends 1977, s 97A(1).
para 4(3)	226(3)–(6), 227(3)	Amends 1977, s 97A(3), (6)–(8).
para 4(4)	226(7)	Amends 1977, s 97A(9).
para 5	227(1), (2)	Amends 1977, s 97AA(1), (3).
para 6	—	Repeals in part 1977, s 97D(1).
para 7(1)	—	Introductory.
para 7(2)	230(1)	Amends 1977, s 97E(1).
para 7(3)	230(3)	Substitutes 1977, s 97E(2A).
para 8	235(1)	Amends 1977, s 104(1).
para 9	236(2); W 181(2)	Amends 1977, s 105(2).
para 12	—	Spent.
para 18	—	Spent.
para 23	—	Introductory.
para 24	—	Spent.
para 25	—	Introductory.
para 26	—	Spent.
para 27	—	Spent.
para 30	—	Spent.
para 31	—	Spent.
para 32	—	Introductory.
para 33	—	Repeals 2001, s 1(4), (5).
para 34	—	Repeals 2001, s 3(3), (4).
para 35	242(1), (4), (5)	Amends 2001, s 11.
para 36	—	Repeals 2001, s 43(5).
para 37	—	Repeals 2001, Sch 5 para 5(12)(b).

Adoption and Children Act 2002 (c 38)

Existing provision	Rewritten provision	Remarks
Sch 3 Minor and consequential amendments		
para 20	270(3); W 201(3)	Repeals in part and amends 1977, s 124A(3).

Nationality, Immigration and Asylum Act 2002 (c 41)

Existing provision	Rewritten provision	Remarks
45 Destitute asylum seeker: supplemental		
(7)	Sch 20 para 2(7); W Sch 15 para 2(7)	Substitutes 1977, Sch 8 para 2(2B).

Health (Wales) Act 2003 (c 4)

Existing provision	Rewritten provision	Remarks
1 Community Health Councils in Wales		
(1)	W 182	Inserts 1977, s 20A.
(3)	W Sch 10	Inserts 1977, Sch 7A.
(4)	—	Repeals 1977, s 20 and Sch 7.
Sch 1 Schedule 7A to be inserted in the National Health Service Act 1977		
	W Sch 10	Inserts 1977, Sch 7A.
Sch 3 Minor and consequential amendments		
para 3	—	Repeals in part 1977, s 18(1A).
para 4	—	Repeals 1977, s 98(2A).
para 6	9(4); W 7(4)	Amends 1990, s 4(2).
para 9	—	Repeals in part Government of Wales Act 1998 (c 38) s 27(7).

Health and Social Care (Community Health and Standards) Act 2003 (c 43)

Existing provision	Rewritten provision	Remarks
Part 1 NHS foundation trusts		
1 NHS foundation trusts		
(1)	30(1)	
(2)	30(2)	
2 Independent Regulator of NHS Foundation Trusts		
(1)	31(1)	
(2)	31(2)	
3 General duty of regulator		
	32	
4 Application by NHS trusts		
(1)	33(1)	
(2)	33(2)	
(3)	33(3)	
(4)	33(4)	
5 Other applications		
(1)	34(1)	
(2)	34(2)	
(3)	34(3)	
(4)	34(4)	
(5)	34(5)	
(6)	34(6)	

Existing provision	Rewritten provision	Remarks
(7)	34(7)	
6 Authorisation of NHS foundation trusts		
(1)	35(1)	
(2)	35(2)	
(3)	35(3)	
(4)	35(4)	
(5)	35(5)	
(6)	35(6)	
(7)	35(7)	
7 Effect of authorisation		
(1)	36(1)	
(2)	36(1)	
(3)	36(2)	
(4)	36(3)	
(5)	36(4)	Amended 2006 para 53.
(6)	36(5)	
(7)	36(6)	
8 Amendments of constitution		
	37	
9 Variation of authorisation		
(1)	38(1)	
(2)	38(2)	
10 Register of NHS foundation trusts		
(1)	39(1)	
(2)	39(2)	
(3)	39(3)	
(4)	39(4)	
(5)	39(5)	
11 Power of Secretary of State to give financial assistance		
(1)	40(1)	
(2)	40(2)	
(3)	40(3), (4)	
12 Prudential borrowing code		
(1)	41(1)	
(2)	41(2), (3)	
(3)	41(4)	
(4)	41(5)	
(5)	41(1), (2), (4)	
13 Public dividend capital		
(1)	42(1)	
(2)	42(2)	
(3)	42(3)	
(4)	42(4)	
(5)	42(5)	
(6)	42(6)	
14 Authorised services		
(1)	43(1)	
(2)	43(2)	
(3)	43(3)	
(4)	43(4)	
(5)	65(2)	

Existing provision	Rewritten provision	Remarks
(6)	43(5)	
(7)	43(6)	
(8)	43(7)	
15 Private health care		
(1)	44(1)	
(2)	44(2)	
(3)	44(3)	
(4)	44(4)	
(5)	44(5)	
16 Protection of property		
(1)	45(1), (2)	
(2)	45(3)	
(3)	45(4)	
(4)	45(5)	
(5)	45(6)	
17 Financial powers		
(1)	46(1)	
(2)	46(2)	
(3)	46(3)	
(4)	46(4)	
(5)	46(5)	
(6)	46(6)	
18 General powers		
(1)	47(1)	
(2)	47(2)	
(3)	47(3)	
19 Information		
(1)	48(1)	
(2)	48(2)	
20 Entry and inspection of premises		
	49	
21 Fees		
	50	
22 Trust funds and trustees		
(1)	51(1)	
(2)	51(2)	
(3)	51(3)	
(4)	51(4)	
23 Failing NHS foundation trusts		
(1)	52(1)	
(2)	52(2)	
(3)	52(3)	
(4)	52(4)	
(5)	52(5)	
24 Voluntary arrangements		
(1)	53(1)	
(2)	53(2), (3), (4)	
25 Dissolution etc		
(1)	54(1)	
(2)	54(2), (3)	
(3)	54(4)	

Existing provision	Rewritten provision	Remarks
(3A)	54(5)	Inserted 2006, s 74(6).
(4)	54(6)	
(5)	54(7)	
(6)	54(8)	
(7)	54(9)	
26 Sections 24 and 25: supplementary		
(1)	55(1)	
(2)	55(2)	
(3)	55(3)	
(4)	55(4)	
(5)	55(5)	
27 Mergers		
(1)	56(1)	
(2)	56(2)	
(3)	56(3)	
(4)	56(4)	
(5)	56(5)	
(6)	56(6)	
(7)	56(7)	
(8)	56(8)	
(9)	56(9)	
(10)	56(10)	
(11)	56(11)	
28 Section 27: supplementary		
(1)	57(1)	
(2)	57(2)	
(3)	57(3)	
(3A)	57(4)	Inserted 2006, s 74(7).
(4)	57(5)	
(5)	57(6)	
29 Co-operation between NHS bodies		
	72	Amends 1999, s 26.
30 Public involvement and consultation		
	242(1)	Amends 2001, s 11(2).
31 Patients' Forums		
(1)	—	Introductory.
(2)	237(1), (9)	Amends 2002, s 15(1), (9).
(3)	239(1)	Amends 2002, s 17(1).
(4)	240(2)	Amends 2002, s 18(2).
(5)	241(2), (4)	Amends 2002, s 19(2), (4).
32 Commission for Patient and Public Involvement in Health		
(1)	—	Introductory.
(2)	243(10)	Amends 2002, s 20(10).
(3)	243(12)	Amends 2002, s 20(12).
33 Taxation		
(2)	58	
35 Conduct of elections		
(1)	59(1)	
(2)	59(2)	
(3)	59(3)	
(4)	59(4)	

Existing provision	Rewritten provision	Remarks
(5)	59(5)	
36 Offence		
(1)	60(1)	
(2)	60(2)	
(3)	60(3)	
(4)	60(4)	
(5)	60(5)	
(6)	60(6)	
(7)	60(7)	
37 Representative membership		
	61	
38 Audit		
	62	
39 General duty of NHS foundation trusts		
	63	
40 Interpretation of Part 1		
(1)	65(1)	
(2)	—	Unnecessary.
(3)	47(4), 51(5)	
(4)	65(2)	
Part 4 Dental and Medical Services		
170 Provision of primary dental services		
	99; W 56	Inserts 1977, s 16CA.
171 Dental public health		
(1)	111; W 67	Inserts 1977, s 16CB.
(2)	—	Repeals 1977, s 5(1A).
172 General dental services contracts		
(1)	100–105; W 57–62	Inserts 1977, ss 28K, 28L, 28M, 28N, 28O, 28P
(2)	—	Repeals 1977, ss 36, 37
174 Provision of primary medical services		
	83; W 41	Inserts 1977, s 16CC
175 General medical services contracts		
(1)	84–90; W 42–48	Inserts 1977, ss 28Q, 28R, 28S, 28T, 28U, 28V, 28W
(2)	—	Repeals 1977, ss 29, 29A, 29B, 31, 32, 33, 34A.
177 Arrangements under s 28C of the 1977 Act		
(1)	—	Introductory

Existing provision	Rewritten provision	Remarks
(2)	93(1), 108(1); W 51(1), W 65(1)	Amends 1977, s 28D(1).
(3)	93(2), 108(2); W 51(2), W 65(2)	Inserts 1977, s 28D(1A).
(4)	93(3), 108(3); W 51(3), W 65(3)	Amends 1977, s 28D(2).
(5)	93(3), 108(3); W 51(3), W 65(3)	Amends 1977, s 28D(2).
(6)	93(3), 108(3); W 51(3), W 65(3)	Amends 1977, s 28D(2).
(7)	94(3), 109(3); W 52(3), W 66(3)	Amends 1977, s 28E(3).
(8)	94(4), (5), 109(4), (5); W 52(4), (5), W 66(4), (5)	Inserts 1977, ss 28E(3A), 28E(3B).
(9)	94(6), 109(6); W 52(6), W 66(6)	Inserts 1977, s 28E(3C).
(10)	94(7), 109(7); W 52(7), W 66(7)	Inserts 1977, s 28E(3D).
(11)	94(8), (9), 109(8), (9), W 52(8), (9), W 66(8), (9)	Inserts 1977, ss 28E(3E), 28E(3F).

Existing provision	Rewritten provision	Remarks
(12)	—	Repeals 1977, ss 28F, 28G, 28H.
178 Abolition of pilot schemes		
(1)	—	Repeals 1997 Pt 1.
(2)	—	Spent.
179 Persons performing primary medical and dental services		
(1)	91, 106, 123, 146; W 49, W 63	Inserts 1977, s 28X
(2)	158(8); W 114(8)	Amends 1977, s 49M(7)
180 Assistance and support		
	96, 112, 124, 147; W 53, W 68	Inserts 1977, s 28Y.
181 Abolition of Dental Practice Board		
	—	Abolishes Dental Practice Board.
182 Special Health Authorities		
(1)	19(5), (6)	Inserts 1977, s 16B(4).
(2)	W 13(5), (6)	Inserts 1977, s 16BC(4).
183 Charges for dental services		
(1)	176; W 125	Substitutes 1977, s 79.
(2)	177; W 126	Inserts 1977, Sch 12ZA.
(3)	—	Spent.
(4)	—	Spent.
Sch1 Constitution of public benefit corporations		
para 1	Sch 7 para 1	
para 2	Sch 7 para 2	
para 3	Sch 7 para 3	
para 4	Sch 7 para 4	
para 5	Sch 7 para 5	
para 6	Sch 7 para 6	
para 7	Sch 7 para 7	
para 8	Sch 7 para 8	
para 9	Sch 7 para 9	
para 10	Sch 7 para 10	
para 11	Sch 7 para 11	
para 12	Sch 7 para 12	
para 13	Sch 7 para 13	
para 14	Sch 7 para 14	
para 15	Sch 7 para 15	
para 16	Sch 7 para 16	
para 17	Sch 7 para 17	

Existing provision	Rewritten provision	Remarks
para 18	Sch 7 para 18	
para 19	Sch 7 para 19	
para 20	Sch 7 para 20	
para 21	Sch 7 para 21	
para 22	Sch 7 para 22	
para 23	Sch 7 para 23	
para 24	Sch 7 para 24	
para 25	Sch 7 para 25	
para 26	Sch 7 para 26	
para 27	Sch 7 para 27	
para 28	Sch 7 para 28	
para 29	Sch 7 para 29	
Sch 2 Independent regulator of NHS foundation trusts		
para 1	Sch 8 para 1	
para 2	Sch 8 para 2	
para 3	Sch 8 para 3	
para 4	Sch 8 para 4	
para 5(1)	Sch 8 para 5(1)	
para 5(2)	Sch 8 para 5(2)	
para 5(4)	Sch 8 para 5(3)	
para 6	Sch 8 para 6	
para 7	Sch 8 para 7	
para 8	Sch 8 para 8	
para 9	Sch 8 para 9	
para 10	Sch 8 para 10	
para 11	Sch 8 para 11	
para 12	Sch 8 para 12	
para 13	Sch 8 para 13	
para 14	Sch 8 para 14	
para 15	Sch 8 para 15	
para 16	Sch 8 para 16	
Sch 3 Transfer of staff		
para 1	Sch 9 para 1	
para 2	Sch 9 para 2	
para 3	Sch 9 para 3	
para 4	Sch 9 para 4	
para 5	Sch 9 para 5	
para 6	Sch 9 para 6	
Sch 4 Amendments relating to NHS foundation trusts		
para 23	—	Introductory.
para 24	21(6)	Amends 1977, s 18A(6).
para 25	82	Amends 1977, s 22(1A).
para 26	74(1), (3); W 32(3)	Amends 1977, s 28(2).
para 27	256(4); W 194(4)	Amends 1977, s 28A(2B).
para 28	189(3); W 137(3)	Amends 1977, s 63(1C).

Existing provision	Rewritten provision	Remarks
para 29	Sch 2 para 15(5), Sch 6 para 11(5); W Sch 2 para 15(5), W Sch 5 para 11(5)	Amends 1977, s 65(4).
para 30	185(2); W 133(2)	Amends 1977, s 81(a).
para 31	186(2); W 134(2)	Amends 1977, s 82(a).
para 32	183; W 131	Amends 1977, s 83A(1).
para 34	218(4)	Amends 1977, s 91(3).
para 35	213(2), 214(3); W 161(2), W 162(3)	Amends 1977, s 92(1A), (7).
para 36	217(1); W 165(1)	Extends 1977, s 96.
para 37	215(2), (3), (4), 222(1)	Inserts 1977, s 96A(12).
para 38	234(4)	Amends 1977, s 103.
para 39	236(2); W 181(2)	Amends 1977, s 105(2).
para 40	191(1); W 139(1)	Amends 1977, s 122(1).
para 41	69(1), (2)	Amends 1977, s 125.
para 42	275(1); W 206(1)	Amends 1977, s 128(1).
para 43	Sch 3 para 23(1)	Amends 1977, Sch 5A para 20(1).
para 44	Sch 12 para 1(6); W Sch 7 para 1(7)	Amends 1977, Sch 8A para 1(8).
para 45	Sch 14 para 4(3)	Amends 1977, Sch 12A para 7(3).
para 83	—	Introductory.
para 84	71(2)–(6); W 30(3), (5)	Amends 1990, s 21.
para 85(a)	44(6), (7)	Extends 1990, Sch 2 para 14 to NHS foundation Trusts.
para 85(b)	Sch 4 para 29(1); W Sch 3 para 29(1)	Amends 1990, Sch 2 para 30(1).
para 85(c)	Sch 4 para 31	Amends 1990, Sch 2 para 32.

Existing provision	Rewritten provision	Remarks
para 108	—	Introductory.
para 109	75(8); W 33(8)	Amends 1999, s 31(8).
para 115	—	Introductory.
para 116	244(2), (3); W 184(2), (3)	Amends 2001, s 7(3), (4).
para 117	134(6); W 92(6)	Amends 2001, s 28(7).
para 118	139(1); W 97(1)	Amends 2001, s 33(1).
para 123	—	Introductory.
para 124	249(1); W 188(1)	Amends 2002, s 23(5).
Sch 5 Audit of accounts of NHS foundation trusts		
para 1	Sch 10 para 1	
para 2	Sch 10 para 2	
para 3	Sch 10 para 3	
para 4	Sch 10 para 4	
para 5	Sch 10 para 5	
para 6	Sch 10 para 6	
para 7	Sch 10 para 7	
para 8(1)	Sch 10 para 8(1)	
para 8(2)	Sch 10 para 8(2)	
para 8(3)	Sch 10 para 8(3)	
Sch 9 Part 2: Minor and consequential amendments		
para 9	248(2); W 187(2)	Inserts 1977, s 19A(2)(aa).
Sch 11 Part 4: Minor and consequential amendments		
para 7	—	Introductory.
para 8	3(2); W 3(2)	Inserts 1977, s 3(4).
para 9	22; W 15	Amends 1977, s 15(1).
para 10	W 12(3)	Amends 1977, s 16BB(4).
para 12	21(3)	Amends and repeals in part 1977, s 18A(3).
para 13	80(5), (7); W 38(5), (7)	Amends 1977, s 26(2), (4).
para 14	92, 107; W 50, W 64	Amends 1977, s 28C.

Existing provision	Rewritten provision	Remarks
para 15	93(1), (3), 108(1), (3); W 51(1), (3), W 65(1), (3)	Amends 1977, s 28D.
para 16	95(1), 110(1)	Amends 1977, s 28EE.
para 18	126(3); W 80(3)	Amends 1977, s 41.
para 19	132(1); W 86(1)	Amends 1977, s 43.
para 20	150(2); W 106(2)	Amends 1977, s 43D.
para 21	W 78(1), W 90(1)	Amends 1977, s 44.
para 22	167(12), (13); W 78(4)–(9), W 90(4)–(9)	Amends 1977, s 45. Repealed in part PCO 2006.
para 23	97, 113; W 54, W 69	Inserts 1977, s 45A, s 45B.
para 24	159(1); W 115(1)	Amends 1977.49N(1).
para 25	—	Repeals 1977, s 53.
para 26	259	Amends 1977, s 54.
para 27	267(5), (6); W 198(5), (6)	Amends 1977, s 72(5), (6).
para 28	172(3); W 121(3)	Inserts 1977, s 77(4).
para 29	—	Amends 1977, s 78(3). Unnecessary.
para 30	188(1); W 136(1)	Amends 1977, s 83.
para 31	182; W 130	Amends 1977, s 83A.
para 32	—	Repeals in part 1977, s 85(1).
para 35	170(1), Sch 19 para 8; W Sch 13 para 8	Amends 1977, s 100(1). Repeals 1977, s 100(1)(e).

Existing provision	Rewritten provision	Remarks
para 36	234(1); W 180(1)	Amends 1977, s 103(1). Repeals in part 1977, s 103(1).
para 37	236(2); W 181(2)	Amends 1977, s 105(2).
para 39	275(1); W 206(1)	Amends 1977, s 128(1).
para 40	W Sch 10 para 3(1), (2)	Amends 1977, Sch 7A para 3.
para 41	Sch 12 para 1(4); W Sch 7 para 1(4)	Amends 1977, Sch 8A para 1(5).
para 42(1)	—	Introductory.
para 42(2)	Sch 13 para 6(2)	Amends 1977, Sch 9A para 6.
para 42(3)	—	Unnecessary.
para 42(4)	Sch 13 para 10(1), (2)	Amends 1977, Sch 9A para 10.
para 42(5)	Sch 13 para 17	Amends 1977, Sch 9A para 17.
para 43	Sch 21 para 4	Amends 1977, Sch 10, para 3.
para 44	173(1); W 122(1)	Amends 1977, Sch 12, para 1(1).
para 45	Sch 14 para 1(2), 2(2); W Sch 8 paras 1(2), 2(1), (2)	Amends 1977 Sch 12A.
para 69	—	Introductory.
para 70	—	Repeals 2001, s 18.
para 71	134(4); W 92(4)	Amends 2001, s 28(4).
para 72(1)	—	Introductory.
para 72(2)	Sch 17 para, 12, 13(1); W Sch 11 para, 12, 13(1)	Substitutes 2001, Sch 1 para 11.
para 72(3)	Sch 17 para 14; W Sch 11 para 14	Amends 2001, Sch 1 para 13.
para 73	Sch 11 para 5(2); W Sch 6 para 5(2)	
para 74(1)	—	Introductory.
para 74(2)	239(1)	Amends 2002, s 17(1).
para 74(3)	239(2)	Amends 2002, s 17(2).

Sch 13 Amendments consequential on the abolition of the Public Health Laboratory Service Board

para 4(a)	—	Repeals 1977, s 5(4), (5).
para 4(b)	—	Repeals in part 1977, s 127.

Existing provision	Rewritten provision	Remarks
para 4(c)	—	Repeals 1977, Sch 3.
para 6(a)	—	Repeals 1990, s 4(2)(h).
para 6(b)	—	Repeals 1990, s 21(2)(c).

Criminal Justice Act 2003 (c 44)

Existing provision	Rewritten provision	Remarks
Sch 25 Summary offences no longer punishable with imprisonment		
para 74	Sch 22 paras 9(3), 10(5)	Amends 1977, Sch 11 paras 8(3), 9(4).

Health Protection Agency Act 2004 (c 17)

Existing provision	Rewritten provision	Remarks
Sch 3 Amendments		
para 11(1)	—	Introductory.
para 11(2)	9(4); W 7(4)	Amends 1990, s 4(2).
para 11(3)	71(2); W 30(2)	Amends 1990, s 21(2).

Public Audit (Wales) Act 2004 (c 23)

Existing provision	Rewritten provision	Remarks
Sch 2 Minor and consequential amendments		
para 14	Sch 4 para 12(2); W Sch 3 para 12(2)	Amends 1990, Sch 2 para 7(2).

Constitutional Reform Act 2005 (c 4)

Existing provision	Rewritten provision	Remarks
Sch 4 Other functions of the Lord Chancellor and organisation of the courts		
para 95	Sch 13 para 5	Amends 1977, Sch 9A para 5.

Public Services Ombudsman (Wales) Act 2005 (c 10)

Existing provision	Rewritten provision	Remarks
Sch 6 Consequential amendments		
para 20(1)	—	Introductory.
para 20(2)	248(2); W 187(2)	Amends 1977, s 19A(2).
para 20(3)	248(3); W 187(3)	Substitutes 1977, s 19A(3).

Health Act 2006 (c 28)

Existing provision	Rewritten provision	Remarks
34 Power to charge		
	—	Inserts 1977, ss 42A, 42B.
(1)	131; W 85	
(2)	272(7); W 203(9)	Amends 1977, s 126(4).
35 Applications for provision of pharmaceutical services		
	—	Inserts 1977, s 42(2B), (2C).
	129(4), (5); W 83(4), (5)	
36 Arrangements for dispensing of medicines		
(1)	132(2); W 86(2)	Substitutes 1977, s 43(2).
37 Provision of primary ophthalmic services		
	115, 116	Inserts 1977, ss 16CD, 16CE.
38 General ophthalmic services contracts		
	117–122	Inserts 1977, ss 28WA–28WF.
39 Persons performing primary ophthalmic services		
(1)	—	Introductory.
(2)	123(1)	Inserts 1977, s 28X(2A).
(3)	123(2)	Amends 1977, s 28X(3).
(4)	123(6)	Inserts 1977, s 28X(6A).
(5)	—	Unnecessary.
40 Assistance and support		
(1)	—	Introductory.
(2)	96(1), 112(1), 124(1)	Amends 1977, s 28Y(1).
(3)	96(2), 112(2)	Amends 1977, s 28Y(1).
41 Local Optical Committees		
	125	Inserts 1977, s 45C.
42 Payments in respect of optical appliances		
(1)	—	Introductory.
(2)	180(2); W 129(2)	Amends 1977, Sch 12
(3)	181	Inserts 1977, Sch 12 para 2B. Amended PCO 2006, Sch 1 Pt 2 para 15.
44 Compulsory disclosure of documents for purposes of counter fraud or security management functions		
(1)	195(1); W 143(1)	
(2)	195(2); W 143(2)	
(3)	195(3)	

Existing provision	Rewritten provision	Remarks
(4)	195(4); W 143(3)	
(5)	195(5); W 143(4)	
45 Meaning of 'NHS body' etc.		
(1)	196(1); W 144(1)	
(2)	196(2); W 144(2)	
(3)	196(3)	
(4)	196(4); W 144(3)	
(5)	196(5); W 144(4)	
(6)	196(6); W 144(5)	
(7)	196(7); W 144(6)	
46 Notice requiring production of documents		
(1)	197(1); W 145(1)	
(2)	197(2); W 145(2)	
(3)	197(3); W 145(3)	
(4)	197(4); W 145(4)	
(5)	197(5); W 145(5)	
(6)	197(6); W 145(6)	
(7)	197(7); W 145(7)	
(8)	197(8); W 145(8)	

Existing provision	Rewritten provision	Remarks
(9)	197(9); W 145(9)	
(10)	197(10); W 145(10)	
47 Production of documents		
(1)	198(1); W 146(1)	
(2)	198(2); W 146(2)	
(3)	198(3); W 146(3)	
(4)	198(4); W 146(4)	
(5)	198(5); W 146(5)	
(6)	198(6); W 146(6)	
(7)	198(7); W 146(7)	
(8)	198(8); W 146(8)	
48 Delegation of functions		
(1)	199(1); W 147(1)	
(2)	199(2), (3); W 147(2), (3)	
(3)	273(4); W 204(3)	
(4)	199(4); W 147(4)	
(5)	199(5); W 147(5)	
(6)	199(1); W 147(1)	
49 Code of practice relating to delegated functions		

Existing provision	Rewritten provision	Remarks
(1)	200(1); W 148(1)	
(2)	200(2); W 148(2)	
(3)	200(3); W 148(3)	
(4)	200(4); W 148(4)	
(5)	200(5); W 148(5)	
(6)	200(6); W 148(6)	
(7)	200(7); W 148(7)	
(8)	200(8); W 148(8)	

50 Disclosure of information

(1)	201(1); W 149(1)	
(2)	201(2); W 149(2)	
(3)	201(3); W 149(3)	
(4)	201(4); W 149(4)	
(5)	201(5); W 149(5)	
(6)	201(6); W 149(6)	
(7)	201(7); W 149(7)	

51 Protection of personal information disclosed for purposes of proceedings

(1)	202(1); W 150(1)	

Existing provision	Rewritten provision	Remarks
(2)	202(2); W 150(2)	
(3)	202(3); W 150(3)	
(4)	202(4); W 150(4)	
(5)	202(5); W 150(5)	
(6)	202(6); W 150(6)	
(7)	202(7); W 150(7)	
(8)	202(8); W 150(8)	
(9)	202(9); W 150(9)	
52 Offences in connection with production of documents		
(1)	204(1); W 152(1)	
(2)	204(2); W 152(2)	
(3)	204(3); W 152(3)	
(4)	204(4), (5); W 152(4), (5)	
(5)	204(6); W 152(6)	
53 Offences relating to disclosure or use of information		
(1)	205(1); W 153(1)	
(2)	205(2); W 153(2)	
(3)	205(3); W 153(3)	

Existing provision	Rewritten provision	Remarks
(4)	205(4); W 153(4)	
(5)	205(5); W 153(5)	

54 Manner in which disclosure notice may be serviced

(1)	203(1); W 151(1)	
(2)	203(2); W 151(2)	
(3)	203(3); W 151(3)	

55 Interpretation

(1)	210(1); W 158(1)	
(2)	—	Unnecessary.
(3)	210(2); W 158(2)	
(4)	210(4); W 158(4)	
(5)	210(5); W 158(5)	

56 Accounts and audit

(1)	232; W 178	
(2)	Sch 15; W Sch 9	Inserts 1977, Sch 12B.

74 Transfer of criminal liabilities of certain NHS bodies

(1)	13(8), (9)	Inserts 1977, s 8(9), (10).
(2)	28(5), (6); W 22(5), (6)	Inserts 1977, s 11(4A), (4B).
(3)	Sch 3 para 23(2)	Inserts 1977, Sch 5A para 20(1A).
(4)	W Sch 2 para 21(2)	Inserts 1977, Sch 5B para 19(1A).
(5)	Sch 4 para 29(2); W Sch 3 para 29(2)	Inserts 1990, Sch 2 para 30(1A).
(6)	54(5)	Inserts 2003, s 25(3A).
(7)	57(4)	Inserts 2003, s 28(3A).

78 Penalties for offences: transitional modifications

Existing provision	*Rewritten provision*	*Remarks*
(3)	208(2); W 156(2)	
Sch 3 New Sch 12B to the 1977 Act		
	Sch 15; W Sch 9	Inserts 1977, Sch 12B.
Sch 8 Minor and consequential amendments		
para 6	—	Introductory.
para 7(1)	—	Introductory.
para 7(2)	3(1); W 3(1)	Amends 1977, s 3(1).
para 7(3)	3(3); W 3(3)	Amends 1977, s 3(3).
para 7(4)	3(2)	Amends 1977, s 3(4).
para 8	22; W 15	Amends 1977, s 15(1).
para 9	21(3)	Amends 1977, s 18A(3).
para 10	W 190(2)	Amends 1977, s 19(1).
para 11	80(5), (7)	Amends 1977, s 26.
para 12	W 71(1)	Amends 1977, s 38(1).
para 13(1)	—	Introductory.
para 13(2)	—	Repeals in part 1977, s 39(1).
para 13(3)	W 72(1)	Amends 1977, s 39(1).
para 13(4)	W 72(1), (3)	Amends 1977, s 39(1) and (2).
para 13(5)	—	Repeals in part 1977, s 39(1)–(2).
para 13(6)	—	Repeals in part 1977, s 39(3).
para 14	126(4); W 80(4)	Amends 1977, s 41(3).
para 15	149(1)	Amends 1977, s 43D(1).
para 16	—	Repeals in part 1977, s 44(B2).
para 17	97(2), (3)	Amends 1977, s 45A(2), (3).
para 18	W 107(1)	Amends 1977, s 49F(1).
para 19	W 109(1)	Amends 1977, s 49H(1).
para 20	—	Repeals in part 1977, s 49N(4).
para 21(a)	W 198(5)	Amends 1977, s 72(5).
para 21(b)	267(5)	Amends 1977, s 72(5).
para 22	234(1)	Amends 1977, s 103(1).
para 24	275(1); W 206(1)	Amends 1977, s 128(1).
para 25	Sch 13 para 6(1)	Amends 1977, Sch 9A para 6(c).
para 29(1)	—	Introductory.
para 29(2)	11(1), (2); W 9(1), (2)	Amends 1990, s 4A(1).
para 29(3)	W 9(4)	Amends 1990, s 4A(3)

Existing provision	Rewritten provision	Remarks
para 34	—	See National Health Service (Consequential Provisions) Act 2006, Sch 1 paras 167, 293.
para 36(1)	—	Introductory.
para 36(2)	70(1); W 29(1)	Amends National Health Service (Residual Liabilities) Act 1996 (c 15) s 1(1).
para 36(3)	70(2); W 29(2)	Amends National Health Service (Residual Liabilities) Act 1996 (c 15) s 1(2).
para 44(5)	—	See National Health Service (Consequential Provisions) Act 2006, Sch 1 para 299.
para 46	Sch 17 paras 12, 13(1); W Sch 11 paras 12, 13(1)	Substitutes 2001, Sch 1 para 11(a).
para 50	239(1), (2)	Amends 2002, s 17(1).
para 51	—	Repeals 2002, Sch 6 para 6.
para 54	36(4)	Amends 2003, s 7(5).

Family Practitioner Committees (Consequential Modifications) Order 1985 (SI 1985/39)

Existing provision	Rewritten provision	Remarks
art 7 National Health Service Act 1977		
(11)	W 71(1)	Amends 1977, s 38.
(22)	Sch 2 para 9;, Sch 6 para 5; W Sch 5 para 5	Amends 1977, Sch 5 para 12.

Pharmaceutical Qualifications (EEC Recognition) Order 1987 (SI 1987/2202)

Existing provision	Rewritten provision	Remarks
art 4 National Health Service Act 1977		
	129(6); W 83(6)	Amends 1977, s 42.

Health and Personal Social Services (Northern Ireland Consequential Amendments) Order 1991 (SI 1991/195)

Existing provision	Rewritten provision	Remarks
art 7 Amendment of the National Health Service and Community Care Act 1990		
(1)	—	Introductory.
(3)	9(4); W 7(4)	Amends 1990, s 4(2).
(4)	—	Repeals in part 1990, s 4(9).
(5)	10(1), (2); W 8(1), (2)	Inserts 1990, s 4(10).
(9)	—	Spent.

Housing Act 1996 (Consequential Provisions) Order 1996 (SI 1996/2325)

Existing provision	Rewritten provision	Remarks
Sch 2 Consequential amendments		
para 9(2)	256(2); W 194(2)	Substitutes 1977, s 28A(2)(e)(i).
para 9(3)	W 196(2)	Substitutes 1977, s 28B(1)(b)(i).

Health Act 1999 (Supplementary, Consequential etc Provisions) Order 2000 (SI 2000/90)

Existing provision	Rewritten provision	Remarks
Sch 1 Consequential amendments coming into force on 8 February 2000		
para 13(1)	—	Introductory.
para 13(2)	12(4); W 10(4)	Amends 1977, s 23(2).
para 13(3)	185(2), 186(2)	Amends 1977, s 81, 82.
para 13(4)	188(2)	Amends 1977, s 83.
para 13(5)	183	Amends 1977, s 83A.
para 13(7)	69(1)	Amends 1977, s 125.

Financial Services and Markets Act 2000 (Consequential Amendments and Repeals) Order 2001 (SI 2001/3649)

Existing provision	Rewritten provision	Remarks
art 319 Schemes for meeting losses and liabilities of certain health service bodies		
	71(8); W 30(7)	Substitutes 1990, s 21(5).

Nursing and Midwifery Order 2001 (SI 2002/253)

Existing provision	Rewritten provision	Remarks
Sch 5 Consequential amendments to primary legislation		
para 6	—	Amends 1977, s 41 (subsequently substituted 2001, s 42(1)).

National Health Service Reform and Health Care Professions Act 2002 (Supplementary, Consequential etc Provisions) Regulations 2002 (SI 2002/2469)

Existing provision	Rewritten provision	Remarks
Sch 1 Amendments consequential on Pt 1 of the National Health Service Reform and Health Care Professions Act 2002		
para 21	70(1), (2); W 29(2)	Amends National Health Service (Residual Liabilities) Act 1996 (c 15) s 1.
para 30	129(6)	Amends 1977, s 42(3).

National Health Service Act 1977 and National Health Service and Community
Care Act 1990 (Amendment) Regulations 2002 (SI 2002/2759)

Existing provision	Rewritten provision	Remarks
reg 1 Citation, commencement and extent		
	—	Spent.
reg 2 Interpretation		
	—	Spent.
reg 3 Amendment of the 1977 Act		
(1)	6(1); W 6(1)	Inserts 1977, s 3(1A).
(2)	—	Repeals 1977, s 5(2)(b).
reg 4 Amendment of the 1990 Act		
	Sch 4 para 21; W Sch 3 para 21	Inserts 1990, Sch 2 para 15A.

Health, Social Care and Well-being Strategies (Wales) Regulations 2003
(SI 2003/154)

Existing provision	Rewritten provision	Remarks
Schedule		
para 5	—	Introductory.
para 6	W 17(1)	Amends 1999, s 28(1).
para 7	W 17(2)	Amends 1999, s 28(2).
para 8	W 17(3)	Amends 1999, s 28(3).
para 9	W 17(4)	Amends 1999, s 28(4).
para 10	W 17(4)	Amends 1999, s 28(4).
para 11	W 17(5)	Amends 1999, s 28(5).
para 12	W 17(6)	Amends 1999, s 28(6).
para 13	24(5); W 17(6)	Amends 1999, s 28(6).
para 14	24(5); W 17(6)	Amends 1999, s 28(6).
para 15	W 17(7)	Amends 1999, s 28(7).
para 16	W 17(8)	Amends 1999, s 28(8).
para 17	W 17(8)	Amends 1999, s 28(8).
para 18	W 17(8)	Amends 1999, s 28(8).
para 19	—	Unnecessary.

General and Specialist Medical Practice (Education, Training and Qualifications)
Order 2003 (SI 2003/1250)

Existing provision	Rewritten provision	Remarks
Sch 9 Consequential amendments to primary legislation		
para 2	—	Repeals in part 1977, ss 102, 126.
para 6(c)(i)	—	Repeals 1977, s 28E(6) (by repealing in part 1997, s 22(1)). 1977, s 28E(6) subsequently repealed 2003, Sch 14 Pt 4.

Health Professions Order 2001 (Consequential Amendments) Order 2003 (SI 2003/1590)

Existing provision	Rewritten provision	Remarks
Schedule Consequential amendments to primary legislation and secondary legislation		
para 3	126(4); W 80(4)	Amends 1977, s 41(3).

National Health Service Reform and Health Care Professions Act 2002 (Supplementary, Consequential etc Provisions) Regulations 2003 (SI 2003/1937)

Existing provision	Rewritten provision	Remarks
Schedule Amendments consequential on Pt 1 of the National Health Service Reform and Health Care Professions Act 2002		
para 1	Sch 3 para 16(1)	Amends 1977, Sch 5A para 13(1).

Primary Medical Services (Scotland) Act 2004 (Consequential Modifications) Order 2004 (SI 2004/957)

Existing provision	Rewritten provision	Remarks
Schedule Modification of public general Acts		
para 3	93(1), 108(1); W 51(1), W 65(1)	Amends 1977, s 28D.

Health Act 1999 (Consequential Amendments) (Nursing and Midwifery) Order 2004 (SI 2004/1771)

Existing provision	Rewritten provision	Remarks
Schdule Consequential amendments to primary legislation		
para 8	126(4); W 80(4)	Amends 1977, s 41(3).

Health and Social Care (Community Health and Standards) Act 2003 (Commission for Healthcare Audit and Inspection and Commission for Social Care Inspection) (Consequential Provisions) Order 2004 (SI 2004/2987)

Existing provision	Rewritten provision	Remarks
art 2 Consequential amendments, repeals and revocations		
(1)(c)	9(4), 71(2); W 7(4), W 30(2)	Substitutes 1990, ss 4(2)(ff), 21(2)(bb).
(1)(d)	243(7)	Substitutes 2002, s 20(7)(b).

Opticians Act 1989 (Amendment) Order 2005 (SI 2005/848)

Existing provision	Rewritten provision	Remarks
Sch 1 Minor and consequential amendments		

Existing provision	Rewritten provision	Remarks
para 9	275(1); W 206(1)	Amends 1977, s 128(1).

Dentists Act 1984 (Amendment) Order 2005 (SI 2005/2011))

Existing provision	Rewritten provision	Remarks
Sch 6 Minor and consequential amendments		
para 1(1)	—	Introductory.
para 1(2)	—	Spent.
para 1(3)	126(4); W 80(4)	Amends 1977, s 41(3).
para 1(4)	Sch 2 para 7(9)–(11), Sch 6 para 3(9)–(11); W Sch 5 para 3(9)–(11)	Amends 1977, Sch 5 para 10.
para 1(5)	Sch 3 para 10	Substitutes 1977, Sch 5A para 10A.

Freedom of Information (Removal and Relaxation of Statutory Prohibitions on Disclosure of Information) Order 2004 (SI 2004/3363)

Existing provision	Rewritten provision	Remarks
art 7 National Health Service Act 1977		
	Sch 22 para 6	Inserts 1977, Sch 11 para 5A.

Smoking, Health and Social Care (Scotland) Act 2005 (Consequential Modifications) (England, Wales and Northern Ireland) Order 2006 (SI 2006/1056)

Existing provision	Rewritten provision	Remarks
Schedule Minor and consequential amendments		
para 3	128(2); W 82(2)	Amends 1977, s 41B.
para 5(a)	11(1); W 9(1)	Amends 1990, s 4A(1).
para 5(b)	—	Repeals in part 1990, s 4A(3).
para 5(c)	11(5); W 9(5)	Inserts 1990, s 4A(4).

National Health Service (Pre-consolidation Amendments) Order 2006 (SI 2006/1407)

Existing provision	Rewritten provision	Remarks
art 1 Citation, commencement and application		
	—	Spent.
art 2 Amendments of the legislation relating to the health service in England and Wales		
	—	Spent.
art 3 Repeals and revocations of legislation relating to the health service in England and Wales		
	—	Spent.

Existing provision	Rewritten provision	Remarks
art 4 Saving		
	—	Saved, see National Health Service (Consequential Provisions) Act 2006, Sch 2 para 13.
art 5 National Assembly for Wales (Transfer of Functions) Order 1999		
	—	Spent.
Sch 1 Part 1 Amendments to the National Health Service Act 1977		
para 1	—	Introductory.
para 2	3(1); W 3(1)	Amends 1977, s 3(1).
para 3	22; W 15	Amends 1977, s 15(1)(a).
para 4	—	Repeals in part 1977, s 16(1).
para 5	W 13(1)	Amends 1977, s 16BC(1).
para 6	—	Repeals in part 1977, s 16D
para 7	—	Repeals 1977, s 17(2)(a).
para 8	—	Repeals in part 1977, s 18(3)(b).
para 9	254(2); W 192(2)	Inserts 1977, s 21(4).
para 10	—	Repeals 1977, ss 23(4), 27(5).
para 11	80; W 38	Amends 1977, s 26.
para 12	—	Repeals in part 1977, s 28A(2)(b).
para 13	108(3); W 65(3)	Amends 1977, s 28D(2).
para 14	110(1)	Amends 1977, s 28EE(2).
para 15	98, 114, 168; W 55, W 70	Substitutes 1977, s 28I.
para 16	102(4); W 59(4)	Amends 1977, s 28M(4).
para 17	146	Amends 1977, s 28X.
para 18	147	Amends 1977, s 28Y(1).
para 19	164; W 76, W 88	Substitutes 1977, ss 43A, 43B.
para 20	167	Amends 1977, s 44.
para 21	167(6)	Amends 1977, s 45.
para 22	153(1); W 109(1)	Amends 1977, s 49H(1)(b).

Existing provision	Rewritten provision	Remarks
para 23	183; W 131	Amends 1977, s 83A(1).
para 24	68; W 28	Amends 1977, s 85(1).
para 25	253; W 191	Amends 1977, s 86.
para 26	—	Repeals 1977, s 89.
para 27	217(1); W 165(1)	Inserts 1977, s 96(4).
para 28	—	Repeals 1977, s 99.
para 29	170, Sch 19 para 10	Amends and Repeals in part 1977, s 100.
para 30	—	Repeals in part 1977, s 102.
para 31	234	Amends 1977, s 103(1).
para 32	—	Repeals in part 1977, s 123(2).
para 33	269(5); W 200(5)	Amends 1977, s 124(4).
para 34	69	Amends 1977, s 125.
para 35	272(7); W 203(9)	Amends 1977, s 126(4).
para 36	—	Repeals 1977, s 126(4A) (both provisions).
para 37	—	Repeals 1977, s 127(c).
para 38	256(9), 275(1); W 194(9), W 206(1)	Amends 1977, s 128.
para 39	Sch 2, Sch 6; W Sch 5	Amends 1977, Sch 5.
para 40	Sch 13 para 6	Amends 1977, Sch 9A.
para 41	Sch 22 para 3	Amends 1977, Sch 11.
para 42	173, 179, 180; W 122, W 128, W 129	Amends 1977, Sch 12.

Sch 1 Part 2 Amendments to other legislation relating to the health service

para 1	—	Repeals the Ministry of Health Act 1919.
para 2	—	Repeals 1990, s 3.
para 3	—	Provides for the commencement of certain provisions of 1997.
para 4	—	Repeals in part 1997, s 40(2).

Existing provision	Rewritten provision	Remarks
para 5	24(8); W 17(9)	Amends 1999, s 28(10).
para 6	—	Provides for the commencement of certain provisions of 1999.
para 7	145(3); W 103(3)	Inserts 2001, s 41(2A).
para 8	—	Provides for the commencement of certain provisions of 2001.
para 9	—	Repeals in part 2002, s 38(11).
para 10	—	Repeals 2002, Sch 3 para 9.
para 11	—	Repeals 2002, Sch 6 para 11(3).
para 12	—	Provides for the commencement of certain provisions of 2002.
para 13	—	Provides for the commencement of certain provisions of 2003.
para 14	64(6)	Amends 2003, s 195(2).
para 15	181(9)	Amends 2006, s 41(3).
Sch 2 Repeals		
	—	Spent.

2039　National Health Service (Wales) Act 2006

The National Health Service (Wales) Act 2006 consolidates certain enactments relating to the health service. The Act received the royal assent on 8 November 2006 and comes into force, with certain exceptions, on 1 March 2007. For details of commencement, see the commencement table in the title STATUTES.

2040　NHS Redress Act 2006

The NHS Redress Act 2006 makes provision about arrangements for redress in relation to liability in tort in connection with services provided as part of the health service in England and Wales. The Act received the royal assent on 8 November 2006 and came into force in part on that day. The remaining provisions come into force on a day or days to be appointed. For details of commencement, see the commencement table in the title STATUTES.

Section 1 empowers the Secretary of State to establish redress schemes, which apply only to cases involving liability in tort arising out of qualifying services provided as part of the NHS in England, whether provided in England, in another part of the United Kingdom or abroad. Section 2 provides that a scheme may make provisions defining the cases to which it applies, and s 3 sets out in more detail the type of provision that the Secretary of State may make in respect of a scheme, and includes some provisions that the Secretary of State must make. A scheme may include such provision as the Secretary of State thinks fit about how proceedings under the scheme are to be started: s 4. Under s 5, the Secretary of State can by regulations make provision as to how and when particular bodies or persons must consider whether a case is eligible under the redress scheme, and the steps that it must take if it identifies such a case. Section 6 specifies certain provisions that a scheme must contain and further provisions which a scheme may make in relation to sets proceedings under the scheme. A scheme must provide for the period of time when a case is being considered to be disregarded when calculating whether any time limit for bringing court proceedings has expired: s 7. Section 8 enables a scheme to make provision for free legal advice to be provided to individuals seeking redress under the scheme. By virtue of s 9, the Secretary of State is required to arrange, to such extent as he considers necessary, for the provision of assistance to individuals seeking redress, or intending to seek redress, under a scheme. Section 10 provides that a scheme may make provision about membership of the scheme and the functions of members. Section 11 requires the Secretary of State to make provision in a scheme as to the functions of the scheme authority. A general duty to promote resolution under the scheme is imposed by s 12, and a duty of co-operation between the scheme authority and the Healthcare Commission, and the scheme authority and the National Patient Safety Agency is established under s 13. Section 14 enables the Secretary of State to make regulations providing for the handling of complaints about maladministration in the exercise of functions under, or relating to proceedings under a scheme, or about maladministration in connection with settlement agreements under a scheme. Section 15 broadens the remit of the Health Service

Commissioner for England to include complaints relating to maladministration in relation to the exercise of functions under the scheme, in connection with a settlement agreement under the scheme or in the exercise of any functions in relation to complaints made under regulations under s 14. Section 16 makes further provision about the Secretary of State's regulation-making powers under the Act, and s 17 gives the National Assembly for Wales a broad power to make regulations establishing arrangements for redress in respect of Wales. Section 18 provides for interpretation and s 19 deals with short title, commencement and extent.

Amendments, repeals and revocations
The list below, which is not exhaustive, mentions amendments which are or will be effective when the Act if fully in force.

Specific provisions of the Health Service Commissioners Act 1993 are amended. These include ss 3(1F), 4, 7, 11, 12, 14(2G), (2H).

2041   Pension scheme—compensation for premature retirement

The National Health Service (Pension Scheme and Compensation for Premature Retirement) Amendment Regulations 2006, SI 2006/2919 (in force on 1 December 2006), further amend the National Health Service Pension Scheme Regulations 1995, SI 1995/300, so as to (1) add references in various provisions in relation to the provision for early retirement pension and the termination of employment by the employing authority; (2) replace the early retirement pension provisions which deal with (a) members who are made redundant before 1 October 2011; (b) members whose pensionable employment is terminated by their employing authority, whether before or after that date; (c) a member's notification as to whether he wishes specified provisions to apply to him; (d) special provisions for special classes; and (e) the right of a member who is entitled to a specified pension to claim a pension under certain provisions. The regulations also amend the National health Service (Compensation for Premature Retirement) Regulations 2002, SI 2002/1311, in relation to (i) the persons to whom the regulations apply; and (ii) the crediting of an additional period of service, in respect of the calculation of additional periods of service for those who are made redundant on or after 1 December 2006 but before 1 July 2007, and those who are made redundant on or after 1 July 2007 but before 1 October 2011.

2042   Pension scheme—entitlement and additional voluntary contributions

The National Health Service (Pension Scheme, Injury Benefits and Additional Voluntary Contributions) Amendment Regulations 2006, SI 2006/600 (in force in part on 1 April 2006 and in part on 6 April 2006), further amend the National Health Service Pension Scheme Regulations 1995, SI 1995/300, so as to (1) add various definitions relating to the types of dental services provided, and the persons or bodies who provide them; (2) replace certain references to dental pilot scheme employees by a reference to employees of new contractors; (3) revise the definition of 'personal pension scheme' to take into account the change in status of such schemes to registered schemes; (4) provide that, in relation to the early retirement pension (ill-health) provision, any lump sum payment is consistent with the Pension Schemes Act 1993 provisions, and provide for the calculation of such a lump sum; (5) in relation to the early retirement pensions provisions, refer to those who are to have the normal retirement pension age of 55 or, where provided for under the Finance Act 2004, a lower protected pension age; (6) provide that, where a member of the National Health Service Pension Scheme has attained the age of 75, he is no longer entitled to a lump sum but instead has his pension increased in lieu of thet lump sum; (7) provide that, in relation to a member dying after the pension becomes payable, a member may notify the Scheme administrator that he wishes a lump sum to be treated as a pension protection lump sum death benefit; (8) provide that, in certain cases, the dependent child provision refers to a child aged 17 years or over but who has not reached the age of 23; (9) require a member of the Scheme who wishes to allocate part of his pension to another person to do so before the date on which the pension becomes payable to him; (10) provide that the preserved pension provision refers to a normal minimum pension age or, where the 2004 Act provides, a protected pension age; (11) provide that a member of the Scheme who becomes entitled to a refund of his contributions is to receive a lump sum tax at 20 per cent on such part of that sum which does not exceed £10,800 and at 40 per cent on such part of that sum which exceeds that limit; (12) provide that a member of the Scheme may, within 12 months of joining the Scheme, request the Secretary of State to accept a transfer payment in respect of his rights under other schemes except rights under a free-standing additional voluntary contribution scheme; (13) replace references to a health authority with references to a local health board; (14) add a provision relating to the deduction of tax; (15) provide that any commutation of trivial pensions must be consistent with the lump sum and lump sum death benefit rules provided for in the Finance Act 2004; (16) provide for the change in terminology from 'principal practitioners' to 'type 1 medical practitioners'; (17) give effect to changes, in relation to medical and dental practitioners, required by the introduction of the general dental contract; and (18) provide that, in relation to pension sharing on divorce or nullity of marriage or, on the dissolution or nullity of a civil partnership, any pension credit benefit which is to be commuted has to satisfy the requirements of the 2004 Act in respect of trivial commutation of lump sums. The regulations also further amend the

National Health Service (Injury Benefits) Regulations 1995, SI 1995/866, so as to give effect to changes required by the introduction of the general dental contract, and provide that the local health board or primary care trust is responsible for the costs of providing injury benefits to practitioners. The regulations also further amend the National Health Service Pension Scheme (Additional Voluntary Contributions) Regulations 2000, SI 2000/619, so as to (a) provide that the investments of an additional voluntary contribution scheme may be realised to provide for either an annuity or a pension commencement lump sum or a lump sum and an annuity on retirement; (b) enable a person to make contributions to an additional voluntary contribution scheme which do not exceed 100 per cent of his salary; (c) provide that a person who has paid contributions to a registered additional voluntary contribution scheme can give notice to the Secretary of State saying that he wishes the Secretary of State to accept a transfer from that scheme; (d) provide that a lump sum payable on death cannot exceed the limits set out in the 2004 Act; (e) clarify that any benefits paid are limited by reference to the person's lifetime allowance; (f) impose an obligation on a person who wishes to take advantage of an entitlement to an enhanced lifetime allowance to provide the additional voluntary contributions provider with certain information; (g) clarify that benefits are paid net of tax and that benefit limits are now subject to the 2004 Act; and (h) reflect the fact that an additional voluntary contribution investment, in relation to pension sharing on divorce or nullity of marriage or, on dissolution or nullity of civil partnership, may be realised so as to provide a pension commencement lump sum, and to allow for a percentage of the proceeds of any investment specified in a notice of election to be used in that manner.

2043   Pharmaceutical services—fees and charges—Wales

The National Health Service (Pharmaceutical Services) (Amendment) (Wales) Regulations 2006, SI 2006/2985 (in force on 16 November 2006), further amend the 1992 Regulations, SI 1992/662, so as to make provision in respect of fees and charges payable to a doctor who is authorised or required to provide drugs or appliances under pharmaceutical services or provides any additional service associated with the dispensing of such drugs and appliances.

2044   Pharmaceutical services—local services—England

The National Health Service (Local Pharmaceutical Services etc) Regulations 2006, SI 2006/552 (in force on 1 April 2006), govern the arrangements for the provision of local pharmaceutical services in England under agreements, known as LPS schemes, between primary care trusts, which commission the services, and independent contractors, which provide them. Such schemes must be made in accordance with the provisions of the regulations and of the National Health Service Act 1977 Sch 8A. In particular, the regulations (1) provide for the application with modifications of certain provisions of the 1977 Act and the Health Service Commissioners Act 1993 that already deal with arrangements for personal medical or dental services and with local pharmaceutical services pilot schemes so that those provisions apply in relation to LPS schemes in a similar way; (2) deal with designation of priority neighbourhoods or premises, and the review, variation and cancellation of such designations; where a neighbourhood, premises or type of premises are designated, primary care trusts may defer consideration of applications for inclusion in a pharmaceutical list in relation to the same neighbourhood or premises, and, notice of designations, and of the variation and cancellation of designations, has to be given to interested parties; (3) set out the general requirements in relation to contractors; specified categories of individuals, partnerships and companies are prevented from entering into LPS schemes and if the primary care trust determines that an applicant falls within one of those categories, the applicant has a right to the reasons for that determination and a right of appeal; contractors are given health service body status, meaning that their contract is an NHS contract, unless they elect otherwise; (4) set out the general requirements in relation to LPS schemes, which include a requirement for certain information relating to the suitability of the applicant to be included in the proposal and requirements as to the terms to be specified including mandatory terms, which relate to such matters as the dispensing arrangements, clinical governance, professional standards, inducements, the provision of information about fitness to practise matters, NHS charges, remuneration, complaints, dispute resolution and termination; the primary care trust must also determine whether any potential contractor is to be given a right of return to its pharmaceutical list; (5) make provision for arrangements which allow primary care trusts to share information that they receive about the suitability of contractors or the fitness to practise of pharmacists under the regulations with other primary care trusts and, where appropriate, the Royal Pharmaceutical Society of Great Britain; and (6) contain transitional and consequential provisions including a duty on former pilot scheme contractors to provide primary care trusts with certain information about their suitability to be a contractor, although some corporate bodies are exempt from this requirement; generally, pilot scheme agreements all become LPS schemes, or for a transitional period, transitional agreements, but pilot schemes that come under the special arrangements for essential small pharmacies will continue as pilot schemes; the pilot schemes that become LPS schemes must, however, be modified so that they comply with the requirements of the regulations.

The National Health Service (Pharmaceutical Services) (Amendment) Regulations 2006, SI 2006/3373 (in force on 19 January 2007), amend the principal regulations supra, by clarifying that notices have to be in writing and making it clear that an LPS scheme must include dispensing services. The regulations also make miscellaneous amendments to the National Health Service (Pharmaceutical Services) Regulations 2005, SI 2005/641.

2045 Pharmaceutical services—suppliers—supplies from listed premises—recovery of overpayments

The respondent chemist supplied the appellant trust with medical and surgical appliances. Payment was made out of public funds at a rate fixed under statutory powers. The rate of payment diminished if the number of appliances supplied from any registered premise exceeded a specified amount. The respondent supplied fewer than the specified number of appliances from several different premises, thereby avoiding payment at the diminished level. The appellant concluded that this practice was an artifice designed to enhance the respondent's income and withheld payment. When the respondent brought proceedings, the respondent claimed that it had a defence of set off in respect of overpayments made over a number of years. The respondent's claim was allowed, and it fell to be determined whether recovery of overpayments was barred unless such overpayments had been established in accordance with the National Health Service (Pharmaceutical Services) Regulations 1992, SI 1992/662, reg 24 and whether, for the purposes of reg 4, goods were supplied 'from' listed premises only if something of substance happened to them there. *Held*, the effect of reg 4 was that a trust which wished to recover overpayments from a pharmaceutical supplier had to either secure a dispensation or take the issue to a disciplinary committee, the decision of which would be binding. To establish that an appliance had been supplied 'from' listed premises for the purposes under reg 4, more was required than transient presence in a building. The word 'from' was not the same as 'through'. Some material contribution to the supply had to be made in the building, such as modification to or preparation of the appliances which it was not reasonable to make at source. However, this was not a matter for the High Court but the disciplinary committee. Accordingly, the appeal would be dismissed.

Central Liverpool Primary Care Trust v Charles S Bullen Stomacare Ltd [2005] EWCA Civ 1514, (2006) 89 BMLR 130 (Court of Appeal: Buxton, Sedley and Parker LJJ).

1992 Regulations regs 4, 24 now National Health Service (Pharmaceutical Services) Regulations 2005, SI 2005/641, regs 4, 57.

2046 Pre-consolidation amendments

The National Health Service (Pre-consolidation Amendments) Order 2006, SI 2006/1407 (in force immediately before the National Health Service Act 2006 comes into force), amends the National Health Service Act 1977 and other health service legislation which facilitate, or are otherwise desirable in connection with, the consolidation of that legislation. The order is revoked by the National Health Service (Consequential Provisions) Act 2006 Sch 4.

2047 Prescriptions—independent prescribing—England

The National Health Service (Miscellaneous Amendments Relating to Independent Prescribing) Regulations 2006, SI 2006/913 (in force on 1 May 2006), (1) amend the National Health Service (Charges for Drugs and Appliances) Regulations 2000, SI 2000/620, so as to take account of the fact that the revised and new categories of independent prescribers may be acting as prescribers in walk-in centres, and possibly issuing repeatable prescriptions; (2) amend the National Health Service (Pharmaceutical Services) Regulations 2005, SI 2005/641, so as to take account of the revised and new categories of prescribers, and in particular, of the possibility that pharmacists will be dispensing against prescriptions, including repeatable prescriptions, issued by them; and (3) amend the National Health Services (Local Pharmaceutical Services etc) Regulations 2006, SI 2006/552, so as to to take account of the terminology that is to be used for annotations in the register maintained by the Nursing and Midwifery Council to describe the qualifications for the various types of independent nurse prescriber.

2048 Primary care trusts—functions—dental public health—England

The Functions of Primary Care Trusts (Dental Public Health) (England) Regulations 2006, SI 2006/185 (in force on 1 April 2006), set out the functions to be exercised by primary care trusts in relation to oral health promotion programmes, dental inspection of pupils in schools maintained by local education authorities and oral health surveys.

2049 Primary care trusts—performers lists—hearings—procedure

Two primary care trusts intended to hold hearings to consider whether they should remove the names of the applicant doctors from their performers lists. The doctors sought judicial review of the manner in which the hearings were to be conducted. *Held*, while the National Health Service (Performers Lists) Regulations 2004, SI 2004/585, did not provide for a right to legal representation, it was not prohibited, and whether representation was necessary depended on the nature of the case. In cases where an important point of primary fact was in dispute between a doctor and a witness, the panel ought to hear and see the witness to assist in their decision-making process. Where cross-examining would materially advance the decision-making process, it would be permissible. Accordingly, the applications would be allowed.

R (on the application of S) v Knowsley NHS Primary Care Trust [2006] EWHC 26 (Admin), (2006) Times, 2 February (Queen's Bench Division: Toulson J).

2050   Primary care trusts—refusal to fund treatment using unlicensed drug—compatibility with guidance of Secretary of State

The claimant was diagnosed with breast cancer and, as part of her treatment, she began taking an unlicensed drug on a private basis. The Secretary of State subsequently issued guidance to the defendant and other primary care trusts, stating that trusts were not to rule out treatment using the drug as a matter of policy, but were to consider each individual case on its merits. The claimant became unable to afford continued treatment with the drug, and applied to the defendant for funding. The defendant decided that the claimant's case contained no exceptional circumstances justifying funding, and rejected her application. The claimant argued that the refusal to fund her treatment was unlawful in view of the Secretary of State's guidance, and also contrary to her rights under the European Convention on Human Rights art 3, which prohibited inhuman or degrading treatment. The claimant's application for judicial review was dismissed and she appealed. *Held*, once the defendant had decided that it would fund the drug for some patients and that cost was irrelevant, the only reasonable approach was to focus on the patient's clinical needs and fund patients within the eligible group who were properly prescribed the drug by their physician. Therefore, the policy adopted by the defendant in the present case was irrational and unlawful. It followed that the decision of the defendant to refuse to fund the claimant's treatment with the drug had to be quashed. The court could not and should not order the defendant to fund treatment. It was a matter for the defendant to reconsider its policy and to formulate a lawful policy on which to base decisions in particular cases, including that of the claimant, in the future.

R (on the application of Rogers) v Swindon NHS Primary Care Trust [2006] EWCA Civ 392, [2006] 1 WLR 2649 (Court of Appeal: Sir Anthony Clarke MR, Brooke and Buxton LJJ). Decision of Bean J [2006] EWHC 171 (Admin), [2006] All ER (D) 180 (Feb) reversed.

2051   Primary medical services—miscellaneous provisions—Wales

The National Health Service (Primary Medical Services) (Miscellaneous Amendments) (Wales) Regulations 2006, SI 2006/358 (in force on 1 March 2006), which apply in relation to Wales only, amend the National Health Service (General Medical Services Contracts) (Wales) Regulations 2004, SI 2004/48, by (1) widening the definition of 'general medical practitioner' to cover all medical practitioners who (a) are included in the general practitioner register; (b) prior to the coming into force of the register, were suitably experienced within the meaning of the National Health Service Act 1977 s 31; or (c) have an acquired right to practise; (2) providing that provisions that relate to a spouse also relate to a civil partner; (3) enabling chiropodists, podiatrists, physiotherapists and radiographers and optometrists to be recognised as supplementary prescribers; (4) restricting the categories of general medical practitioner who can act as the mandatory medical practitioner for the purposes of a general medical services contract, by excluding from that role practitioners who, prior to 1 April 2004, were restricted services principals or who were not considered to be suitably experienced for the purposes of operating as a principal in the provision of general medical services under s 29; (5) banning the use of telephone services for the purposes of general medical services contracts which make use of national rate numbers, premium rate numbers or personal numbers; (6) disapplying the provisions relating to clinical reports in the case of out of hours services; (7) authorising the supply of medicines to patients by providers of out of hours services where certain conditions are met; (8) enabling a contractor's list of patients which has been closed as a result of a determination by an assessment panel to reopen by agreement before the end of the closure period specified by that panel and, in certain circumstances, to re-close again during that period; (8) removing the restrictions preventing supplementary prescribers from prescribing controlled drugs or unlicensed medicines; (9) altering the circumstances in which a GP registrar can perform medical services under a contract without being included in a medical performers' list; (10) remove the requirement for the National Assembly for Wales to consent to the employment of a GP registrar; (11) removing provision relating to the Quality Information Preparation Scheme; (12) imposing a timescale for the provision of information by contractors to the local health board; (13) clarifying the timescale for the submission of annual returns to local health boards; (14) requiring contractors who are companies limited by shares to notify the local health board of a change of director or secretary, and enabling the board to terminate the contract if untrue information is given about the compliance of that director or secretary with certain conditions; (15) disapplying rules relating to the provision of information about complaints in the case of out of hours services which are covered by the quality requirements; (16) enabling a local health board to vary a contract to allow it to continue at least for an interim period after the death of a partner in a two-handed partnership, even where the remaining individual is not a medical practitioner; (17) providing that a contract with an individual medical practitioner must terminate seven days after that practitioner's death unless, before then, arrangements have been made for it to continue for a further short period; (18) enabling a local health board to continue a contract for a limited period with a medical practitioner who no longer meets prescribed conditions if (a) the reason for that failure is an immediate or interim suspension or health suspension under the Medical Act 1983; (b) adequate arrangements are in place to provide clinical services during the period of suspension, and (c) immediate termination is not necessary on grounds of patient safety or to protect public funds; (19) clarifying that the grounds for termination of the contract apply only to partners, shareholders and directors who join the contracting body after the start of the contract in respect of circumstances which arise after they have so joined; and (20) providing that, for the purpose of meeting its obligation of holding adequate insurance, a contractor can rely on insurance held by a person engaged by it as well as by an employee. SI 2004/1020 is also amended.

2052   Primary medical services and pharmaceutical services—miscellaneous provisions— England

The National Health Service (Primary Medical Services and Pharmaceutical Services) (Miscellaneous Amendments) Regulations 2006, SI 2006/1501 (in force on 24 July 2006), further amend the National Health Service (General Medical Services Contracts) Regulations 2004, SI 2004/291, and the National Health Service (Personal Medical Services Agreements) Regulations 2004, SI 2004/627, so as to (1) reflect changes to the arrangements for independent prescribing by pharmacists and nurses; (2) add a new category of prescriber known as a pharmacist independent prescriber; and (3) make provision in respect of a new category of post medical training to provide that doctors undergoing such a programme may perform medical services even though they are not on a primary care trust's performers list and have not provided two clinical references. The regulations also amend the National Health Service (Pharmaceutical Services) Regulations 2005, SI 2005/641 so as to clarify the definition of 'PMS contractor' and to make further provision in respect of fees and charges payable to a dispensing doctor.

2053   Public benefit corporation—register of members

The Public Benefit Corporation (Register of Members) Amendment Regulations 2006, SI 2006/361 (in force on 23 March 2006), amend the 2004 Regulations, SI 2004/539, so as to provide that the relevant part of the register of members, where it provides for a patients' constituency, is not to be available for inspection by members of the public in circumstances where the constituency member has not consented to his details being made available.

2054   Public consultation—failure to consult—proposals for changes in health services

The Health and Social Care Act 2001 s 11(1) provides that it is the duty of specified health bodies to make arrangements with a view to securing, as respects health services for which they are responsible, that persons to whom those services are being or may be provided are, directly or through representatives, involved in and consulted on the planning of the provision of those services, the development and consideration of proposals for changes in the way those services are provided, and decisions to be made by that body affecting the operation of those services.

The defendant NHS trust decided to close the in-patient wards at a hospital without any public consultation. The claimant, a nurse who lived in the area and who had worked at the hospital, applied for judicial review of the defendant's decision on the grounds that the closures were in breach of the 2001 Act s 11. Held, the duty to consult was of high importance. The public would expect to be involved in decisions by healthcare bodies, particularly where the issues involved were contentious. The need to close the wards had not been so urgent that it was right that no consultation should take place. There should have been consultation about the closure of the wards, and without it the decision to close the wards was unlawful and would be quashed. However, it would not be right to order the reopening of the wards. The defendant had accepted that it was right to hold a full public consultation about the closure of the wards, which could be done quickly, but which might legitimately decide to close the wards. Accordingly, the application would be allowed.

R (on the application of Morris) v Trafford Healthcare NHS Trust [2006] EWHC 2334 (Admin), [2006] All ER (D) 107 (Sep) (Queen's Bench Division: Hodge J).

The Health and Social Care Act 2001 s 11(1), (2) provides that it is the duty of every primary care trust to make arrangements with a view to securing, as respects health services for which it is responsible, that persons to whom those services are being or may be provided are, directly or through representatives, involved in and consulted on (1) the planning of the provision of those services; (2) the development and consideration of proposals for changes in the way those services are provided; and (3) decisions to be made by that body affecting the operation of those services.

The claimant applied for judicial review of the defendant's decision to appoint a certain body to provide general practitioner services in two villages, including the village in which the claimant resided. The application was dismissed on the basis that, although the defendant had failed to comply with the consultation requirements prescribed by the 2001 Act s 11, there was an alternative remedy open to the claimant other than judicial review, and it was unlikely that the defendant would have reached a different decision even if the statutory consultations had been carried out. The claimant appealed, restating its case that there had been a failure to perform the s 11 duty. The defendant submitted that s 11 did not apply to a decision to negotiate with the health provider, and that the claimant had had the option of mobilising a patient's forum as an alternative remedy and had failed to so. Held, it was clear that the defendant had a statutory duty to consult with the claimant and other patients and that it had failed to do so. The defendant could not mitigate performance of that duty by relying on the fact that the claimant had had the option of mobilizing a patient's forum. It was not the claimant's duty to do so, nor would it have provided her with a remedy. It was not enough to show that it was probable that the defendant's decision would have remained the same if it had carried out the statutory consultations. The defendant would have had to have shown that its decision would inevitably have been the same. In the instant case it was clear that it could not be said that there might not have been a different preferred bidder if the proper consultation had been made. Accordingly, the appeal would be allowed.

R (on the application of Smith) v North Eastern Derbyshire Primary Care Trust [2006] EWCA Civ 1291, [2006] 1 WLR 3315 (Court of Appeal: May and Keene LJJ). *R v Chief Constable of the Thames Valley Police, ex p Cotton* [1990] IRLR 344, CA; and *R v Secretary of State for the Environment, ex p Brent LBC* [1982] QB 593 considered.

2055 Scope of services—medical care—medical expenses incurred in another member state—entitlement to reimbursement

See Case C-372/04 *R (on the application of Watts) v Bedford Primary Care Trust*, para 2624.

2056 Social security

See SOCIAL SECURITY.

2057 Special health authorities—abolition

The Special Health Authorities Abolition Order 2006, SI 2006/635 (in force on 1 April 2006), abolishes the Counter Fraud and Security Management Service, the Dental Vocational Training Authority, the National Health Service Logistics Authority and the Prescription Pricing Authority. The order also makes provision for the transfer of staff rights, liabilities and property of those authorities to the NHS Business Services Authority. The regulations amend SI 1986/975, 1990/2024, 1996/707, 708, 1997/980, 2000/704, 2002/881, 2375, 2469, 2861, 2003/172, 1324, 3171, 3172, 2004/585, 696, 865, 1119, 1771, 2005/249, 251, 480 and 848. SI 1990/1718, 1719, 1991/2002, 1993/2210, 1995/2457, 2000/603 and 2002/3040 are revoked.

2058 Special health authorities—audit

The Special Health Authorities (Audit) Order 2006, SI 2006/960 (in force on 30 March 2006), (1) makes the Comptroller and Auditor General the auditor of the accounts of the Health and Social Care Information Centre, NHS Blood and Transplant, NHS Business Services Authority, and the NHS Institute for Innovation and Improvement; (2) require, under the National Health Service Act 1977 s 98(1C), that the bodies listed under head (1) supra lay its accounts before Parliament together with the Comptroller and Auditor General's report on the accounts.

2059 Special health authorities—investigation

The Health Service Commissioner for England (Special Health Authorities) Order 2006, SI 2006/305 (in force on 1 April 2006), designates the special health authority, the NHS Business Services Authority (Awdurdod Gwasanaethau Busnes y GIG), as a health service body subject to investigation by the Health Service Commissioner under the Health Service Commissioners Act 1993 s 2.

The Health Service Commissioner for England (Special Health Authorities) (Revocation) Order 2006, SI 2006/3332 (in force on 22 January 2007), revokes the Health Service Commissioner for England (Rural Dispensing Committee) Order 1983, SI 1983/1115, the Health Service Commissioner for England (National Blood Authority) Order 1994, SI 1994/2954, and the Health Service Commissioner for England (Special Health Authorities) Order 2004, SI 2004/1119, thereby removing the United Kingdom Transplant, the Retained Organs Commission, the National Blood Authority and the Rural Dispensing Committee from the list of special health authorities which are subject to investigation by the Health Service Commissioner.

2060 Special health authorities—NHS Blood and Transplant—suspension and disqualification

The NHS Blood and Transplant (Gwaed a Thrawsblaniadau'r GIG) (Amendment) Regulations 2006, SI 2006/640 (in force on 1 April 2006), amend the 2005 Regulations, SI 2005/2531, so as to (1) add a definition of 'sentence of imprisonment'; (2) provide that where a person is suspended from his appointment as the chief executive of NHS Blood and Transplant ('the Authority') he is also suspended form performing his duties as a member of the Authority; (3) provide that a person is disqualified for appointment as the chairman or as a non-officer member of the Authority if he has within the previous five years been convicted of an offence in any jurisdiction which if committed in the United Kingdom would constitute a criminal offence and he has received a sentence for that offence of a period of imprisonment, whether suspended or not, and the conviction has not been quashed or the sentence reduced to a sentence other than a sentence of imprisonment, whether suspended or not, on appeal; and (4) apply the easement to disqualifications to persons who fall within the 2005 Regulations specified.

2061 Special health authorities—NHS Business Services Authority—establishment and constitution

The NHS Business Services Authority (Awdurdod Gwasanaethau Busnes y GIG) (Establishment and Constitution) (Amendment) Order 2006, SI 2006/632 (in force on 1 April 2006), amends the 2005 Order, SI 2005/2414, so as to confer on the NHS Business Services Authority (Awdurdod Gwasanaethau Busnes y GIG) ('the Authority'), functions previously carried out by the NHS Pensions Agency (Asiantaeth Pensiynau'r GIG), the Prescription Pricing Authority, the Dental Vocational Training Authority, the National Health Service Logistics Authority, the Counter Fraud and Security Management Service and the Dental Practice Board. The order also amends the constitution of the Authority and in particular provides that the non-officer members of the Authority must include a person with particular experience suited to the interests of Wales.

2062 Special health authorities—NHS Business Services Authority—membership and procedure

The NHS Business Services Authority (Awdurdod Gwasanaethau Busnes y GIG) (Amendment) Regulations 2006, SI 2006/633 (in force on 1 April 2006), amend the 2005 Regulations, SI 2005/2415, so as to (1) provide for a new definition of the NHS Pension Scheme and add a related definition of the NHS Injury Benefits Scheme; (2) provide that where a person is suspended from his appointment as chief executive of the Authority he is also suspended from performing his duties as a member of the Authority; and (3) provide that a person is disqualified from appointment as the chairman or as a non-officer member of the Authority if he has been convicted of an offence in any jurisdiction which would constitute a criminal offence in the United Kingdom and has received a sentence of imprisonment.

2063 Special health authorities—NHS Pensions Agency—abolition

The NHS Pensions Agency (Asiantaeth Pensiynau'r GIG) Abolition Order 2006, SI 2006/634 (in force on 1 April 2006), abolishes the NHS Pensions Agency and makes provision for the transfer of its staff, rights, liabilities and property to the NHS Business Services Authority. SI 2004/667 and 668 are revoked.

2064 Special health authorities—summarised accounts—exemption

The Special Health Authorities (Summarised Accounts) Order 2006, SI 2006/250 (in force on 24 March 2006), disapplies the requirement under the National Health Service Act 1977 s 98(4) for the Secretary of State to prepare in respect of each financial year, summarised accounts of certain Special Health Authorities and to send those accounts to the Comptroller and Auditor General to be audited. Specially, the order provides that the requirement will not apply to the Health and Social Care Information Centre, the NHS Business Services Authroity (Awdurdod Gwasanaethau Busnes y GIG) and the NHS Institute for Innovation and Improvement, for the financial year ending 31st March 2006.

2065 Strategic health authorities—establishment and abolition—England

The Strategic Health Authorities (Establishment and Abolition) (England) Amendment Order 2006, SI 2006/1448 (in force on 30 June 2006), amends the Strategic Health Authorities (Establishment and Abolition) (England) Order 2006, SI 2006/1408, by correcting the name of the County of North Somerset.

2066 Strategic health authorities—functions—England

The National Health Service (Functions of Strategic Health Authorities and Primary Care Trusts and Administration Arrangements) (England) (Amendment) Regulations 2006, SI 2006/359 (in force on 1 April 2006), further amend the 2002 Regulations, SI 2002/2375, so as to provide for the circumstances in which a primary care trust must continue to provide or secure certain services for the benefit of a person aged 18 or over who is provided with accommodation in a care home or independent hospital in the area of another primary care trust to meet his community care needs.

2067 Travelling expenses—remission of charges—entitlement—England

The National Health Service (Travel Expenses and Remission of Charges) Amendment Regulations 2006, SI 2006/1065 (in force on 1 May 2006), further amend the 2003 Regulations,

SI 2003/2382, so as to increase the amounts used as the basis for calculating entitlement to the payment of travel expenses and the remission of charges.

The National Health Service (Travel Expenses and Remission of Charges) Amendment (No 2) Regulations 2006, SI 2006/2171 (in force on 1 September 2006), amend the 2003 Regulations, SI 2003/2382, Sch 1, which makes provision for establishing entitlement to the remission of NHS charges and the payment of NHS travel expenses, so as to take account of changes to the provision of financial support to students made by the Education (Student Support) Regulations 2006, SI 2006/119, and the Assembly Learning grants and Loans (Higher Education) (Wales) Regulations 2006, SI 2006/126.

See para ASB0675

2068 Travelling expenses—remission of charges—entitlement—Wales

The National Health Service (Travelling Expenses and Remission of Charges) (Amendment) (Wales) Regulations 2006, SI 2006/1389 (in force on 24 May 2006), further amend the 1988 Regulations, SI 1988/551, by increasing the capital limits used in the calculation of entitlement to remission of NHS charges and repayment of travelling expenses.

The National Health Service (Travelling Expenses and Remission of Charges) (Amendment) (No 2) Regulations 2006, SI 2006/2791 (in force on 18 October 2006), further amend the 1988 Regulations supra to take account of changes to the provision of financial support to students made by the Assembly Learning Grants and Loans (Higher Education) (Wales) Regulations 2006, SI 2006/126, and the Education (Student Support) Regulations 2006, SI 2006/119, and consequential changes to the way in which a student's entitlement to income support will be calculated.

2069 Vaccine damage payments—specified diseases

The Vaccine Damage Payments (Specified Diseases) Order 2006, SI 2006/2066 (in force on 4 September 2006), adds pneumococcal infection to the diseases to which the Vaccine Damage Payments Act 1979 applies.

NEGLIGENCE

Halsbury's Laws of England (4th edn) vol 33 (Reissue) paras 601–700

Articles

For articles relating to this title please refer to the Table of Articles at the beginning of the Abridgment.

2070 Compensation Act 2006

See para 2771.

2071 Duty of care—architects

See BUILDING CONTRACTS, ARCHITECTS, ENGINEERS, VALUERS AND SURVEYORS.

2072 Duty of care—bank—freezing order obtained by third party against customer of bank—duty of care owed by bank to third party

The defendant bank had been notified of asset-freezing injunctions in relation to its customers' accounts. The customers transferred money out of their accounts after the defendant was notified of the injunctions and the defendant failed to stop them doing so. Negligence proceedings brought by the Commissioners of Customs and Excise against the defendant succeeded and the defendant appealed. *Held*, the relationship between the defendant and the Commissioners following the notification of the order was not that of hostile litigating parties but it was adverse. The defendant was bound by law to comply with the order and did not assume any responsibility towards the Commissioners, who could not be said to rely on the defendant, as they were no doubt confident that the defendant would comply promptly with the order. Reliance was usually taken to mean that, if one party had not relied on another, he would have acted differently, but the Commissioners could not have done so as they had availed themselves of the only legal remedy available to them. The freezing injunction jurisdiction developed as one exercised by court order and did not hint at the existence of any other remedy. The regime made sense on the assumption that the only duty owed by the notified party was to the court. The customer owed no duty of care to the party who obtained the order as no duty was owed by a litigating party to its opponent. A duty in tort might co-exist with a similar duty in contract or a statutory duty, and a tortious duty of care to the Commissioners could co-exist with a duty of compliance owed to the court, but there was no instance in which a non-consensual court order had been held to give rise to a duty of care owed to the party obtaining the order. It was unjust and unreasonable that, on being notified of an order which it had no opportunity to resist, the defendant should become exposed to a liability which in this case was a few million pounds but could in another case be for much more. The only protection the defendant had was the Commissioners' undertaking to make good, if so ordered, any loss which the order might cause it, which was not consistent with a duty of care owed by the Commissioners. Accordingly, the appeal would be allowed.

Customs and Excise Comrs v Barclays Bank plc [2006] UKHL 28, [2006] 4 All ER 256 (House of Lords: Lords Bingham of Cornhill, Hoffmann, Rodger of Earlsferry, Walker of Gestingthorpe and Mance). *Hedley Byrne & Co Ltd v Heller & Partners Ltd* [1964] AC 465, HL; *Caparo Industries plc v Dickman* [1990] 2 AC 605, HL (1990 Abr para 294); and *Phelps v Hillingdon LBC* [2001] 2 AC 619, HL (2000 Abr para 1324), considered. Decision of Court of Appeal, [2004] EWCA Civ 1555, [2005] 3 All ER 852 (2004 Abr para 2081) reversed.

2073 Duty of care—bank—income fund—valuation of leases—relevance of contractual structure

The defendant established through its Islamic investment banking unit an income fund whose assets were invested in operating leases of equipment. The first claimant was a major commercial bank based in Saudi Arabia, and the second claimant was one of its subsidiaries, incorporated in England. Following negotiations, it was agreed that the claimants would set up a similar fund to that of the defendant, with the defendant providing technical assistance. The fund was modelled closely on that of the defendant. The fund was eventually suspended, and the claimants issued proceedings against the defendant. A question arose whether the defendant owed a duty of care to the fund to exercise proper care in relation to the valuation of the leases. The judge decided that it did, and the defendant appealed, submitting that it was inappropriate to permit the fund to invoke the law of tort in order to sue the defendant directly for negligent valuation advice when the parties had structured their contractual relationship so that the defendant's duty in respect of that advice was not owed to the fund, but to the second claimant, which in turn owed a similar duty to the fund. *Held*, the findings of the judge were decisive, and in the light of those findings the judge's conclusion was correct. The defendant owed a duty of care to the fund in relation to the valuation of the leases it offered to the second claimant for the fund to buy. The judge was right to conclude that the defendant had assumed responsibility to the fund in relation to the advice and other assessments it had agreed to provide under the technical services agreement notwithstanding the contractual structure the parties had adopted. Accordingly, the appeal would be dismissed.

Riyad Bank v Ahli United Bank (UK) plc [2006] EWCA Civ 780, [2006] 2 All ER (Comm) 777 (Court of Appeal: Buxton, Longmore and Neuberger LJJ).

2074 Duty of care—consultant orthopaedic surgeon—duty owed to person outside doctor/patient relationship—proximity

A football player of the claimant, a football club, suffered an injury on account of which he was referred to the defendant, a consultant orthopaedic surgeon, who recommended reconstructive surgery. The surgery was unsuccessful and the player retired. The advice that the knee should be reconstructed was negligent. The claimant instituted proceedings in both contract and tort for the losses that it alleged it had suffered as a result of the defendant's negligent advice. The court found that there was no contract between the parties or any intention to create legal relations and that, while it was reasonably foreseeable that the claimant club might suffer some loss if the player was negligently treated, there was insufficient proximity between the parties for the imposition of a duty of care in tort. The claimant appealed. *Held*, it was plain that there was no express contract between the claimant and the defendant. It was not necessary to imply a contract under which the defendant agreed to advise the claimant on treatment for the player and undertook a retainer by which he accepted the risk that, if his advice or treatment had been negligent, he would be liable to the claimant for consequential financial loss. The danger of a conflict of interest between a sports employer and a sportsman militated against implying a contract with the employer rather than with the patient, or with the employer as well as the patient. Even if it was assumed that there was foreseeability by the defendant, and reliance by the claimant, none of the other necessary elements for liability in tort were satisfied. The immediate interest in the advice had been medical rather than financial. The question of conflicts of interest emphasised that the defendant's concerns were or ought to have been not only primarily, but exclusively, with the patient's well-being. Therefore, there was no reason to find the proximity necessary to the creation of a duty of care. It would not be fair, just and equitable to impose liability for financial loss on the defendant in favour of the claimant. Accordingly, the appeal would be dismissed.

West Bromwich Albion Football Club Ltd v El-Safty [2006] EWCA Civ 1299, (2006) 92 BMLR 179 (Court of Appeal: Mummery and Rix LJJ and Peter Smith J). *Baird Textiles Holdings v Marks & Spencer plc* [2001] EWCA Civ 274, [2002] 1 All ER (Comm) 737 applied. Decision of Royce J [2005] EWHC 2866 (QB), (2006) 88 BMLR 196 affirmed.

2075 Duty of care—employer—asbestos exposure—several tortfeasors—apportionment of damages

The claimants had contracted mesothelioma after being wrongfully exposed to asbestos dust at different times by various employers, some of which were now insolvent. Additionally, the first claimant had been exposed to asbestos dust during a period of self-employment. It was held that the claimants could recover damages from the employers, subject to a reduction for contributory negligence in the case of the first claimant, and that liability was joint and several. The basis of liability was the application of the exceptional rule that, where an employee had contracted mesothelioma after being wrongfully exposed to asbestos by a number of employees, he could sue any of them, notwithstanding that he could not prove which exposure caused the disease. On the claimants' appeals, the question arose whether each defendant should be liable for the whole of the damage or only for an aliquot share. *Held*, Lord Rodger of Earlsferry dissenting in part, the purpose of the exceptional rule was to provide a cause of action against a defendant who had materially increased the risk that the claimant would suffer damage and might have caused that damage, but could not be proved to have done so because it was impossible to show, on a balance of probability that some other exposure to the same risk might not have caused it instead. It was an essential condition for the operation of the exception that the impossibility of proving that the defendant caused the damage arose out of the existence of another potential causative agent which operated in the same way. The attribution of liability according to the relative degree of contribution to the chance of the disease being contracted would smooth the roughness of the justice that a rule of joint and several liability created. The defendant was a wrongdoer and should not be allowed to escape liability altogether, but he should not be liable for more than the damage which he had caused. Since science could deal only in probabilities where mesothelioma was concerned, the law should accept that position and attribute liability according to probabilities. The justification for the joint and several liability rule was that, if you caused harm, there was no reason why your liability should be reduced because someone else also caused the same harm. However, when liability was exceptionally imposed because the defendant might have caused harm, the same considerations did not apply and fairness suggested that, if more than one person might have been responsible, liability should be divided according to the probability that one or other caused the harm. Accordingly, the appeals would be allowed in part.

Barker v Corus (UK) Ltd; Murray v British Shipbuilders (Hydrodynamics) Ltd; Patterson v Smiths Dock Ltd [2006] UKHL 20, [2006] 2 AC 572 (House of Lords: Lords Hoffmann, Scott of Foscote, Rodger of Earlsferry and Walker of Gestingthorpe and Baroness Hale of Richmond). *McGhee v National Coal Board* [1972] 3 All ER 1008, HL; and *Fairchild v Glenhaven Funeral Services Ltd; Fox v Spousal (Midlands) Ltd; Matthews v Associated Portland Cement Manufacturers (1978) Ltd* [2002] UKHL 22, [2002] 3 All ER 305 (2002 Abr para 1545) considered. Decision of Court of Appeal [2005] EWCA Civ 545, [2005] 3 All ER 661 (2004 Abr para 1392) reversed in part.

2076 Duty of care—employer—bullying at work—failure to take effective remedial action—foreseeability of depression

See *Green v DB Group Services (UK) Ltd*, para 2781.

2077 Duty of care—employer—industrial injury leading to suicide—recoverability of damages

The deceased, the claimant's husband, who was employed by the defendant, was badly injured in a factory accident on the defendant's premises. The defendant admitted that the accident was caused by its negligence or breach of statutory duty. Thereafter, the deceased suffered post-traumatic stress disorder, and lapsed into a deep depression. He was treated for depression, and was admitted to hospital after taking an overdose. He later committed suicide. The claimant brought a claim under the Fatal Accidents Act 1976. The claim was dismissed, the judge deciding that the defendant's duty to the deceased did not extend to a duty to take care to prevent his suicide, and that his suicide was not reasonably foreseeable. The claimant appealed. *Held*, there was no prior ground of legal logic, and no surviving ground of legal policy, for excluding suicide from the compensable consequences of actionable negligence. If a case of suicide were to be excluded, it would have to be because the evidence had failed to establish that the judgment and volition of the deceased were overwhelmed by depression consequent on the injury. That was, in each case, a matter of factual inquiry. If psychological injury had to be distinctly predictable before any liability fell on a tortfeasor in respect of it, the policy of the law would have drawn its line at a point which shut out any damages for the deceased's post-accident depression. However, once the law accepted, as it did, the foreseeability of psychological harm as a concomitant of foreseeable physical harm, it was only if a break dictated by logic or policy or, of course, by evidence, intervened that it was possible today to exclude death by suicide from the compensable damage where that was what the depression had led to. Once it was accepted that suicide by itself did not place a clinically depressed individual beyond the pale of the law of negligence, the relationship of his eventual suicide to his depression became a pure question of fact. The evidence in the instant case amply established that it was depression which had driven the deceased to suicide. Accordingly, the appeal would be allowed.

Corr (Administratrix of Corr deceased) v IBC Vehicles [2006] EWCA Civ 331, [2007] QB 46 (Court of Appeal: Ward, Sedley and Wilson LJJ). Decision of Nigel Baker QC [2005] All ER (D) 418 (Apr) (2005 Abr para 1372) reversed.

2078   Duty of care—employer—nurse in special hospital—assault by violent patient

See *Buck v Nottinghamshire Healthcare NHS Trust*, para 1219.

2079   Duty of care—highway authority—duty to maintain highway—tilting manhole cover

See *Atkins v Ealing LBC*, para 1465.

2080   Duty of care—Home Office—prisoner suffering psychiatric injury consequent to witnessing suicide—nature of claim

The claimant was on remand at prison and claimed that he had been, to the knowledge of the prison authorities, psychiatrically vulnerable as he was in an unstable condition, suffering from depression, and had threatened self-harm and at one time was suicidal. Despite this alleged knowledge, the authorities placed him in a cell with another remand prisoner who was a known suicide risk and did commit suicide. He claimed that the fact that he had been placed with a suicidal prisoner who committed suicide, that a prison officer had blamed him for the suicide, and he had been subsequently placed with another suicidal prisoner, had resulted in him suffering psychiatric harm. He commenced proceedings against the Home Office on the ground that his psychiatric state was caused by a breach of the duty of care it owed to him while he was in custody. The Home Office's application to strike out his claim was dismissed and the Home Office appealed. *Held*, the claim was not narrowly based on the psychiatric injury the claimant had suffered as a witness to the prisoner's suicide, and he was not required to show that he had close ties of love and affection with the deceased. The particulars of claim made it clear that the claimant alleged he had ultimately suffered psychiatric injury as a result of a breach of a primary duty of care owed to him by the defendant. Accordingly, the appeal would be dismissed.

Butchart v Home Office [2006] EWCA Civ 239, [2006] 1 WLR 1155 (Court of Appeal: May, Latham and Longmore LJJ). *Frost v Chief Constable of South Yorkshire Police* [1997] QB 254, [1997] 1 All ER 540, CA (1996 Abr para 2238) considered.

2081   Duty of care—local authority—adoption proceedings—duty to maintain confidentiality of identity of adopters

The defendant local authority had given an undertaking to the parents of two adopted children that their identity and area in which they and their adopted children lived would not be disclosed to the birth parents of the second child. The adoptive parents and the two children contended that, contrary to the undertaking, their identity and locality had been revealed to the second child's mother and grandmother. They claimed that they had been subjected to a campaign of harassment by the second child's birth family and sought damages from the defendant for psychiatric injury and loss and damage which arose from that claim on the basis that the defendant had been negligent. It was held that the defendant had owed the claimants a duty of care to keep their identity confidential, and had breached that duty, but the action was dismissed on the ground that the claimants had not proved that they had been subjected to a campaign of harassment as alleged. The claimants appealed and the defendant cross-appealed on the finding that it owed the claimants a duty of care. *Held*, having regard to the relevant criteria of foreseeability, proximity and 'fair, just and reasonable', the defendant owed a duty of care towards the parents to ensure that the terms of its undertaking in relation to anonymity were respected by its employees. If proved, the alleged conduct of the birth family and its effect on the claimants would be recoverable as damage of the foreseeable type. In relation to proximity, the parties were plainly in a close relationship with each other, whatever was asked for or given in relation to confidentiality, and they had remained in that relationship throughout the process. Although a specific undertaking had been given, the starting point in any adoption would be confidentiality of the identity of the adopters. If a local authority feared that it might not be able to maintain that confidentiality, or it reached a stage where there might be good reason for revealing the identity of the adopters, then the course it should take was to discuss the implications of that with the potential adopters before the latter committed themselves. Similarly, if the authority thought that such an assurance on its part might not be of much use to the adopters because their names might become known from other sources, then the implications of that had also to be discussed with the potential adopters before any assurance was given. However, the trial judge had been justified in his finding that the claimants had failed to prove that they were the victims of a campaign of harassment by the second child's birth family. Accordingly, the appeal and cross-appeal would be dismissed.

B v A CC [2006] EWCA Civ 1388, [2006] 3 FCR 568 (Court of Appeal: Buxton and Sedley LJJ and Bodey J).

2082   Duty of care—local authority—child care proceedings—duty owed to parent and child

A child suffered fractures while in the care of his parents, and was placed with foster parents for four months pursuant to an interim care order. After it was discovered that the child suffered from brittle bone disease, he was returned to his parents. The claimants, the mother and child, brought a claim against the defendant local authority for negligence and damage suffered as a result of the care proceedings. The claim was dismissed and the claimants appealed. *Held*, care professionals had to be free to exercise their functions in relation to questions of protecting children in relation to doubts about injury or abuse without the thought of being exposed to claims from distressed parents if the doubts were unfounded. This freedom lasted throughout the care proceedings process. The interim care order was part of the continuing investigation of the care proceedings. During the proceedings, the defendant did not owe the mother a common law duty of care in respect of its investigation. The defendant admitted that it owed the child a duty of care to carry out its reasonable plans of child protection in a professional manner. However there was no indication that he had suffered any identifiable or psychological harm while with the foster parents that could give rise to an action for damages. Any damage the child had suffered was transient and non-justiciable. Accordingly, the appeal would be dismissed.

D v Bury MBC; H v Bury MBC [2006] EWCA Civ 1, [2006] 1 WLR 917 (Mummery, Laws and Wall LJJ). *D v East Berkshire Community Health NHS Trust* [2005] UKHL 23, [2005] 2 AC 373 (2005 Abr para 2272).

2083   Duty of care—local authority—duty owed to parent suspected of child abuse—effect of human rights legislation

The social services department of the defendant local authority placed the claimant's children's names on the child protection register, but reversed its decision 14 months later. The claimant issued proceedings alleging negligence and a breach of her right, under the European Convention on Human Rights art 8, to family life. She claimed that the children's names should never have been placed on the register, and that she had suffered psychiatric injury as a result. The defendant applied to strike out the claim in negligence, or alternatively for summary judgment in respect of it, on the basis that it was established law that doctors or social workers who failed to exercise reasonable care and skill in erroneously concluding that a child was at risk of abuse from a parent were not liable in negligence to that parent. *Held*, the principal policy consideration which underlay the principle that doctors and social workers should not be liable in negligence to the wrongly accused parent was the avoidance of conflicting duties which could prejudice the interests of the child. This consideration was not rendered invalid or otherwise inapplicable by the fact that a parent might have a claim under art 8. If it was against the public interest that professionals investigating child abuse should owe a duty of care to parents suspected of such abuse, the common law should not pretend otherwise merely to keep pace with Convention jurisprudence. Even if the Convention dictated that a remedy should be available in such circumstances, the claimant should be restricted to a claim under the Human Rights Act 1998. Justice did not require that the claimant should also be able to sue in negligence. The claim in negligence was bad in law and, accordingly, the application would be allowed.

Lawrence v Pembrokeshire CC [2006] EWHC 1029 (QB), [2006] 2 FCR 363 (Queen's Bench Division: Field J). *X (Minors) v Bedfordshire CC* [1995] 2 AC 633, HL (1995 Abr para 2833), followed. *D v East Berkshire Community Health NHS Trust; MAK v Dewsbury Healthcare NHS Trust; RK v Oldham NHS Trust* [2005] UKHL 23, [2005] 2 AC 373 (2005 Abr para 2272) considered.

2084   Duty of care—medical practitioner—private laboratory engaged to perform tissue testing—proximity to patient

The claimants were Jordanian nationals who were healthy carriers of a particular genetic condition. When the first claimant became pregnant for the third time, the claimants wished to establish whether the foetus had that condition. A Jordanian doctor took a tissue sample from the developing placenta and it was sent to the defendant hospital for DNA analysis. The sample required culturing before the testing could be carried out, so the defendant engaged a private laboratory, the Pt 20 defendant, by way of letter for that purpose. The Pt 20 defendant duly returned the cultured sample and the result of the defendant's DNA analysis was that the condition was not present. A child was subsequently born with the condition and the claimants brought proceedings for damages on the basis that the pregnancy would have been terminated had they known that the child had the condition. A preliminary issue arose as to whether the Pt 20 defendant owed a common law duty of care to the claimants. *Held*, applying settled principles, there was a sufficient relationship of proximity to give rise to a duty of care, it was fair, just and reasonable to impose such a duty, and the damage suffered was foreseeable. The lack of direct communication between the claimants and the Pt 20 defendant did not of itself mean that there was insufficient proximity to found a duty of care. Whatever the claimants' precise knowledge of the processes involved, they would have relied on each of the persons involved in carrying out those processes to exercise due care and skill in the performance of his function. Whether the processes were carried out by a laboratory technician employed by the defendant or by an employee of an independent organisation retained by the defendant, the claimants' expectation would have been the same. Furthermore, parents in the claimants' position who received a favourable report of DNA testing would have inferred, in the absence of information to the contrary, that the sample used for testing had been of appropriate quality to yield a reliable result, and would have relied on that fact when making any decision based on the results. In those circumstances, the Pt 20 defendant ought to have been aware that such parents would rely, whether directly or indirectly, on their skill and care. Accordingly, the application would be allowed.

Farraj v King's Healthcare NHS Trust [2006] EWHC 1228 (QB), [2006] 2 FCR 804 (Queen's Bench Division: Swift J). *Smith v Eric S Bush (a firm); Harris v Wyre Forest DC* [1990] 1 AC 831, HL (1989 Abr para 2499); and *Caparo Industries plc v Dickman* [1990] 2 AC 605, HL (1990 Abr para 294), applied.

2085   Duty of care—occupier—duty owed to sub-contractor's employee—knowledge of execution of dangerous work

The third defendant, a hotel company, appointed the second defendant as the main contractor for electrical work involved in the refurbishment of one of the third defendant's hotels, but required the second defendant to sub-contract the installation of the fire alarm system to the first defendant. The deceased, the claimant's husband, was an experienced installation engineer employed by the first defendant. When the first defendant started work, the route for the new electrical cables for the fire alarm system had not been decided. The first defendant decided to route them externally. This involved gaining access to a walkway between a roof and an external wall. The deceased tripped in the course of the installation, fell through a plate glass window and died from his injuries. The claimant brought a claim against the defendants for damages for negligence and breach of statutory duty. The first defendant admitted liability and then sought contribution from the second and third defendants. The judge found that the second and third defendant had relevant knowledge that the first defendant was considering routing the cables externally and that they had been negligent in failing to forbid or ensure the safety of the work, and apportioned responsibility accordingly. The second and third defendants appealed. *Held,* there could be no doubt that, in certain circumstances, both an independent contractor and the occupier of a building could owe a duty of care to the employee of a sub-contractor. The question was one of mixed fact and law, and it was unnecessary and unhelpful to attempt to formulate any specific test for deciding when such a duty arose. The judge had been entitled to hold that, in the circumstances, the second defendant had owed such a duty of care to the deceased. However, it would not be fair, just and reasonable to impose a duty of care on the third defendant, which had engaged a competent contractor to carry out the work through the medium of a competent sub-contractor on a part of the building which the judge found was obviously dangerous. On the evidence, the judge had erred in finding that the second or third defendant had been aware that the first defendant had chosen to route the cables externally, and so the second defendant had not breached its duty of care. Accordingly, the appeals would be allowed.

Gray v Fire Alarm Fabrication Services Ltd [2006] EWCA Civ 1496, [2006] All ER (D) 133 (Nov) (Court of Appeal: May, Gage and Hallett LJJ). *Ferguson v Welsh* [1987] 3 All ER 777, HL (1987 Abr para 1871), considered.

2086   Duty of care—occupier—duty owed to trespassers—state of premises

The claimant, an 11-year-old boy, fell while climbing a fire escape connected to a building owned and occupied by the defendant. The defendant knew that the area was used by the public as a means of access to adjacent streets, and by children as a play area. The claimant fractured his arm and suffered significant brain injury which led to loss of intellectual functioning and a personality change which allegedly caused him to be convicted of various sexual offences. The claimant brought proceedings against the defendant. It was accepted that the claimant had to be treated as a trespasser. The judge determined that there had existed a danger due to the state of the premises within the meaning of the Occupiers' Liability Act 1984 s 1(1)(a) and that the defendant was in breach of duty to the claimant but that the claimant should carry the major proportion of blame and was two-thirds responsible for what had occurred. The defendant appealed. *Held,* the claimant had not passed the threshold requirement of s 1(1)(a). The fire escape was required by law and was a normal fire escape that was not dangerous in itself. The danger was the result of the claimant's activities on the premises, not the state of the premises themselves. Accordingly, the appeal would be allowed.

Keown v Coventry Healthcare NHS Trust [2006] EWCA Civ 39, (2006) Independent, 10 February 2006 (Mummery and Longmore LJJ and Lewison J).

2087   Duty of care—occupier—leisure centre—use of exercise equipment—equipment maintained by independent contractor—pre-contractual inspection

The claimant, a paying visitor to the defendant's leisure centre, was injured while using one of its exercise machines. He brought personal injury proceedings against the defendant and the supplier of the machine, claiming that the accident had been caused by a defect in the machine. The machine had been inspected by one of the supplier's engineers six weeks before the accident, and found to require no maintenance. That inspection had been carried out before the supplier had entered into a full service agreement with the defendant. The judge found that the defendant had been in breach of an implied term in its contract with the claimant that the machine would be reasonably safe for its purpose. The judge decided that that duty was wider than the common duty of care imposed by the Occupiers' Liability Act 1957 s 2, and that the case fell outside the terms of s 5, which applied the s 2 duty to situations where a person used premises in exercise of a right conferred by contract with a person occupying or having control of the premises. He also found that the defendant was in breach of the common duty of care in s 2, on the basis that it had been unreasonable for the defendant to rely on the supplier's pre-contractual inspection, undertaken for the supplier's own purposes. The defendant appealed. *Held*, the defendant had not breached an implied term of its contract with the claimant. It was clear that ss 2, 5 had been intended to impose a single common duty of care, whether arising within or outside a contract, subject to contrary agreement. It followed that the defendant could not be held liable for any default of the supplier, if it had acted reasonably in relying on it. Moreover, the defendant had not breached the common duty of care imposed by s 2. At the time of the pre-contractual inspection, it had been entitled to rely on the supplier, as the best of all experts, to perform a proper inspection, even though that inspection had been carried out before the inception of the service agreement, and for the supplier's own purposes. It followed that the judge had erred in concluding that the defendant had failed to take all reasonable steps to ensure that the claimant had been reasonably safe in using the machine. Accordingly, the appeal would be allowed.

Maguire v Sefton MBC [2006] EWCA Civ 316, [2006] PIQR P378 (Court of Appeal: Rix, Carnwath and Jacob LJJ). *Sole v WJ Hallt Ltd* [1973] QB 574 applied.

2088   Duty of care—research body—testing of toxicity of water in wells—duty owed to general public—proximity

The defendant prepared a report which assessed the hydrochemical character of the main aquifer units of central and north-eastern Bangladesh and possible toxicity of ground water to fish and humans. Most of the samples were taken from deep tube wells but more than a third came from hand-pumped shallow wells which were commonly sunk to provide drinking water. The samples were not tested for arsenic. The claimant, who lived in a region of Bangladesh from which some of the samples were taken, alleged that he had suffered personal injury from arsenic poisoning as a result of drinking the water in his village. He brought proceedings against the defendant for negligence in issuing the report which had induced the health authorities in Bangladesh not to take steps which would have ensured that his drinking water was not contaminated by arsenic. He alleged that the defendant had caused or materially contributed to his illness, by issuing a report which represented that his water was safe to drink. The defendant challenged the contention that it owed a duty of care to the claimant, submitting that it did not have a relationship of proximity with the population of Bangladesh which could make it liable. That application was refused, but the defendant's appeal was allowed, the court deciding that the claimant had no reasonable prospect of satisfying a court that the defendant owed him a duty of care. The claimant appealed. *Held*, the relationship between the claimant and the defendant was not sufficiently proximate to give rise to a duty of care. There had to be proximity in the sense of a measure of control over and responsibility for the potentially dangerous situation. The defendant had no control, whether in law or in practice, over the supply of drinking water in Bangladesh, nor was there any statute, contract or other arrangement which imposed on it responsibility for ensuring that it was safe to drink. Accordingly, the appeal would be dismissed.

Sutradhar v Natural Environment Research Council [2006] UKHL 33, [2006] 4 All ER 490 (House of Lords: Lords Nicholls of Birkenhead, Hoffmann, Walker of Gestingthorpe, Brown of Eaton-under-Heywood and Mance). Decision of Court of Appeal [2004] EWCA Civ 175, [2004] All ER (D) 357 (Feb) (2004 Abr para 2099) affirmed.

2089   Duty of care—Revenue—issue of sub-contractor's tax certificate—delay—losses caused by delay

See *Neil Martin Ltd v Revenue and Customs Comrs*, para 1635.

2090   Duty of care—solicitor

See SOLICITORS.

2091   Duty of care—veterinary surgeon—duty owed when asked to attend and observe treatment of animal

The appellant, an experienced equine veterinary surgeon, had been asked to attend and observe orthopaedic treatment of a horse by another veterinary surgeon and to intervene if it was inappropriate or contrary to the horse's welfare. The horse died in consequence of an overdose of drugs administered in the treatment. The court rejected the appellant's claim for unpaid fees and apportioned some of the liability to him. He appealed. *Held*, Ward LJ dissenting, the judge was correct to hold that the appellant had rendered himself unable to judge whether the proposed treatment was inappropriate by failing to make any inquiry as to the type or dosage of the corticosteroid drugs that were to be administered. The appellant had been asked to be present as the owner's veterinary surgeon. As such, he had a duty to make himself aware of the precise detail of the treatment which was to be carried out and to discuss it with the other vet. Had he done so, he would have discovered that it was unreasonably high and would have known that the treatment was inappropriate. Accordingly, the appeal would be dismissed.

Glyn v McGarel-Groves [2006] EWCA Civ 998, (2006) Times, 22 August (Court of Appeal: Ward, Rix and Gage LJJ).

2092 Nervous shock—liability—employer—police officer participating in armed raid—raid resulting in fatality—unfounded disciplinary proceedings

The claimants were police officers who took part in an armed raid which led to the fatal shooting of a person by another officer. None of the claimants witnessed the shooting itself. An investigation was ordered into the incident, and the claimants were served with disciplinary notices and were suspended. All but one of the claimants were charged with misfeasance in public office. The claimants were acquitted of the misfeasance charges after the prosecution offered no evidence, and the suspensions were lifted following the trial. Disciplinary charges were subsequently brought against some of the claimants, but they too were largely dropped. The claimants commenced proceedings for psychiatric injury caused by the negligence of the defendant Chief Constable as their employer. They claimed that there had been systemic failures in relation to their training and the collection of criminal intelligence in connection with the use of firearms to respond to dangerous criminals, which had foreseeably led to the shooting of the deceased, the various disciplinary and criminal proceedings brought, without justification, against the claimants, the attendant stresses on the claimants and the resultant psychiatric injuries. The judge dismissed the claim and the claimants appealed. *Held,* the claimants were seeking to make a significant extension to the ambit of the duty of care not to cause psychiatric injury. It was not uncommon for systemic failures on the part of undertakings to lead to adverse events which, in their turn, led to public inquiries or other proceedings, such as prosecutions for corporate manslaughter. In such proceedings, fault was commonly alleged against the employees of the undertaking. To be the object of such allegations could be highly stressful, and it was arguably foreseeable that such stress was capable of causing psychiatric injury. However, the claimants' case involved postulating a duty of care on the part of employers towards their employees not to cause or permit an untoward event to occur that could foreseeably lead to proceedings in which the employees' conduct would be in issue. It would not be appropriate for a lower court to make such an extension to the law of negligence and no prospect could be seen that the House of Lords would be minded to do so. The impact of the death on the minds and senses of the claimants was not direct. It had affected them because it had set in train subsequent events, criminal and disciplinary proceedings, which had placed them under stress. It would not be inappropriate to describe them as secondary victims of the deceased's death, but the causative link between his death and their injury was more remote than in the classic case of secondary victims. The judge had rightly taken the view that, if police officers who had witnessed the shooting would have no claim as secondary victims, it necessarily followed that the claimants, who were more remotely affected, could have no claim either. Accordingly, the appeal would be dismissed.

French v Chief Constable of Sussex Police [2006] EWCA Civ 312, [2006] All ER (D) 407 (Mar) (Court of Appeal: Lord Phillips of Worth Matravers CJ, Tuckey and Laws LJJ). *White v Chief Constable of South Yorkshire Police* [1999] 2 AC 455, HL (1998 Abr para 2345); and *Barber v Somerset CC* [2004] UKHL 13, [2004] 2 All ER 385 (2004 Abr para 1177) distinguished.

2093 Occupier's liability—duty owed to persons employed on premises—building work

The defendant was carrying out construction works at his home. The claimant, a delivery driver, was delivering blocks to a location, specified by the defendant, which was a few feet from a deep excavation. When blocks began to fall from his lorry, the claimant stepped back and fell into the pit, seriously injuring his back. He brought personal injury proceedings against the defendant under the Occupiers Liability Act 1957, and asserted that the Construction (Health, Safety and Welfare) Regulations 1996, SI 1996/1592, had applied to him. The claimant joined his employers at the delivery firm, contending that they had been in breach of health and safety regulations. The defendant relied on the fact that he had erected a warning fence. The judge, finding the defendant liable, found that the hazard represented by the pit was extreme, and concluded that the defendant had been under a duty to erect a strong fence around it so as to prevent someone falling in. However, the judge declined to hold that the 1996 Regulations imposed any duty on the defendant, but concluded that it had been reasonable to join the employers as defendants and acceded to an application that the defendant should pay their costs. The defendant appealed against the decision on liability, and the claimant cross-appealed. *Held,* applying settled principles, the judge, having heard the action and assessed the witnesses, was in the best position to make an assessment as to the reasonable care that should have been exercised by the defendant. Further, it could not be said that the judge had exercised his discretion to award the employers their costs against the defendant on any wrong basis. He had taken into account the way in which the defendant had responded to the claim, and had been right to conclude that it was reasonable to join the employers. They might not have been liable in the one sense of that word, but they were parties who might have been found liable, and were parties on whom the defendant sought to place the blame. Accordingly, the appeal would be dismissed and the cross-appeal allowed.

Moon v Garrett [2006] EWCA Civ 1121, [2006] BLR 402 (Court of Appeal: Waller and Jacob LJJ and Sir Peter Gibson).

2094 Trustee—exclusion or limitation of liability—exemption clause—disclosure—Law Commission recommendations

See para 2887.

NORTHERN IRELAND

Halsbury's Laws of England (4th edn) vol 8(2) (Reissue) paras 67–100

Articles

For articles relating to this title please refer to the Table of Articles at the beginning of the Abridgment.

2095 Northern Ireland Act 2006

The Northern Ireland Act 2006 makes provision for preparations for the restoration of devolved government in Northern Ireland, for the selection of persons to be ministers on such restoration, and for the consequences of selecting or not selecting such persons. The Act received the royal assent on 8 May 2006 and came into force on that day.

Section 1 provides the framework for the preparations for devolved government to be undertaken by members of the Northern Ireland Assembly, including for the Secretary of State to refer to them the election of the First Ministers and deputy First Ministers and nominations for ministerial office. Section 1 also gives effect to Sch 1, which makes more detailed provision about the composition and procedure of the Assembly. Three conditions for the restoration of devolved government in Northern Ireland are imposed by s 2: the election of ministers, the making of nominations for other Ministerial offices and the affirmation of the pledge of office by those persons elected or nominated. Section 2 also gives effect to Schs 2 and 3, which specify what is to happen in the event of the conditions either being met or not being met. The Secretary of State is entitled to make supplementary or consequential provision in relation to these matters: ss 3 and 4. Section 5 deals with interpretation, and s 6 with the short title.

2096 Northern Ireland (Miscellaneous Provisions) Act 2006

The Northern Ireland (Miscellaneous Provisions) Act 2006 makes provision about registration of electors and the Chief Electoral Officer for Northern Ireland, amends the Northern Ireland Act 1998, makes provision about donations for political purposes and extends the amnesty period for arms decommissioning in Northern Ireland. The Act received the royal assent on 25 July 2006 and came into force in part on that day and on 25 September 2006. Further provisions come into force on 1 November 2007. The remaining provisions come into force on a day or days to be appointed.

Part 1 (ss 1–7) Registration of electors
Section 1 enables anonymous registration to be introduced by Order in Council in Northern Ireland in respect of district, Assembly, European and Parliamentary elections. The legal requirement to conduct an annual canvass in Northern Ireland is removed: s 2. Section 3 provides that a canvass may take place in 2010 and every tenth year following 2010, and s 4 sets out the relevant registration objectives. Section 5 retains the default requirement that a revised and updated register must be published on or before 1 December in a year in which a canvass has been held. By virtue of s 6, electors are allowed to register closer to the date of the poll. Section 7 enables regulations to be made that give the Chief Electoral Officer the power to obtain information from public authorities to help him to meet the relevant registration objectives.

Part 2 (ss 8, 9) The Chief Electoral Officer
Under s 8, the appointment of the Chief Electoral Officer may be for a term of up to five years and no person may hold the post for more than ten years. Section 9 imposes a duty on the Chief Electoral Officer to prepare an annual report on how he has discharged his functions in the year to which the report relates and send a copy of the report to the Secretary of State.

Part 3 (ss 10–15) Donations for political purposes
Section 10 provides for the commencement of certain provisions. Section 11 extends the disapplication, until 31 October 2007, of the Political Parties, Elections and Referendums Act 2000 Pt 4 (ss 50–71Y) in relation to Northern Ireland. The 2006 Act s 12 provides that Northern Ireland parties and Northern Ireland regulated donees will still be able to accept donations from Irish citizens and other Irish bodies who are entitled to donate to Irish parties. Supplementary provision, including provision to prevent Northern Ireland parties from making donations to candidates

standing for election in Great Britain is made: s 13. By virtue of s 14, the modifications set out in Sch 1 apply to Northern Ireland recipients during a prescribed period. Section 15 gives the Secretary of State power to make an order modifying legislation connected with permissible donors or donations for political purposes.

Part 4 (ss 16–20) Devolution of policing and justice etc
Section 16 sets out the conditions for devolving policing and justice matters. Section 17 adds provisions to the 1998 Act that apply where an Act of the Northern Ireland Assembly establishes a new department responsible for devolved policing and justice functions. Under s 18, the Assembly is prevented from calling ministers of the Crown or civil servants to give evidence or to produce documents in relation to the discharge of functions devolved by an Order in Council or the discharge of statutory functions transferred from a minister of the Crown to a Northern Ireland department or minister during the period before they were transferred. By virtue of s 19, amendments may be made by Order in Council to legislation relevant to extradition. Section 20 enables an Order in Council to entrench additional enactments, or to provide that entrenchments cease to have effect.

Part 5 (ss 21–28) Miscellaneous
Section 21 extends from 27 February 2007 to 27 February 2010 the latest permitted end date of an amnesty period, during which paramilitary arms may be decommissioned. Limits on loans to the Consolidated Fund of Northern Ireland are increased: s 22. Section 23 enables Her Majesty, by Order in Council, to give legal effect to any agreement or arrangement between the British and Irish governments on the creation of a single wholesale electricity market in Northern Ireland and Ireland. By virtue of s 24, financial assistance for specified energy purposes may be provided. Section 25 imposes a duty on Northern Ireland departments and district councils to carry out their functions in a way which contributes to sustainable development. Section 26, Sch 3 provide for the extension to Northern Ireland of certain provisions of the Serious Organised Crime and Police Act 2005 relating to the investigatory powers of the Director of Public Prosecutions and the Director of Revenue and Customs Prosecutions. Section 27 provides a person who holds the office of Chief Constable of the Police Service of Northern Ireland with corporation sole status and amends relevant health and safety legislation in relation to Northern Ireland. Section 28 requires appointments to the office of Lord Chief Justice or Lord Justice of Appeal to be made on the recommendation of the Prime Minister and appointments to the office of High Court judge to be made on the recommendation of the Lord Chancellor.

Part 6 (ss 29–33) Supplementary
Section 29 contains financial provisions. Section 30 introduces Sch 4, which contains minor and consequential amendments, and Sch 5 which deals with repeals and revocations. Section 31 provides for commencement, s 32 deals with extent and s 33 deals with short title.

2097   Northern Ireland (St Andrews Agreement) Act 2006

The Northern Ireland (St Andrews Agreement) Act 2006 makes provision for preparations for the restoration of devolved government in Northern Ireland in accordance with the St Andrews Agreement, and makes provision as to the consequences of compliance or non-compliance with the St Andrews Agreement timetable and about district policing partnerships. The Act received the royal assent on 22 November 2006 and came into force in part on that day.

Part 1 (ss 1–4) Preparations for restoration of devolved government
Section 1, Sch 1 make provision for a Transitional Assembly in preparation for the restoration of devolved government in Northern Ireland. Section 2, Schs 3–5 deal with the consequences of compliance and non-compliance with the St Andrews Agreement timetable, and provide for the restoration of the devolved government and for the repeal of the Northern Ireland Act 2000, provided that a restoration order is made. The 2006 Act s 3 makes provision for the election of the Northern Ireland Assembly and s 4 provides for remuneration of members of the Assembly before and after the election.

Part 2 (ss 5–19) Amendments of the Northern Ireland Act 1998
Part 2 will come into force if the devolved government is restored. Section 5 provides for a new ministerial code and places certain duties on ministers and junior ministers and provides for which matters relating to the ministerial code are to fall to the Executive Committee for discussion and agreement. Section 6 provides for the Assembly to refer important ministerial decisions to the Executive Committee and s 7 amends the pledge of office, which all ministers must affirm before taking up office. New arrangements for the appointment of the First and deputy First ministers are created: ss 8, 9, Schs 5, 6. Section 10 provides for the establishment of a statutory committee to advise and assist the First and deputy First ministers in the formulation of policies in relation to their responsibilities as ministers and s 11 provides for a committee to review the functioning of the Assembly and the Executive Committee. Section 12 makes provision in relation to the North-South Ministerial Council and the British-Irish Council. Situations where a member of the Assembly may change his community designation are dealt with in s 13 and s 14 confers a power on the Executive

Committee to call for witnesses and documents. Sections 15 and 16 place duties on the Executive Committee to adopt strategies relating to the Irish and Ulster Scots languages, Ulster Scots heritage and culture, poverty, social exclusion and patterns of deprivation. Section 17 deals with the preservation of the exercise of the right to vote where there is a vacancy in the Assembly and s 18 places an obligation on the Assembly to provide a report to the Secretary of State on its consideration of policing and justice matters. Section 19 introduces Sch 7, which makes minor and consequential amendments.

Part 3 (ss 20–21) Other amendments
Section 20 introduces Schs 8, 9, which deal with district policing partnerships and the Belfast subgroups and s 21 makes provision in relation to the abolition of academic selection.

Part 4 (ss 22–28) Supplemental
Section 22 deals with repeals, s 23 confers a power on the Secretary of State to make by order any consequential provision that may be needed and s 24 provides for parliamentary procedure for orders made under s 23. Section 25 provides for interpretation, s 26 deals with extent, s 27 with commencement and s 28 with short title.

NOTARIES

Halsbury's Laws of England (4th edn) vol 33 (Reissue) paras 701–734

Articles

For articles relating to this title please refer to the Table of Articles at the beginning of the Abridgment.

NUISANCE

Halsbury's Laws of England (4th edn) vol 34 (Reissue) paras 1–100

Articles

For articles relating to this title please refer to the Table of Articles at the beginning of the Abridgment.

2098   Private nuisance—abatement—encroachment of tree roots—tree preservation order

See *Perrin v Northampton BC*, para 2819.

2099   Statutory nuisance—abatement notice—appeal—England

The Statutory Nuisance (Appeals) (Amendment) (England) Regulations 2006, SI 2006/771 (in force on 6 April 2006), amend the 1995 Regulations, SI 1995/2644, so as to enable reliance to be placed, on an appeal to the magistrates' court against an abatement notice which cites either an insect or artificial light statutory nuisance, on best practicable means having been used to abate, or to counteract the effect of, such a nuisance; best practicable means are a ground of appeal against an abatement notice in respect of this nuisance where the artificial light is emitted either from industrial, trade or business premises, or by lights used for the purpose only of illuminating an outdoor relevant sports facility.

2100   Statutory nuisance—abatement notice—watercourse—obstruction

The Public Health Act 1936 s 259(1)(b) provides that a statutory nuisance exists for the purposes of the Environmental Protection Act 1990 where any part of a watercourse is so choked up as to obstruct or impede the proper flow of water and thereby cause a nuisance.

The claimant lived in a house subject to flooding from a river. He considered that the cause of the flooding was a bridge for which the highway authority was responsible. The claimant sought to persuade the defendant district council to serve an abatement notice under the Environmental Health Act 1990 on the authority. The defendant decided not to serve an abatement notice. The claimant made an application for judicial review of the decision, seeking a mandatory order that the defendant serve such a notice and a declaration that the word 'choked', under s 259, was capable in law of including an obstruction to the proper flow of the river by a bridge constructed in it. Following the grant of permission, the defendant served an abatement notice on the authority which appealed against the notice and sought directions on whether there was any matter that properly remained to be decided in the proceedings. It fell to be determined as a preliminary issue whether the declaration sought could properly be made. *Held,* as the application for a declaration was wholly dependent on, and subsidiary to, the application for the mandatory order, the declaration as to the meaning of the word 'choked' would be refused. The application was academic and it sought an advisory opinion from the court, which the authorities established should be rejected. However, on the true construction of s 259(1)(b), where there was an obstruction or an artificial obstruction in a watercourse causing a statutory nuisance, the watercourse could be said to be 'choked' within the meaning of s 259. Where a flooding occurred from a watercourse due to the presence of an obstruction in the watercourse, a statutory nuisance was caused. Judgment would be given accordingly.

R (*on the application of Robinson*) *v Torridge DC* [2006] EWHC 977 (Admin), [2006] 3 All ER 1148 (Queen's Bench Division: Hodge J).

2101   Statutory nuisance—artificial lighting—relevant sports—designation—England

The Statutory Nuisances (Artificial Lighting) (Designation of Relevant Sports) (England) Order 2006, SI 2006/781 (in force on 6 April 2006), designates relevant sports for the purposes of the Environmental Protection Act 1990 s 80(8A).

2102   Statutory nuisance—insects—England

The Statutory Nuisances (Insects) Regulations 2006, SI 2006/770 (in force on 6 April 2006), prescribe land in respect of which payments are made under any of the specified land management schemes.

OPEN SPACES AND ANCIENT MONUMENTS

Halsbury's Laws of England (4th edn) vol 34 (Reissue) paras 101–500

Articles

For articles relating to this title please refer to the Table of Articles at the beginning of the Abridgment.

2103   Access to the countryside—exclusions and restrictions—England

The Access to the Countryside (Exclusions and Restrictions) (England) (Amendment) Regulations 2006, SI 2006/990 (in force on 24 April 2006), amend the 2003 Regulations, SI 2003/2713, so as to provide that, where an appeal has been made against a decision of a relevant authority not to act in accordance with an application for a direction to exclude or restrict access for the purpose of fire prevention, and the hearing of the appeal has been determined by the Secretary of State, the Secretary of State must ensure that a copy of the amended notice of appeal with the decision indorsed on it is made available for inspection on the Planning Inspectorate Executive Agency's website for three months.

2104   Ancient Monuments Board for Wales—abolition

The Ancient Monuments Board for Wales (Abolition) Order 2006, SI 2006/64 (in force on 1 April 2006), abolishes the Ancient Monuments Board for Wales and transfers its property, rights and liabilities to the National Assembly for Wales.

2105   Countryside and Rights of Way Act 2000—commencement

The Countryside and Rights of Way Act 2000 (Commencement No 8 and Transitional Provisions) (Wales) Order 2006, SI 2006/1279, brings into force, in relation to Wales, on 11 May 2006, ss 47–50, 51 (in part), 57 (in part), 69(2), 102 (in part), Sch 5 paras 1, 5, 6, 9, 12–17, Sch 6 para 23(8), and certain repeals in Sch 16. Transitional provision is also made.

The Countryside and Rights of Way Act 2000 (Commencement No 9 and Saving) (Wales) Order 2006, SI 2006/3257, brings into force, in relation to Wales, (1) on 6 December 2006, (a) ss 57 (in part), 107 (in part), Sch 6 para 26 and a repeal in Sch 16 Pt II; (b) for certain purposes, s 69(1), (3); and (c) so far as they are not already in force Sch 6 paras 1, 6, 9(5) and a repeal in Sch 16 Pt I; and (2) on 1 April 2007, s 69 (so far as not already in force). A saving is also made.

The Countryside and Rights of Way Act 2000 (Commencement No 11 and Savings) Order 2006, SI 2006/1172, brings into force, on 2 May 2006, ss 47–50, 51 (in part), 102 (in part), Sch 5 paras 1, 6, 7, 9, 12–17, and a repeal in Sch 16 Pt II. Savings are also made.

For a summary of the Act, see 2000 Abr para 2405. See also the commencement table in the title STATUTES.

2106   Environmental and countryside stewardship

The Environmental Stewardship (England) and Countryside Stewardship (Amendment) Regulations 2006, SI 2006/991 (in force on 30 April 2006), further amend (1) the Environmental Stewardship (England) Regulations 2005, SI 2005/621, by (a) adding definitions of 'native breed at risk' and 'traditional farm building'; (b) making provision in respect of (i) the maintenance of traditional farm buildings; (ii) the stocking of land with cattle and sheep; and (iii) cattle grazing for conservation purposes and the grazing of native breeds at risk; and (c) revising the maximum payment rate for entry from £500 per environmental stewardship agreement to £500 per year; and (2) the Countryside Stewardship Regulations 2000, SI 2000/3048, by (a) providing, in respect of the temporary removal of sheep from upland grassland, that the maximum payment rate is changed from £1,100 per agreement year to £100 per visit; and (b) adding a new entry in respect of base payments for permitting access to agreement land for educational visits, specifying the maximum payment rate as £500 per agreement year.

2107   Historic Buildings Council for Wales—abolition

See para 2801.

2108   National park—national park authority—membership—England

The National Park Authorities (England) Order 2006, SI 2006/3165 (in force on 8 May 2007), further amends the 1996 Order, SI 1996/1243, so as to (1) alter the number of members appointed to the national park authorities for each of the national parks in England other than Northumberland and the New Forest; (2) reduce from 38 to 30 the total membership of the Peak District National Park Authority, and reduce from 26 to 22 the membership of each of the other authorities; and (3) make changes, in the case of each authority, to the numbers of members appointed by the Secretary of State and by local authorities.

2109   Natural Environment and Rural Communities Act 2006

The Natural Environment and Rural Communities Act 2006 makes provision about bodies concerned with the natural environment and rural communities, in connection with wildlife, sites of special scientific interest and national parks and the Broads. It also amends the law relating to rights of way, makes provision as to the Inland Waterways Amenity Advisory Council and provides for flexible administrative arrangements in connection with functions relating to the environment and rural affairs. The Act received the royal assent on 30 March 2006 and came into force in part on that day. Further provisions came into force on and between 2 May and 1 October 2006: SI 2006/1176, 1382, 2541, 2992. The remaining provisions come into force on a day or days to be appointed. For details of commencement, see commencement table in the title STATUTES.

Part 1 (ss 1–30) Natural England and the Commission for Rural Communities

Chapter 1 (ss 1–16) Natural England
Section 1 establishes Natural England, dissolves the Countryside Agency and English Nature and transfers the functions of those bodies to Natural England. The constitution of Natural England is set out in Sch 1. Natural England's general purpose is to ensure that the natural environment is conserved, enhanced and managed for the benefit of present and future generations, thereby contributing to sustainable development: s 2. Natural England must keep under review matters relating to its general purpose, and may undertake research which relates to its general purpose: s 3. Section 4 specifies Natural England's duties and powers to provide advice to public authorities and others in relation to its general purpose. Under s 5, Natural England may carry out proposals which appear to it to further its general purpose, and may assist, coordinate and promote the carrying out of such proposals by others. Natural England may give financial assistance to any person, if doing so appears to it to further its general purpose: s 6. Section 7 allows Natural England to make management agreements with people who have an interest in land about the management or use of land to further its general purpose. Natural England may make and carry out experimental schemes designed to establish ways in which its general purpose might be furthered: s 8. Under s 9, Natural England must publish documents and provide information relating to its general purpose, and, under s 10, it may provide consultancy and training services. Section 11 allows Natural England to charge for specified services and allows the Secretary of State to make provision requiring charges to be paid in respect of licences. Natural England may institute criminal proceedings: s 12. Natural England may do anything that appears to it to be conducive or incidental to the discharge of its functions, including entering into agreements, acquiring and disposing of property, borrowing money, forming bodies corporate, accepting gifts, and investing money: s 13. Section 14 allows the Secretary of State to make grants to Natural England, s 15 empowers and requires the Secretary of State to give guidance to Natural England in the exercise of its functions, and s 16 empowers the Secretary of State to give Natural England directions as to the exercise of its functions.

Chapter 2 (ss 17–25) Commission for Rural Communities
Section 17 establishes the Commission for Rural Communities and Sch 2 sets out its constitution. The Commission's general purpose is to promote awareness among relevant persons and the public of rural needs, and to promote the meeting of those needs in ways that contribute to sustainable development: s 18. The Commission's main functions are representing rural needs to relevant persons, providing relevant persons with information and advice about issues connected with rural needs or ways of meeting them, and monitoring and making reports on the way in which relevant persons' policies are developed, adopted and implemented: s 19. Section 20 empowers the Commission to undertake, commission and support research which relates to its general purpose. Section 21 allows the Commission to publish documents or provide information about any matter

relating to its general purpose, s 22 allows the Commission to charge for its services, and s 23 makes provision for incidental powers. Section 24 empowers the Secretary of State to make grants to the Commission, and allows him to impose conditions when giving such a grant. By virtue of s 25, the Secretary of State may give the Commission directions as to the exercise of its functions.

Chapter 3 (ss 26–30) Supplementary
Section 26 allows the Secretary of State to make schemes for the transfer of property, rights and liabilities in connection with the dissolution of English Nature and the Countryside Agency, and s 27 provides for continuing powers to make transfer schemes. Detailed provision relating to the making of transfer schemes under ss 26, 27 is made by s 28, Sch 3. The Secretary of State may require English Nature or the Countryside Agency to provide staff, premises or other facilities, on a temporary basis, to Natural England or the Commission: s 29. Section 30 is interpretational.

Part 2 (ss 31–39) Nature conservation in the United Kingdom
Section 31 provides for the continued existence of the Joint Nature Conservation Committee, but for the Joint Committee to be reconstituted in accordance with Sch 4. The terms 'UK conservation bodies' and 'GB conservation bodies' are defined by s 32. The Joint Committee is given functions for the purpose of nature conservation and fostering the understanding of nature conservation: s 33. Section 34 sets out functions of the UK conservation bodies that can be discharged only through the Joint Committee. By virtue of s 35, the Joint Committee may provide advice to the UK conservation bodies in connection with their functions or on a matter of national or international significance. Certain functions of the GB conservation bodies under the Wildlife and Countryside Act 1981 must be discharged through the Joint Committee: 2006 Act s 36. Section 37 empowers the UK conservation bodies to do anything conducive or incidental to their functions, and s 38 enables the Secretary of State to give the Joint Committee directions about the exercise of certain functions. Section 39 is interpretational.

Part 3 (ss 40–54) Wildlife etc
Section 40 imposes a duty on public authorities to have regard to the purpose of conserving biodiversity. Section 41 places a duty on the Secretary of State to publish, review and revise lists of living organisms and types of habitat in England that are of principal importance for the purpose of conserving English biodiversity, and to consult Natural England before doing so, and s 42 places an equivalent duty on the National Assembly for Wales in relation to Wales, requiring the Assembly to consult the Countryside Council for Wales. It is an offence to possess a pesticide containing an ingredient which the Secretary of State has prescribed on the ground that it is necessary or expedient to do so in the interests of protecting wild birds or animals from harm: s 43. Provision for enforcement powers in connection with pesticides is made by s 44. Under s 45, the Secretary of State may issue a code of practice in connection with pesticides. Section 46 provides for the interpretation of ss 44, 45. It is an offence to take, damage or destroy the nest of specified types of wild birds: s 47. Section 48 extends the protection afforded to wild birds under the 1981 Act to birds which have been bred in captivity and lawfully released into the wild as part of a re-population or re-introduction programme. A person may not keep or have in his possession any prescribed bird for five years after being convicted of an offence of keeping or having in his possession any such bird without that bird being properly registered and ringed or marked: 2006 Act s 49. Section 50 makes it an offence to sell, offer or expose for sale, have in one's possession or transport for the purpose of sale, certain specified invasive species of animals and plants, or anything from which such animals or plants can be propagated. By virtue of s 51, the Secretary of State may issue or approve codes of practice relating to non-native animal and plant species. Section 52, Sch 5 make provision relating to enforcement of the 1981 Act, and apply enforcement provisions under the 1981 Act to the Destructive Imported Animals Act 1932, the Conservation of Seals Act 1970, the Deer Act 1991 and the Protection of Badgers Act 1992. The 2006 Act s 53 introduces Sch 6, which contains provisions extending the time limit for summary proceedings for certain offences relating to wildlife. By virtue of s 54, certain provisions of the 1981 Act apply to the Crown.

Part 4 (ss 55–58) Sites of special scientific interest
Section 55 makes it an offence for a relevant authority to fail to comply with its obligations to notify Natural England or, as the case may be, the Countryside Council for Wales, before permitting operations likely to damage a site of special scientific interest, unless it has a reasonable excuse. The intentional or reckless destruction or damage of the listed features of a site of special scientific interest or the disruption of its listed fauna, without reasonable excuse, is also an offence by virtue of s 55. Section 56 allows the relevant conservation body to denotify a site of special scientific interest, or part of a site, where it is not of special interest. The validity of any specified notice relating to a site of special scientific interest is not affected by the relevant conservation body's failure to serve on every owner and occupier where it has taken all reasonable steps to: s 57. By virtue of s 58, Natural England or, in Wales, the Countryside Council for Wales, may erect, maintain and remove signs or notices about a site of special scientific interest on land included in that site.

Part 5 (ss 59–65) National Parks and the Broads
Section 59 clarifies the requirements for designating land in a national park and s 60 amends provision concerning the procedure for orders designating national parks. Section 61 amends

provisions relating to the membership of national park authorities. The duty of national park authorities not to incur significant expenditure in support of their socio-economic duty has been removed by s 62. Section 63 transfers from the Secretary of State to a national park authority the power to make an order placing a temporary prohibition on ploughing, and on other specified agricultural or forestry operations on moor or heath in national parks. Section 64 alters the functions of the Broads Authority. By virtue of s 65, any national park authority and the Broads Authority may apply to a fund for emergency assistance following a natural disaster.

Part 6 (ss 66–72) Rights of way
Section 66 provides that no public right of way for mechanically propelled vehicles may be created unless it is created either on terms that expressly provide for it to be a right of way for such vehicles or by the construction under statutory powers of a road intended to be used for such vehicles. Certain existing rights of way for mechanically propelled vehicles which are not shown in a definitive map and statement, or which are shown in a definitive map and statement only as a footpath, bridleway or restricted byway, are extinguished by s 67. Section 68 enables the use of a way by a non-mechanically propelled vehicle to give rise to a public right of way for such vehicles. Where the right of the public to use a way is brought into question by an application to modify the definitive map and statement, the date on which right of the public is brought into question is to be treated as being the date on which the application is made: s 69. Section 70 allows the recording on the definitive map and statement for the area of a newly discovered right of way which is a restricted byway and creates an exception to the offence of driving a mechanically propelled vehicle on a footpath, bridleway or restricted byway. Section 71 is interpretational. The national park authorities are empowered by s 72 to make traffic regulation orders and other traffic-related orders in relation to roads in a national park that are either byways, footpaths or bridleways shown in a definitive map and statement or unsealed carriageways.

Part 7 (ss 73–77) Inland waterways
Section 73 changes the name of the Inland Waterways Amenity Advisory Council to the Inland Waterways Advisory Council. The arrangements governing the composition of the Council and the procedures to be adopted for the appointment of the chairman and members are set out by s 74. Section 75 sets out the terms under which the members of the Council hold office, the procedure for the appointment of regional and other committees, and provides for the payment of members' expenses and allowances, and the remuneration of the chairman. The Council must provide the Secretary of State and navigation authorities with advice about matters relevant to inland waterways in England and Wales, and may provide any other interested person with such advice: s 76. Section 77 applies to Scotland.

Part 8 (ss 78–98) Flexible administrative arrangements

Chapter 1 (ss 78–86) Agreements with designated bodies
Section 78 empowers the Secretary of State to enter into an agreement with a designated body authorising that body to carry out a function of the Department for Environment, Food and Rural Affairs. One designated body may enter into an agreement with another designated body authorising that second body to carry out a function of the first that is related to or connected with a function of the Department for Environment, Food and Rural Affairs: s 79. Section 80 provides that a designated body is a body listed in Sch 7, and allows the Secretary of State to amend that list. An agreement under s 78 or 79 ('a Chapter 1 agreement') cannot authorise a designated body to perform any of the specified reserved functions: s 81. Section 82 provides that the maximum duration of a Chapter 1 agreement is 20 years. Supplementary provision concerning the conferment and performance of functions under Chapter 1 agreements is made by s 83. Where a function is to be discharged on behalf of the Secretary of State or another designated body by a local authority under a Chapter 1 agreement, s 84 provides that the existing allocation of responsibility for the performance of that type of function under the Local Government Act 2000 and subordinate legislation applies. The 2006 Act s 85 sets out certain procedural provisions concerning a Chapter 1 agreement, and provides that no power of a Minister of the Crown to give directions to a statutory body extends to require the body to enter into a Chapter 1 agreement, or to prohibit it from doing so. Section 86 is interpretational.

Chapter 2 (ss 87–97) Powers to reform agricultural etc bodies
Section 87 empowers the Secretary of State and the National Assembly for Wales to make an order establishing a board, and requiring such an order to specify the geographical area in relation to which assigned functions are to be exercised. Schedule 8 contains provisions about the constitution of boards and related matters. The permissible purposes for which a board may be established are specified by s 88 and the permissible functions of a board are specified by s 89, Sch 9. Section 90 introduces Sch 10, which contains ancillary provisions relating to boards. Sections 91, 92 give the Secretary of State and the Assembly the power to make an order for the dissolution of any existing levy body and any board established under Chapter 2. Such an order may deal with the transfer of any property, rights or liabilities of the existing body or board: s 93. Under s 94, the Secretary of State and the Assembly may make grants to a board under such conditions as he or it sees fit, and

under s 95 the Secretary of State and the Assembly may give a board directions as to the exercise of its functions, and may revoke or amend such directions. Section 96 is interpretational and s 97 contains procedural provision.

Chapter 3 (s 98) Financial assistance
Section 98 enables the Secretary of State to provide financial assistance in respect of expenditure incurred or to be incurred in any matter related to or connected with a function of the Department for Environment, Food and Rural Affairs, subject to any specified condition.

Part 9 (ss 99–101) Miscellaneous
Section 99 provides that, for the purpose of any enactment, the fact that land is used for agriculture, woodlands, as a park or its flora, fauna or physiographical features have been derived, in part, from human intervention in the landscape, does not prevent it from being regarded as land in an area of natural beauty or outstanding natural beauty. Section 100 amends byelaw making powers relating to land drainage so as to integrate environmental issues into the byelaw decision-making process. Section 101 abolishes certain redundant agricultural and other committees.

Part 10 (ss 102–109) Final provisions
Section 102 provides that the appropriate authority responsible for Crown land may enter into management agreements under s 7 in relation to the Crown's interests in Crown land. Section 103 make provision in relation to functions devolved to the National Assembly for Wales. The Secretary of State may make such supplementary, incidental, consequential, transitory, transitional or saving provisions as he considers necessary or expedient for the purposes of, in consequence of, or for the giving of full effect to any provision of the Act: s 104. Section 105 introduces Sch 11, which contains minor and consequential amendments, and Sch 12, which deals with repeals and revocations. Section 106 contains financial provisions, s 107 provides for commencement, s 108 deals with extent and s 109 deals with short title.

Amendments, repeals and revocations
The list below, which is not exhaustive, mentions repeals and amendments which are or will be effective when the Act is fully in force.
Specific provisions of a number of Acts are amended or repealed. These include: Hill Farming Act 1946 ss 32, 34; Industrial Organisation and Development Act 1947 ss 5, 9; National Parks and Access to the Countryside Act 1949 ss 1(2), 3, 4A, 5–7, 9(2), 11A, 15, 15A, 16, 17–22, 50A, 51, 52, 55, 64(5), 65, 85, 86, 86A, 90, 91, 103, 106, 114, Sch 1; Agricultural Marketing Act 1958 ss 19(1)–(5), (9), 20, 21, 32, 47, 53, Sch Pt 2 paras 2, 3, Pt 5 paras 2, 3, Pt 6 paras 2, 3; Cereal Marketing Act 1965 ss 6, 17(2); Agriculture Act 1967 s 24; Countryside Act 1968 ss 1, 2, 4, 8, 12, 13, 15(6A), 15A(5), 23, 37, 38, 41, 45, 46, 49; Local Government Act 1974 s 9; Wildlife and Countryside Act 1981 ss 10, 15, 16, 19, 19ZA, 19ZB, 21(4A), (4D), 22, 24, 27, 27A, 27AA, 28, 28E, 28G, 29–34, 34A, 35–37, 37A, 39, 41, 41A, 43, 45, 47, 49–52, 71, Sch 13; Derelict and Act 1982 s 1; Miscellaneous Financial Provisions Act 1983 s 1; National Heritage Act 1983 s 24(7), (8); Road Traffic Regulation Act 1984 s 22; Environmental Protection Act 1990 ss 36, 128–130, 131(5), 132, 133, 134(2), 135–138, 161, Schs 6–10; Water Industry Act 1991 ss 4, 5, 156, Sch 1A para 11; Agriculture Act 1993 s 20; Environment Act 1995 ss 4, 8, 9, 66, 72, 99, Sch 7; Government of Wales Act 1998 Sch 4 para 6, Sch 5 para 21; Countryside and Rights of Way Act 2000 ss 1, 4, 20, 26, 33, 58, 61, 73, 74, 80, 82–84, 86, 87, 90–92, 101, Schs 4 para 5, Sch 7 paras 6, 7, Sch 8 paras 1, 2, Sch 11, Sch 12 para 8, Sch 13, Sch 15 para 1.

PARLIAMENT

Halsbury's Laws of England (4th edn) vol 34 (Reissue) paras 501–1027

Articles

For articles relating to this title please refer to the Table of Articles at the beginning of the Abridgment.

2110   Legislation—post-legislative scrutiny—Law Commission recommendations

The Secretary of State for Constitutional Affairs and Lord Chancellor has presented to Parliament a report by the Law Commission, *Post-Legislative Scrutiny* (Cm 6945, Law Com No 302). For the purposes of the report, the term 'post-legislative scrutiny' is treated as meaning a broad form of review whose purpose is to address the effects of legislation in terms of whether the intended policy objectives have been met by the legislation and, if so, how effectively. The Commission recognises the case for more systematic post-legislative scrutiny although it would have some limitations. It suggests that the policy objectives of legislation should be clearly set out in the appropriate regulatory impact assessment, together with criteria for monitoring and review. It recommends that consideration should be given to establishing a new parliamentary joint committee on post-legislative scrutiny although, in the first instance, select committees would retain their powers to undertake a review if they wished to exercise such in any particular instance and government departments would continue their practice of reviewing legislation. The joint committee might involve independent experts, for example, the National Audit Office, in its work. The proposed joint committee might also consider Bills and whether and how they might be reviewed after enactment, including the possible inclusion of an appropriate review clause in a Bill. Looking ahead, the Commission envisages the possible extension of post-legislative scrutiny to secondary legislation.

2111   Parliamentary corporate bodies—Crown immunities

The Parliamentary Corporate Bodies (Crown Immunities etc) (Amendment) Order 2006, SI 2006/1457 (in force on 10 July 2006), amends the 1992 Regulations, SI 1992/1732, so as to make consequential amendments, in relation to Crown interests, from the enforcement of the Planning (Application to the Houses of Parliament) Order 2006, SI 2006/1469.

2112   Parliamentary Costs Act 2006

The Parliamentary Costs Act 2006 consolidates the House of Commons Costs Taxation Act 1847, the House of Lords Costs Taxation Act 1849, the Parliamentary Costs Act 1865, the Parliamentary Costs Act 1867, the Parliamentary Costs Act 1871 and the House of Commons Costs Taxation Act 1879, with amendments to give effect to recommendations of the Law Commission and the Scottish Law Commission. The Act received the royal assent on 8 November 2006 and comes into force on 1 April 2007.

DESTINATION TABLE

1. This table shows how enactments proposed to be repealed are dealt with by the consolidation.

2. The following abbreviations are used:

Acts of Parliament

1847	House of Commons Costs Taxation Act 1847 (c 69)
1849	House of Lords Costs Taxation Act 1849 (c 78)
1865	Parliamentary Costs Act 1865 (c 27)
1867	Parliamentary Costs Act 1867 (c 136)
1871	Parliamentary Costs Act 1871 (c 3)
1879	House of Commons Costs Taxation Act 1879 (c 17)

3. 1847, 1849, 1865, 1867, 1871 and 1879 were applied by the Private Bill Procedure Act (Northern Ireland) 1924 (NI c 9). But that Act was subsequently repealed by the Northern Ireland (Modification of Enactments—No 1) Order 1999, SI 1999/663, Sch 2.

House of Commons Costs Taxation Act 1847 (c 69)

Existing provision	Rewritten provision	Remarks
General		
		Applied 1879, ss 1, 3; applied Statutory Orders (Special Procedure) Act 1945 (c 18) s 7(2); modified Solicitors' Incorporated Practices Order 1991, SI 1991/2684, art 4(a), Sch 1.
Preamble		
	—	Repealed Statute Law Revision Act 1891 (c 67) Schedule
1 Repeal		
	—	Repealed Statute Law Revision Act 1875 (c 66) Schedule
2 Parliamentary Agent, Attorney, or Solicitor not to sue for Costs until One Month after delivery of his Bill		
	—	Repealed Statute Law (Repeals) Act 1993 (c 50) Sch 1 Pt 11.
3 Taxing Officer to be appointed by the Speaker		
	s 1	
4 The Speaker to prepare List of Charges thenceforth to be allowed		
	s 2	Repealed in part Statute Law Revision Act 1894 (c 56) Sch 1.
5 Taxing Officer empowered to examine Parties and Witnesses on Oath		

Existing provision	Rewritten provision	Remarks
	s 13(1)	Repealed in part Statute Law (Repeals) Act 1993 (c 50), Sch 1 Pt 11 Group 1.

6 Taxing Officer empowered to call for Books and Papers

| | s 13(1) | Proviso unnecessary. |

7 Taxing Officer to take such Fees as may be allowed by the House of Commons

| | s 14 | |

8 On Application of Party chargeable, or on Application of Parliamentary Agent, Attorney, or Solicitor, the Taxing Officer to tax the Bill

| | ss 3(1), (2), (4), (5), 4, 13(2), (3) | Repealed in part Statute Law Revision Act 1894 (c 56) Sch 1; repealed in part Statute Law (Repeals) Act 1993 (c 50) Sch 1 Pt 11 Group 1; amended Statute Law (Repeals) Act 1993 (c 50) Sch 2 Pt 2 para 13. |

9 Taxing Officer to report to the Speaker

| | ss 6(1), (2), 7, 8 | Repealed in part Statute Law (Repeals) Act 1993 (c 50) Sch 1 Pt 11 Group 1. |

10 Construction of certain Words in this Act

| | — | Repealed in part (definition of 'oath') Statute Law (Repeals) Act 1981 (c 19) Sch 1 Pt 8. Otherwise unnecessary (see Interpretation Act 1978 (c 30) Sch 1). |

11 Form of citing the Act

| | — | Unnecessary. |

12 Act may be amended, &c

| | — | Repealed Statute Law Revision Act 1875 (c 66) Schedule |

House of Lords Costs Taxation Act 1849 (c 78)

Existing provision	Rewritten provision	Remarks
General		
	—	Applied Statutory Orders (Special Procedure) Act 1945 (c 18) s 7(2); modified Solicitors' Incorporated Practices Order 1991, SI 1991/2684, art 4(a), Schs 1, 2.
Preamble		
	—	Repealed Statute Law Revision 1891 (c 67) Schedule
1 Repeal		
	—	Repealed Statute Law Revision Act 1875 (c 66) Schedule

2 Parliamentary Agent, Attorney, or Solicitor not to sue for Costs until One Month after Delivery of his Bill

| | — | Repealed Statute Law (Repeals) Act 1993 (c 50) Sch 1 Pt 11 Group 1. |

3 Taxing Officer to be appointed by the Clerk of Parliaments to Clerk Assistant

| | s 1 | Repealed in part Statute Law (Repeals) Act 1993 (c 50) Sch 1 Pt 11 Group 1. |

4 The Clerk of Parliaments or Clerk Assistant to prepare List of Charges thenceforth to be allowed

Existing provision	Rewritten provision	Remarks
	s 2	Repealed in part Statute Law Revision Act 1892 (c 19) Schedule; repealed in part Statute Law Revision Act 1894 (c 56) Sch 1; repealed in part Statute Law (Repeals) Act 1993 (c 50) Sch 1 Pt 11 Group 1.
5 Taxing Officer empowered to examine Parties and Witnesses on Oath		
	s 13(1)	Repealed in part Statute Law (Repeals) Act 1993 (c 50) Sch 1 Pt 11 Group 1.
6 Taxing Officer empowered to call for Books and Papers		
	s 13(1)	
7 Taxing Officer to take such fees as may be allowed by House of Lords		
	s 14	
8 On Application of Party chargeable, or on Application of Parliamentary Agent, Attorney, or Solicitor, the Taxing Officer to tax the Bill		
	ss 3(1), (2), (4), (5), 4, 13(2), (3)	Repealed in part Statute Law Revision Act 1892 (c 19) Sch; repealed in part Statute Law (Repeals) Act 1993 (c 50) Sch 1 Pt 11 Group 1; amended Statute Law (Repeals) Act 1993 (c 50) Sch 2 para.13.
9 Taxing Officer to report to the Clerk of Parliaments		
	ss 6(1), (2), 7 and 8	Repealed in part Statute Law (Repeals) Act 1993 (c 50) Sch 1 Pt 11 Group 1.
10 Taxing Officer of either House may tax Costs not otherwise taxable under the Act by virtue of which any Bill shall be taxed; and may request other Officers to assist him		
	s 5(1)–(3), (5)–(7)	
11 Taxing Officers to include certain Costs in their Reports, and Certificates of the Amount to be delivered		
	s 6(3)	
12 Officers of other Courts may request the Taxing Officer of either House to tax Parts of Bills		
	s 5(5)–(7)	
13 Taxing Officer of either House may take an Account between the Parties		
	s 13(4)	
14 Construction of certain Words in this Act		
	—	Repealed in part (definition of 'oath') Statute Law (Repeals) Act 1981 (c 19) Sch 1 Pt 8. Otherwise unnecessary (see Interpretation Act 1978 (c 30) Sch 1).
15 Form of citing the Act		
	—	Unnecessary.
16 Act may be amended, &c		
	—	Repealed Statute Law Revision Act 1875 (c 66) Schedule

Parliamentary Costs Act 1865 (c 27)

Existing provision	Rewritten provision	Remarks
General		
		Applied 1871, s 2; applied Private Legislation Procedure (Scotland) Act 1936 (c 52) s 9(3); applied Statutory Orders (Special Procedure) Act 1945 (c 18) s 7(1); modified Solicitors' Incorporated Practices Order 1991, SI 1991/2684, art 4(a), Sch 1.

Existing provision	Rewritten provision	Remarks
Preamble		
		Repealed Statute Law Revision Act 1893 (c 14) Schedule
1 When Committee report 'Preamble not proved', Opponents to be entitles to recover Costs		
	s 10(1), (2)	Applied Private Legislation Procedure (Scotland) Act 1936 (c 52) s 6(6) (amended by Statute Law (Repeals) Act 1993 (c 50) Sch 1 Pt 11 Group 1).
2 When Committee report unanimously 'Opposition unfounded', Promoters to be entitled to recover Costs		
	s 9(1)–(4)	Applied Private Legislation Procedure (Scotland) Act 1936 (c 52) s 6(6) (amended by Statute Law (Repeals) Act 1993 (c 50) Sch 1, Pt 11, Group 1).
3 Costs to be taxed		
	ss 11, 12	Applied Private Legislation Procedure (Scotland) Act 1936 (c 52) s 6(6) (amended by Statute Law (Repeals) Act 1993 (c 50) Sch 1 Pt 11 Group 1).
4 Powers of Taxing Officer		
	ss 13(1), 14	Applies 1847 and 1849.
5 Recovery of Costs when taxed		
	—	Repealed Statute Law (Repeals) Act 1993 (c 50) Sch 1 Pt 11 Group 1.
6 Form of Action in Scotland		
	—	Repealed Statute Law (Repeals) Act 1993 (c 50) Sch 1 Pt 11 Group 1.
7 Persons paying Costs may recover a Proportion from other Persons liable thereto		
	—	Repealed Statute Law (Repeals) Act 1993 (c 50) Sch 1 Pt 11 Group 1.
8 When Committee report 'Preamble not proved', Promoters to pay Costs out of Deposits		
	—	Repealed Statute Law Revision Act 1966 (c 5) Schedule
9 Definition of Promoters		
	s 18, definition of 'promoter'	
10 Meaning of Private Bill		
		Unnecessary.
11 Commencement of Act		
	—	Repealed Statute Law Revision Act 1893 (c 14) Schedule

Parliamentary Costs Act 1867 (c 136)

Existing provision	Rewritten provision	Remarks
Preamble		
	—	Repealed Statute Law Revision Act 1893 (c 14) Schedule
1 Power of Court of Referees to administer Oaths to Witnesses		
	s 16	
2 Witnesses falsely deposing guilty of Perjury		

Existing provision	Rewritten provision	Remarks
	—	Repealed Statute Law (Repeals) Act 1993 (c 50) Sch 1 Pt 11 Group 2.
3 Power to award Costs		
	—	Repealed Statute Law (Repeals) Act 1993 (c 50) Sch 1 Pt 11 Group 1.

Parliamentary Costs Act 1871 (c 3)

Existing provision	Rewritten provision	Remarks
General		Applied Statutory Orders (Special Procedure) Act 1945 (c 18) s 7(1).
1 Repeal		
	—	Repealed Statute Law Revision Act 1883 (c 39) Sch.
2 Power of Select Committees on Bills confirming Provisional Orders to Award costs		
	15(4), (5)	Applies 1865.
3 Power to Committees of the House of Commons to examine witnesses on oath		
	—	Repealed Parliamentary Witnesses Oaths Act 1871 (c 83) s 2.
4 Interpretation of 'Provisional Order'		
	18, definition of 'provisional order'	Repealed in part Statute Law (Repeals) Act 1986 (c 12) Sch 1 Pt 10.

House of Commons Costs Taxation Act 1879 (c 17)

Existing provision	Rewritten provision	Remarks
General		Modified Solicitors' Incorporated Practices Order 1991 (SI 1991/2684) art 4, Sch 1.
Preamble		
	—	Repealed Statute Law Revision Act 1894 (c 56) Sch 1.
1 Powers of 1947 extended to provisional orders and other costs		
	15(1)–(3)	Applies 1847; repealed in part Statute Law (Repeals) Act 1986 (c 12) Sch 1 Pt 10.
2 Taxing officer of House of Commons to tax costs or orders and Bills on request from proper authority		
	5(3), (5)	Applied Statutory Orders (Special Procedure) Act 1945 (c 18) s 7(2); repealed in part Statute Law (Repeals) Act 1986 (c 12) Sch 1 Pt 10.
3 Fees under this Act to be received as directed by 1847		
	13(2), (3), 15(1)–(3)	Applies 1847.
4 Short title		
	—	Unnecessary.

Statute Law (Repeals) Act 1993 (c 50)

Existing provision	Rewritten provision	Remarks
Sch 2 Consequential and Connected Provisions		
Pt 2 Other provisions		
para 13	4(2)	Amends 1847 s 8, 1849 s 8.

Solicitors' Incorporated Practices Order 1991 (SI 1991/2684)

Existing provision	Rewritten provision	Remarks
Sch 1 Statutes which apply to recognised bodies		
Entries relating to 1847, 1849, 1865 and 1879	18, definition of 'solicitor'	Modifies 1847, 1849, 1865 and 1879.
Sch 2 Statutes which apple to recognised bodies with additions, omissions and modifications		
Entry relating to 1849	18, definition of 'solicitor'	Modifies 1849.

2113 Parliamentary pensions—general

The Parliamentary Pensions (Amendment) Regulations 2006, SI 2006/920 (in force on 6 April 2006), further amend the Parliamentary Pensions (Consolidation and Amendment) Regulations 1993, SI 1993/3253, so as to (1) update the definition of 'the index' and make the definition of 'permitted maximum' independent of the Income and Corporation Taxes Act 1998 without changing its meaning; (2) add a definition of the pension value of retained benefits which is relevant to the maximum pension that can be paid to participants; (3) provide that additional voluntary contributions are not taken into account in determining maximum contributions, and benefits purchased as a result of such contributions are not taken into account in determining maximum benefits; (4) limit the total contributions to buy added years, whether periodical or by way of lump sum, to not more than ten per cent of a parliamentary pensions member's salary in a tax year; (5) provide that pensions are payable despite a person being a candidate in an election; (6) provide that pensions are reduced to nil during further service as a member of the House of Commons; (7) impose limits on pension commencement lump sums; (8) provide a special option for members reaching the age of 75 before 6 April 2006 to opt to cease to be participants and to become entitled to commute their pensions for a lump sum despite continuing in office as a member of the House of Commons or as an office holder; (9) provide that, where such a member decides to opt to cease to be a participant, a special ten year pension guarantee will be given where certain specified conditions are satisfied; (10) restrict the amount of pensions payable so that they qualify as dependants' scheme pensions; (11) change the definition of 'child' for the purposes of children's pensions; (12) provide that death in service lump sums can only be paid to members who have reached the age of 75 if they are pensioners on 6 April 2006; (13) remove the discretion to pay lump sums on the death of a pensioner member; (14) provide that, where a pensioner member dies before receiving his five years' pension, one or more pensions are payable to the pensioner's dependants for the remainder of the five year period that are equal to the member's own pension; (15) provide that the right to a lump sum will only continue where the member had no dependants and, unless he was a pensioner on 5 April 2006, he has not reached 75; (16) provide that the ill-health pension provisions mirror requirements about cessation of occupation and medical evidence about incapacity; (17) enable persons who are participants on or after 2 April 1991 to take early retirement despite having less that 15 years' reckonable service; (18) impose general obligations on statements of investment principles; (19) extend the provisions relating to the chairman of select committees to all chairmen of such committees who are eligible for additional salary as such and all chairmen of standing committees; (20) provide for the scheme administrator to pay the lifetime allowance charge on behalf of participants in some circumstances, and for benefits to be reduced where the scheme administrator has done so without the participant having made a payment to cover the tax; (21) provide for the payment of the short service refund lump sum charge and the special lump sum death benefits charge to be deducted from payments liable to those charges; (22) reflect changes in the law relating to transfer out and restricts the time within which certain transfers from other pension schemes can be accepted; (23) in relation to refunds of contributions, align the requirements with those for short service refund lump sums; (24) make provision in relation to enhanced protection of pension rights; (25) enable people who become a participant for a second or subsequent time on or after 6 April 2006 to elect for their new term of service to be treated separately from earlier service; and (26) extend the pension sharing provisions to cases where civil partnerships are dissolved and to prevent payments being made in cases where the ex-spouse or civil partner dies before liability in respect of pension credit is discharged but after reaching 75 years of age. The regulations also amend the Parliamentary Pensions (Additional Voluntary Contributions) Regulations 1993, SI 1993/3252, so as to (a) remove restrictions on amounts of contributions and the benefits attributable to them and restrict the kinds of transfers in that may be accepted by the additional voluntary contribution scheme; (b) prevent participants in the parliamentary pension scheme who are over 75 from joining the additional voluntary scheme; (c) enable any benefits to be paid that are authorised for registered schemes; (d) require lump sums to be taken at retirement or at a later time up to the member's 75th birthday, subject to the limits imposed; (e) provide that the amounts that can be taken as benefits or transferred out include the realisable value of amounts transferred in; (f) enable transfers out to be applied in any way permitted, and to bring payments by way of return of contributions within the requirements for short service refund lump sums; (g) provide for the trustees to pay the lifetime allowance charge in some circumstances and for the contributor's fund to be reduced where they have done so; (h) extend the pension sharing provisions where civil partnerships are dissolved to prevent payments being made in cases where the ex-spouse or civil partner dies before liability in respect of pension credit is discharged but after reaching 75 years of age; and (i) make various consequential amendments.

The Parliamentary Pensions (Amendment) (No 2) Regulations 2006, SI 2006/1965 (in force on 18 August 2006), further amend the 1993 Regulations, SI 1993/3253, supra by extending the class of members so as to allow the holder of the office of Speaker of the House of Lords to participate in the parliamentary pension scheme.

PARTNERSHIP

Halsbury's Laws of England (4th edn) vol 35 (Reissue) paras 1–300

Articles

For articles relating to this title please refer to the Table of Articles at the beginning of the Abridgment.

2114   Dissolution—indemnity of outgoing partner—liability for losses arising from business introduced after dissolution

The defendant's partnership applied to the claimant to act as its intermediary for the purposes of selling its insurance products. An agreement was entered into whereby the partnership would sell the claimant's medical insurance in return for a commission. The claimant agreed to pay commission in advance before the premiums were paid. If the premiums were not paid, those advance commissions would be repaid, pursuant to an indemnity clause, under which liability arose to indemnify the claimant for any losses incurred as a result of business introduced by the intermediary. The defendant left the partnership, which was then dissolved. When the claimant brought proceedings against the defendant seeking repayment of unearned commission, the issue arose as to whether the defendant was liable for unearned commission paid in relation to business introduced after the partnership had been dissolved. The claimant submitted that the defendant was liable under the Partnership Act 1890 s 17(2), since the obligation to repay had arisen at the time the contract had been entered into, and not when the advance commissions had been paid. The judge found that the defendant's indebtedness had arisen both prior to and after the date on which he had dissolved the partnership. The defendant appealed. *Held*, the defendant was not liable under the agreement to repay the unearned commissions arising from policies issued after the claimant had been notified of the dissolution of partnership. It was clear that the agreement was with the partnership, and that therefore the partnership was the intermediary for the purposes of the indemnity clause, under which liability arose for any losses suffered by the claimant in respect of business introduced by the intermediary. As the partnership had ceased to exist when the defendant had left, and the claimant had been notified of that by the defendant, any business introduced after that notification had not been introduced by the intermediary. It followed that the indemnity clause did not extend to business introduced after the dissolution of the partnership. Accordingly, the appeal would be allowed.

Friends Provident Life and Pensions Ltd v Evans [2006] All ER (D) 388 (Mar) (Court of Appeal: Chadwick and Arden LJJ).

2115   Insolvency

See COMPANY AND PARTNERSHIP INSOLVENCY.

2116   Partners—registration of partnership for value added tax purposes—taxable persons

See *Revenue and Customs Comrs v Pal*, para 2920.

2117   Trading losses—set-off

See para 1694.

PATENTS AND REGISTERED DESIGNS

Halsbury's Laws of England (4th edn) vol 35 (Reissue) paras 301–900

Articles

For articles relating to this title please refer to the Table of Articles at the beginning of the Abridgment.

2118   Patent—address for service

See para 2853.

2119   Patent—entitlement—dispute—proceedings—guidance

Guidance has been given in relation to patent entitlement disputes, and the following observations were made: (1) entitlement disputes inevitably gave rise to many issues of fact and could readily become overheated and prolix; (2) such disputes were more likely where the parties' relationships had not been reduced to writing; (3) since it was clearly unsatisfactory for a dispute to be in two different tribunals, the jurisdiction of the Comptroller General of Patents, Designs and Trade Marks should be reserved for relatively straightforward cases, and he should refer complex cases to the High Court or a county court at an early stage; (4) in some cases it could make sense for a claimant to initiate proceedings simultaneously before the court and the Comptroller, with a view to making an immediate application to the Comptroller for transfer; (5) parties should realise that such disputes, if fully fought, were potentially protracted, very expensive and emotionally draining, and that it would often have been better to settle early for a smaller share; and (6) such a dispute was particularly apt for early mediation going well beyond conventional mediation, where a mediator trusted by both sides was given the authority to decide the terms of a binding settlement agreement.

University of Southampton's Applications [2006] EWCA Civ 145, [2006] RPC 567 (Court of Appeal: Ward, Jacob and Wilson LJJ).

2120   Patent—intellectual property—enforcement of rights

The Intellectual Property (Enforcement, etc) Regulations 2006, SI 2006/1028 (in force on 29 April 2006), make various amendments and repeals to primary and secondary legislation so as to implement or further implement (1) EC Parliament and Council Directive 2004/48 on the enforcement of intellectual property rights; (2) the Agreement establishing the World Trade Organisation, including the Agreement on Trade-Related Aspects of Intellectual Property Rights; (3) EC Parliament and Council Directive 98/71 on the legal protection of designs; (4) EC Council Regulation 6/2002 on Community designs; and (5) the European Economic Area Agreement.

2121   Patent—licence—grant

On the application of one co-proprietor of a patent, it has been held that the Comptroller General of Patents, Designs and Trade Marks has jurisdiction under the Patents Act 1977 s 37(1) to order that licences under the patent be granted. The whole point of the patent system is to encourage innovation and the exploitation of inventions. Parliament cannot have intended that the exploitation of inventions can be frustrated by a deadlock situation. The comptroller has to act rationally, fairly and proportionately so that the wide discretion conferred on him under s 37(1) does not violate the principle of legal certainty. The power is not arbitrary but produces a fair commercial solution when co-owners cannot agree.

Paxman v Hughes [2006] EWCA Civ 818, [2007] RPC 34 (Court of Appeal: Sir Anthony Clarke MR, Jacob and Neuberger LJJ).

2122   Patent—ownership—application for licence following failed proprietorship claim— jurisdiction

The Patents Act 1977 s 37(1) provides that after a patent has been granted any person having or claiming a proprietary interest in or under the patent may refer to the comptroller the question who is the true proprietor or whether the patent should have been granted to the person to whom it was granted. Without prejudice to the generality of s 37(1), an order under s 37(1) may contain provision granting any licence or other right in or under the patent: s 37(2)(c).

Following the court's refusal to make a declaration that the claimant was entitled to be registered as the proprietor of a patent, the claimant sought a licence under the 1977 Act s 37(2)(c) to enable it to continue using the invention. The question arose whether the court had jurisdiction to grant a licence to the claimant notwithstanding the failed proprietorship claim. *Held*, the purpose of s 37 was to resolve conflicts between genuine proprietary claims. Entitlement was dealt with by s 37(1), (2) provided for relief available to those who had established that they came within those entitled under s 37(1). If those who shared an interest in property could not agree what should happen to or in relation to it, the comptroller decided the question and was given a reasonably free hand in deciding what to do. If a party's claims to a proprietary interest had been held to be bad, then it was no longer a person claiming a proprietary interest for those purposes, and s 37 was not available. The claimant's proprietary claim had failed, albeit because of an estoppel, and so it ceased to be a claimant for the purposes of s 37. Accordingly, the court had no jurisdiction to grant a licence and the application would be dismissed.

Cinpres Gas Injection Ltd v Melea Ltd [2006] EWHC 2950 (Ch), [2006] All ER (D) 305 (Nov) (Chancery Division: Mann J). *Rhone-Poulenc Rorer International Holdings Inc v Yeda Research and Development Co Ltd* [2006] EWCA Civ 1094, [2007] RPC 167 considered. For previous proceedings see *Cinpres Gas Injection Ltd v Melea Ltd* [2005] All ER (D) 209 (Dec).

2123   Patent—ownership—transfer to rightful owner after grant—claim for sole ownership after expiry of time limit

The Patents Act 1977 s 37(5) provides that, where a reference has been made to determine who owns a patent, no order may be made transferring the patent to which the reference relates if the reference was made after the end of the period of two years beginning with the date of the grant. Legal proceedings for the transfer of a patent to its true owner may be instituted only within a period of not more than two years after the date on which the European Patent Bulletin mentions the grant of the European patent: Convention for the European Patent for the Common Market art 23.

A reference was made to the comptroller to determine who owned a certain patent for a medicine. The proceedings were initiated within the two-year time limit specified by the 1977 Act s 37(5). A proposed amended statement, in which sole ownership was claimed, was subsequently filed outside the time limit. The registered proprietor of the patent and a licensee under the patent objected to the amendments on the ground that they were made outside the time limit. The amendment was permitted, and the proprietor and licensee appealed. The judge reversed the decision, deciding that the limitation periods in the 1977 Act did not permit new claims to be raised out of time. The respondent company appealed, and an issue arose as to the relevance of the Community Patent Convention art 23 to the construction of the 1977 Act s 37(5). *Held*, Parliament had intended s 37(5) to have the same meaning as the Convention art 23, envisaging that, where the provisions were in force, the same result would be reached whatever member state the case was started in. The fact that the Convention was not in force was immaterial. Moreover, the judge had been correct in deciding that the 1977 Act s 37(5) barred the making of a new claim out of time, and that that included amending a statement to make a novel claim for sole ownership. Where a patentee was assailed by a claim to sole ownership, he would be aware that he might be dispossessed entirely. It was sufficient for the purposes of the present case to say that the unamended statement did not disclose a case of sole inventorship. The proposed amendment had added, for the first time, a claim to sole ownership. In so far as the proposed amended reference claimed sole ownership and sought to set up facts in support of that remedy, it was a reference made after the expiry of the limitation period. Accordingly, the appeal would be dismissed.

Rhone-Poulenc Rorer International Holdings Inc v Yeda Research and Development Co Ltd [2006] EWCA Civ 1094, [2007] RPC 167 (Court of Appeal: Sir Anthony Clarke MR, Keene and Jacob LJJ).

2124   Patent—protection of industrial property—Convention countries

The Patents (Convention Countries) Order 2006, SI 2006/315 (in force on 6 April 2006), replaces the 2004 Order, SI 2004/3335, and declares specified countries to be Convention countries for the purpose of the protection of industrial property. With the exception of the Comoros all of the specified countries are already considered to be Convention countries.

2125   Patent—validity—anticipation

The Patents Act 1977 s 1(2)(c), (d) provides that (1) a scheme, rule or method for performing a mental act, playing a game or doing business, or a program for computer; or (2) the presentation of information, is not an invention for the purposes of the 1977 Act.

The defendant was the proprietor of a patent relating to various ways in which web pages might be 'pre-treated' before being downloaded to machines of modest processing capacity so as to save time and prolong battery life. The claimant company commenced proceedings against the defendant for revocation of the patent on the grounds of anticipation or obviousness. The claimant submitted alternatively that the invention consisted of a computer program and method of displaying information, and was therefore excluded from patentability pursuant to the 1977 Act s 1(2). *Held*, for a prior documentary disclosure to anticipate, it had both to disclose the invention and enable the skilled man to perform it. In cases of anticipation by inevitable result, the prior art disclosed those things which, if the skilled man did them, would fall within the claim. If the skilled person was given a target, in the shape of a disclosure of the invention, the law of enablement permitted reasonable experimentation and error correction while still holding that the prior disclosure was enabling. If the only target the skilled man was given was a course of action, then following that course of action would inevitably result in something within the claim, and there was no space for experimentation except in getting what was disclosed to work in accordance with the terms of the prior document. In the instant case, the claims of the patent at issue were invalid, having regard to the prior art cited by the claimant. The right approach to determining whether material was excluded pursuant to s 1(2) was to take the claims of the patent, correctly construed, and consider what the claimed invention contributed to the art outside the excluded subject matter. That test was to be applied on a case-by-case basis and little benefit was to be gained by drawing analogies with other cases decided on different facts in relation to different inventions. The objection on the part of the claimant that the invention lay in excluded subject matter failed. Accordingly, the application would be allowed.

Inpro Licensing Sarl's Patent (Application for revocation by Research in Motion UK Ltd) [2006] EWHC 70 (Pat), [2006] RPC 517 (Chancery Division: Pumfrey J). *Fujitsu Ltd's Application* [1997] RPC 608, CA (1987 Abr para 2496); and *Halliburton Energy Services Inc v Smith International (North Sea) Ltd* [2005] EWHC 1623 (Pat), [2006] RPC 25 applied.

2126   Patent—validity—exclusions from patentability—invention

The European Patent Convention art 52(2) provides that (1) discoveries, scientific theories and mathematical methods; (2) aesthetic creations; (3) schemes, rules and methods for performing mental acts, playing games or doing business, and programs for computers; and (4) presentations of information are not inventions in relation to which European patents may be granted. Article 52(2) excludes patentability of the subject matter or activities referred to only to the extent to which a European patent application or European patent relates to such subject matter or activities as such: art 52(3).

Two appeals heard together concerned certain of the categories declared by the European Patent Convention art 52(2) not to be inventions and so unpatentable. The first appeal related to a method of making telephone calls using a prepayment system that involved customers calling a central office before being routed to the number they ultimately wished to call. The judge ordered revocation of the patent, deciding that it was a method of doing business 'as such' within the meaning of art 52(2) and (3). The second appeal involved an automated method of acquiring the documents necessary to incorporate a company, under which a user sitting at a computer communicated with a remote server. The judge ruled that the alleged invention fell within the computer program and mental act exclusions in art 52(2). The applicants for the patent in each case appealed. *Held*, the correct approach in determining whether an invention was unpatentable within the terms of art 52(2) and (3) was to (a) construe the claim properly; (b) identify the actual contribution; (c) ask whether it fell solely within the excluded subject matter; and (d) check whether the actual or alleged contribution was actually technical in nature. That was a structured and more helpful way of reformulating the statutory test. In the first appeal, the system claimed as a whole in the patent was new in itself, so the contribution was a new system. It was clear that there was more than just a method of doing business as such, and the system was clearly technical in nature. In the second appeal, the patent was both for a method of doing business as such and for a computer program as such. The method was for the very business itself, the business of advising on and creating appropriate company formation documents, and there was nothing technical about the contribution beyond the mere fact of the running of a computer program. Accordingly, the first appeal would be allowed and the second appeal would be dismissed.

Aerotel Ltd v Telco Holdings Ltd; Re Macrossan's Application [2006] EWCA Civ 1371, [2007] 1 All ER 225 (Court of Appeal: Chadwick, Jacob and Neuberger LJJ). *Merrill Lynch's Application* [1989] RPC 561, CA (1989 Abr para 1705); *Gale's Application* [1991] RPC 305, CA; and *Fujitsu Ltd's Application* [1997] RPC 608, CA, applied.

2127   Patent—validity—obviousness—knowledge of skilled person

The claimant patentee was a pharmaceutical company marketing a formulation of cyclosporin, a pharmaceutical of particular utility in producing immunosuppression in recipients of allogenic organ transplants. The defendant intended to launch a cyclosporin formulation in the United Kingdom under a certain brand name. The claimant commenced proceedings alleging infringement by the defendant of two patents relating to the formulation of cyclosporine, the first, a microemulsion patent and the second, a component patent. Validity of the first patent was challenged on the basis of a United States patent and the common general knowledge. In respect of the second patent, the defendant alleged its own formulation was distinct on the basis that it was not a microemulsion pre-concentrate, it was not an emulsion pre-concentrate, it had no second component, and it had no lipophilic component. *Held*, it was artificial and incorrect to construe the word 'lipophilic' otherwise than as meaning substantially immiscible with the hydrophilic phase and destined to form a dispersed phase in the resulting microemulsion. There was no separately identifiable lipophilic phase in the defendant's formulation. 'Lipophilic' should be given its natural meaning when the underlying physical system, the microemulsion, was not part of the common general knowledge and the skilled person was relying on the patent itself, and the references it contained, to construct his view of how a microemulsion was to be characterised and how it worked. The claimant had failed to show that it was obvious to the skilled person that the particle size of the emulsion could be reduced, and that the obvious way to reduce it was to formulate a microemulsion. It followed that the attack on the first patent failed. Moreover, the allegation of infringement of the second patent failed on the basis that the term 'emulsion' did not cover the product's liquid crystal nature, as there was no lipophilic component, as that phrase had to be construed. However, on the evidence, the second patent stood as invalid on obviousness grounds. Accordingly, the application would be allowed in part.

Novartis AG v Ivax Pharmaceuticals UK Ltd [2006] EWHC 2506 (Pat), [2006] All ER (D) 172 (Oct) (Chancery Division: Pumfrey J).

2128   Patent—validity—specification of invention—sufficiency

The claimant patentee was the proprietor of two European patents relating to the design and use of drill bits for drilling in rock. The claimant brought proceedings in respect of both patents against the defendants, who had designed allegedly infringing bits using modelling software to simulate the performance of different designs of bits under defined conditions. The defendants counterclaimed for the revocation of the patents, disputing the sufficiency of the patents. The judge found that both patents were insufficient, in the case of the second patent because it required too much work to implement, and ordered the revocation of the patents. On appeal against the revocation of the second patent, *held*, patents were meant to teach people how to do things and if what was taught involved too much to be reasonable, allowing for the circumstances, including the nature of the art, then the patent could not be regarded as an enabling disclosure. In deciding whether the amount of work involved to perform the invention was too much, the line had to be drawn by an exercise of judgment, taking into account all of the relevant factors, including the nature of the invention itself and its field of technology, as well as the width of the patent claim or whether it had functional limitations which required too much work to explore. The setting of a gigantic project, even if merely routine, would not do. The patent required an extraordinary amount of work, going beyond the agony of the work required to produce an original scientific paper worthy of publication after peer review, and it was not surprising the judge found it insufficient. Accordingly, the appeal would be dismissed.

Halliburton Energy Services Inc v Smith International Inc [2006] EWCA Civ 1715, [2006] All ER (D) 246 (Dec) (Court of Appeal: Chadwick, Rix and Jacob LJJ). *Biogen Inc v Medeva plc* [1997] RPC 1, HL (1996 Abr para 2283), applied.

2129   Patent Office—electronic communications

The Registered Designs Act 1949 and Patents Act 1977 (Electronic Communications) Order 2006, SI 2006/1229 (in force on 1 October 2006), amends the Registered Designs Act 1949 and the Patents Act 1977, so as to facilitate the use of electronic communications with the Patent Office. In particular, the order (1) provides that the registrar has the power to (a) direct the form and manner in which a document is delivered to the registrar where the document is to be delivered in electronic form or using electronic communications; (b) require a document which is to be delivered in electronic form or using electronic communications to be accompanied by one or more additional documents; (c) treat a document as not having been delivered if the form and manner of its delivery does not comply with directions; (d) give directions as to how a fee must be paid and when the fee is to be deemed to have been paid where a document is delivered using electronic communications and there is a requirement for a fee to accompany the document; (e) direct that a person delivering a document to the registrar in electronic form or using electronic communications cannot treat it as having been delivered unless its delivery has been acknowledged; and (f) direct how the time of delivery is to be accorded to a document which is sent to the registrar in electronic form or using electronic communications; (2) provides that 'electronic communication' in the 1949 Act is to have the same meaning as in the Electronic Communications Act 2000; and (3) makes amendments to the 1977 Act s 124A to bring it into line with the 1949 Act s 37A.

2130   Registered designs—address for service

See para 2853.

2131   Registered designs—Community design—infringement—different overall impression

The parties were both multi-national corporations whose business included selling domestic air spray fresheners. The claimant's product was packaged in a custom designed canister surmounted by a trigger within a housing. Up to that time it had been conventional for aerosol air fresheners to deliver a spray vertically released by pushing a button on the top of the canister. The design of the package was registered as a Community design. The defendant's marketers subsequently designed a new freshener which involved fitting a cap onto a standard cylindrical aerosol container. The claimant brought proceedings alleging that this product infringed its registered Community design contrary to EC Council Regulation 6/2002, which by virtue of art 10 extended protection conferred on a Community design to any design which did not produce on the informed user a different overall impression. The defendant submitted that, if its product would otherwise infringe the registered design, the differences between that product and the registered design were such that, in the light of pre-existing products and designs, the registered design should be invalid. *Held*, having considered the relevant pieces of prior art, they created a very different overall visual impression from the registered design. The dominant features of the registered design were found in the defendant's canister and top. Although there were some differences, those were relatively insignificant details and did not detract from the same overall impression created by each of the two designs. The similarities between the two were overwhelmingly greater than the differences, and the fact that the registered design was of a far greater quality and more integrated than the defendant's canister did not mean that the latter escaped infringement. Accordingly, the application would be allowed.

Proctor & Gamble Co v Reckitt Benckiser (UK) Ltd [2006] EWHC 3154 (Ch), [2006] All ER (D) 243 (Dec) (Chancery Division: Lewison J). *Woodhouse UK v Architectural Lighting Systems* [2006] RPC 1 considered.

2132 Registered designs—fees

The Registered Designs (Fees) (No 2) Rules 2006, SI 2006/2617 (in force on 1 October 2006), prescribe the fees payable in respect of matters arising under the Registered Designs Act 1949 and reflect the changes made by the Regulatory Reform (Registered Designs) Order 2006, SI 2006/1974, and the new procedures under the Registered Designs Rules 2006, SI 2006/1975. SI 2006/2424 is revoked.

2133 Registered designs—intellectual property—enforcement rights

See para 2120.

2134 Registered designs—protection of industrial property—Convention countries

The Designs (Convention Countries) Order 2006, SI 2006/317 (in force on 6 April 2006), replaces the 2004 Order, SI 2004/3336, and declares specified countries to be Convention countries for the purpose of the protection of industrial property. With the exception of the Comoros all of the specified countries are already considered to be Convention countries.

2135 Registered designs—regulatory reform

The Regulatory Reform (Registered Designs) Order 2006, SI 2006/1974 (in force on 1 October 2006), amends the Registered Designs Act 1949, so as to (1) repeal provisions which set out the substantive grounds for refusing to register a design; (2) repeal provisions, which gave the registrar the power to make searches for determining whether a design was new or had individual character; (3) make new provision setting out the remaining substantive grounds for refusing to register a design; (4) make consequential amendments; (5) permit an application to include multiple designs; (6) repeal provisions in order to remove restrictions on inspecting certain registered designs; and (7) provide that an applicant will only have to show that their failure to pay the renewal fee on time was unintentional, instead of having to prove that they exercised reasonable care to see that the renewal fee was paid on time.

2136 Registered designs—rules

The Registered Designs Rules 2006, SI 2006/1975 (in force on 1 October 2006), replace the 1995 Rules, SI 1995/2912, so as to regulate the business of the Patent Office in relation to designs. In particular, the rules (1) contain provisions relating to applications for registered designs, which include the requirements as to form, disclaimers and special provisions for convention applications, as well as provisions relating to substantive examination of applications and their publication; (2) contain provisions relating to designs after registration, which include provisions on publication of a representation of the registered design, extending the duration of the right in a registered design and restoration of a lapsed registration; (3) contain provisions relating to proceedings before the registrar, which include provisions relating to applying for a declaration of invalidity, evidence rounds and the registrar's decision, as well as provisions on the conduct of such proceedings; (4) contain provisions relating to the register and other information, which include provisions on the certificate of registration, the registration of interests, inspection and information on registered designs and provisions on altering names and addresses or rectifying the register; and (5) contain miscellaneous provisions, including provisions on agents, advisers, correction of irregularities, extension of times or periods, furnishing an address for service, the journal and hours of business.

PENSIONS AND SUPERANNUATION

Halsbury's Laws of England (4th edn) vol 44(2) (Reissue) paras 551–1000

Articles

For articles relating to this title please refer to the Table of Articles at the beginning of the Abridgment.

2137 Armed forces—pensions

See ARMED FORCES.

2138 Employer-financed retirement benefits—excluded benefits—tax

The Employer-Financed Retirement Benefits (Excluded Benefits for Tax Purposes) Regulations 2006, SI 2006/210 (in force on 6 April 2006), prescribe a lump sum benefit as an excluded benefit for income tax purposes if it meets the conditions that (1) it is paid by an employer-financed retirement benefit scheme in respect of an employee's non-accidental death in service; and (2) payment of such a lump sum benefit is already provided for under the rules of the scheme on 6th April 2006.

2139   European Parliamentary pensions—United Kingdom representatives

The European Parliamentary (United Kingdom Representatives) Pensions (Amendment) Order 2006, SI 2006/919 (in force on 6 April 2006), further amends the European Parliamentary (United Kingdom Representatives) Pensions (Consolidation and Amendment) Order 1994, SI 1994/1662, and amends the European Parliamentary (United Kingdom Representatives) Pensions (Additional Voluntary Contributions) Order 1995, SI 1995/739. The order amends the 1994 Order (1) so as to update the definition of 'the index' and make the definition of 'permitted maximum' independent of the Income and Corporation Taxes Act 1988 s 590C without changing its meaning; it also inserts a definition of the pension value of retained benefits which is relevant to the maximum pension that can be paid to participants; (2) so that the total contributions to buy added years, whether periodical or by way of lump sum, must not exceed 10 per cent of the participant's salary in the tax year; (3) so that pensions are payable despite a person being a candidate in an election and so that pensions are reduced to nil during further service as a representative, rather than becoming non-payable, which is not permitted under the pension rules in the Finance Act 2004 s 165; (4) in order to enable pensions to be commuted for lump sums, so as to apply the limits imposed by the 2004 Act on pension commencement lump sums; (5) in order to make provision relating to death benefits under the 1994 Order; (6) so as to mirror requirements imposed by the 1994 Order Pt 4 about cessation of occupation and medical evidence about incapacity; (7) in order to provide for the scheme administrator to pay the lifetime allowance charge on behalf of participants in some circumstances, and for benefits to be reduced where the scheme administrator has done so without the participant having made a payment to cover the tax; (8) in order to reflect changes in the law relating to transfers out as set out in the Pension Schemes Act 1993 Pt 4 Ch 4, to update certain references in consequence of the 2004 Act Pt 4, and to refer to the public sector transfer arrangements; (9) in relation to refunds of contributions, in order to align the requirements with those for short service refund lump sums, which are authorised payments for the purposes of Pt 4; (10) in relation to restrictions on the application of pensions; (11) in order to give 'protected individuals' the right to cease making contributions, to surrender certain rights so as to obtain enhanced protection, or to surrender rights to which they have a prospective entitlement so as to avoid relevant benefit accrual; and (12) in order to enable people who become a participant for a second or subsequent time on or after 6 April 2006 to opt for their service when they do so to be treated separately from earlier service; the result of this will often be that the rights in respect of old service will be less valuable than if the service had been aggregated, and accordingly the option may benefit a person whose rights would otherwise breach limits above which tax charges apply under Pt 4. The order amends the 1995 Order (a) so as to remove restrictions on amounts of contributions and the benefits attributable to them, which do not need to apply once the 2004 Act Pt 4 is in force, and to restrict the kinds of transfers in that may be accepted by the AVC scheme; (b) so as to prevent participants in the scheme who are over 75 from joining the AVC scheme; (c) in relation to the provision of benefits under the AVC scheme, so as to enable any benefits to be paid that are authorised for registered schemes under the 2004 Act Pt 4; the existing provisions about the benefits are then amended so as to achieve conformity with Pt 4; a specific provision for lump sums to be taken at retirement or at a later time up to the participant's 75th birthday, subject to the limits imposed by Pt 4 on pension commencement lump sums is also added; (d) so as to enable transfers out to be applied in any way permitted under the Pension Schemes Act 1993 Pt 4 Ch 4 and to bring payments by way of return of contributions within the requirements for short service refund lump sums, which are authorised payments for the purposes of the 2004 Act Pt 4; and (e) so as to provide for the managers to pay the lifetime allowance charge on behalf of contributors in some circumstances, and for benefits to be reduced where they have done so without the contributor having made a payment to them to cover the tax.

2140   Financial provision on divorce—earmarking of pensions

See MATRIMONIAL LAW.

2141   Firefighters—pension scheme

See FIRE SERVICES.

2142   Health service pensions

See NATIONAL HEALTH SERVICE.

2143   Investment-regulated pension schemes—exception of tangible movable property

The Investment-regulated Pension Schemes (Exception of Tangible Movable Property) Order 2006, SI 2006/1959 (in force on 11 August 2006), provides that the following property is not to be regarded as taxable property for the purposes of the taxable property provisions of the Finance Act 2004 Sch 29A relating to registered pension schemes: (1) investment grade gold bullion; and (2) property, not worth more than £6,000, held by an investment vehicle, in which the relevant pension scheme holds a direct or indirect interest, where the item of property is used solely for the purposes of the administration or management of the vehicle, and no member of the pension scheme or a person connected with such a member occupies or uses, or has any right to occupy or use, the property. The order has effect from 6 April 2006, retrospective provision for which is conferred by Sch 29A para 11(2).

2144 Judicial pensions

See COURTS.

2145 Local government pensions

See LOCAL GOVERNMENT.

2146 Occupational pension schemes—benefit—retirement benefits scheme—payment in connection with past service

The defendant bank had run a scheme to provide its former employees with free assistance in the preparation of their annual tax returns, which it then withdrew in return for a one-off cash payment to those who had been entitled to the service. Notices of determination had been issued under the Income Tax (Employments) Regulations 1993, SI 1993/774, which the bank successfully appealed to a Special Commissioner. The Commissioners for Her Majesty's Revenue and Customs appealed. *Held*, the bank accepted that the payments made constituted a 'scheme' as defined under the Income and Corporation Taxes Act 1988 s 611. The Special Commissioner had erred in law in determining that the payments were not made in connection with past service and so were not a relevant benefit, which included a lump sum in connection with past service. The fact that it was a lump sum did not necessarily mean it was a deferred reward. However, a sum paid in connection with past service that replaced a free tax service by way of compensation was a relevant benefit provided under a retirement benefit scheme and chargeable to tax under s 596A. Accordingly the appeal would be allowed.

Revenue and Customs Comrs v Barclays Bank plc [2006] EWHC 2118 (Ch), [2006] All ER (D) 67 (Aug) (Chancery Division: David Richards J).

1988 Act ss 596A, 611 repealed: Finance Act 2004 s 326, Sch 42 Pt 3. See now Income Tax (Earning and Pensions) Act 2003 s 394.

2147 Occupational pension schemes—consultation by employers—miscellaneous amendment

The Occupational and Personal Pension Schemes (Consultation by Employers and Miscellaneous Amendment) Regulations 2006, SI 2006/349 (in force in part on 16 February 2006 and in part on 6 April 2006), prohibit the making of certain changes to occupational or personal pension schemes unless consultation about the change is carried out beforehand. In particular, the regulations (1) specify the persons to whom they apply; for all occupational or personal pension schemes, these are relevant employers; (2) prohibit the making of any listed change without consultation having been carried out by each relevant employer in relation to the scheme; (3) specify certain changes that are excluded; (4) require the person who proposes the change to notify all employers in relation to the scheme; if an employer is a relevant employer and has employees who are affected by the change, he is required to consult in accordance with specified provisions; (5) make provision for the way in which consultations are to be conducted; (6) make provision for employment rights and protections in relation to persons who are consulted; (7) make provision as to the role of the Pensions Regulator in enforcing the regulations; (8) amend the Pensions Act 2004 so that any decision of the Pensions Regulator to make an order to waive or relax a requirement of the regulations must be taken by the Determinations Panel established under the 2004 Act Pt 1 (ss 1–106); and (9) amend the Financial Assistance Scheme (Internal Review) Regulations 2005, SI 2005/1994, so as to correct a typographical error.

2148 Occupational pension schemes—consultation by employers—modification for multi-employer schemes

The Occupational Pension Schemes (Consultation by Employers) (Modification for Multi-employer Schemes) Regulations 2006, SI 2006/16 (in force on 2 February 2006), amend the Pensions Act 2004 ss 259, 261, in its application to occupational pension schemes in relation to which there is more than one employer, so as to enable regulations made under ss 259, 261, to extend to any other person who has power to make decisions in relation to a multi-employer scheme.

2149 Occupational pension schemes—cross-border activities

The Occupational Pension Schemes (Cross-border Activities) (Amendment) Regulations 2006, SI 2006/925 (in force on 28 March 2006), further amend the 2005 Regulations, SI 2005/3381, so as to allow an occupational pension scheme which carries out cross-border activity within the European Union until 15 May 2006 to submit some of the information which must be included as part of its application to the Pensions Regulator for authorisation and approval as such a scheme.

2150   Occupational pension schemes—deed of trust—rules of scheme—amendment

See *Trustee Solutions Ltd v Dubery*, para 1047.

2151   Occupational pension schemes—early leavers—cash transfer sums—contribution refunds

The Occupational Pension Schemes (Early Leavers: Cash Transfer Sums and Contribution Refunds) Regulations 2006, SI 2006/33 (in force on 6 April 2006), apply only where the pensionable service of a member, who leaves after three months pensionable service in an occupational pension scheme and is entitled to a cash transfer sum which might be used to acquire rights under another occupational pension scheme or personal pension scheme or to a refund of his employee contributions, terminates on or after 6 April 2006. In particular, the regulations (1) provide for the calculation and verification of the cash transfer sum; cash transfer sums are calculated in a similar manner to cash equivalents under the Pensions Schemes Act 1993 Pt 4 Chap 4; (2) provide for the contribution refund to be increased by any interest payable on the member's contributions to the scheme, and where the contributions have been invested, for the refund to represent the value of the invested contributions; (3) make provision for the cash transfer sum to be reduced where the scheme is under-funded and provide for the cash transfer sum and the contribution refund to be reduced where the scheme is being wound up to the extent necessary to meet any preferential liabilities; and where the member has incurred a monetary obligation due to the employer or to the scheme as a result of a criminal, negligent or fraudulent act or omission; (4) make provision for the cash transfer sum and contribution refund to be increased where the trustees or managers of the scheme fail to carry out what the member requires within a reasonable period and, where the failure is without reasonable excuse, provide for interest to be payable on the cash transfer sum and contribution refund; (5) set out the requirements which an occupational pension scheme or personal pension scheme must satisfy if the cash transfer sum is to be used to acquire rights under that scheme; and (6) prescribe additional information which the trustees or managers of the scheme must provide in the statement which they are required to give to the member explaining the nature of his rights; and provide for the trustees and managers of a transferring scheme when requested by the trustees and managers of a scheme under which transfer credits have been allowed to the member, to provide information as to the amount of employee contributions made by or on behalf of the member as they relate to the transfer payment.

2152   Occupational pension schemes—financial assistance—general

The Financial Assistance Scheme (Miscellaneous Amendments) Regulations 2006 SI 2006/3370 (in force on 16 December 2006), further amend (1) the 2005 Regulations, SI 2005/1986, so as to (a) revise the definition of 'multi-employer scheme'; (b) provide that a scheme manager may treat an insolvency event as having occurred in relation to a scheme that (i) has not formally had an insolvency event, as long as the scheme manager is satisfied that (A) the value of the employer's assets are less than the amount of its liabilities; (B) the employer cannot pay its debts as they fall due or have fallen due; and (C) the employer is unlikely to continue as a going concern; and (ii) has had an overseas insolvency event that the scheme manager is satisfied substantially corresponds to a qualifying insolvency event, and is also satisfied that the employer is unlikely to continue as a going concern; (c) clarify (i) that a member of a qualifying pension scheme who satisfies the relevant conditions is still a qualifying member even if he died before the coming into force of the 2005 Regulations, SI 2005/1986, and extend eligibility for assistance to members who were within 15 years of their normal retirement age for their scheme on 14 May 2004; (ii) that initial payments are on account of annual payment; and (iii) the circumstances under which overpayments will be recoverable; (d) provide that (i) a scheme manager may deem a member or survivor to be receiving an interim pension for the purposes of calculating the amount of initial payments in certain circumstances; and (ii) some of the members to whom the extension in applies will not be eligible for initial payments; and (e) revise how the amount of annual payment is calculated for the members and survivors to whom the extension applies; (2) the Financial Assistance Scheme (Internal Review) Regulations 2005, SI 2005/1994, by (a) clarifying the definition of potential beneficiary; and (b) allowing for a right of review and appeal of a decision as to whether a member is terminally ill by adding a new reviewable determination, and providing that the scheme manager may issue certain notices via the FAS website where in his opinion that it is reasonable to do so; and (3) the Financial Assistance Scheme (Appeals) Regulations 2005, SI 2005/3273, by making consequential revisions to take account of the new reviewable determination in relation to terminal illness, and to ensure consistency as to when an interested person is to be treated as a party to the appeal.

2153   Occupational pension schemes—fraud compensation levy

The Occupational Pension Schemes (Fraud Compensation Levy) Regulations 2006, SI 2006/558 (in force on 1 April 2006), make provision for the imposition of a fraud compensation levy ('the levy') on occupational pension schemes, under the Pensions Act 2004 s 189. In particular, the regulations (1) provide for the imposition of the levy on the reference day and for the maximum rate of the levy; (2) define the reference day; (3) provide for the times when the levy is payable; (4) make provision relating to levy notices; (5) make provision relating to the circumstances in which any amount payable by way of levy may be waived; (6) make provision in relation to any scheme which is a multi-employer scheme or has a partial guarantee from a relevant public authority; (7) make provision to avoid duplication of payments where the levy is payable under corresponding provisions which have effect in Northern Ireland; (8) set out civil penalties which the Regulator may impose where the levy has not been paid; and (9) amend the Occupational Pension Schemes (Employer Debt) Regulations 2005, SI 2005/678, so that any unpaid levy in respect of a money purchase scheme is treated as a debt due from the employer to the trustees or managers of the scheme.

2154 Occupational pension schemes—guaranteed minimum pension—increase

The Guaranteed Minimum Pensions Increase Order 2006, SI 2006/673 (in force on 6 April 2006), specifies 2.7 per cent as the percentage by which that part of any guaranteed minimum pension attributable to earnings factors for the tax years 1988–89 to 1996–97 and payable by contracted-out, defined benefit occupational pension schemes is to be increased.

2155 Occupational pension schemes—levies

The Occupational Pension Schemes (Levies) (Amendment) Regulations 2006, SI 2006/935 (in force on 1 April 2006), amend the 2005 Regulations, SI 2005/842, so as to (1) provide that the Pension Protection Fund Ombudsman levy is not payable in respect of the financial year ending 31 March 2007; (2) provide that, for the financial year beginning on 1 April 2006, in respect of the administration levy, the general rule for determining the reference day for a scheme is to apply; (3) make provision for the amount payable in respect of the administration levy for the financial year ending 31 March 2007; (4) provide that, other than in relation to multi-employer schemes, a reference to 'the levies' in the 2005 Regulations includes a reference to the pension protection levy; and (5) provide that reg 15 does not apply to any pension protection levy.

2156 Occupational pension schemes—levy ceiling—amount

The Occupational Pension Schemes (Levy Ceiling) Order 2006, SI 2006/742 (in force on 14 March 2006), provides, for the purposes of the Pensions Act 2004 s 177, that the levy ceiling for the financial year beginning on 1 April 2006 is £775,000,000.

2157 Occupational pension schemes—levy ceiling—earnings percentage increase

The Occupational Pension Schemes (Levy Ceiling—Earnings Percentage Increase) Order 2006, SI 2006/3105 (in force on 18 December 2006), specifies that, for the purposes of the Pensions Act 2004 s 178(3), the earnings percentage for the 12 month period ending with 31 July 2006 is 3.8 per cent.

2158 Occupational pension schemes—member-nominated trustees and directors

The Occupational Pension Schemes (Member-nominated Trustees and Directors) Regulations 2006, SI 2006/714 (in force on 6 April 2006), make provision in relation to member-nominated trustees and directors under the Pensions Act 2004 ss 241, 242. In particular, the regulations prescribe the types of scheme where the minimum proportion of member-nominated trustees and directors is not required and modify ss 241, 242 in respect of schemes whose existing scheme rules require a higher proportion of trustees or directors to be member-nominated.

2159 Occupational pension schemes—miscellaneous provisions

The Occupational and Personal Pension Schemes (Miscellaneous Amendments) Regulations 2006, SI 2006/778 (in force on 6 April 2006), (1) further amend the Occupational Pension Schemes (Contracting-out) Regulations (Northern Ireland) 1996, SI 1996/493, so as to consequentially update such regulations on the provisions of the Pensions (Northern Ireland) Order 2005, SI 2005/255; (2) further amend the Occupational Pension Schemes (Contracting-out) Regulations 1996, SI 1996/1172, so as to consequentially update such regulations on the provisions of the Pensions Act 2004; (3) further amend the Occupational Pension Schemes (Scheme Administration) Regulations 1996, SI 1996/1715, and the Occupation Pension Schemes (Requirement to obtain Audited Accounts and a Statement from the Auditor) Regulations 1996, SI 1996/1975, so as to correct errors and update references; (4) further amend the Occupation Pension Schemes (Assignment, Forfeiture, Bankruptcy etc) Regulations 1997, SI 1997/785, so as to clarify the procedure by which the trustees of a scheme may discharge rights derived from equivalent pension benefits under the National Insurance Act 1965 Pt 3; (5) amend the Pension Sharing (Pension Credit Benefit) Regulations 2000, SI 2000/1054, so as to correct an error; (6) further amend the Personal Pension Schemes (Payments by Employers) Regulations 2000, SI 2000/2692, so as to preserve the requirement for trustees or managers of a personal pension scheme or a stakeholder pension scheme to send an employee statement of payments made where direct payment arrangements exist between the employee and his employer; (7) amend the Occupational Pension Schemes (Investment) Regulations 2005, SI 2005/3378, so as to correct errors; and (8) amend the

Occupational and Personal Pension Schemes (Consultation by Employers and Miscellaneous Amendment) Regulations 2006, SI 2006/349, so that in relation to their application to small employers they are consistent with the Information and Consultation of Employees Regulations 2004, SI 2004/3426.

2160   Occupational pension schemes—modification of schemes

The Occupational Pension Schemes (Modification of Schemes) Regulations 2006, SI 2006/759 (in force in part on 30 March 2006 and in part on 6 April 2006), prescribe certain requirements which must be met where an occupational pension scheme is modified using a power conferred on any person by a scheme and where the subsisting rights provisions, which are contained in the Pensions Act 1995 ss 67–67I, apply. The regulations also enable trustees, in prescribed circumstances, to modify a trust scheme by way of a resolution. In particular, the regulations (1) exempt categories of schemes from the subsisting rights provisions; (2) exempt from the subsisting rights provisions modifications made in a prescribed manner; (3) prescribe the qualifications and experience required for a person providing an actuarial equivalence statement, where a modification of a scheme must comply with the actuarial equivalence requirements; (4) prescribe requirements for calculating the actuarial value of an affected member's subsisting rights, where the actuarial equivalence requirements apply to a modification of a scheme; (5) prescribe that the trustees of a trust scheme may by resolution modify the scheme for the purposes of achieving the same effect as all of the modifications in the Registered Pension Schemes (Modification of the Rules of Existing Schemes) Regulations 2006, SI 2006/364, regs 3–8; (6) prescribe that the trustees of a trust scheme may by resolution modify the scheme for the purposes of providing benefits to surviving civil partners so that they may be treated in the same way as widows or widowers; such modifications must not be made without the consent of the employer where the modification confers rights in excess of what is required to comply with the Civil Partnership Act 2004; and (7) exempt certain schemes from the provisions which allow trustees of trust schemes to modify the scheme by resolution. SI 1996/2517 is revoked.

2161   Occupational pension schemes—normal retirement date—representation of reduced normal retirement date

See *Hutchinson v Steria Ltd*, para 1289.

2162   Occupational pension schemes—payments to employer

The Occupational Pension Schemes (Payments to Employer) Regulations 2006, SI 2006/802 (in force on 6 April 2006), replace the 1996 Regulations, SI 1996/2156, and prescribe the circumstances in which, and the extent to which, payments may be made from certain pension schemes to the employer in relation to that scheme ('the relevant employer'). In particular, the regulations (1) prescribe that no payment may be made under the Pensions Act 1995 s 37 except in the case of the specified types of scheme; (2) prescribe that in the case of a scheme which is subject to the requirements of the Pensions Act 2004 Pt 3 (ss 221–233), which is not a regulatory own funds scheme and which is not winding up, prior to a payment to the relevant employer being made the scheme must conduct an actuarial valuation of its assets and liabilities and prescribe the assets and liabilities that are to be taken into account when making this valuation; (3) prescribe the manner in which the actuary must value the assets and estimate the value of the liabilities of the scheme; (4) prescribe the qualifications required for a person to prepare and sign a written valuation; (5) prescribe that where a valuation shows that the assets of the scheme exceed the liabilities of the scheme, then the maximum payment that may be made to the employer is the amount of that excess and that where this is the case the actuary must certify this on a form; (6) prescribe that in the case of a money purchase scheme that holds each member's fund under a separate insurance policy a scheme may consider making a payment to the relevant employer where the liabilities in relation to any particular member have been paid in full, and the payment to the employer represents the excess of the assets produced by the insurance policy, over and above the member's entitlement to scheme benefits; (7) provide that a valuation certificate must be valid for a maximum period of either 12 or 15 months from the date it is prepared; (8) prescribe the information that the trustees of the scheme must provide to the scheme members where the trustees propose to exercise a power to make a payment to the relevant employer; (9) prescribe the information that the trustees of the scheme must provide to the Regulator where a payment to the relevant employer is to be made; (10) provide for exceptions to the requirements contained in the regulations in respect of schemes which are not prescribed in the regulations and Crown guaranteed and partially guaranteed schemes; (11) modify the 1995 Act s 37 in the case of an earmarked scheme; (12) prescribe requirements in accordance with which notice must be given to scheme members where the trustees plan to distribute a scheme surplus when a scheme is winding up; (13) provide for circumstances where the Regulator must be satisfied that the provisions of s 76 are satisfied; (14) provide that where they have not received notification from the Regulator that the power to pay excess assets to the employer should not be exercised, then the trustees or employers in relation to the scheme should obtain written confirmation from the Regulator that it has not received any representations or information that could impact on payment of a surplus assets on wind up; and (15) provide for the application of ss 36, 37 in relation to a scheme with more than one employer.

2163 Occupational pension schemes—pension protection levies—modification for multi-employer schemes

The Occupational Pension Schemes (Pension Protection Levies) (Transitional Period and Modification for Multi-employer Schemes) Regulations 2006, SI 2006/566 (in force on 30 March 2006), (1) provide that the transitional period for the pension protection levy is a period of 12 months beginning on 1 April 2006; and (2) amend the Pensions Act 2004 s 175 in relation to segregated schemes, non-segregated schemes, and to multi-employer sections of segregated schemes for the financial year beginning on 1 April 2006.

2164 Occupational pension schemes—revaluation percentage—revaluation period

The Occupational Pensions (Revaluation) Order 2006, SI 2006/3086 (in force on 1 January 2007), specifies the revaluation percentages for the purpose of the revaluation on or after 1 January 2007 of benefits under occupational pension schemes, as required by the Pension Schemes Act 1993 s 84, Sch 3.

2165 Occupational pension schemes—taxation—consequential amendments

The Taxation of Pension Schemes (Consequential Amendments of Occupational and Personal Pension Schemes Legislation) Order 2006, SI 2006/744 (in force on 6 April 2006), amends various legislation as a consequence of changes to the tax system in relation to pension schemes made by the Finance Act 2004 Pt 4 (ss 149–284), makes provision for the tax registration of occupational and personal pension schemes, and prescribes the circumstances in which an occupational pension may be commuted. Specifically, the order amends or further amends (1) the Occupational Pension Schemes (Managers) Regulations 1986, SI 1986/1718, by prescribing the person who is to be treated as the manager of a scheme established outside the United Kingdom; (2) the Personal Pension Schemes (Disclosure of Information) Regulations 1987, SI 1987/1110, so as to make provision for the registration of schemes; (3) the Personal Pension Schemes (Transfer Values) Regulations 1987, SI 1987/1112, by prescribing that a member's transfer credits and rights must be acquired under a registered scheme; (4) the Personal and Occupational Pension Schemes (Perpetuities) Regulations 1990, SI 1990/1143, by prescribing the schemes excepted from the rules of law relating to perpetuities; (5) the Occupational Pension Schemes (Preservation of Benefit) Regulations 1991, SI 1991/167, by removing the provision relating to refunds on additional voluntary contributions; (6) the Occupational Pension Schemes (Discharge of Protected Rights on Winding Up) Regulations 1996, SI 1996/775, so as to enable the amount secured by a policy of insurance in respect of a member's protected rights to be commuted where the payment satisfies requirements contained in the Finance Act 2004 for lump sum payments by pension schemes; (7) the Occupational Pension Schemes (Contracting-out) Regulations 1996, SI 1996/1172, by (a) prescribing that an unregistered scheme cannot be a contracted-out scheme or certified as a salary-related contracted-out scheme; and (b) enabling benefits which are payable under an occupational pension scheme to be commuted into lump sum payments in certain circumstances; (8) the Contracting-out (Transfer and Transfer Payment) Regulations 1996, SI 1996/1462, by modifying the interpretation provisions; (9) the Personal and Occupational Pension Schemes (Protected Rights) Regulations 1996, SI 1996/1537, so as to (a) substitute new definitions of 'employee share' and 'grossed-up equivalent'; and (b) enable a member's protected rights to be commuted into a lump sum payment if the payment satisfies the requirements for lump sum payments by pension schemes contained in the Finance Act 2004; (10) the Occupational Pension Schemes (Indexation) Regulations 1996, SI 1996/1679, by modifying the interpretation provision; (11) the Occupational Pension Schemes (Transfer Values) Regulations 1996, SI 1996/1847, so as to provide for registered schemes and prescribe the requirement an annuity must satisfy; (12) the Occupational Pension Schemes (Discharge of Liability) Regulations 1997, SI 1997/784, by prescribing the requirements which must be satisfied before the amount secured by a policy of insurance or annuity contract may be commuted; (13) the Occupational Pension Schemes (Assignment, Forfeiture and Bankruptcy etc) Regulations 1997, SI 1997/785, by modifying the interpretation provision and prescribing a further exception from the inalienability provisions and the circumstances in which an occupational pension may be commuted; (14) the Pensions on Divorce etc (Provision of Information) Regulations 2000, SI 2000/1048, by modifying the interpretation provisions; (15) the Pension Sharing (Valuation) Regulations 2000, SI 2000/1052, by modifying the interpretation provision and prescribing the rights which are not shareable; (16) the Pension Sharing (Implementation and Discharge of Liability) Regulations 2000, SI 2000/1053, by (a) prescribing a further condition on which liability may be discharged in relation to pension credit benefit; (b) enabling an occupational pension to be commuted; and (c) providing that, for an annuity contract or insurance policy to be a destination for a pension credit, it must provide that benefits secured by the contract or policy may be commuted if the payment qualifies as a trivial commutation lump sum payment under the Finance Act 2004; (17) the Pension Sharing (Pension Credit Benefit)

Regulations 2000, SI 2000/1054, so as to (a) make provision for the registration of schemes; and (b) enable schemes to provide for the payment of pension credit benefit in the form of a lump sum before normal benefit age where the payment qualifies as either a serious ill-health lump sum payment or a trivial commutation lump sum payment under the Finance Act 2004; (18) the Pension Sharing (Safeguarded Rights) Regulations 2000, SI 2000/1055, so as to (a) specify the circumstances in which pension credit benefit arising from safeguarded rights can be paid by a registered scheme; and (b) require benefits payable in consequence of serious ill-health to have satisfied provisions of the Finance Act 2004 for the commutation of lump sum payments; (19) the Stakeholder Pension Schemes Regulations 2000, SI 2000/1403, so as to make provision for registered schemes; and (20) the Occupational and Personal Pension Schemes (Bankruptcy) (No 2) Regulations 2002, SI 2002/836, so as to substitute new arrangements which qualify as approved pension arrangements and unapproved pension arrangements. The order also makes provision for Northern Ireland.

2166   Occupational pension schemes—transfer values—Coal Staff and Mineworkers' Schemes

The Occupational Pension Schemes (Transfer Values etc) (Coal Staff and Mineworkers' Schemes) (Amendment) Regulations 2006, SI 2006/34 (in force on 6 February 2006), (1) amend the Occupational Pension Schemes (Transfer Values) Regulations 1996, SI 1996/1847, the Pension Sharing (Pension Credit Benefit) Regulations 2000, SI 2000/1054, and the Pension Sharing (Valuation) Regulations 2000, SI 2000/1052, so as to provide that where a cash equivalent transfer value is being calculated for a member of the British Coal Scheme or the Mineworkers' Scheme and such a member has been awarded a bonus, or bonuses, the amount of the cash equivalent transfer value payable in respect of such bonuses must reflect that the bonuses are not guaranteed and could be reduced in the future, as a result of the scheme's funding position.

2167   Occupational pension schemes—trustees' knowledge and understanding

The Occupational Pension Schemes (Trustees' Knowledge and Understanding) Regulations 2006, SI 2006/686 (in force on 6 April 2006), (1) provide an exemption for trustees of small schemes from the requirements under the Pensions Act 2004 ss 247, 248; (2) provide that individual trustees and persons who exercise functions of corporate trustees have, from the date of their appointment, a six month period of grace from the trustee requirements; and (3) provide that such a period of grace will not apply if the person is an independent trustee for the purpose of the Pensions Act 1995 s 23 or was appointed as a consequence of holding himself out as having expertise in any of the matters specified in the 2004 Act.

2168   Occupational pension schemes—winding up procedure

The Occupational Pension Schemes (Winding up Procedure Requirement) Regulations 2006, SI 2006/1733 (in force on 24 July 2006), amend the Pensions Act 2004 so as to provide that trustees or managers of a scheme must prepare a winding up procedure as soon as reasonably practicable after a scheme begins to wind up during the recovery period. The regulations also amend (1) the Occupational Pension Schemes (Disclosure of Information) Regulations 1996, SI 1996/1655, so as to require trustees or managers of a scheme to disclose an outline of the winding up procedure to members of the scheme and their representatives; (2) the Register of Occupational and Personal Pension Schemes Regulations 2005, SI 2005/597, so as to prescribe that where a scheme begins to wind up during the recovery period, the date the winding up of the scheme commenced is registrable information for the purposes of the 2004 Act; and (3) the Occupational Pension Schemes (Scheme Funding) Regulations 2005, SI 2005/3377, so as to remove the duty to notify the Pensions Regulator of the winding up of an eligible scheme during the recovery period.

2169   Pension benefits—insurance company—liability—scheme administrator

The Pension Benefits (Insurance Company Liable as Scheme Administrator) Regulations 2006, SI 2006/136 (in force on 6 April 2006), (1) provide that an insurance company which makes lump sum death benefit payment falling under the Finance Act 2004 s 273A(1) is to be treated as the scheme administrator for the purposes of the special lump sum death benefit charge to income tax under s 206; and (2) provide that the insurance company is liable to account for such a charge under s 254 and is liable to penalties for failing to make a return for fraudulently or negligently making an incorrect return.

2170   Pension Protection Fund—assets and liabilities—valuation

The Pension Protection Fund (Valuation of the Assets and Liabilities of the Pension Protection Fund) Regulations 2006, SI 2006/597 (in force on 1 April 2006), provide for the manner in which the assets and liabilities of the Pension Protection Fund are to be determined for the purposes of preparing an actuarial valuation which the Board of the Pension Protection Fund must include in its annual statement of accounts prepared in accordance with the Pensions Act 2004 Sch 5 para 22(1)(b). Specifically, the regulations (1) provide that the basis for the actuarial valuation is to be the asset values contained in the most recent Fund accounts kept in accordance with the 2004 Act Sch 5 para 22(1)(a); (2) provide that liabilities included in the actuarial valuation are to be any liability that falls to be paid, or transferred, out of the Fund under s 173(3), and the value of the liabilities is to be the present value of the liabilities on the valuation date; (3) provide that certain assets of the Fund are to be excluded from the valuation by the appointed actuary; (4) provide that certain types of asset and liability must be valued otherwise than on the value set out in the relevant accounts; and (5) prescribe the qualifications required for a person to be appointed as the actuary to the Fund.

2171   Pension Protection Fund—benefits—entitlement

See para 2615.

2172   Pension Protection Fund—disclosure of restricted information—specified persons

The Pensions Act 2004 (Disclosure of Restricted Information) (Amendment of Specified Persons) Order 2006, SI 2006/2937 (in force on 7 December 2006), amends the Pensions Act 2004 Schs 3, 8 so as to enable the Pensions Regulator and the Board of the Pension Protection Fund to disclose restricted information to certain persons to facilitate the exercise of certain regulatory functions by those persons. The order (1) adds, as specified persons, any bodies carrying on activities concerned with any of the matters set out under the Companies (Audit, Investigations and Community Enterprise) Act 2004 s 16(2), and any subsidiaries of such bodies and any bodies established under the constitution of any such bodies or subsidiaries; and (2) provides that the functions specified for this purpose are those relating to such bodies' investigatory, disciplinary, supervisory, oversight, direction, standard-setting and enforcement activities in connection with actuarial bodies, their members and actuarial work, the funding of such activities, and functions in connection with any levy payable under s 17.

2173   Pension Protection Fund—dissolution—civil partnership

The Dissolution etc (Pension Protection Fund) Regulations 2006, SI 2006/1934 (in force on 8 August 2006), (1) modify the Civil Partnership Act 2004 Sch 5, so as to allow for cases where a pension attachment order has been made and the Board of the Pension Protection Fund becomes involved with the pension arrangement in question; (2) modify orders including a provision made by virtue of Sch 5 para 25(5), so as to enable the order to be enforced in respect of compensation paid by the Fund; (3) modify Sch 5 in order to allow the court to exercise certain of its powers on an application to vary or an appeal in relation to a pension attachment or a pension sharing order notwithstanding the fact that the Board has assumed responsibility for the pension arrangement in question; and (4) modify the Dissolution etc (Pensions) Regulations 2005, SI 2005/2920, so as to provide for notices of change of circumstances in relation to pension attachment orders to be given to the Board where appropriate and for the Board to be discharged from liability in circumstances where payments cannot be made to the correct party or are made in error due to lack of, or incorrect, information.

2174   Pension Protection Fund—divorce

The Divorce etc (Pension Protection Fund) Regulations 2006, SI 2006/1932 (in force on 8 August 2006), (1) modify the Matrimonial Causes Act 1973 Pt II (ss 21–40A), so as to allow for cases where a pension attachment order has been made and the Board of the Pension Protection Fund becomes involved with the pension arrangement in question; (2) modify orders including a provision made by virtue of s 25B(7), so as to enable the order to be enforced in respect of compensation paid by the Fund; (3) modify Pt II in order to allow the court to exercise certain of its powers on an application to vary or an appeal in relation to a pension attachment or a pension sharing order notwithstanding the fact that the Board has assumed responsibility for the pension arrangement in question; and (4) modify the Divorce etc (Pensions) Regulations 2000, SI 2000/1123, so as to provide for notices of change of circumstances in relation to pension attachment orders to be given to the Board where appropriate and for the Board to be discharged from liability in circumstances where payments cannot be made to the correct party or are made in error due to lack of or incorrect information.

2175   Pension Protection Fund—Financial Assistance Scheme—payments—consequential amendments

The Pensions Act 2004 (PPF Payments and FAS Payments) (Consequential Provisions) Order 2006, SI 2006/343 (in force on 14 February 2006), amends (1) the Social Security Contributions and Benefits Act 1992 so as to provide that Pension Protection Fund periodic payments ('PPF payments') are treated in the same manner as occupational and personal pensions for the purposes of determining whether incapacity benefit and increases of benefit for adult dependants are payable; (2) the Jobseekers Act 1995 so as to specify that, for the purposes of contribution-based jobseeker's allowance, PPF payments and Financial Assistance Scheme payments ('FAS payments') will be taken into account when calculating the rate of contribution-based jobseeker's allowance that is to be paid to a claimant; and (3) the State Pension Credit Act 2002 so as to include periodic PPF payments within the definition of 'retirement provision' to provide that periodic PPF payments are treated in the same manner as occupational and personal pensions for the purposes of the assessed income period.

2176 Pension Protection Fund—general and miscellaneous provisions

The Pension Protection Fund (General and Miscellaneous Amendments) Regulations 2006, SI 2006/580 (in force in part on 1 April 2006 and in part on 6 April 2006), amend the Pension Protection Fund (Entry Rules) Regulations 2005, SI 2005/590; the Pension Protection Fund (Compensation) Regulations 2005, SI 2005/670; and the Pension Protection Fund (Valuation) Regulations 2005, SI 2005/672. The regulations make provision in relation to the administration of the Pension Protection Fund, the assumption of responsibility for an eligible pension scheme by the Board of the Pension Protection Fund, the pension protection levy, which the Board must impose for each financial year by virtue of the Pensions Act 2004 s 175(1).

2177 Pension Protection Fund—levy ceiling

The Pension Protection Fund (Levy Ceiling) Regulations 2006, SI 2006/2692 (in force on 6 November 2006), (1) provide that for the financial year 2007–2008, the first financial year after the transitional period, reference in the Pensions Act 2004 s 177(2) to the levy ceiling for the financial year will be read as if it were a reference to £718,750,000; and (2) prescribe (a) the period before the beginning of which the Secretary of State must discharge the duties imposed in respect of a review period, as the period which begins on 1 March and ends at the time the first financial year after the review period begins; and (b) the manner of the consultation required under the Pensions Act 2004 s 178(9), providing that the Board will (i) include details of how it proposes to decide on its recommendation to the Secretary of State in a consultation document; and (ii) publish on the Pension Protection Fund website, and in paper format, if it is requested to do so (A) the consultation document; and (B) a summary of the non-confidential responses it receives to the consultation.

2178 Pension Protection Fund—pension compensation cap

The Pension Protection Fund (Pension Compensation Cap) Order 2006, SI 2006/347 (in force on 1 April 2006), replaces the 2005 Order, SI 2005/825, and specifies, for the purposes of the Pension Act 2004 Sch 7 paras 26(7), 27(2), (3), the amount of the compensation cap, which determines the amount of compensation payable to a person who is under normal pension age on the assessment date and whose compensation is not derived from a pension payable on the grounds of ill health or a survivor's pension.

2179 Pension Protection Fund—pension sharing

The Pension Protection Fund (Pension Sharing) Regulations 2006, SI 2006/1690 (in force on 1 August 2006), make provision for the Board of the Pension Protection Fund to discharge liability in respect of a pension sharing order or provision which has been made prior to the date the trustees or managers of a scheme receive a transfer notice under the Pensions Act 2004 s 160, but which has either not come into effect by that date or in relation to which the liabilities of the trustees or managers have not been discharged by that date.

2180 Pension Protection Fund—provision of information

The Pension Protection Fund (Provision of Information) (Amendment) Regulations 2006, SI 2006/595 (in force on 6 April 2006), further amend the 2005 Regulations, SI 2005/674, so as to (1) prescribe the information to be provided by the Board of the Pension Protection Fund in connection with a notice under the Pensions Act 2004 s 120(2), where the occupational pension scheme or section of a segregated scheme is not an eligible scheme or section; (2) make provision as to the information to be provided by the Board in connection with an application or notice under s 129(1), (4); (3) require the Board to provide information within 28 days beginning with the date it receives the application, notice or all the information or documents requested, if any; (4) make provision for information to be provided by the Board, on request, to a member who is a party to, or contemplating, civil partnership proceedings; (5) require trustees or managers of a scheme to provide the Board with information relating to each member of the scheme who is entitled to a reviewable ill health pension if the decision to award that ill health pension was made within the previous three years immediately before the assessment date; and (6) make provision regarding the information to be provided by members or beneficiaries to the Board where a member's civil partnership is dissolved.

2181 Pension Protection Fund—reviewable matters—review and reconsideration

The Pension Protection Fund (Reviewable Matters and Review and Reconsideration of Reviewable Matters) (Amendment) Regulations 2006, SI 2006/685 (in force on 6 April 2006), amend the Pensions Act 2004 Sch 9, by adding the following to the list of reviewable matters: (1) the provision of information by the Board of the Pension Protection Fund ('the Board') or the failure to provide such information; (2) any steps taken by the Board to recover the amount of any excess from future pension compensation payments; and (3) any determination by the Board, or a failure to make a determination under the Pension Protection Fund (General and Miscellaneous Amendments) Regulations 2006, SI 2006/580. The regulations also further amend the Pension Protection Fund (Reviewable Matters) Regulations 2005, SI 2005/600, so as to provide for the period during which a failure by the Board to make a determination must occur, and further amend the Pension Protection Fund (Review and Reconsideration of Reviewable Matters) Regulations 2005, SI 2005/669, by adding the issue of a validation notice to the list of matters in respect of which the Board cannot give a review decision if the application for such a decision is made out of time and specifying 'the interested persons'.

2182   Pension Protection Fund—risk-based pension protection levy

The Pension Protection Fund (Risk-based Pension Protection Levy) Regulations 2006, SI 2006/672 (in force on 8 March 2006), provide that, when assessing the amount of the risk-based pension protection levy payable by an eligible scheme in accordance with the Pensions Act 2004 s 175, the Board of the Pension Protection Fund may take into account the nature of, and any risks associated with, any arrangements which may reduce the risk of compensation being payable from the Pension Protection Fund in the event of an insolvency event occurring in respect of an employer in relation to the scheme.

2183   Pension Protection Fund—tax

The Pension Protection Fund (Tax) Regulations 2006, SI 2006/575 (in force on 6 April 2006), make provision, in relation to the Board, the Pension Protection Fund and the Fraud Compensation Fund, for the application of income tax, corporation tax, capital gains tax, inheritance tax, and stamp duty land tax during the period beginning on 6 April 2006. In particular, the regulations (1) make detailed modifications of tax legislation with the object of ensuring that the tax treatment of the Pension Protection Fund is equivalent to the tax treatment of a registered pension scheme; (2) include provision to ensure that gains and losses accruing on disposals of investments held by the Board for the purposes of the Pension Protection Fund or the Fraud Compensation Fund are not chargeable gains or allowable losses; and (3) eliminate any possibility that receipt of a fraud compensation payment or of one of a number of related payments may be liable to capital gains tax or to corporation tax on chargeable gains.

2184   Pension schemes—contributions—deductions

The Social Security (Reduced Rates of Class 1 Contributions, Rebates and Minimum Contributions) Order 2006, SI 2006/1009 (in force on 6 April 2007), (1) alters the percentage to be deducted from secondary Class 1 contributions in respect of members of salary related contracted-out pension schemes; (2) specifies the appropriate flat-rate percentage and the appropriate age-related percentage for members of money-purchase contracted-out percentage schemes; and (3) specifies the appropriate age-related percentage of earnings payable as minimum contributions in respect of members of appropriate personal pension schemes.

2185   Pension schemes—overseas pension schemes—electronic communication—returns and information

See para 2220.

2186   Pension schemes—overseas pension schemes—information requirements

The Pension Schemes (Information Requirements for Qualifying Overseas Pension Schemes, Qualifying Recognised Overseas Pension Schemes and Corresponding Relief) Regulations 2006, SI 2006/208 (in force on 6 April 2006), (1) prescribe information which a qualifying overseas pension scheme must provide to an officer of Revenue and Customs in order to be recognised as such and the time limit by which that information must be provided; (2) prescribe information to be given to such an officer by the scheme manager of a pension scheme, where relief is given in respect of contributions made by an individual; (3) prescribe information which a qualifying recognised overseas pension scheme must provide to an officer of Revenue and Customs to be recognised as such, and the time limits by which that information must be provided; and (4) prescribe circumstances in which an officer of Revenue and Customs may require a pension scheme to provide the information prescribed within 30 days of the issue of a notice, notwithstanding the time limits provided.

See para 2225.

2187   Pension schemes—overseas pension schemes—recognised overseas pension schemes—requirements

The Pension Schemes (Categories of Country and Requirements for Overseas Pension Schemes and Recognised Overseas Pension Schemes) Regulations 2006, SI 2006/206 (in force on 6 April 2006), prescribes the requirements which an overseas pension scheme must satisfy for tax purposes under the Finance Act 2004 Pt 4 (ss 149–284). The regulations also set out the requirements which an overseas pension scheme must satisfy in order to be treated as a recognised overseas pension scheme and provide that (1) a scheme must either be established in another EEA State, or in a country or territory with which the United Kingdom has a double taxation agreement providing for the exchange of information between the fiscal authorities of the United Kingdom and the overseas country or territory and for non-discrimination between United Kingdom nationals and nationals of the overseas country or territory; and (2) if the scheme is not established in such a country or territory a scheme may nonetheless be recognised if it satisfies the specified requirements.

2188   Pension schemes—overseas pension schemes—relevant migrant members

The Pension Schemes (Relevant Migrant Members) Regulations 2006, SI 2006/212 (in force on 6 April 2006), provide that an individual is a relevant migrant member of an overseas pension scheme on condition that he was entitled to tax relief on contributions paid under the pension scheme in the country of residence at any time in the ten years prior to coming to the United Kingdom.

2189   Pension schemes—pension rates—reduction

The Pension Schemes (Reduction in Pension Rates) Regulations 2006, SI 2006/138 (in force on 6 April 2006), prescribe the circumstances in which pensions which have been forfeited or reduced are exempt from the requirement set out under the Finance Act 2004 Sch 28, that the rate of pension payable in respect of any relevant 12 month period is not less than the rate payable in respect of the previous 12 month period.

2190   Pension schemes—relevant non-United Kingdom schemes

The Pensions Schemes (Application of UK Provisions to Relevant Non-UK Schemes) Regulations 2006, SI 2006/207 (in force on 6 April 2006), provide a method of computing the amount to be charged to United Kingdom tax in respect of a payment by a relevant non-United Kingdom pension scheme which is referable to a member's United Kingdom tax-relieved funds, and modify the provisions of the Finance Act 2004 Pt 4 (ss 149–284) in its application to relevant non-United Kingdom schemes. In particular, the regulations (1) provide the method of computing the amount of a member's United Kingdom tax-relieved fund under a relevant non-United Kingdom scheme; (2) provide the method of computing the amount of a member's relevant transfer fund under a relevant non-United Kingdom scheme; (3) provide the rule for attributing payments out of a relevant non-United Kingdom scheme which are made to, or in respect of, a member to the member's United Kingdom tax-relieved fund and the relevant transfer fund; and (4) modify the Finance Act 2004 Pt 4 so as to (a) ensure that the new regime for pensions which are subject to United Kingdom taxation works in the context of relevant non-United Kingdom schemes; and (b) provide the Inland Revenue with a discretionary power to mitigate, in relation to relevant non-United Kingdom schemes, the charges to tax which would otherwise arise, if it appears to them that any difference in the operation of the relevant non-United Kingdom scheme from that prescribed is not material, and that it is appropriate to mitigate the effect of the strict rules.

2191   Pension schemes—taxable property

The Pensions Schemes (Taxable Property Provisions) Regulations 2006, SI 2006/1958 (in force on 11 August 2006), (1) apply certain valuation provisions of the Finance Act 2004 Sch 29A to land outside the United Kingdom; (2) modify taxable property provisions of Sch 29A for licences to use residential property and timeshares at a rent by treating each payment of rent as an acquisition of an interest in taxable property; (3) apply valuation provisions to tangible movable property, licences to use residential property and timeshare arrangements; (4) apply valuation provisions of the Finance Act 2003 Sch 17A for leases that continue after a fixed term and leases for an indefinite term, with modifications where an original fixed term is extended; (5) provide that an unauthorised payment is to be treated as made to a member of an investment-regulated pension scheme where a lease of taxable property is varied to increase the rent by an abnormal amount; and (6) make a member of a registered pension scheme which is established outside the United Kingdom, and holds an interest in taxable property located outside the United Kingdom, liable to pay the scheme sanction charge in respect of income and gains from that property.

2192   Pension schemes—taxation—consequential amendments

The Taxation of Pension Schemes (Consequential Amendments) Order 2006, SI 2006/745 (in force on 6 April 2006), amends various primary and secondary legislation as a consequence of the coming into force of the Finance Act 2004 Pt 4 (ss 149–284), as it relates to the taxation of pension schemes.

The Taxation of Pension Schemes (Consequential Amendments) (No 2) Order 2006, SI 2006/1963 (in force on 11 August 2006), (1) amends the Income Tax (Earnings and Pensions) Act 2003 s 408(1) by adding a reference to an employer-financed retirement benefit scheme; (2) amends the Finance Act 1995 s 128 by replacing the reference to the 2003 Act s 605 (repealed, but having effect until 5 April 2007) with a reference to annuity contracts to which s 605 applied before 6 April 2006 and which fall within the 2004 Act supra Sch 36 para 1(1)(f); and (3) amends the Income and Corporation Taxes Act 1988 s 336 by replacing a reference to annuity contracts with a reference to annuities made under registered pension schemes which fall within the 2004 Act Sch 36 para 1(1)(f).

2193 Pension schemes—taxation—transitional provision

The Taxation of Pension Schemes (Transitional Provisions) Order 2006, SI 2006/572 (in force on 6 April 2006), makes further transitional provision in relation to the new provisions for pension schemes under the Finance Act 2004 Pt 4 (ss 149–284). In particular, the order amends the 2004 Act so as to (1) extend s 161 in relation to pensions, to cover payments made, or benefits provided, from investments purchased by approved schemes before 6 April 2006 ('A day') and exclude certain annuities bought from insurance companies from this extension; (2) provide for staggered dates for the valuation exercise of unsecured pensions or dependant's unsecured pensions which are in payment by way of income withdrawal before A day; (3) provide transitional protection for (a) people who, prior to A day, have rights to life cover lump sums where the rules of the pension scheme included such provisions on 10 December 2003; and (b) individuals who, prior to A day, qualify for primary protection but whose pre-commencement rights may have been undervalued on the day before A day due to the poor performance of investments held by the scheme; (4) prevent individuals who qualify for primary protection and a lifetime allowance enhancement factor in relation to a period of non-residence from qualifying for two lifetime allowance enhancement factors in respect of the same increase in benefits; (5) provide transitional protection to contributions made by employees where those contributions qualified for corresponding relief under the Finance Act 1989 s 76(6A), (6C); (6) exempt an individual whose pension commencement lump sum is determined under enhanced protection from the requirement that the lump sum be payable when all or part of the member's lifetime allowance is available; (7) provide that any pre-commencement pension rights valued under specified provisions are included in the aggregate of the amounts crystallised by each benefit; (8) provide that where a lump sum death benefit is paid in respect of a member who had an actual right to payment of a pre-commencement pension immediately before his death, the pre-commencement pension rights will be taken into account when calculating the available amount of lifetime allowance to be set against the lump sum death benefit; (9) provide for scheme specific lump sum protection to be lost in respect of rights transferred where there had been a partial transfer of those rights away from a scheme; (10) remove the limit on specified dependants scheme pensions where the member in respect of whom the dependent's scheme pension is being paid was actually entitled to one or more relevant existing pensions on the day before A day; (11) provide transitional protection for individuals whose benefits will only be payable as a lump sum with no connected pension; (12) make provision for contracts which had been approved under the Income and Corporation Taxes Act 1988 s 62(1)(b) prior to A day to be added to the list of pensions which are converted to registered pensions and list of 'pre-commencement retirement annuity arrangements'; (13) provide that individuals who have become entitled to a tax-free lump sum before A day but deferred their entitlement to the accompanying pension, will not become entitled to a second tax-free lump sum under the same arrangement; (14) provide that certain types of pension to which the member was entitled immediately before A day will become unsecured pension funds and covered by the new regime; (15) make provision for similar provision as in head (14) above in relation to dependant's pension funds; (16) provide for certain individuals over the age of 75 at A day to be treated as being in an alternatively secured pension from A day; (17) make provision for similar provision as in head (16) for a dependant's alternatively secured pension fund; (18) make provision in relation to serious ill-health lump sums, pension protection lump sum death benefits and annuity protection lump sum death benefits; (19) make provision for transitional protection for dependants over the age of 23 who are in full time education or become incapacitated before that age; (20) provide that transfers to insurance companies which are recognised transfers are permitted transfers; (21) make provision for protection of an individual's right to enhanced protection in the event of a transfer made in connection with a wind-up; and (22) provide transitional provisions in relation to various lump sums which have become payable under the pre A day regime. The order also amends the Income Tax (Earnings and Pensions) Act 2003 s 636B so as to make provision in relation to specified commutation and winding up lump sums.

The Taxation of Pension Schemes (Transitional Provisions) (Amendment) Order 2006, SI 2006/1962 (in force on 11 August 2006), amends SI 2006/572 supra so as to (1) modify the 2004 Act supra s 216 (benefit crystallisation events and amounts crystallised); and (2) extend to two years from the date on which a pension scheme administrator could reasonably have known of the death of the member or dependant concerned, rather than from the date of death, the transitional protection afforded to lump sum death benefits paid by schemes in existence before 6 April 2006 in respect of members, and dependants of members, who died before that day.

The Taxation of Pension Schemes (Transitional Provisions) (Amendment No 2) Order 2006, SI 2006/2004 (in force on 25 July 2006), further amends SI 2006/572 by making further transitional provision relating to the new provisions for pension schemes under the 2004 Act Pt 4, in particular in relation to stand-alone lump sums.

2194 Pension schemes—transfers, reorganisations and winding up

The Pension Schemes (Transfers, Reorganisations and Winding Up) (Transitional Provisions) Order 2006, SI 2006/573 (in force on 6 April 2006), (1) relates to the transfer, or transfers, of an undertaking during the period beginning 10 December 2003 and ending 5 April 2006, and (a) ensures that, where an individual's pension rights are transferred in the prescribed period, and where the Transfer of Undertakings (Protection of Employment) Regulations 1981, SI 1981/1794, apply to the transfers of the undertaking, an employee's right to retire before the normal minimum pension age is preserved; (b) prescribes conditions which must be met before such a right can apply, which are that (i) there must be an original pension scheme whose rules conferred a right to retire before the normal minimum pension age, and the employee must have been entitled to take advantage of that right as it existed in relation to the original pension scheme; (ii) there must be either one transfer of the relevant undertaking or two or more such transfers, which have the overall result that an employee's pension rights are transferred from the original pension scheme to the new pension scheme; and (iii) the new pension scheme must also have rules which confer a right to retire before the normal minimum pension age; (2) relates to reorganisations during the specified period and prescribes conditions which must be met before an employee can benefit from the right to retire before the normal minimum pension age, which are that (a) there must be an original pension scheme whose rules conferred a right to retire before the normal minimum pension age, and the employee must have been entitled to take advantage of that right as it existed in relation to the original pension scheme; (b) there must be a reorganisation which has the overall result that the pension rights of an employee, or former employee, are transferred from the original pension scheme to a new pension scheme; and (c) the new pension scheme must also have rules which confer a right to retire before the normal minimum pension age; and (3) relates to where a pension scheme is being wound up and prescribes conditions for the membership of a new pension scheme, which relate to the rights of members of the pension scheme that is being wound up and to the nature of the annuities purchased for a member, and provide that in such circumstances, an individual's accrued pension rights are secured by providing that the member is to be treated as having become a member of a new pension scheme as the result of a block transfer to it.

2195 Pensionable age—difference in age between men and women—unlawful discrimination

See Application 42735/02 *Barrow v United Kingdom*; Application 8374/03 *Pearson v United Kingdom*; Application 7212/02 *Walker v United Kingdom*, para 1082.

2196 Pensions Act 2004—commencement

The Pensions Act 2004 (Commencement No 9) Order 2006, SI 2006/560, brings into force (1) on 9 March 2006, for the purpose only of conferring power to make regulations, ss 249(2), 250 and 251; (2) on 1 April 2006, so far as they are not already in force, ss 151(8), 173(1)(b), 177(9); and (3) on 6 April 2006, ss 109 (in part), 165, 169(1), (2)(a)–(c), 173(1)(a), (f), 254, 267, 268, 306(2)(j), (k), (4), (5), 319(1) (in part), 321, Sch 12 paras 10, 11(1) (in part), (2), 14–17, 21, 22, 27, 29, 33, 48, 57, 58, 64, 65 and certain repeals in Sch 13, and so far as they are not already in force or for remaining purposes, ss 18, 86, 102, 160(7), 173(3), 204, 247–249, Sch 4, Sch 5 para 18(2), Sch 12 paras 5, 62, 76(3).

The Pensions Act 2004 (Commencement No 10 and Saving Provision) Order 2006, SI 2006/2272, brings into force (1) on 1 September 2006, (a) ss 177(5), (8), 178(5); and (b) for the purpose only of conferring power to make regulations, s 177(4), 178(4), (7), (9); (2) on 1 October 2006, (a) for the purpose only of conferring power to make an order, s 178(6); (b) for the purpose only of conferring power to make regulations, s 319(1) (in part), Sch 12 para 11 (so far as not already in force); and (c) for remaining purposes, ss 177(4), 178(4), (7), (9); (3) on 1 November 2006, for the purpose only of conferring power to make regulations, ss 153(4), (7), 155(1), (4), 156(1), (2), (5), (6), 157(1), (7), (9); (4) on 1 December 2006, for remaining purposes, s 178(6); (5) on 1 January 2007, (a) for the purpose only of conferring power to make regulations or an order, so far as not already in force, ss 117(7), 178; and (b) for remaining purposes, s 319(1) (in part), Sch 12 para 11; (6) on 1 March 2007, for remaining purposes, ss 117(7), 178; and (7) on 6 April 2007, (a) ss 158, 159 and a repeal in Sch 13; (b) so far as not already in force, ss 132, 153–157, 160, 172; and (c) for remaining purposes, ss 153(4), (7), 155(1), (4), 156(1), (2), (5), (6), 157(1), (7), (9). A saving is also made.

For a summary of the Act, see 2004 Abr para 2143. See also the commencement table in the title STATUTES.

2197 Pensions appeal tribunal—scope—war pensions claim

The Pensions Appeal Tribunals (Additional Rights of Appeal) (Amendment) Regulations 2006, SI 2006/2893 (in force on 31 October 2006), amend the 2001 Regulations, SI 2001/1031, by providing that certain decisions made under the Naval, Military and Air Forces etc (Disablement and

Death) Service Pensions Order 2006, SI 2006/606, are specified decisions, for the purpose of the Pensions Appeal Tribunals Act 1943 s 5A, and provide that such decisions attract a right of appeal to the Pensions Appeal Tribunal.

2198   Pensions Ombudsman—determination—discretion

The appellant refused the defendant's application for personal injury benefit under the National Health Service (Injury Benefits) Regulations 1995, SI 1995/866. The defendant complained to the Pensions Ombudsman, who directed, under the Pension Schemes Act 1993 s 151(2), that the appellant should appoint a suitable medical adviser to consider the defendant's claim, rather than relying on its previous medical advisers. The court upheld the ombudsman's determination and the appellant appealed. *Held*, the ombudsman was entitled to exercise his discretionary power under s 151(2). His power to give directions was not limited to cases where it was proved that maladministration or a risk of maladministration had occurred. He could legitimately take into account as a factor the perception of unfairness, even where there was no actual unfairness, and was merely stating that fairness required another doctor to deal with the reconsideration of the claim. Accordingly, the appeal would be dismissed.

NHS Pensions Agency v Suggett [2006] EWCA Civ 10, (2006) Times, 27 January (Court of Appeal: Mummery, Latham and Gage LJJ).

2199   Pensions regulator—codes of practice—early leavers, late payment of contributions and trustee knowledge and understanding

The Pensions Act 2004 (Codes of Practice) (Early Leavers, Late Payment of Contributions and Trustee Knowledge and Understanding) Appointed Day Order 2006, SI 2006/1383 (in force on 22 May 2006), appoints 30 May 2006 as the day, for the purposes of the Pensions Act 2004 s 91(9), for the coming into effect of (1) the Pensions Regulator Code of Practice No 4: Early leavers—reasonable periods; (2) the Pensions Regulator Code of Practice No 5: Reporting late payment of contributions to occupational money purchase schemes; (3) the Pensions Regulator Code of Practice No 6: Reporting late payment of contributions to personal pensions; and (4) the Pensions Regulator Code of Practice No 7: Trustee knowledge and understanding.

2200   Pensions regulator—codes of practice—funding defined benefits

The Pensions Act 2004 (Funding Defined Benefits) Appointed Day Order 2006, SI 2006/337 (in force on 13 February 2006), appoints 15 February 2006 as the day, for the purposes of the Pensions Act 2004 s 91(9), for the coming into force of the Pensions Code of Practice No 03: Funding defined benefits.

2201   Pensions regulator—codes of practice—member-nominated trustees and directors and internal controls

The Pensions Act 2004 (Codes of Practice) (Member-nominated Trustees and Directors and Internal Controls) Appointed Day Order 2006, SI 2006/3079 (in force on 17 November 2006), appoints 22 November 2006 as the day, for the purposes of the Pensions Act 2004 s 91(9), for the coming into effect of (1) the Pensions Regulator Code of Practice No 8: Member-nominated trustees and directors–putting in place and implementing arrangements; and (2) the Pensions Regulator Code of Practice No 9: Internal controls.

2202   Pensions regulator—disclosure of restricted information—specified persons

See para 2172.

2203   Personal pension schemes—appropriate schemes

The Personal Pension Schemes (Appropriate Schemes) (Amendment) Regulations 2006, SI 2006/147 (in force on 6 April 2006), further amend the 1997 Regulations, SI 1997/470, so as to (1) make provision for the tax registration of schemes as a consequence of the Finance Act 2004; (2) add to the forms of scheme which qualify as an appropriate personal pension scheme, specifying that, to qualify as an appropriate personal pension scheme an arrangement must be established by an authorised corporate director of an open-ended investment company; (3) specify that the rules of a scheme may provide for the scheme to hold any pension arrangement in addition to a pension arrangement approved by the Inland Revenue under the Income and Corporation Taxes Act 1988 Pt XIV Ch I (ss 590–612); (4) require that the rules of the scheme must not allow a member's protected rights to be held in a pension arrangement which falls outside a pension arrangement approved by the Inland Revenue under Pt XIV Ch I; and (5) define 'self-invested personal pension scheme.'

2204   Personal pension schemes—consultation by employers—miscellaneous amendment

See para 2147.

2205 Personal pension schemes—miscellaneous provisions

See para 2159.

2206 Personal pension schemes—taxation—consequential amendments

See para 2165.

2207 Police pensions

See POLICE.

2208 Public service pensions—compensatory service—early retirement

See *Chapman v South Holland DC*, para 1845.

2209 Public service pensions—increase—armed forces

The Pensions Increase (Armed Forces Pension Schemes and Conservation Board) Regulations 2006, SI 2006/801 (in force on 7 April 2006), apply the provisions of the Pensions (Increase) Act 1971 to any pension payable under the Armed Forces Pension Scheme 2005, any pension payable under the Reserve Forces Pension Scheme 2005, and any pension payable by a conservation board under the Local Government Pension Scheme or other schemes made under the Superannuation Act 1972, so that the rate of any such pension will be increased annually in accordance with the Retail Prices Index.

2210 Public service pensions—increase—review

The Pensions Increase (Review) Order 2006, SI 2006/741 (in force on 10 April 2006), makes provision for (1) percentage increases in the rates of public service pensions, the increase being the percentage, or a fraction of the percentage, by which the Secretary of State has, by direction given under the Social Security Administration Act 1992 s 151(1), increased the sums referred to in s 150(1)(c); (2) increases in certain deferred lump sums which became payable on or after 11 April 2005 and before 10 April 2006; (3) a reduction in the amount by reference to which any increase in the rate of an official pension is to be calculated where the pensioner is entitled to a guaranteed minimum pension deriving from an employment from which the entitlement to the official pension also arises; and (4) a reduction in the amount by reference to which any increase in a widow's or widower's pension is to be calculated where the pensioner becomes entitled on the death of the deceased spouse to a guaranteed minimum pension.

2211 Public service pensions—miscellaneous offices

The Superannuation (Admission to Schedule 1 to the Superannuation Act 1972) Order 2006, SI 2006/3374 (in force on 2 February 2007), further amends the Superannuation Act 1972 by adding (1) employment by the Commonwealth Parliamentary Association (United Kingdom Branch), the Trustees of the Independent Living (Extension) Fund and the Independent Living (1993) Fund, the NHS Business Services Authority, the Adjudicator to Her Majesty's Land Registry, the Quality Improvement Agency, the School Food Trust and the Scottish Parliamentary Standards Commissioner; and (2) the offices of the Chief Electoral Officer for Northern Ireland and the Scottish Parliamentary Standards Commissioner, to the specified employments and offices. Employment by the Greater London Magistrates' Court Authority, the NHS Pensions Agency (Asianteth Pensiynau'r GIG), and the Wine Standards Board is removed from the specified employments.

2212 Registered pension schemes—annuities

The Registered Pension Schemes (Prescribed Manner of Determining Amount of Annuities) Regulations 2006, SI 2006/568 (in force on 6 April 2006), prescribe the manner in which the amount of increase or decrease in the amount of an annuity paid under a pension scheme is to be determined. In particular, the regulations prescribe the manner of determining (1) the amount of a member's lifetime annuity; (2) a dependant's annuity; and (3) a short-term annuity in relation to members and dependants.

2213 Registered pension schemes—authorised member payments

The Registered Pension Schemes (Authorised Member Payments) Regulations 2006, SI 2006/137 (in force on 6 April 2006), prescribe an additional class of authorised member payments for the purposes of the Finance Act 2004 s 164. In particular, the regulations prescribe as an authorised member payment, a payment made in connection with the demutualisation of an insurance company to (1) a member of a registered pension scheme, not being an occupational pension scheme or a public service pension scheme; or (2) the beneficiary under a qualifying annuity contract. In addition, the regulations provide that the payment must satisfy the following further conditions: (a) it is made in compensation for the loss of the person's rights as a member of the insurance company and; (b) it is made without a reduction in the total value of the sums and assets held for the purposes of the registered pension scheme, or the value or amount of the annuity.

The Registered Pension Schemes (Authorised Member Payments) (No 2) Regulations 2006, SI 2006/571 (in force on 6 April 2006), authorise registered pension schemes to make certain payments to which entitlement accrued before 6 April 2006, with the effect of exempting payments made on or after 6 April 2006, from the unauthorised payments charge imposed by the Finance Act 2004 s 209.

2214   Registered pension schemes—authorised payments—general

The Registered Pension Schemes (Authorised Payments) Regulations 2006, SI 2006/209 (in force on 6 April 2006), prescribe payments a registered pension scheme is authorised to make to, or in respect of, a member of a pension scheme under the Finance Act 2004 s 164(f).

2215   Registered pension schemes—authorised payments—pension arrears

The Registered Pension Schemes (Authorised Payments—Arrears of Pension) Regulations 2006, SI 2006/614 (in force on 6 April 2006), prescribe a payment of arrears of pension which have accrued, to which a member is entitled at the time when the pension begins to be paid, and which is taxable pension income, as an additional description of authorised payment for the purposes of the Finance Act 2004 Pt 4 (ss 149–284).

2216   Registered pension schemes—authorised payments—transfers—Pension Protection Fund

The Registered Pension Schemes (Authorised Payments) (Transfers to the Pension Protection Fund) Regulations 2006, SI 2006/134 (in force on 6 April 2006), prescribe transfers of property, rights and liabilities of a scheme to the Board of the Pension Protection Fund, for the purposes of the Finance Act 2004 s 164(f).

2217   Registered pension schemes—authorised surplus payments

The Registered Pension Schemes (Authorised Surplus Payments) Regulations 2006, SI 2006/574 (in force on 6 April 2006), prescribe, for the purposes of the Finance Act 2004 s 177, authorised surplus payments and the conditions which must be satisfied for a payment to be an authorised surplus payment, with regards to payments falling under the Pensions Act 1995 ss 37 or 76.

2218   Registered pension schemes—block transfers—permitted membership period

The Registered Pension Schemes (Block Transfers) (Permitted Membership Period) Regulations 2006, SI 2006/498 (in force on 6 April 2006), provide that, for the purposes of the Finance Act 2004 Sch 36 para 22(6)(b), in relation to a block transfer, the prescribed period is 12 months ending with the date on which the transfer is made, in which an individual's rights in a pension scheme is protected when transferred out of the original pension scheme on or after 6 April 2006.

2219   Registered pension schemes—co-ownership of living accommodation

The Registered Pension Schemes (Co-ownership of Living Accommodation) Regulations 2006, SI 2006/133 (in force on 6 April 2006), apply where living accommodation is owned partly by a registered pension scheme and partly by other persons, and provide for a charge to income tax to arise in certain circumstances. The regulations also (1) provide for a living accommodation benefit to be apportioned, with the amount apportioned to the registered pension scheme being called 'the pension scheme owner's benefit'; (2) provide for the pension scheme owner's benefit to be apportioned, with the amount finally apportioned to a scheme member being referred to as 'the private owner's benefit'; and (3) provide that the registered pension scheme is to be treated as having made an unauthorised payment to the scheme member to whom an amount has been apportioned.

2220   Registered pension schemes—electronic communication—returns and information

The Registered Pension Schemes and Overseas Pension Schemes (Electronic Communication of Returns and Information) Regulations 2006, SI 2006/570 (in force on a day or days to be appointed in the London, Edinburgh and Belfast Gazettes), make provision about the use of approved methods of electronic communication for the purposes of delivery of information required under the Finance Act 2004 Pt 4 (ss 149–284). The regulations (1) deal with information which must be delivered to Revenue and Customs by an approved method of electronic communications; (2) deal with information which may be delivered either to or by Revenue and Customs by an approved method of electronic communications; and (3) deal with evidential matters.

2221   Registered pension schemes—enhanced lifetime allowance

The Registered Pension Schemes (Enhanced Lifetime Allowance) Regulations 2006, SI 2006/131 (in force on 6 April 2006), contain provisions which enable an individual to rely on the enactments providing for an enhanced lifetime allowance and on the Finance Act 2004 Sch 36 para 12. The regulations also contain additional provisions of an administrative nature. In particular, the regulations (1) provide that an individual who wishes to rely on the relevant enactment must give a notification to Her Majesty's Revenue and Customs on or before the closing date; (2) provide that if Her Majesty's Revenue and Customs issues a certificate to the individual in response to the giving of the notification, the individual may rely on the relevant enactment until the certificate is revoked, or until an amended certificate is issued; (3) provide that the individual may then rely, to the same extent, on the amended certificate; (4) make provision for an individual ceasing to have the benefit of the Finance Act 2004 Sch 36 para 12, and operate to protect the individual from suffering disproportionate loss; (5) deal with the form of notifications and provide that an individual must preserve documents relating to the information given in the notification; (6) deal with the case where an individual gives a notification to Her Majesty's Revenue and Customs after the closing date, but had a reasonable excuse for not giving the notification before the closing date, and gives the notification without undue delay after the reasonable excuse ceased; (7) provide that if Her Majesty's Revenue and Customs do not take any objection to the information provided in the notification, they must issue a certificate to the individual; if Her Majesty's Revenue and Customs take an objection, they must return the notification to the individual; (8) deal with the case where there is a dispute as to whether Her Majesty's Revenue and Customs is entitled to take an objection to the information provided in the notification; the individual may appeal to Commissioners for Her Majesty's Revenue and Customs; (9) permit an individual, in certain circumstances, to require information contained in two notifications or certificates to be combined in a single certificate (an 'aggregate certificate'); (10) provide for the case where incorrect information is given in the notification, or in connection with the notification; (11) provide for the case where incorrect information is given in the certificate; (12) provide that an individual may require the Revenue and Customs to provide information which the individual no longer possesses; (13) provide that the Revenue and Customs may begin a review of information given in the notification, or in connection with the notification, at any time within the year beginning with the day on which the notification was given; (14) provide that the Revenue and Customs may begin a review at any time if the Revenue and Customs have reason to believe that the information given in the notification, in connection with the notification, or in the certificate, either was incorrect or has become incorrect; (15) deal with the procedure to be followed on reviews whereby the Revenue and Customs must give notice to the individual requiring the production of information and documents and the individual may appeal against the notice; (16) provide that Her Majesty's Revenue and Customs may revoke or amend a certificate in certain circumstances; the Revenue and Customs must give notice to the individual, who may appeal to the Commissioners; (17) make special provision for persons incapable, by reason of mental disorder, of managing and administering their property and affairs, and for persons suffering from physical disabilities; and (18) provide that if an individual dies, then anything under the regulations which could have been done by the individual may be done by the individual's personal representatives.

The Registered Pension Schemes (Enhanced Lifetime Allowance) (Amendment) Regulations 2006, SI 2006/3261 (in force on 28 December 2006), amend the principal 2006 Regulations supra so as to take account of provisions in the Finance Act 2006 which provide for an enhanced lifetime allowance or for enhanced protection. In particular, the regulations (1) provide that the procedure to be followed in the case of the new provisions differs from that applying in other cases; and (2) ensure that separate provision is made for the form of notification to be given, the procedure on the giving of a notification and for an appeal hearing if there is a dispute about the validity of the notification.

2222   Registered pension schemes—existing schemes—modifications

The Registered Pension Schemes (Modification of the Rules of Existing Schemes) Regulations 2006, SI 2006/364 (in force on 6 April 2006), modify the rules of existing pension schemes during the period beginning with 6 April 2006 and ending in accordance with the Finance Act 2004 Sch 36. The regulations (1) limit the application of the specified later provisions of these regulations and provide that each of the later provisions will apply unless (a) the scheme has, prior to 6 April 2006, amended its rules in a way which corresponds to the provision in question; or (b) the rules are framed in such a way that amendment to reflect the provision in question is unnecessary; (2) provide that if an existing scheme's rules would otherwise require the trustees or managers of an existing scheme to make an unauthorised payment, the rules will instead be construed as conferring on them a discretion to choose whether to make such a payment; (3) preserve the effect of the Income and Corporation Taxes Act 1988 s 590C in relation to the indexation of the permitted maximum during the transitional period; (4) make provision in the case of existing scheme rules where benefits are restricted by reference to the scheme's approval by the Inland Revenue or Her

Majesty's Revenue and Customs; and (5) provide that the rules of an existing scheme are to be read as authorising reduction of a member's benefits in respect of the administrator's liability for the lifetime allowance charge.

2223 Registered pension schemes—extension of migrant member relief

The Registered Pension Schemes (Extension of Migrant Member Relief) Regulations 2006, SI 2006/1957 (in force on 11 August 2006), extend eligibility for migrant member relief to cases where a person was not resident in the United Kingdom at the time that he joined a scheme, so as to apply where (1) the member's rights have been subject to one or more block transfers, with the effect that reference to the pension scheme is read as including the scheme from which the transfer occurred; (2) a series of block transfers have occurred, so that reference to the pension scheme is read to include any of the schemes from which any of the transfers forming part of the series have occurred; and (3) the scheme to which the member originally belonged is closed to new accruals for existing members and a further scheme for members of that scheme is set up, in which case reference to the pension scheme to which the member belonged when non-resident is read as a reference to either the new scheme or the original scheme.

2224 Registered pension schemes—pension commencement lump sum

The Registered Pension Schemes (Meaning of Pension Commencement Lump Sum) Regulations 2006, SI 2006/135 (in force on 6 April 2006), provide that the prescribed circumstances, where incorrect income tax has been paid by a scheme administrator in relation to a member by way of a lifetime allowance charge, are circumstances in which the scheme administrator has made an overpayment by way of the lifetime allowance charge in relation to the member, and Her Majesty's Revenue and Customs refund the overpayment to the scheme administrator. The regulations also provide that the prescribed circumstances in which a lump sum subsequently paid to the member is to be treated as a pension commencement lump sum, are circumstances in which Her Majesty's Revenue and Customs refund such an overpayment to the scheme administrator, and the scheme administrator pays part or all of the overpayment to the member within three months of receiving it.

2225 Registered pension schemes—provision of information

The Registered Pension Schemes (Provision of Information) Regulations 2006, SI 2006/567 (in force on 6 April 2006), specify the requirements for the provision of information in connection with registered pension schemes under the Finance Act 2004 Pt 4 (ss 149–284). In particular, the regulations prescribe (1) information which a scheme administrator is required to provide to the Commissioners for Her Majesty's Revenue and Customs in the form of an annual event report, and prescribe the information to be included in the form in respect of various events; (2) other information which is required to be given in connection with the administration of a scheme; and (3) requirements in respect of the keeping of records.

The Registered Pension Schemes (Provision of Information) (Amendment) Regulations 2006, SI 2006/1961 (in force on 11 August 2006), amend (1) the principal 2006 Regulations supra so as to (a) provide for reportable events (i) when a stand-alone lump sum is paid, (ii) when a scheme becomes, or ceases to be, an investment-regulated pension scheme, (iii) when a scheme chargeable payment arises, (iv) when there is a change in the country or territory in which a scheme is established, and (v) where a scheme becomes, or ceases to be, an occupational pension scheme; (b) require members to provide information in relation to recycling of lump sums and the available portion of the member's lump sum allowance; and (2) the Pension Schemes (Information Requirements for Qualifying Overseas Pension Schemes, Qualifying Recognised Overseas Pension Schemes and Corresponding Relief) Regulations 2006, SI 2006/208, so as to require an overseas pension scheme to report unauthorised payments in relation to recycling provisions and investment-regulated pension schemes.

2226 Registered pension schemes—relevant annuities

The Registered Pension Schemes (Relevant Annuities) Regulations 2006, SI 2006/129 (in force on 6 April 2006), provide definitions for the terms 'relevant annuity' and 'annual amount', which are relevant in calculating the basis amount in the Finance Act 2004.

2227 Registered pension schemes—splitting of schemes

The Registered Pension Schemes (Splitting of Schemes) Regulations 2006, SI 2006/569 (in force on 6 April 2006), provide for certain registered pension schemes to be treated as if they were a number of separate registered pension schemes pursuant to the Finance Act 2004 s 247A. In particular, the regulations (1) prescribe the pension schemes that are to be treated as separate pension schemes; and (2) provide that scheme administrators of sub-schemes are to assume the liabilities and responsibilities specified and that the scheme administrator of the split scheme will cease to have responsibility for those matters.

2228   Registered pension schemes—surrender of relevant excess

The Registered Pension Schemes (Surrender of Relevant Excess) Regulations 2006, SI 2006/211 (in force on 6 April 2006), (1) provide that, for the purposes of the Finance Act 2004 Sch 36, the rights that are to be treated as representing the relevant excess are those that meet the qualification condition specified and are valued in accordance with the computation condition specified; (2) deal with the qualification condition and the computation condition; (3) provide that a surrender of rights that are to be treated as representing the relevant excess, are not to be treated as an unauthorised payment, and, accordingly, as a payment chargeable to income tax, except to the extent that the value of the rights surrendered is greater than the relevant excess; and (4) provide that the rules of any existing pension scheme, to which the deemed registration of existing pension schemes provision applies, are modified, so as to provide that a member may surrender rights that are to be treated as representing the relevant excess to the extent that the value of the rights surrendered does not exceed the relevant excess.

2229   Registered pension schemes—transfer of sums and assets

The Registered Pension Schemes (Transfer of Sums and Assets) Regulations 2006, SI 2006/499 (in force on 6 April 2006), make provision in relation to the transfer of sums and assets by registered pension schemes and insurance companies under the Finance Act 2004 Pt 4 (ss 149–284). In particular, the regulations make provision (1) in relation to scheme pensions payable by registered pension schemes and provide that a transfer of sums or assets in respect of an original scheme pension from one registered pension scheme to another where the new scheme pension is provided is a recognised transfer, and further provide that the new scheme pension is to be treated as the original scheme pension for the purposes prescribed in Table 1; (2) in relation to scheme pensions payable by insurance companies and provide for a new scheme pension payable by an insurance company following a transfer of sums or assets to be treated as the original scheme pension for the purposes prescribed in Table 1; (3) for certain specified transfers to avoid an unauthorised payments charge on the transfer; (4) in relation to lifetime annuities and provide that where a new lifetime annuity is payable following a transfer of sums or assets it is treated as the original lifetime annuity for the purposes prescribed in Table 2, and provide that other transfers are treated as unauthorised payments; (5) in relation to short-term annuities and provide that where a short-term annuity ceases to be paid on a transfer of sums and assets the transfer is treated as an unauthorised payment except where a new short-term annuity becomes payable; (6) in relation to dependants' scheme pensions payable by registered pension schemes and provide that a transfer of sums or assets in respect of a dependants' scheme pension from one registered pension scheme to another where another dependants' scheme pension is provided is a recognised transfer; (7) in relation to dependants' scheme pensions payable by insurance companies and provide that where a dependants' scheme pension ceases to be paid on a transfer of sums and assets the transfer is treated as an unauthorised payment except where a new dependants' scheme pension becomes payable; (8) in relation to dependants' annuities and provide that where a dependants' annuity ceases to be paid on a transfer of sums and assets the transfer is treated as an unauthorised payment except where a new dependants' annuity becomes payable; (9) in relation to dependants' short-term annuities and provide that where a dependants' short-term annuity ceases to be paid on a transfer of sums and assets the transfer is treated as an unauthorised payment except where a new dependants' short-term annuity becomes payable; (10) in relation to unsecured pension funds, alternatively secured pension funds, dependants' unsecured pension funds and dependants' alternatively secured pension funds and provide that a transfer of sums and assets from one arrangement to a new arrangement under which no other sums or assets are held is a recognised transfer. The sums and assets transferred are treated as remaining sums and assets held under the old arrangement for the purposes prescribed in Tables 3–6.

2230   Registered pension schemes—unauthorised payments

The Registered Pension Schemes (Unauthorised Payments by Existing Schemes) Regulations 2006, SI 2006/365 (in force on 6 April 2006), describe a payment which is exempted from being a scheme chargeable payment. The regulations (1) provide that a payment, made by an existing pension scheme falling under the Finance Act 2004 Sch 36, on or after 6 April 2006, is a payment of a description prescribed for the purposes of s 241(2); and (2) provide that such a payment is only a payment of such a description to the extent that it is referable to subsisting rights which have accrued under defined benefits arrangements before that day, or to contributions which have been paid to a scheme under money purchase arrangements on or before that day.

2231   Registered pension schemes—uprating—defined benefits arrangements—enhanced protection limits

The Registered Pension Schemes (Uprating Percentages for Defined Benefits Arrangements and Enhanced Protection Limits) Regulations 2006, SI 2006/130 (in force on 6 April 2006), prescribe alternative percentages by reference to which the opening value of defined benefits arrangements and enhanced protection limits under the Finance Act 2004 s 235(3)(c) and Sch 36 respectively, are increased.

2232 Retirement pension—entitlement—discrimination

See Case C-423/04 *Richards v Secretary of State for Work and Pensions*, para 1083.

2233 Social security pensions—deferral

The Social Security (Deferral of Retirement Pensions etc) Regulations 2006, SI 2006/516 (in force on 6 April 2006), apply in relation to the deferral of retirement pensions, shared additional pension and graduated retirement benefit. In particular, the regulations (1) amend the Social Security (Widow's Benefit and Retirement Pensions) Regulations 1979, SI 1979/642, so as to (a) ensure that days of increment may, in respect of periods of deferment ending on or after 6 April 2006, accrue in respect of days where a person is both deferring entitlement to his category A or category B retirement pension and receiving graduated retirement benefit; and (b) remove an otiose reference to injury benefit; (2) ensure that in calculating the amount of a lump sum payable to a person whose period of deferment spans 6 April 2005, in all cases, the amount of any increase of retirement pension payable under the Social Security Contributions and Benefits Act 1992, ss 83–85, in respect of an adult dependant, is excluded when determining the total amount of retirement pension which would have been payable to the person in the previous 12 months if his entitlement had not been deferred; (3) correct erroneous cross references to provisions in the Social Security (Claims and Payments) Regulations 1987, SI 1987/1968, relating to changes of elections to receive either an increase in a pension or benefit or a lump sum; and (4) amend the Social Security (Payments on account, Overpayments and Recovery) Regulations 1988, SI 1988/664, so that sums paid following deferral of entitlement to retirement pension, shared additional pension or graduated retirement benefit and which are made under a decision which is subsequently revised, superseded or overturned on appeal, must be offset against such payments as are due under the subsequent determination.

2234 Social security pensions—low earnings threshold—increase

The Social Security Pensions (Low Earnings Threshold) Order 2006, SI 2006/500 (in force on 6 April 2006), directs that, for the purposes of the Social Security Contributions and Benefits Act 1992, the low earnings threshold for the tax years following the tax year 2005–06 is £12,500.

2235 Teachers—pensions

See EDUCATION.

PERPETUITIES AND ACCUMULATIONS

Halsbury's Laws of England (4th edn) vol 35 (Reissue) paras 1001–1200

Articles

For articles relating to this title please refer to the Table of Articles at the beginning of the Abridgment.

POLICE

Halsbury's Laws of England (4th edn) vol 36(1) (Reissue) paras 201–600

Articles

For articles relating to this title please refer to the Table of Articles at the beginning of the Abridgment.

2236 Codes of practice

See CRIMINAL EVIDENCE AND PROCEDURE

2237 Conditions of service—general

The Police (Amendment) (No 2) Regulations 2006, SI 2006/3449 (in force on 1 February 2007), further amend the 2003 Regulations, SI 2003/527, by (1) providing that (a) where a business interest is held by a relative of an officer, then the duty to give written notification of that interest arises only in cases where the officer believes that it could interfere with the impartial discharge of his duties; (b) in determining whether a business interest is incompatible, the chief officer must have regard to whether, as a result of the interest, the member's conduct fails to meet the appropriate standards of the statutory Code of Conduct; and (c) in the circumstances where substantive reasons have been adduced as to why the business interest should be permitted, and those reasons have not yet been considered by the chief officer, or in reaching his determination the chief officer failed to apply fair procedures, then a police authority may remit a decision back to the chief officer for redetermination, rather than itself determining an appeal; (2) extending the category of persons whose interests may be incompatible with an officer's membership of a police force so as to include a civil partner or a co habitee of the officer; (3) providing that a personal record kept of each police officer must contain particulars of any civil partnership; (4) revising the circumstances in which an officer's maternity leave counts as service for the purposes of her pay, and setting out the circumstances in which periods of adoption leave, maternity support leave and adoption support leave are to count; and (5) giving the Secretary of State the power to make a determination (a) relating to adoption support leave and career breaks; and (b) that would give police authorities a discretion to reimburse to chief officers the tax payable in relation to removal or relocation expenses associated with their appointment.

The Police (Amendment) Regulations 2006, SI 2006/1467 (in force on 1 July 2006), further amend the 2003 Regulations supra by (1) providing for the abolition of fixed-term appointments for commanders in the metropolitan and City of London police forces and for assistant chief constables in other forces; (2) specifying, in relation to other senior ranks, a maximum period of five years for a fixed term appointment, and a maximum period by which such appointments can be extended; and (3) providing that existing fixed-term appointments of commanders in the metropolitan and City of London police forces and of assistant chief constables become indefinite.

2238   Criminal records—registration

The Police Act 1997 (Criminal Records) (Registration) Regulations 2006, SI 2006/750 (in force on 6 April 2006), replace the 2001 Regulations, SI 2001/1194, as amended, and (1) set out the information to be included in the register maintained by the Secretary of State under the Police Act 1997 s 120; (2) require a body or statutory office holder which has registered person status to submit the names of those persons who are authorised to countersign applications for criminal record and enhanced criminal record certificates; (3) set out the fee payable on application for inclusion in the register; (4) set out additional fees which are payable by a registered person which is a body or a statutory office holder for the inclusion in the register of second and subsequent names of those authorised to countersign applications for criminal record and enhanced criminal record certificates; (5) set out conditions which are attached to registration; (6) require registered persons and countersignatories to allow the Secretary of State access to their premises for the purpose of assessing compliance with the conditions attached to registration; (7) enable the Secretary of State to remove from the register any person who fails to comply with the conditions of registration; (8) prescribe a limit on the number of countersignatories and provide that the Secretary of State may refuse to accept the nomination of a countersignatory if the maximum number is already registered; and (9) enable the Secretary of State to remove any excess countersignatories from the register.

2239   Duty of care—duty owed to police officer—nervous shock—unjustified disciplinary proceedings brought following fatal shooting by different officer

See *French v Chief Constable of Sussex Police*, para 2092.

2240   Independent Police Complaints Commission—bodies subject to investigation—Her Majesty's Revenue and Customs

The Revenue and Customs (Complaints and Misconduct) (Amendment) Regulations 2006, SI 2006/1748 (in force on 27 July 2006), amend the 2005 Regulations, SI 2005/3311, so as to (1) specify the conditions subject to which a duty to refer a complaint or conduct matter to the Independent Police Complaints Commission ('IPCC') arises; and (2) provide for the appropriate authority to appoint an officer of Her Majesty's Revenue and Customs to investigate a complaint or conduct matter which the IPCC has determined should be investigated by the appropriate authority on its own behalf.

2241   Judicial privilege—protected proceedings—police disciplinary hearing

See *Lake v British Transport Police*, para 2249.

2242   Local policing summaries

The Police Act 1996 (Local Policing Summaries) Order 2006, SI 2006/122 (in force on 1 April 2006), specifies matters which must be included in local policing summaries issued by police authorities pursuant to the Police Act 1996 s 8A.

2243   National Crime Squad—abolition

The NCIS and NCS (Abolition) Order 2006, SI 2006/540 (in force on 1 April 2006), provides that the National Criminal Intelligence Service and the National Crime Squad and their service authorities cease to exist on 1 April 2006.

2244   National Criminal Intelligence Service—abolition

See para 2243.

2245   Police and Justice Act 2006

The Police and Justice Act 2006 establishes a National Policing Improvement Agency, makes provision about police forces and police authorities and about police pensions, makes provision about police powers and about the powers and duties of community support officers, weights and measures inspectors and others, makes provision about the supply to the police and others of information contained in registers of death, makes further provision for combating crime and disorder, makes further provision about certain inspectorates, amends the Criminal Justice Act 2003 and the Computer Misuse Act 1990, makes provision about the forfeiture of indecent images of children, provides for the conferring of functions on the Independent Police Complaints Commission in relation to the exercise of enforcement functions by officials involved with immigration and asylum, amends the Extradition Act 2003, and makes further provision about the use of live links in criminal proceedings. The 2006 Act received the royal assent on 8 November 2006 and certain provisions came into force on that day. Further provisions came into force on 8 November 2006 and 15 January 2007: SI 2006/3364. The remaining provisions come into force on a day or days to be appointed. For details of commencement, see the commencement table in the title STATUTES.

Part 1 (ss 1–9) Police reform
The 2006 Act s 1 establishes the National Policing Improvement Agency (the Agency), and abolishes the Central Police Training and Development Authority and the Police Information Technology Organisation. Schedule 1 makes further provision about the Agency and sets out details of its constitution, objects and powers. Section 2 gives effect to Sch 2, which makes amendments to the Police Act 1996 regarding the composition and functions of police authorities and other matters. The 2006 Act s 3 amends the Local Government Act 1972 so as to allow police authorities additional flexibility in the delegation of their functions. The extent to which the best value provisions contained in the Local Government Act 1999 apply to police authorities is limited by the 2006 Act s 4. Section 5, Sch 3 provide the power to make provision replacing existing pensions regulations so as to create a single, unified pension scheme for persons who became members of one of the original police schemes before a specified date. Section 6, Sch 4 require the Secretary of State to consult with the Association of Police Authorities and the Association of Chief Police Officers before exercising certain powers in relation to policing. The standard powers and duties of community support officers are dealt with in s 7, and s 8 provides community support officers with a new power to deal with truants. Section 9, Sch 5 make amendments to the Police Reform Act 2002 as a result of the standardisation of powers of community support officers, and in connection with the exercise of police powers by civilians.

Part 2 (ss 10–18) Powers of police etc
The 2006 Act s 10, Sch 6 amend the Police and Criminal Evidence Act 1984 so as to allow police officers to attach conditions to bail granted at a police station before charge, and also to street bail, granted elsewhere than at a police station. The 2006 Act ss 11, 12 further amend the Police and Criminal Evidence Act 1984 by allowing police to detain a suspect pending a decision by the Director of Public Prosecutions about charging, and to stop and search, without warrant, any person, vehicle or aircraft in any area of an aerodrome, for stolen or prohibited articles, where an officer has reasonable grounds to suspect that he will find such articles. The Registrar General may supply information from death registers to the police and certain other organisations by virtue of the 2006 Act s 13. Section 14 extends police powers to gather information relating to flights or voyages to include information relating to domestic flights and voyages. The Police Reform Act 2002 is further amended by the 2006 Act ss 15, 16, Sch 7. Section 15 makes provision for the accreditation of weights and measures inspectors and Sch 7 sets out the powers exercisable by accredited inspectors. Section 16 empowers the Secretary of State to apply the accreditation provisions to persons of a description specified by order. Section 17 amends the Criminal Justice Act 2003 so as to widen the scope of the conditions that can be attached to a conditional caution, and a power of arrest for breach of a conditional caution is introduced by the 2006 Act s 18.

Part 3 (ss 19–27) Crime and anti-social behaviour
Section 19 requires a local authority to ensure that it has a crime and disorder committee with power to review and scrutinise, and make reports or recommendations, regarding the functioning of the local Crime and Disorder Reduction Partnership ('CDRP')/Community Safety Partnership ('CSP'). Further provision about crime and disorder committees of certain local authorities is contained in Sch 8. The Secretary of State may issue guidance regarding the overview and scrutiny of CDRPs and make regulations regarding crime and disorder matters under s 20. Section 21 amends the Crime and Disorder Act 1998 by empowering the Secretary of State to require councils for certain local government areas to appoint a joint committee to carry out crime and disorder scrutiny functions where CDRP mergers have taken place. The 2006 Act s 22, Sch 9 further amend the Crime and Disorder Act 1998 in relation to crime and disorder strategies and other matters relating to the reduction of crime and disorder. The 2006 Act ss 23–25 amend the Anti-social Behaviour Act 2003. The 2006 Act s 23 enables a local authority or a registered social landlord to enter into a parenting contract with a parent of a child or young person where it has reason to believe that the child or

young person has engaged, or is likely to engage, in anti-social behaviour. A local authority or registered social landlord may apply for a parenting order against a parent of a child or young person where it has reason to believe that the child or young person has engaged, or is likely to engage, in anti-social behaviour by virtue of s 24. The Secretary of State may by order enable a local authority to contract out to a specified person the functions of entering into parenting contracts and applying for parenting orders: s 25. Section 26 amends legislation relating to anti-social behaviour injunctions contained in the Housing Act 1996, so that a housing related anti-social behaviour injunction may be granted without any requirement to name a particular individual as someone adversely affected by the conduct referred to in the injunction. The 2006 Act s 27, Sch 10 deal with powers of arrest and remand relating to anti-social behaviour injunctions in local authority proceedings, and give the courts power to remand a person in custody pending trial, where he has been arrested for breach of an anti-social behaviour injunction.

Part 4 (ss 28–33) Inspectorates
Section 28 confers additional powers and duties on Her Majesty's Chief Inspector of Prisons, which relate to the delegation of functions, inspection programmes and inspection frameworks, inspections by other inspectors of organisations within the Chief Inspector's remit, cooperation, joint action, and assistance for other public authorities. Sections 29–32 make equivalent provision in respect of Her Majesty's Inspectors of Constabulary, Her Majesty's Chief Inspector of the Crown Prosecution Service, Her Majesty's Chief Inspector of the National Probation Service for England and Wales, and Her Majesty's Inspectorate of Court Administration. Transitional provision is dealt with in s 33.

Part 5 (ss 34–48) Miscellaneous
Section 34 amends the Criminal Justice Act 2003 so that sentencing arrangements for prison sentences of less than 12 months do not apply to offences of absconding while released on bail. The 2006 Act ss 35–37 amend the Computer Misuse Act 1990. The offence of unauthorised access to computer material is extended by the 2006 Act s 35 so that the offence is also committed where a person's intention is to enable someone else to secure unauthorised access to a computer or to enable the person himself to secure unauthorised access to a computer at some later time. The offence is made indictable, and the maximum sentence increased from six months' imprisonment to two years. By virtue of s 36, it is an offence for a person to commit any unauthorised act in relation to a computer, knowing it to be unauthorised, if by doing the act he intends to impair the operation of a computer, prevent or hinder access to programs or data, impair the operation of programs or the reliability of data, or is reckless as to such a result occurring. The maximum penalty for this offence is an unlimited fine and/or ten years' imprisonment. Section 37 creates offences of: making, adapting, supplying or offering to supply an article intending it to be used to commit, or to assist in the commission of a computer misuse offence mentioned above, supplying or offering to supply an article believing that it is likely to be used in this way, and obtaining an article with a view to its being supplied for use in this way. Transitional arrangements relating to ss 35–37 are dealt with in s 38. Section 39, Sch 11 facilitate the forfeiture of indecent photographs of children irrespective of the power under which they were seized, and s 40, Sch 12 make equivalent provision in relation to Northern Ireland. The remit of the Independent Police Complaints Commission ('IPCC') is expanded by s 41, which empowers the Secretary of State to confer functions on the IPCC enabling them to investigate complaints and alleged misconduct regarding the exercise of specified immigration and asylum enforcement functions. Section 42, Sch 13 make various amendments to the Extradition Act 2003 in connection with requests for extradition of persons unlawfully at large, restrictions on extradition following transfer from the International Criminal Court and in cases where trial in the United Kingdom is more appropriate, remand and extradition of persons serving a sentence in the United Kingdom, remands in connection with appeal proceedings, time limits and warrants. The requirement for the United States to provide prima facie evidence with its extradition requests to the United Kingdom is restored by the 2006 Act s 43, and s 44 provides for the transfer of prisoners under international arrangements without their consent. Section 45 amends the Crime and Disorder Act 1998 to make provision for the use of live links, with a defendant's consent, at certain preliminary and sentencing hearings. The 2006 Act s 46 amends the Police and Criminal Evidence Act 1984 so as to allow the police to grant bail subject to a duty to appear at a police station for the purpose of a live link hearing ('live link bail'). By virtue of the 2006 Act s 47, which amends the Youth Justice and Criminal Evidence Act 1999, the court may in criminal proceedings, on application by an accused, direct that any evidence given by the accused is to be given over a live video link, where it is considered it to be in the interests of justice. The 2006 Act s 48 provides that certain appeal hearings may also be conducted by way of a live link.

Part 6 (ss 49–55) Supplemental
Section 49 makes general provision as to the making of orders and regulations by the Secretary of State, while s 50 deals with expenses under the Act. A power to make consequential amendments and transitional provision is provided by s 51, and s 52, Sch 14 deal with minor and consequential amendments and repeals. Section 53 deals with commencement, s 54 with extent and s 55 with the short title.

Amendments, repeals and revocations

The list below, which is not exhaustive, mentions repeals and amendments which are or will be effective when the Act is fully in force.

Specific provisions of a number of Acts are added, amended or repealed: Prison Act 1952 s 5A, Sch A1; Criminal Justice Act 1967 s 22; Criminal Appeal Act 1968 ss 22, 23, 31; Local Government Act 1972 s 107; Bail Act 1976 s 4; Protection of Children Act 1978 ss 4, 5, 11–14, 16, 17, Schedule; Aviation Security Act 1982 ss 24B, 27; Police and Criminal Evidence Act 1984 ss 30A, 30B, 30CA, 30CB, 30D, 34, 37, 37A, 37CA, 37D, 46A, 46ZA, 47, 54, 67; Repatriation of Prisoners Act 1984 s 1; Criminal Justice Act 1988 Sch 15 para 62; Computer Misuse Act 1990 ss 1, 3, 3A; Criminal Justice Act 1991 s 47; Bail (Amendment) Act 1993 s 1; Criminal Justice and Public Order Act 1994 Sch 10; Criminal Procedure and Investigations Act 1996 s 21A; Employment Rights Act 1996 s 50(6); Housing Act 1996 s 153A; Police Act 1996 ss 4, 5C, 6, 6A, 6ZA, 6ZB, 6ZC, 7, 8, 8A, 9, 9A, 10, 11A, 12A, 15, 16, 19, 24, 27, 30, 36A, 37, 37A, 38, 39A, 40, 40A, 40B, 41, 41A, 41B, 42A, 53, 53A, 54, 57, 96, 96B, 97, 101, Schs 2, 2A, 3, 3A, 4A, 6; Police Act 1997 ss 109–111, Schs 8, 9; Crime and Disorder Act 1998 ss 5, 6, 6A, 17, 17A, 57, 57A–57E, 114, 115; Greater London Authority Act 1999 s 310(2), Schs 26, 27; Local Government Act 1999 ss 1, 24; Youth Justice and Criminal Evidence Act 1999 s 33A–33C; Criminal Justice and Court Services Act 2000 s 7, Sch 1A; Crown Prosecution Service Inspectorate Act 2000 s 2, Schedule; Insolvency Act 2000 Sch 4 para 20; Powers of Criminal Courts (Sentencing) Act 2000 s 101, Sch 9 para 199; Criminal Justice and Police Act 2001 ss 87–96, 97, 101(1), 104–7, Schs 2–4; Police Reform Act 2002 ss 1, 5, 22, 24, 38, 38A, 39, 40(7), 41A, 41B, 42, 43, 45, 51, 92, 94, 96–99, 102, 105, 106, 108, Schs 4, 5, 5A, 7; Anti-social Behaviour Act 2003 ss 13, 25A, 25B, 26A–26C, 28A, 29, 91; Courts Act 2003 s 61A, Schs 3A, 4, 8; Criminal Justice Act 2003 ss 22, 23A, 24A, 24B, 195, 237, 243, 257, 258, 305, 330; Extradition Act 2003 ss 2, 7–9, 11, 12–19, 19A, 19B, 21, 23, 24, 29, 30, 32, 33, 33A, 35, 37, 38, 44, 46, 50, 51, 52, 59, 67, 68A, 70, 72, 74, 77, 79, 82, 83A, 89, 90, 92, 93, 96A, 99, 104, 106, 107, 111, 112, 114, 115, 115A, 119, 132, 139, 140A, 141–143, 146, 148, 155A, 179, 187–189, 197A, 202, Sch 1; Energy Act 2004 Sch 14 para 9; Clean Neighbourhoods and Environment Act 2005 s 1; Constitutional Reform Act 2005 Sch 9; Serious Organised Crime and Police Act 2005 Schs 4, 16; Immigration Asylum and Nationality Act 2006 ss 32, 36, 38, 63.

2246   Police authority—best value authority—performance indicators

See para 1841.

2247   Police authority—membership—lay justice members—extension of appointments

The Police and Justice Act 2006 (Supplementary and Transitional Provisions) Order 2006, SI 2006/3365 (in force on 15 January 2007), provides that existing lay justice members of police authorities whose appointments are due to expire on or after 15 January 2007 are to remain members of those authorities until 31 March 2008, or, in the case of lay justice members of the Metropolitan Police Authority, 2 July 2008, so as to avoid the need to appoint further lay justice members for a short time only until a new regime in relation to membership of police authorities comes into force.

2248   Police authority—special police services—entitlement to payment—request for services—police attendance at music festival

The defendant organised an annual three-day music festival within the claimant police authority's area. For each festival the defendant requested and paid for 'special police services' provided by the claimant under the terms of the Police Act 1996 s 25(1). After several years of operating under this arrangement, a dispute arose as to whether payment was due for such services in relation to the festival. The defendant refused to pay, and the claimant commenced proceedings. The judge concluded that the defendant had requested special police services, but observed that a claim in contract could not have succeeded because there was no meeting of minds between the parties as to how those services were to be deployed and paid for. He therefore ruled in favour of the claimant, and the defendant appealed, contending that there had been no request for special police services and that the services in fact provided were not special police services within the meaning of s 25(1). *Held*, the judge had not been entitled on the facts to rule there had been a request by the defendant for special police services. Once he had concluded that a claim based on contract could not succeed, the claimant's claim was then bound to fail. Had there been agreement about what special services the police were to provide, all operational decisions under the umbrella of the agreement would have been a matter for the police. However, it was for the defendant to decide, albeit after negotiation, what special police services it wanted even though it was for the police to decide how they would provide them. If the judge's approach was correct, a promoter who put on a sporting event or a festival would effectively have no choice but to pay the police for whatever operation it chose to mount. Accordingly, the appeal would be allowed.

West Yorkshire Police Authority v Reading Festival Ltd [2006] EWCA Civ 524, [2006] 1 WLR 2005 (Court of Appeal: Scott Baker, Jacob and Neuberger LJJ).

2249   Police disciplinary board—judicial immunity—proceedings—unfair discrimination

An employee, a police officer, made a complaint of bullying against another officer. At the same time, the employee made a separate allegation that the officer in question had retained a piece of skull, described as a souvenir, from an accident scene several years previously. The employee stated that he had a CCTV tape of the incident but had never revealed it. The employer carried out an investigation into the allegations, but decided that they had not been proven. Following an investigation into the employee's conduct, internal disciplinary proceedings were brought against him for failing to disclose immediately the initial complaint and the CCTV tape, and for making false accusations against a colleague. The Police Disciplinary Board decided that the employee should be dismissed, and that decision was upheld by the chief constable. The employee maintained that the reason, or one of the principal reasons for his dismissal, had been the protected disclosure which he had made in relation to the alleged conduct of his fellow officer. He therefore brought a complaint before an employment tribunal that his dismissal had been automatically unfair under the Employment Rights Act 1996 s 103A. At a pre-hearing review, it was directed that the proceedings before the board could not form the basis of the claim because that decision had been protected by judicial immunity. The employee appealed. *Held*, the scope of the immunity from suit afforded to judicial and quasi-judicial bodies applied to the final decisions of those bodies, in addition to their conduct and comments during the course of hearings before them. If the immunity had not extended in that way, their decisions would have been subject to endless collateral challenges. Furthermore, nothing contained within the provisions of the 1996 Act militated against that conclusion. Although that created several anomalies in the present case, the end result was that the employee had been entitled to challenge every stage in the process of his dismissal, albeit by different mechanisms. The board was, for very good reason, a more formal body than a private employer's domestic tribunal. It had been established by statute, and recognised as having the status of a quasi-judicial body. Once those facts had been accepted, public policy dictated that challenges, whether directly or by collateral attack, to its decisions should be restrained. That immunity had not extinguished the employee's claim, since he had been entitled to challenge both the decision to prosecute him, and the decision of the chief constable to uphold his dismissal, and, in those circumstances, the tribunal had been correct to hold that the decision of the board could form no part of the employee's claim. Accordingly, the appeal would be dismissed.

Lake v British Transport Police [2006] All ER (D) 04 (Oct) (Employment Appeal Tribunal: Judge Serota QC presiding). *Heath v Metropolitan Police Comr* [2004] EWCA Civ 943, [2005] ICR 329 (2004 Abr para 2174) considered.

2250   Police officer—abolition of fixed-term appointments—senior ranks

See para 2237.

2251   Police officer—code of conduct—complaints

The Police (Complaints and Misconduct) (Amendment) Regulations 2006, SI 2006/1406 (in force on 22 June 2006), amend the 2004 Regulations, SI 2004/643, (1) so that they apply to death or serious injury matters, which concern cases where a person has died or has been seriously injured following some form of contact with the police and where there has been no complaint and no indication that a criminal or disciplinary offence has been committed; and (2) by changing the time within which a chief officer or police authority must refer complaints and conduct matters to the Commission so that the matters are now to be referred by the end of the day, whether or not a working day, following the day on which that duty arises.

2252   Police officer—injury benefit

See para 2621.

2253   Police officer—minimum age for appointment

The Police (Minimum Age for Appointment) Regulations 2006, SI 2006/2278 (in force on 19 September 2006), further amend the Special Constables Regulations 1965, SI 1965/536, and the Police Regulations 2003, SI 2003/527, to lower, from eighteen years and six months to eighteen years, the age that a candidate for appointment as a special or regular constable must have attained.

2254   Police officer—powers—caution of suspect—compatibility with police policy

See *R (on the application of Mondelly) v Metropolitan Police Comr*, para 747.

2255   Police officer—powers—preventing breach of the peace—anti-war demonstration—coach containing suspected protesters—power to prevent access to site

The claimant was travelling on a coach which contained passengers who were going to an air base to take part in an anti-war demonstration. Acting on intelligence that hard-line protesters intended to attend the demonstration, and pursuant to a stop and search authorisation granted under the Criminal Justice and Public Order Act 1994 s 60, the police stopped the coach at a lay-by. Several of the passengers, including the claimant, refused to co-operate with the police, including declining to disclose their names and addresses. The police concluded that the passengers were travelling to the air base and were likely to cause a breach of the peace. The coach was returned to London with a police escort, which prevented them from stopping or leaving the motorway. On the claimant's application for judicial review of the police's actions, the court found that the decision to prevent the claimant from travelling to the air base was lawful, but that the decision to return the claimant to London was not. The claimant's appeal against the first finding and the defendant chief constable's appeal against the second finding were dismissed and, on the parties' further appeal, *held*, no action short of arrest might be taken to prevent a breach of the peace which was not sufficiently imminent to justify arrest. While it was entirely reasonable to suppose that some of those on board the coaches might have wished to cause damage and injury to the air base, and to enter the base with a view to causing further damage and injury, it was not reasonable to suppose that even those passengers simply wanted a violent confrontation with the police, which they could have had in the lay-by. Nor was it reasonable to anticipate an outburst of disorder on arrival of those passengers in the assembly area or during the procession to the base, during which time the police would be in close attendance and well able to identify and arrest those who showed a violent propensity or breached the conditions to which the assembly and procession were subject. There had been no reason (other than her refusal to give her name, which however irritating to the police was entirely lawful) to view the claimant as other than a committed, peaceful demonstrator. It was wholly disproportionate to restrict her exercise of her human rights because she was in the company of others, some of whom might, at some time in the future, breach the peace. Accordingly, the appeal would be allowed and the cross-appeal would be dismissed.

R (on the application of Laporte) v Chief Constable of Gloucestershire Constabulary [2006] UKHL 55, [2006] All ER (D) 172 (Dec) (House of Lords: Lords Bingham of Cornhill, Rodger of Earlsferry, Carswell, Brown of Eaton-under-Heywood and Mance). Decision of Court of Appeal [2004] EWCA Civ 1639, [2005] QB 678 (2004 Abr para 2180) reversed in part.

2256 Police officer—powers—stop and search—authorisation

See *R (on the application of Gillan) v Metropolitan Police Comr*, para 892.

2257 Police officer—promotion

The Police (Promotion) (Amendment) Regulations 2006, SI 2006/1442 (in force on 1 July 2006), further amend the 1996 Regulations, SI 1996/1685, so as to correct errors in relation to the alternative to Part II of the qualifying examination.

2258 Police officer—vicarious liability of chief constable—exemplary damages

The claimant brought an action against the police for assault, false imprisonment and malicious prosecution. She was awarded damages for physical and psychiatric injury, in the form of post-traumatic stress disorder. However, the judge rejected her claims for aggravated damages in respect of the affront to her dignity and exemplary damages in respect of what she alleged were the arbitrary, oppressive and unconstitutional actions of the police on the basis that aggravated damages would result in over-compensation. The claimant appealed, and the question arose as to whether it would be wrong in law to make an award of exemplary damages against the chief constable who, although vicariously liable under the Police Act 1996 s 88, was not personally at fault. *Held*, the fact that the basic award included an element to compensate for psychiatric harm did not preclude an award of aggravated damages. Whether damages awarded to compensate the claimant for distress, humiliation and injury to feelings were treated as part of the basic damages or were separately identified by the name of aggravated damages, the important factor was that they were primarily intended to be compensatory rather than punitive. While the claimant had been entitled to compensation for the psychiatric injury resulting from the circumstances of her arrest, harm of that kind was not to be equated with the humiliation and injury to pride and dignity that might follow from the particular circumstances of the arrest or with the feelings of anger and resentment induced by the insulting or arrogant conduct of those by whom it was made and by their subsequent attempts to obtain an unjustified conviction through false evidence. The judge had erred in withdrawing from the jury consideration of aggravated damages. A substantial award of exemplary damages could be made against a chief officer of police under s 88. While the common law recognised a power to award exemplary damages in respect of wrongdoing by servants of the government of a kind that had a direct effect on civil liberties, it was desirable as a matter of policy that the courts should be able to make punitive awards against those who were vicariously liable for the conduct of their subordinates without being constrained by the financial means of those who committed the wrongful acts in questions. Accordingly, the appeal would be allowed.

Rowlands v Chief Constable of Merseyside Police [2006] EWCA Civ 1773, [2006] All ER (D) 298 (Dec) (Court of Appeal: Ward, Moore-Bick and Richards LJJ). *Thompson v Metropolitan Police Comr* [1998] QB 498, CA (1997 Abr para 1030); *Cassell & Co Ltd v Broome* [1972] AC 1027, HL; *Kuddus v Chief Constable of Leicestershire Constabulary* [2001] UKHL 29, [2002] 2 AC 122 (2001 Abr para 948) considered.

2259   Police pensions—civil partnerships

See para 2260.

2260   Police pensions—general

The Police Pensions (Amendment) Regulations 2006, SI 2006/740 (in force on 5 April 2006), further amend the 1987 Regulations, SI 1987/257, and the Police Pensions (Additional Voluntary Contributions) Regulations 1991, SI 1991/1304, so as to ensure parity of treatment between police officers who form civil partnerships and those who marry, and so as to restrict the ability of a police officer who has opted out of the police pension scheme to opt back into it. In particular, the regulations (1) modify provisions which previously applied to married couples so that they also apply to couples who form a civil partnership; (2) enable payments to be made by women members to enhance widowers' and surviving civil partners' awards in cases where members with service before 17 May 1990 did not elect to make such payments because they related only to widowers' benefits; (3) enable such elections to be made (a) within a period of three months from 5 April 2006 where the woman's contributions became payable again on or before that date; or (b) where they became payable again on a later date, within a period of three months after that date; and (4) impose a cut-off date of 5 April 2006 for cancelling elections not to pay pension contributions due to the introduction of a new police pension scheme.

The Police Pensions Regulations 2006, SI 2006/3415 (in force on 1 February 2007), (1) amend the Police (Injury Benefit) Regulations 2006, SI 2006/932, in relation to the calculation of pensionable and average pensionable pay and aggregate pensions contributions, and disablement gratuities; (2) require pension contributions to be paid by police officers to the police authority, subject to an election not to do so; (3) provide for the reckoning of pensionable services; (4) govern the time of voluntary retirement, the minimum age for which is set at 55 years, and compulsory retirement; (5) specify the method to calculate pensionable pay, and the aggregate pension contributions for the purposes of awards; (6) provide for the pension awards which may be payable to police officers or in respect of a deceased officer, and for the circumstances in which awards may be reviewed, withdrawn or forfeited; (7) enable officers to purchase increased benefits or added years; (8) make provision (a) in relation to cases where there is a pension sharing order under the Welfare Reform and Pensions Act 1999 or the Civil Partnership Act 2004; (b) for the determination of medical questions related to eligibility for awards; and (c) for special cases involving chief officers affected by alterations in police areas, servicemen and transfers of police officers to or from a Scottish police force or the Police Service of Northern Ireland; and (9) make financial provision, including provisions on transfer values.

2261   Police pensions—right to pension—disablement—permanent disablement—member of police force

The applicant, a police officer, was injured with CS gas while on duty. As a consequence, she claimed that she was permanently disabled within the meaning of the Police Pensions Regulations 1987, SI 1987/257, reg A12. The Police Medical Appeal Board decided that, although the applicant was permanently disabled from carrying out the ordinary duties of a member of her police force, she was not permanently disabled within the meaning of reg A12(2) as she could still perform duties in another force which did not use CS gas. The applicant sought judicial review of the Board's decision. *Held*, the term 'member of a police force' under reg A12 referred to membership of a particular force and not the police service as a whole. The statutory reference to a police force in the Police Act 1996 was most naturally read as a reference to a particular police force. Also, since it was a rule that terms used in a statutory instrument had the same meaning as in its parent statute unless a contrary intention appeared, the definition of police force in the Police Pensions Act 1976 s 11(3) had to be imported into the 1987 Regulations. Such a conclusion was also right as a matter of policy. However, where a police officer was genuinely disabled from serving in the particular force to which he belonged, it did not seem fair that he should be disentitled to a pension because he might be fit to serve in another force, which might be in an entirely different part of the country and be quite different in character from the force which he chose to join. Accordingly, the application would be allowed.

R (on the application of Corkindale) v Police Medical Appeal Board [2006] EWHC 3362 (Admin), [2006] All ER (D) 334 (Dec) (Queen's Bench Division: Underhill J).

2262   Police pensions—widow's pension—forfeiture—widow convicted of manslaughter of husband

The appellant pleaded guilty to the manslaughter of her husband, having stabbed him while she was drunk. The trial judge was of the opinion that the appellant had acted in temper with no intention to cause serious harm. At the time of his death, the husband was a retired police sergeant who was in receipt of a pension under the Police Pensions Act 1976 and the Police Pensions Regulations 1987, SI 1987/257. Following her conviction, the respondent informed the appellant that she was not entitled to a widow's pension under the 1987 Regulations by virtue of the common law rule of forfeiture as stated in the Forfeiture Act 1982 s 1(1), which operated to preclude a person who had unlawfully killed another from acquiring a benefit as a consequence of that killing. The appellant appealed unsuccessfully against that decision and, on her further appeal, she argued that, having regard to the discretion to forfeit pensions that had been introduced in the Police Pensions Act 1921 and the Police Pensions Act 1948, and which was maintained in the 1976 Act s 1(3), (4) and the 1987 Regulations reg K5(1)–(4), the common law forfeiture rule was excluded. *Held*, the common law rule was long-standing and well understood at the time of the 1921 and 1948 Acts. It was a rule of public policy of fundamental importance. Parliament would not have intended at that time to sweep it away simply in the case of a particular type of public service pension while it remained in force in all other aspects of the law of inheritance and related matters. It was much more likely that the common law rule was taken as read, but Parliament was concerned to confer a further limited discretion to withdraw pension entitlements in particular cases of bad behaviour by the potential beneficiary. Similarly, there was nothing in the 1976 Act or the 1987 Regulations to indicate that the common law rule had been in any way abrogated by their provisions. It followed that the common law rule applied to the appellant's case and, accordingly, the appeal would be dismissed.

Glover v Staffordshire Police Authority [2006] EWHC 2414 (Admin), [2006] All ER (D) 77 (Oct) (Queen's Bench Division: McCombe J). *R v Chief National Insurance Comr, ex p Connor* [1981] QB 758, DC (1980 Abr para 2799), applied.

2263   Police surveillance—covert surveillance—video recording made available to police—admissibility in evidence

The defendant's neighbour informed a police officer that he had a video camera trained on the defendant's house and that he was recording events there. Although the officer warned the neighbour that his conduct amounted to a violation of the defendant's right to privacy, when offered a tape from the recordings, the officer accepted it. The tape included footage that appeared to show the defendant engaged in unwrapping packets of drugs. Police officers attended the defendant's address and found a quantity of drugs. At the defendant's trial for possession of a Class A drug with intent to supply, the prosecution sought to rely on the recordings made by the neighbour of the defendant's house. An application was made to exclude the video evidence. The defendant contended that the surveillance had been directed by the police, either directly or tacitly, and that there had been a breach of the Regulation of Investigatory Powers Act 2000. She was convicted of possessing a Class A drug with intent to supply. On her appeal against conviction, *held*, while the police had been complicit in the surveillance to the extent that they had known of it and had been prepared to use it in a criminal prosecution, it could not be regarded, for the purposes of the 2000 Act, as police surveillance. The police had neither initiated the surveillance nor had they encouraged it. While the degree of police involvement could be a factor in deciding on admissibility under the Police and Criminal Evidence Act 1984 s 78, the warning that had been given to the neighbour did not convert the recordings into police surveillance. The warning might have been a sensible piece of advice, given the history of trouble between the defendant and her neighbour, but that did not convert the police acceptance of the videos into a breach by them of the European Convention on Human Rights art 8 which conferred the right to respect for private life, or of the 1984 Act. There could be no breach of the 2000 Act s 26 as the surveillance was not 'covert' within the meaning of the provision. The camera had been of the most ostentatious type, and it could not be said that the surveillance had been carried out in a manner calculated to ensure that the defendant was unaware that it might have been taking place. The conviction was not unsafe and, accordingly, the appeal would be dismissed.

R v Rosenberg [2006] EWCA Crim 6, [2006] All ER (D) 127 (Jan) (Court of Appeal: Pill LJ, Newman and Lloyd Jones JJ).

2264   Serious organised crime—abolition of National Criminal Intelligence Service and National Crime Squad—consequential amendments

The Serious Organised Crime and Police Act 2005 (Consequential and Supplementary Amendments to Secondary Legislation) Order 2006, SI 2006/594 (in force on 1 April 2006), omits references in specified secondary legislation to the National Criminal Intelligence Service and the National Crime Squad and their service authorities consequential on the abolition of those bodies by the Serious Organised Crime and Police Act 2005. The order also ensures that specified traffic provisions apply to the Serious Organised Crime Agency in the same manner as they apply to the police and other emergency services.

POST OFFICE

Halsbury's Laws of England (4th edn) vol 36(2) (Reissue) paras 1–200

2265   Postal services—Jersey

The Postal Services (Jersey) Order 2006, SI 2006/1918 (in force on 20 July 2006), revokes the 1969 Order, SI 1969/1366, the Postal Service (Channel Islands Consequential Provisions) Order 1969, SI 1969/1368, and the Postal Services (Isle of Man Consequential Provisions) Order 1973, SI 1973/960, in so far as they extend to Jersey.

2266   Public procurement—award of contracts—procedure

See para 396.

POWERS

Halsbury's Laws of England (4th edn) vol 36(2) (Reissue) paras 201–400

Articles

For articles relating to this title please refer to the Table of Articles at the beginning of the Abridgment.

PRACTICE AND PROCEDURE

Halsbury's Laws of England (4th edn) vol 37 (Reissue) paras 1–1558

Articles

For articles relating to this title please refer to the Table of Articles at the beginning of the Abridgment.

2267   Abuse of process—striking out—withdrawal of admission

The claimant injured his knee while at work and brought a claim against the defendant, his employer. The defendant referred the matter to its loss adjusters whose employee admitted liability on behalf of the defendant. The loss adjusters, having found the employee's work to be unsatisfactory, dismissed him. The claimant's file was reviewed and the defendant's solicitors sought to rescind the admission of liability. The defendant filed a defence denying liability. The case was then assigned to the multi-track. The claimant applied under CPR 3.4(2) to strike out the defence on the ground that it was an abuse of process of the court or was otherwise likely to obstruct the just disposal of the proceedings. The matter came before a deputy district judge, who was referred to CPR 14, concerning the court's jurisdiction to allow a party to amend or withdraw an admission made in the course of proceedings, and not to CPR 3.4(2). The judge proceeded on the basis that CPR 14 applied to pre-action admissions and did not apply the provisions of CPR 3.4(2). He considered that the defendant should be bound by its admission, and granted the application to strike out the defence. His decision was affirmed on substantially the same basis. The Court of Appeal subsequently decided that CPR 14 did not apply to pre-action admissions, for which a defendant did not need the permission of the court to withdraw, although the pre-action admission would retain evidential significance. On the defendant's appeal, it fell to be determined whether its defence was an abuse of process or was otherwise likely to obstruct the just disposal of the case. *Held*, for a claimant to show that the withdrawal of an admission would amount to an abuse of the process of the court for the purposes of an application to strike out a defence under CPR 3.4(2), it would usually be necessary to show that the defendant had acted in bad faith. Although the loss adjusters had not managed their staff as well as they should have done, it could not be said that they had acted in bad faith. In order to show that the withdrawal of a pre-action admission was likely to obstruct the just disposal of the case, it would usually be necessary for the claimant to show that he would suffer some prejudice that would affect the fairness of the trial. Funding difficulties might give rise to real prejudice, if the evidence were to show that the claimant had changed his position in reliance on the pre-action admission. Such evidence should be put in at the outset. However, there was no evidence that this was the case, and any effect on the funding of the withdrawal of the admission would not be likely to obstruct the fair disposal of the case. The claimant's feelings of disappointment at the withdrawal could not be said to obstruct the just disposal of the case. The matter would be remitted back to the county court for case management with a view to arranging a hearing as soon as practicable and, accordingly, the appeal would be allowed.

The court added that, now that the position was clear under the CPR regime, there was great force in giving the status of an admission of liability in response to a pre-action protocol letter before action in a multi-track claim more powerful effect than it at present enjoyed. Now that such a valuable pre-action procedure had been introduced in advance of the formalities of litigation procedure, anything that lent uncertainty to the value of a pre-action admission of liability appeared to run against the grain of the overriding objective, and would be likely to lead to avoidable delay, expense and worry.

Stoke-on-Trent City Council v Walley [2006] EWCA Civ 1137, [2007] PIQR P55 (Court of Appeal: Brooke, Smith and Wall LJJ). *Gale v Superdrug Stores plc* [1996] 3 All ER 468, CA (1996 Abr para 2369; *Flaviis v Pauley (t/a Banjax Bike Hire)* [2002] All ER (D) 436 (Oct); and *Sowerby v Charlton* [2005] EWCA Civ 1610, [2005] All ER (D) 343 (Dec) (para 2268) considered.

2268 Admission—pre-action admission—defendant's ability to resile from admission

The claimant became paraplegic as a result of personal injuries suffered when falling from a platform at the defendant's property. The defendant's solicitors made an admission of liability in a without prejudice letter and made a proposal for settlement of the contributory negligence issue. After the claimant rejected the proposal and commenced proceedings, the defendant withdrew the admission. The claimant applied successfully to strike out parts of the defence, and the defendant appealed. *Held*, the CPR made some provision as to pre-action activity, but were primarily concerned with the settlement of disputes without resorting to proceedings. It was clear that CPR Pt 14 was not intended to apply to pre-action admissions of liability. Where the court was satisfied that a complete denial of primary liability had no real prospect of success, it could uphold the judgment on liability. In the circumstances of this case, no judge would fail to find the defendant at least partly liable. Accordingly, the appeal would be dismissed.

Sowerby v Charlton [2005] EWCA Civ 1610, [2006] 1 WLR 568 (Court of Appeal: Sir Anthony Clarke MR, Brooke and May LJJ). *Braybrook v Basildon and Thurrock University NHS Trust* [2004] EWHC 3352 (QB), [2005] All ER (D) 320 (Apr) considered.

2269 Appeal—evidence—fresh evidence—admissibility—test to be applied

See *Miklis v Deputy Prosecutor General of Lithuania*, para 1314.

2270 Appeal—leave to appeal—case raising hypothetical question only

It has been held that leave to appeal to the Court of Appeal should not be given where the substantive argument and the appeal raise what is in truth a hypothetical question. The court's business is to decide real issues which arise on facts which have been found or are capable of being determined in the court, or sometimes on facts which are assumed in favour of a party who asserts them for the purpose of a properly structured preliminary issue. Its business is not to conduct and determine academic seminars.

Menary-Smith v Secretary of State for Work and Pensions [2006] EWCA Civ 1689, [2006] All ER (D) 199 (Dec) (Court of Appeal: May, Carnwath and Gage LJJ).

2271 Appeal—permission to appeal—application—adjournment

It has been held that applications for permission to appeal are not to be adjourned for the convenience of counsel. In order to avoid undue delay in proceedings, such applications should be dealt with by junior counsel where necessary.

Bracknell Forest Borough v N (2006) Times, 6 November (Court of Appeal: Thorpe, Smith and Wall LJJ).

2272 Appeal—permission to appeal—committal order

CPR 52.3(1)(a) provides that an appellant or respondent requires permission to appeal where the appeal is from a decision of a judge in a county court or the High Court, except where the appeal is against (1) a committal order; (2) a refusal to grant habeas corpus; or (3) a secure accommodation order.

The defendant was found to have breached a non-molestation and occupation order, and was committed to prison for 28 days suspended on the condition that the defendant did not enter a defined area where the claimant, his former partner, lived and worked. The claimant appealed against that decision, proceeding on the basis that, pursuant to CPR 52.3(1)(a)(i), permission to appeal was not needed from either the judge or the Court of Appeal. She contended that, in the circumstances, the suspended committal order had been unduly lenient and that nothing other than a term of immediate custody could be justified. The defendant contended that permission to appeal was needed, submitting that, as the wording used in CPR 52.3(1)(a)(ii) and (iii) was restrictive to a person or about a person whose liberty had been restricted, CPR 52.3(1)(a)(i) should be read in a similar way. *Held*, on the proper construction of CPR 52.3(1)(a)(i), permission to appeal was not required by either an applicant or a contemnor. The right of appeal without permission against a committal order was not to be considered as restricted to the contemnor. It followed that the claimant had been entitled to appeal against the judge's decision as of right. Further, as the defendant had committed repeated breaches of the order and threatened and intimidated the claimant, the sentence of 28 days' imprisonment had been unduly lenient. Judgment would be given accordingly.

Wood v Collins [2006] EWCA Civ 743, [2006] All ER (D) 165 (May) (Court of Appeal: Thorpe and Gage LJJ and Hedley J). *Lomas v Parle* [2003] EWCA Civ 1804, [2004] 1 All ER 1173 (2003 Abr para 1816) applied. *Government of Sierra Leone v Davenport* [2002] EWCA Civ 230, [2002] All ER (D) 160 (Jan) considered.

2273   Appeal—permission to appeal—grant—lower court's power

CPR 52.3(2) provides that an application for permission to appeal may be made to the lower court at the hearing at which the decision to be appealed was made or to the appeal court in an appeal notice.

The court handed down a substantive judgment in favour of the defendant and the claimant decided not to appeal. However, the claimant changed its mind and sought an order extending time for making an application for permission to appeal to the judge or to the Court of Appeal under CPR 52.3(2). *Held*, after the trial court had given its decision, a party could apply to the lower court when the decision was made or, if he needed more time, he could ask for an adjournment of the hearing at which the decision was made in order to apply for permission to appeal on that later date. If he did neither, he had to apply to the appeal court. The claimant had neither asked for permission to appeal nor sought an adjournment so as to enable it to make such an application. The hearing, therefore, had finished and the lower court could no longer grant permission to appeal. It followed that the claimant could not be granted an extension of time in order to make an application for permission to appeal to the lower court. However, an extension of time would be granted in order to allow the claimant to file an appellant's notice at the Court of Appeal. Judgment would be given accordingly.

Balmoral Group Ltd v Borealis (UK) Ltd [2006] All ER (D) 135 (Aug) (Queen's Bench Division: Christopher Clarke J).

2274   Appeal—permission to appeal—grant—power to revoke

It has been held that the Court of Appeal has the power to revoke the grant of permission to appeal where the judge granting permission has been misled.

Angel Airlines SA v Dean & Dean Solicitors [2006] All ER (D) 280 (Oct) (Court of Appeal: Auld, Rix and Moses LJJ).

2275   Appeal—reopening of decision—avoidance of real injustice—misleading Court of Appeal

The claimants were sheep farmers and exporters who for several years had been subject to a European Community scheme which required them to pay a premium on the sale for slaughter of certain lambs. In the case of lambs exported to other Community countries, the premium was repaid under a clawback system in order to avoid a competitive disadvantage arising. A dispute between the claimants and the defendant board over the recovery of clawback resulted in judgment in favour of the defendant in a counterclaim. The claimants' appeal against the decision was dismissed. The claimants subsequently sought to reopen the appeal pursuant to CPR 52.17, contending that the Court of Appeal had been misled by an official of the defendant in relation to the way in which the system for claiming clawback was operated and with regard to the underlying documentation which went to support the original counterclaim. *Held*, it had been established that the amounts claimed in the counterclaim by way of clawback were excessive and that the judgment below and that of the Court of Appeal had led to an erroneous result. The fact that the Court of Appeal was led to that conclusion was not the fault of the claimants. The defendant had produced a statement which was untruthful and which seriously misled the Court of Appeal. In such circumstances, a serious injustice would result were the claimants not permitted to reopen the appeal and challenge the counterclaim. Accordingly, the application would be allowed.

Feakins v Intervention Board for Agricultural Produce [2006] EWCA Civ 699, [2006] All ER (D) 49 (Jun) (Court of Appeal: Dyson, Smith and Moses LJJ).

2276   Appeal—reopening of decision—avoidance of real injustice—mistake of fact—importance

The claimants sought permission to apply for judicial review of the grant of planning permission and hazardous substances consents for two large natural gas terminals at a port. The judge refused permission on the basis that the challenge had not been brought promptly and that granting permission to seek judicial review would cause very substantial prejudice to the developers and be detrimental to good administration. The claimants' application for permission to appeal against that decision was refused on the grounds that the judge was entitled to conclude that the merits of the claimants' case did not outweigh the undue delay and the prejudice flowing from permission to proceed, that he had made no error of principle, and that his decision had not been obviously wrong. The court stated that, although it was not strictly necessary to scrutinise in greater depth the decisions of the local authority, it appeared that the Health and Safety Executive ('HSE') had carried out sufficient studies to negate concerns about the risk of an escape. It subsequently emerged that the assessments undertaken by the HSE were not as extensive as believed at the time of the judgment. The claimants therefore applied pursuant to CPR 52.17 to reopen the decision refusing permission to appeal, submitting that the error as to the extent of the assessments had given rise to real injustice. *Held*, the hurdle to be surmounted by a party seeking to invoke the jurisdiction to reopen a decision was high, since it was a jurisdiction which, if exercised, would undermine the important principle that there had to be finality in litigation. The effect on others of reopening the appeal was an important consideration in any such application. In the present case, the mistake of fact now relied on by the claimants had not occurred in an essential part of the court's reasoning when it had refused the application for permission to appeal. The grounds given for refusing the application had not turned on any assumption about the precise studies carried out by the HSE. Even assuming that the mistake of fact had occurred in a necessary part of the reasons for the decision, the factual error would not have amounted to a critical undermining of the integrity of the earlier appeal, since the factual point that could now be seen to have been mistaken was of limited significance. Accordingly, the application would be dismissed.

Hardy v Pembrokeshire CC [2006] EWCA Civ 1008, [2006] All ER (D) 252 (Jul) (Court of Appeal: Chadwick and Keene LJJ and Sir Peter Gibson).

2277 Appeal—special statutory provisions—appeal against boundary dispute award

It has been held that an appeal to a county court made under the Party Wall etc Act 1996 s 10(17) is a statutory appeal governed by CPR Pt 52, rather than CPR Pt 8. CPR Pt 52 is intended to cover a form of statutory appeal such as that provided for by the 1996 Act s 10(17), and the provisions of CPR Pt 52 are amply sufficient to allow justice to be done.

Zissis v Lukomski [2006] EWCA Civ 341, [2006] 1 WLR 2778 (Court of Appeal: Brooke and Wilson LJJ and Sir Peter Gibson). *EI Du Pont de Nemours & Co v ST Dupont* [2003] EWCA Civ 1368, [2004] FSR 293 considered.

2278 Case management directions—expert evidence—soft tissue injuries—road traffic accidents

The Court of Appeal gave the following guidance in relation to the grant of permission to adduce expert evidence on questions of causation in personal injury claims where it was alleged that soft tissue injuries were caused by a low vehicles velocity impact in a road traffic accident. Where a defendant wished to raise the causation issue, he should notify all other parties in writing within three months of receipt of the letter of claim that he considered that the matter was a low impact case and that he intended to raise the causation issue. The issue should be expressly identified in the defence, supported by a statement of truth. The defendant should serve on the court and the other parties a witness statement which clearly identified the grounds on which the issue was raised within 21 days of serving a defence raising the causation issue. The statement would be expected to deal with the defendant's evidence relating to the issue, including the circumstances of the impact and the resulting damage. On receipt of the witness statement, the court would, if it was satisfied that the issue has been properly identified and raised, generally give permission for the claimant to be examined by a medical expert nominated by the defendant. Where the court, on receipt of any medical evidence served by the defendant following such examination, was satisfied on the entirety of the evidence submitted by the defendant that he had properly identified a case on the causation issue, which had a real prospect of success, then the court would generally give the defendant permission to rely on such evidence at trial. However, in certain circumstances the judge might decide that despite this, the overriding objective nevertheless required permission for expert evidence to be refused. Although single joint experts had an invaluable role to play in litigation generally, especially in low value litigation, judges should be slow to direct that expert evidence on the causation issue be given by a single joint expert, as the causation issue was controversial.

Casey v Cartwright [2006] EWCA Civ 1280, [2007] 2 All ER 78 (Court of Appeal: Keene, Dyson and Hallett LJJ). *Kearsley v Klarfeld* [2005] EWCA Civ 1510, [2006] 2 All ER 303 (2005 Abr para 2490) considered.

2279 Civil Procedure Rule Committee—appointment of judges

The Civil Procedure Act 1997 (Amendment) Order 2006, SI 2006/1847 (in force on 1 September 2006), amends the Civil Procedure Act 1997 s 2 so that the Lord Chief Justice may appoint one or two district judges to the Civil Procedure Rule Committee.

2280 Civil Procedure Rules 1998

The Civil Procedure (Amendment) Rules 2006, SI 2006/1689 (in force on 2 October 2006), further amend the CPR so as to (1) deal with the supply of documents to parties and non-parties; (2) make general provision regarding access to court documents; (3) make provision in relation to claims by and against partnerships; (4) make provision for the costs of appeals from small claims; (5) allow the Court of Appeal to make an order that a person refused permission to appeal may not request the decision to be reconsidered at a hearing; (6) specify the documents to be filed with a notice to the High Court; (7) implement a procedure for notifying the High Court that an appellant wishes to continue with an immigration appeal which would otherwise be deemed to be abandoned; and

(8) make provision for the procedure to be followed when applying for an order under the Partnership Act 1890 s 23. A number of Rules of the Supreme Court and County Court Rules are revoked

The Civil Procedure (Amendment No 2) Rules 2006, SI 2006/3132 (in force on 18 December 2006), further amend the CPR so as to make provision about statements of case filed at court before 2 October 2006.

The Civil Procedure (Amendment No 3) Rules 2006, SI 2006/3435 (in force on 6 April 2007), further amend the CPR so as to (1) remove the requirement for defendants to make payments into court, and provide that the defendant can make an offer to settle a claim, in writing, by payment of a single sum of money within 14 days of the date of acceptance of the offer; (2) clarify the process for offers to settle, so that the permission of the court is not generally required to accept an offer or to withdraw it; (3) make provision in relation to admissions made as to the truth of the whole or any part of another party's case before the commencement of proceedings, with the effect that pre-action admissions are given equal weight to those made during the proceedings; and (4) introduce provision for applications for drinking banning orders under the Violent Crime Reduction Act 2006. CPR Sch 1 RSC Ord 93 rr 2, 5(2) and (3), Ord 94 rr 1–3, 14 and 15, Ord 95 rr 2 and 3, Ord 96 rr 2–8, Ord 110 and CPR Sch 2 CCR Ord 46, Ord 49 rr 7 and 12 are revoked.

2281 Claim form—issue of claim form—time limit

CPR 7.2(1) provides that proceedings are started when the court issues a claim form at the request of the claimant. A claim form is issued on the date entered on the form by the court: CPR 7.2(2).

The claimant brought proceedings against the defendant local education authority alleging negligence and breach of statutory duty. On the day before the three-year limitation period in relation to the claim was due to expire, the claimant's solicitor delivered the requisite paperwork to the county court, and the documents were duly stamped with the date. However, owing to industrial action at the court, the claim form was not issued until four days later, meaning the proceedings were not started for the purpose of CPR 7.2 until that date, which was after the primary limitation period had expired. However, the practice direction issued in relation to CPR 7.2 stated that, where the claim form was received by the court on a date earlier than the date on which it was issued by the court, proceedings were commenced for limitation purposes on that earlier date. The judge decided that the practice direction was correct so that the claim had been brought in time. On the defendant's appeal, *held*, the Limitation Act 1980 could perfectly properly be construed so that, in the context of the CPR, a claim was brought when the claimant's request for the issue of a claim form was delivered with the court fee to the correct court office during the hours in which that office was open. The practice direction gave sensible guidance to ensure that the actual date of delivery was readily ascertainable by recording the date of receipt. The claimant was thus given the full period of limitation in which to bring the claim and did not take the risk that the court would fail to process it in time. Accordingly, the appeal would be dismissed.

St Helens MBC v Barnes [2006] EWCA Civ 1372, [2007] PIQR P118 (Court of Appeal: Tuckey, Arden and Lloyd LJJ).

2282 Claim form—service of claim form—address for service—principles

In four appeals issues arose as to the proper construction of CPR 6.4(2), 6.5, the meaning of 'no solicitor acting' in CPR 6.5(6) and paper applications made without notice under CPR 23.8. *Held*, where a defendant had nominated a solicitor for service, the business address of that solicitor was the defendant's address for service. There was no requirement for the solicitor to have notified the claimant in writing that he was authorised to accept service before service could be effected. On the face of it CPR 6.5(2), (4) were plain and unqualified. A party had to give an address for service and any document to be served by post, or by one of the other methods stated in CPR 6.5(4), had to be sent to the address for service given by the defendant. CPR 6.4 was concerned with personal service only and CPR 6.4(2) was only concerned with preventing personal service. There was no need to provide for an address for service if service was to be effected personally. If a claimant wished to use one of the types of service referred to in CPR 6.5(4), then if he had been provided with a solicitor's address as the address for service, he would not be able to post the document to the defendant himself. Therefore, where a defendant gave the claimant a solicitor's address for service, the claim form might validly be served at that address by one of the permitted methods of service. The phrase 'no solicitor acting' in CPR 6.5(6) had to be interpreted as meaning 'no solicitor acting so that he can be served'. Otherwise a claimant would not be able safely to use the table in CPR 6.5(6) and would have to have recourse to personal service under CPR 6.4 or to apply to the court for service by an alternative method. If that were the position CPR 6.5(6) would be emasculated. If a claimant knew that a solicitor was authorised to accept service, then it was right that the methods of service set out in CPR 6.5(5) should not be available. The word 'agree' in CPR 23.8(b) referred to an agreement between the parties to the application, rather than to an agreement between one party and the court whereas CPR 23.8(c) gave the court jurisdiction to dispose of any application without a hearing. Judgment would be given accordingly.

Collier v Williams [2006] EWCA Civ 20, [2006] 1 WLR 1945 (Court of Appeal: Waller, Dyson and Neuberger LJJ).

2283 Claim form—service of claim form—extension of time—discretion of court

CPR 7.6(3) provides that, if the claimant applies for an order to extend the time for service of the claim form after the end of the period specified by CPR 7.5 or by an order made under CPR 7.6, the court may make such an order only in certain prescribed circumstances.

The claimant sought to challenge parts of the local plan adopted by the defendant authority. Due to an error on the part of the agents for the claimant's solicitors, the claim form to commence the proceedings was served on the defendant after the expiry of the prescribed six-week time limit. The claimant applied for an extension of time for service of the claim form, and an issue arose as to whether the court's discretion to extend time arose under CPR 7.6 or its general discretion in CPR 3.1(2)(a). The defendant submitted that, having regard to the relevant practice direction, which provided that CPR Pt 7 and the practice direction applied to all claims, including those to which CPR Pt 8 applied, it was appropriate to apply CPR 7.6. The judge rejected that contention and granted the extension sought. The defendant appealed. *Held*, the provisions of CPR 7.6 were only engaged in a case for which the period for serving the claim form specified by CPR 7.5 applied, which was four months after the date of issue, and six months where the claim form was to be served outside the jurisdiction. CPR 7.5 did not specify any other period. Applications under the Town and Country Planning Act 1990 s 287 were, however, subject to the six-week time limit pursuant to RSC Ord 94 r 1.2. There was no justification for rewriting CPR 7.5 so as to interpret the period specified by CPR 7.5 as referring to the time for service given by RSC Ord 94 r 1.2. It followed that CPR 3.1(2)(a) applied, since there was nothing else to displace it. Judges would exercise their discretion as to whether to extend time for service under CPR 3.1(2)(a) in accordance with the overriding objective, which would require them to have regard to the statutory policy that those cases be subject to minimum delay, a policy demonstrated by the absolute six-week time limit for the issue of proceedings. On the other hand, they would also have regard to the general public interest in having viable challenges to decisions of public authorities ventilated in proceedings. It followed that the judge's construction of the CPR was correct and, accordingly, the appeal would be dismissed.

Corus UK Ltd v Erewash BC [2006] EWCA Civ 1175, [2006] All ER (D) 91 (Nov) (Court of Appeal: Ward, Laws and Longmore LJJ). Decision of McCombe J [2005] EWHC 2821 (Admin), [2005] All ER (D) 145 (Dec) (2005 Abr para 2498) affirmed.

2284 Claim form—service of claim form—power to dispense with service—court first seised of proceedings

The claimant administrators issued proceedings in England against the first defendant, a Swiss resident, and the second defendant, a company owned by the first defendant. Documents were subsequently served on the first defendant in connection with the English proceedings, except for the copy claim form. Shortly afterwards, the defendants instituted proceedings against the claimants in Switzerland, in which the defendants sought declaratory relief which mirrored the relief sought in the English proceedings. The claimants applied for an order under CPR 6.9 to have the court's sanction for dispensing with service of the copy of the claim on the first defendant, on the basis that that would enable the English proceedings to obtain priority over the Swiss proceedings pursuant to the Lugano Convention on Jurisdiction and the Enforcement of Judgments in Civil and Commercial Matters 1988 art 21. The judge decided that, although there was binding authority for the proposition that the English courts were not seised of proceedings against a foreign defendant until that defendant had been served with the copy claim form in those proceedings, he had the discretion pursuant to CPR 6.9 to dispense with its service, and that the English proceedings thereby achieved priority over the Swiss proceedings. The defendants appealed. *Held*, although the court would have granted the claimants relief under CPR 6.9 had the case been a domestic one, it could not be right to do so in a case where the sole purpose of the relief sought was to enable the inadequately served English proceedings to achieve priority over Swiss proceedings which had already obtained such priority. Once that reason for making the order under CPR 6.9 was discarded, nothing was left. It was not possible for the English court, once the Swiss court had become the first seised of the proceedings, to invoke its discretionary jurisdiction under a domestic rule of procedure such as CPR 6.9 to enable those proceedings to reclaim priority for the purposes of the Convention art 21. Accordingly, the appeal would be allowed.

Phillips v Nussberger [2006] EWCA Civ 654, [2006] All ER (D) 296 (May) (Court of Appeal: Pill, Neuberger and Wilson LJJ). *Dresser UK Ltd v Falcongate Freight Management Ltd* [1992] QB 502, CA (2001 Abr para 421), applied.

2285 Claim form—service of documents—service by facsimile—failure to obtain consent—power of court to dispense with service

Practice Direction—Service (2000) PD 6A para 3.1 provides that where a document is to be served by facsimile, the party who is to be served or his legal representative must previously have indicated in writing to the party serving that he is willing to accept service by facsimile.

The claimant sought to bring proceedings against the defendant. On the last day for service of the claim form, the claimant sent a copy of the form to the defendant by courier and also by fax. The defendant maintained that the claim form had not been properly served and the claimant applied under CPR 6.9 for an order that such service be dispensed with. The application was successful, with the judge finding that the failure to obtain the defendant's advance written consent to service of the claim form by fax, as stipulated by the *Practice Direction—Service* (2000) PD 6A para 3.1, was a comparatively minor departure from the requirements of CPR 6.2(1). The defendant appealed. *Held*, service by fax, without the written consent of the defendant, could not be described as 'service by one of the methods allowed' by CPR 6.2, nor could it be characterised as no more than a 'minor departure' from CPR 6.2(1). Moreover, prejudice to the defendant was a reason for not dispensing with service, but the absence of prejudice could not usually, if ever, be a reason for dispensing with service. Therefore, the order dispensing with service of the claim form would be set aside. Accordingly, the appeal would be allowed.

Kuenyehia v International Hospitals Group Ltd [2006] EWCA Civ 21, [2006] All ER (D) 169 (Jan) (Court of Appeal: Waller, Dyson and Neuberger LJJ).

2286   Committal for contempt—proceedings in High Court—criminal or civil proceedings

The claimants brought proceedings in the High Court to commit the defendant for contempt for breach of freezing and search orders and for verifying defences without an honest belief in the truth of the statements made. The judge rejected the defendant's contention that the proceedings were criminal and, as such, hearsay evidence should not be admitted. He found the defendant was in contempt of court and committed him to prison. The defendant appealed. *Held*, High Court proceedings for contempt of court were civil rather than criminal in relation to the admission of hearsay evidence. The provision concerning the exclusion of admissible hearsay evidence in the Criminal Justice Act 1988 Act s 25 (repealed) only applied in Crown Court, the criminal division of the Court of Appeal and magistrates' courts. This was a powerful indication that proceedings in the High Court were not to be regarded as criminal, but instead as civil proceedings, to which the Civil Evidence Act 1995 applied. However, the right to a fair trial under the European Convention on Human Rights art 6 applied in High Court contempt proceedings, and proof of contempt to the criminal standard was required. Accordingly, the appeal would be dismissed.

Daltel Europe Ltd v Makki [2006] EWCA Civ 94, [2006] 1 WLR 2704 (Court of Appeal: Auld, Lloyd and Wilson LJJ). *Savings and Investment Bank Ltd v Gasco Investments (Netherlands) BV (No 2)* [1988] Ch 422 (Abr 1987 para 398) applied.

As to the admissibility of hearsay evidence in criminal proceedings, see now Criminal Justice Act 2003 ss 114–136.

2287   Conditional fee agreements

See COSTS.

2288   Costs—criminal cases

See CRIMINAL EVIDENCE AND PROCEDURE.

2289   Costs

See COSTS.

2290   Criminal cases

See CRIMINAL EVIDENCE AND PROCEDURE.

2291   Disclosure—communications between solicitor and client—legal professional privilege—waiver

The defendant, a firm of solicitors, had acted for the claimant in relation to its purchase of an interest in a football club. The claimant alleged that the transaction had been completed on a footing which gave minority shareholders greater rights than they should have had and commenced proceedings against the defendant for professional negligence. Certain invoices were disclosed by the claimant in respect of legal fees of a second firm of solicitors incurred in trying to sort out the position of the minority shareholders. The defendant contended that it followed that the claimant had waived privilege in a category of documents, which was opened up to disclosure and inspection, and applied for disclosure of documents setting out the instructions received and work carried out by the second firm. *Held,* it was not open to a waiving party to say that the transaction was simply what that party had chosen to disclose. The court would determine what the real transaction was so that the scope of the waiver could be determined. If only part of the material involved in that transaction had been disclosed, then further disclosure would be ordered and it could not be resisted on the basis of privilege. In determining an application for disclosure, in circumstances such as those in the present case, the court had first to identify the transaction in respect of which the disclosure had been made, which might be identifiable simply from the nature of the disclosure made. However, it might be apparent that the transaction was wider than that which was immediately apparent, in which case the whole of the wider transaction had be disclosed. Further disclosure would then be ordered if it was necessary in order to avoid unfairness or misunderstanding of what had been disclosed. The claimant was entitled to draw the waiver line more or less where it had been drawn. Accordingly, the application would be dismissed.

Fulham Leisure Holdings Ltd v Nicholson Graham & Jones [2006] EWHC 158 (Ch), [2006] 2 All ER 599 (Chancery Division: Mann J).

2292 Disclosure—documents—application against non-party

CPR 31.16(3) provides that the court may make an order for disclosure before proceedings have started only where (1) the respondent is likely to be a party to subsequent proceedings (CPR 31.16(3)(a)); (2) the applicant is also likely to be a party to those proceedings (CPR 31.16(3)(b)); and (3) disclosure before proceedings have started is desirable in order to dispose fairly of the anticipated proceedings, assist the dispute to be resolved without proceedings, or save costs (CPR 31.16(3)(d)). The court may make an order for disclosure by a person who is not a party to the proceedings only where (a) the documents of which disclosure is sought are likely to support the case of the applicant or adversely affect the case of one of the other parties to the proceedings (CPR 31.17(3)(a)); and (b) disclosure is necessary in order to dispose fairly of the claim or to save costs (CPR 31.17(3)(b)).

The Secretary of State brought proceedings for negligence and breach of contract against the defendant engineering company which he had engaged to carry out certain motorway works, and the defendant consultancy which he had also engaged to work on the project. The consultancy became aware that the engineering company was in possession of certain categories of documents and applied for disclosure of those documents from the engineering company as a non-party to the litigation under the Supreme Court Act 1981 and CPR 31.17. The consultancy argued that disclosure was necessary to put the parties on an equal footing in the light of the voluntary disclosure that had taken place between it and the Secretary of State. Issues arose as to whether the proper approach to the condition in CPR 31.17(3)(b) was by way of references to authorities on CPR 31.16(3)(d) and as to how the court should exercise its discretion under CPR 31.17(3). *Held*, 'likely' in CPR 31.17(3)(a) was to be interpreted in the same way as 'likely' in CPR 31.16(3)(a) and (b), but authorities concerning CPR 31.16(3)(d) were not relevant to CPR 31.17(3)(d) despite the similarities between those provisions. Most cases under CPR 31.17(3)(b) were likely to involve considerations such as whether the documents added significantly to what was already known or whether the likely benefits of disclosure justified the expense. CPR 31.17(3)(a) and (b) were necessary, not just sufficient conditions to the ordering of disclosure. The court might need, in some cases, to strike a balance between the applicant's need for access and some other competing interest such as public interest immunity or the respondent's legitimate interest in keeping them private. The court was entitled to consider whether it was necessary to infringe a person's privacy in order to enable a party to legal proceedings to prosecute his case. The court had to take great care not to impose a heavy burden on non-parties. The interests arising under CPR 31.16 were different to those that needed to be weighed up under CPR 31.17. CPR 31.16 was concerned with whether early disclosure ought to be granted in circumstances where it was unlikely that the documents would be withheld forever whereas CPR 31.17 was concerned with whether disclosure ought to be granted at all. This general condition militated in favour of ordering disclosure under CPR 31.17. Moreover parties to an application under CPR 31.16 were already in an existing legal dispute whereas parties in an application under CPR 31.17 usually were not. The respondent to such an application might have no interest in the applicant's litigation, only in protecting the confidentiality of the documents of which disclosure had been sought. That militated against ordering discovery under CPR 31.17. It would have been appropriate to order disclosure if the arbitration between the Secretary of State and the engineering company had not come to any end. However it was inevitable that the court would order either that the cases should be heard together or that they should be consolidated. This would allow the consultancy to become entitled to standard disclosure from the engineering company in the relatively near future, which would likely include the documents sought. While it would be advantageous for the consultancy and experts to have access to the documents earlier, it was outweighed by the cost and inconvenience of the engineering company giving disclosure twice and the volume of documents involved in the project. None of the matters relied on by the consultancy made the disclosure necessary within the meaning of CPR 31.17(3)(b). Accordingly, the application would be dismissed.

Secretary of State for Transport v Pell Frischmann Consultants Ltd [2007] BLR 46 (Queen's Bench Division: Jackson J). *Three Rivers DC v Bank of England (No 4)* [2002] EWCA Civ 1182, [2002] 4 All ER 881 (2002 Abr para 2387); *Frankson v Home Office; Johns v Home Office* [2003] EWCA Civ 655, [2003] 1 WLR 1953 (2003 Abr para 2123); and *Black v Sumitomo Corpn* [2001] EWCA 1819, [2003] 3 All ER 643 (2001 Abr para 2536) applied.

2293 Disclosure—documents—confidentiality—public interest defence—proportionality

The defendants published an article in a newspaper in which an unnamed, former director of the claimant made revelations about his experience of employment with the claimant. The claimant alleged that the article disclosed confidential information relating to the internal workings of the claimant and commenced proceedings for breach of confidentiality on the ground that the defendant knew, or ought to have known, that the information disclosed in the article was confidential. The defendants argued that the claimant was projecting a false public image as a benevolent employer when in reality its culture was autocratic and there was a high turnover of staff, particularly among senior employees. The defendants sought disclosure of information about the departure from the claimant company of certain senior members of staff after the date of publication of the article. It fell to be determined whether a defendant relying on a public interest defence was limited to what he knew at the date of publication or whether he could rely on matters which had come to light since that date. *Held*, although there had to be something to justify the allegations made by a defendant, there was nothing to suggest that he could only base a public interest defence on what was known at the date of publication. Where a defendant could rely on matters that came to light after publication, the court had jurisdiction to order disclosure under the Civil Procedure Rules. The question of proportionality was important as it would be wrong to order disclosure which was disproportionate to the information reasonably expected to be discovered. Accordingly, the court would make orders for specific disclosure as sought by the defendant.

Harrods Ltd v Times Newspapers Ltd [2006] EWHC 83 (Ch), [2006] All ER (D) 147 (Jan) (Chancery Division: Warren J). *A-G v Observer Ltd; A-G v Times Newspapers Ltd)* [1990] 1 AC 109, HL (1988 Abr para 1934); and *Gartside v Outram* (1856) 26 LJ Ch 113 applied.

2294   Disclosure—documents—judicial review proceedings—proportionality

Northern Ireland

The applicant gave notice to the police on behalf of the local Orange lodge of a proposed public procession to be held on Easter Sunday. The defendant commission received a police report in respect of the proposed procession and situation reports from its authorised officers. On the basis of that information the defendant decided that, in view of the potential adverse impact on community relations, the parade could only go ahead subject to a number of restrictions. The applicant sought judicial review of that decision, arguing that the relevant legislation and guidelines followed by the defendant were incompatible with the European Convention on Human Rights arts 9–11. The applicant sought specific discovery of five documents, including the police report and two situation reports, held by the defendant. The judge allowed the application and ordered discovery of the documents, subject to any public interest immunity requirements. He concluded that, in a case where proportionality was in issue, disclosure of the full documents should take place. The defendant successfully appealed on the ground that it was premature to require disclosure until the validity of the relevant guidelines had been established. The applicant appealed. *Held*, the time had come to do away with the rule that there had to be a demonstrable contradiction or inconsistency in the respondent's affidavit before disclosure would be ordered. It would not arise in most applications for judicial review, for they generally raised legal issues which did not call for disclosure of documents. For that reason the courts were correct in not ordering disclosure in the same routine manner as it was given in actions commenced by writ. Even in cases involving issues of proportionality disclosure should be carefully limited to the issues which required it in the interests of justice. Disclosure orders were likely to remain exceptional in judicial review proceedings, even in proportionality cases, and the courts should continue to guard against what appeared to be merely 'fishing expeditions' for adventitious further grounds of challenge. The proportionality issue formed part of the context in which the court had to consider whether it was necessary for fairly disposing of the case to order disclosure of such documents. It did not give rise automatically to the need for disclosure of such documents. In the present case, it was appropriate to make an order for disclosure of the requested documents. Accordingly, the appeal would be allowed.

Tweed v Parades Commission for Northern Ireland [2006] UKHL 53, [2006] All ER (D) 175 (Dec) (House of Lords: Lords Bingham of Cornhill, Hoffmann, Rodger of Earlsferry, Carswell and Brown of Eaton-under-Heywood).

2295   Disclosure—documents—public interest defence

See *Ackroyd v Mersey Care NHS Trust (No 2)*, para 580.

2296   Disclosure—documents—unused material—criminal trials

See para 766.

2297   Disclosure—pre-action disclosure

In proceedings for infringement of design right and copyright, it fell to be determined whether and in what circumstances a would-be claimant who was unable to plead and prove its case on the evidence before it might seek to employ the powers of the court under CPR 31.16 in order to discover whether it had a good cause of action. *Held*, only if there was at least a clear and convincing evidential basis for the belief that acts of infringement might have taken place and the court could be satisfied that the pre-action disclosure sought was highly focused could CPR 31.16 be applied as a means of examining a competitor's secret designs. The power under CPR 31.16 had to be exercised with a view to deciding whether pre-action disclosure should be granted to the applicant. The court was far from convinced that it could overcome the real objection to the grant of the relief sought by, in effect, rewriting the rule so as to introduce a quite different procedure designed to allow the court to look at the documents to see whether they were potentially incriminating before deciding on whether to make the order actually sought. That lay outside the scope of CPR 31.16 and would lead in almost every case to invitations being made to the court to intervene in the adversarial process by, in effect, ignoring the evidence and looking to see if the documents sought did in fact reveal what was alleged. The court had no power to do that. Judgment would be given accordingly.

BSW Ltd v Balltec Ltd [2006] EWHC 822 (Ch), [2007] FSR 1 (Chancery Division: Patten J). *Black v Sumitomo Corpn* [2001] EWCA Civ 1819, [2003] 3 All ER 643 (2001 Abr para 2536) applied.

2298   Expert evidence—agreed opinion between experts—dissatisfaction with amended opinion—evidence from new expert

See *Stallwood v David*, para 1297.

2299   Expert evidence—joint statement of issues—privilege

In the course of litigation, the claimant and defendant sought mediation. The judge stayed the proceedings and ordered that the parties' experts should prepare a joint statement of issues setting out the issues on which they agreed and those on which they did not agree. The order was in the standard form for orders made under CPR 35.12, which provided for a statement of experts in the course of litigation. The claimant, its solicitors and its expert proceeded with the statement of issues on the basis that it would be made without prejudice. The mediation failed. The claimant's expert signed a statement that the joint statement was not privileged and the claimant sought to amend its pleadings. The defendant sought a declaration that the joint statement was not subject to privilege, but the application was dismissed. The defendant appealed. *Held*, when a joint statement was ordered under CPR 35.12(3), the experts were obliged to produce it. Such a statement was for use in the proceedings, and was not protected by privilege. It did not, however, bind the parties, and was not strictly speaking an admission. It was certainly not an admission by the parties, nor could it be characterised as an admission by the experts. It was a statement pursuant to an order of the court. Although it was possible for a party to instruct an expert not to proceed in accordance with the order, the expert would be obliged to decline to act or to seek the court's directions. It would be an instruction not to perform his duties to the court; an instruction to disobey the order of the court; and an instruction not to perform his overriding duty. Accordingly, the appeal would be allowed.

Aird v Prime Meridian Ltd [2006] EWCA Civ 1866, [2006] All ER (D) 358 (Dec) (Court of Appeal: May and Smith LJJ and Sir Martin Nourse). Decision of Judge Peter Coulson QC [2006] EWHC 2338 (TCC), (2006) 108 Con LR 1 reversed.

2300   Family Division—guidance—vacation business

Senior district judge Philip Waller, has issued the following *Practice Direction (Family Division: Guide to Vacation Business)* [2006] 2 FCR 840, which applies to all long vacation business at the Royal Courts of Justice with effect from the long vacation 2006 on 26 July 2006 with the approval of the President.

1. Business taken at the Royal Courts of Justice during the long vacation will be (a) injunctions; (b) committals to, and release from, prison; (c) any application relating to children provided that the estimated length of hearing does not exceed one day; (d) any matter which has been certified by a district judge as being fit for vacation business subject to the estimated length of hearing not exceeding one day; and (e) if so directed by a High Court judge, any matters where the estimated length of hearing is in excess of one day.

2. In any case under head 1(c), above, the time estimate must be signed by the solicitor making the application or by counsel if instructed. It will be only in rare circumstances that a case, accepted for vacation business on a basis of an estimate of not more than one day but which takes longer, will continue to be heard during the vacation after the first day.

3. In any case under head 1(d), above, a certificate signed by the solicitor making the application or by counsel if instructed, must be supplied to the district judge stating that, in his opinion, and giving reasons, the matter is such that it should be dealt with during the vacation and giving the time estimate.

4. Whether the Clerk of the Rules lists an application within head 1(c), above, or a district judge accepts an application within head 1(d), above, as vacation business, will be entirely a matter for his or her discretion.

5. In cases falling within head 1(e), above, application for the appropriate direction should be made to the applications judge.

2301   Family Division—proceedings pending or treated as pending in county court—allocation to judiciary—amendments

The Lord Chancellor, in exercise of the powers conferred on him by the Courts and Legal Services Act 1990 s 9, has issued the following *Family Proceedings (Allocation to Judiciary) (Amendment No 1) Directions* [2006] 1 FLR 1147 with the concurrence of the President on 10 August 2005.

1. These *Directions* come into force on 5 September 2005.

2. These *Directions* amend the *Family Proceedings (Allocation to Judiciary) Directions* 1999 para 7 [1999] 2 FLR 799 (1999 Abr para 2716).

3. For the 1999 Directions Schedule paras (h), (i), (j) substitute:

'(h)		
Proceedings under any of the following provisions of the Children Act 1989:	A circuit judge nominated for public family law proceedings;	All circumstances.
s 25 (secure accommodation);	a district judge of the Principal Registry of the Family Division of the High Court; or	All circumstances.
s 31 (care and supervision orders); s 33(7) (change of child's name or removal from jurisdiction); s 39(1), (2) or (4) (discharge and variation of care and supervision orders); Sch 3, para 6 (supervision order); s 34 (parental contact etc with child in care); Sch 2 para 19(1) (arrangement to assist children to live abroad).	a district judge nominated for public family law proceedings. a district judge nominated for public family law proceedings and who is also nominated to hear and determine all proceedings described in this paragraph; or a recorder nominated for public family law proceedings.	(1) Interlocutory matters; or (2) unopposed hearings; or (3) opposed hearings where the application is for an order under s 34 (a contact order) and the principle of contact is unopposed. All circumstances.
(i)		
Proceedings under the 1989 Act s 38 (interim care or supervision orders).	A circuit judge nominated for public family law proceedings;	All circumstances.
	a district judge of the Principal Registry of the Family Division of the High Court;	All circumstances.
	a district judge nominated for public family law proceedings; a recorder nominated for public family law proceedings.	All circumstances. All circumstances.
(j)		
Proceedings under any of the following provisions of the 1989 Act:	A circuit judge nominated for public family law proceedings;	All circumstances.

'(h)		
s 39(3) (variation of supervision order);	a district judge of the Principal Registry of the Family Division of the High Court; or	All circumstances.
Sch 3, para 15(2) or 17(1) (extension and discharge of education supervision order); s 43 (child assessment order); ss 44, 45(4), 45 (8), 46(7), 48(9) (order for emergency protection of child); s 50 (recovery order); applications for leave under s 91(14), (15) or (17) (further applications); applications under the Adoption Act 1976 s 21 (substitution of adoption agencies).'	a district judge nominated for public family law proceedings; or	All circumstances.

The Lord Chancellor has issued the following *Family Proceedings (Allocation to Judiciary) (Amendment No 2) Directions* [2006] 1 FLR 1150 in exercise of the powers conferred by the Courts and Legal Services Act 1990 s 9 with the concurrence of the President of the Family Division on 10 October 2005.

1. This *Practice Direction* comes into force for the purposes of heads 2(b), 3, 5, 8, below, and this head on 5 December 2005, and for all other purposes on 30 December 2005.

2. The provisions in the *Family Proceedings (Allocation to Judiciary) Directions* 1999 Schedule [1999] 2 FLR 799 (1999 Abr para 2716) is to continue to apply as if the amendments in this *Practice Direction* had not been made

(a) to an application under the following sections of the Adoption Act 1976:
   (i) s 12 (adoption order);
   (ii) s 18 (freeing for adoption);
   (iii) s 20 (revocation of a s 18 order);
   (iv) s 21 (variation of a s 18 order so as to substitute one adoption agency for another);
   (v) s 27(1) or (2) (restriction on removal of child where adoption pending or application made under s 18); and
   (vi) s 29 (return of child taken away in breach of s 27);
   (vii) s 53 (annulment etc. of overseas adoptions); and
   (viii) s 55 (adoption of children abroad); and

(b) to an application under the Children Act 1989 s 4(1)(a) (applications for parental responsibility by father) made before 1 December 2003.

3. (a) In the 1999 Directions Schedule para (d) col (i) after 'nullity' insert 'of marriage'.
   (b) After Schedule para (d) insert:

'(da)		
Hearing of contested petition for an order of dissolution, nullity of civil partnership or separation.	A circuit judge, deputy circuit judge or a recorder nominated for private or public family law proceedings;	All circumstances.'

4. For Schedule para (e), substitute:

'(e)

Proceedings under any of the following sections of the Adoption and Children Act 2002:	A circuit judge nominated for adoption proceedings; or	All circumstances.
Section 22 (applications for placement orders);	a deputy circuit judge or recorder nominated for adoption proceedings; or	All circumstances.
s 24 (revoking placement orders); s 26 (application for contact); s 27 (variation or revocation of contact order); s 28(2) (change child's surname or remove the child from the United Kingdom); s 29 (leave to apply for order);	a circuit judge nominated for public family law proceedings; or	All circumstances where proceedings under s 21 (placement orders) are heard in conjunction with care proceedings under the 1989 Act s 31 and relate to the same child.
s 30(2), 37, 38, 39 or 40 (restrictions on removal of child); s 41 (recovery orders);	a district judge of the Principal Registry of the Family Division of the High Court; or	All circumstances.
s 42(6) or 44(4) (leave to make application for adoption order); s 47(3) or (5) (leave to oppose the making of an adoption order);	a district judge nominated for adoption proceedings; or	Interlocutory matters.
s 50 (adoption by couple); s 51 (adoption by one person);	a deputy district judge nominated for adoption proceedings; or	Interlocutory matters.
s 55 (revocation of adoption on legitimisation); s 79(4) (disclosure of information kept by Registrar General); An application under the 1989 Act s 8 for a residence order where the 2002 Act s 28(1) or 29(4) applies; An application under the 1989 Act s 14A for a special guardianship order where the 2002 Act s 28(1) or 29(5) applies.	a district judge nominated for public family law proceedings.	Interlocutory matters where proceedings under s 21 (placement orders) are heard in conjunction with care proceedings under the 1989 Act s 31 and relate to the same child.

5. In the 1999 Directions Schedule para (f) col (i), for 's 4(1)(a) (applications for parental responsibility by father)' substitute 's 4(1)(c) (applications for parental responsibility by father); s 4A(1)(b) (applications for parental responsibility by step-parent)'.

6. In the 1999 Directions Schedule para (g) col (i), after the entry relating to s 13(1) insert:
   's 14A (special guardianship orders);
   s 14C(3) (change of child's name or removal from jurisdiction);
   s 14D (variation and discharge of special guardianship orders);'

7. In the 1999 Directions Schedule para (j) col (i), for the entry relating to the 1976 Act s 21 substitute 'application under the 2002 Act s 23 (varying placement orders).'

8. After the 1999 Directions Schedule para (o), insert:

'(p)		
Proceedings under the Civil Partnership Act 2004 s 58 (declarations).	A circuit judge nominated for private or public family law proceedings; or a district judge of the Principal Registry of the Family Division of the High Court; or a district judge.	All circumstances. Interlocutory matters.'

2302   Freezing orders
See INJUNCTIONS.

2303   Injunctions
See INJUNCTIONS.

2304   Judgment—draft judgment—publication before judgment officially pronounced—contempt of court
See *Baigent v Random House; Re The Lawyer*, para 645.

2305   Judgment—final judgment—format
It has been held that a judge's determination should be produced in a format which enables the determination to be clearly understood and analysed, with the reasons set out in manageable paragraphs and sub-paragraphs, with cross-headings where appropriate.

Jasim v Secretary of State for the Home Department [2006] EWCA Civ 342, [2006] All ER (D) 453 (Mar) (Court of Appeal: Pill and Sedley LJJ and Sir Peter Gibson).

2306   Judgment—merger of causes of action—wrongful dismissal—separate employment tribunal and High Court claims
See *Fraser v HLMAD Ltd*, para 1280.

2307   Judgment—publication—proceedings compromised before judgment sent to parties—discretion to publish
See *Gurney Consulting Engineers (a firm) v Gleeds Health and Safety Ltd (No 2)*, para 2336.

2308   Judgment—summary judgment—party confining application to one of several issues
It has been held that the court has power to give summary judgment on one or more of the issues raised in an action. Where a party chooses to confine its application to a single issue and the judge thinks it appropriate to give summary judgment on that issue, the Court of Appeal should not interfere unless some unfairness has been seen to result from the course taken by the judge.

Wrexham Association Football Club Ltd v Crucialmove Ltd [2006] EWCA Civ 237, (2006) Independent, 10 April (Court of Appeal: Sir Igor Judge P, Dyson LJ and Sir Peter Gibson).

2309   Judgment—summary judgment—recovery under counter-indemnity—fraud defence—test
See *Banque Saudi Fransi v Lear Siegler Services Inc*, para 1440.

2310   Judgment in default—setting aside—application of claimant—discretion of court
The claimant obtained judgment in default of acknowledgment of service against the defendant in a claim to recover a guarantee payment under the claimant's right of subrogation. The judgment could not be enforced in India where the defendant's assets were situated. The claimant applied to have the judgment in default set aside and substituted by summary judgment in its favour, which could be enforced there. The defendant asserted that once judgment in default had been entered, the claim had merged in the judgment so that the defendant could not be forced to comply with it. *Held*, the common law principle of merger had the consequence that, unless the judgment was set aside, the cause of action to which it gave rise could not be pursued. The underlying policy of the principle was to avoid multiplicity of proceedings and achieve finality; it was not an intended consequence that a claimant should be deprived of the good of the claim. The court had an unconditional discretionary power to set aside the default judgment under CPR 13.3, the purpose of which was to

avoid injustice. Where a claimant could demonstrate that it had a good claim which would be lost unless a default judgment was set aside, that claimant could be taken to have shown a good reason why the judgment should be set aside. Accordingly, the application would be allowed.

Messer Griesheim GmbH v Goyal MG Gases PVT Ltd [2006] EWHC 79 (Comm), (2006) Times, 7 February (Queen's Bench Division: Langley J).

2311   Jurisdiction—disputing jurisdiction of court—actions constituting submission to jurisdiction

After receipt of the claim form, the defendant's solicitors corresponded with the claimant's solicitors as to the time for filing the acknowledgment of service. The defendant's solicitors filed an acknowledgment of service ticking the box indicating that defendant intended to defend the claim but not ticking the box indicating that he intended to contest the jurisdiction of the court. After the time for challenge to the court's jurisdiction under CPR Pt 11 had expired the defendant's solicitors wrote to the solicitors for the claimant giving first indication of the defendant's intention to challenge jurisdiction. The defendant issued an application to extend time for the making of an application to dispute the jurisdiction of the court to try the claim against him. The claimant resisted the application on the basis that the defendant had submitted to the jurisdiction. *Held*, the test applied in the determination of whether any particular conduct amounted to a submission to the jurisdiction was an objective one. The question was whether the only possible explanation for the conduct relied on was an intention on the part of the defendant to have the case tried in England. To any objective outsider the conduct of the defendant's solicitors and accordingly that of defendant from the receipt of instructions to the letter giving the claimant's solicitors notice of an intention to challenge jurisdiction, a period of over five weeks, was only consistent with an acceptance of the court's jurisdiction to determine the claim on its merits. The defendant had therefore submitted to the jurisdiction before its solicitor had given notice of its intention to challenge jurisdiction and before his application for an extension of time was issued. Accordingly, the application would be dismissed.

Global Multimedia International Ltd v Ara Media Services [2006] All ER (D) 324 (Jul) (Chancery Division: Sir Andrew Morritt QC).

2312   Order—compliance—power to extend or shorten time

CPR 3.1(2)(a) provides that the court may extend or shorten the time for compliance with any rule, practice direction or court order, except where otherwise provided. Where a party has failed to comply with a rule, practice direction or court order, any sanction for failure to comply imposed by the rule, practice direction or court order has effect unless the party in default applies for and obtains relief from the sanction: CPR 3.8(1).

The claimants sought permission to appeal from a decision. The judge made an order requiring the claimants to lodge a transcript of the original decision by a certain date and providing that, in default, permission to appeal would be refused. The claimants, through no fault of their own, were unable to comply with the order. The judge held that he had jurisdiction to extend time retrospectively for filing a transcript of the original judgment, and he allowed the appeal. The defendant appealed. *Held*, it could not be said that the court's general case management powers to extend time and to act on its own initiative were reduced by CPR 3.8 with the consequence that the court was powerless to extend time in such cases unless and until an application for relief under CPR 3.8 was made by the party in default. Such an interpretation would be perverse and fly in the face of the overriding objective. There was no sensible reason why the court should be deprived of jurisdiction to extend time or otherwise grant relief from sanction unless, or until, the party who would otherwise be in default applied for relief from sanction. The judge had had jurisdiction to grant permission to appeal. Accordingly, the appeal would be dismissed.

Keen Phillips (a firm) v Field [2006] EWCA Civ 1524, [2006] All ER (D) 160 (Nov) (Court of Appeal: Jonathan Parker and Moore-Bick LJJ).

2313   Parties—addition—expiry of limitation period—mistake

CPR 19.5(1), (3) provides that the addition or substitution of a party after the end of a period of limitation is necessary only if the court is satisfied that (1) the new party is to be substituted for a party who was named in the claim form in mistake for the new party; and (2) the claim cannot properly be carried on by or against the original party unless the new party is added or substituted as claimant or defendant.

The claimant, who was the sole director of a company which had property interests in Spain, alleged that he had been the victim of a fraudulent scheme consisting of the preparation and notarisation of a document, purportedly but not actually signed by him, which adversely affected his company's interests. His purported signature had been notarised by the first defendant, and confirmed by the second defendant. The claimant brought proceedings against the second defendant in negligence and alleging misfeasance in public office. The second defendant successfully applied to strike out the particulars of claim against it in relation to the property on the basis that any legal duties were owed to the company as owner of the property rather than to the claimant. The claimant therefore applied to add the company as claimant, albeit after the period of limitation had expired. The judge allowed the application to the extent of enabling the claimant to maintain a claim based on an alleged two-thirds beneficial interest owned by him under a trust of which the company was said to have been a trustee. The claimant appealed, submitting that, while he had made a conscious decision to sue in his own name rather than that of the company, that choice had been made on a mistaken basis and was thus within the scope of CPR 19.5(3)(a). *Held*, it was not the case that a claim based on a two-thirds beneficial interest could not properly be carried on by the claimant unless the company was added or substituted as claimant. The claim based on a two-thirds beneficial interest could not be carried on because the judge had held that it was bad in law, since no duty was owed to the claimant. Moreover, a convenient test to apply in deciding whether a party could be added or substituted pursuant to CPR 19.5(3)(a) might to be to ask whether the identity of the claimant or, as the case might be, the defendant, could be changed without significantly altering the claim. In the present case, the amendments that would be necessary to the formulation of the particulars of claim, as they stood at the time of the hearing before the judge, would be too substantial to pass that test. The substitution of the company for the claimant could not be made without significant alteration to the formulation of the claim to enable it to be asserted on behalf of the company. Accordingly, the appeal would be dismissed.

Weston v Gribben [2006] EWCA Civ 1425, [2006] All ER (D) 29 (Nov) (Court of Appeal: Sedley, Lloyd and Hallett LJJ).

2314 Parties—capacity to litigate—patient—compromise reached before start of proceedings

The claimant suffered severe head injuries in a road traffic accident, and agreed liability on a 50/50 basis prior to commencing proceedings. Medical evidence subsequently suggested that he lacked mental capacity, and a litigation friend was appointed. The claimant sought to set aside the agreement on the ground that he was a 'patient', defined by CPR 21.1(2)(b) as a person who was, by reason of mental disorder, incapable of managing and administering his property and affairs. It was held that the claimant had been a patient at the time of commencement of proceedings, but not when liability was agreed, and the judge directed that the 50/50 apportionment should stand. The claimant appealed, contending that, at the time of the pre-action agreement, he had been a patient and that, under CPR 21.10(1), the agreement was invalid without the permission of the court. *Held*, the claimant had to understand all aspects of the proceedings in order to make an informed decision. If he understood what was meant by a 50/50 split but lacked the capacity to understand the concept of resultant damages, he lacked capacity to conduct the proceedings. However, the claimant's case was that the judge had applied the wrong test for establishing whether the claimant was a patient. A 'patient' was a creature of the CPR, and the earliest moment at which a person could become a patient was at the commencement of proceedings. A party might have all the attributes of a patient before proceedings were begun but, until they had commenced. he could not be a 'patient'. The claimant was not a patient at the time of the pre-action agreement and, accordingly, the appeal would be dismissed.

Bailey (by his litigation friend Ashton) v Warren [2006] EWCA Civ 51, [2006] WTLR 753 (Court of Appeal: Ward, Arden and Hallett LJJ). *Masterman-Lister v Brutton and Co* [2002] EWCA Civ 1889, [2003] 1 WLR 1511 (2003 Abr para 2135) applied.

2315 Parties—joinder—group litigation order—extent of court's power to join parties

CPR 19.2 provides that the court may order a person to be added as a new party (1) if it is desirable to add the new party so that the court can resolve all the matters in dispute in the proceedings; or (2) if there is an issue involving the new party and an existing party which is connected to the matters in dispute in the proceedings, and it is desirable to add the new party so that the court can resolve that issue.

The claimants had sustained chronic knee injuries while working for various contractors engaged by the British Coal Corporation and the National Coal Board. They intended to claim against the defendant, which had inherited the liabilities of those bodies, by way of a group litigation order. The contractors concerned wished to be involved in the litigation from the outset as they were concerned that they might be faced with contribution claims by the defendant if the defendant was found liable. They therefore applied to be joined as parties. The claimants and the defendant resisted joinder. The judge decided it was not right to join the contractors, and indicated that such a decision should be postponed until the court had a better idea of the allegations against the defendant and of how many of the claimants had been employees of the contractors as well as the defendant. The contractors appealed, submitting that there was a power, under CPR 19.2, in relation to any proceedings to join a party on that party's application where that party had an interest in any issue. The issue for the court was whether the judge had misdirected himself as to his powers or had acted wrongly in the exercise of his discretion. *Held*, the judge had not misdirected himself as to his powers. Although the very wide power contained in CPR 19.2 to join parties who might be affected by a finding in proceedings was available where proceedings had not yet commenced, the court had to be entitled to look at the proceedings which at that stage were threatened and to take a view on whether the relevant party should be joined. With regard to discretion, the judge had very properly said that the matter should be kept under review. The court would be better able to assess whether its initial view was correct when proceedings had been properly pleaded by the claimants and registered under the group litigation order and when the court had seen the defences pleaded. It followed that the exercise of discretion could not be impugned and, accordingly, the appeal would be dismissed.

Davies v Secretary of State for Trade and Industry [2006] EWCA Civ 1360, [2007] 1 All ER 518 (Court of Appeal: Waller, Longmore and Maurice Kay LJJ).

2316   Parties—substitution—expiry of limitation period—mistake

See *O'Byrne v Aventis Pasteur MSD Ltd*, para 1816.

2317   Parties—substitution—public law proceedings—challenge to award of planning permission

CPR 19.2 provides that the court may order a new party to be substituted for an existing one if the existing party's interest or liability has passed to the new party, and it is desirable to substitute the new party so that the court can resolve the matters in dispute in the proceedings.

An environmental society sought to challenge, pursuant to the Town and Country Planning Act 1990 s 288, the decision of the Secretary of State to grant planning permission in relation to the redevelopment of an old power station. The society subsequently decided to withdraw its challenge, but the claimant, the vice-chairman of the society, wished to continue the proceedings. She therefore applied to be substituted for the society as the claimant in the proceedings, and sought a protected costs order in view of the potential high cost of bringing the claim. The defendant developers argued that the court had no jurisdiction to order the substitution, on the basis that CPR Pt 19 did not apply to public law proceedings, and that, if the court did have such jurisdiction, substitution of the claimant would undermine the strict time limits governing challenges under the 1990 Act s 288. *Held*, CPR Pt 19 was not intended to cover public law cases. While, in one sense, claimants in public law proceedings were required to have an 'interest' in the dispute, it was an interest of a different kind from a private law interest. It was hard to see how an interest in public law proceedings could be transferred. Moreover, a defendant in public law proceedings did not have a liability which could be passed. However, while the court had no jurisdiction under CPR Pt 19 to substitute the claimant in the challenge, it had the inherent jurisdiction to do so. Moreover, there was no clear line delineating cases in which there was a sufficient identity of interest between a claimant and a person seeking to be substituted so that such substitution could not be said to undermine the principles of the 1990 Act s 288. Although the present case was not the paradigm case where one member of a pressure group sought to be substituted for another, it was far from the case of a stranger who had failed to bring his challenge within the time limit, and had sought to take advantage of existing proceedings. The applicant was the vice-president of the society, and, if the society had not brought a challenge under s 288, she would have done so. Moreover, the society had provided some limited financial support for the proceedings. It followed that to allow the substitution would not conflict with the principles of s 288. Judgment would be given accordingly.

River Thames Society v First Secretary of State [2006] All ER (D) 105 (Sep) (Queen's Bench Division: Underhill J). *Eco-Energy (GB) Ltd v First Secretary of State* [2004] EWCA Civ 1566, [2005] 2 P & CR 78 considered.

2318   Parties—unincorporated association—representative of association

The claimants had been attempting to build a bio-medical research laboratory which had been the subject of a campaign by an animal rights association to obstruct or prevent the project. The claimants had been granted injunctive relief against the campaigners and sought to continue such relief. The association was an unincorporated organisation. It fell to be determined whether its spokesperson should be a defendant to the action as a representative of the association or as a person in his own right or both. *Held*, an organisation as coherent as the association could be represented in a legal action. While it deliberately lacked the trappings of an organisation, the truth of the matter was that it was an organisation with a consistent and coherent body of people at its heart. The device of concealment should not permit the association to avoid the effects of civil law. The spokesperson should continue as a defendant as a representative of the association. It was difficult to see who could better represent an unincorporated association than its public spokesman. It was clear that he was a central and pivotal figure who was fully adherent to the association's aims, strategy and tactics. There was a world of difference between a reputable journalist reporting extremist views and a concerted and considered attempt to build up a threat so as to apply pressure to people as part of a strategy linked directly to those committing crimes. He was a propagandist who strove to maximise and potentiate the effect of criminal acts on the minds of those whom he wished to frighten. His activities went far beyond legitimate self-expression. There was nothing in the injunction sought to be continued that impinged on his legitimate freedom of speech. It was appropriate that he should continue as a defendant in his own right. Accordingly, the injunction would be continued.

Chancellor, Masters and Scholars of the University of Oxford v Broughton [2006] EWHC 2490 (QB), [2006] All ER (D) 157 (Oct) (Queen's Bench Division: Irwin J). *United Kingdom Nirex Ltd v Barton* (1986) Times, 14 October (1986 Abr para 2021); and Application 23927/94 *Surek v Turkey* (1999) 7 BHRC 339, ECtHR, considered.

2319 Payment into court—interest—claimant a patient—date interest starts to accrue

The claimant was injured in an accident and as a consequence of his injuries became a patient. Proceedings were commenced on his behalf against the defendant companies. The defendants made a Pt 36 payment, but the claimant's solicitors only notified the defendants' solicitors that the claimant wished to accept the payment into court after the prescribed period for acceptance. The matter subsequently came before the court on an application by the claimant for the court's approval of the decision to accept the money paid into court. The defendants also sought leave to take the money out of court because of what they contended had been a change in the claimant's life expectancy. The matter was adjourned. In the event, the defendants decided not to apply to take the money out of court, and a settlement was eventually approved. A dispute arose as to which party should be entitled to receive the interest on the money which had been paid into court in respect of the period until the hearing. *Held*, a claimant who was a patient could only receive the interest on money paid into court after the court's approval was obtained. There was nothing unjust about that state of affairs as a claimant could take that factor into account in deciding whether to accept a payment in and solicitors for claimants should be able to ensure that a judge was available to approve the acceptance of the money paid into court very speedily after a claimant had decided to accept the money. A claimant was not bound by an intimation of acceptance until the court approved the acceptance. The terms of CPR 21.10 meant that a payment into court in respect of a person under a disability was not validly accepted until the court approved it. Moreover, in accordance with the relevant practice direction, the payee was entitled to interest on the payment into court until the court had approved the acceptance of the payment in. Judgment would be given accordingly.

Brennan v Eco Composting Ltd [2006] EWHC 3153 (QB), [2006] All ER (D) 94 (Dec) (Queen's Bench Division: Silber J). *Dietz v Lennig Chemicals Ltd* [1969] 1 AC 170, HL; and *Drinkall v Whitwood* [2003] EWCA Civ 1547, [2004] 4 All ER 378 (2004 Abr para 401) considered.

2320 Pleadings—application to amend—late application

A tenant brought proceedings for the grant of a new business tenancy. The landlord wished to have the option of redeveloping the property and, on the last working day before the trial, sought the court's permission to amend its acknowledgment of service by including a break clause in the new lease. The recorder refused the application, referring to the legitimate expectations of the parties and stating that there ought to be a compelling explanation where such an application came to the court so close to the trial date. The landlord appealed. *Held*, the phrase 'legitimate expectations' was a public law concept and the recorder was wrong to have brought it into civil procedure. There was nothing in the CPR which required an applicant to provide a compelling explanation of the need for an amendment or the reason for the lateness. The fact that circumstances might change during the course of an application for the grant of a new tenancy was not unusual and should not be a reason for refusing to allow an amendment to the pleadings. Accordingly, the appeal would be allowed.

Davies Attbrook (Chemists) Ltd v Benchmark Group plc [2005] EWHC 3413 (Ch), [2006] 1 WLR 2493 (Chancery Division: Lewison J).

2321 Precedent—conflicting decisions of co-ordinate courts—earlier decision fully considered but not followed

The applicant, an administrator, sought a discharge of the administration and authorisation for a distribution to creditors who would have been preferential creditors in the event of a winding up. The question arose as to whether, in the light of conflicting authorities on the point, the court had jurisdiction to authorise such a distribution under the provisions of the Insolvency Act 1986 before its amendment by the Enterprise Act 2002. Recently, the issue had been determined on eight occasions. On six of those occasions it was held that such a jurisdiction had existed, and on two occasions the jurisdiction had been held not to have existed. The issue to be decided was where, in the light of those authorities, the law ought to have been taken as settled at first instance. *Held*, it was generally desirable that the law enjoyed the benefit of certainty. To that end, and in relation to cases where there existed conflicting decisions at first instance, questions of law were to be taken as having been settled at first instance when the earlier decision had been fully considered but not followed by a later judge. An exception would only arise where a third judge was convinced that the second had erred in failing to follow the first decision. In the present case, the two most recent decisions had fully considered the previous authorities and had concluded that the jurisdiction to authorise the payments existed both under the 1986 Act s 18(3) and under the court's inherent jurisdiction. Therefore, those conclusions fell to be treated as the settled law at first instance. Accordingly, the application would be granted.

Re Cromptons Leisure Machines Ltd [2006] All ER (D) 178 (Dec) (Chancery Division: Lewison J).

2322   Precedent—Court of Appeal—Community law—binding effect of previous ruling

A VAT and duties tribunal refused the taxpayer's claim for repayment of input tax, and the High Court dismissed the taxpayer's appeal. On the taxpayer's appeal to the Court of Appeal, the Commissioners of Customs and Excise sought a reference to the European Court of Justice. A question arose as to the binding effect of a previous ruling of the Court of Appeal in which a judgment of the European Court of Justice had been considered. *Held*, there might be circumstances in which the obligation imposed on courts by the European Communities Act 1972 s 3(1) would require the Court of Appeal to refuse to follow its own earlier decision as to the meaning and effect of a Community instrument, including the effect of a judgment of the European Court of Justice. This would include a case in which the European judgment under consideration by the Court of Appeal in the earlier case had been the subject of further consideration and consequent interpretation, explanation or qualification by the European Court in a later judgment. However, the Court of Appeal should not substitute its own view as to the effect of a judgment of the European Court for the view taken by the Court of Appeal in an earlier decision where there had been no opportunity for the European Court to review the decision. Where the Court of Appeal had been persuaded that there were strong grounds for thinking that the earlier decision was wrong as a matter of Community law, it might think it right to refer the point to the European Court for a preliminary ruling or it might follow the earlier decision and give permission to appeal. However, it should not refuse to follow the earlier decision merely because it was satisfied that a different conclusion should have been reached on the same material and the same arguments. The application for a reference would be refused and, accordingly, the appeal would be allowed.

Condé Nast Publications Ltd v Customs and Excise Comrs [2006] EWCA Civ 976, [2006] STC 1721 (Court of Appeal: Chadwick, Arden and Smith LJJ). *Kay v Lambeth LBC* [2006] UKHL 10 (para 1539), [2006] 2 WLR 570 considered. *Fleming (t/a Bodycraft) v Customs and Excise Comrs* [2006] EWCA Civ 70, [2006] All ER (D) 199 (Feb) (para 2914) applied. Decision of Warren J [2005] EWHC 1167 (Ch), [2005] STC 1327 (2005 Abr para 3146) reversed.

2323   Precedent—Privy Council—power to overrule decision of House of Lords

Two appeals against conviction were heard together because each turned on the true interpretation of the Homicide Act 1957 Act s 3, which provided that it was for a jury to decide in a murder trial whether the provocation of the defendant was enough to cause a reasonable man to do as he did. The House of Lords had ruled that the question for the jury was whether the loss of the defendant's self control was sufficiently 'excusable' to reduce the gravity of the offence from murder to manslaughter. However, in a later case the Privy Council had doubted the correctness of that ruling. An issue arose as to whether the decision of the Privy Council had effectively overruled the decision of the House of Lords. *Held*, the Privy Council had altered the established approach to precedent. While there were possible constitutional issues in postulating that a Board of the Privy Council, however numerous or distinguished, was in a position, on an appeal from Jersey, to displace and replace a decision of the Appellate Committee on an issue of English law, the principles in relation to precedent were common law principles. Putting to one side the position of the European Court of Justice, the Lords of Appeal in Ordinary had never hitherto accepted that any other tribunal could overrule a decision of the Appellate Committee. Uniquely, a majority of the Lords in the relevant case before the Privy Council had decided that they could do so, and proceeded to do so in their capacity as members of the Judicial Committee of the Privy Council. It followed that it was not for the Court of Appeal to rule that it was beyond their powers so to alter the common law rules of precedent. Also, the rule that the Court of Appeal had always to follow a decision of the House of Lords and one of its own decisions, rather than a decision of the Privy Council, had been established at a time when no tribunal other than the House of Lords itself could rule that a previous decision of the House was no longer good law. Once one postulated that there were circumstances in which a decision of the Judicial Committee of the Privy Council could take precedence over the House of Lords, the Court of Appeal was bound, in those circumstances, to prefer the decision of the Privy Council to the prior decision of the House of Lords. In the circumstances of the instant case, there were exceptional features which justified preferring the decision in the Privy Council case to that in the earlier case before the House of Lords. All nine of the Lords of Appeal in Ordinary on the board in the Privy Council case had agreed in the course of their judgments that the result reached by the majority had clarified definitively English law on the question of provocation. The majority in the Privy Council case had constituted half of the Appellate Committee of the House of Lords. In the circumstances, the result of any appeal on the issue to the House of Lords was a foregone conclusion. It was unlikely that the Court of Appeal would ever again be presented with the circumstances that had arisen in the instant case. The instant case should not, therefore, be taken as a licence to decline to follow a decision of the House of Lords in any other circumstances. Judgment would be given accordingly.

R v James; R v Karimi [2006] EWCA Crim 14, [2006] QB 588 (Court of Appeal: Lord Phillips of Worth Matravers CJ, Sir Igor Judge P, Poole, Bean and Dobbs JJ). *R v Holley* [2005] UKPC 23, [2005] 2 AC 580, PC (para 05/1582), followed. *R v Smith (Morgan)* [2000] 4 All ER 289, HL (2000 Abr para 957), not followed.

2324 Procedure—terrorism cases—management

See para 900.

2325 Procedure—vacation business—guidance

See para 2300.

2326 Proceedings—vexatious proceedings—restraint—refusal of leave to institute proceedings without oral hearing

Both of the claimants had been made the subject of a civil proceedings order under the Supreme Court Act 1981 s 42 on the ground that they had habitually and persistently and without any reasonable ground instituted vexatious civil proceedings in the High Court. Consequently, they could only bring civil proceedings where the High Court was satisfied that the application was not an abuse of process of the court. Both claimants sought leave to institute civil proceedings. The first claimant's application was dismissed without a hearing and the second claimant's application was outstanding. They brought proceedings for judicial review of the decisions, contending that *Practice Direction—Striking out a Statement of Case* (2001) PD 3A para 7.6(3), which provided that a High Court judge could refuse an application without an oral hearing, was ultra vires the applicable provisions of the Civil Procedure Act 1997. They also argued that CPR PD 3A para 7.6(3) was contrary to natural justice and in violation of their right, under the European Convention on Human Rights art 6, of access to a court. *Held*, the 1981 Act s 42 gave the court the right to place limitations on access to a court; CPR PD 3A merely dealt with the machinery for putting that into effect so as to prevent an abuse of its own process. As both the 1981 Act and the CPR were silent as to the procedure to be adopted by the court when dealing with an application for leave to institute proceedings, the regulation of the procedure fell within the court's inherent power to regulate its own procedure. Therefore, CPR PD 3A para 7.6(3) was not ultra vires the 1997 Act. In stating that rules 'may, instead of providing for any matter' and in cross-referring to provisions contained in practice directions, Sch 1 para 6 implicitly accepted that the court had an inherent jurisdiction to make such directions, but it did not confer that jurisdiction. CPR PD 3A para 7.6(3) was not contrary to natural justice. The purpose of the 1981 Act s 42 was to protect those persons who might otherwise be subject to vexatious litigation. In deciding whether to give leave the court would not be resolving contested issues between the parties. Rather, in most cases, the court would be considering whether the claim was abusive and whether there were reasonable grounds for the application, and these matters could be determined without recourse to an oral hearing. Furthermore, the court could direct an oral hearing in a case where fairness required it. Finally, given that a person subject to a civil proceedings order could seek permission to commence proceedings before a judge at High Court level who had an unfettered discretion to direct a hearing, and that such an order pursued the legitimate aim of preventing vexatious litigation in the interests of the proper administration of justice, there was no violation of the person's right, under the Convention art 6(1), of access to the court. Accordingly, the application would be dismissed.

R (on the application of Ewing) v Department for Constitutional Affairs [2006] EWHC 504 (Admin), [2006] 2 All ER 993 (Queen's Bench Division: Sullivan J).

2327 Service of process—incorrect service of documents—election petition

See *Ali v Haques*, para 1183.

2328 Service of process—service out of the jurisdiction—claim form

The claimant bank had obtained permission to serve its claim form for reimbursement in respect of payments under two confirmed letters of credit on the officials of the respondent bank in Khartoum. *Held*, the function of CPR 6.24 was not to prevent service by a method which the law of the place of service did not permit. It was implicit that the court could permit any alternative method of service under CPR 6.8 so long as it did not contravene the law of the country where service was to be effected. There was no authority for the proposition that service abroad had to be expressly permitted by the foreign jurisdiction for it to be good service. Accordingly, the claim would be allowed.

Habib Bank Ltd v Central Bank of Sudan [2006] EWHC 1767 (Comm), [2007] 1 All ER (Comm) 53 (Queen's Bench Division: Field J). *Shiblaq v Sadikoglu* [2004] EWHC 1890 (Comm), [2004] 2 All ER (Comm) 596 (2004 Abr para 2243) considered.

2329 Service of process—service out of the jurisdiction—determination of jurisdiction— commencement of fraud proceedings—wording of insurance policy

See *Dornoch Ltd v Mauritius Union Assurance Co Ltd*, para 601.

2330   Service of process—service out of the jurisdiction—enforcement of foreign award— existence of assets

The claimant was a Turkish public legal entity with authority to restructure and administer banks and banking institutions in Turkey whose banking licences had been revoked. The action in England was brought to enforce at common law three judgments entered in the claimant's favour by the Turkish courts obtained in civil actions in the civil courts in Turkey against the first defendant, which was the owner of three banks which had collapsed and been taken over by the claimant. The claimant's case was that the first defendant had misappropriated large sums of money from the banks. The claimant was given permission to serve the first defendant with the proceedings out of the jurisdiction and was granted a worldwide freezing injunction. The first defendant applied to set aside the grant of permission outside the jurisdiction in relation to the claim and discharge of the injunction, arguing that he had no assets within the jurisdiction so that no judgment obtained against him in Turkey could be enforced against him within the jurisdiction. The first defendant contended that it was a pre-condition of the existence of jurisdiction under CPR 6.20(9) that there should be assets within the jurisdiction, and since there were no assets of the first defendant in England, the court had no jurisdiction. *Held*, the presence of assets was not a pre-condition to the exercise of jurisdiction under CPR 6.20(9). It was added as a ground for jurisdiction to fill a gap revealed in cases where judgment creditors sought to enforce at common law judgments emanating from countries whose judgments were not capable of registration in England. Prior to its addition, where the judgment creditor wished to proceed against assets in England, and the judgment debtor was not present or domiciled in England, there was no basis for service out of the jurisdiction even though the judgment debtor had assets in England which could be attached to satisfy the judgment. There was no reason for applying a requirement that there be assets within the jurisdiction. There was nothing in the CPR Pt 74 procedure for registration which required the presence of assets within the jurisdiction, and it would be odd if CPR 6.20(9) were so interpreted. Judgment would be given accordingly.

Tasarruff Meduati Sigorta Fonu v Demirel [2006] EWHC 3354 (Ch), [2006] All ER (D) 364 (Dec) (Chancery Division: Lawrence Collins J).

2331   Service of process—service out of the jurisdiction—proceedings purportedly served by invalid method in foreign jurisdiction—power of court to rectify

CPR 3.10 provides that, where there has been an error of procedure such as a failure to comply with a rule or practice direction, the error does not invalidate any step taken in the proceedings unless the court so orders, and the court may make an order to remedy the error.

The claimant issued proceedings in defamation against the defendant, a resident of Iceland. The proceedings were purportedly served personally on the defendant at an address in Reykjavik by a member of staff of the British Embassy in Iceland. Beyond receiving the envelope containing the documents, opening and reading the contents, the defendant took no other steps. He did not sign a written receipt. There having been no acknowledgment of service, and the court being satisfied that the documents had been served, the master ordered judgment in default in favour of the claimant. The defendant subsequently applied to set aside that judgment, and the claimant sought relief under CPR 3.10. The master held that there had been an error regarding service in that no written receipt had been obtained. However, he decided to dismiss the application to set aside, and exercised his discretion under CPR 3.10 to correct the error in respect of service. The defendant appealed, contending that simple personal service was not a permitted method of service in Iceland, that the claimant therefore had not used a valid method of service, and that there had been a fundamental flaw in the purported service which was of no effect and which could not be rendered valid by retrospective application of CPR 3.10. *Held*, CPR 3.10 could not be used in circumstances such as those of the present case to effect an error in service where proceedings had been purportedly served out of the jurisdiction, but in a method which was not valid in the relevant jurisdiction. The master had fallen into error in using that provision to correct the defect in the purported service. Accordingly, the appeal would be allowed.

Olafsson v Gissurarson [2006] EWHC 3162 (QB), [2006] All ER (D) 116 (Dec) (Queen's Bench Division: Mackay J).

2332   Service of process—service out of the jurisdiction—property within jurisdiction

The claimants had brought proceedings against the defendants following a commercial dispute. The claimants discovered that spyware had been installed on their computer system in London and that it had been accessed remotely. They considered that the defendants had been responsible and brought proceedings for breach of confidence. The defendants sought to have the proceedings set aside, denied responsibility and contended that, in any case, the alleged tort had occurred in Russia. *Held*, CPR 6.20(10), which allowed service out of the jurisdiction where the whole subject matter of a claim related to property within the jurisdiction, extended to claims for breach of confidence where it could be established that the confidential information was located in the jurisdiction. Information stored in London in digital form on a server satisfied the test. CPR 6.20(8) provided that a claim is made in tort where damage was sustained within the jurisdiction. Here, the substance of the tort was committed within the jurisdiction where the computer server was located within the jurisdiction, and this was so even though the attack emanated outside the jurisdiction. Accordingly, the application would be refused.

Ashton Investments Ltd v OJSC Russian Aluminium (RUSAL) [2006] EWHC 2545 (Comm), [2006] All ER (D) 209 (Oct) (Queen's Bench Division: Jonathan Hirst QC).

2333 Service of process—service out of the jurisdiction—tort—damage sustained within the jurisdiction

See *Newsat Holdings Ltd v Zani*, para 608.

2334 Service of process—service through agencies—service by post—relationship between methods of transmission and service

Questions were referred to the European Court of Justice on the interpretation of EC Council Regulation 1348/2000 arts 4–11, on the service of documents through agencies, and art 14, on the service of documents by post. *Held*, there was nothing in the wording of Regulation 1348/2000 to indicate that it introduced a hierarchy between service through agencies and service by post. Neither recitals in its preamble nor its provisions stated that a method of transmission and service, used in accordance with the rules of Regulation 1348/2000, would rank below the method of service through agencies. Moreover, it followed from the spirit and purpose of Regulation 1348/2000 that it was intended to ensure that judicial documents were served effectively, while respecting the legitimate interests of the person on whom they were served. Regulation 1348/2000 had to be interpreted as meaning that, where transmission and service were effected by both methods, reference had to be made to the date of the first service validly effected. In order not to render meaningless the provisions of Regulation 1348/2000 governing methods of service, all the legal effects that followed when one of the methods was validly effected had to be taken into account, irrespective of subsequent successful service by another method. Regulation 1348/2000 was intended to expedite the transmission of judicial documents for service and, therefore, the conduct of judicial proceedings. If, for the purposes of computing a procedural time limit, the first service of the document in question was taken into consideration, the person on whom that document was served was required to defend judicial proceedings earlier, which could enable the competent court to give a ruling within shorter time limits.

Case C-473/04 *Plumex v Young Sports NV* [2006] All ER (D) 120 (Feb) (ECJ: Third Chamber).

2335 Settlement of proceedings—Part 36 offer—withdrawal of offer—offeror seeking to accept offer after conclusion of hearing

In a claim for assault, it had been held that the first defendant was vicariously liable and that his liability was covered by his public liability insurance policy provided by the third defendant. The first defendant appealed and the third defendant cross-appealed. Before the hearing of the appeal and cross-appeal, the third defendant made a CPR Pt 36 offer to settle to the first defendant on the basis that the parties agreed to a 50:50 division of liability. On the second day of the appeal hearing, the first defendant made a Pt 36 offer to the third defendant, offering to accept a 40:60 division of liability. The third defendant rejected the offer, and stated that it followed that the offer to split liability equally was no longer available. After the appeal hearing had ended and judgment had been reserved, the first defendant purported to accept the original offer of the 50:50 split in liability, and sought a declaration that the offer had been validly accepted. *Held*, the third defendant had explicitly withdrawn its offer on the second day of the appeal hearing, so it was no longer open for acceptance. If the first defendant had been in any doubt as to the meaning of the words in the withdrawal it could have asked for clarification. Even if the offer had been open for acceptance after the beginning of the appeal hearing, it carried an implied term that it would not be available for acceptance after the hearing had ended and the court had reserved judgment. Accordingly, the application would be dismissed.

Hawley v Luminar Leisure plc [2006] EWCA Civ 30, [2006] All ER (D) 12 (Feb) (Court of Appeal: Brooke and Kay LJJ). For related proceedings see [2005] EWHC 5 (QB), [2005] Lloyd's Rep IR 275 (2005 Abr para 3002).

2336 Settlement of proceedings—settlement between reserving and delivery of judgment—duty of parties to notify court

It has been held that parties engaging in meaningful settlement discussions between the reserving and delivery of judgment have a duty to inform the court of that fact, as a failure to do so results in a waste of judicial resources which has an adverse effect on other court users. In particular, judicial time is wasted in drafting judgments which become superfluous on settlement. Further, where parties have compromised their dispute after the hearing but before the delivery of the judgment or draft judgment, it is doubtful whether a first instance judge has a discretion to publish the judgment.

Gurney Consulting Engineers (a firm) v Gleeds Health and Safety Ltd [2006] EWHC 536 (TCC), (2006) 108 Con LR 43 (Queen's Bench Division: Judge Peter Coulson QC).

2337   Statement of claim—amendment—breach of fiduciary duty

The first defendant was sole director of a company which imported goods from suppliers in the European Union. The goods were sold to various United Kingdom purchasers, including two English companies. The first defendant gave instructions for the company to divert the bulk of the moneys due from the English companies to overseas companies. In respect of two transactions, the company directed payments to the second defendant, a Spanish company, with which the company had not previously dealt. This resulted in the company's insolvency and it was unable to discharge its value added tax liabilities. Subsequently, the company was wound up following a petition presented by the Commissioners for Her Majesty's Revenue and Customs in respect of a VAT assessment. The second claimant was appointed liquidator of the company. The company commenced proceedings against the first and second defendants, alleging that the first defendant was liable to account for breach of fiduciary duty and that the second defendant was liable for knowingly receiving moneys in breach of trust. The original particulars of claim were amended and draft reamended particulars of claim were served but the master directed that the claimants' application to reamend their particulars of claim should be stood over. In their reamended particulars of claim, the claimants sought to allege that the second defendant was knowingly a party to the VAT fraud perpetuated by the first defendant. The second defendant objected to the proposed reamendments. *Held*, it could not be accepted that the amendments had not set out matters of fraud. The claimants had assumed the mantle of challenging the entirety of the transactions in which the second defendant had participated and that would require extensive disclosure. To categorise the action as merely a private claim was to ignore the reality that the action was for indirect recovery of the VAT due to the Revenue that the company had received but for which it had failed to account. In any event, United Kingdom legislation, such as the Finance Act 1989 s 182, the Insolvency Act 1986 s 236, the Enterprise Act 2002 s 237 and the Commissioners of Revenue and Customs Act 2005 s 18 had been passed to enable it to be used by the Revenue to assist the litigation. Taking those statutory provisions together, everything that had been disclosed had been disclosed lawfully. Even if that was not the case, CPR 32.1 gave the court a discretion to control evidence, including the exclusion of evidence which would otherwise be admissible. Since the factors were in favour of allowing the claimants to rely on the evidence provided that full disclosure of the material was obtained, the claimants would be given permission to reamend their particulars of claim, and accordingly, the application would be allowed.

   Silversafe Ltd (in liquidation) v Hood [2006] EWHC 1849 (Ch), [2006] All ER (D) 350 (Jul) (Chancery Division: Peter Smith J).

**2338   Stay of proceedings—earlier proceedings dismissed—costs order not satisfied—
          jurisdiction to stay current proceedings—assignee**

The defendant contracted with a company, whose business was sold to a second company. The debts disputed between the defendant and the original company were assigned to the second company and it presented a petition seeking to have the defendant wound up. The petition was dismissed as an abuse of process and the second company was ordered to pay the defendant its costs. The second company then began proceedings against the defendant. Subsequently, the claimant bought the second company's liabilities and obtained an assignment in respect of them. The second company did not comply with the order for costs and the defendant sought an order that the second company provide security for those costs and also, for the costs of the present proceedings. The second company transferred the disputed debts to the claimant, and an application was made to join the claimant to the proceedings. That order was granted and in respect of the defendant's applications the judge ordered that, unless the second company made a payment into court, its claim should be struck out. Finally, the judge stayed further proceedings and ordered the second company to pay the costs of the present applications. The second company did not comply and its remaining claims were struck out. The defendant applied for an order that the claimant's claim be struck out unless it paid or provided security for the total amount ordered to be paid by the second company. The claimant contended that as the assignment had been made for genuine reasons, it would not be right to impose such terms. However, the judge held that the claim should be stayed until the second company had paid the sum into court. On the claimant's appeal, *held,* there was a clear distinction between imposing on a new party to litigation as a condition of joinder a requirement to provide security for costs and staying the proceedings until a previous order for costs had been satisfied. The former was concerned with costs that were likely to be incurred in the future and with the ability of the party to pay them, the latter was concerned with preventing an abuse of the court's process. In cases concerning the commencement by the same person of a second set of proceedings while the costs of the first remained unpaid, the court would consider it unjust to allow a claimant whose action had failed to put the defendant to the expense of a second action until those costs had been paid. To pursue a second action in those circumstances would be an abuse of the court's process. In the present case, therefore, the judge had jurisdiction to make the order he had, even if its effect had been to impose on the claimant the burden of ensuring that the second company discharged its liability for costs. The judge had taken into account the fact that the claimant was suing as the assignee of the second company and the circumstances of the case. In light of the way in which matters had developed, the order made had been within the scope of his discretion. Accordingly, the appeal would be dismissed.

Investment Invoice Financing Ltd v Limehouse Board Mills Ltd [2006] EWCA Civ 9, [2006] 1 WLR 985 (Court of Appeal: Tuckey and Moore-Bick LJJ).

2339 Stay of proceedings—lawfulness—exercise of court's case management powers

CPR 3.1(2)(f), (m) entitles the court, except where the CPR provide otherwise, to stay the whole or part of any proceedings either generally or until a specified date or event, or take any other step or make any other order for the purpose of managing the case and furthering the overriding objective.

By order of court, a two-year moratorium was imposed on parties involved in protracted ongoing proceedings, under which the claimant's proceedings in relation to accounts and inquiries were stayed together with the entirety of the present action and the majority of associated actions. The liquidators of the first defendant's company appealed against the order, contending that it was a civil restraint order that had been imposed improperly. *Held*, the court had exercised its discretionary case management powers under CPR 3.1(2) to ensure that the overriding objective was achieved in the context of the present proceedings. Pursuant to CPR 1.1, the court had a duty to take into account matters of proportionality and the allotment of the court's resources in respect of particular proceedings. Accordingly, the appeal would be dismissed.

Phillips v Symes [2006] All ER (D) 170 (Oct) (Chancery Division: Peter Smith J).

2340 Trial—conduct of proceedings—intervention by judge on examination of witnesses—fairness of trial

The claimant local authority sought possession of a flat occupied by the defendant, who was a secure tenant, on the grounds that she had been continuously in arrears and had been guilty of causing a nuisance to a neighbour. The issue arose whether it was reasonable to make a possession order if the grounds were made out. During the trial the judge frequently intervened in a contentious manner during the oral evidence. He held that it would be unreasonable to make an outright order for possession. The authority appealed, submitting that the judge's findings in relation to housing benefit had been irrational and that he had failed to address the credibility of the defendant's evidence in his judgment or to explain why he rejected the neighbour's evidence. *Held*, a first instance judge was entitled to a wide degree of latitude in the way in which he conducted proceedings in his court. That latitude, however, was not unlimited. Although first instance judges rightly tended to be very much more proactive than their predecessors, it remained the case that interventions by a judge in the court of oral evidence, as opposed to interventions during counsel's submissions, had inevitably to carry the risk of depriving himself of the advantage of calm and dispassionate observation. The greater the frequency of the interventions the greater the risk, and where the interventions took the form of lengthy interrogation of the witnesses, the risk became a serious one. The risk was that the judge's descent into the arena might so hamper his ability properly to evaluate the evidence before him as to impair his judgment, and might for that reason render the trial unfair. In the present case, the manner in which the judge conducted the trial led to a failure on his part to discharge his judicial function. The judge had arrogated to himself a quasi-inquisitorial role which was entirely at odds with the adversarial system. Therefore, a retrial would be ordered. Accordingly, the appeal would be allowed.

Southwark LBC v Kofi-Adu [2006] EWCA Civ 281, [2006] HLR 599 (Court of Appeal: Laws and Jonathan Parker LJJ and Sir Martin Nourse).

2341 Trial—failure to attend trial—claim form not served on defendant—order made against defendant—defendant's right to have order set aside

CPR 39.3(3) provides that where a party does not attend and the court gives judgment against him, the party who failed to attend may apply for the judgment or order to be set aside. Where an application is made under CPR 39.3(3) by a party who failed to attend the trial, the court may grant the application only if the applicant acted promptly when he found out that the court had exercised its power to enter judgment against him, had a good reason for not attending the trial, and has a reasonable prospect of success at the trial: CPR 39.3(5).

The claimants issued a claim form for possession of a residential property and arrears of rent. However, the address of the defendant was stated incorrectly and the defendant did not acknowledge or respond to the claim form and had been unaware of the proceedings until it learned of the judgment in the claimants' favour. The defendant sought to have the judgment set aside on the basis that the claim form had not been served at its address. The judge rejected the defendant's contention that it was entitled to have the judgment set aside as of right, holding that it had to satisfy the provisions of CPR 39.3(5) in order to have judgment set aside. On appeal the judgment was set aside, and the first claimant appealed to the Court of Appeal. *Held*, to hold that CPR 39.3 applied where the defendant had not been served with the proceedings in accordance with the CPR and had no knowledge of the proceedings would involve disregarding the complex provisions for service of process under the CPR and would involve placing on the defendant the burden of satisfying the criteria in CRP 39.3(5). The CPR could not have been intended that the stringent requirements of CPR 39.3(5) should apply to applications to set aside judgments irregularly obtained, in the sense of being obtained without service of the claim form in accordance with the CPR. The whole of CPR 39.3(5) contemplated a trial in the absence of a party who had been served under the CPR or in respect of whom service had been dispensed with. Further, in the case of a judgment for a sum of money, interest could be payable from the date of judgment until payment. That would be an unjust result where the judgment had been obtained without service of process and without any order dispensing with service. CPR 39.3(5) therefore did not apply to a case where the defendant had not been served with proceedings and was ignorant of them. Although a defendant who could show that he had not been served with a claim form at all would normally be entitled to an order setting the judgment aside, he would not be entitled to have the judgment set aside as of right. Where a claimant could show that the defendant had been guilty of inexcusable delay since learning that the judgment had been entered against him, the court would be entitled to make no order on the defendant's application for that reason, and would be entitled to make an appropriate order in relation to statutory interest accruing due on the judgment or otherwise. Accordingly, the appeal would be dismissed.

Nelson v Clearsprings (Management) Ltd [2006] EWCA Civ 1252, [2006] All ER (D) 109 (Sep) (Court of Appeal: Sir Anthony Clarke MR, Brooke and Waller LJJ).

2342   Trial—failure to attend trial—order made against party—application to set aside order—discretion

The tenants held a lease in respect of a property. They moved out but failed to notify the landlord. The landlord wrote to them at the property, demanding payment for ground rent, maintenance contributions and insurance premiums. The landlord commenced proceedings for possession and arrears of rent. The claim form was served in accordance with CPR 6.5(6) at the property, being the tenants' 'usual or last known address'. The tenants, having no knowledge of the proceedings, failed to appear at the hearing, where the judge ordered them to give possession of the property and pay rent arrears. The tenants applied to the judge to have the order set aside under CPR 39.3(5). The judge concluded that the tenants had acted promptly when they found out that the order had been made against them and that they had a good reason for not attending. Therefore, he set aside the order. The landlord appealed successfully and the tenants appealed. *Held,* if the reason for a party's non-attendance was that he had not known that the hearing was taking place on that particular day, it would usually be necessary to ask why the party was unaware in that regard. It would usually be relevant to inquire whether the party was aware that proceedings had been issued and served. It would be difficult for a party to argue that he had a good reason for not attending if he had deliberately avoided receiving such communication in order to frustrate the litigation process. However, a person was under no obligation to make himself amenable to potential claims of which he had no notice. In the present case, the approach that had been adopted by the judge had produced a result that was unjust, and had denied a fair hearing to a party who, by definition, had a reasonable prospect of success on the merits and had acted promptly to make the application. The tenants had done nothing to avoid receipt of communications, for the purpose of frustrating the proceedings, having left the property on account of health problems. Although they might well have been misguided in not forwarding their new address to the landlord, they had not failed to take any steps in order to avoid their contractual responsibilities. Therefore, they had a good reason for not attending the hearing, and accordingly, the appeal would be allowed.

Estate Acquisition and Development Ltd v Wiltshire [2006] All ER (D) 50 (May) (Court of Appeal: Dyson, Jacob and Moses LJJ). *Brazil v Brazil* [2002] EWCA Civ 1135, [2002] All ER (D) 508 (Jul) (2002 Abr para 2441) applied.

2343   Trial—submission of no case to answer—putting defendant to its election

The claimant brought an action for negligence against the defendant local authority following an accident in her garden. At trial, the judge decided that there was no case to answer without putting the defendant to its election, and directed that judgment be entered for the defendant on the basis that, given the varying explanations for the accident that had been advanced, the court could not possibly find on the balance of probabilities that the accident had happened in the way the claimant had described it. On the claimant's appeal, issues arose as to whether the judge had erred in failing to put the defendant to its election before being willing to entertain a submission of no case to answer, and whether the judge had applied the correct standard of proof when dismissing the claim. *Held,* it was only in exceptional circumstances that a judge in a civil action should entertain a submission of no case to answer without putting the defence to its election. That position had not been altered by the introduction of the CPR. Moreover, the judge should not have judged the merits of the claim at the half-way stage on the balance of probabilities. He should have asked himself whether the claimant had advanced a prima facie case. If the course adopted by the judge were to be followed, the claimant would simultaneously be deprived of the opportunity of making a weak case stronger by eliciting favourable evidence for the defendant's witnesses, and of the opportunity of inviting the court to draw adverse inferences from the defendant's failure to give evidence, because the judge had not put the defendant to its election. Judgment would be given accordingly.

Graham v Chorley BC [2006] EWCA Civ 92, [2006] PIQR P367 (Court of Appeal: Brooke, Rix and Maurice Kay LJJ). *Benham Ltd v Kythira Investments Ltd* [2003] EWCA Civ 1794, [2003] All ER (D) 252 (Dec) applied.

2344 Witness summons—summons to produce documents in court—confidentiality

See *R (on the application of B) v Stafford Combined Court*, para 1624.

PRESS, PRINTING AND PUBLISHING

Halsbury's Laws of England (4th edn) vol 36(2) (Reissue) paras 401–500

Articles

For articles relating to this title please refer to the Table of Articles at the beginning of the Abridgment.

2345 Internet—publication on internet—libel—publication within jurisdiction of court

See *Al Amoudi v Brisard*, para 1799.

2346 Press—duty to disclose source of information

See CONFIDENCE AND DATA PROTECTION.

2347 Press—duty to impart information to public—confidential information about individual—right to respect for private life

See *HRH Prince of Wales v Associated Newspapers Ltd*, para 583.

2348 Publishing—publication of book—disclosure of sensitive personal data—balance between right to privacy and freedom of expression

See *McKennitt v Ash*, para 584.

2349 Reports of judicial proceedings—draft judgment—publication before judgment officially pronounced—contempt of court

See *Baigent v Random House; Re The Lawyer*, para 645.

2350 Reports of judicial proceedings—reporting restrictions—family proceedings—claim of miscarriage of justice—previous media attention

See *Re Webster (A Child)*, para 467.

2351 Reports of judicial proceedings—reporting restrictions—risk of prejudice to further proceedings

The defendants were arrested and charged with conspiracy to murder. The charges related to alleged plots to commit acts of terrorism. The judge ordered that the 23 counts on indictment be severed. The fist defendant pleaded guilty, but on the basis that that was no admission of conspiracy with his co-defendants. The trials of the co-defendants were due to commence five months after the first defendant fell to be sentenced. The co-defendants applied for an order preventing the publication of any report of the first defendant's sentencing hearing till after their trials, pursuant to the Contempt of Court Act 1981 s 4(1). The first defendant's conviction would be admissible as evidence against the co-defendants since his acts were central to the trials of the co-defendants. The evidence against the first defendant would also be admissible against the co-defendants. However, the judge's sentencing remarks would not be admissible and the co-defendants submitted that their publication could prejudice their trials. Therefore, the judge decided to order reporting restrictions on the sentencing hearing, postponing any reporting of the hearing until the conclusion of the co-defendants' trials. Several media organisations appealed against the order pursuant to the Criminal Justice Act 1988 s 159. *Held*, the court's power under the 1981 Act s 4(2) was intended to be used to deal with reports of its proceedings which were fair and accurate but should none the less be postponed. Therefore, it would be an abuse of that power to pronounce an order not for the purpose of warding off an anticipated consequence of the fair and accurate reporting of proceedings but for the purposes of warding off prejudicial comment which those proceedings might prompt. If such comment did actually create a substantial risk that the course of justice would be seriously impeded, the strict liability rule would apply in terms of s 2(2). In that event, the court would have power to punish the publisher. The responsibility for ensuring that publicity did not prejudice the course of a trial rested fairly and squarely with those responsible for that publicity. The risk of being in contempt of court was not one which any responsible editor would wish to run. The two safeguards to the fairness of the co-defendants' trial were the responsibility of the media to avoid inappropriate comment, and the trial process, including the jury itself. Therefore, the order would be set aside. Accordingly, the appeal would be allowed.

Re B [2006] EWCA Crim 2692, [2007] EMLR 145 (Court of Appeal: Sir Igor Judge P, Penry-Davey and Mackay JJ).

PRISONS

Halsbury's Laws of England (4th edn) vol 36(2) (Reissue) paras 501–800

Articles

For articles relating to this title please refer to the Table of Articles at the beginning of the Abridgment.

2352   Parole Board—application for parole—child—provision of adult assistance

The applicant had been convicted when 14 years old of five serious offences and sentenced to a period of detention. He applied for parole as soon as he was eligible, but was rejected. He had seen reports and written a letter making submissions without any adult assistance, and received no visit from the defendant, the Parole Board. The applicant made an application for judicial review, in which he complained that the Board's procedure had been unfair. *Held*, the Board was obliged to ensure that the applicant had at least the offer of adult assistance with his representations and if that offer was declined, the Board ought to know of it before it reached its decision. The possibility of the parole dossier being gone through scrupulously by an adult with the child for the strengths and weakness of the case to be identified and the possibility of assistance in formulation and reviewing any written representations was the minimum standard of fairness. The final product should also be looked at by an adult and advice given where appropriate before any document was delivered to the Board. The failure to assist rendered the applicant's right to make representations null, especially compared to the safeguards given to children during police interviews. The United Convention on the Rights of the Child art 12(1), (2) envisaged that the opportunity to be heard had to be rendered effective by the provision of appropriate adult assistance where possible. The obligation to provide assistance fell on the prison authorities and no such assistance had been forthcoming. The applicant had never been told that an oral hearing might have been possible and it appeared that the question of the desirability of such a hearing might never have been addressed by the Board. The Board had also indicated that he would be visited before any decision was made, but no visit took place. Accordingly, the application would be granted.

R (on the application of K) v Parole Board [2006] EWHC 2413 (Admin), [2006] All ER (D) 75 (Oct) (Queen's Bench Division: McCombe J).

2353   Prisoner—deportation—eligibility period—duty to consider matter expeditiously before period elapses

The Criminal Justice Act 1991 s 46A(1) provides that, where a short-term or long-term prisoner is liable to removal from the United Kingdom, the Secretary of State may remove him from prison at any time after he has served the requisite period. For this purpose, 'the requisite period' means, in relation to a term of 18 months or more, a period that is 135 days less than one-half of the term: s 46(5)(c).

The claimant, a national of Antigua, was convicted of a drugs offence and sentenced to imprisonment. A recommendation for deportation was made, and by virtue of the 1991 Act s 46A he was eligible to be removed to Antigua within the timeframe specified in s 46(5)(c). Owing to administrative delays, no action was taken in that regard for several months, and he was eventually deported one day before the expiration of his eligibility period. The claimant sought judicial review to challenge the manner in which his deportation had been handled, alleging that the Secretary of State had been in breach of a duty to consider the matter expeditiously, that the delay had been unreasonable, and that the claimant had had a legitimate expectation that the Secretary of State would be prompt in his disposal of the matter. The claimant relied on the failure of the Secretary of State to follow Prison Service Order 6000 Chapter 9, which prescribed a timetable for such cases. *Held*, the 1991 Act was clear. It imposed no duty to exercise the discretion to release a deportee early in any particular way save that it had to be within the eligibility period. It was not possible to graft into the relevant provisions a duty to do so by reference to the Prison Service Order. The legitimate expectation arising, as much from the 1991 Act as the Prison Service Order, was that foreign prisoners would have their case considered within the specified eligibility period. Moreover, the Prison Service Order was, by its nature and aspirations, merely instructions and directions to the Prison Service to achieve desired standards of administration. Properly interpreted, the timetable was not a promise in character, but an internal administrative direction to the Prison Service. Accordingly, the application would be dismissed.

R (on the application of Christian) v Secretary of State for the Home Department [2006] All ER (D) 35 (Jul) (Queen's Bench Division: Newman J).

1991 Act s 46A repealed by Criminal Justice Act 2003 Sch 37 Pt 7.

2354 Prisoner—detention on remand—attempted suicide—investigation

See *R (on the application of D) v Secretary of State for the Home Department*, para 1586.

2355 Prisoner—duty of care owed to prisoner by Home Office—psychiatric injury

See *Butchart v Home Office*, para 2080.

2356 Prisoner—release on licence—licence conditions—home detention curfew—recall for breach

The claimants, who were serving short prison sentences, were released on licence under home detention curfew pursuant to the Criminal Justice Act 2003 s 246. The claimants both breached general licence conditions imposed in relation to their release, and the defendant Secretary of State therefore recommended their recall under s 254. The Parole Board confirmed the first claimant's recall and declined to recommend her release. In relation to the second claimant, the board set a review date of which a decision was pending at the date of the judicial review hearing. The consequence of recalling under s 254 was that the claimants were not released at the halfway point of their sentences, which was a general right under s 244. The claimants applied for judicial review of the Secretary of State's continuing decision to detain, submitting that the decision made by the Secretary of State under s 254 was unlawful as the s 255 power had been open to him, which would have led to their releases at the halfway point of their respective sentences under s 244. The claimants sought to argue that ss 254 and 255 were mutually exclusive. *Held*, on the proper construction of ss 254 and 255, it was clear that mutual exclusivity was not intended by the drafters. The Secretary of State had separate powers under the two provisions when considering whether to release a prisoner who had breached a licence condition. Section 254 was a stronger power and was therefore subject to the scrutiny of the Parole Board, whereas s 255 was not. The powers existed for the interests of public protection, and also involved a prisoner's loss of liberty. When considering which provision was to be invoked, a balancing exercise had to be taken between the public interest and a prisoner's liberty, and the stronger power was to be used if the public interest so required. In the circumstances of the case, the Secretary of State had acted lawfully in invoking his s 254 power in relation to both claimants. Accordingly, the applications would be dismissed.

R (on the application of Ramsden) v Secretary of State for the Home Department; R (on the application of Naylor) v Secretary of State for the Home Department [2006] All ER (D) 167 (Dec) (Queen's Bench Division: Toulson J).

2357 Prisoner—release on licence—long-term prisoners and prisoners liable to deportation—power to release vested in Secretary of State rather than Parole Board—discrimination

The first claimant was a British national who had been sentenced to 18 years' imprisonment. The second and third claimants were foreign nationals who were liable to removal from the United Kingdom. In general, the Parole Board could recommend the release of a prisoner and the Secretary of State would be obliged to follow such a recommendation. However, the effect of the Criminal Justice Act 1991 ss 33(2), (5), 35, 46(1) and 50(2), and the Parole Board (Transfer of Functions) Order 1998, SI 1998/3218, art 2 was that power to order the early release of the claimants was vested solely in the Secretary of State. In the case of the first claimant, this was because he had been sentenced to a term of 15 years or more, and in the case of the second and third claimants, this was because the Parole Board had no power to recommend the release of prisoners liable to deportation. The claimants sought judicial review on the basis that the statutory regime discriminated against them in breach of their right to liberty under the European Convention of Human Rights art 5 in conjunction with art 14, which provided that the enjoyment of the rights and freedoms in the Convention had to be secured without discrimination on any ground such as 'sex, race, colour, language, religion, political or other opinion, national or social origin, association with a national minority, property, birth or other status'. The applications were refused and their appeals were dismissed. They further appealed. *Held*, the right to seek early release, where domestic law provided for such a right, was clearly within the ambit of art 5, and differential treatment of one prisoner as compared with another, otherwise than on the merits of their respective cases, gave rise to a potential complaint under art 14. However, a difference in treatment based on the seriousness of an offence fell outside the grounds proscribed by art 14. The words 'or other status' were not intended to cover differential treatment on any ground whatever. The reason for the distinction was not a personal characteristic of the offender but what the offender had done. In the case of the first claimant, his classification as a prisoner serving a determinate sentence of 15 years or more was not a personal characteristic. The differential treatment of prisoners serving 15 years or more and those who were serving indeterminate sentences and were liable for removal had become anomalies for which there was no justification. It had been recognised that assessment of the risk presented by any individual prisoner, in the application of publicly promulgated criteria, was a task with no political content and one to which the Secretary of State could not claim to bring any superior expertise. A declaration would be made that, to the extent that the 1991 Act ss 46(1) and 50(2) prevented prisoners liable for removal from having their cases reviewed by the Parole Board in the same manner as other longer term prisoners, those sections were incompatible with the Convention art 14 in conjunction with art 5. Accordingly, the first claimant's appeal would be dismissed and the second and third claimants' appeals would be allowed.

R (on the application of Clift) v Secretary of State for the Home Department; R (on the application of Hindawi) v Secretary of State for the Home Department [2006] UKHL 54, [2007] 2 All ER 1 (House of Lords: Lords Bingham of Cornhill and Hope of Craighead, Baroness Hale of Richmond, Lords Carswell and Brown of Eaton-under-Heywood). Decision of Court of Appeal [2004] EWCA Civ 514, [2004] 3 All ER 338 (2004 Abr para 2481) affirmed. Decision of Court of Appeal [2004] EWCA Civ 1309, [2005] 1 WLR 1102 (2004 Abr para 2263) reversed.

1991 Act ss 33(2), (5), 35, 46(1), 50(2) repealed: Crime (Sentences) Act 1997 Sch 6; Criminal Justice Act 2003 Sch 37 Pt 7. SI 1998/3218 lapsed.

2358   Prisoner—release on licence—recall to custody—power to exclude prisoner from hearing

The Parole Board Rules 2004 r 19(2) provides that the panel of the Parole Board must conduct the hearing of a prisoner's case in such manner as it considers most suitable to the clarification of the issues before it and generally to the just handling of the proceedings. The parties are entitled to appear and be heard at the hearing and to take such part in the proceedings as the panel thinks fit, and may hear each other's evidence: r 19(3).

The claimant was serving a life sentence for murder. He was released on licence and, subsequently, had his licence revoked on the ground that he represented a risk of harm to his ex-wife. As a result, the Secretary of State was required to refer the matter to the Parole Board to consider whether to direct the claimant's release. The claimant's former wife was unwilling to give evidence in front of the claimant. Consequently, the panel directed his removal from the room while she gave evidence, although the claimant's legal representative remained so that he saw and heard her give evidence, and later cross-examined her. The Board determined that the claimant ought to remain in custody. He sought judicial review of the decision to exclude him from the hearing, and his application was dismissed. The claimant appealed. *Held*, the procedural code set out in the 2004 Rules r 19 contained the essential features of fairness, but was obviously not designed to deal expressly with every eventuality. Rather, it was designed to confer the widest possible procedural discretion to enable the tribunal to discharge its duties. If an essential witness was too frightened to give evidence in the presence of the prisoner, r 19(2) permitted the panel to exclude the prisoner from the hearing while evidence was given, otherwise it might be deprived of relevant information as to the level of risk of the prisoner. The same approach was to be adopted for the construction of r 19(3). In contrast to the opening words of that provision, which gave the parties the right to appear and be heard, the words which gave the parties the right to hear each other's evidence was preceded by the word 'may'. This indicated that in a particular case the panel could decide that a party would not be able to take a full part in proceedings. Moreover, the requirements of the rule could be met where the rights were afforded to the prisoner's legal representative. The claimant had known what his ex-wife was going to say, he had been able to give instructions to his legal representative who had been present throughout, and his legal representative had been able to challenge the ex-wife's account. His position had been amply protected despite his temporary exclusion, and in all the circumstances he had had a fair hearing. Accordingly, the appeal would be dismissed.

R (on the application of Gardner) v Parole Board [2006] EWCA Civ 1222, [2006] All ER (D) 12 (Sep) (Court of Appeal: Mummery, Tuckey and Wilson LJJ). Decision of Munby J [2005] EWHC 2981 (Admin), [2005] All ER (D) 350 (Dec) (2005 Abr para 2557) affirmed.

2359   Prisoner—release on licence—recall to custody—reasons for recall

The claimant was convicted of manslaughter and sentenced to life imprisonment. He was eventually released on licence, but was recalled to prison pursuant to the Crime (Sentences) Act 1997 s 32. On his recall, the claimant was supplied with the appropriate recall dossier, but it was a further three weeks before he was given the reasons for his recall. An oral hearing into the matter was held, at which it was decided that, although the claimant's recall was fully justified, he should be released. The claimant sought judicial review to challenge various procedural aspects of his recall to custody. The judge decided that, contrary to the European Convention on Human Rights art 5(2), there was impermissible delay in the process by which the claimant was informed of the reasons for his recall and also that there was further such delay, contrary to art 5(4), in the provision of the appropriate recall dossier. However, the judge dismissed the claimant's primary challenge that the entire statutory scheme for recall was incompatible with art 5. On the claimant's appeal against that ruling, *held*, in the interests of the both the public and the offender, the process of achieving a final determination into the validity of the preliminary view formed either by the Secretary of State or the board should be completed as quickly as possible. Without a preliminary view that recall was appropriate, a recall order should not be made. It was difficult to conceive of a process consistent with public safety which could enable a recall order to take effect while the offender remained at large. That would not be a recall at all, it would be an inquiry into the question of whether there should be a recall. Provided that the necessary causal connection existed, the essential requirement was that the remaining parts of the process should take place as rapidly as possible, consistent with doing justice to all the relevant elements of the individual case. Moreover, the fact that there had been breaches of an offender's Convention rights did not render the scheme as a whole incompatible with art 5. The claimant's recall was justified in law by the link between the discretionary sentence of life imprisonment imposed following his conviction for manslaughter and his behaviour during the short period while he was living in the community on licence, which gave rise to realistic concerns for public safety. Accordingly, the appeal would be dismissed.

R (on the application of Hirst) v Secretary of State for the Home Department [2006] EWCA Civ 945, [2006] All ER (D) 59 (Jul) (Court of Appeal: Judge P, Scott Baker and Hallett LJJ). Application 9787/82 Weeks v United Kingdom (1987) 10 EHRR 293, ECtHR (1987 Abr para 1193); and Application 46295/99 Stafford v United Kingdom (2002) 35 EHRR 32, ECtHR (2002 Abr para 2466) considered. Decision of Crane J [2005] EWHC 1480 (Admin), [2005] All ER (D) 223 (Jun) (2005 Abr para 1758) affirmed.

2360   Prisoner—release on licence—recall to custody—transitional arrangements

The applicant was released from prison on licence and became subject to the revocation and recall provisions contained in the Criminal Justice Act 1991 Pt II, as amended. The applicant's licence was revoked by the Home Secretary and the applicant sought judicial review on the ground the Home Secretary lacked the power to make the order to recall him to prison. The application was refused and the applicant appealed on the ground that the system for revocation and recall had not merely been modified by the new legislation, but that, unless saved by transitional provisions, the effect of legislation simultaneously repealing the 1991 Act and bringing the equivalent provisions of the Criminal Justice Act 2003 into force had brought an immediate end to the power of the Home Secretary to revoke his licence, and that the transitional provisions, namely the Criminal Justice Act 2003 (Commencement No 8 and Transitional and Saving Provisions) Order 2005, SI 2005/950, Sch 2 para 23(1), were not effective for that purpose. Held, the only realistic approach was to construe para 23(1) so that the words 'after 4 April 2005' in para 23(1) governed both 23(1)(a), (b) and to regard the words 'falls to be released under the provisions of Pt II of the 1991 Act' as applying to all prisoners released in accordance with the provisions of the 1991 Act, whether the release had taken place before or after 4 April. If so, the 2003 Act s 254 would apply to the applicant, and the Home Secretary was entitled to recall him notwithstanding his release on licence under the 1991 Act Pt II before the relevant date. That interpretation would do justice to the purpose of the legislation. It would maintain a coherent system of release of prisoners on licence and it would safeguard the public interest by providing sanctions against non-compliance by the applicant with his licence conditions, or in the public interest generally. Accordingly, the appeal would be dismissed.

R (on the application of Buddington) v Secretary of State for the Home Department [2006] EWCA Civ 280, [2006] 2 Cr App Rep (S) 715 (Court of Appeal: Sir Igor Judge P and May LJ and Sir Peter Gibson). Decision of Silber and Leveson JJ [2005] EWHC 2198 (QB), [2005] All ER (D) 158 (Oct) affirmed.

2361   Prisoner—release on licence—refusal—directions given by Secretary of State to Parole Board

The Criminal Justice Act 1991 s 32(6) provides that the Secretary of State may give to the Parole Board directions as to the matters to be taken into account by it in discharging its functions.

The applicant was serving a sentence for life imprisonment. He sought judicial review of the Parole Board's decision not to recommend his release after the expiry of his minimum term. In dismissing the claim, the judge made a declaration that the 1991 Act s 32(6) should be construed not to apply to the judicial functions of the Board. He held that the power conferred on the Secretary of State by s 32(6) to give directions to the Board when exercising its judicial functions was incompatible with it acting in an independent judicial capacity. The Secretary of State and the Board appealed. Held, s 32(6) stated that the Secretary of State was to give the Board directions as to matters to be taken into account. Parliament could not have intended to give the Secretary of State power to give mandatory directions to the Board which would conflict with or otherwise usurp the responsibility of the Board to determine the question whether to direct the release of a prisoner in accordance with the law. Rather, s 36(2) empowered the Secretary of State to give directions, so as to provide guidance to the Board as to matters to be taken into account, so far as they were legally relevant, in order to assist the Board to reach a structured decision on the question which it was its duty to decide. Accordingly, the appeal would be allowed.

R (on the application of Girling) v Parole Board [2006] EWCA Civ 1779, [2006] All ER (D) 344 (Dec) (Court of Appeal: Sir Anthony Clarke MR, Sir Igor Judge P and Carnwath LJ). Decision of Paul Walker J [2006] 1 All ER 11 (2005 Abr para 2549) reversed.

2362   Prisoner—release on licence—release due to administrative error—treatment of period spent out of custody

The claimant was convicted of burglary and sentenced to two and a half years' imprisonment, with the sentence to run consecutively with the unexpired period of an existing prison term. Owing to an administrative error, the order for imprisonment stated that the two terms were to run concurrently. The claimant was therefore classified as a short-term prisoner, and he was later released on licence on that basis. The mistake was eventually discovered and an amended order was made which correctly reflected the sentence passed by the judge. The offender was arrested, having been at large for 65 days, and returned to prison. The effect of the amended order was that the offender became a long-term prisoner, so that it was necessary to recalculate the dates on which he would become eligible for parole and release on licence. The prison governor considered that, since the offender had only been released as the result of a mistake, and since his release had been contrary to the relevant statutory provisions, he had been unlawfully at large during the 65 days, which therefore had to be disregarded for the purpose of the calculation. The offender's application for judicial review of that decision was dismissed, and he appealed. *Held*, it was an important principle of the administration of justice that an order of a court of competent jurisdiction made in the exercise of that jurisdiction was valid and binding until it was varied or set aside, either on appeal or in the proper exercise of the court's own jurisdiction. It was the duty of the prison governor to carry out the order of the court in accordance with its terms and the relevant statutory provisions. In those circumstances, having regard to the terms of the only order in existence at time of the offender's release, he had not been unlawfully at large between the date of his release and the date of the amended order. Accordingly, the appeal would be allowed.

R (on the application of Lunn) v Governor of HM Prison Moorland [2006] 1 WLR 2870 (Court of Appeal: Latham, Neuberger and Moore-Bick LJJ). Decision of Queen's Bench Divisional Court [2005] EWHC 2558 (Admin), [2005] All ER (D) 304 (Oct) (2005 Abr para 2559) reversed.

2363   Prisoner—rights and privileges—correspondence with legal advisers—correspondence opened by prison officers

See *Watkins v Secretary of State for the Home Department*, para 2778.

2364   Young offender—secure training centres—custody officer's certificate—suspension

The Criminal Justice and Public Order Act 1994 (Suspension of Custody Officer Certificate) (Amendment) Regulations 2006, SI 2006/1050 (in force on 2 May 2006), amend the 1998 Regulations, SI 1998/1050, so as to clarify that the type of allegation that must be made before a custody's officer's certificate authorising the performance of escort functions or custodial duties may be suspended by the escort monitor or person in charge of a secure training centre, pending a decision of the Secretary of State as to whether to revoke the certificate under the Criminal Justice and Public Order Act 1994 Sch 2 para 4, must be one of misconduct.

2365   Young offender—young offender institution—remand—prevention of commission of imprisonable offence

The claimant, a 16-year-old boy, was refused bail and remanded to a young offender institution after being charged with attempted robbery, on the basis that only such remand would prevent him from committing imprisonable offences. The Children and Young Persons Act 1969 s 23(5) had been modified by the Crime and Disorder Act 1998 s 98(3) to make different provision in relation to 15 or 16 year old males by allowing them to be remanded to a young offender institution where such remand was necessary to protect the public from serious harm from the claimant. The Criminal Justice and Police Act 2001 s 130 amended the unmodified 1969 Act s 23(5) so as to refer to s 23(5AA), which allowed the court to impose a security requirement in respect of the young person to prevent the commission of an imprisonable offence. The 2001 Act inserted s 23(5AA) into the unmodified and modified s 23, but did not amend the modified s 23(5) so as to refer to s 23(5AA). The claimant applied for judicial review on the ground that the judge should have only remanded him to a young offender institution if he was of the opinion that such remand was necessary to protect the public from serious harm from the claimant. *Held*, the 1969 Act s 23(5), as modified and in relation to males of the age of 15 or 16, should be construed to incorporate the condition in s 23(5AA). It was therefore sufficient that the court was of the opinion that only remand to a young offender institution would be adequate to prevent the commission of an imprisonable offence by the claimant. Accordingly, the application would be refused.

R (on the application of M) v Crown Court at Inner London [2006] EWHC 2497 (Admin), [2006] 1 WLR 3406 (Queen's Bench Division: Latham LJ and McCombe J).

PROTECTION OF ENVIRONMENT AND PUBLIC HEALTH

Halsbury's Laws of England (4th edn) vol 38 (2006 Reissue) paras 1–801

Articles

For articles relating to this title please refer to the Table of Articles at the beginning of the Abridgment.

2366   Building—energy efficiency

The Building and Approved Inspectors (Amendment) Regulations 2006, SI 2006/652 (in force in part on 6 April 2006 and in part on 1 October 2006), amend the Building Regulations 2000, SI 2000/2531, by (1) adding new categories of energy efficiency requirements in relation to building work; (2) providing that the new energy efficiency requirements need only comply with specified requirements concerning the conservation of fuel and power; (3) requiring persons carrying out renovation or replacement work on the fabric of a building to meet specified requirements; (4) requiring work to be carried out to a building which has ceased to be exempt from the energy efficiency requirements; (5) requiring work on buildings to meet specified energy efficiency requirements; (6) removing local authorities' power to dispense or relax certain pollution and energy efficiency requirements; (7) allowing a person proposing to carry out specified types of emergency repairs to give a building notice after starting work where it is impractical to do so beforehand; (8) making provision in relation to the energy performance of buildings; (9) making provision in relation to pressure testing of new buildings; and (10) requiring a person carrying out the work to provide the local authority with a notice that specifies the target carbon dioxide emission rate for the building and the calculated emission rate for the building as constructed. The order also amends the Building (Approved Inspectors etc) Regulations 2000, SI 2000/2532, by making provision in relation to (a) self-certification schemes for building work; (b) pressure testing of new buildings; and (c) carbon dioxide emission rate calculations. Specified provisions of the Building Regulations 2000 are applied to educational buildings and buildings of statutory undertakers.

2367   Clean Neighbourhoods and Environment Act 2005—commencement

The Clean Neighbourhoods and Environment Act 2005 (Commencement No 2, Transitional Provisions and Savings) (England and Wales) (Amendment) Order 2006, SI 2006/1002, amends the Clean Neighbourhoods and Environment Act 2005 (Commencement No 2, Transitional Provisions and Savings) (England and Wales) Order 2005, SI 2005/2896, so as to limit certain savings provisions.

The Clean Neighbourhoods and Environment Act 2005 (Commencement No 1, Transitional and Savings Provisions) (England) Order 2006, SI 2006/795, brings into force, in relation to England, (1) on 14 March 2006, ss 6 (for certain purposes), 8 (for certain purposes), 9, 19(1) (in part), (6), 55 (for certain purposes), 56, 57 (for certain purposes), 59 (for certain purposes), 60 (for certain purposes), 66, 67, 74 (for certain purposes), 75 (for certain purposes), 80, 81, 83 (so far as not already in force), 84 (for certain purposes), 96 (for certain purposes), 97, 98, Sch 1 para 12(1); (2) on 1 April 2006, s 2; and (3) on 6 April 2006, 6 (so far as not already in force), 7, 8 (so far as not already in force), 10, 19 (so far as not already in force), 20–25, 28, 29, 30(1), 31, 34, 37 (for certain purposes), 38, 45, 48, 50, 52, 55 (so far as not already in force), 57 (so far as not already in force), 58, 59 (so far as not already in force), 60 (so far as not already in force), 61–65, 69–73, 74 (so far as not already in force), 75 (so far as not already in force), 76–79, 82, 84 (for certain purposes), 86, 96 (so far as not already in force), 99–103, Sch 1 paras 2, 7(2)(a), (3), 8(2), 12(2), (5), (6) and certain repeals in Sch 5.

The Clean Neighbourhoods and Environment Act 2005 (Commencement No 2) (England) Order 2006, SI 2006/1361, brings into force, on 4 August 2006, s 104, Sch 5 Pt 10, in so far as they amend the Environmental Protection Act 1990 s 78L so far as they relate to appeals against remediation notices served by a local authority in England or by the Environment Agency in relation to land in England.

The Clean Neighbourhoods and Environment Act 2005 (Commencement No 3) (England) Order 2006, SI 2006/2006, brings s 84 into force, so far as it is not already in force, in relation to England on 1 October 2006.

The Clean Neighbourhoods and Environment Act 2005 (Commencement No 4) Order 2006, SI 2006/656, brings into force (1) on 7 March 2006, s 49(1) (2) (for certain purposes), (3), (6) (for certain purposes); and (2) on 6 April 2006, ss 49(2) (so far as not already in force), (6) (so far as not already in force), (8) (for certain purposes), (9), 106 (in part), Sch 4 para 3(1)–(4), (6) (in part).

The Clean Neighbourhoods and Environment Act 2005 (Commencement No 1 and Savings) (Wales) Order 2006, SI 2006/768, brings into force, in relation to Wales, on 16 March 2006, ss 47, 53, Sch 4 para 4, certain repeals in Sch 5 Pt 4 and, so far as confers on the National Assembly a power or imposes a duty to make or make provision by regulations or orders, or to give directions or give or issue guidance, or make provision with respect to the exercise of any such power or performance of any such duty, ss 2, 6, 8, 10, 13, 17, 19, 20, 24, 28, 30, 37, 38, 45, 46, 48, 52, 55–60, 67, 73–75, 82, 96–98, 101, 103, 104.

The Clean Neighbourhoods and Environment Act 2005 (Commencement No 2, Transitional Provisions and Savings) (Wales) Order 2006, SI 2006/2797, brings into force on 27 October 2006, in relation to Wales, ss 11, 12, 13 (so far as not already in force), 15, 16, 17 (so far as not already in force), 34, 37 (in part), 50, 56 (so far as not already in force), 66, 67 (so far as not already in force), 80, 81, 83 (so far as not already in force), 84 (in part), 86, 99, 100, Sch 1 paras 2, 7(2)(a), (3), 8(2), 12(2), (5), (6), and certain repeals in Sch 5 Pt 1. The commencement of other provisions is related to regulations which have not yet been made. Transitional provisions and savings are also made.

For a summary of the Act, see 2005 Abr para 1270. See also the commencement table in the title STATUTES.

2368 Climate Change and Sustainable Energy Act 2006

See para 1415.

2369 Contaminated land—liability to remediate—statutory successor to actual contaminator

The defendant body decided that the claimant gas company was an 'appropriate person' for the purposes of the Environmental Protection Act 1990 Pt IIA (ss 78A–78YC) in respect of contaminated land on which a gas works formerly stood. The claimant was the statutory successor to the land on which the contamination had originally occurred. The effect of the decision was that the claimant was liable for a proportion of the costs of remediating the contamination. The claimant applied for judicial review of the decision, contending that 'person' in Pt IIA did not extend to any body which succeeded to the liabilities of the undertaking which had actually caused or knowingly permitted the contaminating substances to be in, on or under the land. *Held*, on a purposive construction, the provisions of Pt IIA imposed a liability for remediating contamination on a person where contaminating substances had been brought onto land by his statutory predecessors. Parliament's intention was that primary responsibility for contamination should rest with the original polluter. In normal cases, where the company responsible for the contamination had been dissolved and its assets sold or distributed to other persons, the original polluter could not be found for the purposes of the 1990 Act. However, that was not the case where assets, rights and liabilities were transferred under a clear chain of statutory provisions which ensured continuity. In the circumstances, the defendant had been entitled to find that the claimant was an appropriate person within Pt IIA. Accordingly, the application would be dismissed.

R (on the application of National Grid Gas plc) v Environment Agency [2006] EWHC 1083 (Admin), [2007] 1 All ER 1163 (Queen's Bench Division: Forbes J).

2370 Contaminated land—radioactivity—England

The Radioactive Contaminated Land (Modification of Enactments) (England) Regulations 2006, SI 2006/1379 (in force on 4 August 2006), make provision for the Environmental Protection Act 1990 Pt 2A (ss 78A–78YC) to have effect with modification for the purpose of the identification and remediation of radioactive contaminated land other than in circumstances where the operator of a nuclear installation is liable under the Nuclear Installations Act 1965, or in related circumstances. In particular, the regulations (1) modify various definitions; (2) ensure that the local authority's duty of inspection only applies in relation to land that it has reasonable grounds for believing may be contaminated; (3) restrict the discretion of an enforcing authority to determine what is reasonable by way of remediation so as to require the enforcing authority to weigh up the benefit of any intervention against the health detriment and costs arising from such intervention and maximise the benefit from such intervention; (4) require the enforcing authority to carry out remediation itself in certain circumstances; (5) provide that the 1990 Act Pt 2A does not apply where land is contaminated land by reason of substances being in or under the land, in so far as by reason of that presence damage to any property occurs in breach of certain duties under the 1965 Act, or in related circumstances; and (6) ensure that the powers of the Environment Agency or local authority extend to their functions under the 1990 Act Pt 2A as it applies to harm attributable to radioactivity.

2371 Contaminated land—radioactivity—Wales

The Radioactive Contaminated Land (Modification of Enactments) (Wales) Regulations 2006, SI 2006/2988 (in force in part on 16 November 2006 and in part on 10 December 2006), apply in relation to Wales, and make provision for the Environmental Protection Act 1990 Pt 2A (ss 78A–78YC) to have effect with modification for the purpose of the identification and remediation of radioactive contaminated land other than in circumstances where the operator of a nuclear installation is liable under the Nuclear Installations Act 1965, or in related circumstances. In particular, the regulations (1) modify various definitions; (2) ensure that the local authority's duty of inspection only applies in relation to land that it has reasonable grounds for believing may be contaminated; (3) restrict the discretion of an enforcement authority to determine what is reasonable by way of remediation so as to require the enforcement authority to weigh up the benefit of any intervention against the health detriment and costs arising from such intervention and maximise the benefit from such intervention; (4) require the enforcing authority to carry out remediation itself in certain circumstances; (5) provide that the 1990 Act Pt 2A does not apply where land is contaminated land by reason of substances being in, on or under the land, in so far as by reason of that presence damage to any property occurs in breach of certain duties under the 1965 Act, or in related circumstances; and (6) ensure that the powers of the Environment Agency or local authority under the Environment Act 1995 s 108 extend to their functions under the 1990 Act Pt 2A as it applies to harm attributable to radioactivity.

2372 Contaminated land—remediation notices—England

The Contaminated Land (England) Regulations 2006, SI 2006/1380 (in force on 4 August 2006), replace the 2000 Regulations, SI 2000/227 and the 2001 Regulations, SI 2001/663, and (1) identify those categories of site, known as special sites, in relation to which the Environment Agency is the enforcing authority; (2) provide for the content and services of copies of remediation notices which are notices served by a local authority or the Environment Agency specifying what is to be done by way of remediation and the time for taking any action; (3) make provision in relation to the compensation which is to be paid to a person who grants, or joins in granting, rights of entry and other rights required to enable a person to comply with a remediation notice; (4) make provision with respect to appeals against remediation notices, including grounds of appeal and the procedure to be followed; and (5) prescribe the particulars of matters which are required to be placed on a register maintained by local authorities or, in the case of special sites, by the Environment Agency.

2373 Contaminated land—remediation notices—Wales

The Contaminated Land (Wales) Regulations 2006, SI 2006/2989 (in force on 10 December 2006), which apply in relation to Wales, replace the 2001 Regulations, SI 2001/2197, and set out further provisions relating to the identification and remediation of contaminated land under the Environmental Protection Act 1990 Pt 2A (ss 78A–78YC). In particular, the regulations (1) make provision for an additional description of contaminated land that is required to be designated as a special site: that is land which is contaminated land as a result of radioactive substances in, on or under that land; (2) remove provisions relating to appeals against remediation notices to a magistrates' court; (3) identify those categories of site (known as 'special sites') for which the Environment Agency is to be the enforcing authority; local authorities are the enforcing authority in relation to any other type of site; (4) provide for the content and service of copies of 'remediation notices' which are notices served by a local authority or the Environment Agency specifying what is to be done by way of remediation and the time within which any action must be taken; (5) make provision in relation to the compensation which is to be paid to a person who grants, or joins in granting, rights of entry and other rights required to enable a person to comply with a remediation notice; (6) make provision with respect to appeals against remediation notices, including the grounds of appeal and the procedure to be followed; and (7) prescribe the particulars of matters which are required under the 1990 Act s 78R to be placed on a register maintained by local authorities or, in the case of special sites, by the Environment Agency.

2374 Environment Act 1995—commencement

The Environment Act 1995 (Commencement No 23) (England and Wales) Order 2006, SI 2006/934, brings into force, on 15 May 2006, s 120(1) (in part), (3) (in part), Sch 22 paras 27(b), (c), 88 and 95. For a summary of the Act, see 1995 Abr para 1289. For details of commencement, see commencement table in the title STATUTES.

2375 Environmental impact assessment—agriculture

The Environmental Impact Assessment (Agriculture) (England) (No 2) Regulations 2006, SI 2006/2522 (in force in part on 30 September 2006 and in part on 10 October 2006), implement EC Council Directives 85/337 and 1992/43. In particular, the regulations (1) set out the types of projects which are excluded from the scope of the regulations; (2) enable the Secretary of State to exclude certain projects from the scope of the regulations; (3) prohibit any person from beginning or carrying out certain uncultivated land projects or restructuring projects unless that person has obtained a screening decision allowing the project to go ahead; (4) set out how to calculate the appropriate threshold for a project; (5) set out provisions relating to the service of screening notices which allow Natural England to remove the application thresholds from areas of land; (6) set out what must be included in an application for a screening decision, and allow Natural England to ask for further information; (7) make provision for the factors to be taken into consideration by Natural England when it makes a screening decision, and the procedures relating to a screening decision; (8) prohibit a person from beginning or carrying out a project likely to have significant effects on the environment unless he has first obtained consent from Natural England; (9) provide for the procedure by which Natural England can give an applicant an opinion on the scope of an environmental statement; (10) set out the duties of consultation bodies from whom information is sought in connection with applications and scoping opinions; (11) provide that applications for consent must include an environmental statement and set out consultation procedures relating to the application; (12) set out further procedures relating to any further information that is required; (13) prescribe the procedures to be followed where a significant project in England might affect another EEA State, and a significant project in another EEA State might affect England; (14) set out the factors to be taken into consideration when Natural England makes a consent decision, including the situation where a project is likely to affect a European Site, and provide for the timing of consent decisions; (15) specify the conditions which must be applied to a consent and set out the procedures following the consent decision; (16) make provision on the treatment of transborder projects; (17) make provision for the situation where, following a decision permitting the commencement of a project, the relevant land becomes a European site; (18) make it an offence to begin or carry out a project without obtaining a screening decision or a consent decision where these are required; (19) make it an offence to breach a condition of consent and to procure a decision by deception or the supply of false or misleading information or documents; (20) enable Natural England to (a) issue stop notices and make it an offence to contravene a stop notice; and (b) issue remediation notices requiring a person in breach of the regulations to return his land to the condition it was in before the breach, or to good environmental condition and make it an offence to fail to comply with a remediation notice without reasonable excuse; (21) provide for prosecutions to be brought within six months of the date sufficient evidence comes to the prosecutor's knowledge, but they must be brought within two years of the date on which the offence is committed; (22) confer powers on persons authorised by the Secretary of State or Natural England to enforce the regulations; and (23) make provision in respect of notices and decisions given under the regulations. SI 2006/2362 is revoked.

2376   Environmental impact assessment—land drainage improvement works

The Environmental Impact Assessment (Land Drainage Improvement Works) (Amendment) Regulations 2006, SI 2006/618 (in force on 30 March 2006), amend the 1999 Regulations, SI 1999/1783, so as to clarify that drainage bodies may substitute, for one of the notices required to be placed in at least two newspapers, a notice on the site of the proposed improvement works.

2377   Environmental impact assessment—water resources

The Water Resources (Environmental Impact Assessment) (England and Wales) (Amendment) Regulations 2006, SI 2006/3124 (in force on 31 December 2006), amend the 2003 Regulations, SI 2003/164, and implement amendments to EEC Council Directive 85/337 on the assessment of the effects of certain public and private projects on the environment. In particular, the regulations (1) provide that projects involving abstraction of water will only fall within the scope of the 2003 Regulations where the abstraction is one which requires a licence under the Water Resources Act 1991; where the amount abstracted in any 24 hours in aggregate exceeds 20 cubic metres; (2) provide that notices publicising an environmental statement and further information must be published by the Environment Agency on its website, must specify any other arrangements that have been made for informing the public of an application and must also make available to the public other information which only becomes available to it after it has published the notice; and (3) require the Environment Agency to publish, with a notice of its decision on the application, information regarding the public participation process that has taken place, any right to challenge the decision, and the procedures for doing so.

2378   Environmental offences—fixed penalties—England

The Environmental Offences (Fixed Penalties) (Miscellaneous Provisions) Regulations 2006, SI 2006/783 (in force on 6 April 2006), prescribe the ranges within which the amounts of certain fixed penalties that are capable of being specified by a local authority are required to fall They also prescribe the minimum amount of fixed penalty that a local authority may treat as full payment where that lesser amount is paid within 14 days. Where a local authority has been categorised as either 'excellent' or 'good', certain fixed penalty receipts may be used for any functions of that authority. Before a person can be an authorised officer of a parish council for the purposes of giving certain fixed penalty notices, he must successfully complete an approved training course.

2379   Environmental offences—fixed penalty receipts—England

The Environmental Offences (Use of Fixed Penalty Receipts) Regulations 2006, SI 2006/1334 (in force on 6 April 2006), (1) provide that any fixed penalty receipts paid to (a) an authority, other than a parish council; or (b) a primary authority, in pursuance of notices issued under specified legislation, may, for as long as such an authority is categorised as either 'excellent' or 'good', be used for any functions of that authority; (2) provide that in the event that such an authority ceases to be categorised as excellent or good, it may continue to use its fixed penalty receipts for any of its functions for one year; and (3) make provision for parish councils.

2380   Environmental protection—dangerous substances and preparations—control

The Controls on Dangerous Substances and Preparations Regulations 2006, SI 2006/3311 (in force on 7 January 2007), give effect to restrictions on the marketing and use of certain of the dangerous substances and preparations set out in EEC Council Directive 76/769, by (1) listing the substances and preparations subject to marketing and usage restrictions; (2) providing (a) that the enforcement authorities, the Environment Agency, the Scottish Environment Protection Agency and the Department of the Environment for Northern Ireland, will enforce the restrictions; (b) that the enforcement authorities will have powers of entry, inspection and seizure, in addition to powers issued under a warrant and in relation to notices, and may appoint persons to act on their behalf in respect of enforcement; and (c) for the enforcement authorities to bring civil proceedings instead of proceedings for offences where the latter would afford an ineffectual remedy; (3) making it an offence to contravene the specified restrictions on the marketing and use of the dangerous substances, or cause or permit another person to do so, and setting out the penalties in respect of the offences; (4) setting out offences in relation to the intentional obstruction of, or failure to comply without reasonable excuse with, an authorised person in exercise of his powers or duties, and specifying the penalties in respect of the offences; and (5) providing (a) that the court has the power to order a person to remedy matters where that person has been convicted of an offence; (b) that a person can appeal against an enforcement notice or a prohibition notice; and (c) the information that must be included in relation to the use of leaded paint where its use is permitted. The Control of Pollution (Anti-Fouling Paints and Treatments) Regulations 1987, SI 1987/783, the Environmental Protection (Controls on Injurious Substances) Regulations 1992, SI 1992/31 and SI 1992/1583, the Environmental Protection (Controls on Injurious Substances) Regulations, SI 1993/1 (as amended) and SI 1993/1643, the Environmental Protection (Controls on Dangerous Substances) Regulations 2003, SI 2003/3274, and Controls on Pentabromodiphenyl Ether and Octobromophenyl Ether SI 2004/1816 and SI 2004/3278 are revoked.

2381   Environmental protection—financial assistance

The Financial Assistance for Environmental Purposes Order 2006, SI 2006/1735 (in force on 31 July 2006), further amends the Environmental Protection Act 1990 s 153(1) so as to give financial assistance to, or for the purposes of, the World Summit on Sustainable Development Implementation Fund ('WIF'), and to, or for the purposes of, the Envirowise Programme in relation to its activities in England.

2382   Environmental protection—gaseous and particulate pollutants—agricultural or forestry tractors

The Agricultural or Forestry Tractors (Emission of Gaseous and Particulate Pollutants) (Amendment) Regulations 2006, SI 2006/2393 (in force on 12 October 2006), amend the 2002 Regulations, SI 2002/1891, in order to implement European Commission Directive 2005/13 in relation to the entry into service of tractors and tractor engines. Specifically, the regulations (1) alter the categories of engines, relevant dates and limit values; (2) revise various definitions; (3) remove the exemption for replacement engines; (4) create an exemption with regard to engines placed on the market under a flexibility scheme; (5) prevent requirements from being imposed retroactively; (6) apply some requirements to tractors as well as to their engines; (7) clarify that powers of enforcement available in relation to engines are also available in relation to tractors; and (8) set out the requirements for the United Kingdom flexibility scheme.

2383   Environmental protection—gaseous and particulate pollutants—non-road mobile machinery

The Non-Road Mobile Machinery (Emission of Gaseous and Particulate Pollutants) (Amendment) Regulations 2006, SI 2006/29 (in force on 17 February 2006), further amend the 1999 Regulations, SI 1999/1053, so as to implement European Parliament and EC Council Directive 2004/26. In particular, the regulations (1) make changes to the list of engines to which the regulations apply; (2) provide for compression ignition engines to be dealt with separately from spark ignition engines; (3) make provision in relation to compression ignition engines to determine which category a compression ignition engine falls into and how to determine the limit values that apply to emissions of gaseous and particulate pollutants from the engine; (4) set out the requirements that a compression ignition engine must meet before it can be placed on the market; (5) specify the circumstances in which engines which do not comply with some or all of those requirements may nevertheless be placed on the market, and where a type approval certificate from the UK competent authority is needed, the requirements that need to be met before the certificate will be issued; (6) exclude certain engines from provisions relating to replacement engines; (7) make provision in relation to the EEA; and (8) prohibit the Secretary of State from issuing a Declaration of Compliance with the technical requirements applying to inland waterway vessels in any case where the engine or engines installed in a vessel do not comply with EC Directive 1997/68.

2384 Environmental protection—hazardous substances—ozone depleting substances

The Ozone Depleting Substances (Qualifications) Regulations 2006, SI 2006/1510 (in force on 10 July 2006), give effect to EC European Parliament and Council Regulation 2037/2000 on substances that deplete the ozone layer. In particular, the regulations (1) define various terms; (2) make it an offence for a person to carry out relevant work involving controlled substances or work with methyl bromide unless he is competent to do so; (3) contain provision making it an offence for an employer to employ a person to carry out relevant work or work with methyl bromide unless that person is competent to do so; and (4) make provision for the appointment of authorised persons to enforce the regulations. SI 2002/528 is amended.

2385 Environmental protection—hazardous substances—restriction of use—electrical and electronic equipment

The Restriction of the Use of Certain Hazardous Substances in Electrical and Electronic Equipment Regulations 2006, SI 2006/1463 (in force on 1 July 2006), replace the 2005 Regulations, SI 2005/2748, which implemented EC European Parliament and Council Directive 2002/95 on the restriction of the use of certain hazardous substances in electrical and electronic Equipment, as amended by EC Commission Decision 2005/818. The regulations incorporate further amendments to Directive 2002/95 by EC Commission Decisions 2005/717, 2005/747 and 2006/310. Specifically, the regulations (1) apply to specified new electrical and electronic equipment, and to electric light bulbs and luminaries for use in households that are put on the market on or after 1 July 2006; (2) provide that new equipment put on the market must not contain more than the permissible maximum concentration values of hazardous substances; (3) set out the requirements relating to technical documentation; (4) provide that the Secretary of State has the duty of enforcing the regulations and may appoint any person to act on his behalf; (5) provide that the Secretary of State has the power to serve a compliance notice and make test purchases; (6) provide for offences, penalties and defences; and (7) amend the Enterprise Act 2002 (Part 9 Restrictions on Disclosure of Information) (Specification) Order 2004, SI 2004/693, by substituting the reference to the 2005 Regulations for a reference to these regulations.

2386 Environmental protection—household waste—duty of care—Wales

The Waste (Household Waste Duty of Care) (Wales) Regulations 2006, SI 2006/123 (in force on 26 January 2006), implement EEC Council Directive 75/442 art 8 on waste as respects an occupier of domestic property in relation to the household waste produced on the property. The regulations amend the Environmental Protection Act 1990 s 34, so as to extend a duty on an occupier of domestic property in Wales as respects the household waste produced on the property to take all such measures available to him, as are reasonable in the circumstances, to secure that any transfer by him of household waste produced on the property is only to an authorised person, or to a person for authorised transport purposes. The regulations also make consequential amendments to the Controlled Waste Regulations 1992, SI 1992/588, reg 2.

2387 Environmental protection—Isles of Scilly

The Environmental Protection Act 1990 (Isles of Scilly) Order 2006, SI 2006/1381 (in force on 4 August 2006), applies, to the Isles of Scilly (1) the Environmental Protection Act 1990 Pt 2A (ss 78A–78YC) in relation to harm attributable to radioactivity possessed by any substance; and (2) the Environment Agency's powers under the Environment Act 1995 ss 108–110 in relation to functions under the 1990 Act Pt 2A.

2388 Environmental stewardship—England

See para 150.

2389 Finance Act 2006

See para 2465.

2390 Landfill tax—administration

The Landfill Tax (Amendment) Regulations 2006, SI 2006/865 (in force on 1 April 2006), further amend the 1996 Regulations, SI 1996/1527, so as to increase the maximum credit that landfill site operators may claim against their annual landfill tax liability in the scheme whereby operators are entitled to credit based on the contributions they give to approved bodies with objects concerned with the environment.

2391 Natural Environment and Rural Communities Act 2006

See para 2109.

2392 Noise—environmental noise—assessment and management—England

The Environmental Noise (England) Regulations 2006, SI 2006/2238 (in force on 1 October 2006), which apply in relation to England only, implement European Parliament and EC Council Directive 2002/49 relating to the assessment and management of environmental noise. The regulations (1) require the Secretary of State to (a) identify the noise sources for which strategic noise maps must be made; (b) make strategic noise maps for agglomerations, major roads, major railways and major airports designated under the Civil Aviation Act 1982 s 80; and (c) from time to time, and whenever a major development occurs, review (and if necessary, revise) strategic noise maps; (2) require airport operators to make strategic noise maps for airports that are not designated under the 1982 Act; (3) provide that strategic noise maps must be made for (a) all non-designated major airports; and (b) noise in agglomerations arising from any other airports, if aircraft noise exceeds specified levels; (4) prescribe the noise indicators and supplementary noise indicators that must be used in making the strategic noise maps; (5) set out the assessment methods to be used in calculating the values of noise indicators, which vary according to the noise source; (6) require the Secretary of State to identify quiet areas in first round agglomerations and in agglomerations; (7) provide that action plans must be drawn up in 2008 and in 2013, following the preparation of the relevant strategic noise maps; (8) require the Secretary of State to publish guidance on how the priorities in action plans should be identified, and to compile and publish a consolidated noise map; (9) set out the requirements for action plans; (10) require the Secretary of State to (a) draw up action plans for places near to major roads and major railways, and for first round agglomerations and agglomerations; and (b) review (and revise, if necessary) the action plans every five years, or sooner if a major development occurs; (11) require airport operators to (a) draw up action plans in relation to major airports and other airports if aircraft noise exceeds specified levels; (b) review (and revise, if necessary) the action plans every five years, or sooner if a major development occurs; (c) submit the plan to the Secretary of State for adoption; (12) specify the public participation required during the preparation and revision of action plans; (13) require public authorities to treat action plans as policy in so far as the action plan identifies them as being responsible for a particular action; (14) permit public authorities to depart from such policies in specified circumstances; (15) require competent authorities in England to cooperate with their counterparts in Northern Ireland, Scotland and Wales when necessary in order to meet their obligations in relation to the assessment and management of environmental noise; (16) set out the mechanism by which the Secretary of State adopts strategic noise maps and action plans; (17) empower the Secretary of State to require competent authorities to provide information in relation to their obligations or to step in and carry out the functions of competent authorities under specified circumstances; (18) give the Secretary of State power to reclaim certain expenses from competent authorities; (19) set out requirements for the publication of strategic noise maps, a consolidated noise map and action plans prepared by airport operators and approved by the Secretary of State; and (20) require competent authorities to have regard to any guidance published by the Secretary of State.

2393 Noise—environmental noise—assessment and management—Wales

The Environmental Noise (Wales) Regulations 2006, SI 2006/2629 (in force on 4 October 2006), implement EC European Parliament and Council Directive 2002/49, relating to the assessment and management of environmental noise. The regulations (1) require the National Assembly for Wales to identify noise sources for which strategic noise maps must be made, and to make strategic noise maps for agglomerations, major roads, major railways and major airports designated under the Civil Aviation Act 1982; (2) require airport operators to make strategic noise maps for airports that are not designated under the 1982 Act; (3) require the Assembly to review strategic noise maps from time to time and whenever a major development occurs; (4) specify which noise indicators and supplementary noise indicators must be used in making strategic noise maps; (5) set out assessment methods to be used in calculating values of noise indicators; (6) require the Assembly to identify quiet areas in agglomerations; (7) require the Assembly to publish guidance on how priorities in action plans should be identified, and set out requirements for action plans; (8) require the Assembly to draw up action plans for places near to major roads, major railways, and for agglomerations, and to review, and revise, if necessary, the action plans every five years or sooner if a major development occurs; (9) require airport operators to draw up action plans in relation to major airports, and to review, and revise, if necessary, the action plans every five years or sooner if a major development occurs and submit it to the assembly for adoption; (10) specify the public participation required during preparation and revision of action plans; (11) require public authorities to treat action plans as policy insofar as the action plan identifies them as being responsible for a particular action; (12) set out the mechanism by which the Assembly adopts strategic noise maps and action plans; (13) confer a power on the Assembly to require competent authorities to provide information in relation to their obligations or to carry out functions of competent authorities under specified circumstances; (14) confer a power on the Assembly to reclaim expenses from competent authorities; (15) set out requirements for the publication of strategic noise maps and action plans; and (16) require competent authorities to have regard to any guidance published by the Assembly.

2394   Pollution—air pollution—Emissions Trading Scheme—carbon dioxide emissions—allocation of allowances—fairness

The claimant company, a global producer of cement, operated under strict allowances for the carbon dioxide emissions of its cement plants. The allocation of those allowances was governed by the UK National Allocation Plan which was made by the defendant pursuant to the scheme established under EC Council Directive 2003/87. Following a consultation exercise, the defendant replaced the 'first year of operations rule' with the 'commissioning rule', which resulted in a reduced allocation to the claimant's plant. The claimant applied for judicial review of that decision, submitting that a new rule could have been formulated to treat all relevant sectors consistently, and that a special rule was not needed, particularly as the commissioning rule applied only to three installations. It argued that the new allocation infringed the EC principle of equality or non-discrimination. The defendant contended that it had been entitled to replace the commissioning rule even though it had little material to objectively justify that decision. *Held*, provided that a rule was capable of applying to all installations in a particular sector which justified different treatment, it would not matter that only a limited number of installations would benefit from that rule. The desire to simplify, to treat all sectors consistently, and to retain only essential rules, provided no justification for a rule which treated two unlike sectors in the same way. The desire for 'administrative tidiness' provided no justification for discrimination. However, where a rule treating two sectors differently had been adopted for a pilot phase of a scheme on the basis of very limited material by way of objective justification, the revocation of that rule would require commensurately little by way of objective justification. The material that the defendant had relied on as justification for not continuing the commissioning rule, although not extensive, had been more substantial than the material which persuaded the defendant that the adoption of the original rule was justified. The introduction of a new allocation rule had not infringed the EC principle of equality or non-discrimination. Accordingly, the application would be dismissed.

R (on the application of Cemex UK Cement Ltd) v Department for Environment Food and Rural Affairs [2006] EWHC 3207 (Admin), [2006] All ER (D) 181 (Dec) (Queen's Bench Division: Sullivan J).

2395   Pollution—air pollution—partial prohibition of heavy goods vehicles—free movement of goods

See Case C-320/03 *EC Commission v Austria*, para 925.

2396   Pollution—control—water—protection against agricultural nitrate pollution

The Protection of Water Against Agricultural Nitrate Pollution (England and Wales) (Amendment) Regulations 2006, SI 2006/1289 (in force on 1 June 2006), implement, in part, EC European Parliament and Council Directive 2003/35 art 2 on public participation in respect of drawing up certain plans and programmes relating to the environment. In particular, the regulations (1) further amend the 1996 Regulations, SI 1996/888, so as to (a) require provision to be made for public participation in the preparation, review or revision of any action programme in England or Wales; and (b) require the Secretary of State to make provision where an action programme relates to a nitrate vulnerable zone in England, and require the National Assembly for Wales to also make such a provision in regards to Wales; and (2) amend the Nitrate Vulnerable Zones (Additional Designations) (England) (No 2) Regulations 2002, SI 2002/2614, so as to ensure that the new public participation obligations apply in relation to action programmes for the nitrate vulnerable zones in England.

2397   Pollution—greenhouse gas—emissions—trading scheme

The Greenhouse Gas Emissions Trading Scheme (Amendment) Regulations 2006, SI 2006/737 (in force on 6 April 2006), amend the 2005 Regulations, SI 2005/925, so as to (1) provide a mechanism for installations which began operating before 2004 but which have not received an allocation of allowances, to apply for an allocation; (2) add to the types of charges which may be included in a charging scheme made by the Secretary of State relating to offshore installations; (3) confer a power on the regulator to delay the allocation of allowances each year to an operator who has been allocated allowances from either the new entrant reserve or the late installation reserve, where certain conditions in the approved national allocation plan are fulfilled; (4) require the payment of a fee by a verifier or an organisation which wishes to be appointed as an additional authorised representative to be included in the registry; (5) vary the circumstances in which a holder of a person holding account is required to pay a fee when nominating a person to be one of his authorised representatives; (6) permit the use of information held or collected for the purposes of the regulations to be used for the purpose of preparing and publishing energy and emissions statistics; and (7) make a number of new provisions relating to the surrender and revocation of greenhouse gas emissions permits and payment of subsistence fees.

2398   Pollution—prevention and control—permits—England

The Pollution Prevention and Control (England and Wales) (Amendment) (England) Regulations 2006, SI 2006/2311 (in force on 1 October 2006), which apply in relation to England only, further amend the Pollution Prevention and Control (England and Wales) Regulations 2000, SI 2000/1973, by (1) adding motor vehicle refuelling activities to the list of activities that require a permit; (2) clarifying that incineration incidentally in the course of burning of landfill gas is not subject to permission; and (3) making transitional provision in connection with the exemption of certain operators of coin-operated dry cleaning machines.

2399 Pollution—prevention and control—permits—landfill site—condition prohibiting emission of odours

The respondent ran a landfill facility. A condition of the respondent's pollution prevention and control permit prohibited the emission of odours at levels which were likely to cause pollution outside the permitted installation boundary, as perceived by an authorised officer of the Environment Agency. The Agency preferred an information which alleged that the respondent had failed to comply with the condition. The district judge held that the words 'as perceived by an officer of the agency' rendered the offence dependent on the subjective opinion of an authorised officer, and thus undermined clarity and foreseeability. He ruled that the condition offended the principles of certainty and had the effect of usurping the fact-finding and adjudicative roles of the court by bestowing on an authorised officer the functions of establishing the relevant facts and obliging the court to convict whenever it was satisfied that the officer had honestly perceived those facts. The Agency appealed by way of case stated. *Held*, the closing words of the condition required evidence from the authorised officer as a necessary ingredient of the case put against the respondent. The condition did not limit the jurisdiction of the court on the basis of all the evidence presented to it to decide whether the odours emitted were at a level offending against the condition, and did not offend against the principles of clarity required by the criminal law. The power and duty of the court to form its own view on the evidence before it was not usurped. Accordingly, the appeal would be allowed.

Environment Agency v Biffa Waste Services Ltd [2006] All ER (D) 155 (Dec) (Queen's Bench Division: Pill LJ and Tugendhat J).

2400 Pollution—prevention and control—permits—Wales

The Pollution Prevention and Control (England and Wales) (Amendment) (Wales) Regulations 2006, SI 2006/2802 (in force on 25 October 2006), further amend the Pollution Prevention and Control (England and Wales) Regulations 2000, SI 2000/1973, by (1) increasing the maximum penalty a magistrates' court may impose in respect of specified offences; (2) adding motor vehicle refuelling activities to the list of activities that require a permit; (3) clarifying that incineration incidentally in the course of burning of landfill gas is not subject to permission; and (4) providing for the exemption of certain operators of coin operated dry cleaning machines who choose not to make an application for a permit before 31 October 2006 from the permit requirements of EC Solvent Emissions Directive 1999/13, on the basis that the operators agree to cease carrying out operations that fall within the scope of that Directive at the installation before 31 October 2007.

2401 Sewers and drains—public sewer—discharge of trade effluent into public sewers—authorisation

The respondent company was charged with discharging trade effluent into the public sewer without authorisation, contrary to the Water Industry Act 1991 s 118(5). The respondent accepted that the discharges had been made, but argued that it had been authorised by an oral agreement with the appellant water and sewerage undertaker's predecessor. The respondent argued that any such agreement had been terminated by a letter giving the respondent three months' notice to that effect. The judge found that there was an agreement between the parties and that the agreement had not been terminated because three months' notice was unreasonable. The judge refused to make detailed findings as to the terms of the agreement and the appellant appealed. *Held*, the respondent had the evidential burden of establishing the existence of an agreement and, having done so, it was for the appellant to prove that the discharges were not in accordance with that agreement. In the present case, the appellant had not obtained from the judge the findings that would require a guilty verdict. An acquittal was justified on the findings that had been made. Further, it was not clear what kind of finding as to the terms of the agreement could touch on the question of adequate notice. Although the judge had failed to make detailed findings as to the terms of the agreement, the respondent's acquittal would be affirmed. Accordingly, the appeal would be dismissed.

United Utilities Water plc v Moss Rose Piggeries Ltd [2006] All ER (D) 338 (Jun) (Queen's Bench Division: Laws LJ and Walker J).

2402 Smoke control areas—authorised fuels—England

The Smoke Control Areas (Authorised Fuels) (England) (Amendment) Regulations 2006, SI 2006/1869 (in force on 14 August 2006), further amend the 2001 Regulations, SI 2001/3745, by adding Briteflame briquettes and ZIP Firelogs to the list of authorised fuels for the purposes of the Clean Air Act 1993 Pt III (ss 18–29).

2403   Smoke control areas—authorised fuels—Wales

The Smoke Control Areas (Authorised Fuels) (Wales) Regulations 2006, SI 2006/2979 (in force on 24 November 2006), specify all fuels which are currently authorised for use in Wales for the purposes of the Clean Air Act 1993 s 20. They consolidate and replace the 2001 Regulations, SI 2001/3762, 3996 and the 2002 Regulations, SI 2002/3160. Most of the fuels in the regulations have previously been authorised fuels. However, the description of Ancit briquettes, Phurnacite briquettes and Taybright briquettes has been revised to reflect changes in their manufacture. Briteflame briquettes, Duraflame Firelogs, Multiheat briquettes, Stoveheat Premium briquettes, ZIP Cracklelog firelogs, ZIP Crackle-log firelogs, ZIP Crackling Log firelogs, and ZIP Firelogs are authorised for use for the first time.

2404   Smoke control areas—exempted fireplaces—England

The Smoke Control Areas (Exempted Fireplaces) (England) (No 2) Order 2006, SI 2006/2704 (in force on 10 November 2006), exempts certain classes of fireplace, subject to specified conditions, from the provisions of the Clean Air Act 1993 s 20, which prohibits smoke emissions in smoke control areas. SI 2005 /2304 and SI 2006/1152 are revoked.

2405   Smoke control areas—exempted fireplaces—Wales

The Smoke Control Areas (Exempted Fireplaces) (Wales) Order 2006, SI 2006/2980 (in force on 24 November 2006), applies in relation to Wales only, and exempts certain classes of fireplace, subject to specified conditions, from the provisions of the Clean Air Act 1993 s 20, which prohibits smoke emissions in smoke control areas.

2406   Smoke-free premises—definitions—England

The Smoke-free (Premises and Enforcement) Regulations 2006, SI 2006/3368 (in force on 1 July 2007), apply in relation to England only, and specify the meanings of 'enclosed' and 'substantially enclosed' premises for the purposes of the Health Act 2006 Pt 1 Ch 1 (ss 1–12). Premises are 'enclosed' if they have a ceiling or roof and, except for doors, windows and passageways, they are wholly enclosed either permanently or temporarily. Premises are 'substantially enclosed' if they have a ceiling or roof and less than half of their perimeter consists of openings in the walls, other than windows, doors or openings which can be shut. 'Roof' is defined so as to include any fixed or movable structure which is capable of covering all or part of the premises. The regulations also specify enforcement authorities and make other provision relating to enforcement.

2407   Statutory nuisance

See NUISANCE.

2408   Sustainable and Secure Buildings Act 2004—commencement

The Sustainable and Secure Buildings Act 2004 (Commencement No 1) Order 2006, SI 2006/224, brings into force, on 1 February 2006, ss 2, 7 (for the purpose only of conferring power to make regulations), 8 and 9. For a summary of the Act, see 2004 Abr para 337. For details of commencement, see commencement table in the title STATUTES.

2409   Waste—collection and disposal—recycling payments—England

The Environmental Protection (Waste Recycling Payments) Regulations 2006, SI 2006/743 (in force on 6 April 2006), replace the 2004 Regulations, SI 2004/639, and make provision for the determination of the amounts payable, under the Environmental Protection Act 1990 s 52(1) or (3), by waste disposal authorities to waste collection authorities and other persons in respect of waste retained or collected for recycling within a waste disposal authority's area. In particular, the regulations (1) provide that such recycling payments consist of amounts representing a waste disposal authority's net saving of expenditure on the disposal of waste retained or collected by a waste collection authority or other persons for recycling; (2) provide for the general mechanism for the determination of a waste disposal authority's net saving of expenditure, including specific determination provisions which are applicable in respect of the period beginning on 6 April 2006 and ending on 31 March 2007; and (3) provide that if a determination cannot be made, a waste disposal authority's net savings of expenditure is to be determined by reference to specified figures, which will be increased on an annual basis. SI 2005/415 is revoked.

2410   Waste—controlled waste—disposal—offence—need to prove failure of exercise of duty of care

The Environmental Protection Act 1990 s 34(1)(b) provides that it is the duty of any person who disposes of controlled waste to take all such measures as are reasonable in the circumstances to prevent the escape of the waste from his control.

A local authority had informed the defendant, a producer of controlled waste, the times during which waste could be placed on a public highway for collection. Waste had been observed outside the specified hours and the authority brought a summons alleging that the defendant had contravened the 1990 Act s 34(1)(b). The justices determined, on the way the case was presented to them, that the depositing of waste on the highway did not constitute an escape under s 34(1)(b). The authority appealed. *Held*, there had been no escape under s 34(1)(b). However, the justices had not been asked the right question as the offence was the failure to take reasonable measures as required by the duty imposed under s 34(1). The authority had to establish that there had been a failure to exercise the statutory duty of care, not that an escape had taken place. An escape by itself was not a prerequisite of liability. However the justices had given the correct answer to the case that was presented to them and, accordingly, the appeal would be dismissed.

Camden LBC v Mortgage Times Group Ltd [2006] EWHC 615 (Admin), (2006) Times, 15 August (Queen's Bench Division: Latham LJ and McCombe J). *Gateway Professional Services (Management) Ltd v Kingston upon Hull CC* [2004] EWHC 597 (Admin), [2004] All ER (D) 133 (Mar), DC (2005 Abr para 2610) considered.

2411   Waste—electrical and electronic equipment

The Waste Electrical and Electronic Equipment Regulations 2006, SI 2006/3289 (in force in part on 2 January 2007, in part on 1 April 2007 and in part on 1 July 2007) (1) amend the Environment Act 1995 to extend the definition of 'environmental licence' to cover specified functions of the Environment Agency and the Scottish Environment Protection Agency; (2) provide that (a) all producers who put electrical and electronic equipment on the market in the United Kingdom in a compliance period will be responsible for financing the costs of collection, treatment, recovery and environmentally sound disposal of waste electrical and electronic equipment from (i) private households that is deposited at a designated collection facility, or returned in that compliance period to the system that has been set up by an operator of a scheme and approved for the purposes of complying with that operator's obligations; or (ii) users other than private households that arises during that compliance period; (b) any producer who puts electrical and electronic equipment on the market in the United Kingdom must join an approved compliance scheme, and will be exempt from complying with any obligation for the period that his membership of that scheme subsists; and (c) where a scheme's approval is withdrawn, the obligations will fall back on the producer, until the date that a new scheme is joined, who will be notified of any obligations by the appropriate authority, and the producer must supply a declaration of compliance to the Environment Agency, the Scottish Environment Protection Agency or the Department of the Environment in Northern Ireland; (3) require (a) a producer to mark all electrical and electronic equipment that he puts on the market with the crossed out wheeled bin symbol, a producer identification mark and a date mark, and provide information on reuse and environmentally sound treatment for each new type of electrical and electronic equipment he puts on the market; and (b) an operator of an approved compliance scheme to (i) register or notify each producer who is a member of that scheme with the appropriate authority; (ii) meet the financing obligations that its members would have had, but for their membership of the scheme; (iii) ensure that obligations in relation to the reuse of whole appliances, treatment and recovery are complied with; and (iv) fulfil specified reporting, compliance and record keeping obligations; and (4) set out (a) the procedure to apply for, or withdraw, approval (i) from an authorised scheme; (ii) as an authorised treatment facility; or (iii) as an exporter for the purpose of issuing evidence of producer or scheme compliance; (b) the powers and duties of the Secretary of State; and (c) the duties of the appropriate authorities to maintain and make available a register of producers, and to monitor the performance of specified obligations of the producers, operators of schemes, approved authorised treatment facility and approved exporters.

2412   Waste—joint waste disposal authorities—recycling payments—disapplication—England

The Joint Waste Disposal Authorities (Recycling Payments) (Disapplication) (England) Order 2006, SI 2006/651 (in force on 1 April 2006), disapplies the requirement under the Environmental Protection Act 1990 s 52(1) for joint waste disposal authorities to make payments to a waste collection authority for the waste which the collection authority retains and recycles in the waste disposal authority's area.

2413   Waste—waste management—controlled waste

The Waste Management (England and Wales) Regulations 2006, SI 2006/937 (in force on 15 May 2006) implement, in part, EEC Council Directive 75/442 and EC Council Directive 1999/31. In particular, the regulations amend (1) the Environmental Protection Act 1990 so as to (a) require establishments and undertakings to comply with specified requirements and persons who are not establishments or undertakings to comply with only some of such requirements; (b) provide that a person who is not an establishment or undertaking and who commits a relevant offence will be ordered by a magistrates' court to pay not more than £5,000 in clean-up costs; (c) disapply certain provisions where a person who is not an establishment or undertaking is convicted of a specified offence; (2) the Environment Act 1995 so that, in relation to agricultural waste, no charges may be imposed under a charging scheme in respect of a relevant environmental licence; (3) the Controlled

Waste (Registration of Carriers and Seizure of Vehicles) Regulations 1991, SI 1991/1624, so as to replace the specified registration requirements which apply to those who only transport animal by-products waste, mines or quarries waste, or agricultural waste on a professional basis; (4) the Controlled Waste Regulations 1992, SI 1992/588, so as to disapply specified requirements in relation to waste which comprises animal by-products collected and transported in accordance with specified regulations, and provide that certain waste is to be classified as industrial waste if it is not classified as household or commercial waste; and (5) the 1994 Regulations, SI 1994/1056, so as to (a) set out certain record-keeping requirements in relation to activities which are exempt from waste management licensing; and (b) provide for exemptions from waste management licensing for activities involving the recovery of animal by-products, the treatment of land with liquid milk, and the deposit of plant tissue.

2414   Waste—waste management—treatment of sewage sludge—requirement for permit

The claimant was a statutory water and sewerage undertaker within the meaning of the Water Industry Act 1991. It sought declarations that certain waste treatment plants did not require permits under the Pollution Prevention and Control (England and Wales) Regulations 2000, SI 2000/1973, which were intended to transpose into domestic law EC Council Directive 96/61. The judge found that four plants at which sludge was produced for disposal as an intermediate step before further treatment elsewhere required a permit, whereas two plants at which industrial effluent was treated, having been piped from nearby industrial sites, did not. On the claimant's appeal, it fell to be determined whether the operations carried out at the sludge plants amounted to treatment that resulted in final compounds that were discarded by way of disposal within the meaning of the 2000 Regulations; and whether the operations at the industrial effluent plants were 'directly associated activities' with the activities carried on at the industrial sites that fed them. Held, treatment processes at intermediate plants were not excluded from the permit regime. The general purpose of the legislation was that of environmental protection in the course of waste disposal operations. Directive 96/61 tended to demonstrate that the reach of that purpose touched immediate as surely as final operations. The notion that the permit regime might be less interested in the process than in the product because, where the process resulted in recovery rather than disposal, there was no question of a permit being required was refuted by the proposition that intermediate treatment might affect the quality of the product sent for disposal regardless of whether some of the same product went to recovery. Given the legislative context, the difference between intermediate and final operations was not a principled distinction. By no stretch of the imagination were the two sets of premises, being at least a mile and a half apart and connected only by pipeline, on the 'same site'. Accordingly, the appeal would be dismissed.

United Utilities Water plc v Environment Agency for England and Wales [2006] EWCA Civ 633, [2006] 21 EG 131 (CS) (Court of Appeal: Sir Anthony Clarke MR, Laws and Smith LJJ).

2415   Waste—waste management licensing—electrical and electronic equipment

The Waste Electrical and Electronic Equipment (Waste Management Licensing) (England and Wales) Regulations 2006, SI 2006/3315 (in force on 5 January 2007), transpose the permit requirements of EC Council Directive 2002/96 on waste electrical and electronic equipment, and further amend the Waste Management Licensing Regulations 1994, SI 1994/1056. The regulations provide for exemptions from permit requirements for treatment of waste electrical and electronic equipment, together with exemptions from the permit requirements of EC Council Directive 2006/12 on waste for the purposes of storing such equipment.

RAILWAYS, INLAND WATERWAYS AND PIPELINES
Halsbury's Laws of England (4th edn) vol 39(1) (Reissue) paras 1–600

Articles

For articles relating to this title please refer to the Table of Articles at the beginning of the Abridgment.

2416   Channel tunnel—security—electronic communications
See para 2878.

2417   Natural Environment and Rural Communities Act 2006
See para 2109.

2418   Railways—access to training services
The Railways (Access to Training Services) Regulations 2006, SI 2006/598 (in force on 10 April 2006), implement, in part, EC Council Directive 2004/49 art 13 on safety of the Community's railways. In particular, the regulations (1) confer a right of access to training services provided by

other bodies on railway undertakings applying for a safety certificate, infrastructure managers and staff performing safety critical tasks; (2) provide that access to such training services must be provided in a fair and non-discriminatory fashion and where the services are provided by only one railway undertaking or infrastructure manager, the price for the use of those services must be reasonable and non-discriminatory; (3) provide that where relevant experience is gained with another employer, the experience must be taken into account by railway undertakings recruiting certain categories of staff and, for that purpose, employees are granted access to, and the right to obtain copies of, the relevant documentation; and (4) provide for a right of appeal to the Office of Rail Regulation where railway undertakings, infrastructure managers or their employees are denied access to the specified entitlements, or if the price charged for such access is contrary to those specified.

2419 Railways—closures guidance—England and Scotland

The Closures Guidance (Railway Services in Scotland and England) Order 2006, SI 2006/2837 (in force on 1 December 2006), gives effect to the closures guidance which is required to be published by the Secretary of State and Scottish ministers, which relate to proposals to discontinue any service or services, network or part of a network, or the use or operation of any railway station, in Scotland, or cross border services between England and Scotland.

2420 Railways—closures guidance—England and Wales

The Closures Guidance (Railway Services in England and Wales) Order 2006, SI 2006/2836 (in force on 1 December 2006), gives effect to the closures guidance which is required to be published by the Secretary of State and by the Secretary of State jointly with the National Assembly for Wales, which relate to proposals to discontinue any service or services, network or part of a network, or the use or operation of any railway station, in England or Wales.

2421 Railways—infrastructure—maintenance—public authority function

See *Cameron v Network Rail Infrastructure Ltd*, para 1533.

2422 Railways—interoperability

The Railways (Interoperability) Regulations 2006, SI 2006/397 (in force in part on 20 March 2006 and in part on 2 April 2006), replace the Railways (Interoperability) (High-Speed) Regulations 2002, SI 2002/1166, and implement EC Parliament and Council Directives 2001/16 and 2004/50 and include the prior implementation of EC Council Directive 96/48, concerning railway interoperability for the purpose of establishing conditions for the inter-working, interoperability, of the trans-European rail system. In particular, the regulations (1) apply, with exceptions, to the trans-European rail system in the United Kingdom, their subsystems and interoperability constituents; (2) restrict the placing in service of structural subsystems that are new or have undergone major renewal or upgrade to those authorised by a safety authority or ruled by a competent authority as not requiring authorisation; (3) require that, for those subsystems for which an authorisation is needed, an application to a safety authority for authorisation must be made with the complete technical file and the contracting entity's verification declaration; (4) in relation to major upgrade or renewal works, require a competent authority to decide whether an authorisation is required for the subsystem to be placed in service, and compel the authority to requires authorisation where there may be an adverse effect on safety; (5) provide that if such authorisation is required and the subsystem is part of the conventional trans-European rail system, the competent authority can decide the extent to which the requirements of relevant technical specifications for interoperability ('TSI') apply; (6) allow for derogations from conformity with the TSIs, whether for subsystems or interoperability constituents in specified circumstances; (7) specify how the essential requirements are to be met by a subsystem where authorisation is required; (8) require the contracting entity to appoint a notified body to carry out the verification assessment procedure and to draw up a verification declaration where the specified conditions are satisfied; (9) provide that a structural subsystem, for which there is a verification declaration, is to be taken to meet the essential requirements unless there are reasonable grounds for believing it does not; (10) specify the content of the technical file and provide for its retention and updating after it has been lodged with the contracting entity; (11) place obligations on the operator of an authorised subsystem that has been placed in services to continue to meet the essential requirements, TSIs and notified national technical rules; (12) permit, with exceptions, a safety authority and a competent authority to charge for certain work; (13) contain requirements for interoperability constituents; (14) provide that an EC declaration of conformity or suitability for use indicates the interoperability constituent satisfies the requirements, which are comprised in European specifications and TSIs; (15) provide a presumption that an interoperability constituent for which an EC declaration has been made satisfies the essential requirements and requisite standards; (16) set out the assessment procedure; (17) prohibit an interoperability constituent being placed on the trans-European rail system market without the manufacturer of the constituent, or other appropriate person, having drawn up the EC declaration; (18) place continuing requirements on an operator using an interoperability constituent on the trans-European rail system in the United Kingdom; (19) allow for the drawing up of an EC declaration after the interoperability constituent has been placed on the market; (20) provide for recognition of assessments carried out in other member states and notification to the EC Commission and other member states where it appears to a safety authority that a declaration is incorrect; (21) provide for the appointment of notified bodies; (22) place duties on notified bodies when appointed to carry out the appropriate assessment processes for subsystems and interoperability constituents; (23) make provision for those cases where the notified body is not minded to draw up a certificate of conformity in relation to a project subsystem or confirm that an EC declaration in relation to an interoperability constituent can be drawn up; (24) require notified bodies to consult with other notified bodies in the European Community in a co-ordination group; (25) provide for the recovery of fees by notified bodies and the Secretary of State; (26) provide for the keeping of registers of authorised rolling stock and infrastructure and a national vehicle register; (27) provide for a defence of due diligence; and (28) make provision for liabilities on persons other than the principal offender.

2423 Railways—Office of Rail Regulation—health and safety law—enforcement

The Health and Safety (Enforcing Authority for Railways and Other Guided Transport Systems) Regulations 2006, SI 2006/557 (in force on 1 April 2006), make the Office of Rail Regulation responsible for the enforcement of health and safety law in relation to the operation of railways, tramways and certain other systems of guided transport in place of the Health and Safety Executive. The scope of the Office of Rail Regulation's enforcement responsibilities is subject to specified exceptions and is limited in relation to construction work. The regulations also make consequential amendments to various enactments.

2424 Railways—railway safety purposes

The Railways Act 2005 (Amendment) Regulations 2006, SI 2006/556 (in force on 1 April 2006), amend the definition of 'railway safety purposes' in the Railways Act 2005, so as to exclude from the remit of the Office of Rail Regulation, fairground equipment, guided bus systems and trolley vehicle systems.

2425 Railways—safety critical work

The Railways and Other Guided Transport Systems (Safety) Regulations 2006, SI 2006/599 (in force in part on 10 April 2006 and in part on 1 October 2006), replace the Railways and Other Transport Systems (Approval of Works, Plant and Equipment) Regulations, SI 1994/157, the Railways (Safety Critical Work) Regulations 1994, SI 1994/299, and the Railways (Safety Case) Regulations 2000, SI 2000/2688, and impose prohibitions and requirements in relation to safety on railways and other guided transport systems in implementation of European Parliament and EC Council Directive 2004/49. The regulations (1) impose prohibitions in relation to the operation of trains or vehicles on railways and other guided transport systems and the management and use of infrastructure, except where a person has established and is maintaining a safety management system and in specified cases has a safety certificate in relation to the operation of vehicles or a safety authorisation in relation to the management and use of infrastructure; (2) make provision in relation to the requirements for a safety management system and the issuing, amendment and revocation of safety certificates and authorisations by, and for the giving of notices to, the Office of Rail Regulation; (3) impose general duties on transport operators to carry out risk assessment, to co-operate with each other and certain other persons, and to prepare an annual safety report to the Office of Rail Regulation; (4) detail requirements in relation to the preparation of annual reports for the European Railway Agency and for the issuing, keeping and public inspection of documents; (5) make provision in relation to the carrying out of safety critical work on guided transport systems, including imposing obligations on those controlling the carrying out of such work to ensure that it is only carried out by fit and competent persons, and that safety critical workers do not carry out such work when fatigued; (6) make provision for appeals in relation to decisions relating to safety certificates and authorisations; and (7) provide for a defence in relation to the safety verification requirements.

The Railways and Other Guided Transport Systems (Safety) (Amendment) Regulations 2006, SI 2006/1057 (in force in part on 10 April 2006 and in part on 1 October 2006), amend SI 2006/599 supra in order to update the list of legislation in the Enterprise Act 2002 Sch 4.

2426 Railways—safety levy

The Railway Safety Levy Regulations 2006, SI 2006/1010 (in force on 1 April 2006), place an obligation on railway service providers to pay a levy to the Office of Rail Regulation to meet the expenses it incurs in performing activities relating to railway safety. The regulations enable the Office of Rail Regulation to (1) determine, in respect of each financial year (a) the total amount of the levy; (b) the railway service providers that are liable to pay the levy; (c) when the levy is to be paid; and (d) the criteria for determining the proportion of the levy to be paid by each railway service provider; (2) revise a determination of any of the specified matters, it then being a requirement that publication of each determination or revision of a determination is made; and (3) make reasonable requests to the railway service provider for information for the purpose of revising a determination or calculating the amount of levy payable by each railway service provider. Where information requested is financial information, the information must be accompanied by a certificate signed by an auditor attesting to its accuracy. If the railway service provider has a relevant turnover of less than £10,000,000 it can provide a statement regarding the accuracy of the information signed by or on behalf of the railway service provider rather than by an auditor. The regulations also provide (i) that where information is requested but is not supplied the Office of Rail Regulation may make assumptions concerning the information as are reasonable in all the circumstances, but must provide the railway service provider with written notice of any assumption it intends to make and the reasons for making that assumption. The railway service provider may make representations to the Office of Rail Regulation regarding that assumption within 21 days of the date of the notice, after which the Office of Rail Regulation may apply the assumption with or without modifications; (ii) for the payment of the levy to the Office of Rail Regulation, and for the recovery of that which is not paid, and (iii) for the refund of any payment by the Office of Rail Regulation.

2427 Railways—security—electronic communications

See para 2878.

2428 Railways—Strategic Rail Authority—abolition

The Railways (Abolition of the Strategic Rail Authority) Order 2006, SI 2006/2925 (in force on 1 December 2006), provides for the abolition of the strategic Rail Authority.

2429 Railways—substitute road services—exemptions

The Railways (Substitute Road Services) (Exemptions) Order 2006, SI 2006/1935 (in force on 1 October 2006), relates to the obligations of operators of railway passenger services pursuant to the Transport Act 2000 s 248. In particular, the order exempts relevant operators from their obligations in respect of all substitute road services other than those relating to the railway passenger services specified.

2430 Railways—track access—charge—discrimination

The claimant train operating company provided passenger services pursuant to franchising agreements. The defendant, the independent statutory body charged with regulating the railway industry, granted two other train operating companies, which were 'open access operators', track access rights to enable them to operate passenger services on the same line as the claimant. Pursuant to the defendant's criteria and procedures for the approval of passenger track access contracts, open access operators, unlike franchise operators, were not charged a fixed track charge under the charging regime for track access. The claimant applied for judicial review of the decision to grant the interested parties track access rights, alleging that the charging regime was contrary to the Railways Infrastructure (Access and Management) Regulations 2005, SI 2005/3049, and EC Council Directive 2001/14 on the allocation of railway infrastructure capacity and the levying of charges for the use of railway infrastructure and safety certification because it unlawfully discriminated between franchise operators and open access operators. The claimant also contended that the regime amounted to an unlawful grant of state aid in favour of open access operators. *Held*, in the circumstances, the defendant's approach was consistent with Directive 2001/14 and with the 2005 Regulations, purposively construed as a whole, and had not unlawfully discriminated against the claimant. The focus of the 2005 Regulations, which implemented Directive 2001/14, was clearly on the need to ensure that all railway undertakings had equal and non-discriminatory access to rail infrastructure. If the defendant's charging scheme had not reflected differences between the ability of franchise operators and open access operators, who were in fundamentally different positions, to obtain access to the rail infrastructure, then it would not have achieved the objectives of Directive 2001/14. Further, the charging regime viewed as a whole did not distort competition by favouring franchise operators or open access operators, it simply treated them differently on the grounds that they were in a different position regarding access to the rail infrastructure. Accordingly, the application would be dismissed.

R (on the application of Great North Eastern Railway Ltd) v Office of Rail Regulation [2006] EWHC 1942 (Admin), [2006] All ER (D) 414 (Jul) (Queen's Bench Division: Sullivan J).

2431 Railways Act 2005—commencement

The Railways Act 2005 (Commencement No 5) Order 2006, SI 2006/266, brings into force (1) on 7 February 2006, s 2 (in part), Sch 3 paras 1, 12; and (2) on 1 April 2006, s 2 (in part), 3(1) (in part), (2) (so far as not already in force), (4), (8)(a) (so far as not already in force), (9) (in part), (10) (so far as not already in force), (11)(b) (so far as not already in force), 51(1)(b), (5), 59(1) (in part), (6) (in part), Sch 3 (so far as not already in force), Sch 12 paras 4, 6, 12, and certain repeals in Sch 13 Pt 1.

The Railways Act 2005 (Commencement No 6) Order 2006, SI 2006/1951, brings into force, on 1 August 2006, ss 1(10), 42, 43, 45(1) (in part), (2), 56 (so far as not already in force), 59(1) (in part), Sch 12 paras 17(1) (in part), (4)–(6) and a repeal in Sch 13 Pt 1.

The Railways Act 2005 (Commencement No 7, Transitional and Saving Provisions) Order 2006, SI 2006/2911, brings into force, on 1 December 2006, ss 1(1) (in part), 3(1) (in part), (5), (6) (so far as not already in force), 22–39, 41, 44, 45 (so far as not already in force), 54(4), 59(1) (in part), (6) (in part), (7) (in part), Sch 1 (so far as not already in force, except Sch 1 para 32(2) (which is commenced in part)), Schs 7, 8, Sch 11 para 1 (in part), 2–5, 7(1), (3)–(6), 10, 11, 13, Sch 12 paras 1 (so far as not already in force), 14 (so far as not already in force), certain repeals in Sch 13 Pt 1 and certain savings in Sch 13 Pt 2.

For a summary of the Act, see 2005 Abr para 2624. See also the commencement table in the title STATUTES.

2432 Transport and works—assessment of environmental effects

The Transport and Works (Assessment of Environmental Effects) Regulations 2006, SI 2006/958 (in force on 20 April 2006), implement certain provisions of EC European Parliament and Council Directive 2003/35, which relate to the assessment of the effects of certain public and private projects on the environment. The regulations amend the Transport and Works Act 1992 in relation to orders relating to the construction or operation of railways, tramways, trolley vehicle systems or inland waterways so as to (1) enable rules to be made as to the publicity to be given to any environmental information provided in relation to an application for such an order; (2) require the Secretary of State to publish a notice in the London Gazette and a local newspaper for any draft order which is to be made otherwise than on application; (3) require the Secretary of State to publish a notice in a local newspaper for all proposals which he considers to be of national significance; and (4) require the notice of a determination to state the main reasons and considerations on which the determination is based together with information regarding the public participation process and the process for challenging the validity of the determination.

2433 Transport and works—model clauses for railways and tramways

The Transport and Works (Model Clauses for Railways and Tramways) Order 2006, SI 2006/1954 (in force on 8 August 2006), replaces the 1992 Order, SI 1992/3270, and prescribes model clauses for inclusion in orders made under the Transport and Works Act 1992 s 1, which authorise the construction and operation of certain systems of transport.

RATING AND COUNCIL TAX

Halsbury's Laws of England (4th edn) vol 39(1) (Reissue) paras 601–999

Articles

For articles relating to this title please refer to the Table of Articles at the beginning of the Abridgment.

2434 Council tax—calculation of precepts—Greater London Authority

See para 1863.

2435 Council tax—demand notices—electronic communications—England

The Non-Domestic Rating and Council Tax (Electronic Communications) (England) Order 2006, SI 2006/237 (in force on 1 March 2006), further amends (1) the Non-Domestic Rating (Collection and Enforcement) (Central Lists) Regulations 1989, SI 1989/2260, so as to allow the notices which are required to be served by the Secretary of State, to be served electronically; and (2) the Non-Domestic Rating (Collection and Enforcement) (Local Lists) Regulations 1989, SI 1989/1058, and the Council Tax (Administration and Enforcement) Regulations 1992, SI 1992/613, so as to reflect the definition of 'electronic communication' under the Electronic Communications Act 2000 s 15.

2436 Council tax—demand notices—England

The Council Tax and Non-Domestic Rating (Demand Notices) (Amendment) (England) Regulations 2006, SI 2006/492 (in force on 31 March 2006), further amend the 2003 Regulations, SI 2003/2613, so as to provide that the explanatory notes of the former agricultural premises relief are amended to reflect the coming to an end of such a relief. The regulations also provide that the explanatory notes relating to such a relief are to be omitted for financial years 2007/2008 and beyond.

2437 Council tax—discount disregards—England

The Council Tax (Discount Disregards) (Amendment) (England) Order 2006, SI 2006/3396 (in force on 31 January 2007), which applies in relation to billing authorities in England, and financial years beginning on or after 1 April 2007, further amends the 1992 Order, SI 1992/548, so as to (1) amend the definition of an apprentice by (a) providing that an apprentice's salary and allowances must now be no more than £195 per week; and (b) removing the requirement that an apprentice's salary and allowances must be substantially less than the salary he would be likely to receive if he had achieved the relevant qualification; and (2) amend the definition of a youth trainee. In particular, to be a youth trainee any training undertaken by a person must be funded by the Learning and Skills Council for England.

2438 Council tax—discounts—sole or main residence

The taxpayer owned a cottage which he let out while he worked abroad. During that time, he had the legal status of a Spanish resident, paid Spanish taxes and rented Spanish accommodation. The tenancy came to an end prematurely and the cottage remained empty until the taxpayer returned. The defendant council considered that, for the purposes of the Local Government Finance Act 1992 s 6, the cottage was the taxpayer's sole or main residence while it remained empty so that he was liable for 75 per cent of the council tax due for that period. The taxpayer appealed to a valuation tribunal, contending that the cottage was not his main residence and consequently, that he was only liable for 50 per cent of the council tax due. The tribunal upheld the defendant's decision. On the taxpayer's appeal, *held,* the fact that a legal impediment to residence by the freehold owner was removed did not, of itself, result in his residing in the dwelling. Section 6(2) distinguished between residence and ownership of a dwelling. The issue of residence was a question of fact, not simply of law. The tribunal had failed to consider whether it could sensibly be said that the taxpayer was resident in the cottage during the period in question when he lived and was resident in Spain. It was impossible to say that the taxpayer resided solely in the cottage, or that he had his main residence there, while he lived in Spain. It seemed anomalous that the taxpayer should be non-resident in the United Kingdom for income tax purposes, but mainly resident in the cottage for the purpose of liability for council tax. Accordingly, the appeal would be allowed.

Parry v Derbyshire Dales DC [2006] EWHC 988 (Admin), [2006] All ER (D) 70 (May) (Queen's Bench Division: Stanley Burnton J).

2439 Council tax—exempt dwellings—England

The Council Tax (Exempt Dwellings) (Amendment) (England) Order 2006, SI 2006/2318 (in force on 1 April 2007), further amends the 1992 Order, SI 1992/558, by clarifying that, where a planning condition prevents the occupancy of a dwelling, and the dwelling is unoccupied, the dwelling is exempt from council tax.

2440 Council tax—general provisions—England

The Council Tax and Non-Domestic Rating (Amendment) (England) Regulations 2006, SI 2006/3395 (in force on 31 January 2007), make amendments to a number of regulations concerning council tax and non-domestic rating. In particular, the regulations (1) further amend the Non-Domestic Rating (Collection and Enforcement) (Local Lists) Regulations 1989, SI 1989/1058, so as to increase the charges connected with distress, and costs connected with committal, in line with inflation; (2) make a minor amendment to the Billing Authorities (Anticipation of Precepts) Regulations 1992, SI 1992/3239; (3) further amend the Council Tax (Additional Provisions for Discount Disregards) Regulations 1992, SI 1992/552, so as to increase from £36 to £44 a week the discount disregard for care workers; (4) further amend the Council Tax (Administration and Enforcement) Regulations 1992, SI 1992/613, so as to increase, in line with inflation, the deductions to be made under attachments of earnings orders, charges connected with distress and costs connected with committal; (5) further amend the Council Tax (Alteration of Lists and Appeals) Regulations 1993, SI 1993/290, so that (a) alterations to reflect a material increase in the value of a dwelling; and (b) alterations to correct an inaccuracy which shows as one dwelling property which should have been treated as two or more dwellings, take effect on the day they are entered in the list; and (6) further amend the Council Tax and Non-Domestic Rating (Demand Notices) (England) Regulations 2003, SI 2003/2613, so as to (a) provide that new information must be included in council tax demand notices where a combined fire and rescue authority has been created and the demand notice concerns the financial year when the combined authority first exercises its functions; (b) provide that revised explanatory information concerning small business rate relief, following amendments to the application process for that relief, and rate relief for businesses in rural areas must be included in non-domestic rates demand notices where relevant; and (c) provide that information about a parish council's budget requirement must be included in a council tax demand notice if the budget requirement is £140,000 or more and the dwelling to which the notice relates is within the parish council's area.

2441   Council tax benefit

See SOCIAL SECURITY.

2442   Council Tax (New Valuation Lists for England) Act 2006

The Council Tax (New Valuation Lists for England) Act 2006 makes provision about the dates on which new valuation lists for the purposes of council tax must be compiled in relation to billing authorities in England. The Act received the royal assent on 30 March 2006 and came into force on that day.

Section 1 amends the Local Government Finance Act 1992 and the Local Government Act 2003 so as to (1) provide a power for the Secretary of State to specify by order, in relation to England, the year in which each new valuation list must be compiled; and (2) remove the requirement for a new list to be compiled (a) in relation to billing authorities in England on 1 April 2007; and (b) ten years after the first revaluation for billing authorities in England. Short title and extent are provided for by s 2.

2443   Non-domestic rating—amendments—England

See para 2440.

2444   Non-domestic rating—billing authorities—contributions—England

The Non-Domestic Rating Contributions (Amendment) (England) Regulations 2006, SI 2006/3167 (in force on 31 December 2006), further amend the 1992 Regulations, SI 1992/3238, by replacing certain figures used in the calculation of the non-domestic rating contributions which billing authorities in England are required to pay to the Secretary of State.

2445   Non-domestic rating—billing authorities—contributions—Wales

The Non-Domestic Rating Contributions (Wales) (Amendment) Regulations 2006, SI 2006/3347 (in force on 31 December 2006), which apply in relation to Wales only, further amend the 1992 Regulations, SI 1992/3238, by (1) removing the 90 per cent discretionary rate relief reduction in respect of ratepayers who occupy hereditaments to which the Local Government Finance Act 1988 s 43(4B) applies (hereditaments which receive mandatory small business rate relief); (2) adjusting the multiplier to be used when calculating the amount for the billing authority in accordance with the prescribed assumptions as to the gross amount; and (3) updating the list of adult population figures.

2446   Non-domestic rating—central rating list—England

The Central Rating List (Amendment) (England) Regulations 2006, SI 2006/495 (in force on 1 April 2006), amend the 2005 Regulations, SI 2005/551, so as to provide that British Telecommunications plc will continue to be treated as being in occupation of unbundled local loops until 1 April 2008.

2447   Non-domestic rating—chargeable amounts—England

The Non-Domestic Rating (Chargeable Amounts) (Amendment) (England) Regulations 2006, SI 2006/3394 (in force on 14 December 2006), which apply in relation to England only, further amend the 2004 Regulations, SI 2004/3387, so that hereditaments which had a rateable value of zero on 31 March 2005 are added to the category of defined hereditaments.

2448   Non-domestic rating—demand notices—electronic communications—England

See para 2435.

2449   Non-domestic rating—demand notices—England

See para 2436.

2450   Non-domestic rating—demand notices and discretionary relief—Wales

The Non-Domestic Rating (Demand Notices and Discretionary Relief) (Wales) (Amendment) Regulations 2006, SI 2006/3392 (in force on 1 April 2007), which apply in relation to Wales, further amend (1) the Non-Domestic Rating (Discretionary Relief) Regulations 1989, SI 1989/1059, by removing the need for billing authorities (county and county borough councils) to send a 12 months notice to ratepayers if the effect of the coming into force of the Local Government Act 2003 s 63, and the consequent revocation of the rural rate relief scheme in Wales and removal of billing authorities' discretion to provide rate relief under the Local Government Finance Act 1988 s 47 in relation to rural settlements, is that ratepayers would be required to pay a greater chargeable amount; and (2) the Non-Domestic Rating (Demand Notices) (Wales) Regulations 1993, SI 1993/252, by requiring billing authorities to insert in demand notices for non-domestic rates a note regarding the effect of the introduction of the small business rate relief scheme.

2451   Non-domestic rating—rating lists—alteration of lists—appeals—England

The Non-Domestic Rating (Alteration of Lists and Appeals) (England) (Amendment) Regulations 2006, SI 2006/2312 (in force on 1 October 2006), amend the 2005 Regulations, SI 2005/659, so that (1) where a person makes a proposal in one capacity, he may make a duplicate proposal if he changes capacity; (2) a proposal to alter a rating list in respect of a hereditament as a result of a decision in relation to another hereditament of a valuation tribunal, the Lands Tribunal or a court, may be made at any time until six months after new rating lists have been compiled; (3) an interested person who makes a proposal is required to state what their capacity is; (4) the classes of proposal are extended in respect of which the ratepayer must provide the valuation officer with information about the amount payable in respect of a lease, easement or licence to occupy the hereditament; (5) there is clarification as to what information must be provided by different classes of proposer where there is such a lease, easement or licence; (6) the period of time for which a valuation officer may serve notice that a proposal has been invalidly made is extended; (7) where an alteration to a rating list falls to be made with effect from the day the proposal was served on the valuation officer, if that proposal replaced a previous proposal in respect of which an invalidity notice has been served, the alteration will have effect from the day on which the original proposal was served; and (8) the right to make a proposal to alter a 1995 local rating list following a revision to a 2000 list instigated by a valuation officer on the grounds of a split or merger is re-established.

2452   Non-domestic rating—rating lists—alteration of lists—appeals—Wales

The Non-Domestic Rating (Alteration of Lists and Appeals) (Wales) (Amendment) Regulations 2006, SI 2006/1035 (in force on 5 April 2006), amend the 2005 Regulations, SI 2005/758, so as to (1) remove references to the Valuation and Community Charge Tribunals Regulations 1989, SI 1989/439, which were disapplied in respect of tribunals in Wales by the Valuation Tribunals (Wales) Regulations 1995, SI 1995/3056; and (2) insert gender-neutral provisions where required.

2453   Non-domestic rating—small business rate relief—England

The Non-Domestic Rating (Small Business Rate Relief) (Amendment) (England) Order 2006, SI 2006/2313 (in force on 1 October 2006), amends the 2004 Order, SI 2004/3315, by (1) replacing a condition that ratepayers annually apply for small business rate relief so as to now require an application to be made in respect of the five year period between revaluations of non-domestic hereditaments in England, or so much of such a period as remains when the application is made; (2) providing that, where such relief is granted, certain changes in circumstances must be notified to the billing authority by the ratepayer, which are (a) the ratepayer taking up occupation of property they did not occupy at the time of making their application for relief; and (b) an increase in the rateable value of a property occupied by the ratepayer in an area other than the area of the billing authority which granted the relief; (3) providing that, notification that the ratepayer has taken up occupation of an additional property must be by way of a fresh application for relief and that a notice of an increase in rateable value must be in writing; (4) providing that, where such changes are notified within four weeks of the day after the day on which they occurred and the ratepayer continues to be entitled to relief, they will continue to benefit from the relief uninterrupted; and (5) prescribing the form of application for relief.

2454   Non-domestic rating—small business relief—Wales

The Non-Domestic Rating (Small Business Relief) (Wales) Order 2006, SI 2006/3345 (in force on 1 April 2007), provides for a small business rate relief scheme for Wales following the coming into force of the Local Government Act 2003 s 63. In particular, the order (1) defines hereditaments which are excepted from the small business rate relief scheme; (2) prescribes a maximum rateable value of £12,000 for hereditaments which might be eligible for relief; (3) prescribes conditions of eligibility; (4) prescribes the amount of E in the formula contained in the Local Government Finance Act 1988 s 43(4A)(b); (5) has the effect of granting (a) 50 per cent mandatory rate relief to hereditaments which have a rateable value of £2,000 or less, which are not excepted hereditaments, and are wholly occupied; and (b) 25 per cent mandatory rate relief to hereditaments which have a rateable value of more than £2,000 but not more than £5,000, which are not excepted hereditaments, and are wholly occupied; and (6) has the effect of granting 100 per cent mandatory relief to post offices which have a rateable value of £9,000 or less, and of granting 50 per cent mandatory relief to post offices which have a rateable value of more than £9,000 but not more than £12,000.

REAL PROPERTY

Halsbury's Laws of England (4th edn) vol 39(2) (Reissue) paras 1–300

Articles

For articles relating to this title please refer to the Table of Articles at the beginning of the Abridgment.

2455　Conveyancing

See CONVEYANCING.

REGISTRATION CONCERNING THE INDIVIDUAL

Halsbury's Laws of England (4th edn) vol 39(2) (Reissue) paras 501–750

2456　Registration of births and deaths—electronic communications—electronic storage

The Registration of Births and Deaths (Electronic Communications and Electronic Storage) Order 2006, SI 2006/2809 (in force on 13 November 2006), amends the Births and Deaths Registration Act 1953 to allow for the electronic communication and storage of copies of entries in the registers of births and deaths, to enable local registrars to transmit those copies to the Registrar General electronically and to allow the Registrar General to use the copies in the same way as paper copies.

2457　Registration of births and deaths—general

The Registration of Births and Deaths (Amendment) Regulations 2006, SI 2006/2827 (in force on 13 November 2006), further amend the 1987 Regulations, SI 1987/2088, and the Registration of Births and Deaths (Welsh Language) Regulations 1987, SI 1987/2089, by (1) amending the procedure for the registration of births and deaths following the introduction of an electronic method of communication between registrars, superintendent registrars and the Registrar General; (2) making provision for more detailed marginal notes when corrections are made to entries; and (3) allowing a registrar to give a certificate for disposal of a deceased person prior to burial or cremation.

RESTITUTION

Halsbury's Laws of England (4th edn) vol 40(2) (Reissue) paras 1301–1484

Articles

For articles relating to this title please refer to the Table of Articles at the beginning of the Abridgment.

2458　Mistake—mistake of law—payment of tax—extent to which claim statute-barred

The claimant company issued a claim seeking compensation or restitution with regard to advance corporation tax payments. The Revenue contended that the claims were time-barred by the Limitation Act 1980. The judge found for the claimant and the Revenue appealed. The appeal raised a question as to the scope of the principle in *Kleinwort Benson v Lincoln CC*, in which the House of Lords abrogated the common law rule that no restitutionary claim lay in respect of money paid under a mistake of law, namely whether the principle applied where the payment in question was a payment to the Revenue on account of a supposed liability to tax. The Revenue contended that it did not apply to such a payment, given that statute provided for the recovery of tax overpaid by error or mistake in certain, limited circumstances and that, as the House of Lords held in *Woolwich Equitable Building Society v IRC*, a taxpayer who had made a payment to the Revenue pursuant to an unlawful demand was entitled as of right to a restitutionary remedy, regardless of whether in making the payment the taxpayer had acted under any mistake of law. The court accepted the Revenue's contentions, and the claimant appealed. *Held*, English law recognised a restitutionary claim for tax paid under a mistake of law. The remedy in restitution that was available for payments under a mistake was not subject to an exception in the case of taxes paid under a mistake of law to the Revenue. Moreover, it made no difference that the payments were made in accordance with a settled understanding of the law. The payments were made under a mistake of law and a cause of action at common law for their recovery was available. Accordingly, the appeal would be allowed.

Deutsche Morgan Grenfell Group plc v IRC [2006] UKHL 49, [2007] 1 All ER 449 (House of Lords: Lords Hoffmann, Hope of Craighead, Scott of Foscote, Walker of Gestingthorpe and Brown of Eaton-under-Heywood). *Woolwich Equitable Building Society v IRC (No 2)* [1993] AC 70, HL (1992 Abr para 1401), applied. *Kleinwort Benson Ltd v Lincoln CC* [1998] 4 All ER 513, HL (1998 Abr para 2243), considered. Decision of Court of Appeal [2005] EWCA Civ 78, [2006] Ch 243 (2005 Abr para 2657) reversed.

2459　Unjust enrichment—defence—change of position—good faith—bank having general suspicion that account might be used for money laundering from time to time

A number of fraudsters entrapped the claimants in a fraudulent scheme which involved the supposed investment in an overseas family trust. Under the scheme, the claimants made payments into a bank account run by a foreign bank, for onward transfer to a client. No trust money ever materialised, the fraudsters disappeared and the money was cleared out of the client's account. The claimants brought a claim for restitution of money had and received against the bank. It was held that the bank could maintain a change of position defence and the claimants appealed. *Held*, Rix LJ dissenting, the trial judge had found that the manager of the bank had suspected in a general way that the fraudsters might be involved in money laundering in the course of their business. However, he had found that there was no evidence that he had any suspicions about the particular transactions which constituted the fraud, and that the failure to make further inquiries did not amount to unacceptable commercial conduct and therefore bad faith. Although a change of position defence was dependent on good faith, the lack of good faith had to be related to the change of position. Therefore, the manager's general suspicions of money laundering did not amount to lack of good faith when those suspicions did not relate to the specific payments in consideration. Accordingly, the appeal would be dismissed.

Abou-Ramah v Abacha [2006] EWCA Civ 1492, [2007] WTLR 1 (Court of Appeal: Pill, Rix and Arden LJJ). *Twinsectra Ltd v Yardley* [2002] UKHL 12, [2002] 2 All ER 377 (2002 Abr para 3025); and *Barlow Clowes International Ltd (in liq) v Eurotrust International Ltd* [2005] UKPC 37, [2006] 1 All ER 333 (2005 Abr para 973) considered. Decision of Treacy J [2006] 1 All ER (Comm) 247 affirmed.

REVENUE

Halsbury's Laws of England (4th edn) vols 5(1) (Reissue), 12(2) (Reissue), 19(1), (2) (Reissue), 23(1) (Reissue), 23(2) (Reissue), 24 (Reissue), 44(2) (Reissue), 49(1) (Reissue)

2460 Appropriation Act 2006

The Appropriation Act 2006 authorises the use of resources for the service of the year ending with 31 March 2005 to the amount of £188,157,000, and for the year ending 31 March 2006 to the amount of £9,947,340,000. It also authorises the issue out of the Consolidated Fund of the United Kingdom and the application to the service of the year ending with 31 March 2006 the sum of £7,637,727,000. The Act received the royal assent on 30 March 2006 and came into force on that date.

2461 Appropriation (No 2) Act 2006

The Appropriation (No 2) Act 2006 authorises the use of resources for the service of the year ending with 31 March 2007 to the amount of £226,955,376,000. It also authorises the issue out of the Consolidated Fund of the United Kingdom and the application to the service of the year ending with 31 March 2007 the sum of £211,924,284,000. The Act received the royal assent on 19 July 2006 and came into force on that date.

2462 Capital gains tax

See CAPITAL GAINS TAXATION.

2463 Consolidated Fund Act 2006

The Consolidated Fund Act 2006 authorises the use of resources for the service of the year ending with 31 March 2007 to the amount of £6,284,598,000, authorises the issue out of the Consolidated Fund of the United Kingdom and applies to the service of the year ending with 31 March 2007 the sum of £7,831,205,000, authorises the use of resources for the year ending 31 March 2008 to the amount of £181,206,923,000, and authorises the issue out of the Consolidated Fund and applies to the service of the year ending with 31 March 2008 the sum of £171,368,021,000. The Act received the royal assent on 19 December 2006 and came into force on that date.

2464 Finance Act 2004—appointed day

The Finance Act 2004 (Duty Stamps) (Appointed Day) Order 2006, SI 2006/201, brings into force the amendments made by s 4 in relation to retail containers containing alcoholic liquor if the excise duty point for that alcoholic liquor falls on or after 22 February 2006.

The Finance Act 2004, Section 77(1) and (7), (Appointed Day) Order 2006, SI 2006/3240, appoints 6 April 2007 for the purposes of s 77(1).

For a summary of the Act, see 2004 Abr para 2364. See also the commencement table in the title STATUTES.

2465 Finance Act 2006

The Finance Act 2006 grants certain duties, alters other duties, amends the law relating to the national debt and the public revenue, and makes further provision in connection with finance. The Act received the royal assent on 19 July 2006 and certain provisions came into force on that day. For details of commencement, see the commencement table in the title STATUTES.

Part 1 (ss 1–15) Excise duties
Section 1 provides for an increase in the rates of excise duty on tobacco products, and s 2 imposes a duty on tobacco manufacturers not to facilitate smuggling. Section 3 provides for an increase in the rate of excise duty charged on beer, and s 4 provides for an increase in the rate of excise duty charged on still wine and still made-wine. A number of provisions of the Alcoholic Liquor Duties Act 1979 that are of no practical utility or are entirely obsolete cease to have effect by virtue of the 2006 Act s 5. The adjustments made by certain statutory instruments affecting the liabilities to duty under the Hydrocarbon Oil Duties Act 1979 are consolidated and the rates of duty and rates of rebate applicable to products charged to duty under that Act are amended: 2006 Act ss 6, 7. Section 8 confers power on the Treasury to amend the schedule of excepted vehicles for the purposes of the Hydrocarbon Oil Duties Act 1979 that are entitled to run on rebated heavy oil. The charging provision for general betting duty in the Betting and Gaming Duties Act 1981 to exclude specifically any bets that are made on a gaming machine and are charged with value added tax is amended by the 2006 Act s 9, and s 10 increases the rates of gaming duty. Section 11 revises the definition of 'gaming machine' in the 1981 Act. The description of gaming machine categories and rates of duty for the purposes of amusement machine licence duty are also amended: 2006 Act s 12. Section 13 provides for changes in the rates of vehicle excise duty, and s 14 extends the Secretary of State's regulation-making powers in respect of reduced pollution certificates. Section 15 provides for the recovery in Scotland of supplements payable under continuous registration.

Part 2 (ss 16–22) Value added tax
The definition of gaming machines for valuation purposes is amended by s 16. The Treasury is empowered by s 17 to substitute the Value Added Tax Act 1994 Sch 10 for the purpose of rewriting it with amendments and to make related provision or savings, and to repeal certain redundant provisions. Changes to the valuation for value added tax purposes of certain importations of works of art, antiques and collector's pieces from outside the European Union are made by the 2006 Act s 18 so that where any such goods have been entered to a temporary importation regime and sold by auction while within it, any commissions payable to the auctioneer are to be excluded from the value of the goods for VAT where the goods are then finally imported into the European Union. By virtue of s 19, the VAT registered customer, rather than the seller, is to account for and pay the VAT on the supply of certain goods of a kind used in missing trader intra-community fraud. The power of officers of Revenue and Customs to enter premises and inspect goods for VAT purposes is extended by s 20 to include a right to mark the goods or their packaging for the purposes of indicating that they have been inspected, and to record by electronic means any information relating to the goods. Power is conferred on the Commissioners for Her Majesty's Revenue and Customs to direct individual businesses to keep specified records relating to specified goods, in addition to the current records that are required to be kept for VAT purposes, where they have reasonable grounds for believing that the records might assist in identifying taxable supplies in respect of which the VAT chargeable might not be paid: s 21. Under s 22, the Treasury may specify the circumstances in which the supply of credit vouchers is not to be disregarded for VAT purposes.

Part 3 (ss 23–102) Income tax, corporation tax and capital gains tax

Chapter 1 (ss 23–26) Income tax and corporation tax charge and rate bands
For the year 2006–07, the starting, basic, and higher rates of tax are 10 per cent, 22 per cent, and 40 per cent: s 23. Corporation tax for the financial year beginning 1 April 2007 remains at 30 per cent (s 24) and the small companies' rate of corporation tax for the financial year beginning 1 April 2006 is 19 per cent, and the marginal-relief fraction remains at 11/400ths (s 25). Section 26 provides for the abolition of the corporation tax starting rate and non-corporate distribution rate.

Chapter 2 (ss 27–30) Reliefs for business
Section 27, Sch 1 make provision for group relief where the surrendering company is not resident in the United Kingdom, s 28, Sch 2 expand the expenditure qualifying for research and development reliefs to include payments to volunteers participating in clinical trials, and s 29, Sch 3 amend provisions relating to claims for relief for research and development. Section 30 increases to 50 per cent, for one year, the rate of first-year capital allowances for spending by small businesses on most plant and machinery.

Chapter 3 (ss 31–53) Films and sound recordings
Definitions are provided of 'film' and the circumstances in which a series of films is to be treated as a single film, and when a film is treated as having been completed (s 31), 'film production company' (s 32), 'film making activities' (s 33), 'production expenditure', 'core expenditure' and 'limited-budget film' (s 34), 'UK expenditure' (s 35), and 'qualifying co-production' and 'qualifying co-producer' (s 36). Section 37, Sch 4 provide for the computation by film production companies of their profits and gains for tax purposes. The three conditions that films need to meet in order to qualify for film tax relief are set out in s 38. A film must be intended for theatrical release, it must be certified as a British film and not less than 25 per cent of the core production expenditure on the film must be UK expenditure: ss 39–41. Section 42, Sch 5 set out how film tax relief is to operate. A restriction is imposed by s 43 as to the way in which a film production company may use trading losses, which may be carried forward only while the film is in production. A film production

company may use its losses, including those brought forward from earlier periods, more widely in the period during which the film is completed or abandoned (s 44) and any losses remaining, when the trade of the film production company making a film that qualifies for film tax relief ceases, may be transferred to another similar trade of the same company, or within the same group (s 45). Section 46 sets out how and when the current basic treatment of expenditure on the production or acquisition of films and of preliminary expenditure on film production, and the special relief for British films, is to be disapplied for corporation tax purposes, and s 47 sets out how and when the current basic treatment of expenditure on the production or acquisition of films and of preliminary expenditure on film production, and the special relief for British films, is to be disapplied for income tax purposes. By virtue of s 48, expenditure on the production or acquisition of the original master version of a sound recording is treated as expenditure of a revenue nature and receipts from disposal of the master version, rights in it or money derived from the original master version are treated as revenue receipts for corporation tax purposes and are brought into account in calculating the profits for the accounting period in which they are received. The way in which expenditure on the original master version of a sound recording is allocated to accounting periods for the computation of taxable profits is set out in s 49. Section 50 provides for the interpretation of 'sound recording', 'original master version' and 'relevant period the purposes of ss 48 and 49. Provision is made by s 51 for the modification of the exclusion of films so far as acquisition expenditure is concerned. The Treasury may make regulations providing for the tax treatment of films that are already in production (s 52) and to appoint a day for the commencement of Pt 3 Ch 3 and amend key dates (s 53).

Chapter 4 (ss 54–58) Charities
Restrictions are imposed by s 54 on the transactions in which a charity may participate with a substantial donor that benefit from tax exemption or relief. A mechanism that restricts tax reliefs granted to a charity where it incurs non-charitable expenditure is excepted by s 55. Section 56 removes the risk that a charity with a trade that is only partly carried on for a primary charitable purpose of the charity, or is not mainly carried on by the beneficiaries of the charity, might, if the non-charitable part of the trade is large, lose tax relief on the profits of the whole of the trade. Under s 57, subsidiary companies that are wholly owned by one or more charities may donate their profits to those charities and obtain tax relief for the donation using company gift aid. Restrictions on gift aid payments by close companies are extended by s 58.

Chapter 5 (ss 59–64) Personal taxation
From 2008–09, the lower threshold for company car tax rates is to be reduced and a new 10 per cent band for cars with CO_2 emissions of 120g/km or below is introduced: s 59. The exemption for employer provided mobile telephones is replaced so that no tax will be due when employers make only one mobile telephone available for private use; the availability to family or household tax-free is removed, and the provision of a non-cash voucher or credit token used to facilitate the private use of a mobile telephone that would otherwise be exempt from a tax charge on the benefit in kind is exempt from tax: s 60. The exemption for computer equipment made available to employees for private use is removed: s 61. By virtue of s 62, the provision by employers of eye tests and/or corrective glasses for visual display units use to their employees and the provision of a non-cash voucher or credit-token used to facilitate the provision of such eyecare tests and corrective glasses are exempt form tax. Under s 63, the Treasury may exempt from tax the use of a voucher or credit-token to provide a benefit in kind that would otherwise be exempt from tax. Tax payments made by United Kingdom and foreign banks and building societies to Holocaust victims or their heirs for dormant accounts are exempt from tax: s 64.

Chapter 6 (ss 65–68) London Olympic Games and Paralympic Games
The London Organising Committee of the Olympic Games Ltd ('LOCOG') is exempt from corporation tax with retrospective effect and the Treasury may apply the exemption, as appropriate, to a wholly-owned subsidiary of LOCOG and make further provision in relation to LOCOG and another person where LOCOG is acting in concert with a third party: ss 65, 66. Regulations may be made under s 67 in relation to the tax treatment of the International Olympic Committee ('IOC') and certain persons owned or controlled by it. Regulations may be made in relation to the tax treatment of non-United Kingdom resident athletes and other non-resident persons temporarily in the United Kingdom to carry out Olympic-related business: s 68.

Chapter 7 (ss 69–74) Chargeable gains
Section 69 amends the definition of an allowable capital loss for corporation tax purposes so as to exclude losses generated by a company as part of a tax avoidance scheme. A company is prevented by s 70 from being bought and sold primarily in order to allow one group of companies to access the capital losses that were suffered by another company or group where the ownership of the company changes as part of arrangements that have a main purpose of tax avoidance. Section 71 prevents the use of a company's capital losses in tax avoidance schemes intended to reduce the income profits chargeable to corporation tax. Section 72 repeals the Taxation of Capital Gains Act 1992 s 106. Provisions relating to capital gains and losses arising on disposals of rights conferred by certain types of insurance policiy and annuity contract are amended so as to clarify how the rules apply in relation to capital redemption policies: 2006 Act s 73. Schemes to avoid capital gains tax are amended so that,

in certain circumstances, the 'bed and breakfasting' rules do not identify 'securities' (including shares or other assets that cannot be separately identified), that have been disposed of, with identical assets acquired within the following 30 days if the person who makes the disposal is not resident in the United Kingdom for tax purposes at the time of the acquisition: s 74.

Chapter 8 (ss 75–80) Avoidance: miscellaneous
Where an individual who pays interest on a loan used to buy into a partnership carrying on a film-related trade (a 'film partnership'), s 75 restricts relief to 40 per cent of the interest paid where the individual's loan is secured on an investment in another partnership (an 'investment partnership') in which his right to a share of the taxable income is disproportionately low compared to his capital contribution to the investment partnership. Section 76, Sch 6 make provision in relation to tax avoidance involving financial arrangements. Changes are made by s 77 to the legislation that deals with companies' intangible fixed assets, and by s 78 to the controlled foreign company rules. Section 79, Sch 7 amend the anti-avoidance legislation on the transfer of assets abroad. An existing exemption from the charge to income tax on the benefit of enjoying pre-owned assets will not apply where the chargeable person disposes of an asset, continues to enjoy it, and is given an interest in possession in it: s 80.

Chapter 9 (ss 81–102) Miscellaneous provisions
A new regime for the taxation of long funding leases of plant or machinery is introduced by s 81, Sch 8, and Sch 9 makes amendments relating to such leases. Section 82, Sch 10 make provision about the sale etc of lessor companies carrying on a business on their own or in partnership where there is a change of ownership of the company or a change in the arrangements for sharing partnership profits. Section 83 restricts the use of losses arising from a leasing business carried on by a company in partnership where there are unusual profit sharing arrangements. Provision is made by s 84 as to the disposal value to be used when a piece of plant or machinery subject to a lease is sold and the right to all or some of the income from the lease is retained. Restrictions are imposed by s 85, for corporation tax purposes, on the effect of an election where the transferor and transferee are both carrying on a business of leasing plant or machinery. Section 86, Sch 11 make a number of changes to the taxation of companies carrying on life assurance business by ensuring that losses cannot be created or profits reduced by paying bonuses etc out of untaxed surplus transferred to a company on a demutualisation, by preventing the potentially indefinite deferral of taxation on investment return in non-profit, and by removing unintended charges to tax where there is a transfer of business, including a demutualisation. Insurance companies and friendly societies are enabled by s 87 to agree certain types of variation in the terms of life insurance policies with their holders without attracting undesirable tax consequences for the policyholders. Section 88, Sch 12 provide for the amendment of legislation relating to chargeable gains in respect of settlements, and s 89, Sch 13 provide for the amendment of legislation relating to income taxation in respect of trustees and settlements. Income arising from service charges held on trust by certain social landlords is excluded by s 90 from being taxed at the special trust rates. The Enterprise Investment Scheme, the Venture Capital Trust Scheme and the Corporate Venturing Scheme are amended: s 91, Sch 14. Changes relating to employment-related securities are made to counter avoidance schemes which use options over shares and securities to deliver employment reward: s 92. The rules on corporation tax relief for shares acquired under Enterprise Management Incentive options are amended by s 93. Provision is made by s 94 for PAYE to be applicable prospectively on retrospective notional payments of employment income. The legislation on alternative finance arrangements is extended to provide for an agency-style alternative finance arrangement, which is economically equivalent to a deposit at interest, to be taxed in the same way as a conventional deposit (s 95), and to provide for a partnership-style alternative finance arrangement, used to finance the purchase of property or other asset, to be taxed in a similar way to conventional arrangements (s 96). Section 97 provides for certain low-cost alternative finance arrangements made by employers to employees to be taxed as a benefit in kind in the same way as conventional low-interest loans to employees. Arrangements similar to alternative finance arrangements which equate in substance to a loan or deposit but do not give rise to the payment or receipt of interest may be brought into the existing legislation by Treasury order: s 98. The Energy Act 2004 is amended so that accounting entries made by certain publicly owned companies in the British Nuclear Fuels Group, arising from the recognition of the Nuclear Decommissioning Authority taking responsibility for nuclear decommissioning and cleaning-up, are not to be brought into account for corporation tax purposes (2006 Act s 99) and certain accounting entries made by the Nuclear Decommissioning Authority on taking responsibility for nuclear decommissioning and cleaning-up should not be brought into account for corporation tax purposes (s 100). The temporary regime under which securitisation companies remain on old UK generally accepted accounting practice for tax purposes is extended for a further year to cover periods of account ending before 1 January 2008: s 101. Certain taxable adjustments, which arise from a change in accounting policy required to comply with the interpretation of UK generally accepted accounting practice, may be spread for income tax and corporation tax purposes over between three and six years: s 102, Sch 15.

Part 4 (ss 103–145) Real Estate Investment Trusts

Section 103 introduces Pt 4, which enables a company or group of companies, a Real Estate Investment Trust ('REIT'), which carries on property rental business and which satisfies specified requirements to opt to benefit from exemptions from corporation tax on profits and gains and have liabilities to tax imposed on the company or group and the recipients of distributions made by it. 'Property rental business' is defined by s 104, and Sch 16 sets out the classes of business and of income or profit that are excluded form the definition. Other key concepts relating to REITs are defined by s 105. Section 106 sets out the conditions for giving notice to join the REIT regime, and the conditions that a company must fulfil in order to join and remain in it. Details are provided by s 107 of the conditions that a company must satisfy in relation to the type of business that it carries out in order to be eligible for the REIT regime. Section 108 provides details on the proportion of a company's business that must be qualifying property rental business by reference to profits and assets in order to qualify for the REIT regime. The mechanism through which a company may inform the Commissioners for Her Majesty's Revenue and Customs that it wishes to opt for the REIT legislation to apply to it is set out by s 109. Once Pt 4 has begun to apply to a company, it continues to apply until a termination event occurs: s 110. Section 111 describes the effect on the existing business of a company when it enters the REIT regime. The amount and nature of the charge levied when a company first enters the REIT regime is 2 per cent of the value of the company's assets that transfer to the tax-exempt property rental busiiness: s 112. A separation is provided by s 113 for tax purposes between the pre-conversion company, the post-conversion company, and the tax-exempt business and non tax-exempt business during the time of application of REIT legislation to the company. The Treasury, under s 114, may impose a tax charge on the REIT if it pays out distributions to investors with 10 per cent or more of the company's dividends, share capital or voting rights. Provision is made by s 115 of an interest cover ratio that an REIT must meet if it is to avoid the imposition of a tax charge, which is to be set out in regulations. Treasury regulations under s 116 may provide for minor or inadvertent breaches of some of the REIT regime membership conditions as an alternative to requiring the company to leave the regime. Section 117 allows for the cancellation of the tax advantage, when an REIT tries to obtain a tax advantage, and for the imposition of an additional charge to tax equal to the advantage sought. Where cash arising from the disposal of an asset used in the tax-exempt business is not immediately reinvested in an asset of the tax-exempt business and is instead invested in short term funds, debits or credits arising from any resulting loan relationships, it falls to be relieved or taxed as part of the non tax-exempt business: s 118. Section 119 sets out the exemption from corporation tax that applies to the property rental business of an REIT and the rate of tax applicable to other activities, and s 120 provides the mechanism for the calculation of profits of the tax-exempt business of an REIT. A distribution from the tax-exempt profits of an REIT is taxable under Schedule A, in the case of a shareholder chargeable to corporation tax, and as profits of a UK property business, in the case of a shareholder chargeable to income tax: s 121. Section 122 provides powers to set out the detailed requirements concerning deduction of basic rate income tax from distributions of profits of the tax-exempt business of an REIT, and s 123 sets out how an REIT identifies which of its distributions are treated as paid out of profits of its tax-exempt property rental income. Rules are set out by s 124 for exempting from corporation tax some or all of the gain on the disposal of an asset that has been used at some time for the purposes of the tax-exempt business of an REIT. Section 125 provides that, where an asset is transferred from the tax-exempt business to the non tax-exempt business of an REIT, the transfer is treated as a disposal by the tax-exempt business for a consideration equal to the market value of the asset as defined for chargeable gains purposes, and the sale and reacquisition take place at tax written-down value for capital allowances purposes. Where an asset is transferred from the non tax-exempt business to the tax-exempt business of an REIT, the transfer is treated as a disposal by the non tax-exempt business for a consideration equal to the market value of the asset for chargeable gains purposes, and the transfer takes place at tax written-down value for capital allowances purposes: s 126. By virtue of s 127, the capital gains provisions in ss 124–126 supra are to be construed as one with the Taxation of Chargeable Gains Act 1992: 2006 Act s 127. A company that is an REIT may give notice to the Commissioners that it wishes to leave the REIT regime: s 128. They may issue a notice to an REIT that the regime is to cease to apply to it if the REIT has repeatedly failed to meet certain conditions of the regime or been involved in tax avoidance: s 129. By virtue of s 130, the REIT regime ceases automatically to apply to a company when it breaches certain conditions of the regime. Section 131 describes what happens for tax purposes to the tax-exempt business that was carried on by the company while it was an REIT. Rules that apply if a company leaves the REIT regime within ten years of entering it are set out in s 132, and rules for when the REIT regime ceases to apply to a company if it leaves the regime early as the result of breaching one of the conditions the company has to meet to remain in the regime are set out in s 133. Section 134 defines the group of companies that may join the regime to become a group REIT, and introduces Sch 17 which modifies the single-company REIT rules so that they may apply to groups of companies. In relation to a single company which has elected into the REIT, the normal capital gains group rules which enable a transfer of assets between members of the group at no gain or loss do not apply between the tax-exempt and non tax-exempt parts of the company:

s 135. Section 136 sets out the availability of group reliefs. For the purposes of the taxation of chargeable gains, where shares in REITs are held by an insurance company as part of its long term insurance fund. the company is deemed to have sold the shares and immediately reacquired them at market value at the end of each accounting period: s 137. Section 138 allows provision to be made in regulations to accommodate joint ventures in which an REIT is an investor being included within the REIT regime, and s 139 applies the provisions of the manufactured payments regime to distributions paid out of the tax-exempt profits of an REIT. Provision is made by s 140 for penalties in cases where an REIT fails to comply with certain provisions of the legislation. Section 141 deals with the effect of deemed disposal and re-acquisition of an asset under Pt 4. Section 142 defines various terms used in Pt 4, s 143 repeals the legislation relating to Housing Investment Trusts, s 144 describes how the powers to make regulations provided in relation to the REIT provisions may be used, and s 145 sets out when a company may first enter the REIT regime, and sets the date for repeal of the Housing Investment Trust legislation.

Part 5 (ss 146–154) Oil
Section 146, Sch 18 provide a new basis for determining the market value of oil, and s 147 provides for the commencement of those provisions and makes transitional provisions. The Commissioners may make regulations for determining to which fields and in what proportions blended oil is attributable for oil pricing for tax purposes: s 148. Section 149 revises the terms of the nomination scheme in the way in which nomination excesses are calculated. Section 150 provides for changes to the way oil disposed of is valued for tax purposes. Provision is made by s 151 for an excess of nominated proceeds to be brought into charge for the purposes of ring fence corporation tax and supplementary charge. The supplementary charge in respect of ring fence trades is increased by s 152 to 20 per cent. Under s 153, a company may elect to defer capital allowances for capital expenditure in respect of a ring fence trade. A new supplement, known as ring fence expenditure supplement, extends and replaces the existing exploration expenditure supplement: s 154, Sch 19.

Part 6 (ss 155–157) Inheritance tax
The inheritance tax threshold is increased to £312,000 in 2008–09 and to £325,000 in 2009–10: s 155. Section 156, Sch 20 align the inheritance tax rules for assets held in trust. The exemption from inheritance tax of settled property situated outside the United Kingdom that applies unless the settlor was domiciled in the United Kingdom at the time the settlement was made no longer extends to holdings in authorised unit trusts and open-ended investment companies where a person domiciled in the United Kingdom has acquired an interest in possession in the property as a result of a money transaction: s 157.

Part 7 (ss 158–161) Pensions
Section 158, Sch 21 remove tax advantages for investment-regulated pension schemes on investments in residential or tangible movable. An anti-avoidance rule counters the use of tax-free lump sums from registered pension schemes to fund further tax-relieved pension contributions: s 159. Section 160, Sch 22 clarify how inheritance tax is applied to members of registered pension schemes when the new tax rules for pension schemes take effect. The pensions tax simplification legislation is amended to give schemes, employers and pension savers additional flexibility, and to provide measures dealing with the transition to the new regime and to prevent abuse of the new rules: s 161, Sch 23.

Part 8 (ss 162–169) Stamp taxes
Stamp duty land tax on residential transactions is increased by s 162 to £125,000, and the threshold for stamp duty on documents effecting land transactions is increased to £125,000. Further provision is made for the stamp duty land tax treatment of transactions between partners and partnerships and transactions in partnership interests (s 163, Sch 24) and for the stamp duty land tax treatment of leases (s 164, Sch 25). Section 165 prevents a charge to stamp duty land tax arising when trust property is reallocated between beneficiaries. Provision is made for the stamp duty land tax treatment of transfers of assets to the trustees of a unit trust scheme (s 166) and for relief from stamp duty land tax on the demutualisation of an insurance company (s 167). The current reliefs from stamp duty land tax for alternative financing transactions are extended by s 168 to persons other than individuals. The stamp duty reconstruction and acquisition reliefs are amended by s 169 so that the acquiring company is no longer required to have its registered office in the United Kingdom and the rules requiring the proportion of shares held by each shareholder to remain unaltered are revised.

Part 9 (ss 170–177) Miscellaneous provisions
The standard rate of landfill tax is increased by s 170 to £21 per. The rates of climate change levy are increased with effect from 1 April 2007: s 171. Section 172 abolishes the temporary half-rate of climate change levy for energy used by the horticulture sector, and s 173 provides for international agreements about mutual assistance in the enforcement of taxes, covering exchange of information, assistance in tax collection and the service of documents. The powers available to the Commissioners to obtain information for the purposes of a liability to income tax, corporation tax and capital gains tax are adapted by s 174 so that they may be used to obtain information in respect of a liability to any foreign tax included in agreements provided for in s 173. By virtue of s 175, foreign tax debts arising from the international agreements provided for in s 174 may be recovered in the United Kingdom.

Section 176 aligns the parliamentary procedures applying to Orders in Council that give effect to agreements concerning the avoidance of double taxation with the procedures applying to orders made under s 174. A criminal sanction is incurred for the wrongful disclosure of information provided by the Commissioners that has been passed to the Gambling Commission, or other specified persons or bodies, in accordance with information sharing provisions in the Gambling Act 2005: 2006 Act s 177.

Part 10 (ss 178–180) Supplementary provisions
Section 178, Sch 26 deal with repeals, s 179 provides for interpretation, and s 180 deals with short title.

2466   Finance (No 2) Act 2005—commencement

The Finance (No 2) Act 2005, Section 17(1), (Appointed Day) Order 2006, SI 2006/982, brings s 17(1) into force (1) for the purposes of income tax, (a) for the year 2006–07 and subsequent years of assessment, and (b) for distributions made on or after 6 April 2006; and (2) for the purposes of corporation tax, (a) on income, for accounting periods beginning on or after 1 April 2006, (b) on chargeable gains, in relation to disposals made on or after 1 April 2006, and (c) for distributions made on or after 1 April 2006. For a summary of the Act, see 2005 Abr para 2670. See also the commencement table in the title STATUTES.

2467   Income and corporation tax

See INCOME TAXATION.

2468   Inheritance tax

See INHERITANCE TAXATION.

2469   Stamp duties

See STAMP DUTIES AND STAMP DUTY RESERVE TAX.

2470   Value added tax

See VALUE ADDED TAX.

ROAD TRAFFIC

Halsbury's Laws of England (4th edn) vol 40(1) (Reissue) paras 1–672, vol 40(2) (Reissue) paras 673–1484

Articles

For articles relating to this title please refer to the Table of Articles at the beginning of the Abridgment.

2471   Accident—personal injury claim—causation—permission to adduce expert evidence

See *Casey v Cartwright*, para 2278.

2472   Dangerous driving—causing death by dangerous driving—aiding and abetting

The defendant was charged with aiding and abetting causing death by dangerous driving. The co-accused had been drinking all day, and later in the evening, the defendant permitted the co-accused to drive. The co-accused drove erratically and at excessive speed. The vehicle left the road and the deceased was thrown from the vehicle. The co-accused pleaded guilty to causing death by dangerous driving. The prosecution case against the defendant was that the defendant had known that it was dangerous to permit the co-accused to drive because of his state of intoxication, or alternatively that the defendant had appreciated that the co-accused was driving dangerously, and that he ought to have intervened. The defendant was convicted. On appeal against conviction, *held,* it was not sufficient to rely on the condition of the driver in order to prove the offence of dangerous driving or of causing death by dangerous driving. In order to prove that a defendant was guilty of aiding and abetting a principal to drive dangerously, the prosecution had to prove that, at the time he had permitted him to drive, he had foreseen that the principal was likely to drive in a dangerous manner. Evidence that the defendant had known that the co-accused had not only been drinking, but appeared to be intoxicated, was powerful evidence that he had foreseen that the co-accused was likely to drive in a dangerous manner at the time that he had permitted him to drive. However, the evidence of the co-accused's intoxication did not determine the issue. In relation to the defendant's potential liability for failing to intervene when the co-accused was driving dangerously, the prosecution had to prove knowledge of what was actually happening at the time. In the present case, the judge's directions and the way in which the prosecution had put its case were incorrect and the conviction would be quashed. Accordingly, the appeal would be allowed.

R v Webster [2006] EWCA Crim 415, [2006] All ER (D) 41 (Mar) (Court of Appeal: Moses LJ, Jack and Royce JJ).

2473 Dangerous driving—causing death by dangerous driving—plea of guilty to all charges—withdrawal of one charge

See *DPP v Revitt*, para 806.

2474 Disqualification from holding licence—previous conviction—certificate of disqualification—proof of identity

See *Pattison v DPP*, para 796.

2475 Drink-driving—breath test—specimen of breath—unreliable result—further specimens

The claimant was stopped by police while driving a motor vehicle. He provided a positive breath test and was taken to a police station. At the police station he was requested to give two further specimens of breath and warned, pursuant to the Road Traffic Act 1988 s 7(7), that a failure to provide such specimens might render him liable to prosecution. Specimens were taken, but they gave such variable readings that the police officer invited the claimant to provide further specimens. No fresh s 7(7) warning was given and the claimant agreed to provide the specimens. The specimens were taken and the claimant was subsequently convicted of driving a motor vehicle after consuming excess alcohol. The judge rejected the claimant's contention that the procedure by which he had provided two further specimens of breath had been defective because the police officer had failed to give a fresh s 7(7) warning. The claimant appealed. *Held*, where further specimens of breath had been requested it was not necessary for the police officer to give the claimant a further warning under s 7(7). After the first set of specimens had proved unreliable the officer had not required the claimant to provide further specimens. Rather, the officer had invited the claimant to provide a further set of specimens and the claimant had agreed to do so. Therefore, s 7(7) had not applied in that situation. The purpose of s 7(7) was to warn that failure to provide a specimen as required might render a person liable to prosecution. However, a failure to provide a specimen when invited, rather than required, to do so, could not render a person liable to prosecution. In the circumstances, the procedure adopted by the police officer had not been defective. Accordingly, the appeal would be dismissed.

Edmond v DPP [2006] EWHC 463 (Admin), [2006] All ER (D) 287 (Mar) (Queen's Bench Division: Richards LJ and David Clarke J).

2476 Drink-driving—defence—breath-testing device—lawfulness of type approval

See *DPP v Wood; DPP v McGillicuddy* and *Murphy v DPP*, para 768.

2477 Driving instruction—licence

The Motor Cars (Driving Instruction) (Amendment) Regulations 2006, SI 2006/525 (in force on 1 April 2006), further amend the 2005 Regulations, SI 2005/1902, so as to (1) provide that a candidate for a written examination, driving ability and fitness test, or instructional ability and fitness test is no longer permitted to give proof of his or her identity by producing a cheque guarantee or credit card bearing his or her photograph and signature; the only permitted forms of identification in all cases are (a) a photocard licence and its counterpart; or (b) a licence in a form other than a photocard and a current passport; for the instructional ability and fitness test a candidate may alternatively provide a licence in a form other than a photocard and a licence issued under the Road Traffic Act 1988 s 129(2); and (2) require a candidate for a driving ability and fitness test, the instructional ability and fitness test or the practical part of the continued ability and fitness test to allow a person authorised by the Secretary of State to travel in the motor car provided for the test for the purpose of supervising the test or otherwise.

2478 Driving licence—requirements

The Motor Vehicles (Driving Licences) (Amendment) Regulations 2006, SI 2006/524 (in force in part on 1 April 2006 and in part on 1 July 2007), amend the 1999 Regulations, SI 1999/2864, so as to (1) restore the minimum period for which a qualified driver who supervises a provisional licence holder must hold a licence in respect of certain categories of vehicle; (2) provide that a qualified driver supervising a provisional licence holder driving, broadly, a coach, bus or lorry, must have held a licence of a type specified for a minimum period of three years provided that licence also authorises the driving of vehicles in the same category as the vehicle being driven by the provisional licence holder and he has held that entitlement for a minimum period of one year; (3) remove a spent provision; (4) allow instructors of drivers of motor cars to make block bookings for theory driving tests for their pupils; (5) remove a spent provision concerning tests conducted before 4 January 2000; (6) remove an error in the 1999 Regulations specifying fees for theory tests by substituting 'motor vehicle' for 'motor car'; (7) specify that the fee for taking theory and practical or unitary tests is determined according to whether the application for the test is made before 1 April 2006, or on or after that date, rather than according to whether the test is to be conducted before 1 April 2006, or on or after that date; (8) require category C and C+E vehicles, broadly lorries with or without trailers, that are provided for practical driving tests to be fitted with seat belts for use by the examiner and any person authorised by the Secretary of State to be present at the test for the purpose of supervising it or otherwise; (9) require certain vehicles, broadly cars, lorries and buses with or without trailers, provided for practical driving tests to be fitted with nearside and offside mirrors that give the examiner adequate rearward vision; and (10) make the requirement relating to seatbelts apply also in respect of category D and D+E vehicles (broadly buses).

2479   Driving offence—dangerous driving—meaning of 'driving dangerously'—high speed as sufficient condition

The Road Traffic Act 1988 s 2A(1) provides that a person is to be regarded as driving dangerously if, and only if (1) the way he drives falls far below what would be expected of a competent and careful driver; and (2) it would be obvious to a competent and careful driver that driving in that way would be dangerous.

The defendant was a police officer and grade 1 advanced driver. In the early hours of one morning when he was on duty, he drove an unmarked police car, without using its sirens or flashing lights, at average speeds of 91 miles per hour on a road in a built-up area with a 30 miles per hour speed limit, and of 148/9 miles per hour on a motorway. He was charged with one count of dangerous driving, contrary to the 1988 Act s 2. The district judge accepted the defendant's contention that he was 'honing his driving skills' in an unfamiliar car that he might be required to drive in operational conditions pursuant to instructions that he had been given. Having watched a video of the driving in question, he found that the weather was fine, that visibility was good, that the roads were 'more or less deserted', and that there was no evidence that another road user had been endangered. He therefore acquitted the defendant of dangerous driving. The prosecution appealed, submitting that driving at twice the speed limit was dangerous whatever the context. *Held*, speed alone was not sufficient to found a conviction for dangerous driving; it had to be a question of speed in the context of all the circumstances. To hold otherwise would mean that any driver of an emergency vehicle would be liable to be found guilty of dangerous driving, and would have to rely on the Crown Prosecution Service exercising its discretion not to prosecute. However, the district judge had failed to conduct an adequate review of the facts. He appeared to have made no distinction between the different speeds on the different types of road and to have ignored hazards identified by the prosecution. Different considerations might apply to doing 90 miles per hour in a built-up area than to doing 150 miles per hour on a motorway. The fact that the defendant was travelling without warning siren or lights distinguished the instant case from one in which a police officer was responding to an emergency call, and the district judge had failed to take into account that a driver pulling out into the path of the defendant's vehicle would be taken completely by surprise. Accordingly, the appeal would be allowed.

DPP v Milton [2006] All ER (D) 04 (Feb) (Queen's Bench Division: Hallett LJ and Owen J). *R v Collins* [1997] RTR 439, CA (1997 Abr para 2825), applied.

2480   Driving Standards Agency—funding—maximum borrowing

See para 616.

2481   Motor cycles—type approval

The Motor Cycles Etc (EC Type Approval) (Amendment) Regulations 2006, SI 2006/2935 (in force on 11 December 2006), further amend the 1999 Regulations, SI 1999/2920, by amending the definition of 'the Framework Directive' and adding EC Commission Directive 2005/30 to the list of amending separate directives, so as to implement amendments to EC Parliament and Council Directives 97/24 and 2002/24 for the purposes of EC type approval procedures.

2482   Motor insurance

See INSURANCE.

2483   Motor vehicles—registration—ownership rights

The claimant had received a letter from a bankrupt which he believed transferred the ownership rights of a vehicle registration mark to him. The trustee in bankruptcy successfully applied for a declaration from the registrar that the letter had no effect under the Retention of Registration Marks Regulations 1993, SI 1993/987. The claimant appealed. *Held*, a vehicle registration mark was assigned to a motor vehicle by a government agency for regulatory reasons, and so was an item of property only in a qualified sense. The right to the mark was the ability to use the regulatory machinery to obtain the transfer of a mark from one vehicle to another, which could not be described as a chose in action. Even if it could, it could not be assigned, as distinct from being exercised in accordance with the 1993 Regulations. There had been no legal or equitable assignment of the mark and, accordingly, the appeal would be dismissed.

Goel v Pick [2006] EWHC 833 (Ch), [2007] 1 All ER 982 (Chancery Division: Sir Francis Ferris).

2484   Motor vehicles—registration—two cars with same registration number

The claimant and the defendant owned historic racing cars. Both cars bore the same chassis and registration number. Both cars had, at various times, been registered at the Driver and Vehicle Licensing Agency ('DVLA'), which eventually discovered that there were two cars bearing the same chassis and registration numbers. The DVLA was asked to decide which car should retain the registration number. It took the view that both parties had complex and contradictory claims, and decided to withdraw the registration number from both vehicles. The claimant sought declaratory relief and the defendant counterclaimed. An issue arose as to the justiciability of the claim. *Held*, the claim and counterclaim did not concern any right which could be the subject of adjudication. There was no common law right to a particular registration mark. The system of registration marks was a creature of statute, and any right to a particular mark had to be found in statute. Apart from certain exceptions, there was no general statutory right to a particular registration mark. Further, the DVLA had been entrusted by Parliament with making decisions in relation to registration numbers, and the decision which it had reached in the present case appeared to have been lawful. The genealogy of motor cars was not of itself a proper subject for the court to investigate unless the investigation was for the purpose of deciding on justiciable rights of the parties. There were no established principles to apply to the determination of the issue raised, precisely because a registration mark was not a right of property. Accordingly, both the claim and counterclaim would be dismissed.

Lloyd v Svenby [2006] EWHC 315 (QB), [2006] All ER (D) 380 (Feb) (Queen's Bench Division: Stanley Burnton J).

2485   Motor vehicles—tests

The Motor Vehicles (Tests) (Amendment) Regulations 2006, SI 2006/1998 (in force on 8 September 2006), amend the 1981 Regulations, SI 1981/1694, so as to (1) modify the procedures for the re-examination of vehicles, other than those in class VI or VIA, which have failed the MOT test so that no fee is payable in respect of a re-examination carried out within ten working days by the same authorised examiner after the completion of repairs at the vehicle testing station; (2) provide that the re-examination of class VI or VIA vehicles will be charged at a maximum of one-half of the full fee where such vehicles are returned to the same testing station before the expiration of ten working days starting from the day after the day of the original examination; (3) remove the reference to class IVA and VA vehicles from the exclusion to the re-examination provisions so as to allow such classes of vehicles to continue to benefit from the re-examination provisions, so long as there has been no change to the authorised examiner at the vehicle testing station between the original examination and the re-examination; and (4) permit those requiring an examination of class IVA and VA vehicles, in specified circumstances, to be charged a maximum of one-half of the fee chargeable for a class IV or V vehicle.

The Motor Vehicles (Tests) (Amendment) (No 2) Regulations 2006, SI 2006/2680 (in force on 7 November 2006), further amend the 1981 Regulations supra, so as to (1) increase the fees payable for test examinations of vehicles; and (2) provide for an increase, from £1·44 to £1·71, in the charge for the making of entries in the computerised record in respect of vehicles which pass the MOT test.

2486   Motor vehicles—type approval

The Motor Vehicles (EC Type Approval) (Amendment) Regulations 2006, SI 2006/142 (in force on 21 April 2006), further amend the 1998 Regulations, SI 1998/2051, by adding EC Parliament and Council Directives 2005/39, 2005/40 and 2005/41 to the list of amending separate directives, thereby implementing them for the purposes of the type approval of light vehicles.

The Motor Vehicles (EC Type Approval) (Amendment No 2) Regulations 2006, SI 2006/1695 (in force on 30 July 2006), further amend the 1998 Regulations supra so as to encompass, in the definition of 'Framework Directive', the further amendments made to ECC Council Directive 70/156 by EC Commission Directives 2005/49 and 2006/28. The regulations also require a type of light passenger vehicle to comply with the requirements of the Directives to receive EC type approval.

The Motor Vehicles (EC Type Approval) (Amendment No 3) Regulations 2006, SI 2006/2409 (in force on 13 October 2006), further amend the 1998 Regulations by adding references to EC Council Directive 2005/66, which imposes new frontal protection requirements on light passenger vehicles of a total technically permissible laden mass less than or equal to 3·5 tonnes and on goods vehicles with a maximum mass not exceeding 3·5 tonnes, to the list of Directives which lay down technical requirements for vehicle components or features of construction to receive EC type approval.

The Motor Vehicles (EC Type Approval) (Amendment No 4) Regulations 2006, SI 2006/2816 (in force on 30 November 2006), further amend the 1998 Regulations supra so as to encompass, in the definition of 'Framework Directive', further amendments made to EEC Council Directive 70/156 by EC European Parliament and Council Directive 2005/55, and EC European Commission Directives 2005/78 and 2006/51, which relate to the type approval of light passenger vehicles.

2487 Motor vehicles—type approval and approval marks—fees

The Motor Vehicles (Type Approval and Approval Marks) (Fees) (Amendment) Regulations 2006, SI 2006/1638 (in force on 9 August 2006), further amend the 1999 Regulations, SI 1999/2149, by increasing the fees payable for examinations of vehicles or parts, the examination of complete vehicles and the issue of documents in connection with type approval.

2488 Motor vehicles—wearing of seat belts

The Motor Vehicles (Wearing of Seat Belts) (Amendment) Regulations 2006, SI 2006/1892 (in force on 18 September 2006), amend the Road Traffic Act 1988, the Road Traffic Offenders Act 1988, and the 1993 Regulations, SI 1993/176, so as to implement EC Council Directive 2003/20, and make provision relating to the wearing of seat belts and other restraints by children and adults in motor vehicles. In relation to the wearing of seat belts by children in the front or rear of motor vehicles, the regulations (1) provide that a child should not be transported in the front of a motor vehicle other than a bus using a rear-facing child restraint, unless any front air bag has been deactivated entirely or is designed or adapted in such a way that it cannot inflate enough to pose a risk of injury to a child travelling in a rear-facing child restraint; (2) create an offence of transporting a child in a motor vehicle other than a bus in circumstances where the front air bag has not been so deactivated or is not so designed; (3) prohibit, with exceptions, the driving of a motor vehicle with a child under the age of three years in the rear unless the child is restrained by an acceptable seat belt; (4) apply the same prohibition to a child over the age of three years but under the age of 14 years where any seat belt is fitted in the rear of the vehicle; (5) amend the definition of 'small child' for the purposes of the 1993 Regulations, so that it refers to a child under the age of 12 years and under 135 cm in height; and (6) provide for further exemptions from the prohibition against driving a motor vehicle with a child in the rear who is not wearing an appropriate restraint. In relation to the wearing of seat belts by adults and children in the rear of buses, the regulations (a) require bus operators to take reasonable steps to ensure that bus passengers are notified that they are required to wear a seat belt, which may be done by means of an announcement by the driver or by a courier, conductor or group leader, by means of an audio-visual presentation or by specified signs displayed at every seating position; (b) create an offence for operators of failing to take reasonable steps to ensure passengers are notified as such; (c) make provision in relation to offences by bodies corporate; (d) amend the definition of an 'appropriate' seat belt in the 1993 Regulations so as to exclude the possibility of an adult seat belt being 'appropriate' in relation to small children; (e) require adults and children over the age of 13 years to wear seat belts, where available, in the rear of all classes of motor vehicle except where a large or small bus is being used to provide a local service in a built-up area, or where the bus is constructed or adapted for the carriage of standing passengers and standing is permitted; and (f) require children aged three years or over but under the age of 14 years to wear seat belts where available in the rear of all classes of motor vehicle except large buses.

2489 Motor vehicles—wearing of seat belts—children in front seats

The Motor Vehicles (Wearing of Seat Belts by Children in Front Seats) (Amendment) Regulations 2006, SI 2006/2213 (in force on 18 September 2006), amend the 1993 Regulations, SI 1993/31, so as to implement EC Council Directive 2003/20, and make provision relating to the wearing of seat belts and other restraints by children in the front of motor vehicles. In particular, the regulations (1) prescribe the types of seat belt or child restraints to be worn in the front seats of motor vehicles by children under the age of 14 of different ages and sizes; (2) remove the exemption which allows small children aged three or above to wear adult belts in cases where no appropriate child restraint is available, except in relation to buses; (3) remove the exemption for children under the age of one year travelling in a carry cot and for children riding unrestrained in the front seat of a motor car first used before 1 January 1965, where that car has no rear seat and no seat belt is provided which is appropriate for the child; (4) replace the existing exemption for a child riding in a vehicle which is being used to provide a local service, with an exemption for a child riding in a bus, which is (a) providing a local service in a built up area; or (b) constructed or adapted for the carriage of standing passengers and on which standing is permitted; and (5) amend the description of the types of child restraint, or adult belt, in the case of large children, which may be worn in order to permit restraints or belts approved by other member states to be worn in all classes of motor vehicle.

**2490   Offence—causing danger to other road users—placing object in road—
dangerousness—reasonable person**

The respondent placed a metal road sign in the carriageway of a public road during the hours of
darkness. A car crashed into a tree some distance beyond the position of the sign, and both occupants
of the car were killed. The respondent was charged with an offence of causing anything to be on or
over a road in such circumstances that it would be obvious to a reasonable person that to do so
would be dangerous, contrary to the Road Traffic Act 1988 s 22A(1)(a). The judge ruled that the
term 'reasonable person' in that provision had to be construed in the context of a reasonable road
user and that the dangerousness must relate to injury to a person or serious damage to property, and
must be a real and significant danger, not simply a fanciful possibility. He concluded that he could
not be satisfied that it would have been obvious to a reasonable person that causing the sign to be in
the road would be dangerous. On the prosecutor's appeal, *held*, the reasonable person would have
realised that an obstruction of the sort described could play a part in causing an accident,
notwithstanding that the primary cause of such an accident might be bad driving on the part of a
motorist, whether in the form of excessive speed or a failure to keep a proper lookout, or following
other traffic too closely, or a combination of such factors. The question to consider was whether a
reasonable bystander would consider that what had been placed on the road represented an obvious
danger, irrespective of whether that reasonable bystander was a motorist. In the instant case, the
reasonable bystander would have been fully aware that not all drivers do drive carefully and well.
Accordingly, the appeal would be allowed.

DPP v D [2006] EWHC 314 (Admin), [2006] RTR 461 (Queen's Bench Division: Richards LJ
and David Clarke J).

2491   Road Safety Act 2006

The Road Safety Act 2006 makes provision about road traffic, registration plates, vehicle and driver
information, hackney carriages and private hire vehicles and trunk road picnic areas. The Act
received the royal assent on 8 November 2006 and certain provisions came into force on that day.
Further provisions came into force on 8 January 2007. The remaining provisions come into force on
a day or days to be appointed. For details of commencement, see the commencement table in the
title STATUTES.

The Secretary of State may pay road safety grants to local and other authorities, and may make
regulations allowing the use of surplus road safety camera income by public authorities for road
safety purposes: ss 1, 2. Sections 3, 4 enable the Secretary of State to impose graduated fixed
penalties and graduated fixed penalty points, so as to take account of the circumstances and
seriousness of offences, and s 5, Sch 1 empower vehicle examiners to issue fixed penalty notices for
offences which they have the power to enforce. Provision is also made by ss 6, 7 for fixed penalty
notices in respect of heavy goods vehicles and public service vehicles to be made notifiable to the
traffic commissioners by an applicant for, or a holder of, a goods vehicle operator's licence or, as the
case may be, a public service vehicle operator's licence. Section 8 introduces the concept of a driving
record in relation to each person, which must be maintained by the Secretary of State and is
endorseable with particulars of road traffic offences committed by that person. Such driving records
are to have effect in relation to foreign and unlicensed drivers (s 9, Sch 2), and subsequently in
relation to all drivers (s 10, Sch 3). Section 11 empowers the police and vehicle examiners to require
a deposit towards the payment of a fixed penalty notice to be paid by a person they believe has
committed a relevant offence but has no satisfactory address in the United Kingdom, and provides
that an immediate prohibition on driving may be imposed on failure to pay such a deposit. Vehicles
issued with an immediate prohibition may be immobilised by an enforcement officer or other
authorised person: s 12, Sch 4. By virtue of s 13, high risk offenders are no longer entitled to drive
while awaiting the outcome of medical inquiries relevant to the return of a licence, and s 14 provides
that an endorsement in respect of a failure to allow a specimen to be subjected to a laboratory test
will remain on a person's licence for 11 years. Provision is made by ss 15, 16 for alcohol ignition
interlock programmes to be offered to offenders in certain circumstances over an experimental
period, with the effect that completion of such a programme will reduce an offender's overall period
of disqualification. Section 17 extends the range of penalty points available and provides for a more
graduated arrangement of fixed penalties in respect of specified speeding offences and s 19 enables
the Secretary of State to prescribe new purposes for which vehicles are exempted from speed limits.
Section 18 allows for the prohibition of speed assessment equipment detection devices. New
offences of causing death by careless, or inconsiderate, driving (s 20), causing death by driving while
unlicensed, disqualified or uninsured (s 21) and keeping a vehicle which does not meet insurance
requirements (s 22, Sch 5) are created. Penalties are also increased by ss 23–29 for the offences of
careless, and inconsiderate, driving, contravening requirements relating to the wearing of seat belts
by children in the rear of vehicles, using a vehicle in a dangerous condition, breaching requirements
as to vehicle control and the use of mobile telephones, failing to stop a mechanically propelled
vehicle, furious driving and breaching the duty to give information as to driver identity in certain
circumstances. The meaning of careless, or inconsiderate, driving is clarified by virtue of s 30 and
s 31 extends the application of the offence of causing death by dangerous driving when under the

influence of drink or drugs to drivers who have not consented to blood being subjected to a laboratory test. Section 33 enables convictions for specified offences to be made available as alternative verdicts where a prosecution for manslaughter in connection with the driving of a mechanically propelled vehicle has been unsuccessful. Penalty points and periods of disqualification imposed in respect of specified offences may be reduced where an offender successfully completes a prescribed course: ss 34, 35. Provision is made in relation to driving tests and extended tests by ss 36, 37. Section 38 empowers the Secretary of State to impose further conditions on the grant of a full driving licence and s 39 makes provision in relation to the compulsory surrender of old-form driving licences. The Secretary of State may charge a fee for the renewal of photocard licences and certain other driving licences (s 40) and may make regulations so as to make available information about persons providing or giving instruction on driver training courses (s 41). Section 42, Sch 6 impose new requirements in relation to paid driving instruction, relating in particular to the registration of driving instructors, and s 43 makes provision in relation to a statutory scheme regulating the use of persons who may assist certain driving test candidates. Provision is made by ss 44, 45 in relation to the regulation of number plate suppliers. Particulars to be included in the register of vehicles held by the Driver and Vehicle Licensing Agency may be prescribed by regulations and may relate to a vehicle or to its keeper: s 47. The effect of s 48 is to require the Secretary of State to maintain records relating to the testing of goods vehicles, and s 49 provides for the disclosure of certain data to foreign vehicle licensing authorities. Sections 50, 51 enable the Secretary of State to place requirements on a local traffic authority when making a level crossing order and concern the delegation of the Secretary of State's powers to make such orders. A licensing authority may suspend or revoke the licence of a taxi or private hire vehicle driver with immediate effect if it appears that the interests of public safety require such action to be taken: s 52. Sections 53, 54 extend the existing licensing requirements for drivers of public hire vehicles. The Secretary of State may enter into arrangements with a view to providing picnic areas and conveniences on land adjoining motorways (s 55), may make a scheme requiring modified vehicles running on fuels stored under pressure to have certificates verifying satisfactory modification (s 56) and may impose further regulation relating to the transport of radioactive material (s 57). Section 58 makes minor corrections to legislation and s 59, Sch 7 set out repeals and revocations. The Secretary of State is empowered by s 60 to make amendments to other legislation as a consequence of the coming into force of a provision of the 2006 Act. Sections 61–63 deal with commencement, extent and short title.

Amendments, repeals and revocations
The list below, which is not exhaustive, mentions amendments which are or will be effective when the Act is fully in force.

Specific provisions of a number of Acts are substituted, added or repealed. These include: Road Traffic Regulation Act 1984 s 87; Road Traffic Act 1988 ss 2B, 3ZA, 3ZB, 40, 41C, 41D, 49A, 98A, 123–125, 125ZA, 126, 128, 128A, 129, 130, 132, 133, 133ZA, 134, 135, 141A, 142, 144A–144D, 159A, 162A; Road Traffic Offenders Act 1988 ss 30A–30D, 32, 34A–34G, 41B, 44A, 45, 45A, 57, 57A, 58, 58A, 61, 61A, 77, 77A, 90A–90F, 91ZB, 91B, 97A; Road Traffic (Driving Instruction by Disabled Persons) Act 1993 s 2; Railways and Transport Safety Act 2003 s 109.

2492 Road traffic offences—sentencing

See SENTENCING.

2493 Road vehicles—construction and use

The Road Vehicles (Construction and Use) (Amendment) Regulations 2006, SI 2006/1756 (in force on 1 August 2006), further amend the 1986 Regulations, SI 1986/1078, by revising the definition of 'the emissions publication' so as to refer to the most recent edition of the publication entitled 'In Service Exhaust Emission Standards for Road Vehicles'.

2494 Road vehicles—construction and use—motor vehicles—type approval

The Road Vehicles (Construction and Use) and Motor Vehicles (Type Approval for Goods Vehicles) (Great Britain) (Amendment) Regulations 2006, SI 2006/2565 (in force in part on 20 October 2006 and in part on 9 November 2006), further amend the Road Vehicles (Construction and Use) Regulations 1986, SI 1986/1078, so as to incorporate the requirements of EC Directive 2005/55 and EC Directive 2005/78 on vehicle emissions into the domestic requirements concerning the design, construction, equipment and use of vehicles. The regulations also amend the provisions relating to emissions requirements for end-of-series vehicles to ensure that European law is fully implemented and align the calculation of the maximum number of vehicles that may enter into service under the emissions end-of-series provisions, both in the 1986 Regulations and under the Motor Vehicles (Type Approval for Goods Vehicles) (Great Britain) 1982, SI 1982/1271, with that used in European law, and, in particular, EEC Directive 70/156. In particular, the regulations (1) replace the reference to the Directives previously listed in the 1986 Regulations reg 61A Table item 2 with a reference to Directive 2005/55, Directive 2005/78 and EC Directive 2006/51, in order to implement these Directives; (2) make the same substitutions with respect to the definition of 'vehicle' for the purposes of the meaning of 'non-type approval end-of-series vehicles'; (3) amend the 1986 Regulations to take into account the fact that some Directives specify more than one stage of emission limit values, or other requirements; these amendments ensure that an end-of-series vehicle can be exempted from one stage only; (4) ensure that end-of-series exemptions granted in other member states and in Northern Ireland are recognised in Great Britain; (5) ensure that end-of-series vehicles under the Motor Vehicles (EC Type Approval) Regulations 1998, SI 1998/2051 are covered by the exemptions in the 1986 Regulations; (6) in relation to vehicles not subject to type approval, the maximum number of vehicles that can enter into service under the 1986 Regulations is increased to either 30 per cent of the vehicles registered by the manufacturer in the 12 months before the date when the new set of requirements came into effect, or 100, whichever is the greater; and (7) in relation to vehicles subject to the 1982 Regulations, the maximum number of vehicles which may be regarded as end-of-series vehicles is increased to 30 per cent of those registered in the 12 months before the date when the new set of requirements came into effect, or 100, whichever is the greater.

2495   Road vehicles—registration and licensing

The Road Vehicles (Registration and Licensing) (Amendment) Regulations 2006, SI 2006/2320 (in force on 1 October 2006), further amend the 2002 Regulations, SI 2002/2742, so as to (1) provide that eligible vehicles which are registered before 1 October 2006 must satisfy the reduced pollution requirements; (2) provide that a reduced pollution certificate is conclusive evidence that the reduced pollution requirements are satisfied by a registered eligible vehicle; and (3) provide that, where an applicant furnishes a reduced pollution certificate in respect of a vehicle which is not registered, the Secretary of State must revoke the certificate if he is satisfied that the vehicle is not an eligible vehicle which satisfies the reduced pollution requirements.

2496   Roads—quiet lanes and home zones—designation—England

The Quiet Lanes and Home Zones (England) Regulations 2006, SI 2006/2082 (in force on 21 August 2006), provide for the making, variation and revocation of designations of roads as quiet lanes or home zones under the Transport Act 2000 s 268, and of use orders and speed orders in respect of those roads. Specifically, the regulations (1) require the local traffic authority to give persons in the area of the relevant road an opportunity to make representations before a proposal for designation is developed and provide that at least one public meeting must be held; (2) require an authority, before designating a road, to consult prescribed persons, to publish details of the designation proposals and to consider objections; (3) provide for the making of use orders and speed orders in respect of designated roads; (4) require an authority, before making such an order, to consult prescribed persons, to publish details of the order proposals and to consider objections; (5) permit the modification of proposed designations or orders, subject to persons affected by substantial changes being given an opportunity to object; (6) require notices to be given by an authority after it has made a designation or use or speed order and provide for the variation or revocation of a designation or order subject to similar procedures as those for designation or making an order; (7) require a map showing a designation to be kept by the authority; and (8) require traffic signs informing road users of the designation to be placed appropriately.

2497   Speeding—traffic signs—indication of speed limit—signs not visible

The Road Traffic Regulations Act 1984 s 85(1) provides that for the purpose of securing that adequate guidance is given to drivers of motor vehicles as to whether any, and if so what, limit of speed is to be observed on any road, it is the duty of the Secretary of State, in the case of a road for which he is the traffic authority, to erect and maintain traffic signs in such positions as may be requisite for that purpose. It is the duty of the local traffic authority to erect and maintain traffic signs in such positions as may be requisite in order to give effect to general or other directions given by the Secretary of State: s 85(2). Under s 85(4), where no such system of street or carriageway lighting is provided on a road, but a limit of speed is to be observed on the road, a person will not be convicted of driving a motor vehicle on the road at a speed exceeding the limit unless the limit is indicated by means of specified traffic signs.

The defendant was convicted of an offence of speeding. He had driven down a stretch of road subject to a 30 mph speed limit at 46 mph. He claimed not to have seen the road signs indicating the speed limit. The court found that the stretch of road in question was preceded by a stretch of road that was subject to a 40 mph speed limit, and while the roadside signs were in the correct place and of the correct size, height and shape, they were only visible at the point at which the defendant drove past them as they were obscured by overgrown hedgerows. The Crown Court dismissed the defendant's appeal and he appealed against that decision. *Held,* under the 1984 Act s 85(4), two tests had to be met before the defendant could be convicted, the first being that at the time the offence was said to have been committed there were such signs as were mentioned in the 1984 Act s 85(1) or (2), and the second being that those signs indicated the relevant speed limit. The second test required that at the geographical point where the motorist exceeded the limit, the signs could reasonably be expected to have conveyed the limit to an approaching motorist to give him sufficient time to reduce from a previous lawful speed to a speed within the limit. The objective of s 85(4) was to prevent motorists being convicted in the absence of adequate guidance as to the relevant limit. It was impossible to conclude that the second test had been met. Accordingly, the appeal would be allowed.

Coombe v DPP [2006] EWHC 3263 (Admin), [2006] All ER (D) 296 (Dec) (Queen's Bench Division: Keene LJ and Waller J). *Wawrzynczyk v Chief Constable of Staffordshire Constabulary* (2000) Times, 16 March, DC (2000 Abr para 2804), considered.

2498 Tractors—emission of gaseous and particulate pollutants

See para 2382.

2499 Tractors—type approval

The Tractor etc (EC Type-Approval) (Amendment) Regulations 2006, SI 2006/2533 (in force on 18 October 2006), amend the 2005 Regulations, SI 2005/390, so as to (1) amend the definitions of 'separate directive' and 'the Tractor Type Approval Directive' so that EC Directive 2003/37 and amending Community instruments are taken into account; and (2) provide that, in deciding whether to grant or amend type-approval, the United Kingdom type-approval authority must make any decision in accordance with Directive 2003/37 and any relevant separate directive. SI 1988/1567, 1989/2275, 1990/2336, 1992/80, 2000/828, 2001/1710 and 2002/1890 are revoked.

2500 Traffic signs—quiet lanes

The Traffic Signs (Amendment) Regulations 2006, SI 2006/2083 (in force on 21 August 2006), amend the Traffic Signs Regulations and General Directions 2002, SI 2002/3113, by adding new diagrams to indicate quiet lanes in England, and by revising the requirements regarding the illumination of signs.

2501 Traffic signs—school crossing patrol sign

The School Crossing Patrol Sign (England and Wales) Regulations 2006, SI 2006/2215 (in force on 4 September 2006), replace the 2002 Regulations, SI 2002/3020, and prescribe the size, colour and type of sign which, in accordance with the Road Traffic Regulation Act 1984 s 28, a school crossing patrol may exhibit in order to require traffic to stop when approaching a place where a person is crossing or seeking to cross a road. In particular, the regulations increase the permissible size of the perimeter strip and increase the flexibility with regard to the colouring and illumination requirements of the patrol signs.

SALE OF GOODS AND SUPPLY OF SERVICES

Halsbury's Laws of England (4th edn) vol 41 (2005 Reissue) paras 1–930

Articles

For articles relating to this title please refer to the Table of Articles at the beginning of the Abridgment.

2502 Consumer contracts—unfair terms—water

The Unfair Terms in Consumer Contracts (Amendment) and Water Act 2003 (Transitional Provision) Regulations 2006, SI 2006/523 (in force on 1 April 2006), amend the Unfair Terms in Consumer Contracts Regulations 1999, SI 1999/2083, so as to substitute a reference to the 'authority' for a reference to the 'director'.

2503 Consumer protection—contractual terms—unfairness—implied terms

The defendant company purchased a property including a static caravan park, whose caravans were owned by the claimants who had contractual licences to pitch their caravans on the property. The defendant sent letters to the claimants purporting to give them six months' notice of the termination of their rights to occupy. The claimants brought proceedings, claiming that they had a contractual right to occupy their pitches for ten years. The question arose as to whether a term was to be implied into the licences based on a common but unexpressed understanding, and whether the Unfair Terms in Consumer Contracts Regulations 1999, SI 1999/2083 applied to terms implied at common law. *Held*, while reg 4(2) excluded terms which reflected mandatory statutory or regulatory provisions, it did not explicitly exclude terms implied by common law. Such terms were implied to make contracts work by filling a technical lacuna in the contract. It was difficult to see how these terms could be seen to be unfair. Further, terms could be implied to give effect to the common but unspoken intention of the parties and again, it was difficult to see how such a term could be unfair. It was highly unlikely that the 1999 Regulations were intended to apply to implied terms.

Schedule 2 provided a list of indicative and non-exhaustive terms which might be regarded as unfair, but none obviously fell within the category of implied terms. Accordingly, the claim would be dismissed.

Baybut v Eccle Riggs Country Park Ltd [2006] All ER (D) 161 (Nov) (Chancery Division: Pelling J).

2504 Consumer protection—enforcement—Community infringements—specified laws

The Enterprise Act 2002 (Part 8 Community Infringements Specified UK Laws) Order 2006, SI 2006/3372 (in force on 8 January 2007), specifies, for the purposes of the Enterprise Act 2002 s 212, (1) the Control of Misleading Advertisements Regulations 1988, SI 1988/3372, reg 4A as the law which gives effect to EC European Parliament and Council Directive 97/55 amending EEC Council Directive 84/450; (2) the Price Marking Order 2004, SI 2004/102, as the law which gives effect to EC European Parliament and Council Directive 98/6; and (3) the Civil Aviation (Denied Boarding, Compensation and Assistance) Regulations 2005, SI 2005/975, as the law which gives effect to European Parliament and EC Council Regulation 261/2004.

2505 Consumer protection—general provisions

The Enterprise Act 2002 (Amendment) Regulations 2006, SI 2006/3363 (in force on 8 January 2007), amend (1) the Enterprise Act 2002 by (a) adding entry and inspection to the powers of an officer of a Consumer Protection Co-operation enforcer ('CPC enforcer'), and providing that such powers do not apply to the Crown; (b) providing (i) procedural safeguards in relation to the exercise of the CPC enforcers' powers; and (ii) that it is a criminal offence to obstruct without reasonable excuse, or fail to co-operate with, an officer of a CPC enforcer who is seeking to exercise the powers conferred; (c) giving (i) details of the bodies which are entitled to exercise the powers as a CPC enforcer, but restricting the scope of the CPC enforcers' activities by providing that they may only apply for an enforcement order in relation to Community infringements; and (ii) CPC enforcers the power to publish (or to obtain an undertaking to publish) an undertaking obtained other than in connection with proceedings to obtain an enforcement order; (d) extending the power to give notice to enable an enforcer to acquire information in any form; (e) clarifying how references to the bodies which already act as enforcers are to be interpreted; and (f) ensuring that certain powers and protections which the Financial Services Authority enjoys under the Financial Services and Markets Act 2000 apply to the discharge of its functions under European Parliament and EC Council Regulation 2006/2004 (as amended); (2) the Criminal Justice and Police Act 2001 by (a) applying the enhanced seizure powers to the power of entry and inspection under warrant; and (b) ensuring that the definition of 'legal professional privilege' applies where the issue of privilege arises in the context of powers under the 2001 Act by CPC enforcers; and (3) the Data Protection Act 1998 by ensuring that the subject access provisions do not obstruct the proper functioning of Regulation 2006/2004.

2506 Consumer protection—liability for defective products—supply of goods

A company incorporated under French law produced vaccines and supplied them to its subsidiary, incorporated in the United Kingdom, which then sold them to hospitals. In proceedings against the first respondent, the applicant contended that he had suffered harm as a result of being vaccinated with a defective vaccine supplied by the first respondent. The action was discontinued when it became clear that the proceedings should have been commenced against the second respondent. A fresh action was duly initiated against the second respondent, which was resisted on limitation grounds since more than ten years had elapsed since the product had been put into circulation by delivery to the first respondent. The applicant contended that the action was not statute-barred, as the putting into circulation of the product had not taken place until the moment when it had been supplied by the first respondent to a hospital nominated by the Department of Health, a time less than ten years prior to the bringing of the action. The court stayed proceedings and referred to the European Court of Justice for a preliminary ruling the questions of whether, in the case where a product was transferred by a producer company to a distribution subsidiary to a third party, EC Council Directive 85/374 art 11 was to be interpreted as meaning that the putting into circulation of the product occurred at the time of the transfer of the product from the production company to the subsidiary, or instead when that product was transferred by the subsidiary to the third party, and whether, when an action was brought against a company mistakenly considered to be the producer of a product, it was open to the national courts to view such an action as being brought against the actual production company and to substitute the latter, as defendant to the action, for the company initially proceeded against. *Held*, art 11 was to be interpreted as meaning that a product was put into circulation when it was taken out of the manufacturing process operated by the producer and entered a marketing process in the form in which it was offered to the public in order to be used or consumed. When an action was brought against a company mistakenly considered to be the producer of a product, whereas, in reality, it was manufactured by another company, it was as a rule for national law to determine whether the conditions in accordance with which one party might be substituted for another in the context of such an action. A national court examining the conditions governing such a substitution had, however, to ensure that due regard was had to the personal scope of Directive 85/374.

Case C-127/04 *O'Byrne v Sanofi Pasteur MSD Ltd* [2006] All ER (EC) 674 (ECJ: First Chamber).

2507   Consumer protection—packaging—essential requirements

The Packaging (Essential Requirements) (Amendment) Regulations 2006, SI 2006/1492 (in force on 1 July 2006), further amend the 2003 Regulations, SI 2003/1941, by revising the definition of packaging to reflect the wording in European Parliament and EC Council Directive 2004/12, and by removing the expiry date for the derogation for glass packaging in relation to the heavy metal concentration levels.

2508   Consumer protection—supply of goods—liability for defective goods—eggs with salmonella poisoning

After eating eggs from a shop, the claimants fell ill with salmonella poisoning. They brought proceedings against the supplier, the owner of the shop, which joined the producer of the eggs in the proceedings. The court found that the eggs had been defective, that there was a causal link between the defect and the damage suffered, and that no fault on the part of the claimants had been shown. The supplier was ordered to pay compensation to the claimants, and the producer was ordered to reimburse the supplier for that compensation. The supplier and the producer appealed. A ruling was sought from the European Court of Justice as to whether EC Council Directive 85/374 on the approximation of the laws, regulations and administrative provisions of the member states concerning liability for defective products, was to be interpreted as precluding a national rule under which the supplier was answerable without restriction for the no-fault liability which Directive 85/374 established and imposed on the producer, and whether Directive 85/374 precluded a national rule under which the supplier was answerable without restriction for the fault-based liability of the producer where damage was caused by a defective product. *Held,* Directive 85/374 had to be interpreted as precluding a national rule under which the supplier was answerable, beyond the cases listed exhaustively in art 3(3), for the no-fault liability which Directive 85/374 established and imposed on the producer, and not precluding a national rule under which the supplier was answerable without restriction for the producer's fault-based liability.

Case C-402/03 *Skov AEG v Bilka Lavprisvarehus A/S Bilka Lavprisvarehus A/S v Mikkelsen* [2006] 2 CMLR 455 (ECJ: Grand Chamber).

2509   Consumer protection—tobacco products—advertising and promotion—information society services

The Tobacco Advertising and Promotion Act 2002 etc (Amendment) Regulations 2006, SI 2006/2369 (in force on 28 September 2006), give effect to EC European Parliament and Council Directive 2000/31 and 2003/33 by amending the Tobacco Advertising and Promotion Act 2002. The amendments (1) create new offences in relation to publishing, devising or distributing a tobacco advertisement in the EEA by information society services ('ISS') from an establishment in the United Kingdom; (2) provide that it is only where the publisher carries on business outside the EEA that it is not an offence to publish a tobacco advertisement on a website which is accessible in the United Kingdom; (3) create new offences in relation to any proprietor or editor of an ISS which contains a tobacco advertisement and in relation to any person who directly or indirectly commissioned the offending advertisement; (4) limit the exclusion from the tobacco advertising offences to publications printed outside the EEA whose principal market is not any of the EEA states, or any part of them; (5) exclude from the offences under the 2002 Act information on tobacco products provided by ISS only in reply to a particular request by a person for such information or to persons who have initiated a purchase of a tobacco product from an ISS; (6) exclude from the prohibition of free distributions ISS providers who act as a mere conduit, or who are caching or hosting information containing a tobacco advertisement; (7) extend the defences in the 2002 Act to the new offences; and (8) provide for maximum penalties for the new offences. The regulations also amend the Electronic Commerce (EC Directive) (Extension) Regulations 2003, SI 2003/115.

2510   Consumer protection—weights and measures—prosecutions—notice

The Enterprise Act 2002 (Part 8 Notice to OFT of Intended Prosecution Specified Enactments) Order 2006, SI 2006/3371 (in force on 8 January 2007), specifies the Civil Aviation (Denied Boarding, Compensation and Assistance) Regulations 2005, SI 2005/975, as legislation under which prosecutions by local weights and measures authorities must be notified to the Office of Fair Trading.

2511   Consumer safety—cosmetic products

The Cosmetic Products (Safety) (Amendment) Regulations 2006, SI 2006/1198 (in force on 22 May 2006), further amend the 2004 Regulations, SI 2004/2152, by adding further substances classified as carcinogenic, mutagenic or toxic to reproduction to the list of substances which cosmetic products may not contain, and by revising the list of substances which cosmetic products must not contain except subject to specified restrictions.

The Cosmetic Products (Safety) (Amendment) (No 2) Regulations 2006, SI 2006/2231 (in force on 1 September 2006), further amend the 2004 Regulations supra by revising the list of substances which cosmetic products may not contain so as to add further substances which are banned from use in hair dyes, and by extending to 30 December 2007 the date until which certain substances may be used.

The Cosmetic Products (Safety) (Amendment) (No 3) Regulations 2006, SI 2006/2907, further amend the 2004 Regulations, in order to correct an error in SI 2006/2231 supra, so as to prohibit the placing on the market or the supply of certain substances in hair dyes after 30 November 2006.

2512   Consumer safety—dangerous substances and preparations—safety

The Dangerous Substances and Preparations (Safety) Regulations 2006, SI 2006/2916 (in force in part on 4 December 2006, in part on 24 August 2007, in part on 16 January 2007, and in part on 24 August 2007), prohibit, subject to exceptions, the supply of certain dangerous substances and preparations. They revoke the 1994 Regulations, SI 1994/2844 and implement EC Commission Directives 2005/59, 2005/84 and 2005/90. The regulations also implement EEC Council Directive 76/769, as last amended by EC Directive 2005/90, so far as the amended directive concerns substances and preparations prohibited for supply to consumers. In particular, the regulations, which do not apply to supply for research and development or analysis (1) prohibit, with exceptions, the supply of substances or preparations containing benzene in concentrations equal or greater than 0.1 per cent by mass; (2) prohibit, with exceptions, the supply to a member of the general public, or for the purposes of sale to such a person, of substances which are carcinogenic, mutagenic or toxic for reproduction; (3) prohibit the supply of textile articles intended to come into contact with the skin and children's dressing gowns treated with certain substances; (4) prohibit, with exceptions, the supply to a member of the general public, or for supply for the purposes of sale to such a person, of substances or preparations containing specified chlorinated solvents; (5) prohibit, with exceptions, the perfuming or colouring of certain liquid substances supplied as fuel for decorative lamps; (6) prohibit the supply of ornamental objects, tricks, jokes and games containing specified substances which are 'dangerous for supply'; (7) prohibit the supply of dangerous substances and preparations intended to cause amusement, for example stink bombs and sneezing powder; (8) prohibit the supply of childcare articles containing greater than a specified percentage of phthalates; and (9) prohibit the supply to a member of the general public, or supply for the purposes of sale to such a person, of toluene or adhesives or spray paints containing toluene in a concentration equal to or greater than 0.1 per cent by mass.

2513   Sale of goods—advertising—comparative advertising—substantial duplication of product identification codes

EC Council Directive 84/450 art 3a(1)(g) provides that comparative advertising is permitted when it does not take unfair advantage of the reputation of a trade mark, trade name or other distinguishing marks of a competitor or of the designation of origin of competing products.

The claimant company manufactured and distributed programmable controllers. The order numbers for the controllers and add-on components followed a particular system designed by the claimant. The defendant company manufactured and sold components that were compatible with the claimant's controllers. The defendant's own product identification system was virtually identical to that used by the claimant, with each product code largely corresponding to that of the equivalent product manufactured by the claimant. The codes were displayed on the products themselves and in the defendant's product catalogue. The claimant brought proceedings against the defendant, alleging that the defendant's product identification system took unfair advantage of the reputation of the claimant's products. It fell to be determined whether the use by a competing supplier of the core elements of a manufacturer's distinguishing mark, which was known in trade circles, constituted taking unfair advantage of the reputation of that distinguishing mark within the meaning of Directive 84/450 art 3a(1)(g). *Held*, art 3a(1)(g) had to be interpreted as meaning that, in circumstances such as those in the main proceedings, by using in its catalogues the core element of a manufacturer's distinguishing mark which was known in specialist circles, a competing supplier had not taken unfair advantage of the reputation of that distinguishing mark. In the present case, there had been no unfair advantage because the products at issue were intended for a specialist public which was much less likely than final consumers to associate the reputation of the claimant's products with that of the defendant's products, and the use of the defendant's acronym in the order numbers made it possible to distinguish between the parties' products and prevented a false impression being created either as to the origin of the defendant's products or as to the existence of any association between the two companies.

Case C-59/05 *Siemens AG v VIPA GmbH* [2006] 2 CMLR 865 (ECJ: First Chamber).

2514   Sale of goods—contract—risk—delivery on a carriage and insurance paid basis

Scotland

It has been held that the use of the expression 'CIP' (Carriage and Insurance Paid) in a contract for the sale of goods is not, in itself, determinative of when risk passes.

Stora Enso OYJ v Port of Dundee (2006) Times, 11 April (Outer House).

2515   Sale of goods—doorstep selling—prohibition—free movement of goods

See Case C-441/04 *A-Punkt Schmuckhandels GmbH v Schmidt*, para 924.

2516   Sale of goods—international sale contracts—c i f and related contracts—place of delivery and performance—jurisdiction

See *Scottish and Newcastle International Ltd v Othon Ghalanos Ltd*, para 598.

2517   Tobacco Advertising and Promotion Act 2002—commencement

The Tobacco Advertising and Promotion Act 2002 (Commencement No 9) Order 2006, SI 2006/2372, brings the Act, so far as it is not already in force, into force on 26 September 2006. For a summary of the Act, see 2002 Abr para 2614. For details of commencement, see the commencement table in the title STATUTES.

2518   Trade descriptions—textile products—composition

The Textile Products (Determination of Composition) Regulations 2006, SI 2006/3298 (in force on 6 January 2007), replace the 1976 Regulations, SI 1976/202, and specify that the test methods to be used to analyse certain textile products are those set out in European Parliament and EC Council Directive 96/73 and EEC Council Directive 73/44.

2519   Trade descriptions—textile products—indications of fibre content

The Textile Products (Indications of Fibre Content) (Amendment and Consolidation of Schedules of Textile Names and Allowances) Regulations 2006, SI 2006/3297 (in force on 6 January 2007), further amend the Textile Products (Indications of Fibre Content) Regulations 1986, SI 1986/26, so as to (1) set out a replacement list of the names to be used for different types of textile fibres and fibre descriptions; and (2) set out the replacement percentage allowances to apply to the anhydrous mass of each fibre when determining composition of mixtures by weight.

SALE OF LAND

Halsbury's Laws of England (4th edn) vol 42 (Reissue) paras 1–400

Articles

For articles relating to this title please refer to the Table of Articles at the beginning of the Abridgment.

See

conveyancing.

SENTENCING

Halsbury's Laws of England (4th edn) vol 11(4) (2007 Reissue) paras 1558–1836

Articles

For articles relating to this title please refer to the Table of Articles at the beginning of the Abridgment.

2520   Anti-social Behaviour Act 2003—commencement

The Anti-Social Behaviour Act 2003 (Commencement No 4) (Amendment) Order 2006, SI 2006/835, amends the Anti-social Behaviour Act 2003 (Commencement No 4) Order 2004, SI 2004/2168, so as to extend, for a further period of six months, the period of eighteen months for which s 85(5) has been brought partially into force in relation to juveniles, for the purpose of conducting a pilot. This makes possible the continued conduct of the pilot for the extended period in relation to applications for anti-social behaviour orders in specified county courts.

The Anti-social Behaviour Act 2003 (Commencement No 5) (Wales) 2006, SI 2006/1278, brings into force, in relation to Wales, on 11 May 2006, ss 19–22 and 24.

The Anti-social Behaviour Act 2003 (Commencement No 6) (England) Order 2006, SI 2006/393, brings ss 48–52 into force, so far as they are not already in force, on 6 April 2006.

For a summary of the Act, see 2003 Abr para 2320. See also the commencement table in the title
STATUTES.

2521   Anti-social behaviour order—application for order—relevant authorities and relevant persons

The Crime and Disorder Act 1998 (Relevant Authorities and Relevant Persons) Order 2006,
SI 2006/2137 (in force on 1 September 2006), provides that the Environment Agency and Transport
for London are to be relevant authorities for the purposes of the Crime and Disorder Act 1998 ss 1,
1B, 1CA, 1CA and 1E, with the effect that they are bodies which, after consultation with the local
authority and the police, can apply to a magistrates' court for an anti-social behaviour order, or to a
county court for a similar order, for the purpose of protecting the persons specified from further
anti-social acts.

2522   Anti-social behaviour order—breach—jurisdiction to determine validity of order

The respondent was made the subject of an anti-social behaviour order which prohibited him from
acting in an anti-social manner in a specified city. The respondent subsequently committed an
interference with a motor vehicle, and proceedings were brought alleging that he had breached the
order. The district judge decided that the prohibition in the order, which he had himself made, was
too vague and too widely drawn, and was therefore invalid. The prosecution appealed, submitting
that any order made by a court of competent jurisdiction was valid on its face and that any challenge
to it should have been by way of appeal against the making of the order or by application to vary it.
Held, the normal rule in relation to an order of the court was that it had to be treated as valid and be
obeyed unless and until it was set aside. Even if the order should not have been made in the first
place, a person might be liable for any breach of it committed before it was set aside. The person
against whom an anti-social behaviour order was made had a full opportunity to challenge that order
on appeal or to apply to vary it. During the intervening period it could not be treated as a nullity
and of no legal effect. In so far as any question arose as to the validity of an order of the court, there
was no obvious reason why the person against whom the order was made should be allowed to raise
that issue as a defence in subsequent breach proceedings. If the magistrates' court was in error in
including a provision that was too broad, that did not have the consequence of taking the order
outside the court's jurisdiction; and if the order was within the court's jurisdiction, it would remain
valid even if there were errors in it that were open to correction on appeal. It followed that it had
not been open to the district judge, as a matter of jurisdiction, to rule that the original order was
invalid. Accordingly, the appeal would be allowed.

DPP v T [2006] EWHC 728 (Admin), [2006] 3 All ER 471 (Queen's Bench Division: Richards LJ
and David Clarke J). *Hadkinson v Hadkinson* [1952] 2 All ER 567, CA, considered. *Boddington v
British Transport Police* [1999] 2 AC 143, HL (1998 Abr para 1); and *R (on the application of W) v DPP*
[2005] EWCA Civ 1333, (2005) 169 JP 435 (2005 Abr para 2726) distinguished.

2523   Anti-social behaviour order—breach—reasonable excuse—terms of order

The defendant, an animal rights activist, was charged with breaching an anti-social behaviour order
('ASBO') whose terms prohibited her from being within 500 metres of a proposed primate testing
laboratory. Some months later, she attended a demonstration authorised by order of the High Court
and which had complied with the order. She was subsequently arrested for breaching the ASBO, as
the demonstration had occurred within 500 metres of the laboratory. The defendant contended that
she had not carefully checked the terms of the order, that she had no recollection of having heard
any reference to the particular address as the address of the laboratory, and that she had mistakenly
believed that she was entitled to attend the demonstration. On a preliminary ruling, the judge found
that the offence was one of strict liability and that ignorance of, or forgetfulness as to, or
misunderstanding of, an order's terms could not amount to a reasonable excuse. In the light of the
ruling, the defendant pleaded guilty and was sentenced to four months' imprisonment. On appeal
against conviction, *held*, in the context of an ASBO, ignorance, forgetfulness or misunderstanding,
whether arising from an error as to the terms of the order or lack of knowledge of where the
defendant was at the material time, might be capable of constituting a defence of reasonable excuse.
Those issues of fact and the value judgment as to reasonableness were a matter for the jury rather
than the judge. The judge should have left the issue to the jury and should have allowed the
defendant to present a defence based on ignorance or misunderstanding as to the terms of the order.
While policy considerations raised concern as to the ease with which a defendant's claiming
ignorance or forgetfulness might frustrate the effective enforcement of the law in relation to ASBOs,
there was a line to be drawn in the particular circumstances of each case. The issue raised in the
present case was likely very often to be highly fact sensitive, an eminently desirable reason to leave
such issues to the jury rather than the judge, or before the facts on which the defendant relied had
been deployed and articulated at trial. Accordingly, the appeal would be allowed and the conviction
quashed.

R v Nicholson [2006] EWCA Crim 1518, [2006] 1 WLR 2857 (Court of Appeal: Auld LJ, Gibbs J
and Sir Michael Wright). *R v Wang* [2005] UKHL 9, [2005] 1 All ER 782 (2005 Abr para 950); *R v*

Glidewell (1999) 163 JP 557, CA (1999 Abr para 975); *R v Bird* [2004] EWCA Crim 964, [2004] All ER (D) 75 (May); *R v Jolie* [2003] EWCA Crim 1543, [2004] 1 Cr App Rep 44 (2003 Abr para 753); *R v Quayle; A-G's Reference (No 2 of 2004); R v Kenny; R v Taylor; R v Wales* [2005] EWCA Crim 1415, [2006] 1 All ER 988 (2005 Abr para 964); and *R v Evans* [2004] EWCA Crim 3102, [2005] 1 WLR 1435 (2004 Abr para 794) considered.

2524 Anti-social behaviour order—breach—sentence—imposition of sentence more severe than available for offence involved in breach

The defendant was made subject to an anti-social behaviour order which prohibited him from being drunk in a public place and from defecating or urinating in a public place other than a public toilet. He had many previous convictions for alcohol-related offences and theft. He admitted breaching the order, having been found drunk and incontinent in a public place. The judge deferred sentence but, two months later, the defendant appeared before the same judge for breaching the order again. The judge imposed a sentence of nine months' imprisonment for the breach of the order. The defendant appealed against sentence, submitting that it was wrong in principle for a sentence of imprisonment to be imposed in respect of breach of an anti-social behaviour order where the conduct amounting to that breach constituted an offence for which the statutory maximum sentence was merely a fine. *Held,* it was obvious that, when passing sentence for breach of an anti-social behaviour order, it was a sentence for the offence of breaching the order. Plainly, however, any sentence had to be proportionate, or 'commensurate'. It followed that, where conduct constituting breach of the order was also a distinct criminal offence for which the statutory maximum sentence might be, for example, six months' imprisonment, that was a factor to be borne in mind when considering proportionality. However, it could not be right for the court's power to be limited to imposing that maximum six-month sentence. Breach of an anti-social behaviour order was an offence in its own right, created by Parliament, and which attracted a statutory maximum sentence of five years' imprisonment. It was not wrong in principle, therefore, for the judge to have imposed a custodial sentence for breach of the order, albeit where the maximum sentence for the 'offence' was a fine. That principle should not be taken to suggest that anti-social behaviour orders should be imposed as a kind of device to circumvent a maximum penalty for an offence which might be believed to be too modest. That was a distinct issue which related to the circumstances in which it was proper to make an order, and did not relate to the consequences which followed breach of an order properly made. The judge had been correct to pass a custodial sentence and, accordingly, the appeal would be dismissed.

R v Stevens [2006] EWCA Crim 255, (2006) 170 JP Jo 362 (Court of Appeal: Sir Igor Judge P, Dobbs J and Sir Douglas Brown).

2525 Anti-social behaviour order—intervention order

The Crime and Disorder Act 1998 (Intervention Orders) Order 2006, SI 2006/2138 (in force on 1 October 2006), (1) provides that a relevant authority must consult a National Health Service trust, a primary care trust, a National Health Service foundation trust and a local authority, other than a relevant authority, before applying for an intervention order pursuant to the Crime and Disorder Act 1998 s 1G; (2) provides that such trusts or authorities are responsible for the provision or supervision of 'appropriate activities' under an intervention order, where they provide or supervise, or arrange for the provision or supervision of, those activities; and (3) prescribes the 'appropriate activities' and who constitutes an 'appropriately qualified person' to compile a report for the purposes of an application.

2526 Anti-social behaviour order—likelihood of causing harassment, alarm or distress—lack of evidence—no victim present

The defendant was seen riding a jet ski personal watercraft. Witnesses provided statements that he rode the jet ski at excessive speeds. The witness statements did not mention that harassment, alarm or distress was caused to any person. The judge refused to impose an anti-social behaviour order since the defendant's behaviour had only been likely to be dangerous to himself. The applicant local authority sought judicial review of the judge's decision. *Held,* in the absence of a potential victim, a person could not behave in an anti-social manner. Accordingly, the application would be dismissed.

R (on the application of Gosport BC) v Fareham Magistrates' Court [2006] EWHC 3047 (Admin), (2007) 171 JP Jo 102 (Queen's Bench Division: Bean J).

2527 Anti-social behaviour order—procedure—guidance

The Court of Appeal has issued the following guidance in relation to applications to the Crown Court for anti-social behaviour orders ('ASBO') under the Crime and Disorder Act 1998 s 1C. (1) It is imperative that the prosecution identifies the particular facts said to constitute anti-social behaviour. If the offender accepts those facts, they should be put in writing. If the facts are not accepted, they must be proved to the criminal standard of proof before they can be acted on. The judge should state his findings of fact expressly, and they should be recorded in writing on the ASBO. (2) The Magistrates' Courts (Hearsay Evidence in Civil Proceedings) Rules 1999,

SI 1999/681, are not the correct rules to follow in adducing hearsay evidence in support of an ASBO in the Crown Court. On the assumption that such proceedings are civil in nature and so subject to the Civil Evidence Act 1995, hearsay evidence is capable of being adduced in support of an application in the Crown Court for an ASBO under the 1998 Act s 1C. An offender must have a proper opportunity to consider the evidence advanced by the prosecution in support of an ASBO, especially where the prosecution wishes to rely on material that goes wider than the evidence concerning the particular offence for which the offender was convicted. An offender must be given proper time to challenge such material, and principles analogous to those in the 1999 Rules should therefore be followed. (3) The terms of an ASBO should be precise and capable of being understood by the offender, and the conditions in the ASBO should be enforceable in the sense that they should allow a breach to be readily identified and capable of being proved. Each ASBO must be specifically fashioned to deal with the offender concerned. Not all the conditions set out in an ASBO have to run for the full term of the order. The test must always be what is necessary to deal with the particular anti-social behaviour of the offender and what is proportionate to the circumstances. An ASBO must not be used merely to increase the sentence of imprisonment that the offender is to receive.

R v W [2006] EWCA Crim 686, [2006] 3 All ER 562 (Court of Appeal: Longmore LJ, Aikens J and Henry Globe QC). *R (on the application of McCann) v Crown Court at Manchester* [2002] UKHL 39, [2002] 4 All ER 593 (2002 Abr para 2616); *R v P* [2004] EWCA Crim 287, [2004] 2 Cr App Rep (S) 343; and *R v Boness; R v Bebbington* [2005] EWCA Crim 2395, (2005) 169 JP 621 (2005 Abr para 2722) applied.

2528 Anti-social behaviour order—procedure—variation or discharge of order

See para 1876.

2529 Breach of statutory duty—employer—fine

See *R v Balfour Beatty Rail Infrastructure Services Ltd*, para 1452.

2530 Compensation order—power to make—time limit

The defendant was found guilty of conspiracy to defraud and sentenced to 12 months' imprisonment. The Crown gave notice of its intention to seek a confiscation order pursuant to the Criminal Justice Act 1988 s 71, and a date for the hearing was duly set by the trial judge. The Crown indicated that it would raise the question of a compensation order at the same time as the confiscation proceedings. However, the confiscation hearing did not take place until two months after its scheduled date. The judge decided that the six-month time limit under s 72A(3)(b) for bringing confiscation proceedings had expired, and he therefore dismissed the confiscation proceedings and adjourned the question of compensation. Two months after that decision, and more than seven months after the passing of the custodial sentence, submissions were eventually heard as to whether a compensation order could be made. The judge decided that it could, and made an order accordingly. The defendant appealed against the order, contending that it was a part, or a variation, of the initial custodial sentence, and should therefore have been made no later than 28 days after the dismissal of the confiscation proceedings. *Held*, although the 1988 Act imposed no time limit on the making of a compensation order by the Crown Court, that was not to say such an order could be made at any time, however long had elapsed since the sentence had been imposed. Compensation orders should be made as soon as possible, for the benefit of the victim. However, in so far as the 1988 Act contemplated the order being made at the time of sentencing, that did not raise any expectation in the mind of the defendant that, if it were not so made, he could expect to keep his ill-gotten gains. Parliament could not have intended that a defendant could legitimately expect that, after 28 days from the dismissal of confiscation proceedings, he could retain for himself the proceeds of crime of which he had deprived the victims. At both hearings the judges had indicated that it was their intention that the making of a compensation order should be adjourned. There could be no suggestion of any abuse of process or prejudice to the defendant. Accordingly, the appeal would be dismissed.

R v Hussain [2006] EWCA Crim 2405, [2006] All ER (D) 01 (Oct) (Court of Appeal: Silber and Tugendhat LJJ). *R v Soneji* [2005] UKHL 49, [2006] 1 AC 340 (2005 Abr para 2738) followed. 1988 Act ss 71, 72A replaced by Proceeds of Crime Act 2002 ss 6, 14.

2531 Confiscation order—basis for proceedings—fraudulent evasion of value added tax

See *R v Hashash*, para 2938.

2532 Confiscation order—delay in confiscation proceedings—reasonable time requirement

See *R v Norman*, para 1565.

2533   Confiscation order—postponement—invalid forfeiture order made in postponement period—court's jurisdiction to subsequently make confiscation order

The offender pleaded guilty to the possession of a controlled Class A drug with intent to supply. Confiscation proceedings were initiated but postponed, and a forfeiture order was made. However, the forfeiture order was invalid because the Proceeds of Crime Act 2002 s 15(2)(b) prohibited the court from making a forfeiture order during the postponement period of confiscation proceedings. The court subsequently made a confiscation order and the offender appealed. *Held*, nothing in s 15(2) or s 14(11) or (12), stated that, on a forfeiture order being made in contravention of the prohibition in s 15(2), the court was thereafter deprived of jurisdiction to make a confiscation order. It would frustrate the purpose of the 2002 Act if, for example, the erroneous imposition of a trivial fine or the forfeiture of drug-dealing paraphernalia rendered the court powerless to proceed with the substantial confiscation proceedings. Accordingly, the appeal would be dismissed.

R v Donahoe (2006) Times, 20 October (Court of Appeal: Sir Igor Judge P, Gray and McCombe JJ).

2534   Confiscation order—proceeds of crime—benefit derived form offence—pecuniary advantage

The defendant withdrew himself along with another from a conspiracy to rob shortly before the robbery took place. He was convicted of conspiracy to rob and was sentenced to three-and-a-half years' imprisonment. The judge also imposed a confiscation order on the ground that although the defendant had withdrawn from the conspiracy, he had been prepared to take part at the outset, and that it was a reasonable inference that, had the conspiracy consisted only of two, the enterprise would not have begun. The defendant appealed contending that he had not benefited from the conspiracy and that he could not be said to have been instrumental in getting the property or in any real sense of having had control over it. *Held*, it was settled law that a person benefited if he obtained property as a result or in connection with his criminal conduct. The law did not require him to retain or otherwise keep the benefit. All that was required was that a defendant's acts should have contributed, to a non-trivial extent, to the getting of the property. While there was a separate requirement that a defendant had to be shown to have had control over the property, in reality if he had been instrumental in getting it he would in some sense have had control over it. In the instant case, the judge had reached the wrong conclusion as to the defendant's benefit. The defendant had not obtained a benefit. At the stage at which the defendant had withdrawn, no robbery had taken place. In the circumstances, it could not be said that he had been instrumental in obtaining the cash in any realistic way. Accordingly, the appeal would be allowed.

R v Byatt [2006] EWCA Crim 904, [2006] 2 Cr App Rep (S) 779 (Court of Appeal: Richards LJ and Collins J and Judge Goddard QC). *R v Olubitan* [2003] EWCA Crim 2940, [2004] 2 Cr App Rep (S) 70 (2003 Abr para 2324); *Jennings v Crown Prosecution Service* [2005] EWCA Civ 746, [2005] 4 All ER 391 (2005 Abr para 936) considered.

The defendant was the chairman and chief executive officer of a company listed on the London Stock Exchange. The company issued a trading statement which took into account three putative contracts which had not in fact been entered into, thereby giving a misleading impression of the company's turnover and profit. The company's share price then rose so that the value of the defendant's shareholding increased significantly. The defendant did not realise or otherwise benefit from this increase as Stock Exchange rules prohibited him from selling shares in that period. Corrective announcements were made in relation to the contracts, and the company's share price fell dramatically. The defendant was convicted of recklessly making a statement, promise or forecast which was misleading, false or deceptive in a material particular, contrary to the Financial Services and Markets Act 2000 s 397(1)(c). A confiscation order was made against him and, on his appeal against the order, he contended that, for the purposes of s 71(5), the temporary and unrealised increase in the value of the shareholding did not constitute a pecuniary advantage which he had derived as a result or in connection with the commission of the offence. Held, the defendant had not in any ordinary sense derived a pecuniary advantage, because he had not sold his shares at the top of the market. The increase in the share price was neither the proceeds of the offence of which he was convicted nor the positive consequence of the offending. It followed that the increase should not have been included in his benefit from the offence for the purposes of confiscation proceedings. Accordingly, the appeal would be allowed.

R v Rigby [2006] EWCA Crim 1653, [2006] All ER (D) 156 (Jul) (Court of Appeal: May LJ, Rafferty J and Judge Diehl QC).

1988 Act s 71(5) replaced by Proceeds of Crime Act 2002 s 7(1).

2535   Confiscation order—proceeds of drug trafficking—benefit derived from offence—value of drugs—courier

The defendant was arrested for attempting to import cocaine into the United Kingdom from Nigeria, having been found in possession of a large amount of the drug. She pleaded guilty to being knowingly concerned in the fraudulent evasion of the prohibition on the importation of a Class A drug. During confiscation proceedings brought pursuant to the Proceeds of Crime Act 2002, the judge assessed the benefit to the defendant on the basis of the 'wholesale value' of the drugs, in other words their realisable value as illegal drugs. The defendant appealed, contending that the judge's approach had been incorrect. *Held*, the judge had erred in finding that the amount of the defendant's benefit from her criminal conduct was the wholesale value of the drugs found in her possession on her arrest. In view of the fact that the defendant had merely been a courier of the drugs, he had wrongly treated the controlled drugs as having a lawful market value for the purposes of the 2002 Act. The value of the property was to be taken as its market value, which had to be the market value were the property to be sold lawfully. It was obvious that the drugs could not be sold lawfully, and therefore they had no market value. While different considerations might have applied had the defendant not been a courier, and had instead purchased the drugs or incurred an expense in obtaining them, in the instant case the judge had wrongly assessed the defendant's benefit. Accordingly, the appeal would be allowed.

R v Ajibade [2006] All ER (D) 54 (Feb) (Court of Appeal: Pill LJ, Swift J and Judge Radford). *R v Dore* [1997] 2 Cr App Rep (S) 152, CA (1997 Abr para 2932), considered.

2536   Confiscation order—proceeds of drug trafficking—realisable property—certificate of inadequacy

The appellant was convicted of conspiring to supply a Class A drug. He was sentenced to seven years' imprisonment and a confiscation order was made against him. Of the amount deemed by the court to be realisable property, approximately two-fifths was held to be in the form of hidden assets. The amount specified in the order was subsequently reduced on appeal, and the appellant applied pursuant to the Drug Trafficking Act 1994 s 17 for a certificate of inadequacy, claiming that he did not possess the hidden assets in question. The judge decided that it was not open to the appellant to challenge the court's findings as to his realisable assets. The appellant appealed, submitting that any person was prima facie entitled to a certificate of inadequacy whenever he could satisfy the court that his assets were inadequate to pay the amount of the confiscation order. The Crown contended that the certificate of inadequacy procedure under s 17 was intended to be used only where there had been a genuine change in a defendant's financial circumstances since the confiscation order had been made, where, for example, an asset had dropped in value, as could be the case with a property or shares. *Held*, the court did not have jurisdiction in certificate of inadequacy proceedings to go behind the basis of the confiscation order made by the Crown Court. Any attempt to do so was an abuse of the process of the court. A close examination of s 17 against the background of the 1994 Act as a whole pointed strongly to the construction that the court was limited to consideration of post-confiscation order events and was not entitled to go behind the confiscation order even if there had been a manifest error. Accordingly, the appeal would be dismissed.

Re McKinsley [2006] EWCA Civ 1092, [2006] 1 WLR 3420 (Court of Appeal: Sir Igor Judge P, Scott Baker and Hallett LJJ).

1994 Act s 17 repealed: Proceeds of Crime Act 2002 Sch 11 para 25(2)(a), Sch 12.

2537   Cruelty to a child—mitigation—no malice—deluded belief

The defendants had been convicted of offences relating to cruelty to a child contrary to the Children and Young Persons Act 1933 s 1(1) and two of them were sentenced to the maximum sentence of ten years' imprisonment. The defendants appealed against their sentences, contending that their ill-treatment of the child was not due to malice, but their belief that she was possessed by spirits. *Held*, the court believed that the defendants had acted out of a deluded belief rather than malice, but this was no mitigation and could not reduce the culpability of the defendants. While the crime was truly shocking, it was possible to conceive of worse cases. Accordingly, their appeals would be allowed in part.

R v P; R v K; R v M (2006) Times, 17 March (Court of Appeal: Dyson LJ, Grigson J and Sir Douglas Brown).

2538   Custodial sentence—duration—causing or allowing death of child or vulnerable adult

The second defendant and the deceased were married in China. They came to the United Kingdom where the deceased requested a divorce. The second defendant informed the deceased that he would allow her to return to China only after she had repaid, by way of two years' unpaid labour, the debt which she owed him as a result of his marrying her and assisting her entry into the United Kingdom. It then became apparent that the deceased was being assaulted by the first defendant, the second defendant's mistress, but the second defendant refused to obtain medical treatment for the deceased. The deceased's body was subsequently found in the defendants' garden where she had been left outside in freezing conditions. An autopsy revealed that the deceased had sustained bruising to her head, arms, legs, torso and feet, and that she had defensive knife wounds on her hands. She had also sustained a deep stab wound to the elbow which had become infected but had not been treated. The cause of death was stated to have been haemorrhaging and shock due to multiple injuries. The first defendant admitted striking the deceased with a broom, a copper pipe, a piece of wood with nails in it, a wok and a ladle. She pleaded guilty to manslaughter and causing grievous bodily harm with intent. The second defendant was convicted of causing or allowing the death of a vulnerable adult, contrary to the Domestic Violence, Crime and Victims Act 2004 s 5, and was sentenced to six years' imprisonment. He sought leave to appeal against sentence. *Held*, the facts of the case were horrific and distinctive, and it was hoped that they would never be repeated. The deceased had been kept as a slave by the second defendant for the repayment of a perceived debt, and had been ill-treated, assaulted and abused to her death by the first defendant while the second defendant had stood idly by and done nothing. The sentence imposed on the second defendant had been richly deserved and was not a day too long. Accordingly, the application would be dismissed.

R v Liu [2006] All ER (D) 242 (Nov) (Court of Appeal: Laws LJ, Penry-Davey and Royce JJ).

2539 Custodial sentence—duration—mitigation argued after sentencing

The claimant was granted a non-molestation order against the defendant, the claimant's former husband, who was aged 52. The order was subsequently extended to protect the claimant's children. The defendant had a number of other children by other women and had remarried. He breached the conditions of the order on a number of occasions. The most serious breaches included threatening the claimant at her children's school, slashing her mother's car tyres, and pushed a note containing an unpleasant threat under the claimant's door. A further serious breach occurred following the commencement of committal proceedings for the previous breaches, when the defendant's wife attacked the claimant while the defendant shouted encouragement and prevented the claimant from reaching her car. At the committal proceedings, the judge found the defendant in contempt of court and immediately sentenced him to fifteen months' imprisonment. The sentence was reduced to twelve months following mitigation arguments from the defendant's counsel, but the judge refused to suspend the sentence in view of what he considered to be a campaign of harassment. The defendant appealed. *Held*, the judge had been entitled to impose an immediate sentence of imprisonment. The most serious breaches were all different in quality, and the acts of the defendant, given the circumstances, his age and experience of the world, warranted an immediate sentence of imprisonment. The defendant had been aware of what he was doing: making a number of threats directly and indirectly. The appropriate bracket of sentence was below twelve months and between six and nine months. Had the judge heard mitigation prior to passing sentence, he would not have passed a sentence of twelve months. The appropriate sentence was one of eight months. Accordingly, the appeal would be allowed.

Goldsmith v Goldsmith [2006] All ER (D) 380 (Oct) (Court of Appeal: Wall and Lloyd LJJ). *Hale v Tanner* [2000] 1 WLR 2377, CA (2000 Abr para 717), considered.

2540 Custodial sentence—duration—treatment of time served on remand

The Criminal Justice Act 2003 s 240(3) provides that, subject to s 240(4), the court must direct that the number of days for which an offender was remanded in custody in connection with the offence or a related offence is to count as time served by him as part of the sentence. Section 240(3) does not apply if and to the extent that it is in the opinion of the court just in all the circumstances not to give such a direction: s 240(4)(b).

The defendant, having been originally indicted for robbery, pleaded guilty to assault occasioning actual bodily harm. He had served 161 days on remand in custody. In sentencing the defendant, the judge stated that, bearing in mind the defendant's pleas of guilty and the period of 161 days that he had spent in custody, there would be a sentence of six months' imprisonment. Both prosecuting and defence counsel understood the judge to intend that the time spent on remand should be discounted in order that the defendant be released immediately. In the event, that did not happen. The defendant appealed against sentence. *Held*, in most cases, the court might be expected to give a direction under the 2003 Act s 240(3) that the whole of the period of remand would count as time served as part of the sentence. The court would then impose a sentence of imprisonment that reflected the seriousness of the offence for which the defendant had been convicted. Section 240 did not contain an explicit requirement that a judge who was considering departing from the usual practice of making a direction under s 240(3) should state in advance that he was considering doing so. Nevertheless, it was plainly good practice for a judge to inform defence counsel where he was considering making no direction and thus give counsel the opportunity to address him on that issue and to seek to persuade him that the circumstances were not such that it would be just for the period spent in custody on remand not to count as part of the sentence. Otherwise, mitigation might proceed with defence counsel and the judge at cross purposes as to the effect of the period spent on remand. Where there was any reason to suppose that a judge might be considering not making a direction under s 240(3), or making a limited direction, defence counsel should seek clarification so as to be sure that he was able fully to address the issue. Accordingly, the appeal would be allowed.

R v Barber [2006] EWCA Crim 162, [2006] 2 Cr App Rep (S) 539 (Court of Appeal: Pill LJ, Swift J and Judge Radford QC). *R v Oosthuizen* [2005] EWCA Crim 1978, [2005] Crim LR 979 (2005 Abr para 2779) followed.

Custodial sentences had been imposed on the defendants but no direction or correct direction as to the amount of time for which they had been remanded in custody had been given. They appealed. *Held*, the failure to identify or correctly identify the period which should be treated as served, as required under the Criminal Justice Act 2003 s 240, rendered the sentence wrong in principle. The defendants were entitled to a direction as to the number of days for which they had been remanded in custody that were to count as time served. If the Powers of Criminal Courts (Sentencing) Act 2000 s 155, which gave power to vary or rescind a sentence within 28 days of the order, or an administrative correction was not available, the only route available was an appeal. Accordingly, the appeals would be allowed and the sentences varied.

R v Norman [2006] EWCA Crim 1792, (2006) Times, 4 August (Court of Appeal: Latham LJ, Forbes and Irwin JJ).

2541   Custodial sentence—evasion of immigration law—seriousness of offence—forgery of identity card to obtain employment in United Kingdom

After the expiry of her limited leave to remain in the United Kingdom, the offender applied for a job at a supermarket. She used a forged French identity card in order to obtain employment. On a guilty plea to a count of obtaining a pecuniary advantage by deception, despite being of previous good character, the offender was sentenced to 14 months' imprisonment. She appealed against sentence, contending that the offence had not been sufficiently serious to justify a custodial sentence or, alternatively, that the length of the custodial sentence was manifestly excessive. *Held*, a deterrent element was required in sentences for offences motivated by the desire to evade immigration law. Although the present case had crossed the custody threshold, it fell at the lower end of the range of offences. After the guilty plea, the appropriate sentence was four months' imprisonment. Accordingly, the appeal would be allowed.

R v Mwangi [2006] All ER (D) 114 (Sep) (Court of Appeal: Moses LJ, Gibbs and Cooke JJ). *R v Kolawole* [2004] EWCA Crim 3047, [2005] 2 Cr App Rep (S) 71 (2004 Abr para 2467) applied.

2542   Custodial sentence—imprisonment for public protection—prohibition on punishment for offences of which defendant not convicted

The defendant, aged 22, pleaded guilty to child abduction and sexual assault following an incident with a six-year-old boy. The defendant had been involved in several previous incidents with young boys, but none had resulted in prosecution. Pursuant to the Criminal Justice Act 2003 s 225, the judge decided to hear evidence as to one of those earlier incidents as being relevant to the assessment of the defendant's dangerousness, stating that he would make findings to the criminal standard of proof. He decided that the conduct had been such as to make the defendant guilty of indecent assault on the basis of the law as it then stood, had he been tried by a jury. He then found, taking into account his findings as to the earlier alleged incident, that the defendant had displayed a pattern of behaviour for the purposes of s 229(2)(b) and that, in all the circumstances, a sentence of imprisonment for public protection was required with a minimum term of 18 months. The defendant appealed against sentence, and an issue arose as to whether the judge had erred in principle in holding a trial of an issue as to a previous allegation not previously pursued by the prosecution and had thereby deprived the defendant of his right to trial by jury. *Held*, the law as it stood before the enactment of the 2003 Act was that a defendant was not to be convicted of any offence with which he was charged unless and until his guilt was proved. Such guilt might be proved by his own admission or, on indictment, by the verdict of a jury. He might be sentenced only for an offence proved against him or which he had admitted and asked the court to take into consideration when passing sentence. On the basis of those basic principles underlying the administration of the criminal law, it was not easy to see how a defendant could lawfully be punished for offences for which he had not been indicted and which he had denied or declined to admit. Nothing in the 2003 Act expressly overturned that principle and, as a matter of necessary implication, there was no logic or express language in s 229 which had the effect of permitting a judge alone to decide that a defendant was guilty of discrete offences separate to that for which the defendant was being sentenced, nor was it compellingly clear that Parliament had intended to deprive a defendant of his right to a trial by jury or justices in such circumstances. It followed that the judge had erred in principle. However, the sentence could not be said to be manifestly excessive, and, accordingly, the appeal would be dismissed.

R v Farrar [2006] All ER (D) 204 (Dec) (Court of Appeal: Latham LJ, Mitting and Teare JJ). *R v Kidd; R v Canavan; R v Shaw* [1998] 1 All ER 42, CA (1997 Abr para 2982), applied.

2543   Custodial sentence—interception of communications—intention to secure substantial commercial advantage

See *R v Stanford*, para 862.

2544   Custodial sentence—two offences committed under differing sentencing regimes—concurrent sentences on identical terms—release on licence falling on different dates

The defendant pleaded guilty to a count concerning the possession of criminal property and a count of facilitating the use of criminal property. He was sentenced to five years' imprisonment on both counts to run concurrently. The first offence had been committed before the sentencing provisions of the Criminal Justice Act 2003 had come into force, and so he was sentenced in accordance with the Criminal Justice Act 1991 s 33 in relation to that offence, while the sentence for the second offence was governed by the 2003 Act. The effect was that the defendant would be released on licence after serving two-thirds of his sentence in relation to the first offence but released after serving one-half of his sentence in relation to the second offence. The judge declined either to impose no separate penalty in relation to the first offence or to reduce the sentence so that the defendant could be released after serving two-and-a-half years. The defendant appealed against sentence. *Held*, a defendant being sentenced for offences committed both before and after the commencement of the sentencing provisions of the 2003 Act was required to be sentenced by reference to two different regimes. It would generally be preferable to pass sentence on the later offences by reference to the new regime, imposing no separate penalty for the earlier offences, albeit that might not be possible if the later offences were less serious than the earlier ones. The second offence had involved a greater sum of money and was more serious than the first. The judge should have considered the consequences of the sentences that he had imposed so as to make the release date the same, or to impose no separate penalty in relation to the first offence. The judge had failed to take into account the guidance in the authorities and had been wrong to decline the opportunity to adjust the sentences. The defendant's sentence would be reduced and, accordingly, the appeal would be allowed.

R v Ahmet [2006] All ER (D) 73 (Oct) (Court of Appeal: Hooper LJ, Simon and Lloyd Jones JJ). *R v Lang* [2005] EWCA Crim 2864, [2006] 2 All ER 410 (2005 Abr para 2787) applied.

2545　Deportation order—recommendation—duty of court to consider human rights

The defendant received a sentence of 15 months' imprisonment for offences of dishonesty, and the judge made a recommendation for deportation. The defendant appealed against the recommendation, contending that the court, when considering whether to recommend deportation, was obliged to consider the defendant's rights under the European Convention on Human Rights and the effect of deportation on the defendant's family. *Held*, there was no need for a sentencing court to consider the Convention rights of an offender whose offences justified a recommendation for deportation. It was undesirable that the court should undertake an assessment for which it was not qualified or equipped, and which would, in any event, be undertaken by the Home Secretary and the Asylum and Immigration Tribunal. The defendant's Convention rights would be considered where a deportation order was made, against which the defendant could appeal to the tribunal. In the case of non-EU citizens, sentencing courts should consider only whether the offence committed by the offender, in the light of information before the court, justified the conclusion that his continued presence in the United Kingdom was contrary to the public interest. Moreover, it was unnecessary and undesirable for a judge to consider the effect of the recommendation for deportation, if implemented, on the defendant's family. Since the coming into force of the Human Rights Act 1998 Act, the prescription in previous authority that sentences should have regard to the effect of deportation on the offender's family would be regarded as a requirement to consider the family's rights under the Convention art 8. It was settled law that, although deportation might involve or risk a breach of the defendant's rights under arts 2 and 3, a sentencing judge was precluded from considering such risks. A recommendation could only impact on rights to family life if it was followed, a matter which was not for the court to decide. It would also be irrational for the sentencing judge to be required to consider the art 8 rights of the offender's family but be debarred from considering the more important Convention rights of the offender. Accordingly, the appeal would be dismissed.

R v Carmona [2006] EWCA Crim 508, [2006] 1 WLR 2264 (Court of Appeal: Keane LJ, Stanley Burnton and Simon JJ). *R v Nazari* [1980] 3 All ER 880, CA (1980 Abr para 1506); *R v B* [2001] EWCA Crim 765, [2001] 2 Cr App Rep (S) 46; *R v Cravioto* (1990) 12 Cr App Rep (S) 71, CA; and *R v Shittu* (1993) 14 Cr App Rep (S) 283, CA, considered.

2546　Driving offences causing a fatality—statutory increase in maximum sentences—renewal of guidelines

The Court of Appeal and Courts-Martial Appeal Court considered the effect of the increase in maximum sentences for aggravated vehicle taking involving an accident causing death, causing death by dangerous driving and causing death by careless driving when under the influence of drink or drugs on the sentencing guidelines in *R v Cooksley*. It was held: (1) the primary object of the increase in the maximum sentence was to address cases of the most serious gravity. However, even in such cases it was not intended that the increase in sentence should reflect the consequences of the increase in a strictly mathematical proportion. It had long been recognised that mathematics did not provide the appropriate answer to a sentencing decision. That said, if the level of sentence in cases of the utmost gravity was significantly increased, there should be some corresponding increase in sentences immediately below that level of gravity, continuing down the scale. (2) Some proportion had to be maintained between the levels of sentences for the present offences and those which were thought appropriate for other offences of crimes of violence resulting in death, such as sentences for manslaughter following a deliberate blow, and manslaughter arising from gross negligence. While not identical these offences were certainly not far removed from negligent conduct which fell 'far below' expected standards, which was the criminal ingredient for dangerous driving. (3) At the lowest levels of seriousness, it should be borne in mind that the Criminal Justice Act 2003 required the sentencer only to impose a custodial sentence if such a sentence was necessary, and that the sentence should be no longer than necessary to fulfil the statutory purposes of sentencing laid down in s 142. For those reasons, at those levels there would continue to be cases in which the broad guidance in *R v Cooksley* would remain appropriate and exceptional situations where even shorter sentences, or non-custodial sentences, might be appropriate. (4) The four bands of culpability identified in *R v Cooksley* would continue to be expressed in the same terms. These were (a) where the offender intended to cause the harm; (b) where he was reckless; (c) where he knew of the specific risk of harm, although the harm was unintentional; and (d) where he was negligent. However, the relevant starting points should be reassessed as follows: (i) no aggravating circumstances, 12 months' to 2 years' imprisonment; (ii) intermediate culpability, two to four-and-a-half years' imprisonment; (iii) higher culpability, four-and-a-half to seven years' imprisonment; (iv) most serious culpability, 7 to 14 years' imprisonment. (5) Where death had arisen from a road traffic accident caused when the driver had voluntarily consumed excess alcohol, in culpability terms that was and should be equated with causing death by dangerous driving. If there was a consequent road traffic accident in which death resulted, the consequences were catastrophic for the deceased and his family, and however excellent the character of the offender, and genuine his remorse, for all effective purposes, a custodial sentence was inevitable. (6) Taken on its own, and wholly excluding any element of drink or drugs, careless driving was hugely less culpable than dangerous driving, and fell in the fourth, lowest category of negligence. Depending on the facts, dangerous driving and driving with excess alcohol would fall in the second or third category. However, the precise level of culpability would be determined by such factors as motivation, whether the offence was planned or spontaneous or whether the offender was in a position of trust. (7) Although the offences of causing death by dangerous driving and by careless driving when under the influence of drink or drugs were currently regarded on an equal basis, this might not be appropriate when the new offences of causing death by careless driving without having consumed excess alcohol and causing death when the driver was unlicensed, disqualified or uninsured come into force. (8) The maximum sentence for causing death by dangerous driving or causing death having consumed excess alcohol was identical. The natural implication was that they were equated in seriousness. If the level of impairment was only just in excess of the permitted limit, and the driving was otherwise careless rather than dangerous, the consumption of alcohol provided the most significant aggravating element of the offence. If there were no others, it would normally fall in the category of offences of causing death by dangerous driving which lacked any additional aggravating features.

R v Richardson; R v Robertson [2006] EWCA Crim 3186, [2006] All ER (D) 255 (Dec) (Court of Appeal; Courts-Martial Appeal Court: Sir Igor Judge P, Forbes and Royce JJ). *R v Cooksley; R v Stride; R v Cook; A-G's Reference (No 152 of 2002)* [2003] EWCA Crim 996, [2003] 3 All ER 40 (2003 Abr para 2322) considered.

2547   Drug offences—controlled drug—importation—Class C drug—maximum sentence— drugs other than cannabis

The defendant was involved in the illegal importation of a very large quantity of diazepam, a Class C drug, into the United Kingdom. The defendant's role in the operation was to collect three boxes of the drug from an airport, the boxes in question purportedly containing electrical goods. When the defendant was first arrested, he maintained that he had thought that the boxes contained electrical goods, but subsequently he pleaded guilty to being knowingly concerned in the illegal importation of a Class C drug. He had no previous convictions within the United Kingdom. He was sentenced to a five-year custodial sentence, on the basis that, although he was not the ringleader of the operation, he had been sent to the United Kingdom with the express task of organising the distribution of the drugs. The judge had heard expert evidence that diazepam was used by heroin addicts to control the side effects of their addiction. In selecting his starting point, he had also had regard to authority on sentencing for the importation of cannabis that pre-dated the reclassification of cannabis from a Class B drug to a Class C drug, and the increase in the maximum sentence for the illegal importation of Class C drugs from 5 years to 14 years. The defendant appealed against sentence, submitting that, in increasing the maximum sentence for the importation of Class C drugs, Parliament had had only cannabis in mind, and sentencing for other Class C drugs remained unaffected. *Held*, by making the maximum sentence for the importation of all Class C drugs 14 years, Parliament had not intended to distinguish between cannabis and diazepam. The increase in sentence related to the importation of all Class C drugs, and it reflected the extreme seriousness with which Parliament viewed offences of that type. The instant case had been a relatively sophisticated illegal importation of a very large amount of drugs. Although the defendant had pleaded guilty, an importation on such a large scale had to result in a lengthy sentence. Accordingly, the appeal would be dismissed.

R v Parekh [2006] All ER (D) 225 (Apr) (Court of Appeal: Langstaff J and Judge Stewart QC). *R v Golder* [2000] 1 Cr App Rep (S) 59, CA, considered.

2548 Handling stolen goods—custodial sentence—excessive sentence

The defendant bought a car which had been hijacked by masked robbers. He was aware that the car had been hijacked, and had had false number plates put on it, but he was not involved in the commission of the offences. He pleaded guilty to handling stolen goods and driving a vehicle without insurance. He had a number of previous convictions, including taking a vehicle without consent, but all his relevant previous convictions were more than five years' old. He had also had a drugs problem at the time of the present offences. He was sentenced to 12 months' imprisonment for handling stolen goods, with no separate penalty for the offence of driving without insurance, apart from having his driving licence endorsed with six penalty points. He appealed against sentence. *Held*, only three of the aggravating factors identified by the relevant guideline authority had been present in the offence. Those factors were the seriousness of the original offence in which the goods were stolen, the high level of profit which the defendant had made and the high value of the property to the victim. The defendant had not been linked to the primary offence, nor had he been linked to the fixing of false licence plates. The defendant's previous relevant convictions were old and, although he had had a drugs problem, he was free of drugs. It followed that, although the judge had been right to conclude that the offences passed the custody threshold, the sentence of 12 months' imprisonment was manifestly excessive. A sentence of six months' imprisonment was appropriate and, accordingly, the appeal would be allowed.

R v Heyes [2006] All ER (D) 113 (Sep) (Court of Appeal: Moses LJ, Gibbs and Cooke JJ). *R v Webbe* [2001] EWCA Crim 1217, [2002] 1 Cr App Rep (S) 22 (2001 Abr para 2807) applied.

2549 Life sentence—mandatory life sentence—minimum term—conduct in prison

The defendant had been convicted of murder and his life sentence was subject to a minimum term of 14 years. He applied for a review of his minimum term under the Criminal Justice Act 2003 Sch 22 para 3. *Held*, while commendable, the defendant's good conduct in prison was not a relevant factor to the setting of the minimum term of imprisonment. The judge was required by Sch 22 para 4(1)(a) to have regard to the seriousness of the offence, not the behaviour of the offender after conviction. He was also required to have regard to the general principles on aggravating and mitigating features set out in Sch 21 which, sensibly, did not include conduct after conviction. A convicted defendant being sentenced at the conclusion of his trial could not have his minimum term set under Sch 21 by reference to his conduct after the minimum term had been set. The minimum term was intended to reflect deterrence and retribution only. Accordingly, the application would be dismissed.

Re Waters [2006] EWHC 355 (QB), [2006] 3 All ER 1251 (Queen's Bench Division: Mitting J). *R (on the application of Cole) v Secretary of State for the Home Department* [2003] EWHC 1789 (Admin), [2003] All ER (D) 173 (Jul), DC, considered.

2550 Life sentence—mandatory life sentence—minimum term—mental abnormality of offender

The offender killed two people in a frenzied attack. He was convicted of murder. The judge recommended a minimum term of 15 years but the Lord Chief Justice recommended a shorter punitive term of 10 to 11 years. That conviction was set aside by the Court of Appeal on the ground that the prosecution expert changed her mind and stated that the offender was entitled to a diminished responsibility defence. A retrial was ordered. The offender's defence of diminished responsibility was rejected and he was convicted again. The judge recommended a minimum term of 15 years. The Lord Chief Justice said that he had to accept that two juries had convicted and two judges had recommended a minimum term of 15 years. The offender's application for judicial review of the Secretary of State's decision to set the tariff at 15 years was dismissed. The offender applied for a review of his minimum term pursuant to the Criminal Justice Act 2003 Sch 22 para 3. *Held*, it was necessary to consider the seriousness of the offence and the culpability of the offender. Those had not changed since the Secretary of State's first tariff setting exercise. Notwithstanding the appalling nature of the double murder, considering the relevant guidance, the outstanding feature of the case acting to reduce the starting point of 14 years was the obvious sub-normality or mental abnormality of the offender, which was alone sufficient to require a significant reduction from that starting point down to 11 years. The early release provisions would apply to the offender after a minimum term of 11 years had passed less the amount of time spent on remand in custody.

Re Cole (application pursuant to the Criminal Justice Act 2003 Sch 22 para 3) [2006] EWHC 3036 (QB), [2006] All ER (D) 274 (Dec) (Queen's Bench Division: Mackay J).

2551 Life sentence—mandatory life sentence—minimum term—murder

The defendant seized the 16-year-old deceased and strangled her. At the trial for her murder, the defendant pleaded guilty and was sentenced to life imprisonment. The judge recommended a minimum term of 25 years. The Lord Chief Justice recommended a minimum term of 20 years. The Secretary of State for the Home Department referred the case to the High Court for it to set a minimum term pursuant to the Criminal Justice Act 2003 Sch 22 para 6. Subsequently, the defendant pleaded guilty to further offences of rape in respect of which he was also sentenced to life imprisonment. The issue to be decided was whether the defendant's rape convictions could be taken into account in determining the minimum tariff, when those offences had not been known to the judge when he had made his original recommendation. *Held,* Sch 22 para 10(a) did not prevent previous crimes from being taken into account, even where they came to light only after the defendant had been sentenced for murder. They were to be taken into consideration to the same extent that the judge and the Lord Chief Justice would have considered them had they known about them at the relevant time. In the present case, the offence had been aggravated by the fact that the victim was a child, that it had involved sexual maltreatment and that the defendant had a substantial record of serious violence. There were no circumstances that served to mitigate the offence. Therefore, the early release provisions would apply to the defendant when he had served 30 years less the period he had spent on remand.

Re Taylor (reference under para 6 of Sch 22 to the Criminal Justice Act 2006) [2006] EWHC 2944 (QB), [2006] All ER (D) 285 (Dec) (Queen's Bench Division: Openshaw J).

2552   Life sentence—mandatory life sentence—minimum term—murder—aggravating factor—intention to kill

The defendant had pleaded guilty to murder and been sentenced to 15 years' imprisonment, the appropriate starting point under the Criminal Justice Act 2003 Sch 21 para 6, to which the judge added two years by reference to the intention to kill. The defendant appealed. *Held,* the intention to kill was assumed in the 15-year starting point and was not an aggravating factor. This proposition was supported by the fact that the intention to cause bodily harm rather than to kill was one of the mitigating factors listed in Sch 21 para 11. The judge was entitled to increase the starting point in light of other factors such as the ferocity of the attack and the fact that it took place in the victim's home. Accordingly, the appeal was dismissed.

R v Ainsworth (2006) Times, 13 September (Court of Appeal: Gage LJ, Dobbs J and Judge Mettyear).

2553   Life sentence—mandatory life sentence—minimum term—progress of offender

See *Re Bingham (application under para 3 of Sch 22 to the Criminal Justice Act 2003)*, para 2554.

The offender was convicted of the murder of three elderly persons in the course of burgling their homes. The trial judge recommended a minimum term of 15 years' imprisonment. Subsequently, the Lord Chief Justice recommended a minimum term of 18 years on the basis of the number of victims. The Secretary of State, following representations from the offender, set his minimum term at 25 years. Following the coming into force of the Criminal Justice Act 2003, the offender applied to have that term reviewed. Issues arose as to the appropriate minimum term having regard, pursuant to Sch 22, to that recommended by the Lord Chief Justice and that set by the Secretary of State, and whether there should be any reduction in respect of 'exceptional' progress while in custody. *Held,* the starting point under Sch 21 was 30 years' imprisonment, as the case concerned the murder of two or more people for gain. Aggravating features were that three persons, rather than two, had been murdered, and that the victims were particularly vulnerable. The only mitigating factor was the offender's age. In all the circumstances, having regard to the recommendation of the Lord Chief Justice, and the notified minimum term, the offender's minimum term would be set at 21 years' imprisonment, subject to any reduction for exceptional progress. In that respect, it would seem unlikely that Parliament had impliedly decided when enacting the 2003 Act that exceptional progress in custody should be excluded from consideration. However, the 2003 Act did not justify increases in reductions to be made on account of exceptional progress beyond a reduction of one or two years that it was the practice of the Secretary of State to make. Faced with the reports, with no indication that the authors had misunderstood either the meaning or the import of 'exceptional progress', a judge should be slow to reach, and would have to justify, a different conclusion. The applicant's exceptional progress did not diminish the seriousness of the terrible offences that he had committed. However, his progress had been 'exceptional' and his minimum term would be reduced by two years. Judgment would be given accordingly.

Re Cadman (application under para 3 of Sch 22 to the Criminal Justice Act 2003) [2006] All ER (D) 342 (Mar) (Queen's Bench Division: Stanley Burnton J). *R (on the application of Cole) v Secretary of State for the Home Department* [2003] EWHC 1789 (Admin), [2003] All ER (D) 173 (Jul), DC, applied.

The Court of Appeal has issued the following guidance in relation to the provisions in the Criminal Justice Act 2003 Sch 22, which relate to transitional mandatory life cases. The first feature which the court has to address when hearing an application as to the appropriate minimum term of a life sentence pursuant to Sch 22 is the seriousness of the offence analysed in the context of the general principles in Sch 21, and for the purposes of Sch 22, the general principles extend to and include the 'starting points' under Sch 21 themselves. The remaining statutory guidance in Sch 22 directs the judge hearing the application to have regard to the recommendations of the trial judge and the Lord Chief Justice before the original tariff was fixed by the Secretary of State. The transitional provisions in Sch 22 apply irrespective of the guidance in force when the original minimum period was fixed. The guidance further requires the judge to reflect on the length of the notified term fixed by the Secretary of State, again uninfluenced by Sch 21. The express terms of Sch 22 rule out the possibility of an application being decided by reference only to the general principles in Sch 21 and the original judicial recommendations, ignoring the decision of the Secretary of State. The views of the Secretary of State as reflected in the notified minimum period are relevant first, to ensure that the eventual order made by the judge does not produce a longer minimum period than before, and second, in the context of exceptional progress by the prisoner. They should not otherwise influence the outcome of the review. In hearing a Sch 22 application, the judge is making a sentencing decision; he is not conducting an appeal from the judicial recommendations, or the decision of the Secretary of State, nor is he passing sentence as such. While there might be inevitable difficulties, and indeed some illogicality, in re-examining the tariff fixed for the purpose of punishment and deterrence by reference to exceptional behaviour post sentence, exceptional progress in prison by a prisoner serving a mandatory life sentence might nevertheless be taken into account when the notified minimum term is reconsidered under Sch 22. The applicant prisoner may well have spent a significant part of his sentence under a regime in which exceptional progress provided a recognised basis for a reduction in the minimum term. Moreover, the review required by Sch 22 is unusual and specific for transitional purposes and the exclusion of the Secretary of State, who would otherwise have continued to allow for exceptional progress against the minimum term, is deliberate. If the reduction for exceptional progress is to operate effectively, it must do so against the fixed minimum term, not against the newly assessed, albeit notional tariff. As exceptional progress is properly to be taken into account, it should be productive of real benefit for the prisoner. Good behaviour is not enough to constitute exceptional progress. The standard should be very high, and even where the necessary high standard is reached, the impact on the total tariff period is likely to be very modest. Further, it is a prerequisite to any reduction that the risk assessment should be favourable. When the court is considering whether exceptional progress has been made, it would be helpful for the information to include the observations from the governors of the last two prisons in which the offender was serving his sentence.

R v Caines; R v Roberts [2006] EWCA Crim 2915, [2006] All ER (D) 334 (Nov) (Court of Appeal: Sir Igor Judge P, Holland and Goldring JJ).

2554   Life sentence—mandatory life sentence—minimum term—reconsideration in light of European Convention on Human Rights

The offender killed his wife by striking her several times on the head with an iron bar or spike. The offender then took steps to make it appear that his wife had been killed by an intruder. He admitted to the police that he had killed his wife and, although he originally entered a plea of not guilty, he pleaded guilty on re-arraignment. No record of the hearing, which took place 16 years ago, was available. In his report to the Secretary of State, the trial judge stated that the murder had been coldly premeditated and carefully planned and that the motive had been financial gain, and he recommended a minimum term of 18 years' imprisonment with which the Lord Chief Justice agreed. The offender sought a review of that term under the Criminal Justice Act 2003 Sch 22 para 3. *Held*, notwithstanding that the trial judge might have considered material that was no longer available, it would be inconsistent with the 2003 Act and its purpose of ensuring compliance with the European Convention on Human Rights art 6 to simply adopt the trial judge's conclusions on questions of premeditation and financial motivation. Furthermore, given that heavier retrospective penalties were prohibited by the Convention, the court had to ask itself what minimum term the Secretary of State would have set on any different factual basis adopted by the court and limit the minimum term it set accordingly, even though the 2003 Act contained no transitional provisions to that effect. The phrase 'murder done for gain' in Sch 21 para 5(2)(c) was directed to the purpose or motive for the murder. It was not restricted to those who made a living out of killing, but also applied to domestic murders committed in order to solve debt problems. In all the circumstances, there was insufficient evidence that the murder was financially motivated or that it had been carefully planned over some days. However, there was a degree of planning that could properly be regarded as significant and which aggravated the offence. On the other hand, in view of his admissions, the credit given for the offender's guilty plea should not be the less either because he did not plead guilty when first arraigned or because there was strong evidence against him. Further, as the offender's progress in prison had been exceptional, he was entitled to a six-month reduction to his minimum term. The appropriate minimum term would be 13 and a-half years, and the offender's application would be allowed accordingly.

Re Bingham (application under para 3 of Sch 22 to the Criminal Justice Act 2003) [2006] EWHC 2591 (QB), [2006] All ER (D) 262 (Oct) (Queen's Bench Division: Andrew Smith J). *R (on the application of Cole) v Secretary of State for the Home Department* [2003] EWHC 1789 (Admin), [2003] All ER (D) 173 (Jul), DC, applied.

2555   Life sentence—mandatory life sentence—minimum term—reference to High Court—High Court judge same as trial judge—right to fair trial

The defendant was convicted of murder and sentenced to life imprisonment. The judge recommended to the Secretary of State that the minimum term of imprisonment should be 12 years, and that recommendation was indorsed by the Lord Chief Justice. By the time the new regime for setting minimum terms under the Criminal Justice Act 2003 Sch 22 para 6 had come into force, the Secretary of State had not notified the defendant of her minimum term, and the case was therefore referred to the High Court for the minimum term to be set. The Lord Chief Justice had directed that, in cases where the trial judge was a High Court judge, the matter should be referred to him. By the time of the defendant's reference, the trial judge had been elevated to the High Court bench, so the matter came back to him. He took a starting point of 14 years and, in view of the mitigating circumstances, ordered that the minimum term be set at 12 years. The defendant appealed, submitting that the fact that the judge who had set the minimum term on her reference to the High Court was also the trial judge violated her right to a fair trial under the European Convention on Human Rights art 6. *Held*, the fact that the judge who set the minimum term was the trial judge put him in a better place to exercise the function of reviewing the sentence. It was of course necessary that the judge reconsider the sentence and have regard to any additional relevant factors that were not before him the first time, but a judge was well capable of doing that. It would even be appropriate for the same judge to consider the matter if it was alleged that he had overlooked something or not given a matter sufficient weight. However, a sentence of ten years was appropriate and, accordingly the appeal would be allowed.

R v Sampson [2006] All ER (D) 284 (Oct) (Court of Appeal: Lord Phillips of Worth Matravers CJ, Pitchford and Calvert-Smith JJ).

2556 Life sentence—mandatory life sentence—minimum term—time served on remand for separate offence arising from same facts

The defendant attacked a man in a public house, fracturing the man's spinal cord and causing his legs and arms to become paralysed. The defendant pleaded guilty to causing grievous bodily harm with intent and was sentenced to ten years' imprisonment. The man subsequently died from his injuries and from complications arising from a tracheotomy performed after he began to experience breathing difficulties. The Attorney General gave his consent to a murder charge being brought against the defendant. The defendant was convicted of murder and given a life sentence. He had not spent any time on remand for murder, all his time in custody before receiving his life sentence having been in respect of his earlier conviction. After passing sentence, but before the commencement of the Criminal Justice Act 2003, the trial judge reported to the Home Secretary in accordance with the practice then in operation, recommending a tariff period of 12 years. The Lord Chief Justice recommended a period of nine to ten years. By the time that the 2003 Act had come into force, the Home Secretary had not notified the defendant of the minimum period which he thought he should serve before his release on licence. The case was therefore referred to the High Court under Sch 22 para 6 for the making of an order under s 269(2) or (4). *Held*, since the defendant had not been remanded in custody at all for murder, he was not entitled as of right to have any credit for time spent on remand prior to sentence. However, as a matter of justice, he clearly should not serve longer in custody because he had been sentenced for two offences based on identical facts. The proper way of dealing with that problem was to reduce the minimum term itself by the amount of time spent on remand for serving a sentence for the earlier offence. In reducing the trial judge's minimum term, the Lord Chief Justice had identified the earlier proceedings as a substantial mitigating factor, but had not said what part of that mitigation was attributable to the fact that the defendant had served time which would not count towards his minimum term for murder. There being doubt, it had to be resolved in the way most favourable to the defendant. Judgment would be given accordingly.

Re Brown (reference under paragraph 6 of Schedule 22 to the Criminal Justice Act 2003) [2006] All ER (D) 280 (Mar) (Queen's Bench Division: Pitchers J).

2557 Life sentence—manslaughter—mentally ill offender

The defendant pleaded guilty to manslaughter. In sentencing her, the judge stated that medical reports indicated that she was suffering from a psychopathic disorder, and that the nature of that disorder made it appropriate for her to be detained in a hospital. He stated that the defendant presented a risk of serious danger to the public and that it was not possible to know when it would be safe to release her. The judge decided that it was necessary to ensure that, were the defendant incapable of responding to hospital treatment, she would be returned to prison until it was safe for her to be released. He imposed custody for life with a hospital direction and a limitation direction under the Mental Health Act 1983 Act ss 41, 45A. The defendant applied for permission to appeal against her sentence. Subsequently, a mental health review tribunal found that she was suffering from mental illness as well as psychopathic disorder. *Held*, s 45A did not preclude its application in cases where the offender suffered from a psychopathic disorder and a mental illness. It could not be said that the presence of mental illness would serve to allay a judge's fear that lack of treatability might result in release, at a time when there remained a risk of serious danger to the public, and thus militate against an order pursuant to s 45A. It might be thought that the genesis of s 45A was not simply the problem posed by those suffering from psychopathic disorder alone, but rather, the situation which would arise where neither a sentence of imprisonment nor a hospital order alone might be appropriate. In the present case, it was the view of the medical team that the defendant would prove to be treatable in the long-term, and they had been proved right. It had not been shown that the continuing option of a return to prison was proving so significant an impediment to the defendant's successful treatment that the sentence should be quashed. The fact that the defendant had proved to be treatable did not establish that the concerns expressed by the judge had been proved wrong. Orders under s 45A had been so rarely made that there was no experience on which to draw as to the procedure which should be followed in the event of an offender reaching the stage at which release into the community could be considered. Accordingly, the appeal would be dismissed.

R v Staines [2006] EWCA Crim 15, [2006] 2 Cr App Rep (S) 376 (Court of Appeal: Dyson LJ, Tomlinson and Andrew Smith JJ).

2558   Life sentence—murder—tariff—minimum term

The victim was subjected to a sustained and horrific assault over a period of hours culminating in his murder. The defendants pleaded guilty to murder. The prosecution contended that the offence had been a sadistic killing under the Criminal Justice Act 2003 Sch 21 para 5(2)(e) which referred to 'a murder involving sexual or sadistic conduct'. Therefore, the prosecution submitted that the 30-year starting point for a minimum term of a life sentence applied. The judge stated that the conduct had not been sadistic because the word 'sadism' required a form of 'sexual perversion' when pleasure was gained from the infliction of pain on others. Therefore, he reached a starting point of 15 years and sentenced the first and second defendants to life imprisonment with minimum terms of 20 years and 15 years respectively. The Attorney General was granted leave to refer the sentences to the Court of Appeal as being unduly lenient. *Held,* the meaning of the word 'sadistic' did not require a form of sexual perversion. While sadistic conduct might be sexually fuelled, it could not be said that, nowadays, whether in relation to its ordinary meaning or in its statutory context, the word 'sadistic' implied a sexual element. In the present case, the fundamental question was whether the offence was of such seriousness as to require a starting point of 30 years rather than the 15-year starting point taken by the judge. The circumstances of the murder made it clear that it was of great seriousness. By reference to the statute, it had plainly called for a starting point of 30 years. It followed that the 15-year starting point taken by the judge had been unduly lenient. Accordingly, adjustments would be made to the starting point of 30 years to allow for mitigating factors and periods spent on remand in custody, and the sentences would be varied to a minimum term of 28 years, in the case of the first defendant, and 22 years, in the case of the second defendant.

A-G's References (Nos 108 and 109 of 2005); R v Swindon [2006] EWCA Crim 513, [2006] 2 Cr App Rep (S) 531 (Court of Appeal: Rose LJ, Rafferty J and Sir Richard Curtis).

2559   Life sentence—murder—tariff—minimum term—mitigation—no intent to kill

The defendant gained entry to the victim's home in the early hours of the morning. The victim was disturbed by the defendant and went downstairs to investigate. The defendant grabbed a large knife from the kitchen and plunged it into the victim's chest, killing him. He then fled, making off with an item belonging to the victim's wife. The defendant was convicted of murder. In sentencing the defendant, the judge concluded that the murder had been committed for gain within the meaning of the Criminal Justice Act 2003 Sch 21 para 5 and took a starting point of 30 years. He sentenced the defendant on the basis that he had intended to cause serious harm rather than kill, and that the murder had not been pre-meditated. He gave the defendant a sentence of life imprisonment with a minimum term of 27 years, less time spent on remand. The defendant appealed against his sentence, submitting that the judge had erred in his choice of starting point in that the murder had not been committed for gain. He contended that, although the murder had occurred in the course of a burglary, it had not been to facilitate that burglary but rather to facilitate his escape. Alternatively, he submitted that the judge had failed adequately to reflect his mitigation by applying only a three-year discount from the 30-year starting point. *Held,* a defendant's escape after committing a burglary was an integral part of the enterprise and it followed that, where a murder was committed in the course of a burglary, that was properly to be characterised as a murder for gain within the meaning of Sch 21 para 5. To enter a person's house to steal, and to kill a member of the household in order to escape was, for the purpose of setting a minimum term, unquestionably extremely serious. However, a lack of intention to kill could constitute a mitigating factor. In the present case, the judge had rightly taken the 30-year starting point. Taking into account the defendant's mitigation, the fact that the murder had not been pre-meditated and the judge's acceptance of the fact that he had had no intention to kill, the minimum term would be reduced to 24 years. Accordingly, the appeal would be allowed.

R v Bouhaddaou [2006] All ER (D) 37 (Dec) (Court of Appeal: Lord Phillips of Worth Matravers CJ, Jackson and Walker JJ).

2560   Murder—mitigating factors—previous good character—availability as mitigating factor

The defendant was convicted of murdering a man whom he believed to have raped the defendant's former girlfriend. He had no previous convictions. The judge sentenced him to life imprisonment with a minimum term of 18 years. He noted that the premeditation and dismemberment of the body constituted aggravating features. However, he found that the defendant's lack of previous convictions did not constitute a mitigating feature within the meaning of the Criminal Justice Act 2003 Sch 21 para 11. The defendant appealed against sentence. *Held*, it could not be said that a defendant's good character was irrelevant in all offences of murder and that it had always to be ignored altogether. However, that was not to say that previous good character would always be a mitigating factor. There might be cases in which little, if any, weight could be attached to a defendant's lack of previous convictions. It followed that there were circumstances in which positive good character could be taken into account as a mitigating factor sufficient to reduce a minimum term. While it was true that bad character was expressly to be treated as an aggravating feature pursuant to s 143(2), and that good character was not listed as a mitigating feature in Sch 21 para 11, that provision was not, and was not intended by Parliament to be, exhaustive. Schedule 21 para 11 specified that the mitigating factors might include those listed. However, in all the circumstances, the instant case was not one of those cases in which the defendant's lack of previous convictions could constitute a mitigating factor. The defendant's lifestyle could hardly be described as unblemished and he had decided to become judge, jury and executioner of the victim. There were at least two statutory aggravating features. Accordingly, the judge had been entirely justified in finding that there were no mitigating factors, and no complaint could be made of the minimum term imposed. The appeal would be dismissed accordingly.

R v Simmons [2006] EWCA Crim 1259, [2007] 1 Cr App Rep (S) 140 (Court of Appeal: Hallett LJ, Gibbs J and Judge Stewart QC). *R v Jones* [2005] EWCA Crim 3115, [2006] Crim LR 262; and *R v Last* [2005] EWCA Crim 106, [2005] 2 Cr App Rep (S) 381 (2005 Abr para 2763) considered.

2561   Plea of guilty—discount for plea—sentencing principles

The defendant was stopped as she entered the United Kingdom and was found to be carrying cocaine which she told customs officers she thought was cannabis. She also claimed that although she was to be paid for picking up the purported cannabis she had also been coerced into the offence. The defendant pleaded guilty to importing Class A drugs into the country at the earliest opportunity. The sentencing judge indicated that he would not sentence the defendant on the basis that she had thought that she was carrying cannabis without the benefit of a *Newton* hearing. However, counsel for the defendant indicated that he had been instructed that the defendant would not be willing to give evidence on oath that she had not known that she had been carrying cocaine. There was therefore no *Newton* hearing, and the judge sentenced her on the basis that she had known that she had been carrying cocaine. The defendant was sentenced to nine years' imprisonment. She appealed, submitting that the judge had erred in failing to give the defendant sufficient credit for a guilty plea at the earliest opportunity, having regard to the Criminal Justice Act 2003 s 144, which provided for a reduction in sentence for a guilty plea, the relevant definitive guidelines of the Sentencing Guidelines Council, and the court's duty under s 172 to consider such guidelines. *Held*, sentencing was not a mathematical exercise. It involved the weighing up of sometimes conflicting mitigating and aggravating factors. In this regard, s 144 did not add anything new. No one could doubt that a plea of guilty called for a reduction in the sentence. Further, although the court had a duty to consider 'definitive' guidelines under s 172, the guidelines of the Sentencing Guidelines Council remained guidelines and the term 'definitive guidelines' meant simply guidelines that had been through the process outlined in s 170. In the present case, it would be wrong not to reduce the sentence, given the indication given by the court in granting leave to appeal. Accordingly, the appeal would be allowed and a sentence of eight years' imprisonment substituted.

R v Martin [2006] EWCA Crim 1035, [2007] 1 Cr App Rep (S) 14 (Court of Appeal: Sir Igor Judge P, Mackay and Gross JJ).

2562   Proceeds of crime—receiving order—interim order—separate unlawful conduct—information relating to conduct—treatment of information

The applicant obtained an interim receiving order against the defendant. While performing her duties under the order, the interim receiver obtained information relating to alleged different wrongdoings and some of that information led to the applicant obtaining a second interim receiving order against the defendant. The latter applied for the discharge of the second order on a limited basis. Issues arose as to whether, on an application for the appointment of an interim receiver over certain property under the civil recovery provisions in the Proceeds of Crime Act 2002 Pt V (ss 240–316), an enforcement agency such as the applicant was entitled to rely on information about that property which had come to light only as a result of investigations conducted pursuant to a previous interim receiving order but which related to different wrongdoing by the proposed defendant. *Held*, the interim receiver and the enforcement agency were entitled to use in the application for the second order information which had come to light only as a result of information obtained pursuant to the first order but which related to different wrongdoing by the defendant from that relied on to obtain the first order. Sections 247(2)(b) and 255(1)(c) specifically contained the words 'in relation to the same unlawful conduct', with the effect that, under the terms of his interim receiving order, the receiver was obliged to take steps which the court deemed necessary to establish whether any other property was recoverable property in relation to the same unlawful conduct and, if it was, who held it. It followed that, where an interim receiver discovered realisable property in relation to the same unlawful conduct, he had first, pursuant to s 255(1)(c), to inform the court and the enforcement authority as soon as reasonably practicable if he thought that any property to which the order did not apply was recoverable property or associated property. The 2002 Act was silent on the consequences of the receiver finding in the execution of the order recoverable property which did not relate to the same unlawful conduct which had led to the interim receiving order being made but which related to different unlawful conduct. The absence of provisions on that issue did not mean that the receiver could not use that information.

Director of the Assets Recovery Agency v Szepietowski [2006] EWHC 2406 (Admin), [2006] All ER (D) 147 (Sep) (Queen's Bench Division: Silber J). *Chic Fashions (West Wales) Ltd v Jones* [1968] 2 QB 299, CA; and *LT Piver Sarl v S & J Perfume Co Ltd* [1987] FSR 159 considered.

2563   Restraint order—refusal to vary or discharge—jurisdiction of Crown Court to hear appeal

The Magistrates' Courts Act 1980 s 108(1) provides that a person convicted by a magistrates' court may appeal to the Crown Court against the sentence.

The applicant was convicted by a magistrates' court of an offence contrary to the Protection from Harassment Act 1997 and a restraining order was imposed by a district judge. The applicant applied unsuccessfully for the restraining order to be varied or discharged. He then appealed to the Crown Court against that refusal, but the recorder ruled that the Crown Court had no jurisdiction to hear the appeal. The applicant brought proceedings for judicial review, contending that the Crown Court had jurisdiction because the decision of the district judge was a 'sentence' within the meaning of the word in the 1980 Act s 108. *Held*, there was no right of appeal to the Crown Court against the refusal to vary or discharge a restraining order which had been made following conviction of an offence of harassment in a magistrates' court. On the ordinary meaning of the word 'sentence' in s 108 such a refusal could not of itself constitute a sentence. The appropriate remedy would be by way of judicial review or case stated in an appropriate case where an error of law in the decision making process could be demonstrated. Accordingly, the application would be dismissed.

R (on the application of Lee) v Crown Court at Leeds [2006] All ER (D) 18 (Oct) (Queen's Bench Division: Maurice Kay LJ and Bean J).

2564   Review of sentence—unduly lenient sentence—power of review—extension

The Criminal Justice Act 1988 (Reviews of Sentencing) Order 2006, SI 2006/1116 (in force on 16 May 2006), extends the range of cases which the Attorney General may refer to the Court of Appeal where he considers that a sentence imposed in the Crown Court was unduly lenient to include (1) serious fraud offences which have been transferred to the Crown Court by way of a notice of transfer made under the Criminal Justice Act 1987 s 5, and serious fraud offences in which proceedings were brought by way of a voluntary bill of indictment following dismissal of charges which were the subject of a notice of transfer; (2) certain triable either way offences under the Sexual Offences Act 2003 and attempting to commit or inciting the commission of certain of those offences; and (3) certain other specified offences. SI 1994/119, 1995/10, 2000/1924, 2003/2267 are revoked.

2565   Sentencing principles—considerations relevant to sentence—provision of evidence or information relating to another suspect

The defendant was charged with harbouring a large quantity of Class A drugs. He contended that he had acted under duress, and gave details of the persons allegedly involved. Those persons were arrested but subsequently absconded, with the result that the defendant was tried alone. He was convicted and sentenced to 13 years' imprisonment. After his trial and sentence, one of the persons originally arrested was apprehended. The defendant agreed to give evidence against him, and he was duly convicted. The defendant then appealed against his own sentence, submitting that the court was entitled pursuant to the Criminal Appeal Act 1968 s 11(3) to substitute a lower sentence on the basis of events subsequent to sentence such as the giving of vital testimony against a co-accused. *Held*, the general principle in cases where a defendant was prepared to give evidence or information in relation to criminal activity of others was that he would be entitled to a discount in his sentence, depending on the quality and nature of the material, and the way in which it was provided, and that that discount could be as high as two-thirds. The level of reduction depended on the quality of the material provided and, importantly, the extent to which the defendant was prepared to provide it despite the risk of danger to himself or his family. In view of the importance of the information and testimony given, the present case justified a substantial discount in sentence. Moreover, s 11(3) permitted the court to consider material arising subsequent to sentence, notwithstanding the general principle that, where a defendant had denied his guilt but had been convicted and sentenced, he could not expect the court to intervene in what was otherwise a proper sentence by thereafter deciding to give information to the police, and that, generally speaking, the court was a court of review and should not reopen a sentence properly given at the time. The defendant had maintained the same story throughout and should not be prohibited from relying on subsequent events in support of a claim for a reduced sentence. In the circumstances, a five-year term of imprisonment was appropriate. Accordingly, the appeal would be allowed.

R v A [2006] All ER (D) 348 (Jun) (Court of Appeal: Latham LJ, Forbes and Irwin JJ).

2566   Sentencing principles—duty of counsel to assist judge

It has been held that both defence and prosecuting advocates have a duty to assist the judge at the sentencing stage. Although judges have a duty to impose lawful sentences, sentencing has become a complex matter and a judge will very often not see the papers very long before the hearing and will not have the time for preparation that the advocates should enjoy. In these circumstances, a judge relies on advocates to assist him with sentencing. It is unacceptable for advocates not to ascertain and be prepared to assist the judge with the legal restrictions on the sentence that he can impose on the defendant. In particular, it is unsatisfactory for a prosecuting advocate, having secured a conviction, to sit back and leave sentencing to the defence, nor can an advocate, when appearing for the prosecution for the purpose of sentence on a plea of guilty, limit the assistance that he provides to the court to providing an outline of the facts and details of the defendant's previous convictions. The advocate for the prosecution should always be ready to assist the court by drawing attention to any statutory provisions that govern the court's sentencing powers. It is the duty of prosecuting counsel to ensure that the judge does not, through inadvertence, impose a sentence which is outside his powers. The advocate for the prosecution should also be in a position to offer to draw the judge's attention to any relevant sentencing guidelines or guideline decisions of the Court of Appeal. These principles are equally applicable to those appearing for prosecution and defence before the justices.

R v Cain [2006] All ER (D) 113 (Dec) (Court of Appeal: Lord Phillips of Worth Matravers CJ, Rafferty and Walker JJ). *A-G's Reference (No 52 of 2003)* [2003] EWCA Crim 3731, [2004] Crim LR 306 (2003 Abr para 212); and *R v Pepper* [2005] EWCA Crim 1181, [2006] 1 Cr App Rep (S) 111 (2005 Abr para 2786) considered.

2567   Sentencing principles—matters to be taken into account—other offences

It has been held that the court cannot, when sentencing an offender, take into consideration other offences committed by the offender unless he expressly agrees to it. The court is not, however, obligated to take such offences into consideration notwithstanding that the offender wishes it. The sentence is intended to reflect the defendant's overall criminality, and for that purpose all offences committed are relevant. The court may take into account the fact that an offender co-operated with the police and thereby helped to clear up offences that might not otherwise have been brought to justice. On the other hand, the fact that the offender has committed more offences may persuade the court to impose a harsher sentence.

R v Miles [2006] EWCA Crim 256, [2006] All ER (D) 176 (Mar) (Court of Appeal: Sir Igor Judge P, Nelson J and Sir Douglas Brown).

2568   Sexual offence—administering a substance with intent—excessive sentence

The defendant was convicted of administering a substance with intent to engage in sexual activity, contrary to the Sexual Offences Act 2003 s 61, and sentenced to five years' imprisonment. On his appeal against sentence, the court considered the proper approach to be taken in sentencing offences contrary to s 61. *Held*, lacing the drinks of young women in pubs and nightclubs so as to make them anaesthetized and vulnerable was on the increase. Given the short time in which the drug passed through the body, detection was made more difficult. Such drugs were apparently relatively easy to acquire and relatively easy to use. The offence was very serious indeed and any sentence imposed had to include a strong deterrent element. Those who used drugs in order to commit crime had to understand that such conduct would attract very substantial terms of imprisonment. In the present case, while the victim had not, in fact, been at risk of death, aggravating features still justified the sentence imposed. There had unquestionably been a breach of trust and the dose given had to be regarded as an aggravating feature. Moreover, knowing what he had done, the defendant had failed to act when the victim had suffered an adverse reaction. Therefore five years' imprisonment was, in all the circumstances, entirely appropriate and accordingly, the appeal would be dismissed.

R v Wright [2006] All ER (D) 228 (Oct) (Court of Appeal: Latham LJ, Henriques and Gloster JJ).

2569   Sexual offence—notification order—application to conditionally discharged offender

The Powers of Criminal Courts (Sentencing) Act 2000 s 14(1) provides that a conviction of an offence for which an order is made discharging the offender absolutely or conditionally is to be deemed not to be a conviction for any purpose other than the purposes of the proceedings in which the order is made.

The defendant was charged on two counts of making indecent photographs of children, contrary to the Protection of Children Act 1978 s 1(1)(a), and of possessing indecent photographs of children, contrary to the Criminal Justice Act 1988 s 160(1). The judge imposed 12-month conditional discharges under the 2000 Act s 12 for each offence, and also ruled that there was a requirement to notify under the Sex Offenders Act 1997 for a period of five years from the date of conviction. The defendant's appeal against the judge's finding that the defendant was subject to the notification requirements was dismissed, but the court certified that the question of whether the 2000 Act s 14(1) had the effect of preventing an order for conditional discharge made on conviction for an offence other than under the 1997 Act from being classed as a conviction for the purposes of the 1997 Act, thereby avoiding the notification requirements under the 1997 Act, was a question of general importance involved in its decision. The defendant appealed. *Held*, it was outside the power of the judge and of the Court of Appeal to determine that the defendant was subject to notification requirements and to require him to register under the 1997 Act. It was accepted that, if there was any requirement to notify under s 1 in consequence of the defendant's convictions in the proceedings under the 1978 and 1988 Acts, it arose independently of anything provided in that legislation and of any order which was or could be made by the court in the proceedings or on the convictions under it. It was also accepted that the only statutory sanction for failure to register was to be found in the 1997 Act s 3. It followed that, if and in so far as the judge in the instant case had heard submissions and purported to determine whether any and what notification requirements arose under the 1997 Act consequent on the orders of conditional discharge which he had made, he had had no power to do so. The fact that he had purported as part of the sentencing exercise to determine the issue entitled the defendant to appeal. However, on the appeal, if the issue regarding the judge's power to rule had been identified, the judge's ruling should have been set aside without more as having been beyond his power. Accordingly, the appeal would be allowed.

R v Longworth [2006] UKHL 1, [2006] 1 All ER 887 (House of Lords: Lords Nicholls of Birkenhead, Hoffmann, Hope of Craighead, Rodger of Earlsferry and Mance). *R v Cain* [1984] 2 All ER 737, HL (1984 Abr para 552), applied.

2570 Sexual offence—rape—indecent photographs of children—aggravating factors—plea of guilty

The defendants carried out a series of horrifying acts of sexual abuse and rape on a three-month old baby, who had been entrusted to the care of the first defendant. The second defendant had also committed an indecent assault on a 14-year-old girl and had downloaded a number of pornographic images involving children. The second defendant pleaded guilty to four counts of rape. The first defendant pleaded guilty to rape and indecent assault. The second defendant was sentenced to life imprisonment on each of the four counts of rape. Since the defendants had pleaded guilty at the first available opportunity, the judge reduced the minimum term of 18 years by one third resulting in a minimum term of six years for the second defendant. The first defendant was sentenced to an extended sentence of ten years comprising a custodial term of five years and an extension period of five years. The Attorney General was granted leave to refer the sentences to the Court of Appeal as being unduly lenient. *Held*, the extraordinary and abhorrent features of the treatment of the baby, called, in the case of the second defendant, for a starting point of longer than 18 years. The offending had gone beyond that envisaged by the guideline authorities. It had combined the aggravating features of repeated rape over a period of time, breach of trust, and rape of the most vulnerable victim possible. Further aggravating factors were the assault on the 14 year-old complainant and the downloading of indecent photographs. In all the circumstances, the appropriate starting point was 24 years. Whilst there might be circumstances which justified awarding less than a discount of one third where the defendant had pleaded guilty at the first opportunity, it was difficult to see how a judge could comply with the Criminal Justice Act 2003 s 172 where he deliberately flouted the guideline by granting less than a full discount on the ground of the strength of the case against a defendant. In the circumstances of the present case, it would not be right to reduce the discount. Accordingly, the first defendant's sentence would stand, but the minimum term to be served by the second defendant before any consideration for early release would be increased from six years to eight years.

A-G's References (Nos 14 and 15 of 2006); R v French [2006] EWCA Crim 1335, [2006] All ER (D) 47 (Jun) (Court of Appeal: Lord Phillips of Worth Matravers CJ, Sir Igor Judge P, Henriques, Roderick Evans and Fulford JJ).

2571 Sexual offence—sexual activity with person with a mental disorder—relevance of consent to sentence

The defendant pleaded guilty to engaging in sexual activity with a person with a mental disorder, and where he was involved in her care, contrary to the Sexual Offences Act 2003 s 38. The judge found that the fact that the complainant had been willing was irrelevant to sentence. The defendant was sentenced to 17 months' imprisonment. He appealed on the ground that the judge had erred in imposing a custodial sentence as the custody threshold had not been passed. Alternatively, he submitted that the sentence was manifestly excessive in all the circumstances. Consideration was given to the Sentencing Guideline Council recommendation that the starting point on conviction for offences contrary to s 38 where penetration had been involved was three years' imprisonment. *Held*, s 38 had created a new offence, the aim of which was to protect people who, because of their mental disorder, were vulnerable to sexual advances from those who looked after them. The rationale of the offence was that because the victim suffered from a mental disorder, they would not be able to make an informed choice about sexual activity. The issue of consent was not relevant to whether the offence had been committed. In all the circumstances, the judge had passed a perfectly proper sentence. The defendant had taken advantage of an extremely vulnerable person and had led her into a sexual relationship which had devastating effects on her. Further, there had been an element of planning on the defendant's part. Accordingly, the appeal would be dismissed.

R v Bradford [2006] All ER (D) 258 (Oct) (Court of Appeal: Hooper LJ, Aikens and Lloyd Jones JJ).

2572   Sexual offence—sexual offences prevention order—distinction from custodial sentencing provisions

The defendant, who had previous convictions for gross indecency, was convicted of exposure. The judge sentenced the defendant to six months' imprisonment and concluded that it was also necessary to make him subject to a sexual offences prevention order pursuant to the Sexual Offences Act 2003 s 104. The defendant appealed against the order, and the question arose whether it was open to the sentencing judge to impose a sexual offences prevention order under s 104 when an extended sentence was not required pursuant to the Criminal Justice Act 2003 s 227. Held, the schemes under the Sexual Offences Act 2003 and the Criminal Justice Act 2003 were intended to be and were distinct. The two Acts had been enacted on the same date and contained no provision which required the court to impose an extended custodial sentence whenever it imposed a sexual offences prevention order. The list of offences to which the relevant provisions of the two Acts applied were different and other fine distinctions served to fortify the conclusion that the two Acts were not intended to be linked so as to enable the provisions of one of them to override the other. It followed that it was not a pre-condition to the making of a sexual offences prevention order that the judge should be satisfied that the defendant would also qualify for an extended sentence, life imprisonment or imprisonment for public protection. Accordingly, the appeal would be dismissed.

R v Richards [2006] EWCA Crim 2519, [2006] All ER (D) 338 (Oct) (Court of Appeal: Sir Igor Judge P, Holland and Tugendhat JJ).

2573   Sexual or violent offence—custodial sentence—public protection—guidance

Three appeals were heard together since each raised issues as to whether a sentence of imprisonment for public protection under the Criminal Justice Act 2003 s 225 could be ordered to run consecutively with another sentence of imprisonment for public protection. Held, while there was no provision which prohibited the imposition of consecutive indeterminate sentences or the imposition of an indeterminate sentence consecutive to another period of imprisonment, it was undesirable that that should be done. Common sense suggested that a sentence of life imprisonment or of imprisonment for public protection would start immediately on its imposition. Given the difficulties that might arise in determining when a prisoner should be released or was eligible for parole, it was easier not to compound those difficulties by making indeterminate sentences consecutive to other sentences or periods in custody. Where a judge intended to order that the period before which the defendant would become eligible for parole should be served consecutive to an existing sentence or to follow a period imposed under the Powers of Criminal Courts (Sentencing) Act 2000 s 116, in order to ensure that a sentence imposed included the balance of an existing sentence under s 116, he should increase the notional determinate term to reflect that balance or that period. In cases to which the 2003 Act s 244 applied, the notional determinate sentence should be divided by half to arrive at the specified minimum term. Any period under the 2000 Act s 116 would attract the same treatment, namely, by adding it to the notional determinate term which the judge would otherwise have set. Judgment would be given accordingly.

R v O'Brien; R v Moss; R v Llewellyn [2006] EWCA Crim 1741, [2006] 4 All ER 1012 (Court of Appeal: Hooper LJ, Penry-Davey and Walker JJ).

2574   Sexual or violent offence—imprisonment for public protection—guidance

The Court of Appeal heard together several cases which raised issues concerning the imprisonment of sexual or violent offenders for public protection pursuant to the Criminal Justice Act 2003 ss 224–229. The court gave the following guidance: (1) The judgment in R v Lang represents an attempt to summarise the approach to sentencing which the 2003 Act requires and to give guidance as to its meaning, but warns against treating it as if it were a substitute for looking at the provisions of the 2003 Act. Until recently, the sentencing options available to deal with defendants who posed a continuing danger were limited. However, the 2003 Act provided a new sentence, imprisonment for public protection ('the sentence'). A cursory glance at the provisions makes it plain that the sentence is concerned with future risk and public protection. Although punitive in its effect, with far-reaching consequences for the defendant on whom it is imposed, strictly speaking, it does not represent punishment for past offending. As any such assessment of future risk has to be based on the information available to the court when sentence is passed, the potential for distraction from the real issue is obvious. Nevertheless, when the information before the court is evaluated, for the purposes of this sentence, the decision is directed not to the past, but to the future, and the future protection of the public. The words 'the assessment of dangerousness' in the headnote to s 229 do not appear in ss 224–229, and it seems clear that 'dangerousness' is intended to represent a convenient shorthand to describe, in the words of s 225(1)(b), those cases where 'the court is of the opinion that there is a significant risk to members of the public of serious harm occasioned by the commission of further specified offences'. That provision is common to ss 225–228. While 'dangerousness' was, therefore, shorthand, it is emphasised that there are two distinct requirements to a finding of dangerousness for the purposes of s 225. (2) It is a prerequisite to the sentence that the defendant has been convicted of a 'specified offence', one of 153 categories of violent or sexual offences listed in Sch 15. Some specified offences are serious offences for the purposes of s 224. Where, in the judgment of the court, there is a significant risk that the defendant will commit further specified (but not necessarily serious) offences, and that the consequence of any such offence would be serious harm (death or serious personal injury, whether physical or psychological) to members of the public, then, in brief, he is to be regarded as a dangerous defendant. Indeed, if the judge is satisfied that the defendant is properly to be described as dangerous for the purposes of the 2003 Act, then he is required to impose either a sentence of life imprisonment or imprisonment for public protection. The effect of s 225(1), (3) is that the court is left with no alternative. (3) In contrast to, for example, s 225, s 229 does not confirm or create any new sentence, but rather it provides statutory direction on the approach to the assessment of dangerousness which should be adopted by the sentencing court. Section 229(2) is concerned with defendants aged over 18, without previous convictions for specified offences. In reality, this provision adds nothing to the approach which the sentencer would normally take, that is, to consider all the information available to the court. Although the court has what is described as a 'discretion' to take into account any information about the 'pattern of behaviour' or indeed 'any information about the defendant', it is difficult to see how any sentencer, properly forming his judgment, would fail to take all matters of possible relevance into account. However, what s 229(2) highlights is that it is not a prerequisite to a finding of dangerousness that the defendant should be an individual with previous convictions. A man of good character may properly qualify for this sentence. (4) Section 229(3) addresses the familiar situation of the adult defendant with previous convictions for specified offences. Here, the court is directed to approach the dangerousness issue by treating it as established unless that conclusion would be unreasonable. The analysis is for the sentencer. The use of language like 'assumption', 'conclusion' and 'unreasonable' in a provision directing the method of approach to the assessment of dangerousness does not produce helpful clarity. The decision in *R v Lang* explained that sentencers should not allow the language of s 229(3) to obscure the ultimate responsibility of the sentencer to make the necessary assessment. The effect of *R v Lang* is that, in the end, the question of whether it is unreasonable to make the assumption of dangerousness on the basis of previous convictions for specified offences is left to his judgment. The sentencer is entitled to conclude that, notwithstanding the statutory assumption, the defendant with previous convictions, even for specified offences, does not necessarily satisfy the requirements of dangerousness. Much of the argument in *R v Lang* itself, and many of the submissions in the instant cases, on the issue of dangerousness focussed on s 229(3), and whether, and, if so in what circumstances, the assumption of dangerousness should be disapplied. Nothing in the instant cases is intended to undermine the guidance provided in *R v Lang*. (5) Just as the absence of previous convictions does not preclude a finding of dangerousness, the existence of previous convictions for specified offences does not compel such a finding: there is a presumption that it does, which may be rebutted. (6) If a finding of dangerousness can be made against a defendant without previous specified convictions, it also follows that previous offences, not in fact specified for the purposes of s 229, are not disqualified from consideration. Accordingly, for example, as indeed the 2003 Act recognises, a pattern of minor previous offences of gradually escalating seriousness may be significant. In other words, it is not right that, unless the previous offences were specified offences, they were irrelevant. (7) Where the facts of the instant offence, or indeed any specified offences for the purposes of s 229(3) are examined, it may emerge that no harm actually occurred. That may be advantageous to the defendant, and some of the cases examined in *R v Lang* exemplify the point. On the other hand, the absence of harm may be entirely fortuitous. A victim cowering away from an armed assailant may avoid direct physical injury or serious psychological harm. Faced with such a case, the sentencer considering dangerousness may wish to reflect, for example, on the likely response of the defendant if his victim, instead of surrendering, resolutely defended himself. It does not automatically follow from the absence of actual harm caused by the defendant to date that the risk that he will cause serious harm in the future is negligible. In particular, *R v Shaffi*, where it was accepted, on the facts, that the judge had erred in finding that there was a risk of serious harm on the facts, is not authority for the proposition that, as a matter of law, offences which do not result in harm to the victim should be treated as irrelevant. (8) Characteristics such as the inadequacy, suggestibility, or vulnerability of the defendant may serve to produce or reinforce the conclusion that the defendant is dangerous. In one of the instant cases it was suggested that the sentence was wrong because an inadequate defendant had suffered what was described as an 'aberrant moment'. But, as experience shows, aberrant moments may be productive of catastrophe. The sentencer is right to be alert to such risks of aberrant moments in the future, and their consequences. (9) In *R v Lang*, it was suggested that the prosecution should be in a position to describe the facts of previous specified offences. That was plainly desirable, but is not always practicable. There is no reason why the prosecution's failure to comply with this good practice, even when it can and should, should either make an adjournment obligatory, or indeed preclude the imposition of the sentence, when appropriate. In any such case, counsel for the defendant should be in a position to explain the circumstances on the basis of his instructions. If the Crown is not in a position to challenge those instructions, then the court may proceed on the information it has. Equally, there are some situations in which the sentence imposed by the court dealing with earlier specified offences may enable the sentencer to draw inferences about its seriousness, or otherwise. In short, failure to comply with best practice on this point should be discouraged, but it does not normally preclude the imposition of the sentence. (10) It is not obligatory for the sentencer to spell out all the details of the earlier specified offences. To the extent that a judge is minded to rely on a disputed fact in reaching a finding of dangerousness, he should not rely on that fact unless the dispute can fairly be resolved adversely to the defendant. In the end, the requirement is that the sentencing remarks should explain the reasoning which has led the sentencer to the conclusion. (11) The Court of Appeal will not normally interfere with the conclusions reached by a sentencer who has accurately identified the relevant principles, and applied his mind to the relevant facts. It cannot be too strongly emphasised that the question to be addressed in the Court of Appeal is not whether it is possible to discover some words used by the sentencer which may be inconsistent with the precise language used in *R v Lang*, or indeed some failure on his part to deploy identical language to that used in *R v Lang*, but whether the imposition of the sentence was manifestly excessive or wrong in principle. Notwithstanding the labyrinthine provisions of ss 224–229, and the guidance offered by *R v Lang*, these essential principles are not affected. They apply with equal force to references by the Attorney General, where the question is whether the decision not to impose the sentence, in the circumstances, was unduly lenient. (12) In cases to which s 229(3) applies, where the sentencer has applied the statutory assumption, to succeed the defendant should demonstrate that it was unreasonable not to disapply it. Equally, where the Attorney General has referred such a case because the sentencer has decided to disapply the assumption, the reference will not succeed unless it is shown that the decision was one which the sentencer could not properly have reached.

R v Johnson [2006] EWCA Crim 2486, [2006] All ER (D) 257 (Oct) (Court of Appeal: Sir Igor Judge P, Goldring and Owen JJ). *R v Lang* [2005] EWCA Crim 2864, [2006] 2 All ER 410 (2005 Abr para 2787); and *R v Shaffi* [2006] EWCA Crim 418, [2006] All ER (D) 103 (Mar) explained.

2575 Sexual or violent offence—life imprisonment—public protection—rape

The Criminal Justice Act 2003 s 255(1), (2) provides that, where (1) the court is of the opinion that a person convicted of a serious offence poses a significant risk to members of the public of serious harm occasioned by the commission of further specified offences; (2) the offence is one in respect of which the offender would apart from s 255 be liable to imprisonment for life; and (3) the court considers that the seriousness of the offence, or of the offence and one or more offences associated with it, is such as to justify the imposition of a sentence of imprisonment for life, the court must impose a sentence of imprisonment for life.

During the course of burgling the home of the 65-year-old complainant, the defendants threatened the complainant with a knife and screwdriver, bound her legs and wrists with tape, put a sock into her mouth, put tape on her head, mouth, eyes and ears and struck the complainant several times. She was also raped by both defendants while a sharp object was held to her neck. Both defendants had previous convictions for dishonesty offences, assault and criminal damage. They pleaded guilty to two counts of rape and aggravated burglary, and were sentenced to life sentences pursuant to the Criminal Justice Act 2003 with minimum terms of six years. They appealed against sentence, submitting that s 225 did not apply as rape was not an offence in relation to which a defendant was liable to be imprisoned for life, and that in any event the judge could not reasonably have concluded that they presented a significant risk of serious harm to the public by the commission by them of further specified offences. *Held*, rape was an offence in respect of which a defendant was liable to be imprisoned for life. It was not appropriate in the course of the inquiry under s 225(2) to consider whether, applying particular guidelines, a sentence of life imprisonment would in fact have been imposed, but rather the question was whether the defendant was liable to such a sentence. Moreover, the judge had had sufficient material on which to conclude that the defendants presented a significant risk of serious harm to the public by the commission by them of further specified offences. Accordingly, the appeals would be dismissed.

R v Beazley [2006] All ER (D) 175 (Oct) (Court of Appeal: Latham LJ, Henriques and Gloster JJ). *R v Millberry; R v Morgan; R v Lackenby* [2002] EWCA Crim 2891, [2003] 2 All ER 939 (2002 Abr para 2658); and *R v Lang* [2005] EWCA Crim 2864, [2006] 2 All ER 410 (2005 Abr para 2787) considered.

2576 Supervision order—seriousness of offence—sexual offence—mistaken identity

The Sexual Offences Act 2003 s 2(1) provides that a person (A) commits an offence if (a) he intentionally penetrates the vagina or anus of another person (B) with a part of his body or anything else, (b) the penetration is sexual, (c) B does not consent to the penetration, and (d) A does not reasonably believe that B consents. Whether a belief is reasonable is to be determined having regard to all the circumstances, including any steps A has taken to ascertain whether B consents: s 2(2).

The offender was invited by the complainant's son to a party at their home. In the course of the evening, the offender became friendly with a woman. In due course, the offender was shown to the room in which he was to sleep. However, he went into a room which he thought was occupied by the woman but was in fact occupied by the complainant and her sister. The complainant woke up to find the offender behind her putting his fingers into her vagina. She told him to stop, at which the offender apologised and left. In interview, the offender stated that he had understood from conversations with the woman that she would have sexual intercourse with him and that he had subsequently gone into what he thought was the woman's room, removed his glasses, climbed into the bed and begun making sexual advances to the person in the bed. He was charged with rape, contrary to the 2003 Act s 1, and assault by penetration, contrary to s 2. The judge ruled that the account put forward by the offender did not amount to a defence because s 2 was limited to whatever had taken place between the offender and the named complainant in the indictment so that the jury were not entitled to consider mistaken identity as a relevant circumstance in assessing whether the offender reasonably believed that consent had been given. The offender pleaded guilty to assault by penetration as an alternative to rape. He had no previous convictions and was sentenced to a supervision order for three years, with a requirement that he attend a sexual offender group work programme. The Attorney General sought leave to refer the sentence to the Court of Appeal on the ground that it was unduly lenient, arguing that the proper sentence would have been in the region of four years' imprisonment on a guilty plea and that the violation of the complainant's right not to be assaulted by penetration had to be marked by a substantial immediate custodial sentence, even if the sole reason for the offence was the offender's mistaken belief as to the identity of the woman in the bed. *Held*, on the basis that the offender would not have been committing any offence had the woman been in the bed and that a reasonable and sober person would have realised that the person in the bed was not the woman, it could not be said that the sentence of four years' imprisonment as suggested by the Attorney General was the proper sentence. The present case was far from the normal case. In all the circumstances, including the offender's mitigation, it could not be said that the sentence was unduly lenient and, accordingly, leave to appeal would be refused.

A-G's Reference (No 79 of 2006); R v Whitta [2006] EWCA Crim 2626, [2006] All ER (D) 383 (Oct) (Court of Appeal: Hooper LJ, Aikens and Lloyd Jones JJ). *A-G's Reference (No 104 of 2004); R v Garvey* [2004] EWCA Crim 2672, [2005] Crim LR 150 (2004 Abr para 2488) considered.

2577 Unduly lenient sentence—reference by Attorney General—cheating the public revenue

Four offenders were involved in a 'missing trader' fraud which resulted in several million pounds' worth of valued added tax revenue being lost. They were convicted of cheating the public revenue, and the first three offenders were sentenced to four-and-a-half years' imprisonment and the fourth offender to two-and-a-half years' imprisonment. The sentencing judge stated that the sentences in relation to the first three offenders would have been a year longer had there not been a long delay in bringing the case to trial. The Attorney General applied pursuant to the Criminal Justice Act 1988 s 36 for leave to refer the sentences as being unduly lenient, submitting also that the had erred by failing to impose directors disqualification orders on the offenders. *Held*, those who organised fraudulent activity such as missing trader frauds could and should expect sentences well into double figures. Authorities upholding a sentence of nine years' imprisonment in such a case should not be taken as suggesting that it was an appropriate sentence, but rather that the sentence was not manifestly excessive or wrong in principle. In the present case, the offenders' roles had been limited to running buffer companies which handed over VAT to the organisers of the fraud. They had not, on the evidence, been involved in any deeper way in the planning, organising or running of the scheme. In the case of the first three offenders, the appropriate bracket was seven to eight years' imprisonment. That more than adequately reflected the seriousness of the offending and the need to deter people from becoming involved in activity which could be easy for a company to be tempted to join. While it could be said that the sentence ultimately imposed by the judge was unduly lenient, it was not necessary in the interests of justice to interfere with them. The fourth offender, by contrast, had been involved in the fraud for a limited period and the sums involved had been substantially less. The appropriate sentence in his case was three years' imprisonment. However, in all the circumstances, while the judge's starting point was lenient, it was not unduly lenient. The judge should have made directors disqualifications in the present case. The offenders were directors of companies and who had involved those companies in dishonest fraudulent activity of a significant sort. Judgment would be given accordingly.

A-G's References (Nos 88, 89, 98 and 91 of 2006); R v Meehan [2006] All ER (D) 105 (Dec) (Court of Appeal: Latham LJ, Mitting and Teare JJ).

2578 Unduly lenient sentence—reference by Attorney General—gross indecency with child

The offender, aged 81, was a friend of the complainant's family, for whom he also did some gardening. On a number of occasions when the complainant was aged between six and ten, the offender touched the complainant's genitals over his clothing. The offences came to light when the complainant later suffered a breakdown, albeit one caused only in part by the abuse. The offender admitted touching the complainant and explained that he had stopped because he had realised that what he was doing was wrong. He subsequently pleaded guilty to five counts of gross indecency with a child, and asked for a further five similar offences in respect of the same complainant to be taken into consideration. The offender was of previous good character and had recently undergone a triple heart bypass. The judge imposed a community order with the requirement of both supervision and attendance at a sex offender programme. The offender was also made subject to a sexual offences prevention order, prohibiting him from having unsupervised contact with a child under the age of 16. The Attorney General applied for leave pursuant to the Criminal Justice Act 1998 s 36 to refer the sentence to the Court of Appeal as being unduly lenient. *Held*, it had always to be remembered that sentencing was an art rather than a science, that the trial judge was particularly well placed to assess the weight to be given to various competing considerations, and that leniency was not in itself a vice. That mercy should season justice was a proposition as soundly based in law as it was in literature. If the sentence imposed had been merciful, in all the circumstances the present case was a salutary reminder that a sentencing judge could, on occasion, and in the right case, temper justice with mercy. Faced with difficult features, the judge had had to consider precisely where the level of sentence should be. To his credit, and somewhat unusually in such a class of case, the offender had himself brought his misconduct to an end. When interviewed, his immediate reaction was to be frank, open and honest about what he had done, and to express genuine remorse. While the offences were serious, and had involved a serious breach of trust, the offender's mitigation was compelling. The judge had carefully balanced all relevant considerations, including the need to protect children. The requirement under the community order of attendance at a sex offender programme was far from being a soft option. Accordingly, the application would be dismissed.

A-G's Reference (No 73 of 2006); R v M [2006] All ER (D) 106 (Oct) (Court of Appeal: Sir Igor Judge P, Holland and Goldring JJ). *A-G's Reference (No 4 of 1989)* [1990] 1 WLR 41, CA, considered.

2579   Unduly lenient sentence—reference by Attorney General—gross negligence manslaughter—failure to implement health and safety safeguards—appropriateness of custodial sentence

The offender was the managing director of a company which manufactured fireplace surrounds using stone and marble. Three stone-cutting machines installed by the company were fully automated and operated in response to computer programmes that were set by the operators. The operating manual warned that under no circumstances should a person enter a clearly defined 'danger zone' while the machine was in operation. The danger zone was indicated by beams of light emitted from the machine, and the machine automatically switched off if a beam was broken by someone entering the zone. However, due to the cost to the business of the machine being rendered inactive for that reason, the offender decided that the safety mechanisms should be deactivated. An employee was fatally injured by one of the stone-cutting machines, and the offender was charged with manslaughter and offences contrary to the Health and Safety at Work etc Act 1974. He was convicted of the health and safety offences, but the jury was unable to reach a verdict in relation to manslaughter. The offender subsequently pleaded guilty to manslaughter by gross negligence. The judge imposed a sentence of two years' imprisonment, suspended for two years. The offender's mitigation included the fact that he had suffered from a heart attack since the offence and that his company had suffered financially. The Attorney General was granted permission pursuant to the Criminal Justice Act 1988 s 36 to refer the sentence to the Court of Appeal as being unduly lenient. *Held*, the consideration that imprisonment might result in the collapse of the offender's business and the unemployment of his employees could not be treated as an exceptional circumstance for the purpose of determining whether the suspension of a sentence of imprisonment was justified. There would be occasions in which it might well be relevant to take into account the consequences of imprisonment to a business run by the offender. However, where the offence had arisen directly from the offender's misconduct of his business, different considerations would apply. While many small businesses with a 'hands-on boss' might operate without regard to health and safety obligations, and imprisonment of the boss might jeopardise the business or the livelihood of employees, to take into account such consequences would serve as no incentive to ensure that health and safety obligations were complied with. There was nothing in the case which could be said to justify the suspension of a custodial sentence. A sentence of 15 months' imprisonment was appropriate. Judgment would be given accordingly.

A-G's Reference (No 89 of 2006); R v Shaw [2006] All ER (D) 45 (Oct) (Court of Appeal: Sir Igor Judge P, Goldring and Henriques JJ).

2580   Unduly lenient sentence—reference by Attorney General—possession of Class A drug with intent to supply—factors relevant to sentencing decision—prison overcrowding

The defendant pleaded guilty to possessing a Class A controlled drug with intent to supply. The judge, commenting that jails were full to overflowing, imposed a suspended sentence of 12 months in a young offender institution, 100 hours of unpaid community work and an 18-month supervision order. The Attorney General referred the sentence for review, under the Criminal Justice Act 1988 s 36, as being unduly lenient. *Held*, by virtue of the Criminal Justice Act 2003 s 152(2) a court could not pass a custodial sentence unless it was of the opinion that the offence was so serious that a community sentence could not be justified. When deciding whether a community sentence could be justified, a sentencer had to have regard to the importance of imposing a sentence that would bring about the reformation and rehabilitation of the offender and, consequently, the reduction of crime. When prisons were overcrowded this could hinder or prevent the valuable work of rehabilitation that prisons should normally provide. Prison overcrowding could, therefore, be a relevant factor where the decision as to whether a community sentence could be justified over a custodial sentence was a particularly difficult one to make. However, in the instant case, the question of whether prisons were overcrowded was not relevant. The defendant had been retailing drugs for profit on a considerable scale and a suspended sentence was unduly lenient. Accordingly, the application would be allowed.

A-G's Reference (No 11 of 2006); R v Scarth [2006] EWCA Crim 856, [2006] 2 Cr App Rep (S) 705 (Court of Appeal: Lord Phillips of Worth Matravers CJ, McCombe and Gross JJ).

**2581   Unduly lenient sentence—reference by Attorney General—sexual offence—
           community penalty**

The offender pleaded guilty to the attempted rape of the 16-year-old complainant. Immediately following the offence, the offender called the police and confessed to committing attempted rape. He had no previous convictions, and was aged 20 at the time of sentence. The judge concluded that he was not dangerous and would not require imprisonment for public protection. If the offender had been an adult, then the appropriate sentence would have been four to five years' imprisonment on conviction but the sentence would have to be reduced to three years' imprisonment on account of the offender's age and circumstances. The sentence, following credit for the offender's guilty plea and reduction for time spent on remand in custody, would be less than what was required to help the offender. The judge also found that the offender had expressed genuine remorse and that it was astonishing that he had informed the police himself. The judge imposed a community penalty involving unpaid work and supervision for 36 months. The Attorney General asked the court to review the sentence as being unduly lenient. *Held*, to impose a community penalty for such a serious offence as attempted rape was unusual and would be rarely justified. While sentences should deter other offenders from committing an offence, there was always room for the courts, in particular circumstances, to conclude that the imposition of a determinate custodial sentence would not achieve sufficient benefit as to outweigh the consequences of a relatively short determinate custodial sentence. The judge's exercise in determining the sentence had been correct. The judge had rightly concluded that a very short period of custody, falling far shorter than that which could enable any sort of assistance by way of education to be provided to the offender, would have remained. Even if the sentence could be said to be unduly lenient, the fact that the offender had completed the penal portion of his sentence and the issue of double jeopardy had to be taken into account. It was not only inappropriate to interfere with the sentence but it would be wrong to do so. The problems with sentencing had justified the judge's conclusion that an exceptional course could and should be taken. Accordingly, the application would be dismissed.

R v Miles; A-G's Reference (No 96 of 2006) [2006] All ER (D) 133 (Dec) (Court of Appeal: Latham LJ, Mitting and Teare JJ).

**2582   Unduly lenient sentence—reference by Attorney General—sexual offence—
           discretionary life sentence**

The defendant was charged with a series of sexual offences. He pleaded guilty to seven counts of rape, two counts of taking indecent photographs of children, two counts of sexual activity with a child, five counts of making indecent photographs of a child and two counts of indecent assault. He was sentenced to a total of 13 years' imprisonment. The Attorney General sought leave, pursuant to the Criminal Justice Act 1988 s 36, to refer the sentence to the Court of Appeal as being unduly lenient. Psychiatric reports were prepared in which the offender was described as a 'highly deviant psychopathically disordered individual', a predatory paedophile, and of high risk of further sexual offences against children. The Attorney General submitted that, while the terms of s 36 precluded recourse to the new material in relation to making the assessment as to whether the sentence was unduly lenient, it had been open to the judge, in the absence of psychiatric evidence, to conclude that the offender presented a risk of harm, and thus to have found that an indeterminate sentence was appropriate. *Held*, while the psychiatric material available after sentence strongly pointed in the direction of an indeterminate sentence being appropriate in the present case, it was not the court's function under s 36 to substitute, in the light of that material, its own view as to what sentence ought to have been imposed. While the criteria for the imposition of a discretionary life sentence were, on the fresh material, met, particularly in relation to the offences of rape, and a discretionary life sentence might well be appropriate, the judge had been entitled, in the material before him, to reach the conclusion that a determinate sentence was appropriate. The judge had been alert to matters in relation to the possibility of a discretionary life sentence, but had reached a conclusion that had been open to him on the material before him. In all the circumstances, the sentence could not properly be characterised as unduly lenient. Accordingly, the application would be dismissed.

A-G's Reference (No 19 of 2005); R v B [2006] All ER (D) 247 (Mar) (Court of Appeal: Rose LJ, Aikens and Walker JJ).

2583   Unduly lenient sentence—reference by Attorney General—suspended sentence— exceptional circumstances

The offender pleaded guilty to three counts of sexual activity with a child. The judge passed a sentence of 51 weeks' imprisonment on the three counts, each to be served concurrently, and each suspended for a period of two years. On a reference to the Court of Appeal on the ground that the sentence was unduly lenient, the Attorney General contended that the sentence had failed to mark appropriately the gravity of the offences to which the offender had pleaded guilty and that the appropriate starting point for sentence was three years so that the judge should not have suspended the sentence. The Attorney General also submitted that, even if a sentence of two years or less was appropriate, there were no exceptional circumstances justifying a suspension of sentence. *Held*, taking into account all the relevant factors such as the victim impact statement, the evidence of the child, the offender's plea and basis on which the plea was entered, two years' imprisonment was not an unduly lenient sentence. There was, however, no justification for a further reduction to 51 weeks. In addition, there were no exceptional circumstances which could justify the suspension of any sentence. In the circumstances, the appropriate sentence was one of immediate imprisonment. The sentence passed was unduly lenient but, given the need to mitigate for double jeopardy, a sentence of 18 months' imprisonment would be substituted.

A-G's Reference (No 59 of 2006); R v D [2006] EWCA Crim 2096, [2006] All ER (D) 240 (Nov) (Court of Appeal: Latham LJ, Stanley Burnton and Dobbs JJ).

2584   Young offender—detention and training order—duration—maximum equivalent term for adult

The Powers of Criminal Courts (Sentencing) Act 2000 s 101(2) provides that the term of a detention and training order may not exceed the maximum term of imprisonment that the Crown Court could, in the case of an offender aged 21 or over, impose for the offence.

The defendant, who was aged 17, appeared before a youth court and pleaded guilty to an offence of criminal damage. The defendant had numerous previous convictions for similar offences. The district judge sentenced him to a four-month detention and training order. The defendant appealed against sentence, arguing that the 2000 Act s 101(2) prohibited the court from imposing a custodial sentence longer than three months, which was the maximum sentence an adult could receive for the same offence. *Held*, a youth court had no power to impose a sentence which was greater than that which could be imposed were an adult to be charged with a similar offence in the magistrates' court. Parliament could not have intended such a result; youth was a mitigating not an aggravating feature. It followed that the detention and training order was unlawful and, accordingly, the appeal would be allowed.

Pye v Leeds Youth Court [2006] All ER (D) 16 (Oct) (Queen's Bench Division: Maurice Kay LJ and Bean J).

2585   Young offender—indeterminate sentence—detention for life

The defendant, aged 15 at the time of the offence and 16 at the time of sentence, was a pupil at a boys' school at which the complainant, aged 28, was a teacher. The defendant carried out a violent sexual assault on the complainant and pleaded guilty to one count of rape, contrary to the Sexual Offences Act 2003 s 3, the charge having related to the act of forced oral sex. Pre-sentence and psychological reports indicated that the defendant presented a high risk of harm to the public, and a high risk of violent re-offending, although the degree to which the risk could be alleviated could not be predicted. In particular, he was described as non-compliant and unco-operative. Victim impact statements from the complainant stated that her confidence and social life had been devastated, that she had been unable to teach, and that she lived in fear of returning to her vocation. The judge imposed an indeterminate sentence of detention for life, with a notional determinate term of nine years' imprisonment. The defendant appealed against sentence, contending that it had been wrong in principle to impose an indeterminate sentence. Alternatively, he submitted that the notional determinate period of nine years was excessive. *Held*, while it was correct for the court to examine guideline authorities, they formed guidelines only in that it was essential that, having taken such guidance into account, the court should look back to the circumstances of the individual case as a whole, and should then impose a sentence that was appropriate in all those circumstances. It was wrong to take a mechanistic approach to such guidelines, otherwise inappropriately high or low sentences might be passed. In the circumstances of the present case, a sentence of detention for life could not be described as either wrong in principle or manifestly excessive, but rather as appropriate. While there were undoubtedly mitigating features, including the defendant's age, guilty plea, intelligence and disturbed childhood, those factors had to be weighed in the balance with the seriousness of the offences. There were substantial and grave aggravating features, including the serious psychological effect on the victim and the forceful, violent, and degrading nature of the rape itself. Moreover, the violence used by the defendant had been over and above that which was necessary for him to commit the offence. While the guideline indicated that a sentence should, in the case of young offenders, be significantly shorter than otherwise would be imposed in the case of an adult, that was a broadly general observation, which nevertheless admitted exceptions. It was not designed to be of invariable and inevitable application. Therefore, while the age of a defendant was important, the extent to which it justified a reduction, particularly a significant reduction in the sentence that was otherwise appropriate for an adult, remained to be assessed by reference to the circumstances of the case. Although the defendant was a very young man and an indeterminate sentence did not provide him with a fixed date at which to aim, it could not be a matter that prevented an appropriate sentence being imposed in the circumstances. Since the offence was very grave and was within the upper range of seriousness, there could be no challenge to the notional determinate period. Even considering the defendant's guilty plea and his mitigation, a nine-year determinate sentence could not be described as manifestly excessive. Accordingly, the appeal would be dismissed.

R v Best [2006] EWCA Crim 330, [2006] All ER (D) 134 (Jan) (Court of Appeal: Hallett and Nelson LJJ and Jack J). *R v Storey* (1984) 6 Cr App Rep (S) 104, CA; *R v Evans* (1986) 8 Cr App Rep (S) 253, CA; and *R v Millberry; R v Morgan; R v Lakenby* [2002] EWCA Crim 2891, [2003] 2 All ER 939 (2002 Abr para 2658) considered.

2586   Youthful offender—custodial sentence—restriction on imprisonment of defendant under certain age

The defendant was charged with possessing a firearm, contrary to the Firearms Act 1968 s 5(1)(aba). Section 51A imposed a statutory minimum sentence of five years' imprisonment. In relation to an offender aged 18 or over, s 51(4)(a)(i) provided that the appropriate custodial sentence was imprisonment. However, the defendant was 19 at the time of the offence and 20 at appeal, and it followed that the Powers of Criminal Courts (Sentencing) Act 2000 s 89(1), expressly prohibiting the imposition of imprisonment on a person aged under 21 at the time of conviction, applied. While provisions of the Criminal Justice and Courts Services Act 2000 provided for the amendment of the Powers of Criminal Courts (Sentencing) Act 2000 s 89(1) to read those 'under 18' rather than 'under 21', that provision had not yet come into force. Further, the Secretary of State had not exercised his powers under the Criminal Justice Act 2003 s 333 to make supplementary provisions relating to the issue. The defendant pleaded guilty, and the judge imposed the statutory minimum of five years' detention. The defendant appealed against his sentence. *Held,* the judge should not have imposed the mandatory sentence. Parliament's expressed legislative intention was that those aged under 21 years should not be imprisoned. Despite the fact that Parliament had empowered the Secretary of State to make transitional and consequential provisions in relation to those aged 18 to 20, no provisions relating to the circumstances arising in the present case had been made. It followed that, whatever the Secretary of State might or might not have intended, it was impossible to say that Parliament had intended that a transitional regime in accordance with the 1968 Act s 51A should prevail, particularly in the light of the clear prohibition on the imprisonment of those under 21. Bearing in mind that the statute in the present case was a penal statute, no basis could properly be interpreted in the way interpreted by the judge. The sentence of five years' detention in a young offender institution would be quashed and a sentence of four years' detention substituted. Accordingly, the appeal would be allowed.

R v Campbell [2006] EWCA Crim 726, [2006] 2 Cr App (S) 779 (Court of Appeal: Rose LJ and Stanley Burnton and Hedley JJ).

SET-OFF AND COUNTERCLAIM

Halsbury's Laws of England (4th edn) vol 42 (Reissue) paras 401–600

2587   Set-off—set-off against claims for rent—assignment of reversion—damages for defective construction

The owner of a former colliery contracted with the defendant to build a factory on the site, the defendant being required to take a lease of the premises once construction was completed. When the factory was built, the defendant brought proceedings against the owner, submitting that the factory was seriously defective and inadequate for its purposes. While the proceedings were pending, the reversion in the site was assigned to the claimant. The claimant issued proceedings for rack rent and insurance premiums said to be due under the terms of the lease. A preliminary issue was ordered to be tried as to whether the defendant had a right to set off its damages claim against the original owner against the claimant's claim for rack rent and insurance premiums. The judge decided the preliminary issue in the claimant's favour. On the defendant's appeal, *held,* where the freehold owner of a site agreed with a future tenant to construct a building on the site and to grant a long lease of the premises to the tenant, and after the lease had begun, assigned the reversion, a claim by the tenant against the original freeholder for damages for defective construction of the building could not be set off against the rent due to the assignee for periods after the assignment of the reversion. A tenant's right to claim damages against a predecessor in title of the present landlord, whether or not it arose under a covenant in the lease, was a personal right which was not an interest in land. While it was true that the claim in the present case was being invoked to impeach a liability which did not arise under the lease, it was not a claim which could be said in any way to be proprietary in character. The very nature of an equitable set-off was that it was personal in nature, in that it was a claim raised against the claimant, which impeached his right to sue, and did not run against third parties. Accordingly, the appeal would be dismissed.

Edlington Properties Ltd v JH Fenner & Co Ltd [2006] EWCA Civ 403, [2006] 3 All ER 1200 (Court of Appeal: Pill, Scott Baker and Neuberger LJJ). Decision of Bean J [2005] EWHC 2158 (QB), [2005] All ER (D) 216 (Oct) (2005 Abr para 2799) affirmed.

SETTLEMENTS

Halsbury's Laws of England (4th edn) vol 42 (Reissue) paras 601–1100

2588   Trustees of land—powers—application to court—order for sale of land

See *Nicholls v Lan*, para 281.

SHERIFFS

Halsbury's Laws of England (4th edn) vol 42 (Reissue) paras 1101–1152

Articles

For articles relating to this title please refer to the Table of Articles at the beginning of the Abridgment.

SHIPPING AND NAVIGATION

Halsbury's Laws of England (4th edn) vol 43(1) (Reissue) paras 1–1100, vol 43(2) (Reissue) paras 1101–1996

Articles

For articles relating to this title please refer to the Table of Articles at the beginning of the Abridgment.

2589   Charterparty—construction—laytime—commencement—notice of readiness

Shipowners let their vessel to charterers on Asbatankvoy standard terms, amended to include the charterers' standard voyage chartering conditions. The Asbatankvoy form included stipulations that laytime was not to commence before the given date except with the charterers' sanction, and that, on arrival at customary anchorage at each port of loading or discharge, the master or his agent should give the charterer or his agent notice of readiness, with laytime to commence six hours after receipt of such notice or on the vessel's arrival in berth, whichever occurred first. The charterers' standard terms stipulated that laytime was to commence before the stipulated date only where the charterers consented in writing and that, if the charterers permitted the vessel to tender notice of readiness and berth prior to the commencement of the lay days, all time from berthing until commencement of lay days was to be credited to the charterers. The shipowners made a claim with the charterers in respect of demurrage incurred on the voyage. A dispute arose when the charterers contended that, pursuant to the charter, laytime should not start to count until six hours had elapsed on the first of the lay days. The shipowners issued proceedings, arguing that consent to laytime commencing had been given expressly by e-mail and also impliedly by loading having commenced with the knowledge and consent of the charterers. The judge dismissed the claim, and the shipowners appealed, submitting that the consent to an early notice of readiness, and the instruction to begin loading before the earliest lay day, amounted to consent to the early commencement of laytime. *Held*, the relevant Asbatankvoy standard terms meant that the start of the laytime was postponed to the beginning of the earliest lay day unless the charterers sanctioned otherwise. The charterers order to, or request of, the vessel to load before the beginning of the earliest lay day constituted such a sanction. The charterers were not obliged to commence loading before the earliest lay day if they did not want to load, but if they did so, they were entitled to, once the vessel was presented as ready to load. In doing so, they sanctioned the earlier commencement of laytime and the protection of the provision regarding the earliest lay day was spent. The charterers' own terms made better and more commercial sense if they were construed as providing that time used in loading or discharging, from berthing, was prima facie to count against the charterers who were using it for their purposes, but was to be credited back to them to the extent that it occurred before the earliest agreed lay day. Accordingly, the appeal would be allowed.

Tidebrook Maritime Corpn v Vitol SA of Geneva, The Front Commander [2006] EWCA Civ 944, [2006] 2 Lloyd's Rep 251 (Court of Appeal: Buxton, Rix and Scott Baker LJJ). *Pteroti Compania Naviera SA v National Coal Board* [1958] 1 QB 469 distinguished. *Glencore Grain Ltd v Flacker Shipping Ltd, The Happy Day* [2002] EWCA Civ 1068, [2002] 2 All ER (Comm) 896 (2002 Abr para 2671) considered.

2590   Charterparty—frustration—exclusion—standard clause in charterparty—discharge of cargo becoming illegal

Shipowners chartered their vessel to the charterers for the carriage of a cargo of vegetable oil for discharge at Lagos. The charter was on the Vegoilvoy standard form of Tanker Voyage Charter Party. However, before the time for performance had become due, the charterers informed the shipowners that they had to cancel the voyage on the ground that the Nigerian authorities had been preventing vessels from discharging their cargo in Lagos in view of the ban on the importation of vegetable oil into Nigeria. In the event, no cargo was ever made available for loading and the shipowners did not call for a cargo to be loaded. The charterers argued that the authorities' ban had frustrated the charterparty. The shipowners took the view that the doctrine of frustration was excluded from the charterparty by a standard clause in the contract which provided that the shipowners were entitled, where a situation arose which made it unlawful to discharge the cargo, to require the party taking delivery to undertake any of various alternative forms of action. An arbitrator decided that the charterparty would have been frustrated but for the clause relied on by the shipowners. The charterers appealed. *Held*, on its true construction, the clause did not exclude the doctrine of frustration in circumstances in which no cargo had been brought forward for loading. It made no provision for those circumstances at all. It did not make full and complete provision for all of the effects of the illegality which supervened in the instant case, still less did it provide for a permitted alternative means of performance. On the facts, no cargo existed. The clause did not require the charterers to produce a cargo simply so that the shipowners could then require the shipper to take delivery of it and not load it on board. The purpose of the clause was to compensate the shipowners when they had rendered unusual protection or services to the cargo in transit or at any port or place. Accordingly, the appeal would be allowed.

Select Commodities Ltd v Valdo SA; 'The Florida' [2006] EWHC 1137 (Comm), [2006] 2 All ER (Comm) 493 (Queen's Bench Division: Tomlinson J).

2591   Charterparty—safe port—duty to nominate safe port

Charterers chartered a ship from the shipowners for the carriage of goods to a port which the charterers had nominated as a safe port. The ship was delayed due to two vessels running aground, one after the other, in the access channel to the port. The shipowners claimed from the charterers the amount of their loss resulting from the delay on the ground that the loss resulted from the breach by the charterers of the safe port provisions in the charter. An arbitration panel upheld the claim and the charterers appealed. *Held*, the arbitrators had implicitly held that the port was an unsafe port to nominate for the ship at the time of nomination. A port would not lack the characteristics of a safe port merely because some delay, insufficient to frustrate the adventure, might be caused to the vessel in her attempt to reach, use and leave the port, by some temporary evident obstruction or hazard. The hazards in the access channel had not been of a temporary nature. The grounding of the second vessel was caused by characteristics which made the port an unsafe port to nominate. It was not an independent event which broke the chain of causation between the breach of contract and the shipowners' loss. Accordingly, the appeal would be dismissed.

Independent Petroleum Group Ltd v Seacarriers Count Pte Ltd, The Count [2006] EWHC 3173 (Comm), [2006] All ER (D) 149 (Dec) (Queen's Bench Division: Toulson J). *Unitramp v Garnac Grain Co Inc, The Hermine* [1979] 1 Lloyd's Rep 212, CA (1978 Abr para 2593), considered.

2592   Charterparty—stowage of cargo causing unseaworthiness—duty of shipowner to intervene

The appellants chartered a vessel owned by the respondent shipowner, which was seriously damaged by an explosion. The shipowner contended that the explosion had been caused by the improper stowage of a container of calcium hypochlorite. The charterparty placed responsibility for stowage on the charterers. The shipowner successfully brought an arbitral claim for loss of hire and loss and damage. On appeal, it fell to be determined whether, if the cargo had been stowed in such a way as to render the vessel unseaworthy, the shipowner had owed a duty to the appellant charterers to intervene. *Held*, the shipowner did not owe the appellants a duty to intervene in the loading process. While the shipowner, through its master, was entitled to seek to protect its vessel from stowage which rendered it unsafe, whether or not the charterparty expressly conferred such a right, there was clearly a difference between a right to supervise and require reloading and a duty to do so. That principle applied even if the stowage caused unseaworthiness. Accordingly, the appeal would be dismissed.

Compania Sud American Vapores v Hamburg [2006] EWHC 483 (Comm), [2006] 2 All ER (Comm) 1 (Queen's Bench Division: Morison J). *Canadian Transport Co Ltd v Court Line Ltd* [1940] AC 934, HL, applied. *CHZ Rolimpex v Eftavrysses Compania Naviera SA, The Panaghia Tinnou* [1986] 2 Lloyd's Rep 586; and *Transocean Liners Reederei GmbH v Euxine Shipping Co Ltd, The Imvros* [1999] 1 All ER (Comm) 724 (1999 Abr para 3012) considered.

2593   Hovercraft—fees

The Hovercraft (Fees) (Amendment) Regulations 2006, SI 2006/2053 (in force on 11 September 2006), further amend the 1997 Regulations, SI 1997/320, so as to increase certain of the hourly rates charged in respect of surveys and inspections.

2594   Marine insurance

See INSURANCE.

2595   Merchant shipping—boatmasters—qualifications and hours of work

The Merchant Shipping (Inland Waterway and Limited Coastal Operations) (Boatmasters' Qualifications and Hours of Work) Regulations 2006, SI 2006/3223 (in force in part on 22 December 2006 and in part on 1 January 2007), provide for standards of competence which must be attained by masters of passenger vessels carrying no more than 250 passengers engaged on short voyages close to the coast, and implement EC Council Directive 96/50 on the harmonisation of conditions for obtaining national boatmasters' certificates for the carriage of goods and passengers by inland waterway. The regulations also re-enact provisions made in relation to self-employed masters' hours of work. SI 1993/1213 and 2002/2125 are further amended and SI 2003/3049 is amended.

2596   Merchant shipping—fees

The Merchant Shipping (Fees) Regulations 2006, SI 2006/2055 (in force on 11 September 2006), replace the 1996 Regulations, SI 1996/3243, and prescribe the revised fees payable for services and functions performed by or on behalf of the Maritime Coastguard Agency under the Merchant Shipping Act 1995. SI 1996/1820, 1998/1609, 2004/302 are amended.

The Merchant Shipping (Fees) (Amendment) Regulations 2006, SI 2006/3225 (in force on 1 January 2007), amend the principal 2006 Regulations supra by replacing the schedule of fees payable in respect of examinations for, and the issue of, boatmasters' licences, and for related matters, so as to reflect the replacement of the Merchant Shipping (Local Passenger Vessels) (Masters' Licences and Hours, Manning and Training) Regulations 1993, SI 1993/1213, by the Merchant Shipping (Inland Waterway and Limited Coastal Operations) (Boatmasters' Qualifications and Hours of Work) Regulations 2006, SI 2006/3223.

2597   Merchant shipping—lifting operations and lifting equipment

The Merchant Shipping and Fishing Vessels (Lifting Operations and Lifting Equipment) Regulations 2006, SI 2006/2184 (in force on 24 November 2006), replace the Merchant Shipping (Hatches and Lifting Plant) Regulations 1988, SI 1988/1639, so as to (1) extend the duties imposed by the regulations to provide that where a person on whom a duty is imposed does not have control of a matter, because he does not have responsibility for the operation of the ship, the duty extends to any person having control of that matter; (2) specify requirements as to the strength of and stability of lifting equipment; (3) make provision in relation to lifting equipment for lifting persons, and the positioning and installation of permanently installed lifting equipment; (4) require (a) lifting equipment to be marked with its safe working loads; and (b) lifting operations to be properly planned and supervised, and for the employer to provide a safe system of work in specified circumstances; (5) provide for the testing, examination and inspection of lifting equipment; (6) make provision in respect of hatch covers used on a ship and require account to be taken of the principles and guidance in the Code of Safe Working Practices for Merchant Seaman; and (7) require every worker to (a) comply, in relation to use by him of lifting equipment, with any reasonable instruction that may be given to him by his employer for the purpose of securing compliance with any of the specified obligations on the employer; and (b) make full and proper use of any system of work provided for his use by his employer in compliance with the specified obligations on the employer.

2598   Merchant shipping—light dues

The Merchant Shipping (Light Dues) (Amendment) Regulations 2006, SI 2006/649 (in force on 1 April 2006), further amend the 1997 Regulations, SI 1997/562, so as to (1) provide that per voyage payments of general light dues are only to be payable in respect of voyages ending at a port or place in the United Kingdom; (2) reduce the light dues per voyage from 39p to 35p per ton; and (3) remove the exemption from dues for vessels navigating in ballast.

2599 Merchant shipping—lighthouses—beacons

The General Lighthouse Authorities (Beacons: Automatic Identification System) Order 2006, SI 2006/1977 (in force on 20 July 2006), specifies equipment provided for broadcasts in the frequency range 156.025–162.025 MHz where such equipment forms part of a system for providing information to ships about the type, position and functioning of aids to navigation, or for assisting the general lighthouse authorities in the efficient provision of aids to navigation.

2600 Merchant shipping—local passenger vessels—crew

The Merchant Shipping (Local Passenger Vessels) (Crew) Regulations 2006, SI 2006/3224 (in force on 1 January 2007), prescribe the qualifications which must be held by members of crew of passenger ships operating on inland waterways and on certain short coastal voyages. The regulations also create offences and empower relevant inspectors to detain any vessel in relation to which any such offence is committed. SI 1993/1213 is amended.

2601 Merchant shipping—prevention of air pollution

The Merchant Shipping (Prevention of Air Pollution from Ships) Order 2006, SI 2006/1248 (in force on 12 June 2006), enables the Secretary of State to make regulations for the prevention of air pollution from ships to give effect to Annex VI to the International Convention for the Prevention of Pollution from Ships 1973.

2602 Merchant shipping—prevention of oil pollution—bunker oil

The Merchant Shipping (Oil Pollution) (Bunkers Convention) Regulations 2006, SI 2006/1244 (in force on various dates), further amend the Merchant Shipping Act 1995 in order to implement EC Council Decision 2002/762 authorising the member states, in the interests of the Community, to sign, ratify or accede to the International Convention on Civil Liability for Bunker Oil Pollution Damage 2001 (the 'Bunkers Convention'). In particular, the regulations amend the 1995 Act so as to (1) insert definitions of 'the Bunkers Convention' and related expressions; (2) add new provision so that (a) where, as a result of any occurrence, any bunker oil is discharged or escapes from a ship, the owner of the ship is liable for any damage caused outside the ship in the territory of the United Kingdom by contamination resulting from the discharge or escape; (b) the owner is also liable for the cost of any measures reasonably taken for the purpose of preventing or minimising the damage and for any damage caused by the measures taken; and (c) where there is a grave and imminent threat of contamination by bunker oil, the owner is liable for the cost of measures taken to prevent or minimise damage and for damage caused by those measures; (3) provide that where, as a result of any occurrence, any oil is discharged or escapes from a vessel which is not sea-going the owner is liable for any damage caused outside the ship in the territory of the United Kingdom by resulting contamination, for the cost of measures to minimise or prevent damage and for damage caused by any such measures taken; liability also arises where there is a relevant threat of contamination; (4) create certain restrictions on the liability of the owner, salvors and others in the case of bunker oil spills; (5) make provision for compulsory insurance in respect of bunker oil contamination for ships having a gross tonnage greater than 1,000 tons; (6) make provision in respect of the rights of third parties against insurers where it is alleged that the owner of a ship has incurred a liability for pollution by bunker oil; (7) make provision in respect of the jurisdiction of United Kingdom courts and the registration of foreign judgments and make provision in respect of Government ships; and (8) provide that any liability incurred for pollution by bunker oil is to be deemed to be a liability to damages in respect of such damage to property as is mentioned in the Convention on Limitation of Liability for Maritime Claims 1976 art 2 para 1(a).

2603 Merchant shipping—prevention of oil pollution—Supplementary Fund Protocol

The Merchant Shipping (Oil Pollution) (Supplementary Fund Protocol) Order 2006, SI 2006/1265 (in force on a date to be notified in the London Gazette), further amends the Merchant Shipping Act 1995 to give legal effect in the United Kingdom to the Protocol of 2003 to the International Convention on the Establishment of an International Fund for Compensation for Oil Pollution Damage, 1992 ('the Supplementary Fund Protocol'). The order also further amends the Supreme Court Act 1981 to include a reference to the Supplementary Fund Protocol.

2604 Merchant shipping—prevention of pollution—sewage and garbage

The Merchant Shipping (Prevention of Pollution by Sewage and Garbage) Order 2006, SI 2006/2950 (in force on 12 December 2006), replaces the 1988 Regulations, SI 1988/2252, and enables regulations to be made to give effect to the International Convention for the Prevention of Pollution from Ships 1973, for the prevention of pollution by sewage and garbage from ships. SI 1997/2569, 1998/254 are amended.

2605   Merchant shipping—provision and use of work equipment

The Merchant Shipping and Fishing Vessels (Provision and Use of Work Equipment) Regulations 2006, SI 2006/2183 (in force on 24 November 2006), replace, for the purposes of consolidation, the Merchant Shipping (Guarding of Machinery and Safety of Electrical Equipment) Regulations 1988, SI 1988/1636, the Merchant Shipping (Safe Movement on Board Ships) Regulations 1988, SI 1988/1641, reg 10 and the Merchant Shipping (Safety at Work) (Non-UK Ships) Regulations 1988, SI 1988/2274, reg 2, so as to impose health and safety requirements with respect to the provision and use of work equipment on merchant ships and fishing vessels, with the effect of (1) extending the duties imposed by the 2006 Regulations, so that where a person on whom a duty is imposed does not have control of a matter, because he does not have responsibility for the operation of the ship, the duty will extend to any person who has control of that matter; (2) specifying requirements as to the suitability of work equipment made available to workers on the ship; (3) requiring work equipment to be maintained in an efficient state and in good repair; (4) providing (a) for the inspection of work equipment where its safety depends on the installation conditions; (b) for the use of work equipment which involves a specific risk to health or safety; (c) that employers must ensure that all workers who use equipment have available to them adequate health and safety information and instructions, and training in the use of work equipment; (d) for dangerous parts of ship's work equipment to have guards or protection devices; (e) for protection against (i) electrical hazards; (ii) specified hazards; and (iii) injury as a consequence of high or very low temperatures; and (f) for controls in respect of mobile work equipment; and (5) placing duties on self-employed persons (a) in respect of work equipment on a ship which he provides for use and uses himself, or provides for use by another person; or (b) in respect of his own use of work equipment on a ship, whether provided by him or not.

2606   Merchant shipping—training and certification—safety communications—minimum standards

The Merchant Shipping (Training and Certification and Minimum Standards of Safety Communications) (Amendment) Regulations 2006, SI 2006/89 (in force on 20 February 2006), give effect to EC Council Directive 2003/103 on the minimum level of training for seafarers, by permitting the Secretary of State to recognise certificates issued by those states which are not EEA member states but who are parties to the International Convention on Standards of Training, Certification and Watchkeeping 1978 ('third party states'). The regulations also amend the Merchant Shipping (Training and Certification) Regulations 1997, SI 1997/348, so as to provide for the decision on whether to recognise the certificates issued to officers by a third party state to be made by the Commission. In particular, the regulations (1) make such recognition a pre-condition for the Secretary of State to recognise particular certificates; (2) provide that the Secretary of State may also recognise certificates issued by a third party state where those certificates were recognised by a member state of the EEA as at 14 June 2005 and that recognition has not been withdrawn by the Commission, or a request has been made by the Secretary of State to the Commission to recognise those certificates and three months has elapsed since the request was made without a decision having been made; and (3) permit the holder of a valid certificate issued by a third party state to serve in an appropriate capacity for a maximum period of three months provided that person has made an application to the Secretary of State for recognition of his certificates. The regulations also amend the Merchant Shipping (Minimum Standards of Safety Communications) Regulations 1997, SI 1997/529, so as to make it the duty of the master and company to ensure that English is used as the language of communication in ship to ship and ship to shore communications and in communications with the pilot, except where those directly involved in the communication speak a common language other than English.

2607   Merchant Shipping (Pollution) Act 2006

The Merchant Shipping (Pollution) Act 2006 enables effect to be given to the Supplementary Fund Protocol 2003 and to future revisions of the international arrangements relating to compensation for oil pollution from ships, enables effect to be given to the MARPOL Convention Annex VI, and amends the Merchant Shipping Act 1995 s 178(1). The Act received the royal assent on 30 March 2006 and the following provisions came into force on that day: ss 1 (in part), 2, 4. The following provisions came into force on 30 May 2006: ss 1 (in part), 3. For details of commencement, see the commencement table in the title STATUTES.

Section 1 enables Her Majesty by Order in Council to give effect to revisions of the international arrangements relating to compensation for oil pollution from ships. Her Majesty by Order in Council is enabled under s 2 to implement the MARPOL Convention Annex VI, which provides regulations for the prevention of air pollution from ships. Section 3 makes it clear that the time limit contained in the 1995 Act is consistent with the text of the Convention. The 2006 Act s 4 deals with short title, commencement and extent.

2608   Safety—security—electronic communications

See para 2878.

2609 Towage contract—delay—reason for delay—failure to proceed with proper despatch

The claimant entered into a towage contract with the defendant, under which the defendant was to use its best endeavours to have a vessel towed to China. The defendant in turn entered into a sub-contract with the Pt 20 defendant, a tug owner, to deliver the vessel. The vessel was delivered later than required. The claimant issued proceedings, seeking damages on the grounds that the tug had failed to proceed with proper despatch and, accordingly, that the defendant was in breach of the towage contract. The claimant alleged that the delay was due to the fact that the tug had only used two of its four engines for much of the voyage. The defendant contended that the delay had been caused because the vessel had been heavier than expected. The defendant also issued proceedings against the Pt 20 defendant on the ground that if the defendant was liable to the claimant, this was because the Pt 20 defendant had been in breach of the sub-contract. *Held*, the vessel had been in light ballast condition and carrying no more than was necessary. It had not been heavier than expected. Further, the tug had not used all engines at all times, and had therefore not proceeded with proper despatch. Accordingly, the claimant's application against the defendant and the defendant's application against the Pt 20 defendant would be allowed.

Ease Faith Ltd v Leonis Marine Management Ltd [2006] EWHC 232 (Comm), [2006] 2 All ER (Comm) 422 (Queen's Bench Division: Andrew Smith J).

SOCIAL SECURITY

Halsbury's Laws of England (4th edn) vol 44(2) (Reissue) paras 1–550

Articles

For articles relating to this title please refer to the Table of Articles at the beginning of the Abridgment.

2610 Benefits—claims and payments

The Social Security (Claims and Payments) Amendment Regulations 2006, SI 2006/551 (in force on 1 April 2006), further amend the 1987 Regulations, SI 1987/1968, so as to increase the fee, which qualifying lenders pay for the purpose of defraying administrative expense incurred by the Secretary of State in making payments in respect of mortgage interest direct to qualifying lenders, from £0·31 to £0·51.

The Social Security (Claims and Payments) Amendment (No 2) Regulations 2006, SI 2006/3188 (in force on 27 December 2006), further amend the 1987 Regulations supra so as to enable the Secretary of State to make deductions from benefit and make payments on behalf of the beneficiary for the purpose of repaying certain loans.

2611 Benefits—earnings factors

The Social Security Revaluation of Earnings Factors Order 2006, SI 2006/496 (in force on 6 April 2006), directs that earnings factors relevant to the calculation of the additional pension in the rate of any long-term benefit or any guaranteed minimum pension, or to any other calculation required under the Pension Schemes Act 1993 Pt III (ss 7–68), are to be increased for the tax years specified by the percentage of their amount specified.

2612 Benefits—entitlement—adult learning option

The Social Security (Adult Learning Option) Amendment Regulations 2006, SI 2006/2144 (in force on 1 September 2006), further amend (1) the Income Support (General) Regulations 1987, SI 1987/1967, so that a full-time student remains entitled to income support if he attends a scheme known as the adult learning option; and (2) the Social Security (Incapacity Benefit) Regulations 1994, SI 1994/2946, so that a person remains entitled to incapacity benefit if he attends the adult learning option and receive a training premium.

2613 Benefits—entitlement—conditions—appearances in court

The Social Security (Income Support and Jobseeker's Allowance) Amendment Regulations 2006, SI 2006/1402 (in force on 30 May 2006), amend (1) the Jobseeker's Allowance Regulations 1996, SI 1996/207, by (a) changing the entitlement conditions for the receipt of benefit to take into account situations in which the claimant is required to attend a court or tribunal as a justice of the peace, a party to any proceedings, a witness or a juror, or where the claimant is detained in custody in specified circumstances; and (b) altering the circumstances in which a carer does not have to meet the requirement to be available for work immediately; and (2) the Income Support (General) Regulations 1987, SI 1987/1967, to change the circumstances in which a person can be entitled to income support where they are required to attend a court or tribunal as a justice of the peace, a party to any proceedings, a witness or a juror.

2614   Benefits—entitlement—habitual residence—nationals of Bulgaria and Romania

The Social Security (Bulgaria and Romania) Amendment Regulations 2006, SI 2006/3341 (in force on 1 January 2007), amend the Income Support (General) Regulations 1987, SI 1987/1967, the Jobseeker's Allowance Regulations 1996, SI 1996/207, the State Pension Credit Regulations 2002, SI 2002/1792, the Housing Benefit Regulations 2006, SI 2006/213, the Housing Benefit (Persons who have attained the qualifying age for state pension credit) Regulations 2006, SI 2006/214, the Council Tax Benefit Regulations 2006, SI 2006/215, and the Council Tax Benefit (Persons who have attained the qualifying age for state pension credit) Regulations 2006, SI 2006/216, in consequence of the accession to the European Union on 1 January 2007 of Bulgaria and Romania. The regulations insert a new category of persons who are exempt from the habitual residence test, namely nationals of Bulgaria and Romania who are subject to the worker authorisation scheme established by the Accession (Immigration and Worker Authorisation) Regulations 2006, SI 2006/3317, and who are treated as workers pursuant to those regulations.

2615   Benefits—entitlement—Pension Protection Fund—Financial Assistance Scheme

The Social Security (PPF Payments and FAS Payments) (Consequential Amendments) Regulations 2006, SI 2006/1069 (in force on 5 May 2006), further amend the Social Security Benefit (Dependency) Regulations 1977, SI 1977/343, the Social Security (Incapacity Benefit-Increases for Dependants) Regulations 1994, SI 1994/2945, and the Social Security (Incapacity Benefit) Regulations 1994, SI 1994/2946, so as to allow Pension Protection Fund ('PPF') periodic payments to be included in the calculation of entitlement to benefit in the same way as pension payments are included. The regulations also further amend the Jobseeker's Allowance Regulations 1996, SI 1996/207, so as to allow PPF payments or Financial Assistance Scheme ('FAS') payments to be included in the calculation of entitlement to contribution-based jobseeker's allowance in the same way as pension payments are included, and further provides for PPF payments or FAS payments to be disregarded where they are made to the survivor of a person entitled to such payments, in the same circumstances as pension payments would be.

2616   Benefits—entitlement—person designated by United Nations Sanctions Committee— spouse of designated person—indirect provision of economic resources

EC Council Regulation 881/2002 art 2(2), (3) provides that no funds or economic resources may be made available to, or for the benefit of, a natural or legal person group or entity designated by the Sanctions Committee.

The claimants, who were housewives in receipt of various social security benefits, were each married to and lived with a person listed under United Nations Security Council Resolution 1390, which laid down measures to be directed against members of the Al-Qa'ida network and the Taliban. The Al-Qa'ida and Taliban (United Nations Measures) Order 2002, SI 2002/111, art 7 provided that a person was guilty of an offence where, except under the authority of a licence granted by the Treasury, he made funds available to or for the benefit of a listed person. Funds were defined as financial assets, economic benefits and economic resources of any kind. Licences granted by the Treasury to the Commissioners for Her Majesty's Revenue and Customs and to the Secretary of State permitted them to continue to make payments to each claimant with a view to ensuring that the claimants did not engage in conduct which would offend the United Nations Resolution, the 2002 Regulations, or Regulation 881/2002, which imposed specific restrictive measures against certain persons and entities associated with the Taliban. The Treasury then decided that the payment of the benefits to the claimants fell within the scope of the applicable legislative provisions. The claimants sought judicial review of the decision. *Held*, the narrow interpretation that the purpose of Regulation 881/2002 was to prevent listed persons from having access to or control over funds or economic resources, since those could be used to obtain items and services of use for terrorism, was incorrect. The payment of the relevant social security benefits fell squarely within the plain language of art 2(2), since significant funds would be paid in benefits on a regular basis to the non-listed person in circumstances where it could reasonably be expected that the non-listed person would use the funds to confer significant economic benefits on the listed person. Moreover, it was clear that the intention of the Security Council was to remove, in principle and subject to humanitarian considerations, all economic support from listed persons, with a view to achieving public policy objectives of the highest importance, namely, combating international terrorism and promoting peace, security and safety. For that reason, the prohibitions were deliberately draconian. Accordingly, the application would be dismissed.

R (on the application of M) v HM Treasury [2006] EWHC 2328 (Admin), [2006] All ER (D) 108 (Sep) (Queen's Bench Division: Kenneth Parker QC).

2617   Benefits—entitlement—person living in another member state—citizen of European Union

The claimant, a Belgian national, was in receipt of unemployment benefit, having obtained an exemption from the requirement to sign on, so that he was no longer subject to the requirement of having been available to work. He declared that he was unemployed and living in Belgium when he had in fact been residing in France. When this was discovered, the claimant was notified of a decision refusing him unemployment allowance on the ground that he no longer satisfied the requirement under Belgian law under which eligibility was conditional on habitual and actual residence in Belgium. The claimant contested that decision and certain questions, concerning whether the obligation to actually reside in Belgium, imposed under national legislation, amounted to a fetter on the freedom of movement and residence of citizens of the European Union, were referred to the European Court of Justice for a preliminary ruling. *Held,* freedom of movement and residence did not preclude a residence clause which was imposed on an unemployed person over 50 years of age who was exempt from the requirement of proving that he was available for work, as a condition for the retention of his entitlement to unemployment benefit. The right of residence afforded by the EC Treaty art 18 was conferred subject to the limitations and conditions laid down by the EC Treaty. It had been established that the Belgian legislation which placed certain Belgian nationals at a disadvantage because they resided in another member state was a restriction on freedom which could only be justified if it was based on objective considerations of public interest proportionate to the legitimate objective of the national provisions. In the present case, the residence clause reflected the need to monitor the employment and family situation of unemployed persons and could be seen as a restriction. However, it was based on objective considerations of public interest independent of the nationality of the persons concerned. Further, the obligation to reside in the member state in which the institution responsible for payment was situated, which was justified in domestic law by the need to monitor compliance with the statutory conditions governing the compensation paid to unemployed persons, satisfied the requirement of proportionality.

Case C-406/04 *De Cuyper v Office National de L'Emploi* [2006] All ER (EC) 947 (ECJ: Grand Chamber).

2618 Benefits—entitlement—work-focused interviews—working neighbourhoods

The Social Security (Working Neighbourhoods) Miscellaneous Amendments Regulations 2006, SI 2006/909 (in force on 24 April 2006), largely revoke the Social Security (Working Neighbourhoods) Regulations 2004, SI 2004/959, which imposed requirements to take part in work-focused interviews on certain persons who reside in specified areas.

2619 Benefits—general

The Social Security (Miscellaneous Amendments) Regulations 2006, SI 2006/588 (in force in part on and between 31 March 2006 and 10 April 2006), further amend the Income Support (General) Regulations 1987, SI 1987/1967, the Jobseeker's Allowance Regulations 1996, SI 1996/207, the Housing Benefit Regulations 2006, SI 2006/213, and the Council Tax Benefit Regulations 2006, SI 2006/215 so as to (1) provide that a person aged under 60, who does not take a payment from the Board of the Pension Protection Fund ('PPF') that would be available to them is not treated as possessing the amount of any income or capital deferred; (2) provide that payments made by the Board of the PPF to a third party may be regarded as notional income and notional capital; (3) provide that payments from the Board of the PPF are not regarded as notional income or notional capital where the payment is not received by the claimant due to his bankruptcy. The regulations also (a) amend the 1987 Regulations and the l996 Regulations so as to provide that a person aged 60 or over, who opts not to take a payment from the PPF available to him, is to be treated as possessing the amount of any income or capital foregone from the date on which it could be expected to be acquired were an application to be made; (b) amend the 1987 Regulations to remove provisions which make transitional provision for claimants who were either in board and lodging accommodation or hostel dwellers following the changes to income support and housing benefit in 1989; (c) amend the State Pension Credit Regulations 2002, SI 2002/1792, by adding PPF periodic payments, as defined in the State Pension Credit Act 2002 s 17(1), to the descriptions of income which are prescribed for the purposes of s 15(1)(j) and protect transitional amounts paid to patients whose benefit is no longer reduced from 10 April 2006; (d) amend the Social Fund Maternity and Funeral Expenses (General) Regulations 2005, SI 2005/3061, so that a person in respect of whom child benefit may be paid is a person who is excluded from the 'immediate family member' and the 'nature and extent of contact' tests for the purposes of a claim for a funeral payment; (e) amend the Social Security (Hospital In-Patients) Regulations 2005, SI 2005/3360, to provide for paying a beneficiary's increase for a dependant on a third party for the benefit of a child of the beneficiary if the beneficiary and dependant have been in hospital for 52 weeks or more; (f) amend SI 2006/213 and SI 2006/215 so as to exclude payments made by the Board of the PPF from the regulations relating to notional capital; and make further amendments to ensure that SI 2006/213 and the Housing Benefit (Persons who have attained the qualifying age for state pension credit) Regulations 2006, SI 2006/214 make equivalent provision in relation to the possession of housing benefit at an altered rate and in relation to the date on which entitlement to housing benefit begins for people who live in hostels where rent is paid daily; (g) make revocations and clarificatory amendments to ensure that SI 2006/215 and the Council Tax Benefit (Persons who have attained the qualifying age for state pension credit) Regulations 2006, SI 2006/216 make equivalent provision in relation to the circumstances in which persons can qualify for the highest rate of alternative maximum council tax benefit; this is a form of council tax benefit payable in certain circumstances to persons who are not eligible for council tax benefit, or are entitled to less benefit, under the ordinary rules; the regulations also ensure that all types of reduction are taken into account when calculating alternative maximum council tax benefit and that discounts are also taken into account in cases where the highest rate of alternative maximum council tax benefit applies; and (h) amend SI 2006/214 and SI 2006/216 so as, for people to whom those regulations apply, to make provision to take into account as income payments made by the Board of the PPF and to provide that payments made by the Board of the PPF to a third party may be regarded as notional income.

The Social Security (Miscellaneous Amendments) (No 2) Regulations 2006, SI 2006/832 (in force in part on 10 April 2006 and in part on 24 July 2006), further amend (1) the Social Security (Claims and Payments) Regulations 1987, SI 1987/1968, so as to (a) remove provisions which provide for instrument for benefit payment; (b) allow claims for a disability living allowance and a carer's allowance to be made at offices other than offices of the Department for Work and Pensions which have been approved by the Secretary of State; (c) provide that where a person first notifies an appropriate office that he intends to claim incapacity benefit and his properly completed claim is received in such an office within one month, the date of claim is the date of the first notification; (d) provide that a person who has attained the qualifying age for state pension credit may notify his intention and may send or deliver his claim to an office approved by the Secretary of State; (e) allow a claim for carer's allowance to be treated as made on the first day for which the qualifying benefit is payable, where the claim is made within three months of the date of the award of that qualifying benefit; (f) provide that where a person subject to work-focused interviews notifies an appropriate office of his intention of making a claim for incapacity benefit and a properly completed claim is received within one month, the date of claim is the date of first notification; (g) provide for an appointee, or other specified persons acting on behalf of a person claiming or entitled to benefit, to arrange for it to be paid by direct credit transfer; (h) increase the amount allowed for personal expenses for a person in accommodation for which benefit is paid to his accommodation provider; and (i) enable a persons to claim state pension credit by telephone unless the Secretary of State directs that the claimant must approve a written statement of his circumstances provided for the purpose by the Secretary of State; (2) SI 1996/207 supra so as to provide that a change in circumstances affecting the continuance of entitlement to, or the payment of, jobseeker's allowance is to be notified to the Secretary of State in writing or by telephone or, if he so requires in a class of case, the change to be notified in writing unless he accepts another means of notification in any particular case; (3) the Social Security (Notification of Change of Circumstances) Regulations 2001, SI 2001/3252, so as to make similar provision as that made to the 1996 Regulations for the purposes of offences relating to failure to notify changes of circumstances; and (4) the Social Security and Child Support (Decisions and Appeals) Regulations 1999, SI 1999/991, so as to (a) allow the Secretary of State to revise a decision where a determination necessary to it has been revised or overturned on appeal; (b) remove the exception from the general rule for determining the effective date of a change of circumstances which is not advantageous; and (c) provide that where the claimant, who would otherwise be a severely disabled person, ceases to have a non-dependant, the effective date is the date the claimant ceased to have a non-dependant. SI 1994/3196 is revoked.

The Social Security (Miscellaneous Amendments) (No 3) Regulations 2006, SI 2006/2377 (in force on 2 October 2006), further amend (1) SI 1987/1968 supra by providing that (a) the Secretary of State can extend the time in which defective claims for state pension credit may be corrected; (b) the date of a claim for a relevant benefit made following the termination of an earlier award of that benefit is the date of entitlement to that qualifying benefit where the qualifying benefit is re-awarded or awarded on a claim made before the termination of the award of the relevant benefit, provided the claim for the relevant benefit is made within three months of the date of the award of the qualifying benefit; (c) the time for claiming income support or jobseeker's allowance may be extended by a period not exceeding one month where the claimant was unable to notify the appropriate office of his intention of making a claim because the telephone lines were busy or inoperative; and (d) where a claimant receives child tax credit, the amount that may be deducted from his income support or jobseeker's allowance without his consent may not exceed 25 per cent of the sum of his applicable amount, child benefit and the child tax credit he or his partner is entitled to; where the claimant receives state pension credit, deductions may not, without his consent, exceed 25 per cent of the sum of the appropriate minimum guarantee less any housing costs and the amount of child benefit and child tax credit he or his partner is entitled to; and (2) SI 1999/991 supra providing that (a) where a decision is superseded in connection with the cessation of payment of a carer's allowance, the decision takes effect from the day after the day in respect of which the carer's allowance was paid; and (b) where a decision superseding a decision concerning persons in certain accommodation other than hospitals applies or ceases to apply to the claimant for a period of less than one week, it takes effect from the date of the change.

The Social Security (Miscellaneous Amendments) (No 4) Regulations 2006, SI 2006/2378 (in force on and between 1 and 9 October 2006), (1) further amend SI 1987/1967 and SI 1996/207 supra so as to include new definitions relating to disabled children in the Tax Credits Act 2002 and provide that certain charitable and voluntary payments of income are disregarded in full; (2) further amend SI 1987/1967 and SI 1996/207, and amend the Housing Benefit Regulations 2006, SI 2006/213, and the Council Tax Benefit Regulations 2006, SI 2006/215, so as to (a) create a disregard for any payment made in consequence of any personal injury to a claimant or his or her partner for a period of up to 52 weeks from the day of receipt of the first payment; (b) enable awards of certain damages to be disregarded where such awards are not administered by the court but are held subject to the order or direction of the court; (c) provide that income derived from such capital is no longer to be treated as capital; and (d) take into account changes to the linking term for welfare to work beneficiaries; (3) further amend the Social Security (Incapacity Benefit-Increases for Dependants) Regulations 1994, SI 1994/2945, so as to provide for entitlement to an increase in incapacity benefit where the claimant lives with an adult who is entitled to child benefit in respect of a child or young person who is living with him; (4) further amend the Social Security (Incapacity for Work) (General) Regulations 1995, SI 1995/311, so as to (a) remove reference to procedures which are no longer in use; (b) increase from one week to one month after entitlements cease, the period within which a person must become engaged in remunerative work after cessation of benefit in order to be a welfare to work beneficiary and to remove the requirement to give notice; (c) extend to 104 weeks the linking term which applies to welfare to work beneficiaries; and (d) change the definition of 'immediate past period of incapacity for work' so that it refers to the most recent period of incapacity for work; (5) further amend SI 1994/2945 supra, the Social Security (Widow's Benefit and Retirement Pensions) Regulations 1979, SI 1979/642, and the Social Security (Incapacity Benefit) (Transitional) Regulations 1995, SI 1995/310, so as to increase to 104 weeks the linking term which applies to relevant welfare to work beneficiaries; (6) amend the State Pension Credit Regulations 2002, SI 2002/1792, the Housing Benefit (Persons who have attained the qualifying age for state pension credit) Regulations 2006, SI 2006/214, and the Council Tax Benefit (Persons who have attained the qualifying age for state pension credit) Regulations 2006, SI 2006/216, so as to clarify the treatment of certain types of notional income and enable awards of certain damages to be disregarded where such awards are not administered by the court but are held subject to the order or direction of the court; and (7) in relation to certain claimants of incapacity benefit, severe disablement allowance, attendance allowance and disability living allowance, who receive income on which they do not have to pay tax in the United Kingdom, remove certain conditions relating to presence in Great Britain.

The Social Security (Miscellaneous Amendments) (No 5) Regulations 2006, SI 2006/3274 (in force on 8 January 2007), further amend (1) the Income Support (General) Regulations 1987, SI 1987/1967; (2) the Jobseeker's Allowance Regulations 1996, SI 1996/207; (3) the State Pension Credit Regulations 2002, SI 2002/1792; (4) the Housing Benefit Regulations 2006, SI 2006/213; and (5) the Housing Benefit (Persons who have attained the qualifying age for state pension credit) Regulations 2006, SI 2006/214, so as to clarify the start date of the four benefit week period during which housing costs in relation to income support, jobseeker's allowance and state pension credit, and rent in relation to housing benefit, may be paid in respect of two dwellings where a claimant is treated as occupying both dwellings as his home and could not have avoided liability in respect of both dwellings.

2620 Benefits—income-related benefit—habitual residence test—excepted persons

The Social Security (Lebanon) Amendment Regulations 2006, SI 2006/1981 (in force on 25 July 2006), further amend the Income Support (General) Regulations 1987, SI 1987/1967, the Jobseeker's Allowance Regulations 1996, SI 1996/207, the State Pension Credit Regulations 2002, SI 2002/1792, the Housing Benefit Regulations 2006, SI 2006/213, the Housing Benefit (Persons who have attained the qualifying age for state pension credit) Regulations 2006, SI. 2006/214, the Council Tax Benefit Regulations 2006, SI 2006/215, and the Council Tax Benefit (Persons who have attained the qualifying age for state pension credit) Regulations 2006, SI 2006/216, by adding, until 31 January 2007, a new category, namely persons in Great Britain who left Lebanon on or after 12 July 2006 because of the armed conflict there, to the list of persons who are excepted from having to satisfy the habitual residence test in order to be eligible for income-related benefit.

2621 Benefits—injury—police officers

The Police (Injury Benefit) Regulations 2006, SI 2006/932 (in force on 20 April 2006), replace the 1987 Regulations, SI 1987/156, and amend the Police Pensions (Supplementary Provisions) Regulations 1987, SI 1987/256, and the Police Pensions Regulations 1987, SI 1987/257. The regulations make provision for payments to police officers who are permanently disabled as a result of an injury received in the execution of duty or, where death results from such an injury, to surviving spouses or civil partners, children or other dependent relatives of the deceased officer. In particular, the regulations (1) include definitions of 'injury received in the execution of duty' and 'disablement', (2) make provision for the awards payable on injury or death, (3) govern the circumstances in which an award may be revised, withdrawn or forfeited, (4) provide procedures for the determination of medical questions which arise, and (5) contain provision in respect of the payment of awards.

2622   Benefits—occupational disease—worker resident in another member state—calculation of average earnings

EC Council Regulation 1408/71 art 58(1) provides that the competent institution of a member state whose legislation provides that the calculation of cash benefits is to be based on average earnings must determine such average earnings exclusively by reference to earnings confirmed as having been paid during the periods completed under the said legislation.

The applicant had lived and worked in France for several years, during which time he had been exposed to asbestos at his place of work. The applicant received social security benefits from the French authorities in respect of that occupational disease. He later began to work in Belgium, but remained resident in France and continued to pay taxes there. The French authorities decided that the amount of the applicant's occupational disease benefit was to be assessed on the basis of the average pay earned by him in the last 12 months of his employment in France. The applicant challenged that assessment before a social security tribunal, arguing that the authorities had failed to take account of the pay he had most recently earned in Belgium, which was higher than that used to calculate the benefits. The tribunal stayed the proceedings and referred the questions to the European Court of Justice of whether the authorities' assessment constituted an infringement of Regulation 1408/71 art 58(1) when interpreted in the light of the principle of free movement of workers set out in the EC Treaty art 42. *Held*, the obligation not to put migrant workers who had availed themselves of their right to free movement at a disadvantage did not mean that Regulation 1408/71 art 58(1) should be regarded as contrary to the objective set down in the EC Treaty art 42. That obligation merely implied that those benefits should be the same for the migrant worker as they would have been if he had not availed himself of his right to free movement. It followed that, although account was to be taken only of the pay earned in the member state in which the competent institution was situated, the amount of that pay should be updated to correspond to the pay the person concerned might reasonably have been able to earn had he continued to work in the member state.

Case C-205/05 *Nemec v Caisse regionale d'assurance maladie du Nord-Est* [2006] All ER (D) 110 (Nov) (ECJ: Second Chamber).

2623   Benefits—prescribed benefits

The Social Security Act 1998 (Prescribed Benefits) Regulations 2006, SI 2006/2529 (in force on 16 October 2006), prescribe benefits for the purpose of the definition of 'relevant benefit' under the Social Security Act 1998 s 8(3).

2624   Benefits—sickness benefit—entitlement to have treatment in another member state and claim reimbursement

EC Council Regulation 1408/71 art 22(1)(c)(i) provides that a person who satisfies the conditions of the legislation of the competent state for entitlement to benefits and is authorised by the competent institution to go to another member state to receive treatment is entitled to benefits provided on behalf of the competent institution. The authorisation required under art 22(1)(c) may not be refused where the treatment is a benefit provided for by the legislation of the member state where the person resides and where he cannot be given such treatment within the time normally necessary for obtaining it in that member state taking account of his current state of health and the probable course of his disease: art 22(2).

The applicant suffered from arthritis of the hips which hampered her mobility and caused her to be in constant pain. Initially the respondent health trust put the applicant's case in a category which would result in a wait of approximately one year, although three months later her case was reclassified so that the waiting time was reduced to three or four months. Her application for authorisation to undergo surgery abroad was rejected by the respondent on the ground that the time condition set out in Regulation 1408/71 art 22(2) was not satisfied because it appeared likely she would be treated within the government's national health services targets. The applicant underwent a hip replacement operation in France at her own expense, and then sought reimbursement of the medical fees. The Court of Appeal stayed the proceedings and referred to the European Court of Justice questions concerning the scope of art 22 and of the prohibition of restrictions on freedom to provide services in the EC Treaty art 49. *Held*, in order to be entitled to refuse to grant the authorisation referred to in Regulation 1408/71 art 22(1)(c)(i) on the ground that there was a waiting time for hospital treatment, the competent institution was required to establish that that time did not exceed the period which was acceptable on the basis of an objective medical assessment of the clinical needs of the person concerned in the light of all of the factors characterising his medical condition. The EC Treaty art 49 had to be interpreted as meaning that, where the legislation of a member state provided that hospital treatment provided under the national health service was to be free of charge but did not provide for the reimbursement in full of the cost of treatment of a patient, the competent institution had to reimburse that patient the difference between the cost of equivalent treatment in a hospital covered by the service up to the total cost of the treatment provided. Further, art 49 had to be interpreted as meaning that a patient who was authorised to go to another member state for hospital treatment was entitled to seek from the competent institution reimbursement of the ancillary costs associated with that cross-border movement for medical purposes, in addition to the cost of medical services he could receive under Regulation 1408/71 art 22, provided that the legislation of the member state imposed a corresponding obligation on the national system to reimburse in respect of treatment provided in a local hospital covered by that system.

Case C-372/04 R (*on the application of Watts*) *v Bedford Primary Care Trust* [2006] QB 667 (ECJ: Grand Chamber).

2625 Benefits—students and income-related

The Social Security (Students and Income-related Benefits) Amendment Regulations 2006, SI 2006/1752 (in force on 1 August 2006), further amend the Income Support (General) Regulations 1987, SI 1987/1967, the Jobseeker's Allowance Regulations 1996, SI 1996/207, the Housing Benefit Regulations 2006, SI 2006/213, and the Council Tax Benefit Regulations 2006, SI 2006/215, so as to (1) increase the amounts of grant and loan income to be disregarded in respect of travel costs and the costs of books and equipment; and (2) take account of the changes to the provision of support to students by introducing a disregard for tuition fee loans from the calculation of a student's income.

2626 Benefits—up-rating

The Social Security Benefits Up-rating Order 2006, SI 2006/645 (in force on various dates in April 2006), replaces the 2005 Regulations, SI 2005/522, and (1) alters the benefits and increases of benefits under the Social Security Contributions and Benefits Act 1992; (2) increases the rates and amounts of certain pensions and allowances under the 1992 Act; (3) increases the sums payable as part of a Category A or Category B retirement pension under the Pension Schemes Act 1993 on account of increases in guaranteed minimum pensions; (4) specifies the dates from which the sums specified for rates or amounts of benefit under the 1992 Act, or the 1993 Act are altered; (5) increases the rates of certain workmen's compensation and industrial injuries benefits in respect of employment before 5 July 1948; (6) specifies earnings limits for child dependency increases; (7) increases the weekly rate of statutory sick pay; (8) specifies the weekly rate of statutory maternity pay; (9) specifies the weekly rates of statutory paternity pay and statutory adoption pay; (10) increases the rate of graduated retirement benefit; (11) increases the rates of disability living allowance; (12) increases the weekly rates of age addition to long-term incapacity benefit; (13) increases the weekly rates of transitional invalidity allowance in long-term incapacity benefit cases; (14) states the amount of sums relevant to the applicable amount for the purposes of income support, and sets out the personal allowances and premiums; (15) provides for the percentage increase of sums payable by way of special transitional additions to income support; (16) states the sum by which any income support of a person involved in a trade dispute is reduced; (17) states the amount of the sums relevant for the purposes of housing benefit, council tax benefit and income-based jobseeker's allowance, including the amount of sums relevant for certain persons over the qualifying age for state pension credit, and sets out the personal allowances and premiums; (18) increases the age-related amounts for contribution-based jobseeker's allowance; (19) states the sum by which any jobseeker's allowance of a person involved in a trade dispute is reduced; and (20) specifies the amounts relevant to state pension credit.

The Social Security Benefits Up-rating Regulations 2006, SI 2006/712 (in force on 10 April 2006), replace the 2005 Regulations, SI 2005/632, and (1) provide that where a question has arisen about the effect of the 2006 Order, SI 2006/645 supra, on a benefit already in payment, the altered rates do not apply until that question is determined by the Secretary of State, an appeal tribunal or a social security commissioner; (2) restrict the application of the increases specified in SI 2006/645 in cases where the beneficiary lives abroad; (3) raise, from £170 to £175 and from £22 to £23, the earnings limits for child dependency increases payable with a carer's allowance.

2627 Child benefit—administration

The Child Benefit and Guardian's Allowance (Miscellaneous Amendments) Regulations 2006, SI 2006/203 (in force on 10 April 2006), amend the Child Benefit and Guardian's Allowance (Administration) Regulations 2003, SI 2003/492, and the Child Benefit and Guardian's Allowance (Administrative Arrangements) Regulations 2003/494, so as to (1) make provision in relation to the introduction of the concept of a qualifying young person, introduced by the Child Benefit Act 2005; and (2) modify the definition of 'the Board' to reflect the transfer of the functions of the Board of Inland Revenue to the Commissioners for Her Majesty's Revenue and Customs and the use of a specified facility for the electronic processing of claims and notifications.

2628 Child benefit—general

The Child Benefit (General) Regulations 2006, SI 2006/223 (in force on 10 April 2006 immediately after the Child Benefit Act 2005), replace the 2003 Regulations, SI 2003/493, with amendments reflecting the extension of child benefit authorised by the Child Benefit Act 2005, and make general provisions relating to child benefit. The regulations (1) contain provisions specifying the age which a person must not have attained, and the conditions which must be satisfied, in order to be a qualifying young person; (2) contain provisions determining who is the person responsible for a child or qualifying young person for the purposes of entitlement to child benefit; (3) contain provisions relating to exclusions from entitlement to child benefit and priority between persons entitled to child benefit; (4) contain a provision concerning entitlement to child benefit after the death of a child; and (5) prescribe circumstances in which a person is to be treated as being, or as not being, in the United Kingdom.

2629   Child benefit—qualifying young persons

The Social Security (Provisions relating to Qualifying Young Persons) (Amendment) Regulations 2006, SI 2006/692 (in force on 10 April 2006), amend the Social Security Benefit (Dependency) Regulations 1977, SI 1977/343, the Social Security (Widow's Benefit and Retirement Pensions) Regulations 1979, SI 1979/642, and the Social Security (Incapacity Benefit— Increases for Dependants) Regulations 1994, SI 1994/2945, so that persons in respect of whom child benefit is payable after their sixteenth birthday are no longer referred to as children, but as qualifying young persons.

2630   Child benefit—rates

The Child Benefit (Rates) Regulations 2006, SI 2006/965 (in force on 10 April 2006), prescribe, subject to specified circumstances, the weekly rate of child benefit payable in respect of a child or qualifying young person to be (1) £17·45 where in any week a child or qualifying young person is the only person or, if not the only person, the elder or eldest person; and (2) £11·70 in any other case. The regulations amend SI 1993/965, 1996/1803, 2000/1483 and 2005/2913, and revoke SI 1976/1267, 1991/502 and 1998/1581.

2631   Child support

See CHILDREN AND YOUNG PERSONS.

2632   Child tax credit—entitlement

The Child Tax Credit (Amendment) Regulations 2006, SI 2006/222 (in force on 6 April 2006), amend the 2002 Regulations, SI 2002/2007, so as to align the treatment of qualifying young persons, for the purposes of the 2002 Regulations, with that contained in the Child Benefit (General) Regulations 2006, SI 2006/223.

2633   Contributions—categorisation of earners—civil partners

See para 501.

2634   Contributions—categorisation of earners—withdrawal of exemptions

The Social Security (Categorisation of Earners) (Amendment) Regulations 2006, SI 2006/1530 (in force on 5 July 2006), further amend the 1978 Regulations, SI 1978/1689, (1) by omitting employment as a Queen's Gurkha officer or any other member of the Brigade of Gurkhas recruited in Nepal from the list of employments which are to be disregarded in relation to liability for National Insurance, with the effect that Gurkhas recruited in Nepal will be liable to pay National Insurance contributions in the same way as other serving members of the United Kingdom armed forces, and the Ministry of Defence will also become liable to pay secondary National Insurance contributions on the Gurkhas' earnings; and (2) by providing that the exemption conferred on members of visiting forces and international defence organisations does not extend to members of the naval, military or air forces of the Crown, if the force is raised in the United Kingdom or has its depot or headquarters in the United Kingdom.

2635   Contributions—general provisions

The Social Security (Contributions) (Amendment) Regulations 2006, SI 2006/127 (in force on 6 April 2006), amend the 2001 Regulations, SI 2001/1004, so as to (1) specify the levels of the lower and upper earnings limits for primary Class 1 contributions and the primary and secondary threshold for primary and secondary Class 1 contributions for the tax year beginning 6 April 2006; and (2) provide for the equivalents of the primary and secondary threshold where the earnings period is a month or a year.

The Social Security (Contributions) (Amendment No 2) Regulations 2006, SI 2006/576 (in force on 6 April 2006), further amend the 2001 Regulations supra in consequence of the income tax provisions relating to pensions and pension contributions contained in the Finance Act 2004 Pt 4 (ss 149–284). The regulations also make two amendments to the computation of amounts by reference to which employers are entitled to make payments on account of national insurance contributions to HM Revenue and Customs quarterly rather than monthly, both of which are consequential on the abolition of payment by employers of tax credits to their employees.

The Social Security (Contributions) (Amendment No 3) Regulations 2006, SI 2006/883 (in force on 6 April 2006), further amend the 2001 Regulations so as to increase the maximum value of childcare vouchers which may be disregarded in computing an earner's earnings for the purpose of Class 1 National Insurance contributions.

The Social Security (Contributions) (Amendment No 4) Regulations 2006, SI 2006/2003 (in force on 14 August 2006), further amend the 2001 Regulations so as to provide for two items to be added to the list of non-cash vouchers which are to be disregarded in the calculation of earnings for the purposes of earnings-related national insurance contributions. The items are non-cash vouchers for one mobile telephone and for eye tests and special corrective appliances.

The Social Security (Contributions) (Amendment No 5) Regulations 2006, SI 2006/2829 (in force on 16 November 2006), further amend the 2001 Regulations so as to extend the list of situations in which contributions to, and payments from, registered pension schemes and relevant non-United Kingdom schemes, in each case within the meaning of the Finance Act 2004 Pt 4 (ss 149–284) fall to be disregarded. The regulations also extend the disregard in respect of superannuation funds established in the United Kingdom to which the Income and Corporation Taxes Act 1988 s 615(3) applies, so as to cover both contributions to, and pensions payable by, such funds.

The Social Security (Contributions) (Amendment No 6) Regulations 2006, SI 2006/2924 (in force on 14 November 2006), further amend the 2001 Regulations so as to provide disregards, in the computation of an earner's liability to Class 1 National Insurance contributions, for payments of operational allowances made by the Secretary of State to members of Her Majesty's forces.

2636 Contributions—national insurance numbers

The Social Security (National Insurance Numbers) Amendment Regulations 2006, SI 2006/2897 (in force in part on 11 December 2006 and in part on 1 March 2007), amend the Social Security (Crediting and Treatment of Contributions, and National Insurance Numbers) Regulations 2001, SI 2001/769, so as to (1) provide that a person who is required to apply for a national insurance number because he is an employed earner or self-employed earner must provide the prescribed document; and (2) require a person to apply for a national insurance number if he is required to produce one when he qualifies for a student loan under the Teaching and Higher Education Act 1998 or the Education (Scotland) Act 1980.

2637 Contributions—recovery—limitation period

The taxpayer appealed against the decision of the Commissioners for Her Majesty's Revenue and Customs that certain transactions were subject to National Insurance contributions. The commissioners subsequently commenced proceedings in the county court in order not to fall foul of the six-year limitation period under the Limitation Act 1980 s 9(1). A district judge adjourned the proceedings pending the taxpayer's appeal since, under the Social Security Administration Act 1992 s 117A, the taxpayer's liability was to be determined by the commissioners. A district judge, again of his own motion, ordered that the claim be struck out. The commissioners failed to respond to the order and, by a further order made by another district judge, their application to have the action reinstated was dismissed. They appealed against the orders contending that the court had no discretion to make them as s 117A(5) did not require the court to do anything other than adjourn. The judge rejected the argument and dismissed the appeal. A single Lord Justice granted permission for a second appeal. *Held*, s 117A did not deprive the court of jurisdiction but it was not possible to conceive of any circumstances where the court could refuse a stay when it was first applied for, pending statutory appeals as contemplated by s 117, unless the proceedings were issued outside the limitation period and the taxpayer chose to seek dismissal of the same as opposed to an adjournment. The fact that a stay could not be refused did not mean that the court thereafter was not entitled to be kept informed of progress. It did not mean that, if an order was made, one or other of the parties should supply information to the court and, if one or other of the parties refused to obey that order, the court did not retain its jurisdiction to sanction that party and ultimately by strikeout if appropriate. It would only be possible to interfere with the judge's order, on appeal, if he should have decided that the district judge had erred in principle or was wholly wrong, or if it could be shown that he had erred in principle, had failed to take into account some feature which he should have taken into account or was wholly wrong because the court was forced to the conclusion that he had not balanced the various factors fairly in the scale. Accordingly, the appeal would be allowed and the action would be reinstated in the county court.

Revenue and Customs Comrs v Hyde Industrial Holdings Ltd [2006] EWCA Civ 502, [2006] All ER (D) 281 (Apr) (Court of Appeal: Waller, Longmore and Lloyd LJJ).

2638 Contributions—re-rating and national insurance funds payments

The Social Security (Contributions) (Re-rating and National Insurance Funds Payments) Order 2006, SI 2006/624 (in force on 6 April 2006), amends the Social Security Contributions and Benefits Act 1992 so as to increase (1) from £7·35 to £7·55, the amount of a Class 3 contribution; (2) from £4,345 to £4,465, the amount of earnings below which an earner may be excepted from liability for Class 2 contributions; (3) from £4,895 to £5,035 and from £32,760 to £33,540, the lower and upper limits of profits or gains between which Class 4 contributions are payable. The order also provides for the Social Security Act 1993 s 2(2) to have effect for the tax year 2006–07 and provides that the amount of any money that may be provided by Parliament to be paid into the National Insurance Fund in that year must not exceed in aggregate two per cent of the estimated benefit expenditure for the financial year ending 31 March 2007.

2639   Council tax benefit—calculation of income—modification

See para 2654.

2640   Council tax benefit—consequential provisions

See para 2648.

2641   Council tax benefit—entitlement to benefit—refusal of application—appeal— independent and impartial tribunal

The applicant was an Ethiopian asylum-seeker who had moved into housing association accommodation. A member of the association's staff helped her to fill in an application for housing and council tax benefit and the application was successful. The applicant was required to renew her application for housing and council tax benefit on an annual basis. Due to her lack of familiarity with the benefits system and her poor English, she failed to submit a benefit renewal form within the required time. She then submitted both a prospective and backdated claim for housing and council tax benefit. The prospective claim was successful, but the backdated claim was refused on the basis that the applicant had failed to show good cause why she had not claimed the benefits earlier. The decision was upheld by the local authority and the applicant's appeal to the housing benefit and council tax benefit review board also failed. The applicant complained to the European Court of Human Rights that the board was not an independent and impartial tribunal as required by the European Convention on Human Rights art 6(1). *Held*, in contrast to some other decisions which were amenable to judicial review which required a measure of professional knowledge and the exercise of administrative discretion, the decision of the board in the present case had been a question of fact as to whether there had been good cause for the applicant's delay in making a claim. The board was not merely lacking in independence from the executive, but was directly connected with one of the parties to the dispute. That connection of the councillors to the party resisting entitlement to housing benefit might infect the independence of judgment in relation to the finding of fact in a manner which could not be adequately scrutinised. The safeguards built into the board's procedure were not adequate to overcome that fundamental lack of impartiality. On an application for judicial review, the High Court would not have jurisdiction to rehear the evidence. It followed that there had been a violation of art 6 for which the applicant would be awarded a sum in respect of non-pecuniary damage.

Application 60860/00 *Tsfayo v United Kingdom* [2007] LGR 1 (European Court of Human Rights).

2642   Council tax benefit—general provisions

The Council Tax Benefit Regulations 2006, SI 2006/215 (in force on 6 March 2006), consolidate existing provision relating to council tax benefit for claimants who have not attained the qualifying age for state pension credit, as well as for those who have attained that age and are receiving either income support or income-based jobseeker's allowance. The regulations, in particular, (1) specify the circumstances in which a child or young person under the age of 19 is to be treated as a member of a family, and who is to be treated as a member of the same household as a claimant for council tax benefit; (2) provide for the calculation of a person's applicable amount in respect of his entitlement to council tax benefit by reference to which the amount of his benefit is calculated; (3) make provision in relation to polygamous marriages and persons receiving free in-patient treatment in hospitals; (4) provide for the calculation of the income and capital of a claimant for council tax benefit, the earnings of employed and self-employed earners, the treatment of income other than earnings, including notional income and the sums to be disregarded from such income; (5) deal with the calculation of capital, and capital to be disregarded; (6) provide for the treatment of students in relation to council tax benefit; (7) specify the maximum amount of council tax benefit to which a person is entitled and any deductions which are to be made from that maximum; (8) provide for the cases in which the alternative maximum council tax benefit is to apply; (9) detail when council tax benefit is to begin and end, in particular on a relevant change in a claimant's circumstances; (10) provide for the making of claims and for a person's duty to notify changes of circumstances affecting entitlement to benefit; (11) provide for decisions on questions relating to council tax benefit and for the payment of council tax benefit; (12) provide for the recovery of excess benefit; (13) make provision for the collection, recording and holding of information by local authorities and for the forwarding of information held by them to other authorities or persons providing services to those authorities; and (14) specify the circumstances in which information held by a local authority is to be disclosed to another local authority.

The Council Tax Benefit (Persons who have attained the qualifying age for state pension credit) Regulations 2006, SI 2006/216 (in force on 6 March 2006), consolidate existing provision relating to council tax benefit for claimants who have attained the qualifying age for state pension credit, except where the claimant or his partner is in receipt of income support or an income-based jobseeker's allowance. The regulations, in particular, (1) specify the circumstances in which a child or young person under the age of 19 is to be treated as a member of a family, and who is to be treated as a member of the same household as a claimant for council tax benefit; (2) provide for the calculation of a person's applicable amount in respect of his entitlement to council tax benefit by reference to which the amount of his benefit is calculated; (3) make provision for the determination of a person's income and capital for the purposes of entitlement to council tax benefit, in particular that (a) a person entitled to a guarantee credit in state pension credit is to be treated as having neither income nor capital; and (b) a person whose entitlement to state pension credit is restricted to the savings credit will have his income calculated by reference to the assessment made by the Secretary of State for the purpose of determining the award of state pension credit; and (c) separate rules apply to persons who are not entitled to state pension credit; (4) provide for the appropriate maximum council tax benefit; (5) make provision for non-dependant deductions, council tax benefit taper, extended payments of council tax benefit and the alternative council tax benefit; (6) detail when council tax benefit is to begin and end, in particular on a relevant change in a claimant's circumstances; (7) make provision for claims for council tax benefit; (8) provide for decisions on questions relating to council tax benefit and for the payment of council tax benefit; (9) provide for the recovery of excess benefit; (10) make provision for the collection, recording and holding of information by local authorities and for the forwarding of information held by them to other authorities or persons providing services to those authorities; and (11) specify the circumstances in which information held by a local authority is to be disclosed to another local authority.

See paras 2620, 2660.

2643   Guardian's allowance—general provisions

The Guardian's Allowance (General) (Amendment) Regulations 2006, SI 2006/204 (in force on 10 April 2006), further amend the 2003 Regulations, SI 2003/495, so as to (1) reflect the fact that persons in respect of whom child benefit is payable after their sixteenth birthday are no longer referred to as children but as qualifying young persons, by virtue of the Child Benefit Act 2005; and (2) vary the manner of making a guardian's allowance election under the Social Security Contributions and Benefits Act 1992 s 77, to reflect (a) the transfer of functions of the Board of Inland Revenue to the Commissioners for Her Majesty's Revenue and Customs; and (b) the use of a specified facility for electronic processing of notifications.

2644   Guardian's allowance—up-rating

The Guardian's Allowance Up-rating Order 2006, SI 2006/957 (in force on 10 April 2006), further amends the Social Security Contributions and Benefits Act 1992 Sch 4 Pt III by increasing, from £12.20 to £12.50, the weekly rate of guardian's allowance.

The Guardian's Allowance Up-rating Regulations 2006, SI 2006/1034 (in force on 10 April 2006), (1) provide that, where a question has arisen about the effect of the 2006 Order, SI 2006/957 supra, or the Guardian's Allowance Up-rating (Northern Ireland) Order 2006, SI 2006/956, on a guardian's allowance already in payment, the altered rates do not apply until that question is determined by Her Majesty's Revenue and Customs, an appeal tribunal or a Commissioner; and (2) restrict the application of the increases in cases where the beneficiary lives abroad.

2645   Housing benefit—application—refusal—requirement to provide partner's national insurance number

The claimant, a British citizen, was a local authority tenant. He was in receipt of income support and housing benefit and, following his marriage to a Thai national with whom he lived, he submitted a renewed claim for housing benefit. His wife had entered the United Kingdom on a visitor's visa and was not permitted to work or have recourse to public funds, and she had not applied for a national insurance number. The authority rejected the claim as the claimant had not provided information about his wife's national insurance number as required by the Social Security Administration Act 1992 s 1(1B). The Secretary of State appealed following the social security commissioner's decision that the authority had wrongly refused housing benefit. *Held*, in a claim for housing benefit, a claimant's partner was taken into account in the quantification of the benefit, whichever partner made the claim. In general, the applicable amount in the case of a couple was a larger amount than in respect of an individual. Therefore, where a benefit was claimed by one member of a couple, it was claimed in respect of the claimant's partner, and the requirement to provide a national insurance number related to both of them. The fact that the claimant was on income support and there was no requirement for a separate calculation for housing benefit was not required made no difference. The wife could have claimed for a national insurance number without prejudice to her immigration status or application for leave to remain, as she eventually did.

Entitlement to benefit depended on the claimant providing information about his own and his partner's national insurance number. Accordingly, the appeal would be allowed.

Secretary of State for Work and Pensions v Wilson [2006] EWCA Civ 882, (2006) Times, 4 July (Court of Appeal: Waller, Moore-Bick and Richards LJJ).

2646   Housing benefit—application—telephone communications

See para 2654.

2647   Housing benefit—calculation of income—modification

See para 2654.

2648   Housing benefit—consequential provisions

The Housing Benefit and Council Tax Benefit (Consequential Provisions) Regulations 2006, SI 2006/217 (in force on 6 March 2006), make provision consequential on the coming into force of the Housing Benefit Regulations 2006, SI 2006/213, the Housing Benefit (Persons who have attained the qualifying age for state pension credit) Regulations 2006, SI 2006/214, the Council Tax Benefit Regulations 2006, SI 2006/215, and the Council Tax Benefit (Persons who have attained the qualifying age for state pension credit) Regulations 2006, SI 2006/216, and replace the Housing Benefit (General) Regulations 1987, SI 1987/1971, the Council Tax Benefit (General) Regulations 1992, SI 1992/1814, and the Housing Benefit and Council Tax Benefit (State Pension Credit) Regulations 2003, SI 2003/325. SI 1988/662, 1995/1644, 1997/584, 2435, 2619, 2001/537, 2002/499, 1132, 2004/154 are revoked.

2649   Housing benefit—electronic communications

The Housing Benefit and Council Tax Benefit (Electronic Communications) Order 2006, SI 2006/2968 (in force on 20 December 2006), further amends the Housing Benefit Regulations 2006, SI 2006/213, the Housing Benefit (Persons who have attained the qualifying age for state pension credit) Regulations 2006, SI 2006/214, the Council Tax Benefit Regulations 2006, SI 2006/215, and the Council Tax Benefit (Persons who have attained the qualifying age for state pension credit) Regulations 2006, SI 2006/216, in order to enable the use of electronic communications in connection with claims for and awards of housing benefit and council tax benefit.

2650   Housing benefit—entitlement—deemed occupation of dwelling as home—trial period in residential accommodation—intention to return to dwelling

The Housing Benefit (General) Regulations 1987, SI 1987/1971, reg 5(7B), (7C) provides that a person who enters residential accommodation (1) for the purpose of ascertaining whether the accommodation suits his needs; (2) with the intention of returning to the dwelling which is normally occupied by him as his home should, in the event, the residential accommodation prove not to suit his needs; and (3) while the part of the dwelling which is normally occupied by him as his home is not let or sub-let, is to be treated as if he is occupying the dwelling he normally occupies as his home for a period not exceeding 13 weeks.

The tenant of a property received housing benefit from his local authority. He was in frail health, and entered residential care accommodation for the purpose of determining whether it would be suitable for his needs. He decided that it was suitable, and the authority was informed that the landlord had been given four weeks' notice to terminate the tenancy. The authority terminated the tenant's entitlement to housing benefit as from the date of his decision that the residential accommodation was suitable for his needs, and sought to recover the overpayment that had been made. The tenant died, and his appointee appealed against the request for overpaid benefit. The appeal tribunal ruled that the tenant had been entitled to receive housing benefit until the expiration of the notice given to the landlord. The authority appealed to the Social Security Appeal Commissioner, who decided that the entitlement to housing benefit ceased from the first day of the benefit week after the change in circumstances, namely when the tenant decided that the residential accommodation was suitable. The Secretary of State appealed against the decision, seeking to rely on the 1987 Regulations reg 5(7B), (7C). *Held*, on the true construction of reg 5(7B), (7C), a claimant for housing benefit who entered residential care accommodation on a trial basis with the intention of returning to his home should the accommodation not meet his needs was, while that home was not let or sub-let, entitled to housing benefit for a period of up to 13 weeks, regardless of whether during that period he took the decision to remain in the residential accommodation. Regulation 5(7B) prescribed the conditions that had to operate before reg 5(7C) came into effect, and the language of reg 5(7B)(b), being in the present tense, required that the intention of returning to the dwelling be present at the time the claimant entered residential accommodation. It did not apply to the whole of the period spent in residential accommodation, unlike reg 5(7B)(c). Accordingly, the application would be allowed.

Secretary of State for Work and Pensions v Selby DC [2006] All ER (D) 154 (Feb) (Court of Appeal: Ward, Latham and Hooper LJJ).

2651 Housing benefit—entitlement—European Economic Area national in receipt of income support

It has been held that European Economic Area nationals who live on income support in the United Kingdom are entitled to housing benefit as homeless persons subject to immigration control. Such persons are to be regarded as being subject to immigration control for the purposes of the Homelessness (England) Regulations 2000, SI 2000/701, reg 3, with the effect that they qualify for housing benefit pursuant to the Housing Act 1996 s 185(2).

Barnet LBC v Ismail [2006] EWCA Civ 383, [2007] 1 All ER 922 (Court of Appeal: Buxton, Lloyd and Richards LJJ).

2652 Housing benefit—entitlement—foreign national with visitor status—application by British spouse

The Social Security Administration Act 1992 s 1(1A), (1B) provides that no person whose entitlement to any benefit depends on his making a claim is entitled to the benefit unless, in relation both to the person making the claim and to any other person in respect of whom he is claiming benefit, the claim is accompanied by a statement of the person's national insurance number.

The respondent, a British citizen, was a council tenant and had been in receipt of housing benefit and council tax benefit for some time. He married a Thai national who had entered the United Kingdom on a visitor's visa with a condition that she neither worked nor had recourse to public funds. She lived with the respondent in his council property. The respondent submitted a renewal claim for housing benefit. In the claim form he named himself as the claimant but also referred to his wife and made clear that he was living at the property with her. However, the local authority refused to process the claim as no national insurance number had been supplied in relation to the wife, as required under the 1992 Act s 1(1A), (1B). The respondent informed the authority that he had been advised that his wife should not apply for housing benefit or a national insurance number as she did not wish to claim any form of benefit because of her immigration status. The authority notified the respondent that he was not entitled to housing benefit. The respondent appealed to an appeal tribunal, which ruled that the respondent was making a claim only for himself. The Social Security Commissioner then dismissed the authority's appeal, concluding that, where a claimant's partner was not allowed by law to have recourse to public funds, she was not 'a person in respect of whom he is claiming benefit' for the purposes of s 1(1A) so that the requirements of s 1(1B) did not have to be satisfied in relation to her. The Secretary of State appealed against that decision. *Held*, as a matter of ordinary language, benefit was claimed 'in respect of' a person if the benefit claimed was referable in some way to that person, as where the benefit or some component of it was defined or quantified by reference to that person. There was no reason to depart from that ordinary meaning when considering s 1(1A). In the ordinary course, therefore, where benefit was claimed by one member of a couple, it was claimed in respect of the claimant's partner as well as the claimant and the relevant condition in s 1(1B) had to be satisfied in relation to both of them. It would make no difference that a claimant was on income support and no separate calculation was carried out for the purposes of housing benefit, beyond a simple assessment of the amount of housing costs eligible for housing benefit. Accordingly, the appeal would be allowed.

Secretary of State for Work and Pensions v Wilson [2006] EWCA Civ 882, [2007] 1 All ER 281 (Court of Appeal: Waller, Moore-Bick and Richards LJJ).

2653 Housing benefit—entitlement—refusal of application—appeal—independent and impartial tribunal

See Application 60860/00 *Tsfayo v United Kingdom*, para 2641.

2654 Housing benefit—general provisions

The Housing Benefit Regulations 2006, SI 2006/213 (in force on 6 March 2006), consolidate provisions relating to housing benefit for claimants who have not attained the qualifying age for state pension credit and for those who have attained that age and are receiving, or have a partner who is receiving, income support or income-based jobseeker's allowance. In particular, the regulations (1) make provision with regard to the circumstances in which a person is or is not to be treated as occupying a dwelling as his home and is or is not to be treated as liable to make payments for a dwelling; (2) specify the payments by way of rent which are eligible for the payment of housing benefit and for determinations and redeterminations by rent officers in rent allowance cases; (3) specify the circumstances in which a person is or is not to be treated as responsible for another person, and specify who is to be treated as a member of the same household as a housing benefit claimant; (4) provide for the calculation of the applicable amount in respect of a person's entitlement to housing benefit, by reference to which the amount of that person's benefit is calculated; (5) make provision in respect of polygamous marriages and persons receiving free in-patient treatment in a hospital; (6) make provision as to the calculation of the income and capital of a housing benefit claimant, the earnings of employed and self-employed earners, the treatment of income other than earnings, including notional income, and the sums of income and capital which are to be disregarded for these purposes; (7) provide for the treatment of students, their entitlement to housing benefit and the calculation of their income; (8) specify the maximum amount of housing benefit payable in any case, and any deductions which must be made from that maximum; (9) contain provisions as to when housing benefit begins, together with provisions relating to changes in circumstances and the date on which they take effect; (10) provide for the making, amendment and withdrawal of claims, the evidence and information required in connection with claims, and the duty to notify the designated office of changes in circumstances; and (11) make provision for (a) the determination of questions arising on claims and the notification of decisions by authorities; (b) the payment, and withholding, of housing benefit, and persons to whom payments are to be made; (c) the recovery and method of recovery of overpaid housing benefit, and what constitutes a recoverable overpayment; (d) the collection, recording and holding of information, and the supply of information between local authorities; and (e) modifications of the housing benefit scheme in respect of Pathfinder authorities.

The Housing Benefit (Persons who have attained the qualifying age for state pension credit) Regulations 2006, SI 2006/214 (in force on 6 March 2006), consolidate provisions relating to housing benefit for claimants who have attained the qualifying age for state pension credit. In particular, the regulations (1) make provision with regard to the circumstances in which a person is or is not to be treated as occupying a dwelling as his home and is or is not to be treated as liable to make payments for a dwelling; (2) specify the payments by way of rent which are eligible for the payment of housing benefit and for determinations and redeterminations by rent officers in rent allowance cases; (3) specify the circumstances in which a person is or is not to be treated as responsible for another person, and specify who is to be treated as a member of the same household as a housing benefit claimant; (4) provide for the calculation of the applicable amount in respect of a person's entitlement to housing benefit, by reference to which the amount of that person's benefit is calculated; (5) make provision in relation to the determination of income and capital of a person to whom the regulations apply, the earnings of employed and self-employed earners, the treatment of income other than earnings, including notional income, and appropriate disregards, and provide that (a) a person entitled to a guarantee credit in state pension credit is to be treated as having neither income nor capital; (b) a person whose entitlement to state pension credit is restricted to the savings credit will have his income calculated by reference to the assessment made by the Secretary of State for the purpose of determining the award of state pension credit; and (c) persons to whom the regulations apply but who have no entitlement to state pension credit are to have their income and capital determined in accordance with other specified provisions; (6) provide for the appropriate maximum housing benefit, non-dependant deductions, housing benefit taper and extended payments; (7) contain provisions as to when housing benefit begins, together with provisions relating to changes in circumstances and the date on which they take effect; (8) provide for the making, amendment and withdrawal of claims, the evidence and information required in connection with claims, and the duty to notify the designated office of changes in circumstances; and (9) make provision for (a) the determination of questions arising on claims and the notification of decisions by authorities; (b) the payment, and withholding, of housing benefit, and persons to whom payments are to be made; (c) the recovery and method of recovery of overpaid housing benefit, and what constitutes a recoverable overpayment; (d) the collection, recording and holding of information, and the supply of information between local authorities; and (e) modifications of the housing benefit scheme in respect of Pathfinder authorities.

The Housing Benefit and Council Tax Benefit (Amendment) Regulations 2006, SI 2006/2813 (in force on 20 November 2006), amend the Housing Benefit Regulations 2006 supra, the Housing Benefit (Persons who have attained the qualifying age for state pension credit) Regulations 2006 supra, the Council Tax Benefit Regulations 2006, SI 2006/215, and the Council Tax Benefit (Persons who have attained the qualifying age for state pension credit) Regulations 2006, SI 2006/216, so as to grant authorities the power to modify those regulations to provide that certain payments made under the Armed Forces and Reserve Forces (Compensation Scheme) Order 2005, SI 2005/439, may be disregarded from the calculation of income for housing benefit or council tax benefit purposes.

The Housing Benefit and Council Tax Benefit (Amendment) (No 2) Regulations 2006, SI 2006/2967 (in force on 20 December 2006), further amend the Housing Benefit Regulations 2006, the Housing Benefit (Persons who have attained the qualifying age for state pension credit) Regulations 2006, the Council Tax Benefit Regulations 2006, and the Council Tax Benefit (Persons who have attained the qualifying age for state pension credit) Regulations 2006, so that a person may (1) claim housing benefit and council tax benefit by telephone; (2) amend, by telephone, the claim he made by telephone; and (3) notify a change of circumstances by telephone or by other means.

The Housing Benefit (Amendment) Regulations 2006, SI 2006/644 (in force on 3 April 2006), further amend the Housing Benefit Regulations 2006 and the Housing Benefit (Persons who have attained the qualifying age for state pension credit) Regulations 2006 so as to prescribe the cases in which housing benefit is to take the form of a rent allowance with the effect that the occupier of a dwelling is liable to make payments to a local authority and not the landlord of the dwelling.

See paras 2620, 2660.

2655 Housing benefit—subsidy—rates

The Income-related Benefits (Subsidy to Authorities) Amendment Order 2006, SI 2006/54 (in force on 9 February 2006), amends the 1998 Order, SI 1998/562, so as to (1) make provision for balancing what has been paid by way of interim subsidy with what it is estimated will be the amount of final subsidy before the claim has been audited; (2) provide that the payment of final subsidy should take into account the amounts paid or recovered pursuant to the new provisions, as well as interim subsidy that has been paid; (3) provide an addition to subsidy in recognition of the operation by local authorities of schemes under the Social Security Administration Act 1992 ss 134(8), 139(6) to disregard the income of those who receive war disablement and war widow's pensions; (4) provide for a new rate of subsidy of 100 per cent of qualifying expenditure attributable to housing benefit and council tax benefit; (5) increase the rates of subsidy for backdated benefits and for homeless and short lease rebate cases to 100 percent; (5) abolish regulated rent allowance thresholds; (6) provide for increases to rates of subsidy where there has been a departmental error overpayment; (7) clarify how much subsidy is payable where there has been an overpayment and that authorities can reclassify overpayments in-year; (8) refer to the Housing Benefit and Council Tax Benefit Security Manual, which encompasses those circulars which were previously listed; (9) substitute the figures to be used in the calculation of subsidy which are outlined; (10) clarify that subsidy will be payable in certain circumstances where the local authority has not referred to the rent officer; and (11) provide that the definition of 'dwelling' is the same definition as is used in the Housing Revenue Account Subsidy Determination.

The Income-related Benefits (Subsidy to Authorities) Amendment (No 2) Order 2006, SI 2006/559 (in force on 1 April 2006), further amends the 1998 Order supra so as to (1) substitute, in relation to England, (a) the GDP deflator, the annual factor and the weekly rent limit for the purposes of determining whether an authority is liable to a deduction from subsidy payable for 2006–07; and (b) a rebate proportion for 2006–07 for the purpose of calculating the amount of the deduction; and (2) substitute, in relation to Wales, (a) a specified amount and the guideline rent increase for the purposes of determining whether an authority is liable to a deduction from subsidy payable for 2006–07; and (b) a rebate proportion for 2006–07 for the purpose of calculating the amount of the deduction; and (3) amend the manner for calculating a dwelling's average weekly rent and service charges.

2656 Incapacity benefit—entitlement—computation of earnings—average earnings

The claimant applied for incapacity benefit under the Social Security Contributions and Benefits Act 1992 Pt II (ss 20–62). Her application was refused on the ground that her average net weekly income from student lodgers for whom she shopped, cooked and cleaned was such that she was capable of work. She appealed to a social security commissioner, who was of the opinion that there was no statutory regime which governed the calculation of the claimant's earnings. Based on his own computation of her earnings, the commissioner found that the claimant was to be treated as having been capable of work only in the eight weeks of the year of claim in which her earnings had exceeded the limit set by the Social Security (Incapacity for Work) (General) Regulations 1995, SI 1995/311, reg 17. The respondent appealed, contending that the correct method of calculating earnings so as to decide entitlement to incapacity benefit was dictated by the Social Security Benefit (Computation of Earnings) Regulations 1996, SI 1996/2745, which required an average of earnings to be taken. *Held*, the purpose of determining whether a claimant was entitled to incapacity benefit was a purpose prescribed by the 1992 Act Pt II. The 1996 Regulations reg 3 required such a purpose to be carried out, where it involved computation, in accordance with those regulations. Accordingly, the appeal would be allowed and the matter remitted to the commissioner to be determined in accordance with the court's judgment.

Doyle v Secretary of State for Work and Pensions [2006] EWCA Civ 466, [2006] All ER (D) 263 (Apr) (Court of Appeal: Buxton, Lloyd and Richards LJJ).

2657 Incapacity benefit—incapacity for work

The Social Security (Incapacity for Work) Amendment Regulations 2006, SI 2006/757 (in force on 10 April 2006), further amend the 1995 Regulations, SI 1995/311, so as to (1) change the requirement to give notice and the definition of 'immediate past period of incapacity for work'; (2) substitute the provision which describes persons who are treated as capable of work; and (3) substitute the provision which describes categories of exempt work.

2658   Incapacity benefit—work-focused interviews

The Social Security (Incapacity Benefit Work-focused Interviews) Amendment Regulations 2006, SI 2006/536 (in force on 3 April 2006), further amend the 2003 Regulations, SI 2003/2439, so as to increase the numbers of persons that can be required to attend work-focused interviews as a condition of their continued entitlement to full benefit. In particular, the regulations (1) extend the dates a claim for a specified benefit will bring some claimants within the 2003 Regulations; (2) create an area of the country in which a claim for a specified benefit on any date brings a claimant within the 2003 Regulations; and (3) amend the places in which a claimant must live to fall within the 2003 Regulations.

The Social Security (Incapacity Benefit Work-focused Interviews) Amendment (No 2) Regulations 2006, SI 2006/3088 (in force on 29 December 2006), further amend the 2003 Regulations supra, so as to increase the numbers of persons who can be required to attend work-focused interviews as a condition of their continued entitlement to full benefit. In particular, the regulations (1) amend the places in which a person must live to fall within the 2003 Regulations, so that they apply to an increased number of persons; (2) provide that, in addition to living in those new places, a person must make his claim for a specified benefit at a particular Department for Work and Pensions office; those particular offices are whichever offices the Secretary of State decides to designate as a 'Pathways to Work office'; and (3) provide that where a person is subject to the 2003 Regulations because he lives in a specified area, and meets the other relevant conditions, he can continue to be subject to the 2003 Regulations when he moves to another specified area; the date he claimed benefit is not relevant to whether he continues to be subject to the 2003 Regulations.

2659   Income support—entitlement—advance award—claimant not satisfying habitual residence requirement

The Social Security (Claims and Payments) Regulations 1987, SI 1987/1968, reg 13(1) provides that where, although a person does not satisfy the requirements for entitlement to benefit on the date on which a claim is made, the Secretary of State is of the opinion that unless there is a change of circumstances the person will satisfy those requirements, the Secretary of State may award benefit.

The claimant, who had previously lived in the United Kingdom, returned to the United Kingdom with a view to settling permanently. Five days later, she made a claim for income support. The Secretary of State disallowed the claim on the ground that the claimant had not been in the United Kingdom for an appreciable amount of time so as to show a settled intention to stay. An appeal tribunal accepted that the claimant had a settled intention to remain but dismissed her appeal because she had not been resident in the United Kingdom for an 'appreciable period of time'. The claimant appealed to a social security commissioner who found that the tribunal had erred in failing to consider whether the Secretary of State had power to make an advance award of income support under the 1987 Regulations reg 13(1) and allowed the appeal. The Secretary of State appealed. *Held*, whether a person was habitually resident involved an assessment as to whether, at the time of the decision to grant or refuse income support, he had genuinely adopted the United Kingdom as his normal place of residence. In each case, there was a very broad spectrum of facts that might enable a decision maker to determine the point at which he could be reasonably confident that a claimant had both the intention to remain and a reasonable foreseeability of fulfilling that intention. Where reasonable confidence as to the continuance of such an intention became speculation in such decision-making was essentially a matter of fact for the decision maker. However, the mere possibility that later unforeseen developments might affect the will or the ability of a claimant to adhere to an intention to settle should not prevent the Secretary of State from deciding in his favour. It followed that it was not necessary where a claim for an advance award was made that there should be certainty or near certainty of the claimant achieving whatever 'appreciable period' of actual residence was considered appropriate by the decision-maker. It was plain from the wording of reg 13(1) that something less than certainty was required, since it empowered the Secretary of State to make such an award where, in his opinion, the claimant would satisfy the requirement at a future date unless there was a change of circumstances. The commissioner's conclusion that the tribunal had erred in not considering whether the Secretary of State could have made an advance award was correct and, accordingly, the appeal would be dismissed.

Bhakta v Secretary of State for Work and Pensions [2006] EWCA Civ 65, [2006] All ER (D) 195 (Feb) (Court of Appeal: Auld, Longmore and Hallett LJJ). *Nessa v Chief Adjudication Officer* [1998] 2 All ER 728, CA (1998 Abr para 2947), considered.

2660   Income support—general provisions

The Social Security (Young Persons) Amendment Regulations 2006, SI 2006/718 (in force on 10 April 2006), amend the following social security legislation in consequence of changes made by the Child Benefit Act 2005 and the Child Benefit (General) Regulations 2006, SI 2006/223, to the conditions of entitlement to child benefit, in particular the conditions relating to a person's age and the education or training in which he is engaged: (1) the Income Support (General) Regulations 1987, SI 1987/1967, in relation to (a) the circumstances in which (i) a person is treated as receiving relevant education, (ii) a disabled person receiving relevant education may be entitled to income support, and (iii) a person may be entitled to income support by virtue of being engaged in training; and (b) the definitions of 'young person' and 'full-time student'; (2) the Jobseeker's Allowance Regulations 1996, SI 1996/207, so as to (a) revise the definitions of 'full-time student', 'child benefit extension period' and 'young person'; (b) revise the circumstances in which (i) a joint-claim couple may be entitled to a jobseeker's allowance, (ii) a person is treated as receiving relevant education, and (iii) a person may be entitled to a jobseeker's allowance when he is engaged in training; (3) the Housing Benefit Regulations 2006, SI 2006/213, and the Housing Benefit (Persons who have attained the qualifying age for state pension credit) Regulations 2006, SI 2006/214, so as to revise the definition of 'young person' and the circumstances in which a student is entitled to housing benefit; (5) the Council Tax Benefit Regulations 2006, SI 2006/215, and the Council Tax Benefit (Persons who have attained the qualifying age for state pension credit) Regulations 2006, SI 2006/216, so as to revise the definition of 'young person' and the circumstances in which a student is entitled to council tax benefit; and (6) the State Pension Credit Regulations 2002, SI 2002/1792, by revising the definition of 'young person'.

See para 2620.

2661   Industrial injuries—disablement pension with unemployability supplement—permitted earnings limit

The Social Security (Industrial Injuries) (Dependency) (Permitted Earnings Limits) Order 2006, SI 2006/663 (in force on 12 April 2006), further amends the Social Security Contributions and Benefits Act 1992, so as to increase the amount which the spouse or civil partner, or person living as spouse or civil partner with the beneficiary, may earn and still receive any increased disablement pension with unemployability supplement in respect of one or more children or qualifying young persons.

2662   Industrial injuries—prescribed diseases

The Social Security (Industrial Injuries) (Prescribed Diseases) Amendment Regulations 2006, SI 2006/586 (in force on 6 April 2006), further amend the 1985 Regulations, SI 1985/967, so as to make alterations to the list of prescribed diseases and to provide, on a claim for disablement pension in respect of certain prescribed diseases, that entitlement may arise from the first day a person suffers from a loss of faculty due to that disease and prescribes lung impairment caused by primary carcinoma of the lung as a loss of faculty from which the resulting disabilities are to be taken as amounting to 100 per cent disablement.

The Social Security (Industrial Injuries) (Prescribed Diseases) Amendment (No 2) Regulations 2006, SI 2006/769 (in force on 5 April 2006), amend the principal 2006 Regulations supra so as to provide that reg 3 does not apply to claims made before those regulations come into force.

2663   Industrial injuries—reduced earnings allowance—age limits for entitlement—discrimination

The applicants had been injured at work. They received reduced earnings allowance administered under the terms of the Social Security Contributions and Benefits Act 1992. A cut-off point for receipt of the allowance applied to workers who had reached retirement age. This was based on the state pension age of 65 years of age for men and 60 for women until 1996, tapering up to eventual equality at 65 years of age in 2020. When eligibility for reduced earnings allowance ended, a retirement allowance was paid. That allowance started at 65 years of age for men and 60 for women, where the recipient had ceased to work. The applicants complained to the European Court of Human Rights that the allowance schemes were discriminatory, in breach of the European Convention on Human Rights art 14 taken in conjunction with the First Protocol art 1. *Held*, art 14 did not prohibit contracting states from treating groups differently in order to correct factual inequalities between them. A difference of treatment was, however, discriminatory if it had no objective and reasonable justification. The contracting state enjoyed a margin of appreciation in assessing whether and to what extent differences in otherwise similar situations justified a different treatment. The difference in state pensionable age between men and women in the United Kingdom was originally intended to correct the disadvantaged economic position of women. It continued to be reasonably and objectively justified on that ground until such time as social and economic changes removed the need for special treatment for women. The government's decisions as to the precise timing and means of putting right the inequality were not so manifestly unreasonable as to exceed the wide margin of appreciation which it was allowed. Similarly, the decision to link eligibility for reduced earnings allowance to the pension scheme was reasonably and objectively justified, given that the benefit was intended to compensate for reduced earnings capacity during a person's working life. There had been no violation of art 14 taken in conjunction with the First Protocol art 1. Accordingly, the application would be dismissed.

Applications 65731/01 and 65900/01 *Stec v United Kingdom* [2006] 43 EHRR 1017 (European Court of Human Rights).

2664   Jobseeker's allowance—employment zones—allocation to contractors

The Employment Zones (Allocation to Contractors) Pilot Regulations 2006, SI 2006/962 (in force on 24 April 2006), make provision for a pilot scheme for jobseeker's allowance claimants to participate in a compulsory employment zone programme with a particular employment zone contractor. In particular, the regulations, (1) specify those people who may be selected by an employment officer to participate in an employment zone programme with a particular employment zone contractor; (2) make provision for certain jobseeker's allowance claimants who are at a significant disadvantage in the labour market to apply voluntarily to an employment officer for selection; (3) provide for jobseeker's allowance claimants who have begun but not completed an employment zone programme in the previous 12 months to be required to complete an employment zone programme with the same employment zone contractor; (4) set out the two stages of an employment zone programme; (5) make provision for certain conditions for entitlement to a jobseeker's allowance relating to availability for work, a jobseeker's agreement and actively seeking work to be suspended while people are participating in an employment zone programme; (6) enable a sanction to be imposed under the Jobseekers Act 1995 s 19 or 20A if a person without good cause refuses or fails to participate in an employment zone programme with a particular employment zone contractor; (7) provide that where the Secretary of State is satisfied that such a person is no longer ordinarily resident in, or his address for payment is no longer in, an employment zone, that if a sanction has been incurred it will end and the regulations will cease to apply except where a person who has already begun an employment zone programme requests to be allowed to complete it; and (8) require a person who was participating in an employment zone programme under the 2005 Regulations, SI 2005/1125, before 24 April 2006 to complete the programme under the regulations. The regulations cease to have force on 23 April 2007.

2665   Jobseeker's allowance—employment zones—programmes

The Employment Zones (Amendment) Regulations 2006, SI 2006/1000 (in force on 24 April 2006), further amend the 2003 Regulations, SI 2003/2438, so as to (1) provide for a jobseeker who does not have a fixed address to participate in the employment zone programme where the address for payment of his jobseeker's allowance is within an employment zone; (2) ensure that time previously spent on an employment zone programme is taken into account; and (3) require a jobseeker aged under 25 years to have taken part in a new deal for young people programme before applying for early entry to an employment zone programme.

2666   Jobseeker's allowance—entitlement—migrant worker—habitual residence

See *Collins v Secretary of State for Work and Pensions*, para 2992.

2667   Jobseeker's allowance—general provisions

See paras 2620, 2660.

2668   National Insurance Contributions Act 2006

The National Insurance Contributions Act 2006 makes provision about national insurance contributions in cases where there is a retrospective change to the law relating to income tax, enables related provision to be made for the purposes of contributory benefits, statutory payments and other matters, and makes provision about the disclosure of information in relation to arrangements for the avoidance of national insurance contributions. The Act received the royal assent on 30 March 2006 and came into force on that day.

Section 1 enables existing regulation-making powers to be exercised so as to create a retrospective liability for national insurance contributions where there have been retrospective tax enactments, relating to those parts of the Income Tax (Earnings and Pensions) Act 2003 dealing with employment income, and the Treasury consider it appropriate to make regulations for the purpose of reflecting the whole or part of the retrospective tax provision. The extended powers allow for liability for national insurance contributions to be charged back to 2 December 2004. Wide powers to make consequential changes or other changes that may be required through exercise of the powers described above are also introduced for the purposes of contributions, contributory benefits, statutory payments, contracted-out pension rebates or other purposes. Corresponding provision is made in relation to Northern Ireland: s 2. Section 3 allows regulations to be made in relation to matters affecting the law relating to Class 1A national insurance contributions where this is expedient in consequence of retrospective tax legislation affecting a person's general earnings. Section 4 makes corresponding provision in relation to Northern Ireland. Section 5 prevents existing rules on agreements and elections being used so as to allow employers to recover from, or pass on to, employees any secondary liability for national insurance contributions due on certain employment income from shares and securities acquired by employees, which is created retrospectively by virtue of the powers created by this Act. Corresponding provision is made in relation to Northern Ireland: s 6. Section 7 provides for the tax disclosure rules to apply to proposals and arrangements relating to national insurance contributions as they apply to income tax schemes. Section 8 deals with extent, s 9 with commencement, and s 10 with short title.

Amendments, repeals and revocations

The list below, which is not exhaustive, mentions repeals and amendments which are or will be effective when the Act is fully in force.

Specific provisions of a number of Acts are added or amended. These include: Social Security Contributions and Benefits Act 1992: ss 4B, 4C, 10ZC, 176, Sch 1; and Social Security Administration Act 1992 ss 132A, 190, 192.

2669   Pensions

See PENSIONS AND SUPERANNUATION.

2670   Persons from abroad—exclusions from entitlement

The Social Security (Persons from Abroad) Amendment Regulations 2006, SI 2006/1026 (in force on 30 April 2006), amend or further amend, in consequence of EC Council Directive 2004/38, (1) the Council Tax Benefit Regulations 2006, SI 2006/215; (2) the Council Tax Benefit (Persons who have attained the qualifying age for state pension credit) Regulations 2006, SI 2006/216; (3) the Housing Benefit Regulations 2006, SI 2006/213; (4) the Housing Benefit (Persons who have attained the qualifying age for state pension credit) Regulations 2006, SI 2006/214; (5) the Income Support (General) Regulations 1987, SI 1987/1967; (6) the Jobseeker's Allowance Regulations 1996, SI 1996/207; (7) the State Pension Credit Regulations 2002, SI 2002/1792; and (8) the Social Fund Maternity and Funeral Expenses (General) Regulations 2005, SI 2005/3061. In particular, the regulations (a) restate more simply the definition of 'persons from abroad'; (b) set out afresh the categories of persons who are excluded from that definition so as to reflect the terms of the Directive; (c) modify the right to reside requirement in the habitual residence test and provide that where a person's right of residence is of a specified type, he is not to be treated as habitually resident for the purposes of entitlement to income support, jobseeker's allowance, housing benefit, council tax benefit and state pension credit; (d) add Switzerland to the list of places where a funeral can take place in the 2002 Regulations, SI 2002/1792; and (e) ensure that a national of Norway, Iceland, Liechtenstein or Switzerland is treated as a national of a member state in certain circumstances. SI 1994/1807, 1996/2006, 2000/979, 2004/1232 are revoked.

The Social Security (Persons from Abroad) Amendment (No 2) Regulations 2006, SI 2006/2528 (in force on 9 October 2006), amend or further amend (1) SI 1987/1967 supra; (2) SI 1996/207 supra; (3) SI 2002/1792 supra; (4) SI 2006/213 supra; (5) SI 2006/214 supra; (6) SI 2006/215 supra; and (7) SI 2006/216 supra. In particular, the regulations (a) amend an existing category which exempts those with exceptional leave to enter the United Kingdom granted by an immigration officer, or to remain in the United Kingdom granted by the Secretary of State, which defines exceptional leave as being leave to enter or remain granted outside of the rules made under the Immigration Act 1971 s 3(2) and no longer refers to the person who grants the leave; and (b) add a category of persons who are exempt from the habitual residence test, namely those who have humanitarian protection.

2671   Pneumoconiosis, byssinosis and miscellaneous diseases—benefit scheme

The Pneumoconiosis, Byssinosis and Miscellaneous Diseases Benefit (Amendment) Scheme 2006, SI 2006/638 (in force on 6 April 2006), further amends the 1983 Regulations, SI 1983/136, so as to provide that where a claim is made in relation to the diseases listed, the disablement is to be regarded as being total.

2672   Retirement benefit—graduated retirement benefit—up-rating

The Social Security (Graduated Retirement Benefit) (Consequential Provisions) Order 2006, SI 2006/2839 (in force on 26 October 2006), amends the Social Security Administration Act 1992 s 150, so as to allow the lump sum payable to a surviving spouse or civil partner whose spouse or civil partner died while they were deferring entitlement to graduated benefit, to be up-rated in line with the annual up-rating orders made under that provision for the years that the surviving spouse or civil partner was below state pension age.

2673   Social fund—cold weather payments—general

The Social Fund Cold Weather Payments (General) Amendment Regulations 2006, SI 2006/2655 (in force on 1 November 2006), further amend the 1988 Regulations, SI 1988/1724, so as to revise (1) the list of primary weather stations, which are relevant to determining whether there is a recorded, or forecasted, period of cold weather, by assigning postcodes from Coltishall Weather Station, which has closed, to a new weather station, Weybourne, which is added to the scheme; and (2) the list specifying alternative weather stations, used to determine the information where the primary weather station is unable to do so, by providing Mumbles as the specified alternative weather station for St Athan, replacing the Cardiff weather station that has closed.

2674   Social fund—determination of claims—review procedure

The Social Fund (Application for Review) (Amendment) Regulations 2006, SI 2006/961 (in force on 24 April 2006), amend the 1988 Regulations, SI 1988/961, so as to provide that an application for review by a social fund inspector may be made to the Independent Review Service, or, until 2 April 2007, to the Department for Work and Pensions.

2675   Social fund—funeral payments—claim for funeral abroad—discrimination

In each of four appeals, the claimants and their late partners had relatively recent family origins in overseas Muslim countries and continuing personal ties with those countries. In each case the choice was made for social, family or religious reasons, or a combination of all three, that the deceased should be returned to the country of family origin to be buried there in accordance with Muslim practice. In each case, a claim was made for a funeral payment under the Social Fund Maternity and Funeral Expenses (General) Regulations 1987, SI 1987/481, reg 7(1)(b)(ii). However, under reg 7(1), a payment for funeral expenses was to be made only where a funeral was held in the United Kingdom. The Secretary of State therefore refused the claims. The claimants appeal to a social security commissioner, submitting that the condition relating to the place where the funeral was held discriminated against them within the meaning of the European Convention on Human Rights art 14. The commissioner rejected the appeals, deciding that, although the refusal of their claims involved indirect discrimination, their treatment did not fall within the ambit of any of the substantive articles of the Convention, so that art 14 did not apply. On the claimants' further appeal, *held*, it was impossible to see the instant case as one of discrimination in any relevant sense. The state made provision for a suitable burial in the United Kingdom for all those of inadequate means, regardless of personal characteristics or status. There was no obligation on the state to do so, and certainly no obligation to do more. It had been open to each claimant to take advantage of the provision, but each had chosen not to do so for understandable, but entirely personal, reasons. The only way in which it could be represented as discriminatory was by characterising the claimants as members of a group, that of recent migrants to the country, and then finding indirect discrimination in that as a group they were more likely than other comparable groups to have retained family links with their countries of origin, and therefore more likely to want their loved ones to be buried there. Such reasoning was, however, wholly artificial. Without demeaning the strength and sincerity of the wishes of the claimants as individuals, it was not obvious that recent migrants, as a group, were particularly likely to prefer a burial in their country of origin rather than in the country they had made their home. In any event, there might be many other categories of people resident in the United Kingdom who, given the choice, might elect for a burial abroad for themselves or their loved ones, whether for religious, family, social or purely sentimental reasons. Such wishes were understandable and to be respected, but it was not the job of the state to satisfy them, nor did the sharing of such desires render those who had them a 'group' requiring special protection under art 14. Accordingly, the appeal would be dismissed.

Esfandiari v Secretary of State for Work and Pensions [2006] EWCA Civ 282, [2006] All ER (D) 339 (Mar) (Court of Appeal: Tuckey, Carnwath and Jacob LJJ).

2676   Social Security Act 1998—commencement

The Social Security Act 1998 (Commencement Nos 9 and 11) (Amendment) Order 2006, SI 2006/2540, (1) further amends the Social Security Act 1998 (Commencement No 9, and Savings and Consequential and Transitional Provisions) Order 1999, SI 1999/2422, by adding a further definition of 'relevant benefit' and making consequential amendments to the Social Security (Incapacity Benefit) (Transitional) Regulations 1995, SI 1995/310; and (2) amends the Social Security Act 1998 (Commencement No 11, and Savings and Consequential and Transitional Provisions) Order 1999, SI 1999/2860, by adding a further definition of 'relevant benefit' and making consequential amendments to the Social Security (Introduction of Disability Living Allowance) Regulations 1991, SI 1991/2891. The effect of the amendments is that decisions of the adjudication officer in respect of the relevant benefits are treated as decisions of the Secretary of State.

The Social Security Act 1998 (Commencement No 14) Order 2006, SI 2006/2376, appoints 1 October 2006 for the coming into force of s 67 in respect of women whose expected week of confinement falls on or after 1 April 2007.

For a summary of the Act, see 1998 Abr para 2970. See also the commencement table in the title STATUTES.

2677   Social security tribunal—reduced benefit direction—mother refusing to seek child support—undue distress

A mother gave up her part-time job and applied for income support for herself and her son. She stated that she did not want to pursue the father for child support as she was afraid of retribution, although she said that violence was not an issue. An official considered the application and decided that the reasons given by the mother could not be accepted, and the Secretary of State made a reduced benefit direction as there were no reasonable grounds to believe that the mother or the son would suffer harm or undue distress if child support was recovered from the father. On appeal to a social security tribunal, the mother claimed for the first time that there had been an incident of violence as a result of an argument about support for the son. The tribunal rejected the appeal on the basis that it did not believe the mother was telling the truth. The mother appealed to a social security commissioner who concluded that there was a failure of logic in the tribunal's reasoning process and that there would have been a risk of the mother suffering undue distress as a result of having to recover child support. The Secretary of State appealed. *Held*, the tribunal was permitted to determine that the mother was deliberately lying. Fear could generate distress, and irrational fear might generate greater distress, but it did not necessarily evidence undue distress. The exaggeration by the mother had been found to be deliberate and the approach of the tribunal revealed no error of law or failure of logic. The tribunal had then considered whether there was a realistic prospect of such an incident or undue distress to the mother or the son and had decided that there was not. The tribunal had been entitled to reach the conclusion of fact that it had and the commissioner had no basis in law for preferring his alternative analysis. Accordingly, the appeal would be allowed.

Roach v Secretary of State for Work and Pensions [2006] EWCA Civ 1746, [2007] 1 FCR 238 (Court of Appeal: Mummery, Smith and Leveson LJJ). *Tote Bookmakers v Development and Property Holding Co Ltd* [1985] Ch 261 (1985 Abr para 123) considered.

2678 State pension credit—general provisions

See paras 2620, 2660.

2679 Statutory maternity pay—maternity allowance—overlapping benefits

See para 1253.

2680 Statutory sick pay—general

The Statutory Sick Pay (General) Amendment Regulations 2006, SI 2006/599 (in force on 10 April 2006), further amend the 1982 Regulations, SI 1982/894, so as to provide that a person is deemed incapable of work if he is excluded or abstains from work in accordance with a request or notice in writing made under an enactment, or is otherwise prevented from working pursuant to an enactment, in order to prevent the spread of a relevant disease.

2681 Tax credits—claims and notifications

The Tax Credits (Claims and Notifications) (Amendment) Regulations 2006, SI 2006/2689 (in force in part on 1 November 2006 and in part on 6 April 2007), further amend the 2002 Regulations, SI 2002/2014, so as to (1) set out the changes in circumstances which must be notified to HM Revenue and Customs for the purposes of Working Tax Credit and Child Tax Credit; (2) revise the notification requirement by providing that the period for giving notice begins from the date on which the claimant first became aware of the change in circumstances; (3) reduce the period for notification from three months to one month; and (4) add an additional circumstance which may be notified in advance to HM Revenue and Customs, where a child is expected to become a qualifying young person for the purposes of tax credits.

2682 Tax credits—miscellaneous amendments

The Tax Credits (Miscellaneous Amendments) Regulations 2006, SI 2006/766 (in force on 6 April 2006), amend or further amend (1) the Tax Credits (Claims and Notifications) Regulations 2002, SI 2002/2014, by changing the date when a claim for tax credit is treated as made and changing the specified date for the purposes of a notice under the Tax Credits Act 2002 s 17; (2) the Child Tax Credit Regulations 2002, SI 2002/2007, which prescribe conditions and the maximum age for a person who has either left full-time education or approved training; (3) the Tax Credits (Residence) Regulations 2003, SI 2003/654, so as to update the application of European legislation; (4) the Tax Credits (Residence) (Amendment) Regulations 2004, SI 2004/1243, by removing the date limitation on the requirement to have a right to reside in the United Kingdom for the purposes of the Tax Credits Act 2002 Pt 1 (ss 1–48); (5) the Tax Credits (Definition and Calculation of Income) Regulations 2002, SI 2002/2006, so as to (a) update references to taxable income derived from tax legislation as a result of the entry into force of the Income Tax (Trading and Other Income) Act 2005; (b) update definitions; (c) provide that for tax credit purposes a trading loss is not available unless the trade is carried on a commercial basis and with a view to realising a profit; (d) update references to any adult dependants' grant in relation to student income to take account of new student support regulations in England and Wales; and (e) update references in relation to income which is exempt from income tax, and references in the definitions of various types of different income and in the provisions under which claimants are treated as having income; and (6) the Working Tax Credit (Entitlement and Maximum Rate) Regulations 2002, SI 2002/2005, so as to update references in various legislation.

2683　Tax credits—up-rating

The Tax Credits Up-rating Regulations 2006, SI 2006/963 (in force on 6 April 2006), prescribe increases in certain sums required to be reviewed under the Tax Credits Act 2002 s 41 and, in consequence, amend (1) the Child Tax Credit Regulations 2002, SI 2002/2007, by increasing the maximum rate of the elements of a child tax credit; (2) the Working Tax Credit (Entitlement and Maximum Rate) Regulations 2002, SI 2002/2005, by prescribing new maximum rates for the elements of working tax credit other than the child care element; and (3) the Tax Credits (Income Thresholds and Determination of Rates) Regulations 2002, SI 2002/2008, by increasing the first income thresholds for those entitled to child tax credit.

2684　Tax Credits Act 2002—commencement

The Tax Credits Act 2002 (Commencement and Transitional Provisions) Order 2006, SI 2006/3369, amends (1) the Tax Credits Act 2002 (Commencement No 4, Transitional Provisions and Savings) Order 2003, SI 2003/962, so that the 2002 Act s 1(3)(d) comes into force on 31 December 2008 instead of on 31 December 2006; and (2) the Tax Credits Act 2002 (Transitional Provisions) Order 2005, SI 2005/773, by extending, from 31 December 2006 to 31 December 2008, the period during which a person entitled to the child premia in respect of income support or income-based jobseeker's allowance is not also entitled to a tax credit. SI 2005/776, 1106 are revoked. For a summary of the Act, see 2002 Abr para 2787. See also the commencement table in the title STATUTES.

2685　Welfare foods—free milk and vitamins

See para 2698.

2686　Workers' compensation—pneumoconiosis—amount of payments

The Pneumoconiosis etc (Workers' Compensation) (Payment of Claims) (Amendment) Regulations 2006, SI 2006/829 (in force on 1 April 2006), further amend the 1998 Regulations, SI 1988/668, so as to increase, by 2.7 per cent, the lump sum payable under the Pneumoconiosis etc (Workers' Compensation) Act 1979 to certain persons disabled by a relevant disease, or to dependants of persons who were so disabled before they died.

2687　Workmen's compensation—supplementation

The Workmen's Compensation (Supplementation) (Amendment) Scheme 2006, SI 2006/738 (in force on 12 April 2006), further amends the 1982 Scheme, SI 1982/1489, by making adjustments to the rate of lesser incapacity allowance which are consequential on the increase in the maximum rate of that allowance made by the Social Security Benefits Up-rating Order 2006, SI 2006/645. Transitional provision is also made.

SOCIAL SERVICES AND COMMUNITY CARE

Halsbury's Laws of England (4th edn) vol 44(2) (Reissue) paras 1001–1081

Articles

For articles relating to this title please refer to the Table of Articles at the beginning of the Abridgment.

2688　Adult placement schemes—England

See para 2689.

2689　Care homes—England

The Care Standards Act 2000 (Establishments and Agencies) (Miscellaneous Amendments) Regulations 2006, SI 2006/1493 (in force in part on 1 July 2006 and in part on 1 September 2006), which apply to establishments and agencies in England, further amend the Care Homes Regulations 2001, SI 2001/3965, so as to (1) include a definition of 'working day'; (2) require greater detail to be included in a service user's guide relating to the standard package of services provided in a care home, the terms and conditions which apply to key services and fee levels and payment arrangements and require the guide to state whether the terms and conditions, including fees, would be different in circumstances where a service user's care is funded, in whole or in part, by someone other than the service user; (3) enable a person to request an extract of the information contained in the service user's guide instead of a copy of the whole guide; (4) provide that the copy, or the extract, must be provided within five working days of any request being received by the care home; (5) revise provisions as to information about fees to be given to service users so as to apply to all care homes, and not only to those where nursing is provided; (6) require any notice of increase of fees to be accompanied by a statement of the reasons for such an increase and to qualify the requirement that any increase in fees must be notified at least one month in advance, to reflect the fact that such notice may not always be practicable; (7) require a system to be put in place by the registered provider for evaluating the quality of services provided at the care home, and for reports based on such system to be given to the Commission for Social Care Inspection on request; (8) provide that, if the Commission so requests, the registered person in respect of a care home must produce an improvement plan detailing how he intends to improve the services provided in the home; and (9) require a written copy of the plan to be provided to the Commission and made available to service users and their representatives and to the parents and placing authorities of children accommodated in a care home.

The Nurses Agencies Regulations 2002, SI 2002/3212, the Domiciliary Care Agencies Regulations 2002, SI 2002/3214, and the Adult Placement Schemes (England) Regulations 2004, SI 2004/2071, are also amended so as to (a) replace provisions dealing with the review of quality of service provision with provisions, in similar terms to those described in head (7) supra, dealing with the assessment of quality of services; and (b) require an improvement plan in the same terms as described in head (8) supra.

2690   Commission for Social Care Inspection—fees—adoption agencies and adoption support agencies

The National Care Standards Commission (Commission for Social Care Inspection) (Fees) (Adoption Agencies, Adoption Support Agencies and Local Authority Fostering Functions) (Amendment) Regulations 2006, SI 2006/578 (in force on 1 April 2006), further amend the National Care Standards Commission (Fees and Frequency of Inspections) (Adoption Agencies) Regulations 2003, SI 2003/368, so as to (1) increase by 15 per cent the amount of fees that voluntary adoption agencies and adoption support agencies must pay to the Commission for Social Care Inspection under the Care Standards Act 2000 Pt 2 (ss 11–42); and (2) prescribe the functions of the Commission, for the purposes for the Health and Social Care (Community Health and Standards) Act 2003 s 86(1), so as to allow the Commission to make provision for charging local authorities fees for the inspection of local authority adoption and fostering services.

2691   Commission for Social Care Inspection—fees and frequency of inspections

The Commission for Social Care Inspection (Fees and Frequency of Inspections) (Amendment) Regulations 2006, SI 2006/517 (in force on 1 April 2006), further amend the 2004 Regulations, SI 2004/662, so as to (1) increase the amount of fees payable to the Commission for Social Care Inspection by establishments and agencies, with the exception of voluntary adoption agencies, adoption support agencies, independent hospitals, independent clinics, independent medical agencies and local authority fostering services; and (2) make changes to the minimum required frequency for inspection by the Commission of premises used for the purposes of care homes, domiciliary care agencies, nurses agencies and adult placement schemes, from once in every 12 months to once in every three years. SI 2005/575 is revoked.

2692   Commissioner for Older People (Wales) Act 2006

The Commissioner for Older People (Wales) Act 2006 establishes and makes provision about the office of Commissioner for Older People in Wales and makes provision in relation to the functions of the Commissioner. The Act received the royal assent on 25 July 2006 and came into force in part on that day. The remaining provisions came into force on 14 October 2006: SI 2006/2699. For details of commencement, see the commencement table in the title STATUTES.

Section 1, Sch 1 establish the office of the Commissioner for Older People in Wales ('the Commissioner') and make further provision about the office of the Commissioner, and s 2 sets out the general functions of the Commissioner. The Commissioner may review the effect on older people in Wales of the discharge or proposed discharge of functions of the National Assembly for Wales or of specified persons, or the effect of a failure to discharge such functions (s 3, Sch 2), and the Assembly may by order amend the list of specified persons (s 4). The Commissioner may review any advocacy, complaints or whistle-blowing arrangements for the purpose of ascertaining whether, and to what extent, they are effective in safeguarding and promoting the interests of relevant older people in Wales: s 5. 'Relevant older people' is defined by s 6, with reference to the persons listed in Sch 3, and s 7 empowers the Assembly to amend that list of persons. The Assembly may make regulations empowering the Commissioner to assist an older person in Wales who is making certain complaints or representations (s 8) and to examine the cases of particular older people in Wales in connection with certain of his functions (s 10). Section 9 makes provision for the Commissioner to undertake, commission or provide assistance for another to undertake or commission research or educational activities in connection with any of his functions. Section 11 enables the Commissioner to issue a certificate to the High Court in the event of a person obstructing him in the exercise of his functions, and s 12 allows the Commissioner to issue guidance on best practice to the Assembly and to specified persons. The Commissioner, or a person authorised by him, may enter premises that are not private dwellings in order to interview older people with their consent: s 13. Sections 14, 15 enable regulations to be made conferring further functions on the Commissioner and providing for the making by the Commissioner of reports following the discharge of certain of his functions. Provision is made by ss 16, 17 for the Commissioner to work jointly with the Public Services Ombudsman for Wales, and collaboratively with other ombudsmen, in specified circumstances. The Commissioner has a duty not to disclose information obtained by him in the discharge of his functions, or obtained from other commissioners or ombudsmen, other than for specified purposes: s 18. Provision is made for certain publications to be absolutely privileged: s 19. Section 20 requires the Commissioner to establish a procedure for dealing with complaints made about the discharge of his functions, and s 21 prevents the Commissioner from discharging his functions in specified circumstances. Section 22, Sch 4 make minor and consequential amendments and s 23 provides for commencement. Sections 24, 26, 27 contain interpretative provisions. The Commissioner must have regard to the United Nations Principles for Older Persons in considering what constitutes the interests of older people in Wales: s 25. Section 28 deals with the making of orders and regulations by the Assembly, s 29 with extent and s 30 with short title.

Amendments, repeals and revocations

Specific provisions of a number of Acts are added or amended. These include: Care Standards Act 2000 ss 75ZA, 76; Public Services Ombudsman (Wales) Act 2005 ss 25A, 25B, 26, 41.

2693 Community care, services for carers and children's services—direct payments—Wales

The Community Care, Services for Carers and Children's Services (Direct Payments) (Wales) Amendment Regulations 2006, SI 2006/2840 (in force on 1 October 2006), amend the 2004 Regulations, SI 2004/1748, so as to (1) provide that all persons for whom Welsh local authorities have decided to provide community care services are prescribed persons for the purposes of the 2004 Regulations; and (2) provide that direct payments must be made by local authorities, instead of the direct provision of services, to all persons prescribed, as specified, if such persons have consented to such payments and are not otherwise excluded from receiving them.

2694 Complaints—England

The Local Authority Social Services Complaints (England) Regulations 2006, SI 2006/1681 (in force on 1 September 2006), set out the procedure for the handling of complaints about local authority social services. In particular, the regulations (1) describe when the duty on a local authority to handle a complaint arises; (2) allow a complaint to be made by a service user, a prospective service user or, in certain circumstances, another person on his behalf; (3) provide that complaints will not be considered if they (a) are withdrawn; (b) are repeat complaints which have already been investigated; (c) relate to care provided by an establishment or agency registered under the Care Standards Act 2000; (d) relate to legal or disciplinary proceedings; (e) relate to criminal proceedings or proceedings under s 59; (f) relate to matters over a year old at the date of the complaint which cannot be handled effectively or fairly because of the delay; or (g) are unclear, frivolous or vexatious; (4) provide for complaints which relate to care provided by an establishment or agency registered under the 2000 Act to be referred to the registered person in respect of that establishment or agency where a complainant so wishes; (5) require the local authorities to try to resolve complaints informally within 20 working days; (6) provide for the formal investigation of a complaint if a complainant does not want it to be investigated informally or is not satisfied with the outcome of the informal investigation; (7) require a local authority which has investigated a complaint to send a report of its investigation to the complainant and, where it finds the complaint to be well-founded, explain to the complainant what action, if any, it proposes to take; (8) enable a complainant to require his case to be referred to a three-person review panel, which must include at least two members independent of the local authority, once his complaint has been formally investigated or the period for such an investigation has expired without a report on the outcome of the complaint being made; (9) provide that, where a local authority is found by the review panel not to have dealt with a complaint adequately, it must notify the complainant of what action, if any, it proposes to take and must provide guidance to the complainant as to the powers of a Local Commissioner to investigate a complaint under the Local Government Act 1974 s 26(1); (10) require a local authority to send any complaint which is sent to it and which relates to an NHS body to the NHS body if the complainant so wishes and require the local authority and the NHS body to co-operate with a view to providing the complainant with a comprehensive response to both elements of the complaint; and (11) require each local authority to (a) appoint a complaints manager to assist it in the co-ordination of its consideration of complaints; (b) assist complainants to comply with the complaints procedure as necessary or to explain where such assistance can be found; and (c) monitor and report on the discharge of its functions.

2695 Domiciliary care agencies—England

See para 2689.

2696 Fees—abolition—Wales

The Care Standards Act 2000 and the Children Act 1989 (Abolition of Fees) (Wales) Regulations 2006, SI 2006/878 (in force on 1 April 2006), abolish (1) all requirements under the Care Standards Act 2000 and the Children Act 1989 for fees to be paid in respect of registration to the National Assembly for Wales; (2) the requirement for annual fees to be paid in respect of inspections by the Assembly of local authority adoption and fostering services under the Health and Social Care (Community Health and Services) Act 2003 and of boarding schools and colleges under the Children Act 1989; and (3) as a ground for cancellation of registration, the non payment of fees by providers.

2697 Healthy start scheme—description of healthy start food—Wales

The Healthy Start Scheme (Description of Healthy Start Food) (Wales) Regulations 2006, SI 2006/3108 (in force on 27 November 2006), describe the healthy start food and healthy start vitamins that will apply in relation to the operation of the healthy start scheme in Wales.

2698 Healthy start scheme—welfare foods scheme

The Healthy Start Scheme and Welfare Food (Amendment) Regulations 2006, SI 2006/589 (in force on 6 April 2006), further amend the Welfare Food Regulations 1996, SI 1996/1434, and amend the 2005 Regulations, SI 2005/3262, so as to raise to £14,155 the upper income level that determines whether a person receiving child tax credit but not working tax credit and who meets other conditions is entitled to milk or dried milk and vitamins under the welfare food scheme and the healthy start scheme.

The Healthy Start Scheme and Welfare Food (Amendment No 2) Regulations 2006, SI 2006/2818 (in force on 27 November 2006), further amend the 2005 Regulations supra so as to (1) extend the healthy start scheme to the whole of Great Britain; (2) lower to the age of four the age under which a child who satisfies the conditions stated is a person entitled to benefit; (3) provide for healthy start vitamins and payments in lieu of healthy start vitamins; and (4) provide for information to be disclosed to and used by persons carrying out functions on behalf of the Secretary of State for enforcement of the 2005 Regulations. The regulations also amend the 1996 Regulations supra so as to bring to an end entitlement to milk, dried milk or vitamins under those regulations, except for milk or dried milk for children in day care.

2699 National assistance—accommodation—infirm destitute asylum-seeker

The National Assistance Act 1948 s 21(1)(a) provides that a local authority may make arrangements for providing residential accommodation for persons who, by reason of age, illness, disability or any other circumstances, are in need of care and attention which is not otherwise available to them. A person to whom the Immigration and Asylum Act 1999 s 115 applies may not be provided with residential accommodation under the 1948 Act s 21(1)(a) if his need for care and attention has arisen solely because he is destitute or because of the physical effects of his being destitute: s 21(1A).

The claimant, a citizen of Zimbabwe, arrived in the United Kingdom on a six-month visa. He was subsequently diagnosed as being HIV-positive and claimed that, in view of his medical condition and the lack of suitable treatment in Zimbabwe, the Secretary of State could not return him to that country without breaching his rights under the European Convention on Human Rights art 3. The claimant also requested the defendant local authority to undertake an assessment with a view to his being provided with accommodation under the 1948 Act s 21. The defendant local authority rejected the s 21 application, and the claimant applied for judicial review. The judge allowed the application on the ground that someone suffering from the claimant's condition was more vulnerable than the able-bodied, and in need of care and attention not solely because he was destitute. The defendant appealed. *Held*, it had been established that all asylum-seekers, whether infirm or able-bodied, were potential beneficiaries of s 21, and it was implicit that 'care and attention' was not to be interpreted in a narrow way, but could extend to the provision of shelter, warmth, food and other basic necessities. The judge had therefore been entitled to conclude that s 21 applied, and that, if the claimant were to lose the accommodation currently provided by the defendant, he would be a 'destitution-plus' case in the context of s 21(1A). Accordingly, the appeal would be dismissed.

R (on the application of M) v Slough BC [2006] EWCA Civ 655, [2006] All ER (D) 364 (May) (Court of Appeal: Ward and Maurice Kay LJJ and Sir Peter Gibson). Decision of Collins J [2004] EWHC 1109 (Admin), [2004] LGR 657 affirmed.

2700 National assistance—assessment of resources—England

The National Assistance (Sums for Personal Requirements and Assessment of Resources) (Amendment) (England) Regulations 2006, SI 2006/674 (in force on 10 April 2006), further amend the National Assistance (Sums for Personal Requirements) (England) Regulations 2003, SI 2003/628, so as to prescribe £19.60 as the weekly sum which local authorities in England are to assume, in the absence of special requirements, that a resident in accommodation arranged under the National Assistance Act 1948 Pt III (ss 21–36) will need for his personal requirements. The regulations also amend the National Assistance (Assessment of Resources) Regulations 1992, SI 1992/2977, so as to (1) increase the capital limit above which a resident is not entitled to be assessed as unable to pay for accommodation; (2) provide that weekly tariff income is now to be calculated on a resident's capital between £12,750 and £21,000; (3) add references to 'qualifying young person' in relation to the payment of child benefit; and (4) provide for an increase to £5·05, or £7·50 if a resident has a partner, (a) in the amount of any savings credit to be disregarded where a resident has qualifying income not exceeding the standard minimum guarantee; and (b) in the amount to be disregarded if a resident has qualifying income that exceeds the standard minimum guarantee.

2701 National assistance—assessment of resources—Wales

The National Assistance (Assessment of Resources and Sums for Personal Requirements) (Amendment) (Wales) Regulations 2006, SI 2006/1051 (in force on 10 April 2006), prescribe £20 as the weekly sum which local authorities are to assume, in the absence of special circumstances, that residents who are in accommodation arranged under the National Assistance Act 1948 Pt III (ss 21–36) will need for their personal requirements. The regulations also further amend the National Assistance (Assessment of Resources) Regulations 1992, SI 1992/2977, so as to (1) provide for civil partners to be treated in the same way as spouses; (2) provide for adoption and support payments under the Adoption and Children Act 2002 to be disregarded both as capital and income; and (3) increase the capital limits and the disregard for those in receipt of pension credit. SI 2005/663 is revoked.

2702 National assistance—person lacking finances to secure deposit—provision of accommodation

See *R (on the application of Conville) v Richmond upon Thames LBC*, para 1484.

2703 National assistance—sums for personal requirements—England

See para 2700.

2704 National assistance—sums for personal requirements—Wales

See para 2701.

2705 Pensions

See PENSIONS AND SUPERANNUATION.

2706 Private and voluntary health care—England

The Private and Voluntary Health Care (England) (Amendment) Regulations 2006, SI 2006/539 (in force on 1 April 2006), which apply in relation to England only, further amend the 2001 Regulations, SI 2001/3968, so as to amend the minimum frequency of inspections of premises used for the purposes of health care and establishments and agencies. SI 2004/661 is revoked.

The Private and Voluntary Health Care (England) (Amendment No 2) Regulations 2006, SI 2006/1734 (in force on 1 August 2006), which apply in relation to England only, further amend the 2001 Regulations supra, by prescribing the time for payment of an annual fee by health care establishments and agencies under the Care Standards Act 2000 s 16(3). SI 2004/661 and SI 2005/647 are revoked.

2707 Private and voluntary health care—Wales

The Private and Voluntary Health Care and Miscellaneous (Wales) (Amendment) Regulations 2006, SI 2006/1703 (in force on 6 July 2006), extend the Private and Voluntary Health Care (Wales) Regulations 2002, SI 2002/325, so that they apply to independent medical agencies in Wales; and consequentially amend the Registration of Social Care and Independent Health Care (Wales) Regulations 2002, SI 2002/919.

2708 Safeguarding Vulnerable Groups Act 2006

See para 490.

2709 Social care—quality of care—monitoring and review—Wales

The Care Standards Act 2000 and the Children Act 1989 (Regulatory Reform and Complaints) (Wales) Regulations 2006, SI 2006/3251, amend various regulations made under the Children Act 1989 and the Care Standards Act 2000. Provision is inserted which requires registered persons to establish and maintain systems for monitoring, reviewing and improving the quality of care provided by various care services at least once a year. Provision is made for the registered person to ascertain the views of service users and their representatives, purchasing authorities and staff of the service. Reports of this review must be prepared by the registered person. At the request of the National

Assembly for Wales the registered person must undertake an assessment of the service provided. The National Assembly can require the registered person to take such action as it considers is necessary in order to meet statutory provision and the registered person must advise the National Assembly when this action has been completed. Amendment is also made to the requirements in relation to the handling of complaints by registered persons. A failure to meet any of these requirements is an offence. The regulations amended are (1) the Care Homes (Wales) Regulations 2002, SI 2002/324; (2) the Children's Homes (Wales) Regulations 2002, SI 2002/327; (3) the Child Minding and Day Care (Wales) Regulations 2002, SI 2002/812; (4) the Fostering Services (Wales) Regulations 2003, SI 2003/237; (5) the Residential Family Centres (Wales) Regulations 2003, SI 2003/781; (6) the Nurses Agencies (Wales) Regulations 2003, SI 2003/2527; (7) the Adult Placement Schemes (Wales) Regulations 2004, SI 2004/1756; (8) the Domiciliary Care Agencies (Wales) Regulations 2004, SI 2004/219;and (9) the Adoption Support Agencies (Wales) Regulations 2005, SI 2005/1514.

2710 Vulnerable adults—protection—care worker—alleged misconduct

Under the Care Standards Act 2000 s 82(1), a person who provides care for vulnerable adults must refer a care worker to the Secretary of State if certain conditions are fulfilled. If it appears from the information submitted with a reference under s 82(1) that it may be appropriate for the worker to be included in the list of individuals who are considered unsuitable to work with vulnerable adults, the Secretary of State must determine that reference and, pending that determination, provisionally include the worker in the list: s 82(4).

The applicant care workers had been placed on the Protection of Vulnerable Adults list on the basis of their alleged misconduct which predated the coming into force of the relevant statutory provisions. The applicants sought judicial review of the decision to place them on the list and issues arose as to whether the respondent Secretary of State might include a person in the list under the 2000 Act s 82 on reference from the employer where the alleged misconduct took place before the coming into force of s 82, and whether the provisions of Pt VII (ss 80–104), which provided for the creation and maintenance of the list, was compatible with the rights to a fair trial and to respect for private and family life guaranteed by the European Convention on Human Rights arts 6 and 8. *Held*, a reference by a care provider based on an act that took place before the coming into force of the 2000 Act was a reference under s 82(1) and, therefore, the Secretary of State could put the person on the list if he thought it might be appropriate. The wholesale copying of the wording of the Protection of Children Act 1999 s 2, which clearly had retrospective effect, in the 2000 Act s 82 led to the conclusion that Parliament had intended s 82 to have retrospective effect. The provisions of the 2000 Act in relation to provisional listings were not compatible with the Convention arts 6 and 8. The procedures were unfair and did not meet the requirements of art 6. While the suspension was temporary, art 6 was still engaged. The rights and obligations of an employment contract of a care worker were civil rights and obligations. The listing of a care worker had a clear and decisive effect on the contract of employment, even though there was no statutory obligation for the employer to suspend or transfer the care worker. The Secretary of State was not an independent and impartial tribunal. A provisionally listed care worker had to wait nine months to make an application to set aside the termination of his employment, and an application for judicial review would only result in the quashing of the decision to list the care worker. It was for the employer to re-engage the care worker and there was no way of obliging him to do so. The care worker's employment could be terminated without him being heard on the ground of suspected misconduct. The 2000 Act was also disproportionate and unfair in addressing the problem as different systems were used for other health professionals. The basis of provisional listing was suspicion of misconduct serious enough to indicate that a person constituted a risk to vulnerable persons that was calculated to interfere with his relationships with colleagues and others, which engaged the Convention art 8. The procedures in the 2000 Act in relation to provisional listings were unfair and did not ensure the respect for the interests of care workers. Those provisions were incompatible with the Convention art 8. Accordingly, the application would be allowed.

R (on the application of Wright) v Secretary of State for Health [2006] EWHC 2886 (Admin), [2007] 1 All ER 825 (Queen's Bench Division: Stanley Burnton J). *Antonelli v Secretary of State for Trade and Industry* [1998] 1 All ER 997, CA (1997 Abr para 66), considered.

2711 Vulnerable adults—protection—tribunal—proceedings

See para 485.

SOLICITORS

Halsbury's Laws of England (4th edn) vol 44(1) (Reissue) paras 1–800

Articles

For articles relating to this title please refer to the Table of Articles at the beginning of the Abridgment.

2712   Conditional fee agreements

See COSTS.

2713   Costs—wasted costs—personal liability of solicitor—proceedings brought to delay payment of tax

See *Morris v Roberts (Inspector of Taxes)*, para 709.

2714   Costs—wasted costs—personal liability of solicitor—unauthorised acceptance of service of claim

See *Regent Leisuretime Ltd v Skerrett*, para 708.

2715   Disciplinary proceedings—Solicitors Disciplinary Tribunal—consideration of representations following order

The Solicitors Act 1974 s 48(1) provides that an order of the Solicitors Disciplinary Tribunal must be filed with the Law Society, and a statement of the Tribunal's findings, signed by the chairman or by some other member of the Tribunal authorised by him in that behalf, must either be prefaced to the order or added to the file containing the order as soon as may be after the order has been made.

The claimant solicitor was charged with conduct unbefitting a solicitor. The charge comprised two separate allegations. The Solicitors Disciplinary Tribunal dismissed the first allegation, but decided to impose a three-year suspension in relation to the second allegation. The solicitor made further representations following the making of the order, which the Tribunal refused to take into account on the basis that it was functus officio. The solicitor appealed. *Held*, once the Tribunal had made its order pursuant to the 1974 Act s 48, it was functus officio. Section 48 made it clear that the Tribunal's statutory function was to make an order, and that reasons might be made at the same time or later. Further, the mere fact that it was essential to give reasons, as part of a fair judicial process, did not lead to the conclusion that, until such time as a tribunal or court had given its reasons, it might change them at any time. Although there were occasions when a court might choose to reconsider its decision, usually when it itself had identified an error, there was no warrant for an unending process continuing up until the time of giving reasons. Accordingly, the appeal would be dismissed.

Baxendale-Walker v Law Society [2006] EWHC 643 (Admin), [2006] All ER (D) 439 (Mar) (Queen's Bench Division: Moses LJ and Stanley Burnton J).

2716   Duty to disclose—formation of partnership—partner suspended from practice—non-disclosure to other partner—fraudulent misrepresentation—damages

See *Conlon v Simms*, para 1984.

2717   Fee—commission paid on conveyancing searches—non-disclosure to client

A firm of solicitors entered into an arrangement with a company under which the company was to carry out local authority and other searches for the firm in conveyancing matters. Under the arrangement, the firm's clients would be charged the nominal full cost of the searches, but after that fee had been paid by the firm, the firm would invoice the company for 'commission' of a certain fixed amount. No mention of the arrangement for the payment of the commission was made to the firm's clients. The Law Society was critical of the failure to tell the clients of the full cost of the searches, but later issued guidance which appeared to authorise the firm to retain the commission and not disclose it to their clients. When the firm's books were inspected, the report raised no issues of compliance with the Solicitors' Accounts Rules 1991. In subsequent correspondence, the solicitors maintained that they thought the arrangement was beneficial to their clients, the charges being less than those which would otherwise be made by local authorities, but without prejudice to that position amended their letters and terms of business. The Society made an application to the Solicitors' Disciplinary Tribunal, contending that the arrangement amounted to conduct unbefitting a solicitor. The tribunal acceded to an application to strike out the proceedings on the ground that the Society could not succeed. The Society appealed under the Solicitors Act 1974 s 49. *Held*, on the true construction of the 1991 Rules r 10, the arrangement did not give rise to commission properly earned but rather a discount dressed up as a commission. On the facts, given the confusion in the Society, the solicitors could hardly have been called dishonest and the charge should never have been made. Nor had they acted in a way unbefitting of a solicitor. Accordingly, the appeal would be dismissed.

Law Society v Adcock [2006] EWHC 3212 (Admin), [2006] All ER (D) 322 (Dec) (Queen's Bench Division: Waller LJ and Treacy J).

2718   Law Society—notice of intervention—application for withdrawal of notice

The applicant solicitor was the sole practitioner at her firm. The defendant Law Society informed the applicant that it would be attending her office to investigate the firm's books. After the investigation the defendant sent the applicant a letter particularising allegations of professional failures to which she did not reply even though the letter requested her response by a certain date. Subsequently, the matter was referred to the Adjudication Panel of the Compliance Board. The Panel decided that there was reason to suspect dishonesty on the applicant's part and that she had failed to comply with the rules, so that there should be an intervention. Notice of the intervention was sent to the applicant's office. The applicant made an application for an order directing the defendant to withdraw the intervention. She contended that there was no reason to suspect dishonesty in any respect which justified intervention. The defendant argued, in support of the intervention, that there was a cash shortage on a client bank account and that transfers had been made from the client account to the office account. The court decided there was insufficient evidence to justify the drastic step of intervention. On the defendant's appeal, *held,* it was unnecessary and inappropriate in the instant case for the judge to make a finding of honesty or dishonesty. The question which he had to decide was whether the suspicion of dishonesty raised by the material on which the defendant relied had been dispelled by the evidence so that he could safely direct withdrawal of the intervention notices. If the judge had intended to suggest that there was, or should be, a general rule that, absent grounds to suspect dishonesty, the defendant should not exercise intervention powers on the basis of a solicitor's failure to comply with the accounts rules, he had gone too far. If he had intended only to suggest that, in a case where there was no reason to suspect dishonesty, the defendant should give careful consideration to the question whether the need for compliance with the relevant rules could be met by the exercise of powers short of intervention, his observation could not be criticised. However, on that question, the court had to give proper respect to the view of the defendant. If, after consideration, the defendant had taken the view that, in the particular case, compliance with the rules could not be achieved by the exercise of powers short of intervention, the court should be slow to substitute its own view on a question which was peculiarly within the experience and expertise of the defendant. Accordingly, the appeal would be allowed.

Sheikh v Law Society [2006] EWCA Civ 1577, [2006] All ER (D) 316 (Nov) (Court of Appeal: Chadwick, Tuckey and Moore-Bick LJJ). Decision of Park J [2005] EWHC 1409 (Ch), [2005] 4 All ER 717 (2005 Abr para 2941) reversed.

2719   Law Society—solicitors' compensation fund—trust funds—classification of trust

The Law Society maintained and acted as the trustee of a compensation fund, under the Solicitors' Compensation Fund Rules 1995, into which all practising solicitors made contributions. The purpose of the fund was the payment of discretionary grants to clients of solicitors who had suffered through solicitors' dishonesty. Under the 1995 Rules, the Society was empowered in certain circumstances to vest in itself all the money in solicitors' client accounts, and was obliged to pay all such money into a special account and to hold the money on trust for the persons beneficially entitled to it. In many cases, solicitors' records were incomplete or fraudulent and it was difficult to determine who was entitled to the funds. The Society brought a number of test cases in order to determine whether the trust created by the 1995 Rules was a private law trust or a statutory purpose trust. *Held,* when the word 'trust' was used in a statute, it did not necessarily bring with it the full range of trust obligations attendant on a traditional private law trust, particularly where the trust was imposed by statute in the context of the exercise of a public function. In respect of the application of funds under the 1995 Rules, the duties of a private trustee would be unduly onerous and, in the cases where intervention was needed most, a private law trust could be void for uncertainty as to the beneficiaries. Accordingly, the Society was not an assignee of the trusts of the client accounts, but took the funds subject to new statutory trusts, and the exercise of its discretion as trustee would be subject to review on public law grounds.

Re Ahmed & Co; Re Biebuyck Solicitors; Re Dixon & Co; Re Zoi [2006] EWHC 480 (Ch), (2006) 8 ITELR 779 (Chancery Division: Lawrence Collins J).

2720   Legal Services Ombudsman—jurisdiction

The Legal Services Ombudsman (Jurisdiction) (Amendment) Order 2006, SI 2006/3362 (in force on 5 January 2007), further amends the 1990 Order, SI 1990/2485, by adding the Association of Law Costs Draftsmen to the list of public bodies over which the Legal Services Ombudsman has jurisdiction.

2721   Rights of audience—right to conduct litigation—Association of Law Costs Draftsmen

The Association of Law Costs Draftsmen Order 2006, SI 2006/3333 (in force on 1 January 2007), designates the Association of Law Costs Draftsmen as an authorised body for the purposes of the Courts and Legal Services Act 1990 ss 27 and 28, so as to enable it to grant rights of audience and the right to conduct litigation.

2722   Solicitor and client—authority—silence

See *Northstar Land Ltd v Brooks*, para 1290.

STAMP DUTIES AND STAMP DUTY RESERVE TAX

Halsbury's Laws of England (4th edn) vol 44(1) (Reissue) paras 1001–1200

Articles

For articles relating to this title please refer to the Table of Articles at the beginning of the Abridgment.

2723   Finance Act 2006

See para 2465.

2724   Open-ended investment company—definition

The Stamp Duty and Stamp Duty Reserve Tax (Definition of Unit Trust Scheme and Open-ended Investment Company) (Amendment) Regulations 2006, SI 2006/746 (in force on 6 April 2006), amend the 2001 Regulations, SI 2001/964, in consequence of the changes made to the taxation of pensions by the Finance Act 2004 Pt 4 (ss 149–284). In particular, the regulations provide that (1) an open-ended investment company has the meaning given under the Financial Services and Markets Act 2000 s 236; and (2) a unit trust scheme has the meaning given under s 237.

2725   Stamp duty—recognised exchanges—exceptions—extension

The Stamp Duty and Stamp Duty Reserve Tax (Extension of Exceptions relating to Recognised Exchanges) Regulations 2006, SI 2006/139 (in force on 16 February 2006), extend the stamp duty and stamp duty reserve tax exemptions for sales of stock to intermediaries and for repurchase and stock lending under the Finance Act 1986 to the prescribed multilateral trading facilities listed in the 2005 Regulations, SI 2005/1990.

2726   Stamp duty land tax—administration

The Stamp Duty Land Tax (Administration) (Amendment) Regulations 2006, SI 2006/776 (in force on 17 April 2006), further amend the 2003 Regulations, SI 2003/2837, so as to provide for a new form SDLT 60 in connection with land transactions for the purposes of stamp duty land tax.

2727   Stamp duty land tax—anti-avoidance rule

The Stamp Duty Land Tax (Variation of the Finance Act 2003) Regulations 2006, SI 2006/3237 (in force on 6 December 2006), amend the Finance Act 2003 Pt 4 (ss 42–124), so as to introduce an anti-avoidance rule which treats a series of linked transactions, which have the effect of transferring from a vendor to a purchaser the vendor's interest, as a notional land transaction, and revise the rules on the treatment of partnerships for stamp duty land tax purposes.

2728   Stamp duty land tax—chargeable consideration—land transactions and grant of leases

The Stamp Duty Land Tax (Amendment to the Finance Act 2003) Regulations 2006, SI 2006/875 (in force on 12 April 2006), amend the Finance Act 2003 in relation to (1) land transactions where the purchaser bears any inheritance tax, capital gains tax or costs of enfranchisement; and (2) the grant of leases where the tenant bears the costs of the grant and where the lease includes a covenant that any payment entitlement be transferred to the landlord on termination of the lease.

2729   Stamp duty land tax—electronic communications

The Stamp Duty Land Tax (Electronic Communications) (Amendment) Regulations 2006, SI 2006/3427 (in force on 31 January 2007), amend the 2005 Regulations, SI 2005/844, so as to make provision in connection with the introduction by the Keeper of the Registers of Scotland of an automated system for land registration.

2730   Stamp duty reserve tax—recognised exchanges—exceptions—extension

See para 2725.

2731   Unit trust scheme—definition

See para 2724.

STATUTES

Halsbury's Laws of England (4th edn) vol 44(1) (Reissue) paras 1201–1526

Articles

For articles relating to this title please refer to the Table of Articles at the beginning of the Abridgment.

2732   Commencement of statutes

The following table contains detailed commencement provisions of all statutes passed in 2006. Repealed provisions are omitted. Schedules are included but not those sections which simply introduce schedules. The table also contains details of all commencement orders made in 2006, which in certain cases relate to statutes passed before 2006. Revoked orders are omitted.

An asterisk (★) indicates that a section, subsection or schedule is in force only in part or only for certain purposes.

The table refers to statutes only in so far as they relate to England and Wales.

STATUTE	IN FORCE	AUTHORITY
Animal Welfare Act 2006		
• ss 1–45, 51, 52, 54–60, 62, 63, 66	no date	s 68(3)
• ss 61, 67, 68(1), (3), (4), 69	8 November 2006	s 68(1)
• Schs 1–4	no date	s 68(3)
Anti-social Behaviour Act 2003		
• ss 19–22★, 24★	11 May 2006	s 93(1); SI 2006/1278
• ss 48–52★	6 April 2006	s 93(1); SI 2006/393
Appropriation Act 2006	30 March 2006	
Appropriation (No 2) Act 2006	19 July 2006	
Armed Forces Act 2001		
• s 30	25 August 2006	s 39(2); SI 2006/2309
• ss 32(1)–(8), (9)★, 33	3 February 2006	s 39(2); SI 2006/235
• Sch 4	25 August 2006	s 39(2); SI 2006/2309
• Sch 5 (paras 1–4, 5(1), (2)(a), (3), 6, 7)	3 February 2006	s 39(2); SI 2006/235
Armed Forces Act 2006		
• ss 1–180, 182, 183, 185–205, 207–271, 272(1), 273–320, 322–350, 352, 354–357, 360–372, 374–377, 379–381, 385	no date	s 383(2)
• ss 359, 373, 382–384, 386	8 November 2006	s 383(1)
• Schs 1–16, 17★	no date	s 383(2)
• Sch 17★	8 November 2006	s 383(1)
Asylum and Immigration (Treatment of Claimants, etc) Act 2004		
• s 13	29 June 2006	s 48(3); SI 2006/1517
Care of Cathedrals (Amendment) Measure 2005		
• ss 8(4)(a), 12(1)	7 February 2006	s 20(3); instrument dated 6 February 2006
• Schs 1 (paras 1–8, 12), 2, 3 (paras 4(b), (e), (g), (i), 7)	7 February 2006	s 20(3); instrument dated 6 February 2006
Charities Act 2006		
• ss 1–11, 13(1)–(3), 14–33, 35–73, 75(6), 76	no date	s 79(2), (3)

STATUTE	IN FORCE	AUTHORITY
• ss 13(4), (5), 74, 75(4), (5), 77–80	8 November 2006	s 79(1)
• Schs 1 (paras 1, 2), 3, 3 (paras 1, 2, 4, 5), 4–7, 8 (paras 1–89, 90(1), (3), (4), 91–103, 104★, 105–173, 174(a)–(c), 175–208, 212), 9, 10	no date	s 79(2), (3)
• Sch 8 (paras 90(2), 104★, 174(d))	8 November 2006	s 79(1)
Childcare Act 2006		
• ss 1★, 2–10, 11–13★, 14–17, 22–38, 40, 47, 49–61, 62–64★, 65, 66, 67★, 68, 69★, 70, 72, 73, 74★, 76–82, 83★, 84★, 85–88, 90★, 91, 92★, 93–95, 96★, 97, 99★, 101, 102★	no date	s 109(2)
• ss 1★, 11–13★, 18–21, 39, 41–46, 62–64★, 67★, 69★, 71, 74★, 75, 83★, 84★, 89, 90★, 92★, 96★, 98, 99★, 100, 102★	20 December 2006	s 109(2); SI 2006/3360
• ss 104–111	11 July 2006	s 109(1)
• Schs 1, 2 (paras 2–44), 3	no date	s 109(2)
• Sch 2 (para 1)	11 July 2006	s 109(1)
Children Act 2004		
• ss 13★, 14★, 15, 16★, 56★	1 April 2006	s 67(2); SI 2006/927
• ss 25, 27	1 September 2006	s 67(3); SI 2006/870, 885
• s 26	31 March 2006	s 67(3); SI 2006/885
• ss 28(1)(a)–(c), (i), (2)★, (3), (4), 44★, 53–55★, 61	1 April 2006	s 67(3); SI 2006/885
• ss 30–34, 50★, 52★	1 October 2006	s 67(3); SI 2006/870, 885
• Schs 4 (paras 1–4, 6–9)★, 5 (Pts 1, 2, 4)★	1 April 2006	s 67(3); SI 2006/885
• Sch 5 (Pt 1)	1 September 2006	s 67(3); SI 2006/885
Children and Adoption Act 2006		
• ss 1–14, 16	no date	s 17(2)
• s 17	21 June 2006	
• Schs 1–3	no date	s 17(2)
Church of England (Miscellaneous Provisions) Measure 2006		
• ss 3–9, 11, 13, 16	1 October 2006	s 16(2); instrument dated 27 September 2006
• Sch 1	no date	
• Schs 2–6	1 October 2006	s 16(2); instrument dated 27 September 2006
Civil Aviation Act 2006		
• ss 1–5, 7–11	no date	s 14(3)–(5)
• s 14	8 November 2006	s 14(2)
• Sch 2	no date	s 14(3)–(5)
• Sch 1	8 November 2006	s 14(2)

STATUTE	IN FORCE	AUTHORITY
Civil Partnership Act 2004		
• Schs 5 (paras 30–37), 7 (para 10(4)(b), (5)(b), (9)(c))	6 April 2006	s 263; SI 2006/639
Clean Neighbourhods and Environment Act 2005		
• s 2★	1 April 2006	s 108(3); SI 2006/795
• ss 2★, 6★, 8★, 10★, 13★, 17★, 19★, 20★, 24★, 28★, 30★, 37★, 38★, 45–48★, 52★, 53★, 55–60★, 67★, 73–75★, 82★, 96–98★, 101★, 103★, 104★	16 March 2006	s 108(3); SI 2006/768
• ss 6★, 8★, 9★, 19(1)★, (6)★, 30(2)★, 55–57★, 59★, 60★, 66★, 67★, 74★, 75★, 80★, 81★, 83(1)★, (3)★, 96–98★	14 March 2006	s 108(3); SI 2006/795
• s 49(1), (2)★, (3), (6)★	7 March 2006	s 108(3); SI 2006/656
• ss 6–8★, 10★, 19–25★, 28★, 29★, 30(1)★, 31★, 34★, 37★, 38★, 45★, 48★, 49(2)★, (4), (6)★, (8)★, (9), 50★, 52★, 55★, 57–65★, 69–79★, 82★, 84★, 86★, 96★, 99–103	6 April 2006	s 108(3); SI 2006/656, 795
• ss 11–13★, 15–17★, 34★, 37★, 50★, 56★, 86★, 99★, 100★	27 October 2006	s 108(3); SI 2006/2797
• s 104★	4 August 2006	s 108(1), (2); SI 2006/1361
• Sch 1 (para 12(4)★)	14 March 2006	s 108(3); SI 2006/795
• Schs 1 (paras 2, 7(2)(a), (3), 8(2), 12(2), (5), (6))★, 4 (para 3(1)–(4), (6)★), 5 (Pts 2, 3, 5, 7, 9)★	6 April 2006	s 108(3); SI 2006/656, 795
• Sch 1 (paras 1, 3–6, 7(1), (2)(b), 8(1), (3), 9–11, 12(1), (3), 13, 14)★	1 October 2006	s 108(1)(a); SI 2006/2006
• Schs 4 (para 4★), 5 (Pt 4★)	16 March 2006	s 108(3); SI 2006/768
• Sch 5 (Pt 1★)	27 October 2006	s 108(3); SI 2006/2797
Climate Change and Sustainable Energy Act 2006		
• ss 15, 16	no date	s 28(3)
• ss 1, 3–5, 7–11, 13, 14, 18–21, 23–25	21 August 2006	s 28(1)
• ss 2, 6, 12, 22	1 January 2007	s 28(2)
• ss 26–29	21 June 2006	
• Schedule	no date	s 28(3)
Commissioner for Older People (Wales) Act 2006		
• ss 1–21	14 October 2006	s 23; SI 2006/2699
• ss 23–30	25 July 2006	
• Schs 1–4	14 October 2006	s 23; SI 2006/2699
Commons Act 2006		
• ss 1–8, 10–21, 24–44, 45★, 46, 47★, 48, 49★, 50, 51★	no date	s 56(1)
• ss 9, 57	28 June 2005	ss 9(7), 57(4)

STATUTE	IN FORCE	AUTHORITY
• ss 45★, 47★, 49★, 51★	1 October 2006	s 56(1); SI 2006/2504
• ss 54, 55	19 September 2006	s 56(2)
• ss 56, 58–63	19 July 2006	
• Schs 2, 3 (paras 1–8, 9★), 4 (paras 1–5, 6★, 7), 5 (paras 1–6, 7(1)★, (2)–(4), (5)★, 8), 6 (Pts 1–3★, 4, 5)	no date	s 56(1)
• Schs 3 (para 9★), 4 (para 6★), 5 (para 7(1), (5))★, 6 (Pts 1–3★)	1 October 2006	s 56(1); SI 2006/2504
• Sch 1	28 June 2005	s 9(7)
Companies Act 2006		
• ss 1–307★, 310–332★, 334–462★, 464–790★, 811(4)★, 812★, 814★, 829–867★, 869–1062★, 1064–1067★, 1069–1076★, 1081–1084★, 1093–1101★, 1108–1110★, 1112–1123★, 1125–1142★, 1149–1173★, 1180–1263★	no date	s 1300(2)
• ss 2★, 1068(1)–(4)★, (5), (6)★, (7)★, 1077–1080, 1085–1092, 1102–1107, 1111, 1114★, 1117★, 1120★, 1168★, 1173★	1 January 2007	s 1300(2); SI 2006/3428
• ss 1–307★, 308, 309, 310–332★, 333, 334–462★, 463, 464–790★, 791–810, 811(1)–(3), (4)★, 812★, 813, 814★, 815–828, 829–867★, 869–1062★, 1064–1067★, 1069–1076★, 1081–1084★, 1093–1101★, 1108–1110★, 1112–1123★, 1125–1142★, 1143–1148, 1149–1173★, 1180–1263★	20 January 2007	s 1300(2); SI 2006/3428
• ss 1063★, 1176–1179★, 1281★	6 April 2007	s 1300(2); SI 2006/3428
• ss 1265–1271, 1273, 1274, 1288–1294, 1296–1300	8 November 2006	s 1300(1)
• Schs 1–3★, 6–14★, 15 (para 11(2)★), 16★	no date	s 1300(2)
• Schs 1–3★, 4, 5, 6–14★, 15 (para 11(2)★), 16★	20 January 2007	s 1300(2); SI 2006/3428
• Sch 16★	6 April 2007	s 1300(2); SI 2006/3428
• Sch 15 (paras 1–10, 11(1), (3), 12–15)	8 November 2006	s 1300(1)
Compensation Act 2006		
• ss 4(1), (4), 7, 8(1)–(7), 10–13	no date	s 16(1)
• ss 1–3	25 July 2006 (*s 3 deemed always to have had effect, subject to a saving*)	s 16(3), (4)
• ss 4(2), (3), (5), (6), 5, 6, 8(8), 9, 14, 15	1 December 2006	s 16(1); SI 2006/3005
• Schedule	1 December 2006	s 16(1); SI 2006/3005
Consolidated Fund Act 2006	19 December 2006	

STATUTE	IN FORCE	AUTHORITY
Constitutional Reform Act 2005		
• ss 1–3, 5(1), (2), (5), 7, 9, 12, 13, 15★, 16, 17, 61★, 62–64, 65(4), 85(1)(b), (c), (2), 86–96, 98–114, 115–118★, 119, 122, 139, 145★, 146★	3 April 2006	s 148(1); SI 2006/1014
• ss 45, 46	27 February 2006	s 148(1); SI 2006/228
• ss 67–84	2 October 2006	s 148(1); SI 2006/1014
• s 85(1)(a)	2 April 2007	s 148(1); SI 2006/1014
• Schs 1, 2, 3 (paras 1, 2. 3(1), (2)★, (3)★, (4), (5)★, 4–6), 4 (paras 1–6, 13, 15–17, 19–41, 43–114, 115(1), (2)(a), (b), (d), (3), (4), (5)(a), 116, 117(1), (2)(a), (3), (4)(a), 118(1), (2), (4)–(6), 119, 120(1), (2), (3)(a), 121, 122(1), (2)(b), (3), (5), 123(1)–(3), 124, 126–141, 143–158, 160–211, 212(1), (2), (4), 213–215, 217–228, 230–279, 280(1), (3), 281–308, 310–330, 331(1), (2)(a), (b)(i), (ii), (iv), (v), (vii)–(ix), (3)–(5), 332–344, 346–350, 352–407), 12, (paras 1–25, 26★, 27–36), 13, 14★, 17 (paras 1–6), 18 (Pts 1, 2★, 3, 4)	3 April 2006	s 148(1); SI 2006/1014
Consumer Credit Act 2006		
• ss 1, 2, 3★, 4★, 5, 6★, 7(3), 8, 9★, 10★, 11, 12★, 13, 14(3), 15, 16, 17★, 19–23, 24(1), (3), (5), 25(1), (3), (4), 26, 27(1)★, (2)–(4), 28★, 29–33, 34(1), (2)★, (3)–(7), (8)★, (9), 35★, 36★, 37–58, 62, 64, 69	no date	s 71(2)
• ss 3★, 4★, 6★, 7(1), (2), 9★, 10★, 12★, 14(2), 17★, 18, 24(2), (4), (6), 25(2), (5), 27(1)★, 28★, 34(2)★, (8)★, 35★, 36★, 59–61, 63, 65–68, 69(2)–(5)	16 June 2006	s 71(2); SI 2006/1508
• s 14(1)	1 October 2006	s 71(2); SI 2006/1508
• s 71	30 March 2006	s 71(2)
• Schs 1, 3 (paras 1(2), 2–9, 11–29), 4	no date	s 71(2)
• Schs 2, 3 (para 1(1))	16 June 2006	s 71(2); SI 2006/1508
• Sch 3 (para 10)	1 October 2006	s 71(2); SI 2006/1508
Council Tax (New Valuation Lists for England) Act 2006	30 March 2006	
Countryside and Rights of Way Act 2000		
• ss 47–50★	2 May 2006	s 103(3); SI 2006/1172
• ss 47–50★, 69(2)★	11 May 2006	s 103(3); SI 2006/1279
• s 69(1)★, (3)★	6 December 2006	s 103(3); SI 2006/3257
• s 69(1)★, (3)–(5)★	1 April 2007	s 103(3); SI 2006/3257
• Schs 5 (paras 1, 6, 7, 9, 12–17)★, 16 (Pt II★)	2 May 2006	s 103(3); SI 2006/1172

STATUTE	IN FORCE	AUTHORITY
● Schs 5 (paras 1, 5, 6, 9, 12–17)★, 6 (para 23(8)★), 16 (Pt II★)	11 May 2006	s 103(3); SI 2006/1279
● Sch 6 (paras 1, 6, 9(5), 26)★	6 December 2006	s 103(3); SI 2006/3257
Crime (International Co-operation) Act 2003		
● ss 32–36, 42–46	1 November 2006	s 94(1); SI 2006/2811
Criminal Defence Service Act 2006		
● ss 1–4	2 October 2006	s 5(2); SI 2006/2491
● s 5	30 March 2006	s 5(2)
Criminal Justice Act 2003		
● ss 14★, 15(1)★, (2)★	1 January 2007	s 336(3); SI 2006/3217
● ss 33(1)★, 44–47, 48★	24 July 2006	s 336(3); SI 2006/1835
● Schs 35 (paras 5★, 6, 8, 9, 12), 37 (Pt 11★)	6 April 2006	s 336(3); SI 2006/751
● Sch 36 (para 3)	1 January 2007	s 336(3); SI 2006/3217
● Sch 36 (paras 40–42, 44, 47–55, 62–78)	24 July 2006	s 336(3); SI 2006/1835
Disability Rights Commission Act 1999		
● Sch 5★	4 December 2006	s 16(2); SI 2006/3189
Domestic Violence, Crime and Victims Act 2004		
● ss 17–20, 30, 56	8 January 2006	s 60; SI 2006/3423
● s 55	4 October 2006	s 60; SI 2006/2662
● Sch 10 (para 62)	8 January 2006	s 60; SI 2006/3423
Drugs Act 2005		
● s 20	1 October 2006	s 24(3); SI 2006/2136
Education Act 2002		
● ss 18(1)★, 134(2)★, (3)★, 136–138★, 140★, 146★, 154(3)★, 158(3)★, 178(2)★	6 November 2006	s 216(4), (5); SI 2006/2895
● ss 35–37★	1 April 2006	s 216(4), (5); SI 2006/879
● ss 47★, 48★	1 February 2006	s 216(4), (5); SI 2006/172
● s 175★	1 September 2006	s 216(4), (5); SI 2006/172
● Schs 2, 3 (paras 6–8★), 21 (paras 30, 107, 110(3)(b), (c))★, 22 (Pt 3★)	1 April 2006	s 216(4), (5); SI 2006/879
● Schs 4 (paras 3(6), 5–7, 12(2), (6), 13, 14)★, 22 (Pt 3★)	1 February 2006	s 216(4), (5); SI 2006/172
● Sch 12 (paras 3(1), (5), 4(2), 5)★	31 May 2006	s 216(4), (5); SI 2006/1336
● 12 (paras 3(3), (5), 4(2), (4), 5, 8, 10, 12(3))★, 21 (paras 5, 6, 10, 15, 55, 79, 125)★, 22★	6 November 2006	s 216(4), (5); SI 2006/2895

STATUTE	IN FORCE	AUTHORITY
Education Act 2005		
● ss 19–40, 41★, 42★, 43, 44★, 45★, 47★, 50, 51★, 52, 58–60★, 64, 65★, 66(1)–(5), (7)–(9), (11), (12), (14), 68, 69, 70★, 71, 73, 105★, 106★, 115★, 116★, 118★	1 September 2006	s 125(4); SI 2006/1338, 2129
● ss 55–57	1 April 2007	s 125(4); SI 2006/1338
● ss 65★, 66(6), (10), (13)	1 August 2006	s 125(4); SI 2006/2129
● Schs 2–4, 5★, 6, 7 (paras 5, 6–24★), 8★, 9 (paras 6, 7, 8–21★, 22, 24, 25, 27, 28–30★), 10 (paras 1–3, 4(1)–(3), (5)–(7), 5–7, 9–15), 11, 12 (paras 1–8, 9★, 10–13, 14★, 15, 16), 18 (paras 1, 6, 15)★, 19 (Pt 1, 2) ★	1 September 2006	s 125(4); SI 2006/1338
● Schs 10 (paras 4(4), 8)	1 August 2006	s 125(4); SI 2006/2129
● Sch 19 (Pt 1★)	1 April 2007	s 125(4); SI 2006/1338
Education and Inspections Act 2006		
● ss 1–3, 4★, 5★, 7–29, 31–35, 37, 38, 39★, 40★, 43–45★, 47★, 53★, 54(3)(a), 55, 56, 59–69, 72–84, 88–108, 109(8), 110, 113★, 114★, 116(1)(c)★, (2)★, 118–148★, 150–156★, 160, 164–167, 169–171, 173★, 176	no date	s 188(3)
● ss 6, 43★, 45★, 48–52, 54(1), (2), (3)(b), 58, 162, 163, 168, 172, 173★, 174, 177–179	8 January 2007	s 188(2), (3); SI 2006/3400
● s 5★	8 February 2007	s 188(3); SI 2006/3400
● ss 4★, 39★, 41, 42, 44★, 46, 47★, 53★	27 February 2007	s 188(3); SI 2006/3400
● ss 40★, 112(1)–(3), 116(1)(a)★, (b)★, 117★, 159★	12 December 2006	s 188(3); SI 2006/2990
● ss 86, 87, 109(1)–(7), (9)–(11), 111, 112–114★, 116–148★, 150–156★, 159★, 180–183, 185–191	8 November 2006	s 188(1)
● Schs 2–4, 5★, 6–10, 11 (paras 2(2)★, (3), 4, 5(2)–(4), 6(5), 7(2), (3), 12(4)), 12–14, 15 (paras 1–6, 8, 9★), 17, 18 (Pts 3–5, 6★)	no date	s 188(3)
● Schs 1, 18 (Pts 2, 6★)	8 January 2007	s 188(2), (3); SI 2006/3400
● Schs 5★, 18 (Pt 6★)	8 February 2007	s 188(3); SI 2006/3400
● Sch 18 (Pt 6★)	27 February 2007	s 188(3); SI 2006/3400
● Schs 11 (paras 1, 2(1), (2)★, 3, 5(1), 6(1)–(4), 7(1), 8–11, 12(1)–(3), 13), 15 (paras 7, 9★), 18 (Pt 6★)	12 December 2006	s 188(3); SI 2006/2990
● Schs 16, 18 (Pt 1)	8 November 2006	s 188(1)

STATUTE	IN FORCE	AUTHORITY
Electoral Administration Act 2006		
• ss 1(2), (5), 2(2), (4)–(9), (12), 5(10), 7, 13(2), (3), 31(4)★, 38(4), (5), 42–44★, 52(4)–(6)★, 58, 59, 61(1)★, (5)★, 68, 73(3)	no date	s 77(2)
• ss 1(1), (3), (4), (6)–(11), 2(1), (3), (10), (11), (13), 3, 4, 5(1)–(9), 6, 8, 75–79	11 July 2006	s 77(1)
• ss 9, 15, 23(1), (3)★, 25, 27, 39, 40, 47★, 48, 50, 51, 52(1)–(3), 53–57, 61(1)★, (2)–(4), (5)★, 62, 64, 65, 67	11 September 2006	s 77(2); SI 2006/1972, 2268
• ss 10–12, 13(1), 14, 16–22, 23(2), (3)★, (4), 24, 26, 28, 30, 31(1)–(3), (4)★, (5)–(9), 32–37, 38(1)–(3), (6), 41(1)–(6), (8), (9), 45, 46, 47★, 49, 52(4)–(6)★, 66, 69–72, 73(1), (2), 75★	1 January 2007	s 77(2); SI 2006/3412
• s 29	31 January 2007	s 77(2); SI 2006/3412
• Schs 1 (paras 75(1)★, 90, 95, 99★, 107, 110, 134, 135, 143(3)), 2★	no date	s 77(2)
• Schs 1 (paras 1–44, 49–54, 69, 70, 72–74, 75(1)★, (2), 76–81, 86–89, 91–94, 103, 105, 106, 108, 109, 113–115, 128–132, 136, 137), 2★	1 January 2007	s 77(2); SI 2006/3412
• Schs 1 (paras 71, 97, 98, 99★, 100–102, 104, 111, 112, 116–127, 138–142, 143(1), (2), 144–156), 2★	11 September 2006	s 77(2); SI 2006/1972, 2268
• Sch 1 (paras 82–85)	31 January 2007	s 77(2); SI 2006/3412
Emergency Workers (Obstruction) Act 2006		
• ss 1–6	no date	s 7(2)
• s 7	8 November 2006	s 7(2)
Energy Act 2004		
• ss 145(2), (4), 147(5), 149(2), (4), (10), 151, 153	14 August 2006	s 198(2); SI 2006/1964
Environment Act 1995		
• Schs 22 (paras 27(b), (c), 88, 95), 24★	15 May 2006	s 125(2); SI 2006/934
Equality Act 2006		
• ss 6–32, 44–51, 52(1)–(5), (7)–(9), 53–69, 72–80	no date	s 93(1)
• ss 1, 3–5, 33–39, 52(6), 70, 71, 81, 84★, 85★, 87–90, 92	18 April 2006	s 93(1); SI 2006/1082
• ss 41, 42, 86, 93–95	16 February 2006	s 93(1)
• ss 83, 84★, 85★	6 April 2007	s 93(1); SI 2006/1082
• Schs 2, 3 (paras 1–4, 6–38, 40–61), 4	no date	s 93(1)
• Schs 1, 3 (para 35(b))	18 April 2006	s 93(1); SI 2006/1082
European Union (Accessions) Act 2006	16 February 2006	

STATUTE	IN FORCE	AUTHORITY
Finance Act 2004		
• appointed date for the purposes of s 77(1)	6 April 2007	s 77(1); SI 2006/3240
• appointed date for the purposes of s 4	22 February 2006	s 4(5); SI 2006/201
Finance Act 2006		
• appointed date for the purposes of ss 19, 94, 172(8)–(15)	no date	ss 19(8), 94(5), 172(16)
• appointed date for the purposes of s 2	1 October 2006	s 2(3); SI 2006/2367
• appointed date for the purposes of s 18(1)–(3)	1 September 2006	s 18(4); SI 2006/2149
• appointed date for the purposes of s 53(1)	1 January 2007	s 53(1); SI 2006/3399
• s 1	22 March 2006 (*at 6 pm*)	s 1(2)
• ss 3, 4	26 March 2006 (*at midnight*)	ss 3(2), 4(2)
• s 7	1 September 2006	s 7(9)
• s 157	5 December 2005	s 157(6)
• s 159	6 April 2006	s 159(2)
• appointed date for the purposes of Sch 2	no date	s 28(3)
• Schs 21–23	6 April 2006	ss 158(2), 160(2), 161(2)
• remaining provisions	19 July 2006	see specific provisions of the Act
Finance (No 2) Act 2005		
• appointed date for the purposes of s 17(1)★	1 April 2006	s 19(1); SI 2006/982
• appointed date for the purposes of s 17(1)★	6 April 2006	s 19(1); SI 2006/982
Fraud Act 2006		
• ss 1–13	15 January 2007	s 15(1); SI 2006/3200
• ss 15, 16	8 November 2006	s 15(1)
• Schs 1–3	15 January 2007	s 15(1); SI 2006/3200
Gambling Act 2005		
• ss 7(5)–(7), 150–153, 154(1)★, (2)(a), (b)★, (c), (3)–(5), 155–158, 159–165★, 167–171, 174(1), 176(1), (2), 181, 184, 186–190, 192, 194–196, 204★, 205–213, 235(2)(a), (3)(f), (4), 236, 303, 304, 309(1), 311(1), 313(1), 317–326, 342★, 343, 346(1)(l), (2), (3)	30 April 2007	s 358(1); SI 2006/3272, 3361

STATUTE	IN FORCE	AUTHORITY
• ss 10(3), 24(9), 27, 28★, 29, 33–64, 65(1)★, (3)–(5)★, 66–74★, 82, 83, 89(2), (3), 108, 110–112, 116(1), (2)(a), 117–120★, 121, 123, 128★, 130★, 131, 134, 135, 137–139, 172, 173, 174(2)–(8), 176(3), 177–180, 182, 183, 185, 191, 193, 197–203, 214–232, 234, 242–246, 247(1), 248(1), 249, 250, 258(1)–(4), (5)★, 259–265, 269, 270, 271(1), (3)–(7), 272, 273(1), (3)–(5), 275, 279–282, 283(1), (3), (4), 286, 287, 289(1), (3)★, 290, 291★, 292–294, 296–302, 305–308, 309(2), 310(2), 311(2), 312(1)–(3), 313(2), 314–316, 327–340, 341★, 344, 345★, 346(1)(a)–(k), (m)–(o), 347, 348, 356(3)	1 September 2007	s 358(1); SI 2006/3272
• ss 28★, 65(1)★, (3)–(5)★, 66–74★, 75(3), 76(4)–(6), 77, 78, 79★, 80★, 81, 84–88, 89(1), (4)–(7), 90–107, 109, 113–115, 116(2)(b), (c), (3)–(5), 117–120★, 122, 124–126, 128★, 129, 130★, 132, 133, 136, 140–149, 235(1), (2)(b)–(i), (3)(a)–(e), (5), 237–241, 248(2), 251–257, 288, 291★, 341★, 342★, 345★, 350, 351, 353	1 January 2007	s 358(1); SI 2006/3272, 3361
• ss 154(1)★, (2)(b)★, 247(2), 289(2), (3)★	13 November 2006	s 358(1); SI 2006/2964
• ss 159–165★, 175, 204★, 266–268, 271(2), 273(2), 276–278, 283(2), 284, 310(1), 312(4)	1 June 2007	s 358(1); SI 2006/3272
• ss 166, 349	31 March 2006	s 358(1); SI 2006/631
• Schs 3 (paras 1, 3), 10 (paras 2–6★, 8–11★, 12(b), 14, 18–20, 22★), 11 (paras 1–8★, 9, 10–12★, 13–19, 20★, 21–29, 30★, 31★, 32–63), 12 (paras 1–11★, 12–14, 22, 24, 25★), 13 (paras 1–7★, 8–10, 21★), 14 (paras 3–7★, 9–12★, 13(b), 18–20, 22★), 15, 16 (paras 1, 2, 4, 8, 10, 11, 12★, 15, 17, 18, 20, 21), 17★	1 September 2007	s 358(1); SI 2006/3272
• Schs 7 (paras 1–22), 8, 16 (para 12★)	1 January 2007	s 358(1); SI 2006/3272, 3361
• Sch 7 (para 23)	5 December 2006	s 358(1); SI 2006/3220
• Schs 9, 12 (paras 1–11★, 15–21, 23, 25★, 26–31), 13 (paras 1–7★, 11–20, 21★, 22, 23)	1 June 2007	s 358(1); SI 2006/3272
• Schs 10 (paras 1, 7(1), (2), (3)★), 14 (paras 1, 8(1), (2), (3)★)	13 November 2006	s 358(1); SI 2006/2964
• Sch 10 (paras 2–6★, 7(3)★, 8–11★, 12(a), 13, 15–17, 21, 22★, 23, 24), 14 (paras 2, 3–7★, 8(3)★, 9–12★, 13(a), 14–17, 21, 22★, 23, 24)	30 April 2007	s 358(1); SI 2006/3272, 3361

STATUTE	IN FORCE	AUTHORITY
Gangmasters (Licensing) Act 2004		
• ss 6(1)★, 11, 12★, 13(3), 14, 27★	1 October 2006	s 29(1); SI 2006/2406
• s 13(1)★, (2)★, (4)★	1 December 2006	s 29(1); SI 2006/2906
Government of Wales Act 2006		
• Sections 1–94, 97–106, 116, 123, 127, 130–156, Sch 1, Sch 2 paras 1–4, 7–11, Schs 3, 4, 6, 8, 9, Sch 10 paras 1–11, 13–20, 22–32, 34–40, 62–97, and certain repeals in Sch 12 come into force immediately after the 2007 election (except for specified purposes) or otherwise on the day on which the first appointment is made under s 46: s 161(1), (4), (6). Schedule 10 paras 41–55 come into force on the day on which the first appointment is made under s 46: s 161(4)(c).	no date	
• ss 107, 108, 110–115	no date	s 105
• ss 95, 96, 109, 119, 120(3), (7), 125, 157–159, 160(2)–(4), 161, 162, 164–166	25 July 2006	s 161(2)
• ss 117, 118, 120(1), (2), (4)–(6), (8), 121, 122, 124, 126, 128, 129	1 April 2007	s 161(3)
• Schs 2 (paras 5, 6, 12), 5, 7, 10 (para 61), 11, 12★	25 July 2006	s 161(2)
• Schs 10 (paras 12, 21, 33), 12★	1 April 2007	s 161(3)
Health Act 2006		
• ss 1–15, 17–25★, 26–32, 34★, 35★, 36–56, 72, 76–78	no date	s 83(3)–(8)
• ss 74, 75, 79, 80(3), (7), (8), 81–84 and any other provision of the Act in so far as it confers power to make an order or regulations or defines any expression relevant to the exercise of any such power	19 July 2006	s 83(1)
• ss 14–16, 33, 57, 58–62★, 63–69, 70★, 71★	1 October 2006	s 83(1); SI 2006/2603
• ss 17–25★	1 January 2007	s 83(1); SI 2006/3125
• ss 34★, 35★	28 February 2007	s 83(1); SI 2006/3125
• ss 58–62★, 70★, 71★	28 September 2006	s 83(1); SI 2006/2603
• s 73	29 January 2007	s 83(1); SI 2006/3125
• Schs 1–3, 8 (paras 6–25, 29, 30, 32–34, 37–44, 45(1)★, (2), 46, 49★, 50, 55, 62), 9★	no date	s 83(3)–(8)
• Schs 4, 5★, 6★, 7, 8 (paras 1–4, 26–28, 31, 35, 45(1)★, (3), 47, 48, 49★, 51, 52, 56–61), 9★	1 October 2006	s 83(1); SI 2006/2603
• Schs 5★, 6★	28 September 2006	s 83(1); SI 2006/2603
• Sch 8 (paras 36, 53, 54)	19 July 2006	s 83(1)

STATUTE	IN FORCE	AUTHORITY
Health and Social Care Act 2001		
• s 40★	28 February 2006	s 70(2); SI 2006/481
• s 40★	1 April 2006	s 70(2); SI 2006/481
• Sch 3★	28 February 2006	s 70(2); SI 2006/481
• Schs 3★, 5 (paras 5(12)(a), 11(4))★, 6★	1 April 2006	s 70(2); SI 2006/481
Health and Social Care (Community Health and Standards) Act 2003		
• ss 170★, 171(1)★, (2)★, 172(2)★, 177★, 178★, 183★	1 April 2006	s 199; SI 2006/345
• s 105(1)★, (3)–(7)★	1 August 2006	s 199; SI 2006/1680
• s 105(1)★, (6)★	27 June 2006	s 199; SI 2006/1680
• ss 113(1)★, (3)★, (4)★, 114(1)★, (2)★, (5)★, (6)★, 115★	1 September 2006	s 199; SI 2006/1680
• s 150(1)–(7)★, (10)–(14)★	28 January 2007	s 199; SI 2006/3397
• ss 151–164, 166, 168, 169	29 January 2007	s 199; SI 2006/3397
• ss 170★, 171(1)★, 172(1)★, 173★, 177(1)–(11)★, 179(1)★, 180★, 182(2), 183★	15 February 2006	s 199; SI 2006/345
• s 185★	27 October 2006	s 199; SI 2006/2817
• Sch 9 (para 15)	15 January 2007	s 199; SI 2006/3397
• Schs 10, 14★	29 January 2007	s 199; SI 2006/3397
• Schs 11 (paras 2, 3, 7, 11, 17–20, 21(1), (5), 22(1), (3)(b), 24(b), 28–31, 36(b), 45, 46(1), (2)(b), (3)(b), (c), 50, 66, 67(b), 69, 72)★, 14★	1 April 2006	s 199; SI 2006/345
• Schs 11 (paras 7, 14, 15, 39)★, 14★	15 February 2006	s 199; SI 2006/345
Higher Education Act 2004		
&qsse23, 24(1)–(5), (6)★, 25, 43, 45	14 January 2006	s 52(2); SI 2006/51
• Sch 6 (paras 7–9★), 7★	14 January 2006	s 52(2); SI 2006/51
Housing Act 2004		
• ss 1★, 3★, 5–8★, 10–17★, 19–26★, 28–30★, 32–54★, 55(3–(6)★, 58–70★, 72–78★, 82–93★, 95–122★, 124–133★, 135–147★, 229–231★, 232, 235, 236, 238–243	16 June 2006	s 270(4), (5); SI 2006/1535
• 1★, 3–8★, 10–17★, 19–26★, 28–30★, 32–52★, 54★, 55(3)★, (4)★, (5)(c)★, (6)★, 58–70★, 72(2)★, (3)★, (5)–(7)★, 75–78★, 82–93★, 95(2)★, (4)★, (6)★, 96–122★, 124–133★, 135–147★, 232★, 235★, 236★, 238–243★	6 April 2006	s 270(4), (5); SI 2006/1060
• ss 72(1)★, (4)★, (8)–(10)★, 73★, 74★, 95(1)★, (3)★, (5)★, (7)–(9)★, 96★, 134★	6 July 2006	s 270(4), (5); SI 2006/1060
• ss 225★, 226★	2 January 2007	s 270(4), (5); SI 2006/3191
• Schs 1–7★, 13★, 15 (paras 2–6, 9–34, 36, 38–44), 16★	16 June 2006	s 270(4), (5); SI 2006/1535

STATUTE	IN FORCE	AUTHORITY
• Schs 1–7★, 15 (paras 2–6, 8–36, 38–44)★, 16★	6 April 2006	s 270(4), (5); SI 2006/1060
Sch 15 (para 47★)	2 January 2007	s 270(4), (5); SI 2006/3191
Housing Corporation (Delegation) etc Act 2006	19 July 2006	
Human Tissue Act 2004		
• ss 1–4★, 6★, 7★, 9–12★, 16–25★, 30★, 31★, 33★, 34★, 37★, 39–41★, 43–46★, 49★, 50★, 52–54★, 58(1)★, (2)★	1 September 2006	s 60(2); SI 2006/1997, 2169
• ss 5★, 8★	1 December 2006	s 60(2); SI 2006/1997, 2169
• ss 16–25★, 37★, 39★, 41★, 44★, 48–54★, 56★, 58(1)★, (2)★	1 March 2006	s 60(2); SI 2006/404
• ss 16–25★	7 April 2006	s 60(2); SI 2006/404
• ss 16–24★, 37★, 39–41★, 44★, 52–54★, 58(1)★, (2)★	31 July 2006	s 60(2); SI 2006/1997, 2169
• Schs 3–5★, 6 (paras 1–5, 7)★, 7★	1 September 2006	s 60(2); SI 2006/1997, 2169
• Schs 3★, 5★, 6 (para 5★)	1 March 2006	s 60(2); SI 2006/404
• Schs 3★, 5★, 6 (para 5★)	7 April 2006	s 60(2); SI 2006/404
Identity Cards Act 2006		
• ss 1(1)–(4), (5)–(8)★, 2–24, 27–29, 31–35, 39, 41, 42★	no date	s 44(3)
• ss 1(5)–(8)★, 25, 26, 30(1)–(3), 40, 42★	7 June 2006	s 44(3); SI 2006/1439
• ss 36, 38	30 May 2006	s 44(5)
• s 37	30 September 2006	s 44(3); SI 2006/2602
• s 44	30 March 2006	
• Sch 1	no date	s 44(3)
• Sch 2	7 June 2006	s 44(3); SI 2006/1439
Immigration, Asylum and Nationality Act 2006		
• ss 4, 8, 12, 13, 15–18, 20–22, 24–26, 31–39, 44, 47, 50–52	no date	s 62
• ss 1–3, 5–7, 11, 19, 23, 27–29, 40–42, 46, 49, 53–55, 59	31 August 2006	s 62; SI 2006/2226
• s 9	13 November 2006	s 62; SI 2006/2838
• ss 10, 30, 43(1)–(4), (7), 48, 56, 57, 60	16 June 2006	s 62; SI 2006/1497
• s 45	30 June 2006	s 62; SI 2006/1497
• s 58	4 December 2006	s 62; SI 2006/2838
• ss 62–64	30 March 2006	
• Schs 1 (para 11), 2, 3★	no date	s 62
• Schs 1 (paras 1–10, 12–14), 3★	31 August 2006	s 62; SI 2006/2226
• Sch 3★	16 June 2006	s 62; SI 2006/1497

STATUTE	IN FORCE	AUTHORITY
International Development (Reporting and Transparency) Act 2006		
• ss 1–6	25 October 2006	s 9(2)
• ss 7–9	25 July 2006	
• Schedule	25 October 2006	s 9(2)
Investment Exchanges and Clearing Houses Act 2006	20 December 2006	s 5(2)
Legislative and Regulatory Reform Act 2006	8 January 2007	s 33
Local Government Act 2003		
• s 63	1 April 2007	s 128(4); SI 2006/3339
London Olympics Games and Paralympic Games Act 2006		
• ss 13–16, 39(1)	no date	s 40(2)
• ss 1, 3–5, 34, 35(1), (2), 36(3)(a), (d), 40–42	30 March 2006	s 40(1)
• ss 2, 6, 7, 8(1)–(8), 9–12, 17–31, 35(3)–(5), 36(1), (2), (3)(b), (c), (4), (5)	30 May 2006	s 40(2); SI 2006/1118
• Sch 3 (paras 12–14)	no date	s 40(2)
• Schs 1, 3 (paras 1–11), 4	30 March 2006	s 40(1)
• Sch 2	30 May 2006	s 40(2); SI 2006/1118
Mental Capacity Act 2005		
• ss 30–34★	1 July 2007	s 68; SI 2006/2814, 3473
• ss 30–34★	1 October 2008	s 68; SI 2006/2814, 3473
• ss 35–41★	1 November 2006	s 68; SI 2006/2814
• ss 35–41★	1 April 2007	s 68; SI 2006/2814
Merchant Shipping (Pollution) Act 2006		
• ss 1(1), (2)(a), (3)–(6), 2, 4	30 March 2006	
• ss 1(2)(b), 3	30 May 2006	s 4(2)
National Health Service Act 2006		
• *To the extent that this Act re-enacts a provision to which s 277(4) applies, and the provision has not come into force before 1 March 2007, the re-enactment by this Act of the provision does not come into force until the provision which is re-enacted comes into force; and the re-enactment comes into force immediately after, and to the extent that, the provision which is re-enacted comes into force.*	no date	s 277(4)
• remaining provisions	1 March 2007	s 277(1)

STATUTE	IN FORCE	AUTHORITY
National Health Service (Consequential Provisions) Act 2006		
• To the extent that this Act repeals or revokes a provision to which s 8(5) applies, and the provision has not come into force before 1 March 2007, the repeal or revocation by this Act of the provision does not come into force until the provision which is repealed or revoked comes into force; and the repeal or revocation comes into force immediately after, and to the extent that, the provision which is re-enacted comes into force.	no date	s 8(5)
• remaining provisions	1 March 2007	s 8(2)
National Health Service (Wales) Act 2006		
• To the extent that this Act re-enacts a provision to which s 208(4) applies, and the provision has not come into force before 1 March 2007, the re-enactment by this Act of the provision does not come into force until the provision which is re-enacted comes into force; and the re-enactment comes into force immediately after, and to the extent that, the provision which is re-enacted comes into force.	no date	s 208(4)
• remaining provisions	1 March 2007	s 208(1)
National Insurance Contributions Act 2006	30 March 2006	s 9
National Lottery Act 2006		
• ss 5, 7(3)★, 9, 13★	no date	s 22(1)
• ss 1–4, 8, 10–12	1 October 2006	s 22(1); SI 2006/2630
• ss 6, 16, 22–24	11 July 2006	s 22(1)
• ss 7(1), (2), (3)★, 13★, 15, 17–20	1 December 2006	s 22(1); SI 2006/3201
• s 14	1 August 2006	s 22(1); SI 2006/2177
• Sch 1	no date	s 22(1)
• Sch 2	1 August 2006	s 22(1); SI 2006/2177
• Sch 3	1 December 2006	s 22(1); SI 2006/3201
Nationality, Immigration and Asylum Act 2002		
• s 9★	5 June 2006	s 162(1); SI 2006/1498
• s 9★	1 July 2006	s 162(1); SI 2006/1498
• s 10(5)(b)	21 December 2006	s 162(1); SI 2006/3144
Natural Environment and Rural Communities Act 2006		
• ss 61(1)★, (2)–(5), 72–76	no date	s 107
• ss 1(1)–(3), (5), 2, 5, 9, 11(1), (2)(b), 13, 14, 15(2)–(6), 16, 29, 66–71★, 98	2 May 2006	s 107; SI 2006/1176
• ss 1(4), 3, 4, 6–8, 10, 11(2)(a), (c), (3)–(7), 12, 15(1), 17–28, 30–46, 48–51, 54, 55, 58, 60, 61(1)★, (6), 62–65, 87–89, 91–97, 101	1 October 2006	s 107; SI 2006/2541

STATUTE	IN FORCE	AUTHORITY
• ss 47, 56, 57, 78, 79, 81–86	31 May 2006	s 107; SI 2006/1382
• ss 59, 99	30 May 2006	s 107(3)(a), (7)(a)
• ss 66–71★	16 November 2006	s 107; SI 2006/2992
• ss 100, 102–104, 106–109	30 March 2006	
• Schs 11 (paras 174–176), 12★	no date	s 107
• Schs 1, 11 (paras 34(1), (2), 39(1), (2), 58(1), (2), 60(1), (2), 61(1), (3), 105, 153(1), (2))★, 12★	2 May 2006	s 107; SI 2006/1176
• Schs 2–4, 8–10, 11 (paras 1–33, 34(1)★, (2)★, (3), 35–38, 39(1)★, (2)★, (3), 40–57, 58(1)★, (2)★, (3), 59, 60(1)★, (2)★, (3), 61(1)★, (2), (3)★, (4), (5), 62–99, 102–104, 105★, 107–152, 153(1)★, (2)★, (3), 154–170, 172), 12★	1 October 2006	s 107; SI 2006/2541
• Schs 5–7	31 May 2006	s 107; SI 2006/1382
NHS Redress Act 2006		
• ss 1–17	no date	s 19(3), (4)
• ss 18, 19	8 November 2006	s 19(2)
Parliamentary Costs Act 2006	1 April 2007	s 19(1)
Pastoral (Amendment) Measure 2006	1 January 2007	s 2(2); instrument dated 22 December 2006
Pensions Act 2004		
• ss 18(3)(b), (4)(b), 86(2), 160(7)★, 165, 169(1), (2)(a)–(c), 173(1)(a), (f), (3)(a), (e)–(g), (j), 204(3), 247, 248, 249(1), (2)★, (3)★, 250★, 251★, 254, 267, 268, 306(2)(j), (k), (4), (5), 321	6 April 2006	s 322(1); SI 2006/560
• ss 117(7)(b)★, 178(3)★, (8)★	1 January 2007	s 322(1); SI 2006/2272
• ss 117(7)(b)★, 178(3)★, (8)★	1 March 2007	s 322(1); SI 2006/2272
• s 132(6), 153(1)–(3), (4)★, (5), (6), (7)★, (8), 154(2)(b), (3)–(5), 155(1)★, (2), (3), (4)★, 156(1)★, (2)★, (3), (4), (5)★, (6)★, 157(1)★, (2)–(6), (7)★, (8), (9)★, 158, 159, 160(4), 172(5)(d)	6 April 2007	s 322(1); SI 2006/2272
• ss 151(8)★, 173(1)(b)★, 177(9)(b)	1 April 2006	s 322(1); SI 2006/560
• ss 153(4)★, (7)★, 155(1)★, (4)★, 156(1)★, (2)★, (5)★, (6)★, 157(1)★, (7)★, (9)★	1 November 2006	s 322(1); SI 2006/2272
• ss 177(4)★, (5), (8), 178(4)★, (5), (7)★, (9)★	1 September 2006	s 322(1); SI 2006/2272
• ss 177(4)★, 178(4)★, (6)★, (7)★, (9)★	1 October 2006	s 322(1); SI 2006/2272
• s 178(6)★	1 December 2006	s 322(1); SI 2006/2272
• ss 249(2)★, 250★, 251★	9 March 2006	s 322(1); SI 2006/560
• Schs 4 (para 18), 5 (para 18(2)(a)–(e)), 12 (paras 5(2), 10, 11(1)★, (2), 14–17, 21, 22, 27, 29, 33, 48, 57, 58, 62(a), (b), 64, 65, 76(3)★), 13★	6 April 2006	s 322(1); SI 2006/560
• Sch 12 (para 11(1), (3))★	1 October 2006	s 322(1); SI 2006/2272
• Sch 12 (para 11(1), (3))★	1 January 2007	s 322(1); SI 2006/2272

STATUTE	IN FORCE	AUTHORITY
● Sch 13★	6 April 2007	s 322(1); SI 2006/2272
Planning and Compulsory Purchase Act 2004		
● ss 40★, 41★, 49★	10 May 2006	s 121; SI 2006/1061
● ss 42(1)★, (5)–(9)★	10 August 2006	s 121; SI 2006/1061
● s 53★	1 April 2006	s 121; SI 2006/931
● ss 79–83★, 84–88, 111(1), 112	7 June 2006	s 121; SI 2006/1281
● Sch 1★	10 May 2006	s 121; SI 2006/1061
● Sch 3 (paras 1–5, 6–8★, 9, 10–12★, 13–27), 4, 6 (para 2), 9★	7 June 2006	s 121; SI 2006/1281
● Sch 9★	10 August 2006	s 121; SI 2006/1061
Police and Justice Act 2006		
● ss 1, 3, 4, 6–8, 12–21, 23–39, 41, 43(1), 45★, 46	no date	s 53
● ss 11, 44, 45★, 47, 48	15 January 2007	s 53(1); SI 2006/3364
● ss 43(2)–(6), 49–51, 53–55	8 November 2006	s 53(2)
● Schs 1 (paras 1–55, 57–72, 74–92), 2 (paras 7(1), (2), (3)(b), (c), (4), 9–13, 16–23, 27–30), 3–11, 13 (paras 4, 5), 14 (paras 1, 2, 5, 7–24, 26, 29–33, 35–38, 40–46, 48, 50–58, 60, 62), 15 (Pts 1(A), (B)★, 2–4)	no date	s 53
● Schs 2 (paras 7(3)(a), 14, 15, 24–26), 13 (para 6), 14 (paras 34, 39, 47, 49, 59), 15 (Pt 1(B)★)	8 November 2006	s 53(2)
● Schs 2 (paras 1–6, 8), 13 (paras 1–3, 7–29, 31–35), 14 (paras 3, 4, 61), 15 (Pt 1(B)★)	15 January 2007	s 53(1); SI 2006/3364
Political Parties, Elections and Referendums Act 2000		
● s 143	1 January 2007	s 163(2); SI 2006/3416
● Sch 18 (para 14)	1 January 2007	s 163(2); SI 2006/3416
Private Security Industry Act 2001		
● ss 14, 15(1), (2)(a)–(e), (f)(i), (ii)★, (g), (3)(a)★, (b)★, (c), (d), (4)★, (5)–(7), (8)★, 16, 18	20 March 2006	s 26(2); SI 2006/392
Racial and Religious Hatred Act 2006	no date	s 3(2)
Railways Act 2005		
● ss 1(10), 42, 43, 45(1)★, 56(3)(b), (c)	1 August 2006	s 60(2); SI 2006/1951
● ss 3(1)★, (2)★, (4), (8)(a)★, (9)★, (10)★, (11)(b)★, 51(1)(b), (5)	1 April 2006	s 60(2); SI 2006/266
● ss 3(1)★, (5), (6)★, 22–39, 41, 44, 45(1)★, (3)–(9)	1 December 2006	s 60(2); SI 2006/2911
Schs 1 (paras 12, 21(1)★, (3), (4)–(8)★, 22–26★, 32(2)★, 34, 36(b)), 7, 8, 11 (paras 1★, 2–5, 7(1), (3)–(6), 10, 11, 13), 12 (paras 1(1)★, (2), 14(1)★, (2), (5)(a)), 13★	1 December 2006	s 60(2); SI 2006/2911

STATUTE	IN FORCE	AUTHORITY
• Sch 3 (paras 1, 12)	7 February 2006	s 60(2); SI 2006/266
• Schs 3 (paras 2–11, 13–15), 12 (paras 4, 6, 12), 13★	1 April 2006	s 60(2); SI 2006/266
• Schs 12 (para 17(1)★, (4)–(6)), 13★	1 August 2006	s 60(2); SI 2006/1951
Road Safety Act 2006		
• ss 2–4, 6–41, 43–48, 50, 52–57	no date	s 61(1), (8)
• ss 1, 49(1)	8 January 2007	s 61(7)
• ss 51, 58, 60–63	8 November 2006	s 61(9)
• Schs 1–6, 7★	no date	s 61(1)
• Sch 7★	8 November 2006	s 61(9)
Safeguarding Vulnerable Groups Act 2006		
• ss 1–54, 56–61, 64, 66, 67	no date	s 65
• s 65	8 November 2006	s 65
• Schs 1–10	no date	s 65
Serious Organised Crime and Police Act 2005		
• ss 1(1)★, 6, 43, 44(1), 55(2)	1 March 2006	s 178(8); SI 2006/378
• s 1(1)★, 2–5, 7, 11–16, 19–26, 28–38, 40, 41, 45–51, 53, 56, 57, 71–76, 78–81, 157	1 April 2006	s 178(8); SI 2006/378
• s 102	15 May 2006	s 178(8); SI 2006/1085
• s 161(1)	8 May 2006	s 178(8); SI 2006/1085
• appointed date for the purposes of s 161(2)	8 May 2006	s 161(4); SI 2006/1085
• ss 163(1)–(3)★, 165(1)(b), (2), (3)	6 April 2006	s 178(8); SI 2006/378
• s 163(2)★	25 September 2006	s 178(8); SI 2006/2182
• Schs 1 (paras 1–8, 9(1)–(3), 10, 11, 14, 15(1)–(4), 16–21)★, 2 (para 8)	1 March 2006	s 178(8); SI 2006/378
• Schs 1 (paras 9(4), 12, 13, 15(5)), 2 (paras 1–7, 9–11), 4 (paras 1–11, 17–20, 22–24, 28–35, 41, 43–87, 93–106, 111, 112, 122–169, 173–200), 17 (Pt 2★)	1 April 2006	s 178(8); SI 2006/378
• Sch 10 (paras 1–6)★	20 July 2006	s 178(8); SI 2006/1871, 2182
• Schs 13 (paras 9, 10, 12), 17 (Pt 2★)	8 May 2006	s 178(8); SI 2006/1085
Social Security Act 1998		
• s 67	1 October 2006	s 87(2); SI 2006/2376
Sustainable and Secure Buildings Act 2004		
• ss 2, 7★, 8, 9	1 February 2006	s 11(3); SI 2006/224
Terrorism Act 2006		
• ss 1–22, 26–36, 37(1)–(4), 38	13 April 2006	s 39(2); SI 2006/1013
• ss 23–25	25 July 2006	s 39(2); SI 2006/1936
• s 39	30 March 2006	s 39(2)
• Schs 1, 2, 3★	13 April 2006	s 39(2); SI 2006/1013
• Sch 3★	25 July 2006	s 39(2); SI 2006/1936

STATUTE	IN FORCE	AUTHORITY
Tobacco Advertising and Promotion Act 2002		
• s 2★	26 September 2006	s 22(1); SI 2006/2372
Traffic Management Act 2004		
• ss 5(4)★, (5)★, 10★, 16–31★, 72–90★, 92–95★, 96	26 October 2006	s 99(1); SI 2006/2826
• s 94★	29 September 2006	s 99(1); SI 2006/1736
• Sch 12 (Pt 2★)	26 October 2006	s 99(1); SI 2006/2826
Transport Act 2000		
• s 248	1 October 2006	s 275(1); SI 2006/1933
Transport (Wales) Act 2006		
• ss 1, 2, 4–11	26 May 2006	s 12; SI 2006/1403
• ss 12–17	16 February 2006	
• Schedule	26 May 2006	s 12; SI 2006/1403
Violent Crime Reduction Act 2006		
• ss 1–24, 26–50, 52–54, 57, 58, 59(1), 61, 62, 64	no date	s 66(2)
• ss 25, 56, 60, 63, 66	8 November 2006	s 66(2)
• Schs 1, 3, 4, 5★	no date	s 66(2)
• Sch 5★	8 November 2006	s 66(2)
Water Act 2003		
• ss 1–4, 8(1)★, (3)–(7), 11–14, 19(1)–(3), (5), (6), 21–23, 25(1)★, (3), 30, 33, 62★, 100(2)(c), (g)★, (4)(b)(iii), (6)★, (7)★	1 April 2006	s 105(3); SI 2006/984
• Schs 7 (paras 4, 7, 8, 10–13, 15), 9★	1 April 2006	s 105(3); SI 2006/984
Wireless Telegraphy Act 2006	8 February 2007	s 126(2)
Work and Families Act 2006		
• ss 3–10, 11(2), (3)	no date	s 19(2)
• ss 1★, 2★	27 June 2006	s 19(2); SI 2006/1682
• ss 1★, 2★, 13, 14	1 October 2006	s 19(2); SI 2006/1682
• s 12	6 April 2007	s 19(2); SI 2006/1682
• ss 16, 18–20	21 June 2006	s 19(1)
• Schs 1 (paras 1–5, 10–15, 16(1)★, (2), 17–20, 22, 24–30, 35–61), 2★	no date	s 19(2)
• Schs 1 (paras 6, 7, 9, 21, 31–34)★, 2★	27 June 2006	s 19(2); SI 2006/1682
• Schs 1 (paras 6★, 7★, 8, 9★, 16(1)★, (3), 21★, 23, 31–34★), 2★	1 October 2006	s 19(2); SI 2006/1682, 2232
• Sch 2★	6 April 2007	s 19(2); SI 2006/1682
Youth Justice and Criminal Evidence Act 1999		
• Sch 6★	6 December 2006	s 68(3); SI 2006/2885

2733 Interpretation—purposive construction—repeal of legislation prior to implementation of replacement legislation—drafting error

Five individuals were charged with offences contrary to the Forgery and Counterfeiting Act 1981 s 5(2). At the contested committal hearing in the magistrates' court, the district judge concluded that the Identity Cards Act 2006 s 44(2), Sch 2 operated to repeal, as from 30 March 2006, the 1981 Act s 5(5)(f), (fa), so that the offences with which the individuals were charged were not known to the criminal law. The judge, therefore, discharged them. The Crown Prosecution Service sought judicial review of the decision, arguing that the draftsman of the 2006 Act s 44(3), which provided for the commencement of the 2006 Act, with specified exceptions including s 44, had not used language apt to achieve the clear intention of Parliament, namely to effect a smooth transition in replacing the 1981 Act s 5(5)(f), (fa) with the new provisions contained in the 2006 Act ss 25 and 26, which created a series of offences similar to those contained in the 1981 Act s 5(5)(f), (fa), so that it was permissible for the court to use its interpretative powers to read words into the 2006 Act s 44(3) in order to give effect to that intention. *Held*, in order to give effect to the intention of Parliament, s 44(2) should be excluded from the excepted provisions specified in s 44(3). Parliament had clearly intended that the repeal of the relevant provisions of the 1981 Act s 5 should be consequential on the coming into force of the new provisions contained in the 2006 Act ss 25 and 26, and s 44(3) was intended to achieve that purpose. However, as a result of an error and inadvertence on the part of the draftsman and Parliament, the terms of s 44(3) failed to give effect to that intended purpose because s 44(2) was not excluded from the list of excepted provisions specified in s 44(3). It was a plain case of a drafting mistake. That construction did not inflict any detriment or greater detriment on any of the five individuals or any other person as the proper construction of s 44(3) merely continued the existing law until its replacement by the new provisions and no increase in penalty was involved at any stage. Accordingly, the application would be allowed.

R (on the application of the Crown Prosecution Service) v Bow Street Magistrates' Court (James and others, interested parties) [2006] EWHC 1763 (Admin), [2006] 4 All ER 1342 (Queen's Bench Division: May LJ and Forbes J). *Inco Europe Ltd v First Choice Distribution (a firm)* [2000] 2 All ER 109, HL (2000 Abr para 209), applied.

2734   Primary legislation—post-legislative scrutiny—Law Commission recommendations

See para 2110.

2735   Ministers—transfer of functions—statutory instruments

See para 625.

2736   Statutory duty—breach—Revenue—delay in issuing sub-contractor's tax certificate

See *Neil Martin Ltd v Revenue and Customs Comrs*, para 1635.

2737   Subordinate legislation—power to make—enabling words—interpretation

The claimants sought to recover damages from the defendants in respect of damage to property and loss of profit suffered as a result of fires in their premises. They alleged that the fires were caused by a defective type of printing machinery containing a dryer supplied by the defendants. The fires destroyed three presses and caused other significant damage. Proceedings were brought for breach of duty in contract and tort and for breach of statutory duty under the Health and Safety at Work etc Act 1974. The claimants relied on s 47(2), contending that the Supply of Machinery (Safety) Regulations 1992, SI 1992/3073, were health and safety regulations for the purposes of the 1974 Act s 47(2). The defendants applied to strike out the claims under the 1974 Act, arguing that the Secretary of State could not make health and safety regulations so as to give rise to a claim for damages to property. The judge dismissed the claims and the claimants appealed. An issue arose as to whether general enabling words such as 'and of all his other enabling powers' when used in a statutory instrument, covered all the powers that might have been invoked to make the statutory instrument, or whether they were apt to denote only the powers that had necessarily to be utilised if the statutory instrument was to take effect according to the terms in which it was enacted. *Held*, general enabling words in the preamble to a statutory instrument might be interpreted as referring to an enabling power, not expressly invoked, in situations such as the following: (1) where, in order for the statutory instrument to have effect, the maker of the instrument had necessarily to have invoked that power; (2) where the operative provisions of the statutory instrument made it clear that its maker had to have invoked that power; or (3) where it was necessary to adopt that interpretation in order to make the statutory instrument conform to Community law or if that interpretation would make the statutory instrument compatible with the rights conferred by the European Convention on Human Rights. However, the general enabling words would not be interpreted as including an enabling power simply because the maker of the statutory instrument could have used that power. The general enabling words in the preamble to the 1992 Regulations did not invoke the enabling power contained in the 1974 Act s 15(1) and, accordingly, the appeal would be dismissed.

Polestar Jowetts v Komori UK Ltd; Vibixa v Komori UK Ltd [2006] EWCA Civ 536, [2006] 4 All ER 294 (Court of Appeal: Sir Anthony Clarke MR, Brooke and Arden LJJ). Decision of Field J [2005] EWHC 1674 (QB), [2005] All ER (D) 480 (Jul) (2005 Abr para 1617) affirmed.

TELECOMMUNICATIONS AND BROADCASTING

Halsbury's Laws of England (4th edn) vol 45(1) (2005 Reissue) paras 1–768

Articles

For articles relating to this title please refer to the Table of Articles at the beginning of the Abridgment.

2738   Broadcasting—radio—multiplex services—digital capacity

The Radio Multiplex Services (Required Percentage of Digital Capacity) Order 2006, SI 2006/2130 (in force on 25 July 2006), amends the Broadcasting Act 1996 s 54(2A) so as to change, from 80 per cent to 70 per cent, the minimum proportion of the digital capacity on the frequency or frequencies on which a radio multiplex service is broadcast and which the Office of Communications may specify as being used or reserved for certain broadcasting services.

2739   Broadcasting—television—digital terrestrial sound—technical service—definition

The Broadcasting Digital Terrestrial Sound (Technical Service) Order 2006, SI 2006/2793 (in force on 13 November 2006), amends the 1998 Order, SI 1998/685, by extending the meaning of a 'technical service' to a service consisting of the transmission of electronic signals controlling access to programmes or other information included in television licensable content services.

2740   Broadcasting—television—licence fees

The Communications (Television Licensing) (Amendment) Regulations 2006, SI 2006/619 (in force on 1 April 2006), further amend the 2004 Regulations, SI 2004/692, so as to (1) increase, from £42 to £44, the fee for a basic black and white only TV licence, and, from £126·50 to £131·50, the fee for a basic colour TV licence; (2) increase the issue fee and subsequent instalments for the premium instalment licence so that the total payable rises from £131·50 to £136·50; (3) increase, from £126·50 to £131·50, the total amount payable in relation to the instalments payable for the budget instalment licence and the easy entrance licence; (4) revise the provisions relating to the interim TV licence by increasing the fee payable in respect of each month, or part of a month, from £3·500 to £3·666, in the case of a black and white only TV licence, and from £10·541 to £10·958, in the case of a colour TV licence; and (5) revise the provisions relating to TV licence fees for hotels, hospitality areas and mobile units in order to reflect the rise in the fees payable for basic black and white only and colour TV licences under head (1) supra. The regulations also amend the definition of a 'television set' so as to exempt mobile telephones from the television dealer notification requirements set out in the Wireless Telegraphy Act 1967.

2741   Broadcasting—television—licensable content services

The Television Licensable Content Services Order 2006, SI 2006/2131 (in force on 25 July 2006), amends the Communications Act 2003 and the Broadcasting Act 1996, so as to (1) revise the definition of 'television licensable content service' in the 2003 Act so that television programme services falling within that definition can be carried on a radio multiplex service; and (2) in relation to the 1996 Act (a) ensure that television licensable content services, digital programme services and digital additional services are defined in a manner that is mutually exclusive; (b) make provision in relation to television licensable content services in the advertising, award and issuing by OFCOM of licences to provide radio multiplex services; and (c) make provision to take account of television licensable content services in the calculation of multiplex revenue.

2742   Broadcasting—television and radio—advertising—restriction on political advertising—unjust interference

See *R (on the application of Animal Defenders International) v Secretary of State for Culture, Media and Sport*, para 1548.

2743   Telecommunications—electronic communications networks and services—persistent misuse—maximum penalty

The Communications Act 2003 (Maximum Penalty for Persistent Misuse of Network or Service) Order 2006, SI 2006/1032 (in force on 6 April 2006), amends the Communications Act 2003 s 130(4) so as to increase, from £5,000 to £50,000, the maximum penalty which the Office of Communications can impose in respect of persistent misuse of electronic communications networks or electronic communications services.

2744   Telecommunications—interception of communications—person with right to control communication system

See *R v Stanford*, para 862.

2745 Telecommunications—offences—improper use of public electronic communications network—grossly offensive message

The defendant had made various telephone calls to the constituency and Westminster offices of a member of Parliament to give vent to financial and political grievances. He had spoken to members of staff or left offensive messages on an answering machine, and had used racially offensive terms. The defendant was acquitted of a charge of improper use of a public electronic communications network contrary to the Communications Act 2003 s 127(1)(a), and the prosecution appealed. *Held*, the purpose of s 127(1)(a) was to prohibit the use of a service provided and funded by the public, for the benefit of the public, for transmission of communications which contravened the basic standards of society. The actus reus of the offence was the sending of a message of the proscribed character by the defined means. The offence was complete when the message was sent, and it would make no difference if the message was never received. It was agreed by the parties that it was for the court of first instance to determine as a matter of fact whether a message was grossly offensive, applying the standards of an open and just multiracial society, and the words had to be judged taking into account their context and all relevant circumstances. Section 127(1)(a) provided no explicit guidance on the state of mind of the defendant that had to be proved to establish an offence. The defendant was entitled to make his views known and express them strongly. The question was whether he used language which was beyond the pale of what was tolerable. Some of the language used by the defendant could only have been chosen because of its highly abusive and offensive character. The defendant's messages were grossly offensive and would be found by a reasonable person to be so. The messages were sent by means of a public electronic communications network and so fell within s 127(1)(a) and the defendant should have been convicted. Accordingly, the appeal would be allowed.

DPP v Collins [2006] UKHL 40, [2006] 4 All ER 602 (House of Lords: Lords Bingham of Cornhill and Nicholls of Birkenhead, Baroness Hale of Richmond, Lords Carswell and Brown of Eaton-under-Heywood. Decision of Queen's Bench Divisional Court [2005] EWHC 1308 (Admin), [2005] 3 All ER 326 (2005 Abr para 2972) reversed.

2746 Wireless telegraphy—Guernsey

The Wireless Telegraphy (Guernsey) Order 2006, SI 2006/3325 (in force on 8 February 2007), extends to the Bailiwick of Guernsey provisions of the Wireless Telegraphy Act 2006, which consolidates all the provisions relating to wireless telegraphy formerly contained in a number of Acts of Parliament.

2747 Wireless telegraphy—Jersey

The Wireless Telegraphy (Jersey) Order 2006, SI 2006/3324 (in force on 8 February 2007), extends to the Bailiwick of Jersey provisions of the Wireless Telegraphy Act 2006, which consolidates all the provisions relating to wireless telegraphy formerly contained in a number of Acts of Parliament.

2748 Wireless telegraphy—licence—limitation—Concurrent Spectrum Access

The Wireless Telegraphy (Limitation of Number of Concurrent Spectrum Access Licences) Order 2006, SI 2006/341 (in force on 10 March 2006), specifies frequency bands for the use of which the Office of Communications will grant only a limited number of wireless telegraphy licences falling within the licence class known as Concurrent Spectrum Access.

2749 Wireless telegraphy—licence—limitation—Spectrum Access

The Wireless Telegraphy (Limitation of Number of Spectrum Access Licences) Order 2006, SI 2006/1809 (in force on 7 August 2006), (1) specifies frequency bands for the use of which the Office of Communications will grant a limited number of wireless telegraphy licences which will fall within the licence class known as Spectrum Access; and (2) makes reference to the Wireless Telegraphy (Licence Award) (No 2) Regulations 2006, SI 2006/1806, which sets out the procedure applied by the Office of Communications for determining the limit on the number of licences at such frequencies and the persons to whom licences will be granted.

2750 Wireless telegraphy—licence—register

The Wireless Telegraphy (Register) (Amendment) Regulations 2006, SI 2006/340 (in force on 10 March 2006), amend the 2004 Regulations, SI 2004/3155, by adding to the public register, the Concurrent Spectrum Access class of licence and relevant frequency bands.

The Wireless Telegraphy (Register) (Amendment) (No 2) Regulations 2006, SI 2006/1808 (in force on 7 August 2006), further amend the 2004 Regulations supra by adding to the public register, the Spectrum Access class of licence and relevant frequency bands.

2751 Wireless telegraphy—licence—spectrum trading

The Wireless Telegraphy (Spectrum Trading) (Amendment) Regulations 2006, SI 2006/339 (in force on 10 March 2006), amend the 2004 Regulations, SI 2004/3154, so as to authorise the transfer of all rights and obligations arising by virtue of a wireless telegraphy licence in the Concurrent Spectrum

Access class within the frequency bands specified if the rights and obligations of the person making the transfer become rights and obligations of the transferee to the exclusion of the person making the transfer.

The Wireless Telegraphy (Spectrum Trading) (Amendment) (No 2) Regulations 2006, SI 2006/1807 (in force on 7 August 2006), further amend the 2004 Regulations supra so as to authorise the transfer of rights and obligations arising by virtue of a wireless telegraphy licence in the Spectrum Access class within the frequency bands specified.

2752   Wireless telegraphy—licence award

The Wireless Telegraphy (Licence Award) Regulations 2006, SI 2006/338 (in force on 10 March 2006), set out the procedure that will apply to the grant of wireless telegraphy licences at the frequency bands 1781.7 MHz to 1785.0 MHz and 1876.7 MHz to 1880.0 MHz. In particular, the regulations (1) provide that, to apply for a grant, a body corporate must deliver specified documents to the Office of Communications ('OFCOM') on a day specified on their website and pay an initial deposit of £25,000; (2) provide for a procedure under which, overlaps between applicants' bidder groups can be drawn to the attention of the applicants and that time is to be allowed for applicants to notify OFCOM of any changes to bidder groups which have the effect that such overlaps are removed; (3) provide that an applicant will not be qualified to bid where a member of its bidder group is also a member of another bidder group; (4) prescribe that OFCOM will determine which applicants are qualified to bid in the auction and that notification will be given to applicants of the last day when they may withdraw their application without forfeiture of the initial deposit; (5) prescribe that, where the number of bidders is more than seven, OFCOM will give each bidder a notice setting out the delivery period within which the completed bid documentation must be provided and that a further deposit must be paid; (6) procure that winning bidders will be given provisional award notices setting out the licence fee payable by that bidder; (7) provide that licences not granted due to a failure by a winning bidder to make a payment may be offered to other bidders; and (8) provide that an applicant who is qualified to bid or a bidder will forfeit sums on deposit and may be excluded from the award process if OFCOM is satisfied that any specified event is occurring or has occurred and that the occurrence would materially affect the outcome of the award process.

The Wireless Telegraphy (Licence Award) (No 2) Regulations 2006, SI 2006/1806 (in force on 7 August 2006), set out the procedure that will apply to the grant of wireless telegraphy licences at the frequency bands 412.0 MHz to 414.0 MHz and 422.0 MHz to 424.0 MHz. In particular, the regulations (1) set out the procedure for applications for a licence; (2) provide for the assessment of whether bidders qualify to take part in the award process; (3) set out the procedure for granting a licence where there is only one bidder, and where there is more than one bidder; and (4) specify circumstances in which a deposit may be forfeited by the applicant or bidder, and in which that applicant or bidder may be excluded from the award process.

2753   Wireless telegraphy—licences—charges

The Wireless Telegraphy (Licence Charges) (Amendment) Regulations 2006, SI 2006/2894 (in force on 1 December 2006), amend the 2005 Regulations, SI 2005/1378, by (1) removing the concession that applies to registered charities that apply for ship radio and ship portable radio licences; (2) removing the waiver of licence fees for applicants for amateur radio licences who are under 21 years of age; (3) removing the licence fees for amateur radio, ship radio and ship portable radio licences where applicants apply for these classes of licences electronically; and (4) set the licence fees in the amount of £20 for amateur radio, ship radio and ship portable radio licences that are not applied for electronically.

2754   Wireless telegraphy—licences—exemption

The Wireless Telegraphy (Exemption) (Amendment) Regulations 2006, SI 2006/2994 (in force on 8 December 2006), further amend the 2003 Regulations, SI 2003/74, so as to widen the classes of wireless telegraphy apparatus whose establishment, installation and use are exempted from the provisions of the Wireless Telegraphy Act 1949. The regulations do not specify the detailed technical requirements directly, but instead refer to published interface requirements ('IRs') where those technical requirements are fully set out. In particular, the regulations (1) make minor drafting and updating changes to the 2003 Regulations; (2) amend the interface requirement in relation to land-mobile satellite service stations, so as to refer to the updated IR 2016, which makes provision for Inmarsat BGAN terminals; (3) amend the interface requirement in relation to short range devices, so as to refer to the updated IR 2030, which makes provision for 'micro' FM transmitters designed to facilitate easy connection between audio sources and normal FM broadcast receivers, and makes provision for radar level gauges; these amendments also ensure compliance with EC Commission Decision 2006/771 on harmonisation of the radio spectrum for use by short-range devices and EC Commission Decision 2005/928 on the harmonisation of the 169,4–169,8125 MHz frequency band in the Community with regard to harmonisation of the low power part of the 169.4–169.8125 MHz frequency band in the Community; (4) amend the 2003 Regulations so as to implement the changes that are required to ensure compliance with EC Commission Decision 2005/513 on the harmonised use of radio spectrum in the 5 GHz frequency band for the implementation of wireless access systems including radio local area networks, and so as to refer to the updated IR 2005 and IR 2006; and (5) provide for Citizens' Band Radio Equipment, as defined, to be exempt from the licensing requirement.

2755 Wireless telegraphy—licences—limitation of number

The Wireless Telegraphy (Limitation of Number of Licences) (Amendment) Order 2006, SI 2006/2786 (in force on 16 November 2006), amends the 2003 Order, SI 2003/1902, so as to reflect changes in the wireless telegraphy licence classes which are now available. In particular, changes have been made in respect of the following uses of spectrum: (1) broadcasting; (2) fixed links; (3) satellite services; (4) aeronautical; (5) maritime; and (6) science and technology, formerly called test and development.

2756 Wireless telegraphy—licences—procedures

The Wireless Telegraphy (Licensing Procedures) Regulations 2006, SI 2006/2785 (in force on 16 November 2006), prescribe the procedures for the determination by OFCOM of an application for a grant of a wireless telegraphy licence. In particular, the regulations (1) make provision for time limits within which OFCOM will make, notify to the applicant, and publish a decision on an application for the grant of a licence; (2) set out the requirements that must be met for the grant of every licence, whether in respect of a station or apparatus, and contain specific requirements that must be met for the grant of a licence in respect of a station; and (3) give particulars of the terms, provisions and limitations to which a licence are made subject.

2757 Wireless telegraphy—pre-consolidation amendments

The Wireless Telegraphy (Pre-Consolidation Amendments) Order 2006, SI 2006/1391 (in force immediately before the commencement of the Act resulting from the Wireless Telegraphy Bill introduced in the House of Lords on 20 April 2006), amends various enactments relating and referring to the management of the radio spectrum. In particular, the order (1) modifies the Wireless Telegraphy Act 1949 s 14(7) so that it has effect in relation to conduct rendered unlawful by the Wireless Telegraphy Act 1967; (2) modifies the 1949 Act so that it applies to the provisions of s 1D, which relate to the procedure for granting wireless telegraphy licences; (3) amends the Telecommunications Act 1984 so that the powers of the court are disapplied as regards offences under the Marine, &c., Broadcasting (Offences) Act 1967; (4) amends the Wireless Telegraphy Act 1998 s 4(5) so as to provide for revocation of variation of wireless telegraphy licences where it is necessary or expedient to do so for the purpose of complying with international obligations of the United Kingdom; (5) modifies references to 'broadcast', 'frequency', 'information', and 'international obligation of the United Kingdom' as they appear in various enactments; and (6) makes provision in relation to the powers to make an Order in Council.

2758 Wireless Telegraphy Act 2006

The Wireless Telegraphy Act 2006 consolidates certain enactments relating to wireless telegraphy. The Act received the royal assent on 8 November 2006 and came into force on 8 February 2007.

DESTINATION TABLE

1. This Table shows how enactments proposed to be repealed or revoked are dealt with by the Wireless Telegraphy Act 2006.

2. The following abbreviations are used in the Table:

Acts of Parliament

1949	Wireless Telegraphy Act 1949 (c 54)
1967(M)	Marine, &c, Broadcasting (Offences) Act 1967 (c 41)
1967(W)	Wireless Telegraphy Act 1967 (c 72)
1984	Telecommunications Act 1984 (c 12)
1990	Broadcasting Act 1990 (c 42)
1998	Wireless Telegraphy Act 1998 (c 6)
2000	Regulation of Investigatory Powers Act 2000 (c 23)
2003	Communications Act 2003 (c 21)

Statutory Instruments

Order	Wireless Telegraphy (Pre-Consolidation Amendments) Order 2006 (SI 2006/1391)

3. The functions of the Postmaster General under 1949 and 1967(W) were transferred to the Minister of Posts and Telecommunications by the Post Office Act 1969 (c 48), s 3(1). The functions

of that Minister were transferred to the Secretary of State by the Ministry of Posts and Telecommunications (Dissolution) Order 1974 (SI 1974/691) art 2.

Wireless Telegraphy Act 1949 (c 54)

Existing provision	Rewritten provision	Remarks
1 Licensing of wireless telegraphy		
(1)	ss 8(1), 35(1)	Amended 1990, Sch 18, Pt 1, para 1(2), 2003, Sch 17, para 6(2).
(1) proviso	s 8(3)	Amended 1990, Sch 18, Pt 1, para 1(2), 2003, Sch 17, para 6(2).
(1AA)	s 8(2)	Inserted 2003, Sch 17, para 6(3).
(1A)	—	Inserted Deregulation (Wireless Telegraphy) Order 1996 (SI 1996/1864) art 3; repealed 2003, Sch 19.
(2)	ss 9(1), (2), (3), 115(1)	Amended 1990, Sch 18, Pt 1, para 1(3), 2003, Sch 17, para 6(4).
(2A)	s 9(4)	Inserted 2003, s 165.
(2B)	s 9(5)	Inserted 2003, s 165.
(2C)	s 9(6)	Inserted 2003, s 165.
(3)	Sch 1, para 5	Amended 1990, Sch 18, Pt 1, para 1(4), 2003, Sch 17, para 6(5).
(4)	Sch 1, para 6	Amended 1990, Sch 18, Pt 1, para 1(5), 2003, Sch 17, para 6(6); repealed in part 2003, Sch 19.
(5)	s 11(1), (3)	Amended 2003, Sch 17, para 6(7).
(5) proviso	ss 11(2), 115(1)	
(6)	—	Repealed 2003, Sch 19.
(7)	—	Inserted 1990, Sch 18, Pt 1, para 1(6); repealed 2003, Sch 19.
1AA Exemption from the need for wireless telegraphy licence		
		Inserted 2003, s 166.
(1)	s 8(4)	
(2)	s 8(5)	
1A Offence of keeping wireless telegraphy station or apparatus available for unauthorised use		
	s 36(1)	Inserted 1990, s 168.
1B Offence of allowing premises to be used for purpose of unlawful broadcasting		
		Inserted 1990, s 169.
(1)	s 37(1), (5)	
(2)	s 37(4)	
(3)	s 37(6)	
(4)	s 37(7)	
1C Prohibition of acts facilitating unauthorised broadcasting		
		Inserted 1990, s 170.
(1)	s 38(1), (2)	
(2)	s 38(2), (3)	
(3)	s 38(5)	
(4)	s 38(4)	Substituted 2003, Sch 17, para 7.
(5)	s 115(6)	
(6)	ss 38(8), 115(1)	
1D Procedures for the grant of licences for providing a telecommunications service		
		Inserted Telecommunications (Licensing) Regulations 1997 (SI 1997/ 2930) reg 4(2).
(1), (2)	—	Repealed 2003, Sch 17, para 8(3).
(3)	Sch 1, para 1(1)	Substituted 2003, Sch 17, para 8(4).

Existing provision	Rewritten provision	Remarks
(4)	Sch 1, para 1(2)	Amended 2003, Sch 17, para 8(5).
(4A)	Sch 1, para 2(1)	Inserted 2003, Sch 17, para 8(6). Words 'made after the coming into force of this subsection' unnecessary.
(4B)	Sch 1, para 2(2)	Inserted 2003, Sch 17, para 8(6).
(4C)	Sch 1, para 2(3)	Inserted 2003, Sch 17, para 8(6).
(5)	Sch 1, para 3	Amended 2003, Sch 17, para 8(2),(7).
(6)	Sch 1, para 4	Amended 2003, Sch 17, para 8(2),(8).
(7), (8)	—	Repealed 2003, Sch 17, para 8(9).
(9)	s 9(7)	Substituted 2003, Sch 17, para 8(10).

1E Variation or revocation of a licence

		Inserted Telecommunications (Licensing) Regulations 1997 (SI 1997/ 2930) reg 4(2); substituted 2003, s 169(1).
(1)	Sch 1, para 7(1)	
(2)	Sch 1, para 7(2)	
(3)	Sch 1, para 7(3)	
(4)	Sch 1, para 7(4)	
(5)	Sch 1, para 7(5)	
(6)	Sch 1, para 7(6)	
(7)	Sch 1, para 7(7)	
(8)	Sch 1, para 7(12)	
(9)	Sch 1, para 7(8)	Words 'For the purposes of this section' unnecessary.
(10)	Sch 1, para 7(9)	
(11)	Sch 1, para 7(10)	
(12)	Sch 1, para 7(11)	
(13)	Sch 1, para 7(13)	
(14)	s 115(1)	

1F Appeals

		Inserted Telecommunications (Appeals) Regulations 1999 (SI 1999/ 3180) reg 4(3); repealed 2003, Sch 19.

2 Fees and charges for wireless telegraphy services

		Repealed 2003, Sch 19.
	—	

3 Regulations as to wireless telegraphy

(1)	s 45(1), (2), (3), (4), (5), (6)	Amended 2003, Sch 17, para 9(2); repealed in part 2003, Sch 19.
(1) proviso	ss 45(8), 115(1)	
(2)	s 46(1)	
(2A)	s 45(9)	Inserted 2003, Sch 17, para 9(3).
(2B)	s 45(10)	Inserted 2003, Sch 17, para 9(3).

3A Restriction on revocation or variation of certain wireless telegraphy licences

	—	Inserted 1984, s 74; repealed 1998, Sch 2, Pt 1.

4 Experimental Licences

	—	Repealed 1998, Sch 1, para 2.

5 Misleading messages and interception and disclosure of messages

		1949, s 5 renumbered as, s 5(1) 2000, s 73(1).
(1)(a)	s 47(1), (2), (3)	

Existing provision	Rewritten provision	Remarks
(1)(b)	s 48(1), (2), (3)	Amended 2000, s 73(2). Certain functions of Secretary of State treated as exercisable in or as regards Scotland by Scotland Act 1998 (Functions Exercisable in or as Regards Scotland) Order 1999 (SI 1999/1748) art 3, Sch 1, para 1 (later amended by Scotland Act 1998 (Transfer of Functions to the Scottish Ministers etc) (No 2) Order 2000 (SI 2000/3253) art 4(2)(b)). Certain functions of Secretary of State transferred to Scottish Ministers by Scotland Act 1998 (Transfer of Functions to the Scottish Ministers etc) Order 1999 (SI 1999/1750) art 2, Sch 1 (later amended by Scotland Act 1998 (Transfer of Functions to the Scottish Ministers etc) (No 2) Order 2000 (SI 2000/3253) art 4(3)(a)) (effect saved by, Sch 8, para 4 to consolidation).
(2)	s 49(1), (2)	Inserted 2000, s 73(3). Words 'by any person' in, paras (c), (d) unnecessary.
(3)	s 49(3)	Inserted 2000, s 73(3).
(4)	s 49(4), (12)	Inserted 2000, s 73(3).
(5)	s 49(5)	Inserted 2000, s 73(3).
(6)	s 49(6)	Inserted 2000, s 73(3).
(7)	s 49(7)	Inserted 2000, s 73(3). Reference to Commissioners of Customs and Excise taken as reference to Commissioners for Her Majesty's Revenue and Customs Commissioners for Revenue and Customs Act 2005 (c 11), s 50(1). Certain functions of Secretary of State transferred to Scottish Ministers by Scotland Act 1998 (Transfer of Functions to the Scottish Ministers etc) (No 2) Order 2000 (SI 2000/3253), Sch 3, Pt 1, paras 1, 2 (effect saved by, Sch 8, para 4 to consolidation).
(8)	s 49(8)	Inserted 2000, s 73(3).
(9)	s 49(9)	Inserted 2000, s 73(3).
(10)	s 49(10)	Inserted 2000, s 73(3).
(11)	s 49(11)	Inserted 2000, s 73(3).
(12)	ss 48(5), 49(12)	Inserted 2000, s 73(3). Reference to Commissioners of Customs and Excise taken as reference to Commissioners for Her Majesty's Revenue and Customs Commissioners for Revenue and Customs Act 2005 (c 11), s 50(1).

6 Territorial extent of previous provisions

(1)	ss 105(1), (2), 119(1), (2)	Extended 1967(W), s 10(3); repealed in part 1967(W), s 9(2). Words 'Subject to the provisions of this section' unnecessary.
(1) proviso	s 105(3)	
(2)	s 50(1), (2), (3), (5), (6)	Amended 1967(W), s 9(3), Criminal Justice Act 1982 (c 48), s 50(1)(a); extended 1967(W), s 9(4); repealed in part Statute Law (Repeals) Act 1993 (c 50), Sch 1, Pt XIV Group 2.
(3)	s 119(3)	Repealed in part 1967(W), s 9(2). Words 'British protectorate or British protected state' unnecessary.

Existing provision	Rewritten provision	Remarks
(4)	—	Inserted Criminal Justice Act 1982 (c 48), s 50(1)(b); repealed Fines and Penalties (Northern Ireland) Order 1984 (SI 1984/703 (NI 3)), Sch 7.
7 Powers of Secretary of State as to wireless personnel		
(1)	s 52(1), (2)	
(2)	s 52(3), (4)	
(3)	s 52(5), (6)	
(4)	s 53(1), (2)	
(5)	s 52(7)	
8 Commencement of Part 1		
	—	Repealed Post Office Act 1969 (c 48), Sch 8, Pt 1.
9 Appeal tribunal		
	—	Repealed 2003, Sch 17, para 10.
10 Regulations as to radiation of electro-magnetic energy, etc.		
(1)	s 54(1), (2)	Amended 2003, Sch 17, para 11(2); repealed in part 1984, Sch 7, Pt 4.
(2)	s 54(3), (4)	Amended 2003, Schedule 17, para 11(3); words after, para (b) repealed 2003, Sch 19.
(3)	ss 54(1), (2), (5), 61	Repealed in part 1967(W), s 10(2).
(4)	s 54(6)	
(4A)	s 54(7)	Inserted 2003, Sch 17, para 11(4).
(4B)	s 54(8)	Inserted 2003, Sch 17, para 11(4).
11 Enforcement of regulations as to use of apparatus		
(1)	s 55(1), (2), (3), (4), (5)	Amended 2003, Sch 17, para 12(2).
(1) proviso	s 55(6)	Amended 2003, Sch 17, para 12(2); repealed in part 2003, s 178(1)(a), Sch 19.
(2)	s 55(7)	Amended 2003, Sch 17, para 12(3).
(2) proviso	s 55(8)	
(2A)	s 57(1), (2)	Inserted 2003, s 178(1)(b).
(2B)	s 57(3)	Inserted 2003, s 178(1)(b).
(2C)	s 57(4)	Inserted 2003, s 178(1)(b).
(2D)	s 57(5)	Inserted 2003, s 178(1)(b).
(3)–(6)	—	Repealed 2003, s 178(1)(b).
(7)	s 58(1)	Amended 2003, Sch 17, para 12(4). Words 'from OFCOM' unnecessary.
12 Enforcement of regulations as to sales, etc, by manufacturers and others		
(1)	s 56(1), (2)	Amended 2003, Sch 17, para 13(2).
(1A)	s 57(1), (2)	Inserted 2003, s 178(2).
(1B)	s 57(3)	Inserted 2003, s 178(2).
(1C)	s 57(4)	Inserted 2003, s 178(2).
(1D)	s 57(5)	Inserted 2003, s 178(2).
(2)–(4)	—	Repealed 2003, s 178(2).
(5)	s 58(4)	Amended 2003, Sch 17, para 13(3).
12A Regulations with respect to resistance to interference		
	—	Inserted 1984, s 78; repealed Electromagnetic Compatibility Regulations 1992 (SI 1992/2372) reg 2(1).
13 Deliberate interference		
(1)	s 68(1)	
(2)	s 68(2)	
13A Information requirements		

Existing provision	Rewritten provision	Remarks
		Inserted 2003, s 171(1).
(1)	s 32(1), (2)	
(2)	s 32(3)	
(3)	s 32(4)	
(4)	s 32(5)	
(5)	s 33(1)	
(6)	s 33(2)	
(7)	s 33(4)	
13B Statement of policy in information gathering		
		Inserted 2003, s 171(1).
(1)	s 34(1)	
(2)	s 34(2)	
(3)	s 34(3)	
(4)	s 34(4)	
14 Penalties and legal proceedings		
(1)	ss 35(2), (7), 36(2), 37(2), 38(6), 47(4), 68(3)	Substituted 1984, Sch 3, para 1; amended 1990, s 172(2), 2003, s 179(1), Sch 17, para 14(2); modified (E,W) Criminal Justice Act 2003 (c 44), s 282(3).
(1A)	ss 11(4), 33(3), 35(4), 36(4), 46(2), 51(5), 53(3), 58(2), (5), (6), 115(1)	Substituted 1984, Sch 3, para 1; amended 1990, s 172(3), 2003, s 171(2), Sch 17, para 14(3)(a); para (e) repealed 2003, Sch 17, para 14(3)(b). Words 'otherwise than under and in accordance with a wireless telegraphy licence' in, para (a) unnecessary (see prohibition in, s 8(1) of consolidation).
(1AA)	ss 35(5), 36(5)	Inserted 2003, s 179(2); modified (E,W) Criminal Justice Act 2003 (c 44), s 281(5).
(1B)	s 58(2)	Substituted 1984, Sch 3, para 1; para (a) repealed 1990, Sch 21; repealed in part (E,W) Criminal Justice Act 2003 (c 44), Sch 37, Pt 9 (as consequence of Criminal Justice Act 2003 (c 44), Sch 25, para 29).
(1C)	ss 33(5), 46(3), 48(4), 58(5), 60(2), 66(3), 98(2), 100(2)	Substituted 1984, Sch 3, para 1.
(2)	—	Repealed 2003, s 404(5).
(3)	Sch 5, para 1	Substituted 1990, s 172(4); amended 2003, Sch 17, para 14(4)(b); para (b) repealed 2003, Sch 17, para 14(4)(a), para (d) (in part) spent.
(3AA)	Sch 5, para 1	Inserted 1990, s 172(4).
(3AB)	Sch 5, para 1	Inserted 1990, s 172(4).
(3A)	Sch 5, para 2	Inserted 1984, s 82; amended 2003, Sch 17, para 14(5).
(3B)	Sch 5, paras 3, 4	Inserted 1984, s 82; amended 2003, Sch 17, para 14(5), (6).
(3C)	Sch 5, para 6	Inserted 1984, s 82.
(3D)	Sch 5, para 5	Inserted 1984, s 82; amended 2003, Sch 17, para 14(5), (7).
(3E)	Sch 5, para 5	Inserted 1984, s 82; amended 1990, s 172(5), 2003, Sch 17, para 14(5).
(4)	—	Repealed Post Office Act 1969 (c 48), Sch 8, Pt 2.
(5)	—	Repealed Post Office Act 1969 (c 48), Sch 8, Pt 1.
(6)	s 106(1), (2), (3)	

Existing provision	Rewritten provision	Remarks
(7)	s 108(1), (2), (3)	Amended 2003, Sch 17, para 14(8), Order, Schedule, para 2.
(8), (9)	—	Inserted 1984, Sch 3, para 2; repealed Statute Law (Repeals) Act 1993 (c 50), Sch 1, Pt XIV Group 2.
15 Entry and search of premises, etc		
(1)	s 97(1), (2), (3), (9)	Amended 1990, s 173(1)(a), Sch 18, Pt 1, para 3, 2003, Sch 17, para 15(2), (E,W) Serious Organised Crime and Police Act 2005 (c 15), Sch 16, para 3; modified Justice (Northern Ireland) Act 2002 (c 26), Sch 4, para 6; repealed in part 1990, s 173(1)(b).
(1A)	s 97(5)	Inserted 2003, Sch 17, para 15(3).
(2)	s 59(1), (5), (6), (10)	Amended 2003, Sch 17, para 15(4); modified Justice (Northern Ireland) Act 2002 (c 26), Sch 4, para 6; repealed in part 1990, s 173(2).
(2) proviso	s 59(2), (3), (4), (10)	Amended 2003, Sch 17, para 15(4).
(2A)	ss 59(7), (8), 97(6), (7)	Inserted 1990, s 173(3); amended 2003, Sch 17, para 15(5). Words '(as the case may be)' unnecessary.
(3)	ss 59(9), 97(8)	
(4)	ss 60(1), 98(1)	Amended 1984, s 92(2); repealed in part Post Office Act 1969 (c 48), Sch 8, Pt 2.
16 Regulations and orders		
(1)	—	Unnecessary (see Interpretation Act 1978 (c 30), s 14(b)).
(1A)	s 122(1)	Inserted 2003, Sch 17, para 16(2).
(2)	s 121(1), (2)	Amended 2000, s 73(4), 2003, Sch 17, para 16(3); repealed in part Post Office Act 1969 (c 48), Sch 8, Pt 1.
17 Financial provisions		
(1)	s 109(1), (2)	Repealed in part Post Office Act 1961 (c 15), Schedule Remainder repealed (NI) Northern Ireland Act 1962 (c 30), Sch 2; superseded (E, W) Powers of Criminal Courts (Sentencing) Act 2000 (c 6), s 140(6), Courts Act 2003 (c 39), s 38.
(2)	—	Repealed Transfer of Functions (Local Government, etc) (Northern Ireland) Order 1973 (S.R. & O. (NI) 1973/256), Sch 2.
18 Transitional provisions, etc.		
	—	Repealed Post Office Act 1969 (c 48), Sch 8, Pt 1.
19 Interpretation		
(1)	ss 116(1), (2), 117(1), (2)	Proviso repealed Cable and Broadcasting Act 1984 (c 46), Sch 6.
(2)	ss 115(1), 117(2)	Amended Electricity Act 1989 (c 29), Sch 16, para 6.
(2AA)	s 115(1)	Inserted 2003, Sch 17, para 17.
(2A)	—	Inserted 1990, Sch 18, Pt 1, para 4; repealed 2003, Sch 19.
(3)	s 115(2)	
(4)	s 115(1), (3)	
(5)	s 115(4)	Substituted 2003, s 183.
(5A)	s 115(5)	Substituted 2003, s 183.
(6)	s 115(7)	
(7)	s 115(1)	Amended Merchant Shipping Act 1995 (c 21), Sch 13, para 24.

Existing provision	Rewritten provision	Remarks
(8)	s 115(8)	
(9)	—	Repealed 2003, Sch 19.
(10)	—	Unnecessary (see Interpretation Act 1978 (c 30), s 20(2)).
20 Short title and extent		
(1)	—	Unnecessary.
(2)	s 118(1)	
(3)	s 118(3)	Extended Post Office Act 1969 (c 48), s 3(6), 1990, s 174, 1998, s 9(2), Order, Schedule, para 3.
Sch 1 Procedure in relation to supervision and revocation of authorities to wireless personnel		
para 1	Sch 3, para 1	
para 2	Sch 3, paras 2, 3	
para 3	Sch 3, para 4	Substituted 2003, Sch 17, para 18.
Sch 2 Provisions as to the appeal tribunal		
	—	Repealed 2003, Sch 19.

Marine &c, Broadcasting (Offences) Act 1967 (c 41)

Existing	Rewritten	Remarks
1 Prohibition of broadcasting from ships and aircraft		
(1)	ss 77(1), 95(1)	
(2)	s 77(2), (3)	
(3)	s 77(4)	
(4)	s 77(5)	
2 Prohibition of broadcasting from marine structures		
(1)	s 78(2), (3), (4)	Amended 1990, Sch 16, para 1(2).
(2)	s 78(5)	
(3)	ss 78(1), 95(1)	Inserted 1990, Sch 16, para 1(3).
2A Unlawful broadcasting from within prescribed areas of the high seas		
		Inserted 1990, Sch 16, para 2.
(1)	ss 79(1), (5), 95(1)	
(2)	s 79(2)	
(3)	s 79(3)	
(4)	s 79(4)	
(5)	s 121(1), (2)	
3 Prohibition of acts connected with broadcasting from certain ships and aircraft, and from marine structures outside the United Kingdom		
(1)	ss 80(1), 95(1)	Amended 1990, Sch 16, para 3(a); words 'Subject to subsection (1A) below' unnecessary.
(1A)	s 80(2)	Inserted 1990, Sch 16, para 3(b).
(2)	s 80(3)	
(3)	s 95(2)	Amended British Nationality Act 1981 (c 61), Sch 7, Hong Kong (British Nationality) Order 1986 (SI 1986/948), Sch 1.
3A Prohibition of management of stations broadcasting from ships, aircraft, etc		
		Inserted 1990, Sch 16, para 4.
(1)	s 81(1)	
(2)	s 81(2)	
4 Prohibition of facilitating broadcasting from ships, aircraft, etc		

Existing	Rewritten	Remarks
(1)	ss 82(1), (2), (3), 83(1), (2), 84(1), 86(1), (2), (3), (4), (5), (6), 95(1)	Amended 1990, Sch 16, para 5(2).
(2)	s 87	
(3)(a)	s 82(1)	
(3)(b)	s 82(2)	
(3)(c)	s 82(2)	
(3)(d)	s 83(1), (7)	
(3)(e)	s 84(1)	Amended 1990, Sch 16, para 5(3).
(3)(f)	s 82(3)	
(3)(g)	s 83(2), (7)	
(3A)	s 115(6)	Inserted 2003, Sch 17, para 32.

5 Prohibition of acts relating to matter broadcast from marine structures

Existing	Rewritten	Remarks
(1)	ss 85(1), 86(1), (2), (3), (4), (5), (6), 95(1)	Amended 1990, Sch 16, para 6(2).
(2)	s 87	
(3)	s 85(1), (2), (3)	Amended Copyright, Designs and Patents Act 1988 (c 48), Sch 7, para 9(a), 1990, Sch 16, para 6(3), 2003, Sch 17, para 33(2).
(3A)	s 115(6)	Inserted 2003, Sch 17, para 32.
(4)	s 85(4)	Substituted 2003, Sch 17, para 33(3).
(5)	s 85(5)	
(6)	s 115(1)	Amended Copyright, Designs and Patents Act 1988 (c 48), Sch 7, para 9(b).

6 Penalties and legal proceedings

Existing	Rewritten	Remarks
(1)	s 93(1)	Amended 1990, Sch 16, para 7(2); modified Magistrates' Courts Act 1980 (c 43), s 32(2), Fines and Penalties (Northern Ireland) Order 1984 (SI 1984/703 (NI 3) art 4, Criminal Procedure (Consequential Provisions) (Scotland) Act 1995 (c 40), Sch 1, para 2, (E,W) Criminal Justice Act 2003 (c 44), s 282(3).
(2)	—	Repealed 2003, Sch 19.
(3)	s 107(1)	
(4)	s 93(5)	Words 'Notwithstanding anything in any enactment relating to courts of summary jurisdiction' unnecessary. Sub, s does not apply in England and Wales or Northern Ireland (Magistrates' Courts Act 1980 (c 43), s 127(2)(b), Magistrates' Courts (Northern Ireland) Order 1981 (SI 1981/1675 (NI 26)) art 19(2)).
(5)	s 93(3), (4)	Amended 1990, Sch 16, para 7(3), Justice (Northern Ireland) Act 2002 (c 26), Sch 7, para 25, 2003, Sch 17, para 34; repealed in part Criminal Jurisdiction Act 1975 (c 59), Sch 6, Pt 1.
(6)	s 107(2), (3)	
(7)	—	Repealed 2003, Sch 19.
(8)	s 107(4)	Reference to Royal Ulster Constabulary modified Police (Northern Ireland) Act 2000 (c 32), s 78(2).

7 Special defence available in proceedings for carrying goods or persons in contravention of s 4

Existing	Rewritten	Remarks
(1)	s 82(4)	

Existing	Rewritten	Remarks
(2)	s 83(3)	
(3)	ss 82(7), 83(6)	
(4)	ss 82(5), (6), 83(4), (5)	

7A Powers of enforcement in relation to marine offences under 1967(M)

		Inserted 1990, Sch 16, para 8.
(1)	s 88(1), (3)	Amended 2003, Sch 17, para 35(2); repealed in part Reserve Forces Act 1996 (Consequential Provisions etc) Regulations 1998 (SI 1998/3086) reg 10(2). Reference to officers commissioned by Commissioners of Customs and Excise under Customs and Excise Management Act 1979, s 6(3) taken as reference to officers of Revenue and Customs Commissioners for Revenue and Customs Act 2005 (c 11), s 50(2).
(2)	ss 89(1), (2), (3), 95(1)	Amended 2003, Sch 17, para 35(2). Words 'subject to subsections (6) and (7) below' unnecessary.
(3)	s 90(1), (2)	Amended 2003, Sch 17, para 35(2). Words 'subject to subsections (6) and (7) below' unnecessary.
(4)	s 90(3), (4), (5)	Amended 2003, Sch 17, para 35(2). Words 'subject to subsections (6) and (7) below' unnecessary.
(5)	s 89(4), (5)	
(6)	s 91(1)	
(7)	ss 91(2), (3), 95(1)	Amended 2003, Sch 17, para 35(5).
(8)	s 92(1)	
(9)	s 92(2)	
(10)	s 92(3)	
(11)	s 92(4)	

8 Saving for things done under wireless telegraphy licence

	s 94	

9 Interpretation

(1)	ss 95(1), 115(1), 116(1), (2), 117(1)	Amended 2003, Sch 17, para 36.
(2)	—	Repealed Territorial Sea Act 1987 (c 49), Sch 2.

10 Power to extent Act to Isle of Man and Channel Islands

(1)	s 118(3)	Extended 1990, s 174.
(2)	—	Unnecessary (see Interpretation Act 1978 (c 30), s 14(b)).

11 Short title and commencement

(1)	—	Unnecessary.
(2)	—	Spent.

Wireless Telegraphy Act 1967 (c 72)

Existing	Rewritten	Remarks
7 Restriction on dealings in and custody of certain apparatus		
		Substituted 1984, s 77(1).
(1)	s 62(1)	
(2)	s 62(2)	Amended 2003, Sch 17, para 37(2).
(3)	s 62(3)	
(4)	s 62(4)	

Existing	Rewritten	Remarks
(5)	s 62(5)	Amended 2003, Sch 17, para 37(3); para (b) repealed 2003, s 182(7).
(6)	s 63(1)	Amended 2003, Sch 17, para 37(3).
(7)	s 63(2)	Amended 2003, Sch 17, para 37(3).
(8)	s 63(3)	Amended 2003, Sch 17, para 37(3).
(9)	ss 64, 115(1)	Amended 2003, Sch 17, para 37(3), (4).
(10)	s 65(1), (2), (3)	Reference to Commissioners of Customs and Excise taken as reference to Commissioners for Her Majesty's Revenue and Customs Commissioners for Revenue and Customs Act 2005 (c 11), s 50(1); reference to person commissioned by Commissioners of Customs and Excise taken as reference to officer of Revenue and Customs Commissioners for Revenue and Customs Act 2005 (c 11), s 50(2).
(11)	s 66(1), (2), (4)	Amended 2003, Sch 17, para 37(3).
(11A)	s 122(1)	Inserted 2003, Sch 17, para 37(5).
(11B)	s 62(6)	Inserted 2003, Sch 17, para 37(5).
(11C)	s 62(7)	Inserted 2003, Sch 17, para 37(5).
(11D)	s 115(1)	Inserted 2003, Sch 17, para 37(5).
(12)	s 67	
8 Provisions for securing enforcement of 1949 s 1(1) in relation to vehicles		
(1)	s 51(1), (2), (3)	Amended Vehicle Excise and Registration Act 1994 (c 22), Sch 3, para 3(a), 2003, Sch 17, para 38(2). The 'appropriate authority' is the Secretary of State (see Vehicle and Driving Licences Act 1969 (c 27), s 1 and Vehicle Excise and Registration Act 1994 (c 22), s 6).
(2)	s 51(4)	Amended 2003, Sch 17, para 38(3).
(3)	s 51(6)	Amended Vehicle Excise and Registration Act 1994 (c 22), Sch 3, para 3(b).
(4)	—	Repealed Vehicle Excise and Registration Act 1994 (c 22), Sch 5, Pt 1.
9 Amendments as to territorial extent of 1949 Pt 1		
(1)	—	Repealed Territorial Sea Act 1987 (c 49), Sch 2.
(2)	—	Words before semi-colon introductory; remainder repeals in part 1949, s 6(1), (3).
(3)	s 50(1), (5), (6)	Part amends 1949, s 6(2); remainder repealed 1984, Sch 7, Pt 4.
(4)	ss 50(4), 121(3)	Extends 1949, s 6(2).
(5)	—	Spent.
10 Amendments as to scope and territorial extent of 1949 Pt 2		
(1)	—	Introductory.
(2)	—	Words before semi-colon introductory; remainder repeals in part 1949, s 10(3).
(3)	ss 105(1), 119(2)	Extends 1949, s 6.
11 Amendments as to penalties for offences under 1949		
	—	Repealed 1984, Sch 7, Pt 4.
12 Enforcement of 1949		
(1)	s 107(1)	Reference to territorial sea modified Territorial Sea Act 1987 (c 49), s 1.
(2)	s 107(2), (3)	

Existing	Rewritten	Remarks
(3)	s 107(4)	Reference to Royal Ulster Constabulary modified Police (Northern Ireland) Act 2000 (c 32), s 78(2).
13 Regulations and orders		
words in (4)	—	Unnecessary (see Interpretation Act 1978 (c 30), s 14(b)).
15 Short title, citation, interpretation and extent		
(2)	—	Unnecessary (citation of Wireless Telegraphy Acts).
(3)	ss 115(3), (5), 116(1), (2), 117(1)	Definition of 'the principal Act' unnecessary (see amendment of 1967(W), s 5(1) in, Sch 7, para 2 to consolidation).
words in (6)	s 118(4)	

Post Office Act 1969 (c 48)

Existing	Rewritten	Remarks
3 Transfer to the Minister of the Postmaster General's functions with respect to wireless telegraphy, and provisions consequential thereon		
words in (1)		See Note 3. Applied passim. Word 'rules' in paragraph (ii) unnecessary (see repeal of 1949, s 9(2), s 11(4), s 12(3) by 2003, s 178(1)(b), (2), Sch 17, para 10). Effect of words in paragraph (ii) saved by, Sch 8, para 14 to consolidation.
3(6)	s 118(3)	Extends 1949, s 20(3). Repealed in part Merchant Shipping Act 1995 (c 21), Sch 12.

British Nationality Act 1981 (c 61)

Existing	Rewritten	Remarks
Sch 7 Consequential amendments		
para relating to 1967(M)	s 95(2)	Substitutes 1967(M), s 3(3)(a) to (c).

Criminal Justice Act 1982 (c 48)

Existing	Rewritten	Remarks
50 Fines for offences against regulations relating to wireless telegraphy apparatus on foreign ships and aircraft		
(1)	s 50(3)	Para (a) amends 1949, s 6(2); para (b) repealed Fines and Penalties (Northern Ireland) Order 1984 (SI 1984/703 (NI 3)), Sch 7.
(2)	—	Spent.
81 Citation and extent		
entry in (5)	—	Unnecessary (relates to Criminal Justice Act 1982 (c 48), s 50).
(12)(c)(v)	S 118(3)	

Telecommunications Act 1984 (c 12)

Existing	Rewritten	Remarks
74 Restriction on revocation or variation of certain wireless telegraphy licences		
	—	Repealed 1998, Sch 2, Pt 1.
75 Alteration of penalties and mode of trial for certain offences under 1949		
(1)	—	Amends 1949, s 14 (see 1984, Sch 3, para 1).

Existing	Rewritten	Remarks
(2)	—	Introduces 1984, Sch 3.
(3)	—	Spent.
76 Arrest without warrant for certain offences under 1949		
	—	Repealed Police and Criminal Evidence Act 1984 (c 60), s 26(1).
77 Substitution of new section for 1967(W) s 7		
(1)	ss 63(1), (2), (3), 64, 65(1), (2), (3), 66(1), (2), (4), 67	Substitutes 1967(W), s 7.
(2)	—	Spent.
78 Regulations with respect to resistance to interference		
	—	Repealed Electromagnetic Compatibility Regulations 1992 (SI 1992/ 2372) reg 2(1).
79 Seizure of apparatus and other property used in committing certain offences under 1949		
(1)	s 99(1)	Amended 1990, s 173(4), 2003, s 179(3). Words 'otherwise than under and in accordance with a wireless telegraphy licence' in, para (b) unnecessary (see description of offences in, s 36 of consolidation).
(2)	s 99(2), (7)	Amended, and repealed in part, 1990, s 173(5); amended 2003, Sch 17, para 64.
(3)	s 99(3), (7)	Amended 2003, Sch 17, para 64.
(4)	s 99(6)	Amended 2003, Sch 17, para 64.
(4A)	s 99(4), (5)	Inserted 1990, s 173(6); amended 2003, Sch 17, para 64.
(5)	s 100(1)	
(6)	s 99(7)	Amended 2003, Sch 17, para 65.
80 Proceedings in England and Wales or Northern Ireland for forfeiture of restricted apparatus		
	—	Repealed 2003, Sch 19.
81 Proceedings in Scotland for forfeiture of restricted apparatus		
	—	Repealed 2003, Sch 19.
82 Amendments with respect to forfeiture on conviction		
	Sch 5, paras 2, 3, 4, 5, 6	Substitutes 1949, s 14(3) to (3E).
83 Disposal of apparatus and other property seized by virtue of s 79		
(1)	s 101(1), (2)	Amended 2003, Sch 17, para 64, para 66(2).
(2)	s 101(3)	Amended 2003, Sch 17, para 64, para 66(2). Words '(which includes provision for forfeiture of wireless telegraphy apparatus used in the commission of certain offences)' unnecessary.
(3)	s 101(4)	Amended 2003, Sch 17, para 64, para 66(3).
(4)	s 101(5)	Amended 2003, Sch 17, para 66(4).
(5)	s 101(6)	Amended 2003, Sch 17, para 64.
84 Approval of wireless telegraphy apparatus etc		
(1)	ss 69(1), (2), (3), 76	Amended 2003, Sch 17, para 67(2).
(2)	s 69(4)	Amended 2003, Sch 17, para 67(2).
(3)	s 69(5)	
(4)	s 69(6), (7)	
(5)	s 69(8)	Amended 2003, Sch 17, para 67(2), (3).
(6)	s 70(1)	Amended 2003, Sch 17, para 67(2).
(7)	s 70(2), (4)	Amended 2003, Sch 17, para 67(2); modified Finance Act 1990 (c 29), s 128.
(8)	s 70(5)	Amended 2003, Sch 17, para 67(2), (4).

Existing	Rewritten	Remarks
(8A)	s 71(1)	Inserted 2003, Sch 17, para 67(5).
(8B)	s 71(2)	Inserted 2003, Sch 17, para 67(5).
(9)	s 70(6)	

85 Information etc to be marked on or to accompany apparatus

(1)	s 72(1), (2), (3)	Amended 2003, Sch 17, para 64.
(2)	s 72(4)	
(3)	s 74(1), (4)	Words 'subject to section 87 below' unnecessary.
(4)	s 74(2)	
(5)	ss 76, 115(6)	Para (b) amended Consumer Protection Act 1987 (c 43), Sch 4, para 9(1).

86 Information etc to be given in advertisements

(1)	s 73(1), (2)	Amended 2003, Sch 17, para 64.
(2)	s 73(3)	
(3)	s 74(3), (4)	Words 'subject to section 87 below' unnecessary.
(4)	ss 76, 115(6)	

87 Offences under s 85 or 86 due to default of third person

(1)	s 75(1)	
(2)	s 75(2)	Words 'subject to subsection (3) below' unnecessary.
(3)	s 75(3)	
(4)	s 75(4)	

88 Wireless telegraphy functions of Director

	—	Repealed 2003, Sch 19.

89 Abolition of advisory committee

	—	Repealed Statute Law (Repeals) Act 2004 (c 14), Sch 1, Pt 5 Group 19.

90 Radio interference service

	—	Repealed 2003, Sch 17, para 68.

91 Construction of references to conclusion of proceedings

(1)	s 102(1), (2), (5)	Amended 2003, Sch 17, para 69(2).
(2)	s 102(3)	Repealed in part 2003, Sch 19.
(3)	s 102(4)	
(4)	s 102(6)	Repealed in part 2003, Sch 19.

92 Interpretation of Part 6 and minor amendments

(1)	ss 115(2), (3), 116(1), (2), 117(1)	
(2)	ss 60(1), 98(1)	Amends 1949, s 15(4).
(3)	—	Repealed Cable and Broadcasting Act 1984 (c 46), Sch 6.
(4)	—	Repealed 2003, Sch 19.

101 General restrictions on disclosure of information

Words in (1)	—	Inserted 2003, Sch 17, para 72(2). See, s 111 of consolidation.
Words in (2)	—	Inserted 2003, Sch 17, para 72(3). See, s 111 of consolidation.
Words in (3)	—	Inserted 2003, Sch 17, para 72(5); modified Order, Schedule, para 7(4). See, s 111 of consolidation.

104 Orders and schemes

(1B)	ss 72(5), 73(4)	Inserted 2003, Sch 17, para 73.
(1C)	ss 72(6), 73(5)	Inserted 2003, Sch 17, para 73.

Sch 3 Penalties and mode of trial under 1949

Existing	Rewritten	Remarks
para 1	ss 11(4), 33(3), (5), 35(4), 36(2), (4), 37(2), 38(6), 46(2), (3), 47(4), 48(4), 51(5), 53(3), 58(2), (5), (6), 60(2), 66(3), 68(3), 98(2), 100(2), 115(1)	Substitutes 1949, s 14(1) to (1C).
para 2	—	Repealed Statute Law (Repeals) Act 1993 (c 50), Sch 1, Pt XIV Group 2.
para 3	Sch 5, para 7	Amended Order, Schedule, para 4, para (a) substituted Powers of Criminal Courts (Sentencing) Act 2000 (c 6), Sch 9, para 92, para (b) amended Criminal Justice (Northern Ireland) Order 1994 (SI 1994/2795 (NI 15)), Sch 2, para 10, Criminal Procedure (Consequential Provisions) (Scotland) Act 1995 (c 40), Sch 4, para 48(4), Powers of Criminal Courts (Sentencing) Act 2000 (c 6), Sch 9, para 92.

Consumer Protection Act 1987 (c 43)

Existing	Rewritten	Remarks
Sch 4 Minor and consequential amendments		
para 9(1)	s 115(6)	Amends 1984, s 28(6), s 85(5)(b). Repealed as regards 1984, s 28(6) 2003, Sch 19.

Copyright, Designs and Patents Act 1988 (c 48)

Existing	Rewritten	Remarks
Sch 7 Consequential amendments: general		
para 9	ss 85(1), 115(1)	Amends 1967(M), s 5(3)(a), (6).

Electricity Act 1989 (c 29)

Existing	Rewritten	Remarks
Sch 16 Minor and consequential amendments		
para 6	s 115(1)	Amends 1949, s 19(2).

Broadcasting Act 1990 (c 42)

Existing	Rewritten	Remarks
168 Offences of keeping wireless telegraphy station or apparatus for unauthorised use		
	s 36(1)	Inserts 1949, s 1A.
169 Offence if allowing premises to be used for purpose of unlawful broadcasting		
	s 37(1), (5), (6), (7)	Inserts 1949, s 1B.
170 Prohibition of acts facilitating unlawful broadcasting		
	ss 38(1), (2), (3), (4), (5), (8), 115(1), (6)	Inserts 1949, s 1C.
171 Amendments of 1967(M)		

Existing	Rewritten	Remarks
	Introduces 1990, Sch 16.	
172 Amendments of provisions of 1949 relating to penalties and forfeiture		
(1)	—	Introductory.
(2)	ss 35(2), (7), 37(2), 38(6)	Inserts 1949, s 14(1)(aa) to (ac).
(3)	ss 36(2), (4), 115(1)	Inserts 1949, s 14(1A)(aa).
(4)	Sch 5, para 1	Substitutes 1949, s 14(3) to (3AB).
(5)	Sch 5, para 5	Amends 1949, s 14(3E).
173 Extension of search and seizure powers in relation to unlawful broadcasting etc		
(1)	s 97(1)	Amends, and repeals in part, 1949, s 15(1).
(2)	—	Repeals in part 1949, s 15(2).
(3)	ss 59(7), (8), 97(6), (7)	Inserts 1949, s 15(2A).
(4)	s 99(1)	Inserts 1984, s 79(1)(ba), (bb).
(5)	s 99(2)	Amends, and repeals in part, 1984, s 79(2).
(6)	s 99(4), (5)	Inserts 1984, s 79(4A).
174 Application of Part 8 to Isle of Man and Channel Islands		
	s 118(3)	Extends 1949, s 20(3), 1967(M), s 10.
180 Transfer to BBC of functions connected with television licences		
(1)	—	Introduces 1990, Sch 18, Pt 1.
Sch 16 Amendments of 1967(M)		
para 1	ss 78(1), (2), 95(1)	Amends 1967(M), s 2(1)(a); inserts 1967(M), s 2(3).
para 2	ss 79(1), (2), (3), (4), (5), 95(1), 121(1), (2)	Inserts 1967(M), s 2A.
para 3	s 80(2)	Amends 1967(M), s 3(1); inserts 1967(M), s 3(1A).
para 4	s 81(1), (2)	Inserts 1967(M), s 3A.
para 5	ss 84(1), 86(4), (5)	Inserts 1967(M), s 4(1)(aa), (ab); amends 1967(M), s 4(3)(e).
para 6	ss 85(2), 86(4), (5)	Inserts 1967(M), s 5(1)(aa), (ab); amends 1967(M), s 5(3)(a), (4).
para 7	s 93(1), (3), (4)	Amends 1967(M), s 6(1)(a), (5).
para 8	ss 88(1), (3), 89(1), (2), (3), (4), (5), 90(1), (2), (3), (4), (5), 91(1), (2), (3), 92(1), (2), (3), (4), 95(1)	Inserts 1967(M), s 7A.
Sch 18 Transfer of functions connected with television licences		
Pt 1, para 1	ss 8(1), 9(1)	Amends 1949, s 1(1), (2). Sub-paras (4), (5), (6) repealed 2003, Sch 19.
para 3	s 97(2)	Amends 1949, s 15(1).

Vehicle Excise and Registration Act 1994 (c 22)

Existing	Rewritten	Remarks
Sch 3 Consequential amendments		
para 3	s 51(3), (6)	Amends 1967(W), s 8(1), (3), para (a)(i) repealed 2003, Sch 19.

Merchant Shipping Act 1995 (c 21)

Existing	Rewritten	Remarks
Sch 13 Consequential amendments		
para 24	s 115(1)	Amends 1949, s 19(7).

Criminal Procedure (Consequential Provisions) (Scotland) Act 1995 (c 40)

Existing	Rewritten	Remarks
Sch 4 Minor and consequential amendments		
para 48	Sch 5, para 7	Sub-para (1) introductory. Sub-paras (2), (3) repealed 2003, Sch 19. Sub-, para (4) amends 1984, Sch 3, para 3(b).

Wireless Telegraphy Act 1998 (c 6)

Existing	Rewritten	Remarks
1 Charges for wireless telegraphy licences		
(1)	s 115(1)	Amended 2003, s 161(2)(a); repealed in part 2003, Sch 19.
(2)	ss 12(1), (2), 21(1), (2)	Amended 2003, s 161(2)(b), Sch 17, paras 145, 146.
(3)	ss 12(3), 21(3)	Amended 2003, Sch 17, para 146; repealed in part 2003, Sch 19.
(4)	ss 12(4), 21(4)	Amended 2003, s 161(2)(c), Sch 17, para 146.
(5)	ss 12(5), 21(5)	Amended 2003, Sch 17, para 146.
(6)	—	Spent.
(7)	Sch 8, para 11	
2 Matters to be taken into account		
		Substituted 2003, Sch 17, para 147.
(1)	ss 13(1), 22(1)	
(2)	ss 13(2), 22(2)	
(3)	ss 13(3), 22(3), 115(1)	
3 Bidding for licences		
(1)	s 14(1)	Amended 2003, Sch 17, para 145; repealed in part 2003, s 167(2).
(2)	—	Repealed 2003, s 167(2).
(3)	s 14(2), (3)	Amended 2003, s 162(3); para (h) repealed 2003, s 167(3).
(4)	s 14(4)	Substituted 2003, s 167(4).
(5)	s 14(5)	Substituted 2003, s 167(5).
(5A)	s 14(6)	Inserted 2003, s 167(6).
(5B)	s 14(7)	Inserted 2003, s 167(6).
(6)	s 14(8)	Substituted 2003, s 167(6).
(7)	ss 9(8), 45(7)	Amended 2003, Sch 17, para 145.
(8)	s 17	
3A Bidding for grants of recognised spectrum access		
		Inserted 2003, s 161(3).
(1)	s 23(1)	
(2)	s 23(2)	
(3)	s 23(3)	
(4)	s 23(4)	
(5)	s 23(5)	

Existing	Rewritten	Remarks
(6)	s 23(6)	
(7)	s 23(7)	
(8)	s 23(8)	
4 Restriction on revocation or variation of licences		
(1)	Sch 1, para 8(1)	Amended 2003, Sch 17, paras 145, 148.
(2)	Sch 1, para 8(2)	
(3)	Sch 1, para 8(3)	
(4)	Sch 1, para 8(4)	
(5)	Sch 1, para 8(5)	Amended 2003, Sch 17, paras 145, 148.
4A Recovery of sums payable to OFCOM		
	ss 15(1), (2), 24(1), (2)	Inserted 2003, Sch 17, para 149.
5 Promotion of efficient use and management of spectrum		
	—	Repealed 2003, Sch 19.
6 Regulations		
		Substituted 2003, Sch 17, para 150.
(1)	ss 16(1), 25(1), 122(1)	
(2)	ss 16(2), 25(2)	
(3)	ss 16(3), 25(3)	
7 Minor and consequential amendments and repeals		
	—	Introduces 1998 Schs 1, 2.
8 Interpretation		
	ss 17, 26, 115(1), 116(1), (2)	Amended 2003, Sch 17, para 151.
9 Extent and application		
(1)	s 118(1)	
(2)	s 118(3)	Extends 1949, s 20(3).
(3)	s 118(3)	
10 Short title and commencement amendments		
(1)	—	Unnecessary.
(2)	—	Spent.
Sch 1 Minor and consequential amendments		
	—	Repealed 2003, Sch 19.
Sch 2 Repeals and revocations		
	—	Spent.

Powers of Criminal Courts (Sentencing) Act 2000 (c. 6)

Existing	Rewritten	Remarks
Sch 9 Consequential amendments		
para 92	Sch 5, para 7	Amends 1984, Sch 3, para 3.

Regulation of Investigatory Powers Act 2000 (c 23)

Existing	Rewritten	Remarks
73 Conduct in relation to wireless telegraphy		
(1)	—	Renumbers 1949, s 5 as, s 5(1).
(2)	s 48(1)	Amends 1949, s 5(1)(b).

Existing	Rewritten	Remarks
73 Conduct in relation to wireless telegraphy		
(3)	ss 48(5), 49(1), (2), (3), (4), (5), (6), (7), (8), (9), (10), (11), (12)	Inserts 1949, s 5(2) to (12).
(4)	s 121(2)	Amends 1949, s 16(2).

Justice (Northern Ireland) Act 2002 (c 26)

Existing	Rewritten	Remarks
Sch 7 Functions of Advocate General		
para 25	s 93(4)	Amends 1967(M), s 6(5).

Communications Act 2003 (c 21)

Existing	Rewritten	Remarks
152 General functions of OFCOM in relation to radio spectrum		
(1)	s 1(1)	
(2)	s 1(2)	
(3)	s 1(3)	
(4)	s 1(4)	
(5)	s 1(5)	
(6)	s 1(6)	
(7)	s 1(7)	
(8)	s 1(8)	
(9)	s 1(9)	
153 United Kingdom Plan for Frequency Authorisation		
(1)	s 2(1)	
(2)	s 2(2)	
154 Duties of OFCOM when carrying out spectrum functions		
(1)	s 3(1)	
(2)	s 3(2)	
(3)	s 3(3), (4)	
(4)	s 3(5)	
(5)	s 3(6)	
155 Advisory service in relation to interference		
(1)	s 4	
(2)	s 115(3)	
156 Directions with respect to the radio spectrum		
(1)	s 5(1)	
(2)	s 5(2)	
(3)	s 5(3)	
(4)	s 5(4)	
(5)	s 5(5)	
157 Procedure for directions under s 156		
(1)	s 6(1)	
(2)	s 6(2)	
(3)	s 6(3)	
(4)	s 6(4)	
(5)	s 6(5)	
(6)	s 6(6)	

Existing	Rewritten	Remarks
(7)	s 6(7)	
158 Special duty in relation to television multiplexes		
(1)	s 7(1)	
(2)	s 7(2)	
(3)	s 7(3)	
(4)	s 7(4)	
(5)	s 7(5)	
159 Grant for recognised spectrum cases		
(1)	s 18(1), (2)	
(2)	s 18(3)	
(3)	s 18(4)	
(4)	s 18(5)	
(5)	s 18(6)	
(6)	s 18(7)	
(7)	s 18(8)	
(8)	s 19	
(9)	s 122(1)	
(10)	ss 115(1), (2), 116(1), (2), 117(1), (2)	
160 Effect of grant of recognised spectrum access		
(1)	s 20(1)	
(2)	s 20(2)	
161 Charges in respect of grants of recognised spectrum access		
(1)	—	Introductory.
(2)	ss 12(1), (4), 21(1), (4), 115(1)	Amends 1998, s 1.
(3)	s 23(1), (3), (4), (5), (6), (7), (8)	Inserts 1998, s 3A.
162 Conversion into and from wireless telegraphy licences		
(1)	s 27	
(2)	s 122(1)	
163 Payments for use of radio spectrum by the Crown		
(1)	s 28(1)	
(2)	s 28(2)	
(3)	s 117(1), (2)	
164 Limitations on authorised spectrum use		
(1)	s 29(1)	
(2)	s 29(2)	
(3)	s 29(3)	
(4)	s 29(4)	
(5)	s 29(5)	
(6)	s 29(6)	
(7)	s 29(7)	
(8)	s 29(8)	
(9)	s 122(1)	
165 Terms etc of wireless telegraphy licences		
	s 9(4), (5), (6)	Inserts 1949, s 1(2A), (2B), (2C).
166 Exemption from need for wireless telegraphy licence		
	s 8(4), (5)	Inserts 1949, s 1AA.
167 Bidding for wireless telegraphy licences		

Existing	Rewritten	Remarks
(1)	—	Introductory.
(2)	—	Repeals in part 1998, s 3(1); repeals 1998, s 3(2).
(3)	s 14(3)	Amends, and repeals in part, 1998, s 3(3).
(4)	s 14(4)	Substitutes 1998, s 3(4).
(5)	s 14(5)	Substitutes 1998, s 3(5).
(6)	s 14(6), (7), (8)	Substitutes 1998, s 3(5A), (5B), (6).

168 Spectrum trading

(1)	s 30(1)	
(2)	s 30(2)	
(3)	s 30(3)	
(4)	s 30(4)	
(5)	s 30(5)	
(6)	s 30(6)	
(7)	s 122(1)	

169 Variation and revocation of wireless telegraphy licences

(1)	s 115(1), Sch 1, para 7(1), (2), (3), (4), (5), (6), (7), (8), (9), (10), (11), (12), (13)	Substitutes 1949, s 1E.
(2)	—	Spent.

170 Wireless telegraphy register

(1)	s 31(1)	
(2)	s 31(2)	
(3)	s 31(3)	
(4)	s 31(4)	
(5)	s 122(1)	

171 Information requirements in relation to wireless telegraphy licences

(1)	ss 32(1), (2), (3), (4), (5), 33(1), (2), (4), 34(1), (2), (3), (4)	Inserts 1949, s 13A, s 13B.
(2)	s 33(3)	Inserts 1949, s 14(1A)(ea).

172 Contraventions of use of wireless telegraphy

(1)	s 39(1)	
(2)	s 39(2)	
(3)	s 39(3)	
(4)	s 39(4)	
(5)	s 39(5)	
(6)	s 39(6)	
(7)	s 39(7)	

173 Meaning of 'repeated contravention' in s 172

(1)	s 40(1)	
(2)	s 40(2)	
(3)	s 40(3)	
(4)	s 40(4)	
(5)	s 40(5)	
(6)	s 40(6)	
(7)	s 40(7)	
(8)	s 40(8)	
(9)	s 40(9)	

Existing	Rewritten	Remarks
174 Procedure for prosecutions of wireless telegraphy offences		
(1)	s 41(1)	
(2)	s 41(2), Sch 8, para 15	
(3)	s 41(3), Sch 8, para 15	
(4)	s 41(4)	
(5)	s 41(5)	
(6)	s 41(6)	
(7)	s 41(7), (8)	
(8)	s 117(1), (2)	
175 Special procedure for contraventions by multiplex licence holders		
(1)	s 42(1)	
(2)	s 42(2)	
(3)	s 42(3)	
(4)	s 42(4)	
(5)	s 42(5)	
(6)	s 42(6)	
176 Amount of penalty under s 175		
(1)	s 43(1), (2)	
(2)	s 43(3)	
(3)	s 43(4)	
(4)	s 43(5)	
177 'Relevant amount of gross revenue' for the purposes of s 176		
(1)	s 44(1)	
(2)	s 44(2)	
(3)	s 44(3)	
(4)	s 44(4)	
(5)	s 44(5)	
(6)	s 44(6)	
(7)	s 44(7)	
(8)	s 44(8)	
(9)	s 44(9)	
(10)	s 44(10)	
(11)	s 44(11)	
178 Proceedings for an offence relating to apparatus use		
(1)	s 57(1), (2), (3), (4), (5)	Repeals 1949, s 11(1), proviso, para (i); substitutes 1949, s 11(2A), (2B), (2C), (2D). Effect of part saved by, Sch 8, para 13 to consolidation.
(2)	s 57(1), (2), (3), (4), (5)	Substitutes 1949, s 12(1A), (1B), (1C), (1D). Effect of part saved by, Sch 8, para 13 to consolidation.
179 Modification of penalties for certain wireless telegraphy offences		
(1)	ss 35(2), (7), 36(2)	Substitutes 1949, s 14(1)(aa), (ab).
(2)	ss 35(5), 36(5)	Inserts 1949, s 14(1AA).
(3)	s 99(1)	Inserts 1984, s 79(1)(bza).
(4)	Sch 8, paras 17, 21	
180 Fixed penalties for certain wireless telegraphy offences		
	s 96	Introduces 2003, Sch 6.
181 Power of arrest		
(1)	—	Repealed Serious Organised Crime and Police Act 2005 (c 15), Sch 17.

Existing	Rewritten	Remarks
(2)	—	Inserts Police and Criminal Evidence (Northern Ireland) Order 1989 (SI 1989/1341 (NI 12)) art 26(2)(j). (See amendment of 1989 (SI 1989/1341 (NI 12)), Sch 7, para 8 to consolidation.)
182 Forfeiture etc of restricted apparatus		
(1)	s 104(1)	
(2)	s 104(2)	
(3)	s 104(3)	
(4)	s 104(4)	Introduces 2003, Sch 7.
(5)	Sch 8, para 22	
(6)	—	Repeals 1984 s, s 80, 81 in relation to apparatus seized after coming into force of 2003, s 182.
(7)	—	Spent.
183 Modification of definition of 'undue influence'		
	s 115(4), (5)	Substitutes 1949, s 19(5), (5A).
184 Modification of definition of 'wireless telegraphy'		
(1)	s 116(3)	Words '(at the passing of this Act, 3,000 GHz)' unnecessary.
(2)	s 116(4)	
393 General restrictions on disclosure of information		
(1)(b)	—	See, s 111 of consolidation.
(5)(a), (b), (l)	—	See, s 111 of consolidation.
394 Service of notifications and other documents		
(2)(c)	—	See, s 112 of consolidation.
402 Power of Secretary of State to make orders and regulations		
(2)(b)	—	See, s 121 of consolidation.
404 Criminal liability of company directors etc.		
(4)(b), (c)	—	See, s 110 of consolidation.
(5)	—	Repeals 1949, s 14(2).
407 Pre-consolidation amendments		
(1)(a), words in	—	Power exercised (see Order).
(1)(c)		
Sch 1 Functions transferred to OFCOM		
para 1	—	Transfers functions from Secretary of State to Office of Communications Applied passim.
para 2	—	Transfers functions under 1967(M), s 7A from Secretary of State to Secretary of State concurrently with Office of Communications See s, s 88, 89, 90, 91 of consolidation.
Sch 5 Procedure for grants of recognised spectrum access		
para 1	s 122(1), Sch 2, para 1	
para 2	Sch 2, para 2	
para 3	Sch 2, para 3	
para 4	Sch 2, para 4	
para 5	Sch 2, para 5	
para 6	Sch 2, para 6	
para 7	Sch 2, para 7	
para 8	s 117(1), (2)	
Sch 6 Fixed penalties for wireless telegraphy offences		
para 1	Sch 4, para 1, Sch 8, para 20	

Existing	Rewritten	Remarks
para 2	Sch 4, para 2	
para 3	Sch 4, para 3	
para 4	Sch 4, para 4	
para 5	Sch 4, para 5	
para 6	Sch 4, para 6	
para 7	Sch 4, para 7	
para 8	Sch 4, para 8	
para 9	Sch 4, para 9	
para 10	Sch 4, para 10	
para 11	Sch 4, para 11	
para 12	Sch 4, para 12	
para 13	Sch 4, para 13	Amended Courts Act 2003 (Consequential Provisions) Order 2005 (SI 2005/886), Schedule, para 95.
Sch 7 Seizure and forfeiture of apparatus		
para 1	Sch 6, para 1, Sch 8, para 22	
para 2	Sch 6, para 2	
para 3	Sch 6, para 3	
para 4	Sch 6, para 4	
para 5	Sch 6, para 5	
para 6	Sch 6, para 6	
para 7	Sch 6, para 7	
para 8	Sch 6, para 8	
para 9	Sch 6, para 9	
para 10	Sch 6, para 10	
para 11	Sch 6, para 11	
para 12	Sch 6, para 12	
para 13	Sch 6, para 13	
para 14	Sch 6, para 14	
para 15	Sch 6, para 15	
para 16	Sch 6, para 16	
para 17	Sch 6, para 17	
Sch 8 Decisions not subject to appeal		
paras 13–36	—	See Sch 7, para 36 to consolidation.
Sch 17 Minor and consequential amendments		
para 6	ss 8(1), (2), (3), 9(1), 11(1), (3), Sch 1, paras 5, 6	Amends 1949, s 1(1), (1) proviso, (2), (3), (4), (5); inserts 1949, s 1(1AA).
para 7	s 38(4)	Substitutes 1949, s 1C(4).
para 8	s 9(7), Sch 1, paras 1(1), (2), 2(1), (2), (3), 3	Amends 1949, s 1D(4), (5), (6); inserts 1949, s 1D(4A), (4B), (4C); substitutes 1949, s 1D(3), (9); repeals 1949, s 1D(1), (2), (7), (8).
para 9	s 45(1), (3), (5), (6), (9), (10)	Amends 1949, s 3(1); inserts 1949, s 3(2A), (2B).
para 10	—	Repeals 1949, s 9 in respect of decisions made after coming into force of 2003, s 192.
para 11	s 54(1), (2), (3), (7), (8)	Amends 1949, s 10(1), (2); inserts 1949, s 10(4A), (4B).
para 12	ss 55(1), (3), (4), (6), (7), 58(1)	Amends 1949, s 11(1), (2), (7).
para 13	ss 56(1), (2), 58(4)	Amends 1949, s 12(1), (5).

Existing	Rewritten	Remarks
para 14	ss 47(4), 58(6), 108(2), (3), Sch 5, paras 1, 2, 4, 5	Amends 1949, s 14(1), (1A), (3), (3A), (3B), (3D), (3E), (7); repeals 1949, s 14(1A)(e), (3)(b).
para 15	ss 59(1), (3), (5), (7), 97(2), (5), (6)	Amends 1949, s 15(1), (2), (2A); inserts 1949, s 15(1A).
para 16	ss 121(1), 122(1)	Amends 1949, s 16(2); inserts 1949, s 16(1A).
para 17	s 115(1)	Inserts 1949, s 19(2AA).
para 18	Sch 3, para 4	Substitutes 1949, Sch 1, para 3.
para 32	s 115(6)	Inserts 1967(M), s 4(3A), s 5(3A).
para 33	s 85(1), (4)	Amends 1967(M), s 5(3); substitutes 1967(M), s 5(4).
para 34	s 93(3), (4)	Amends 1967(M), s 6(5).
para 35	ss 88(1), 89(3), 90(1), (5), 91(3)	Amends 1967(M), s 7A(1), (2), (3), (4), (7).
para 36	s 115(1)	Amends 1967(M), s 9(1).
para 37	ss 63(1), (2), (3), 64, 66(2), 115(1), 122(1)	Amends 1967(W), s 7(2), (5), (6), (7), (8), (9), (11); inserts 1967(W), s 7(11A), (11B), (11C), (11D).
para 38	s 51(1), (3), (4)	Amends 1967(W), s 8(1), (2).
para 64	ss 72(1), (2), 73(1), (2), 99(2), (3), (4), 101(1), (3), (4), (5), (6)	Amends 1984 s, s 79, 83, 85, 86.
para 65	s 99(7)	Amends 1984, s 79(6)(b).
para 66	s 101(2), (3), (4), (5)	Amends 1984, s 83(1), (2), (3), (4).
para 67	ss 69(3), (4), (8), 70(1), (2), (5), 71(1), (2)	Amends 1984, s 84(1), (2), (5), (6), (7), (8); inserts 1984, s 84(8A), (8B).
para 68	—	Repeals 1984, s 90.
para 69	s 102(1)	Amends 1984, s 91(1).
para 72(2)	—	Amends 1984, s 101(1)(a) (see note on that provision).
para 145	ss 12(2), 14(1), (3), 21(2), Sch 1, para 8(1), (5)	Amends 1998 s, s 1, 3, 4.
para 146	ss 12(2), (3), (4), 21(2), (3), (4), (5)	Amends 1998, s 1(2), (3), (4), (5).
para 147	ss 13(1), (2), (3), 22(1), (2), (3), 115(1)	Substitutes 1998, s 2.
para 148	Sch 1, para 8(1), (5)	Amends 1998, s 4(1), (5).
para 149	ss 15(1), (2), 24(1), (2)	Inserts 1998, s 4A.
para 150	ss 16(1), (2), (3), 25(1), (2), (3), 122(1)	Substitutes 1998, s 6.
para 151	ss 17, 26, 115(1)	Amends 1998, s 8.

Sch 18 Transitional Provisions

para 6	—	See, Sch 8, para 10 to consolidation.
para 20	—	See, Sch 8, para 12 to consolidation.

Existing	Rewritten	Remarks
para 21	—	See, Sch 8, para 12 to consolidation.
para 23(1) (c)(i), words in (2), (3)	—	Spent as regards 2003, Sch 18, para 23(3); otherwise effect saved by, Sch 8, para 23 to consolidation.
para 55	—	Spent.
para 63	—	Effect saved by, Sch 8, para 25 to consolidation.
Sch 19 Repeals		
Note 1	—	See, Sch 8, para 7 to consolidation.
Note 3	—	See, Sch 8, para 7 to consolidation.

Criminal Justice Act 2003 (c 44)

Existing	Rewritten	Remarks
Sch 25 Summary offences no longer punishable with imprisonment		
para 29	—	See note on 1949, s 14(1B).

Serious Organised Crime and Police Act 2005 (c 15)

Existing	Rewritten	Remarks
Sch 16 Remaining minor and consequential amendments (search warrants)		
para 3	s 97(3)	Amends 1949, s 15(1).

Transfer of Functions (Local Government, etc) (Northern Ireland) Order 1973, SR & O (NI) 1973/256

Existing	Rewritten	Remarks
Sch 1 Functions transferred		
Entry relating to 1949	—	Transfers functions under 1949, s 2 from welfare authorities to health and social services boards (see note on that provision).
Sch 2 Amendments		
Entry relating to 1949	—	Amends 1949, s 2(2)(d) (see note on that provision); repeals 1949, s 17(2).

Hong Kong (British Nationality) Order 1986, SI 1986/948

Existing	Rewritten	Remarks
Sch 1 Consequential amendments		
para relating to 1967(M)	s 95(2)	Amends 1967(M), s 3(3).

Police and Criminal Evidence (Northern Ireland) Order 1989, SI 1989/1341 (NI 12)

Existing	Rewritten	Remarks
art 26 Arrest without warrant for arrestable offences		
para (2)(j) relating to 1949, s 14(1)	—	See, Sch 7, para 8 to consolidation.

Criminal Justice (Northern Ireland) Order 1994, SI 1994/2795 (NI 15)

Existing	Rewritten	Remarks
Sch 2 Minor and consequential amendments		
para 10	Sch 5, para 7	Amends 1984, Sch 3, para 3(b).

Deregulation (Wireless Telegraphy) Order 1996, SI 1996/1864

Existing	Rewritten	Remarks
art 3 Licensing of television dealers		
	—	Inserts 1949, s 1(1A) (see note on that provision).

Telecommunications (Licensing) Regulations 1997, SI 1997/2930

Existing	Rewritten	Remarks
reg 4 Amendments of 1949		
(1)	—	Introductory.
(2)	Sch 1, paras 1(2), 3	Inserts 1949 s, s 1D, 1E.

Transfer of Functions (Lord Advocate and Advocate General for Scotland) Order 1999, SI 1999/679

Existing	Rewritten	Remarks
Sch Functions transferred from the Lord Advocate to the Advocate General for Scotland		
Entry relating to 1949, s 14(7)	—	Superseded by amendment of 1949, s 14(7) by 2003, Sch 17, para 14(8).

Telecommunications (Appeals) Regulations 1999, SI 1999/3180

Existing	Rewritten	Remarks
reg 4 Amendments of 1949		
(1)	—	Introductory.
(2)	—	Amends 1949, s 1D(1) (see note on that provision).
(3)	—	Inserts 1949, s 1F (see note on that provision).

Courts Act 2003 (Consequential Provisions) Order 2005, SI 2005/886

Existing	Rewritten	Remarks
Sch Consequential amendments		
para 95	Sch 4, para 13	Amends 2003, Sch 6, para 13.

Wireless Telegraphy (Pre-Consolidation Amendments) Order 2006, SI 2006/1391

Existing	Rewritten	Remarks
art 1 Citation and commencement		
	—	Unnecessary.
art 2 Pre-consolidation amendments		
	—	Introduces Schedule.
Sch Modifications of enactments		
para 1	—	Introductory.
para 2	s 108(1), (2)	Amends 1949, s 14(7).
para 3	s 118(3)	Modifies 1949, s 20(3).
para 4	Sch 5, para 7	Amends 1984, Sch 3, para 3.
para 5	Sch 1, para 8(5)	Amends 1998, s 4(5).
para 6	s 115(1)	Modifies references to 'broadcast', 'frequency', 'information', 'international obligation of the United Kingdom' in 1949, 1967(W), 1984.

Existing	Rewritten	Remarks
para 7	—	Modifies references to 1984, 2003, in Water Act 1989 (c 15), Water Industry Act 1991 (c 56), Water Resources Act 1991 (c 57), Railways Act 1993 (c 43), Greater London Authority Act (c 29), Postal Services Act 2000 (c 26), Utilities Act 2000 (c 27), Transport Act 2000 (c 38), Enterprise Act 2002 (c 40), Energy (Northern Ireland) Order 2003 (SI 2003/419 (NI 6)).
para 8	s 121(3)	Modifies 1949 s, s 5, 6(2), 1967(M), s 2A(1), 1984, s 84.
para 9	s 118(5)	Modifies 1949, s 20(3), 1967(M), s 10(1), 1967(W), s 15(6), 1984, s 108, 1998, s 9(3).

THEATRES AND OTHER FORMS OF ENTERTAINMENT

Halsbury's Laws of England (4th edn) vol 45(2) (Reissue) paras 1–200

2759   Films—British films—certification

The Films (Certification) (Amendment) Regulations 2006, SI 2006/642 (in force on 1 April 2006), further amend the 1985 Regulations, SI 1985/994, so as to require an application for certification of a film as a British film to include particulars relating to how the film meets the requirement to pass the cultural test.

The Films (Certification) Regulations 2006, SI 2006/3281 (in force on 1 January 2007), prescribe the particulars and evidence required to satisfy the Secretary of State that a film is a British film for the purposes of the Films Act 1985 Sch 1 and make provision in relation to the making of a statutory declaration on behalf of a company.

2760   Films—British films—definition

The Films (Definition of 'British Film') Order 2006, SI 2006/643 (in force on 1 April 2006), removes two of the current requirements to be satisfied by a film to meet the definition, that is, the requirements that at least 70 per cent of the expenditure on the film is incurred on film production activity carried out in the United Kingdom, and that not less than a requisite amount of labour costs of the film represents payments for the services of residents or citizens of Commonwealth countries or member states. The order introduces a new requirement to be satisfied, namely that a film passes a points-based 'cultural test', by which points are awarded on the basis of the content of the film, where certain work on the film is carried out, and the residence or citizenship of the personnel involved in the making of the film.

The Films (Definition of 'British Film') (No 2) Order 2006, SI 2006/3430 (in force on 1 January 2007), amends the definition of 'British film' in the Films Act 1985 Sch 1 by modifying the points-based test introduced by the principal 2006 Order supra.

2761   Films—British films—European Convention on Cinematographic Co-production

The European Convention on Cinematographic Co-production Order 2006, SI 2006/2656 (in force on 11 October 2006), provides that a film is to be treated as a British film for the purposes of the Films Act 1985 Sch 1 where it is made in accordance with the European Convention on Cinematographic Co-production, and (1) where there are two co-producers, one is established in the United Kingdom and the other is established in a state which is a contracting party to the Convention; or (2) where there are three or more co-producers, one is established in the United Kingdom and at least two others are established in different states each of which is a contracting party to the Convention.

2762   Films—co-production agreements

The Films Co-Production Agreements (Amendment) Order 2006, SI 2006/1921 (in force on 20 July 2006), amends the 1985 Regulations, SI 1985/960, and (1) extends the specified list of co-production agreements so as to include an agreement with South Africa; and (2) removes, from the specified list, certain agreements with Italy which have been terminated. SI 1985/2001, 1990/1513, 1991/1725, 1993/1805, 1994/3222, 2000/740 are revoked.

2763   Football—spectators—2006 World Cup control period

The Football Spectators (2006 World Cup Control Period) Order 2006, SI 2006/988 (in force on 24 April 2006), describes the control period for the 2006 FIFA World Cup in Germany which is to commence on 30 May 2006, being ten days before the first match in the tournament, and ends when the last match in the tournament is finished or cancelled.

2764   Football—spectators—prescription

The Football Spectators (Prescription) (Amendment) Order 2006, SI 2006/761 (in force on 10 April 2006), amends the 2004 Order, SI 2004/2409, so as to prescribe additional matches for the purposes of the Football Spectators Act 1989 Pt II (ss 14–22A). In particular, the order (1) adds to those football matches which are regulated matches in England and Wales any match in which a participating team represents a club from outside England and Wales; and (2) makes two additions to those football matches which are regulated outside England and Wales, the first being any match involving a country or territory whose football association is a member of the Federation Internationale de Football Associations ('FIFA'), where the match is part of a competition or tournament organised by or under the authority of FIFA or the Union des Associations Europeennes de Football ('UEFA'), and where the competition or tournament is one in which the England or Wales national team is eligible to participate or has participated, and the second being any match involving a club whose national football association is a member of FIFA, where the match is part of a competition or tournament organised by or under the authority of FIFA or UEFA, and where the competition or tournament is one in which a club from the Football League, the Football Association Premier League, the Football Conference or the League of Wales is eligible to participate or has participated.

2765   London Olympic Games and Paralympic Games Act 2006

The London Olympic Games and Paralympic Games Act 2006 makes provision in connection with the Olympic and Paralympic Games that are to take place in London in the year 2012 and amends the Olympic Symbol etc (Protection) Act 1995. The 2006 Act received the royal assent on 30 March 2006 and certain provisions came into force on that day. Further provisions came into force on 30 May 2006: SI 2006/1118. The remaining provisions come into force on a day or days to be appointed. For details of commencement, see the commencement table in the title STATUTES.

Section 1 deals with interpretation and, in particular, defines the term 'London Olympics', so as to include events which are held outside London as part of the Games. By virtue of s 2, the Secretary of State may by order amend a reference in the Act to any document referred to in s 1 if he thinks that the reference has ceased to be accurate by reason of the amendment or substitution of that document.

Provision is made for the establishment of a body corporate to be known as the Olympic Delivery Authority ('the ODA'): s 3, Sch 1. Section 4 sets out the functions of the ODA, which are to do anything necessary or expedient for the purpose of (1) preparing for the London Olympics; (2) making arrangements in preparation for, or in connection with, the use or management before, during or after the Games of premises and facilities acquired, constructed or adapted in preparation for the Games; or (3) ensuring that adequate arrangements are made for the provision, management and control of facilities for transport in connection with the Games. Under s 5, the Secretary of State may, by order, appoint the ODA as the local planning authority for an area specified in that order. Under s 6, the ODA must, in exercising all its functions, have regard to safety and security, in consultation with the police. The ODA may take action with regard to the cleaning or lighting of specified areas during the London Olympics period: s 7. Section 8 allows for the creation of a 'transfer scheme' to transfer specified property, rights and liabilities to the ODA simultaneously, where the Secretary of State thinks it expedient in order to enable the ODA to carry out its functions, and introduces Sch 2, which sets out in more detail what may and may not be included in a transfer scheme. Dissolution of the ODA by order made by the Secretary of State is dealt with in s 9.

The ODA will be required to prepare and keep under review an Olympic Transport Plan ('OTP'), which will set out the transport plans for the Games, and details of how they are to be implemented: s 10. The Olympic Route Network ('ORN') will consist of roads within England that will be used for travel to and from events venues and accommodation: s 11. Section 12 allows the ODA to co-ordinate the delivery of the transport needs of the Games, and imposes an obligation on various authorities and bodies to co-operate with the ODA for the purpose of implementing the OTP. Section 13 gives the ODA has a degree of 'negative control' over the roads for the purposes of the Games by requiring the ODA to be notified of the exercise of any highway, traffic or street functions that might reasonably be expected to affect transport needs connected to the Games: s 13. By virtue of s 14, the ODA may make traffic regulation orders over roads that are part of the Olympic Route Network ('ORN'), although only with the consent of the Secretary of State, and only for Olympic purposes. Section 15 provides for the enforcement of traffic regulation orders made for Olympic purposes. Section 16 amends, for Olympic purposes, the provisions relating to special events orders, under which roads may be restricted or closed in connection with sporting events, social events and entertainments. There is a new objective given to the Office of Rail Regulations to facilitate the provision, management and control of transport facilities related to the Olympics and to consult the ODA as to how to do so: s 17. Interpretation and definition of the principal terms in ss 10–17 are set out in s 18.

Section 19 imposes a duty on the Secretary of State to make regulations about advertising in the vicinity of Olympic venues, and s 20 sets out in more detail what restrictions and flexibilities will apply to the making of such regulations. By virtue of s 21, it is a criminal offence to contravene such regulations, punishable by a fine. Section 22 gives a constable, or an enforcement officer designated by the ODA, the power to enter land or premises in order to prevent or stop unauthorised advertising as defined in the regulations. Under s 23, a duty is placed on the ODA, to inform those people likely to be affected by the regulations about the effect of the regulations, and the ODA is allowed to provide assistance to persons so that they can comply with the regulations. Section 24 allows the Secretary of State to make an order that requires certain local planning authorities to notify those people to whom they grant consents, in relation to advertisements, of the nature of regulations made and obligations imposed under s 19.

Section 25 imposes a duty on the Secretary of State to make regulations to control trading in the vicinity of Games venues, and s 26 sets out in more detail what restrictions and flexibilities will apply to regulations made under s 25. Contravention of a regulation made under s 25 will be an offence, punishable by a fine: s 27. By virtue of s 28, a constable, or enforcement officer designated by the ODA, is given the power to enter premises on which they reasonably believe a contravention of the regulations is occurring. Section 29 places a duty on the ODA to inform those people likely to be affected by the regulations about the effect of the regulations. The Secretary of State may make an order requiring those persons who grant authorisations to trade to notify recipients that their rights will be superseded by any relevant regulations made under s 25: s 30. Section 31 creates a criminal offence of touting tickets for the 2012 Olympic Games.

The Olympic Symbol etc (Protection) Act 1995, which creates the Olympic association right, protecting the Olympic symbol, motto and other words relating to the Olympics, is amended, so as to allow for joint proprietorship of the Olympic association right, afford increased protection for the Olympic words, symbols and motto, clarify exceptions to the 2005 Act and create a Paralympic association right: s 32, Sch 3. A specific event association right in relation to the 2012 London Olympic and Paralympic Games is created, and it is sought to prevent those who use innovative ways of making an association with the Games from doing so: s 33, Sch 4. Section 34 enables the Greater London Authority ('GLA') to play its part in delivering the 2012 Olympic Games and gives the GLA the power to do anything for the purpose of complying with the obligations which are placed on the Mayor of London in the Host City Contract or to prepare for and manage the London Olympics. When giving financial support to others for activity connected with the London Olympics, the GLA may do so on specific terms or conditions, in particular as regards the payment of interest: s 35. Section 36 amends the purposes of a regional development agency as listed in the Regional Development Agencies Act 1998 to include the purpose of preparing for the London Olympics.

The 2005 Act ss 37, 38 modify the provisions of the Act in their application to Scotland and Northern Ireland. Section 39 adds the offences of breach of the advertising and street trading regulations in ss 21, 27, respectively, and of ticket touting created by s 31, to the Police and Criminal Evidence Act 1984 Sch 1A, so as to make those offences arrestable. The 2005 Act s 40 deals with commencement, s 41 with extent, and s 42 with short title.

Amendments, repeals and revocations
The list below, which is not exhaustive, mentions repeals and amendments which are or will be effective when the Act is fully in force.

Specific provisions of a number of Acts are amended or repealed. These include: Police and Criminal Evidence Act 1984 Sch 1A; Olympic Symbol etc (Protection) Act 1995 ss 1, 3(1), 4, 5, 7(3), 18.

2766 Performing arts—funding—ancillary funding activities—cultural exemptions—link between input and taxable supplies

See *Mayflower Theatre Trust Ltd v Revenue and Customs Comrs*, para 2913.

2767 Video recordings—supply of restricted videos—offer to supply

The Video Recordings Act 1984 s 12(1) provides that, where a classification certificate issued in respect of a video work states that no video recording containing that work is to be supplied other than in a licensed sex shop, a person who at any place other than in a licensed sex shop supplies a video recording containing the work, or offers to do so, is guilty of an offence unless the supply is, or would if it took place be, an exempted supply. 'Supply' means supply in any manner, whether or not for reward, and, therefore, includes supply by way of sale, letting on hire, exchange or loan: s 1(4).

In two separate cases the defendant owners of licensed sex shops were convicted of offences under the 1984 Act s 12(1). All of the offences concerned supplying or offering to supply video recordings which, pursuant to s 7(2)(c), had been given R18 certificates, by virtue of which the recordings in question were not to be supplied to any person below the age of 18 years and could only be supplied in a licensed sex shop. In the first case, orders for recordings were placed by post and telephone to the shop and deliveries were made to an office, which was not a sex shop. In the second case, orders were made via the shop's website and by telephone and were delivered to an office together with catalogues. On the defendants' conjoined appeals, issues arose whether there were supplies of videos in a licensed sex shop and whether there were offers to supply by way of the catalogues. *Held*, a licensed sex shop could not lawfully supply video recordings with R18 certificates by way of mail or telephone order. Supply could only be made to a person physically in the shop. Section 12(1) was to be interpreted according to the purpose of s 7(2)(c), namely to prevent children viewing unsuitable material. The requirement that the event of supply was to be confined to a licensed sex shop gave heightened protection, reducing the opportunity for the material to be viewed by children. The words 'offers to do so' in s 12(1) referred to an offer to make a supply other than in a licensed sex shop. The phrase 'or would if it took place be an exempted supply' was there to ensure that the offence of offering to supply did not extend to an offer to supply an exempted supply where no supply had taken place. The meaning of s 12(1) was that it was an offence in connection with a video recording to offer to make the supply, not to make the offer, other than in a licensed sex shop. Moreover, the words 'supply in any manner' in s 1(4) indicated that there could be a supply where there had been no binding contract to supply. Supply, therefore, meant the actual supply, and the underlying transaction which gave rise to the supply was of no importance. The catalogue and the terms and conditions forming part of the catalogue amounted to an offer, at the conclusion of the sale, to deliver the recordings to the address. Judgment would be given accordingly.

Interfact Ltd v Liverpool CC; Pabo v Liverpool CC [2005] EWHC 995 (Admin), [2005] 1 WLR 3118 (Queen's Bench Division: Maurice Kay LJ and Newman J).

TIME

Halsbury's Laws of England (4th edn) vol 45(2) (Reissue) paras 201–300

2768   Computation of time—date of court order—order made after normal business hours—permitted period for lodging notice of appeal

See *R (on the application of Amoako) v DPP*, para 1313.

TORT

Halsbury's Laws of England (4th edn) vol 45(2) (Reissue) paras 301–849

Articles

For articles relating to this title please refer to the Table of Articles at the beginning of the Abridgment.

2769   Breach of statutory duty—local authority—allegation of child abuse—duty to parent to investigate claim competently

The first claimant was a father who had been suspected of sexually abusing his daughter, the second claimant, when she was very young. The allegations were later held to be unfounded, and the claimants sought damages for the actions of the social workers and the police officers involved. The court struck out certain parts of the pleading which alleged that the social workers who had been investigating the allegations of abuse had owed the first claimant a duty of care. The first claimant applied to amend the particulars of claim to plead breaches of the direct duty of care owed to him by the first and second defendant local authorities. It was alleged that, in order to fulfil its statutory functions, a local authority was obliged to put in place systems and policies which would ensure (1) that allegations of abuse of children were investigated competently by staff who were properly managed and supervised; (2) that such staff were aware of the relevant local and national guidance relating to the investigation of such allegations and were properly trained in their application; and (3) that records relating to such investigations, and to the management, supervision and training of staff carrying out those investigations, were properly kept and maintained. An issue also arose as to whether the imposition of such a duty was inconsistent with the established principle that no duty of care was owed by individual social workers to parents in respect of an investigation into the abuse of children. *Held*, in general, the imposition of a duty of care of the sort which the first claimant proposed to plead did not create the conflict of interest of the kind which applied to social workers when they carried out allegations of child abuse. It was in the interests of parents just as much as the interests of children that investigations were carried out competently by staff who were properly managed and supervised, that such staff were aware of the relevant local and national guidance relating to the investigation of such allegations and were properly trained in their application, and that proper records were kept and maintained of such investigations and of the management, supervision and training of staff who carried them out. There was no basis on which it could be said that if duties of that kind were owed to children suspected of having been abused, they would conflict with duties of that kind being owed to the parents suspected of having abused them. In the instant case, it was sufficiently arguable that the relevant authority owed the first claimant a 'direct' duty of care. Accordingly, the application would be allowed.

L v Reading BC [2006] EWHC 3206 (QB), [2006] All ER (D) 183 (Dec) (Queen's Bench Division: Keith J).

2770   Breach of statutory duty—Revenue—delay in issuing sub-contractor's tax certificate

See *Neil Martin Ltd v Revenue and Customs Comrs*, para 1635.

2771   Compensation Act 2006

The Compensation Act 2006 specifies certain factors that may be taken into account by a court determining a claim in negligence or breach of statutory duty, makes provision about damages for mesothelioma and makes provision for the regulation of claims management services. The Act received the royal assent on 25 July 2006 and certain provisions came into force on that day. Further provisions came into force on 1 December 2006 (SI 2006/3005) and the remaining provisions come into force on a day or days to be appointed. For details of commencement, see the commencement table in the title STATUTES.

Part 1 (ss 1–3) Standard of care
Section 1 provides that in considering a claim in negligence or breach of statutory duty, a court may, in determining whether the defendant should have taken particular steps to meet a standard of care, whether by taking precautions or otherwise, have regard to whether a requirement to take those steps might prevent a desirable activity from taking place, or might discourage persons from undertaking functions in connection with a desirable activity. An apology, offer of treatment or other redress does not of itself amount to an admission of negligence or breach of statutory duty: s 2. Section 3 contains provisions establishing joint and several liability in cases where a person has contracted mesothelioma as a result of being negligently exposed to asbestos.

Part 2 (ss 4–15) Claims management services
The provisions of regulated claims management services by those who are not authorised, exempted from authorisation or subject to a waiver, or an individual acting otherwise than in the course of a business is prohibited by s 4. Section 5 permits the Secretary of State to designate, by order, an existing individual or body to carry out regulatory functions, including authorising persons to provide claims management services, regulating the conduct of authorised and other functions which are conferred on the regulator by or under Pt 2. The Secretary of State may, by order, specify bodies whose members may offer claims management services without the need for authorisation: s 6. Section 7 creates an offence of providing regulated claims management services in contravention of s 4. Section 8 empowers the regulator to apply to the High Court or a county court for an injunction restraining a person from providing regulated claims management services if he is not authorised, exempted by the Secretary of State or subject to a waiver by the regulator. Section 9, Schedule give the Secretary of State the power to make regulations about authorisations under s 5 and the functions of the regulator. It is a criminal offence to obstruct the regulator, without reasonable excuse, in the course of investigating whether any of the offences in s 7 or 11 have been committed: s 10. Section 11 makes it a criminal offence for an unauthorised individual or body to pretend that it is authorised, exempted by the Secretary of State or subject to a waiver from the regulator. Section 12 establishes the Claims Management Services Tribunal and makes provision about its constitution and proceedings. The circumstances in which appeals and references may be made to the tribunal are specified: s 13. Section 14 deals with interpretation. Under s 15, general information as to the procedure for making orders and regulations under Pt 2 is provided.

Part 3 (ss 16–18) General
Section 16 provides for commencement, s 17 deals with extent and s 18 with short title.

2772   Deceit

See MISREPRESENTATION AND FRAUD.

2773   Harassment—vicarious liability of employer—elements of tort—act within course of employment

An employee commenced proceedings against his employer, claiming damages for breach of statutory duty. He alleged that he had been bullied and harassed by his manager, acting in the course of her employment by the employer. He pleaded his claim under the Protection from Harassment Act 1997. The judge struck out the claim, holding that the 1997 Act was not designed to create another level of liability in employment law. The employee's appeal was allowed and the employer appealed. *Held,* neither the terms nor the practical effect of the 1997 Act indicated that Parliament had intended to exclude the ordinary principle of vicarious liability. By s 3, Parliament had created a new cause of action. Section 3 had spelled out particular features of a new civil wrong, including that anxiety was a head of damage. Those features did not indicate an intention to exclude vicarious liability, which only arose if the new wrong was committed by an employee in the course of his employment. If an employee's acts of harassment met the 'close connection' test, there was no reason why the particular features of the newly created wrong should place it in a special category in which an employer was exempt from vicarious liability. It was true that the new wrong usually comprised conduct of an intensely personal character, but that feature might also be present with other wrongs which attracted vicarious liability, such as assault. Vicarious liability for an employee's harassment of another person, whether a fellow employee or not, would to some extent increase employers' burdens. However, that did not suffice to show that Parliament had intended to exclude the ordinary common law principle of vicarious liability. Accordingly, the appeal would be dismissed.

Majrowski v Guy's and St Thomas's NHS Trust [2006] UKHL 34, [2006] 4 All ER 395 (House of Lords: Lords Nicholls of Birkenhead and Hope of Craighead, Baroness Hale of Richmond, Lords Carswell and Brown of Eaton-under-Heywood). Decision of Court of Appeal [2005] EWCA Civ 251, [2005] QB 848 (2005 Abr para 2989) affirmed.

2774   Interference with contractual relations—inducing breach of contract—voidable contract—contract with minor

The claimant and the defendants were engaged in the provision of management and agency services for professional football players. The claimant entered into a representation agreement with a 15-year-old player under which the claimant was appointed to act as the player's executive agent for two years during which time the player was not permitted to appoint any other agents. The agreement was signed by the player and his father. Before the two-year period had elapsed, the defendants telephoned the claimant expressing their desire to represent the player. The claimant replied that it was not interested in the proposal. The following month, and still within the term of the contract, a letter signed by the player and his parents was sent to the claimant advising it that the player had made the decision not to renew the representation agreement at the end of the two-year period. Less than a month later, the player and his parents entered into a purported representation agreement with the defendants. The player then wrote to the claimant and informed it that, on the ground that the agreement was voidable at the option of the player by virtue of the fact that he had been a minor at the time he signed the agreement, that letter was to be taken as notice that the agreement had been terminated. He then signed a further representation agreement with the defendants. The claimant issued proceedings alleging that the defendants had procured a breach of the contract between the claimant and the player. *Held*, there was no liability for the tort of interference with, or inducing the breach of, a contract that was voidable on the ground that a party to the contract was a minor. That was the position notwithstanding the fact that the contract remained valid until it was avoided. The fact that the contract was voidable was, in principle, a defence to any claim under those torts. It was not in dispute that the player had been a minor at the time of the agreement. An agreement pursuant to which a party was to act as a minor's executive agent and to carry out all the functions in respect of personal representation on behalf of his work as a professional football player did not fall to be considered as analogous to the class of contacts that were enforceable against a minor. It followed that the agreement had been voidable at the option of the player and, accordingly, the application would be dismissed.

Proform Sports Management Ltd v Proactive Sports Management Ltd [2006] EWHC 2812 (Ch), [2007] 1 All ER 542 (Chancery Division: Judge Hodge QC). *Shears v Mendeloff* (1914) 30 TLR 342 considered. *Doyle v White City Stadium Ltd* [1935] 1 KB 110, CA; and *Chaplin v Leslie Frewin (Publishers) Ltd* [1966] Ch 71, CA, distinguished.

2775   Liability—mesothelioma claims—contribution

The Compensation Act 2006 (Contribution for Mesothelioma Claims) Regulations 2006, SI 2006/3259 (in force on 7 December 2007), further amend the Financial Services and Markets Act 2000 (Transitional Provisions, Repeals and Savings) (Financial Services Compensation Scheme) Order 2001, SI 2001/2967, and provide the Financial Services Authority (the 'FSA') with an additional power to make rules for the Financial Services Compensation Scheme (the 'FSCS'). In particular, the amendments (1) enable a person who is liable in tort, or an insurer of such a person, for having exposed a person to asbestos who goes on to develop mesothelioma to recover a contribution from the FSCS, and set out the circumstances where a contribution can be paid to such a person by the FSCS; (2) provide a power for the FSA to make rules, and to give guidance on those rules, having similar effect in relation to claims other than those dealt with in the 2001 Order; and (3) relieve the FSA of its specific statutory duty to consult on the first occasion on which it makes rules or guidance in relation to mesothelioma claims under the regulations.

2776   Malicious procurement of search warrant—elements of tort—proof of malice

See Application 28867/03 *Keegan v United Kingdom*, para 1619.

2777   Misfeasance in public office—ingredients of tort—loss of liberty–prisoner moved from open conditions to closed conditions

On an appeal against part of an order which struck out the claimant's claim against the defendant for misfeasance in public office, issues arose as to whether a person who lost his freedom as a result of misfeasance had suffered damage sufficient to entitle him to recover damages from the defendant and, if so, whether a prisoner who was moved from open conditions to closed conditions was such a person. *Held*, loss of liberty was a form of special or material damage sufficient to support a claim for misfeasance in public office, if the other ingredients of the tort were made out. A person who was unlawfully detained and lost his freedom as a result of the tort of false imprisonment was entitled to general damages, including for damage suffered by loss of liberty. It was incorrect in principle to distinguish between what was injury or damage for the purposes of the tort of false imprisonment on the one hand and for the purposes of the tort of misfeasance on the other, as loss of liberty should either be an injury or damage in both cases or in neither case. There was also no reason to distinguish between misfeasance and malicious prosecution. In principle, a prisoner who was moved from open conditions because of misfeasance in public office was entitled to general damages for the further restriction on his liberty caused by that move. Accordingly, the appeal would be allowed.

Karagozlu v Metropolitan Police Comr [2006] EWCA Civ 1691, [2006] All ER (D) 166 (Dec) (Court of Appeal: Sir Anthony Clarke MR, Scott Baker and Thomas LJJ). *Gregory v Portsmouth City Council* [2000] 1 AC 419, HL (2000 Abr para 3151); *Watkins v Secretary of State for the Home Department* [2006] UKHL 17, [2006] 2 AC 395; and *Thompson v Metropolitan Police Comr* [1998] QB 498, CA (1997 Abr para 1030), considered.

2778   Misfeasance in public office—ingredients of tort—necessity to prove loss or damage

The claimant, a serving prisoner, brought proceedings against the defendants, the Secretary of State and three prison officers, alleging misfeasance in public office. It was found that the officers had acted in bad faith and in contravention of the relevant rules by opening the claimant's correspondence with his legal advisers. However, because the claimant had not suffered any loss or damage, which was found to be an essential ingredient of the tort of misfeasance in public office, the claim was dismissed. The claimant's appeal was allowed. On the defendants' appeal, the issue to be determined was whether the tort of misfeasance in public office was actionable without proof of financial loss or physical or mental injury, and if so, in what circumstances. *Held*, the tort of misfeasance in public office was never actionable without proof of material damage, an expression which included financial loss, or physical or mental injury and psychiatric illness but not distress, injured feelings, indignation or annoyance. The importance of the claimant's right to enjoyment of his right to confidential legal correspondence did not require the modification of a rule that material damage had to be proved to establish a cause of action. Further, the lack of a remedy in tort for someone in the position of the claimant, who had suffered a legal wrong but no material damage, did not leave him without a legal remedy. Parliament had intended that infringements of the core human rights protected by the Human Rights Act 1998 should be remedied under it and not by development of parallel remedies. It was accepted that exemplary damages might be awarded where a compensatory award was insufficient to mark the court's disapproval of proven misfeasance in public office and deter repetition. The policy of the law was not in general to encourage the award of exemplary damages and the law of tort should not be developed to make it an instrument of punishment in cases where there was no material damage for which to compensate. Accordingly, the appeal would be allowed.

Watkins v Secretary of State for the Home Department [2006] UKHL 17, [2006] 2 AC 395 (House of Lords: Lords Bingham of Cornhill, Hope of Craighead, Rodger of Earlsferry, Walker of Gestingthorpe and Carswell). Decision of Court of Appeal [2004] EWCA Civ 966, [2005] QB 883 (2004 Abr para 2728) reversed.

2779   Trespass—trespass to the person—self-defence—burden of proof

One of the claimants' relatives had been shot by a police constable during an armed police raid on the deceased's flat. The claimants brought a claim for battery against the defendant chief constable. The judge found that the claimants had failed to negate the contention that the constable had acted in self-defence and gave summary judgment for the defendant. The claimants appealed. *Held*, several textbooks supported the view that the burden of proof in relation to self-defence rested with the defendant. Formerly, criminal law required a defendant relying on self-defence to demonstrate both an honest and reasonable belief that self-defence was necessary, and that the force used was reasonable. Under criminal law, the reasonable belief requirement had been removed. However, in civil proceedings, the test had not been changed, so that a defendant who mistakenly but honestly believed that it was necessary to act in self-defence, had also to have a reasonable belief. The judge had erred in concluding that the burden of negativing self-defence was on the claimant, and so the defendant had not been entitled to summary judgment. The claim should have proceeded to trial. Accordingly, the appeal would be allowed.

Ashley v Chief Constable of Sussex Police [2006] EWCA Civ 1085, [2006] All ER (D) 268 (Jul) (Court of Appeal: Sir Anthony Clarke MR, Auld and Arden LJJ). *R v Fennell* [1971] 1 QB 428, CA, considered.

2780   Vicarious liability—dual liability—power to make finding

The claimant suffered a fractured skull after being struck by a doorman outside a club owned by the first defendant. The doorman was hired pursuant to a contract between the first defendant and the second defendant. The claimant brought proceedings against the first and second defendants on the basis that they were each responsible for the doorman's actions. Judgment in default was entered against the second defendant, which had gone into liquidation. The third defendant, which was the second defendant's insurer, declined to indemnify the second defendant, and the claimant therefore sought a declaration that he could recover under the terms of the policy between the second and third defendants. The judge ruled that the first defendant was vicariously liable, on the ground that it had sufficient control over the second defendant's employees to make them temporary deemed employees. The judge also decided that the injury came within the terms of the second defendant's insurance policy, and therefore granted a declaration that the third defendant was liable to indemnify the second defendant for any damages and costs awarded to the claimant against the second defendant. In relation to the first defendant's claim against the second defendant for a contribution pursuant to the Civil Liability (Contribution) Act 1978, arising out of the second defendant's failure to make proper inquiries about the doorman at the time of his employment, the judge assessed the second defendant's contribution as nil. The first and third defendants appealed against the judge's decisions. *Held*, a judge was entitled in appropriate circumstances to find more than one set of employers vicariously liable. Every case was fact specific and many factors might be relevant. While the question of control might not be wholly determinative, it would, however, remain at the heart of the test to be applied. In the present case, where there had been effectively and substantially a transfer of control and responsibility from the second defendant to the first defendant, it would not be appropriate to attribute vicarious liability to both of those defendants. Also, the lack of fault of a person vicariously liable for the wrongful act of his employee was not relevant for the purposes of determining contribution proceedings between that person and another wrongdoer. The first defendant had to stand in the shoes of its deemed employee, and the judge had been obliged to assess the responsibility for the fateful blow as between the doorman and the second defendant, his general employer. Any failing on the second defendant's part in not making proper inquiries about the doorman was far removed from the incident giving rise to the claim, and it had been open to the judge to find that, as between the defendants, the second defendant's negligence had had a negligible causative effect. Accordingly, the appeal would be dismissed.

Hawley v Luminar Leisure Ltd [2006] EWCA Civ 18, [2006] Lloyd's Rep IR 307 (Court of Appeal: Latham, Neuberger and Hallett LJJ). *Viasystems (Tyneside) Ltd v Thermal Transfer (Northern) Ltd* [2005] EWCA Civ 1151, [2005] 4 All ER 1181 (2005 Abr para 2999) considered.

2781   Vicarious liability—employer—bullying at work—connection between employment and tort

An employee had suffered depression as a result of a deeply troubled childhood. She was appointed to a position with the employer, a commercial bank, and during the course of the interviewing process she disclosed that she had been treated for depression. Subsequently, the employee claimed that she had been subjected to bullying and harassment by a group of women with whom she worked in close proximity. She complained to her manager and the human resources department, but they failed to take any effective steps to deal with the problem. The employee also experienced difficulties with a male colleague who occupied a co-ordinate post to her. She claimed that his behaviour was hostile and offensive, and that he undermined and humiliated her. She again informed her manager and the human resources department. The manager told the individual concerned to stop interfering with the employee's work, but no formal steps were taken to ensure that he did so. The employee developed a major depressive disorder and was unable to return to work. She brought proceedings against the employer claiming damages for personal injury on the basis that her psychiatric injury was caused by harassment and bullying by her work colleagues for whom the employer was vicariously liable, and further alleged that the employer had been negligent in failing to take adequate steps to protect her from such conduct. *Held*, the employee had been subjected to a relentless campaign of mean and spiteful behaviour designed to cause her distress by the group of women. Additionally, the male colleague had pursued a course of conduct that was disrespectful and designed to belittle her. The cumulative effect of both courses of conduct amounted to bullying, and it was reasonable that those involved ought to have known that their conduct was likely to cause anxiety and depression. In both the case of the individual perpetrator and the group there was a close connection between their employment and the behaviour in issue which gave rise to vicarious liability. Moreover, the employee's manager knew what was going on and had failed to stop the bullying. The stress caused by the bullying went beyond that which was normally to be expected in a workplace. The employer's knowledge of the situation coupled with its knowledge of the employee's history of depression gave rise to a foreseeable risk of psychiatric injury. Accordingly, the employee's claim would succeed.

Green v DB Group Services (UK) Ltd [2006] EWHC 1898 (QB), [2006] IRLR 764 (Queen's Bench Division: Owen J). *Bernard v A-G of Jamaica* [2004] UKPC 47, [2005] IRLR 398 (2005 Abr para 3000) applied.

2782   Vicarious liability—Revenue—officer of Revenue and Customs—duty of care—breach—liability of Revenue

See *Neil Martin Ltd v Revenue and Customs Comrs*, para 1635.

TOWN AND COUNTRY PLANNING

Halsbury's Laws of England (4th edn) vol 46(1) (Reissue) paras 1–550, 46(2) (Reissue) paras 551–1008 and 46(3) (Reissue) paras 1009–1508

Articles

For articles relating to this title please refer to the Table of Articles at the beginning of the Abridgment.

2783   Advertisements—control of display—sale or letting of property—deemed permission—removal within fourteen days

The claimant estate agency was convicted of five counts of unlawfully displaying advertisements, contrary to the Town and Country Planning Act 1990 s 224. The defendant local authority had complained that five signs relating to the letting of flats had remained displayed at premises outside the period of deemed permission granted by the Town and Country Planning (Control of Advertisements) Regulations 1992, SI 1992/666, Sch 3 Pt I. The deemed permission was subject to the condition that signs should be removed within 14 days of a tenancy being granted. In each case the defendant stated that a sign indicating that the premises had been 'let by' the claimant had remained in situ well after 14 days from the date on which the respective tenancies had been granted. The claimant appealed, and an issue arose as to whether the magistrates were entitled to conclude that the change in the sign from 'to let' to 'let by' was prima facie evidence that a tenancy of the relevant premises had been granted. *Held*, in the circumstances, the magistrates were entitled to conclude that the change in sign to 'let by' had been an unambiguous assertion without any qualification that the premises had been let which, in ordinary parlance, indicated prima facie that a tenancy had been granted. Accordingly, the appeal would be dismissed.

Barbara Rees Ltd v Cardiff CC [2006] EWHC 1617 (Admin), [2006] All ER (D) 13 (Jul) (Queen's Bench Division: Latham LJ and McCombe J).

2784   Caravan sites—England

The Caravan Sites Act 1968 and Social Landlords (Permissible Additional Purposes) (England) Order 2006 (Definition of Caravan) (Amendment) (England) Order 2006, SI 2006/2374 (in force on 1 October 2006), amends the definition of 'caravan' in the Caravan Sites Act 1968 and the Social Landlords (Permissible Additional Purposes) (England) Order 2006, SI 2006/1968, so as to substitute larger dimensions for twin-unit structures designed or adapted for human habitation.

2785   Crown application—subordinate legislation

The Town and Country Planning (Application of Subordinate Legislation to the Crown) Order 2006, SI 2006/1282 (in force on 7 June 2006), applies to the Crown various subordinate legislation subject, in certain cases, to modification.

2786   Development—appeal—determination by appointed person—prescribed classes—England

The Town and Country Planning (Determination of Appeals by Appointed Persons) (Prescribed Classes) (Amendment) (England) Regulations 2006, SI 2006/2227 (in force on 1 October 2006), amend the 1997 Regulations, SI 1997/420, in relation to England, by excluding from the reserved classes of appeal, determined by a person appointed by the Secretary of State, listed building consent appeals and listed building enforcement notice appeals concerned with Grade I and Grade II listed buildings.

2787   Development—environmental impact assessment—duty to consider need for assessment—reserved matters

A local planning authority granted outline planning permission for a leisure facility development, reserving certain matters for subsequent approval. The authority decided that no environmental impact assessment was required in respect of the reserved matters under the Town and Country

Planning (Assessment of Environmental Effects) Regulations 1988, SI 1988/1199, which were intended to implement EC Council Directive 85/337. The decision was affirmed by the Court of Appeal, which rejected the contention that there was a lacuna in the implementation of the directive by the 1988 Regulations. On appeal, the House of Lords referred a number of questions to the European Court of Justice for a preliminary ruling. It ruled that an environmental impact assessment was required if, in the case of grant of consent comprising more than one stage, it became apparent, in the course of the second stage, that the project was likely to have significant effects on the environment. In light of this ruling, the House of Lords *held*, the 1988 Regulations precluded any consideration for the need for an environmental impact assessment at the stage when, following the grant of outline planning permission, consideration was being given to an application for approval of reserved matters. Outline planning permission and the decision approving reserved matters constituted, as a whole, a multi-stage development consent process. Although any environmental impact assessment undertaken at the outline permission stage may be sufficient, it was possible that potential significant effects on the environment might have been overlooked or might not emerge until the reserved matters stage, in which case a further assessment would be necessary. It followed that the 1988 Regulations failed fully and properly to implement the directive. Accordingly, the appeal would be allowed.

R (on the application of Barker) v Bromley LBC [2006] UKHL 52, [2006] 3 WLR 1209 (House of Lords: Lords Bingham of Cornhill and Hope of Craighead, Baroness Hale of Richmond, Lords Carswell and Brown of Eaton-under-Heywood). Case C-508/03 *EC Commission v United Kingdom* [2006] All ER (D) 62 (May), ECJ, applied. For previous proceedings see Case C-290/03 *R (on the application of Barker) v Bromley LBC* [2006] QB 764, ECJ. Decision of Court of Appeal [2001] EWCA Civ 1766, [2002] 2 P & CR 96 (2001 Abr para 3042) reversed.

1988 Regulations replaced by Town and Country Planning (Environmental Impact Assessment) (England and Wales) Regulations 1999, SI 1999/293.

2788   Development—environmental impact assessment—procedure—England

The Town and Country Planning (Environmental Impact Assessment) (Amendment) Regulations 2006, SI 2006/3295 (in force on 15 January 2007), which apply mostly in relation to England, further amend the 1999 Regulations, SI 1999/293, so as to give effect to EC Parliament and Council Directive 2003/35 art 3, in so far as it affects public participation in the decision-making process for applications and appeals relating to development for which environmental impact assessment is required, and so as to apply EC Council Directive 85/337, which requires the assessment of the likely environmental effects of major new development, to local development orders. In particular, the regulations (1) amend the definitions of 'consultation bodies', 'environmental information' and 'exempt development', and insert new definitions of various terms; (2) amend the Secretary of State's power to exempt particular proposed developments from the application of the 1999 Regulations; (3) insert provisions requiring persons and environmental organisations likely to be affected by or to have an interest in an application to be notified of it; (4) reduce the number of copies of an environmental statement or further information that are to be sent to the Secretary of State; (5) extend the requirements in relation to further information so that they apply to any other information provided by an applicant which relates to an environmental statement; (6) require more extensive notification of decisions and information to be provided on the right to challenge a decision; (7) provide that the requirement to assess the likely environmental effects of major new development does not apply to projects serving national defence purposes in Wales where that requirement might have an adverse effect on those purposes, and require the Secretary of State to notify the National Assembly for Wales where this is the case; and (8) make amendments consequential on the introduction of a new category of project, namely a change to or extension of a specified project where the change or extension itself meets specified thresholds for that type of project.

2789   Development—environmental impact assessment—procedure—Wales

The Town and Country Planning (Environmental Impact Assessment) (Amendment) (Wales) Regulations 2006, SI 2006/3099 (in force on 30 November 2006), further amend the 1999 Regulations, SI 1999/293, so as to give effect to EC Parliament and Council Directive 2003/35 art 3, in so far as it effects public participation in the decision-making process for applications and appeals relating to development for which environmental impact assessment is required, and so as to apply EC Council Directive 85/337, which requires the assessment of the likely environmental effects of major new development, to local development orders. In particular, the regulations (1) amend the definitions of 'consultation bodies', 'environmental information' and 'exempt development', and insert new definitions of various terms; (2) amend the National Assembly for Wales' power to exempt particular proposed developments from the application of the 1999 Regulations; (3) insert provisions requiring persons and environmental organisations likely to be affected by or to have an interest in an application to be notified of it; (4) reduce the number of copies of an environmental statement or further information that are to be sent to the National Assembly; (5) extend the requirements in relation to further information so that they apply to any other information provided by an applicant which relates to an environmental statement; (6) require more extensive notification of decisions and information to be provided on the right to challenge a decision; (7) make minor changes in relation to unauthorised development; and (8) relate to projects likely to have transboundary effects.

2790   Development—general development order—procedure—England

The Town and Country Planning (General Development Procedure) (Amendment) (England) Order 2006, SI 2006/1062 (in force in part on 10 May 2006 and in part on 10 August 2006), further amends the 1995 Order, SI 1995/419, so as to (1) amend the definition of 'reserved matters' and specify what needs to be included in applications for outline planning permission in relation to those matters; (2) provide that operations which increase the gross floor space of a building used for the retail sale of goods, other than hot food, by more than 200 square metres will constitute development and will require planning permission; (3) make provision for the preparation and revocation of local development orders by local planning authorities and specify the type of development for which a local development order cannot grant planning permission; (4) provide for registers of local development orders; (5) make provision for design and access statements which are required to accompany certain applications for planning permission; and (5) provide that the time period within which a local planning authority must determine an application for planning permission for major developments is 13 weeks.

The Town and Country Planning (General Development Procedure) (Amendment) (No 2) (England) Order 2006, SI 2006/2375 (in force on 1 October 2006), further amends the 1995 Order supra by introducing further requirements to consult the Environment Agency before applications for development involving (1) the carrying out of works or operations in the bed of, or within 20 metres of the top of a bank of, a main river which has been notified to the local planning authority by the Environment Agency as a main river for these purposes; (2) the culverting or control of flow of any river or stream; and (3) development, other than minor development, which is carried out on land in an area within Flood Zones 2 or 3, or in an area within Flood Zone 1 which has critical drainage problems that have been notified to the local planning authority by the Environment Agency.

2791   Development—general development order—procedure—Wales

The Town and Country Planning (General Development Procedure) (Amendment) (Wales) Order 2006, SI 2006/3390 (in force on 30 June 2007), further amends, in relation to Wales, the 1995 Order, SI 1995/419, so as to make provision for access statements which are required to accompany certain applications for planning permission.

2792   Development—general permitted development—England

The Town and Country Planning (General Permitted Development) (Amendment) (England) Order 2006, SI 2006/221 (in force on 6 April 2006), further amends the 1995 Order, SI 1995/418, so as to give casinos permitted development rights to change to use for assembly and leisure without the need for planning permission.

2793   Development—general permitted development—prior approval not required— subsequent designation of site as conservation area

The respondent telecommunications companies had applied to the appellant planning authority, under the Town and Country Planning (General Permitted Development) Order 1995, SI 1995/418, Sch 2 Pt 24, for prior approval for the installation of antennae, dishes and other equipment on land at a telephone exchange. The appellant gave notice that prior approval was not required. The site was subsequently designated as part of a conservation area and the appellant issued withdrawal notices. The respondents sought and were granted judicial review of the decision. On appeal, the respondents submitted that their rights accrued when the development order came into effect, but the appellant maintained that this only occurred on substantial completion of the work. *Held*, it would be unjust if permission granted to developers could be defeated by the adventitious arrival of a conservation area. Where no prior approval for development was required, the advent of a conservation order would not affect planning permission. Where prior approval for development had to be sought, the analogue to the commencement of work was the application for prior approval and the receipt of a notice. Accordingly, the appeal would be dismissed.

R (on the application of Orange Personal Communications Services Ltd) v Islington LBC (2006) Times, 24 January (Court of Appeal: Laws, Jonathan Parker and Richards LJJ).

2794   Development—general permitted development—Wales

The Town and Country Planning (General Permitted Development) (Amendment) (Wales) Order 2006, SI 2006/124 (in force on 31 January 2006), further amends the 1995 Order, SI 1995/418, so as to (1) in relation to Class H and B developments, (a) increase to two the number of permitted antennas; (b) extend the permitted development rights to all types of antennas;

(c) provide for a size limit of 60cm for one of the permitted antennas, and 100cm for the other; (d) permit roof mounted antenna to protrude above a roof with a chimney and restrict the height of the antenna or antennas to the highest part of the chimney, or 60cm measured from the ridge tiles of the roof, whichever is lower; (e) provide for a maximum cubic capacity of 35 litres for individual antennas; and (f) relax restrictions in respect of antenna on specified land to permit antenna on roof slopes, walls or chimneys that are not visible from a highway; (2) in relation to class A developments, (a) extend the permitted development rights to all types of antennas, and increase the number of permitted antenna to four; (b) provide for a size limit for chimney mounted antenna of 60cm when measured in any linear direction; (c) provide for a maximum cubic capacity of 35 litres for individual antennas; and (d) relax restrictions in respect of antenna on specified land to permit antenna on roof slopes, walls or chimneys that are not visible from a highway; and (3) provide that in assessing the maximum permitted antennas account must now be taken of any small antenna.

2795   Development—London Thames Gateway—planning functions

The London Thames Gateway Development Corporation (Planning Functions) (Amendment) Order 2006, SI 2006/2186 (in force on 7 September 2006), amends the 2005 Order, SI 2005/2721, by restating the portions of the urban development area in which planning functions were conferred on the development corporation, and by replacing the maps that describe the planning functions areas, to ensure that there is no overlap with the area for which the Olympic Delivery Authority is the local planning authority by virtue of the Olympic Delivery Authority (Planning Functions) Order 2006, SI 2006/2185.

2796   Development—planning permission—refusal—provision of parking spaces

The claimant applied for planning permission to develop a property into two separate dwellings. Permission was refused on the basis that the proposed development had not provided for parking spaces and was therefore in contravention of local planning policy. The claimant's appeal was refused by the local planning inspector. The claimant applied to challenge that decision under the Town and Country Planning Act 1990 s 288. The claimant submitted that the inspector had erred in law in basing her decision on the local planning policy, and failing to consider the Planning Policy Guidelines ('the PPG') that had been issued by the Secretary of State, and which post-dated the local policy in question. *Held*, the PPG expressly stated that local authorities should refrain from requiring potential developers to provide additional car parking spaces, over and above those that had been put forward in the developers' proposals, except for in exceptional circumstances. In the present case, the inspector had based her decision on the local planning policy and had failed to consider the PPG. The decision of the inspector was not one that could have been reached within a reasonable interpretation of the PPG, and that decision would therefore be quashed. Accordingly, the application would be allowed.

R (on the application of Lovelock) v First Secretary of State [2006] EWHC 2423 (Admin), [2007] JPL 600 (Queen's Bench Division: Judge Gilbart QC).

2797   Development—regional planning—regional spatial strategies—England

The Town and Country Planning (Regional Spatial Strategies) (Examinations in Public) (Remuneration and Allowances) (England) (Revocation) Regulations 2006, SI 2006/3320 (in force on 21 January 2007), revoke the 2004 Regulations, SI 2004/2209.

2798   Development—urban development and regeneration—acquisition of land

See *Pascoe v First Secretary of State*, para 2851.

2799   Development—use classes—exclusion—England

The Town and Country Planning (Use Classes) (Amendment) (England) Order 2006, SI 2006/220 (in force on 6 April 2006), further amends the 1987 Order, SI 1987/764, so as to exclude use as a casino from the specified use classes under the Town and Country Planning Act 1990 s 55(2)(f).

2800   Enforcement notice—time limit—breach of condition of planning permission

The Town and Country Planning Act 1990 s 171B(2) provides that, where there has been a breach of planning control consisting in the change of use of any building to use as a single dwelling house, no enforcement action may be taken after the end of the period of four years beginning with the date of the breach.

Planning permission was granted to the defendant to build an extension to form accommodation for a dependent relative. The permission was subject to two conditions: the first, that only the relative would occupy the extension, and the second, that, on vacation, the extension would not be occupied as a separate independent unit. The extension was rented out to students in contravention of the second condition and, over seven years after the date of the breach, the claimant local authority served an enforcement notice on the defendant. On appeal, the inspector found that that the case fell within the 1990 Act s 171B(2) so that the enforcement notice had been served outside the four-year time limit. The authority's appeal against the decision succeeded and the defendant appealed. *Held*, when read with s 171A(1) and the remainder of s 171B, s 171B(2) applied the four-year time limit to a breach of a condition as to, or limitation on, a change of use to a single dwelling house, irrespective of whether that change was a material change. While s 171B(1) repeated the definition of operational development in s 55(1), s 171B(2) did not repeat the reference in s 55(1) to 'material' change of use. That omission allowed s 171B(2) to include changes of use that were not sufficiently material to amount to a breach of planning control by way of development without planning permission under s 171A(1)(a), but which did amount to such a breach by way of failure to comply with a condition or limitation under s 171A(1)(b). Furthermore, change of use to a dwelling house, whether being development without planning permission or simply being in breach of condition, had been treated in the same way as operational development in the predecessors to the 1990 Act. Such an outcome was logical in that, whichever form the breach of planning control took, it should be subject to the same time limit for enforcement action. Accordingly, the appeal would be allowed.

First Secretary of State v Arun DC [2006] EWCA Civ 1172, [2006] All ER (D) 56 (Aug) (Court of Appeal: Auld, Sedley and Carnwath LJJ). Decision of Mole J [2005] EWHC 2520 (Admin), [2006] 1 WLR 365 (2005 Abr para 3020) reversed.

2801   Historic Buildings Council for Wales—abolition

The Historic Buildings Council for Wales (Abolition) Order 2006, SI 2006/63 (in force on 1 April 2006), abolishes the Historic Buildings Council for Wales and transfers its property, rights and liabilities to the National Assembly for Wales.

2802   Independent examinations—costs—standard daily amount—England

The Town and Country Planning (Costs of Independent Examinations) (Standard Daily Amount) (England) Regulations 2006, SI 2006/3227 (in force on 3 January 2007), specify a standard daily amount, which may be charged for each day the person appointed to hold an independent examination is engaged in the holding of the examination, or is otherwise engaged on work connected with it. The amount is £779 per day in relation to independent examinations opening on or after 3 January 2007 and before 31 March 2007. The amount is £879 per day in relation to independent examinations opening on or after 31 March 2007 and before 31 March 2008. The amount is £993 per day in relation to independent examinations opening on or after 31 March 2008.

2803   Inquiries—national security directions—appointed representatives—England

The Planning (National Security Directions and Appointed Representatives) (England) Rules 2006, SI 2006/1284 (in force on 7 June 2006), make provision, in relation to planning inquiries, as to the procedure to be followed by the Secretary of State when he is considering giving a national security direction, including provisions on publicity, written representations, hearings and notification of his decision. The rules also set out the functions of appointed representatives.

2804   Inquiries—national security directions—appointed representatives—Wales

The Planning (National Security Directions and Appointed Representatives) (Wales) Regulations 2006, SI 2006/1387 (in force on 7 June 2006), provide, in relation to Wales, (1) that all planning inquiries are to be held in public except to the extent to which the National Assembly for Wales or the Secretary of State otherwise directs that it would be contrary to national security on the grounds of national interest or security of premises or property; and (2) for the Counsel General to the National Assembly to appoint persons to represent the interests of any person who will be prevented from hearing or inspecting any evidence at a local inquiry if a direction is given by the National Assembly or Secretary of State. The regulations also make provision as to the procedure to be followed by the directing authority relating to publicity, written representations, hearings and notification of the directing authority's decision, when it is considering whether to give a national security direction.

2805   Mobile homes—England

The Mobile Homes Act 1983 (Amendment of Schedule 1) (England) Order 2006, SI 2006/1755 (in force on 1 October 2006), amends the Mobile Homes Act 1983 Sch 1, so as to imply additional terms into relevant agreements made on or after 30 September 2006. The effects of the amendments to the 1983 Act are that (1) the court is required, before it makes an order terminating an agreement on the basis that an occupier is not occupying a mobile home as his only or main residence, to be satisfied that it is reasonable for the agreement to be terminated; (2) owners are able to apply to the court to terminate an agreement forthwith if the mobile home is having a detrimental effect on the amenity of the site; (3) where an occupier wishes to sell his mobile home, the owner may not impose conditions when giving their approval; (4) the owner may not require any payment on the gift of a mobile home; (5) an owner can only require a mobile home to be stationed on another pitch if the court is satisfied that the other pitch is broadly comparable and that it is reasonable for the mobile home to be stationed there, or if the mobile home needs to be moved so that the owner can carry out essential repair or emergency work; (6) an occupier is entitled to quiet enjoyment of the mobile home during the continuance of the agreement; (7) the owner's rights to enter the pitch, but not the mobile home are set out; (8) the procedure to be followed when reviewing and determining the new pitch fee is described; (9) the occupier's obligations to the owner are described; (10) a requirement to consult the occupier and any qualifying residents' association about improvements to the protected sites is included; (11) the owner's obligation to inform the occupier and any qualifying residents' association of his name and address generally and when giving any written demand or notice to them is specified; and (12) the criteria that a residents' association must satisfy if it is to be a qualifying resident's association are listed.

2806 Olympic Delivery Authority—planning functions

The Olympic Delivery Authority (Planning Functions) Order 2006, SI 2006/2185 (in force on 7 September 2006), (1) specifies the development area in respect of which the Olympic Delivery Authority has planning functions; (2) makes the Authority the local planning authority in relation to development for the purposes of the Town and Country Planning Act 1990 Pt 3 (ss 55–106B); (3) confers on the Authority the functions of the Town and Country Planning Act 1990 and such functions of the Planning (Listed Buildings and Conservation Areas)Act 1990 as are specified in the Local Government, Planning and Land Act 1980 Sch 29 Pt 1; (4) applies to the Authority and the development area, with modifications, all the provisions of the Town and Country Planning Act 1990 and such provisions of the Planning (Listed Buildings and Conservation Areas) Act 1990 as are specified in the 1980 Act Sch 29 Pt 2; (5) provides for the former local planning authority to transmit to the Olympic Delivery Authority for determination applications received but not determined by the former authority prior to 7 September 2006; and (6) leaves responsibility for the payment of compensation under the Town and Country Planning Act 1990 ss 107, 108, 115, 186, 203 and 204 or the Planning (Listed Buildings and Conservation Areas) Act 1990 s 28 or 29 with the local planning authority which took the action giving rise to the right of compensation.

2807 Planning and Compulsory Purchase Act 2004—commencement

The Planning and Compulsory Purchase Act 2004 (Commencement No 4 and Consequential, Transitional and Savings Provisions) (Wales) (Amendment) Order 2006, SI 2006/842, amends transitional provisions in the Planning and Compulsory Purchase Act 2004 (Commencement No 4 and Consequential, Transitional, Transitional and Savings Provisions) (Wales) Order 2005, SI 2005/2722, in order to make it clear that the transitional arrangements continue to apply to the specified local planning authorities.

The Planning and Compulsory Purchase Act 2004 (Commencement No 4 and Consequential, Transitional and Savings Provisions) (Wales) (Amendment No 2) Order 2006, SI 2006/1700, further amends SI 2005/2722 supra so as to remove the Isle of Anglesey County Council from the list of local planning authorities in relation to whose area certain transitional provisions do not apply.

The Planning and Compulsory Purchase Act 2004 (Commencement No 4 and Consequential, Transitional and Savings Provisions) (Wales) (Amendment No 3) Order 2006, SI 2006/3119, further amends SI 2005/2722 so that each of the two specified local planning authorities in Wales is now required to prepare a local development plan for its area under the 2004 Act instead of being able to continue with the process for the adoption of its unitary development plan under the Town and Country Planning Act 1990.

The Planning and Compulsory Purchase Act 2004 (Commencement No 7) Order 2006, SI 2006/931, brings into force in relation to Wales, on 1 April 2006, s 53 (so far as not already in force).

The Planning and Compulsory Purchase Act 2004 (Commencement No 8 and Saving) Order 2006, SI 2006/1061, brings into force, in relation to England, (1) on 10 May 2006, in so far as they are not yet in force, ss 40, 41, 49 and Sch 1; and (2) on 10 August 2006, s 42(1), (5)–(9) and a repeal in Sch 9.

The Planning and Compulsory Purchase Act 2004 (Commencement No 9 and Consequential Provisions) Order 2006, SI 2006/1281, brings into force, on 7 June 2006, ss 79–89 (so far as not already in force), 111(1), 112, Sch 3 (so far as not already in force), Sch 4, Sch 6 para 2, and certain repeals in Sch 9. Consequential provisions are also made.

For a summary of the Act, see 2004 Abr para 2751. See also the commencement table in the title STATUTES.

2808 Planning permission—application—fees—England

The Town and Country Planning (Fees for Applications and Deemed Applications) (Amendment) (England) Regulations 2006, SI 2006/994 (in force on 6 April 2006), further amend the 1989 Regulations, SI 1989/193, so as to (1) provide for the payment of fees in respect of site visits carried out by local planning authorities to mining sites and landfill sites to monitor compliance with the planning permissions to which they are subject; and (2) provide for situations where there is more than one operator on site, where the site is inactive, and where two or more sites are grouped together for the purpose of monitoring, and limit the number of chargeable visits in any one year.

2809 Planning permission—application—fees—Wales

The Town and Country Planning (Fees for Applications and Deemed Applications) (Amendment) (Wales) Regulations 2006, SI 2006/948 (in force on 1 April 2006), further amend the 1989 Regulations, SI 1989/193, so as to (1) increase certain fees payable for planning applications and deemed applications by 20 per cent from 1 April 2006 and by a further ten per cent from 1 April 2007; and (2) require an applicant to pay a fee for making a further application to a local planning authority where the further application relates to an application for which planning permission has previously been granted. SI 2004/2736 is revoked.

The Town and Country Planning (Fees for Applications and Deemed Applications) (Amendment No 2) (Wales) Regulations 2006, SI 2006/1052 (in force on 6 April 2006), further amend the 1989 Regulations supra so as to (1) provide for the payment of fees in respect of site visits carried out by local planning authorities to mining sites and landfill sites to monitor compliance with the planning permissions to which they are subject; (2) make provision for situations where there is more than one operator on site, where a site is inactive, and where two or more sites are grouped together for the purpose of monitoring; and (3) limit the number of chargeable visits in any one year.

2810 Planning permission—application—Houses of Parliament—England

The Planning (Application to the Houses of Parliament) Order 2006, SI 2006/1469 (in force on 7 June 2006), specifies as Crown interests the interests of the two speakers and one or both of the corporate officers in particular parts of the Palace of Westminster and its precincts and provides that the appropriate authority in relation to that land is one or both of the corporate officers, as the case may be.

2811 Planning permission—application—listed buildings and conservation areas—England

The Planning (Applications for Planning Permission, Listed Buildings and Conservation Areas) (Amendment) (England) Regulations 2006, SI 2006/1063 (in force on 10 August 2006), amend the Town and Country Planning (Applications) Regulations 1988, SI 1988/1812, so as to define 'outline planning permission' and specify what constitutes 'reserved matters'. The regulations also amend the Planning (Listed Buildings and Conservation Areas) Regulations 1990, SI 1990/1519, so as to make provision for design and access statements which are required to accompany applications for listed building consent.

2812 Planning permission—Crown land—modification of statutory provisions—Wales

The Town and Country Planning (Miscellaneous Amendments and Modifications relating to Crown Land) (Wales) Order 2006, SI 2006/1386 (in force on 7 June 2006), modifies the Town and Country Planning (Use Classes) Order 1987, SI 1987/764, (1) by adding a new class of development, secure residential institutions; and (2) by adding use as a law court to class D1 which covers non-residential institutions. The order also modifies the Town and Country Planning (General Permitted Development) Order 1995, SI 1995/418, so as to (a) give the National Assembly for Wales planning permission in relation to works carried out under the Highways Act 1980; and (b) add new provisions to give the Crown planning permission for certain activities including aviation development, Crown railways, dockyards and lighthouses, development for emergency purposes and development for national security or national defence purposes.

2813 Planning permission—decision of planning officer—exercise of delegated powers

The claimant's neighbour applied for planning permission to demolish and replace a single storey dwelling. The dwelling was within a conservation area to which planning guidance containing a presumption against the demolition of such buildings applied. The claimant wrote to the local planning authority objecting to the neighbour's proposal. The authority had adopted a scheme of delegation and allocation of its delegated powers under the Town and Country Planning Act 1990 between its planning committee and officers. The application was approved by a planning officer and the claimant sought judicial review of the decision. This was refused, and he appealed. Issues arose as to the nature and exercise of the delegated power exercised by the officer. *Held*, there was no general principle that, where there was any real issue about the meaning or application of a planning policy, it was unlawful for a planning officer to exercise delegated powers of decision-making. If a planning officer was of the view that he could make sense of the policies and identify the relevant facts so as to enable him to apply the former to the latter, there was no basis, short of illegality or Wednesbury irrationality, why the courts should intrude further on the arrangements local planning authorities made for their decision-making. It was for local planning authorities to determine the policy or basis of their schemes of delegation. Further, the presumption against development in the wording of the authority's relevant policy in the present case contained within it an acceptance that, even when capable of application, it might, as a matter of planning judgment, be rebutted by the circumstances. Accordingly, the appeal would be dismissed.

R (on the application of Springhall) v Richmond upon Thames LBC [2006] EWCA Civ 19, [2006] All ER (D) 153 (Jan) (Court of Appeal: Auld and Moore-Bick LJJ and Sir Peter Gibson). *R (on the application of Carlton-Conway) v Harrow LBC* [2002] EWCA Civ 927, [2002] JPL 1216 (2002 Abr para 2921) distinguished. Decision of Richards J [2005] EWHC 52 (Admin), [2005] All ER (D) 117 (Jan) affirmed.

2814   Planning permission—determination—material consideration—fear of crime—gipsy caravan site

A site had been used as an unauthorised gipsy caravan park for a number of years. After the local authority had taken steps to remove the occupants from the site, the claimant sought planning permission to retain some of the plots. The applications were refused and an inspector dismissed the claimant's appeal. On further appeal, the claimant challenged the inspector's reasoning in relation to the fear of crime. *Held*, fear and concern about crime had to be real; concerns which rested on assumptions not supported by evidence as to the characteristics of the future occupiers could not be taken into account. The number of incidents of crime had diminished and those reported could not be reliably attributed to the site or its occupants. Further, the incidents could not be taken into account unless they were attributable not merely to the individuals concerned but also to the use of the land. A caravan site was not like a polluting factory or bail hostel, likely of its very nature to produce difficulties for its neighbours, and it was not right to view land use for the purpose of a gipsy caravan site as inherently creating the real concern that attached to an institution such as a bail hostel. Accordingly, the appeal would be allowed.

Smith v First Secretary of State [2005] EWCA Civ 859, [2006] JPL 386 (Court of Appeal: Buxton, Sedley and Rimmer LJJ).

2815   Planning permission—grant of permission—reasons for grant

The Town and Country Planning (General Development Procedure) Order 1995, SI 1995/419, art 22(1)(b) provides that when the local planning authority gives notice of a decision or determination on an application for planning permission or for approval of reserved matters and planning permission is granted subject to conditions, the notice must include a summary of its reasons for the grant together with a summary of the policies and proposals in the development plan which are relevant to the decision to grant permission, and state clearly and precisely its full reasons for each condition imposed, specifying all policies and proposals in the development plan which are relevant to the decision. Under art 22(1)(c), where planning permission is refused, the notice must state clearly and precisely the authority's full reasons for the refusal, specifying all policies and proposals in the development plan which are relevant to the decision.

The defendant local planning authority granted the claimant planning permissions in relation to the claimant's fun park. The grant of the permissions followed recommendations made in the reports of the defendant's officer, with an additional condition that would lessen the potential for loss of privacy by neighbouring properties. The claimant sought judicial review of the decision, arguing that, having regard to the 1995 Order art 22(1), and by reference to the standard of reasons expected when refusing planning permission, the reasons given for the grant of the permissions were not adequate. *Held*, the standard expected of reasons for a grant of permission was not the same as that expected of reasons for the refusal of permission. Article 22(1)(b) only required a summary of the reasons for the grant of permission, not a summary of the reasons for rejecting the objections to the grant of permission. The summary could be shortly stated in appropriate cases, but planning authorities should guard against the temptation to provide a standard formula for reasons for the grant of permission. The difference in statutory language was stark and significant. 'Full' reasons were required under art 22(1)(c) when permission was refused, whereas only 'summary' reasons were required when permission was granted. If the officer's report recommended refusal and the members of the authority decided to grant permission, a fuller summary of reasons would be appropriate than would be the case where they had simply followed the officer's recommendation. The reasons given for the grant of the permissions were really as short as they could be. Anything less would be inappropriate, but they did reflect the conclusion in the officer's report for each permission. Accordingly, the application would be dismissed.

R (on the application of Ling (Bridlington) Ltd) v East Riding of Yorkshire Council [2006] EWHC 1604 (Admin), [2007] JPL 396 (Queen's Bench Division: Sir Michael Harrison). *English v Emery Reimbold & Strick Ltd* [2002] EWCA Civ 605, [2002] 3 All ER 385 (2002 Abr para 2366); and *R (on the application of Wall) v Brighton and Hove CC* [2004] EWHC 2582 (Admin), [2005] 1 P & CR 566 (2004 Abr para 2763) considered.

2816   Planning permission—listed buildings and conservation areas—access statements— Wales

The Planning (Listed Buildings and Conservation Areas) (Amendment) (Wales) Regulations 2006, SI 2006/3316 (in force on 30 June 2007), further amend the 1990 Regulations, SI 1990/1519, in relation to Wales, so as to add new provision in respect of the requirement for access statements to accompany applications for listed building consent.

2817 Planning permission—listed buildings and conservation areas—hazardous substances—Crown land—England

The Planning (Listed Buildings, Conservation Areas and Hazardous Substances) (Amendment) (England) Regulations 2006, SI 2006/1283 (in force on 7 June 2006), amend the Planning (Listed Buildings and Conservation Areas) Regulations 1990, SI 1990/1283, so as to prescribe the publicity requirements in relation to applications for works to buildings on Crown land.

2818 Planning permission—listed buildings and conservation areas—hazardous substances—Crown land—Wales

The Planning (Listed Buildings, Conservation Areas and Hazardous Substances) (Amendments Relating to Crown Land) (Wales) Regulations 2006, SI 2006/1388 (in force on 7 June 2006), amend the Planning (Listed Buildings and Conservation Areas) Regulations 1990, SI 1990/1519, so as to prescribe the publicity requirements relating to urgent applications for works to buildings on Crown land which are listed or which are in conservation areas. The regulations also further amend the Planning (Hazardous Substances) Regulations 1992, SI 1992/656, so as to prescribe the form and content of a claim for deemed hazardous substances consent and the conditions to which a deemed consent will be subject.

2819 Tree preservation order—exemption—abatement of nuisance

The Town and Country Planning Act 1990 s 198(6)(b) provides that, without prejudice to any other exemptions for which provision may be made by a tree preservation order, no order is to apply to the cutting down, uprooting, topping or lopping of any trees in compliance with any obligations imposed by or under an Act of Parliament or so far as may be necessary for the prevention or abatement of a nuisance.

The claimants' house was being affected by roots from a tree on the defendant local authority's land. The tree was the subject of a tree preservation order issued by the defendant which had also issued a certificate precluding the claimants from applying for compensation. The claimants sought a declaration that the tree could be lawfully felled under the 1990 Act s 198(6)(b). *Held*, the principal purpose of s 198 was to preserve trees through the mechanism of a tree preservation order and the exemption in s 198(6)(b) had to be carefully construed so as to ensure that the principal purpose of the legislation was not frustrated by too wide a construction of the exemption. The word 'nuisance' meant an actionable nuisance where damage had been caused or, if no action was taken to prevent it, would imminently be caused, rather than simple encroachment. The word 'necessary' governed the extent of the work to the tree and nothing more. Whether the lopping or felling of the tree was necessary to prevent or abate a nuisance was a question of fact, to be decided on the everyday sensible approach of a prudent citizen looking at the tree and deciding in his own mind whether he could properly say that lopping or felling was necessary. Something more than simple encroachment had to be required in order for the tree preservation order not to apply; that would be something significant which balanced the primary purpose of tree protection with the right of an individual to live in a safe and unthreatened home. It would be impossible to operate s 198(6) in a clear and coherent way if a man was guilty of an offence if he cut down a tree protected by a tree preservation order where the nuisance he was anxious to prevent or abate might have been dealt with by carrying out expensive underpinning work instead. Accordingly, the order would be granted.

Perrin v Northampton BC [2006] EWHC 2331 (TCC), [2007] 1 All ER 929 (Queen's Bench Division: Judge Peter Coulson QC). *Smith v Oliver* [1989] 2 PLR 1, DC, applied. *Delaware Mansions Ltd v Westminster CC* [2001] UKHL 55, [2002] 1 AC 321 (2001 Abr para 2374) considered.

TRADE, INDUSTRY AND INDUSTRIAL RELATIONS

Halsbury's Laws of England (4th edn) vol 47 (2001 Reissue) paras 1–1616

Articles

For articles relating to this title please refer to the Table of Articles at the beginning of the Abridgment.

2820 Competition—agreements preventing, restricting or distorting competition—EC Commission decision—effect on national proceedings

See *Crehan v Inntrepreneur Pub Co*, para 2985.

2821　Competition—Competition Appeal Tribunal—remission of matter to competition authority—power to impose time limit

The claimant company complained to the predecessor of the defendant regulator that a rival company had abused its dominant position in the market for telecommunications services. The claim was rejected, but an appeal to the Competition Appeal Tribunal was allowed. The tribunal decided to set aside the decision and to remit the whole matter to the defendant for reinvestigation. The defendant offered an undertaking to reinvestigate on the basis that, if it decided there was no infringement, it would come to that decision within six months, and if it did not come to that conclusion it would set out its case, by a statement of objections, within twelve months. The tribunal sought an undertaking from the defendant to issue a non-infringement decision or statement of objections within five months, in default of which it would make an order remitting the matter to the defendant in those terms. The defendant appealed, and issues arose as to whether the tribunal had power to set a time limit for the investigation, and whether it could fix a case management conference. *Held*, the tribunal was wrong to hold that it had the power to direct the time within which the new investigation was to be carried out following the setting aside of the original decision. It could certainly express its own view as to the urgency of the matter, but by its order it had disposed of the appeal and could neither impose time limits under the Competition Appeal Tribunal Rules 2003, SI 2003/1372, r 19 nor give such a direction under the Competition Act 1998 Sch 8 para 3(2)(d), which was limited to directions or other steps which could be the subject of an appeal, being decisions within the meaning of s 46. There was no power to give such a direction as an implied incident of Sch 8 para 3(2)(a), nor could the tribunal direct the hearing of a case management conference under the 2003 Rules r 19 or 20, since there would be no subsisting appeal in relation to which the case management conference could be held. Also, the tribunal had no role in relation to the time taken by a regulator over an initial investigation even if, as in the instant case, the right to a fair hearing without undue delay under the European Convention on Human Rights art 6 applied at that stage. If the complainant considered that the defendant was guilty of unreasonable delay in pursuing the initial investigation, its remedy would be to apply for judicial review. Judgment would be given accordingly.

Floe Telecom Ltd v Office of Communications [2006] EWCA Civ 768, [2006] 4 All ER 688 (Court of Appeal: Chadwick, Sedley and Lloyd LJJ).

2822　Competition—disclosure of information—restrictions

The Enterprise Act 2002 (Part 9 Restrictions on Disclosure of Information) (Amendment) Order 2006, SI 2006/2909 (in force on 1 December 2006), amends the Enterprise Act 2002, by adding the Gambling Act 2005 to the list of enactments conferring functions under the 2002 Act Sch 15.

2823　Competition—enforcement undertakings

The Enterprise Act 2002 (Enforcement Undertakings) Order 2006, SI 2006/354 (in force on 10 March 2006), specifies certain undertakings accepted by a minister of the Crown in relation to merger situations under the Fair Trading Act 1973 s 75G for the purposes of specified provisions under the Enterprise Act 2002. In particular, the order provides for consequential amendments to the terms of the undertakings so that the Office of Fair Trading may provide consent, approval or agreement in place of the Secretary of State.

The Enterprise Act 2002 (Enforcement Undertakings) (No 2) Order 2006, SI 2006/3095 (in force on 20 December 2006), specifies certain undertakings accepted by a minister of the Crown in relation to merger and monopoly situations under the 1973 Act supra s 88, for the purposes of specified provisions under the Enterprise Act 2002. In particular, the order provides that, where certain undertakings refer to action requiring the consent, approval or agreement of the Secretary of State, the Office of Fair Trading may give such consent, approval or agreement in place of the Secretary of State.

2824　Competition—enforcement undertakings and orders

The Enterprise Act 2002 (Enforcement Undertakings and Orders) Order 2006, SI 2006/355 (in force on 10 March 2006), specifies certain undertakings accepted by a minister of the Crown in relation to merger and monopoly situations under the Fair Trading Act 1973 s 88 and orders made by a minister of the Crown under s 56 for the purposes specified under the Enterprise Act 2002. In particular, the order provides for consequential amendments to the terms of the undertakings and orders so that the Office of Fair Trading may give directions or consent in place of the Secretary of State.

2825　Competition—exclusion—public policy

The Competition Act 1998 (Public Policy Exclusion) Order 2006, SI 2006/605 (in force on 3 April 2006), excludes any agreement where the purpose of the agreement is to enable the parties to provide or receive maintenance and repair services for surface warships and the agreement does not have as its object or effect the prevention, restriction or distortion of competition within the United Kingdom except in relation to the market for maintenance and repair of surface warships.

2826 Competition—merger—Competition Commission—powers

The first applicant was a company, incorporated in the United States, which operated in the United Kingdom through the second applicant, a wholly owned subsidiary of the first applicant. The second applicant merged with the third applicant, a company incorporated in the Republic of Ireland. The Office of Fair Trading was not pre-notified and referred the merger to the Competition Commission. The Commission gave directions under the Enterprise Act 2002 s 81 for the applicants to appoint a hold separate manager from outside their business to perform functions in relation to the merged companies. The Commission found that their proposals in relation to sales and marketing, operations and finance did not meet the Commission's concerns. The applicants sought judicial review of the Commission's decision. *Held,* s 81 gave the Commission wide powers for the purpose of preventing pre-emptive action, including the appointment of a hold separate manager to conduct or supervise the conduct of any activities. When the Commission considered whether to exercise its powers, it could not be sure whether any action being taken or proposed by the merging or merged parties would impede any action being taken by it as a result of the reference. The power enabled the Commission to intervene where it considered that there was at least some risk of that happening. While the Commission had to exercise its powers reasonably and proportionately, it had a considerable margin of appreciation under s 81. Since the outcome of a reference might well require a remedy to restore the status quo, the Commission, when exercising its powers under s 81, might have regard to the need to safeguard the effectiveness of any divestiture that might ultimately by ordered. The Commission had had regard to relevant considerations, had weighed the options available and had given reasons for its decision. It was reasonable for it to decide that the applicants' proposals in relation to sales and marketing, operation and finance did not fully meet its concerns. Without a hold separate manager during the period of inquiry, there would not be a demonstrably independent chief executive officer operating at arm's length from the merged companies to whom the executives responsible for those functions would report. It could not be assumed that there would be no matters arising in those areas requiring a decision by the chief executive officer to be taken in the interests of the applicants. The Commission had not acted outside its margin of appreciation in deciding that the appointment of a hold separate manager was necessary in order to ensure that the directing mind ultimately responsible for the merged companies was, and was seen to be, entirely independent of the applicants during the remainder of the Commission's inquiry. Accordingly, the application would be dismissed.

Stericycle International LLC v Competition Commission [2006] CAT 21, [2006] All ER (D) 116 (Sep) (Competition Appeal Tribunal).

2827 Competition—scope of Community law—sport—anti-doping rules

The applicants were professional athletes. Following a positive test for a banned substance, the applicants were suspended. The applicants filed a complaint with the Commission of the European Communities alleging that the rules on doping control were not compatible with and infringed Community rules on competition pursuant to the EC Treaty arts 81, 82. The applicants argued that the threshold of the banned substance in the body was too low. The Commission rejected the complaint. The applicants' action to have the decision set aside before the Court of First Instance was dismissed, the court holding that sport was subject to Community law only in so far as it constituted an economic activity. The applicants made an appeal before the European Court of Justice. *Held,* the fact that a rule was purely sporting in nature did not have the effect of removing from the scope of the EC Treaty the person engaged in the activity governed by that rule. Where a sporting activity took the form of gainful employment or provision of services for remuneration it fell within the scope of art 49. However, it had been held that the provisions of the Treaty on freedom of movement for persons and freedom to provide services did not affect rules concerning questions which were of purely sporting interest and, as such, had nothing to do with economic activity. It the sporting activity in question fell within the scope of the Treaty, the conditions for engaging in it were then subject to all the obligations which resulted from the various provisions of the Treaty. It followed that the rules which governed that activity satisfied the requirements of those provisions, which sought to ensure freedom of movement for workers, freedom of establishment, freedom to provide services, or competition. Therefore, even if those rules did not constitute restrictions on freedom of movement because they concerned questions of purely sporting interest and, as such, had nothing to do with economic activity, that fact meant neither that the sporting activity necessarily fell outside the scope of arts 81, 82, nor that the rules had not satisfied the specific requirements of those articles. Therefore, the Court of First Instance had erred in law. However, the applicants had failed to establish that the anti-doping rules at issue were disproportionate and accordingly, the appeal would be dismissed.

Case C-519/04 *Meca-Medina v European Commission (Finland Intervening)* [2006] All ER (EC) 1057 (ECJ: Third Chamber). Decision of Court of First Instance Case T-313/02 *Meca-Medina v European Commission* [2004] 3 CMLR 1314 (2004 Abr para 2779) affirmed.

2828   Customs—control—technical assistance

The Technical Assistance Control Regulations 2006, SI 2006/1719 (in force on 30 July 2006), provide for criminal offences, penalties and enforcement in respect of the prohibition on the acceptance of technical assistance in EC Council Regulation 1236/2005 concerning trade in certain goods which could be used for capital punishment, torture or other cruel, inhuman or degrading treatment or punishment.

2829   Export of goods—control—embargoed arms—Bosnia and Herzegovina

The Export Control (Bosnia and Herzegovina) Order 2006, SI 2006/300 (in force on 6 March 2006), amends the Export of Goods, Transfer of Technology and Provision of Technical Assistance (Control) Order 2003, SI 2003/2764, and the Trade in Controlled Goods (Embargoed Destinations) Order 2004, SI 2004/318, so as to remove the arms embargo in relation to Bosnia and Herzegovina.

2830   Export of goods—control—general

The Export Control Order 2006, SI 2006/1331 (in force on 6 June 2006), further amends, (1) the Export of Goods, Transfer of Technology and Provision of Technical Assistance (Control) Order 2003, SI 2003/2764, the Trade in Goods (Control) Order 2003, SI 2003/2765, and the Trade in Controlled Goods (Embargoed Destinations) Order 2004, SI 2004/318, so as to remove references to the address of the Export Control Organisation; and (2) SI 2003/2764 supra, so as to (a) make a number of revisions as a consequence of changes to the control list of the Wassenaar Arrangement, an international non-proliferation regime, including (i) removing 'the General Technology Note'; (ii) revising the definition of 'riot control agents' and control entries concerning technology (ML22), chemical or biological agents (ML7) and electronic equipment (ML11); (iii) providing a new definition for 'lighter than air vehicles'; and (iv) making minor amendments to the control entries concerning bombs, torpedoes etc (ML4), ground vehicles (ML6), chemical or biological agents (ML7), vessels (ML9), aircraft (ML10), military helmets (ML13), software (ML21), security and para-military goods (PL5001) and explosive related goods and technology (PL8001); and (b) provide a General Technology Note concerning prohibited dual-use goods, software and technology.

2831   Export of goods—control—radioactive sources

The Export of Radioactive Sources (Control) Order 2006, SI 2006/1846 (in force on 1 October 2006), controls the export of certain high-activity radioactive sources by (1) prohibiting, except under licence, the export of controlled radioactive sources; (2) excluding from such control, with limited exceptions, controlled radioactive sources in transit; (3) providing for the granting of licences, record keeping and appeals against the refusal of a licence application; (4) making provision in respect of misleading applications for licences and failure to comply with licence conditions; (5) empowering the Commissioners for Her Majesty's Revenue and Customs to require evidence of the destination to which a controlled radioactive source was delivered; and (6) setting out the purposes for which information obtained by the Secretary of State, or the Commissioners, may be disclosed.

2832   Export of goods—control—restrictive measures

See FOREIGN RELATIONS LAW.

2833   Export of goods—control—security and para-military goods

The Export Control (Security and Para-military Goods) Order 2006, SI 2006/1696 (in force on 30 July 2006), further amends the Export of Goods, Transfer of Technology and Provision of Technical Assistance (Control) Order 2003, SI 2003/2764, the Trade in Goods (Control) Order 2003, SI 2003/2765, and the Trade in Controlled Goods (Embargoed Destinations) Order 2004, SI 2004/318, so as to provide for licensing, enforcement and penalties in relation to goods controlled by EC Council Regulation 1236/2005 concerning trade in certain goods which could be used for capital punishment, torture or other cruel, inhuman or degrading treatment or punishment.

2834   Export of goods—control—technical and financial assistance—Liberia

The Export Control (Liberia) Order 2006, SI 2006/2065 (in force on 27 July 2006), makes provision in respect of Liberia in consequence of EC Council Regulation 234/2004 which prohibits technical or financial assistance relating to military activities being given to Liberia. In particular, the order (1) provides that breaches of certain provisions of Regulation 234/2004 are criminal offences; (2) provides for the licensing of specified transactions; (3) provides penalties in respect of criminal offences; and (4) provides for the enforcement of such penalties. SI 2004/432 is revoked.

2835   Export of goods—control—trade with Channel Islands

The Export Control (Amendment) Order 2006, SI 2006/2271 (in force on 23 August 2006), further amends (1) the Export of Goods, Transfer of Technology and Provision of Technical Assistance (Control) Order 2003, SI 2003/2764, to specify that certain security and paramilitary goods are prohibited to be exported to any of the Channel Islands and to provide for a control on transit to and from any of the Channel Islands; and (2) the Trade in Goods (Control) Order 2003, SI 2003/2765, with the effect that the controls therein will not apply to the removal of certain goods from a member state to the Channel Islands or from the Channel Islands to a member state.

2836   Export of goods—control—trade with Lebanon

The Export Control (Lebanon etc) Order 2006, SI 2006/2683 (in force on 11 October 2006), (1) further amends the Export of Goods, Transfer of Technology and Provision of Technical Assistance (Control) Order 2003, SI 2003/2764, by providing that gangchains, leg-irons and portable devices that administer an electric shock are prohibited to be exported when they are goods in transit to destinations outside the European Community or any of the Channel Islands; and (2) makes provision in respect of an arms embargo to Lebanon by adding it (a) to the list of destinations to which the exportation of aircraft, vessels and fire arms, in specified circumstances, are prohibited; and (b) to the list of embargoed destinations in the Trade in Controlled Goods (Embargoed Destinations) Order 2004, SI 2004/318.

2837   Industrial relations—information and consultation of employees

The Information and Consultation of Employees (Amendment) Regulations 2006, SI 2006/514 (in force on 6 April 2006), amend the 2004 Regulations, SI 2004/3426, so as to provide that the obligations to inform and consult on 'listed changes' arising either as a result of a negotiated agreement entered into before the regulations come into force, or pursuant to the 2004 Regulations reg 20, do not apply where the employer is under a duty under the Occupational and Personal Pension Schemes (Consultation by Employers and Miscellaneous Amendment) Regulations 2006, SI 2006/349, regs 7(3), 11–13 and he has notified the information and consultation representatives appointed under a negotiated agreement or employees (where the agreement requires they be informed and consulted directly) or the information and consultation representatives appointed under the 2004 Regulations, as appropriate, in writing that he will be complying with that duty.

2838   Industrial relations—redundancy—duty to consult trade union—consultation in good time

The claimant trade union was recognised by the employer, a local authority, for the purposes of collective bargaining. A decision was made to establish a unified pay structure which would cover all local authority grades. This resulted in some staff being upgraded and others being downgraded, and the employer decided to proceed by terminating its employees' contracts and simultaneously offering them new contracts. The claimant complained to an employment tribunal that it had not been consulted by the defendant in good time pursuant to the Trade Union and Labour Relations (Consolidation) Act 1992 s 188(1), which applied where the employer was proposing to dismiss, as redundant, employees. The tribunal upheld the complaint that in relation to the downgraded group there had been an intentional failure to consult, an intentional delay in informing the claimant of the proposal to dismiss and only partial compliance with the requirement to provide information. Therefore, the tribunal made a protective award for the maximum period of 90 days in respect of that group. In respect of the upgraded group, the tribunal decided that a protective award for a period of 20 days was appropriate. On appeal, the employer sought to challenge the tribunal's construction of the phrase 'in good time' in s 188(1A), submitting that it did not mean speedily, but rather meant in good time before the proposed dismissals took effect. The Employment Appeal Tribunal decided that there were no exceptional circumstances to justify it considering the new point. However, in relation to the enhanced group it reduced the protective award from 20 days to 10 days. The employer appealed and the claimant cross-appealed. *Held*, it was well established that the Employment Appeal Tribunal could entertain a new point of law only in exceptional circumstances. The employer had failed to demonstrate that the present case was of an exceptional nature, and the high value of the case could not make it so. Whether consultation took place in good time was a matter of fact and degree. Even if all necessary primary facts were already found, the judgment whether the consultation would have been begun in good time on the basis of the employer's construction had to require an evaluation of the detailed facts which had not yet been undertaken, and could only properly be undertaken by the specialist first instance tribunal. The employment tribunal had not erred in making a protective award for a period of 20 days in respect of the enhanced group of employees. Neither was the view that the appropriate period should be 20 days or 10 days perverse. It followed that the Employment Appeal Tribunal had erred in reducing the protective award. Accordingly, the appeal would be dismissed and the cross-appeal would be allowed.

Leicestershire CC v Unison [2006] EWCA Civ 825, [2006] IRLR 810 (Court of Appeal: Brooke, Laws and Scott Baker LJJ). Decision of Employment Appeal Tribunal [2005] IRLR 920 (2005 Abr para 3053) reversed.

2839　Industrial relations—redundancy—failure to consult trade union—protective award—employee remaining employed during protected period

The Trade Union and Labour Relations (Consolidation) Act 1992 s 190(4) provides that an employee is not entitled to remuneration under a protective award in respect of a period during which he is employed by the employer unless he would be entitled to be paid by the employer in respect of that period either by virtue of his contract of employment or by virtue of the Employment Rights Act 1996 ss 87–91, if that period falls within the period of notice required to be given by s 86(1).

An employer made approximately 90 employees redundant in two stages. Certain employees who were made redundant towards the end of that period brought proceedings alleging that the employer was in breach of its duty to consult, and that they were therefore entitled to a protective award under the 1992 Act s 189. The tribunal allowed the claim and ordered the employer to pay 70 days' pay to each employee. The Employment Appeal Tribunal dismissed an appeal by the employer, and the employees brought proceedings for the ascertainment of their awards. The employer argued that, by virtue of s 190(4), they were not entitled to compensation, as they had continued in employment throughout the 70-day protected period. The tribunal found in favour of the claimants, and the employer appealed, arguing that an employee who remained employed during a protected period and who was not under notice was entitled to receive a protective award. *Held*, on the true construction of s 190(4), an employee who remained employed during a protected period and who was not under notice was entitled to receive a protective award. It was necessary to construe s 190(4) in a manner which was consistent with compliance by the United Kingdom with its obligations under EC Council Directive 77/187. The 1992 Act s 190(4) was dealing with the position of persons who had not received pay because, for example, they were on long-term sick leave or leave of absence and possibly those where an employer was in financial difficulties. It followed that the tribunal had reasoned correctly, and, accordingly, the appeal would be dismissed.

Beall v Cranswick Country Foods plc [2006] All ER (D) 315 (Dec) (Employment Appeal Tribunal: Judge Serota QC presiding).

2840　Industrial relations—redundancy—failure to consult trade union—protective award—entitlement to benefit of award

A trade union complained to an employment tribunal, under the Trade Union and Labour Relations (Consolidation) Act 1992 s 189(1)(c), that the employer had failed to fulfil its consultation obligations, under s 188, in respect of proposed redundancies. The tribunal found that the trade union's complaints had been made out and made a protective award in relation to the employees in respect of whom the trade union was recognised by the employer. The trade union appealed, arguing that, where a protective payment had been awarded by a tribunal in respect of proceedings brought by a trade union under s 189(1)(c), all employees were entitled to the benefit of the award, notwithstanding that they did not fall within the class of employees in respect of which the trade union was recognised by the employer. It also argued that an employment tribunal was entitled to make findings in relation to failures to consult under s 189(1)(a), by virtue of which, in the case of a failure relating to the election of employee representatives, any of the affected employees or any of the employees who had been dismissed as redundant could present a complaint, and under s 189(1)(b), by virtue of which, in the case of a failure relating to representatives of a trade union, the trade union could present the complaint, if evidence of such failures arose in relation to proceedings brought by a trade union under s 189(1)(c). *Held*, where a claim was brought by a trade union, it had to have been based on a breach of the obligation owed to the trade union under s 189(1)(c). The trade union was not entitled to bring claims under s 189(1)(a) or (b) and any protective award made under s 189(1)(c) was applicable only to those employees in respect of whom the trade union was recognised by the employer. The employment tribunal had been right to hold that the protective award was only applicable to those employees. It was clear from s 189(1)(a)–(c) that the legislation had not intended that protective awards made in respect of one of the avenue of complaints to be applicable to those who might have had a complaint down one of the alternative avenues. Further, there had been no evidence on which the tribunal could have concluded that there had been breaches under s 189(1)(a) and (b) in addition to those complained of under s 189(1)(c) and, in any event, the tribunal would not have been entitled to make such a finding having regard to the express statutory provisions. The protective award made by the tribunal was applicable only in respect of the employees in relation to whom the trade union was recognised by the employer. Accordingly, the appeal would be dismissed.

Transport & General Workers Union Ltd v Brauer Coley [2007] IRLR 207 (Employment Appeal Tribunal: Burton J presiding).

2841　Private security industry—activities—amendments

The Private Security Industry Act 2001 (Amendments to Schedule 2) Order 2006, SI 2006/1831 (in force on 11 July 2006), amends the Private Security Industry Act 2001, so as to (1) remove from the definition of the manned guarding activities of a security operative those activities carried out by persons in circumstances relating to prisons and to immigration and police matters; (2) include within the scope of the activities of a security operative which relate to the immobilisation, restriction and removal of vehicles the following related activities: (a) the removal of any such immobilisation or restriction; (b) the return of a vehicle so removed to the control of the person who would otherwise be entitled to remove it; and (c) the demand or collection of a charge for those activities; (3) remove the activities of certain bailiffs and a number of activities relating to police matters; (4) remove the vehicle removal activities of persons operating under contracts entered into with local authorities and the police; (5) remove activities which involve only the use of CCTV equipment; and (6) ensure that manned guarding activities carried out in relation to a specified licensed premises are only subject to additional controls when they are carried out at a time when alcohol is being served for consumption on those premises or when entertainment is being provided on those premises respectively.

2842   Private security industry—approved contractor scheme

The Private Security Industry Act 2001 (Approved Contractor Scheme) Regulations 2006, SI 2006/425 (in force on 20 March 2005), prescribe (1) a requirement under the Private Security Industry Act 2001 s 15(3)(a) which the Security Industry Authority must be satisfied will be met before granting an approval under s 15 for the purpose of the Approved Contractor Scheme; (2) the fee that must be paid by a person on application for approval under s 15; and (3) the annual fee which must be paid by an approved person in respect of each person undertaking licensable conduct on his behalf or under his direction.

2843   Private security industry—designated activities

The Private Security Industry Act 2001 (Designated Activities) Order 2006, SI 2006/426 (in force on 20 March 2006), designates, for the purposes of the Private Security Industry Act 2001 s 3, (1) the activities of security operatives engaged in manned guarding on licensed premises at or in relation to times when those premises are open to the public and (2) the activities of security operatives engaged in immobilisation, restriction and removal of vehicles, and keyholding activities. SI 2005/2251 is revoked.

The Private Security Industry Act 2001 (Designated Activities) (Amendment No 2) Order 2006, SI 2006/1804 (in force on 11 July 2006), removes the amendments made to the principal 2006 Order supra by the 2006 Order, SI 2006/824, which is revoked. Consequently, the principal order designates all specified manned guarding activities for the purposes of the Private Security Industry Act 2001 s 3.

2844   Private security industry—exemption—aviation security

The Private Security Industry Act 2001 (Exemption) (Aviation Security) Regulations 2006, SI 2006/428 (in force on 20 March 2006), (1) exempt certain persons from the licensing requirement in the Private Industry Act 2001 s 3 on the basis that suitable alternative arrangements are in place which make it unnecessary for those persons to be so licensed; and (2) specify that an operative, supervisor or manager undertakes, supervises or manages certain activates relating to aviation security, which are undertaken by virtue of a Direction under the Aviation Security Act 1982 s 14 having been recruited in accordance with the Aviation Security (Aircraft Operators, Aerodrome Managers, Listed Security Approved Air Cargo Agents and Catering Undertakings) (selection of aviation security staff) Direction 2002 and, in the case of operators and supervisors, trained in accordance with the Aviation Security (Aircraft Operators, Aerodrome Managers) (training of aviation security staff) Direction 1993, will be exempt.

2845   Private security industry—licence—categories

The Private Security Industry (Licences) (Amendment) Regulations 2006, SI 2006/3410 (in force on 1 February 2007), further amend the 2004 Regulations, SI 2004/255, so as to (1) subject to certain exceptions, extend the 2004 Regulations to Scotland; (2) substitute the definition of 'category of licensable activity' so as to clarify the relationship between the categories of Door Supervisor, Cash and Valuables in Transit and Close Protection; (3) amend the Public Space Surveillance (CCTV) category to ensure it applies to contractors on licensed premises; (4) amend the Security Guard category to clarify that it will apply to contractors on licensed premises in certain circumstances; (5) enable a front line licence issued in respect of the 'Public Space Surveillance (CCTV)' category of licensable activities to cover the use of CCTV equipment which would otherwise fall under, and require a licence for, the 'Security Guard' category of licensable activities; (6) enable a non-front line licence in respect of any category of licensable activity to cover non-front line conduct in respect of any other category of licensable activities; and (7) substitute a new form of licence to act as manager, director, employer or partner.

2846   Private security industry—licence—duration

The Private Security Industry Act 2001 (Duration of Licence) (No 2) Order 2006, SI 2006/3411 (in force on 1 February 2007), makes provision in respect of the duration of licences issued by the

Security Industry Authority under the Private Security Industry Act 2001 s 8. In particular, the order (1) provides that where such a licence is issued to persons engaged in front line licensable conduct in respect of the immobilisation of vehicles or the restriction and removal of vehicles, it is to remain in force for a period of one year beginning on the day on which it is granted; and (2) provides that where such a licence is issued to persons by way of renewal, it is to remain in force for the sum of the period of time for which a new licence in respect of that licensable conduct would be issued were it not for the renewal and, subject to a maximum period of three months, the maximum period for which the previous licence could have remained in force after the renewal was granted had that previous licence remained in force for the full period of time for which it was issued. For this purpose, a renewal is granted where the old licence is valid, when applying for renewal, for no more than four months and where the new licence covers the same category of licensable activity and the same category of licensable conduct as the previous licence. SI 2006/427 is revoked save in respect of applications received before 1 February 2007.

2847   Private Security Industry Act 2001—commencement

The Private Security Industry Act 2001 (Commencement No 10) Order 2006, SI 2006/392, brings ss 14, 15 (so far as not already in force), 16 and 18 into force on 20 March 2006. For a summary of the Act, see 2001 Abr para 3083. See also the commencement table in the title STATUTES.

2848   Trade restrictions—trade with Burma—European Community common foreign and security policy—penalties and licences

The Burma (Sale, Supply, Export, Technical Assistance, Financing and Financial Assistance) (Penalties and Licences) Regulations 2006, SI 2006/2682 (in force on 11 October 2006), replace the 2004 Regulations, SI 2004/1315, and make provision in respect of Burma for offences, penalties and enforcement in respect of EC Council Regulation 817/2006. In particular, the regulations (1) provide for criminal offences in relation to the prohibitions in Regulation 817/2006 arts 2, 3; (2) provide offences for breach of the prohibitions on technical assistance, financing and financial assistance related to military activities, and on activities circumventing these prohibitions; (3) provide offences for breach of the prohibitions on the sale, supply, transfer or export of equipment, connected technical assistance, financing or financial assistance, and on activities circumventing these prohibitions; (4) provide for the licensing of the activities set out in Regulation 817/2006 arts 2, 3; (5) provide for an offence in connection with the provision of false statements related to the obtaining of a licence; (6) provide penalties in respect of the criminal offences created; and (7) provide for the enforcement of these regulations by the Commissioners for Her Majesty's Revenue and Customs.

2849   Trade restrictions—trade with Lebanon—European Community common foreign and security policy—technical and financial assistance—penalties and licences

The Lebanon (Technical Assistance, Financing and Financial Assistance) (Penalties and Licences) Regulations 2006, SI 2006/2681 (in force on 11 October 2006), make provision in respect of Lebanon for penalties and enforcement in respect of EC Council Regulation 1412/2006. The regulations (1) provide for criminal offences in relation to prohibitions on technical assistance, financing and financial assistance related to military activities, and on activities circumventing such prohibitions; (2) provide for an offence in connection with the provision of false statements related to the obtaining of a licence; and (3) provide for enforcement of the regulations by the Commissioners for Her Majesty's Revenue and Customs.

2850   Trade union—collective bargaining—reference to Central Arbitration Committee—approval of collective labour agreements by employees

Scotland
The claimant was employed by the defendant local authority. In the course of negotiations with employees under the Information and Consultation of Employees Regulations 2004, SI 2004/3426, the defendant notified the claimant that it intended to hold a ballot pursuant to reg 8(2). The defendant sought to rely on three pre-existing agreements which applied to teachers and all other staff for the purpose of conducting consultations with employees under the 2004 Regulations. The claimant contended that those agreements did not satisfy the demands of reg 8, which required that a pre-existing agreement should cover all the employees of an undertaking, because they only provided for consultation with trade union representatives and there was no procedure for ensuring that the interests of employees who were not trade union members would be taken into consideration. The matter was referred to the Central Arbitration Committee, which held that the agreements did not meet all the conditions in reg 8 because one of the agreements failed to set out the manner in which the defendant communicated information to the employees caught by the scheme. The defendant appealed. *Held*, save for the provisions of reg 8(1)(b), each of the requirements of reg 8 had to be met by each individual agreement. There was no justification in reg 8 to suggest that it was sufficient for the conditions to be met only by agreements covering the majority of the employees. The committee had been right to find that reg 8(1)(d) had not been

satisfied with respect to one of the pre-existing agreements. The question of whether an employee was a union member was irrelevant. The requirement that the agreements were approved by the employees was a requirement that the majority of the employees approved the agreements. All that was required was evidence from which employee approval could be inferred. In the present case, there had been evidence that at the time of the application the majority of the defendant's employees had been trade union members and in those circumstances the committee had been entitled to find that the agreements had been approved by the majority of the employees. Accordingly, the appeal would be dismissed.

Stewart v Moray Council [2006] IRLR 592 (Employment Appeal Tribunal: Elias J presiding).

2851   Urban Regeneration Agency—acquisition of land—underused or ineffectively used land

Pursuant to the Leasehold Reform, Housing and Urban Development Act 1993 s 162(1), a compulsory purchase order was drafted in relation to an area of land. Following a public inquiry into the matter, an inspector of the defendant Secretary of State produced a report recommending without qualification the confirmation of the order, on the basis that a compelling case in the public interest had been demonstrated and that this justified the interference with the human rights of those affected. In particular, the inspector concluded that the land was predominantly underused or ineffectively used within the meaning of s 159(2)(b). The defendant duly confirmed the order. The claimant, who owned a residential property named in the order, challenged the confirmation of the order under the Land Acquisition Act 1981 s 23(1), arguing that the defendant had misdirected itself in law in finding that the requirements of the 1993 Act s 159(2)(b) had been satisfied, and that the order also thereby constituted an unjustified interference with her rights, under the European Convention on Human Rights art 8 and the First Protocol art 1, to respect for her private life and to peaceful enjoyment of her possessions. *Held*, the concept in the 1993 Act s 159(2)(b) of land being underused or ineffectively used expressly contemplated that some of the land to be acquired was being used, as otherwise the land would fall within the terms of unused land in s 159(2)(a). In practical terms, the regeneration of a complete area would often require an entire area to be taken over in order for a coherent and effective plan of redevelopment to be implemented. In order to meet the requirements of s 159(2)(b), it was therefore necessary to establish that the land, when considered as a unified and coherent whole, was underused or ineffectively used. However, the inspector had concluded that the land was merely predominantly underused or ineffectively used. It followed that both he and the defendant, who had concurred with the inspector's reasoning, had erroneously applied s 159(2)(b). Moreover, the order had constituted an interference with the claimant's rights under the Convention art 8 and the First Protocol art 1, since it deprived her of her home and put the onus on the public authority to justify that interference. Given that the defendant had erred in confirming the order, it followed that the interference was not in accordance with the law, was not justified, and constituted a breach of the claimant's Convention rights. Accordingly, the application would be allowed.

Pascoe v First Secretary of State [2006] EWHC 2356 (Admin), [2006] 4 All ER 1240 (Queen's Bench Division: Forbes J).

TRADE MARKS AND TRADE NAMES

Halsbury's Laws of England (4th edn) vol 48 (2000 Reissue) paras 1–500

Articles

For articles relating to this title please refer to the Table of Articles at the beginning of the Abridgment.

2852   Passing off—goodwill—misleading marketing practices—misrepresentation by conduct

See *British Sky Broadcasting Group plc v Sky Home Services Ltd*, para 1986.

2853   Trade mark—address for service

The Patents, Trade Marks and Designs (Address For Service and Time Limits, etc) Rules 2006, SI 2006/760 (in force on 6 April 2006), amend the Design Right (Proceedings Before Comptroller Rules) 1989, SI 1989/1130, the Patent Rules 1995, SI 1995/2093, the Registered Designs Rules 1995, SI 1995/2912, and the Trade Marks Rules 2000, SI 2000/136, so as to allow applicants for registered rights to provide an address for service in the United Kingdom, the Channel Islands or another EEA state, although, during any proceedings before the comptroller or registrar an address for service in the United Kingdom will be required unless the comptroller or registrar otherwise directs. The rules also (1) liberalise the provisions in both of the 1995 Rules and the 2000 Rules relating to any delays caused by 'interrupted days', which are days where there are disruptions at the

Patent Office or in the postal system; (2) amend provisions in SI 1995/2912 relating to the registration of interest; and (3) add a provision to the 2000 Rules so as to facilitate electronic communications by the registrar.

The Trade Marks and Designs (Address For Service) (Amendment) Rules 2006, SI 2006/1029 (in force on 6 April 2006), further amend SI 1995/2912 supra and SI 2000/136 supra so as to substitute the word 'registrar' for the word 'comptroller' in the provisions specified.

2854   Trade mark—Community trade mark—infringement—order prohibiting defendant from proceeding with infringing behaviour

EC Council Regulation 40/94 art 98(1) provides that, where a Community trade mark court finds that the defendant has infringed or threatened to infringe a Community trade mark, it must (1) issue an order prohibiting the defendant from proceeding with the acts which infringed or would infringe the Community trade mark, unless there are special reasons for not doing so; and (2) take such measures in accordance with its national law as are aimed at ensuring that the prohibition is complied with.

The appellant was the proprietor of a trade mark for mobile telephones and their accessories. The respondent imported devices which were intended to be attached to mobile telephones and contained a light-emitting diode which flashed when the telephone rang. A number of those devices bore the trade mark owned by the appellant, and the appellant therefore brought infringement proceedings in a Swedish district court. The court decided that infringement had been established and issued a prohibition with a fine attached as the court was of the opinion that there was a risk that the defendant might in the future commit the same infringement. On the defendant's appeal, the court found that he had committed the infringement, but that, as he had never committed such acts before and could only be accused of carelessness, there was no need to impose on him a prohibition and fine. The appellant appealed, and the court decided to stay the proceedings and refer questions to the European Court of Justice for a preliminary ruling on the interpretation of Regulation 40/94 art 98(1). *Held*, art 98(1) had to be interpreted as meaning (a) that the mere fact that the risk of further infringement or threatened infringement of a Community trade mark was not obvious or was otherwise merely limited did not constitute a special reason for a Community trade mark court not to issue an order prohibiting the defendant from proceeding with those actions; (b) that the fact that the national law included a general prohibition of the infringement of Community trade marks and provided for the possibility of penalising further infringement or threatened infringement, whether intentional or due to gross negligence, did not constitute a special reason for a Community trade mark court not to issue an order prohibiting the defendant from proceedings with those acts; (c) that a Community trade mark court which had issued an order prohibiting the defendant from proceeding with infringement or threatened infringement of a Community trade mark was required to take such measures, in accordance with its national law, as were aimed at ensuring that that prohibition was complied with, even if the national law included a general prohibition of infringement of Community trade marks and provided for the possibility of penalising further infringement or threatened infringement, whether intentional or due to gross negligence; and (d) that a Community trade mark court which had issued an order prohibiting the defendant from proceeding with infringement or threatened infringement of a Community trade mark was required to take, from among the measures provided for under national law, such as were aimed at ensuring that that prohibition was complied with, even if those measures could not, under that law, be taken in the case of a corresponding infringement of a national trade mark.

Case C-316/05 *Nokia Corp v Wardell* [2006] All ER (D) 219 (Dec) (ECJ: First Chamber).

2855   Trade mark—Community trade mark—international registration

The Community Trade Mark Regulations 2006, SI 2006/1027 (in force on 29 April 2006), replace the 1996 Regulations, SI 1996/1908, and make new provision for the operation of EC Council Regulation 40/94 on the Community trade mark. In particular, the regulations, which also largely apply to international trade marks (EC), (1) prescribe the procedure for determining the invalidity, or liability to revocation, of the registration of a trade mark over which a Community trade mark claims seniority; (2) set out the sanctions available for the infringement of a Community trade mark and apply to such marks the Trade Marks Act 1994 ss 15–19, which deal with infringement proceedings; (3) apply s 21, which deals with groundless threats of infringement proceedings, to Community trade marks; (4) apply to Community trade marks the provisions of the 1994 Act which relate to the importation of infringing goods, material or articles and to offences and forfeiture; (5) make it an offence to falsely represent that a mark is a Community trade mark or to make false representations as to the goods and services for which a Community trade mark is registered; (6) provide for the conversion of Community trade marks or applications for Community trade marks into applications for registration under the 1994 Act; (7) provide for the privilege from disclosure of certain communications with professional trade marks representatives; and (8) designate certain United Kingdom courts as Community trade mark courts with jurisdiction over proceedings arising out of the Regulation. SI 2004/2332 is amended and SI 2004/949, 2005/440 are revoked.

2856 Trade mark—infringement—defence—defence raised in opposition proceedings—power to plead

The claimant company was the assignee of a word mark which was registered under the Trade Marks Act 1994 s 40(1). Pursuant to s 38, the first defendant gave notice of its opposition to the registration, but its objection was dismissed by the hearing officer for the registrar. The claimant subsequently commenced proceedings against the first defendant and its United Kingdom subsidiary, the second defendant, alleging that they had infringed the mark by the use of a similar brand. The defendants opposed the claim, arguing pursuant to s 47 that the registration of the mark was invalid. An issue arose as to whether the defendants were precluded on the ground of cause of action or issue estoppel from challenging the validity of the mark. *Held*, there was no relevant difference between the practice and procedure of the registry in opposition proceedings under s 38(2) and in invalidity proceedings under s 47(1). The former took place before registration and the latter afterwards, but in each case the issues were whether any objection to registration could be made out under ss 3 and 5. It followed that the issues underlying the two sets of proceedings in the present case were identical and, as it was established that cause of action estoppel applied where a cause of action in the second action was identical to a cause of action in the first, the defendants were estopped from pleading invalidity as a defence in the second set of proceedings. Judgment would be given accordingly.

Special Effects v L'Oreal SA [2006] EWHC 481 (Ch), [2006] RPC 849 (Chancery Division: Sir Andrew Morritt C). *Hormel Foods Corpn v Antilles Landscape Investments NV* [2005] EWHC 13 (Ch), [2005] RPC 657 (2005 Abr para 3086) applied.

This decision has been reversed on appeal: [2007] EWCA Civ 1, [2007] All ER (D) 29 (Jan).

2857 Trade mark—infringement—goods marketed within European Economic Area

The Trade Marks Act 1994 s 12(1) provides that a registered trade mark is not infringed by the use of the trade mark in relation to goods which have been put on the market in the European Economic Area under that trade mark by the proprietor or with his consent. Section 12(1) does not apply where there exist legitimate reasons for the proprietor to oppose further dealings in the goods, in particular, where the condition of the goods has been changed or impaired after they have been put on the market: s 12(2).

The claimant manufactured garments in relation to which it used a word mark and a related graphic mark. Under an agreement between the claimant and a distributor, the distributor had exclusivity within its territory. The defendant obtained and sold garments manufactured by the claimant from a source other than the distributor. The claimant commenced proceedings against the defendant alleging infringement of its trade mark and applied to strike out certain paragraphs of the defence relating to such allegations. The application was allowed on the basis that there was no adequate nexus between the distribution agreement and the issue of whether the claimant had legitimate reasons to oppose further distribution under the 1994 Act s 12(2). The defendant appealed. *Held*, it was arguable that to be able to prove that a relevant agreement was in breach of the EC Treaty art 81 would give a defendant a stronger basis for saying that the claimant did not have legitimate reasons to oppose further dealings in the goods, within the meaning of the 1994 Act s 12(2). Having regard to recent references to the European Court of Justice relating to the issue of parallel imports and relabelling, certain issues of Community law arising in relation to those matters remained unresolved. The judge should not have been satisfied that the defence was necessarily bound to fail. The paragraphs of the defence struck out were not unarguable for lack of a legally sufficient nexus. Whether such nexus as was proved at trial would be held to be sufficient in law and in fact was a matter for the trial judge. Accordingly, the appeal would be allowed.

Sportswear SpA v Stonestyle [2006] EWCA Civ 380, [2006] IP & T 769 (Court of Appeal: Waller, Longmore and Lloyd LJJ). *Glaxo Group Ltd v Dowelhurst Ltd* [2000] FSR 371 considered.

2858 Trade mark—infringement—identical mark—perfume

The Trade Mark Act 1994 s 10(1) provides that a person infringes a registered trade mark if he uses, in the course of trade, a sign which is identical with the trade mark in relation to goods or services which are identical with those for which it is registered. A person also infringes a registered trade mark if he uses, in the course of trade, a sign which is identical with or similar to the trade mark, where the trade mark has a reputation in the United Kingdom and the use of the sign, being without due cause, takes unfair advantage of, or is detrimental to, the distinctive character or the repute of the trade mark: s 10(3).

The claimants, who were manufacturers of high quality perfumes and other beauty products, complained that the defendants had imported and distributed a range of perfumes which were 'smell-alikes' and were marketed in packaging which took unfair advantage of its own product names, packaging and brand image contrary to the 1994 Act s 10(3). The claimants also contended that lists comparing the claimants' marked brands with the defendants' products, which were used when selling the defendants' products and when dealing with customers' queries, were contrary to s 10(1). *Held*, the correct comparison to make was a contextual one between the mark and the sign, having first identified both the mark and the sign. In the present case, the extent of the similarity was deliberate, with the two fragrances chosen as comparators both well-promoted and extensively advertised brands. There was no question that part of the reward for the costs of promoting, maintaining and enhancing a particular trade mark had been received by the defendants, which amounted to taking an unfair advantage. Both the box and bottle were sufficiently similar to the respective competing marks to give rise to an association in the mind of the average consumer. The marks in question enjoyed a reputation and the relevant signs of the defendants took unfair advantage of the character or reputation of the registered marks. It followed that infringement under s 10(3) had been established. Further, the use of the claimants' word marks on comparison lists and in response to customers' queries amounted to infringement within the meaning of s 10(1). Accordingly, the application would be allowed.

L'Oreal SA v Bellure NV [2006] EWHC 2355 (Ch), [2007] IP & T 232 (Chancery Division: Lewison J).

2859   Trade mark—intellectual property—enforcement

See para 2120.

2860   Trade mark—international registration

The Trade Marks (International Registration) (Amendment) Order 2006, SI 2006/763 (in force on 6 April 2006), further amends the 1996 Order, SI 1996/714, so as to (1) allow applicants for an international trade mark to provide an address for service in the United Kingdom, another EEA state or the Channel Islands; and (2) provide that during any proceedings before the registrar, an address for service in the United Kingdom will be required unless the registrar otherwise directs.

The Trade Marks (International Registration) (Amendment No 2) Order 2006, SI 2006/1080 (in force on 12 April 2006), further amends the 1996 Order supra so as to substitute the word 'registrar' for the word 'comptroller' in the provisions specified.

2861   Trade mark—Olympics and Paralympics association right—appointment of proprietors

The Olympics and Paralympics Association Rights (Appointment of Proprietors) Order 2006, SI 2006/1119 (in force on 12 May 2006), replaces the 1995 Order, SI 1995/2473, and appoints the British Olympic Association and the London Organising Committee as the proprietors of the Olympics and Paralympics association rights, thereby allowing them the rights provided by the Olympic Symbol etc (Protection) Act 1995 in relation to the Olympic and Paralympic symbols and mottos, the words 'Olympiad', 'Olympian', 'Olympic', 'Paralympiad', 'Paralympian', 'Paralympic' and their plural forms, and confusingly similar symbols, mottos or words.

2862   Trade mark—Paralympics association right—Paralympic symbol

The Paralympics Association Right (Paralympic Symbol) Order 2006, SI 2006/1120 (in force on 12 May 2006), sets out the symbol of the International Paralympic Committee for the purposes of the Olympic Symbol etc (Protection) Act 1995 s 18(1).

2863   Trade mark—registration—application—examination of facts

The applicant applied for a Community trade mark under EC Council Regulation 40/94 in respect of the word sign 'EUROHYPO'. The application was refused pursuant to art 7(1)(b), (c), (2), and the applicant appealed. The respondent trade mark authority upheld the appeal in part, and the applicant appealed, contending that, in coming to its decision, the respondent had infringed art 74(1) by failing to carry out an exhaustive examination of the facts. *Held*, according to settled case law, the examination carried out by the competent trade mark authority had to be a stringent and full examination in order to prevent trade marks from being improperly registered. However, art 74(1) did not state how such an authority was to carry out the examination. It was therefore sufficient if an authority applied the descriptiveness test, as interpreted by case law, in order to reach a decision, and it was not obliged to justify its action by the production of evidence. The respondent had analysed the meaning of the elements 'euro' and 'hypo' for the German consumer and the possible meanings of the compound word 'EUROHYPO'. The finding that there had been no references to further research in the statement of reasons of the contested decision was not sufficient to establish that the respondent had substituted its own interpretation of the word at issue for that of the relevant public. Accordingly, the application would be dismissed.

Case T-439/04 *Eurohypo AG v Office for Harmonisation in the Internal Market (Trade Marks and Designs)* [2006] 3 CMLR 364 (CFI: Third Chamber).

2864   Trade mark—registration—distinctive character

The applicant objected to the respondent's attempt to register 'Easy.com' as a trade mark. The applicant contended that the respondent's proposed trade mark was caught by the Trade Marks Act 1994 s 3, on the ground that it was merely descriptive of the nature of the products and services offered, and that therefore, the proposed trade mark was not capable of registration. The objection was unsuccessful and the applicant appealed, submitting that the individual elements of the proposed mark should have been considered and the mark would only have been capable of registration if, as a whole, it had an unusual or distinctive effect. *Held,* where a proposed trade mark consisted of two purely descriptive elements, the correct test under s 3 was whether the whole was greater than merely the sum of its parts. If the proposed mark remained purely descriptive it would fail. However, there was no separate requirement for the existence of some unusual characteristic. In the present case, the decision had had regard to the relevant authorities. The decision-making process had involved consideration of the individual descriptive elements of the proposed mark and the effect of the whole. Accordingly, the appeal would be dismissed.

Easynet Group Ltd v Easygroup IP Licensing Ltd [2007] EWHC 1872 (Pat), [2007] RPC 107 (Chancery Division: Mann J).

2865 Trade mark—registration—grounds for refusal—identical or similar mark for dissimilar goods or services

The applicant was the proprietor of a large number of registrations in respect of the marks 'INTEL' and 'INTEL INSIDE'. The respondent applied for registration of the mark 'INTELMARK' for a specification of marketing and telemarketing services. The applicant applied for a declaration of invalidity against registration of that mark under the Trade Marks Act 1994 s 47 on the ground that its use without due cause would take unfair advantage of or be detrimental to the distinctive character or the repute of its own marks, contrary to s 5(3). The hearing officer was not satisfied that there would be any material damage to the distinctiveness or repute of the INTEL brand if INTELMARK was used in a normal and fair manner in relation to the services for which it was registered, and therefore dismissed the application. The applicant appealed, contending that the hearing officer had considerably underestimated the reputation and distinctive character of the INTEL mark and that that had a significant impact on his subsequent assessment of the challenge to validity on the s 5(3) grounds. *Held,* the emphasis in a s 5(3) inquiry was on the reputation enjoyed by the earlier mark and the use or misuse of that reputation by the owners of the later mark either for their own benefit or at the expense of the earlier mark. The first step in the exploitation of the distinctive character of the earlier mark was necessarily the making of the association or link between the two marks. The making of the association was not necessarily to be treated as a detriment or the taking of an unfair advantage in itself and in cases of unfair advantage it was likely to be necessary to show that the making of the link between the marks had economic consequences beneficial to the user of the later mark. In relation to detriment, the position was more complicated. The association between the marks and therefore potentially between the products or services to which they related might be detrimental to the strength and reputation of the earlier mark if it tarnished it by association or made it less distinctive. That was likely to take place as a consequence of the same mental process which linked the two marks in the minds of consumers and was essentially a negative reaction and effect. In the present case, the difference between the goods and the services could not be bridged simply by the strength of the INTEL mark itself. Accordingly, the appeal would be dismissed.

Intel Corpn Inc v CPM United Kingdom Ltd [2006] EWHC 1878 (Ch), [2006] All ER (D) 399 (Jul) (Chancery Division: Patten J).

2866 Trade mark—registration—rules

The Trade Marks (Amendment) Rules 2006, SI 2006/3039 (in force on 1 January), further amend the 2000 Rules, SI 2000/136, so as to formally prescribe the Nice Classification as the prescribed system of classification under the Trade Marks Act 1994. In particular, the rules (1) set out minor and consequential amendments; (2) make provision so as to enable the registrar to re-classify a registered trade mark where the Nice Classification has changed for some or all of the goods and services in respect of which the mark has been registered; and (3) revoke provisions which set out two previous systems of classification, both of which were based on earlier versions of the Nice Classification system.

2867 Trade mark—registration—validity—shape—shape necessary to obtain a technical result

The Trade Marks Act 1994 s 3(2)(b) provides that a sign may not be registered as a trade mark if it consists exclusively of the shape of goods which is necessary to obtain a technical result.

The claimant brought trade mark infringement proceedings against the defendant following the sale by the defendant of three-headed rotary shavers with heads alleged to be identical or confusingly similar to the claimant's registered trade mark. The defendant contended that as the claimant's mark consisted exclusively of features of the shape of the goods which were necessary to obtain a technical result, it was invalid under the 1994 Act s 3(2)(b). The judge concluded that the essential features of the mark were attributable only to the technical result obtained and the mark was invalid. The judge also ruled that the declaration of invalidity covered the claimant's other trade marks which were all device marks. The claimant appealed. *Held,* the important factor in trade mark law was the impact of the mark on the eye of the average customer. The perception of the average customer for the goods in question would not depend on the dissection of the mark and on an examination of each feature of the mark. It turned on the feature which contributed most to the overall impression. The question was one of fact and degree for the judge. The judge had been entitled to find that the particular feature of the claimant's mark was not an essential feature of the shape at issue and he had made no error of law in that conclusion. Taking account of the essential elements of the mark, an assessment had to be made as to its functionality. The judge's assessment of the functionality of the first mark had not been flawed and he had been entitled to find that the mark was invalid. However, the device marks had all been images of an abstract, non-technical and non-functional nature. None of them amounted to 'a shape of goods' as they were shapes only in a figurative sense. It could not be said that they were descriptive or devoid of any distinctive character and so precluded by s 3(1)(c) or (b). The device marks were not invalid. Accordingly, the appeal would be allowed in part.

Koninklijke Philips Electronics NV v Remington Consumer Products Ltd [2006] EWCA Civ 16, [2007] IP & T 209 (Court of Appeal: Mummery, Neuberger and Lloyd LJJ). Decision of Rimer J [2004] All ER (D) 301 (Oct), [2004] All ER (D) 301 (Oct) (2004 Abr para 2832) reversed in part.

TRANSPORT

2868   Goods vehicle—road tanker—drivers' hours—temporary exception

See para 1279.

2869   Goods vehicle—weight limit—exceeding weight limit—defence—travelling to nearest available weighbridge

The Road Traffic Act 1988 s 41B(2)(a)(i) provides that in any proceedings for an offence under s 41B in which there is alleged a contravention of a construction and use requirement as to any description of weight applicable to a goods vehicle, it is a defence to prove that at the time when the vehicle was being used on the road it was proceeding to a weighbridge which was the nearest available one to the place where the loading of the vehicle was completed for the purpose of being weighed.

The defendant company was charged with using a goods vehicle on a road when its maximum permissible weight had been exceeded, contrary to the Road Vehicles (Construction and Use) Regulations 1986, SI 1986/1078, reg 80 and the 1988 Act s 41B. The charge was dismissed on the basis that the defendant had a defence under s 41B(3)(a)(i) because it had proved that the vehicle was proceeding to the nearest available weighbridge known to the driver for the purpose of being weighed. On appeal, the prosecution submitted that the defence was not available because the weighbridge to which the driver claimed he was proceeding was not the nearest available weighbridge. *Held*, as a matter of statutory construction, the concept of the 'nearest available weighbridge' had to be construed to mean the nearest available weighbridge that was actually available as a matter of objective fact regardless of the knowledge of the driver. If Parliament had intended an element of mens rea to be imported into the statutory defence then it would have been simple to include the necessary words in the statute. Moreover, to allow such an element to be imported would create difficulties of enforcement and would be detrimental to Parliament's objective of protecting the public. Accordingly, the appeal would be allowed.

Vehicle and Operator Services Agency v F & S Gibbs Transport Services Ltd [2006] EWHC 1109 (Admin), (2006) 170 JP 586 (Queen's Bench Division: Keene LJ and Jack J).

2870   Guided transport systems—safety

See para 2425.

2871   Passenger and goods vehicles—recording equipment—fitting date

The Passenger and Goods Vehicles (Recording Equipment) (Fitting Date) Regulations 2006, SI 2006/1117 (in force on 1 May 2006), amend the Transport Act 1968 s 97, so as to set the date to 1 May 2006, from which the new digital tachograph must be fitted to a new vehicle which requires a tachograph.

2872   Passenger and goods vehicles—recording equipment—general

The Passenger and Goods Vehicles (Community Recording Equipment Regulation) Regulations 2006, SI 2006/3276 (in force on 3 January 2007), amend the definition of 'the Community Recording Equipment Regulation' in the enactments specified. SI 2005/1904 is amended. SI 1996/941 is revoked.

2873   Passenger and goods vehicles—recording equipment—tachograph card

The Passenger and Goods Vehicles (Recording Equipment) (Tachograph Card) Regulations 2006, SI 2006/1937 (in force on 21 August 2006), make provision in relation to the cards used by digital tachographs. In particular, the regulations (1) prohibit (a) the use by a person (i) of more than one driver card; (ii) of a driver card of which he is not the holder; (iii) of a forged or altered card; (iv) of a card issued as a result of an incorrect application; (v) of more than one workshop card, or PIN, for each workshop in which he works; (vi) of a workshop card or PIN of which he is not the holder or in a place which is not his workplace; and (vii) of a forged or altered card and of a card issued as a result of an incorrect application; (b) making a false statement in an application for a card; and (c) the divulging of a PIN; (2) provide that a breach of the prohibitions under head (1) is an offence; (3) prohibit causing or permitting a person to breach the prohibitions under head (1), the maximum penalty being, if the offender is convicted on indictment, two years and a fine, or if the offender is convicted summarily, the statutory maximum; (4) require a card holder to notify the Secretary of State of details on the card requiring correction and to return it for correction and provide that the Secretary of State may also require the return of cards issued erroneously for correction; (5) provide that failure to comply with head (4) is an offence punishable by a level 5 fine; (6) provide that a card which identifies another person as the holder, which has been falsified or which has been issued as a result of a false application, must be surrendered or may be confiscated by a constable or VOSA examiner; and (7) provide that it is an offence punishable by a level 5 fine to fail to surrender a card under head (6).

2874   Railways

See RAILWAYS, INLAND WATERWAYS AND PIPELINES.

2875   Road traffic

See ROAD TRAFFIC.

2876   Transport Act 2000—commencement

The Transport Act 2000 (Commencement No 12) Order 2006, SI 2006/1933, brings s 248 into force on 1 October 2006. For a summary of the Act, see 2000 Abr para 3297. For details of commencement, see the commencement table in the title STATUTES.

2877   Transport for London

See LONDON GOVERNMENT.

2878   Transport security—electronic communications

The Transport Security (Electronic Communications) Order 2006, SI 2006/2190 (in force on 30 September 2006), modifies the Aviation Security Act 1982, the Aviation and Maritime Security Act 1990, the Railways Act 1993, the Channel Tunnel (Security) Order 1994, SI 1994/570 and the Ship and Port Facility (Security) Regulations 2004, SI 2004/1495. In particular, the order (1) enables documents to be served using electronic communication, where the intended recipient has provided in advance an electronic address for services and the document is served on that person at that address in a form agreed by the recipient; (2) amends the 1993 Act so that it relates only to documents served by the Secretary of State; (3) requires a document, in order for service to be effective, to be in a sufficiently permanent form so that it can be used for subsequent reference; (4) provides that, unless the contrary is proved, service is deemed to have been effected at the time the electronic communication is transmitted, except where an electronic communication is received outside a person's normal business hours, when it is to be treated as having been received on the next working day; (5) enables the recipient to withdraw his permission to accept service electronically by giving not less than 14 days' written notice; (6) makes provision for documents to be treated as served where the intended recipient has agreed in advance that he will have access to such documents on a website maintained by the Secretary of State, and the Secretary of State notifies him, in a manner agreed in advance, of the publication of the website of the document being served and how to access it; (7) provides that any person who has agreed to such a method of service may withdraw his permission by giving not less than 14 days' written notice; and (8) provides for new definitions of 'address' and 'electronic communications'.

2879   Transport (Wales) Act 2006

The Transport (Wales) Act 2006 makes provision about transport to, from and within Wales. The Act received the royal assent on 16 February 2006 and the following provisions came into force in part on that day. The remaining provisions came into force on 26 May 2006: SI 2006/1403. For details of commencement, see the commencement table in the title STATUTES.

Section 1 imposes on the National Assembly for Wales a general duty ('the general transport duty') to develop policies for the promotion and encouragement of safe, integrated, sustainable, efficient and economic transport facilities and services to, from and within Wales, and s 2 requires the Assembly to prepare and publish a document known as the Wales Transport Strategy, which must set out its policies and proposals for discharging the general transport duty. Provision is made in relation to local transport plans by s 3, Schedule. The Assembly is empowered to give directions to two or more local authorities in Wales to enter into specified arrangements in relation to the discharge of transport functions: s 4. Section 5 provides for the establishment of joint transport authorities, which will discharge specified transport functions of two or more local authorities in Wales, and s 6 empowers the Assembly to give direct financial assistance to authorities discharging transport functions in Wales. The Assembly may secure the provision of any public passenger transport service which it considers appropriate for the purpose of meeting any public transport requirements within Wales that would not, in its view, otherwise be met: s 7. Sections 8–10 provide for the establishment and functions of, and guidance and directions given to, the Public Transport Users' Committee for Wales, and s 11 empowers the Assembly to give financial assistance in relation to air transport services in Wales. Section 12 deals with commencement, s 13 with the making of orders, and s 14 with interpretation. Provision is also made in relation to money (s 15), extent (s 16) and short title (s 17).

Amendments, repeals and revocations
Subscribers should note that the list below mentions repeals and amendments which are or will be effective when the Act is fully in force. Please refer to the top of this summary for details of the in-force dates of the provisions of the Act. This information may also be found in the Commencement of Statutes table in *Halsbury's Laws Current Service*. Please also note that this list is not exhaustive.

Specific provisions of the Transport Act 2000 are added or amended, including ss 108, 109, 109A–109C, 113A, 113B.

TRUSTS

Halsbury's Laws of England (4th edn) vol 48 (2000 Reissue) paras 501–1025

Articles

For articles relating to this title please refer to the Table of Articles at the beginning of the Abridgment.

2880 Breach of trust—loss to beneficiaries—participation of third party—dishonesty—test

An offender, through the claimant company, operated a fraudulent off-shore investment scheme purporting to offer high returns from investment in United Kingdom gilt-edged securities. Some of the investors' funds were paid through bank accounts maintained by companies administered from the Isle of Man by the first defendant company. The second and third defendants were the principal directors of the first defendant. The claimant brought proceedings claiming that the second and third defendants and, through them, the first defendant, dishonestly assisted the offender to misappropriate the investors' funds. The judge held that the second defendant was liable for dishonestly assisting in the misappropriation of certain sums on account of the second defendant strongly suspecting that the funds passing through his hands was money which the claimant had received from members of the public who thought they were subscribing to a scheme of investment in gilt-edged securities. If those suspicions were correct, no honest person could have assisted the offender to dispose of the funds for their personal use. The judge also found that the first and third defendants were similarly liable. The defendants appealed and the first and third defendants' appeals were dismissed. The second defendant's appeal was allowed. The claimant appealed. *Held,* liability for dishonest assistance required a dishonest state of mind on the part of the person who assisted in a breach of trust. Such a state of mind might consist of knowledge that the transaction was one in which he could not honestly participate, or it might consist of suspicion combined with a conscious decision not to make inquiries which might result in knowledge. Although a dishonest state of mind was a subjective mental state, the standard by which the law determined whether it was dishonest was objective. If by ordinary standards a defendant's mental state would be characterised as dishonest, it was irrelevant that the defendant had different standards. Judged by ordinary standards the second defendant's state of mind was dishonest. There was no evidence that the second defendant had tried to seek any explanation for disposals about which he had reason to be suspicious and the original judge was fully justified in concluding that that was the result of a dishonest decision. Accordingly, the appeal would be allowed.

Barlow Clowes International Ltd (in liquidation) v Eurotrust International Ltd [2005] UKPC 37, [2006] 1 All ER (Comm) 478 (Privy Council: Lords Nicholls of Birkenhead, Steyn, Hoffmann, Walker of Gestingthorpe and Carswell).

2881 Constructive trust—acquisition of property—contribution to purchase price—detrimental reliance—common intention—beneficial interest

The transferees, the claimant, her husband and their son, the defendant, purchased a property jointly. The transfer document did not set out their beneficial interests. All three transferees made payments under the mortgage, which was in all of their names. Following the death of the husband, legal ownership of the property vested in the claimant and the defendant. The claimant sought a declaration under the Trusts of Land and Appointment of Trustees Act 1996 s 14 that she was the sole beneficial owner of the property. The judge found that, after the death of the husband, the beneficial interest had passed to the surviving joint tenants in shares equivalent to their existing interests so that the claimant and the defendant each held a 50 per cent beneficial interest. The claimant appealed.

Held, the judge had to consider whether there had been any agreement, arrangement or understanding reached between the transferees as to the beneficial ownership of the property. Her conclusion had plainly been that there was a common communicated understanding that the defendant would acquire a beneficial interest. While there had been a failure to consider whether the person relying on the agreement, arrangement or understanding had acted to his detriment or significantly altered his position, such detrimental reliance could be inferred from the defendant's undertaking of joint and several liability under the mortgage, as well as his apparent acceptance of liability under a related endowment policy. It followed that he could claim a beneficial interest in the property under a constructive trust and, accordingly, the appeal would be dismissed.

Crossley v Crossley [2005] EWCA Civ 1581, [2006] 2 FLR 813 (Court of Appeal: May LJ and Sir Peter Gibson). *Lloyds Bank plc v Rosset* [1991] 1 AC 107, HL (1990 Abr para 1414); *Oxley v Hiscock* [2004] EWCA Civ 546, [2005] Fam 211 (2004 Abr para 2862); and *Mortgage Corpn v Shaire* [2001] Ch 743 (2000 Abr para 3318) applied.

2882 Constructive trust—married couple—matrimonial home—beneficial interest—intention of parties

A matrimonial home was registered in the joint names of a husband and wife. The husband was declared bankrupt, and the registrar made a declaration that the matrimonial home was owned in equal shares by the parties, and made an order for vacant possession and sale. The wife appealed against that decision, arguing that she owned 85 per cent of the property, which the husband did not dispute. At the time of the transfer of the property, no express declaration was made as to the parties' respective shares in the property. However, they had made statements in connection with the husband's individual voluntary arrangement that they owned the property in equal shares. Furthermore, it was common ground before the registrar and on appeal that their respective beneficial interests arose under a constructive trust rather than an express or resulting trust. Therefore, the only issue was the respective sizes of their beneficial interests as tenants in common. *Held*, the size of the parties' beneficial shares was determined by their actual or assumed common intention at the time of purchase, though recourse could be had to later conduct where it gave an indication of what that earlier intention was. In the instant case, the statements made at the time of the individual voluntary arrangement were not declarations of trust in relation to the property. Neither party purported to create a trust where either no trust or some different trust had existed before. They were merely statements made for the purpose of informing the husband's creditors as to the nature and extent of his assets and as to his wife's readiness to co-operate in the sale of the property and the realisation of his beneficial interest for the benefit of those creditors. It would not be satisfactory to infer purely from those statements that the husband and wife had a shared common intention of equal beneficial ownership at the time of purchase. However, the registrar was right to describe the statements as a compelling factor in determining what was fair. It would be very unfair if the wife, having made a written statement that she and her husband were equal beneficial owners in the property, should then be able to obtain a determination from the court that her interest exceeded 50 per cent. Accordingly, the appeal would be dismissed.

Supperstone v Hurst [2005] EWHC 1309 (Ch), [2006] 1 FCR 352 (Chancery Division: Michael Briggs QC).

2883 Constructive trust—oral arrangements—father transferring property to daughter and third party

The first claimant transferred a property he owned into the names of the second claimant, his daughter, and the defendant. Their title was registered at the Land Registry. Subsequently, the second claimant executed a general power of attorney in the defendant's favour, purportedly in order to enable the defendant to sell the property. Neither the defendant nor the second claimant lived at the property, it having been let to a private company. The defendant then received a letter from the first claimant stating that he had agreed to transfer the property to the defendant in order that he manage the property for the first claimant whilst he was abroad and that that agreement had been on the understanding that the defendant would re-convey the property to the first claimant on his request. The defendant denied that the transfer had proceeded on that basis. Both parties issued proceedings, the claimants seeking the vesting of the property in the first claimant or a declaration that the defendant and the second claimant held the property on trust for the first claimant. The defendant asserted that the second claimant had agreed to relinquish her interest in the property in return for the defendant meeting the future responsibilities on the property. *Held*, in the present case, there had been no evidence on which it could be held that the first claimant had transferred the property to the defendant and the second claimant on the terms contended for by the claimants. Further, such an agreement would have made little commercial sense to any of the concerned parties. On the other hand, the defendant had failed to demonstrate that the second claimant had relinquished her interest in the property. Therefore, the defendant and the second claimant each held a one-half share in the property. Judgment would be given accordingly.

Akhtar v Arif [2006] EWHC 2726 (Ch), [2006] 3 FCR 526 (Chancery Division: Suart Isaacs QC).

2884   Resulting trust—contribution to purchase price—property acquired pursuant to profit-sharing agreement

The parties made an agreement under which the defendant contributed to the purchase price and development costs of two properties. The agreement provided for the money to be repaid with interest and for payment to the defendant of a percentage of the profits of any sale. Both projects went into deficit. The defendant claimed that he had a beneficial interest in the two properties on the basis that his contribution to the purchase price and development costs gave rise to a resulting trust. The claimants applied for summary judgment, seeking a declaration that the defendant had no such entitlement in the properties and damages for slander of title. *Held*, the fact that a person was entitled to a profit share did not entitle him to an equitable interest in a property. A resulting trust arose where there was a perceived gap in the interest in a property, which would be filled by equity. However, where the interest was regulated by contract there was no gap for equity to fill. Under the terms of the agreement, the defendant contributed towards the purchase price and development costs and in return would receive, not an equitable interest in the properties, but a potential interest in the eventual profits. Accordingly, the defendant had no arguable basis for the claim that he had a beneficial interest in the properties and a declaration to that effect would be made. The action for slander of title required proof that the defendant had no reasonable belief in his claim for beneficial title. The defendant's solicitors had advised him that he had a claim to an interest in the property. Notwithstanding the fact that the defendant had no arguable claim that he had an interest in the properties, his reliance on the legal advice gave him an arguable defence to the slander of title action. Accordingly, the claimant's application for summary judgment would be refused.

Assured Quality Construction Ltd v Thompson [2006] All ER (D) 181 (Mar) (Chancery Division: Lewison J).

2885   Trustee—powers and duties—classification of trust—statutory trust

See *Re Ahmed & Co; Re Biebuyck Solicitors; Re Dixon & Co; Re Zoi*, para 2719.

2886   Trustee—powers and duties—fraudulent breach of trust—dishonest assistance claim—limitation

See *Cattley v Pollard*, para 1817.

2887   Trustee—powers and duties—restriction of liabilities—trustee exemption clauses— Law Commission recommendations

The Law Commission has published a report, *Trustee Exemption Clauses* (Cm 6874, Law Com No 301), setting out its recommendations regarding exemption clauses in trust instruments. In the course of the parliamentary passage of the Trustee Act 2000, a question was raised as to the need to restrict the use of exemption clauses in trust instruments, and the Lord Chancellor asked the Law Commission to examine the law governing clauses which restrict the liabilities of trustees either by excluding liability for breach of their duties or by limiting the duties to which the trustees are subject, the latter type of clauses being dubbed 'duty modification clauses'. The Commission felt that the nub of the problem lay with the possibility of a failure on the part of settlors to be aware of any trustee exemption clauses in the trust instruments. This is a matter which particularly applies in the case of trustees who are remunerated for their services. Following extensive consultation, the Commission decided that this failure could not be dealt with satisfactorily by legislation, particularly with regard to duty modification clauses, and has adopted a practice-based approach. The Commission recommends that regulatory and professional bodies should adopt a rule of practice as to the proper disclosure of exemption clauses. This would be enforced in accordance with their codes of conduct and would be applicable not only to paid trustees but to draftsmen of trust instruments. The Commission recommends that the main elements of the rule should state that any paid trustee who causes a settlor to include a clause in a trust instrument which has the effect of excluding or limiting liability for negligence must, before the creation of the trust, take such steps as are reasonable to ensure that the settlor is aware of the meaning and effect of the clause.

VALUE ADDED TAX

Halsbury's Laws of England (4th edn) vol 49(1) (2005 Reissue) paras 1–400

Articles

For articles relating to this title please refer to the Table of Articles at the beginning of the Abridgment.

2888   Accounting—fraud—joint and several liability—Community law

In the course of an application for judicial review in proceedings regarding the compatibility of Community law with the provisions of the Finance Act 2003 ss 17 and 18, which were enacted to deal with the fraudulent abuse of the system of value added tax, the Court of Appeal referred for a preliminary ruling questions concerning the interpretation of EC Council Directive 77/388 arts 21(3) and 22(8). *Held*, art 21(3) was to be interpreted as allowing a member state to enact legislation, such as that in issue in the main proceedings, which provided that a taxable person to whom a supply of goods or services had been made and who knew, or had reasonable grounds to suspect, that some or all of the VAT payable in respect of that supply, or any previous or subsequent supply, would go unpaid, might be made jointly and severally liable with the person who was liable for payment of that tax. However, such legislation had to comply with the general principles of law which formed part of the Community legal order and which included, in particular, the principles of legal certainty and proportionality. Moreover, art 22(8) was to be interpreted as not allowing a member state to enact either (1) legislation, such as that in issue in the main proceedings, which provided that a taxable person, to whom a supply of goods or services had been made and who knew or had reasonable grounds to suspect that some or all of the VAT payable in respect of that joint supply, or any previous or subsequent supply, would go unpaid, might be made jointly and severally liable with the person who was liable for payment of that tax; or (2) legislation which provided that a taxable person might be required to provide security for the payment of that tax which was or could become payable by the taxable person to whom he supplied those goods or services or by whom they were supplied to him. By contrast, that provision did not preclude a national measure which imposed on any person who was, pursuant to a national measure adopted on the basis of art 21(3), jointly and severally liable for payment of VAT, a requirement to provide security for the payment of that tax which was due.

Case C-384/04 *Customs and Excise Comrs v Federation of Technological Industries* [2006] 3 CMLR 337 (ECJ: Third Chamber).

2889   Exempt supply—betting, gaming and lotteries—call centre services—provision of facilities for placing bets

A call centre received and recorded telephone bet instructions from the public on behalf of a telephone betting operator and bore no financial risk. The Commissioners of Customs and Excise refused to regard the call centre's activities as exempt from value added tax under EC Council Directive 77/388 art 13(B)(f), which exempted betting, lotteries and other forms of gambling. The House of Lords referred the matter to the European Court of Justice. *Held*, the call centre's activity in providing the staff, premises, telephone and computer equipment necessary to take bets could not be said to be characterised by an offer to customers placing bets of a chance of winning in consideration for accepting the risk of having to pay for winnings. Therefore the activity could not be classified as a betting transaction within the meaning of art 13(B)(f). That was not affected by the fact that the acceptance by the call centre's staff was a stage in the placing of the bets. It followed that the provision of call centre services to a telephone bookmaking organiser which entailed the staff or the supplier of those services accepting bets on behalf of the organiser, did not constitute a betting transaction and so could not qualify for the VAT exemption.

Case C-89/05 *United Utilities plc v Comrs of Customs and Excise* [2006] STC 1423 (ECJ: Second Chamber). For previous proceedings see *United Utilities plc v Customs and Excise Comrs* [2004] EWCA Civ 245, [2004] STC 727 (2004 Abr para 2875).

2890   Exempt supply—betting, gaming and lotteries—game of chance

The Value Added Tax (Betting, Gaming and Lotteries) Order 2006, SI 2006/2685 (in force on 1 November 2006), replaces the 2005 Order, SI 2005/3328, and amends the Value Added Tax Act 1994 Sch 9 Pt 2 Group 4, which exempts from value added tax certain types of betting, gaming and lotteries. In particular, the order amends the definition of 'a game of chance' and changes the scope of the exemption by restricting it to games of chance played for prizes.

2891   Exempt supply—betting, gaming and lotteries—gaming machine

The Value Added Tax (Gaming Machines) Order 2006, SI 2006/2686 (in force on 1 November 2006), updates the definition of a gaming machine in the Value Added Tax Act 1994 s 23, which restricts the amount on which value added tax is charged to the net takings after deduction of any winnings paid out by the machine, and replaces the definition of gambling so that it refers to the definition of a game of chance.

2892   Exempt supply—cultural services—eligible body—bodies managed and administered on an essentially voluntary basis—remuneration of director

The taxpayer was an orchestra that operated as a company limited by guarantee; the musicians were all employed by the taxpayer, as were a number of administrative staff. The articles of association provided for a council, which had few significant functions other than the appointment of some of the directors to the board, which essentially equated to the board of a commercial company. The membership of the board included a number of people, most of whom clearly participated on a voluntary basis. One of the members was the managing director, a paid employee of the taxpayer. His salary included payment for his participation in the management and administration of the orchestra as a member of the board. The taxpayer claimed to be exempt to the charge to value added tax under EC Council Directive 77/388 art 13(A)(1)(n), which provided for the exemption from VAT of the supply of certain cultural services and goods closely linked thereto supplied by bodies governed by public law or by other recognised cultural bodies. In implementing art 13(A)(1)(n) the United Kingdom required, under the Value Added Tax Act 1994 Sch 9 Group 13, that a taxpayer which sought to claim the cultural services exemption should be managed or administered on a voluntary basis by persons who had no direct or indirect financial interest in its activities. The Commissioners for Her Majesty's Revenue and Customs refused to accept that the taxpayer was entitled to be treated as making exempt supplies within the scope of Directive 77/388 art 13(A)(1)(n) because the managing director was paid a salary to manage and administer the taxpayer. On the taxpayer's appeal, it was held that the managing director had no financial interest in the results of the taxpayer's activities, but since he was not a volunteer and overall the managerial body was not essentially voluntary, it was not entitled to the exemption. The taxpayer appealed further. *Held*, the managing director's remuneration and his participation in the highest decision-making processes of the taxpayer made it impossible to say that the management and administration of the taxpayer was conducted on an essentially voluntary basis. Accordingly, the appeal would be dismissed.

Bournemouth Symphony Orchestra v Revenue and Customs Comrs [2006] EWCA Civ 1281, [2006] All ER (D) 101 (Oct) (Court of Appeal: Chadwick, May and Lloyd LJJ). Case C-267/00 *Customs and Excise Comrs v Zoological Society of London* [2002] STC 521, ECJ (2002 Abr para 3034), considered. Judgment of Mann J [2005] EWHC 1566 (Ch), [2005] STC 1406 (2005 Abr para 3125) affirmed.

2893   Exempt supply—cultural services—eligible body—persons having financial interest in body's activities—person undertaking to pay any debts incurred

The Value Added Tax Act 1994 Sch 9 Pt II Group 13 note 2(c) provides that an eligible body is a body which is managed and administered on a voluntary basis by persons who have no direct or indirect financial interest in its activities.

The founders of an opera were the owners and directors of a property and development company. Initially, the opera performances were produced and managed by the company on a commercial basis. However, one of the directors considered that the quality of the opera performances could be improved if it operated as a charity. To this end, he set up and became a director of a company and registered it as a charity which took over the management of the opera. The company allowed the charity to use the opera premises on a rent-free basis. Concerns were raised that the charity could make losses in its first season and the director provided two letters of comfort which confirmed that he and his company would provide the appropriate funds to cover any deficit. The property and development company and the director made interest-free loans to the charity. A VAT and Duties tribunal rejected the charity's claim that it was entitled to exemption from value added tax on the basis that it was an eligible body within the meaning of the 1994 Act Sch 9 Pt II Group 13 note 2. On appeal, *held*, the disqualifying 'financial interest' in Sch 9 Pt II Group 13 note 2(c) was directed at potential enrichment. It was not designed to preclude participation in management by persons who for the benefit of the cultural body assumed responsibility for some liability of the body and, therefore, the risk of an actual impoverishment. It followed that any liability of the director under the letters of comfort would not disqualify the charity from being an eligible body. Still less could the letters disqualify because they were not legally enforceable as guarantees. For the same reason, the grant of interest-free loans could not give rise to a disqualifying financial interest. Further, a body was not disqualified because it could legally and in fact did enter commercial contracts with a director so long as the contract did not confer any interest in the body's results or profits, for example by calculating his remuneration by reference to the results. Commercial contracts which provided the essentials for the conduct by the charity of its business need not do so. Accordingly, the appeal would be allowed.

Longborough Festival Opera v Revenue and Customs Comrs [2006] EWHC 40 (Ch), [2006] STC 818 (Chancery Division: Lightman J). *Bournemouth Symphony Orchestra v Customs and Excise Comrs* [2005] EWCA 1566 (Ch), [2005] STC 1406 applied.

2894   Exempt supply—finance—special investment fund—management

EC Council Directive 77/388 art 13(B)(d)(6) requires member states to exempt from value added tax transactions for the management of special investment funds.

In the course of two sets of proceedings concerning the taxation of services supplied by the depositaries of a number of authorised unit trusts and of an open-ended investment company, reference was made to the European Court of Justice for a preliminary ruling on various questions concerning the interpretation of Directive 77/388 art 13(B)(d)(6). *Held*, the concept of 'management' of special investment funds in art 13(B)(d)(6) had its own independent meaning in Community law whose content the member states could not alter. It was settled law that the exemptions provided for in art 13 had their own independent meaning in Community law which had to be given a Community definition whose purpose was to avoid divergences in the application of the VAT system from one member state to another. While art 13(B)(d)(6) conferred on the member states the task of defining the meaning of 'special investment funds', that task had not been extended to 'management'. Also, art 13(B)(d)(6) was to be interpreted as meaning that the concept of 'management of special investment funds' covered the services performed by a third-party manager in respect of the administrative management of the fund, if, viewed broadly, they formed a distinct whole and were specific to, and essential for, the management of those funds. However, services corresponding to the functions of a depositary were not covered by that concept. Moreover, interpreting the provision in the light of the context in which it was used and of the aims and scheme of Directive 77/388, having particular regard to the underlying purpose of the exemption which it established, the transactions covered by the exemption were those which were specific to the business of undertakings for collective investment. It followed that the management services performed by a third-party manager came generally within the scope of the provision, while the functions of depositary did not fall under the management of undertakings for collective investment but under the control and supervision of their activities and were therefore not within the scope of the provision.

Case C-169/04 *Abbey National plc v Customs and Excise Comrs* [2006] 2 CMLR 1587 (ECJ: Third Chamber). Case C-2/95 *Sparekassernes Datacenter (SDC) v Skatteministeriet* [1997] All ER (EC) 610, ECJ, considered. Case C-358/97 *European Commission v Ireland* [2000] ECR I-6301, ECJ, applied.

2895 Exempt supply—financial services—payments and transfers—card handling charge

EC Council Directive 77/388 art 13(B)(d)(3) provides for the exemption from value added tax of transactions concerning payments and transfers.

The taxpayer was a subsidiary of a company which owned a chain of cinemas. The taxpayer provided a service whereby a customer could reserve tickets for a film and pay for them, together with a handling charge, by credit or debit card. In each transaction, the taxpayer would take details from the customer's card, verify its validity and transmit the card and security information and the card issuer's identification codes to a bank. The bank would then process the payment and credit the price of the cinema ticket and the handling charge to the taxpayer, which then transmitted the price of the ticket to its parent company. The taxpayer claimed that its services were financial services which were exempt from VAT. However, the Commissioners for Her Majesty's Revenue and Customs decided that the services were liable to VAT on the handling charges. The taxpayer's appeal against their decision succeeded on the basis that its services were separately remunerated by the card handling charge. The Commissioners appealed. *Held*, services would have to have the effect of transferring funds and change the legal and financial situation if their supply fell within the exemption concerning payments or transfers under Directive 77/388 art 13(B)(d)(3). The transmission of the card and security information to a bank had the effect of transferring funds and entailed changes in the legal and financial situation. There was no requirement that the transfer of funds effected by that component of the services had to be a transfer of funds by the taxpayer itself. In requesting and accepting the taxpayer's services, the customer would have contemplated and intended that some payment would be made that would enable him to collect his tickets, and that the taxpayer would arrange for that. The services supplied by the taxpayer had that effect, and it was irrelevant that the customer was indifferent to the machinery by which it was achieved. Accordingly, the appeal would be dismissed.

Bookit Ltd v Revenue and Customs Comrs [2006] EWCA Civ 550, [2006] STC 1367 (Court of Appeal: Chadwick, Sedley and Arden LJJ).

2896 Exempt supply—health and welfare—childcare—intermediary service putting parents in contact with parents offering childcare

The respondent foundation was a non-profit making organisation that provided pre-schooling and after-school childcare and maintained a list of 'host parents' who provided childcare in their own homes. The respondent acted as an intermediary by putting parents who needed childcare in touch with host parents and charged parents an hourly rate for the services of a host parent. Parents also paid the host parents a separate hourly rate for each child. The question arose during proceedings in relation to the reimbursement value added tax paid by the respondent as to whether such services as the respondent offered were exempt from VAT as being services closely linked to welfare and social security work, the protection of children or young persons and/or children's or young people's education under EC Council Directive 77/388 art 13(A)(1)(g)–(i). The question was referred to the European Court of Justice. *Held*, childcare provided by host parents could be regarded as the provision of a service falling within the scope of the welfare and social security work and protection of children and young persons' exemption of the directive. While it could not be established with certainty whether host parents provided education, it was unnecessary to do so as childcare was capable of being covered by at least two categories of exemption. The exemption of the respondent's services as an intermediary presupposed that the childcare offered between the host parents and the parents were exempt from VAT. As the host parents were independent persons and not regarded as bodies under public law, the childcare services were only exempt to the extent that they were provided by organisations recognised as charitable by the member states concerned. It was for national courts to determine whether the childcare services provided by host parents satisfied the conditions for exemption, in particular whether the service provider fulfilled the criteria of being charitable. The mere provision of a list of people known to offer childcare and making it available to parents could not be described as an essential service, which was a requirement for the intermediary services of the respondent to be considered exempt. It was for national courts to determine whether the respondent's services as an intermediary, which resulted in only host parents who were competent and trustworthy, was of such a nature that it would be impossible to obtain a service of the same value without the assistance of an intermediary service such as that offered by the respondent.

Case C-415/04 *Staatssecretaris van Financiën v Stichting Kinderopvang Enschede* [2006] 2 CMLR 1395 (ECJ: Third Chamber).

2897 Exempt supply—hospital and medical care—closely related activities

EC Council Directive 77/388 art 13(A)(1)(b) provides for the exemption from value added tax of hospital and medical care and closely related activities.

Following an audit of the taxpayer's records, the authorities concluded that income earned by the taxpayer from the provision of telephone services and the hiring out of television sets to in-patients in hospitals, and the provision of beds and meals to persons accompanying in-patients did not fall within the exemption from value added tax set out in Directive 77/388 art 13(A)(1)(b). On the taxpayer's appeal, it fell to be determined whether its supplies fell within the exemption for activities closely related to hospital and medical care. *Held*, services fell within activities closely related to hospital and medical care only when they were actually supplied as a service ancillary to the hospital and medical care received by the patients and constituting the principal service. A service could be considered ancillary to the principal service where it constituted not an end in itself but a means of enhancing the enjoyment or benefit of the principal service. Services which constituted closely related activities would be services which were logically part of the provision of hospital or medical services and were an indispensable stage in the process of the supply of those services to achieve their therapeutic objectives. Provision of services which by their nature improved the comfort and well-being of in-patients would not generally qualify for the exemption provided for by art 13(A)(1)(b).

Cases C-394/04 and C-395/04 *Diagnostiko & Therapeftiko Kentro Athinon-Ygeia AE v Ipourgos Ikonomikon* [2006] STC 1349 (ECJ: Third Chamber).

2898 Exempt supply—land—election to waive exemption—meaning of 'occupation'

The Value Added Tax Act 1994 Sch 10 para 3A(7) provides that, for the purposes of Sch 10 para 2(3AA), land is exempt land if the grantor or a person connected with the grantor is in occupation of the land without being in occupation of it wholly or mainly for eligible purposes.

The taxpayer college decided to rebuild and refurbish its library. Pursuant to professional advice it received, the taxpayer formed a wholly owned subsidiary and elected to waive exemption from value added tax in respect of the main college building (including the library) on the college site. At the conclusion of the construction work, the taxpayer granted a formal lease of the building to the subsidiary. The taxpayer also entered into other agreements with the subsidiary, including arrangements relating to the sale of library books and other library assets of the college, an agreement for the secondment of library staff from the taxpayer to the subsidiary, an administration agreement for the running of the library (by the seconded staff) and an agreement for the management of rare books. The Commissioners for Her Majesty's Revenue and Customs decided that the taxpayer no longer remained in occupation of the land after the grant of the lease so that it was not exempt land for the purposes of the 1994 Act Sch 10 para 2(3AA). A VAT and duties tribunal upheld that decision, and the taxpayer appealed. *Held*, for the purposes of Sch 10 para 3A(7), to be in 'occupation' of land required more than simply having a right to use the land. It required some degree of control over the user by others, namely, some degree of control over what those who were not also in occupation of the land could do on the land. In the absence of any element of control by students and fellows of the taxpayer over access to and use of the library by others, it was impossible to sustain the reasoning given by the tribunal. The fact that the library staff remained employees of the taxpayer was not sufficient to support the conclusion that the taxpayer was in occupation of the library. Their presence and control was as persons acting under the direction of the subsidiary. Further, the arrangements reflected the true intent of the parties and had to be given the effect which, in law, they had, notwithstanding that had no commercial purpose other than to enable the taxpayer to recover input tax. Accordingly, the appeal would be allowed.

Principal and Fellows of Newnham College in the University of Cambridge v Revenue and Customs Comrs [2006] EWCA Civ 285, [2006] All ER (D) 368 (Mar) (Court of Appeal: Sir Andrew Morritt C, Chadwick and Lloyd LJJ).

2899 Exempt supply—land—election to waive exemption—notification

A company acquired a property which it let to an associated company. The purchase price of the property had included an element of value added tax, and the company had charged VAT on the rent of the premises. It then agreed a sale to the purchaser. By virtue of the Value Added Tax Act 1994 Sch 10 para 2(1), the company was entitled to elect to bring the property into the VAT regime, which would have the consequence that it would be required to charge VAT on the disposal consideration. Schedule 10 para 3 provided that such an election was to have effect from the beginning of the day on which it was made and that a notification of the election had to be made to Her Majesty's Commissioners of Revenue and Customs within 30 days or a longer period if allowed. Although notification had not taken place by the time of completion, the company subsequently wrote a letter to the Commissioners that appeared to have been accepted as late notification. A VAT and duties tribunal accepted that the company had made an election when it owned the property, and went on to find that the company's purported notification of election was capable of operating retrospectively so as to make the sale to the purchaser one which was subject to VAT. The purchaser appealed. *Held*, there had been material on which the tribunal had been entitled to reach the conclusion that there had been an election. The legislation supposed a two-stage process: firstly, an election and, secondly, notification within 30 days. By virtue of Sch 10 para 3(1) the election had effect from the beginning of the day on which it was made, and Sch 10 para 3(6) provided that the election only had effect once notification had been given. It was clear that notification could be given after the election, and that the subsequent notification gave effect retrospectively to the election. Nothing in the legislation suggested a different conclusion where there had been a disposal of the land following the election. It followed that there had been a valid notification and, accordingly, the appeal would be dismissed.

Marlow Gardner & Cooke Ltd Directors' Pension Scheme v Revenue and Customs Comrs [2006] EWHC 1612 (Ch), [2006] STC 2014 (Chancery Division: Mann J). *Fencing Supplies Ltd v Customs and Excise Comrs* [1993] VATTR 302 considered.

2900 Exempt supply—land—leasing or letting of immovable property—deduction of input tax—fiscal neutrality

The taxpayer was a sports club classed as a non-profit making organisation. It constructed an annexe to its clubhouse, which included a refreshment bar intended to be let to a tenant. The taxpayer claimed a deduction in respect of the input tax paid exclusively for the part of the annex which included the bar and was to be let. The Austrian authorities refused to allow the deduction on the ground that the taxpayer was exempt from tax, did not have the right to make deductions under Austrian law and could not choose to waive its exemption in respect of turnover resulting from the leasing and letting of immovable property. The national court referred the case to the European Court of Justice for a preliminary ruling on whether EC Council Directive 77/388 arts 13(B)(b), 13(C) precluded national legislation which, by exempting generally the transactions of non-profit making sports clubs, restricted the right to opt for the taxation of leasing and letting transactions. *Held*, art 13(C) did not specify on what conditions and by what means the scope of the right of option provided by it might be restricted. It was therefore for each member state to specify the scope of that right of option. However, any decision of a member state to restrict, pursuant to art 13(C), the scope of the right to opt for taxation of leasing of immovable property had to observe the principle of fiscal neutrality. It was for the national court to determine whether the application of a general exemption to all transactions, including the leasing of immovable property, effected by non-profit making sports clubs entailed a breach of the principle of fiscal neutrality. There could be a breach of fiscal neutrality if such a club could not opt for taxation where other taxable persons carrying out comparable activities in competition with those of the club were permitted to do so.

Case C-246/04 *Turn- und Sportunion Waldburg v Finanzlandsdirektion für Oberösterreich* [2006] STC 1506 (ECJ: Third Chamber). Case 8/81 *Becker v Finanzamt Münster-Innenstadt* [1982] ECR 53, ECJ (1982 Abr para 1344), considered.

2901 Exempt supply—land—leasing or letting of immovable property—grant of interest or right over land—virtual assignment

The taxpayer agreed to transfer its property portfolio to the transferee, a company, with the intention that the transferee would manage the property and lease back the properties which the taxpayer required to conduct its business. In the case of some of the shorter leasehold properties, a 'virtual assignment', under which the economic benefits and burdens associated with the property, but no actual proprietary interest, were transferred to the transferee, was made. In those cases, the taxpayer paid a sum to the taxpayer that was equivalent to the rent it would have paid under a formal lease. In relation to premises which the taxpayer had sublet, a virtual assignment, under which the taxpayer held the benefit of each sublease in trust for the transferee, was made. The transferee was entitled to receive rent from the underlessees. The Commissioners for Her Majesty's Revenue and Customs decided that in neither case was there an exempt supply consisting of the 'leasing or letting of immovable property' within the meaning of EC Council Directive 77/388 art 13(B)(b), but rather a standard-rated supply of agency and property management services. The taxpayer's appeal against that decision was dismissed in relation to the principal fee paid by the taxpayer to the transferee, but allowed in relation to the rent paid by the underlessees to the transferee. The taxpayer appealed against the first ruling, and the Commissioners cross-appealed against the second ruling. An issue arose as to whether a contractual arrangement relating to real property which, under domestic law, fell short and was intended to fall short of being a transaction of leasing or letting was nevertheless to be treated as if it were such a transaction for value added tax purposes, with the consequence that it was an exempt supply. *Held*, Community law authorities left no room for doubt that a right of occupation was an essential element of a transaction of leasing or letting for the purposes of art 13(B)(b). That provision could not include a situation where no right of occupation was in fact granted. As the transferee acquired no right of occupation of the properties, the subject of the virtual assignment, and hence was never in a position to transfer such a right back to the taxpayer, the supply made by the transferee to the taxpayer under the contractual arrangements was not a supply of leasing or letting within the meaning of art 13(B)(b) and therefore was not exempt from VAT. It followed that the Commissioners were correct in characterising the supply by the transferee as a standard-rated supply of agency and property management services and that the tribunal reached the right decision on the art 13(B)(b) issue and did so for the right reasons. Judgment would be given accordingly.

Abbey National plc v Revenue and Customs Comrs [2006] EWCA Civ 886, [2006] STC 1961 (Court of Appeal: May and Jonathan Parker LJJ and Sir Peter Gibson).

2902   Exempt supply—land—supplies of facilities incidental to occupation of land

The taxpayer owned and leased a massage parlour from which self-employed masseuses offered their services to clients. A written contract between the taxpayer and each masseuse provided for the rent to the masseuse of a room on the day chosen by her at a specified rate per day. The rent paid included costs towards the use of laundry facilities, charges for credit card payments and advertising. The taxpayer was responsible for security, cleaning and maintaining the premises and for heating and lighting. A VAT and duties tribunal determined that the supplies by the taxpayer were not of licences to occupy land, which would be exempt, but were supplies of the various facilities which the taxpayer provided in the course of its business and to which the occupation licences were merely incidental. The taxpayer appealed. *Held*, having regard to the evidence and applying the appropriate tests, the other services were not ancillary to the licence to use the room. Although it could be said that the relevant services were provided as a means to enable a masseuse to operate her business, it did not follow that they were provided as a means to enable the better enjoyment of the licence to use the room. The services identified were to be contrasted with cleaning and lighting which could properly be regarded as ancillary to the use of the room, as could the use of common parts for access to the rooms. The provision of laundry services, the use of the day room and the provision of receptionist services were all services which assisted a masseuse in the conduct of her business in the room, but they were not provided to enjoy the room itself. The over-arching single supply was not to be treated as a supply of a licence to occupy land. The description which reflected economic and social reality was a supply of massage parlour services one element of which was the provision of the room. This was a case where the tax treatment of the supply was self-evident once it was established that the other service elements were not ancillary to the provision of the licence. Accordingly, the appeal would be dismissed.

Byrom (t/a Salon 24) v Revenue and Customs Comrs [2006] EWHC 111 (Ch), [2006] STC 992 (Chancery Division: Warren J). Case C-349/96 *Card Protection Plan Ltd v Customs and Excise Comrs* [1999] 3 WLR 203, ECJ (1999 Abr para 3419), applied. *Customs and Excise Comrs v FDR Ltd* [2000] STC 672, CA (2000 Abr para 3332), considered.

2903   Exempt supply—property—leasing or letting of immovable property—deduction of input tax—apportionment between grant of lease and transfer of freehold reversion

A university sold the freehold of a newly built property to the taxpayer as a standard-rated supply of a new commercial building. In return, the taxpayer elected to waive exemption from value added tax in respect of the property and granted a short lease to the university, which was able to reclaim VAT on the construction costs, although it became liable for VAT on the rent paid. The taxpayer subsequently granted a 999-year lease at a premium to an unregistered subsidiary of the university. This exempt transaction was followed by the taxable transfer of the freehold reversion to the university. The taxpayer cancelled its VAT registration. A question arose as to how to apply the rules of adjustment of the deduction of input tax paid on the taxpayer's acquisition of the building under the Value Added Tax Regulations 1995, SI 1995/2518, reg 115(3). The Commissioners of Customs and Excise considered that reg 115(3), implementing EC Council Directive 77/388 art 20(3), required an apportionment between the grant of the 999-year lease and the transfer of the freehold reversion in proportion to their respective values, resulting in a substantial VAT liability. The taxpayer argued that it had disposed of its entire interest in the building by the transfer of the freehold reversion, giving a much smaller VAT liability. A VAT and duties tribunal concluded that the proper application of the 1995 Regulations reg 115(3) required an apportionment between the reversionary lease and the transfer. On the taxpayer's appeal, the court referred the case to the European Court of Justice for a preliminary ruling on the proper application of Directive 77/388 art 20(3). *Held*, because the grant of the lease and the transfer of the freehold reversion were inextricably linked and constituted supplies that were, respectively, exempt and taxable for VAT purposes, account had to be taken of the two supplies in proportion to their respective values for the purposes of the adjustment required by art 20(3). The system of deductions and adjustments provided for in arts 17–20 was intended to establish a close and direct relationship between the right to deduct input VAT and the use of the goods and services concerned for taxable transactions. In the circumstances of the case, taking into account each of the two supplies proportionately was most likely satisfactorily to attain that objective. Judgment would be given accordingly.

Case C-63/04 *Centralan Property Ltd v Customs and Excise Comrs* [2006] STC 1568 (ECJ: Third Chamber).

2904 Exempt supply—works of art—relief on importation

The European Commission sent the United Kingdom a formal notice and initiated the procedure for infringement provided for under the EC Treaty art 226 EC after establishing that the United Kingdom did not tax at the standard rate the profit margin of auctioneers on the sale by auction of imported works of art. The main issue was whether the auctioneer's profit margin on those sales imported under the arrangements for temporary importation had to be taxed as a transaction within the territory of the country in accordance with the conditions referred to in EC Council Directive 77/388 art 16(1). *Held*, where a work of art was sold by auction under the arrangements for temporary importation and following that transaction was imported into the territory of the Community, it was necessary to draw a distinction between the sale by auction and the importation. In order to tax both the importation and the sale by auction, it was necessary to draw a distinction between that part of the auction price which corresponded to the auctioneer's commission and that which corresponded to the customs value of the imported goods. The former constituted the taxable amount for the sale by auction and was to be levied at the standard rate. The latter corresponded to the customs value of the goods which was subject to VAT on imports and was to be levied at an effective reduced rate applicable in the United Kingdom. That interpretation was in accordance with the objective of art 16(1), which was to ensure, in particular, fiscal neutrality between goods placed under the arrangements for temporary importation and subsequently imported, on the one hand, and those concerning goods which were already within the territory of the Community, on the other. Having regard to the fact that the sale by auction of works of art under the arrangements for temporary importation had to be regarded as a transaction effected within the territory of the country and had to be taxed as such, the Commission's complaint relating to infringement of art 16(1) was well-founded. Judgment would be given accordingly.

Case C-305/03 *European Commission v United Kingdom* [2006] All ER (D) 123 (Feb) (ECJ: Third Chamber).

2905 Finance Act 2006

See para 2465.

2906 General regulations

The Value Added Tax (Amendment) Regulations 2006, SI 2006/587 (in force in part on 1 April 2006 and in part on 6 April 2006), further amend the 1995 Regulations, SI 1995/2518, in relation to the annual accounting scheme, so as to (1) increase, from £660,000 to £1,350,000, the maximum turnover limit for entrants to the value added tax annual accounting scheme; (2) remove the requirement that a taxable person with a turnover above £150,000 must have been registered for VAT for 12 months before he is eligible to apply to use annual accounting; and (3) increase, from £825,000 to £1,600,000, the maximum turnover limit for those already operating the scheme. The regulations also replace the provisions for returned goods relief in the 1995 Regulations by (a) aligning certain rules for import VAT relief with those for the returned goods relief from import duty by enabling adapted import duty provisions to apply, including rules for adjusting the amount of VAT relief to take account of the existing VAT status of transactions involving the goods in the European Community VAT territory; (b) providing that any VAT deductible or refundable through the VAT system, such as input tax, is disregarded; and (c) providing that the VAT relief continues not to apply in the case of goods zero-rated for VAT under the United Kingdom's personal export schemes.

The Value Added Tax (Amendment) (No 2) Regulations 2006, SI 2006/2902 (in force on 1 December 2006), further amend the 1995 Regulations supra by replacing the application form for value added tax registration.

The Value Added Tax (Amendment) (No 3) Regulations 2006, SI 2006/3292 (in force on 1 January 2007), further amend the 1995 Regulations so as to (1) revise the definition of 'alphabetical code' to take account of the accession to the European Union of Bulgaria and Romania; (2) update references to EEC Council Regulation 2913/92 and EEC Commission Regulation 2454/93; and (3) treat certain goods supplied in the course of a tax free export in Bulgaria or Romania before 1 January 2007, and which arrive in the United Kingdom on or after that date, or goods which are removed on or after 1 January 2007 from specified customs arrangements or procedures under which they were placed before that date, as if they were imported into the United Kingdom.

2907   Input tax—attribution—calculation—decision to change method used—jurisdiction of VAT and duties tribunal

The taxpayer companies were part of a group which operated a well known chain of high street opticians stores. The Commissioners for Her Majesty's Revenue and Customs terminated the use by the taxpayers of a partial exemption special method which had previously been approved under the Value Added Tax Regulations 1995, SI 1995/2518, reg 102(1), causing it to be replaced with the standard method under reg 101. A VAT and duties tribunal dismissed the taxpayers' appeal against that decision and, on their further appeal, they submitted that the tribunal was wrong in law to conclude that its jurisdiction was limited to consideration of whether the Commissioners had acted reasonably in deciding that the standard method should be substituted for the former method. *Held*, the jurisdiction of the tribunal on the appeals by the taxpayers was not a limited one. Nothing in the Value Added Tax Act 1994 or the 1995 Regulations conferred on the Commissioners alone the right to decide whether a particular method would in fact achieve the statutory objective, to the exclusion of the tribunal on an appeal. There was no practical or jurisprudential difficulty in conferring on the tribunal a full appellate jurisdiction to determine, on the basis of all the facts and matters found by it at the time of its decision, whether a decision of the Commissioners under reg 102 substituted, in place of an existing method, a method which secured, or at least better secured, a fair and reasonable attribution of input tax to taxable supplies for the purposes of the 1994 Act s 26(3). Accordingly, the appeal would be dismissed.

Banbury Visionplus Ltd v Revenue and Customs Comrs [2006] EWHC 1024 (Ch), [2006] All ER (D) 105 (May) (Chancery Division: Etherton J).

2908   Input tax—deduction—motor cars—purchase for purpose of business—intention to make available for private use

The taxpayer claimed input tax in relation to the purchase of a company car. The claim was refused by the Commissioners of Customs and Excise on the basis that, pursuant to the Value Added Tax (Input) Order 1992, SI 1992/3222, art 7(1), input tax on the acquisition of cars was not recoverable. The Commissioners considered that the taxpayer could not bring itself within one of the exceptions to the 1992 Order in art 7(2) because it could not satisfy the 'relevant condition' as defined by art 7(2E). The 'relevant condition' was that the taxpayer intended to use the motor car exclusively for the purposes of a business. The tribunal allowed the taxpayer's appeal, taking the view that the taxpayer had satisfied the 'relevant condition', since there was no intention that the car should be made available for private use. The commissioners' appeal was dismissed. On the commissioners' further appeal, *held,* a purposive approach had to be applied to the overall scheme in art 7. The object of the scheme was to prevent claims to deduct tax on cars purchased for business save where the possibility of private use was excluded. Parliament had not said in art 7(2G) that to show that there was no intention to make a car available for private use the taxpayer had to show that it was not physically available. Parliament had neither said that any particular circumstance constituted making a car 'available', nor had it excluded any evidence from the determination of whether a car was or was not made available. Therefore, it was a question of fact as to whether the taxpayer intended not to make the car available for private use by whatever means. Therefore, there was no reason why a car could not be made unavailable for private use by suitable contractual restraints. Accordingly, the appeal would be dismissed.

Customs and Excise Comrs v Elm Milk Ltd [2006] EWCA Civ 164, [2006] ICR 880 (Court of Appeal: Ward, Arden and Moore-Bick LJJ). Decision of Park J [2005] EWHC 366 (Ch), [2005] STC 776 (2005 Abr para 3140) affirmed.

2909   Input tax—deduction—right to deduct—economic activity—abusive practice—transactions carried out with sole aim of obtaining tax advantage

The taxpayers, a company and two of its subsidiaries, assigned certain leases under a scheme designed to reduce the tax burden of the group of companies. The Commissioners of Customs and Excise rejected their claim for relief from value added tax and the taxpayers appealed. A VAT and duties tribunal referred to the European Court of Justice the questions whether a transaction would constitute a supply of goods or services and an economic activity when it was effected for the sole purpose of obtaining a tax advantage, and whether a taxable person had the right to deduct VAT where the transactions on which that right was based constituted an abusive practice. *Held*, transactions which satisfied the objective criteria set out in the relevant provisions of EC Council Directive 77/388 constituted supplies of goods or services and economic activities, even where they were carried out with the sole aim of obtaining a tax advantage. However, a taxpayer would not be entitled to deduct input VAT where the transactions from which that right derived constituted an abusive practice. A finding of abusive practice should not lead to a penalty, for which a clear and unambiguous legal basis would be necessary, but rather to an obligation to repay. Where an abusive practice had been found to exist, the transactions involved had to be redefined so as to re-establish the situation that would have prevailed in the absence of the transactions constituting that abusive practice. Judgment would be given accordingly.

Case C-255/02 *Halifax plc v Customs and Excise Comrs*; Case C-223/03 *University of Huddersfield Higher Education Corpn v Customs and Excise Comrs* [2006] Ch 387 (ECJ: Grand Chamber).

2910 Input tax—deduction—right to deduct—economic activity—series of transactions constituting carousel fraud

The taxpayers carried on the business of buying central processing units for computers from companies established in the United Kingdom and selling them to purchasers in other member states. Unbeknown to the taxpayers, some of the purchases formed part of a fraudulent series of transactions under which the goods would be sold from company to company, and eventually sold back to the original suppliers, and certain companies in the chain would deduct input tax but not account for value added tax. The Commissioners of Customs and Excise disallowed the taxpayers' claim to deduct input tax on the relevant purchases on the ground that the transactions, viewed as a whole, were devoid of economic substance and so fell outside the scope of VAT. In the course of appeals by the claimants, the High Court referred for a preliminary ruling from the European Court of Justice questions raised relating to EC Council Directive 77/388. *Held,* the definitions in Directive 77/388 and in case law showed that the term 'economic activity' in art 4(1) was very wide in scope and objective in character, in that such an activity was considered per se and without regard to its purpose or results. An obligation on the tax authorities to carry out inquiries into the intention of a taxable person or to take account of the intention of other traders in the same chain of supply, of which the taxable person had no knowledge or means of knowledge, would be contrary to the objectives of the common system of VAT of ensuring legal certainty and facilitating the application of VAT. Each transaction had to be regarded on its own merits and the character of a particular transaction in the chain could not be altered by subsequent or earlier events. The right of a taxable person to deduct input tax in respect of a particular transaction was to be determined with reference to that transaction alone, and it was immaterial whether another transaction in the series of which the transaction in question formed a part was, without the knowledge of the taxable person, fraudulent.

Cases C-354/03, C-355/03, C-484/03 *Optigen Ltd v Customs and Excise Comrs* [2006] Ch 218 (ECJ: Third Chamber).

2911 Input tax—deduction—right to deduct—economic activity—series of transactions constituting carousel fraud—rate of interest on sums claimed

The taxpayers carried on business buying mobile telephones and selling them to persons outside the United Kingdom. Such exports were exempt from value added tax, but the taxpayers could deduct the input tax incurred when purchasing the phones. The Commissioners of Customs and Excise refused claims to credit for input tax by the taxpayers on the ground that the transactions formed part of a carousel fraud where some of the transactions were part of a chain of supply which involved a trader who incurred liability to VAT but went missing without discharging that liability. The Commissioners took the view that no trader in the chain should be regarded as supplying goods or services as a taxable person or as carrying on an economic activity, with the result that all transactions within the chain were outside the scope of VAT, even where a trader did not know or had no means of knowing of the fraud. The taxpayers brought proceedings against the Commissioners' decision. Following a decision of the European Court of Justice that transactions, which were not themselves vitiated by VAT fraud, constituted supplies of goods or services effected by a taxable person and an economic activity, regardless of the possible fraudulent nature of another transaction in the chain of which that taxable person had no knowledge and no means of knowledge, the Commissioners agreed to pay the sums claimed by the taxpayers. However, issues regarding the rate of interest and when interest should run from arose. *Held,* the transactions were commercial and therefore a commercial rate of interest should be applied under the Supreme Court Act 1981 s 35A(1). The standard for the commercial rate was base plus one per cent. Further, it was also proper to have regard to the Value Added Tax Act 1994 s 78, although it did not follow that the s 78 rate was the rate which had to apply. It was material that Parliament had prescribed the rate of four per cent where, due to an error, the Commissioners had not paid what was due. In the light of the evidence, base plus one per cent was too low a rate and a figure of base plus two and a half per cent producing a figure of some seven per cent overall would be suitable. As to the date from which interest would run, a reasonable period was needed to enable the Commissioners to investigate whether the claim for repayment was tainted with fraud. Therefore a 30-day period would be applicable. Judgment would be given accordingly.

R (on the application of Mobile Export 365 Ltd) v Revenue and Customs Comrs [2006] EWHC 311 (Admin), [2006] STC 1069 (Queen's Bench Division: Collins J).

2912 Input tax—deduction—right to deduct—publicly funded research

The taxpayer was a charity which carried on the business of making supplies of education and undertaking commercial research. Approximately three-quarters of the research grants and contracts were in the form of publicly funded research ('PFR'), meaning research funded in whole or in part by way of a grant provided by one or more public sponsors for which the taxpayer had applied for the purposes of carrying out a particular research project. The taxpayer was assessed to value added tax in respect of six consecutive accounting periods on the ground that the PFR was not a business activity. On that basis, the Commissioners for Her Majesty's Revenue and Customs concluded that the taxpayer was not entitled to input tax credit pursuant to the Value Added Tax Act 1994 in respect of tax on the supply of goods or services which were used for the purposes of PFR. The taxpayer appealed to a VAT and duties tribunal, submitting that PFR was an integral part of its business, which included the supply of education, undertaking research for commercial sponsors, the exploitation of intellectual property, an active conference trade, and publishing and consultancy. The tribunal rejected that argument, taking the view that PFR was completely distinct from the taxpayer's other activities. The taxpayer appealed. *Held*, for the purposes of VAT, PFR was a separate economic activity or business from the taxpayer's other activities so that tax on goods and services used exclusively for PFR was not deductible or recoverable, and tax on goods and services used partly for PFR and partly for business purposes fell to be apportioned under s 24(5). Applying the relevant legal principles, the tribunal's decisions that PFR had not formed part of the taxpayer's VAT business, and that PFR had not been an activity the costs of which could be recovered as an overhead of the taxpayer's VAT business, had been conclusions which the tribunal could properly have reached on the facts as found by it. Accordingly, the appeal would be dismissed.

University of Southampton v Revenue and Customs Comrs [2006] EWHC 528 (Ch), [2006] STC 1389 (Chancery Division: Warren J). Case C 4–94 *BLP Group plc v Customs and Excise Comrs* [1995] All ER (EC) 401, ECJ (1995 Abr para 3167); Case C-408/98 *Abbey National plc v Customs and Excise Comrs* [2001] All ER (EC) 385, ECJ (2001 Abr para 3176); and Case C-465/03 *Kretztechnik AG v Finanzant Linz* [2005] 1 WLR 3755, ECJ (2005 Abr para 3145), considered.

2913   Input tax—deduction—right to deduct—theatre making taxable and non-taxable supplies

The taxpayer ran a theatre which put on various performances for the purposes of encouraging the arts. The performances were funded partly through ticket sales, and partly through ancillary activities such as the sale of programmes, refreshments and sponsorship rights. It was accepted that the taxpayer's sales of tickets to the public were exempt supplies for value added tax purposes, coming within the cultural exemptions established by EC Council Directive 77/388 art 13(A)(1)(n). The other supplies made were, however, taxable. On the taxpayer's application for a deduction in the input tax it had paid, the Commissioners for Her Majesty's Customs and Revenue took the view that the whole of the services supplied by the production companies were used by the taxpayer exclusively in making the exempt supplies represented by the sale of the tickets so that, by virtue of the Value Added Tax Regulations 1995, SI 1995/2518, reg 101(2)(c), no part of the input tax was deductible. The taxpayer appealed to a VAT and duties tribunal, arguing that there was a case for attributing a proportion of the tax pursuant to reg 101(2)(d). The tribunal concluded that the consideration paid was used exclusively in making exempt supplies of ticket sales for productions. On the taxpayer's appeal against that decision, *held*, the decisive question was whether a particular input had been used exclusively in making exempt supplies. If the input had not been exclusively so used, then, unless it had been exclusively used in making taxable supplies, by virtue of reg 101(2)(d) the residual tax could be deducted. In the instant case, there had been taxable supplies of the right to see the productions, and the production costs had been linked to those supplies in precisely the same way as to the exempt supplies. It followed that there had been a sufficient direct and immediate link between the relevant inputs and any of the taxable supplies to make it impossible for it to be said that the inputs had been used exclusively for the exempt supplies. Accordingly, the appeal would be allowed.

Mayflower Theatre Trust Ltd v Revenue and Customs Comrs [2006] EWHC 706 (Ch), [2006] STC 1607 (Chancery Division: Hart J).

2914   Input tax—deduction—time limit

The taxpayer was the proprietor of a business engaged in the purchase and servicing of cars. The Commissioners of Customs and Excise refused his claim for the recovery of input tax on the purchase of three motor cars on the ground that the claim had been made outside the three-year time limit imposed by the Value Added Tax Regulations 1995, SI 1995/2518, reg 29(1A). The time limit had been introduced after the taxpayer's claim arose and there was no transitional provision contained in reg 29(1A). The taxpayer appealed. *Held*, reg 29(1A) was incompatible with the principle of effectiveness because it did not include transitional arrangements allowing an adequate period after the enactment of the legislation for lodging claims for repayment. The court had a duty to read legislation in such a way that it gave proper effect to Community rights as far as possible and, therefore, reg 29(1A) would have to be disapplied. Accordingly, the appeal would be allowed.

Fleming (t/a Bodycraft) v Customs and Excise Comrs [2006] EWCA Civ 70, (2006) Independent, 17 February (Court of Appeal: Ward, Arden and Hallett LJJ). Case C-62/00 *Marks and Spencer plc v Customs and Excise Comrs* [2003] 2 WLR 665, ECJ (2002 Abr para 3057); and *Ghaidan v Mendoza* [2004] UKHL 30, [2004] 2 AC 557 (2004 Abr para 1757) applied.

2915 Overpayment—recovery—defence—unjust enrichment

The taxpayer, which was registered for value added tax and accounted for VAT on the price charged for its services to its customers, was engaged in the business of providing debt management services. The taxpayer had originally contended that its business was exempt for VAT purposes but the Commissioners for Her Majesty's Revenue and Customs disagreed and the taxpayer did not pursue the point. However, a VAT and duties tribunal held that services indistinguishable from those that the taxpayer was providing were exempt from VAT. Subsequently, the taxpayer was treated as exempt and it sought to recover the net amount of VAT for which it had accounted. The Commissioners relied in defence on unjust enrichment, pursuant to the Value Added Tax Act 1994 s 80(3). On appeal the tribunal held that the defence had been made out. On the taxpayer's appeal, the judge remitted the claim in respect of certain years to the tribunal for reconsideration. The Commissioners appealed and the taxpayer cross-appealed. The taxpayer argued that it would have charged the same amount for its services even if it had been treated as exempt, so that the burden of the tax for which it accounted was pure loss. *Held*, there was insufficient evidence as to what charge the taxpayer might have imposed. The taxpayer had claimed that it would have charged the exact amount as VAT and it did not have an alternative position that it might have charged between 15 per cent and the full VAT equivalent. That stance did not relieve the Commissioners of the need to put forward an intermediate case as to what the taxpayer's charge would have been, in case it was unable to make good a case that the rate would have been 15 per cent. Therefore, while the tribunal's finding that the whole of the tax was passed on had to be set aside, the judge had been incorrect to remit the case back to the tribunal. The defence of unjust enrichment could not be made out and the Commissioners should not be allowed another opportunity to seek to persuade the tribunal that the defence was made out. Accordingly, the appeal would be dismissed and the cross-appeal allowed.

Baines & Ernst Ltd v Revenue and Customs Comrs [2006] EWCA Civ 1040, [2006] STC 1632 (Court of Appeal: May, Gage and Lloyd LJJ). Decision of Warren J [2005] EWHC 2300 (Ch), [2006] STC 654 reversed.

2916 Penalty proceedings—right to fair and public hearing—competence of lay representative

See *Khan v Revenue and Customs Comrs*, para 1561.

2917 Reduced rate charge—contraceptive products—welfare advice and information

The Value Added Tax (Reduced Rate) Order 2006, SI 2006/1472 (in force on 1 July 2006), amends the Value Added Tax Act 1994 Sch 7A Pt 2 by adding Group 8 and Group 9. In particular, the order extends the reduced rate of value added tax to (1) qualifying supplies of contraceptive products; and (2) supplies of welfare advice or information provided by a charity or a state-regulated welfare institution or agency.

2918 Refund—entitlement—specified bodies

The Value Added Tax (Refund of Tax) Order 2006, SI 2006/1793 (in force on 1 August 2006), specifies the London Pensions Fund Authority and regional Transport Partnership in Scotland for the purposes of the Value Added Tax Act 1994 s 33, so that they are entitled to claim refunds of VAT on supplies to, or acquisitions or importations by, them, provided the supplies, acquisitions or importations are not for the purpose of any business carried on by them.

2919 Registration—liability to be registered—increase of limits

The Value Added Tax (Increase of Registration Limits) Order 2006, SI 2006/876 (in force on 1 April 2006), amends the Value Added Tax Act 1994 by increasing (1) from £60,000 to £61,000, the value added tax registration limits for taxable supplies and for acquisitions from other member states; and (2) from £58,000 to £59,000, the limit for cancellation of registration in the case of taxable supplies, and from £60,000 to £61,000 in the case of acquisitions from other member states.

2920 Registration—partners—registration in name of firm—status of registered partnership

The Value Added Tax Act 1994 s 45(1) provides that the registration of persons (a) carrying on business in partnership, or (b) carrying on in partnership any other activities in the course or furtherance of which they acquire goods from other member states, may be in the name of the firm, and no account may be taken, in determining whether goods or services are supplied to or by such persons or are acquired by such persons from another member state, of any change in the partnership.

The taxpayer was one of four business partners who ran a bar and restaurant. In the application form for value added tax registration, a name was given as the trading name of the partnership. The Commissioners for Her Majesty's Revenue and Customs exercised the power contained in the 1994 Act s 45 and completed registration in that name. The partnership had made no VAT returns and the Commissioners made an assessment against it. The taxpayer appealed to a VAT and duties tribunal, contending that he had not been involved in the making of taxable supplies at the relevant time and that the assessment was excessive. The tribunal decided that the assessment was invalid. The Commissioners appealed, arguing that the tribunal had failed to recognise that the partners, including the taxpayer, had all registered for VAT by virtue of the registration in the name of the partnership and were, therefore, all taxable persons for VAT purposes and liable to account for VAT. *Held*, in the light of established authority, it was clear that it was not the partnership as such that was the taxable person nor was registration pursuant to s 45(1) the separate registration of each of the partners as an individual. They were deemed to be registered on a collective basis so that one or other of them would become liable to separate registration as the taxable person in relation to another business carried on solely or in a different combination. The registration could only take effect in relation to those on the application form who were partners and could therefore constitute a taxable person for VAT purposes. Although not all of the partners could constitute the 'taxable person', the taxpayer and another clearly could. Only a 'person' who made taxable supplies might be registered and the inclusion of non-partners on the application form was of no effect in relation to other individuals. It followed that the registration had correctly been raised against the taxpayer. There were no grounds for interfering with the tribunal's finding. Accordingly, the appeal would be allowed in part.

Revenue and Customs Comrs v Pal [2006] EWHC 2016 (Ch), [2006] All ER (D) 480 (Jul) (Chancery Division: Patten J). *Customs and Excise Comrs v Glassborow* [1975] 1 QB 465 (1974 Abr para 3352), DC, applied. *Nationwide Building Society v Lewis* [1998] Ch 482 (1998 Abr para 2398), CA, considered.

The Value Added Tax Act 1994 s 45(1) provides that the registration of persons carrying on a business in partnership may be in the name of the firm. Until the date on which a change in the partnership is notified to the Commissioners for Her Majesty's Revenue and Customs, a person who has ceased to be a member of a partnership is to be regarded as continuing to be a partner for the purpose of any liability for VAT: s 45(2).

A partnership had traded under a particular name which it subsequently changed. The Commissioners notified the partners of their decision to register the partnership compulsorily for value added tax purposes under the partnership's more recent name, pursuant to the 1994 Act s 45(1). The partners failed to file their VAT returns and the Commissioners raised an assessment and penalty notice. Although the partnership had traded under both names during the period to which the assessment and penalty notice related, the Commissioners specified only the current name. The partners appealed against the compulsory registration and the issue of the assessment and penalty notice. It fell to be determined whether the notice of assessment was valid given that the partnership was not known by the name specified in the notice at the commencement of the period under assessment. A VAT and duties tribunal ruled that it was valid and the partners appealed. *Held*, a partnership did not acquire a distinct personality on its registration for VAT. Under s 3, a person was a taxable person when he was registered or when he was required to be registered, and so it followed that the compulsory registration of the partners as individuals was not a prerequisite for their liability to make returns. It was apparent from s 45(1), (2) and the Partnership Act 1890 ss 6, 9, which provided that partners were bound by acts done in the firm's name and that partners were jointly liable for the firm's debts and obligations, that the liability for VAT was that of the members of the partnership and not of the partnership as a distinct entity. The assessment had been notified to each of the partners so that they became jointly liable under s 9, whatever the name of the partnership. Accordingly, the appeal would be dismissed.

Scrace v Revenue and Customs Comrs [2006] EWHC 2646 (Ch), [2007] STC 269 (Chancery Division: Blackburne J).

2921   Reliefs—legacies imported from third countries—application for relief

See para 917.

2922   Supply of goods and services—composite supply—different rates applicable to different parts of supply

EC Council Directive 77/388 art 28(2)(a) contained transitional provisions allowing member states to maintain existing exemptions with refund of tax paid. At the applicable date, the supply of caravans was zero-rated and the supply of their removable contents was excluded from the exemption. The zero-rating of caravans was now detailed in the Value Added Tax Act 1994 Sch 8 Pt II Group 9 item 1 and the exclusion from the exemption of their removable contents was specified by Sch 8 Pt II Group 9 note (a). Part of the taxpayer's business activities involved the sale of fitted caravans. The Commissioners for Her Majesty's Revenue and Customs concluded that the zero-rate applied only to the caravans themselves and that the standard rate of applied to their contents. The taxpayer, however, disputed this view on the basis that caravans and their contents comprised a single supply, and as such could be subject to only one rate of value added tax. The matter was referred to the European Court of Justice and it fell to be determined whether, where specific goods were counted as a single supply which included both a zero-rated principal item and items excluded from the scope of that zero-rating, a member state was precluded from charging VAT at the standard rate on the supply of the excluded items. *Held,* under the provisions of the 1994 Act it was clear that an exemption with refund of the tax paid applied to caravans and that items supplied with the caravans were excluded from the scope of that exemption. Therefore, if, notwithstanding the national legislation, the Directive art 28(2) required the exemption to apply to the items supplied with the caravans, the effect would extend the scope of the exemption. Clearly, such an interpretation of art 28(2)(a) would run counter to the wording and purpose of that provision. Exceptions in the Directive to the general principle that VAT was to be levied on all goods or services were to be interpreted strictly. Article 28(2)(a) provided for the maintenance of existing exemptions and could not cover items which had been excluded from such an exemption by the national legislature before the applicable date. The fact that the supply of the caravan and its contents might be characterised as a single supply did not affect that conclusion. Therefore, the fact that specific goods were counted as a single supply, including both a principal item which was zero-rated and items which were excluded from the scope of that zero-rating, did not prevent the member state concerned from levying VAT at the standard rate on the supply of those excluded items.

Case C-251/05 *Talacre Beach Caravan Sales Ltd v Customs and Excise Comrs* [2006] STC 1671 (ECJ: First Chamber). Case C-173/88 *Skatteministeriet v Henriksen* [1990] STC 768, ECJ (1990 Abr para 2689), distinguished.

2923 Supply of goods and services—credit card company—assignment of customer debts to third party

The appellant bank provided credit card facilities to its customers. In order to raise working capital, the appellant employed a securitisation scheme under which the beneficial interest in the debts ('receivables') payable by its credit card-holding customers were assigned to a trust company. The appellant was obliged to service the accounts of the credit card holders, and the trust was entitled to borrow in capital markets, using the assigned receivables as security, and pass the proceeds back in order temporarily to swell the cash flow, and, therefore, the working capital of the appellant. The Commissioners for Her Majesty's Revenue and Customs took the view that the assignment of the receivables constituted a supply for value added tax purposes, and that the supply of services by the appellant, in performing its obligation under the assignment agreement to continue to service the accounts of its credit card holders, incurred attributable inputs on the basis that the payment received from the credit card holders for the service of their accounts had already incurred attributable inputs. A VAT and duties tribunal upheld that decision and the appellant appealed. *Held,* the appellant's assignment of the receivables constituted a new class of exception to the general rule that any transaction whereby goods or services were transferred or provided for consideration was a supply. The assignments were, viewed separately from the rest of the securitisation scheme, capable in theory of having constituted supplies, but because those assignments were no more than a necessary pre-condition to the supply of a securitisation service to the appellant, performed by the third part entities created specifically for that purpose, they were thereby deprived of the character of a supply by the appellant. Also, where a single business activity constituted the supply of a service to two different persons who each paid separately for what they had received, there existed no reason why the inputs incurred in the carrying out of that single activity should have been solely attributable to the supply to the one of them. The fact that the supply had consisted of a promise to go on making a continuing supply to a third party might have been relevant to the fair and reasonable apportionment of the inputs as between each supply but that had not justified the conclusion that no parts of the input could have been attributed to the supply to the promisee. Accordingly, the appeal would be allowed.

MBNA Europe Bank Ltd v Revenue and Customs Comrs [2006] EWHC 2326 (Ch), [2006] STC 2089 (Chancery Division: Briggs J). *Customs and Excise Comrs v Redrow Group plc* [1999] 2 All ER 1, HL; *Tesco plc v Customs and Excise Comrs* [2002] EWHC 2131 (Ch), [2003] 1 CMLR 116 (2002 Abr para 3069); and Case C-465/03 *Kretztechnik AG v Finanzamt Linz* [2005] 1 WLR 3755, ECJ (2005 Abr para 3145), considered.

2924 Supply of goods and services—fuel for private use—consideration for fuel—reduction

The Value Added Tax (Consideration for Fuel Provided for Private Use) Order 2006, SI 2006/868 (in force on 1 May 2006), increases, by an average of ten per cent in relation to fuel for diesel vehicles, and 11 per cent in relation to vehicles using other fuels, the fixed scales used as the basis for charging value added tax on road fuel provided by businesses for private motoring, set out in the Value Added Tax Act 1994 s 57 Table A, in relation to any prescribed accounting period starting after 30 April 2006.

2925 Supply of goods and services—goods—cars

The Value Added Tax (Cars) (Amendment) Order 2006, SI 2006/874 (in force on 13 April 2006), further amends the 1992 Order, SI 1992/3122, so as to (1) introduce an exception to the treatment of supply of goods and services in art 4(1)(a), where the supplier makes an adjustment to the consideration accounted for on the original sale of a motor car, whether that adjustment is required to be made under the Value Added Tax Regulations 1995, SI 1995/2518, or is made in any other way; (2) limit the application of this exception to agreements where the motor cars delivered under those agreements are delivered on or after 1 September 2006; and (3) define a finance agreement.

2926 Supply of goods and services—goods—special provisions

The Value Added Tax (Special Provisions) (Amendment) Order 2006, SI 2006/869 (in force on 13 April 2006), further amends the 1995 Order, SI 1995/1268, so as to (1) introduce an exception to the treatment of supply of goods and service where the supplier makes an adjustment to the consideration accounted for on the original sale of relevant goods, whether that adjustment is required to be made under the Value Added Tax Regulations 1995, SI 1995/2518, or is made in any other way; (2) limit the application of the exception under head (1) supra to agreements where the goods delivered under such agreements are delivered on or after 1 September 2006; and (3) define a finance agreement.

See para 2937.

2927 Supply of goods and services—place of supply—consultancy services provided in United Kingdom—supplier with headquarters outside United Kingdom

The taxpayer was a Swiss company which had its headquarters in Zurich and a large operation in the United Kingdom. The taxpayer engaged a Swiss consultancy firm to complete work in connection with the implementation of a new software system at its United Kingdom operations. The consultancy firm sub-contracted performance to its United Kingdom branch. All, or substantially all, of the services were physically provided at the taxpayer's business premises in the United Kingdom. The invoices raised by the Swiss consultancy firm did not include any charge to value added tax under the law of the United Kingdom or any other member state. If the taxpayer's United Kingdom operations had obtained the same or similar consultancy services from a supplier based in the United Kingdom, it would have invoiced for them at their basic contractual price plus 17·5 per cent. The supplier of the services would have been liable to account to the Commissioners for Her Majesty's Revenue and Customs for the 17·5 per cent output tax. The Commissioners took the view that the reverse provisions of the Value Added Tax Act 1994 s 8 meant that the taxpayer's United Kingdom operations were liable to pay VAT to them. The taxpayer's appeal to a VAT and duties tribunal was allowed on the basis that the United Kingdom operation was not a 'fixed establishment to which the service is supplied' within the meaning in EC Council Directive 77/388 art 9(2)(e), meaning that Switzerland rather than the United Kingdom was the place of supply. The Commissioners appealed. *Held*, on a proper application of art 9(2)(e), the supplies were made to the taxpayer's establishment in the United Kingdom. It followed that the result of applying the reverse charge provision in the 1994 Act s 8 was the same as the result required to be brought about by Directive 77/388, making the taxpayer liable to the commissioners for VAT in respect of those services. The tribunal's view that the most important consideration was the place at which the contract for the services to be supplied was made could not be supported. Value added tax was not charged on the supply of the service of making a contract for services, but on the supply of the services which had been contracted to be supplied. Although the tribunal had been right to ask whether the services had been supplied to the taxpayer at its head office or at its United Kingdom establishment, the answer it gave to that question had been incorrect. On the facts of the case, the only tenable answer to that question was that the services had been supplied to the taxpayer at its United Kingdom establishments. Accordingly, the appeal would be allowed.

Zurich Insurance Co v Revenue and Customs Comrs [2006] EWHC 593 (Ch), [2006] STC 1694 (Chancery Division: Park J).

This decision has been affirmed on appeal: [2007] EWCA Civ 218, (2007) Times, 5 April.

2928 Supply of goods and services—place of supply—fairs and shows

The respondent, a United Kingdom company, organised two boat shows in France. It supplied exhibitors with inclusive services including setting up stands and means of communication and making them available for use, providing staff to welcome visitors, and renting and arranging surveillance of mooring areas for boats on show. The respondent applied in France for a refund of value added tax paid on the price of goods and services which it purchased in France in order to organise the boat shows. The tax authority rejected the application on the basis that the organisation of shows and fairs, since it was physically carried out in France, was a service deemed to be provided in France pursuant to the national provision by which EC Council Directive 77/388 art 9(2)(c) was transposed into domestic law. Under art 9(2)(c), the place of the supply of services relating to cultural, artistic, sporting, educational, entertainment or similar activities, including the activities of the organisers of such activities, and where appropriate the supply of ancillary services, was the place where those services were physically carried out. The authority considered that the conditions required for a refund of VAT had not been met. The respondent successfully challenged that decision and an appeal was dismissed. On a further appeal by the appellant minister, the court sought a preliminary ruling from the European Court of Justice. *Held*, art 9(2)(c) had to be interpreted as meaning that an inclusive service provided by an organiser to exhibitors at a fair or in an exhibition hall fell within the category of relevant services. The overall purpose of art 9(2) was to establish a special system for services provided between taxable persons where the cost of the services was included in the price of the goods. The Community legislature considered that, in so far as the supplier provided his service in the state in which such services were physically carried out, and the organiser of the event charged the final consumer VAT in the same state, the VAT charged on the basis of all those services had to be paid to that state, and not to the state in which the supplier of the service was established. No particular artistic or sporting level was required by art 9(2)(c), and services similar to artistic, sporting and entertainment activities fell within its scope. A show or fair, whatever its theme, was intended to provide to a number of recipients in a single place and on a single occasion with a variety of complex services, with the particular purpose of presenting information, goods or events in such a way as to promote them to visitors. Such a show or fair could be regarded as a similar activity within the meaning of art 9(2)(c).

Case C-114–05 *Ministre de l'Economie, des Finances et de l'Industrie v Gillian Beach Ltd* [2006] STC 1080 (ECJ: Sixth Chamber).

2929 Supply of goods and services—place of supply—services

The Value Added Tax (Place of Supply of Services) (Amendment) Order 2006, SI 2006/1683 (in force on 1 August 2006), further amends the 1992 Order, SI 1992/3121, so as to clarify the place of supply of a right to services.

2930 Supply of goods and services—place of supply—telecommunications services

The claimant was a supplier of multifunction phone cards from Ireland to distributors and retailers within the United Kingdom. Customers who had purchased the cards from United Kingdom retailers obtained telecommunication services from a company established in Ireland. In general, Ireland imposed value added tax on the supply of phone cards and avoided double taxation by providing that no further VAT was due when access to the telecommunications was obtained on redemption of the card. The United Kingdom did not impose VAT on the supply of the phone card, which was regarded as a face-value voucher, the consideration for which was disregarded for the purposes of VAT pursuant to the Value Added Tax Act 1994 Sch 10A para 31. Instead, VAT was charged on the supply of the telecommunication services when a card was redeemed. However, under EC Council Directive 77/388 art 9(2), telecommunication services provided to non-business users were regarded as supplied from the member state in which the supplier had established its business, and therefore supplies of telecommunications by an Irish supplier to non-business users in the United Kingdom could not be charged in the United Kingdom. The Commissioners for Her Majesty's Revenue and Customs determined that the consequence of the claimant's arrangements was that a situation of complete non-taxation was established in relation to the supply of both the phone cards and the telecommunication services, which was contrary to the United Kingdom's duty under Directive 77/388 to prevent non-taxation. The Commissioners decided, therefore, that the exclusion from VAT on the supply of the phone cards was disapplied by the 1994 Act Sch 10A para 3(3), since the person from whom services were obtained by the use of the voucher, namely the Irish company, had failed to account for the VAT due on the supply of those services to the person using the voucher to obtain them. The claimant successfully applied for judicial review of that decision, and the commissioners appealed. *Held*, if neither the issue of phonecards for telecommunications services nor the supply of those services to persons within the Community was subject to VAT, the principle of the avoidance of non-taxation was necessarily infringed. Likewise, in that case, the principle that VAT law should not distort competition applied and was on the facts infringed because the provider of the services and its distributors were able to market the services without having to account for VAT. The issue of the phonecards was no more than a promise to make the telecommunications services available, and therefore constituted a supply of telecommunications services within art 9(2)(e). The 1994 Act Sch 10A para 3 had to be interpreted in conformity with that provision in order to prevent the non-taxation of the supplies to the United Kingdom distributors of the taxpayer's phonecards, or other taxpayers in the same position. The appropriate interpretation was to read in words to widen the disapplication in Sch 10 para 3(3) of the disregard in Sch 10 para 3(2) so that the disapplication applied where the disregard would result in the non-taxation, contrary to the objectives of Directive 77/388, of a taxable supply of goods or services in the United Kingdom. Accordingly, the appeal would be allowed.

Revenue and Customs Comrs v IDT Card Services Ireland Ltd [2006] EWCA Civ 29, [2006] STC 1252 (Court of Appeal: Pill, Latham and Arden LJJ). Decision of Moses J [2004] EWHC 3188 (Admin), [2005] STC 314 (2005 Abr para 3158) reversed.

2931 Supply of goods and services—single supply or separate supplies—CD books

The taxpayer was a direct marketing company supplying a series of CD books, comprising a CD in a wallet with the works of a single composer and 12 pages of text regarding the composer, all bound together. A VAT and duties tribunal dismissed the taxpayer's appeal against a ruling that the supply of the product was standard rated for value added tax purposes, holding that the CD book was a single supply, principally of the CD. On the taxpayer's appeal, the issue arose whether, in a case where a taxpayer argued that a mixed supply of goods or services could be treated either as a single supply or as separate supplies of the individual components consisting of the mixed supply, a finding by the tribunal that the supply consisted of a principal element and an ancillary element concluded the issue as to whether there were separate supplies. *Held*, to determine the correct treatment for VAT purposes of mixed supplies, the question was not just whether one of the elements of the supply was the principal element of a single supply and the other the ancillary element of that supply. The other possible view in the case of multiple supplies was that there were two separate supplies. In order to determine whether the supply was a mixed supply, where each supply should be treated as a separate supply but not artificially split, the court had to examine all relevant circumstances. The tribunal had given reasons that it was satisfied that the two elements of the supply were the principal and ancillary elements of a single supply, which logically excluded the possibility of separate supplies. The tribunal had not made an error of law by not dealing with that possibility as a separate issue. Accordingly, the appeal would be dismissed.

International Masters Publishers Ltd v Revenue and Customs Comrs [2006] EWCA Civ 1455, [2007] STC 153 (Court of Appeal: Pill, Rix and Arden LJJ). Case C-349/96 *Card Protection Plan Ltd v Customs and Excise Comrs* [1999] All ER (EC) 339, ECJ (1999 Abr para 3419), applied. Decision of Collins J [2006] EWHC 127 (Admin), [2006] STC 1450 affirmed.

2932   Supply of goods and services—single supply or separate supplies—reward scheme delegated to company

The taxpayer, a boiler manufacturing company and representative member of a VAT group, delegated the operation of a reward scheme to a company which operated such schemes. The scheme rewarded installers of the taxpayer's boilers with points which could be redeemed for goods and services provided by the company. The company invoiced the taxpayer at the full recommended retail price for what had been provided to the installers, and charged value added tax on the invoiced amount. The taxpayer paid the amount and completed its VAT returns on the basis that it was not entitled to deduct as input tax the VAT thus charged to it and paid by it to the company. However, the taxpayer's accountants made a voluntary disclosure, claiming to deduct as input tax for the relevant periods the VAT paid to the company. The Commissioners for Her Majesty's Revenue and Customs rejected the disclosure but were willing to allow the deduction of such part of the overall sums paid to the company as it represented only the associated marketing services which the company supplied to the taxpayer. A VAT and duties tribunal dismissed the taxpayer's appeal on the basis that, under the scheme, there was, for VAT purposes, a supply of goods by the company to the taxpayer and then another supply to installers by the taxpayer, so that the taxpayer was entitled to recover as input tax the VAT included in the company's invoices but had to account for output tax on the value of such individual distributed rewards as had acquisition costs exceeding £50. The taxpayer appealed, arguing that the scheme represented an indivisible single supply of marketing services to it, albeit a supply to it of a service which included provision of goods and services, the rewards, to others, namely, the installers. *Held*, in order to determine whether a supply was a composite or mixed supply from an economic point of view, one had to identify the essential features to determine whether the supplier was supplying a typical customer with separate services, or a single service. Looking at the acts performed under the scheme from an economic and commercial standpoint, they were not economically dissociable from the provision of goods but a mechanism without which the provision of goods to installers could not achieve its purpose. The taxpayer was entitled to have all its VAT paid to the company under the scheme in the relevant periods treated as part of its input tax in those periods. Accordingly, the appeal would be allowed.

Baxi Group v Revenue and Customs Comrs [2006] EWHC 3353 (Ch), [2006] All ER (D) 359 (Dec) (Chancery Division: Lindsay J). *Customs and Excise Comrs v British Telecommunications plc* [1999] 3 All ER 961, HL (1999 Abr para 3433); and *Customs and Excise Comrs v Telemed Ltd* [1992] STC 89 considered.

2933   Supply of goods and services—supply for a consideration—gift vouchers under a promotional scheme

It has been held that a promotional sales scheme, providing motorists with vouchers which may be redeemed at various retail shops, allows the taxpayer, who has awarded the vouchers, to reduce its value added tax liability by the level of expense incurred by it when purchasing the vouchers.

Total UK Ltd v Revenue and Customs Comrs [2006] EWHC 3422 (Ch), [2007] STC 564 (Chancery Division: Sir Andrew Park). Case C-317/94 *Elida Gibbs Ltd v Customs and Excise Comrs* [1996] STC 1387, ECJ (1996 Abr para 3375), applied.

2934   Supply of goods and services—time of supply—prepayment for future supplies— unascertained goods

EC Council Directive 77/388 art 10(2) provides that tax becomes chargeable when the goods are delivered but, where a payment is to be made on account before the goods are delivered, the tax becomes chargeable on receipt of the payment.

The taxpayer operated a large number of private hospitals. The value added tax status of supplies by health providers was changed from zero-rated to exempt, which meant that health providers could no longer deduct input tax on purchases of medical supplies. Before the change was introduced, the taxpayer set up a scheme in reliance of the prepayment provision in Directive 77/388 art 10(2) to take maximum advantage of the right to make deductions. Under the scheme, in consideration of an immediate payment, an associated company agreed to make supplies of drugs and prostheses listed in a schedule, which could be amended by agreement. Either party was entitled to terminate the contract, in which case the taxpayer was entitled to recover the value not delivered. The Commissioners of Customs and Excise refused the taxpayer's claim to recover input tax. On a reference to the European Court of Justice, it fell to be determined whether the prepayment arrangements set up by the taxpayer fell within the scope of art 10(2). *Held*, as a derogation from the ordinary rule that VAT was chargeable on delivery, the provision in art 10(2) which allowed VAT to become chargeable on receipt of a prepaid sum had to be interpreted strictly. In order for VAT to become chargeable under art 10(2) on receipt of a prepayment, the goods which were to be supplied had to be precisely identified when the payment was made. It was not sufficient that the goods were referred to in general terms in a list which could be altered by agreement and from which the buyer could select articles, on the basis of an agreement from which he could unilaterally resile at any time. It followed that VAT chargeable under the taxpayer's scheme under art 10(2) was not chargeable at the time of the prepayment.

Case C-419/02 *BUPA Hospitals Ltd v Customs and Excise Comrs* [2006] Ch 446 (ECJ: Grand Chamber).

2935 Supply of goods and services—time of supply—sale on approval—online sales

Scotland
The taxpayer, an electrical goods retailer, appealed to a VAT and duties tribunal against a notice of assessment issued by the Revenue and Customs Commissioners. It was common ground that the taxpayer had to account for output VAT on the price of goods purchased by customers through their online service, since these were distance contracts governed by the Consumer Protection (Distance Selling) Regulations 2000, SI 2000/2334. It fell to be determined when the tax point occurred. The Commissioners argued that the date of payment was the tax point, whereas the taxpayer submitted that it was the date on which the customer ceased to be entitled to cancel the contract under the 2000 Regulations. The tribunal allowed the appeal and the Commissioners appealed. *Held*, reg 10 gave the customer an unqualified right to cancel the sale. It did not change the nature of the contract of sale by making all distance contracts transactions of sale on approval, as the tribunal's approach implied. Under this kind of transaction, a taxable supply took place when the online payment was made. Accordingly, the appeal would be allowed.

Revenue and Customs Comrs v Robertson's Electrical Ltd 2005 SLT 1149 (Inner House). Decision of VAT and duties tribunal [2004] V & DR 481 reversed.

2936 Supply of goods and services—tour operator—language and study trips aboard

EC Council Directive 77/388 art 26(1) provides that member states must apply value added tax to the operations of travel agents in accordance with the provisions of art 26 where the travel agents deal with customers in their own name and use the supplies and services of other taxable persons in the provision of travel facilities. If transactions entrusted by the travel agent to other taxable persons are performed by such persons outside the Community, the travel agent's service is to be treated as an exempted intermediary activity: art 26(3).

The taxpayer, a German company, provided language and study trips abroad. Those services had originally been classified as 'travel services' under domestic law, but the German tax authority subsequently decided that they were in fact educational or training services which were exempt from VAT. As a consequence of the reclassification, the authority reduced the VAT excesses declared by the taxpayer for three tax years. The taxpayer sought an increase in the amount of tax on inputs for those years. It fell to be determined whether the conditions for the application of Directive 77/388 art 26(1) were met in such cases. *Held*, art 26 had to be interpreted as applying to a trader such as the taxpayer which habitually offered to its customers, in addition to services associated with the language training and education of those customers, services, such as travel to the host state and/or stay in that state, bought in from other taxable persons. Although the taxpayer was not a travel agent or tour operator within the normal meaning of those terms, in the course of its activities in relation to the offered programmes it provided services which were identical or at least comparable to those of a travel agent or tour operator, in that it offered to its customers services involving travel by plane. Where a trader such as the taxpayer habitually offered its customers travel services, in addition to services associated with the language training and education of its customers, which could not be carried out without a substantial effect on the package price charged, such services were not to be equated with purely ancillary services. It was clear that the services in question did not represent a marginal share in relation to the corresponding services associated with the language training and education which the taxpayer offered.

Case C-200/04 *Finanzamt Heidelberg v iSt internationale Sprach- und Studienreisen GmbH* [2006] 1 CMLR 672 (ECJ: Second Chamber). Case C-163/91 *Van Ginkel Waddinxveen BV and Reis-en Passagebureau Van Ginkel BV v Inspecteur der Omzetbelasting te Utrecht* [1996] STC 825, ECJ (1996 Abr para 3368) considered. Joined Cases C-308/96 and C-94/97 *Customs and Excise Comrs v Madgett and Baldwin (trading as Howden Court Hotel)* [1998] STC 1189, ECJ (1998 Abr para 3297) applied.

2937   Supply of goods and services—treatment of transactions

The Value Added Tax (Treatment of Transactions and Special Provisions) (Amendment) Order 2006, SI 2006/2187 (in force on 1 September 2006), further amends (1) the Value Added Tax (Treatment of Transactions) Order 1995, SI 1995/958, by removing from its scope sales by auction of works of art, antiques, collections and collector's pieces, and the provision of any services relating to a transfer of ownership, if the goods are then treated as imported, for value added tax purposes, following their removal from the customs temporary importation procedure, so that such sales and the provision of the related services are treated for those purposes as supplies of goods or services; and (2) the Value Added Tax (Special Provisions) Order 1995, SI 1995/1268, by enabling auctioneers to account for VAT on the profit margin only, using the existing scheme for dealers and auctioneers, instead of by reference to the value of the supply.

2938   Taxable person—economic activity—fraudulent evasion of value added tax—evasion effected through lawful trade—basis for confiscation proceedings

EC Council Directive 77/388 art 4(1) provides that 'taxable person' means any person who independently carries out in any place any specified economic activity, whatever the purpose or results of that activity.

The defendant was charged with being knowingly concerned in the fraudulent evasion of value added tax, contrary to the Value Added Tax Act 1994 s 72. The prosecution case was that the defendant had been involved in a missing trader fraud, which involved the sale and purchase of goods between companies in different member states. The defendant was convicted. His application for permission to appeal against conviction was dismissed, though the prosecution conceded that, in the light of a recent decision by the Court of Appeal, it should not have charged the defendant with a breach of s 72. Nevertheless, the prosecution obtained a confiscation order. The defendant appealed, contending that now the prosecution accepted that no VAT was due in relation to the transactions, the defendant could not have benefited from any crime. *Held,* activities which could constitute economic activities in Directive 77/388 art 4(1) were broadly defined, and so should be viewed objectively and applied without regard to the purpose or results of the transactions concerned. The subjective intention of the party carrying out the transaction or chain of transactions was on the whole irrelevant. A wide interpretation had to be given to the criteria for economic activity. If the criteria were satisfied, then the purpose behind the activity was not relevant, save in respect of whether the trader had the right to deduct input tax. The fact that the Revenue would be entitled to withhold a repayment where fraud could be proved against the taxable person did not mean that the fraudulent economic activity was not subject to the VAT regime. Viewed objectively, the transactions to which the defendant and his company had been parties constituted supplies of goods by taxable persons and so constituted economic activities within the meaning of art 4(1), and were therefore subject to VAT. It followed that the defendant had been rightly convicted of the offence of being knowingly concerned in the fraudulent evasion of VAT and that the concession made by the prosecution had been wrongly made. It followed that there had been a proper basis for the confiscation proceedings and, accordingly, the appeal would be dismissed.

R v Hashash [2006] EWCA Crim 2518, [2006] All ER (D) 78 (Nov) (Court of Appeal: Hooper LJ, Simon and Lloyd Jones JJ).

2939   Taxable person—public authority—activities engaged in as public authority— operation of a crematorium

EC Council Directive 77/388 art 4(5) provides that local government authorities are not to be considered taxable persons in respect of activities in which they engage as public authorities, but that they are to be considered as taxable persons in respect of such activities when their engagement in those activities would lead to significant distortions of competition.

The applicant, which operated a crematorium, sought information from the tax office concerning the treatment for value added tax purposes of a local authority which also operated a crematorium. The applicant asserted that if the local authority was treated as a non-taxable person it would be able to offer crematorium services at lower prices than the applicant charged. The tax office refused to disclose the information on the ground that such tax matters were confidential. The applicant brought the matter before a finance court, which held that an action by the applicant against the local authority's tax assessments would be admissible if the treatment of the authority as a non-taxable person would lead to 'significant distortions of competition' within the meaning of EC Council Directive 77/388 art 4(5). The matter was referred to the European Court of Justice. *Held,* a private person was entitled to rely on the direct effect of art 4(5). It followed that a private person alleged to be in competition with a public body in respect of the activities in which it engaged as a public authority was entitled to rely on art 4(5) in proceedings before a national court. It would be for the national court to determine whether the treatment of a public body as a non-taxable person was justified in the particular case.

Case C-430/04 *Finanzamt Eisleben v Feuerbestattungsverein Halle eV* [2006] STC 2043 (ECJ: Second Chamber).

2940　Taxable person—public authority—activities engaged in as public authority—supply of further education courses

Scotland
The taxpayer was a college whose core activity was the supply of further education courses. The courses were funded by central government through the Scottish Education Funding Council under the Further and Higher Education (Scotland) Act 1992, which governed the provision of further education courses which qualified for funding. The taxpayer incurred input tax on the construction of a new campus for which it claimed repayment on the ground that it was not a taxable person, pursuant to EC Council Directive 77/388 art 4(5), as it was a body governed by public law whose activities or transactions were engaged in as a public authority. Although it was agreed that the taxpayer was a body governed by public law for the purposes of art 4(5), a VAT and duties tribunal found that the taxpayer was operating under a private law regime rather than engaging in activities as a public authority and that accordingly, art 4(5) did not apply to it. As a result, the taxpayer fell to be regarded as a private trader supplying exempt supplies. The taxpayer appealed, contending that in providing funded further education courses, it was pursuing an activity under a special legal regime applicable to it and was not acting under the same legal conditions as a hypothetical private trader providing a similar service. *Held*, it was established that bodies governed by public law within art 4(5) engaged in activities as public authorities within the meaning of art 4(5) when they did so under a special legal regime applicable to them. There was no real difficulty in identifying the existence of a special legal regime arising from the provisions of the 1992 Act. Once it was accepted that the taxpayer was a public authority, it was clear that in providing the funded courses it did so as an act of public administration and not as an act governed solely by the rules of private law. In providing the funded core activity, it did not act as a hypothetical private trader providing such courses might. Accordingly, the appeal would be allowed.

Edinburgh Telford College v Revenue and Customs Comrs [2006] CSIH 13, [2006] STC 1291 (Inner House). Joined Cases 231/87 and 129/88 *Ufficio Distrettuale delle Imposte Dirette di Fiorenzuola d'Arda v Comune di Carpaneto Piacentino; Ufficio Provinciale Imposta sul Valore Aggiunto di Piacenza v Comune di Rivergaro* [1991] STC 205, ECJ (1989 Abr para 2592), applied.

2941　Zero rating—caravans—removable contents

See Case C-251/05 *Talacre Beach Caravan Sales Ltd v Customs and Excise Comrs*, para 2922.

2942　Zero rating—construction of buildings—relevant charitable purpose

The taxpayer, a housing association, was both a limited company registered under the Industrial and Provident Societies Act 1965 and a charity registered as a social landlord under the Housing Act 1996. It generally held the freehold or the long leasehold of properties which had been transferred to it by local authorities or which it had built. It let the properties on assured tenancies to residential occupiers. The taxpayer's income was principally derived from rents but properties were occasionally sold to tenants in accordance with right to buy provisions or when the properties became surplus to requirements. The taxpayer built a new divisional head office and requested approval for the issue of a certificate of zero rating, pursuant to the Value Added Tax Act 1994 Sch 8 in respect of the construction. On its appeal against the refusal of its request, a VAT and duties tribunal decided that the letting of property in return for payment was an economic activity whether it was pursued for social or for philanthropic reasons so that it constituted 'business' for the purposes of s 4 and was, therefore, chargeable to tax. On the taxpayer's further appeal, it fell to be determined whether its use of the new head office was 'in the course or furtherance of business' under s 4. *Held*, 'business' was a word of wide meaning, and the absence of one common attribute of ordinary businesses, trades, professions or vocations, such as the pursuit of profit, did not necessarily mean that the activity was not a business or trade. On the evidence and in light of the trend of case authorities, the tribunal had been entitled to come to its well-reasoned decision that the activities of the taxpayer were in the course or furtherance of a business. Accordingly, the appeal would be dismissed.

Riverside Housing Association Ltd v Revenue and Customs Comrs [2006] EWHC 2383 (Ch), [2006] STC 2072 (Chancery Division: Lawrence Collins J). *Customs and Excise Comrs v Yarburgh Children's Trust* [2002] STC 207 (2002 Abr para 3078); *Customs and Excise Comrs v St Paul's Community Project Ltd* [2004] EWHC 2490 (Ch), [2005] STC 95; and *Cardiff Community Housing Association Ltd v Customs and Excise Comrs* [2000] V & DR 346 (2001 Abr para 3214) considered.

2943   Zero rating—food—exceptions—supply in the course of catering—supply of cold foods

The taxpayer provided cold prepared foods from retail outlets at the premises of a company for its employees and visitors. The Commissioners for Her Majesty's Revenue and Customs determined that the taxpayer's supplies of cold prepared food, including where the food was consumed elsewhere on the company's premises than at the retail outlet, did not qualify for zero-rated supplies of food for value added tax purposes as they had been made 'in the course of catering' under the Value Added Tax Act 1994 Sch 8 Pt II Group 1 item 1. The taxpayer's appeal to a VAT and duties tribunal succeeded on the basis that the supplies were indistinguishable from those made by high street sandwich shops, which were regarded as zero-rated. The Commissioners appealed. *Held*, Sir Charles Mantell dissenting, while there was no exhaustive list of circumstances in which supplies of food were 'in the course of catering', Sch 8 Pt II Group 1 note (3) gave an indication of the importance attached to the place of consumption, as eating food on the premises at which it was supplied was considered a supply in the course of catering. For a supply of food to be considered 'in the course of catering', it would generally be a part of, or associated with, a broader activity where the supply of food was accompanied by an additional element which would usually add something to the experience of buying and consuming food. The terms of the outsourcing contract had little impact, and there was no satisfactory reason why an individual's liability to VAT should depend on whether the supply was from an outlet subject to outsourcing arrangements. Objectively, the taxpayer's supplies made to individual customers were not in the course of catering. The customers were simply buying and being supplied with food in the same way as if they were buying them and being supplied with them zero-rated from another available retail outlet. Where food was consumed at locations within the company other than at the retail outlets, it was not supplied for consumption on the premises on which it was supplied. Accordingly, the appeal would be dismissed.

Revenue and Customs Comrs v Compass Contract Services UK Ltd [2006] EWCA Civ 730, [2006] STC 1999 (Court of Appeal: Mummery and Scott Baker LJJ and Sir Charles Mantell). *Customs and Excise Comrs v Safeway Stores plc* [1997] STC 163, DC, affirmed.

2944   Zero-rating—lifeboats—supply of fuel

The Value Added Tax (Lifeboats) Order 2006, SI 2006/1750, (in force on 1 August 2006), amends the Value Added Tax Act 1994 Sch 8 Pt II Group 8 item 3 so that the supply of fuel to sea rescue charities is zero-rated where the fuel is for use in a lifeboat.

WAR AND ARMED CONFLICT

Halsbury's Laws of England (4th edn) vol 49(1) (2005 Reissue) paras 401–627

Articles

For articles relating to this title please refer to the Table of Articles at the beginning of the Abridgment.

2945   International agreement—power to detain suspected terrorist without charge—British citizen in Iraq—right to liberty

See *R (on the application of Al-Jedda) v Secretary of State for Defence*, para 1581.

2946   Northern Ireland

See NORTHERN IRELAND.

2947   Prisoner of war—compensation scheme—eligibility criteria—country of birth— discrimination

During the 1939–45 war, the claimant was interned in Hong Kong by the Japanese on the basis that she was a British subject. Several years after the end of the war, she moved to the United Kingdom. A compensation scheme was introduced for British civilians who had been interned by the Japanese during the war. The claimant applied for a payment under the scheme, which was refused on the ground that she did not fulfil the eligibility criteria because neither she, nor one or more of her parents or grandparents, was born in the United Kingdom. In judicial review proceedings brought by the claimant, the judge decided that the eligibility criteria indirectly discriminated against the claimant on racial grounds, and that, although the criteria had a legitimate aim, the indirect discrimination was not objectively justified as the criteria were disproportionate. However, the judge rejected the claim that the claimant had suffered direct discrimination on the grounds of her national origin. He also decided that the Secretary of State had not unlawfully fettered his discretion by failing to consider the possibility of making ex gratia payments to those who fell outside the criteria, but were exceptional cases. The parties appealed against each of those rulings. Appeals were also brought against a separate ruling under the Race Relations Act 1976 s 57 awarding the claimant damages for the injury to her feelings inflicted by indirect racial discrimination, but no aggravated or exemplary damages. *Held*, the eligibility criteria did not directly discriminate against the claimant on racial grounds, but they did indirectly discriminate against her on those grounds. While the eligibility criteria had a legitimate aim, they were not proportionate to the aim to be achieved, were not objectively justified and were therefore unlawful. Moreover, it was lawful for the Secretary of State to refuse to make an exception to the eligibility criteria in the case of the claimant, and there was no unlawful fettering of his common law powers in refusing to depart from the eligibility criteria and to recognise her claim as an exceptional case. The quashing of the eligibility criteria on the ground of indirect discrimination did not entitle the claimant to payment of any compensation under the compensation scheme or to damages for race discrimination. Also, the claim for financial loss for race discrimination had been rightly dismissed. As the unlawful eligibility criteria could be replaced by lawful criteria excluding her from the compensation scheme, she had not suffered and would not suffer any financial loss. As for damages for injury to feelings, there was no error of legal principle in the award made. Judgment would be given accordingly.

R (on the application of Elias) v Secretary of State for Defence [2006] EWCA Civ 1293, [2006] 1 WLR 3213 (Court of Appeal: Mummery, Arden and Longmore LJJ). Decision of Elias J [2005] EWHC 1435 (Admin), [2005] IRLR 788 (2005 Abr para 96) affirmed.

2948 War pensions—civilians

The Personal Injuries (Civilians) (Amendment) Scheme 2006, SI 2006/765 (in force on 10 April 2006), further amends the 1983 Scheme, SI 1983/686, by increasing the rates of allowances, pension and awards payable to, or in respect of, civilians who were killed or injured during the 1939–45 war, and by increasing the amounts of income to be disregarded for the purposes of determining eligibility for certain pensions and allowances. The 2006 Scheme (1) omits provisions relating to unemployability allowances with the effect that a person in receipt of a retirement pension (other than a retirement pension which consists of certain additions) is no longer prevented from being eligible for unemployability allowance; (2) makes revisions to the provision relating to the maintenance of a hospital or institution so as to only require deductions to be made from constant attendance allowance and severe disablement occupational allowance while a person to whom those allowances are paid is in hospital or an institution; and (3) gives the Secretary of State power to suspend, and later cancel, a pension, gratuity or supplement where a person, having been required to provide information, or to attend for a medical examination, fails to do so after being given reasonable notice.

2949 War pensions—services—disablement and death

The Naval, Military and Air Forces Etc (Disablement and Death) Service Pensions (Amendment) Order 2006, SI 2006/303 (in force on 13 March 2006), further amends the 1983 Order, SI 1983/883, so as to correct an error in relation to part-time treatment allowances which was introduced in the 2005 Order, SI 2005/851, by substituting £59 for £60·20 The change has retrospective effect from 11 April 2005.

2950 War pensions—war pensions committees

The War Pensions Committees (Amendment) Regulations 2006, SI 2006/3152 (in force on 1 January 2007), amend the 2000 Regulations, SI 2000/3032, so as to make changes to the constitution and functions of the war pensions committees, which were established by the 2000 Regulations. In particular, the regulations (1) remove the war pensions committees' power to monitor the Veterans Agency and other organisations and replace it with a power to monitor the welfare service of the Veterans Agency and liaise with other organisations; (2) replace the reference to the War Pensions Agency with the Veterans Agency to reflect the change in its name; and (3) replace the table of war pensions committees for regions in England.

WATER

Halsbury's Laws of England (4th edn) vol 49(2) (2004 Reissue) paras 1–399, Vol 49(3) (2004 Reissue) paras 400–806.

Articles

For articles relating to this title please refer to the Table of Articles at the beginning of the Abridgment.

2951 Consumer contracts—unfair terms

See para 2502.

2952 Flood defence—regional committee—composition—Wales

The Welsh Regional Flood Defence Committee (Composition) Order 2006, SI 2006/980 (in force on 1 April 2006), provides that the Welsh regional flood defence committee is to consist of (1) eight members, including the chairperson, appointed by the National Assembly for Wales; (2) two members appointed by the Environment Agency, neither of whom may be a member of the Agency; and (3) eight members appointed by specified groups of councils or, where a group of councils acting jointly is unable to appoint a member, by the Assembly on behalf of that group. The order also amends the Environment Act 1995 so as to provide that the term of office of the first members appointed by the groups of councils is to run from April until 31 May 2010, and thereafter from June. SI 1996/538 is revoked.

2953 Public procurement—award of contracts—procedure

See para 396.

2954 Water Act 2003—commencement

The Water Act 2003 (Commencement No 6, Transitional Provisions and Savings) Order 2006, SI 2006/984, brings into force, on 1 April 2006, ss 1–4, 8(1) (in part), (3)–(7), 11–14, 19 (for all remaining purposes), 21–23, 25, 30, 33, 62 (in part), 100(2)(c), (g) (in part), (4)(b)(iii), (6) (in part), (7) (in part), 101 (in part). Transitional and savings provisions are also made. For a summary of the Act, see 2003 Abr para 2802. See also the commencement table in the title STATUTES.

2955 Water resources—abstraction and impounding

The Water Resources (Abstraction and Impounding) Regulations 2006, SI 2006/641 (in force in part on 1 April 2006 and in part on a day to be appointed), make provision relating to the licensing of abstraction and impounding of water in England and Wales in the light of amendments made by the Water Act 2003 to the Water Resources Act 1991. In particular, the regulations (1) provide for procedural requirements, including time limits in relation to the making of licence applications and in relation to appeals from decisions on licence applications for the abstraction or impounding of water; (2) require that all applications for an abstraction licence or an impounding licence, other than those seeking to vary such a licence so as to reduce the quantity of water authorised to be abstracted, must be made to the Environment Agency containing specified information in a specified manner; (3) prescribe the manner in which notice of such applications must be published; (4) provide exceptions to the requirement to advertise; (5) require the Agency to acknowledge receipt of an application, providing the applicant with specified information within the prescribed time; (6) make special provision where the application relates to abstraction or impounding in a National Park or the Broads; (7) provide that the Agency must make a decision on an application and serve notice of that decision on an applicant or refer the matter to the Secretary of State or the National Assembly for Wales within specified time limits; (8) make provision as to the content of enforcement notices in relation to a breach of a restriction on the abstraction or impounding of water and works notices in relation to the protection of the environment; (9) modify the 2003 Act, as it applies to abstraction or impounding by the Agency, to provide that the Agency must follow similar procedures and comply with similar requirements as any other applicant; and (10) prescribe procedures, requirements and time limits in relation to the process of making, deciding and challenging Agency licence applications; (11) provide for the application of procedures in the Anti-Pollution Works Regulations 1999, SI 1999/1006, to appeals which may be brought against enforcement, works and conservation notices; (12) prescribe the content of and the procedure for publishing notices of proposals by the Agency to modify a licence; (13) permit the Agency to determine the form of a notice to be given by an owner of fishing rights applying to modify a licence; (14) specify a 21 day time-limit for serving a notice of appeal against a notice requiring existing, unlicensed impounding works to be licensed and provide for the application of appeals provisions under SI 1999/1006 for such an appeal; and (15) prescribe what information must be contained on the register of abstraction and impounding licences.

2956 Water resources—environmental impact assessment

See para 2377.

2957 Water services—regulation authority

The Enterprise Act 2002 (Water Services Regulation Authority) Order 2006, SI 2006/522 (in force on 1 April 2006), amends the Enterprise Act 2002 (Super-complaints to Regulators) Order 2003, SI 2003/1368, and the Enterprise Act 2002 (Part 8 Designated Enforcers: Criteria for Designation, Designation of Public Bodies as Designated Enforcers and Transitional Provisions) Order 2003, SI 2003/1399, so as to substitute references to the 'authority' for references to the 'director'.

WEIGHTS AND MEASURES

Halsbury's Laws of England (4th edn) vol 50 (2005 Reissue) paras 1–300

2958   Authorities—prosecutions—notice

See para 2510.

2959   Measuring equipment—liquid fuel and lubricants

The Measuring Equipment (Liquid Fuel and Lubricants) (Amendment) Regulations 2006, SI 2006/2234 (in force on 30 October 2006), further amend the 1995 Regulations, SI 1995/1014, so as to replace the requirement to label measuring equipment with the appropriate British Standard with an obligation to label such equipment clearly to enable the buyer to identify the product that the equipment delivers. The obligation does not arise where measuring equipment is used in the absence of the buyer.

2960   Measuring instruments—active electrical energy meters

The Measuring Instruments (Active Electrical Energy Meters) Regulations 2006, SI 2006/1679 (in force in part on 30 May 2006 and in part on 30 October 2006), implement EC European Parliament and Council Directive 2004/22 on measuring instruments in relation to active electrical energy meters. In particular, the regulations (1) apply, with certain exceptions, to active electrical energy meters for use for trade which are first placed on the market or put into use on or after 30 October 2006; (2) specify the requirements for the placing on the market and putting into use of active electrical energy meters which are that such meters (a) must be in compliance with the essential requirements and the manufacturer must demonstrate such compliance; and (b) must have the CE marking, the M marking and the identification number of the relevant notified body affixed to them; (3) contain provisions relating to the eligibility and designation of persons as notified bodies and with the administrative procedures relating to their appointment, functions and fees; (4) set out the requirements relating to the marking of active electrical energy meters; (5) provide for a presumption of conformity of an active electrical energy meter with other applicable directives conferred by the CE marking; (6) must be enforced by the Gas and Electricity Markets Authority ('GEMA'), in relation to England; (7) detail the offences relating to the unauthorised application of authorised marks; (8) confer powers on the enforcement authorities to take action in respect of non-compliant active electrical energy meters; (9) provide powers of entry and inspection for enforcement officers; (10) provide for offences relating to the obstruction of an enforcement officer; (11) permit a review by the GEMA of notices issued by other enforcement authorities; (12) provide for offences and defences; and (13) make consequential amendments to the existing legislation governing active electrical energy meters.

2961   Measuring instruments—amendments

The Measuring Instruments (Amendment) Regulations 2006, SI 2006/2625 (in force on 30 October 2006), amend (1) the Measuring Instruments (Non-Prescribed Instruments) Regulations 2006, SI 2006/1270, (a) by providing that, in the case of the designation of notified bodies for the assessment of volume conversion devices, the designating authority may charge fees to recover its reasonable costs of designating those bodies and for carrying out periodic inspections of the activities of those bodies; and (b) by deleting the requirements relating to the putting into use of water meters and heat meters; (2) the Measuring Instruments (Automatic Rail-weighbridges) Regulations 2006, SI 2006/1256, by indicating that in the case of an automatic rail-weighbridge which falls within accuracy class one in column one of the specified table, the maximum permissible error in column two is 1.0 per cent; (3) the Measuring Instruments (Automatic Catchweighers) Regulations 2006, SI 2006/1257, by providing that the conformity assessment procedures to be used for mechanical systems are those set out in EC European Parliament and Council Directive 2004/22; and (4) the Measuring Instruments (Cold-water Meters) Regulations 2006, SI 2006/1268, by placing directly on the distributor, or person legally designated for installing the cold-water meter, the obligation to verify that the requirements relating to flowrate range, temperature range and relative pressure are met.

2962   Measuring instruments—automatic catchweighers

The Measuring Instruments (Automatic Catchweighers) Regulations 2006, SI 2006/1257 (in force in part on 30 May 2006 and in part on 30 October 2006), implement EC European Parliament and Council Directive 2004/22 on measuring instruments in relation to the class of automatic catchweighers within the category of automatic weighing instruments. In particular, the regulations (1) apply, with certain exceptions, to automatic catchweighers for use for trade which are first placed on the market or put into use on or after 30 October 2006; (2) specify the requirements for the placing on the market and putting into use of automatic catchweighers which are that automatic catchweighers (a) must be in compliance with the essential requirements and the manufacturer must demonstrate such compliance; and (b) must have the CE marking, the M marking and the identification number of the relevant notified body affixed to them; (3) contain provisions relating to the designation by the Secretary of State of bodies as notified bodies and with the administrative procedures relating to their appointment, functions and fees; (4) set out the requirements relating to the marking of instruments; (5) provide for a presumption of conformity of an automatic catchweigher with other applicable directives conferred by the CE marking; (6) must be enforced by every local weights and measures authority within its area; (7) confer certain powers on the enforcement authorities to take action in respect of non-compliant instruments; (8) permit a review by the Secretary of State of notices issued by other enforcement authorities; (9) provide for the disqualification of instruments; (10) provide for the testing of automatic catchweighers by an inspector otherwise than for the purposes of re-qualification; (11) detail the offences relating to the unauthorised application of authorised marks; (12) provide powers of entry and inspection for enforcement officers; and (13) provide for offences and defences.

2963   Measuring instruments—automatic discontinuous totalisers

The Measuring Instruments (Automatic Discontinuous Totalisers) Regulations 2006, SI 2006/1255 (in force in part on 30 May 2006 and in part on 30 October 2006), implement EC European Parliament and Council Directive 2004/22 on measuring instruments in relation to the class of automatic discontinuous totalisers within the category of automatic weighing instruments. In particular, the regulations (1) apply, with certain exceptions, to automatic discontinuous totalisers for use for trade which are first placed on the market or put into use on or after 30 October 2006; (2) specify the requirements for the placing on the market and putting into use of automatic discontinuous totalisers which are that such totalisers (a) must be in compliance with the essential requirements and the manufacturer must demonstrate such compliance; and (b) must have the CE marking, the M marking and the identification number of the relevant notified body affixed to them; (3) contain provisions relating to the designation by the Secretary of State of persons as notified bodies and with the administrative procedures relating to their appointment, functions and fees; (4) set out the requirements relating to the marking of instruments and identification; (5) provide for a presumption of conformity with other applicable directives conferred by the CE marking; (6) must be enforced by every local weights and measures authority within its area; (7) confer certain powers on the enforcement authorities; (8) permit a review by the Secretary of State of notices issued by other enforcement authorities; (9) provide for the disqualification of instruments; (10) provide for the testing of automatic discontinuous totalisers otherwise than for the purposes of re-qualification; (11) detail the offences relating to the unauthorised application of authorised marks; (12) provide powers of entry and inspection for enforcement officers; and (13) provide for offences and defences.

2964   Measuring instruments—automatic gravimetric filling instruments

The Measuring Instruments (Automatic Gravimetric Filling Instruments) Regulations 2006, SI 2006/1258 (in force in part on 30 May 2006 and in part on 30 October 2006), implement EC European Parliament and Council Directive 2004/22 on measuring instruments in relation to the class of automatic gravimetric filling instruments within the category of automatic weighing instruments. In particular, the regulations (1) apply, with certain exceptions, to automatic gravimetric filling instruments for use for trade which are first placed on the market or put into use on or after 30 October 2006; (2) specify the requirements for the placing on the market and putting into use of automatic gravimetric filling instruments which are that such instruments (a) must be in compliance with the essential requirements and the manufacturer must demonstrate such compliance; and (b) must have the CE marking, the M marking and the identification number of the relevant notified body affixed to them; (3) contain provisions relating to the eligibility and designation of persons as notified bodies and with the administrative procedures relating to their appointment, functions and fees; (4) set out the requirements relating to the marking of automatic gravimetric filling instruments; (5) provide for a presumption of conformity of an automatic gravimetric filling instrument with other applicable directives conferred by the CE marking; (6) must be enforced by every local weights and measures authority within its area; (7) confer certain powers on the enforcement authorities to take action in respect of non-compliant automatic gravimetric filing instruments; (8) permit a review by the Secretary of State of notices issued by other enforcement authorities; (9) provide for the disqualification of automatic gravimetric filling instruments; (10) provide for the testing of an automatic gravimetric filling instrument by an inspector for purposes otherwise than for re-qualification; (11) detail the offences relating to the unauthorised application of authorised marks; (12) provide powers of entry and inspection for enforcement officers; and (13) provide for offences and defences.

2965   Measuring instruments—automatic rail-weighbridges

The Measuring Instruments (Automatic Rail-weighbridges) Regulations 2006, SI 2006/1256 (in force in part on 30 May 2006 and in part on 30 October 2006), implement EC European Parliament and Council Directive 2004/22 on measuring instruments in relation to automatic rail-weighbridges. In particular, the regulations (1) apply, with certain exceptions, to automatic rail-weighbridges for use for trade, which are first placed on the market or put into use on or after 30 October 2006; (2) specify the requirements for the placing on the market and putting into use of automatic rail-weighbridges which are that automatic rail-weighbridges (a) must be in compliance with the essential requirements and the manufacturer must demonstrate such compliance; and (b) must have the CE marking, the M marking and the identification number of the relevant notified body affixed to them; (3) contain provisions relating to the eligibility and designation of persons as notified bodies and with the administrative procedures relating to their appointment, functions and fees; (4) set out the requirements relating to the marking of automatic rail-weighbridges; (5) provide for a presumption of conformity of an automatic rail-weighbridge with other applicable directives conferred by the CE marking; (6) must be enforced by every local weights and measures authority within its area; (7) confer certain powers on the enforcement authorities to take action in respect of non-compliant automatic rail-weighbridges; (8) permit a review by the Secretary of State of notices issued by other enforcement authorities; (9) provide for the disqualification of automatic rail-weighbridges; (10) provide for the testing of automatic rail-weighbridges by an inspector otherwise than for the purposes of re-qualification; (11) detail the offences relating to the unauthorised application of authorised marks; (12) provide powers of entry and inspection for enforcement officers; and (13) provide for offences and defences.

2966 Measuring instruments—beltweighers

The Measuring Instruments (Beltweighers) Regulations 2006, SI 2006/1259 (in force in part on 30 May 2006 and in part on 30 October 2006), implement EC European Parliament and Council Directive 2004/22 on measuring instruments in relation to the class of beltweighers, also known as continuous totalisers, within the category of automatic weighing instruments. In particular, the regulations (1) apply, with certain exceptions, to beltweighers for use for trade which are first placed on the market or put into use on or after 30 October 2006; (2) specify the requirements for the placing on the market and putting into use of beltweighers which are that beltweighers (a) must be in compliance with the essential requirements and the manufacturer must demonstrate such compliance; and (b) must have the CE marking, the M marking and the identification number of the relevant notified body affixed to them; (3) contain provisions relating to the eligibility and designation of persons as notified bodies and with the administrative procedures relating to their appointment, functions and fees; (4) set out the requirements relating to the marking of instruments; (5) provide for a presumption of conformity of a beltweigher with other applicable directives conferred by the CE marking; (6) must be enforced by every local weights and measures authority within its area; (7) confer certain powers on the enforcement authorities to take action in respect of non-compliant instruments; (8) permit a review by the Secretary of State of notices issued by other enforcement authorities; (9) provide for the disqualification of instruments; (10) provide for the testing of beltweighers by an inspector for purposes otherwise than for re-qualification; (11) detail the offences relating to the unauthorised application of authorised marks; (12) provide powers of entry and inspection for enforcement officers; and (13) provide for offences and defences.

2967 Measuring instruments—capacity serving measures

The Measuring Instruments (Capacity Serving Measures) Regulations 2006, SI 2006/1264 (in force in part on 30 May 2006 and in part on 30 October 2006), implement EC European Parliament and Council Directive 2004/22 on measuring instruments in relation to capacity serving measures covered by the Directive in so far as they are prescribed. In particular, the regulations (1) apply, with certain exceptions, to capacity serving measures for use for trade which are first placed on the market or put into use on or after 30 October 2006; (2) specify the requirements for the placing on the market and putting into use of capacity serving measures which are that such measures (a) must be in compliance with the essential requirements and the manufacturer must demonstrate such compliance; and (b) must have the CE marking, the M marking and the identification number of the relevant notified body affixed to them; (3) contain provisions relating to the eligibility and designation of persons to be notified bodies and with the administrative procedures relating to their appointment, functions and fees; (4) set out the requirements relating to the marking of capacity serving measures; (5) provide for a presumption of conformity with other applicable directives conferred by the CE marking; (6) must be enforced by every local weights and measures authority within its area; (7) confer certain powers on the enforcement authorities to take action in respect of non-compliant capacity serving measures; (8) permit a review by the Secretary of State of notices issued by other enforcement authorities; (9) provide for the disqualification of capacity serving measures; (10) detail the offences relating to the unauthorised application of authorised marks; (11) provide powers of entry and inspection for enforcement officers; and (12) provide for offences and defences.

2968 Measuring instruments—cold-water meters

The Measuring Instruments (Cold-water Meters) Regulations 2006, SI 2006/1268 (in force in part on 30 May 2006 and in part on 30 October 2006), implement EC European Parliament and Council Directive 2004/22 on measuring instruments in relation to cold-water meters. In particular, the regulations (1) apply, with certain exceptions, to cold-water meters which are first placed on the market or put into use on or after 30 October 2006, for use for trade for the supply of cold water to domestic premises; (2) specify the requirements for the placing on the market and putting into use of cold-water meters which are that such meters (a) must be in compliance with the essential requirements and the manufacturer must demonstrate such compliance; and (b) must have the CE marking, the M marking and the identification number of the relevant notified body affixed to them; (3) contain provisions relating to the eligibility and designation of persons as notified bodies and with the administrative procedures relating to their appointment, functions and fees; (4) set out the requirements relating to the marking of cold-water meters; (5) provide for a presumption of conformity of a cold-water meter with other applicable directives conferred by the CE marking; (6) must be enforced by every local weights and measures authority within its area; (7) confer powers on the enforcement authorities to take action in respect of non-compliant cold-water meters; (8) permit a review by the Secretary of State of notices issued by other enforcement authorities; (9) provide for the disqualification of cold-water meters; (10) provide for the testing of cold-water meters by an inspector otherwise than for the purposes of re-qualification; (11) detail the offences relating to the unauthorised application of authorised marks; (12) provide powers of entry and inspection for enforcement officers; and (13) provide for offences and defences.

2969   Measuring instruments—EEC requirements—fees

The Measuring Instruments (EEC Requirements) (Fees) (Amendment) Regulations 2006, SI 2006/604 (in force on 1 April 2006), amend the 2004 Regulations, SI 2004/1300, so as to (1) prescribe the fee to be charged by the Secretary of State for the approval of a manufacturer's quality system and the carrying out of EC surveillance under the Non-automatic Weighing Instruments Regulations 2000, SI 2000/3236; (2) replace the hourly rate element of the variable fee for all services specified, with a different hourly rate, depending on which service is being performed; and (3) amend the titles of grade of officers to reflect more accurately the nature of their work.

The Measuring Instruments (EEC Requirements) (Fees) (Amendment No 2) Regulations 2006, SI 2006/2679 (in force on 30 October 2006), further amend the 2004 Regulations supra, so as to (1) extend the fees charged by the Secretary of State for services provided in relation to the designation and inspection of approved bodies under the Non-automatic Weighing Instruments Regulations 2000, SI 2000/1930, to services provided in relation to the designation and inspection of notified bodies under the specified Measuring Instruments Regulations 2006 and the Measuring Instruments (Non-Prescribed Instruments) Regulations 2006, SI 2006/1270; and (2) prescribe fees to be charged by the Secretary of State for the carrying out of the conformity assessment of measuring instruments under the specified Measuring Instruments Regulations 2006 and the 2006 Regulations, SI 2006/1270.

2970   Measuring instruments—exhaust gas analysers

The Measuring Instruments (Exhaust Gas Analysers) Regulations 2006, SI 2006/2164 (in force in part on 7 September 2006 and in part on 30 October 2006), implement EC European Parliament and Council Directive 2004/22 on measuring instruments in relation to exhaust gas analysers. In particular, the regulations (1) apply, with certain exceptions, to exhaust gas analysers intended for use for the protection of the environment and public health which are first placed on the market or put into use on or after 30 October 2006; (2) specify the requirements for the placing on the market and putting into use of exhaust gas analysers which are that such analysers (a) must be in compliance with the essential requirements and the manufacturer must demonstrate such compliance; and (b) must have the CE marking, the M marking and the identification number of the relevant notified body affixed to them; (3) contain provisions relating to the eligibility and designation of persons as notified bodies and with the administrative procedures relating to their appointment, functions and fees; (4) set out the requirements relating to the marking of instruments; (5) provide for a presumption of conformity of an exhaust gas analyser with other applicable directives conferred by the CE marking; (6) provide that the Secretary of State may act as an enforcement authority; (7) confer powers on the enforcement authorities to take action in respect of non-compliant exhaust gas analysers; (8) permit a review by the Secretary of State of notices issued by other enforcement authorities; (9) detail the offences relating to the unauthorised application of authorised marks; (10) provide powers of entry and inspection for enforcement officers; and (11) provide for offences and defences.

2971   Measuring instruments—gas meters

The Measuring Instruments (Gas Meters) Regulations 2006, SI 2006/2647 (in force on 30 October 2006), implement EC European Parliament and Council Directive 2004/22 on measuring instruments in relation to gas meters. In particular, the regulations (1) apply, with certain exceptions, to gas meters for use for trade which are first placed on the market or put into use on or after 30 October 2006; (2) specify the requirements for the placing on the market and putting into use of gas meters which are that such meters (a) must be in compliance with the essential requirements and the manufacturer must demonstrate such compliance with the essential requirements; (b) must have the CE marking, the M marking and the identification number of the relevant notified body affixed to them; and (c) must be put to use in the manner set out in the regulations; (3) contain provisions relating to the eligibility and designation of persons as notified bodies and the administrative procedures relating to their appointment, functions and fees; (4) set out the requirements relating to the marking of gas meters; (5) provide for a presumption of conformity of a gas meter with other applicable directives conferred by the CE marking; (6) provide for enforcement of the regulations by the Gas and Electricity Markets Authority ('GEMA') in relation to England; (7) detail the offences relating to the unauthorised application of authorised marks; (8) confer powers on the enforcement authorities to take action in respect of non-compliant gas meters; (9) provide powers of entry and inspection for enforcement officers; (10) provide for offences relating to the obstruction of an enforcement officer; (11) permit a review by GEMA of notices issued by other enforcement authorities; (12) provide for offences and defences; and (13) make consequential amendments to the existing legislation governing gas meters.

2972 Measuring instruments—material measures of length

The Measuring Instruments (Material Measures of Length) Regulations 2006, SI 2006/1267 (in force in part on 30 May 2006 and in part on 30 October 2006), implement EC European Parliament and Council Directive 2004/22 on measuring instruments in relation to the class of material measures of length within the category of material measures. In particular, the regulations (1) extend, with certain exceptions, to specified material measures of length for use for trade which are first placed on the market or put into use on or after 30 October 2006; (2) specify the requirements for the placing on the market and putting into use of material measures of length which are that such measures (a) must be in compliance with the essential requirements and the manufacturer must demonstrate such compliance; and (b) must have the CE marking, the M marking and the identification number of the relevant notified body affixed to them; (3) contain provisions relating to the eligibility and designation of persons as notified bodies and with the administrative procedures relating to their appointment, functions and fees; (4) set out the requirements relating to the marking of material measures of length and identification; (5) provide for a presumption of conformity with other applicable directives conferred by the CE marking; (6) must be enforced by every local weights and measures authority within its area; (7) confer powers on the enforcement authorities to take action in respect of non-compliant material measures of length; (8) permit a review by the Secretary of State of notices issued by other enforcement authorities; (9) provide for the disqualification of material measures of length; (10) detail the offences relating to the unauthorised application of authorised marks; (11) provide powers of entry and inspection for enforcement officers; and (12) provide for offences and defences.

2973 Measuring instruments—measuring systems—liquid fuel and lubricants

The Measuring Instruments (Liquid Fuel and Lubricants) Regulations 2006, SI 2006/1266 (in force in part on 30 May 2006 and in part on 30 October 2006), implement EC European Parliament and Council Directive 2004/22 on measuring instruments in relation to measuring systems. In particular, the regulations (1) apply, with certain exceptions, to measuring systems which are placed on the market or put into use on or after 30 October 2006, for use for trade in the making of a continuous and dynamic measurement of liquid fuel in a quantity equal to or less than 100 litres or 100 kilograms; (2) specify the requirements for the placing on the market and putting into use of measuring systems which are that such systems (a) must be in compliance with the essential requirements and the manufacturer must demonstrate such compliance; and (b) must have the CE marking, the M marking and the identification number of the relevant notified body affixed to them; (3) contain provisions relating to the eligibility and designation of persons as notified bodies and with the administrative procedures relating to their appointment, functions and fees; (4) set out the requirements relating to the marking of measuring systems; (5) provide for a presumption of conformity of a measuring system with other applicable directives conferred by the CE marking; (6) must be enforced by every local weights and measures authority within its area; (7) confer powers on the enforcement authorities to take action in respect of non-compliant measuring systems; (8) permit a review by the Secretary of State of notices issued by other enforcement authorities; (9) provide for the disqualification of measuring systems; (10) provide for the testing of measuring systems by an inspector otherwise than for the purposes of re-qualification; (11) detail the offences relating to the unauthorised application of authorised marks; (12) provide powers of entry and inspection for enforcement officers; and (13) provide for offences and defences.

2974 Measuring instruments—meter measuring systems—liquid fuel delivered from road tankers

The Measuring Instruments (Liquid Fuel delivered from Road Tankers) Regulations 2006, SI 2006/1269 (in force in part on 30 May 2006 and in part on 30 October 2006), implement EC European Parliament and Council Directive 2004/22 on measuring instruments in relation to meter measuring systems. In particular, the regulations (1) apply, with certain exceptions, to meter measuring systems which are first placed on the market or put into use on or after 30 October 2006, for use for trade in the making of a continuous and dynamic measurement of liquid fuel in a quantity exceeding 100 litres or 100 kilograms delivered from a road tanker; (2) specify the requirements for the placing on the market and putting into use of meter measuring systems which are that such systems (a) must be in compliance with the essential requirements and the manufacturer must demonstrate such compliance; and (b) must have the CE marking, the M marking and the identification number of the relevant notified body affixed to them; (3) contain provisions relating to the eligibility and designation of persons as notified bodies and with the administrative procedures relating to their appointment, functions and fees; (4) set out the requirements relating to the marking of meter measuring systems; (5) provide for a presumption of conformity of a meter measuring system with other applicable directives conferred by the CE marking; (6) must be enforced by every local weights and measures authority within its area; (7) confer powers on the enforcement authorities to take action in respect of non-compliant meter measuring systems; (8) permit a review by the Secretary of State of notices issued by other enforcement authorities; (9) provide for the disqualification of meter measuring systems; (10) provide for the testing of meter measuring systems by an inspector otherwise than for the purposes of re-qualification; (11) detail the offences relating to the unauthorised application of authorised marks; (12) provide powers of entry and inspection for enforcement officers; and (13) provide for offences and defences.

2975   Measuring instruments—non-prescribed instruments

The Measuring Instruments (Non-Prescribed Instruments) Regulations 2006, SI 2006/1270 (in force in part on 30 May 2006 and in part on 30 October 2006), implement EC European Parliament and Council Directive 2004/22 on measuring instruments in relation to those measuring instruments the legal metrological control of which is not regulated in the United Kingdom other than for use for trade for certain specified instruments. In particular, the regulations (1) authorise the appointment of notified bodies to conduct conformity assessments of such instruments intended to be placed on the market or put into service in other member states; (2) contain provision relating to the eligibility and designation of applicants to be notified bodies and with the administrative procedures relating to their appointment, functions and fees; (3) set out the ways by which manufacturers can demonstrate compliance with the essential requirements for placing on the market and putting into use; (4) list the different conformity assessment procedures available to a manufacturer to demonstrate compliance in relation to each measuring instrument; (5) set out the requirements relating to the marking of instruments and identification; and (6) provide for a presumption of conformity with other applicable directives conferred by the CE marking.

2976   Measuring instruments—taximeters

The Measuring Instruments (Taximeters) Regulations 2006, SI 2006/2304 (in force in part on 29 September 2006 and in part on 30 October 2006), implement EC European Parliament and Council Directive 2004/22 on measuring instruments in relation to taximeters. In particular, the regulations (1) apply, with certain exceptions, to taximeters intended for use for the protection of the consumers which are first placed on the market or put into use on or after the 30 October 2006; (2) specify the requirements for the placing on the market and putting into use of taximeters, which are (a) that taximeters must comply with the essential requirements and that the manufacturer has demonstrated such compliance; and (b) that taximeters must have the CE marking, the M marking and the identification number of the relevant notified body affixed to them; (3) contain provisions relating to the eligibility and designation of persons as notified bodies and the administrative procedures relating to their appointment, functions and fees; (4) set out the requirements relating to the marking of taximeters; (5) provide for a presumption of conformity of a taximeter with other applicable directives conferred by the CE marking; (6) provide for enforcement of the regulations by the Secretary of State and such persons as he appoints to act on his behalf; (7) detail the offences relating to the unauthorised application of authorised marks; (8) confer powers on the enforcement authorities to take action in respect of non-compliant taximeters; (9) provide powers of entry and inspection for enforcement officers; (10) provide for offences relating to the obstruction of an enforcement officer; and (11) provide for offences and penalties, and a defence of due diligence.

2977   Units of measurement—packaged goods

The Weights and Measures (Packaged Goods) Regulations 2006, SI 2006/659 (in force on 6 April 2006), replace the Weights and Measures Act 1985 Pt V (ss 47–68). The regulations provide for the control of packages containing products packed in constant nominal quantities by providing for the average system to apply to the quantity contained in each batch of packages which is made up and the implementation of European Union Directives on pre-packaged goods and on the units of measurement to be applied to such packages. In particular, the regulations (1) set out the three rules with which packers must comply in making up packages; (2) set out the information which must be marked on packages and outer containers and the circumstances in which the E-mark may be marked on a package or outer container; (3) provide that a person other than a packer or importer who marks an indication of nominal quantity on a package will become liable under the regulations as though he were a packer or importer; (4) set out specific requirements as to the marking of weight or volume on packages; (5) impose duties on packers and importers as to the measurement of the contents of packages, the checking of the contents and keeping of records; (6) provide for the enforcement of the regulations by local weights and measures authorities and matters connected therewith; (7) lay down penalties in respect of the making up and marking of packages and outer containers and keeping records of proposed markings; (8) lay down penalties in respect of the knowing sale of packages containing short measure or of packages which come from a batch that has failed the reference test; (9) prohibit the marking of the E-mark on packages except as permitted by the regulations; and (10) make the unauthorised disclosure of information concerning trade secrets and secret manufacturing processes an offence. SI 1986/2049 and SI 1992/1580 are revoked.

WILLS

Halsbury's Laws of England (4th edn) vol 50 (2005 Reissue) paras 301–763

Articles

For articles relating to this title please refer to the Table of Articles at the beginning of the Abridgment.

2978   Testamentary disposition—donee—disqualification from benefiting—wrongful act of donee—manslaughter

The Forfeiture Act 1982 s 3(1) provides that the rule in s 1, under which in certain circumstances a person who has unlawfully killed another is precluded from acquiring a benefit in consequence of the killing ('the forfeiture rule'), is not to be taken to preclude any person from making an application under any provision of the Inheritance (Provision for Family and Dependants) Act 1975 or the making of any order on the application.

The claimant was the only child of the deceased and the sole executor and beneficiary under her will. He lived with her throughout his life and cared for her in her latter years, leaving his job in order to be able to do so. The deceased refused to accept medical care but was eventually admitted to hospital suffering from severe bed sores consistent with her having been lying in one place for an extended period of time in her own excrement and urine. She died shortly afterwards. The claimant pleaded guilty to the manslaughter of his mother. He later sought a declaration that the rule against forfeiture did not apply to him, or that an order be made for the reasonable financial provision from the net estate of the deceased under the 1975 Act s 2. *Held*, the forfeiture rule applied to the type of manslaughter to which the claimant had pleaded guilty, with the result that the success of the claim turned on the court's interpretation of the 1982 Act s 3. On its true construction, s 3 had to be read in a way that enabled the court to deprive the wrongdoer of benefit from the estate when it was in the public interest to do so, but to confer a discretion to mitigate the harshness of the absolute rule where it was not in the public interest to deprive the wrongdoer of all benefit from the estate. Section 3 was designed to make clear that, even though the forfeiture rule had deprived unlawful killers of their succession rights, the forfeiture rule did not preclude the making of an application under the 1975 Act nor the making of an order. It followed that the 1982 Act s 3 permitted the court to make an order under the 1975 Act even though it was the forfeiture rule, and not the terms of the will itself, that meant no provision was made for the claimant. On the facts, the forfeiture rule did not serve the public interest. It deprived the one person who had devoted himself to the deceased's care without significant outside support of the benefit she intended for him and conferred it on remote relations most of whom had done nothing for her. In the circumstances the claimant's conduct did not disentitle him to the relief sought under the 1975 Act. Judgment would be given accordingly.

Land v Land [2006] EWHC 2069 (Ch), [2007] 1 All ER 324 (Chancery Division: Judge Norris QC). *Dunbar v Plant* [1998] Ch 412, CA (1997 Abr para 1942), applied. *Re Royse (deceased); Royse v Royse* [1985] Ch 22, CA (1984 Abr para 1057), considered.

2979   Testamentary intent—legacy—entitlement to further financial provision—domicile of testator

See *Cyganik v Agulian*, para 1303.

EUROPEAN COMMUNITIES

Halsbury's Laws of England (4th edn) vols 51 and 52

Articles

For articles relating to this title please refer to the Table of Articles at the beginning of the Abridgment.
The arrangement of the material conforms with vols 51 and 52.

THE COMMUNITIES

2980   Community treaty—agreement between member states and Swiss Confederation—agreement to combat fraud

The European Communities (Definition of Treaties) (Co-operation Agreement between the European Community and its Member States and the Swiss Confederation to Combat Fraud) Order 2006, SI 2006/307 (in force on a date to be notified in the London, Edinburgh and Belfast Gazettes), declares the Co-operation Agreement between the European Community and its member states and the Swiss Confederation, on the combat of fraud and any other illegal activity to the detriment of their financial interests to be a Community treaty as defined in the European Communities Act 1972 s 1(2).

THE COURT OF JUSTICE

2981   Actions—damages—admissibility—action having same effect as action for annulment

The applicants had repeatedly refused to comply with an obligation to disclose the annual accounts of two companies of which they were managers. The Austrian authorities imposed penalties on the applicants in accordance with Austrian law. The applicants contested some of the penalties on the basis that they had been imposed pursuant to the implementation of certain provisions of two invalid EC directives. Their action was dismissed and they brought an action for damages under the EC Treaty art 288, which required the European Community to make good any damage caused by its institutions. *Held*, art 288 differed from an action for annulment in that its end was not the abolition of a particular measure but compensation for damage caused by a Community institution. An action under art 288 was therefore inadmissible where it was aimed at securing the withdrawal of a measure which had become definitive and which would, if upheld, nullify the legal effects of that measure. The applicants were seeking compensation for loss suffered in consequence of the penalties imposed on them on the basis of national law implementing the disputed provisions of the directives. It followed that they were seeking the same result as would be obtained if the penalties decisions taken by the Austrian authorities were annulled, a matter which fell outside the jurisdiction of the European Court of First Instance. The action was inadmissible and, accordingly, it would be dismissed.

Case T-47/02 *Danzer v EU Council* [2006] 3 CMLR 633 (CFI: Third Chamber). Case T-178/98 *Fresh Marine Co SA v European Commission* [2001] 3 CMLR 743, CFI, applied.

2982   Reference from national court—power to refer question—level of doubt concerning validity of law

The applicants were an international airline association and an unincorporated association, which represented the interests of certain European low-fare airlines. The applicants made an application for judicial review against the respondent Department for Transport relating to the implementation of EC Parliament and Council Regulation 261/2004. The court ordered a stay of proceedings and referred certain questions to the European Court of Justice for a preliminary ruling on the validity of Regulation 261/2004 arts 5, 6, 7, and on whether EC Treaty art 234 required a national court to refer a question on the validity of Community legislation only if there was more than a certain degree of doubt concerning its validity. *Held*, where a court, against whose decisions there was a judicial remedy under national law, considered that arguments, as to the validity of Community legislation, which had been put forward by the parties or raised by its own motion were well founded, it had to stay proceedings and make a reference to the European Court of Justice for a preliminary ruling on the validity of the legislation. In the present case, examination of the questions referred to the court had revealed no factor so as to affect the validity of Regulation 261/2004 arts 5, 6, 7. Article 6 was not inconsistent with provisions of the Montreal Convention, which recognised the importance of the interests of consumers in international carriage by air and the need for equitable compensation based on the principle of restitution, where Regulation 261/2004 art 6 enhanced the protection afforded to passengers' interests and improved the conditions under which the principle of restitution was applicable to passengers. Further, arts 5, 6, 7 were not invalid by reason of breach of the principle of legal certainty, or of the obligation to state reasons, or by reason of an infringement of the principle of proportionality. Judgment would be given accordingly.

Case C-344/04 R (*on the application of International Air Transport Association*) *v Department for Transport* [2006] 2 CMLR 557 (ECJ: Grand Chamber).

APPLICATION OF COMMUNITY LAW IN NATIONAL COURTS

2983   Community law—consultation—insider dealing

See Case C-384/02 *Criminal proceedings against Grongaard*, para 537.

2984 Community obligation—infringement—liability of state to make good damage caused to individuals—infringement by court decision

The applicant's claim before an Italian court of unfair competition failed. He appealed, contending that the court had interpreted Community rules on state aid incorrectly so that a preliminary ruling should be made to the European Court of Justice for guidance on the matter. The appeal court refused the request, and the applicant then instituted proceedings against the respondent state for compensation for damage suffered as a result of the errors of interpretation committed by the original court and the breach of its obligation to make a reference for a preliminary ruling. It fell to be determined whether national legislation relating to state liability for judicial errors impeded affirmation of that liability where it precluded liability in relation to the interpretation of provisions of law and assessment of facts and of the evidence adduced in the course of the exercise of judicial functions, and limited state liability solely to cases of intentional fault and serious misconduct on the part of the court. *Held*, Community law precluded national legislation which excluded state liability, in a general manner, for damage caused to individuals by an infringement of Community law attributable to a court adjudicating at last instance by reason of the fact that the infringement in question resulted from an interpretation of provisions of law or an assessment of facts or evidence carried out by that court. Community law also precluded national legislation which limited such liability solely to cases of intentional fault and serious misconduct on the part of the court, if such a limitation were to lead to exclusion of the liability of the member state concerned in other cases where a manifest infringement of the applicable law was committed.

Case C-173/03 *Traghetti del Mediterraneo SpA v Italy* [2006] All ER (EC) 983 (ECJ: Grand Chamber). Case C-224/01 *Köbler v Austria* [2004] QB 848, ECJ (2003 Abr para 2823), considered.

2985 European Commission decision—duty of domestic court to follow—primacy over judgment of European Court of Justice

The claimant contracted to take leases of two public houses from the defendant. The leases contained ties which obliged the claimant to buy his beer from the second defendant at its list prices. The claimant was unable to compete with public houses which were able to sell beer at lower prices, and his business failed. The second defendant brought proceedings against the claimant for the sum outstanding on his beer account. The claimant counterclaimed against the defendants for damages, alleging that the losses had been caused by the tie agreement which had the effect of restricting or distorting competition contrary to the EC Treaty art 81. In reliance on a European Court of Justice case concerning beer supply agreements, the judge decided that there had been no infringement of art 81. However, that decision conflicted with the view taken by the European Commission in a review of beer-tie agreements in the United Kingdom. The claimant appealed, arguing that the view of the Commission should take precedence and that the judge should have treated it as effectively, albeit not formally, binding on him. The court accepted that argument and allowed the appeal. On the defendant's appeal against that ruling, *held*, when there was no question of a conflict of decisions, the decision of the Commission was simply evidence properly admissible before the English court which, given the expertise of the Commission, might well be regarded by that court as highly persuasive. As a matter of law, however, it was only part of the evidence which the court would take into account. If, on assessment of all the evidence, the judge came to the conclusion that the view of the Commission was wrong, he could not, consistently with his judicial oath, say that as a matter of deference he proposed nevertheless to follow the Commission. In the present case, the judge was right in deciding that he could decide on the relevance of the Court of Justice case for himself, and the appellate court was wrong to reverse his decision on the ground that he should have followed the Commission. Accordingly, the appeal would be allowed.

Crehan v Inntrepreneur Pub Co (CPC) [2006] UKHL 38, [2006] 4 All ER 465 (House of Lords: Lords Bingham of Cornhill, Nicholls of Birkenhead, Hoffmann, Rodger of Earlsferry and Walker of Gestingthorpe). Decision of Court of Appeal [2004] EWCA Civ 637, [2004] All ER (D) 322 (May) (2004 Abr para 1715) reversed.

2986 European Commission decision—requirement to state reasons—scope of obligation

The French post office entered into an agreement with a company incorporated under private law in which it had a shareholding ('the subsidiary'), which had been entrusted with the management of the post office's international express delivery service, to provide it with logistical and commercial assistance. This included the transfer of the client base of a post office company to the subsidiary. The applicants were a group of delivery companies which were in competition with the subsidiary and their trade association. The applicants lodged a complaint with the Commission alleging that the assistance provided by the post office to the subsidiary constituted a state aid within the meaning of the EC Treaty art 92. The Commission considered that, in essence, the assistance given was that given from a parent to a subsidiary under normal market conditions and adopted EC Commission Decision 98/365, which stated that various measures of logistical and commercial assistance provided by the post office to the subsidiary did not constitute state aid. The applicants applied to the Court of First Instance for annulment of that decision. *Held*, where the Commission adopted a decision art 190 required it to state the reasons on which it was based. The scope of the obligation to provide a statement of reasons had to be assessed by reference to the circumstances of each case which could, in an appropriate case, justify a more detailed statement of reasons. The disputed decision dealt with the complex question, in the context of the application of the provisions on state aid, of the calculation of the costs of a parent company operating in a reserved market which provided logistical and commercial assistance to a subsidiary which did not operate in a reserved market. In these circumstances a more detailed statement of reasons was justified. As the Commission's statement of reasons had been limited to a very general explanation of the method it had followed, the contested decision had to be annulled for defective reasoning in so far as it concluded that the logistical and commercial assistance provided by the post office to the subsidiary did not constitute state aid. The concept of state aid had a very wide scope. The aim of art 92 was to prevent trade between member states from being affected by advantages granted by public authorities which distorted or threatened to distort competition by favouring certain undertakings or certain products. It followed that aid covered not only positive benefits, such as subsidies, but also interventions which mitigated the charges which were normally included in the budget of an undertaking and which were similar in character to subsidies and had the same effect. The supply of goods or services on preferential terms was one of the indirect advantages which had the same effects as subsidies. The client base transferred to the subsidiary by the post office was an intangible asset which had an economic value and its transfer constituted a state aid. Consequently, the contested decision had to be annulled in so far as it provided that the transfer of the client base had not constituted state aid.

Case T-613/97 *Union Française de L'express (UFEX) v European Commission* [2006] 3 CMLR 527 (CFI: Third Chamber).

EC Treaty arts 92, 190 now arts 87, 253.

INDUSTRIAL POLICY AND INTERNAL MARKET

2987   Industrial policy—harmonisation of national laws—validity of Community legislation

The applicant sought to annul EC Parliament and Council Regulation 2065/2003 on the ground that the EC Treaty art 95 had not been a correct legal basis for the adoption of Regulation 2065/2003. It argued that the purpose of Regulation 2065/2003 was the establishment of a centralised procedure for the authorisation at Community level of smoke flavourings for food, rather than the harmonisation of national laws, and that the EC Treaty art 95 provided a power to harmonise national laws, not to establish Community bodies or confer tasks on such bodies. Further, it argued that, since the measures provided for by Regulation 2065/2003 left open the question of which smoke flavourings were authorised, the essential aspects of the use and marketing of the smoke flavourings were not thereby harmonised. The respondent submitted that the EC Treaty art 95 did not require all the details of measures approximating the laws of the member states to be set out, and left a discretion as to the legislative technique to be followed, provided that the essential elements of the matter to be regulated were contained in the legislation. *Held*, the expression 'measures for the approximation' was intended to confer on the Community legislature a discretion, depending on the general context and the specific matter to be harmonised, as to the harmonisation technique most appropriate for achieving the desired result. Where the legislature provided for a harmonisation which comprised several stages, two conditions had to be satisfied. Firstly, the legislature had to determine the essential elements of the harmonising measure in question. Secondly, the mechanism for implementing those elements had to be designed in such a way as to lead to a harmonisation within the meaning of the EC Treaty art 95. Regulation 2065/2003 contained the essential elements typifying a harmonisation measure. For example, it defined the parameters for the evaluation and authorisation of primary smoke condensates and primary tar fractions used or intended for use as such in or on foods. It also provided for a procedure which constituted an appropriate method of achieving the desired approximation. Regulation 2065/2003 was rightly based on the EC Treaty art 95 and, accordingly, the application would be dismissed.

Case C-66/04 *United Kingdom v European Parliament* [2006] All ER (EC) 487 (ECJ: Grand Chamber).

STATE AIDS AND REGIONAL POLICY

2988   State aid—concept of state aid—Commission decision that activity was not state aid—national post office providing commercial subsidiary with commercial and logistical assistance

See Case T-613/97 *Union Française de L'express (UFEX) v European Commission*, para 2986.

ENVIRONMENT AND CONSUMERS

See PROTECTION OF ENVIRONMENT AND PUBLIC HEALTH; SALE OF GOODS AND SUPPLY OF SERVICES.

CUSTOMS UNION AND FREE MOVEMENT OF GOODS

See CUSTOMS AND EXCISE.

AGRICULTURE
See AGRICULTURE.

FREEDOM OF MOVEMENT FOR WORKERS

2989   European Union (Accessions) Act 2006

The European Union (Accessions) Act 2006 makes provision consequential on the treaty ('the Accession Treaty') concerning the accession of the Republic of Bulgaria and Romania to the European Union, signed at Luxembourg on 25 April 2005, and in relation to the entitlement of nationals of those states to enter or reside in the United Kingdom as workers. The Act received the royal assent on 16 February 2006 and came into force on that day.

Section 1 includes the Accession Treaty within the list of treaties implemented by the European Communities Act 1972 in United Kingdom law, and approves, for the purpose of the European Parliamentary Elections Act 2002, the provisions of the Accession Treaty in so far as they relate to the powers of the European Parliament. By virtue of the 2006 Act s 2, the Secretary of State is empowered to make regulations implementing the transitional arrangements concerning the free movement of Bulgarian and Romanian workers. Section 3 deals with short title.

2990   Material scope—discriminatory taxation—double taxation agreement between member states

The taxpayers were assessed to income tax in Germany where they were employed. They owned and lived in a private house in France and requested that negative income deriving from their use of the house be taken into account. A double taxation agreement between Germany and France provided that, while income derived from the use of immovable property was taxable only in the state in which it was situated, the German authorities retained the right to take account of such income for the purpose of determining the rate applicable to taxes payable in Germany. However, German law stated that, in the absence of positive income from the letting of property in another state, no account would be taken of income losses of the same kind incurred in that state for the purpose of determining the rate of taxation. The taxpayers' appeal against the assessment was dismissed. A question was referred to the European Court of Justice as to whether the rules of the EC Treaty relating to freedom of establishment or freedom of capital precluded the national legislation. *Held, art* 39 had to be interpreted as precluding national legislation which did not permit natural persons in receipt of income from employment in one member state, and assessable to tax on their total income there, to have income losses relating to their own use of a private dwelling in another member state taken into account for the purposes of determining the rate of taxation applicable to their income in the former state, whereas positive rental income relating to such a dwelling was taken into account. Neither the rules relating to freedom of establishment nor those relating to free movement of capital were applicable. However, any Community national who had exercised the right to freedom of movement for workers and who had been employed in a member state other than that of residence fell within the scope of art 39. Even though the national legislation was not directed at non-residents, the latter were more likely to own a home outside Germany. Therefore, the treatment of non-workers was less favourable than that afforded to workers who resided in Germany in their own homes and, accordingly, the legislation was contrary to art 39.

Case C-152/03 *Ritter-Coulais v Finanzamt Germersheim* [2006] All ER (EC) 613 (ECJ: Grand Chamber).

2991   Material scope—migrant worker—incapacity benefit for disabled young people—residence requirement

The claimants received work-incapacity benefit pursuant to a Dutch law which established compulsory general insurance for the whole of the population against the financial consequences of long-term incapacity for work. That benefit was later converted into one aimed at protecting disabled young people against the financial consequences of long-term incapacity for work. The claimants took up residence in other member states, on the basis of which the defendant, the management board of the body entrusted with implementing employee insurance contributions, decided the claimants had become ineligible to receive the benefit. The claimants challenged the decision in the national court, which stayed the proceedings and referred to the European Court of Justice the question of whether a benefit for disabled young people, which was listed in EC Council Regulation 1408/71 Annex IIa, constituted a special non-contributory benefit, as referred to in art 4(2a), with the result that the position of individuals such as the claimants was governed exclusively by the coordinating regime introduced by art 10a so that the benefit could be paid only to persons normally resident in the member state. *Held*, such a benefit could not be paid to any person residing outside the member state. Having regard to case law, a 'special benefit' within the meaning of art 4(2a) was defined by its purpose. It had to either replace or supplement a social security benefit and be by its nature social assistance justified on economic and social grounds and fixed by legislation setting objective criteria. By guaranteeing a minimum income to a socially disadvantaged group (disabled young people), the benefit in question was by its nature social assistance justified on economic and social grounds, granted according to objective criteria defined by law. Moreover, the resources necessary for financing the benefit were from public funds, were not financed, either directly or indirectly, from contributions, and were therefore not contributory in nature.

Case C-154/05 *Kersbergen-Lap v Raad van Bestuur van het Uitvoeringsinstituut Werknemersverzekeringen* [2006] All ER (D) 62 (Jul) (ECJ: Third Chamber).

2992 Material scope—migrant worker—jobseeker's allowance—habitual residence

The claimant was born in the United States of America and had dual United States and Irish nationality. He had spent some time in the United Kingdom doing casual and part-time work, and later decided to settle in the United Kingdom and find full-time work. He applied for jobseeker's allowance, which was refused by the defendant on the ground that the claimant was not habitually resident in the United Kingdom. The claimant appealed to a social security commissioner, who stayed the proceedings and sought a preliminary ruling from the European Court of Justice on the interpretation of the EC Treaty art 48, EC Council Regulation 1612/68 and EC Council Directive 68/360. The European Court ruled that member states were not precluded from making legislation which made entitlement to jobseeker's allowance conditional on a residence requirement, in so far as that requirement might be justified on the basis of objective considerations that were independent of the nationality of the person concerned. The commissioner then decided that a habitual residence test was not the only method of establishing the requisite link between a claimant for jobseeker's allowance and the United Kingdom employment market, and that the application of a habitual residence test should be subject to the proviso that, if the relevant authority was satisfied on other grounds that the requisite link existed, then there was no legitimate role for any additional test of habitual residence. The commissioner again refused the claim, and the claimant appealed. *Held*, the question whether the search for work was genuine was not the sole question to be considered; there was an additional and different question as to whether a genuine link had been established with the United Kingdom employment market. Facts which were relevant to the latter issue might not be relevant to the former issue. Hence there was, in principle, scope for a residence test which imported factors which might be irrelevant to the question of whether the search for work was genuine. A habitual residence test simpliciter as a means of establishing the requisite genuine link between an applicant for jobseeker's allowance and the United Kingdom employment market was fully compatible with Community law. However, a requirement of residence in a particular member state as a condition of eligibility for an allowance in the nature of a social advantage which was available in that member state was conceptually at odds with the status of a citizen of the European Union and the rights attaching to that status. It followed that any consideration of the extent to which such a requirement was compatible with Community law called for an approach which tended towards restricting the scope of the requirement, rather than widening it. In the context of the jobseeker's allowance, while there was a logical connection between a requirement of residence in the United Kingom and the establishment of a genuine link with the United Kingdom employment market, there was no logical connection between such a requirement and a requirement that an applicant for jobseeker's allowance should be actively seeking work in the United Kingdom. In every case, it had to be question of fact whether the claimant was actively seeking work in the United Kingdom, and it was not possible to see how the fact that the claimant might have met a requirement of residence in the United Kingdom could assist in the resolution of that question. Accordingly, the appeal would be dismissed.

Collins v Secretary of State for Work and Pensions [2006] EWCA Civ 376, [2006] 1 WLR 2391 (Court of Appeal: Brooke, Jonathan Parker and Maurice Kay LJJ).

2993 Material scope—migrant worker—right of residence—child of Turkish migrant worker—deportation order following imprisonment

The applicant was born in Germany to a migrant Turkish worker. After finishing a period of vocational training the applicant had periods of employment and unemployment. He developed a drug addiction and was sentenced to a total of over three years' imprisonment on his conviction of armed robbery and the illegal acquisition of narcotics. The local authorities ordered his expulsion from Germany and threatened to deport him. He challenged that decision and the court sought a ruling from the European Court of Justice. *Held*, under the EEC-Turkey Association Council Decision 1/80 art 7, children of a Turkish worker who had completed a vocational course of training in the host state were entitled to take up employment there. It was established that art 7 had direct effect, that the rights conferred by the provision were necessarily a concomitant right of residence for the child and that the right of residence could only be restricted in accordance with art 14(1), which referred to grounds of public policy, public security and public health, or because the child had left the territory for a significant period of time. It followed that, in contrast to the position of a Turkish worker whose right of residence was conferred by art 6, a child of a Turkish worker could not be deprived of his rights under art 7 because he was unemployed on account of being imprisoned for three years.

Case C-502/04 *Torun v Stadt Augsburg* [2006] 2 CMLR 1287 (ECJ: Second Chamber).

2994   Material scope—non-Community national married to Community national—residence in third country—right to work in spouse's state

See Case C-10/05 *Mattern v Ministre du Travail et de l'Emploi*, para 364.

2995   Material scope—social security benefits—occupational disease—calculation of average earnings

See Case C-205/05 *Nemec v Caisse regionale d'assurance maladie du Nord-Est*, para 2622.

RIGHT OF ESTABLISHMENT AND FREEDOM TO PROVIDE SERVICES

2996   Freedom to provide services—control measures—conditions imposed on undertakings posting nationals of non-member states—proportionality

German law provided that nationals of non-member states had to obtain a residence permit in the form of a visa to enter and stay on German territory. Such individuals who intended to reside in Germany for more than three months and pursue salaried employment were required to be in possession of a specific residence visa. Undertakings which intended to provide services in Germany were required to ensure that their workers from third countries obtained a visa at the German diplomatic representation in the member state where the undertaking was established. The application had to fulfil various criteria, such as the specification of the beginning and end dates of the worker's posting and the provision of an assurance that worker had been employed for at least a year and would continue to be employed after the posting. The Commission of the European Communities sought a declaration that the legislation was incompatible with the EC Treaty art 49, which prohibited restrictions on the freedom to provide services. *Held*, legislation which made the provision of services by an undertaking established in another member state subject to the issue of an administrative visa constituted a restriction on the freedom to provide services. However, member states were entitled to impose control measures relating to the public interest where that interest was not already otherwise safeguarded and in so far as it was appropriate and necessary for securing the attainment of the objective being pursued. The public interest grounds relied on by the German government related to the prevention of abuse of the freedom to provide services and the protection of workers. A requirement that the service provider furnished a simple prior declaration certifying that the situation of the workers concerned was lawful would be less restrictive but as effective to guarantee that those workers' situation was lawful. Additionally, a requirement that the undertaking should at the same time report to the local authorities on the presence of the workers, the anticipated duration of their presence and the service justifying their deployment would be a more proportionate means than the check in advance of posting, and would enable the authorities to monitor compliance with German social welfare legislation during the deployment. The control measures requiring checks in advance of posting therefore exceeded what was necessary to prevent abuse of the freedom to provide services and to pursue the objective of protection of the workers.

Case C-244/04 *Re Work Visa Regime; EC Commission v Germany* [2006] 2 CMLR 631 (ECJ: First Chamber).

2997   Freedom to provide services—legal services—registration—appeal—composition of appellate body

European Parliament and EC Council Directive 98/5 art 3 provides that a lawyer who wishes to practise in a member state other than that in which he obtained his professional qualification must register with the competent authority in that state. Decisions not to effect the registration referred to in art 3 or to cancel such registration and decisions imposing disciplinary measures must state the reasons on which they are based, and a remedy must be available against such decisions before a court or tribunal in accordance with the provisions of domestic law: art 9.

The applicant was a United Kingdom national who had practised as a lawyer in Luxembourg for several years. The Bar Council of the Grand Duchy of Luxembourg refused to register him in the list of lawyers practising under its home-country professional title in the Bar Register, stating that he had refused to attend a hearing and that it was therefore not in a position to ascertain whether he was proficient in languages, as required by statute. By law, where registration was refused the lawyer could appeal to a disciplinary committee, which was to include five lawyers. An appeal could also be made against the committee's decision. The applicant's appeal against the refusal of his registration was stayed and a number of questions concerning the interpretation of Directive 98/5 arts 3 and 9 were referred to the European Court of Justice. *Held*, art 9 had to be interpreted as precluding an appeal procedure in which the decision refusing registration, referred to in art 3, had to be challenged at first instance before a body composed exclusively of lawyers practising under the professional title of the host member state and on appeal before a body composed for the most part of such lawyers, where the appeal before the Supreme Court of that member state permitted judicial review of the law only and not the facts. The guarantees of independence and impartiality required rules, particularly as regards the composition of that body and appointment, length of service and the grounds for abstention, rejection and dismissal of its members, in order to dismiss any reasonable doubt in the minds of individuals as to the imperviousness of that body to external factors and its neutrality with respect to the interest before it. Moreover, art 3 had to be interpreted as meaning that the registration of a lawyer with the competent authority of a member state other than the state where he had obtained his qualification in order to practise there under his home country professional title could not be made subject to a prior examination of his proficiency in the languages of the host member state. Directive 98/5 was intended to put an end to the differences in national rules on the conditions for registration with the competent authorities which gave rise to inequalities and obstacles to free movement.

Case C-506/04 *Wilson v Ordre des avocats du barreau de Luxembourg* [2006] All ER (D) 89 (Sep) (ECJ: Grand Chamber).

2998　Freedom to provide services—medical care—entitlement to receive treatment in another member state and claim reimbursement of costs

See Case C-372/04 *R (on the application of Watts) v Bedford Primary Care Trust*, para 2624.

2999　Freedom to provide services—public service contracts—tendering procedure—failure to meet prescribed obligations

See Case C-226/04 *La Cascina Soc Coop arl v Ministero della Difesa*; Case C-228/04 *Consorzio GFM v Ministero della Difesa*, para 397.

3000　Freedom to provide services—services provided by non-resident—retention of tax at source by recipient

The taxpayer, a concert organiser with a registered office in Germany, concluded a contract with a person who made a music group available to it. That person was established in the Netherlands but of unknown nationality. The taxpayer paid for the services provided but did not make the retention of tax at source prescribed by German law. In proceedings by the tax authority for payment of the tax, questions arose as to the interpretation of the EC Treaty arts 49, 50. *Held*, arts 49, 50 did not preclude national legislation under which a procedure of retention of tax at source was applied to payments made to providers of services not resident in the member state in which the services were provided, but not to payments made to providers of services who were resident in that member state, or national legislation under which liability was incurred by a recipient of services who had failed to make the required retention at source. However, arts 49, 50 precluded national legislation which did not allow a taxpayer which had paid for and received services provided by a non-resident to deduct business expenses directly linked to the activity in question, and incurred in the member state in which the services were provided, when making a retention of tax at source.

Case C-290/04 *FKP Scorpio Konzertproduktionen GmbH v Finanzamt Hamburg-Eimsbuttel* [2006] All ER (D) 31 (Oct) (ECJ: Grand Chamber).

3001　Freedom to provide services—tax advice and assistance—exclusive right of tax advice centres

The claimant, a company established in Italy, provided accounting advice. It decided to change its constitution to reflect the fact that it was also providing tax assistance. However, the defendant, a notary, refused to file the company's decision in the local companies registry on the ground that the amendment would be contrary to national law, which provided that tax advice centres had exclusive authority to assist taxpayers and to deliver and file tax declarations. A tax advice centre had to be constituted as a public limited company which carried on its business under authorisation from the Ministry of Finance. The ability to set up a tax advice centre was limited to specified types of legal entity, and appeared to be limited to those established in Italy. The claimant's application for an order that the decision be filed was dismissed. On its appeal, a preliminary ruling was sought from the European Court of Justice on whether the exclusivity rule was a restriction on the right of establishment and the freedom to provide services contrary to the EC Treaty arts 43, 49. *Held*, the restriction on the ability to form a tax advice centre to certain types of legal entity made it difficult or impossible for economic operators from other member states to establish themselves in Italy to provide tax assistance. Although some of the work undertaken by tax advice centres was complex, the organisations authorised to set up tax advice centres did not appear to offer any guarantees of particular professional abilities to accomplish those tasks. It followed that the grant of the exclusive power to provide certain tax advice and assistance services to tax advice centres was not justified in the public interest, and so contravened arts 43, 49.

Case C-451/03 *Servizi Ausiliari Dottori Commercialisti Srl v Calafiori* [2006] 2 CMLR 1135 (ECJ: Third Chamber).

3002　General—prohibition of discrimination—tax exemption—exemption applicable where parent company resident in United Kingdom—double taxation agreement

United Kingdom corporation tax legislation provided that advance corporation tax was to be paid when a company distributed dividends. A United Kingdom subsidiary company which made a distribution to its parent company could elect to make a joint declaration with its parent company and avoid the advanced corporation tax payment if the parent company was based in the United

Kingdom. The claimants were the subsidiaries of companies based in Italy and the Netherlands as well as the Italian and Dutch companies themselves. Following a ruling by the European Court of Justice, which held that the denial of the right of election to holding companies established in member states other than the United Kingdom was contrary to the freedom of establishment conferred by the EC Treaty art 43, the claimants brought an action for compensation in respect of advance corporation tax that they had paid. The Revenue contended that the double taxation agreements between the United Kingdom and Italy and the Netherlands entitled the Italian and Dutch companies to a tax credit in respect of dividends paid to them by their subsidiaries which constituted an advantage that extinguished or reduced the claimants' compensation. The judge rejected the Revenue's submissions and the Revenue appealed. The appeal was dismissed. On the Revenue's further appeal, *held,* on the true construction of the double taxation agreements the parent companies would not have been entitled to tax credits in respect of dividends paid to them by the United Kingdom holding company as group income under a group income election and, therefore, without incurring any liability to pay advance corporation tax. There was no doubt about the character of the dividends assumed to have been received by the parent companies and in respect of which it was to be assumed that they had claimed tax credits. They were dividends assumed to have been paid under a group income election jointly made by the subsidiaries and the parents. An individual company had to be attributed with the ability to receive dividends of that character. If that was the right approach, the individual company which had received dividends of that character would not have been entitled to a tax credit and, consequently, nor would the parent companies. The correct analysis was that the infringements of which the claimants complained were infringements of the parent companies' rights to freedom of establishment in the United Kingdom. The primary measure of the loss thus caused was the financial detriment to their United Kingdom subsidiary caused by its liability to pay advance corporation tax but its inability to make group income elections. However, the benefit of the tax credits that the parent companies would not have received but for the infringements should be brought into account. Accordingly the appeal would be allowed.

Pirelli Cable Holdings NV v IRC [2006] UKHL 4, [2006] 77 TC 409 (House of Lords: Lords Nicholls of Birkenhead, Hope of Craighead, Scott of Foscote, Walker of Gestingthorpe and Brown of Eaton-under-Heywood). Decision of Court of Appeal [2003] EWCA Civ 1849, [2003] STC 250, (2004 Abr para 2972) reversed.

Advance corporation tax abolished by Finance Act 1998 s 31 as from 6 April 1999.

3003   Right of establishment—companies—cross-border mergers

See Case C-411/03 *Re SEVIC Systems AG,* para 523.

3004   Right of establishment—companies—subsidiaries established in another member state—tax avoidance

See Case C-196/04 *Cadbury Schweppes plc v IRC,* para 1642.

3005   Right of establishment—discriminatory taxation—corporation tax—branch of company established in another member state

See Case C-253/03 *CLT-UFA SA v Finanzamt Köln-West,* para 1644.

3006   Right of establishment—discriminatory taxation—corporation tax—deduction of costs relating to shareholdings

See Case C-471/04 *Finanzamt Offenbach am Main-Land v Keller Holding GmbH,* para 1645.

3007   Right of establishment—mutual recognition of qualifications—engineer

An Italian national who held a diploma in civil engineering specialising in hydraulics applied to the Spanish Ministry of Development for recognition of his diploma in order to take up the profession of civil engineer in Spain. The ministry recognised the diploma and granted the national unconditional permission to take up the profession. The applicant, an institution of civil engineers, brought an action for annulment of the decision. The action was dismissed on the basis that the diploma of civil engineer specialising in hydraulics conferred, in Italy, the right to take up the same profession as that of civil engineer in Spain. On appeal by the applicant, the court decided that there were important material differences between the two courses of education and training so that the lower court's assessment was incorrect. It fell to be determined whether (1) when the holder of a diploma awarded in one member state applied for permission to take up a regulated profession in another member state, the competent authorities of that member state were precluded by EC Council Directive 89/48 from partly allowing that application, subject to certain conditions, by limiting the scope of the permission to the activities which that diploma allowed to be taken up in the member state in which it was obtained; and (2) in the present case, the EC Treaty arts 39 and 43 prevented the host member state from excluding the possibility of the partial taking up of a regulated profession, restricted to the pursuit of one or more activities covered by that profession. *Held,* when the holder of a diploma awarded in one member state applied for permission to take up a regulated profession in another member state, the competent authorities of that member state were not precluded by Directive 89/48 from partly allowing that application, if the holder of the diploma so requested, by limiting the scope of the permission to those activities which that diploma allowed to be taken up in the member state in which it was obtained. Moreover, the EC Treaty arts 39 and 43 did not preclude a member state from not allowing a partial taking up of a profession, where shortcomings in the education or training of the party concerned in relation to that required in the host member state might be effectively made up for through the application of the compensatory measures provided for in Directive 89/49 art 4(1). However, the EC Treaty arts 39 and 43 did preclude a member state from not allowing that partial taking up when the party concerned so requested and the differences between the fields of activity were so great that, in reality, a full programme of education and training was required, unless the refusal for that partial taking up was justified by overriding reasons based on the general interest, suitable for securing the attainment of the objective which it pursued and not going beyond what was necessary in order to attain that objective.

Case C-330/03 *Colegio de Ingenieros de Caminos, Canales y Puertos v Administracion del Estrado* [2006] 2 CMLR 709 (ECJ: First Chamber).

3008   Right of establishment—specific sectors—auctioneers—mutual recognition of qualifications

The applicant held a qualification which was accredited by the Royal Institute of Chartered Surveyors. He wished to pursue the profession of director of voluntary sales in France. He submitted an application to the respondent, which was the authority for voluntary sales of chattels by public auction in France, for the recognition of diplomas, certificates or other evidence of education. The respondent requested that the applicant undergo an aptitude test. The applicant brought proceedings in the French appeal court against the decision, claiming that it deprived him of the opportunity to choose between an adaptation period and an aptitude test and therefore infringed EC Council Directive 92/51, on the recognition of diplomas awarded on completion of professional education and training. The respondent claimed to be entitled, under art 4(1)(b), to retain the right to choose between an adaptation period and an aptitude test because the pursuit of the profession concerned required a precise knowledge of domestic law and had as an essential characteristic the provision of advice and assistance concerning domestic law. The court referred the case to the European Court of Justice for a preliminary ruling on whether the Directive applied to the profession and, if so, whether the respondent could exercise the right to choose between imposing an adaptation period or an aptitude test. *Held*, Directive 92/51 did not apply to an applicant relying on qualifications such as those on which the applicant was relying and wishing to pursue the profession of director of voluntary sales of chattels by public auction in France. However, EC Council Directive 89/48 might apply to such an applicant if the profession was not a regulated profession, within the meaning of Directive 89/48, in the member state in which the applicant acquired the qualifications on which he was relying. It was for the domestic court to determine whether that was the case.

Case C-149/05 *Price v Conseil des Ventes Volontaires de Meubles aux Enchères Publiques* [2006] All ER (D) 42 (Sep) (ECJ: First Chamber).

3009   Right of establishment—tax advice and assistance—exclusive right of tax advice centres

See Case C-451/03 *Servizi Ausiliari Dottori Commercialisti Srl v Calafiori*, para 3001.

3010   Specific sectors—insurance—insurance services—insurance company—failure to implement directive

The claimants were underwriting names at Lloyd's who each participated in the writing of insurance business by Lloyd's syndicates. The liabilities of each syndicate included liabilities incurred but not reported in respect of insurance business written in previous years and necessitated the fixing of reserves at a level sufficient to meet all liabilities. The claimants brought proceedings against the defendant claiming that they had suffered economic loss because of the failure of the government to implement promptly EC Council Directive 73/239 on the co-ordination of laws, regulations and administrative provisions relating to the taking-up and pursuit of the business of direct insurance other than life assurance. The claimants contended that, by reason of the failure to implement the Directive 73/239, the defendant had failed to secure that there was an adequate system of accounting for ensuring that the reserves of syndicates were sufficient to meet liabilities. Had the defendant acted as it was alleged that it should have done, the names would not have joined Lloyd's or increased their underwriting and so not suffered the loss alleged. The defendant argued that, if Directive 73/239 entailed any grant of rights to individuals, it was limited to a grant to insurers of the right of freedom of establishment and did not grant rights to the claimants and that, in any event, the claims were time-barred. The claimants argued that time did not begin to run until the date on which Directive 73/239 had been fully transposed or that it did not begin to run earlier than the date on which the claimants knew or were in a position to have known of the failure of the defendant to transpose Directive 73/239. *Held*, the result prescribed by Directive 73/239 did not entail the grant of rights to persons in the position of the claimants. The European Community, acting through the European

Commission, had the right to require transposition of directives into national law. Individuals had no such right. In any event, the claims would have been time barred. Prior to the relevant limitation date, the claimants had been aware of the Community requirements and their possible relevance to the alleged regulatory failures by the state, which they believed had, at least in part, caused the losses. Accordingly, the claims would be dismissed.

Poole v Her Majesty's Treasury [2006] EWHC 2731 (Comm), [2007] 1 All ER (Comm) 255 (Queen's Bench Division: Langley J).

3011 Specific sectors—professional qualifications—recognition

The European Communities (Recognition of Qualifications and Experience) (Third General System) (Amendment) Regulations 2006, SI 2006/2228 (in force on 2 October 2006), further amend the 2002 Regulations, SI 2002/1597, so as to provide that the Secretary of State delegates the function of issuing certificates of experience to ECCTIS Limited.

The European Communities (Recognition of Professional Qualifications) (Second General System) (Amendment) Regulations 2006, SI 2006/3214 (in force on 1 January 2007), further amend the 2002 Regulations supra, so as to give effect in the United Kingdom to EC Council Directive 2006/100 adapting certain directives in the field of freedom of movement of persons, by reason of the accession of the Republics of Bulgaria and Romania to the European Union.

FREEDOM OF MOVEMENT OF CAPITAL

3012 Capital movement—prohibition on restriction of movement—tax on dividends—set-off

The Belgian tax authorities decided that the applicants were not entitled to set off 15 per cent of their foreign tax pursuant to the double taxation convention between Belgium and France. The applicants brought proceedings alleging that this constituted an infringement of the EC Treaty art 56(1) on the free movement of capital. The national court stayed the proceedings and sought a preliminary ruling from the European Court of Justice as to whether art 56(1) had to be interpreted as prohibiting a restriction resulting from a provision in the income tax legislation of a member state which subjected dividends from resident companies and dividends from companies resident in another member state to the same uniform tax rate, without in the latter case providing for the setting off of tax levied at source in that other member state. *Held*, Community law, in its current state and in a situation such as that in the main proceedings, did not lay down any general criteria for the attribution of areas of competence between the member states in relation to the elimination of double taxation within the Community. Consequently, it was for the member states to take the measures necessary to prevent situations such as that at issue in the main proceedings by applying, in particular, the apportionment criteria followed in international tax practice. The purpose of the double taxation convention was essentially to apportion fiscal sovereignty between France and Belgium in those situations. However, that convention was not at issue in the preliminary reference at hand. It followed that the EC Treaty art 56 did not preclude the legislation in question.

Case C-513/04 *Kerckhaert v Belgium* [2006] All ER (D) 168 (Nov) (ECJ: Grand Chamber).

3013 Capital movement—prohibition on restriction of movement—tax relief—different rates of tax for residents and non-residents

The taxpayer, a resident in France, received a payment from a company resident in Sweden on the occasion of a purchase of its shares in connection with a reduction in its share capital. Under Swedish legislation resident shareholders who repurchased shares were taxed on them as a capital gain at a rate of 30 per cent and the cost of acquisition of the repurchased shares could be deducted. For non-resident shareholders however, the repurchase was treated as a distribution of a dividend and the cost of acquisition could not be deducted. The taxpayer paid 15 per cent tax on the whole amount of payment in accordance with a Franco-Swedish agreement for the avoidance of double taxation. The taxpayer applied to the responsible tax office for a refund of the whole amount of the dividend tax paid and was refused. She brought proceedings against the tax office and the court referred the question to the European Court of Justice as to the compatibility of the law with the freedom of movement of capital and the effect of the double taxation agreement. *Held*, a resale of shares to the issuing company constituted a capital movement within the meaning of EC Council Directive 88/361 and fell within the scope of the Community rules relating to the free movement of capital. The right to deduct the cost of acquisition of the shares was a tax advantage that constituted a form of tax relief. By having different rules for residents and non-residents the national legislation made cross-frontier transfer of capital less attractive by deterring non-resident investors from buying shares in resident companies and by restricting the opportunities available to resident companies to raise capital from non-resident investors. The refusal to allow a non-resident shareholder to deduct the cost of acquisition of the shares was a restriction on the movement of capital. There was no objective difference in this area between the situation of a resident or non-resident to justify different treatment between the two categories of taxpayer. The discrimination was arbitrary and prohibited under EC Treaty arts 56, 58 in so far as non-residents were taxed more onerously than resident shareholders in an objectively comparable situation. It was for the national court to determine whether the treatment of non-resident shareholders under national legislation which derived from the double taxation agreement was not less favourable than that afforded to resident shareholders. Articles 56, 58 were to be interpreted as precluding national legislation in relation to double taxation agreements except where such an agreement treated non-resident shareholders less favourably than resident shareholders.

Case C–265/04 *Bouanich v Skatteverket* [2006] 3 CMLR 417 (ECJ: Third Chamber). Case C–319/02 *Proceedings brought by Manninen* [2005] Ch 236, ECJ (2004 Abr para 1621); and Case C–80/94 *Wielock v Inspecteur der Directe Belastingen* [1996] 1 WLR 84, ECJ (1995 Abr para 3143), applied.

3014   Capital movement—prohibition on restriction of movement—transfer of land— authorisation requirement

The applicant, the owner of a dwelling and land situated in Austria, brought proceedings to obtain the eviction of the respondent, a German national, who held a long lease on the property and claimed a right to acquire title to it under agreements concluded with the applicant's parents. The courts took the view that, since certain domestic legislation came into force, foreign purchasers were no longer required to obtain prior authorisation from the competent land transfer authority, but had merely to make a declaration to that authority within a period of two years, failing which the transaction would be retroactively invalid. The courts decided that, in the absence of a declaration provided by the respondent within a period of two years, the agreements had to be regarded as void and that the respondent had therefore to vacate the premises. The respondent appealed against that decision, and the court stayed the proceedings and referred to the European Court of Justice for a preliminary ruling the question of whether the EC Treaty art 56 on the right to free movement of capital should be interpreted as precluding national legislation by which, in the case of a land purchase transaction that did not require the authorisation of the land transfer authority, failure by the acquirer to declare by the due date that the land was built on, that the acquisition was not for holiday purposes, and that he was, or should be treated as, an Austrian national, resulted in the retrospective invalidity of the transaction. *Held*, art 56(1) precluded such legislation. The declaration system provided for by the national legislation in the instant case had, by its very purpose, the effect of restricting the free movement of capital. Such restrictions might nevertheless be permitted provided that the national measures in question pursued an objective in the public interest, were applied in a non-discriminatory manner and complied with the principle of proportionality, that was to say, were appropriate for securing the attainment of that objective and did not go beyond what was necessary in order to attain it. The penalty under national law was not proportionate to the objectives pursued in the public interest in the instant case. Such a measure was excessive in so far as it had automatic consequences for late submissions of the declaration, prohibiting that authority from examining whether, on the merits, the proposed acquisition complied with the applicable planning rules. Such a penalty would not, therefore, be regarded as absolutely necessary to ensure that the obligation to make a declaration of acquisition was complied with and to attain the objective in the public interest pursued by the national legislation.

Case C–213/04 *Burtscher v Stauderer* [2006] 2 CMLR 382 (ECJ: Third Chamber).

COMPETITION

See TRADE, INDUSTRY AND INDUSTRIAL RELATIONS.

TAXATION

3015   Value added tax

See VALUE ADDED TAX.

SOCIAL POLICY

3016   Employment

See EMPLOYMENT.

3017   Equal pay and treatment

See DISCRIMINATION.

3018   Social security—benefits

See SOCIAL SECURITY.

3019   Social security—care allowance—residence in one member state—employment in another member state—entitlement to benefits

The claimant, a German national, was a frontier worker employed in Austria where he paid taxes and social security contributions and was affiliated to sickness insurance. He resided in Germany with his daughter who was severely disabled. After the child's mother ceased to be entitled to care allowance in Germany, the claimant made an application for care allowance under Austrian legislation. The application was refused on the ground that the person reliant on care had to have their main residence in Austria in order to receive the allowance. The action brought against that decision was dismissed but, on appeal, the court held that the allowance constituted a sickness benefit under EC Council Regulation 1408/71 art 4(1)(a) and that the cash benefit had to be exported in accordance with the principles applicable to federal care allowance. On appeal, questions relating to the interpretation of Regulation 1408/71 were referred to the European Court of Justice. *Held,* a care allowance such as that provided for by the Austrian legislation did not constitute a special non-contributory benefit within the meaning of art 4(2)(b) but constituted a sickness benefit within the meaning of art 4(1)(a). As provisions which derogated from the principle that social security benefits were exportable had to be interpreted strictly, it had to be ascertained whether the other conditions in art 4(2)(b) were satisfied. Benefits which were granted objectively on the basis of a legally defined position and were intended to improve the state of health and life of persons reliant on care had to be regarded as 'sickness benefits' within the meaning of art 4(2)(a). The grant of care allowance granted under the Austrian legislation was such a benefit. Therefore, the condition that the benefit in question was classified as a 'special' benefit was not satisfied. A member of the family of a worker employed in Austria who lived with his family in Germany could, where he fulfilled the other conditions of grant, claim from the competent institution of the worker's place of employment payment of a care allowance such as that in question, as a sickness benefit in cash, in so far as the member of the family was not entitled to a similar benefit under the legislation of the state in whose territory he resided.

Case C-286/03 *Hosse v Land Salzburg* [2006] All ER (EC) 640 (ECJ: Grand Chamber).

INDEX

The titles under which the Abridgment is arranged are listed on pp 9–10. The references in the list are to paragraphs, not pages.

Index